50

D0355155

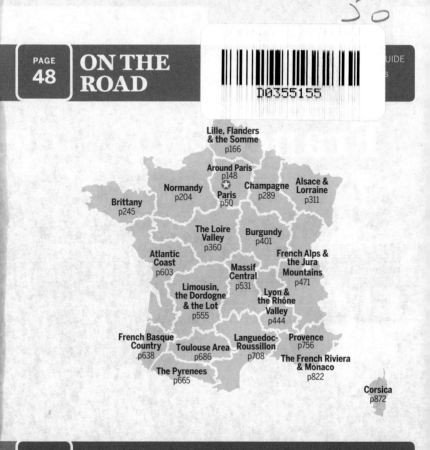

Lille, Flanders & the Somme
p166

Around Paris
p148

Normandy
p204

Paris
p50

Champagne
p289

Alsace & Lorraine
p311

Brittany
p245

The Loire Valley
p360

Burgundy
p401

Atlantic Coast
p603

Massif Central
p531

French Alps & the Jura Mountains
p471

Limousin, the Dordogne & the Lot
p555

Lyon & the Rhône Valley
p444

French Basque Country
p638

Toulouse Area
p686

Languedoc-Roussillon
p708

Provence
p756

The French Riviera & Monaco
p822

The Pyrenees
p665

Corsica
p872

Language

THIS EDITION WRITTEN AND RESEARCHED BY

Nicola Williams,

Oliver Berry, Stuart Butler, Jean-Bernard Carillet, Kerry Christiani,
Gregor Clark, Emilie Filou, Catherine Le Nevez

welcome to
France

Cultural Savoir Faire

France is all about world-class art and architecture, Roman temples and Renaissance châteaux, iconic landmarks known the world over, and rising stars few yet know. Stroll the lily-clad gardens Monet painted and savour *un café* (an espresso) at the Parisian cafe where Sartre and Simone de Beauvoir met to philosophise. See glorious pasts blaze forth and imagine the life of a French king at bourgeois Versailles. View tomorrow's art stars in squats secreted in abandoned 19th-century Haussmann mansions in Paris, or at new headline-grabbing museums up north. Drink cocktails in a shabby-chic Nantes warehouse. Listen to Marseille rap and Parisian jazz. Sense the subtle infusion of language, music and mythology in Brittany, brought by 5th-century Celtic invaders. Yes, French culture offers never-ending possibilities to fill any stay in France.

Gastronomic Art de Vivre

Or perhaps it is the French feast of fine food and wine that woos so many travellers. (This is, after all, the country that entices more than any other: with more than 80 million visitors a year, it ranks as the world's top tourist destination.) But know that gastronomic France goes far deeper than Parisian bistro dining, long lunches outside, shopping for fruit and veg at the

> *A country that seduces travellers with its unfalteringly familiar culture woven around cafe terraces, village-square markets and lace-curtained bistros with their* plat du jour *(dish of the day) chalked on the board.*

(left) St-Cirq Lapopie, Lot Valley (p597)
(below) The St-Michel metro station entrance, Latin Quarter (p83), Paris

market and wolfing down croissants hot from the *boulangerie* (bakery) for breakfast. Learn how to make petits fours with the kids in Paris or flip crêpes in Brittany; taste wine with one of the world's top sommeliers in Bordeaux; visit an Atlantic Coast oyster farm; drink Champagne in ancient cellars in Reims; tour a Provençal melon farm; harvest olives, peaches and cherries in the hot south...and understand that food is as much an *art de vivre* (art of living) for the French as it is essential for survival.

Lyrical Landscape

Then there is the *terroir* (land) and the startlingly varied journey it weaves from northern France's cliffs and sand dunes to the bright-blue sea of the French Riviera and Corsica's green oak forests. Outdoor action is what this lyrical landscape calls for, be it fast-paced and pulse-racing, slow and relaxed, solo or en famille. Walk barefoot across wave-rippled sand to Mont St-Michel; ride the cable car to mindblowing glacial panoramas above mountaineering mecca Chamonix; cartwheel down Europe's highest sand dune; surf in Biarritz; ski the Alps; hike from one extinct volcano to another in the Massif Central; float between locks or pedal the towpath along the Canal du Midi. The action is endless and the next adventure just begging to be had.

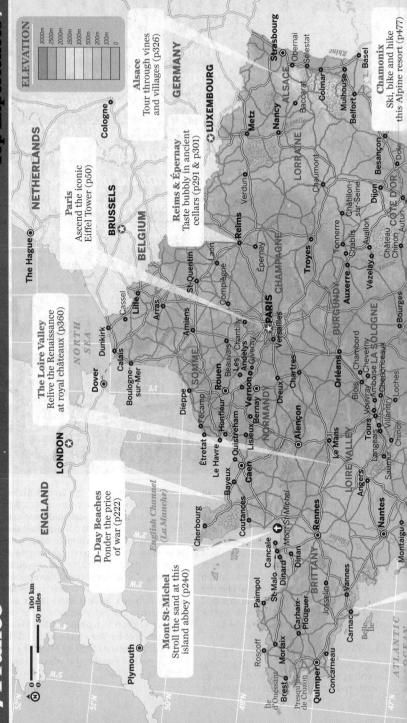

France

Top Experiences

ELEVATION
3000m
2500m
2000m
1500m
1000m
500m
200m
100m
0

Alsace
Tour through vines and villages (p326)

Paris
Ascend the iconic Eiffel Tower (p50)

Reims & Épernay
Taste bubbly in ancient cellars (p291 & p301)

Chamonix
Ski, bike and hike this Alpine resort (p477)

The Loire Valley
Relive the Renaissance at royal châteaux (p360)

D-Day Beaches
Ponder the price of war (p222)

Mont St-Michel
Stroll the sand at this island abbey (p240)

NETHERLANDS
The Hague
GERMANY
Cologne
LUXEMBOURG
BRUSSELS
BELGIUM
Strasbourg
Obernai
Sélestat
ALSACE
Basel
Colmar
Baccarat
Mulhouse
Belfort
Metz
Nancy
LORRAINE
Moselle
Besançon
Dole
Verdun
Chaumont
CÔTE D'OR
Dijon
Châtillon-sur-Seine
Autun
Reims
Épernay
Laon
St-Quentin
Compiègne
Troyes
CHAMPAGNE
Tonnerre
Chablis
Avallon
Château Chinon
Auxerre
BURGUNDY
Vézelay
Bourges
Yonne
ENGLAND
NORTH SEA
Cassel
Lille
Arras
Dunkirk
Calais
Boulogne-sur-Mer
SOMME
Amiens
Beauvais
Chantilly
Les Andelys
Giverny
Dieppe
Rouen
Vernon
PARIS
Versailles
Dreux
Chartres
Orléans
Chambord
LA SOLOGNE
Cheverny
Amiens
Blois
Vouvray
Amboise
Chenonceaux
LOIRE VALLEY
Loches
LONDON
Dover
English Channel (La Manche)
Fécamp
Étretat
Honfleur
Le Havre
Ouistreham
Lisieux
Bernay
NORMANDY
Alençon
Le Mans
Tours
Langeais
Villandry
Chinon
Saumur
Angers
Plymouth
Cherbourg
Bayeux
Caen
Coutances
Mont St-Michel
Rennes
BRITTANY
Nantes
Montaigu
Paimpol
Roscoff
Morlaix
Île d'Ouessant
Brest
Presqu'île de Crozon
Carhaix-Plouguer
Josselin
Vannes
Quimper
Concarneau
Belle Île
Carnac
St-Malo
Dinard
Cancale
Dinan
ATLANTIC OCEAN
Rhine
L. Basel

0 100 km
0 50 miles

52°N
51°N
50°N
49°N
47°N
5°W
4°W
3°W
2°W

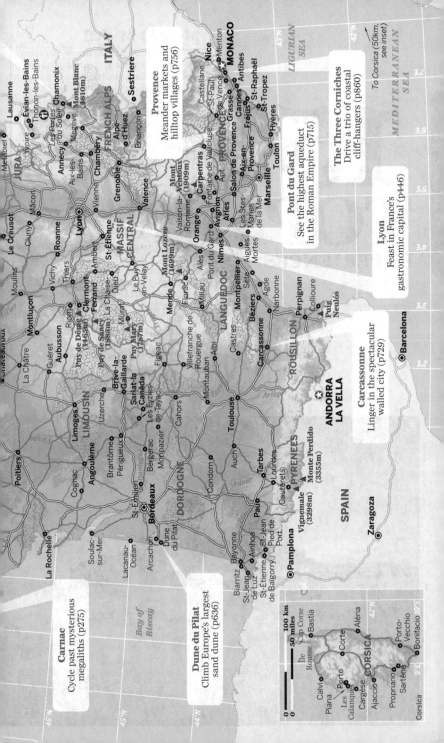

Provence
Meander markets and hilltop villages (p756)

The Three Corniches
Drive a trio of coastal cliff-hangers (p860)

Pont du Gard
See the highest aqueduct in the Roman Empire (p715)

Lyon
Feast in France's gastronomic capital (p446)

Carcassonne
Linger in the spectacular walled city (p729)

Carnac
Cycle past mysterious megaliths (p275)

Dune du Pilat
Climb Europe's largest sand dune (p636)

To Corsica (50km, see inset)

LIGURIAN SEA

MEDITERRANEAN SEA

ITALY

FRENCH ALPS

Mont Blanc (4810m)

JURA

MASSIF CENTRAL

Mont Lozère (1699m)

LANGUEDOC

ROUSSILLON

ANDORRA LA VELLA

PYRENEES

Monte Perdido (3355m)

Vignemale (3298m)

DORDOGNE

LIMOUSIN

PROVENCE

Mont Ventoux (1909m)

SPAIN

Bay of Biscay

MONACO

Puy de Dôme (1465m)
Puy Mary (1787m)
Puy de Sancy (1885m)

100 km
50 miles

CORSICA

Cap Corse
Île Rousse
Bastia
Calvi
Porto
Piana
Les Calanques
Cargèse
Ajaccio
Corte
Aléria
Propriano
Sartène
Porto-Vecchio
Bonifacio

Corsica

Lausanne
Évian-les-Bains
Thonon-les-Bains
Chamonix
Sestriere
Méribel
Yvoire
Les Gets
Megève
Annecy
Aix-les-Bains
Mâcon
Le Creusot
Cluny
Moulins
Montluçon
Vichy
Thiers
Ambert
Riom
Clermont-Ferrand
La Chaise-Dieu
Murat
Le Puy-en-Velay
Florac
Mende
Millau
Villefranche-de-Rouergue
Albi
Castres
Castellane
St-Paul-de-Vence
Nice
Menton
Antibes
Cannes
St-Raphaël
Grasse
Éze
Fréjus
St-Tropez
Hyères
Toulon
Marseille
Aix-en-Provence
Salon-de-Provence
Arles
Avignon
Les Stes-Maries-de-la-Mer
Aigues-Mortes
Nîmes
Pont du Gard
Alès
Orange
Carpentras
Fontaine-de-Vaucluse
Apt
Vaison-la-Romaine
Sète
Agde
Béziers
Montpellier
Narbonne
Collioure
Perpignan
Puig Neulós
Barcelona
Zaragoza
Pamplona
Biarritz
Bayonne
St-Jean-de-Luz
Ainhoa
St-Étienne-de-Baïgorry
St-Jean-Pied-de-Port
Pau
Lourdes
Cauterets
Tarbes
Auch
Condom
Toulouse
Foix
Carcassonne
Cahors
Montauban
Montpazier
Bergerac
Les Eyzies-de-Tayac
Sarlat-la-Canéda
Brive-la-Gaillarde
Uzerche
Limoges
Brantôme
Périgueux
Angoulême
Cognac
St-Émilion
Bordeaux
Arcachon
Dune du Pilat
Lacanau-Océan
Soulac-sur-Mer
La Rochelle
Poitiers
La Châtre
Guéret
Aubusson
Châteauroux
Alpe d'Huez
Briançon
Chambéry
Grenoble
Vienne
Valence
Lyon
Roanne
St-Étienne

46°N
45°N
44°N
43°N
42°N

3.z
3.z
3.3
3.4
3.5
3.6

15
TOP
EXPERIENCES

Mont St-Michel

1 The dramatic play of tides on this abbey-island in Normandy is magical and mysterious. Said by Celtic mythology to be a sea tomb to which souls of the dead were sent, Mont St-Michel (p240) is rich in legend and history, keenly felt as you make your way barefoot across rippled sand to the stunning architectural ensemble. Walk around it alone or, better still, hook up with a guide in nearby Genêts for a dramatic day hike across the bay.

Eiffel Tower

2 Seven million people visit the Eiffel Tower (p55) annually but few disagree that each visit is unique. From an evening ascent amid twinkling lights to lunch at 58 Tour Eiffel (p114) in the company of a staggering city panorama, there are 101 ways to 'do' it. Pedal beneath it, skip the lift and hike up, buy a crêpe from a stand here or a key ring from the street, snap yourself in front of it, visit it at night or – our favourite – on the odd special occasion when all 324m of the tower glows a different colour.

OLIMPIO FANTUZ/SIME/4CORNERS©

Champagne

3 Name-brand Champagne houses, such as Mumm (p294), Mercier (p301) and Moët & Chandon (p301) in the main towns of Reims and Épernay, are known the world over. But – our tip – much of Champagne's best liquid gold is made by almost 5000 small-scale *vignerons* (wine-growers) in 320-odd villages. Dozens of *maisons* (Champagne houses) welcome visitors for a taste, tipple and shopping at producer prices, rendering the region's scenic driving routes (p297) the best way to taste fine bubbly amid rolling vineyards and drop-dead-gorgeous villages. Our favourite: tasting in Le Mesnil-sur-Oger and lunch at Le Mesnil (p301). Champagne barrel, Mercier, above

Loire Valley Châteaux

4 If it's aristocratic pomp and architectural splendour you're after, this regal valley is the place to linger. Flowing for more than 1000km into the Atlantic Ocean, the Loire is one of France's last *fleuves sauvages* (wild rivers) and its banks provide a 1000-year snapshot of French high society. The valley is riddled with beautiful châteaux sporting glittering turrets and ball-rooms, lavish cupolas and chapels. If you're a hopeless romantic seeking the perfect fairy-tale castle, head for moat-ringed Azay-le-Rideau (p387), Villandry (p386) and its gardens, and less-visited Beauregard (p375).

Adrenalin Kick, Chamonix

5 Sure, 007 did it, but so can you: skiing the Vallée Blanche (p480) is a once-in-a-lifetime experience. You won't regret the €75-odd it costs to do the 20km off-piste descent from the spike of the Aiguille du Midi to mountaineering mecca Chamonix – every minute of the five hours it takes to get down will pump more adrenalin in your body than anything else you've ever done. Craving more? Hurl yourself down Europe's longest black run, La Sarenne, at Alpe d'Huez (p516).

Dune du Pilat

6 The Dune du Pilat (p636) is a 'mountain' that just has to be climbed. Not only is the coastal panorama from the top of Europe's largest sand dune a stunner – it takes in the Banc d'Arguin bird reserve and Cap Ferret across the bay – but also the nearby beaches have some of the Atlantic Coast's best surf. Cycle here from Arcachon and top off the heady trip with a dozen oysters, shucked before your very eyes and accompanied by *crepinettes* (local sausages).

Pont du Gard

7 This Unesco World Heritage Site (p715) near Nîmes in southern France is gargantuan: 35 arches straddle the Roman aqueduct's 275m-long upper tier, containing a watercourse that was designed to carry 20,000 cu metres of water per day. View it from afloat a canoe on the River Gard or pay extra to jig across its top tier. Oh, and don't forget your swimming gear for a spot of post-Pont daredevil diving and high jumping from the rocks nearby – a plunge that will entice the most reluctant of young historians.

Three Corniches, Nice

8 It's impossible to drive this dramatic trio of coastal roads (p860), each one higher and with more hairpin bends than the next, without conjuring up cinematic images of Grace Kelly, Hitchcock, the glitz of Monaco high life, and the glamour of the royal family – all while absorbing big view after big view of sweeping blue sea fringing Europe's most mythical coastline. To make a perfect day out of it, shop for a picnic at the Cours Saleya (p827) morning market before leaving Nice.

Alsatian Wine Route

9 It is one of France's most popular drives – and for good reason. Motoring in this far northeast corner of France takes you through a kaleidoscope of lush green vines, perched castles and gentle mist-covered mountains. The only pit stops en route are half-timbered villages and roadside wine cellars, where fruity Alsace vintages can be swirled, tasted and bought. To be truly wooed, drive the Route des Vins d'Alsace (p326) in autumn, when vines are heavy with grapes waiting to be harvested and colours are at their vibrant best.

D-Day Beaches

10 This is one of France's most emotional journeys. The broad stretches of fine sand and breeze-blown bluffs are quiet now, but early on 6 June 1944 the beaches of northern Normandy were a cacophony of gunfire and explosions, the bodies of Allied soldiers lying in the sand as their comrades-in-arms charged inland. Just up the hill from Omaha Beach, the long rows of symmetrical gravestones at the Normandy American Cemetery & Memorial (p227) bear solemn, silent testimony to the horrible price paid for France's liberation from Nazi tyranny. Gun bunker, Omaha Beach, above

GLENN BEANLAND /GETTY IMAGES ©

Provençal Markets

11 No region is more of a market-must than this one. Be it fresh fish by the port in seafaring Marseille, early summer's strings of pink garlic, melons from Cavaillon all summer long or wintertime's earthy 'black diamond' truffles, Provence thrives on a bounty of fresh produce – grown locally and piled high each morning at the market. Every town and village has one, but those in Carpentras (p806) and Aix-en-Provence (p773) are the best known. While you're here, stock up on dried herbs, green and black olives marinated a dozen different ways, courgette flowers and oils.

Carnac Megaliths

12 Pedalling past open fields dotted with the world's greatest concentration of mysterious megaliths (p275) gives a poignant reminder of Brittany's ancient human inhabitants. No one knows for sure what inspired these gigantic menhirs, dolmens, cromlechs, tumuli and cairns to be built. A sun god? Some phallic fertility cult? It's a mystery.

Carcassonne at Dusk

13 That first glimpse of La Cité's sturdy, stone, witch's-hat turrets above Carcassonne (p729) in the Languedoc is enough to make your hair stand on end. To properly savour this fairy-tale walled city, linger at dusk after the crowds have left, when the old town belongs to its 100 or so inhabitants and the few visitors staying at the handful of lovely hotels within its ramparts. Don't forget to look back when you leave to view the old city, beautifully illuminated, glowing in the warm night.

Hilltop Villages

14. Impossibly perched on a rocky peak above the Mediterranean, gloriously lost in back country, fortified or château-topped... southern France's portfolio of *villages perchés* is vast and impressive, and calls for go-slow touring – on foot, by bicycle or car. Most villages are medieval, built from golden stone and riddled with cobbled lanes, flower-filled alleys and hidden squares silent but for the glug of a fountain. Combine a village visit with lunch al fresco – La Table de Ventabren (p781) near Aix-en-Provence and Les Deux Frères (p867) in Roquebrune are two dreamy addresses. View from Èze hilltop village, below

Lyonnais Bouchons

15. The red-and-white checked table-cloths, closely packed tables and decades-old bistro decor could be anywhere in France. It's the local cuisine that makes *bouchons* in Lyon (p457) unique, plus the quaint culinary customs, such as totting up the bill on the paper tablecloth, or serving wine in a glass bottle wrapped with an elastic band to stop drips, or the 'shut weekends' opening hours. Various piggy parts drive Lyonnais cuisine, but have faith – this French city is said to be the gastronomic capital of France. Dine and decide. Chez Paul *bouchon*, below

GLENN VAN DER KNIJFF /GETTY IMAGES ©

HEMIS/ALAMY ©

need to know

Currency
» Euro (€)

Language
» French

When to Go

Brittany & Normandy •
GO Apr–Sep

Paris
• GO May & Jun

• **French Alps**
GO late Dec–early Apr (skiing)
or Jun & Jul (hiking)

French Riviera •
GO Apr–Jun, Sep & Oct

Corsica •
GO Apr–Jun, Sep & Oct

Warm to hot summers, mild winters
Warm to hot summers, cold winters
Mild year-round
Mild summers, cold winters
Polar climate

High Season
(Jul & Aug)
» Queues at big sights and on the road, especially August.

» Christmas, New Year and Easter equally busy.

» Late December to March is high season in French Alpine ski resorts.

Shoulder
(Apr–Jun & Sep)
» Accommodation rates drop in southern France and other hot spots.

» Spring: warm weather, flowers, local produce.

» The *vendange* (grape harvest) is reason to visit in autumn.

Low Season
(Oct–Mar)
» Prices up to 50% less than high season.

» Sights, attractions and restaurants open fewer days and shorter hours.

Your Daily Budget

Budget up to
€100
» Dorm bed: €15–€25

» Double room in a budget hotel: €60–€80

» Free admission to many attractions first Sunday of month

» Set lunches: €12–€18

Midrange
€100-€200
» Double room in a midrange hotel: €80–€180

» Lunch *menus* (set meals) in gourmet restaurants: €20–€40

Top end over
€200
» Double room in a top-end hotel: €180–€300

» Lower weekend rates in business hotels

» Top restaurant dinner: *menu* €50, à la carte €100–€150

Money

» ATMs at every airport, most train stations and every second street corner in towns and cities. Visa, MasterCard and Amex widely accepted.

Visas

» Generally not required for stays of up to 90 days (or at all for EU nationals); some nationalities need a Schengen visa.

Mobile Phones

» European and Australian phones work, but only American cells with 900 and 1800 MHz networks are compatible. Use a French SIM to call with a cheaper French number.

Driving

» Drive on the right; steering wheel is on the left side of the car. Be aware of potentially hazardous 'priority to the right' rule.

Websites

» **France Guide** (www.franceguide. com) Official French government tourist-office website.

» **France.fr** (www. france.fr) Official country website.

» **French Word-a-Day** (http://french-word-a -day.typepad.com) Fun language learning.

» **Lonely Planet** (www. lonelyplanet.com/ france) Destination information, bookings and traveller forum.

» **Paris by Mouth** (www.parisbymouth. com) Dining and drinking; one-stop site for eating and snagging an advance table.

Exchange Rates

Australia	A$1	€0.79
Canada	C$1	€0.79
Japan	¥100	€0.98
New Zealand	NZ$1	€0.63
UK	UK£1	€1.24
US	US$1	€0.77

For current exchange rates, see www.xe.com

Important Numbers

France country code	☏33
International access code	☏00
Europe-wide emergency	☏112
Ambulance (SAMU)	☏15
Police	☏17

Arriving in France

» **Paris – Aéroport Roissy Charles de Gaulle**

Trains, Buses & RER – to Paris centre every 15 to 30 minutes, 5am to 11pm

Night Bus – hourly, 12.30am to 5.30am.

Taxis – €50–€60; 30 minutes to Paris centre

» **Paris – Aéroport d'Orly**

Orlyval Rail, RER & Buses – at least every 15 minutes, 5am to 11pm

Taxis – €45–€60; 25 minutes to Paris centre

In France to Shop!

OK, so Paris is the bee's knees for luxury goods like haute couture, high-quality fashion accessories (Hermès silk scarf, Madame?), lingerie, perfume and cosmetics. Lovely as they are, they most probably aren't any cheaper to buy in France than at home.

Time your trip right and pick up designer and street fashion for a snip of the usual price at France's *soldes* (sales), by law held twice a year for three weeks in January and again in July. Other times look for the words *degriffés* (name-brand products with the labels cut out), *bonnes affaires* (cut-price deals) and *dépôt-vente* (secondhand). Away from the capital, Troyes and Calais in northern France are known for their fantastic factory-outlet shops.

Take along your own bag or basket when shopping for fresh fruit, vegetables and other edible goodies at the local weekly market. Ditto for supermarkets where the bagless can exchange a few centimes for *un sachet* (near-to-useless, thin plastic carrier bag).

first time

Everyone needs a helping hand when visiting a country for the first time. There are phrases to learn, customs to get used to and etiquette to understand. The following section will help demystify France so your first-time trip goes as smoothly as your fifth.

Language

A substantial chunk of visitors to France get around without speaking a word of French. But just a few phrases go a long way in making friends, inviting service with a smile, and ensuring a rich and rewarding travel experience. English is increasingly widespread in Paris, Nice and other big tourist-busy cities, but step into *la France profonde* (rural France) and you'll need those French phrases you mastered before setting off. Irrespective of where you travel in France, know that all-essential *'Bonjour'* (Hello) – a simple greeting exchanged upon entering shops, hotels, restaurants, bakeries and so on.

Booking Ahead

Reserving accommodation in advance is highly recommended, particularly in high season. Most hotel staff speak and read some English, staff in restaurants less so. To ensure you get what you want, use these phrases when booking by telephone or email.

» **Hello.**	Bonjour.
» **I'd like to book a room.**	Je voudrais réserver une chambre.
» **a single room**	une chambre à un lit
» **a double room**	une chambre avec un grand lit
» **My name is ...**	Je m'appelle...
» **from ... to... (date)**	du... au...
» **How much is it?**	C'est combien?
» **per night/person**	par nuit/personne
» **Thank you (very much).**	Merci (beaucoup).

What to Wear

Paris, cradle of haute couture, is chic, so don your smarter threads (think Parisian, think accessories!). The further south you go, the more relaxed fashion becomes, although it's still sassy, especially on the French Riviera. Avoid shorts and flip-flops unless you're at the beach, and dress up rather than down at restaurants, clubs and bars – no jeans and trainers, unless you're at the local village bar. Bring a sweater (jumper) and rain jacket, and something to protect your skin from peckish mosquitoes. Take sensible shoes whatever the season – cobbled streets simply don't marry with high heels or thin soles.

What to Pack

- » Passport
- » Credit cards
- » This guidebook
- » Phrasebook
- » Driver's licence
- » Travel plug (adaptor)
- » Mobile phone (cell phone) and charger
- » Earplugs
- » Sunscreen, sunhat and sunglasses
- » Umbrella (northern France)
- » Rainproof jacket
- » Torch (flashlight)
- » Pocketknife with corkscrew
- » Camera
- » Medical kit
- » Comfortable walking shoes
- » Light scarf or sarong
- » Book or e-reader
- » iPod (with French music playlist)

Checklist

» Check passport validity

» Check if you need a visa (p965)

» Arrange travel insurance (p959)

» Check airline baggage restrictions

» Book ahead for accommodation and big-name restaurants

» Buy tickets online for the Louvre, Eiffel Tower etc

» Organise international roaming on your phone if needed (p963)

» Download France-related travel apps and music playlist

Etiquette

» **Greetings**
Shake hands and say *'Bonjour'* (Hello) or *'Bonsoir'* (Good evening) to strangers, and exchange two cheek-skimming kisses – right cheek first – with casual acquaintances and friends. Use the polite *'vous'* form, as in *'Comment allez-vous?'* (How are you?) to address anyone older than you or who you don't know well, and *'tu'* for close friends and family. For more on kissing etiquette, see p923.

» **Asking for help**
Say *'excusez-moi'* (excuse me) to attract attention, *'pardon'* (sorry) to apologise.

» **Churches**
Dress modestly (cover shoulders) and be respectful of any religious service going on.

» **Dining**
When dining in a French home, wait for your host to start first. Use your cutlery, never your fingers, to eat and always eat everything on your plate. When dining out, never use *'garçon'* to summon a waiter, rather *'Monsieur'*, *'Mademoiselle'* or *'Madame'*.

» **Coffee**
The only acceptable type of coffee to end a meal with is *un café* (an espresso).

Tipping

» **Taxis**
Optional, but most passengers round up to the nearest euro.

» **Restaurants**
A 15% service charge is usually in the bill, but many still leave a few euros. *'Service non compris'* means service is not included.

» **Bars & Cafes**
For drinks at the bar, no need to tip. If drinks are brought to your table, tip as you would in a restaurant.

» **Hotels**
Bellhops usually expect €1 to €2 per bag; it's not necessary to tip the concierge, cleaners or front-desk staff.

Money

Credit and debit cards are widely accepted, but there's often a minimum purchase of €15. Visa and MasterCard are most popular; American Express is only accepted by international chain hotels, luxury boutiques and department stores. Check if bars, cafes and restaurants accept cards before ordering; places in Corsica and rural villages don't. Chip-and-pin is the norm for card transactions; few places accept signatures. ATMs *(points d'argent* or *distributeurs automatiques de billets)* are everywhere, offering withdrawal from savings accounts and cash advances on credit cards. Both incur international transaction fees. If you don't want to rely on plastic, you can change cash and travellers cheques at some banks, post offices and *bureaux de change* (money-exchange offices). Ask for *un mélange* (an assortment) of banknotes; many shops don't accept €200 and €500 bills.

what's new

Our authors have hunted down the fresh, the revamped, the transformed, the hot and the happening. Here are a few of our favourites. For up-to-the-minute reviews and recommendations, see lonelyplanet.com/france.

Art in Paris

1 The new 'flying carpet' Islamic art gallery at the Louvre, the Louis Vuitton arts centre à la Frank Gehry, the Musée Picasso. Oh, what capital openings art lovers are enjoying! (p63; p62; p76)

Gourmet Burgers

2 The burger trend sweeping Paris is, unsurprisingly, *très gourmet ma chère*. Hot on the heels of Blend, with its hand-cut meat in brioche buns, comes the achingly cool Beef Club. (p118; p115)

Louvre-Lens

3 Ingenius. France's latest temple to fine art – aka the Louvre-Lens in northern France – also lets visitors peek into its restoration workshops and store-rooms. (p192)

Au 36

4 Never has Champagne *dégustation* been so chic. This inventive new wine bar in one of Champagne's prettiest hilltop villages has a tasting wall of fizz arranged by aroma. (p299)

Annecy Hostel

5 The chic shores of one of France's most beautiful, flower-strung lakes have suddenly become affordable: enter Annecy's shiny new hostel. (p493)

The Confluence, Lyon

6 The urban renaissance of this former industrial wasteland, where the Rhône and Saône rivers meet, continues: the Pôle de Commerces et de Loisirs Confluence entertains all the family. (p452)

MuséoParc Alésia, Burgundy

7 Julius Caesar's crushing of Vercingétorix at Alésia in 52 BC ended centuries of conflict between the Gauls and the Romans. This new sight is where it happened. (p423)

Puy de Dôme, Massif Central

8 Summiting the volcanic cap of Puy de Dôme has never been easier thanks to the spiffy new cogwheel railway that lumbers up its pea-green slopes. (p541)

Marseille, European Capital of Culture 2013

9 The makeover of this mythical Mediterranean port will climax with a new national museum on European and Mediterranean civilisations inside 13th-century Fort St-Jean. (p761)

A New National Park

10 It's absolutely right that Les Calanques, spectacular cliffs rising from bright turquoise waters east of Marseille, should be protected as a national park. Explore by sea kayak.

Musée d'Art Classique de Mougins

11 Never has the French Riviera village that seduced Picasso been so top-drawer. This art creation of collector and British entrepreneur Christian Levett only adds to its natural panache. (p847)

Jean Nouvel in Sarlat-la-Canéda

12 Architect of Paris' Arab World Institute and Musée du Quai Branly strikes gold again, this time with a panoramic lift inside a village-church turned market in the Dordogne. (p580)

if you like...

Gorgeous Villages

There is no humbler French pleasure than meandering through villages of gold stone, pink granite or whitewash. Cobbled lanes twist and turn to reveal sculpted fountains, hidden squares and shuttered houses strung with purple wisteria, vines or drying peppers.

St-Émilion A medieval village perched dramatically above Bordeaux vines (p632)

St-Jean Pied de Port Ancient pilgrim outpost en route to Santiago de Compostela, Spain (p661)

Yvoire On the shore of Lake Geneva, this flowery Savoy village is a privileged address (p490)

The Luberon A part of Provence lavishly strewn with hilltop villages; red-rock Roussillon is pure brilliance (p808)

Èze Fuses stunning hilltop village with sweeping Riviera panorama – wow! (p862)

The Dordogne Beautiful *bastides* (fortified hilltop towns) at every turn (p588)

Route des Vins d'Alsace Count off gorgeous half-timbered villages like rosary beads on this vine-draped, castle-ruin-dotted driving route: Obernai, Bergheim, Ribeauvillé and Riquewihr are lovely (p326)

Wine Tasting

Be it by tasting in cellars, watching grape harvests or sleeping *au château,* French wine culture demands immediate road-testing.

Bordeaux The Medoc, St-Émilion and Cognac set connoisseurs' hearts aflutter (p622)

Burgundy Sample renowned vintages in Beaune, the Côte d'Or and Chablis (p415, p411 and p427)

Châteauneuf-du-Pape Vines planted by 14th-century popes yield southern France's most illustrious red (p799)

Gigondas Taste raved-about reds in this gold-stone village in Provence, or try its equally luxuriant Jurassien counterpart, **Pupillin** (p808 and p525)

Vin Jaune Something different: liquid gold in the Jura; or go for pea-green chartreuse not far from Chambéry (p526 and p499)

Bandol and Cassis Wine tasting in these two Riviera villages is as much about the majestic Med setting as the wonderful wine (p860 and p775)

Castles

The Loire Valley is the prime stop for French châteaux dripping in period gold leaf. But venture elsewhere and you'll be surprised by what hides behind lumbering stone walls.

Versailles France's largest and grandest château, a stone's throw from Paris (p152)

Chambord Renaissance country-getaway castle where French kings and queens had a ball (p372)

Azay-le-Rideau Classic French château with moat, turrets and sweeping staircase (p387)

Villandry The formal French gardens framing this Renaissance Loire Valley château are glorious (p386)

Cathar fortresses, Languedoc Now ruined, these dramatic, heat-sizzled hilltop castles evoke 13th-century persecution (p751)

Château des Comtes Foix, Vallée de l'Ariège A château with amazing views of the Pyrenees (p685)

» Cycling by the River Loire in Tours, Loire Valley (p375)

Coastal Paths

From bijou pebble-strewn fishing coves to seemingly endless sand, France's coastline has it all. Walk one of France's many windswept *sentiers du littoral* (coastal footpaths) scented with salty air and wild herbal scrub.

St-Tropez This *sentier du littoral* leads from fishing coves to celebrity-laced sands (p853)

Bandol Stride the coast between inland vines and waterfront rock formations (p860)

Chemin de Nietzsche Spectacular, steep rocky footpath near Nice where the German philosopher hung out (p862)

Corsica Hike from Bonifacio to a lighthouse, or past Genoese watchtowers along Cap Corse's rugged Customs Officers' Trail (p893 and p880)

Northern France Trace the Norman coast to Le Havre on the GR21, or see opal blues along northern France's GR120 (p213 and p180)

Breton island capers Lap up seafaring Brittany on much-loved Belle Île and the smaller, more rugged Île d'Ouessant, or hobnob with Parisians on chic Île de Ré (p278, p266 and p619)

Île de Porquerolles Mediterranean island beauty strung with sea-facing cycling and hiking trails (p858)

Markets

Art nouveau hangar, stall-packed street, plane tree–shaded village square... French markets spill across an enticing mix of public spaces. Every town, village and hamlet has one – usually mornings and at least once or twice a week. Take your own bag or basket.

Lyonnais markets Les Halles and Croix Rousse are Lyon's two buxom market divas, endowed with stalls heaving with fruit, veg, meat and runny St Marcellin cheese (p459)

Place des Lices No town square is as celebrity-studded as the one in St-Tropez (p853)

Marché des Capucins Enjoy oysters and white wine at Bordeaux' Saturday-morning market (p630)

Marché Couvert Once a bishop's palace, now temple to local produce in Metz (p354)

Uzès Languedoc's most splendid farmers market (p716)

Carpentras No French region is as known for its markets as Provence, but it's this Friday-morning *marché* that steals the Provençal show (p806)

Islands & Beaches

The country's 3200km-long coastline morphs from white chalk cliffs (Normandy) to treacherous promontories (Brittany) to broad expanses of fine sand (Atlantic Coast) and pebbly or sandy beaches (Mediterranean Coast).

Îles d'Hyères France's only marine national park and a pedestrian paradise fringed with near-tropical beaches (p858)

Plage de Pampelonne Stars love this hip beach in St-Tropez, darling, and for good reason – it's glam and golden. Or try Cannes. (p853 and p840)

Île de Ré Follow the flock from Paris to this chic, beach-laced island off France's west coast (p619)

Belle Île Its name means 'Beautiful Island' and that is just what this island off the coast of Brittany is (p278)

Corsica Plage de Palombaggia and Plage de Santa Giulia near Porto-Vecchio are to die for (p895)

Les Landes Surfers' secret backed by dunes on the Atlantic Coast (p645)

Côte d'Opale Rousing, wind-buffeted beaches across from the white cliffs of Dover (p180)

If you like... dramatic driving, the trio of hairpin-laced *corniches* (coastal roads) near Nice are sure to thril. Or go to Corsica.

Incredible Train Journeys

There is nothing quite like watching mountains, valleys, gorges and rivers jog past kalaidescope-style from the window of an old-fashioned steam train or mountain railway.

Tramway du Mont Blanc Travel in the shade of Europe's biggest mountain by hopping aboard France's highest train in Megève (p486)

Mer de Glace Ride a red mountain train from Chamonix to Montenvers (1913m), from where a cable car whisks to you to this glacial sea of ice (p478)

Train Jaune Mind-blowing Pyreneen scenery aboard a mountain train in Roussillon (p753)

Pine Cone Train Narrow-gauge railway from Nice (p837)

Chemin de Fer Touristique du Haut-Quercy Savour the sun-baked vineyards, oak forests and rivers of the Lot in southwest France aboard a vintage steam train (p601)

La Vapeur du Trieux Journey riverside on this steam train from Breton harbour to an artists village (p260)

Great Outdoors

With seven national parks and loads of protected areas, the French landscape begs outdoor action. The Alps and Pyrenees offer a gamut of activities, but countrywide there's mountains to choose from. *Allez!*

White-water sports Favourite gorges to ride wild waters: Gorges de l'Ardèche, Gorges de l'Allier and Gorges du Verdon (p469, p553 and p818)

Corsica Bonifacio diving, Porto hiking, boat trips everywhere – Corsica is one big outdoor fest (p872)

Mountain biking Knuckle-whitening descents in Morzine, Alpe d'Huez and Cauterets (p487, p516 and p679)

Sea kayaking Do it in France's newest national park, Les Calanques, near Marseille (p775)

Auvergne Hiking trails in this part of central France – around extinct volcanoes coloured soft pastoral green – are astonishing (p540)

Cycling the Loire Valley In a landscape littered with Renaissance châteaux, can pedalling get any more rewarding? (p363)

Gorge floating Squeeze into a wetsuit, strap on a buoyancy bag and float between rocks – the big thrill of Provence's Gorges du Verdon (p818)

Mountain Vistas

On sunny days views atop France's highest mountains are, quite literally, breathtaking. Cable cars and mountain railways often take out the legwork.

Aiguille du Midi, Chamonix If you can handle the height (3842m), unforgettable summit views of the French, Swiss and Italian Alps await (p477)

Pic du Lac Blanc, Alpe d'Huez Scale 3330m year-round by cable car – magical views ripple across the French Alps into Italy and Switzerland (p516)

Massif de l'Estérel, French Riviera Stupendous views of red rock, green forest and big blue – only on foot! (p850)

Ballon d'Alsace See where Alsace, Franche-Comté and Lorraine converge from this rounded, 1247m-high mountain (p340)

Puy de Dôme, Auvergne Gulp at extinct volcanoes, now pea green and grassy, from this icy summit reached by foot or cog railway (p541)

Cirque de Gavarnie Near Lourdes, a mind-blowing mountain amphitheatre ringed by icy Pyrenean peaks (p682)

Pic du Midi Eye-popping panorama of entire Pyrenees; cable car from La Mongie (p682)

month by month

January

With New Year festivities done and dusted, it's time to head to the Alps. Crowds on the slopes thin out once school's back, but January remains a busy month. On the Mediterranean, mild winters are wonderfully serene in a part of France mad busy the rest of the year.

Vive le Ski!
Grab your skis, hit the slopes. Resorts in the Alps, Pyrenees and Jura open in mid- to late December, but January is the start of the French ski season in earnest. Whether a purpose-built station or lost Alpine village, there's a resort to match every mood and moment.

Hunting Black Diamonds
No culinary product is more aromatic or decadent than black truffles. Hunt them in the Dordogne and Provence – the season runs from late December to March, but January is the prime month.

February

Crisp cold weather in the mountains – lots of china-blue skies now – translates as ski season in top gear. Alpine resorts get mobbed by families during the February school holidays and accommodation is at its priciest.

Nice Carnival
Nice makes the most of its mild climate with this crazy Lenten carnival (p832) (www.nicecarnaval.com). As well as parade and costume shenanigans, merrymakers pelt each other with blooms during the legendary flower battles. Dunkirk in northern France is another French city to celebrate Mardi Gras with gusto (p187).

Citrus Celebrations
It's no surprise that Menton on the French Riviera was once Europe's biggest lemon producer, given its exotic Fête du Citron (Lemon Festival; p870). These days it has to ship in a zillion lemons from Spain to sculpt into gargantuan carnival characters.

March

The tail end of the ski season stays busy thanks to ongoing school holidays (until mid-March) and warmer temperatures. Down south, spring ushers in the bullfighting season and *Pâques* (Easter).

Féria Pascale
No fest sets passions in France's hot south blazing more than Féria de Pâques (p783), held at Easter in Arles to open the bullfighting season (www.feriaarles.com). Four days of street dancing, music, concerts al fresco and bullfighting is what this exuberant event is all about. Not all bulls die.

April

Dedicated ski fiends can carve glaciers in the highest French ski resorts until mid-April. Otherwise, it's off with the ski boots and on with the hiking gear as peach and almond trees flower pink against a backdrop of snow-capped peaks.

Counting Sheep

During the ancient Fête de la Transhumance in late April or May, shepherds walk their flocks of sheep up to lush green summer pastures; St-Rémy de Provence's fest is among the best known. Or you could head to villages in the Pyrenees (p675) and Massif Central (p544) to witness this transit.

May

As the first melons ripen in Provence, and outdoor markets burst with new-found colour, there is no lovelier month to travel. Spring is always in.

May Day

No one works on 1 May, a national holiday that incites summer buzz with its *muguets* (lilies of the valley) sold at roadside stalls and given to friends for good luck. In Arles, Camargue cowboys show off their bull-herding and equestrian skills at the Fête des Gardians (p783).

Pèlerinage des Gitans

Roma flock to the Camargue on 24 and 25 May and again in October for a flamboyant fiesta (p788) of street music, dancing and dipping their toes in the sea (www.gitans.fr).

Starring at Cannes

In mid-May, film stars and celebrities walk the red carpet at Cannes (p843), Europe's biggest cinema extravaganza (www.festival-cannes.com).

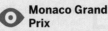 Monaco Grand Prix

How fitting that Formula One's most glamorous rip around the streets of one of the world's most glam countries at the Monaco Grand Prix (www.grand-rix-monaco.com; p863).

June

As midsummer approaches, the festival pace quickens alongside a rising temperature gauge, which tempts the first bathers into the sea. Looking north, nesting white storks shower good luck on farmsteads in Alsace.

Fête de la Musique

Orchestras, crooners, buskers and bands fill streets with free music during France's vibrant nationwide celebration of music on 21 June (www.fetedela musique.culture.fr).

Paris Jazz Festival

No festival better evokes the brilliance of Paris' interwar jazz age than this annual fest (p102) in the Parc de Floral (http://parisjazz festival.paris.fr).

July

If lavender's your French love, now is the time to catch it flowering in Provence. But you won't be the only one. School's out for the summer, showering the country with teems of tourists, traffic and too many *complet* **(full) signs strung in hotel windows.**

Tour de France

The world's most prestigious cycling race (p517) ends on av des Champs-Élysées in Paris on the third or fourth Sunday of July, but you can catch it for two weeks before all over France – the route changes each year but the French Alps are a hot spot (www.letour.fr).

Bastille Day

Join the French in celebrating the storming of the Bastille on 14 July 1789 – countrywide there are firework displays, balls, processions, parades and lots of hoo-ha all round.

Festival d'Avignon

Rouse your inner thespian with Avignon's legendary performing-arts festival (p793) (www.festival-avignon.com). Street acts in its fringe fest are as inspired as those on official stages.

Jazz à Juan

Jive to jazz cats in Juan-les-Pins at this mythical Riviera music fest (p838), which has been around for 50-odd years. Jazz à Juan (www.jazzajuan.fr) commands tickets, but the fringe 'Off' part of the music festival does not.

Festival de Cornouaille

Traditional Celtic music takes over the Breton town of Quimper during this inspiring summer festival (p271) in late July (www.festival-cornouaille.com).

August

It's that mad summer month when the French join everyone else on holiday. Paris, Lyon and other big cities empty; traffic jams at motorway toll booths test the patience of a saint; and temperatures soar. Avoid. Or don your party hat and join the mad crowd!

Celts Unite!

Celtic culture is the focus of the Festival Interceltique de Lorient (p277) (www.festival-interceltique. com), when hundreds of thousands of Celts from Brittany and abroad flock to Lorient to celebrate just that.

September

As sun-plump grapes hang heavy on darkened vines and that August madness drops off as abruptly as it began, a welcome tranquillity falls across autumnal France. This is the start of France's *vendange* (grape harvest).

The Rutting Season

Nothing beats getting up at dawn to watch mating stags, boar and red deer at play. Observatory towers are hidden in woods around Château de Chambord (p372) but when a valley like the Loire is so choc-a-bloc with Renaissance hunting pads, who cares which one?

Braderie de Lille

The mountains of empty mussel shells engulfing the streets after three days of mussel-munching have to be seen to be believed. Then there's the real reason for visiting Lille the first weekend in September – its huge flea market (p176) is Europe's largest.

October

The days become shorter, the last grapes are harvested and the first sweet chestnuts fall from trees. With the changing of the clocks on the last Sunday of the month, there's no denying it's winter.

Nuit Blanche

In one last-ditch attempt to stretch out what's left of summer, Paris museums, monuments, cultural spaces, bars, clubs and so on rock around the clock during Paris' so-called 'White Night' (p102), aka one fabulous long all-nighter!

November

It's nippy now. Toussaint (All Saints' Day) on 1 November ushers in the switch to shorter winter opening hours for many sights. Many restaurants close two nights a week now, making dining out on Monday a challenge in some towns.

Beaujolais Nouveau

At the stroke of midnight on the third Thursday in November the first bottles of cherry-red Beaujolais *nouveau* wine are cracked open – and what a party it can be in Beaujolais, Lyon and other places nearby!

December

Days are short and it's cold everywhere bar the south of France. But there are Christmas school holidays and festive celebrations to bolster sun-deprived souls, not to mention some season-opening winter skiing in the highest-altitude Alpine resorts from mid-December.

Alsatian Christmas Markets

Visitors meander between fairy-light-covered craft stalls, mug of *vin chaud* (warm mulled wine) in gloved hand, at Alsace's traditional pre-Christmas markets.

Fête des Lumières

France's biggest and best light show (p455), on and around 8 December, transforms the streets and squares of Lyon into an open stage (www.lumieres. lyon.fr).

itineraries

Whether you've got five days or 50, these itineraries provide a starting point for a fantastic French trip. Want more inspiration? Head online to lonelyplanet.com/thorntree to chat with other travellers.

10 Days
Essential France

No place screams 'France!' more than **Paris**. Spend two days in the capital, allowing for plenty of time between iconic sights to lounge on cafe terraces, savour long bistro lunches and take romantic strolls along the Seine and Canal St-Martin. Day three, enjoy Renaissance royalty at **Château de Chambord** and **Château de Chenonceau** in the Loire. Or skip this fabled valley, which gives such a fabulous nod to French architecture, and spend two days in Normandy instead, marvelling at **Rouen's** Notre Dame cathedral, the **Bayeux** tapestry, sea-splashed **Mont St-Michel** and – should modern history be your love – the **D-Day landing beaches**.

Day five venture south through the **Bordeaux** wine region, staying overnight in an eco-friendly *chambre d'hôte* in Bordeaux's old wine-merchant quarter and perhaps enrolling in a wine-tasting course at the Maison du Vin de Bordeaux. Then it's a three-hour drive to the walled city of **Carcassonne**, Roman **Nîmes** and the **Pont du Gard**. Finish on the French Riviera with a casino flutter in Grace Kelly's **Monaco**, a portside aperitif in Brigitte Bardot's **St-Tropez** and a stroll around Matisse's **Nice**.

Two Weeks
The Atlantic to the Med

> Step off the boat in **Calais** and be seduced by 40km of cliffs, sand dunes and windy beaches on the spectacular **Côte d'Opale**. Speed southwest, taking in a fish lunch in **Dieppe**, a sensational cathedral visit in **Rouen**, or a picturesque cliffside picnic in **Étretat** en route to your overnight stop: your choice of the pretty Normandy seaside resorts of **Honfleur**, **Deauville** or **Trouville**. Spend two days here exploring: a boat trip beneath the gargantuan and breathtaking Pont de Normandie, shopping for fresh fish and seafood at Trouville's waterfront Poissonnerie, and hobnobbing with Parisians on Deauville's chic star-studded boardwalk are essentials.

Devote day three to Normandy's **D-Day landing beaches**. Start with the Mémorial – Un Musée pour la Paix in **Caen**, the best single museum devoted to the Battle of Normandy and a must-see, then follow a westward arc along the beach-laced coast, taking in the caisson-strewn sands at **Arromanches**, gun installations at **Longues-sur-Mer**, and the now-serene 7km-long stretch of 'bloody **Omaha**'. Come dusk, rejuvenate spent emotions over fresh scallops and *calvados* (apple-flavoured brandy). Or, if art is more your cup of tea, skip the beaches and go for the stunning representation of 11th-century warfare embroidered across 70m of tapestry in **Bayeux**.

Day four and the iconic, postcard-perfect **Mont St-Michel** and its beautiful sandy bay beckon – hiking barefoot across the sands here is an exhilarating experience. End the week in Brittany with a flop in an old-fashioned beach tent in **Dinard** and a bracing stroll on spectacular headlands around **Camaret-sur-Mer**.

Week two begins with a long drive south to chic **La Rochelle** for a lavish seafood feast. Spend a night here, continuing the gourmet theme as you wend your way south through Médoc wine country to **Bordeaux**. Next morning, stop in 'ville rose' **Toulouse** and/or **Carcassonne** before hitting the Med. The **Camargue** – a wetland of flamingos, horses and incredible bird life – is a unique patch of coast to explore and Van Gogh thought so too. Follow in his footsteps around **Arles**, breaking for a gastronomic lunch at L'Atelier or La Chassagnette before continuing on to gritty **Marseille**.

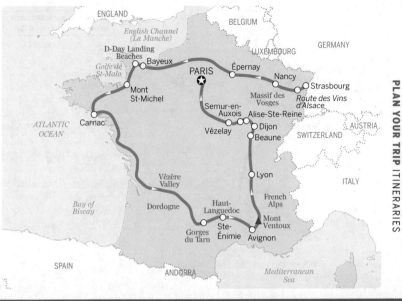

Three Weeks
Tour de France

Get set in **Strasbourg**, ambling around its cathedral and canal-clad Petite France and dining in a traditional *winstub* (tavern). Then move onto greener climes, picking up the **Route des Vins d'Alsace** (Alsace Wine Route) to tipple your way around the **Massif des Vosges** foothills. Keep a clear head for art nouveau architecture in **Nancy**, where at least one night is obligatory in order to enjoy romantic place Stanislas lit after dark. End the week sampling the wares of the Champagne cellars of **Épernay**.

Week two features the pick of Normandy and Brittany: **Bayeux** and its tapestry; Monet's flower-filled garden at **Giverny**; the **D-Day landing beaches**, **Mont St-Michel** and **Carnac** in France's Celtic land of legends. Then zoom south for more prehistory in the form of some of the world's most precious cave art in the **Vézère Valley**. Key sites are around the towns of **Les Eyzies-de-Tayac-Sireuil** and **Montignac**. Or consider **Sarlat-la-Canéda**, showcase to some of France's best medieval architecture, as a base.

The pace hots up in the third week. From the Dordogne, wiggle through **Haut-Languedoc** (Upper Languedoc), not missing the spectacular **Gorges du Tarn**; grab a canoe to drift lazily down its waters in **Ste-Énimie**. Continue southeast to the papal city of **Avignon** with its vast empty palace, vibrant cafe culture and relaxed Provençal air. Slog like a Tour de France cyclist up **Mont Ventoux** for magnificent views of Provence's white stone-capped king of mountains, then speed north to the majestic city of **Lyon**, an unexpected oasis of culture, gastronomy and urban vibe. Should you have another week at hand, a mountain adventure in the **French Alps**, a comfortable two-hour dash from Lyon, is a dandy idea.

The last leg of this ambitious itinerary embraces wine-rich Burgundy: **Beaune**, **Dijon** and **Vézelay** are the obvious desirable places to stop en route to **Paris**. If you're travelling en famile or history-mad, the outstanding **MuséoParc Alésia** – the camp where Julius Caesar defeated Gaulish chief Vercingétorix in 52 BC – near the village of **Alise-Ste-Reine** in the Pays d'Auxois, is well worth the drive from **Dijon** or **Semur-en-Auxois**.

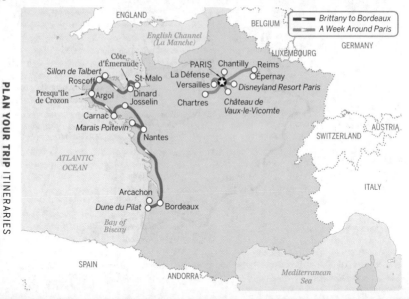

One Week
Brittany to Bordeaux

This trip starts fresh off the boat in **St-Malo**, a walled city with sturdy Vauban ramparts that beg exploration at sunset. Linger at least a day in this gritty port. Walk across at low tide to Île du Grand Bé and lap up great views atop a 14th-century tower in pretty St-Servan. Motor along the **Côte d'Émeraude** the next day, stopping in **Dinard** en route to **Roscoff** 200km west – try to spot local seaweed harvesters around **Sillon de Talbert**. Devote day four to discovering Brittany's famous cider in **Argol** on the **Presqu'île de Crozon**, megaliths around **Carnac**, and a turreted medieval castle in **Josselin**. Push south next along the Atlantic coast, stopping in **Nantes** if you like big cities (and riding mechanical elephants), or continuing to the peaceful waterways of Green Venice, aka the **Marais Poitevin**. **Bordeaux** is your final destination for day six, from where a bevy of Bordeaux wine-tasting trips tempt. End the journey on a high atop Europe's highest sand dune, **Dune du Pilat**, near oyster-famed **Arcachon**.

One Week
A Week Around Paris

Start in **Paris**, from where a journey of magnificent French icons, Renaissance châteaux and sparkling wine unfurls. Day one has to be France's grandest castle, **Château de Versailles**, and its vast gardens. The second day, feast on France's best-preserved medieval basilica and the dazzling blue stained glass in **Chartres**, an easy train ride away. Small-town **Chantilly** is a good spot to combine a laid-back lunch with a Renaissance château, formal French gardens and – if you snagged tickets in advance – an enchanting equestrian performance. Day four, catch the train to elegant **Reims** in the heart of the Champagne region. Scale its cathedral for breathtaking views before tucking into the serious business of Champagne tasting. Dedicated bubbly aficionados can hop the next day to **Épernay**, France's other great Champagne city. On day six enjoy a lazy start then catch an afternoon fountain show at less crowded **Château de Vaux-le-Vicomte**, followed by a candlelit tour of the château. End the week with a look at futuristic **La Défense** or, for those with kids, **Disneyland Resort Paris**.

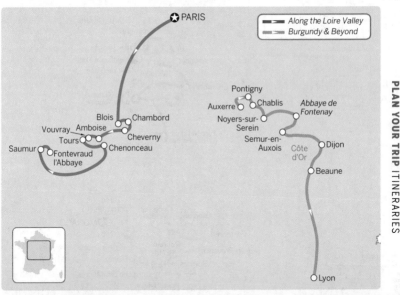

Legend:
- Along the Loire Valley
- Burgundy & Beyond

Five Days
Along the Loire Valley

From France's soulful capital **Paris** head west to its regal surrounds – the magnificent, château-studded Loire Valley. First up is the Unesco-hallmarked city of **Blois**. Day two, make the most of the limited time you have by hooking up with an organised château tour from here: queen of all castles **Château de Chambord** and the charmingly classical **Château de Cheverny**, with its hound-packed kennels, make a great combo. On the third day, continue southwest along France's longest river, the Loire, to **Amboise**, final home of Leonardo da Vinci; and solidly bourgeois **Tours**, from where **Château de Chenonceau**, beautifully strung across the River Cher 34km east, is an easy hop the next morning. If wine is a love, try to build into your itinerary some *dégustation* (tasting) of some local **Vouvray** wines in vineyards east of Tours. End your trip with France's elite riding school in **Saumur** and the movingly simple abbey church of **Fontevraud l'Abbaye**. **Château de Verrières** is a fabulous overnight address in this château-rich neck of the woods.

Six Days
Burgundy & Beyond

Red-wine lovers can enjoy the fruits of Burgundy with this itinerary, which begins in the Roman river-port of **Auxerre**, 170km southeast of Paris. Explore its ancient abbey, Gothic cathedral and cycle along towpaths in the afternoon. On day two consider an easy bike ride to Burgundy's last surviving example of Cistercian architecture in pretty **Pontigny**, 25km north. Stay overnight or push on to nearby **Chablis**, where bags more bike rides and gentle hikes between Burgundy vineyards await – allow plenty of time here to taste the seven *grands crus* of this well-known wine-making town. Day four, meander south to the picture-postcard village of **Noyers-sur-Serein**, then head east to the breathtaking, Unesco-listed **Abbaye de Fontenay**, before winding up for the night in **Semur-en-Auxois**, 25km south. **MuséoParc Alésia**, located where Julius Caesar defeated Gaulish chief Vercingétorix in 52 BC, is not far from here and makes for a fascinating day out . On the last day discover **Dijon** and its beautiful medieval and Renaissance buildings. From here, should you have more time, take a road trip through the winemaking area of **Côte d'Or** to **Beaune**, or south to **Lyon** in the Rhône Valley.

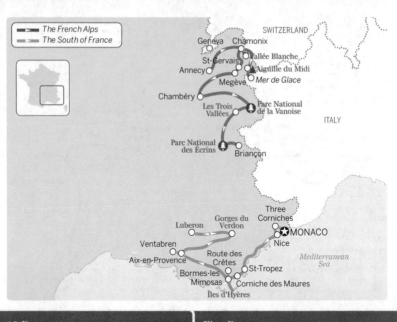

SWITZERLAND

Geneva · Chamonix
St-Gervais · Vallée Blanche
Annecy · Aiguille du Midi
Megève · Mer de Glace
Chambéry
Les Trois Vallées · Parc National de la Vanoise

ITALY

Parc National des Écrins · Briançon

Three Corniches
Luberon · Gorges du Verdon
Ventabren · ☆ MONACO
Aix-en-Provence · Nice
Route des Crêtes · Mediterranean Sea
Bormes-les-Mimosas · St-Tropez
Îles d'Hyères · Corniche des Maures

The French Alps
The South of France

10 Days
The South of France

Hit the country's hot south in **Nice**, star of the coastline that unfurls in an extravagant pageant of belle époque palaces and celebrity sands. Drive along the Riviera's trio of legendary **corniches** – coastal views are mind-blowing – and day three take the train to glitzy **Monaco**. Then move on to the fishing port of **St-Tropez**, where millionaire yachts jostle for space with peddling street artists. Rise early the next morning for the Place des Lices market and frolic away the afternoon on the sand at Plage de Pampelonne. Day six is a toss-up between a dramatic drive along the **Corniche des Maures** to **Bormes-les-Mimosas** and the staggering **Route des Crêtes** mountain pass, or a boat trip to the *très belle* **Îles d'Hyères**. Head inland next to **Aix-en-Provence**, a canvas of graceful 19th-century architecture, stylish cafés and hidden squares; from Aix, a hop and a skip to **Ventabren** for lunch or dinner al fresco at La Table de Ventabren will remind you what eating in Provence is all about. Devote your last two days to the wild **Gorges du Verdon**, Europe's largest canyon, two hour's drive northeast, or the gentler **Luberon**, with its bounty of photogenic hilltop villages.

Five Days
The French Alps

Warm up with some gentle old-town ambling, lakeside strolling and summertime swimming in fairy-tale **Annecy**, just 45km from Geneva, Switzerland. On day, two move on to **Chamonix** at the foot of Mont Blanc, Western Europe's highest peak: ride a cable car to the **Aiguille du Midi** or a train to the **Mer de Glace** glacier, or (in winter) ski the legendary **Vallée Blanche**, off-piste all the way. Yet more unforgettable views of the Mont Blanc massif are cooked up on the ski slopes and hiking trails of **St-Gervais** and **Megève**, chic, picturesque Alpine villages with some exceptional dining addresses to boot – Megève's Flocons de Sel was the only Michelin three-star newbie in 2012. Let the adrenalin rip or push on via **Chambéry** to the **Parc National de la Vanoise**, where spectacular skiing and hiking in **Les Trois Vallées** easily pleases outdoor junkies. A fitting finale to your Alpine foray is the dizzying and staggeringly beautiful drive through **Parc National des Écrins** to **Briançon**, the loveliest of all the medieval villages in the French Alps and famous for its well-preserved Vauban fortifications.

Eat & Drink Like a Local

When to Go
Feasting happens year-round, and the menu changes with the seasons.

Spring
Markets burst with asparagus, artichokes and fresh goat's cheese. Easter cooks up traditional lamb for lunch. The first strawberries turn red.

Summer
Melons, cherries, peaches, apricots, fresh figs, garlic and tomatoes brighten market stalls. Breton shallots are hand-harvested, and on the Atlantic and Mediterranean coasts, food lovers indulge in seafood and shellfish.

Autumn
The Camargue's nutty red rice is harvested. Normandy apples fall from trees to make France's finest cider and the chestnut harvest begins in the Ardèche, Cévennes and Corsica. In damp woods, mushrooming and the game season begins.

Winter
Nets are strung beneath silvery groves in Provence and Corsica to catch olives. Pungent markets in the Dordogne and Provence sell black truffles, and in the Alps skiers dip into cheese fondue. Christmas means Champagne and oysters, foie gras, chestnut-stuffed turkey and yule logs.

Food Experiences
Indulging in the country's extraordinary wealth and variety of gastronomic pleasures is reason alone to travel in France. From north to south, every region safeguards its own unique culinary products and traditions, while dining well is a value shared by all. For more on food and wine, see Bon Appétit (p926) and French Wine (p928).

Dare to Try
» **Andouillette** Big fat sausage made from minced pig intestine; try it in Lyon, France's gastronomic heart and known for its piggy cuisine.

» **Oursins** (sea urchins) Caught and eaten west of Marseille in February.

» **Epoisses de Bourgogne** Create a stink with France's undisputed smelliest cheese from Burgundy.

» **Escargots** (snails) Eat them in Burgundy, shells stuffed with garlic and parsley butter, and oven-baked.

» **Cuisses de grenouilles** (frogs' legs) Catching wild frogs and frog farming has been outlawed in France since 1980, but frogs' legs are imported from Southeast Asia, ensuring that this French culinary tradition is alive and kicking.

» **Foie** (liver) Die-hard afficionados in the Dordogne eat fresh fattened duck or goose liver, raw and chilled, with a glass of sweet Monbazillac wine.

» **Pieds de cochon** (pig trotters) Just that, or go for the oven-baked trotters of a *mouton* (sheep) or *veau* (calf).

Meals of a Lifetime

» **L'Astrance** (p113) Pure, unadulterated gastronomic extravagance in the capital.

» **Restaurant Pierre Reboul** (p777) Aix-en-Provence's latest culinary star.

» **Restaurant Hostellerie de Plaisance** (p634) Twin-star gastronomy in St-Émilion by chef Philippe Etchebest.

» **La Ribaudière** (p621) Michelin-starred cuisine packed with homegrown veggies near Cognac.

» **Les Vieilles Luges** (p483) Dreamy centuries-old Alpine farmhouse in Les Houches, reached only on skis or by foot.

» **L'Essentiel** (p573) Local Dordogne products, including seasonal truffles, in Périgueux.

In the Making

» **Écoles de Treblec** (p286) Crêpe-making school near Rennes in Brittany.

» **Musée du Cidre du Bretagne** (p268) Cider in the making at this stone dairy-turned-*cidrerie* in Argol.

» **Moulin Jean-Marie Cornille** (p790) The olive oil produced at this mill in Les Alpilles is among Provence's best – watch, learn, taste, buy.

» **Confiserie Kerry Aptunion** (p808) Tour the world's largest crystallised fruits factory in Apt.

» **Fromagerie du Mont d'Or** (p529) Arrive with the milk lorry at 9am to see cheese being made in Métabief.

» **Flocons de Sel** (p487) Join the workforce in the swish Alpine kitchen of a Michelin three-star chef in Megève.

» **Ferme Marine** (p257) Visit a Breton oyster farm in Cancale.

Cheap Treats

» **Croque monsieur** Grilled ham and toasted cheese sandwich; cheesey 'madames' are egg-topped.

» **Chestnuts** Served piping hot in paper bags on street corners in winter.

» **Socca** Chickpea-flour pancake typical to Nice, French Riviera.

» **Pan Bagnat** Crusty Niçois tuna sandwich dripping in fruity green olive oil.

» **Flammekueche** (*tarte flambée* in French) Alsatian thin-crust pizza dough topped with sour cream, onions and bacon.

» **Ice cream** by the best *glaciers* in France: Berthillon (p122) in Paris, Fenocchio (p833) in Nice, and Glaces Geronimi (p886) or Raugi (p878) in Corsica. Myrtle, chestnut or lavender ice anyone?

» **Crêpes** Large, round, thin pancakes cooked at street-corner stands while you wait.

Picnic Perfect

» **Baguette** French simplicity at its best: buy a baguette from the *boulangerie* (bakery), stuff it with a chunk of of Camembert, pâté and *cornichons* (miniature gherkins), or a few slices of *rosette de Lyon* or other salami and, *voilà*, picnic perfection! If you're sweet-toothed, do it the French-kid way – wedge a slab of milk chocolate inside.

» **Macarons** No sweeter way to end a gourmet picnic, most famously from Ladurée (p114) in Paris.

» **Kouign amann** The world's most buttery, syrupy cake, aka Breton butter cake.

» Big juicy black **cherries** from Apt, **peaches**, **apricots** and **tomatoes** from the Rhône Valley, Provence and the Riviera.

» **Provençal olives or peppers**, marinated and stuffed with a multitude of edible sins from market stands.

» Alsatian **Kougelhopf** (sugared, ring-shaped raisin cake) and **gingerbread**.

» **Champagne** from Reims and *biscuits roses*.

» Country **pâté**, **walnuts** and **foie gras** from the Dordogne.

Local Specialities

Gourmet appetites know no bounds in France, paradise for food lovers with its varied cuisine, markets and local gusto for dining well. Go to Burgundy for hearty wine-based cooking, Brittany and the Atlantic Coast for seafood, and Basque Country for a slice of Spanish spice.

Normandy

Cream, apples and cider are the essentials of Norman cuisine, which sees mussels simmered in cream and a splash of cider to make *moules à la crème normande* and tripe thrown in the slow pot with cider and vegetables to make *tripes à la mode de Caen*. Creamy Camembert is the local cow's milk cheese, and on the coast *coquilles St-Jacques* (scallops) and *huîtres* (oysters) rule the seafood roost. Apples are the essence of the region's main tipples: tangy cider and the potent apple-brandy *calvados,* exquisite straight or splashed on apple sorbet.

Burgundy

Vine-wealthy Burgundy honours a culinary trinity of beef, red wine and Dijon mustard. Savour bœuf bourguignon (beef marinated and cooked in young red wine with mushrooms, onions, carrots and bacon), followed by the pick of Burgundy AOC (Appellation d'Origine Contrôlée) cheeses. Or eat a snail, traditionally served by the dozen and oven-baked in their shells with butter, garlic and parsley – mop the juices up with bread.

The Dordogne

This southwest region is fabulously famous for its black truffles and poultry, especially ducks and geese, whose fattened livers are turned into *pâté de foie gras* (duck- or goose-liver pâté), which, somewhat predictably, comes straight or flavoured with Cognac and truffles. *Confit de canard* and *confit d'oie* are duck or goose joints cooked very slowly in their own fat. Snails are another tasty treat – savour one stuffed with foie gras.

Lyon

All too often it is dubbed France's gastronomic capital. And while it hardly competes with France's real capital when it comes to sheer variety of international cuisine, it certainly holds its own when it comes to titillating taste buds with the unusual and inventive. Take the age-old repertoire of feisty, often pork-driven dishes served in the city's legendary *bouchons* (small bistros): breaded fried tripe, big fat *andouillettes* (pig-intestine sausage), silk-weaver's brains (a herbed cheese spread, not brains at all) – there is no way you can ever say Lyonnais cuisine is run-of-the-mill. A lighter, less meaty speciality is *quenelle de brochet,* a poached dumpling made of freshwater fish (usually pike) and served with sauce Nantua (a cream and freshwater-crayfish sauce).

Alsace

No Alsatian dish is more classic than *choucroute alsacienne* – sauerkraut flavoured with juniper berries and served hot with sausages, bacon, pork and/or ham knuckle. It's meaty, Teutonic and served in *winstubs* (traditional Alsatian taverns). *Wädele braisé au pinot noir* (ham knuckles braised in wine) also come with sauerkraut. Crack open a bottle of chilled riesling or Alsatian pinot noir to accompany either and round off the filling feast with a *tarte alsacienne,* a scrumptious custard tart made with local fruit like mirabelles (sweet yellow plums) or *quetsches* (a variety of purple plum). Beer is big in Alsace but a big no-no when it comes to sauerkraut. Munster is the cheese to try.

Provence & the Riviera

Cuisine in this sun-baked land is laden with tomatoes, melons, cherries, peaches, olives, Mediterranean fish and Alpine cheese. Farmers gather at the weekly market to sell their fruit and vegetables, olives, woven garlic plaits and dried herbs displayed in stubby coarse sacks. *À la Provençal* still means anything with a generous dose of garlic-seasoned tomatoes; while a simple filet mignon sprinkled with olive oil and rosemary fresh from the garden makes the same magnificent Sunday lunch it did generations ago.

Yet there are exciting culinary contrasts in this region, which see fishermen return with the catch of the day in seafaring Marseille; grazing bulls and paddy fields in the Camargue; lambs in the Alpilles; black truffles in the Vaucluse; cheese made from cow's milk in Alpine pastures; and an Italianate accent to cooking in seaside Nice.

Bouillabaisse, Marseille's mighty meal of fish stew, is Provence's most famous contribution to French cuisine. The chowder must contain at least three kinds of fresh saltwater fish, cooked for about 10 minutes in a broth containing onions, tomatoes, saffron and various herbs, and eaten as a main course with toasted bread and *rouille,* a spicy red mayonnaise of olive oil, garlic and chilli peppers.

Brittany

Brittany is a paradise for seafood-lovers (think lobster, scallops, sea bass, turbot, mussels and oysters from Cancale) and kids, thanks to the humble crêpe and *galette,* an ancient culinary tradition that has long ruled Breton cuisine. Pair a sweet wheat-flour pancake or savoury buckwheat *galette* with *une bolée* (a stubby terracotta goblet) of apple-rich Breton cider, and taste buds enter gourmet heaven.

Cheese is not big, but *la beurre de Bretagne* (Breton butter) is. Traditionally sea-salted and creamy, a knob of it naturally goes into crêpes, *galettes* and the most outrageously buttery cake you're likely to ever taste in your life – *kouign amann* (Breton butter cake). Bretons, unlike the rest of the French, even butter their bread. Butter handmade by Jean-Yves Bourdier – you can buy it at his shop in St-Malo – ends up on tables of top restaurants around the world.

Seaweed is another Breton culinary curiosity, and 80% of French shallots are grown here.

Languedoc-Roussillon

No dish better evokes Languedoc than cassoulet, an earthy cockle-warming stew of white beans and meat that fires passionate debate (and yes, people do eat it in summer too). Everyone knows best which type of bean and meat hunk should be thrown in the *cassole*, the traditional earthenware dish it is cooked and brought to the table in. The version made in Toulouse adds *saucisse de Toulouse*, a fat, mild-tasting pork sausage.

Otherwise this region's trademark cuisine *campagnarde* (country cooking) sees fishermen tend lagoon oyster beds on the coast, olives pressed in gentle hills inland, blue-veined 'king of cheeses' ripening in caves in Roquefort, fattened geese and gaggles of ducks around Toulouse, sheep in salty marsh meadows around Montpellier, and mushrooms in its forests.

A Spanish accent gives the cuisine in neighbouring Roussillon a fiery twist of exuberance.

Basque Country

Among the essential ingredients of Basque cooking are the deep-red Espelette chillies that add bite to many dishes, including the dusting on the signature *jambon de Bayonne,* the locally prepared Bayonne ham. Eating out in this part of France near Spain is a delight thanks to its many casual *pintxo* bars serving garlic prawns, spicy chorizo sausages and other local dishes tapas-style.

Basques love cakes, especially *gâteau basque* (layer cake filled with cream or cherry jam). Then there's Bayonne chocolate...

How to Eat & Drink Like a Local

It pays to know what and how much to eat, and when – adopting the local culinary pace is key to savouring every last exquisite moment of the French day.

When to Eat

» **Petit déjeuner (breakfast)** The French kick-start the day with a *tartine* (slice of baguette smeared with unsalted butter and jam) and *un café* (espresso), long milky *café au lait* or – especially kids – hot chocolate. In hotels you get a real cup but in French homes, coffee and hot chocolate are drunk from a cereal bowl – perfect bread-dunking terrain. Urbanites might grab a coffee and croissant on the way to work, but otherwise croissants (eaten straight, never with butter or jam) are a weekend treat along with brioches (sweet breads), *pains au chocolat* (chocolate-filled croissants) and other *viennoiserie* (sweet baked goods).

» **Déjeuner (lunch)** A meal no French would traditionally go without. The traditional main meal of the day, lunch translates as a starter and main course with wine, followed by a short sharp *café*. Sunday lunch is a long, languid affair when several hours are devoted to enjoying the many courses it entails. Indeed, a fully fledged, traditional French meal – lunch or *dîner* – often comprises six distinct *plats* (courses), each accompanied by a different wine to complement the cuisine. Standard restaurant lunch hours are noon to 2.30pm.

» **Apéritif** Otherwise known as an *apéro,* the pre-meal drink is sacred. Paris cafes and bars get packed out from around 5pm onwards as Parisians wrap up work for the day and relax over a chit-chat-fuelled *kir* or beer. Drinks frequently come with a complimentary ramekin of olives, peanuts or crisps.

» **Dîner (dinner)** Traditionally lighter than lunch, but a meal that is being treated more and more as the main meal of the day. Standard restaurant times are 7pm to 11pm.

Choosing Your Restaurant

» **Auberge** Country inn serving traditional fare, often attached to a B&B or small hotel.

» **Ferme auberge** Working farm that cooks up meals – only dinner usually – from local farm products.

» **Bistro** (also spelled *bistrot*) Anything from a pub or bar with snacks and light meals to a small, fully fledged restaurant.

» **Neobistro** Particularly trendy in the capital where this contemporary take on the traditional bistro embraces everything from checked-tablecloth tradition to contemporary minimalism.

» **Brasserie** Much like a cafe except it serves full meals, drinks and coffee from morning until 11pm or later. Typical fare includes *choucroute* (sauerkraut) and *moules frites* (mussels and fries).

» **Restaurant** Born in Paris in the 18th century, restaurants today serve lunch and dinner five or six days a week.

» **Buffet** (or *buvette*) Kiosk, usually at train stations and airports, selling drinks, filled baguettes and snacks.

» **Cafe** Basic light snacks as well as drinks.

» **Crêperie** (also *galetteries*) Casual address specialising in sweet crêpes and savoury *galettes* (buckwheat crêpes).

» **Salon de Thé** Trendy tearoom often serving light lunches (quiche, salads, cakes, tarts, pies and pastries) as well as black and herbal teas.

» **Table d'hôte** (literally 'host's table') Some of the most charming B&Bs serve *table d'hôte* too, a delicious homemade meal of set courses with little or no choice.

» **Winstub** Cosy wine tavern in Alsace serving traditional Alsatian cooking and local wines.

» **Estaminet** Flemish-style eatery of Flanders and *le nord*, cooking up regional fare.

Menu Advice

» **Carte** Menu, as in the written list of what's cooking, listed in the order you'd eat it: starter, main course, cheese then dessert.

» **Menu** Not at all what it means in English, *le menu* in French is a two- or three-course meal at a fixed price. It's by far the best-value dining there is and most bistros and restaurants chalk one on the board. Lunch *menus* occasionally include a glass of wine and/or coffee, and dinner *menus* in top-end gastronomic restaurants sometimes pair each course with a perfectly matched glass of wine.

» **À la carte** Order whatever you fancy from the menu (as opposed to opting for a fixed menu).

» **Formule** Not to be confused with a *menu*, *une formule* is a cheaper lunchtime option comprising a main plus starter or dessert.

» **Plat du jour** Dish of the day, invariably good value.

» **Menu enfant** Two- or three-course kids' meal (generally up to the age of 12) at a fixed price; usually includes a soft drink.

» **Menu touristique** Good value as it might appear, the dreaded 'tourist *menu*' is a pale reflection of authentic fare consumed by locals.

» **Menu dégustation** Fixed-price tasting *menu* served in many top-end restaurants, consisting of five to seven modestly sized courses.

» **Amuse-bouche** A complimentary savoury morsel intended to excite and ignite tastebuds, served in top-end and gastronomic restaurants at the very beginning of a meal.

» **Entrée** Starter, appetiser.

» **Plat** Main course, fish or meat.

» **Fromage** Cheese, accompanied with fresh bread (never crackers and no butter); always served after the main course and *before* dessert.

» **Dessert** Just that, invariably accompanied by a glass of Champagne when *un gâteau* (a cake).

Etiquette

» **Table reservations** To snag a table in the best addresses, particularly at weekends, booking a table in advance by telephone or by email is essential; try at least a week in advance.

» **Bread** Order a meal and within seconds a basket of fresh bread will be brought to the table. Butter is rarely an accompaniment, and when it is (occasionally in top-end addresses), it will be *doux* (unsalted). Except in the most upmarket of places, don't expect a side plate – simply put it on the table. And yes, in bistros and other casual dines, it is perfectly acceptable to mop up what's left of that delicious sauce on your plate with a bread chunk.

» **Water** Asking for *une carafe d'eau* (jug of tap water) is perfectly acceptable. Should bubbles be more your cup of tea, ask for *de l'eau gazeuze* (some fizzy mineral water). Perrier is the most popular French brand.

» **Coffee** Never end a meal with a cappuccino, *café au lait* or cup of tea, which, incidentally, never comes with milk in France. Go local and order *un café* (espresso).

» **Dress** Smart casual is best, particularly in Paris and chic spots on the French Riviera like St-Tropez and Cannes, where local hipsters dress up to go out for dinner. In provincial towns and most of rural France, anything goes providing you're reasonably well covered. No bikini tops or bare male chests *s'il vous plaît*.

Travel with Children

Which Region?

Not sure which bit of France to visit? Here's our pick of regions and their main appeal.

Paris

Interactive museums, choice dining for every taste and budget, and beautiful green parks at seemingly every turn make the French capital a top choice for families.

Normandy

Beaches, boats and some great stuff for history-mad kids and teens give this northern region plenty of family lure.

Brittany

More beaches, boats, pirate-perfect islands and bags of good old-fashioned outdoor fun.

French Alps & the Jura Mountains

Winter in this mountainous region in western France translates as one giant outdoor (snowy) playground – for all ages. Parents, you can't go wrong.

French Riviera & Monaco

A vibrant arts scene, a vivacious cafe culture and a beach-laced shore filled with seafaring activities keeps kids of all ages on their toes.

Corsica

Sailing, kayaking, walking, biking or simply dipping your toes in clear turquoise waters: life on this island is fairy-tale *belle* (beautiful).

France for Kids

Once in situ there is no stopping the most zealous of sightseeing, activity-driven families from exploring. France has plenty to suit every age and interest. Throughout this book there are bags of ideas on what to do with kids in Paris (p103), Chamonix (p480), the Loire Valley (p361) and on the Atlantic coast (p604).

Savvy parents can find kid appeal in every sight in France, must-sees included. Skip the formal guided tour of Mont St-Michel, for example, and hook up with a walking guide to take you and the kids barefoot across the sand to the abbey; trade the daytime queues at the Eiffel Tower for a tour after dark with teens; don't dismiss wine tasting in Provence or Burgundy outright – rent bicycles and turn it into a family bike ride instead. The opportunities are endless.

Museums & Monuments

It pays to pick the right one. Most Paris museums organise imaginative *ateliers* (workshops) for children, solo and parent-accompanied. Workshops are themed, require advance booking, last 1½ to two hours, and cost €5 to €10 per child. French children have no school Wednesday, meaning most workshops happen Wednesday, weekends and daily during school holidays. Most cater for kids aged seven to 14 years, although in Paris art tours at the Louvre start at four years and at the Musée d'Orsay, five years.

Countrywide, check what activity sheets museums and monuments have when buying admission tickets – most have something to keep kids interested. Another winner is to arm your gadget-mad child (aged from six years) with an audioguide – or street-cool Nintendo 3DS in the case of the Louvre!

Outdoor Activities

Once the kids are out of nappies, skiing in the French Alps is the obvious family choice. Ski school École du Ski Français (p955) initiates kids in the art of snow plough (group or private lessons, half- or full day) from four years old, and many resorts open their fun-driven *jardins de neige* (snow gardens) to kids from three years old. Families with kids aged under 10 will find smaller resorts like Les Gets, Avoriaz (car-free), La Clusaz, Chamrousse and Le Grand Bornand easier to navigate and better value than larger ski stations. Then, of course, there is all the fun of the fair off-piste: ice skating, sledging, snowshoeing and mushing.

The French Alps and Pyrenees are prime walking areas. Tourist offices have information on easy, well-signposted family walks – or get in touch with a local guide. In Chamonix the cable-car ride and two-hour hike to Lac Blanc followed by a dip in the Alpine lake is a DIY family favourite; as are the mountain-discovery half-days for ages three to seven, and outdoor-adventure days for ages eight to 12 run by Cham' Aventure (p481), based inside Chamonix' Maison de la Montagne. As with skiing, smaller places like the Parc Naturel Régional du Massif des Bauges (essentially set up for a local French audience) cater much better to young families than the big names everyone knows.

Invariably as (if not more) entertaining than the final destination is a ride in one of the Alps' many *rémontées mécaniques* (lifts and cable cars). A particularly memorable trip is the mountain train from Chamonix to Montenvers (1913m), from where a cable car whisks adventurers up to France's largest glacier, the Mer de Glace. Both journey and what's at the top – ice cave, crystal gallery and Glaciorium exhibition dedicated to glacial history – captivates young minds every time.

White-water sports and canoeing are doable for children aged seven and older; the French Alps, Provence and Massif Central are key areas. Mountain biking is an outdoor thrill that teens can share – try Morzine. Or dip into some gentle sea-kayaking around *calanques* (deep rocky inlets), below cliffs and into caves in the Mediterranean,

a family activity suitable for kids aged four upwards. Marseille in Provence and Bonifacio on Corsica are hot spots to rent the gear and get afloat.

Entertainment

France's repertoire is impressive: puppet shows al fresco, children's theatres, children's films at cinemas Wednesday afternoon and weekends, street buskers, illuminated monuments after dark, an abundance of music festivals and so on. A sure winner are the *son et lumière* (sound-and-light) shows projected on some Renaissance châteaux in the Loire Valley and cathedral facades in Rouen, Chartres and Amiens. In Paris, weekly entertainment magazine *L'Officiel des Spectacles* is the key to what's on – or ask at tourist offices.

Dining Out

French children, accustomed to three-course lunches at school, expect a starter *(entrée)*, main course *(plat)* and dessert as their main meal of the day. They know the difference between Brie and Camembert, and are quite accustomed to eating green lettuce, grated carrot and other salads as *entrée*. Main meals tend to be meat 'n' veg or pasta, followed by dessert and/or a slice of cheese; many families end with a square of *chocolat noir* (dark chocolate). Classic French mains loved by children include *gratin dauphinois* (sliced potatoes oven-baked in cream), *escalope de veau* (breaded pan-fried veal) and *boeuf bourguignon* (beef stew). Fondue and *raclette* (melted cheese served with potatoes and cold meats) become favourites from about five years, and *moules frites* (mussels and fries) a couple of years later.

Across the board, children's *menus* (fixed meal at a set price) are common, although anyone in France for more than a few days will soon tire of the ubiquitous spaghetti bolognaise or *saucisse* (sausage), or *steak haché* (beef burger) and *frites* (fries) followed by ice cream that most *menus* feature. Don't be shy in asking for a half-portion of an adult main – most restaurants, top-end places included, usually oblige. Ditto in budget and midrange places, where you might ask for a plate of *pâtes au beurre* (pasta with butter) for fussy or very young eaters.

Bread, specifically slices of baguette, accompanies every meal and in restaurants is brought to the table before or immediately after you've ordered – to the glee of children who wolf it down while they wait. Watch for the fight to ensue over who gets the *quignon* (the knobbly end bit, equally a hit with teething babies!).

It is perfectly acceptable to dine *en famille* after dark providing the kids don't run wild. Few restaurants open their doors, however, before 7.30pm or 8pm, making brasseries and cafes – many of which serve food continuously from 7am or 8am until midnight – more appealing for families with younger children. Many restaurants have high chairs and some supply paper and pens for the kids to draw with while waiting for their meal to arrive.

France is fabulous snack-attack terrain. Parisian pavements are rife with crêpe stands and wintertime stalls selling hot chestnuts. Savoury *galettes* (pancakes) make for an easy light lunch, as does France's signature *croque monsieur* (toasted cheese and ham sandwich) served by most cafes and brasseries. *Goûter* (afternoon snack), devoured after school around 4.30pm, is golden for every French child and *salons de thé* (tea rooms) serve a mouth-watering array of cakes, pastries and biscuits. Or go local: buy a baguette, rip off a chunk and pop a slab of chocolate inside. True, really!

Baby requirements are easily met. The choice of infant formula, soy and cow's milk, nappies (diapers) and jarred baby food in supermarkets and pharmacies is similar to any developed country, although opening hours are more limited (few shops open Sunday). Organic *(bio)* baby food is hard to find.

Drinks

Buy a fizzy drink for every child sitting at the table and the bill swiftly soars. Opt instead for a free *carafe d'eau* (jug of tap water) with meals and *un sirop* (flavoured fruit syrup) in between. Every self-respecting cafe and bar in France has dozens of syrup flavours to choose from: pomegranate-fuelled grenadine and pea-green *menthe* (mint) are French-kid favourites, but there are peach, raspberry, cherry, lemon and a rainbow of others to pick from. Syrup is served diluted with water and, best up, costs a good €2 less than a coke. Expect to pay around €1.50 a glass.

Children's Highlights
Gastronomic Experiences

» Afternoon tea to remember at 58 Tour Eiffel or Ladurée, Paris

» Breton crêpes

» Berthillon or Pozzetto icecream, Paris

» Waffles with sweet vanilla cream, served since the 18th century, at Meert tearoom, Lille

» Oysters on an oyster farm, Gujan Mestras, near Bordeaux

» Grape-juice tasting (while parents taste the alcoholic equivalent), La Balance Mets et Vins, Arbois

» Frogs' legs and a lakeside bike ride, La Bicyclette Bleue, La Dombes

» Snail discovery and tasting at Languedoc snail farm-museum, La Caracole, near Alès

» Joining in the chestnut harvest at La Ferme de la Borie, an organic farm in Haut-Languedoc

» Hand-milling mustard seeds with stone at mustard factory Moutarderie Fallot in Beaune

Entertaining Dines

» Pizza picnic with a Pink Flamingo pink balloon, Canal St-Martin, Paris

» Watching noodles be hand-pulled at Les Pâtes Vivantes, Paris

» Digging into a four-course picnic hamper of Breton delicacies from Chez Michel in a favourite city park, Paris

» Dining between frogs – on frogs legs – at Roger la Grenouille, Paris

» Dipping into a cheese fondue or scraping your own *raclette* anywhere in the French Alps

» Filling your own water jug at the 'village fountain' while Corsican music plays at rustic Le 20123, Ajaccio

» Scoffing chocolate soup sprinkled with gingerbread croutons, Bistrot et Chocolat, Strasbourg

Energy Burners

» Skiing, snowboarding, sledging and dog-mushing (over fours), French Alps and Pyrenees

» Scaling Aiguille du Midi by gondola and crossing glaciers into Italy (over fours), Chamonix

» Around an island by bike (over fives) or parent-pulled bike trailer (over ones), Île de Ré and Île de Porquerolles

» White-water sports (over sevens), Gorges du Verdon, Gorges du Tarn and Gorges de l'Ardèche

» Canoeing (over sevens) beneath the Pont du Gard, near Nîmes

» Donkey treks (over 10s) like Robert Louis Stevenson in the wild Cévennes

» Horse-riding with cowboys in the Camargue

Wildlife Watch

» Vultures in Parc National des Pyrénées

» Wolves in Parc National du Mercantour and Parc Animalier des Monts de Guéret

» Whistling marmots in Chamonix

» Sharks at aquariums in Paris, Monaco, Boulogne-sur-Mer, St-Malo, Brest, La Rochelle, Lyon and Biarritz

» Dancing horses in Saumur, Versailles and Chantilly

» Bulls and flamingos in the Camargue

» Storks and kingfishers at Le Teich Parc Ornithologique, near Arcachon, and Alsace's Centre de Réintroduction Cigognes et Loutres

» Fish (through a snorkelling mask) at the Domaine du Rayol and off island shores (Porquerolles, Port-Cros and Corsica)

Rainy Days

» Build a house, Bob-style (over threes), Cité des Sciences, Paris

» Romp through sewage tunnels with rats, Musée des Égouts de Paris

» Create your own perfume at Le Studio des Parfums, Paris

» Ride a house-sized, mechanical elephant (any age), Les Machines de l'Île de Nantes, Nantes

» Ogle at skulls (teens), Les Catacombes, Paris

» Play cave dwellers (any age) in caves riddled with prehistoric art, Vézère Valley

» Delve into the depths of the ocean at Cité de l'Océan, Biarritz

» Learn all about chocolate at Planète Musée du Chocolat, Biarritz

Hi-Tech Experiences

» Discover something new with science-experiment workshops (over 10s) at the Palais de la Découverte, Paris

» Learn how planes are built (over sixes), Jean Luc Lagardère Airbus factory, Toulouse

» Discover V2 rocket technology in a subterranean bunker (teens), La Coupole, St-Omer

» Enter wannabe-mechanic heaven (any age), Cité de l'Automobile and Cité du Train, Mulhouse

» Meddle in science at Strasbourg's interactive Le Vaisseau science and technology museum

» Spin in a fish on a hi-tech vintage carousel or climb aboard a giant mechanical elephant at Les Machines de l'Île de Nantes, Nantes

TOP WEBSITES

» **Familiscope** (www.familiscope.fr) Definitive family-holiday planner: endless activity, outing and entertainment listings.

» **Bienvenue à la Ferme** (www.bienvenue-a-la-ferme.com) Cooking courses, animals, nature activities and accommodation on farms France-wide.

» **Tots to Travel** (http://totstotravel.co.uk) Self-catering properties vetted by a team of trained mums.

» **Baby-friendly Boltholes** (www.babyfriendlyboltholes.co.uk) 'Stylish escapes – perfect for pre-schoolers' is the strapline of this London-based enterprise specialising in sourcing charming and unique family accommodation.

» **Baby Goes 2** (www.babygoes2.com) Why, where, how-to travel guide aimed squarely at families.

» **Mumsnet** (www.mumsnet.com) No question is unanswerable for this UK-based gang of mothers: online discussion, advice, tips, open forum and so on, much of it France-related.

WHAT TO PACK

Babies & Toddlers

» A front or back sling for baby and toddler: France's cobbled streets, metro stairs and hilltop villages were not built with pushchairs (strollers) in mind. Several must-see museums, moreover, notably Château de Versailles, don't let pushchairs in.

» A portable changing mat, handwash gel etc (baby-changing facilities are a rarity)

» A canvas screw-on seat for toddlers (not many restaurants have high chairs)

» Kids' car seats: rental companies rent them but at proportionately extortionate rates. In France children under 10 years or less than 1.40m in height must, by law, be strapped in an appropriate car seat.

Six to 12 Years

» Binoculars for young explorers to zoom in on wildlife, sculpted cathedral facades, stained-glass windows etc

» A pocket video camera to inject fun into 'boring' grown-up activities

» Activity books, sketchpad and pens, travel journal and kid-sized day pack; a water bottle is also handy and great fun to fill up at the many stone-sculpted water fountains found all over France (marked 'eau potable')

» Fold-away microscooter and/or rollerblades if you're doing lots of city walking

» Kite (for beaches, particularly in Brittany, Normandy and on the Atlantic coast where winds blow particularly well)

Teens

» France-related iPhone apps

» French phrasebook

» Mask, snorkel and flippers to dive in from a multitude of magnificent beaches on the Atlantic coast and Med; only two or three marked trails countrywide rent the gear.

Hands-On History & Culture

» Delve behind the scenes of a world-class art museum with a visit to the restoration and storerooms of the groundbreaking Louvre-Lens, northern France

» Pretend you're back in 1920s Paris: chase vintage sailboats with a stick in Jardin du Luxembourg, just like Parisian kids did a century ago

» Relive the battle between Julius Caesar and Vercingétorix at Alésia in 52 BC, with reconstructed Roman fortification lines et al, at Burgundy's first-class MuséoParc Alésia

» Become acquainted with the fine art of perfumerie in Grasse (perfume studios, museum, workshops) and nearby Mouans-Sartoux (flower gardens)

» Play medieval builders at Chantier Médiéval de Guédelon, Burgundy

» Go Roman (over fives) at Ludo, Pont du Gard, near Nîmes

» Watch Victorian-era machines clatter and clank to turn thread into lace at Calais' Cité Internationale de la Dentelle et de la Mode

» Explore the beachfront site of a derelict dynamite factory in Paulilles, Roussillon

Theme Parks

» Cité de l'Espace (outer space), Toulouse

» Disneyland, Paris

» Vulcania (volcanoes), Massif Central

» Le Bioscope (eco-conscious theme park), near Mulhouse

» Futuroscope (film), Poitiers

» Insectopia (insects), Lot Valley

» Micropolis (insects), near Millau, Languedoc

Boat Trips

» Canal boating, Burgundy

» Sailing around caves and pearly-white cliffs, Bonifacio, Corsica

» Sea-kayaking in Les Calanques, Marseille

» River boating aboard a flat-bottomed *gabarre* (barge), Périgord and Lot Valleys

» White-water rafting on green waters in the Gorges du Verdon, Provence

» Ferry trips from Marseille to Château d'If and Îles du Frioul

» Underground river tours inside Gouffre de Padirac, Lot Valley

Planning

From France's kid-friendly extraordinaire capital to its rural hinterland, families are spoilt with a rich mix of cultural sights, activities and entertainment – some paid for, some free. To get the most out of travelling en famille, plan ahead.

When to Go

Consider the season and what you want to do/see: teen travel is a year-round affair (there's always something to entertain, regardless of the weather), but parents travelling with younger kids will find the dry, pleasantly warm days of spring and early summer best suited to kidding around the park – every town has at least one *terrain de jeux* (playground) – and indulging in other energy-burning, outdoor pursuits.

France's fabulous festival repertoire is another planning consideration. Kids of all ages will be particularly enchanted by Avignon's fringe Festival Off, Lyon's Fête des Lumières and the Carnival de Nice – three freebie events worth planning a trip around.

Accommodation

In Paris and larger towns and cities, serviced apartments equipped with washing machine and kitchen are suited to families with younger children. Countrywide, hotels with family or four-person rooms can be hard to find and need booking in advance. Functional, if soulless, chain hotels like Formule 1, found on the outskirts of most large towns, always have a generous quota of family rooms and make convenient overnight stops for motorists driving from continental Europe or the UK (Troyes is a popular stopover for Brits en route to the Alps). Parents with just one child and/or a baby in tow will have no problem finding hotel accommodation – most midrange hotels have baby cots and are happy to put a child's bed in a double room for a minimal extra cost.

In rural France, family-friendly B&Bs and *fermes auberges* (farmstays), some of which cook up tasty evening meals, are the way to go. Or what about a hip baby-and-toddler house party in a château in Burgundy or a chalet retreat in the French Alps? For older children, tree houses decked out with bunk beds and Mongolian yurts create a real family adventure; see the Accommodation section of the Directory A–Z (p952) for more.

Camping is huge with French families: check into a self-catering mobile home, wooden chalet or family tent; sit back on the verandah with glass of wine in hand and watch as your kids – wonderfully oblivious to any barriers language might pose – run around with new-found French friends. Campgrounds require booking well in advance, especially during high season.

regions at a glance

Paris

Food ✓✓✓
Art ✓✓✓
Shopping ✓✓✓

Bistro Dining
Tables are jammed tight, chairs spill onto busy pavements outside, dishes of the day are chalked on the blackboard and cuisine is simple and delicious. Such is the timeless joy of bistro dining in the capital.

Museums & Galleries
All the great masters star in Paris' priceless portfolio of museums. Not all the booty is stashed inside: buildings, metro stations, parks and other public art give *Mona* a good run for her money.

Fashion & Flea Markets
Luxury fashion houses, edgy boutiques, Left Bank designer-vintage and Europe's largest flea market: Paris really is the last word in fabulous shopping.

p50

Around Paris

Châteaux ✓✓✓
Cathedrals ✓✓
Green Spaces ✓

A Taste of Royalty
Château de Versailles – vast, opulent and *very* shimmery – has to be seen to be believed. Fontainebleau, Chantilly and Vaux-le-Vicomte are other fabled addresses in French royalty's little black book.

Sacred Architecture
The other heavyweight near Paris is Chartres' cathedral, one of Western architecture's greatest achievements, with stained glass in awesome blue.

Paris' Lungs
Parisians take air in thick forests outside the city: Forêt de Fontainebleau, an old royal hunting ground, is a hot spot for rock climbing and family walks. Chantilly means manicured French gardens and upper-class horse racing.

p148

Lille, Flanders & the Somme

Architecture ✓✓
History ✓✓✓
Coastline ✓✓✓

Flemish Style
Breaking for a glass of strong local beer between old-town meanders around extravagant Flemish Renaissance buildings is a highlight of northern France. Lille and Arras are the cities to target.

Gothic to WWI
Amiens evokes serene contemplation inside one of France's most awe-inspiring Gothic cathedrals, and emotional encounters in WWI cemeteries.

Coastal Capers
Hiking along the Côte d'Opale – a wind-buffeted area of white cliffs, gold sand and ever-changing sea and sky – is dramatic and beautiful, as is a Baie de Somme bicycle ride past lounging seals.

p166

Normandy

Food ✓✓
Coastline ✓✓✓
Battlefields ✓✓✓

Calvados & Camembert
This coastal chunk of northern France is a pastoral land of butter and soft cheeses. Its exotic fruits: Camembert, cider, fiery apple brandy and super-fresh seafood.

Cliffs & Coves
Chalk-white cliff to dune-lined beach, rock spire to pebble cove, coastal path to tide-splashed island-abbey Mont St-Michel: few coastlines are as inspiring.

D-Day Beaches
Normandy has long played a pivotal role in European history. But it was during WWII's D-Day landings that Normandy leaped to global importance. Museums, memorials, cemeteries and endless stretches of soft golden sand evoke that dramatic day in 1944.

p204

Brittany

Food ✓✓
Walking ✓✓✓
Islands ✓✓

Crêpes & Cider
These two Breton culinary staples are no secret but who cares? Devouring caramel-doused buckwheat pancakes in the company of homemade cider is a big reason to visit Brittany.

Wild Hikes
With its wild dramatic coastline, islands, medieval towns and thick forests laced in Celtic lore and legend, this proud and fiercely independent region promises exhilarating walks.

Breton Beauties
Brittany's much-loved islands, dotted with black sheep and crossed with craggy coastal paths and windswept cycling tracks, are big draws. Don't miss dramatic Île d'Ouessant or the very aptly named Belle Île.

p245

Champagne

Champagne ✓✓✓
Walking ✓✓
Drives ✓✓✓

Bubbly Tasting
Gawp at a Champagne panorama from atop Reims' cathedral then zoom in close with serious tasting at the world's most prestigious Champagne houses in Reims and Épernay.

Vineyard Trails
Nothing quite fulfils the French dream like easy day hikes through neat rows of vineyards, exquisite picture-postcard villages bedecked in flowers and a gold-stone riverside hamlet right out of a Renoir painting.

Majestic Motoring
No routes are more geared to motorists and cyclists than the Champagne Routes, fabulously picturesque and well-signposted driving itineraries taking in the region's wealthy winemaking villages, hillside vines and traditional cellars.

p289

Alsace & Lorraine

Battlefields ✓✓✓
City Life ✓✓
Villages ✓✓✓

Emotional Journeys
Surveying the dazzling symmetry of crosses on the Verdun battlefields is painful. Memorials, museums, cemeteries, forts and an ossuary mark out the emotional journey.

Urban Icons
With the sublime (Strasbourg's cathedral) to the space-age (Centre Pompidou in Metz), this northeast chunk of France steals urbanite hearts with its city squares, architecture, museums and Alsatian dining.

Chocolate-box Villages
There is no lovelier way of getting acquainted with this part of France than travelling from hilltop castles to stork-nest-blessed farms to half-timbered villages framed by vines.

p311

The Loire Valley

Châteaux ✓✓✓
History ✓✓✓
Cycling ✓✓

Royal Architecture

Endowed with dazzling structural and decorative gems from medieval to Renaissance and beyond, the Loire's lavish châteaux sweep most visitors off their feet.

Tempestuous Tales

This region is a dramatic story teller: through spectacular castles, fortresses, apocalyptic tapestries and court paintings, the gore and glory, political intrigue and sex scandals of medieval and Renaissance France fabulously unfold.

Riverside Trails

The River Loire is France's longest, best-decorated river. Pedalling riverside along the flat from château to château is one of the valley's great joys.

p360

Burgundy

Wine ✓✓✓
History ✓✓✓
Activities ✓✓

Reds & Whites

Mooch between vines and old-stone villages along Burgundy's *grand cru* wine route. But this region is not just about Côte d'Or reds. Taste whites in Chablis and Mâcon.

Medieval History

Nowhere is Burgundy's past as one of medieval Europe's mightiest states evoked more keenly than in the dashingly handsome capital Dijon. Complete the medieval history tour with abbeys Cluny and Cîteaux.

Great Outdoors

Hiking and biking past vineyards or cruising in a canal boat is the good life. Pedal the towpath to gloriously medieval Abbaye de Fontenay, open a bottle of Chablis and savour the best of Burgundy.

p401

Lyon & the Rhône Valley

Food ✓✓✓
Roman Sites ✓✓
Cycling ✓

Famous Flavours

No city in France excites taste buds more than Lyon. Savour local specialities in a checked-tableclothed *bouchon* (Lyonnais bistro).

Roman Remains

Not content with lavishing two majestic amphitheatres on Lyon (catch a concert al fresco after dark during Les Nuits de Fourvière – magical!), the Romans gifted the Rhône Valley with a third in jazz-famed Vienne.

Two-wheel Touring

Pedalling between vineyards in Beaujolais country or around frog-filled lakes swamped with bird life in La Dombes is one of life's simple pleasures.

p444

French Alps & the Jura Mountains

Food ✓✓
Outdoors ✓✓✓
Farmstays ✓✓✓

Culture & Cuisine

Fondue is the tip of the culinary iceberg in this Alpine region, where cow's milk flavours dozens of cheeses. Around chic Lake Annecy, chefs woo with wild herbs and lake perch.

Adrenalin Rush

Crowned by Mont Blanc (4810m), the French Alps show no mercy in their insanely challenging ski trails and mountain-bike descents. Did we mention Europe's longest black downhill piste?

Back to Nature

Feel the humble rhythm of the land with an overnight stay on a farm. Bottle-feed calves, collect the eggs, have breakfast in a fragrant garden or before a wood-burning stove, and feel right at home.

p471

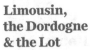

Massif Central

Volcanoes ✓✓✓
Architecture ✓
Outdoors ✓✓✓

Volcanoes
The last one erupted in 5000 BC but their presence is still evident: mineral waters bubble up from volcanic springs in Vichy and Volvic; volcanic stone paints Clermont-Ferrand black and there's the razzmatazz of Vulcania.

Belle Époque
A string of early 20th-century spa towns including Vichy add understated elegance to this region's otherwise deeply provincial bow.

Hiking & Skiing
Walking is the best way to explore this unique landscape – an uncanny, grass-green moonscape of giant molehills crossed with trails. Then there are the little-known ski slopes of Le Mont-Dore.

p531

Limousin, the Dordogne & the Lot

Food ✓✓✓
Hilltop Towns ✓✓
Cruises ✓✓✓

Mouth-watering Markets
Black truffles, foie gras and walnuts... Gourmets, eat your heart out in this fertile part of central and southwest France, where the fruits of the land are piled high at a bevy of atmospheric weekly markets.

Mighty *Bastides*
Not only is Dordogne's prized collection of fortified 13th-century towns and villages a joy to explore, valley views from the top of these clifftop *bastides* are uplifting. Start with Monpazier and Domme.

Meandering Waterways
Be it aboard a canoe, raft or flat-bottomed *gabarre* (barge), cruising quietly along the region's rivers is an invitation to see *la belle France* at her most serene.

p555

Atlantic Coast

Port Towns ✓✓
Wine ✓✓✓
Activities ✓✓✓

Sea View
Hip dining rendez-vous in an old banana-ripening warehouse in Nantes, limestone arcades and islands in La Rochelle, and brilliant art museums in wine-rich Bordeaux.

Wonderful Wines
France's largest winegrowing region, Bordeaux encompasses the Médoc with its magnificent châteaux and medieval hamlet of St-Émilion. The wine (and Cognac) is wonderful.

Rural Retreats
Paddling emerald-green waterways in the Marais Poitevin, pedalling sun-baked Île de Ré and wandering between weathered, wooden oyster shacks in Arcachon Bay is what this tranquil region is all about – slowing the pace right down.

p603

French Basque Country

Food ✓✓
Activities ✓✓✓
Culture ✓✓✓

Culture & Cuisine
This exuberant region beneath the mist-soaked Pyrenees evokes Spain with its fiestas, bullfights, traditional *pelota* (ball games), tapas and famous Bayonne ham.

Surf's Up
Riding waves in the glitzy beach resort of Biarritz or on surfer beaches in Les Landes is good reason to visit this sun-slicked coastal region, snug in France's most southwestern corner.

A Timeless Pilgrimage
For centuries pilgrims have made their way across France to the quaint walled town of St-Jean Pied de Port, just across the border from Santiago de Compostela in Spain. Do the same, on foot or by bicycle.

p638

The Pyrenees

Outdoors ✓✓✓
Scenery ✓✓✓
History ✓✓

Adrenalin Rush

Make Parc National des Pyrénées your playground. Vigorous hikes to lofty heights, good-value downhill skiing and racy white-water sports will leave you wanting more.

Jaw-dropping Views

France's last wilderness has rare flora and fauna, snow-kissed peaks, vulture-specked skies, waterfalls and lakes. Top views include those from Pic du Jer, Pic du Midi, Lescun, Cirque de Gavarnie, Lac de Gaube and pretty much every valley going.

Rare & Holy Cities

That same elegance that saw well-to-do 19th-century English and Americans winter in Pau still attracts guests today. Then there is sacred Lourdes, a provincial pilgrim city.

p665

Toulouse Area

Food ✓✓
History ✓✓✓
Cruises ✓✓

Cassoulet & Armagnac

Try Emile restaurant for Toulouse's best cassoulet, though this classic bean-stew dish simmers on the stove in most kitchens. Begin the experience with an aperitif and end with an Armagnac brandy.

Towns with Tales

Red-brick Toulouse's historic mansions, quintessential fortified town Montauban, Gothic Albi, Moissac's Romanesque abbey: this compact region is packed with historical tales and historic architecture.

Canal du Midi

Pop a cork out of a bottle of Vin de Pays d'Oc and savour the go-slow, lush-green loveliness of the Canal du Midi. Stroll or pedal its towpaths, soak in a spa or simply rent a canal boat and drift.

p686

Languedoc-Roussillon

Culture ✓✓
Roman Sites ✓✓
Activities ✓✓

So Near Spain

Roussillon is a hot, dusty, lively region, long part of Catalonia at the eastern end of the Pyrenees. Celebrate a traditional fiesta in Perpignan, or modern art and *sardane* folk dances in Céret.

Aqueducts & Amphitheatres

Nîmes' amphitheatre and the gracefully arched Pont du Gard are two of the Roman Empire's best-preserved sites.

Footpaths & Waterways

Try canoeing beneath the Pont du Gard, biking towpaths to Carcassonne, boating the Canal du Midi, climbing up to Cathar fortresses, donkey trekking in the Cévennes or hiking gorges in Haut-Languedoc (Upper Languedoc).

p708

Provence

Food ✓✓✓
Villages ✓✓✓
Modern Art ✓✓✓

Eating & Drinking

Sip pastis over *pétanque*, spend all evening savouring *bouillabaisse* (fish stew), mingle over buckets of herbs and marinated olives at the market, hunt truffles, and taste Bandol reds and Côtes de Provence rosé.

Sensual Sauntering

Travelling *à la Provençal* is a sensual journey past scented lavender fields and chestnut forests, through apple-green vineyards and silvery olive groves, around markets, chapels and medieval villages perched on rocky crags.

Avant-garde

Provence is an art museum and has the roll-call to prove it: Matisse, Renoir, Picasso, Cézanne, Van Gogh and Signac all painted and lived here.

p756

The French Riviera & Monaco

Resorts ✓✓✓
Glamour ✓✓✓
Coastline ✓✓✓

Coastal Queen
Urban grit, old-world opulence, art that moves and a seaside promenade everyone loves – Nice, queen of the French Riviera, will always be belle of the seaside ball.

Party Time
Enjoy the Riviera high life: trail film stars in Cannes, see Formula One meet high society in Monaco, guzzle champers in St-Tropez, frolic in famous footsteps on sandy beaches, dine between priceless art, dance til dawn...

Magnificent Scenery
With its glistening sea, idyllic beaches and coastal paths, this part of the Med coast begs wonderful walks. Cicadas sing on Cap Ferrat, while the sun turns the Massif de l'Estérel brilliant red.

p822

Corsica

Coast Roads ✓✓✓
Hiking ✓✓
Boat Trips ✓✓✓

Postcard Home
Corsican coastal towns are impossibly picturesque – alley-woven Bastia, celeb-loved Île Rousse, chichi Calvi – but it's the hair-raising coastal roads that wend their way past medieval Genoese watchtowers and big blue views that scream 'Send a postcard home!'.

Great Outdoors
Hiking high-altitude mountain trails once the preserve of bandits and *bergers* (shepherds) is a trail-junkie favourite, as are the cliff-hanging Gorges de Spelunca and pink, ochre and ginger Les Calanques de Piana.

The Big Blue
Nowhere does the Med seem bluer. Hop on deck in Porto, Bonifacio, Calvi or Porto-Vecchio for a boat excursion or view sapphire waters while diving and snorkelling.

p872

> **Every listing is recommended by our authors, and their favourite places are listed first**

> **Look out for these icons:**

 Our author's top recommendation

 A green or sustainable option

FREE No payment required

See the Index for a full list of destinations covered in this book.

On the Road

Paris

Includes »

Best Places to Eat

» Septime (p66)
» Au Passage (p120)
» L'AOC (p122)
» Derrière (p121)
» Bouillon Racine (p126)

Best Places to Stay

» Hôtel Crayon (p104)
» Le Pradey (p104)
» Mama Shelter (p107)
» L'Hôtel (p111)
» Hôtel Particulier Montmartre (p106)

Why Go

In the springtime, the fall, the winter (when it drizzles) or the summer (when it sizzles!), to paraphrase Cole Porter, France's romanticised capital seduces every moment of the year.

No matter the season, Paris has a timeless familiarity, with more recognisable landmarks than any other city. The wrought-iron Eiffel Tower, the Arc de Triomphe standing sentinel above the Champs-Élysées, ethereal Notre Dame, lamplit bridges spanning the Seine, art nouveau cafes spilling onto wicker-chair-lined terraces, and graceful parks, gardens and esplanades: they are indelibly etched in the minds of anyone who's visited – and the imaginations of anyone who hasn't (yet).

Equally alluring is Paris' fabulous food – from cosy neighbourhood bistros through to triple-Michelin-starred temples to gastronomy, and from scrumptious patisseries, *boulangeries* (bakeries) and *fromageries* (cheese shops) to heady street markets – as well as its stylish shopping and its priceless artistic treasures, showcased in incomparable museums.

When to Go

Paris

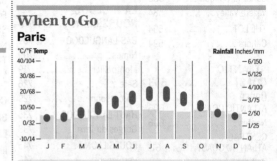

Jun & Jul Concerts every Saturday and Sunday afternoon during the Paris Jazz Festival.

Mid-Jul–mid-Aug The Seine's riverbanks become a sandy beach with sunbeds, parasols and palm trees.

Oct Museums, bars and more stay open all night during Nuit Blanche.

Cooking & Wine-Tasting Courses

If dining in the city's sublime restaurants whets your appetite, there are stacks of cookery schools (p101) – from famous institutions to private Parisian homes – offering courses that suit all abilities, itineraries and pockets. Many courses include shopping and market visits.

Where there's food in France, wine is never more than an arm's length away, and plenty of places in the capital offer wine tastings and instruction for all schedules, levels and budgets.

Some cooking and wine-tasting courses (p101) are run in English, while those that are in French usually offer at least some level of English translation; confirm language requirements when you book.

FOR FIRST-TIMERS

The pinch-yourself panorama from place de la Concorde – taking in the Tuileries, the length of av des Champs-Élysées to the Arc de Triomphe, and the Eiffel Tower – is an unforgettable introduction to the French capital, as is the view from the Palais de Chaillot's terrace across the Jardins du Trocadéro to the tower (especially when it's sparkling at night).

The tower is also an ideal spot to board a river cruise (or the hop-on, hop-off Batobus) along the Seine, and float past Parisian landmarks like the Louvre and Notre Dame.

Other vantage points perfect for acquainting yourself with the city include the rooftops of the Centre Pompidou cultural centre and the art nouveau department store Galeries Lafayette, as well as the steps of Sacré-Cœur basilica.

Top Five Signature Splurges

» Flit between flagship *haute couture* (high fashion) houses in the Triangle d'Or (Golden Triangle; bordered by avs Georges V, Champs-Élysées and Montaigne), St-Germain's storied shops, and emerging designers in the Haut Marais (p137).

» Feast on *baiser Ladurée* (layered almond cake with strawberries and cream) at Champs-Élysées patisserie Ladurée (p60).

» Concoct your own personal fragrance at Le Studio des Parfums (p142).

» Sip a decadent hot chocolate at *salon de thé* (tea room) Angelina (p129).

» Spend an evening at Paris' oldest and most palatial opera house, the Palais Garnier (p137).

ARRONDISSE-MENTS

Paris is spit into 20 *arrondissements* (districts), and addresses always include the *arrondissement* number – 1er for *premier* (1st), 2e for *deuxième* (2nd), 3e for *troisième* (3rd) etc.

Fast Facts

» **Population** 2.2 million
» **Area** 105 sq km
» **Hotel overnights/year** 35.7 million
» **Signature drink** France's finest are all here; don't miss a Bloody Mary from its inventor, Harry's New York Bar.

Need to Know

Most museums close Monday, but some, including the Louvre and Centre Pompidou, close Tuesday instead.

Resources

» Paris Info (www.parisinfo.com)
» Secrets of Paris (www.secretsofparis.com)
» Paris By Mouth (http://parisbymouth.com)
» My Little Paris (www.mylittleparis.com)

Paris Highlights

1 Indulge in an exquisitely Parisian moment in the sculpture-filled gardens of the **Musée Rodin** (p41).

2 Listen to a classical music concert in the sublime stained-glass surrounds of **Ste-Chapelle** (p82).

3 Sip a *café crème* on the terrace of famous literary cafe **Les Deux Magots** (p132).

4 Stroll through Parisian history at the **Musée Carnavalet** (p77), secreted in two sumptuous Marais mansions.

5 Marvel at Monet's extraordinary *Water Lilies* at the **Musée de l'Orangerie** (p69).

6 Pay your respects to the rich, famous and infamous at **Cimetière du Père Lachaise** (p75).

7 Relive the *ooh là là* Paris of cancan and windmills on a **Montmartre** walking tour (p90).

8 Join Parisians at play in the city's most popular park, the **Jardin du Luxembourg** (p99).

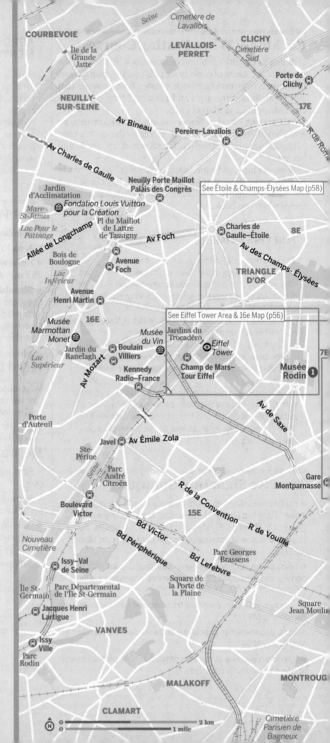

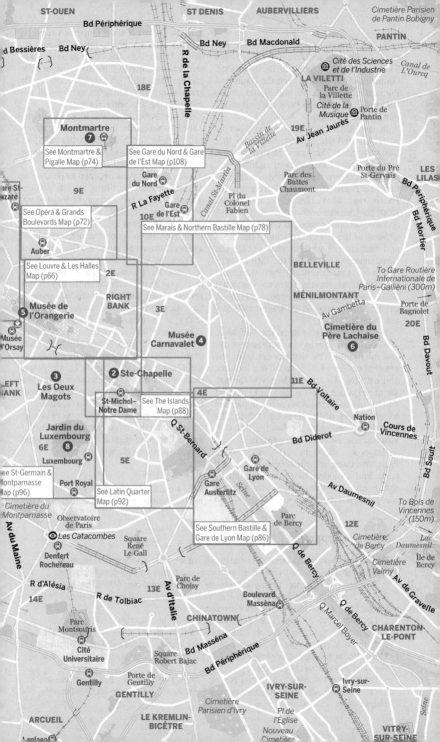

History

Paris was born in the Seine in the 3rd century BC, when the Parisii tribe of Celtic Gauls settled on what is now the Île de la Cité. Centuries of conflict between the Gauls and Romans ended in 52 BC, and in 508 Frankish king Clovis I made Paris the seat of his united Gaul kingdom.

In the 9th century France was beset by Scandinavian Vikings. In the centuries that followed, these 'Norsemen' started pushing towards Paris, which had risen rapidly in importance. Construction had begun on the cathedral of Notre Dame in the 12th century, the Louvre was built as a riverside fortress around 1200, Ste-Chapelle was consecrated in 1248 and the Sorbonne opened its doors in 1253.

Many of the city's most famous buildings and monuments were erected during the Renaissance at the end of the 15th century. But in less than a century, Paris was again in turmoil, as clashes between Huguenot (Protestant) and Catholic groups increased, culminating in the St Bartholomew's Day massacre in 1572.

Louis XIV, also known as the Sun King, ascended the throne in 1643 at the age of five and ruled until 1715, virtually emptying the national coffers with his ambitious building and battling. His greatest legacy is the palace at Versailles. The excesses of Louis XVI and his queen, Marie Antoinette, in part led to an uprising of Parisians on 14 July 1789 and the storming of the Bastille prison – kick-starting the French Revolution.

Emperor Napoleon III 'modernised' Paris, installing wide boulevards, sculpted parks and a modern sewer system, but he also became involved in a costly and unsuccessful war with Prussia in 1870. When Parisians heard of their emperor's capture, they demanded a republic. Despite its bloody beginnings, the Third Republic ushered in the glittering, highly creative belle époque (beautiful age), celebrated for its graceful art nouveau architecture and advances in the arts and sciences.

By the 1930s, Paris was a centre for the artistic avant-garde, but the movement was cut short by the Nazi occupation of 1940. Paris was liberated in 1944 by an Allied force spearheaded by Free French units.

After the war, Paris regained its position as a creative centre, nurturing a revitalised liberalism that reached a climax in the student-led uprisings of 1968. The Sorbonne was occupied, the Latin Quarter barricaded and some nine million people nationwide joined a general strike that paralysed the country.

From the latter half of the 20th century on, France's presidents have made their mark on the cityscape by initiating *grands projets* (great projects or works), such as the Mitterand-instigated book-shaped Bibliothèque Nationale de France (national library) and the city's second opera house, Opéra Bastille, and Chirac's Musée du Quai Branly. Sarkozy's national history museum, the Maison de l'Histoire de France (www.maison-histoire.fr), is due to open in the Marais in 2016. Stay tuned, too, for initiatives by current French president François Hollande.

In 2001 Bertrand Delanoë, a socialist with support from the Green Party, became Paris' – and a European capital's – first openly gay mayor. He was re-elected in 2008.

⊙ Sights

Paris straddles the Seine fairly evenly. In this book, neighbourhoods start with the one sur-

---

ⓘ IT'S FREE

Permanent collections at most city-run museums are free, including the Maison de Victor Hugo and the Musée Carnavalet. Temporary exhibitions usually command a fee.

Admission to national museums is reduced for those aged over 60 and between 18 and 25, and completely free for EU residents under 26 years and anyone under 18 years, so don't buy a Paris Museums Pass if you qualify.

National museums are also free for everyone on the first Sunday of each month. These include: the Louvre, the Musée National d'Art Moderne in the Pompidou, Musée de l'Orangerie, Musée du Quai Branly, Musée d'Orsay, Musée Guimet des Arts Asiatiques, Musée Rodin, Musée National du Moyen Âge, Cité de l'Architecture et du Patrimoine and the Musée des Arts et Métiers.

Ditto for the following, except they're only free the first Sunday of the month November to March: Arc de Triomphe, Conciergerie, Panthéon, Ste-Chapelle and the Tours de Notre Dame.

DON'T MISS

MUSÉE MARMOTTAN MONET

Housed in the duc de Valmy's former hunting lodge (well, let's call it a mansion), the intimate Musée Marmottan Monet (☎01 44 96 50 33; www.marmottan.com; 2 rue Louis Boilly, 16e; adult/7-25yr €10/5; ⊙10am-6pm Tue-Sun, to 9pm Thu; MLa Muette) houses the world's largest collection of Monet paintings and sketches. It provides an interesting if patchy cross-section of his work, beginning with paintings such as the seminal *Impression Soleil Levant* (1873) and *Promenade près d'Argenteuil* (1875), passing through numerous water-lily studies, before moving on to the rest of the collection, which is considerably more abstract and dates to the early 1900s. Some of the masterpieces to look out for include: *La Barque* (1887), *Cathédrale de Rouen* (1892), *Londres, le Parlement* (1901) and the various *Nymphéas* – many of which were smaller studies for the works now on display in the Musée de l'Orangerie (p19).

Also on display are a handful of canvases by Renoir, Pissarro, Gauguin and Morisot, and a collection of 15th- and 16th-century illuminations, which are quite lovely if somewhat out of place.

rounding the city's most famous sight, the Eiffel Tower, and move clockwise around the Right Bank to the Islands and the Left Bank.

EIFFEL TOWER AREA & 16E

Paris' iconic spire is surrounded by open areas on both banks of the Seine, which take in both the 7e and 16e. Both are home to *very* well-heeled Parisians and some outstanding museums.

Eiffel Tower   LANDMARK
(Map p56; ☎01 44 11 23 23; www.tour-eiffel.fr; lift to 3rd fl adult/12-24yr/4-12yr €14/12.50/9.50, lift to 2nd fl €8.50/7/4, stairs to 2nd fl €5/3.50/3; ⊙lifts & stairs 9am-midnight mid-Jun–Aug, lifts 9.30am-11pm, stairs 9.30am-6pm Sep–mid-June; MBir Hakeim or RER Champ de Mars–Tour Eiffel) No one could imagine Paris today without its signature spire. But Gustave Eiffel only constructed this graceful tower – the world's tallest, at 320m, until it was eclipsed by Manhattan's Chrysler Building some four decades later – as a temporary exhibit for the 1889 Exposition Universelle (World Fair). Luckily, the tower's popularity assured its survival beyond the fair, and its elegant art nouveau webbed-metal design has become the defining fixture of the city's skyline.

Lifts/elevators yo-yo up and down the north, west and east pillars to the tower's three platforms (57m, 115m and 276m); change lifts on the 2nd level for the final ascent to the top, from where views extend up to 60km. (There's wheelchair access to the 1st and 2nd levels.) If you're feeling athletic, you can take the south pillar's 1665 stairs as far as the 2nd level. Prebook tickets online to avoid monumentally long ticket queues.

Refreshment options in the tower include the 1st-level 58 Tour Eiffel (p114), the sublime 2nd-level Le Jules Verne, and, at the top, the new Bar à Champagne.

Palais de Chaillot   PALACE
(Map p56; 17 place du Trocadéro et du 11 Novembre, 16e; MTrocadéro) The two curved, colonnaded wings of the Palais de Chaillot, built for the 1937 Exposition Universelle, and the terrace in between them afford an exceptional panorama of the Jardins du Trocadéro (named after a Spanish stronghold near Cádiz captured by the French in 1823), the Seine and the Eiffel Tower.

In the palace's eastern wing is the standout Cité de l'Architecture et du Patrimoine (Map p56; www.citechaillot.fr; 1 place du Trocadéro et du 11 Novembre, 16e; adult/18-25yr/under 18yr €8/5/free; ⊙11am-7pm Wed-Mon, to 9pm Thu; MTrocadéro), a mammoth 23,000 sq metres of space spread over three floors and devoted to French architecture and heritage. The highlight is the light-filled ground floor, which contains a beautiful collection of 350 plaster and wood *moulages* (casts) of cathedral portals, columns and gargoyles, and replicas of murals and stained glass originally created for the 1878 Exposition Universelle. The views of the Eiffel Tower from the windows are equally monumental.

In the western wing are two other museums. The Musée de la Marine (Maritime Museum; Map p56; www.musee-marine.fr; 17 place du Trocadéro et du 11 Novembre, 16e; adult/18-25yr/under 18yr €7/5/free; ⊙11am-6pm Wed-Mon, to 7pm Sat & Sun; MTrocadéro), to the right of the main entrance, examines France's naval adventures from the 17th century to today and has

Eiffel Tower Area & 16e

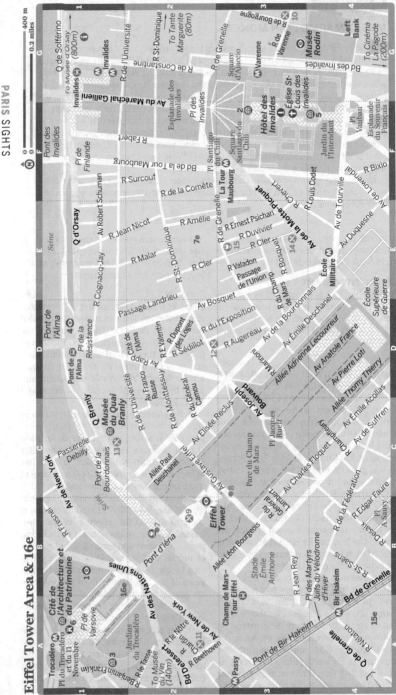

400 m
0.2 miles

one of the world's finest collections of model ships, as well as ancient figureheads, compasses, sextants, telescopes and paintings.

The Musée de l'Homme (Museum of Humankind; Map p56; www.mnhn.fr), focuses on human development, ethnology and population growth. It is closed for renovations until 2015.

Cinéaqua   AQUARIUM
(Map p56; www.cineaqua.com; av des Nations Unies, 16e; adult/child €20/13; ⊙10am-7pm; MTrocadéro) On the eastern side of the Jardins du Trocadéro is Paris' largest aquarium. It's a decent rainy-day destination for families, with a shark tank and some 500 species of fish on display. There are also, somewhat oddly, three cinemas inside (only one of which shows ocean-related films); non-French-speaking kids will need to be able to read subtitles, as almost everything is dubbed in French.

Eiffel Tower Area & 16e

Musée du Quai Branly   ART MUSEUM
(Map p56; www.quaibranly.fr; 37 quai Branly, 7e; adult/child €8.50/free; ⊙11am-7pm Tue, Wed & Sun, to 9pm Thu-Sat; MAlma-Marceau or RER Pont de l'Alma) No other museum in Paris provides such inspiration for travellers, armchair anthropologists and those who simply appreciate the beauty of traditional craftsmanship. A tribute to the incredible diversity of human culture, the Musée du Quai Branly, which opened in 2006, presents an overview of indigenous and folk art from around the world.

Divided into four main sections – Oceania, Asia, Africa and the Americas – the museum showcases an impressive array of masks, carvings, weapons, jewellery and more, all displayed in a refreshingly unique interior without rooms or high walls. Be sure to check out the temporary exhibits and performances, both of which are generally excellent.

Musée des Égouts de Paris   SEWERS
(Map p56; place de la Résistance, 7e; adult/child €4.20/3.40; ⊙11am-5pm Sat-Wed May-Sep, to 4pm Sat-Wed Oct-Dec & Feb-Apr; MAlma Marceau or RER Pont de l'Alma) Raw sewage flows beneath your feet as you walk through 480m of odoriferous tunnels in this working sewer museum. Exhibitions cover the development of Paris' waste-water disposal system, including its resident rates (an estimated one sewer rat for every Parisian above ground). Enter via a rectangular maintenance hole topped with a kiosk across the street from 93 quai d'Orsay, 7e.

The sewers keep regular hours except – God forbid – when rain threatens to flood the tunnels. Toy rats are sold at its gift shop.

ÉTOILE & CHAMPS-ÉLYSÉES

A dozen avenues radiate out from place de l'Étoile (officially called place Charles de Gaulle). First among them is av des Champs-Élysées. This broad boulevard, the name of which refers to the 'Elysian Fields' ('heaven' in Greek mythology), links place de la Concorde with the Arc de Triomphe. To its north, rue du Faubourg St-Honoré (8e), the western extension of rue St-Honoré, is home to renowned couture houses, jewellers, antique shops and the 18th-century Palais de l'Élysée, official residence of the French president.

Arc de Triomphe   LANDMARK
(Map p58; www.monuments-nationaux.fr; place Charles de Gaulle; adult/18-25yr €9.50/6; ⊙10am-10.30pm, to 11pm Apr-Sep; MCharles de

Étoile & Champs-Élysées

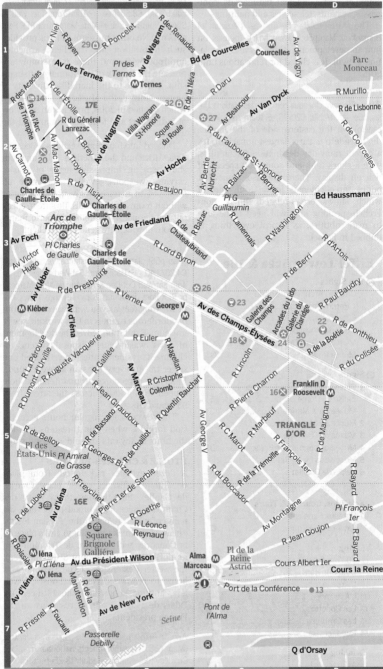

Av N'iel
R Bayen
29
R Poncelet
R des Renaudes
Bd de Courcelles
Courcelles
Av de Vigny
Parc Monceau

Av des Ternes
Pl des Ternes
Av de Wagram
Ternes
R Daru
R de la Néva
R Murillo
R de Lisbonne

R des Acacias
14
R de l'Étoile
17E
Villa Wagram St-Honoré
32
R de la Néva
27
Av Van Dyck
R de Courcelles

R de l'Arc de Triomphe
R du Général Lanrezac
Square du Roule
R du Faubourg St-Honoré
R Beaucour

Av Carnot
20
Av Mac Mahon
R Brey
R Troyon
Av de Wagram
Av Hoche
Av Bertie Albrecht
R Balzac
R Berryer
Bd Haussmann

Charles de Gaulle–Étoile
R de Tilsitt
R Beaujon
Pl G Guillaumin
R Balzac
R Lamennais
R Washington
R d'Artois

Arc de Triomphe
Charles de Gaulle–Étoile
Av de Friedland
R de Chateaubriand

Av Foch
Pl Charles de Gaulle
Charles de Gaulle–Étoile
R Lord Byron
R de Berri

Av Victor Hugo
R de Presbourg
26
Galerie des Champs
R Paul Baudry

Av Kléber
R Yernet
George V
23
Galerie du Lido
Arcades du Lido
22
R de Ponthieu

Kléber
Av d'Iéna
Av des Champs-Élysées
18
24
30
R de la Boétie
R du Colisée

R La Pérouse
R Galilée
R Euler
R Magellan
R Lincoln
R Pierre Charron
Franklin D Roosevelt
16
R de Marignan

R Dumont d'Urville
R Auguste Vacquerie
R Jean Giraudoux
Av Marceau
R Cristophe Colomb
R Quentin Bauchart
R C Marot
R Marbeuf
TRIANGLE D'OR
R François 1er

R de Belloy
R de Bassano
R Georges Bizet
Av George V
R du Boccador
R de la Trémoille
R Bayard

Pl des États-Unis
Pl Amiral de Grasse
R Goethe
Pl François 1er

R de Lübeck
Av d'Iéna
16E
R Freycinet
Av Pierre 1er de Serbie
R Léonce Reynaud
Av Montaigne
R Jean Goujon
R Bayard

3
7
6
Square Brignole Galliéra
Av du Président Wilson
9
Alma Marceau
Pl de la Reine Astrid
Cours Albert 1er
Cours la Reine

Iéna
Pl d'Iéna
Iéna
R de la Manutention
Av de New York
2
Port de la Conférence
13

Av d'Iéna
R Fresnel
R Foucault
Seine
Pont de l'Alma
Q d'Orsay

Passerelle Debilly

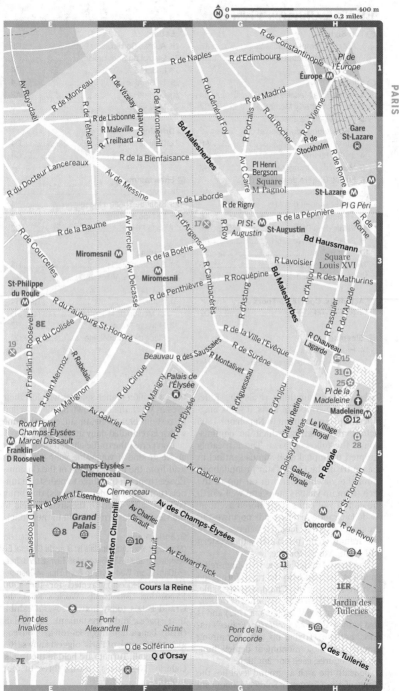

N 0 ———————— 400 m
0 ———————— 0.2 miles

R de Constantinople
R de Naples
R d'Edimbourg
Pl de l'Europe
Europe M
Av Ruysdael
R de Monceau
R de Vézelay
R de Téhéran
R de Lisbonne
R Maleville
R Treilhard
R Corvetto
R de Miromesnil
R du Général Foy
R de Madrid
R Portalis
R du Rocher
R de Vienne
Bd Malesherbes
Gare St-Lazare
R de Stockholm
R de la Bienfaisance
R du Docteur Lancereaux
Av de Messine
Av C Caire
Pl Henri Bergson
Square M Pagnol
R de Rome
M
St-Lazare M
R de Laborde
R de Rigny
Pl G Péri
R de la Baume
Av Percier
R d'Argenson
17 ✕
Pl St-Augustin
R Roy
M
St-Augustin
R de la Pépinière
R de Rome
Miromesnil M
R de la Boétie
Av Delcassé
R Cambacérès
R Lavoisier
Square Louis XVI
Bd Haussmann
R de Courcelles
Miromesnil M
R de Penthièvre
R Roquépine
Bd Malesherbes
R des Mathurins
R d'Anjou
St-Philippe du Roule M
R du Faubourg St-Honoré
R d'Astorg
R de la Ville l'Evêque
R Pasquier
R de l'Arcade
8E
R du Colisée
Pl Beauvau
R des Saussaies
R de Surène
R Chauveau Lagarde
📋**15**
19 ✕
Av Franklin D Roosevelt
R Jean Mermoz
R Rabelais
R du Cirque
R de Marigny
Palais de l'Élysée 🏛
R Montalivet
R d'Aguesseau
R d'Anjou
31 🏨
25 ☆
Pl de la Madeleine 🛈 **1**
Madeleine M
📷**12**
Rond Point Champs-Élysées M Marcel Dassault
Franklin D Roosevelt
Av Gabriel
Av de Marigny
R de l'Élysée
Cité du Retiro
Le Village Royal
28
Av Franklin D Roosevelt
Champs-Élysées – Clemenceau M
Pl Clemenceau
Av Gabriel
R Boissy d'Anglas
Galerie Royale
R Royale
R St-Florentin
Av du Général Eisenhower
Av des Champs-Élysées
Concorde M
R de Rivoli
Grand Palais 🏛
🏛**8**
Av Charles Girault
🏛**10**
Av Dutuit
📷**11**
🏛**4**
21 ✕
Av Edward Tuck
1ER
Cours la Reine
Jardin des Tuileries
Pont des Invalides
Pont Alexandre III
Seine
Pont de la Concorde
🏛**5**
Q des Tuileries
7E
Q de Solférino
Q d'Orsay

Étoile & Champs-Élysées

Gaulle–Étoile) If anything rivals the Eiffel Tower as the symbol of Paris, it's this magnificent 1836 monument to Napoleon's 1805 victory at Austerlitz, which he commissioned the following year. The intricately sculpted triumphal arch stands sentinel in the centre of the Étoile ('star') roundabout. From the viewing platform on top of the arch (50m up via 284 steps and well worth the climb) you can see the dozen avenues. Av de la Grande Armée heads northwest to the skyscraper district of La Défense, where the Grande Arche (p150) marks the western end of the Axe Historique.

The most famous of the four high-relief panels at the base is to the right, facing the arch from the av des Champs-Élysées side. It's entitled *Départ des Volontaires de 1792* (Departure of the Volunteers of 1792) and is also known as *La Marseillaise* (France's national anthem). Higher up, a frieze running around the whole monument depicts hundreds of figures, each one 2m high.

Beneath the arch at ground level lies the Tomb of the Unknown Soldier. Honouring the 1.3 million French soldiers who lost their lives in WWI, the Unknown Soldier was laid to rest in 1921, beneath an eternal flame which is rekindled daily at 6.30pm.

Don't cross the traffic-choked roundabout above ground if you value your life! Stairs lead from the northern side of the Champs-Élysées beneath the Étoile to pedestrian tunnels (not linked to metro tunnels) that bring you out safely beneath the arch. Tickets to the viewing platform are sold in the tunnel.

Grand Palais GALLERY
(Map p58; www.grandpalais.fr; 3 av du Général Eisenhower; adult/13-25yr/under 13yr €12/8/free; ☺10am-10pm Wed-Mon, to 8pm Thu; Ⓜ Champs-Élysées-Clemenceau) Erected for the 1900 Exposition Universelle (World's Fair), the Grand Palais today houses several exhibition spaces and a restaurant, Minipalais (p115), beneath its huge 8.5-ton art nouveau glass roof. Some of Paris' biggest shows (Renoir, Chagall, Turner) are held in the Palais' Galeries Nationales, lasting three to four months.

Other exhibition spaces include the imaginative Nef – which plays host to concerts, art installations, a seasonal amusement park and horse shows – and several other minor galleries. Renovations are ongoing, and the monument will continue to develop its layout in the coming years, though it will remain open. Hours, prices and exhibition dates vary significantly for all galleries. Those listed here generally apply to the Galeries Nationales, but be sure to always check the website for exact details. Reserving a ticket online for any show is strongly advised.

FREE **Petit Palais** ART MUSEUM
(Map p58; www.petitpalais.paris.fr; av Winston Churchill; permanent collections free; ☉10am-6pm Tue-Sun; ⓜChamps-Élysées-Clemenceau) Like the Grand Palais, this architectural stunner was also built for the 1900 Exposition Universelle, and is home to the Paris municipality's Museum of Fine Arts. It specialises in medieval and Renaissance objets d'art such as porcelain and clocks, tapestries, drawings and 19th-century French painting and sculpture. There are also paintings here by such artists as Rembrandt, Colbert and Cézanne.

Palais de la Découverte SCIENCE MUSEUM
(Map p58; www.palais-decouverte.fr; av Franklin D Roosevelt, 8e; adult/senior & 6-25yr/under 6yr €8/6/free; ☉9.30am-6pm Tue-Sat, 10am-7pm Sun; ⓜChamps-Élysées-Clemenceau) Attached to the Grand Palais, this children's science museum has excellent temporary exhibits (eg moving lifelike dinosaurs) as well as a hands-on, interactive permanent collection focusing on astronomy, biology, physics and the like. Some of the older exhibits have French-only explanations, but overall this is a dependable family outing.

Palais de Tokyo ART MUSEUM
(Map p58; www.palaisdetokyo.com; 13 av du Président Wilson, 16e; adult/18-25yr/under 18yr €8/6/free; ☉noon-midnight Tue-Sun; ⓜléna) The Tokyo Palace, created for the 1937 Exposition Universelle and now a contemporary-art space, has no permanent collection. Instead, its shell-like interior of polished concrete and steel is the stark backdrop for rotating, interactive art installations: the rooftop, for example, has been the setting for attention-getting projects like the transient Hotel Everland and the see-through restaurant Nomiya. Exhibition space was tripled in 2012.

Musée Guimet des Arts Asiatiques ART MUSEUM
(Map p58; www.museeguimet.fr; 6 place d'Iéna, 16e; adult/18-25yr/child €7.50/5.50/free; ☉10am-6pm Wed-Mon; ⓜléna) France's foremost Asian art museum has a superb collection of sculptures, paintings and religious articles that originated in the vast stretch of land between Afghanistan and Japan. It's possible to observe the gradual transmission of both Buddhism and artistic styles along the Silk Road in some of the museum's pieces, from the 1st-century Gandhara Buddhas from Afghanistan and Pakistan to the later Central Asian, Chinese and Japanese Buddhist sculptures and art.

Part of the collection, comprised of Buddhist paintings and sculptures, is housed in the nearby **Galeries du Panthéon Bouddhique du Japon et de la Chine** (Map p58; 19 av d'Iéna, 16e). Don't miss the wonderful **Japanese garden** here.

Place de la Concorde CITY SQUARE
(Map p58; ⓜConcorde) With is majestic vistas in just about every direction – the Arc de Triomphe, the Assemblée Nationale (the lower house of Parliament) and even a rare swath of open sky above – place de la Concorde is one of Paris' most impressive squares. It was first laid out in 1755 and originally named after King Louis XV, but its associations with royalty meant that it would go on to take centre stage during the Revolution.

Louis XVI was the first to be guillotined here in 1793; during the next two years, 1343 more people, including Marie Antoinette, Danton and Robespierre, lost their heads here as well. The square was given its present name after the Reign of Terror in the hope that it would become a place of

---

ⓘ **PARIS MUSEUM PASS**

The **Paris Museum Pass** (www.paris museumpass.fr; 2/4/6 days €39/54/69) is valid for entry to over 60 museums and monuments in and around Paris – including the Louvre, Centre Pompidou, Musée d'Orsay and parts of the châteaux at Versailles and Fontainebleau. Buy the pass online, at participating venues, Paris Convention & Visitors Bureau branches, Fnac outlets, RATP information desks and major metro stations.

peace and harmony. In the centre, atop the site of one of the former guillotines, stands a 3300-year-old Egyptian obelisk engraved with hieroglyphics. It originally stood in the Temple of Ramses at Thebes (now Luxor) and was presented to France in 1831. The corners of the square are marked by eight statues representing what were once the largest cities in France.

Place de la Madeleine   CITY SQUARE

(Map p58; M Madeleine) Ringed by fine-food shops, place de la Madeleine is named after the 19th-century neoclassical church at its centre, the Église de la Madeleine (Church of St Mary Magdalene; Map p58; www.eglise-lamadeleine.com; ⊙9.30am-7pm). Constructed in the style of a massive Greek temple, what is now simply called 'La Madeleine' was consecrated in 1842 after almost a century of design changes and construction delays.

The monumental staircase on the south side affords one of the city's most quintessential Parisian panoramas: down rue Royale to place de la Concorde and its obelisk and across the Seine to the Assemblée Nationale. The gold dome of the Invalides appears in the background.

The church is a popular venue for classical music concerts (some free); check the posters outside or the website for dates.

La Pinacothèque   ART MUSEUM

(Map p72; www.pinacotheque.com; 28 place de la Madeleine, 8e; adult/12-25yr/under 12yr €10/8/free; ⊙10.30am-6pm daily, to 9pm Wed & Fri; M Madeleine) The top private museum in Paris, La Pinacothèque organises three to four major exhibitions per year. Its nonlinear approach to art history – with shows that range from exhibitions of Mayan masks to retrospectives of artists such as Edvard Munch – has shaken up the otherwise rigid Paris art world and won over residents who are used to more formal presentations elsewhere.

Flame of Liberty Memorial   MEMORIAL

(Map p58; place de l'Alma; M Alma-Marceau) This bronze sculpture, a replica of the one topping the Statue of Liberty, was placed here in 1987 on the centenary of the launch of the *International Herald Tribune*, as a symbol of friendship between France and the USA.

The sculpture is located on the place de l'Alma, near the end of the Pont de l'Alma bridge. On 31 August 1997 in the place d'Alma underpass, Diana, Princess of Wales,

---

WORTH A TRIP

BOIS DE BOULOGNE

On Paris' western edge, the 845-hectare Bois de Boulogne (bd Maillot; M Porte Maillot) owes its informal layout to Baron Haussmann, who planted 400,000 trees here in the 19th century. Along with various gardens and attractions, the park has 15km of cycle paths and 28km of bridle paths through 125 hectares of forested land.

Be warned that the area becomes a distinctly adult playground after dark, especially along the Allée de Longchamp running northeast from the Étang des Réservoirs (Reservoirs Pond), where all kinds of prostitutes cruise for clients.

Vélib' stations are found near most of the park entrances, but not within the park itself; Paris Cycles (✆01 47 47 76 50; per hr €5; ⊙10am-7pm mid-Apr-mid-Oct) rents bikes. Rowing boats (per hr €15; ⊙10am-6pm mid-Mar–mid-Oct; M Av Henri Martin) can be hired at Lac Inférieur, the largest of the Bois' lakes and ponds.

Families with young kids flock to amusement park Jardin d'Acclimatation (www.jardindacclimatation.fr; av du Mahatma Gandhi; admission €2.90, activity tickets €2.90, under 3yr free; ⊙10am-7pm Apr-Sep, to 6pm Oct-Mar; M Les Sablons), with puppet shows, boat rides, a small water park, pony rides, art exhibits and sometimes special movies. Most activities cost extra (on top of the admission price).

The Bois de Boulogne is home to the Roland Garros (www.billetterie.fft.fr; 2 av Gordon Bennett, Bois de Boulogne; M Porte d'Auteuil) stadium, home to the French Open. The world's most extravagant tennis museum, the Tenniseum-Musée de Roland Garros (www.fft.fr; 2 av Gordon Bennett; adult/child €7.50/4, with stadium visit €15/10; ⊙10am-6pm Tue-Sun; M Porte d'Auteuil), traces the sport's 500-year history through paintings, sculptures and posters. Tours of the stadium take place at 11am and 3pm in English; reservations are required.

Designed by Frank Gehry, the fine arts centre Fondation Louis Vuitton pour la Création (www.fondationlouisvuitton.fr) was under construction at the time of writing.

was killed in a devastating car accident along with her companion, Dodi Fayed, and their chauffeur, Henri Paul.

Musée Galliera de la Mode de la Ville de Paris FASHION MUSEUM
(Map p58; www.galliera.paris.fr; 10 av Pierre 1er de Serbie, 16e; ◷10am-6pm Tue-Sun; Ⓜléna) Paris' Fashion Museum has been undergoing renovations but should be open by the time you read this.

LOUVRE & LES HALLES
Louis VI created *halles* (markets) for merchants who converged on the city centre to sell their wares, and for over 800 years they were, in the words of Émile Zola, the 'belly of Paris'. Although the wholesalers moved out to the suburb of Rungis in 1971 (and were replaced by the soulless subterranean shopping mall Forum des Halles, currently undergoing a much-anticipated makeover), the markets' spirit lives on here. To the southwest is the world's mightiest museum, the Louvre.

Musée du Louvre ART MUSEUM
(Map p66; ☎01 40 20 53 17; www.louvre.fr; rue de Rivoli & quai des Tuileries, 1er; permanent/temporary collection €11/12, both €15, under 18yr free; ◷9am-6pm Mon, Thu, Sat & Sun, to 9.45pm Wed & Fri; ⓂPalais Royal–Musée du Louvre) The vast Palais du Louvre was constructed as a fortress by Philippe-Auguste in the early 13th century and rebuilt in the mid-16th century as a royal residence. The Revolutionary Convention turned it into a national museum in 1793.

The paintings, sculptures and artefacts on display in the Louvre Museum have been amassed by subsequent French governments. Among them are works of art and artisanship from all over Europe and collections of Assyrian, Etruscan, Greek, Coptic and Islamic art and antiquities. The Louvre's *raison d'être* is essentially to present Western art from the Middle Ages to about 1848 (at which point the Musée d'Orsay takes over), as well as works from ancient civilisations that formed the starting point for Western art.

When the museum opened in the late 18th century it contained 2500 paintings and objets d'art; today some 35,000 are on display. The 'Grand Louvre' project inaugurated by the late President Mitterrand in 1989 doubled the museum's exhibition space, and both new and renovated galleries have opened in recent years devoted to objets d'art such as the crown jewels of Louis XV (Room 66, 1st floor, Apollo Gallery, Denon

Wing). Late 2012 saw the opening of the new Islamic art galleries in the restored Cour Visconti, topped with an elegant, shimmering gold 'flying carpet' roof designed by Italian architects Mario Bellini and Rudy Ricciotti.

The richness and sheer size of the place (the south side facing the Seine is 700m long and it's estimated it would take nine months just to *glance* at every work) can be overwhelming. However, there's an array of innovative, entertaining self-guided thematic trails (1½ to three hours; download trail brochures in advance from the website) ranging from a Louvre masterpieces trail to the art of eating, plus several for kids (hunt lions, galloping horses). Equally entertaining are the Louvre's new, self-paced multimedia guides (€5). More-formal, English-language guided tours (☑reservations 01 40 20 51 77; ◷11am & 2pm Wed-Mon except 1st Sun of month) depart from the Hall Napoléon, which also has free English-language maps.

For many, the star attraction is Leonardo da Vinci's *La Joconde*, better known as *Mona Lisa* (Room 6, 1st floor, Denon Wing). The most famous works from antiquity include the *Seated Scribe* (Room 22, 1st floor, Sully Wing), the *Code of Hammurabi* (Room 3, ground floor, Richelieu Wing) and that armless duo, the *Venus de Milo* (Room 16, ground floor, Sully Wing) and the *Winged Victory of Samothrace* (top of Daru staircase, 1st floor, Denon Wing). From the Renaissance, don't miss Michelangelo's *The Dying Slave* (Room 4, ground floor, Denon Wing) and works by Raphael, Botticelli and Titian (1st floor, Denon Wing). French masterpieces of the 19th century include Ingres' *The Turkish Bath* (off Room 60, 2nd floor, Sully Wing), Géricault's *The Raft of the Medusa* (Room 77, 1st floor, Denon Wing) and works by Corot, Delacroix and Fragonard (2nd floor, Sully Wing).

The main entrance and ticket windows are covered by the 21m-high Grande Pyramide (Map p66; place du Louvre), a glass pyramid designed by the Chinese-born American architect IM Pei. You can avoid the queues outside the pyramid or at the Porte des Lions entrance by entering the Louvre complex via the underground shopping centre Carrousel du Louvre, at 99 rue de Rivoli.

Buy your tickets in advance from the ticket machines in the Carrousel du Louvre, by phoning 08 92 68 46 94 or 01 41 57 32 28 or from the *billeteries* (ticket offices) of Fnac

Continued on p68

The Louvre

A HALF-DAY TOUR

Successfully visiting the Louvre is a fine art. Its complex labyrinth of galleries and staircases spiralling three wings and four floors renders discovery a snakes-and-ladders experience. Initiate yourself with this three-hour itinerary – a playful mix of *Mona Lisa* obvious and up-to-the-minute unexpected.

Arriving by the stunning main entrance, pick up colour-coded floor plans at the lower-ground-floor **information desk 1** beneath IM Pei's glass pyramid, ride the escalator up to the Sully Wing and swap passport for multimedia guide (there are limited descriptions in the galleries) at the wing entrance.

The Louvre is as much about spectacular architecture as masterly art. To appreciate this zip up and down Sully's Escalier Henri II to admire **Venus de Milo 2**, then up parallel Escalier Henri IV to the palatial displays in **Cour Khorsabad 3**. Cross room 1 to find the escalator up to the 1st floor and staircase-as-art **L'Esprit d'Escalier 4**. Next traverse 25 consecutive galleries (thank you, floor plan!) to flip conventional contemplation on its head with Cy Twombly's **The Ceiling 5**, and the hypnotic **Winged Victory of Samothrace sculpture 6** – just two rooms away – which brazenly insists on being admired from all angles. End with the impossibly famous **The Raft of Medusa 7**, **Mona Lisa 8** and **Virgin & Child 9**.

Mission Mona Lisa

If you just want to venerate the Louvre's most famous lady, use the Porte des Lions entrance (closed Tuesday and Friday), from where it's a five-minute walk. Go up one flight of stairs and through rooms 26, 14 and 13 to the Grande Galerie and adjoining room 6.

L'Esprit d'Escalier
Escalier Lefuel, Richelieu
Discover the 'Spirit of the Staircase' through François Morel-let's contemporary stained glass, which casts new light on old stone. DETOUR» Napoleon III's gorgeous gilt apartments.

Rue de Rivoli Entrance

Jardin du Carrousel

Galerie du Carrousel Entrances

Porte des Lions Entrance

The Raft of the Medusa
Room 77, 1st Floor, Denon
Decipher the politics behind French romanticism in Théodore Géricault's *Raft of the Medusa*.

TERRY SMITH IMAGES/ALAMY ©

TOP TIPS

» **Floor Plans** Don't even consider entering the Louvre's maze of galleries without a *Plan/Information Louvre* brochure, free from the information desk in the Hall Napoléon

» **Crowd dodgers** The Denon Wing is always packed; visit on late nights Wednesday or Friday or trade Denon in for the notably quieter Richelieu Wing

» **2nd floor** Not for first-timers: save its more specialist works for subsequent visits

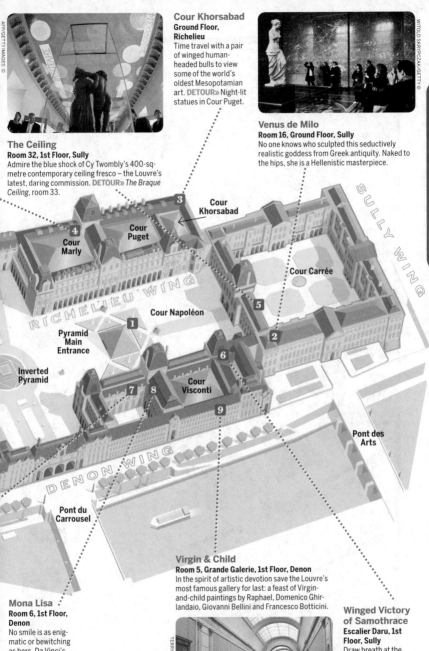

Cour Khorsabad
Ground Floor, Richelieu
Time travel with a pair of winged human-headed bulls to view some of the world's oldest Mesopotamian art. DETOUR» Night-lit statues in Cour Puget.

Venus de Milo
Room 16, Ground Floor, Sully
No one knows who sculpted this seductively realistic goddess from Greek antiquity. Naked to the hips, she is a Hellenistic masterpiece.

The Ceiling
Room 32, 1st Floor, Sully
Admire the blue shock of Cy Twombly's 400-sq-metre contemporary ceiling fresco – the Louvre's latest, daring commission. DETOUR» *The Braque Ceiling*, room 33.

Virgin & Child
Room 5, Grande Galerie, 1st Floor, Denon
In the spirit of artistic devotion save the Louvre's most famous gallery for last: a feast of Virgin-and-child paintings by Raphael, Domenico Ghirlandaio, Giovanni Bellini and Francesco Botticini.

Mona Lisa
Room 6, 1st Floor, Denon
No smile is as enigmatic or bewitching as hers. Da Vinci's diminutive *La Joconde* hangs opposite the largest painting in the Louvre – sumptuous, fellow Italian Renaissance artwork *The Wedding at Cana*.

Winged Victory of Samothrace
Escalier Daru, 1st Floor, Sully
Draw breath at the aggressive dynamism of this headless, handless Hellenistic goddess. DETOUR» The razzle-dazzle of the Apollo Gallery's crown jewels.

Louvre & Les Halles

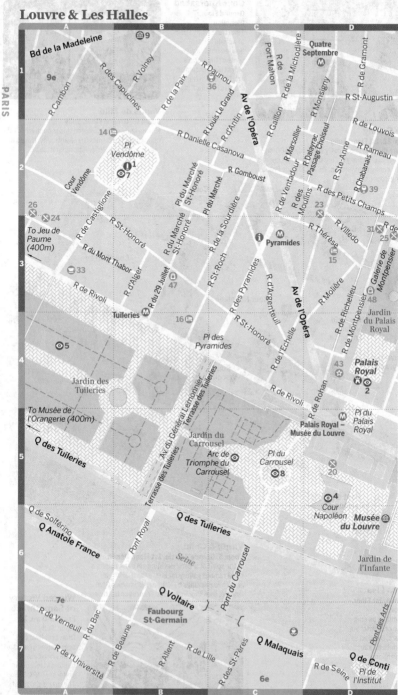

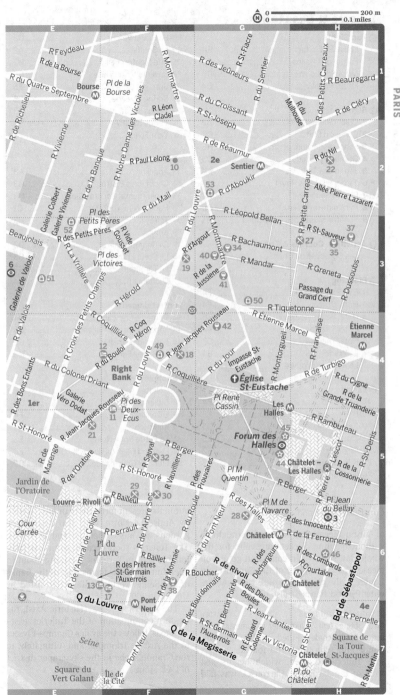

Louvre & Les Halles

Continued from p63

or Virgin Megastores, and walk straight in without queuing. Tickets are valid for the whole day, so you can come and go as you please. The centrepiece of the Carrousel du Louvre is the glass Pyramide Inversée (Inverted Pyramid; Map p66), also by Pei.

Jardin des Tuileries GARDEN
(Map p66; ⊙7am-7.30pm, later in summer; Ⓜ Tuileries or Concorde) Filled with fountains, ponds and sculptures, the formal, 28-hectare Tuileries Garden, which begins just west of the Jardin du Carrousel, was laid out in its present form, more or less, in 1664 by André Le Nôtre, who also created the gardens at Vaux-le-Vicomte and Versailles. The Tuileries soon became the most fashionable spot in Paris for parading about in one's finery. It now forms part of the Banks of the Seine World Heritage Site listed by Unesco in 1991.

The Axe Historique (Historic Axis), the western continuation of the Tuileries' east–west axis, follows the av des Champs-Élysées to the Arc de Triomphe and, ultimately, to the Grande Arche in the skyscraper district of La Défense.

Jeu de Paume
GALLERY

(Map p58; ☎01 47 03 12 50; www.jeudepaume.org; 1 place de la Concorde, 8e; adult/18-25yr/under 18yr €7.50/5/free; ◉noon-9pm Tue, noon-7pm Wed-Fri, 10am-7pm Sat & Sun; Ⓜ Concorde) This former royal tennis court is now France's national photography centre. Rotating photography, cinema, video exhibitions and installations span the 19th to 21st centuries.

Musée de l'Orangerie
ART MUSEUM

(Map p58; www.musee-orangerie.fr; quai des Tuileries & rue de Rivoli; adult/child €7.50/5.50; ◉9am-6pm Wed-Mon; Ⓜ Tuileries or Concorde) Monet's prized cycle of eight enormous *Water Lilies*, which he conceived specifically for this former palace greenhouse, wrap around two skylit oval rooms. The lower level houses an astonishing collection of additional works by Monet and many by Sisley, Renoir, Cézanne, Gauguin, Picasso, Matisse and Modigliani.

Place Vendôme
CITY SQUARE

(Map p66; Ⓜ Tuileries or Opéra) Octagonal place Vendôme and the arcaded and colonnaded buildings around it were constructed between 1687 and 1721. In March 1796 Napoleon married Josephine, viscountess Beauharnais, in the building at No 3. Today the buildings surrounding the square house the posh Hôtel Ritz Paris (closed for renovations until 2014) and some of the city's most fashionable boutiques.

The 43.5m-tall Colonne Vendôme (Vendôme Column; Map p66) in the centre of the square consists of a stone core wrapped in a 160m-long bronze spiral made from hundreds of Austrian and Russian cannons captured by Napoleon at the Battle of Austerlitz in 1805. The statue on top depicts Napoleon in classical Roman dress.

Palais Royal
PALACE

(Map p66; place du Palais Royal; Ⓜ Palais Royal–Musée du Louvre) The Royal Palace, which accommodated a young Louis XIV for a time in the 1640s, lies to the north of place du Palais Royal and the Louvre. Construction was begun in 1624 by Cardinal Richelieu, though most of the present neoclassical complex dates from the latter part of the 18th century. Today it contains the governmental Conseil d'État (State Council; Map p66) and is closed to the public.

The colonnaded building facing place André Malraux is the Comédie Française (p137); founded in 1680, it's the world's oldest national theatre.

Just north of the palace is the Jardin du Palais Royal (Map p66; 2 place Colette, 1er; ◉7.30am-10pm Apr & May, 7am-11pm Jun-Aug, 7am-9.30pm Sep, 7.30am-8.30pm Oct-Mar; Ⓜ Palais Royal–Musée du Louvre), an exquisite park surrounded by two arcades. On the eastern side, Galerie de Valois shelters designer fashion shops, art galleries and jewellers, while Galerie de Montpensier on the western side still has a few old shops remaining.

At the southern end there's a controversial sculpture of black-and-white striped columns of various heights by Daniel Buren. It was started in 1986, interrupted by irate Parisians and finished – following the

---

PARIS IN...

Two Days

Kick off with a morning cruise or tour, then concentrate on the most Parisian of sights and attractions: **Notre Dame**, the **Louvre**, the **Eiffel Tower** and the **Arc de Triomphe**. In the late afternoon have a coffee or glass of wine on the av des Champs-Élysées before making your way to Montmartre for dinner. The following day take in such sights as the **Musée d'Orsay**, **Ste-Chapelle**, **Conciergerie**, **Musée National du Moyen Âge** or **Musée Rodin**. Dine in the hip Marais area before checking out its nightlife.

Four Days

Be sure to visit at least one Parisian street market and consider a cruise along **Canal St-Martin**, bookended by visits to **Cimetière du Père Lachaise** and **Parc de la Villette**. By night, take in a concert, opera or ballet at the **Palais Garnier** or **Opéra Bastille**, and a bar and club crawl along rue Oberkampf in Ménilmontant or the Bastille area.

A Week

With one week in the French capital, you can see a good many of the major sights covered in this chapter and take excursions from Paris proper further afield to surrounding areas such as **Versailles**.

METRO ART

Almost half of the city's 300-plus metro stations were given a facelift to mark the centenary of the world-famous *Métropolitain* at the turn of the millennium, many being assigned themes relating to the *quartier* (neighbourhood) or name of the station.

The following is just a taste of the most interesting stations from an artistic perspective. For stations served by more than one line, the specific platform is noted.

» **Abbesses** (line 12) The noodlelike pale-green metalwork and glass canopy of the station entrance is one of the finest examples of the work of Hector Guimard (1867–1942), the celebrated French art nouveau architect whose signature style once graced most metro stations.

» **Arts et Métiers** (line 11 platform) The copper panelling, portholes and mechanisms of this station recall Jules Verne, Captain Nemo and collections of the nearby Musée des Arts et Métiers.

» **Bastille** (line 5 platform) A 180-sq-metre ceramic fresco features scenes taken from newspaper engravings published during the Revolution, with illustrations of the destruction of the infamous prison.

» **Chaussée d'Antin-Lafayette** (line 7 platform) Large allegorical painting on the vaulted ceiling recalls the Marquis de Lafayette (1757–1834) and his role as general in the American Revolution.

» **Cluny–La Sorbonne** (line 10 platform) A large ceramic mosaic replicates the signatures of intellectuals, artists and scientists from the Latin Quarter through history, including Molière, Rabelais and Robespierre.

» **Concorde** (line 12 platform) What look like children's building blocks in white-and-blue ceramic on the walls of the station are 45,000 tiles that spell out the text of the Déclaration des Droits de l'Homme et du Citoyen (Declaration of the Rights of Man and of the Citizen), the document setting forth the principles of the French Revolution.

» **Louvre Rivoli** (line 1 platform and corridor) Statues, bas-reliefs and photographs offer a small taste of what to expect at the Musée du Louvre above ground.

» **Palais Royal–Musée du Louvre** (line 1) The zany entrance on the place du Palais by Jean-Michel Othoniel is composed of two crown-shaped cupolas (one representing the day, the other night) consisting of 800 red, blue, amber and violet glass balls threaded on an aluminium structure.

intervention of the Ministry of Culture and Communication – in 1995.

Forum des Halles SHOPPING MALL
(Map p66; www.forumdeshalles.com; 1 rue Pierre Lescot, 1er; ⊙shops 10am-8pm Mon-Sat; Ⓜ Les Halles or RER Châtelet–Les Halles) Dramatic change (for the better) is afoot: the dodgy park and dated arbours topping this underground shopping mall have been demolished and cranes, diggers and an army of builders are busy at work creating La Canopée – a contemporary, glass-topped, curvilinear building by architects Patrick Berger and Jacques Anziutti, inspired by the natural shade canopy of a rainforest. Spilling out from the translucent, leaflike rooftop will be state-of-the-art gardens by landscape designer David Mangin. It will be completed in 2016.

The mall itself will receive a relatively light renovation in stages; hence business should continue more or less as usual, with minimal disruption to city's largest metro/RER hub. Follow the project at www.parisleshalles.fr or pop into the information centre on place Jean du Bellay, a pretty square pierced by the Fontaine des Innocents (Map p66). The multitiered fountain (built in 1549) is named after the Cimetière des Innocents, a cemetery formerly on this site from which two million skeletons were disinterred after the Revolution and transferred to the Catacombes.

Église St-Eustache CHURCH
(Map p66; www.st-eustache.org; 2 impasse St-Eustache, 1er; admission free; ⊙9.30am-7pm Mon-Fri, 10am-7pm Sat, 9am-7pm Sun; Ⓜ Les Halles) This majestic church, one of the most beautiful in Paris, is just north of the Forum des

Halles. Constructed between 1532 and 1637, St-Eustache is primarily Gothic, though a neoclassical façade was added on the western side in the mid-18th century. Inside, some exceptional Flamboyant Gothic arches hold up the ceiling of the chancel, though most of the ornamentation is Renaissance and even classical. Above the western entrance, the gargantuan organ, with 101 stops and 8000 pipes dating from 1854, is used for concerts (long a tradition here) and at Sunday Mass at 11am and Sunday recitals at 5.30pm.

OPÉRA & GRANDS BOULEVARDS

Palais Garnier   OPERA HOUSE
(Map p72; ☎08 25 05 44 05; www.operadeparis. fr; cnr rues Scribe & Auber; adult/10-25yr/under 10yr unguided tour €9/6/free, guided tour €13.50/9.50/6.50; ⊙10am-4.30pm; MOpéra) From Degas' ballerinas to Gaston Leroux's phantom and Chagall's ceiling, the layers of myth painted on gradually over the decades have bestowed a particular air of mystery and drama to the Palais Garnier's ornate interior. Designed in 1860 by Charles Garnier – then an unknown 35-year-old architect – the opera house was part of Baron Haussmann's massive urban renovation project.

The opera is open for visits during the day; highlights include the opulent Grand Staircase, the library-museum (1st fl), where you'll find old show posters, costumes and original music scores, and the horseshoe-shaped auditorium (2nd fl), with its extravagant gilded interior and red velvet seats. Above the massive chandelier is Chagall's gorgeous ceiling mural (1964), which depicts scenes from 14 operas. Alternatively, reserve a spot on an English-language guided tour (http://visites. operadeparis.fr; ⊙11.30am & 2.30pm Wed, Sat & Sun). Note that the auditorium cannot be visited when daytime rehearsals or matinees are scheduled; try to arrive before 1pm or check the website for the exact schedule.

Interestingly, a prop man at the opera set up beehives on the roof some 20 years ago – the honey is now sold at the gift shop when available.

FREE Musée du Parfum   PERFUME MUSEUM
(Map p72; www.fragonard.com; 9 rue Scribe, 2e; ⊙9am-6pm Mon-Sat, to 5pm Sun; MOpéra) If the art of perfume-making entices, stop by this collection of copper distillery vats and antique flacons and test your nose on a few basic scents. It's run by the parfumerie Fragonard and located in a beautiful

old *hôtel particulier* (private mansion); free guided visits are available in multiple languages. A separate wing is a short distance south, in the Théâtre-Musée des Capucines (Map p66; 39 bd des Capucines; ⊙9am-6pm Mon-Sat; MOpéra).

Passage Couverts   SHOPPING ARCADES
Step back back into the sepia-toned Paris of the early 19th century in several covered shopping arcades off bd Montmartre. The passage des Panoramas (Map p72; 10 rue St-Marc, 2e; MBourse), which was opened in 1800 and received Paris' first gas lighting in 1817, was expanded in 1834 with the addition of four other interconnecting passages: Feydeau, Montmartre, St-Marc and Variétés.

On the northern side of bd Montmartre, between Nos 10 and 12, is passage Jouffroy (Map p72), which leads across rue de la Grange Batelière to passage Verdeau (Map p72). Both contain shops selling antiques, old postcards, used and antiquarian books, gifts and much more.

MONTMARTRE & PIGALLE

Montmartre's slinking streets lined with crooked ivy-clad buildings retain a fairy tale charm, despite their popularity. Crowned by the Sacré-Cœur basilica, Montmartre has lofty views, wine-producing vines and hidden village squares that have lured painters from the 19th century on.

To its southwest, lively, neon-lit Pigalle (9e and 18e) is one of Paris' main red-light districts. The area has plenty of trendy nightspots too, including clubs and cabarets.

Basilique du Sacré-Cœur   BASILICA
(Map p74; www.sacre-coeur-montmartre.com; place du Parvis du Sacré Cœur; Basilica dome admission €5, cash only; ⊙6am-10.30pm, dome 9am-7pm Apr-Sep, to 5.30pm Oct-Mar; MAnvers) Crowning the Butte de Montmartre (Montmartre Hill), Sacred Heart Basilica was built from contributions pledged by Parisian Catholics as an act of contrition after the humiliating Franco-Prussian War of 1870–71. Construction began in 1876, but the basilica was not consecrated until 1919. In a way, atonement here has never stopped; a perpetual prayer 'cycle' that began at the consecration of the Basilica continues round the clock to this day.

Some 234 spiralling steps lead you to the basilica's dome, which affords one of Paris' most spectacular panoramas – up to 30km on a clear day. Weighing in at 19 tonnes, the bell called La Savoyarde in the tower above is the largest in France. The chapel-lined

Opéra & Grands Boulevards

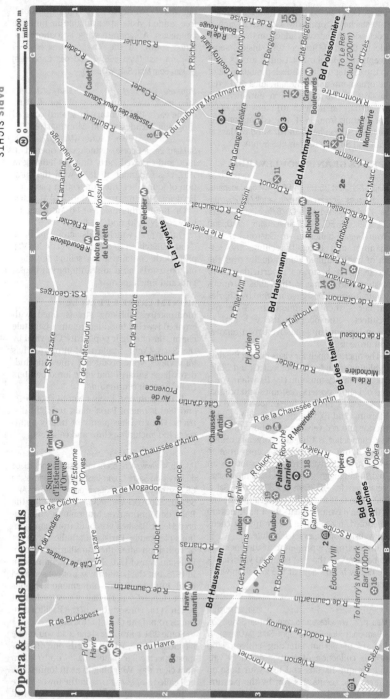

0 — 200 m
0 — 0.1 miles

Opéra & Grands Boulevards

crypt, visited in conjunction with the dome, is huge.

If you don't want to walk the hill, you can use a regular metro ticket aboard the funicular.

Place du Tertre CITY SQUARE
(ⓂAbbesses) It would be hard to miss the place du Tertre, one of the most touristy spots in all of Paris. Though today it's filled with visitors, buskers and portrait artists, it was originally the main square of the village of Montmartre before it was incorporated into the city proper.

FREE **Cimetière de Montmartre** CEMETERY
(Map p74; ◎8am-5.30pm Mon-Fri, from 8.30am Sat, from 9am Sun; ⓂPlace de Clichy) Established in 1798, this 11-hectare cemetery is perhaps the most celebrated necropolis in Paris after Père Lachaise. It contains the graves of writers Émile Zola (whose ashes are now in the Panthéon), Alexandre Dumas (fils) and Stendhal, composers Jacques Offenbach and Hector Berlioz, artist Edgar Degas, film director François Truffaut and dancer Vaslav Nijinsky, among others.

The entrance closest to the Butte de Montmartre is at the end of av Rachel, just off bd de Clichy, or down the stairs from 10 rue Caulaincourt. Free maps are available at the conservation office (Map p74; 20 av Rachel) at the cemetery's entrance.

Musée de Montmartre HISTORY MUSEUM
(Map p74; www.museedemontmartre.fr; 12 rue Cortot, 18e; adult/18-25yr/10-17yr €8/6/4; ◎10am-6pm; ⓂLamarck–Caulaincourt) The Montmartre Museum displays paintings, lithographs and documents mostly relating to the area's rebellious and bohemian past. It's located in the oldest structure in Montmartre, a 17th-century manor house where over a dozen artists, including Renoir and Utrillo, once lived. There's an excellent bookshop here that sells small bottles of the wine produced from grapes grown in the Clos Montmartre (Map p74; 18 rue des Saules, 18e) vineyard.

Musée de l'Érotisme ART MUSEUM
(Map p74; www.musee-erotisme.com; 72 bd de Clichy, 18e; adult/student €10/6; ◎10am-2am; ⓂBlanche) The Museum of Erotic Art attempts to raise around 2000 titillating statuary, stimulating sexual aids and fetishist items to a loftier plane, with antique and modern erotic art from four continents spread out across several floors. Some of the exhibits are, well, breathtaking, to say the least.

LA VILLETTE
The forested Parc des Buttes-Chaumont (rue Manin & rue Botzaris, 19e; ◎7.30am-11pm May-Sep, to 9pm Oct-Apr; ⓂButtes-Chaumont or Botzaris), the Canal de l'Ourcq and especially the Parc de la Villette, with its wonderful museums and other attractions, create a winning trifecta in the 19e *arrondissement*.

Montmartre & Pigalle

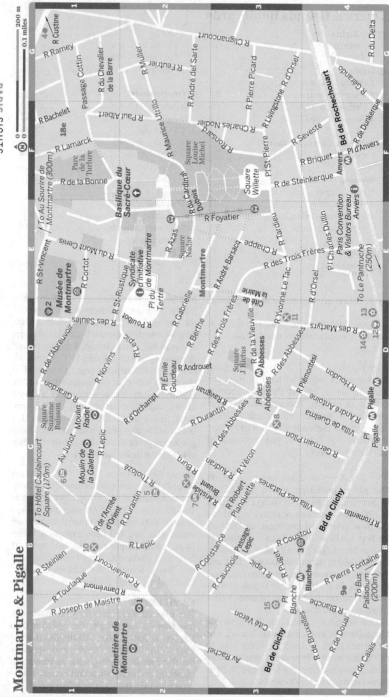

G **F** **E** **D** **C** **B** **A**

200 m
0.1 miles

Cimetière de
Montmartre

Basilique du
Sacré-Cœur

Musée de
Montmartre

Montmartre

Syndicate
d'Initiative

Pl du
Tertre

Moulin de
la Galette

Moulin
Radet

Parc de
la Turlure

Square
Louise
Michel

Square
Willette

Square
Nadar

Square
J Rictus

Square
Suzanne
Buisson

Paris Convention
& Visitors Bureau

R Custine
R Ramey
R Bachelet
R Lamarck
R de la Bonne
R St-Vincent
R du Mont Cenis
R Cortot
R des Saules
R de l'Abreuvoir
R Norvins
R St-Rustique
R Poulbot
R Lepic
R Gabrielle
R Berthe
R Andouet
R d'Orchampt
R Durantin
R Ravignan
Pl Émile
Goudeau
R des Trois Frères
R des Abbesses
Villa des Platanes
R Germain Pilon
R André Antoine
Villa de Guelma
R des Martyrs
R d'Orsel
R Yvonne Le Tac
Cité de
la Mairie
Pl des
Abbesses
R de la Vieuville
R Houdon
R Piémontesi
R des Abbesses
R Durantin
R Audran
R Véron
R Robert
Planquette
R Burq
R Aristide
Bruant
R Tholozé
Av Junot
R Girardon
Passage Cottin
R du Chevalier
de la Barre
R Muller
R Feutrier
R Paul Albert
R Maurice Utrillo
R du Cardinal Dubois
R Azaïs
R Foyatier
R Chappe
R André Barsacq
R Tardieu
R Clignancourt
R André del Sarte
R Pierre Picard
R Livingstone
R d'Orsel
R Charles Nodier
R Ronsard
Pl St-Pierre
R de Steinkerque
R Seveste
R Briquet
Bd de Rochechouart
R de Dunkerque
Pl d'Anvers
R du Delta
R de Gérando
Anvers
Anvers
Pl Charles Dullin
To Le Pantruche
(250m)
R d'Orsel
R des Trois Frères
To Au Sourire
de Montmartre (300m)
To Hôtel Caulaincourt
Square (170m)
R de l'Armée
d'Orient
R Caulaincourt
R Steinlen
R Tourlaque
R Damrémont
R Joseph de Maistre
R Lepic
R Constance
R Cauchois
Passage
Lepic
R Puget
R Coustou
Cité Véron
Av Rachel
Bd de Clichy
Pl
Blanche
R Pierre Fontaine
Blanche
R de Douai
R de Bruxelles
R de Calais
R Fromentin
R Blanche
R Lepic
Bd de Clichy
Bd de Clichy
Pigalle
Pigalle
Pl
Pigalle
Pigalle
Blanche
9e
18e
To Bus
Palladium
(200m)

1 2 3 4

2 3 4

Parc de la Villette   PARK
(www.villette.com; MPorte de la Villette or Porte de
Pantin) The largest park in Paris, the Parc
de la Villette is a cultural centre, kids' playground and landscaped urban space at the
intersection of two canals, the Ourcq and
the St-Denis. Its futuristic layout includes
the colossal mirrorlike sphere of the Géode
cinema and the bright-red cubical pavilions
known as *folies*. Among its themed gardens
are the Jardin du Dragon (Dragon Garden),
with a giant dragon's tounge slide for kids,
the Jardin des Dunes (Dunes Garden) and
Jardin des Miroirs (Mirror Garden).

Events are staged in the wonderful old
Grande Halle (formerly a slaughterhouse –
the Parisian cattle market was located here
from 1867 to 1974), Le Zénith, the Cabaret
Sauvage, the Cité de la Musique and the
Conservatoire National Supérieur de
Musique et de Danse. The new Paris Philharmonic hall is due to be completed here
in 2015.

Cité des Sciences   SCIENCE MUSEUM
(☎01 40 05 12 12; www.cite-sciences.fr; Parc de la
Villette; adult/under 26yr €8/6; ⊙10am-6pm Tue-
Sat, to 7pm Sun; MPorte de la Villette) This is the
city's top museum for kids, with three floors
of hands-on exhibits for children ages two and
up, plus two special-effects cinemas, a planetarium and a retired submarine. The only
drawback is that each exhibit has a separate
admission fee (though some combined tickets
do exist), so you'll have to do some pretrip research to figure out what's most appropriate.

Make sure to reserve tickets in advance
via the website if you plan on coming on a
weekend or during school holidays. Packing
a picnic is also a good idea.

Cité de la Musique   MUSIC MUSEUM
(www.cite-musique.fr; 221 av Jean Jaurès, 19e;
⊙noon-6pm Tue-Sat, 10am-6pm Sun; MPorte de
Pantin) The Cité de la Musique, on the southern edge of Parc de la Villette, is a striking,
triangular-shaped concert hall; its mission is
to introduce music from around the world
to Parisians. The Musée de la Musique (Music Museum; adult/under 26yr €8/free) inside displays some 900 rare musical instruments;
you can hear many of them being played on
the audioguide.

MÉNILMONTANT & BELLEVILLE
A solidly working-class *quartier* (neighbourhood) until just a few years ago, Ménilmontant in the 11e now heaves with restaurants,
bars and clubs. Multicultural Belleville (20e)
remains for the most part gritty and unpretentious. Superb views over the area and the
city extend from the hilltop Parc de Belleville (MCouronnes) almost 200m above sea
level amid 4.5 hectares of greenery.

Cimetière du Père Lachaise   CEMETERY
(☎01 43 70 70 33; www.pere-lachaise.com; 16 rue
du Repos & bd de Ménilmontant, 20e; admission
free; ⊙8am-6pm Mon-Fri, from 8.30am Sat, from
9am Sun; MPère Lachaise or Philippe Auguste) The
world's most visited cemetery, Père Lachaise
(named after a confessor of Louis XIV)
opened its one-way doors in 1804. Its 69,000
ornate, even ostentatious, tombs of the rich
and/or famous form a verdant, 44-hectare
sculpture garden. Among those buried here

Montmartre & Pigalle

are composer Chopin; playwright Molière; poet Apollinaire; writers Balzac, Proust, Gertrude Stein and Colette; actors Sarah Bernhardt and Yves Montand; painters Pissarro, Seurat, Modigliani and Delacroix; *chanteuse* Édith Piaf; and dancer Isadora Duncan.

Particularly visited graves are those of Oscar Wilde, interred in division 89 in 1900, and 1960s rock star Jim Morrison, who died in a flat at 17–19 rue Beautreillis (4e) in the Marais in 1971 and is buried in division 6.

On 27 May 1871, the last of the Communard insurgents, cornered by government forces, fought a hopeless, all-night battle among the tombstones. In the morning, the 147 survivors were lined up against the Mur des Fédérés (Wall of the Federalists), shot and buried where they fell in a mass grave.

Père Lachaise has five entrances, two of which are on bd de Ménilmontant. Free maps of noteworthy graves are available from the conservation office (16 rue du Repos, 20e).

LE MARAIS & BASTILLE

Paris' *marais* (marsh) was converted to farmland in the 12th century. In the early 17th century, Henri IV built the place Royale (today's place des Vosges), turning the area into Paris' most fashionable residential district and attracting wealthy aristocrats who then erected their own luxurious *hôtels particulier*. Today many of them are house museums and government institutions.

Funky bars and restaurants, designers' boutiques and the city's thriving gay and Jewish communities all squeeze into this vibrant neighbourhood's medieval laneways. And while the lower Marais has long been fashionable, the real buzz these days is in Haut Marais (upper or northern Marais; NoMa), showcasing rising design talent, vintage fashion, hip art and cool eateries. Watch for new openings – pop-up and permanent – on rue de Bretagne, rue Dupetit Thouars, rue Charles François Dupuis and rue Charlot among others.

The contiguous Bastille district (11e and 12e) has also undergone a fair degree of gentrification and is another buzzing nightlife district.

Centre Pompidou
ART MUSEUM

(Map p78; ✆01 44 78 12 33; www.centrepompidou.fr; place Georges Pompidou, 1er; museum, exhibitions & panorama adult/child €13/free; ☺11am-9pm Wed-Mon; MRambuteau) Former French President Georges Pompidou wanted an ultracontemporary artistic hub, and he got

it: competition-winning architects Renzo Piano and Richard Rogers effectively designed the building inside out, with utilitarian features such as plumbing, pipes, air vents and electrical cables forming part of the external façade, freeing up the interior space for exhibitions and events. Paris' premier cultural centre has amazed visitors since it was inaugurated in 1977.

On the ground floor, the Forum du Centre Pompidou has temporary exhibitions and information desks, while the 4th and 5th floors house the Musée National d'Art Moderne (Map p78; adult/child €12/free; ☺11am-9pm Wed-Mon), France's national collection of art dating from 1905 onward. A fraction of the 65,000-plus works by 5700 artists – including the work of the surrealists and cubists, as well as pop art and contemporary works – are on display.

The huge Bibliothèque Publique d'Information (BPI; Map p78; ✆01 44 78 12 33; www.bpi.fr; ☺noon-10pm Mon & Wed-Fri, 11am-10pm Sat & Sun), entered from rue du Renard, takes up part of the 1st and the entire 2nd and 3rd floors. The 6th floor has two galleries for temporary exhibitions and a chic, hyperindustrial restaurant, Georges, with panoramic views of Paris, which is accessed by a free lift/elevator (look for the red door to the left of the main entrance).

Rooftop admission is included in museum and exhibition admission – or buy a panorama ticket (€3; 11am to 11pm, Wed-Mon) for just the roof.

Admission to the museum is free on the first Sunday of each month.

There are cinemas and other entertainment venues on the 1st floor and in the basement.

West of the centre, Place Georges Pompidou and the nearby pedestrian streets attract buskers, musicians, jugglers and mime artists. South of the centre on place Igor Stravinsky are fanciful mechanical fountains of skeletons, hearts, treble clefs and a big pair of ruby-red lips, created by Jean Tinguely and Niki de Saint Phalle.

Musée Picasso
MUSEUM

(Map p78; ✆01 42 71 25 21; www.musee-picasso.fr; 5 rue de Thorigny; MSt-Paul or Chemin Vert) The Picasso Museum, housed in the stunning mid-17th-century Hôtel Salé, will reopen after extensive renovations in mid-2013. Its collection includes more than 3500 drawings, engravings, paintings, ceramic works and sculptures by the *grand maître* (great

DON'T MISS

CANAL ST-MARTIN

The shaded towpaths of the tranquil, 4.5km-long Canal St-Martin are a wonderful place for a romantic stroll or a bike ride.

Dug out in 1825, the canal was a major cargo thoroughfare by the time Marcel Carné's 1938 film *Hôtel du Nord* was set in the canalside hotel – now a cafe/bar (Map p78; www.hoteldunord.org; 102 quai de Jemmapes, 10e; ⏰9am-2.30am; ☎⛄; ⓂJacques Bonsergent) – of the same name. Although the film (about a Romeo-and-Juliet-style suicide pact) was shot in a studio, author Eugène Dabit, whose stories formed the basis of the film, lived here when the hotel was run by his parents.

The canal's fortunes fell in the 1960s when barge transportation declined. It was slated to be concreted over and turned into a roadway until local residents rallied to save it. When the title character of *Amélie* skipped stones here in 2001, the cheap rents and quaint setting were just starting to lure artists, designers and students, who set up artists' collectives, vintage and offbeat boutiques, and a bevy of neoretro cafes and bars.

Today Canal St-Martin is the centre of Paris' *bobo* (bohemian bourgeois) life, but maritime legacies endure, including old swing-bridges that still pivot 90 degrees when barges pass through the canal's double-locks. Take a canal boat cruise (☎01 42 39 15 00; www.canauxrama.com; adult/student & senior/4-12yr €16/12/8.50) to savour the full flavour.

master), Pablo Picasso (1881–1973), which his heirs donated to the French government in lieu of paying inheritance taxes. Also here is Picasso's personal art collection, which includes works by Braque, Cézanne, Matisse, Modigliani, Degas and Rousseau.

FREE **Hôtel de Ville**   ARCHITECTURE
(Map p78; www.paris.fr; place de l'Hôtel de Ville, 3e; ⓂHôtel de Ville) Paris' beautiful town hall was gutted during the Paris Commune of 1871 and rebuilt in luxurious neo-Renaissance style between 1874 and 1882. The ornate façade is decorated with 108 statues of illustrious Parisians. Free temporary exhibitions held inside in the Salle St-Jean (Map p78; 5 rue de Lobau) generally have a Paris theme.

From December to early March, an iceskating rink (Patinoire de l'Hôtel de Ville; Map p78; admission free, skate hire €5; ⏰noon-10pm Mon-Fri, 9am-10pm Sat & Sun, Dec-Mar; ⓂHôtel de Ville) sets up outside.

FREE **Place des Vosges**   CITY SQUARE
(Map p78; place des Vosges, 4e; ⓂSt-Paul or Bastille) Inaugurated in 1612 as place Royale, Paris' oldest square is a strikingly elegant ensemble of 36 symmetrical houses with ground-floor arcades, steep slate roofs and large dormer windows. They're arranged around the large and leafy square with four symmetrical fountains.

Writer Victor Hugo lived here between 1832 and 1848; his former home is now the small museum Maison de Victor Hugo (Map p78; www.musee-hugo.paris.fr; admission free; ⏰10am-6pm Tue-Sun; ⓂSt-Paul or Bastille), with an impressive collection of his personal drawings and portraits.

FREE **Musée Carnavalet**   HISTORY MUSEUM
(Map p78; www.carnavalet.paris.fr; 23 rue de Sévigné, 3e; ⏰10am-6pm Tue-Sun; ⓂSt-Paul, Chemin Vert or Rambuteau) This enormous museum, subtitled Histoire de Paris (History of Paris), is housed in two *hôtels particuliers*: the mid-16th-century Renaissance-style Hôtel Carnavalet and the late-17th-century Hôtel Le Peletier de St-Fargeau.

Displays chart the history of Paris from the Gallo-Roman period to modern times on the 1st floor and fill more than 100 rooms. Some of the nation's most important documents, paintings and other objects from the French Revolution are here; so are Georges Fouquet's stunning art nouveau jewellery shop from the rue Royale and Marcel Proust's cork-lined bedroom from his apartment on bd Haussmann, where he wrote most of the 7350-page literary cycle *À la Recherche du Temps Perdu* (In Search of Lost Time).

Musée des Arts et Métiers   MUSEUM
(Map p78; www.arts-et-metiers.net; 60 rue de Réaumur, 3e; adult/student/child €6.50/4.50/ free; ⏰10am-6pm Tue, Wed & Fri-Sun, to 9.30pm

PARIS

Le Marais & Northern Bastille

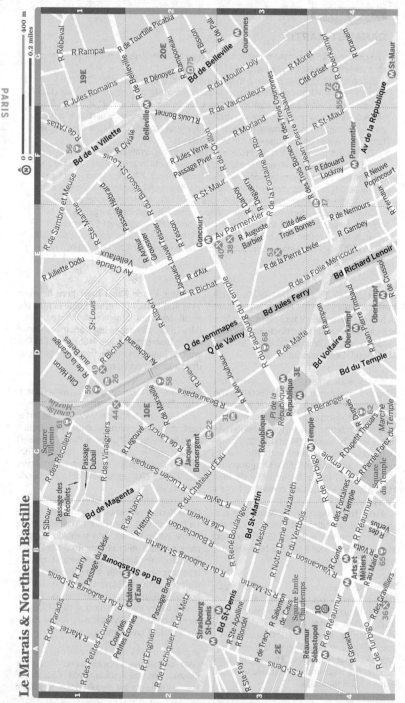

0 0.2 miles

0 400 m

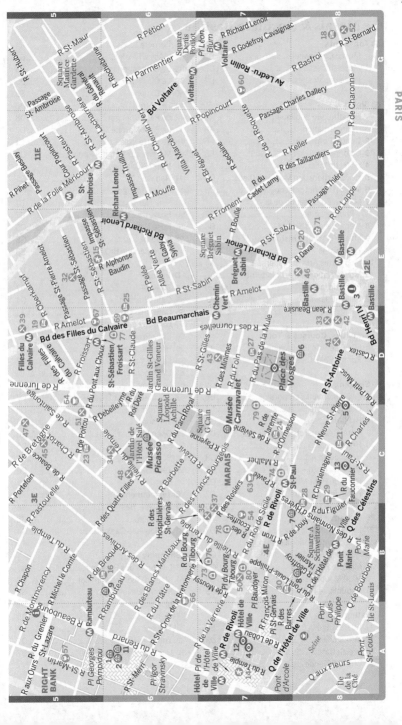

Le Marais & Northern Bastille

Thu; MArts et Métiers) The Arts & Crafts Museum, dating to 1794 and the oldest museum of science and technology in Europe, is a must for anyone with an interest in how things tick or work. Housed inside the sublime 18th-century priory of St-Martin des Champs, some 3000 instruments, machines and working models from the 18th to 20th centuries are displayed according to theme (from Construction and Energy to Transportation) across three floors.

Musée d'Art et d'Histoire du Judaïsme
MUSEUM

(Map p78; www.mahj.org; 71 rue du Temple; adult/under 26yr €6.80/free; ◷11am-6pm Mon-Fri, 10am-6pm Sun; MRambuteau) Housed in the sumptuous Hôtel de St-Aignan (1650), the Museum of the Art & History of Judaism traces the evolution of Jewish communities from the Middle Ages to the present, with particular emphasis on the history of Jews in France but also that of communities in other parts of Europe and North Africa. Highlights include documents relating to the Dreyfus Affair and works by Chagall, Modigliani and Soutine.

FREE Mémorial de la Shoah
MUSEUM

(Map p78; www.memorialdelashoah.org; 17 rue Geoffroy l'Asnier, 4e; ◷10am-6pm Sun-Wed & Fri, to 10pm Thu; MSt-Paul) Established in 1956, the Memorial to the Unknown Jewish Martyr has metamorphosed into the Memorial of the Shoah – a Hebrew word meaning 'catastrophe' and synonymous with the Holocaust – and an important documentation centre. The permanent collection and temporary exhibitions relate to the Holocaust and the German occupation of parts of France and Paris during WWII; the film clips of contemporary footage and interviews are heart-rending and the displays instructive and easy to follow. The actual memorial to the victims of the Shoah stands at the entrance, where a wall is inscribed with the names of 76,000 men, women and children deported from France to Nazi extermination camps.

Maison Européenne de la Photographie
PHOTOGRAPHY MUSEUM

(Map p78; www.mep-fr.org; 5-7 rue de Fourcy, 4e; adult/child/under 8yr €7/4/free; ◷11am-8pm Wed-Sun; MSt-Paul or Pont Marie) The European House of Photography, housed in the overly renovated Hôtel Hénault de Cantorbe (dating – believe it or not – from the early 18th

century), has cutting-edge temporary exhibitions (usually retrospectives on individual photographers), as well as an enormous permanent collection on the history of photography and its connections with France.

Place de la Bastille
CITY SQUARE

(Map p78; MBastille) The Bastille, a 14th-century fortress built to protect the city gates, is the most famous monument in Paris that no longer exists. Transformed into a dreaded state prison under Cardinal Richelieu, it was demolished shortly after a mob stormed it on 14 July 1789 and freed a total of just seven prisoners.

The *place* still resonates with the French as a symbol of revolutionary change, but first impressions of today's busy traffic circle can be a bit underwhelming. The most obvious monument is the Colonne de Juillet (Map p78), a lone bronze column topped with the gilded *Spirit of Liberty*, but upon closer inspection you'll notice that the column has little to do with the famous storming of the prison; it instead commemorates the victims of the later revolutions of 1830 and 1848.

If you're interested in finding the Bastille's one-time foundations, look for a triple row of paving stones that trace the building's outline on the ground between bd Henri IV and rue St-Antoine. The foundations are also marked below ground in the Bastille metro station, on the platform of line 5.

Promenade Plantée
PARK

(Map p86; ◷8am-9.30pm May-Aug, to 5.30pm Sep-Apr; MBastille or Gare de Lyon) The most innovative green space in the city, the elevated Promenade Plantée was built atop the old Vincennes Railway, which was in operation from 1859 to 1969. Three stories above ground level, it provides all the usual park amenities – benches, rose trellises, corridors of bamboo – but its real attraction is the unique aerial views of city life and the surrounding architecture.

The viaduct drops back to street level at the Jardin de Reuilly (1.5km), but it's possible to follow the line all the way to the Bois de Vincennes at the city's edge. This latter section, known as the Coulée Verte (3km), can also be done on a bike or in-line skates. Access to the elevated section is via staircase; there is usually at least one per city block. Beneath the park at street level is the Viaduc des Arts (Map p86; MGare de Lyon or Daumesnil), a series of artisan workshops and galleries, which runs along av Daumesnil.

THE ISLANDS

Paris' two inner-city islands could not be more different. The bigger Île de la Cité is full of sights, including Notre Dame, while little Île St-Louis is residential and much quieter, with a scattering of boutiques and restaurants – and legendary ice-cream maker Berthillon.

ÎLE DE LA CITÉ

The site of the first settlement in Paris, around the 3rd century BC, and later the Roman town of Lutèce (Lutetia), the Île de la Cité remained the centre of royal and ecclesiastical power even after the city spread to both banks of the Seine during the Middle Ages. The buildings on the middle part of the island were demolished and rebuilt during Baron Haussmann's great urban renewal scheme of the late 19th century.

FREE **Cathédrale de Notre Dame de Paris**   CATHEDRAL

(Map p88; www.cathedraledeparis.com; 6 place du Parvis Notre Dame, 4e; ☉ 7.45am-7pm; M Cité) This is the heart of Paris – so much so that distances from Paris to every part of metropolitan France are measured from place du Parvis Notre Dame, the square in front of the Cathedral of Our Lady of Paris. A bronze star across the street from the cathedral's main entrance marks the exact location of *point zéro des routes de France*.

Notre Dame, the most visited unticketed site in Paris, with upwards of 14 million people crossing its threshold a year, is not just a masterpiece of French Gothic architecture; it was also the focus of Catholic Paris for seven centuries.

Built on a site occupied by earlier churches and, a millennium before that, a Gallo-Roman temple, it was begun in 1163 according to the design of Bishop Maurice de Sully and largely completed by the early 14th century. The cathedral was badly damaged during the Revolution; architect Eugène Emmanuel Viollet-le-Duc carried out extensive renovations between 1845 and 1864. The cathedral is on a very grand scale; the

interior alone is 130m long, 48m wide and 35m high and can accommodate more than 6000 worshippers.

Notre Dame is known for its sublime balance, though if you look closely you'll see all sorts of minor asymmetrical elements introduced to avoid monotony, in accordance with standard Gothic practice. These include the slightly different shapes of each of the three main portals. One of the best views of Notre Dame is from square Jean XXIII, the little park behind the cathedral, where you can better appreciate the forest of ornate flying buttresses that encircle the chancel and support its walls and roof.

Inside, exceptional features include three spectacular rose windows – the most renowned of which is the 10m-wide one over the western façade above the 7800-pipe organ – and the window on the northern side of the transept, which has remained virtually unchanged since the 13th century. The central choir, with its carved wooden stalls and statues representing the Passion of the Christ, is also noteworthy. There are free 1½-hour guided tours of the cathedral in English.

The trésor (treasury; adult/student/child €4/2/1; ☉ 9.30am-6pm Mon-Fri, 9.30am-6.30pm Sat, 1.30-6.30pm Sun) in the southeastern transept contains artwork, liturgical objects and first-class relics. Among these is the Ste-Couronne, the 'Holy Crown', which is purportedly the wreath of thorns placed on Jesus' head before he was crucified, brought here in the mid-13th century. It's exhibited between 3pm and 4pm on the first Friday of each month, 3pm to 4pm every Friday during Lent, and 10am to 5pm on Good Friday.

The entrance to the Tours de Notre Dame (Notre Dame Towers; rue du Cloître Notre Dame, 4e; adult/18-25yr/under 18yr €8.50/5.50/free; ☉ 10am-6.30pm daily Apr-Jun & Sep, 10am-6.30pm Mon-Fri, 10am-11pm Sat & Sun Jul & Aug, 10.30am-5.30pm daily Oct-Mar) is from the North Tower (Map p88). Climb the 422 spiralling steps to the top of the western façade, where you'll find yourself face-to-face with the cathedral's most frightening gargoyles, the 13-tonne bell Emmanuel (all of the cathedral's bells are named) in the South Tower and, last but not least, a spectacular view of Paris from the Galerie des Chimères (Dreams Gallery).

Ste-Chapelle   CHURCH

(Map p88; 4 bd du Palais, 1er; adult/under 18yr €8.50/free; ☉ 9.30am-5pm Nov-Feb, to 6pm Mar-Oct; M Cité) Try to save Ste-Chapelle for a

---

NEW NOTRE DAME BELLS

As part of 2013's celebrations for Notre Dame's 850th anniversary, nine new bells replicating the original medieval chimes replaced the previous bells, which were melted down to create them.

WORTH A TRIP

BOIS DE VINCENNES

Originally royal hunting grounds, the Bois de Vincennes (blvd Poniatowski, 12e; M Porte de Charenton or Porte Dorée), just east of the 12e, was annexed by the army following the Revolution and then donated to the city in 1860 by Napoleon III. Its 995 hectares encompass the Château de Vincennes (www.chateau-vincennes.fr; av de Paris, Vincennes; adult/18-25yr/under 18yr €8.50/5.50/free; ☉10am-6.15pm Apr-Sep, to 5.15pm Oct-Mar; M Château de Vincennes), a 12th-century hunting lodge-turned-castle. Also here is the magnificent botanical park, the Parc Floral de Paris (Esplanade du Chateau de Vincennes; adult/7-18yr/under 7yr €5/2/free; ☉9.30am-9pm May-Aug, shorter hr rest of year; M Château de Vincennes). The woods' largest lake, the Lac Daumesnil (M Porte Dorée) is a popular destination for walks and rowboat excursions in warmer months. Its zoo, the Parc Zoologique de Paris (M Porte Dorée) is expected to reopen after renovations in spring 2014.

sunny day, when Paris' oldest, finest stained glass is at its dazzling best. Enshrined within the Palais de Justice (Law Courts), this gem-like Holy Chapel is Paris' most exquisite Gothic monument. Ste-Chapelle was built in just six years (compared with nearly 200 years for Notre Dame) and consecrated in 1248. The chapel was conceived by Louis IX to house his personal collection of holy relics, including the famous Holy Crown (now in Notre Dame). Peek at its exterior from across the street, by the law courts' magnificently gilded 18th-century gate facing rue de Lutèce.

A combined ticket with the Conciergerie costs €12.50.

Conciergerie   HISTORIC SITE†
(Map p88; www.monuments-nationaux.fr; 2 bd du Palais, Île de la Cité, 1er; adult/under 18yr €8.50/free, 1st Sun of month Nov-Mar free; ☉9.30am-6pm; M Cité)
The Conciergerie was built as a royal palace in the 14th century, but later lost favour with the kings of France and became a prison and torture chamber. During the Reign of Terror (1793–94), it was used to incarcerate (in various 'classes' of cells) alleged enemies of the Revolution before they were brought before the Revolutionary Tribunal, next door in the Palais de Justice.

Among the almost 2800 prisoners held in the dungeons here before being sent in tumbrils to the guillotine were Queen Marie Antoinette (see a reproduction of her cell) and, as the Revolution began to turn on its own, the radicals Danton, Robespierre and, finally, the judges of the Tribunal themselves. The 14th-century Salle des Gens d'Armes (Cavalrymen's Hall), a fine example of Rayonnant Gothic style, is Europe's largest surviving medieval hall.

A joint ticket with Ste-Chapelle costs €12.50.

Pont Neuf   HISTORIC SITE
(Map p88; M Pont Neuf) Paris' oldest bridge (called 'New Bridge', ironically) has linked the western end of Île de la Cité with both river banks since 1607, when the king inaugurated it by crossing the bridge on a white stallion. The occasion is commemorated by an equestrian statue of Henri IV.

ÎLE ST-LOUIS
In the early 17th century, the smaller of the Seine's two islands, Île St-Louis, was actually two uninhabited islets called Île Notre Dame (Our Lady Isle) and Île aux Vaches (Cows Island). A building contractor and two financiers worked out a deal with Louis XIII to create a single island and build two stone bridges to the mainland in exchange for the right to subdivide and sell the newly created real estate. By 1664 the entire island was covered with fine new and airy houses facing the quays and the river.

Today the island's 17th-century, greystone houses and the shops that line the streets and quays impart a villagelike, provincial calm. The only sight as such, French baroque Église St-Louis en l'Île (Map p88; 19bis rue St-Louis en l'Île; ☉9am-1pm & 2-7.30pm Tue-Sat, to 7pm Sun; M Pont Marie), was built between 1664 and 1726.

LATIN QUARTER
The centre of Parisian higher education since the Middle Ages, the Latin Quarter is so called because conversation between students and professors until the Revolution was in Latin. It still has a large population of students and academics affiliated with

Notre Dame

TIMELINE

1160 Maurice de Sully becomes bishop of Paris. Mission: to grace growing Paris with a lofty new cathedral.

1182–90 The **choir with double ambulatory** 1 is finished and work starts on the nave and side chapels.

1200–50 The **west facade** 2, with rose window, three portals and two soaring towers, goes up. Everyone is stunned.

1345 Some 180 years after the foundation stone was laid, the Cathédrale de Notre Dame is complete. It is dedicated to *notre dame* (our lady), the Virgin Mary.

1789 Revolutionaries smash the original **Gallery of Kings** 3, pillage the cathedral and melt all its bells except the great bell Emmanuel. The cathedral becomes a Temple of Reason then a warehouse.

1831 Victor Hugo's novel *The Hunchback of Notre Dame* inspires new interest in the half-ruined Gothic cathedral.

1845–50 Architect Viollet-le-Duc undertakes its restoration. Twenty-eight new kings are sculpted for the west facade. The heavily decorated **portals** 4 and **spire** 5 are reconstructed. The neo-Gothic **treasury** 6 is built.

1860 The area in front of Notre Dame is cleared to create the *parvis*, an alfresco classroom where Parisians can learn a catechism illustrated on sculpted stone portals.

1935 A rooster bearing part of the relics of the Crown of Thorns, St Denis and St Geneviève is put on top of the cathedral spire to protect those who pray inside.

1991 The architectural masterpiece of Notre Dame and its Seine-side riverbanks become a Unesco World Heritage Site.

2013 Notre Dame celebrates 850 years since construction began with a bevy of new bells and restoration works.

Virgin & Child
Spot all 37 artworks representing the Virgin Mary. Pilgrims have revered the pearly-cream sculpture of her in the sanctuary since the 14th century. Light a devotional candle and write some words to the *Livre de Vie* (Book of Life).

North Rose Window
See prophets, judges, kings and priests venerate Mary in vivid blue and violet glass, one of three beautiful rose blooms (1225–70), each almost 10m in diameter.

Flying Buttresses

Choir Screen
No part of the cathedral weaves biblical tales more evocatively than these ornate wooden panels, carved in the 14th century after the Black Death killed half the country's population. The faintly gaudy colours were restored in the 1960s.

Treasury
This was the cash reserve of French kings, who ordered chalices, crucifixes, baptism fonts and other sacred gems to be melted down in the Mint during times of financial strife – war, famine and so on.

Great Bell
Navigate an elf-sized door and 22 wooden steps to reach the bell Emmanuel: its peal is so pure thanks to the precious gems and jewels Parisian women threw into the pot when it was recast from copper and bronze in 1631.

Chimera Gallery
Scale the north tower for a Paris panorama admired by birds, dragons, grimacing gargoyles and grotesque chimera. Nod to celebrity chimera Stryga, who has wings, horns, a human body and sticking-out tongue. This bestial lot warns off demons.

5

Spire

6

North Tower

South Tower

Great Gallery

West Rose Window

2

3

4

Transept

North Tower Staircase

The 'Mays'
On 1 May 1630, city goldsmiths offered a 3m-high painting to the cathedral – a tradition they continued every 1 May until 1707 when their bankrupt guild folded. View 13 of these huge artworks in the side chapels.

Three Portals
Play I spy (Greed, Cowardice et al) beneath these sculpted doorways, which illustrate the seasons, life and the 12 vices and virtues alongside the Bible.

Portal of the Virgin
Exit

Portal of the Last Judgement

Portal of St-Anne
Entrance

Parvis Notre Dame

Southern Bastille & Gare de Lyon

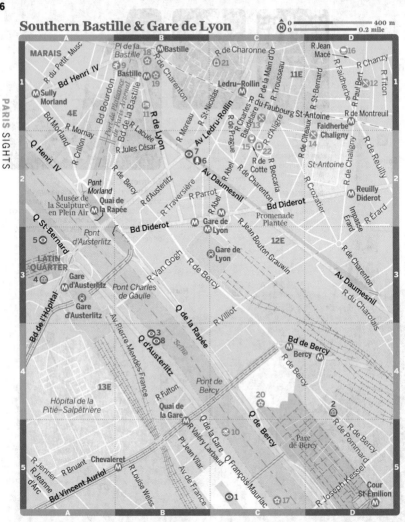

institutions that include the world-famous Sorbonne university. To the southeast is the city's beautiful botanic gardens, the Jardin des Plantes.

Musée National du Moyen Âge

HISTORY MUSEUM

(Map p92; www.musee-moyenage.fr; 6 place Paul Painlevé; adult/18-25yr/under 18yr €8.50/6.50/free; ⊗9.15am-5.45pm Wed-Mon; Ⓜ Cluny–La Sorbonne) The National Museum of the Middle Ages occupies both a *frigidarium* (cooling room), which holds remains of Gallo-Roman *thermes* (baths) dating from around AD 200, and the 15th-century Hôtel des Abbés de Cluny, Paris' finest example of medieval civil architecture. Inside, spectacular displays include statuary, illuminated manuscripts, weapons, furnishings and objets d'art made of gold, ivory and enamel. But nothing compares with *La Dame à la Licorne* (The Lady with the Unicorn), a sublime series of late-15th-century tapestries from the southern Netherlands.

Small gardens northeast of the museum, including the Jardin Céleste (Heavenly Garden) and the Jardin d'Amour (Garden of Love), are planted with flowers, herbs and

Southern Bastille & Gare de Lyon

PARIS SIGHTS

shrubs that appear in masterpieces hanging throughout the museum. To the west the Forêt de la Licorne (Unicorn Forest) is based on the illustrations in the tapestries.

Sorbonne   UNIVERSITY
(Map p92; 12 rue de la Sorbonne, 5e; MCluny–La Sorbonne or RER Luxembourg) The *crème de la crème* of academia flock to this distinguished university. Founded in 1253 by Robert de Sorbon, confessor to Louis IX, as a college for 16 impoverished theology students, the Sorbonne soon grew into a powerful body with its own government and laws.

Today, 'La Sorbonne' embraces most of the 13 autonomous universities – 35,500-odd students in all – created when the University of Paris was reorganised after the student protests of 1968. Until 2015, parts of the complex are under renovation.

Place de la Sorbonne links blvd St-Michel and the Chapelle de la Sorbonne, the university's distinctive domed church, built between 1635 and 1642. The remains of Cardinal Richelieu (1585–1642) lie in a tomb with an effigy of a cardinal's hat suspended above.

Panthéon   MAUSOLEUM
(Map p92; www.monum.fr; place du Panthéon; adult/under 18yr €8.50/free; ⊙10am-6.30pm Apr-Sep, to 6pm Oct-Mar; MMaubert-Mutualité, Cardinal Lemoine or RER Luxembourg) The Panthéon is a superb example of 18th-century neoclassicism. The domed landmark was commissioned by Louis XV around 1750 as an abbey,

but due to financial and structural problems it wasn't completed until 1789 – not a good year for church openings in Paris. Two years later the Constituent Assembly turned it into a secular mausoleum.

Louis XV originally dedicated the church to Sainte Geneviève in thanksgiving for his recovery from an illness. It reverted to its religious duties twice more after the Revolution but has played a secular role ever since 1885, and now is the resting place of some of France's greatest thinkers. Among its 80 or so permanent residents are Voltaire, Jean-Jacques Rousseau, Louis Braille, Émile Zola and Jean Moulin. The first woman to be interred in the Panthéon was the two-time Nobel Prize winner Marie Curie (1867–1934), reburied here, along with her husband, Pierre, in 1995.

Jardin des Plantes   GARDEN
(Map p86; www.jardindesplantes.net; 57 rue Cuvier, 5e; adult/child €6/4; ⊙7.30am-7.45pm Apr–mid-Oct, 8.30am-5.30pm mid-Oct–Mar; MGare d'Austerlitz, Censier Daubenton or Jussieu) Founded in 1626 as a medicinal herb garden for Louis XIII, Paris' 24-hectare botanical gardens are a serious institute rather than a leisure destination, but fascinating all the same and idyllic to stroll or jog around.

Sections include a winter garden, tropical greenhouses and an alpine garden with 2000 mountainous plants, as well as the gardens of the École de Botanique, used by students of the School of Botany and green-fingered Parisians

The Islands

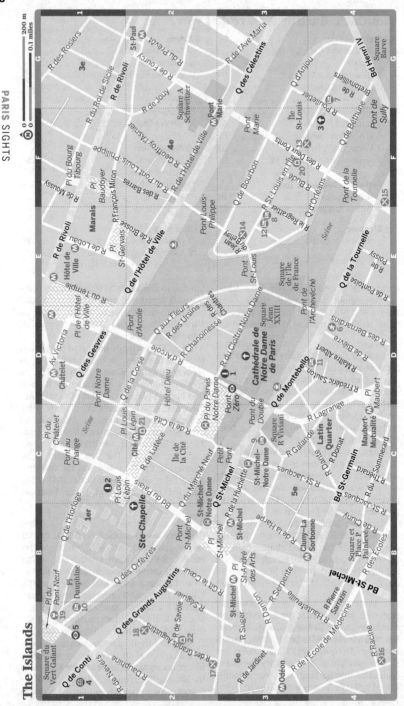

200 m
0.1 miles

G 1
R des Rosiers
St-Paul
R du Prévôt
3e
R de Sicile
R du Roi de Sicile
R de Fourcy
R de l'Ave Maria
Q des Célestins
Square Barve
Bd Henri IV

R de Rivoli
R de Joly
Square A Schweitzer
Pont Marie
Île St-Louis
R d'Anjou
Q d'Anjou
R de Bretonvilliers
7

Pl du Bourg Tibourg
R Baudoyer
R François Miron
R de l'Hôtel de Ville
4e
R Geoffroy l'Asnier
Pont Marie
3
Q de Béthune
Pont de Sully

Marais
R des Barres
R du Pont-Louis-Philippe
R de Brosse
Q de Bourbon
R St-Louis en l'Île
13
20
R des Deux Ponts
Q d'Orléans
Pont de la Tournelle
15

R de Rivoli
Pl St-Gervais
Pont Louis-Philippe
14
R Jean du Bellay
8
12
R Regrattier
Seine

Hôtel de Ville
Q de l'Hôtel de Ville
Pont St-Louis
Square de l'Île de France
Pont de l'Archevêché
Q de la Tournelle
R de Poissy
Q de Pontoise

Pl de l'Hôtel de Ville
Av Victoria
Châtelet
Q des Gesvres
Pont d'Arcole
Q aux Fleurs
R des Ursins
R des Chanoinesses
R du Cloître Notre Dame
Square Jean XXIII
Cathédrale de Notre Dame de Paris
R des Bernardins

Pl du Châtelet
Pont Notre Dame
Q de la Corse
Hôtel Dieu
Pl Louis Lépin
Pl de la Cité
1
Pont Zéro
Pl du Parvis Notre Dame
Pont au Double
R de Bièvre

Pont au Change
Seine
Pl du Châtelet
Île de la Cité
Cité
21
Pl Louis Lépin
Petit Pont
Q de Montebello
R Maître Albert
R Frédéric Sauton
11
Pl Maubert

1er
Pl Dauphine
Pont Neuf
2
Bd du Palais
R de Lutèce
R du Marché Neuf
St-Michel-Notre Dame
9
Square R Viviani
R Lagrange
R Galande
Latin Quarter
Maubert-Mutualité
R Domat

Ste-Chapelle
Q des Orfèvres
Pont St-Michel
Q du Marché Neuf
Notre Dame
St-Michel
R de la Huchette
R St-Jacques
R Dante
5e
R Thénard
R du Sommerard
Bd St-Germain

Pl du Pont Neuf
19
10
Pl Dauphine
R du Petit Pont
St-Michel
Pl St-Michel
St-Michel
R de la Harpe
R St-Jacques
Cluny-La Sorbonne
Square et Place P Painlevé
R des Écoles
Bd St-Michel

5
4
Q de Conti
Q des Grands Augustins
R Séguier
R Git le Cœur
Pl St-André des Arts
St-Michel
R Suger
R Serpente
Hautefeuille
R Pierre Sarrazin
R de Cluny

R de Nevers
R Dauphine
Q des Grands Augustins
18
22
R de Savoie
6e
17
R Dauphin
R de Jardinet
Odéon
R de l'École de Médecine
R Racine
16

Square du Vert Galant

A 1
B 2
C 3
D
E
F
G 4

The Islands

studying up on horticultural techniques. It also encompasses a zoo, the **Ménagerie du Jardin des Plantes** (Map p92; www.mnhn.fr; 57 rue Cuvier & 3 quai St-Bernard, 5e; adult/child €9/7; ◎9am-5pm; MGare d'Austerlitz, Censier Daubenton or Jussieu), and the Musée National d'Histoire Naturelle (p89), three separate centres comprising France's natural history museum. Some sections are free; a two-day pass covering access to all areas of the Jardin des Plantes costs €25/20 per adult/child.

**Musée National
d'Histoire Naturelle** HISTORY MUSEUM
(Map p92; www.mnhn.fr; 57 rue Cuvier, 5e; MCensier Daubenton or Gare d'Austerlitz) France's

National Museum of Natural History, within the Jardin des Plantes, incorporates the **Galerie de Minéralogie et de Géologie** (Mineralogy & Geology Gallery; Map p92; 36 rue Geoffroy St-Hilaire; adult/child €8/6; ◎10am-6pm Wed-Mon), which was closed for renovations at the time of research; the **Galerie de Paléontologie et d'Anatomie Comparée** (Gallery of Paleontology & Comparative Anatomy; Map p86; 2 rue Buffon; adult/child €7/5; ◎10am-5 or 6pm Wed-Mon), covering anatomy and fossils; and the **Grande Galerie de l'Évolution** (Great Gallery of Evolution; Map p92; 36 rue Geoffroy St-Hilaire; adult/child €7/5; ◎10am-6pm Wed-Mon), highlighting humanity's effect on the planet's ecosystems.

The National Museum of Natural History was created in 1793 and became a site of significant scientific research in the 19th century. Of its three museums, the Grande Galerie de l'Évolution is a particular winner if you're travelling with kids: life-size elephants, tigers and rhinos play safari, and imaginative exhibits on evolution and global warming fill 6000 sq metres.

**Institut du Monde
Arabe** ARCHITECTURE, MUSEUM
(Institute of the Arab World; Map p92; www.imarabe. org; 1 place Mohammed V; adult/under 26yr €8/ free; ◎10am-6pm Tue-Fri, to 7pm Sat & Sun; MJussieu) The Institute of the Arab World, set up by France and 20 Arab countries to promote cultural contacts between the Arab world and the West, is housed in a highly praised building designed by Jean Nouvel; it opened in 1987. Its new-look museum, showcasing Arab art, artisanship and science, was unveiled in 2012.

Inspired by traditional latticed-wood windows, the stunning building blends modern and traditional Arab and Western elements, with thousands of *mushrabiyah* (or *mouche-arabies*) – photoelectrically sensitive apertures built into the glass walls that allow you to see out without being seen. The apertures are opened and closed by electric motors in order to regulate the amount of light and heat that reach the interior of the building.

From the 9th-floor **observation terrace**, incredible views stretch across the Seine as far as Sacré-Cœur. In addition to a panoramic restaurant here, the building also contains a cafe and a cafeteria, as well as a cinema and library.

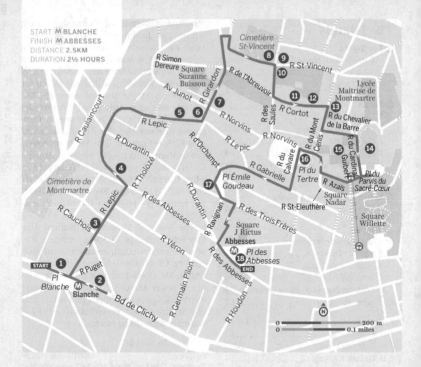

START M BLANCHE
FINISH M ABBESSES
DISTANCE 2.5KM
DURATION 2½ HOURS

Walking Tour
Montmartre Art Attack

❯ Montmartre has been a place of legend ever since St Denis was executed here in about AD 250 and began his headless journey on foot to the village north of Paris that still bears his name (p150). In recent times the Montmartre of myth has been resurrected by music, books and especially films like *Le Fabuleux Destin d'Amélie Poulain* (*Amélie*; 2002), which presented the district in various shades of rose, and *Moulin Rouge* (2001), which also made it pretty but gave it a bit more edge.

For centuries Montmartre was a simple country village filled with the *moulins* (mills) that supplied Paris with its flour. When it was incorporated into the capital in 1860, its picturesque charm and low rents attracted painters and writers – especially after the Communard uprising of 1871, which began here. The late 19th and early 20th centuries were Montmartre's heyday, when Toulouse-Lautrec drew his favourite cancan dancers and Picasso, Braque and others introduced cubism to the world.

After WWI such creative activity shifted to Montparnasse, but Montmartre retained an upbeat ambience. The real attractions here, apart from the great views from the Butte de Montmartre (Montmartre Hill), are the area's little parks and steep, winding cobblestone streets, lined with houses that seem about to be engulfed by creeping vines and ivy.

Begin the walk outside the Blanche metro station on place Blanche ('White Square'). The name of this square derives from the plaster (made from the locally mined gypsum) that was carted through the area. To the northwest is the legendary ❶ **Moulin Rouge** beneath its trademark red windmill. To the right is the ❷ **Musée de l'Érotisme**, an institution that portrays itself as educational rather than titillating. Yeah, right.

Walk up rue Lepic, lined with food shops, and halfway up on the left you'll find ❸ **Café des Deux Moulins** where heroine Amélie worked in the eponymous film. Follow the curve to the west: Théo van Gogh owned the ❹ **house at No 54**, and his brother, the artist Vincent, stayed with him on the 3rd floor from 1886 to 1888.

Further along rue Lepic are Montmartre's famous twinned windmills. The better-known **5** **Moulin de la Galette** was a popular open-air dance hall in the late 19th century and was immortalised by Pierre-Auguste Renoir in his 1876 tableau *Le Bal du Moulin de la Galette* (Dance at the Moulin de la Galette). About 100m to the east, at the corner of rue Girardon is the **6** **Moulin Radet** (now a restaurant confusingly called Le Moulin de la Galette).

Crossing through place Marcel Aymé you'll see a curious sculpture of a man emerging from a stone wall, the **7** **Passe-Muraille statue**. It portrays Dutilleul, the hero of Marcel Aymé's short story *Le Passe-Muraille* (The Walker through Walls) who awakes one fine morning to discover he can do just what he's shown doing here. Aymé lived in the adjacent apartment building from 1902 to 1967.

Cross the street to leafy square Suzanne Buisson, turn left (north) onto rue Girardon, and pass Allée des Brouillards (Fog Alley), named after the adjacent 'Fog Castle' where several artists squatted in the late 19th century – Renoir lived at No 8 from 1890 to 1897. Descend the stairs from place Dalida into rue St-Vincent: on the other side of the wall is **8** **Cimetière St-Vincent**, final resting place of Maurice Utrillo (1883–1955), the 'painter of Montmartre'.

Just over rue des Saules is the celebrated cabaret **9** **Au Lapin Agile**. Although its name seems to suggest a 'nimble rabbit', it actually comes from *Le Lapin à Gill*, a mural of a rabbit jumping out of a cooking pot by caricaturist André Gill, which can still be seen on the western exterior wall.

Turn right (south) onto rue des Saules. Just opposite is **10** **Clos Montmartre**, a small vineyard dating from 1933; its 2000 vines produce an average 800 bottles of wine each October, which is then auctioned off for charity. The **11** **Musée de Montmartre** is at 12–14 rue Cortot, the first street on the left after the vineyard. The museum is housed in Montmartre's oldest building, a manor house built in the 17th century, and was the one-time home to painters Renoir, Utrillo

and Raoul Dufy. Further along at No 6 is the **12** **house of Eric Satie** where the celebrated composer lived from 1892 to 1898.

At the end of rue Cortot turn right (south) onto rue du Mont Cenis – the attractive **13** **water tower** just opposite dates from the early 20th century – then left onto rue de Chevalier de la Barre and right onto rue du Cardinal Guibert. The entrance to the **14** **Basilique du Sacré Cœur** and the stunning vista over Paris from the steps are just to the south.

From the basilica follow rue Azaïs west, then turn north to **15** **Église St-Pierre de Montmartre**. This church was built on the site of a Roman temple to Mars (or Mercury) – some say that the name Montmartre is derived from 'Mons Martis' (Latin for Mount of Mars), others prefer the Christian 'Mont Martyr' (Mount of the Martyr).

Across from the church is **16** **place du Tertre**, arguably Paris' most touristy place but buzzy and fun nonetheless. Cossack soldiers allegedly first introduced the term *bistro* (Russian for 'quickly') into French at No 6 (La Mère Catherine) in 1814. On Christmas Eve 1898, Louis Renault's first car was driven up the Butte to place du Tertre, marking the start of the French auto industry.

From place du Calvaire take the steps onto rue Gabrielle, turning right (west) to reach place Émile Goudeau. At No 11b is the **17** **Bateau Lavoir** where Kees Van Dongen, Max Jacob, Amedeo Modigliani and Pablo Picasso once lived in an old piano factory later used as a laundry. It was dubbed the 'Laundry Boat' because of the way it swayed in a strong breeze. Picasso painted his seminal *Les Demoiselles d'Avignon* (1907) here. Originally at No 13, the real Bateau Lavoir burned down in 1970 and was rebuilt in 1978.

Take the steps down from place Émile Goudeau and follow rue des Abbesses south into place des Abbesses, where you can't miss the **18** **metro station** entrance designed by Hector Guimard. In the 18th century gypsum miners excavated significant amounts of the Butte, which is why the Abbesses metro station was dug so deeply.

Latin Quarter

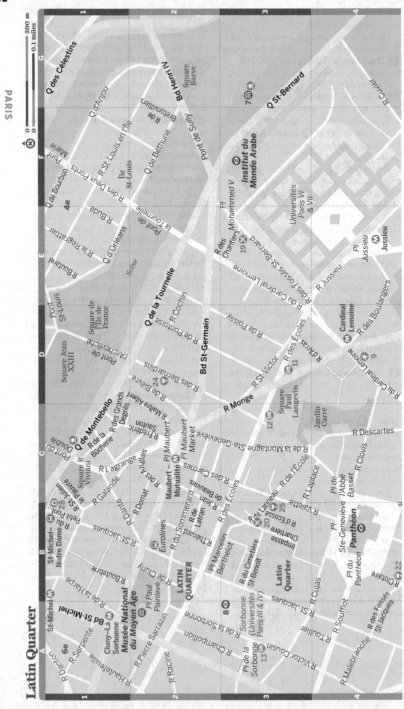

200 m
0.1 miles

Q des Célestins
Bd Henri IV
Square Barye
Q St-Bernard
7

Q d'Anjou
R de Bretonvilliers
Pont de Sully

Institut du Monde Arabe

Q de Bourbon
R St-Louis en l'Île
Île St-Louis
Q de Béthune
Pl Mohammed V
Universités Paris VI & VII

Pont Marie
R des Deux Ponts
4e
R Budé
Q d'Orléans
Pont de la Tournelle
R des Chantiers
19

Pl Jussieu
Jussieu

R Boulard
R le Regrattier
Q de la Tournelle
R du Cardinal Lemoine
R des Fossés St-Bernard
R Jussieu
R des Boulangers

Pont St-Louis
Square de l'Île de France
R Cochin
Q de la Tournelle
R de Pontoise
R de Poissy
R St-Victor
R des Écoles
R d'Arras
Cardinal Lemoine

Square Jean XXIII
Pont de l'Archevêché
R Maître Albert
R de Bièvre
24
R des Bernardins
Bd St-Germain
R Monge
11
Square Paul Langevin
Jardin Carré
R Descartes
9

Pont du Double
Q de Montebello
R des Grands Degrés
Frédéric Sauton
R Maubert
Pl Maubert
Maubert Market
Pl Maubert Mutualité
Rue de la Montagne Ste-Geneviève
12
R de l'École
R Laplace
R Clovis

Square R Viviani
R de la Bûcherie
R Lagrange
R des Anglais
R Galande
R Dante
R Domat
R des Carmes
R des Écoles
R Valette
Pl de l'Abbé Basset

St-Michel–Notre Dame
Petit Pont
R St-Julien le Pauvre
28
R St-Jacques
Eurolines
R du Sommerard
R Jean de Beauvais
R Latran
R de Lanneau
25
R d'Écosse
20
Ste-Geneviève
Panthéon

St-Michel
Bd St-Michel
Cluny–La Sorbonne
Musée National du Moyen Âge
Pl Paul Painlevé
LATIN QUARTER
R Boutebrie
R de Cluny
Pl Marcelin Berthelot
R du Cimetière St-Benoît
Impasse Chartière
Latin Quarter
R St-Jacques
R Cujas
Pl Ste-Geneviève
Pl du Panthéon
22

6e
R Danton
R Serpente
R Hautefeuille
R de la Harpe
8
Sorbonne (Universités Paris III & IV)
R Soufflot
R des Fossés St-Jacques

R Champollion
Pl de la Sorbonne
13
R de la Sorbonne
R Victor Cousin
R Toullier
Pl du Panthéon
R Clotaire
R Malebranche

R Racine
R Pierre Sarrazin

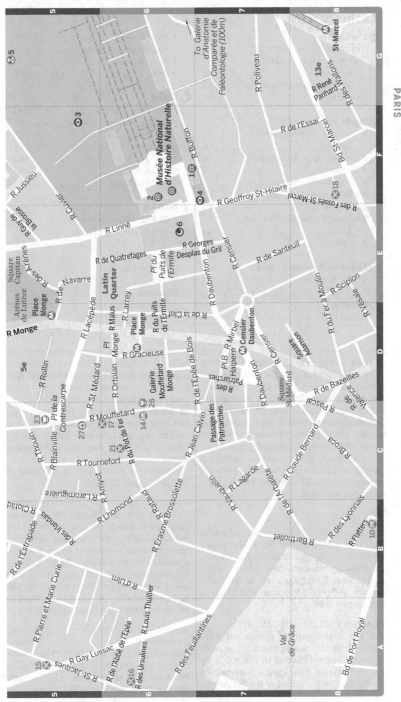

⊛ 5

🎯 3

To Galerie
d'Anatomie
Comparée et de
Paléontologie (100m)

St-Marcel

R Poliveau

13e

R René
Panhard

R des Wallons

R de l'Essai

R Buffon

Musée National
d'Histoire Naturelle

2

1

🎯 4

R Geoffroy St-Hilaire

R des Fossés St-Marcel

18

R Jussieu

R Linné

🎯 6

R Georges
Desplas du Gril

R Censier

R de Santeuil

R Cuvier

R de Quatrefages

Latin
Quarter

Pl du
Puits de
l'Ermite

R Daubenton

R du Fer à Moulin

R Scipion

Square
Capitan

R des Arènes

R de Navarre

R Larrey

R Malus

R du Puits
de l'Ermite

R de la Clef

R Vésèse

Arènes
de Lutèce

Place
Monge

R de Navarre

R Lacépède

Place
Monge

Pl B Mirbel

Censier
Daubenton

R Censier

Square
Adanson

R Monge

R Monge

Pl
Monge

R Gracieuse

Pl des
Patriarches

R Daubenton

5e

R Rollin

R-St-Médard

R Ortolan

Galerie
Mouffetard
Monge

R de l'Epée de Bois

R des
Patriarches

Square
St-Médard

R de Bazeilles

R Pascal

R de
Valence

Pl de la
Contrescarpe

R Mouffetard

26

17

R Jean Calvin

23

27

21

14

R du Pot de Fer

Passage des
Patriarches

R Broca

R Thouin

R Blainville

R Tournefort

R Lagarde

R Claude Bernard

R Laromiguière

R Amyot

R l'Aquelin

R de la l'Abalée

R des Lyonnais

R Clotild

R des Irlandais

R Lhomond

R Erasme Brossolette

R Rataud

R Berthollet

R Flatters

10

R de l'Estrapade

R Pierre et Marie Curie

R d'Ulm

R Louis Thuillier

R des Feuillantines

Val
de Grâce

Bd de Port Royal

15

16

R St-Jacques

R Gay Lussac

R de l'Abbé de l'Epée

R des Ursulines

Latin Quarter

Mosquée de Paris MOSQUE
(Map p92; ☑01 45 35 97 33; www.la-mosquee.com; 2bis place du Puits de l'Ermite, 5e; adult/child €3/2; ⊙mosque 9am-noon & 2-6pm Sat-Thu, souk 11am-7pm daily; Ⓜ Censier Daubenton or Place Monge) Paris' central mosque, with a striking 26m-high minaret, was built in 1926 in an ornate art deco Moorish style. The complex includes a wonderful North African–style *salon de thé* and restaurant; a *hammam* (a traditional Turkish-style bathhouse); as well as a vibrant Moroccan-style *souk* (market). Visitors must be modestly dressed.

FREE **Musée de la Sculpture en Plein Air** SCULPTURE MUSEUM
(Map p92; quai St-Bernard, 5e; ⊙24hr; Ⓜ Gare d'Austerlitz) Along quai St-Bernard, this open-air sculpture museum (also known as the Jardin Tino Rossi) has over 50 late-20th-century unfenced sculptures, and makes a great picnic spot.

PLACE D'ITALIE & CHINATOWN

The 13e arrondissement spirals out from Place d'Italie. It's undergone a renaissance in recent years, heralded in the 1990s by the controversial Bibliothèque Nationale de France and by the arrival of the high-speed Météor metro line. Many other additions followed, including the MK2 entertainment complex, the floating Piscine Joséphine Baker swimming pool on the Seine, and – Paris' most recent bridge – the Passerelle Simone de Beauvoir (2006), which provides a cycle and pedestrian link to the Right Bank. And the changes aren't slated to stop until 2020, when the ZAC Paris Rive Gauche redevelopment project ends.

Between av d'Italie and av de Choisy is the city's largest Chinatown.

Docks en Seine CULTURAL CENTRE
(Cité de la Mode et du Design; Map p86; www.paris-docks-en-seine.fr; 36 quai d'Austerlitz, 13e; Ⓜ Gare d'Austerlitz) Don't miss this 20,000-sq-metre riverside warehouse, which has been transformed into a state-of-the-art cultural, fashion-design and entertainment centre; its hip 'creative space', Wanderlust (Map p86; 32 Quai d'Austerlitz, 13e; ⊙noon-6am, Wed-Sun; Ⓜ Gare d'Austerlitz), has Paris' biggest terrace.

Bibliothèque Nationale de France LIBRARY
(Map p86; ☑01 53 79 40 41, 01 53 79 53 79; www.bnf.fr; 11 quai François Mauriac, 13e; temporary exhibitions adult/18-26yr from €7/5; ⊙10am-7pm Tue-Sat, 1-7pm Sun; Ⓜ Bibliothèque) The

National Library of France, with four glass towers shaped like open books, was one of President Mitterand's most ambitious and costliest *grands projets*. The national library contains around 12 million tomes stored on some 420km of shelves and can hold 2000 readers and 2000 researchers. It's well worth visiting for its excellent temporary exhibitions (entrance E), which revolve around 'the word' – from storytelling to bookbinding and French heroes.

ST-GERMAIN & LES INVALIDES

Despite gentrification since its early 20th century bohemian days, there remains a startling cinematic quality to this soulful part of the Left Bank, where artists, writers, actors and musicians cross paths and *la vie germanopratine* (St-Germain life) is *belle*. To St-Germain's west is the refined Les Invalides area.

This is one of those neighbourhoods whose very fabric is an attraction in itself, so allow plenty of time to stroll its side streets and stop at its fabled literary cafes and storied shops.

Musée d'Orsay
ART MUSEUM

(www.musee-orsay.fr; 62 rue de Lille, 7e; adult/18-25yr/under 18yr €9/6.50/free; ⊙9.30am-6pm Tue, Wed & Fri-Sun, to 9.45pm Thu; MAssemblée Nationale or RER Musée d'Orsay) Fresh from renovations that incorporate richly coloured walls, a re-energised layout and increased exhibition space, the home of France's national collection from the impressionist, postimpressionist and art nouveau movements spanning the 1840s and 1914 is the glorious former Gare d'Orsay railway station – itself an art nouveau showpiece – where a roll-call of masters and their world-famous works are on display.

Top of every visitor's must-see list is the museum's painting collections, centred on the world's largest collection of impressionist and post-impressionist art. Just some of its highlights are Manet's *On The Beach* and *Woman With Fans*; Monet's gardens at Giverny; Cézanne's card players and still lifes; Renoir's *Ball at the Moulin de la Galette* and *Girls at the Piano*; Degas' ballerinas; Toulouse-Lautrec's cabaret dancers; Pissarro's *The Harvest*; Sisley's *View of the Canal St-Martin*; and Van Gogh's self-portraits, *Bedroom in Arles* and *Starry Night*. There are also some magnificent decorative arts, graphic arts and sculptures.

Save time by prepurchasing tickets online or at Kiosque du Musée d'Orsay (⊙9am-5pm Tue-Fri school holidays, Tue only rest of year), in front of the museum, and head to entrance C. Admission drops to €6.50 after 4.30pm (after 6pm on Thursday). Combined tickets with the Musée de l'Orangerie (p69) cost €14 to visit both within four days.

Musée Rodin
GARDEN, MUSEUM

(Map p56; www.musee-rodin.fr; 79 rue de Varenne, 7e; permanent exhibition adult/under 25yr €7/5, garden €1/free; ⊙10am-5.45pm Tue-Sun; MVarenne) Sculptor, painter, sketcher, engraver and collector Auguste Rodin donated his entire collection to the French state in 1908 on the proviso that they dedicate his former workshop and showroom, the beautiful 1730 Hôtel Biron, to displaying his works. They're now installed not only in the mansion itself, but in its rose-clambered garden – one of the most peaceful places in central Paris and a wonderful spot to contemplate his famous work *The Thinker*. Other sculptural highlights are *The Gates of Hell*, the 180 figures of which comprise an intricate scene from Dante's *Inferno*; Rodin's marble monument to love, *The Kiss*; and some 15 works by sculptor Camille Claudel, sister of writer Paul Claudel and Rodin's muse, protégé and mistress. Purchase tickets online to avoid queuing.

Hôtel des Invalides
HISTORIC SITE, MUSEUM

(Map p56; www.invalides.org; 129 rue de Grenelle, 7e; adult/child €9/free; ⊙10am-6pm Mon & Wed-Sun, 10am-9pm Tue, to 5pm Oct-Mar, closed 1st Mon of month; MInvalides) Fronted by a 500m-long expanse of lawn known as the Esplanade des Invalides, the Hôtel des Invalides was built in the 1670s by Louis XIV to provide housing for 4000 *invalides* (disabled war veterans). On 14 July 1789, a mob forced its way into the building and, after fierce fighting, seized 32,000 rifles before heading on to the prison at Bastille and the start of the French Revolution. At the southern end of the esplanade, laid out between 1704 and 1720, is the final resting place of Napoleon.

In the Cour d'Honneur, the Musée de l'Armée (Army Museum; Map p56; www.invalides.org; 129 rue de Grenelle, 7e; ⊙10am-6pm Mon & Wed-Sat, to 9pm Tue) holds the nation's largest collection on the history of the French military. South is Église St-Louis des Invalides, once used by soldiers, and Église du Dôme (Map p56; ⊙10am-7pm Jul & Aug, to 6pm Sep & Apr-Jun, to 5pm Oct-Mar) which, with its sparkling golden dome (1677–1735), is one of the finest religious edifices erected under Louis XIV and was the inspiration for the United States Capitol building. It

St-Germain & Montparnasse

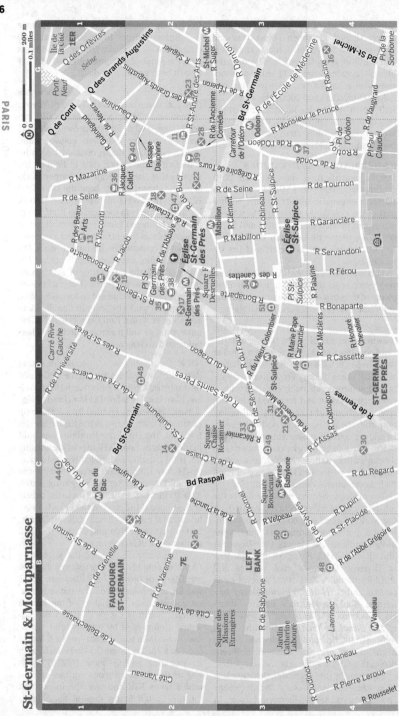

200 m
0.1 miles

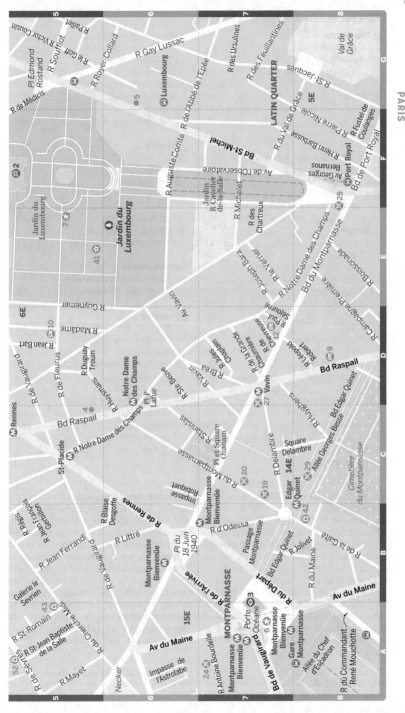

St-Germain & Montparnasse

received the remains of Napoleon in 1840. The extravagant Tombeau de Napoléon 1er (Napoleon I's Tomb; Map p56; ◷10am-6pm Apr-Sep, to 5pm Oct-Mar), in the centre of the church, comprises six coffins fitting into one another like a Russian doll.

Admission includes entry to all the sights in Hôtel des Invalides, including the Musée des Plans-Reliefs (Map p56; ☏01 45 51 95 05; http://plans-reliefs.monuments-nationaux.fr; ◷10am-6pm Apr-Sep, to 5pm Oct-Mar, closed 1st Mon of month), an esoteric museum full of scale models of towns, fortresses and châteaux across France.

Musée de la Monnaie de Paris MINT MUSEUM
(Map p88; ☏01 40 46 55 35; www.monnaiede paris.fr; 11 quai de Conti, 6e; Ⓜ Pont Neuf) Closed

for renovations at the time of writing, the Parisian Mint Museum traces the history of French coinage from antiquity onwards, with displays that help to bring to life this otherwise niche subject. It's housed in the 18th-century royal mint, the Hôtel de la Monnaie, which is still used by the Ministry of Finance to produce commemorative medals and coins. The overhaul of this magnificent neoclassical building with one of the longest façades on the Seine is slated to incorporate triple-Michelin-starred chef Guy Savoy's new cafe and restaurant.

Église St-Germain des Prés CHURCH
(Map p96; www.eglise-sgp.org; 3 place St-Germain des Prés, 6e; ◷8am-7pm Mon-Sat, 9am-8pm Sun; Ⓜ St-Germain des Prés) Paris' oldest stand-

ing church, the Romanesque St Germanus of the Fields, was built in the 11th century on the site of a 6th-century abbey and was the dominant place of worship in Paris until the arrival of Notre Dame. It has since been altered many times, but the Chapelle de St-Symphorien (to the right as you enter) was part of the original abbey and is believed to be the resting place of St Germanus (AD 496–576), the first bishop of Paris. The Merovingian kings were buried here during the 6th and 7th centuries, but their tombs disappeared during the Revolution. Over the western entrance, the bell tower has changed little since 990, although the spire dates only from the 19th century.

Église St-Sulpice   CHURCH
(Map p96; www.paroisse-saint-sulpice-paris.org; place St-Sulpice, 6e; ⊙7.30am-7.30pm; MSt-Sulpice) Work started on the twin-towered Church of St Sulpicius in 1646 and took six architects 150 years to finish. What draws most people today is not its striking Italianate façade with two rows of superimposed columns, Counter-Reformation-influenced neoclassical decor or even the frescoes by Delacroix – but its setting for a murderous scene in Dan Brown's *The Da Vinci Code.*

Jardin du Luxembourg   PARK
(Map p96; numerous entrances; ⊙hours vary; MSt-Sulpice, Rennes or Notre Dame des Champs, or RER Luxembourg) This inner-city oasis of formal terraces, chestnut groves and lush lawns has a special place in the hearts of Parisians. Napoleon dedicated the 23 gracefully laid-out hectares of the Luxembourg Gardens to the children of Paris, and many residents spent their childhood prodding 1920s wooden sailboats (per 30/60min €2/3.20; ⊙Apr-Oct) with long sticks on the octagonal Grand Bassin pond, watching puppets perform Punch & Judy–type shows at the Théâtre des Marionnettes du Jardin du Luxembourg (Map p96; ☑01 43 26 46 47; admission €4; ⊙3.30pm Wed, 11am & 3.30pm Sat & Sun, daily during school holidays), and riding the *carrousel* (merry-go-round) or Shetland ponies (Map p96). All those activities are still here today, as are modern playgrounds (adult/child €1.20/2.50; ⊙10am-park close) and sporting and games venues.

Dozens of apple varieties grow in the orchards in the gardens' south, while bees have produced honey in the nearby Rucher du Luxembourg since the 19th century;

don't miss the two-day Fête du Miel (Honey Festival) in late September.

The gardens are a backdrop to the Palais du Luxembourg, built in the 1620s for Marie de Médici, Henri IV's consort, to assuage her longing for the Pitti Palace in Florence, where she had spent her childhood. Since 1958 the palace has housed the Sénat (Senate; Map p96; ☑01 44 54 19 49; www.senat.fr; rue de Vaugirard; adult/18-25yr €8/6), the Upper House of French Parliament, which is occasionally visitable by guided tour. East of the palace is the Italianate Fontaine des Médici (1630), an ornate fish pond.

Prestigious temporary art exhibitions, such as 'Cézanne et Paris', take place in the Musée du Luxembourg (Map p96; www.musee duluxembourg.fr; 19 rue de Vaugirard, 6e; most exhibitions adult/child around €13.50/9; ⊙10am-8pm Sun-Thu, to 10pm Fri & Sat). Around the back of the museum, lemon and orange trees, palms, grenadiers and oleanders shelter from the cold in the palace's orangery. Nearby the heavily guarded Hôtel du Petit Luxembourg was the modest 16th-century pad where Marie de Médici lived while Palais du Luxembourg was being built. The president of the Senate has called it home since 1825.

If you're planning on picnicking, forget bringing a blanket – the elegantly manicured lawns are off limits apart from a small wedge on the southern boundary. Instead, do as Parisians do, and corral one of the iconic 1923-designed sage-green metal chairs and find your own favourite part of the park.

Opening hours vary greatly throughout the year; seasonal entry times are posted at entrance gates.

MONTPARNASSE
After WWI, writers, poets and artists of the avant-garde – Cocteau, Chagall and Picasso among them – abandoned Montmartre on the Right Bank and crossed the Seine, shifting the centre of artistic ferment to the area around bd du Montparnasse. Montparnasse remained a creative centre until the mid-1930s. Since the construction of the Gare Montparnasse complex, there's little to remind visitors of the area's bohemian past except cafes and brasseries where bohemians hung out – and some famous graves in Montparnasse cemetery.

Tour Montparnasse   VIEWPOINT
(Map p96; www.tourmontparnasse56.com; rue de l'Arrivée, 15e; adult/child €13/7.50; ⊙9.30am-

11.30pm daily Apr-Sep, to 10.30pm Sun-Thu, to 11pm Fri & Sat Oct-Mar; Ⓜ Montparnasse Bienvenüe) The 210m-high Montparnasse Tower, built in 1973 with steel and smoked glass and housing offices for 5000 workers, affords spectacular views over the city. (Bonus: its observation floor and terrace are about the only spots in Paris you can't see this startlingly ugly skyscraper.)

Europe's fastest lift/elevator whisks visitors up in 38 seconds to the indoor observatory on the 56th floor, with exhibition centre, video clips, multimedia terminals and Paris' highest restaurant, Le Ciel de Paris. Finish with a hike up the stairs to the open-air terrace on the 59th floor.

Cimetière du Montparnasse   CEMETERY
(www.paris.fr; bd Edgar Quinet & rue Froidevaux, 14e; ⊗8am-6pm Mon-Fri, 8.30am-6pm Sat, 9am-6pm Sun; Ⓜ Edgar Quinet or Raspail) Opened in 1824, Montparnasse Cemetery, Paris' second largest after Père Lachaise, sprawls over 19 hectares shaded by 1200 trees, including maples, ash, lime trees and conifers. Among its illustrious 'residents' are poet Charles Baudelaire, writer Guy de Maupassant, playwright Samuel Beckett, sculptor Constantin Brancusi, painter Chaim Soutine, photographer Man Ray, industrialist André Citroën, Captain Alfred Dreyfus of the infamous affair, actress Jean Seberg, and philosopher-writer couple Jean-Paul Sartre and Simone de Beauvoir, as well as singer Serge Gainsbourg. Free maps are available from the conservation office.

Les Catacombes   HISTORIC SITE
(www.catacombes.paris.fr; 1 av Colonel Henri Roi-Tanguy, 14e; adult/13-26yr/under 13yr €8/4/free; ⊗10am-5pm Tue-Sun; Ⓜ Denfert Rochereau) Paris' most gruesome and macabre sight is its series of underground tunnels lined with skulls and bones exhumed from the city's overflowing cemeteries. In 1785 it was decided to solve the hygiene and aesthetic problems posed by Paris' overflowing cemeteries by exhuming the bones and storing them in the tunnels of three disused quarries, and the Catacombes were created in 1810.

The route through the Catacombes begins at a small, dark-green belle époque building in the centre of a grassy area of av Colonel Henri Roi-Tanguy, adjacent to Place Denfert Rochereau. After descending 20m (130 steps) from street level, you follow 2km of subterranean passages where the bones and skulls of millions of Parisians are neatly packed along each and every wall. During WWII these tunnels were used as Resistance headquarters; thrill-seeking *cataphiles* are often caught (and fined) roaming the tunnels at night.

Renting an audioguide greatly enhances the experience. In the tunnels, the temperature is a cool 14°C – bring a jacket, even in summer. The exit is back up 83 steps on rue Remy Dumoncel (Mouton-Duvernet), 700m southwest of av Colonel Henri Roi-Tanguy.

🏃 Activities

Cycling

Paris is set to expand its cycling lanes to 700km by 2014. Additionally many sections of road are shut to motorised traffic on Sunday as part of the Paris Respire (p146) scheme. Pick up wheels with Vélib (http://en.velib.paris.fr), join an organised tour or hire your own wheels and DIY. Most hire places require a deposit; take ID and a credit card.

Gepetto et Vélos   CYCLING
(Map p92; www.gepetto-et-velos.com; 59 rue du Cardinal Lemoine, 5e; bicycles per day €15; ⊗9am-1pm & 2-7.30pm Tue-Sat; Ⓜ Cardinal Lemoine)

Paris à Vélo, C'est Sympa!   CYCLING
(Map p78; www.parisvelosympa.com; 22 rue Alphonse Baudin, 11e; bicycles per day €20; ⊗9.30am-1pm & 2-6pm Mon-Fri, 9am-1pm & 2-7pm Sat & Sun; Ⓜ St-Sébastien–Froissart)

Skating

Paris' most popular activity after cycling has to be skating, whether on the street or on ice. Rent a pair of in-line skates at Nomades (Map p86; www.nomadeshop.com; 37 bd Bourdon, 4e; half-/full day from €5/8, weekend/week €15/30; Ⓜ Bastille). Then join the Friday-evening skate Pari Roller (Map p96; www.pari-roller.com; place Raoul Dautry, 14e; admission free; ⊗10pm-1am Fri, arrive 9.30pm; Ⓜ Montparnasse Bienvenüe) through the Paris streets, or join the more laid-back Sunday-afternoon skate, Rollers & Coquillages (☏01 44 54 07 44; www.rollers-coquillages.org).

In winter temporary outdoor rinks are installed in front of the Hôtel de Ville and on the 1st floor of the Eiffel Tower. See www.paris.fr for other locations.

Swimming

Paris has some 37 public swimming pools, including the glamorous Piscine Joséphine Baker (Map p86; ☏01 56 61 96 50; www.paris.fr;

quai François Mauriac, 13e; pool adult/child €3/1.70, sauna €10/5; ☺1-9pm Mon, Wed & Fri, 1-11pm Tue & Thu, noon-8pm Sat, 10am-8pm Sun; MBibliothèque or Quai de la Gare) floating on the Seine. Visit www.paris.fr for a complete list. Swimmers need to don a *bonnet de bain* (bathing cap), generally sold at pools. Men are required to wear skin-tight trunks (Speedos); loose-fitting Bermuda shorts are not allowed.

🍴 Courses

Culinary

» **Les Coulisses du Chef** (Map p66; ☎01 40 26 14 00; www.coursdecuisineparis.com; 2nd fl, 7 rue Paul Lelong, 2e; MBourse) Popular courses for beginners.

» **Cook'n With Class** (Map p74; www.cooknwithclass.com) Seven international chefs, small classes and a Montmartre location.

» **La Cuisine Paris** (Map p96; www.lacuisineparis.com) A variety of courses, from bread and pastries to market classes and 'foodie walks'.

» **École Le Cordon Bleu** (☎01 53 68 22 50; www.cordonbleu.edu; 8 rue Léon Delhomme, 15e; MVaugirard or Convention) One of the world's foremost culinary arts schools.

» **Patricia Wells** (www.patriciawells.com) Five-day movable feast from the former *International Herald Tribune* food critic.

Wine Tasting

» **Ô Chateau** (Map p66; ☎01 44 73 97 80; www.o-chateau.com; 68 rue Jean-Jacques Rousseau, 1er; MLouvre Rivoli) Young fun-charged company offering the full range of tastings and experiences near the Louvre. Tastings start from €30 for one hour through to *grand cru* (wine of exceptional quality) master classes (€120); there are also lunches, dinners, champagne cruises and excursions.

» **Musée du Vin** (☎01 45 25 63 26; www.museeduvinparis.com; 5 sq Charles Dickens, 16e; adult/child €12/free; ☺10am-6pm Tue-Sun; MPassy) In addition to displays, Paris' wine museum offers instructive tastings (€59 for two hours).

🚶 Tours

Bicycle

Fat Tire Bike Tours   CYCLING
(Map p56; ☎01 56 58 10 54; www.fattirebiketours.com) Daytime bike tours of the city (€28; four hours) start at 11am daily from mid-February to early January, with an ad-ditional departure at 3pm from April to October. Night bicycle tours depart at 7pm from April to October and 6pm (not always daily) in low season. Other tours go to Versailles, Monet's garden in Giverny and the Normandy beaches. Participants generally meet opposite the Eiffel Tower's South Pillar at the start of the Champ de Mars; look for the yellow signs. Reserve in advance.

Boat

Bateaux-Mouches   BOAT TOUR
(Map p58; ☎01 42 25 96 10; www.bateauxmouches.com; Port de la Conférence, 8e; adult/4-12yr €11/5.50; ☺Apr-Dec; MAlma Marceau) The largest river cruise company in Paris and a favourite with tour groups, Bateaux-Mouches runs frequent cruises (70 minutes) from 10.15am to 11pm April to September and 13 times a day between 11am and 9pm the rest of the year. Commentary is in French and English. It's located on the Right Bank, just east of the Pont de l'Alma.

Bateaux Parisiens   BOAT TOUR
(Map p56; www.bateauxparisiens.com; Port de la Bourdonnais, 7e; adult/child €12/6; ☺every 30min 10am-10.30pm Apr-Sep, hourly 10am-10pm Oct-Mar; MBir Hakeim or RER Pont de l'Alma) Runs smaller boats that do one-hour river circuits with recorded commentary in 13 different languages. There are two locations: one northwest of the Eiffel Tower, the other south of Notre Dame.

Bus

L'Open Tour   BUS TOUR
(Map p72; www.pariscityrama.com; 2-day passes adult/child €32/15) This hop-on, hop-off bus tour runs daily open-deck buses along four circuits (central Paris; Montmartre–

HAVE YOUR SAY

Found a fantastic restaurant that you're longing to share with the world? Disagree with our recommendations? Or just want to talk about your most recent trip?

Whatever your reason, head to lonelyplanet.com, where you can post a review, ask or answer a question on the Thorntree forum, comment on a blog, or share your photos and tips on Groups. Or you can simply spend time chatting with like-minded travellers. So go on, have your say.

Grands Boulevards; Bastille–Bercy; and Montparnasse–St-Germain) year-round.

Walking

Paris Greeter   WALKING TOUR
(www.parisiendunjour.fr; by donation) See Paris through local eyes with these two- to three-hour city tours. Volunteers lead groups (max six people) to their favourite spots in the city. Minimum two weeks' advance notice required.

Ça Se Visite   WALKING TOUR
(www.ca-se-visite.fr; €12) Meet local artists and craftspeople on resident-led 'urban discovery tours' of the northeast.

Free Tour   WALKING TOUR
(neweuropetours.eu; by donation) This group tour of the city's main highlights takes 3½ hours, with two departures a day. It also runs daily two-hour tours of Montmartre for €12.

Paris Walks   WALKING TOUR
(www.paris-walks.com; adult/child €12/8) Long established and highly rated by Lonely Planet readers, Paris Walks offers thematic tours (fashion, chocolate, the French Revolution).

✩ Festivals & Events

Innumerable festivals, cultural and sporting events and trade shows take place in Paris throughout the year. Check 'What's On' on the website of the Paris Convention & Visitors Bureau, www.parisinfo.com.

January & February

Fashion Week   FASHION
(www.pretparis.com; MPorte de Versailles) Prêt-à-Porter, the ready-to-wear fashion salon held twice a year in late January and again in September, is held at the Parc des Expositions at Porte de Versailles, 15e.

Salon International de l'Agriculture   FOOD FESTIVAL
(www.salon-agriculture.com) A 10-day international agricultural fair with produce and animals turned into starter and main-course fare from all over France, held at the Parc des Expositions at Porte de Versailles, 15e, from late February.

March & April

Foire du Trône   FUN FAIR
(www.foiredutrone.com; MPorte Dorée) Huge fun fair dating back some 1000 years, held from early April to late May on the Pelouse de Reuilly of the Bois de Vincennes.

Marathon International de Paris   SPORTS
(www.parismarathon.com) The Paris International Marathon, usually held on the second Sunday in April, starts on the av des Champs-Élysées, 8e, and finishes on av Foch, 16e.

May & June

French Tennis Open   SPORTS
(www.rolandgarros.com) The glitzy Internationaux de France de Tennis – the Grand Slam – is a two-week affair from late May to mid-June at Stade Roland Garros.

Gay Pride March   GAY
(www.gaypride.fr) A colourful, Saturday-afternoon parade in late June through the Marais to Bastille celebrates Gay Pride Day, with flamboyant floats and costumes.

Paris Jazz Festival   MUSIC FESTIVAL
(www.parcfloraldeparis.com) Free jazz concerts every Saturday and Sunday afternoon in June and July in Parc Floral de Paris. Park entry applies.

July & August

Paris Plages   BEACH
(www.paris.fr) 'Paris Beaches' transforms waterfront areas into sand-and-pebble 'beaches', complete with sun beds, beach umbrellas, atomisers, lounge chairs and palm trees from mid-July to mid-August.

Cinéma au Clair de Lune   FILM FESTIVAL
(www.forumdesimages.fr) Themed film screenings take place under the stars around town during Paris' free 'moonlight cinema'.

Rock en Seine   MUSIC FESTIVAL
(www.rockenseine.com) Headlining acts rock the Domaine National de St-Cloud on the city's southwestern edge.

September & October

Jazz à la Villette   MUSIC FESTIVAL
(www.villette.com) This 10-day jazz festival in early September has sessions in Parc de la Villette, at the Cité de la Musique and in surrounding bars.

Nuit Blanche   EVENT
(www.paris.fr) From sundown until sunrise on the first Saturday and Sunday of October, museums and recreational facilities like swimming pools, along with bars and clubs, stay open for one 'White Night' (ie 'All Nighter').

Fête des Vendanges de Montmartre   HARVEST
(www.fetedesvendangesdemontmartre.com) The grape harvest from the Clos Montmartre in

PARIS FOR CHILDREN

Paris is extraordinarily kid-friendly, and on a family trip, you'll find no shortage of things to do – from playing tag around the Palais Royal's black-and-white columns to sailing down the Seine or resting younger legs with a DIY city sightseeing tour aboard one of Paris' two partially above-ground metro lines (2 and 6).

Check the What's On directory of www.parisinfo.com. *Pariscope* and *L'Officiel des Spectacles* both have decent 'Enfants' sections for the low-down on current exhibitions and events with kids in mind.

For more on travelling with kids, see Travel with Children (p36).

These are the top five Parisian attractions for kids:

» Jardin du Luxembourg (p45) Puppet shows, pony rides and more.
» Cité des Sciences (p75) Interactive exhibits make science fun.
» Cinéaqua (p57) Shark tank!
» Ménagerie du Jardin des Plantes (p89) Central zoo.
» Jardin d'Acclimatation (p62) Delightful amusement park for tots.

early October is followed by five days of festivities, including a parade.

November & December

Christmas Eve Mass — CHRISTMAS
Celebrated at midnight on Christmas Eve at many Paris churches, including Notre Dame.

New Year's Eve — NEW YEAR
Bd St-Michel (5e), place de la Bastille (11e), the Eiffel Tower (7e) and especially av des Champs-Élysées (8e) are the Parisian hot spots for welcoming in the new year.

Sleeping

Paris has a huge choice of accommodation, from hostels through to budget hotels, excellent midrange hotels and deluxe hotels, some of which rank among the finest in the world. Yet although the city has more than 150,000 beds in over 1500 establishments, you'll still need to book well ahead during the warmer months (April to October) and for all public and school holidays.

Accommodation outside central Paris is marginally cheaper than within the city itself, but it's almost always a false economy, particularly as travelling into the city will eat up precious time. Choose somewhere within Paris' 20 *arrondissements*, where you can experience Parisian life the moment you step out the door.

Good hotel-booking websites include the well-organised Paris Hotel (www.hotels-paris.fr), with lots of user reviews, and Paris Hotel Service (www.parishotelservice.com), specialising in boutique hotel gems.

B&B accommodation (*chambres d'hôte* in French) is increasingly popular. The city of Paris has inaugurated a scheme called Paris Quality Hosts (www.hqp.fr) to foster B&Bs – not just to offer an alternative choice of accommodation, but also to ease the isolation of some Parisians, half of whom live alone. There's often a minimum stay of three or four nights.

ÉTOILE & CHAMPS-ÉLYSÉES

Hidden Hotel — BOUTIQUE HOTEL €€€
(Map p58; 01 40 55 03 57; www.hidden-hotel.com; 28 rue de l'Arc de Triomphe, 17e; r from €376; ❄@☎; MCharles de Gaulle-Étoile) The Hidden is one of the Champs-Élysées' best secrets: an ecofriendly boutique hotel, it's serene, stylish, reasonably spacious and it even sports green credentials. The earth-coloured tones are the result of natural pigments (there's no paint), and all rooms have handmade wooden furniture, stone basins for sinks and linen curtains surrounding the beds. The Emotion rooms are among the most popular.

Hôtel Amarante Beau Manoir — HOTEL €€€
(Map p58; 01 53 42 28 28; www.amarantebeaumanoir.com; 6 rue de l'Arcade, 8e; r €216-255; ❄@☎; MMadeleine) Among the cosier hotels in the 8e, the Amarante has traditional-style rooms, with exposed rafters, wooden furniture and oak panelling, and it has a prime location just around the corner from place Madeleine. There's a small fitness room downstairs. Note that wi-fi access here costs an additional €22.

WANT MORE?

For in-depth information, reviews and recommendations at your fingertips, head to the Apple App Store to purchase Lonely Planet's *France* or *Paris City Guide* iPhone app.

Alternatively, head to Lonely Planet (www.lonelyplanet.com/france/paris) for planning advice, author recommendations, traveller reviews and insider tips.

LOUVRE & LES HALLES

The upsides of this neighbourhood are its central location, excellent transport links and proximity to major museums and shopping. However, the immediate area around the Forum des Halles (p70) may be noisy or inconvenient during construction works.

TOP CHOICE Hôtel Crayon BOUTIQUE HOTEL €€
(Map p66; ☎01 42 36 54 19; www.hotelcrayon. com; 25 rue du Bouloi, 1er; s €129-249, d €149-299; ❉❜; ⓂLes Halles or Sentier) Line drawings by French artist Julie Gauthron bedeck walls and doors at this creative boutique hotel – a work of art. The pencil (*le crayon*) is the theme, with rooms sporting a different shade of each floor's chosen colour – we love the coloured-glass shower doors and the books on the bedside table that guests can swap and take home.

Hôtel Tiquetonne HOTEL €
(☎01 42 36 94 58; www.hoteltiquetonne; 6 rue Tiquetonne, 2e; d €65, with shared shower €45; ❜; ⓂÉtienne Marcel) What heart-warmingly good value this 45-room vintage cheapie is. This serious, well-tended address in the heart of party land has been in the hotel biz since the 1900s and is much-loved by a loyal clientele of all ages. Rooms straddling seven floors are spick and span and sport an inoffensive mix of vintage decor – roughly 1930s to the 1980s. Recently renovated rooms have brand-new bathrooms and parquet flooring.

Ask for a room in the rooftops with a view of the Sacré-Cœur (Nos 701, 702 or 703) or Eiffel Tower (Nos 704 and 705). Shared shower *jeton* (tokens) are €5; ask at reception.

Le Pradey DESIGN HOTEL €€€
(Map p66; ☎01 42 60 31 70; www.lepradey.com; 5 rue St-Roch, 1er; d from €220; ❉@❜; ⓂTuileries) Enviably tucked behind the Louvre and Jardin des Tuileries by boutique-smart rue St-Honoré, this exclusive new address is the last word in luxury hotel design. Guests linger over glossy art books in the understatedly chic, mezzanine lounge – if they can drag themselves away from whichever individually themed suite they are staying in. Exuberant Cabaret evokes the theatrical glamour of the Moulin Rouge, with its frilly-skirt bedspread, deep red walls and heart-shape door frame; while Opéra, elegantly dressed in pretty pinks and greys, treats guests to a magical night at the ballet.

Hôtel Thérèse HOTEL €€€
(Map p66; ☎01 42 96 10 01; www.hoteltherese. com; 5-7 rue Thérèse, 1er; s €165-185, d €195-295; ⓂPyramides) Ideal for those with a fetish for Japanese food, this chic address is steps from rue Ste-Anne and Japantown. Rooms are individually decorated – classical yet eclectic in design – with stylish linen panels on the windows and tubs in the bathroom (cheaper, smaller rooms – and they are small – have showers). Highlight: the clubby library lounge.

Hôtel Ritz Paris HOTEL €€€
(Map p66; ☎01 43 16 30 30; www.ritzparis.com; 15 place Vendôme, 1er; d from €735; ❉❜❉; ⓂOpéra) So famous it has lent its name to the English lexicon, the Ritz is closed for major renovations until autumn 2014.

Le Relais du Louvre BOUTIQUE HOTEL €€€
(Map p66; ☎01 40 41 96 42; www.relaisdulouvre. com; 19 rue des Prêtres St-Germain l'Auxerrois, 1er; s €135-170, d €195-220, tr €235-250; ❉❜; ⓂPont Neuf) If you like style in a traditional sense, choose this lovely 21-room hotel just west of the Louvre and across the street from Église St-Germain l'Auxerrois, with its melodious chime of bells. The nine rooms facing the street and church are petite. Room 2 has access to the garden, and the top-floor apartment sleeps five, has a fully equipped kitchen and memorable views across the rooftops.

Hôtel de la Place du Louvre BOUTIQUE HOTEL €€
(Map p66; ☎01 42 33 78 68; www.paris-hotel-place-du-louvre.com; 21 rue des Prêtres St-Germain l'Auxerrois, 1er; d €140-185; ❉❜; ⓂPont Neuf) Not to be confused with the Relais du Louvre next door, this fairly recent addition to the Parisian hotel scene is warmly welcomed. It has just 20 rooms split across

five floors, and a couple on each floor are lucky enough to ogle at the majestic Louvre across the street.

BVJ Paris-Louvre HOSTEL €
(Map p66; ☎01 53 00 90 90; www.bvjhotel.com; 20 rue Jean-Jacques Rousseau, 1er; dm/d incl breakfast €30/70; @🖀; MLouvre Rivoli) This modern, 200-bed hostel run by the Bureau des Voyages de la Jeunesse (BVJ; Youth Travel Bureau) has doubles and bunks in a single-sex room for four to 10 people with showers down the corridor. Guests should be aged 18 to 35. Rooms are accessible from 2.30pm on the day you arrive. There are no kitchen facilities. Wi-fi costs €3/5 per two/four hours.

OPÉRA & GRANDS BOULEVARDS

W Paris – Opéra DESIGN HOTEL €€€
(Map p72; ☎01 77 48 94 94; www.wparisopera.fr; 4 rue Meyerbeer, 9e; d €340-500; 🖀@; MChaussée d'Antin–La Fayette) Melding 1870s Haussmann style with modern design, this sleek new hotel has the plushest rooms on the Grands Boulevards. Don't sell yourself short with a Cozy or Wonderful room: what you want is a Spectacular room – or maybe even a Wow suite – with superlative views of the Palais Garnier next door.

Hôtel Joyce DESIGN HOTEL €€€
(☎01 55 07 00 01; www.hotel-joyce.com; 29 rue La Bruyère, 9e; r €259-294; 🖀@🖀; MSt-Georges) This design hotel is in a lovely residential area in between Montmartre and l'Opéra. It's got all the modern design touches (iPod docks, a skylit breakfast room fitted out with old seats from a 4WD) and even makes some ecofriendly claims – it relies on 50% renewable energy and uses organic products when available. Rates drop significantly outside high season.

Hôtel Langlois HISTORIC HOTEL €€
(Map p72; ☎01 48 74 78 24; www.hotel-langlois.com; 63 rue St-Lazare, 9e; s €110-120, d €140-150; 🖀@🖀; MTrinité) If you're looking for a bit of belle époque Paris, the Langlois won't let you down. Built in 1870, this 27-room hotel has kept its charm, from the tiny caged elevator to sandstone fireplaces in many rooms (sadly decommissioned) as well as original bathroom fixtures and tiles. Room 64 has wonderful views of Montmartre's rooftops.

Hôtel Monte Carlo HOTEL €
(Map p72; ☎01 47 70 36 75; www.hotelmontecarlo.fr; 44 rue du Faubourg Montmartre, 9e; s €45-120, d €59-147, tr €119-179; 🖀; MLe Peletier) A unique budget hotel, the Monte Carlo is a steal, with colourful, personalised rooms and a great neighbourhood location. The owners go the extra mile and even provide a partly organic breakfast. The cheaper rooms come without bathroom or shower, but overall it outclasses many of the other choices in its price range. Rates vary with the season.

Hôtel Chopin HISTORIC HOTEL €
(Map p72; ☎01 47 70 58 10; www.hotelchopin.fr; 46 passage Jouffroy, 9e; s €72-88, d €98-114, tr €136;

PARISIAN APARTMENT RENTAL

Families – and anyone wanting to self-cater – should consider renting a short-stay apartment. Paris has a number of excellent apartment hotels, such as the international chain Apart'hotels Citadines (www.citadines.com/Apart_hotels).

For an even more authentic Parisian experience, apartment rental agencies offer furnished residential apartments for stays of a few days to several months. Apartments often include facilities such as wi-fi and washing machines, and can be superb value. Beware of direct-rental scams.

Paris Attitude (www.parisattitude.com) Thousands of apartment rentals; professional service, reasonable fees.

Guest Apartment Services (Map p35; www.guestapartment.com) Romantic apartment rentals on and around Paris' islands.

Room Sélection (www.room-selection.com) Select apartment rentals centred on the Marais.

À La Carte Paris Apartments (www.alacarte-paris-apartments.com) Designer apartment rentals.

Allô Logement Temporaire (Map p78; www.allo-logement-temporaire.asso.fr) Nonprofit organisation linking property owners with foreigners seeking furnished apartments for one week or more.

@; MGrands Boulevards) Dating to 1846, the 36-room Chopin is down one of Paris' most delightful 19th-century arcades. The rooms don't have much in the way of personality, but the belle époque location is fabulous.

MONTMARTRE & PIGALLE

Montmartre, encompassing the 18e and the northern part of the 9e, is one of Paris' most charming neighbourhoods with loads of variety, from boutique to bohemian and from hostel to *hôtel particulier*. Many have views of some kind – whether of the streets of Montmartre and Sacré-Cœur or the Paris skyline stretching away to the south – and top-floor availability is a good factor to take into account when choosing your room. The flat area around the base of the Butte Montmartre has some surprisingly good budget deals.

Hôtel Amour   BOUTIQUE HOTEL €€
(☎01 48 78 31 80; www.hotelamourparis.fr; 8 rue Navarin, 9e; s €105, d €155-215; 🛜; MSt-Georges or Pigalle) Planning a romantic escape to Paris? Say no more. One of the 'in' hotels of the moment, the inimitable black-clad Amour (formerly a by-the-hour love hotel) features original design and artwork in each of the rooms and is very much worthy of the hype – you won't find a more original place to lay your head in Paris at these prices. Of course, you have to be willing to forgo television, but who needs TV when you're in love?

Au Sourire de Montmartre   B&B €€
(☎06 64 64 72 86; www.sourire-de-montmartre. com; rue du Mont Cenis, 18e; r €125-170, apt per week €600; MJules Joffrin) This charming B&B on the far side of Montmartre has four rooms and one studio, each individually decorated with either French antiques or Moroccan motifs. The surrounding neighbourhood is delightful, though slightly out of the way. The owners also rent out an apartment that sleeps up to four in a separate building.

Hôtel Particulier
Montmartre   BOUTIQUE HOTEL €€€
(Map p74; ☎01 53 41 81 40; http://hotel-particulier -montmartre.com; 23 av Junot, 18e; ste €390- 590; ❄🛜; MLamarck-Caulaincourt) An 18th-century mansion hidden down a private alleyway, this VIP bijou sparkles from every angle. Much more than an exclusive hotel, it's the equivalent of staying in a modern art collector's personal residence, with rotating exhibitions, five imaginative suites designed by top French artists (Philippe

Mayaux, Natacha Lesueur) and a lush garden landscaped by Louis Benech of Jardin des Tuileries fame.

Hôtel Eldorado   HOTEL €
(☎01 45 22 35 21; www.eldoradohotel.fr; 18 rue des Dames, 17e; s €39-65, d €58-85, tr €75-93; 🛜; MPlace de Clichy) This bohemian hotel is one of Paris' greatest finds: a welcoming, reasonably well-run place with 23 colourfully decorated and (often) ethnically themed rooms, with a private garden at the back. Rooms 1 and 2 in the garden annexe and rooms 16 and 17 in the main building are the picks of the bunch. Cheaper-category singles have washbasin only.

Hôtel des Arts   HOTEL €€
(Map p74; ☎01 46 06 30 52; www.arts-hotel-paris. com; 5 rue Tholozé, 18e; s €105, d €140-165; 🛜; MAbbesses or Blanche) The Hôtel des Arts is a friendly, attractive 50-room hotel, convenient to both place Pigalle and Montmartre. It has comfortable midrange rooms that are excellent value; consider spending an extra €25 for the superior rooms, which have nicer views. Just up the street is the old-style windmill, Moulin de la Galette.

Plug-Inn Hostel   HOSTEL €
(Map p74; ☎01 42 58 42 58; www.plug-inn.fr; 7 rue Aristide Bruant, 18e; dm/d/tr €25/60/90; @🛜; MAbbesses or Blanche) This 2010 hostel has several things going for it, the first of which is its central Montmartre location. Then, the four- to five-person rooms all have their own showers; there's a kitchen and free breakfast; and the staff are friendly. No curfew.

Hotel Caulaincourt Square   HOSTEL €
(☎01 46 06 46 06; www.caulaincourt.com; 2 square Caulaincourt, 18e; dm €30, s €59-69, d €70-80, tr €97; @🛜; MLamarck-Caulaincourt) This hotel with dorm rooms is perched on the far side of Montmartre, beyond the tourist hoopla in a real Parisian neighbourhood. The rooms are in decent condition, with parquet floors and a funky design, though there is no lift. Wi-fi in the reception area only.

GARE DU NORD & GARE DE L'EST

The budget-to-midrange hotels around the Gare du Nord and Gare de l'Est train stations in the 10e are convenient for early birds headed to London or those wanting to crash on arrival. Nearby, the area around place de la République – transformed from a hectic roundabout to a leafy, pedestrian square in 2013 – is handy for Ménilmontant nightlife.

TOP
CHOICE Le Citizen Hotel   BOUTIQUE HOTEL €€
(Map p78; ☎01 83 62 55 50; www.lecitizenhotel. com; 96 quai de Jemmapes, 10e; d €177-275, q €450; ☎; MGare du Nord) A team of forward-thinking creative types put their heads together to open Le Citizen Hotel in 2011, and the result is 12 alluring rooms equipped with niceties such as iPads, filtered water and warm minimalist design. Artwork is from Oakland's Creative Growth Art Center for artists with disabilities.

Hôtel du Nord – Le Pari Vélo   HOTEL €
(Map p78; ☎01 42 01 66 00; www.hoteldunord -leparivelo.com; 47 rue Albert Thomas, 10e; s/d/q €71/85/110; ☎; MRépublique) This particularly charming place has 24 personalised rooms decorated with flea-market antiques. Beyond the bric-a-brac charm (and the ever popular dog, Pluto), Hôtel du Nord's other winning attribute is its prized location near place République. Bikes are on loan for guests.

République Hôtel   HOTEL €€
(Map p78; ☎01 42 39 19 03; www.republiquehotel. com; 31 rue Albert Thomas, 10e; s €82, d €95-120, tr €120, q €169; ☎; MRépublique) This hip spot is heavy on pop art – local street artists did some of the paintings here – and features what is possibly the narrowest elevator in Paris, if not the world. Regardless of what you think about the garden gnomes in the breakfast room, you won't be able to fault the inexpensive rates and fantastic location off place République.

St Christopher's Inn   HOSTEL €
(☎01 40 34 34 40; www.st-christophers.co.uk/ paris-hostels; 68-74 quai de la Seine, 19e; dm €22-40, d from €70; @☎; MRiquet or Jaurès) This is certainly one of Paris' best, biggest (300 beds) and most up-to-date hostels. It features a modern design, four types of dorms (12-bed, 10-bed, eight-bed, six-bed), and doubles with or without bathrooms. Other perks include a canal-side cafe, a female-only floor and bar. Seasonal prices vary wildly; check the website for an accurate quote. No kitchen.

A new branch (Map p108; rue de Dunkerque) across from the Gare du Nord should be open by the time you read this. Although larger than its sibling at La Villette, the rooms here were designed to accommodate fewer people and thus should be more private.

MÉNILMONTANT & BELLEVILLE

TOP
CHOICE **Mama Shelter**   DESIGN HOTEL €
(☎01 43 48 48 48; www.mamashelter.com; 109 rue de Bagnolet, 20e; r €80-200; ❄@☎; ☐76, MAlexandre Dumas or Gambetta) Coaxed into its zany new incarnation by uberdesigner Philippe Starck, this former car park offers what is surely the best-value accommodation in the city. Its 170 super-comfortable rooms feature computers, trademark Starck details (like a chocolate-and-fuchsia colour scheme), cool concrete walls and even microwave ovens, while a rooftop terrace and cool pizzeria add to its street cred.

The only drawback? Mama Shelter is a hike from both central Paris and the nearest metro stop.

Hôtel Beaumarchais   DESIGN HOTEL €
(Map p78; ☎01 53 36 86 86; www.hotelbeaumarchais.com; 3 rue Oberkampf, 11e; s/d/tr from €75/90/160; MFilles du Calvaire) This brighter-than-bright 31-room design hotel, with its emphasis on sunbursts and bold primary colours, is just this side of kitsch. But it makes for a different Paris experience. There are monthly art exhibitions, and guests are invited to the *vernissage* (opening night).

LE MARAIS & BASTILLE

Buzzing nightlife, hip shopping and a great range of eating options make the centrally situated Marais neighbourhood popular. The nearby Bastille has far fewer tourists, allowing you to see the 'real' Paris up close.

TOP
CHOICE **Hôtel Jeanne d'Arc**   HOTEL €
(Map p78; ☎01 48 87 62 11; www.hoteljeannedarc. com; 3 rue de Jarente, 4e; s €65, d €81-96, tr €149, q €164; ☎; MSt-Paul) About the only thing wrong with this gorgeous address is that everyone knows about it, meaning you need to book well in advance to snag one of its cosy, excellent-value rooms. Games, a painted rocking chair for tots in the bijou lounge, knick-knacks everywhere, and the most extraordinary mirror in the breakfast room create a real 'family home' air in this 35-room house.

Le Pavillon de la Reine   HISTORIC HOTEL €€€
(Map p78; ☎01 44 59 80 40; www.pavillondela reine.com; 28 place des Vosges, 3e; d from €330; MChemin Vert) Dreamily set on Paris' most beautiful and elegant square, place des Vosges, this sumptuous address loaded with history doesn't come cheap. But who cares when you can sleep like a queen? (Indeed,

PARIS SLEEPING

Gare du Nord & Gare de l'Est

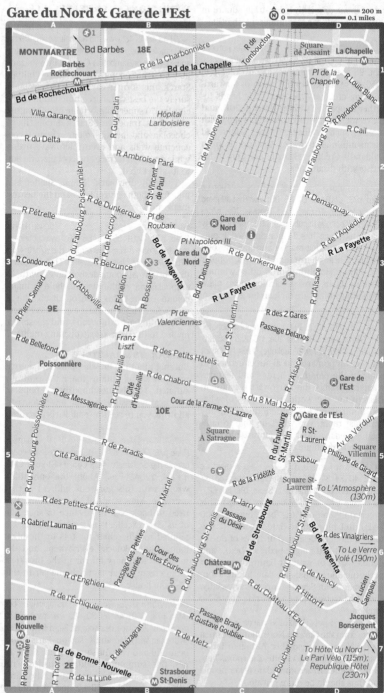

N
0 ———————— 200 m
0 ———————— 0.1 miles

Gare du Nord & Gare de l'Est

the hotel is named after Anne of Austria, queen to Louis XIII from 1615, who stayed here.)

Its cobbled stoned courtyard gardens are as pretty as a picture, especially in summer when they are a real country retreat from the hubbub of urban Paris. Its spa is equally revitalising.

Hôtel Les Jardins du Marais HOTEL €€€
(Map p78; ☎01 40 21 20 00; www.lesjardinsdu marais.com; 74 rue Amelot, 4e; d from €320; ⓂChemin Vert) A real summer address, the Marais Gardens is just that: a handful of buildings designed by Gustave Eiffel (of Tower fame) and nestled in beautiful courtyard cobblestone gardens strung with flowers and tables and chairs. Interior design gives a nod to art deco – lots of blacks, whites, purples and straight lines – and the hotel is always busy despite its size (more than 200 rooms). Communicating doubles make it a perfect family choice.

Cosmos Hôtel HOTEL €
(Map p78; ☎01 43 57 25 88; www.cosmos-hotel -paris.com; 35 Jean-Pierre Timbaud, 11e; s/d/tr €55/62/78; ☜; ⓂRépublique) Cheap, brilliant-value and just footsteps from the fun and happening bars, cafes and music clubs of increasingly trendy rue JPT, Cosmos is a shiny star with retro style on the budget-hotel scene. It has been around for 30-odd years, but, unlike most other hotels in the same price bracket, Cosmos has been treated to a thoroughly modern makeover this century. Enjoy.

Hôtel du Petit Moulin BOUTIQUE HOTEL €€€
(Map p78; ☎01 42 74 10 10; www.hoteldupetitmoulin. com; 29-31 rue du Poitou, 3e; d €190-350; ⓂFilles du Calvaire) This scrumptious 17-room hotel, a bakery at the time of Henri IV, was designed from head to toe by Christian Lacroix. Pick

from the medieval and rococo Marais, sporting exposed beams and dressed in toile de Jouy wallpaper, to more modern surrounds with contemporary murals and heart-shape mirrors just this side of kitsch.

Hi Matic HOTEL €€
(Map p78; ☎01 43 67 56 56; www.hi-matic.net; 71 rue de Charonne, 11e; r €110-160; ❋ @ ☜; ⓂBastille) This odd place has staked its claim as the 'urban hotel of the future', though there is both good and bad in that statement. The plus side is that it has some ecofriendly aspects (LED energy-saving lights, natural pigments instead of paint) and a colourful, imaginative space-saving design (mattresses are rolled out onto tatamis at night) that some will find kind of fun.

The drawback is that service is kept to a minimum – check-in is via computer, and the organic breakfast comes out of a vending machine. There is a manager on the premises to help with any problems, but it's safe to say this is definitely a spot that caters to independent personalities.

Hôtel Paris Bastille HOTEL €€€
(Map p86; ☎01 40 01 07 17; www.hotelparisbastille. com; 67 rue de Lyon, 12e; s €188, d €200-247, tr €247, q €263; ❋☜; ⓂBastille) A haven of serenity near busy Bastille, this comfortable hotel has a range of modern rooms. Although it feels slightly chainlike, it's nonetheless one of the nicest and most dependable options in the neighbourhood.

Maison Internationale de la Jeunesse et des Étudiants HOSTEL €
(MIJE; Map p78; ☎01 42 74 23 45; www.mije.com; 6 rue de Fourcy, 4e; dm incl breakfast €31; ⓂSt-Paul) Sweep through the elegant front door with brass knob and pride yourself on finding such magnificent digs. The MIJE runs three hostels in attractively renovated 17th- and

18th-century *hôtels particuliers* in the heart of the Marais – the other two are MIJE Le Fauconnier (Map p78; 11 rue du Fauconnier, 4e; M St-Paul or Pont Marie) and MIJE Maubuisson (Map p78; 12 rue des Barres, 4e; M Hôtel de Ville or Pont Marie) – and it's difficult to think of a better budget deal in Paris. Rooms are closed from noon to 3pm, and the curfew is 1am to 7am. Annual membership costs €2.50.

Hôtel Daval   HOTEL €
(Map p78; ☎01 47 00 51 23; www.hoteldaval.com; 21 rue Daval, 11e; s/d/tr/q €86/92/112/131; ✳☎; M Bastille) This 23-room hotel is a very central option if you're looking for budget accommodation just off place de la Bastille. Rooms and bathrooms are on the small side; to ensure peace and quiet, choose a back room (eg room 13).

Hôtel du 7e Art   HOTEL €€
(Map p78; ☎01 44 54 85 00; www.paris-hotel-7art.com; 20 rue St-Paul, 4e; s €75, d €100-180, tr €180, q €200; ☎; M St-Paul) Just across the road from the Village St-Paul, *le septième art* (or seventh art, as the French know cinema) is a fun place for film buffs, with its jaunty 1950s and '60s movie posters and cinematic B&W bathroom tiling. Ground-floor reception doubles as a cosy cafe-bar selling postcards and figurines.

THE ISLANDS
The Île St-Louis is the more romantic of the islands and has a string of excellent top-end hotels, while Île de la Cité has just one (budget) hotel.

[TOP CHOICE] Hôtel St-Louis en l'Île BOUTIQUE HOTEL €€
(Map p88; ☎01 46 34 04 80; www.saintlouisenlisle.com; 75 rue St-Louis en l'Île, 4e; d €169-199, with balcony €239-259, tr €279; ✳@☎; M Pont Marie) One of several hotels lining posh rue St-Louis en l'Île, this elegant abode has a pristine taupe façade and a perfectly polished interior to match. Spot-on home comforts like the kettle with complimentary tea and coffee in each room or the iPod docking station next to the bed make St-Louis stand out from the crowd.

Hôtel Henri IV   HOTEL €
(Map p88; ☎01 43 54 44 53; www.henri4hotel.fr; 25 place Dauphine, 1er; s/d/tr incl breakfast from €67/72/88; M Pont Neuf or Cité) It would be impossible to find a hotel more romantically located at such a price in all of Paris – much less on the tip of the Île de la Cité! Rooms at this much-loved budget hotel have

been freshened up with countrified colour schemes, and all but one has its own private bathroom. The views over the square are wonderful. Book well in advance (phone reservations only).

Hôtel de Lutèce   HOTEL €€
(Map p88; ☎01 43 26 23 52; www.paris-hotel-lutece.com; 65 rue St-Louis en l'Île, 4e; d €165-179; ✳☎; M Pont Marie) A lobby-salon with ancient fireplace, wood panelling, antique furnishings and terracotta tiles set the inviting tone of the lovely Lutèce, an exquisite hotel with tastefully decorated rooms and one of the city's most desirable locations.

LATIN QUARTER
This energetic area's popularity with students and visiting academics makes rooms hardest to find during conferences and seminars from March to June and in October.

Five Hotel   DESIGN HOTEL €€€
(Map p92; ☎01 43 31 74 21; www.thefivehotel-paris.com; 3 rue Flatters, 5e; d €202-342; ✳☎; M Les Gobelins) Choose from one of five perfumes to fragrance your room at this contemporary romantic sanctum (the cheapest 'standard' rooms are especially conducive to romance, ie small). Its private apartment, One by The Five, has a phenomenal 'suspended' bed.

Hôtel Minerve   HOTEL €€
(Map p92; ☎01 43 26 26 04; www.parishotelminerve.com; 13 rue des Écoles, 5e; s €99, d €129-165, tr €165; ✳@☎; M Cardinal Lemoine) Oriental carpets, antique books, frescos of French monuments and reproduction 18th-century wallpaper make this family-run hotel a charming place to stay. Some rooms have small balconies with views of Notre Dame, and two have tiny courtyards that are swooningly romantic.

Select Hôtel   BOUTIQUE HOTEL €€€
(Map p92; ☎01 46 34 14 80; www.selecthotel.fr; 1 place de la Sorbonne, 5e; s €165, d €215-299, tr €309-320; ✳@☎; M Cluny−La Sorbonne) In the heart of the studenty Sorbonne area, the Select is a very Parisian art deco mini-palace, with an atrium and cactus-strewn winter garden, an 18th-century vaulted breakfast room and 67 small but stylish bedrooms with ingenious design solutions to maximise their limited space. The 1920s-style cocktail bar with an attached 'library' just off the lobby is a delight.

Hôtel les Degrés de Notre Dame HOTEL €€

(Map p88; ✆01 55 42 88 88; www.lesdegreshotel. com; 10 rue des Grands Degrés, 5e; d incl breakfast €115-170; ☎; Ⓜ Maubert-Mutualité) Wonderfully old-school, with a winding timber staircase (no lift) and charming staff, this hotel a block from the Seine is unbeatable value. Breakfast comes with fresh-squeezed OJ. Rooms 47 and the spacious 501 have romantic views of Notre Dame.

Hôtel Résidence Henri IV HOTEL €€€

(Map p92; ✆01 44 41 31 81; www.residencehenri4. com; 50 rue des Bernadins, 5e; d €260-330; ❄@☎; Ⓜ Maubert-Mutualité) This exquisite late 19th-century cul-de-sac hotel has eight generously sized rooms (minimum 17 sq metres) and five two-room apartments (minimum 25 sq metres). All are equipped with kitchenettes (hot plates, fridge, microwave and dishes), making them particularly handy for families.

Hôtel Esmeralda HOTEL €

(Map p88; ✆01 43 54 19 20; www.hotel-esmeralda. fr; 4 rue St-Julien le Pauvre, 5e; s €75, d €100-115, tr €130, q €150; Ⓜ St-Michel) Tucked away in a quiet street with million-dollar views of Notre Dame (choose room 12!), this no-frills place is about as central to the Latin Quarter as it gets. At these prices, the 19 rooms – the cheapest singles have washbasin only – are no great shakes, but they're popular: book well ahead by phone (no online bookings).

Young & Happy HOSTEL €

(Map p92; ✆01 47 07 47 07; www.youngandhappy.fr; 80 rue Mouffetard, 5e; dm €20-33, d €70-90; @☎; Ⓜ Place Monge) This friendly if frayed Latin Quarter favourite was Paris' first independent hostel. The self-catering kitchen gets a workout from guests trawling rue Mouffetard's markets and food shops, and rates include breakfast in the dark stone-vaulted cellar. Beds are in cramped rooms with washbasins, but gals are in luck with an en suite female dorm (€29 to €38).

PLACE D'ITALIE & CHINATOWN

Oops HOSTEL €

(✆01 47 07 47 00; www.oops-paris.com; 50 av des Gobelins, 13e; dm/d incl breakfast €30/70; @☎; Ⓜ Gobelins) A lurid candyfloss-pink lift scales the six floors – each painted a different bold colour – of Paris' first 'design hostel'. Well-sized doubles and modern but lockerless four- to six-bed dorms all have attached bath and some have Eiffel Tower views, though they're offlimits from 11am to

4pm. There's no kitchen. No credit cards accepted; no alcohol allowed.

ST-GERMAIN & LES INVALIDES

Staying in the chic Left Bank neighbourhoods of St-Germain des Prés (6e) and the quieter 7e *arrondissement* next door is a delight, especially for those mad about boutique shopping.

TOP CHOICE L'Hôtel BOUTIQUE HOTEL €€€

(Map p96; ✆01 44 41 99 00; www.l-hotel.com; 13 rue des Beaux Arts, 6e; d €285-795; ❄@☎❄; Ⓜ St-Germain des Prés) In a quiet quayside street, this award-winning hostelry is the stuff of romance, Parisian myths and urban legends. Rock- and film-star patrons fight to sleep in room 16, where Oscar Wilde died in 1900 (it's now decorated with a peacock motif), or in the art deco room 36 of dancer Mistinguett, with its huge mirrored bed.

A stunning, modern swimming pool occupies the ancient cellar. Guests and non-guests can soak up the fantastic atmosphere of the bar (often with live music by up-and-coming new talent) and restaurant under a glass canopy.

TOP CHOICE L'Apostrophe DESIGN HOTEL €€

(Map p96; ✆01 56 54 31 31; www.apostrophe -hotel.com; 3 rue de Chevreuse, 6e; d €150-350; ❄@☎; Ⓜ Vavin) A street work-of-art with its stencilled façade, this art hotel's 16 dramatically different rooms pay homage to the written word. Spray-painted graffiti tags cover one wall of room U (for '*urbain*'), which has a ceiling shaped like a skateboard ramp. Room P (for 'Paris parody') sits in the clouds overlooking Paris' rooftops. Inspired design features include double sets of imprinted curtains (one for day, one for night) and a 'bar table' on wheels that slots over the bed.

Le Bellechasse DESIGN HOTEL €€

(✆01 45 50 22 31; www.lebellechasse.com; 8 rue de Bellechasse, 7e; d from €161; ❄☎; Ⓜ Solférino) Fashion designer (and, increasingly, interior designer) Christian Lacroix's entrancing room themes make you feel like you've stepped into a larger-than-life oil painting. Themes include 'St-Germain', with brocades, zebra striping and faux-gold leafing, 'Tuileries', with trompe l'œil and palms, and 'Jeu de Paume', with giant playing-card motifs. Mod cons include iPod docks and 200 TV channels.

Hôtel Perreyve HOTEL €€
(Map p96; ☑0145483501; www.hotel-perreyve.com; 63 rue Madame, 6e; d €145-165; ❈☎; MRennes) A hop, skip and a jump from the Jardin du Luxembourg, this warmly welcoming 1920s hotel is superb value given its coveted location. Cosy, carpeted rooms have patterned wallpaper and sleek furniture, and an elegant breakfast room is done in gold hues.

Hôtel d'Angleterre HISTORIC HOTEL €€€
(Map p96; ☑01 42 60 34 72; www.hotel-dangleterre. com; 44 rue Jacob, 6e; s €160, d €220-260; @☎; MSt-Germain des Prés) If the walls could talk... The garden of the beautiful 27-room 'England Hotel' – a former British Embassy – is where the Treaty of Paris ending the American Revolution was prepared in 1783. Hemingway lodged here in 1921, as did Charles Lindbergh in 1927 after completing the world's first solo nonstop flight from New York to Paris. Rooms are individually – and exquisitely – decorated; rates include breakfast.

Hôtel St-André des Arts HOTEL €
(Map p96; ☑01 43 26 96 16; 66 rue St-André des Arts, 6e; s/d/tr/q incl breakfast €75/95/119/132; ☎; MOdéon) Located on a lively, restaurant-lined thoroughfare, this 31-room hotel is a veritable bargain in the centre of the action. The rooms are basic, and there's no lift, but the public areas are very evocative of *vieux Paris* (old Paris), with beamed ceilings and ancient stone walls.

MONTPARNASSE

Just east of mammoth train station Gare Montparnasse, there are several budget and lower-end midrange places on rue Vandamme and rue de la Gaîté – though the latter street is rife with sex shops and peep shows.

La Maison BOUTIQUE HOTEL €€
(☑01 45 42 11 39; www.lamaisonmontparnasse. com; 53 rue de Gergovie, 14e; s/d/tr €110/130/160; ❈@☎; MPernety) The House goes all out to re-create home, with homemade cakes and jams for breakfast in the open-plan kitchen-lounge or little courtyard garden. A candy-striped staircase leads to its 36 rooms (there's a box-size lift too) with bold pinks, violets and soft neutral tones. Ask for an Eiffel Tower–view room. Rates tumble into budget range on weekends.

Hôtel de la Paix DESIGN HOTEL €€
(Map p96; ☑01 43 20 35 82; www.hotelparispaix. com; 225 bd Raspail, 14e; s €105-125, d €140-150, tr €190-210; ❈@☎; MMontparnasse Bienvenüe)

A hip mix of industrial workshop and *côte maison* (home-like), this restyled hotel is stacked on seven floors of a 1970s building. Its 39 light-filled modern rooms have at least one vintage feature in each – old pegs to hang coats on, old-fashioned school desk, wooden-slat house shutters recycled as bed head... Cheaper rooms are simply smaller than dearer ones.

Aloha Hostel HOSTEL €
(☑01 42 73 03 03; www.aloha.fr; 1 rue Borromée, 15e; per person dm/d incl breakfast €28/32; @☎; MVolontaires) An aubergine staircase is among the rainbow of colours brightening this laid-back crash pad, which has opera music in the hybrid reception-lounge and a stone-walled self-catering kitchen. You'll need a credit card to reserve four- to eight-bed dorms (reservations for doubles aren't guaranteed) but you must pay cash on arrival. Rooms are locked from 11am to 5pm, curfew is at 2am.

Hôtel Carladez Cambronne HOTEL €
(☑01 47 34 07 12; www.hotelcarladez.com; 3 place du Général Beuret, 15e; s/d/tr/q €94/97/167/180; @☎; MVaugirard) On a quintessential cafe-clad square, this accommodating hotel rents coffee- and tea-making facilities for you to make yourself at home. Room No 11 opens onto a tiny courtyard with table for two.

🍴 Eating

Some people rally around local sports teams, but in Paris, they rally around *la table* – and everything on it. Pistachio macarons, shots of tomato consommé, decadent bœuf bourguignon, a gooey wedge of Camembert running onto the cheese plate: food is not fuel here – it's the reason you get up in the morning.

Rather than being known for regional specialties as elsewhere in the country, the city is the crossroads for the regional flavours of France. And, as a multicultural melting pot, it's also a fantastic place to experience cuisine from around the globe.

Neobistros offer some of the most exciting dining options in Paris today. Generally small and relatively informal, they're run by young, talented chefs who aren't afraid to experiment and push the envelope of traditional French fare.

EIFFEL TOWER AREA & 16E

The museum- and monument-rich 16e *arrondissement* has some fine places to dine. Near the Eiffel Tower, grab picnic supplies on foodie street rue Cler or choose from several restaurants on rue de Montessuy.

L'Astrance GASTRONOMIC €€€
(Map p56; ☎01 40 50 84 40; 4 rue Beethoven, 16e;
lunch/dinner menus €70/210; ⊗Tue-Fri; MPassy)
It's been over a decade now since Pascal
Barbot's dazzling cuisine at the three-
star L'Astrance made its debut, but it has
shown no signs of losing its cutting edge.
Look beyond the complicated descriptions
on the menu – what you should expect are
teasers of taste that you never even knew
existed, and a presentation that is an art
unto itself.

You'll need to reserve two months in advance (one month for lunch) for this culinary experience unique to Paris.

Les Ombres MODERN FRENCH €€€
(Map p56; ☎01 47 53 68 00; www.lesombres
-restaurant.com; 27 quai Branly, 7e; lunches €26-38,
dinners €65; ⊗daily; Mléna or RER Pont de l'Alma)
Paris gained not only a museum in the
Musée du Quai Branly but also this glass-
enclosed rooftop restaurant on the 5th floor.
Named 'The Shadows' for the patterns cast
by the Eiffel Tower's webbed ironwork, it has
dramatic views complemented by the kitch-
en's creations, such as *gambas* (prawns)
with black rice and fennel, or sea bream in a
parmesan crust.

Stop by between 3pm and 5pm to sample pastry chef Pascal Chanceau's decadent

DON'T MISS

PARISIAN FOOD MARKETS

Nowhere encapsulates Paris' village atmosphere more than its markets. Not simply places to shop, the city's street markets are social gatherings for the entire neighbourhood.
Nearly every little quarter has its own street market at least once a week, and the city
also has some wonderful covered markets and commercial streets with stalls. No markets take place on Mondays. The website www.paris.fr lists every market by *arrondissement*, including speciality markets.

The following are Paris' top 10 markets:

Marché aux Enfants Rouges (Map p78; 39 rue de Bretagne, 3e; ⊗8.30am-1pm & 4-7.30pm
Tue-Fri, 4-8pm Sat, 8.30am-2pm Sun; MFilles du Calvaire) Paris' oldest covered market with
communal tables for lunch.

Marché Bastille (Map p78; bd Richard Lenoir, 11e; ⊗7am-2.30pm Thu & Sun; MBastille or
Richard Lenoir) Arguably the best open-air market in Paris.

Marché Couvert Beauvau (Map p86; place d'Aligre, 12e; ⊗8am-1pm & 4-7.30pm Tue-Sat,
8am-1pm Sun; MLedru Rollin) Colourful Arab and North African covered market.

Marché Belleville (Map p78; bd de Belleville, btwn rue Jean-Pierre Timbaud & rue du Faubourg
du Temple, 11e & 20e; ⊗7am-2.30pm Tue & Fri; MBelleville or Couronnes) Fascinating entry
into the large communities of the eastern neighbourhoods, home to artists, students and
immigrants from Africa, Asia and the Middle East.

Marché Couvert St-Quentin (Map p108; 85 bd de Magenta, 10e; ⊗8am-1pm & 3.30-
7.30pm Tue-Sat, 8.30am-1pm Sun; MGare de l'Est) Iron-and-glass covered market built in
1866; lots of gourmet and upmarket food stalls.

Marché Edgar Quinet (Map p96; bd Edgar Quinet, 14e; ⊗7am-2pm Wed & Sat; MEdgar
Quinet or Montparnasse Bienvenüe) Local open-air market with some great stalls sizzling up
snacks to eat on the run.

Marché Raspail (Map p96; bd Raspail btwn rue de Rennes & rue du Cherche Midi, 6e; ⊗regu-
lar market 7am-2.30pm Tue & Fri, organic market 9am-3pm Sun; MRennes) Especially popular
on Sundays, when it's filled with organic produce.

Rue Cler (Map p56; rue Cler, 7e; ⊗8am-7pm Tue-Sat, to noon Sun; MÉcole Militaire) Fabulous
commercial street that almost feels like a party on weekends, when the whole neighbourhood seemingly shops en masse.

Rue Montorgueil (Map p66; rue Montorgueil, 2e) A splinter of the historic Les Halles –
Paris' wholesale markets, which relocated after some 800 years to the suburb of Rungis
in 1971. Today grocery and speciality stalls set up along the pedestrian street.

Rue Mouffetard (Map p92; rue Mouffetard, 5e; ⊗8am-7.30pm Tue-Sat, to noon Sun; MCensier Daubenton) Paris' most photogenic commercial street.

INTERNATIONAL EAT STREETS

One of Paris' largest concentrations of international restaurants squeezes into a labyrinth of narrow streets across the Seine from Notre Dame in the 5e – between rue St-Jacques, bd St-Germain and bd St-Michel, including rue de la Huchette. Its eateries attract mainly tourists, often under the mistaken impression that this little maze is the whole of the famous 'Latin Quarter'. But for the best global cuisine, try the following:

» **Av de Choisy, av d'Ivry and rue Baudricourt, 13e** Cheap Chinese and Southeast Asian (especially Vietnamese) eateries.

» **Bd de Belleville, 11e & 20e** North African food, especially couscous.

» **Passage Brady, 10e** (Map p108) Covered passage crammed with Indian, Pakistani and Bangladeshi specialities.

» **Rue Au Maire, 3e** (Map p78) Small Chinese noodle shops and restaurants.

» **Rue Cadet, rue Richer and rue Geoffroy Marie, 9e** (Map p72) Triangle of streets with Jewish (mostly Sephardic) and kosher food.

» **Rue Cail, 10e** (Map p108) Fabulous array of Indian restaurants.

» **Rue de Belleville, 20e** Dine on Chinese, Southeast Asian or Middle Eastern.

» **Rue Ste-Anne, 2e** (Map p66) The heart of Paris' Japantown.

» **Rue des Rosiers, 4e** (Map p78) Jewish restaurants (some Ashkenazic, some Sephardic, not all kosher) serving specialities from Central Europe, North Africa and Israel. Many are closed Friday evenings, Saturdays and Jewish holidays.

afternoon tea menu, or in the evening when the tower is all a glitter.

58 Tour Eiffel
BRASSERIE €€
(Map p56; ☎01 45 55 20 04; www.restaurants-tour eiffel.com; 1st level, Champ de Mars, 7e; lunch menus €18-23, dinner menus €67-150; ⊗11.30am-4.30pm & 6.30-11pm; ⓂBir Hakeim or RER Champ de Mars–Tour Eiffel) If you're intrigued by the idea of a meal in the Tower, the 58 Tour Eiffel is a pretty good choice. It may not be the caviar and black truffles of Le Jules Verne (on the 2nd level), but Alain Ducasse did sign off on the menu, ensuring that this is much more than just another tourist cafeteria.

For lunch, go first to the restaurant's outside kiosk (near the north pillar); for dinner, reserve online or by telephone.

ÉTOILE & CHAMPS-ÉLYSÉES
This area is renowned for *haute cuisine* – and *haute* prices – but if you choose to eat at one of the finer restaurants for lunch on a weekday, you'll save a bundle and still get to treat your tastebuds to an extraordinary meal. Make sure to reserve. Under-the-radar restaurants are scattered in the back streets; gourmet food and drink shops, some with attached eateries, garland place de la Madeleine (p143).

TOP CHOICE Ladurée
PATISSERIE €
(Map p58; www.laduree.fr; 75 av des Champs-Élysées, 8e; pastries from €1.50; ⊗7.30am-11pm; ⓂGeorge V) One of the oldest patisseries in Paris, Ladurée has been around since 1862. The tearoom here is the classiest spot to indulge your sweet tooth on the Champs; alternatively, pick up some pastries to go – from croissants to the trademark macarons, it's all quite heavenly.

Le Boudoir
TRADITIONAL FRENCH €€€
(Map p58; ☎01 43 59 25 29; www.boudoirparis.fr; 25 rue du Colisée, 8e; lunch menus €25, mains €25-29; ⊗lunch Mon-Fri, dinner Tue-Sat; ⓂSt-Philippe du Roule or Franklin D Roosevelt) Spread across two floors, the quirky salons here – Marie Antoinette, Palme d'Or, le Fumoir – are individual works of art with a style that befits the name. Expect classy bistro fare (quail stuffed with dried fruit and foie gras, chateaubriand steak with chestnut purée) prepared by chef Arnaud Nicolas, a recipient of France's top culinary honour.

Le Hide
TRADITIONAL FRENCH €€
(Map p58; ☎01 45 74 15 81; www.lehide.fr; 10 rue du Général Lanrezac, 17e; menus from €24; ⊗lunch Mon-Fri, dinner Mon-Sat; ⓂCharles de Gaulle–Étoile) A reader favourite, Le Hide is a tiny neighbourhood bistro serving scrumptious

traditional French fare: snails, baked shoulder of lamb with pumpkin purée or monkfish in lemon butter. Unsurprisingly, this place fills up faster than you can scamper down the steps at the nearby Arc de Triomphe. Reserve well in advance.

Aubrac Corner   DELICATESSEN €
(Map p58; www.aubrac-corner.com; 37 rue Marbeuf, 8e; sandwiches from €5, burgers from €9; ◷7.30am-6.30pm Mon-Sat; Ⓜ Franklin D Roosevelt) Burgers? On the Champs-Élysées? It might not sound all that French, but rest assured, this isn't fast food – it's actually the gourmet deli of a famous steakhouse. The burgers come with bowls of fries or *aligot* (mashed potatoes with melted cheese); take it all downstairs into the hidden wine cellar, a welcome refuge from the nonstop commotion outside.

Minipalais   MODERN FRENCH €€
(Map p58; ☑ 01 42 56 42 42; www.minipalais.com; av Winston Churchill, 8e; lunch menus €28, mains €15-35; ◷10am-1am; Ⓜ Champs-Élysées-Clemenceau or Invalides) Set inside the fabulous Grand Palais (p60), the Minipalais resembles an artist's studio on a colossal scale, with unvarnished hardwood floors, industrial lights suspended from ceiling beams and a handful of plaster casts on display. Its sizzling success, however, means that the crowd is anything but bohemian; dress to impress for a taste of the lauded modern cuisine.

LOUVRE & LES HALLES
Trendy restaurants are on the rise in this central area.

TOP CHOICE Beef Club   BISTRO €€
(Map p66; ☑ 09 54 37 13 65; www.eccbeefclub.com; 58 rue Jean-Jacques Rousseau, 1er; mains €20-45; ◷dinner daily; Ⓜ Les Halles) No steakhouse is chicer or hipper than this. Packed out ever since it threw its first T-bone on the grill in spring 2012, this beefy spot is all about steak, prepared to sweet perfection by legendary Paris butcher Yves-Marie Le Bourdonnec. The vibe is hip New York and the downstairs cellar bar, the Ballroom du Beef Club, shakes a mean cocktail (€12 to €15) courtesy of the cool guys from the Experimental Cocktail Club. An address not to be missed – if you are lucky enough to score a table that is!

TOP CHOICE Frenchie   BISTRO €€
(Map p66; ☑ 01 40 39 96 19; www.frenchie-restaurant.com; 5-6 rue du Nil, 2e; menus €34, €38 & €45; ◷dinner Mon-Fri; Ⓜ Sentier) Tucked down an alley you wouldn't venture down otherwise, this bijou bistro with wooden tables and old stone walls is iconic. Frenchie is always packed and for good reason: excellent-value dishes are modern, market-driven (the menu changes daily, with a choice of two dishes by course) and prepared with just the right dose of unpretentious creative flair by French chef Gregory Marchand.

The only hiccup is snagging a table: reserve for one of two sittings (7pm or 9.30pm) two months in advance, arrive at 7pm and pray for a cancellation, or – failing that – share tapas-style small plates with friends across the street at Frenchie's **Bar à Vin**. No reservations: write your name on the sheet of paper strung outside, loiter in the alley and wait for your name to be called.

Yam'Tcha   FUSION €€€
(Map p66; ☑ 01 40 26 08 07; www.yamtcha.com; 4 rue Sauval, 1er; lunch/dinner menus from €50/85; ◷lunch Wed-Sun, dinner Wed-Sat; Ⓜ Louvre Rivoli) Adeline Grattard's ingeniously fused French and Chinese flavours recently earned the chef a Michelin star. Pair dishes on the frequently changing menu with wine or exotic teas. Book well ahead.

Passage 53   MODERN FRENCH €€€
(Map p72; ☑ 01 42 33 04 35; www.passage53.com; 53 Passage des Panoramas, 2e; lunch/dinner menus €60/110; ◷lunch & dinner Tue-Sat; Ⓜ Grands Boulevards or Bourse) No address inside Passage des Panoramas contrasts more dramatically with the outside hustle and bustle than this elegant restaurant at No 53. An oasis of calm and tranquillity (with window blinds pulled firmly down when closed), this gastronomic address is an ode to the best French produce – worked to perfection in a series of tasting courses by Japanese chef Shinichi Sato. Advance reservations recommended.

Spring   MODERN FRENCH €€
(Map p66; ☑ 01 45 96 05 72; www.springparis.fr; 6 rue Bailleul, 1er; lunch/dinner menus €44/76; ◷lunch & dinner Wed-Fri, dinner Tue & Sat; Ⓜ Palais Royal–Musée du Louvre) A 'talk-of-the-town' address with an American in the kitchen and stunning food. Spring has no printed menu, meaning hungry gourmets put their appetites in the hands of the chef and allow the multilingual wait staff to reveal what's cooking as each course is served. Advance reservations essential.

At lunchtime, nip to the **Spring Épicerie** (Map p66; 52 rue de l'Arbre Sec, 1er; ◷noon-8pm Tue-Sat), a tiny wine shop that serves steaming bowls of market-inspired, 'hungry worker-style' *bouillon du poule* (chicken soup).

Kunitoraya
INTERNATIONAL €

(Map p66; www.kunitoraya.com; 39 rue Ste-Anne, 1er; mains €12-14; ⊙11.30am-10pm; MPyramides) Some of the best-value *udon* (handmade Japanese noodles) is what this buzzing address in Paris' food-rich Japantown is all about. Grab a stool at the kitchen bar and watch the hip young chefs strut their stuff over steaming bowls of soup, *grands bols de riz* (big bowls of rice) laced with battered prawns, sweet duck or beef, and other meal-in-one dishes. In summer go for one of the cold noodle dishes served on bamboo. No credit cards.

TOP CHOICE Claus
BISTRO, DELICATESSEN €

(Map p66; ✆01 42 33 55 10; www.clausparis.com; 14 rue Jean-Jacques Rousseau, 1er; breakfasts €13-18, lunches €19; ⊙7.30am-6pm Mon-Fri, 9.30am-5pm Sat & Sun; MÉtienne Marcel) Dubbed the 'haute-couture' breakfast specialist' in Parisian foodie circles, this inspired *épicerie du petit-déjeuner* (breakfast grocery shop) has everything you could possibly desire for the ultimate gourmet breakfast and brunch – organic mueslis and cereals, fresh juices, jams, honey and so on.

Breakfast or brunch on site, shop at Claus to create your own or ask for a luxury breakfast hamper to be delivered to your door. Its lunchtime salads, soups and tarts are equally tasty.

Le Grand Véfour
TRADITIONAL FRENCH €€€

(Map p66; ✆01 42 96 56 27; www.grand-vefour. com; 17 rue de Beaujolais, 1er; lunch/dinner menus €96/282; ⊙lunch Mon-Fri, dinner Mon-Thu; MPyramides) This 18th-century jewel on the northern edge of the Jardin du Palais Royal has been a dining favourite of the Parisian elite since 1784; just look at who gets their names ascribed to each table – from Napoleon to Victor Hugo and Colette (who lived next door). The food is tip-top; expect a voyage of discovery in one of the most beautiful restaurants in the world.

L'Ardoise
BISTRO €€

(Map p66; ✆01 42 96 28 18; www.lardoise-paris. com; 28 rue du Mont Thabor, 1er; menus €35; ⊙lunch Tue-Sat, dinner Tue-Sun; MConcorde or Tuileries) This is a lovely little bistro with no menu as such (*ardoise* means 'blackboard', which is all there is), but who cares? The food – fricassee of corn-fed chicken with morels, pork cheeks in ginger, hare in black pepper, all prepared dexterously by chef Pierre Jay (ex-Tour d'Argent) – is superb. The menu changes every three weeks and the three-course *prix fixe* (set menu) offers good value.

Le Soufflé
TRADITIONAL FRENCH €€

(Map p66; ✆01 42 60 27 19; www.lesouffle.fr; 36 rue du Mont Thabor, 1er; lunch/dinner menus €25/35; ⊙lunch & dinner Mon-Sat; MConcorde or Tuileries) The faintly vintage, aqua-blue façade of this concept kitchen is reassuringly befitting of the timeless French classic it serves inside – the soufflé. The light fluffy dish served in white ramekins comes in dozens of different flavours, both savoury and sweet; *andouillette* (pig-intestine sausage) is the top choice for fearless gourmets.

Café Marly
CAFE €€

(Map p66; ✆01 46 26 06 60; www.maisonthierry costes.com; 93 rue de Rivoli, 1er; mains €18-39; ⊙8am-2am; MPalais Royal–Musée du Louvre) This chic venue facing the Louvre's inner courtyard

---

TOP FIVE PATISSERIES

Ladurée (p60) Specialities include macarons (especially the chocolate and pistachio variety).

Le Nôtre (Map p78; www.lenotre.fr; 10 rue St-Antoine, 4e; MBastille) Some of Paris' most delectable pastries and chocolate; 10 more outlets across the capital.

La Pâtisserie des Rêves (Map p96; www.lapatisseriedesreves.com; 93 rue du Bac, 7e; ⊙10am-8.30pm Tue-Sat, 8.30am-2pm Sun; MRue du Bac) Extraordinary cakes and seasonal fruit tarts, far too beautiful to eat, showcased beneath glass domes.

Boulangerie Bruno Solques (Map p92; 243 rue St-Jacques, 5e; ⊙6.30am-8pm Mon-Fri; ⛾; MPlace Monge or RER Luxembourg) Fabulous flat tarts with mashed fruit, and fruit-filled brioches.

Arnaud Delmontel (39 rue des Martyrs, 9e; ⊙7am-8.30pm Wed-Mon; MPigalle) Not only award-winning baguettes, but gorgeous pastries and cakes too.

serves contemporary French fare throughout the day under the palace colonnades. Views of the glass pyramid are priceless.

Saveurs Végét'Halles VEGETARIAN €

(Map p66; ☎01 40 41 93 95; www.saveursveget halles.fr; 41 rue des Bourdonnais, 1er; salads €11.90; ⊙lunch & dinner Mon-Sat; ☑; MⓂChâtelet) This vegan eatery offers quite a few mock-meat dishes like *poulet végétal aux champignons* ('chicken' with mushrooms). No alcohol.

OPÉRA & GRANDS BOULEVARDS

L'Opéra marks the start of the Grands Boulevards and the 9e *arrondissement*, where shoppers break for coffee between shops at Galeries Lafayette. Just north of here the area becomes more residential, and the diversity increases, with kosher delis, handmade Chinese noodles, organic cafes and Michelin-starred chefs.

Le J'Go SOUTHWEST FRENCH €€

(Map p72; ☎01 40 22 09 09; www.lejgo.com; 4 rue Drouot, 9e; lunch/dinner menus €16/35; ⊙Mon-Sat; MⓂRichelieu Drouot) This contemporary Toulouse-style bistro is meant to magic you away to southwestern France for a spell (perfect on a grey Parisian day). Its bright yellow walls are decorated with bullfighting posters, and the flavourful regional cooking is based around the rotisserie – not to mention other Gascogne standards like cassoulet and foie gras.

For the full experience, it's best to go in a small group with time to spare: the roasting takes a minimum 20 minutes, which gives you the opportunity to sample its choice selection of sunny southern wines.

Les Pâtes Vivantes INTERNATIONAL €

(Map p72; 46 du Faubourg Montmartre, 9e; noodles €9.50-12; ⊙Mon-Sat; MⓂLe Peletier) This is one of the only spots in Paris for hand-pulled noodles (*là miàn*), made to order in the age-old northern Chinese tradition. It packs in a crowd, so arrive early to stake out a table on the ground floor and watch as the nimble noodle-maker works his magic.

Le Zinc des Cavistes CAFE €

(Map p72; ☎01 47 70 88 64; 5 rue du Faubourg Montmartre, 9e; lunch menus €16, mains €11-19; ⊙8am-10.30pm; MⓂGrands Boulevards) Don't tell the masses standing dutifully in the Chartier queue that there's a much better restaurant right next door – your formerly friendly waiter will probably run off screaming. A local favourite, Le Zinc des Cavistes is as good

for a full-blown meal – *confit de canard* (confit of duck), salads – as it is for sampling new vintages.

Chez Plume ROTISSERIE €

(Map p72; 6 rue des Martyrs, 9e; dishes €4.50-8.50; ⊙10am-3pm & Tue-Sun, 5.30-8.30pm Tue-Sat; MⓂNotre Dame de Lorette) This gourmet rotisserie specialises in free-range chickens from southwest France, prepared in a variety of fashions: simply roasted, as a crumble, or even in a quiche or sandwich. It's wonderfully casual: add a side or two (potatoes, polenta, seasonal vegies) and pull up a counter seat.

MONTMARTRE & PIGALLE

Neobistros, wine bars and world cuisine all feature in this area. Choose carefully to avoid tourist traps.

TOP CHOICE / **Cul de Poule** MODERN FRENCH €€

(☎01 53 16 13 07; 53 rue des Martyrs, 9e; 2-/3-course menus lunch €15/18, dinner €23/28; ⊙closed Sun lunch; MⓂPigalle) With plastic orange cafeteria seats outside, you probably wouldn't wander into the Cul de Poule by accident. But the light-hearted spirit (yes, there is a mounted chicken's derrière on the wall) is deceiving; this is one of the best and most affordable kitchens in the Pigalle neighbourhood, with excellent neobistro fare that emphasises quality ingredients from the French countryside.

Le Miroir BISTRO €€

(Map p74; ☎01 46 06 50 73; 94 rue des Martyrs, 18e; lunch menus €18, dinner menus €25-40; ⊙lunch Tue-Sun, dinner Tue-Sat; MⓂAbbesses) This unassuming modern bistro is smack in the middle of the Montmartre tourist trail, yet it remains a local favourite. There are lots of delightful pâtés and rillettes to start off with – guinea hen with dates, duck with mushrooms, haddock and lemon – followed by well-prepared standards like stuffed veal shoulder.

The lunch special includes a glass of wine, coffee and dessert; the Sunday brunch also gets the thumbs up. Afterwards, pop into its wine shop across the street.

Le Pantruche BISTRO €€

(☎01 48 78 55 60; www.lepantruche.com; 3 rue Victor Masse, 9e; lunch/dinner menus €17/32; ⊙Mon-Fri; MⓂPigalle) Named after a nearby 19th-century theatre, classy Pantruche has been making waves in the already-crowded dining hot spot of South Pigalle. No surprise,

BURGER MANIA

The burger trend sweeping Paris is, unsurprisingly, *très* gourmet. Sizzling new openings include Blend (Map p66; www.blendhamburger.com; 44 rue d'Argout, 2e; burgers €10, lunch menus €15 & €17; ⏾lunch & dinner Mon-Sat; Ⓜ Sentier), on happening little rue d'Argout, serving burgers with house-baked brioche buns, homemade ketchup and hand-cut meat.

then, that it hits all the right notes: seasonal bistro fare, reasonable prices and an intimate setting. The menu runs from classics (steak with Béarnaise sauce) to more daring creations (scallops served in a parmesan broth with cauliflower mousseline). Reserve well in advance.

La Mascotte SEAFOOD, CAFE €€
(Map p74; ☑01 46 06 28 15; www.la-mascotte-montmartre.com; 52 rue des Abbesses, 18e; lunch/dinner menus €25/41; ⏾7am-midnight; Ⓜ Abbesses) Founded in 1889, this unassuming bar is about as authentic as it gets in Montmartre. It specialises in quality seafood – oysters, lobster, scallops – and regional dishes (Auvergne sausage), but you can also pull up a seat at the bar for a simple glass of wine and a plate of charcuterie.

Chez Toinette FRENCH €€
(Map p74; ☑01 42 54 44 36; 20 rue Germain Pilon, 18e; mains €16-25; ⏾dinner Mon-Sat; Ⓜ Abbesses) The atmosphere of this convivial restaurant is rivalled only by its fine cuisine. In the heart of one of the capital's most touristy neighbourhoods, Chez Toinette has kept alive the tradition of old Montmartre with its simplicity and culinary expertise.

Le Café qui Parle MODERN FRENCH €€
(Map p74; ☑01 46 06 06 88; 24 rue Caulaincourt, 18e; 2-/3-course lunch menus €12.50/17, mains €17-25; ⏾8.30am-11pm Mon-Sat, lunch Sun; ☎; Ⓜ Lamarck Caulaincourt or Blanche) The Café qui Parle is a fine example of where modern-day eateries are headed in Paris. It offers inventive, reasonably priced dishes prepared by owner-chef Damian Moeuf amid comfortable surroundings. Regulars love the art on the walls and ancient safes down below (the building was once a bank), but not as much as the brunch, served from 10am on Saturdays and Sundays.

Rose Bakery VEGETARIAN €€
(☑01 42 82 12 80; 46 rue des Martyrs, 18e; mains €14.50-17.50; ⏾9am-6.30pm Tue-Sat; ☎; Ⓜ St-Georges) Savoury tarts, salads, risotto, great breakfasts, feisty organic fruit juices and lots of different teas at this hip, English-style daytime eating address. Another branch is in the Marais (Map p78; ☑01 49 96 54 01; 30 rue Debelleyme, 3e; mains €7-18; ⏾9am-6.30pm Tue-Sun; Ⓜ Filles du Calvaire or St-Sébastien–Froissart).

GARE DU NORD & GARE DE L'EST

Indian and Pakistani eateries are concentrated in and around Passage Brady; traditional brasseries and bistros cluster around Gare du Nord and Gare de l'Est; and great things await along Canal St-Martin's creative banks.

TOP CHOICE Le Verre Volé WINE BAR €
(Map p78; ☑01 48 03 17 34; 67 rue de Lancry, 10e; mains €13-16; ⏾lunch & dinner; Ⓜ Jacques Bonsergent) The tiny 'Stolen Glass' – a wine shop with a few tables – is just about the most perfect wine bar/restaurant in Paris, with excellent wines and expert advice. Unpretentious and hearty *plats du jour* (dishes of the day) are excellent. Reserve well in advance for meals, or stop by just for a tasting.

Chez Michel BRETON, SEAFOOD €€€
(Map p108; ☑01 44 53 06 20; 10 rue Belzunce, 10e; menus €50; ⏾lunch Tue-Fri, dinner Mon-Fri; Ⓜ Gare du Nord) If all you know about Breton cuisine is crêpes and cider, a visit to Chez Michel is in order. The only option is to order the four-course *menu*, which features excellent seafood (scallop tartare, hake with Breton white beans) as well as specialities like *keuz breizh* (Breton cheeses) and *kouign* (butter cake). If you can't book a table, don't despair: it also offers four-course picnic baskets (€52 for two people) if you order ahead. Two doors down is little brother Chez Casimir (Map p108; 6 rue Belzunce, 10e; menus €24-32; ⏾lunch & dinner Mon-Fri, 10am-7pm Sat & Sun), with decent bistro fare.

L'Office MODERN FRENCH €€
(Map p108; ☑01 47 70 67 31; 3 rue Richer, 9e; lunch menus €19-24, dinner menus €27-33; ⏾Mon-Fri; Ⓜ Poissonière or Bonne Nouvelle) Straddling the east-west Paris divide, L'Office is off the beaten track but unusual enough to merit a detour for those serious about their food. The market-inspired menu is mercifully short – as in, there are only two choices for lunch – but outstanding. Don't judge this one by the menu; the simple chalkboard descriptions

('beef/polenta') belie the rich and complex flavours emerging from the kitchen.

Pink Flamingo — PIZZA €

(Map p78; ☑01 42 02 31 70; www.pinkflamin gopizza.com; 67 rue Bichat, 10e; pizzas €10.50-16; ☺lunch Tue-Sun, dinner daily; Ⓜ Jacques Bonsergent) Not another pizza place? *Mais non, chérie!* Once the weather warms up, the Flamingo unveils its secret weapon – pink helium balloons that the delivery guy uses to locate you and your perfect canal-side picnic spot (GPS not needed). Order a Poulidor (duck, apple and chèvre) or a Basquiat (gorgonzola, figs and cured ham), pop into Le Verre Volé (p118) across the canal for the perfect bottle of vino, and you're set. There's also a **Marais branch** (Map p78; ☑01 42 71 28 20; 105 rue Vieille du Temple, 3e; pizzas €10.50-16; ☺noon-3pm & 7-11.30pm; Ⓜ St-Sébastien-Froissart).

MÉNILMONTANT & BELLEVILLE

In the northern section of the 11e and into the 19e and 20e *arrondissements*, rue Oberkampf and its extension, rue de Ménilmontant, are popular with diners and denizens of the night. Rue Jean-Pierre Timbaud, running parallel to the north, has been giving them a bit of competition, though.

TOP
CHOICE
Le Dauphin — BISTRO €€

(Map p78; ☑01 55 28 78 88; 131 av Parmentier, 11e; 2-/3-course lunch menus €23/27; ☺lunch & dinner Tue-Fri, dinner Sat; Ⓜ Goncourt) Advance reservations are essential at this buzzing wine bar. Run by the same team as Le Chateaubriand a few doors down, the stark white space, with marble floor, marble bar, marble ceiling and marble walls (and the odd mirror), is a temple to taste. Lunch is a choice of two starters and two mains (one fish, one meat), presented like a work of art on (predictably) white china. But the pièce de résistance is evening dining, when foodies pick and choose their way through an exquisite succession of *petites assiettes comme tapas* (small tapas-style dishes).

Soya Cantine BIO — VEGETARIAN €€

(Map p78; ☑01 48 06 33 02; www.soya75.fr; 20 rue de la Pierre Levée, 11e; mains €15-20, 2-/3-course lunch menus €16/19; ☺lunch & dinner Tue-Sat, lunch Sun; ✍; Ⓜ Goncourt) A real favourite for its hip location in an old industrial atelier (think bare cement, metal columns and big windows), Soya is a full-on vegetarian eatery in what was once a staunchly working-

class district. Dishes, many tofu-based, are 95% organic and the weekend brunch buffet (€23.50) is a deliciously lazed, languid and organic affair. A glass floor floods the basement area with light.

Le Chateaubriand — MODERN FRENCH €€€

(Map p78; ☑01 43 57 45 95; www.lechateaubriand. fr; 129 av Parmentier, 11e; mains €27-46; ☺lunch & dinner Tue-Sat; Ⓜ Goncourt) The quintessential neobistro, Le Chateaubriand is a simple but elegantly tiled art deco dining room with some of the most imaginative cuisine in town. Chef Iñaki Aizpitarte – a name that could only be Basque – is well travelled and his dishes show that global exposure again and again in its odd combinations (watermelon and mackerel, milk-fed veal with langoustines and truffles). Dinner is a five-course tasting menu with no choices. Divine. Advance reservations essential.

Chatomat — MODERN FRENCH €€

(☑01 47 97 25 77; 6 rue Victor Letalle, 20e; mains €15-20; ☺dinner Wed-Sun; Ⓜ Ménilmontant, Couronnes or Père Lachaise) No dinner address is worth the trek to lesser known Ménilmontant more than this contemporary bistro, with signature plain white walls, pinch of postindustrial flavour and bags of foodie buzz. Fronted with flare by Brazilian Antonio and manned with much creativity in the kitchen by Alice and Victor, the old shop-turned-restaurant cooks up just three starters, three mains and three desserts each night – and none disappoint. Book at least a few days in advance.

Le Clown Bar — TRADITIONAL FRENCH €

(Map p78; ☑01 43 55 87 35; 114 rue Amelot, 11e; plats du jour €10.50; ☺lunch & dinner Mon-Sat; Ⓜ Filles du Calvaire) A wonderful wine-bar-cum-bistro next to the **Cirque d'Hiver** (1852), the Clown Bar is like a museum, with its painted ceilings, mosaics on the wall, lovely zinc bar and circus memorabilia that touches on one of our favourite themes of all time: the evil clown. The food is simple and unpretentious traditional French. *Parmentier de boudin à la normande* (black pudding Parmentier with apple) is its most popular dish.

LE MARAIS & BASTILLE

The Marais spills over with small restaurants of every imaginable type, and is one of Paris' premier neighbourhoods for eating out. Traditional French and neobistros vie for supremacy in Bastille.

TOP CHOICE Septime   MODERN FRENCH €€€

(Map p78; ✆01 43 67 38 29; 80 rue de Charonne, 11e; lunch/5-course menus €26/55; ⊗lunch Tue-Fri, dinner Mon-Fri; MCharonne) Reading the menu at Septime won't get you far – it looks mostly like an obscure shopping list (hanger steak/chicory/roots, chicken's egg/foie gras/*lardo*). But rest assured, the alchemists in the kitchen here, run by Bertrand Grébaut, are capable of producing some truly beautiful creations. The Northern European bistro feel (hardwood tables, blue-smocked waitstaff) marries well with the modern cuisine. Reserve in advance – particularly for the unbeatable lunch deal.

Le Siffleur de Ballons   WINE BAR €

(Map p86; www.lesiffleurdeballons.com; 34 rue de Citeaux, 12e; lunch menus €14, mains €7-15; ⊗10.30am-3pm & 5.30-10pm Tue-Sat; MFaidherbe Chaligny) With Tom Waits on the stereo and a few cacti atop the register, this contemporary wine bar clearly has a dash of California in its soul. The wines, though, are all French – and all natural – and paired with a quality selection of simple but delicious offerings: tartines, soups, lentil salad with truffle oil, cheeses and Iberian charcuterie plates. Look out for the weekly tastings with winemakers. No reservations, so don't waltz in too late.

Bistrot Paul Bert   BISTRO €€

(Map p86; ✆01 43 72 24 01; 18 rue Paul Bert, 11e; 3-course lunch/dinner menus €18/36; ⊗lunch & dinner Tue-Sat; MFaidherbe-Chaligny) When food writers make lists of the best Paris bistros, one of the names that almost always pops up is Paul Bert. The timeless decor and perfectly executed classic dishes guarantee that you'll need to reserve well in advance, even if the service isn't always up to snuff. Favourites here include the *steak-frites* (steak and chips) and the *Paris-Brest* (a cream-filled pastry).

La Gazzetta   MODERN FRENCH €€€

(Map p86; ✆01 43 47 47 05; www.lagazzetta.fr; 29 rue de Cotte, 12e; lunch menus €17, 5-/7-course dinner menus €42/56; ⊗lunch Tue-Sat, dinner to 11pm Mon-Sat; MLedru-Rollin) This fabulous neobrasserie has gained a substantial following under the tutelage of Swedish chef Petter Nilsson, who is as comfortable producing daring creations (milk-fed lamb confit and ice bleu d'Auvergne cheese) as he is more subtle ones (gnocchi with roasted almonds and lemon). Nilsson's penchant for unusual flavour combinations is quite a polariser, so

sample the lunch menu before splashing out for a five-course dinner.

Au Passage   BISTRO €€

(Map p78; ✆01 43 55 07 52; www.facebook.com/aupassage; 1bis passage de St-Sébastien, 11e; 2-/3-course lunch menus €13.50/19.50, dinners €20-35; ⊗lunch & dinner Sat; MSt-Sébastien-Froissart) Have faith in talented Australian chef James Henry at this raved-about *petit bar de quartier* (neighbourhood bar) with vegetable crates piled scruffily in the window and a fridge filling one corner of the old-fashioned dining room.

The lunch menu – a good-value, uncomplicated choice of two starters and two mains – is chalked on the blackboard, while dinner sees waiting staff in jeans twirl in and out the pocket-size kitchen with tapas-style starters to share, followed by a feisty shoulder of lamb, side of beef or other meaty cut for the entire table. Advance reservations essential.

Chez Marianne   JEWISH €

(Map p78; 2 rue des Hospitalières St-Gervais, 4e; mains €19-24; ⊗noon-midnight; MSt-Paul) Absolutely heaving at lunchtime, Chez Marianne translates as elbow-to-elbow eating beneath age-old beams on copious portions of falafel, hummus, purées of aubergine and chickpeas, and 25-odd other *zakouski* (hors d'œuvres; €12/14/16 for plate of 4/5/6). Fare is Sephardic rather than Ashkenazi (the norm at most Pletzl eateries), not Beth Din kosher, and a hole-in-the-wall window sells falafel in pita (€6) to munch on the move.

Nanashi   FUSION €

(Map p78; ✆09 60 00 25 59; www.nanashi.fr; 57 rue Charlot, 3e; bento €14-16; ⊗noon-midnight Mon-Fri, to 6pm Sat & Sun; MFilles du Calvaire) A fabulous lunch and after-dark address wedged between boutiques in the Haut Marais, this hip industrial space with large street-facing windows and concrete floor is ubercool, ultrahealthy and great value. Pick from creative salads, soups and bento boxes chalked on the board, and whatever you do, don't miss out on the amazing and astonishing freshly squeezed fruit and veg cocktails. Weekend brunch €17.

Breizh Café   CAFE €

(Map p78; www.breizhcafe.com; 109 rue Vieille du Temple, 3e; crêpes & galettes €4-12; ⊗lunch & dinner Wed-Sun; MSt-Sébastien Froissart) It may use a minority language in its name (*breizh* is 'Breton' in Breton), but you won't hear much of that Celtic tongue spoken here. Concen-

A HIDDEN KITCHEN

So successful were their twice-weekly dinners held in their apartment that American duo Braden and Laura shut their Hidden Kitchen supper club and opened Verjus (Map p66; ☑01 42 97 54 40; www.verjusparis.com; 52 rue de Richelieu, 1er; 4-/6-course tasting menus €55/70, with wine pairings €85/110; ⊘dinner Mon-Fri; Ⓜ Bourse or Palais Royal–Musée du Louvre), a hidden but hyped restaurant you need to know about to find. Cuisine is contemporary and international – think brown butter monkfish with brussel sprouts, apple and Tabasco broth or hangar steak with hazelnuts and horseradish. Walk-ins Monday to Wednesday often end up with a table.

Alternatively, Braden and Laura's pocket-size wine bar Verjus Bar à Vin (Map p66; 47 rue de Montpensier, 1er; ⊘6-11pm Mon-Fri; Ⓜ Bourse or Palais Royal-Musée du Louvre) cooks up superb and affordable food like fried buttermilk chicken. No reservations: arrive early to snag one of 10 bar stools.

trate instead on the sound of Cancale oysters being sucked, crêpes of organic flour prepared on a grill *autrement* (in a different way) and any of the 20 types of cider on offer being uncorked. This is definitely a cut-above *crêperie*.

Derrière
MODERN FRENCH €€

(Map p78; ☑01 44 61 91 95; www.derriere-resto.com; 69 rue des Gravilliers, 3e; lunch menus €25, mains €17-24; ⊘lunch & dinner Mon-Fri & Sun, dinner Sat; Ⓜ Arts et Métiers) Play ping pong between courses, sit on the side of the bed, glass of champers in hand, lounge between bookcases, or entertain a dinner party of 12 – such is the nature of this apartment restaurant, which has courtyard seating in summer. Its vibe might be chilled in a trendy 'shoes-off' kind of way, but Derrière (literally 'Behind') is deadly serious in the kitchen. Classic French bistro dishes and more inventive creations are excellent, as is its Sunday brunch. Advance reservations for dinner essential.

Pozzetto
ICE CREAM €

(Map p78; www.pozzetto.biz; 39 rue du Roi de Sicile, 4e; ⊘11.30am-9pm Mon-Thu, to 11.30pm Fri-Sun; Ⓜ St-Paul) This gelato maker opened when a group of friends from northern Italy couldn't find their favourite ice cream in Paris and so imported the ingredients to create it from scratch. The gelato is spatula'd, not scooped; flavours include *gianduia torinese* (hazelnut chocolate from Turin) and *zabaione* (made from egg yolks, sugar and sweet Marsala wine), along with the more usual peach, pistachio and Poire William. Great Italian coffee too.

Le Petit Marché
BISTRO €

(Map p78; ☑01 42 72 06 67; 9 rue de Béarn, 3e; mains €17-20; Ⓜ Chemin Vert) A faintly fusion

cuisine is what makes this cosy bistro, with old cream beams, candles on the tables and mirrors on the walls, stand out. Raw tuna wrapped in sesame seeds, ginger-spiced prawns, and monkfish medallions with figs give a creative Asian kick to a menu that otherwise reassures with old French bistro favourites that have been around for centuries.

Bofinger
BRASSERIE €€

(Map p78; ☑01 42 72 87 82; www.bofingerparis. com; 5-7 rue de la Bastille, 4e; mains €20-38; ⊘lunch & dinner; Ⓜ Bastille) Founded in 1864, Bofinger is reputedly the oldest brasserie in Paris, though the polished art nouveau brass, glass and mirrors throughout flags a redecoration a few decades later. As at most Parisian brasseries, specialities include Alsatian-inspired dishes such as *choucroute* (sauerkraut with assorted meats; from €20) and seafood dishes. Ask for a seat downstairs and under the *coupole* (stained-glass dome): it's the prettiest part of the restaurant. Just opposite, Le Petit Bofinger (Map p78; ☑01 42 72 05 23; 6 rue de la Bastille, 4e; mains €15-26, menus with wine €18 & €26; ⊘lunch & dinner to midnight daily; Ⓜ Bastille) is the brasserie's less brash (and cheaper) little sister.

L'As du Felafel
JEWISH €

(Map p78; 34 rue des Rosiers, 4e; takeaway dishes €5-8; ⊘noon-midnight Sun-Thu, to 5pm Fri; Ⓜ St-Paul) The lunchtime queue stretching halfway down the street from this place says it all! The Parisian favourite, 100% worth the inevitable wait, is *the* address for kosher, perfectly deep-fried chickpea balls and turkey or lamb shawarma sandwiches. Do as every Parisian does and take away.

THE ISLANDS

Famed more for its ice cream than dining options, Île St-Louis can be a pricey place to eat, although there are a couple of fine places. On the Île de la Cité, a handful of places ring pretty Place Dauphine.

Café Saint-Régis   CAFE
(Map p88; http://cafesaintregisparis.com; 6 rue du Jean de Bellay, 4e; ⊗daily; 🖰; Ⓜ Pont Marie) A deliciously Parisian hang-out any time of day.

⭐ TOP CHOICE Berthillon   ICE CREAM €
(Map p88; 31 rue St-Louis en l'Île, 4e; ice cream from €2; ⊗10am-8pm Wed-Sun; Ⓜ Pont Marie) Berthillon is to ice cream what Château Lafite Rothschild is to wine and Valhrona is to chocolate. And with nigh on to 70 flavours to choose from, you'll be spoiled for choice. While the fruit-flavoured sorbets (cassis, blackberry etc) produced by this celebrated *glacier* (ice-cream maker) are renowned, the chocolate, coffee, *marrons glacés* (candied chestnuts), Agenaise (Armagnac and prunes), *noisette* (hazelnut) and *nougat au miel* (honey nougat) are richer. Eat in or grab a cone with one/two/three/four small scoops (€2.30/3.60/4.90/6.20) to take away.

Mon Vieil Ami   TRADITIONAL FRENCH €€€
(Map p88; ☑01 40 46 01 35; www.mon-vieil-ami. com; 69 rue St-Louis en l'Île, 4e; plats du jour €13, menus €41; ⊗lunch & dinner Wed-Sun; Ⓜ Pont Marie) Alsatian chef Antoine Westermann is the creative talent behind this sleek black neobistro where guests are treated like old friends (hence the name) and vegetables get royal treatment. The lunchtime *plat du jour* (dish of the day) is especially good value and a perfect reflection of the season.

For dinner try artichokes and potatoes cooked with lemon confit and pan-fried skate. Unusually for Paris, Mon Veil Ami opens for dinner at 6.30pm – handy for those seeking an early dinner.

LATIN QUARTER

From cheap-eat student haunts to chandelier-lit palaces loaded with history, the 5e has something to suit every budget and culinary taste. Rue Mouffetard is famed for its food market and food shops, while its side streets, especially pedestrianised rue du Pot au Fer, cook up some fine budget dining.

⭐ TOP CHOICE L'AOC   REGIONAL CUISINE €€
(Map p92; ☑01 43 54 22 52; www.restoaoc.com; 14 rue des Fossés St-Bernard, 5e; 2-/3-course lunch menus €21/29, mains €18-32; ⊗lunch & dinner Tue-Sat; Ⓜ Cardinal Lemoine) '*Bistrot carnivore*' is the strapline of this ingenious restaurant concocted around France's most respected culinary products. The concept here is AOC (Appellation d'Origine Contrôlée): everything has been reared or made according to strict guidelines designed to protect products that are unique to a particular village, town or area. The result? Only the best!

La Tour d'Argent   GASTRONOMIC €€€
(Map p88; ☑01 43 54 23 31; www.latourdargent. com; 15 quai de la Tournelle, 5e; lunch menus €65, dinner menus €170-190; ⊗lunch & dinner Tue-Sat; Ⓜ Cardinal Lemoine or Pont Marie) The venerable 'Silver Tower' is famous for its *caneton* (duckling), rooftop garden with glimmering Notre Dame views and a fabulous history harking back to 1582 – from Henry III's inauguration of the first fork in France to the inspiration for the winsome animated film *Ratatouille*. Its wine cellar is one of Paris' best; dining is dressy and exceedingly fine.

Reserve eight to 10 days ahead for lunch, three weeks ahead for dinner – and don't miss its chocolate and coconut sphere with banana and lime sorbet for dessert. Buy fine food and accessories in its boutique directly across the street.

L'Agrume   NEOBISTRO €€
(Map p92; ☑01 43 31 86 48; 15 rue des Fossés St-Marcel, 5e; 2-/3-course lunch menus €19/24, mains €26-39; ⊗lunch & dinner Tue-Sat; Ⓜ Censier Daubenton) Snagging a table at L'Agrume – meaning 'Citrus Fruit' – is tough; reserve several days ahead. The reward is watching chefs work with seasonal products in the open kitchen while you dine – at a table, bar-stool or *comptoir* (counter) – at this pocket-size contemporary bistro on a little-known street on the Latin Quarter's southern fringe. Lunching is magnificent value and a real gourmet experience. Evening dining is an exquisite, no-choice *dégustation* (tasting) melody of five courses, different every day.

Le Coupe-Chou   TRADITIONAL FRENCH €€
(Map p92; ☑01 46 33 68 69; www.lecoupechou. com; 9 & 11 rue de Lanneau, 5e; 2-/3-course lunch menus €27, mains €18-25; ⊗Mon-Sat; Ⓜ Maubert-Mutualité) This maze of candle-lit rooms inside a vine-clad 17th-century townhouse is overwhelmingly romantic. Ceilings are beamed, furnishings are antique, and background classical music mingles with the intimate chatter of diners. As in the days when Marlene Dietrich et al dined here, advance

reservations are essential. Timeless French dishes include Burgundy snails, steak tartare and bœuf bourguignon, finished off with fabulous cheeses sourced from *fromagerie* Quatrehomme and a silken crème brûlée.

Bistrot Les Papilles
BISTRO €€

(Map p92; ☎01 43 25 20 79; www.lespapillesparis. com; 30 rue Gay Lussac, 5e; lunch/dinner menus from €22/31; ☺10.30am-midnight Mon-Sat; MRaspail or RER Luxembourg) This hybrid bistro, wine cellar and *épicerie* (specialist grocer) with sunflower-yellow façade is one of those fabulous dining experiences that packs out the place. Dining is at simply dressed tables wedged beneath bottle-lined walls, and fare is market-driven: each weekday cooks up a different *marmite du marché* (market casserole). But what really sets it apart is its exceptional wine list.

It only seats around 15 people; reserve a few days in advance to guarantee a table. After your meal, stock your own *cave* (wine cellar) at Les Papilles' *cave à vin*.

Chez Nicos
CRÊPERIE €

(Map p92; 44 rue Mouffetard, 5e; crêpes €3.50-6; ☺10am-2am; ☷; MPlace Monge) The signboard outside crêpe artist Nicos' unassuming little shop chalks up dozens of fillings, but ask by name for his masterpiece, 'La Crêpe du Chef', stuffed with aubergines, feta, mozzarella, lettuce, tomatoes and onions. There's a handful of tables inside; otherwise get it wrapped up in foil and head to a nearby park.

Le Pot de Terre
TRADITIONAL FRENCH €

(Map p92; ☎01 43 31 15 51; www.lepotdeterre.com; 22 rue du Pot de Fer, 5e; lunch/dinner menus from €9/18; ☺lunch & dinner daily; ☷; MPlace Monge) Le Pot de Terre was built in 1539, and legend has it that d'Artagnan and the musketeers slaked their thirst here between sword duels. The great-value fare – *tartatouille* (puff pastry-encased ratatouille), *magret de canard aux framboises* (duck breast in raspberry sauce) and old-fashioned desserts like chocolate mousse – make it worth hunting down on this restaurant-clad street.

PLACE D'ITALIE & CHINATOWN

Foodies hot-foot it to the 13e's Chinatown in search of authentic Asian food. Near Place d'Italie, the villagey Butte aux Cailles is chock-a-block with interesting addresses.

L'Auberge du 15
GASTRONOMIC €€

(☎01 47 07 07 45; www.laubergedu15.com; 15 Rue de la Santé, 13e; lunch menus €26, mains €28-50; ☺lunch & dinner Tue-Sat; MSt-Jacques or RER Port Royal) Rising chef Nicolas Castelet and his *pâtissier* brother Florent run this charming 'inn', where rough-hewn stone walls, chocolate-toned decor and classic dishes evoke a country retreat. Choose dining companions who share your culinary tastes – most mains must be ordered by a minimum of two people, and the €68 *dégustation* menu by the entire table. Definitely one to watch.

Le Temps des Cerises
TRADITIONAL FRENCH €

(☎01 45 89 69 48; www.cooperativetempsdes cerises.eu; 18-20 rue de la Butte aux Cailles, 13e; mains €11-20; ☺lunch Mon-Fri, dinner Mon-Sat; MCorvisart or Place d'Italie) Run by a workers' cooperative for over three decades, the 'Time of Cherries' (ie 'days of wine and roses') is an easygoing restaurant (provided you switch off your phone, lest there be hell to pay) serving faithfully solid fare in a quintessentially Parisian atmosphere. Buy its *coton-bio* T-shirt upon departure.

L'Avant Goût
NEOBISTRO €€

(☎01 53 80 24 00; www.lavantgout.com; 26 rue Bobillot, 13e; lunch/dinner menus €14/31, mains €16.50; ☺lunch & dinner Tue-Sat; MPlace d'Italie) A prototype of the Parisian neobistro, the 'Foretaste' has chef Christophe Beaufront serving some of the most inventive modern cuisine around. Tables count little more than a dozen and the place gets noisy. But the food is different and divine – don't miss his signature dish, *pot au feu au cochon aux épices* (spicy pork stew).

Advance reservations are vital but, should you miss out, you can get takeaway dishes from its nearby wine shop, **L'Avant-Goût Coté Cellier** (☎01 53 81 14 06; www.lavant gout.com; 37 rue Bobillot, 13e; ☺noon-8pm Tue-Fri, 10.30am-1.30pm & 3.30-8.30pm Sat; MPlace d'Italie).

Chez Gladines
FRENCH BASQUE €

(☎01 45 80 70 10; 30 rue des Cinq Diamants, 13e; mains €8.50-13; ☺lunch daily, dinner Mon-Sat; ☷; MCorvisart) Colossal 'meal-in-a-metal-bowl' salads are the prime draw of this down-to-earth Basque bistro with red-and-white-checked tablecloths in Buttes aux Cailles. It buzzes with students and thrifty diners and is always a hoot. Traditional Basque specialities include *pipérade* (spicy soup) and *poulet basque* (chicken cooked with tomatoes, onions, peppers and white wine). Arrive early to grab a seat.

The Seine

Dividing Paris neatly in two, the River Seine only adds to the fun and romance of the city. And never more so than in July and August, when sand is dumped on 5km of its riverbanks to create Paris Plages – yes, a riverside beach with water fountains, sprays, sun loungers and parasols.

Year-round, the Seine riverbanks are where Parisians come for cycling, jogging and taking a simple stroll to savour a river sufficiently precious to be in Unesco's World Heritage treasure trove. Stand on one of the bridges leading to the Seine's two elegant islands and watch lovers mingle with cello-playing buskers and teenaged skateboarders.

After dark, watch the river dance with the watery reflections of street lights, headlamps, stop signals, the dim glow of curtained windows and – occasionally – the superbright flood lamps of a tourist boat. You are in Paris.

BEST SEINE-SIDE PICNIC SPOTS

» **Musée de la Sculpture en Plein Air** (p94) A baguette beside a Brancusi at the Open-Air Sculpture Museum is picnic class

» **Square du Vert Gallant** Bijou park at the tip of Île de la Cité (p82)

» **Square Jean XXIII** Flowery park beneath the magnificent flying buttresses of Notre Dame (p82)

» **Pont St-Louis** Picnic on this pedestrian bridge linking Paris' two islands (p82) and be entertained by buskers, bands and street performers

» **Pont au Double** The other bridge, linking Notre Dame with the Left Bank, that guarantees a free show while you picnic

» **Jardin des Tuileries** (p68) Formal 17th-century gardens near the Louvre

Clockwise from top left
1. The Seine and Eiffel Tower at night 2. Cruising the Seine at sunset 3. Ferry at Square du Vert Gallant 4. The sun shines on Paris Plages

WILL SALTER/GETTY IMAGES ©

JEAN-BERNARD CARILLET/GETTY IMAGES ©

LOCAL KNOWLEDGE

PATRICIA WELLS' CULINARY SHOPPING SECRETS

Cookery teacher and author of *The Food Lover's Guide to Paris*, American Patricia Wells (www.patriciawells.com) has lived, cooked and shopped in Paris since 1980, and is considered to have truly captured the soul of French cuisine.

What is it that makes Paris so wonderful for culinary shopping? The tradition, the quality, the quantity, the atmosphere and physical beauty!

Where do you shop? All over: the Sunday organic market at Rennes (Marché Raspail; p61) – I love the dried fruits and nuts; Poilâne (p127) for bread; Quatrehomme (Map p96; 62 rue de Sèvres, 6e; ⊙8.45am-1pm & 4-7.45pm Tue-Thu, 8.45am-7.45pm Fri & Sat; MVanneau) for cheese; and Poissonnerie du Bac (Map p96; 69 rue du Bac, 7e; ⊙9am-1pm & 4-7.30pm Tue-Sat, 9.30am-1pm Sun; MRue du Bac) for fish. I shop regularly at Le Bon Marché's La Grande Épicerie de Paris (p142); for special meals I always order things in advance and go from shop to shop – La Maison du Chocolat (Map p96; www.lamaison-duchocolat.com; 19 rue de Sèvres, 6e; ⊙10am-7.30pm Mon-Sat, to 1pm Sun; MSèvres-Babylone) and Pierre Hermé (p142) for chocolate and cakes, and La Dernière Goutte (Map p96; www.laderniegoutte.net; 6 rue du Bourbon le Château, 6e; ⊙10am-1.30pm & 3.30-8.30pm; MMabillon) for wine. That is the fun of Paris and of France.

A perfect culinary souvenir from Paris? Fragonard (Map p96; ☎01 42 84 12 12; 196 bd St-Germain; ⊙11am-9pm Mon-Sat, 2-7.30pm Sun; MRue du Bac or St-Germain des Prés), the perfume maker, has a great shop on bd St-Germain. It has a changing litany of *great* things for the home. Nothing is very expensive and the offerings change every few months. The gift wrapping is worth it alone!

La Tropicale   ICE CREAM €
(www.latropicaleglacier.com; 180 bd Vincent Auriol, 13e; ice cream from €2.50, lunch menus €8-12; ⊙noon-7pm Mon-Sat, closed mid- to late Aug; ☝; MPlace d'Italie) All-natural flavours like lychee, guava, mango and papaya, honey and pine nut, as well as a Pina Colada–like coconut, rum and pineapple transport you to the tropics at this mint-coloured *glacier-salon de thé*. It also serves seasonally changing lunchtime quiches, flans and a *plat du jour*.

ST-GERMAIN & LES INVALIDES
The picnicking turf of the Jardin du Luxembourg is complemented by some fabulous places to pick up picnic ingredients. But even if it's not picnic weather, the neighbourhood's streets are lined with places to dine – from quintessential Parisian bistros to chic designer restaurants. Rue St-André des Arts and its continuation, rue du Buci, are good hunting grounds, as is the area between Église St-Sulpice and Église St-Germain des Prés.

TOP
CHOICE Bouillon Racine   BRASSERIE €€
(Map p96; ☎01 44 32 15 60; www.bouillonracine.com; 3 rue Racine, 6e; lunch menu €14.50, menus €30-41; ⊙noon-11pm; MCluny–La Sorbonne) Inconspicuously situated in a quiet street, this

heritage-listed 1906 art nouveau 'soup kitchen', with mirrored walls, floral motifs and ceramic tiling, was built in 1906 to feed market workers. Despite the magnificent interior, the food – inspired by age-old recipes – is by no means an afterthought. Superbly executed dishes include stuffed, spit-roasted suckling pig, pork shank in Rodenbach red beer, and scallops and shrimps with lobster coulis. Finish off your foray in gastronomic history with an old-fashioned sherbet.

Ze Kitchen Galerie   GASTRONOMIC €€€
(Map p88; ☎01 44 32 00 32; www.zekitchengalerie.fr; 4 rue des Grands Augustins, 6e; lunch/dinner menus €26.50/65; ⊙lunch & dinner Mon-Fri, dinner Sat; MSt-Michel) William Ledeuil's passion for Southeast Asian travel shows in the feisty dishes he creates in his Michelin-starred glass-box kitchen. Hosting three to five art exhibitions a year, the restaurant/gallery's menu is a vibrant feast of broths loaded with Thai herbs and coconut milk, meat and fish cooked *à la plancha* (on a hot plate) and inventive desserts like white chocolate and wasabi ice cream.

Café Constant   NEOBISTRO €€
(Map p56; www.cafeconstant.com; 139 rue Ste-Dominique, 7e; 2-/3-course menus €16/23; ⊙lunch & dinner Tue-Sun; MÉcole Militaire or RER Port de

l'Alma) Take a former Michelin-star chef and a simple corner cafe and what do you get? This jam-packed address, with original mosaic floor, wooden tables and huge queues every meal time. The pride and joy of Christian and Catherine Constant, it doesn't take reservations but you can enjoy a drink at the bar (or on the pavement outside) while you wait.

Nearby, Les Cocottes (Map p56; www.leviolondingres.com; 135 rue Ste-Dominique, 7e; 2-/3-course lunch menus €9/15, mains €14-28; ☺lunch & dinner Mon-Sat; Ⓜ École Militaire or RER Port de l'Alma) is another Constant hit.

KGB
FUSION €€

(Map p96; ✆01 46 33 00 85; http://zekitchengalerie.fr; 25 rue des Grands Augustins, 6e; 2-/3-course lunch menus €27/34, mains €27-32; ☺lunch & dinner Tue-Sat; Ⓜ St-Michel) Overtly art gallery in feel, KGB ('Kitchen Galerie Bis', in reference to Ze Kitchen Galerie (p126) draws a hip crowd for its casual platters of Asian-influenced hors d'oeuvres; creative pastas such as orecchiette studded with octopus, squid and crab; and mains spanning roast pigeon with ginger and cranberry condiment, suckling lamb, and grilled seabass with lemongrass and mandarin dressing.

Cuisine de Bar
SANDWICH BAR €

(Map p96; 8 rue du Cherche Midi, 6e; dishes €7.50-13; ☺8.30am-7pm Tue-Sat; Ⓜ Sèvres-Babylone) Next-door neighbour to one of Paris' most famous bakers, this is not any old sandwich bar. Rather, it is an ultrachic spot to lunch between designer boutiques. Open sandwiches are cut from bread baked by the celebrated Poilâne (Map p96; www.poilane.fr; 8 rue du Cherche Midi, 6e; ☺7.15am-8.15pm Mon-Sat; Ⓜ Sèvres-Babylone) and fabulously topped with gourmet goodies such as foie gras, smoked duck, gooey St-Marcellin cheese and Bayonne ham.

Au Pied de Fouet
BISTRO €

(Map p96; ✆01 43 54 87 83; www.aupieddefouet.com; 50 rue St-Benoît, 6e; mains €9-12.50; ☺Mon-Sat; Ⓜ St-Germain des Prés) Wholly classic bistro dishes such as entrecôte (steak), confit de canard (duck cooked slowly its own fat) and foie de volailles sauté (pan-fried chicken livers) at this busy bistro are astonishingly good value. Round off your meal with a tarte Tatin (upside-down apple tart), wine-soaked prunes or bowl of fromage blanc (a cross between yoghurt, sour cream and cream cheese).

Cosi
SANDWICH BAR €

(Map p96; 54 rue de Seine, 6e; sandwich menus €10-15; ☺noon-11pm; ♿; Ⓜ Odéon) An institution in the 6th for a quick, cheap eat in its upstairs dining room or to take to a park, Cosi might just be Paris' most imaginative sandwich maker, with sandwich names like Stonker, Tom Dooley and Naked Willi chalked on the blackground. Classical music plays in the background, and homemade focaccia bread is still warm from the oven.

Brasserie Lipp
BRASSERIE €€

(Map p96; ✆01 45 48 53 91; 151 bd St-Germain, 6e; mains €17-24; ☺11.45am-12.45am; Ⓜ St-Germain des Prés) Waiters in black waistcoats, bow ties and long white aprons serve brasserie favourites like choucroute garnie (sauerkraut with pork, frankfurters and potatoes) and jarret de porc aux lentilles (pork knuckle with lentils) at this celebrated wood-panelled establishment. Opened by Léonard Lipp in 1880, it achieved immortality when Hemingway sang its praises in A Moveable Feast. Arrive hungry: salads aren't allowed as meals.

Roger la Grenouille
TRADITIONAL FRENCH €€

(Map p88; ✆01 56 24 24 34; 26-28 rue des Grands Augustins, 6e; lunch/dinner menus from €19/24; ☺lunch Tue-Sat, dinner Mon-Sat; Ⓜ St-Michel) Nine varieties of frogs' legs are served at the time-worn institution 'Roger the Frog'. À la Provençale is with tomato, Orientale sees the pin-sized legs spiced with pine kernels and fresh mint, while Indienne has a splash of curry. If you're squeamish about devouring Roger and his mates, dishes like roast pheasant with dried figs are also on the menu.

Frog sculptures and statues are scattered throughout the restaurant, along with B&W pictures of 1920s Paris on the whitewashed walls and an array of old lamps illuminating the low sepia-coloured ceiling.

Polidor
TRADITIONAL FRENCH €€

(Map p88; ✆01 43 26 95 34; www.polidor.com; 41 rue Monsieur le Prince, 6e; menus from €22; ☺lunch & dinner; Ⓜ Odéon) A meal at this quintessentially Parisian crèmerie-restaurant is like a trip to Victor Hugo's Paris: the restaurant and its decor date from 1845. Menus of tasty, family-style French cuisine ensure a never-ending stream of diners eager to sample bœuf bourguignon, blanquette de veau à l'ancienne (veal in white sauce) and Polidor's famous tarte Tatin. Expect to wait.

Grom
ICE CREAM €

(Map p96; www.grom.fr; 81 rue de Seine, 6e; ice cream from €3.50; ☺1-10.30pm Mon-Wed, 1pm-

PARIS EATING

midnight Thu-Sat, noon-10.30pm Sun; 🚻; Ⓜ Mabillon) Flavours change monthly at France's only outlet of prestigious Turin gelato-maker Grom. All include sustainably sourced, high-grade ingredients like Syrian pistachio nuts and Venezuelan chocolate chips.

Le Square — REGIONAL CUISINE €€

(📞01 45 51 09 03; www.restaurant-lesquare.com; 31 rue St-Dominique, 7e; lunch/dinner menus from €19.50/26; ⊙lunch & dinner Mon-Sat; ⓂSolférino) The terrace tables along rue Casimir-Périer are the best seats in the house for views of the neighbouring twin-spired Basilique Ste Clotilde, which resembles a mini-Notre Dame. Inside, autumnal-hued banquettes and wood panelling create an elegant spot to dine on classical dishes with a southwestern accent, such as beef with Béarnaise sauce and potato gratin. To drink in the views, the bar opens from 8am to 11pm.

L'Arpège — GASTRONOMIC €€€

(Map p56; 📞01 47 05 09 06; www.alain-passard.com; 84 rue de Varenne, 7e; menus from €120; ⊙lunch & dinner Mon-Fri; ⓂVarenne) Triple Michelin-starred chef Alain Passard specialises in vegetables and inspired desserts, like his signature tomatoes stuffed with a veritable orchard of a dozen dried and fresh fruits and served with aniseed ice cream. Book at least two weeks ahead.

Tante Marguerite — REGIONAL CUISINE €€€

(📞01 45 51 79 42; www.bernard-loiseau.com; 5 rue de Bourgogne, 7e; lunch/dinner menus €38/52; ⊙lunch & dinner Mon-Fri; ⓂAssemblée Nationale) Opened by one of France's most decorated chefs, the late Bernard Loiseau, and helmed by chef Pedro Gomes, this elegant wood-panelled restaurant celebrates the rich flavours of Burgundy. Immortal Loiseau recipes include snail ragout.

MONTPARNASSE

In the 1920s the area around bd du Montparnasse became one of Paris' premier avenues for enjoying cafe life, and it still has a handful of legendary brasseries and cafes warranting a culinary visit.

TOP CHOICE La Cabane à Huîtres — SEAFOOD €

(Map p96; 📞01 45 49 47 27; 4 rue Antoine Bourdelle, 14e; dozen oysters €14.50, menus €19.50; ⊙lunch & dinner Wed-Sat; ⓂMontparnasse Bienvenüe) Wonderfully rustic, this wooden-styled *cabane* (cabin) with just nine tables is the pride and joy of fifth-generation oyster farmer Francis Dubourg, who splits his week between the capital and his oyster farm in Arcachon on the Atlantic Coast. The fixed menu includes a dozen oysters, foie gras, *magret de canard fumé* (smoked duck breast) or smoked salmon and scrumptious desserts.

Jadis — NEOBISTRO €€

(📞01 45 57 73 20; www.bistrot-jadis.com; 202 rue de la Croix Nivert, 15e; lunch/dinner menus from €29/36; ⊙lunch & dinner Mon-Fri; ⓂBoucicaut) This upmarket neobistro on the corner of a very unassuming street in the 15e is one of Paris' most raved about (ie reserve in advance). Traditional French dishes pack a modern punch thanks to the daring of rising-star chef Guillaume Delage, who braises pork cheeks in beer and uses black rice instead of white. The lunch *menu* is extraordinarily good value, and the chocolate soufflé – order it at the start of your meal – is divine.

Le Dôme — BRASSERIE €€€

(Map p96; 📞01 43 35 25 81; 108 bd du Montparnasse, 14e; mains €37-49, seafood platters €54; ⊙lunch & dinner; ⓂVavin) A 1930s art deco extravaganza, Le Dôme is a monumental place for a meal service of the formal white-tablecloth and bow-tied waiter variety. It's one of the swishest places around for shellfish platters piled high with fresh oysters, king prawns, crab claws and so on, followed by traditional creamy homemade mille-feuille for dessert, wheeled in on a trolley and cut in front of you.

La Closerie des Lilas — BRASSERIE €€

(Map p96; 📞01 40 51 34 50; www.closeriedeslilas.fr; 171 bd du Montparnasse, 6e; restaurant mains €23-49, brasserie mains €23-27; ⊙restaurant lunch & dinner, brasserie noon-1am, piano bar 11am-1am; ⓂVavin or RER Port Royal) As anyone who has read Hemingway knows, what is now the American Bar at the 'Lilac Enclosure' is where Papa did a lot of writing (including much of *The Sun Also Rises*), drinking and oyster slurping; brass plaques tell you exactly where he and luminaries such as Picasso, Apollinaire, Man Ray, Jean-Paul Sartre and Samuel Beckett stood, sat or fell. La Closerie des Lilas is split into a late-night piano bar, chic restaurant and more lovable (and cheaper) brasserie with a hedged-in pavement terrace.

🍸 Drinking

In a country where eating and drinking are as inseparable as cheese and wine, it's inevitable that the line between bars, cafes and bistros is blurred at best.

PARIS' OLDEST RESTAURANT & CAFE

St-Germain claims both the city's oldest restaurant and its oldest cafe.

À la Petite Chaise (Map p42; ☎01 42 22 13 35; www.alapetitechaise.fr; 36 rue de Grenelle, 6e; lunch/dinner menus from €27/33; ⊙lunch & dinner Mon-Sat; ⓂSèvres- Babylone) hides behind an iron gate that's been here since it opened in 1680, when wine merchant Georges Rameau served food to the public to go with his wares. Classical decor and cuisine to match (onion soup, foie gras, duck, lamb and unexpected delights like truffled asparagus) make it worth a visit above and beyond its history.

Hot on the heels of À la Petite Chaise's opening, Le Procope (Map p96; www.procope. com; 13 rue de l'Ancienne Comédie, 6e; 2-/3-course menus from €21/28; ⊙11.30am-midnight; ♿; ⓂOdéon) welcomed its first patrons in 1686, and was frequented by Voltaire, Molière and Balzac et al. Its chandeliered interior also has an entrance to the 1735-built glass-roofed passageway Cour du Commerce St-André. Along with house specialities like coq au vin, calf's head casserole in veal stock, and calf kidneys with violet mustard, it serves its own sorbets and ice creams, which it's been making here since 1686 too.

Drinking in Paris essentially means paying the rent for the space you take up, meaning it costs more sitting at tables than standing at the counter, more on a fancy square than a backstreet, more in the 8e than in the 18e. Come 10pm, many cafes apply a pricier *tarif de nuit* (night rate).

Expect to pay at least €3 to €5 for a glass of wine or *demi* (half-pint) of beer, €10 to €15 for a cocktail and substantially more in chic bars and clubs.

ÉTOILE & CHAMPS-ÉLYSÉES

Charlie Birdy   PUB
(Map p58; 124 rue de la Boétie, 8e; ⊙noon-5am; ⓂFranklin D Roosevelt) This kick-back brick-walled pub just off the Champs-Élysées is easily the most inviting spot in the neighbourhood for a drink. The usual array of bar food is served; DJs hit the decks on weekend nights.

LOUVRE & LES HALLES

Angelina   TEAROOM
(Map p66; 226 rue de Rivoli, 1er; ⊙daily; ⓂTuileries) This beautiful, high-ceilinged tearoom has exquisite furnishings, mirrored walls and fabulous fluffy cakes. More importantly, it serves the best and most wonderfully sickening 'African' hot chocolate in the history of time (€7), served with a pot of whipped cream. It's a positive meal replacement. Branches include two at Versailles.

Harry's New York Bar   COCKTAIL BAR
(Map p66; www.harrysbar.fr; 5 rue Daunou, 2e; ⊙daily; ⓂOpéra) One of the most popular American-style bars in the prewar years, Harry's once welcomed writers like F Scott Fitzgerald and Ernest Hemingway, who no doubt sampled the bar's unique cocktail and creation: the Bloody Mary. The Cuban mahogany interior dates from the mid-19th century and was brought over from a Manhattan bar in 1911.

There's a basement piano bar called Ivories where Gershwin supposedly composed *An American in Paris* and, for the peckish, old-school hot dogs and generous club sandwiches to snack on. The advertisement for Harry's that occasionally appears in the papers still reads 'Tell the Taxi Driver Sank Roo Doe Noo' and is copyrighted.

Experimental Cocktail Club   COCKTAIL BAR
(Map p66; www.experimentalcocktailclub.com; 37 rue St-Saveur, 2e; ⊙daily; ⓂRéaumur-Sebastopol) Called ECC by trendies, this fabulous speakeasy, with grey façade and old-beamed ceiling, is effortlessly hip. Oozing spirit and soul, the cocktail bar – with retro-chic decor by American interior designer Cuoco Black – is a sophisticated flashback to those *années folles* (crazy years) of Prohibition New York. DJs set the space partying until dawn at weekends.

Jefrey's   COCKTAIL BAR
(Map p66; www.jefreys.fr; 14 rue St-Saveur, 2e; ⊙Tue-Sat; ⓂRéaumur-Sebastopol) Oh, how dandy is this trendy drawing room, with wooden façade, leather Chesterfields and old-fashioned gramophone! Gentlemen's club in soul, yes, but creative cocktails are shaken for both him and her, and never more so during happy hour (7pm to 10.30pm Tuesdays and Thursdays), when cocktails (€11 to €13) dip to €9. Favourites include 'I Wanna be This Drink' (rum, strawberry juice, fresh raspberries and

LITTLE BRITTANY

Gare Montparnasse's transport links to Brittany have ensured a high Breton population, and rue du Montparnasse, 14e, is lined with over a dozen authentic Breton crêperies. Two of the best are the cosy, dark-timbered Crêperie Josselin (Map p96; ☑01 43 20 93 50; 67 rue du Montparnasse, 14e; crêpes €4-9.50; ◔lunch & dinner Tue-Fri, noon-11pm Sat & Sun; ♿; MEdgar Quinet), and Crêperie Plougastel (Map p96; ☑01 01 42 79 90 63; 47 rue du Montparnasse, 14e; 2-/3-course menus €15/17; ◔11am-midnight; ♿; MEdgar Quinet), which makes sublime *caramel au beurre salé* (salty caramel sauce; *salidou* in Breton). One block west of rue du Montparnasse, rue Odessa, 14e, also has a handful of crêperies.

balsamic vinegar caramel) and the Grand Marnier–based 'Cucumber Cooler'.

Kong
BAR

(Map p66; www.kong.fr; 1 rue du Pont Neuf, 1er; ◔daily; MPont Neuf) Late nights at this Philippe Starck–designed place – containing a riot of iridescent champagne-coloured vinyl booths, Japanese cartoon cut-outs and garden gnome stools – see Paris' glam young set guzzling Dom Pérignon, nibbling on tapas-style platters (mains €20 to €40) and shaking their designer-clad booties on the tables. If you can, try to snag a table *à l'étage* – upstairs in the partly glass-roofed terrace-gallery. Light floods across the giant geisha swooning horizontal across the ceiling, and the stunning river views (particularly at sunset) will make you swoon.

MONTMARTRE & PIGALLE

TOP
CHOICE La Fourmi
BAR, CAFE

(Map p74; 74 rue des Martyrs, 18e; ◔8am-1am Mon-Thu, to 3am Fri & Sat, 10am-1am Sun; MPigalle) A Pigalle institution, La Fourmi hits the mark with its high ceilings, long zinc bar and unpretentious vibe. Get up to speed on live music and club nights or sit down for a reasonably priced meal and drinks.

GARE DU NORD & GARE DE L'EST

TOP
CHOICE L'Atmosphère
BAR, CAFE

(Map p78; 49 rue Lucien Sampaix, 10e; ◔9.30am-1.45am Mon-Sat, to midnight Sun; MJacques Bonsergent or Gare de l'Est) A nod to the 1938 flick *Hôtel du Nord*, this timber-and-tile cafe along the canal has an arty, spirited ambience, well-priced drinks and good food.

Chez Prune
BAR, CAFE

(Map p78; 71 quai de Valmy, 10e; ◔8am-2am Mon-Sat, 10am-2am Sun; MRépublique) This Sohoboho cafe put Canal St-Martin on the map a decade ago, and its good vibes and rough-

around-the-edges look show no sign of fading in the near future.

Chez Jeanette
BAR, CAFE

(Map p108; www.chezjeannette.com; 47 rue du Faubourg Saint-Denis, 10e; ◔11am-11.30pm; MChâteau d'Eau) Cracked tile floors and original 1950s decor have turned Chez Jeanette into one of the 10e's most popular hot spots. It's MacBooks by day, pints by night and reasonably priced meals around the clock.

Swinging Londress
BAR, CAFE

(Map p108; 97 rue du Faubourg St-Denis, 10e; ◔7am-2am daily; ☎; MGare de l'Est) The latest addition to the St-Denis drinking scene, Swinging Londress is a funky ode to 1960s design, with tripped-out wallpaper that will have you seeing things before the night is through. Cheap drinks, decent grub and a sense of humour make this place a winner.

MÉNILMONTANT & BELLEVILLE

Café Charbon
BAR, CAFE

(Map p78; www.lecafecharbon.com; 109 rue Oberkampf, 11e; ◔daily; ☎; MParmentier) With its postindustrial belle époque ambience, the Charbon was the first of the hip cafes and bars to catch on in Ménilmontant. It's always crowded and it's worth heading to for the distressed decor with high ceilings, chandeliers and perched DJ booth. Food (mains €12.50 to €15) and evening tapas (€6) are all good.

Café Chéri(e)
BAR, CAFE

(Map p78; 44 bd de la Villette, 19e; ◔noon-1am; MBelleville) An imaginative, colourful bar with its signature red lighting, infamous mojitos and caipirinhas, and commitment to quality tunes, Chéri(e) is everyone's darling in this part of town. Gritty art-chic crowd and electro DJs Thursday to Saturday.

Zéro Zéro
BAR

(Map p78; www.radiozerozero.com; 89 rue Amelot, 11e; ◔Mon-Sat; MSt-Sébastien–Froissart) A heaving Saturday-night address on rue Amelot, Zéro Zéro screams Berlin, with its banquet seating and tag-covered walls (and ceiling, and windows, and bar...). Electro and house is the sound, and the house cocktail, a potent rum-and-ginger concoction, ensures a wild party spirit.

LE MARAIS & BASTILLE

TOP CHOICE Le Baron Rouge   WINE BAR

(Map p86; 1 rue Théophile Roussel, 12e; ⊘10am-2pm & 5-10pm Mon-Fri, to 10pm Sat, to 4pm Sun; MLedru-Rollin) Just about the ultimate Parisian wine-bar experience, this place has a dozen barrels of the stuff stacked up against the bottle-lined walls. As unpretentious as you'll find, it's a local meeting place where everyone is welcome and is especially busy on Sundays after the Aligre Market wraps up. All the usual suspects – cheese, charcuterie and oysters – will keep your belly full. For a small deposit, you can even fill up one-litre bottles straight from the barrel for under €5.

Le Pure Café   CAFE

(Map p86; 14 rue Jean Macé, 11e; ⊘daily; MCharonne) A classic Parisian haunt, this rustic, cherry-red corner cafe featured in the arthouse film *Before Sunset*, but it's still a refreshingly unpretentious spot for a drink or for well-crafted fare like veal with chestnut purée.

Le Loir dans La Théière   CAFE

(Map p78; 3 rue des Rosiers, 4e; ⊘daily; MSt-Paul) Its cutesy name ('Dormouse in the Teapot') notwithstanding, this is a wonderful old space filled with retro toys, comfy couches and scenes of *Through the Looking Glass* on the walls. It serves up to a dozen different types of tea, excellent savoury tarts and sandwiches (€8.50 to €12), desserts like apple crumble (€6.50), and brunch (€19.50) at the weekend.

La Fée Verte   BAR

(Map p78; 108 rue de la Roquette, 11e; dishes €10-16; ⊘daily; 🛜; MVoltaire) You guessed it, the 'Green Fairy' specialises in absinthe (served traditionally with spoons and sugar cubes), but this fabulously old-fashioned neighbourhood cafe and bar also serves terrific food, including Green Fairy cheeseburgers.

Le Barav   WINE BAR

(Map p78; 📞01 48 04 57 59; www.lebarav.fr; 6 rue Charles-François Dupuis, 3e; ⊘Tue-Sat; MTemple) This hipster *bar à vin* (wine bar), on one of the trendiest streets in the Haut Marais, oozes atmosphere – and has one of the city's loveliest pavement terraces. Its extensive wine list is complimented by tasty food (lunch *plat du jour* €10.50); seating is at vintage bistro tables or on bar stools; and its wine shop a few doors down hosts great *dégustations à thème* (themed wine tastings; reserve in advance).

Panic Room   BAR

(Map p78; www.panicroomparis.com; 101 rue Amelot, 11e; ⊘Mon-Sat; MSt-Sébastien–Froissart) This brazenly wild bar just east of the Haut Marais is not quite as terrifying or forbidding as its name suggests. A wildly flavoured cocktail – such as gin shaken with strawberries and basil, or a cognac-based creation mixing cucumber, coriander and ginger – is the thing to sip here, especially during happy hour (6.30pm to 8.30pm). Check its website for DJ sets, gigs and happenings.

Le Progrès   CAFE

(Map p78; 1 rue de Bretagne, 3e; ⊘Mon-Sat; MSt-Sébastien–Froissart or Filles du Calvaire) This sunlit, art deco–style corner cafe is a sociable

---

RUE MONTMARTRE

In the Louvre & Les Halles neighbourhood, rue Montmartre is dotted with appealing places to sip a *café* or cocktail. Start at the southern end with heritage-listed, hole-in-the-wall **Christ Inn's Bistrot** (Map p66; 📞01 42 36 07 56; 15 rue Montmartre, 1er; ⊘Tue-Sat; MLes Halles), a historic gem, with railway-carriage-style slatted wooden seats and belle époque tiles featuring market scenes of Les Halles. Equally 'vintage' is **Le Tambour** (Map p66; 📞01 42 33 06 90; 41 rue Montmartre, 2e; ⊘8am-6am; MÉtienne Marcel or Sentier), a Mecca for Parisian night owls with its long hours (food served until 3.30am or 4am), recycled street furniture and old metro maps. The Crazy Heart, aka **Le Cœur Fou** (Map p66; 📞01 42 33 91 33; 55 rue Montmartre, 2e; ⊘5pm-2am; MÉtienne Marcel), a few doors up, is a tiny gallery-bar with candles nestled in whitewashed walls and a *très bobo* (bohemian bourgeois), late-20s crowd.

TOP FIVE BAR-HOPPING STREETS

The following prime Parisian streets (and their surrounds) are perfect for evening meandering to soak up the scene:

» **Rue Vieille du Temple, 4e** Marais cocktail of gay bars and chic cafes.

» **Rue Oberkampf, 11e** Hip bars and bohemian hang-outs.

» **Rue de Lappe, 11e** Lively bars and clubs.

» **Rue Montmartre, 2e** Atmospheric cafes.

» **Rue Princesse, 6e** Student and sports bars.

spot to chat with locals over strong coffee, inexpensive bistro fare and pitchers of wine.

Café La Fusée   BAR

(Map p78; 168 rue St-Martin, 3e; ⊘daily; MRambuteau or Étienne Marcel) A short walk from the Pompidou, the Rocket is a lively, laid-back hang-out with red-and-white-striped awnings strung with fairy lights outside and paint-peeling, tobacco-coloured walls inside. Its wine selection by the glass (€2.70–€5.50) is notably good.

THE ISLANDS

Taverne Henri IV   WINE BAR

(Map p88; 13 place du Pont Neuf, 1er; ⊘Mon-Fri; MPont Neuf) One of the very few places to drink on Île de la Cité, this is a serious wine bar dating back to 1885. A tasty choice of inexpensive *tartines* (open sandwiches), charcuterie, and cheese platters complement its extensive wine list, making it a lovely riverside place to drink with friends.

LATIN QUARTER

Café de la Nouvelle Mairie   WINE BAR

(Map p92; 19 rue des Fossés St-Jacques, 5e; ⊘9am-8pm Mon-Fri; MCardinal-Lemoine) Shhhh... Just around the corner from the Panthéon but hidden away on a small, fountained square, the narrow wine bar Café de la Nouvelle Mairie is a neighbourhood secret, serving blackboard-chalked wines by the glass as well as bottles. Accompanying tapas-style food is simple and delicious.

Curio Parlor Cocktail Club   COCKTAIL BAR

(Map p92; www.curioparlor.com; 16 rue des Bernardins, 5e; ⊘7pm-2am Mon-Thu, to 4am Fri-Sun; MMaubert-Mutualité) Run by the same switched-on, chilled-out team as the Experimental Cocktail Club et al, this hybrid bar-club looks to the interwar *années folles* (crazy years) of 1920s Paris, London and New York for inspiration. Its racing-green

façade with a simple brass plaque on the door is the height of discretion.

Le Pub St-Hilaire   PUB

(Map p92; www.pubsainthilaire.com; 2 rue Valette, 5e; ⊘3pm-2am Mon-Thu, 3pm-4am Fri, 4pm-4am Sat, 4pm-midnight Sun; MMaubert-Mutualité) 'Buzzing' fails to do justice to the pulsating vibe inside this student-loved pub. Generous happy hours last several hours, and board games, a trio of pool tables, music on two floors, hearty bar food and various gimmicks (a metre of cocktails, 'be your own barman' etc) to rev up the party crowd keep the place packed.

Le Vieux Chêne   BAR

(Map p92; 69 rue Mouffetard, 5e; ⊘9am-2am Sun-Thu, to 5am Fri & Sat; MPlace Monge) This rue Mouffetard institution is reckoned to be Paris' oldest bar. Indeed, a revolutionary circle met here in 1848 and it was a popular *bal musette* (dancing club) in the late 19th and early 20th centuries. These days it's a student favourite, especially during happy 'hour' (4pm to 9pm Tuesday to Sunday, and from 4pm until closing on Monday). Resident DJs mix it up on Friday and Saturday nights.

Café Delmas   CAFE

(Map p92; www.cafedelmasparis.com; 2 place de la Contrescarpe, 5e; ⊘8am-2am Sun-Thu, to 4am Fri & Sat; MPlace Monge) Enviably situated on tree-studded place de la Contrescarpe, the Delmas is a hot spot for chilling over *un café*, cappuccino or all-day breakfast. Cosy up beneath overhead heaters outside to soak up the street atmosphere or snuggle up between books in the library-style interior – awash with students from the nearby universities.

ST-GERMAIN & LES INVALIDES

TOP
CHOICE **Les Deux Magots**   CAFE

(Map p96; www.lesdeuxmagots.fr; 170 bd St-Germain, 6e; ⊘7.30am-1am; MSt-Germain des

Prés) If ever there was a cafe that summed up St-Germain des Prés' early-20th-century literary scene, it's this former hang-out of anyone who was anyone. You will spend *beaucoup* (a lot) to sip a coffee in a wicker chair on the terrace shaded by dark-green awnings and geraniums spilling from window boxes, but it's an undeniable piece of Parisian history. If you're feeling decadent, order the famous shop-made hot chocolate, served in porcelain jugs. The name refers to the two *magots* (grotesque figurines) of Chinese dignitaries at the entrance.

Au Sauvignon   WINE BAR
(Map p96; 80 rue des Saints Pères, 7e; ⊙8.30am-10pm; ⓂSèvres-Babylone) There's no more authentic *bar à vin* than this. Grab a table in the evening sun or head to the quintessential bistro interior, with an original zinc bar, tightly packed tables and hand-painted ceiling celebrating French viticultural tradition. Order a plate of *casse-croûtes au pain Poilâne* – toast with ham, pâté, terrine, smoked salmon, foie gras and so on.

Alain Milliart   JUICE BAR
(Map p56; ☑01 45 55 63 86; www.alain-milliat.com; 159 rue de Grenelle, 7e; ⊙10am-10pm Tue-Sat; ⓂLa Tour Maubourg) Alain Milliart's fruit juices, bottled in the south of France, were until recently reserved for ultra-exclusive hotels and restaurants. But the opening of his Parisian juice bar/bistro means you can pop in to buy one of 33 varieties of juices and nectars, or sip them in-house. Milliart's jams and compotes are equally lush.

Stunning flavours include rosé grape or green tomato juice and white peach nectar. There's also a short but stellar, regularly changing blackboard menu (*menus* €22 to €36), influenced by the markets and seasons; be sure to book ahead for dinner.

Prescription Cocktail Club   COCKTAIL BAR
(Map p96; www.prescriptioncocktailclub.com; 23 rue Mazarine, 6e; ⊙7pm-1am Mon-Thu, to 4am Fri & Sat; ⓂOdéon) With bowler and flat-top hats as lampshades and a 1930s New York speakeasy air to the place, this cocktail club – run by the same massively successful team as Curio Parlor and Experimental – is very Parisian-cool. Getting past the doorman can be tough, but, once in, it's friendliness and old-fashioned cocktails all round. Watch its Facebook page for events such as Sunday-afternoon Mad Hatters pyjama parties.

Le 10   PUB
(Map p96; 10 rue de l'Odéon, 6e; ⊙6pm-2am; ⓂOdéon) A local institution, the poster-plastered cellar pub 'Le Dix' is a student favourite, not least for its cheap sangria. An eclectic selection emerges from the jukebox; everything from jazz and the Doors to traditional French *chansons* (à la Édith Piaf). It's the ideal spot for plotting the next revolution or conquering a lonely heart.

Brasserie O'Neil   MICROBREWERY
(Map p96; www.oneilbar.fr; 20 rue des Canettes, 6e; ⊙noon-2am; ⓂSt-Sulpice or Mabillon) Paris' original microbrewery brews four fabulous beers (blond, amber, bitter brown and citrusy white) on the premises. Soak 'em up with thin-crusted *flammekueches* (Alsatian pizzas).

Café de Flore   CAFE
(Map p96; www.cafedeflore.fr; 172 bd St-Germain, 6e; ⊙7am-1.30am; ⓂSt-Germain des Prés) The red upholstered benches, mirrors and marble walls at this art deco landmark haven't changed much since the days when Jean-Paul Sartre and Simone de Beauvoir essentially set up office here, writing in its warmth during the Nazi occupation.

Les Étages St-Germain   BAR
(Map p96; 5 rue de Buci, 6e; ⊙noon-2am; ⓂOdéon) Busy and bustling on shop-lined rue de Buci, this shabby-chic terrace bar with retro stools makes a fabulous people-watching pit stop between boutiques. Grab a coffee or summer-time strawberry mojito in the sun, or plump for happy hour (3pm to 8pm) when the price of cocktails plummets.

Café La Palette   CAFE
(Map p96; www.cafelapaletteparis.com; 43 rue de Seine, 6e; ⊙6.30am-2am Mon-Sat; ⓂMabillon) In the heart of gallery land, this fin de siècle cafe and erstwhile stomping ground of Paul Cézanne and Georges Braque attracts a grown-up set of fashion people and local art dealers. Its summer terrace is beautiful.

☆ Entertainment

From sipping cocktails in swanky bars to grooving at hip clubs, from rocking to live bands to being awed by spectacular operas, ballets and classical concerts, from being entertained by films to being dazzled by high-kicking cabarets, from being intrigued by avant-garde theatre productions to listening to smooth jazz sessions or stirring *chansons* – a night out in Paris promises a night to remember.

Cabaret

Whirling lines of feather boa–clad, high-kicking dancers are a quintessential fixture on Paris' entertainment scene – for everyone but Parisians. Still, the dazzling sets, costumes and routines guarantee an entertaining evening (or matinée). Tickets to major cabarets start from around €90 (from €130 with lunch, from €150 with dinner), and usually include a half-bottle of champagne. Reservations are essential; venues sell tickets online.

Moulin Rouge   CABARET
(Map p74; ☎01 53 09 82 82; www.moulinrouge.fr; 82 bd de Clichy, 18e; MBlanche) Immortalised in the posters of Toulouse-Lautrec and later on screen by Baz Luhrmann, the Moulin Rouge twinkles beneath a 1925 replica of its original red windmill.

Le Lido de Paris   CABARET
(Map p58; ☎01 40 76 56 10; www.lido.fr; 116bis av des Champs-Élysées, 8e; MGeorge V) Founded at the close of WWII, this show-stopping cabaret gets top marks for its lavish costumes.

Live Music

Cosmopolitan Paris is a first-class stage for classical music and big-name rock, pop and independent acts. A musical culture deeply influenced by rich immigration, vibrant sub-cultures and progressive audiences make it a fervent breeding ground for experimental music: Paris-bred World Music is renowned. The city became Europe's most important jazz centre after WWII, and clubs and cellars still lure international stars. You'll also find fantastically atmospheric *chansons* (heartfelt, lyric-driven music typified by Édith Piaf) venues.

Palais Omnisports de Paris-Bercy (Map p86; www.bercy.fr; 8 bd de Bercy, 12e; MBercy), **Le Zénith** (☎01 55 80 09 38, 08 90 71 02 07; www.le-zenith.com; 211 av Jean Jaurès, 19e; MPorte de Pantin) and **Stade de France** (☎08 92 39 01 00; www.stadefrance.com; rue Francis de Pressensé, ZAC du Cornillon Nord, St-Denis La Plaine; MSt-Denis-Porte de Paris) are Paris' big-name venues.

But it's the smaller concert halls loaded with history and charm that most fans favour: **La Cigale** (Map p74; ☎01 49 25 81 75; www.lacigale.fr; 120 bd de Rochechouart, 18e; admission €25-60; MAnvers or Pigalle) and **L'Olympia** (Map p72; ☎08 92 68 33 68; www.olympiahall.com; 28 bd des Capucines, 9e; MOpéra) are two of many.

Salle Pleyel   CLASSICAL
(Map p58; ☎01 42 56 13 13; www.sallepleyel.fr; 252 rue du Faubourg St-Honoré, 8e; ☺box office

---

GAY & LESBIAN PARIS

The Marais (4e), especially around the intersection of rue Ste-Croix de la Bretonnerie and rue des Archives, and eastwards to rue Vieille du Temple, has been Paris' main centre of gay nightlife for over two decades. There are also a few bars and clubs within walking distance of bd de Sébastopol. Other venues are scattered throughout the city.

The lesbian scene is less public than its gay counterpart, and centres on a few cafes and bars in the Marais, especially along rue des Écouffes.

The **Centre Gai et Lesbien de Paris** (CGL; ☎01 43 57 21 47; www.centrelgbtparis.org; 61-63 rue Beaubourg, 3e; ☺6-8pm Mon, 3.30-8pm Tue-Thu, 1-8pm Fri & Sat; MRambuteau or Arts et Métiers), with a large library and sociable bar, is the single best source of information in Paris for gay and lesbian travellers.

Our top choices include:

» **Open Café** (Map p78; www.opencafe.fr; 17 rue des Archives, 4e; ☺daily; MHôtel de Ville) The wide, white-seated terrace is prime for talent-watching.

» **Scream Club** (Map p78; www.scream-paris.com; 18 rue du Faubourg du Temple, 11e; ☺daily; MBelleville or Goncourt) Saturday night's the night at 'Paris' biggest gay party'.

» **3W Kafé** (Map p78; 8 rue des Écouffes, 4e; ☺Tue-Sat; MSt-Paul) The name of this sleek spot stands for 'women with women'.

» **Queen** (Map p58; ☎01 53 89 08 90; www.queen.fr; 102 av des Champs-Élysées, 8e; admission €20; ☺11.30pm-10am; MGeorge V) Don't miss disco night!

» **La Champmeslé** (Map p66; www.lachampmesle.com; 4 rue Chabanais, 2e; ☺daily; MPyramides) Cabaret nights, fortune-telling and art exhibitions attract an older lesbian crowd.

» **Le Tango** (Map p78; www.boite-a-frissons.fr; 13 rue au Maire, 3e; ☺Fri-Sun; MArts et Métiers) Historic 1930s dancehall hosting legendary gay tea dances.

noon-7pm Mon-Sat, to 8pm on day of performance; MTernes) This highly regarded hall dating from the 1920s hosts many of Paris' finest classical music recitals and concerts, including those by the celebrated Orchestre de Paris (www.orchestredeparis.com).

Point Éphémère   LIVE MUSIC

(www.pointephemere.org; 200 quai de Valmy, 10e; ⏰noon-2am Mon-Sat, to 10pm Sun; 🔊; MLouis Blanc) This ubercool cultural centre by the Canal St-Martin attracts an underground crowd from noon till past midnight, for drinks, meals, concerts, dance nights and cutting-edge art exhibitions.

Le Nouveau Casino   LIVE MUSIC

(Map p78; www.nouveaucasino.net; 109 rue Oberkampf, 11e; ⏰Tue-Sun; MParmentier) This club-concert annexe of Café Charbon (p130) has made a name for itself amid the bars of Oberkampf with its live-music concerts (usually Tuesday, Thursday and Friday) and lively club nights on weekends. Electro, pop, deep house, rock – the program is eclectic, underground and always up to the minute. Check the website for up-to-date listings.

Le Vieux Belleville   LIVE MUSIC

(www.le-vieux-belleville.com; 12 rue des Envierges, 20e; MPyrénées) This old-fashioned bistro and *bal musette* (dancing club) at the top of Parc de Belleville is an atmospheric venue for performances of *chansons* featuring accordions and an organ grinder three times a week. It's a lively favourite with locals, though, so booking ahead is advised. The 'Old Belleville' serves classic bistro food (open for lunch Monday to Friday, dinner Tuesday to Saturday).

Cabaret Sauvage   LIVE MUSIC

(www.cabaretsauvage.com; 221 av Jean Jaurès, 19e; MPorte de la Villette) This very cool space in the Parc de la Villette (it looks like a gigantic yurt) is host to African, reggae and raï concerts as well as DJ nights that last till dawn. There are also occasional hip hop and indie acts that pass through.

Le Baiser Salé   LIVE MUSIC

(Map p66; www.lebaisersale.com; 58 rue des Lombards, 2e; ⏰daily; MChâtelet) One of several stellar jazz clubs located on this street, the *salle de jazz* (jazz room) on its 1st floor has concerts of jazz, Afro and Latin jazz and jazz fusion. Combining big names and unknown artists, it's known for its relaxed vibe and has a gift for discovering new talents.

PARIS ENTERTAINMENT

Sets start at 7.30pm and 10pm. The Monday night *soirée bœuf* (jam session) is free.

Au Limonaire   LIVE MUSIC

(Map p72; ☎01 45 23 33 33; http://limonaire.free. fr; 18 cité Bergère, 9e; ⏰7pm-midnight; MGrands Boulevards) This little wine bar is one of the best places to listen to traditional French *chansons* and local singer-songwriters. Performances begin at 10pm Tuesday to Saturday and 7pm on Sunday. Entry is free, the wine is good and dinner is served (*plat du jour* €7). Reservations are recommended if you plan on dining.

Nightclubs

Paris' residential make-up means clubs aren't ubiquitous. Still, electronica, laced with funk and groove, is its strong suit. DJs tend to have short stints in venues – look for flyers or check www.gogoparis.com. Salsa and Latino also maintain a huge following. Admission to clubs is free to around €20; entry is often cheaper before 1am.

La Scène Bastille   NIGHTCLUB

(Map p78; www.scenebastille.com; 2bis rue des Taillandiers, 11e; ⏰Thu-Sun; MBastille or Ledru-Rollin) The 'Bastille Scene' puts on a mixed bag of concerts but focuses on electro, funk and hip hop.

Le Batofar   NIGHTCLUB

(Map p86; www.batofar.org; opposite 11 quai François Mauriac, 13e; ⏰9pm-midnight Mon & Tue, to 4am or later Wed-Sun; MQuai de la Gare or Bibliothèque) This incongruous, much-loved, red-metal

ℹ THEATRE & CONCERT TICKETS

Buy tickets for concerts, theatre performances and other cultural events at *billetteries* (box offices) in Fnac (☎08 92 68 36 22; www.fnactickets.com) or Virgin Megastore (place Raoul Dautry, Gare Montparnasse; ⊙7am-8.30pm Mon-Thu, to 9pm Fri, 8am-8pm Sat; Ⓜ Montparnasse Bienvenüe) branches. Fnac has branches at Forum des Halles (Map p16) and on av des Champs-Élysées (Map p58; 74 av des Champs-Élysées; ⊙10am-midnight Mon-Sat, noon-midnight Sun; Ⓜ Franklin D Roosevelt). Both accept reservations by phone and the internet, and take most credit cards. Tickets generally cannot be returned or exchanged unless a performance is cancelled. Or try Paris' oldest ticket agency, Agence Marivaux (Map p72; ☎01 42 97 46 70; 7 rue de Marivaux, 2e; ⊙11am-7.30pm Mon-Fri, noon-4pm Sat; Ⓜ Richelieu-Drouot), just opposite the Opéra Comique (Map p72; www.opera-comique.com; 1 place Boïeldieu, 2e; Ⓜ Richelieu Drouot).

Come the day of a performance, snag a half-price ticket (plus €3 commission) for ballet, theatre, opera etc at discount-ticket outlet Kiosque Théâtre Madeleine (Map p58; opposite 15 place de la Madeleine, 8e; ⊙12.30-8pm Tue-Sat, to 4pm Sun; Ⓜ Madeleine).

tugboat has a rooftop bar with a respected restaurant that's terrific in summer. The club underneath provides memorable underwater acoustics between its metal walls and portholes. Le Batofar is known for its edgy, experimental music policy and live performances – mostly electro-oriented but also incorporating hip hop, new wave, rock, punk or jazz. Hours can vary.

Several other floating bars/nightclubs are moored nearby.

Le Divan du Monde   LIVE MUSIC
(Map p74; www.divandumonde.com; 75 rue des Martyrs, 18e; ⊙Fri & Sat, open for events Mon-Fri; Ⓜ Pigalle) Cinematographic events, Gypsy gatherings, *nouvelles chansons françaises* (new French songs), air-guitar face-offs, soul/funk fiestas, and rock parties all feature at this inventive, open-minded cross-cultural venue.

Le Balajo   NIGHTCLUB
(Map p78; www.balajo.fr; 9 rue de Lappe, 11e; ⊙daily; Ⓜ Bastille) A mainstay of Parisian nightlife since 1936, this ancient ballroom is devoted to salsa classes and Latino music during the week, with an R&B slant on weekends. At times it can be somewhat tacky, but it scores a mention for its historical value and its old-fashioned *musette* (accordion music) gigs on Monday afternoons.

Le Rex Club   NIGHTCLUB
(Map p108; www.rexclub.com; 5 bd Poissonnière, 2e; ⊙Wed-Sat; Ⓜ Bonne Nouvelle) Attached to the art deco Grand Rex cinema, this is Paris' premier house and techno venue, where some of the world's hottest DJs strut their stuff on a 70-speaker, multidiffusion sound system.

Bus Palladium   NIGHTCLUB
(www.lebuspalladium.com; 6 rue Pierre Fontaine, 9e; ⊙11pm-5am Tue, Fri & Sat; Ⓜ Blanche) The place to be back in the 1960s, the Bus is now back in business 50 years later, with funky DJs and a mixed bag of performances by indie and pop groups.

Cinema

The film-lover's ultimate city, Paris has some wonderful movie houses. Both *Pariscope* and *L'Officiel des Spectacles* list the full crop of Paris' cinematic pickings and screening times; online see http://cinema.leparisien.fr. Expect to pay around €10 for a first-run film (€13 for 3D). Foreign films (including English-language films) screened in their original language with French subtitles are labelled 'VO' (*version originale*). Films labelled 'VF' (*version française*) are dubbed in French.

Cinemas showing films set in Paris are the centrepiece of the city's film archive, the Forum des Images (Map p66; www.forumdesimages.net; 1 Grande Galerie, Porte St-Eustache, Forum des Halles, 1er; ⊙12.30-11.30pm Tue-Fri, from 2pm Sat & Sun; Ⓜ Les Halles). Film buffs also shouldn't miss the Cinémathèque Française (Map p86; www.cinemathequefrancaise.com; 51 rue de Bercy, 12e; exhibits adult/18-25yr/under 18yr €6/5/3; ⊙noon-7pm Mon & Wed-Sat, to 8pm Sun; Ⓜ Bercy), with two museums, a film library and screenings.

Cinéma La Pagode   CINEMA
(☎01 45 55 48 48; www.etoile-cinema.com; 57bis rue de Babylone, 7e; Ⓜ St-François Xavier) This 19th-century Japanese pagoda was converted into a cinema in the 1930s and remains the most atmospheric spot in Paris to catch art-house

and classic films. Don't miss a moment or two in its bamboo-enshrined garden.

Theatre

Most theatre productions, including those originally written in other languages, are performed in French. Very occasionally, English-speaking troupes play at smaller venues around town.

Comédie Française   THEATRE
(Map p66; www.comedie-francaise.fr; place Colette, 1er; MPalais Royal–Musée du Louvre) Founded in 1680 under Louis XIV, the 'French Comedy' theatre bases its repertoire around the works of classic French playwrights. The theatre has its roots in an earlier company directed by Molière at the Palais Royal – the French playwright and actor was seized by a convulsion on stage during the fourth performance of the *Imaginary Invalid* in 1673 and died later at his home on nearby rue de Richelieu.

Opera & Ballet

France's Opéra National de Paris and Ballet de l'Opéra National de Paris perform at Paris' two opera houses, the Palais Garnier and Opéra Bastille. The season runs between September and July.

Palais Garnier   OPERA
(Map p72; 08 92 89 90 90; www.operadeparis.fr; place de l'Opéra, 9e; MOpéra) The city's original opera house is smaller than its Bastille counterpart, but boasts perfect acoustics. Due to its odd shape, however, some seats have limited or no visibility. Ticket prices and conditions (including last-minute discounts) are available at the box office (Map p72; cnr rues Scribe & Auber; 11am-6.30pm Mon-Sat).

Opéra Bastille   OPERA, BALLET
(Map p86; 08 92 89 90 90; www.operadeparis.fr; 2-6 place de la Bastille, 12e; MBastille) Tickets at this monolithic 3400-seat venue, which opened in 1989, go on sale online two weeks before they're available by telephone or at the box office (Map p86; 01 40 01 19 70; 130 rue de Lyon, 12e; 2.30-6.30pm Mon-Sat). Standing-only tickets (*places débouts;* €5) are available 90 minutes before performances begin. Unsold seats are sometimes available 45 minutes before the curtain goes up to people aged under 28 or over 60.

🛍 Shopping

The most exclusive designer boutiques require customers to buzz to get in – don't be shy about ringing that bell. Winter *soldes* (sales) start mid-January; summer ones, the second week of June.

Many larger stores hold *nocturnes* (late nights) on Thursday, remaining open until around 10pm. For Sunday shopping, the Champs-Élysées, Montmartre, the Marais and Bastille areas are the liveliest.

TOP CHOICE Didier Ludot   FASHION
(Map p66; www.didierludot.fr; 19-20 & 23-24 Galerie de Montpensier, 1er; MPalais Royal–Musée du Louvre) In the rag trade since 1975, collector Didier Ludot sells the city's finest couture creations of yesteryear in his exclusive twinset of boutiques. He also hosts exhibitions and has published a book portraying the evolution of the little black dress, brilliantly brought to life

---

DON'T MISS

BUSKERS IN PARIS

Paris' eclectic gaggle of clowns, mime artists, living statues, acrobats, rollerbladers, buskers and other street entertainers can be bags of fun and cost substantially less than a theatre ticket (a few coins in the hat is appreciated). Some excellent musicians perform in the long, echo-filled corridors of the metro, a highly prized privilege that artists audition for. Outside, you can be sure of a good show at the following spots:

» **Place Georges Pompidou, 4e** The huge square in front of the Centre Pompidou.

» **Pont St-Louis, 4e** The bridge linking Paris' two islands (best enjoyed with Berthillon ice cream).

» **Pont au Double, 4e** The pedestrian bridge linking Notre Dame with the Left Bank.

» **Place Jean du Bellay, 1er** Musicians and fire-eaters near the Fontaine des Innocents.

» **Parc de la Villette (p75), 19e** African drummers on the weekend.

» **Place du Tertre (p73), 18e** Montmartre's original main square wins hands down as Paris' busiest busker stage.

in his boutique that sells just that, La Petite Robe Noire (Map p66; 125 Galerie de Valois, 1er; MPalais Royal-Musée du Louvre).

Adam Montparnasse ART SUPPLIES
(Map p96; www.adamparis.com; 11 bd Edgar Quinet, 14e; ⊙9.30am-12.30pm & 1.30-7pm Mon, 9.30am-7pm Tue-Sat; MEdgar Quinet) If Paris' glorious art galleries have awoken your inner artist, pick up paint brushes, charcoals, pastels, sketchpads, watercolours, oils, acrylics, canvases and all manner of art supplies at this historic shop. Picasso, Brancusi and Giacometti were among Édouard Adam's clients. Another seminal client was Yves Klein, with whom Adam developed the ultramarine 'Klein blue' – the VLB25 'Klein Blue' varnish is sold exclusively here.

Shakespeare & Company BOOKS
(Map p92; www.shakespeareandcompany.com; 37 rue de la Bûcherie, 5e; ⊙10am-11pm Mon-Fri, from 11am Sat & Sun; MSt-Michel) A kind of spell descends as you enter this enchanting bookshop, where nooks and crannies overflow with new and secondhand English-language books. Fabled for nurturing writers, at night its couches turn into beds where writers stay in exchange for stacking shelves. Readings by emerging to illustrious authors take place at 7pm most Mondays; it also hosts workshops and literary festivals.

The bookshop is the stuff of legends. The original shop (12 rue l'Odeon; closed by the Nazis in 1941) was run by Sylvia Beach and became the meeting point for Hemingway's 'Lost Generation'. American-born George Whitman opened the present incarnation in 1951, attracting a beat poet clientele, and scores of authors have since passed through

SECRET SHOPPING IN THE MARAIS

Some of the Marais' sweetest boutique shopping is hidden down peaceful alleyways and courtyards, free of cars, as they were centuries ago.

Don't miss Village St-Paul (Map p78; rue St-Paul, des rue Jardins St-Paul & rue Charlemagne, 4e; MSt-Paul), a designer set of five vintage courtyards, refashioned in the 1970s from the 14th-century walled gardens of King Charles V, with tiny artisan boutiques, galleries and antique shops.

its doors. George died in 2011, aged 98; he is buried in Division 73 of Cimetière du Père Lachaise. Today his daughter, Sylvia Beach Whitman, maintains Shakespeare & Company's serendipitous magic.

Merci CONCEPT STORE
(Map p78; www.merci-merci.com; 111 bd Beaumarchais, 3e; MSt-Sébastien–Froissart) The landmark Fiat Cinquecento in the courtyard marks the entrance to this unique multistorey concept store; its rallying cry is one-stop shopping. Fashion, accessories, linens, lamps and various other nifty designs for the home (a kitchen brush made from recycled egg shells and coffee grounds anyone?). A trio of inspired eating-drinking spaces complete Paris' hippest shopping experience. All proceeds go to a children's charity in Madagascar.

Maison Georges Larnicol CHOCOLATE
(Map p78; www.chocolaterielarnicol.fr; 9 rue du Roi de Sicile & 14 rue de Rivoli, 4e; ⊙9.30am-10pm; MChemin Vert) Coco-ginger bites, buttery caramels and chocolate objects (a pair of red stilettos perhaps? an alarm clock or football?) are among the sweet treats displayed so enticingly at this master chocolate maker and pastry chef from Brittany. But it is his syrupy, chewy *kouignettes*, traditional Breton butter cakes unusually made in mini dimensions and 16 different flavours (€2.50 per 100g), that are the real reason to come here.

Trésor FASHION
(Map p78; 5 rue du Trésor, 4e; MHôtel de Ville or St-Paul) Tucked at the end of pedestrian rue du Trésor, this bohemian boutique by Brigitte Masson injects a fresh, individual take on women's fashion. From its catchy salmon-orange façade strung with old-fashioned fairy lights to its overtly retro ambience inside, this address is Paris-perfect for picking up something a little different. Great accessories.

Galeries Lafayette DEPARTMENT STORE
(Map p72; www.galerieslafayette.com; 40 bd Haussmann, 9e; ⊙9.30am-8pm Mon-Sat, to 9pm Thu; MAuber or Chaussée d'Antin) Probably the best known of the big Parisian department stores, Galeries Lafayette is spread across three buildings: the main store (its historic dome turned 100 in 2012), the men's store and the home-design store. You can check out modern art in the gallery (1st fl; ⊙11am-7pm Mon-Sat), take in a fashion show (☏bookings 01 42 82 30 25; ⊙Mar-Jul & Sep-Dec) at 3pm on Fridays, or ascend to the rooftop for a windswept Parisian panorama (free).

DISCOUNT DESIGNER OUTLETS & SECONDHAND CHIC

You can save up to 70% off previous seasons' collections, surpluses, prototypes and seconds by name-brand designers – for men, women and kids – at the discounted outlet stores along rue d'Alésia, 14e, particularly between av de Maine to rue Raymond-Losserand. Exiting the Alésia metro station, walk west along rue d'Alésia to uncover its line-up of outlets. For slashed prices on *grandes marques* (big names) under one roof, head to the 15e's Mistigriff (www.mistigriff.fr; 83-85 rue St-Charles, 15e; MCharles Michels).

When well-heeled Parisians spring clean their wardrobes, they take their designer and vintage cast-offs to *dépôt-vente* (secondhand) boutiques, where savvy locals snap up serious bargains. A superb place to start is at Chercheminippes (Map p96; www.chercheminippes.com; 102, 109-111 & 124 rue du Cherche Midi, 6e; 11am-7pm Mon-Sat; MVaneau), which has five beautifully presented boutiques on one street selling secondhand pieces – including menswear and childrenswear – by current designers.

When your legs need a break, head to one of the many restaurants and cafes inside.

E Dehillerin   HOMEWARES
(Map p66; www.dehillerin.com; 18-20 rue Coquillière, 1er; 9-12.30pm Mon & Wed-Fri, 8am-6pm Tue & Sat; MLes Halles) Founded in 1820, this extraordinary two-level store – think old-fashioned warehouse rather than shiny chic boutique – carries an incredible selection of professional-quality *matériel de cuisine* (kitchenware). Poultry scissors, turbot poacher, old-fashioned copper pot or Eiffel Tower–shaped cake tin – it's all here.

Colette   CONCEPT STORE
(Map p66; www.colette.fr; 213 rue St-Honoré, 1er; MTuileries) Uberhip is an understatement. Ogle at designer fashion on the 1st floor; and streetwear, limited-edition sneakers, art books, music, gadgets and other hi-tech, inventive and/or plain unusual items on the ground floor. End with a drink in the basement 'water bar' and pick up free design magazines and flyers for some of the city's hippest happenings by the door upon leaving.

Guerlain   COSMETICS
(Map p58; www.guerlain.com; 68 av des Champs-Élysées, 8e; 10.30am-8pm Mon-Sat, noon-7pm Sun; MFranklin D Roosevelt) Guerlain is Paris' most famous *parfumerie*, and its shop (dating from 1912) is one of the most beautiful in the city. With its shimmering mirror and marble art deco interior, it's a reminder of the former glory of the Champs-Élysées. For total indulgence, make an appointment at its decadent spa (01 45 62 11 21).

Un Chien dans le Marais   FASHION
(Map p78; www.unchiendanslemarais.com; 35bis rue du Roi de Sicile, 4e; MSt-Paul) Only in Paris: this pocket-size boutique has to be seen to be believed: ballerina tutus, fur coats, woolly jumpers, black-tailed coats, hoodies, frilly blouses and sweaters with 101 different logos – all for your dog.

Clair de Rêve   TOYS
(Map p88; www.clairdereve.com; 35 rue St-Louis en l'Île, 4e; MPont Marie) This shop is all about wind-up toys, music boxes and puppets – mostly marionettes, which sway and bob, suspended from the ceiling.

Legrand Filles & Fils   FOOD, DRINK
(Map p66; www.caves-legrand.com; 1 rue de la Banque, 2e; MPyramides) This shop, tucked inside Galerie Vivienne since 1880, sells fine wine and all the accoutrements: corkscrews, tasting glasses, decanters etc. It also has a fancy wine bar, *école du vin* (wine school) and *éspace dégustation* with several tastings a month; check its website for details.

Librairie Gourmande   BOOKS
(Map p66; www.librairie-gourmande.fr; 92 rue Montmartre, 1er; 11am-7pm Mon-Sat; MSentier) The city's leading bookshop dedicated to things culinary and gourmet.

Isabel Marant   FASHION
(Map p86; www.isabelmarant.tm.fr; 16 rue de Charonne, 11e; Mon-Sat; MBastille) Great cardigans and trousers, interesting accessories, ethnic influences and beautiful fabrics: just a few reasons why Isabel Marant has become the darling of Paris fashion. Bohemian and stylish, these are clothes that people actually look good in.

JB Guanti   FASHION
(Map p96; www.jbguanti.fr; 59 rue de Rennes, 6e; 10am-7pm Mon-Sat; MSt-Sulpice or Mabillon) For the ultimate finishing touch, the men's and women's gloves at this boutique, which

Shopping

Paris has it all: large boulevards with international chains, luxury avenues with designer fashion, famous *grands magasins* (department stores) and fabulous markets (p142). But the real charm resides in a peripatetic stroll along side streets where tiny speciality shops and cutting-edge boutiques, selling everything from strawberry-scented Wellington boots to candles scented like heaven, mingle with cafés, galleries and churches.

If you're after what the French do best – fashion – tread the haute-couture, luxury jewellery and designer perfume boardwalks in the Étoile and Champs-Élysées. For original fashion, street and vintage, head for the Marais and St-Germain des Prés.

But it's not just fashion. Paris is an exquisite treasure chest of fine food, wine, tea, books, beautiful stationery, fine art, antiques and original collectables. You won't be stuck for gifts and souvenirs to take home.

SHOP LIKE A PARISIAN FOR...

» **A rainbow of macarons** from Left Bank *chocolatier* Pierre Hermé (p142)

» **Designer fashion** from an edgy boutique or concept store in the Marais or an haute-couture label in the Triangle d'Or (p137)

» **Perfume** from Fragonard (p126) or Guerlain (p139)

» **Postcards of Old Paris** from the *bouquinistes* (antiquarian-book sellers) who've set up stalls on the quays near Notre Dame since the 16th century

» **Parisian curios** from Marché aux Puces de la Porte de Vanves (p142), the most intimate of Paris' made-for-Sunday-mooching flea markets

---

Clockwise from top left
1. Fashion boutique in the Marais 2. Inside *grand magasin* Galeries Lafayette 3. A bright display of macarons

142

specialises solely in gloves, are the epitome of both style and comfort, whether unlined, silk-lined, cashmere-lined, lambskin-lined or trimmed with rabbit fur.

Pierre Hermé   FOOD, DRINK
(Map p96; www.pierreherme.com; 72 rue Bonaparte, 6e; ☺10am-7pm Sun-Fri, to 8pm Sat; MOdéon or RER Luxembourg) It's the size of a chocolate box, but once you're in, your tastebuds will go wild. Pierre Hermé is one of Paris' top chocolatiers, and this boutique is a veritable feast of perfectly presented petits fours, cakes, chocolate, nougats, macarons and jam.

Le Bon Marché   DEPARTMENT STORE
(Map p96; www.bonmarche.fr; 24 rue de Sèvres, 7e; ☺10am-8pm Mon-Wed & Fri, to 9pm Thu & Sat; MSèvres Babylone) Built by Gustave Eiffel as Paris' first department store in 1852, Le Bon Marché translates as 'good market' but also means 'bargain', which it isn't. But it is the epitome of style, with a superb concentration of men's and women's fashions, beautiful homewares, stationery and a good range of books and toys as well as chic dining options.

The icing on the cake is its glorious food hall, La Grande Épicerie de Paris (Map p96; www.lagrandeepicerie.fr; 36 rue de Sèvres, 7e; ☺8.30am-9pm Mon-Sat; MSèvres Babylone).

Le Printemps   DEPARTMENT STORE
(Map p72; www.printemps.com; 64 bd Haussmann, 9e; ☺9.30am-8pm Mon-Sat, to 10pm Thu; MHavre Caumartin) This is actually three separate stores – Le Printemps de la Mode (women's fashion), Le Printemps de l'Homme (for men) and Le Printemps de la Beauté et Maison (for beauty and household goods) – offering a staggering display of perfume, cosmetics and

accessories, as well as established and up-and-coming designer wear.

Fromagerie Alléosse   FOOD, DRINK
(Map p58; www.alleosse.com; 13 rue Poncelet, 17e; ☺9am-1pm & 4-7pm Tue-Thu, 9am-6pm Fri & Sat; MTernes) Although there are cheese shops throughout the city, this one is actually worth a trip across town. Cheeses are sold as they should be, grouped into five main categories: fromage de chèvre (goat's milk cheese), fromage à pâte persillée (veined or blue cheese), fromage à pâte molle (soft cheese), fromage à pâte demi-dure (semihard cheese) and fromage à pâte dure (hard cheese).

Kiliwatch   FASHION
(Map p66; http://espacekiliwatch.fr; 64 rue Tiquetonne, 2e; ☺2-7.15pm Mon, 11am-7.45pm Tue-Sat; MÉtienne Marcel) A Parisian institution, Kiliwatch gets jam-packed with hip guys and gals rummaging through racks of new and used streetwear. Startling vintage range of hats and boots, plus art/photography books, eyewear and the latest sneakers.

Le Studio des Parfums   COSMETICS
(Map p78; ☎01 40 29 90 84; www.artisanparfumeur.com; 23 rue du Bourg Tibourg, 4e; MSt-Paul) Learn how a perfume maker's organ – with more than 150 different scents – works and create your own fragrance (€95/175 for one/three hours) at this charming perfume studio. Little ones will love the scent workshops for children (45 minutes, €30).

Tumbleweed   TOYS, FASHION
(Map p78; www.tumbleweedparis.com; 19 rue de Turenne, 4e; ☺11am-7pm; MSt-Paul or Chemin Vert) This little shop specialises in leather slippers

DON'T MISS

FLEA MARKETS

» Marché aux Puces de Montreuil (av du Professeur André Lemière, 20e; ☺8am-7.30pm Sat-Mon; MPorte de Montreuil) A 19th-century marché aux puces (flea market) particularly known for its secondhand clothing, designer seconds, engravings, jewellery, linen, crockery, old furniture and appliances.

» Marché aux Puces de St-Ouen (www.marcheauxpuces-saintouen.com; rue des Rosiers, av Michelet, rue Voltaire, rue Paul Bert & rue Jean-Henri Fabre; ☺9am-6pm Sat, 10am-6pm Sun, 11am-5pm Mon; MPorte de Clignancourt) Founded in the late 19th century and said to be Europe's largest.

» Marché aux Puces de la Porte de Vanves (http://pucesdevanves.typepad.com; av Georges Lafenestre & av Marc Sangnier, 14e; ☺from 7am Sat & Sun; MPorte de Vanves) The Porte de Vanves flea market is the smallest and one of the friendliest of the lot. Av Georges Lafenestre has lots of 'curios' that don't quite qualify as antiques. Av Marc Sangnier is lined with stalls of new clothes, shoes, handbags and household items.

for kids and *l'artisanat d'art ludique* (crafts of the playing art): think handmade wooden toys and exquisitely made brain-teasers and puzzles for adults, such as Japanese 'spin' and 'secret' boxes that defy entry.

Deyrolle   ANTIQUES, HOMEWARES
(Map p96; www.deyrolle.com; 46 rue du Bac, 7e; ☺10am-7pm Tue-Sat; MRue du Bac) Overrun with creatures including lions, tigers, zebras and storks, taxidermist Deyrolle opened in 1831. In addition to stuffed animals (for rent and sale), it stocks minerals, shells, corals and crustaceans, stand-mounted ostrich eggs and pedagogical storyboards. There are also rare and unusual seeds (including many old types of tomato), gardening tools and accessories.

Mariage Frères   DRINK
(Map p78; www.mariagefreres.com; 30, 32 & 35 rue du Bourg Tibourg, 4e; ☺daily; MHôtel de Ville) Founded in 1854, this is Paris' first and arguably finest tea shop. Choose from more than 500 varieties of tea sourced from some 35 countries. Mariage Frères has four other outlets, including the **6e branch** (Map p88; ☑01 40 51 82 50; 13 rue des Grands Augustins; MOdéon) and the **8e branch** (Map p58; ☑01 46 22 18 54; 260 rue du Faubourg St-Honoré; MTernes).

Place de la Madeleine   FOOD, DRINK
(Map p58; place de la Madeleine, 8e; MMadeleine) Ultragourmet food shops are the treat here; if you feel your knees start to go all wobbly in front of a display window, you know you're in the right place. The most notable names include truffle dealers **La Maison de la Truffe** (Map p58; ☑01 42 65 53 22; www.maison-de-la-truffe.com; 19 place de la Madeleine; ☺10am-10pm Mon-Sat; MMadeleine); luxury food shop **Hédiard** (Map p58; 21 place de la Madeleine, 8e; ☺9am-9pm Mon-Sat; MMadeleine); mustard specialist **Boutique Maille** (Map p58; ☑01 40 15 06 00; www.maille.com; 6 place de la Madeleine; ☺10am-7pm Mon-Sat; MMadeleine); and Paris' most famous caterer, **Fauchon** (Map p72; ☑01 70 39 38 00; www.fauchon.fr; 26 & 30 place de la Madeleine; ☺8.30am-7pm Mon-Sat; MMadeleine), selling incredibly mouth-watering delicacies, from foie gras to jams, chocolates and pastries.

Marché aux Fleurs   MARKET
(Map p88; place Louis Lépin, 4e; ☺8am-7.30pm Mon-Sat; MCité) Blooms have been sold at this flower market since 1808, making it the oldest market of any kind in Paris. On Sunday, between 9am and 7pm, it transforms into a twittering *marché aux oiseaux* (bird market).

ℹ Information

Dangers & Annoyances

Paris is generally a safe city. Metro stations probably best avoided late at night include: Châtelet–Les Halles and its seemingly endless corridors; Château Rouge; Gare du Nord; Strasbourg St-Denis; Réaumur Sébastopol; and Montparnasse Bienvenüe. *Bornes d'alarme* (alarm boxes) are located in the centre of each metro/RER platform and some station corridors.

Pickpocketing and thefts from handbags and packs is a problem wherever there are crowds (especially of tourists). Be particularly alert around Sacré-Cœur; Pigalle; the areas around Forum des Halles and Centre Pompidou; the Latin Quarter (especially the rectangle bounded by rue St-Jacques, bd St-Germain, bd St-Michel and quai St-Michel); below the Eiffel Tower; and on the metro during rush hour. In an increasingly common ruse, scammers pretend to 'find' a gold ring (by subtly dropping it on the ground) then offer it to you as a diversionary tactic to surreptitiously reach into your pockets or bags, or to demand money. Don't fall for it!

Take care crossing roads, as Parisian drivers frequently ignore green pedestrian lights.

Internet Access

Wi-fi is widely available at accommodation in Paris and is increasingly free. The city has 400 free wi-fi points (some time-limited) at popular locations, including parks, libraries, local town halls and tourist hot spots. Locations are mapped at www.paris.fr. Free wi-fi is available on Paris' metro.

Parisian internet cafes include several along bd St-Michel opposite the Jardin du Luxembourg.

Medical Services

American Hospital of Paris (☑01 46 41 25 25; www.american-hospital.org; 63 bd Victor Hugo, Neuilly-sur-Seine; MPont de Levallois) Private hospital offering emergency 24-hour medical and dental care.

Hertford British Hospital (☑01 47 59 59 59; www.ihfb.org; 3 rue Barbès, Levallois; MAnatole France) A less-expensive private English-speaking option than the American Hospital.

Hôpital Hôtel Dieu (☑01 42 34 82 34; www.aphp.fr; 1 place du Parvis Notre Dame, 4e; MCité) One of the city's main government-run public hospitals; after 8pm use the emergency entrance on rue de la Cité.

Pharmacie Les Champs (☑01 45 62 02 41; 84 av des Champs-Élysées, 8e; ☺24hr; MGeorge V)

Tourist Information

Paris Convention & Visitors Bureau (Office de Tourisme et de Congrès de Paris; ☑08 92 68 30 00; www.parisinfo.com; 25-27 rue des

Pyramides, 1er; ⊙9am-7pm Jun-Oct, shorter hours rest of year; MPyramides) Main tourist office with a clutch of smaller centres elsewhere in the city.

❶ Getting There & Away

Air

Aéroport Roissy Charles de Gaulle (CDG; ☑01 70 36 39 50; www.aeroportsdeparis.fr) Paris' biggest airport has three terminal complexes – Aérogare 1, 2 and 3 – 30km northeast of the centre in the suburb of Roissy.

Aéroport d'Orly (ORY; ☑01 70 36 39 50; www.aeroportsdeparis.fr) Aéroport d'Orly is the older, smaller of Paris' two major airports, 19km south of the city.

Aéroport Beauvais (BVA; ☑08 92 68 20 66; www.aeroportbeauvais.com) Beauvais is 75km north of Paris: before you snap up that low-cost flight, consider if the postarrival journey is worth it.

Bus

Eurolines (☑01 43 54 11 99; www.eurolines. fr; 55 rue St-Jacques, 5e; ⊙9.30am-6.30pm Mon-Fri, 10am-1pm & 2-5pm Sat; MCluny–La Sorbonne) Connects Paris with all major European capitals.

Gare Routiére Internationale de Paris-Galliéni (☑08 92 89 90 91; 28 av du Général de Gaulle; MGalliéni) The city's international bus terminal is in the eastern suburb of Bagnolet; it's about a 15-minute metro ride to the more central République metro station.

Train

Paris has six major train stations. For mainline train information available round the clock, contact **SNCF** (☑08 91 36 20 20, timetables 08 91 67 68 69; www.sncf.fr).

Gare du Nord (rue de Dunkerque, 10e; MGare du Nord) The terminus for the Eurostar and Thalys trains, serving London and Amsterdam, respectively, as well as northbound domestic trains. Located in northern Paris.

Gare de l'Est (blvd de Strasbourg, 10e; MGare de l'Est) The terminus for eastbound trains, including services to Strasbourg, Berlin and Vienna. Located in northern Paris.

Gare de Lyon (blvd Diderot, 12e; MGare de Lyon) The terminus for southeast-bound trains, with destinations including Provence, the Alps, the Riviera and Italy. Also serves Geneva. Located in eastern Paris.

Gare d'Austerlitz (blvd de l'Hôpital, 13e; MGare d'Austerlitz) The terminus for a handful of southbound trains, including services to Orléans and Limoges. Currently no TGV services, though renovations are under way. Located on the Left Bank.

Gare Montparnasse (av du Maine & blvd de Vaugirard, 15e; MMontparnasse Bienvenüe) The terminus for southwest- and westbound trains, including services to Brittany, the Loire, Bordeaux, Toulouse and Spain and Portugal. Located in southern Paris.

Gare St-Lazare (rue St-Lazare & rue d'Amsterdam, 8e; MSt-Lazare) The terminus for Normandy-bound trains. Located in northwestern Paris.

❶ Getting Around

To/From the Airports

Getting into town is straightforward and inexpensive thanks to a fleet of public-transport options; the most expedient are listed here. Bus drivers sell tickets. Children aged four to 11 years pay half price on most of the services.

AÉROPORT ROISSY CHARLES DE GAULLE

A **taxi** to the city centre takes approximately 40 minutes, assuming no traffic jams. During the day, expect to pay around €50; the fare increases 15% between 5pm and 10am and on Sundays. Only take taxis at a clearly marked rank. Never follow anyone who approaches you at the airport and claims to be a driver.

RER B (☑32 46; www.ratp.fr; one-way €9; ⊙5am-11pm) Departs every 10 to 15 minutes, serving the Gare du Nord, Châtelet-Les Halles and St-Michel Notre Dame stations in the city centre. Journey time is approximately 35 minutes.

Air France Bus 2 (☑08 92 35 08 20; http:// videocdn.airfrance.com/cars-airfrance; one-way €15; ⊙6am-11pm) To the Arc de Triomphe.

Air France Bus 4 (☑08 92 35 08 20; http:// videocdn.airfrance.com/cars-airfrance; adult €16.50; ⊙6am-10pm from Roissy Charles de Gaulle, 6am-9.30pm from Paris) Links the airport with Gare de Lyon (50 minutes) in eastern Paris and Gare Montparnasse (55 minutes) in southern Paris.

Noctilien Buses 140 & 143 (☑32 46; www. noctilien.fr; adult €7.60; ⊙12.30am-5.30am) Part of the RATP night service, Noctilien bus 140 from Gare de l'Est and 143 from Gare de l'Est and Gare du Nord go to Roissy-Charles de Gaulle hourly.

RATP Bus 350 (☑32 46; www.ratp.fr; adult €5.10 or 3 metro tickets; ⊙5.30am-11pm) Links the airport with Gare de l'Est in northern Paris every 30 minutes. Journey time is one hour.

Roissybus (☑32 46; www.ratp.fr; adult €10; ⊙5.30am-11pm) Direct bus every 15 minutes to/from Opéra (corner of rue Scribe and rue Auber, 9e). Journey time is 45 minutes to one hour.

AÉROPORT D'ORLY

There is no direct train to/from Orly; you'll need to change transport halfway.

The **RER B** (€11, 35 minutes, every four to 12 minutes) connects Orly with the St-Michel–Notre Dame, Châtelet–Les Halles and Gare du Nord stations in the city centre. To get from Orly to the RER station (Antony), you must first take the **Orlyval** automatic train. The service runs from 6am to 11pm; there are fewer trains on weekends. You only need one ticket. Note that while it is possible to take a shuttle to the RER C line, this service is quite long and not recommended.

A **taxi** to the city centre takes roughly 30 minutes, assuming no traffic jams. During the day, expect to pay around €45; the fare increases 15% between 5pm and 10am and on Sundays. Only take taxis at a clearly marked rank. Never follow anyone who approaches you at the airport and claims to be a driver.

Air France Bus 1 (☑08 92 35 08 20; http://videocdn.airfrance.com/cars-airfrance; adult €11.50; ⊙5am-10.20pm from Orly, 6am-11.20pm from Invalides) This bus runs to/from the Gare Montparnasse (35 minutes) in southern Paris, Invalides in the 7e, and the Arc de Triomphe.

Orlybus (☑32 46; www.ratp.fr; adult €6.90; ⊙6am-11.20pm from Orly, 5.35am-11.05pm from Paris) RATP bus every 15 to 20 minutes to/from metro Denfert Rochereau (30 minutes) in the 14e.

BETWEEN ORLY & CHARLES DE GAULLE

Air France Shuttle Bus 3 (www.cars-airfrance.com; adult €20; ⊙6am-10.30pm) Every 30 minutes; journey time is 30 to 45 minutes.

AÉROPORT PARIS-BEAUVAIS

Navette Officielle (Official Shuttle Bus; ☑08 92 68 20 64, airport 08 92 68 20 66; adult €15) The Beauvais shuttle links the airport with the metro station Porte de Maillot in western Paris. See the airport website for details.

Bicycle

The **Vélib'** (Map p108; www.velib.paris.fr) bike-share scheme has revolutionised how Parisians get around. There are some 1800 stations throughout the city, each with anywhere from 20 to 70 bike stands. The bikes are accessible around the clock.

» To get a bike, you first need to purchase a daily/weekly subscription (€1.70/8). There are two ways to do this: either at the terminals (which require a credit card with an embedded smartchip) at docking stations or online.

» After you authorise a deposit (€150) to pay for the bike should it go missing, you'll receive an ID number and PIN code and you're ready to go.

» Bikes are rented in 30-minute intervals: the 1st half-hour is free, the 2nd is €2, the 3rd and each additional half-hour is €4. If you return a bike before a half-hour is up and then take a new one, you will not be charged.

» If the station you want to return your bike to is full, log in to the terminal to get 15 minutes for free to find another station.

» Bikes are geared to cyclists aged 14 and over, and are fitted with gears, an antitheft lock with key, reflective strips and front/rear lights. Bring your own helmet, though!

Boat

Batobus (www.batobus.com; 1-/2-/5-day pass €15/18/21; ⊙10am-9.30pm Apr-Aug, to 7pm rest of year) Fleet of glassed-in trimarans dock at eight small piers along the Seine; buy tickets at each stop or tourist offices and jump on and off as you like. Its eight stops are the Eiffel Tower, Musée d'Orsay, St-Germain des Prés, Notre Dame, Jardin des Plantes, Hôtel de Ville, Louvre and the Champs-Élysées.

Car & Motorcycle

Driving in Paris is defined by the triple hassle of navigation, heavy traffic and parking. If you must drive, the fastest way to get across the city is usually via the bd Périphérique, the ring road that encircles the city.

Major car-hire companies have offices at airports and train stations.

Parking meters in Paris do not accept coins but require either a chip-enabled credit card or a Paris Carte, available at any *tabac* (tobacconist) for €10 to €30. Municipal public car parks, of which there are more than 200 in Paris, charge between €2 and €3.50 an hour or €20 to €25 per 24 hours. Most are open 24 hours.

Want to look like you've just stepped into (or out of) a 1950s French film? Grab a pastel-coloured Vespa XLV 50cc scooter from **Left Bank Scooters** (☑06 82 70 13 82; www.leftbankscooters.com). They'll deliver/pick up from your hotel and arrange tours (from €130) as far as Versailles. Renters must be at least 30 years old and hold a motorcycle license. Credit-card deposit is €1000. **Freescoot** (Map p88; ☑01 44 07 06 72; www.scooter-rental-paris.com; 63 quai de la Tournelle; bike/tandem half-day €10/22, day €15/32; ⊙9am-1pm & 2-7pm Mon-Sat year-round, plus Sun mid-Apr–mid-Sep; Ⓜ Maubert-Mutualité) also rents scooters; no license is required for smaller scooters.

Public Transport

Paris' public-transit system, mostly operated by the **RATP** (www.ratp.fr) is one of Europe's cheapest and most efficient. View and download transport maps from RATP's website.

BUS

Paris' RATP-operated bus system runs from 5.30am to 8.30pm Monday to Saturday; after that, certain evening-service lines continue until between midnight and 12.30am. Services are drastically reduced on Sunday and public holidays, when buses run from 7am to 8.30pm.

Normal bus rides in one or two bus zones cost one metro ticket; longer rides require two or even three tickets. Transfers to other buses – but not the metro – are allowed on the same ticket as long as the change takes place 1½ hours between the first and last validation. Validate single-journey tickets in the ticket machine near the driver. If you don't have a ticket, the driver can sell you one for €1.90. If you have a Mobilis or Paris Visite pass, flash it at the driver when you board.

The RATP runs 47 **Noctilien** (www.noctilien.fr) night bus lines, which depart hourly from 12.30am to 5.30pm: look for navy-blue N or Noctilien signs at bus stops. Noctilien services are included on your Mobilis or Paris Visite pass for the zones in which you are travelling. Otherwise you pay a certain number of standard €1.70 metro/bus tickets, depending on the length of your journey. Transfers require a separate ticket.

METRO & RER

Paris' underground network, run by the RATP, consists of two separate but linked systems: the metro and the RER suburban train line. The metro has 14 numbered lines; the RER has five main lines, designated A to E and then numbered, that pass through the city centre.

» Each metro train is known by the name of its terminus. On maps and plans each line has a different colour and number (from 1 to 14). Signs in stations indicate the way to the platform for your line. The *direction* signs on each platform indicate the terminus. On lines that split into several branches (such as lines 7 and 13), the terminus served by each train is indicated on the cars, and signs on each platform give the number of minutes until the next train.

» Signs marked *correspondance* (transfer) show how to reach connecting trains. At stations with many intersecting lines, such as Châtelet and Montparnasse Bienvenüe, the connection can take a long time.

» Each metro line has its own schedule, but trains usually start at around 5.30am, with the last train beginning its run between 12.35am and 1.15am (2.15am on Friday and Saturday).

» The same RATP tickets are valid on the metro, RER (for travel within the city limits), buses, trams and the Montmartre funicular. A ticket – called *Le Ticket t+* – costs €1.70 (half-price for children aged four to nine years) if bought individually and €12.70 for adults for a *carnet* (book) of 10. Ticket windows and vending machines accept most – but not all – credit cards.

» One ticket lets you travel between any two metro stations – no return journeys – for a period of 1½ hours, no matter how many transfers are required. You can also use it on the RER for travel within zone 1. A single ticket can be used to transfer between daytime buses and trams, but not from the metro to bus or vice versa.

» Always keep your ticket until you exit from your station; you may be stopped by a *contrôleur* (ticket inspector) and will have to pay a fine if you don't have a valid ticket.

TOURIST PASSES

The **Mobilis** and **Paris Visite** passes are valid on the metro, RER, SNCF's suburban lines, buses, night buses, trams and Montmartre funicular railway. No photo is needed, but write your card number on the ticket. Passes are sold at larger metro and RER stations, SNCF offices in Paris, and the airports.

The Mobilis card allows unlimited travel for one day and costs €6.40 (two zones) to €14.20 (five zones). Buy it at any metro, RER or SNCF station in the Paris region. Depending on how many times you plan to hop on/off the metro in a day, a *carnet* might work out cheaper.

Paris Visite allows unlimited travel (including to/from airports) as well as discounted entry to certain museums and other discounts and bonuses. Passes are valid for either three or five zones. The zone 1 to 3 pass costs €10/16/22/31 for one/two/three/five days. Children aged four to 11 years pay half-price.

TRAVEL PASSES

If you're staying for longer than a few days, the cheapest and easiest way to use public transport in Paris is to get a combined travel pass that allows unlimited travel on the metro, RER and buses for a week, a month or even a year. You can get passes for travel in two to five zones but, unless you'll be using the suburban commuter lines extensively, the basic ticket valid for zones 1 and 2 should be sufficient.

PARIS BREATHES

'Paris Respire' (Paris Breathes) kicks motorised traffic off certain streets – including areas by the Seine and in the Latin Quarter, Bastille, Montmartre and Canal St-Martin – on Sundays to let pedestrians, cyclists, in-line skaters and other nonmotorised cruisers take over and, well, breathe. For details see www.velo.paris.fr.

AUTOLIB'

In December 2011 Paris launched the world's first electric-car-share programme, Autolib' (www.autolib.eu). The premise is quite similar to Vélib' (the bike-share scheme): you pay a subscription (day/week €10/15) and then rent a GPS-equipped car in 30-minute intervals and drop it off at one of the 1000 available stations when you're done. Unfortunately, it's really only good for short hops, because renting a car overnight would be exorbitant – the rates are €7 for the 1st half hour, €6 for the 2nd half-hour and €8 for subsequent intervals. The car battery is good for 250km, which means you can take it into the surrounding countryside (eg Fontainebleau), but no further. You'll need a driver's license and photo ID.

Navigo (www.navigo.fr) is a system that provides you with a refillable weekly, monthly or yearly unlimited pass that you can recharge at machines in most metro stations; to pass through the station barrier, swipe the card across the electronic panel as you go through the turnstiles. Standard Navigo passes, available to anyone with an address in Île de France, are free but take up to three weeks to be issued; ask at the ticket counter for a form or visit the Navigo website. Otherwise pay €5 for a Navigo Découverte (Navigo Discovery) card, which is issued on the spot but (unlike the standard Navigo pass) is not replaceable if lost or stolen. Both passes require a passport photo.

A weekly pass costs €19 for zones 1 and 2 and is valid from Monday to Sunday. It can be purchased from the previous Friday until Thursday; from the next day weekly tickets are available for the following week only. Even if you're in Paris for three or four days, it may work out cheaper than buying *carnets* and will certainly cost less than buying a daily Mobilis or Paris Visite pass. The monthly pass (€63 for zones 1 and 2) begins on the first day of each calendar month; you can buy one from the 20th of the preceding month. Both are sold in metro and RER stations from 6.30am to 10pm and at some bus terminals.

Taxi

» The *prise en charge* (flagfall) is €2.40. Within the city limits, it costs €0.96 per kilometre for travel between 10am and 5pm Monday to Saturday (*Tarif A*; white light on taxi roof and meter).

» At night (5pm to 10am), on Sunday from 7am to midnight, and in the inner suburbs the rate is €1.21 per km (*Tarif B*; orange light).

» Travel in the outer suburbs is at *Tarif C*, €1.47 per kilometre (blue light).

» There's a €2.95 surcharge for taking a fourth passenger, but drivers sometimes refuse for insurance reasons. The first piece of baggage is free; additional pieces over 5kg cost €1 extra. When tipping, round up to the nearest €1 or so.

» Flagging down a taxi in Paris can be difficult; it's best to find an official taxi stand.

» To order a taxi, call or reserve online with **Taxis G7** (☑01 41 27 66 99; www.taxisg7.fr), **Taxis Bleus** (☑01 49 36 10 10; www.taxis-bleus.com) or **Alpha Taxis** (☑01 45 85 85 85; www.alphataxis.com).

Around Paris

Best Places to Eat

» Dardonville (p159)

» Le Saint-Hilaire (p165)

» La Capitainerie (p161)

» La Chocolaterie (p165)

» Côté Sud (p159)

Best Tours

» Paris City Vision (p156)

» City Discovery (p156)

Why Go?

Whether you're taking day trips from Paris or continuing further afield, a trove of treasures awaits in the areas around the French capital.

The Île de France *région* – the 12,000-sq-km 'Island of France' shaped by five rivers – and surrounding areas count some of the most extravagant châteaux in the land. At the top of everyone's list is the palace at Versailles, the opulence and extravagance of which partly spurred the French Revolution, but the châteaux in Fontainebleau and Chantilly are also breathtaking. Many of the nation's most beautiful and ambitious cathedrals are also here, including the mighty basilica in St-Denis and the cathedral crowning the medieval old town of Chartres.

But Paris' surrounds aren't stuck in the past. The futuristic cityscape of La Défense stands in sharp contrast to the France of legend. And then there's every kid's favourite, Disneyland, which now has more attractions than ever.

When to Go
Chartres

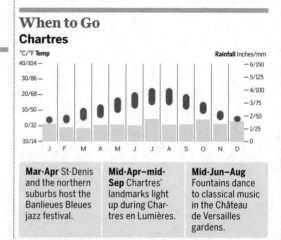

Mar-Apr St-Denis and the northern suburbs host the Banlieues Bleues jazz festival.

Mid-Apr–mid-Sep Chartres' landmarks light up during Chartres en Lumières.

Mid-Jun–Aug Fountains dance to classical music in the Château de Versailles gardens.

La Défense

POP 21,000

The ultramodern architecture of La Défense, the skyscraper district 3km west of the capital, is strikingly different from the rest of centuries-old Paris. When development of the 160-hectare site began in the late 1950s, it was one of the world's most ambitious civil-engineering projects. Its first major structure was the vaulted, largely triangular Centre des Nouvelles Industries et Technologies (CNIT; Centre for New Industries and Technologies), a giant 'pregnant oyster' inaugurated in 1958, extensively rebuilt three decades later and then reborn as a shopping

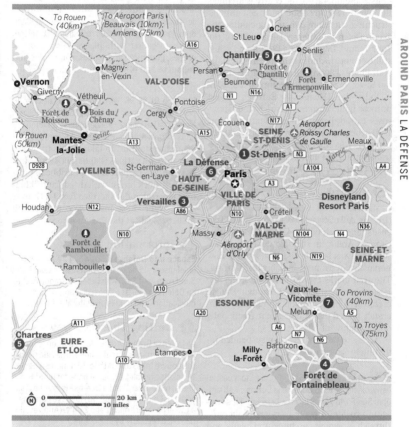

Around Paris Highlights

❶ Take a behind-the-scenes tour of the nation's premier sports stadium, the **Stade de France** (p151) in St-Denis

❷ Share a fiesta of magical moments with Mickey and his mates at **Disneyland Resort Paris** (p151)

❸ Relive the glory of the 17th- and 18th-century kingdom of France at the opulent **Château de Versailles** (p152)

❹ Walk, cycle, horse ride or rock climb in one of France's loveliest woods, the **Forêt de Fontainebleau** (p158)

❺ Gaze at the hypnotic blue stained-glass windows at the **Cathédrale Notre Dame de Chartres** (p162)

❻ Search out sculptures by Miró, César and other modern masters amid the forest of glass-and-steel skyscrapers in **La Défense** (p150)

❼ Visit the interior of **Château de Vaux-le-Vicomte** (p159) by candlelight

---

ÎLE DE FRANCE INFO

The official **Paris Île de France** (www. nouveau-paris-ile-de-france.fr) website is a treasure trove of information on the area.

---

and conference centre in 2008. Like many of its contemporaries, the centre is architecturally uninspiring. But later generations' structures are more dynamic, including the Cœur Défense (Défense Heart; 2001), the Tour T1 and Tour Granite (2008) and many still to come, including the record-breaking Tour Phare, a 300m-tall double office and retail tower, expected to be completed in 2017.

Today La Défense is Europe's largest purpose-built business district and showcases extraordinary monumental art. Some 1500 companies employ around 150,000 people across 3,500,000 sq metre of offices, transforming the nocturnal ghost town into a hive of high-flying commercial activity by day.

⊙ Sights

Grande Arche de la Défense   LANDMARK
(1 Parvis de la Défense; Ⓜ La Défense) La Défense's landmark edifice is the white marble Grande Arche, a striking cubelike structure that was built in the 1980s and is now home to government and business offices. The arch marks the western end of the Axe Historique (Historic Axis), though Danish architect Johan-Otto von Sprekelsen deliberately placed the Grande Arche fractionally out of alignment.

Access to the roof has been suspended indefinitely for security reasons.

FREE **Musée de la Défense**   HISTORY MUSEUM
(www.ladefense.fr; 15 place de la Défense; ⊙10am-6pm Sun-Fri, to 7pm Sat; Ⓜ La Défense) This museum provides a good overview of the area through drawings, architectural plans and scale models. Pick up tourist info and maps on the ground floor.

Gardens & Monuments   GARDENS, SCULPTURES
The Parvis, place de la Défense and Esplanade du Général de Gaulle – a pleasant 1km walkway – is an open-air contemporary art gallery. Calder, Miró, Agam, César and Torricini are among the international artists behind the colourful and often surprising sculptures and murals on Voie des Sculptures (Sculptures Way), the Quartier du Parc (Park District), west of the Grande

Arche, and Jardins de l'Arche, a 2km-long extension of the Axe Historique. La Défense is named not for military connections but for the 1883 La Défense de Paris monument here, commemorating the defence of Paris during the Franco-Prussian war of 1870–71.

✗ Eating

La Défense is mostly fast-food territory. The shopping centre Les Quatre Temps (www .les4temps.com; 15 parvis de la Défense; ⊙10am-8pm Mon-Sat, 11am-7pm Sun, restaurants 10am-11pm daily) is loaded with places serving pizza, crêpes, gourmet sandwiches, soup, juice and Japanese and other Asian cuisine.

Globetrotter   INTERNATIONAL €€
(✆01 55 91 96 96; www.globetrottercafe.com; 16 place de la Défense; mains €16.25-34.50; ⊙lunch Mon-Fri; Ⓜ La Défense Grande Arche) La Défense's *gens d'affaires* (businesspeople) come to this tropical restaurant to take a culinary world tour through various islands, via dishes such as swordfish carpaccio with Caribbean pineapple or duck breast with dried fruit. Tables on the wooden-deck terrace face La Grande Arche while those inside woo diners with first-row seats at the Bassin Agam.

ⓘ Information

Espace Info-Défense (✆01 47 74 84 24; www. ladefense.fr; 15 place de la Défense; ⊙10am-6pm Sun-Fri, to 7pm Sat; Ⓜ La Défense Grande Arche) La Défense's tourist office has reams of free publications and details on cultural activities.

ⓘ Getting There & Away

La Défense Grande Arche metro station is the western terminus of metro line 1. The ride from the Louvre takes about 15 to 20 minutes; regular t+ tickets are valid. If you take the faster RER line A, remember that La Défense is in zone 3 so you must buy a ticket (€2.50) if you're carrying a travel pass for zones 1 and 2 only. (And yes, it's patrolled regularly by inspectors.)

St-Denis

POP 102,000

For 1200 years the hallowed burial place of French royalty, St-Denis today is a multicultural suburb a short metro ride north of Paris' 18e *arrondissement*. The ornate royal tombs, adorned with some truly remarkable statuary, and the Basilique de St-Denis containing them, are well worth the trip, as is the Stade de France, the futuristic stadium just south of Canal de St-Denis.

◉ Sights

FREE **Basilique de St-Denis**   CATHEDRAL
(www.monuments-nationaux.fr; 1 rue de la Légion
d'Honneur; tombs adult/senior & 18-25yr €7.50/4.50,
basilica free; ◷10am-6.15pm Mon-Sat, noon-6.15pm
Sun Apr-Sep, to 5.15pm Oct-Mar; MBasilique de St-
Denis, line 13) St-Denis Basilica was the burial
place for all but a handful of France's kings
and queens from Dagobert I (r 629–39) to
Louis XVIII (r 1814–24), constituting one of
Europe's most important collections of funer-
ary sculpture; today the remains of 43 kings
and 32 queens repose here. The single-tow-
ered basilica, begun around 1136, was the first
major structure to be built in the Gothic style,
serving as a model for other 12th-century
French cathedrals, including the one at
Chartres. Features illustrating the transition
from Romanesque to Gothic can be seen in
the choir and double ambulatory, which
are adorned with a number of 12th-century
stained-glass windows. The narthex (the
portico running along the western end of the
basilica) also dates from this period. The nave
and transept were built in the 13th century.

During the Revolution and the Reign of
Terror, the basilica was devastated; remains
from the royal tombs were dumped into two
big pits outside the church. The mausoleums
were put into storage in Paris, however, and
survived. They were brought back in 1816,
and the royal bones were reburied in the
crypt a year later. Restoration of the structure
was begun under Napoleon, but most of the
work was carried out by the Gothic Revival-
ist architect Eugène Viollet-le-Duc from 1858
until his death in 1879. The tombs in the
crypt are decorated with life-sized figures of
the deceased. Those built before the Renaissance are adorned with *gisants* (recumbent
figures). Those made after 1285 were carved
from death masks and are thus fairly, well,
lifelike; the 14 figures commissioned under
Louis IX (St Louis; r 1214–70) are depictions
of how earlier rulers *might* have looked. The
oldest tombs (from around 1230) are those
of Clovis I (d 511) and his son Childebert I (d
558). Don't miss the white marble catafalque
tomb of Louis XII and Anne of Bretagne
dating from 1597. If you look carefully you'll
see graffiti etched on the arms of the seated
figures dating from the early 17th century.
The Bourbon sepulchral vault contains the
remains of Louis XVI and Marie-Antoinette
but not of the king's younger brother Charles
X; there's a tomb, but his bones lie in a
church in Nova Gorica in Slovenia.

Stade de France   STADIUM
(www.stadefrance.com; rue Francis de Pressensé;
adult/student/child €15/12/10; ◷tours in French
hourly 10am-5pm, in English 10.30am & 2.30pm
daily during school holidays, reduced hrs rest of year;
MSt-Denis-Porte de Paris) The 80,000-seat Stadium of France, just south of central St-Denis
and in full view from rue Gabriel Péri, was
built for the 1998 football World Cup, which
France won by miraculously defeating Brazil
3-0. The futuristic and quite beautiful structure, with a roof the size of place de la Concorde, is used for football and rugby matches,
major gymnastic events and big-ticket music
concerts. One-hour guided tours take you
behind the scenes including the presidential box, the change rooms and through the
tunnel to the pitch. Tickets include entry to
the superbly renovated four-room museum
with sporting and concert memorabilia.

❶ Information

**Office de Tourisme de St-Denis Plaine Com-
mune** (☑01 55 87 08 70; www.saint-denis
-tourisme.com; 1 rue de la République;
◷9.30am-1pm & 2-6pm Mon-Sat, 10am-1pm &
2-4pm Sun; MBasilique de St-Denis) St-Denis'
helpful tourist office is 100m west of the basilica.

❶ Getting There & Away

You can reach St-Denis in 20 minutes on metro
line 13: take it to Basilique de St-Denis station for
the basilica and tourist office, and to St-Denis-
Porte de Paris station for the Stade de France
(the latter can also be reached via RER line B;
alight at La Plaine Stade de France station).
Make sure to board a metro heading for St-Denis
Université and *not* for Asnières-Gennevilliers Les
Courtilles, as the line splits at La Fourche station.

Disneyland Resort Paris

It took almost €4.6 billion to turn the beet
fields 32km east of Paris into Europe's first
Disney theme park. What started out as
Euro-Disney in 1992 today comprises the
traditional Disneyland Park theme park, the
film-oriented Walt Disney Studios Park, and
hotel-, shop- and restaurant-filled Disney
Village. And kids – and kids at heart – can't
seem to get enough.

◉ Sights

One-day admission fees at Disneyland
Resort Paris (☑hotel booking 01 60 30 60 30,
restaurant reservations 01 60 30 40 50; www.disney
landparis.com; 1-day admission adult/child €59/53;

⊘hours vary; ⓜMarne-la-Vallée/Chessy) include unlimited access to attractions in *either* Disneyland Park or Walt Disney Studios Park. The latter includes entry to Disneyland Park three hours before it closes. A multitude of multiday passes, special offers and packages are always available.

Disneyland Park
THEME PARK

(⊘10am-8pm Mon-Fri, 9am-8pm Sat & Sun Sep-May, 9am-11pm Jun-Aug, hours can vary) Disneyland Park has five themed *pays* (lands): the 1900s-styled Main Street USA; Frontierland, home to the legendary Big Thunder Mountain ride; Adventureland, which evokes exotic lands in rides like the Pirates of the Caribbean; Fantasyland, crowned by Sleeping Beauty's castle; and the high-tech Discoveryland, with massive-queue rides such as Space Mountain: Mission 2 and Buzz Lightyear Laser Blast.

Walt Disney Studios Park
THEME PARK

(⊘9am-7pm late Jun-early Sep, 10am-7pm Mon-Fri & 9am-7pm Sat & Sun early Sep-late Jun) The sound stage, production back lot and animation studios provide an up-close illustration of how films, TV programs and cartoons are produced, with behind-the-scenes tours, larger-than-life characters and spine-tingling rides like the Twighlight Zone Tower of Terror.

🛏 Sleeping

The resort's seven American-styled hotels (☑central booking 01 60 30 60 30) are linked by free shuttle bus to the parks. Rates vary hugely, according to the season and promotional deals.

✖ Eating

No picnics are allowed at Disneyland Resort Paris, but there are ample themed restaurants (☑central reservations 01 60 30 40 50).

❶ Information

Espace du Tourisme d'Île de France et de Seine et Marne (☑01 60 43 33 33; www.nouveau-paris-ile-de-france.fr; place François Truffaut; ⊘9am-8.30pm) Near the RER and TCV train stations.

❶ Getting There & Away

Marne-la-Vallée/Chessy, Disneyland's RER station, is served by line A4; trains run frequently from central Paris (€7.10).

By car, follow route A4 from Porte de Bercy (direction Metz-Nancy) and take exit 14.

Versailles
POP 88,930

Louis XIV transformed his father's hunting lodge into the monumental Château de Versailles in the mid-17th century, and it remains France's most famous, grandest palace. Situated in the prosperous, leafy and bourgeois suburb of Versailles, 28km southwest of Paris, the baroque château was the kingdom's political capital and the seat of the royal court from 1682 up until the fateful events of 1789 when revolutionaries massacred the palace guard and dragged Louis XVI and Marie Antoinette back to Paris, where they were ingloriously guillotined.

◉ Sights

Château de Versailles
PALACE

(☑01 30 83 78 00; www.chateauversailles.fr; admission passport for estate-wide access €18, with musical events €25, palace €15; ⊘8am-6pm Tue-Sat, 9am-6pm Sun Apr-Oct, 8.30am-5.30pm Tue-Sat, 9am-5.30pm Sun Nov-Mar) This splendid and enormous palace was built in the mid-17th century during the reign of Louis XIV – the Roi Soleil (Sun King) – to project the absolute power of the French monarchy, which was then at the height of its glory. Its scale and decor reflect Louis XIV's taste for profligate luxury and his boundless appetite for grandstanding. Some 30,000 workers and soldiers toiled on the structure, the bills for which all but emptied the kingdom's coffers. The château has undergone relatively few alterations since its construction, though almost all the interior furnishings disappeared during the Revolution and many of the rooms were rebuilt by Louis-Philippe (r 1830–48). The current €400-million restoration program is the most ambitious yet and until it's completed in 2020 at least a part of the palace is likely to be clad in scaffolding when you visit.

Work began in 1661 under the guidance of architect Louis Le Vau (Jules Hardouin-Mansart took over from Le Vau in the mid-1670s); painter and interior designer Charles Le Brun; and landscape artist André Le Nôtre, whose workers flattened hills, drained marshes and relocated forests as they laid out the seemingly endless gardens, ponds and fountains.

Le Brun and his hundreds of artisans decorated every moulding, cornice, ceiling and door of the interior with the most luxurious and ostentatious of appointments: frescos, marble, gilt and woodcarvings, many with

TOP DISNEY TIPS

Long queues can make a Disney visit hard going but the following tips will help you minimise waiting times and get the most out of your visit.

» Before hot-footing it to Disney, devote a good hour on its website planning your day – which rides, shows, characters etc you really want to see.

» Buy your tickets in advance to at least avoid the ticket queue.

» Once in, reserve your time slot on the busiest rides using FastPass, the park's ride-reservation system (limited to one reservation at a time).

» To avoid another queue, choose a restaurant online and reserve a table in advance.

» Consider staying overnight: guests at Disney's hotels are often entitled on designated days to two 'Magic hours' in Disneyland Park when the park is closed to regular visitors. Advance online reservations yield savings of up to 30% off hotel and park admission packages.

themes and symbols drawn from Greek and Roman mythology. The King's Suite of the Grands Appartements du Roi et de la Reine (King's and Queen's State Apartments), for example, includes rooms dedicated to Hercules, Venus, Diana, Mars and Mercury. The opulence reaches its peak in the recently restored Galerie des Glaces (Hall of Mirrors), a 75m-long ballroom with 17 huge mirrors on one side and, on the other, an equal number of windows looking out over the gardens and the setting sun.

Château de Versailles Gardens & Park

(admission free except during musical events; ☺gardens 8.30am-8.30pm Apr-Oct, 8am-6pm Nov-Mar, park 7am-7pm Apr-Oct, 8am-6pm Nov-Mar) The section of the vast gardens nearest the palace, laid out between 1661 and 1700 in the formal French style, is famed for its geometrically aligned terraces, flowerbeds, tree-lined paths, ponds and fountains. The 400-odd statues of marble, bronze and lead were made by the most talented sculptors of the era. The English-style Jardins du Petit Trianon are more pastoral and have meandering, sheltered paths.

The Grand Canal (Chateau gardens), 1.6km long and 62m wide, is oriented to reflect the setting sun. It is traversed by the 1km-long Petit Canal, creating a cross-shaped body of water with a perimeter of more than 5.5km.

The Orangerie, built under the Parterre du Midi (Southern Flowerbed) on the southwestern side of the palace, shelters tropical plants in winter.

The gardens' largest fountains are the 17th-century Bassin de Neptune (Chateau gardens), a dazzling mirage of 99 spouting gushers 300m north of the palace, and the Bassin

d'Apollon, built in 1688 at the eastern end of the Grand Canal. The straight side of the Bassin de Neptune abuts a small round pond graced by a winged dragon. Emerging from the water in the centre of the Bassin d'Apollon is Apollo's chariot, pulled by rearing horses.

Domaine de Marie-Antoinette

(Marie-Antoinette's Estate; admission €10; ☺noon-6.30pm Tue-Sat Apr-Oct, to 5.30pm Tue-Sat Nov-Mar) Northwest of the main palace is the Domaine de Marie-Antoinette. Tickets include the pink-colonnaded Grand Trianon (adult before/after 3.30pm €5/3, child free; ☺noon-6.30pm Apr-Oct, to 5.30pm Nov-Mar), built in 1687 for Louis XIV and his family as a place of escape from the rigid etiquette of the court, and the ochre-coloured, 1760s Petit Trianon (☺noon-6.30pm Apr-Oct, to 5.30pm Nov-Mar), redecorated in 1867 by consort of Napoleon III, Empress Eugénie, who added Louis XVI-style furnishings, as well as the Hameau de la Reine (Queen's Hamlet), a mock village of thatched cottages completed in 1784, where Marie-Antoinette played milkmaid; admission is included in passport tickets.

Versailles Stables

Today Versailles' school of architecture and restoration workshops fill the Petites Écuries (Little Stables), while the Grandes Écuries (Big Stables) house the Académie du Spectacle Équestre (Academy of Equestrian Arts; ☑01 39 02 07 14; www.acadequestre.fr; 1 av Rockefeller, Grandes Écuries). In addition to its 45-minute Les Matinales (morning training sessions; adult/13-18yr/under 13yr €12/10/6.50; ☺11.15am Sat & Sun & some Thu), the academy presents spectacular Reprises Musicales (Musical Equestrian Shows; adult/13-18yr/under 13yr €25/22/16; ☺6pm Sat, 3pm Sun & some Thu), which sell out weeks in advance.

Versailles

A DAY IN COURT

Visiting Versailles – even just the State Apartments – may seem overwhelming at first, but think of it as a house where people ate, drank, worked, slept and conspired and you'll be on the right path.

Some two decades into his long reign, Louis XIV began turning his father's hunting lodge into a palace large enough to house his entire court (to keep closer tabs on the 6000-strong army of courtiers). Sparing no expense, the Sun King employed the greatest artists and craftspeople of the day and by 1682 he'd created the most extravagant dormitory in history.

The royal schedule was as accurate and predictable as a Swiss watch. By following this itinerary of rooms you can recreate the king's day, starting with the **King's Bedchamber 1** and the **Queen's Bedchamber 2**, where the royal couple was roused at about the same time. The royal procession then leads through the **Hall of Mirrors 3** to the **Royal Chapel 4** for morning Mass and returns to the **Council Chamber 5** for late-morning meetings with ministers. After lunch the king might ride or hunt or visit the **King's Library 6**. Later he could join courtesans for an 'apartment evening' starting from the **Hercules Drawing Room 7** or play billiards in the **Diana Drawing Room 8** before supping at 10pm.

VERSAILLES BY NUMBERS

- » **Rooms** 700 (11 hectares of roof)
- » **Windows** 2153
- » **Staircases** 67
- » **Gardens and parks** 800 hectares
- » **Trees** 200,000
- » **Fountains** 50 (with 620 nozzles)
- » **Paintings** 6300 (measuring 11km laid end to end)
- » **Statues and sculptures** 2100
- » **Objets d'art and furnishings** 5000
- » **Visitors** 5.3 million per year

Queen's Bedchamber
Chambre de la Reine
The queen's life was on constant public display and even the births of her children were watched by crowds of spectators in her own bedchamber. DETOUR » The Guardroom, with a dozen armed men at the ready.

Lunch Break
Diner-style food at Sister's Café, crêpes at Le Phare St-Louis or picnic in the park.

Guardroom

South Wing

King's Library
Bibliothèque du Roi
The last resident, bibliophile Louis XVI, loved geography and his copy of *The Travels of James Cook* (in English, which he read fluently) is still on the shelf here.

Savvy Sightseeing
Avoid Versailles on Monday (closed), Tuesday (Paris' museums close, so visitors flock here) and Sunday, the busiest day. Also, book tickets online so you don't have to queue.

Hall of Mirrors
Galerie des Glaces
The solid-silver candelabra and furnishings in this extravagant hall, devoted to Louis XIV's successes in war, were melted down in 1689 to pay for yet another conflict. **DETOUR»** The antithetical Peace Drawing Room, adjacent.

King's Bedchamber
Chambre du Roi
The king's daily life was anything but private and even his *lever* (rising) at 8am and *coucher* (retiring) at 11.30pm would be witnessed by up to 150 sycophantic courtiers.

Council Chamber
Cabinet du Conseil
This chamber, with carved medallions evoking the king's work, is where the monarch met his various ministers (state, finance, religion etc) depending on the days of the week.

Peace Drawing Room

2

3

Hall of Mirrors

1   5

Apollo Drawing Room

Marble Courtyard

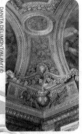

6

8

Entrance

Entrance

North Wing

Diana Drawing Room
Salon de Diane
With walls and ceiling covered in frescos devoted to the mythical huntress, this room contained a large billiard table reserved for Louis XIV, a keen player.

7

To Royal Opera

4

Royal Chapel
Chapelle Royale
This two-storey chapel (with gallery for the royals and important courtiers, and the ground floor for the B-list) was dedicated to St Louis, patron of French monarchs. **DETOUR»** The sumptuous Royal Opera.

Hercules Drawing Room
Salon d'Hercule
This salon, with its stunning ceiling fresco of the strong man, gave way to the State Apartments, which were open to courtiers three nights a week. **DETOUR»** Apollo Drawing Room, used for formal audiences and as a throne room.

Salle du Jeu de Paume

(www.versailles-tourisme.com; 1 rue du Jeu de Paume; guided tour €9; ⊙3pm Sat) Built in 1686, the Salle du Jeu de Paume played a pivotal role in the Revolution a century later. It was in Versailles that Louis XVI convened the États-Généraux made up of more than 1000 deputies representing the nobility, clergy and the so-called Third Estate (ie the middle classes) in May 1789 in a bid to deal with national debt and to moderate dissent by reforming the tax system. But when the Third Estate's reps were denied entry, they met separately on the tennis court, formed a National Assembly and took the famous Serment du Jeu de Paume (Tennis Court Oath), swearing not to dissolve it until Louis XVI had accepted a new constitution. This act of defiance sparked demonstrations of support and, less than a month later, a mob in Paris stormed the prison at Bastille. It's visitable by guided tour in French only.

Tours

Take a tour if you're pressed for time.

Paris City Vision BUS TOUR
(☎01 45 15 45 96; www.pariscityvision.com) Half-day minibus trips from Paris to Versailles (from €95), and full-day coach tours including Versailles/Fontainebleau (from €123).

City Discovery BUS TOUR
(☎09 70 44 52 90; www.city-discovery.com) Various Versailles tours; other options include Versailles/Giverny, Champagne, Vaux-le-Vicomte, and Disneyland.

Eating

Eateries within the estate include tearoom **Angelina** (www.angelina-versailles.fr; mains €10-24; ⊙10am-6pm Tue-Sat Apr-Oct, to 5pm Tue-Sat Nov-Mar), famed for its decadent hot chocolate. In addition to the branch by the Petit Trianon, there's another inside the palace. In the Louis XIV–created town of Versailles, rue de Satory is lined with restaurants serving cuisine from all over the globe. For an enjoyable culinary experience, check out La Cuisine de Bertrand (p960), where you can learn traditional French cooking in Bertrand's Versailles home, followed by a meal with his family. Produce is from the château's Potager du Roi.

À la Ferme SOUTHWEST FRENCH €€
(☎01 39 53 10 81; www.alaferme-versailles.com; 3 rue du Maréchal Joffre; lunch menus €13.80-23.90, dinner menus €19.50-23.90; ⊙Wed-Sun) Cow-hide seats and rustic garlands strung from old wood beams add a country air 'At the Farm', a temple to grilled meats and cuisine from southwest France.

ℹ TOP VERSAILLES TIPS

Versailles is one of the country's most popular destinations, with over five million visitors annually; advance planning will make visiting more enjoyable.

» Monday is out for obvious reasons (it's closed).

» By noon queues for tickets and entering the château spiral out of control: arrive early morning and avoid Tuesday and Sunday, its busiest days.

» Save time by prepurchasing tickets on the château's website or at Fnac branches and head straight to Entrance A.

» To access areas that are otherwise off limits and to learn more about Versailles' history, take a 90-minute guided tour (☎01 30 83 77 88; tours €16; ⊙English-language tours 9.30am & 2pm Tue-Sun) of the Private Apartments of Louis XV and Louis XVI and the Opera House or Royal Chapel. Tour tickets include access to the most famous parts of the palace, such as the Galerie des Glaces (Hall of Mirrors) and the Grands Appartements du Roi et de la Reine (King's and Queen's State Apartments); prebook online.

» The estate is so vast that the only way to see it all is to hire a four-person electric car (☎01 39 66 97 66; per hr €30) or hop aboard the shuttle train (www.train-versailles.com; adult/child €6.70/5); you can also rent a bike (☎01 39 66 97 66; per hr €6.50) or boat (☎01 39 66 97 66; per hr €15).

» Try to time your visit for the Grandes Eaux Musicales (adult/child €7.50/6.50; ⊙11am-noon & 3.30-5pm Tue, Sat & Sun Apr-Sep) or the after-dark Grandes Eaux Nocturnes (adult/child €23/19; ⊙9-11.20pm Sat mid-Jun–Aug), truly magical 'dancing water' displays – set to music composed by baroque- and classical-era composers – throughout the grounds in summer.

❶ Information

Tourist office (☎01 39 24 88 88; www.
versailles-tourisme.com; 2bis av de Paris;
🕑10am-6pm Mon, 9am-7pm Tue-Sun Apr-
Sep, 11am-5pm Sun & Mon, 9am-6pm Tue-Sat
Oct-Mar) Sells the passport to Château de
Versailles and detailed visitor's guides and has
information on lectures.

❶ Getting There & Away

BUS RATP bus 171 (€1.70 or one t+ metro/bus
ticket, 35 minutes) links Paris' Pont de Sèvres
metro station (15e) with place d'Armes at least
every 15 minutes from around 6am to 1am.

CAR Follow the A13 from Porte d'Auteuil and
take the exit marked 'Versailles Château'.

TRAIN RER Line C5 (€3.20, 45 minutes, frequent) goes from Paris' Left Bank RER stations
to Versailles-Rive Gauche station. Less convenient, RER line C8 links Paris with Versailles-
Chantiers station, a 1.3km walk from the
château. SNCF operates trains from Paris' Gare
Montparnasse to Versailles-Chantiers, and from
Paris' Gare St-Lazare to Versailles-Rive Droite,
1.2km from the château.

Fontainebleau

POP 21,800

Fresh air fills your lungs on arriving in the
smart town of Fontainebleau. It's enveloped
by the 20,000-hectare Forêt de Fontainebleau, which is as big a playground today as it
was in the 16th century, with superb walking
and rock-climbing opportunities. The town
grew up around its magnificent château, one
of the most beautifully decorated and furnished in France. Although it's less crowded
and pressured than Versailles, exploring it
can still take the best part of a day. You'll also
find a cosmopolitan drinking and dining
scene, thanks to the town's lifeblood, the international graduate business school Insead.

◎ Sights

Château de Fontainebleau PALACE
(☎01 60 71 50 70; www.musee-chateau-fontaine
bleau.fr; place Général de Gaulle; château adult/
child €10/free, guided tours of the Petits Appartements or Musée Napoleon each €14.50, both €21,
gardens free; 🕑château 9.30am-6pm Wed-Mon
Apr-Sep, to 5pm Wed-Mon Oct-Mar, gardens 9am-
7pm May-Sep, to 6pm Mar, Apr & Oct, to 5pm Nov-
Feb) The resplendent, 1900-room Château
de Fontainebleau's list of former tenants
and their guests reads like a who's who of
French royalty and aristocracy. Every square
centimetre of wall and ceiling space is richly
adorned with wood panelling, gilded carvings, frescos, tapestries and paintings.

The first château on this site was built in
the early 12th century and enlarged by Louis
IX a century later. Only a single medieval
tower survived the energetic Renaissance-
style reconstruction undertaken by François
I (r 1515–47), whose superb artisans, many
of them brought from Italy, blended Italian
and French styles to create what is known as
the First School of Fontainebleau. The *Mona
Lisa* once hung here amid other fine works
of art in the royal collection.

During the latter half of the 16th century,
the château was further enlarged by Henri
II (r 1547–59), Catherine de Médicis and
Henri IV (r 1589–1610), whose Flemish and
French artists created the Second School of
Fontainebleau. Even Louis XIV got in on the
act: it was he who hired landscape artist
André Le Nôtre, celebrated for his work at
Versailles, to redesign the gardens.

Fontainebleau was beloved by Napoléon
Bonaparte, who had a fair bit of restoration
work carried out. Napoléon III was another
frequent visitor. During WWII the château
was turned into a German headquarters. After it was liberated by Allied forces under US
General George Patton in 1944, part of the
complex served as the Allied and then NATO
headquarters from 1945 to 1965.

Château
(🕑9.30am-6pm Wed-Mon Apr-Sep, to 5pm Wed-Mon
Oct-Mar) Visits take in the Grands Appartements (State Apartments), which contain
several outstanding rooms. An informative
1½-hour audioguide (included in the price)
leads visitors around the main areas.

The spectacular Chapelle de la Trinité
(Trinity Chapel), with ornamentation that
dates from the first half of the 17th century,
is where Louis XV married Marie Leczinska
in 1725 and where the future Napoléon III
was christened in 1810. Galerie François
1er, a jewel of Renaissance architecture, was
decorated from 1533 to 1540 by Il Rosso, a
Florentine follower of Michelangelo. In the
wood panelling, François I's monogram appears repeatedly along with his emblem, a
dragon-like salamander. The Musée Chinois de l'Impératice Eugénie (Chinese
Museum of Empress Eugénie) consists of
four drawing rooms created in 1863 for
the oriental art and curios collected by Napoléon III's wife.

The Salle de Bal, a 30m-long ballroom
dating from the mid-16th century that was

also used for receptions and banquets, is renowned for its mythological frescos, marquetry floor and Italian-inspired coffered ceiling. The large windows afford views of the Cour Ovale (Oval Courtyard) and the gardens. The gilded bed in the 17th- and 18th-century Chambre de l'Impératrice (Empress' Bedroom) was never used by Marie-Antoinette, for whom it was built in 1787. The gilding in the Salle du Trône (Throne Room), which was the royal bedroom before the Napoléonic period, is decorated in golds, greens and yellows.

Daily 1¼-hour guided tours (in French) take visitors through the Petits Appartements, the private rooms of the emperor and empress, and the Musée Napoléon 1er, which contains uniforms, hats, coats, ornamental swords and bric-a-brac that belonged to Napoléon and his relatives. Tickets for either tour include admission to the main part of the château.

As successive monarchs added their own wings to the château, five irregularly shaped courtyards were created. The oldest and most interesting is the Cour Ovale (Oval Courtyard), no longer oval but U-shaped due to Henri IV's construction work. It incorporates the keep, the sole remnant of the medieval château. The largest courtyard is the Cour du Cheval Blanc (Courtyard of the White Horse), from where you enter the château. Napoléon, about to be exiled to Elba in 1814, bade farewell to his guards from the magnificent 17th-century double-horse-shoe staircase here. For that reason the courtyard is also called the Cour des Adieux (Farewell Courtyard).

Château Gardens
(🕙9am-7pm May-Sep, to 6pm Mar, Apr & Oct, to 5pm Nov-Feb) The gardens are quite extraordinary. On the northern side of the château is the Jardin de Diane, a formal garden created by Catherine de Médicis. Le Nôtre's formal, 17th-century Jardin Français (French Garden), also known as the Grand Parterre, is east of the Cour de la Fontaine (Fountain Courtyard) and the Étang des Carpes (Carp Pond). The informal Jardin Anglais (English Garden), laid out in 1812, is west of the pond. The Grand Canal was excavated in 1609 and predates the canals at Versailles by more than half a century. The palace park is open 24 hours.

🛌 Sleeping

Hôtel de Londres   HOTEL €€
(☎01 64 22 20 21; www.hoteldelondres.com; 1 place Général de Gaulle; d €100-180; 🏧@🛜) Classy, cosy and beautifully kept, the 16-room 'Hotel London' is charmingly furnished in warm reds and royal blues. The priciest rooms (eg room 5) have balconies with dreamy château views.

La Guérinière   B&B €
(☎06 13 50 50 37; balestier.gerard@wanadoo.fr; 10 rue de Montebello; d incl breakfast €70; @) This charming B&B provides some of the best-value accommodation in town. Owner Monsieur Balestier speaks English and has five rooms, each named after a different flower and dressed in white linens and period wooden furniture. Breakfast includes homemade jam.

> **WORTH A TRIP**
>
> ## FORÊT DE FONTAINEBLEAU
>
> Beginning just 500m south of the château and surrounding the town, the 200-sq-km Forêt de Fontainebleau (Fontainebleau Forest) is one of the prettiest woods in the region. The many trails – including parts of the GR1 and GR11 – are excellent for jogging, walking, cycling and horse riding; Fontainebleau's tourist office stocks maps and guides.
>
> Rock-climbing enthusiasts have long come to the forest's sandstone ridges, rich in cliffs and overhangs, to hone their skills before setting off for the Alps. There are different grades marked by colours, starting with white ones, which are suitable for children, and going up to death-defying black boulders. The website Bleau (http://bleau.info) has stacks of information in English on climbing in Fontainebleau. Two gorges worth visiting are the Gorges d'Apremont, 7km northwest near Barbizon, and the Gorges de Franchard, a few kilometres south of Gorges d'Apremont. If you want to give it a go, contact Top Loisirs (☎01 60 74 08 50; www.toploisirs.fr; 16 rue Sylvain Collinet) about equipment hire and instruction. The tourist office also sells comprehensive climbing guides.

✕ Eating

There are lovely cafe terraces on place Napoléon Bonaparte and some appealing drinking options on rue de la Corne. Rue de Montebello tours the world with Indian, Lebanese and other international cuisines. For fabulous *fromageries* (cheese shops), head to rue des Sablons and rue Grande.

TOP
CHOICE **Dardonville**　　PATISSERIE, BOULANGERIE €
(24 rue des Sablons; ☺7am-1.30pm & 3.15-7.30pm Tue-Sat, 7am-1.30pm Sun) Melt-in-your-mouth macarons in flavours like poppy seed and gingerbread cost just €4.50 per dozen (per *dozen*!) at this exceptional patisserie-*boulangerie*. Queues also form out the door for its amazing breads and savoury petits fours such as tiny pastry-wrapped sausages and teensy coin-size quiches that are perfect picnic fare.

Côté Sud　　REGIONAL CUISINE €€
(✆01 64 22 00 33; 1 rue Montebello; lunch menu €14.50, mains €16.50-22; ☺lunch & dinner daily) Dishes at this welcoming bistro have a southern accent, such as *daube de sanglier* (wild boar stew) and *salade landoise* (an enormous salad of fresh and cooked vegetables, goose liver and preserved gizzards). Bring your appetite.

Le Franklin Roosevelt　　BRASSERIE €€
(✆01 64 22 28 73; 20 rue Grande; starters €6-13, mains €15.50-22; ☺10am-1am Mon-Sat) With wooden panelling, red banquette seating and oodles of atmosphere, the Franklin keeps locals well fed too: the *salades composées* (salads with meat or fish) are healthy and huge.

Le Ferrare　　BRASSERIE €
(✆01 60 72 37 04; 23 rue de France; 2-/3-course menus €11.50-13; ☺7.30am-4pm Mon, to 10.30pm Tue-Thu, to 1am Fri & Sat) Locals pile into this quintessential bar-brasserie, which has a blackboard full of Auvergne specialities and bargain-priced *plats du jour* (daily specials).

① Information

Tourist office (✆01 60 74 99 99; www. fontainebleau-tourisme.com; 4 rue Royale; ☺10am-6pm Mon-Sat, 10am-12.30pm & 3-5pm Sun May-Oct, 10am-6pm Mon-Sat, 10am-1pm Sun Nov-Apr) Although poorly signposted, once you find it, Fontainebleau's tourist office (in a converted petrol station west of the château) is a fount of information on the town and forest, and hires bikes (€5/15/19 per hour/half-day/24 hours; advance reservations required).

① Getting There & Around

Importantly, train tickets to Fontainebleau Avon are sold at Gare de Lyon's SNCF Transilien counter/Billet Ile-de-France machines, *not* SNCF mainline counters/machines. On returning to Paris, tickets include travel to any metro station.

Up to 40 daily **SNCF Transilien** (www.transilien. com) commuter trains link Paris' Gare de Lyon with Fontainebleau-Avon station (€8.55, 35 to 60 minutes).

Local bus line A links the train station with Château de Fontainebleau (€1.90), 2km southwest, every 10 minutes; the stop is opposite the main entrance.

Vaux-le-Vicomte

The privately owned Château de Vaux-le-Vicomte (✆01 64 14 41 90; www.vaux-le-vicomte. com; adult/child €14/11, incl private apartments €16/13; ☺10am-6pm, closed early Nov–mid-Mar) and its magnificent formal gardens, 20km north of Fontainebleau and 61km southeast of Paris, were designed and built by Le Brun, Le Vau and Le Nôtre between 1656 and 1661 as a precursor to their more ambitious work at Versailles.

Candlelight visits (adult/child €17/15, incl private apartments €19/17) of the château, lasting four hours, take place at 8pm on Saturday from May to early October. During the same period there are elaborate jeux d'eau (fountain displays) in the gardens from 3pm to 6pm on the second and last Saturday of the month.

The beauty of Vaux-le-Vicomte turned out to be the undoing of its original owner, Nicolas Fouquet, Louis XIV's minister of finance. It seems that Louis, seething that he'd been upstaged at the château's official opening, had Fouquet thrown into prison, where the unfortunate *ministre* died in 1680.

Today visitors swoon over the château's beautifully furnished interior, including its fabulous dome. In the vaulted cellars an exhibition looks at Le Nôtre's landscaping of the formal gardens. A collection of 18th- and 19th-century carriages in the château stables forms the Musée des Équipages (Carriage Museum); entry is included in the château admission price.

① Getting There & Away

Vaux-le-Vicomte is not an easy place to reach by public transport. The château is 6km northeast of Melun, which is served by RER line D2 from Paris (€7.80, 45 minutes). The Châteaubus shuttle (€3.50 each way) links Melun station with the château four to six times daily at weekends from early April to early November; at other times you'll have to take a **taxi** (☑01 64 52 51 50; €15, evening & Sun €19).

By car, follow the A6 from Paris and then the A5 (direction Melun), and take the 'St-Germain Laxis' exit. From Fontainebleau take the N6 and N36.

Chantilly

POP 11,350

The elegant old town of Chantilly, 50km north of Paris, is small and select. Its imposing, heavily restored château is surrounded by parkland, gardens and the Forêt de Chantilly, offering a wealth of walking opportunities. Chantilly's racetrack is one of the most prestigious hat-and-frock addresses in Europe, and that deliciously sweetened thick *crème* called Chantilly was created here. Just don't come on Tuesday, when the château is closed.

◉ Sights

Château de Chantilly   PALACE

(☑03 44 27 31 80; www.chateaudechantilly.com; domain pass adult/child €20/8, show pass €29.50/16.50, park & gardens only €7/3; ☺château 10am-6pm Wed-Mon, gardens 10am-8pm Wed-Mon) Left in a shambles after the Revolution, today the Château de Chantilly is of interest mainly because of its superb paintings and gardens. The château consists of two attached buildings, the Petit and Grand Châteaux, which are entered through the same vestibule.

Containing the Appartements des Princes (Princes' Suites), the Petit Château was built around 1560 for Anne de Montmorency (1492–1567), who served six French kings as *connétable* (high constable), diplomat and warrior, and died doing battle with Protestants in the Counter-Reformation. The highlight here is the Cabinet des Livres, a repository of 700

manuscripts and more than 30,000 volumes, including a Gutenberg Bible and a facsimile of the *Très Riches Heures du Duc de Berry,* an illuminated manuscript dating from the 15th century that illustrates the calendar year for both the peasantry and the nobility. The chapel, to the left as you walk into the vestibule, has woodwork and stained-glass windows dating from the mid-16th century.

The attached Renaissance-style Grand Château, completely demolished during the Revolution, was rebuilt by the Duke of Aumale, son of King Louis-Philippe, from 1875 to 1885. It contains the Musée Condé, a series of unremarkable 19th-century rooms adorned with paintings and sculptures haphazardly arranged according to the whims of the duke – he donated the château to the Institut de France on the condition the exhibits were not reorganised and would remain open to the public. The most remarkable works, hidden in the Sanctuaire (Sanctuary), include paintings by Filippino Lippi, Jean Fouquet and Raphael, though the authenticity of the last is now disputed.

The château's fabulous gardens encompass the formal Jardin Français (French Garden), with flowerbeds, lakes and a Grand Canal all laid out by Le Nôtre in the mid-17th century, northeast of the main building; and the 'wilder' Jardin Anglais (English Garden), begun in 1817, to the west. East of the Jardin Français is the rustic Jardin Anglo-Chinois (Anglo-Chinese Garden), created in the 1770s. Its foliage and silted-up waterways surround the hameau, a mock village dating from 1774, whose mill and half-timbered buildings inspired the Hameau de la Reine at Versailles. *Crème Chantilly* was born here.

The Grandes Écuries (Grand Stables), built between 1719 and 1740 to house 240 horses and more than 400 hounds, stand apart from the château to the west and close to Chantilly's famous hippodrome (race-

---

CHÂTEAU DE WHIPPED CREAM

Like every self-respecting French château three centuries ago, the palace at Chantilly had its own *hameau* (hamlet) complete with *laitier* (dairy), where the lady of the household and her guests could play at being milkmaids. But the cows at the Chantilly dairy took their job rather more seriously than their fellow bovines at other faux *crémeries* (dairy shops), and the *crème Chantilly* (sweetened whipped cream) served at the hamlet's teas became the talk (and envy) of aristocratic 18th-century Europe. The future Habsburg emperor Joseph II paid a clandestine visit to this 'temple de marbre' (marble temple), as he called it, to taste it himself in 1777. Chantilly (or more properly *crème Chantilly*) is whipped unpasteurised cream with a twist. It's beaten with icing and vanilla sugars to the consistency of a mousse and dolloped on berries. Try it in any cafe or restaurant in town.

course), inaugurated in 1834. Today the stables house the Musée Vivant du Cheval (Living Horse Museum; 03 44 27 31 80; www.museevivantducheval.fr; adult/child incl demonstration €11/8, stables only €4/free; 10am-5pm Wed-Mon), included in domain and show pass admission. Its pampered equines live in luxurious wooden stalls built by Louis-Henri de Bourbon, the seventh Prince de Condé, who was convinced he would be reincarnated as a horse (hence the extraordinary grandeur!). Displays include everything from riding equipment to rocking horses and portraits, drawings and sculptures of famous nags from the past.

Every visitor, big and small, will be mesmerised by the one-hour equestrian show (2.30pm Wed-Mon). Even more magical and highly sought-after are the handful of special equestrian shows (€22/16.50) performed in the stables year-round; tickets should be reserved online. The show pass includes one of the special shows.

Forêt de Chantilly FOREST

South of the château is the 63-sq-km Forêt de Chantilly, once a royal hunting estate and now criss-crossed by a variety of walking and riding trails. Long-distance trails here include the GR11, which links the château with the town of Senlis and its cathedral; the GR1, which goes from Luzarches (famed for its cathedral, parts of which date from the 12th century) to Ermenonville; and the GR12, which heads northeast from four lakes known as the Étangs de Commelles to the Forêt d'Halatte. The tourist office stocks maps and guides.

✖ Eating

La Capitainerie TRADITIONAL FRENCH €€

(03 44 57 15 89; www.chateaudechantilly.com; 2-/3-course menus €27/32; lunch Wed-Mon) Enviably nestled beneath the vaulted stone ceiling of the château kitchens, La Capitainerie is pricey but captures history's grandeur and romance. Fare is traditional and includes *crème Chantilly* at every opportunity.

Le Boudoir TEAROOM €

(03 44 55 44 49; www.leboudoir-chantilly.fr; 100 rue du Connétable; lunch menu €11.50; 11am-6pm Mon, 10am-7pm Tue-Sat, 11am-7pm Sun) As a certified partner of Parisian gourmet emporium Fauchon, you can be sure of the quality at this charming tearoom. Strewn with comfy sofas, it's a perfect place to try *crème Chantilly* in all its decadence (on hot chocolate topped with lashings of the stuff) or to enjoy a light lunch (salads, savoury tarts and so on).

Le Vertugadin TRADITIONAL FRENCH €€

(03 44 57 03 19; www.restaurantlevertugadin.fr; 44 rue du Connétable; menus €28; lunch Tue-Sun, dinner Tue-Sat) Old-style and elegant, this ode to regional cuisine – meat, game and terrines accompanied by sweet onion chutney – fills a white-shuttered town house. A warming fire roars in the hearth in winter, and summer welcomes diners to its walled garden.

Le Goutillon BISTRO €€

(03 44 58 01 00; 61 rue du Connétable; 2-/3-course menus €15/25; lunch & dinner) With its red-and-white checked tablecloths, simple wooden tables and classic bistro fare, this cosy, very friendly French affair is as much a wine bar as a place to dine.

Marché Decouvert MARKET

(Place Omer Vallon; 8.30am-12.30pm Wed & Sat) Twice-weekly open-air market.

ℹ Information

Office de Tourisme de Chantilly (03 44 67 37 37; www.chantilly-tourisme.com; 60 av du Maréchal Joffre; 9.30am-12.30pm & 1.30-5.30pm Mon-Sat, 10am-1.30pm Sun) Ample information on Chantilly, including accommodation and walks through town, along Chantilly's two canals and around the racecourse. It also has information on walking and mountain-bike trails in the forest.

ℹ Getting There & Away

Château de Chantilly is just over 2km northeast of the train and bus stations. The most direct route is to walk along av de la Plaine des Aigles through a section of the Forêt de Chantilly. You will get a better sense of the town, however, by following av du Maréchal Joffre and rue de Paris to connect with rue du Connétable, Chantilly's principal thoroughfare.

Paris Gare du Nord links with Chantilly-Gouvieux train station (€7.80, 25 to 40 minutes) by hourly-or-better SNCF commuter trains.

Driving from Paris, the fastest route is via the Autoroute du Nord (A1/E19); use exit 7 ('Survilliers-Chantilly'). The N1 then N16 from Porte de la Chapelle/St-Denis is cheaper.

Senlis

POP 21,000

Just 10km northeast of Chantilly (53km north of Paris), Senlis is an attractive medieval town of winding cobblestone streets, Gallo-Roman ramparts and towers. It was a royal seat from the time of Clovis in the 5th and 6th centuries to Henri IV (r 1589–1610), and contains four small but well-formed museums (adult/child €4.25/2.15) devoted to subjects as diverse as art and archaeology, local history, hunting and the French cavalry in North Africa.

The real reason to come is to see the Gothic Cathédrale de Notre Dame (place du Parvis Notre Dame; admission free; ◷8am-6pm), built between 1150 and 1191. The cathedral is unusually bright, but the stained glass, though original, is unexceptional. The magnificent carved-stone Grand Portal (1176), on the western side facing place du Parvis Notre Dame, has statues and a central relief relating to the life of the Virgin Mary. It is believed to have been the inspiration for the portal at the cathedral in Chartres.

The Office de Tourisme de Senlis (◷03 44 53 06 40; www.senlis-tourisme.fr; place du Parvis Notre Dame; ◷10am-12.30pm & 2-6.15pm) is just opposite the cathedral.

Buses (€2, 25 minutes) link Senlis with Chantilly's bus station, next to its train station, about every half-hour on weekdays and hourly on Saturday, with around half a dozen departures on Sunday.

Chartres

POP 45,600

Step off the train in Chartres, 91km southwest of Paris, and the two very different spires – one Gothic, the other Romanesque – of its glorious 13th-century cathedral beckon. Follow them to check out the cathedral's brilliant-blue stained-glass windows and its collection of relics, including the Sainte Voile (Holy Veil) said to have been worn by the Virgin Mary when she gave birth to Jesus, which have lured pilgrims since the Middle Ages.

After visiting the town's museums, don't miss a stroll around Chartres' carefully preserved old town. Adjacent to the cathedral, staircases and steep streets lined with half-timbered medieval houses lead downhill to the narrow western channel of the Eure River, romantically spanned by footbridges.

◉ Sights & Activities

Allow 1½ to two hours to walk the signposted *circuit touristique* (tourist circuit) taking in Chartres' key sights. Free town maps from the tourist office also mark the route.

Cathédrale Notre Dame   CATHEDRAL
(www.diocese-chartres.com; place de la Cathédrale; ◷8.30am-7.30pm, to 10pm Tue, Fri & Sun Jun-Aug) One of the crowning architectural achievements of Western civilisation, the 130m-long Cathédrale Notre Dame de Chartres was built in the Gothic style during the first quarter of the 13th century to replace a Romanesque cathedral that had been devastated by fire – along with much of the town – in 1194. Because of effective fundraising and donated labour, construction took only 30 years, resulting in a high degree of architectural unity. It is France's best-preserved medieval cathedral, having been spared postmedieval modifications, the ravages of war and the Reign of Terror.

The cathedral's west, north and south entrances have superbly ornamented triple portals, but the west entrance, known as the Portail Royal, is the only one that predates the fire. Carved from 1145 to 1155, its superb statues, whose features are elongated in the Romanesque style, represent the glory of Christ in the centre, and the Nativity and the Ascension to the right and left, respectively. The structure's other main Romanesque feature is the 105m-high Clocher Vieux (Old Bell Tower; also called the Tour Sud or 'South Tower'). Construction began in the 1140s; it remains the tallest Romanesque steeple still standing.

A visit to the 112m-high Clocher Neuf (New Bell Tower; adult/child €7/free; ◷9.30am-12.30pm & 2-6pm Mon-Sat, 2-6pm Sun May-Aug, 9.30am-12.30pm & 2-5pm Mon-Sat, 2-5pm Sun Sep-Apr), also known as the Tour Nord (North Tower), is worth the ticket price and the climb up the long spiral stairway (350 steps). Access is just behind the cathedral bookshop. A 70m-high platform on the lacy flamboyant Gothic spire, built from 1507 to 1513 by Jehan de Beauce after an earlier wooden spire burned down, affords superb views of the three-tiered flying buttresses and the 19th-century copper roof, turned green by verdigris.

The cathedral's 172 extraordinary stained-glass windows, almost all of which date back to the 13th century, form one of the most important ensembles of medieval stained glass in the world. The three most exquisite windows, dating from the mid-12th century, are in the wall above the west entrance and below the rose window. Survivors of the fire of 1194 (they were made some four decades before), the windows are renowned for the depth and intensity of their tones, famously known as 'Chartres blue'.

In Chartres since 876, the venerated Sainte Voile (p164) – a yellowish bolt of

Chartres

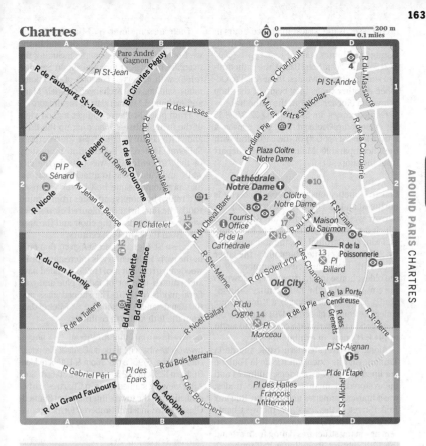

Chartres

silk draped over a support – is displayed at the end of the cathedral's north aisle behind the choir.

The cathedral's 110m **crypt** (adult/child €2.70/2.10; ⊙tours 11am Mon-Sat & 2.15pm, 3.15pm, 4.30pm & 5.15pm daily late Jun-late Sep, 11am Mon-Sat & 2.15pm, 3.30pm, 4.30pm & 5.15 daily Apr-late Jun & late Sep-Oct, 11am Mon-Sat & 4.15pm Nov-Mar), a tombless Romanesque structure built in 1024 around a 9th-century predecessor, is the largest in France. Tours in French (with a written English translation) lasting 30 minutes start at La Crypte (⏁02 37 21 56 33; 18 Cloître Notre Dame), the cathedral-run shop selling souvenirs, from April to October. At other times they begin at the shop below the Clocher Neuf in the cathedral.

Guided tours in English (⏁02 37 28 15 58; millerchartres@aol.com; tour €10; ☺noon & 2.45pm Mon-Sat Apr-Oct) of the cathedral with the incomparable Malcolm Miller depart from the shop.

Old City   HISTORIC QUARTER

Chartres' meticulously preserved old city is northeast and east of the cathedral along the narrow western channel of the River Eure, which is spanned by a number of footbridges. From rue Cardinal Pie, the stairways Tertre St-Nicolas and rue Chantault – the latter lined with medieval houses (number 29 is the oldest house in Chartres) – lead down to the empty shell of the 12th-century Collégiale St-André (place St-André), a Romanesque collegiate church closed in 1791 and severely damaged in the early 19th century and again in 1944. It's now an exhibition centre.

Along the river's eastern bank, rue de la Tannerie and its extension rue de la Foulerie are lined with flower gardens, millraces and the restored remnants of riverside trades: wash houses, tanneries and the like. Rue aux Juifs (Street of the Jews), on the west bank, has been extensively renovated. Rue des Écuyers has many structures dating from around the 16th century, including a half-timbered, prow-shaped house at number 26, with its upper section supported by beams. Escalier de la Reine Berthe (Queen Bertha's Staircase; 35 rue des Écuyers) is a towerlike covered stairwell clinging to a half-timbered house that dates back to the early 16th century.

HOLY VEIL

The most venerated object in Chartres cathedral is the Sainte Voile, the 'Holy Veil' said to have been worn by the Virgin Mary when she gave birth to Jesus. It originally formed part of the imperial treasury of Constantinople but was offered to Charlemagne by the Empress Irene when the Holy Roman Emperor proposed marriage to her in 802. Charles the Bald presented it to the town in 876; the cathedral was built because the veil survived the 1194 fire.

There are some lovely half-timbered houses north of here on rue du Bourg and to the west on rue de la Poissonnerie, including the magnificent 16th-century Maison du Saumon (p165), with its carved consoles of the eponymous salmon, the Archangel Gabriel, Mary, and Archangel Michael slaying the dragon.

From place St-Pierre you get a good view of the flying buttresses holding up the 12th-and 13th-century Église St-Pierre (place St-Pierre). Part of a Benedictine monastery in the 7th century, it was outside the city walls and vulnerable to attack; its fortress-like, pre-Romanesque bell tower was used as a refuge by monks and dates from around 1000. The fine, brightly coloured clerestory windows in the nave, the choir and the apse date from the early 14th century.

Église St-Aignan (place St-Aignan), first built in the early 16th century, is interesting for its wooden barrel-vault roof (1625), arcaded nave and painted interior of faded blue-and-gold floral motifs (c 1870). The stained glass and the Renaissance Chapelle de St-Michel date from the 16th and 17th centuries.

Centre International du Vitrail   MUSEUM

(www.centre-vitrail.org; 5 rue du Cardinal Pie; adult/child €4/free; ☺9.30am-12.30pm & 1.30-6pm Mon-Fri, 10am-12.30pm & 2.30-6pm Sat, 2.30-6pm Sun) After viewing stained glass in Chartres' cathedral, nip into the town's International Stained-Glass Centre, in a half-timbered former granary, to see superb examples close up.

Musée des Beaux-Arts   MUSEUM

(29 Cloître Notre Dame; adult/child €3.20/free; ☺2-6pm Wed, Sat & Sun May-Oct, to 5pm Wed, Sat & Sun Nov-Mar) Chartres' fine-arts museum, accessed via the gate next to Cathédrale Notre Dame's north portal, is in the former Palais Épiscopal (Bishop's Palace), built in the 17th and 18th centuries. Its collections include 16th-century enamels of the Apostles made for François I, paintings from the 16th to 19th centuries and polychromatic wooden sculptures from the Middle Ages.

Le Petit Chart' Train   TOURIST TRAIN

(www.promotrain.fr/gbcircuit.htm; adult/child €6/3; ☺10.30am-7pm Apr-Oct) Departing from the tourist office, Chartres' electric tourist 'train' covers the main sights in 35 minutes.

★☆ Festivals & Events

Chartres en Lumières   LIGHTS FESTIVAL

(www.chartresenlumieres.com) From mid-April to mid-September, 27 of Chartres' landmarks are spectacularly lit every night. You can also catch them aboard **Le Petit Chart' Train late circuits** (adult/child €6.50/3; ⊙daily Jul & Aug, Fri & Sat May, Jun & Sep) or on **night walking tours** (adult/child €12/8; ⊙Jul & Aug) in English.

🛏 Sleeping

Chartres is a convenient stop en route to the Loire Valley.

Best Western Le Grand Monarque   HOTEL
(✆02 37 18 15 15; www.bw-grand-monarque.com; 22 place des Épars; d/tr from €132/195; ❄@🕾) With its teal blue shutters gracing its 1779 facade, lovely stained-glass ceiling and treasure trove of period furnishings, old B&W photos and knick-knacks, the refurbished Grand Monarque (with air-con in some rooms) is a historical gem and very central. Its restaurant has a Michelin star; check the website for its program of three-hour cooking lessons (€55).

Hôtel du Bœuf Couronné   HOTEL
(✆02 37 18 06 06; www.leboeufcouronne.com; 15 place Châtelet; s €65-85, d €75-109; @🕾) The red-curtained entrance lends a vaguely theatrical air to this two-star Logis guesthouse in the centre of everything. Its summer-time terrace restaurant cooks up cathedral-view dining and the Dickens music bar is right next door.

🍴 Eating & Drinking

Food shops surround the **covered market** (place Billard; ⊙7am-1pm Wed & Sat), just off rue des Changes south of the cathedral.

TOP CHOICE Le Saint-Hilaire   REGIONAL CUISINE €€
(✆02 37 30 97 57; www.restaurant-saint-hilaire. fr; 11 rue du Pont Saint-Hilaire; 2-/3-course menus from €27/42; ⊙lunch & dinner Tue-Sat) Local products are ingeniously used in to-die-for dishes – like stuffed mushrooms with lentils, snails in puff pastry with leek fondue, a seasonal lobster menu, and aromatic cheese platters – at this pistachio-painted, wood-beamed charmer.

La Chocolaterie   PATISSERIE, TEAROOM €
(14 place du Cygne; ⊙8am-7.30pm Tue-Sat, 10am-7.30pm Sun & Mon) Soak up local life overlooking the open-air **flower market** (place du Cygne; ⊙8am-1pm Tue, Thu & Sat). This tearoom-patisserie's hot chocolate and macarons (flavoured with orange, apricot, peanut, pineapple and so on) are sublime, as are

its sweet homemade crêpes and miniature madeleine sponge cakes (dishes from €3.35).

La Passacaille   ITALIAN €
(✆02 37 21 52 10; www.lapassacaille.fr; 30 rue Ste-Même; 2-/3-course menus €15/18, pizzas €7.50-11.50, pasta €9; ⊙lunch & dinner Thu-Tue; 🎔) This welcoming spot has particularly good pizzas (try the Montagnarde with tomato, mozzarella, soft, nutty-flavoured Reblochon cheese, potatoes, red onions, cured ham and *crème fraîche*) and homemade pasta with toppings including *pistou* (pesto) also made on the premises.

Le Serpente   BRASSERIE, TEAROOM €
(✆02 37 21 68 81; www.leserpente.com; 2 Cloître Notre Dame; mains €16-18.50; ⊙11am-11pm) Its location slap-bang opposite the cathedral ensures this traditional brasserie and *salon de thé* (tearoom) – one of the oldest in Chartres – is always full. Specialities span pig's trotters and veal kidneys to fresh fish and meal-sized salads.

Le Bistro de la Cathédrale   BISTRO, BAR €€
(✆02 37 36 59 60; 1 Cloître Notre Dame; menus €22-24; ⊙lunch & dinner Thu-Tue) In the shadow of the cathedral, this stylish wine bar is ideally situated for a long lazy lunch of pâté, duck breast and the like over a glass or three of wine. Service is friendly and efficient.

ℹ Information

Tourist office (✆02 37 18 26 26; www. chartres-tourisme.com; place de la Cathédrale; ⊙9am-7pm Mon-Sat, 9.30am-5.30pm Sun Apr-Sep, 9am-6pm Mon-Sat, 9.30am-5pm Sun Oct-Mar) Hires out 1½-hour English-language audioguide tours (€5.50/8.50 for one/two) of the medieval city as well as binoculars (€2), fabulous for seeing details of the cathedral close up.

Maison du Saumon (8-10 rue de la Poissonnerie; ⊙10am-1pm & 2-6pm Mon-Sat Apr-Oct, 10am-noon & 1-6pm Mon-Sat Nov-Mar) This historic building now houses a branch of the tourist office with an exhibition on Chartres' history.

ℹ Getting There & Away

Frequent SNCF trains link Paris' Gare Montparnasse (€14.40, 55 to 70 minutes) with Chartres, some of which stop at Versailles-Chantiers (€12.10, 45 to 60 minutes).

If you're driving from Paris, follow the A6 from Porte d'Orléans (direction Bordeaux–Nantes), then the A10 and A11 (direction Nantes) and take the 'Chartres' exit.

Lille, Flanders & the Somme

Why Go?

True, a tan is easier to come by along the Mediterranean, but when it comes to culture, cuisine, beer, shopping and dramatic views of land and sea – not to mention good old-fashioned friendliness – the Ch'tis (residents of France's northern tip) and their region compete with the best France has to offer. In Lille and French Flanders, the down-to-earth Flemish vibe mixes easily with French sophistication and savoir-faire. And in the Somme, although WWI has been over for almost a century, the British, Canadians and Australians who perished in the trenches of the Western Front have not been forgotten. The moving memorials and cemeteries marking the front lines of 1916 remain places of pilgrimage and reflection.

If you snag a promotional fare on the Eurostar, Lille, Flanders and the Somme make for a superb short trip from London – with a much smaller carbon footprint than flying.

Best Places to Eat

» Het Kasteelhof (p186)
» Chez la Vieille (p173)
» Histoire Ancienne (p179)

Best Places to Stay

» L'Hermitage Gantois (p171)
» Grand Hôtel de l'Univers (p189)
» Maison St-Vaast (p192)

When to Go
Lille

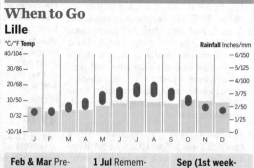

Feb & Mar Pre-Lenten carnivals bring out marching bands and costumed revellers.

1 Jul Remembrance ceremonies at Thiepval on the anniversary of the Battle of the Somme.

Sep (1st weekend) The world's largest flea market, the Braderie, takes over Lille.

To Dover
To Dover
To Dover
North Sea
Channel Tunnel
Strait of Dover
Côte d'Opale
Cap Gris-Nez
Bray Dunes
Dunes Flamandes
St-Pol-sur-Mer
Leffrinckoucke
Zuydecoote
Loon Plage
Dunkirk
Malo-les-Bains
Bergues
Blériot Plage
Calais
Sangatte
Cap Blanc-Nez
Wissant
Audinghen
Ambleteuse
Wimereux
Boulogne-sur-Mer
Parc Naturel Régional des Caps et Marais d'Opale
Clairmarais
St-Omer
Wizernes
Arques
La Coupole
Aire-sur-la-Lys
Le Touquet-Paris-Plage
Montreuil
Agincourt (Azincourt)
Berck-sur-Mer
Parc Ornithologique du Marquenterre
St-Quentin-en-Tourmont
Rue
Baie de la Somme
Le Crotoy
Crécy-en-Ponthieu
Point du Hourdel
St-Valéry-sur-Somme
Abbeville
Hesdin
St-Pol-sur-Ternoise
Avesnes-le-Comte
Beaurains
La Herlière
Doullens
Ayette
Ervillers
Le Tréport
To Dieppe (24km)
Gamaches
Blagny-sur-Bresle
HAUTE-NORMANDIE
SEINE-MARITIME
To Rouen (38km)
Neufchâtel-en-Bray
Picardie
SOMME
Amiens
Australian Corps Memorial Park
Corbie
Villers-Bretonneux
Framerville-Rainecourt
Nesle
Ham
Roye
Montdidier
To Paris (95km)
To Laon (40km); Reims (91km)
St-Quentin
AISNE
To Château de Blérancourt (Musée Franco-Américain) (6.5km)
Somm America Cemete
Péronne
Bapaume
Cambrai
Beaumont-Hamel Newfoundland Memorial
Beamont
Thiepval Memorial
Hamel
South African National Memorial
Puchevillers
La Boisselle
Contay
Albert
La Grande Mine
BELGIUM
Veurne
Adinkerke
Diksmuide
Roeselare
Poperinge
Ypres
Kortrijk
Menen
Mouscron
Tourcoing
Roubaix
Cassel
Dranouter
Bailleul
Armentières
FLANDERS
Fromelles
Lille
Indian Memorial
La Bassée
Carvin
NORD
Lens
Louvre-Lens
Vimy Ridge Canadian National Historical Site
Hénin-Beaumont
Douai
St-Laurent-Blangy
Arras
PAS-DE-CALAIS
ARTOIS

0   20 km
0   10 miles

A16 A25 D940 N42 N43 A26 D901 D1001 A28 N29 A16 N25 D929 N17 N30 A1 D939 A2 N41 A1 A23 A26 D917 D6 D1029 N29

Lille, Flanders & the Somme Highlights

1 Stroll around the chic and photogenic centre of **Lille** (p168) and explore the city's trio of superb art museums

2 Marvel at Amiens' breathtaking Gothic **cathedral** (p188) both inside and out

3 Ramble along the spectacular, windswept **Côte d'Opale** (p180), facing the white cliffs of Dover

4 Be among the first to visit the brand-new **Louvre-Lens museum** (p192) in Lens

5 Enjoy a hefty dose of Flemish culture and tour a working windmill in the pretty hilltop town of **Cassel** (p186)

6 Join the bustle of the **Saturday market** (p194) in Arras' gorgeous Flemish-style Place des Héros

7 Watch clacking machinery turn thread into lace at **Cité Internationale de la Dentelle et de la Mode** (p177) in Calais

8 Ponder the sacrifices and horror of WWI at **Vimy** (p200)

History & Geography

In the Middle Ages the Nord *département* (the sliver of France along the Belgian border; www.cdt-nord.fr), together with much of Belgium and part of the Netherlands, belonged to a feudal principality known as Flanders (Flandre or Flandres in French, Vlaanderen in Flemish). Today many people in the area still speak Flemish – essentially Dutch with some variation in pronunciation and vocabulary – and are very proud of their *flamand* culture and cuisine. Along with the neighbouring *département* of Pas-de-Calais (www.pas-de-calais.com), which runs inland from the Pas de Calais (Strait of Dover), the Nord forms the *région* of Nord-Pas de Calais (www.tourisme-nordpasdecalais.fr).

The area south of the Somme estuary and Albert forms the *région* of Picardy (Picardie; www.picardie.fr), historically centred on the Somme *département* (www.somme-tourisme.com), which saw some of the bloodiest fighting of WWI. The popular British WWI love song 'Roses of Picardy' was penned here in 1916 by Frederick E Weatherley.

ⓘ Getting There & Away

Lille, Flanders and the Somme are a hop, skip and a jump from southwest England. By train on the **Eurostar** (www.eurostar.com) – promotional fares Lille–London start at just €88 return – Lille is just 70 minutes from London's St Pancras International train station. **Eurotunnel** (www.eurotunnel.com) can get you and your car from Folkestone to Calais, via the Channel Tunnel, in a mere 35 minutes. For those with sturdy sea legs, car ferries link Dover with Calais and Dunkirk. At present, the only sailings open to foot passengers are those run by P&O Ferries, during daylight hours, between Dover and Calais.

On the Continent, superfast Eurostar and TGV trains link Lille with Brussels (35 minutes), and TGVs make travel from Lille to Paris' Gare du Nord (one hour) and Charles de Gaulle airport (one hour) a breeze.

Lille

POP 233,210

Lille (Rijsel in Flemish) may be France's most underrated major city. In recent decades this once-grimy industrial metropolis, its economy based on declining industries, has transformed itself – with generous government help – into a glittering and self-confident cultural and commercial hub. Highlights for the visitor include an attractive old town with a strong Flemish accent, three renowned art museums, stylish shopping, some excellent dining options and a cutting-edge, student-driven nightlife scene. The Lillois have a well-deserved reputation for friendliness – and are so proud of being friendly that they often mention it!

THE GIANTS

In far northern France and nearby Belgium, *géants* (giants) – wickerwork body masks up to 8.5m tall animated by someone (or several someones) inside – emerge for local carnivals and on feast days to dance and add to the general merriment. Each has a name and a personality, usually based on the Bible, legends or local history. Giants are born, baptised, grow up, marry and have children, creating, over the years, complicated family relationships. They serve as important symbols of town, neighbourhood and village identity.

Medieval in origin – and also found in places such as the UK (www.giants.org.uk), Catalonia, the Austrian Tyrol, Mexico, Brazil and India – giants have been a tradition in northern France since the 16th century. More than 300 of the creatures, also known as *reuze* (in Flemish) and *gayants* (in Picard), now 'live' in French towns, including Arras, Boulogne, Calais, Cassel, Dunkirk and Lille. Local associations cater to their every need, while transnational groups such as the International Circle of Friends of the Giant Puppets (www.ciag.org) promote the creatures worldwide. France and Belgium's giants were recognised by Unesco as 'masterpieces of the oral and intangible heritage of humanity' in 2005.

Giants make appearances year-round but your best chance to see them is at pre-Lenten carnivals, during Easter and at festivals held from May to September, often on weekends. Dates and places – as well as the latest marriage and birth announcements – appear in the free, annual, French-language brochure *Le Calendrier des Géants*, available at tourist offices and online at www.geants-carnaval.org, in French.

Thanks to the Eurostar and the TGV, Lille makes an easy, environmentally sustainable weekend destination from London, Paris or Brussels.

History

Lille owes its name – once spelled L'Isle – to the fact that it was founded, back in the 11th century, on an island in the River Deûle. In 1667 the city was captured by French forces led personally by Louis XIV, who promptly set about fortifying his prize, creating the Lille Citadelle. In the 1850s the miserable conditions in which Lille's 'labouring classes' lived – the city was long the centre of France's textile industry – were exposed by Victor Hugo.

◉ Sights & Activities

Palais des Beaux Arts   ART MUSEUM
(Fine Arts Museum; www.pba-lille.fr; place de la République; adult/student/child €6.50/4/free; ⊘2-6pm Mon, 10am-6pm Wed-Sun; Ⓜ République Beaux Arts) Lille's world-renowned Fine Arts Museum displays a truly first-rate collection of 15th- to 20th-century paintings, including works by Rubens, Van Dyck and Manet. Exquisite porcelain and faience (pottery), much of it of local provenance, is on the ground floor, while in the basement you'll find classical archaeology, medieval statuary and 18th-century scale models of the fortified cities of northern France and Belgium. Tickets are valid for the whole day. Information sheets in French, English and Dutch are available in each hall.

Musée d'Art Moderne Lille-Métropole   ART MUSEUM
(📞 03 20 19 68 68; www.musee-lam.fr; 1 allée du Musée; adult/student/child €7/5/free; ⊘10am-6pm Tue-Sun) Colourful, playful and just plain weird works of modern and contemporary art by masters such as Braque, Calder, Léger, Miró, Modigliani and Picasso are the big draw at this renowned, newly renovated museum and sculpture park in the Lille suburb of Villeneuve-d'Ascq, 9km east of Gare Lille-Europe. Take metro line 1 to Pont de Bois, then bus 41 (10 minutes) to Parc Urbain-Musée.

La Piscine Musée d'Art et d'Industrie   ART MUSEUM
(www.roubaix-lapiscine.com; 23 rue de l'Espérance, Roubaix; adult/child €4.50/free; ⊘11am-6pm Tue-Thu, 11am-8pm Fri, 1-6pm Sat & Sun; Ⓜ Gare Jean Lebas) If Paris can turn a disused train station into a world-class museum (the Musée

---

LILLE CITY PASS

Available in one-/two-/three-day versions (€20/30/45), the Lille Métropole pass gets you into almost all the museums in greater Lille (www.destination-lille-metropole.eu) and affords unlimited use of public transport. The three-day version throws in sites in six cities in the Nord-Pas de Calais *région* and free use of regional TER trains. Available at the Lille tourist office.

---

d'Orsay), why not transform an art deco municipal swimming pool (built 1927–32) – an architectural masterpiece inspired by civic pride and hygienic high-mindedness – into a temple of the arts? This innovative museum, 12km northeast of Gare Lille-Europe, showcases fine arts, applied arts and sculpture in a delightfully watery environment.

Wazemmes   NEIGHBOURHOOD
(Ⓜ Gambetta) For an authentic taste of grassroots Lille, head to the ethnically mixed, family-friendly *quartier populaire* (working-class quarter) of Wazemmes, 1.7km southwest of place du Général de Gaulle, where African immigrants and old-time proletarians live harmoniously alongside penurious students and trendy *bobos* (bourgeois bohemians).

The neighbourhood's focal point is the cavernous Marché de Wazemmes, Lille's favourite food market. The adjacent outdoor market (place de la Nouvelle Aventure; ⊘7am-1.30pm Tue, Thu & Sun) is *the* place to be on Sunday morning – it's a real carnival scene! Rue des Sarrazins and rue Jules Guesde are lined with shops, restaurants and Tunisian pastry places, many owned by, and catering to, the area's North African residents; they intersect in the southeastern corner of place de la Nouvelle Aventure, one periphery of which is sprinkled with cafes.

Wazemmes is famed for its many outdoor concerts and street festivals, including La Louche d'Or (Golden Ladle; 1 May), a soup festival that has spread to cities across Europe.

Maison Natale de Charles de Gaulle   HOUSE MUSEUM
(www.maison-natale-de-gaulle.com; 9 rue Princesse; adult/student/child incl audioguide €6/4/free; ⊘10am-1pm & 2-6pm Wed-Sat, 2-6pm Sun) The upper-middle-class house in which Charles de Gaulle was born in 1890 is now a museum presenting the French leader in the

Lille

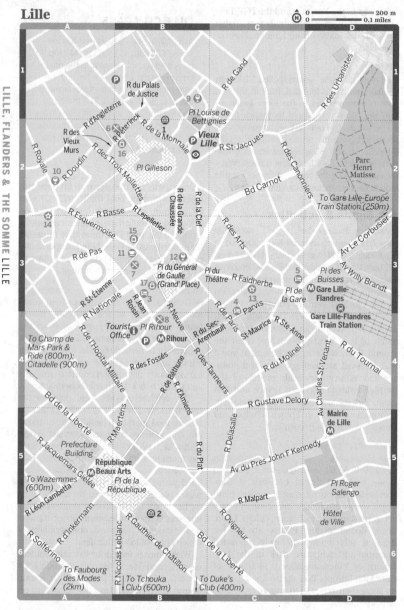

0   200 m
0   0.1 miles

R du Palais de Justice

Pl Louise de Bettignies

R de Gand

R des Urbanistes

Vieux Lille

R St-Jacques

R d'Angleterre

R Peterinck
R de la Monnaie

R des Vieux Murs

R Royale

R Doudin

R des Trois Mollettes

Pl Gilleson

R des Canonniers

Bd Carnot

Parc Henri Matisse

To Gare Lille-Europe Train Station (250m)

R Esquermoise

R Basse

R Lepelletier

R de la Grande Chaussée

R de la Clef

R des Arts

Av Le Corbusier

R de Pas

Pl du Général de Gaulle (Grand' Place)

Pl du Théâtre

R Faidherbe

Pl des Buisses

Av Willy Brandt

R St-Étienne

R Nationale

R Jean Roisin

R Neuve

R de Paris

Parvis

Pl de la Gare

Gare Lille-Flandres

Gare Lille-Flandres Train Station

Tourist Office

Pl Rihour

Rihour

R du Sec Arembault

St-Maurice

R Ste-Anne

R du Molinel

R Charles St-Venant

R du Tournai

To Champ de Mars Park & Ride (800m); Citadelle (900m)

R de l'Hôpital Militaire

R des Fossés

R de Béthune

R d'Amiens

R des Tanneurs

R Gustave Delory

Av Mairie de Lille

Bd de la Liberté

R Maertens

Prefecture Building

R Jacquemars Giélée

République

Beaux Arts

Pl de la République

R du Plat

R Delasalle

Av du Pres John F Kennedy

Pl Roger Salengo

To Wazemmes (600m)

R Léon Gambetta

R Malpart

Hôtel de Ville

R Solférino

R d'Inkermann

R Nicolas Leblanc

R Gauthier de Châtillon

Bd de la Liberté

R Ovigneur

To Faubourg des Modes (2km)

To Tchouka Club (600m)

To Duke's Club (400m)

context of his times, with an emphasis on his connection to French Flanders. Displays include de Gaulle's dainty baptismal robe and some evocative newsreels. The museum is 1.5km northwest of Lille's central square, place du Général de Gaulle.

Musée de l'Hospice Comtesse ART MUSEUM
(www.mairie-lille.fr; 32 rue de la Monnaie; adult/student/child €3.50/2.50/free; ◷10am-12.30pm & 2-6pm, closed Mon morning & Tue) Housed in a remarkably attractive 15th- and 17th-century poorhouse, this museum features ce-

Lille

ramics, earthenware wall tiles, religious art and 17th- and 18th-century paintings and furniture. A rood screen separates the Salle des Malades (Hospital Hall) from a mid-17th century chapel (look up to see a mid-19th century painted ceiling).

Citadelle FORTRESS
(☏03 20 21 94 39; Vauban-Esquermes; ▣12) At the northwestern end of bd de la Liberté, this massive star-shaped fortress was designed by renowned 17th-century French military architect Vauban (p941) after France captured Lille in 1667. Made of some 60 million bricks, it still functions as a French and NATO military base. Guided tours (below) are available on Sundays in summer. Outside the 2.2km-long ramparts is the city centre's largest park, where children will love the amusement park, playground and small municipal zoo (admission free; ◷9am-6pm, closed mid-Dec–mid-Feb).

☞ Tours

The tourist office (p176) runs various guided tours.

Citadelle WALKING TOUR
(adult €7; ◷3pm & 4.30pm Sun Jun-Aug) This is the only way to see the inside of the Citadelle, usually a closed military zone. Sign up for the tour (in French) at least 72 hours ahead and bring a passport or national ID card.

Vieux Lille WALKING TOUR
(Map p170; adult/child €9/7.50; ◷tours in English 10.15am Sat) Departing from the tourist office, this walking tour takes in all the highlights of Lille's 17th- and 18th-century Old Town.

Flanders Battlefields Tour WWI HISTORY TOUR
(adult €42; ◷tours in English 1pm Sat) Four-hour tour of several important WWI battle sites around Ypres (just across the Belgian border).

✿ Festivals & Events

The Braderie (p176), a flea-market extraordinaire, is held on the first weekend in September. The varied art exhibitions associated with Lille 3000 (www.lille3000.com) 'explore the richness and complexities of the world of tomorrow'. Christmas decorations and edible goodies are sold at the Marché de Noël (Christmas Market; www.noel-a-lille.com; place Rihour; ◷late Nov-30 Dec).

⌂ Sleeping

Most Lille hotels are at their fullest, and priciest, from Monday to Thursday.

TOP CHOICE **L'Hermitage Gantois** DESIGN HOTEL €€€
(☏03 20 85 30 30; www.hotelhermitagegantois.com; 224 rue de Paris; d €219-455; @⌂; ⓜMairie de Lille) This five-star hotel creates enchanting, harmonious spaces by complementing its rich architectural heritage – such as a Flemish-Gothic facade – with refined ultramodernism. The 67 rooms are huge and sumptuous, with Starck accessories next to Louis XV–style chairs and bathrooms that sparkle with Carrara marble. One of the four courtyards is home to a 220-year-old wisteria that's been declared a historic monument. The still-consecrated chapel was built in 1637.

Grand Hôtel Bellevue HISTORIC HOTEL €€
(☏03 20 57 45 64; www.grandhotelbellevue.com; 5 rue Jean Roisin; d €115-215; ✳@⌂; ⓜRihour) Grandly built in the early 20th century, this

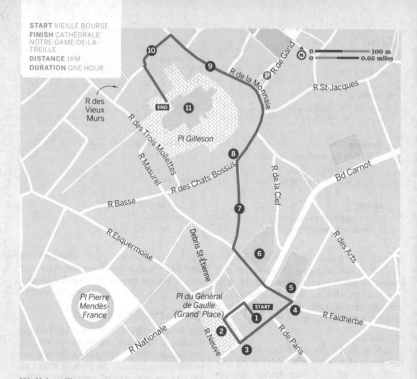

START VIEILLE BOURSE
FINISH CATHÉDRALE NOTRE-DAME-DE-LA-TREILLE
DISTANCE 1KM
DURATION ONE HOUR

Walking Tour
Lille Discovery Stroll

❯ The best place to begin a discovery stroll through the Flemish heart of Lille is the ① **Vieille Bourse**, a Flemish Renaissance extravaganza ornately decorated with caryatids and cornucopia. Built in 1653, it consists of 24 separate houses set around a richly ornamented interior courtyard that hosts a used-book market. In warm weather locals often gather here to play *échecs* (chess).

Just west of the Vieille Bourse is ② **place du Général de Gaulle**, where you can admire the 1932 art deco home of ③ **La Voix du Nord** (the leading regional newspaper), crowned by a gilded sculpture of the Three Graces. The goddess-topped victory column (1845) in the fountain commemorates the city's successful resistance to the Austrian siege of 1792. On spring and summer evenings, Lillois come here by the thousands to stroll, take in the atmosphere and sip a local beer.

Just east of the Vieille Bourse, impressive ④ **place du Théâtre** is dominated by the Louis XVI–style ⑤ **Opéra** and the neo-Flemish ⑥ **Chambre de Commerce**, topped by a 76m-high spire that sports a gilded clock. Both were built in the early 20th century. Look east along rue Faidherbe and you'll see Gare Lille-Flandres way at the other end.

Vieux Lille (Old Lille), justly proud of its restored 17th- and 18th-century brick houses, begins just north of here. Hard to believe, but in the late 1970s this quarter was a half-abandoned slum dominated by empty, dilapidated buildings. Head north along ⑦ **rue de la Grande Chaussée**, lined with Lille's chicest shops, and take a peek at ⑧ **À l'Huîtrière** restaurant, an art deco masterpiece. Continue north along ⑨ **rue de la Monnaie** (named after a mint constructed here in 1685), the old brick residences of which now house boutiques and the Musée de l'Hospice Comtesse.

Turning left (west) on tiny ⑩ **rue Péterinck** and then left again will take you to the 19th-century, neogothic ⑪ **Cathédrale Notre-Dame-de-la-Treille**, which has a strikingly modern (some would say 'jarring') west facade (1999) that looks better from inside or when illuminated at night.

Best Western–affiliated establishment has a charmingly creaky belle époque lift that trundles guests up to 60 spacious rooms equipped with marble bathrooms, gilded picture frames and flat-screen TVs. It's well worth springing for one of the better rooms with views of place du Général de Gaulle (from €130).

Hotel Kanaï HOTEL €
(☑03 20 57 14 78; www.hotelkanai.com; 10 rue de Bethune; s €47-98, d €65-115; ❋@☎; MRihour) In the heart of Lille's pedestrian zone, this newer hotel offers reasonably priced rooms with a clean modern design, ranging from a cozy single tucked away on the top floor to spacious doubles with queen beds and couches; all come with coffee-makers, attractive tiled bathrooms and cable internet connections. Wi-fi only reaches the lounge and breakfast area.

Hôtel Brueghel HOTEL €€
(☑03 20 06 06 69; www.hotel-brueghel-lille.com; 5 parvis St-Maurice; s €79-95, d €89-105; ☎; MGare Lille-Flandres) At this dependable midrange hotel halfway between Gare Lille-Flandres and the Grande Place, the 65 rooms mix vaguely antique furnishings with modern styling (though none of them offers as much Flemish charm as the lobby). Some south-facing rooms have sunny views of the adjacent church.

Hôtel Flandre-Angleterre HOTEL €€
(☑03 20 06 04 12; www.hotel-flandreangleterre-lille. com; 13 place de la Gare; s/d Mon-Thu from €71/85, Fri-Sun from €60/69; ☎; MGare Lille-Flandres) Directly opposite Gare Lille-Flandres, this practical, lift-equipped establishment offers 44 comfortable, if slightly faded and claustrophobic, rooms; the best have full-on views of bustling place de la Gare and the train station's attractive façade.

Auberge de Jeunesse HOSTEL €
(☑03 20 57 08 94; www.fuaj.org; 12 rue Malpart; dm incl breakfast €21, d €42; ☺Feb–mid-Dec; @☎; MMairie de Lille, République-Beaux-Arts) This central former maternity hospital has 163 beds in rooms for two to eight, kitchen facilities and free parking. A few doubles have en suite showers. Lockout 11am to 3pm (to 4pm Friday to Sunday).

✗ Eating

Lille (especially Vieux Lille) has a flourishing culinary scene, with great new places opening up all the time. Keep an eye out for *es-taminets* (traditional Flemish eateries, with antique knick-knacks on the walls and plain wooden tables) serving Flemish specialities such as *carbonade* (braised beef stewed with Flemish beer, spice bread and brown sugar) and *potjevleesch* (jellied chicken, pork, veal and rabbit).

Dining hot spots in Vieux Lille include: rue de Gand – home to a dozen small, moderately priced French and Flemish restaurants; rue de la Monnaie and its side streets – a good place to look for quirky, moderately priced restaurants; and rue Royale – *the* place to come for ethnic cuisine (couscous, Japanese etc).

There are heaps of cheap eats along lively, student-dominated rue Solférino and rue Masséna. Good-value *restaurants populaires* can be found in Wazemmes.

⬛ TOP CHOICE Chez la Vieille FLEMISH €
(☑03 28 36 40 06; 60 rue de Gand; mains €10-14; ☺dinner Mon, lunch & dinner Tue-Sat) Old-time prints, antiques and fresh hops hanging from the rafters create the cozy ambience of a Flemish village c 1900 at this beloved *estaminet* (Flemish-style eatery). Its sister restaurant **Au Vieux de la Vieille** (www. estaminetlille.fr; 2-4 rue des Vieux Murs; mains €10-14; ☺lunch & dinner daily) serves an identical menu, with outdoor seating on picturesque cobblestoned place de l'Oignon. The vibe at both is informal, but it's best to call ahead.

À l'Huîtrière SEAFOOD €€€
(☑03 20 55 43 41; www.huitriere.fr; 3 rue des Chats Bossus; lunch/dinner menus €45/110, oyster bar items from €15; ☺lunch & dinner Mon-Sat, lunch Sun Sep-Jul) On the 'Street of the Hunchback Cats', this sophisticated restaurant is well known for its fabulous seafood and wine cellar. For a lighter meal with a lower price tag, sit at the oyster bar up front, where stunning art deco trappings – including sea-themed mosaics and stained glass – create a colourful, more relaxed atmosphere.

Le Pain Quotidien BOULANGERIE €
(www.lepainquotidien.com; 35 place Rihour; sandwiches & salads €9-14; ☺8am-10pm; MRihour) At this popular bakery, the high-ceilinged interior rooms are flanked by display cases stacked floor to ceiling with jams, organic juices and delicious baked goods; in warm weather there's also outdoor seating on place Rihour, making this a prime spot for morning bowls of coffee, midday sandwiches and salads, and afternoon snacks.

NORTHERN BREWS

French Flanders brews some truly excellent *bière blonde* (lager) and *bière ambrée* (amber beer) with an alcohol content of up to 8.5%. While in the area, beer lovers should be sure to try some of these brands, which give the Belgian brewers a run for their money: 3 Monts, Amadeus, Ambre des Flandres, Brasserie des 2 Caps, Ch'ti, Enfants de Gayant, Grain d'Orge, Hellemus, Jenlain, L'Angellus, La Wambrechies, Moulins d'Ascq, Raoul, Septante 5, St-Landelin, Triple Secret des Moines and Vieux Lille.

Crêperie Beaurepaire CRÊPERIE €
(www.creperiebeaurepaire.com; 1 rue St-Étienne; crêpes €5-9; ⊙lunch & dinner Mon-Sat; MRihour) With its sunny beamed dining room, stonewalled cellar and sweet little outdoor courtyard, this hideaway just steps from place Charles de Gaulle is a lovely spot to enjoy crispy buckwheat *galettes* (savoury pancakes), salads and flaming dessert crêpes, accompanied by ceramic bowls full of cider.

La Source ORGANIC, VEGETARIAN €
(☎03 20 57 53 07; www.denislasource.com; 13 rue du Plat; menus €9.50-16; ⊙11.30am-2pm Mon-Sat, 7-9pm Fri; ✍; MRépublique Beaux Arts) This Lille institution serves delicious vegetarian, fowl and fish *plats du jour*, each accompanied by five hot veggie side dishes. The light, airy ambience and the diners exude health, well-being and cheer.

Self-Catering

Marché de Wazemmes FOOD MARKET €
(place de la Nouvelle Aventure; ⊙8am-2pm Tue-Thu, to 8pm Fri & Sat, to 3pm Sun & holidays; MGambetta) Beloved foodie space, 1.7km southwest of the tourist office in Lille's working-class quarter of Wazemmes.

Marché Sébastopol FOOD MARKET €
(place Sébastopol; ⊙7am-2pm Wed & Sat; MRépublique Beaux Arts) A popular food market.

🍷 Drinking

Lille has several drinking and nightlife areas. In Vieux Lille the small, stylish bars and cafes along streets such as rue Royale, rue de la Barre and rue de Gand are a big hit with chic 30-somethings. Especially on Friday and Saturday nights, in the rue Masséna student zone a university-age crowd descends on dozens of high-decibel bars along rue Masséna (750m southwest of the tourist office) and almost-perpendicular rue Solférino (as far southeast as Marché Sébastopol). London-style excess is not unknown here.

A number of edgy (and undercapitalised) cafes are tucked away around the periphery of place de la Nouvelle Aventure in Wazemmes, site of the Wazemmes food market.

In the warm season, sidewalk cafes make the square in front of the Opéra, the place du Théâtre, a fine spot to sip beer and soak up the Flemish atmosphere.

Meert TEAROOM
(www.meert.fr; 27 rue Esquermoise; ⊙9.30am-7.30pm Tue-Sat, 9am-1pm & 3-7pm Sun; MRihour) A delightful spot for morning coffee or mid-afternoon tea, this elegant tearoom dating to 1761 is beloved for its retro decor and its *gaufres* (waffles; €3) filled with sweet Madagascar vanilla paste. The tearoom's 1830s-vintage chocolate shop (chocolate €95 per kg) next door has a similarly old-fashioned atmosphere.

L'Illustration Café BAR, CAFE
(www.bar-lillustration.com; 18 rue Royale; ⊙12.30pm-3am Mon-Sat, 3pm-3am Sun) Adorned with art nouveau woodwork and changing exhibits by local painters, this laid-back bar attracts artists, musicians, budding intellectuals and teachers in the mood to read, exchange weighty ideas, or just shoot the breeze. The mellow soundtrack mixes Western classical with jazz, French *chansons* (heart-felt, lyric driven music) and African beats.

Morel & Fils BAR, CAFE
(31-33 place du Théâtre; ⊙8am-11pm Mon-Sat, 3-11pm Sun; MRihour) This bar-cafe diagonally across from Lille's Opéra features eclectic historical decor incorporating mannequins from its former life as a lingerie shop. For French-speakers, its biggest claim to fame is its cameo role in the 2008 blockbuster film *Bienvenue Chez les Ch'tis* (p925). Scan the facade for cannonballs dating back to the Austrian siege of 1792 (including one suggestively painted pink one).

Café Oz PUB
(33 place Louise de Bettignies; ⊙4pm-3am Mon-Fri, noon-3am Sat & Sun) Footy and rugby on a wide screen, Australiana on the walls and cold bottles of Toohey's Extra Dry – what more could you ask for? Popular with English-

speakers, including students, this place is packed when DJs do their thing from 9pm to 3am on Thursday, Friday and Saturday nights. Opens at noon daily in nice weather and has a great warm-season terrace. Happy hour is 6pm to 9pm Monday to Saturday.

☆ Entertainment

Lille's free French-language entertainment guide *Sortir* (www.lille.sortir.eu, in French) comes out each Wednesday and is available at the tourist office, cinemas, event venues and bookshops.

Tickets for Lille's rich cultural offerings can be bought at the Fnac Billetterie (www.fnacspectacles.com; 16 rue du Sec-Arembault; ⊙10am-7.30pm Mon-Sat; Rihour). Events details are posted by category on the walls and on flat screens.

Cinemas

Cinéma Majestic CINEMA
(☏08 36 68 00 73; www.cinemaslumieres.com; 56 rue de Béthune; MRihour) Nondubbed films on six screens.

Cinéma Métropole CINEMA
(☏08 36 68 00 73; www.cinemaslumieres.com; 26 rue des Ponts de Comines; MGare Lille-Flandres) An art-house cinema with nondubbed films on four screens.

Nightclubs

Network Café DISCO
(www.network-cafe.net; 15 rue du Faisan; ⊙10.30pm-5.30am Tue & Wed, 9.30pm-5.30am Thu, 10.30pm-7am Fri & Sat, 7pm-5am Sun; MRépublique Beaux Arts) At Lille's hottest discotheque, you can sip beer and boogie in the main hall, presided over by two 5m-high statues from faraway lands, or in the baroque Venetian room, decked out with velvet settees and crystal chandeliers. The door policy is pretty strict – locals dress up – but tends to be a bit more relaxed for tourists. Situated 600m northwest of the Palais des Beaux-Arts.

Duke's Club DISCO
(www.dukesclub.fr; 6-8 rue Gosselin; admission free; ⊙9pm-dawn Wed-Sat; MRépublique Beaux Arts) A traditional disco with three bars and three dance spaces on three levels (used simultaneously only on Saturday night), theme nights (see the website) and black light that makes white shirts glow a radioactive purple. Most of the bouncing bods are in the 30-to-50 age range. Situated 600m southeast of the Palais des Beaux-Arts.

Gay & Lesbian

Tchouka Club GAY DISCO
(www.tchoukaclub.org; 80 rue Barthélemy Delespaul; ⊙11pm-7am Fri, Sat & holiday eves; MRépublique Beaux Arts) This till-dawn gay and lesbian disco has photo-montage wall murals, plenty of flashing lights, buff barmen in tank tops and a soundtrack that's heavy on electro, house and techno. So packed after 1am that you may have trouble getting in. Relaxed dress code. Situated 700m due south of the Palais des Beaux-Arts.

Vice & Versa GAY BAR
(3 rue de la Barre; ⊙3pm-3am Mon-Sat, 4pm-3am Sun) The rainbow flies proudly at this well-heeled, sophisticated bar, which is as gay as it is popular (and it's very popular). Decor includes brick walls, a camp crystal chandelier and lots of red and green laser dots. Has '80s-themed nights from 10pm every Tuesday, a house-and-electro DJ from 10pm on Friday and Saturday, and a soirée from 9pm on Sunday.

🛍 Shopping

Lille's snazziest clothing and housewares boutiques are in Vieux Lille, in the area bounded by rue de la Monnaie, rue Esquermoise, rue de la Grande Chausée (a window-shopper's paradise!) and rue d'Angleterre. Keep an eye out for shops (eg at 23 rue Masurel) specialising in French Flemish edibles, including cheeses. For midrange prices, locals often head to the hugely popular pedestrians-only zone south of place du Général de Gaulle (all near Rihour metro), including rue Neuve, rue de Béthune, rue des Tanneurs and rue du Sec-Arembault.

Maisons de Mode FASHION
(www.maisonsdemode.com) Cool, cutting-edge couture by promising young designers can be found in two clusters of studio-boutiques, Faubourg des Modes (58-60 rue du Faubourg des Postes; MPorte des Postes), about 2.5km southwest of the Palais des Beaux-Arts, and around La Piscine Musée d'Art et d'Industrie (p169), 12km northeast of Gare Lille-Europe.

L'Abbaye des Saveurs FOOD & WINE
(www.abbayedessaveurs.com; 13 rue des Vieux Murs; ⊙2-7pm Mon & Tue, 11am-7pm Wed-Sat, 11am-1.30pm Sun) A beer-lover's dream, this little shop features dozens of famous and more obscure local brews, from both the French and Belgian sides of the border.

BRADERIE DE LILLE

On the first weekend in September, Lille's entire city centre – 200km of footpaths – is transformed into the Braderie de Lille, billed as the world's largest flea market. The extravaganza – with stands selling antiques, local delicacies, handicrafts and more – dates from the Middle Ages, when Lillois servants were permitted to hawk their employers' old garments for some extra cash.

The city's biggest annual event, the Braderie runs nonstop – yes, all night long – from 2pm on Saturday to 11pm on Sunday, when street sweepers emerge to tackle the mounds of mussel shells and old *frites* (French fries) left behind by the merrymakers. Before the festivities you can make room for all those extra calories by joining in the semi-marathon (www.semimarathon-lille.fr) that begins at 9am on Saturday, or a 10km run at 11am; both set off from place de la République. Lille's tourist office can supply you with a free map of the festivities.

Fromagerie Philippe Olivier FOOD & WINE
(☑03 20 74 96 99; 3 rue du Curé St-Étienne; ☺9.30am-7.15pm Tue-Sat, 2.30-7.15pm Mon; Ⓜ️Rihour) This shop near place de Gaulle is an excellent source for local cheeses.

Le Furet du Nord BOOKS
(15 place du Général de Gaulle; Ⓜ️Rihour) One of Europe's largest bookshops. Has a good selection of English-language books, including a few Lonely Planet guides and other titles on Flanders and France.

Euralille MALL
(www.euralille.com; cnr av Le Corbusier & av Willy Brandt; ☺10am-8pm Mon-Sat; Ⓜ️Gare Lille-Flandres or Gare Lille-Europe) A vast shopping mall with 120 popularly priced shops.

❶ Information

Hôpital Roger Salengro (☑03 20 44 61 40/41; rue du Professeur Émile Laine; ☺24hr; Ⓜ️CHR B Calmette) The *accueil urgences* (emergency room/casualty ward) of Lille's vast, 15-hospital Cité Hospitalière is 4km southwest of the city centre.

International Currency Exchange (☺7.30am-8pm Mon-Sat, 10am-8pm Sun; Ⓜ️Gare Lille-Europe) Currency exchange in Gare Lille-Europe, next to *accès* (track access) H.

SOS Médecins (☑03 20 29 91 91; www.sosmedecins-france.fr; 3 av Louise Michel; ☺24hr; Ⓜ️Porte de Douai) Round-the-clock medical clinic (call ahead from 11pm to 9am) and house calls by doctors

Tourist office (from abroad ☑03 59 57 94 00, in France ☑08 91 56 20 04; www.lilletourism.com; place Rihour; ☺9am-6pm Mon-Sat, 10am-noon & 2-5pm Sun & holidays; Ⓜ️Rihour) Occupies what's left of the Flamboyant Gothic–style Palais Rihour, built in the mid-1400s for Philip the Good, duke of Burgundy; a war memorial forms the structure's eastern side. Has free maps and an excellent map-brochure (€3) outlining walking tours of five city *quartiers*. Can exchange small amounts of foreign currency but the rate is poor.

❶ Getting There & Away

Bus

Eurolines (☑08 92 89 90 91; www.eurolines.com; 23 parvis St-Maurice; Ⓜ️Gare Lille-Flandres) serves cities such as Brussels (€18, 1½ hours), Amsterdam (€43, five hours) and London (€36, 5½ hours; by day via the Channel Tunnel, at night by ferry). The bus stop is a 10-minute walk from Eurolines' ticket office; follow av Le Corbusier just past Gare Lille-Europe, then look for the stop on your left, beyond the taxi rank on bd de Leeds.

Car

Driving into Lille is incredibly confusing, even with a good map. To get to the city centre, the best thing to do is to suspend your sense of direction and blindly follow the 'Centre Ville' signs.

Parking at the **Champ de Mars** (bd de la Liberté; ☺10am-6pm, closed Sat & Sun Sep or Oct-Mar), a P+R (park-and-ride) car park 1.2km northwest of the tourist office (next to the Citadelle), costs €3.25 a day, including return travel (for up to five people) to central Lille on bus line 12 (just show the driver the card issued at the entrance barrier). On Sundays, holidays and evenings between 8pm and 7am, parking is free, but you don't get the free bus ticket .

Parking is free along some of the streets southwest of rue Solférino and up around the Maison Natale de Charles de Gaulle.

Avis, Europcar, Hertz and National-Citer have car-hire offices in Gare Lille-Europe, while domestic rental companies such as **DLM** (☑03 20 06 18 80; www.dlm.fr; 32 place de la Gare; Gare Lille-Flandres) can be found in the backstreets around Gare Lille-Flandres.

Train

Lille's two main train stations, old-fashioned Gare Lille-Flandres and ultramodern Gare Lille-Europe, are 400m apart on the eastern edge of the city centre. They are one stop apart on metro line 2 (in the Gare Lille-Europe metro station, look for the fabulous mural). Lille has been linked to Paris by rail since 1846.

Gare Lille-Flandres (MGare Lille-Flandres) Used by almost all intraregional services and almost all TGVs to Paris' Gare du Nord (€42 to €58, one hour, 14 to 18 daily).

Gare Lille-Europe (MGare Lille-Europe) Topped by what looks like a 20-storey ski boot, this ultramodern station handles province-to-province TGVs, including services to Charles de Gaulle airport (€42 to €58, one hour, at least hourly), Nice (€124 to €147, 7½ hours, two direct daily) and Strasbourg (€102 to €114, 3¼ to four hours, three direct daily); Eurostar trains to London (€82 to €133, departures are from the station's far northern end); and TGVs/Eurostars to Brussels-Nord (Monday to Friday €25, weekend & holidays €18, 35 minutes, a dozen daily).

ⓘ Getting Around

Bicycle & Segway

Station Oxygène (☑03 20 81 44 02; teamsegway@transpole; bd de la Liberté; per 30min/half-day/full day Segway €4/15/20, electric bicycle €1.50/7/10, discounted with bus ticket stamped within the hour; ☺10am-6pm Mon-Sat, 1-6pm Sun) Cruising around Lille by Segway or electric bike – it's so noughties but still really cool! Rentals are available at this shiny glass structure that resembles a hovering flying saucer, next to the Citadelle. First-time Segway riders (minimum age 18; if accompanied by an adult, 16) must take an intro lesson (€4) to get a licence (we're not kidding). Credit card deposit of €500 required. It's run by Transpole (Lille's public transport company).

Transpole Information Office (Gare Lille-Flandres, track level, place des Buisses exit; daily/weekly/yearly sign-up fee €1.40/7/36; ☺7.30am-6.30pm Mon-Fri; MGare Lille-Flandres) For information and maps regarding V'lille, Lille's ever-expanding municipal bike-hire program, visit this office just outside Gare Lille-Flandres. To hire a bike, new users (including short-term visitors) must register by paying an initial sign-up fee, either online at vlille.fr, or by using a chip-equipped credit card at one of dozens of hire depots around town. Once registered, simply pick up a bike at any hire location, then drop it off at any other location. The first half-hour of each rental is free; subsequent half-hour periods cost €1 each.

Bus, Tram & Metro

Lille's two speedy metro lines (1 and 2), two tramways (R and T), two Citadine shuttles (C1, which circles the city centre clockwise, and C2, which goes counterclockwise) and many urban and suburban bus lines – several of which cross into Belgium – are run by **Transpole** (www.transpole.fr). In the city centre, metros run every two to four minutes until about 12.30am. Useful metro stops include those at the train stations, Rihour (next to the tourist office), République Beaux Arts (near the Palais des Beaux-Arts), Gambetta (near the Wazemmes food market) and Gare Jean Lebas (near La Piscine).

Tickets (€1.40; valid for transfers for up to one hour) are sold on buses but must be purchased (and validated in the orange posts) *before* boarding a metro or tram. A *carnet* (pack) of 10 tickets costs €11.40. A Pass' Journée (all-day pass) costs €4.10 and needs to be time-stamped just once. A Pass Soirée, good for unlimited travel after 7pm, costs €2.05.

Taxi

Taxi Gare Lille (☑03 20 06 64 00; ☺24hr)
Taxi Rihour (☑03 20 55 20 56; ☺24hr)

Calais

POP 75,240

As Churchill might have put it, 'never in the field of human tourism have so many travellers passed through a place and so few stopped to visit'. There would seem to be few compelling reasons for the 15 million people who travel by way of Calais each year to stop and explore – pity the local tourist office, whose job it is to snag a few of the Britons racing south to warmer climes – but in fact the town *is* worth at least a brief stopover.

The city, a mere 34km from the English town of Dover (Douvres in French), makes a convenient base for exploring the majestic Côte d'Opale by car or public transport.

⊙ Sights & Activities

TOP CHOICE **Cité Internationale de la Dentelle et de la Mode** LACE MUSEUM (International Centre of Lace & Fashion; ☑03 21 00 42 30; www.cite-dentelle.fr; 135 quai du Commerce; adult/child €5/2.50; ☺10am-6pm Wed-Mon) Enter the intricate world of lace-making, the industry that once made Calais a textile powerhouse. The informative, cutting-edge exhibits trace the history of lace from the early centuries of hand-knotting (some stunning samples are on display). The highlight is watching a century-old mechanical

Calais

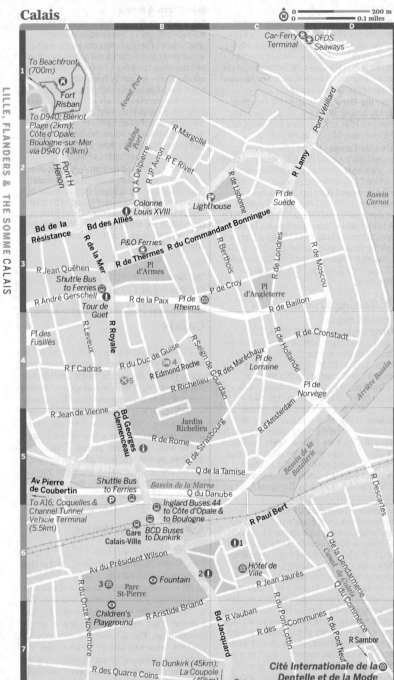

N 0 ———————— 200 m
   0 ———————— 0.1 miles

To Beachfront
(700m)

Fort Risban

To D940; Blériot Plage (2km);
Côte d'Opale;
Boulogne-sur-Mer
via D940 (43km)

Car-Ferry Terminal

DFDS Seaways

Pont H Henon

Avant Port

Fishing Port

R Margollé

Q A Delpierre

R JP Avron

R E Rivet

R de Listonne

Pont Vétillard

R Lamy

Bassin Carnot

Colonne Louis XVIII

Lighthouse

Pl de Suède

Bd de la Résistance

Bd des Alliés

R de la Mer

R Jean Quéhen

Shuttle Bus to Ferries

R André Gerschell

Tour de Guet

P&O Ferries

R de Thermes

R du Commandant Bonningue

R Berthois

R de Londres

R de Moscou

Pl d'Armes

R de la Paix

P de Croy

Pl de Rheims

Pl d'Angleterre

R de Baillon

Pl des Fusillés

R Leveux

R Royale

R F Cadras

R du Duc de Guise

R Edmond Roche

4

5

R Seign de Gourdan

R Richelieu

R des Maréchaux

Pl de Lorraine

R de Cronstadt

R de Hollande

Pl de Norvège

Arrière Bassin

R Jean de Vienne

Bd Georges Clemenceau

R de Rome

Jardin Richelieu

R de Strasbourg

R d'Amsterdam

Bassin de la Batellerie

Av Pierre de Coubertin

Shuttle Bus to Ferries

To A16; Coquelles & Channel Tunnel Vehicle Terminal (5.5km)

Q de la Tamise

Bassin de la Marne

Q du Danube

Inglard Buses 44 to Côte d'Opale & to Boulogne

Gare Calais-Ville

BCD Buses to Dunkirk

R Paul Bert

R Descartes

Q de la Gendarmerie

Canal de Calais

Q du Commerce

1

Av du Président Wilson

Fountain

2

Hôtel de Ville

R Jean Jaurès

3

Parc St-Pierre

Children's Playground

R du Onze Novembre

R Aristide Briand

R Vauban

R des Communes

R du Pont Lottin

R du Pont Neuf

R des Quarre Coins

Bd Jacquard

To Dunkirk (45km);
La Coupole (49km)

R de Vic

R Sambor

Cité Internationale de la Dentelle et de la Mode

Calais

loom with 3500 vertical threads and 11,000 horizontal ones bang, clatter and clunk according to instructions given by perforated Jacquard cards. Signs are in French, English and Dutch. Situated 500m southeast of the *hôtel de ville* (town hall building).

Burghers of Calais   SCULPTURE

In front of Calais' Flemish Renaissance-style town hall (1911–25) is Rodin's famous statue *Les Bourgeois de Calais* (The Burghers of Calais; 1895), honouring six local citizens who, in 1347, held off the besieging English forces for more than eight months. Edward III was so impressed he ultimately spared the Calaisiens and their six leaders.

Beffroi de Calais   BELL TOWER

(Town Hall Belfry; adult/child €5/3; ⊙10am-noon & 2-5.30pm, closed Mon Oct-Apr) An imposing landmark visible from anywhere in town, Calais' town hall belfry was recognised as a Unesco World Heritage Site in 2005 and opened to the public in 2011. An elevator whisks you to the top, where you can admire 360-degree views of the town and surrounding landscape.

Musée Mémoire 1939–1945   WAR MUSEUM

(✆03 21 34 21 57; adult/child incl audioguide €6/5; ⊙10am-6pm, closed Dec & Jan) Housed in a concrete bunker built as a German naval headquarters, this WWII museum displays thousands of period artefacts, including weapons, uniforms and proclamations. It's situated incongruously in flowery Parc St-Pierre, next to a boules ground and a children's playground.

Beachfront   BEACH

The unique attraction at Calais' cabin-lined beach, which begins 1km northwest of place d'Armes, is watching huge car ferries as they sail majestically to and from Dover. The sand continues westward along 8km-long, dune-lined Blériot Plage, named after the pioneer aviator Louis Blériot, who began the first ever trans-Channel flight from here in 1909. Both beaches are served by buses 3, 5 and 9.

🛏 Sleeping

Lots of budget hotels can be found along, and just east of, rue Royale. Coquelles' main claim to fame is that it's a convenient place to grab a night's sleep, thanks to the abundance of chain hotels just off the autoroute near the tunnel entrance.

Hôtel Meurice   HOTEL €€

(✆03 21 34 57 03; www.hotel-meurice.fr; 5-7 rue Edmond Roche; d €92-162; @ⓢ) This veteran downtown hotel with 39 rooms offers plenty of atmosphere, thanks to its grand lobby staircase, antique furnishings, Hemingway-esque bar and breakfast room with garden views.

Auberge de Jeunesse   HOSTEL €

(✆03 21 34 70 20; www.auberge-jeunesse-calais.com; av Maréchal de Lattre de Tassigny; dm/s/tw incl breakfast €21/28/42; ⓢ; ⎙3, 5, 9) Modern, well equipped and just 200m from the beach.

🍴 Eating

Restaurants ring place d'Armes and are plentiful just south of there along rue Royale.

TOP CHOICE **Histoire Ancienne**   BISTRO €€

(✆03 21 34 11 20; www.histoire-ancienne.com; 20 rue Royale; lunch menus €15, dinner menus €19-28; ⊙lunch & dinner Tue-Sat, lunch Mon) Specialising in French and regional dishes, some grilled over an open wood fire, this 1930s Paris-style bistro offers excellent-value lunch and dinner *menus* (fixed-price meals) in a classy dining room at the heart of town.

🛍 Shopping

Cité Europe   MALL

(www.citeeurope.com; 1001 bd du Kent; ⊙10am-8pm Mon-Thu & Sat, to 9pm Fri) Has 20 restaurants, 12 cinema screens and 140 shops, including a vast Carrefour supermarket. Situated next to the vehicle-loading area for the Channel Tunnel; from the A16, take exits 41 or 43.

L'Usine Côte d'Opale FACTORY OUTLETS
(www.usinecotedopale.fr; bd du Parc; ⊙10am-7pm Mon-Sat) Discount clothing and accessories from 80 name brands. From the A16, take exit 41.

❶ Information

Exchange rates aboard car ferries and in the terminals are atrocious. You'll find banks with cash machines downtown, but inexplicably, the ferry terminal still lacks an ATM.

Tourist office (☑03 21 96 62 40; www.calais -cotedopale.com; 12 bd Georges Clemenceau; ⊙10am-6pm Mon-Sat, to 5pm Sun) Just across the bridge (north) from the train station.

❶ Getting There & Away

You can cross the English Channel by ferry or rail.

Boat

Each day, over three dozen car ferries from Dover dock at Calais' bustling car-ferry terminal, situated about 1.5km northeast of place d'Armes.

P&O Ferries (www.poferries.com; 41 place d'Armes) and **DFDS Seaways** (☑03 28 59 01 01; www.dfdsseaways.co.uk; Ferry Terminal) both operate regular trans-Channel service. P&O accepts foot passengers; DFDS only takes passengers with vehicles.

Shuttle buses (€2, roughly hourly from 11am to 6pm) link Gare Calais-Ville (the train station) and place d'Armes (the stop is in front of Café de la Tour) with the car-ferry terminal. Departure times are posted at the stops.

Bus

Bus 44, run by **Inglard-Colvert** (☑03 21 96 36 12), makes four runs daily (except Sunday) along the breathtaking Côte d'Opale coastal road (D940), stopping in Wissant (40 minutes) and other coastal communes en route to Boulogne-sur-Mer (1½ hours). The fare is only €1 for any stop along this route.

Ligne BCD (☑08 00 62 00 59; www.ligne -bcd.com) links Calais' train station (hours posted) with Dunkirk (€8.20, 50 minutes, six daily Monday to Friday, three on Saturday).

Car & Motorcycle

To reach the Channel Tunnel's vehicle-loading area at Coquelles, about 6km southwest of Calais' town centre, follow the road signs on the A16 to 'Tunnel Sous La Manche' (Tunnel Under the Channel) and get off at exit 42.

ADA, Europcar, Hertz and National-Citer have offices inside the car-ferry terminal but they're not always staffed. Avis hires cars from the train station downtown.

Train

Calais has two train stations, linked by trains and a navette (shuttle bus; €2, free with train ticket).

Gare Calais-Ville, in the city centre, has direct services to Amiens (€25.30, 2½ to 3½ hours, six or seven daily), Boulogne (€7.70, 30 minutes, 19 daily Monday to Friday, 11 on Saturday, six on Sunday), Dunkirk (€8.60, 50 minutes, four to six Monday to Friday, two Saturday) and Lille-Flandres (€17.30, 1¼ hours, 19 daily Monday to Friday, eight to 10 daily on weekend).

Gare Calais-Fréthun, a TGV station 10km southwest of town near the Channel Tunnel entrance, is served by TGVs to Paris' Gare du Nord (€44 to €61, 1¾ hours, six daily Monday to Saturday, three on Sunday) as well as Eurostars to London St Pancras (from €96, one hour, three daily).

Côte d'Opale

For a dramatic and beautiful introduction to France, head to the 40km of cliffs, sand dunes and beaches between Calais and Boulogne, known as the Côte d'Opale (Opal Coast) because of the ever-changing interplay of greys and blues in the sea and sky. The coastal peaks (frequently buffeted by gale-force winds), wide beaches and rolling farmland are dotted with the remains of Nazi Germany's Atlantic Wall, a chain of fortifications and gun emplacements built to prevent the Allied invasion that in the end took place in Normandy. The seashore has been attracting British beach lovers since the Victorian era.

Part of the Parc Naturel Régional des Caps et Marais d'Opale (www.parc-opale. fr), the Côte d'Opale area is criss-crossed by hiking paths, including the GR120 trail (red-and-white trail markings) that hugs the coast – except where the cliffs are in danger of collapse. Some routes are also suitable for mountain biking and horse riding. Each village along the Côte d'Opale has at least one campground, and most have places to eat.

By car, the D940 offers some truly spectacular vistas.

The Channel Tunnel slips under the Strait of Dover 8km west of Calais at the village of Sangatte, known for its wide beach. Southwest of there, the coastal dunes give way to cliffs that culminate in windswept, 134m-high Cap Blanc-Nez, which affords breathtaking views of the Bay of Wissant, the port of Calais, the Flemish countryside (pock-marked by Allied bomb craters) and the distant cliffs of Kent. The grey obelisk (erected 1922), a short walk up the hill from the parking area, honours the WWI Dover Patrol. Paths lead to a number of massive, concrete German bunkers and gun emplacements.

The tidy and very French seaside resort of Wissant is a good base for walks in the rolling countryside and along the beach between Cap Blanc-Nez and Cap Gris-Nez; pick up a free trail map and check the tides at the tourist office (☎08 20 20 76 00; ☺9.30am-noon & 2-6pm Mon-Sat, 10am-1pm & 3-6pm Sun) before setting out or you may get trapped between a rock and a wet place. Wissant boasts a vast fine-sand beach where you can admire England from afar – in 55 BC Julius Caesar launched his invasion of Britain from here.

Hôtel Le Vivier (☎03 21 35 93 61; www.le vivier.com; place de l'Église; d incl breakfast €60-90; ☎), opposite Wissant's church and a couple of blocks from the beach, has 39 nicely appointed rooms. Nearby are several other hotels and a pair of delightfully down-to-earth restaurants: Le Charlemagne (☎03 21 35 90 67; rue Gambetta; menus €15; ☺lunch & dinner daily), with its bustling bar and homey back dining room, and Chez Nicole (☎03 21 35 90 42; rue Gambetta; mussels & frites €9; ☺lunch & dinner daily), which serves ridiculously large and reasonably priced heaps of local mussels and *frites* (chips). For those with a vehicle, the family-friendly Hôtel-Restaurant L'Escale (☎03 21 85 25 09; www.hotel-lescale. com; rue de la Mer; s from €36, d €64-82, q €95; ☎) in neighbouring Escalles is another good option, tucked into a deep, verdant valley that leads straight down to the ocean.

Historic farm buildings in the countryside 5km south of Wissant house one of northern

France's best microbreweries, Brasserie Artisanale des 2 Caps (☎03 21 10 56 53; www.2caps.fr; Ferme de Belle Dalle, Tardinghen; tours €4.50; ☺10am-7pm Fri & Sat Sep-Jun, daily Jul & Aug). The shop and tasting room is open Fridays and Saturdays year-round, and brewmaster Christophe Noyon offers occasional 90-minute tours of the premises.

Topped by a lighthouse and a radar station serving the 600 ships that pass by each day, the 45m-high cliffs of Cap Gris-Nez are only 28km from the white cliffs of the English coast. The name – Grey Nose – is a corruption of the archaic English 'craig ness', meaning 'rocky promontory'. The area is a stopping-off point for millions of migrating birds.

Oodles of WWII hardware, including a massive, rail-borne German artillery piece with a range of 86km, are on display at the Musée du Mur de l'Atlantique (Atlantic Wall Museum; ☎03 21 32 97 33; www.batterietodt.com; adult/child €8/4; ☺10am-noon & 2-5pm Mon-Fri, 2-6pm Sat & Sun, closed mid-Nov–mid-Feb), housed in a Brobdingnagian German pillbox. It is just southwest of Audinghen, 500m off D940.

The village of Ambleteuse, on the northern side of the mouth of the River Slack, is blessed with a lovely beach that was once defended from attack by the 17th-century Fort d'Ambleteuse, designed by Vauban (that's why it's also known as Fort Vauban). Just south of town is a protected area of grass-covered dunes known as Dunes de la Slack.

The neatly organised Musée 39-45 (☎03 21 87 33 01; www.musee3945.com; adult/ child €7.40/5; ☺10am-6pm, weekends only Mar & Nov, closed Dec-Feb), at the northern edge

LA COUPOLE

A top-secret subterranean V2 rocket launch site just five minutes' flying time from London – almost (but not quite) put into operation in 1944 – now houses La Coupole (☎03 21 12 27 27; www.lacoupole-france.com; adult/child/family incl audioguide €9.50/6.50/24; ☺9am-6pm Sep-Jun, 10am-7pm Jul & Aug, closed 2 weeks in Dec), an innovative museum that uses film and images to present information on the following:

» Nazi Germany's secret programs to build V1 and V2 rockets, which could fly at 650km/h and an astounding 5780km/h respectively

» Life in northern France during the Nazi occupation

» The postwar conquest of space with the help of V2 rocket technology – and seconded V2 engineers

La Coupole is 49km southeast of Calais just outside the town of Wizernes, near the intersection of D928 and D210. From the A26, take exit 3 or 4.

of Ambleteuse, features realistic tableaux of WWII military and civilian life, and a 25-minute film. The dashing but wildly impractical French officers' dress uniforms of 1931 hint at why France fared so badly on the battlefield in 1940. Popular wartime songs accompany your visit.

Boulogne-sur-Mer

POP 44,070

The most interesting of France's Channel ports, Boulogne makes a pretty good first stop in France, especially if combined with a swing north through the Côte d'Opale. The Basse Ville (Lower City) is an uninspiring assemblage of postwar structures but the attractive Ville Haute (Upper City), perched high above the rest of town, is girded by a 13th-century wall. The biggest draw is Nausicaä, one of Europe's premier aquariums.

Auguste Mariette (1821–81), the archaeologist who founded Cairo's Egyptian Museum, was born here, which is why Boulogne has a number of sculptures and artefacts related to the Pharaohs.

◉ Sights

Nausicaä   AQUARIUM
(French Sea Experience Centre; ☑03 21 30 99 99; www.nausicaa.fr; bd Ste-Beuve; adult/student/child €17.95/12.50/11.70, audioguide €3.50; ⊙9.30am-6.30pm, closed 3 weeks in Jan) This superb aquarium complex, a few hundred metres north of the fishing port along quai Gambetta, lets you get up close and personal with see-through jellyfish, 250kg adult sharks (compare them to the shark eggs and hatchlings housed in a tiny tank), toothy speckled caimans (in the Submerged Forest), North Sea fish you usually see *au beurre* or *au gratin*, and arawanas, fish that can hop out of the water to pluck birds from overhanging branches (wearers of fancy feathered hats, beware!). Kid-friendly activities include feeding sessions and fish petting. Also a hit with younger visitors: California sea lions and African penguins, including young 'uns hatched right here. Details on the day's activities appear on flat-screen bulletin boards. All signs are in French and English.

Ville Haute   HISTORIC QUARTER
You can walk all the way around the Upper City – a hilltop island of centuries-old buildings and cobblestone streets – atop the rectangular, tree-shaded ramparts, a distance

of just under 1.5km. Among the impressive buildings around place Godefroy de Bouillon are the neoclassical **Hôtel Desandrouin** (17 rue du Puits d'Amour), built in the 1780s and later used by Napoléon, and the brick **Hôtel de Ville** (1735), with its square medieval belfry (ground floor accessible through the lobby).

The cultures of the world mix and mingle inside the **Château-Musée** (Castle Museum; ☑03 21 10 02 20; adult/child €3/free; ⊙museum 10am-12.30pm & 2-5.30pm, closed Tue, courtyard 7am-7pm daily), one of the few places on earth where you can admire Egyptian antiquities (including a mummy) next to 19th-century Inuit masks and compare Andean ceramics with Grecian urns, with an in-situ 4th-century Roman wall thrown in for good measure – all inside a 13th-century fortified castle.

Basilique Notre Dame (rue de Lille; ⊙10am-noon & 2-5pm), its towering, Italianate dome visible from all over town (and best admired from the ramparts), is an odd structure built from 1827 to 1866 with little input from trained architects. The partly Romanesque crypt and treasury are eminently skippable.

FREE **Museo Libertador San Martín**   MUSEUM
(www.ambassadeargentine.net; 113 Grande Rue; ⊙10am-noon & 2-6pm Tue-Sat, closed Jan & 2 weeks Jul) Boulogne's most unexpected sight is the house where José de San Martín, the exiled hero of Argentine, Chilean and Peruvian independence, died in 1850. Ring the bell to visit an expatriated slice of 19th-century South America, complete with memorabilia related to San Martín's life and lots of gaudy military uniforms. Owned by the Argentine government, it is staffed by Argentine army personnel.

Basse Ville   NEIGHBOURHOOD
Boulogne's Basse Ville is dominated by its fishing port (quai Gambetta). Hungry seagulls dive and squawk overhead as they survey the fishing boats and the *poissonniers* (fishmongers) selling freshly landed *cabillaud* (Atlantic cod), *carrelet* (plaice) and sole – Boulogne's most important commercial fish – as well as *bar* (sea bass), mullet, *raie* (skate) and turbot. Take a good look so you know what you're getting next time you order *poisson* (fish).

Also in the Lower Town, a few blocks inland from the port, you'll find Boulogne's lively shopping precinct, centred on rue Victor Hugo and rue Adolphe Thiers.

Seashore
BEACHES

Boulogne's beach begins just north of Nausicaä, across the mouth of the Liane from a whirring wind farm on the one-time site of a steelworks.

There are other fine beaches 4km north of town at Wimereux (served two to four times per hour by buses 1 and 2 from place de France), a partly belle époque–style resort founded by Napoléon in 1806; 2.5km southwest at Le Portel (bus 23 from place de France); and 5km south at Equihen Plage (bus Ea or Eb from the train station or place de France). Note: Sunday bus numbers end in 'd'.

🛏 Sleeping

Hôtel La Matelote
HOTEL €€

(✆03 21 30 33 33; www.la-matelote.com; 70 bd Ste-Beuve; d Sun-Thu €100-160, Fri, Sat & holidays €125-195; ✿🀫🛜🎱) Boulogne's plushest hotel has a luxurious jacuzzi, *hammam* (Turkish steambath) and dry sauna. The 35 spacious rooms, many decorated in rich shades of red and gold, have ultramodern bathrooms and classic wood furnishings, and some come with balconies. Wheelchair access available. It's situated a few hundred metres north of the fishing port along quai Gambetta.

Les Terrasses de l'Enclos
B&B €€

(✆03 91 90 05 90; www.enclosdeleveche.com; 6 rue Pressy; d €85-120) Charmingly situated at the top of the old town, this five-room B&B in a converted 19th-century mansion offers high-ceilinged rooms, parquet wood floors and an attached restaurant with a pleasant stone-paved courtyard.

Auberge de Jeunesse
HOSTEL €

(✆03 21 99 15 30; www.fuaj.org; place Rouget de Lisle; dm/s incl breakfast & sheets €21/33; ✿closed 22 Dec-31 Jan; @🛜) Facing the train station, about 1km south of the Basse Ville, this 137-bed outfit has a bar, kitchen facilities, a lounge area and spacious two- to five-bed rooms with en suite bathrooms.

🍴 Eating & Drinking

Thanks to its ready supply, Boulogne is an excellent place for fresh fish (everything except the salmon is likely to have been landed locally). In the Basse Ville you can build a gourmet picnic in the shops surrounding the biweekly market at place Dalton: cheese from Fromagerie Gérard Delpierre (23 Grande Rue; ✿closed Mon morning & Sun), wine from Trésor de Vin (12 rue Adolphe Thiers; ✿closed Sun & Mon) and delicious baked goods from Dessert ou Dessert Autrement (35 Grande Rue; ✿closed Sun afternoon, Mon & Tue).

La Matelote
SEAFOOD €€

(✆03 21 30 17 97; 80 bd Ste-Beuve; menus €31-75; ✿restaurant closed lunch Thu, bistro closed dinner Mon, plus dinner Sun Sep-May) A stylish Michelin-starred establishment with white tablecloths, paper-thin wine glasses, fine porcelain and a focus on fish and seafood, La Matelote also runs the excellent beach-view bistro inside Nausicaä.

L'îlot Vert
SEAFOOD

(36 rue de Lille; menus €17; ✿closed Wed & Sun) One of several eateries lining rue de Lille, just above the *hôtel de ville* in the upper town.

Marché
FOOD MARKET €

(place Dalton; ✿morning Wed & Sat) Boulogne's lively biweekly fruit and vegetable market.

ℹ Information

Several commercial banks can be found on or near rue Victor Hugo.

Tourist office (✆03 21 10 88 10; www.tourisme-boulognesurmer.com; parvis de Nausicaä; ✿10am-12.30pm & 1.45-6pm Mon-Sat, 10.30am-1pm & 2.30-5pm Sun; 🛜) Helpful staff, English brochures and free wi-fi.

Tourist office annexe (forum Jean Noël; ✿9.30am-12.30pm & 1.45-6pm Mon-Sat) In an octagonal pavilion 600m south of the main tourist office.

ℹ Getting There & Around

BOAT At the time of research, all ferries from Boulogne to England had been indefinitely discontinued, leaving Calais and Dunkirk (Dunkerque) as the only ports in the region with trans-Channel passenger service. Check with the tourist office for updates.

BUS Buses go to Calais via the gorgeous Côte d'Opale. For details, see p180.

TAXI To order a cab, call ✆03 21 91 25 00.

TRAIN The main train station, Gare Boulogne-Ville, is 1.2km southeast of the centre. Destinations include Amiens (€19.70, 1½ hours, seven to nine daily), Calais-Ville (€7.70, 30 minutes, 19 daily Monday to Friday, 11 on Saturday, six on Sunday), Gare Lille-Flandres or Gare Lille-Europe (€22.90, one to two hours, nine to 12 daily) and Paris' Gare du Nord (€35, 2¾ hours, four or five direct daily).

Boulogne-sur-Mer

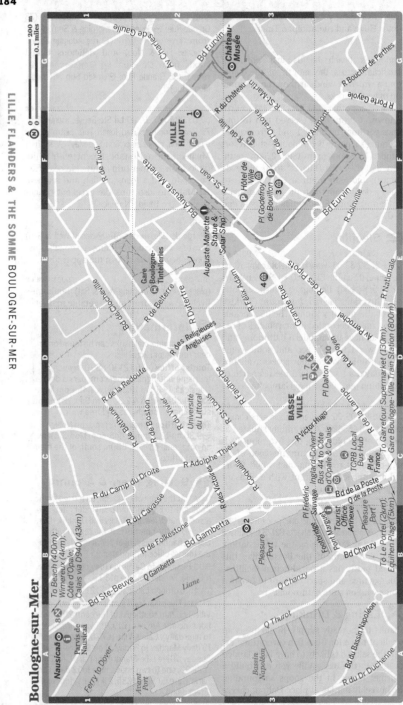

N
0   200 m
0   0.1 miles

VILLE HAUTE

BASSE VILLE

Château-Musée

Gare Boulogne-Tintelleries

Auguste Mariette Statue & 'Solar Ship'

Hôtel de Ville

Pl Godefroy de Bouillon

Pl Dalton

R Victor Hugo

Pl Frédéric Sauvage

Pont Marguet

Footbridge

Tourist Office Annexe

Pl de France

TCRB Local Bus Hub

Pleasure Port

Pleasure Port

Liane

Bassin Napoléon

Avant Port

Parvis de Nausicaä

Nausicaä

To Beach (400m); Wimereux (4km); Côte d'Opale; Calais via D940 (43km)

To Garrefour Supermarket (130m); Gare Boulogne-Ville Train Station (800m)

To Le Portel (2km); Équihen Plage (5km)

Inglard-Colvert Bus 44 to Côte d'Opale & Calais

Boulogne-sur-Mer

◎ Top Sights
Château-Musée G3
Nausicaä...A1

◎ Sights
1 Basilique Notre Dame F2
2 Fishing Port B3
3 Hôtel Desandrouin..............................F3
4 Museo Libertador San Martín............E3

◎ Sleeping
Hôtel La Matelote ....(see 8)
5 Les Terrasses de l'Enclos F2

◎ Eating
6 Dessert ou Dessert Autrement D3
7 Fromagerie Gérard Delpierre D3
8 La Matelote A1
9 L'îlot Vert F3
10 Marché D4

◎ Drinking
11 Trésor de Vin.......................................D3

Dunkirk

POP 94,450

In 1940 Dunkirk (Dunkerque) – the name means 'church of the dunes' in Flemish – became world famous and was flattened, almost simultaneously. Rebuilt during one of the most uninspired periods in the entire history of Western architecture, the modern city has precious little charm but does offer visitors worthwhile museums, a family-popular beach and colourful pre-Lent carnivals.

◉ Sights & Activities

The Musée Portuaire (Harbour Museum; www.museeportuaire.com; 9 quai de la Citadelle; adult/child/family €5/4/13; ⊙10am-12.45pm & 1.30-6pm Wed-Mon), housed in a one-time tobacco warehouse, will delight fans of maritime history and, especially, of model ships. Guided tours (adult/child/family incl museum €12.50/10/30; ⊙3.30pm Wed & Sun) of the adjacent harbor take visitors aboard a lighthouse ship, a *peniche* (barge) and the *Duchesse Anne*, a three-masted training ship built for the German merchant marine in 1901 and acquired by France as WWII reparations. Some signs are in English. It's situated 500m northwest of the tourist office.

To get a feel for the 1940 evacuation of Dunkirk, drop by the not-for-profit Mémo-

rial du Souvenir (www.dynamo-dunkerque. com; Courtines du Bastion 32; adult/child €4.50/ free; ⊙10am-noon & 2-5pm Apr-Sep), staffed by dedicated volunteers, most with personal ties to this period in history. Highlights include a 12-minute film, scale models, evocative period uniforms, weapons, photos and an ever-expanding collection of WWII-related objects discovered in the Dunkirk area.

The Dunkirk British Memorial (D601), honouring over 4500 British and Commonwealth soldiers 'with no known grave', is next to a Commonwealth military cemetery 1.5km southeast of the tourist office.

Malo-les-Bains, 2km northeast of Dunkirk's city centre, is a faded turn-of-the-20th-century seaside resort; its broad, sandy beach, Plage des Alliés, is named in honour of the Allied troops evacuated to England during Operation Dynamo. A bit to the northeast, off Zuydecoote, the wrecks of vessels sunk in 1940 can be visited on scuba dives, and a handful are accessible on foot during especially low tides (the tourist office has details of guided tours).

Stretching east from Malo-les-Bains to the Belgian border, the Dunes Flamandes (Flemish Dunes) represent a unique ecosystem harbouring hundreds of plant species, including rare orchids. Tides permitting, you can walk or cycle along the wet sand or the GR path from Malo-les-Bains to Leffrinckoucke, Zuydcoote and Bray-Dunes.

✗ Eating

Restaurants can be found along quai de la Citadelle and facing the beach in Malo-les-Bains (along digue des Alliés and digue de Mer).

⊙ Information

Tourist Office (☏03 28 66 79 21; www. ot-dunkerque.fr; ⊙9.30am-12.30pm & 1.30-6.30pm Mon-Sat, 10am-noon & 2-4pm Sun & holidays) Has a free brochure, *Dunkirk Wartime Memories,* on WWI and WWII. It's situated in the base of a 58m-high belfry (adult/child €2.90/2) erected around 1440, with spectacular views and a renovated 50-bell carillon that sounds every quarter-hour.

⊙ Getting There & Away

DFDS Seaways (www.dfdsseaways.co.uk) offers regular ferry service from Dover (England) to Dunkirk's car-ferry port, about 15km west of the town centre at Loon Plage (A16 exit 53).

EVACUATION OF DUNKIRK

In late May of 1940, as Nazi armies closed in, 1400 naval vessels and 'little ships' – fishing boats and pleasure craft crewed by civilian volunteers – braved intense German artillery and air attacks to ferry 340,000 Allied soldiers to the safety of England. Conducted in the difficult first year of WWII, this unplanned and chaotic evacuation – dubbed Operation Dynamo – failed to save any heavy equipment but was nevertheless seen as a heroic demonstration of Britain's resourcefulness and determination.

Buses travel to/from Calais. For details, see p180.

Dunkirk's train station is 1km southwest of the tourist office. Rail destinations include Lille (mainly to Gare Lille-Flandres; €14.30, 30 to 75 minutes, 20 direct daily Monday to Friday, 10 to 13 daily weekends) and Calais (€8.60, 50 minutes, four to six daily Monday to Friday, two or three on Saturday).

Cassel

POP 2390

At the summit of French Flanders' highest hill (though at 176m it's hardly Mont Blanc), the fortified, quintessentially Flemish village of Cassel offers panoramic views of the verdant Flanders plain.

Thanks to its elevated position, Cassel served as Maréchal Ferdinand Foch's headquarters at the beginning of WWI. In 1940 it was the site of intensive rearguard resistance by British troops defending Dunkirk during the evacuation.

The main square, fringed by austere brick buildings with steep slate roofs, is where you'll find the newly renovated Musée Départemental de Flandre (22 Grand' Place; adult/child €5/free; 10am-12.30pm & 2-6pm Tue-Sat, 10am-6pm Sun), which spotlights Flanders' rich heritage and showcases Flemish art both old and new.

Ten generations ago, wheat flour was milled and linseed oil pressed just as it is today at the wooden moulin (windmill; adult/child €3/2.50; 2-6pm Mon-Sat, 10am-12.30pm & 2-6pm Sun, weekends only Oct-Mar), perched on the highest point in town to catch the wind. Knowledgeable mill-keeper Franck Becquart offers excellent 45-minute tours in which he demonstrates the internal workings of the mill and explains the historical and cultural context of windmills in French Flanders; during the 19th century the region's skyline was dotted with 2000 such windmills! Nearby, you can peer into Belgium from a flowery park; two orientation tables point to cities near and far.

Cassel's citizens are enormously proud of Reuze Papa and Reuze Maman, the resident giants (see boxed text, p168), who are feted on Easter Monday. A bagpipe festival is held in Cassel on a weekend in early to mid-June.

On Cassel's main square, Hôtel Le Foch (03 28 42 47 73; www.hotel-foch.net; 41 Grand' Place; s/d €60/69;) has six spacious rooms with antique-style beds, some with views of the square. The town also boasts a few superbly atmospheric estaminets, home-style restaurants serving Flemish specialities. Best of all is Het Kasteelhof (03 28 40 59 29; http://lvermeersch.free.fr/kasteelhof; 8 rue St-Nicolas; mains €10-12; lunch & dinner Thu-Sun), the self-proclaimed 'highest estaminet in Flanders'. Directly across from Cassel's hilltop windmill, it's got two cozy and crowded rooms connected by a ridiculously narrow and steep staircase which waitresses somehow manage to navigate with glasses of walnut liqueur, mugs of Flemish beer and plattersful of sausages, hearty soups and casseroles. For dessert, don't miss its Speculoos ice cream, and as you exit, peek in its store downstairs for uniquely Flemish treats that you're unlikely to find elsewhere in France. Other worthwhile Flemish eateries on the main square include Kerelshof (03 28 48 06 75; 31 Grand' Place; mains €7.50-11.50; lunch & dinner Thu-Sun), with folksy decor, beamed ceilings, a pair of fireplaces trimmed in cheery shades of blue and several local beers on tap, and Taverne Flamande (03 28 42 42 59; 34 Grand' Place; menus €27; closed Wed & dinner Tue), the classic 1933 dining room of which has red banquettes, red-and-white checked tablecloths and, on cold days, a crackling fire.

The tourist office (03 28 40 52 55; www.cassel-horizons.com; 20 Grand' Place; 8.30am-noon & 1.30-5.45pm Mon-Sat, 2-6pm Sun) is on the main square.

Cassel is 57km southeast of Calais. Cassel's train station, 3km down the hill from the centre, has direct services to Dunkirk (€6.20, 25 minutes, nine daily Monday to Friday, two or three daily on weekends).

Baie de Somme

The **Somme Estuary** (www.baiedesomme.org) affords delightfully watery views as the cycle of the tides alternately hides and reveals vast expanses of sand. **Le Crotoy** (population 2300), a modest beach resort on the northern bank, and **St-Valery-sur-Somme** (population 2910), with its attractive tree-lined promenade and medieval quarter on the southern bank, both make good bases for exploring the area. The towns are linked by a **bike path** (www.baiecyclette.com) and a **tourist train** (www.cfbs.eu; adult/child €12.60/9.50), or by a knee-deep slog through the bay at low tide year-round; the latter should only be undertaken with a guide, as the area is notorious for strong currents and galloping tides; contact **Promenade en Baie** (✆03 22 27 47 36; www.promenade-en-baie.com; 5 allée des Soupirs, Le Crotoy). Numerous operators offer kayak trips around the estuary, affording views of duck-hunting huts and the colony of sandbank-lounging seals at Pointe du Hourdel.

Le Crotoy's **tourist office** (www.tourisme-crotoy.com; 1 rue Carnot; ⏲9.30am-12.30pm & 2-6pm Wed-Mon) can supply you with an *horaire des marées* (tide schedule).

Sleeping & Eating

Les Tourelles €

(✆03 22 27 16 33; www.lestourelles.com; 2-4 rue Pierre Guerlain; s €60, d €75-106; @📶) Overlooking Le Crotoy's beach, this sprawling family-run hotel has a bracing Victorian feel. Kids aged four to 14 can stay in a room with 14 bunk beds (€28 per child including breakfast). The attached restaurant (mains €24 to €36) serves French cuisine with Channel Coast touches and offers veggie and locavore options.

Le Relais Guillaume de Normandie HOTEL €

(✆03 22 60 82 36; www.relais-guillaume-de-normandy.com; Quai du Romerel; s €58, d €68-82; 📶) Perfectly positioned between St-Valery's medieval town and the tree-lined bay, this gingerbread mansion houses a hotel and an acclaimed restaurant.

Parc Ornithologique du Marquenterre

An astonishing 360 species of bird have been sighted at the 2.6-sq-km **Marquenterre Ornithological Park** (✆03 22 25 68 99; www.parcdumarquenterre.com; adult/child/family €10.50/7.90/33.80, binoculars €4; ⏲10am-7.30pm, last entry 5pm), an important migratory stopover between the UK, Iceland, Scandinavia and Siberia and the warmer climes of West Africa. Three marked **walking circuits** (2km to 6km) take you to marshes, dunes, meadows, freshwater ponds, a brackish lagoon and 14 observation posts, or you can tour the park by horse-drawn cart. It's in St-Quentin-en-Tourmont, a circuitous 10km northwest of Le Crotoy.

Amiens

POP 137,030

One of France's most awe-inspiring Gothic cathedrals is reason enough to spend time in Amiens, the comfy, if reserved, former capital of Picardy, where Jules Verne spent the last two decades of his life. The mostly pedestrianised city centre, rebuilt after WWII, is complemented by lovely green spaces along the Somme river. Some 25,000 students give the town a youthful feel.

Amiens is an excellent base for visits to the Battle of the Somme Memorials.

CROSS-DRESSING & AIRBORNE HERRINGS *DANIEL ROBINSON*

Dunkirk's carnivals, held both before and (mischievously) after the beginning of Lent, originated as a final fling for the town's cod fishermen before they set out for months in the frigid waters off Iceland. The biggest celebration is the *bande* (parade) held on the Sunday before Mardi Gras, when men traditionally dress up as women, costumed citizens of all genders march around town behind fife-and-drum bands, and general merriment reigns. At the climax of the festivities, the mayor and other dignitaries stand on the *hôtel de ville* (town hall building) balcony and pelt the assembled locals with dried salted herrings.

Once, in the Dunkirk suburb of St-Pol-sur-Mer, I caught one of Hizzoner's flying herrings. I was so very pleased with myself that, while I repeatedly deemed the fish unsuitable for lunch, I couldn't quite bring myself to throw it out either. So there it stayed, on the floor of my car, for weeks on end, with predictably unpleasant results...

⊙ Sights & Activities

TOP CHOICE Cathédrale Notre Dame CATHEDRAL
(place Notre Dame; audioguide 1st/2nd person €4/3, north tower adult/child €5.50/free; ☉cathedral 8.30am-6.15pm daily, north tower afternoon only Wed-Mon) The largest Gothic cathedral in France (it's 145m long) and a Unesco World Heritage Site, this magnificent structure was begun in 1220 to house the skull of St John the Baptist, shown – framed in gold and jewels – in the northern outer wall of the ambulatory. Connoisseurs rave about the soaring Gothic arches (42.3m-high over the transept), unity of style and immense interior, but for locals, the 17th-century statue known as the Ange Pleureur (Crying Angel), in the ambulatory directly behind the over-the-top Baroque (18th-century) high altar, remains a favourite.

The octagonal, 234m-long labyrinth on the black-and-white floor of the nave is easy to miss as the soaring vaults draw the eye upward. Plaques in the south transept arm honour American, Australian, British, Canadian and New Zealand soldiers who perished in WWI.

To get a sense of what you're seeing, it's worth hiring a one-hour audioguide, available in six languages, at the tourist office (across the street). Weather permitting, it's possible to climb the north tower; tickets are sold in the boutique to the left as you approach the west facade.

A free 45-minute light show bathes the cathedral's facade in vivid medieval colours nightly from mid-June to mid-September and December to 1 January; the photons start flying at 7pm in winter and sometime between 9.45pm (September) and 10.45pm (June) in summer.

Hortillonnages BOAT TOUR
(☎03 22 92 12 18; 54 bd Beauvillé; adult/child €5.90/5.20; ☉1.30-4.30pm) Amiens' market gardens – some 3 sq km in extent – have

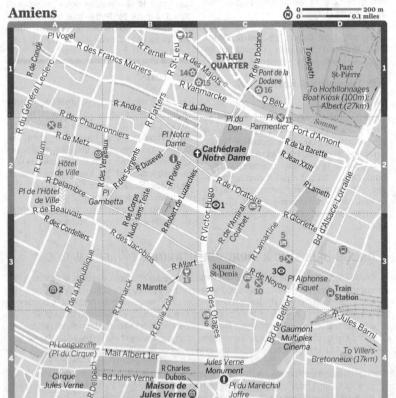

Amiens

supplied the city with vegetables and flowers since the Middle Ages. Today their peaceful *rieux* (waterways), home to seven working farms, over 1000 private gardens and countless water birds, can be visited on 12-person boats the raised prows of which make them look a bit like gondolas. Available later (to 6.30pm) if weather and demand allow.

Maison de Jules Verne   HOUSE MUSEUM
(Home of Jules Verne; ☑03 22 45 45 75; www.jules-verne.net; 2 rue Charles Dubois; adult/child €7/3.50, audioguide €2; ☉10am-12.30pm & 2-6.30pm Mon & Wed-Fri, 2-6.30pm Tue, 11am-6.30pm Sat & Sun) Jules Verne (1828–1905) wrote many of his best-known works of brain-tingling – and eerily prescient – science fiction under the eaves of this turreted Amiens home. The models, prints, posters and other items inspired by Verne's fecund imagination afford a fascinating opportunity to check out the future as he envisioned it over a century ago, when going around the world in 80 days sounded utterly fantastic – and before WWI dashed Europeans' belief in a world destined to improve thanks to 'progress'. Signs are in French and English.

Musée de Picardie   MUSEUM
(☑03 22 97 14 00; www.amiens.fr/musees; 48 rue de la République; adult/child €5/free; ☉10am-12.30pm & 2-6pm Tue-Sat, to 9pm Thu, 2-7pm Sun) Housed in a dashing Second Empire structure (1855–67) with a jaw-droppingly impressive central room, the Picardy Museum is surprisingly well endowed with archaeological exhibits, medieval art and Revolution-era ceramics.

Galerie du Vitrail Claude Barre   STAINED GLASS
(☑03 22 91 81 18; 40 rue Victor Hugo; adult/child €6/3; ☉tours 3pm Mon-Sat) Ever wonder how stained glass is designed and put together? You can see firsthand at this workshop, the artisans of which fill commissions from churches and private collectors.

Tour Perret   ARCHITECTURE
(place Alphonse Fiquet) Long the tallest building in western Europe, the reinforced concrete Perret Tower (110m), facing the train station, was designed by Belgian architect Auguste Perret (who also planned postwar Le Havre) and completed in 1954. Not open to visitors.

🛏 Sleeping
Amiens' hotels offer excellent value for money but often fill up with businesspeople from Monday to Thursday.

Grand Hôtel de l'Univers   HOTEL €€
(☑03 22 91 52 51; www.hotel-univers-amiens.com; 2 rue de Noyon; s €67-89, d €88-156; @🛜) This venerable, Best Western–affiliated hostelry has an enviable parkside location in the city's pedestrianised heart, one block from the train station. The 41 rooms, set around a four-storey atrium, are immaculate and very comfortable; some on the 4th floor even come with views of the cathedral.

Hôtel Victor Hugo   HOTEL €
(☑03 22 91 57 91; www.hotel-a-amiens.com; 2 rue de l'Oratoire; r €46-70; 🛜) Just a block from the cathedral, this friendly, family-run two-star hotel has 10 simple but comfortable rooms. Best value, if you don't mind a long stair climb, are the welcoming top-floor units

LILLE, FLANDERS & THE SOMME AMIENS

(rooms 7 and 8) with rooftop views and lots of natural light.

Hôtel Le St-Louis   HOTEL €
(☎03 22 91 76 03; www.le-saintlouis.com; 24 rue des Otages; d €67-71, q €108; 🕲) All the mod cons combined with more than a dash of 19th-century French class. The 24 rooms, some off a decklike inner courtyard, are spacious and tasteful.

Hôtel Central & Anzac   HOTEL €
(☎03 22 91 34 08; www.hotelcentralanzac.com; 17 rue Alexandre Fatton; s €35-51, d €41-57; 🕲) Founded decades ago by an Australian ex-serviceman, this place near the train station has 26 clean, well-maintained rooms, including five cheapies with shared bathroom.

✕ Eating

The St-Leu Quarter (quai Bélu) – picturesque, though not quite the 'northern Venice' it's touted to be – is lined with neon-lit riverside restaurants and pubs, many featuring warm-season terraces with views up to the cathedral. There are more places to eat across the river at place du Don.

Le T'chiot Zinc   BISTRO €
(☎03 22 91 43 79; 18 rue de Noyon; menus €13-27; ⊘closed Sun, also closed Mon Jul & Aug) Inviting, bistro-style decor reminiscent of the belle époque provides a fine backdrop for the tasty French and Picard cuisine, including fish dishes and *caqhuse* (pork in a cream, wine vinegar and onion sauce). The proper, Picard pronunciation of the restaurant's name is 'shtyoh-zang'.

Le Bouchon   FRENCH €€
(☎03 22 92 14 32; www.lebouchon.fr; 10 rue Alexandre Fatton; lunch menus Mon-Fri €18, other menus €20-42; ⊘closed dinner Sun) The decor is a bit sparse but the traditional cuisine is good value, encompassing French classics such as white asparagus and roast duck breast with new potatoes, followed by tasty desserts including a raspberry, almond and mascarpone cake.

La Tante Jeanne   CRÊPERIE €
(www.restaurant-tantejeanne.com; 1 rue de la Dodane; menus €12-16; ⊘lunch & dinner daily) Down in the Saint-Leu neighborhood, this is a good spot for an afternoon snack or a lighter meal, with crispy galettes, a variety of salads and views from the footpath tables in warm weather.

Self-Catering

Marché sur l'eau   FOOD MARKET €
(place Parmentier; ⊘to 12.30pm Sat, to 1pm in summer) Fruit and vegetables grown in the Hortillonnages are sold at this one-time floating market, now held on dry land on Saturday mornings throughout the year. A special market is also held on the third Sunday in June, when producers don traditional outfits and bring their produce downriver in high-prowed, gondola-like boats.

Covered Market   FOOD MARKET €
(rue de Metz; ⊘9am-1pm & 3-7pm Tue-Thu, 9am-7pm Fri & Sat, 8.30am-12.30pm Sun) Amiens' popular covered market features two dozen vendors selling fresh fruit, vegetables, seafood and baked goods.

🍷 Drinking

TOP CHOICE **Café Bissap**   CAFE, BAR
(☎03 22 92 36 41; 50 rue St-Leu; ⊘4pm-1am Mon-Fri, 6pm-1am Sat & Sun) An ethnically mixed crowd, including students, sips rum cocktails and West African beers (eg Guinness Foreign Extra, brewed in Cameroon) amid decor from the Senegalese-born proprietor's native land. The soundtrack is African, Caribbean and Latin American, the atmosphere superfriendly.

Marott' Street   WINE BAR
(☎03 22 91 14 93; 1 rue Marotte; ⊘11am-1am, closed Sun) Designed by Gustave Eiffel's architectural firm in 1892, this exquisite ex-insurance office now attracts chic, well-off 30-somethings who sip Champagne while suspended – on clear-glass tiles – over the wine cellar.

☆ Entertainment

La Lune des Pirates   CONCERT VENUE
(☎03 22 97 88 01; www.lalune.net; 17 quai Bélu) Hosts cutting-edge concerts a dozen times a month.

Chés Cabotans d'Amiens   MARIONETTES
(☎03 22 22 30 90; www.ches-cabotans-damiens.com; 31 rue Édouard-David) A theatre whose stars are all traditional Picard marionettes. Great fun even if you don't speak Picard or French.

Ciné St-Leu   CINEMA
(☎03 22 91 61 23; www.cine-st-leu.com; 33 rue Vanmarcke) An art-house cinema with non-dubbed films, some in English.

ℹ Information

Banks can be found around place René Goblet and rue des Trois Cailloux.

Bibliothèque (☎03 22 97 10 10; 50 rue de la République; ☺2-7pm Mon, 9.30am-7pm Tue-Fri, to 6pm Sat) Free internet access in a grand public library built in the 1820s.

Tourist office (☎03 22 71 60 50; www.amiens -tourisme.com; 40 place Notre Dame; ☺9.30am-6pm Mon-Sat, 10am-noon & 2-5pm Sun) Can supply details on the Somme memorials (including minibus tours) and cultural events.

ℹ Getting There & Around

BICYCLE **Velam** (www.velam.amiens.fr; daily/ weekly sign-up fee €1/5) Amiens' municipal bicycle program has outlets all over town. Once you've paid the small sign-up fee, the first half-hour of each rental is free; after that, an escalating surcharge (€1 to €4 per half-hour) applies.

Vélo Service (Buscyclette; ☎03 22 72 55 13; http://amiensveloservice.fubicy.org; per day/ weekend €3/7; ☺9am-7pm Mon-Sat) A non-profit organisation that hires out bikes from the courtyard of Tour Perret, behind the main entrance.

CAR There's free parking one or two blocks north of the Victor Hugo and Central & Anzac hotels, along rue Lameth, rue Cardon, rue Jean XXIII and rue de la Barette.

To hire a car to tour the memorials, try **Avis** (☎03 22 91 31 21; train station).

TRAIN Amiens is an important rail hub. Accessed through a dramatic modern entrance, the downtown train station offers direct services to all cities listed below. SNCF buses (€10, 45 minutes, 15 to 20 daily) also go to the Haute Picardie TGV station, 42km east of the city.

Arras €11.90, 45 minutes, six to 12 daily

Boulogne €19.70, 1½ hours, seven to nine daily

Calais-Ville €25.30, two to 2½ hours, six or seven daily

Compiègne €12.90, 1¼ hours, eight to 12 daily

Laon €17.30, 1¾ hours, four to nine daily

Lille-Flandres €20.20, 1½ hours, six to 12 daily

Paris' Gare du Nord €20.70, 1¼ to 1¾ hours, 14 to 30 daily

Rouen €19.40, 1¼ hours, five daily

Arras

POP 43,690

Arras (the final *s* is pronounced), former capital of Artois and *préfecture* (capital) of the *département* of Pas-de-Calais, is worth seeing mainly for its harmonious ensemble of Flemish-style arcaded buildings and two subterranean WWI sites.

The city makes a good base for visits to the Battle of the Somme Memorials.

◉ Sights & Activities

Grand' Place & Petite Place   ARCHITECTURE
Arras' two ancient market squares, the Grand' Place and the almost-adjacent, smaller Petite Place (officially known as place des Héros), are surrounded by 17th- and 18th-century Flemish-baroque houses topped by curvaceous 'Dutch' gables. Although the structures vary in decorative detail, their 345 sandstone columns form a common arcade unique in France. The squares, especially handsome at night, are about 600m northwest of the train station. As picture-perfect as they look today, both squares were heavily damaged during WWI and most of the gorgeous facades had to be reconstructed from scratch!

Hôtel de Ville   BELFRY, CELLARS
(Petite Place; belfry adult/child €2.90/1.90, boves tour adult/child €5.20/3, combined ticket adult/ child €6.80/3.70; ☺belfry 10am-noon & 2-6pm, boves closed 3 weeks in Jan) Arras' Flemish-Gothic city hall dates from the 16th century but was completely rebuilt after WWI. Three giants (see p168) – Colas, Jacqueline and their son Dédé – make their home in the lobby.

For a panoramic view, hop on a lift to the top of the Unesco World Heritage–listed, 75m-high belfry, or for a truly unique perspective on Arras head into the slimy souterrains (tunnels) that fan out underneath the building. Also known as *boves* (cellars), they run under the Petite Place and were turned into British command posts, hospitals and barracks during WWI. Each spring, in a brilliant juxtaposition of underground gloom and horticultural exuberance, plants and flowers turn the tunnels into the Jardin des Boves (Cellar Gardens), designed around a different theme each year. Tours lasting 45

ARRAS CITY PASS

Arras' tourist office sells the City Pass Argent (adult/student €11.40/5.60), a combo ticket valid for the belfry, the tunnels and Carrière Wellington. The City Pass Or (adult/student €19/10) is also valid for the Musée des Beaux-Arts (Fine Arts Museum) and Cité Nature (a science museum focusing on food, health and nature).

THE LOUVRE'S GREAT MIGRATION NORTH

After years of anticipation, Europe's most ballyhooed new art museum has opened its doors in the northern town of Lens. On 4 December 2012 the innovative Louvre-Lens (www.louvrelens.fr; 6 rue Charles Lecocq, Lens; Galerie du Temps & Pavillon de Verre free through 2013; ⊙10am-6pm Wed-Mon) welcomed its first visitors, showcasing hundreds of treasures from Paris' venerable Musée du Louvre in a purpose-built, state-of-the-art new exhibition space.

A World-Famous Collection Reconfigured

Designed to give museumgoers a completely different experience than its Parisian cousin, the Louvre-Lens is all about making art accessible to new audiences, while showing off the Louvre's remarkable holdings in exciting new ways. The location, in a former coal mining town at the crossroads of two international superhighways, was carefully chosen to to make a statement that art is for everyone. The same 'accessible is beautiful' vision is reflected in the Louvre-Lens' open architecture (visitors are invited behind the scenes to view the museum's storerooms and watch art-restoration personnel at work), its engagement with local residents and school groups through hands-on workshops and seminars, and the museum's spacious grounds, intended to become a flourishing community green space.

In stark contrast to the grandiosity of the Parisian original, the new Louvre branch is about keeping things simple. There's no permanent collection here. Instead, the museum's centrepiece, a 120m-long exhibition space called the Galerie du Temps, displays a limited but significant, ever-rotating collection of 200-plus pieces from the original Louvre, spanning that museum's full breadth and diversity of cultures and historical periods. Early ads for Louvre-Lens showed dozens of artworks whisked skywards from Paris, caught up in a whirlwind like Dorothy's house in *The Wizard of Oz*, then raining down gently on a wonderstruck new crop of Lens museumgoers. The idea is to give ancient treasures and modern masterpieces a chance to rub shoulders with each other – in chronological order and in the same long corridor – creating a tangible timeline of world art history rather than keeping everything segregated in the monumental and largely monocultural period rooms of the Parisian mother ship.

minutes (in English upon request) focus on the gardens when they're there, or on the tunnels' history the rest of the year. Tours generally begin at 11am and run at least twice in the afternoon from Monday to Friday, or every 30 minutes on Saturday and Sunday.

TOP CHOICE Carrière Wellington   HISTORIC SITE
(Wellington Quarry; ☑Arras tourist office 03 21 51 26 95; www.carriere-wellington.com; rue Delétoille; adult/child €6.80/3.10; ⊙tours begin 10am-12.30pm & 1.30-5pm, closed Christmas–mid-Jan; ▣1, 4) The staging ground for the spring 1917 offensive in which the poet Siegfried Sassoon was wounded, Wellington Quarry is a 20m-deep network of old chalk quarries expanded during WWI by tunnellers from New Zealand. Hour-long guided tours in French and English combine imaginative audiovisuals, evocative photos and period artefacts. It's easy to tell who wrote which graffiti when: signs painted in black are British and from WWI, those in red are French from WWII, when the site was used as a bomb shelter. The quarry is about 1km south

of the train station; by car, follow the 'Carrière' signs from the northeast corner of the Grand' Place (bd Faidherbe).

🛏 Sleeping

Place du Maréchal Foch, in front of the train station, also has a number of hotels.

Hôtel de l'Univers   HOTEL €€
(☑03 21 71 34 01; www.hotel-univers-arras.com; 3-5 place de la Croix Rouge; d €139-179; 🖘) Ensconced in a 16th-century former Jesuit monastery, this Best Western–affiliated hostelry is arrayed in a U around a quiet neoclassical courtyard. Classic draperies and bedspreads give each of the 38 rooms a touch of French class – civilised comfort at reasonable prices. It's situated four blocks southwest of the *hôtel de ville;* by car, take one-way rue Baudimont from the west and follow the orange hotel signs; reserve ahead for parking in the hotel's courtyard (€9).

Maison St-Vaast   HOSTEL €
(☑03 21 21 40 38; http://arras.catholique.fr/page-15065.html; 103 rue d'Amiens; dm/s/d €23/27/44;

Initial Exhibits

The museum's grand opening featured European masterpieces such as Delacroix's *Liberty Leading the People* and Raphael's *Portrait of Baldassare Castiglione* displayed alongside works as diverse as ancient Mesopotamian tablets, Persian glazed tiles, Greek statues, Pompeiian frescos, Roman bronzes, Islamic art from Spain to Syria and 11th-century Italian mosaics. These will be gradually swapped out over the next five years for other Louvre holdings until the whole collection has been replaced with new treasures (although if you're hoping to see the *Mona Lisa* or *Winged Victory* in Lens anytime soon, don't hold your breath – certain works have been deemed too precious to travel!).

Complementing this core collection, a second building, the glass-walled Pavillon de Verre, will display annually changing themed exhibits – 2013's theme is the Renaissance, including Leonardo's *Saint Anne* among other works. Rounding out the museum are 1800 sq metre of galleries housing summer and winter temporary exhibits, educational facilities, and an auditorium, restaurant and park. The futuristic ensemble of buildings and surrounding parkland, designed to look like five river boats that have drifted haphazardly together on the grassed-over site of a former coal mine, are the product of an international design competition that was won by a triumvirate of architects and landscape architects from France, Japan and the United States.

Practicalities

To celebrate Louvre-Lens' grand opening, the main collections will be free of charge through 2013 (temporary exhibits cost €9). Lens, 18km north of Arras and 40km southwest of Lille, is accessible by regular TGV trains from Paris' Gare du Nord (€28 to €46, 65 to 70 minutes), as well as regional trains from Lille (€7.60, 40 minutes) and Arras (€4.20, 15 minutes). (Who knows – depending on where you're staying and the length of the Paris museum lines, you may be able to get from Paris to Louvre-Lens faster than to the original Louvre!)

☎) Arras' Catholic diocese welcomes visitors to its dorm facilities; the 43 rooms (91 beds), for one to four people, are spartan (the floors are pine planks) but clean and practical, with disabled access. Constructed as a convent in the 1600s and rebuilt after WWI, the atmospheric building has a fine cloister and a 1920s chapel with lovely stained glass and an organ that's frequently played for practice. If you're checking in after 7pm or on a weekend or holiday, call or write ahead to arrange for the watchperson to let you in.

Hôtel Diamant HOTEL €€

(☎03 21 71 23 23; www.arras-hotel-diamant.com; 5 place des Héros; r €75-86, apt for 2/4/6 people €125/145/165) This small hotel is an excellent option if you can snag one of the cozy rooms overlooking the Petite Place and the belfry; regular serenades from the chiming bells and the bustle of the Saturday market just outside your window may be pluses or minuses, depending on your perspective! The hotel also rents a fully equipped apartment in the townhouse next door, sleeping up to six people with kitchen and laundry facilities.

Ostel Les 3 Luppars HOTEL €

(☎03 21 60 02 03; www.ostel-les-3luppars.com; 49 Grand' Place; s/d/q €62/77/92; ☎) Occupying the Grand' Place's only non-Flemish-style building (it's Gothic and dates from the 1400s), this hotel has a private courtyard and 42 rooms, including 10 with fine views of the square and two fitted out for families. The decor and breakfast are uninspired but the atmosphere is homey. Has a sauna (€5 per person for a half-hour).

✗ Eating

Many places to eat are tucked away under the arches of the Grand' Place and along adjacent rue de la Taillerie, which leads to the Petite Place.

Carpe Diem REGIONAL CUISINE €

(☎03 21 51 70 08; 8bis, rue des Petits Viéziers; mains €14-16; ☻closed Sun & dinner Mon) With a cosy beamed-ceiling downstairs room and another dining area hidden away upstairs, this informal place serves delicious grilled meats, accompanied by your choice of eight sauces and six side dishes (green beans, basmati rice, beer-braised endives etc). The good-value lunch *menu* (€12) includes main dish, drink and coffee.

Le Mamounia   NORTH AFRICAN €€

(☑03 21 07 99 99; 9 rue des Balances; mains €13-25; ☺dinner Tue-Sat, lunch Tue-Fri & Sun) The elegant, brightly coloured decor mixes the Maghreb with Provence but the couscous and *tajines* are 100% Moroccan.

Café Georget   CAFE €

(☑03 21 71 13 07; 42 place des Héros; plat du jour €9; ☺lunch Mon-Sat) An authentic neighbourhood cafe. Madame Delforge, who speaks English with a charmingly thick French accent, has been serving hearty, home-style French dishes to people who work in the neighbourhood since 1985. It's situated 100m west of the *hôtel de ville*.

La Cave des Saveurs   FRENCH €

(☑03 21 59 75 24; 36 Grand' Place; mains €11-20, menus €19-33; ☺lunch & dinner Mon-Sat) In a vaulted brick cellar that served as a brewery before WWII, this popular restaurant serves traditional French dishes as well as a low-fat *bien-être* (well-being) *menu* (€19). Flemish specialties include *potjevleesch* (€12).

Self-Catering

Open-Air Market   FOOD MARKET €

(place des Héros, Grand' Place & place de la Vacquerie; ☺7am-1pm Wed & Sat) Around the *hôtel de ville*. The Saturday market is really huge.

ⓘ Information

Banks can be found along rue Gambetta and its continuation, rue Ernestale.

Tourist office (☑03 21 51 26 95; www.ot-arras.fr; place des Héros; ☺9am-noon & 2-6pm Mon-Sat, 10am-12.30pm & 2.30-6.30pm Sun & holidays) Inside the *hôtel de ville*.

ⓘ Getting There & Around

BICYCLE **Cycloville** (☑06 81 73 24 28; www.cycloville.com; per person €1 plus per km €1,

---

MOVING ON?

For tips, recommendations and reviews, head to shop.lonelyplanet.com to purchase a downloadable PDF of the Western Flanders chapter from Lonely Planet's *Belgium & Luxembourg* guide.

---

half-hour city tour €10; ☺10am-6pm Mon-Sat) Bicycle taxi service that also offers city tours.

Arras Vélo (www.arrasavelo.com; place des Héros; per 2hr/day €8/20) Hires out electric bicycles, convenient for getting to the Vimy battlefields 12km north of town.

CAR **Avis** (☑03 21 51 69 03; 8 rue Gambetta) Half a block northwest of the train station.

Europcar (☑03 21 07 29 54; 5 rue de Douai) Half a block to the right as you exit the train station.

TAXI **Alliance Arras Taxis** (☑03 21 23 69 69; ☺24hr) Can take you to Somme battlefield sites (eg Vimy).

TRAIN Arras' station is 750m southeast of the two main squares.

Amiens €11.90, 45 minutes, six to 12 daily

Calais-Ville €21, two hours, 13 daily Monday to Friday, seven on Saturday, four on Sunday

Lens €4.20, 20 minutes, 13 daily Monday to Friday, seven on Saturday, four on Sunday

Lille-Flandres €10.50, 35 minutes, nine to 16 daily

Paris Gare du Nord TGV €31 to €47, 50 minutes, 11 to 15 daily

Battle of the Somme Memorials

Almost 750,000 soldiers, airmen and sailors from Great Britain, Australia, Canada, the Indian subcontinent, Ireland, New Zealand, South Africa, the West Indies and other parts of the British Empire died during WWI on the Western Front, two-thirds of them in France. They were buried where they fell, in more than 1000 military cemeteries and 2000 civilian cemeteries that dot the landscape along a wide swath of territory – 'Flanders Fields' – running roughly from Amiens and Cambrai north via Arras and Béthune to Armentières and Ypres (Ieper) in Belgium.

The focal point of each Commonwealth cemetery, now tended by the Commonwealth War Graves Commission (www.cwgc.org), is the Cross of Sacrifice. Many of the headstones, made of Portland limestone, bear moving personal inscriptions composed by family members. Most cemeteries have a bronze Cemetery Register box that contains a visitors book, in which you can record your impressions, and a booklet with biographical details on each of the identified dead (Americans who died fighting with British forces can be spotted by their addresses). Some larger cemeteries also have a bronze plaque with historical information.

Battle of the Somme Memorials

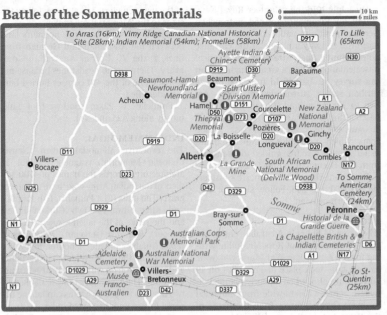

American war dead of the world wars were either repatriated (61%) or reburied in large cemeteries near where they fell (39%).

Area tourist offices can supply you with some excellent English-language brochures, including *The Vistor's Guide to the Battlefields* and *Australians in the Somme*, as well as the free multilingual map *The Great War Remembered*. For online information, see www.somme-battlefields.com and www.somme14-18.com.

Sights

AUSTRALIAN CORPS MEMORIAL PARK

This memorial (⊘vehicle access 9am-6pm Apr-Oct, to 4pm Nov-Mar, pedestrians 24hr) stands on the hilltop site of the Battle of Le Hamel (4 July 1918), fought by Australian and American troops under the command of Australian Lieutenant General John Monash. The German air ace Baron Manfred von Richthofen, aka the Red Baron, was shot down a bit northwest of here – Australian ground forces claimed credit but so did a Canadian pilot.

Inaugurated in 2008, the Australian Corps Memorial is 7km northeast of Villers-Bretonneux; follow the signs to 'Monument Australien/Memorial Park'.

AYETTE INDIAN & CHINESE CEMETERY

Towards the end of WWI, tens of thousands of Chinese labourers of were recruited by the British government to perform noncombat jobs in Europe, including the gruesome task of recovering and burying Allied war dead. Some of these *travailleurs chinois* (Chinese labourers) died in the Spanish flu epidemic of 1918–19 and are buried in this Commonwealth cemetery beneath gravestones etched in Chinese and English with inscriptions such as 'a good reputation endures forever', 'a noble duty bravely done' and 'faithful unto death'. Nearby are the graves of Indians who served with British forces, marked in Hindi or Arabic, and the tomb of a single German.

The cemetery is 29km northeast of Albert, just off the D919 at the southern edge of the village of Ayette.

BEAUMONT-HAMEL NEWFOUNDLAND MEMORIAL

Like Vimy, the evocative Mémorial Terre-Neuvien de Beaumont-Hamel preserves part of the Western Front in the state it was in at fighting's end. The zigzag trench system, which still fills with mud in winter, is clearly visible, as are countless shell craters and the remains of barbed-wire barriers.

On 1 July 1916 the volunteer Royal Newfoundland Regiment stormed entrenched German positions and was nearly wiped out; until recently a plaque at the entrance noted bluntly that 'strategic and tactical miscalculations led to a great slaughter'. You can survey the battlefield from the bronze caribou statue, surrounded by plants native to Newfoundland. Canadian students based at the Welcome Centre (☑03 22 76 70 86; www.veterans.gc.ca/eng/memorials; ☉10am-6pm), which resembles a Newfoundland fisher's house, give free guided tours (except from mid-December to mid-January).

Beaumont-Hamel is 9km north of Albert via the D50 and D73. Follow signs for 'Memorial Terreneuvien'.

FROMELLES

'The worst 24 hours in Australia's entire history' – in the words of Ross McMullin, writing for the Australian War Memorial (www.awm.gov.au) – took place at Fromelles on 19 and 20 July 1916, when a poorly planned offensive across a 3.6km-wide front, intended to divert German forces from the Battle of the Somme, turned into a disastrous rout: 1917 men of the Australian Imperial Force and 519 British soldiers were killed and another 3146 Australians and 977 British were wounded. It seems likely that one of the soldiers on the victorious German side was a 27-year-old corporal in the 16th Bavarian Reserve Infantry Regiment named Adolf Hitler.

After the battle, the Germans buried many of the Australian and British dead in mass graves behind their lines. Most were reburied after the war, but eight pits containing the remains of 250 men were not found until 2008. To provide them with a dignified final resting place, the hexagonal Fromelles (Pheasant Wood) Military Cemetery (www.cwgc.org) – the first new Commonwealth cemetery in half a century – was dedicated on 19 July 2010, the 94th anniversary of the catastrophic and pointless assault. DNA testing established the identity of 109 Australians.

After the surviving Australians retreated to their prebattle front lines, hundreds of their comrades-in-arms lay wounded in no-man's land. For three days the survivors made heroic efforts to rescue them, acts of bravery commemorated by the sculpture *Cobbers* in the Fromelles Memorial Park. Inaugurated in 1998, it is situated atop a row of German blockhouses 2km northwest of the new cemetery; to get there, follow the signs to the 'Mémorial Australien'.

Nearby, in what was once no-man's land between the Australian and German front lines, is the VC Corner Australian Cemetery. There are no headstones because not a single one of the 410 corpses buried here was identified.

Fromelles is 22km southwest of Lille, mostly along A25 and N41.

INDIAN MEMORIAL

The evocative Mémorial Indien (Neuve-Chapelle Memorial), vaguely Moghul in architecture, records the names of 4700 soldiers of the Indian Army who 'have no known grave'. The units (31st Punjabis, 11th Rajputs, 2nd King Edward's Own Gurkha Rifles) and the ranks of the fallen – *sowar* (cavalry trooper), *havildar* (sergeant), *naik* (chief), *sepoy* (infantry private), labourer, follower – engraved on the walls evoke the pride, pomp and exploitation on which the British Empire was built. The 15m-high column, flanked by two tigers, is topped by a lotus capital, the Imperial Crown and the Star of India.

This seldom-visited – and poorly signposted – memorial is 20km southwest of Lille. To get there from La Bassée, head north along D947 for 5km.

LA GRANDE MINE

Just outside the hamlet of La Boisselle, this enormous crater looks like the site of a meteor impact. Some 100m across and 30m deep, the Lochnagar Crater Memorial (as it's officially known) was created on the morning of the first day of the First Battle of the Somme (1 July 1916) by about 25 tonnes of ammonal laid by British sappers in order to create a breach in the German lines – and is a testament to the boundless ingenuity human beings can muster when determined to kill their fellow creatures.

La Grande Mine is 4km northeast of Albert along the D929.

PÉRONNE

The best place to begin a visit to the Somme battlefields – especially if you're interested in WWI's historical and cultural context – is the outstanding Historial de la Grande Guerre (Museum of the Great War; ☑03 22 83 14 18; www.historial.org; Château de Péronne; adult/child incl audioguide €7.50/3.80; ☉10am-6pm, closed mid-Dec–mid-Jan). Tucked inside Péronne's massively fortified château, this award-winning museum tells the story of the war chronologically, with equal space given to the German, French and British perspectives on what happened, how and why. A great deal of visually engaging material, including period films and the bone-chilling engravings by Otto Dix, capture the aesthetic sensibilities, enthusiasm, naive patriotism and unimaginable violence of the time. The proud uniforms of various units and armies are shown laid out on the ground, as if on freshly – though bloodlessly – dead soldiers. Not much glory here. The lake behind the museum is a fine place for a stroll or picnic.

Excellent English brochures on the battlefields can be picked up at Péronne's tourist office (☎03 22 84 42 38; www.hautesomme-tourisme.com; 16 place André Audinot; ⊙10am-noon & 2-6pm Mon-Sat), 100m from the museum entrance.

On the D1017 at the southern edge of town (towards St-Quentin), La Chapellette British & Indian Cemeteries have multi-faith, multilingual headstones, with a section for the fallen of units such as the 38th King George's Own Central India Horse.

Péronne (pop 8450) is about 60km east of Amiens; from the D1029 or A29, follow the D1017 the last few kilometres into town.

SOMME AMERICAN CEMETERY

In late September 1918, just six weeks before the end of WWI, American units – flanked by their British, Canadian and Australian allies – launched an assault on the Germans' heavily fortified Hindenburg Line. One regiment of the 27th Infantry Division, a National Guard unit from New York, suffered 337 dead and 658 wounded on a single day.

Some of the fiercest fighting took place near the village of Bony, on the sloping site now occupied by the 1844 Latin Crosses and Stars of David of the Somme American Cemetery (www.abmc.gov; ⊙9am-5pm). The names of 333 men whose remains were never recovered are inscribed on the walls of the Memorial Chapel, reached through massive bronze doors. The small Visitors' Building (turn left at the flagpole) has information on the battle.

The cemetery is 24km northeast of Péronne, mostly along the D6, and 18km north of St-Quentin along the D1044. From A26, take exit 9 and follow the signs for 17km.

SOUTH AFRICAN NATIONAL MEMORIAL

The Mémorial Sud-Africain stands in the middle of shell-pocked Delville Wood, which was almost captured by a South African brigade in the third week of July 1916. The avenues through the trees are named after streets in London and Edinburgh. The star-shaped museum (www.delvillewood.com; ⊙10am-5.30pm Tue-Sun, closed Dec & Jan) is a replica of Cape Town's Castle of Good Hope.

The memorial is 13km east-northeast of Albert, mostly along the D20.

The New Zealand National Memorial is also in this area, 1.5km due north of Longueval.

THIEPVAL MEMORIAL

Dedicated to 'the Missing of the Somme', this Commonwealth memorial – its distinctive outline visible for many kilometres in all directions – is the region's most visited place of pilgrimage. Situated on the site of a German stronghold that was stormed on 1 July 1916 with unimaginable casualties, it was designed by Sir Edwin Lutyens and dedicated in 1932. The columns of the arches are inscribed with the names of 73,367 British and South African soldiers whose remains were never recovered or identified. The glass-walled visitors centre (☎03 22 74 60 47; admission free; ⊙10am-6pm, closed 2 weeks around New Year) is discreetly below ground level. Thiepval is 7.5km northeast of Albert along the D151.

THIRTY-SIXTH (ULSTER) DIVISION MEMORIAL

Built on a German frontline position assaulted by the overwhelmingly Protestant 36th (Ulster) Division on 1 July 1916, the Ulster Tower Memorial (☎03 22 74 87 14; ⊙museum 10am-5pm Tue-Sun Mar-Nov, to 6pm May-Sep) is an exact replica of Helen's Tower at Clanboye, County Down, where the unit did its training. Dedicated in 1921, it has long been a Unionist pilgrimage site; a black obelisk known as the Orange Memorial to Fallen Brethren (1993) stands in an enclosure behind the tower. In a sign that historic wounds are finally healing, in 2006 the Irish Republic issued a €0.75 postage stamp showing the 36th Division in action on this site, to commemorate the 90th anniversary of the Battle of the Somme.

Virtually untouched since the war, nearby Thiepval Wood can be visited on a guided tour (donation requested) at 11am and/or 3pm; call ahead for dates of scheduled group tours.

The monument is on the D73 between Beaumont-Hamel and Thiepval; follow the signs to the 'Mémorial Irlandais'.

Battle of the Somme

The First Battle of the Somme, a WWI Allied offensive waged in the villages and woodlands northeast of Amiens, was designed to relieve pressure on the beleaguered French troops at Verdun. On 1 July 1916, British, Commonwealth and French troops 'went over the top' in a massive assault along a 34km front. However, German positions proved virtually unbreachable, and on the first day of the battle – the bloodiest day in the history of the British army – an astounding 21,392 Allied troops were killed and another 35,492 were wounded. Most casualties were infantrymen mown down by German machine guns.

By the time the offensive was called off in mid-November, a total of 1.2 million lives had been lost on both sides. The British had advanced 12km, the French 8km. The Battle of the Somme has become a symbol of the meaningless slaughter of war, and its killing fields remain sites of pilgrimage.

PLACES OF PILGRIMAGE

» **Historial de la Grande Guerre** (p196), a superb introduction to WWI and its context

» **Vimy Ridge Canadian National Historic Site** (p200), a cratered slice of the Western Front undisturbed since the day the guns fell silent

» **Thiepval Memorial** (p197), honouring Commonwealth soldiers who rest in unknown graves

» **Musée Franco-Australien** (p200), an intimate look at Anzac life on the Western Front

» **Somme American Cemetery** (p197), final resting place for soldiers of a New York regiment

Clockwise from top left
1. Somme American Cemetery 2. Flags flying over the Australian Corps Memorial Park 3. Headstone of an Australian soldier

DANIEL ROBINSON/GETTY IMAGES ©

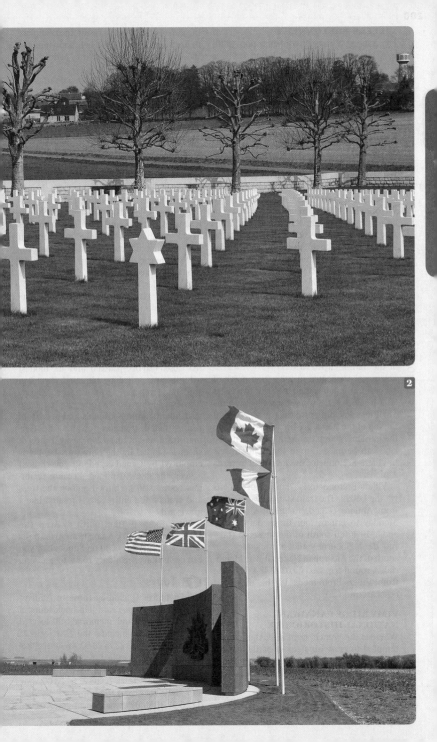

VILLERS-BRETONNEUX

For Aussies, Villers-Bretonneux (pop 4220) is a heart-warming place. Billing itself as *l'Australie en Picardie,* the town religiously commemorates Anzac Day (www.anzac-france.com) on 25 April and is home to the Musée Franco-Australien (Franco-Australian Museum; ☑03 22 96 80 79; www.museeaustralien.com; 9 rue Victoria; adult/child €5/3; ⊗9.30am-5.30pm Mon-Sat), which displays highly personal WWI Australiana including letters and photographs that evoke life on the Western Front. It is housed in a primary school that was built with funds donated by schoolchildren in the Australian state of Victoria. In 1993 the unidentified remains of an Australian soldier were transferred from Adelaide Cemetery, on the D1029 at the western edge of town, to the Australian War Memorial in Canberra.

During WWI 313,000 Australians (out of a total population of 4.5 million) volunteered for overseas military service; 46,000 met their deaths on the Western Front (14,000 others perished elsewhere; www.ww1westernfront.gov.au). The names of 10,982 Australian soldiers whose remains were never found are engraved on the base of the 32m-high Australian National War Memorial, dedicated in 1938, 2km north of Villers-Bretonneux along the D23; two years later its stone walls were scarred by the guns of Hitler's invading armies. The views from the top of the tower are breathtaking; when the gardeners aren't present to open it, the keys can be picked up at the Gendarmerie in Villers-Bretonneux, on the D1029 towards Amiens.

Villers-Bretonneux is 17km east of Amiens via the D1029. The train station, well served from Amiens (€3.60, 10 minutes, 11 daily Monday to Friday, four to six daily weekends), is 600m south of the museum (take rue de Melbourne) and a walkable 3km south of the Australian National War Memorial. A round-trip taxi (☑03 22 48 49 49) ride from Villers-Bretonneux to the memorial costs around €20.

VIMY RIDGE CANADIAN NATIONAL HISTORIC SITE

Whereas the French, right after the war, attempted to erase all signs of battle and return the Somme region to agriculture and normalcy, the Canadians decided that the most evocative way to remember their fallen was to preserve part of the crater-pocked battlefield exactly the way it looked when the guns fell silent. As a result, the best place to get some sense of the hell known as the Western Front is the chilling, eerie moonscape of Vimy.

Of the 66,655 Canadians who died in WWI, 3598 lost their lives in April 1917 taking 14km-long Vimy Ridge (Crête de Vimy). Its highest point – site of a heavily fortified German position – was later chosen as the site of Canada's WWI memorial, designed by Walter Seymour Allward and built from 1925 to 1936. The 20 allegorical figures, carved from huge blocks of white Croatian limestone, include a cloaked, downcast female figure representing a young Canada grieving for her fallen. The two striking columns represent Canada and France. The names of 11,285 Canadians who 'died in France but have no known graves', listed alphabetically and within each letter by rank, are inscribed around the base. The peaceful, 1-sq-km park also includes two Canadian cemeteries and, at the vehicle entrance to the main memorial, a monument to France's Moroccan Division (in French and Arabic).

The rust-coloured Welcome Centre (☑03 22 76 70 86; www.veterans.gc.ca/eng/memorials; ⊗10am-6pm Mar-Oct, 9am-5pm Nov-Feb, closed mid-Dec–mid-Jan) and its modest exhibits are staffed by bilingual Canadian students. From here, guided tours (⊗hourly 10am-5pm Tue-Sun Feb-Nov) offer the chance to visit infantry supply tunnels and peer from reconstructed trenches towards the German front line, a mere 25m away. Herds of sheep - tended by the only two shepherds employed by Canada's federal government - keep the grass trimmed. Because countless bodies still lie buried among the trees and craters, the entire site is treated like a graveyard.

Vimy Ridge is 11km north of Arras (towards Lens via N17). A taxi from Arras costs about €25 one way (€30 on Sunday), or you can cycle along secondary roads to get here.

☞ Tours

Tourist offices (including those in Amiens, Arras and Péronne) can help book tours of battlefield sites and memorials. Respected tour companies include the Battlefields Experience (☑03 22 76 29 60; www.thebattleofthesomme.co.uk), Western Front Tours (www.westernfronttours.com.au; ⊗mid-Mar–mid-Nov), Terres de Mémoire (☑03 22 84 23 05; www.terresdememoire.com), Chemins d'Histoire (☑06 31 31 85 02; www.cheminsdhistoire.com)

and True Blue Digger Tours (☎03 22 51 56 21; www.trueblue-diggertours.com).

❶ Getting There & Away

You'll need your own transport to visit most of the Somme memorials (one exception is Villers-Bretonneux, which is accessible by train; see that section for details).

Compiègne

POP 42,690

The *cité imperiale* (imperial city) of Compiègne reached its glittering zenith under Emperor Napoléon III (r 1852–70), whose legacy is alive and well in the château – the star attraction – and its park. A forest clearing near the city was the site of the armistice that ended WWI and the French surrender in 1940.

On 23 May 1430 Joan of Arc (Jeanne d'Arc) – honoured by two statues in the city centre – was captured at Compiègne by the Burgundians, who later sold her to their English allies.

◉ Sights

Château de Compiègne   PALACE, MUSEUMS
(☎03 44 38 47 00; www.musee-chateau -compiegne.fr; place du Général de Gaulle; adult/ child €6.50/free) Napoléon III's dazzling hunting parties drew aristocrats and wannabes from all around Europe to his 1337-room palace, built around eight courtyards. The sumptuous Grands Appartements (Imperial Apartments; ⊙10am-12.30pm & 1.30-5.45pm Wed-Mon, last admission 30min before closing), including the empress's bedroom and a ballroom lit by 15 chandeliers, can be visited with an audioguide (available in French, English, German and Japanese). The same ticket grants access – without audio commentary – to the adjacent Musée du Second Empire, which illustrates the lives of Napoléon III and his family.

Two other attractions inside the palace require you to join a French-language guided tour (also included in the ticket price): the Musée de la Voiture, which features vehicles that predate the internal combustion engine as well as early motorcars such as the Jamais Contente, a torpedo-shaped contraption from 1899; and the Musée de l'Impératrice, which stars Eugénie (Napoléon III's wife) and includes mementos of her dashing, exiled son who was 'killed by the Zulus, in Zululand, Africa' in 1879 while serving, with Queen Victoria's express permission, in the British army.

Stretching east from the château, the 20-hectare, English-style Petit Parc links up with the Grand Parc and the Forêt de Compiègne, a forest that surrounds Compiègne on the east and south and is criss-crossed by rectilinear paths. The area is a favourite venue for hiking and cycling (maps available at the tourist office) as well as horse riding. Napoléon I had the 4.5km Allée des Beaux-Monts laid out so that Empress Marie-Louise wouldn't miss Vienna's Schönbrunn palace quite so much.

[TOP CHOICE] **Mémorial de l'Internement et de la Déportation**   MUSEUM
(Internment & Deportation Memorial; ☎03 44 96 37 00; http://memorial.compiegne.fr; 2bis av des Martyrs de la Liberté; adult/child incl English audioguide €3/1.50; ⊙10am-6pm Wed-Mon) The French military base of Royallieu was used as a Nazi transit camp from 1941 to 1944; several of the original buildings have housed this profoundly moving memorial museum since 2008. Of the more than 53,000 men, women and children held here (Resistance fighters, political prisoners, prisoners of war, Jews – kept in a special section – and American civilians arrested after Pearl Harbour), 48,000 were marched through town to the train station for the trip east to concentration and extermination camps, including Auschwitz.

The memorial is 2.5km southwest of the city centre, easily accessible by bus 5.

Clairière de l'Armistice   HISTORIC SITE
(Armistice Clearing; ☎03 44 85 14 18; www.musee -armistice-14-18.fr; adult/child €5/3; ⊙10am-5.30pm, closed Tue Oct-Mar) The armistice that came into force on the 11th hour of the 11th day of the 11th month – the year was 1918 – and finally put an end to WWI was signed 7km northeast of Compiègne (towards Soissons) inside the railway carriage of the Allied supreme commander, Maréchal Ferdinand Foch.

On 22 June 1940, in the same railway car, the French – with Hitler looking on smugly – were forced to sign the armistice that recognised Nazi Germany's domination of France. Taken for exhibition to Berlin, the carriage was destroyed in April 1945 on the Führer's personal orders lest it be used for a third surrender – his own.

In the middle of a thick forest, Clairière de l'Armistice – staffed by volunteers (mainly French army veterans) – commemorates these events with monuments, memorabilia, newspaper clippings and stereoscopic (3D) photos that capture all the mud, muck and misery of WWI. The wooden rail wagon now on display is of the same type as the original; some of the furnishings, hidden away during WWII, were the ones actually used in 1918.

🛏 Sleeping

Compiègne's rather lacklustre collection of hotels is concentrated near the train station and along the River Oise.

Hôtel de Flandre HOTEL €
(☎03 44 83 24 40; www.hoteldeflandre.com; 16 quai de la République; d with shared/private bathroom €35/70) A block from the station, this straightforward two-star hotel offers more convenience than charm. Some of the 37 rooms have river views.

🍴 Eating

Restaurants and cafes are sprinkled around the city centre, including rue Magenta, rue de l'Étoile and narrow, ancient rue des Lombards, which form a triangle two blocks south of the tourist office.

Bistrot des Arts BISTRO €€
(35 cours Guynemer; menus €18-28; ⊙closed Sun & lunch Sat) An old-time bistro with traditional French meat dishes and a selection of fresh fish (consult the blackboard). Midway between the tourist office and the train station, facing the river.

ℹ Information

Tourist office (☎03 44 40 01 00; www.compiegne-tourisme.fr; place de l'Hôtel de Ville; ⊙9.15am-12.15pm & 1.45-6.15pm Mon-Sat) This centrally located office (600m southwest of the château and 1km southeast of the train station) abuts the Flamboyant Gothic 16th-century *hôtel de ville* and faces a tulip-filled square with a *Joan of Arc* statue.

ℹ Getting There & Away

Compiègne, 65km northeast of Paris, can be easily visited on a day trip from the capital.

Compiègne is linked by train to Paris' Gare du Nord (€14, 40 to 70 minutes, 13 to 26 daily) and Amiens (€12.90, one to 1¼ hours, eight to 12 daily). As you exit the station towards the tracks, look about 80m down the platform to your right for a poignant deportation memorial, which includes two train carriages of the type used during WWII to ship Royallieu prisoners to concentration camps.

ℹ Getting Around

Local buses, which depart from the train station, are free Monday to Saturday, and cost €1 Sunday and holidays. Buses 1 and 2 serve the tourist office and château.

There's free parking in front of the château (place du Général de Gaulle), southeast of there along av Royale and av de la Résistance, and along the river (cours Guynemer).

Laon
POP 27,090

The walled, hilltop Ville Haute (Upper City) – an architectural gem – boasts a magnificent Gothic cathedral and commands fantastic views of the surrounding plains. About 100 vertical metres below sits the Ville Basse (Lower City), completely rebuilt after being flattened in WWII. Laon (the name, as pronounced locally, has one syllable and rhymes with *enfant*) makes a great spot for a romantic getaway.

Laon served as the capital of the Carolingian empire until it was brought to an end in 987 by Hugh Capet, who for some reason preferred ruling from Paris.

◉ Sights & Activities

The claw-shaped Ville Haute has no less than 84 listed historic monuments, the densest concentration in France. Laon's narrow streets, alleyways (some less than 1m wide) and courtyards are particularly rewarding territory for keen-eyed wandering.

Cathédrale Notre Dame CATHEDRAL
(south tower adult €4 ; ⊙cathedral 9am-8pm, south tower tours 2.30pm Wed-Sun, daily during school holidays, also at 4pm early Jul-early Sep) A model for a number of its more famous Gothic sisters (Chartres, Reims and Dijon among them), this medieval jewel was built (1150–1230) in the transitional Gothic style on Romanesque foundations. The 110m-long interior, remarkably well lit, has three levels of columns and arches and a gilded wrought-iron choir screen; some of the stained glass dates from the 12th century. A memorial plaque for Commonwealth WWI dead hangs just inside the west facade. The structure is best appreciated with an audioguide, available next door at the tourist office, which is also the place to sign up for a guided tour of the south tower.

TOP CHOICE City Ramparts

RAMPARTS

To get a sense of the city and its commanding position, take a walk around the Ville Haute's 7km-long wall, pierced by three fortified gates. For some of the finest panoramic views, head to the 13th-century Porte d'Ardon (one of the gates); circular Batterie Morlot, a one-time optical telegraph station; and rue du Rempart St-Rémi. Over 80 paths, known as *grimpettes,* take you down the steep forested slopes in every direction.

🛏 Sleeping & Eating

The pedestrianised section of rue Châtelaine (linking the cathedral with place du Général Leclerc) is home to several restaurants and shops selling nutritional basics such as bread (at No 54) and chocolate (at No 27).

Hôtel Les Chevaliers

HOTEL €

(✆03 23 27 17 50; hotelchevaliers@aol.com; 3-5 rue Sérurier; s/d €57/63; 🛜) Parts of this friendly 16-room hostelry, right around the corner from the Haute Ville's *hôtel de ville*, date from the Middle Ages. Recent renovations have opened up two new suites under the eaves with exposed beams and brick walls; rooms 6 and 7 downstairs enjoy nice views.

Estaminet Saint-Jean

REGIONAL CUISINE

(www.estaminetsaintjean.com; 23 rue St-Jean; mains €12-15; ⏱lunch Tue-Sun, dinner Tue & Thu-Sat) Specialising in traditional Flemish and Picard cuisine accompanied by your choice of 30 beers, this homey eatery near the *hôtel de ville* is especially good value at lunch-time, when *plats du jour* go for €8 and full meals for €12.50.

❶ Information

Tourist office (✆03 23 20 28 62; www.tourisme-paysdelaon.com; place de la Cathédrale; ⏱9.30am-1pm & 2-6.30pm) Can supply you with a free town map and excellent English brochures on Laon and the surrounds. Also offers audioguides (€4) for excellent one- to three-hour walking tours of the Ville Haute and the cathedral, guided tours (in French, with guides who speak English) and free internet access. It's situated next to the cathedral in a 12th-century hospital decorated with 14th-century frescos.

❶ Getting There & Around

Laon is 67km northwest of Reims (in Champagne).

CAR The Ville Haute's one-way streets circle round and round – if they don't drive you crazy they'll at least make you dizzy. Parking is available at the eastern end of the Ville Haute, around the Citadelle.

TRAIN The train station, in the Ville Basse, is linked to Amiens (€17.30, 1½ hours, four to nine daily), Paris' Gare du Nord (€21.90, 1½ hours, 14 daily Monday to Friday, nine on Saturday and Sunday) and Reims (€9.50, 45 minutes, three to eight daily).

The Ville Haute is a steep 20-minute walk from the train station – the stairs begin at the upper end of av Carnot – but it's more fun to take the automated, elevated **Poma funicular railway** (1 way/return €1.10/1.20; ⏱every 5min 7am-8pm Mon-Sat, closed holidays, closed 2 wks late Jul-early Aug), which links the train station with the upper city in 3½ minutes flat.

Normandy

Includes »

Best Places to Eat

» Le Bouchon du Vaugueux (p232)

» Les Voiles d'Or (p212)

» La Petite Auberge (p217)

» Les Nymphéas (p210)

» Hôtel & Restaurant de la Chaîne d'Or (p218)

Best Places to Sleep

» Hôtel & Restaurant de la Chaîne d'Or (p218)

» La Maison de Famille (p231)

» Hôtel Vent d'Ouest (p216)

» La Maison de Lucie (p236)

» Hôtel de Bourgtheroulde (p209)

Why Go?

Ever since the armies of William the Conqueror set sail from its shores in 1066, Normandy has played a pivotal role in European history, from the Norman invasion of England to the Hundred Years War and the D-Day beach landings of 1944. This rich and often brutal past is what draws travellers to the region today, though the pastoral landscapes, small fishing ports, dramatic coastline and waistline-expanding cuisine are all equally good reasons to include this accessible and beautiful chunk of France on any trip.

The standout highlights of Normandy are world-renowned sights such as the Bayeux Tapestry, the D-Day beaches, Monet's garden at Giverny and the spectacular Mont St-Michel, but the region's lesser-known charms include a variety of stunning beaches and coastal landscapes, some excellent and little-known art museums, quaint villages in the hinterland, and architectural gems ranging from classic beauty Honfleur to postwar oddball Le Havre.

When to Go

Rouen

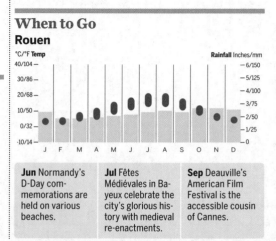

Jun Normandy's D-Day commemorations are held on various beaches.

Jul Fêtes Médiévales in Bayeux celebrate the city's glorious history with medieval re-enactments.

Sep Deauville's American Film Festival is the accessible cousin of Cannes.

Route du Cidre

Normandy's signposted 40km Route du Cidre (Cider Route; www.larouteducidre.fr), about 20km east of Caen, wends its way through the Pays d'Auge, a rural area of orchards, pastures, hedgerows, half-timbered farmhouses and stud farms, through picturesque villages such as Cambremer and Beuvron-en-Auge. Signs reading Cru de Cambremer indicate the way to about 20 small-scale, traditional producers who are happy to show you their facilities and sell you their home-grown cider (€3 a bottle) and calvados (apple-flavoured brandy).

Traditional Normandy cider takes about six months to make. The apples are shaken off the trees or gathered from the ground between early October and early December. After being stored for two or three weeks, they are pressed, purified, slow-fermented, bottled and naturally carbonated, just like Champagne.

Normandy's AOC (Appellation d'Origine Contrôlée) cider is made with a blend of apple varieties and is known for being fruity, tangy and slightly bitter. You'll be able to enjoy it in any crêperie or restaurant throughout Normandy.

ITINERARIES

One Week

Coming from Paris, **Giverny** will be your first stop for Monet's Garden, with perhaps a side trip to gorgeous **Les Andelys**, before continuing to **Rouen**, **Honfleur**, **Bayeux** and the **D-Day beaches**, ending at **Mont St-Michel**.

Two Weeks

With an extra week, follow the same route but take more time to explore places on the way. **Côte d'Albâtre** and **Le Havre** are all well worth detouring for, as are pretty **Trouville** and **Deauville**, interesting **Caen** and **Coutances**. You could also lose yourself in pastoral Normandy – make a beeline for **Camembert country**.

Getting There & Around

Ferries to and from England and Ireland dock at Cherbourg, Dieppe, Le Havre and Ouistreham (Caen). The Channel Islands (Jersey and Guernsey) are most accessible from the Breton port of St-Malo but from April to September there are passenger services from the Normandy towns of Granville, Carteret and Diélette.

Normandy is easily accessible by train from Paris – Rouen is just 70 minutes from Paris Gare St-Lazare. Most major towns are accessible by rail, and with the **Carte Sillage Loisirs** (www.ter-sncf.com) travel around the Basse Normandie region is remarkably cheap on weekends and holidays. However, bus services between smaller towns are infrequent at best. To really explore Normandy's rural areas you need either two or four wheels.

DRIVING NORMANDY

Though public transport in Normandy is good, driving here is highly recommended if you plan to visit the D-Day beaches independently or explore some of the region's lesser-known areas.

Fast Facts

» **Population** 3.3 million
» **Area** 24,317 km2
» **Hotel Overnights/yr** 1.58 million
» **Signature drink** Calvados

Top 5 Museums

» Musée d'Art Moderne André Malraux (p216), Le Havre
» Musée des Impressionnismes Giverny (p219), Giverny
» Bayeux Tapestry (p220), Bayeux
» Musée Eugène Boudin (p236), Honfleur
» Musée des Beaux-Arts (p231), Caen

Resources

» Tourism and travel links: www.normandie-tourisme.fr and www.normandie-qualite-tourisme.com
» Calvados facts: vimoutiers.net/AppleCider Calvados.htm
» Cheese fan? www.fromage-normandie.com

NORMANDY

Normandy Highlights

1 Admire the architecture, art and antiques of **Rouen's old town** (p207)

2 Dive into an Impressionist masterpiece by visiting **Monet's garden** (p219) at Giverny

3 Travel back 1000 years with the world's oldest comic strip, the **Bayeux Tapestry** (p220)

4 See Normandy's historic **D-Day beaches** (p222) and the moving war cemeteries

5 Watch the tide come in from the summit of the extraordinary abbey of **Mont St-Michel** (p240)

6 Savour superfresh seafood at the harbourside restaurants

7 Wander the spectacular coastline and marvel at the famous cliffs at **Étretat** (p215)

8 Enjoy some rich **Norman cuisine** (p211), from creamy Camembert and fresh oysters to cider and calvados

of beautiful **Honfleur** (p235) and glamorous **Trouville** (p232)

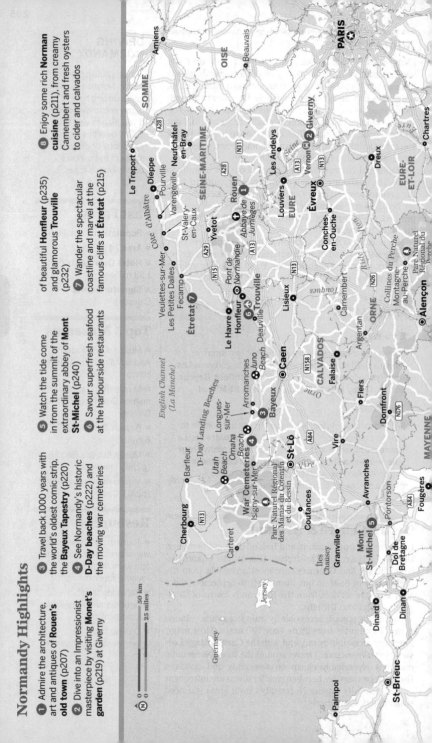

History

The Vikings invaded present-day Normandy in the 9th century, and some of invaders established settlements and adopted Christianity. In 911 French king Charles the Simple, of the Carolingian dynasty, and Viking chief Hrölfr agreed that the area around Rouen should be handed over to these Norsemen – or Normans, as they came to be known.

Throughout the Hundred Years War (1337–1453), the duchy seesawed between French and English rule. England dominated Normandy for some 30 years until France gained permanent control in 1450. In the 16th century, Normandy, a Protestant stronghold, was the scene of much fighting between Catholics and Huguenots.

SEINE-MARITIME

The Seine-Maritime *département* stretches along the chalk-white cliffs of the Côte d'Albâtre (Alabaster Coast) from Le Tréport via Dieppe to Le Havre, the second-busiest port in France. It's a region whose history is firmly bound up with the sea, and is ideal for coastal exploring and clifftop walks. When you fancy a break from the bracing sea air, head inland to the lively, lovely metropolis of Rouen, a favourite haunt of Monet and Simone de Beauvoir, and one of the most intriguing cities in France's northeastern corner.

Rouen

POP 119,927

With its elegant spires, beautifully restored medieval quarter and soaring Gothic cathedral, the ancient city of Rouen is one of Normandy's highlights. Rouen has had a turbulent history – it was devastated several times during the Middle Ages by fire and plague, and was occupied by the English during the Hundred Years War. The young French heroine Joan of Arc (Jeanne d'Arc) was tried for heresy and burned at the stake in the central square in 1431. During WWII, Allied bombing raids laid waste to large parts of the city, especially the area south of the cathedral, but over the last six decades the city has been meticulously rebuilt.

◎ Sights & Activities

Place du Vieux Marché　　　TOWN SQUARE

Rue du Gros Horloge runs from the cathedral west to this square, where 19-year-old Joan of Arc was executed for heresy in 1431. Dedicated in 1979, the thrillingly bizarre Église Jeanne d'Arc (place du Vieux Marché; ◎10am-noon & 2-6pm Apr-Oct), with its fish-scale exterior, marks the spot where Joan was burned at the stake. The church's soaring modernist interior, lit by some marvellous 16th-century stained glass, is well worth a look.

Gros Horloge　　　CLOCK TOWER

(rue du Gros Horloge; adult/child €6/3; ◎10am-1pm & 2-6pm Tue-Sun) Rue du Gros Horloge is spanned by this impressive structure, a Gothic belfry with one-handed medieval clocks on each side.

Palais de Justice　　　ARCHITECTURE

(place Maréchal Foch) The ornately Gothic Law Courts, little more than a shell at the end of WWII, have been restored to their early 16th-century Gothic glory. The courtyard, with its impossibly delicate spires, gargoyles and statuary, is accessible via a metal detector from rue aux Juifs.

Under the staircase at the courtyard's eastern end is the Monument Juif (Jewish Monument), the oldest Jewish communal structure in France and the only reminder of Rouen's medieval Jewish community, which was expelled by Philippe le Bel in 1306.

Cathédrale Notre Dame　　　CATHEDRAL

(place de la Cathédrale; ◎2-6pm Mon, 7.30am-7pm Tue-Sat, 8am-6pm Sun) Rouen's stunning Gothic cathedral, with its polished, brilliant-white façade, is the famous subject of a series of paintings by Monet. Its 75m-tall Tour de Beurre (Butter Tower) was financed by locals who donated to the cathedral in return for being allowed to eat butter during Lent – or so the story goes.

Musée des Beaux-Arts　　　ART MUSEUM

(☎02 35 71 28 40; www.rouen-musees.com; esplanade Marcel Duchamp; adult/child €5/free; ◎10am-6pm Wed-Mon) Housed in a grand structure erected in 1870, Rouen's fine-arts museum features canvases by Caravaggio, Rubens, Modigliani, Pissarro, Renoir, Sisley (lots) and (of course) several works by Monet.

NORMANDY ROUEN

Rouen

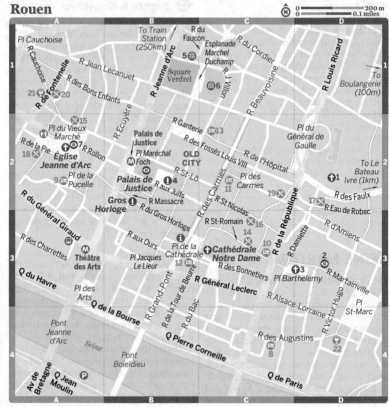

Rouen

Musée de la Céramique   PORCELAIN MUSEUM
(☑02 35 07 31 74; www.rouen-musees.com; 1 rue du Faucon; adult/child €3/free; ⊙10am-1pm & 2-6pm Wed-Mon) Housed in a 17th-century building with a fine courtyard, the Ceramics Museum is known for its 16th- to 19th-century faience (decorated earthenware) and porcelain.

Église St-Maclou   CHURCH
(place Barthelemy; ⊙10am-noon & 2-6pm Fri-Mon) This Flamboyant Gothic church was built between 1437 and 1521 but much of the decoration dates from the Renaissance. It is partly surrounded by half-timbered houses inclined at curious angles.

Abbatiale St-Ouen   CHURCH
(place du Général de Gaulle; ⊙10am-noon & 2-6pm Tue-Thu, Sat & Sun) This 14th-century abbey is a marvellous example of the Rayonnant Gothic style. The entrance is through a lovely garden along rue des Faulx.

FREE **Aître St-Maclou**   HISTORIC QUARTER
(186 rue Martainville; ⊙8am-8pm Apr-Oct, 8am-7pm Nov-Mar) For a macabre thrill, check out the courtyard of this curious ensemble of half-timbered buildings built between 1526 and 1533. Decorated with lurid woodcarvings of skulls, crossbones, gravediggers' tools and hourglasses, it was used as a burial ground for plague victims as recently as 1781.

🛏 Sleeping

TOP CHOICE **Hôtel de Bourgtheroulde**   HOTEL €€€
(☑02 35 14 50 50; www.hotelsparouen.com; 15 place de la Pucelle; r €240-380; ❋🅿🎐) This stunning conversion of an old private mansion brings a dash of glamour and luxury to Rouen's hotel scene. Rooms are large, gorgeously designed and feature beautiful bathrooms. There's a pool (you can see through the lobby bar's glass floor down into it), a sauna and spa in the basement, two restaurants and a sleek lobby bar.

La Boulangerie   B&B €
(☑06 12 94 53 15; www.laboulangerie.fr; 59 rue St-Nicaise; d €77-92, q €150; 🎐) Tucked into a quiet side street slightly off the historic quarter, this adorable B&B occupying a former bakery offers three pleasingly decorated rooms. The largest 'Levain' room can sleep up to four people, while the smaller 'Patte d'Ours' features exposed beams. Your charming hosts, Franck and Aminata, are a mine of local information.

Hôtel de la Cathédrale   HOTEL €
(☑02 35 71 57 95; www.hotel-de-la-cathedrale.fr; 12 rue St-Romain; s €66-86, d €76-104, q €143; @🎐) Hiding behind a 17th-century half-timbered façade, this atmospheric hotel has 27 stylishly refitted rooms, mostly overlooking a quiet plant-filled courtyard. Most of the bathroom fixtures are new, and the place remains a pleasant combination of modern and traditional.

Hôtel Alive de Québec   HOTEL €
(☑02 35 70 09 38; www.hotel-rouen.com; 18-24 rue de Québec; s €49-53, d €57-75; 🎐) You wouldn't guess from the outside, but this muscular building on a quiet backstreet near the Seine shelters modern, clean-as-a-pin rooms, all in beiges, maroons or greys, that offer tranquil havens for businesspeople and travellers. A good surprise. Private parking €8.

Hôtel le Cardinal   HOTEL €€
(☑02 35 70 24 42; www.cardinal-hotel.fr; 1 place de la Cathédrale; s €75-95, d €85-160; 🎐) After a top-to-bottom makeover in 2012, this 15-room hotel facing the cathedral now ranks as one of the best deals in central Rouen. The 4th-floor rooms have fantastic private terraces overlooking the square.

Hôtel des Carmes   HOTEL €
(☑02 35 71 92 31; www.hoteldescarmes.com; 33 place des Carmes; d €57-74, ste €82-107; 🎐) Occupying an elegant building on a central square (very handy for exploring the old streets of the city centre), this sweet little abode offers simple but pleasant rooms that are cheaper the higher you climb (no lift). Bathrooms are petite, though. A wiser option is the annex just down the street; opened in 2011, it features two beautifully appointed and spacious suites – a steal at the price.

Le Vieux Carré   HOTEL €
(☑02 35 71 67 70; www.hotel-vieux-carre.com; 34 rue Ganterie; r €60-68; 🎐) Set around a cute little garden courtyard, this quiet half-timbered hotel has a delightfully old-fashioned *salon de thé* (tearoom) and 13 smallish yet practical rooms, many of which have been freshly renovated. Ask for rooms 31, 32 or 33 if you want a view of the cathedral.

Auberge de Jeunesse Robec   HOSTEL €
(☑02 35 08 18 50; www.fuaj.org; 3 rue de la Tour; dm/s/d incl breakfast €22/33/56; 🎐) The two- to eight-bed rooms at this modern hostel are comfortable and functional. Sadly, it's some

way from the centre of town, off route de Darnétal – take bus T2 or T3 from Rouen's city centre and get off at the 'Auberge de Jeunesse' stop. The happy news is that prices include breakfast. Check in is from 5pm to 10pm only.

✕ Eating

Little eateries crowd the north side of rue Martainville, facing Église St-Maclou. More restaurants can be found along rue de Fontenelle (a block west of Église Jeanne d'Arc), and a few blocks east along rue Ecuyère.

TOP CHOICE Les Nymphéas   TRADITIONAL FRENCH €€
(✆02 35 89 26 69; www.lesnympheas-rouen.com; 7-9 rue de la Pie; mains €29-37, menus €34-52; ⊙lunch & dinner Tue-Sat) Its formal table settings arrayed under 16th-century beams, this fine restaurant serves cuisine based on fresh ingredients. Let chef Patrick Kukurudz and his team seduce you with meat and fish dishes accompanied with divinely inspired sauces. Even the cheaper lunch menu (€34) is exquisite.

Minute et Mijoté   BISTRO €
(58 rue de Fontenelle; mains €20, menus €13-30; ⊙lunch & dinner Mon-Sat) This smart bistro is one of our favourite finds in Rouen. The trademark here is freshness and great value for money, hence its fast-growing reputation. There's outdoor seating in summer.

Dame Cakes   PASTRIES €
(✆02 35 07 49 31; www.damecakes.fr; 70 rue St-Romain; mains €11, menus €14-22; ⊙10.30am-7pm Mon-Sat) This gourmet emporium is a veritable feast of perfectly presented pastries, cakes and chocolates. Best of all, there's a *salon de thé* (tearoom) attached, where you can tuck into well-prepared quiches and salads at lunchtime. Save a cranny for the exquisite *tarte tatin* (upside-down apple pie). Lovely.

L'Espiguette   BISTRO €
(✆02 35 71 66 27; 25 place St-Amand; mains €13-19, lunch menu €11; ⊙lunch & dinner Tue-Sat) A growing number of local connoisseurs are enthusiastic about this place, which overlooks a picturesque square. No culinary acrobatics here, just pared-down classics such as *joue de bœuf* (ox cheek), beef sirloin and salads. Its fixed-priced menu, with loads of good choices, is a great deal.

La Rose des Vents   MODERN FRENCH €
(✆02 35 70 29 78; 37 rue St-Nicolas; mains €9-13; ⊙lunch Tue-Sat) Hidden out the back of a sec-

ondhand shop, this discreet venture is recommended by local foodies who rave about the delicious lunch menu, which changes every week to match the mood of market stalls.

Gill Côté Bistro   BISTRO €
(✆02 35 89 88 72; 14 place du Vieux Marché; mains €14-22, menu €22; ⊙lunch & dinner daily) Market cuisine, new good-value wines, and sleek contemporary design are the rules of thumb at this popular operation under the tutelage of renowned chef Gilles Tournadre.

Brasserie Paul   BRASSERIE €
(✆02 35 71 86 07; www.brasserie-paul.com; 1 place de la Cathédrale; mains €10-16, menus €16-24; ⊙breakfast, lunch & dinner) The classic Rouennaise brasserie, favoured by artists and philosophers for over a century and still going strong. All the decorative trappings are there – starchy service, plush red seats and spinning overhead fans – and the menu is crammed with regional dishes.

Le P'tit Bec   BISTRO €
(✆02 35 07 63 33; www.leptitbec.com; 182 rue Eau de Robec; mains €9-15, menus €13-16; ⊙lunch Mon-Sat, dinner Thu & Sat, also open dinner Tue & Wed Jun-Aug) The down-to-earth menu here is stuffed with *gratins* (cheese-topped dishes), salads, *œufs cocottes* (eggs with grated cheese baked in cream) and homemade pastries. Its summer terrace sits on one of Rouen's most picturesque side streets.

♟ Drinking & Entertainment

The old town has no shortage of bars and cafes that buzz with students from midday until the early hours. Rouen is also the centre of Normandy's gay life – there are a couple of bars around rue St-Etienne des Tonneliers, south of rue Général Leclerc.

La Boîte à Bières   BAR
(www.laboiteabieres.fr; 35 rue Cauchoise; ⊙5pm-2am Tue-Sat) Affectionately known as BAB, this lively, half-timbered corner bar is a good place to down a few local *bières artisanales* (microbrews) in the company of a loyal student following.

Le Saxo   BAR
(✆02 35 98 24 92; 11 place St-Marc; ⊙9am-1am) This place swings to the rhythm of jazz and blues – it's a must on the nightcrawler's itinerary, especially on weekends when there are often live concerts. It serves a wide array of beers and prices are very reasonable.

NORMAN CUISINE

Normandy may be the largest region of France not to contain a single vineyard, but its culinary wealth more than makes up for what it lacks in the wine department – besides, any self-respecting Norman would far rather partake of a locally produced cider or calvados. This is a land of soft cheeses, apples, cream and an astonishingly rich range of seafood and fish. You simply shouldn't leave Normandy without trying classics like *coquilles St-Jacques* (scallops) and *sole dieppoise* (Dieppe sole). And whatever you do, don't forget your *trou normand* ('Norman hole') – the traditional break between courses of a meal for a glass of calvados to cleanse the palate and improve the appetite for the next course!

Le Bateau Ivre LIVE MUSIC
(http://bateauivre.rouen.free.fr; 17 rue des Sapins; ⏱9pm or 10pm-4am Wed-Sat, closed Wed in summer) A longstanding live venue with a varied program of concerts (French *chansons,* blues, rock reggae etc) except on Thursday, when anyone can join in the jam session.

ℹ Information

Post Office (45 rue Jeanne d'Arc) Changes foreign currency.
Tourist Office (☏02 32 08 32 40; www.rouentourisme.com; 25 place de la Cathédrale; ⏱9am-7pm Mon-Sat, 9.30am-12.30pm & 2-6pm Sun & holidays) Inside a Renaissance building from the 1500s. Hotel reservations cost €3 and audioguides (€5) are available in seven languages.

ℹ Getting There & Away

BUS Rouen is not very well served by buses, although there's a useful service to Le Havre (€2, three hours, four to five daily) from the bus station.
CAR Most car rental companies have desks in the train-station complex.
TRAIN The train station is just north of the city centre. Trains running from Rouen include:
Amiens From €19.40, 1¼ hours, four or five daily
Caen From €24.90, 1½ hours, eight to 10 daily
Dieppe From €11.10, 45 minutes, 14 to 16 daily Monday to Saturday, six Sunday
Le Havre €14.60, 50 minutes, 20 daily Monday to Saturday, 10 Sunday
Paris St-Lazare €21.90, 1¼ hours, about 27 daily Monday to Friday, 14 to 19 Saturday and Sunday

ℹ Getting Around

BICYCLE **Cy'clic** (☏08 00 08 78 00; http://cyclic.rouen.fr), Rouen's version of Paris' Vélib', lets you rent a city bike from 14 locations around town. Credit card registration for one/seven days costs €1/5. Use is free for the first 30 minutes; the 2nd/3rd/4th and subsequent half-hours cost €1/2/4 each.
BUS Rouen's bus lines are operated by **TCAR** (☏02 35 52 52 52; www.tcar.fr). The most useful routes for travellers are the T2 and T3, which serve the Auberge de Jeunesse Robec. A single-journey ticket costs €1.50.
CAR Free parking is available across the Seine from the city centre, along and below quai Jean Moulin.
METRO Rouen's **metro** (☏02 35 52 52 52; www.tcar.fr) runs from 5am (6am on Sunday) to about 11pm and is useful for getting from the train station to the centre of town. One ticket costs €1.50. There are Espace Métrobus ticket offices inside the train station.

Dieppe

POP 34,450
Sandwiched between limestone cliffs, Dieppe – a seaside resort since 1824 – is salty and a bit shabby but authentic, the kind of place where leather-skinned herring fishermen rub shoulders with British day trippers and summertime tourists licking oversized ice creams.

History

The early European settlers in Canada included many Dieppois and the town was one of France's most important ports during the 16th century, when ships regularly sailed to West Africa and Brazil.

On 19 August 1942 a mainly Canadian force of over 6000 landed on the Dieppe beaches, in part to help the Soviets by drawing Nazi military power away from the Eastern Front. The results were nothing short of catastrophic, but lessons learned here proved useful in planning the Normandy landings two years later.

◉ Sights & Activities

Château-Musée MUSEUM
(☎02 35 06 61 99; www.dieppe.fr; rue de Chastes; adult/child €4/2; ☺10am-noon & 2-6pm, closed Tue Oct-May) High above the city on the western cliff, this 15th-century château is Dieppe's most imposing landmark. The museum inside is devoted to the city's maritime and artistic history and hosts ivory carvings as well as paintings of local scenes by artists such as Courbet and Renoir.

Cité de la Mer MARITIME MUSEUM
(☎02 35 06 93 20; www.estrancitedelamer.fr; 37 rue de l'Asile Thomas; adult/child €7/3.50; ☺10am-noon & 2-6pm) Exhibits on fishing, shipbuilding, the tides, Dieppe's cliffs and the Channel's sea and seaside habitats. An English-language brochure is available at the ticket desk.

Dieppe Port HISTORIC QUARTER
Still used by fishing vessels but dominated by pleasure craft, the port makes for a bracing sea-air stroll.

Église St-Jacques CHURCH
(place St-Jacques) Two blocks west of the port, this Norman Gothic church has been reconstructed several times since the early 13th century.

Beach BEACH
Dieppe's often-windy, 1.8km-long beach is ideal if you love smooth, round pebbles. The vast lawns were laid out in the 1860s by that seashore-loving imperial duo, Napoléon III and his wife, Eugénie.

Canadian Military Cemetery CEMETERY
To visit the Canadian military cemetery 4km towards Rouen, take av des Canadiens (the continuation of av Gambetta) south and follow the signs.

Le Carré AQUATIC CENTRE
(☎02 35 82 80 90; www.lecarre-dieppe.fr; 101 bd de Verdun; day pass from €13; ☺10am-8pm) Established in the 1800s and completely renovated in 2007, the baths have several seawater pools heated to 28°C, including a 50m outdoor pool, and plenty of facilities for kids. Also boasts a fitness centre and a spa.

☞ Tours

Ville de Dieppe BOAT TOUR
(☎06 09 52 37 38; www.bateau-ville-de-dieppe. com; harbour; adult/child from €8/5; ☺weekends, school holidays & mid-Jul–mid-Aug) This operator offers boat excursions along the coast, which take in the dramatic cliffs of Côte d'Albâtre, and fishing trips aboard a well-equipped vessel.

⊨ Sleeping

Les Arcades HOTEL €
(☎02 35 84 14 12; www.lesarcades.fr; 1-3 arcades de la Bourse; d €69-85; 🛜) Perched above a colonnaded arcade, this well-managed hotel enjoys an advantageous location right in the heart of town and features 21 well-equipped rooms with salubrious bathrooms. Angle for a room with a port view. Double-glazed windows help with street noise. There's an onsite restaurant.

Villa Les Capucins B&B €
(☎02 35 82 16 52; www.villa-des-capucins.fr; 11 rue des Capucins; d €75, q €110-126) This B&B run by a retired lady is a good surprise, not least for the marvellous sense of peacefulness that wraps the property – yet just a two-minute walk east of the harbour. The four rooms are cosy, tidy and uncomplicated, and the ravishing landscaped garden is a great spot to unwind after a bout of sightseeing.

Au Grand Duquesne HOTEL €
(☎02 32 14 61 10; http://augrandduquesne.free.fr; 15 place St-Jacques; s €62-75, d €70-83, s/d without bathroom €57/65, incl breakfast; 🛜) Lacking excitement, maybe, but this central establishment overlooking Église St-Jacques is a safe bet, with neat rooms, prim bathrooms and good bedding. Alas, no harbour views. Seafood and regional dishes are served in the appealing dining room.

Hôtel de la Plage HOTEL €€
(☎02 35 84 18 28; http://plagehotel.fr.st; 20 bd de Verdun; d €65-110; 🛜) One of several somewhat faded places along the seafront, this hotel has 40 modern, mod-con rooms of varying shape and size; those at the front have balconies and afford knock-out views of the sea. Parking €8.

✗ Eating & Drinking

The harbour, especially quai Henri IV, is chock-full of touristy restaurants that double as bars.

Les Voiles d'Or GASTRONOMIC €€€
(☎02 35 84 16 84; www.lesvoilesdor.fr; 2 chemin des Falaises; mains €27-33, lunch menu €35, dinner menu €52; ☺lunch Wed-Sun, dinner Wed-Sat) If you want to savour cutting-edge cuisine

JUMIÈGES

Following the Seine valley west of Rouen, the D982 road winds through little towns, occasionally following the banks of the Seine as it climbs and descends. About 27km west of Rouen, in Jumièges. The Abbaye de Jumièges (☑02 35 37 24 02; Jumièges; adult/child €5/free; ☉9.30am-6.30pm Jul-Aug, 9.30am-1pm & 2.30-5.30pm Sep-Jun) is an absolute must-see, even if you're not a history buff. With its ghostly white stone set off by a backdrop of trees, it's one of the most evocative ruins in Normandy. The church was begun in 1020, and William the Conqueror attended its consecration in 1067. It declined during the Hundred Years War and then enjoyed a renaissance under Charles VII. It continued to flourish until the 18th-century revolutionaries booted out the monks and allowed the buildings to be mined for building materials. Should you be tempted to overnight in Jumièges, consider staying at Le Clos Fleuri (☑06 16 72 29 53, 02 35 81 49 00; www.closfleuri76.fr; 2196 route du Mesnil; s/d €42/48), an economical B&B just one kilometre away from the abbey.

made from top-quality ingredients, this is the place to go. Chef Christian Arhan has a soft spot for local seafood but the menu also includes savoury meat dishes. Just next door is Villa Bali-Dieppe (same owners), an excellent B&B featuring three rooms decorated in a Balinese style. It's near Église Notre-Dame de Bon Secours.

Le Turbot   NORMAN €
(☑02 35 82 63 44; 12 quai Cale; mains €11-23, menu €14; ☉Tue-Sun) This family-run Norman bistro decked out in sea paraphernalia is a bargain. Fresh-from-the-sea dishes, such as monkfish, Dover sole and ray in cream sauce, vie with deftly prepared meat dishes. At €14, the prix-fixed menu (also available at dinner and on weekends) is impressive value.

A La Marmite Dieppoise   SEAFOOD €€
(☑02 35 84 24 26; 8 rue St Jean; mains €12-35, menus €30-44; ☉lunch Tue-Sun, dinner Tue-Sat) A Dieppe institution, this eatery is celebrated for its hearty *marmite dieppoise* (stew consisting of four kinds of fish, mussels and prawns in cream sauce) served in a rustic dining room complete with exposed beams and stone walls.

❶ Information

Post Office (2 bd Maréchal Joffre) Changes foreign currency.

Tourist Office (☑02 32 14 40 60; www.dieppetourisme.com; Pont Jehan Ango, Quai du Carénage; ☉9am-1pm & 2-7pm Mon-Sat, 10am-1pm & 2-5pm Sun) Has useful English brochures on Dieppe and nearby parts of the Côte d'Albâtre.

❶ Getting There & Away

BOAT Car ferries run from the ferry terminal to Newhaven. **LD Lines** (www.ldlines.fr) plies the route between Dieppe and Newhaven.

TRAIN Trains running from Dieppe:
Le Havre €23.10, two to four hours, four to seven daily
Paris St-Lazare €29.40, two to three hours, nine to 10 daily
Rouen €11.10, 45 minutes, 12 to 16 daily

Côte d'Albâtre

No part of Normandy has more allure than this wedge of coast stretching 130km from Le Tréport southwest to Étretat. The bone-white cliffs of the Côte d'Albâtre (Alabaster Coast) are strikingly reminiscent of the limestone cliffs of Dover, just across the Channel. The dramatic coastline is dotted with small villages, fishing ports and resort towns, lovely gardens, several pebbly beaches, and two nuclear power plants (Paluel and Penly).

Without a car, the Côte d'Albâtre is pretty inaccessible, though walkers can take the coastal GR21 hiking trail (www.gr-infos.com/gr21.htm), which follows the Côte d'Albâtre all the way from Le Tréport to Le Havre. If you're driving west from Dieppe, take the coastal roads (D75, D68 and D79) rather than the inland D925. Toast your trip with oysters in Pourville before cruising west to scenic Varangeville and delightful St Valery en Caux with its fishing port and lovely beach. Then drive west to Veulettes-sur-Mer and Les Petites Dalles before reaching Fécamp.

🛏 Sleeping & Eating

Hôtel-Restaurant La Terrasse   HOTEL €
(☎02 35 85 12 54; www.hotel-restaurant-la-terrasse.
com; route de Vasterival, Varangeville; r incl half board
per person €62; ☎) You keep expecting Hercule
Poirot to pop his head around the corner of
this charmingly old-world hotel. The simply
finished rooms are accentuated by warm,
pale colours, and laminate floors; don't even
consider one without a sea view. The onsite
restaurant specialises in hearty regional
cuisine.

La Maison des Galets   HOTEL €
(☎02 35 97 11 22; www.lamaisondesgalets.com; 22
cours Le Perrey, St Valery en Caux; s €53, d €65-80;
☎) Surprisingly, St Valery en Caux is short
on quality sleeps, but this solid two-starrer
on the seafront makes up for the shortfall.
Most of the rooms have had a modern-day
refit and feature squeaky-clean bathrooms.
The sea views are worth the outlay. The
onsite restaurant (☎02 35 97 11 22; 22 cours
Le Perrey; mains €15-18, menus €19-35; ⊙lunch &
dinner Fri-Tue) is well worth considering for
its meaty dishes and seafood, often prepared with a creative twist. A big picture
window gives lovely views of the beach.

Restaurant du Port   SEAFOOD €€
(☎02 35 97 08 93; 18 quai d'Amont, St Valery en
Caux; mains €13-38, menus €26-46; ⊙lunch Tue-
Sun, dinner Tue-Wed, Fri-Sun) A gem for seafood
lovers. The à la carte offerings might include
oysters, fresh crab or turbot marinated in
cream. The seafood platters (€38) are a real
sight to behold.

L'Huîtrière   SEAFOOD €
(☎02 35 84 36 20; rue de la Mer, Pourville; mains
€10-30; ⊙10am-8pm Easter-Sep) An extension
of a fish shop, this 1st-floor restaurant in
a charmless concrete building offers views
over the beach and the freshest seafood for
miles around.

FÉCAMP
POP 19,630

Fécamp was an ordinary fishing village until
the 6th century, when a few drops of Christ's
blood miraculously found their way here
and attracted hordes of pilgrims. Benedictine monks soon established a monastery,
and the fiery 'medicinal elixir' that a Venetian monk concocted in 1510 (using East
Asian herbs) helped keep Fécamp on the
map. The recipe, lost during the Revolution,
was rediscovered in an old book in the 19th

century. Today, Bénédictine is one of the
most widely marketed *digestifs* in the world.

⊙ Sights & Activities

The port, still used by fishing craft, is connected to the sea by the narrow *avant port*
(outer harbour). North of the port rises Cap
Fagnet (110m), which offers fantastic views
of the town and the coastline, while to the
south is the beach, where you can rent catamarans, kayaks and windsurfers in summer.

Abbatiale de la Ste-Trinité   ABBEY
(place des Ducs Richard; ⊙9am-5pm) Built from
1175 to 1220 by Richard the Lionheart, this
attractive abbey, 1.5km east of the beach,
was the most important pilgrimage site in
Normandy until the construction of Mont
St-Michel, thanks to the drops of holy blood
that miraculously floated to Fécamp in the
trunk of a fig tree. Across from the abbey are
the remains of the fortified château built
by the earliest dukes of Normandy in the
10th and 11th centuries.

Palais de la Bénédictine   LIQUEUR FACTORY
(☎02 35 10 26 10; www.benedictinedom.com; 110
rue Alexandre Le Grand; adult/child €7.20/3.20;
⊙tickets sold 10am-noon & 2-5.30pm, no midday
closure Jul-Aug, closed Jan) Opened in 1900,
this unusually ornate factory is where all the
Bénédictine liqueur in the world is made.
Tours take you to a surprisingly interesting
collection of 13th- to 19th-century religious
art and paintings assembled by the company's visionary founder, Alexandre Le Grand.
They continue to the production facilities,
where you can admire copper alembics and
touch and smell the natural ingredients
used to make Bénédictine. There's a shop.

🛏 Sleeping & Eating

Quite a few restaurants are situated on the
south side of the port, along quai de la Vi-
comté and nearby parts of quai Bérigny.

Hôtel Normandy   HOTEL €
(☎02 35 29 55 11; www.normandy-fecamp.com; 4
av Gambetta; s/d €61/68; ☎) In a smart fin-de-
siècle building just up the hill from the train
station, this quiet place has 32 recently refurbished rooms – some quite spacious – with
rather bland furnishings and lots of light.
Rooms are often cheaper from October to
June.

La Ferme de la Chapelle   HOTEL €€
(☎02 35 10 12 12; www.fermedelachapelle.fr; Côte
de la Vierge; d €85-95; ☎🎇) High above town
near Cap Fagnet, this renovated farm has

rather ordinary rooms and kitchenette-equipped apartments that overlook a grassy central courtyard, so there's no sea view – for that you'll have to step outside the compound. There were plans to renovate the rooms at the time of research.

Camping de Renéville CAMPGROUND €
(☑02 35 28 20 97; www.campingderaneville.com; chemin de Nesmond; tent & 2 adults from €12; ☺Apr-mid-Nov) Dramatically situated on the western cliffs overlooking the beach, this campground also rents out two- and six-people chalets (€264 to €654 per week). In July and August the tent rate goes up to €15.70.

Café de la Boucane NORMAN, SEAFOOD €€
(☑02 35 10 50 50; 12 Grand Quai; mains €10-20, menus €12-25; ☺10am-midnight Jul-Aug, closed Tue Sep-Jun) A much-loved locals' hangout occupying a converted smokehouse, Café de la Boucane is as much a restaurant as a bar. Its specialities include mussels, oysters and *morue* (cod fish). The interior is super atmospheric but the terrace overlooking the marina is a great spot to just chill out in summer.

La Marée SEAFOOD €€
(☑02 35 29 39 15; 77 quai Bérigny; mains €17-36, menus €29-36; ☺lunch Tue-Sun, dinner Tue-Sat) Fish, fish and fish – that's all that matters at La Marée, Fécamp's premier address for *fruits de mer*. The rather staid atmosphere might not be to everyone's taste, but you won't find better seafood anywhere in Fécamp.

❶ Information
Tourist Office (☑02 35 28 51 01; www.fecamp tourisme.com; quai Sadi Carnot; ☺10am-6pm, closed Sun Sep-Mar) Situated at the southern end of the pleasure port, across the parking lot from the train station, the tourist office has useful English-language brochures.

❶ Getting There & Away
BUS Bus 24, operated by **Keolis** (☑02 35 28 19 88; www.keolis-seine-maritime.com), goes to Le Havre (€2, 1½ hours, eight to 10 daily) via Étretat.

TRAIN Train destinations include Le Havre (€8.50, 45 to 75 minutes, seven to 10 daily) and Rouen (€13.90, 1¼ hours, seven to 10 daily).

ÉTRETAT
POP 1550
The small village of Étretat, 20km southwest of Fécamp, is known for its twin cliffs, the Falaise d'Aval and the Falaise d'Amont, positioned on either side of the pebbly beach.

The dramatic scenery made Étretat a favourite of painters Camille Corot, Boudin, Gustave Courbet and Monet. With the vogue for sea air at the end of the 19th century, fashionable Parisians came and built extravagant villas. Étretat has never gone out of style and swells to bursting point with visitors every weekend.

◉ Sights & Activities
The Falaise d'Aval is renowned for its free-standing arch – compared by French writer Maupassant to an elephant dipping its trunk in the sea – and the adjacent Aiguille, a 70m-high spire of chalk-white rock rising from the surface of the waves. Further along the cliff is a second impressive arch, known as La Manneporte, reached by a steep path up the cliff from the western end of Étretat's beach. On the Falaise d'Amont, a memorial marks the spot where two aviators were last seen before their attempt to cross the Atlantic in 1927.

The tourist office has a map of the cliff trails.

🛏 Sleeping & Eating
There are plenty of accommodation and dining options in Étretat but most places are overpriced and overbusy.

Detective Hotel HOTEL €
(☑02 35 27 01 34; www.detectivehotel.com; 6 av Georges V; s €39, d €45-79; ☎) Run by a former detective, this place has to be one of Côte d'Albâtre's best bargains. Despite the bottom-of-the-barrel price tag, it's packed with thoughtful touches and each room has its own design scheme inspired by Cluedo, the famous board game. Utterly original.

DON'T MISS

VEULES-LES-ROSES

One of Côte d'Albâtre's gems is the village of Veules-les-Roses, a few kilometres east of St Valery en Caux. With its wonderfully relaxing atmosphere and lovely setting, it's sure to win your heart. The pebbly beach is never too crowded, and the village is utterly picturesque, with its elegant manors and imposing church. The fact that it's traversed by a small river adds to the bucolic appeal. Also look out for the *cressonnières* (ponds where watercress is grown).

ℹ Information

Tourist Office (☑02 35 27 05 21; www.etretat. net; place Maurice Guillard; ☺10am-noon & 2-6pm Mon-Sat) This tourist office has accommodation lists for the area (also available on the website).

ℹ Getting There & Away

Bus 24, operated by **Keolis** (☑02 35 28 19 88; www.keolis-seine-maritime.com), goes to Le Havre (€2, one hour, eight to 10 daily) and Fécamp (€2, 30 minutes, eight to 10 daily).

Le Havre

POP 182,400

All but obliterated in September 1944 by Allied bombing raids that killed 3000 civilians, Le Havre's city centre was totally rebuilt after the war by Belgian architect Auguste Perret. What emerged from the rubble is a most unexpected love letter to modernism, and an evocative portrait of France's postwar energy and optimism. It's a love-it or hate-it kind of place, but even if vast municipal squares and architectural quirks such as Oscar Niemeyer's Le Volcan aren't your thing, it's not hard to see why Unesco listed Le Havre as a World Heritage Site in 2005. With its fantastic Malraux museum and friendly, progressive feel, Le Havre is far more than just another ferry port.

◉ Sights & Activities

TOP **CHOICE** **Musée d'Art Moderne André Malraux**   ART MUSEUM
(☑02 35 19 62 62; 2 bd Clemenceau; adult/child €5/ free; ☺11am-6pm Mon-Fri, 11am-7pm Sat & Sun) At the city centre's southwestern tip, this fantastic modern space houses a truly fabulous collection of Impressionist works – the finest in France outside of Paris – by luminaries such as Degas, Monet, Pissarro, Renoir, Sisley and Le Havre native Eugène Boudin. A section is devoted to Fauvist Raoul Dufy, also born in Le Havre.

Église St-Joseph   CHURCH
(bd François 1er) The city is dominated by Perret's centrepiece, the magnificent 107m-high Église St-Joseph, which was begun in 1951 and inaugurated in 1959. Its 13,000 panels of coloured glass make the interior particularly striking when it's sunny.

Appartement Témoin   ARCHITECTURE
(adult/child €3/free; ☺tours 2pm, 3pm, 4pm & 5pm Wed, Sat & Sun, plus 2pm & 3pm Mon, Tue, Thu & Fri

Jul-Aug) Furnished in impeccable 1950s style, this perfectly preserved apartment within an ensemble of six striking Perret-designed residential buildings facing the town hall can be visited on a one-hour guided tour that starts at 181 rue de Paris (Maison du Patrimoine).

Le Volcan   CULTURAL CENTRE
(The Volcano; Espace Oscar Niemeyer; www.levolcan .com; av Lucien Corbeaux) Le Havre's most famous landmark is also its premier cultural venue and boasts concert halls and an excellent art cinema. One look and you'll understand how it got its name. It was conceived by Brazilian architect Oscar Niemeyer.

FREE **Jardins Suspendus**   GARDENS
(rue du Fort; ☺10.30am-6pm Mon-Fri, 10.30am-8pm Sat & Sun) An old hilltop fortress a bit over 1km north of the tourist office has been transformed into a beautiful set of gardens, whose greenhouses and outdoor spaces feature rare plants and cacti from five continents.

⏸ Sleeping

TOP **CHOICE** **Hôtel Vent d'Ouest**   BOUTIQUE HOTEL €€
(☑02 35 42 50 69; www.ventdouest.fr; 4 rue de Caligny; d €110-170, q €184; ☎) This stylish establishment is decorated in maritime fashion, with nautical memorabilia downstairs and a range of posh cream-walled, sisal-floored rooms upstairs; ask for one with a balcony. Facilities include a restaurant, a fashionable tearoom, a bar and a sparkling spa. Parking €8.

Hôtel Oscar   HOTEL €
(☑02 35 42 39 77; www.hotel-oscar.fr; 106 rue Voltaire; s €60-68, d €70-78; ☎) A treat for architecture aficionados, this hotel in a Perret-designed building is an opportunity to experience the Belgian architect's legacy inside and out. The superior rooms are larger and marginally dearer than the standard ones and offer great views of the Volcan.

Hôtel Le Richelieu   HOTEL €
(☑02 35 42 38 71; www.hotellerichelieu.fr; 132 rue de Paris; s €54-57, d €58-62, tr €74; ☎) Inside one of the architecturally interesting buildings along the rue de Paris, Le Richelieu offers spotless, bright and often bizarrely decorated rooms that are great value for their comfort and location. Bathrooms are tiny, though, and there's no lift. Parking €8.

🍴 Eating

In Quartier St-François, rue du Général Faidherbe and perpendicular rue Jean de la Fontaine are lined with eateries. There's also a great selection at the Docks Vauban.

La Petite Auberge   TRADITIONAL FRENCH €€
(☏02 35 46 27 32; www.lapetiteauberge-lehavre.fr; 32 rue de Ste Adresse; mains €13-25, menus €20-40; ⊗lunch & dinner Tue & Thu-Sat, dinner Wed, lunch Sun) This absolute gem of a place is possibly Le Havre's most charming dining option, with a low-beamed dining room that whispers of romance. Seafood dominates the inventive yet traditional menu but there's plenty of room for meaty dishes, too.

Cafeteria du Musée Malraux   MODERN FRENCH €€
(☏02 35 19 62 62; 2 bd Clémenceau; mains €14, menus €20-25; ⊗lunch Wed-Mon) Inside the museum this is a great place to tuck into well-executed French classics, with the added bonus of ample harbour views.

La Taverne Paillette   BRASSERIE €
(☏02 35 41 31 50; www.taverne-paillette.com; 22 rue Georges Braques; mains €11-44, lunch menu €14; ⊗noon-midnight daily) Solid brasserie food is the order of the day at this Le Havre institution – think big bowls of mussels, generous salads and gargantuan seafood platters, or be adventurous with tripes *à la normande* or maybe some *choucroute* (sauerkraut).

ℹ Information

Normandie Change (41 chaussée Kennedy; ⊗9am-12.30pm & 2-6.30pm Mon-Fri, to 5pm Sat) An exchange bureau half a block west of the southern end of rue de Paris.

Microminute (☏02 35 22 10 15; 7 rue Casimir Periér; per hr €3.60; ⊗2-6.30pm Mon, 9.30am-noon & 1-6.30pm Tue-Sat) Internet access a block east of the Hôtel de Ville.

Post Office (place des Halles Centrales)

Tourist Office (☏02 32 74 04 04; www.lehavretourisme.com; 186 bd Clemenceau; ⊗9am-6.45pm Mon-Sat, 10am-12.30pm & 2.30-5.45pm Sun & holidays) Can supply you with an English map/brochure for a two-hour self-guided walking tour of the city centre's architectural highlight.

ℹ Getting There & Away

BOAT Ferry services are available to Portsmouth. **LD Lines** (www.ldlines.fr) has ferry services between Portsmouth and Le Havre.

BUS Bus 20, run by **Bus Verts** (☏0810 214 214; www.busverts.fr), runs from the bus station (next to the train station) to Caen (€10.80, 2½ hours), Deauville and Trouville (€6.60, one hour) and Honfleur (€4.35, 35 minutes). Express buses (Prestobus, line 39) also run to Caen (€15.15, 1½ hours, about three daily Monday to Saturday, two Sunday) via Honfleur. Bus 24, operated by **Keolis** (☏02 35 28 19 88; www.keolis-seine-maritime.com) goes to Fécamp (€2, 1½ hours, eight to 10 daily) via Étretat.

TRAIN The **train station** (www.voyages-sncf.com; cours de la République) is 2km east of the Hôtel de Ville at the eastern end of bd de Strasbourg. Services run to Fécamp (€8.50, 45 to 75 minutes, seven to 11 daily), Paris St-Lazare (€32.10, 2¼ hours, at least hourly) and Rouen (€14.60, 50 minutes, 20 daily Monday to Saturday, 10 Sunday).

ℹ Getting Around

Year-round, **Vélocéane bicycles** (www.bus-oceane.com; per 2hr/half-day/full day €2/3/5) can be hired at five sites, including the tourist office and the train station.

EURE

Lovely day trips can be made from Rouen, particularly in the landlocked Eure (www.eure-tourisme.fr) *département*. The beautiful gardens of Claude Monet are at Giverny, while the 12th-century Château Gaillard in Les Andelys affords a breathtaking panorama of the Seine.

Les Andelys

POP 8440

Some 40km southeast of Rouen, on a hairpin curve in the Seine, lies Les Andelys (the 's' is silent), crowned by the ruins of Château Gaillard, the 12th-century hilltop fastness of Richard the Lionheart.

◉ Sights

Château Gaillard   CASTLE
(☏02 32 54 41 93; adult/child €3.15/2.60; ⊗10am-1pm & 2-6pm Wed-Mon mid-Mar–mid-Nov) Built from 1196 to 1197, Château Gaillard secured the western border of English territory along the Seine until Henry IV ordered its destruction in 1603. Fantastic views of the Seine's white cliffs can be enjoyed from the platform a few hundred metres up the one-lane road from the castle. The tourist office has details on tours (€4.50, in French with

CLAUDE MONET

Everyone discusses my art and pretends to understand, as if it were necessary to understand, when it is simply necessary to love.

Claude Monet

The undisputed leader of the Impressionists, Claude Monet was born in Paris in 1840 and grew up in Le Havre, where he found an early affinity with the outdoors. Monet disliked school and spent much of his time sketching his professors in the margins of his exercise books. By 15 his skills as a caricaturist were known throughout Le Havre, but Eugène Boudin, his first mentor, convinced him to turn his attention away from portraiture towards the study of colour, light and landscape.

In 1860 military service interrupted Monet's studies at the Académie Suisse in Paris and took him to Algiers, where the intense light and colours further fuelled his imagination. The young painter became fascinated with capturing a specific moment in time, the immediate impression of the scene before him, rather than the precise detail.

From 1867 Monet's distinctive style began to emerge, focusing on the effects of light and colour and using the quick, undisguised broken brushstrokes that would characterise the Impressionist period. His contemporaries were Pissarro, Renoir, Sisley, Cézanne and Degas. The young painters left the studio to work outdoors, experimenting with the shades and hues of nature, and arguing and sharing ideas. Their work was far from welcomed by critics; one of them condemned it as 'impressionism', in reference to Monet's *Impression: Sunrise* (1874). Much to the critic's chagrin, the name stuck.

From the late 1870s Monet concentrated on painting in series, seeking to re-create a landscape by showing its transformation under different conditions of light and atmosphere. *Haystacks* (1890–91) and *Rouen Cathedral* (1891–95) are some of the best-known works of this period. In 1883 Monet moved to Giverny, planting his property with a variety of flowers around an artificial pond, the Jardin d'Eau, in order to paint the subtle effects of sunlight on natural forms. It was here that he painted the *Nymphéas* (Water Lilies) series. The huge dimensions of some of these works, together with the fact that the pond's surface takes up the entire canvas, meant the abandonment of composition in the traditional sense and the virtual disintegration of form. A *Nymphéas* canvas from 1919, likely to be the last ever to come up for auction, sold in June 2008 for an astounding US$80 million.

For more info on Monet and his work, visit www.giverny.org.

English-speaking guides). Entry to the château grounds is free.

Sleeping & Eating

Hôtel & Restaurant de la Chaîne d'Or TRADITIONAL HOTEL **€€**
(☎02 32 54 00 31; www.hotel-lachainedor.com; 27 rue Grande, Petit Andely; r €94-149; ⊗closed Jan; 🕸) Right on the Seine, this little rural hideaway, packed with character, is rustically stylish without being twee. The 12 rooms are spacious, tasteful and romantic, with antique wood furnishings and plush rugs; some are so close to the river you could almost fish out the window. The classy French *restaurant* (lunch menus €20-65; ⊗restaurant lunch & dinner Thu-Tue mid-Apr–mid-Oct, Wed-Sat mid-Oct–mid-Apr, lunch Sun mid-Oct–mid-Apr) is one of the best for miles around – specialities include lobster and *ris de veau*. Top it off, if you can, with a local favourite, *tarte aux pommes flambées au* calvados (flambéed apple pie).

❶ Information

Tourist Office (☎02 32 54 41 93; http://office-tourisme.ville-andelys.fr; 24 rue Philippe Auguste; ⊗10am-noon & 2-6pm Mon-Sat, 10am-noon & 2-5pm Sun) In Petit Andely.

Giverny

POP 530

The tiny country village of Giverny, 15km south of Les Andelys, is a place of pilgrimage for devotees of Impressionism, and can feel swamped by the tour-bus crowd in the summer months. Monet lived here from

1883 until his death in 1926, in a rambling house – surrounded by flower-filled gardens – that's now the immensely popular Maison et Jardins de Claude Monet.

◉ Sights

Maison et Jardins de Claude Monet
MUSEUM, GARDENS

(☎02 32 51 28 21; www.fondation-monet.com; adult/child €9/5; ⏱9.30am-5.30pm Apr-Oct) Monet's home for the last 43 years of his life is now a delightful house-museum. His pastel-pink house and Water Lily studio stand on the periphery of the Clos Normand, with its symmetrically laid-out gardens bursting with flowers. Monet bought the Jardin d'Eau (Water Garden) in 1895 and set about creating his trademark lily pond, as well as the famous Japanese bridge (since rebuilt).

Draped with purple wisteria, the bridge blends into the asymmetrical foreground and background, creating the intimate atmosphere for which the 'painter of light' was renowned.

Seasons have an enormous effect on Giverny. From early to late spring, daffodils, tulips, rhododendrons, wisteria and irises appear, followed by poppies and lilies. By June, nasturtiums, roses and sweet peas are in flower. Around September, there are dahlias, sunflowers and hollyhocks.

Musée des Impressionnismes Giverny
ART MUSEUM

(☎02 32 51 94 65; www.mdig.fr; 99 rue Claude Monet; adult/child €6.50/3; ⏱10am-5.30pm Apr-Oct) Giverny's not-to-be-missed attraction, this museum is surrounded by beautiful gardens and displays works by various Impressionists as well as temporary exhibitions. It's 100m down the road from the Maison de Claude Monet.

🛏 Sleeping & Eating

La Pluie de Roses
B&B €€

(☎02 32 51 10 67; www.givernylapluiederoses.fr; 14 rue Claude Monet; d €120-130; 🛜) You'll be won over by this adorable private home cocooned in a dreamy, peaceful garden. Inside, the three rooms are so comfy it's hard to wake up. Superb breakfast in a veranda awash with sunlight. Payment is by cash only.

La Musardière
HOTEL €€

(☎02 32 21 03 18; www.lamusardiere.fr; 123 rue Claude Monet; d €83-97; ⏱hotel Feb–mid-Dec, restaurant daily Apr-Oct; 🛜) This two-star 10-room hotel dating back to 1880 and evocatively

called the 'Idler' is set amid a lovely garden less than 100m north-east of the Maison de Claude Monet. Savouring a crêpe in its summer restaurant (menus €26 and €36) is a pleasure.

❶ Getting There & Away

BICYCLE Facing the train station in Vernon, you can rent a bike at the Café L'Arrivée de Giverny (☎02 32 21 16 01; 1 pl de la Gare; per day €14; ⏱7am-11pm).

BUS Shuttle buses (€6.50 round trip, three to six daily April to October) meet most trains to and from Paris.

TAXI Taxis usually wait outside the train station in Vernon and charge around €12 for a ride to Giverny.

TRAIN From Paris Gare St-Lazare there are up to 15 daily trains to Vernon (€13.30, 50 minutes), 7km to the west of Giverny. From Rouen (€10.80, 40 minutes), seven trains leave for Vernon before noon; to get back to Rouen, there's about one train every hour between 5pm and 8pm.

CALVADOS

The département of Calvados (www.calvados-tourisme.com) stretches from Honfleur in the east to Isigny-sur-Mer in the west and includes Caen, Bayeux – world-renowned for its tapestry – and the D-Day beaches. The area is famed for its rich pastures and farm products, including butter, cheese, cider and the distinctive apple brandy calvados, which bears the name of the département.

Bayeux

POP 14,350

Bayeux has become famous throughout the English-speaking world thanks to a 68m-long piece of painstakingly embroidered cloth: the 11th-century Bayeux Tapestry, whose 58 scenes vividly tell the story of the Norman invasion of England in 1066. But there's more to Bayeux than this unparalleled piece of needlework. The first town to be liberated after D-Day (on the morning of 7 June 1944), it is one of the few in Calvados to have survived WWII practically unscathed. A great place to soak up the Norman atmosphere, Bayeux' delightful city centre is crammed with 13th- to 18th-century buildings, including lots of wood-framed Norman-style houses, and a fine Gothic cathedral. Bayeux also makes an ideal launch pad for exploring the D-Day beaches just to the north.

NORMANDY BAYEUX

◉ Sights

TOP CHOICE **Bayeux Tapestry** TAPESTRY
(Map p220; ☑ 02 31 51 25 50; www.tapisserie-ba yeux.fr; rue de Nesmond; adult/child incl audioguide €7.80/3.80; ⊙9am-6.30pm mid-Mar–mid-Nov, to 7pm May-Aug, 9.30am-12.30pm & 2-6pm mid-Nov–mid-Mar) The world's most celebrated embroidery recounts the conquest of England from an unashamedly Norman perspective. Fifty-eight scenes fill the central canvas, and religious allegories and illustrations of everyday 11th-century life fill the borders. The final showdown at the Battle of Hastings is depicted in graphic fashion, complete with severed limbs and decapitated heads (along the bottom of scene 52); Halley's Comet, which blazed across the sky in 1066, appears in scene 32. Scholars believe the 68.3m-long tapestry was commissioned by Bishop Odo of Bayeux, William the Conquerer's half-brother, for the opening of Bayeux' cathedral in 1077.

Cathédrale Notre Dame CATHEDRAL
(Map p220; rue du Bienvenu; ⊙8.30am-6pm) Most of Bayeux' spectacular Norman Gothic cathedral dates from the 13th century, though the crypt (accessible from the north side of the choir), the arches of the nave and the lower portions of the entrance towers are 11th-century Romanesque. The central tower was added in the 15th century; the copper dome dates from the 1860s. First prize for tackiness has got to go to 'Litanies de la Sainte Vierge', a 17th-century retable in the first chapel on the left as you enter the cathedral.

FREE **Conservatoire de la Dentelle** LACE WORKSHOP
(Lace Conservatory; Map p220; ☑ 02 31 92 73 80; http://dentelledebayeux.free.fr; 6 rue du Bienvenu; ⊙9.30am-12.30pm & 2.30-5pm Mon-Sat) This workshop is dedicated to the preservation of traditional Norman lacemaking, and you can watch some of France's most celebrated

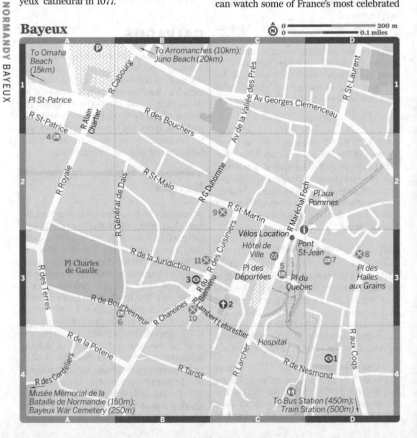

Bayeux

lacemakers create intricate designs using dozens of bobbins and hundreds of pins. At its height, the local lace industry employed 5000 lacemakers.

Musée Mémorial de la Bataille de Normandie
WAR MUSEUM

(Battle of Normandy Memorial Museum; bd Fabien Ware; adult/child €7/3.80; ◎9.30am-6.30pm May-Sep, 10am-12.30pm & 2-6pm Oct-Apr) Using well-chosen photos, personal accounts, dioramas and wartime objects, this first-rate museum offers an excellent introduction to WWII in Normandy. Don't miss the 25-minute film on the Battle of Normandy, screened in English up to five times daily.

Bayeux War Cemetery
CEMETERY

(bd Fabien Ware) This peaceful cemetery is the largest of the 18 Commonwealth military cemeteries in Normandy. It contains 4848 graves of soldiers from the UK and 10 other countries, including, rather surprisingly, Germany. Across the road is a memorial for 1807 Commonwealth soldiers whose remains were never found; the Latin inscription across the top reads: 'We, whom William once conquered, have now set free the conqueror's native land'.

Mémorial des Reporters
MEMORIAL

Just beyond the cemetery and easily missed (the entrance is not on bd Fabien Ware itself), a landscaped promenade lists the names of nearly 2000 journalists killed in the line of duty around the world since 1944.

🛌 Sleeping

The tourist office has a list of *chambres d'hôte* (B&Bs; €50 to €90) around Bayeux.

Bayeux

◎ Sights

TOP CHOICE **Les Logis du Rempart**
B&B €

(Map p220; ☑02 31 92 50 40; www.lecornu.fr; 4 rue Bourbesneur; d €60-80, q €130; ☎) What a find. This *maison de famille* shelters three rooms that ooze old-fashioned cosiness. Our favourite, the Bajocasse, has parquet floor and Toile de Jouy wallpaper. Best of all, your hosts run a tasting shop downstairs – the perfect place to stock up on top-quality, homemade calvados and cider. Breakfast is extra (€6) and features – you guessed it – organic apple juice and apple jelly.

Villa Lara
BOUTIQUE HOTEL €€€

(Map p220; ☑02 31 92 00 55; www.hotel-villalara. com; 6 place de Québec; d €180-280, ste €290-450; ❊☎) Luxury and sophistication are the hallmarks of this 28-room boutique hotel, which opened in 2012. Clean lines, trendy colour schemes, top-quality fabrics and minimalist motifs distinguish the rooms, while other facilities include a bistro and a gym. The best rooms are blessed with views of the cathedral.

Hôtel d'Argouges
TRADITIONAL HOTEL €€

(Map p220; ☑02 31 92 88 86; www.hotel-dargoug es.com; 21 rue St-Patrice; d €134-149; ◎closed Dec-Jan; ☎) This graceful venture, in a stately 18th-century residence, has 28 comfortable rooms with old-time touches, such as exposed beams, thick walls and old-fashioned furniture, and a deliciously lush little garden. Most bathrooms have been recently upgraded. Breakfast is served in an enchanting room complete with a 18th-century tapestry, period wood panels and parquet floors.

Hôtel Reine Mathilde
HOTEL €€

(Map p220; ☑02 31 92 08 13; www.hotel-bayeux-reine mathilde.fr; 23 rue Larcher; d €70-105; ☎) Above a bustling local cafe of the same name, this family-run hotel is an excellent bet, right in the centre of town, with smallish but comfortable rooms. Better yet, the annexe which was opened in 2012, behind the main building, sports six sleek, spacious and sparkling rooms in a converted barn by the river.

🍴 Eating

Local specialities to keep an eye out for include *cochon de Bayeux* (Bayeux-style pork). Rue St-Jean and rue St-Martin are home to a variety of cheap eateries and food shops.

La Rapière
NORMAN €€

(Map p220; ☑02 31 21 05 45; 53 rue St-Jean; menus €15-33.50; ◎lunch & dinner Fri-Tue) Housed in a late-1400s mansion composed of stone walls and big wooden beams, this atmospheric restaurant specialises in Normandy staples such as terrines, duck and veal with Camembert. Four fixed-price menus assure a splendid meal on any budget.

La Reine Mathilde CAKE SHOP €
(Map p220; 47 rue St-Martin; cakes from €2.50; ⊙8.30am-7.30pm Tue-Sun) A sumptuous, c 1900-style patisserie and *salon de thé* (tearoom) that's ideal if you've got a hankering for something sweet. There's seating here, making it prime breakfast and afternoon-tea terrain.

Le Pommier NORMAN €€
(Map p220; ☑02 31 21 52 10; www.restaurantlepommier.com; 38-40 rue des Cuisiniers; menus €15-30; ⊙closed Sun Nov-Mar & mid-Dec–mid-Jan; ☑) A celebration of all things Norman, Le Pommier's menus include such classics as Caen-style tripe and steamed pollock. A vegetarian menu – a rarity in Normandy – is also available, with deeply satisfying dishes like soya beans steak in Norman cream. The restaurant has a romantic setting, with bare stone walls, warm feature walls and hardwood floors.

L'Assiette Normande NORMAN €
(Map p220; ☑02 31 22 04 61; www.lassiettenormande.fr; 1-3 rue des Chanoines; menus €10-35; ⊙lunch Tue-Sat, dinner daily) Crammed at lunchtime and on weekends, this lively eatery beside the cathedral is about uncomplicated food at fair prices, from meat and fish dishes to oysters and mussels. There's an interesting menu with a focus on Bayeux-style pork (€16).

ℹ Information

Post Office (14 rue Larcher) Changes foreign currency.

Tourist Office (☑02 31 51 28 28; www.bessin-normandie.com; pont St-Jean; ⊙9.30am-12.30pm & 2-6pm) Covers both Bayeux and the surrounding Bessin region, including the D-Day beaches. Has a walking tour map of town, English books on the D-Day landings and the Bayeux Tapestry, and bus and train schedules. Charges €2 to book hotels and B&Bs.

ℹ Getting There & Away

BUS **Bus Verts** (☑08 10 21 42 14; www.busverts.fr) bus 30 links the train station and place St-Patrice with Caen (€4.50, one hour, three or four daily Monday to Friday except holidays).

Bus Verts also runs regular buses to the D-Day beaches.

TRAIN To get to Deauville, change at Lisieux. For Paris Gare St-Lazare and Rouen, change at Caen.

Destinations include Caen (€6.20, 20 minutes, at least hourly), Cherbourg (€16.50, one hour, 15 daily Monday to Friday, eight to 10 on weekends) and Pontorson (Mont St-Michel; €22.30, 1¾ hours, two or three direct daily).

ℹ Getting Around

Taxi (☑02 31 92 92 40; www.bayeux-taxis.com) Can take you around Bayeux or out to the D-Day sites.

Vélos Location (☑02 31 92 89 16; 5 rue Larcher; per half-/full day €7.50/10; ⊙8.30am-8pm) Offers year-round bike rental from a grocery store near the tourist office.

D-Day Beaches

Code-named 'Operation Overlord', the D-Day landings were the largest military operation in history. On the morning of 6 June 1944, swarms of landing craft – part of an armada of over 6000 ships and boats – hit the northern Normandy beaches and tens of thousands of soldiers from the USA, the UK, Canada and elsewhere began pouring onto French soil.

The majority of the 135,000 Allied troops stormed ashore along 80km of beaches north of Bayeux code-named (from west to east) Utah, Omaha, Gold, Juno and Sword. The landings on D-Day – known as 'Jour J' in French – were followed by the 76-day Battle of Normandy, during which the Allies suffered 210,000 casualties, including 37,000 troops killed. German casualties are believed to have been around 200,000; another 200,000 German soldiers were taken prisoner. About 14,000 French civilians also died.

Caen's Mémorial (p228) and Bayeux' Musée Mémorial (p221) provide a comprehensive overview of the events of D-Day, and many of the villages near the landing beaches (eg Arromanches) have local museums with insightful exhibits.

If you've got wheels, you can follow the D514 along the D-Day coast or several signposted circuits around the battle sites; look for signs for 'D-Day–Le Choc' in the American sectors and 'Overlord–L'Assaut' in the British and Canadian sectors. The area is also sometimes called the Côte de Nacre (Mother-of-Pearl Coast). A free booklet

The Battle of Normandy

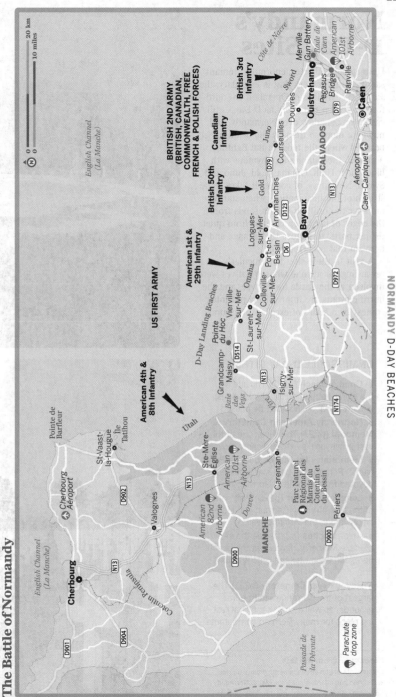

20 km
10 miles

N

English Channel
(La Manche)

English Channel
(La Manche)

Cherbourg

Pointe de
Barfleur

N13

D901

D904

Cherbourg
Aéroport

D902

St-Vaast-
la-Hougue

Île de
Tatihou

Valognes

Cotentin Peninsula

N13

**American 4th &
8th Infantry**

Utah

Ste-Mère-
Église

American 101st
Airborne

American
82nd
Airborne

Douve

MANCHE

D900

Carentan

Parc Naturel
Régional des
Marais du
Cotentin et
du Bessin

Périers

D900

D972

Passage de
la Déroute

Parachute
drop zone

Baie
des
Veys

Grandcamp-
Maisy

D514

St-Laurent-
sur-Mer

Pointe
du Hoc

D-Day Landing Beaches

Vierville-
sur-Mer

Omaha

Colleville-
sur-Mer

Isigny-
sur-Mer

N13

N174

Vire

**American 1st &
29th Infantry**

US FIRST ARMY

Longues-
sur-Mer

Port-en-
Bessin

Arromanches

D123

Bayeux

D6

**British 50th
Infantry**

Gold

D79

**Canadian
Infantry**

Juno

Courseulles

**BRITISH 2ND ARMY
(BRITISH, CANADIAN,
COMMONWEALTH, FREE
FRENCH & POLISH FORCES)**

Douvres

**British 3rd
Infantry**

Sword

Merville
Gun Battery

Rade de
Caen

American
101st
Airborne

Pegasus
Bridge

Ranville

Ouistreham

D79

Caen

CALVADOS

Aéroport
Caen-Carpiquet

N13

Côte de Nacre

Normandy's D-Day Sites

Unimaginable danger, enormous human sacrifice and bravery that is legendary, the June 1944 landings of Operation Overlord – forever known to history as D-Day – still cast a long shadow over Normandy, and nowhere more so than on the beautiful beaches where the most brutal fighting occurred, their names synonymous with bloodshed: Utah, Omaha, Gold, Juno and Sword. Nowadays, of course, it takes some stretch of the imagination, when staring out over the brilliant golden sands from the edges of the green cliffs or from quiet fishing ports, to picture the carnage and heroism that occurred here.

A visit to these sites is particularly rewarding for anyone whose relatives were involved in the Battle for Europe, and the horrific events are impressively put into context by a series of excellent museums.

UNMISSABLE D-DAY SITES

» **Omaha Beach** (p227) The site of the worst fighting during the landings, 'bloody Omaha' shouldn't be missed

» **Normandy American Cemetery & Memorial** (p227) The sheer size of this vast graveyard is extraordinarily moving

» **Mémorial – Un Musée pour la Paix** (p227) Perhaps the best single museum devoted to the Battle of Normandy

» **Longues-sur-Mer** (p226) Visit some of the few surviving German gun installations along the 'Atlantic Wall'

» **Arromanches** (p226) See the incredible Mulberry Harbour at the beach here, and even walk out onto it at low tide

» **Bayeux War Cemetery** (p221) The largest of the Commonwealth burial grounds, as well as being the final resting place for many German combatants

Clockwise from top left

1. Remnants of gun emplacements, Pointe du Hoc
2. German gun near Longues-sur-Mer 3. Normandy American Cemetery & Memorial, overlooking Omaha Beach

2

called *The D-Day Landings and the Battle of Normandy,* available from tourist offices, has details on the eight major visitors' routes.

Maps of the D-Day beaches are available at *tabacs* (tobacconists), newsagents and bookshops in Bayeux and elsewhere. All the towns along the coast have plenty of small hotels.

For more details on D-Day and its context, see www.normandiememoire.com and www.6juin1944.com.

☞ Tours

An organised minibus tour is an excellent way to get a sense of the D-Day beaches and their place in history. The Bayeux tourist office (p222) can handle reservations.

Normandy Sightseeing Tours D-DAY TOUR
(☎02 31 51 70 52; www.normandywebguide.com) From May to October (and on request the rest of the year), this experienced outfit offers morning (adult/child €45/25) tours of various beaches and cemeteries. These can be combined into an all-day excursion (€90/50).

Normandy Tours D-DAY TOUR
(☎02 31 92 10 70; 26 place de la Gare, Bayeux; adult/child €48/41) This local operator offers five-hour tours of the main sites from 1pm to 6pm most days, as well as personally tailored trips. Based at Bayeux' Hotel de la Gare.

Mémorial MINIBUS TOURS
(www.memorial-caen.fr; adult/child €77/61) Excellent year-round minibus tours (four to five hours). Rates include entry to Mémorial – Un Musée pour la Paix (p228). Book online.

❶ Getting There & Away

BUS Bus Verts (www.busverts.fr) runs bus 70 (two or three daily Monday to Saturday, more frequently and on Sunday and holidays in summer), which goes northwest from Bayeux to Colleville-sur-Mer (Omaha Beach and the American Cemetery; €2.30, 35 minutes), Pointe du Hoc (€4.50) and Grandcamp-Maisy. Bus 74 (bus 75 in summer; three or four daily Monday to Saturday, more frequently and on Sunday and holidays in summer) links Bayeux with Arromanches (€2.30, 30 minutes), Gold and Juno Beaches, and Courseulles (€3.40, one hour).

ARROMANCHES

In order to unload the vast quantities of cargo needed by the invasion forces without having to capture – intact! – one of the heavily defended Channel ports (a lesson of the 1942 Dieppe Raid), the Allies set up prefabricated marinas, code-named Mulberry Harbour, off two of the landing beaches. These consisted of 146 massive cement caissons towed over from England and sunk to form a semicircular breakwater in which floating bridge spans were moored. In the three months after D-Day, the Mulberries facilitated the unloading of a mind-boggling 2.5 million men, four million tonnes of equipment and 500,000 vehicles.

The harbour established at Omaha was completely destroyed by a ferocious gale just two weeks after D-Day, but the remains of the second, Port Winston (named after Churchill), can still be seen near Arromanches, 10km northeast of Bayeux. At low tide you can walk out to one of the caissons from the beach. The best view of Port Winston and nearby Gold Beach is from the hill east of town, marked with a statue of the Virgin Mary.

Down in Arromanches itself and right on the beach, the Musée du Débarquement (Landing Museum; ☎02 31 22 34 31; www.normandy1944.com; place du 6 Juin; adult/child €7/5; ⊙9am-6pm, closed Jan), redesigned in 2004 for the 60th anniversary of D-Day, makes an informative stop before visiting the beaches. Dioramas, models and two films explain the logistics and importance of Port Winston. Written material is available in 18 languages.

JUNO BEACH

Dune-lined Juno Beach, 12km east of Arromanches, was stormed by Canadian troops on D-Day. A Cross of Lorraine marks the spot where General Charles de Gaulle came ashore shortly after the landings. He was followed by Winston Churchill on 12 June and King George VI on 16 June.

The area's only Canadian museum, Centre Juno Beach (☎02 31 37 32 17; www.junobeach.org; adult/child €6.50/5; ⊙9.30am-7pm Apr-Sep, reduced hours out of season, closed Jan) has multimedia exhibits on Canada's role in the war effort and the landings. Guided tours of Juno Beach (€5) are available from April to October.

LONGUES-SUR-MER

Part of the Nazis' Atlantic Wall, the massive casemates and 150mm German guns near Longues-sur-Mer, 6km west of Arromanches, were designed to hit targets some 20km away, including both Gold Beach (to the east) and Omaha Beach (to the west). Over six decades later, the mammoth artillery pieces are still in their colossal concrete emplacements – the only in situ large-calibre weapons in Normandy. For details on the tours in English available from April to October, contact the Longues tourist office (☎02 31 21 46 87; www.bessin-normandie.com).

Parts of the classic D-Day film, *The Longest Day* (1962), were filmed both here and at Pointe du Hoc. On clear days, Bayeux' cathedral, 8km away, is visible to the south.

OMAHA BEACH

The most brutal fighting on D-Day took place on the 7km stretch of coastline around Vierville-sur-Mer, St-Laurent-sur-Mer and Colleville-sur-Mer, 15km northwest of Bayeux, known as 'Bloody Omaha' to US veterans. Sixty years on, little evidence of the carnage unleashed here on 6 June 1944 remains except for concrete German bunkers, though at very low tide you can see a few remnants of the Mulberry Harbour.

These days Omaha is a peaceful place, a glorious stretch of fine golden sand partly lined with sand dunes and summer homes. Near the car park in St-Laurent-sur-Mer, a memorial marks the site of the first US military cemetery on French soil. There's also a sculpture on the beach called *Les Braves,* by the French sculptor Anilore Banon, commissioned to commemorate the 60th anniversary of the landings in 2004. Circuit de la Plage d'Omaha, trail-marked with a yellow stripe, is a self-guided tour along Omaha Beach.

On a bluff above the beach, the huge Normandy American Cemetery & Memorial (www.abmc.gov; Colleville-sur-Mer; ⊗9am-5pm), 17km northwest of Bayeux, is the largest American cemetery in Europe. Featured in the opening scenes of Steven Spielberg's *Saving Private Ryan,* it contains the graves of 9387 American soldiers, including 41 pairs of brothers, and a memorial to 1557 others whose remains were never found. White marble crosses and Stars of David stretch off in seemingly endless rows, surrounded by an immaculately tended expanse of lawn. The cemetery is overlooked by a large colonnaded memorial, centred on a statue dedicated to the spirit of American youth. Nearby is a reflective pond and a small chapel.

Opened in 2007, the visitor center, mostly underground so as not to detract from the site, has an excellent free multimedia presentation on the D-Day landings, told in part through the stories of individuals. Be prepared for airport-type security. Visitor centre tours of the cemetery (one in the afternoon year-round, a second in the morning in summer) focus on personal stories.

POINTE DU HOC RANGER MEMORIAL

At 7.10am on 6 June 1944, 225 US Army Rangers commanded by Lt Col James Earl Rudder scaled the 30m cliffs at Pointe du Hoc, where the Germans had a battery of huge artillery guns perfectly placed to rain shells onto the beaches of Utah and Omaha. Unbeknown to Rudder and his team, the guns had already been transferred inland, and they spent the next two days repelling fierce German counterattacks. By the time they were finally relieved on 8 June, 81 of the rangers had been killed and 58 more had been wounded.

Today the site (☎02 31 51 90 70; admission free; ⊗9am-5pm), which France turned over to the US government in 1979, looks much as it did more than half a century ago. The ground is pockmarked with bomb craters, and the German command post (no longer open to the public because it's too close to the eroding cliff) and several of the concrete gun emplacements are still standing, scarred by bullet holes and blackened by flame-throwers.

As you face the sea, Utah Beach is 14km to the left.

UTAH BEACH

This beach is marked by memorials to the various divisions that landed here and the Musée du Débarquement (Landing Museum; ☎02 33 71 53 35; www.utah-beach.com; Ste-Marie du Mont; adult/child €7.50/3; ⊗9.30am-7pm).

Caen

POP 112,500

Founded in the 11th century by William the Conqueror, Caen – the capital of the Basse Normandie region – was 80% destroyed during the 1944 Battle of Normandy. Rebuilt in the 1950s and '60s in a typically utilitarian style, modern-day Caen nevertheless offers visitors some great sights: a

THE BATTLE OF NORMANDY

In early 1944 an Allied invasion of continental Europe seemed inevitable. Hitler's disastrous campaign on the Russian front and the Luftwaffe's inability to control the skies over Europe had left Germany vulnerable. Both sides knew a landing was coming – the only questions were where and, of course, when.

Several sites were considered. After long deliberation, it was decided that the beaches along Normandy's northern coast – rather than the even more heavily fortified coastline further north around Calais, where Hitler was expecting an attack – would serve as a surprise spearhead into Europe.

Code-named 'Operation Overlord', the invasion began on the night of 5 June 1944 when three paratroop divisions were dropped behind enemy lines. At about 6.30am on the morning of 6 June, six amphibious divisions stormed ashore at five beaches, backed up by an unimaginable 6000 sea craft and 13,000 aeroplanes. The initial landing force involved some 45,000 troops; 15 more divisions were to follow once successful beachheads had been established.

The narrow Straits of Dover had seemed the most likely invasion spot to the Germans, who'd set about heavily reinforcing the area around Calais and the other Channel ports. Allied intelligence went to extraordinary lengths to encourage the German belief that the invasion would be launched north of Normandy: double agents, leaked documents and fake radio traffic, buttressed by phoney airfields and an entirely fictitious American army group, supposedly stationed in the southeast of England, all suggested the invasion would centre on the Pas de Calais.

Because of the tides and unpredictable weather patterns, Allied planners had only a few dates available each month in which to launch the invasion. On 5 June, the date chosen, the worst storm in 20 years set in, delaying the operation. The weather had only marginally improved the next day, but General Dwight D Eisenhower, Allied commander-in-chief, gave the go-ahead: 6 June would be D-Day.

In the hours leading up to D-Day, teams of the French Resistance set about disrupting German communications. Just after midnight on 6 June, the first Allied troops were on French soil. British commandos and glider units captured key bridges and destroyed German gun emplacements, and the American 82nd and 101st Airborne Divisions landed west of the invasion site. Although the paratroops' tactical victories were few, they caused confusion in German ranks and, because of their relatively small numbers, the German high command was convinced that the real invasion had not yet begun.

Omaha & Utah Beaches

The assault by the US 1st and 29th Infantry Divisions on Omaha Beach (Vierville-sur-Mer, St-Laurent-sur-Mer and Colleville-sur-Mer) was by far the bloodiest of the day. From the outset, the Allies' best-laid plans were thrown into chaos. The beach was heavily defended by three battalions of heavily armed, highly trained Germans supported by mines, underwater obstacles and an extensive trench system. Strong winds blew many of the landing craft far from their carefully planned landing sectors. Many troops, overloaded with equipment, disembarked in deep water and simply drowned; others were cut to pieces by machine-gun and mortar fire from the cliffs. Only two of the 29 Sherman tanks expected to support the troops made it to shore, and it proved almost impossible to advance up the beach as planned.

By noon the situation was so serious that General Omar Bradley, in charge of the Omaha Beach forces, considered abandoning the attack; but eventually, metre by metre, the GIs

walled medieval château, two ancient abbeys, several very attractive 19th-century areas and a clutch of excellent museums, including a groundbreaking museum of war and peace.

👁 Sights

Mémorial – Un Musée pour la Paix   MEMORIAL
(Memorial – A Museum for Peace; ☎02 31 06 06 45; www.memorial-caen.fr; esplanade Général Eisen-

gained a precarious toehold on the beach. Assisted by naval bombardment, the US troops blew through a key German strongpoint and at last began to move off the beach. But of 2500 American casualties sustained there on D-Day, more than a thousand were fatalities, most of which occurred within the first hour of the landings.

The soldiers of the US 4th and 8th Infantry Divisions who landed at Utah Beach fared much better than their comrades at Omaha. Most of the landing craft came ashore in a relatively lightly protected sector, and by noon the beach had been cleared and soldiers of the 4th Infantry had linked with paratroopers from the 101st Airborne. By nightfall, some 20,000 men and 1700 vehicles had arrived on French soil via Utah Beach. However, during the three weeks it took to get from this sector to Cherbourg, US forces suffered one casualty for every 10m they advanced.

Sword, Juno & Gold Beaches

These beaches, stretching for about 35km from Ouistreham to Arromanches, were attacked by the British Second Army, which included significant Canadian units and smaller groups of Commonwealth, Free French and Polish forces.

At Sword Beach, initial German resistance was quickly overcome and the beach was secured within hours. Infantry pushed inland from Ouistreham to link up with paratroops around Ranville, but they suffered heavy casualties as their supporting armour fell behind, trapped in a massive traffic jam on the narrow coastal roads. Nevertheless, they were within 5km of Caen by 4pm, but a heavy German counterattack forced them to dig in and Caen was not taken on the first day as planned.

At Juno Beach, Canadian battalions landed quickly but had to clear the Germans trench by trench before moving inland. Mines took a heavy toll on the infantry, but by noon they were south and east of Creuilly.

At Gold Beach, the attack by British forces was at first chaotic, as unexpectedly high waters obscured German underwater obstacles. By 9am, though, Allied armoured divisions were on the beach and several brigades pushed inland. By afternoon they'd linked up with the Juno forces and were only 3km from Bayeux.

The Beginning of the End

By the fourth day after D-Day, the Allies held a coastal strip about 100km long and 10km deep. British Field Marshal Montgomery's plan successfully drew the German armour towards Caen, where fierce fighting continued for more than a month and reduced the city to rubble. The US Army, stationed further west, pushed northwards through the fields and *bocage* (hedgerows) of the Cotentin Peninsula.

The prized port of Cherbourg fell to the Allies on 27 June after a series of fierce battles. However, its valuable facilities were sabotaged by the retreating Germans and it remained out of service until autumn. Having foreseen such logistical problems, the Allies had devised the remarkable Mulberry Harbours, two huge temporary ports set up off the Norman coast.

By the end of July, US army units had smashed through to the border of Brittany. By mid-August, two German armies had been surrounded and destroyed near Argentan and Falaise (the so-called 'Falaise Pocket'), and on 20 August US forces crossed the Seine at several points, around 40km north and south of Paris. Led by General Charles de Gaulle, France's leader-in-exile, both Allied and Free French troops arrived on the streets of the capital on 25 August and by that afternoon the city had been liberated.

hower; adult/child €18.80/16.30; ☺9am-6.30pm, closed Jan & Mon mid-Nov–mid-Dec) Situated 3km northwest of the city centre, this innovative memorial/museum provides an insightful and vivid account of the Battle of Normandy. Tickets bought after 1pm can be used to re-enter until 1pm the next day. All signs are in French, English and German.

The visit begins with a whistle-stop overview of Europe's descent into total war, tracing events from the end of WWI and the Treaty of Versailles, through the rise of

Caen

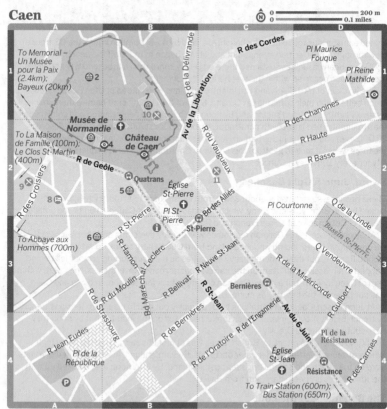

Caen

fascism in Europe and the German occupation of France, right up through the Battle of Normandy. It's a hugely impressive affair, using sound, lighting, film, animation and audio testimony, as well as a range of artefacts and exhibits, to graphically evoke the realities of war, the trials of occupation and the joy of liberation.

A second section focuses on the Cold War. There's also an underground gallery dedicated to winners of the Nobel Peace Prize, located in bunkers used by the Germans in 1944.

To get here, take bus 2 from place Courtonne. By car, follow the signs marked 'Mémorial'.

FREE **Château de Caen** CHÂTEAU
(www.chateau.caen.fr) Looming above the centre of the city and surrounded by a dry moat and massive battlements, the castle was established by William the Conqueror, Duke of Normandy, in 1060 and extended by his son Henry I. Visitors can walk around the ramparts, and visit the 12th-century Église St-Georges (open during temporary exhibitions) and the Échiquier (Exchequer), which dates from about 1100 and is one of the oldest civic buildings in Normandy. The Jardin des Simples (Château de Caen) is a garden of medicinal and aromatic herbs cultivated during the Middle Ages – some of them poisonous.

Near the château are two of the only prewar buildings left in the city centre: the half-timbered, 16th-century Musée de la Poste (Postal Museum; 52 rue St-Pierre) and the 15th-century Maison des Quatrans (25 rue de Geôle).

Musée de Normandie

(☏02 31 30 47 60; www.musee-de-normandie.caen.fr; adult from €3.10, child free; ◷9.30am-6pm, closed Tue Oct-May) This two-part museum looks at traditional life in Normandy and the region's history and archaeology. Admission prices depend on temporary exhibitions.

Musée des Beaux-Arts

(Fine Arts Museum; ☏02 31 30 47 70; www.mba.caen.fr; Château de Caen; adult/child from €3.10/2.10; ◷9.30am-6pm Wed-Mon) This excellent and well-curated museum takes you on a tour through the history of Western art from the 15th to 21st centuries. The collection includes works by Rubens, Tintoretto, Géricault, Monet, Bonnard, Braque, Balthus and Dubuffet, among many others.

FREE **Abbaye aux Hommes** ABBEY
(Men's Abbey; ☏02 31 30 42 81; ◷9am-1pm & 2-6.30pm Mon-Sat, 2-6.30pm Sun) Caen's two Romanesque abbeys were founded in the mid-11th century by William the Conqueror and his wife, Matilda of Flanders, as part of a deal in which the Church pardoned these fifth cousins for having semi-incestuously married each other. With its magnificent and multiturreted Église St-Étienne, the Abbaye aux Hommes is near the western end of rue Écuyère. This was William's final resting place, though the original tomb was destroyed by a 16th-century Calvinist mob and, in 1793, by fevered Revolutionaries – a solitary thighbone is all that's left of Will's mor-

tal remains. Today, the 18th-century convent buildings house the town hall, and tours of the abbey (adult/child €4/free, free on Sundays) run at 9.30am, 11am, 2.30pm and 4pm.

FREE **Abbaye aux Dames** ABBEY
(Women's Abbey; ☏02 31 06 98 98; ◷tours 2.30pm & 4pm) The counterpoint of the Abbaye aux Hommes is the Abbaye aux Dames at the eastern end of rue des Chanoines. The complex includes the Église de la Trinité. Look for Matilda's tomb behind the main altar and for the striking pink stained-glass windows beyond. Free twice-daily tours take you through the interior in some detail, though you can snoop around yourself at other times outside of Mass.

🛏 Sleeping

TOP
CHOICE **La Maison de Famille** B&B €€
(☏06 61 64 88 54; www.maisondefamille.sitew.com; 4 rue Elie de Beaumont; d €70-90, q €105-130; 🛜) Wow! This four-room B&B enlivens three floors of an imposing townhouse not far from the centre. Each room has its own personality; romantics love La Baldaquin, which comes with a four-poster bed, wooden floors and an old fireplace, while families plump for the large La Sous Les Toits ('Under the roof') or, if you don't want to lug your suitcase up the steep staircase, the soothing La Suite Jardin. Added perks include a peaceful garden and private parking. Probably the best value of its kind.

Le Clos St-Martin B&B €€
(☏01 31 50 08 71; www.leclosaintmartin.com; 18bis place St-Martin; d €105-155; 🛜) Eighteenth-century grace is offered at this delightfully atmospheric *maison d'hôtes* where the four rooms are of standard that puts many top-class hotels to shame. The building's antique character has been lovingly preserved during refurbishment – ask for Albane with its beamed ceilings and exposed stone walls, or Louise with its sloping roof. A luxurious cocoon.

Hôtel des Quatrans HOTEL €€
(☏02 31 86 25 57; www.hotel-des-quatrans.com; 17 rue Gémare; s €68-81, d €80-95; 🛜) It might look like a set of concrete boxes piled up on top of each other from outside, but inside this typically modern hotel you'll find a surprising range of comfy, unfussy rooms, handy for exploring the city centre. Frequent online promotional deals provide real value.

NORMANDY CAEN

✕ Eating

A variety of eateries line rue du Vaugueux and the streets running off it, home to some of Caen's few surviving medieval buildings. More restaurants can be found three blocks to the southeast along quai Vandeuvre.

TOP CHOICE Le Bouchon du Vaugueux

NORMAN €€

(☑02 31 44 26 26; www.bouchonduvaugueux.com; 4 rue Graindorge; menus €15-28; ☺lunch & dinner Tue-Sat) Look no further for Caen's most popular and buzzing restaurant. Le Bouchon is well worth reserving ahead for, though you may squeeze in if you simply turn up. You may well be the only foreigners here and certainly should't expect a translation of the chalk-board menu – but if your French is up to it, come and savour some spectacular modern Norman cooking and enjoy a wonderful choice of well-priced wines, which the manager will very passionately help you choose.

A Contre Sens

MODERN FRENCH €€

(☑02 31 97 44 48; www.acontresenscaen.fr; 8 rue Croisiers; mains €28-32, menus €22-48; ☺lunch Wed-Sat, dinner Tue-Sat) A Contre Sens' stylish interior and serene atmosphere belie the hotbed of seething creativity that is the kitchen. Under the helm of young chef Anthony Caillot, meals are thoughtfully crafted and superbly presented. Given its quality, A Contre Sens is remarkably affordable, especially at lunchtime.

Café Mancel

NORMAN €

(☑02 31 86 63 64; www.cafemancel.com; Château de Caen; mains €12-20, menus €18-24; ☺lunch Tue-Sun, dinner Tue-Sat) In the same building as the Musée des Beaux-Arts, Café Mancel offers a menu that veers from straightforward beef steaks and salads to hearty Caen-style tripes. Outside, it has a sun-trap terrace for when the weather's good.

❶ Information

Tourist Office (☑02 31 27 14 14; www.tourisme.caen.fr; place St-Pierre; ☺9.30am-6.30pm Mon-Sat, 10am-1pm Sun)

❶ Getting There & Away

BUS Run by Caen-based **Bus Verts** (☑08 10 21 42 14; www.busverts.fr; place Courtonne; ☺7.30am-7pm Mon-Fri, 9am-7pm Sat), bus 20 goes to Le Havre (€11, 2½ hours) via Deauville, Trouville and Honfleur. The Caen–Le Havre route is also served by an express bus (€15.15, 1½

hours, four daily Monday to Saturday, two Sunday) via Honfleur.

Bus 30 goes to Bayeux (€4.50, one hour, three or four daily Monday to Friday except holidays); bus 1 serves the ferry port at Ouistreham; and bus 3 will get you to Courseulles.

In Caen, most buses stop at the bus station and place Courtonne. When arriving or departing, your Bus Verts ticket is valid for an hour on Caen's buses and trams.

CAR Many car rental agencies have a desk at the train station.

FERRY **Brittany Ferries** (www.brittany-ferries.co.uk) has services from Portsmouth to Ouistreham, 14km northeast of Caen.

TRAIN The train station is about 1.2km southeast of Château de Caen. Train services include:

Bayeux €6.20, 20 minutes, at least hourly

Cherbourg €20.80, 1¼ hours, 10 to 15 daily

Deauville €8.90, one hour, at least hourly

Paris Gare St-Lazare €33.30, two hours, 14 daily

Pontorson (Mont St-Michel) €26.10, two hours, two to three daily

Rouen From €24.90, 1½ hours, eight to 10 daily

❶ Getting Around

BIKE **V'eol** (☑08 00 20 03 06; www.veol.caen.fr; 1st 30min free), Caen's answer to Paris' Velib', has 350 bicycles available at 40 automatic stations. The only problem is you need to sign up (one week/year €1/15).

BUS **Twisto** (www.twisto.fr) runs the city's buses and the two tram lines, A and B, which link the train station with the city centre.

Trouville & Deauville

The twin seaside towns of Trouville (population 5075) and Deauville (population 4100), 15km southwest of Honfleur, are hugely popular with Parisians, who flock here year-round on weekends and all week long from April to September.

Chic Deauville has been a playground of the wealthy ever since it was founded by Napoléon III's half-brother, the Duke of Morny, in 1861. Exclusive, expensive and brash, it's packed with designer boutiques, deluxe hotels and public gardens of impossible neatness, and is home to two racetracks and a high-profile American film festival.

Trouville, another veteran beach resort, is also a working fishing port and, in many ways, a much more attractive place to visit. The town was frequented by painters and

WILLIAM CONQUERS ENGLAND

Born out of wedlock to Robert the Magnificent, future Duke of Normandy, and Arlette, daughter of a furrier, William the Bastard (1027–87) – better known to posterity as William the Conqueror – became Duke of Normandy at the tender age of eight when his father died while on the way back from Jerusalem. Having survived several assassination attempts by rivals, including members of his own family, William assumed full control of the province at age 15 and set about regaining his lost territory and quashing rebellious vassals.

One of several pretenders to the English throne on the death of Edward the Confessor, William crossed the Channel with an army of about 6000 men to claim the throne from Harold Godwinson, Edward the Confessor's apparent death-bed choice of successor. William's forces landed at Pevensey before marching to Hastings, where, on 13 October 1066, Harold faced off against William with about 7000 men from a strong defensive position. The battle began the next day.

Although William's archers scored many hits, the Saxon army's ferocious defence ended a charge by the Norman cavalry and drove them back in disarray. Summoning the experience and tactical ability he had gained in numerous campaigns against rivals back in Normandy, William used the cavalry's rout to draw the Saxon infantry out of their defensive positions, whereupon the Norman infantry turned and caused heavy casualties among the undisciplined Saxon troops. Late in the afternoon the battle started to turn against Harold, who was slain – by an arrow through the eye, according to the Bayeux Tapestry. The embattled Saxons fought on until sunset and then fled. William immediately marched to London, ruthlessly quelled the opposition, and was crowned king of England on Christmas Day.

William thus became the ruler of two kingdoms, bringing England's feudal system of government under the control of Norman nobles. Ongoing unrest among the Saxon peasantry soured William's opinion of the country and, after 1072, he spent the rest of his life in Normandy, only going to England when compelled to do so. In 1087 William was injured during an attack on Mantes. He died in Rouen a few weeks later and was buried in Caen.

NORMANDY TROUVILLE & DEAUVILLE

writers during the 19th century, including Mozin and Flaubert, and many French celebrities have holiday homes here, lured by the 2km-long sandy beach and the laid-back seaside ambience.

The towns are linked by pont des Belges, just east of Deauville's train and bus stations, and by a low-tide footpath near the river's mouth.

Sights & Activities

In Deauville, the rich and beautiful strut their stuff along the beachside Promenade des Planches, a 643m-long boardwalk lined with cabins named after famous Americans (mainly film stars), before swimming in the nearby 50m covered Piscine Olympique (Olympic swimming pool; bd de la Mer, Deauville; adult from €4; ⊙closed 3 weeks in Jan & 2 weeks in Jun) or losing a wad at the casino 200m inland.

Trouville, too, has a casino and a 583m boardwalk where you can swim in freshwater swimming pools, rent sailboats, windsurf

and even surf. Nearby are lots of imposing 19th-century villas.

Musée de Trouville   MUSEUM
(☏02 31 88 16 26; 64 rue du Général Leclerc; adult/child €2/1.50; ⊙11am-1pm & 2pm-5.30pm Wed-Mon Easter–mid-Nov) In the fine Villa Montebello, Trouville's museum is 1km to the northeast of the town's tourist office. With a panoramic view over the beach, the museum recounts Trouville's history and features works by Charles Mozin and Eugène Boudin.

Natur' Aquarium   AQUARIUM
(☏02 31 88 46 04; www.natur-aquarium.fr; promenade des Planches; adult/child €8/6; ⊙10am-noon & 2-6.30pm) Trouville's beach is home to an aquarium packed with multicoloured fish, fearsome reptiles and weird insects.

Festivals & Events

Deauville is renowned for its horse racing in July, August and October – with a few

PONT DE NORMANDIE

Opened in 1995, this futuristic bridge (€5 each way per car) stretches in a soaring 2km arch over the Seine between Le Havre and Honfleur. It's a typically French affair, as much sophisticated architecture as engineering, with two huge V-shaped columns holding aloft a delicate net of cables. Crossing it is quite a thrill – and the views of the Seine are magnificent. In each direction there's a narrow footpath and a bike lane.

winter races – at two *hippodromes* (racetracks; see www.hippodromesdedeauville. com, in French): La Touques for flat races, and Clairefontaine (see www.hippodrome -deauville-clairefontaine.com) for flat, trotting and jumping races (steeplechases and hurdles).

Asian Film Festival　　　　FILM FESTIVAL
(www.deauvilleasia.com) Deauville's Asian film festival runs for five days in mid-March.

American Film Festival　　　FILM FESTIVAL
(www.festival-deauville.com) Deauville's 10-day film festival is an altogether more welcoming affair than its better-known cousin at Cannes. Tickets for most screenings are on sale to the public, and you're bound to catch glimpses of a few Hollywood stars when the festival's in full swing in early September.

🛏 Sleeping

Trouville offers much better accommodation value than Deauville. Prices are highest in July and August and on weekends, and lowest from October to Easter except during Paris' school holidays.

Le Fer à Cheval　　　　　　HOTEL €€
(☏02 31 98 30 20; www.hotel-trouville.com; 11 rue Victor Hugo, Trouville; s €86-98, d €92-104, q €177; 🕾) Occupying three beautiful turn-of-the-20th-century buildings, this modern hotel has 34 comfortable rooms with big windows, horse-themed decor and bright bathrooms. The breakfast (€11) is a real spoil and includes homemade bread and croissants. The prices outside July and August are very generously reduced.

L'Espérance　　　　　　　　HOTEL €€
(☏02 31 88 26 88; www.lesperancehoteldeauville. com; 32 rue Victor Hugo, Deauville; d €77-110; 🕾) Compact and bijou are the watchwords at this elegant townhouse right in the centre of Deauville. While the 10 rooms are hardly spacious, they're well equipped and brim with character. No two rooms are alike. Top choices are the 'Victor Hugo' and the 'Van Gogh', which are decked out in earthy tones. The 'Lamartine', with its black and lilac colour scheme, might not be to everyone's taste.

La Maison Normande　　　　HOTEL €
(☏02 31 88 12 25; 4 place de Lattre de Tassigny, Trouville; d €50-75, apt €95; 🕾) Stay in this late 17th-century Norman house and you'll feel like you're visiting your new Norman grandma. The 17 rooms vary considerably in size and comfort; some have been recently modernised. We found the mattresses a tad saggy but they will do for a night's kip.

🍴 Eating

In Trouville, there are lots of restaurants and buzzing brasseries along bd Fernand Moureaux. Their menus offer few surprises – fresh fish, mussels and seafood are the mainstays – but the atmosphere is fantastic on a summer evening. It's also worth seeking out some lesser-known ventures in the backstreets. Deauville also has a good selection of eateries scattered around town.

Bistrot Les Quatre Chats　　　BISTRO €
(☏02 31 88 94 94; 8 rue d'Orléans, Trouville; mains €11-25; ⏰lunch Mon, Fri-Sun, dinner Mon, Thu, Fri-Sun) This character-laden bistro is beloved by all who come here. The blackboard menus feature plenty of flavourful fish and meat classics, some with an exotic twist (think lamb in saffron sauce). Try the *rôti de cœur d'aloyau au gros sel* (beef sirloin), the house's signature dish.

Tivoli Bistro　　　　　　　BISTRO €€
(☏02 31 98 43 44; 27 rue Charles Mozin, Trouville; mains €12-28; ⏰lunch & dinner Fri-Tue) You won't find a cosier place in Trouville than this much-loved hideaway, tucked away just off the seafront. It's famous for its delicious *sole meunière* (Dover sole) and exquisite homemade terrine.

Le Comptoir et la Table　　MODERN FRENCH €€
(☏02 31 88 92 51; 1 quai de la Marine, Deauville; mains €18-35, lunch menu €21; ⏰lunch & dinner daily Jul-Aug, closed Wed Sep-Jun) This smart bistro on the waterfront in Deauville has

long been one of the city's *bonnes adresses*. Ingredients fresh from the market are whipped into shape by the talented chef and served in appealing surroundings.

☆ Entertainment

Nightlife is centred on Deauville.

Le Zoo   BAR
(www.lezoo.fr; 53 rue Désiré-le-Hoc, Deauville; ⊙6pm-3am) A sleek and sophisticated urban-style hang-out, tailor-made for cocktails (€9) and checking out the beautiful people. Has a DJ from 10pm on Friday and Saturday, when you can dance in the cellar. The website has details on theme nights.

🔒 Shopping

Shopping in Deauville (for instance right around the casino and along rue Eugène Colas) tends towards well-known Parisian brand names, while Trouville features less-glitzy wares along its main commercial street, rue des Bains.

ℹ Information

Deauville Post Office (rue Robert Fossorier) Exchanges currency.

Deauville Tourist Office (☎02 31 14 40 00; www.deauville.org; place de la Mairie; ⊙10am-6pm Mon-Sat, 10am-1pm & 2-5pm Sun) Situated about 400m west of the train station, Deauville's tourist office can supply you with an English-language walking tour brochure and a Deauville map.

Trouville Tourist Office (☎02 31 14 60 70; www.trouvillesurmer.org; 32 bd Fernand Moureaux; ⊙9.30am-6.30pm Mon-Sat & 10am-1pm Sun) Situated about 200m north of pont des Belges, Trouville's tourist office has a free (Deauville-less) map of Trouville and sells maps for a self-guided architectural tour and two rural walks (7km and 11km).

ℹ Getting There & Around

AIR A useful **CityJet** (www.cityjet.com) service was introduced in mid-2010, linking Deauville's tiny airport to London City Airport three to four days a week.

BUS From next to Deauville's train station, **Bus Verts** (☎08 10 21 42 14; www.busverts.fr) has hourly services to Caen (€5.40, 1¼ hours), Honfleur (€2.20, 40 minutes) and Le Havre (€6.60, 1¼ hours).

TRAIN Rail travel to and from Deauville and Trouville requires a change at Lisieux (€6.20, 20 minutes, eight to 12 daily). There is, however, a handful of direct trains to Paris Gare St-Lazare (from €15, 2¼ hours, two to four weekly). Destinations from Lisieux include Caen (€8.90, 30 minutes, at least hourly) and Rouen (€18.50, 1¼ hours, hourly).

Honfleur

POP 8350

Long a favourite with painters but now more popular with the Parisian jet set, Honfleur is arguably Normandy's most charming seaside town. Even though it can be overrun with tourists in the summer months, it's hard not to love its graceful beauty.

Its heart is the Vieux Bassin (Old Harbour), from where explorers once set sail for the New World. Now filled with pleasure vessels, this part of the port is surrounded by a jumble of brightly coloured buildings that evoke maritime Normandy of centuries past.

🔘 Sights

Église Ste-Catherine   CHURCH
(place Ste-Catherine; ⊙9am-6pm) Initially intended as a temporary structure, this extraordinary church has been standing in the square for over 500 years. Built by the people of Honfleur during the late 15th and early 16th centuries, after its stone predecessor had been destroyed during the Hundred Years War, wood was used in an effort to save funds for strengthening the fortifications around the walled Enclos. The structure is particularly notable for its double-vaulted roof and its twin naves, which from the inside resemble a couple of overturned ships' hulls.

Across the square is the church's free-standing wooden bell tower, Clocher Ste-Catherine, supposedly built away from the

NORMANDY HONFLEUR

DON'T MISS

SEAFOOD PICNIC

The Marché aux Poissons (Fish Market; bd Fernand Moureaux; ⊙9am-6pm) is *the* place in Trouville to head for a waterfront picnic of fresh oysters with lemon (from €9 a dozen) – or for whelks, prawns and shrimps. Everything is fresh, so no energy is wasted on freezing, and since there are almost no middlemen, you pay reasonable prices and the fishermen get a fair share of the proceeds. It's housed in the market building.

church in order to avoid lightning strikes and damage to the clock's clanging bells.

Old Harbour
HISTORIC QUARTER

On the west side of the Vieux Bassin, with its many pleasure boats, quai Ste-Catherine is lined with tall, taper-thin houses – many protected from the elements by slate tiles – dating from the 16th to 18th centuries. The Lieutenance, at the mouth of the old harbour, was once the residence of the town's royal governor. The Avant Port, just northeast of the Lieutenance, is home to Honfleur's 30 or so fishing vessels, which moor in the area northeast of quai de la Quarantaine.

Musée Eugène Boudin
ART MUSEUM

(☎02 31 89 54 00; www.musees-honfleur.fr; 50 rue de l'Homme de Bois; adult/child €5.10/3.40, Jul-Sep €5.80/4.30; ☉10am-noon & 2-6pm Wed-Mon mid-Mar–Sep, 2.30-5.30pm Mon & Wed-Fri, 10am-noon & 2.30-5.30pm Sat-Sun Oct–mid-Mar) Named in honour of Eugène Boudin, an early Impressionist painter born here in 1824, this museum features a collection of Impressionist paintings from Normandy, including works by Dubourg, Dufy and Monet. One room is devoted to Boudin, whom Baudelaire called the 'king of skies' for his luscious skyscapes.

Les Maisons Satie
MUSEUM

(☎02 31 89 11 11; 67 bd Charles V; adult/child €5.70/4.20; ☉10am-6pm Wed-Mon) The quirky Maisons Satie capture the spirit of the eccentric, avant-garde composer Erik Satie (1866–1925), who lived and worked in Honfleur and was born in the half-timbered house that now contains the museum. Visitors wander through the museum with a headset playing Satie's music and excerpts from his writings (in French or English). Each room is a surreal surprise – winged pears and self-pedalling carousels are just the start.

Musée de la Marine
MARITIME MUSEUM

(☎02 31 89 14 12; quai St-Etienne; adult/child €3.60/2.40; ☉10am-noon & 2-6.30pm Tue-Sun, closed mid-Nov-Feb) Located in the Enclos quarter, the Maritime Museum has nautically themed displays of model ships, carpenters' tools and engravings. It is inside the deconsecrated 13th- and 14th-century Église St-Étienne.

Musée d'Ethnographie et d'Art Populaire Normand
MUSEUM

(rue de la Prison; adult/child €3.50/2.30; ☉10am-noon & 2-6.30pm Tue-Sun, closed mid-Nov–mid-Feb) This museum occupies a couple of period houses and a former prison. Its nine rooms re-create the world of Honfleur during the 16th to 19th centuries, using a mix of costumes, furniture and artefacts.

Scenic Walks
WALKS

Honfleur is superb for aimless ambling. One option is to head north from the Lieutenance along quai des Passagers to Jetée de l'Ouest (Western Jetty), which forms the west side of the Avant Port, out to the broad mouth of the Seine. Possible stops include the Jardin des Personnalités, a park featuring figures from Honfleur history; Naturospace (☎02 31 81 77 00; www.naturospace.com; bd Charles V; adult/child €8.20/6.40; ☉9.30am-6.30pm Jul & Aug, 9.30am-1pm & 2-5.30pm Sep-Nov & Feb-Jun), a tropical greenhouse filled with 60 different species of free-flying butterflies; and the beach.

Chapelle Notre Dame de Grâce
CHURCH

Built between 1600 and 1613, Chapelle Notre Dame de Grâce is at the top of the Plateau de Grâce, a wooded, 100m-high hill about 2km west of the Vieux Bassin. There's a great view of the town and port.

☞ Tours

Walking Tours
WALKING TOUR

(€5 to €6) Some of the tourist office's 1½- to two-hour walking tours of Honfleur are in English (contact the tourist office for details). Atmospheric night-time tours begin at 9pm Saturday from May to October.

Boat Tours
BOAT TOUR

(adult/child €7.50/5) From about March to mid-October, you can take a boat tour from the Avant Port (across the street from the Lieutenance) out to the Seine Estuary and the Pont de Normandie – look for the *Cap Christian, L'Évasion III* or the larger *Jolie France*.

⌨ Sleeping

TOP CHOICE La Maison de Lucie
BOUTIQUE HOTEL €€€

(☎02 31 14 40 40; www.lamaisondelucie.com; 44 rue des Capucins; d €150-200, ste €250-315; ☜) This marvellous little hideaway has just 10 rooms and two suites, which ensures intimacy. Some of the bedrooms, panelled in oak, have Moroccan-tile bathrooms and boast fantastic views across the harbour to the Pont de Normandie. The shady terrace is a glorious place for a summer breakfast. There's a chic jacuzzi in the old brick-vaulted cellar. No lift.

CAMEMBERT COUNTRY

Some of the most enduring names in the pungent world of French *fromage* come from Normandy, including Pont L'Évêque, Livarot and, most famous of all, Camembert, all of which are named after towns south of Honfleur, on or near the D579.

It's thought that monks first began experimenting with cheesemaking in the Pays d'Auge sometime in the 11th century, but the present-day varieties didn't emerge until around the 17th century. The invention of Camembert is generally credited to Marie Harel, who was supposedly given the secret of soft cheesemaking by an abbot from Brie on the run from Revolutionary mobs in 1790. Whatever the truth of the legend, the cheese was a huge success at the local market in Vimoutiers, and production of Camembert quickly grew from a cottage industry into an international operation. The distinctive round wooden boxes, in which Camembert is wrapped, have been around since 1890; they were designed by a local engineer to protect the soft disc during long-distance travel.

If you're interested in seeing how the cheese is made, you can take a guided tour of the Président Farm (02 33 36 06 60; www.fermepresident.com; adult/child €3/2; 10am-6pm Jun-Aug, 10am-6pm Apr & Sep-Oct, 10am-5pm Mar, closed Nov-Feb), an early 19th-century farm restored by Président, one of the region's largest Camembert producers. It's in the centre of the town of Camembert, which is about 60km south of Honfleur.

L'École Buissonnière
B&B €€

(06 16 18 43 62; www.a-lecole-buissonniere.com; 4 rue de la Foulerie; d €100-130;) Right in the centre, this old primary school, lovingly restored and decorated, is pristine and convivial, with biggish, comfortable and airy rooms overlooking a courtyard. The owner knows about nutrition and serves generous, organic breakfasts. Bikes are available for hire.

Le Fond de la Cour
B&B €€

(09 62 31 24 30; www.lefonddelacour.com; 29 rue Eugène Boudin; d €85-130;) No language barrier in this charming B&B – it's run by energetic Amanda, a native of Scotland, who goes to great lengths to make you feel at home. The three rooms and two studios are light, airy and immaculate, with gleaming bathrooms. There's a communal kitchen, too.

La Petite Folie
B&B €€

(06 74 39 46 46; www.lapetitefolie-honfleur.com; 44 rue Haute; d €145-185;) Penny Vincent, born in the US, and her French husband welcome you in their elegant mansion right in the heart of Honfleur. The house is spotlessly clean, neat and cosy, and Penny willingly shares her great knowledge of all things Norman – in perfect English, of course. The garden at the rear is a plus. There's a two-night minimum.

Hôtel du Dauphin
TRADITIONAL HOTEL €

(02 31 89 15 53; www.hoteldudauphin.com; 10 place Pierre-Berthelot; d €70-155, q €165;) Right in the heart of Honfleur behind a 17th-century slate and half-timbered façade, this very well-run hotel has 34 modern, eclectically decorated rooms. There's a nearby annexe. Our favourite rooms include 'La Macaron', 'La Pavé de Rue' and 'La Pont de Normandie', with a quirky decor and stupendous views of Église Ste-Catherine. There's no lift in either building.

Etap Hôtel
HOTEL €

(08 92 68 07 81; www.etaphotel.com; rue des Vases; tr €42-47;) This almost comically anonymous chain hotel has 63 charmless rooms with bunk beds and functional bathrooms. It's included here as, in the absence of a youth hostel, it's the cheapest bed in town.

Eating

Le Gambetta
MODERN FRENCH €€

(02 31 87 05 01; 58 rue Haute; mains €15-20, menu €23; lunch Sat-Wed, dinner Fri-Wed) Honfleur's latest addition to the restaurant scene, Le Gambetta is well worth seeking out. The decor is a lovely mix of traditional and modern touches, and the food is deliberately eclectic; seafood predominates, but everything's laced with a creative twist. *Andouilles à la plancha* (grilled tripe sausage)? More please.

REGIONAL PARK

Inland from Utah Beach, to the south and southwest, is the 1450-sq-km **Parc Naturel Régional des Marais du Cotentin et du Bessin** (www.parc-cotentin-bessin.fr), with its waterways, marshes, moors and hedgerows. For details on hiking and cycling in the park and elsewhere in the Manche *département*, see www.mancherandonnee.com (in French).

Le Bréard   GASTRONOMIC €€€
(☑02 31 89 53 40; www.restaurant-lebreard.com; 7 rue du Puits; menus €29-55; ☺lunch & dinner Wed-Sun) *The* place to go in Honfleur for *gastronomique* specialities of the highest order, served in two chic, modern dining rooms. The cuisine is wonderfully imaginative and permeated from every region of France.

L'Écailleur   NORMAN €€
(☑02 31 89 93 34; www.lecailleur.fr; 1 rue de la République; mains €16-24, menus €29-42; ☺lunch & dinner Fri-Tue) Overlooking the Vieux Bassin, this quietly stylish restaurant makes a lovely haven from the hustle. The wood-panelled dining room, which resembles a ship's interior, is easy on the eye. Menuwise, look out for turbot and monkfish or roasted tenderloin of pork.

Au Bouillon Normand   NORMAN €€
(☑02 31 89 02 41; www.aubouillonnormand.fr; 7 rue de la Ville; menus €18-26; ☺lunch & dinner Fri-Tue) There's nothing remotely pretentious about this cute bistro slightly off the Vieux Bassin, but the food has charmed many culinary critics. Small tables and wooden floors make for a cosy setting, and the menu specialises in hearty Norman fare – think tripes or codfish cooked in cider.

Au P'tit Mareyeur   NORMAN €€
(☑02 31 98 84 23; 4 rue Haute; menus €26-48; ☺lunch & dinner Wed-Sun) With its snug, low-beamed dining room, Au P'tit Mareyeur could be a movie set for a typical Norman inn. With the scene in place, prepare for the traditional Norman meal. Hungry? Opt for the *bouillabaisse honfleuraise* (fish stew).

L'Homme de Bois   NORMAN €€
(☑02 31 89 75 27; 30-32 rue de L'Homme de Bois; mains €18-35, menus €21-32; ☺lunch & dinner daily) A rustic interior complete with a fire-

place sets the tone for this much-lauded address near the Vieux-Bassin. Unsurprisingly in Honfleur, fishy flavours feature heavily, but you'll also find excellent meat dishes. The *homard breton* (lobster) is a must for seafoodies.

Drinking

L'Albatros   CAFE-BAR
(32 quai Ste-Catherine; ☺8am-2am) Sailors, students, philosophers and layabouts are all at home at this cafe–bar.

Le Perroquet Vert   BAR
(52 quai Ste-Catherine; ☺8am-2am) The brick-vaulted 'Green Parrot' has an excellent selection of beers and a fine terrace for people-watching. Serves breakfast, afternoon sandwiches and evening tapas.

Information

Post Office (7 cours Albert Manuel; ☺8.30am-noon & 1.45-5.45pm Mon-Fri, 8.30am-noon Sat) Changes foreign currency.

Tourist Office (☑02 31 89 23 30; www.ot-honfleur.fr; quai Lepaulmier; ☺9.30am-12.30pm & 2pm-6pm Mon-Sat) Situated inside the Médiathèque (library) building. Has a free map detailing a 2km walking circuit. Internet access costs €1 for 15 minutes.

Getting There & Around

BUS The **bus station** (☑02 31 89 28 41) is two blocks east of the tourist office. **Bus Verts** (☑08 10 21 42 14; www.busverts.fr) services include an express bus to Caen (€11, one hour):

Caen €7.95, two hours, 12 daily Monday to Saturday, six Sunday

Deauville & Trouville €2.30, 30 minutes

Le Havre €4.50, 35 minutes, eight daily Monday to Saturday, four Sunday

CAR Free parking is available next to Naturospace, which is 600m from the Avant Port on bd Charles V.

TRAIN To catch the train (eg to Paris), take the bus to Deauville or Le Havre.

MANCHE

The Manche *département* (www.manchetourisme.com) encompasses the entire Cotentin Peninsula, stretching from Utah Beach northwest to Cherbourg and southwest to the magnificent Mont St-Michel. The peninsula's northwest corner is especially captivating, with unspoiled stretches of rocky coastline sheltering tranquil bays and villages. The fertile inland areas, crisscrossed with hedgerows, produce an abundance of cattle, dairy products and apples. The British crown dependencies of Jersey and Guernsey lie 22km and 48km offshore, respectively.

Cherbourg

POP 41,560

At the top of the Cotentin Peninsula sits Cherbourg, the largest town in this part of Normandy. Transatlantic cargo ships, passenger ferries from Britain and Ireland, yachts and warships pass in and out of Cherbourg's monumental port. During WWII, most of the petrol used by the Allied armies during the Normandy campaign was supplied by an underwater pipeline laid from England to Cherbourg shortly after D-Day.

Modern-day Cherbourg – now united with adjacent Octeville – is a far cry from the romantic city portrayed in Jacques Demy's 1964 film *Les Parapluies de Cherbourg* (The Umbrellas of Cherbourg) but you may pass through if you're crossing the Channel by ferry.

◉ Sights

Cité de la Mer　　　　　　　AQUARIUM
(☑02 33 20 26 26; www.citedelamer.com; Gare Maritime Transatlantique; adult/child €18/13; ◷9.30am-6pm) Housed in Cherbourg's art deco transatlantic ferry terminal, this fascinating place was built in the 1930s and is both an aquarium – the deepest in Europe – and a showcase for French submarine prowess. This may be your only chance to go inside a French nuclear submarine, *Le Redoubtable,* in service from 1967 to 1991.

⌂ Sleeping

La Régence　　　　　　　HOTEL €€
(☑02 33 43 05 16; www.laregence.com; 42-44 quai de Caligny; d €73-115; ☎) The façade does a good impersonation of an upmarket London pub, with black paint at street level and colourful window boxes above. Inside are 21 cosy rooms, some with dashing harbour views, and a well-regarded restaurant.

Hôtel de la Renaissance　　　　HOTEL €
(☑0233432390; www.hotel-renaissance-cherbourg.com; 4 rue de l'Église; s €50-65, d €57-72; ☎) Friendly staff, affordable rates, well-kept rooms and a convenient location make this trim hotel a highly desirable option. The up-

stairs rooms have terrific port views. Book ahead.

Auberge de Jeunesse　　　　　HOSTEL €
(☑02 33 78 15 15; www.fuaj.org; 55 rue de l'Abbaye; dm incl breakfast €21; @) Situated 1km northwest of the tourist office, this excellent 99-bed hostel is housed in the French navy's old archives buildings and has a small kitchen for self-caterers. Rooms have two to five beds. Take bus 3 or 5 to the Hôtel de Ville stop. Check-in is 9am to 1pm and 6pm to 11pm.

✕ Eating

Le Pily　　　　　　GASTRONOMIC €€€
(☑02 33 10 19 29; www.restaurant-le-pily.com; 39 Grande Rue; menus €22-69; ◷lunch Thu, Fri & Sun-Tue, dinner Thu-Sat & Mon, Tue) The young chef Pierre Marion is at the helm of Cherbourg's best restaurant. Expect a lively menu of seafood and meat dishes, with great care taken in the balancing of flavours.

Le Plouc 2　　　　　　NORMAN €€
(☑02 33 01 06 46; 59 rue du Blé; mains €13-22, menus €18-34; ◷lunch Tue-Fri & Sun, dinner Mon-Sat) A crowd of regulars keeps this place humming, returning for hearty serves of homespun cooking served in a cosy, wood-beamed dining room. Try the so-tender-they-fall-apart pork cheeks.

Au Tire-Bouchon　　　　　BISTRO €
(☑02 33 53 54 69; 17 rue Notre-Dame; mains €10-16, menus €11-28; ◷lunch & dinner Tue-Sat) This convivial bistro and wine bar is much appreciated by locals who prize good value. It serves good salads, tartines (open sandwiches) as well as wines by the glass. In summer, the small outdoor terrace is a plus.

ℹ Information

Post Office (1 rue de l'Ancien Quai; ◷8am-7pm Mon-Fri, 8am-noon Sat) Exchanges currency.

Tourist Office (☑02 33 93 52 02; www.cherbourgtourisme.com; 2 quai Alexandre III; ◷10am-7pm, closed Sun mid-Sep–mid-June) Has useful information on visiting the city, the Cotentin Peninsula and D-Day sites.

ℹ Getting There & Away

FERRY There are car ferry services from Cherbourg's **ferry terminal** (www.port-cherbourg.com) to Poole, Portsmouth and Rosslare (Ireland). **Brittany Ferries** (www.brittany-ferries.co.uk) has services between Cherbourg and Poole and Portsmouth, while **Irish Ferries** (www.irishferries.com) and **Celtic Link** (www.

WORTH A TRIP

COUTANCES

The lovely old Norman town of Coutances makes for a good detour when travelling between the D-Day beaches and Mont St-Michel. At the town's heart is its Gothic **Cathédrale de Coutances** (parvis Notre-Dame, Coutances; admission free; ⊙9am-7pm). Interior highlights include several 13th-century windows, a 14th-century fresco of St Michael skewering the dragon, and an organ and high altar from the mid-1700s. You can climb the lantern tower on a **tour** (adult/child €7/4; ⊙in French 11am & 3pm Mon-Fri, 3pm Sun Jul & Aug). Note that children under 10 are not allowed to climb the tower.

celticlinkferries.com) sail between Cherbourg and Rosslare.

TRAIN The train station is at the southern end of the central waterway, the Bassin du Commerce. Direct trains include:

Bayeux €16.50, one hour, 15 daily Monday to Friday, eight to 10 on weekends

Caen €20.80, 1¼ hours, 10 to 15 daily

Paris St-Lazare €47.20, three hours, four to seven direct daily

Pontorson €28.10, three hours, two to three daily, change at Lison

ⓘ Getting Around

BUS In the warm months, a shuttle-bus service links the ferry terminal with the town centre and train station.

TAXI For a taxi, call ☑02 33 53 36 38. A daytime trip between the train station and ferry terminal costs about €10.

Mont St-Michel

POP 43

It's one of France's most iconic images: the slender towers and sky-scraping turrets of the abbey of Mont St-Michel rising from stout ramparts and battlements, the whole ensemble connected to the mainland by a narrow causeway (which will be replaced by a bridge by 2014; see www.projetmont saintmichel.fr for more information on the changes that are under way). Fortunately, although it's visited by huge numbers of tourists, both French and foreign, the Mont still manages to whisk you back to the Middle Ages, its fantastic architecture set against the backdrop of the area's extraordinary tides.

The bay around Mont St-Michel is famed for having Europe's highest tidal variations; the difference between low and high tides can reach an astonishing 15m. The Mont is only completely surrounded by the sea every month or two, when the tidal coefficient is above 100 and high tide is above 14m. Regardless of the time of year, the waters sweep in at an astonishing clip, said to be as fast as a galloping horse. At low tide the Mont is surrounded by bare sand for kilometres around, but at high tide, barely six hours later, the whole bay can be submerged.

Be prepared for lots of steps, some of them spiral – alas, the Mont is one of the least wheelchair-accessible sites in France. Be prepared also for big crowds; come early in the morning to miss the worst of them, though the Mont is never entirely free of visitors.

History

Bishop Aubert of Avranches is said to have built a devotional chapel on the summit of the island in 708, following his vision of the Archangel Michael, whose gilded figure, perched on the vanquished dragon, crowns the tip of the abbey's spire. In 966 Richard I, Duke of Normandy, gave Mont St-Michel to the Benedictines, who turned it into a centre of learning and, in the 11th century, into something of an ecclesiastical fortress, with a military garrison at the disposal of the abbot and the king.

In the 15th century, during the Hundred Years War, the English blockaded and besieged Mont St-Michel three times. The fortified abbey withstood these assaults and was the only place in western and northern France not to fall into English hands. After the Revolution, Mont St-Michel was turned into a prison. In 1966 the abbey was symbolically returned to the Benedictines as part of the celebrations marking its millennium. Mont St-Michel and the bay became a Unesco World Heritage Site in 1979. It may be removed from the Unesco list because of the planned construction of offshore wind farms some 20km off the Mont.

⊙ Sights

Abbaye du Mont St-Michel ABBEY
(☑02 33 89 80 00; www.monuments-nationaux.fr; adult/child incl guided tour €9/free; ⊙9am-7pm, last entry 1hr before closing) The Mont's major

attraction is the stunning architectural ensemble of the Abbaye du Mont St-Michel, towards which you'll be swept by a human tide ascending the Grande Rue and a steep stairway. From Monday to Saturday in July and August, there are illuminated *nocturnes* (night-time visits) with music from 7pm to 10pm.

Most rooms can be visited without a guide but it's worth taking the one-hour tour included in the ticket price. The frequency of English tours ranges from twice a day (11am and 3pm) in the dead of winter to hourly in summer; the last leaves at least 1½ hours before closing time. Audioguides are available in six languages.

Église Abbatiale

(Abbey Church) The Église Abbatiale was built on the rocky tip of the mountain cone. The transept rests on solid rock, while the nave, choir and transept arms are supported by the rooms below. The church is famous for its mix of architectural styles: the nave and south transept (11th and 12th centuries) are solid Norman Romanesque, while the choir (late 15th century) is Flamboyant Gothic.

La Merveille

(The Marvel) The buildings on the northern side of the Mont are known as La Merveille. The famous cloître (cloister) is surrounded by a double row of delicately carved arches resting on granite pillars. The early 13th-century, barrel-roofed réfectoire (dining hall) is illuminated by a wall of recessed windows – remarkable, given that the sheer drop precluded the use of flying buttresses. The Gothic Salle des Hôtes (Guest Hall), dating from 1213, has two enormous fireplaces. Look out for the promenoir (ambulatory), with one of the oldest ribbed vaulted ceilings in Europe, and the Chapelle de Notre Dame sous Terre (Underground Chapel of Our Lady), one of the abbey's oldest rooms, rediscovered in 1903.

The masonry used to build the abbey was brought to the Mont by boat and pulled up the hillside using ropes.

☞ Tours

When the tide is out, you can walk all the way around Mont St-Michel, a distance of about 1km. Straying too far from the Mont can be very risky: you might get stuck in wet sand – from which Norman soldiers are depicted being rescued in one scene of the Bayeux Tapestry – or be overtaken by the incoming tide.

Guided Walks   WALKING TOUR
(Guided Bay Crossing adult/child €6.50/4.50) Experienced outfits offering guided walks into – or even across – the bay include Découverte de la Baie du Mont-Saint-Michel (☎02 33 70 83 49; www.decouvertebaie.com; Genêts; adult/child from €6/4) and Chemins de la Baie (☎02 33 89 80 88; www.cheminsdelabaie.com; adult/child from €6.50/4.50), both based across the bay from Mont St-Michel in Genêts. Local tourist offices have details.

🛏 Sleeping

Hôtel Du Guesclin   HOTEL €€
(☎02 33 60 14 10; www.hotelduguesclin.com; Grande Rue, Mont St-Michel; d €77-93; ☺mid-Mar–mid-Nov) This hotel on the Mont is worth recommending for its affordable rates, even in high season – a rarity on the Mont. Best of all, five rooms have views of the bay – priceless! The onsite restaurant also features large windows with fantastic bay vistas.

NORMANDY MONT ST-MICHEL

ℹ KNOW BEFORE YOU BOOK

Basing yourself in one of the rather pricey hotels on the Mont itself is not a bad idea provided you can get a room with a bay view (surprisingly, few hotels offer rooms with a view). Take note that you'll have to leave your car in the new car park in La Caserne on the mainland, and take a (free) shuttle bus to the Mont. You could also stay (or leave your car) in Beauvoir, a village slightly further inland, from where it's an easy 25-minute walk along the Coüesnon River to the departure of the shuttle buses in La Caserne. Thus, you'd save the €8.50 parking fees. A third option includes the chain-style hotels in La Caserne but they generally don't offer rooms with views of the Mont. Some visitors choose to stay in the rather ordinary town of Pontorson, 9km due south of the Mont, but it's less convenient.

Mont St-Michel

TIMELINE

708 Inspired by a vision from **St Michael 1**, Bishop Aubert is compelled to 'build here and build high'.

966 Richard I, Duke of Normandy, gives the Mont to the Benedictines. The three levels of the **abbey 2** reflect their monastic hierarchy.

1017 Development of the abbey begins. Pilgrims arrive to honour the cult of St Michael. They walk barefoot across the mudflats and up the **Grande Rue 3** to be received in the almonry (now the bookshop).

1203 The monastery is burnt by the troops of Philip Augustus, who later donates money for its restoration and the Gothic 'miracle', **La Merveille 4**, is constructed.

1434 The Mont's **ramparts 5** and fortifications ensure it withstands the English assault during the Hundred Years War. It is the only place in northern France not to fall.

1789 After the Revolution, Monasticism is abolished and the Mont is turned into a prison. During this period the **treadmill 6** is built to lift up supplies.

1878 The **causeway 7** is created. It allows modern-day pilgrims to visit without hip-high boots, but it cuts off the flow of water and the bay silts up.

1979 The Mont is declared a Unesco World Heritage Site.

2012 The car park is set up on the mainland. The Mont is only accessed on foot or by shuttle bus.

TOP TIPS

» Bring a packed lunch from Pontorson to avoid the poor lunch selection on the Mont

» Leave the car – it's a pleasant walk from Beauvoir, with spectacular views

» Pay attention to the tides – they are dangerous

» Take the excellent audioguide – it tells some great stories

JOHN ELK III/GETTY ©

Îlot de Tombelaine

Occupied by the English during the Hundred Years War, this islet is now a bird reserve. From April to July it teems with exceptional birdlife.

Treadmill
The giant treadmill was powered hamsterlike by half a dozen prisoners, who, marching two abreast, raised stone and supplies up the Mont.

The West Terrace

Chapelle St-Aubert

Tour Gabriel

5

Les Fanils

Ramparts
The Mont was also a military garrison surrounded by machicolated and turreted walls, dating from the 13th to 15th centuries. The single entrance, Porte de l'Avancée, ensured its security in the Hundred Years War. Tip: Tour du Nord (North Tower) has the best views.

ROCCO FASANO/GETTY ©

Abbey

The abbey's three levels reflect the monastic order: monks lived isolated in church and cloister, the abbot entertained noble guests at the middle level, and lowly pilgrims were received in the basement. Tip: night visits run in July and August.

St Michael Statue & Bell Tower

A golden statue of the winged St Michael looks ready to leap heavenward from the bell tower. He is the patron of the Mont, having inspired St Aubert's original devotional chapel.

1

La Merveille

The highlights of La Merveille are the vast refectory hall lit through embrasured windows, the Knights Hall with its elegant ribbed vaulting, and the cloister (above), which is one of the purest examples of 13th-century architecture to survive here.

The Gardens

2

4

6

Église St-Pierre

Cemetery

3

Toilets

Tour de l'Arcade

Tour du Roi

Tourist Office

Porte de l'Avancée (Entrance)

7

Grande Rue

The main thoroughfare of the small village below the abbey, Grande Rue has its charm despite its rampant commercialism. Don't miss the famous Mère Poulard shop here, for souvenir cookies.

Causeway

In 2014 the causeway will be replaced by a new bridge, which will allow the water to circulate and will return the Mont to an island. Tip: join a barefoot walking tour and see the Mont as pilgrims would.

Best Views

The view from the Jardin des Plantes in nearby Avranches is unique, as are the panoramas from Pointe du Grouin du Sud near the village of St-Léonard.

La Bourdatière
B&B €

(☎02 33 68 11 17; www.la-bourdatiere.com; 8 rue Maurice Desfeux, Beauvoir; d €39-43; ☉Apr-Sep) This charming stone farmhouse in Beauvoir is excellent value. The decor of the four rooms could do with updating, but the rural setting and blissful gardens are tough to top.

Hôtel Formule Verte
HOTEL €

(☎02 33 60 14 13; www.hotelformuleverte-mont saintmichel.com; route du Mont St-Michel, Beauvoir; d €49-65) Yes, the Formule Verte is a motel-like venture with bland rooms, but it's economical and conveniently located a few metres away from the shuttle stop in Beauvoir.

Auberge de Jeunesse
HOSTEL €

(Centre Duguesclin; ☎02 33 60 18 65; www.fuaj.org; 21 bd du Général Patton, Pontorson; dm €15; ☉May-Sep) The cheapest venture for miles around, this 62-bed hostel has four- to six-bed rooms and kitchen facilities. Reception closes from noon to 5pm.

✖ Eating

It's a good idea to bring your lunch with you to Mont St-Michel – many options on the Mont are overpriced, overbooked and overbusy, and serve rather bland food. The Grande Rue is jammed with sandwich shops and crêperies. Consider having lunch in Beauvoir, which has better-value options.

Crêperie La Sirène
CRÊPERIE €

(Grande Rue; crêpes €3.50-10; ☉9am-10.30pm) Not a bad budget option, with a good selection of sweet crêpes and savoury galettes

and salads. Up an ancient spiral staircase from a souvenir shop.

❶ Information

Post Office (Grande Rue) Changes currency and has an ATM.

Tourist Office – Mont St-Michel (☎02 33 60 14 30; www.ot-montsaintmichel.com; ☉9am-12.30pm & 2-6.30pm Mon-Sat, 9am-noon & 2-6pm Sun, no midday closure Jul & Aug) Just inside Porte de l'Avancée, up the stairs to the left. An *horaire des marées* (tide table) is posted just inside the door and you can also change money here. A detailed map of the Mont costs €3. Just next door are toilets (€0.40) and an ATM.

❶ Getting There & Around

BUS Mont St-Michel is linked to Beauvoir (€2.20, eight minutes) and Pontorson (€2.20, 13 minutes) by bus 6, operated by **Manéo** (☎08 00 15 00 50; www.vtni50.com), six to eight times daily (more frequently in July and August). Buses will drop you in La Caserne, from where you can take free shuttles buses to the Mont itself. Times are coordinated with the arrival in Pontorson of some trains from Caen and Rennes.

Keolis Emeraude (☎02 99 19 70 80; www.destination-montsaintmichel.com) links Rennes' railway station with Mont St-Michel (€12.10, 1¼ hours, four to six daily); times are coordinated with the arrival in Rennes of TGVs from Paris.

TRAIN The town of Pontorson is the transport hub for travellers arriving by train.

Destinations from Pontorson include Bayeux (€22.30, 1¾ hours, three direct daily), Cherbourg (€28.10, three hours, two to three daily) and Rennes (€13.30, 50 minutes, two to four daily).

Brittany

Includes »

Best Places to Eat

» Le Bistro de Jean (p253)

» Au Crabe Tamboure (p274)

» Le Coquillage (p260)

» Le Moulin de Rosmadec (p279)

» Saveurs et Marées (p279)

Best Places to Stay

» La Rance Hotel (p252)

» Hotel Quic en Groigne (p249)

» Plume au Vent (p277)

» Hôtel Arvor (p258)

» Dihan (p280)

Why Go?

Brittany is for explorers. Its wild, dramatic coastline, medieval towns and thick forests make an excursion here well worth the detour from the beaten track. This is a land of prehistoric mysticism, proud tradition and culinary wealth, where fiercely independent locals celebrate Breton culture and Paris feels a long way away indeed.

The entire region has a wonderfully undiscovered feel once you go beyond world-famous sights such as stunning St-Malo, regal Dinard and charming Dinan. Unexpected Breton gems – including the little-known towns of Roscoff, Quimper and Vannes, the megaliths of Carnac, the rugged coastlines of Finistère, the Presqu'île de Crozon and the Morbihan Coast – all demonstrate that there's far more to Brittany than delicious crêpes and homemade cider. Brittany's much-loved islands are also big draws – don't miss its two real stars, dramatic Île d'Ouessant and the aptly named Belle Île.

When to Go
Brest

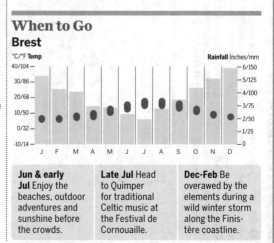

Jun & early Jul Enjoy the beaches, outdoor adventures and sunshine before the crowds.

Late Jul Head to Quimper for traditional Celtic music at the Festival de Cornouaille.

Dec-Feb Be overawed by the elements during a wild winter storm along the Finistère coastline.

Brittany Highlights

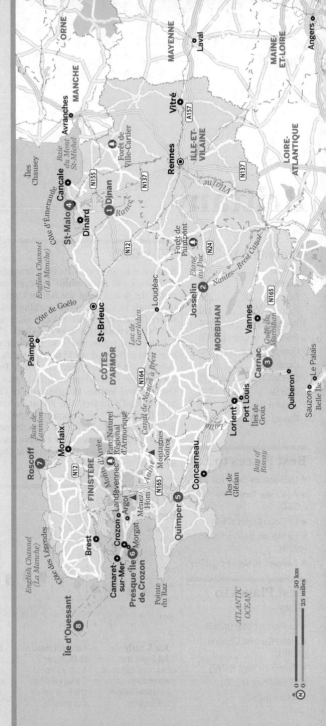

1 Get lost in the higgledy-piggledy old town of **Dinan** (p258)

2 Tour the turreted medieval castle over the fairy-tale forest village of **Josselin** (p282)

3 Cycle past fields full of prehistoric **megaliths** (p275) around Carnac

4 Stroll along the ramparts at sunset for panoramic views over **St-Malo** (p247)

5 Explore the often overlooked Breton city of **Quimper** (p270), with its wonderful cathedral and old town

6 Walk the coastal paths of the diverse and beautiful **Presqu'île de Crozon** (p268)

7 Take in the relaxed mood and unusual church in **Roscoff** (p261), a charming port town

8 Hike around the barren coastline of the dramatic **île d'Ouessant** (p266), home to some of Finistère's most appealing scenery

History

Brittany's earliest known neolithic tribes left a legacy of menhirs and dolmens that continue to baffle historians. Celts arrived in the 6th century BC, naming their new homeland Armor ('the land beside the sea'). The region was conquered by Julius Caesar in 56 BC. Following the withdrawal of the Romans in the 5th century AD, Celts – driven from what is now Britain and Ireland by the Anglo-Saxon invasions – settled in Brittany, bringing Christianity with them.

In the 9th century, Brittany's national hero Nominoë revolted against French rule. Wedged between two more-powerful kingdoms, the duchy of Brittany was continually contested by France and England until a series of strategic royal weddings finally saw the region become part of France in 1532.

Brittany has retained a separate regional identity. There's currently a drive for cultural and linguistic renewal, and a consciousness of Brittany's place within a wider Celtic culture embracing Ireland, Wales, Scotland, Cornwall and Galicia in Spain.

❶ Getting There & Around

Ferries link St-Malo with the Channel Islands and the English ports of Portsmouth and Poole. From Roscoff there are ferries to Plymouth (UK) and Cork (Ireland). Alternatively, airports in Brest, Dinard and, to the south, Nantes, serve the UK and Ireland, as well as other European and domestic destinations.

Brittany's major towns and cities have rail connections but routes leave the interior poorly served. The bus network is extensive, if generally infrequent, meaning that your own wheels are the best way to see the area, particularly out-of-the-way destinations.

With gently undulating, well-maintained roads, an absence of tolls and relatively little traffic outside the major towns, driving in Brittany is a real pleasure. Cycling is also extremely popular, and bike-rental places are never hard to find.

NORTH COAST

Enveloped by belle époque beach resorts, fishing villages and wave-splashed headlands, Brittany's central north coast spans the *départements* of Ille-et-Vilaine and Côtes d'Armor. Green shallows give rise to the name Côte d'Émeraude (Emerald Coast) to the east; westwards, boulders blush along the Côte de Granit Rose.

St-Malo

POP 48,800

The enthralling mast-filled port town of St-Malo has a cinematically changing landscape. With one of the world's highest tidal ranges, brewing storms under blackened skies see waves lash the top of the ramparts ringing its beautiful walled city. Hours later, the blue sky merges with the deep marine-blue sea, exposing beaches as wide and flat as the clear skies above and creating land bridges to the granite outcrop islands.

Construction of the walled city's fortifications began in the 12th century. The town became a key port during the 17th and 18th centuries as a base for both merchant ships and government-sanctioned privateers (pirates, basically) against the constant threat of the English. These days English arrivals are tourists, for whom St-Malo, a short ferry hop from the Channel Islands, is a summer haven.

◉ Sights

INTRA MUROS

St-Malo's first inhabitants originally lived in St-Servan but later moved to this former island, which became linked to the mainland by the sandy isthmus of Le Sillon in the 13th century. For the best views of the walled city, either stroll along the jetty that pokes out to sea off the southwestern tip of Intra muros (from the end of which you'll get the wide angle view) or, to zoom in, clamber along the top of the 1.8km stretch of ramparts, constructed at the end of the 17th century under military architect Vauban.

Though you'd never guess it from the cobblestone streets and reconstructed 17th-and 18th-century-style monuments, during August 1944 the battle to drive German forces out of St-Malo destroyed around 80% of the old city, which has been lovingly restored since then.

Cathédrale St-Vincent CATHEDRAL
(Map p252; place Jean de Châtillon; ☉9.30am-6pm) The city's centrepiece was constructed between the 12th and 18th centuries. Damage to the cathedral was particularly severe during the 1944 battle to liberate St-Malo. A mosaic plaque on the floor of the nave marks the spot where Jacques Cartier received the blessing of the bishop of St-Malo before his 'voyage of discovery' to Canada in 1535.

St-Malo & St-Servan

St-Malo & St-Servan

◎ Top Sights
Mémorial 39–45 .... A5

◎ Sights
1 Fort National B1
2 Île du Grand Bé A2
3 Musée International du Long
    Cours Cap-Hornier B5

🛏 Sleeping
4 Camping Aleth A5
5 Hôtel de la Plage B4
6 La Rance Hotel B5
7 Le Valmarin B5

✕ Eating
Le Bulot .... (see 6)

Guided tours are in French but descriptions are available in English. Tours run more frequently during school holidays (10am, 11.30am, 2.30pm & 5.30pm).

ÎLE DU GRAND BÉ

At low tide, cross the beach to walk out via the Porte des Bés to the rocky islet of Île du Grand Bé (Map p248; www.petit-be.com), where the great St-Malo–born 18th-century writer Chateaubriand is buried. Once the tide rushes in, the causeway remains impassable for about six hours; check tide times with the tourist office. Depths can be deceptive; if you get caught out, stay on the islet until the tide subsides.

About 100m beyond the Île du Grand Bé is the Vauban-built 17th-century Fort du Petit Bé (☎06 08 27 51 20), also accessible at low tide.

BEYOND THE WALLS

The pretty fishing port of St-Servan sits south of the walled city.

Fort National   RUIN
(Map p248; www.fortnational.com; adult/child €5/3; ⊙Easter, school holidays & Jun–mid-Sep) The ramparts' northern stretch looks across to the remains of this former prison, built by Vauban in 1689. Standing atop a rocky outcrop, the fort can only be accessed at low tide. Ask at the tourist office for times of tours.

Mémorial 39–45   MONUMENT
(Map p248; ☎02 99 82 41 74; adult/child €6/3; ⊙guided visits 10.15am, 11am, 2pm, 3pm, 4pm & 5pm) Constructed in the mid-18th century,

Musée du Château   MUSEUM
(Map p252; ☎02 99 40 71 57; adult/child €6/3; ⊙10am-noon & 2-6pm Apr-Sep, Tue-Sun Oct-Mar) Within Château de St-Malo, built by the dukes of Brittany in the 15th and 16th centuries, this museum looks at the life and history of the city.

La Maison de Corsaire   HISTORIC MANSION
(Map p252; ☎02 99 56 09 40; www.demeure-de-corsaire.com; 5 rue d'Asfeld; adult/child €5.50/4; ⊙guided tours 3pm, closed Mon winter, Dec & Jan) You can visit this 18th-century mansion and historic monument, once owned by corsair (privateer) François Auguste Magon.

Fort de la Cité was used as a German base during WWII. One of the bunkers now houses the Mémorial 39–45, which depicts St-Malo's violent WWII history and liberation, and includes a 45-minute film in French (not shown on every tour – ask at the tourist office or entrance gate for exact times). Some guided visits are conducted in English; call ahead to confirm times. Outside July and August tour frequency drops and it's closed Mondays.

Musée International du Long Cours Cap-Hornier
MARITIME MUSEUM

(Museum of the Cape Horn Route; Map p248; ☑02 99 40 71 58; adult/child €6/3; ◷10am-noon & 2-6pm, closed Mon Oct-Mar) Housed in the 14th-century **Tour Solidor**, this museum presents the life of the hardy sailors who followed the dangerous Cape Horn route around the southern tip of South America. The top of the tower also offers superb views.

Grand Aquarium
AQUARIUM

(☑02 99 21 19 00; www.aquarium-st-malo.com; av Général Patton; adult/child €16/11.50; ◷9.30am-10pm mid-Jul–mid-Aug, 9.30am-8pm early-Jul & late Aug; ☑; ☐C1) The Atlantic coast of France has a couple of superb aquariums (those in Brest and La Rochelle being the other major ones). Of the three, this is the smallest but also the best one for children, who will simply adore the submarine ride (and adults will think this is pretty cool as well). The exhibits on local marine life and mangrove forests are also very strong and everyone will be captivated by the tiny cartoon-like Cow Fish, as well as seahorses, turtles and sharks. Allow around two hours for a visit. It's about 4km south of the city centre and bus C1 from the train station passes by every half-hour.

Activities

Ferries & Boat Excursions
Compagnie Corsaire
CRUISE

(Map p252; ☑08 25 13 81 00; www.compagniecorsaire.com) Compagnie Corsaire runs *pêche en mer* (deep-sea fishing) trips for about four hours (€40, Monday, Wednesday and Friday, July and August), and runs ferries from just outside Porte de Dinan to the following: **Bay of St-Malo** (adult/child €19.50/11.50, 2½ hours), **Bay of Cancale** (adult/child €29/17.50, 2½ hours), **Dinan** (adult/child return €31/18.50, April to September), **Île Cézembre** (adult/child return €14.50/8.50, two to seven departures per week daily April to September) and **Îles Chausey** (adult/

child return €32/19, two to five departures per week April to September).

Courses

To learn how to windsurf (lessons from €35 for one hour) or sail a catamaran (lessons from €50 for one hour), contact **Surf School** (☑02 99 40 07 47; www.surfschool.org).

Sleeping

St-Malo has plenty of hotels, but accommodation books up quickly in summer and it's essential to reserve in advance. If you get stuck, the tourist office has regular updates of availability. For *chambres d'hôte* (B&Bs), try the nearby towns of Cancale, Dinan and their surrounds.

INTRA MUROS

TOP CHOICE Hôtel Quic en Groigne
BOUTIQUE HOTEL €€

(Map p252; ☑02 99 20 22 20; www.quic-en-groigne.com; 8 rue d'Estrées; s €64-72, d €79-102; ◷closed mid-Nov–Feb; ☎) This exceptional hotel has 15 rooms that are the epitome of clean, simple style, and many a hotel twice the price should be envious of this place. If straight-out good value for money isn't enough then consider also staff who could hardly be more accommodating, an ideal location on a quiet old-town street just a few metres from a (low tide only) beach and secure lock-up parking.

Hôtel San Pedro
HOTEL €

(Map p252; ☑02 99 40 88 57; www.sanpedro-hotel.com; 1 rue Ste-Anne; s €58-60, d €69-79; ☎) Tucked at the back of the old city, the San

---

ST-MALO & ST-SERVAN BEACHES

You can splash in the protected tidal pool west of the city walls at **Plage de Bon Secours** or climb its ladder to jump off into the sea.

St-Servan's **Plage des Bas Sablons** has a cement wall to keep the sea from receding completely at low tide.

The much larger **Grande Plage** stretches northeast along the isthmus of Le Sillon. Spectacular sunsets can be seen along the stretch from Grande Plage to Plage des Bas Sablons. Less-crowded **Plage de Rochebonne** is another 1km to the northeast.

The Breton Coast

Brittany's rugged coastline is one of the region's best-kept secrets. With brilliant sand beaches framing traditional fishing villages, rocky cliffs towering above the churning swell of the North Atlantic, and lots of activities to keep you occupied, there's plenty to discover.

Superb Stretches of Sand

1 Don't associate Brittany with beaches? Think again... Yes the water may be freezing, but the sand is spectacular and the backing sublime at St-Malo (p247), or Quiberon (p277). Alternatively, find your own patch of sand on the beaches of Belle Île (p278).

Hiking the Coasts

2 Get out into nature on the coastal hiking trail from Morgat to Cap de la Chèvre (p268). For a challenge, walk the 45km coastal path on Île d'Ouessant (p266) or the 95km path around Belle Île (p278).

Coastal Villages

3 Find your own quiet bliss in the village life of the fishing port of Roscoff (p261), charming Camaret-sur-Mer (p270) and our personal favourite, chic hideaway Cancale (p257).

Island Life

4 Take the ferry to Île d'Ouessant (p266), with its rugged coastal path and great activities, or head out of season to Belle Île (p278), the southern coast's standout star. To get off the beaten track, head to Île de Batz (p262).

Get Active!

5 You can dive, windsurf and hire catamarans in Dinard (p255), canoe or kayak in Paimpol (p260), and hire bikes pretty much anywhere, though we recommend Presqu'Île de Crozon (p268) and any of Brittany's islands.

Clockwise from top left
1. The beach at St-Malo 2. Brittany's rugged coastline
3. Boats in the harbour of Camaret-sur-Mer

Intra Muros

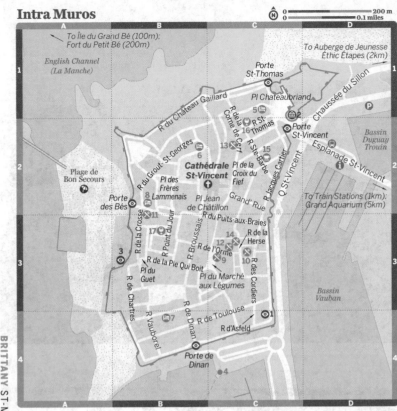

Pedro has a cool, crisp, neutral-toned decor with subtle splashes of colour, friendly service and superb sea views. Private parking is €10 per day.

Hôtel du Palais   HOTEL €€

(Map p252; ☎02 99 40 07 30; www.hoteldupalais
-stmalo.com; 8 rue Toullier; d €53-86; @☎) Strikingly coloured rooms with strategically positioned bunches of flowers make this a decent choice and it's large enough to mean there's always the chance of a bed here when everywhere else is full. The top-floor rooms have huge sunlight windows built into the roof.

Hôtel de l'Univers   HOTEL €€

(Map p252; ☎02 99 40 89 52; www.hotel-univers
-saintmalo.com; pl Chateaubriand; r from €99; ☎) Right by the most frequently used gateway to the old city (Porte St-Vincent), this cream-coloured place with 63 rooms is perfectly poised for all of St-Malo's attractions. Rooms are compact, in dark tones and with crisp linens. The whole place has a very club-like country-hotel feel, especially in the all-wood maritime bar. For two weeks in early August the miniumn room price rises to €120.

BEYOND THE WALLS

TOP CHOICE La Rance Hotel   BOUTIQUE HOTEL €€

(Map p248; ☎02 99 81 78 63; www.larancehotel.
com; 15 quai Sébastopol; r €65-84; ☎) This is a fabulous little hotel with searing white rooms decorated with han-l-painted wooden ship communication flags and smart blue-and-white tiled bathrooms. Hosts Chantal and Thierry are warm and helpful, there's a nice little garden, a charming breakfast room and it's just a few metres from the Tour Solidor and the cute Port-Solidor.

Le Valmarin   HISTORIC HOTEL €€

(Map p248; ☎02 99 81 94 76; www.levalmarin.
com; 7 rue Jean XXIII; r €100-145; ☎) If you're

Intra Muros

yearning for a bit of aristocratic class then this sober 18th-century mansion should do the job nicely. It has 12 rooms dressed in a refined late-19th-century style, attentive service and glorious gardens full of spring flowers and shady trees. It's well positioned on the edge of the village-like St-Servan quarter.

Hôtel de la Plage   BOUTIQUE HOTEL €
(Map p248; ☑02 99 81 61 05; 3 rue Dauphine; s/d from €59/65; ☎) This smart, family-run place is set just back from the beach on a road filled with neighbourhood restaurants. It has a handful of soft, marine-coloured rooms with tiny bathrooms.

Auberge de Jeunesse
Éthic Étapes   HOSTEL €
(Off map p252; ☑02 99 40 29 80; www.centrevar angot.com; 37 av du Père Umbricht; dm incl breakfast €21; @; ☐3) This efficient place has a self-catering kitchen and free sports facilities. Take bus 3 from the train station.

Camping Aleth   CAMPGROUND €
(Map p248; ☑06 78 96 10 62; www.camping-aleth .com; allée Gaston Buy, St-Servan; per 2-person tent €14.50; ☎) Perched on a peninsula, Camping Aleth has panoramic 360-degree views and is close to beaches and some lively bars.

✕ Eating

St-Malo has some superb places to eat, but it also has a lot of mediocre tourist-style eateries (mainly those around the Porte St-Vincent and Grande Porte).

TOP CHOICE **Le Bistro de Jean**   BISTRO €
(Map p252; ☑02 99 40 98 68; 6 rue de la Corne de Cerf; mains €15-19, menus from €12; ☺closed Wed & Sat lunch, all day Sun) Want to know where the locals choose to eat inside the walls? Peer through the windows of this lively and authentic bistro and you'll get your answer. The place is packed at lunchtime with loyal regulars, and there's rarely a foreign tourist in sight, which is strange, because for the price you simply won't get a better proper French meal in St-Malo.

Le Chalut   SEAFOOD €€
(Map p252; ☑02 99 56 71 58; 8 rue de la Corne-du-Cerf; menus €26-70; ☺Wed-Sun) This unremarkable-looking establishment is, in fact, St-Malo's most celebrated restaurant. Its kitchen overflows with the best the Breton coastline has to offer – buttered turbot, line-caught sea bass and scallops in Champagne sauce.

Le Bulot   BISTRO €
(Map p248; ☑02 99 81 07 11; www.lebulot.com; 13 quai Sébastopol; menus €10-15, mains €8-14; ☺closed dinner Sun Oct-May) A laid-back neighbourhood bistro with a modern feel and views over the Port-Solidor (best appreciated on sunny days from the restaurant's raised wooden terrace). There's a short menu of delicious fusion dishes at bargain prices and they'll even serve you lunch after 2pm (a rare occurrence in anything other than tourist-class restaurants).

La Bouche en Folie
MODERN FRENCH €€

(Map p252; ☎06 72 49 08 89; 14 rue du Boyer; menus €13-29; ⊘Wed-Sun) Well off the tourist trail, this sleek joint oozes Gallic gorgeousness and casts a modern spin on traditional French staples – lamb is fricasséed with garlic and artichokes; monkfish is partnered by peas, black olives and asparagus.

Restaurant l'Atelier
MODERN FRENCH €€

(Map p252; ☎02 23 18 34 55; www.restaurant-l-atelier.fr; 18 rue de la Herse; mains €19-25, plat du jour €10) With bottles of wine stood in a bubbling fish tank there's a slightly playful edge to this quality oldtown restaurant specialising in modern French cuisine. Dishes could be anything from salmon with foie gras and truffle oil to a simple fish cooked on a plancha. The waiter is happy to advise on wine and food combinations and the dish of the day is a bargain, although some think the à la carte options a little overpriced.

Crêperie Margaux
CRÊPERIE €

(Map p252; ☎02 99 20 26 02; www.creperie-margaux.com; 3 place du Marché aux Légumes; crêpes €2.50-10; ⊘closed Tue & Wed Sep-Jun) Watch the owner of this wonderful little crêperie on violet-filled place du Marché aux Légumes making traditional crêpes by hand (her motto: 'If you're in a hurry, don't come here'). The aromas wafting through the timber-lined dining room and the scads of happy diners prove it's well worth the wait.

Self-Catering

Cheeses and butters handmade by Jean-Yves Bordier's **La Maison du Beurre** (Map p252; 9 rue de l'Orme; ⊘Tue-Sat, closed Wed afternoon) are shipped to famous restaurants all over the world. Just down the street is the covered market, **Halle au Blé** (Map p252; rue de la Herse; ⊘8am-noon Tue & Fri).

🍷 Drinking

L'Alchimiste
BAR

(Map p252; 7 rue St-Thomas; ⊘5pm-2am, closed Mon Oct-Apr) Ben Harper–style music creates a mellow backdrop at this magical place filled with old books and a toy flying fox. Take a seat at the bar draped with a red tasselled theatre curtain, on the carved timber mezzanine (including a pulpit) or in the wood-heated basement.

L'Aviso
LIVE MUSIC

(Map p252; 12 rue Point du Jour; ⊘6pm-3am) Regular live music features at this cosy place, which has more than 300 beers on offer, with over 10 – including Breton beer – on tap. If you can't decide, ask the friendly owner/connoisseur. It's the old-fashioned place with the Duvel Beer sign.

❶ Information

Tourist Office (☎€0.15 per min 08 25 13 52 00; www.saint-malo-tourisme.com; esplanade St-Vincent; ⊘9am-7.30pm Mon-Sat, 10am-6pm Sun) Just outside the walls.

❶ Getting There & Away

BOAT **Brittany Ferries** (www.brittany-ferries.com) sails between St-Malo and Portsmouth, and **Condor Ferries** (www.condorferries.co.uk) runs to/from Poole via Jersey or Guernsey. Car ferries leave from the Gare Maritime du Naye.

In July and August **Compagnie Corsaire** (☎08 25 13 80 35; www.compagniecorsaire.com; adult/child €7.50/5) run a Bus de Mer shuttle service (10 minutes, at least half-hourly) between St-Malo and Dinard. Outside the July–August peak season both frequency, and cost, falls. **Taxi de la Mer** (www.taxibateau.fr; adult/child €5/free) run a similar service.

COUNTING THE BEAT

Celtic culture is synonymous with music and Brittany is no exception. A wealth of indoor and outdoor festivals and concerts feature traditional instruments through to electronica, and everything in between, with some big-name international acts. Keep your finger on the pulse by picking up the free monthly zine **Ty Zicos** (www.tyzicos.com) in cafes and bars.

In addition to an array of festivals and events, tune in to the region's top musical trio each year.

Les Vieilles Charrues de Carhaix (www.vieillescharrues.asso.fr) Old-school crooners, electronic beats and much more attract crowds of 300,000-plus to Carhaix in mid-July.

Astropolis (www.astropolis.org) Brest's electronic music fest in early August, with the main event atmospherically set in a castle.

Les Transmusicales de Rennes (www.lestrans.com) Groundbreaking indie bands in Rennes, in early December.

LA CAFE DU COIN D'EN BAS DE LA RUE DU BOUT DE LA VILLE D'EN FACE DU PORT... LA JAVA

The word 'eccentric' must have been coined to describe the extraordinary and insanely named La Cafe du Coin d'en Bas de la Rue du Bout de la Ville d'en Face du Port... La Java (Map p252; ☑02 99 56 41 90; www.lajavacafe.com; 3 rue Sante-Barbe). Think part-museum, part-toyshop and the work of art of an ever-so-slightly-twisted mind. Traditional French accordion music plays in the background and the beady eyes of hundreds of dolls and puppets keep watch from shelves and alcoves in the walls. Customers sit on swings, not chairs, and fake elephant tusks reach down out of the lamp shades. Even the opening times are odd: it opens at 8.31am on the dot during the week and 8.33am on weekends. And the drinks? Ah, well they're actually quite sane – there's 100 different kinds of coffee and a quality beer range.

BUS All intercity buses stop by the train station. **Keolis Emeraude** (www.keolis-emeraude.com) has services to Cancale (€2, 30 minutes). **Illenno** (www.illenoo-services.fr) services run to Dinard (€2, 30 minutes, hourly) and Rennes (€4.30, one to 1½ hours, three to six daily). **Tibus** (☑08 10 22 22 22; www.tibus.fr) buses go to Dinan (€2, 50 minutes, three to eight daily).

CAR Various hire-car firms can be found at the train station and the Gare Maritime du Naye. There are plenty of pay carparks (€5 per day) around the edge of Intra muros.

TRAIN TGV trains run from St-Malo:

Dinan €8-9.50, one hour, 10 daily (requiring a change in Dol de Bretagne)

Paris Montparnasse €52 to €64, three hours, up to 10 daily

Rennes €13.50, one hour, roughly hourly

❶ Getting Around

BUS St-Malo city buses (single journey €1.20, 24-hour pass €3.50) operate until about 8pm, with some lines extending until around midnight in summer. Between esplanade St-Vincent and the train station, take buses C1 or C2.

TAXI Call ☑02 99 81 30 30.

Dinard

POP 11,230

Visiting Dinard 'in season' is a little like stepping into one of the canvases Picasso painted here in the 1920s. Belle époque mansions built into the cliffs form a timeless backdrop to the beach dotted with blue-and-white striped bathing tents and the beachside carnival. Out of season, when holidaymakers have packed up their buckets and spades, the town is decidedly dormant, but wintry walks along the coastal paths are spectacular.

◉ Sights & Activities

Scenic Walks   WALKING
(☺guided walks 2.30pm) The romantically named promenade du Clair de Lune (moonlight promenade) has views across the Rance River estuary to St-Malo's walled city, and nightly sound-and-light spectacles in summer.

Two-hour guided walks (adult/child €5/3) explaining the town's history, art and architecture (in English and French) depart from the tourist office. The tourist office also doles out maps and leaflets detailing self-guided walking tours taking in the best of the town's architecture.

Beautiful seaside trails extend along the coast in both directions. Walkers can follow the shoreline from Plage du Prieuré to Plage de St-Énogat via Pointe du Moulinet, while cyclists can shadow the coastline on the road.

Barrage de la Rance   BRIDGE
This 750m bridge over the Rance estuary carries the D168 between St-Malo and Dinard, lopping a good 30km off the journey. A feat of hydroelectrics, the Usine Marémotrice de la Rance (below the bridge) generates electricity by harnessing the lower estuary's extraordinarily high tidal range – a difference of 13.5m between high and low tide.

FREE Espace Découverte   MUSEUM
(☺10am-6pm Jul-Aug) On the Dinard bank, Espace Découverte is good for the mechanically minded. It illustrates the power station's construction and environmental impact, with a film in English.

Beaches & Swimming SWIMMING

Framed by fashionable hotels, a casino and neo-Gothic villas, Plage de l'Écluse is the perfect place to shade yourself in style by renting one of Dinard's trademark blue-and-white striped bathing tents; you can also hire parasols and deckchairs. Reproductions of Picasso's paintings are often planted in the sand here in high summer.

Filled with heated seawater, the Olympic-sized indoor Piscine Municipale (local pool; ☑02 99 46 22 77; promenade des Alliés; admission €3.40) is beside the beach.

Less chic (and less crowded) than the Plage de l'Écluse is Plage du Prieuré, 1km to the south. Plage de St-Énogat is 1km west of Plage de l'Écluse, on the far side of Pointe de la Malouine.

Water Sports WATER SPORTS

At Plage de l'Écluse, Wishbone Club (☑02 99 88 15 20; www.wishbone-club-dinard.com; ☺9am-7pm Jun-Sep) rents windsurfing boards from €15 per hour, and can arrange lessons. The company also organises catamaran and kayak rental.

Dive trips are run by CSD (Club Subaquatique Dinardais; ☑02 99 46 25 97; from €25).

🛏 Sleeping

Dinard's prices match its cachet: budget travellers may want to consider staying in St-Malo and catching the ferry or strolling across.

Hôtel Printania HOTEL €€

(☑02 99 46 13 07; www.printaniahotel.com; 5 av George V; s/d from €70/83; ☎) This is a charming Breton-style hotel, complete with wood-and-leather furniture, and it has a superb location overlooking the Baie du Prieuré. Guest rooms with a sea view cost more; otherwise get your fill of the grand views across the water to St-Servan at breakfast (€10.50). There's an annexe of the hotel on the road that you may come to before you get to the main building – there's no reception here, so keep on going until you see the hotel proper. The waitresses in the in-house restaurant wear traditional Breton dress – possibly the only time you're likely to see anyone actually wearing it!

Grand Hôtel Barrière LUXURY HOTEL €€€

(☑02 99 88 26 26; www.lucienbarriere.com; 46 av George V; d from €212; ❋☎🏊) Dinard's most fabulous address is this old-timer, which has been given a very smart facelift. The rooms are spacious, and many have balconies and magnificent sea views, though the decor style is very much anonymous chic. There's a large swimming pool (covered most of the year) and a glamorous lawn area for taking an evening cocktail.

Hôtel de la Plage HOTEL €€

(☑02 99 46 14 87; www.hoteldelaplage-dinard. com; 3 bd Féart; d €70-142; ☎) Refreshingly unpretentious, this traditional seaside hotel has red-and-gold furnishings and heavy timber furniture, including sleigh beds. A handful of the 18 rooms here have huge timber decks looking out to the sea, a few footsteps away.

Camping Municipal du Port Blanc CAMPGROUND €

(☑02 99 46 10 74; www.camping-port-blanc.com; rue du Sergeant Boulanger; site per 2 adults from €24; ☺Apr-Sep) You'll find this campground close to the beach, about 2km west of Plage de l'Écluse. There's direct access to the sand.

🍴 Eating

Some of Dinard's best restaurants are attached to hotels, such as Hôtel Printania (menus €25-38), which serves top-notch fish and seafood.

TOP CHOICE La Balafon MODERN FRENCH €

(☑02 99 46 14 81; 31 rue de la Vallée; menu from €17, mains €9-15; ☺closed dinner Sun & Thu, lunch Mon) Away from the tourist hustle and bustle of the seafront, this is a quality modern neighbourhood bistro serving freshly made meals using produce from the nearby market. The daily lunch menu consists of a couple of well-chosen and presented dishes, usually one fish and one meat. It's totally unpretentious, well priced and many locals rate it as the best place in town.

La Passerelle-du-Clair-de-Lune MODERN FRENCH €€

(☑02 99 16 96 37; Promenade du Clair-de-Lune, 3 av George V; menus €20-35, mains €19; ☺dinner only Jul-Aug, closed Mon & Tue Sep-Jun, all Jan) Creative, modern seafood is served up at this intimate little restaurant with stunning views over the former home of the fish now sitting on your plate.

ℹ Information

Tourist Office (☑02 99 46 94 12; www.ot -dinard.com; 2 bd Féart; ☺9.30am-12.15pm &

2-6pm Mon-Sat) Staff book accommodation for free.

❶ Getting There & Away

AIR **Ryanair** (www.ryanair.com) has daily flights to and from London Stansted as well as flights to Bradford-Leeds and East Midlands. It's also possible to fly from here to Guernsey. There's no public transport from Dinard airport (5km from Dinard) to town (or to neighbouring St-Malo); a daytime/evening taxi from Dinard to the airport costs around €15/22.

BOAT **Compagnie Corsaire** (🖋08 25 13 81 00; www.compagniecorsaire.com) run a **Bus de Mer** (Sea Bus; adult/child return €7.50/4.90, 10 minutes, half-hourly) shuttle service between St-Malo and Dinard. Outside the July–August peak season both frequency, and cost, falls. A similar service is offered by **Taxi de la Mer** (www.taxibateau.fr; adult/child €5/free).

BUS **Illenoo** (www.illenoo-services.fr) buses connect Dinard and the train station in St-Malo (€1.90, 30 minutes, hourly). Le Gallic bus stop, outside the tourist office, is the most convenient. Several buses travel to Rennes (€4.30, two hours).

❶ Getting Around

TAXI Call 🖋06 64 98 59 59.

Cancale

POP 5440

The idyllic little fishing port of Cancale, 14km east of St-Malo, is famed for its offshore *parcs à huîtres* (oyster beds). There's no real beach here but the waterfront is a fun place to stroll and take in all the comings and goings of the fisherfolk.

The town is split into two parts, with the locals' day-to-day life taking place up the hill in the town centre, while most of the tourist facilities are down by the seashore.

◉ Sights

Ferme Marine　FARM
(🖋02 99 89 69 99; www.ferme-marine.com; corniche de l'Aurore; adult/child €7/3.70; ⊘guided tours in French 11am, 3pm & 5pm Jul-Aug, in English 2pm, in German 4pm) Entry to this small museum and working oyster farm is by guided tour only. Tour frequency decreases out of season.

🍽 Sleeping & Eating

Accommodation is expensive and most of it not even remotely worth the asking price. Fortunately, the town is an easy day trip from St-Malo or Dinard and there are dozens of cheap and excellent *chambres d'hôte* in the region – ask at the tourist office for a full list.

Maison de la Marine　B&B €€
(🖋02 99 89 88 53; www.maisondelamarine.com; 23 rue de la Marine; d with breakfast €145; 🛜) This *chambre d'hôte*, opposite the church in the town centre, is all understated elegance. There are five rooms with wooden four-poster beds, calming colour tones and free-standing bath tubs. If all that doesn't sound relaxing enough then simply sit back in a wicker chair in the pretty gardens and listen to the birdsong. Don't miss out on a meal in the excellent attached restaurant.

La Pastourelle　B&B €
(🖋02 99 89 10 09; www.baie-saintmichel.com; Les Nielles; r €67-76; 🛜) This is a delightful *chambre d'hôte* inside a vine-covered traditional Breton *longère* (long house) looking out to sea. Rooms are crisp and countrified, and convivial *tables d'hôte* (€25 per person) are available by reservation. It's on the (sometimes noisy) D155, 7km from town.

Le Duguay-Trouin　HOTEL €€
(🖋02 23 15 12 07; www.hotelduguaytrouin.com; 11 quai Duguay-Trouin; d €90-110) Easily the best portside option, this small hotel has sun-filled rooms that have been tastefully decorated and come complete with DVD players and flat-screen TVs.

Marché aux Huîtres　MARKET €
(lunch platters €20; ⊘9am-6pm) Clustered by the Pointe des Crolles lighthouse, stalls at this market sell oysters from €3 per dozen for small *huîtres creuses* (oysters on the half shell).

❶ Information

Tourist Office (🖋02 99 89 63 72; www.cancale-tourisme.fr; ⊘9.30am-1pm & 2.30-7pm) At the top of rue du Port. In July and August there's an annexe in the wooden house where the fish auction takes place on quai Gambetta.

❶ Getting There & Around

BUS Buses stop behind the church on place Lucidas and at Port de la Houle, next to the pungent fish market. **Keolis Emeraude** (www.keolis-emeraude.com) has year-round services to and from St-Malo (€2, 30 minutes). In summer, at least three daily Keolis Emeraude buses continue to Port Pican and Port Mer, near Pointe du Grouin.

Dinan

POP 11,600

Set high above the fast-flowing Rance River, the narrow cobblestone streets and squares lined with crooked half-timbered houses of Dinan's old town are straight out of the Middle Ages – something that's not lost on the deluge of summer tourists; by around 6pm though someone waves a magic wand and most of them vanish and a sense of calm befalls the town. Needless to say, it's well worth sticking around for a night or two.

◉ Sights

Château de Dinan MUSEUM

(☏02 96 39 45 20; rue du Château; adult/child €4.60/1.90; ◷10am-6.30pm, closed Jan) The town's museum is atmospherically housed in the keep of Dinan's ruined 14th-century château. It showcases the town's history and has information sheets in various languages. Just east of the church, beyond the tiny Jardin Anglais (English Garden), a former cemetery and nowadays a pleasant little park, is the 13th-century Tour Ste-Cathérine, with great views down over the viaduct and port.

Basilique St-Sauveur CHURCH

(place St-Sauveur; ◷9am-6pm, closed during services) With its soaring Gothic chancel, the Basilique St-Sauveur contains a 14th-century grave slab in its north transept reputed to contain the heart of Bertrand du Guesclin, a 14th-century knight noted for his hatred of the English and his fierce battles to expel them. Ironically, Dinan today has one of the largest English expat communities in Brittany!

Tour de l'Horloge Tower TOWER

(☏02 96 87 02 26; rue de l'Horloge; adult/teenager/child €3.10/2/free; ◷10am-6.30pm Jun-Sep) The half-timbered houses overhanging place des Cordeliers and place des Merciers mark the heart of the old town. A few paces south, climb up to the little balcony of this 15th-century clock tower whose chimes ring every quarter hour.

Vieux Pont HISTORIC QUARTER

Rue du Jerzual, which is one of the oldest streets in town, and its continuation, the steep stone rue du Petit Fort, are both lined with art galleries, antiques shops and restaurants, and lead down to the Vieux Pont (Old Bridge). From here the pretty little port, hemmed by restaurants and cafes, extends northwards, while the 19th-century Viaduc de Dinan soars high above to the south.

✦ Activities

Compagnie Corsaire CRUISE

(☏08 25 13 81 00; www.compagniecorsaire.com) Between May and September boats sail along the Rance River to Dinard and St-Malo (return trip adult/child €31/18.50, 2½ hours). Sailing schedules vary according to the tides. From Dinard or St-Malo you can easily return to Dinan by bus (and from St-Malo, by train too).

Jaman IV CRUISE

(☏02 96 39 28 41; www.vedettejamaniv.com; adult/child €12.50/8.50) This converted barge offers one-hour cruises up river past the Abbaye Sant-Magloire. There are four departures daily in high summer from the port in Dinan.

Self-Guided Walks WALKING

Ask at the tourist office for the free map and leaflet, available in several languages (including English), which plots two walking itineraries around town.

⚑ Festivals & Events

Fête des Remparts MEDIEVAL FESTIVAL

(www.fete-remparts-dinan.com) No fewer than 100,000 visitors turn up to join Dinannais townsfolk dressed in medieval garb for the two-day Fête des Remparts, held in late July every even-numbered year.

⌦ Sleeping

In summer, advance reservations are recommended. Ask the tourist office for a list of *chambres d'hôte* in the surrounding area.

Hôtel Arvor BOUTIQUE HOTEL €€

TOP CHOICE

(☏02 96 39 21 22; www.hotelarvordinan.com; 5 rue Pavie; s/d from €85/95; ☎) Back in the 18th century the building that the Hôtel Arvor now occupies was a Jacobin convent – we can only think that the former occupants must be cursing the fact that they were born 200 years too soon and that they can't stay here now. Each room is a unique work of art, painted in striking shades and with anything from big soft hearts to wooden shutters hung like paintings on the walls. Service is excellent and it's an all-round good deal.

BRETON LANGUAGE REDUX

Throughout Brittany you'll see bilingual Breton street and transport signs, and many other occurrences of the language popping up. Even though all Breton speakers also speak French, it is seen as an important gesture to normalising the use of a language that has been stigmatised (and even banned) throughout much of the early and mid-20th century.

Historically speaking, Breton is a Celtic language related to Cornish and Welsh, and more distantly to Irish and Scottish Gaelic. Following on from the French Revolution, the government banned the teaching of Breton in schools, punishing children who spoke their mother tongue. As happened with other marginalised Celtic cultures, speakers of all ages were stigmatised. For the next century and a half it remained a language spoken in the sanctum of private homes. Education, post-WWII economics, mass media and, most of all, fluid transportation between Brittany and the rest of the country also saw French rapidly gain ground. Between 1950 and 1990 there was an 80% reduction in Breton usage.

But what constitutes 'Breton' these days is trickier to pin down. The seeds of the language's revival were planted in the 1960s, particularly after France's May 1968 protests, driven by the younger generation rebelling against their oppressed cultural heritage. Bringing about the rebirth of the language, no longer passed on generationally, wasn't straightforward. Settling on a standardised Breton for teaching in schools is still a complex issue, as the language is more often spoken than written, with regional differences in both areas.

There's also a distinct difference between the Breton of first-generation speakers and 'neo-Breton', particularly as the new incarnation often replaces French words long intermingled with Breton with completely Breton ones. Case in point: *Aotrou* and *Itron* are now used for the French *Monsieur* and *Madame*. Traditionally, though, they denote someone of exceedingly high rank (*Itron* is the respectful term of address for the Virgin Mary) – creating another generational language gap. (Bizarrely, it would be like being greeted by a stranger, without irony, as 'Hello, Exalted One'.) Some older Breton speakers also find it hard to shake the ostracism inflicted on them for their language and aren't comfortable conversing in it openly.

Breton now extends beyond its historic boundaries. Originally, Basse Bretagne (Lower Brittany, in the west) spoke variants of the Breton language, while Haute Bretagne (Upper Brittany, in the east, including areas such as St-Malo) spoke Gallo, a language similar to French. But today you'll find Breton signage in Rennes' metro stations and in many other parts of the east, symbolising Brittany's culture across the entire region.

BRITTANY DINAN

La Villa Côté Cour   B&B €€€

(☑02 96 39 30 07; www.villa-cote-cour-dinan .com; 10 rue Lord Kitchener; d €99-239; ☜) And feel those stress levels drop! Opening onto a delightful garden, this exquisite *chambre d'hôte* has just five countrified rooms (with names like 're-birth', 'harmony' and 'vitality') with checked fabrics, scrubbed floorboards and a decadant sauna. Rooms also have their own jacuzzis.

Le Logis du Jerzual   B&B €€

(☑02 96 85 46 54; www.logis-du-jerzual.com; 25-27 rue du Petit Fort; s incl breakfast €70, d incl breakfast €80-110; @☜) A higgledy-piggledy little B&B halfway down an ancient cobbled street, the rooms here are stuffed with a family's knick-knacks and there's a beautiful flower garden

to relax in. However, there's not much parking nearby and it's a long walk down hill from town – and then back up again!

Hôtel de la Tour de l'Horloge   HOTEL €€

(☑02 96 39 96 92; www.hotel-dinan.com; 5 rue de la Chaux; s €70-80, d €72-86; ☜) In the centre of the old town, the 12-room Horloge occupies a charming 18th-century house on a cobbled, car-free lane, which contrasts with its colourful North African style. Head to the top floor, where rooms have exposed wooden beams and a lofty view of the hotel's namesake clock tower.

Camping Municipal Châteaubriand   CAMPGROUND €

(☑02 96 39 11 96; 103 rue Châteaubriand; per adult/tent/car €2.80/3.10/2.25; ☼Jun-Sep) This

LE COQUILLAGE

Super chef Olivier Roellinger's latest project is his sumptuous restaurant Le Coquillage (☑02 99 89 64 76; www .maisons-de-bricourt.com; 1 rue Duguesclin; menus €27-135; ☉Mar-Dec) and hotel, housed in the impressive Château Richeux, 4km to the south of Cancale. Roellinger's creations have earned him Michelin-star approval and you won't have trouble understanding why if you're lucky enough to bag a table here. The food takes in the culinary highlights of both Brittany and Normandy, from fresh scallops to regional dishes, all beautifully cooked and imaginatively served. Booking well ahead is essential. As well as offering rooms at Château Richeux, Roellinger offers a range of cottages and other deluxe accommodation around Cancale. See the website for details.

campground at the foot of the ramparts is the closest to the old town.

🍴 Eating & Drinking

The old city has some really charming (and surprisingly good-value) eateries and bars, with more along the river at the old port.

Le Cantorbery   TRADITIONAL FRENCH €€
(☑02 96 39 02 52; 6 rue Ste-Claire; menus €26-37; ☉closed Wed) Occupying a magnificent 17th-century house, this elegant, intimate restaurant is perfect for wining and dining your beloved over a romantic lunch or dinner. Its traditional menu – based on beef, grilled fish and seafood, including *coquilles St-Jacques* (scallops) from St-Brieuc – changes in accordance with the seasons.

Crêperie Ahna   CRÊPERIE €
(☑02 96 39 09 13; 7 rue de la Poissonnerie; crêpes €6.50-9; ☉closed Sun) Run by the same family for four generations and with such unusual delights as a *galette* with duck and snail butter (better than it sounds!), this place deserves its reputation as one of the best crêperies in town. It's never less than heaving with happy customers, making it a good idea to reserve a table.

ℹ️ Information

Tourist Office (☑02 96 87 69 76; www.dinan -tourisme.com; 9 rue du Château; ☉9.30am-

7pm Mon-Sat, 10am-12.30pm & 2-6pm Sun) Offers internet access.

ℹ️ Getting There & Around

BUS Buses leave from place Duclos and the bus station. **Illenoo** (☑08 10 35 10 35; www.illenoo -services.fr) runs several daily services:
Dinard €2.80, 40 minutes
Rennes €4.30, 1¼ hours
TAXI Call ☑06 08 00 80 90.
TRAIN Change in Dol de Bretagne:
Rennes from €14.50, one hour
St-Malo €9.50, one hour, five daily

Paimpol

POP 8240

Set around a working fishing harbour and ringed by half-timbered buildings, Paimpol (Pempoull in Breton) is rich in history. It was the one-time home port of the Icelandic fishery, when the town's fishermen would set sail to the seas around Iceland for seven months or more at a stretch. It's also rich in legends – the fishermen lost at sea are recalled in folk tales and *chants de marins* (sea shanties).

◎ Sights & Activities

Enquire at the tourist office about canoeing and kayaking operators.

TOP CHOICE **La Vapeur du Trieux**   STEAM TRAIN
(☑08 92 39 14 27; www.vapeurdutrieux.com; adult/ child return €23/11.50; ☉May-Sep) This 1922 steam train chuffs along the riverbank on a beautiful journey from Paimpol's station to the artists' town of Pontrieux, where there's time for a pleasant meal and a stroll before the return journey. Reserve at least one day ahead.

Abbaye de Beauport   ABBEY
(Beauport Abbey; ☑02 96 55 18 58; www.abbaye -beauport.com; adult/child/family €6/3.50/12; ☉10am-7pm) If you have wheels (or you're up for a glorious 1½-hour walk along the seashore from the town harbour), head 3.5km east of Paimpol to this romantic 18th-century abbey that plays host to frequent art and sculpture exhibitions. En route, stop at the Pointe de Guilben for beautiful bay views. The tourist office has a free map.

Musée de la Mer   MARITIME MUSEUM
(Sea Museum; ☑02 96 22 02 19; rue Labenne; adult/child €4.90/2; ☺10.30am-12.30pm & 2-6.30pm) This splendid little museum charts the Paimpol region's maritime history and is, rather appropriately, set in a former cod-drying factory.

Musée du Costume Breton   CLOTHING MUSEUM
(☑02 96 22 02 19; rue Raymond Pellier; adult/child €2.90/1.40; ☺3-6pm Tue-Sun Jul & Aug, weekends only Sep) In the summer months this rather curious museum displays traditional Breton clothing items. Think lots of big lace hats.

Île de Bréhat   ISLAND
Paimpol is the closest port to Île de Bréhat (Enez Vriad in Breton), a tiny, car-free island 8km offshore to the north. With a population of 350, it stretches just 5km from north to south. The most idyllic time to visit is in spring, when Mediterranean wildflowers bloom in its gentle microclimate (indeed it's known as the island of flowers). There are a number of *chambres d'hôte* on the island; contact Paimpol's tourist office for information.

Vedettes de Bréhat (☑02 96 55 79 50; www.vedettesdebrehat.com) operates ferries (adult/child return €9/7.50, 15 minutes, around fifteen sailings daily July–August, less frequent rest of year) to Île de Bréhat from Pointe L'Arcouest, 6km north of Paimpol. Bikes cost an extra €15 return to transport, which is only possible on certain in- and out-bound journeys. It's cheaper to rent a bike on the island; shops line the right-hand side of the road when you get off the boat. The best way to enjoy the vibe of the island, however, is to walk.

For more on the island see www.brehat -infos.fr (in French).

✰ Festivals & Events

Festival du Chant de Marin   CULTURAL FESTIVAL
(www.paimpol-festival.com) Traditional Breton dancing takes place on the quays in August every odd-numbered year.

🛏 Sleeping & Eating

Hôtel Le Terre-Neuvas   HOTEL €
(☑02 96 55 14 14; www.le-terre-neuvas.com; 16 quai Duguay Trouin; d €46-80; ☺mid-Jan–mid-Dec; 🔊) Perched right beside the harbour, and a few steps from the historic town centre as well as the seafront, the Terre-Neuvas has comfortable, inexpensive rooms, some with views out to sea. Its excellent restaurant

(*menus* from €12) is a popular port of call for guests and nonguests.

ℹ Information

Tourist Office (☑02 96 20 83 16; www .paimpol-goelo.com; place de la République; ☺9.30am-7.30pm Mon-Sat, 9.30am-12.30pm & 4-6pm Sun) Sells local rambling guides.

ℹ Getting There & Around

BUS Tibus (☑08 10 22 22 22; www.tibus.fr) runs buses to and from St-Brieuc (€2, 1½ hours). In summer most continue to Pointe L'Arcouest.

TRAIN There are several trains or SNCF buses daily between Paimpol and Guingamp (€7, 45 minutes), where you can pick up connections to Brest, St-Brieuc and Rennes.

FINISTÈRE

The country's westernmost *département*, Finistère has a wind-whipped coastline scattered with lighthouses and beacons lashed by waves. Finistère's southern prow, Cornouaille, takes its name from early Celts who sailed from Cornwall and other parts of Britain to settle here, and today it harbours the Breton language, customs and culture.

Wild and mysterious, this is, for many people, the most enticing corner of an enticing region.

Roscoff
POP 3780

Unlike many of its industrial and less-than-beautiful sister Channel ports, Roscoff (Rosko in Breton) provides a captivating first glimpse of Brittany. Granite houses dating from the 16th century wreathe the pretty docks, which are surrounded by emerald-green fields producing cauliflowers, onions, tomatoes, new potatoes and artichokes.

Once upon a time, Roscoff farmers known as 'Johnnies', wearing distinctive horizontally striped tops, loaded up their boats with plaited strings of locally grown small pink onions and crossed the Channel to the UK. They peddled – and pedalled – with their onions hanging from their bikes' handlebars, creating the traditional British stereotype of the French today. This trade began in the early 19th century, reaching its peak in the 1920s. Today, Johnnies have a near-mythical status in the area, with a number still continuing the trade and a new wave of

BRITTANY ROSCOFF

younger-generation Johnnies ensuring the survival of this iconic tradition.

Roscoff's waters conceal beds of *goémon* (algae), harvested for foodstuffs as well as for *thalassothérapie* health and beauty treatments.

◉ Sights & Activities

Église Notre Dame de Kroaz-Batz   CHURCH
(place Lacaze-Duthiers; ☺9am-noon & 2-6pm) The most obvious sight in Roscoff is this unusual church at the heart of the old town. With its Renaissance belfry rising above the flat landscape, the 16th-century Flamboyant Gothic structure is one of Brittany's most impressive churches.

Maison des Johnnies   MUSEUM
(✑02 98 61 25 48; 48 rue Brizeux; adult/over 10yr/child €4/2.50/free; ☺tours 11am, 3pm & 5pm Mon-Fri) Photographs trace Roscoff's roaming onion farmers from the early 19th century at this popular museum. A visit is by guided tour only and there's an extra tour at 9.30am on Thursdays. Call ahead for tour times, as they change frequently.

Le Jardin Exotique de Roscoff   GARDEN
(www.jardinexotiqueroscoff.com; adult/child €5/2; ☺10am-7pm, closed Dec-Feb) Wander through 3000 species of exotic plants (many from the southern hemisphere) at this impressive exotic garden. It's a well sign-posted half-hour walk southeast from the town centre.

FREE Centre de Découverte des Algues   MUSEUM
(✑02 98 69 77 05; www.thalado.fr; 5 rue Victor Hugo; walks per adult/child €6/3; ☺9am-12pm & 2.15-7pm Mon-Fri, 9am-12pm & 2-6.30pm Sat) You can learn about local seaweed harvesting at this enthusiastically run museum, which also organises guided walks and gives regular free lectures (often in English and German).

Île de Batz   ISLAND
(www.iledebatz.com) Bordering what is basically a 4-sq-km vegetable garden fertilised by seaweed, the beaches on the Île de Batz (pronounced 'ba, Enez Vaz' in Breton) are a peaceful place to bask. The mild island climate supports the luxuriant Jardins Georges Delaselle (✑02 98 61 75 65; www

GET YOUR MOTOR RUNNING AROUND BRITTANY'S COASTLINE
CATHERINE LE NEVEZ

Sillon de Talbert Brittany's best coastal drives let you see long-standing traditions in action. West of Paimpol on the north coast, you may spot the local seaweed harvesters tossing strands of kelp into their carts.

Côte de Granit Rose The otter-inhabited coastline known as the Pink Granite Coast glows with pink granite cliffs, outcrops and boulders sculpted over millennia by wind and waves. Their fiery colours are even more impressive when you're scaling them while following the 5km walking path, *sentier des douaniers* (custom officers' trail), just near the area's main town, the seaside resort of **Perros-Guirec**. Local fisherfolk sell their catch each morning at Peros' Marché des Pêcheurs on place du Marché. Offshore, head out on a boat trip to the **Sept-Îles** (Seven Islands), home to more than 20,000 marine birds including puffins, razorbills and fulmars. Check out www.armor-de couverte.fr for boat info.

Pays Bigouden If you're lucky enough to catch one of the cultural celebrations here in Finistère's southwestern corner, you might see women wearing the *coiffe bigoudène,* the area's traditional lace headdress that's up to 30cm tall. And if you're brave enough, you might want to join the surfers riding the waves off **Pointe de la Torche**. Near the car park, surf shops rent gear and offer advice.

Côte Sauvage On the western edge of the peninsula en route to Quiberon, the aptly named 'wild coast' swoops between barren headlands and sheer cliffs. Bonus: you'll avoid the choked main-road traffic here – partly because the coast road (the D186a) isn't well signed. Heading south, turn off just before you reach St-Pierre-Quiberon, in the direction of Kemiscob and Kervozès.

Golfe du Morbihan (Morbihan Coast) Most people visiting Morbihan's megaliths never make it to this part of the gulf. But swinging southwest from Vannes to **Port Navalo** rewards you with stupendous views over the gulf and its islands. Picnic benches perch at Port Navalo's tip – bring a hamper and a bottle of Breton cider.

.jardin-georgesdelaselle.fr; adult/child €5/2.50; ⊘1-6.30pm Jul & Aug, 2-6pm Wed-Mon Apr-Oct), founded in the 19th century, with over 1500 plants from all over the world.

Ferries (adult/child return €8/4, bike €8, 15 minutes each way) between Roscoff and Île de Batz run every 30 minutes between 8am and 8pm in July and August, with less-frequent sailings the rest of the year.

Bicycles can be rented on the island for around €10 per day.

🛏 Sleeping & Eating

TOP CHOICE **Hôtel la Residence**   BOUTIQUE HOTEL €
(☑02 98 69 74 85; www.hotelroscoff-laresidence. fr; 14 rue des Johnnies; d from €69; ⊘closed Dec-Jan; 🐾) This superb new hotel ticks all the boxes for a good place to stay. With colour-coordinated, bright and modern decor, all the rooms here are slightly different and there's a piano in the arty reception area. The staff are helpful and it's on a central, quiet street (close to a free car park), making this place very good value for money.

Hôtel du Centre   BOUTIQUE HOTEL€€
(☑02 98 61 24 25; www.chezjanie.com; Le Port; s/d from €64/100; ⊘mid-Feb–mid-Nov; 🐾) The minimalist, sleek rooms at this boutique hotel look like they've been lifted from a magazine, and indeed they've featured in many. For a sea-view room looking out over the postcard-pretty old port, add a further €25. It's perhaps best known for its restaurant, Chez Janie (menu €24), serving Breton classics such as *kig ha farz* – a farmers' family meal based on the Breton cake *far,* cooked in a linen bag within a boiling bacon-and-vegetable stew.

Hotel aux Tamaris   BOUTIQUE HOTEL €€
(☑02 98 61 22 99; www.hotel-aux-tamaris.com; 49 rue Edouard Corbière; d from €85; 🐾) This smart, family-run place in an old granite building overlooking the water at the western end of town is an excellent choice, with spacious, light- and seabreeze-filled rooms and yacht sails for ceilings (don't worry, there's a proper ceiling as well!). Rooms with sea views cost a lot more.

Le Temps de Vivre   BOUTIQUE HOTEL €€
(☑02 98 19 33 19; www.letempsdevivre.net; 19 place Lacaze Duthiers; d from €145; 🐾) This glamorous place is hidden away in a lovely stone mansion complete with its own tower just opposite the church. With fantastic sea views from some rooms, decor that blends modernity with tradition, plus friendly staff, this is one of Roscoff's best options. Breakfast costs €15.

Camping Aux Quatre Saisons   CAMPGROUND €
(☑02 98 69 70 86; www.camping-aux4saisons.fr; Le Ruguel; sites €14; ⊘Easter-Sep; 🐾🏊) Close to a sandy beach in the grounds of a lovely 19th-century mansion, this campground is approximately 3km southwest of Roscoff.

L'Écume des Jours   GOURMET €€
(☑02 98 61 22 83; quai d'Auxerre; menus €15-55; ⊘closed Wed Jul & Aug, Tue Sep-Jun) Regarded as the best restaurant in town, this elegant pace is housed inside a former ship-owner's house and serves magnificent and inventive local dishes that marry seafood tastes with land-lubbers' delights. There's also an excellent wine list. It's quite formal so dress smart.

Le Surcouf   BRASSERIE €€
(☑02 98 69 71 89; 14 rue Amiral Réveillère; menus €11-55) Smart without being snooty, there's top-notch seafood here and you can choose your own crab and lobster from the window tank or tuck into the classic fish soup. Opening hours and days can vary.

Crêperie Ty Saozon   CRÊPERIE €
(☑02 98 69 70 89; 30 rue Gambetta; €5.50-8.50; ⊘dinner, closed Sun & Wed) Watch and then devour handmade artisan crêpes from this award-winning crêperie in the heart of the old town. Reservations are a good idea.

❶ Information

Tourist Office (☑02 98 61 12 13; www.roscoff -tourisme.com; quai d'Auxerre; ⊘9am-12.30pm & 1.30-7pm Mon-Sat, 10am-12.30pm & 2.30-7pm Sun Jul-Aug, 9.15am-noon & 2-6pm Mon-Sat Sep-Jun) Next to the lighthouse.

❶ Getting There & Away

BUS The combined bus and train station is on rue Ropartz Morvan. Buses depart from the ferry terminal (Port de Bloscon) and pass by the town centre.

Brest €2, 1½ to two hours, up to four daily

Morlaix €2, 40 minutes, several daily

FERRY Brittany Ferries (☑reservations in France 08 25 82 88 28, reservations in UK 0871 244 0744; www.brittany-ferries.com) links Roscoff to Plymouth in England (five to nine hours, one to three daily year-round) and Cork in Ireland (14 hours, once weekly June to September).

Boats leave from Port de Bloscon, about 2km east of the town centre.

TRAIN There are regular trains and SNCF buses to Morlaix (€6, 35 minutes), where you can make connections to Brest, Quimper and St-Brieuc.

Morlaix

POP 15,605

Positioned at the bottom of a deep valley sluicing through northeastern Finistère, Morlaix is an engaging town that makes a good gateway to the coast. In the small villages to the south of Morlaix are a number of parish churches surrounded by rich sculptures. These are known as the *enclos paroissiaux* (enclosed parishes) and for a particularly fine one check out the 16th-century masterpiece in the village of Pleyben.

The narrow, finger like town centre is filled with ancient half-timbered houses that spill down to a small port. Towering above all else in the town is an arched 58m-high railway viaduct dating from 1863. During daylight hours you can walk along the lower level for a great view of the town.

◎ Sights & Activities

Église St-Melaine CHURCH
(6 place des Otages; ◎9am-noon & 2-6pm) The late-15th-century Flamboyant Gothic Église St-Melaine features a star-studded barrel-vault roof and polychrome wooden statues, including those of St Peter and the eponymous St Melaine.

Musée de Morlaix MUSEUM
(②02 98 88 07 75; www.musee.ville.morlaix.fr; place des Jacobins; adult/child/family €4.10/free/6.50; ◎10am-12.30pm & 2-6pm Jul-Sep) The area's history, archaeology and art are showcased at Musée de Morlaix. The museum also incorporates the beautifully preserved half-timbered house nearby, La Maison à Pondalez (②02 98 88 68 88; 9 Grand' Rue). Tickets are valid for both the museum and the house.

Maison de la Duchesse Anne MUSEUM
(33 rue de Mur; admission €1.80; ◎11am-6pm Mon-Sat) This 15th-century home (which, despite the name, really has nothing to do with Duchess Anne) is one of the finest examples of the local building style. The highlight is a staircase engraved with the faces of the building's patron saints.

Le Léon à Fer et à Flots BOAT TOUR
(②02 98 62 07 52; www.aferaflots.org; adult/child €26/13; ◎Apr-Sep) A great way to see the area by land and sea, this tour combines a boat trip through the islands of the Baie de Morlaix and a picturesque train trip between Roscoff and Morlaix.

🍴 Sleeping & Eating

Rue Ange de Guernisac has several enticing restaurants.

TOP CHOICE **Manoir de Ker-Huella** HISTORIC HOTEL €€
(②02 98 88 05 52; http://manoirdekerhuella.monsite-orange.fr; 78 voie d'accès au port; d with breakfast €83-88; 🕑) Built in 1898 by the then-director of the railways (the train station is very close by), this wonderful grey stone manor house set in park-like gardens above the town is now a well-run *chambre d'hôte*. Despite the size of the building there are actually only four guestrooms, all named after heroines from classic novels, although there's nothing classic about the rooms, with the sort of decoration that includes 'plants' climbing the posts of the four-poster beds. Children will enjoy sharing the gardens with the odd sheep. Call ahead if arriving outside the reception hours of 6pm to 8pm.

Ty Pierre B&B €
(②02 98 63 25 75; http://lenaj.free.fr/typierre/index.htm; 1bis place de Viarmes; s/d/tr with shared bathroom €34/50/65; 🕑) Artworks and artefacts picked up by Pierre-Yves Jacquet on his Asian travels now decorate the 10 spacious rooms of this *chambre d'hôte*. At this price there's no lift (count on climbing three or four floors), and most rooms don't have their own bathroom (they're just along the wide corridors). Bikes are available for rent from €15 per day.

Hôtel de l'Europe HOTEL €€
(②02 98 62 11 99; www.hotel-europe-com.fr; 1 rue d'Aiguillon; d from €85; 🕑) Regal, refined, yet still relaxed, the Hôtel de l'Europe occupies an elegant 19th-century building. Moulded ceilings, carved panelling and sculpted woodwork fill the sweeping public areas. The guestrooms, by contrast, are pretty dull and, in some cases, rather dated.

Grand Café de la Terrasse BRASSERIE €
(②02 98 88 20 25; 31 place des Otages; mains €12.50-16.50; ◎8am-midnight Mon-Sat) In the heart of town, Morlaix' showpiece is this

stunning 1872-established brasserie with an original central spiral staircase. Sip tea, coffee or something stronger, or sup on classical brasserie fare such as rabbit and leek crumble.

❶ Information

Tourist Office (☑02 98 62 14 94; www .tourisme.morlaix.fr; place des Otages; ☺9am-7pm Mon-Sat, 10am-12.30pm Sun Jul-Aug, 9am-12.30pm & 2-6.30pm Mon-Sat Jun & Sep) A few steps southwest below the railway viaduct. From the train station, take rue de Léon south, then turn left and descend the stairs of rue Courte.

❶ Getting There & Away

TRAIN Morlaix has frequent train services, including to the following destinations:
Brest €10, 35 minutes
Paris Montparnasse from €55, four hours
Roscoff €6, 30 minutes

Brest

POP 144,500

A major port and military base, Brest is big, bold and dynamic. Destroyed by Allied air attacks during WWII, Brest was swiftly rebuilt after the war, with little thought given to aesthetics. However, it's a lively port and university town, home to a fantastic aquarium and it's the gateway to the sea-swept Île d'Ouessant.

◉ Sights & Activities

TOP CHOICE **Océanopolis** AQUARIUM
(☑02 98 34 40 40; www.oceanopolis.com; adult/child €17/12; ☺10am-7pm Jul-Aug, reduced hours rest of year; ⊕; ☐15) Using the word aquarium to describe this enormous space-age 'aquatic world' does Brest's Océanopolis an injustice. Divided into three pavilions containing polar, tropical and temperate ecosystems, this is much more than just a traditional aquarium. Highlights are the shark tanks, mangrove and rainforest sections, colourful tropical reefs, seals and (probably everyone's favourite) the icy-cold penguin display. In addition to the animals, there are numerous films and interactive displays and it's educational for both children and adults alike (although it helps to understand French). An otter display was under construction at the time of research. Allow at least half a day for a visit. Tip: buying your ticket online for the same

price allows you to skip the queues (which can be very long on wet summer days). It's about 3km east of the city centre; take bus 15 from place de la Liberté.

Musée de la Marine MUSEUM
(Naval Museum; ☑02 98 22 12 39; www.musee -marine.fr; adult/child €5.50/free; ☺10am-6.30pm, closed Jan) Learn about Brest's maritime military history at this museum, housed within the fortified 13th-century Château de Brest, which was built to defend the harbour, on the Penfeld River. Following the 1532 union of Brittany and France, both the castle and its harbour became a royal fortress. From its ramparts there are striking views of the harbour and the naval base. Based on the museum alone (which is fairly small) the admission fee is a bit steep, but the château and its viewpoints are worth exploring.

FREE **Tour Tanguy** TOWER
(☑02 98 00 87 93; place Pierre Péron; ☺10am-noon & 2-7pm Jun-Sep, Wed, Thu, Sat & Sun afternoon Oct-May) A sobering reminder of what Brest looked like on the eve of WWII can be seen at this 14th-century tower. Other exhibits on the town's history include the documented visit of three Siamese ambassadors in 1686, who presented gifts to the court of Louis XIV; rue de Siam was named in their honour.

Les Vedettes Azenor CRUISE
(☑02 98 41 46 23; www.azenor.fr; adult/child €15/11; ☺Apr-Sep) This well-regarded cruise operator offers 1½-hour cruises around the harbour and the naval base two or three times daily from both the Port de Commerce (which is near the castle) and the Port de Plaisance (which is opposite Océanopolis).

🎊 Festivals & Events

Les Jeudis du Port MUSIC FESTIVAL
(Harbour Thursdays; ☺7.30pm-midnight Thu mid-Jul–late Aug) Plan to be in Brest on a Thursday night during summer, when Les Jeudis du Port fills the port with live rock, reggae and world music, as well as street performances and children's events.

🛏 Sleeping

TOP CHOICE **Hôtel St Louis** BOUTIQUE HOTEL €
(☑02 98 44 23 91; www.brest-hotel.com; 6 rue Algésiras; d €37-52; ☏) This sassy hotel has a boutique-on-a-budget feel. The spartan

BRITTANY BREST

rooms are livened by eccentric flourishes such as pop art prints, brightly painted walls and retro bathrooms tucked away within cupboards. Simple and cheap, but remarkably cool, so reserve ahead. Breakfast costs €6.

Hôtel de la Rade HOTEL €
(☑02 98 44 47 76; www.hoteldelarade.com; 6 rue de Siam; s €51-65, d €56-70; ☎) Right in the centre of town, this good-value place has smart and stylishly simple rooms with tiny yet functional bathrooms. Some rooms have good views onto the harbour and the couple who manage it are very welcoming.

Hôtel Continental HOTEL €€
(☑02 98 80 50 40; www.oceaniahotels.com; rue Émile Zola; r from €137; ☀☎) Every business person's favourite base in Brest, this reliable place has big rooms with big desks to work at, big beds to sleep in and big wardrobes to hang your suit in. What it's not big on, though, is any defining character. There are considerable reductions on room rates at weekends. Breakfast costs €15.

✖ Eating

Le Ruffé BISTRO €€
(☑02 98 46 07 70; 1bis rue Yves-Collet; menus €15-36; ☼closed dinner Sun & Mon) Described by *L'Express* (a French national newspaper) as the best place to eat cheap traditional food in Brest, this city-centre place is something of a mix between classic bistro dining and a gourmet cuisine experience. For the price you won't get much better.

❶ Information

Tourist Office (☑02 98 44 24 96; www.brest-metropole-tourisme.fr; place de la Liberté; ☼9.30am-7pm Mon-Sat & 10am-1pm Sun)

❶ Getting There & Away

AIR Brest's newly expanded **airport** (www.brest.aeroport.fr) has regular Ryanair flights to/from Marseille; Flybe flights to/from Birming-ham and Southampton; easyJet to Paris; and Air France flights to Paris, London and Lyon.

BOAT Ferries to Île d'Ouessant leave from Port de Commerce. **Azénor** (☑02 98 41 46 23; www.azenor.com) connects Brest with Le Fret on the Crozon Peninsula (one way adult/child €7/5, 30 minutes, three daily Tuesday to Sunday).

BUS Brest's **bus station** (☑02 98 44 46 73) is beside the train station.
Le Conquet €2, 45 minutes, six daily
Roscoff €2, 1½ hours, four daily
TRAIN For Roscoff, change trains at Morlaix.
Morlaix from €9.50, 45 minutes
Paris Montparnasse from €72, 4½ hours, around 15 daily
Quimper €16.50, 1¼ hours
Rennes from €28, two hours

❶ Getting Around

BUS & TRAM Shuttle buses (one way €4.50) connect the train station and airport approximately hourly; you can buy tickets on the bus. The local bus network **Bibus** (☑02 98 80 30 30) sells tickets good for two hours for €1.35 and day passes for €3.70. There's an information kiosk on place de la Liberté. The same people also run the city's new **tram** service and tickets are interchangeable with the bus system.
TAXI Call ☑02 98 80 18 01. A taxi for the 10km airport trip costs around €18.

Île d'Ouessant

POP 950

There is an old Breton saying that goes 'Qui voit Molène, voit sa peine, qui voit Ouessant, voit son sang' (those who see Molène see their sorrow, those who see Ouessant see their blood), and it's true that on a wild stormy winter day there's a real end-of-the-world feeling to the Île d'Ouessant (Enez Eusa in Breton, meaning 'Island of Terror'; Ushant in English) and its smaller neighbouring island of Molène. However, if you come on a sunny day the place can seem like a little paradise, with turquoise waters, abundant wildflowers and not much to do but walk and picnic. The peace and calm of the island is best experienced by hiking its 45km craggy coastal path or hiring a bike and cycling across the island. While the island can be visited as a day trip (as masses of people do) it's best savoured over several slow days.

ÎLE D'OUESSANT BEACHES

Plage de Corz, 600m south of Lampaul, is the island's best beach. Other good spots to stretch out are Plage du Prat, Plage de Yuzin and Plage Ar Lan. All are easily accessible by bike from Lampaul or Port du Stiff.

◉ Sights

Musée des Phares et des Balises　MUSEUM
(Lighthouse & Beacon Museum; ☑02 98 48 80 70; adult/child €4.30/3; ⏰10.30am-6pm Jul-Aug, 11am-5pm Apr-Jun & Sep) The black-and-white-striped Phare de Créac'h is the world's most powerful lighthouse. Beaming two white flashes every 10 seconds and visible for over 50km, it serves as a beacon for over 50,000 ships entering the Channel each year. Beneath is the island's main museum, which tells the story of these vital navigation aids. There are also displays devoted to the numerous shipwrecks that have occurred off this island and, for something completely different, a look back at the island's Bronze Age past. You'll definitely get more out of a visit if you speak French.

Écomusée d'Ouessant　MUSEUM
(Maison du Niou; ☑02 98 48 86 37; adult/child €3.50/2.40; ⏰10.30am-6pm Jul-Aug, 11am-5pm Apr-Jun & Sep, closed Mon Oct-Mar) Two typical local houses make up this small 'ecomuseum'. One re-creates a traditional homestead, furnished like a ship's cabin, with furniture fashioned from driftwood and painted in bright colours to mask imperfections; the other explores the island's history and customs. A combined ticket for both the lighthouse museum and the ecomuseum costs €7/4.50 for an adult/child. Check ahead as schedules are liable to change.

⊨ Sleeping & Eating

Ti Jan Ar C'hafe　BOUTIQUE HOTEL €€
(☑02 98 48 82 64; www.tijan.fr; Kerginou; r €79-99; ⏰closed mid-Nov–mid-Feb; 🛜) This hotel feels more like a *chambre d'hôte* than a proper hotel and it's all the better for it. Rooms come in a swirl of different colours but they're normally loud and vivid; we were especially taken with the purple room. There's a nice garden with cane furniture where you can have your breakfast on sunny mornings (a sunshine guarantee is not included in the price!). It's on the road into town from the port.

Hôtel Roc'h Ar Mor　HOTEL €
(☑02 98 48 80 19; http://rocharmor.pagesperso -orange.fr; s/d from €59/70; ⏰mid-Feb–mid-Nov; 🛜) In a superb location next to Baie de Lampaul, this hotel has sunlit blue-and-white rooms and also boasts a good restaurant with a terrace overlooking the ocean. Thanks to the hotel's very own smokehouse,

WORTH A TRIP

ÎLE MOLÈNE

Scarcely 1km across, Île Molène feels even more remote than its neighbour Île d'Ouessant. It's carless, virtually treeless, home to just 270 people and its electricity supply comes from a single diesel generator. The island's only village is Le Bourg, a huddle of white-washed fishermen's cottages clustered around a granite quay. Needless to say, the island is best (and can only be) explored on foot and a half-day is all you really need to walk the circumference of the island. Another option, which also allows you to investigate the nearby islets, is to hire a kayak or canoe, which can be arranged from the port on arrival. Small though the island is, it's well worth staying overnight in one of the *chambres d'hôte* or the only hotel. Getting to the island is easy enough, with all ferries to Ouessant stopping off here en route.

excellent smoked fish and meats regularly appear on the imaginative evening menu.

Auberge de Jeunesse　HOSTEL €
(☑02 98 48 84 53; http://auberge-ouessant.com; dm incl breakfast €19; ⏰closed Dec-Jan) This friendly hostel, on the hill above Lampaul, has two- to six-person rooms. It's popular with school and walking groups; reservations are essential. Under 26s and students stay for €17.

Camping Municipal　CAMPGROUND €
(☑02 98 48 80 06; Stang Ar Glan; per person €3.20, per tent €3.15; ⏰Apr-Sep) About 500m east of Lampaul, this sprawling 100-pitch place looks more like a football field than a campground.

Ty Korn　SEAFOOD €€
(☑02 98 48 87 33; lunch/dinner menus €16/32; ⏰closed Sun & Mon) The ground floor of this hyperfriendly place is a bar, serving Breton black-wheat beers (made from the same *blé noire* as Breton galettes). Upstairs there's an excellent restaurant where seafood is a speciality. Opening hours can vary, though the bar stays open until 1am.

❶ Information

Tourist Office (☑02 98 48 85 83; www.ot -ouessant.fr; place de l'Église; ⏰9am-12.30pm

& 1.30-6.30pm Mon-Sat, 9.30am-12.30pm Sun) Sells walking brochures and can hook you up with operators offering horse riding, sailing and other activities.

① Getting There & Away

AIR **Finist'air** (☑02 98 84 64 87; www.finistair .fr) flies from Brest's airport to Ouessant in a mere 15 minutes. There are two flights daily in the week and one on Saturdays (one way adult/child under 13 €65/47).

BOAT Ferries depart from Brest and the tiny town (and Brittany's most westerly point) of Le Conquet (Konk Leon in Breton). Buses operated by **Les Cars St-Mathieu** (☑02 98 89 12 02) link Brest with Le Conquet (€2, 45 minutes, six daily). In high summer it's a good idea to reserve at least two days in advance and to check in 30 minutes before departure. Transporting a bicycle costs €14.

Penn Ar Bed (☑02 98 80 80 80; www .pennarbed.fr) sails from the Port de Commerce in Brest (adult/under 26/child return €32/25.50/19.50, 2½ hours) and from Le Conquet (same prices, 1½ hours). Boats run between each port and the island two to five times daily from May to September and once daily between October and April. Prices fall in winter.

Finist'mer (☑08 25 13 5235; www.finist-mer .fr) runs high-speed boats from Le Conquet (adult/child €22/18, 40 minutes) and Lanildut (€25/22, 35 minutes) once a day.

① Getting Around

BICYCLE Bike-hire operators have kiosks at the Port du Stiff ferry terminal and compounds just up the hill, as well as outlets in Lampaul. The going rate for town/mountain bikes is €10/14 per day. You can save by booking and prepaying for a mountain bike (€10) at the Brest tourist office. Cycling on the coastal footpath is forbidden – the fragile turf is strictly reserved for walkers.

MINIBUS Islander-run minibus services such as **Ouessant Voyage** (☑06 07 90 07 43) meet the ferry at Port du Stiff and will shuttle you to Lampaul or your accommodation for a flat fare of €2 (to guarantee a seat in July and August, book ahead at the island tourist office or at the tourist office in Brest). For the return journey, the pick-up point is the car park beside Lampaul's church. Minibus owners also offer two-hour guided tours (€15 per person) of the island, in French.

Presqu'île de Crozon

The anchor-shaped Crozon Peninsula is part of the Parc Naturel Régional d'Armorique and one of the most scenic spots in Brittany. The partly forested peninsula is criss-crossed by some of 145km of signed walking trails and excellent biking terrain, with crêperies in traditional stone buildings tucked in and around the hinterland.

LANDÉVENNEC
POP 358

The Aulne River flows into the Rade de Brest beside the pretty village of Landévennec, home to the ruined Benedictine Abbaye St-Guenolé. The abbey museum (adult/child €4/3; ⊙10am-6.30pm, closed Sat May-Jun & late Sep) records the history of the settlement, founded by St Guenolé in 485 and the oldest Christian site in Brittany. Nearby, a new abbey is home to a community of monks, who run a little shop selling homemade fruit jellies.

Landévennec-based Vedettes Rosmeur (☑06 98 11 93 33, 06 85 95 55 49; www.vedettes -rosmeur.fr; adult/child €16.50/11) operates nature boat trips up the estuary behind Landévennec.

ARGOL
POP 833

Argol is a quaint village in its own right, but its main draw is the Musée du Cidre du Bretagne (Breton Cider Museum; ☑02 98 17 21 67; www.maisonducidredebretagne.fr; adult/child €5/free; ⊙10am-noon & 2-7pm Jul-Aug, 2-7pm Apr-Jun & Sep). This former dairy's old stone buildings have been transformed into a working *cidrerie* producing over 300,000 bottles annually. A visit (allow around an hour, including a French-language but understandable film) takes you through the history of cider in Brittany and present-day production. And, of course, you get to taste it too. In July and August, one of the barns is used as a crêperie (crêpes €4.50-7.50; ⊙noon-10pm).

CROZON & MORGAT
POP 7950

The area's largest town, Crozon is the engine room for the peninsula. The town centre is pleasant enough but there's little reason to hang around. On the water 2km south, Morgat was built in the 1930s by the Peugeot brothers (of motor-vehicle fame) as a summer resort and it retains something of the feel of that period. It's one of the prettier resorts in this part of Brittany, with colourful houses piled up at one end of a long sandy beach that has very safe bathing.

🏃 Activities

Coastal Hike   WALKING
Morgat is the launching pad for a fine day-long coastal walk. Beyond the marina at

the southern end of Morgat's beach, the coastal path offers an excellent 13km hike (part of the GR34) along the sea cliffs to Cap de la Chèvre. The route takes you past an old fort and through sweet-scented pine forests overlooking numerous little coves (most inaccessible) with water that on a sunny day glows electric blue. It's hard not to think you've somehow walked to the Mediterranean. These lazy summer-day images are shattered on reaching Cap de la Chèvre and the exposed, western side of the peninsula. Here the coastline is much wilder and the sea is slate-grey and clearly Atlantic.

Vedettes Sirènes   CRUISE
(06 85 95 55 49; adult/child €11/8) Vedettes Sirènes operate 45-minute boat trips to the colourful sea caves along the coast. Tours depart from Morgat harbour several times daily from April to September.

Festivals & Events
Every Tuesday during July and August free concerts take place on place d'Ys.

Festival du Bout du Monde   MUSIC FESTIVAL
(Festival of the End of the World; www.festivalduboutdumonde.com) The place d'Ys area hosts the Festival du Bout du Monde in early August, which features world music.

Sleeping & Eating
Morgat's seafront and place d'Ys are good spots to trawl for seafood restaurants.

Villa Ker-Maria   B&B €€
(02 98 26 20 02; www.kermaria.com; 1 bd de la Plage; r with breakfast €90-125;) This spectacular five-room chambre d'hôte overlooking the sea and just outside Morgat's centre has pastel-coloured rooms full of fine furnishings. Its seaward-sloping gardens are the perfect spot to while away an afternoon relaxing on one of the sun loungers.

Hôtel de la Baie   HOTEL €
(02 98 27 07 51; www.hoteldelabaie-crozon-morgat.com; 46 bd de la Plage; s €45-65, d €63-88;) One of the very few places to remain open year-round, this friendly, family-run spot on Morgat's promenade has recently renovated rooms, some with views over the ocean, and is one of the best deals around. There are tea- and coffee-making facilities in the rooms.

ECOBUZZ

Tucked away on the road to Crozon, 8km west of Le Faou, Ferme Apicole de Terenez (02 98 81 06 90; www.ferme-apicole-de-terenez.com; Rosnoën) is abuzz with live bees that you can view in its honey museum (admission free; 9am-7pm). Depending on the season, you might also see apiculteurs (beekeepers) Irène and Stéphane Brindeau using environmentally friendly cold-extraction methods to extract the all-natural honey, produced with the pollen of flowers and trees, from giant combs in the workshop here. You can buy honey, nougat and other home-made honey products like hydromel (chouchen in Breton; a fermented alcoholic drink made from honey and water).

Camping Les Pieds dans l'Eau   CAMPGROUND €
(02 02 35 46 26 12; http://lespiedsdansleau.free.fr; St-Fiacre; per person/tent/car from €4/4/2.30; mid-Jun–mid-Sep) 'Camping feet in the water' (almost literally, at high tide) is one of 16 campgrounds along the peninsula.

Saveurs et Marées   TOP CHOICE   SEAFOOD €€
(02 98 26 23 18; 52 bd de la Plage; menus €14-45; closed Feb) Our pick of Morgat's clutch of restaurants is this lemon-yellow cottage overlooking the sea with its breezy dining room, sunny terrace and consistently good, locally caught seafood (including succulent lobster).

Le Kreisker   SEAFOOD €€
(02 98 26 15 49; 2 rue du Kreisker; mains from €14) This waterfront place in Crozon has a laid-back vibe but a chef who races about creating seafood magic in the kitchen – all for a price you can't knock. The Breton seafood salad comes highly recommended.

Information
Crozon Tourist Office (02 98 27 07 92; www.crozon.com; bd Pralognan; 9.30am-1pm & 2-7pm Mon-Sat, 10am-noon Sun) Housed in the former railway station, on the main road to Camaret.

Morgat Tourist Office (02 98 27 29 49; www.officedetourisme-crozon-morgat.fr; 9.30am-1pm & 2-7pm Mon-Sat, 10am-noon Sun) Overlooks the promenade at the corner of bd de la Plage and doubles as the town's post office.

CAMARET-SUR-MER
POP 2600

At the western extremity of the Crozon Peninsula, Camaret (unusually in French, the final 't' is pronounced) is a classic fishing village – or at least it was until early in the 20th century, when it was France's then-biggest crayfish port. Abandoned fishing-boat carcasses now decay in its harbour, but it remains an enchanting place that lures artists. There's an ever-increasing number of galleries dotted around town, particularly along rue de la Marne and around place St-Thomas, one block north of the waterfront.

◉ Sights

Pointe de Pen-Hir   MEMORIAL
Three kilometres south of Camaret, this is a spectacular headland bounded by steep, sheer sea cliffs, with two WWII memorials. On a peninsula full of breathtaking scenery this might be the most impressive lookout of them all. On a stormy day, with giant waves hurling themselves at the cliff faces, it feels like the end of the world. There are plenty of opportunities for short walks around here as well as a handful of little cove beaches and some ancient megalithic sites.

Chapelle Notre-Dame-
de-Rocamadour   CHURCH
(⊙school hols) Its timber roof like an inverted ship's hull, the Chapelle Notre-Dame-de-Rocamadour is dedicated to the sailors of Camaret, who have adorned it with votive offerings of oars, lifebuoys and model ships.

🍴 Sleeping & Eating

Hôtel Vauban   HOTEL €
(☑02 98 27 91 36; 4 quai du Styvel; d €41-60; ⊙Feb-Nov; 🛜) Its airy rooms are contemporary but the Vauban's old-fashioned hospitality extends to its large rear garden, with a barbecue to grill your own fish and a piano to play. Its bar remains a favourite with Camaret's old-timers too. There are two similar places nearby.

Del Mare   SEAFOOD €€
(☑02 98 27 97 22; 16 quai Gustave Toudouze; menus €13-26.50; ⊙closed Tue & Wed early Apr-Jun & Sep–mid-Nov) Seafood is the order of the day at this marine-styled place on the main stretch of waterfront, with a clutch of tables on its little timber terrace. Service is prompt and friendly.

❶ Information

Tourist Office (☑02 98 27 93 60; www .camaretsurmer-tourisme.fr; 15 quai Kléber; ⊙9am-noon & 2-6pm Mon-Sat) On the waterfront.

❶ Getting There & Around

BOAT Azénor (☑02 98 41 46 23; www.azenor .com) runs seasonal ferries between Brest and the Presqu'île de Crozon.

From mid-April to mid-September, Penn Ar Bed (☑02 98 80 80 80; www.pennarbed. fr) sails between Camaret and Île d'Ouessant (adult/child return from €32/25.50).

BUS Five buses daily run from Quimper to Crozon (€2, 1¼ hours), continuing to Camaret (€2), and up to four go from Camaret and Crozon to Brest (€2, 1¼ hours, daily). Buses also run between Morgat, Crozon and Camaret several times daily (€2, 10 minutes).

Quimper
POP 66,911

Small enough to feel like a village, with its slanted half-timbered houses and narrow cobbled streets, and large enough to buzz as the troubadour of Breton culture and arts, Quimper (kam-pair) is Finistère's thriving capital. Derived from the Breton word *kemper,* meaning 'confluence', Quimper sits at the juncture of the small Rivers Odet and Steïr, criss-crossed by footbridges with cascading flowers. Despite being one of Brittany's most charming towns, it is often overlooked by visitors.

◉ Sights

Cathédrale St-Corentin   CHURCH
(⊙8.30am-noon & 1.30-6.30pm Mon-Sat, 8.30am-noon & 2-6.30 Sun) At the centre of the city is its cathedral with its distinctive kink, said to symbolise Christ's inclined head as he was dying on the cross. Construction began in 1239 but the cathedral's dramatic twin spires weren't added until the 19th century. Look out for an equestrian statue of King Gradlon, the city's mythical 5th-century founder, located high on the west facade.

Musée Départemental Breton   MUSEUM
(☑02 98 95 21 60; 1 rue du Roi Gradlon; adult/child €4/free; ⊙9am-6pm) Beside the cathedral, recessed behind a magnificent stone courtyard, this superb museum showcases Breton history, furniture, costumes, crafts and archaeology, in a former bishop's palace.

Centre d'Art Contemporain de Quimper
GALLERY

(📞02 98 55 55 77; www.le-quartier.net; 10 esplanade François Mitterrand; admission €2; ⏰10amnoon & 1-6pm Tue-Sat, 2-6pm Sun) A splendid temple to modern art, with cutting-edge and sometimes-challenging temporary exhibitions on display. Note that when exhibitions are being changed over it may be closed for a few days. Entry on Sundays is free.

Musée des Beaux-Arts
GALLERY

(📞02 98 95 45 20; 40 place St-Corentin; adult/child €5/free; ⏰10am-7pm Jul-Aug, 9.30am-noon & 2-6pm Wed-Mon Apr-Jun & Sep-Oct) The groundfloor halls are home to some fairly morbid 16th- to 20th-century European paintings, but things lighten up on the upper levels of the town's main art museum. A room dedicated to Quimper-born poet Max Jacob includes sketches by Picasso.

👉 Tours

Vedettes de l'Odet
BOAT TOUR

(📞02 98 57 00 58; www.vedettes-odet.com) From June to September, Vedettes de l'Odet runs boat trips (adult/child €27/16, 1¼ hours one way) from Quimper along the serene Odet estuary to Bénodet, departing from quai Neuf. You can stop for a look about Bénodet and then hop on a boat back.

🎉 Festivals & Events

Festival de Cornouaille
CELTIC FESTIVAL

(www.festival-cornouaille.com) A celebration of traditional Celtic music, costumes and culture takes place over six days in late July. After the traditional festival, classical-music concerts are held at different venues around town.

🛏 Sleeping

Unfortunately, Quimper has a chronic shortage of inexpensive accommodation; there's none in the old town.

Hôtel Manoir des Indes
MANOR HOUSE €€

(📞02 98 55 48 40; www.manoir-hoteldesindes.com; 1 allée de Prad ar C'hras; s/d from €105/133; 📶🏊) This stunning hotel conversion, located in an old manor house just a short drive from the centre of Quimper, has been restored with the globe-trotting original owner in mind. Decor is minimalist and modern, with Asian objets d'art, lots of exposed wood and a couple of fake elephants outside. It's located a five-minute drive west of Quimper, a little way north of the D100.

Hôtel Gradlon
HOTEL €€

(📞02 98 95 04 39; www.hotel-gradlon.com; 30 rue de Brest; s €101-119, d €109-135; ⏰closed mid-Dec–mid-Jan; 📶) This place may not look like much from the street, but its rather bland and modern facade belies a charming country-manor interior. The smallish but well-furnished rooms all differ but at the same time all have plenty of character and individual touches. It's a short walk from the old town and secure parking is available.

Hôtel Kregenn
DESIGN HOTEL €€

(📞02 98 95 08 70; www.hotel-kregenn.fr; 13 rue des Réguaires; r €100-180, ste €220; 📶📶) A timberdecked courtyard and a guest lounge with outsized mirrors and white leather sofas give you the initial impression that Quimper's coolest hotel is contemporary in style, but the plush rooms (in pistachio green, ocean blue or chocolate) evoke a traditional feel, as does the warm-hearted welcome. Higherpriced rooms have air-con; two rooms are equipped for wheelchairs and everyone gets to fuss over the podgy black-and-white dog who lives in the reception area.

Camping Municipal
CAMPGROUND €

(📞02 98 55 61 09; av des Oiseaux; sites €0.79, person €3.70, car €1.85; ⏰Jun-Oct; 📶1) This wooded park is 1km west of the old city and 3km from the train station. From quai de l'Odet, follow rue Pont l'Abbé northwestwards and continue straight ahead where it veers left. Alternatively, take bus 1 from the train station to the Chaptal stop.

🍴 Eating & Drinking

You'd better like crêpes because as a bastion of Breton culture, Quimper has some exceptional crêperies, but little else. Rue du Frout near the cathedral has a couple of small pubs that attract a Breton-speaking clientele.

Crêperie du Quartier
CRÊPERIE €

(📞02 98 64 29 30; 16 rue du Sallé; menus from €6, galettes €5-7) In a town where the humble crêpe is king, this cosy stone-lined place is one of the best. Its wide-ranging menu includes a *galette* of the week and, to follow up, you can go for the full monty, such as a crêpe stuffed with apple, caramel, ice-cream, almonds and chantilly. Wash it all down with a tipple from their range of local ciders.

L'Ambroisie
GASTRONOMIC €€€

(📞02 98 95 00 02; www.ambroisie-quimper.com; 49 rue Elie Fréron; menus €25-62; ⏰lunch & dinner

Quimper

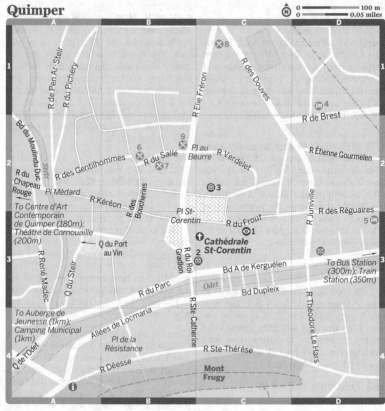

Tue-Sat, lunch Sun) Quimper's most celebrated gastronomic restaurant is sumptuously decorated with contemporary art and features elegant china on snow-white tablecloths. Regional produce provided by chef Gilbert Guyon's friends is used in the creation of house specials such as turbot with eschalots and there are lots of those Breton favourites, scallops. Cooking classes are available on request.

Le Cosy Restaurant   BRETON CUISINE €
(📞02 98 95 23 65; 2 rue du Sallé; mains €10-14.50; ⊘closed Sun, lunch Mon & dinner Tue) Make your way through the *épicerie* crammed with locally canned sardines, ciders and other Breton specialities to this eclectic dining room, where you can tuck into top-quality gratins and *tartines* (open sandwiches).

Crêperie La Krampouzerie   CRÊPERIE €
(9 rue du Sallé; galettes €2-7; ⊘Tue-Sat, dinner Sun) Crêpes and *galettes* made from organic flours and regional ingredients like *algues d'Ouessant* (seaweed), Roscoff onions and homemade ginger caramel are king here. Tables on the square out front create a real street-party atmosphere.

☆ Entertainment

From mid-June to mid-September traditional Breton music and dance takes place in the Jardin de l'Évêché (admission €5; ⊘9pm Thu).

Check posters and leaflets pasted up around town or ask the tourist office for times and venues of a local *fest-noz* (night festival). On average there's one in or near Quimper every couple of weeks.

TOP CHOICE Théâtre de Cornouaille   PERFORMING ARTS
(📞02 98 55 98 55; www.theatre-cornouaille .fr; 1 esplanade François Mitterrand; tickets €15-25) This forward-thinking theatre stages

Quimper

a wide array of performances that take in everything from classic French theatre through to West African music, Chinese opera, puppet shows and Latin American dance.

❶ Information

Tourist Office (☏02 98 53 04 05; www .quimper-tourisme.com; place de la Résistance; ☺9am-7pm Mon-Sat, 10am-12.45pm & 3-5.45pm Sun Jul-Aug, 9.30am-12.30pm & 1.30-6.30pm Mon-Sat, 10am-12.45pm Sun Jun & Sep) Sells the Pass' Quimper (€12) whereby you can access four attractions or tours of your choosing (from a list of participating organisations).

❶ Getting There & Away

BUS **CAT/Viaoo** (www.viaoo29.fr) has regular buses to Brest (€6, 1¼ hours). **Autocars l'Été** runs buses to Concarneau (€2, 45 minutes, seven to 10 daily); three buses that depart daily continue to Quimperlé (€2, 1½ hours).

TRAIN Frequent services:
Brest €16.50, 1¼ hours, up to 10 daily
Paris Montparnasse €70-86, 4¾ hours, hourly
Rennes €28-34, 2½ hours, hourly
Vannes €19.50-23, 1½ hours, hourly

❶ Getting Around

BUS **QUB** (www.qub.fr; 2 quai de l'Odet), the Quimper bus network, has an information office opposite the tourist office; a single/day ticket costs €1/3.30.

TAXI Call ☏02 98 90 21 21.

Concarneau

POP 21,000

The sheltered harbour of Concarneau (Konk-Kerne in Breton), 24km southeast of Quimper, radiates out from its trawler port, which brings in close to 200,000 tonnes of *thon* (tuna) from the Indian Ocean and off the African coast (the adjacent Atlantic's too cold). Jutting out into the port, the old town, Ville Close, is circled by medieval walls.

◉ Sights

The walled town, fortified in the 14th century and modified by the architect Vauban two centuries later, huddles on a small island linked to place Jean Jaurès by a footbridge. Once you're within the walls, rue Vauban and place St-Guénolé outside are enchanting for their old stone houses converted into shops, restaurants and galleries.

Musée de la Pêche MUSEUM
(Fisheries Museum; ☏02 98 97 10 20; www.musee delapeche.eu; 3 rue Vauban; adult/child €6.50/4; ☺9.30am-8pm Jul-Aug, 10am-6pm Apr-Jun & Sep, closed Nov-Feb) Concarneau's seafaring traditions, offshore fishing trawlers, model ships and fishing exhibits feature at the ever-popular Musée de la Pêche, in the middle of the walled town.

Marinarium AQUARIUM
(☏02 98 50 81 64; www.mnhn.fr/concarneau; place de la Croix; adult/child €5/3; ☺10am-noon & 2-6pm) Founded in 1859, Concarneau's Marinarium is the world's oldest institute of marine biology. While not as flash as some aquariums in the region, this is first and foremost a research centre. Besides, other aquarium don't have things like a dolphin embryo on display! Alongside this and its 10 aquariums are exhibits on oceanography and marine flora and fauna.

Château de Keriolet CHÂTEAU
(☏02 98 97 36 50; www.chateaudekeriolet.com; adult/child €5.50/3; ☺10.30am-1pm & 2-6pm Sun-Fri, 10.30am-1pm Sat Jun-Sep, by reservation Easter-May) This impressive building is an exquisite example of 19th-century architecture. Its intriguing Russian connections are revealed during a guided tour. The castle is a well-signed five-minute drive from town (turn right just before the large Leclerc supermarket).

CONCARNEAU BEACHES

Plage des Sables Blancs is on Baie de la Forêt, 1.5km northwest of the town centre; take bus 2 or 3 northbound from the tourist office. For **Plage du Cabellou**, 5km south of town, take bus 4 southbound.

🏃 Activities

Walking & Cycling
WALKING, CYCLING

The tourist office can provide information on walking and cycling circuits in the area, covering everything from easy two-hour rambles to much more demanding day hikes and rides.

Vedettes Glenn
BOAT TRIP

(☎02 98 97 10 31; www.vedettes-glenn.fr; 17 av du Dr Nicolas) In July and August four-hour river trips (adult/child €27/13, departures 2.15pm Tuesday, Thursday and Sunday) sail from Concarneau along the gorgeously scenic estuary of the **River Odet**. Boat trips also operate to the **Îles de Glénan** (adult/child €28/13) – a cluster of nine islands surrounded by waters so blue they look like they've dropped out of the South Pacific. The islands sit about 20km south of Concarneau and offer good diving and kayaking opportunities.

🛏 Sleeping

Hôtel des Halles
HOTEL €

(☎02 98 97 11 41; www.hoteldeshalles.com; place de l'Hôtel de Ville; s €50-85, d €65-85; 🛜) A few steps from Ville Close, this 22-room hotel looks plain on the outside but its renovated rooms come in a rainbow of colour combinations and are decorated with a suitably nautical air (think life bouys and pictures of pebbles on the walls). The all-organic breakfast (€9) includes homemade jams and bread straight from the oven.

Les Sables Blancs
BOUTIQUE HOTEL €€

(☎02 98 50 10 12; www.hotel-les-sables-blancs .com; place des Sables Blancs; s/d from €115/120; 🛜) Right on the 'white sands' of the beach from which it takes its name, this ultrachic hotel has spacious rooms and an excellent restaurant, with good deals on half-board.

Hôtel de France et d'Europe
HOTEL €

(☎02 98 97 00 64; www.hotel-france-europe.com; 9 av de la Gare; r €65-88; 🛜) The sardine tins stuck to the room doors add a bit of local character to what is otherwise a fairly sterile but very comfortable and good-value place, a very short walk back from the waterfront.

Auberge de Jeunesse Éthic Étapes
HOSTEL €

(☎02 98 97 03 47; www.ajconcarneau.com; quai de la Croix; dm incl breakfast €17) Fall asleep listening to the waves at this welcoming waterfront hostel next to the Marinarium. Extras include a wraparound barbecue terrace, a self-catering kitchen and pastries for breakfast.

🍴 Eating

Cafes, pizzerias and crêperies line the waterfront, and there are more inside the walls of Ville Close.

TOP CHOICE Au Crabe Tamboure
SEAFOOD €€

(☎02 98 60 52 84; 6 rue Sant Guénole; mains from €18) The French are renowned for their love and knowledge of food (and all the finer things in life) and as such it takes a very special meal for them to heap praise upon a restaurant, but the Au Crabe Tamboure receives near-universal applause from everyone who eats here. It's seafood (primarily crab, oysters and other shellfish) all the way and it's as fresh as you could hope for. Find it in the Ville Close, just below the chapel with the crazy Alice in Wonderland clock.

ℹ Information

Tourist Office (☎02 98 97 01 44; www.tourisme concarneau.fr; quai d'Aiguillon; ⊘9am-7pm)

ℹ Getting There & Away

BOAT A small **passenger ferry** (fare €0.80; ⊘8am-11pm Jul-Aug, 8am-6.30pm Mon-Sat, 9am-12.30pm & 2-7.30pm Sun Sep-Jun) links Ville Close with place Duquesne on the eastern side of the harbour.

BUS **L'Été Évasion** (☎02 98 56 82 82; www .autocars-ete.com) runs up to 10 buses daily between Quimper and Quimperlé, calling by Concarneau (€2 from Quimper).

TAXI Call ☎02 98 97 10 93.

MORBIHAN COAST

In the crook of Brittany's southern coastline, the Golfe du Morbihan (Morbihan Coast) is a haven of islands, oyster beds and bird life. But the area is perhaps best known for its proliferation of mystifying Celtic megaliths, which are strewn throughout most of the *département*.

Carnac

POP 4362

With enticing beaches and a pretty town centre, Carnac would be a popular tourist town even without its collection of magnificent megalithic sites, but when these are thrown into the mix you end up with a place that is unmissable on any ramble through Brittany. Predating Stonehenge by around 100 years, Carnac (Garnag in Breton) also tops it with the sheer number of ancient sites found in the vicinity, making this the world's greatest concentration of megalithic sites. There are no fewer than 3000 of these upright stones, most around thigh-high, erected between 5000 and 3500 BC.

Carnac, some 32km west of Vannes, comprises the old stone village Carnac-Ville and the seaside resort of Carnac-Plage, 1.5km south, bordered by the 2km-long sandy beach. Its megaliths stretch 13km north from Carnac-Ville and east as far as the village of Locmariaquer.

MORBIHAN'S MIGHTY MEGALITHS

Two perplexing questions arise from the Morbihan region's neolithic menhirs, dolmens, cromlechs, tumuli and cairns. Just *how* did the original constructors hew, then haul, these blocks (the heaviest weighs 300 tonnes), millennia before the wheel and the mechanical engine reached Brittany? And *why*?

Theories and hypotheses abound, but the vague yet common consensus is that they served some kind of sacred purpose – the same spiritual impulse behind so many monuments built by humankind.

The best way to appreciate the stones' sheer numbers is to walk or bike between the Le Ménec and Kerlescan groups, with menhirs almost continuously in view. Between June and September seven buses per day run between the two sites and both Carnac-Ville and Carnac-Plage.

Sign up for a one-hour guided visit at the Maison des Mégalithes (02 97 52 29 81; rte des Alignements; tour adult/child €6/free; ⊗10am-8pm Jul & Aug, to 5.15pm Sep-Apr, to 7pm May & Jun). Tour times vary considerably depending on time of year but they run regularly in French in the summer and at least once or twice per day at other times. English tours are usually held at 3pm Wednesday, Thursday and Friday from early July to late August. Because of severe erosion the sites are fenced off to allow the vegetation to regenerate. However, between 9am and 5pm from October to March you can wander freely through parts (ask at the Maison des Mégalithes for updates).

Opposite the Maison des Mégalithes, the largest menhir field – with 1099 stones – is the Alignements du Ménec, 1km north of Carnac-Ville; the eastern section is accessible in winter. From here, the D196 heads northeast for about 1.5km to the equally impressive Alignements de Kermario (which is open year-round). Climb the stone observation tower midway along the site to see the alignment from above. Another 500m further are the Alignements de Kerlescan, a smaller grouping also accessible in winter.

Tumulus St-Michel, at the end of rue du Tumulus and 400m northeast of the Carnac-Ville tourist office, dates back to at least 5000 BC and offers sweeping views.

Between Kermario and Kerlescan, 500m to the south of the D196, deposit your fee in an honour box at Tumulus de Kercado (admission €1), dating from 3800 BC and the burial site of a neolithic chieftain. From the parking area 300m further along the D196, a 15-minute walk brings you to the Géant du Manio, the highest menhir in the complex.

Near Locmariaquer, 13km southeast of Carnac-Ville, the major monuments are the Table des Marchands, a 30m-long dolmen, and the Grand Menhir Brisé (adult/child €5/free; ⊗10am-6pm), the region's largest menhir, which once stood 20m high but now lies broken on its side. Both are off the D781, just before the village. Just south of Locmariaquer by the sea is the Dolmen des Pierres Plates, a 24m-long chamber with still-visible engravings.

For some background, the Musée de Préhistoire (02 97 52 22 04; www.museede carnac.fr; 10 place de la Chapelle, Carnac-Ville; adult/child €5/2.50; ⊗10am-6pm) chronicles life in and around Carnac from the Palaeolithic and neolithic eras to the Middle Ages.

Morbihan Coast

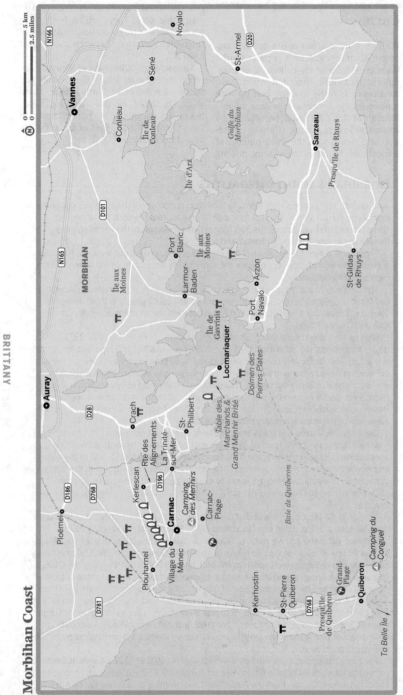

N166

Vannes

N165

N165

Noyalo

St-Armel

D20

Séné

Gulfe du Morbihan

Conleau

Île de Conleau

Sarzeau

Île d'Arz

D101

MORBIHAN

Presqu'île de Rhuys

Port Blanc

Île aux Moines

Île aux Moines

Larmor-Baden

St-Gildas de Rhuys

Île de Gavrinis

Port Navalo

Arzon

Auray

Locmariaquer

Dolmen des Pierres Plates

D28

Crach

St-Philibert

Table des Marchands & Grand Menhir Brisé

Rte des Alignements

Kerlescan

La Trinité-sur-Mer

D196

Camping des Menhirs

D186

D768

Baie de Quiberon

Ploëmel

Carnac

Carnac-Plage

Plouharnel

Village du Ménec

Camping du Conguel

D781

Kerhostin

St-Pierre Quiberon

Grand Plage

Quiberon

D768

Presqu'île de Quiberon

To Belle Île

5 km

2.5 miles

🛏 Sleeping & Eating

TOP CHOICE Plume au Vent
B&B €€

(☎06 16 98 34 79; www.plume-au-vent.com; 4 venelle Notre Dame; d with breakfast €90) Forget about tacky seaside hotels, as this two-room *chambre d'hôte* in the town centre (it's a bit tricky to find, but it's on the little street behind the very central Hotel de la Marine) is more like something from an interior design magazine. It's all mellow shades of blues and greys, hundreds of neatly bound books, knick-knacks discovered washed up on the high-tide line and polished cement showers and sinks. All up it's something of a work of art. Advance booking is essential in season.

Hotel Restaurant Les Rochers
HOTEL €€

(☎02 97 52 10 09; www.les-rochers.com; 6 Blvd de la Base Nautique; s/d half-board from €72/144; ☎) This hotel has 15 sea-blue rooms, many of which directly overlook the port at the western end of Carnac plage, and is an ideal base for families with children who prefer to build megaliths made of sand rather than peer at the real thing. Downstairs is a good seafood restaurant (mains €12 to €18).

Auberge Le Ratelier
B&B €

(☎02 97 52 05 04; www.le-ratelier.com; 4 chemin du Douet; d €56-66; ☉Feb-Dec; ☎) This vine-clad former farmhouse, now an eight-room inn with low ceilings and traditional timber furnishings, is in a quiet street one block southwest of place de l'Église. The cheapest rooms have showers only and shared toilets. Lunch and dinner *menus* (€23 to €48) at its whitewashed, wood-beamed restaurant (closed Tuesday and lunchtime Wednesday October to December and from February to April) revolve around fresh seafood, particularly lobster.

Camping des Menhirs
CAMPGROUND €

(☎02 97 52 94 67; www.lesmenhirs.com; 7 allée St-Michel; adult/site €8/30.50; ☉mid-Apr–late Sep; ☎▧) Carnac and its surrounds have over 15 campgrounds, including this luxury complex of 100-sq-metre sites. Just 300m north of the beach, this is very much the glamorous end of camping, with amenities such as a sauna and cocktail bar!

ℹ Information

Tourist Office (☎02 97 52 13 52; www.ot-carnac.fr; 74 av des Druides; ☉9am-7pm Mon-Sat & 3-7pm Sun)

ℹ Getting There & Away

BICYCLE Hire bikes from **A Bicyclette** (☎02 97 52 75 08; http://velocarnac.com; 93bis av des Druides; per day from €7) down near the beach.

BUS The main bus stops are in Carnac-Ville, outside the police station on rue St-Cornély, and in Carnac-Plage, beside the tourist office. **Keolis Atlantique** (☎02 97 47 29 64; www.keolis-atlantique.com) runs a daily bus to Auray, Vannes and Quiberon (€2).

TAXI Call ☎02 97 52 75 75.

TRAIN The nearest useful train station is in Auray, 12km to the northeast. SNCF has an office in the Carnac-Plage tourist office where you can buy advance tickets.

Quiberon

POP 5200

Quiberon (Kiberen in Breton) sits at the southern tip of a sliver-thin, 14km-long peninsula flanked on the western side by the rocky, wave-lashed Côte Sauvage (Wild Coast). The setting is nice, but the town itself quite tacky, and finding a parking spot is like looking for a pot of gold at the end of a rainbow. Even so, it's wildly popular in summer and is also the departure point for ferries to Belle Île.

🏃 Activities

FREE Conserverie La Belle-Iloise
CANNERY TOUR

(☎02 97 50 08 77; www.labelleiloise.fr; rue de Kerné; ☉10-11am & 3-4pm Mon-Fri, 11am-3pm Sat) Located north of the train station, guided visits around this former sardine cannery run hourly in summer, with bargain-priced sardines available from the adjacent shop.

CELTIC FESTIVAL

Celtic communities from Ireland, Scotland, Wales, Cornwall, the Isle of Man and Galicia in northwest Spain congregate with Bretons at the Festival Interceltique de Lorient (☎02 97 21 24 29; www.festival-interceltique.com) over 10 days in early August. Upwards of 600,000 people descend on the city of Lorient, about 30km northwest of Carnac, so book well ahead if you're planning to stay in town for the festival.

BRITTANY QUIBERON

La Grande Plage
BEACH

La Grande Plage is a family-friendly beach, with bathing spots towards the peninsula's tip larger and less crowded. The Côte Sauvage on the opposite coast is great for a windy walk, but you'll need a permit for any nautically based activity (such as a diving certificate) or risk a fine.

🛏 Sleeping

Hôtel de l'Océan
HOTEL €

(☎02 97 50 07 58; www.hotel-de-locean.com; 7 quai de l'Océan; r €62-84; ☺Easter-Sep; 🛜) Overlooking the harbour and a small beach, this huge white house with multicoloured shutters is something of a local landmark. The cheapest of its 37 rather twee rooms don't have TVs, but rooms at the other end of the price scale get you a fabulous harbour view. Parking (very welcome in summer) costs €8.

Camping du Conguel
CAMPGROUND €

(☎02 97 50 19 11; www.campingduconguel.com; bd de la Teignouse; sites €45, electricity €3; ☺Apr-Oct; ⛱) This splashy option, with an aqua park that has water slides, is one of the peninsula's 15 campgrounds. Just 2km east of the town centre, it's beside Plage du Conguel, and also has caravans to rent.

🍴 Eating & Drinking

TOP CHOICE Villa Margot
SEAFOOD €€

(☎02 97 50 33 89; www.villamargot.fr; 7 rue de Port Maria; menus €25-40; ☺Thu-Mon) The interior of this stunning stone restaurant looks like it'd be at home in a chic Parisian *quartier*, with original art (painted on adjacent Belle Île) on the walls, flower-shaped opaque glass light fittings, hot-pink and brown colour schemes, and lobsters clawing in the live tank (caught the night before, along with the fish). That is, until you head out onto the timber deck, which has direct access to the beach for a post-repast stroll.

ℹ Information

Tourist Office (☎02 97 50 07 84; www .quiberon.com; 14 rue de Verdun; ☺9am-7pm Mon-Sat, 10am-1pm & 2-5pm Sun) Between the train station and La Grande Plage.

ℹ Getting There & Away

BOAT There are ferries between Quiberon and Belle Île.

BUS Quiberon is connected by **Keolis Atlantique** (☎02 97 47 29 64; www.keolis-atlantique .com) with Carnac (45 minutes), Auray (1¼

hours) and Vannes (1¾ hours). The flat fare is €2. Buses stop at the train station and at place Hoche, near the tourist office and the beach.

CAR High-summer traffic is hellish – consider leaving your vehicle at the 1200-place Sémaphore car park (€3.60 for up to four hours, €12.50 for 24 hours), 1.5km north of the beach, and walking or taking the free shuttle bus into town.

TRAIN In July and August only, a train runs several times a day between Auray and Quiberon (€6, 45 minutes). From September to June an SNCF bus service links Quiberon and Auray train stations (€2, 50 minutes) at least seven times a day.

Belle Île
POP 5200

Accessed by ferries from Quiberon, Belle Île (in full, Belle-Île-en-Mer) sees its population swell ten-fold in summer. But as it's Brittany's largest island (at 20km by 9km), there's room to escape the crowds and yes, in case you're wondering, the name Belle Île is very appropriate.

🔘 Sights & Activities

Musée Historique
MUSEUM

(☎02 97 31 85 54; www.citadellevauban.com; adult/ child €6.50/3.50; ☺9am-6pm) The dramatic citadel, strengthened by the architect Vauban in 1682, dominates little Le Palais port. Inside, the various displays concentrate on the history of the island's defensive system, though there are also interesting sections on the various celebrities who were regular visitors here, the local fish trade and island life.

Grotte de l'Apothicairerie
CAVE

Belle Île's fretted southwestern coast has spectacular rock formations and caves including Grotte de l'Apothicairerie (Cave of the Apothecary's Shop), where waves roll in from two sides.

Beaches & Swimming
BEACH

Plage de Donnant has awesome surf, though swimming here is dangerous. Sheltered Port Kérel, to the southwest, is better for children, as is the 2km-long Plage des Grands Sables, the biggest and busiest strand, spanning the calm waters of the island's eastern side.

Walking & Cycling
WALKING, CYCLING

The tourist office sells walking and cycling guides. The ultimate hike is the 95km coastal path that follows the island's coastline.

🛏 Sleeping & Eating

Citadelle Vauban

Hôtel Musée   HISTORIC HOTEL €€

(☎02 97 31 84 17; www.citadellevauban.com; r from €147; ⊙closed mid-Oct–May; 🛜) Definitely the best hotel on the island, this fantastic conversion within the historic citadel is Belle Île's top address and boasts 53 stunning rooms with antique furniture, stylish trimmings and an awful lot of history.

Hôtel Vauban   HOTEL €€

(☎02 97 31 45 42; http://hotel-vauban-belleile.com; 1 rue des Ramparts; r €86-107; ⊙Mar–mid-Nov; 🛜) This comfy place, with 16 multicoloured rooms splashed with driftwood, is perched high on the coastal path, with views of the ferry landing below. They also do special hiking packages, which include several nights' stay and all meals, including a picnic lunch.

Auberge de Jeunesse

Haute Boulogne   HOSTEL €

(☎02 97 31 81 33; www.fuaj.org; Haute Boulogne; dm incl sheets & breakfast €15.50; ⊙closed Oct; @) This modern 96-bed HI-affiliated hostel with a self-catering kitchen is to the north of the citadel. Its rooms are all twins with bunkbeds and shared toilets.

La Table du Gouverneur   GASTRONOMIC €€

(☎02 97 31 82 57; www.citadellevauban.com; menus €20-35; ⊙closed mid-Oct–May) You may literally eat off the governor's table here,

---

DON'T MISS

PONT-AVEN

Once the railway pushed through in the 19th century, the tiny Breton village of Pont-Aven (population 3000), nestled in the 'valley of willows', was discovered by artists. American painters were among the first to uncover it, but things really took off when France's Paul Gaugin and Émile Bernard set up a colony here in the 1850s. Their work, and that of their disciples, morphed into a movement known today as the Pont-Aven School.

There is some debate in artistic and sociological circles as to whether these works folklorised the local Breton people, but they certainly captured the beauty of the little village and the surrounding countryside. For an insight into the town's place in art history, stop by the Musée des Beaux-Arts de Pont-Aven (☎02 98 06 14 43; www.museepont aven.fr; place de l'Hôtel de Ville; adult/child €4.50/free; ⊙10am-12.30pm & 2pm-6.30pm, closed Jan). To see the spots where the masters set up their easels, pick up a free walking-trail map from the nearby tourist office (☎02 98 06 04 70; place de l'Hôtel de Ville; ⊙10am-12.30pm & 2-6pm Mon-Sat), which can also help with accommodation if you want to spend the night.

There are several places to stay, including Les Ajoncs d'Or (☎02 98 06 02 06; www .ajoncsdor-pontaven.com; 1 place de l'Hotel de Ville; d from €60; 🛜) which has small, colourful and good-value rooms. Twenty minutes' drive north of Pont-Aven (and 4km north of the village of Bannalec) is Le Manoir du Menec (☎02 98 39 47 47; www.manoirdumenec .fr; Bannalec; d with breakfast €100; 🛜🏊). Hidden away under a veil of trees this converted manor house ticks all the 'rural escape' boxes. The rooms themselves are fairly drab but the facilities, which include a heated indoor pool and a decent inhouse restaurant (evening only; menus €30) make up for this. Charming spots for a drink or a meal include the bar-restaurant Auberge de la Fleur d'Ajonc (☎02 98 06 10 65; place de l'Hôtel de Ville; menus €16-23; ⊙lunch Tue-Sun, daily Jul-Aug), in an atmospheric medieval building of sloping stone floors and low ceilings held up by hefty beams, and Le Moulin de Rosmadec (☎02 98 06 00 22; www.moulinderosmadec.com; menus €30-79; ⊙closed Sun evening & all day Mon), serving gastronomic fare overlooking the town's namesake pont (bridge) and aven (river in Breton). Le Moulin de Rosmadec also has four delightful guestrooms upstairs (doubles €98, apartment €120).

Since the 1960s Pont-Aven has again become a magnet for artists, with no fewer than 60 galleries here in summer. Even in winter, you'll still find around 20 galleries open on weekends.

Pont-Aven is an easy 18km drive southeast of Concarneau. Buses (☎02 98 44 46 73; €2) – five Monday to Saturday and two on Sunday – connect Pont-Aven with Quimperlé in the east (30 minutes), Concarneau (30 minutes) and Quimper (one hour).

TREETOP SLEEPING

For the ultimate eco-escape, don't miss eccentric Dihan (☏02 97 56 88 27; www.dihan -evasion.org; Kerganiet; d guestroom/yurt incl breakfast €82/102, d tree house €142-152, table d'hôte from €25; ☎), a guesthouse secluded in a leafy dell just outside Ploëmel (follow the black signs from the village).

Run by a fun-loving young couple, Myriam and Arno Le Masle, the property was originally Myriam's grandparents' working farm. The farmhouse and barns now house guestrooms, while the grounds shelter a couple of yurts imported from Mongolia and five tree houses, reached by climbing ladders (the highest – at 12m – requires you to strap on a harness to reach it and children are not allowed to stay in it). Should nature call, there are biodegradable dry toilets up here, as well as conserved water (you'll find brightly tiled bathrooms and a sauna in the reception building).

Rates include breakfast, which is a combination of organic, fair-trade and local artisan produce, such as caramel au beurre salé (Breton salted caramel spread). Fabulous tables d'hôte (meals that are a combination of Myriam's Breton, Mauritian and Indian heritage; by reservation) take place in the converted cidrerie (cidery), where pianist Arno hits the keys and bands sometimes drop by. Otherwise, guests can fire up the barbecue and dine beneath a bamboo-sheltered pergola.

All of this would be enough to recommend it heartily, but you can also rent bikes (€12 per day), book a massage (from €80) or even an onsite beauty treatment with organic cosmetics. Both guests and nonguests can saddle up, with horse riding starting at €20 per hour (there are also ponies for kids).

Note that the quoted accommodation prices are weekend rates. Prices are lower during the week.

given that this hugely atmospheric and formal place is housed in his former residence. The gastronomic menus are heavily focused on seafood, inventively combining flavours as disparate as lobster, grapefruit and celery to sublime effect.

ⓘ Information

Turn left as you leave the ferry in Le Palais to get to the **tourist office** (☏02 97 31 81 93; www .belle-ile.com; quai Bonnelle; ☺8.45am-7pm Mon-Sat, to 1pm Sun). There's a summer-only **information kiosk** (☏02 97 31 69 49; ☺5-7.30pm Mon-Thu & Sat mid-Apr–mid-Sep) on the quay in Sauzon.

ⓘ Getting There & Away

BOAT Travelling to Belle Île can involve a bit of planning, as taking a car on the ferry is prohibitively expensive for a short trip and needs to be booked well ahead, even outside peak season.

The shortest crossing to Belle Île is from Quiberon. **Compagnie Océane** (☏08 20 05 61 56; www.compagnie-oceane.fr) operates car/passenger ferries (45 minutes, year-round) and fast passenger ferries to Le Palais and Sauzon in July and August. An adult return passenger fare is €29.50; a bike costs €17.50; transporting a small car costs a hefty €161 return plus

passenger fares. There are five crossings a day (up to 13 in July and August). A couple of other companies also travel this route with less frequency.

It is also possible to make the trip from Vannes. **Navix** (☏08 25 13 21 00; www.navix.fr) operates ferries (adult/child one way €22/13) between May and mid-September.

ⓘ Getting Around

BICYCLE Lots of places in Le Palais rent out bicycles (about €11 per day) and motor scooters (about €45 per day).

BUS Seasonal buses run by **Taol Mor** (☏02 97 31 32 32; www.cars-verts.fr/taolmor.html) criss-cross the island. A single journey costs €2.50.

CAR Car-rental rates on the island are expensive and start at about €80 for 24 hours; you'll find outlets at the harbour as you disembark.

Vannes

POP 53,000

Street art, sculptures and intriguing galleries pop up unexpectedly throughout the half-timbered, cobblestoned city of Vannes (Gwened in Breton), which has a quirky, creative bent.

The city's integral role in Brittany's history stretches back to pre-Roman times, when it was the capital of the Veneti, a Gaulish tribe of sailors who fortified the town. Conquered by Julius Caesar in the 1st century BC, it became the centre of Breton unity in the 9th century under Breton hero Nominoë, and in 1532 the union of the duchy of Brittany with France was proclaimed here. These days it's a vibrant hub for students attending the city's Université de Bretagne-Sud.

⊙ Sights

Surrounding Vannes' walled old town is a flower-filled moat. Inside, you can weave through the web of narrow alleys ranged around the 13th-century Gothic Cathédrale St-Pierre. Tucked away behind rue des Vierges, stairs lead to the accessible section of the ramparts. From here, you can see the black-roofed Vieux Lavoirs (Old Laundry Houses), though you'll get a better view from the Tour du Connétable or from the Porte Poterne to the south.

Musée de la Cohue MUSEUM
(⏰02 97 01 63 00; 9-15 place St-Pierre; combined ticket with Musée d'Histoire et d'Archéologie adult/child €6/5; ⊙10am-6pm) Since the 14th century, the building now housing the Musée de la Cohue has variously been a produce market, a law court and the seat of the Breton parliament. Today it's a museum of fine arts, displaying mostly 19th-century paintings, sculptures and engravings.

☞ Tours

Navix BOAT TOUR
(⏰08 25 13 21 00; www.navix.fr; from €15) From April to September, Navix runs a range of cruises on the Golfe du Morbihan (Morbihan Coast), departing from the Gare Maritime, 2km south of the tourist office. It's also possible to visit the two largest of the gulf's 40 inhabited islands, Île aux Moines and Île d'Arz.

✦ Festivals & Events

Festival de Jazz MUSIC FESTIVAL
(www.jazzavannes.fr) Vannes swings for four days in late July or early August.

Les Musicales du Golfe MUSIC FESTIVAL
(www.musicalesdugolfe.com) Classical music concerts take place in early August.

Fêtes d'Arvor CULTURAL FESTIVAL
(www.fetes-arvor.org) This three-day celebration of Breton culture from 13 to 15 August

includes parades, concerts and *festoù-noz* (night festivals).

🛏 Sleeping

TOP CHOICE **Hôtel Villa Kerasy** BOUTIQUE HOTEL €€€
(⏰02 97 68 36 83; www.villakerasy.com; 20 av Favrel-et-Lincy; d €141-198; ⊙closed mid-Nov–mid-Dec; 🛜) From the outside this looks like nothing more than a standard Breton town house, but once beyond the entrance you'll discover an exotic world of spices and far-away tropical sea ports. Rooms are individually decorated in Indian and Far Eastern styles and the garden, which is crowded with Buddha statues and ponds filled with lazy koi carp, are a little slice of Sri Lanka or Japan. Indian-inspired cuisine is served in the evening. It's just 100m from the train station.

Hôtel Le Marina HOTEL €
(⏰02 97 47 22 81; www.hotellemarina.fr; 4 place Gambetta; s €38-57, d €41-61; 🛜) By far the best-located place in town, this friendly hotel is run by the same team operating the busy downstairs cafe. There are 14 simple and rather cramped rooms here in hues of Atlantic blue and blinding white, the cheapest of which have bathroom facilities in the corridor.

Le Branhoc HOTEL €
(⏰02 97 56 41 55; www.hotel-auray.fr; 5 rte du Bono; d €47-69; 🛜) Located 17km west of Vannes, just outside the pretty riverside town of Auray (itself well worth a wander), this peacefully situated, family-run hotel is a handy base for exploring both Vannes and Morbihan's megalithic sites. Rooms are bright, spacious and spotlessly clean.

🍴 Eating & Drinking

Rue des Halles and its offshoots are lined with tempting eateries, while classical and contemporary brasseries arc around the port.

Côte et Saveurs MODERN FRENCH €
(⏰02 97 47 21 94; 8 rue Pierre-René Rogues; mains €8-18; ⊙lunch & dinner Thu-Mon, lunch Tue) A spiral staircase winds through the centre of the ground-floor dining room to the upper level of this airy, contemporary restaurant serving dishes such as *magret de canard* (duck breast) in rhubarb sauce.

Afghan Cafe
AFGHANI €

(☑02 97 42 77 77; 12 rue Fontaine; mains €12-14; ⊘closed Mon) There's little doubting the quality of the local cuisine in Brittany, but sometimes you just need a break from seafood or *galettes,* so thank goodness for this excellent little restaurant serving delicious rice-based dishes and Afghani curries all suffused with just a little Frenchness! It's one of those rare restaurants in France that's not afraid to use chilli.

Dan Ewen
CRÊPERIE €

(☑02 97 42 44 34; 3 place du Général de Gaulle; crêpes €3-8; ⊘Mon-Sat) A near-life-size statue of a sweet, smiling and wrinkled Breton lady bearing a tray greets you at the entrance of this stone and dark-wood crêperie, which serves up fillings such as frangipane, and flambéed options topped with *crème Chantilly.*

Brasserie des Halles et des Arts
BRASSERIE €€

(☑02 97 54 08 34; 9 rue des Halles; menus €15-25, mains €9.50-18; ⊘noon-midnight) You can eat at this buzzing brasserie, but it's an equally good spot for a drink while browsing the art – which includes the Breton images made from tiles that adorn its colourful walls.

❶ Information

Tourist Office (☑08 25 13 56 10; www .tourisme-vannes.com; quai de Tabarly; ⊘9.30am-7pm Mon-Sat, 10am-6pm Jul-Aug, 9.30am-12.30pm & 1.30-6pm Mon-Sat Sep-Jun) In a smart modern building on the newly developed marina.

❶ Getting There & Away

BUS The small bus station is opposite the train station. Services include **Keolis Atlantique** (www.keolis-atlantique.com), which runs to Carnac (€2, 1¼ hours) and on to Quiberon (€2, a further 45 minutes).

TRAIN Frequent trains:

Auray €4 to €5.50, 10 minutes

Nantes €21, 1½ hours

Quimper €19.50 to €23, 1¼ hours

Rennes €20 to €24, 1 to 1½ hours

❶ Getting Around

BUS TPV (www.tpv.fr; tickets €1.30) runs eight city bus lines until 8.15pm. Its Infobus kiosk is on place de la République. Bus 8 links the train station with place de la République.

TAXI Call ☑02 97 54 34 34.

EASTERN & CENTRAL BRITTANY

The one-time frontier between Brittany and France, fertile eastern Brittany fans out around the region's lively capital, Rennes. Central Brittany conceals the enchanting Forêt de Paimpont, sprinkled with villages and ancient Breton legends.

Josselin
POP 2600

In the shadow of an enormous, witch's-hat-turreted 14th-century castle that was the long-time seat of the counts of Rohan, the story-book village of Josselin lies on the banks of the River Oust, 43km northeast of Vannes. Today, visitors in their thousands continue to fall under its spell. Place Notre Dame, a beautiful square of 16th-century half-timbered houses, is the little town's heart. The castle, the tourist office and the river are south, below rue des Trente, the main through street.

◉ Sights

TOP CHOICE **Château de Josselin**
CHÂTEAU

(☑02 97 22 36 45; www.chateaujosselin.com; adult/child €8/5; ⊘11am-6pm mid-Jul-Aug, 2-6pm Apr–mid-Jul, 2-5.30pm Sep) Guarded by its three round towers, the extraordinary town château is an incredible sight that remains the home of the Rohan family today. As such, it can only be visited by guided tour: one English-language tour departs daily (2.30pm) from June to September; otherwise you can ask for a leaflet in English. The château is filled with treasures, including an ornate writing desk of which only two others exist (one in Windsor Castle), a clock that has so many gadgets it must have been considered the iPhone of its time and a magnificent library containing 3000 books, some of which date back to the 17th century. Within the château is the **Musée de Poupées** (Doll Museum; adult/child €7/4.90; ⊘11am-6pm mid-Jul-Aug, 2-6pm Apr–mid-Jul, 2-5.30pm Sep) – a museum of puppets and dolls that is more interesting than it sounds! A combination ticket for both costs €13/8.50 per adult/child.

Basilique Notre Dame du Roncier
CHURCH

(place Notre Dame) Parts of the Basilique Notre Dame du Roncier date from the 12th century; superb 15th- and 16th-century stained glass illuminates the south aisle.

✈️ Festivals & Events

Medieval Josselin   MEDIEVAL FESTIVAL

(www.medieval-josselin.com) The hulking Château de Josselin makes an evocative backdrop for the village's two-day Medieval Josselin festival featuring feasting and fireworks, held in mid-July in even-numbered years.

🛏️ Sleeping & Eating

Maison de l'Oiseau   B&B €

(✆02 97 73 98 07; www.thebirdhouse.eu; 6 rue de Caradec; d with breakfast €60; 🛜) On first arriving here, one sunny spring day, our immediate thought was what a gorgeous English country garden this *chambre d'hôte* has. Therefore it came as no surprise to learn that the owners of this two-room place are indeed English and that they have spent the past seven years renovating this old village cottage and turning it into a delightfully cute place to stay. French-speaking guests may want to bear in mind that the owners don't speak much French.

Hôtel-Restaurant du Château   HOTEL €

(✆02 97 22 20 11; www.hotel-chateau.com; 1 rue Général de Gaulle; d from €75; 🛜) This fantastically located hotel is the smartest choice in town; it's well worth paying the extra euros for a magnificent view of the château across the Oust River. Its restaurant *menus* range from €10 to €37 and regional specialities abound – bag a table on the delightful terrace overlooking the river and the château if the weather is good.

Domaine de Kerelly Camping   CAMPGROUND €

(✆02 97 22 22 20; www.camping-josselin.com; sites for 2 people, tent & car €13; ⏰Apr-Oct; 🏊) This peaceful spot is 2km west of Josselin, on the south bank of the Oust.

La Table d'O   MODERN FRENCH €€

(✆02 97 70 61 39; 9 rue Glatinier; menus €13-46; ⏰lunch & dinner Mon & Thu-Sat, lunch Tue) This pleasant family-run place offers an interesting and varied menu of local cooking with a sprinkle of fusion on top, making it a local favourite. The sweeping views of the town and valley from the terrace are fantastic for a summer lunch. It's a short walk beyond the château.

ℹ️ Information

Tourist Office (✆02 97 22 24 90; www.josselin-communaute.fr; 3 place des Remparts; ⏰10am-6pm Jul-Aug, 1.30-5.30pm Mon, 10am-noon & 1.30-5.30pm Tue-Sat Apr-Jun & Sep) Not far from the castle entrance and with a useful list of local *gites* and *chambres d'hôtes*.

ℹ️ Getting There & Away

BUS Viaoo (www.viaoo29.fr) runs several daily buses to Rennes (€2, 1½ hours).

Forêt de Paimpont

Also known as Brocéliande, the Paimpont Forest is about 40km southwest of Rennes, and legendary for being the place where King Arthur received Excalibur, his magic sword. (Forget that these stories are thought to have been brought to Brittany by Celtic settlers and hence probably took place offshore – it's a magical setting all the same.)

The best base for exploring the forest is the lakeside village of Paimpont. Some 95% of the forest is private land, but the tourist office (✆02 99 07 84 23; www.tourisme-broceliande.com; ⏰10am-noon & 2-6pm, closed Mon Oct-Mar), beside the 12th-century Église Abbatiale (Abbey Church), has a free brochure outlining a 62km-long driving circuit with numerous short walks along the way that are accessible to the public. It also sells more-detailed walking and cycling guides.

In April, July and August the tourist office leads guided tours (adult/child from €7/4) of the forest (the availability of English-speaking guides varies).

Campers can set up their tents at the lakeside Camping Municipal de Paimpont (✆02 99 07 89 16; www.camping-paimpont-broceliande.com; rue du Chevalier Lancelot du Lac; sites €3, adult €3.30, car €1.60; ⏰Apr-Sep). La Maison du Graal (✆02 99 07 83 82; 21 rue du Général de Gaulle; d incl breakfast without/with bathroom €45/50) is a cheery little *chambre d'hôte* that has just two rooms decorated with twee paintings depicting the Arthurian legends. A formal option is the Hôtel Le Relais de Brocéliande (✆02 99 07 84 94; www.le-relais-de-broceliande.fr; 5 rue des Forges; r from €99; 🛜), which has smart rooms, comfortable mattresses and good bathrooms. Its onsite restaurant (*menus* €16 to €38) specialises in local river-caught fish. Illenoo (www.illenoo.fr) runs buses to/from Rennes (€2, one hour) from Monday to Saturday.

BRITTANY FORÊT DE PAIMPONT

Rennes

POP 212,200

A crossroads since Roman times, Brittany's vibrant capital sits at the junction of highways linking northwestern France's major cities. It's a beautifully set-out city, with an elaborate and stately centre and a charming old town that's a joy to get lost in. At night, this student city has no end of lively places to pop in for a pint and its restaurants are also superb.

◉ Sights & Activities

Cathédrale St-Pierre   CATHEDRAL
(◷9.30am-noon & 3-6pm) Crowning Rennes' old town is the 17th-century cathedral, which has an impressive, if dark, neoclassical interior. Much of the surrounding old town was gutted by the great fire of 1720, started by a drunken carpenter who accidentally set alight a pile of shavings. Surviving half-timbered houses that survived line the old city's cobbled streets, such as rue St-Michel and rue St-Georges.

Palais du Parlement de Bretagne   LAW COURTS
(place du Parlement de Bretagne; adult/child €7/ free) This 17th-century former seat of the rebellious Breton parliament has in more recent times been home to the Palais de Justice. In 1994 this building was destroyed by

Rennes

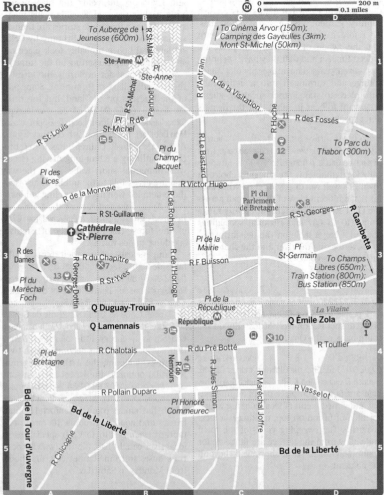

a fire started by demonstrating fishermen. Now restored, it houses the Court of Appeal. Daily guided tours (request in advance for a tour in English) take you through the ostentatiously gilded rooms. Tour bookings must be made through the tourist office.

Musée des Beaux-Arts   GALLERY
(☑02 23 62 17 45; www.mbar.org; 20 quai Émile Zola; adult/child €6/free; ☺10am-6pm Tue, 10am-noon & 2-6pm Wed-Sun) Rooms devoted to the Pont-Aven school are the highlight of the Musée des Beaux-Arts, which also has a 'curiosity gallery' of antiques and illustrations amassed in the 18th century. It also hosts numerous temporary exhibitions: note that when there is no temporary exhibition entrance fees are a little lower than those quoted here.

Champs Libres   CULTURAL CENTRE
(☑02 23 40 66 00; www.leschampslibres.fr; 10 cours des Alliés; ☺noon-9pm Tue, noon-7pm Wed-Fri, 2-7pm Sat-Sun) Rennes' futuristic cultural centre is home to the Musée de Bretagne (☑02 23 40 66 00; www.musee-bretagne.fr), with displays on Breton history and culture. Under the same roof is Espace des Sciences (☑02 23 40 66 40; www.espace-sciences.org), an interactive science museum, along with a

Rennes

planetarium, a temporary exhibition space and a library. A combined ticket for all sections costs €10/7 per adult/under 26.

★ Festivals & Events

Les Mercredis du Thabor   CULTURAL FESTIVAL
Traditional Breton dancing and music take place in Rennes' beautiful Parc du Thabor on Wednesdays during June and July.

Tombées de la Nuit   CULTURAL FESTIVAL
(www.lestombeesdelanuit.com) Rennes' old town comes alive during this music and theatre festival in the first week of July.

🛏 Sleeping

There's a dire lack of accommodation in Rennes and most of what there is falls squarely into the chain hotel category. If you're planning on visiting during the week it's absolutely vital that you make advance reservations, as the town's few hotels are frequently booked solid. During the weekend demand drops hugely and many of the chain hotels offer cut-price rates.

TOP CHOICE **Hôtel de Nemours**   BOUTIQUE HOTEL €
(☑02 99 78 26 26; www.hotelnemours.com; 5 rue de Nemours; s/d from €61/72; ❉🛜) Lined with historic black-and-white photographs of Rennes, sumptuous Hôtel de Nemours is an understatement in elegance, with cream, chocolate and caramel furnishings, high thread-count white linens and flat-screen TVs. In short, this place stands head and shoulders above any other option in town.

Angelina Hôtel   HOTEL €
(☑02 99 79 29 66; www.angelina-hotel.com; 1 quai Lamennais; d €48-90; 🛜) It doesn't get more central than this cavernous hotel next to République, with the old city and shopping district on the doorstep. Reception's on the 3rd floor of this creaking old building (there's a lift), but the wicker-furnished rooms are well kept and have bright modern bathrooms. Book ahead for the two large double corner rooms – a great deal.

Hôtel des Lices   HOTEL €
(☑02 99 79 14 81; www.hotel-des-lices.com; 7 place des Lices; s/d from €70/74; ❉🛜) You can peer down from the steel balconies or through the floor-to-ceiling glass doors to see the Saturday-morning market, which snakes right past the front door of this modern six-storey hotel. Inside, rooms are small but sleek, with contemporary furnishings and

textured walls. Breakfast (€8.50) is served in a sunlit ground-floor salon with limed floorboards, white tables and fresh flowers.

Auberge de Jeunesse
HOSTEL €

(☑02 99 33 22 33; www.fuaj.org; 10-12 canal St-Martin; dm incl breakfast €20.50; ☉7am-1am, closed late-Dec–mid-Jan) Rennes' well-equipped youth hostel has a self-catering kitchen and a canalside setting 2km north from the centre. Take bus 18 from place de la Mairie.

✕ Eating

Rennes has a wide choice of restaurants. Rues St-Malo and St-Georges are the city's two main 'eat streets'; the latter in particular specialises in crêperies.

Léon le Cochon
PORK €€

(☑02 99 79 37 54; 1 rue Maréchal Joffre; menu €25, mains €11-25) Basking in the plaudits of almost every French gastronomic guidebook, but still fun and informal, 'Leon the Pig' specialises not just in pork but porcine products in all their many and varied manifestations.

L'Épicerie
CAFE €

(☑02 99 38 76 70; 2 rue des Fossés; tartines €5-9; ☉noon-midnight) This fantastic old-town eatery is riotously popular with a student-style crowd, who pile in to enjoy the generous *tartines* (open sandwiches, including some rather unusual ones, such as one with 'vanishing pears' – *trois fromages avec ou sans poire*) and flasks of beer on the buzzing terrace outside.

Le Café du Port
BISTRO €

(☑02 99 30 01 43; 3 rue le Bouteiller; menu €12-15; ☉closed Sun) Market fresh produce and great value is the name of the game at this laid-back, modern bistro that also doubles up as a popular spot for an early evening drink.

Café Babylone
MODERN FRENCH €

(☑02 99 85 82 99; 12 rue des Dames; mains €7-18; ☉closed dinner Mon) Despite being virtually built into the walls of Rennes' cathedral, this charming contemporary, yet traditional, place is a surprisingly tourist-free zone, favoured by locals enjoying a mixed plate of

---

LOCAL KNOWLEDGE

BRETON CRÊPES

Crêpes are Brittany's traditional staple, and they are ubiquitous throughout the region. Unlike the rolled-up crêpes sold at stalls on Paris' street corners, Breton crêpes are folded envelope-style at the edges, served flat on a plate and eaten using cutlery.

Rennes has dozens of enticing crêperies, including La Ville d'Ys (☑02 99 36 70 28; 5 rue St-Georges; crêpes €2.20-8.40), one of the town's better known crêperies, named for the fabled Atlantis-style submerged city of Breton legend. Tucked inside a two-storey 15th-century house with a slanted wooden staircase and colourful crockery displayed on the walls, La Ville d'Ys serves up mouth-watering buckwheat pancakes with sublime taste combinations.

We spoke to the crêperie's owner-chef, **Claudine Thomas**, as she cooked in her open kitchen, to find out the secrets behind making Breton crêpes.

What are the essential ingredients in a basic galette?

Blé noir (buckwheat flour) – *sarrasin* in Breton – and salted Breton butter. It's important to keep the Breton tradition; locals take crêpes very seriously. Well, crêpes are crêpes!

What are your favourite toppings?

Andouille (local sausage) and for sweet crêpes, *caramel au beurre salé* (salty caramel sauce) – *salidou* in Breton – which I make here with ingredients from the market.

What's the ideal cooking temperature?

A *galettier* (the hotplate) – *bilig* in Breton – has no temperature dial, only numbers from one to eight. It can't be too hot – the crêpe needs to be brown at the edges, crispy but not burnt.

Do you use a particular recipe?

I use a recipe from Finistère – the crêpes are a finer texture and crispier than other recipes. People always come in because of this recipe; they don't want any other kind.

If you want to learn how to create your own crêpes, the Écoles de Treblec (☑02 99 34 86 76; www.ecole-maitre-crepier.com; 66 rue de Guer), 38km southwest of Rennes, runs a variety of courses and classes.

tapas or one of the finely produced dishes of rich home cooking on the terrace.

La Saint-Georges CRÊPERIE €
(☑02 99 38 87 04; www.creperie-saintgeorges.com; 11 rue du Chapitre; galettes €7-10; ☺closed Sun & Mon) Whereas most crêperies play on the twee old Breton style, this one takes a totally novel approach: with its fuscia, green and gold furnishings and luxurious chairs this place looks more like a glam Ibizan chill-out club. The crêpes aren't bad either, though prices are somewhat inflated.

Drinking

Rue St-Michel – nicknamed rue de la Soif (Thirsty St) for its bars, pubs and cafes – is the best-known drinking strip, but it can get rowdy late at night.

Le Nabuchodonosor WINE BAR
(12 rue Hoche) The favoured haunt of arty and intellectual types in Rennes, this charming wine bar is a great place for an evening drink in buzzing surroundings.

Oan's Pub PUB
(1 rue Georges Dottin; ☺2pm-1am Mon-Sat) Locals habitually turn up with instruments for impromptu Celtic jam sessions at this cosy cave-like, stone-walled pub with Brittany-brewed Coreff beer on tap.

Entertainment

Cinéma Arvor CINEMA
(☑09 71 38 52 63; www.cinema-arvor.fr; 29 rue d'Antrain) Screens nondubbed films.

Information

Tourist Office (☑02 99 67 11 11; www .tourisme-rennes.com; 11 rue St-Yves; ☺9am-7pm Mon-Sat, 11am-1pm & 2-6pm Sun) This tourist office offers an audioguide to the city, which takes you on a walking tour of eight sights for €4.50 (or it can be downloaded for free from the website). Staff can book accommodation at no cost.

Getting There & Away

BUS Among Rennes' many bus services, **Illenoo** (☑08 10 35 10 35; www.illenoo.fr) runs regular daily services:
Dinan €4.30, 1½ hours
Dinard €4.30, two hours
Mont St-Michel €11, 80 minutes
Paimpont €3.50, one hour
TRAIN Destinations with frequent services:
Brest €34 to €38, two hours

Dinan €12 to €15, one hour including a change
Nantes €24, 1¼ hours
Paris Montparnasse €58, 2¼ hours
Quimper €34 to €38, 2½ hours
St-Malo €14, one hour
Vannes €20 to €24, 1½ hours

Getting Around

BUS Rennes has an efficient local bus network run by **STAR** (☑09 70 82 18 00; www.star.fr; 12 rue Pré Botté). Bus tickets (single journey €1.20, 10-trip carnet €11, 24-hour pass €3.50) are interchangeable with the metro.

METRO Incredibly for a city its size, Rennes has its own single-line metro system, run by STAR. The metro line runs northwest to southeast. Main stations include République (place de la République) in the centre and Ste-Anne (old town).

TAXI Call ☑02 99 30 79 79.

Vitré

POP 17,300

With its narrow cobbled streets, half-timbered houses and colossal castle topped by witch's-hat turrets, Vitré rivals Dinan as one of Brittany's best-preserved medieval towns – with far fewer tourists and a more laissez-faire village air.

Sights & Activities

Musée du Château CASTLE MUSEUM
(☑02 99 75 04 54; place du Château; adult/child €4/2.50; ☺10.30am-12.30pm & 2pm-6.30pm) From outside, Vitré's medieval castle, which rises on a rocky outcrop overlooking the River Vilaine, is one of the most impressive in Brittany – a real fairytale of spires and drawbridges. However, once beyond the twin-turreted gateway you'll find the triangular inner courtyard somewhat bare. The château was originally built in 1060 and expanded in the 14th and 15th centuries. A small museum sits in the château's southern corner. The town hall stands in the opposite corner.

The entrance ticket to the château also covers the **Musée Saint-Nicholas** (15 rue Pasteur), which houses a collection of sacred art, and the **Château Rochers-Sévigné** (☑02 99 75 04 54), 6 km south of Vitré on the D88, which is surrounded by beautiful parkland.

Opening times are the same for all the sites though to visit the Château Rochers-Sévigné you have to go on one of the frequent (French) guided tours.

BRITTANY VITRÉ

🛏 Sleeping

Vitré has a shortage of accommodation, so it's worth booking ahead any time of year.

Le Minotel   HOTEL €

(📞02 99 75 11 11; www.leminotel.fr; 47 rue de la Poterie; s €45-62, d €54-66; 🛜) In the heart of the old quarter, this hotel is as minisized as the name suggests. It has just 15 rooms, which are very cosy indeed (read: small), but nonetheless smart and cheerful.

Hôtel du Château   HOTEL €

(📞02 99 74 58 59; www.hotelduchateauvitre.fr; 5 rue Rallon; s €46-59, d €52-65; 🛜) Wake up to the aroma of freshly baked bread and, on upper floors, fantastic vistas of the castle at this family-run hotel at the base of the ramparts. The rooms are a bit dated, but the friendly owners are a great source of local information; there's good wheelchair access and a pleasant courtyard for breakfast (€8.50).

Le Petit Billot   HOTEL €

(📞02 99 75 02 10; www.petit-billot.com; 5bis place du Général Leclerc; s/d from €48/51; 🛜) This friendly hotel, which is close to the station and on the edge of the old town, has neat and functional rooms that lack character, but for the price it offers superb value for money.

🍴 Eating & Drinking

Quaint crêperies and gastronomic restaurants are tucked away throughout the old town.

Le Potager de Louise   MODERN FRENCH €€

(📞02 99 74 68 88; 5 place du Général Leclerc; menus €15-32; ⊙closed Sun & Mon) The food from Le Potager de Louise (Louise's vegetable garden) is assured and, as the name would suggest, all locally grown or sourced. It has a classic small-town bistro feel but with more imaginative taste combinations.

Le Barabis   MICROBREWERY

(3 rue de la Trémouille; ⊙3pm-3am Mon-Sat, to 10pm Sun) Vitré's funky, laid-back microbrewery creates artisan beers in its gleaming copper boilers, then serves them on tap. In summer try the *blanche,* brewed with citrus zest; in winter, go for the robust *noire* (stout).

ℹ Information

Tourist Office (📞02 99 75 04 46; www .ot-vitre.fr; place Général de Gaulle; ⊙9.30am-12.30pm & 2-6.30pm Mon-Sat, 10am-12.30pm & 3-6pm Sun) Right outside the train station.

ℹ Getting There & Away

TRAIN Frequent trains travel between Vitré and Rennes (from €7.50, 20 to 35 minutes).

Champagne

Includes »

Best Places to Eat

» Le Foch (p296)

» La Grillade Gourmande (p302)

» La Table Anna (p296)

» Le Valentino (p307)

» Aux Tables des Peintres (p307)

Best Places to Stay

» Les Telliers (p295)

» Maison de Rhodes (p305)

» La Parenthèse (p295)

» Le Clos Raymi (p302)

» Le Relais St-Jean (p305)

Why Go?

Champagne arouses all of the senses: the eyes feast on vine-covered hillsides and vertical processions of tiny, sparkling bubbles; the nose is tantalised by the damp soil and the heavenly bouquet of fermentation; the ears rejoice at the clink of glasses and the barely audible fizz; and the palate tingles with every sip. The imagination and the intellect are engaged as Champagne cellar visits reveal the magical processes – governed by the strictest of rules – that transform the world's most pampered pinot noir, pinot meunier and chardonnay grapes into this region's most fabled wines.

Happily, despite the prestige of their vines, the people of Champagne offer visitors a warm and surprisingly easygoing welcome, both in the stylish cities and along the Champagne Routes, which wend their way through vineyards and villages to family-run cellars, where perfectly aged sparklers can be sampled, savoured, compared and purchased.

When to Go

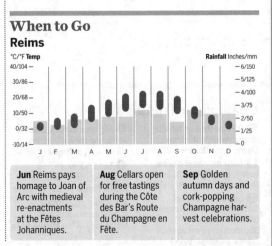

Reims

°C/°F Temp | Rainfall Inches/mm

Jun Reims pays homage to Joan of Arc with medieval re-enactments at the Fêtes Johanniques.

Aug Cellars open for free tastings during the Côte des Bar's Route du Champagne en Fête.

Sep Golden autumn days and cork-popping Champagne harvest celebrations.

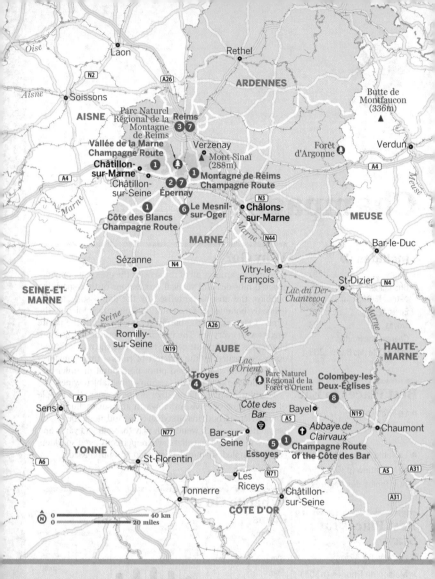

Champagne Highlights

1 Ramble through hillside vineyards along the scenic **Champagne Routes** (p297)

2 Toast the end of a **cellar tour** in Épernay (p301) or Reims (p291) with a glass of fizz

3 Climb the tower of **Cathédrale Notre Dame** (p291) in Reims for 360-degree views across France's flattest region

4 Slip back to the Middle Ages wandering the half-timbered backstreets of **Troyes** (p303)

5 Tread in Renoir's impressionistic footsteps at **Atelier Renoir** (p310) in Essoyes

6 Marvel at Champagne-making techniques and technology at the **Musée de la Vigne et du Vin** (p300) in Le Mesnil-sur-Oger

7 Revel in the lordly mansions and Champagne houses lining Épernay's **Avenue de Champagne** (p301)

8 Experience in mid-20th-century France at the **Mémorial Charles de Gaulle** (p309) in Colombey-les-Deux-Églises

History

Champagne's most famous convert to Christianity was the Merovingian warrior-king Clovis I, who founded the Frankish kingdom in the late 5th century and began the tradition of holding royal coronations in Reims. In the Middle Ages, the region – especially Troyes – grew rich from commercial fairs at which merchants from around Europe bought and sold products from as far afield as the Mediterranean.

In more recent history, the region was host to the end of WWII in Europe when Nazi Germany surrendered unconditionally to Allied Supreme Commander General Dwight D Eisenhower in Reims on 7 May 1945.

Today, the *paysages du Champagne* (landscapes of Champagne) are on the Tentative List for inscription as a Unesco World Heritage Site.

ℹ️ Getting There & Around

Champagne, just north of Burgundy's Châtillonnais and Chablis wine regions, makes a refreshing stopover if you're driving from the Channel ports, Lille or Paris eastward to Lorraine or Alsace, or southeastward towards Dijon, Lyon or Provence.

France's rail lines radiate out from Paris like the spokes of a wheel and, as it happens, Reims, Épernay and Troyes are each on a different spoke (more or less). Although there are pretty good rail connections between Reims and Épernay, the best way to get from Reims to Troyes is by bus. Thanks to the TGV Est Européen line, Reims can be visited on a day trip from Paris.

Reims

POP 184,984

No matter what you have read, nothing can prepare you for that first skyward glimpse of Reims' gargantuan Gothic cathedral. Rising golden and imperious above the city, the cathedral is where, over the course of a millennium (816 to 1825), some 34 sovereigns – among them two dozen kings – began their reigns.

Meticulously restored after WWI and again following WWII, Reims is endowed with handsome pedestrian boulevards, Roman remains, art deco cafes and a flourishing fine-dining scene that counts four Michelin-starred restaurants. Along with Épernay, it is the most important centre of Champagne production and a fine base for exploring the Montagne de Reims Champagne Route.

◉ Sights

TOP CHOICE Cathédrale Notre Dame   CATHEDRAL
(www.cathedrale-reims.culture.fr; place du Cardinal Luçon; tower adult/child €7.50/free, incl Palais du Tau €11/free; ⊙7.30am-7.30pm, tower tours hourly 10am-5pm Tue-Sat, 2-5pm Sun Apr-Sep) Imagine the egos, extravagance and the over-the-top costumes of a French royal coronation... The focal point of all the bejewelled pomposity was Reims' cathedral, a Gothic edifice begun in 1211 – and mostly completed 100 years later – on a site occupied by churches since the 5th century. The single most famous event to take place here was the coronation of Charles VII, with Joan of Arc at his side, on 17 July 1429. The structure, a Unesco World Heritage Site since 1991, celebrated its 800th anniversary in 2011. To get the most impressive first view, approach the cathedral from the west, along rue Libergier.

MAKING FIZZ

Champagne is made from the red pinot noir (38%), the black pinot meunier (35%) or the white chardonnay (27%) grape. Each vine is vigorously pruned and trained to produce a small quantity of high-quality grapes. Indeed, to maintain exclusivity (and price), the designated areas where grapes used for Champagne can be grown and the amount of wine produced each year are limited.

Making Champagne according to the traditional method (*méthode champenoise*) is a complex procedure. There are two fermentation processes, the first in casks and the second after the wine has been bottled and had sugar and yeast added. Bottles are then aged in cellars for two to five years, depending on the *cuvée* (vintage).

During the two months in early spring when the bottles are aged in cellars kept at 12°C, the wine turns effervescent. The sediment that forms in the bottle is removed by *remuage*, a painstakingly slow process in which each bottle, stored horizontally, is rotated slightly every day for weeks until the sludge works its way to the cork. Next comes *dégorgement*: the neck of the bottle is frozen, creating a blob of solidified Champagne and sediment, then removed.

Reims

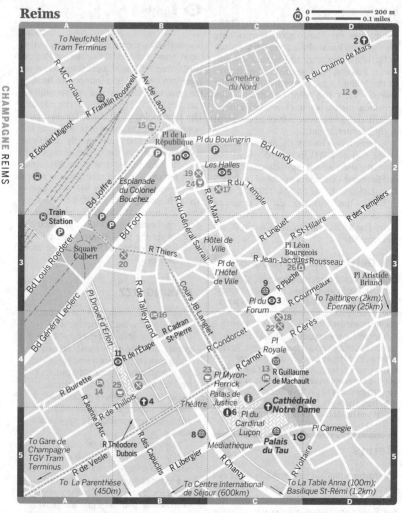

Seriously damaged by artillery and fire during WWI, the 139m-long cathedral is more interesting for its dramatic history than its heavily restored architectural features – repaired during the interwar years, thanks, in part, to significant donations from the American Rockefeller family.

The finest stained-glass windows are the western façade's 12-petalled great rose window; its cobalt-blue neighbour below; and the rose window in the north transept (to the left as you walk from the entrance to the high altar), above the Flamboyant Gothic organ case (15th and 18th centuries) topped with a figure of Christ. Nearby is a 15th-century wooden astronomical clock. There are windows by Chagall (1974; a sign explains each panel) in the central axial chapel (directly behind the high altar) and, two chapels to the left, you'll find a statue of Joan of Arc in full body armour (1901); there's a second statue of her outside on the square, to the right as you exit the cathedral. The tourist office rents audioguides (€6) with self-paced tours of the cathedral. The cathedral is close during Sunday morning Mass.

Feeling as strong as Goliath? (Look for his worn figure up on the west façade, held

Reims

in place with metal straps.) Then consider climbing 250 steps up the cathedral tower on a one-hour tour. Book at the Palais du Tau.

Palais du Tau   MUSEUM
(http://palais-tau.monuments-nationaux.fr; 2 place du Cardinal Luçon; adult/child €7.50/free, incl cathedral tower €11/free; ⊙9.30am-6.30pm Tue-Sun) A Unesco World Heritage Site, this former archbishop's residence, constructed in 1690, was where French princes stayed before their coronations – and where they hosted sumptuous banquets afterwards. Now a museum, it displays exceptional statuary, liturgical objects and tapestries, some in the impressive, Gothic-style Salle de Tau (Great Hall).

Basilique St-Rémi   BASILICA
(place du Chanoine Ladame; ⊙8am-nightfall, to 7pm summer) This 121m-long former Benedictine abbey church, a Unesco World Heritage Site, mixes Romanesque elements from the mid-11th century (the worn but stunning nave and transept) with early Gothic features from the latter half of the 12th century (the choir, with a large triforium gallery and, way up top, tiny clerestory windows). It is named in honour of Bishop Remigius, who baptised Clovis and 3000 Frankish warriors in 498. The 12th-century-style chandelier has 96 candles, one for each year of the life of St Rémi, whose tomb (in the choir) is marked

by a mausoleum from the mid-1600s. The basilica is situated about 1.5km south-southeast of the tourist office; take the Citadine 1 or 2 or bus A or F to the St-Rémi stop. Next door, **Musée St-Rémi** (53 rue Simon; adult/child €3/ free; ⊙2-6.30pm Mon-Fri, to 7pm Sat & Sun), in a 17th- and 18th-century abbey, features local Gallo-Roman archaeology, tapestries and 16th- to 19th-century military history.

Musée des Beaux-Arts   ART MUSEUM
(8 rue Chanzy; adult/child €3/free; ⊙10am-noon & 2-6pm Wed-Mon) This institution's rich collection, housed in an 18th-century abbey, boasts one of only four versions of Jacques-Louis David's world-famous *Death of Marat* (yes, the bloody corpse in the bathtub), 27 works by Camille Corot (only the Louvre has more), 13 portraits by German Renaissance painters Cranach the Elder and the Younger, lots of Barbizon School landscapes, some art-nouveau creations by Émile Gallé, and two works each by Monet, Gauguin and Pissarro.

Place Drouet d'Erlon   CITY SQUARE
Lit up like Las Vegas after dark, Reims' pedestrianised main square draws locals in the mood for a bite, a beer or a bit of shopping. Its centrepiece is the Subé Fountain, built in 1907 and crowned by a gleaming gold statue of Winged Victory. The 12th- to 14th-century Église St-Jacques (rue Marx

Dormoy), the city's only remaining medieval parish church, has some 1960s stained glass that's so awful it has to be seen to be believed. The blue and white windows in the nave were added in 2010.

Musée Hôtel Le Vergeur   MUSEUM
(36 place du Forum; adult/child €5/free; ⊙2-6pm Tue-Sun) In a 13th- to 16th-century town house, highlights include a series of furnished period rooms (kitchen, smoking room, Napoléon III's bedroom), engravings by Albrecht Dürer and a stunning Renaissance façade facing the interior garden.

Musée de la Reddition   MUSEUM
(Surrender Museum; 12 rue Franklin Roosevelt; adult/child €3/free; ⊙10am-noon & 2-6pm Wed-Mon) The original Allied battle maps are still affixed to the walls of US General Dwight D Eisenhower's headquarters, where Nazi Germany, represented by General Alfred Jodl, surrendered unconditionally at 2.41am on 7 May 1945. Displays include military uniforms and photographs. A 12-minute film is screened in French, English and German.

Roman Reims   ROMAN SITES
For a quick trip back to Roman Gaul, check out the massive Porte de Mars (Mars Gate; place de la République), a three-arched triumphal gate built in the 2nd century AD, and the below-street-level Cryptoportique (place du Forum; admission free; ⊙interior 2-6pm Jun-Sep), thought to have been used for grain storage in the 3rd century AD. Cultural events are held in the adjacent amphitheatre (place du Forum), inaugurated in 2010.

Art Deco Reims   ARCHITECTURE
The vaulted Halles du Boulingrin (rue de Mars) were a symbol of Reims' emergence from the destruction of WWI when they began service as the city's main food market in

---

1929. Following a major restoration project, the Halles were reopened in all their art deco glory in September 2012. Besides sheltering a food market, they provide a unique backdrop for exhibitions and cultural events.

Thanks to a donation from the US-based Carnegie Foundation, the lobby of the Bibliothèque (Library; 2 place Carnegie) boasts gorgeous 1920s mosaics, stained glass, frescos and an extraordinary chandelier – duck inside for a look!

The tourist office also has a brochure on art deco sites in Reims.

Chapelle Foujita   CHAPEL
(33 rue du Champ de Mars; adult/child €3/free; ⊙2-6pm, closed Wed) The last great work by the Japanese-born artist Tsuguharu (Léonard) Foujita (1886–1968). Inaugurated in 1966.

☞ Tours

The musty *caves* (cellars) and dusty bottles of 10 Reims-area Champagne houses (known as *maisons* – literally, 'houses') can be visited on guided tours. The following places both have fancy websites, cellar temperatures of 10°C to 12°C (bring warm clothes!) and frequent English-language tours that end, *naturellement*, with a tasting session.

Mumm   CHAMPAGNE HOUSE
(☏03 26 49 59 70; www.mumm.com; 34 rue du Champ de Mars; tours €11; ⊙tours begin 9am-11am & 2-5pm daily, closed Sun Nov-Feb) Mumm (pronounced 'moom'), the only *maison* in central Reims, was founded in 1827 and is now the world's third-largest producer (almost eight million bottles a year). Engaging and edifying one-hour tours take you through cellars filled with 25 million bottles of fine bubbly. Wheelchair accessible. Phone ahead if possible.

Taittinger   CHAMPAGNE CELLAR
(☏03 26 85 84 33; www.taittinger.com; 9 place St-Niçaise; tours €16; ⊙tours begin 9.30-11.50am & 2pm-4.20pm, closed Sat & Sun Dec–mid-Mar) The headquarters of Taittinger is an excellent place to come for a clear, straightforward presentation on how Champagne is actually made – there's no claptrap about 'the Champagne mystique' here. Parts of the cellars occupy 4th-century Roman stone quarries; other bits were excavated by 13th-century Benedictine monks. No need to reserve. Situated 1.5km southeast of Reims centre; take the Citadine 1 or 2 bus to the St-Niçaise or Salines stops.

CHAMPAGNE SAVOIR-FAIRE

Buying and tasting Champagne for the first time? These tips will have you talking fizz, popping corks and swirling like a pro in no time.

Champagne Types

» **Blanc de Blancs** Champagne made using only chardonnay grapes. Fresh and elegant, with very small bubbles and a bouquet reminiscent of 'yellow fruits' such as pear and plum.

» **Blanc de Noirs** A full-bodied, deep golden Champagne made solely with black grapes (despite the colour). Often rich and refined, with great complexity and a long finish.

» **Rosé** Pink Champagne (mostly served as an aperitif), with a fresh character and summer fruit flavours. Made by adding a small percentage of red pinot noir wine to white Champagne.

» **Prestige Cuvée** The crème de la crème of Champagne. Usually made with grapes from *grand cru* vineyards and priced and bottled accordingly.

» **Millésimé** Vintage Champagne produced from a single crop during an exceptional year. Most Champagne is non-vintage.

Champagne Sweetness

» **Brut** Dry, most common style, pairs well with food.

» **Extra Sec** Fairly dry but sweeter than Brut, nice as an aperitif.

» **Demi Sec** Medium sweet, goes well with fruit and dessert.

» **Doux** Very sweet, a dessert Champagne.

Serving & Tasting

» **Chilling** Chill Champagne in a bucket of ice 30 minutes before serving. The ideal serving temperature is 7°C to 9°C.

» **Opening** Grip the bottle securely and tilt it at a 45° angle facing away from you. Rotate the bottle slowly to ease out the cork – it should sigh, not pop.

» **Pouring** Hold the flute by the stem at an angle and let the Champagne trickle gently into the glass – less foam, more bubbles.

» **Tasting** Admire the colour and bubbles. Swirl your glass to release the aroma and inhale slowly before tasting the Champagne.

🛌 Sleeping

TOP CHOICE Les Telliers   B&B €€
(☏09 53 79 80 74; http://telliers.fr; 18 rue des Telliers; s €76, d €87-110, tr €123, q €142; 🛜) Enticingly positioned down a quiet alley near the cathedral, this bijou B&B extends one of Reims' warmest *bienvenues*. The high-ceilinged rooms are big on art-deco character, and have been handsomely decorated with ornamental fireplaces, polished oak floors and the odd antique. Breakfast is a generous spread of pastries, fruit, fresh-pressed juice and coffee.

La Parenthèse   B&B €€
(☏03 26 40 39 57; www.laparenthese.fr; 83 rue Clovis; 2-night stay d €170-220; 🛜) Tucked away in the backstreets of old Reims, this little

B&B has got everything going for it. The rooms are tastefully done out with wood floors and bursts of pastel colour, and all come with kitchenettes. The good-natured owner will squeeze in a cot if you ask.

Chambre d'Hôte Cathédrale   B&B €
(☏03 26 91 06 22; 21 place du Chapitre; s/d/tr without bathroom €50/60/75) The cathedral bells are your wake-up call at this sweet and simple B&B. Rooms are immaculate and old-fashioned, with stripy wallpaper, heavy wood furnishings and shared bathrooms.

Hôtel de la Paix   HOTEL €€
(☏03 26 40 04 08; www.bestwestern-lapaix-reims. com; 9 rue Buirette; d €170-220; ✳@🛜🏊) Outclassing most of Reims' midrange options,

this contemporary, Best Western–affiliated hotel is just off cafe-lined place Drouet d'Erlon. To mellow out, head to the pool, jacuzzi, hammam, fitness room or the Zen-like courtyard garden.

Hôtel Porte Mars   HOTEL €€
(☎03 26 40 28 35; www.hotelportemars.com; 2 place de la République; s/d/tr/q €92/103/ 135/152; ☎) True, the decor has seen better days, but the super-central location, friendly service and homely touches like tea-making facilities make this a decent choice.

Centre International de Séjour   HOTEL €
(☎03 26 40 52 60; www.cis-reims.com; chaussée Bocquaine; s/d/q €49/60/84, with shared bathroom s/d €37/46; ☎) Good-value and well-kept (if charmless) digs, with a shared kitchen, lounge and free parking. Situated 200m south of the Comédie tram stop.

✕ Eating

Place Drouet d'Erlon is lined with inexpensive restaurants and pub/cafes but, as one local matron put it with arched eyebrows, its eateries are *populaire, ordinaire* and *touristique*. More discerning diners often head to the stretch of rue de Mars facing Halles du Boulingrin and adjacent rue du Temple, and to the bistros flanking place du Forum.

TOP CHOICE Le Foch   GASTRONOMIC €€€
(☎03 26 47 48 22; www.lefoch.com; 37 bd Foch; lunch menus €31, dinner menus €48-80; ⊘lunch Tue-Fri & Sun, dinner Tue-Sat) Described as 'one of France's best fish restaurants' by the food critic Michael Edwards, Michelin-starred Le Foch serves up cuisine that is as beautiful as it is delicious. Specialities like scallops with Jerusalem artichokes, pistachios and truffle emulsion are expertly paired with wines and presented with panache.

La Table Anna   TRADITIONAL FRENCH €€
(☎03 26 89 12 12; 6 rue Gambetta; lunch menus €17, dinner menus €25-42; ⊘lunch Tue-Sun, dinner Tue & Thu-Sun) So what if the decor is chintzy? There is a reason why this bistro is as busy as a beehive. Friendly service and a menu packed with well-executed classics – guinea fowl cooked with herbs, fillet of veal in a rich, earthy morel sauce – hit the mark every time. The three-course, €17 lunch is a steal.

Brasserie Le Boulingrin   BRASSERIE €€
(☎03 26 40 96 22; www.boulingrin.fr; 48 rue de Mars; menus €18.50-29; ⊘lunch & dinner Mon-Sat) A genuine, old-time brasserie – the de-cor and zinc bar date back to 1925 – whose ambience and cuisine make it an enduring favourite. From September to June, the culinary focus is on *fruits de mer* (seafood).

Le Millénaire   GASTRONOMIC €€€
(☎03 26 08 26 62; www.lemillenaire.com; 4-6 rue Bertin; mains €32-87; ⊘lunch Mon-Fri, dinner Mon-Sat) Sand and claret hues and contemporary artworks create an air of intimate sophistication at this Michelin-starred haunt. Chef Laurent Laplaige keeps flavours crisp and seasonal in specialities such as smoked haddock carpaccio with herby mascarpone and tangy green apple sorbet.

Le Gaulois   BRASSERIE €€
(☎03 26 47 35 76; 2 place Drouet d'Erlon; mains €10-15; ⊘lunch & dinner daily; ⏵) Solid choice for brasserie fare like *moules frites* (mussels and chips) and steaks. There's a €6.50 children's menu.

Le Bocal   SEAFOOD €€
(☎03 26 47 02 51; 27 rue de Mars; mains €12-21; ⊘lunch & dinner Tue-Sat) Winningly fresh seafood is the big deal at this tiny eatery: try sardines tossed in chilli butter or hot oysters with parmesan.

La Cave aux Fromages   CHEESE €
(12 place du Forum; ⊘8am-1pm & 3.30-8pm Tue-Sat) Fromage heaven.

🍷 Drinking

Café du Palais   CAFE
(www.cafedupalais.fr; 14 place Myron-Herrick; ⊘Tue-Sat) Run by the same family since 1930, this art-deco cafe is *the* place to sip a glass of Champagne and see and be seen, at least if you're a *bon bourgeois* or a theatre type. Lit by a skylight is an extraordinary collection of bric-a-brac ranging from the inspired to the kitsch.

Hall Place   WINE BAR
(23bis rue de Mars; ⊘Mon-Sat) Relax and sip Champagne at this wine bar, a huge hit with Reims' in-crowd. Cheese and charcuterie tasting plates (around €12) go nicely with regional wines. Streetside butcher-block tables look out on the curves of Halles du Boulingrin.

Waïda   TEAROOM
(5 place Drouet d'Erlon; ⊘Tue-Sun) A tea room and confectioner with old-fashioned mirrors, mosaics and marble. A good place to pick up a box of Reims' famous *biscuits roses*, traditionally nibbled with Champagne (€6 to

€7.50 a glass), rainbow-bright macarons and divine *religieuses* (cream-filled puff pastries).

🛍 Shopping

Vins CPH   WINE
(www.vinscph.com; 3 place Léon Bourgeois) Shop for wines the way savvy locals do. At the end of the courtyard, head down into the cellar for a huge selection (some 1000 vintages are on offer), including over 150 Champagnes.

ℹ Information

Tourist Office (☎08 92 70 13 51; www.reims -tourisme.com; 2 rue Guillaume de Machault; ⊙9am-7pm Mon-Sat, 10am-6pm Sun)

ℹ Getting There & Away

BUS The best way to get to Troyes (€26, 1¾ to 2¼ hours, two to five daily) is to take a bus operated by **TransChampagneArdenne** (www.std marne.fr). The stop is outside the train station's northern (back) entrance; hours are posted.

CAR Rental agencies:

ADA (☎03 26 82 57 81; www.ada.fr; train station car park) Also rents out bicycles (from €17) and electric bicycles (€24 a day).

Avis (☎03 26 47 10 08; train station car park)

Hertz (☎03 26 47 98 78; 26 bd Joffre)

Rent a Car Système (☎03 26 77 87 77; www. rentacar.fr; 28 bd Joffre)

TRAIN Reims train station is 1km northwest of the cathedral. Frequent services run to Paris Gare de l'Est (€26 to €34, 45 minutes to 3¾ hours, 12 to 17 daily). Direct services also go to Épernay (€6.50, 21 to 50 minutes, seven to 18 daily) and Laon (€9.50, 35 to 50 minutes, three to nine daily).

In the city centre, train information and tickets are available at the **Boutique SNCF** (1 cours Jean-Baptiste Langlet; ⊙9am-7pm Mon-Fri, 9am-6pm Sat).

ℹ Getting Around

BICYCLE Holiday Bikes (www.holiday-bikes. com; train station car park) Rents out city/ mountain/electric bikes for €14/23/35 per day.

BUS & TRAM Launched in April 2011, Reims' first tram line links the city centre (rue de Vesle and cours JB Langlet) and the train station with Gare de Champagne-Ardenne TGV, on the Paris–Strasbourg TGV Est Européen line.

Two circular bus lines, the clockwise Citadine 1 and the anticlockwise Citadine 2 (single ticket €1.30, all-day ticket *journée* €3.20) serve most of the major sights of Reims. Most TUR lines begin their last runs at about 9.50pm; five night lines operate until 12.15am.

TAXI Call ☎03 26 47 05 05.

Champagne Routes of the Marne

The Champagne Routes (www.tourisme-en -champagne.com, in French) of the Marne *département* wend their way among neat rows of hillside vines, through hilltop forests and across lowland crop fields. Along the way, they call on winemaking villages and hamlets, some with notable churches or speciality museums, others quite ordinary, most without a centre or even a cafe. At almost every turn, beautiful panoramas unfold and small-scale, family-run Champagne wineries welcome travellers in search of bubbly.

Area tourist offices can supply you with details on B&Bs and on the opening times (and English capabilities) of various Champagne producers – but bear in mind that their map-brochures are far from exhaustive. Many producers prefer that visitors phone ahead but, if you haven't, don't be shy about knocking on the door. Almost all producers are closed around the *vendange* (grape harvest, ie from very late August into October), when bringing in the crop by hand – mechanical harvesters are forbidden here – eclipses all other activities. More and more young *vignerons* (winegrowers) speak English.

The Champagne Routes of the Marne map shows three serpentine itineraries – Montagne de Reims, Vallée de la Marne and Côte des Blancs. The routes are not designed to be driven in their entirety in a single day so pick and choose segments that suit your mood; we've covered just a few of the villages and highlights.

The Champagne Routes, which follow secondary and tertiary rural roads, are signposted but there are so many twists and turn-offs that setting off without a map would be unwise. Bookshops and tourist offices sell Michelin's yellow-jacketed, 1:150,000-scale *Aisne, Ardennes, Marne* map (No 306; €4.50).

MONTAGNE DE REIMS CHAMPAGNE ROUTE

Linking Reims with Épernay by skirting the Parc Natural Régional de la Montagne de Reims, a regional park covering the forested Reims Mountain plateau, this meandering, 70km route passes through vineyards planted mainly with pinot noir vines. Villages are listed in the order you'll encounter them if starting out from Reims.

Routes of the Marne

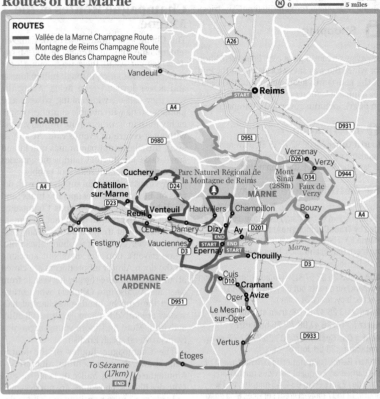

ROUTES
— Vallée de la Marne Champagne Route
— Montagne de Reims Champagne Route
— Côte des Blancs Champagne Route

VERZENAY

For the region's best introduction to the art of growing grapes and the cycles of the seasons, head to the **Phare de Verzenay** (Verzenay Lighthouse; www.lepharedeverzenay. com; D26; lighthouse adult/child €3/2, incl museum €7/4; ⏱10am-5pm Tue-Fri, to 5.30pm Sat & Sun, closed Jan-Mar), on a hilltop at the eastern edge of the village. Exactly 101 spiral stairs lead to the top of the lighthouse, constructed as a publicity stunt in 1909, which rewards visitors with unsurpassed 360-degree views of vine, field and forest – and, if you're lucky, a tiny TGV zipping by in the distance. The Sillery sugar mill, visible on the horizon, turns an astounding 16,000 tonnes of beets (a major regional crop) into 2600 tonnes of sugar each day! Stop by the **Jardin Panoramique** (admission free) to get a look at the four authorised techniques for tying grape vines to horizontal wires (can you make out the differences?). The ticket counter can provide an English translation of the wall texts.

The **Moulin de Verzenay** (Verzenay Windmill; D26), on the western edge of town, was used as an observation post during WWI and by the US Army during WWII. The interior is closed but the nearby hill offers fine valley views.

PARC NATURAL RÉGIONAL DE LA MONTAGNE DE REIMS

The 500 sq km Montagne de Reims Regional Park is best known for a botanical curiosity, 800 mutant beech trees known as **faux de Verzy** (see http://verzy.verzenay.online.fr for photos). To get a good look at the trees, which have torturously twisted trunks and branches that hang down like an umbrella, take the Balade des Faux **forest walk** from 'Les Faux' parking lot, 2km up D34 from Verzy (situated on D26).

Across D34, a 500m gravel path leads through the forest to a *point de vue* (panoramic viewpoint) – next to a concrete WWI bunker – atop 288m-high **Mont Sinaï**.

VALLÉE DE LA MARNE CHAMPAGNE ROUTE

A stronghold of pinot meunier vines, this 90km itinerary winds from Épernay to Dormans, heading more or less west along the hillsides north of the River Marne; it then circles back to the east along the river's south bank. The GR14 long-distance walking trail and its variants (eg GR141) pass through the area.

HAUTVILLERS

Perching above a sea of emerald vines and ablaze with forsythia and tulips in spring, Hautvillers (population 790) is where Dom Pierre Pérignon is popularly believed to have created Champagne. The good Dom's tomb is in front of the altar of the Église Abbatiale (Abbey Church; ☺daily), adorned with 17th-century woodwork. The village is one of Champagne's prettiest, with ubiquitous medieval-style wrought-iron signs providing pictorial clues to the activities taking place on the other side of the wall.

The attractive main square, place de la République, is where you'll find the Café d'Hautvillers (mains €11.50-14.50; ☺daily), which serves drinks and classic bistro grub on a people-watching terrace. You'll also find the helpful tourist office (☎03 26 57 06 35; www.tourisme-hautvillers.com; ☺9.30am-1pm & 1.30-5.30pm Mon-Sat, 10am-4pm Sun), where you can pick up excellent free maps for several vineyard walks. One-hour guided tours cost €3 (with a Champagne tasting €5).

Steps away is Au 36 (www.au36.net; 36 rue Dom Pérignon; ☺10.30am-1pm & 3-7pm Thu-Tue), a slinky wine boutique with a 'wall' of Champagne, innovatively arranged by aroma, and a laid-back upstairs tasting room. A two-/three glass tasting costs €10/15.

Astonishing vineyard views await a few hundred metres north of the centre along route de Fismes (D386); south along route de Cumières (a road leading to D1); and along the GR14 long-distance walking trail (red-and-white markings) and local vineyard footpaths (yellow markings).

Hautvillers is twinned with the Alsatian town of Eguisheim, which explains why three storks live in the Volière des Cigognes Altavilloises (D386; admission free), an easy 500m walk towards Épernay from place de la République. If you're not expecting a baby, this may be your only chance to get a close-up view of these majestic birds. In most years, storklings hatch here in May.

Hautvillers is 6km north of Épernay.

CUCHERY

You're assured a warm – and English-speaking – welcome and a fascinating cellar tour at Albert Levasseur (☎03 26 58 11 38; www. champagne-levasseur.fr; 6 rue Sorbier, Cuchery), which run by a friendly Franco-Irish couple and turns grapes grown on 4.2 hectares into 35,000 to 40,000 bottles of Champagne each year. Try to phone or email ahead if possible; but if not just drop by and knock. Situated in the hamlet of Cuchery (population 410), 18km northwest of Épernay on D24.

CHÂTILLON-SUR-MARNE

The highest point in this sloping village (population 850) is crowned by a 25m-high

---

MORE BUBBLES FOR EVERYONE

Around 55% of the 320 million bottles of Champagne sold each year are popped open, sipped and savoured in France itself. That doesn't leave much for the rest of us, especially when you consider how many bottles are wasted naming ships and showering victorious football players. But help is at hand. Faced with rising worldwide demand, the government body that regulates where Champagne can be grown has proposed expanding the area – currently 327 sq km – for the first time since 1927. Starting in about 2017, 40 lucky villages are likely to start planting their very first official Champagne vines. Not surprisingly, the exact delineation of the new vineyards has been hugely controversial, not least because the value of land declared Champagne-worthy will rise by up to 30,000%, to about €1 million per hectare!

Large maisons (Champagne houses) with global brand recognition send a high percentage of their production to other countries (Moët & Chandon, for example, exports 80% of its bubbly). But the region's 4800 small producers (known as récoltants-manipulants because they both harvest the grapes and turn the juice into wine) continue to serve an almost exclusively domestic clientele. Global sales were up 13% in 2011, with notable increases in demand in the UK, America, Germany, Russia, China and South America.

statue of Pope Urban II (dedicated in 1887), a particularly successful local boy (1042–99) best known to history for having launched the bloody First Crusade. The orientation table near the base offers excellent views of the Marne Valley and is a super spot for a picnic.

The tourist office (☎03 26 58 32 86; www.otchatillon51.com; 4 rue de l'Eglise; ⊙10am-12.30pm & 2-6pm, closed morning Mon) is very near the partly Romanesque church. A map panel right next to the post office details an 11km, four-hour vineyard walk.

Châtillon is 19km west of Épernay, on D23.

ŒUILLY

To get a sense of winegrowing life a century ago, drop by the Écomusée d'Œuilly (www. ecomusee-oeuilly.fr; adult/child €6.50/4; ⊙tours 10.30am, 2pm & 6pm, closed Tue), whose three sections include a schoolroom, c 1900. Behind the sturdy 13th-century Église St-Memmie, the panoramic churchyard is the final resting place of five members of a RAF air crew downed in 1944; each grave bears a moving personal inscription.

Œuilly (population 636) is 15km west of Épernay, just off D3.

CÔTE DES BLANCS CHAMPAGNE ROUTE

This 100km route, planted almost exclusively with white chardonnay grapes (the name means 'hillside of the whites'), begins along Épernay's majestic av du Champagne and then heads south to Sézanne and beyond. The gently rolling landscape is at its most attractive in late summer and autumn.

CRAMANT

For views of the neatly tended vines and the patchwork colours of the Champagne countryside, check out the view from the ridge above this village (population 890), whose northern entrance is adorned by a two-storey-high champagne bottle. Situated on D10 7.5km southeast of Épernay on D10.

AVIZE

Many past, present and future Champagne makers learned, or are learning, their art and science at the Lycée Viticole de la Champagne (Champagne High School of Winemaking; www.les-enfants-de-la-viti.com), run by the Ministry of Agriculture. As part of their studies, students produce quite excellent bubbly, made with grapes from some of Champagne's most prestigious parcels and sold under the

label Champagne Sanger (www.sanger.fr). Sanger was established shortly after WWI, which is why the name is pronounced *sans guerre* ('without war'), ie sahn-GHER.

At the Sanger Cellars (☎03 26 57 79 79; www.sanger.fr; 33 rue du Rempart du Midi; ⊙8am-noon & 2-5pm Mon-Fri), free tours of the high school's impressive production facilities take in both traditional production and the latest high-tech machinery. Champagnes are sold at the discounted *prix départ cave* (cellar-door price); profits are reinvested in the school. The entrance is on D19; if the door is locked, push the intercom button.

Once the abbey church of a Benedictine convent, Église St-Nicolas, on rue de l'Église (D10), mixes Romanesque, Flamboyant Gothic and Renaissance styles. From there, aptly named rue de la Montagne leads up the hill (towards Grauves) – past another oversized Champagne bottle – to Parc Vix (D19), which affords panoramic vineyard views; a map sign details a 6.5km, two-hour walk through forest and field.

OGER

Oger (population 588) is known for its *grand cru* fields, prize-winning flower gardens and the Musée du Mariage (Wedding Museum; www.mariage-et-champagne.com; 1 rue d'Avize/D10; adult/child €6/free; ⊙9.30am-noon & 2-6pm Tue-Sun). Featuring colourful and often gaudy objects associated with 19th-century marriage traditions, highlights include a tableau of newlyweds in their nuptial bed – but they're not alone, for they've been woken up early by family and friends bearing Champagne, chocolate and broad smiles. The collection was assembled by the parents of the owner of Champagne Henry de Vaugency (founded 1732), an eighth-generation Champagne grower. The visit concludes with a Champagne tasting.

LE MESNIL-SUR-OGER

Musée de la Vigne et du Vin (☎03 26 57 50 15; www.champagne-launois.fr; 2 av Eugène Guillaume, cnr D10; adult incl 3 flutes Champagne €7.50; ⊙tours 10am Mon-Fri, 10.30am Sat & Sun) is so outstanding that it's worth planning your day around a tour.

Assembled by a family that has been making Champagne since 1872, this extraordinary collection of century-old Champagne-making equipment includes objects so aesthetically ravishing that you'll want to reach out and touch them. Among the highlights is a massive 16-tonne oak-beam grape press from

1630. Reservations can be made by phone or through the website; tours are not necessarily in English.

For an excellent French meal, head to **Le Mesnil** (☎03 26 57 95 57; www.restaurantlemesnil.com; 2 rue Pasteur; menus €19.50-26; ⏰lunch & dinner Thu-Sat & Mon-Tue, lunch Sun). This refined contemporary restaurant spotlights seasonal flavours in dishes from suckling pig goulash to lobster terrine with scallops. Wine and restaurant critic Michael Edwards calls Le Mesnil 'the greatest Chardonnay commune in Champagne'.

Épernay

POP 25,000

Prosperous Épernay, the self-proclaimed *capitale du champagne* and home to many of the world's most celebrated Champagne houses, is the best place for touring cellars and sampling bubbly. The town also makes an excellent base for exploring the Champagne Routes.

Beneath the streets in 110km of subterranean cellars, more than 200 million bottles of Champagne, just waiting to be popped open on some sparkling occasion, are being aged. In 1950 one such cellar – owned by the irrepressible Mercier family – hosted a car rally without the loss of a single bottle!

Épernay is 25km south of Reims and can be visited by train or car as a day trip from Reims.

Sights

TOP CHOICE Avenue de Champagne — STREET

Épernay's handsome and eminently strollable avenue de Champagne fizzes with *maisons de champagne* (Champagne houses). The boulevard is lined with turreted mansions and neoclassical villas, rebuilt after the devastation of WWI. Peek through wrought-iron gates at Moët's private **Hôtel Chandon**, an early 19th-century pavilion-style residence set in landscaped gardens, which counts Wagner among its famous past guests. Notice, too, the haunted-looking **Château Perrier**, a redbrick mansion built in 1854 in neo-Louis XIII style and aptly placed at number 13! The roundabout presents photo-ops with its giant cork and bottle-top.

Comtesse Lafond — CHAMPAGNE HOUSE

(☎03 86 39 18 33; www.deladoucette.net; 79 av de Champagne; 3-glass tasting €9, incl cellar tour €14; ⏰10am-noon & 2-5.30pm daily) Owned by wine magnate Baron Patrick de Ladoucette, the whimsically turreted Comtesse Lafond is the most intimate and charming of all the *maisons* on the avenue de Champagne. Tastings of three Champagnes, including the excellent Blanc des Blancs, take place in the elegant salon or in manicured gardens overlooking vine-streaked hills.

Moët & Chandon — CHAMPAGNE HOUSE

(☎03 26 51 20 20; www.moet.com; 20 av de Champagne; adult incl 1/2 glasses €16.50/23, 10-18yr €9.50; ⏰tours 9.30am-11.30am & 2-4.30pm, closed Sat & Sun mid-Nov–mid-Mar) Flying the Moët, French, European and Russian flags, this prestigious *maison* offers frequent one-hour tours that are among the region's most impressive. At the shop you can pick up a 15L bottle of Brut Impérial for just €1500; a standard bottle will set you back €31.

Mercier — CHAMPAGNE HOUSE

(☎03 26 51 22 22; www.champagnemercier.fr; 68-70 av de Champagne; adult incl 1/2/3 glasses €11/16/19, 12-17yr €5.50; ⏰tours 9.30-11.30am & 2-4.30pm, closed mid-Dec–mid-Feb) France's most popular brand was founded in 1847 by Eugène Mercier, a trailblazer in the field of eye-catching publicity stunts and the virtual creator of the cellar tour. Everything here is flashy, including the 160,000L barrel that took two decades to build (for the Universal Exposition of 1889), the lift that transports you 30m underground and the laser-guided touring train.

De Castellane — CHAMPAGNE HOUSE

(☎03 26 51 19 11; www.castellane.com; 64 av de Champagne; adult incl 1 glass €10, under 12yr free; ⏰tours 10am-noon & 2-6pm, closed Christmas–mid-Mar) The 45-minute tours, in French and English, take in a bubbly museum dedicated to elucidating the *méthode champenoise* and its diverse technologies. The reward for climbing the 237 steps up the 66m-high tower (built 1905) is a fine panoramic view.

Hôtel de Ville — CITY HALL

(City Hall; 7bis av de Champagne; ⏰8.30am-noon & 1.30-6pm Mon-Fri) In the neoclassical Hôtel de Ville, you can take a peek at the ornate, Louis XV-style **Salle de Conseil** (city council room) and **Salle de Mariages** (marriage hall). The adjacent, flowery park is perfect for a picnic.

Église Notre-Dame — CHURCH

(Place Flodoard) Crowned by a fairy-tale silver spire, this late 19th-century church bears Romanesque and Gothic influences and is lit from within by a rose window.

DOM PÉRIGNON

Everyone who visits Moët & Chandon invariably stops to strike a pose next to the statue of **Dom Pérignon** (c 1638–1715), after whom the *prestige cuvée* is named. The Benedictine monk played a pivotal role in making Champagne what it is – perfecting the process of using a second, in-the-bottle fermentation to make ho-hum wine sparkle. Apparently, he was so blown away by the result that he rhapsodised about 'tasting the stars'. While his contribution was undoubtedly significant, bubbly didn't come to dominate Champagne's wine production until over a century after his death.

Théâtre Gabrielle Dorziat   HISTORIC SITE
(www.lesalmanazar.fr; place Mendès-France) The north side of Théâtre Gabrielle Dorziat, built in 1902, still shows shell and bullet marks from WWII.

👉 Tours

Champagne Domi Moreau   VINEYARD TOUR
(☎06 30 35 51 07, after 7pm 03 26 59 45 85; www.champagne-domimoreau.com; tours €20; ⏰tours 9.30am & 2.30pm except Wed & late Aug) Runs scenic and insightful three-hour minibus tours, in French and English, of nearby vineyards. Pick-up is across the street from the tourist office. It also organises two-hour vineyard tours by bicycle (€15). Call ahead for reservations.

🛏 Sleeping

Épernay's hotels fill up fast on weekends from Easter to September and on weekdays, too, in May, June and September.

TOP CHOICE **Le Clos Raymi**   HISTORIC HOTEL €€
(☎03 26 51 00 58; www.closraymi-hotel.com; 3 rue Joseph de Venoge; s €115, d €155-175; 🛜) Staying at this atmospheric place is like being a personal guest of Monsieur Chandon of Champagne fame, who occupied this luxurious town house over a century ago. The seven romantic rooms – styles include Provençal, Tuscan and colonial – have giant beds, high ceilings, French windows and parquet floors. In winter there's often a fire in the cosy art deco living room. Perfect for a honeymoon.

Parva Domus   B&B €€
(☎03 26 32 40 74; www.parvadomusrimaire.com; 25 av de Champagne; d €90, ste €110; 🛜) Bril-liantly situated on the avenue de Champagne, this vine-swathed B&B is kept spick and span by the amiable Rimaire family. Rooms have a countrified feel, with wood floors, floral fabrics and pastel colours. Sip a glass of house Champagne on the terrace or in the elegant living room.

Hôtel Jean Moët   HISTORIC HOTEL €€
(☎03 26 32 19 22; www.hoteljeanmoet.com; 7 rue Jean Moët; r €125-190; ❄🛜🏊) Housed in a beautifully converted 18th-century mansion, this old-town hotel is big on atmosphere, with its skylit tea room, antique-meets-boutique-chic rooms and cellar, C. Comme (p302). Spa treatments and a swimming pool await after a hard day's Champagne tasting.

La Villa St-Pierre   HOTEL €
(☎03 26 54 40 80; www.villasaintpierre.fr; 14 av Paul Chandon; d €51-61; 🛜) In an early 20th-century mansion, this homey place, with 11 simple rooms, retains some of the charm of yesteryear.

Hôtel de la Cloche   HOTEL €
(☎03 26 55 15 15; www.hotel-la-cloche.com; 5 place Mendès-France; d €49-59, tr €59-69; 🛜) A slightly stiff hotel with 19 rooms decorated in bright, dissonant colours. Some rooms have park or church views.

🍴 Eating & Drinking

Épernay's main eat street is rue Gambetta and adjacent place de la République. For picnic fixings, head to rue St-Thibault.

La Grillade Gourmande   REGIONAL CUISINE €€
(☎03 26 55 44 22; www.lagrilladegourmande.com; 16 rue de Reims; menus €19-55; ⏰lunch & dinner Tue-Sat) This chic, red-walled bistro is an inviting spot to try char-grilled meats and dishes rich in texture and flavour, such as crayfish pan-fried in Champagne and lamb cooked until meltingly tender in rosemary and honey. Diners spill out onto the covered terrace in the warm months.

C. Comme   CHAMPAGNE BAR
(8 rue Gambetta; light meals €7.50-12, 6-glass Champagne tasting €33; ⏰10am-8.30pm Sun-Wed, 10am-11pm Thu, 10am-midnight Fri-Sat) The downstairs cellar has a stash of 300 different varieties of Champagne; sample them (from €5.50 a glass) in the softly lit bar/bistro upstairs. Accompany with a tasting plate of regional cheese, charcuterie and *rillettes* (pork pâté). We love the funky bottle-top tables and relaxed ambience.

Chez Max TRADITIONAL FRENCH €€
(☎03 26 55 23 59; www.chez-max.com; 13 av AA
Thevenet, Magenta; menus €13.50-38.50; ⊗lunch &
dinner Tue-Sun, closed dinner Sun & Wed) No fuss,
no frills, just good old-fashioned French
cooking and a neighbourly vibe is what
you'll get at Chez Max. Dishes like confit
of duck leg and sea bass with Champagne
sauce hit the mark every time.

La Table Kobus INTERNATIONAL €€
(☎03 26 51 53 53; www.latablekobus.com; 3 rue
du Docteur Rousseau; menus €19.50-45; ⊗lunch &
dinner Tue-Sun, closed dinner Sun & Thu) French
cuisine in versions traditional and creative
are served amid fin-de-siècle Paris bistro
decor. Specialities like sea bream tartar with
fennel and lime and flaky *pastilla* (Moroccan pie) of pork tenderloin with spices are
presented with flair.

La Cave à Champagne REGIONAL CUISINE €€
(☎03 26 55 50 70; www.la-cave-a-champagne.com;
16 rue Gambetta; menus €18-34; ⊗lunch & dinner
Thu-Mon, lunch Tue) 'The Champagne Cellar' is
well regarded by locals for its *champenoise*
cuisine (artichoke hearts with snails in
parsley-cream, duck cooked in grape juice),
served in a warm, traditional, bourgeois
atmosphere. You can sample four different
Champagnes for €24.

Cook'In FUSION €€
(☎03 26 54 89 80; www.restaurant-cookin.com; 18
rue Porte Lucas; menus €15-21; ⊗lunch Mon-Sat,
dinner Wed-Sat) A sparky chef came up with the
idea of combining French and Thai flavours
at this sleek bistro. Go for well-spiced dishes
like satay of guinea fowl in banana leaf with
a peanut sauce and tournedos of beef in red
curry. The day's wok dish costs €9.50.

Le Sardaigne PIZZERIA €
(1 place Mendès-France; pizzas €8-12; ⊗lunch &
dinner daily) Best pizza in town.

Covered Market FOOD MARKET €
(Halle St-Thibault; rue Gallice; ⊗7.30am-12.30pm
Wed & Sat) Picnic treats galore.

Charcutier-Traiteur GOURMET FOOD €
(rue Gallice, Halle St-Thibault; ⊗7.30am-12.30pm
Wed & Sat) Scrumptious prepared dishes.

La Cloche à Fromage CHEESE €
(19 rue St-Thibault; ⊗8.30am-1pm & 2.30pm-
7.30pm Tue-Thu, 8am-7.30pm Fri, 7.30am-7.30pm
Sat) Has been selling cheeses at this location
for over a century.

ℹ️ Information

Tourist Office (☎03 26 53 33 00; www.
ot-epernay.fr; 7 av de Champagne; ⊗9.30am-
12.30pm & 1.30-7pm Mon-Sat, 11am-4pm Sun)
Has excellent English brochures and maps on
cellar visits, walking and cycling options and
car touring. It also rents out a GPS unit (€7 per
day) with self-guided vineyard driving tours in
French, English and Dutch.

ℹ️ Getting There & Around

BICYCLE Bicycles can be rented at Épernay's
municipal swimming pool, **Espace Aquatique
Bulléo** (rue Dom Pérignon, Roger Menu; per
half-day/day/week €11/16.50/77.50; ⊗10am-
6pm Mon-Fri, 10am-12.30pm & 3-6pm Sat & Sun
mid-Apr–Oct), situated about 700m south of the
covered market.

The tourist office sells cycling maps and map-
cards (€0.50).

CAR **Europcar** (www.europcar.com; 20 rempart Perrier)

TRAIN The **train station** (place Mendès-France)
has direct services to Reims (€6.40, 20 to 90
minutes, seven to 18 daily) and Paris Gare de
l'Est (€22, 1¼ hours, five to 10 daily).

Troyes

POP 62,810

Troyes – like Reims, one of the historic capitals of Champagne – has a lively centre that's
graced with one of France's finest ensembles
of half-timbered houses and Gothic churches. Often overlooked, it's one of the best places in France to get a sense of what Europe
looked like back when Molière was penning
his finest plays and the *Three Musketeers*

WORTH A TRIP

TASTE LIKE A PRO

You can taste Champagne anywhere
but you might get more out of one of the
two-hour workshops at Villa Bissinger
(☎03 26 55 78 78; www.villabissinger.com;
15 rue Jeanson, Ay; 2hr workshop in English/
French €38/23; ⊗2.30pm Sat Apr-Oct),
home to the International Institute
for the Wines of Champagne. Besides
covering the basics like names, producers, grape varieties and characteristics,
the workshop includes a tasting of four
different Champagnes. The institute is
in Ay, 3.5km northeast of Épernay. Call
ahead to secure your place.

DID YOU KNOW...?

Chances are Troyes has already played at least a cameo role in your life:

» If you've ever read or seen a story about Lancelot or the search for the Holy Grail, you've enjoyed creations of the 12th-century poet and troubadour Chrétien (Chrestien) de Troyes (1135–83), who was, as his name indicates, a local boy.

» If you've ever purchased gold bullion, you've done so using the troy ounce, a unit of measure derived from exchange standards established in Troyes in the 12th and 13th centuries.

» Every time you've admired a Lacoste shirt, Petit Bateau kids clothing or sexy Dim underwear, you've paid homage to a brand name created right here in France's historic knitwear capital.

were swashbuckling. Several unique and very worthwhile museums are another lure.

Troyes does not have any Champagne cellars. However, you can shop in its scores of outlet stores stuffed with brand-name clothing and accessories, a legacy of the city's long-time role as France's knitwear capital.

⊙ Sights

Panels posted around the old city provide tidbits on Troyes' history in French and English.

TOP CHOICE **16th-Century Troyes**   HISTORIC QUARTER
Half-timbered houses – some with lurching walls and floors that aren't quite on the level – line many streets in the old city, rebuilt after a devastating fire in 1524. The best place for aimless ambling is the area bounded by (clockwise from the north) rue Général de Gaulle, the Hôtel de Ville, rue Général Saussier and rue de la Pierre; of special interest are (from southwest to northeast) rue de Vauluisant, rue de la Trinité, rue Champeaux and rue Paillot de Montabert.

Off rue Champeaux (between No 30 and 32), a stroll along tiny ruelle des Chats (Alley of the Cats), as dark and narrow as it was four centuries ago – the upper floors almost touch – is like stepping back into the Middle Ages. The stones along the base of the walls were designed to give pedestrians a place to stand when horses clattered by.

One of the founders of the Canadian city of Montréal, Paul Chomeday de Maisonneuve (1612–76), once lived in the Hôtel du Chaudron (4 rue Chrestien de Troyes).

TOP CHOICE **Maison de l'Outil et de la Pensée Ouvrière**   TOOL MUSEUM
(Museum of Tools & Crafts; www.maison-de-l-outil.com; 7 rue de la Trinité; adult/child €6.50/3; ⊙10am-6pm daily, closed Tue Oct-Mar) Worn to a sensuous lustre by generations of skilled hands, the 10,000 hand tools on display here – each designed to perform a single, specialised task with exquisite efficiency – bring to life a world of manual skills made obsolete by the Industrial Revolution. The collection is housed in the magnificent Renaissance-style Hôtel de Mauroy, built in 1556. Videos show how the tools were used and what they were used for. A catalogue in English is available at the reception.

Cathédrale St-Pierre et St-Paul   CATHEDRAL
(place St-Pierre; ⊙9am-noon & 1-5pm Mon-Sat, 11.30am-5pm Sun) Troyes' most important house of worship, 114m long, incorporates elements from every period of *champenois* Gothic architecture. The Flamboyant west façade, for instance, dates from the mid-1500s, while the choir and transepts are more than 250 years older. The interior is illuminated by a spectacular series of some 180 stained-glass windows (13th to 17th centuries) that shine like jewels when it's sunny. Also of interest: a fantastical baroque organ (1730s) sporting musical putti (cherubs), and a tiny treasury (open July and August only) with enamels from the Meuse Valley. Back in 1429, Joan of Arc and Charles VII stopped off here on their way to his coronation in Reims.

Musée d'Art Moderne   ART MUSEUM
(place St-Pierre; adult/child €5/free; ⊙10am-1pm & 2-7pm Tue-Fri, 11am-7pm Sat & Sun, to 5pm Oct-Apr) The highlights here are French painting (including lots of fauvist works) created between 1850 and 1950, glass (especially the work of local glassmaker and painter Maurice Marinot) and ceramics. Featured artists include Derain, Dufy, Matisse, Modigliani, Picasso and Soutine. Housed in a 16th- to 18th-century bishop's palace, this place owes its existence to all those crocodile-logo shirts, whose global success allowed Lacoste entrepreneurs Pierre and Denise Lévy to amass this outstanding collection.

Église Ste-Madeleine   CHURCH

(rue Général de Gaulle; ⊙10am-1pm & 2-7pm Tue-Sat, 2-7pm Sun) Troyes' oldest and most interesting neighbourhood church has an early Gothic nave and transept (early 13th century) and a Renaissance-style choir and tower. The highlights here are the splendid Flamboyant Gothic rood screen (early 1500s), dividing the transept from the choir, and the 16th-century stained glass in the presbytery portraying scenes from Genesis. In the nave, the statue of a deadly serious Ste-Marthe (St Martha), around the pillar from the wooden pulpit, is considered a masterpiece of the 15th-century Troyes School.

Basilique St-Urbain   CHURCH

(place Vernier; ⊙10am-noon & 2-4.30pm Tue-Sat, 2-4.30pm Sun) Begun in 1262 by the Troyes-born Pope Urban IV, whose father's shoemaker shop once stood on this spot, this church is exuberantly Gothic both inside and out, and has some fine 13th-century stained glass. In the chapel off the south transept arm is La Vierge au Raisin (Virgin with Grapes), a graceful, early 15th-century stone statue of Mary and the Christ Child.

Église St-Pantaléon   CHURCH

(rue de Vauluisant; ⊙10.30am-noon & 2-4.30pm Tue-Sat) Faded with age and all the more enigmatic for it, this Renaissance-style, cruciform church, with its vaulted wood ceiling, is a great place to see the work of the 16th-century Troyes School – check out the sculptures attached to the columns of the nave. The west façade was added in the 18th century. History sheets are available.

Hôtel de Vauluisant   MUSEUM

(☑03 25 43 43 20; 4 rue de Vauluisant; adult/child €3/free; ⊙2-7pm Wed, 10am-1pm & 2-7pm Thu & Fri, 11am-1pm & 2-7pm Sat & Sun, shorter hrs in winter) This haunted-looking, Renaissance-style mansion, which looks as though it has been asleep for 100 years, houses two unique museums: Musée de l'Art Troyen and Musée de la Bonneterie. Plants used to make dyes and oil paints in the Middle Ages grow in the courtyard.

Musée de l'Art Troyen

Redesigned in 2009, the Museum of Troyes Art features the evocative paintings, stained glass and statuary (stone and wood) of the Troyes School, which flourished here during the economic prosperity and artistic ferment of the early 16th century.

Musée de la Bonneterie

The Hosiery Museum showcases the sock-strewn story of Troyes' 19th-century knitting industry, with exhibits from knitting machines and looms to bonnets and embroidered silk stockings.

Apothicairerie de l'Hôtel-Dieu-le-Comte   APOTHECARY MUSEUM

(quai des Comtes de Champagne; adult/child €2/free; ⊙2-7pm Wed, 10am-1pm & 2-7pm Thu & Fri, 11am-1pm & 2-7pm Sat & Sun, shorter hrs in winter) If you come down with an old-fashioned malady – scurvy, perhaps, or unbalanced humours – the place to go is this fully outfitted, wood-panelled pharmacy from 1721. Rare pharmaceutical jars share shelf space with decorative pill boxes and bronze mortars.

🛏 Sleeping

ⓣ Maison de Rhodes   HISTORIC HOTEL €€€

(☑03 25 43 11 11; www.maisonderhodes.com; 18, rue Linard Gonthier; d €154-250; ☎) Once home to the Knights Templar, this half-timbered pile sits proudly on its 12th-century foundations. Creaking staircases lead to 11 spacious rooms, with beams and stone floors, which positively ooze medieval character; iPod docks and wi-fi suddenly wing you back into the 21st century. The gardens, courtyard and gourmet restaurant invite lingering.

Le Relais St-Jean   HISTORIC HOTEL €€

(☑03 25 73 89 90; www.relais-st-jean.com; 51 rue Paillot de Montabert; d €95-150; ✳@☎) On a narrow medieval street in the heart of the old city, this hotel combines half-timbered charm with 24 contemporary rooms, a mini-tropical hothouse, a musical jacuzzi with coloured underwater lights, a small fitness centre and facilities for the disabled. There's direct access from the underground car park (€10).

Hôtel Les Comtes de Champagne   HISTORIC HOTEL €

(☑03 25 73 11 70; www.comtesdechampagne.com; 56 rue de la Monnaie; s €62, d €68-90, q €130, d with

Troyes

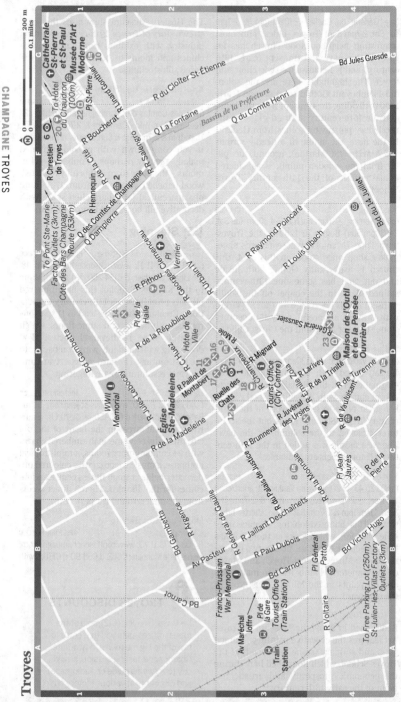

0 ⊚——— 200 m
0 ⊚——— 0.1 miles

G

Cathédrale St-Pierre et St-Paul
Musée d'Art Moderne 10
To Hôtel du Chaudron (100m) 20
R Chrestien de Troyes 6
R Boucherat
Pl St-Pierre 22
R Linard Gonthier
R du Cloître St-Étienne
Q La Fontaine
Bassin de la Préfecture
Bd Jules Guesde
Q du Comte Henri

F

To Pont-Ste-Marie; Factory Outlets (3km); Côte des Bars Champagne Route (53km)
R de Hennequin la Cité 2
Q des Comtes de Champagne
Q Dampierre
R R Salengro
R Raymond Poincaré
R Louis Ulbach
Bd du 14 Juillet

E

R Pithou 19
Pl Clémenceau 3
R Georges Vernier
R Urbain IV
Maison de l'Outil et de la Pensée Ouvrière 13
R Général Saussier 23
7

D

Bd Gambetta
Pl de la Halle 14
R de la République
Hôtel de Ville 16
R Clemenceau 6
R Mignard
R Larivey
R de la Trinité
R de Turenne

C

Église Ste-Madeleine
R de la Madeleine
R Paillot de Montabert 11 17
Ruelle des Chats 12
Tourist Office (City Centre) 18 21
R Champeaux 1
R Juvénal des Ursins
R Émile Zola
R de Vauluisant 4
R de Vauluisant 5
15
8
Pl Jean Jaurès
R de la Pierre
R de la Monnaie

B

WWII Memorial
R Jules Lebocey
R Leclerc
Bd Gambetta
R Argence
R Brunneval
R du Palais de Justice
R Jaillant Deschaînets
R Paul Dubois
Bd Carnot
Pl Général Patton
Bd Victor Hugo
To Free Parking Lot (250m); St-Julien-les-Villas Factory Outlets (3km)

A

Bd Carnot
Franco-Prussian War Memorial
Av Pasteur
R Général de Gaulle
Av Maréchal Joffre
Pl de la Gare Tourist Office (Train Station)
Train Station
R Voltaire

Troyes

washbasin €45; ☎) The same massive wooden beams have kept this trio of pastel-hued half-timbered houses vertical since the 16th century. We love the bright courtyard lobby, the flower boxes and the 12th-century cellar. A huge and very romantic double goes for €90. No lift.

Hôtel Arlequin HOTEL €
(☎03 25 83 12 70; www.hotelarlequin.com; 50 rue de Turenne; s €47-65, d €78-88; ✿☎) Lovingly kept and efficiently run, this charming hostelry shows good taste all round, from the smart custard façade to the cheerful rooms with antique furnishings, high ceilings and *commedia dell'arte* playfulness. No lift.

✕ Eating

Rue Champeaux has the city's highest concentration of restaurants, cafes and crêperies, though few rise much above the ordinary. Student-oriented eateries can be found just west of the cathedral along rue de la Cité.

Locals are enormously proud of the city's specialities: *andouillettes de Troyes* (sausages made with strips of pigs' intestines) and *tête de veau* (calf's head served without the brain). As far as most non-locals are concerned, they're an acquired taste.

TOP CHOICE Le Valentino GASTRONOMIC €€
(☎03 25 73 14 14; 35 rue Paillot de Montabert; menu €25-56; ⊙lunch & dinner Tue-Sat) What could be more romantic than a *table à deux* in the cobbled courtyard of this rose-hued, 17th-century restaurant? The chef juggles flavours skilfully in palate-awakening specialities like fried char with parsnips and citrus reduction, and scallops with tart Granny Smith apple, white radish and cilantro.

Aux Tables des Peintres BISTRO €
(☎03 25 73 59 94; 23 rue des Quinze Vingts; 2-course menu €12; ⊙lunch & dinner Tue-Sat, lunch Sun) This endearingly eccentric gallery-bistro does a great-value *menu* for €12, with specials from honey-glazed chicken to beef lasagne. The 18th-century courtyard is a quaint taste of country life with its overhanging beams, wagon wheels and cobbles polished smooth over centuries.

La Table de François BISTRO €€
(☎03 25 73 83 53; www.latabledefrancois.fr; 18 rue Juvénal des Ursins; lunch menus €17-22, dinner menus €33-45; ⊙lunch & dinner Tue-Sat) Crisp white linen, brick walls and high-back chairs create a backdrop of understated elegance at this bistro. The menu delivers spot-on classics like Charolais beef with creamy *gratin dauphinois*, *andouillettes de Troyes* in Chablis sauce and green-tea creme brûlée.

SELF-GUIDED TOUR

The tourist offices in Troyes can supply you with an **audioguide tour** (€5.50) of the old city in French, English, German, Italian or Dutch.

Au Jardin Gourmand TRADITIONAL FRENCH €€
(☎03 25 73 36 13; 31 rue Paillot de Montabert; menus €17-30; ☺lunch & dinner Mon-Fri, lunch Sat) Elegant without being overly formal, this intimate restaurant – with a summer terrace – uses only the freshest ingredients for its classic French and *champenois* dishes; among the latter are no fewer than 11 varieties of *andouillette*. About 20 vintages from the estimable wine list are available by the glass.

Pizzeria Guiseppino PIZZA €
(26 rue Paillot de Montabert; pizza €8-10; ☺lunch & dinner Tue-Sat) Thin and crisp, the pizza at this no-frills, big-smiles pizzeria is the real deal.

Clef de Voûte FONDUE €
(☎03 25 73 72 07; 33 rue Général Saussier; menus €10.50-19; ☺lunch & dinner Tue-Sat) A rustic Savoyard-style bolthole, with fondue and *raclette* to warm the cockles on winter days.

Covered Market FOOD MARKET €
(place de la Halle; ☺8am-12.45pm & 3.30-7pm Mon-Thu, 9am-7pm Fri & Sat, 9am-1pm Sun) Fruit, veggies, bread, charcuterie, fish and cheese glorious cheese.

Drinking & Entertainment

The hum of chatter fills the open-air bars and cafes around rue Champeaux and half-timbered place A Israël on warm evenings.

Dixi Café BAR
(12 rue Pithou; ☺5pm-3am Tue-Sat) A convivial neighbourhood bar that draws an arty crowd, including students. The house speciality is *rhum arrangé* (fruit-infused rum). Has live music – rock, reggae, jazz, French *chansons* – every Friday and Saturday from about 10pm.

Rive Gauche Café BAR
(59 rue de la Cité; ☺daily; ☎) Attracts a lively crowd with its Belgian beer, terrace overlooking the cathedral, free wi-fi and occasional live music.

Café de l'Union CAFE
(34 rue Champeaux; ☺daily) Venerable old-town cafe with a perfect people-watching terrace.

La Maison du Boulanger TICKET OFFICE
(☎03 25 40 15 55; www.maisonduboulanger.com; 42 rue Paillot de Montabert; ☺closed Sun) Sells tickets to concerts, plays and other cultural events.

Shopping

In the city centre, handsome rue Émile Zola is lined with big-name high-street shops. Antique shops and galleries huddle along rue de la Cité.

Sarah Dollé ACCESSORIES
(23 rue Larivey; ☺2-7pm Tue-Sat) Hidden down a narrow backstreet, this is where you will find Sarah's marvellous hat-making workshop. Squeeze into her tiny boutique, jam-packed with bonnets, woolly winter numbers, top hats and other fancy headwear, and slip back to a more glamorous age.

Cellier St-Pierre WINE
(www.celliersaintpierre.fr; 1 place St-Pierre; ☺closed Sun & Mon) A fine place to purchase bubbly and Aube wines such as *rosé des Riceys*. The cellar has been used since 1840 to distil *Prunelle de Troyes* (€21 per bottle), a 40 per cent liqueur made with sloe (blackthorn fruit) that's great on ice cream. The modest production facilities, which you can visit, are often fired up on Friday and Saturday mornings.

Magasins d'Usine FACTORY OUTLETS
(☺closed Sun) Troyes is famous across France for its factory outlets, which attract bargain-hunters by the coachload. These include **Marques Avenue** (www.marquesavenue.com; av de la Maille), which is home to 240 brand names and located 3km south of the centre along bd de Dijon; **McArthur Glen Troyes** (www.mcarthurglen.fr), a mall with over 100 shops and situated 3km northeast of the centre in Pont Ste-Marie; and **Marques City** (www.marquescity.fr), also in Pont Ste-Marie, with scores of brands in nine buildings.

Information

Tourist Office (www.tourisme-troyes.com) Has two helpful bureaux: **train station** (☎03 25 82 62 70; www.tourisme-troyes.com; 16 bd Carnot; ☺9am-12.30pm & 2-6pm Mon-Sat, also 10am-1pm Sun Nov-early Apr) and **city centre** (☎03 25 73 36 88; www.tourisme-troyes.com; rue Mignard; ☺10am-1pm & 2-6pm Mon-Sat,10-noon & 2-5pm Sun, closed Nov-early Apr). The latter faces the west façade of Église St-Jean.

Getting There & Around

BUS The best way to get to Reims is by bus. Departures are from the very last bus berth to the right as you approach the train station; a schedule is posted. The **bus station office** (☎03 25 71 28 42; ⏱8.30am-noon & 2-5.30pm Mon-Fri), run by Courriers de l'Aube, is in the side of the train station.

CAR There's a huge free car park three blocks south of the Hôtel Arlequin – take rue de Turenne, cross the roundabout and turn right. **National Citer** (☎03 25 73 27 37; 10 rue Voltaire) rents cars. Find it a block south of the train station, near place Général Patton.

TAXI Call ☎03 25 78 30 30.

TRAIN Troyes is on the rather isolated train line that links Mulhouse (€42.90, 3½ hours) in Alsace with Paris Gare de l'Est (€25.40, 1½ hours, 10 to 14 daily). To get to Dijon (€31, 2¾ hours), change in Chaumont.

Champagne Route of the Côte des Bar

Although the Aube *département* (www. aube-champagne.com), of which Troyes is the capital, is a major producer of Champagne (it has about 67 sq km of vineyards, 85% of them pinot noir and 15% chardonnay), it gets a fraction of the recognition accorded to the Marne. Much of the acrimony dates back to 1909, when winemakers of the Aube were excluded from the growing area for Champagne's AOC (Appellation d'Origine Contrôlée). Two years later, they were also forbidden to sell their grapes to producers up north, provoking a revolt by local *vignerons*, months of strikes and a situation so chaotic that the army was called in. Only in 1927 were the Aube growers fully certified as producers of genuine Champagne, but by then the Marne had established market domination.

Today, Champagne production in the southeastern corner of the Aube – just north of Burgundy's Châtillonnais vineyards – is relatively modest in scale, though the reputation of the area's wines has been on an upward trajectory in recent years.

The 220km Côte des Bar Champagne Route does curlicues and loop-the-loops through austere fields, neat vineyards and forestland in an area 30km to 50km east and southeast of Troyes. Great for a deliciously leisurely drive, it passes through stone-built villages that are bedecked with flowers in the spring. Tourist offices, including the one in Troyes, can supply map-brochures. The selected highlights that follow are listed from northeast to southwest.

COLOMBEY-LES-DEUX-ÉGLISES
POP 700

Charles de Gaulle lived in this village (www. colombey-les-deux-eglises.com, in French) from 1934 – except, obviously, during WWII – until his death in 1970. It is named after two historic *églises* (churches), one a parish church, the other a Cluniac priory.

Coachloads of (mostly older) French people flock here to visit CDG's home, La Boisserie (www.charles-de-gaulle.org; adult/child €4.50/3, incl Mémorial Charles de Gaulle €14.50/13; ⏱10am-12.30pm & 2-5.30pm daily), its furnishings unchanged since he was laid to rest in the village-centre cimetière (churchyard). Tours (English brochure available; price included in admission) begin at the ticket office, situated across D23 from the house, on the Colombey's southern edge.

The hill just north of town (on D619) is crowned by a 43.5m-high Croix de Lorraine (Lorraine Cross; erected 1972), symbol of France's WWII Resistance. Nearby is the impressive Mémorial Charles de Gaulle (http://memorial-charlesdegaulle.fr; adult/child €12.50/10, incl La Boisserie €14.50/13; ⏱9.30am-7pm daily May-Sep, 10am-5.30pm Wed-Mon Oct-Apr), opened in 2008, whose graphic, easily digestible exhibits, rich in photos, form an admiring biography of France's greatest modern statesman. Displays help visitors untangle such complicated mid-20th-century events as the Algerian war and the creation of the Fifth Republic, and consider the ways in which De Gaulle's years in power (1958–69) affected French culture, style and economic growth. Audioguides are available. The site affords breathtaking, sublime views of the Haute-Marne countryside.

Colombey-les-Deux-Églises is 72km east of Troyes along D619; taking A5 to exit 23 (88km) is a bit faster.

BAYEL
POP 868

Thanks to the Cristallerie Royale de Champagne (adult/child €6/3; ⏱9.30 & 11am Mon-Fri), established by a family of glassmakers from Murano, Italy, this quiet village has been a centre of crystal manufacture since 1678. To see the production process, take a factory tour. Tours are in French unless the group is predominantly English-speaking. For even more insight into how crystal is made, tie this in with a visit to the Musée du Cristal (Crystal Museum | Écomusée; adult/child €4/2, combined with tour €8/4; ⏱9.15am-6pm Mon-Fri, 9am-5.30pm Sat, 2-5.30pm Sun); a 15-minute film highlights the different stages involved

DON'T MISS

PARTY POPPER

If you're in the Côte des Bar on the first weekend in August, you're in luck, as this is when the region hosts the Route du Champagne en Fête (http://2012. routeduchampagne.com). A celebratory flute, which costs €15 and is sold at local tourist offices, is your ticket to free tastings at the caves ouvertes (open cellars) of more than 20 top Champagne houses. Exhibitions, live music, dinners and shows feature on the programme, which can be viewed in its entirety online.

in crystal production. For lovely but fragile gifts, head to the Cristalleries de Champagne outlet shop (⊙closed Sun).

Bayel is 11km southwest of Colombey-les-Deux-Églises.

ABBAYE DE CLAIRVAUX

Bernard de Clairvaux (1090–1153), nemesis of Abelard and preacher of the Second Crusade, founded this hugely influential Cistercian monastery (www.abbayedeclairvaux.com; adult €7/4; ⊙tours 11am & 2.30pm or 3pm, additional tours Wed-Sun Mar-Oct, closed Mon & Tue Nov-Feb) in 1115. Since the time of Napoléon, the complex has served as one of France's highest-security prisons. Past 'guests' have included Carlos the Jackal; two prisoners who staged a revolt here in 1971 were guillotined.

Several historic abbey buildings have recently been opened to the public. Tours take in some 12th-century structures, built in the austere Cistercian tradition, but more interesting is the half-abandoned, 18th-century Grand Cloître, where you can see collective 'chicken coop' cells (from the 1800s) and individual cells (used until 1971). For security reasons, visitors need to bring ID, mobile phones must be off, and photography is prohibited.

The abbey is on D396, 8km south of Bayel and 6km north of A5 exit 23.

ESSOYES
POP 716

It's easy to see why Renoir loved Essoyes, so much that he spent his last 25 summers here: it's one of the area's comeliest villages, with neat stone houses, a riverfront that glows golden in the late afternoon sun and landscapes of vineyards and flower-flecked meadows that unfold in a gentle, almost artistic way.

You can slip into the shoes of the great Impressionist on Essoyes' standout *circuit découverte*, a marked trail that loops around the village, taking in viewpoints that inspired the artist, the family home and the cemetery where he lies buried, his grave marked by a contemplative bronze bust. The trail begins at the Espace du Renoir (www.renoir-essoyes. fr; place de la Mairie, Renoir Centre; adult/child €8/4; ⊙10am-12.30pm & 1.30-6.30pm daily, closed Tue Oct-Mar), which also houses the tourist office (☑03 25 29 21 27; www.essoyes.fr; place de la Mairie, Renoir Centre; ⊙same hrs). Opened in 2011, the centre screens a 15-minute film about the artist and displays temporary exhibitions of mostly contemporary art. Marking the end of the tour and covered by the same ticket is the Atelier Renoir (Renoir's Studio; ⊙10am-12.30pm & 1.30-6.30pm daily, closed Tue Oct-Mar), with displays zooming in on the hallmarks of Renoir's work (the female form, the vibrant use of colour and light), alongside original pieces such as his antiquated wheelchair and the box he used to carry his paintings to Paris. Perhaps loveliest of all is the studio garden, particularly in spring to early summer when it bursts forth with tulips, anemones and roses.

Prettily set above the village, on the D67, the Hôtel des Canotiers (☑03 25 38 61 08; www.hoteldescanotiers.com; d/q €77/120, menus lunch/dinner €15/25-46; ❀☷) has 14 upbeat, spacious and practical rooms, each named after a famous Renoir canvas. The restaurant pairs well-executed regional dishes with local Champagnes.

Essoyes is 49km southeast of Troyes.

LES RICEYS
POP 1403

Running along both banks of the picturesque River Laigne, the commune of Les Riceys consists of three adjacent villages (Ricey-Bas, Ricey-Haute-Rive and Ricey-Haut) and is famous for its three churches, and for growing grapes belonging to three different AOC wines. Its best-known product is rosé des Riceys, an exclusive pinot noir rosé that can be made only in particularly sunny years and was a special favourite of Louis XIV. Annual production of this – when there is any – hovers around 65,000 bottles. Lots of Champagne wineries are nestled along and near D70.

For more information, including details on walking circuits through vine and vale, contact the tourist office (www.lesriceys -champagne.com; 14 place des Héros de la Résistance, Ricey-Haut; ⊙9am-noon & 2-5pm Thu-Tue).

Les Riceys is 47km southeast of Troyes and 18km southwest of Essoyes.

Alsace & Lorraine

Best Places to Eat

» Le Gavroche (p322)

» Au Trotthus (p332)

» L'Atelier du Peintre (p337)

» La Primatiale (p348)

» Le Bistro des Sommeliers (p353)

Best Places to Stay

» Maison de Myon (p347)

» Cour du Corbeau (p320)

» Chez Leslie (p335)

» Hôtel de la Cathédrale (p351)

Why Go?

Alsace is a one-off cultural hybrid. With its Germanic dialect and French sense of fashion, love of foie gras and *choucroute* (sauerkraut), fine wine *and* beer, this distinctive region often leaves you wondering quite where you are. Where are you? Why, in the land of living fairy tales of course, where vineyards fade into watercolour distance, hilltop castles send spirits soaring higher than the region's emblematic storks and half-timbered villages look fresh-minted for a Disney film set. If the locals' way with geraniums and pastels seems impossibly twee, take heart – beneath that oh-so-traditional exterior, your average Alsatian is an eccentric just itching to get out.

Lorraine has high culture and effortless grace thanks to its historic roll call of dukes and art nouveau pioneers, who had an eye for grand designs and good living. Its blessedly underrated cities, cathedrals and art collections leave visitors spellbound, while its WWI battlefields render visitors speechless time and again with their painful beauty.

When to Go
Strasbourgh

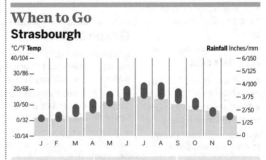

July Fireworks, street parties and cathedral illuminations at L'Été à Strasbourg.

September Toast the grape harvest with new wine and autumn colour on the Route des Vins d'Alsace.

December Mulled wine, gingerbread and carols galore at Christmas markets throughout Alsace.

BATTLEFIELDS

Take a guided walk of the WWI battlefields with Jean-Paul de Vries and be touched by the real-life stories of soldiers at Romagne '14-'18 (p359) near Verdun.

Fast Facts

» **Population** 4.2 million

» **Area** 31,827 sq km

» **Hotel overnights/yr** 9.5 million

» **Signature drinks** sylvaner white wine; Kronenbourg beer

Grand Designs

» Strasbourg's sublimely Gothic Cathédrale Notre-Dame (p316)

» The space-age curves of gleaming white Centre Pompidou-Metz (p350)

» Nancy's ever-so-grand neoclassical place Stanislas (p344)

» The light fantastic Cathédrale St-Étienne (p350) in Metz

» Vauban's star-shaped citadel in Neuf-Brisach (p340)

Resources

» Northern Alsace Tourism (www.tourisme67.com)

» Southern Alsace Tourism (www.tourisme68.com)

» Lorraine Tourism (www.tourism-lorraine.com)

Glorious Food & Wine

With its chocolate-box villages and lusciously green vineyards, Alsace doesn't only *look* good enough to eat. The Alsatians dine with French finesse and drink with German gusto, and every corner leads to mouth-watering surprises: shops doing a brisk trade in homemade foie gras, gingerbread and macarons; entire regions dedicated to cheese; mile upon glorious mile of country lanes given over to the life-sweetening pleasures of wine and chocolate. So take the lead of locals: go forth and indulge!

Kick-start your gourmet adventure by visiting www.tourisme-alsace.com and http://gastronomie.vins.tourisme-alsace.com. Local tourist boards can help you fine-tune your visit, be it a stay on a working dairy farm, a chocolate-tasting road trip or a *dégustation* (tasting) of *grand cru* (the official designation for superior or highest grade French wines) wines.

FOODIE TRAILS

Whether you're planning to get behind the wheel for a morning or pedal leisurely for a week through the vineyards, the picture-book Route des Vins d'Alsace (Alsace Wine Route) is a must. Swinging 170km from Marlenheim to Thann, the road is like a 'greatest hits' of Alsace, with its pastoral views, welcoming *caves* (wine cellars) and half-timbered villages. Go to www.alsace-route-des-vins.com to start planning.

Fancy some cheese to go with that wine? Head to Munster to taste the pungent, creamy *fromage* first made by Benedictine monks. The Munster tourist office can arrange farmstays and dairy tours.

Having polished off the cheese and wine, it would be rude not to pass the chocolates, not to mention the gingerbread and macarons, on the Route du Chocolat et des Douceurs d'Alsace, 200km of mmmm...

Grape & Grain

» Vignoble Klur (p334) is a friendly, family-run winery producing excellent organic wines. Linger for guided vineyard walks, Alsatian cookery classes and tastings.

» Cave de Ribeauvillé (p331), France's oldest winegrowers' cooperative, opens its doors for tastings of all seven varieties of Alsatian wine.

» Brasseries Kronenbourg (p320) sells 700 million litres of beer a year in France. Phone ahead for tours that include a, hic..., tasting.

» Cave des Hospices de Strasbourg (p320), deep below Strasbourg's hospital, has been curing all ills with its prized vintages since the 14th century.

» Domaine Gilg (p327), in the quaint village of Mittelbergheim, pops a cork on award-winning wines, including *grand cru* sylvaners, pinots and rieslings.

ALSACE

History

Though settled since prehistoric times and cultivated by the Celts in 1500 BC, it wasn't until the Romans arrived in 58 BC that Alsace really made the history books. Alsace formed part of Germania Superior in the Roman Empire, and the Romans made their mark building forts and camps such as Argentoratum (modern-day Strasbourg).

As the influence of the Roman Empire waned, the Alemanni (Germanic tribes from the Upper Rhine) seized power, bringing with them the dialect that forms the basis of present-day Alsatian, but they were soon ousted by Frankish Merovingians in the 5th century.

Under Charlemagne (742–814), the church gained influence and Alsace flourished. Over the following eight centuries, Alsace prospered as part of the Holy Roman Empire. Thanks to the imperial clout of the Hohenstaufen emperors, the 12th and 13th centuries signalled a golden age, with the rise of guilds and a prosperous merchant class, the expansion of towns and cities, and the construction of Romanesque churches. Alsace became a cradle of intellectual and artistic activity in the 15th century. The final stone was laid on its Gothic crowning glory, Strasbourg Cathedral, in 1439.

French influence in Alsace began during the Wars of Religion (1562–98) and increased during the Thirty Years War (1618–48). Most of the region was attached to France in 1648 under the Treaty of Westphalia.

By the time of the French Revolution, Alsatians felt more connected to France than to Germany, but time did little to dampen Germany's appetite for the region they called Elsass. When the Franco-Prussian War ended in 1871, an embittered France was forced to cede Alsace to the Kaiser. The region was returned to France following Germany's defeat in WWI but it was reannexed by Nazi Germany in 1940.

After WWII Alsace was once again returned to France. Intra-Alsatian tensions ran high, however, as 140,000 Alsatians – as annexed citizens of the Third Reich – had been conscripted into Hitler's armies. These conscripts were known as the 'Malgré-Nous' (literally 'despite ourselves') because the majority went to war against their will. To make Alsace a symbol of hope for future Franco-German (and pan-European) cooperation, Strasbourg was chosen as the seat of the

Council of Europe (in 1949) and, later, of the European Parliament.

The Mémorial de l'Alsace-Moselle (www.memorial-alsace-moselle.org; adult/child €10/8; ☺10am-6.30pm Tue-Sun), 50km southwest of Strasbourg in Schirmeck, takes an unblinking but reconciliatory look at the region's traumatic modern history, which saw residents change nationality four times in 75 years.

❶ Getting There & Around

BICYCLE Alsace is interwoven with bike trails. Bicycles can be taken on virtually all regional TER trains (but not SNCF buses).

CAR & MOTORCYCLE From Strasbourg, the A4 heads northwest towards Metz and Paris, while from Mulhouse the A36 goes southwest towards the Jura and Dijon. The A31 connects Metz and Nancy with Luxembourg to the north and Dijon to the south. The Massif des Vosges gets snowy in winter so winter tyres and/or chains may be required.

TRAIN & BUS TER regional trains and TGV high-speed trains make up the region's fast and efficient rail network. Getting between major towns and cities is straightforward, but train services thin out in rural Alsace, where small towns and villages are connected by just a handful of buses, often making getting around by car a quicker, easier option.

Those aged 12 to 25 can get 50% off on all regional rail travel with an annual Tonus Alsace pass (€16). The great-value Réflexe Alsace ticket, available for those aged 26 and over, costs €26 for a year and gets you a 30% discount on travel on weekdays and a huge 70% reduction at weekends.

Strasbourg

POP 276,136

Strasbourg is the perfect overture to all that is idiosyncratic about Alsace – walking a fine tightrope between France and Germany and between a medieval past and a progressive future, it pulls off its act in inimitable Alsatian style.

Tear your gaze away from that mesmerising Gothic cathedral for just a minute and you'll be roaming the old town's twisting alleys lined with crooked half-timbered houses à la Grimm; feasting in the cosiest of *winstubs* (Alsatian taverns) by the canalside in Petite France; and marvelling at how a city that does Christmas markets and gingerbread so well can also be home to the glittering EU Quarter and France's second-largest

Alsace & Lorraine Highlights

1 Saunter around canal-laced **Petite Venise** (p334) as Colmar starts to twinkle

2 Get a gargoyle's-eye view of Strasbourg from the platform of Gothic **Cathédrale Notre-Dame** (p316)

3 Survey the cross-studded **Verdun Battlefields** (p357) in the early morning silence

4 Be amazed by art-nouveau and rococo grace in **Nancy** (p344)

5 Gaze across the vines from the giddy heights of medieval **Château du Haut Kœnigsbourg** (p330)

6 Wish for luck (or lots of babies!) spotting storks in **Hunawihr** (p331)

7 Immerse yourself in modern art at the architecturally innovative **Centre Pompidou-Metz** (p350)

8 Tiptoe through the enchanting forests of the misty **Vosges** (p339) mountains

9 Go dairy-hopping in the verdant **Vallée de Munster** (p339)

10 Save the storybook lanes of half-timbered **Riquewihr** (p331) until dusk

THE LOCAL LINGO

The roots of Alsatian (Elsässisch; see www.heimetsproch.org, in French and German) go back to the 4th century, when Germanic Alemanni tribes assimilated the local Celts (Gauls) and Romans. Similar to the dialects spoken in nearby Germany and Switzerland, it has no official written form (spelling is something of a free-for-all) and pronunciation varies considerably. Yet despite heavy-handed attempts by the French and Germans to impose their language on the region by restricting (or even banning) Alsatian, you'll still hear it used in everyday life by people of all ages, especially in rural areas.

student population. But that's Strasbourg for you: all the sweeter for its contradictions and cross-cultural quirks.

History

Founded by the Merovingians in the 5th century, Strasbourg was long an important trade centre on the route between northern Europe and the Mediterranean. The city was ruled by democratic guilds in medieval times, when the cathedral, once the highest in Christendom, was built between 1015 and 1439. Johannes Gutenberg developed the first printing press with moveable type here in 1450.

Strasbourg witnessed the Reformation in the 16th century, the founding of its university in 1567 and the debut of *La Marseillaise* (the French national anthem) in 1792. Over ensuing centuries, the city ping-ponged between France and Germany. Strasbourg's prominent place in Europe's heart was confirmed when it became the seat of the Council of Europe in 1949 and of the European Parliament in 1992.

⊙ Sights

TOP CHOICE **Cathédrale Notre-Dame**   CATHEDRAL
(place de la Cathédrale; astronomical clock adult/child €2/1.50, platform adult/child €5/2.50; ⊙7am-7pm; astronomical clock tickets sold from 11.45am, platform 9am-7.15pm; 🚋Langstross) Victor Hugo declared it a 'gigantic and delicate marvel'; Goethe professed that its 'loftiness is linked to its beauty'; and, no matter the angle or time of day, you too will be capti-

vated by Strasbourg's centrepiece Gothic cathedral. At once immense and intricate, the red-sandstone cathedral is a riot of filigree stonework and flying buttresses, leering gargoyles and lacy spires.

The west facade, most impressive if approached from rue Mercière, was completed in 1284, but the 142m spire – the tallest of its time – was not in place until 1439; its southern companion was never built.

On a sunny day, the 12th- to 14th-century stained-glass windows – especially the rose window over the western portal – shine like jewels. To appreciate the cathedral in peace, visit in the early evening when the crowds have thinned and stay to see its façade glow gold at dusk.

The 30m-high Gothic-meets-Renaissance astronomical clock strikes solar noon at 12.30pm with a parade of carved wooden figures portraying the different stages of life and Jesus with his apostles.

A spiral staircase twists up to the 66m-high platform above the facade, from which the tower and its Gothic openwork spire soar another 76m. As Hugo put it: 'From the belfry, the view is wonderful. Strasbourg lays at your feet, the old city of tiled triangular roof tops and gable windows, interrupted by towers and churches as picturesque as those of any city in Flanders.'

Grande Île   HISTORIC QUARTER
(🚋Langstross) History seeps through the twisting lanes and cafe-rimmed plazas of Grande Île, Strasbourg's Unesco World Heritage–listed island bordered by the River Ill. These streets – with their photogenic line-up of wonky, timber-framed houses in sherbet colours – are made for aimless ambling. They cower beneath the soaring magnificence of the cathedral and its sidekick, the gingerbready 15th-century **Maison Kammerzell** (rue des Hallebardes), with its ornate carvings and leaded windows. The alleys are at their most atmospheric when lantern-lit at night.

Petite France   HISTORIC QUARTER
Criss-crossed by narrow lanes, canals and locks, Petite France is where artisans plied their trades in the Middle Ages. The half-timbered houses, sprouting veritable thickets of scarlet geraniums in summer, and the riverside parks attract the masses, but the area still manages to retain its Alsatian atmosphere and charm, especially in the early morning and late evening.

Drink in views of the River Ill and the mighty 17th-century Barrage Vauban (Vauban Dam), undergoing renovation at the time of writing, from the much-photographed Ponts Couverts (Covered Bridges) and their trio of 13th-century towers.

Musée d'Art Moderne et Contemporain
ART MUSEUM

(www.musees.strasbourg.org; place Hans Jean Arp; adult/child €7/free; ☺noon-7pm Tue, Wed & Fri, noon-9pm Thu, 10am-6pm Sat & Sun, Art Café Tue-Sun; ⊞Musée d'Art Moderne) This striking glass-and-steel cube showcases an outstanding collection of fine art, graphic art and photography. Kandinsky, Picasso, Magritte and Monet canvases hang out alongside curvaceous works by Strasbourg-born abstract artist Hans Jean Arp. Find details on temporary exhibitions on the website.

Don't leave without enjoying a drink at the glass-fronted Art Café, graced by bold frescoes by Japanese artist Aki Kuroda. The terrace commands terrific views of the River Ill and Petite France.

Palais Rohan
HISTORIC RESIDENCE

(2 place du Château; adult/child €6/free; ☺noon-6pm Mon & Wed-Fri, 10am-6pm Sat & Sun; ⊞Langstross) Hailed a 'Versailles in miniature', this opulent 18th-century residence was built for the city's princely bishops, and Louis XV and Marie-Antoinette once slept here.

The basement Musée Archéologique takes you from the Palaeolithic period to AD 800. On the ground floor is the Musée des Arts Décoratifs, where rooms adorned with Hannong ceramics and gleaming silverware evoke the lavish lifestyle of the nobility in the 18th century. On the 1st floor, the Musée des Beaux-Arts' collection of 14th- to 19th-century art reveals El Greco, Botticelli and Flemish Primitive works.

Musée de l'Œuvre Notre-Dame
ECCLESIASTICAL MUSEUM

(www.musees.strasbourg.org; 3 place du Château; adult/child €6/free; ☺10am-6pm Tue-Sun, to 8pm Thu; ⊞Langstross) Occupying a cluster of sublime 14th- and 16th-century buildings, this museum harbours one of Europe's premier collections of Romanesque, Gothic and Renaissance sculptures (including many originals from the cathedral), plus 15th-century paintings and stained glass. *Christ de Wissembourg* (c 1060) is the oldest work of stained glass in France.

Hollywood gore seems tame compared to the tortures back when Hell really was hell.

Sure to scare you into a life of chastity is *Les Amants Trépassés* (the Deceased Lovers), painted in 1470, showing a grotesque couple being punished for their illicit lust: both of their entrails are being devoured by dragon-headed snakes.

Musée Historique
HISTORY MUSEUM

(www.musees.strasbourg.org; 2 rue du Vieux Marché aux Poissons; adult/child €6/free; ☺noon-6pm Tue-Fri, 10am-6pm Sat & Sun; ⊞Langstross) Trace Strasbourg's history from its beginnings as a Roman military camp called Argentoratum at this engaging museum housed in a 16th-century slaughterhouse. Highlights include a famous painting of the first-ever performance of *La Marseillaise,* France's stirring national anthem, which – despite its name – was written in Strasbourg in 1792; a 1:600-scale model of the city, created in the 1720s to help Louis XV visualise the city's fortifications; and a Gutenberg Bible from 1485. Kids can try on medieval-style knights' helmets and touch ancient pots and 18th-century cannons.

Musée Alsacien
FOLK MUSEUM

(www.musees.strasbourg.org; 23 quai St-Nicolas; adult/child €6/free; ☺noon-6pm Mon & Wed-Fri, 10am-6pm Sat & Sun; ⊞Porte de l'Hôpital) Spread across three typical houses from the 1500s and 1600s, this museum affords a fascinating glimpse into Alsatian life over the centuries. Kitchen equipment, children's toys, colourful furniture and even a tiny 18th-century synagogue are on display in the museum's two dozen rooms.

Musée Tomi Ungerer
MUSEUM

(www.musees.strasbourg.org; 2 av de la Marseillaise; adult/child €6/free; ☺noon-6pm Mon & Wed-Fri, 10am-6pm Sat & Sun; ⊞République) A tribute to one of Strasbourg's most famous sons – award-winning illustrator and cartoonist Tomi Ungerer – this museum, just northeast of Grande Île, is housed in the fetching Villa Greiner. The collection discloses the artist's love of dabbling in many genres, from children's book illustrations to satirical drawings and erotica.

Place de la République
CITY SQUARE

(⊞République) Many of Strasbourg's grandest public buildings, constructed when the city was ruled by the German Reich, huddle northeast of Strasbourg's Grande Île area around place de la République. The neighbourhood that stretches eastwards to Parc de l'Orangerie is dominated by sturdy stone

ALSACE & LORRAINE STRASBOURG

Strasbourg

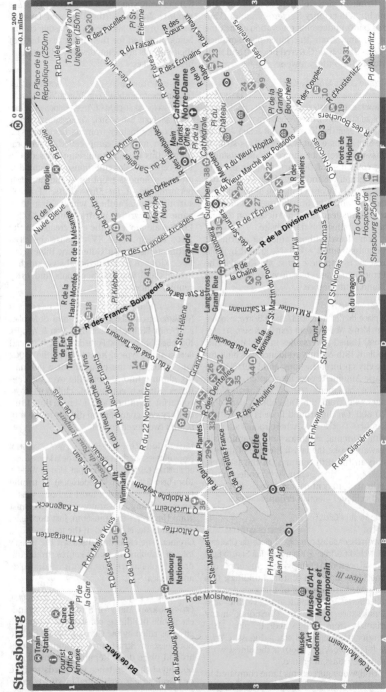

200 m
0.1 miles

To Place de la
République (250m)

To Musée Tomi
Ungerer (150m)

Train Station
Gare
Centrale

Tourist
Office
Annexe

Bd de Metz

Homme
de Fer
Tram Hub

R des Pucelles
Pl St-
Étienne

R Brûlée

R du Faisan

R des
Sœurs

R des Frères

R des Écrivains

Q des Bateliers

Cathédrale
Notre-Dame

R de la
Râpe

Pl d'Austerlitz

R des Couples

R d'Austerlitz

Pl de la
Grande
Boucherie

Pl du
Château

R des Bouchers

Porte de
l'Hôpital

R du Dôme

R des Hallebardes

Main
Tourist
Office

Pl de la
Cathédrale

R du Vieux Hôpital

R du Vieux Marché aux Poissons

R Mercière

R des
Tonneliers

Q St-Nicolas

Q des Hallebardes

R du Sanglier

Broglie
Pl Broglie

R des Orfèvres

Pl
Gutenberg

R du
Vieux Marché aux Vins

R de la
Nuée Bleue

R de la Mésange

R d'Outre

Pl du
Marché
Neuf

R des Grandes Arcades

R Gutenberg

Grande
Île

R des Serruriers

R de l'Épine

R de la Division Leclerc

R de l'Ail

Q St-Thomas

To Cave des
Hospices de
Strasbourg (250m)

R du Dragon

R de la
Chaîne

R de la
Haute Montée

Pl Kléber

R des Francs-Bourgeois

R Ste-Barbe

Langstross
Grand Rue

R de
la Chaine

R de la
Monnaie

R St-Martin du Pont

R Salzmann

R M Luther

Pont
St-Thomas

Q St-Thomas

R Finkwiller

R des Glacières

R du Fossé des Tanneurs

R Ste-Hélène

Grand'R

R des Dentelles

R du Bouclier

Homme
de Fer
Tram Hub

R de la
Haute Montée

R du 22 Novembre

R du Jeu des Enfants

R du Vieux Marché aux Vins

Quai St-Jean

Passage du pont Rempart

Q Desaix

Alt
Winmärik

Q Adolphe Seyboth

Q Turckheim

R du Bain aux Plantes

Petite
France

R des Moulins

R Kuhn

R Kageneck

R Thiergarten

R du Maire Kuss

R Déserte

R de la Course

Faubourg
National

R Ste-Marguerite

Q Altorffer

R du Bain aux Plantes

Pl de
la Gare

Musée d'Art
Moderne et
Contemporain

Pl Hans
Jean Arp

River III

Musée
d'Art
Moderne

R de Molsheim

R du Faubourg National

R de Moisheim

Tourist
Office

Strasbourg

buildings inspired by late-19th-century Prussian tastes.

Parc de l'Orangerie PARK
(zoo admission free; 🚇Droits de l'Homme) Across from the Council of Europe's Palais de l'Europe, 2km northeast of Grande Île, this flowery park, designed in the 17th century by Le Nôtre of Versailles fame, is a family magnet with its playgrounds and swan-dotted lake. In summer you can rent row boats on Lac de l'Orangerie. Kids can get up close to storks and goats at the park's mini zoo.

Le Vaisseau SCIENCE MUSEUM
(www.levaisseau.com; 1bis rue Philippe Dollinger; adult/child €8/7; ⊙10am-6pm Tue-Sun; 🚇Winston Churchill) Science is *never* boring at this interactive science and technology museum,

2.5km southeast of central Strasbourg. There are plenty of hands-on activities to amuse little minds, from crawling through an ant colony to creating cartoons and broadcasting the news.

Jardin des Deux Rives GARDEN
(Two-Shores Garden; 🚇Aristide Briand) An expression of flourishing Franco-German friendship, Strasbourg and its German neighbour Kehl have turned former customs posts and military installations into this 60-hectare garden, whose play areas, promenades and parkland straddle both banks of the Rhine. The centrepiece is Marc Mimram's sleek (and hugely expensive) suspension bridge, which has proved a big hit with pedestrians and cyclists. From the

tram stop, walk east or take bus 21 for three stops. It is 3km southeast of central Strasbourg (Grande Île).

River Ill   RIVERFRONT
(🚋Langstross) The leafy paths that shadow the River Ill and its canalised branch, the Fossé du Faux Rempart, are great for an impromptu picnic or a romantic stroll.

Place Gutenberg   CITY SQUARE
(🚋Langstross) Well worth a peek for its Renaissance-style Chambre de Commerce (Chamber of Commerce).

👉 Tours

Take a DIY spin of Strasbourg's cathedral and the old city with one of the tourist office's 1½-hour audio guides (adult/child €5.50/2.75), available in five languages.

Batorama   BOAT TOUR
(www.batorama.fr; rue de Rohan; adult/child €9.20/4.80; ⏱tours half-hourly 9.30am-7pm, hourly 8-10pm; 🚋Langstross) This outfit runs scenic 70-minute boat trips, which glide along the storybook canals of Petite France, taking in the Vauban Dam and the glinting EU institutions. Tours depart on Rue de Rohan, the quay behind Palais Rohan.

FREE Cave des Hospices
de Strasbourg   WINERY
(www.vins-des-hospices-de-strasbourg.fr; 1 place de l'Hôpital; ⏱8.30am-noon & 1.30-5.30pm Mon-Fri,

9am-12.30pm Sat; 🚋Porte de l'Hôpital) Founded in 1395, this brick-vaulted wine cellar nestles deep in the bowels of Strasbourg's hospital. A hospice back in the days when wine was considered a cure for all ills, today the cellar bottles first-rate Alsatian wines from rieslings to sweet muscats. One of its historic barrels is filled with a 1472 vintage. Take tram A or D to Porte de l'Hôpital. From here it is a three-minute walk south on Rue d'Or.

Brasseries Kronenbourg   BREWERY
(📞03 88 27 41 59; www.brasseries-kronenbourg.com; 68 rte d'Oberhausbergen; adult/child €6/4.50; ⏱tours 1.30pm Tue-Sat; 🚋Ducs d'Alsace) Selling 700 million litres of beer in France every year – enough to fill about 250 Olympic swimming pools! – this brewery is in Cronenbourg, 2.5km northwest of Strasbourg's Grande Île. Call ahead to join a thirst-quenching 1½-hour tour (some in English), which includes a tasting. Take tram A to Ducs d'Alsace. From here it is a five-minute walk north along Rue des Ducs and Route d'Oberhausbergen.

🎉 Festivals & Events

Mulled wine, spicy *bredele* (biscuits) and a Santa-loaded children's village are all part and parcel of Strasbourg's sparkly Marché de Noël (Christmas Market; www.noel.strasbourg.eu), running from the last Saturday in November until 31 December. Strasbourg slides into summer with fireworks, fairs and striking cathedral illuminations at L'Été à Strasbourg (www.ete.strasbourg.eu) from late June to August. Raise a glass to Alsatian beer at October's Mondial de la Bière (www.mondialbierestrasbourg.com) and wine at the Riesling du Monde (www.portail-vins-du-monde.com) in mid-April.

🛏️ Sleeping

It can be tricky to find last-minute accommodation from Monday to Thursday when the European Parliament is in plenary session (see www.europarl.europa.eu for dates). Book ahead for December when beds are at a premium because of the Christmas market. The tourist office can advise about same-night room availability; if you drop by, staff are happy to help reserve a room.

Cour du Corbeau   BOUTIQUE HOTEL €€€
(📞03 90 00 26 26; www.cour-corbeau.com; 6-8 rue des Couples; r €190-330; ❄️@🖥; 🚋Porte de l'Hôpital) A 16th-century inn lovingly converted into a boutique hotel, Cour du Corbeau

wins you over with its half-timbered charm and location, just steps from the river. Gathered around a courtyard, rooms blend original touches like oak parquet and Louis XV furnishings with mod cons like flat-screen TVs.

Hôtel du Dragon HOTEL €€
(03 88 35 79 80; www.dragon.fr; 12 rue du Dragon; s € 84-159, d €92-159; @🛜; 🚇Porte de l'Hôpital) Step through a tree-shaded courtyard and into the, ahhh...blissful calm of this bijou hotel. The Dragon receives glowing reviews for its crisp interiors, attentive service and prime location near Petite France.

Hôtel Régent Petite France DESIGN HOTEL €€
(03 88 76 43 43; www.regent-hotels.com; 5 rue des Moulins; r €159-460; ❋@🛜; 🚇Alt Winmärik) Once an ice factory and now Strasbourg's hottest design hotel, this waterfront pile is quaint on the outside and ubercool on the inside. The sleek rooms dressed in muted colours and plush fabrics sport shiny marble bathrooms. Work your relaxed look in the sauna, chic restaurant and Champagne bar with dreamy River Ill views.

Hôtel Gutenberg HISTORIC HOTEL €€
(03 88 32 17 15; www.hotel-gutenberg.com; 31 rue des Serruriers; r €85-170; ❋@🛜; 🚇Langstross) Nestled in the flower-strewn heart of Petite France, this hotel is a harmonious blend of 250 years of history and contemporary design, combining clean lines, zesty colours and the occasional antique.

Romantik Hôtel Beaucour HISTORIC HOTEL €€
(03 88 76 72 00; www.hotel-beaucour.com; 5 rue des Bouchers; s €77-112, d €139-169; ❋@🛜; 🚇Porte de l'Hôpital) With its antique flourishes and a cosy salon centred on a fireplace, this place positively oozes half-timbered romance. Rooms are stylishly decked out in warm colours and florals, and most feature (like it!) jacuzzi bathtubs.

Hôtel Hannong BOUTIQUE HOTEL €€
(03 88 32 16 22; www.hotel-hannong.com; 15 rue du 22 Novembre; s €69-119, d €79-178; ❋🛜; 🚇Alt Winmärik) Minimalist chic best describes the rooms at this design-focused hotel, kitted out with hardwood floors and colour schemes ranging from space-age silver to chocolate cream. The skylit lounge bar serves tapas and fine wines.

Hôtel Suisse HOTEL €€
(03 88 35 22 11; www.hotel-suisse.com; 2-4 rue de la Râpe; s €68-95, d €77-105; @🛜; 🚇Langstross) Tucked away in a charming corner of Grande Île, this lemon-fronted hotel exudes Alsatian authenticity with its beams, chandeliers and traditional rooms decorated with solid wood furnishings. Often full.

Hôtel Le Colmar HOTEL €
(03 88 32 16 89; www.hotel-lecolmar.com; 1 rue du Maire Kuss; r with/without shower €43/38; 🚇Gare Centrale) Sandwiched between Petite France and the train station, this central, no-frills hotel is a bargain. The high-ceilinged rooms are bright, clean and generously proportioned, though some beds are so springy they are borderline trampoline. Corner rooms look out across the river.

Royal Lutetia HOTEL €€
(03 88 35 20 45; www.royal-lutetia.fr; 2bis rue du Général Rapp; s €72-80, d €82-90; 🛜; 🚇Parc du Contades) A 10-minute stroll north of the centre, this recently revamped hotel has bright and spacious rooms with above-par perks such as flatscreen TVs and free wi-fi.

DON'T MISS

BIENVENUE CHEZ LES EUROCRATS

Should the inner workings of the EU intrigue, you can sit in on debates ranging from lively to yawn-a-minute at the Parlement Européen (European Parliament; www.europarl.europa.eu; rue Lucien Fèbvre; 🚇Parlement Européen); dates are available from the tourist office or on the website. For individuals it's first come, first served (bring ID).

A futuristic glass crescent, the Council of Europe's Palais de l'Europe (Palace of Europe; 03 88 41 20 29; www.coe.int; 🚇Droits de l'Homme) across the River Ill can be visited on free one-hour weekday tours; phone ahead for times and reservations.

It's just a hop across the Canal de la Marne to the swirly silver Palais des Droits de l'Homme (European Court of Human Rights; www.echr.coe.int; 🚇Droits de l'Homme), the most eye-catching of all the EU institutions.

The EU buildings sit 2km northeast of Grande Île (central Strasbourg), close to Parc de l'Orangerie.

EAT ALSATIAN

Here's what is probably cooking in the kitchen of that cosy *winstub* (Alsatian tavern):

» **Baeckeoffe** Beef, pork, lamb, vegetable and potato stew, marinated in riesling or pinot blanc and slow-cooked in a ceramic dish.

» **Choucroute garnie** Sauerkraut garnished with salty bacon, ham hock and Alsatian-style sausage. Bring an appetite.

» **Fleischnacka** Herby minced beef and egg pasta rolls shaped like *schnacka* (snails).

» **Flammekueche** (*tarte flambée* in French) A thin-crust pizza dough topped with crème fraîche, onions and lardons. Fingers are allowed!

» **Kougelhopf** Brioche-style raisin cake, baked in its namesake mould, with a hole in the middle and a dusting of icing sugar.

» **Lewerknepfle** Ground liver, shallot and parsley quenelles (dumplings).

» **Spätzle** Thick egg noodles, usually served with onions and/or cheese.

» **Wädele** Pork knuckles, often braised in pinot noir or beer and served with lashings of *choucroute*.

Le Kléber Hôtel
HOTEL €€

(☑03 88 32 09 53; www.hotel-kleber.com; 29 place Kléber; r €62-95; 🖥; 🚇Homme de Fer) So what will sweeten your dreams tonight? Pistachio, Pavlova or maybe Meringue? Highly original and supercentral, Le Kléber's rooms are named and decorated after fruits, spices and other calorific treats – pick one to suit your taste.

Hôtel Au Cerf d'Or
HISTORIC HOTEL €€

(☑03 88 36 20 05; www.cerf-dor.com; 6 place de l'Hôpital; s €70-99, d €85-115; ❈🖥📶; 🚇Porte de l'Hôpital) A golden *cerf* (stag) hangs proudly out front at this half-timbered Logis de France hotel, with simple, spotless rooms. Best of all it has a jacuzzi, a swimming pool, a sauna (half-hour €8) and a homely French restaurant.

✖ Eating

Restaurants abound on Grande Île: try canalside Petite France for Alsatian fare and half-timbered romance; Grand' Rue for curbside kebabs and *tarte flambée;* and rue des Veaux or rue des Pucelles for hole-in-the-wall eateries serving the world on a plate. Stepping across the river, pedestrianised rue d'Austerlitz is lined with patisseries and bistros.

Le Gavroche
MEDITERRANEAN €€

(☑03 88 36 82 89; www.restaurant-gavroche.com; 4 rue Klein; menu €38; ⏱Mon-Fri; 🖥; 🚇Porte de l'Hôpital) Bistro food is given a pinch of creativity and southern sunshine at intimate, softly lit Le Gavroche. Mains like veal in a mint crust with crispy polenta and coriander-

infused artichoke tagine are followed by zingy desserts like lime tart with lemon-thyme sorbet. There's a menu for *les petits.*

Kobus
BISTRO €€

(☑03 88 32 59 71; www.restaurantkobus.com; 7 rue des Tonneliers; lunch/dinner menus €19.50/39.50; ⏱Tue-Sat; 🚇Langstross) Graphic artworks lend a contemporary feel to this stone-walled bistro. The menu goes with the seasons, be it rich, earthy wild mushroom risotto in autumn or herb-crusted spring lamb. The €19.50 lunch includes a main, glass of wine and *café gourmand* (coffee with an array of bite-sized desserts).

Umami
FUSION €€€

(☑03 88 32 80 53; 8 rue des Dentelles; menus €37-60; ⏱lunch Sat, dinner Mon-Sat; 🚇Langstross) Simplicity is the ethos at Michelin-starred Umami, loosely translatable as 'savoury', the fifth taste in Japanese cuisine. A clean-lined, art-strewn bistro sets the scene for taste sensations like escargots tossed in Thai herbs and served with a red curry jus, and tender veal sliding into a black mushroom risotto.

Le Stras'
INTERNATIONAL €

(☑03 88 35 34 46; 9 rue des Dentelles; mains €19-24; ⏱Tue-Sat; 🚇Langstross) The chef puts an innovative spin on seasonal ingredients at this beamed, gallery-style bistro in Petite France. It's a terrific choice for an intimate dinner. Med-infused dishes such as swordfish samosas with nut and endive salad and scallop-Parma ham rolls flambéed in pastis are expertly matched with Alsatian wines.

Bistrot et Chocolat
CAFE €

(www.bistrotetchocolat.net; 8 rue de la Râpe; snacks €5-8, brunch €10-26; ⊙11am-7pm Tue-Fri, 10am-7pm Sat & Sun; 🖼🐾; 🚇Langstross) This boho-flavoured bistro is hailed for its solid and liquid organic chocolate (ginger is superb). The terrace is a local hangout for light bites like tofu tapas, wok dishes and weekend brunches. The website has details on children's cooking classes.

La Cloche à Fromage
TRADITIONAL FRENCH €€

(☎03 88 23 13 19; www.cheese-gourmet.com; 27 rue des Tonneliers; fondue €24-28; 🚇Langstross) *Au revoir* diet. Loosen a belt notch or three for Strasbourg's gooiest fondues and *raclette* at this temple to *fromage* (cheese), saving an inch for the 200-variety cheese board of *Guinness Book of World Records* fame.

Au Crocodile
GASTRONOMIC €€€

(☎03 88 32 13 02; www.au-crocodile.com; 10 rue de l'Outre; lunch menus €38-69, dinner menu €94-143; ⊙Tue-Sat; 🚇Broglie) This hushed temple of French gastronomy is named after a stuffed toothy critter brought back from Egypt by one of Napoléon's generals. Artistically presented seasonal specialities like fillet of venison served on date leaves with oyster plant and root vegetable puree have won Au Crocodile a Michelin star.

Au Petit Tonnelier
FUSION €€

(☎03 88 32 53 54; www.aupetittonnelier.com; 16 rue des Tonneliers; menus €33, mains €17.50-22; 🚇Langstross) Look for the wellies in the window of this slick, monochromatic bistro. On the menu: specialities like octopus ceviche-style and beef millefeuille with onion compote and *gratin dauphinois* (thinly sliced potatoes baked slowly with cream and melted cheese) – all skilfully cooked and presented. Occasionally hosts live jazz and blues.

L'Assiette du Vin
BISTRO €€

(☎03 88 32 00 92; www.assietteduvin.fr; 5 rue de la Chaîne; menus €26-50; ⊙closed lunch Mon, Sat & Sun; 🚇Langstross) Market-fresh cuisine with a twist, discreet service and an award-winning wine list lure discerning foodies to this rustic-chic bistro in the old town. The *plat du jour* (dish of the day) is a snip at €8.50.

La Cambuse
SEAFOOD €€

(☎03 88 22 10 22; 1 rue des Dentelles; mains €23-27; ⊙Tue-Sat; 🚇Langstross) Michelin-starred dining has a maritime flavour at La Cambuse, with its portholes, brass lamps and polished wood interior. The experimental chef infuses seafood with Asian spices in dishes like fish *choucroute* (sauerkraut) with saffron and monkfish with shitake mushrooms.

Maison des Tanneurs
ALSATIAN €

(☎03 88 32 79 70; 42 rue du Bain aux Plantes; mains €16-22; ⊙Tue-Sat; 🚇Alt Winmärik) Even locals book ahead at this former tannery, creaking under the weight of its 16th-century beams and billowing geraniums. *Choucroute* with fat pork knuckles and garlicky Alsatian-style escargot are matched with top-notch pinots and rieslings. Snag a window table for fine views of Petite France's canals.

Au Coin des Pucelles
ALSATIAN €€

(☎03 88 35 35 14; 12 rue des Pucelles; mains €14-24; ⊙dinner Tue-Sat; 🚇Broglie) Snug *winstub* with just six tables, serving solid Alsatian fare such as *choucroute au canard*.

La Tinta
CAFE €

(36 rue du Bain aux Plantes; brunch & lunch menus €9.90-10.90; ⊙Tue-Sat; 🚇Alt Winmärik) Boho-flavoured literary cafe for a gourmet salad, fresh-pressed juice or tea and cake.

Poêles de Carottes
VEGETARIAN €

(2 place des Meuniers; mains €10-12; ⊙Tue-Sat; 🖼; 🚇Langstross) Laid-back cafe dishing up wholesome veggie fare from organic soups to aubergine cordon bleu.

La Cloche à Fromage Boutique
DELICATESSEN

(32 rue des Tonneliers; 🚇Langstross) Sells creamy Tomme, ripe Camembert and other first-rate cheeses.

Farmers' Market
FOOD MARKET

(place du Marché aux Poissons; ⊙7am-1pm Sat; 🚇Porte de l'Hôpital) Stalls are piled high with everything from locally produced foie gras to organic fruit and honey.

🍺 Drinking

Strasbourg's beer-thirsty students keep the scene lively and the bars and clubs pumping at weekends. Among the city's legions of pubs and bars is a glut of student-oriented places on the small streets east of the cathedral such as rue des Juifs, rue des Frères and rue des Sœurs.

Jeannette et les Cycleux
BAR

(www.lenetdejeannette.com; 30 rue des Tonneliers; 🎵; 🚇Langstross) Elvis lives on, baby, at this swinging '50s-themed haunt, where classic motorbikes dangle from the chilli-red walls.

ALSACE & LORRAINE STRASBOURG

We dig the good vibes, retro decor and music from rockabilly to Motown.

Académie de la Bière   PUB
(17 rue Adolphe-Seyboth; ⊗11am-4am; 🔊; 🚇Alt Winmärik) Get the beers in at this chilled Petite France pub before a boogie in the cellar disco. There are hundreds of brews on offer, from Kronenbourg to *krieks* (Belgian beers fermented with sour cherries).

Bar Exils   BAR
(28 rue de l'Ail; 🚇Langstross) This is student central, with darts and billiards, well-worn sofas and plenty of cheap beer on tap.

☆ Entertainment

Cultural event listings appear in the free monthly publication, Spectacles (www.spectacles-publications.com), available at the tourist office.

Boutique Culture   TICKET OUTLET
(place de la Cathédrale, cnr rue Mercière; ⊗Tue-Sat; 🚇Langstross) Ticket outlet for cultural events.

Fnac Billetterie   TICKET OUTLET
(www.fnacspectacles.com; 22 place Kléber, 2nd fl; ⊗Mon-Sat; 🚇Homme de Fer) Ticket outlet for cultural events.

La Laiterie   LIVE MUSIC
(www.laiterie.artefact.org; 11-13 rue du Hohwald; 🚇Laiterie) Reggae, metal, punk, chanson, blues – Strasbourg's premier concert venue covers the entire musical spectrum and stages some 200 gigs a year. Tickets are available at the door and online. La Laiterie is just a five-minute walk (500m) south of Petite France along rue de Molsheim.

L'Artichaut   LIVE MUSIC
(www.lartichaut.fr; 56 Grand' Rue; ⊗Tue-Sun; 🔊; 🚇Langstross) The 'artichoke' is the city's quirkiest arts and culture cafe, hosting free exhibitions, first-rate jazz concerts and jam sessions. The line-up is posted on the door and on the website.

Le Seven   CLUB
(www.lesevenstrasbourg.com; 25 rue des Tonneliers; ⊗Wed-Sat) Hip hop and house dominate the decks at this club, which heaves with students. As its name suggests, it stays open until 7am.

Odyssée   CINEMA
(www.cinemaodyssee.com; 3 rue des Francs-Bourgeois; 🚇Langstross) An art-house cinema.

🔒 Shopping
Strasbourg's swishest shopping street is rue des Hallebardes, whose window displays are real eye candy (luxury crystal brand Baccarat is at No 44). High-street shops punctuate rue des Grandes Arcades and Grand' Rue, while Petite France is crammed with souvenir shops selling stuffed storks and pretzels aplenty. For vintage furniture, hip accessories and works by local creatives, mosey down rue des Veaux.

DON'T MISS

PASS THE CHOCOLATE

Strasbourg is now sweeter than ever, as it's one of the main stops on La Route du Chocolat et des Douceurs d'Alsace (Alsace Chocolate and Sweets Road), stretching 80km north to Bad Bergzabern and 125km south to Heimsbrunn near Mulhouse. Pick up a map at the tourist office to pinpoint Alsace's finest patisseries, chocolatiers, macaron shops and confectioners. The following are three sweet-toothed Strasbourg favourites to get you started.

» Mireille Oster (www.mireille-oster.com; 14 rue des Dentelles; 🚇Langstross) Cherubs adorn this heavenly shop where Strasbourg's *pain d'épices* (gingerbread) fairy Mireille Oster tempts with handmade varieties with figs, amaretto, cinnamon and chocolate. Have a nibble before you buy.

» Christian (www.christian.fr; 12 rue de l'Outre; 🚇Broglie) Sumptuous truffles, pralines and florentines, weightless macarons and edible Strasbourg landmarks – renowned chocolatier Christian's creations are mini works of art.

» Coco LM (www.coco-lm.com; 16 rue du Dôme; 🚇Broglie) Bakes scrumptious Alsatian gingerbread, *beerawecka* (Alsatian fruit cake), raisin-stuffed *kougelhopf* and a startlingly spicy ginger biscuit called a *gingerli*.

ℹ Information

A cluster of places offer discount calls and internet access (around €2) around Quai St-Jean near the train station.

Main Tourist Office (☏03 88 52 28 28; www.otstrasbourg.fr; 17 place de la Cathédrale; ⊙9am-7pm daily; ▣Langstross) A city-centre walking map with English text costs €1; bus/tram and cycling maps are free. *Strolling in Strasbourg* (€4.50) details six architectural walking tours.

Tourist Office Annexe (⊙9am-7pm daily; ▣Gare Centrale) In the train station's southern wing.

ℹ Getting There & Away

Air

Strasbourg's international **airport** (www.strasbourg.aeroport.fr) is 17km southwest of the city centre (towards Molsheim), near the village of Entzheim. The airport is served by major carriers such as Air France, KLM and Iberia. Flights link Strasbourg to European cities including Amsterdam, Madrid, Vienna, and domestic destinations like Paris, Nice, Lille and Lyon.

Ryanair links London Stansted with **Karlsruhe/Baden-Baden airport** (www.badenairpark.de), across the Rhine in Germany, 58km northeast of Strasbourg.

Bus

The **Eurolines office** (www.eurolines.com; 6D place d'Austerlitz; ▣Porte de l'Hôpital) is a few blocks southeast of Grande Île; their buses use a **bus stop** (▣Lycée Couffignal) 2.5km further south on rue du Maréchal Lefèbvre (facing the Citroën garage).

Strasbourg city bus 21 (€1.60) links the Aristide Briand tram terminus with Kehl, the German town just across the Rhine.

Car & Motorcycle

The following rental companies have offices in the south wing of the train station:

» **Avis** (www.avis.com)

» **Europcar** (www.europcar.com)

» **National-Citer** (www.citer.fr)

» **Sixt** (www.sixt.com)

Train

Built in 1883, the Gare Centrale was given a 120m-long, 23m-high glass facade and underground galleries in order to welcome the new TGV Est Européen in grand style. On the Grande Île, tickets are available at the **SNCF Boutique** (www.voyages-sncf.com; 5 rue des Francs-Bourgeois; ▣Langstross).

INTERNATIONAL If you take the Eurostar via Paris or Lille, London is just five hours and 15 minutes away. Cities with direct services include the following:

» **Basel SNCF** €22, 1¼ hours, 25 daily

» **Brussels-Nord** €74, 5¼ hours, three daily

» **Karlsruhe** €25, 40 minutes, 16 daily

» **Stuttgart** €47, 1¼ hours, four TGVs daily

DOMESTIC Destinations within France:

» **Paris** Gare de l'Est; €71, 2¼ hours, 19 daily

» **Lille** €115, four hours, 17 daily

» **Lyon** €71, 4½ hours, 14 daily

» **Marseille** €161, 6¾ hours, 16 daily

» **Metz** €24.50, two hours, 20 daily

» **Nancy** €24, 1½ hours, 25 daily

From Strasbourg, there are trains to Route des Vins destinations including the following:

» **Colmar** €11.50, 30 minutes, 30 daily

» **Dambach-la-Ville** €8.50, one hour, 12 daily

» **Obernai** €6, 30 minutes, 20 daily

» **Sélestat** €8.30, 30 minutes, 46 daily

ℹ Getting Around

TO/FROM THE AIRPORT A speedy shuttle train links the airport to the train station (€3.80, nine minutes, four hourly); the ticket also covers your onward tram journey into the city centre.

Flight Liner Buses (www.flightliner.de) Flight Liner buses link Place de l'Etoile in Strasbourg with Karlsruhe/Baden Baden airport (€18, one hour), across the Rhine. Bus times are coordinated with Ryanair's London services.

BICYCLE A world leader in bicycle-friendly planning, Strasbourg has an extensive and ever-expanding *réseau cyclable* (cycling network). The tourist office stocks free maps.

The city's 24-hour, self-rental **Vélhop** (www.velhop.strasbourg.eu) system can supply you with a bike (per hour/day €1/5). Pay by card and receive a code to unlock your bike. Helmets are not available. There are 11 automatic rental points plus outlets including the following:

» **City Centre** (3 rue d'Or; ▣Porte de l'Hôpital)

» **Train Station** (▣Gare Centrale) Situated on Level -1. Adjacent is an 820-place bicycle parking lot (€1 for 24 hours).

» **Rotonde** (▣Rotonde)

CAR & MOTORCYCLE Virtually the whole city centre is either pedestrianised or a hopeless maze of one-way streets, so don't even think of getting around Grande Île by car, or parking there for more

MUSÉE LALIQUE

A stunning and romantic tribute to French art nouveau designer René Lalique, the Musée Lalique (www.musee-lalique.com; Rue du Hochberg, Wingen-sur-Moder; adult/child €6/3; ⊙10am-7pm daily, closed Mon Oct-Mar) opened on the site of the former Hochberg glassworks in July 2011. A visit affords wonderful insight into how Lalique drew on sinuous, naturalistic forms (flowers, insects, foliage) as well as the curvaceous female form in his work. The collection assembles exquisite gem-encrusted and enamelled jewellery, perfume bottles, stoppers and sculpture. Complementing it are flower and wooded gardens, making the connection, as Lalique did, between art and the natural world.

Located in the Northern Vosges, 60km north of Strasbourg, the museum can easily be visited on a half-day trip by taking the train to Wingen-sur-Moder (€9.50, 40 minutes). Alternatively, it's around an hour's drive.

than a couple of hours. For details on city-centre parking garages see www.parcus.com.

At Strasbourg's eight P+R (park-and-ride) car parks, all on tram routes, the €3.10 all-day fee, payable from 7am to 8pm, gets the driver and each passenger a free return tram or bus ride into the city centre. From the autoroute, follow the signs marked 'P+R Relais Tram'. The safest picks are north of the city centre at Rives de l'Aar, northwest at Rotonde and south at Baggersee.

PUBLIC TRANSPORT Five superefficient tram lines, A through E, form the backbone of Strasbourg's outstanding public transport network, run by **CTS** (www.cts-strasbourg.fr). The main tram hub is Homme de Fer. Trams generally operate until 12.30am; buses – few of which pass through Grande Île – run until about 11pm. Night buses operate from 11.30pm to 5.30am on Fridays and Saturdays, stopping at nightlife hot spots.

Tickets, valid on both buses and trams, are sold by bus drivers and ticket machines at tram stops and cost €1.60 (€3 return). The 24h Individuel (for one person €4) and Trio (for two to three people €5.70) tickets, valid for 24 hours from the moment they are stamped, are sold at tourist offices and tram stops.

In our Strasbourg listings, the nearest tram stops are indicated with a tram icon (🚋).

Route des Vins d'Alsace

Green and soothingly beautiful, the Route des Vins d'Alsace (Alsace Wine Route) is one of France's most evocative drives. Vines march up the hillsides to castle-topped crags and the mist-enshrouded Vosges, and every mile or so is a roadside *cave* (wine cellar) or half-timbered village inviting you to stop, raise a glass and enjoy. Corkscrewing through glorious countryside, the entire route stretches 170km from Marlenheim,

21km west of Strasbourg, southwards to Thann, 46km southwest of Colmar.

Local tourist offices can supply you with the excellent English-language map and brochure *The Alsace Wine Route* (free), and *Alsace Grand Cru Wines,* detailing Alsace's 50 most prestigious Appellation d'Origine Contrôlée (AOC) winegrowing microregions. More information is available online at www.alsace-route-des-vins.com.

The villages mentioned in the following section, listed from north to south, all have plenty of hotels and restaurants, and some have campgrounds. Tourist offices can provide details on local *chambres d'hôte* (B&Bs), which generally cost €40 to €60 for a double.

👉 Tours

For minibus tours of the Route des Vins try these agencies:

LCA Top Tour   BUS TOUR
(✆03 89 41 90 88; www.alsace-travel.com; 8 place de la Gare, Colmar; half-day €56-59) Reservations can be made via Colmar's tourist office. Most tours depart from the office on place de la Gare.

Regioscope   BUS TOUR
(✆03 89 44 38 21; www.regioscope.com; morning/afternoon tour €50/75) Departures are from the tourist office, or your hotel, in Strasbourg.

ⓘ Getting There & Around

The Route des Vins comprises several minor, lightly trafficked roads (D422, D35, D18 and so on). It is signposted but you might want to pick up a copy of Blay's colour-coded map *Alsace Touristique* (€5.50). Cyclists have a wide variety of on- and off-road options (p339), which wend through some highly scenic countryside. Bike hire is available in all the major towns and cities. Expect to pay around €10 per day.

BUS & TRAIN It's entirely possible, if a bit cumbersome, to get around the Route des Vins by public transport, since almost all the towns and villages mentioned here are served by train from Strasbourg or by train and/or bus from Colmar. Bicycles can be taken on virtually all trains. A handy website for checking regional bus connections and timetables is www.vialsace.eu.

CAR & MOTORCYCLE Driving is undoubtedly the quickest and easiest way to reach villages and small towns on the Route des Vins, and the meandering country roads make for a memorable road trip. Car hire is available at airports and in major cities. Parking can be a nightmare in the high season, especially in Ribeauvillé and Riquewihr; your best bet is to park a bit out of the town centre and walk for a few minutes.

OBERNAI
POP 11,321

A vision of half-timbered, vine-draped, ring-walled loveliness, the wine-producing town of Obernai sits 31km south of Strasbourg. Give the summertime crowds the slip by ducking down cool, flower-bedecked alleyways, such as ruelle des Juifs, next to the tourist office.

Sights & Activities

A number of winegrowers have cellars a short walk from town (the tourist office has a map).

Place du Marché TOWN SQUARE
Life spirals around this market square, put to use each Thursday morning, where you'll find the 16th-century hôtel de ville (town hall building) embellished with baroque trompe l'œil; the Renaissance Puits aux Six Seaux (Six Bucket Well) just across rue du Général Gouraud; and the bell-topped, 16th-century Halle aux Blés (Corn Exchange).

Ramparts CITY WALL
Stretch your legs by strolling around Obernai's 13th-century ramparts, accessible from the square in front of twin-spired, neo-Gothic Église St-Pierre et St-Paul.

Sentier Viticole du Schenkenberg WALKING
This 1.5km wine route meanders through vineyards and begins at the hilltop cross north of town; to get there, follow the yellow signs from the cemetery behind Église St-Pierre et St-Paul.

Sleeping & Eating

Le Gouverneur HISTORIC HOTEL €€
(03 88 95 63 72; www.hotellegouverneur.com; 13 rue de Sélestat; s €55-80, d €60-90, tr €70-100, q

€80-110; @) Overlooking a courtyard, this old-town hotel strikes perfect balance between half-timbered rusticity and contemporary comfort. Its petit rooms have a boutiquey feel, with bursts of vivid colour and art-slung walls. The family-friendly team can provide cots and highchairs free of charge.

Winstub La Dîme ALSATIAN €
(03 88 95 54 02; 5 rue des Pélerins; menus €12-22; closed Wed) Precisely as an Alsatian *winstub* should be: beamed and bustling with diners tucking into earthy dishes like fat pork knuckles and *zweibelkuchen* (onion tart).

La Fourchette des Ducs GASTRONOMIC €€€
(03 88 48 33 38; www.lafourchettedesducs.com; 6 rue de la Gare; menus €95-130; dinner Tue-Sat, lunch Sun) Chef Nicolas Stamm adds a pinch of imagination to Alsatian ingredients and serves them with gourmet panache to a food-literate crowd at this two Michelin-starred restaurant.

Information
Tourist Office (03 88 95 64 13; www.obernai.fr; place du Beffroi; 9am-12.30pm & 2-6pm Mon-Sun) Tucked behind the hôtel de ville.

Getting There & Away
The train station is about 300m east of the old town. There are at least hourly TER train connections from Obernai to Colmar (€8.60, 70 minutes) and Strasbourg (€6, 30 minutes).

MITTELBERGHEIM
POP 675

Serene, untouristy and set on a hillside, Mittelbergheim sits amid a sea of sylvaner grapevines and seasonal wild tulips, its tiny streets lined with sand-hued, red-roofed houses.

Sights & Activities
Each of Mittelbergheim's *caves* (wine cellars) has an old-fashioned, wrought-iron sign hanging out front.

Sentier Viticole WALKING
From the car park on the D362 at the upper edge of the village next to the cemetery, a vineyard trail wriggles across the slopes towards the perky twin-towered Château du Haut Andlau and the lushly forested Vosges.

Domaine Gilg WINERY
(www.domaine-gilg.com; 2 rue Rotland; 8am-noon & 1.30-6pm Mon-Fri, to 5pm Sat, 9.30-11.30am Sun) Nip into this friendly, family-run winery

START MARLENHEIM
FINISH COLMAR
DISTANCE 87KM
DURATION ONE TO TWO
DAYS

Driving Tour
Route des Vins d'Alsace

❯ Weaving through lyrical landscapes, this
road trip takes in the best of the vine-
strewn Route des Vins d'Alsace.

From the Route des Vins gateway,
1 Marlenheim, a well-marked country lane,
wriggles through bucolic scenery to medieval
2 Molsheim, centred on a picture-perfect
square dominated by the step-gabled Renaissance *Metzig* (butcher's shop). Continue
south to **3 Rosheim**, where the striking
Romanesque Église St-Pierre-St-Paul raises
eyebrows with its, ahem, lasciviously copulat-
ing gargoyles! Step inside for a moment of
contemplation before meandering south to
pretty, half-timbered **4 Obernai** to explore
the market square and vineyard trail. Views
of the Vosges unfold as you head south to
the sleepy hamlet of **5 Mittelbergheim**,
pausing to taste the local *grand cru* wines
at award-winning Domaine Gilg. Even higher
peaks slide into view as you cruise south
to cellar-studded **6 Dambach-la-Ville**,
embraced by ancient town walls, and catch
your first tantalising glimpse of the turrets of
hilltop **7 Château du Haut Kœnigsbourg**.
After detouring for an astounding panorama
from the castle ramparts, slip back in time
roaming cobbled streets in half-timbered
8 Bergheim and enchanting tower-speck-
led **9 Ribeauvillé**. Stork lovers' hearts are
set aflutter at the Centre de Réintroduction
Cigognes & Loutres in nearby **10 Hunawihr**.
Set aside time for serendipitous strolls and
medieval towers galore in the storybook half-
timbered village of **11 Riquewihr**. Contemplate glass-blowing magic and the house of
Nobel Peace Prize winner Albert Schweitzer
in riverside **12 Kaysersberg**, then wend your
way south to little-known **13 Katzenthal** for
organic wine tasting at Vignoble Klur. Wrap
up your tour with culture and *winstub* (Alsatian tavern) dining in canal-laced **14 Colmar**,
Alsatian wine capital and birthplace of Statue
of Liberty creator Frédéric Auguste Bartholdi.

to taste award-winning wines, including *grand cru* sylvaners, pinots and rieslings.

Sleeping & Eating

Private accommodation is good value and easy to come by – you'll see signs in windows all over town. For information, see www.pays-de-barr.com.

Hôtel Gilg   HISTORIC HOTEL €
(☑03 88 08 91 37; www.hotel-gilg.com; 1 rte du Vin; s €55-65, d €60-90, menus €32-72) For a dose of old-fashioned romance, check into this 17th-century half-timbered pile. A spiral staircase leads up to spacious rooms in pretty pastels, some with wooden beams. The elegantly rustic restaurant serves classic French and Alsatian cuisine.

DAMBACH-LA-VILLE
POP 1996

Ringed by vines and sturdy ramparts, this flowery village has some 60 *caves* (wine cellars) but manages to avoid touristic overload. The renowned Frankstein *grand cru* vineyards cover the southern slopes of four granitic hills west and southwest of Dambach.

Sights & Activities

Some of the eye-catching half-timbered houses, painted in ice-cream colours like pistachio, caramel and raspberry, date from before 1500.

Ramparts   CITY WALL
A gentle stroll takes in the 14th-century, pink-granite ramparts, originally pierced by four gates, three still holding aloft watchtowers and bearing quintessentially Alsatian names: Ebersheim, Blienschwiller and Dieffenthal.

Sentier Viticole du Frankstein   WALKING
It's a pleasant 1½-hour walk through the vineyards on this trail, which begins 70m up the hill from the tourist office on rue du Général de Gaulle. The path meanders among the hallowed vines, passing by hillside Chapelle St-Sébastien (☺9am-7pm), known for its Romanesque tower and Gothic choir.

Sleeping

Le Vignoble   HISTORIC HOTEL €
(☑03 88 92 43 75; www.hotel-vignoble-alsace.fr; 1 rue de l'Église; s/d €60/70; ⓐ) Housed in a beautifully converted 18th-century barn, this hotel has comfortable wood-beamed rooms in fresh lemon and lime hues. It's well situated in the village centre.

Information

Tourist Office (☑03 88 92 61 00; www.pays-de-barr.com; ☺10am-noon & 2-5pm Mon-Fri, 10am-noon Sat) In the Renaissance-style *hôtel de ville*. Hands out walking tour and has details on cycling to Itterwiller.

Getting There & Away

The train station is about 1km east of the old town. Dambach-la-Ville has hourly services to Sélestat (€2, 10 minutes), Colmar (€6.10, 40 minutes) and Strasbourg (€8.50, one hour).

SÉLESTAT
POP 19.677

Wedged between Strasbourg, 50km to the north, and Colmar, 23km to the south, Sélestat is an enticing jumble of colourful half-timbered houses and church spires. The town's claim to cultural fame is its incomparable Humanist Library.

Sights

Bibliothèque Humaniste   LIBRARY
(1 rue de la Bibliothèque; adult/child €4.20/2.70; ☺9am-noon & 2-6pm Mon & Wed-Fri, 9am-noon Sat) Founded in 1452, the Humanist Library's stellar collection features a 7th-century book of Merovingian liturgy, a copy of *Cosmographiae Introductio* (printed in 1507), in which the New World was referred to as 'America' for the first time, and the first written mention of the Christmas tree (1521).

Vieux Sélestat   HISTORIC QUARTER
Church spires rise gracefully above the red rooftops of the old town, which hugs the left bank of the River Ill. Some of the finest examples of half-timbered and trompe-l'œil buildings can be found along the medieval quai des Tanneurs.

Église St-Georges   CHURCH
(place St-Georges; ☺8am-6pm) One of Alsace's most striking churches, this Gothic giant, built from weighty red sandstone and sporting a colourful mosaic-tile roof, is illuminated by curtains of stained glass in the choir.

Montagne des Singes   PARK
(www.montagnedessinges.com; Kintzheim; adult/child €8.50/5; ☺10am-noon & 1-6pm, closed Dec-Mar) Kids love to feed the free-roaming Barbary macaques and their cheeky infants popcorn (special monkey popcorn, of course) at this 6-acre woodland park. Take the D35 to Kintzheim, 7km west of Sélestat.

WORTH A TRIP

NATZWEILER-STRUTHOF

About 25km west of Obernai stands Natzweiler-Struthof (www.struthof.fr; adult/child €6/3; ⊙9am-6.30pm, closed Christmas-Feb), the only Nazi concentration camp on French territory. In all, 40%, or some 22,000, of the total number of prisoners interned here and at nearby annexe camps died; many were shot or hanged. In early September 1944, as US Army forces approached, the 5517 surviving inmates were sent to Dachau.

Today, the sombre remains of the camp are still surrounded by guard towers and concentric, once-electrified, barbed-wire fences. The four crématoire (crematorium ovens), the salle d'autopsie (autopsy room) and the chambre à gaz (gas chamber), 1.7km from the camp gate, bear grim witness to the atrocities committed here. The nearby Centre Européen du Résistant Déporté (⊙9am-6.30pm, closed Christmas-Feb) pays homage to Europe's Resistance fighters.

To get there from Obernai, take the D426, D214 and D130; follow the signs to 'Le Struthof'.

Marché   MARKET
(⊙8am-1pm Tue) A huge outdoor market, held since 1435, takes over the streets around Romanesque Église St-Foy.

Marché du Terroir   MARKET
(place Vanolles; ⊙8am-noon Sat) Local-produce market, on the southern edge of the old town, selling home-grown fruit and veggies.

❶ Information

Tourist Office (☑03 88 58 87 20; www. selestat-tourisme.com; bd du Général Leclerc; ⊙9am-noon & 2-5.45pm Mon-Fri, 9am-noon & 2-5pm Sat) On the edge of the town centre, two blocks from the Bibliothèque Humaniste.

❶ Getting There & Around

The tourist office rents out **bicycles** (two hours/ half-day/day €7/9/14; deposit €150) from June to October.

The train station is 1km west of the Bibliothèque Humaniste. Train is the fastest way to reach destinations including Strasbourg (€8.30, 20 minutes, twice hourly), Colmar (€4.70, 11 minutes, hourly) and Obernai (€4.90, 33 minutes, hourly).

HAUT KŒNIGSBOURG

On its fairy-tale perch above vineyards and hills, the turreted red-sandstone Château du Haut Kœnigsbourg (www.haut-koenigsbourg. fr; adult/child €8/free; ⊙9.15am-5.15pm) is worth the detour for the wraparound panorama from its ramparts, taking in the Vosges, the Black Forest and, on cloud-free days, the Alps. Audioguides delve into the turbulent 900-year history of the castle, which makes a very medieval impression despite having been reconstructed, with German imperial pomposity, by Kaiser Wilhelm II in 1908.

BERGHEIM
POP 1940

Enclosed by a sturdy 14th-century ring wall, overflowing with geraniums and enlivened by half-timbered houses in shocking pastels, Bergheim is a joy to behold. But things have not always been so cheerful: overlords, stampeding invaders, women burnt at the stake for witchcraft – this tiny village has seen the lot.

A stroll through the cobbled streets of the well-preserved medieval centre takes in the early Gothic church, the wall-mounted sundial at 44 Grand' Rue dating from 1711, and the imposing, turreted Porte Haute, Bergheim's last remaining town gate. Outside across the park sits the gnarled Herrengarten linden tree, planted around 1300. A 2km path circumnavigates the town's ramparts. Bergheim's *grands crus* labels are Kanzlerberg and Altenberg de Bergheim.

The tiny tourist office (☑03 89 73 31 98; ⊙9.30-noon & 2-6pm Mon-Sat, 10am-1pm Sun) is between the 18th-century hôtel de ville and the deconsecrated Ancienne Synagogue (rue des Juifs), now a cultural centre.

Just inside the Porte Haute, La Cour du Bailli (☑03 89 73 73 46; www.cour-bailli.com; 57 Grand' Rue; r €86-122, menus €20-31; ☒) is draped around a 16th-century courtyard. The countrified studios and apartments all have kitchenettes. Factor in downtime in the pool and stone-built spa, which pampers with luscious vinotherapy treatments. The atmospheric cellar restaurant serves wine-drenched specialities like *coq au riesling*. There's no lift so be prepared to lug your bags.

RIBEAUVILLÉ
POP 4979

Nestled snugly in a valley, presided over by a castle, its winding alleys brimming with half-timbered houses – medieval Ribeauvillé is a Route des Vins must. The local *grands crus* are Kirchberg de Ribeauvillé, Osterberg and Geisberg.

◉ Sights & Activities

Vieille Ville HISTORIC QUARTER
Along the main street that threads through the old town keep an eye out for the 17th-century Pfifferhüs (Fifers' House; 14 Grand' Rue), which once housed the town's fife-playing minstrels; the hôtel de ville and its Renaissance fountain; and the nearby, clock-equipped Tour des Bouchers (Butchers' Bell Tower).

FREE Cave de Ribeauvillé WINERY
(2 rte de Colmar; ⊙8am-noon & 2-6pm Mon-Fri, 10am-12.30pm & 2.30-7pm Sat & Sun) France's oldest winegrowers' cooperative, founded in 1895, has a viniculture museum, informative brochures and free tastings of its excellent wines, made with all seven of the grape varieties grown in Alsace. On weekends it's staffed by local winegrowers. It's just across two roundabouts north from the tourist office.

Castle Ruins WALK
West and northwest of Ribeauvillé, the ruins of three 12th- and 13th-century hilltop castles – St-Ulrich (530m), Giersberg (530m) and Haut Ribeaupierre (642m) – can be reached on a hike (three hours return) beginning at place de la République (at the northern tip of Grand' Rue).

⊨ Sleeping & Eating

Hôtel de la Tour HISTORIC HOTEL €€
(☎03 89 73 72 73; www.hotel-la-tour.com; 1 rue de la Mairie; s €72-96, d €78-104; ☎) Ensconced in a stylishly converted winery, this half-timbered hotel has quaint and comfy rooms, some with views of the Tour des Bouchers.

Camping Municipal Pierre de Coubertin CAMPGROUND €
(☎03 89 73 66 71; 23 rue Landau; sites €16.50; ☎) This shady campground, with bike and canoe rental and a playground, is 500m east of the town centre.

TOP CHOICE Auberge du Parc Carola INTERNATIONAL €€
(☎03 89 86 05 75; www.auberge-parc-carola.com; 48 rte de Bergheim; lunch menus €17-20, dinner menus €26.50-58; ⊙closed Tue & Wed) Quaint on the outside, slick on the inside, this auberge is all about surprises, not least much-lauded chef Michaela Peters behind the stove. Flavours ring clear and true in seasonal show-stoppers like acacia honey-glazed suckling pig with artichoke hearts and wild garlic polenta. Tables are set up under the trees in summer.

❶ Information

Tourist Office (☎03 89 73 23 23; www.ribeau ville-riquewihr.com; 1 Grand' Rue; ⊙9.30am-noon & 2-6pm Mon-Sat, 10am-1pm Sun) At the southern end of one-way Grand' Rue.

❶ Getting There & Away

A fairly frequent service runs from Ribeauvillé's central bus station to Route des Vins destinations including Colmar (€3.80, 25 minutes) and Riquewihr (€2.50, 13 minutes). Timetables are available online at www.vialsace.eu.

HUNAWIHR
POP 620

You're absolutely guaranteed to see storks in the quiet walled hamlet of Hunawihr, 1km south of Ribeauvillé. On a hillside just outside the centre, the 16th-century fortified church has been a *simultaneum* – serving both the Catholic and Protestant communities – since 1687.

About 500m east of Hunawihr, the delightful Centre de Réintroduction Cigognes & Loutres (Stork & Otter Reintroduction Centre; www.cigogne-loutre.com; adult/child €9/6; ⊙10am-6.30pm, closed mid-Nov–Mar) is home base for 200 free-flying storks; visit in spring to see hatchlings. Cormorants, penguins, otters and sea lions show off their fishing prowess several times each afternoon.

Stroll among exotic free-flying butterflies at the Jardins des Papillons (www.jardinsdes papillons.fr; adult/child €7.50/5; ⊙10am-6pm, closed Nov-Easter), nearby the Centre de Réintroduction Cigognes & Loutres.

Bus 106 runs between Hunawihr and Colmar (€3.80, 33 minutes).

RIQUEWIHR
POP 1273

Competition is stiff but Riquewihr is, just maybe, *the* most enchanting town on the Route des Vins. Medieval ramparts enclose its walkable centre, a photogenic maze of twisting lanes, hidden courtyards and half-timbered houses – each brighter and lovelier than the next. Of course, its chocolate-box looks also make it popular, so arrive in the

ALSACE & LORRAINE ROUTE DES VINS D'ALSACE

STORKS OF ALSACE

White storks (cigognes), prominent in local folklore, are Alsace's most beloved symbols. Believed to bring luck (as well as babies), they winter in Africa and then spend summer in Europe, feeding in the marshes and building twig nests on church steeples and rooftops.

In the mid-20th century, environmental changes reduced stork numbers catastrophically. By the early 1980s only two pairs were left in the wild, so research and breeding centres were set up to establish a year-round Alsatian stork population. The program has been a huge success and today Alsace is home to more than 400 pairs – some of which you are bound to spot (or hear bill-clattering) on the Route de Vins.

early morning or evening to appreciate the town at its peaceful best.

Sights & Activities

Dolder HISTORIC SITE
(admission €3, incl Tour des Voleurs €5; ⊙2-6pm Sat & Sun Apr-Nov, daily Jul–mid-Aug) This late 13th-century stone and half-timbered gate, topped by a 25m bell tower, is worth a look for its panoramic views and small local-history museum.

Tour des Voleurs HISTORIC SITE
(Thieves' Tower; admission €3, incl Dolder €5; ⊙10.30am-1pm & 2-6pm Easter–1 Nov) Rue des Juifs (site of the former Jewish quarter) leads down the hill to this medieval stone tower. Inside is a gruesome torture chamber with English commentary and an old-style winegrower's kitchen.

Maison de Hansi MUSEUM
(16 rue du Général de Gaulle; adult/child €2/free; ⊙10am-12.30pm & 1.30-6pm daily, closed Tue Feb-Jun, Jan) Peer into the imagination of celebrated Colmar-born illustrator Jean-Jacques Waltz (1873–1951), aka Hansi, whose idealised images of Alsace are known around the world. On display are the artist's posters, children's books, engravings and even wine labels.

Sentier Viticole des Grands Crus WALKING
A yellow-marked 2km trail takes you out to acclaimed local vineyards, Schœnenbourg (north of town) and Sporen (southeast of

town), while a 15km trail with red markers takes you to five nearby villages. Both trails can be picked up next to Auberge du Schœnenbourg, 100m to the right of the hôtel de ville.

Sleeping & Eating

Sugary smells of traditional macarons and coconut macaroons – a tradition since coconuts were first brought here in the 1700s – waft through the centre, where you'll find confectioners, winstubs and bakeries selling humongous pretzels.

Hôtel de la Couronne HISTORIC HOTEL €
(☎03 89 49 03 03; www.hoteldelacouronne.com; 5 rue de la Coronne; s €52-66, d €59-120; ☎) With its 16th-century tower and wisteria, this central choice is big on old-world character. Rooms are country-style with crisp floral fabrics, low oak beams and period furnishings; many have views over the rooftops to the hills beyond. There's no lift.

Le Sarment d'Or HISTORIC HOTEL €
(☎03 89 86 02 86; http://riquewihr-sarment-dor.fr; 4 rue du Cerf; d €60-80, tr €90, menus €26-37) Yes, you'll have to schlep your bags up a spiral staircase, but frankly it's a small price to pay for staying at this 17th-century, rose-tinted abode. Rooms are simple with a dash of rusticity, and the restaurant serves regional food cooked with precision and finesse.

Au Trotthus MODERN FRENCH €€
(☎03 89 47 96 47; www.trotthus.com; 9 rue des Juifs; lunch menus €18, dinner menus €26-37; ⊙lunch & dinner Mon & Thu-Sun, dinner Tue, closed Wed) Lodged in a 16th-century winemakers' house, this snug wood-beamed restaurant is overseen by a chef with exacting standards. The market-driven menu might include such delicacies as slow-cooked pork cheeks with argan oil and cabbage-filled spring rolls.

Table du Gourmet GASTRONOMIC €€€
(☎03 89 49 09 09; www.jlbrendel.com; 5 rue de la Première Armée; menus €38-98; ⊙lunch & dinner Mon & Fri-Sun, dinner Thu, closed Tue & Wed) Jean-Luc Brendel is the culinary force behind this Michelin-starred venture. A 16th-century house given a Zen makeover forms the backdrop for specialities prepared with home-grown herbs and vegetables that sing with intense, natural flavours.

Information
Tourist Office (☎03 89 73 23 23; www.ribeauville-riquewihr.com; 2 rue de la Première

Armée; ☺9.30am-noon & 2-6pm Mon-Sat, 10am-1pm Sun) In the centre of the old town.

❶ Getting There & Around

Bus 106 runs several times daily from Riquewihr to Ribeauvillé (€2.50, 18 minutes) and Colmar (€3.05, 25 minutes).

KAYSERSBERG
POP 2773

Kaysersberg, 10km northwest of Colmar, is an instant heart-stealer with its backdrop of gently sloping vines, hilltop castle and 16th-century fortified bridge spanning the gushing River Weiss.

◉ Sights & Activities

Audioguides of the town (1½ to two hours, €5) are available from the tourist office.

Vieille Ville   HISTORIC QUARTER

An old-town saunter brings you to the ornate Renaissance hôtel de ville and the red-sandstone Église Ste Croix (☺9am-4pm), whose altar has 18 painted haut-relief panels of the Passion and the Resurrection. Out front, a Renaissance fountain holds aloft a statue of Emperor Constantine.

Musée Albert Schweitzer   MUSEUM

(126 rue du Général de Gaulle; adult/child €2/1; ☺9am-noon & 2-6pm Easter–early Nov) The house where the musicologist, medical doctor and 1952 Nobel Peace Prize winner Albert Schweitzer (1875–1965) was born is now this museum, with exhibits on the good doctor's life in Alsace and Gabon.

Sentiers Viticoles   WALKING

(☺two hours) Footpaths lead in all directions through glens and vineyards. A 10-minute walk above town, the remains of the massive, crenulated Château de Kaysersberg stand surrounded by vines; other destinations include Riquewihr and Ribeauvillé (four hours). These paths begin through the arch to the right as you face the entrance to the hôtel de ville.

⌂ Sleeping

Hôtel Constantin   HOTEL €

(☑03 89 47 19 90; www.hotel-constantin.com; 10 rue du Père Kohlmann; d €62-78; ☏) Originally a winegrower's house in the heart of the old town, this hotel has 20 clean and modern rooms with wood furnishings.

❶ Information

Tourist Office (☑03 89 71 30 11; www.kaysersberg.com; 37 rue du Général de Gaulle; ☺9am-12.30pm & 2-6pm Mon-Sat, 9am-12.30pm Sun; ☏) Inside the hôtel de ville; supplies walking-tour brochures as well as hiking and cycling maps, and makes bookings free of charge. You can log on to free internet and wi-fi here.

❶ Getting There & Away

Bus 145 runs several times daily between Kaysersberg and Colmar (€3.50, 30 minutes).

ALSACE & LORRAINE ROUTE DES VINS D'ALSACE

LOCAL KNOWLEDGE

FRANCINE KLUR, VIGNOBLE KLUR

Alsatian Wine

There's an Alsatian wine for every occasion. Try a light, citrusy sylvaner with *tarte flambée* or foie gras, or a crisp, dry riesling with fish or *choucroute* (sauerkraut). Gewürztraminer is round and full of exotic fruit and spices, making it the ideal partner for Munster cheese, charcuterie and Asian food. Muscat is aromatic and flowery – great with asparagus or as an aperitif. Pick full-bodied pinot noirs for red meat.

Route des Vins

The Route des Vins is different from France's other wine regions because the villages are small and tight-knit, making it easy for visitors to get acquainted with our wine, food and culture. There are no grand châteaux but there *is* a real neighbourly feel – our doors are always open.

Insider Tips

Take a day to stroll or cycle through the vineyards, stopping for a wine tasting, lunch and to simply enjoy the atmosphere. Visit famous villages like Riquewihr and Ribeauvillé in the evening to have the streets to yourself. My favourite seasons are autumn, when the heady scent of new wine is in the air, and spring, when the cherry trees are in bloom.

KATZENTHAL
POP 564

Close-to-nature Katzenthal, 5km south of Kaysersberg, is great for tiptoeing off the tourist trail for a while. *Grand cru* vines ensnare the hillside, topped by the medieval ruins of Château du Wineck, where walks through forest and vineyard begin.

Organic, family-run winery Vignoble Klur (03 89 80 94 29; www.klur.net; 105 rue des Trois Epis; apt €90-150, min 3-night stay) is a relaxed choice for tastings, Alsatian cookery classes and vineyard walks. The light-drenched, well-equipped apartments are great for back-to-nature holidays, and you can unwind in the organic sauna after a long day's walking and wine tasting.

Colmar
POP 68,843

Alsace wine region capital, Colmar looks for all the world as though it has been plucked from the pages of a medieval folk tale. At times the Route des Vins d'Alsace fools you into thinking it's 1454, but here, in the alley-woven heart of the old town, the illusion is complete. Half-timbered houses in chalk-box colours crowd dark, cobblestone lanes and bridge-laced canals, which have most day-trippers wondering around in a permanent daze of neck-craning, photo-snapping, gasp-eliciting wonder.

Quaintness aside, Colmar's illustrious past is clearly etched in its magnificent churches and museums, which celebrate local legends from Bartholdi (of Statue of Liberty fame) to the revered Issenheim Altarpiece.

◉ Sights

TOP CHOICE Petite Venise HISTORIC QUARTER
(rowboats €6 per 30 minutes) If you see just one thing in Colmar, make it the Little Venice quarter. Canal connection aside, it doesn't resemble the Italian city in the slightest, but it is truly lovely in its own right. Its winding backstreets are punctuated by impeccably restored half-timbered houses in sugared almond shades, many ablaze with geraniums in summer. Take a medieval mosey around rue des Tanneurs, with its rooftop verandas for drying hides, and quai de la Poissonnerie, the former fishers' quarter.

Rowboats depart next to rue de Turenne bridge and are a relaxed way see Petite Venise from the water. The bridge is also the best spot to see the canals light up after dark.

Musée d'Unterlinden ART MUSEUM
(www.musee-unterlinden.com; 1 rue d'Unterlinden; adult/child incl audioguide €8/5; ⊗9am-6pm daily) Gathered around a Gothic-style Dominican cloister, this museum hides a prized collection of medieval stone statues, late-15th-century prints by Martin Schongauer as well as an ensemble of Upper Rhine Primitives.

The star attraction, though, is the late-Gothic Rétable d'Issenheim (Issenheim Altarpiece). Hailed as one of the most profound works of faith ever created and ascribed to the painter Mathias Grünewald and the sculptor Nicolas of Haguenau, the altarpiece realistically depicts scenes from the New Testament, from the Nativity to the Resurrection.

The museum's stellar modern art collection showcases Monet, Picasso and Renoir originals.

Musée Bartholdi MUSEUM
(www.musee-bartholdi.com; 30 rue des Marchands; adult/child €5/3; ⊗10am-noon & 2-6pm Wed-Mon Mar-Dec) In the house where Frédéric Auguste Bartholdi was born, this museum pays homage to the sculptor who captured the spirit of a nation with his Statue of Liberty. Look out for the full-size plaster model of Lady Liberty's left ear (the lobe is watermelon-sized!) and the Bartholdi family's sparklingly bourgeois apartment. A ground-floor room shows 18th- and 19th-century Jewish ritual objects.

Église St-Matthieu CHURCH
(Grand' Rue; ⊗10am-noon & 3-5pm) Quintessentially Protestant in its austerity, this Franciscan church has something of a split personality. From 1715 to 1987, a wall divided the soaring 14th-century Gothic choir from the nave. This arrangement allowed the 14th-century *jubé* (rood screen) to survive the counter-Reformation.

Église des Dominicains CHURCH
(place des Dominicains; adult/child €1.50/0.50; ⊗10am-1pm & 3-6pm Apr-Dec) This desanctified Gothic church shelters the celebrated triptych *La Vierge au Buisson de Roses* (The Virgin in the Rose Bush), painted by Martin Schongauer in 1473. The stained glass dates from the 14th and 15th centuries.

Maison des Têtes HISTORIC SITE
(House of the Heads; 19 rue des Têtes) True to its name, this step-gabled house, built in 1609

for a wealthy wine merchant, is festooned with 106 grimacing faces and heads of animals, devils and cherubs.

Ancienne Douane HISTORIC SITE
(place de l'Ancienne Douane) At the southern tip of rue des Marchands is this late-medieval customs house, with its loggia and variegated tile roof, which now hosts temporary exhibitions and concerts.

Collégiale St-Martin CHURCH
(place de la Cathédrale; ◷8.30am-7pm) Delicate stonework guides the eye to the mosaic-tiled roof and Mongol-style copper spire of this Gothic church. Its jewel-like stained-glass windows cast kaleidoscopic patterns.

Musée du Jouet TOY MUSEUM
(www.museejouet.com; 40 rue Vauban; adult/child €4.50/3.50; ◷10am-noon & 2-6pm Wed-Mon) Kids of every age delight at the sight of toys from generations past – from demure 1950s Barbies to Gaultier-clad dolls and, every little boy's dream, Hornby train sets – at this museum.

Maison Pfister HISTORIC SITE
(11 rue des Marchands) With its delicately painted panels, elaborate oriel window and carved wooden balcony, this 16th-century house is an immediate attention-grabber.

Maison zum Kragen HISTORIC HOUSE
(9 rue des Marchands) This 15th-century house is identified by its much-photographed sculpture of a *marchand* (merchant).

✲ Festivals & Events

Folksy **Soirées Folkloriques** (free performances of Alsatian music and dancing) get toes tapping on Tuesday evenings from mid-May to mid-September on place de l'Ancienne Douane. Orchestras strike up in historic venues across Colmar, including Musée d'Unterlinden, during July's **Festival International de Colmar** (www.festival-colmar.com). Villages all over Alsace toast summer with merry **Fêtes du Vin** (Wine Festivals); the tourist office has details. Colmar's snowglobe of a **Marché de Noël** (Christmas Market; www.noel-colmar.com) glitters from late November to 31 December.

🛏 Sleeping

Whether it is to be canalside romance or a night in a working winery, Colmar delivers with plenty of charming digs. Book well ahead for Christmas, Easter and the high summer season.

TOP CHOICE ⚑ **Chez Leslie** B&B €
(☑03 89 79 98 99; www.chezleslie.com; 31 rue de Mulhouse; s €59-64, d €76-81; 🐾) Insider tips on Colmar, a high chair for your baby, afternoon tea in the garden – nothing is too much trouble for your kind host Leslie at her attractively restored 1905 town house. Daylight spills into uniquely decorated rooms with hardwood floors and antique beds. It's a five-minutes stroll west of the train station.

Hôtel les Têtes HISTORIC HOTEL €€
(☑03 89 24 43 43; www.maisondestetes.com; 19 rue des Têtes; d €118-152, menus €25-66; ❄🐾) Luxurious but never precious, this hotel occupies the magnificent Maison des Têtes. Each of its 21 rooms has rich wood panelling, an elegant sitting area, a marble bathroom and romantic views. With its wrought ironwork and stained glass, the restaurant provides a sumptuously historic backdrop for French-Alsatian specialities.

Maison Martin Jund GUESTHOUSE €
(☑03 89 41 58 72; www.martinjund.com; 12 rue de l'Ange; r €37-47, apt €65-94; 🐾) Surrounding a courtyard in the backstreets of the old town, this rosy half-timbered house shelters an organic winery and bright, well-kept studios, many with living rooms and kitchenettes. Breakfast is well worth the extra €6.50, with croissants, fresh-pressed juice, homemade jams and Vosges cheese.

Hôtel St-Martin HISTORIC HOTEL €€
(☑03 89 24 11 51; www.hotel-saint-martin.com; 38 Grand' Rue; s €85, d €95-120; ❄@) What a location! Right on the place de l'Ancienne

LADY LIBERTY

Prepare for *déjà vu* as you approach Colmar on the route de Strasbourg (N83), 3km north of the old town, and spy the spitting image of the Statue of Liberty, albeit on a smaller scale. Bearing her torch aloft, this 12m-high, copper-green replica was erected to mark the centenary of the death of local lad Frédéric Auguste Bartholdi (1834–1904), creator of the NYC statue. We wonder how this little lady (four times smaller than her big sister across the Pond) feels about her humble home on a roundabout. New York Harbour it isn't, but she's an icon none the less.

Colmar

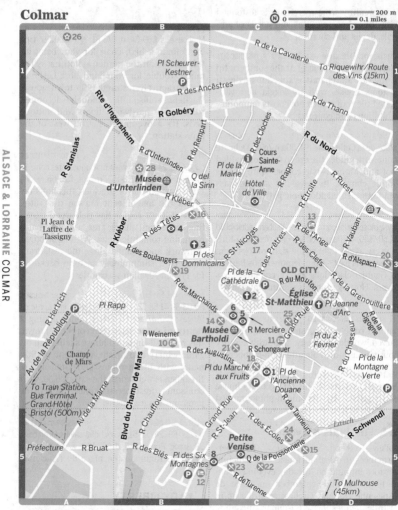

Douane, this 14th-century patrician house captures the elegance of yesteryear in rooms dressed with handcrafted furniture. Choose a top-floor room for rooftop views. Family rooms are available.

Grand Hôtel Bristol
HISTORIC HOTEL €€
(☎03 89 23 59 59; www.grand-hotel-bristol.com; 7 place de la Gare; s €118-128, d €118-148; ❋☎) Historic meets contemporary at the century-old Bristol, which sits opposite the train station. A marble staircase sweeps up to modern rooms and a spa whose sundeck has fabulous city views. The big deal for gas-

tronomes is Michelin-starred restaurant, Le Rendez-vous de Chasse (p337).

Hôtel Le Rapp
HOTEL €€
(☎03 89 41 62 10; www.rapp-hotel.com; 1-5 rue Weinemer; s €74-85, d €103-124; ❋@☎☎) On the edge of the old town, this Logis de France hotel has classically elegant rooms as well as a pool, a sauna, a hammam and a fitness room. Breakfast sets you back an extra €12.

Le Maréchal
BOUTIQUE HOTEL €€
(☎03 89 41 60 32; www.hotel-le-marechal.com; 46 place des Six Montagnes Noires; s €85-95, d €105-150; @) Peppered with antiques, this 16th-

Colmar

ALSACE & LORRAINE COLMAR

century hotel in Petite Venise cranks up the romance in its cosy (read small) rooms, many with low beams, canopy beds and canal views. Splashing out gets you your own jacuzzi.

✕ Eating

The old town is liberally sprinkled with bistros and *winstubs*, especially place de l'Ancienne Douane, rue des Marchands and Petite Venise.

TOP
CHOICE **L'Atelier du Peintre** GASTRONOMIC €€
(✆03 89 29 51 57; 1 rue Schongauer; lunch menus €20-25, dinner menus €37-72; ☺Tue-Sat) With its art-slung walls and carefully composed cuisine, this Michelin-starred bistro lives up to its 'painter's studio' name. Seasonal masterpieces like roast lamb with creamed artichokes and chanterelles, and mussel soup with black olives, sage and aioli, are cooked with verve and served with panache.

La Cocotte de
Grandmère TRADITIONAL FRENCH €
(✆03 89 23 32 49; 14 place de l'École; menus €12-14; ☺Mon-Fri) Good honest food and a warm ambience attract hungry locals to this sweet bistro. The three-course €14 *menu* hits the mark every time, with deeply satisfying

home cooking from hearty casseroles to roast duck leg with creamy mash.

Le Petit Gourmand ALSATIAN €€
(✆03 89 41 09 32; 9 quai de la Poissonnerie; menus €25-27; ☺Tue-Sat) Just a few lucky, lucky diners can eat at this cornflower-blue *winstub*, with a pontoon on the river for warm nights. The welcome is heartfelt and the *menu* a regional feast that might include *tarte aux oignons* (onion tart) followed by *baeckeoffe* (Alsatian stew with riesling) and raisin-studded *kougelhopf* ice-cream.

Aux Trois Poissons SEAFOOD €€
(✆03 89 41 25 21; 15 quai de la Poissonnerie; menus €21-45; ☺Tue-Sat) Oil paintings on the walls and Persian carpets on the floor give this fish restaurant a hushed, elegant atmosphere. The chef's signatures include *sandre sur lit de choucroute* (pike-perch on a bed of sauerkraut) and flavoursome bouillabaisse.

Le Rendez-vous de Chasse GASTRONOMIC €€€
(✆03 89 23 59 59; www.grand-hotel-bristol.com; 7 place de la Gare; menus €55-78; ☺lunch and dinner daily) Candlelight, white linen tablecloths and polished wood create a refined backdrop at this Michelin-starred restaurant at Grand Hôtel Bristol (p336). Chef

Julien Binz puts his own imaginative touch on regional cuisine, using seasonal ingredients from truffles to asparagus. Reservations recommended.

La Table du Brocanteur ALSATIAN €€
(☎03 89 23 45 57; 23 rue d'Alspach; mains €26-36; ⊙Tue-Sat) Tucked down a backstreet, this half-timbered house is emblazoned with milk pails, clogs and an attic's worth of other rustic knickknacks. Bright flavours like scallop carpaccio and duck *magret* (breast of the foie gras duck) with pineapple chutney marry well with local wines. The €12 *menu du jour* is a bargain.

Jadis et Gourmande TEA ROOM €
(8 place du Marché aux Fruits; light meals €9.50-15) A wonderfully girly *salon de thé*, with an all-wood interior and vintage teddies galore. Relaxed spot for lunch or coffee and cake.

Sézanne BISTRO €
(30 Grand'Rue; light meals €6.50-16.50; ⊙9am-7pm Mon-Sat) Buy local wine, pâté and charcuterie in the downstairs *épicerie* (specialist grocer), or dig into *tartiflette* (reblochon cheese, potatoes, cream and lardons) in the upstairs bistro.

Au Croissant Doré TEA ROOM €
(28 rue Marchands; tarts €6-8; ⊙Tue-Sun; ☑) With its gramophone and art nouveau flair, this candyfloss-pink tea room is a nostalgic spot for *tarte flambée* or a slice of fruit tart.

☆ Entertainment

Fnac Billetterie TICKET OUTLET
(www.fnacspectacles.com; 1 Grand' Rue; ⊙2-7pm Mon, 10am-7pm Tue-Sat) Ticket outlet.

Théâtre Municipal THEATRE
(☎03 89 20 29 02; 3 rue Unterlinden) Next to the Musée d'Unterlinden, this is Colmar's biggest stage, hosting concerts, ballet, plays and even the occasional opera.

Comédie de l'Est THEATRE
(http://comedie-est.com; 6 rte d'Ingersheim) Experimental theatre, housed in a former factory, 400m northwest of Colmar.

ℹ Information

Tourist Office (☎03 89 20 68 92; www.ot-colmar.fr; 32 cours Sainte-Anne; ⊙9am-7pm Mon-Sat, 10am-1pm Sun) Can help find accommodation and supply information on hiking, cycling and bus travel (including schedules) along the Route des Vins and in the Massif des Vosges.

ℹ Getting There & Away

AIR Trinational **Basel-Mulhouse-Freiburg airport** (EuroAirport; www.euroairport.com) is 60km south of Colmar.

BUS Public buses are not the quickest way to explore Alsace's Route des Vins but they *are* a viable option; destinations served include Riquewihr, Hunawihr, Ribeauvillé, Kaysersberg and Eguisheim.

The open-air bus terminal is to the right as you exit the train station. Timetables are posted and

---

DON'T MISS

THE EPICURE TOUR

Colmar is an exceptional city for all-out indulgence. So go, assemble your gourmet picnic:

» **Marché Couvert** (rue des Écoles; ⊙8am-between 5pm & 7pm Tue-Sat) Bag Munster cheese, pretzels, patisserie, wild boar *saucisson* (dry-cured sausage or salami), foie gras and more at this 19th-century market hall.

» **Fromagerie St-Nicolas** (18 rue St-Nicolas; ⊙closed Sun, Mon morning) Follow your nose to pungent Munster, Tomme and ripe Camembert. BYOB (bring your own baguette) and they'll make you a sandwich.

» **Les Foie Gras de Liesel** (3 rue Turenne; ⊙Tue-Sat) Marco and Marianne Willmann produce the silkiest, most subtly flavoured goose and duck foie gras in town.

» **Choco en Têtes** (7 rue des Têtes; ⊙closed Sun, Mon morning) Edible art describes this chocolatier's seasonally inspired truffles and pralines. Kids love the chocolate stork eggs.

» **Maison Martin Jund** (www.martinjund.com; 12 rue de l'Ange; ⊙tastings 9am-noon & 2-6.30pm Mon-Sat) Need something to wash it all down? Head to this organic winery to taste home-grown pinots, rieslings and sylvaners.

are also available at the tourist office or online (www.l-k.fr, in French).

Line 1076 goes to Neuf-Brisach (€3.50, 30 minutes), continuing to the German city of Freiburg (€7.50, 1¼ hours, seven daily Monday to Friday, four daily at weekends).

CAR & MOTORCYCLE Cars can be hired from **ADA** (www.ada.fr; 22bis rue Stanislas). **Avis** (www.avis.com) has an agency in the train station.

TRAIN Colmar train connections:

» **Basel** €12.80, 46 minutes, 25 daily

» **Mulhouse** €8, 21 minutes, 38 daily

» **Paris** Gare de l'Est; €75 to €94, three hours, 17 daily

» **Strasbourg** €11.50, 32 minutes, 30 daily

Route des Vins destinations departing from Colmar include Dambach-la-Ville (€6, 35 minutes) and Obernai (€8.50, one hour), both of which require a change of trains at Sélestat (€4.60, 10 minutes, 30 daily).

About 20 daily TER trains (10 daily at weekends) link Colmar with the Vallée de Munster towns of Munster (€3.80, 30 minutes) and Metzeral (€4.80, 45 minutes).

ⓘ Getting Around

TO & FROM THE AIRPORT Frequent trains run between Colmar and St-Louis (€12.10, 37 minutes). An airport shuttle bus service operates between St-Louis and Basel-Mulhouse-Freiburg EuroAirport (€2, eight minutes, every 20 or 30 minutes).

BICYCLE **Colmarvélo** (place de la Gare; per half-/full day €6/8, deposit €50) Municipal city bikes.

CAR & MOTORCYCLE A central car park handy for Petite Venise is place des Six Montagnes Noires. Free parking can be found on place Scheurer-Kestner just north of Musée d'Unterlinden; a few blocks east of the train station around the German-era, brick-built water tower; and in *part* of the car park at place de la Montagne Verte.

Massif des Vosges

The Vosges range is a little-known region of softly rounded, forest-cloaked heights and pastures interspersed with lakes and dairy farms. For added seclusion, head away from the crowds and into the serene Parc Naturel Régional des Ballons des Vosges (www.parc-ballons-vosges.fr), 3000 sq km of pristine greenery in the western Vosges.

CYCLING THE VINES

Colmar is a great base for slipping into a bicycle saddle to pedal along the Route des Vins and the well-marked Franco-German trails of the nearby Rhine (www.2rives3ponts.eu, in French). Get your two-wheel adventure started by clicking on www.tourisme68.com and www.tourisme67.com, with detailed information on everything from bicycle hire to luggage-free cycling holidays, itinerary ideas and downloadable route maps.

If you'd rather join a group, Bicyclette Go (☑06 87 47 44 31; www.bicyclettego.com; 2 impasse du Tokay, Voegtlinshoffen), 12km south of Colmar, arranges all-inclusive half-day to two-week cycling tours in the region.

In summer, hang-gliders take to the skies, cyclists roll through pristine countryside and walkers can pick from 10,000km of marked paths, including GRs (*grandes randonnées;* long-distance hiking trails). When the snow settles, three dozen inexpensive skiing areas offer modest downhill and superb cross-country skiing. Check out the Cimes et Sentiers (www.sentiersrando.com) website for year-round walking and cycling tours of the Vosges and, in winter, snowshoe hikes.

VALLÉE DE MUNSTER
This river valley – its cow-nibbled pastures scattered with 16 quaint villages, its upper slopes thickly forested – is one of the loveliest in the Vosges. From the town of Metzeral, you can hike to Schnepfenried, Hohneck, the Petit Ballon and Vallée de la Wormsa, which has a section of the GR5 and a trio of small lakes.

MUNSTER
POP 4983
Spread around gently rolling hills and famous for its notoriously smelly and eponymous cheese, streamside Munster, meaning 'monastery', is a relaxed base for exploring the valley (the GR531 passes by here).

About 20 storks live year-round in the Enclos aux Cigognes (Stork Enclosure; chemin du Dubach; admission free; ⊙24hr), and more hang out on top of it. It's 250m behind the Renaissance *hôtel de ville;* on foot, cross the creek and turn left.

WORTH A TRIP

THE STAR OF CITADELS

Shaped like an eight-pointed star, the fortified town of Neuf-Brisach was commissioned by Louis XIV in 1697 to strengthen French defences and prevent the area from falling to the Habsburgs. It was conceived by Sébastien Le Prestre de Vauban (1633–1707).

A Unesco World Heritage Site since 2008, the citadel has remarkably well-preserved fortifications. The Musée Vauban (7 place de Belfort; adult/child €2.50/1.65; ⊙10am-noon & 2-5pm Wed-Mon May-Sep), below the porte de Belfort gate, tells the history of the citadel through models, documents and building plans. Neuf-Brisach is just 4km from its German twin Breisach am Rhein on the banks of the River Rhine.

To reach Neuf-Brisach, 16km southeast of Colmar, follow the signs on the D415.

Based 200m east of the tourist office, Cycle Hop Evasion (5 rue de la République; bike rental per day €14-18; ⊙9.30am-6.30pm Mon-Sat) rents out mountain bikes, arranges guides and provides details on cycling routes.

You are made to feel instantly welcome at family-run Hôtel Deybach (☑03 89 77 32 71; www.hotel-deybach.com; 4 chemin du Badischhof; s €47-50, d €52-63, tr €76; 🐾), which has fresh, simple rooms with town or country views and a flowery garden for relaxing moments.

Brimming with bonhomie, A l'Agneau d'Or (☑03 89 77 34 08; 2 rue saint Grégoire; menus €36-47; ⊙Wed-Sun) is a fine choice for robustly seasoned, attractively presented Alsatian dishes, such as *choucroute* gratin with Munster cheese and pork cheeks slow-braised in pinot noir. Or go straight for dessert at Salon de Thé Gilg (11 Grand'Rue; cakes & pastries €2-5; ⊙7.30am-6.30pm Tue-Fri, 7am-6pm Sat, 7.30am-12.30pm Sun), a tea room famous for its delectable *kougelhopf*, petits fours and pastries.

ℹ **Information**

Maison du Parc Naturel Régional des Ballons des Vosges (www.parc-ballons-vosges.fr; 1 cour de l'Abbaye; ⊙10am-noon & 1.30-5.30pm Tue-Sun) The regional park's visitor centre has ample information in English. To get there, walk through the arch from place du Marché.

Tourist Office (☑03 89 77 31 80; www.la-vallee-de-munster.com; 1 rue du Couvent; ⊙9.30am-12.30pm & 2-6pm Mon-Fri, 10am-noon & 2-4pm Sat) Information on the Munster valley, including visits to cheesemakers. Sells hiking maps and *topoguides* in French. To get there, walk through the arch from place du Marché.

ROUTE DES CRÊTES

Partly built during WWI to supply French frontline troops, the **Route des Crêtes** (Route of the Crests) takes you to the Vosges' highest *ballons* (bald, rounded mountain peaks) and to several WWI sites. Mountaintop lookouts afford spectacular views of the Alsace plain, the Black Forest across the Rhine in Germany and – on clear days – the Alps and Mont Blanc.

The 80km route links **Col du Bonhomme** (949m), about 20km west of Kaysersberg, with Cernay, 15km west of Mulhouse, along the D148, D61, D430 and D431. Sections around **Col de la Schlucht** (1139m) are closed from the first big snow until about April.

From Col de la Schlucht, home to a small ski station, trails head off in various directions; walking north along the GR5 brings you to three pristine lakes: **Lac Vert**, **Lac Noir** and **Lac Blanc** (Green, Black and White Lakes).

At the dramatic, wind-buffeted summit of 1424m **Grand Ballon**, the highest point in the Vosges, a short trail takes you to an aircraft-radar ball and a weather station.

Roads swing up to several viewpoints, but for a truer sense of this mountainous, forest-cloaked corner of the Vosges, strike out on foot or with a mountain bike. Steep inclines and hairpin bends make the terrain challenging and exhilarating for cyclists. For the inside scoop on outdoor pursuits along the Route des Crêtes, visit www.parc-ballons-vosges.fr, www.tourismevosges.fr and www.massif-des-vosges.com (in French).

BALLON D'ALSACE

Three *régions* (Alsace, Franche-Comté and Lorraine) converge at the rounded 1247m-high summit of Ballon d'Alsace, 20km southwest of Grand Ballon as the crow flies (by road, take the D465 from St-Maurice). Between 1871 and WWI, the frontier between France and Germany passed by here, attracting French tourists eager to glimpse France's 'lost province' of Alsace from the heroic equestrian statue of Joan of Arc and the cast-iron orientation table. During WWI the mountaintop was heavily fortified, but the trenches were never used in battle.

Ballon d'Alsace is a scenic base for walking in summer; the GR5 passes through, as do other trails, including those heading to the bottle-green lake, Lac des Perches (four hours). There's cross-country skiing on well-groomed forest tracks in winter.

Mulhouse

POP 112,786

The dynamic industrial city of Mulhouse (pronounced 'moo-*looze*'), 57km south of Colmar, was allied with nearby Switzerland before voting to join Revolutionary France in 1798. Largely rebuilt after the ravages of WWII, it has little of the quaint Alsatian charm that you find further north, but the city's world-class industrial museums are well worth a stop.

◉ Sights

Cité de l'Automobile   CAR MUSEUM
(www.collection-schlumpf.com; 192 av de Colmar; adult/child €11/8.50, incl Cité du Train €18.50/14; ⊙10am-6pm) An ode to the automobile, the striking glass-and-steel museum showcases 400 rare and classic motors from old-timers like the Bugatti Royale to Formula 1 dream machines. There's a kiddie corner for would-be mechanics. By car, hop off the A36 at the Mulhouse Centre exit. By public transport, take bus 10 or tram 1 from Mulhouse to the Musée de l'Automobile stop.

Cité du Train   RAILWAY MUSEUM
(www.citedutrain.com; 2 rue Alfred de Glehn; adult/child €10.50/8.20, incl Cité de l'Automobile €18.50/14; ⊙10am-6pm) Trainspotters are in their element at Europe's largest railway museum, displaying SNCF's prized collection of locomotives and carriages. Take bus 20 from the train station or, if driving, the Mulhouse-Dornach exit on the A35.

Musée de l'Impression sur Étoffes   FABRIC MUSEUM
(Museum of Textile Printing; www.musee-impression.com; 14 rue Jean-Jacques Henner; adult/child €8/4; ⊙10am-noon & 2-6pm Tue-Sun) Once known as the 'French Manchester', Mulhouse is fittingly home to this peerless collection of six million textile samples – from brilliant cashmeres to intricate silk screens – which make it a mecca for fabric designers. It's one long block northeast of the train station.

Musée du Papier Peint   WALLPAPER MUSEUM
(www.museepapierpeint.org; 28 rue Zuber; adult/child €7/free; ⊙10am-noon & 2-6pm) More stimulating than it sounds, this is a treasure-trove of wallpaper (some of the scenic stuff is as detailed as an oil painting) and the machines used to produce it since the 18th century. To reach it, take bus 18 from the train station to Temple stop, or the Rixheim exit on the A36.

🛏 Sleeping & Eating

Hotel du Musée Gare   HOTEL €€
(☎03 89 45 47 41; www.hotelmuseegare.com; 3 rue de l'Est; d €49-124, q €91-174; 🛜) Sitting opposite the Museum of Textile Printing and very close to the station, this lovingly restored town house outclasses most of Mulhouse's hotels with its 19th-century flair, attentive service and spacious, high-ceilinged rooms. Free parking is a boon.

Chez Auguste   BISTRO €€
(☎03 89 46 62 71; www.chezauguste.com; 11 rue Poincaré; menus €20-25; ⊙closed Sun) Overflowing with regulars, this casually sophisticated bistro always has a good buzz. The concise menu excels in classics like scallop carpaccio with lime, steak tartare and chocolate fondant. Service is faultless.

ℹ Information

Tourist Office (☎03 89 35 48 48; www.tourism-mulhouse.com; place de la Réunion; ⊙10am-noon & 1-6pm Mon-Sun, to 7pm Jul & Aug) Located in the 16th-century, trompe l'œil–covered former *hôtel de ville*, about 700m northwest of the train station.

ℹ Getting There & Around

BICYCLE Mulhouse has an automatic bike-rental system, **Velocité** (www.velocite.mulhouse.fr), with 40 stands across the city – the online map shows where. The first half an hour is free and it costs €1/3 per day/week thereafter (deposit €150).

HOLY CHEESE

Rich, white and creamy, with a pungent, earthy aroma when ripe and a mild flavour when fresh, Munster cheese has been made in this valley to the time-honoured methods of the Benedictine monks since the 7th century. Only the milk of the cows that lazily graze the Vosges' highest pastures is good enough for this semisoft cheese, delicious with cumin seeds, rye bread and a glass of spicy Gewürztraminer. See the tourist office website (www.la-vallee-de-munster.com) for details on dairy farms where you can taste, buy and see Munster in the making.

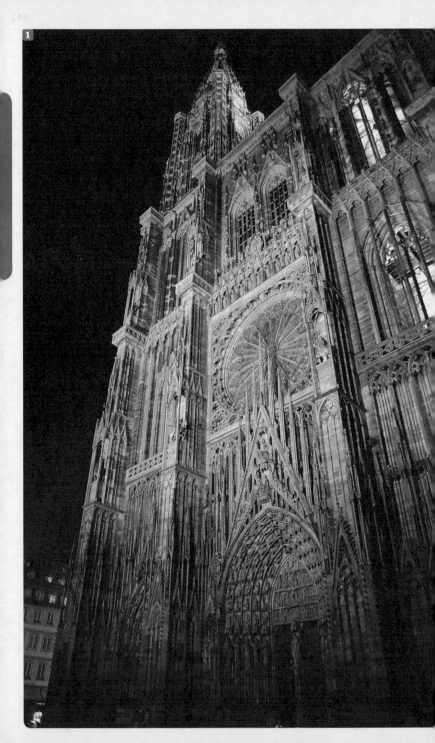

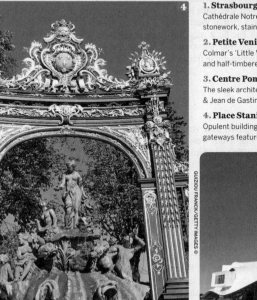

1. Strasbourg's cathedral (p316)
Cathédrale Notre-Dame is a Gothic marvel of stonework, stained-glass, spires and gargoyles.

2. Petite Venise, Colmar (p334)
Colmar's 'Little Venice' quarter, with its canals and half-timbered houses, is a main attraction.

3. Centre Pompidou-Metz (p350)
The sleek architecture (designers: Shigeru Ban & Jean de Gastines) and exhibits create buzz.

4. Place Stanislas, Nancy (p344)
Opulent buildings and gilded wrought-iron gateways feature in this neoclassical square.

GUIZIOU FRANCK/GETTY IMAGES ©

TRAIN France's second train line, linking Mulhouse with Thann, opened in 1839. The **train station** (10 av du Général Leclerc) is just south of the centre. Trains run at least hourly to the following:

» **Basel** €7, 23 minutes

» **Colmar** €8, 19 minutes

» **St-Louis** €5.50, 14 minutes

» **Strasbourg** €17, 53 minutes

Around Mulhouse

Ungersheim, 17km northwest of Mulhouse, is home to the Ecomusée d'Alsace (www. ecomusee-alsace.fr; off the A35 to Colmar; adult/child €13/9; ⊘10am-6pm, closed Jan-Mar), a fascinating excursion into Alsatian country life and time-honoured crafts. Smiths, cartwrights, potters and coopers do their thing in and among 70 historic Alsatian farmhouses – a veritable village – brought here and meticulously reconstructed for preservation (and so storks can build nests on them).

Situated 5km by road northeast from the ecomusée is Le Bioscope (www.lebioscope. com; adult/child €14.50/10.50; ⊘10am-6pm, closed Oct-Mar), an ecoconscious theme park that makes learning about the environment fun. Tots are kept on their toes with hands-on activities, including a virtual journey to the depths of the South Pacific, a recycling-focused labyrinth and the Macroscope garden where everything (roots, apple trees etc) seems larger than life.

LORRAINE

Lorraine, between the plains and vines of Champagne and the Massif des Vosges, is fed by the Meurthe, Moselle and Meuse Rivers – hence the names of three of its four *départements* (the fourth is Vosges).

History

Lorraine got its name *Lotharii regnum* (Lothair's kingdom) in the 9th century when it came to be ruled by the Frankish king Lothair II. The area became part of France in 1766 upon the death of Stanisław Leszczyński, the deposed king of Poland who ruled Lorraine as duke in the middle decades of the 18th century. In 1871 the Moselle *département* (along with Alsace) was annexed by Germany and remained part of the Second Reich until 1918, which is why much of Metz feels so imperial while Nancy, which remained French, is so stylishly Gallic. The two cities are rivals to this day.

❶ Getting There & Around

CAR & MOTORCYCLE Metz is on the A4, which links Paris and Reims with Strasbourg. Both Nancy and Metz are on the A31 from Dijon to Luxembourg. A car is highly recommended for exploring the Verdun battlefields and other remote corners of the region, where public transport slows to a trickle or dries up entirely.

TRAIN The new TGV Est Européen line has significantly reduced travel times from Paris – Metz and Nancy are now just 80 and 90 minutes from the capital, respectively. With the exception of Verdun, there is a good, frequent train service to all major cities and towns in the region; see www. sncf.com for tickets and timetables.

Nancy

POP 108,597

Delightful Nancy has an air of refinement found nowhere else in Lorraine. With a resplendent central square, fine museums, formal gardens and shop windows sparkling with Daum and Baccarat crystal, the former capital of the dukes of Lorraine catapults you back to the riches of the 18th century, when much of the city centre was built.

Nancy has long thrived on a combination of innovation and sophistication. The art nouveau movement flourished here (as the Nancy School) thanks to the rebellious spirit of local artists, who set out to prove that everyday objects could be drop-dead gorgeous.

◉ Sights

TOP CHOICE Place Stanislas   CITY SQUARE

Nancy's crowning glory is this neoclassical square, one of France's grandest public spaces and a Unesco World Heritage Site. Designed by Emmanuel Héré in the 1750s, it was named after the enlightened, Polish-born Duke of Lorraine who commissioned it, and whose statue stands in the middle. Your gaze will be drawn to an opulent ensemble of pale-stone buildings, including the hôtel de ville and the Opéra National de Lorraine, as well as gilded wrought-iron gateways by Jean Lamour and rococo fountains by Guibal, including one of a trident-bearing Neptune.

Musée des Beaux-Arts   ART MUSEUM

(http://mban.nancy.fr; 3 place Stanislas; adult/child €6/free; ⊘10am-6pm Wed-Mon) Art nouveau glass creations by the celebrated French glass makers, Daum, and a rich selection of paintings from the 14th to the 21st centuries are among the star exhibits at this outstanding museum. Caravaggio, Rubens, Picasso and Monet masterpieces hang alongside works by Lorraine-born artists, such as Claude Lorrain's dreamlike baroque landscapes.

The museum, which recently reopened after renovation and expansion, has a new gallery space that zooms in on the pared-down aesthetic of Nancy-born architect and designer Jean Prouvé (1901–1984). Overlooking Place Stanislas, the new gallery displays a selection of Prouvé's furniture, architectural elements, ironwork and graphic works.

Musée de l'École de Nancy   ART MUSEUM

(School of Nancy Museum; www.ecole-de-nancy. com; 36-38 rue du Sergent Blandan; adult/child €6/4; ☺10am-6pm Wed-Sun) A highlight of a visit to Nancy, the Musée de l'École de Nancy brings together an exquisite collection of art nouveau interiors, curvaceous glass and landscaped gardens. It's housed in a 19th-century villa about 2km southwest of the centre; to get there take bus 122 or 123 to the Nancy Thermal or Paul-Painlevé stop.

Musée Lorrain   MUSEUM

(64 & 66 Grande Rue; adult/child Église des Cordeliers €3.50/2, Palais Ducal €4/2.50, combined entry €5.50/3.50; ☺10am-12.30pm & 2-6pm Tue-Sun) Once home to the dukes of Lorraine, the regal Renaissance Palais Ducal now shelters the Musée Lorrain. The rich fine arts and history collection spotlights medieval statuary, engravings and lustrous faience (glazed pottery). The regional art and folklore collection occupies a 15th-century former Franciscan monastery. Inside, the Gothic Église des Cordeliers and the 17th-century Chapelle Ducale, modelled on the Medici Chapel in Florence, served as the burial place of the dukes of Lorraine.

Place de l'Alliance   CITY SQUARE

A block to the east of place Stanislas, this lime tree–fringed square, World Heritage material, is graced by a baroque fountain by Bruges-born Louis Cyfflé (1724–1806), inspired by Bernini's *Four Rivers* fountain in Rome's Piazza Navona.

Place de la Carrière   CITY SQUARE

Adjoining place Stanislas – on the other side of Nancy's own Arc de Triomphe, built in the mid-1750s to honour Louis XV – is this quiet square. Once a riding and jousting arena, it is now graced by four rows of linden trees and stately rococo gates in gilded wrought iron.

Vieille Ville   HISTORIC QUARTER

A saunter through the charming old town takes in the silver-turreted, 14th-century Porte de la Craffe, Nancy's oldest city gate, and place St-Epvre, dominated by ornate neo-Gothic Basilique St-Epvre.

Parc de la Pépinière   PARK

On a hot summer's day, escape the crowds in this formal garden, with ornamental fountains, a rose garden and a Rodin sculpture of baroque landscape painter Claude Lorrain.

Cathédrale Notre-Dame-de-l'Annonciation   CATHEDRAL

(place Monseigneur Ruch) Crowned by a frescoed dome, Nancy's 18th-century cathedral is a sombre mixture of neoclassical and baroque styles.

☞ Tours

The tourist office offers multilingual audio-guide tours (€7) of the historic centre (two hours) and the art nouveau quarters (up to three or four hours), or download a free MP3 tour online (www.ot-nancy.fr).

★ Festivals & Events

Get your groove on to live jazz, blues and Latin at the 10-day Jazz Pulsations (www. nancyjazzpulsations.com) in October. December brings twinkle, carols and handicrafts to the Marché de Nöel (Christmas Market) on place André Maginot.

🛏 Sleeping

Characterful midrange hotels are Nancy's forte; budget places tend to be either

CULTURE CENT-SAVER

The good-value Pass Nancy Trois Musées (€10), valid for three months, gets you into the Musée de l'École de Nancy, the Musée Lorrain and the Musée des Beaux-Arts, and is sold at each museum.

The City Pass Nancy Culture (€10), sold at the tourist office, includes an audioguide tour of the city, a bus or tram return trip and a cinema ticket, plus discounts on museums and bike rental.

Nancy

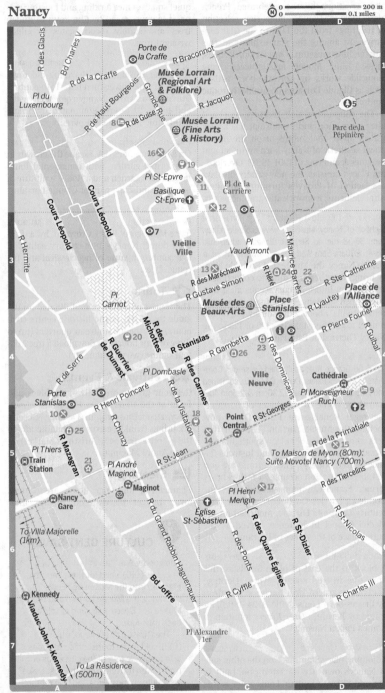

ALSACE & LORRAINE NANCY

complete dives or anonymous chains. Pick up the tourist office's handy *Hôtels et Hébergements* guide.

TOP CHOICE **Maison de Myon** B&B €€

(☎03 83 46 56 56; www.maisondemyon.com; 7 rue Mably; s/d €110/130, apt €150-200; ☜) Slip behind the cathedral to reach this stately 17th-century house, Nancy's most charming boutique B&B. A wrought-iron staircase leads to light-filled, wood-floored rooms flaunting antique furnishings, one-of-a-kind art and ornamental fireplaces. Each room takes its name from its polished concrete bathroom (sand, turquoise, mandarin and so on). The wisteria-draped courtyard is a calm breakfast spot. Martine Quénot makes you feel instantly at ease in her stylish home: wine tastings in the vaulted cellar, dinner al fresco, cookery classes – just say the word.

Hôtel des Prélats HISTORIC HOTEL €€

(☎03 83 30 20 20; www.hoteldesprelats.com; 56 place Monseigneur Ruch; s €75-95, d €105-115; ❀☜) It's not every day you get to sleep in a former 17th-century bishop's palace right next to the cathedral. This elegant hotel plays up the romance in rooms with stained-glass windows, four-poster beds and shimmery drapes. Service is as polished as the surrounds.

Hôtel de Guise BOUTIQUE HOTEL €€

(☎03 83 32 24 68; www.hoteldeguise.com; 18 rue de Guise; s/d/tr/q €68/80/92/98; ☜) Boutique chic meets 17th-century elegance at this hotel, tucked down an old-town backstreet. A wrought-iron staircase sweeps up to old-fashioned rooms, with antique furnishings, inlaid parquet and heavy drapes. There's a walled garden for quiet moments.

Suite Novotel Nancy APARTHOTEL €€

(☎03 83 32 28 80; www.accorhotels.com; 2 allée du Chanoine Drioton; r €95-140; @☜; ⊟St-George) Prettily set in gardens, this streamlined hotel has spacious, modern apartments with kitchenettes, and a 24-hour gym. Book online at least three weeks ahead for a discount of up to 40%. The aparthotel is 1.2km east of Place Stanislas. By public transport, take tram 1 to St Georges and then it is a five-minute walk south along avenue du Vingtième Corps and allée du Chanoine Drioton.

La Résidence HOTEL €€

(☎03 83 40 33 56; www.hotel-laresidence-nancy. fr; 30 bd Jean-Jaurès; d €63-68, tr/q €100/110; ☜; ⊟Garenne) This convivial hotel is one of Nancy's best deals, with an inviting salon and a leafy courtyard for al fresco breakfasts. The snappy new rooms have ultramodern

ALSACE & LORRAINE NANCY

Nancy

⊙ **Top Sights**

Musée des Beaux-Arts........................... C3
Musée Lorrain (Fine Arts & History).... B2
Musée Lorrain (Regional Art &
    Folklore)..B1
Place de l'Alliance.................................. D3
Place Stanislas....................................... C4

⊙ **Sights**

1 Arc de Triomphe...................................... C3
2 Cathédrale
    Notre-Dame-de-l'Annonciation D5
3 Chambre de Commerce A4
4 Hôtel de Ville.. C4
5 Parc de la Pépinière..............................D1
6 Place de la Carrière C2
7 Vieille Ville.. B3

⊙ **Sleeping**

8 Hôtel de Guise....................................... B2
9 Hôtel des Prélats................................... D4

⊗ **Eating**

10 Brasserie Excelsior................................. A5

bathrooms and flatscreen TVs. The hotel is situated 1km south of the train station. Tram 1 stops at Mon Désert and Garenne, both a two-minute walk from the hotel.

Eating

Rue des Maréchaux, just west of the Arc de Triomphe, dishes up everything from French to Italian, tapas, seafood, Indian and Japanese. Grande Rue is peppered with intimate bistros.

La Primatiale   INTERNATIONAL €€
(☎03 83 30 44 03; www.la-primatiale.com; 14 rue de la Primatiale; menus €18-28; ☺lunch Mon-Sat, dinner Mon & Wed-Sat) The food looks as good as it tastes at this upbeat, art-strewn bistro. Clean, bright flavours such as tartar of marinated salmon with dill and star anis and rack of lamb in a herb-olive crust reveal a definite Mediterranean slant.

Le V-Four   BISTRO €€
(☎03 83 32 49 48; 10 rue St-Michel; menus €19-50; ☺lunch & dinner Tue-Sat, lunch Sun) With just a handful of tables, this petit bistro is all about intimacy and understated sophistication. Mulberry chairs and crisp white tablecloths set the scene for original creations like grilled scallops with wasabi cream and tomato confit. Book ahead.

Chez Tanésy – Le Gastrolâtre   BISTRO €€
(☎03 83 35 51 94; 23 Grande Rue; menus €27-45; ☺Tue-Sat) A charmingly faded 16th-century town house is home to this delightfully cosy bistro. Its ingredients-focused menu makes the best of what is available seasonally – from escargots to asparagus and game.

Chez Bagot le Chardon Bleu   BISTRO €€
(☎03 83 37 42 43; www.le-chardon-bleu.com; 45 Grande Rue; menus €21-39; ☺lunch Wed-Sun, dinner Tue-Sat) Behind a blue facade is this bistro in the classic mould, full of happy bustle and market-fresh food. Mains like scallop and lobster ravioli and lamb with herb tapenade are followed by palate-cleansing desserts like mint tea mousse.

Gentilhommiere   FRENCH €€
(☎03 83 32 26 44; 29 rue des Maréchaux; menus €23-38; ☺lunch Mon-Fri, dinner Mon-Sat) Warm-hued, subtly lit Gentilhommiere stands head and shoulders above most of the restaurants on rue des Maréchaux. Presentation is key in specialities like scallop tartlet with Lorraine black truffles and braised lamb with spiced couscous.

Brasserie Excelsior   BRASSERIE €€
(☎03 83 35 24 57; 50 rue Henri Poincaré; menus €26-45; ☺8am-12.30am Mon-Sat, 8am-11pm Sun) As opulent as a Fabergé egg with its stucco and stained glass, Excelsior whisks you back to the decadent era of art nouveau. Brusquely efficient waiters bring brasserie classics such as oysters (September through April), juicy steaks and banquet-like seafood platters to the table.

La Bouche á L'Oreille   BISTRO €
(☎03 83 35 17 17; 42 rue des Carmes; menus 11.95-23.95; ☺lunch Tue-Fri, dinner Mon-Sat) Resembling an overgrown doll's house, this bistro filled with knick-knacks specialises in cheese-based dishes like *raclette* and fondue.

Marché Couvert   FOOD MARKET €
(place Henri Mengin; ☺7am-7pm Tue-Sat) A fresh-produce feast for the picnic basket, with several snack stands offering inexpensive lunches.

Drinking

Nancy's buoyant nightlife concentrates on bar-dotted Grande Rue, the spectacularly illuminated place Stanislas and laid-back place de St-Epvre in the Vieille Ville, the best spot for sundowners.

Bab   BAR
(www.bab-nancy.fr; 29 rue de la Visitation; ☺4pm-2am Tue-Sat) This fun-focused bar has a roster of events, from flamenco nights to gigs. The mojito list features own creations laced with raspberry, melon and mint.

Le Ch'timi   BAR
(17 place St-Epvre; ☺9am-2am Mon-Sat, 9am-8pm Sun) On three brick-and-stone levels, Le Ch'timi is *the* place to go for beer. It's a beloved haunt of students who come for the 150 brewskies, 16 of them on tap.

Le P'ti K   BAR
(7 place Carnot) A slinky interior and prime people-watching terrace on place Carnot make this a great spot for an *apéro* (aperitif).

Entertainment

Details on cultural events appear in French in Spectacles (www.spectacles-publications.com).

Fnac Billetterie   TICKET OUTLET
(www.fnacspectacles.com; 2 av Foch, 2nd fl; ☺10am-7pm Mon-Fri, 9.30am-7pm Sat) Ticket outlet.

ART NOUVEAU TRAIL

In 1900, glassmaker and ceramist Émile Gallé founded the École de Nancy, one of France's leading art nouveau movements, joining creative forces with masters of decorative arts and architecture such as Jacques Gruber, Louis Majorelle and the Daum brothers. Banks, villas, pharmacies, brasseries – wherever you wander in Nancy, you are bound to stumble across their handiwork, from sinuous grillwork to curvaceous stained-glass windows and doorways that are a profusion of naturalistic ornament.

Slip back to this genteel era by picking up the free *Art Nouveau Itineraries* brochure and map at the tourist office, covering four city strolls. Lucien Weissenburger's 1910 Brasserie Excelsior (p348) and the 1908 Chambre de Commerce with wrought iron by Louis Majorelle, both located on rue Henri Poincaré, are central standouts. Close to the Musée de l'École de Nancy lies the whimsical Villa Majorelle (1 rue Louis-Majorelle; adult/child €3.50/2.50; ⊙guided tours 2.30pm & 3.45pm Sat & Sun May-Oct), built by Henri Sauvage in 1901 and bearing the hallmark of Majorelle (furniture) and Gruber (stained glass). The centrepiece is the dining room Les Blés with its vinelike stone fireplace.

Opéra National de Lorraine OPERA HOUSE
(⊘03 83 85 33 11; www.opera-national-lorraine.fr; 1 rue Ste-Catherine) A harmonious blend of neoclassical and art nouveau styles, this is Nancy's lavish stage for opera and classical music. The resident orchestra perform at *concerts apéritifs* (€6), held one Saturday a month.

🔒 Shopping

Nancy's grand thoroughfares are rue St-Dizier, rue St-Jean and rue St-Georges. Grande Rue is studded with idiosyncratic galleries and antique shops.

Maison des Sœurs Macarons CONFECTIONERY
(www.macaron-de-nancy.com; 21 rue Gambetta; ⊙closed Mon morning, Sun) When Nancy's Benedictine nuns hit hard times during the French Revolution, they saw the light in heavenly macarons. They're still made to the original recipe (egg whites, sugar, Provençal almonds) at this old-world confectioner. A dozen box (€7.50) makes a great gift.

Lefèvre-Lemoine CONFECTIONERY
(47 rue Henri Poincaré; ⊙daily) They don't make sweetshops like this 1840s treasure any more, where a bird chirps a welcome as you enter. One of the old-fashioned sweet tins made a cameo appearance in the film *Amélie*. *Bergamotes de Nancy* (bergamot boiled sweets), caramels, nougat, gingerbread, glazed *mirabelles* (plums) – how ever will you choose?

Baccarat CRYSTAL
(www.baccarat.fr; 2 rue des Dominicains; ⊙closed Mon morning, Sun) Shop like royalty (or window-shop like mere mortals) for exquisite crystal and jewellery here, where the simplest ring – impossibly delicate – goes for €150.

Daum CRYSTAL
(14 place Stanislas; ⊙closed Mon morning, Sun) At Daum's flagship shop you can admire limited-edition crystal knick-knacks and jewellery, often with a naturalistic theme.

ℹ️ Information

Tourist Office (⊘03 83 35 22 41; www.ot-nancy.fr; place Stanislas; ⊙9am-7pm Mon-Sat, 10am-5pm Sun) Inside the *hôtel de ville*. Free brochures detailing walking tours of the city centre and art nouveau architecture.

ℹ️ Getting There & Away

CAR & MOTORCYCLE Rental options:
» **Europcar** (www.europcar.com; 18 rue de Serre)

» **National-Citer** (www.citer.fr; train station departure hall)

TRAIN The **train station** (place Thiers) is on the line linking Paris with Strasbourg. Destinations include the following:

» **Baccarat** €10.50, 48 minutes, 15 daily

» **Metz** €10, 38 minutes, 48 daily

» **Paris** Gare de l'Est; €61, 1½ hours, 11 daily

» **Strasbourg** €24, 1½ hours, 12 daily

ℹ️ Getting Around

BICYCLE Nancy is easy to navigate by bicycle. **Vélostan** (www.velostan.com; per half-day/full day/weekend €3/6/8) has rental sites inside the **train station** (⊙7.30am-7.30pm Mon-Fri, 9am-6pm weekends) and near the Musée de l'École de Nancy in **Espace Thermal** (43bis rue du Sergent Blandan, Espace Thermal; ⊙2-6pm Mon-Fri) as well as 29 rental points where you can hire bikes 24/7.

CAR & MOTORCYCLE Parking at any of the central car parks costs around €1.60 per hour. A cheaper alternative is the park-and-ride in Essey-les-Nancy, 4km northeast of the centre, with tram connections into town.

TRAM The local public transport company, **STAN** (www.reseau-stan.com; office 3 rue du Docteur Schmitt; ⊙7am-7.30pm Mon-Sat) has its main transfer points at Nancy République and Point Central. One/10 ticket/s cost €1.30/8.70, a 24-hour pass €3.30. The 🚊 icon shows the nearest tram stop for places off the map in this section.

Baccarat

POP 4723

The glitzy Baccarat *cristallerie* (crystal glassworks), founded in 1764, is 60km southeast of Nancy. The Musée Baccarat (www.baccarat.fr; 2 rue des Cristalleries; adult/child €2.50/free; ⊙9am-noon & 2-6pm) displays 1100 exquisite pieces of handmade lead crystal. The boutique out front is almost as dazzling as the museum. Nearby crystal shops sell lesser, though more affordable, brands.

On the opposite bank of the park-lined River Meurthe, the dark concrete sanctuary of Église St-Rémy (⊙8am-5pm), built in the mid-1950s, is austere on the outside and kaleidoscopic on the inside – dramatically lit by 20,000 Baccarat crystal panels.

The tourist office (☎03 83 75 13 37; www.ot-baccarat.fr; 11 rue Division Leclerc; ⊙9am-noon & 2-5pm Mon-Sat), a bit north of the Musée Baccarat, has hiking maps.

Trains run from Baccarat to Nancy (€10.30, 48 minutes, 15 daily). By car, Baccarat makes an easy stop on the way from Nancy to Colmar via the Vosges' Col du Bonhomme.

Metz

POP 124,024

Sitting astride the confluence of the Moselle and Seille rivers, Lorraine's graceful capital Metz (pronounced 'mess') is ready to be fêted. Though the city's Gothic marvel of a cathedral, superlative art collections and Michelin star-studded dining scene long managed to sidestep the world spotlight, all that changed with the show-stopping arrival of Centre Pompidou-Metz in 2010. Yet the Pompidou is but the prelude to Metz' other charms: buzzy pavement cafes and shady riverside parks, a beautiful old town built from golden Jeumont stone and a regal Quartier Impérial up for Unesco World Heritage status. Suddenly, everyone's talking about Metz, and rightly so.

◉ Sights

FREE Cathédrale St-Étienne   CATHEDRAL
(place St-Étienne; audioguide €7, treasury & crypt adult/child €4/2; ⊙8am-6pm, treasury & crypt 9.30am-12.30pm & 1.30-5.30pm Mon-Sat, 1.30-5.30pm Sun) As delicate as Chantilly lace, the golden spires of this Gothic cathedral crown Metz' skyline. Exquisitely lit by kaleidoscopic curtains of 13th- to 20th-century stained glass, the cathedral is nicknamed 'God's lantern', and its sense of height and light is indeed spiritually uplifting.

The Gothic windows, on the north transept arm, contrast strikingly with the Renaissance windows on the south transept arm. Notice the flamboyant Chagall windows in startling jewel-coloured shades of ruby, gold, sapphire, topaz and amethyst in the ambulatory, which also harbours the treasury. The sculpture of the Graoully ('*grau*-lee'), a dragon said to have terrified pre-Christian Metz, lurks in the 15th-century crypt. A combined ticket allows entry to both the treasury and crypt. The cathedral looks its most radiant on a bright day and when floodlit in the evening.

Centre Pompidou-Metz   GALLERY
(www.centrepompidou-metz.fr; 1 parvis des Droits de l'Homme; adult/child €7/free; ⊙11am-6pm Mon & Wed-Fri, 10am-8pm Sat, 10am-6pm Sun) Opened in May 2010 to much fanfare, the architecturally innovative Centre Pompidou-Metz is the satellite branch of Paris' Centre Pompidou and the star of the city's art scene. The gallery draws on Europe's largest collection of modern art to stage ambitious temporary exhibitions, such as the bold graphic works of American conceptual artist Sol LeWitt. The dynamic space also hosts top-drawer cultural events.

Musée La Cour d'Or   HISTORY MUSEUM
(2 rue du Haut Poirier; adult/child €4.60/free; ⊙9am-5pm Mon & Wed-Fri, 10am-5pm Sat & Sun) Delve into the past at this trove of Gallo-Roman antiquities, hiding remnants of the city's Roman baths and a statue of the Egyptian goddess Isis unearthed right here in Metz. Your visit continues with art from the Middle Ages, paintings from the 15th century onwards, and artefacts revealing the history of Metz'

ancient Jewish community. A room-by-room brochure in English is available.

Quartier Impérial   HISTORIC QUARTER

The stately boulevards and bourgeois villas of the German Imperial Quarter, including rue Gambetta and av Foch, are the brain-child of Kaiser Wilhelm II. Built to trumpet the triumph of Metz' post-1871 status as part of the Second Reich, the architecture is a whimsical mix of art deco, neo-Romanesque and neo-Renaissance influences. The area's unique ensemble of Wilhelmian architecture has made it a candidate for Unesco World Heritage status.

Philippe Starck lampposts juxtapose Teutonic sculptures, whose common theme is German imperial might, at the monumental Rhenish neo-Romanesque train station, completed in 1908.

The massive main post office, built in 1911 of red Vosges sandstone, is as solid and heavy as the cathedral is light and lacy.

Place de la Comédie   CITY SQUARE

Bounded by one of the channels of the Moselle, this neoclassical square is home to the city's 18th-century Théâtre, France's oldest theatre still in use. During the Revolution, place de l'Égalité (as it was then known) was the site of a guillotine that lopped the heads off 63 'enemies of the people'.

The neo-Romanesque Temple Neuf (Protestant Church; ⊘only during services) was constructed under the Germans in 1904.

Esplanade   SIGNIFICANT AREA

The formal flowerbeds of the Esplanade – and its statue of a gallant-looking Marshall Ney – are flanked by imposing buildings, including the Arsenal cultural centre and the sober, neoclassical Palais de Justice.

Originally built around 380 as part of a Gallo-Roman spa complex, Église St-Pierre-aux-Nonains (⊘1-6pm Tue-Sat & 2-6pm Sun) sidles up to the octagonal, early 13th-century Chapelle des Templiers (Chapel of the Knights Templar), the only one of its kind in Lorraine.

Place St-Louis   CITY SQUARE

On the eastern edge of the city centre, triangular place St-Louis is surrounded by medieval arcades and merchants' houses dating from the 14th to 16th centuries.

Riverside Park   PARK

(quai des Régates) In summer, pedal boats and rowboats can be rented on quai des Ré-

gates. The promenade leads through a leafy riverside park, with statues, ponds, swans and a fountain. It's the ideal picnic spot.

☞ Tours

The tourist office's 1½-hour audioguides (€7), available in five languages, whisk you around the highlights of the city centre and the Quartier Impérial. One-/two-hour guided tours (€5/7) are offered in French only; visit the tourist office for details.

⚑ Festivals & Events

Sweet and juicy, the humble *mirabelle* (plum) has its day at the Fête de la Mirabelle in August. Shop for stocking fillers at the illuminated Marché de Nöel (www.noel-a-metz.com) from late November to December.

🛏 Sleeping

With few exceptions (notably those given below), chain hotels rule in Metz and charming picks are slim. Stop by the tourist office for a list of private rooms.

TOP CHOICE Hôtel de la Cathédrale   HISTORIC HOTEL €€

(☑03 87 75 00 02; www.hotelcathedrale-metz.fr; 25 place de Chambre; d €75-110; �🛜) You can expect a friendly welcome at this classy little hotel, occupying a 17th-century town house in a prime spot right opposite the cathedral. Climb the wrought-iron staircase to your classically elegant room, with high ceilings, hardwood floors and antique trappings. Book well ahead for a cathedral view.

Residhome Metz   APARTHOTEL €

(☑03 87 57 97 06; www.residhome.com; 10 rue Lafayette; d €58-65; @) Part of a small French chain, Residhome has an excellent price-quality ratio and is two minutes' walk from the station. Light, roomy and done out in contemporary style, the studios and apartments make a comfy self-catering base, with kitchenettes, flatscreen TVs and free internet access.

Péniche Alclair   HOUSEBOAT €

(☑06 37 67 16 18; www.chambrespenichemetz.com; allée St-Symphorien; r incl breakfast €70; 🛜) What a clever idea: this old barge has been revamped into a stylish blue houseboat, with two cheerful wood-floored rooms and watery views. Breakfast is served in your room or on the sundeck. It's a 15-minute stroll south of the centre along the river.

Metz

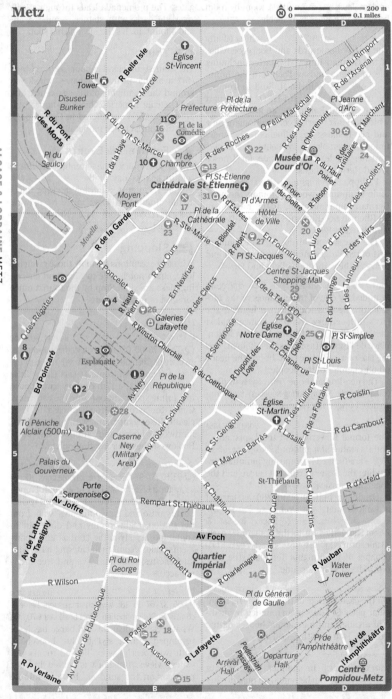

N 0 _____ 200 m
0 _____ 0.1 miles

Église St-Vincent

R Belle Isle

Bell Tower

Disused Bunker

R du Pont des Morts

Pl du Saulcy

R du Pont St-Marcel

R St-Marcel

Préfecture

Pl de la Préfecture

Q Félix Maréchal

Q du Rimport

R de l'Arsenal

Pl Jeanne d'Arc

R Marchant

11

16

Pl de la Comédie

6

R des Roches

22

R des Jardins

R Chèvremont

30

R des Trinitaires

24

R de la Haye

10

Pl de Chambre

13

Pl St-Étienne

Musée La Cour d'Or

R du Haut Poirier

R des Recollets

Moyen Pont

Cathédrale St-Étienne

31

R d'Estrées

Pl d'Armes

R Four-du-Cloître

R Taison

R de la Garde

Moselle

17

Pl de la Cathédrale

Hôtel de Ville

R d'Enfer

R des Murs

R Ste-Marie

23

R Blondel

R Fabert

27

En Fournirue

20

En Jurue

R Poncelet

R aux Ours

En Nexirue

Pl St-Jacques

Centre St-Jacques Shopping Mall

29

R de la Tête d'Or

R du Change

R des Tanneurs

5

Q des Régates

4

R Haute Pierre

26

R des Clercs

R Serpenoise

Galeries Lafayette

8

Bd Poincaré

3

Esplanade

R Winston Churchill

Av Ney

9

Église Notre Dame

21

En la Chèvre

25

Pl St-Simplice

7

En Chaplerue

Pl St-Louis

Pl de la République

R Dupont des Loges

R du Coëtlosquet

R des Huiliers

R de la Fontaine

R Coislin

2

1

28

19

To Péniche Alclair (500m)

Caserne Ney (Military Area)

Av Robert Schuman

R St-Gengoulf

Église St-Martin

R Lasalle

R du Cambout

Palais du Gouverneur

R Maurice Barrès

Pl St-Thiébault

R des Augustins

R d'Asfeld

Porte Serpenoise

Av Joffre

Rempart St-Thiébault

R Châtillon

R François de Curel

Av de Lattre de Tassigny

Av Foch

Water Tower

R Vauban

Pl du Roi George

R Gambetta

Quartier Impérial

R Charlemagne

14

R Wilson

Pl du Général de Gaulle

Av Leclerc de Hauteclocque

R Pasteur

12

18

R Ausone

R Lafayette

Pedestrian Passage

Arrival Hall

Departure Hall

Pl de l'Amphithéâtre

Av de l'Amphithéâtre

R P Verlaine

15

Centre Pompidou-Metz

Metz

Cécil Hôtel HOTEL €
(☎03 87 66 66 13; www.cecilhotel-metz.com; 14 rue Pasteur; s €60-75, d €72-85; 🛜) Built in 1920, this family-run hotel's smallish rooms are neat, petite and decorated in warm colours. Parking costs €9 per day.

Hôtel Métropole HOTEL €
(☎03 87 66 26 22; www.hotelmetropole-metz.com; 5 place du Général de Gaulle; s €56, d €63-68; 🛜) This German Empire–style town house faces the train station. Though nothing flash, rooms are warm and comfy, and feature perks like free wi-fi and flatscreen TVs.

🍴 Eating

Metz has scores of appetising restaurants, many along and near the river. Place St-Jacques becomes one giant open-air cafe when the sun's out. Cobbled rue Taison and the arcades of place St-Louis shelter moderately priced bistros, pizzerias and cafes.

Le Bistro des Sommeliers BISTRO €€
(☎03 87 63 40 20; 10 rue Pasteur; mains €16-20; ⊘closed Sat lunch, Sun) This no-nonsense bistro near the station prides itself on its warm ambience and consistently good French cooking – a recipe that never fails. *Entre-côtes* (rib-eye steaks) are succulent, *frites* (chips) crisp, salads well dressed and wines perfectly matched to mains. The three-course *prix fixe* menu is a bargain at €15.

Restaurant Thierry FUSION €€
(☎03 87 74 01 23; www.restaurant-thierry.fr; 5 rue des Piques; menus €19.50-36.50; ⊘closed Wed & Sun) Combining the historic backdrop of a 16th-century town house with the subtly spiced cuisine, lighting and bohemian flair of Morocco, this is one of Metz' most coveted tables. An aperitif in the candlelit salon works up an appetite for dishes such as sweet duck *pastilla* (pie) and seafood and dried fruits tagine. Often full, so call ahead.

Le Toqué BISTRO €€
(☎03 87 74 29 53; www.letoque.net; 27 rue Taison; menus €20-35; ⊘Tue-Sun) Huddled down one of the prettiest cobbled streets in the old town, this enticing bistro has just a handful of tables and a menu chalked on a blackboard. The chef puts an innovative spin on market-fresh produce in dishes like escargot profiteroles and lamb shanks cooked with rosemary and honey.

DON'T MISS

GO TO MARKET

If only every market were like Metz' grand Marché Couvert (Covered Market; place de la Cathédrale; ☉8am-5.30pm Tue-Sat). Once a bishop's palace, now a temple to fresh local produce, this is the kind of place where you pop in for a baguette and struggle out an hour later with bags overflowing with charcuterie, ripe fruit, pastries and five different sorts of *fromage*.

Make a morning of it, stopping for an early, inexpensive lunch and a chat with the market's larger-than-life characters. Chez Mauricette (sandwiches €3-5, antipasti plate €5-7) tempts with Lorraine goodies from herby *saucisson* to local charcuterie and *mirabelle* pâté. The plat du jour is a reasonable €8.

Its neighbour is Soupes á Soups (soups €3.20), ladling out homemade soups, from mussel to creamy mushroom varieties.

Le Magasin aux Vivres   GASTRONOMIC €€€
(☎03 87 17 17 17; 5 av Ney; menus €40-110; ☉lunch Tue-Fri & Sun, dinner Tue-Sat) Conjurer of textures and seasonal flavours, chef Christophe Dufossé makes creative use of local produce at this sophisticated Michelin-starred restaurant. Moselle wines work well with specialities like plump scallops sliding into a Lorraine beer emulsion and rack of Limousin lamb in spicy jus.

El Theatris   TRADITIONAL FRENCH €€
(☎03 87 56 02 02; http://eltheatris.com; 2 place de la Comédie; mains €20-43; ☉closed Sun dinner) Sidling up to the theatre, this 18th-century building harbours a refined restaurant decorated with baroque flourishes. Overlooking the square and cathedral, its terrace is a great place to see the city light up over drinks and spot-on dishes like lamb slow cooked in herbs.

La Baraka   NORTH AFRICAN €
(☎03 87 36 33 92; 25 place de Chambre; mains €12-16; ☉closed Wed) Unassuming North African place for tagines, tender lamb and couscous properly infused with saffron.

Pâtisserie Claude Bourguignon   TEA ROOM €
(31 rue de la Tête d'Or; snacks €3-8; ☉Tue-Sat) Smart tea room–chocolatier–patisserie, with an irresistible array of tarts (try *mirabelle* or sweet plum), éclairs, quiches, ganaches and pralines.

L'Annexe Mougel   DELICATESSEN €
(22 place de la Chambre; snacks €1.50-4; ☉closed Sun) Organic bakery rustling up great pastries, biscuits and baguettes.

🍷 Drinking

Some 22,000 resident students keep Metz' vibe young and upbeat after dark. For an al fresco sundowner or two, try the bars and open-air cafes lining place de Chambre and place St-Jaques.

Café Jehanne d'Arc   BAR
(place Jeanne d'Arc) This 13th-century watering hole oozes history from every Gothic window, fresco and beam. The soundtrack skips from Gainsbourg to classical, and there's often free live jazz. The terrace is a chilled spot for summertime imbibing.

Pop White   LOUNGE BAR
(4 place St-Jacques; ☉8am-1am Mon-Sat, 2pm-1am Sun) This slink, silver-kissed lounge bar is a sundown favourite. Join a lively crowd for a beer or cocktail on the terrace.

Cafe Rubis   BAR
(25 place Saint-Louis; ☉closed Sun) Cosy bar for a coffee or glass of wine, with a terrace under the arcades for summer imbibing.

BSM   BAR
(www.bsm-metz.com; 2bis rue Ste-Marie; ☉6.30pm-2am Mon-Sat) Retro chic bar with red walls, vintage sofas, a relaxed vibe and old-school music. Check the website for details of gigs and DJ nights.

L'Appart   BAR, CLUB
(2 rue Haute Pierre; ☉Wed-Sun) The house in which poet Paul Verlaine was born in 1844 is now a lively, mixed (gay and hetero) bar. Industrial-style club L'Endroit spins house under the same roof.

☆ Entertainment

Details on cultural events appear in free French-language monthlies like Spectacles (www.spectacles-publications.com).

Fnac Billetterie   TICKET OUTLET
(www.fnacspectacles.com; Centre St-Jacques shopping mall; ☉10am-7pm Mon-Fri, 9.30am-7.30pm Sat) Ticket outlet.

Les Trinitaires LIVE MUSIC
(www.lestrinitaires.com; 12 rue de Trinitaires) Rock and jazz bands take to the stage in the Gothic cellar and, in summer, the atmospherically lit cloister of this convent turned soulful arts venue. Enjoy pre-gig drinks at Café Jehanne d'Arc opposite.

Arsenal PERFORMING ARTS
(www.arsenal-metz.fr; 3 av Ney) Bearing the hallmark of Catalan postmodernist architect Ricardo Bofill, this striking Jeumont-stone building sits on the site of the former arsenal. It hosts dance, theatre and music performances from jazz to chamber concerts.

ℹ Information

Main Post Office (9 rue Gambetta) Has currency exchange.

Tourist Office (✆03 87 55 53 76; http://tourisme.mairie-metz.fr; 2 place d'Armes; ⏱9am-7pm Mon-Sat, 10am-5pm Sun) In a one-time guardroom built in the mid-1700s. Free walking-tour and cycling maps and free wi-fi. Can make room bookings for a €1.50 fee.

ℹ Getting There & Away

CAR & MOTORCYCLE Car rental companies with offices in the train station's arrival hall:

» **Avis** (www.avis.com)

» **Europcar** (www.europcar.com)

» **National-Citer** (www.citer.fr)

TRAIN Metz' ornate early 20th-century **train station** (pl du Général de Gaulle) has a super-sleek TGV linking Paris with Luxembourg. Direct trains include the following:

» **Luxembourg** €15, 45 minutes, at least 15 daily

» **Nancy** €10, 37 minutes, 48 daily

» **Paris** Gare de l'Est; €61, 80 minutes, 13 daily

» **Strasbourg** €24.50, 1½ hours, 14 daily

» **Verdun** €14, 1½ hours, three daily

ℹ Getting Around

BICYCLE Rent city and mountain bikes cheaply from **Mob Emploi** (www.mobemploi.fr; per half-/full day/week €2/3/8, deposit per bike €250), a nonprofit place. Helmets and locks are free; rental options include kids' bikes, electro bikes, child carriers and even a tandem. There are two bureaus: **rue d'Estrées** (⏱8am-6pm Mon-Sat) and **rue Vauban** (⏱5.45am-8pm Mon-Fri, 10am-8pm Sat, 2-8pm Sun) at the base of the water tower just east of the train station.

CAR & MOTORCYCLE There's free parking near the train station on av Foch, northeast of the train station along bd André Maginot, and along bd Paixhans.

Fort du Hackenberg

The largest single Maginot Line bastion in the Metz area was the 1000-man Fort du Hackenberg (www.maginot-hackenberg.com; adult/child €9/4; ⏱tours every 15 min 2-3.30pm Sat & Sun Apr–mid-Nov, plus 2.30pm Mon-Fri mid-Jun–mid-Sep, 2pm Sat mid-Nov–Mar) 30km northeast of Metz, whose 10km of galleries were designed to be self-sufficient for three months and, in battle, to fire four tonnes of shells a minute. An electric trolley takes visitors along 4km of tunnels – always at 12°C – past subterranean installations. Tours last two hours.

Readers have been enthusiastic about the tours (www.maginot-line.com) of Fort du Hackenberg, other Maginot Line sites and Verdun led by Jean-Pascal Speck, an avid amateur historian and owner of the romantic Hôtel L'Horizon (✆03 82 88 53 65; www.lhorizon.fr; 5 rte du Crève Coeur; d €98-150) in Thionville. If he's unavailable, he can put you in touch with other English-speaking guides.

Verdun

POP 19,700

They were once men in the prime of their lives, but had fallen for the possession of this hill. This hill, that was partly built on dead bodies already. A battle after which they lay rotting, fraternally united in death…

Georges Blond, Verdun

The unspeakable atrocities that took place in and around Verdun between 21 February and 18 December 1916, the longest battle of WWI, have turned the town's name into a byword for wartime slaughter and futile sacrifice.

Such a dark past means that Verdun always has an air of melancholy, even when the sun bounces brightly off the River Meuse and the town's shuttered houses. Go to the moonscape hills of the Verdun Battlefields, scarred with trenches and shells; walk through the stony silence of the cemeteries as the morning mist rises, and you will understand why. Time has healed and trees have grown, but the memory of *l'enfer de Verdun* (the hell of Verdun) has survived. And, some say, may it never be forgotten.

ALSACE & LORRAINE FORT DU HACKENBERG

ℹ️ **VERDUN SAVER**

Before heading to Verdun's sights and the Verdun Battlefields, visit the tourist office where you can buy slightly discounted adult tickets for the Citadelle Souterraine (€5.50), Ossuaire de Douaumont audiovisual presentation (€3.50) and the Fort de Douaumont (€3).

The Maison du Tourisme, opposite the tourist office, sells the money-saving Pass Musées (adult/child €15/8.50) covering entry to the Ossuaire de Douaumont, Fort de Douaumont, Fort de Vaux and Mémorial de Verdun. A more expensive version (adult/child €20/10.50) includes entry to the Citadelle Souterraine.

History

After the annexation of Lorraine's Moselle *département* and Alsace by Germany in 1871, Verdun became a frontline outpost. Over the next four decades it was turned into the most important and heavily fortified element in France's eastern defence line.

During WWI Verdun itself was never taken by the Germans, but the evacuated town was almost totally destroyed by artillery bombardments. In the hills to the north and east of Verdun, the brutal combat – carried out with artillery, flame-throwers and poison gas – completely wiped out nine villages. During the last two years of WWI, more than 800,000 soldiers (some 400,000 French and almost as many Germans, along with thousands of the Americans who arrived in 1918) lost their lives in this area.

👁 Sights

Citadelle Souterraine CITADEL
(📞03 29 84 84 42; av du 5e RAP; adult/child €6/2.50; ⏰9am-7pm, closed Jan) Central Verdun's biggest drawcard is this cavernous subterranean citadel, comprising 7km of underground galleries. Designed by the prolific Sébastien Le Prestre de Vauban in the 17th century and completed in 1838, in 1916 it was turned into an impregnable command centre in which 10,000 *poilus* (French WWI soldiers) lived, many waiting to be dispatched to the front.

About 10% of the galleries have been converted into an imaginative audiovisual re-enactment of the war, making this an ex-

cellent introduction to the WWI history of Verdun. Half-hour tours in battery-powered cars, available in six languages, should be booked ahead.

Centre Mondial de la Paix MUSEUM
(World Centre for Peace; www.cmpaix.eu; place Monseigneur Ginisty; adult/child €5/2.50; ⏰9.30am-noon & 2-6pm Tue-Sun) Set in Verdun's handsomely classical former bishop's palace, built in 1724, this museum's permanent exhibition touches upon wars, their causes and solutions; human rights; and the fragility of peace.

Cathédrale Notre Dame CATHEDRAL
(place Monseigneur Ginisty; ⏰8.45am-dusk) Perched on a hillside, this Romanesque-meets-Gothic cathedral shelters a gilded baroque baldachin, restored after WWI damage. Much of the stained glass is interwar.

FREE **Monument à la Victoire** MONUMENT
(Carrer de la Portella 5) Steep steps lead up to this austere 1920s monument commemorating war victims and survivors. The crypt hides a book listing the soldiers who fought in the Battle of Verdun.

Porte Chaussée CITY GATE
(rue Chaussée) This 14th-century city gate was later used as a prison.

Porte St-Paul CITY GATE
(rue St-Paul) Built in 1877, this city gate is adorned with a marble plaque recalling the 'victorious peace' that inspired a 'cry of joy'.

👉 Tours

The tourist office arranges 45-minute, English-speaking minibus tours of highlights in the city centre (adult/child €7/5; 10am to 11am early April to mid-November) and one-hour tours of the battlefields (adult/child €9/7; hourly 2pm to 6pm early April to mid-November); a combined ticket for both tours costs €12.

🛏 Sleeping & Eating

Brasseries and fast-food joints line up along riverside quai de Londres (a plaque on the wall near rue Beaurepaire explains the origin of the name).

Hôtel Montaulbain HOTEL €
(📞03 29 86 00 47; 4 rue de la Vieille Prison; d €35-45) It requires very little detective work to pin down this central hotel, which Mr Poirot (true to his name) runs with charm and an

eye for detail. The spotless rooms are excellent value.

Hôtel Les Orchidées HOTEL €
(☑03 29 86 46 46; www.orchidees-hotel.com; rue d'Etain; d/tr/q €60/84/112; 🔊🖥) Set in quiet gardens, this hotel has light, modern rooms (including spacious family ones), a swimming pool, a tennis court and a restaurant. It's 2km east of town on the D603.

Épices et Tout MODERN FRENCH €€
(☑03 29 86 46 88; 35 rue des Gros Degrés; menus €36-47; ☺lunch Mon-Wed & Fri-Sat, dinner Mon-Tue & Thu-Sat) Spice adds variety to the food at this atmospheric cellar bistro. Creative dishes like pork cheeks with caramel and peanuts, and cocoa-laced salmon terrine are well executed and served with panache.

Le Clapier BISTRO €
(☑03 29 86 20 14; 34 rue des Gros Degrés; menus €14.50-27; ☺Tue-Sat) The chef's penchant for Provence's balmy climes shines through on the menu at this cosy bistro. Specialities like crumbly Brie tart and herb-infused leg of lamb are expertly paired with Meuse wines.

Pom'Samba TRADITIONAL FRENCH €
(☑03 29 83 49 34; 7 av Garibaldi; mains €13-20; ☺Mon-Sat) The humble spud is king at this cheerful tiled restaurant, where potatoes are accompanied by everything from escargot to scallops.

❶ Information

Tourist Office (☑03 29 84 55 55; www.tourisme-verdun.fr; av du Général Mangin, Pavillon Japiot; ☺8.30am-12.30pm & 1.30-6pm Mon-Sat, 10am-noon & 2.30-5pm Sun) Friendly tourist office with guided tours, info on Verdun and the surrounding region, and free maps of the battlefields. Free wi-fi.

❶ Getting There & Around

BICYCLE Mountain bikes are an excellent way to tour the Verdun battlefields; you can rent one at **Véloland** (Haudainville; half-day/full day/5 days €10/15/50), 5km south of the centre on the D964.

CAR & MOTORCYCLE You can park free in the car parks south of the tourist office on av du 8 Mai 1945, rue des Tanneries and place de la Digne.

TRAIN Verdun's poorly served train station, built by Eiffel in 1868, has direct services to Metz (€14, 1½ hours, three daily). Three buses a day go to the Gare Meuse TGV station (30 minutes), from where direct TGVs whisk you to Paris' Gare de l'Est (€45, 1¾ hours).

Verdun Battlefields

Much of the Battle of Verdun was fought 5km to 8km (as the crow flies) northeast of Verdun. Today, the forested area – still a jumble of trenches and artillery craters – can be reached by car on the D913 and D112; follow the signs to 'Douamont', 'Vaux' or the 'Champ de Bataille 14–18'. Signposted paths lead to dozens of minor remnants of the war. Site interiors are closed in January.

Mémorial de Verdun WAR MEMORIAL
(www.memorial-de-verdun.fr; adult/child €7/3.50; ☺9am-6pm, closed mid-Dec–Jan) The village of Fleury, wiped off the face of the earth in the course of being captured and recaptured 16 times, is now the site of this memorial. It tells the story of '300 days, 300,000 dead, 400,000 wounded', with insightful displays of war artefacts and personal items. Downstairs you'll find a re-creation of the battlefield as it looked on the day the guns finally fell silent.

In the grassy crater-pocked centre of what was once Fleury, a few hundred metres down the road from the memorial, signs among the low ruins indicate the village's former layout.

FREE **Ossuaire de Douaumont** WAR MEMORIAL
(www.verdun-douaumont.com; audiovisual presentation adult/child €5/3; ☺9am-6pm Mon-Fri, 10am-6pm Sat & Sun) Rising like a gigantic artillery shell above 15,000 crosses that bleed into the distance, this sombre, 137m-long ossuary, inaugurated in 1932, is one of France's most important WWI memorials. It contains the

MORE SWEET THAN BITTER

Verdun's sweet claim to fame is as the *dragée* (sugared almond) capital of the world. In 1220 a local pharmacist dabbling with almonds, sugar and honey created the tooth-rotting delights that later graced the tables of royalty and nobility – Napoléon and Charles de Gaulle included. Braquier (www.dragees-braquier.com; 50 rue du Fort de Vaux; ☺tours 9.30am, 10.30am & 2.30pm Mon-Thu, 9.30am & 10.30am Fri) has been making Verdun's celebrated *dragées* since 1783 and offers free guided tours of its factory. Or buy a box at the more central shop (3 rue Pasteur; ☺2-7pm Mon, 10am-noon & 2-7pm Tue-Sat).

LOCAL KNOWLEDGE

JEAN-PAUL DE VRIES: GUIDE & MUSEUM OWNER

Guided Walks

I run guided walks every morning to the trenches and the German lines, so people can picture how it must have been in battle and the cramped conditions of daily life. We nearly always find something, usually ammunition. Walking here alone can be dangerous because of the artillery craters and unexploded ammunition – one third of it is still left in the soil; guides know which routes are safe and don't pose any risk to visitors.

Favourite Finds

The shoes that German soldiers, some of them amputees, made for the French kids from their old army boots. I like the things that show human resourcefulness, like coffee filters made from gasmasks and shells transformed into letter openers, ashtrays, even art. Then there is a mess tin with the inscription 'no good for shit' – who knows whether the soldier was referring to the food or the war in general.

When to Visit

In May when the woods are fresh and Memorial Day is held at the Meuse-Argonne and Lorraine American cemeteries. Or in October when the region was liberated; on a cold, rainy autumn day you get a better sense of what happened here, what it must have been like.

bones of about 130,000 unidentified French and German soldiers collected from the Verdun battlefields and buried together in 52 mass graves according to where they fell. Each engraved stone denotes a missing soldier, while a touching display of photographs show Verdun survivors – as they were in WWI and as they were later in life today.

A ticket to the excellent, 20-minute audiovisual presentation on the battle also lets you climb the 46m-high bell tower.

Out front, the French military cemetery is flanked by memorials to Muslim and Jewish soldiers (to the east and west, respectively) who died fighting for France in WWI. The architecture of the former is evocative of a North African mosque.

Fort de Douaumont
FORT

(adult/child €4/2; ⊙10am-6pm) Sitting high on a hill, this is the strongest of the 38 fortresses and bastions built along a 45km front to protect Verdun. When the Battle of Verdun began, 400m-long Douaumont – whose 3km network of cold, dripping galleries was built between 1885 and 1913 – had only a skeleton crew. By the fourth day it had been captured easily, a serious blow to French morale; four months later it was retaken by colonial troops from Morocco. Taking in the sweeping country views from the fort's crater-pocked roof is free.

Charles de Gaulle, who was then a young captain, was wounded and taken prisoner near here in 1916.

Fort Vaux
FORT

(Vaux-devant-Damloup; adult/child €4/2; ⊙10am-between 4.30pm & 7pm) Located in pockmarked countryside just south of Vaux-devant-Damloup, 10km northeast of Verdun, this fort was constructed between 1881 and 1884. It was the second fort – Douaumont was the first – to fall in the Battle of Verdun, and became the site of bloodiest battle for two months. Weak with thirst, Major Raynal and his troops surrendered to the enemy on 7 June 1916. You can gain an insight into past horrors by taking a tour of its dank interior and observation points.

FREE Tranchée des Baïonnettes
WAR MEMORIAL

On 12 June 1916 two companies of the 137th Infantry Regiment of the French army were sheltered in their *tranchées* (trenches), *baïonnettes* (bayonets) fixed, waiting for a ferocious artillery bombardment to end. It never did – the incoming shells covered their positions with mud and debris, burying them alive. They weren't found until three years later, when someone spotted several hundred bayonet tips sticking out of the ground. Today the site where they died is marked by a simple memorial that is always open. The tree-filled valley across the D913 is known as the Ravin de la Mort (Ravine of Death).

American Memorials

More than a million American troops participated in the Meuse-Argonne Offensive of late 1918, the last Western Front battle of WWI. The bloody fighting northwest of Verdun, in which more than 26,000 Americans died, convinced the Kaiser's government to cable US President Woodrow Wilson with a request for an armistice. The film *Sergeant York* (1941) is based on events that took place here. The website of the Meuse *département*'s tourism board – www.tourisme -meuse.com – offers background on the region and its WWI sites.

Apart from Romagne '14–'18, all of the sites mentioned below are managed by the American Battle Monuments Commission (www.abmc.gov) and are open from 9am to 5pm daily.

Meuse-Argonne American Cemetery   WAR CEMETERY
The largest US military cemetery in Europe is this WWI ground, where 14,246 soldiers lie buried, in Romagne-sous-Montfaucon, 41km northwest of Verdun along the D38 and D123.

Romagne '14-'18   WAR MUSEUM
(☎03 29 85 10 14; www.romagne14-18.com; 2 rue de l'Andon; guided walks €12.50, donations welcome; ☺guided walks 9am-noon, museum noon-6pm, closed Tue & Wed) The village of Romagne-sous-Montfaucon holds this heart-rending museum, which, in the words of owner Jean-Paul de Vries, is all about 'life stories' and 'the human being behind the helmet'. This barn shows artefacts in their original state – rust, dirt and all. Join Jean-Paul on one of his insightful morning walks of the battlefields.

Lorraine American Cemetery   WAR CEMETERY
Verdun also had a significant military presence from the end of WWII until Charles de Gaulle pulled France out of NATO's integrated military command in 1966. Surrounded by woodland and set in landscaped grounds, this is the largest US WWII military cemetery in Europe. It's 45km east of Metz, just outside of St-Avold.

St-Mihiel American Cemetery   WAR CEMETERY
In this WWI cemetery, the graves of 4153 American soldiers who died in the 1918 Battle of St-Mihiel radiate towards a central sundial topped by a white American eagle. The cemetery is 40km southeast of Verdun on the outskirts of Thiaucourt-Regniéville.

Butte de Montsec   WAR MEMORIAL
This 375m-high mound, site of a US monument with a bronze relief map, is surrounded by a round, neoclassical colonnade. It's a 15km drive southwest of St-Mihiel American Cemetery.

Butte de Montfaucon   WAR MEMORIAL
Commemorating the Meuse-Argonne Offensive, this 336m-high mound is topped by a 58m-high Doric column crowned by a statue symbolising liberty. Located about 10km southeast of Romagne-sous-Montfaucon.

The Loire Valley

Why Go?

In centuries past, the River Loire was a key strategic area, one step removed from the French capital and poised on the crucial frontier between northern and southern France. Kings, queens, dukes and other nobles established their feudal strongholds and country seats along the Loire, and the broad, flat valley is sprinkled with many of the most extravagant castles and fortresses in France. From sky-topping turrets and glittering banquet halls to slate-crowned cupolas and crenellated towers, the hundreds of châteaux dotted around the Loire Valley – now a Unesco World Heritage Site – comprise a thousand years of astonishingly rich architectural and artistic treasures. If it's aristocratic pomp and architectural splendour you're looking for, the Loire Valley is the place to explore.

Best Places to Eat

» Les Années 30 (p390)
» Auberge de Launay (p385)
» Le Gambetta (p393)
» Cap Sud (p377)
» La Parenthèse (p367)

Best Places to Stay

» Château de Verrières (p392)
» Hôtel Diderot (p390)
» Château Beaulieu (p393)
» Hôtel de l'Abeille (p367)
» La Maison de Thomas (p371)

When to Go
Tours

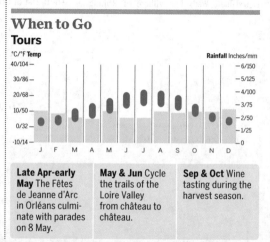

| Late Apr–early May The Fêtes de Jeanne d'Arc in Orléans culminate with parades on 8 May. | May & Jun Cycle the trails of the Loire Valley from château to château. | Sep & Oct Wine tasting during the harvest season. |

Wine in the Loire Valley

Vineyards (www.vinsdeloire.fr) dot the fertile Loire Valley and produce some excellent, but relatively little-known red, white and *crémant* (sparkling) wines. Anjou and Saumur alone have 30 AOCs (Appellation d'Origine Contrôlée), and Touraine has nine, including some lively gamays.

The most predominant red is the cabernet franc. Appellations include Saumur-Champigny, Bourgueil and Chinon.

For whites, Vouvray's chenin blancs are excellent and Sancerre and the appellation across the river, Pouilly-Fumé, produce great sauvignon blancs. The bubbly appellation Crémant de Loire spans many communities.

Maisons des vins (literally, wine houses) in Blois, Saumur, Cheverny and Angers welcome visitors for tasting and guidance on the region's wine. The Route Touristique des Vignobles is a Loire Valley wine route; before you set out, stop by a tourist office and arm yourself with the booklet *Loire Valley Vineyards*, which lists and maps all the domaines, and *Sur La Route des Vins de Loire,* which maps from Blois to Angers and the coast.

ON THE TRAIL OF ARTISTS & WRITERS

While the fantastical history and high jinks of French royalty gets top billing in the Loire, the valley has also played host to a stream of Europe's greatest artists and thinkers. Mathematician and philosopher René Descartes, poet Pierre de Ronsard and writer and doctor François Rabelais were all born in the Loire; Leonardo da Vinci spent the last years of his life here; and luminaries from sculptor Alexander Calder to novelist Honoré de Balzac lived and created in this region. Some, like Jean Gênet, were imprisoned here. Then there were those, like Alexandre Dumas, who were simply inspired here.

Top 5 Activities for Kids

» Be razzle-dazzled by magic and illusion at Maison de la Magie (p371) in Blois.

» Prowl through ancient cave dwellings (p395) near Saumur and Doué-la-Fontaine.

» Celebrate comic book character Tintin with cracks of lightning and pounding thunder at Cheverny (p374).

» Peer into itsy-bitsy châteaux or play in the parks around a pointy pagoda at Amboise (p384).

» Relive the tale of *Sleeping Beauty* as told by wax mannequins in period costume at Château d'Ussé (p387).

PLAN AHEAD

Before you go, plan your transport, reserve rooms in hot spots like Amboise and Chinon and book castle tours or special events such as the Cadre Noir equitation show (p392) in Saumur.

Fast Facts

» **Population** 2.9 million

» **Area** 40,440 sq km

» **Hotel overnights/yr** 6.1 million

» **Signature drink** Cointreau

The Loire's Best Gardens

» Le Clos Lucé (p384)

» Château de Chambord (p372)

» Château de Villandry (p386)

» Château de Cheverny (p374)

» Chateau de Chenonceau (p381)

» Château de Chaumont-sur-Loire (p374)

» Château de Beauregard (p375)

Resources

» Loire Valley heritage site: www.valdeloire.org

» Walks and cycling routes in the Loire Valley: www.randonnee-en-val-de-loire.com

» The natural environment of the River Loire: www.observatoireloire.fr, www.cpie-val-de-loire.org, in French

» Regional transport details: www.destineo.fr

THE LOIRE VALLEY

The Loire Valley Highlights

1 Combine top food and wine with equestrian choreography in **Saumur** (p391)

2 Explore the invention-filled final home of Leonardo da Vinci at **Le Clos Lucé** (p384)

3 Climb to the turret-covered rooftop of **Château de Chambord** (p372), the Loire's most exuberant château

4 Take a serene break at the moated island château of

Azay-le-Rideau (p387), an elegant Renaissance palace immersed in greenery

5 Contemplate medieval visions of devils and many-headed beasts in Angers'

Apocalypse tapestry at **Château d'Angers** (p396)

6 Admire graceful arches at **Château de Chenonceau** (p381) or meticulous floral display at **Château de Villandry** (p386)

7 Imagine dropping hot oil on your enemies – or simply enjoy the view – atop **Loches'** (p388) 11th-century citadel

8 Steep yourself in Joan of Arc lore in **Orléans** (p365)

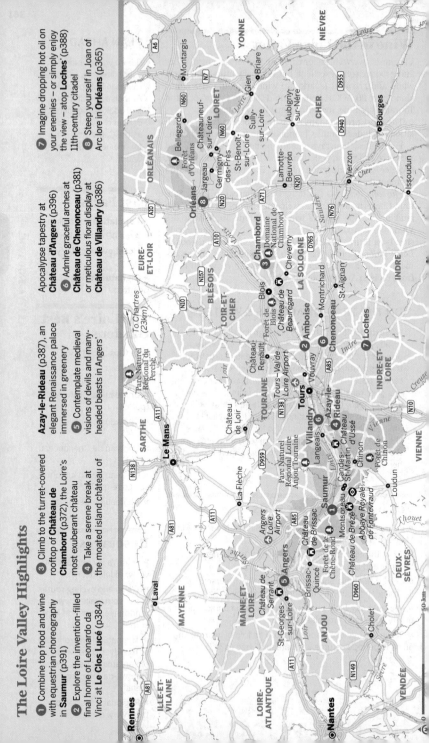

History

The dramas of French history are writ large across the face of the Loire Valley's châteaux. Early on, the Loire was one of Roman Gaul's most important transport arteries and the earliest châteaux were medieval fortresses established in the 9th century to fend off marauding Vikings. By the 11th century massive walls, fortified keeps and moats were all the rage.

During the Hundred Years War (1337–1453) the Loire marked the boundary between French and English forces and the area was ravaged by fierce fighting. After Charles VII regained his crown with the help of Joan of Arc, the Loire emerged as the centre of French court life. Charles took up residence in Loches with his mistress, Agnès Sorel, and the French nobility and bourgeois elite established their own extravagant châteaux as an expression of wealth and power.

François I (r 1515–47) made his mark by introducing ornate Renaissance palaces to the Loire. François' successor Henri II (r 1547–59), his wife Catherine de Médicis and his mistress Diane de Poitiers played out their interpersonal dramas from castle to castle, while Henri's son, Henri III (r 1573–89) used Blois castle to assassinate two of his greatest rivals before being assassinated himself eight months later.

❶ Getting There & Away

AIR Tours' airport has connections to London Stansted, Manchester, Southampton, Dublin, Marseille and Porto, while Angers' small airport offers service to London and Nice.

TRAIN The TGV Atlantique connects St-Pierre-des-Corps, near Tours, with Paris' Gare Montparnasse and Charles de Gaulle Airport in around an hour. The Loire's other cities (including Orléans, Blois, Amboise and Angers) are served by high-speed trains to Paris.

❶ Getting Around

Most main towns and many châteaux are accessible by train or bus, but if you're working to a timetable, having your own wheels allows significantly more freedom.

BICYCLE The Loire Valley is mostly flat, which makes for excellent cycling country. The **Loire à Vélo** (www.loireavelo.fr) scheme maintains a total of 800km of signposted routes from Cuffy near Nevers all the way to the Atlantic. Pick up a free guide from tourist offices, or download material (including route maps, audioguides and bike-hire details) from the website.

Détours de Loire (☑02 47 61 22 23; www.locationdevelos.com) Has bike-rental shops in Tours, Amboise, Blois and Saumur and myriad partners; can deliver bikes; and allows you to pick up and drop off bikes along the route for a small surcharge. Prices include a lock, helmet, repair kit and pump. Classic bikes cost €14 per day; weekly hire costs €59, with extra days at €5. Tandems are €45 per day, or €140 per week.

Les Châteaux à Vélo (☑in Blois 02 54 78 62 52; www.chateauxavelo.com; per day €12-14) Has a bike rental circuit between Blois, Chambord and Cheverny, and 300km of marked trails, and can shuttle you by minibus. Get free route maps and three dozen downloadable MP3 guides from the website, or pick up a brochure at local tourist offices.

TOURS Hard-core indie travellers might balk at the idea of a minibus tour of the châteaux, but don't dismiss it out of hand, especially if you don't have your own transport.

From April through August, the Blois tourist office and **TLC** (☑02 54 58 55 44; www.tlcinfo.net) offer a twice-daily shuttle (€6) from Blois to the châteaux at Chambord, Cheverny and Beauregard.

Many private companies offer a choice of well-organised itineraries, taking in various combinations of Azay-le-Rideau, Villandry, Cheverny, Chambord and Chenonceau (plus wine-tasting tours). Half-day trips cost between €20 and €35; full-day trips range from €45 to €52. Entry to the châteaux isn't included, although you'll likely get a discount on tickets. Reserve via the tourist offices in Tours or Amboise, from where most tours depart.

Acco-Dispo (☑06 82 00 64 51; www.accodispo-tours.com)

Loire Valley Tours (☑02 54 33 99 80; www.loire-valley-tours.com)

Quart de Tours (☑06 30 65 52 01; www.quartdetours.com)

St-Eloi Excursions (☑06 70 82 78 75; www.chateauxexcursions.com)

Touraine Evasion (☑06 07 39 13 31; www.tourevasion.com)

ORLÉANAIS

Taking its name from the historic city of Orléans, famous for its Joan of Arc connections, the Orléanais is the northern gateway to the Loire Valley. In the east are the ecclesiastical treasures of St-Benoît-sur-Loire and Germigny-des-Prés, while to the south lies the marshy Sologne, historically a favourite hunting ground for France's kings and princes.

NEW PERSPECTIVES ON THE VALLEY

Looking for a break from the standard château circuit? Several less conventional tour operators offer alternative perspectives on the Loire Valley, from horseback riding to hot-air ballooning to personal visits to local vintners.

Alain Caillemer (📞02 47 95 87 59; dcaillemer@rand.com; half-day tour €75 per couple)
This excellent bilingual (French-English) guide leads customised wine tours near his native Chinon. On a typical four- to five-hour outing, he'll tour you around the wine-growing region of your choice (Chinon, Cravant, Saumur Champigny, St-Nicolas de Bourgeuil, Touraine) in his own car, stopping en route for visits to his personal favorite vineyards, where you have the opportunity to meet the producers, taste wine extracted straight from the barrel and purchase direct.

Cheval et Châteaux (www.cheval-et-chateaux.com; multi-day tour per person €1062-2124)
Based between Orléans and Blois, experienced equestrian and local guide Anne-France Launay leads four- to seven-day horseback excursions combining visits to several of the Loire's best known châteaux (Chambord, Chinon, Azay-le-Rideau and Saumur among others), with overnights in castle-based B&Bs along the way. Group size is four to 10, with daily rides encompassing vineyards, forests, parks and riverbanks. Rates include gourmet meals, wine, B&B accommodation, horses, gear and guide.

Art Montgolfières (📞02 54 32 08 11; www.art-montgolfieres.fr; solo/duo €205/390) If you've ever dreamed of soaring over the rooftops of Chenonceau in a hot-air balloon, this company founded by Amboise native Charles Aréthuse can take you there. Trips last about three hours, with one hour spent in the air and the rest of the time preparing the balloon, dismantling it and drinking a celebratory glass of champagne (or two).

Orléans

POP 116,830

There's a definite big-city buzz around the boulevards, flashy boutiques and elegant buildings of Orléans, 100km south of Paris. It's a city with enduring heritage: already an important settlement by the time of the Romans' arrival, Orléans sealed its place in history in 1429 when a young peasant girl by the name of Jeanne d'Arc (Joan of Arc) rallied the armies of Charles VII and staged a spectacular rout against the besieging English forces, a key turning point in the Hundred Years War. Six centuries later, the Maid of Orléans still exerts a powerful hold on the French imagination, and you'll discover statues, plaques and museums dedicated to her around town. The city's charming, mostly pedestrianised medieval quarter stretches from the River Loire north to rue Jeanne d'Arc and has an outstanding art museum and fantastical cathedral.

◉ Sights & Activities

The tourist office runs guided walking tours (generally in French, but sometimes in English) of Orléans' sights in July and August, and occasionally the rest of the year. Some are combined with a riverboat cruise. The office also sells the self-guided walking tour brochure *9 Balades Entre Ciel et Loire* (€0.50).

Cathédrale Ste-Croix CATHEDRAL
(place Ste-Croix; ⏰9.15am-noon & 2.15-5.45pm)
In a country of jaw-dropping churches, the Cathédrale Ste-Croix still raises a gasp. Towering above place Ste-Croix, Orléans' Flamboyant Gothic cathedral was originally built in the 13th century and then underwent collective tinkering by successive monarchs, including Henri IV, who started reconstruction in 1601.

Louis XIII (r 1610–43) restored the choir and nave, Louis XIV (r 1643–1715) was responsible for the transept, and Louis XV (r 1715–74) and Louis XVI (r 1774–92) rebuilt the western facade, including its huge arches and wedding-cake towers. Inside, slender columns soar skywards towards the vaulted ceiling and 106m spire, completed in 1895, while a series of vividly coloured stained-glass windows relate the life of St Joan, who was canonised in 1920. Joan came here on 8 May 1429 and was greeted with a procession of thanks for saving the town.

Musée des Beaux-Arts ART MUSEUM
(📞02 38 79 21 55; 1 rue Fernand Rabier; adult/child incl audio guide €4/free; ⏰10am-6pm Tue-Sun)

Orléans' five-storeyed fine-arts museum is a treat, with an excellent selection of Italian, Flemish and Dutch paintings (including works by Correggio, Velázquez and Bruegel), as well as a huge collection by French artists such as Léon Cogniet (1794–1880) and Orléans-born Alexandre Antigna (1817–78). Among the treasures are a rare set of 18th-century pastels by Maurice Quentin de la Tour and Jean-Baptiste Chardin.

Free the first Sunday of each month.

FREE **Hôtel Groslot**　　　　HISTORIC MANSION
(place de l'Étape; ⊙10am-noon & 2-6pm Sun-Fri, 5-7pm Sat) The Renaissance Hôtel Groslot was built in the 15th century as a private mansion for Jacques Groslot, a city bailiff, and later used as Orléans' town hall during the Revolution. The neomedieval interior is extravagant, especially the ornate bedroom in which the 16-year-old King François II died in 1560 (it's now used as a marriage hall). The gardens at the rear are lovely.

Maison de Jeanne d'Arc　　　HISTORY MUSEUM
(☑02 38 68 32 63; www.jeannedarc.com.fr; 3 place du Général de Gaulle; adult/child €4/free;

⊙10am-6pm Tue-Sun Apr-Sep, 2-6pm Tue-Sun Oct-Mar) The best place to get an overview of Joan of Arc's life story is this reconstruction of the 15th-century house that hosted her between April and May 1429 (the original was destroyed by British bombing in 1940).

Completely revamped in 2012 for the 600th anniversary of the French heroine's birth, its main feature is a 15-minute audiovisual presentation (in French or English) tracing her origins, accomplishments and historical impact, reinforced by a wall-sized timeline in the adjoining room. Upstairs are the archives of the world's largest Joan of Arc research centre.

Musée Historique et Archéologique　　ARCHAEOLOGY MUSEUM
(☑02 38 79 25 60; sq Abbé Desnoyers; ⊙1.30-5.45pm Tue-Fri, 9.30am-noon & 1.30-5.45pm Sat, 2-6pm Sun) A ticket to Musée des Beaux-Arts also grants entry to this museum, whose centrepiece is the newly opened Salle Jeanne d'Arc, filled with imaginative representations of the Maid of Orléans, from a late 15th-century Swiss tapestry to

CHOOSING YOUR CHÂTEAU

There's no doubt that for dramatic castles, the Loire Valley is definitely the place, but with so many glorious palaces to choose from, how on earth do you go about selecting which one to visit? Here's our whistle-stop guide to help you decide.

For sheer, unadulterated architectural splendour, you can't top the big three: François I's country getaway Chambord (p372), Renaissance river-spanning Chenonceau (p381) and the supremely graceful Cheverny (p374). Unsurprisingly, these are also far and away the three most visited châteaux; turn up early or late to dodge the hordes.

If it's the medieval, Monty Python and the Holy Grail kind of castle you're after, head for the imposing fortress of Langeais (p386), complete with its original furnishings, battlements and drawbridge; the cylindrical towers of Chaumont-sur-Loire (p374), once owned by Catherine de Médicis; or the austere, ruined 11th-century keep at Loches (p388).

For historical significance, top of the list are the royal residences of Blois (p370), spanning four distinct periods of French history; stately Amboise (p384), home to a succession of French monarchs including Charles VIII and Louis XI; Forteresse Royale de Chinon (p389), where Joan of Arc held her momentous first rendez-vous with the future King Charles VII; black-stoned Château d'Angers (p396) with its fantastic tapestry; and pastoral Le Clos Lucé (p384) in Amboise, where Leonardo da Vinci whiled away his final years.

For literary connections, try the inspiration for *Sleeping Beauty*, Château d'Ussé (p387); Balzac's residence, Saché (p388); or Château de Montsoreau (p394), the setting for a classic Alexandre Dumas novel.

Looking for the picture-perfect setting? Our choices are the moat-ringed Château d'Azay-le-Rideau (p387) and Château de Sully-sur-Loire (p369), and the stunning formal gardens of Château de Villandry (p386).

Lastly, if you're looking for solitude, the chances are that off-the-beaten-track châteaux such as Brissac (p400) and Beauregard (p375) will be much quieter than their bigger, better-known cousins elsewhere in the valley.

THE LOIRE VALLEY ORLÉANS

Orléans

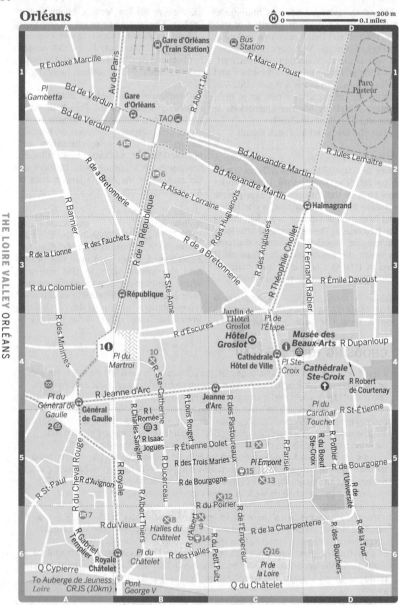

N
0 ————— 200 m
0 ————— 0.1 miles

20th-century mustard jars, inkwells and paintings. Across the courtyard, the museum's Gallo-Roman collection includes several rare bronze figurines recovered from the Loire's sandy bottom.

Place du Martroi CITY SQUARE

Three of Orléans' main boulevards (rue Bannier, rue de la République and rue Royale) converge on place du Martroi, where you'll find a huge bronze **statue** (1855) by Denis Foyatier, depicting St Joan atop a prancing steed.

Orléans

✦ Festivals & Events

Fêtes de Jeanne d'Arc　　CULTURAL FESTIVAL
(www.fetesjeannedarc.com) Since 1430 the Orléanais have celebrated the annual Fêtes de Jeanne d'Arc in late April and early May, commemorating the liberation of the city from the occupying English. A week of street parties, enormous medieval costume parades and concerts ends with a solemn morning Mass at the cathedral on 8 May.

🛏 Sleeping

TOP CHOICE Hôtel de l'Abeille　　HISTORIC HOTEL €€
(✆02 38 53 54 87; www.hoteldelabeille.com; 64 rue Alsace-Lorraine; s €52, d €69-130, ste €135-180; 🛜) Bees buzz, floorboards creak and vintage Orléans posters adorn the walls at this gorgeous turn-of-the-century house, run by the same family for four generations. It's deliciously old-fashioned, from the scuffed pine floors and wildly floral wallpapers to the hefty dressers and bee-print curtains. For breakfast (€11) there's a choice of coffees, teas, juices and exotic jams.

Hôtel d'Arc　　HOTEL €€
(✆02 38 53 10 94; www.hoteldarc.fr; 37ter rue de la République; s €103-141, d €117-181; ✳@🛜) Ride the vintage-style lift to swank guestrooms at this Best Western–affiliated hotel, conveniently placed between the train station and the pedestrianised centre. Rooms vary in size and the Prestige and Deluxe come with plush robes, but all are done up comfortably. Double-glazed windows help with daytime tram noise.

Hôtel Marguerite　　HOTEL €€
(✆02 38 53 74 32; www.hotel-orleans.fr; 14 place du Vieux Marché; s €59-95, d €69-105; 🛜) Recently renovated top to bottom, this basic but solid hotel wins points for its friendly reception and central location. Opt for a superior room if you like your bathroom sparkling and your shower powerful. Free bike parking is available.

Hôtel Archange　　BOUTIQUE HOTEL €
(✆02 38 54 42 42; www.hotelarchange.com; 1 bd de Verdun; d €51-83; 🛜) Gilded mirrors, cherub murals and sofas shaped like giant hands greet you at this station hotel aiming for boutique status. Citrus colour schemes spice up some rooms. Shuttered windows combat daytime tram noise.

Auberge de Jeunesse CRJS　　HOSTEL €
(✆02 38 53 60 06; auberge.crjs45@wanadoo.fr; 7 av de Beaumarchais, La Source; dm/s with HI membership €14/22; ⊙reception 8.30am-7pm) For those on a shoestring budget, this is a bare-bones hostel at the Stade Omnisports (sports stadium), 10km south of Orléans in La Source. Sixty beds in spartan rooms have cardboard mattresses. Jump off the tram or bus 20 at Université L'Indien.

🍴 Eating

TOP CHOICE La Parenthèse　　MODERN FRENCH €€
(✆02 38 62 07 50; www.restaurant-la-parenthese.com; 26 place du Châtelet; lunch menus €13.50-16.50, dinner menus €24-28; ⊙lunch & dinner Tue-Sat) Book ahead for this very popular restaurant, a labour of love for youthful local

RIVER CRUISING

The Loire offers relatively few opportunities to get out on the water: the currents are often too unpredictable to navigate safely. But it's not completely off-limits.

» **Croisières Fluviales La Belandre** (☑02 47 23 98 64; www.labelandre.com; adult/child €8.50/5.50; ☺Apr-Oct) Offers cruises from Chenonceau, with great views of the château.

» **Naviloire** (☑02 47 52 68 88; www.naviloire.com; adult/child €9/6; ☺Apr-Nov) Runs one of the few cruises on the Loire proper, in a 66-seat boat departing from Rochecorbon (7km east of Tours) to wild islets and nature reserves.

» **Observatoire Loire** (☑02 54 56 09 24; www.observatoireloire.fr; 4 rue Vauvert, Blois; adult/child €9/6.50; ☺May-Sep) Sets out from the Blois quayside aboard a traditional *futreau* (flat-bottomed barge).

» **CPIE Val de Loire** (☑02 47 95 93 15; http://bateaux-candes.org; adult €8.50-14, child €6-9; ☺Jul & Aug) Operates two traditional high-cabined Loire vessels known as *toues*, departing from Candes-St-Martin at the confluence of the Loire and the Vienne (14km east of Saumur).

chef David Sterne. Produce from the Halles marketplace across the street forms the basis for ever-changing, bargain-priced *plats du jour* (€9.50), plus creative lunch and dinner menus. Choose from relaxed sidewalk seating or two more refined indoor dining rooms.

Le Dariole   REGIONAL CUISINE €€
(☑02 38 77 26 67; 25 rue Étienne Dolet; menus €19.50-24; ☺lunch Mon-Fri, dinner Tue & Fri) This former *salon de thé* has transformed itself into one of Orléans' smartest restaurants, specialising in regional food. Inventive starters such as gazpacho with an asparagus-avocado charlotte are followed by mains like wine-braised beef with artichokes and new potatoes, and desserts such as vanilla bean *crème brulée* with fresh raspberries.

Les Fagots   TRADITIONAL FRENCH €
(☑02 38 62 22 79; 32 rue du Poirier; menus €12.50-15.60) Delightful smoky smells lure you in from pedestrianised rue du Poirier at this unpretentious eatery whose menu revolves around roasted meat. The Auvergnat owner cooks everything over an open fire, including grilled tomatoes and baked potatoes slathered with crème fraiche and chives. Lunch menus include an aperitif, plus simple, healthy appetizers and desserts (melon with Port wine, or fresh strawberries with mascarpone cheese and crumbled cookies).

Le Brin de Zinc   BISTRO €€
(☑02 38 53 38 77; 62 rue St-Catherine; lunch menus €16, dinner menus €22-27; ☺lunch & dinner daily) Battered signs, old telephones and

even a vintage scooter decorate this old-world bistro, serving French classics till late. On summer evenings, the sunny sidewalk tables are a big draw, as are daily blackboard specials (mussels, frites and a beer for under €12, anyone?).

Les Pissenlits par la Racine   BISTRO €
(☑02 38 53 18 60; 225 rue de Bourgogne; mains €12-19; ☺lunch & dinner Mon-Sat) A popular warm-weather hangout thanks to sidewalk seating on an intimate square, this simple eatery specialises in meal-sized salads and comfort food including burgers, tartiflette and homemade pork stew.

Covered Market   FOOD MARKET €
(place du Châtelet; ☺8.30am-7pm Tue-Sat, 8.30am-12.30pm Sun) Inside the Halles du Châtelet shopping centre.

🍷 Drinking & Entertainment

The free *Orléans Poche* (www.orleanspoche.com, in French) details cultural hot spots and happenings. Rue de Bourgogne and rue du Poirier are chock-a-block with drinking holes.

McEwan's   PUB
(250 rue de Bourgogne; ☺4pm-1am Mon-Sat) This Scottish-themed pub is popular for its wide variety of whiskies and beers on tap, and for its regular rugby and football broadcasts.

Les Becs à Vin   WINE BAR
(8 place du Châtelet; ☺11am-3pm & 6pm-1am Tue-Sat, 11am-3pm Sun) Good place to sample local wines, including several organic varieties.

Cinéma Pathé Orléans CINEMA
(place de la Loire) Centrally located 9-screen cinema with frequent English-language films.

❶ Information

Tourist Office (☑02 38 24 05 05; www.tourisme-orleans.com; 2 place de l'Étape; ⊙9.30am-1pm & 2-6pm Mon-Sat)

❶ Getting There & Away

BUS **Ulys** (www.ulys-loiret.com) brings together information for local bus companies serving the Orléanais area. Buy tickets (€2.10) on board or at the **bus station** (☑02 38 53 94 75; 2 rue Marcel Proust).

Sully-sur-Loire Line 3 or 7, 1½ hours, six daily Monday to Saturday, two Sunday

Châteauneuf-sur-Loire Line 3, 45 minutes to one hour, five daily Monday to Saturday, two on Sunday

TRAIN The city's two stations, Gare d'Orléans and Gare des Aubrais-Orléans (the latter is 2km to the north), are linked by tram and frequent shuttle trains. Trains usually stop at both stations.

Blois €10.50, 35 minutes, hourly

Paris Gare d'Austerlitz €19.40, 65 minutes, hourly

Tours €18.80, 1¼ hours, hourly

❶ Getting Around

TAO (☑08 00 01 20 00; www.reseau-tao.fr) Orléans' public transit authority operates buses and trams throughout the city, including the brand-new tram B (launched in June 2012), which passes in front of the cathedral and tourist office. Information and tickets (single/10-ticket *carnet* €1.40/12.70) are available at TAO's two downtown agencies, **Agence Place d'Arc** (Gare d'Orléans; ⊙6.45am-7.15pm Mon-Fri, 8am-6.30pm Sat) at the train station, and **Agence Martroi** (rue de la Hallebarde; ⊙8.30am-6.30pm Mon-Sat) in the historic centre. Trams run until around 12.30am, buses till 8pm or 9pm.

Vélo+ (☑08 00 00 83 56; www.agglo-veloplus.fr; deposit with credit card €3, first 30min free, next 30min €0.50, per subsequent hr €2) On-street bike-hire system, with stations all over town (eg train station, cathedral).

Orléans to Sully-sur-Loire

The 350-sq-km **Forêt d'Orléans** (one of the few remaining places in France where you can spot wild ospreys) stretches north of Orléans, while east of Orléans lie intriguing churches and little-known châteaux.

Châteauneuf-sur-Loire's **Musée de la Marine de Loire** (☑02 38 46 84 46; 1 place Aristide Briand; adult/child €3.50/2; ⊙10am-6pm Wed-Mon Apr-Oct, 2-6pm Wed-Mon Nov-Mar) explores the history of river shipping on the Loire, with a collection of model boats and riverine artefacts displayed in the former stables of the town's **château**.

Oratoire de Germigny-des-Prés (admission free, guided visit adult/child €3/1.50; ⊙9am-7pm Jun-Sep, 9am-5pm Oct-May), another 6km southeast, is one of France's few Carolingian churches, renowned for its unusual Maltese-cross layout and gilt-and-silver 9th-century mosaic of the Ark of the Covenant.

Five kilometres further southeast, St-Benoît-sur-Loire's Romanesque **Abbaye de Fleury** (☑02 38 35 72 43; www.abbaye-fleury.com; ⊙6.30am-10pm, guided visits 3.15pm Sun, 4pm Mon-Sat Mar-Oct) is still home to a practising Benedictine brotherhood, who conduct summertime tours. Look out for the basilica's famous decorated portal and capitals and the relics of St Benedict (480–547) which the monks fetched from Montecassino, Italy in 672.

Nine kilometres southeast of St-Benoît, the **Château de Sully-sur-Loire** (☑02 38 36 36 86; adult/child €6/3, with guided tour €7/3.50; ⊙10am-6pm Tue-Sun, closed noon-2pm Oct-Mar) is a grand example of a fairy-tale castle. Initiated in 1395, its machicolated ramparts and turrets were designed to defend one of the Loire's crucial crossings. From the outside this is one of the region's most picturesque châteaux, rising from a glassy moat lined by stately bald cypresses (brought from the United States by General Lafayette in the late 1700s). The castle underwent major refurbishment in 2007–08 and has an impressive exposed vaulted roof and historic tapestries depicting the story of Psyche. An outdoor **music festival** (www.festival-sully.com) jams in late May and early June.

La Sologne

For centuries, the boggy wetland and murky woods of La Sologne have been one of France's great hunting grounds, with deer, boars, pheasants and stags roaming the woodland, and eels, carp and pike filling its deep ponds and rivers. François I established it as a royal playground, but years of war and floods turned it into malaria-infested swamp; only in the mid-19th century, after it was drained under Napoléon III, did La Sologne regain its hunting prestige.

In winter it can be a desolate place, with drizzle and thick fog blanketing the landscape, but in summer it's a riot of wildflowers and makes for great country to explore on foot, bike or horseback. Paths and trails criss-cross the area, including the GR31 and the GR3C, but stick to the signposted routes during hunting season to avoid getting buckshot in your backside.

For info on hikes and walks in the Sologne, contact the tourist office (☏02 54 76 43 89; www.tourisme-romorantin.com; place de la Paix; ⏰9.45am-12.15pm & 1.30-6pm Mon-Sat, also 9.45am-12.15pm Sun July & Aug) in Romorantin-Lanthenay, 41km southeast of Blois. Some trails leave from near Saint-Viâtre's Maison des Étangs (☏02 54 88 23 00; www.maison-des-etangs.com/musee; 2 rue de la Poste; adult/child €5/2.50; ⏰10am-noon & 2-6pm Apr-Oct, 2-6pm Wed, Sat & Sun Nov-Mar), a museum exploring La Sologne's 2800 *étangs* (ponds).

On the last weekend in October, the annual Journées Gastronomiques de Sologne (www.romorantin.fr/jgs) fill the streets of Romorantin with local delicacies like stuffed trout, wild-boar pâté and freshly baked *tarte tatin,* the upside-down apple tart accidentally created in 1888 by two sisters in nearby Lamotte-Beuvron.

SNCF operates train-bus combos from Romorantin-Lanthenay to Tours (via Gièvres; €15, 1½ hours, five to seven daily). TLC (p372) bus 4 runs direct to Blois (€2, one hour, two to six daily).

BLÉSOIS

The countryside around the former royal seat of Blois is surrounded by some of the country's finest châteaux, including graceful Cheverny, little-visited Beauregard and the turret-topped supertanker château to end them all, Chambord.

COMBO TICKETS

If you're visiting Blois château, the *son et lumière* show and/or the Maison de la Magie, combination tickets save a bit of cash. Kids under six are free.

» Admission to any two attractions (adult/child €14.50/6.50)

» All three (adult/child €19/10)

Blois

POP 48,110

Looming on a rocky escarpment on the northern bank of the Loire, Blois' historic château (formerly the feudal seat of the powerful counts of Blois) provides a whistle-stop tour through the key periods of French history and architecture. Blois suffered heavy bombardment during WWII, and the modern-day town is mostly the result of postwar reconstruction. The twisting streets of the old town give some idea of how Blois might have looked to its medieval inhabitants.

👁 Sights & Activities

Château Royal de Blois   CHÂTEAU
(www.chateaudeblois.fr; place du Château; adult/child €9.50/4; ⏰9am-6.30pm Apr-Sep, reduced hours rest of year) Intended more as an architectural showpiece than a military stronghold, Blois' Royal Chateau bears the creative mark of several successive French kings. It makes an excellent introduction to the chateaux of the Loire Valley, with elements of Gothic (13th century), Flamboyant Gothic (1498–1503), early Renaissance (1515–24) and classical (1630s) architecture in its four grand wings.

The most famous feature of the Renaissance wing, the royal apartments of François I and Queen Claude, is the loggia staircase, decorated with salamanders and curly 'F's (heraldic symbols of François I). Highlights include the bedchamber in which Catherine de Médicis (Henri II's machiavellian wife) died in 1589. According to Alexandre Dumas, the queen stashed her poisons in secret cupboards behind the elaborately panelled walls of the studiolo, one of the few rooms in the castle with its original decor.

The second-floor king's apartments were the setting for one of the bloodiest episodes in the château's history: in 1588 Henri III had his arch-rival, Duke Henri I de Guise, murdered by royal bodyguards (the king hid behind a tapestry). He had the Duke's brother, the Cardinal de Guise, killed the next day. Henri III himself was himself murdered just eight months later by a vengeful monk. Period paintings chronicle the gruesome events.

In spring and summer, don't miss the nightly son et lumière (Sound & Light Show; ☏02 54 55 26 31; adult/child €7.50/4; ⏰10pm Apr, May & Sep, 10.30pm Jun-Aug), which bring the château's history and architecture to life with dramatic lighting and narration.

LE PASS CHÂTEAUX

Many of the châteaux in the Blésois are covered by the Pass Châteaux, multi-site tickets that can save you a few euros. For information, contact the tourist offices in Blois, Cheverny and Chambord. Below are some of the most popular combinations; additional combos include smaller châteaux at Villesavin and Troussay.

» Blois–Chambord–Cheverny €25
» Blois–Chenonceau–Chambord–Cheverny €35.50
» Blois–Chaumont–Chambord–Cheverny €34
» Blois–Chambord–Amboise–Clos Lucé €38.50
» Chambord–Cheverny–Beauregard €28.20

Maison de la Magie   MUSEUM
(www.maisondelamagie.fr; 1 place du Château; adult/child €8/5; ☺10am-12.30pm & 2-6.30pm Apr-Aug, 2-6.30pm Sep) Opposite the chateau you can't miss the former home of watchmaker, inventor and conjurer Jean Eugène Robert-Houdin (1805–71), whose name was later adopted by American magician Harry Houdini. Dragons emerge roaring from the windows on the hour, while the museum inside hosts daily magic shows, exhibits on the history of magic, displays of optical trickery and a short historical film about Houdini.

Old City   HISTORIC QUARTER
Despite serious damage by German attacks in 1940, Blois' old city is worth exploring, especially around the 17th-century Cathédrale St-Louis (place St-Louis; ☺9am-6pm), with its lovely multistoreyed bell tower, dramatically floodlit after dark. Most of the stained glass inside was installed by Dutch artist Jan Dibberts in 2000.

Across the square, the facade of Maison des Acrobates (3bis place St-Louis) – one of the few 15th-century houses to survive – is decorated with wooden sculptures taken from medieval farces. There's another example around the corner at No 13 rue Pierre de Blois called Hôtel de Villebrême.

Lovely panoramas unfold across town from the peaceful Jardins de l'Évêché and the top of the Escalier Denis Papin.

☞ Tours

Walking Tours   WALKING TOUR
(adult/child €5/3) The tourist office offers English-language walking tour brochures (€0.20) and guided tours in French. Château guides also run 1½-hour French-language city tours (adult/child €5/3) focusing on history.

Carriage Rides   CARRIAGE RIDE
(www.attelagesdeblois.com; adult/child €7/4; ☺2-6pm Apr-Jun & Sep, 11am-7pm Jul & Aug) Horse-drawn carriage rides clop around town from the château's main gate. Book at the tourist office, or wait outside the château for the next carriage.

🛏 Sleeping

La Maison de Thomas   B&B €€
(✆02 54 46 12 10; www.lamaisondethomas.fr; 12 rue Beauvoir; s/d €75/85) Four spacious rooms and a friendly welcome await travelers at this homely bed and breakfast on a pedestrianised street halfway between the château and the cathedral. There's safe bike storage in the interior courtyard and a wine cellar where you can sample local vintages.

Côté Loire   HOTEL €
(✆02 54 78 07 86; www.coteloire.com; 2 place de la Grève; d €57-89; ☎) If it's charm and colours you want, head for the Loire Coast. Its rooms come in cheery checks, bright pastels and the odd bit of exposed brick; and breakfast is served on a wooden deck.

Hôtel Anne de Bretagne   HOTEL €
(✆02 54 78 05 38; www.hotelannedebretagne.com; 31 av du Dr Jean Laigret; s €45-54, d €56-80; ☎) This creeper-covered hotel has friendly staff and a bar full of polished wood and vintage pictures. Modern rooms are finished in flowery wallpaper and stripy bedspreads.

Le Monarque   HOTEL €
(✆02 54 78 02 35; www.lemonarque.fr; 61 rue Porte Chartraine; s €38, d €58-59; ✻☎) Modern, bright and no-nonsense, this hotel sits at the edge of the old city, and offers comfort, cleanliness and a restaurant.

RV Parking   CAMPGROUND €
Contact the tourist office about its two RV parking sites, one near the castle and with waste disposal and showers (€5, May to September), and one on the river (free, October to April).

Eating

L'Orangerie   GASTRONOMIC €€€
(☑02 54 78 05 36; www.orangerie-du-chateau.fr; 1 av du Dr Jean Laigret; menus €35-80; ⊙lunch & dinner Tue-Sat) This acclaimed eatery is cloud nine for connoisseurs of haute cuisine. Plates are artfully stacked (duck liver, langoustine, foie gras) and the sparkling *salon* would make Louis XIV envious. On summer nights, dine in the courtyard.

Les Banquettes Rouges   TRADITIONAL FRENCH €€
(☑02 54 78 74 92; www.lesbanquettesrouges.com; 16 rue des Trois Marchands; menus €17-32; ⊙lunch & dinner Tue-Sat) Handwritten slate menus and wholesome food distinguish the Red Benches: rabbit with marmalade, duck with lentils and salmon with apple vinaigrette, all done with a spicy twist.

Le Castelet   TRADITIONAL FRENCH €€
(☑02 54 74 66 09; 40 rue St-Lubin; lunch menu incl wine €18, dinner menus €19-34; ⊙lunch & dinner daily, closed Wed & Sun; ☑) This country restaurant emphasises seasonal ingredients and hearty traditional dishes such as *fondant de porc au cidre* (pork stewed in cider, accompanied by baked apples and potatoes au gratin). There are also a few vegetarian options.

Au Bouchon Lyonnais   BOUCHON €€
(☑02 54 74 12 87; www.aubouchonlyonnais.com; 25 rue des Violettes; lunch/dinner menus €16/22; ⊙lunch & dinner Tue-Sat) Classic neighbourhood bistro with a flavour of bygone days. The food is straight out of the Lyonnais cookbook: *andouillette* (type of pig-intestine sausage), *quenelles* (pike dumplings), snails and *salade lyonnaise* (green salad topped with croutons, egg and bacon bits).

Food Market   MARKET €
(rue Anne de Bretagne; ⊙8am-1pm Tue, Thu & Sat) Blois' thrice-weekly market.

Drinking

The best bars are in the old town, particularly in the small alleys off rue Foulerie.

Velvet Jazz Lounge   JAZZ BAR
(☑02 54 78 36 32; 15bis rue Haute; ⊙3pm-2am Tue-Sat, 4.30-9.30pm Sun) Lodged under artful lights and 13th-century vaults, Blois' funkiest bar hosts Friday jazz acts from September through May, and in winter offers a selection of 30 (count 'em) hot chocolates in its alternative guise as an afternoon *salon de thé* (tea house).

Information

Tourist Office (☑02 54 90 41 41; www.blois chambord.com; 23 place du Château; ⊙9am-7pm)

Getting There & Away

BUS From April through August, **TLC** (☑02 54 58 55 44; www.tlcinfo.net) runs a château shuttle (Line 18), charging a flat fare of €6 for as many stops as you like on the Blois–Chambord–Bracieux–Cheverny–Beauregard–Blois circuit.

TLC also operates regular buses to the from Blois' train station (tickets €2 on board): Chambord (Line 3; 25 to 40 minutes, two Monday to Saturday) and Cheverny (Line 4; 45 minutes, six to eight Monday to Friday, two Saturday, one Sunday).

CAR Car rental is available at the train station.
Avis (☑02 54 45 10 61; Train station)

TRAIN The train station is 600m uphill from the château, on av Jean Laigret.
Amboise €6.60, 20 minutes, 10 daily
Orléans €10.50, 45 minutes, hourly
Paris Gares d'Austerlitz and Montparnasse from €26.70, 1½ to two hours, 26 daily
Tours €10.20, 40 minutes, 13 daily

Getting Around

BICYCLE The Châteaux à Vélo network offers 17 waymarked cycling routes in the Blois area. Maps are available at the tourist office.
Detours de Loire (☑02 54 56 07 73; www.detoursdeloire.com; 3 rue de la Garenne; per half-/full day €9/14) Hire bikes here, one long block downhill from the train station.

BUS Local buses in Blois and nearby communities, including Cheverny, are run by **TUB** (☑02 54 78 15 66; www.tub-blois.fr). Tickets cost €1.10. Buses run until about 8pm Monday to Saturday, with limited service on Sunday.

TAXI Available at the train station; call ☑02 54 78 07 65.

Château de Chambord

For full-blown château splendour, you can't top Chambord (☑02 54 50 40 00; www.chambord.org; adult/child €9.50/free, parking €3; ⊙9am-6pm Apr–Sep, 10am-5pm Oct-Mar), one of the crowning examples of French Renaissance architecture, and by far the largest, grandest and most visited château in the Loire Valley. It's worth picking up the multilingual audioguide (adult/child version €5/2), if only to avoid getting lost around the endless rooms and corridors.

Begun in 1519 as a weekend hunting lodge by François I, it quickly snowballed into one of the most ambitious (and expensive) architectural projects ever attempted by any French monarch. Though construction was repeatedly halted by financial problems, design setbacks and military commitments (not to mention the kidnapping of the king's two sons in Spain), by the time Chambord was finally finished 30-odd years later, the castle boasted some 440 rooms, 365 fireplaces and 84 staircases, not to mention a cityscape of turrets, chimneys and lanterns crowning its rooftop, and a famous double-helix staircase, reputedly designed by the king's chum, Leonardo da Vinci. Ironically, François ultimately found his elaborate palace too draughty, preferring the royal apartments in Amboise and Blois; he stayed here for only 42 days during his entire reign from 1515 to 1547.

Despite its apparent complexity, Chambord is laid out according to simple mathematical rules. Each section is arranged on a system of symmetrical grid squares around a Maltese cross. At the centre stands the rectangular keep, crossed by four great hallways, and at each corner stands one of the castle's four circular bastions. Through the centre of the keep winds the great staircase, with two intertwining flights of stairs leading up to the great lantern tower and the castle's rooftop, from where you can gaze out across the landscaped grounds and marvel at the Tolkienesque jumble of cupolas, domes, chimneys and lightning rods.

The most interesting rooms are on the 1st floor, including the king's and queen's chambers (complete with interconnecting passages to enable late-night nooky) and a wing devoted to the thwarted attempts of the Comte de Chambord to be crowned Henri V after the fall of the Second Empire. On the 2nd floor the eerie Museum of Hunting exhibits a copious display of weapons and hunting trophies. On the ground floor, an interesting multilanguage film relates the history of the castle's construction.

In a place of such ostentatious grandeur, it's often the smallest things that are most interesting: look out for the display of hundreds of cast-iron keys, one for each door in the château.

Several times daily there are guided tours (adult/child 1hr tour €5/3, 2hr tour €7/5) in English, and during school holidays costumed tours entertain the kids. Outdoor spectacles held throughout summer include a daily equestrian show (www.ecuries-chambord.com; adult/child €15/11; ☺May-Sep).

Domaine National de Chambord

This huge hunting reserve (the largest in Europe) stretches for 54 sq km around the château, and is reserved solely for the use of high-ranking French government personalities (though somehow it's difficult to imagine François Hollande astride a galloping stallion). About 10 sq km of the park is publicly accessible, with trails open to walkers, mountain bikers and horse riders.

It's great for wildlife-spotting, especially in September and October during the deer mating season. Observation towers dot the park; set out at dawn or dusk to spot stags, boars and red deer.

THE LOIRE VALLEY DOMAINE NATIONAL DE CHAMBORD

LUNCH BREAK

Need a moment to collect yourself between châteaux? For a pleasant lunch break, stop at La Madeleine de Proust (☎02 54 20 94 80; 33 rue du Maréchal Leclerc, Chaumont-sur-Loire; menus €21-28; ☺lunch Wed-Sun, dinner daily), halfway between Amboise and Blois, in the shadow of Château de Chaumont. The tasty meals here feature plenty of fresh local produce, in dishes like crispy pan-fried trout with herb-sautéed zucchini or raspberry tiramisù with creamy mascarpone. Alternatively, for a quick chocolate fix, head to sleepy Bracieux, 7km south of Chambord, where the Max Vauché chocolate factory (☎02 54 46 07 96; www.maxvauche-chocolatier.com; 22 Les Jardins du Moulin, Bracieux; tour adult/child €4/3.20; ☺10am-12.30pm & 2-7pm, closed Sun & Mon Sep-Jun) offers tours and a taste test!

STAYING OVER

Only 2km south of Cheverny, amid 3 hectares of grassland, La Levraudière (☎02 54 79 81 99; www.lalevraudiere.fr; 1 chemin de la Levraudière; s €62, d €66-69, tr €85-90) is a perfect blend of the farmstyle and the modern. In a peaceful, renovated 19th-century farmhouse, the B&B has a slab-like wooden table for breakfasts featuring fabulous homemade jams. But the crisp linens and meticulously kept house are the opposite of roughing it.

Hire bikes at a rental kiosk (☎02 54 33 37 54; per hr/half-/full day €7/11/15; ☺Apr-Oct) near the *embarcadère* (jetty) on the River Cosson, where you can also rent boats. Guided bike trips (adult/child €10/6 plus bike hire) depart mid-August to September.

To see the rest of the reserve, jump aboard a Land Rover safari tour (☎02 54 50 50 06; adult/child €20/12; ☺Apr-Sep), conducted by French-speaking guides with an intimate knowledge of where and when to see the best wildlife.

ⓘ Getting There & Away

Chambord is 16km east of Blois, 45km southwest of Orléans and 17km northeast of Cheverny.

Château de Cheverny

Thought by many to be the most perfectly proportioned château of all, Cheverny (☎02 54 79 96 29; www.chateau-cheverny.fr; adult/child €8.70/5.70; ☺9.15am-6.45pm Jul & Aug, 9.15am-6.15pm Apr-Jun & Sep, 9.45am-5.30pm Oct, 9.45am-5pm Nov-Mar) represents the zenith of French classical architecture, the perfect blend of symmetry, geometry and aesthetic order.

Built from gleaming stone from the nearby Bourré quarries and surrounded by lush parkland, Cheverny is one of the few châteaux whose original architectural vision has survived the centuries practically unscathed. Since its construction between 1625 and 1634 by Jacques Hurault, an intendant to Louis XII, the castle has hardly been altered, and its interior decoration includes some of the most sumptuous furnishings, tapestries and objets d'art anywhere in the Loire Valley. The Hurault family has owned (and inhabited) the castle for the last

six centuries and its fabulous art collection includes a portrait of Jeanne of Aragon by Raphael's studio, an 18th-century De la Tour pastel, and a who's who of court painters. Keep your eyes open for the certificate signed by US President George Washington.

The interior was designed by Jean Monier, known for his work on Luxembourg Palace for Queen Marie de Médicis. Highlights include a formal dining room with panels depicting the story of Don Quixote, the king's chamber with murals relating stories from Greek mythology, a bridal chamber and children's playroom (complete with Napoléon III–era toys). The guards' room is full of pikestaffs, claymores and suits of armour – including a tiny one fit for a kid.

Behind the main château, the 18th-century Orangerie, where many priceless artworks, including the *Mona Lisa*, were stashed during WWII, is now a tearoom.

Tintin fans might find the château's facade oddly familiar: Hergé used it as a model (minus the two end towers) for Moulinsart (Marlinspike) Hall, the ancestral home of Tintin's irascible sidekick, Captain Haddock. A dynamic exhibition, Les Secrets de Moulinsart (combined ticket with chateau adult/child €13.20/9.10), explores the Tintin connections with re-created scenes, thunder and other special effects.

Near the château's gateway, the kennels house pedigreed French pointer/English foxhound hunting dogs still used by the owners of Cheverny: feeding time, known as the Soupe des Chiens, takes place daily at 5pm April to September and 3pm October to March.

ⓘ Getting There & Away

Cheverny is on the D102, 16km southeast of Blois and 17km southwest of Chambord.

Château de Chaumont

Set on a defensible bluff behind the Loire, Chaumont-sur-Loire (www.domaine-chaumont.fr; adult/child €10/6, with gardens €15.50/11; ☺10am-6.30pm Apr-Sep, to 5 or 6pm Oct-Mar) presents a resolutely medieval face, with its cylindrical corner turrets and sturdy drawbridge, but the interior mostly dates from the 19th century.

At least two earlier fortresses occupied the site (whose name derives from Chauve Mont, 'Bald Hill'), but the main phase of construction for the present château began sometime around 1465 under Pierre d'Amboise. Originally a strictly defensive fortress, the castle became a short-lived residence for Catherine de Médicis following the death of Henry II in 1560, and later passed into the hands of Diane de Poitiers (Henry II's mistress), who was forced by the ruthless Catherine to swap the altogether grander surroundings of Chenonceau for Chaumont.

The château was thoroughly renovated by Princess de Broglie, heiress to the Say sugar fortune, who bought it in 1875 (and knocked down one entire wing to provide a better view of the river). The most impressive room is the Council Chamber, with its original maiolica-tiled floor, plundered from a palace in Palermo, but the château's finest architecture is arguably reserved for the Écuries (stables), built in 1877 to house the Broglies' horses in truly sumptuous style (the thoroughbreds all had their own personal padded stalls). A collection of vintage carriages is now displayed inside.

Chaumont's English-style gardens can be visited independently or together with the château. They're at their finest during the annual Festival International des Jardins (International Garden Festival; adult/child €11/7.50; ☾9.30am-sunset late Apr–mid-Oct).

❶ Getting There & Away

Chaumont-sur-Loire is 17km southwest of Blois. Onzain, a 2.5km walk from Chaumont across the Loire, has trains to Blois (€3.40, 10 minutes, 13 daily) and Tours (€8, 30 minutes, 10 daily).

Château de Beauregard

Less visited than its sister châteaux, peaceful Beauregard (☏02 54 70 41 65; www.beauregard-loire.com; adult/child €12.50/5; ☾10.30am-6.30pm, closed mid-Nov–mid-Feb), built as yet another hunting lodge by François I, has special charms all of its own. The highlight is an amazing portrait gallery depicting 327 notables of European royalty, clergy and intelligentsia. Spot famous faces including Christopher Columbus, Sir Francis Drake, Cardinal Richelieu, Catherine de Médicis, Anne de Bretagne, Henry VIII of England and his doomed wife Anne Boleyn, and every French king since Philippe VI. The quiet, 40-hectare grounds encompass numerous gardens, including the Garden of Portraits with 12 colour variations.

TOURAINE

Often dubbed the 'Garden of France', the Touraine region is famous for its rich food, tasty cheeses and notoriously pure French accent, as well as a smattering of glorious châteaux: some medieval (Langeais and Loches), others Renaissance (Azay-le-Rideau, Villandry and Chenonceau). The peppy capital, Tours, makes a good base, with castle tours and transportation links.

Tours

POP 138,590

Bustling Tours has a life of its own despite being one of the hubs of castle country. It's a smart, vivacious kind of place, filled with wide 18th-century boulevards, parks and imposing public buildings, as well as a busy university of some 25,000 students. Hovering somewhere between the style of Paris and the conservative sturdiness of central France, Tours makes a useful staging post for exploring the Touraine, with châteaux Azay-le-Rideau, Villandry and Langeais all a short drive away.

◉ Sights & Activities

The old city encircles place Plumereau (locally known as place Plum), about 400m west of rue Nationale.

Musée des Beaux-Arts   ART MUSEUM
(18 place François Sicard; adult/child €4/2; ☾9am-12.45pm & 2-6pm Wed-Mon) Arranged around the courtyard of the archbishop's gorgeous palace, this wheelchair-accessible

---

ROYAL MENAGERIE

As you visit the Loire's splendiferous châteaux, you may see some surprising zoological emblems etched into the walls, ceilings, towers and floors. See if you can spot:

» **porcupine** Louis XII

» **salamander in flames** François I

» **ermine** Queen Claude

» **stag** Jean II

» **winged stag** Charles V and Charles VII

» **genet** (sort of like a spotted civet) Charles VI

fine-arts museum flaunts grand rooms with works spanning several centuries, including paintings by Delacroix, Degas and Monet, as well as a rare Rembrandt miniature and a Rubens *Madonna and Child*. The stately 1804 Lebanese cedar in the courtyard measures a whopping 7.5m around the base.

Cathédrale St-Gatien CHURCH
(place de la Cathédrale; ⊘9am-7pm) With its twin towers, flying buttresses, stained glass and gargoyles, this cathedral is a show-stopper. The interior dates from the 13th to 16th centuries, and the domed tops of the two 70m-high towers are Renaissance. On the north side is the Cloître de la Psallette (adult/child €3/free; ⊘9.30am-12.30pm & 2-6pm Mon-Sat, 2-6pm Sun, closed Mon & Tue Oct-Mar), built from 1442 to 1524.

Musée du Compagnonnage MUSEUM
(www.museecompagnonnage.fr; 8 rue Nationale; adult/child €5.30/3.50; ⊘9am-12.30pm & 2-6pm, closed Tue mid-Sep–mid-Jun) France has long prided itself on its *compagnonnages*, guild organisations of skilled labourers who have been responsible for everything from medieval cathedrals to the Statue of Liberty. Dozens of professions – from pastry chefs to locksmiths – are celebrated here through displays of their handiwork: exquisitely carved chests, handmade tools, booby-trapped locks, vintage barrels, outlandishly ornate cakes and more.

Basilique St-Martin CHURCH
Tours was once an important pilgrimage city thanks to the soldier-turned-evangelist St Martin (c 317–97), bishop of Tours in the 4th century. After his death a Romanesque basilica was constructed above his tomb, but today only the north tower, the Tour Charlemagne, remains. A replacement basilica was built in 1862 to house his relics, while the small Musée St-Martin (☎02 47 64 48 87; 3 rue Rapin; adult/child €2/1; ⊘10am-1pm & 2-5.30pm Wed-Sun) displays artefacts relating to the lost church.

Jardin Botanique GARDEN
(bd Tonnelle; ⊘7.45am-sunset) Tours has several public parks, including the 19th-century botanic garden, a 5-hectare landscaped park with a tropical greenhouse, medicinal herb garden and petting zoo. The park is 1.6km west of place Jean Jaurès; bus 4 along bd Béranger stops nearby.

☞ Tours

Walks WALKING TOURS
The tourist office offers an audioguide (€5) for a two-hour self-guided tour, and also leads several guided walks (€5.80 to €9) in French.

Train TRAIN TOUR
(☎06 63 18 45 68; adult/child €6/4; ⊘daily May-Sep, weekends only Apr & Oct) Forty-minute tours leave the tourist office seven times daily (nine in July & August).

Carriages CARRIAGE TOUR
(rides €1.35; ⊘10am, 11am, 3pm, 4pm & 5pm Tue-Sat, 3pm, 4pm & 5pm Sun May-Sep) Fifty-minute rides depart from place François Sicard near the cathedral. Drivers sell tickets.

🛏 Sleeping
Tours has high-calibre rooms for the prices.

Hôtel Ronsard BOUTIQUE HOTEL €
(☎02 47 05 25 36; www.hotel-ronsard.com; 2 rue Pimbert; s €58-72, d €66-78; ✸@☎) More promising than you'd expect from its bland exterior, this centrally located and recently renovated hotel offers comfort and good value. The halls are lined with colourful photographs, while the sleek, modern and immaculate rooms incorporate muted tones of grey with sparkling white linens.

Hôtel Colbert HOTEL €
(☎02 47 66 61 56; www.tours-hotel-colbert.fr; 78 rue Colbert; s €37-54, d €45-61; ☎) In the heart of Tours' pedestrianised restaurant row, this newly remodelled, family-run hotel offers a welcoming haven amidst the surrounding street life. You're spoiled for choice when dinnertime rolls around, but light sleepers should opt for the 'Calme' rooms facing the peaceful inner courtyard (which also doubles as a pleasant spot to read, drink a glass of wine or park bikes overnight).

Hôtel Val de Loire HOTEL €
(☎02 47 05 37 86; www.hotelvaldeloire.fr; 33 bd Heurteloup; s €45-58, d €55-78; ☎) A prime location near the train station, friendly management and bright remodelled rooms make this an excellent midtown choice. Period features are nicely complemented by modern touches including new showers, double glazing and sound-dampening doors. The nicer back rooms downstairs have high ceilings and pleasant garden views, while the less expensive top-floor rooms are tucked under the eaves.

Hôtel des Arts HOTEL €
(☑02 47 05 05 00; www.hoteldesartstours.com; 40 rue de la Préfecture; s €33-46, d €48-51; ☎) A sweet place, with charming management, it has tiny but fastidious and cheery rooms in oranges and siennas. Get one with a balcony for extra light. There's public parking right across the street.

Hôtel de l'Univers HOTEL €€€
(☑02 47 05 37 12; www.oceaniahotels.com/ hotel-lunivers-tours; 5 bd Heurteloup; d €201-295; ✳@☎) Everyone from Ernest Hemingway to Édith Piaf has bunked at the Universe over its 150-year history. Previous guests gaze down from the frescoed balcony above the lobby, and rooms are appropriately glitzy: huge beds, gleaming bathrooms.

Hôtel Mondial HOTEL €€
(☑02 47 05 62 68; www.hotelmondialtours.com; 3 place de la Résistance; s €56-76, d €58-89; ☎) Overlooking place de la Résistance, this hotel boasts a fantastic city-centre position, with modernised, metropolitan rooms in funky greys, browns and scarlets. Reception is on the 2nd floor and there's no lift.

Auberge de Jeunesse du Vieux Tours HOSTEL €
(☑02 47 37 81 58; www.fuaj.org/Tours; 5 rue Bretonneau; s/tw/tr incl breakfast €23/46/69; ☺reception 8am-noon & 5-11pm; @☎) This friendly, bustling Hostelling International hostel (membership required; youth/adult €7/11) attracts a large foreign-student and young-worker contingent. Most rooms have only one to three beds; all share communal bathrooms, small kitchens and lounges. Bike rental available.

🍴 Eating

Pedestrianised rue Colbert is a great place to stroll and study your options, with eateries ranging from classic French to Asian and Middle Eastern. Place Plumereau is crammed with cheap eats, although the quality can be variable.

TOP CHOICE Cap Sud GASTRO BISTRO €€
(☑02 47 05 24 81; http://capsudrestaurant.fr; 88 rue Colbert; lunch menus €15.50-19, dinner menus €24-36; ☺lunch & dinner Tue-Sat) The hot-mod red interior combines nicely with genial service and refined culinary creations made from the freshest ingredients. Expect stylishly presented dishes such as warm St-Maure cheese with a pistachio-herb crumble and baby vegetables, or mullet fillet with sweet peppers, squid risotto and a ginger-tomato emulsion. Reserve in advance.

L'Atelier Gourmand GASTRO BISTRO €€
(☑02 47 38 59 87; www.lateliergourmand.fr; 37 rue Étienne Marcel; lunch/dinner menus €12/23; ☺lunch Tue-Fri, dinner Mon-Sat) Another foodie address, but bring dark glasses: the puce-and-silver colour scheme is straight out of a Brett Easton Ellis novel. Everything's delivered with a modern spin, and many dishes feature intriguing blends of the sweet and savory: cognac-flambéed prawns with sweet pea and mint risotto, spare ribs with

THE LOIRE VALLEY TOURS

LOIRE VALLEY WINE ROUTES

Splendid scenery and densely packed vineyards make the Loire Valley a classic wine touring destination. Armed with the free map *Sur la Route des Vins de Loire* (*On the Loire Wine Route*), available at area tourist offices, you can put together a never-ending web of good wine-tasting itineraries, drawing from the map's numbered list of 320 'open cellars'.

Two of the most densely packed stretches for wine-tasting along the Loire itself are just outside Tours and Saumur.

Towns to watch for east of Tours include **Rochecorbon** (home to Château Monmousseau and Blanc Foussy), **Vouvray** (Domaine Huet l'Echansonne, Château Moncontour and several others) and **Montlouis-sur-Loire**. You'll find a Cave des Producteurs representing multiple producers in each of the latter two towns.

Towns with multiple tasting rooms near Saumur (from west to east) include **St-Hilaire-St-Florent** (where you'll find Ackerman, Gratien et Meyer, Langlois Château and Veuve Amiot), **Souzay Champigny** (home to Château Villeneuve and Clos des Cordeliers), and **Parnay** (Château de Parnay and Château de Targé).

Either of these two stretches can easily keep you busy for an entire afternoon. So designate a driver (or hop on your bike), grab your map, and go explore!

THE LOIRE VALLEY TOURS

Tours

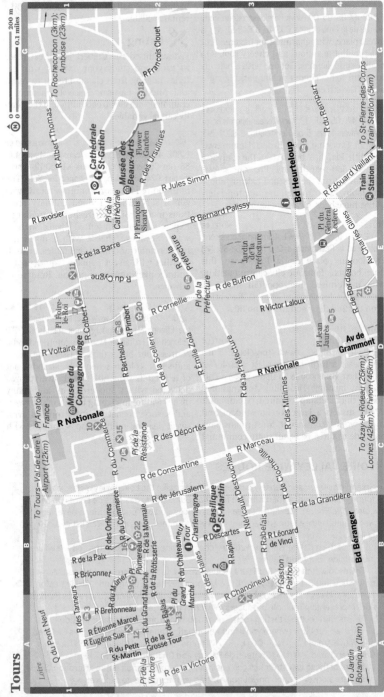

200 m
0.1 miles

Loire

Q du Pont Neuf

To Rochecorbon (3km);
Amboise (23km)

R François Clouet

R Albert Thomas

Cathédrale
St-Gatien

Musée des
Beaux-Arts

Flower
Garden

R des Ursulines

Pl de la
Cathédrale

R Jules Simon

R Lavoisier

R de la Barre

Pl François
Sicard

R Bernard Palissy

R de la
Préfecture

Jardin
de la
Préfecture

R de Buffon

To St-Pierre-des-Corps;
Train Station (5km)

R du Rempart

R Édouard Vaillant

Train
Station

Bd Heurteloup

Pl du
Général
Leclerc

Av Charles Gilles

R du Cygne

Pl Foire-
le-Roi

R Colbert

R Corneille

R de la
Préfecture

R Victor Laloux

R de Bordeaux

Pl Jean
Jaurès

Av de
Grammont

R Voltaire

R Berthelot

R Pimbert

R de la Scellerie

R Émile Zola

R de la Préfecture

R Nationale

Musée du
Compagnonnage

R Nationale

Pl Anatole
France

To Tours–Val de Loire
Airport (12km)

R du Commerce

Pl de la
Résistance

R des Déportés

R des Minimes

R Marceau

To Azay-le-Rideau (26km);
Loches (42km); Chinon (46km)

R de Constantine

R de Jérusalem

R de Cheville

R de la Grandière

R des Orfèvres

R du Commerce

R de la Monnaie

Tour
Charlemagne

Basilique
St-Martin

R Descartes

R Néricault Destouches

R Rabelais

R Léonard
de Vinci

Bd Béranger

Pl
Plumereau

R de la Paix

R Briçonnet

R des Tanneurs

R du Mûrier

R de la Rôtisserie

Tour
Châteauneuf

R du
Grand Marché

R des Halles

R Rapin

Pl Gaston
Paillhou

R du Grand Marché

Pl du
Grand
Marché

R Chanoineau

R Bretonneau

R des Balais

Pl de la
Victoire

R de la
Grosse Tour

R de la Victoire

R Étienne Marcel

R Eugène Sue

R du Petit
St-Martin

To Jardin
Botanique (1km)

Tours

caramelised lemon and ginger, or fish curry with coconut milk and pineapple.

BAC   BISTRO €€
(☎02 47 64 72 68; www.restaurant-bac.com; 3 rue du Commerce; lunch menus €13.90, dinner menus €22-26; ⊙lunch & dinner Mon-Sat) With its bustling street corner location and spacious outdoor terrace, this convivial eatery is a good place for people-watching any time of day. Stop in for the midday *plat du jour* (€8.90), an afternoon tea or cocktail, or inventive twists on French classics: duck breast with mashed sweet potatoes, or honey-and-cumin-marinated lamb roasted with rosemary.

Tartines & Co   BISTRO €
(6 rue des Fusillés; sandwiches €9-13; ⊙lunch Mon-Sat, dinner Wed-Fri) This snazzy little bistro reinvents the traditional *croque* (toasted sandwich) amidst jazz and friendly chatter. Choose your topping (chicken, roasted veg, beef carpaccio, foie gras with artichokes and honey vinaigrette) and it's served up quick as a flash on toasted artisanal bread.

Le Zinc   TRADITIONAL FRENCH €€
(☎02 47 20 29 00; 27 place du Grand Marché; menus €19.50-24.50; ⊙lunch Tue & Thu-Sat, dinner Thu-Tue) More concerned with market-fresh staples (sourced from the nearby Halles) than with Michelin stars and haute cuisine cachet, this bistro impresses with its authentic, attractive presentation of country classics (duck breast, beef fillet, river fish).

Les Halles   MARKET
(www.halles-de-tours.com; place Gaston Pailhou; ⊙7am-7pm Mon-Sat, 7am-1pm Sun) Tours' big daily market.

🍷 Drinking

Place Plumereau and the surrounding streets are plastered with grungy bars and drinking dens, all of which get stuffed to bursting on hot summer nights.

Pale   PUB
(cnr rue Colbert & place Foire-le-Roi; ⊙2pm-2am) This quintessential Irish pub enjoys an enviable location opposite a small park along pedestrianised rue Colbert. Outdoor seating and a plethora of beers on tap make it a prime warm-weather hangout, day and night.

L'Alexandra   ENGLISH BAR
(106 rue du Commerce; ⊙noon-2am Mon-Fri, 3pm-2am Sat & Sun; 🛜) Popular Anglo-Saxon bar crammed with students and late-night boozers.

Le Corsaire   COCKTAIL BAR
(187 av Grammont; ⊙6pm-4am Mon-Sat) Nautically themed cocktail bar serving ridiculously large drinks from an encyclopaedic menu.

☆ Entertainment

Get the low-down from the free monthly *Tours.infos* (www.tours.fr, in French), available all over town. Buy event tickets at Fnac billeterie (☎08 92 68 36 22; 72 rue Nationale).

Le Paradis Vert   BILLIARDS, DISCO
(☏02 47 66 00 94; www.leparadis-vert.com; 9 rue Michelet; adult/student pool table per hr €11/8; ⏰10am-2am; ☎) Fast Eddie eat your heart out! France's biggest pool hall is right here in Tours, with 36 tables and a weekly pool contest open to all comers. On Fridays the attached disco hosts theme dance nights, while Saturdays feature DJs spinning everything from rock to salsa.

Les Trois Orfèvres   MUSIC CLUB
(☏02 47 64 02 73; 3orfevres.com; 6 rue des Orfèvres; ⏰8pm-5am Wed-Sat) Grungy nightspot in the heart of the medieval quarter, where DJs and bands lean towards alternative and indie, and the students hang out in force.

Excalibur   NIGHTCLUB
(☏02 47 64 76 78; www.facebook.com/excalibur.tours; 35 rue Briçonnet; ⏰11pm-6am Tue-Sat) Hot-and-heavy club lodged in a converted ecclesiastical building. Has varied music, from pop to drum-and-bass, which packs in Tourangeaux (residents of Tours) clubbers.

Grand Théâtre   LIVE MUSIC
(☏02 47 60 20 20; www.operadetours.fr; 34 rue de la Scellerie; ⏰box office 10am-noon & 1-5.45pm Tue-Sat) Hosts operas, symphonies, chamber music and other concerts.

Cinémas Studio   CINEMA
(☏02 47 20 27 00; www.studiocine.com; 2 rue des Ursulines) Cinema showing non-dubbed foreign films.

❶ Information

Tourist Office (☏02 47 70 37 37; www.tours-tourisme.fr; 78-82 rue Bernard Palissy; ⏰8.30am-7pm Mon-Sat, 10am-12.30pm & 2.30-5pm Sun) Offers abundant info and sells château tickets at a slight reduction.

Police Station (☏02 47 33 80 69; 70-72 rue Marceau; ⏰24hr)

SOS Médecins (☏02 47 38 33 33) Phone advice for medical emergencies.

❶ Getting There & Away
Air

Tours-Val de Loire Airport (www.tours.aeroport.fr), about 5km northeast of town, is linked to London's Stansted, Manchester, Marseille, Dublin and Porto by Ryanair, and to Southampton by Flybe.

BUS The information desk for **Touraine Fil Vert** (☏02 47 31 14 00; www.tourainefilvert.com; single ticket €1.80) is at the bus station next to the train station. Destinations in the Indre-et-Loire

département include Amboise (40 minutes, 10 daily Monday to Saturday) and Chenonceau (1¼ hours, one daily), both served by Line C.

CAR Tours' perplexing network of one-way streets makes driving a headache, so you'll be glad to park your car. Use an **underground garage** (per 24hr €10) for stays of more than two hours; check opening hours for the garage you choose – many are reduced on Sundays.

Avis (☏02 47 20 53 27; train station, rue Edouard Vaillant) Car-hire option near the train station.

TRAIN Tours is the Loire Valley's main rail hub. Trains from Tours Centre station include:
Amboise €5.20, 20 minutes, 13 daily
Angers €17.30, 1½ hours, 26 daily
Blois €10.20, 40 minutes, 13 daily
Chenonceau €6.40, 25 minutes, eight daily
Loches €8.70, one hour, one or two trains plus several SNCF buses daily
Orléans €18.80, 1¼ hours, hourly
Paris Gare d'Austerlitz €32.90, two to 2¾ hours, five daily (slow trains)
Paris Gare Montparnasse €44 to €82, 1¼ hours, eight daily (high-speed TGVs)
Saumur €11.20, 45 minutes, hourly

TGV trains from St-Pierre-des-Corps (Tours' TGV station, 4km east and linked to Tours by frequent shuttle trains) regularly serve the following:
Bordeaux (€50, 2¾ hours)
La Rochelle (€40.30, 2¼ hours)
Nantes (€29, 1½ hours)
Paris Gare Montparnasse (€44 to €59, one hour).

❶ Getting Around

TO/FROM THE AIRPORT **Alphacars** (www.alphacars.fr) runs a shuttle bus (€5, 20 to 30 minutes) from Tours' bus station to the airport two hours before each departing flight, returning from the airport to the centre half an hour after each arriving flight.

BICYCLE For bicycle hire, try **Détours de Loire** (☏02 47 61 22 23; www.locationdevelos.com; 35 rue Charles Gille; per day/week €14/59; ⏰9am-1pm & 2-7pm Mon-Sat, 9.30am-12.30pm & 6-7pm Sun May-Sep), part of the **Loire à Vélo** (www.loireavelo.fr) network, or **Vélomania** (☏02 47 05 10 11; www.velomaniatours.fr; 109 rue Colbert; per day/week €15/52; ⏰3.30-7.30pm Mon, 10.30am-1.30pm & 3.30-7.30pm Tue-Sat).

BUS Local buses, run by **Fil Bleu** (☏02 47 66 70 70; www.filbleu.fr; 9 rue Michelet; individual ticket/day pass €1.35/3.50; ⏰7.30am-7pm Mon-Fri, 10am-5pm Sun), stop near place Jean-Jaurès. Most lines run until about 8.30pm;

several night buses run until about 1am. The information office is near the train station.

At the time of research, a new tram line was under construction, running south from Pont Wilson along rue Nationale and scheduled to begin service in 2014.

Vouvray

Chenin blanc vineyards carpet the area around Vouvray (population 3180) and Montlouis-sur-Loire, 10km east of Tours, and wine cellars sprinkle the region. Contact the tourist office (☎02 47 52 68 73; 12 rue Rabelais; ⏰9.30am-1pm & 2-6.30pm Mon-Sat, 9.30am-3.30pm Sun May-Sep, closed Sun & Mon Oct-Apr) for a list of local wine sellers, or stop in at Cave des Producteurs de Vouvray (☎02 47 52 75 03; www.cp-vouvray.com; 38 la Vallée Coquette) for a tour and tasting.

Château de Moncontour (☎02 47 52 60 77; www.moncontour.com; ⏰10am-1pm & 2-7pm, closed Sun mid-Sep–Mar) also does tastings and has a small wine museum.

Fil Bleu bus 61 links Tours' train station with Vouvray (€1.35, 20 minutes, 10 daily).

Château de Chenonceau

Spanning the languid Cher River via a series of supremely graceful arches, the castle of Chenonceau (☎02 47 23 90 07; www.chenonceau.com; adult/child €11/8.50, with audioguide €15/12; ⏰9am-7pm Apr-Sep, reduced hours rest of year) is one of the most elegant and unusual in the Loire Valley. You can't help but be swept up in the magical architecture and the glorious surroundings: exquisite formal gardens and landscaped parkland.

This architectural fantasy land is largely the work of several remarkable women (hence its alternative name, Le Château des Dames: 'Ladies' Château'). The initial phase of construction started in 1515 for Thomas Bohier, a court minister of King Charles VIII, although much of the work and design was actually overseen by his wife, Katherine Briçonnet. The château's distinctive arches and one of the formal gardens were added by Diane de Poitiers, mistress of King Henri II. Following Henri's death, Diane was forced to exchange Chenonceau for the rather less grand château of Chaumont by the king's scheming widow, Catherine de Médicis, who completed the construction and added the huge yew-tree labyrinth and the western rose garden. Louise of Lorraine's most in-teresting contribution was her mourning room, on the top floor, all in black, to which she retreated when her husband, Henri III, was assassinated.

Chenonceau had a heyday under the aristocratic Madame Dupin, who made the château a centre of fashionable 18th-century society and attracted guests including Voltaire and Rousseau (the latter tutored her son). Legend also has it that it was she who single-handedly saved the château from destruction during the Revolution, thanks to her popularity with the local villagers.

The château's interior is crammed with wonderful furniture and tapestries, several stunning original tiled floors and a fabulous art collection including works by Tintoretto, Correggio, Rubens, Murillo, Van Dyck and Ribera.

The *pièce de résistance* is the 60m-long window-lined Grande Gallerie spanning the Cher, scene of many a wild party hosted by Catherine de Médicis or Madame Dupin. During WWII the Cher also marked the boundary between free and occupied France; local legend has it that the Grand Gallery was used as the escape route for many refugees fleeing the Nazi occupation.

Skip the drab wax museum (€2) and instead visit the gardens: it seems as if there's one of every kind imaginable (maze, English, vegetable, playground, flower...). In July and August the illuminated château and grounds are open for the Promenade Nocturne (adult/child €5/free).

❶ Getting There & Away

The château is 34km east of Tours, 10km southeast of Amboise and 40km southwest of Blois. From Chenonceaux, the town just outside the château grounds (spelled with an 'x', unlike the château!), seven daily trains run to Tours (€6.40, 24 minutes). Touraine Fil Vert's bus Line C (€1.80) also runs once daily from Chenonceaux to Amboise (25 minutes). Croisières Fluviales La Bélandre (p368) offers 50-minute boat trips along the Cher River in summer, passing directly beneath the château's arches.

Amboise

POP 12,860

The childhood home of Charles VIII and the final resting place of the great Leonardo da Vinci, elegant Amboise is pleasantly perched on the southern bank of the Loire and overlooked by its fortified 15th-century château. With some seriously posh hotels

Châteaux of the Loire Valley

French history is written across the landscape of the Loire. Every castle traces a tale: of wars won and lost, romances embarked upon or destroyed, alliances forged and enemies vanquished. From the shockingly grand to the quietly subdued, there should be a castle to match your own mood.

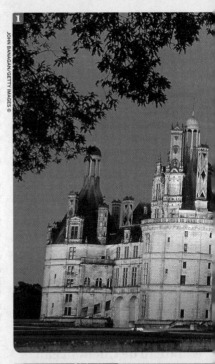

Chambord

1 Château de Chambord gets all the hype for a reason: it's stunning. Visit in the early morning to see it rise, all towers and turrets, from the mist – making it possible to imagine it in the days of François I (p372).

Chenonceau

2 Like an elegant lady, Chenonceau effortlessly occupies its beautiful surroundings. The impressive arches that span the calm Cher River draw you in, while the exquisite decor and the fascinating history keep you captivated (p381).

Azay-le-Rideau

3 A cypress-lined drive leads to this comparatively discreet and certainly romantic castle beautifully reflected in its still, broad moat. Fantastic views of the château from the lush park are lit up at night (p387).

Langeais

4 Over the centuries châteaux change hands, alterations are made...but in the case of Langeais, the details are intact. The 10th-century keep and the intricate medieval interior take you to a time of valiant knights and mysterious ladies (p386).

Angers

5 Whether for its distinctive black stone and watchtowers or for its mind-blowing medieval tapestry, Château d'Angers stands out from the crowd. The forbidding exterior hides a jewel-box of riches (p396).

Clockwise from top left
1. Château de Chambord 2. Château de Chenonceau
3. Château d'Azay-le-Rideau

and a wonderful weekend market, Amboise has become a very popular base for exploring nearby châteaux, and coach tours arrive en masse to visit da Vinci's Clos Lucé.

◉ Sights & Activities

Go to sights early in the day to avoid crowds and buy tickets in advance at the tourist office during high season.

TOP CHOICE Le Clos Lucé HISTORIC MANOR
(www.vinci-closluce.com; 2 rue du Clos Lucé; adult/child €13.50/8.50; ⊙9am-7pm Feb-Oct, 10am-6pm Nov-Jan; ⊕) Leonardo da Vinci took up residence at this grand manor house in 1516 on the invitation of François I, who was greatly enamoured of the Italian Renaissance. Already 64 by the time he arrived, da Vinci spent his time sketching, tinkering and dreaming up new contraptions, scale models of which are now abundantly displayed throughout the home and its expansive gardens. Visitors can see the rooms where da Vinci worked and the bedroom where drew his last breath on 2 May 1519.

Château Royal d'Amboise CASTLE
(www.chateau-amboise.com; place Michel Debré; adult/child €10.20/7, with audioguide €14.20/10; ⊙9am-6pm Apr-Oct, earlier closing Nov-Mar) Sprawling across a rocky escarpment above town, this easily defendable castle presented a formidable prospect to would-be attackers – but saw little military action. It was more often used as a weekend getaway from the official royal seat at nearby Blois. Charles VIII (r 1483–98), born and bred here, was responsible for the chateau's Italianate remodelling in 1492. Today, just a few of the original 15th- and 16th-century structures survive, notably the Flamboyant Gothic wing and Chapelle St-Hubert, believed to be the final resting place of da Vinci. Exit the chateau through the circular Tour Hurtault with its ingenious sloping spiral ramp for easy carriage access.

Pagode de Chanteloup PAGODA
(www.pagode-chanteloup.com; adult/child €8.90/6.90; ⊙10am-7pm May-Sep, reduced hours Oct-Apr) Two kilometres south of Amboise, this curiosity was built between 1775 and 1778 when the odd blend of classical French architecture and Chinese motifs were all the rage. Clamber to the top for glorious views. In summer, picnic hampers (€6.50 to €26) are sold, and you can rent rowing boats and play free outdoor games.

Parc de Mini-Châteaux MINI CASTLES
(⊡08 25 08 25 22; www.mini-chateaux.com; adult/child €14/10.50; ⊙10.30am-6pm Apr–mid-Nov; ⊕) Intricate scale models of 44 of the Loire Valley's most famous châteaux. Squint a bit and it's almost as good as a hot-air balloon trip over the Loire for a fraction of the price.

⌖ Tours

Freemove Segway Tours SEGWAY TOUR
(www.freemove.fr; 45min/90min/2hr tour €27/47/57; ⊙9.30am-1pm & 3-6.30pm May-Sep) Zip around town on a Segway PT; tours leave from a riverside kiosk opposite the tourist office.

Tourist Train TRAIN TOUR
(adult/child €6/4.50; ⊙Apr-Sep) Six departures daily from the château, with French and English commentary.

🛏 Sleeping

Amboise has some of the smartest places to stay in the Loire Valley, but you'll need deep pockets and you should book ahead.

Le Clos d'Amboise HISTORIC HOTEL €€€
(⊡02 47 30 10 20; www.leclosamboise.com; 27 rue Rabelais; r €110-180, ste €210-310; ❀☂▣) Backed by a vast grassy lawn, complete with 200-year-old trees, a heated pool and private parking for cars and bikes, this posh pad offers a taste of country living in the heart of town. Stylish features abound, from luxurious fabrics to wood-panelling to antique beds; the best rooms have separate sitting areas, original fireplaces and/or big windows overlooking the garden. Common spaces include a sauna, gym and multiple *salons*.

Villa Mary B&B €€
(⊡02 47 23 03 31; www.villa-mary.fr; 14 rue de la Concorde; d €90-120, apt per week €1180) Sandwiched between the river and the château walls, this spacious 18th-century town house includes four lovingly restored, old-fashioned rooms plus a 200-sq-m top-floor apartment. The owner, a former economics professor and inveterate world traveller with a passion for history, lives onsite. Pricier rooms have direct views of the Loire, while others gaze up at the château.

Au Charme Rabelaisien B&B €€
(⊡02 47 57 53 84; www.au-charme-rabelaisien.com; 25 rue Rabelais; d €92-175; ⊙late Mar-Oct; ▣) At this calm haven near the town centre,

Sylvie and Richard Viard offer the perfect small B&B experience. Mixing modern fixtures with antique charm, three comfy rooms share a grassy yard, pool and free enclosed parking. Pick of the lot is the spacious Chambre Nature, delightfully secluded away from the main house but only a few steps from the pool.

Le Vieux Manoir   B&B €€€

(☑02 47 30 41 27; www.le-vieux-manoir.com; 13 rue Rabelais; r €160-195; ✿🅿🛜) Set back from the street and fronted by a lovely garden, this restored mansion is stuffed floor to ceiling with period charm. Rooms get lots of natural light, and owners Gloria and Bob (ex-pat Americans who had an award-winning Boston B&B) are generous in sharing their knowledge of the local area.

Le Manoir Les Minimes   DESIGN HOTEL €€€

(☑02 47 30 40 40; www.manoirlesminimes.com; 34 quai Charles Guinot; d €131-205, ste €290; ✿@🛜) This pamper-palace set around a private courtyard would put most châteaux to shame. The best rooms in the main building have tall windows opening onto Loire or château views (corner suite No 10 has both!); some rooms are also wheelchair-accessible.

Hôtel Le Blason   HOTEL €

(☑02 47 23 22 41; www.leblason.fr; 11 place Richelieu; s €50, d €53-63, q €83; ✿@🛜) Quirky, creaky budget hotel on a quiet square with 25 higgledy-piggledy rooms, wedged in around corridors: most are titchy, flowery and timber-beamed. Upstairs units under the eaves come with air-conditioning.

Centre Charles Péguy-Auberge de Jeunesse   HOSTEL €

(☑02 47 30 60 90; www.mjcamboise.fr; Île d'Or; per person incl breakfast €19; @🛜) Efficient 72-bed boarding-school-style hostel on Île d'Or, an island in the middle of the Loire. Private rooms cost the same as dorms, making it an excellent budget option for solo travellers. Discounts for multi-night stays.

Camping Municipal de l'Île d'Or   CAMPGROUND €

(☑02 47 57 23 37; www.camping-amboise.com; sites per adult/child/tent €2.80/1.90/3.70; ☉Apr-Sep; 🏊) Pleasant campground on a peaceful river island opposite the château. Facilities include tennis courts, ping pong and canoe hire.

🍴 Eating & Drinking

TOP CHOICE Auberge de Launay   TRADITIONAL FRENCH €€

(☑02 47 30 16 82; www.aubergedelaunay.com; Le Haut Chantier, Limeray; menus €19.50-38; ☉lunch Tue-Fri, dinner Mon-Sat) Renowned far and wide for its cosy atmosphere and superb food, this country inn 8km east of Amboise merits the detour for anyone with their own wheels. Herbs and vegetables from the garden out back find their way into classic French meat, fish and poultry dishes, accompanied by a superb wine list and finished off with a divine artisanal cheese platter or desserts like wine-poached pears and homemade macaroons.

La Fourchette   TRADITIONAL FRENCH €

(☑06 11 78 16 98; 9 rue Malebranche; lunch/dinner menus €15/24; ☉lunch Tue-Sat, dinner Fri & Sat) Tucked into a back alley behind the tourist office, this is Amboise's favourite address for straightforward, reasonably priced home cooking. Chef Christine makes you feel like you've been invited to her house for lunch, with daily specials including *travers de porc* (spare ribs), *poulet rôti* (roast chicken) and *blanquette de veau* (veal stew).

Bigot   PATISSERIE €

(www.bigot-amboise.com; place du Château; ☉noon-7.30pm Mon, 9am-7.30pm Tue-Fri, 8.30am-7.30pm Sat & Sun) Since 1913 this award-winning chocolaterie and patisserie has been whipping up some of the Loire's creamiest cakes and gooiest treats: multi-coloured *macarons,* buttery biscuits, hand-made chocolates and petits fours, alongside specialty coffees and teas and savoury lunch-time treats including omelettes, salads and excellent quiches.

Chez Bruno   REGIONAL CUISINE €

(☑02 47 57 73 49; place Michel Debré; menus from €15; ☉lunch & dinner Tue-Sat) Uncork a host of local vintages in a coolly contemporary setting, accompanied by honest, inexpensive regional cooking. If you're after Loire Valley wine tips, this is the place.

Food Market   MARKET €

(☉8am-1pm Fri & Sun) Fills the riverbank west of the tourist office.

Le Shaker   BAR

(3 quai François Tissard; ☉6pm-3am) Perfect for a nightcap on a warm summer evening, this low-key bar on the Île d'Or enjoys full-on

views of the château and the river from its Loire-side sidewalk tables. Snacks, beer and cocktails are served late into the night.

ℹ️ Information

Tourist Office (☎02 47 57 09 28; www.amboise-valdeloire.com; ⊙9.30am-6pm Mon-Sat, 10am-1pm & 2-5pm Sun) In a riverside building opposite 7 quai du Général de Gaulle. Sells walking and cycling maps and discount ticket combinations for the château, Clos Lucé and the Pagode de Chanteloup.

ℹ️ Getting There & Around

Amboise is 34km southwest of Blois and 23km northeast of Tours. From the train station, 1.5km north of the château and across the Loire, local trains run 12 to 20 times daily to Tours (€5.20, 20 minutes) and Blois (€6.60, 20 minutes). Four daily express trains also serve Paris Gare d'Austerlitz (€30.10, 1¾ hours).

Bicycle

Détours de Loire (☎02 47 30 00 55; www.locationdevelos.com; quai du Géneral de Gaulle; ⊙9.30am-1pm & 3-6.30pm May-Sep) rents bikes from its brand new branch, across the street from the tourist office.

Train

From the **train station** (bd Gambetta), 1.5km north of the château on the opposite side of the Loire, local trains run 12 to 20 times daily to **Tours** (€5.20, 20 minutes) and **Blois** (€6.60, 20 minutes). Four daily express trains also serve **Paris Gare d'Austerlitz** (€30.10, 1¾ hours).

Château de Villandry

Completed in 1756, one of the last major Renaissance châteaux to be built in the Loire Valley, Villandry (☎02 47 50 02 09; www.chateauvillandry.com; château & gardens adult/child €9.50/5.50, gardens only €6.50/4; ⊙9am-6pm Apr-Oct, earlier rest of year, closed mid-Nov–Dec) is more famous for what lies outside the château's walls than what lies within. Sheltered with enclosing walls, the château's glorious landscaped gardens (closing 30 minutes after the château) are some of the finest in France, occupying over 6 hectares filled with completely manicured lime trees, ornamental vines, razor-sharp box hedges and tinkling fountains.

The original gardens and château were built by Jean le Breton, who served François I as finance minister and Italian ambassador (and supervised the construction of Chambord). During his time as ambassador, le

Breton became enamoured by the art of Italian Renaissance gardening, and created his own ornamental masterpiece at his newly constructed château at Villandry.

Wandering around the pebbled walkways you'll see formal water gardens, a maze, vineyards and the Jardin d'Ornement (Ornamental Garden), which depicts various aspects of love (fickle, passionate, tender and tragic) using geometrically pruned hedges and coloured flowerbeds. The Sun Garden is a looser array of gorgeous multi-coloured and multiscented perennials. But the highlight is the 16th-century potager (kitchen garden), where even the vegetables are laid out in regimental colour-coordinated fashion; plantings change in spring and autumn.

Try to visit when the gardens are in bloom, between April and October; midsummer is most spectacular.

After the gardens, the château's interior is a bit of a let-down compared with others in the region. Nevertheless, highlights include an over-the-top oriental room, complete with a gilded ceiling plundered from a 15th-century Moorish palace in Toledo, and a gallery of Spanish and Flemish art. Best of all are the bird's-eye views across the gardens and the nearby Loire and Cher rivers from the top of the donjon (the only remnant from the original medieval château) and the belvedere. Audio guides cost €3.50.

ℹ️ Getting There & Away

Villandry is 17km southwest of Tours and 11km northeast of Azay-le-Rideau.

BUS Touraine Fil Vert's bus V (€1.80) travels between Tours and Azay-le-Rideau (50 minutes), stopping at Villandry (30 minutes from Tours), twice daily from June to August.

TRAIN From Savonnières, 4km northeast of Villandry, one to three direct trains daily run to Tours (€3.20, 12 minutes) and Saumur (€9.20, 40 minutes).

Château de Langeais

In contrast to the showy splendour of many châteaux, Langeais (☎02 47 96 72 60; www.chateau-de-langeais.com; adult/child €8.50/5; ⊙9.30am-6.30pm Apr–mid-Nov, reduced hours mid-Nov–Mar) was constructed first and foremost as a fortress, built in the 1460s to cut off the likely invasion route from Brittany. It is fantastically preserved inside and out, so it remains every inch the medieval stronghold: crenellated ramparts and defensive towers jut out from the jumbled rooftops of the surrounding village.

One of the few châteaux with its original medieval interior, the castle (reached via a creaky drawbridge) has 15th-century furniture throughout its flag-stoned rooms. Among many fine Flemish and Aubusson tapestries, look out for one from 1530 depicting astrological signs; an intricate *Mille Fleurs;* and the famous *Neuf Preux* series portraying nine 'worthy' knights who represent the epitome of medieval courtly honour.

In one room, a waxwork display illustrates the marriage of Charles VIII and Anne of Brittany, which was held here on 6 December 1491 and brought about the historic union of France and Brittany.

Up top, stroll the castle's ramparts for a soldier's-eye view of the town: gaps underfoot enabled boiling oil, rocks and ordure to be dumped on attackers. Across the château's interior courtyard, climb to the top of the ruined keep, constructed by the 10th-century warlord, Count Foulques Nerra. Built in 944, it's the oldest such structure in France.

🛏 Sleeping & Eating

The village of Langeais (population 4070), with its peaceful walking streets, is a fun pit stop in the midst of the mayhem of castle-hunting. The town's market bustles on Sunday mornings.

Reserve ahead to stay at Anne de Bretagne (🖉02 47 96 08 52; www.chambresdhotes -langeais.fr; 27 rue Anne de Bretagne; d €62-68, ste €75-139), a B&B in a 19th-century town house just down the street from the castle's drawbridge. You can dine around the corner at Au Coin des Halles (🖉02 47 96 37 25; www. aucoindeshalles.com; 9 rue Gambetta; lunch menus €16-19, dinner menus €24-49; ⊙lunch Fri-Tue, dinner Thu-Tue), the village's elegant bistro.

❶ Getting There & Away

Langeais is 14km west of Villandry and about 31km southwest of Tours. Its train station, 400m from the château, is on the line linking Tours (€5.20, 20 minutes, six to eight daily) and Saumur (€7.60, 25 minutes, six to 10 daily).

Château d'Azay-le-Rideau

Romantic, moat-ringed Azay-le-Rideau (🖉02 47 45 42 04; http://azay-le-rideau.monuments -nationaux.fr/en; adult/child €8.50/free; ⊙9.30am-

6pm Apr-Sep, to 7pm Jul & Aug, 10am-5.15pm Oct-Mar) is wonderfully adorned with slender turrets, geometric windows and decorative stonework, wrapped up within a shady landscaped park. Built in the 1500s on a natural island in middle of the River Indre, the château is one of the Loire's loveliest: Honoré de Balzac called it a 'multifaceted diamond set in the River Indre'.

Its most famous feature is its open loggia staircase, in the Italian style, overlooking the central courtyard and decorated with the salamanders and ermines of François I and Queen Claude. The interior is mostly 19th century, remodelled by the Marquis de Biencourt from the original 16th-century château built by Gilles Berthelot, chief treasurer for François I. In July and August, a son et lumière (adult/teen/child €11/8/3), one of the Loire's oldest and best, is projected onto the castle walls nightly. Audioguides (adult/child €4.50/3) are available in five languages, and 45-minute guided tours in French are free.

❶ Getting There & Away

Château d'Azay-le-Rideau is 26km southwest of Tours. The D84 and D17, on either side of the Indre, are a delight to cycle.

BUS Touraine Fil Vert's bus V travels from Tours to Azay-le-Rideau (€1.80, 50 minutes) twice daily June to August. An SNCF bus stops near the château.

TRAIN Azay-le-Rideau's station is 2.5km west of the château. Trains run three to eight times daily to Tours (€5.40, 25 to 30 minutes) and Chinon (€4.80, 20 minutes).

Château d'Ussé

The main claim to fame of the elaborate Château d'Ussé (www.chateaudusse.fr; adult/child €14/4; ⊙10am-6pm, closed early Nov–mid-Feb) is as the inspiration for Charles Perrault's classic fairy tale, *La Belle au Bois Dormant* (better known to English-speakers as *Sleeping Beauty*).

Ussé's creamy white towers and slate roofs jut out from the edge of the glowering forest of Chinon, offering sweeping views across the flat Loire countryside and the flood-prone River Indre. The castle mainly dates from the 15th and 16th centuries, built on top of a much earlier 11th-century fortress. Its most notable features are the wonderful formal gardens designed by Le Nôtre, architect of Versailles. A popular local

MUSÉE BALZAC

Meander down the Indre Valley along the tiny D84, passing mansions, villages and troglodyte caves, and 7km east of Azay-le-Rideau you come to sweet Saché. Once home to American sculptor Alexander Calder (one of his mobiles sits in the town square), it still celebrates the life of long-time inhabitant Honoré de Balzac (1799–1850), author of *La Comédie Humaine*. The lovely Musée Balzac (☑02 47 26 86 50; www.musee-balzac.fr; adult/child €5/4; ☉10am-6pm daily Apr-Sep, 10am-12.30pm & 2-5pm Wed-Mon Oct-Mar) inhabits the town's château where Balzac was a habitual guest of his parents' friend, Jean Margonne. On a quiet slope in the lush river valley, the castle features original furnishings, manuscripts, letters and first editions. Feeling the peace, you can easily imagine Balzac escaping his hectic Parisian life and reclining here in his cosy bed, a board on his knees, writing for 12 hours a day – as he did.

rumour claims Ussé was one of Walt Disney's inspirations when he dreamed up his magic kingdom (check out the Disney logo and you might agree).

You may be satisfied just looking at the château from outside, since refurbished rooms are starting to show their age; they include a series of dodgy wax models recounting the tale of *Sleeping Beauty*.

Ussé is on the edge of the small riverside village of Rigny-Ussé, about 14km northeast of Chinon and 14km west of Azay-le-Rideau. There is no public transport.

Loches

POP 7180

The historic town of Loches spirals around the base of its medieval citadel, another forbidding stronghold begun by Foulques Nerra in the 10th century, and later enlarged by Charles VII. Loches earned a lasting footnote in the history books in 1429, when Joan of Arc persuaded Charles VII to march north from here to belatedly claim the French crown, but these days the town is a sleepy kind of place, best known for its lively Saturday morning market.

◎ Sights

From rue de la République, the old gateway Porte Picois leads through the cobbled Vieille Ville towards the Porte Royale (Royal Gate), flanked by two forbidding 13th-century towers, and the sole entrance to the Cité Royale de Loches, aka the citadel.

As you climb uphill you'll pass the Maison Lansyer (1 rue Lansyer; adult/child €3/2; ☉10am-noon & 2-6pm Wed-Mon), the former home of the landscape painter Emmanuel Lansyer (1838–93), featuring his paintings

alongside works by Canaletto, Millet, Piranese and Delacroix.

Cité Royale de Loches   CITADEL
(☑02 47 59 01 32; www.chateau-loches.fr; adult/child €7.50/5.50; ☉9am-7pm Apr-Sep, 9.30am-5pm Oct-Mar) Loches' vast hilltop citadel comprises several points of interest, all accessible with a single ticket.

At the southern end of the promontory is Loches' original medieval stronghold, the 36m-high donjon built in the 11th century by Foulques Nerra. Though the interior floors have fallen away, several architectural details remain, including remnants of fireplaces and the original chapel; dizzying catwalks allow you to climb right to the top for fantastic views across town.

Next door to the donjon is the notorious Tour Ronde (Round Tower), built during the 15th century by Charles VII and Louis XI. The basement holds a circular chamber where the unfortunate Cardinal Balue was supposedly kept suspended from the ceiling in a wooden cage for betraying Louis XI. (In fact, it was more likely a grain store, although you can see a replica of the cardinal's actual cage back in the donjon.) Other highlights here include the chilling Salle des Questions (a torture chamber), traces of prisoners' graffiti etched into the tower walls, and the rooftop terrace – once a strategic platform for firing artillery, nowadays just a fine vantage point for surveying the surrounding countryside.

In the adjacent courtyard, the Tour Martelet houses additional dungeons, along with a subterranean passageway bearing interesting displays about the 11th-century quarrying of *tuffeau* stone for the construction of the keep.

At the northern end of the citadel sits the **Logis Royal**, royal residence of Charles VII and his successors, built originally for defensive purposes but later converted to a hunting lodge and embellished in Flamboyant Gothic style. Joan of Arc famously passed through here after her victory at Orléans in May 1429 to meet Charlex VII and nudge him towards his coronation in Reims later that year.

Collegiale St-Ours   CHURCH
This church contains the tomb of Agnés Sorel, Charles VII's mistress, who lived in the château during her illicit affair with the king. Notoriously beautiful and fiercely intelligent, Agnés earned many courtly enemies due to her powerful influence over Charles. Having borne three daughters, she died in mysterious circumstances while pregnant with their fourth child. The official cause was dysentery, although some scientists have speculated that elevated levels of mercury in her body indicate she may have been poisoned.

🛏 Sleeping & Eating

Hôtel de France   HOTEL €
(☑02 47 59 00 32; www.hoteldefranceloches. com; 6 rue Picois; d €50-62; ❋ 🐾) Two blocks west of the tourist office in the lower town, an arched gateway leads into the paved courtyard of this old *relais de poste* (post house), now a trim if rather tired Logis de France. The best rooms are above the restaurant, which serves traditional French standbys.

La Gerbe d'Or   TRADITIONAL FRENCH €€
(☑02 47 91 67 63; www.restaurantlagerbedor.fr; 22 rue Balzac; menus €19-27; ⊙lunch daily, dinner Thu-Tue) The time-honoured 'Golden Sheaf' (and no, it's *not* the Golden Gerbil!) specialises in hearty traditional fare using local products, such as foie gras and duck confit terrines with Vouvray wine jelly, or beef with shallots and haricots verts.

Food Market   MARKET €
(⊙8am-12.30pm Wed & Sat) Fills rue de la République and surrounding streets.

ℹ Information

Tourist Office (☑02 47 91 82 82; www.loches -tourainecotesud.com; place de la Marne; ⊙9am-12.30pm & 1.30-6pm Mon-Sat, 10am-12.30pm & 2.30-5pm Sun) Beside the river, one block across the bridge from the train station.

ℹ Getting There & Around

Loches is 67km southwest of Blois and 41km southeast of Tours. Trains and SNCF buses link the train station, across the River Indre from the tourist office, with Tours (€8.70, one hour, six to 15 daily).

Chinon

POP 8450

Peacefully placed along the northern bank of the Vienne and dominated by its hulking hillside château, Chinon is forever etched in France's collective memory as the place where Joan of Arc first met Charles VII in 1429; more recently, it's earned renown as one of the Loire's main wine-producing areas. Chinon AOC (www.chinon.com) cabernet franc vineyards stretch along both sides of the river. Within the steep muddle of white tufa houses and black slate rooftops you'll discover an appealing medieval quarter.

◎ Sights

Forteresse Royale de Chinon   CASTLE
(☑02 47 93 13 45; www.forteresse-chinon.fr; adult/ child €7.50/5.50; ⊙9.30am-7pm May-Aug, shorter hours rest of year) In 2010 the castle emerged from one of the region's largest restoration projects (at a cost of €14.5 million). It is split into three sections separated by dry moats. The 12th-century **Fort St-Georges** and the **Logis Royal** (Royal Lodgings) remain from the time when the Plantagenet court of Henry II and Eleanor of Aquitaine was held here. The 14th-century **Tour de l'Horloge** (Clock Tower) houses a collection of Joan of Arc memorabilia; she came here in 1429 to meet the future Charles VII. There's a wonderful valley panorama from the top of the 13th-century **Fort du Coudray** and a small historical exhibition in the **Château du Milieu** (the Middle Castle).

Entry to the castle is across from the free **lift** (⊙7am-midnight Apr-Sep, to 11pm Oct-Mar) ascending from the lower town.

Old Town   HISTORIC QUARTER
(guided tours adult/child €4.70/2.50) The author François Rabelais (c 1483–1553), whose works include the Gargantua and Pantagruel series grew up in Chinon; you'll see Rabelais-related names dotted all around the old town, which offers a fine cross-section of medieval architecture, best seen along rue Haute St-Maurice and rue Voltaire. Look out for the remarkable **Hôtel du Gouverneur** (rue Haute St-Maurice), an impressive

town house with a double-flighted staircase ensconced behind a carved gateway, and the nearby Gothic Palais du Bailliage, the former residence of Chinon's bailiwick (now occupied by the Hostellerie Gargantua). The tourist office has a free walking-tour leaflet and offers guided tours.

Caves Painctes de Chinon   WINE CELLAR
(☏02 47 93 30 44; impasse des Caves Painctes; admission €3; ⏱guided tours 11am, 3pm, 4.30pm & 6pm Tue-Sun Jul & Aug) Hidden at the end of a cobbled alleyway off rue Voltaire, these former quarries were converted into wine cellars during the 15th century. The Confrérie des Bons Entonneurs Rabelaisiens, a brotherhood of local winegrowers, runs tours of the *caves* in summertime.

Chapelle Ste-Radegonde   CHURCH
(☏02 47 93 17 85; rue du Coteau Ste-Radegonde; adult/child €3/free; ⏱3-6pm Sat & Sun May, Jun & Sep, 3-6pm Wed-Mon Jul & Aug) Built into a cave above town, this atmospheric, half-ruined medieval chapel is noteworthy for its 12th-century 'Royal Hunt' fresco and a staircase that descends to a subterranean spring associated with a pre-Christian cult. From the tourist office, follow rue Rousseau 300m east, then climb rue du Pitoche along the base of the cliffs past several abandoned troglodytic dwellings.

Musée d'Art et d'Histoire   MUSEUM
(☏02 47 93 18 12; 44 rue Haute St-Maurice; adult/child €3/free; ⏱2.30-6pm Fri-Mon mid-Feb–mid-Nov) Art and archaeology exhibits from prehistory to the 19th century relating to Chinon and its environs.

🛏 Sleeping

TOP CHOICE Hôtel Diderot   HISTORIC HOTEL €
(☏02 47 93 18 87; www.hoteldiderot.com; 4 rue de Buffon; s €46-68, d €56-86; 🌐) This gorgeous shady townhouse is tucked amid luscious rose-filled gardens and crammed with polished antiques. The friendly owners impart the kind of glowing charm you'd expect of a hotel twice the price. Rooms are all individually styled, from over-the-top Napoleonic to stripped-back art deco and have large flat-screen TVs. Breakfast (€9) includes a rainbow of homemade jams, plus locally produced apple juice, yogurt and goat cheese served with honey and 'crack-your-own' walnuts. Parking is €7 in the hotel lot, or free just down the street.

Hostellerie Gargantua   HISTORIC HOTEL €€
(☏02 47 93 04 71; www.hotel-gargantua.com; 73 rue Haute St-Maurice; standard/superior d €55/81; 🌐) Harry Potter would feel right at home at this turret-topped medieval mansion. The simple, offbeat hotel has spiral staircases, pitch-dark wood and solid stone. Superior rooms are worth the cash, including Grangousier with its fireplace and four-poster, and Badebec with its oak beams and château views. Parking €5.50.

Hôtel Le Plantagenêt   HOTEL €€
(☏02 47 93 36 92; www.hotel-plantagenet.com; 12 place Jeanne d'Arc; s €60-72, d €67-82, tr €93; ❄🌐) A basic, dated but perfectly serviceable hotel halfway between centre and station, with rooms spread over three buildings. The original *maison bourgeoise* is more charming and less cramped than the motel-like annexe out back. Perks include guest laundry (€8), a pleasant central patio where guests are invited to picnic and a hearty cyclist-friendly breakfast (€9.50). Parking €8.

🍴 Eating & Drinking

Reserve ahead on weekends and during high season.

TOP CHOICE Les Années 30   TRADITIONAL FRENCH €€
(☏02 47 93 37 18; www.lesannees30.com; 78 rue Voltaire; menus €27-43; ⏱lunch & dinner Thu-Mon) Expect the kind of meal you came to France to eat: exquisite attention to flavours and detail, served up in relaxed intimacy. The interior dining room is golden-lit downstairs and cool blue upstairs, with twin fireplaces enhancing the cosy atmosphere in chilly weather; in summer dine under the streetside pergola, in the heart of the old quarter. The menu ranges from traditional *coq au vin* and duck with cherry coulis to unusual choices such as wild boar.

La Bonne France   TRADITIONAL FRENCH €
(☏02 47 98 01 34; www.labonnefrance.com; 4 Place de la Victoire; lunch menus €10-12.50, dinner menus €15.50-31.50; ⏱lunch Fri-Tue, dinner Thu-Tue) Dine al fresco under the patio umbrellas, or reserve ahead for one of the nine indoor tables at this low-key, intimate eatery, tucked into a little square in Chinon's pedestrian zone. Good-value menus balance hearty fare such as stewed pork and *gratin dauphinois* (potatoes with melted cheese) against lighter fish and veggie dishes (ratatouille, salmon-sorrel pâté with lemon cream).

Restaurant au
Chapeau Rouge TRADITIONAL FRENCH €€
(☎02 47 98 08 08; www.restaurant-chapeau-rouge.
fr; 49 place du Général de Gaulle; dinner menus €29-
53; ☺lunch Tue-Sun, dinner Tue-Sat) There's an
air of a Left Bank brasserie hanging around
the Red Hat, sheltered behind red and gold
awnings. Chatting families dig into hare
fondant, smoked fish and other countrified
dishes.

Food Market MARKET €
(place Jeanne d'Arc; ☺Thu morning) Weekly
market.

ℹ Information

Tourist Office (☎02 47 93 17 85; www.chinon
-valdeloire.com; place Hofheïm; ☺10am-7pm
May-Sep, 10am-12.30pm & 2.30-6pm Mon-Sat
Oct-Apr) Has a free walking tour brochure and
details on kayaking and can arrange hot-air
balloon flights.

ℹ Getting There & Away

Chinon is 47km southwest of Tours, 21km southwest of Azay-le-Rideau and 30km southeast of
Saumur.

BUS Touraine Fil Vert's bus TF (€1.80) connects
Chinon, Azay-le-Rideau and Langeais (two or
three Monday to Friday).

TRAIN The train station is 1km east of place
du Général de Gaulle. Trains or SNCF buses run
11 times daily (five at weekends) to Tours (€9,
50 minutes to 1¼ hours) and Azay-le-Rideau
(€4.80, 20 minutes).

ANJOU

In Anjou, Renaissance châteaux give way
to chalky white tufa cliffs concealing an
astonishing underworld of wine cellars,
mushroom farms and art sculptures. Above
ground, black slate roofs pepper the vine-
rich land from which some of the Loire's
best wines are produced.

Angers, the historic capital of Anjou, is
famous for its fortified hilltop château and
its stunning medieval tapestry. Architectural gems in Anjou's crown include Angers'
cathedral and, to the southeast, the Romanesque Abbaye de Fontevraud. Europe's highest concentration of troglodyte dwellings
dot the banks of the Loire around cosmopolitan Saumur.

The area along the Rivers Loire, Authion
and Vienne from Angers southeast to Azay-
le-Rideau form the Parc Naturel Régional
Loire-Anjou-Touraine.

Saumur
POP 29,650

There's an air of Parisian sophistication
around Saumur, but also a sense of laid-back
contentment. The food is good, the wine is
good, the spot is good – and the Saumurites
know it. The town is renowned for its École
Nationale d'Équitation, a national cavalry
school that's been home to the crack riders of the Cadre Noir since 1828. Soft white
tufa cliffs stretch along the riverbanks east
and west of town, pock-marked by the unusual man-made caves known as *habitations
troglodytes*.

◉ Sights & Activities

For wine tasting, drive west of town along
route D751 towards Gennes, or east on
route D947 through Souzay-Champigny and
Parnay.

Château de Saumur CASTLE
(☎02 41 40 24 40; adult/child €9/5; ☺10am-1pm
& 2-5.30pm Tue-Sun Apr-Oct) Soaring above the
town's rooftops, Saumur's fairy-tale château
was largely built during the 13th century by

MUSÉE RABELAIS

Follow the signs 9km southwest of Chinon, to the outskirts of Seuilly to find La Devinière, the farm where François Rabelais – doctor, Franciscan friar, theoretician and
author – was born (sometime between 1483 and 1494; no one is sure). Set among the
fields and vineyards with sweeping views to the private château in Coudray Montpensier, this farm inspired the settings for Rabelais' five satirical, erudite Gargantua and
Pantagruel novels. The rambling buildings of the farmstead hold the Musée Rabelais
(www.musee-rabelais.fr; adult/child €5/4; ☺10am-12.30pm & 2-6pm Apr-Sep, to 7pm Jul & Aug,
to 5pm Oct-Mar, closed Tue Oct-Mar), with thoughtful exhibits including early editions of
Rabelais' work and a Matisse portrait of the author from 1951. The winding cave network
beneath provides an atmospheric setting for special exhibitions.

Louis XI, and has variously served as a dungeon, fortress and country residence. Its defensive heritage took a hefty knock in 2001 when a large chunk of the western ramparts collapsed without warning. After a decade-long restoration project, the castle's decorative arts collection reopened in July 2012 on the first floor, and the second floor, with its impressive collection of vintage equestrian gear, is scheduled to reopen in 2013.

Musée des Blindés
MILITARY MUSEUM
(☑02 41 83 69 95; www.museedesblindes.fr; 1043 rte de Fontevraud; adult/child €7.50/4.50; ☺10am-6pm) Gearheads love this comprehensive museum of over 200 tanks and military vehicles. Children are allowed to climb on some of them. Examples include many WWI tanks such as the Schneider and dozens of WWII models, such as the Hotchkiss H39, Panzers and an Issoise infantry tractor.

FREE Musée de la Cavalerie
CAVALRY MUSEUM
(☑02 41 83 69 23; http://museecavalerie.free.fr; place Charles de Foucauld; ☺9am-noon & 2-5pm Mon-Thu, 2-6pm Sat-Sun) Housed in the old military stables of the Cadre Noir, this museum traces the history of the French cavalry from 1445 in the time of Charles VII to modern tanks.

TOP CHOICE École Nationale d'Équitation
RIDING SCHOOL
(National Equestrian School; ☑02 41 53 50 60; www.cadrenoir.fr; rte de Marson; adult/child €7/5, Cadre Noir presentations adult/child €16/9; ☺mornings Tue-Sat & afternoons Mon-Fri Apr–mid-Nov) Anchored in France's academic-military riding tradition, Saumur has been an equine centre since 1593. Three kilometres west of town, outside of sleepy St-Hilaire-St-Florent, the École Nationale d'Équitation is one of France's foremost riding academies, responsible for training the country's Olympic teams and members of the elite Cadre Noir, distinguished by their special black jackets, caps, gold spurs and three golden wings on their whips. The Cadre Noir train both the school's instructors and horses (which take around 5½ years to achieve display standard) and are famous for their astonishing discipline and acrobatic manoeuvres (like 'airs above ground'), which are all performed without stirrups.

Advance reservations are essential for the one-hour guided visits (four to 10 per day; enquire about the availability of English-language tours). If you happen to be in town for one of the semi-monthly Cadre Noir presentations do not miss it: they are like astonishing horse ballets. Check the website for dates.

Distillerie Combier
DISTILLERY
(☑02 41 40 23 00; www.combier.fr; 48 rue Beaurepaire; adult €4; ☺10am-12.30pm & 2-7pm, closed Mon Oct-May, Sun Nov & Jan-Mar) In business since its invention of Triple Sec in 1834, this distillery has also recently resurrected authentic absinthe, the famous firewater. Taste these alongside other liqueurs including Royal Combier and Pastis d'Antan, and get a behind-the-scenes look at their production facility, with gleaming century-old copper stills, vintage Eiffel machinery and fragrant vats full of Haitian bitter oranges. There are three to five guided visits per day.

Langlois – Chateau
WINE SCHOOL
(☑02 41 40 21 40; www.langlois-chateau.fr; 3 rue Léopold Palustre; classes adult/child €5/free, extended classes €225; ☺guided tours 10.20am, 11.20am, 2.20pm & 4.20pm, tasting 10am-12.30pm & 2-6.30pm Apr–mid-Oct) Founded in 1912 and specialising in Crémant de Loire sparkling wines, this domaine is open for tours, tasting and a visit to the caves, and offers an introduction to winemaking at its wine school.

☞ Tours

Boat Trip
BOAT TOUR
(☑06 63 22 87 00; saumurloire@orange.fr; adult/child €10/5; ☺2pm, 3pm & 4pm daily Jun-Sep, weekends May & Oct) The *Saumur-Loire* embarks on 50-minute afternoon cruises from Quai Lucien Gautier, across from the town hall.

Base de Loisirs Millocheau
KAYAK TOUR
(☑02 41 50 62 72; http://canoe.saumur.free.fr; kayak tours per person €10-28) Organises canoe and kayak tours down the Loire by reservation.

Carriage Rides
CARRIAGE TOUR
(adult/child €8/5; ☺2-5pm Sat-Thu Apr–mid-Oct) Depart from place de la République. Also operate on Fridays in July and August.

🛏 Sleeping

Saumur's accommodation is of a high calibre. Reserve ahead.

TOP CHOICE Château de Verrières
CASTLE HOTEL €€€
(☑02 41 38 05 15; www.chateau-verrieres.com; 53 rue d'Alsace; r €170-240, ste €280-310; ☕🏊)

Every one of the 10 rooms in this impeccably wonderful 1890 château, ensconced within the woods and ponds of a 1.6-hectare English park, is different. But the feel is universally plush and kingly: antique writing desks, original artwork, wood panelling and fantastic bathrooms. Some, like the top-of-the-line Rising Sun suite (with a dash of modish Japanese minimalism), have views of the sun rising over the Saumur château. Regal with a capital R. Parking free.

Château de Beaulieu
B&B €€

(02 41 50 83 52; www.chateaudebeaulieu.fr; 98 rte de Montsoreau; d €85-120, ste €140-200;) Irish expats Mary and Conor welcome you to their sprawling home with a glass of bubbling *crémant*, delicious homemade breakfasts and a wealth of friendly advice on surrounding attractions. Rooms are imaginatively and comfortably done up, and the mood among the generally gregarious clientele is one of extended family. Sun yourself by the pool or play billiards in the grand salon. Parking free.

Hôtel Saint-Pierre
HISTORIC HOTEL €€

(02 41 50 33 00; www.saintpierresaumur.com; 8 rue Haute St-Pierre; r €115-200, ste €200-295;) Squeezed down a minuscule alleyway opposite the cathedral, this effortlessly smart hideaway mixes heritage architecture with modern-day comfort: pale stone, thick rugs and vintage lamps sit happily alongside minibars and satellite TV. Tiled mosaics line the bathrooms, and black-and-white dressage photos enliven the lobby.

Hôtel de Londres
HOTEL €

(02 41 51 23 98; www.lelondres.com; 48 rue d'Orléans; s €48, d €57-85, apt €120;) Snag one of the refurbished rooms in jolly colours, or one of the brand-new, family-friendly apartments, all with big windows, gleaming bathrooms and thoughtful perks including afternoon tea (€3) and a well-stocked comic library. Parking €5.

Camping l'Île d'Offard
CAMPGROUND €

(02 41 40 30 00; www.saumur-camping.com; rue de Verden; sites for 2 people €14-35; Mar–mid-Nov;) Well-equipped and very pretty campground on a natural river island opposite the château. Cyclists get special discounts; riverside and castle-view sites cost extra.

✗ Eating

Saumur is one of the culinary centres of the Loire; book ahead.

TOP CHOICE Le Gambetta
GASTRONOMIC €€

(02 41 67 66 66; www.restaurantlegambetta.com; 12 rue Gambetta; lunch menus €23.50-28.50, other menus €30-96; lunch Tue & Thu-Sun, dinner Tue & Thu-Sat) OK, prepare yourself. This is one to write home about: a fantastic regional restaurant combining refined elegance and knock-your-socks-off creative food. The parade of exquisitely presented dishes ranges from rosemary-and-thyme roasted pork with an asparagus-lemon-parmesan *maki* to surprisingly delicious wasabi *crème brûlée*. Some menus include wine pairings, and all are punctuated by surprise treats from the kitchen.

Le Pot de Lapin
MODERN FRENCH €€

(02 41 67 12 86; 35 rue Rabelais; tapas €1-7, mains €11-24; lunch & dinner Tue-Sat) Jazzy music wafts from the cheery dining room through the wine bar and onto the streetside terrace as Chef Olivier works the tables, proposing perfect wine pairings and serving up tempting platefuls of tapas and French classics. Start with a *soupe saumuroise* – the iconic local aperitif made with triple sec, lemon juice and sparkling wine, then move on to perfectly seasoned shrimp brochettes, coulis-drizzled foie gras or pollock cooked in parchment paper. Somehow the vibe here is, simply put, happiness – happy staff, happy clients.

L'Escargot
TRADITIONAL FRENCH €€

(02 41 51 20 88; 30 rue du Maréchal Leclerc; menus €18-33; lunch Thu, Fri, Sun & Mon, dinner Thu-Mon) A Saumur fixture for over half a century, this place is all about traditional recipes done really well: *escargots* with garlic, parsley and 'three butters' (flavoured with herbs, walnuts and roquefort); red mullet with fresh thyme, olive oil and vegetables; or a frozen triple sec soufflé with *crème anglaise* and a red berry coulis.

L'Alchimiste
MODERN FRENCH €€

(02 41 67 65 18; 6 rue de Lorraine; menus €16-19; lunch & dinner Tue-Sat) Simple, clean flavours are the hallmark of this sleek bistro. As a result, the flavours of the fresh ingredients sing out, from plaice with lemon zest to roasted leg of rabbit with apricots and coriander.

L'Amuse Bouche
TRADITIONAL FRENCH €€

(02 41 67 79 63; www.lamusebouche.fr; 512 rte Montsoreau, Dampierre-sur-Loire; lunch menus €15.50, dinner menus €22-67; lunch Thu-Tue, dinner Mon & Thu-Sat) Tuck into delicious, fresh

meals prepared with creativity, like *chèvre* with a hint of honey where you don't expect it. The crimson and silver dining room with colourful oil paintings manages to be both cheery and homey, and the outside terrace is great in summer. Kids' *menus* €10 to €15.

ⓘ Information

Tourist office (☏02 41 40 20 60; www. saumur-tourisme.com; 8bis quai Carnot; ⏲9.15am-7pm Mon-Sat, 10.30am-5.30pm Sun)

ⓘ Getting There & Around

BICYCLE **Détours de Loire** (☏02 41 53 01 01; 10 rue de Rouen; ⏲9.30am-1pm & 3-6.30pm May-Sep) rents bikes.

BUS **Agglobus** (☏02 41 51 11 87; www. agglobus.fr) runs local buses (tickets €1.35).

TRAIN SNCF offers frequent service to Tours (€11.20, 30 to 50 minutes, 12 daily) and Angers (€8.30, 20 to 35 minutes, 16 daily).

East of Saumur

The tufa bluffs east of Saumur are home to some of the area's main wine producers: you'll see notable vineyards and vintners (www.producteurs-de-saumur-champigny .fr, in French) along the riverside D947, most offering free tasting sessions from around 10am to 6pm from spring to autumn.

MONTSOREAU, CANDES-ST-MARTIN & TURQUANT

Château de Montsoreau (☏02 41 67 12 60; www.chateau-montsoreau.com; adult/child €8.90/5.80; ⏲10am-7pm May-Sep, 2-6pm Apr, Oct–mid-Nov & weekends in Mar, closed mid-Nov–Feb; ♿), beautifully situated on the edge of the Loire, was built in 1455 by one of Charles VII's advisers, and later became famous thanks to an Alexandre Dumas novel, *La Dame de Monsoreau*. A series of exhibits explores the castle's history, the novel and the river trade that once sustained the Loire Valley, although they're all rather sparse and underwhelming compared to the impressive river views from the rooftop. Wine lovers can enjoy free tasting in the castle cellars afterwards (weekends from May to September, daily in July and August).

Maison du Parc (☏02 41 38 38 88; www. parc-loire-anjou-touraine.fr; 15 av de la Loire; ⏲9.30am-7pm) for the Parc Naturel Régional Loire-Anjou-Touraine is a clearinghouse of information on the 2530-sq-km regional park whose mission is to protect both the landscape and the area's extraordinary architectural patrimony.

Just east of Montsoreau, the village of Candes-St-Martin occupies an idyllic spot at the confluence of the Vienne and the Loire. The 12th- to 13th-century church venerates the spot where St Martin died and was buried in 397 (though his body was later moved to Tours). Candes eventually became a major pilgrimage point and hence bears his name. For nice views, wander down to the benches overlooking the waterfront along rue du Confluent, or climb the tiny streets above the church past inhabited cave dwellings for a higher-altitude perspective on the confluence. Near the top, a funky old teahouse and used-book shop, La Brocante Gourmand (20 rue Trochet; sandwich €3; ⏲11am-7pm Tue-Sun), makes a convenient pit stop.

West of Montsoreau, the picturesque village of Turquant has one of the region's highest concentrations of troglodyte dwellings. Many have now been spiffed up and converted into shops, art galleries or restaurants. Local businesses worth investigating include La Grande Vignolle (☏02 41 38 16 44; www.filliatreau.com; Turquant), a domaine and tasting room in grand tufa caves; L'Helianthe (☏02 41 51 22 28; www.restaurant -helianthe.fr; Ruelle Antoine Cristal, Turquant; lunch/dinner menus €21/30; ⏲lunch & dinner Thu-Tue Apr–mid-Nov, lunch Sat & Sun, dinner Fri-Sun mid-Nov–Mar), a cliffside eatery whose menu revolves around traditional ingredients including river fish and 'ancient vegetables' (Jerusalem artichokes, beets, rutabagas, sweet potatoes, etc); and Demeure de la Vignole (☏02 41 53 67 00; www.demeure-vignole. com; 3 impasse Marguerite d'Anjou, Turquant; d €105-145, ste €150-260; ☎♿), an upscale hotel with four gorgeously redecorated troglodyte rooms and a subterranean swimming pool.

FONTEVRAUD-L'ABBAYE

Abbaye Royale de Fontevraud HISTORIC ABBEY (☏02 41 51 73 52; www.abbayedefontevraud.com; adult/child €9/6, tour or audioguide €4; ⏲9.30am-6.30pm Apr-Oct, 10am-5.30pm Tue-Sun Nov-Mar, closed Jan) Until its closure in 1793 this huge 12th-century complex was one of the largest ecclesiastical centres in Europe. Unusually, both nuns and monks were governed by an abbess (generally a lady of noble birth retiring from public life). The extensive grounds include a chapter room with murals of the Passion of Christ by Thomas Pot, dormitories, workrooms and prayer halls, as well as

TROGLODYTE VALLEY

For centuries the creamy white tufa cliffs around Saumur have been a key source of local building materials; in fact, many of the Loire's grandest châteaux were constructed from this soft stone. The rocky bluffs also provided shelter and storage for the local inhabitants, leading to the development of a unique *culture troglodyte* (cave culture), as in the Vézère Valley in the Dordogne. The cool, dank caves were developed into proper houses (*habitations troglodytes*) and perfect natural cellars for everyone from vintners to mushroom farmers. Eat your heart out, Bilbo Baggins!

Find caves lining the Loire east and west of Saumur and radiating from the village of Doué-la-Fontaine; bring a sweater as they remain cool (13°C) year-round.

Château de Brézé (☎02 41 51 60 15; www.chateaudebreze.com; adult/child €11/6; ⏱10am-6.30pm Apr-Sep, to 7.30pm Jul & Aug, 10am-6pm Tue-Sun Oct-Mar, closed Jan) This unique château, 12km south of Saumur, sits atop a network of subterranean rooms and passages that account for more square footage than the castle itself. A self-guided tour takes you through the original troglodyte dwelling directly under the château, then crosses a deep moat to other caves adapted for the castle's owners for use as kitchens, wine cellars and defensive bastions. Finish your visit with a climb to the château's rooftop, followed by *degustation* (tasting) of wines from the surrounding vineyards.

Rochemenier (☎02 41 59 18 15; www.troglodyte.info; adult/child €5.40/3; ⏱9.30am-7pm Apr-Oct, 2-6pm Sat & Sun Nov, Feb & Mar) Inhabited until the 1930s, this abandoned village, 6km north of Doué-la-Fontaine, is one of the best examples of troglodytic culture. You can also explore the remains of two farmsteads (complete with houses, stables and an underground chapel).

Troglodytes et Sarcophages (☎06 77 77 06 94; www.troglo-sarcophages.fr; adult/child €4.80/3.30; ⏱2.30-7pm daily Jun-Aug, Sat & Sun May) A Merovingian mine where sarcophagi were produced from the 6th to the 9th centuries and exported via the Loire as far as England and Belgium. Atmospheric lantern-lit tours (adult/child €7.50/5.50) are conducted on Tuesday and Friday at 8.30pm in July and August, by reservation.

Troglo des Pommes Tapées (☎02 41 51 48 30; www.letroglodespommestapees.fr; 11 rue des Ducs d'Anjou; adult/child €6/3.50; ⏱2-6.30pm Tue, 10am-12.30pm & 2-6.30pm Wed-Sun, closed mid-Nov–mid-Feb) One of the last places in France to produce the traditional dried apples known as *pommes tapées*. Visit and taste 10km southeast of Saumur.

Les Perrières (☎02 41 59 71 29; www.ville-douelafontaine.fr/perrieres; adult/child €4.50/3; ⏱10.30am-6.30pm Jul & Aug, 2-6.30pm Tue-Sun Apr-Jun, Sep & Oct, closed Nov-Mar) Former stone quarries sometimes called the 'cathedral caves' due to their lofty sloping walls that resemble Gothic arches.

Musée du Champignon (Mushroom Museum; ☎02 41 50 31 55; www.musee-du-champignon.com; rte de Gennes; adult/child €8/6; ⏱10am-7pm mid-Feb–mid-Nov) Get acquainted with the fabulous fungus at the museum tucked into a cave at the western edge of St-Hilaire-St-Florent.

You'll also find some unusual pieces of artwork sprinkled around the valley:

La Cave aux Sculptures (☎02 41 59 15 40; adult/child €4/2.50; ⏱10.30am-1pm & 2-6.30pm Tue-Sun Apr-Oct) Full of leering faces, contorted figures and bestial gargoyles carved sometime between the 16th and 17th centuries. Six kilometres north of Doué-la-Fontaine.

Pierre et Lumière (☎02 41 50 70 04; www.pierre-et-lumiere.com; route de Gennes, St-Hilaire St-Florent; adult/child €8/6; ⏱10am-7pm Apr-Sep, 10am-12.30pm & 2-6pm Feb, Mar, Oct & Nov) Modern sculptures of the Loire Valley's most famous monuments, from Tours' cathedral to the château at Amboise, carved in *tuffeau* stone and displayed in a large cave 5km northwest of Saumur.

ANGERS CITY PASS

Swing by the tourist office to buy the Angers City Pass (24/48/72 hours €12.50/22/29), good for entry to the château, museums, the tourist train and other sights, as well as for transport discounts.

a spooky underground sewer system and a wonderful barrel-vaulted refectory, where the monks and nuns would eat in silence while being read the scriptures.

Look out, too, for the multichimneyed, rocket-shaped kitchen, built entirely from stone to make it fireproof.

The highlight is undoubtedly the massive, movingly simple abbey church, notable for its soaring pillars, Romanesque domes and the polychrome tombs of four illustrious Plantagenets: Henry II, King of England (r 1154–89); his wife Eleanor of Aquitaine (who retired to Fontevraud following Henry's death); their son Richard the Lionheart; and his wife Isabelle of Angoulême.

After the Revolution, the buildings became a prison, in use until 1963. Author Jean Gênet was imprisoned at Fontevraud for stealing, and later wrote *Miracle de la Rose* (1946) based on his experiences.

Chez Teresa   TEAROOM €
(☎02 41 51 21 24; www.chezteresa.fr; 6 av Rochechouart; menus €12.50-17.50) Keeping up Fontevraud's English connections, this frilly little teashop is run by an expat English couple with a passion for traditional teatime fare: tea for two with sandwiches, scones and cakes costs €9.50, and there are two cute upstairs rooms (double €60) if you fancy staying overnight.

Angers

POP 151,690

Often dubbed 'Black Angers' due to the local dark slate used for its roofs, the lively riverside city is famous for its tapestries: the 14th-century *Tenture de l'Apocalypse* in the city's château and the 20th-century *Chant du Monde* at the Jean Lurçat museum. A bustling old town, with many pedestrianised streets and a thriving café culture, makes it a good western gateway to the Loire Valley.

◉ Sights & Activities

A small tourist train (☎02 41 23 50 00; adult/child €6/4; ☉daily May-Sep, weekends Apr & Oct), departing from the château, makes a circuit through the city's highlights.

TOP CHOICE Château d'Angers   CHÂTEAU
(☎02 41 86 48 77; http://angers.monuments-nationaux.fr; 2 promenade du Bout-du-Monde; adult/child €8.50/free; ☉9.30am-6.30pm May-Aug, 10am-5.30pm Sep-Apr) This impressive black-stone château, formerly the seat of power for the Counts of Anjou, looms behind quai de Ligny, ringed by battlements and 17 watchtowers. The star of the show is the stunning Tenture de l'Apocalypse (Apocalypse tapestry), a 104m-long series of tapestries commissioned by Louis I, Duke of Anjou around 1375 to illustrate the Book of Revelation. It dramatically recounts the story of the Day of Judgment from start to finish, complete with the Four Horsemen of the Apocalypse, the Battle of Armageddon and the coming of the Beast: look out for graphic depictions of St Michael battling a seven-headed dragon and the fall of Babylon. Audioguides (€4.50) provide useful context, and guided tours are free. That black stone? It's actually called blue schist.

Musée Jean Lurçat et de la
Tapisserie Contemporaine   TAPESTRY MUSEUM
(☎02 41 24 18 45; www.musees.angers.fr; 4 bd Arago; adult/child €4/free; ☉10am-noon & 2-6pm Tue-Sun) Providing an interesting counterpoint to Angers' other famous piece of needlework, this museum collects major 20th-century tapestries by Jean Lurçat, Thomas Gleb and others inside the Hôpital St-Jean, a 12th-century hospital founded by Henry Plantagenet. The centrepiece is the *Chant du Monde* (Song of the World), an amazing series depicting the trials and triumphs of modern humanity, from nuclear holocaust and space exploration to the delights of drinking Champagne. Odd and unmissable.

Galerie David d'Angers   SCULPTURE MUSEUM
(☎02 41 05 38 90; www.musees.angers.fr; 33bis rue Toussaint; adult/child €4/free; ☉10am-noon & 2-6pm Tue-Sun) Angers' most famous son is the sculptor Pierre-Jean David (1788–1856), often just known as David d'Angers. Renowned for lifelike busts and sculptures, his work adorns public monuments all over France, notably at the Panthéon, the Louvre and Père Lachaise cemetery (where he carved many tombstones, including Honoré

de Balzac's). His work forms the cornerstone of this museum, housed in the converted 12th-century Toussaint Abbey and flooded with light through a striking glass-and-girder ceiling.

Musée des Beaux-Arts ART MUSEUM
(☎02 41 05 38 00; www.musees.angers.fr; 14 rue du Musée; adult/child €4/free; ☺10am-noon & 2-6pm) The buildings of the sprawling, fantastic fine-arts museum mix plate glass with the fine lines of the typical Angevin aristocratic house. The museum has a section on the history of Angers and an superior 17th- to 20th-century collection: Monet, Ingres, Lorenzo Lippi and Flemish masters including Rogier van der Weyden.

Quartier de la Cité HISTORIC QUARTER
(🚶) In the heart of the old city, Cathédrale St-Maurice (☺8.30am-7.30pm) is one of the earliest examples of Plantagenet or Angevin architecture in France and is distinguished by its rounded ribbed vaulting, 15th-century stained glass and a 12th-century portal depicting the Day of Judgment. Behind the cathedral on place Ste-Croix is the Maison d'Adam (behind Cathédrale St-Maurice), one of the city's best-preserved medieval houses (c 1500), decorated with a riot of carved, bawdy figurines. From the square in front of the cathedral a monumental staircase, the Montée St-Maurice (Cathédrale St-Maurice), leads down to the river.

Maison du Vin de l'Anjou WINE CENTRE
(☎02 41 88 81 13; mdesvins-angers@vinsdeloire.fr; 5bis place du Président Kennedy; ☺2.30-7pm Mon, 10am-1pm & 2.30-7pm Tue-Sat) Head here for the lowdown on local Anjou and Loire vintages: tasting, sales, tours and tips on where to buy wines.

ORANGE PEEL & ANISEED LIQUEURS

Some of France's most distinctive liqueurs are distilled in the Loire Valley, including bitter orange Cointreau and the aniseedy (and allegedly hallucinogenic) brew known as absinthe.

Cointreau has its origins in the experiments of two enterprising brothers: Adolphe Cointreau, a sweet-maker, and his brother Édouard-Jean Cointreau, who founded a factory in Angers in 1849 to produce fruit-flavoured liqueurs. In 1875 Édouard-Jean's son (also called Édouard) hit upon the winning concoction of sweet and bitter oranges, flavoured with intensely orangey peel. The liqueur was a massive success; by the early 1900s over 800,000 bottles of Cointreau were being produced annually to the top-secret recipe, and a century later every one of the 13 million bottles is still distilled to the same formula at the original factory site in Angers.

Carré Cointreau (☎02 41 31 50 50; www.cointreau.com; 2 bd des Bretonnières; 2hr tour €10, tasting €6.20-9.80; ☺by reservation) offers guided tours, which include a visit to the distillery and entry to the Cointreau archive. It is off the ring road east of Angers. From the train station, take bus 7.

By contrast, absinthe has had a more chequered history. Brewed from a heady concoction of natural herbs, true absinthe includes three crucial components: green anise, fennel and the foliage of *Artemisia absinthium* (wormwood, used as a remedy since the time of the ancient Egyptians). Legend has it that modern-day absinthe was created by a French doctor (wonderfully called Dr Pierre Ordinaire) in the late 1790s, before being acquired by a father-and-son team who established the first major absinthe factory, Maison Pernod-Fils, in 1805.

The drink's popularity exploded in the 19th century, when it was discovered by bohemian poets and painters (as well as French troops, who were given the drink as an antimalarial drug). Seriously potent, absinthe's traditional green colour and supposedly psychoactive effects led to its popular nickname 'the green fairy'; everyone from Rimbaud to Vincent van Gogh sang its praises. Ernest Hemingway invented his own absinthe cocktail: ominously dubbed 'Death in the Afternoon'.

But the drink's reputation was ultimately its own downfall: fearing widespread psychic degeneration, governments around the globe banned it in the early 20th century (France in 1915). In the 1990s a group of dedicated *absintheurs* reverse-engineered the liqueur, chemically analysing century-old bottles that had escaped the ban. Try it at Distillerie Combier (p392) in Saumur.

THE LOIRE VALLEY ANGERS

Angers

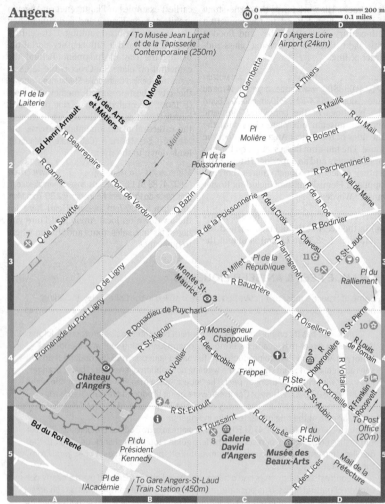

THE LOIRE VALLEY ANGERS

🛏 Sleeping

Hôtel du Mail
HISTORIC HOTEL €€

(☏02 41 25 05 25; www.hoteldumail.fr; 8 rue des Ursules; d €65-85; 🔊) Situated in a converted convent around a quiet courtyard, rooms here have a light, airy feel, even if they are a bit worn. The funky lobby, huge buffet breakfast (€10), friendly staff and thoughtful touches (such as daily newspapers and free umbrellas) make this a peaceful Angers base. Parking is €6. Find it just east of the Quartier de la Cité, near the Hôtel de Ville.

Hôtel Continental
HOTEL €€

(☏02 41 86 94 94; www.hotelcontinental.com; 14 rue Louis de Romain; s €51-82, d €61-86; ❄🔊) Wedged into a triangular corner building in the city centre, this green-certified, metro-style hotel has 25 rooms decked out in cosy checks and sunny colours.

Hôtel Le Progrès
HOTEL €

(☏02 41 88 10 14; www.hotelleprogres.com; 26 rue Denis Papin; s €48-74, d €64-83; 🔊) It's nothing fancy, but this reliable station hotel is solid, friendly and squeaky clean.

Angers

🍴 Eating

Le Favre d'Anne   GASTRONOMIC €€€

(☎02 41 36 12 12; www.lefavredanne.fr; 18 quai des Carmes; lunch menus €25-35, dinner menus €45-95; ⊘lunch & dinner Tue-Sat) Muted tones, crystal, linen and river views call for a romantic night out or a swanky lunch. Ingredients are always fresh (artichokes, asparagus, goat cheese, local fish) and the concoctions creative: a dash of cacao here and a splash of prune coulis there. No wonder it has a Michelin star.

Villa Toussaint   FRENCH FUSION €€

(☎02 41 88 15 64; 43 rue Toussaint; mains €14-23; ⊘lunch & dinner Tue-Sat) With its chic dining room and tree-shaded deck, you know you're in for a treat at this fusion place, combining pan-Asian flavours with classic French ingredients. The *combinaisons* bring together several dishes on one plate, from sushi to Thai chicken and tapas. Reserve ahead.

Chez Toi   BISTRO €

(☎02 41 87 85 58; 44 rue St-Laud; mains €12-21; ⊘9am-12.30am Mon-Sat, 3pm-12.30am Sun; 🛜🅿) Minimalist furniture and technicolour trappings meet head-to-head in this zippy little

lounge-bar, much favoured by the trendy Angevin set. The front terrace along pedestrianised rue St-Laud is great for people-watching.

Food Market   MARKET €

(place Louis Imbach & place Leclerc; ⊘Sat morning) Weekly market.

🍷 Drinking & Entertainment

Le Baroque   BAR

(35 rue St-Laud; ⊘3pm-2am) Specialising in colourful cocktails, this sleek bar with bright modern decor is among the more vibrant nightspots in the St-Laud pedestrian zone.

Grand Théâtre d'Angers   THEATRE

(☎02 41 24 16 40; www.angers-nantes-opera.com; place du Ralliement) Hosts regular theatre, dance and music events.

Les Quatre-Cents Coups   CINEMA

(☎02 41 88 70 95; www.les400coups.org; 12 rue Claveau) Arts cinema showing nondubbed films.

ℹ Information

Tourist Office (☎02 41 23 50 00; www.angersloiretourisme.com; 7 place du Président Kennedy; ⊘10am-7pm Mon, 9am-7pm Tue-Sat, 10am-6pm Sun) Directly across from the château.

ℹ Getting There & Away

Angers is 107km west of Tours and 90km east of Nantes.

AIR At the time of research, **Angers Loire Airport** (☎02 41 33 50 00; www.angersloire aeroport.fr), 25km northeast of the city centre, had just launched flights to London City airport with British Airways and to Nice with Danube Wings.

BUS **Anjou Bus** (☎08 20 16 00 49; www.anjoubus.fr) departs from the Gare Routière, adjacent to the train station.

Brissac-Quincé Bus 5, €1.70, 30 to 40 minutes, 11 daily Monday to Friday, five on Saturday

Doué-La-Fontaine Bus 5, €5.20, 1¼ hours, nine daily Monday to Friday, five on Saturday

Saumur Bus 4, €5.20, 1½ hours, three daily Monday to Saturday

TRAIN From Gare Angers-St-Laud, 500m southwest of the château and tourist office, trains regularly serve the following:

Paris Gare Montparnasse €52 to €67, 1½ to 1¾ hours, hourly

Saumur €8.30, 30 minutes, 16 daily

Tours €18.10, 1¼ hours, nine daily

THE LOIRE VALLEY ANGERS

24 HOURS OF LE MANS

During the second week of June each year, race car aficionados converge on Le Mans (population 146,670) to watch this careening, 24-hour endurance race. Corvettes, Porsches, Ferraris and myriad other souped-up speedsters whip around the 13.629km Circuit de la Sarthe track at the world's oldest sports-car race (www.lemans.org), first run in 1923. The rest of the year, visit the museum (☏02 43 72 72 24; www.lemusee24h.com; 9 place Luigi Chinetti; adult/child €8.50/6; ☉10am-6pm Apr-Sep, 11am-5pm Wed-Mon Oct-Mar), which houses over 150 vehicles from an 1885 De Dion Bouton et Trepardoux steam-driven dog cart to past winners that are just a bit speedier.

❶ Getting Around

BICYCLE The tourist office rents bikes (half-/full day €9/14) from its **Maison du Port annexe** (www.angersloiretourisme.com; 38 bd Henri Arnault) as part of the Détours de Loire network.

BUS & TRAM Local buses are run by **Irigo** (☏02 41 33 64 64; bustram.irigo.fr; single/day ticket €1.40/3.60), along with spiffy new rainbow-coloured trams that began service in June 2011.

CAR Avis, Hertz, Europcar and National have car rental desks inside the train station.

TAXI Call **Allô Anjou Taxi** (☏02 41 87 65 00; www.alloanjoutaxi.com) or **Taxis Angevins** (☏02 41 34 96 52).

Around Angers

South of Angers, the River Maine joins the Loire for the final leg of its journey to the Atlantic. The river banks immediately west of this confluence remain the source of some of the valley's most notable wines, including Savennières and Coteaux du Layon.

CHÂTEAU DE SERRANT

Built from cream-and-fawn tufa stone and topped by bell-shaped, slate-topped towers, the grand Château de Serrant (☏02 41 39 13 01; www.chateau-serrant.net; adult/child €9.50/6.50; ☉tours 9.45am-5.15pm Jun–mid-Sep, hrs vary rest of the year) is a wonderful slice of Renaissance style, reminiscent of Cheverny but on a more modest scale. Begun by the aristocrat Charles de Brie in the 16th century, the château is notable for its 12,000-tome library, huge kitchens and an extravagant domed bedroom known as the Chambre Empire, designed to host an overnight stay by the Emperor Napoléon (who actually only hung around for about two hours).

The château is near St-Georges-sur-Loire, 15km southwest of Angers on the N23. Anjou buses 22 and 24 travel from Angers (€1.70, 30 to 40 minutes, two to four Monday to Saturday).

CHÂTEAU DE BRISSAC

The tallest castle in France, the Château de Brissac (☏02 41 91 22 21; www.chateau-brissac.fr; adult/child incl tour €10/4.50, gardens only €5/free; ☉10am-12.15pm & 2-6pm Wed-Mon Apr-Oct) is 15km south of Angers in Brissac-Quincé. Spread over seven storeys and 204 rooms, this chocolate-box mansion was built by the Duke of Brissac in 1502, and is one of the most luxuriously furnished in the valley, with a riot of posh furniture, ornate tapestries, twinkling chandeliers and luxurious bedrooms – even a private theatre. Around the house, 8 sq km of grounds are filled with cedar trees, 19th-century stables and a vineyard, boasting three AOC vintages. Open 10am to 6pm daily in July and August.

Four of the château's bedrooms are offered as ridiculously extravagant chambres d'hôte (d incl breakfast €390), perfect if you've always dreamt of sleeping on an antique four-poster under priceless tapestries and ancestral portraits.

Anjou bus 5 links Angers with Brissac-Quincé (€1.70, 30 to 40 minutes, 11 daily Monday to Friday, five on Saturday).

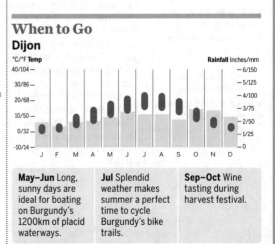

Burgundy

Best Places to Eat

» Les Millésimes (p430)
» La Table d'Héloïse (p441)
» Loiseau des Vignes (p419)
» Le Chambolle (p413)
» Auberge du Pot d'Etain (p435)

Best Places to Stay

» Villa Louise Hôtel (p414)
» La Cimentelle (p434)
» Le Clos de l'Abbaye (p441)
» Moulin Renaudiots (p439)
» La Maison d'Olivier Le-flaive (p414)
» Le Tabellion (p430)

Why Go?

Burgundy (Bourgogne in French) offers some of France's most gorgeous countryside: rolling green hills dotted with medieval villages, and mustard fields blooming in bright contrast. Two great French passions, wine and food, come together here in a particularly rich and enticing form.

The region's towns and its dashingly handsome capital, Dijon, are heirs to a glorious architectural heritage that goes back to the Renaissance, the Middle Ages and beyond, into the mists of Gallo-Roman and Celtic antiquity.

Burgundy is also a paradise for lovers of the great outdoors. You can hike and cycle through the vineyards of the Côte d'Or, on a network of cycling trails, and in the wild reaches of the Parc Naturel Régional du Morvan (Morvan Regional Park); glide along the waterways of the Yonne in a canal boat; or float above the vineyards in a hot-air balloon.

When to Go
Dijon

May–Jun Long, sunny days are ideal for boating on Burgundy's 1200km of placid waterways.

Jul Splendid weather makes summer a perfect time to cycle Burgundy's bike trails.

Sep–Oct Wine tasting during harvest festival.

WINE TOURS

Although Burgundy is covered in vineyards, not many areas offer organised tours of the wineries. The best hubs for picking up a tour are Dijon, Beaune and Chablis.

Fast Facts

» **Population** 1.64 million

» **Area** 31,582 sq km

» **Hotel overnights/year** 4.8 million

» **Signature drink** white wine

Most Atmospheric Castles

» Château d'Ancy-le-Franc (p429)

» Château de Bazoches (p437)

» Château de Sully (p440)

» Château de Maulnes (p430)

Resources

» Biking Burgundy www. burgundy-by-bike.com

» Train and bus options: www.mobigo-bourgogne. com

» Wines of Burgundy: www. bourgogne-wines.com

» Music and events: www. magma-magazine.fr, in French

Top Wine Regions

Burgundy's red and white wines and especially those of the Côte d'Or vineyards, which comprise Côte de Nuits and Côte de Beaune, are world-famous. But don't forget to leave room in your itinerary for a few of the other more laid-back appellations. Charming Irancy is a favourite tasting region for many locals. Nearby Chablis, with its crisp white wines, is wonderful on a hot summer day. To really get off the beaten path, head to the Mâconnais and Châtillonais vineyards.

COOKING COURSES

Burgundy's rich, hearty cuisine combines smoky flavours and fresh ingredients. Why not take the opportunity to learn a few of the local techniques? Courses range from the informal to the chic:

» Use the refurbished 17th-century kitchen at Château d'Ancy-le-Franc (p429) to learn from Judicǎel Ruch of Plaza Athénée in Paris (€120, once per month, April to November).

» Le Charlemagne (p414), in the heart of Côte d'Or wine country, has 1½-hour classes (€80) each Saturday, featuring a fresh, seasonal ingredient and accompanied by a wine tasting and dessert.

» The proprietress of La Cimentelle (p434), Nathalie, will teach you how to make a *repas gastronomique* (gourmet meal) in a half-day course (€90).

» L'Espérance (p436), Marc Meneau's fabulous restaurant near Vézelay, offers two-day cookery classes that include dinner and accommodation at the inn.

The Celts in Burgundy

» Bibracte, the ruins of the capital city of the Aedui people, puts the Celts centre stage at the excellent Museum of Celtic Civilisation (p437).

» Vercingétorix, the chief of the Gauls, was defeated by Julius Caesar at Alésia (p423).

» Trésor de Vix, a stunning collection of Celtic, Greek and Etruscan objects, is the focus of the Musée du Pays Châtillonnais (p422) in Châtillon-sur-Seine.

» The Celtic goddess Sequana is one of the highlights of Dijon's Musée Archéologique (p408).

» Sacred springs and sanctuaries include Fontaines Salées (p436), Fosse Dionne (p429) and Source de la Douix (p422).

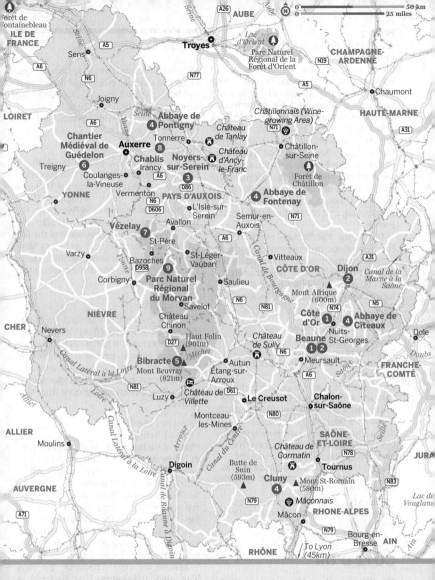

Burgundy Highlights

1 Sample some renowned vintages in **Beaune** (p415) and along the vine-carpeted slopes of the **Côte d'Or** (p411)

2 Gaze at the glories of the late Middle Ages at Dijon's **Musée des Beaux-Arts** (p404) and Beaune's **Hôtel-Dieu** (p415)

3 Explore the quirky village of **Noyers-sur-Serein** (p430)

4 Conjure up monastic life in the Middle Ages at the abbeys of **Cluny** (p440) and **Cîteaux** (p420)

5 Drop back into the early days of humankind at the ancient Celtic ruins of **Bibracte** (p437)

6 Watch a château being built with 13th-century technology at the **Chantier Médiéval de Guédelon** (p426)

7 Explore the winding streets of **Vézelay** (p434)

8 Satisfy your craving for dry white wine in **Chablis** (p427)

9 Walk on the wild side in the remote **Parc Naturel Régional du Morvan** (p437)

History

At its height during the 14th and 15th centuries, the duchy of Burgundy was one of the richest and most powerful states in Europe and encompassed a vast swath of territory stretching from modern-day Burgundy to Alsace and northwest to Lorraine, Luxembourg, Flanders and Holland. This was a time of bitter rivalry between Burgundy and France; indeed, it was the Burgundians who sold Jeanne d'Arc (Joan of Arc) to the English, and for a while it seemed quite possible that the kingdom of France would be taken over by Burgundy. In the end, though, it worked out the other way around, and in 1477 Burgundy became French.

During the Middle Ages two Burgundy-based monastic orders exerted significant influence across much of Christendom. The ascetic Cistercians were headquartered at Cîteaux, while their bitter rivals, the powerful and worldly Benedictines, were based at Cluny.

❶ Getting There & Around

By car or rail (including the TGV Sud-Est), Burgundy makes an easy stopover on the way from the English Channel or Paris to the Alps or southern France.

CAR From Dijon, autoroutes stretch northeast to Alsace (A36), north to Lorraine (A31), north and then west to Champagne (A31, A5 and A26) and south to the Rhône Valley (A6).

BUS & TRAIN The towns and some of the villages in this region are served by trains and buses in high season, though patience and planning are a must as services in many areas are infrequent (especially on Sunday and during school holidays).

Mobigo (✆08 00 10 20 04; www.mobigo-bourgogne.com) has details of buses and trains around Burgundy.

CÔTE D'OR

The Côte d'Or *département* is named after one of the world's foremost wine-growing regions, which stretches from Dijon, bursting with cultural riches, south to the wine town of Beaune and beyond. In the far northwest of the *département*, on the border with Champagne, Châtillon-sur-Seine displays Celtic treasures; in the west you can explore the walled, hilltop town of Semur-en-Auxois.

Dijon

POP 250,000

Dijon is one of France's most appealing cities. Filled with elegant medieval and Renaissance buildings, the lively centre is wonderful for strolling, especially if you like to leaven your cultural enrichment with excellent food, fine wine and shopping.

History

Dijon served as the capital of the duchy of Burgundy from the 11th to 15th centuries, enjoying a golden age during the 14th and 15th centuries under Philippe-le-Hardi (Philip the Bold), Jean-sans-Peur (John the Fearless) and Philippe-le-Bon (Philip the Good). During their reigns, some of the finest painters, sculptors and architects from around the continent were brought to Dijon, turning the city into one of the great centres of European art.

◉ Sights

The Owl's Trail (€3.50), available in 11 languages at the tourist office, details a self-guided city-centre walking tour; the route is marked on the pavement with bronze triangles. All of Dijon's municipal museums are free except, occasionally, for special exhibitions. Major churches are open from 8am to 7pm.

Palais des Ducs et des
États de Bourgogne   PALACE
(Palace of the Dukes & States of Burgundy; place de la Libération) Once home to Burgundy's powerful dukes, this monumental palace with neoclassical façade overlooks place de la Libération, Old Dijon's magnificent central square dating from 1686. The palace's eastern wing houses the outstanding Musée des Beaux-Arts, whose entrance is next to the Tour de Bar, a squat 14th-century tower that once served as a prison.

Just off the Cour d'Honneur, the 46m-high, mid-15th-century Tour Philippe le Bon (adult/child €2.30/free; ⊙guided tours every 45min 9am-noon & 1.45-5.30pm late Nov-Easter, 1.30-3.30pm Wed, 9am-3.30pm Sat-Sun late Nov-Easter) affords fantastic views over the city. Spot Mont Blanc on a clear day.

TOP
CHOICE Musée des Beaux-Arts   ART MUSEUM
(✆03 80 74 52 70; http://mba.dijon.fr; audioguide €4, tours adult/child €6/3; ⊙9.30am-6pm Wed-Mon May-Oct, 10am-5pm Nov-Apr) Housed in the eastern wing of the Palais des Ducs, these

BURGUNDY WINE BASICS

Burgundy's epic vineyards extend approximately 258km from Chablis in the north to the Rhône's Beaujolais in the south and comprise 100 AOCs (Appellation d'Origine Contrôlée). Each region has its own appellations and traits, embodied by a concept called *terroir,* the earth imbuing its produce, like grapes, with unique qualities. However, some appellations, such as *Crémant de Bourgogne* (a light, sparkling white or rosé) and *Bourgogne Aligoté,* are produced in several regions.

Here's an ever-so-brief survey of some of Burgundy's major growing regions:

» **Côte d'Or vineyards** The northern section, the Côte de Nuits, stretches from Marsannay-la-Côte south to Corgoloin and produces reds known for their robust, full-bodied character. The southern section, the Côte de Beaune, lies between Ladoix-Serrigny and Santenay and produces great reds and great whites. Appellations from the area's hilltops are the Hautes-Côtes de Nuits and Hautes-Côtes de Beaune.

» **Chablis & Grand Auxerrois** Four renowned chardonnay white-wine appellations from 20 villages around Chablis. Part of the Auxerrois vineyards, Irancy produces excellent pinot noir reds. The Tonnerrois vineyards produce good, affordable reds, whites and rosés.

» **Châtillonnais** Approximately 20 villages around Châtillon-sur-Seine producing red and white wines.

» **Côte Chalonnaise** The southernmost continuation of the Côte de Beaune's slopes is noted for its excellent reds and whites.

» **Mâconnais** Known for rich or fruity white wines, like the Pouilly-Fuissé chardonnay.

Want to Know More?

Tourist offices provide brochures including *The Burgundy Wine Road* and a useful map, *Roadmap to the Wines of Burgundy*. A handy website is www.bourgogne-wines.com.

Lots of books are available at Beaune's Athenaeum de la Vigne et du Vin. Look for the following:

» *Burgundy* by Anthony Hanson

» *Côte d'Or: A Celebration of the Great Wines of Burgundy* by Clive Coates

» *The Wines of Burgundy* by Sylvain Pitiot and Jean-Charles Servant (excellent overview)

» *Burgundy Wines, 1000 Years of Heritage* (concise, easy-to-use introduction to Burgundy's appellations, with 74 descriptive sheets)

Or take a class!

» École des Vins de Bourgogne (☑03 80 26 35 10; www.ecoledesvins-bourgogne.com; 6 rue du 16e Chasseurs, Beaune) Offers a variety of courses (from a two-hour fundamentals class for €50 to a full weekend course for €365) to refine your vinicultural vocabulary as well as your palate.

» Sensation Vin (☑03 80 22 17 57; www.sensation-vin.com; 1 rue d'Enfer, Beaune; ☺10am-7pm) Offers introductory tasting sessions (no appointment needed) as well as tailor-made courses.

sprawling galleries make up one of the most outstanding museums in France. The rooms themselves are works of art and a special chance to be inside this monumental building. Note that the museum is undergoing major renovation works and some galleries may be closed when you read this.

The star is the wood-panelled Salle des Gardes (Guards' Room), once warmed by a gargantuan Gothic fireplace. It houses the ornate, carved late-medieval sepulchres of dukes John the Fearless and Philip the Bold, as well as three impossibly intricate gilded Gothic retables from the 1300s. The Salle des Gardes was closed for renovation at the time of research; it's scheduled for reopening some time in 2013.

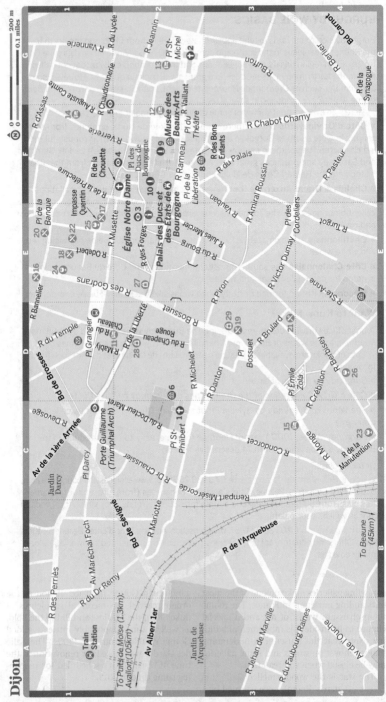

Dijon

Dijon

The modern and contemporary art section, with works by Manet and Monet and sculptures by Matisse and Rodin, harbours a particular delight: the Pompon Room. Tucked off a back staircase, this room is packed with stylised modern sculptures of animals by François Pompon (1855–1933), who was born in Saulieu, Burgundy. Note that the modern and contemporary art galleries close daily from 11.30am to 1.45pm.

Other highlights include a fine collection of primitives that give you a good sense of how artistic and aesthetic sensibilities varied between Italy, Switzerland and the Rhineland in the 13th and 14th centuries; a smattering of old masters such as Lorenzo Lotto; and quite a few naturalistic sculptures by the Dijon-born artist François Rude (1784–1855).

In the courtyard, the ducal kitchens (1433) often host exhibitions of works by local artists.

Église Notre Dame CHURCH
(place Notre-Dame) A block north of the Palais des Ducs, this church was built between 1220 and 1240. Its extraordinary façade's three tiers are lined with leering gargoyles separated by two rows of pencil-thin columns. Atop the church, the 14th-century Horloge à Jacquemart, transported from Flanders in 1383 by Philip the Bold who claimed it as a trophy of war, chimes every quarter-hour.

Around the north side of Notre Dame, rue de la Chouette is named after the small stone *chouette* (owl) carved into the exterior corner of the chapel diagonally across from No 24. Said to grant happiness and wisdom to those who stroke it, it has been worn smooth by generations of fortune-seekers.

Hôtels Particuliers HISTORIC MANSIONS
Many of Dijon's finest houses lie north of the Palais des Ducs on and around rue Verrerie, rue Vannerie and rue des Forges. The names of these streets reflect the industries that once thrived there (glassmaking, basket-weaving and metalsmithery, respectively). The early-17th-century Maison des Cariatides (28 rue Chaudronnerie), its façade a riot of stone caryatids, soldiers and vines, is particularly fine. A bit to the west you'll find the 13th-century Hôtel Aubriot (40 rue des Forges) and the Renaissance-style Maison Maillard (38 rue des Forges), all garlands and lions. Go inside the truly splendid 17th-century Hôtel Chambellan (34 rue des

Forges; admission free); from its courtyard a spiral stone staircase leads up to remarkable vaulting.

Behind Église Notre Dame, the 17th-century Hôtel de Vogüé (8 rue de la Chouette) is renowned for the ornate carvings around its exquisitely proportioned Renaissance courtyard. It's worth walking through the pink stone archway for a peek. Figures of an owl and a cat perch high atop the roof of the 15th-century Maison Millière (10 rue de la Chouette), which was a setting in the 1990 film *Cyrano de Bergerac* with Gérard Depardieu.

Cathédrale St-Bénigne   CHURCH
(place St-Philibert) Built over the tomb of St Benignus (believed to have brought Christianity to Burgundy in the 2nd century), Dijon's Burgundian Gothic-style cathedral was built around 1300 as an abbey church. Some of Burgundy's great figures are buried in its crypt.

Musée Magnin   ART MUSEUM
(☑03 80 67 11 10; www.musee-magnin.fr; 4 rue des Bons Enfants; adult/child incl audioguide €3.50/free; ⊙10am-noon & 2-6pm Tue-Sun) Jeanne and Maurice Magnin turned their historic town house over to the state to display their excellent art collection in perpetuity. Works include fine examples of the Italian Renaissance and Flemish and medieval painting.

FREE Musée
Archéologique   ARCHAEOLOGY MUSEUM
(☑03 80 30 88 54; 5 rue du Docteur Maret; ⊙9am-12.30pm & 1.30-6pm Wed-Mon, closed Mon Sep–mid-May) Truly surprising Celtic, Roman and Merovingian artefacts are displayed here, including a particularly fine 1st-century AD bronze of the Celtic goddess Sequana standing on a dual-prowed boat. Upstairs, the early Gothic hall (12th and 13th centuries), with its ogival arches held aloft by two rows of columns, once served as the dormitory of a Benedictine abbey.

FREE Musée de la Vie
Bourguignonne   MUSEUM
(☑03 80 48 80 90; 17 rue Ste-Anne; ⊙9am-noon & 2-6pm Wed-Mon) Housed in a 17th-century Cistercian convent, this museum explores village and town life in Burgundy in centuries past with evocative tableaux illustrating dress and traditional crafts. On the 1st floor, a whole street has been re-created.

Église St-Michel   CHURCH
(place St-Michel) Originally Gothic, this church subsequently underwent a façade-lift operation in which it was given a richly ornamented Renaissance west front. Its two 17th-century towers are topped with cupolas and, higher still, glittering gold spheres.

Puits de Moïse   MEDIEVAL SCULPTURE
(Well of Moses; 1 bd Chanoine Kir, Centre Hospitalier Spécialisé; admission €3.50; ⊙9.30am-12.30pm & 2-5pm) This famous grouping of six Old Testament figures, carved from 1395 to 1405 by court sculptor Claus Sluter and his nephew Claus de Werve, is on the grounds of a psychiatric hospital 1.2km west of the train station; by bus take line 3 towards Fontaine d'Ouche.

Parks & Gardens   GARDEN
Dijon has plenty of green spaces that are perfect for picnics, including Jardin Darcy and Jardin de l'Arquebuse, the botanic gardens, with a stream and pond.

🅖 Tours

The tourist office has scads of information on tours of the city and the nearby wine regions, and can make bookings.

Walking Tours   HISTORY TOUR
(adult/child €6/1) A slew of different tours depart from the main tourist office. Times vary throughout the year.

Segway Tour   HISTORY TOUR
(adult/child €19/9; ⊙2.30pm & 4pm Mon-Sat) Run by the tourist office, this 1½-hour tour zips around the city centre.

Vineyard Tours   WINE TOUR
Minibus tours in English introduce the Côte d'Or vineyards. Reserve by phone, internet or via the tourist office. Operators include: Alter & Go (☑06 23 37 92 04; www.alterandgo.fr; tours from €70), with an emphasis on history and winemaking methods, Authentica Tour (☑06 87 01 43 78; www.authentica-tour.com; tours €55-125) and Wine & Voyages. (☑03 80 61 15 15; www.wineandvoyages.com; tours from €53)

🛏 Sleeping
Hôtel Le Jacquemart   HOTEL €
(☑03 80 60 09 60; www.hotel-lejacquemart.fr; 32 rue Verrerie; s €52-58, d €60-70; 🖥) In the heart of old Dijon, this two-star hotel is one of our favourite nests in town, with tidy, comfortable rooms and friendly staff. All the rooms are different; the best ones

(Nos 5 and 6) are in a 17th-century annexe just across the street; they're larger and better equipped than those within the hotel's original core, and combine vintage touches (stone walls, beamed ceiling) and modern conveniences.

Hôtel Le Sauvage
HOTEL €

(☑03 80 41 31 21; www.hotellesauvage.com; 64 rue Monge; s €48-59, d €53-64, tr €85; ☎) Set in a 15th-century *relais de poste* (coaching inn) that ranges around a cobbled, vine-shaded courtyard, this little hotel is definitely good value. Rooms 10, 12, 14 and 17, with exposed beams, are the cosiest. It's in a lively area but the hotel is pleasingly quiet. Parking €5.

Hôtel des Ducs
HOTEL €€

(☑info 03 80 67 31 31; www.hoteldesducs.com; 5 rue Lamonnoye; d €83-93; @☎) A modern, three-star hotel that has been recently renovated. Rooms are fresh and airy and the contemporary design scheme is easy on the eye. Comfortable and convenient if you want to stay smack-dab in the centre of things. Parking €10.

Hôtel Le Chambellan
HOTEL €

(☑03 80 67 12 67; www.hotel-chambellan.com; 92 rue Vannerie; s/d without bathroom €33/36, s with bathroom €38-53, d with bathroom €53-58, q €72-81; ☎) Built in 1730, this Old Town address has a vaguely medieval feel. Rooms come in cheerful tones of red, orange, pink and white; some have courtyard views.

B&B Hotel Dijon Centre
HOTEL €

(☑03 80 30 26 81; www.hotel-bb.com; 5 rue du Château; d €54; ✻☎) This abode gets by on its super central location, a waddle away from restaurants, bars, monuments and shops. It offers fairly identical-looking hotel rooms without much character but it's clean, functional and well soundproofed. And it's the only hotel in this price range that has air-con. Look out for internet deals at weekends.

Ethic Étapes Dijon
HOSTEL €

(Centre De Recontres et de Séjour Internationales; CRISD; ☑03 80 72 95 20; www.cri-dijon.com; 1 av Champollion; dm/s/d incl breakfast €21/40/52; @☎) This institutional (though friendly) 219-bed hostel, 2.5km northeast of the centre, is a good choice for budgeteers. Digs are in modern, airy two- to six-bed rooms with private bathrooms. By bus, take line 3 to the Dallas CRI stop. Disabled accessible. Parking free.

✗ Eating

Find loads of restaurants on buzzy rue Berbisey, around place Émile Zola, on rue Amiral Roussin and around the perimeter of the covered market. In warm months, outdoor cafes and brasseries (restaurants) fill place de la Libération.

DZ'Envies
MODERN BURGUNDIAN €€

(☑03 80 50 09 26; www.dzenvies.com; 12 rue Odebert; mains €16-20, lunch menus €13-20, dinner menus €29-36; ☺Mon-Sat) This zinging restaurant with cheery decorative touches is a good choice if you're tired of heavy Burgundian classics. The menu always involves seasonal, fresh ingredients, and dishes are imaginatively prepared and beautifully presented. At €18, the lunchtime *I love Dijon* (yes) *menu* (fixed-price meal) is a steal.

Chez Léon
BURGUNDIAN €

(☑03 80 50 01 07; www.restaurantchezleon.fr; 20 rue des Godrans; mains €11-29, lunch menus €15-21, dinner menus €22-27; ☺Tue-Sat) From bœuf bourguignon (beef marinated in young red wine) to *andouillettes* (chitterling sausages), this is the perfect primer course in hearty regional fare celebrated in a cosy and joyful atmosphere. The dining room is cluttered but there's outdoor seating in warm months.

Chez Nous
BISTRO €

(impasse Quentin; mains €7-8, lunch menus €10-13; ☺lunch noon-2pm Tue-Sat, bar 2pm-1am Mon, 11am-1am Tue-Sat) This quintessentially French *bar du coin* (neighbourhood bar), often crowded, hides down an alleyway near the covered market. At lunchtime join the flock and go for the fabulous-value *plat du jour* (daily special). Wash it all down with a glass of local wine (€2).

Le Piano Qui Fume
MODERN FRENCH €€

(☑03 80 30 35 45; www.lepianoquifume.fr; 36 rue Berbisey; mains €19, lunch menu €16, dinner menus €29-33; ☺lunch Mon, Tue & Thu-Sat, dinner Thu-Sat) Market cuisine, carefully chosen ingredients, good-value wines, ambient lighting and a lovely dining room mixing contemporary design with traditional touches (exposed brick walls and beams) are the rules of thumb at this respectable hideaway. The lunch *menu* is brilliant value.

Le Bistrot des Halles
BISTRO €

(☑03 80 49 94 15; 10 rue Bannelier; mains €12-18, lunch menu €17; ☺Tue-Sat) Under the direction of Jean-Pierre Billoux, Dijon's gastronomic

BURGUNDY DIJON

star, Le Bistrot des Halles serves a range of culinary delights that deliciously represent Burgundy cooking. The *escargots de Bourgogne* (snails) and *jambon à l'os braisé* (braised ham) are two specialities to look for, though the menu is in constant flux according to markets and seasons.

La Maison des Cariatides GASTRONOMIC €€
(☑03 80 45 59 25; www.lamaisondescariatides. fr; 28 rue Chaudronnerie; mains €22-32, lunch menu €21, dinner menus €35-49; ☺lunch & dinner Tue-Sat) Stellar period decor in a renovated 17th-century mansion complete with wood furnishings, exposed beams and stone walls make for an impressive backdrop to delicious French and regional cuisine. If you're on a budget make a beeline for the lunch *menu*.

La Dame d'Aquitaine REGIONAL CUISINE €€
(☑03 80 30 45 65; www.ladamedaquitaine.fr; 23 place Bossuet; mains €21-32, menus €31-46; ☺lunch Tue-Sat, dinner Mon-Sat, closed lunch mid-Jul–mid-Aug) Excellent local cuisine is served under the sumptuously lit bays of a 13th-century *cave* (wine cellar) accessed by a long flight of steps. Classical music filters through and the wine list is extensive.

Self-Catering
Northwest of Palais des Ducs is the covered market, **Les Halles** (rue Quentin; ☺7am-1pm Tue & Thu-Sat).

Drinking

Le Caveau de la Chouette BAR
(39 rue des Godrans; ☺Tue-Sat) Le Caveau de la Chouette is the hang-out of well-connected locals who flock here as much for the jazzy atmosphere as for the inspiring wine list.

Le Cappuccino BAR
(☑03 80 41 06 35; 132 rue Berbisey; ☺Mon-Sat) Coffee isn't even served at this often-packed bar, but wine by the glass and 80 beers are, including Mandubienne, the only beer brewed in Dijon.

Le Quentin BAR
(☑03 80 30 15 05; 6 rue Quentin; ☺daily) This congenial drinking spot looking onto the Halles overflows with friendly regulars enjoying a glass of wine or a cheese platter. The streetside terrace allows for a dash of people-watching on market days.

L'Univers BAR
(☑03 80 30 98 29; 47 rue Berbisey; ☺Mon-Sat) This ground-floor bar, with walls covered in mirrors and beer ads, has its menu on a chalkboard. In the cellar there's live music from 10pm to 1am on Friday and Saturday.

Shopping

The main shopping area is around rue de la Liberté and perpendicular rue du Bourg.

Mulot & Petitjean FOOD
(☑03 80 30 07 10; www.mulotpetitjean.fr; 13 place Bossuet; ☺2-7pm Mon, 9am-noon & 2-7pm Tue-Sat) The sweet-toothed will lose all self-control at this Dijon institution that was founded in 1796. It's famous for its scrumptious *pain d'épices* (gingerbread made with honey and spices).

Moutarde Maille FOOD
(☑03 80 30 41 02; www.maille.com; 32 rue de la Liberté; ☺10am-7pm Mon-Sat) When you enter the factory boutique of this mustard company, tangy odours assault your nostrils. Thirty-six kinds of mustard, like cassis or truffle and celery, including three on tap that you can sample.

Bourgogne Street FOOD, DRINK
(☑03 80 30 26 28; www.bourgognestreet.fr; 61 rue de la Liberté; ☺9am-noon & 2-7pm Mon & Tue, 9am-7pm Wed-Sat, 10am-1pm Sun) No, it's not a tacky souvenir shop. Bourgogne Street sells a wide range of quality Burgundian delicacies from small producers. Stock up on gingerbread, liquors, jams, chocolate, wines and mustard, among others.

Information

Main post office (place Grangier) Exchanges foreign currency.

Tourist office (☑08 92 70 05 58; www.visit dijon.com; 11 rue des Forges; ☺9am-6.30pm Mon-Sat, 10am-6pm Sun) The one- to three-day Dijon Côte de Nuits Pass may save you some cash.

Getting There & Away

A single **train station ticket counter** (☺5.45am-9pm) deals with TER trains, Divia local buses and the *départemental* bus company, Transco.

BUS Transco (☑03 80 11 29 29; www.mobigo -bourgogne.com) Buses stop in front of the train station. Tickets sold on board (€1.50). Bus 44 goes to Nuits-St-Georges and Beaune. Bus 43 goes to Abbaye de Cîteaux.

Eurolines (☑0 892 89 90 91; www.eurolines. fr; 53 rue Guillaume Tell) International bus travel.

CAR Major car-hire companies have desks in the train-station complex.

TRAIN Trains leave the **train station** (www. voyages-sncf.com; rue du Dr Remy) for the following:

Lyon-Part Dieu From €22, 1½ hours, 25 daily

Marseille From €54, 3½ hours by TGV, six direct daily

Paris Gare de Lyon From €49, 1¾ hours by TGV; €42, three hours non-TGV; 25 daily

🛈 Getting Around

BICYCLE The tourist office (p410) rents bikes with free helmets.

Velodi (www.velodi.net), Dijon's version of Paris' Vélib' automatic hire system, has 400 city bikes at 40 sites around town.

BUS Get details of Dijon's bus network, operated by Divia, from **L'Espace Bus** (☏03 80 11 29 29; www.divia.fr; place Grangier; ⏱8am-7pm Mon-Fri, 9am-9pm Sat).

CAR & MOTORCYCLE All city-centre parking is metered. There's a free car park at place Suquet, just south of the police station.

TRAM A **tram system** (www.letram-dijon.fr) was being built at the time of research and should be fully operating by the time you read this.

Côte d'Or Vineyards

Burgundy's most renowned vintages come from the vine-covered Côte d'Or (literally Golden Hillside, but it is actually an abbreviation of Côte d'Orient or Eastern Hillside), the narrow, eastern slopes of a range of hills made of limestone, flint and clay that runs south from Dijon for about 60km. The exquisite terrain with its patchwork of immaculate hand-groomed vines is dotted with peaceful stone villages where every house seems to hold a vintner.

An oenophile's nirvana, the Côte d'Or vineyards are divided into two areas, Côte de Nuits and Côte de Beaune. The Côte de Nuits is noted for its powerful red wines, while the Côte de Beaune produces top-quality dry whites and delicate reds.

CÔTE DE NUITS

The Côte de Nuits wine-growing area extends from Marsannay-la-Côte, just south of Dijion, to Corgoloin, a few kilometres north of Beaune. It includes the picturesque villages of Fixin, Gevrey-Chambertin, Morey-St-Denis, Chambolle-Musigny, Vougeot, Vosnes-Romanée and Nuits-St-Georges.

⊙ Sights

Château du Clos de Vougeot MUSEUM, CASTLE
(☏03 80 62 86 09; www.closdevougeot.fr; Vougeot; adult/child €4/3.10; ⏱9am-5.30pm daily) A mandatory stop on your tour of Burgundy's vineyards, this magnificent wine-producing *château* (estate) provides a wonderful introduction to Burgundy's winemaking techniques. Originally the property of the Abbaye de Cîteaux, the 16th-century country castle served as a getaway for the abbots. Tours offer a chance to discover the workings of enormous ancient wine presses and casks.

Cassissium LIQUEUR FACTORY
(☏03 80 62 49 70; www.cassissium.fr; av du Jura, Nuits-St-Georges; adult/child €8/free; ⏱10am-1pm & 2-7pm, last visits 1½hr before closing) This museum and factory worships all things liqueur, with a particular focus on the blackcurrant, from which cassis is made. There's fun for the whole family: movies, displays, a 30-minute guided tour and a tasting with nonalcoholic fruit syrups for the kids. In the industrial area east of N74.

L'Imaginarium WINE MUSEUM
(☏03 80 62 61 40; www.imaginarium-bourgogne. com; av du Jura, Nuits-St-Georges; adult/child €8/5; ⏱2-7pm Mon, 10am-7pm Tue-Sun) An essential port of call on any wine-tasting itinerary, this gleaming modern museum is a great place to learn about Burgundy wines and winemaking techniques. It's fun and entertaining, with movies, exhibits and interactive displays.

🏌 Activities

Wine Tasting WINE TASTING
The villages of the Côte de Nuits offer innumerable places to sample and purchase world-class wines (especially reds) a short walk from where they were made. Wine can be bought direct from the wine growers, many of whom offer tasting, allowing you to sample two or three vintages, but at many places, especially the better-known ones, you have to make advance reservations. Lists of estates and *caves* (wine cellars) open to the public are available from local tourist offices.

You can also visit wine shops, including Le Caveau des Vignerons (☏03 80 51 86 79; place de l'Église, Morey-St-Denis; ⏱10am-7pm daily), which stocks most Côte de Nuits appellations and offers excellent advice, and Le Caveau des Musignys (☏03 80 62 84 01; 1 rue Traversière, Chambolle-Musigny; ⏱10am-6pm daily), which represents more than 100 Côte de Nuits and Côte de Beaune wine growers.

ON THE GROUND, UPON THE WATER & IN THE AIR

Tasting fine wines often involves hanging out in dimly lit cellars, but Burgundy is also a paradise for lovers of the great outdoors.

The Comité Régional de Tourisme de Bourgogne (Burgundy Regional Tourist Board; www.burgundy-tourism.com) publishes excellent brochures on outdoors options, including *Burgundy by Bike*, available at tourist offices, and has a list of boat hire companies.

Hiking & Cycling

Burgundy has thousands of kilometres of walking and cycling trails, including sections of the GR2, GR7 and GR76. Varied local trails take you through some of the most ravishingly beautiful wine-growing areas in France, among them the vineyards of world-renowned Côte d'Or, Chablis and the Mâconnais (in Saône-et-Loire).

Rural footpaths criss-cross the Parc Naturel Régional du Morvan and some depart from the Morvan Visitors Centre, but you can also pick up trails from the Abbaye de Fontenay, Autun, Avallon, Cluny, Noyers-sur-Serein and Vézelay.

You can cycle on or very near the *chemin de halage* (towpath) of the Canal de Bourgogne all the way from Dijon to Migennes (225km). The section from Montbard to Tonnerre (65km) passes by Château d'Ancy-le-Franc; between Montbard and Pouilly-en-Auxois (58km) spurs go to the Abbaye de Fontenay and Semur-en-Auxois.

For details on Burgundy's planned 800km of *véloroutes* (bike paths) and *voies vertes* (green ways), including maps and guides, see www.burgundy-by-bike.com or stop at a tourist office.

Canal & River Boating

Few modes of transport are as relaxing as a houseboat on Burgundy's 1200km of placid waterways, which include the Rivers Yonne, Saône and Seille and a network of canals, including the Canal de Bourgogne, the Canal du Centre, the Canal Latéral à la Loire and the Canal du Nivernais (www.canal-du-nivernais.com). The following are reliable hire companies that offer boats from late March to 11 November (canals close for repairs in winter, but rivers don't):

» Bourgogne Fluviale (✆03 86 81 54 55; www.bourgogne-fluviale.com; Vermenton) Based in Vermenton, 25km southeast of Auxerre.

» France Afloat (Burgundy Cruisers; ✆03 86 81 67 87, in UK 08700 110 538; www.france afloat.com; 1 quai du Port, Vermenton) Based in Vermenton.

» Locaboat Holidays (✆03 86 91 72 72; www.locaboat.com; Port au Bois) Hires out boats throughout France, including at Joigny (27km northwest of Auxerre).

Hot-Air Ballooning

From about April to October you can take a stunning *montgolfière* (hot-air balloon) ride over Burgundy for around €220 per adult. Book through the Beaune and Dijon tourist offices. The following are some veteran outfits:

» Air Adventures (✆06 08 27 95 39; www.airadventures.fr) Based just outside Pouilly-en-Auxois, 50km west of Dijon.

» Air Escargot (✆03 85 87 12 30; www.air-escargot.com) In Remigny, 16km south of Beaune.

Walking   WALKING

The GR7 and its variant, the GR76, run along the Côte d'Or from a bit west of Dijon to the hills west of Beaune, from where they continue southwards. The Beaune tourist office sells an excellent guide, *Walks in* *the Beaune Countryside*, which details 30 marked routes.

🛏 Sleeping

Hôtel de Vougeot   HOTEL €€

(✆03 80 62 01 15; www.hotel-vougeot.com; 18 rue du Vieux Château, Vougeot; d €64-120; 🛜) What's not to love in this gracious country manor? The 16 rooms are rustically stylish and come with stone walls and exposed beams. Angle for a room with a view of the Vougeot vineyards.

La Colombière B&B €€

(☑03 80 61 07 95; www.maison-lacolombiere.com; 11 rue des Communes, Vosne-Romanée; s/d €75/85, q €140, min 2 nights; ☎) A relaxing place in the heart of the village. Bedrooms are a soothing mix of muted walls, contemporary furnishings and colourful textiles. Your courteous host knows a lot about wine and can organise tasting sessions and vineyard tours. Perfect for wine lovers.

La Closerie de Gilly B&B €€

(☑03 80 62 87 74; www.closerie-gilly.com; 16 av Bouchard, Gilly-lès-Cîteaux; d €85-105, q €120; ☎☒) A homey five-room B&B inside a delightful 18th-century *maison bourgeoise* (mansion) with a huge, flowery garden. Has bicycles for rent and offers wine tasting. It's in Gilly-les-Cîteaux, just 1km east of Vougeot.

Maison des Abeilles B&B €

(☑03 80 62 95 42; www.chambres-beaune.fr; Magny-lès-Villers; d €63-68, q €112; ☎) Sweet and jolly Jocelyne maintains this impeccably clean *chambre d'hôte* (B&B) in Magny-lès-Villers, a small village off rte des Grands Crus; it's at the junction between Côte de Nuits, Haute Côte de Nuits and Côte de Beaune. Rooms have colourful linen and breakfasts are a feast of breads and homemade jams. The flowery garden is a plus.

✗ Eating

Le Millésime MODERN BURGUNDIAN €€

(☑03 80 62 80 37; 1 rue Traversière, Chambolle-Musigny; mains €20-24, lunch menu €19, dinner menus €28-46; ☺Tue-Sat) This renowned venture is located in an exquisitely renovated *maison de village* (village house). The chef combines fresh local ingredients and exotic flavours in his excellent creations. Dark wood floors, well-spaced tables and a warm welcome create an easy air.

Le Chambolle BURGUNDIAN €€

(☑03 80 62 86 26; www.restaurant-lechambolle. com; 28 rue Caroline Aigle, Chambolle-Musigny; mains €13-23, menus €24-30; ☺12.15-1.30pm & 7.15-8.30pm Fri-Tue) This unpretentious backroads gem creates traditional Burgundian cuisine with the freshest ingredients. On the D122, a bit west of Vougeot in gorgeous Chambolle-Musigny.

Chez Guy And Family MODERN FRENCH €€

(☑03 80 58 51 51; www.chez-guy.fr; 3 place de la Mairie, Gevrey-Chambertin; menus €27-44; ☺daily) Its dining room is large and light, and there's a tempting choice of dishes on its fixed-price menus. Along with tender duckling, signature seasonal specialities include rabbit leg and pollack. A long wine list backs up the food.

La Cabotte MODERN FRENCH €€€

(☑03 80 61 20 77; www.restaurantlacabotte.fr; 24 Grand' Rue, Nuits-St-Georges; mains €19-27, menus €29-53; ☺lunch Tue-Fri, dinner Tue-Sat) This intimate restaurant serves up refined, inventive versions of French dishes. No artifice or posing here, just excellent, if sometimes surprising, food.

CÔTE DE BEAUNE

Welcome to one of the most prestigious wine-growing areas in the world. The Côte de Beaune area extends from Ladoix-Serrigny, just a few kilometres north of Beaune, to Santenay, about 18km south of Beaune. It includes the delightful villages of Pernand-Vergelesses, Aloxe-Corton, Savigny-lès-Beaune, Chorey-lès-Beaune, Pommard, Volnay, Meursault, Puligny-Montrachet and Chassagne-Montrachet, which boast Burgundy's most fabled vineyards. If you're looking for an upscale wine château experience, you've come to the right place.

◎ Sights

TOP CHOICE **Château de La Rochepot** CASTLE

(☑03 80 21 71 37; www.larochepot.com; La Rochepot; adult/child €8/4; ☺10am-5.30pm Wed-Mon) Conical towers and multi-coloured tile roofs rise from thick woods above the ancient village of La Rochepot. This marvellous medieval fortress offers fab views of surrounding countryside and the interiors are a fascinating combination of the utilitarian (weapons) and the luxe (fine paintings).

Château de Meursault CASTLE

(☑03 80 26 22 75; www.chateau-meursault.com; Meursault; admission incl tasting €15; ☺9.30am-noon & 2.30-6pm daily, no midday closure Jul-Aug) One of the prettiest of the Côte de Beaune châteaux, Château de Meursault has beautiful grounds and produces some of the most prestigious white wines in the world. Particularly impressive are the 14th-century cellars.

Château de Pommard
CASTLE

(☎03 80 22 12 59; www.chateaudepommard.com; 15 rue Marey-Monge, Pommard; guided tour incl tasting adult/child €21/free; ☉daily 9.30am-6pm Apr-Nov) For many red-wine lovers, a visit to this superb château just 3km south of Beaune is the ultimate Burgundian pilgrimage. The impressive cellars contain many vintage bottles. If the tour has whetted your appetite, you can sample Burgundian specialities at the on-site restaurant.

Château de Savigny
MUSEUM, CASTLE

(☎03 80 21 55 03; www.chateau-savigny.com; Savigny-lès-Beaune; adult/child €8/free; ☉9am-5pm mid-Apr–Oct, 9am-noon & 2-4pm Nov–mid-Apr) Drop in for wine tasting and stay to see the unexpected collection of race cars, motorcycles, aeroplanes and fire trucks.

🏃 Activities

Cycling
CYCLING

The 20km Voie des Vignes (Vineyard Way), a bike route marked by rectangular green-on-white signs, goes from Beaune's Parc de la Bouzaize via Pommard, Volnay, Meursault, Puligny-Montrachet and Chassagne-Montrachet to Santenay, where you can pick up the Voie Verte (see boxed text p442) to Cluny. The Beaune tourist office sells a detailed map.

Wine Tasting
WINE TASTING

You'll find plenty of wine-tasting opportunities in the wine-producing villages. You can stop at the famous wine châteaux or you may prefer to drop in at more laid-back wineries – look for signs.

🛏 Sleeping

La Maison d'Olivier Leflaive
BOUTIQUE HOTEL €€€

(☎03 80 21 37 65; www.olivier-leflaive.com; place du Monument, Puligny-Montrachet; d €160-220; ☉closed Jan) Occupying a tastefully renovated 17th-century village house in the heart of Puligny-Montrachet, this 13-room venture delivers top service and classy comfort. Best of all, it offers personalised wine tours and tastings.

🏆 Villa Louise Hôtel
HOTEL €€

(☎03 80 26 46 70; www.hotel-villa-louise.fr; 9 rue Franche, Aloxe-Corton; d €100-195; @🛜🏊) This tranquil mansion houses elegant, modern rooms, each of them dreamily different. The expansive garden stretches straight to the edge of the vineyard and a separate gazebo shelters the sauna and pool. Genteel Louise

Perrin presides, and has a private *cave,* perfect for wine tastings.

Domaine Corgette
B&B €€

(☎03 80 21 68 08; www.domainecorgette.com; rue de la Perrière, St-Romain; d €85-110; 🛜) The sun-drenched terrace at this renovated winery looks out on the dramatic cliffs. Tucked in the centre of the quiet village of St-Romain, its rooms are light and airy with crisp linen, and retain classic touches like fireplaces and wood floors. Good English is spoken.

🍴 Eating

Excellent restaurants are tucked away in the villages of the Côte de Beaune. Reserve ahead in high season.

Auprès du Clocher
GASTRONOMIC €€€

(☎03 80 22 21 79; www.aupresduclocher.com; 1 rue Nackenheim, Pommard; mains €16-32, lunch menu €25, dinner menus €42-65; ☉lunch & dinner Thu-Mon) Celebrated chef Jean-Christophe Moutet rustles up gastronomic delights at Auprès du Clocher, in the heart of Pommard. The ingredients are Burgundian, but imagination renders them into something new and elegant. Needless to say, the wine list is superb.

Le Chevreuil – La Maison de la Mère Daugier
MODERN BURGUNDIAN €€

(☎03 80 21 23 25; www.lechevreuil.fr; place de la République, Meursault; mains €20-30, menus €23-58; ☉closed Wed & Sun) Chef Tiago is known for his creative take on regional staples. The dining room's country-chic, with plenty of light, wood and stone for that down-home feel, and the menu takes the cream of traditional Burgundian and gives it a 21st-century spin. Try the *terrine chaude de la mère Daugier,* the house's signature offering, and you'll see what we mean.

Le Charlemagne
GASTRONOMIC, FUSION €€€

(☎03 80 21 51 45; www.lecharlemagne.fr; Pernand-Vergelesses; lunch menus Mon, Thu & Fri €31-38, other menus €57-98; ☉noon-1.30pm Thu-Mon, 7-9.30pm Wed-Mon, closed dinner Wed Sep-May) Vineyard views are perhaps even more mind-blowing than the imaginatively prepared dishes melding French cuisine with techniques and ingredients from Japan. At the entrance of Pernand-Vergelesses.

La Table d'Olivier Leflaive
BISTRO €€

(www.olivier-leflaive.com; place du Monument, Puligny-Montrachet; menu €25; ☉lunch & dinner Mon-Sat, closed Jan) This is *the* address to recommend in Puligny-Montrachet. The trademark four-course 'Menu Repas' combines seasonal French classics with global flavours. Add €15 and you'll sample a selection of five local wines chosen by the *sommelier* – a winning formula.

Le Chassagne — GASTRONOMIC €€€
(☎03 80 21 94 94; www.stephaneleger.com; 4 impasse des Chenevottes, Chassagne-Montrachet; mains €31-49, lunch menu €28, dinner menus €58-96; ⊘lunch Tue-Sun, dinner Tue & Thu-Sat) Renowned chef Stéphane Léger has set up shop in quiet Chassagne-Montrachet. He's known for his artful approach to cooking, and it's a pleasure to tuck into his sculptural creations. Expect meat and fish dishes presented with serious panache.

Le Cellier Volnaysien — BURGUNDIAN €
(www.le-cellier-volnaysien.com; place de l'Église, Volnay; menus €18-27; ⊘lunch Thu-Mon, dinner Sat) Solid Burgundian cooking in a cosy stone-walled, vaulted dining room in the heart of Volnay.

❶ Getting There & Around
There is public transport in and around Côte d'Or wine villages.

Beaune
POP 22,720

Beaune (pronounced similarly to 'bone'), 44km south of Dijon, is the unofficial capital of the Côte d'Or. This thriving town's *raison d'être* and the source of its *joie de vivre* is wine: making it, tasting it, selling it, but most of all, drinking it. Consequently Beaune is one of the best places in all of France for wine tasting.

The jewel of Beaune's old city is the magnificent Hôtel-Dieu, France's most splendiferous medieval charity hospital.

◉ Sights
The amoeba-shaped old city is enclosed by thick stone ramparts and a stream which is in turn encircled by a one-way boulevard with seven names. The ramparts, which shelter wine cellars, are lined with overgrown gardens and ringed by a pathway that makes for a lovely stroll.

TOP CHOICE Hôtel-Dieu des Hospices de Beaune — HISTORIC BUILDING
(www.hospices-de-beaune.com; rue de l'Hôtel-Dieu; adult/child €7/3; ⊘9am-5.30pm) Built in 1443, this magnificent Gothic hospital

(until 1971) is famously topped by stunning turrets and pitched rooftops covered in multicoloured tiles. Interior highlights include the barrel-vaulted Grande Salle (look for the dragons and peasant heads up on the roof beams); the mural-covered St-Hughes Room; an 18th-century pharmacy lined with flasks once filled with elixirs and powders; and the multipanelled masterpiece Polyptych of the Last Judgement by 15th-century Flemish painter Rogier van der Weyden, depicting Judgment Day in glorious technicolour.

Moutarderie Fallot — MUSTARD FACTORY
(Mustard Mill; www.fallot.com; 31 rue du Faubourg Bretonnière; adult/child €10/8; ⊘tours 10am & 11.30am Mon-Sat, also afternoons summer, closed Nov-Mar 15) Maison Fallot, Burgundy's last family-run stone-ground mustard company, offers tours of its facilities which include a museum about mustard. Demonstrations include hand-milling mustard seeds – young kids love it! Reserve ahead at the tourist office.

Basilique Collégiale Notre Dame — CHURCH
(place Général Leclerc; ⊘9.30am-5.30pm) Built in the Romanesque and Gothic styles from the 11th to 15th centuries, this church was once affiliated with the monastery of Cluny. It's notable for its extra-large porch and the medieval tapestries that are displayed inside (guided tours cost €3).

🏃 Activities
Underneath Beaune's buildings, streets and ramparts, millions of dusty bottles of wine are being aged to perfection in cool, dark cellars. Wine-tasting options abound; the following places are just a wee sample of what's on offer.

Marché aux Vins — WINE TASTING
(www.marcheauxvins.com; 2 rue Nicolas Rolin; admission €10; ⊘9.30-11.30am & 2-5.30pm, no midday closure Jul-Aug) Using a *tastevin* (wine-tasting cup), sample an impressive 15 wines in the candle-lit former Église des Cordeliers and its cellars. Wandering among the vintages takes about an hour. The finest wines are at the end; look for the *premier crus* and the *grand cru*.

Bouchard Père & Fils — WINE TASTING
(www.bouchard-pereetfils.com; 15 rue du Château; ⊘10am-12.30pm & 2.30-6.30pm Mon-Sat, 10am-12.30pm Sun Apr-Nov, 10am-12.30pm & 2.30-5.30pm Mon-Sat Dec-Mar) The atmospheric

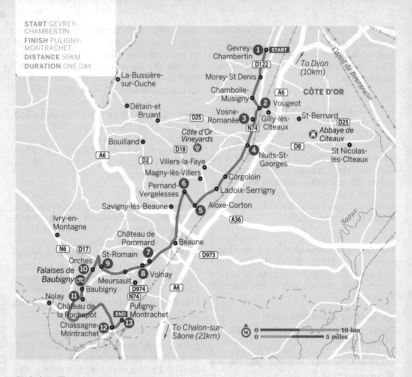

START GEVREY-
CHAMBERTIN
FINISH PULIGNY-
MONTRACHET
DISTANCE 55KM
DURATION ONE DAY

Driving Tour
Route des Grands Crus

❯ Burgundy's most famous wine route, the
Route des Grands Crus, and its often-
narrow variants wend their way between
stone-built villages with steeple-topped
churches or the turrets of a château peep-
ing above the trees. Vines cascade down
the slopes between hamlets – Chambertin,
Chambolle, Chassagne, Montrachet. The
Côte's lower slopes are seas of vineyards; on
the upper slopes, vines give way to forests,
cliffs and breathtaking views. Signposted in
brown, the Route des Grands Crus generally
follows the tertiary roads west of the N74.

Coming from Dijon, the Côte de Nuits
begins in earnest just south of Marsannay-la-
Côte. Most of the area's *grand cru* vineyards
lie between **①** **Gevrey-Chambertin** and
Vosne-Romanée. In **②** **Vougeot**, stop at
the historic château. **③** **Vosne-Romanée** is
famed for its Romanée Conti wines, among
Burgundy's most prestigious and priciest.
Continuing south, visit **④** **Nuits-St-Georges**.

On the Côte de Beaune, the impossibly
steep coloured-tile roof of Château Corton-
André in **⑤** **Aloxe-Corton** is easy to spot,
just off the one-lane main street. **⑥** **Pernand-Vergelesses** is nestled in a little valley
hidden from the N74.

South of Beaune, **⑦** **Château de Pommard**, surrounded by a stone wall, is on the
D973 on the northeast edge of town. Wander
quaint **⑧** **Volnay** to its hillside church. Off
the main track, **⑨** **St-Romain** is a bucolic
village situated right where vineyardland
meets pastureland, forests and cliffs. Hiking trails from here include the spectacular
Sentier des Roches, a circuit that follows
part of the GR7 and the D17l along the top of
the **Falaises de Baubigny** (Baubigny cliffs),
300m above the Saône. Then, via the hillside
hamlet of **⑩** **Orches**, which has breathtaking vineyard views, travel to the fantastic
15th-century **⑪** **Château de La Rochepot**.
For a pretty finale to your journey, drive down
to the villages of **⑫** **Chassagne-Montrachet**
and **⑬** **Puligny-Montrachet**, where you'll
have the chance to sample the world's most
opulent whites.

cellars are housed in a former medieval fortress and feature plenty of prestigious Grands Crus from Côte de Nuits and Côte de Beaune.

Cellier de la Vieille Grange   WINE TASTING
(www.bourgogne-cellier.com; 27 bd Georges Clemenceau; ☺9am-noon & 2-7pm Wed-Sat, by appointment Sun-Tue) This is where locals come to buy Burgundy wines *en vrac* (in bulk) for as little as €4.35 per litre for AOC wines. Tasting is done direct from barrels using a pipette.

Patriarche Père et Fils   WINE TASTING
(www.patriarche.com; 5 rue du Collège; audioguide tour €13; ☺9.30-11.30am & 2-5.30pm) The largest cellars in Burgundy, they are lined with about five million bottles of wine. The oldest is a Beaune Villages AOC from 1904. Visitors sample 13 wines and take the *tastevin* home.

Bourgogne Randonnées   WALKING, CYCLING
(☏03 80 22 06 03; www.bourgogne-randonnees. com; 7 av du 8 Septembre; bikes per day/week €18/96; ☺9am-noon & 1.30-7pm Mon-Sat, 2-7pm Sun) arranges tailor-made self-guided bike and walking tours, including lodging and meals. It also hires out mountain bikes.

Bourgogne Evasion   WALKING, CYCLING
(www.bourgogne-evasion.fr; 6 bd Perpreuil) also runs bike and walking tours in the vineyards, including wine-tasting sessions.

Tours

The small tourist train, Visiotrain (☏06 08 07 45 68; www.visiotrain2000.com; adult/child €7/4; ☺11am-5.30pm, closed Wed & morning Sat), departs six times daily from Rue de l'Hôtel-Dieu and tours the old town.

The tourist office handles reservations for hot-air-balloon rides, and for vineyard tours (from €34) run by the following companies: Chemins de Bourgogne (www.chemins-de -bourgogne.com), Safari Tours (www.burgundy -tourism-safaritours.com) and Vinéatours (www.burgundy-wine-tour.com).

Festivals & Events

Festival International
d'Opéra Baroque   MUSIC FESTIVAL
(www.festivalbeaune.com) In July, this is one of the most prestigious baroque opera festivals in Europe. Performances are held at the Basilique Collégiale Notre-Dame and the Hôtel-Dieu des Hospices de Beaune.

Sleeping

Abbaye de Maizières   HISTORIC HOTEL €€
(☏03 80 24 74 64; www.beaune-abbaye-maizieres. com; 19 rue Maizières; d €118-190; ❄@) This character-laden establishment inside a 12th-century abbey oozes history, yet most rooms have been luxuriously modernised, and decorated with contemporary furnishings. Some rooms boast Cistercian stained-glass windows and exposed beams; those on the top floor offer views over Beaune's famed multicolour tile roofs. There are only nine rooms, which ensures intimacy. No lift, but the friendly staff will help you haul up your luggage to your room.

Hôtel des Remparts   HISTORIC HOTEL €€
(☏03 80 24 94 94; www.hotel-remparts-beaune. com; 48 rue Thiers; d €80-160; ❄☎) Set around two delightful courtyards, rooms in this 17th-century town house have red-tiled or parquet floors and simple antique furniture. Some rooms come with exposed beams and a fireplace while others have air-con. Most bathrooms have been renovated. Friendly staff can also hire out bikes. Parking €10.

Chez Marie   B&B €€
(☏06 64 63 48 20; www.chezmarieabeaune.com; 14 rue Poissonnerie; d €85-110; ☎) All is peace and calm yet only five minutes from the centre of Beaune. Marie and her husband love having people to stay in their comfortable suburban house. They enjoy a chat over the breakfast table, helping you plan the day ahead (especially if you're cycling). The four rooms are impeccably simple and airy; L'Annexe, across the street, is ideal for families. Breakfast is served in a sweet garden. Bikes are available for hire.

Hôtel de la Paix   HOTEL €€
(www.hotelpaix.com; 45 rue du Faubourg Madeleine; s €75, d €85-170, q €145-165; ☎) This hotel has all the hallmarks of a great deal: renovated, squeaky-clean rooms with air-con, modern bathrooms, an ace location near the centre

---

ⓘ **PASS PAYS BEAUNOIS**

If you'll be taking in a lot sights and activities, including wine tasting, in the Beaune area, consider picking up the Pass Pays Beaunois at the Beaune tourist offices. Ticket combos save 5% to 15% depending on the number of sights you plan to visit.

Beaune

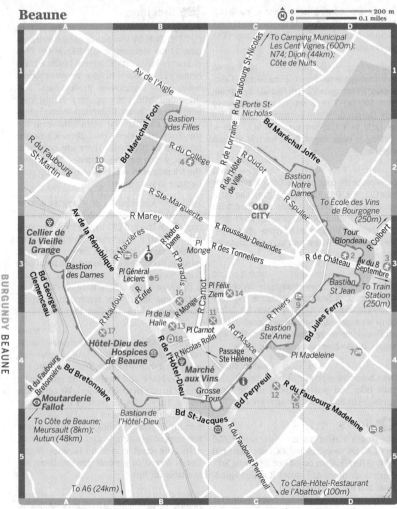

and a tab that won't burn a hole in your pocket. The upstairs rooms get more natural light than the ones on the ground floor. Parking €8.

Café-Hôtel-Restaurant de l'Abattoir   HOTEL €

(☎03 80 22 21 46; 19 rue du Faubourg Perpreuil; d €29; ☎) Everything is simple and laid-back at this unfussy hotel a five-minutes walk from the centre. The rooms are small but tidy; ask for a renovated one. Accommodation with half board (breakfast and dinner) is available (€39 per person). Note that reception is closed on Sunday. Call ahead.

Camping Municipal
Les Cent Vignes   CAMPGROUND €

(☎03 80 22 03 91; campinglescentvignes@mairie-beaune.fr; 10 rue Auguste Dubois; sites per adult/tent €5/4; ⊘mid-Mar–Oct; ☎) A flowery, well-equipped campground 700m north of the centre.

Hôtel le Foch   HOTEL €

(☎03 80 24 05 65; www.hotelbeaune-lefoch.fr; 24 bd Maréchal Foch; d €43-52, q €75) This cheapie on a busy thoroughfare has 10 basic but clean rooms. An acceptable plan B if others are full.

Beaune

✕ Eating

Beaune harbours a host of excellent restaurants; you'll find many around place Carnot, place Félix Ziem and place Madeleine. Reserve ahead in high season.

Loiseau des Vignes　　　GASTRONOMIC €€€
(✆03 80 24 12 06; www.bernard-loiseau.com; 31 rue Maufoux; lunch menus €20-28, dinner menus €59-95; ◷Tue-Sat) For that special meal with your significant other, this culinary shrine is the place to go. Expect stunning concoctions ranging from caramelised pigeon to *quenelles de sandre* (dumplings made from pike fish), all exquisitely presented. And even the most budget-conscious can indulge – lunch *menus* are a bargain. Wines are served only by the glass (from €3). In summer the verdant garden is a plus.

Le Comptoir des Tontons　　MODERN BURGUNDIAN €€
(✆03 80 24 19 64; www.lecomptoirdestontons. com; 22 rue du Faubourg Madeleine; menus €25-36; ◷Tue-Sat) Stylishly decorated in a hip bistro style, this local treasure entices with the passionate Burgundian cooking of chef Pepita. Most ingredients are organic and locally sourced. Does the beef with paprika taste better than the fat duck in aniseed sauce? You be the judge. Service is prompt and friendly.

Caves Madeleine　　TRADITIONAL FRENCH €€
(✆03 80 22 93 30; 8 rue du Faubourg Madeleine; mains €12-25, lunch menu €15; ◷Mon-Wed & Sat, dinner Fri) This is a convivial restaurant where locals tuck into French classics such as *blanquette de veau* (veal stew) at long shared tables surrounded by wine racks.

Koki Food & Shop　　FUSION, FRENCH €
(✆03 80 24 06 61; www.kokifoodshop.com; 10 place Félix Ziem; brunch €11-17, menus €15-18; ◷Thu-Tue) If you think the time has come to give your taste buds something new to sing about, this is the place. This upbeat and colourful eatery run by Laurent Peugeot, a Burgundian chef who worked in Japan for four years, gets kudos for its lip-smacking concoctions that arrive via conveyer belt – you pay by the plate (from €4). Set *menus* are also available.

Le P'tit Paradis　　MODERN BURGUNDIAN €€
(✆03 80 24 91 00; www.restaurantleptitparadis. fr; 25 rue Paradis; mains €18-20, menus €28-36; ◷Thu-Mon) Find this intimate restaurant on a narrow medieval street. It's known for *cuisine elaborée* (creatively transformed versions of traditional dishes) made with fresh local products. Summer terrace.

Self-Catering
Food Market　　MARKET €
(place de la Halle; ◷until 12.30pm Sat) Elaborate weekly market. There's a much smaller *marché gourmand* (gourmet market) on Wednesday morning.

Alain Hess Fromager　　CHEESE SHOP €
(www.fromageriehess.com; 7 place Carnot; ◷9am-12.15pm & 2.30-7.15pm Mon-Sat, plus 10am-12.30pm Sun Easter-Dec) This treasure trove of regional products will tempt the devil in you. It has a wide assortment of gourmet foodstuffs, including cheeses, mustards, wines and dairy products. Don't leave without sampling the Délice de Pommard, the house's signature cheese.

Shopping

Athenaeum de la Vigne et du Vin BOOKS
(☎03 80 25 08 30; www.athenaeumfr.com; 7 rue
de l'Hôtel-Dieu; ☉10am-7pm) Stocks thousands
of titles on oenology (the art and science of
winemaking), including many in English,
as well as recipe books and wine-related
gifts.

Information

Post office (7 bd St-Jacques) Exchanges
currency.
Tourist office (☎03 80 26 21 30; www.
beaune-tourisme.fr; 6 bd Perpreuil; ☉9am-7pm
Mon-Sat, to 6pm Sun) Sells Pass Beaune and
has lots of brochures on Beaune and the nearby
vineyards. You can also get online.

Getting There & Away

BUS **Transco** (☎03 80 11 29 29; www.mobigo
-bourgogne.com) bus 44 links Beaune with Dijon
(€1.50, 1½ hours, two to seven daily), stopping
at Côte d'Or villages such as Vougeot, Nuits-St-
Georges and Aloxe-Corton. Services reduced in
July and August. In Beaune, buses stop along
the boulevards around the old city. Timetables
at the tourist office.

CAR & BICYCLE **ADA** (☎03 80 22 72 90; www.
ada.fr/location-voiture-beaune.htm; 26 av du 8
Septembre) hires cars, scooters (€26 per day)
and bikes (€16).

TRAIN Trains connect the following places:
Dijon €7.30, 25 minutes, 40 daily
Lyon-Part Dieu From €30, 1¾ hours, 16 daily
Mâcon From €13, 50 minutes, 16 daily
Nuits-St-Georges From €4.50, 10 minutes,
40 daily

DON'T MISS

VENTE AUX ENCHÈRES DES VINS DES HOSPICES DE BEAUNE

On the third weekend in November
the Vente aux Enchères des Vins des
Hospices de Beaune (Hospices de
Beaune Wine Auction) is the grandest
of the Côte d'Or's many wine festivals.
As part of this three-day extravaganza,
the Hospices de Beaune holds a *vente
aux enchères* (private auction) of wines
from its endowment, 61 hectares of
prime vineyards bequeathed by ben-
efactors; proceeds go to medical facilities and research.

Paris Gare de Lyon From €41, 2¼ hours by
TGV (non-TGV 3½ hours), 20 daily, two direct
TGVs daily

Getting Around

Parking is free outside the town walls.

Abbaye de Cîteaux

South of Dijon and 13km east of Nuits-
St-Georges (follow the D8 to the east), the
Abbaye de Cîteaux (☎03 80 61 32 58; www.
citeaux-abbaye.com; D996; slide show €3, guided
tour & slide show adult/child under 12 €8.50/
free) is well worth a visit for its historical
significance. In contrast to the showy Benedictines of Cluny, the medieval Cistercian
order was known for its austerity, discipline
and humility, and for the productive manual
labour of its monks, one result of which
was groundbreaking wine-producing techniques. The order was named after Cîteaux
abbey (Cistercium in Latin), where it was
founded in 1098. It enjoyed phenomenal
growth in the 12th century under St Bernard (1090–1153), and some 600 Cistercian
abbeys soon stretched from Scandinavia to
the Near East.

Out in the midst of pastoral mustard
fields, Cîteaux was virtually destroyed during the Revolution and the monks didn't
return until 1898, but today it is home to
about 35 monks. You can visit the monastery
on a 1½-hour guided tour in French with
printed English commentary. It includes an
audiovisual presentation on monastic life.
Phone ahead or email for reservations.

Visitors may attend daily prayers and
Sunday Mass (10.30am). The boutique sells
edibles made at monasteries around France,
including the abbey's own cheese.

Pays d'Auxois

West of Dijon, along and around the Canal
de Bourgogne, the Pays d'Auxois is verdant
and rural. Broad mustard fields, wooded
hills and escarpments are dotted with
fortified hilltop towns, including Semur-
en-Auxois. The recent opening of the
MuséoParc Alésia is another good reason to
explore the area.

SEMUR-EN-AUXOIS
POP 4568

Dont' miss Semur-en-Auxois – this small
fortress town is incredibly picturesque.

CHEESE, GLORIOUS CHEESE

What else would you pair with your dram of wine but one of Burgundy's Appellation d'Origine Protégée (AOP) cheeses? There are three, all made with cow's milk.

» Époisses – invented in the 16th century by the monks at Abbaye de Cîteaux, Époisses is a soft, round, orange-skinned white cheese. It takes a month to make, using washes of salt water, rainwater and Marc de Bourgogne (local pomace brandy), resulting in a strong, creamy flavour.

» Soumaintrain – milder than Époisses, but with a spicy burst at the end of a tasting. Similar in appearance to Époisses.

» Chaource – these elegant little wheels of soft white cheese can be quite fluid when young. A bit like Camembert, they are ideal with sparkling wines.

Perched on a granite spur and surrounded by a hairpin turn in the River Armançon, it is guarded by four massive pink-granite bastions, and the centre is laced with cobbled lanes flanked by attractive houses. At night the ramparts are illuminated, which adds to the appeal.

◉ Sights & Activities

Old City   HISTORIC QUARTER

Most of the old city was built when Semur was an important religious centre boasting no fewer than six monasteries. The tourist office (which has a free walking tour brochure) is next to two concentric medieval gates, Porte Sauvigne (1417) and fortified Porte Guillier (14th century). Through the gates, pedestrianised rue Buffon is lined with 17th-century houses. Be sure to stop at Pâtisserie Coeur (14 rue Buffon; ⊗Tue-Sun), a confectionary shop that produces *semurettes* (delicious dark-chocolate truffles created here a century ago), and *gâteau mont d'auxois*, another treat. The Promenade du Rempart affords panoramic views from atop the western part of Semur's medieval battlements. Fear not if you see some menacing cracks in the 44m-high Tour de la Orle d'Or – they have been there since 1589!

Collégiale Notre Dame   CHURCH

(⊗9am-noon & 2-6.30pm) A stained-glass window (1927) and a plaque commemorating American soldiers who fell in France in WWI are inside this twin-towered, Gothic collegiate church.

🛏 Sleeping & Eating

La Porte Guillier   B&B €€

(☑03 80 97 31 19; www.laporteguillier.com; 5bis rue de l'Ancienne Comédie; d €80-120; 🔊) To really soak up the town's atmosphere, stay at this delightful B&B housed in a forfified stone gateway dating from the 14th century. The three generously sized rooms sport plenty of charming old furniture. Nothing too standard, nothing too studied, a very personal home and good breakfasts brimming with organic specialities.

Hôtel des Cymaises   HOTEL €

(☑03 80 97 21 44; www.hotelcymaises.com; 7 rue du Renaudot; s €63-73, d €68-73, q €85-116; 🔊) Set around a quiet courtyard in a grand 18th-century *maison bourgeoise* are comfortable, slightly worn rooms, some with exposed wooden beams, and a bright verandah for breakfast.

Le Saint-Vernier   BURGUNDIAN €

(☑03 80 97 32 96; 13 rue Févret; mains €11-20; ⊗Tue-Sun) At this cosy bistro in the old town, the menu features simple but inventive offerings that spoil your taste buds without spoiling your budget. Most specialities are made with locally sourced ingredients, such as Époisses cheese.

Les Minimes   BURGUNDIAN €

(☑03 80 97 26 86; www.restaurantlesminimes.fr; 39 rue des Vaux; mains €12-22, lunch menu €13, dinner menus €22-29; ⊗lunch Tue-Sun, dinner Tue & Thu-Sat) Overlooking the river, this restaurant serves an ambitious menu of carefully crafted cuisine. The cheese platter is tempting, and desserts are as artfully caloric, and as stylish, as anything else in Burgundy.

❶ Information

Tourist office (☑03 80 97 05 96; www.ville-semur-en-auxois.fr; 2 place Gaveau; ⊗9am-noon & 2-5pm Mon-Sat, closed Mon Oct-Apr; 🔊) Has a free walking-tour brochure in English and a SNCF train-ticket machine.

BURGUNDY PAYS D'AUXOIS

ESCARGOTS

One of France's trademark culinary habits, the consumption of gastropod molluscs – preferably with butter, garlic, parsley and fresh bread – is inextricably linked in the public mind with Burgundy because *Helix pomatia*, though endemic in much of Europe, is best known as *escargot de Bourgogne* (the Burgundy snail). Once a regular, and unwelcome, visitor to the fine-wine vines of Burgundy and a staple on Catholic plates during Lent, the humble hermaphroditic crawler has been decimated by overharvesting and the use of agricultural chemicals, and is now a protected species. As a result, the vast majority of the critters impaled on French snail forks (the ones with two tines) are now imported from Turkey, Greece and Eastern Europe.

Getting There & Away

BUS **Transco** (☑08 00 10 20 04) bus 49 (two or three daily) goes to Dijon (€1.50, 1¼ hours) and Avallon (40 minutes). Bus 70 goes to Montbard (€1.50, 20 to 60 minutes, three to nine daily) on the Paris–Dijon rail line.

ABBAYE DE FONTENAY

Founded in 1118 and restored to its medieval glory a century ago, Abbaye de Fontenay (Fontenay Abbey; ☑03 80 92 15 00; www.abbaye defontenay.com; adult/child €9.50/5.50; ☉10am-6pm Apr-11 Nov, 10am-noon & 2-5pm 12 Nov-Mar) offers a fascinating glimpse of the austere, serene surroundings in which Cistercian monks lived lives of contemplation, prayer and manual labour. Set in a bucolic wooded valley, the abbey, a Unesco World Heritage Site, includes an unadorned Romanesque church, a barrel-vaulted monks' dormitory, landscaped gardens and the first metallurgical factory in Europe with a forge from 1220. Guided tours (☉hourly 10am-5pm) are in French with printed information in six languages.

From the parking lot, the GR213 trail forms part of two verdant walking circuits: one to Montbard (13km return), the other (11.5km) through Touillon and Le Petit Jailly. Maps and extensive guides to plant life are available in the abbey shop.

Fontenay is 25km north of Semur-en-Auxois. A taxi (☑03 80 92 31 49, 03 80 92 04 79) from the Montbard TGV train station – trains go to Dijon (from €11, 40 minutes) – costs about €13 (30% more on Sunday and holidays).

CHÂTILLON-SUR-SEINE
POP 6257

On the northern outskirts of Burgundy, Châtillon-sur-Seine is a beautifully evocative town, with a picturesque old quarter by the river, well-preserved buildings and a not-to-be-missed archaeology museum. It's also a good base if you want to explore the atmospheric Forêt de Châtillon and the Châtillonnais vineyards.

◉ Sights & Activities

Châtillon's main claim to fame is the Trésor de Vix (Vix Treasure), a collection of Celtic, Etruscan and Greek objects from the 6th century BC on display at the Musée du Pays Châtillonnais (☑03 80 91 24 67; www.musee-vix.fr; 14 rue de la Libération; adult/child €7/3.50; ☉9am-noon & 2-6pm, closed Sun Sep-Jun). The treasure was discovered in 1953 in the tomb of the Dame de Vix, a Celtic princess who controlled the trade in Cornish tin in the 6th century. Mined in Cornwall, the tin was brought by boat up the Seine as far as Vix and then carried overland to the Saône and the Rhône, whence river vessels conveyed it south to Marseille and its most eager consumers, the Greeks. The outstanding collection includes a jaw-droppingly massive bronze Greek krater that can hold 1100L of wine.

The town's commercial centre, rebuilt after WWII, is bordered by two branches of the Seine, here hardly more than a stream. A short walk east, the idyllic Source de la Douix (pronounced 'dwee'), a 600L-a-second artesian spring, flows from a 30m cliff. Perfect for a picnic, it is one of the oldest Celtic religious sites in Europe. Nearby, climb up to crenellated Tour de Gissey (c 1500s), for fine views.

Among the wines produced in the Châtillonnais vineyards, north of town, is Burgundy's own bubbly, Crémant de Bourgogne (www.cremantdebourgogne.fr, in French). Follow the 120km-long Route du Crémant, marked by white-on-brown signs, to the vineyards, and allow plenty of time for a wine tasting. The tourist office can supply you with the useful map/brochure *Route du Crémant* (free). The Champagne region's Côte des Bar vineyards are just a few kilometres further north.

The immense Forêt de Châtillon begins a few kilometres southeast of Châtillon. This peaceful haven is covered mainly by broad-leaved trees, including beeches and hornbeams, and crisscrossed by walking trails.

🛏 Sleeping & Eating

Hôtel de la Côte d'Or   HOTEL €
(✆03 80 91 13 29; www.logishotels.com; 2 rue Charles Ronot; d €60-70) This atmospheric establishment has rooms with antique furnishings and a rustic restaurant (*menus* €20 to €40).

Hôtel Sylvia   HOTEL €
(✆03 80 91 02 44; www.sylvia-hotel.com; 9 av de la Gare; s/d €54/58; @🛜) This elegant mansion offers 17 simple yet welcoming rooms and a delightful garden. Breakfasts (€7.50) come in for warm praise.

ℹ Information

Tourist office (✆03 80 91 13 19; www.chatillonnais-tourisme.fr; place Marmont; ⊙9am-noon & 2-6pm Mon-Sat, plus 10am-noon Sun May-Sep)

ℹ Getting There & Away

Bus 50, run by Transco (✆03 80 11 29 29; www.mobigo-bourgogne.com), goes to Dijon (€1.50, 1¾ hours, two to four daily). SNCF buses go to the TGV train station in Montbard (40 minutes, two to five daily).

YONNE

The Yonne *département* (www.tourisme-yonne.com), roughly midway between Dijon and Paris, has long been Burgundy's northern gateway. The verdant countryside harbours the magical hilltop village of Vézelay, in the Parc Natural Régional du Morvan, and white-wine powerhouse Chablis. Canal boats cruise from ancient river ports such as Auxerre.

ℹ Getting Around

BUS Bus services in the Yonne are cheap but extremely limited. **Les Rapides de Bourgogne** (✆in Auxerre 03 86 94 95 00, in Avallon 03 86 34 00 00; www.rapidesdebourgogne.com; office 39 rue de Paris, Avallon) bus lines run only once or twice a day on school days, with two more daily services available on demand; ie you must make a reservation the day before, prior to 5pm, by internet or phone ✆08 00 30 33 09. Tourist offices have timetables.

Line 1 Links Auxerre with Pontigny.
Line 4 Links Auxerre to Chablis and Tonnerre.

Line 5 Links Avallon's Café de l'Europe taxi stand with Noyers-sur-Serein and Tonnerre.

Auxerre

POP 39,756

The alluring riverside town of Auxerre (pronounced 'oh-sair') has been a port since Roman times. The old city clambers up the hillside on the west bank of the Yonne River. Wandering through the maze of its cobbled streets you come upon Roman remains, Gothic churches and timber-framed medieval houses. Views span a jumble of belfries, spires and steep tiled rooftops.

Auxerre makes a good base for exploring northern Burgundy, including Chablis, and is an excellent place to hire a canal boat.

👁 Sights & Activities

Abbaye St-Germain   ABBEY
(✆03 86 18 05 50; www.auxerre.culture.gouv.fr; place St-Germain; crypt tours adult/child €6/free; ⊙9.45am-6.30pm Wed-Mon, crypt tour departures hourly) This ancient abbey with its dramatic flying buttresses began as a basilica above the tomb of St Germain, the 5th-century bishop who made Auxerre an important Christian centre. By the Middle Ages it was attracting pilgrims from all over Europe.

The crypt, accessible by tour (in French with printed information in English), contains

BURGUNDY AUXERRE

DON'T MISS

MUSÉOPARC ALÉSIA

Opened in 2012, the sensational MuseoParc Alésia (www.alesia.fr; 1 rte des Trois Ormeaux, Alise-Ste-Reine; ⊙9am-9pm Jul-Aug, 9am-6pm Apr-Jun & Sep, 10am-5pm Oct-Dec & Feb-Mar, closed Jan), near the village of Alise-Ste-Reine in the Pays d'Auxois, is well worth the drive from Dijon (67km) or Semur-en-Auxois (16km). This was the site of what was once Alésia, the camp where Vercingétorix, the chief of the Gaulish coalitions, was defeated by Julius Caesar after a long siege. The defeat marked the end of the Gallic/Celtic heritage in France. You can visit the well-organised interpretative centre as well as the vestiges of the Gallo-Roman city that developed after the battle. The MuséoParc Alésia also offers entertaining programs and workshops for kids.

Auxerre

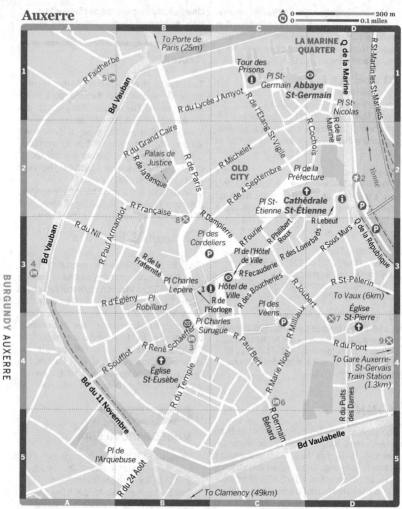

Auxerre

◉ Top Sights

◎ Sights

✦ Activities, Courses & Tours

◉ Sleeping

✖ Eating

some of Europe's finest examples of Carolingian architecture. Supported by 1000-year-old oak beams, the walls and vaulted ceiling are decorated with 9th-century frescos; the far end houses the tomb of St Germain himself.

Housed around the abbey's cloister, the Musée d'Art et d'Histoire (admission free) displays rotating contemporary-art exhibits, prehistoric artefacts and Gallo-Roman sculptures.

Cathédrale St-Étienne   CATHEDRAL
(place St-Étienne; crypt adult/child €3/free, treasury adult/child €1.90/free, son et lumière show €5; ⊙7.30am-6pm, crypt 9am-6pm Mon-Sat, 2-6pm Sun, closed Sun Nov-Easter, son et lumière show 9.30pm or 10pm) This vast Gothic cathedral and its stately 68m-high bell tower dominate Auxerre's skyline. The choir, ambulatory and some of the vivid stained-glass windows date from the 1200s.

The 11th-century Romanesque crypt is ornamented with remarkable frescos, including a scene of Christ à Cheval (Christ on Horseback; late 11th century) unlike any other known in Western art. Upstairs, the treasury has illuminated manuscripts.

From June to September a 70-minute son et lumière (sound-and-light) show is held nightly inside the cathedral.

Tour de l'Horloge   CLOCK TOWER
(btwn place de l'Hôtel de Ville & rue de l'Horloge) In the heart of Auxerre's partly medieval commercial precinct, the golden, spire-topped Tour de l'Horloge was built in 1483 as part of the city's fortifications. On the beautiful 17th-century clock faces (there's one on each side), the sun-hand indicates the time of day; the moon-hand shows the day of the lunar month.

Cycling   CYCLING
Cycling options include the towpath along the Canal du Nivernais to Clamecy (about 60km), just south of town. See www.la-bourgogne-a-velo.com (in French) for a map.

Boating   BOAT HIRE
The main tourist office hires electric boats (per 1hr/half-day/full day €20/48/85; ⊙daily Easter-Sep). It takes at least 1½ hours to get to the locks on the Canal du Nivernais.

☞ Tours

The tourist office offers a tour (adult/child €5/3; ⊙daily Apr-Sep) of the town on an electric vehicle with an audioguide; also the self-guided architectural walking tour brochure *In the Steps of Cadet Roussel* (€1.50).

Across from the tourist office, L'Hirondelle (☎09 75 23 27 89; www.bateauxauxerrois.com; adult/child €9.15/6.10; ⊙Tue-Sun) has river cruises with commentary.

🛏 Sleeping

Hôtel Le Commerce   HOTEL €
(☎03 86 52 03 16; www.hotelducommerceauxerre.fr; 5 rue René Schaeffer; s/d €48/54; ☎) This pleasant hotel is the best of Auxerre's more affordable inns. It's smack in the centre of town, in a former *relais de poste* (coaching inn). Some rooms are enhanced by creative decor inspired by distant sunny lands or quirky themes – room 12 (the 'Africa') and room 26 (the 'Cow') are the quirkiest. There's an on-site restaurant. Parking €7.

Hôtel Le Parc des
Maréchaux   HISTORIC HOTEL €€
(☎03 86 51 43 77; www.hotel-parcmarechaux.com; 6 av Foch; d €100-155; ✳🖨✲) Despite being located off a busy thoroughfare, this mansion of château-like proportions is not a bad choice in this price range. Decorated in an opulent 19th-century style, the rooms may not be to everybody's taste but they brim with character. Opt for the quieter rooms that overlook the private park at the back. The pool is open from May to September. Excellent English is spoken.

Hôtel Normandie   HOTEL €€
(☎03 86 52 57 80; www.hotelnormandie.fr; 41 bd Vauban; d €72-110, q €99-120; ✳🖨) Ivy covers the 19th-century building, and rooms with views make it feel a bit like a country inn. It's tidy and well run, and bathrooms have been recently modernised. Amenities include a cosy lounge bar, workout room and sauna.

La Maison des Randonneurs   HOSTEL €
(☎03 86 41 43 22; www.maison-rando.fr; 5 rue Germain Bénard; dm €18; ☎) Sitting right on the edge of a park, this hostel is amazingly good value. It features a modern design, three types of dorms (six-bed, four-bed and three-bed) as well as doubles and singles with or without bathroom. Other perks include free wi-fi, bike hire and a communal kitchen.

✕ Eating

La P'tite Beursaude   BURGUNDIAN €€
(☎03 86 51 10 21; 55 rue Joubert; mains €15-20, lunch menus €19-21, dinner menus €26-29; ⊙Thu-Mon) Waitresses wearing traditional Morvan

BURGUNDY AUXERRE

dress serve excellent fish and meat dishes. The €21 lunch *menu* is a startling introduction to *cuisine de terroir* (traditional cuisine that's deeply connected to the land), which may include rib steak with Époisses cheese and *œufs en meurette* (poached eggs in red-wine sauce).

Le Flobert BURGUNDIAN €
(☑03 86 51 16 19; www.restaurant-leflobert.fr; 71 rue du Pont; lunch menu €13, mains €9-15; ☺lunch Mon-Sat, dinner Mon & Thu-Sat, Mon-Sat Jul-Aug) The menu at this sweet little spot, just a simple bar and a few tables in an elegant honey-coloured room, changes every day and always involves seasonal, fresh ingredients.

**Le Bistrot du Palais –
Chez Joseph** LYONNAIS, BURGUNDIAN €
(☑03 86 51 47 02; 65 rue de Paris; mains €12, menu €20; ☺Tue-Sat, closed Aug) Housed in a former cinema, this restaurant is high on atmosphere. The walls are adorned with movie posters, and tablecloths are classic red and white. The menu makes good use of local ingredients and also includes Lyonnais specialities.

❶ Information

Post office (place Charles Surugue; ☺noon-6.30pm Mon, 9am-6.30pm Tue-Fri, 9am-12.15pm & 2-5pm Sat) Changes currency.

Tourist office (☑03 86 52 06 19; www.ot-auxerre.fr; 1-2 quai de la République; ☺9am-1pm & 2-7pm Mon-Sat, 9.30am-1pm & 3-6.30pm Sun) Has free wi-fi and will change small amounts of money on weekends and holidays.

❶ Getting There & Away

BUS **Les Rapides de Bourgogne** (☑03 86 94 95 00; www.rapidesdebourgogne.com) schedules are at the tourist office.

TRAIN Trains run from **Gare Auxerre-St-Gervais** (www.voyages-sncf.com; rue Paul Doumer):
Autun €38, 3¼ hours, two daily
Avallon €10, 1¼ hours, five daily
Dijon €27, two hours, 12 daily
Paris Gare de Bercy €27, 1½ to two hours, 13 daily
Sermizelles-Vézelay €8, one hour, eight daily

❶ Getting Around

Hire bicycles at the main tourist office.

La Puisaye

The countryside west of Auxerre, known as La Puisaye, is a lightly populated landscape of woods, winding creeks and dark hills. The area is best known as the birthplace of Colette (1873–1954), author of *La Maison de Claudine* and *Gigi* (and 50 other novels) and is of particular interest because much of her work explores her rural Burgundian childhood.

Colette lived till the age of 18 in the tiny town of St-Sauveur-en-Puisaye, 40km southwest of Auxerre. The Musée Colette (☑03 86 45 61 95; Château de St-Sauveur; adult/child €6/2; ☺10am-6pm Wed-Mon Apr-Oct), in the village château, displays letters, manuscripts, two furnished rooms from her apartment in Paris' Palais Royal and photos featuring her iconic hairdo.

Chantier Médiéval de Guédelon (☑03 86 45 66 66; www.guedelon.fr; D955 near Treigny; adult/child €10/8.50; ☺10am-6pm Jul-Aug, 10am-4.30pm Thu-Tue Mar-Jun & Sep-Oct, closed Oct–mid-Mar) is 45km southwest of Auxerre and 7km southwest of St-Sauveur-en-Puisaye. A team of skilled artisans, aided by archaeologists, has been hard at work building a fortified castle here since 1997 using only 13th-century techniques. No electricity or power

---

GET AWAY FROM IT ALL...

Domaine Dessus Bon Boire (☑03 86 53 89 99; www.dessusbonboire.com; 19 rue de Vallan, Vaux; s/d/tr/q incl breakfast €48/60/72/90; ☎), a family-run organic winery, is perfect for a countryside idyll. In sleepy riverside Vaux, 6km south of Auxerre, Catherine and André Donat maintain impeccable rooms with bright floral accents and plenty of peace and quiet. They also organise tours to their vineyards, and you'll get the opportunity to sample their organic *aligoté* (a dry white wine) or their Côtes d'Auxerre. Breakfast often includes home-baked goodies and excellent grape juice.

Pop over the bridge in the evening for authentic, delicious wood-fired pizza at cheery Pizza-Cotté (☑03 86 53 33 30; 1 rue de la Poire, Champs-sur-Yonne; mains €10-13; ☺dinner Mon-Sat). Grilled meats are also available.

tools here: stone is quarried on-site using iron hand tools forged by a team of blacksmiths, who also produce vital items like door hinges. Clay for tiles is fired for three days using locally cut wood and the mortar, made on-site with lime, is transported in freshly woven wicker baskets.

A very worthwhile guided tour, sometimes in English, costs €2.50 per person. Child-oriented activities include stone carving (using especially soft stone).

The elegant 11th-century Château de Ratilly (☎03 86 74 79 54; www.chateauderatilly.fr; Treigny; adult/child €4/free; ☉10am-noon & 2-6pm Mon-Fri, 3-5pm Sat & Sun, no midday closure 15 Jun-15 Sep) sits in the countryside near Treigny and holds a collection of pottery by the Pierlot family and a changing series of excellent contemporary-art exhibitions and concerts.

Chablis

POP 2580

The well-to-do, picturesque town of Chablis, 19km east of Auxerre, has made its fortune growing, ageing and marketing the dry white wines that have carried its name to the four corners of the earth.

Chablis is made exclusively from chardonnay grapes and originated with the monks of Pontigny. Now it is divided into four AOCs: Petit Chablis, Chablis, Chablis Premier Cru and, most prestigious of all, Chablis Grand Cru. The seven *grands crus* are lovingly grown on just 1 sq km of land on the hillsides northeast of town.

◉ Sights & Activities

Nearby villages worth exploring include Courgis, which offers great views; Chichée and Chemilly, both on the River Serein; and Chitry-le-Fort, famous for its fortified church. The gorgeous hillside village of Fleys has a number of wineries.

Old Town   HISTORIC QUARTER
The 12th- and 13th-century Gothic Église St-Martin (☉Jul & Aug), first founded in the 9th century by monks fleeing the Norman attacks on Tours, is two short blocks northwest of place Charles de Gaulle. Southeast along rue Porte Noël are the twin bastions of Porte Noël (1778), which hosts art exhibitions from June to August. Nearby, the enigmatic 16th-century building known as the synagogue (10-14 rue des Juifs) has been restored. The 12th-century cellar of Petit Pontigny (rue de Chichée) was once used by Pontigny's Cistercian monks to ferment wine.

Wine Tasting   WINE TASTING
Wine can be sampled and purchased at dozens of places (eg along rue des Moulins); the tourist office has a comprehensive list. Some well-established names include Billaud-Simon (☎03 86 42 10 33; www.billaud-simon.com; 1 quai de Reugny; ☉by appointment), on the verdant edge of the canal, William Fèvre (☎03 86 42 12 06; www.williamfevre.fr; 10 rue Jules Rathier; ☉by appointment), Domaine Servin (☎03 86 18 90 00; www.domaine-servin.net; 20 av Oberwesel; ☉by appointment) and Domaine Brocard (☎03 86 41 49 00; www.brocard.fr; 3 route de Chablis, Préhy), a few kilometres south of Auxerre. You can also try La Chablisienne (☎03 86 42 89 98; www.chablisienne.com; 8 bd Pasteur; ☉9am-12.30pm & 2-7pm, no midday closure Jul & Aug), a large cooperative cellar founded in 1923, which carries a variety of vintages, including five of Chablis' seven *grands crus*. Another well-regarded *cave* is La Cave du Connaisseur (www.chablis.net/caveduconnaisseur; 6 rue des Moulins; ☉10am-6pm daily), housed in a 13th-century wine cellar. It offers a wide selection of Chablis wines.

Walking & Cycling   WALKING, CYCLING
Vineyard walks from Chablis include the Sentier des Grands Crus (8km), the Sentier des Clos (13km to 24km, depending on your route) and the Sentier du Moulin des Roches (15.5km to 33km). The tourist office sells topoguides (€3).

Cycling is a great way to tour the Chablis countryside. One flat, lush option is the 45km Chemin de Serein, which follows the old Tacot rail line southeast to Noyers-sur-Serein and L'Isle-sur-Serein. The tourist office hires bikes (per 2hr/half-day/full day €3/10/18)from May to September.

⌖ Tours

For a vineyard tour, call Chablis Vititours (☎06 11 47 82 98; www.chablis-vititours.fr; 90min/half-day/full day €20/45/100) or Au Coeur du Vin (☎06 80 68 23 76, 03 86 18 96 35; www.au coeurduvin.com; half-day from €45).

⌂ Sleeping

Hôtel du Vieux Moulin   BOUTIQUE HOTEL €€
(☎03 86 42 47 30; www.larochehotel.fr; 18 rue des Moulins; d €120-160, ste €245-270; ✷❀) In a one-time mill, the five rooms and two suites, understated and very contemporary, afford luscious views of a branch of the

Serein. The breakfast room has *grand cru* views. The swank restaurant, Le Wine Bar, is downstairs. Note that the hotel is closed on Sundays.

Chambres d'Hôtes du Faubourg St-Pierre
B&B €€

(☎03 86 42 83 90; www.faubourg-saint-pierre.com; rue Jules Rathier; d €75-100; ☎) Chablis' most recent B&B occupies a stately town house and is of a standard that puts many hotels to shame. The mansion's character has been lovingly preserved during refurbishment and the three rooms are large, bright and romantic. Our choice is 'Pauline', with honey-coloured parquet flooring and a marble fireplace.

La Menuiserie
B&B €

(☎03 86 18 86 20; www.chablis-chambresdhotes -lamenuiserie.fr; 11 rue du Panonceau; d €75; ☎) This is a peach of a B&B. Picture this: a former *menuiserie* (joiner's workshop) that has been renovated with a happy respect for the spirit of the place shelters one oh-so-inviting room complete with exposed beams and stone walls. Prices drop by €10 if you stay two nights or more.

Bergerand's – Le Relais de la Belle Étoile
HOTEL €€

(☎03 86 18 96 08; www.chablis-france.fr; 4 rue des Moulins; s incl breakfast €68-118, d incl breakfast €78-128; ☎) This simple rustic hotel with antique wood furniture and cheerful spring colours occupies a heavily ornamented one-time coach inn. All the rooms are different. One minus: the bathrooms could do with some updating. The owner, Nicole de Merteuil, can arrange wine-tasting sessions.

✗ Eating

Le Bistrot des Grands Crus
TRADITIONAL FRENCH €

(☎03 86 42 19 41; www.bistrotdesgrandscrus.com; 8-10 rue Jules Rathier; mains €14-18, weekdays menu €11-21; ☎closed mid-Jan–mid-Feb) A block southeast of Porte Noël, this hip place serves *cuisine du terroir* made with the freshest local ingredients.

La Cuisine Au Vin
MODERN FRENCH €€

(☎03 86 18 98 52; www.lacuisineauvin.fr; 16 rue Auxerroise; mains €16-26, lunch menus €22-25, dinner menus €34-44; ☎lunch Wed-Sun, dinner Wed-Sat) Tuck into exquisitely presented organic meals in a cool 11th-century *cave* highlighted in green neon. An offshoot of the Defaix winery (www.chablisdefaix.com; 16

rue Auxerroise), the restaurant sources its ingredients from its own garden patch. Taste wines upstairs with the very knowledgable Ken Haney.

Le Syracuse
BURGUNDIAN €

(19 rue du Maréchal de Lattre de Tassigny; mains €9-15, weekdays lunch menu €13, dinner menus €19-28; ☎lunch Tue-Sun, dinner Tue-Sat) Dining at this inviting restaurant, housed in a 13th-century vaulted room, is all about having a good time enjoying the finer pleasures of life. The cuisine is resolutely Burgundian, traditional, and well prepared: try the *salade chablisienne* (salad with tripe sausage and Époisses cheese).

ℹ Information

Tourist office (☎03 86 42 80 80; www. chablis.net; 1 rue du Maréchal de Lattre de Tassigny; ☎10am-12.30pm & 1.30-7pm, closed Sun Nov-Mar) Has free English walking-tour booklet and maps of vineyards.

Getting There & Away

Chablis is served by **bus** (www.rapidesde bourgogne.com) between Auxerre and Tonerre (line 4, €2, one per day, Monday to Saturday). The tourist office has schedules.

Abbaye de Pontigny

Founded in 1114, Abbaye de Pontigny (☎03 86 47 54 99; www.abbayedepontigny.eu; ☎9am-7pm), rises from the lush mustard fields 25km north of Auxerre. The spectacular *abbatiale* (abbey church) is one of the last surviving examples of Cistercian architecture in Burgundy. The simplicity and purity of its white-stone construction reflect the austerity of the Cistercian order. On summer days sunshine filtering through the high windows creates an amazing sense of peace and tranquillity. *Discovering Pontigny* (€2.50), on sale in the gift shop, points out fascinating architectural details.

The Gothic sanctuary, 108m long and lined with 23 chapels, was built in the mid-12th century; the wooden choir screen, stalls and organ loft were added in the 17th and 18th centuries.

Monks here were the first to perfect the production of Chablis wine. In summer there are concerts.

The tourist office (☎03 86 47 47 03; www. ot-pontigny.com; 22 rue Paul Desjardins; ☎10am-12.30pm & 2-5.30pm Mon-Sat or Tue-Sat), across

WORTH A TRIP

IRANCY & COULANGES-LA-VINEUSE WINE COUNTRY

Ask locals where they go to taste western Burgundy's wines and many say Irancy (www. irancy.org). This relatively new (1999) Appellation d'Origine Protégée (AOC) predominantly uses a pinot noir grape, and the growing villages are extremely picturesque. Set in rolling hills and spring-blooming cherry orchards, Irancy and nearby Coulanges-la-Vineuse, which has its own appellation, lie 13km south of Auxerre. Explore and you'll find many domaines from which to sample. In Irancy you can try Thierry Richoux (03 86 42 21 60; 73 rue Soufflot), which is converting to all-organic techniques. In Coulanges-la-Vineuse stop by Clos du Roi (03 86 42 25 72; www.closduroi.com; 17 rue André Vilidieu) or, in the heart of the village, Domaine Maltoff (03 86 42 32 48; www.maltoff. com; 20 rue d'Aguesseau; s/d/tr incl breakfast €50/65/85;), which is also a B&B.

the road, has accommodation information and sells hiking maps.

Tonnerre

POP 5509

The town of Tonnerre, on the Canal de Bourgogne, is best known for its Hôtel-Dieu (hoteldieudetonnerre.jimdo.com; rue de l'Hôpital; adult/child €4.50/free; 9am-noon & 2-6pm Mon-Sat, 10am-noon & 2-4.30pm Sun, closed Sun Nov-Mar), a charity hospital founded in 1293 by Marguerite de Bourgogne, wife of Charles d'Anjou. At the eastern end of the barrel-vaulted patients' hall, near the chapel and Marguerite's tomb, is an extraordinary 15th-century *Entombment of Christ,* carved from a single block of stone.

About 400m west, 200L of water per second gushes from Fosse Dionne, a natural spring that was sacred to the Celts. Its blue-green tint hints at its great depth – legend has it that a serpent lurks at the bottom. The pool is surrounded by a mid-18th-century washing house, a semicircle of ancient houses and forested slopes.

In the villages around Tonnerre, the Tonnerrois vineyards produce some good reds, whites and rosés, which are best enjoyed with local dishes or regional cheese. The whites, although much less famous than their Chablis counterparts, are well worth sampling for their slightly fruity aromas.

If you want to stay overnight in Tonnerre, try La Ferme de Fosse Dionne (03 86 54 82 62; www.ferme-fosse-dionne.fr; 11 rue de la Fosse Dionne; d incl breakfast €68). In a late-18th-century farmhouse overlooking Fosse Dionne, this delightful hostelry has a cafe and antique shop.

The tourist office (03 86 55 14 48; www. tourisme-tonnerre.fr; place Marguerite de Bour-gogne; 9.30am-noon & 1.30-6pm, closed Wed & Sun mid-Oct–mid-Apr), at the entrance to the Hôtel-Dieu, has a walking-tour brochure, a map of the Tonnerrois vineyards and hires bicycles (half-/full day €10/18).

By rail, Tonnerre is linked to Dijon (€19, one hour, 12 daily) and, via Laroche-Migennes, to Auxerre (€10.60, 45 minutes, five daily).

Château de Tanlay

The French Renaissance–style Château de Tanlay (03 86 75 70 61; www.chateaude tanlay.fr; Tanlay; adult/child €9/5; tours 10am, 11.30am, 2.15pm, 3.15pm, 4.15pm & 5.15pm Wed-Mon, closed Nov-Mar), an elegant product of the 17th century, is surrounded by a wide moat and elaborately carved outbuildings. Interior highlights include the Grande Galerie, the walls and ceiling of which are completely covered with trompe l'œil. Find it 10km east of Tonnerre in the village of Tanlay.

Château d'Ancy-le-Franc

The Italian Renaissance makes a cameo appearance at Château d'Ancy-le-Franc (03 86 75 14 63; www.chateau-ancy.com; 18 place Clermont-Tonnerre, Ancy-le-Franc; adult/child €9/5; tours 10.30am, 11.30am, 2pm, 3pm, 4pm & 5pm Tue-Sun, closed mid-Nov–Mar), built in the 1540s by the celebrated Italian architect Serlio. The richly painted interior, like the 32m-mural in the Pharsale Gallery, is mainly the work of Italian artists brought to Fontainebleau by François I. Tours are in French with written English translations.

The château is 19km southeast of Tonnerre.

DON'T MISS

CHÂTEAU DE MAULNES

Not your average château, the Château de Maulnes (📞03 86 72 92 00; www. maulnes.fr; Cruzy-le-Châtel; adult/child €2.50/1.50; 🕑2.30-5.30pm Sat & Sun Apr-Oct, 2.30-5.30pm daily Jul-Aug), 24km east of Tonnerre, is a real showstopper. This Renaissance building is the only château in France that's built on a pentagonal plan and buttressed by five towers.

Noyers-sur-Serein

POP 744

A must-see on any Burgundy itinerary, the absolutely picturesque medieval village of Noyers (pronounced 'nwa-yair'), 30km southeast of Auxerre, is surrounded by rolling pastureland, wooded hills and a sharp bend in the River Serein.

⊙ Sights & Activities

Stone ramparts and fortified battlements enclose much of the village and, between the two imposing stone gateways, cobbled streets lead past 15th- and 16th-century gabled houses, wood and stone archways and several art galleries.

Lines carved into the façade of the 18th-century mairie (town hall), next to the library, mark the level of historic floods.

Noyers is a superb base for walking. Just outside the clock-topped southern gate, Chemin des Fossés leads eastwards to the River Serein and a streamside walk around the village's 13th-century fortifications, of which 19 of the original 23 towers are extant. The 9km Balade du Château, trail-marked in red, follows the Serein's right bank past the utterly ruined château just north of Noyers.

✦ Festivals & Events

Classical concerts and jazz sessions are hosted throughout July and August at various venues during the Rencontres Musicales de Noyers (www.musicalesdenoyers.com).

🛏 Sleeping

TOP CHOICE Le Tabellion   B&B €€

(📞06 86 08 39 92, 03 86 82 62 26; www.noyers-tabellion.fr; 5 rue du Jeu de Paume; d €70-74; 🖭) One of the most reliable B&Bs in the area, Le Tabellion occupies a former notary's office right next to the church. The four tastefully furnished and charmingly rustic rooms are rife with personality, and there's a delighful garden at the back. Another draw is Rita Florin, the owner, who is clued-up and speaks excellent English.

Moulin de la Roche   B&B €

(📞03 86 82 68 13; www.bonadresse.com/bourgogne/le-moulin-de-la-roche.htm; rte d'Auxerre; s €62, d €70-80, q €115; 🖭) This welcoming B&B sits on three gorgeous hectares over the River Serein. A renovated mill, it has two beautiful guest rooms and a millwheel in the living room.

La Vieille Tour   B&B €

(📞03 86 82 87 69; place du Grenier à Sel; d €60-80, q €100; 🕑Apr-Sep; 🖭) In a rambling 17th-century house, this Dutch-run venture has several simply furnished *chambres d'hôte* of varying size and shape, loads of local colour and a lovely garden. The best rooms are housed in the 'Tower' annexe.

🍴 Eating

TOP CHOICE Les Millésimes   BURGUNDIAN €€

(📞03 86 82 82 16; www.maison-paillot.com; place de l'Hôtel de Ville; menus €23-42; 🕑lunch & dinner Tue-Sun, closed Jan-Mar) This culinary haven in a meticulously restored medieval house complete with a large fireplace and sturdy wooden tables specialises in *terroir* creations ranging from *jambon au chablis* (ham flavoured with Chablis wine) to *tourte à l'Époisses* (pie with Époisses cheese). It's also renowned for its respectable wine list.

La Vieille Tour   MODERN BURGUNDIAN €

(📞03 86 82 87 36; rue Porte Peinte; mains €12-13, menus €16-23; 🕑lunch Sat-Wed, dinner Fri-Wed, closed Oct-Mar; 🖋) Try the simple, affordable and delicious meals at La Vieille Tour. The menu is unpretentious – a mix of Burgundian staples and exotic interpretations. Vegetarian options are also available.

Ô Marquis Perché   BISTRO €

(📞03 86 75 16 70; 34 place du Grenier à Sel; mains €13-16, menu €12; 🕑lunch & dinner Wed-Mon May-Sep, lunch Wed-Mon, dinner Fri-Sun Oct-Apr) This low-key, low-cost bistro right in the heart of town is a good surprise. Most house specialities are inventive – where else would you get your burger filled with Époisses cheese and Charolais steak? – and the welcome is convivial. The homemade desserts are not to be missed.

🛍 Shopping

Création Maroquinerie   ARTS & CRAFTS
(☑03 86 75 94 60; 24 place de l'Hôtel de Ville; ☺Tue-Sun), a fantastic leather shop full of chic belts and supple handbags. The proprietors, Yazmhil and Brice, do custom work and make everything on-site, sometimes using bison hide.

Diane Calvert   ARTS & CRAFTS
(☑03 86 82 66 01; www.diane-calvert.com; 47 rue de la Petite Étape aux Vins; ☺May-Sep) In this illuminated-painting studio, Diane Calvert grinds her own pigments from semiprecious stones and uses parchment and quill pens.

Maison Paillot   FOOD, DRINK
(☑03 86 82 82 16; www.maison-paillot.com; place de l'Hôtel de Ville; ☺Apr-Dec) Food and wine lovers should head to this charcuterie/deli with a well-stocked wine cellar.

ℹ Information

Tourist Office (☑03 86 82 66 06; www.noyers-et-tourisme.com; 22 place de l'Hôtel de Ville; ☺10am-1pm & 2-6pm, closed Sun Oct-May)

Avallon

POP 7743

The once-strategic walled town of Avallon, on a picturesque hilltop overlooking the green terraced slopes of two River Cousin tributaries, was in centuries past a stop on the coach road from Paris to Lyon. At its most animated during the Saturday-morning market, the city makes a good base for exploring Vézelay and the Parc Naturel Régional du Morvan.

◎ Sights & Activities

The old city is built on a triangular granite hilltop with ravines to the east and west.

TOP CHOICE ◢ Musée de l'Avallonnais   MUSEUM
(☑03 86 34 03 19; place de la Collégiale; ☺2-6pm Wed-Mon Jul-Sep) Founded in 1862, this wonderful small museum displays a series of expressionist watercolours by Georges Rouault (1871–1958) and an excellent art deco silver collection by renowned designer and jeweller Jean Després (1889–1980). Upstairs, don't miss the permanent exhibition on the Yao people.

Collégiale St-Lazare   CHURCH
(rue Bocquillot) Eight centuries ago masses of pilgrims flocked here thanks to a piece of the skull of St Lazarus, believed to provide protection from leprosy. The early-12th-century church once had three portals but one was crushed when the northern belfry came a-tumblin' down in 1633; the two remaining portals are grandly decorated in Romanesque style, though much of the carving has been damaged.

Tour de l'Horloge   CLOCK TOWER
(Grande Rue Aristide Briand) The old city's main thoroughfare, Grande Rue Aristide Briand, is spanned by this solid, 15th-century clock tower.

Walking & Cycling   WALKING, CYCLING
A pathway descends from the ancient gateway Petite Porte, affording fine views over the Vallée du Cousin. You can walk around the walls, with their 15th- to 18th-century towers, ramparts and bastions.

For a bucolic walk or bike ride in the Vallée du Cousin, take the shaded, one-lane D427, which follows the gentle rapids of the River Cousin through dense forests and lush meadows. The tourist office sells hiking maps and has information on Parc Naturel Régional du Morvan.

🛏 Sleeping & Eating

AVALLON

Hôtel Les Capucins   HOTEL €
(☑03 86 34 06 52; www.avallonlescapucins.com; 6 av Paul Doumer; d €52-80; ❋🛜) Sitting on a quiet, plum-lined side street, the professionally run Les Capucins is Avallon's best-value hotel. The 24 rooms are spotless, well-appointed and meet modern standards. The cheerily decorated restaurant (mains €12-16, menus €14-38; ☺daily) here serves up well-prepared French and Burgundian dishes. The icing on the cake? A relaxing garden at the back. There's easy parking on the street. A good pick.

Le Vaudésir   MODERN BURGUNDIAN €
(☑03 86 34 14 60; www.levaudesir.com; 84 rue de Lyon; mains €10-15, menus €13.50-16; ☺lunch Mon, Tue & Thu-Sun, dinner Mon & Thu-Sat) Opened in 2012, Le Vaudésir is a sophisticated bistro that's well worth making a beeline for – it's about 800m away from the centre, on the road to Lyon. The trademark here is freshness and great value for money. Quintessential dishes to try include *jambon à la chablisienne* (ham cooked in Chablis sauce) and *escargots en risotto* (snails). Outdoor seating in summer.

BURGUNDY AVALLON

Medieval Art & Architecture

Burgundy, once a powerful duchy and a major ecclesiastical centre, attracted the foremost European artists and builders of the Middle Ages. Now graced with a bounty of excellent museums and monumental architecture, Burgundy offers a trail of human accomplishment through its rolling emerald hills.

Burgundy's clergy established a series of abbeys and churches that remain some of the world's best examples of Romanesque architecture. The austere Cistercian order was founded at the Abbaye de Cîteaux (p420) in 1098 by monks seeking to live St Benedict's teachings: *pax, ora et labora* (peace, pray and work). Their spectacular 1114 Abbaye de Pontigny (p428) is one of the last surviving examples of Cistercian architecture in Burgundy – the purity of its white stone reflects the simplicity of the order.

Cluny's 12th-century Benedictine abbey (p441), now a sprawling ruin woven into the fabric of the town, once held sway over 1100 priories and monasteries stretching from Poland to Portugal.

The 12th-century Cathédrale St-Lazare (p438) in Autun is world-renowned for its deceptively austere Gislebertus carvings: a fantastic tympanum of the Last Judgement and extraordinary capitals depicting Bible stories and Greek mythology.

Vézelay's Basilique Ste-Madeleine (p434), a Unesco World Heritage Site, was founded in the 880s. It is adorned with Romanesque carvings and attracts both religious and artistic pilgrims. Abbaye de Fontenay (p422), another Unesco World Heritage Site (founded in 1118), sits in a peaceful forested valley perfect for contemplation.

But let's not forget the royals. Dijon was home to the powerful Dukes of Burgundy (with fabulous names like John the Good, Philip the Bold and John the Fearless), and flourished into one of the art capitals of Europe. Explore the dukes' monumental palace (p404) in central Dijon, home to an excellent fine-arts museum. Or head a bit south to Beaune, where Nicolas Rolin, chancellor to Philip the Good, established a hospital-cum-palace (p415) that houses Rogier van der Weyden's fantastic (and fantastical) *Polyptych of the Last Judgement*.

TOP 5 ARCHITECTURAL & ARTISTIC HOTSPOTS

» Hôtel-Dieu des Hospices de Beaune (p415)

» Abbaye de Pontigny (p428)

» Palais des Ducs et des États de Bourgogne (p404)

» Musée Zervos (p435)

» Cathédrale St-Lazare (p438)

Clockwise from top left
1. The village of Cluny 2. Hôtel-Dieu des Hospices de Beaune 3. Relief in the Cathédrale St-Lazare, Autun

Dame Jeanne TEA HOUSE €
(☎03 86 34 58 71; www.damejeanne.fr; 59 Grand Rue Aristide Briand; breakfast €9, snacks €7-9; ⏰8am-7pm Fri-Wed) Folks come from the countryside for delicious lunches or special pastry treats in the garden or 17th-century salon.

AROUND AVALLON

La Cimentelle B&B €€
(☎03 86 31 04 85; www.lacimentelle.com; 2 rue de la Cimentelle; d €80-110, q €130-160; 🐾🏊) Situated on shady, extensive grounds 6km north of Avallon, this château houses luxuriously appointed rooms, each one a bit different. One favourite, Hippolyte, has a free-standing clawfoot tub in front of a fireplace. Three-bedroom family apartments (€140 to €210) are fantastic. Do not skip the *repas* (€35 with wine): Nathalie, your amenable hostess, is a gourmet chef and every meal is a sumptuous delight. The swimming pool sits spectacularly atop the ruins of an old cement factory. English is spoken.

Le Moulin des Ruats HISTORIC HOTEL €€
(☎03 86 34 97 00; www.moulindesruats.com; D427; d €85-160; ⏰closed 15 Nov-20 Feb; 🐾) This romantic former flour mill sits in a gorgeous wooded spot right on the Cousin and has a ravishing waterside terrace. Rooms are a bit disappointing, though – the cheaper ones are small and the furnishings feel a bit tired. Fantastic river views from rooms 4 and 12. Excellent Burgundian dishes are served at its peaceful riverside restaurant.

Camping Municipal Sous Roche CAMPGROUND €
(☎03 86 34 10 39; campingsousroche@ville-avallon.fr; sites per adult/tent/car €3.60/2.70/2.70; ⏰Apr–mid-Oct; 🐾) A woody, well-maintained site 2km southeast of the old city on the forested banks of the Cousin. Has a play structure, RV hook-ups and wastewater disposal.

ⓘ Information

Tourist office (☎03 86 34 14 19; www.avallonnais-tourisme.com; 6 rue Bocquillot; internet per 30min €2, wi-fi free; ⏰9am-7pm, closed Sun mid-Sep–mid-Jun) Has internet access.

ⓘ Getting There & Away

BUS **Transco** (☎03 80 11 29 29; www.mobigo-bourgogne.com) buses leave from the train station to Dijon (€20, two hours, two or three daily), Auxerre and Autun. In July and August there are sometimes services to Vézelay.

TRAIN Trains serve the following destinations:
Autun €18, two hours, one daily
Auxerre €13, 1¼ hours, three daily
Dijon €28, two to 2½ hours, two daily
Paris Gare de Lyon or Gare de Bercy €40, three hours, three daily
Sermizelles-Vézelay €11, 20 minutes, three daily

ⓘ Getting Around

Bikes can be hired from the tourist office (per hour/day €4/10).

Vézelay
POP 486

The tiny hilltop village of Vézelay – a Unesco World Heritage Site – is one of France's architectural gems. Perched on a rocky spur crowned by a medieval basilica and surrounded by a sublime patchwork of vineyards, sunflower fields and cows, Vézelay seems to have been lifted from another age.

One of the main pilgrimage routes to Santiago de Compostela in Spain starts here (see www.amis-saint-jacques-de-compostelle.asso.fr, in French).

History

Thanks to the relics of St Mary Magdalene, Vézelay's Benedictine monastery became an important pilgrimage site in the 11th and 12th centuries. St Bernard, leader of the Cistercian order, preached the Second Crusade here in 1146. King Philip Augustus of France and King Richard the Lionheart of England met up here in 1190 before setting out on the Third Crusade.

Vézelay's vineyards, founded in Gallo-Roman times, were wiped out in the late 1800s by phylloxera and were only reestablished in 1973.

◉ Sights

Basilique Ste-Madeleine LANDMARK, CHURCH
(www.basiliquedevezelay.org) Founded in the 880s on a former Roman and then Carolingian site, Basilique Ste-Madeleine has had a turbulent history. Damaged by fire in 1120, it was rebuilt between the 11th and 13th centuries, then trashed by the Huguenots in 1569, desecrated during the Revolution and, to top off the human ravages, repeatedly struck by lightning. By the mid-1800s it was on the point of collapse. In 1840 the architect Viollet-le-Duc undertook the daunting task of rescuing the structure.

His work, which included reconstructing the western façade and its doorways, helped Vézelay, previously a ghost town, spring back to life.

On the famous 12th-century tympanum, visible from the narthex (enclosed porch), Romanesque carvings show Jesus seated on a throne, radiating his holy spirit to the Apostles. The nave, rebuilt following the great fire of 1120, has round arches and detailed capitals, typical features of the Romanesque style; the transept and choir (1185) have ogival arches, hallmarks of Gothic architecture. Under the transept a mid-12th-century crypt houses a reliquary containing what is believed to be one of Mary Magdalene's bones.

Visitors are welcome to observe prayers or Mass. Concerts of sacred music are held in the nave from June to September; the tourist office and its website have details.

TOP CHOICE Musée Zervos   ART MUSEUM
(☑03 86 32 39 26; www.musee-zervos.fr; rue St-Étienne; adult/child €3/free; ⊙10am-5.30pm Wed-Mon mid-Mar–mid-Nov, daily Jul & Aug) This fantastic museum in the exquisite town house of Nobel Prize–winning pacifist writer Romain Rolland (1866–1944) holds the collection of Christian Zervos (1889–1970), an art critic, gallerist and friend of many modern art luminaries. He and his wife, Yvonne, collected paintings, sculptures and mobiles by Calder, Giacometti, Kandinsky, Léger, Miró and Picasso (for whom he created a pivotal 22-volume catalogue).

FREE Maison Jules Roy   HISTORIC HOME
(☑03 86 33 35 10; admission free; ⊙2-6pm Wed-Sun, 2-5pm Mon, closed Oct-Mar) At the upper end of rue des Écoles, the house of Jules Roy (1907–2000) sits in the shadow of the basilica. Walk around his beautiful gardens and see the Algerian-born writer's study.

Activities

Walking Trails   WALKS
The park behind the basilica affords wonderful views of the Vallée de Cure and nearby villages. A dirt road leads north to the old and new cemeteries. Promenade des Fossés circumnavigates Vézelay's medieval ramparts. A footpath with fine views of the basilica links Porte Neuve, on the northern side of the ramparts, with the village of Asquins (pronounced 'ah-kah') and the River Cure. The GR13 trail passes by Vézelay.

AB Loisirs   OUTDOOR ACTIVITIES
(☑03 86 33 38 38; www.abloisirs.com; rte du Camping; ⊙9.30am-6pm Jul & Aug, phone ahead rest of year) AB Loisirs, based a few kilometres southeast in St-Père, hires bikes (€25 per day) and leads outdoor activities like kayak trips (8/18km from €22/35), rafting (€46), cave exploration (half-day €37) and horse riding (from €18). Bikes can be brought to your hotel. It's best to phone ahead.

Festivals & Events

Rencontres Musicales de Vézelay   MUSIC FESTIVAL
(www.rencontresmusicalesdevezelay.com) This not-to-be-missed festival of classical music is held at various venues in late August.

Sleeping

TOP CHOICE Cabalus   HISTORIC HOTEL €
(☑03 86 33 20 66; www.cabalus.com; rue St-Pierre; d €38-58) Cabalus is an incredibly atmospheric place to stay. This special abode has four rooms in a 12th-century building right next to the cathedral. They're sparsely decorated but come with sturdy beams, ancient tiles and stone walls. Oh, and they're very spacious. Note that the cheaper rooms have outside toilets. Order an organic breakfast (€9) at the cafe downstairs.

Les Glycines   HISTORIC HOTEL €€
(☑03 86 32 35 30; www.glycines-vezelay.com; rue St-Pierre; s €40, d €72-94; ☎) A 1763 bourgeois town house enveloped in ancient wisteria

---

DON'T MISS

AUBERGE DU POT D'ETAIN

You wouldn't necessarily expect to find a gastronomic gem in the modest village of L'Isle-sur-Sereine, halfway between Avallon and Noyers-sur-Serein. But then there is Auberge du Pot d'Etain (☑03 86 33 88 10; www.potdetain.com; rue Bouchardo, L'Isle-sur-Serein; d €60-90, menus €27-53; ⊙noon-1.30pm Wed-Sun, dinner Mon-Sat, Tue-Sun Jul-Aug, closed Feb; ☎), beating all the odds. Delicacies include Marsala veal stew, beef cheeks in red wine and other unlikely surprises. The wine list is epic. The *auberge* (country inn) also shelters nine country-style rooms that are immaculate and comfy.

BURGUNDY VÉZELAY

is now a hotel that's overflowing with old-fashioned character. Hexagonal floor tiles and wooden beams haven't changed in generations. The 11 rooms are all named after famous artists. Good news: there's a lift.

Hôtel Le Compostelle HOTEL €
(☑03 86 33 28 63; www.lecompostellevezelay.com; 1 place du Champ-de-Foire; d €50-66; ☺closed Jan–mid-Feb; 🐾) Eighteen spotless, practical rooms afford romantic views of either the valley or the village.

Auberge de Jeunesse et Camping de Vézelay HOSTEL, CAMPGROUND €
(☑03 86 33 24 18; www.camping-auberge-vezelay. com; rue de l'Étang; dm €15, sites per adult/car €3/1; ☺Apr-Oct) If being right in town isn't a must, this efficiently run venture is manna from heaven for thrifty visitors. After an extensive renovation in 2012, it now shelters well-equipped four- to eight-bed dorms, a communal kitchen and well-maintained sites. About 1km from Vézelay.

✖ Eating

Cabalus CAFÉ €
(☑03 86 33 20 66; www.cabalus.com; rue St-Pierre; dishes €4.50-6; ☺11am-5pm Wed-Sun Easter-Oct, 11am-4pm Fri-Sun Nov-Easter) Crammed with character under ancient arches, this haven of peace displays art and serves snacks, sandwiches and pastry treats as well as tea, coffee and freshly squeezed fruit juices.

Les Glycines TRADITIONAL FRENCH €€
(☑03 86 32 35 30; www.glycines-vezelay.com; rue St-Pierre; mains €16, menus €21-26; ☺lunch Wed-Sun, dinner Fri & Sat, closed mid-Nov–mid-Mar) Expect casual, hearty portions of home-style French food using fresh regional products, such as tripe sausages, snails and truffles. Save room for the excellent homemade desserts. Hmm, the *tarte à l'orange* (orange pie). Bonus: there's a small, shady terrace in warm weather.

Le Bougainville TRADITIONAL FRENCH €€
(☑03 86 33 27 57; 26 rue St-Etienne; menus €26-31; ☺Thu-Mon; 🍴) The smiling owner serves rich French and Burgundian specialities like Charolais beef and tripe sausages. If you're growing weary of heavy regional dishes, fear not – Le Bougainville is also noted for its *Menu du Jardinier* (€26), which features vegetarian options – a rarity in Burgundy!

🛍 Shopping

Vézelay has long attracted artists and writers. About half a dozen art galleries and several wine and crafts shops line rue St-Pierre and rue St-Étienne.

Domaine Maria Cluny WINE
(☑03 86 32 38 50; www.domaine-mariacuny.com; 34 rue St-Étienne; ☺by appointment) Sells organic white wines from the tiny Bourgogne-Vézelay appellation. The friendly owner can also organise vineyard tours around Vézelay.

❶ Information

Tourist office (☑03 86 33 23 69; www.vezelay tourisme.com; 12 rue St-Étienne; ☺10am-1pm & 2-6pm, closed Thu Oct-May & Sun Nov-Easter) Sells hiking maps and has internet access (€2 per 10 minutes).

❶ Getting There & Away

Vézelay is 15km from Avallon (19km if you take the gorgeous D427 via Pontaubert). There's a free car park 250m from place du Champ-de-Foire (towards Clamecy).

BUS In July and August there are sometimes buses to Avallon. Check with the tourist office.

TRAIN About seven trains (or SNCF buses) a day link the Sermizelles-Vézelay train station, about 10km north of Vézelay, with Avallon (€3.20, 15 minutes) and Auxerre (€8, one hour).

TAXI Call ☑03 86 32 31 88 or ☑03 86 33 19 06. From Sermizelles-Vézelay train station to Vézelay costs about €18 (€27 after 7pm and on Sunday).

Around Vézelay

Southeast of Vézelay at the base of the hill, St-Père has a Flamboyant Gothic church.

L'Espérance (☑03 86 33 39 10; www. marc-meneau.com; St-Père; d from €150, lunch menu €60, dinner menus €135-198; ☺lunch Thu-Sun, dinner Wed-Mon, closed mid-Jan–Feb; 🐾🍴), Marc Meneau's legendary French restaurant (and 30-room hotel) with two Michelin stars, however, steals the show. Surrounded by tranquil private gardens, the inn has flawless service and a mood of refined elegance.

Three kilometres south along the D958, the Fontaines Salées (☑03 86 33 26 62; adult/child €4/1.60; ☺10am-12.30pm & 1.30-6.30pm, closed 11 Nov-Mar) are saltwater springs that were the site of a neolithic development and then a Celtic sanctuary (2nd century BC) and Roman baths (1st century AD). Tickets

BIBRACTE

The sprawling archaeological remains of the Celtic city of Bibracte (⊘archaeological sites Jun-Oct) sit atop beautiful Mont Beuvray, 25km west of Autun. Bibracte was the capital of the Celtic Aedui people during the 1st and 2nd centuries BC, and it was here, in 52 BC, that Vercingétorix was declared chief of the Gaulish coalition shortly before his defeat by Julius Caesar at Alésia. Caesar also resided here before the city decamped to Augustodunum (Autun). The site is covered with 1000 hectares of forest, blessed with expansive views and criss-crossed by walking trails, including the GR13. Stone remnants include ancient ramparts and several complexes of buildings, all in varying states of excavation.

The excellent Museum of Celtic Civilisation (✆03 85 86 52 35; www.bibracte. fr; adult/child incl audioguide €6.50/free; ⊘10am-6pm mid-Mar–mid-Nov, to 7pm Jul & Aug) explains the technologies, like a sophisticated system of ramparts, and culture of the Celtic Gauls throughout Europe and also displays finds from the site. During the high season there are guided tours (in English on Mondays at 2.30pm). A Zen-feeling cafe provides set meals and picnic baskets.

allow access to Le Musée Archéologique (⊘10am-12.30pm & 1.30-6.30pm, closed 11 Nov-Mar) in St-Père, which holds finds from the site.

About 2km south, the village of Pierre-Perthuis (literally 'pierced stone') is named after a natural stone arch; nearby, a graceful stone bridge (1770) spans the River Cure underneath a modern highway bridge. The neighbouring hamlet of Soeuvres is home to Au Moulin de Vézelay (✆03 86 32 37 80; www.gite-vezelay.fr; 48 Grand Rue, Soeuvres, C5; d incl breakfast €65-86; 🛜), with cosy rooms, extensive grounds along a stream and nearby walking paths.

Château de Bazoches (✆03 86 22 10 22; www.chateau-bazoches.com; adult/child €8/4; ⊘9.30am-noon & 2.15-6pm, no midday closure Jul & Aug, closed mid-Nov–24 Mar) in Bazoches sits magnificently on a hillside with views to Vézelay 12km to the north. Built in the 13th century and visited by royalty including Richard the Lionheart, it was acquired by field marshal and military strategist Marquis de Vauban in 1675. It is still owned by his descendants.

PARC NATUREL RÉGIONAL DU MORVAN

The 2990-sq-km Morvan Regional Park, bounded more or less by Vézelay, Avallon, Saulieu and Autun and straddling Burgundy's four départements (with the majority in the Nièvre), encompasses 700 sq km of dense woodland, 13 sq km of lakes and vast expanses of rolling farmland broken by hedgerows, stone walls and stands of beech, hornbeam and oak. The sharp-eyed can observe some of France's largest and most majestic birds of prey perched on trees as they scan for field rodents.

⊙ Sights

Six sites around the park explore traditional Morvan life and customs, including one at the village of St-Brisson. There the Maison des Hommes et des Paysages (http:// tourisme.parcdumorvan.org; St-Brisson; adult/ child €3/free; ⊘10am-1pm & 2-6pm, closed 15 Nov-Mar, also Sat morning & Tue except Jul & Aug) has displays in French on the interplay between humans and landscapes. Also, since the Morvan was a major stronghold for the Resistance during WWII, the Musée de la Résistance en Morvan (www.museeresistancemorvan.fr; St-Brisson; adult/child €4/2.50, audioguide €1; ⊘10am-1pm & 2-6pm Wed-Sun, 2-6pm Mon May-Sep, daily & no midday closure Jul-Aug, 10am-1pm & 2-5pm Wed-Mon Apr & Oct-Nov) chronicles key events and characters.

Seven RAF men (the crew of a bomber shot down near here in 1944) and 21 *résistants* are buried in the neatly tended Maquis Bernard Résistance Cemetery (www.ouroux-en-morvan.com). It's surrounded by the dense forests in which British paratroops operated with Free French forces. The nearby drop zone is marked with signs. The cemetery is about 8km southwest of Montsauche-les-Settons (along the D977) and 5.6km east of Oroux-en-Morvan (along the D12), near the hamlet of Savelot.

Activities

The Morvan (a Celtic name meaning 'Black Mountain') offers an abundance of options to fans of outdoor activities. On dry land choose from walking (the park has over 2500km of marked trails), mountain biking, horse riding, rock climbing, orienteering and fishing. There is also Rafting, canoeing and kayaking on several lakes and the Chalaux, Cousin, Cure and Yonne Rivers. Lac de Pannecière, Lac de St-Agnan and Lac des Settons have water-sports centres. Guided walks of the park, some at night (eg to observe owls), are available from April to October, and there are children's activities in July and August. Boat tours are available at Lac des Settons.

In the mood for swimming? Head for Lac des Settons or Lac de St-Agnan, which offer 'beaches' (a loose term by Morvan standards).

The Morvan Visitors Centre has a comprehensive list of outdoor operators.

Sleeping & Eating

There's a good choice of campgrounds and B&Bs, as well as a few hotels, in the park. You'll also find simple eateries and inns. The Morvan Visitors Centre has a list of lodgings and places to eat.

Information

Morvan Visitors Centre (✆03 86 78 79 57; www.parcdumorvan.org; Espace St-Brisson; ⏰tourist office 9.30am-12.30pm & 2-5.30pm Mon-Fri, 10am-12.30pm & 2-5pm Sat, 10am-1pm & 3-5.30pm Sun, closed Sat & Sun mid-Nov–Easter) Surrounded by hills, forests and lakes, Espace St-Brisson is a clearinghouse of park information, including hiking and cycling maps and guides. To get there by car, follow the signs to the 'Maison du Parc' 14km west of Saulieu to St-Brisson. The website has details of local festivals, outdoor activities and lodging. Other useful (though not always up-to-date) websites include www.morvan-tourisme.org and www.patrimoinedumorvan.org, both in French.

SAÔNE-ET-LOIRE

In the southern Saône-et-Loire *département* (www.bourgogne-du-sud.com), midway between Dijon and Lyon, highlights include the Gallo-Roman ruins in Autun, Cluny's glorious Romanesque heritage, and around Mâcon, vineyards galore. Several rivers and the Canal du Centre meander among its forests and pastureland.

Autun

POP 16,310

Autun is a low-key town, but almost two millennia ago (when it was known as Augustodunum) it was one of the most important cities in Roman Gaul, boasting 6km of ramparts, four monumental gates, two theatres, an amphitheatre and a system of aqueducts. Beginning in AD 269, the city was repeatedly sacked by barbarian tribes and its fortunes declined, but things improved considerably in the Middle Ages, making it possible to construct an impressive cathedral. The hilly area around Cathédrale St-Lazare, reached via narrow cobblestone streets, is known as the old city.

If you have a car, Autun is an excellent base for exploring the southern parts of the Parc Naturel Régional du Morvan.

Sights

Napoléon Bonaparte and his brothers Joseph and Lucien studied in Autun as teenagers. Their old Jesuit college is now a high school called Lycée Joseph Bonaparte, on the west side of Champ de Mars. A small train (adult/child €6/3) offers guided town tours in July and August; contact the tourist office.

TOP CHOICE **Cathédrale St-Lazare** CATHEDRAL
(place du Terreau; ⏰8am-7pm Sep-Jun, plus 9-11pm Jul & Aug) Originally Romanesque, this cathedral was built in the 12th century to house the sacred relics of St Lazarus. Later additions include the 15th- to 16th-century bell tower over the transept and the 19th-century towers over the entrance. Over the main doorway, the famous Romanesque tympanum shows the Last Judgement carved in the 1130s by Gislebertus, whose name is inscribed below Jesus' right foot. Look for all manner of symbolism: signs of the zodiac encircling the saved and the damned. Be sure to go upstairs to the Chapter Room where the fantastical capitals, many of them by Gislebertus, are displayed.

Gallo-Roman Sites RUIN
Built during the reign of Constantine, Porte d'Arroux was once one of Augustodunum's four gates. Constructed wholly without mortar, it supports four semicircular arches of the sort that put the 'Roman' in Romanesque: two for vehicles and two for pedestrians. Porte St-André is similar in general design.

Let your imagination run wild at the **Théâtre Romain** (Roman Theatre; ⊙24hr), designed to hold 16,000 people; try picturing the place filled with cheering (or jeering), toga-clad spectators. From the top look southwest to see the **Pierre de Couhard** (Rock of Couhard), the 27m-high remains of a Gallo-Roman pyramid that was probably a tomb.

Long associated (wrongly) with the Roman god Janus, the 24m-high **Temple de Janus** (www.temple-de-janus.net), in the middle of farmland 800m north of the train station, is thought to have been a site for Celtic worship. Only two of its massive walls still stand.

Musée Rolin   MUSEUM
(✆03 85 52 09 76; 5 rue des Bancs; adult/child €5/free; ⊙9.30am-noon & 1.30-6pm Wed-Mon) Explore a worthwhile collection of Gallo-Roman artefacts; 12th-century Romanesque art, including the *Temptation of Eve* by Gislebertus; and 15th-century paintings such as the *Autun Virgin* by the Maître de Moulins. Modern art includes work by Maurice Denis, Jean Dubuffet and Joan Miró.

The adjacent **prison** (2bis place St-Louis; admission €1; ⊙2-6pm Wed-Sun Jul-Sep), a forbidding circular structure built in 1854, was used until 1955.

🏃 Activities

For a stroll along the city walls (part Roman but mostly medieval), walk from av du Morvan south to the 12th-century **Tour des Ursulines** and follow the walls to the northeast. The **Chemin des Manies** leads out to the Pierre de Couhard, where you can pick up the **Circuit des Gorges**, three marked forest trails ranging from 4.7km to 11.5km (map IGN 2925 O). The **watersports centre** based at Plan d'Eau du Vallon (an artificial lake east of the centre) rents kayaks, paddle boats and bikes.

🛏 Sleeping

TOP CHOICE **Moulin Renaudiots**   B&B €€
(✆03 85 86 97 10, 06 16 97 47 80; www.moulin renaudiots.com; chemin du Vieux Moulin; d €125-155; ⊙Apr-Oct; 🐾🏊) The exterior of this old water mill isolated in a verdant property is 17th-century stately; inside, it's a minimalist's dream. This will delight all those who enjoy sobriety, space, charm and functionality at the same time. The vast bedrooms are a symphony of grey, ivory, chocolate and cream and feature luxurious linen. Behind the house is a large, neat, gracious garden with a swimming-pool – perfect for an aperitif before enjoying a *table d'hôte* (set fixed-price menu; €48; available four times a week) expertly prepared by your courteous hosts. Excellent English is spoken. About 3km from Autun off the road to Châlon-sur-Saône.

Maison Sainte-Barbe   B&B €
(✆03 85 86 24 77; www.maisonsaintebarbe.com; 7 place Sainte-Barbe; s/d €72/74; 🐾) Smack in the old city in a 15th-century town house, around a verdant courtyard, some of the rooms of this colourful, spotless B&B have light-filled views of the cathedral. Friendly, knowledgable owners prepare delicious breakfasts. The icing on the cake? A lovely garden at the back.

Hôtel de la Tête Noire   HOTEL €€
(✆03 85 86 59 99; www.hoteltetenoire.fr; 3 rue de l'Arquebuse; s €66-78, d €77-90; ⊙closed mid-Dec–Jan; ❄🐾🅿) Just a short walk down from the cathedral, this well-managed abode is clean, bright and friendly, with a respectable restaurant serving regional dishes on the ground floor. Rooms on the 3rd floor have great views of the town and the countryside.

Les Arcades   HOTEL €
(✆03 85 52 30 03; www.hotel-arcades-autun.com; 22 av de la République; s €41, d €48-51; 🐾) Just across the road from the railway station, Les Arcades is an acceptable plan B, but don't expect the Ritz – rooms are unmemorable and service is lackadaisical. Parking is €5.

🍴 Eating

Restaurant Le Chapitre   MODERN FRENCH €€
(✆03 85 52 04 01; www.restaurantlechapitre.com; 11 place du Terreau; mains €18-23, lunch menus €15-20, dinner menus €29-38; ⊙noon-1.30pm Tue-Sun, 7.30-9.30pm Tue-Sat) The intimate dining room in brushed-grey tones fills up with locals out for a quiet, elegant meal. Le Chapitre offers a creative French-inspired menu, with a good selection of voluptuous fish and meat dishes. It's just a stone's throw from the cathedral.

Le Petit Rolin   CRÊPERIE, BURGUNDIAN €
(✆03 85 86 15 55; www.le-petit-rolin.fr; place St Louis; mains €10-25, lunch menu €13, menus €15-26; ⊙lunch & dinner daily Apr-Sep, Tue-Sun Oct-Dec, closed Jan-Mar) At Le Petit Rolin, with its rustic interior dating back to the 15th century, the Bourguignonne galette is filled with regional ingredients like Époisses (cheese)

CHÂTEAU DE VILLETTE

Set in a 5-sq-km private estate, the delightful 16th- and 18th-century Château de Villette (☑03 86 30 09 13; www.stork-chateau.com; Poil; d incl breakfast €185-245, ste €330-390; ☎❄) offers the luxurious life of Burgundy's landed aristocracy. After waking up in a ravishingly furnished period room, you can ramble, cycle or hunt escargots in the rolling countryside, or simply relax in the stress-melting pool. Feeling mushy? Book the room equipped with a canopied four-poster bed. *Tables d'hôte* (set fixed-price menus; €48; twice a week) come in for warm praise. It's 20km southwest of Autun; call ahead.

and cured meat. Otherwise there are plenty of fish and meat dishes and salads to choose from. In summer tables fill the square outside, right in front of the tympanum of the cathedral.

Le Monde de Don Cabillaud   SEAFOOD €€
(☑07 60 94 21 10; 4 rue des Bancs; menus €22-27; ☉lunch & dinner Tue-Sat) This petite restaurant might not register high on the stylometer, but the convivial atmosphere makes up for it. There's a small selection of seafood dishes, and they're all super fresh, prepared in a variety of styles and presented with a minimum of fuss. Near Musée Rolin.

Le Chalet Bleu   TRADITIONAL FRENCH €€
(☑03 85 86 27 30; www.lechaletbleu.com; 3 rue Jeannin; menus €15-58; ☉lunch Tue & Thu-Sun, dinner Mon & Thu-Sat) Serves classic French gastronomic cuisine in a light, leafy dining room decorated with colourful frescos. Treat yourself to a series of dainty gourmet dishes, such as *pièces de Charolais* (Charolais steak) and *suprême de volaille* (filleted breast of poultry in a white sauce). Takeaway plates sold next door. Near the Hôtel de Ville.

❶ Information

Tourist Office (☑03 85 86 80 38; www.autun -tourisme.com; 13 rue du Général Demetz; ☉9am-12.30pm & 2-6.30pm, closed Mon morning & Sun Oct–mid-May) Sells a self-guided walking-tour brochure (€2) and hiking maps. Information on the Parc Naturel Régional du Morvan. From June to September, it has an annexe in front of the cathedral.

❶ Getting There & Away

BUS Timetables are posted at the bus shelters next to the train station. **Buscéphale** (☑08 00 07 17 10; www.buscephale.fr) serves Le Creusot TGV station (line 5; €1.50, one hour, one to six daily).

TAXI The **train station** (av de la République) is on a slow tertiary line that requires a change of train to get almost anywhere.

Château de Sully

This Renaissance-style château (☑03 85 82 09 86; www.chateaudesully.com; adult/child €7.70/4.80, gardens only €3.70/3; ☉10am-5pm Apr-11 Nov), on the outskirts of the village of Sully (15km northeast of Autun along the D973), has a beautifully furnished interior and a lovely English-style garden. It was the birthplace of Marshall MacMahon, duke of Magenta and president of France from 1873 to 1879, whose ancestors fled Ireland several centuries ago and whose descendents still occupy the property.

Tournus
POP 6276

Tournus, on the Saône, is known for its 10th- to 12th-century Romanesque abbey church, **Abbatiale St-Philibert** (☉8.30am-7pm). In 2002 a superb and extremely rare 12th-century mosaic of the calendar and the zodiac was discovered here by chance.

The scenic roads that link Tournus with Cluny, including the D14, D15, D82 and D56, pass through lots of tiny villages, many with charming churches. The medieval village of Brancion sits at the base of its château, while Chardonnay is, as one would expect, surrounded by vineyards. There's a panoramic view from 579m Mont St-Romain.

Cluny
POP 4872

The remains of Cluny's great abbey – Christendom's largest church until the construction of St Peter's Basilica in the Vatican – are fragmentary and scattered, barely discernible among the houses and green spaces of the modern-day town. But with a bit of imagination, it's possible to picture how things looked in the 12th century, when Cluny's Benedictine abbey, renowned for its wealth and power and answerable only to the Pope, held sway over 1100 priories and monasteries stretching from Poland to Portugal.

Sights

Église Abbatiale
LANDMARK, CHURCH

(Abbey Church; ☎03 85 59 15 93; www.cluny. monuments-nationaux.fr; adult/child €9.50/free; ☺9.30am-6.30pm May-Aug, 9.30am-noon & 1.30-5pm Sep-Apr) Cluny's vast abbey church, built between 1088 and 1130, once stretched from the rectangular map table in front of the Palais Jean de Bourbon all the way to the trees near the octagonal Clocher de l'Eau Bénite (Tower of the Holy Water) and its neighbour, the square Tour de l'Horloge – a distance of 187m!

Buy tickets and begin your visit at the Palais Jean de Bourbon, which hosts the Musée d'Art et d'Archéologie. Displays include a model of the Cluny complex, a 10-minute computer-generated 3D 'virtual tour' of the abbey as it looked in the Middle Ages and some superb Romanesque carvings. It continues on the grounds of the École Nationale Supérieure d'Arts et Métiers (ENSAM; place du 11 Août; ☺9.30am-6.30pm May-Aug, 9.30am-noon & 1.30-5pm Sep-Apr), an institute for training mechanical and industrial engineers that's centred on an 18th-century cloister. You can wander around the grounds at midday and for an hour after the museum closes. Free guided tours in English occur in July and August.

The best place to appreciate the abbey's vastness is from the top of the Tour des Fromages (adult/child €2/free; ☺10am-12.30pm & 2.30-6.45pm, no midday closure Jul & Aug, closed Sun Apr & Sep, Sun & Mon Oct-Mar), once used to ripen cheeses. Access the tower's 120 steps through the tourist office.

Haras National
HORSE STUD

(National Stud Farm; ☎03 85 59 85 19; www.haras-nationaux.fr; 2 rue Porte des Prés; adult/child €6/free; ☺tours 2pm, 3.30pm & 5pm Tue-Sun, closed Dec-Jan) Founded by Napoléon in 1806, the Haras National houses some of France's finest thoroughbreds, ponies and draught horses. Visit on a guided tour.

Église St-Marcel
CHURCH

(rue Prud'hon; ☺closed to public) Topped by an octagonal, three-storey belfry.

Église Notre Dame
CHURCH

(☺9am-7pm) A 13th-century church, across from the tourist office.

Sleeping

ⓣᴼᴾ Le Clos de l'Abbaye
B&B €€

(☎03 85 59 22 06; www.closdelabbaye.fr; 6 place du Marché; d/tr/q €70/85/105, ste €110-170; ☜) The energetic owners have brought vitality to this handsome old house that's right beside the abbey. They have created four comfortable, colour-coordinated bedrooms and modern bathrooms. Three rooms have views of the abbey. Also: a lovely garden with facilities for kids. Your hosts are excellent tour advisers who direct you to little-known treasures.

Hôtel de Bourgogne
HISTORIC HOTEL €€

(☎03 85 59 00 58; www.hotel-cluny.com; place de l'Abbaye; d €93-133; ☺Feb-Nov; ☜) This family-run hotel sits right next to the remains of the abbey. Built in 1817, it has a casual lounge area, 13 antique-furnished rooms and a restaurant. Breakfast is served in an enchanting courtyard. Parking €10.

Hôtel du Commerce
HOTEL €

(☎03 85 59 03 09; www.hotelducommerce-cluny. com; 8 place du Commerce; d with shared bathroom €31-42, d €47; ☺reception closed noon-4.30pm) Blink and you'll miss the tiny entrance of this funky little budget hotel on the main drag. The 17 rooms are monastically plain but clean and tidy.

Cluny Séjour
HOSTEL €

(☎03 85 59 08 83; www.cluny-sejour.blogspot. com; 22 rue Porte de Paris; dm €18, s/d €20/37, incl breakfast; ☺closed mid-Dec–mid-Jan) Clean, bright two- to four-bed rooms, excellent showers and helpful staff are just a few factors that make this place a winner. Towels cost €2.

Eating

The Hôtel de Bourgogne also has a fine restaurant.

ⓣᴼᴾ La Table d'Héloïse
BURGUNDIAN €€

(☎03 85 59 05 65; www.hostelleriedheloise.com; rte de Mâcon; mains €15-22, lunch menu €19, dinner menus €29-49; ☺lunch Fri-Tue, dinner Mon, Tue & Thu-Sat) This family-run restaurant with a charmingly cosy interior is a terrific place to sample firmly traditional Burgundian specialities. The dextrously prepared *fricassée d'escargots* (snail stew) is a stunning entrée, not to be outclassed by the tender Charolais rump steak. The ripe Époisses cheese is sensational and the homemade desserts are every bit as devastatingly delicious as they sound. Book a table in the light-filled verandah overlooking the Grosne river.

Brasserie du Nord BRASSERIE €

(☑03 85 59 09 96; place du Marché; mains €10-19, menus €18-32; ⊙daily 7am-11pm) This surprisingly hip brasserie with a loungey feel has a top-notch location – its terrace is just opposite the Église Abbatiale. The eclectic menu ranges the gamut from salads and pasta to frogs' legs and meat dishes. Better still, it's well priced and stays open late (an exception in sedate Cluny).

Le Bistrot BISTRO €

(☑03 85 59 08 07; 14 place du Commerce; mains €8-17; ⊙8.30am-11pm Wed-Mon) This character-filled bistro which has walls as adorned with cool vintage posters and old clocks is a real charmer. The flavoursome *ravioles* (ravioli with cheese filling) and frondy salads are the house specialities, but there are always imaginative daily specials scrawled on a chalkboard. A wonderful *crème brûlée au chocolat* (cream pie with a caramelised topping) will finish you off sweetly. It doubles as a bar (wine by the glass from €1.80).

Germain TEA HOUSE €

(☑03 85 59 11 21; 25 rue Lamartine; lunch menu €12.50; ⊙daily 7am-8pm) A mouth-watering patisserie-*chocolaterie* with an adjacent *salon de thé* (lunch *menu* €12.50) that serves breakfast and light lunches like quiche and salad.

❶ Information

Tourist office (☑03 85 59 05 34; www.cluny -tourisme.com; 6 rue Mercière; internet per

---

CYCLING THE VOIE VERTE

An old railway line and parts of a former canal towpath have been turned into the Voie Verte (Green Road), a series of paved paths around the Saône-et-Loire *département* that have been designed for walking, cycling and in-line skating. From Cluny, the Voie Verte heads north, via vineyards and valleys, to Givry (42km) and Santenay, where you can pick up the **Voie des Vignes** (p414) to Beaune. Tourist offices have the free cycling map *Voies Vertes et Cyclotourisme – Bourgogne du Sud*. Also log onto www. burgundy-by-bike.com.

15min €1.50; ⊙10am-12.30pm & 2.30-6.45pm, no midday closure Jul & Aug, closed Sun Apr-Nov) Has internet access.

❶ Getting There & Around

BUS The bus stop on rue Porte de Paris is served by **Buscéphale** (☑08 00 07 17 10; www. cg71.fr; tickets €1.50). Lines 7 and 9 (six or seven daily) go to Mâcon (45 minutes), the Mâcon-Loché TGV station (30 minutes) and Cormatin (20 minutes). Schedules are posted at the bus stop and tourist office.

BICYCLE Ludisport (☑06 62 36 09 58; www. ludisport.com; place des Martyrs de la Déportation; per half-/full day from €12/18; ⊙10am-noon & 2-4pm Apr-Nov) is at the old train station, about 1km south of the centre.

Around Cluny

Cormatin, 14km north of Cluny, is home to the Renaissance-style **Château de Cormatin** (☑03 85 50 16 55; www.chateaudecormatin. com; Cormatin; adult/child €9/4.50; ⊙10am-noon & 2-5.30pm, no midday closure mid-Jul–mid-Aug, gardens open till dusk), renowned for its opulent 17th-century, Louis XIII–style interiors and formal gardens.

An interesting side trip from Cluny is **Paray-le-Monial**, about 50km to the west, where the major attraction is the Romanesque **Basilique du Sacré-Cœur**. Its construction began in the 11th century and it has a similar layout and architectural style to that of the Église Abbatiale in Cluny.

Mâcon

POP 35,040

The town of Mâcon, 70km north of Lyon on the west bank of the Saône, is at the heart of the **Mâconnais**, Burgundy's southernmost wine-growing area, which produces mainly dry whites.

Across the street from the 18th-century town hall, the tourist office has information on accommodation and visiting vineyards including the **Route des Vins Mâconnais-Beaujolais**.

The all-wood **Maison de Bois**, facing 95 rue Dombey and built around 1500, is decorated with carved wooden figures, some of them very cheeky indeed.

Musée Lamartine (☑03 85 39 90 38; 41 rue Sigorgne; adult/child €2.50/free; ⊙10am-noon & 2-6pm Tue-Sat, 2-6pm Sun) explores the life and times of the Mâcon-born Romantic poet and left-wing politician Alphonse de Lamartine (1790–1869).

Musée des Ursulines (☎03 85 39 90 38; 5 rue des Ursulines; adult/child €2.50/free; ⏲10am-noon & 2-6pm Tue-Sat, 2-6pm Sun), housed in a 17th-century Ursuline convent, features Gallo-Roman archaeology, 16th- to 20th-century paintings and displays about 19th-century Mâconnais life.

There's no shortage of places to stay in Mâcon, including the three-star Hôtel de Bourgogne (☎03 85 21 10 23; www.hoteldebourgogne.com; 6 rue Victor Hugo; d €70-105; 📶), which has benefited from a partial renovation, and the Hôtel du Nord (www.hotel-dunord.com; 313 quai Jean Jaurès; s €55-67, d €65-77; 📶), with tidy rooms overlooking the Saône.

L'Ethym' Sel (☎03 85 39 48 84; 10 rue Gambetta; mains €16-20, menus €15-46; ⏲Tue-Sat Jul-Aug, lunch Thu-Tue, dinner Thu-Sat & Mon Sep-Jun), two blocks south of the tourist office, is a modern bistro offering French and Burgundian specialities such as locally raised Charolais steak and *souris d'agneau au miel* (lamb in honey sauce). Mâcon's gastronomic sanctuary is Restaurant Pierre (☎03 85 38 14 23; www.restaurant-pierre.com; 7-9 rue Dufour; mains €26-34, lunch menu €25, dinner menus €32-81; ⏲lunch Wed-Sun, dinner Tue-Sat), where chef Christian Gaulin juggles creativity and tradition to conjure up sumptuous culinary surprises.

Information

Tourist office (☎03 85 21 07 07; www.visitezlemaconnais.com; 1 place St-Pierre; ⏲9.30am-12.30pm & 2-6.30pm Mon-Sat, closed Mon Nov-Apr)

Getting There & Around

BUS **Buscéphale** (☎08 00 07 17 10; www.cg71.fr; tickets €1.50) bus lines 7 and 9 serve Cluny.

TRAIN The Mâcon-Ville train station is on the main line (18 daily) linking Dijon (from €17, 1¼ hours), Beaune (from €14, 50 minutes) and Lyon-Part Dieu (from €12, 50 minutes). The Mâcon-Loché TGV station is 5km southwest of town.

Around Mâcon

About 10km west of Mâcon in the wine country, the Musée de Préhistoire de Solutré (☎03 85 35 85 24; www.musees-bourgogne.org; Solutré; adult/child €3.50/free; ⏲10am-6pm Apr-Sep, 10am-noon & 2-5pm Oct-Mar) displays finds from one of Europe's richest prehistoric sites, occupied from 35,000 to 10,000 BC. A lovely 20-minute walk will get you to the top of the rocky outcrop known as the Roche de Solutré, from where Mont Blanc can sometimes be seen, especially at sunset.

If you're after top-quality Mâconnais wines, head to the nearby villages of Fuissé, Vinzelles and Pouilly, which produce the area's best white wines.

Lyon & the Rhône Valley

Best Places to Eat

» Le Bouchon des Filles
(p458)

» L'Ourson qui Boit (p460)

» Restaurant Pic (p468)

» L'Auberge du Pont de
Collonges (p460)

» Le Canut et les Gones
(p460)

Best Places to Stay

» Les Folies de la Serve
(p466)

» Apart'Observatoire St-
Jean (p455)

» Hostellerie de Pérouges
(p466)

» Cour des Loges (p455)

» Péniche Barnum (p456)

Why Go?

At the crossroads of central Europe and the Atlantic, the Rhineland and the Mediterranean, grand old Lyon is France's third-largest metropolis and its gastronomic capital. Savouring lavish dishes and delicacies in timeless, checked-tableclothed *bouchons* (small bistros) or cutting-edge eating spaces creates unforgettable memories – as do Lyon's majestic Roman amphitheatres, its cobbled Unesco-listed old town, the romantic parks and the rejuvenated riverfront, just for starters.

Beaujolais produces illustrious wines, while the picturesque hilltop village of Pérouges turns out traditional sugar-crusted tarts. Downstream, the Rhône forges past centuries-old Côtes du Rhône vineyards yielding some of France's most respected reds, Valence's *pâtisseries* filled with historic shortbread, and Montélimar's artisan nougat factories, eventually reaching the rugged Gorges de l'Ardèche, where the Ardèche River tumbles to the gates of Languedoc and Provence.

When to Go
Lyon

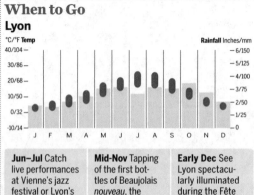

Jun–Jul Catch live performances at Vienne's jazz festival or Lyon's Nuits de Fourvière.

Mid-Nov Tapping of the first bottles of Beaujolais *nouveau*, the third Thursday in November.

Early Dec See Lyon spectacularly illuminated during the Fête des Lumières.

Lyon & the Rhône Valley Highlights

1 Delve into Lyon's hidden labyrinth of **traboules** (secret passageways; p454)

2 Bike the vine-ribboned hills of **Beaujolais** (p466)

3 See dramatic Gallo-Roman ruins, including a perfectly preserved Corinthian-columned **temple** (p467) in Vienne

4 Hop on a boat downstream to the **Confluence** (p463), Lyon's newest neighbourhood near the meeting of the Rhône and Saône rivers

5 Learn about Lyon's silk-weaving heritage in **Croix Rousse** (p452)

6 Canoe beneath the stunning natural stone bridge Pont d'Arc along the **Gorges de l'Ardèche** (p469)

7 Catch a traditional **puppet show** (p461) featuring Lyon's charismatic little raconteur, Guignol

8 See Lyon through the eyes of a local expert on one of the superb **walking tours** (p454) organised by the tourist office

Lyon

POP 487,980

Commercial, industrial and banking power-house for the past 500 years, today Lyon is France's third-largest city.

Outstanding museums, a dynamic cultural life, busy clubbing and drinking scene, thriving university and fantastic shopping lend the city a distinctly sophisticated air, while adventurous gourmets can indulge in their wildest gastronomic fantasies.

Lyon comprises nine *arrondissements* (neighbourhoods); the *arrondissement* number appears after each street address.

History

The Roman military colony of Lugdunum (Lyon) was founded in 43 BC. It served as the capital of the Roman territories known as the Three Gauls under Augustus, but had to wait for fame and fortune until the arrival of movable type in 1473 transformed it into one of Europe's foremost publishing centres.

By the mid-18th century the city's influential silk weavers – 40% of Lyon's total work-force – had developed what had already been a textiles centre since the 15th century into the silk-weaving capital of Europe. A century on, Lyon had tripled in size and boasted 100,000 weaving looms.

In 1870 the Lumière family moved to Lyon, and cinema was born when broth-ers Louis and Auguste shot the world's first moving picture here in 1895.

During WWII some 4000 people (including Resistance leader Jean Moulin) were killed and 7500 others deported to Nazi death camps under Gestapo chief Klaus Barbie (1913–91), the 'butcher of Lyon'. Nazi rule ended in September 1944, when the retreating Germans blew up all but two of Lyon's 28 bridges. Barbie was sentenced to death in absentia in 1952 and again in 1954, but it wasn't until 1987, following his extradition from Bolivia, that he was tried in person in Lyon and sentenced to life imprisonment. He died in prison three years later.

◉ Sights

VIEUX LYON

Lyon's Unesco-listed old town, with its narrow streets and medieval and Renaissance houses, is divided into three quarters: St-Paul (north), St-Jean (middle) and St-Georges (south).

Cathédrale St-Jean   CATHEDRAL
(place St-Jean, 5e; ◷8am-noon & 2-7pm daily; Ⓜ Vieux Lyon) This partly Romanesque cathedral, seat of Lyon's 133rd bishop, was built between the late 11th and early 16th centuries. The portals of its Flamboyant Gothic façade, completed in 1480, are decorated with 280 square stone medallions. Don't miss the astronomical clock in the north transept chiming at noon, 2pm, 3pm and 4pm daily.

LYON IN...

Two Days

If your time's tight, begin with an overview of the city on a guided **tour** before visiting the magnificent **Musée des Beaux-Arts** and lunching on its terrace. Cycle to expansive **Parc de la Tête d'Or** before dinner at a traditional Lyonnais *bouchon* (small bistro), and a drink at the bars aboard the Rhône's *péniches* (barges).

Start your second day on what was long known as 'the hill of work', **Croix Rousse**, browsing its outdoor **market** and discovering its **silk-weaving workshops**. Then cross town and ride the funicular to the 'hill of prayer', basilica-crowned **Fourvière**, to uncover Roman Lyon at the fascinating **Musée de la Civilisation Gallo-Romaine** and **Théâtre Romain**. Dine at **Le Restaurant de Fourvière**, which offers panoramic views, before making your way downhill to Vieux Lyon's lively **bars**.

Four Days

Spend your third day absorbing more of Lyon's lengthy history at its cache of **museums**, catch a **puppet show** featuring famous little Guignol, or hop a ferry south to see the vast new **Confluence** neighbourhood, where you can dine near the riverfront at **Rue Le Bec** restaurant.

Four days gives you enough time for day trips in the surrounding regions such as wine-rich **Beaujolais**, film-star **Pérouges**, design-driven **St-Étienne** or **downstream along the Rhône**.

Medieval & Renaissance
Architecture ARCHITECTURE

(ⓂVieux Lyon) Lovely old buildings line rue du Bœuf, rue St-Jean and rue des Trois Maries. Crane your neck upwards to see gargoyles and other cheeky stone characters carved on window ledges along rue Juiverie, home to Lyon's Jewish community in the Middle Ages.

Musées Gadagne MUSEUMS

(www.museegadagne.com; 1 place du Petit Collège, 5e; single museum adult/child €6/free, both museums €8/free; ☉11am-6.30pm Wed-Sun; ⓂVieux Lyon) Housed in a 16th-century mansion built for two rich Florentine bankers, this twin-themed exhibition space incorporates an excellent local history museum (Musée d'Histoire de Lyon) chronicling the city's layout as its silk-weaving, cinema and transportation evolved, and an international puppet museum (Musée des Marionettes du Monde) paying homage to Lyon's iconic puppet, Guignol. On the 4th floor, a cafe adjoins tranquil, terraced gardens, here since the 14th century and laid out two centuries later.

Le Petit Musée
Fantastique de Guignol PUPPET MUSEUM

(6 rue St-Jean, 5e; adult/child €5/3; ☉11am-1pm & 2-7pm Tue-Sun; ⓂVieux Lyon) Guignol is the star of this tiny, two-room museum with cute, sensor-activated exhibits; ask staff to set up the English soundtrack.

Musée Miniature et Cinéma FILM MUSEUM

(🖉04 72 00 24 77; www.mimlyon.com; 60 rue St-Jean, 5e; adult/child €7/5.50; ☉10am-6.30pm Mon-Fri, to 7pm Sat & Sun; ⓂVieux Lyon) This mazelike museum on tourist-busy rue St-Jean provides an unusual insight into the making of movie sets and special effects achieved with the use of miniatures.

FOURVIÈRE

Over two millennia ago, the Romans built the city of Lugdunum on the slopes of Fourvière. Today it's topped by the Tour Métallique, an Eiffel Tower–like structure (minus its bottom two-thirds) built in 1893 and used as a TV transmitter.

Footpaths wind uphill but the funicular (place Édouard Commette, 5e; return €2.40) is the least taxing way up.

Basilique Notre Dame
de Fourvière CHURCH

(www.fourviere.org; place de Fourvière, 5e; ☉8am-7pm; Fourvière funicular station) Crowning the hill – with stunning city panoramas from its terrace – the 66m-long, 19m-wide and 27m-high basilica is lined with intricate mosaics and a superb example of late-19th-century French ecclesiastical architecture. One-hour discovery visits take in the main features of the basilica and crypt; rooftop tours climax on the stone-sculpted roof.

Musée de la Civilisation
Gallo-Romaine ARCHAEOLOGICAL MUSEUM

(www.musees-gallo-romains.com; 17 rue Cléberg, 5e; adult/child €4/free, Thu free; ☉10am-6pm Tue-Sun; Fourvière funicular station) Ancient artefacts found in the Rhône Valley are displayed at the city's Roman museum.

Théâtre Romain ARCHAEOLOGICAL SITE

(rue Cléberg, 5e; ⓂFourvière funicular station or Minimes funicular station) The Théâtre Romain, built around 15 BC and enlarged in AD 120, sat an audience of 10,000. Romans held poetry readings and musical recitals in the smaller, adjacent odéon.

Musée d'Art Religieux ART MUSEUM

(8 place de Fourvière, 5e; adult/child €6/free; ☉10am-12.30pm & 2-5.30pm; Fourvière funicular station) Works of sacred art and worth-the-trip temporary exhibitions are showcased here.

PRESQU'ÎLE

Lyon's city centre lies on this 500m- to 800m-wide peninsula bounded by the rivers Rhône and Saône.

Musée des Beaux-Arts ART MUSEUM

(www.mba-lyon.fr; 20 place des Terreaux, 1er; adult/child incl audioguide €7/free; ☉10am-6pm Wed, Thu & Sat-Mon, 10.30am-6pm Fri; ⓂHôtel de Ville) This stunning and eminently manageable museum showcases France's finest collection of sculptures and paintings outside Paris from antiquity on. Highlights include works by Rodin, Rubens, Rembrandt, Monet, Matisse and Picasso. Pick up a free audioguide and be sure to stop for a drink or meal on the delightful stone terrace off its café-restaurant or take time out in its tranquil cloister garden.

Place des Terreaux CITY SQUARE

(ⓂHôtel de Ville) The centrepiece of the Presqu'île's beautiful central square is a 19th-century fountain made of 21 tonnes of lead and sculpted by Frédéric-Auguste Bartholdi (of Statue of Liberty fame). The four horses pulling the chariot symbolise rivers galloping seawards. The Hôtel de Ville (Town Hall; place des Terreaux; Hôtel de Ville) fronting the square was built in 1655 but given its

Lyon

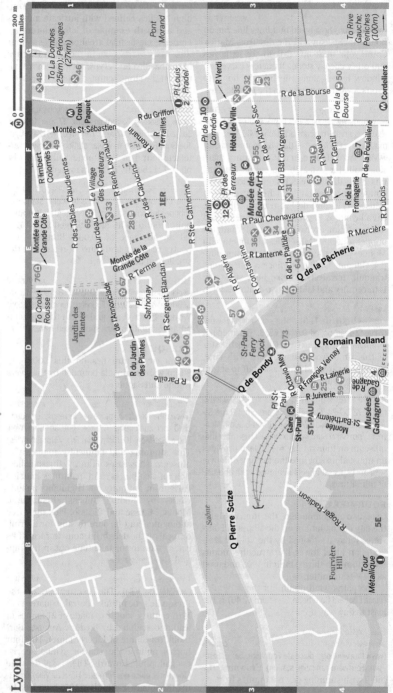

Â

0   200 m
0   0.1 miles

To La Dombes (25km); Pérouges (27km)

To Rive Gauche; Péniches (100m)

Pont Morand

To Croix Rousse

Croix Paquet

Montée St-Sébastien

R de la Grande Côte

R des Tables Claudiennes

Montée de la Grande Côte

R Terme

Jardin des Plantes

Pl Sathonay

R Sergent Blandan

R du Jardin des Plantes

R de l'Annonciade

R Pareille

Q de Bondy

Q Pierre Scize

Saône

R Roger Radison

Fourvière Hill

Tour Métallique

Gare St-Paul

St-Paul

Pl St-Paul

ST-PAUL

Montée St-Barthélemy

St-Paul Ferry Dock

Q Romain Rolland

R Octavio Mey

R François Vernay

R Lainerie

R Juiverie

Musées Gadagne

R de Gadagne

Le Village des Créateurs

R Burdeau

R René Leynaud

R des Capucins

R du Griffon

R Romarin

R Terrailles

1ER

R Ste-Catherine

Fountain

Pl des Terreaux

Musée des Beaux-Arts

R Paul Chenavard

R Constantine

R d'Algérie

R Lanterne

R de la Plâtrière

Q de la Pêcherie

Pl Louis Pradel

R Verdi

Pl de la Comédie

Hôtel de Ville

R de l'Arbre Sec

R du Bât d'Argent

R Neuve

R Gentil

R de la Poulaillerie

R de la Fromagerie

R Mercière

R Dubois

Pl de la Bourse

R de la Bourse

Cordeliers

5E

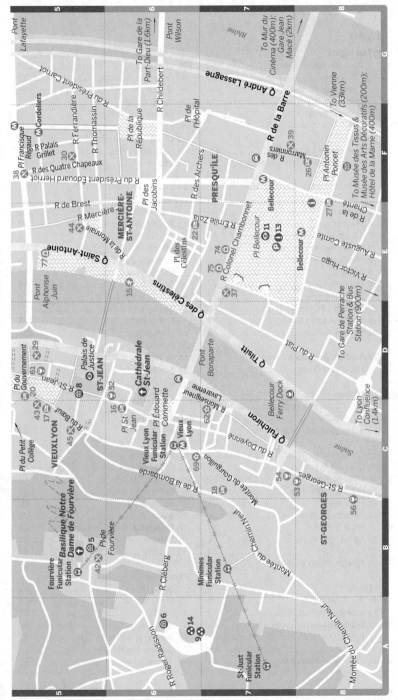

Lyon

present ornate façade in 1702. When Daniel Buren's polka-dot 'forest' of 69 granite fountains (embedded in the ground across much of the square) are on, join the kids in a mad dash as the water dances up, down, disappears for a second and gushes back again.

Place Bellecour
CITY SQUARE

(MBellecour) One of Europe's largest public squares, place Bellecour was laid out in the 17th century. In the centre is an equestrian statue of Louis XIV.

Opéra de Lyon
OPERA HOUSE

(place de la Comédie, 1er; MHôtel de Ville) Lyon's neoclassical 1831-built opera house was modernised in 1993 by renowned French architect Jean Nouvel, who added the striking semicylindrical glass-domed roof. On its northern side, boarders and bladers buzz around the fountains of place Louis Pradel, surveyed by the Homme de la Liberté (Man of Freedom) on roller skates, sculpted from scrap metal by Marseille-born César.

Fresque des Lyonnais
MURAL

(cnr rue de la Martinière & quai de la Pêcherie, 1er; MHôtel de Ville) Well-known Lyonnais peer out from this seven-storey mural, including loom inventor Joseph-Marie Jacquard (1752–1834), Renaissance poet Maurice Scève (c 1499–1560), superstar chef Paul Bocuse (b 1926), puppet Guignol, and the yellow-haired Little Prince, created by author/aviator Antoine de St-Exupéry (1900–44).

Musée des Tissus
SILK MUSEUM

(www.musee-des-tissus.com; 34 rue de la Charité, 2e; adult/child €10/7.50, after 4pm €8/5.50; ⊗10am-5.30pm Tue-Sun; MAmpère) Extraordinary Lyonnais and international silks are showcased here. Ticket includes admission to the adjoining Musée des Arts Décoratifs (free with Musée des Tissus ticket; ⊗10am-noon & 2-5.30pm Tue-Sun), which displays 18th-century furniture, tapestries, wallpaper, ceramics and silver.

Musée de l'Imprimerie
PRINTING MUSEUM

(www.imprimerie.lyon.fr; 13 rue de la Poulaillerie, 2e; adult/child €5/free; ⊗9.30am-noon & 2-6pm Wed-Sun; MCordeliers) Filled with early equipment through to computerised technology, this absorbing museum focuses on the city's extensive printing industry (look for the 1960s airline timetables!).

Aquarium du Grand Lyon
AQUARIUM

(www.aquariumlyon.fr; 7 rue Stéphane Déchant, La Mulatière; adult/child €14/10.50; ⊗11am-7pm Wed-Sun, daily during school holidays) Next to the Confluence, Lyon's well-thought-out aquarium is home to some 280 marine species including over 5000 fish. Bus 15 links it with place Bellecour.

CROIX ROUSSE

Independent until it became part of Lyon in 1852, and retaining its own distinct character with its bohemian inhabitants and lush outdoor food market, the hilltop quarter of Croix Rousse slinks north up the steep *pentes* (slopes).

Following the introduction of the mechanical Jacquard loom in 1805, Lyonnais *canuts* (silk weavers) built tens of thousands of workshops in the area, with large windows to let in light and hefty wood-beamed ceilings more than 4m high to accommodate the huge new machines. Weavers spent 14 to 20 hours a day hunched over their looms breathing in silk dust. Two-thirds were illiterate and everyone was paid a pittance; strikes in 1830–31 and 1834 resulted in the death of several hundred weavers.

Most workshops are chic loft apartments today, but a few have been saved (with more in the process of being saved) by the Soierie Vivante association.

Hidden Croix Rousse gems include place Bertone, a leafy square that doubles as an open-air stage for ad hoc summer entertainment; the Jardin Rosa Mir (http://rosa.mir.free.fr; enter via 87 Grande Rue, 4e; ⊗3-6pm Sat Apr-Nov; MCroix Rousse), a walled garden decorated with thousands of seashells, accessed off a narrow laneway; and the panoramic

LYON CITY CARD

The Lyon City Card (www.lyon-france.com; 1/2/3 days adult €21/31/41, child €12.50/17.50/22.50) covers admission to every Lyon museum and the roof of Basilique Notre Dame de Fourvière, as well as guided city tours, a river excursion (April to October) and discounts on the Aquarium du Grand Lyon and other selected attractions, exhibitions and shops.

The card also includes city-wide transport, offering unlimited travel on buses, trams, the funicular and metro. Buy it online (www.en.lyon-france.com/Lyon-City-Card), from the tourist office, or at some hotels.

Jardin Publique La Cerisaie (rue Chazière, 4e; ⓜCroix Rousse).

Maison des Canuts　　　SILK WORKSHOP
(www.maisondescanuts.com; 10-12 rue d'Ivry, 4e; adult/child €6.50/3.50; ⊙10am-6pm Mon-Sat, guided tours 11am & 3.30pm; ⓜCroix Rousse) On a guided tour, learn about weavers' labour-intensive life and the industry's evolution and see manual looms in use, and browse its silk boutique.

Atelier de Passementerie　　　SILK WORKSHOP
(✆04 78 27 17 13; www.soierie-vivante.asso.fr; 21 rue Richan, 4e; guided tour adult/child €5/3, combined ticket with Atelier de Tissage €8/4; ⊙boutique 2-6.30pm Tue, 9am-noon & 2-6.30pm Wed-Sat, guided tours & demonstrations 2pm & 4pm Tue-Sat; ⓜCroix Rousse) Trimmings workshop that functioned until 1979, weaving braids and intricate pictures. You can browse fabrics in the attached boutique (admission free) any time of day, but to learn the history of the looms and see them at work it's well worth signing up for one of the half-hour afternoon tours.

Atelier de Tissage　　　SILK WORKSHOP
(cnr rue Godart and rue Lebrun, 4e; guided tour adult/child €5/3, combined ticket with Atelier de Passementerie €8/4; ⊙guided tours & demonstrations 3pm & 5pm Thu-Sat; ⓜCroix Rousse) Wonderful old workshop with looms that produce larger fabrics. Access is strictly by guided tour.

Mur des Canuts　　　MURAL
(cnr bd des Canuts & rue Denfert Rochereau, 4e; ⓜHénon) Silk-weaving traditions are illustrated by this fresco.

RIVE GAUCHE
The Rhône's Rive Gauche (Left Bank) harbours superb parks and museums and day-to-day Lyonnais amenities including its main university and transport hubs.

Parc de la Tête d'Or　　　PARK
(www.loisirs-parcdelatetedor.com; blvd des Belges, 6e; ⊙6am-11pm Apr-Sep, to 9pm Oct-Mar; ▣41, 47, ⓜMasséna) Spanning 117 hectares, France's largest urban park was landscaped in the 1860s. It has a lake (rent a row boat), botanic

RIVERSIDE REJUVENATION

The Rhône's Rive Gauche (Left Bank), once the domain of high-speed traffic and car parks, has been extensively redeveloped in the past decade to provide Lyon with fabulously landscaped walking, cycling and inline skating tracks, spanning 10 hectares over 5km of riverfront. Known as the Berges du Rhône, a path separates it from traffic along the upper level, while the lower level incorporates riverside woods, grassy fields and paved areas with tiered seating where locals lounge on sunny days. Starting upstream beneath the Winston Churchill bridge, it passes beneath nine more bridges, and runs past the popular péniches (barges) as it continues downstream to the Lyon Confluence (www.lyon-confluence.fr), where the Rhône and the Saône meet south of Gare de Perrache.

A former industrial wasteland, the Confluence has just emerged from the first stages of a multimillion-euro rejuvenation project. In April 2012 the Pôle de Commerces et de Loisirs Confluence (p463), an enormous complex, including shops, restaurants, movie theatres, a gym and a climbing wall, was officially opened to the public. Other noteworthy structures in the Confluence neighbourhood include the bizarre orange Swiss-cheese-like office building Le Cube Orange (you'll know it when you see it!), the converted sugar warehouse La Sucrerie, now used for art exhibits during the Biennale d'Art Contemporain (p455), the wavy-roofed eating space Rue Le Bec (p458), part of Lyonnais chef Nicolas Le Bec's expanding empire, and the 4-star Novotel Lyon Confluence (www.novotel.com), the first hotel to open in this part of the city.

The biggest attraction yet to come is the ambitious science-and-humanities museum, the Musée des Confluences (www.museedesconfluences.fr), to be housed in a futuristic steel-and-glass transparent crystal (estimated to open in summer 2014, about half a decade behind schedule). The Local d'Information du Musée des Confluences (✆04 78 37 30 00; 86 quai Perrache, 2e; admission free; ⊙1-6pm Wed-Sat, 10am-noon & 1-6pm Sun) offers sneak previews of its future collection on site.

Meanwhile, a new riverside beautification project, Les Rives de Saône (www.lesrives desaone.com), is spreading north along the Saône, with plans to develop an additional 50km of riverbank for recreational use. The first sections are slated to open as early as 2013 – stay tuned!

HÉLÈNE CARLESCHI

Animatrice de Patrimoine (Heritage Communications), Soierie Vivante

Job? The association formed to save the Atelier de Passementerie after Mme Letourneau, who wove here for 54 years, donated it and was furious when it was to be turned into private housing. Most of our volunteers are former textile workers; as a full-time employee I do everything from kids' workshops and guided tours to weaving demonstrations and maintaining the looms.

Best thing about working here? Preserving the area's history – there were once 50,000 silk-weaving workshops in Croix Rousse; I want to help people understand what's behind its architecture and its spirit today.

Life in Croix Rousse? Like a village, it's very sociable, especially the market and my favourite restaurant, Le Cinoche.

And the city as a whole? Lyon's full of culture, it's a really, really living city. Since I was a child, I've visited the crafts market. I like the theatres, drinks at the *péniches* (barges) by the Berges du Rhône and concerts at Transbordeur. I also lead tours at the Musée des Tissus.

Secret spot? The Jardin Public La Cerisaie in Croix Rousse has beautiful views over Lyon.

garden with greenhouses, rose garden, zoo and puppet theatre (☑04 78 93 71 75; www.theatre-guignol.com; Ⓜ Part-Dieu, then ☐41 or 47).

Musée d'Art Contemporain ART MUSEUM
(www.mac-lyon.com; 81 quai Charles de Gaulle, 6e; adult/child €8/free; ☺11am-6pm Wed-Fri, 10am-7pm Sat & Sun) Lyon's contemporary-art museum mounts edgy temporary exhibitions and a rotating permanent collection of post-1960 art. It closes for up to a couple of months between exhibitions, so check to make sure something's on.

Centre d'Histoire de la Résistance et de la Déportation MILITARY MUSEUM
(www.chrd.lyon.fr; 14 av Berthelot, 7e; adult/child €4/free; ☺9am-5.30pm Wed-Sun; ⓂPerrache or Jean Macé) The WWII headquarters of Gestapo commander Klaus Barbie evokes Lyon's role as the 'Capital of the Resistance' through moving multimedia exhibits. Reopened after extensive remodeling in November 2012, the museum's new sections include sound recordings of 30 deportees and Resistance fighters, plus a varied collection of everyday objects associated with the Resistance (including the parachute Jean Moulin used to re-enter France in 1942).

Musée Lumière FILM MUSEUM
(www.institut-lumiere.org; 25 rue du Premier Film, 8e; adult/child €6.50/5.50; ☺10am-6.30pm Tue-Sun; ⓂMonplaisir-Lumière) Cinema's glorious beginnings are showcased at the art nou-

veau home of Antoine Lumière, who moved to Lyon with sons Auguste and Louis in 1870. The brothers shot the first reels of the world's first motion picture, *La Sortie des Usines Lumières* (Exit of the Lumières Factories) here in one of their father's photographic factories in the grounds on 19 March 1895. The former factory is the Hangar du Premier Film cinema today.

Mur du Cinéma MURAL
(cnr cours Gambetta & Grande Rue de la Guillotière, 8e; ⓂGuillotière) Lyon's cinematic story is told in still-image form here in one of the city's many murals.

NORTHERN SUBURBS
Musée Henri Malarte TRANSPORT MUSEUM
(www.musee-malartre.com; 645 rue du Musée, Rochetaillée-sur-Saône; adult/child €6/free; ☺9am-6pm Tue-Sun; ☐40, 70) Jean-Paul II's Renault Espace, Hitler's Mercedes, 50-odd motorbikes, bicycles and historical modes of Lyonnais public transport are showcased inside this 15th-century château, 11km north of Lyon along the D433. Take bus number 40 or 70 to the Rochetaillée stop.

🏃 Activities

Rollerbladers (www.generationsroller.asso.fr) hook up on place Bellecour for a mass scoot around town every Friday at 8.30pm (12km, 1¼ hours) for those with less experience (though you'll need to know how to stop!), and 10pm for speed fiends (25km, 1½ hours).

LYON'S HIDDEN LABYRINTH

Deep within Vieux Lyon and Croix Rousse, dark, dingy *traboules* (secret passages) wind their way through apartment blocks, under streets and into courtyards. In all, 315 passages link 230 streets, with a combined length of 50km.

A couple of Vieux Lyon's *traboules* date from Roman times, but most were constructed by *canuts* (silk weavers) in the 19th century to transport silk in inclement weather. Resistance fighters found them equally handy during WWII.

Genuine *traboules* (derived from the Latin *trans ambulare*, meaning 'to pass through') cut from one street to another, often wending their way up fabulous spiral staircases en route. Passages that fan out into a courtyard or cul-de-sac aren't *traboules* but *miraboules* (two of the finest examples are at 16 rue Boeuf and 8 rue Juiverie, both in Vieux Lyon).

Vieux Lyon's most celebrated *traboules* include those connecting: 27 rue St-Jean with 6 rue des Trois Maries; 54 rue St-Jean with 27 rue du Bœuf (push the intercom button to buzz open the door); 10 quai Romain Rolland with 2 place du Gouvernement; 17 quai Romain Rolland with 9 rue des Trois Maries; and 31 rue du Bœuf with 14 rue de la Bombarde.

Step into Croix Rousse's underworld at 9 place Colbert, crossing cours des Voraces – renowned for its monumental staircase that zigzags up seven floors – and emerging at 29 rue Imbert Colomès. Others include those linking 1 place Colbert with 10 Montée St-Sébastien and 9 place Colbert with 14bis montée St-Sébastien; and the plethora of passages on rue des Capucins – at Nos 3, 6, 13, 22 and 23.

Lyon's tourist office has more information and includes *traboules* on many of its guided walking tours.

Tours

TOP CHOICE Walking Tours WALKING TOUR
(04 72 77 69 69; www.en.lyon-france.com/Visits-and-tours; adult/child €10/5) The tourist office organises a variety of excellent tours through Vieux Lyon and Croix Rousse with local English-speaking guides; several additional tours are available in French. Tours are free with a Lyon City Card; book in advance (online, by phone or in person at the tourist office).

Cyclopolitain CYCLE-TAXI
(info 04 78 30 35 90, reservations 06 80 60 58 04; http://lyon.cyclopolitain.com; 30-/60-/120-min tour 2 people €20/35/60; noon-7pm Tue-Fri, 10.30am-7pm Sat) Tiny and/or tired feet can rest aboard a cycle-taxi tour.

Navig'inter BOAT TOUR
(04 78 42 96 81; www.naviginter.fr; 13bis quai Rambaud, 2e; river excursions adult/child €9.50/6.50; river excursions 1 or 1¼ hr; Bellecour or Vieux Lyon) From April to October, runs river excursions from its dock (3 quai des Célestins, 2e; Bellecour or Vieux Lyon) along the Saône. One free excursion is included with the Lyon City Card. Advance bookings are essential for its lunch and dinner cruises (23 quai Claude Bernard, 7e; transport €20-26 plus menus €27-35; Ampère or Guillotière, T1), which leave from a separate dock on the Rhône.

Jogg'in City JOGGING TOUR
(06 62 67 91 30; www.joggincity.fr; 1hr tour per person for 1/2/3/4 or more people €70/40/30/25) Fast movers (aged over 18) can take in the sights along a 5km to 6km route.

Le Grand Tour BUS TOUR
(04 78 56 32 39; www.lyonlegrandtour.com; adult 1-/2-day ticket €18/20, child 1 or 2 days €5, Lyon by Night adult/child €15/5; 10am-6.15pm Apr-Oct, to 5.15pm Nov-Mar) Hop-on, hop-off double-decker bus tours. On Saturday evenings in July and August, a Lyon by Night tour is also offered at 10pm.

Festivals & Events

Nuits de Fourvière MUSIC FESTIVAL
(Fourvière Nights; www.nuitsdefourviere.fr) A diverse program of open-air concerts atmospherically set in Fourvière's Roman amphitheatre from early June to late July.

Biennale de la Danse DANCE FESTIVAL
(www.labiennaledelyon.com) Month-long dance biennial held between mid-September and early October in even-numbered years.

Biennale d'Art Contemporain ART FESTIVAL
(www.labiennaledelyon.com) Huge contemporary art biennial held from mid-September to December in odd-numbered years.

Fête des Lumières WINTER FESTIVAL
(Festival of Lights; www.lumieres.lyon.fr) Over several days around the Feast of the Immaculate Conception (8 December), sound-and-light shows are projected onto key buildings, while locals illuminate window sills with candles.

🛏 Sleeping

Lyon has a wealth of accommodation to suit every taste and budget.

VIEUX LYON

TOP
CHOICE **Cour des Loges** HOTEL €€€
(☎04 72 77 44 44; www.courdesloges.com; 2-8 rue du Bœuf, 5e; d/ste from €250/530; ✱@☎☀; Ⓜ Vieux Lyon) Four 14th- to 17th-century houses wrapped around a *traboule* (secret passage) with preserved features like Italianate loggias make this an exquisite place to stay. Individually designed rooms woo with Philippe Starck bathroom fittings and a bounty of antiques, while decadent facilities include a spa, an elegant restaurant (menus €75 to €95), swish cafe (mains €17 to €25) and cross-vaulted bar.

Apart'Observatoire St-Jean SELF-CONTAINED €€
(☎04 78 37 47 97; www.gite-de-charme-lyon.com; 70 rue St-Jean, 5e; 2-person apt per night €100-140, per week €490-560; ☎; Ⓜ Vieux Lyon) Smack in the heart of Vieux Lyon, Béatrice Breuilh rents out these two self-catering apartments offering a perfect mix of modern amenities and historic charm. Both have kitchen and laundry facilities, and the south-facing unit boasts full-on cathedral views. Lyon's attractions are all within walking distance or readily accessible from the metro/funicular stop 200m south. The sole disadvantage is a steep stair climb.

Artelit B&B €€
(☎04 78 42 84 83; www.dormiralyon.com; 16 rue du Bœuf, 5e; d €100-190, ste €130-250, apt €150-280; Ⓜ Vieux Lyon) Run by Lyonnais photographer Frédéric Jean, the two tower rooms and self-catering apartment of this *chambre d'hôte* (B&B) have centuries of history behind every nook and cranny. If you fall in love with the artworks, you can buy them to take home. Breakfast is included in the rate for doubles and suites. The apartment is also available for weekly rental at a substantial discount (€590 per week).

Auberge de Jeunesse du Vieux Lyon HOSTEL €
(☎04 78 15 05 50; www.fuaj.org/lyon; 41-45 montée du Chemin Neuf, 5e; dm incl breakfast €22; ☉reception 7am-1pm, 2-8pm & 9pm-1am; @☎; Ⓜ Vieux Lyon) Stunning city views unfold from the terrace of Lyon's only hostel, and from many of the (mostly six-bed) dorms. Bike parking, kitchen and laundry (wash-dry per load €4) facilities are available.

Hôtel St-Paul HOTEL €
(☎04 78 28 13 29; www.hotelstpaul.fr; 6 rue Lainerie, 5e; d €70-85; @☎; Ⓜ Vieux Lyon or Hôtel de Ville) This 20-room hotel with friendly staff is conveniently located on the edge of Vieux Lyon, and only a five-minute walk across the bridge from the Hôtel de Ville. Aim for one of the brighter street-facing rooms; back rooms off the staircase tend to be claustrophobic.

Collège Hotel HOTEL €€
(☎04 72 10 05 05; www.college-hotel.com; 5 place St-Paul, 5e; d €125-155; ✱@☎; Ⓜ Vieux Lyon or Hôtel de Ville) The ultrastark white-on-white minimalism of this hotel's guestrooms is quite startling (which is to say, not everyone will appreciate it). Enjoy breakfast on your balcony, on the rooftop garden terrace, or in the *salle de classe petit dejeuner*, bedecked like a classroom of yesteryear.

PRESQU'ÎLE

TOP
CHOICE **Jardin d'Hiver** B&B €€
(☎04 78 28 69 34; www.guesthouse-lyon.com; 10 rue des Marronniers, 2e; s/d €120/140, 1-/2-bedroom apt per week from €500/550; ✱☎; Ⓜ Bellecour) This chic 3rd-floor B&B (no lift) has just two en suite rooms – one in understated purple and pistachio, and the other in

---

LYON SLEEPS

The tourist-office-run reservation office (☎04 72 77 72 50; resa@lyon-france.com) offers a free booking service and good-value package deals.

Slowly but stylishly, *chambres d'hôte* (B&Bs) are making headway; umbrella organisations include B&B Lyon (☎04 72 32 02 74; www.bb-lyon.com), Chambres Lyon (☎04 72 13 99 35; www.chambreslyon.com) and Gîtes de France (☎04 72 77 17 50; www.gites-de-france-rhone.com).

Many hotels offer cheaper rates at weekends.

much more vivid purple and orange – along with a foliage-filled breakfast room. A pair of apartments with kitchen and laundry facilities are also available.

Hôtel des Célestins
HOTEL €€

(☎04 72 56 08 98; www.hotelcelestins.com; 4 rue des Archers, 2e; s €82-133, d €92-143, ste €174-194; ✳☎; MBellecour) This cosy hotel is surrounded by designer boutiques. The priciest rooms have gorgeous views of the theatre, the cheaper ones face a quiet courtyard.

Le Royal
HOTEL €€€

(☎04 78 37 57 31; www.lyonhotel-leroyal.com; 20 place Bellecour, 2e; d €200-390; ✳☎☎; MBellecour) In business since 1895, this timeless visiting card offers Lyon's ultimate in luxury, enveloping you in its stylish *salons* (lounges) and exquisite fabrics and furnishings. Rates vary wildly depending on dates and availability.

Hôtel Le Boulevardier
HOTEL €

(☎04 78 28 48 22; www.leboulevardier.fr; 5 rue de la Fromagerie, 1er; s €47-56, d €49-59; ☎; MHôtel de Ville or Cordeliers) Newly refurbished and sporting quirky touches like old skis and tennis racquets adorning the hallways, Le Boulevardier is a bargain 11-room hotel with snug, spotless rooms. It's up a steep spiral staircase above a cool little bistro and jazz club of the same name, which doubles as reception.

Hôtel de Paris
HOTEL €€

(☎04 78 28 00 95; www.hoteldeparis-lyon.com; 16 rue de la Platière, 1er; s €52-92, d €64-135; ✳☎☎; MHôtel de Ville) This centrally located, newly remodeled hotel in a 19th-century bourgeois building features bright decor and theme rooms with artsy designs. Some have a funky, retro '70s feel, incorporating a palette of chocolate and turquoise or candyfloss pink.

Hôtel Iris
HOTEL €

(☎04 78 39 93 80; www.hoteliris.fr; 36 rue de l'Arbre Sec, 1er; s €60-79, d €65-86; @; MHôtel de Ville) This basic but colourful dame in a centuries-old convent couldn't be better placed: its street brims with hip places to eat and drink.

Hôtel de la Marne
HOTEL €

(☎04 78 37 07 46; www.hoteldelamarne.fr; 78 rue de la Charité, 2e; s €57-63, d €63-69; MGare de Perrache) Some of the 23 rooms at this stylishly renovated hotel – incorporating smart colour schemes such as chocolate and cherry – open onto a sky-topped courtyard. Wheelchair access is available.

CROIX ROUSSE

Lyon Guesthouse
B&B €€

(☎04 78 30 54 75; www.lyonguesthouse.com; 12 rue de Crimée, 1er; d €100; ☎; MCroix Rousse) Perched on the *pentes*, this B&B with prime views of Fourvière is the creation of art collector and gallery owner Françoise Besson. Its three rooms are modern and minimalist, breakfast is a wholly organic affair, and the gallery's collection hangs on the crisp white walls.

Nos Chambres en Ville
B&B €€

(☎04 78 27 22 30; www.chambres-a-lyon.com; 12 rue René Leynaud, 1er; s/d €70/85; MCroix Paquet or Hôtel de Ville) With an enviable location between Croix Rousse and the Hôtel de Ville, the three rooms in this 18th-century home come with stone walls, exposed wood beams and a nice breakfast. Cash only.

RIVE GAUCHE

Péniche Barnum
B&B €€

(☎06 63 64 37 39; www.peniche-barnum.com; 3 quai du Général Sarrail, 6e; d €120-150; ✳☎; MFoch) Moored on the Rhône between Pont Morand and the Passerelle du Collège footbridge, Lyon's most unique B&B is this navy-and-timber barge with two smart en suite guestrooms, a book-filled lounge, and a shaded terrace up on deck. Organic breakfasts cost €10.

NORTHERN SUBURBS

Camping Indigo Lyon
CAMPGROUND €

(☎04 78 35 64 55; www.camping-indigo.com; Porte de Lyon; sites €17.55-19.90, 5-person chalets €41-61, mobile homes €41-106; @✳) Open year-round, this leafy campground is founded on strict environmental respect. Wooden chalets beneath the trees sleep five, while mobile homes sleep two to six. Family fun includes outdoor and kids' paddling pools, a playground, ping pong and volleyball. The campground is 13km northwest of Lyon, off the A6.

✗ Eating

A flurry of big-name chefs presides over a sparkling restaurant line-up that embraces all genres: French, fusion, fast and international, as well as traditional Lyonnais *bouchons* (see box p457). The website www.lyonresto.com has reviews, videos and ratings.

Many restaurants offer cheaper lunch *menus* (fixed-price meals) on weekdays only.

VIEUX LYON

A surfeit of restaurants, most aimed squarely at tourists, jam the streets of Vieux Lyon.

Les Adrets LYONNAIS €€

(☎04 78 38 24 30; 30 rue du Boeuf, 5e; lunch menu €15.50, dinner menus €23-45; ☺lunch & dinner Mon-Fri; ⓜVieux Lyon) This atmospheric spot on a popular pedestrian thoroughfare serves some of Vieux Lyon's best food any time of day; the lunch *menus* (including wine and coffee) are especially good value at €15.50. The mix is half classic *bouchon* fare, half alternative choices like Parma ham and truffle risotto, or duck breast with roasted pears.

Aux Trois Maries BOUCHON €€

(☎04 78 37 67 28; aux-3-maries.fr; 1 rue des Trois Maries, 5e; menus €22-44; ☺lunch & dinner Tue-Sat, closed Aug; ⓜVieux Lyon) Opening to a table-filled square, this venerable *bouchon* doesn't shy away from traditional dishes like *tête de veau* (jellied calf's head). The chefs also offer dishes including gazpacho, lamb shank with fresh mint or local ravioli with morel mushrooms. Midday *plats du jour* (dishes of the day) are good value at €9.90.

Le Tire Bouchon BOUCHON €€

(☎04 78 37 69 95; 16 rue du Boeuf, 5e; menus €20-25; ☺dinner Tue-Sat; ⓜVieux Lyon) Serving a full range of Lyonnais and French classics

---

BOUCHONS

A *bouchon* might be a 'bottle stopper' or 'traffic jam' elsewhere in France, but in Lyon it's a small, friendly bistro that cooks up traditional city cuisine using regional produce. *Bouchons* originated in the first half of the 20th century when many large bourgeois families had to let go of their in-house cooks, who then set up their own restaurant businesses. The first of these *mères* (mothers) was Mère Guy, followed by Mère Filloux, Mère Brazier (under whom Paul Bocuse trained) and others. Choose carefully – not all *bouchons* are as authentic as they first appear. Many that are have certification with the organisation *Les Authentiques Bouchons Lyonnais* – look for the metal plate on their façades depicting traditional puppet Gnafron (Guignol's mate) with his glass of Beaujolais.

Kick-start a memorable gastronomic experience with a *communard*, an aperitif of red Beaujolais wine and *crème de cassis* (blackcurrant liqueur), named after the supporters of the Paris Commune killed in 1871. Blood red in colour, the mix is considered criminal elsewhere in France. When ordering wine, simply ask for a *pot* – a 46cL glass bottle adorned with an elastic band to prevent wine drips – of local Brouilly, Beaujolais, Côtes du Rhône or Mâcon, costing around €10 to €12; a 25cL version called a *fillette* costs around €6 to €7.

Next comes the entrée, perhaps *tablier de sapeur* ('fireman's apron'; actually meaning breaded, fried tripe), *salade de cervelas* (salad of boiled pork sausage sometimes studded with pistachio nuts or black truffle specks) or *caviar de la Croix Rousse* (lentils in creamy sauce). Hearty main dishes include *boudin blanc* (veal sausage), *boudin noir aux pommes* (blood sausage with apples), *quenelles* (feather-light flour, egg and cream dumplings), *quenelles de brochet* (pike dumplings served in a creamy crayfish sauce), *andouillette* (sausage made from pigs' intestines), *gras double* (a type of tripe) and *pieds de mouton/veau/couchon* (sheep/calf/pig trotters).

The cheese course usually comprises a choice of three things: a bowl of *fromage blanc* (a cross between cream cheese and natural yoghurt) with or without thick whipped cream; *cervelle de canut* ('brains of the silk weaver'; *fromage blanc* mixed with chives and garlic, which originated in Croix Rousse and accompanied every meal for 19th-century weavers); or local St Marcellin ripened to gooey perfection.

Desserts are grandma-style: think *tarte aux pommes* (apple tart) or *fromage blanc* (again) with a fruit coulis dribbled on top.

Recently a new generation of *bouchon*-inspired establishments has started to emerge, putting a lighter, contemporary twist on the traditionally rustic decor and rich cuisine.

Little etiquette is required in *bouchons*. Seldom do you get clean cutlery for each course and mopping your plate with a chunk of bread is fine. In the most popular and traditional spots, you can expect to sit elbow to elbow with your fellow diners, often at a long row of tables wedged side by side (a great way to meet locals and practice your French!). Most *bouchons* serve lunch strictly from noon to 2pm (turn up early if you want a full menu) and don't accept diners after 9.30pm; advance reservations are recommended.

(*andouillette* sausage, quenelles, frogs' legs and foie gras), this iconic *bouchon* has a snug upstairs dining area tucked under the art nouveau lettering of its pretty wine-coloured façade.

FOURVIÈRE

Le Restaurant de Fourvière   LYONNAIS €€
(☎04 78 25 21 15; www.latassee.fr; 9 place de Fourvière, 5e; lunch menus €16, dinner menus €26-36; ☺lunch & dinner daily; funicular station Fourvière) The views are so incredible that it'd be easy for this superbly located restaurant to be a tourist trap, so it's all the more impressive because it's not. Instead it concentrates on well-prepared local specialities including a superb *salade lyonnaise* (lettuce, bacon, poached egg and croutons).

PRESQU'ÎLE

Cobbled rue Mercière, rue des Marronniers and the northern side of place Antonin Poncet – both in the 2e (metro Bellecour) – are chock-a-block with eating options (of widely varying quality), overflowing with pavement terraces in summer. Near the opera house, rue Verdi (1er) is likewise table filled.

TOP CHOICE Le Bouchon des Filles   LYONNAIS €€
(☎04 78 30 40 44; 20 rue Sergent Blandan, 1er; menus €25; ☺dinner daily, lunch Sun; Ⓜ Hôtel de Ville) This contemporary ode to Lyon's legendary culinary *mères* (mother) is run by an enterprising crew of young women with deep roots in the local *bouchon* scene and a flair for fine cooking. The light and fluffy quenelles are among the best you'll find in Lyon, and the rustic atmosphere is warm and welcoming, especially on Sundays when families flock in for lunch.

Le Bistrot du Potager   TAPAS €
(☎04 78 29 61 59; www.lebistrotdupotager.com; 3 rue de la Martinière, 1er; tapas €5-12; ☺lunch & dinner Tue-Sat; Ⓜ Hôtel de Ville) A newly hatched offshoot of the renowned Potager des Halles restaurant next door, this corner tapas bar is a dreamy place to while away a warm spring or summer evening. Throngs of happy diners linger over glasses of wine, sampling Provençal duck carpaccio, grilled vegetables with pistou, stuffed artichokes, octopus salad, Tunisian-style chickpeas and platters of cheeses and charcuterie.

Rue Le Bec   MODERN FRENCH €€
(☎04 78 92 87 87; www.nicolaslebec.com; 43 quai Rambaud, 2e; lunch/dinner menus €18/32, brunch adult/child €50/25 ; ☺lunch & dinner Tue-Sat, brunch 11am-3pm Sun; ☒1, Montrochet stop) Opened in 2009 by Lyon's acclaimed chef Nicolas Le Bec, this was one of the first commercial ventures in the Confluence district. The airy and innovative concept space comprises a covered-market-like layout of shops and eateries (florist, cheese shop, delicatessen, bakery and more) ranged around a tree-filled central 'street'. Sunday brunch here is a family affair: for the kids, there are games and a crêpe stand; for the grown-ups, champagne, wine and an unlimited buffet of gourmet dishes, including cheeses, pastries and desserts. (Oh, and did we forget to mention the riverside garden space with fountains and hammocks for lounging when you're done?)

Café des Fédérations   BOUCHON €€
(☎04 78 28 26 00; www.lesfedeslyon.com; 8-10 rue Major Martin, 1er; lunch/dinner menus €19/25; ☺lunch & dinner Mon-Sat; Ⓜ Hôtel de Ville) Black-and-white photos of old Lyon hang on wood-panelled walls at this Lyonnais bistro, unchanged for decades. From the vast array of appetizers – lentils in mustardy sauce, slices of *rosette de Lyon* sausage, pickles, beets and more – clear through to a classic *baba au rhum* for dessert, this is *bouchon* dining at its finest.

Brasserie Léon de Lyon   BRASSERIE €€
(☎04 72 10 11 12; www.bistrotsdecuisiniers.com; 1 rue Pléney, 1er; menus €20.30-34.90; ☺lunch & dinner daily; Ⓜ Hôtel de Ville) Renowned Lyonnais chef Jean-Paul Lacombe has turned his Michelin-starred gastronomic restaurant into a relaxed brasserie – same 1904 decor, same impeccable service, more affordable prices (the €14.90 *plat du jour* is an excellent deal).

Thomas   FRENCH €€
(☎04 72 56 04 76; www.restaurant-thomas.com; 6 rue Laurencin, 2e; lunch/dinner menus €18/43; ☺lunch & dinner Mon-Fri; Ⓜ Ampère) Ingenious chef Thomas Ponson gives taste buds the choice between formal dining at his eponymous restaurant, more casual fare in his à la carte wine bar, Comptoir Thomas (☎04 72 41 92 99; 3 rue Laurencin; mains for 2 people €21-35; ☺lunch & dinner Mon-Fri), and more casual still at his tapas-inspired Café Thomas (1 rue Laurencin; plat du jour €9, lunch menu €15; ☺lunch & dinner Tue-Sat). His newest venture is the Italian-themed La Cantinetta (☎04 72 60 94 53; 3 rue Laurencin; ☺lunch & dinner Mon-Fri), opened in 2012.

Magali et Martin
LYONNAIS €€

(📞04 72 00 88 01; www.magalietmartin.fr; 11 rue Augustins, 1er; lunch menus €19.50-23, dinner menus €29-35; ⊙lunch & dinner Mon-Fri; Ⓜ️Hôtel de Ville) Watch chefs turn out traditional but lighter, more varied *bouchon*-influenced cuisine, at this sharp dining address.

Boulangerie Pozzoli
BOULANGERIE €

(www.boulangerie-pozzoli.com; 18 Rue Ferrandière, 2e; ⊙7am-8pm Mon-Fri, to 7pm Sat; Ⓜ️Cordeliers) The kind of place foreigners dream of when they hear the words 'French bakery', François Pozzoli's swoon-worthy establishment has been firing up gorgeous breads for decades – from straightforward baguettes to hearty wholegrain loaves studded with nuts and raisins or figs and honey.

Brasserie Georges
BRASSERIE €€

(📞04 72 56 54 54; www.brasseriegeorges.com; 30 cours de Verdun, 2e; menus €19.75-25.50; ⊙11.30am-11.15pm Sun-Thu, 11am-midnight Fri & Sat; Ⓜ️Perrache) Opened as a brewery in 1836 and still in the business (with four brews on tap), Georges' enormous 1924 art deco interior can feed 2000 a day! Famous customers include Rodin, Balzac, Hemingway, Zola, Jules Verne and Piaf; food spans onion soup, sauerkraut, seafood and Lyonnais specialities.

Grand Café des Négociants
BRASSERIE €€

(www.cafe-des-negociants.com; 1 place Francisque Regaud, 2e; breakfast €9, menus €19.90-34; ⊙7am-4am; Ⓜ️Cordeliers) This cafe-style brasserie with mirror-lined walls and tree-shaded terrace has been a favourite meeting point with Lyonnais since 1864. With nonstop service day and night, it makes a classy, convenient spot for breakfast or an afternoon snack (don't miss its thick hot chocolate – cheaper before noon).

La Mère Jean
BOUCHON €€

(📞04 78 37 81 27; 5 rue des Marronniers, 2e; lunch menus €11.50, other menus €15.50-32; ⊙lunch & dinner Tue-Sat; Ⓜ️Bellecour) Its windows plastered with guidebook plaudits, but its tables still packed with loyal locals, this thimble-sized *bouchon* dates back to 1923 and rewards booking ahead for its meat-loaded menu.

L'Épicerie
BISTRO €

(📞04 78 37 70 85; 2 rue de la Monnaie, 2e; tartines €3.80-6.30; ⊙noon-midnight; 🖉🚻; Ⓜ️Cordeliers) Done out like an early-20th-century grocer's, with distressed cupboards full of china and old boxes and canisters, this place serves thick-sliced *tartines* (open-faced sandwiches) with toppings like brie, walnut and honey and delicious desserts like pear-chocolate tart. There's a handful of other branches in Lyon and beyond.

Chez Paul
BOUCHON €€

(📞04 78 28 35 83; www.chezpaul.fr; 11 rue Major Martin, 1er; daily specials €13.50, lunch/dinner menus €19/25; ⊙lunch & dinner Mon-Sat; Ⓜ️Hôtel de Ville) Self-taught Lyonnaise *mère*, Josiane, takes pride that 'people come to eat as if at home or at their parents' house'. Translation: the menu at this iconic *bouchon* is heavily focused on animal parts that may make some squeamish; specialities include a creamier-than-usual *tablier de sapeur* (breaded, fried tripe).

Chez Georges
BOUCHON €€

(📞04 78 28 30 46; 8 rue du Garet, 1er; menus €18-30; ⊙lunch Mon-Fri, dinner Mon-Sat; Ⓜ️Hôtel de Ville) The decor of lace curtains and sepia-toned lighting in this respected *bouchon* retains an intimate ambience. The lunch *menus* and à

LYON FOOD MARKETS

Food shopping in Lyon is an unmissable part of the city's experience. And with so many urban spaces and parks, there are plenty of picnic spots too.

Lyon's famed indoor food market **Les Halles de Lyon** (http://halledelyon.free.fr; 102 cours Lafayette, 3e; ⊙8am-7pm Tue-Sat, to 1pm Sun; Ⓜ️Part-Dieu) has over 60 stalls selling their renowned wares. Pick up a round of impossibly runny St Marcellin from legendary cheesemonger Mère Richard, and a knobbly Jésus de Lyon from pork butcher Collette Sibilia. Or enjoy a sit-down lunch of local produce at the stalls, lip-smacking *coquillages* (shellfish) included.

Lyon has two main outdoor food markets: **Croix Rousse** (bd de la Croix Rousse, 1er; ⊙Tue-Sun morning; Ⓜ️Croix Rousse) and **Presqu'île** (quai St-Antoine, 1er; ⊙Tue-Sun morning; Ⓜ️Bellecour or Cordeliers). If you'd rather have it brought to you, fruit-and-veg service **Potager City** (www.potagercity.fr) shops at markets and delivers by bicycle throughout central Lyon.

la carte dinner choices are likewise tried-and-true to local traditions.

Giraudet
LYONNAIS €

(☎04 72 77 98 58; www.giraudet.fr; 2 rue Colonel Chambonnet, 2e; menus €11-14; ⏱11am-7pm Mon, 9am-7pm Tue-Sat; ✍; Ⓜ Bellecour) Sleek quenelle boutique with seating area to taste the Lyonnais speciality along with homemade soups. There's another branch at Les Halles de Lyon.

CROIX ROUSSE
From December to April, Croix Rousse café life revolves around oyster-and-white-wine breakfasts, with the oysters shucked outdoors on crisp sunny mornings.

TOP CHOICE Le Canut et Les Gones
BISTRO €€

(☎04 78 29 17 23; http://lecanutetlesgones.com; 29 rue de Belfort, 4e; plat du jour €10, lunch menus €14-22, dinner menus €24-26; ⏱lunch & dinner Tue-Sat; Ⓜ Croix Rousse) The first seductions at this neighbourhood bistro are the relaxed atmosphere and funky retro decor (the walls are covered with antique clocks, none of them set to the correct time), but that's just a warm-up for the culinary delights to come. Chef Kazuhito Uchimura draws a savvy local crowd with his creative cuisine built around produce from Croix Rousse's market. From appetisers like Charolais beef with asparagus tips and red curry to the delectable homemade mint, lime and ginger digestif, this is food worth lingering over.

L'Ourson qui Boit
FUSION €€

(☎04 78 27 23 37; 23 rue Royale, 1er; lunch/dinner menus €17/25; ⏱lunch & dinner Mon, Tue & Thu-Sat; Ⓜ Croix Paquet) On the fringes of Croix Rousse, Japanese chef Akira Nishigaki puts his own splendid spin on French cuisine, with plenty of locally sourced fresh vegetables and light, clean flavours (a dash of ginger here, a grapefruit sorbet at dessert time). The ever-changing menu of two daily entrées and two main dishes is complemented by good wines, delicious bread and superb service. Well worth reserving ahead.

Mère Brazier
LYONNAIS €€€

(☎04 78 23 17 20; www.lamerebrazier.fr; 12 rue Royale, 1er; lunch menus €41-45, dinner menus €67-130; ⏱lunch & dinner Mon-Fri, closed 3 weeks Aug & 1 week Feb; Ⓜ Croix Paquet or Hôtel de Ville) Chef Mathieu Vianney has reinvented the mythical early-20th-century restaurant that earned Mère (Eugénie) Brazier Lyon's first trio of Michelin stars in 1933 (a copy of the original guidebook takes pride of place). Brazier was also the first-ever chef to earn two sets of three Michelin stars, a feat only equalled decades later by Alain Ducasse. Vianney is doing admirable justice to Brazier's legacy, claiming two Michelin stars himself for his assured cuisine accompanied by an impressive wine list.

Café Cousu
CAFE €

(☎04 72 98 83 38; www.cafe-cousu.com; Passage Thiaffait, 19 rue René Leynaud, 1er; breakfast €4.50, lunch menus €8.50-11, weekend brunch €8-13; ⏱9am-9pm Tue & Wed, 9am-11pm Thu & Fri, 11am-9pm Sat, 11am-6pm Sun; 🌐✍; Ⓜ Croix Paquet) Wedged between fashion designers in Le Village des Createurs, this hole in the wall entices an arty crowd with its battery-charging breakfasts, healthy lunches and homemade tarts and cakes, as well as its buzzing weekend brunch from 11am until 6pm.

Le Cinoche
CRÊPERIE €

(☎04 72 07 06 99; 7 rue Dumenge, 4e; crêpes from €4, galettes from €9; ⏱lunch & dinner Tue-Sat; ✍; Ⓜ Croix Rousse) Reflecting Lyon's cinema heritage with its old projectors, reels, lights, books and posters, this cosy crêperie specialises in savoury galettes and sweet crêpes named after famous films, such as *Orange Mécanique* (Clockwork Orange), with orange, melted chocolate and vodka-infused Chantilly.

Toutes les Couleurs
VEGETARIAN €€

(☎04 72 00 03 95; www.touteslescouleurs.fr; 26 rue Imbert Colomès, 1er; lunch menus €12.90-18.90, dinner menus €19-30; ⏱lunch Tue-Sat, dinner Fri & Sat; ✍; Ⓜ Croix-Paquet) Lyon's dining scene tends to overlook vegetarians, but its saving grace is this exclusively vegetarian *restaurant bio*, the seasonal menu of which includes *végétalien* (vegan) and gluten-free options. No cow's milk here – only soy, almond or rice.

NORTHERN SUBURBS

TOP CHOICE L'Auberge du Pont de Collonges
FRENCH €€€

(☎04 72 42 90 90; www.bocuse.com; 40 quai de la Plage; menus €145-230; ⏱lunch & dinner daily by reservation) Heading some 6.5km north of central Lyon via quai Georges Clemenceau brings you to this triple-Michelin-starred restaurant of the city's most decorated chef, Paul Bocuse. Classics include the likes of sea bass stuffed with lobster mousse in a puff-pastry shell, and thyme-roasted rack of lamb, as well as Bocuse's signature *soupe*

VGE (truffle soup created for former French president Valéry Giscard d'Estaing in 1975).

🍷 Drinking & Entertainment

Many establishments start as a relaxed place for a drink (and often food too), morphing into jam-packed bars and/or live-music and dancing venues as the night wears on.

VIEUX LYON

Cities the world over have British and Irish pubs, but even by those standards Vieux Lyon has an extraordinary concentration, patronised by expats, visitors and local Lyonnais alike. Firm favourites open daily until at least 1am include the bookshelf-lined Smoking Dog (www.smoking-dog.com; 16 rue Lainerie, 5e; ⊙5pm-1am Mon-Fri, 2pm-1am Sat & Sun; MVieux Lyon) in St Paul; the social James Joyce (68 rue St-Jean, 5e; ⊙daily; MVieux Lyon), and home-from-home St-James (19 rue St-Jean, 5e; ⊙daily; MVieux Lyon) in St-Jean.

Further south in St-Georges, good bets are Johnny's Kitchen (http://johnnyskitchen.fr; 48 rue St-Georges, 5e; ⊙daily; MVieux Lyon) and its sister bar Johnny Walsh's (www.johnnywalshs.com; 56 rue St-Georges, 5e; ⊙Tue-Sun; 🗢; MVieux Lyon), both with frequent live music, and, somewhat off the beaten track, the atmospheric L'Antidote (www.antidote-pub.com; 108 rue St-Georges, 5e; ⊙daily; MVieux Lyon).

If you're still going past closing time, late-night bars open until the *wee* hours are scattered throughout Vieux Lyon – just follow the crowds.

(L'A)Kroche — LIVE MUSIC

(www.lakroche.fr; 8 rue Monseigneur Lavarenne, 5e; ⊙11am-1am Tue-Sat, 3-9pm Sun & Mon; MVieux Lyon) Hip concert cafe-bar with DJs spinning electro, soul, funk and disco; bands too.

PRESQU'ÎLE

Le Wine Bar d'à Côté — WINE BAR

(www.cave-vin-lyon.com; 7 rue Pleney, 1er; ⊙Mon-Sat; MCordeliers) Hidden in a tiny alleyway, this cultured wine bar feels like a rustic English gentlemen's club with leather sofa seating and library. It also doubles as a wine shop, selling local vintages in every size bottle imaginable.

Harmonie des Vins — WINE BAR

(www.harmoniedesvins.fr; 9 rue Neuve, 1er; ⊙10am-2.30pm & 6.30pm-1am Tue-Sat; MHôtel de Ville, Cordeliers) Find out all about French wine at this charm-laden wine bar replete with old stone walls, contemporary furnishings, strong coffee and tasty food.

GUIGNOL: LYON'S HISTORIC PUPPET

The history of Lyon's famous puppet, Guignol, is intertwined with that of the city. In 1797 out-of-work silk-weaver Laurent Mourguet took up dentistry (ie pulling teeth). To attract patients, he set up a puppet show in front of his chair, initially featuring the Italian Polichinelle (who became Punch in England). Success saw Mourguet move into full-time puppetry, creating Guignol in about 1808 and devising shows revolving around working-class issues, the news of the day, social gossip and satire.

Today this little hand-operated glove puppet pops up all over his home town, including on the Fresque des Lyonnais (p451) mural and at puppet museums.

Guignol's highly visual, slapstick-style antics appeal equally to children and adults (theatres also stage some adult-only evening performances). Shows are in French but also incorporate traditional Lyonnais dialect, such as the words *quinquets* (eyes), *picou* (nose), *bajafler* (talking nonstop) and *gones* (kids, and, by extension, all Lyonnais).

In addition to performances at Parc de la Tête d'Or (p452), Lyon has three dedicated Guignol theatres:

Théâtre La Maison de Guignol (☑04 72 40 26 61; www.lamaisondeguignol.fr; 2 montée du Gourguillon, 5e; tickets adult €9.80-15, under 17yr €7.80-12; MVieux Lyon) Quaint St-Georges theatre.

Guignol, un Gone de Lyon (☑04 72 32 11 55; www.guignol-un-gone-de-lyon.com; 65 bd des Canuts, 4e; ⊙Oct-Jun; MHénon) In Croix Rousse.

Théâtre Le Guignol de Lyon (☑04 78 28 92 57; www.guignol-lyon.com; 2 rue Louis Carrand, 5e; tickets adult/under 15yr €10/€7.50; MVieux Lyon) Puppeteers give audiences a behind-the-scenes peek at the props and puppets after certain performances (check ahead for schedules).

More info on Guignol is available at http://amisdeguignol.free.fr.

Le Voxx   BAR
(1 rue d'Algérie, 1er; ☺10am-3am daily; ⓂHôtel
de Ville) Minimalist but lively riverside bar
packed with a real mix of people, from students to city slickers.

Soda Bar   BAR
(http://soda-bar.noziris.com; 7 rue de la Martinière,
1er; ☺Tue-Sat, closed mid-Jul–mid-Aug; ⓂHôtel de
Ville) Spirited bar staff juggle bottles while
mixing cocktails (called 'flair bartending',
apparently).

Café 203   BAR €
(☎04 78 28 66 65; 9 rue du Garet, 1er; ☺7am-2am
Mon-Sat, noon-1am Sun; ⓂHôtel de Ville) This corner bar with a youthful clientele gets especially buzzy at aperitif time and during the
wee hours.

La Fée Verte   CAFE-BAR
(4 rue Pizay, 1er; ☺hours vary; 🖘; ⓂHôtel de Ville)
You guessed it, the green-bedecked Green
Fairy specialises in devilish old absinthe.
There's usually electro and hip hop a couple
of nights a week.

Comptoir de la Bourse   BAR
(www.comptoirdelabourse.fr; 33 rue de la Bourse,
2e; ☺Mon-Sat; ⓂCordeliers) With lounge decor
just as colourful as its potent fruity drinks,
this bar is *très* trendy.

FREE **Péristyle**   LIVE MUSIC
(Programme Jazz de l'Opéra de Lyon; www.opera
-lyon.com/amphiopera/peristyle; Place de la
Comédie, 1er; free; ☺7-11pm Mon-Sat mid-Jun-early
Sep; ⓂHôtel de Ville) This seasonal cafe springs
up under the arches of the Opéra de Lyon
every summer, with free live performances
ranging from swing to blues and funk to
jazz. Hour-long sets start at 7pm, 8.15pm and

10pm, and waiters circulate with drinks as
the music plays; arrive early to snag a table.

Hot Club de Lyon   LIVE MUSIC
(www.hotclubjazz.com; 26 rue Lanterne, 1er; ☺Tue-
Sat; ⓂHôtel de Ville) Lyon's leading jazz club,
around since 1948.

Opéra de Lyon   OPERA HOUSE
(www.opera-lyon.com; place de la Comédie, 1er;
ⓂHôtel de Ville) Premier venue for opera, ballet and classical music.

CNP-Terreaux   CINEMA
(http://ter.cine.allocine.fr; 40 rue du Président Édouard Herriot, 1er; ⓂHôtel de Ville) Screens nondubbed films.

CROIX ROUSSE
Scout out alternative Croix Rousse to find
off-beat bars.

Modernartcafé   BAR
(www.modernartcafe.net; 65 bd de la Croix Rousse,
4e; ☺noon-2pm & 5pm-2am Sun-Fri, 5pm-2am Sat;
🖘; ⓂCroix Rousse) Retro furnishings, changing art on the walls, weekend brunch and
various photography-, music- and video-
driven events make this art bar a linchpin of
Croix Rousse's creative community.

La Bistro fait sa Broc'   BAR
(1-3 rue Dumenge, 4e; ☺Mon-Sat; ⓂCroix Rousse)
A lime-green and candyfloss-pink façade
greets you at this retro wine bar where no
two chairs match. Occasional bands.

Le Club Théâtre   PERFORMING ARTS
(www.thearte.fr; 4 impasse Flesselles, 1er; annual
membership fee €2; ⓂCroix Rousse) Ultrahip
and utterly unique, this cross between a
bar, nightclub and cultural centre opened
its doors in February 2012 in Croix Rousse's
former neighborhood wash house. The big

GAY & LESBIAN LYON

This gay-friendly city has scads of venues. Free publications listing current hot spots are
available from the Forum Gai et Lesbien de Lyon (☎04 78 39 97 72; www.fgllyon.org;
17 rue Romarin, 1er; ⓂCroix Paquet) and ARIS (Accueil Rencontres Informations Service; ☎04
78 27 10 10; www.aris-lyon.org; 19 rue des Capucins, 1er; ⓂHôtel de Ville or Croix Paquet), which
both organise social events.

Guys' favourite places to party include United Café (impasse de la Pêcherie, 1er; ☺daily;
ⓂHôtel de Ville) and the bear bar Station B (http://stationb.fr; 21 place Gabriel Rambaud, 1er;
☺Wed-Sun; ⓂHôtel de Ville), while gals congregate at lesbian Le Domaine Bar (http://le
domainebar.fr; 9 rue du Jardin des Plantes, 1er; ☺daily; ⓂHôtel de Ville, Croix Paquet).

Lyon's Lesbian and Gay Pride (www.fierte.net) march and festivities hit the streets
each year in June.

Online, www.lyongay.net has the low-down on Lyon's scene.

central wash basin doubles as a stage and a dance floor during events that range from book readings to 'new technology' nights, from writing and fine-arts workshops to film screenings and live music.

Le Bec de Jazz   LIVE MUSIC
(19 rue Burdeau, 1er; ⊙Wed-Sat; MCroix Paquet) Ubercool late-night jazz club, presided over by Beninese pianist Tchangodei.

RIVE GAUCHE
In the hip Gare de Brotteaux quarter, start clubbing at ApériKlub (www.first-aperiklub. com; 13-14 place Jules Ferry, 6e; ⊙Wed-Sat; MBrotteaux) and end at adjacent First Revolution (www.first-aperiklub.com; 13-14 place Jules Ferry, 6e; ⊙Wed-Sat; MBrotteaux). Dress sharp for both.

Along the Rhône's left bank, a string of *péniches* (barges) with on-board bars rock until around 3am. Depending on the season you'll find upwards of a dozen moored along quai Victor Augagneur between Pont Lafayette in the north and Pont de la Guillotière in the south. Many have DJs and/ or live bands. Our favourites include the laid-back Passagère (21 quai Victor Augagneur, 3e; ⊙daily; MPlace Guichard - Bourse du Travail), party-hard Le Sirius (www.lesirius.com; 4 quai Victor Augagneur, 3e; ⊙daily; ☎; MPlace Guichard - Bourse du Travail) and electro-oriented La Marquise (www.marquise.net; 20 quai Victor Augagneur, 3e; ⊙Tue-Sun; MPlace Guichard - Bourse du Travail).

Ninkasi Gerland   LIVE MUSIC
(www.ninkasi.fr; 267 rue Marcel Mérieux, 7e; ⊙10am-late; MStade de Gerland) Spilling over with a fun, frenetic crowd, this microbrewery near Lyon's football stadium is one of several Ninkasi addresses around town. Entertainment ranges from DJs and bands to film projections amid a backdrop of fish and chips, build-your-own burgers and other un-French food.

Le Transbordeur   LIVE MUSIC
(www.transbordeur.fr; 3 bd de Stalingrad, Villeurbanne; ⊟Cité Internationale/Transbordeur) In an old industrial building near the northeastern corner of the Parc de la Tête d'Or, Lyon's prime concert venue draws international acts on the European concert-tour circuit.

Hangar du Premier Film   CINEMA
(www.institut-lumiere.org; 25 rue du Premier Film, 8e; MMonplaisir-Lumière) This former factory and birthplace of cinema now screens

LYON WHAT'S ON

Track new nightclub offerings at www. lyonclubbing.com and lyon.2night. fr (both in French). Other what's on guides include Lyon Poche (www. lyonpoche.com) and Le Petit Bulletin (www.petit-bulletin.fr/lyon).

Tickets are sold at Fnac Billetterie (www.fnac.com/spectacles; 85 rue de la République, 2e; ⊙10am-7.30pm Mon-Sat; MBellecour).

films of all genres and eras in their original languages. From approximately June to September, the big screen moves outside.

Auditorium de Lyon   CLASSICAL MUSIC
(⊉04 78 95 95 95; www.auditorium-lyon.com; 149 rue Garibaldi, 3e; ⊙Sep-Jun; MPart-Dieu, ⊟Part-Dieu-Servient, Part-Dieu-Villette) Built in 1975, this spaceshiplike auditorium houses the National Orchestra of Lyon, along with workshops, jazz and world-music concerts.

Maison de la Danse   DANCE CLUB
(www.maisondeladanse.com; 8 av Jean Mermoz, 8e; ⊟Bachut-Mairie du 8ème) Lyon's home of contemporary dance.

🛍 Shopping

VIEUX LYON
Vieux Lyon's narrow streets are dotted with galleries, antiquarian and secondhand bookshops, and quality souvenir shops.

Crafts Market   ARTS & CRAFTS, MARKET
(Marché de la Création; quai de Bondy, 5e; ⊙8am-1.30pm Sun; MVieux Lyon) Along the Saône, meet artists selling their paintings, sculptures, photography and more.

PRESQU'ÎLE
High-street chains line rues de la République and Victor Hugo, while upmarket boutiques and design houses stud rue du Président Édouard Herriot, rue de Brest and the streets between place des Jacobins and place Bellecour. More cluster between art galleries and antique shops around rue Auguste Comte, 2e.

Pôle de Commerces et de Loisirs Confluence   SHOPPING CENTRE
(www.confluence.fr; Cours Charlemagne, 2e; ⊟Montrochet) Opened in April 2012 near the southern tip of Presqu'île, this vast complex of over 100 shops and restaurants is Lyon's showiest new commercial venue. Most

stores here are outlets of major international companies such as Apple, Calvin Klein, Adidas and the like.

In Cuisine BOOKS, FOOD
(www.incuisine.fr; 1 place Bellecour, 2e; MBellecour) This foodie haven has an astonishing selection of culinary, gastronomic and wine titles. It also offers demonstrations, tastings and cooking courses for adults and kids, and serves lunch in its *salon de thé* (tea room).

Book Market BOOKS
(Marché des Bouquinistes; quai de la Pêcherie, 1er; ⊙10am-6pm Sat & Sun; MHôtel de Ville) A treasure trove of hard-to-find titles (most in French).

Decitre BOOKS
(www.decitre.fr; 6 place Bellecour, 2e; MBellecour) Stocks foreign-language fiction including English (very limited travel section).

CROIX ROUSSE

Montée de la Grande Côte ARTS & CRAFTS
(MCroix Rousse or Croix Paquet) Silk, stained glass and other galleries and workshops come and go the length of this walkway linking Croix Rousse with place des Terreaux, 1er. Several more galleries stud the eastern end of rue Burdeau, 1er.

Le Village des Createurs FASHION
(☑04 78 27 37 21; www.villagedescreateurs.com; Passage Thiaffait, 19 rue René Leynaud, 1er; ⊙2-7pm Wed-Sat; MCroix Paquet) Local, just-known or yet-to-make-their-name designer boutiques.

RIVE GAUCHE

Centre Commercial
La Part-Dieu SHOPPING CENTRE
(www.centrecommercial-partdieu.com; MPart-Dieu) Adjacent to the Part-Dieu train station, Lyon's vast indoor shopping centre is dominated by a pencil-shaped tower nicknamed *le crayon*.

Au Vieux Campeur OUTDOORS, TRAVEL
(www.auvieuxcampeur.fr; 43 cours de la Liberté, 3e; MGuillotière) Excellent camping store stocking a mammoth range of maps and travel guides (many in English).

ℹ️ Information

Emergency
Police Station (☑04 78 42 26 56; 47 rue de la Charité, 2e; MPerrache or Ampère)

Medical Services
Hôpital Édouard Herriot (☑08 20 08 20 69; www.chu-lyon.fr; 5 place d'Arsonval, 3e; ⊙24hr; MGrange Blanche) Has an emergency room.

Pharmacie Blanchet (☑04 78 42 12 42; www.lyon-pharmacie.com; 5 place des Cordeliers, 2e; ⊙24hr; MCordeliers) All-night pharmacy.

SOS Médecins (☑04 78 83 51 51; ⊙24hr) Medical emergency hotline.

Money
Global Cash (http://france.globalcash-change.com; 20 rue Gasparin, 2e; ⊙9.30am-6.30pm Mon-Sat; MBellecour) Exchange bureau with three in-town offices and one at the airport.

Tourist Information
Tourist office (☑04 72 77 69 69; www.lyon-france.com; place Bellecour, 2e; ⊙9am-6pm; MBellecour) Excellent tourist office with exceptionally helpful multilingual staff. Offers a variety of city walking tours and sells the Lyon City Card.

Websites
Bulles de Gones (www.bullesdegones.com) Comprehensive guide on what to do with kids (up to 12 years) in and around Lyon.

Lyon (www.lyon.fr) Official city website.

My Little Lyon (www.mylittle.fr/mylittlelyon) Keep up with the city's latest cultural trends.

Le Petit Paume (www.petitpaume.com) Savvy city guide written by local university students.

Rhône-Alpes Tourisme (www.rhonealpes-tourisme.com) Regional tourist information site.

ℹ️ Getting There & Away

Air
Lyon-St-Exupéry Airport (www.lyon.aeroport.fr) Located 25km east of the city, serving 120 direct destinations across Europe and beyond, including many budget carriers.

Bus
In the Perrache complex, **Eurolines** (☑04 72 56 95 30; www.eurolines.fr; Gare de Perrache) and Spain-oriented **Linebús** (☑04 72 41 72 27; www.linebus.com; Gare de Perrache) have offices on the bus-station level of the Centre d'Échange (follow the 'Lignes Internationales' signs).

Car
Major car-hire companies have offices at Gare de la Part-Dieu, Gare de Perrache and the airport.

Train
Lyon has two main-line train stations: **Gare de la Part-Dieu** (MPart-Dieu), 1.5km east of the Rhône, and **Gare de Perrache** (MPerrache). Some local trains stop at **Gare St-Paul** (MVieux Lyon), and **Gare Jean Macé** (MJean Mace). There's also a TGV station at Lyon-St-

FEVER PITCH

Qui ne saute pas n'est pas Lyonnais! (Whoever doesn't jump isn't Lyonnais!) is the rallying cry for multi-championship-winning football (ie soccer) team Olympique Lyonnais (OL; olweb.fr). After decades of playing in the 1920s-built, 40,000-seater Stade de Gerland (04 72 76 01 70; 353 av Jean Jaurès; MStade de Gerland), the team plans to inaugurate its massive new home stadium, Stade des Lumières (www.grandstadeol.com; Décines-Charpieu) in summer 2014. To join the crowds jumping wildly up and down, buy match tickets online, at the stadium or from the club's downtown boutique, OL Store Lyon Centre (http://boutique.olweb.fr/olstores.aspx; cnr rue de Jussieu & rue Grolée, 2e; 10am-7pm Tue-Sat, daily Dec; MCordeliers).

Exupéry Airport. Buy tickets at the stations or at the **SNCF Boutique** (2 place Bellecour; MBellecour)

Destinations by direct TGV include the following:

Dijon From €29, two hours, at least seven daily

Lille-Europe From €90, three hours, at least 11 daily

Marseille From €45, 1¾ hours, every 30 to 60 minutes

Paris Gare de Lyon From €69, two hours, every 30 to 60 minutes

Paris Aéroport Roissy Charles de Gaulle From €69, two hours, at least 11 daily

Strasbourg €88, 3¾ hours, five daily

ℹ Getting Around

To/From the Airport

The **Rhonexpress** (www.rhonexpress.net) tramway links the airport with the Part-Dieu train station in under 30 minutes. It's a five- to 10-minute walk from the arrivals hall – follow the red signs with the Rhonexpress train logo. Trams depart approximately every 15 minutes between 6am and 9.30pm, and every 30 minutes from 5am to 6am and 9.30pm to midnight. One-way tickets cost €14 per adult, €11.50 for youths aged 12 to 25; kids under 12 are free.

By taxi, the 30- to 45-minute minute trip between the airport and the city centre costs around €45 during the day and €60 between 7pm and 7am.

Bicycle

Pick up a red-and-silver bike at one of 200-odd bike stations throughout the city and drop it off at another with Lyon's **Vélo'v** (www.velov.grandlyon.com) scheme. The first 30 minutes are free, the next hour is €1 and subsequent hours €2 with a *carte courte durée* (a short-duration card, costing €1.50 for 24 hours or €5 for seven days), €0.75/1.50 respectively with a *carte longue durée* (long-duration card, costing €25 and valid for one year). Buy either card with a chip-enabled credit card from machines installed at bike stations.

Alternatively, phone for or flag down a chauffeur-driven, soft-roofed tricycle operated by Cyclopolitain (p454).

Boat

Le Vaporetto (08 20 20 69 20; www.confluence.fr/W/do/centre/navette) operates *navettes* (passenger ferry boats) to Lyon's new Pôle de Loisirs et de Commerces Confluence, at the southern extremity of Presqu'île. Boats depart from riverbank docks near place St-Paul and place Bellecour. Travel time is 30 minutes from the **St-Paul dock** (quai de Bondy, 5e; MHôtel de Ville or Vieux Lyon) and 20 minutes from the **Bellecour dock** (quai Tilsitt, 2e; MBellecour or Vieux Lyon); fare is €1.50 each way. First and last boats leave St-Paul at 10am and 9pm, respectively, returning from the Confluence dock half an hour later.

Public Transport

Buses, trams, a four-line metro and two funiculars linking Vieux Lyon to Fourvière and St-Just are operated by **TCL** (www.tcl.fr), which has information offices dispensing transport maps adjacent to several metro stations throughout Lyon, including Bellecour, Croix Rousse, Hôtel de Ville, Part-Dieu, Perrache and Vieux Lyon. Public transport runs from around 5am to midnight.

Tickets valid for all forms of public transport cost €1.60 (€14.30 for a *carnet* of 10) and are available from bus and tram drivers and machines at metro entrances. Tickets allowing unlimited travel for two hours after 9am cost €2.60, for all-day travel €4.90, and a Ticket Liberté Soirée allowing unlimited travel after 7pm is €2.60. Bring coins as machines don't accept notes (or some international credit cards). Time-stamp tickets on all forms of public transport or risk a fine.

Holders of the Lyon City Card (p451) receive free unlimited access to Lyon's transport network for the duration of the card's validity (one, two or three days).

Taxi

Taxis hover in front of both train stations, on the place Bellecour end of rue de la Barre (2e), at the northern end of rue du Président Édouard Herriot (1er) and along quai Romain Rolland in Vieux Lyon (5e).

Allo Taxi (☑04 78 28 23 23; www.allotaxi.fr)

Taxis Lyonnais (☑04 78 26 81 81; www.taxilyonnais.com)

North of Lyon

Lush green hills, lakes and vineyards unfold to the north of cosmopolitan Lyon.

BEAUJOLAIS

Hilly Beaujolais, 50km northwest of Lyon, is a land of streams, granite peaks (the highest is 1012m Mont St-Rigaud), pastures and forests.

The region is synonymous with its fruity red wines, especially its 10 premium *crus,* and the Beaujolais Nouveau, drunk at the tender age of just six weeks. Vineyards stretch south from Mâcon along the right bank of the Saône for some 50km.

At the stroke of midnight on the third Thursday (ie Wednesday night) in November – as soon as French law permits – the *libération* (release) or *mise en perce* (tapping; opening) of the first bottles of cherry-bright Beaujolais Nouveau is celebrated around France and the world. In Beaujeu (population 2050), 64km northwest of Lyon, there's free Beaujolais Nouveau for all as part of the Sarmentelles de Beaujeu (www.sarmentelles.com) – a giant street party that kicks off the day before Beaujolais Nouveau for five days of wine tasting, live music and dancing. During the festival a bus runs between Lyon and Beaujeu but otherwise you'll need your own transport.

For details of wine cellars where you can taste and buy wine, contact Beaujeu's

tourist office (☑04 74 69 22 88; www.beaujolais-vignoble.com; place de l'Église; ⊙9.30am-12.30pm & 2.30-6.30pm, closed Dec-Feb), which can also help with accommodation. Beaujeu's lone hotel closed its doors in 2012, but there are some charming B&Bs in the surrounding countryside.

Les Folies de la Serve (☑04 74 04 76 40; www.lesroulottes.com; La Serve; caravan/d incl breakfast €62/€110; ⊙Apr-Oct), run by traditional caravan-maker Pascal and his hippie wife, Pascaline, has a trio of romantically furnished 1920s to 1950s gypsy caravans amid the B&B's fields (€3 to €5 extra per night for heating). Bathrooms are provided in the main farmhouse, which has two whimsical en suite guestrooms. Reserve at least two days ahead for food baskets and picnic hampers (€15 per person). Follow the road from Avenas to the Col de Crie for 5km, and at the La Serve crossroads, head to Ouroux; after 100m turn right down the track signposted *chambres d'hôtes en roulottes.*

Exploring Beaujolais' (mostly) gentle hills by bike is uplifting. Hire one from Les Sources du Beaujolais (☑04 74 69 20 56; sources.beaujolais@wanadoo.fr; place de l'Hôtel de Ville; per half-/full day €11/16; ⊙Mar-Dec). Walking the area's many footpaths is equally invigorating. The tourist office provides local trail info on its website.

PÉROUGES
POP 1240

French film buffs will recognise photogenic Pérouges. Situated on a hill 30km northeast of Lyon, this enchanting yellow-stone medieval village has long been used as a set for films like *Les Trois Mousquetaires* (The Three Musketeers). It's worth braving the summertime crowds strolling its uneven cobbled alleys, admiring its half-timbered stone houses and 1792-planted liberty tree on place de la Halle and wolfing down *galettes de Pérouges* (warm, thin-pizza-crust-style, sugar-crusted tarts) with cider.

To appreciate Pérouges' charm after the day trippers have left, book a romantic room (try for one with a canopied bed) at the historic Hostellerie de Pérouges (☑04 74 61 00 88; www.hostelleriedeperouges.com; place du Tilleul; s €92-139, d €128-246), which also operates a respected restaurant (menus €38-65).

Pérouges' tiny tourist office (☑04 74 46 70 84; www.perouges.org; ⊙10am-noon & 2-5pm Mon-Fri, 2-5pm Sat & Sun) is on the main road opposite the village entrance.

Cars Philibert (☎04 78 98 56 00; www.
philibert-transport.fr) bus 132 (€2, one hour)
runs two to eight times daily from central
Lyon to the Pérouges turn off on route D4 (a
15-minute walk from the village).

LA DOMBES

Northwest of Pérouges is La Dombes, a
marshy area with hundreds of *étangs* (shallow lakes) that were created from malarial
swamps over the past six centuries by farmers. They are used as fish ponds and then
drained to grow crops on the fertile lake bed.

La Dombes teems with wildlife, particularly waterfowl. Observe local and exotic
birds, including dozens of pairs of storks, at
the Parc des Oiseaux (www.parcdesoiseaux.
com; adult/child €14/11; ☉9.30am-7pm, closed
mid-Nov–Feb), a landscaped bird park on the
edge of Villars-les-Dombes on the N83. The
reserve is a 1.6km walk south of Villars-les-
Dombes' train station, linked to Lyon's Part-
Dieu (€6.80, 40 minutes, at least hourly).

The area is famed for its production
of frogs' legs, which you can taste at La
Bicyclette Bleue (☎04 74 98 21 48; www.la
bicyclettebleue.fr; lunch menus €11, menus €20-
37.50; ☉lunch & dinner Thu-Mon; 🚲), in Joyeux,
7.5km southeast of Villars-les-Dombes on the
D61. Renowned for its *grenouilles fraîches
en persillade* (frogs' legs in butter and parsley), this laid-back family affair also runs
regular cooking courses (€60) and rents bicycles (per half-/full day €12.50/15.50) to explore
11 mapped lakeland circuits, from 12km (one
hour) to 59km (four hours).

Downstream along the Rhône

South of Lyon, vineyards meet nuclear
power plants. Although it doesn't sound like
the most auspicious juxtaposition, there are
several worthwhile stops for Lyon-based day
trippers or the southbound.

VIENNE
POP 30,470

In a commanding position on the Rhône,
30km south of Lyon, the one-time Gallo-
Roman city of Vienne is best known today
for its two-week jazz festival (www.jazzavi
enne.com) in late June/early July.

In the old town, take a look at the superb Corinthian columns of the Temple
d'Auguste et de Livie (place Charles de Gaulle),
built around 10 BC to honour Emperor Augustus and his wife Livia. Across the river

in St-Romain-en-Gal, the excavated remains
of the Gallo-Roman city form the Musée
Gallo-Romain (www.musees-gallo-romains.com;
route D502, St-Romain-en-Gal; adult/child €4/free,
Thu free; ☉10am-6pm Tue-Sun).

Views over Vienne extend from the Belvédère de Pipet, a balcony with a 6m-tall
statue of the Virgin Mary, immediately
above the fabulous Théâtre Romain (rue
du Cirque; adult/child €2.70/free, 1st Sun of month
free; ☉9.30am-1pm & 2-6pm, closed Mon Sep-Mar).
The vast Roman amphitheatre, built around
AD 40–50, is a key jazz-festival venue.

A *billet inter-musées* (combination ticket,
good for six museums and historical sites in
the Viennois area) costs €6; the tourist office (☎04 74 53 80 30; www.vienne-tourisme.com;
3 cours Brillier; ☉10am-noon & 1.30-6pm Mon-Sat,
9am-noon & 2-5pm Sun) has details.

Hôtel de la Pyramide (☎04 74 53 01 96;
www.lapyramide.com; 14 bd Fernand-Point; s €190-
225, d €200-240, ste €390-420; ✳🅿@🛜) overlooking La Pyramide de la Cirque (a 15.5m-
tall obelisk that in Roman times pierced
the centre of a hippodrome), is Vienne's
finest address for eating and/or sleeping.
This apricot-coloured villa with powder-
blue shutters is a haven, especially for foodies. In addition to chef Patrick Henriroux'
two-Michelin-star signature restaurant La
Pyramide (lunch menus €62, dinner menus €117-
172; ☉lunch & dinner Thu-Mon), which serves
lobsters, foie gras, black truffles, scallops
and other seasonal treats, he also helms the
more affordable l'Espace PH (mains €15-
22; ☉lunch & dinner daily), and his Boutique
Patrick Henriroux (☉9am-noon & 2.30-6pm
Thu-Mon), selling tantalisingly packaged
gourmet goodies and chic kitchenware.

Trains link Vienne with Lyon's four stations (€6.60, 20 to 30 minutes, at least hourly) and Valence Centre (€12.50, 50 minutes,
at least hourly). All trains to Valence TGV
station require changing at Valence Centre.

ST-ÉTIENNE, DESIGN CITY

Down-to-business St-Étienne (population 178,530), 62km southwest of Lyon, is drawing on its Industrial Revolution origins and its history of arms, bicycle, textile and ribbon production to reinvent itself as 'design city'. It's worth a brief stop to visit the exceptional collection of 20th-century and contemporary paintings, sculptures and photographs at the Musée d'Art Moderne (MAM; www.mam-st-etienne.fr; rue Fernard Léger, St-Priest-en-Jarez; adult/child €5/4, 1st Sun of month free; ⊗10am-6pm Wed-Mon), the country's second largest after Paris' Centre Pompidou. Tram 4 (direction Hôpital Nord) links it with the centre.

St-Étienne hosts the forward-looking Biennale Internationale Design fair during March in every odd-numbered year (2013's theme is 'empathy'). Find out more and browse exhibitions at the Cité du Design (☑04 77 49 74 70; www.citedudesign.com; 3 rue Javelin Pagnon; adult/child €4/2; ⊗11am-6pm Tue-Sun), in a gleaming glass-and-steel building reached by tram 5 (direction La Terrasse).

The tourist office (☑04 77 49 39 00; www.tourisme-st-etienne.com; 16 av de la Libération; ⊗10am-12.30pm & 2-6.30pm Mon-Sat), 1km southwest of the train station, has accommodation details.

Hourly-or-better trains link St-Étienne with Lyon Gare Part-Dieu (€10.50, 50 minutes).

TOWARDS VALENCE

The Parc Naturel Régional du Pilat spills across 650 sq km southwest of Vienne and offers breathtaking panoramas of the Rhône Valley from its highest peaks, Crêt de l'Œillon (1370m) and Crêt de la Perdrix (1432m). The Montgolfier brothers, who invented the hot-air balloon in 1783 and lent their name to its French term, *montgolfière*, were born and held their first public demonstration on the park's southeastern boundary.

The north section of the Côtes du Rhône winegrowing area stretches from Vienne south to Valence. Two of its most respected appellations, St Joseph and Hermitage, grow around Tain l'Hermitage (population 5933) on the Rhône's left bank.

VALENCE

POP 66.050

Several Rhône Valley towns claim to be the gateway to Provence, including Valence. Valence's quaint old town, Vieux Valence, is crowned by the Cathédrale St-Apollinaire, a late-11th-century pilgrimage church largely destroyed in the Wars of Religion and rebuilt in the 17th century. Allegorical sculpted heads adorn Maison des Têtes (57 Grande Rue), a blend of Flamboyant Gothic and Renaissance from 1530.

🛏 Sleeping & Eating

The city is famed for its crunchy, orange-rind-flavoured shortbread shaped like a Vatican Swiss guard to commemorate Pope Pius VI's imprisonment and death in Valence in 1799. Ask for *un suisse* in any patisserie, including the venerable Maison Nivon (17 av Pierre Semard; suisses €2.20; ⊗6am-7pm Tue-Sun) near the train station, in business since 1856.

Anne-Sophie Pic, France's only three-Michelin-star female chef, reigns over Valence gastronomy, as her father and grandfather (both triple Michelin star-holders) did.

TOP CHOICE Maison Pic   INN €€€
(☑04 75 44 15 32; www.pic-valence.com; 285 av Victor Hugo; d €290-400, ste €410-890; ⊗Feb-Dec; ✿@🛜🌊) The Pic family's truffle-coloured, 1889-established inn has ultrachic rooms and public spaces mixing antique, contemporary and kitsch, alongside a couple of stunning restaurants – top-of-the-line Restaurant Pic (lunch menus €90, menus €210-330; ⊗lunch & dinner Tue-Sat) and less formal bistro Le 7 (menus €18-30; ⊗lunch & dinner daily). Just down the street, their new deli and grocery, L'Épicerie (210 Avenue Victor Hugo; ⊗9am-7pm Mon-Sat, to 12.30pm Sun), features wine and gourmet food items hand-picked by Anne-Sophie Pic. Serious foodies will want to sign up at Pic's cutting-edge cooking school, **Scook** (p960), with 1½-hour courses from €55 through to full-day courses from €250, plus courses for kids aged over six (1½ hours from €39).

ℹ Information

Tourist office (☑04 75 44 90 40; www.valence tourisme.com; 11 bd Bancel; ⊗9.30am-6.30pm Mon-Sat, 10am-3pm Sun) Two blocks north of the train station.

ℹ Getting There & Away

From the central train station, Valence Centre (also known as Valence-Ville), there are trains to/from Montélimar (€8.50, 25 minutes, hourly),

Lyon's Gare Part-Dieu (from €16.90, 1¼ hours, 16 daily), Avignon Centre (€19.90, 1½ hours, 15 daily), Marseille (€34.10, 2½ hours, seven daily) and Grenoble (€15.80, 1¼ hours, hourly). Many stop at Valence TGV Rhône-Alpes Sud station, 10km east.

MONTÉLIMAR
POP 36.870

In the sunny section of the Drôme *département* known as Drôme Provençale, Montélimar, 46km south of Valence, is an appealing town (once you're through its industrial outskirts), with a shaded, grassy promenade lined by cafe terraces carving a C-shape through its centre. The town's biggest claim to fame is its *nougat de Montélimar*, which took off after WWII when motorists travelling to the French Riviera stopped off here to buy the sweeter-than-sweet treat to munch en route.

Authentic Montélimar nougat consists of at least 28% almonds, 25% lavender honey, 2% pistachio nuts, sugar, egg white and vanilla. Texture varies, from *dur* (hard) to *tendre* (light and soft), as does honey strength and crispness of the nuts. Some are coated in chocolate and others have fruit (try the one with figs), but traditional Montélimar nougat is simply off-white.

Nougat factory tours are offered by numerous producers; pick a small (rather than industrial) confectioner, such as Diane-de-Poytiers (☑04 75 01 67 02; www.diane-de-poytiers.fr; 99 av Jean-Jaurès; ☺8am-noon & 2-5.30pm Tue-Sat Jul & Aug, Mon-Fri rest of year), run by the same family for three generations.

The tourist office (☑04 75 01 00 20; www.montelimar-tourisme.com; Montée Saint-Martin; ☺9am-12.15pm & 2-6.30pm Mon-Sat) has a list of nougat and other local producers (lavender, honey and so on), and can help with accommodation.

Montélimar is on the train line linking Valence-Ville (€8.50, 25 minutes, hourly) with Avignon Centre (€13.50, 55 minutes, hourly).

GORGES DE L'ARDÈCHE
The serpentine Ardèche River slithers between towering mauve, yellow and grey limestone cliffs from near Vallon Pont d'Arc (population 2420) to St-Martin de l'Ardèche (population 910), a few kilometres west of the Rhône. En route, it passes beneath the Pont d'Arc, a stunning natural stone bridge created by the river's torrents. The river forms the centrepiece of the 1575-hectare Réserve Naturelle des Gorges de l'Ardèche (www.gorgesdelardeche.

fr/reserve-naturelle.php), a protected area since 1980. Eagles nest in the cliffs and there are numerous caves to explore.

Souvenir-shop-filled Vallon Pont d'Arc is the area's main hub; its tourist office (☑04 75 88 04 01; www.vallon-pont-darc.com; 1 place de l'Ancienne Gare; ☺9am-12.15pm & 1.30-6pm Mon-Fri, to 5pm Sat) is in the village centre. The scenic D579 from the village out along the gorges is lined by campgrounds and canoe- and kayak-hire outlets, including the well-established Base Nautique du Pont d'Arc (☑04 75 37 17 79; www.canoe-ardeche.com; rte des Gorges de l'Ardèche; ☺Apr-Nov). A half-day descent (8km) starts from €16/11 per adult/child (minimum age is seven); longer day and multiday trips are also possible.

SNCF buses link Montélimar's train station with Vallon Pont d'Arc (€11.10, 1¼ hours, four daily).

About 300m above the gorge's waters, the Haute Corniche (D290) has a dizzying series of *belvédères* (panoramic viewpoints), although it can turn into a chaotic traffic jam in midsummer. About halfway between St-Martin and Vallon Pont d'Arc, the Maison de la Réserve (☑04 75 98 77 31; www.gorgesdelardeche.fr; D290) provides information on local flora, fauna and recreational opportunities. A further 2km west along the D290 is the trailhead for the Sentier Aval des Gorges, which descends 2km to the river, then follows the gorge for another 10km. Rough camping (☑04 75 88 00 41; reservation@gorgesdelardeche.fr; campsite per person midweek/weekend €6.50/10; ☺reservation centre 8.30am-1pm & 1.30-3pm) is available (by reservation) at two spots within the protected section of the gorge, Bivouac de Gournier and Bivouac de Gaud. On the plateaux

NUCLEAR-POWERED CROCODILES?

Nuclear energy takes an unlikely twist at the Ferme aux Crocodiles (www.lafermeauxcrocodiles.com; D59; adult/child €14.50/9.50; ☺9.30am-7pm Mar-Sep, to 5pm Oct-Feb), 20km south of Montélimar and just south of Pierrelatte, where 400-odd grouchy Nile crocodiles slumber in exotically landscaped tropical pools heated by the nearby Centre Nucléaire du Tricastin powerplant.

Take the Montélimar Sud or Bollène exit off the A7 and follow the signs.

above the gorges, typical Midi villages are surrounded by *garrigue* (aromatic scrub land), lavender fields and vineyards.

Beyond Vallon Pont d'Arc, the D579 continues northwest to Ruoms (population 2263); across the river, the D4 snakes along the Défilé de Ruoms (a narrow rock tunnel) and the Gorges de la Ligne for 8km.

Northwards from the pretty village of Balazuc (population 340), the D579 leads to Aubenas (population 12,270), from where scenic roads fan into the countryside. This is chestnut land, where the dark-

brown fruit is turned into everything from *crème de châtaigne* (sweet purée served with ice cream, crêpes or cake) to *bière aux marrons* (chestnut beer) and *liqueur de châtaigne* (21% alcohol-by-volume liqueur that makes a sweet aperitif when mixed with white wine). In the area's main town, Privas (population 8850), the tourist office (☎04 75 64 33 35; www.paysdeprivas.com; 3 place Général de Gaulle; ⏱10am-noon & 2-6pm Mon-Sat) has a list of regional producers as well as accommodation.

French Alps & the Jura Mountains

Includes »

Best Places to Eat

» Les Vieilles Luges (p483)

» Flocons de Sel (p487)

» L'Esquisse (p493)

» L'Atelier d'Edmond (p504)

» Le Saint-Pierre (p522)

Best Places to Stay

» Farmhouse (p488)

» Auberge du Manoir (p482)

» Closerie les Capucins (p525)

» Château des Allues (p500)

» Charles Quint Hôtel (p521)

Why Go?

The French Alps are a place of boundless natural beauty. We could rhapsodise about colossal peaks, wondrous white glaciers and sapphire lakes, but seeing really is believing when it comes to Europe's Alpine heartland. Schussing down slopes with Mont Blanc hogging the horizon, driving roller coaster roads up to middle-of-nowhere Alpine passes, hiking to summits where mountain huts perch like eyries: this region will elevate you, make your heart pound and leave you crying 'encore!' like few other places on earth.

As the mountains taper north to Lake Geneva, the picture softens. This is Jura: a soothingly green region of rounded heights and vine-wreathed villages. Lakes are strung like a daisy chain across its forested depths, and wayside farms invite you to stop, relax and sample the tangy delights of Comté and *vin jaune* (yellow wine). Jura's appeal is one of simple, back-to-nature pleasures and 'ahhh, *c'est la vie...*' moments.

When to Go

Grenoble

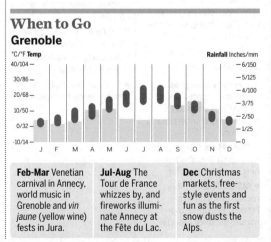

Feb-Mar Venetian carnival in Annecy, world music in Grenoble and *vin jaune* (yellow wine) fests in Jura.

Jul-Aug The Tour de France whizzes by, and fireworks illuminate Annecy at the Fête du Lac.

Dec Christmas markets, freestyle events and fun as the first snow dusts the Alps.

JURA SPECIALITIES

Sip nutty *vin jaune* (yellow wine) on the Route des Vins de Jura (p525) and spoon hot Vacherin Mont d'Or cheese in Métabief Mont d'Or. And that's just for (unusual) starters.

Fast Facts

» **Population** 7.4 million

» **Area** 59,900 sq km

» **Hotel overnights/year** 12.1 million

» **Signature drinks** Chartreuse liqueur; rich, golden *vin jaune*

Planning Your Trip

» Skip the queue by pre-booking your ski pass and ski hire online. One good website is www.ifyouski.com.

» Save by buying a SnowBall Pass (www.snowballpass.com), offering discounts on ski passes, tuition and equipment hire.

» Book your stay at a *refuge* (mountain hut) on the Club Alpin Français website (www.ffcam.fr, in French).

Resources

» **France Montagnes** (http://ski-resort-france.co.uk) For Alps resort guides, maps, snow reports and more.

» **Piste Hors** (http://pistehors.com) If you're planning to head off-piste.

» **Météo France** (www.meteofrance.com, in French) For up-to-the-minute weather reports.

Peak Summer

Peaks spiralling into cobalt blue skies, wildflower-brushed slopes, Alpine lakes – it's all up there for the exploring in summer. Be it scaling Mont Blanc, hiking the multiday Grand Tour de Haute Maurienne through the ruggedly beautiful Parc Nacional de la Vanois, or strolling languidly around Lake Annecy (maximum views, minimum exertion), there's a trail with your name on it. Contact the Club Alpin Français (www.ffcam.fr, in French) for the low-down on *refuges* (mountain huts).

EPIC SKIING

Lift-pass expense and airport distance be damned: the French Alps is a land of infinite world-class pistes, of top-of-Europe elation. Ski touring in the shadow of Mont Blanc; Val d'Isère's roller coaster Olympic runs; big air in Les Deux Alpes; the catwalk slopes of Courchevel, where you'll need to pout as well as you plough – regardless of which you choose, this is one downhill ride you will never forget.

Pre-planning pays off: sidestep school holidays to stretch your euro further, and book lift passes online to skip past the queues. And with the crème de la crème of instructors at the ubiquitous École du Ski Français, you'll go from bending zee knees to freestyle dancing on skis in no time.

Top Five High-Altitude Thrills

» Off-piste skiing in La Vallée Blanche, 20 mind-blowing kilometres from the spike of the Aiguille du Midi to Chamonix.

» Making a knuckle-whitening 3300m mountain-bike descent in Morzine, where the scenery becomes a blur of greenery.

» Skiing breathtakingly sheer La Sarenne – a 16km dive into oblivion on Europe's longest black run.

» Reaching (phew!) the 4810m summit of Mont Blanc, the rooftop of Europe.

» Doing a Tour de France in reverse, hurtling around 21 hairpin bends from Alpe d'Huez to Bourg d'Oisans.

History

Migrant tribes of Celtic, Gaulish and Teutonic origin arrived in the Alps first; by the first century AD, communities were well established, especially around the lakes of Geneva and Annecy.

During the Roman conquest the Alps were a strategic stronghold, falling under Roman control during Augustus' reign. The Frankish kings of the Merovingian and Carolingian empires laid the foundations for the modern Alps with their distinctive dialects, traditions and cultures.

The 13th and 14th centuries saw the feudal houses of Savoy, the Dauphiné and Provence fiercely contesting the Alps. The ensuing centuries were marked by successive wars and occupations, a cycle that ended with the union of Savoy with France in 1860.

Michel-Gabriel Paccard and Jacques Balmat made the first successful ascent of Mont Blanc in 1786, and in the late 19th century holidaymakers began to flock to the area.

German and Italian forces occupied the Alps during WWII, while the mountains became one of the main strongholds for the French Resistance. Modern industry, hydroelectric energy and large-scale tourism all contributed to the regeneration of the Alps in the postwar years.

Skiing & Snowboarding

The 200-plus resorts in the French Alps have carved out their reputation for some of the best – perhaps *the* best – downhill skiing and snowboarding in Europe. The season begins with the first big snow around mid-December and ends in late April or early May.

Dependent on snow conditions, summer Alpine skiing on glaciers in high-altitude resorts Val d'Isère, Les Deux Alpes and Alpe d'Huez runs for anything from two weeks to two months, June to August.

Downhill runs are colour-coded to indicate how kid-easy or killer-hard they are:

» **Green** Beginner
» **Blue** Intermediate
» **Red** Advanced
» **Black** Expert

Summer glacial skiing is on short greens or blues. Snowboarders are brilliantly catered for in larger resorts, with snow parks kitted out with half-pipes, kickers and ramps. Jura excels in scenic rambling *ski de fond* (cross-country skiing) trails.

SKI RENTAL & LESSONS

Skis (alpine, cross-country, telemark), snowboards, boots, poles and helmets can be hired at sport shops in every resort. All-inclusive rental costs around €32/175 per day/six days for alpine equipment or snowboarding gear and €15/65 for cross-country; reserving in advance online typically gets you a 15% discount.

France's leading ski school, the École du Ski Français (ESF; www.esf.net) – its instructors wear red – teaches snowboarding and skiing. It has a branch in every resort and touts competitive rates; a group lesson typically costs €60 per half-day, €150 for four days and €190 for six days. Private instruction is available on request. Kids can start learning from the age of four; from three years old they can play in the *jardin de neige* (snow garden).

LIFT PASSES

You will need a *forfait* (lift pass) to ride the various *remontées mécaniques* (lifts): *téléskis* (chairlifts), *télécabines* (gondolas), *téléphériques* (cable cars) and *funiculaires* (funicular railways).

Passes – €220 or thereabouts for a week – give access to one or more ski sectors. Most lift passes are 'hands-free', with a built-in chip that barriers detect automatically, and can be bought and recharged online. The days of passport-sized photos for multiday/seasonal lift passes are rapidly disappearing; in most resorts these days they simply snap a photo of you with a webcam when you buy the pass.

Children aged under five ski for free but still need a pass; bring along a passport as proof of age.

Cheaper passes – usually around €6 a day – are needed for cross-country ski trails, although these are rarely checked.

INSURANCE

Before you launch yourself like a rocket down that near-vertical black piste, make sure you are properly insured. Accidents happen, and expensive (we're talking five figures here) mountain-rescue costs, medical treatment and repatriation add insult to injury. Rental shops offer insurance for equipment for a small additional charge.

Most packages include insurance. If not, you might try the Carte Neige (www.ffs.fr/site/carteneige), a comprehensive annual policy. It costs €29 to €48 per year (€29 to

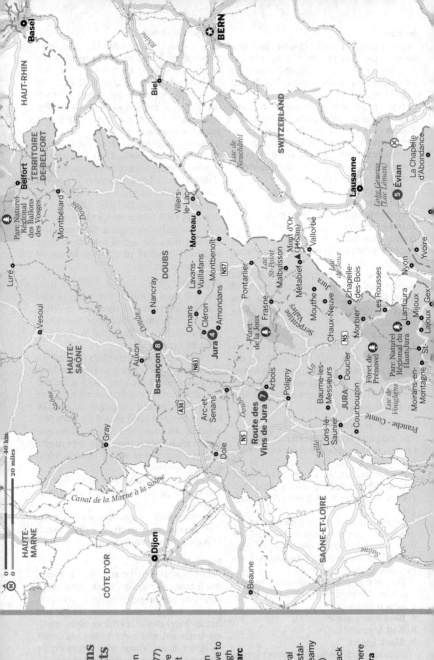

French Alps & the Jura Mountains Highlights

1 Do a Bond, swooshing down the slopes in **Chamonix** (p477) in the distinctive shadow of Mont Blanc

2 Get dizzy on the winding drive to Briançon through the dramatic **Parc National des Écrins** (p514)

3 Delve into castles, medieval lanes and a crystal-clear lake in dreamy **Annecy** (p490)

4 Scamper back to nature at a middle-of-nowhere farm in wild **Jura** (p520)

5 Bathe like royalty in the

mineral-rich waters of **Évian-les-Bains** (p489)

6 Carve legendary slopes and party in the après-ski bars in **Les Trois Vallées** (p500)

7 Sip golden *vin jaune* amid the vines on the bucolic **Route des Vins du Jura** (p525)

8 Seek out the Vauban citadel and the stellar Musée des Beaux-Arts in **Besançon** (p520)

9 Grab your walking boots to explore the glaciated grandeur of **Parc National de la Vanoise** (p505)

TICKET TO GLIDE

RESORT	ELEVATION (M)	LEVEL	RUNS (KM)	1-DAY LIFT PASS (€)	6-DAY LIFT PASS (€)
Chamonix	1037	intermediate, advanced, off-piste	182	52	259
St-Gervais & Megève	810 & 1113	beginner, intermediate	445	40	189
Les Portes du Soleil	1000–2466	all levels	650	44	219
Les Trois Vallées	1450–2300	all levels, especially advanced	600	49	244
Val d'Isère-Espace Killy	1850	intermediate, advanced, off-piste	300	46	230
Les Deux Alpes	1660	intermediate, advanced, snowboarding	225	41	205
Alpe d'Huez	1860	all abilities, snowboarding, Europe's longest black run	245	43	215
La Clusaz	1100	beginner, families	132	32	170
Serre Chevalier	1200	all levels, off-piste	250	43	208
Le Grand Bornand	1000	beginner, intermediate	90	30	150
Chamrousse	1700	beginner, intermediate	90	20	120
Métabief Mont d'Or	1000	cross-country	210	8	40

€33 for cross-country skiing only), depending on the level of coverage you choose. Buy it online or through the ESF in most resorts.

Alternatively, buy the Carré Neige (www. carreneige.com) with your lift pass. Every resort offers the all-inclusive insurance scheme, which costs €2.80 a day.

❶ Getting There & Away

AIR The view through the plane window is the best introduction to the Alps. Chances are you're landing at one of three airports:

» **Lyon St-Exupéry Airport** (www.lyon.aeroport. fr) 25km east of Lyon.

» **Grenoble Airport** (www.grenoble-airport.com) South of Lyon St-Exupéry Airport and southeast of Lyon.

» **Geneva Airport** (www.gva.ch) In neighbouring Switzerland.

BUS From the airports there are buses to numerous ski resorts; fares and frequencies are listed under Getting There & Away for destinations in this chapter.

» **Aeroski-Bus** (www.alpski-bus.com) Geneva.

» **Satobus-Alpes** (http://satobus-alpes.altibus. com) Lyon.

CAR & MOTORCYCLE Traffic on steeply climbing, winding mountain roads can be hellish, especially at weekends. After heavy snowfalls, you may need snow chains. Winter tyres (automatically provided with most hire cars) are a good idea. The Fréjus and Mont Blanc road tunnels connect the French Alps with Italy, as do several mountain passes. Road signs indicate if passes are blocked.

TRAIN Eurostar (www.eurostar.com) ski trains are an environmentally friendly way to travel between London and Moûtiers or Bourg St-Maurice from mid-December to mid-April (return from €185, eight hours, overnight or day service, weekends only). Within France, train services to the Alps are excellent.

SAVOY

'The Alps par excellence' could be the strapline of this northern half of the French Alps, a perfectly executed tableau of wondrous glaciers, titanic peaks, jewel-coloured lakes and dense alpine forests.

Flanked by Switzerland and Italy, Savoy rises from the southern shores of Lake Geneva, Europe's largest alpine lake, and culminates at the roof of Europe, mighty 4810m Mont Blanc. In between is a sprinkling of legendary ski resorts like Chamonix and Val d'Isère, as well as some historical châteaux towns like Chambéry and lakeside Annecy to the southwest.

Rural life, unchanged for centuries, characterises the region's most remote realms, like the Bauges massif (so little known it is often mistaken for the northeastern Vosges region) and the wild Parc National de la Vanoise.

Chamonix

POP 9378 / ELEV 1037M

With the pearly white peaks of the Mont Blanc massif as its sensational backdrop, being an icon comes naturally to Chamonix. First 'discovered' by Brits William Windham and Richard Pococke in 1741, this is the Mecca of mountaineering, its birthplace, its flag-bearer. It is also a wintertime playground of epic proportions that entices Olympic champions and hard-core skiers to its pistes, and party-mad boarders to its boot-stompin' bars.

Even if you and your karabiner aren't quite ready to scale 'the big one' just yet and your technique doesn't *quite* match that of 007 in his stunt-riddled ski chase in *The World Is Not Enough*, there is no resisting the gravitational pull of those mountains. Whether slaloming La Vallée Blanche like a pro or almost colliding with perpendicular cliffs on the vertigo-inducing Aiguille du Midi cable car, there's a whole lot of adrenalin and, yes, a dash of Bond in every trip to Chamonix.

◉ Sights

TOP CHOICE Aiguille du Midi VIEWPOINT

A jagged needle of rock rearing above glaciers, snowfields and rocky crags, 8km from the hump of Mont Blanc, the Aiguille du Midi (3842m) is one of Chamonix' most distinctive landmarks. If you can handle the height, the 360-degree views of the French, Swiss and Italian Alps from the summit are (quite literally) breathtaking.

Year-round the vertiginous **Téléphérique de l'Aiguille du Midi** (place de l'Aiguille du Midi; adult/child return to Aiguille du Midi €46/39, Plan de l'Aiguille €26/22; ⊙8.30am-4.30pm) cable car links Chamonix with the Aiguille du Midi. Halfway up, Plan de l'Aiguille (2317m) is a terrific place to start hikes or paraglide. In summer you'll need to obtain a boarding card (marked with the number of your departing *and* returning cable car) in addition to a ticket. Bring warm clothes, as even in summer the temperature rarely rises above -10°C at the top.

From the Aiguille du Midi, between late June and early September, you can continue for a further 30 minutes of mind-blowing scenery – think suspended glaciers and spurs, seracs and shimmering ice fields – in the smaller bubbles of the **Télécabine Panoramic Mont Blanc** (adult/child return from Chamonix €70/59; ⊙8.30am-3.30pm) to Pointe Helbronner (3466m) on the French–Italian border. From here another cable car descends to the Italian ski resort of Courmayeur.

Le Brévent VIEWPOINT

The highest peak on the western side of the valley, Le Brévent (2525m) has tremendous views of the Mont Blanc massif, myriad

---

AVALANCHES

Avalanches are a serious danger in snowbound areas. You know the golden rule: never ski, hike or climb alone. Off-piste skiers should never leave home without an avalanche pole, transceiver, shovel – and, most importantly, a professional guide. Ski resorts announce the daily risk through signs and coloured flags: yellow (low risk), black and yellow (heightened risk) and black (severe risk). **Henry's Avalanche Talk** (www.henrysavalanchetalk.com) translates the daily avalanche forecast issued by Météo France into English during the ski season.

Chamonix

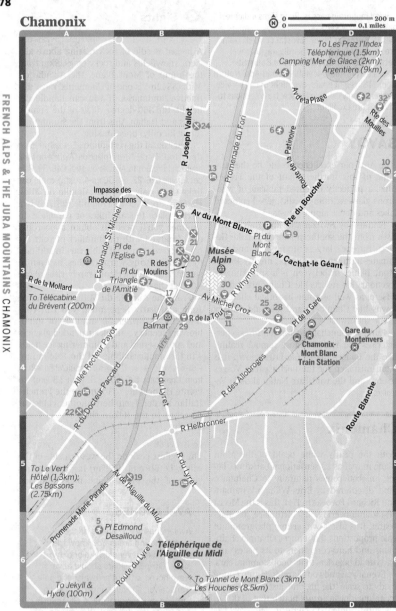

hiking trails, ledges to paraglide from and summit restaurant Le Panoramic. Reach it with the **Télécabine du Brévent** (29 rte Henriette d'Angeville; adult/child return €26/22; ☺8.50am-4.45pm), from the end of rue de la Mollard, via midstation **Planpraz** (2000m).

Mer de Glace   GLACIER

France's largest glacier, the glistening 200m-deep Mer de Glace (Sea of Ice) snakes 7km through mighty rock spires and turrets; it was named by Englishman William Windham, the first foreigner to set eyes on the

Chamonix

FRENCH ALPS & THE JURA MOUNTAINS CHAMONIX

glacier in 1741. The glacier moves up to 90m a year, and has become a popular attraction thanks to the rack-and-pinion railway line opened in 1908.

Wrap up warm to experience the Grotte de la Mer de Glace (☉late Dec–May & mid-Jun–Sep) ice cave, where frozen tunnels and ice sculptures change colour like mood rings.

A quaint red mountain train trundles up from Gare du Montenvers (35 place de la Mer de Glace; adult/child/family €26/22/79; ☉10am-4.30pm) in Chamonix to Montenvers (1913m), from where a cable car takes you down to the glacier and cave. Besides covering the 20-minute journey, the cable car and the ice cave, your ticket gets you entry into the Galerie des Cristaux, glittering with crystals from the Mont Blanc Massif, and the new Glaciorium, spotlighting the birth, life and future of glaciers.

The Mer de Glace can be reached on foot via the Grand Balcon Nord trail from Plan de l'Aiguille. The two-hour uphill trail from Chamonix starts near the summer luge track. Traversing the crevassed glacier requires proper equipment and an experienced guide.

Musée Alpin　　　　ALPINE MUSEUM
(av Michel Croz; adult/child €5/free; ☉2-7pm Wed-Mon) The town's illustrious Alpine history zooms into focus at this museum; from the cliffhanging tale of crystal-hunter Jacques Balmat to the first ascent of Mont Blanc in 1786 and the advent of winter tourism.

Musée des Cristaux　　　CRYSTAL MUSEUM
(Esplanade St-Michel; adult/child €5/free; ☉2-7pm Wed-Mon) As well as cataloguing the region's rich rocks and minerals, this museum hosts intriguing temporary exhibitions on such subjects as the history of mountaineering and the impact of climate change on mountains.

🏃 Activities

Glorious off-piste terrain, thrilling descents and unbeatable Mont Blanc views – skiing in Chamonix is so darn fantastic that skiers don't even mind that accessing the slopes involves lots of transport. Of Chamonix' nine main areas, Le Tour, Les Planards and Les Chosalets are best for beginners. For speed and challenge, it has to be Brévent-Flégère, above Chamonix, and Les Grands

CHILD'S PLAY

There's plenty to amuse *les petits* (the little ones) around Chamonix.

Parc de Merlet (www.parcdemerlet.com; adult/child €6/4; ⊙10am-6pm Tue-Sun May-Sep) is 5km north of Les Houches, and 5km southwest of Chamonix. Kids will enjoy getting close to free-roaming chamois, ibex and whistling marmots in this forested park. Or treat them to a fun-packed day on the trampolines, electric cars, forest-adventure obstacle courses and fun-fair rides at the Parc de Loisirs de Chamonix (www.chamonix parc.com; ⊙10am-7.30pm Jul & Aug, hrs vary Apr-Oct), near the chairlift in Les Planards, 500m east of Gare du Montenvers; the summer luge (Bob Run; 1/8 descents €5.50/31) winds through trees at an electrifying speed.

The ice-skating rink (165 rte de la Patinoire; adult/child €5.50/4.20, skate hire €4; ⊙2-5pm, closed low season) provides amusement when the weather packs up, as do activities at the adjacent Centre Sportif Richard Bozon (214 av de la Plage) with indoor and outdoor swimming pools (adult/child €5.50/4; ⊙10am-7pm).

Montets, accessible from Argentière, 9km north of Chamonix. Boarders seeking big air zip across to the kickers and rails at Les Grands Montets snowpark and the natural half-pipe in Le Tour.

When the snow melts, hikers can take their pick of 350km of spectacular high-altitude trails, many reached by cable car. There's enough light to walk until at least 9pm in June and July.

Maison de la Montagne   OUTDOOR ACTIVITIES
(190 place de l'Église; ⊙8.30am-noon & 3-7pm) Get the Mont Blanc lowdown here, opposite the tourist office. Inside is the highly regarded Compagnie des Guides de Chamonix (p480); the École de Ski Français (ESF; ☎04 50 53 22 57; www.esfchamonix.com); and the Office de Haute Montagne (OHM; ☎04 50 53 22 08; www.ohm-chamonix.com), which has information on trails, hiking conditions, weather forecasts and *refuges*, and topoguides and maps that are free to consult.

Winter Activities
La Vallée Blanche   SKIING
(guided trips per person/group of 4 €75/290) This mythical descent is *the* off-piste ride of a lifetime. A veritable obstacle course of a route, La Vallée Blanche takes four to five hours, leading from Aiguille du Midi over the crevasse-riddled Mer de Glace glacier and back through forest to Chamonix, covering 2800m of jaw-dropping vertical. Because of the obvious risks, it must *only* be tackled with a guide (guides can take a maximum of eight people in a group – add an extra €20 per additional person to the price above). Snowboarders require an even better level

than skiers. Snow coverage is generally best in February and March.

Haute Route   SKIING
(guided trips per person incl full board €990-1495) *Ski de randonnée* (ski touring – like long-distance hiking on skis), at its best between March and May, is big in Chamonix. The backcountry king is this classic six- to seven-day route from Chamonix to Zermatt in Switzerland, stopping en route at *refuges*. To tackle it you need to be superfit and an experienced off-piste skier. Shorter two-day trips are suitable for advanced skiers, but no previous ski touring experience is required.

Compagnie des
Guides de Chamonix   WALKING
(☎04 50 53 00 88; www.chamonix-guides.com; 190 place de l'Église) A pair of *raquettes* (snowshoes) is all you need to go stomping off through virgin powder and glistening forests. The Compagnie des Guides arranges tours around the Mont Blanc range from France to Switzerland and Italy, and romantic twilight tours through the forest with dinner. All prices include snowshoe hire and transport.

Huskydalen   DOGSLEDDING
(☎04 50 47 77 24; www.huskydalen.com; mushing per hr/half-day adult €60/120, child €40/80) Ever fancied trying your hand at mushing (dogsledding)? Huskydalen runs introductory courses from December to April where you can try your hand at dogsledding with some very lovable, very enthusiastic huskies.

Summer Activities
Lac Blanc   WALKING
From the top of Les Praz l'Index Télépherique (cable car; one-way/return €20/24) or La

Flégère (one-way/return €12/14), the line's midway point, gentle 1¼- to two-hour trails lead to 2352m Lac Blanc (literally 'White Lake'), a turquoise-coloured lake surrounded by mountains. Stargazers can overnight at the Refuge du Lac Blanc (☏04 50 47 24 49; dm incl half-board €49; ☉mid-Jun–Sep), a wooden chalet favoured by photographers for its top-of-Europe Mont Blanc views.

Grand Balcon Sud   WALKING
This easygoing trail skirts the western side of the valley, stays at around 2000m and commands a terrific view of Mont Blanc. Reach it on foot from behind Le Brévent's *télécabine* station.

Grand Balcon Nord   WALKING
Routes starting from the Plan de l'Aiguille include the challenging Grand Balcon Nord, which takes you to the dazzling Mer de Glace, from where you can walk or take the Montenvers train down to Chamonix.

Mountaineering & High-Alpine Tours   MOUNTAINEERING
Mountaineers and rock climbers make the pilgrimage to Chamonix in summer, when local guide companies offer exhilarating climbs for those with the necessary skill, experience and stamina, such as five-day rock-climbing courses (€615 to €900) and the incomparable Mont Blanc ascent (€850 to €1760). For hikers, the big draw is the classic six- to 10-day Tour du Mont Blanc (€760 to €1160), taking in majestic glaciers and peaks in France, Italy and Switzerland. Prices usually include half-board in *refuges*, picnics, lift tickets and luggage transport.

Cham' Aventure   WATER SPORTS
(☏04 50 53 55 70; www.cham-aventure.com; Maison de la Montagne, 190 place de l'Église) Thrill-seekers go in for canyoning (half-/full day €68/100 per person), rafting (€38/135 per two hours/day) and hydrospeeding (€48/135 per two hours/day) on Chamonix' River Arve and the Dora Baltea in neighbouring Italy.

Cycling Trails   CYCLING
Lower-altitude trails like the Petit Balcon Sud (250m) from Argentière to Servoz are perfect for biking. Most outdoor-activity specialists arrange guided mountain-biking expeditions.

Paragliding   PARAGLIDING
Come summer, the sky above Chamonix is dotted with paragliders wheeling down from the heights. Tandem flights from Planpraz (2000m) cost €100 per person (€225 from the Aiguille du Midi). Paragliding schools include Summits (☏04 50 53 50 14; www.summits.fr; 81 rue Joseph Vallot) and AirSports Chamonix (☏06 76 90 03 70; www.airsportschamonix.fr; 24 ave de la Plage); contact them ahead for details on meeting points.

★ Festivals & Events

Marathon du Mont Blanc   SPORTS
(www.montblancmarathon.fr) Hard-core runners, phenomenal scenery. Late June.

Fête des Guides   EVENT
Two-day celebrations in mid-August welcome new members to Chamonix' illustrious Compagnie des Guides with a dramatic *son et lumière* (sound-and-light show), fireworks, concerts and mountaineering displays.

ADVENTURE KNOW-HOW

These guide companies have got it. So go, create your adventure:

Compagnie des Guides de Chamonix (p480) The crème de la crème of mountain guides, founded in 1821. Guides for skiing, mountaineering, ice climbing, hiking, mountain biking and every other Alpine pastime.

Association Internationale des Guides du Mont Blanc (☏04 50 53 27 05; www.guides-du-montblanc.com; 85 rue des Moulins) Chamonix-based international guides; extreme skiing, mountaineering, glacier trekking, ice and rock climbing, and paragliding.

Aventure en Tête (☏04 50 54 05 11; www.aventureentete.com; 420 rte du Chapeau, Le Lavancher) Ski touring and ski-Alpinism expeditions; free-ride and off-piste courses; mountaineering and climbing in summer. Le Lavancher is 6km north of Chamonix.

Chamonix Experience (☏09 77 48 58 69; www.chamex.com; 49 place Edmond Desailloud) Courses in off-piste skiing, avalanche awareness, ice climbing and ski touring; in summer, rock and Alpine climbing.

ERIC FAVRET: MOUNTAIN GUIDE

Eric Favret is a guide with Compagnie des Guides de Chamonix and talked to us about his favourite local spots, views and thrills.

Aiguille du Midi

The Aiguille du Midi, with one of the highest cable cars in the world, cannot be missed. Beyond the summit ridge is a world of snow and ice with some of the greatest intermediate terrain in the Alps.

Off-Piste Thrills

The Vallée Blanche has to be seen. But the Aiguille du Midi also has amazing off-piste runs, such as Envers du Plan, a slightly steeper and more advanced version of Vallée Blanche with dramatic views in the heart of the Mont Blanc range. There is also the less frequented run of the 'Virgin' or 'Black Needle'; a striking glacial run, with different views and a close-up look at the Giant's seracs.

Best-Ever Mont Blanc View

No hesitation: the Traverse from Col des Montets to Lac Blanc. It's as popular as the Eiffel Tower for hikers in summer. I love swimming in mountain lakes, so I like to stop at Lac des Chéserys, just below, where it is quieter: What's better that a swim in pure mountain water, looking at Mont Blanc, the Grandes Jorasses and Aiguille Verte? This is what I call mountain landscape perfection!

🛏 Sleeping

That you need to book ahead in winter goes without saying. Many places close from mid-April to May and from November to mid-December. Room rates nosedive up to 50% in the low season and summer.

TOP CHOICE **Auberge du Manoir**   HOTEL €€
(📞04 50 53 10 77; http://aubergedumanoir.com; 8 rte du Bouchet; s €109-122, d €126-176, q €178; 🛜) This beautifully converted farmhouse is ablaze with geraniums in summer. It ticks all the perfect Alpine chalet boxes: pristine mountain views, pine-panelled rooms that are quaint but never cloying, an outdoor hot tub for unwinding tired muscles and a bar where an open fire keeps things cosy. Breakfast is a treat, with fresh fruit, homemade yoghurt, cakes and tarts.

Hotel L'Oustalet   HOTEL €€
(📞04 50 55 54 99; www.hotel-oustalet.com; 330 rue du Lyret; d/q €148/190; 🛜🏊) You'll pray for snow at this Alpine chalet near Aiguille du Midi cable car, just so you can curl up by the fire with a *chocolat chaud* (hot chocolate) and unwind in the sauna and whirlpool. The rooms, including family ones, are snugly decorated in solid pine and open onto balconies with Mont Blanc views. There's a pool in the garden for chilling out during the summertime.

Hotel Slalom   BOUTIQUE HOTEL €€
(📞04 50 54 40 60; www.hotelslalom.net; 44 rue de Bellevue, Les Houches; r €158; 🛜) You'll receive the warmest of welcomes at this gorgeous chalet-style hotel, right at the foot of the slopes in Les Houches (7km west of central Chamonix). Rooms are sleek, spotless and draped with Egyptian cotton linen. A bacon-and-eggs breakfast fires you up for a day's skiing.

Hôtel Faucigny   BOUTIQUE HOTEL €€
(📞04 50 53 01 17; www.hotelfaucigny-chamonix. com; 118 place de l'Église; s/d/q €90/120/170; 🛜) This bijou hotel is a slice of minimalist Alpine cool, with its charcoal-white rooms and slate-walled spa. Your hosts bend over backwards to please: free bike rental and afternoon tea, a summer terrace with Mont Blanc views, an open fire in winter – they've thought of everything. A whirlpool, a sauna and an array of luscious treatments invite post-ski relaxation.

Hôtel Aiguille du Midi   HOTEL €€
(📞04 50 53 00 65; www.hotel-aiguilledumidi.com; 479 chemin Napoléon, Les Bossons; d €75-150, incl half-board €144-220; 🛜🏊) Mont Blanc will most likely be peeking through the window of your cosy, pine-panelled room at this family-run hotel in Les Bossons, 3km from central Chamonix. Come for the Savoyard food, the big mountain views from

the gardens and pool, and the good old-fashioned hospitality.

Chalet Hôtel Hermitage
CHALET €€

(☑04 50 53 13 87; www.hermitage-paccard.com; 63 chemin du Cé; d €156-205, tr/q €229/253; ☜) The trek from the slopes is worth it: Hermitage is a family-run treasure, with an open fire crackling in the bar, a kids' playroom, delicious home cooking and flowery gardens where you can survey Mont Blanc from your sun-lounger. Decked out from top to toe in wood, rooms blend traditional Alpine style with mod cons and afford mountain views.

Grand Hôtel des Alpes
HISTORIC HOTEL €€€

(☑04 50 55 37 80; www.grandhoteldesalpes.com; 75 rue du Docteur Paccard; r €335-390, ste €585-755; ❄@☜❖) This grand old dame goes down in the chronicles of Chamonix history as one of the resort's first (built in 1840) and finest. The wood-panelled rooms exude timeless elegance. What distinguishes this hotel, however, is its friendliness: in winter a scrumptious cake buffet greets skiers back from the slopes.

Le Vert Hôtel
HOTEL €€

(☑04 50 53 13 58; www.verthotel.com; 964 rte des Gaillands; s/d/tr/q €80/103/129/151; ☜) Self-proclaimed 'Chamonix' house of sports and creativity', this party house, 1km south of town, has no-frills rooms, some with microscopically small bathrooms. But what people really come for is the all-happening, ultrahip bar, a regular venue for top DJs and live music. Minimum four-night stay.

Camping Mer de Glace
CAMPGROUND €

(☑04 50 53 44 03; http://chamonix-camping. com; 200 chemin de la Bagna; sites €23.50; ☺late Apr–Sep; ☜) Oh, what a beautiful morning! Draw back your tent flap and be dazzled by Mont Blanc and glaciated peaks at this campground, 2km northeast of Chamonix and an easy 20-minute stroll from the centre. There's ample tree shade, a playground and free wi-fi.

Hôtel Richemond
HOTEL €€

(☑04 50 53 08 85; www.richemond.fr; 228 rue du Docteur Paccard; s/d/tr €71/112/141; ☜) This friendly, supercentral hotel has been run by the same family since 1914. OK, corridors have seen better days and the old-fashioned rooms are floral overload, but the Mont Blanc views and fabulous cast-iron bathtubs (a godsend for sore muscles) more than make up for it.

Hôtel de l'Arve
HOTEL €€

(☑04 50 53 02 31; www.hotelarve-chamonix.com; 60 impasse des Anémones; d €94-125, tr €109-140, q €124-155; ☜) Keeping it sweet and simple is this hotel overlooking the Arve River. The rooms are cheerfully done up in warm hues and pine, and some have Mont Blanc views. Other pluses include a heated ski-boot room, sauna and gym, pool table, and free parking.

✖ Eating

From postpiste burgers to Michelin-starred finery, Chamonix covers all the bases. Most restaurants open seven days a week in season but have reduced hours out of season. Call ahead to check.

Les Vieilles Luges
TOP CHOICE | TRADITIONAL FRENCH €€

(☑06 84 42 37 00; www.lesvieillesluges.com; Les Houches; menus €20-35; ☺lunch daily, dinner by reservation) Like a scene from a snow globe in winter, this childhood dream of a 250-year-old farmhouse can only be reached by slipping on skis or taking a scenic 20-minute hike from the Maison Neuve chairlift. Under low wood beams, Julie and Claude spoil you with their home cooking – dishes such as *grand-mère*'s bœuf bourguignon and creamy *farçon* (a potato bake prepared with prunes, bacon and cream), all washed down with *vin chaud* (mulled wine) warmed over a wood fire. Magic.

La Petite Kitchen
INTERNATIONAL €

(80 place du Poilu; 2-course lunch menus €12.50, mains €18-28; ☺lunch & dinner Wed-Mon) The little kitchen is just that: a handful of tables for the lucky few who get to indulge in its locally sourced feel-good food. Filling English

---

ⓘ PISTES PASS

The **Mont Blanc Unlimited Pass** (www.compagniedumontblanc.com; 1/6 days €52/259) is worth the investment for serious skiers, giving access to 400km of runs, including all ski areas in the Chamonix valley, the Aiguille du Midi cable car and Montenvers train, plus Courmayeur in Italy and Verbier in Switzerland. Cheaper but more limited in scope is the **Chamonix Le Pass** (www.compagniedumontblanc.com; 1/6 days €43/216) with access to most of Chamonix' ski domains. View all options and buy passes online.

CHAMONIX CLIFFHANGERS

Cliffhanging is an understatement for many of the 18 *refuges* (mountain huts) in the Mont Blanc massif that are poised perilously on the mountain edge or teetering precariously over a stomach-churning drop. The Club Alpin Français (☎04 50 53 16 03; www.clubalpin-chamonix.com; 136 av Michel Croz; ☺office for enquiries 4-6.30pm Tue-Sat) owns eight of the *refuges;* the rest are run privately.

Most *refuges* are staffed by a warden from around mid-June to mid-September and must be reserved in advance by telephone or in person at the office. Expect to pay around €25 for a dorm bed and €40 to €50 for half-board. Meals are simple, hearty and prepared by the hut-keeper.

breakfasts, steaks with homemade *frites* (hot chips) and the stickiest of toffee puddings will send you rolling happily out the door.

Le Panier des 4 Saisons
TRADITIONAL FRENCH €€
(☎04 50 53 98 77; www.restaurant-panierdes4saisons.com; 262 rue du Docteur Paccard; menus €30; ☺lunch & dinner Mon-Sat) This warm, woody restaurant brims with chatter and bonhomie. The menu cherry-picks the seasons for the finest ingredients, cooked up into dishes like thick-cut pollack in a bittersweet red-wine sauce and roast venison with quince purée – all expertly matched with wines.

Le Bistrot
GASTRONOMIC €€€
(☎04 50 53 57 64; www.lebistrotchamonix.com; 151 av de l'Aiguille du Midi; lunch menus €17-28, dinner menus €50-85; ☺daily; ☷) Sleek and monochromatic, this is a real foodie's place. Michelin-starred chef Mickey experiments with textures and seasonal flavours to create taste sensations like pan-seared Arctic char with chestnuts, and divine warm chocolate macaroon with raspberry and red pepper coulis.

Le GouThé
TEAROOM €
(95 rue des Moulins; snacks €3-10; ☺9am-7pm daily; ☷) Welcome to the sweetest of tearooms. Smooth hot chocolates with pistachio and gingerbread infusions, macaroons, *galettes* (buckwheat crêpes) and crumbly homemade tarts are just the sugar fix needed for the slopes.

Munchie
FUSION €€
(☎04 50 53 45 41; www.munchie.eu; 87 rue des Moulins; mains €19-24; ☺dinner daily) The style of this trendy Swedish-run hang-out is pan-Asian fusion: sashimi, sushi, tempura and Malaysian yellow curries are authentic and creatively presented. Sittings go faster than musical chairs, so it's worth a try even if you haven't booked.

Tigre Tigre
INDIAN €
(☎04 50 55 33 42; 239 av Michel Croz; mains €11-17; ☺dinner Tue-Sun; ☷) This hip Indian restaurant is all the rage, with its slinky bar perfect for nibbling pappadams and sipping Cobra beers before the main event. Nice and spicy tikka, tandoori and biryani dishes get your tastebuds jumping like a Bollywood film set and service comes with – hurrah! – a smile.

Le Chaudron
SAVOYARD €€
(☎04 50 53 40 34; 79 rue des Moulins; menus €20-31; ☺dinner daily) On a cold winter's day, this chic Alpine chalet is guaranteed to give you that warm inner glow. Funky cowskin-clad benches are the backdrop for a feast of Savoyard fondues and lamb slow-cooked in red wine to melting perfection.

Papillon
CAFE €
(416 rue Joseph Vallot; light meals €4-8; ☺9am-8pm Tue-Sat, 11am-5.30pm Sun) Papillon does great homemade curries, chillis, fat-jacket potatoes and deli-style sandwiches.

Extreme
CAFE €
(21 place Balmat; light meals €3.50-8; ☺9am-9pm daily) Fun snack bar where you can grab a wrap and smoothie and log on to free wi-fi.

Drinking & Entertainment

Chamonix nightlife rocks. In the centre, quaint old riverside rue des Moulins is the best street for a bar crawl, with wall-to-wall drinking holes. Many of these après-ski joints have food and wi-fi as well as booze.

Chambre Neuf
BAR
(272 av Michel Croz; ☺daily; ☷) Cover bands, raucous après-ski drinking and dancing on the tables make Chambre Neuf one of Chamonix' liveliest party haunts. Conversations about epic off-pistes and monster jumps that are, like, totally mental, man, dominate at every table.

MBC
MICROBREWERY
(www.mbchx.com; 350 rte du Bouchet; ☺4pm-2am daily) This trendy microbrewery run by four Canadians is fab. Be it with their burgers,

cheesecake of the week, live music or amazing locally brewed and named beers (Blonde de Chamonix, Stout des Drus, Blanche des Guides etc), MBC delivers.

Elevation 1904   BAR
(259 av Michel Croz; ☉7am-11pm or later daily) Alpine paraphernalia lines the walls of this merry bet by the train station, which has an all-day snack shack. The suntrap terrace is just right for relaxing over a cold one.

La Terrasse   BAR
(www.laterrassechamonix.com; 43 place Balmat; ☉11am-11pm Sun-Thu, to 2am Fri & Sat; ☎) Race the clock for cheap drinks during happy hour (4pm to 7pm and 9pm to 10pm) and take position on the strategically placed terrace on Chamonix' main square. There's live music nightly.

QuartzBar   LOUNGE BAR
(38 rte du Bouchet, Hameau Albert 1er; ☉daily) Inspired by rock crystals, this cleverly backlit hotel bar is a fashionable place for afternoon tea or a Champagne cocktail. There is live music (usually jazz) from 7pm to 11pm Thursdays to Mondays.

Le Privilège   LOUNGE BAR
(www.barleprivilege.com; 52 rue des Moulins; ☉4pm-2am daily) Rustic-chic lounge with great cocktails and live music.

Lapin Agile   LOUNGE BAR
(11 rue Whymper; ☉11.30am-11.30pm daily; ☎) Relaxed wine bar with Italian wines and (like it!) free *aperitivo* tapas from 6.30pm to 8pm daily.

Jekyll & Hyde   PUB
(www.thejekyll.com; 71 rte des Pélerins; ☉4pm-2am daily; ☎) Après-ski mainstay with Irish beer, hearty food (try the Guinness stew), DJs, bands and a friendly vibe.

Office   BAR
(274 rue Charlet Stratton, Argentière; ☉11am-2am daily; ☎) Sunday roast, English footy and a load of Brits, this is Argentière's party headquarters.

Bistrot des Sports   PUB
(182 rue Joseph Vallot; ☉7am-2am daily) This centuries-old bolthole for muleteers, guides and other mountain folk has a street terrace perfect for a mellow drink.

❶ Information

PGHM (☑04 50 53 16 89; 69 rue de la Mollard) Mountain-rescue service for the entire Mont Blanc area.

Post office (89 place Balmat)

Tourist office (☑04 50 53 00 24; www.chamonix.com; 85 place du Triangle de l'Amitié; ☉8.30am-7pm) Accommodation, weather and activity information. The tourist office also has a list of doctors, dentists, pharmacists etc.

❶ Getting There & Away

BUS From the **Chamonix bus station** (www.sat-montblanc.com; place de la Gare), located next to the train station, five buses run daily to/from Geneva airport and bus station (one-way/return €33/55, 1½ to two hours) and Courmayeur (one-way/return €13/20, 45 minutes). Advanced booking is required for both. See the website for timetables and reservations.

CAR & MOTORCYCLE From Italy you'll approach Chamonix via the 11.5km-long **Tunnel de Mont Blanc** (www.atmb.net; toll one-way/return €39/49), which enters town in the southern suburb of Les Pélerins. From France the A40 toll motorway – the Autoroute Blanche – hooks up with the Chamonix-bound N205 dual carriageway for the last leg.

Parking in town can be tricky, although **Parking du Mont-Blanc** (place du Mont Blanc; 1st hr free, then per hr/day/week €2/8/50) is reliable. If you're lucky enough to get a spot, you can park for free on rue Helbronner and allée du Recteur Payot.

Car-hire companies include **Europcar** (www.europcar.com; 36 place de la Gare).

TRAIN The Mont Blanc Express narrow-gauge train trundles from St-Gervais–Le Fayet station, 23km west of Chamonix, to Martigny in Switzerland, stopping en route in Les Houches, Chamonix and Argentière. There are nine to 12 return trips daily between Chamonix and St-Gervais (€10, 45 minutes). Travelling between Servoz and Vallorcine is free if you have the *carte d'hôte* (see boxed text p486).

From St-Gervais–Le Fayet there are trains to most major French cities.

---

❶ **A LOFTY LUNCH**

Crazy as it sounds for a piste restaurant, you might have to book at La Crémerie du Glacier (☑04 50 54 07 52; www.lacremerieduglacier.fr; 766 chemin de la Glacière; menus €12-22; ☉lunch & dinner Thu-Tue) to get a chance to bite into its world-famous *croûtes au fromage* (chunky slices of toasted bread topped with melted cheese). Ski to it on the red Pierre à Ric piste in Les Grands Montets.

🛈 GOING GREEN

Chamonix has long battled with air-pollution problems. In a bid to encourage locals and visitors to leave the car at home, the Chamonix valley offers free public transport on the buses in Chamonix and the train between Servoz (14km west) and Vallorcine (15.5km north). All you have to do is get a *carte d'hôte* from your hotel or campground and on you go for free. The card also offers reductions for a number of activities. Details are listed on the card leaflet.

🛈 Getting Around

BICYCLE You can hire cross-country, mountain and downhill bikes from **Zero G** (www.zerogchx. com; 90 av Ravanel le Rouge; bicycles per day €15-60; ⊙9am-12.30pm & 3.30-7pm), which also rents out snowboard gear.

BUS Local bus transport is handled by **Chamonix Bus** (www.chamonix-bus.com; 591 promenade Marie-Paradis). From mid-December to the end of April, services to the ski lifts and central car parks depart every 10 minutes or so between 7am and 7pm (town-centre shuttles run 8.30am to 6.30pm). All buses are free with the *carte d'hôte* (p486) scheme, except the Chamo' Nuit night buses linking Chamonix with Argentière and Les Houches (last departures from Chamonix 11.30pm or midnight; €2).

TAXI For a taxi, call 📞04 50 53 13 94. Taxis also queue up in front of the train station.

Megève & St-Gervais

Très chic Megève (population 4076, elevation 1113m) was developed in the 1920s for Baroness de Rothschild of the famous banking family, who found Switzerland's overcrowded St-Moritz frankly rather tiresome. Today the ski village looks almost too perfect to be true: horse-drawn sleighs and exquisitely arranged boutique windows spill into its cobbled, medieval-style streets. In winter it attracts a moneyed crowd, but the scene is more laid-back in summer.

Sitting snug below Mont Blanc, 24km west of Chamonix, Megève's neighbour is refreshingly authentic St-Gervais-les-Bains (population 5813, elevation 850m), better known as simply St-Gervais. Its postcard-perfect Savoyard village, centred on a baroque church and old-fashioned carousel, is linked to Chamonix by the legendary Mont Blanc Express.

🏃 Activities

A Mont Blanc massif backdrop makes for fabulously scenic skiing in Megève, where downhill is split into three separate areas: Mont d'Arbois–Princesse (linked to St-Gervais), Jaillet-Combloux and Rochebrune-Côte 2000. Skiing in both resorts is mostly for beginners and cruisy intermediates, and there are 445km of well-groomed pistes to play on. Lift passes are sold online at www.skiamegeve.com.

Panoramic hiking trails in the Bettex, Mont d'Arbois and Mont Joly areas head off from both villages. Some of the best mountain-biking terrain is marked between Val d'Arly, Mont Blanc and Beaufortain.

Maison de la Montagne OUTDOOR ACTIVITIES
(176 rue de la Poste, Megève) Based here are Megève's **ESF** (www.megeve-ski.com; ⊙9am-6.30pm) and **Compagnie des Guides** (www.guides-megeve.com; ⊙9am-6.30pm), which organise activities such as off-piste skiing, ice climbing, rock climbing, paragliding, canyoning and mountain biking excursions.

Tramway du Mont Blanc FUNICULAR
(rue de la Gare, St-Gervais; return to Bellevue/Mont Lachat €28/31; ⊙9am-4.50pm) For spirit-soaring mountain views with zero effort, board France's highest train. Since 1913 it has laboured up to Bellevue (1800m) from St-Gervais–Le Fayet in winter and further up, to 2113m-high Mont Lachat, in summer.

🛏 Sleeping & Eating

The tourist offices in **Megève** (📞04 50 21 29 52; Megève) and **St-Gervais** (📞04 50 47 76 08; St-Gervais) run an **accommodation service**.
Rates drop by up to 50% in summer.

Chalet d'Antoine CHALET €€
(📞04 50 21 05 56; www.chalet-antoine.com; 187 rte Edmond de Rothschild, Megève; d €150-168, q €189; 🛜) This chalet deserves a gold star for its first-class service, supremely comfortable rooms done out in pine and zesty lime and plum shades, and activities, from pro ski tuition to cycle coaching. Post-slope tea and cakes, slap-up breakfasts and massages all add to the feel-good factor.

Le Gai Soleil CHALET €€
(📞04 50 21 00 70; www.le-gai-soleil.fr; 343 rue Crêt du Midi, Megève; d incl breakfast/half-board €142/198; @🛜🛖) Make yourself at home in

this inviting chalet, harbouring warm, spacious rooms, a Jacuzzi and an inviting restaurant. The outdoor pool and sun deck afford sublime mountain views.

La Chaumière   HOTEL €
(☎04 50 93 60 10; www.lachaumierehotel.com; 222 av de Genève, St-Gervais-Le Fayet; s/d/tr/q €42/48/60/69; @🐾) A godsend for cash-strapped skiers, this chalet-style hotel has bright, modern rooms sporting above-par perks like flatscreen TVs and balconies. Family rooms are available. Limber up on the climbing wall or wind down in the Jacuzzi and gym (€5). The hotel is 5km north of St-Gervais-les-Bains.

Les Dômes de Miage   CAMPGROUND €
(☎04 50 93 45 96; www.camping-mont-blanc.com; 197 rte des Contamines, St-Gervais; sites €23-29; ☺May–mid-Sep; 🐾) Mont Blanc is your wake-up call at this well-equipped campground, beautifully set in wooded hills. The first-rate facilities include a restaurant and playground.

TOP CHOICE Flocons de Sel   GASTRONOMIC €€€
(☎04 50 21 49 99; www.floconsdesel.com; 1775 rte de Leutaz, Megève; lunch menus €39-77, dinner menus €147; ☺lunch & dinner Thu-Mon) Emmanuel Renaut, who trained with Marc Veyrat and at Claridges, mans the stove at this triple Michelin-starred restaurant, housed in a stylishly converted farmhouse. He cooks and artistically presents whatever is fresh that day, be it lake fish or pigeon, rounding them out with his signature *flocons de sucre* (sugar snowflakes) dessert. The insightful cooking classes (€60 to €120, 4pm to 6pm Thursday to Saturday) focus on two to three recipes – from simple starters to petits fours.

Le Galeta   SAVOYARD €€
(☎04 50 93 16 11; 150 impasse des Lupins, St-Gervais; menus €25-29; ☺dinner daily; 🚸) Tucked behind the church, this rustic barn-style restaurant radiates Alpine character and warmth. Sylvie and Serge serve up succulent meats grilled over a wood fire and tot up your (rather modest) bill on an antique till.

❶ Information

Megève tourist office (☎04 50 21 27 28; www.megeve.com; 70 rue de Monseigneur Conseil; ☺9am-12.30pm & 2-6.30pm Mon-Sat)

St-Gervais tourist office (☎04 50 47 76 08; www.saintgervais.com; 43 rue du Mont-Blanc;

☺9am-12.30pm & 2-7pm Mon-Fri, 9am-7pm Sat & Sun)

❶ Getting There & Away

BUS From Megève bus station, there are seven daily services to/from St-Gervais-Le Fayet and Sallanches train stations. In winter, **SAT** (www.sat-montblanc.com) buses run at least twice daily between Geneva airport (one-way/return €28/47, 1½ hours) and St-Gervais-Le Fayet.

TRAIN The closest train station to Megève is in Sallanches, 12km north; for information go to the SNCF information desk inside the bus station. St-Gervais is the main train station for Chamonix: the towns are linked by the Mont Blanc Express. Other services include several day trains (€97, 5½ hours) to Paris, plus frequent trains to Lyon (€34, 3½ hours), Annecy (€14.50, 1½ hours) and Geneva (€13, 1½ hours).

Les Portes du Soleil

Poetically dubbed 'the Gates of the Sun' (elevation 1000m to 2466m; www.portesdusoleil.com), this gargantuan ski area – the world's largest – is formed from a chain of 12 villages strung along the French–Swiss border.

The best known of the villages is Morzine (elevation 1000m), which retains some traditional Alpine charm, especially in summer when visits to cheese dairies and traditional slate workshops kick in. Small, trend-conscious Avoriaz (elevation 1800m), a purpose-built ski resort a few kilometres up the valley atop a rock, appeals for its no-cars policy. Horse-drawn sleighs piled high with luggage romantically ferry new arrivals to and from the snowy village centre where wacky 1960s mimetic architecture gets away with an 'avant-garde' tag.

DON'T MISS

POTTER'S FANTASY

His name is Monsieur Baranger, but he prefers to be called 'the potter behind the church' – and that's precisely where you will find his rambling, poster-plastered workshop and gallery in St-Gervais. An eccentric and something of a local legend, M Baranger can often be seen at his wheel, where he throws pots, plates, ornaments and vases, which are then glazed in earthy shades of blue and cream. His workshop is open *quand vous voyez de la lumière* (when the lights are on).

ⓘ MULTIPASS MAGIC

Les Portes du Soleil's hottest summer deal is the Multipass, which costs €1 per day for guests and €6 for day trippers. Available from mid-June to mid-September, the pass covers transport from cable cars and chairlifts to shuttle buses; activities, including tennis courts, ice rinks and swimming pools; and entry to five cultural sites, from heritage museums to abbeys.

Arriving by road via Cluses you hit smaller Les Gets (elevation 1172m), a family favourite.

🏃 Activities

A mind-blowing 650km of downhill slopes and cross-country trails criss-cross Les Portes de Soleil, served by 197 lifts and covered by a single ski pass. Morzine is ideal beginner and intermediate terrain, with scenic tree runs for bad-weather days. The snow-sure slopes of Avoriaz offer more of a challenge. This is freestyle heaven for boarders, with deep powder, several snowparks to play in and a fantastic super-pipe near the top of Prodains cable car. Nursery slopes, toboggan runs, kids' clubs and snow play areas make Les Portes du Soleil a great choice for families.

In summer, the same slopes attract mountain bikers, with invigorating routes like the 90km circular Portes du Soleil tour. Walkers can pick and choose from 800km of marked trails; an extensive lift network takes the slog out of reaching higher altitudes.

Bureau des Guides OUTDOOR ACTIVITIES
(☑04 50 75 96 65; www.bureaudesguides.net) For local know-how on summer activities – hiking, biking, climbing, canyoning and paragliding – and advice on mountain-bike hire and Morzine's heart-stopping 3300m-long bike descent (free; ☺mid-Jun–mid-Sep) from the top of the Plénéy cable car (1/10 ascents €4.50/26).

🛏 Sleeping & Eating

The Morzine tourist office has an accommodation service (☑04 50 79 11 57; www.resa-morzine.com).

TOP CHOICE Farmhouse BOUTIQUE HOTEL €€€
(☑04 50 79 08 26; www.thefarmhouse.fr; Le Mas de la Coutettaz, Morzine; d incl half-board €208-400,

dinner menus €40; ☎) Morzine's oldest pile is this gorgeous 1771 farmhouse run by the charming Dorrien Ricardo. Five rooms (some with Victorian-style bathrooms) are in the main house, and a trio of cottages (including the old *mazot,* a miniature mountain chalet) sit in the lovely grounds. Dining – open to nonguests too – is a lavish affair around one huge banquet table. There is a minimum one-week stay in the peak winter season.

Bonne Valette HOTEL €
(☑04 50 79 04 31; www.hotel-bonne-valette.com; Champs de la Plagne, Morzine; s/d/tr/q €40/80/90/110; ☎🖥) Slap-bang in the heart of Morzine, this family-run hotel has well-kept, old-style rooms heavy on wood and florals. It eclipses most budget options with its sauna, outdoor pool and super-friendly welcome.

Ferme de Montagne BOUTIQUE HOTEL €€€
(☑04 50 75 36 79; www.fermedemontagne.com; Les Gets; r incl half-board per person per week €1950-2400; ☎) This glamourpuss of a spa-clad farmhouse has been tipped as one of Europe's hottest boutique ski hotels by glossy-mag critics. The price tag covers every imaginable luxury: personalised ski guides, afternoon tea with homemade cakes by a roaring fire, a bubble in the hot tub surrounded by snowy peaks, you name it.

Fleur des Neiges CHALET €€
(☑04 50 79 01 23; www.chalethotelfleurdesneiges.com; 227 Taille de Mas de Nant Crue, Morzine; d incl half-board €90; ☎🖥) A cheery welcome and solid home cooking await at this family-run chalet, snuggled at the foot of forested mountains. The sauna invites post-ski steams, and the pool summertime swims.

Le Clin d'Oeil TRADITIONAL FRENCH €
(☑04 50 79 03 10; www.restaurant-leclin.com; 63 rte du Plan, Morzine; mains €14-22, 3-course lunch menus €15; ☺lunch & dinner daily; 🍴) Bringing a pinch of the southwest's herby aromas to the Alps is this seasoned people-pleaser. The all-wood interior is inviting for rich, brothy *cassoulet* (stew) in winter, while the flowery patio is ideal for lighter dishes like risottos and seafood in summer.

ⓘ Information

Avoriaz tourist office (☑04 50 74 02 11; www.avoriaz.com; 44 promenade des Festivals; ☺8.30am-7pm daily; ☎) Can book self-catering chalets and studios. Internet costs €5 per hour.

Les Gets tourist office (☑04 50 75 80 80, accommodation service 04 50 75 80 51; www.lesgets.com; place de la Mairie; ⊙8.30am-7pm)

Morzine tourist office (☑04 50 74 72 72; www.morzine-avoriaz.com; place du Baraty; ⊙8.30am-7.30pm)

❶ Getting There & Away

Free shuttle buses serve the lifts of Télécabine Super Morzine, Télécabine du Pléney and Téléphérique Avoriaz.

During the ski season a regular bus service runs between Geneva airport, about 50km west, and Morzine (one-way/return €36/59), Avoriaz (€39/65) and Les Gets (€33/55). From Morzine there are frequent **SAT buses** (www.sat-montblanc.com) to Les Gets and Avoriaz. There are also buses from Morzine to its closest train stations: Thonon-les-Bains and Cluses (one-way/return €11/22).

Thonon-les-Bains

POP 34,823 / ELEV 430M

Just across the water from Lausanne on the French side of Lake Geneva (Lac Léman), Thonon-les-Bains – a fashionable spa town during the belle époque – sits on a bluff above the lake. Winter is deathly dull, but its summer cruises and lakeside strolls appeal.

◉ Sights & Activities

Château de Ripaille   CASTLE
(www.ripaille.fr; adult/child €7/3.50; ⊙10am-6.30pm, closed Nov-Mar) Once home to the dukes of Savoy, this turreted castle, rebuilt in the 19th century on the site of its 15th-century ancestor, is 1km east of town along quai de Ripaille. It has vineyards, a garden for summer dining and forested grounds to explore.

Fontaine de la Versoie   FOUNTAIN
(Parc Thermal de Thonon) You can fill your bottle with Thonon mineral water for free at this mosaic-lined fountain.

Funicular Railway   FUNICULAR
(rue du Funiculaire; rides one-way/return €1/1.80; ⊙8am-9pm) This nostalgic 230m-long funicular links the upper town with the marina.

CGN   LAKE CRUISES
(www.cgn.ch) Regular services from the port in Thonon-les-Bains to destinations around the lake include Geneva (one-way/return €31.50/54), Évian-les-Bains (€14/24.50), Yvoire (€16/27) and Lausanne (€28/48). See the website for an up-to-date timetable and other themed cruises.

🛏 Sleeping

L'Arc en Ciel   HOTEL €
(☑04 50 71 90 63; www.hotelarcencielthonon.com; 18 place de Crête; s/d/tr/q €69/79/86/104; ☎⊠) Kind-hearted owners, fresh, spacious rooms with balconies and a quiet garden with a pool make this budget option stand out from the crowd. It's a 10-minute amble south of town.

Hôtel à l'Ombre des Marronniers   HOTEL €
(☑04 50 71 26 18; www.hotellesmarronniers.com; 17 place de Crête; s/d/tr/q €62/64/74/98; ☎⊠) Sitting in flowery gardens, L'Arc en Ciel's chalet-style neighbour is another bargain,

ÉVIAN, ÉVIAN EVERYWHERE

Trot 9km east from Thonon along the lake and you hit the elegant belle époque spa town of Évian-les-Bains, of mineral-water fame. Discovered in 1790 and bottled since 1826, the water takes 15 years to trickle down through the Chablais Mountains, gathering minerals en route, before emerging at 11.4°C. A favourite country retreat of the dukes of Savoy, Évian was reinvented as a luxury spa resort in the 18th century, when wallowing in tubs of mineral water was all the rage. You can wallow yourself in the thermal pools at Les Thermes Évian (☑04 50 75 02 30; www.lesthermesevian.com; place de la Libération; journée découverte €65; ⊙9am-8pm Mon-Fri, to 6.30pm Sat). The journée découverte (discovery day) includes a dip in the thermal pool with Évian jets and a 20-minute essential oil massage. This and all other hydrotherapy and beauty treatments must be prebooked online or by calling ahead.

Fill your bottle with Évian water for free at art nouveau spring Buvette Cachat (20 av des Sources). For total immersion, call ahead to arrange a tour (☑04 50 84 80 29; adult/child €3/free; ⊙Jun-Sep) of the Évian bottling plant, 5km out of town. The tourist office (www.eviantourism.com; place d'Allinges) can also help.

with modest, well-kept rooms and an outdoor pool.

❶ Information

Lakeside tourist office (◷10am-12.30pm & 2-6.30pm Jul & Aug) A chalet where you can also buy boat tickets with CGN (p489).

Thonon-les-Bains tourist office (✆04 50 71 55 55; www.thononlesbains.com; 2 rue Michaud, Château de Sonnaz; ◷9am-12.15pm & 1.45-6.30pm Mon-Fri, from 10am Sat) In the upper town.

❶ Getting There & Away

BUS From Thonon bus station (place des Arts), **SAT** (www.sat-leman.com) runs regular buses to/from Évian-les-Bains (€1.50, 20 minutes) and into the Chablais Mountains, including to Morzine (€11, one hour).

TRAIN The train station (place de la Gare) is southwest of place des Arts, the main square. Trains run to/from Évian-les-Bains (€2.30, eight minutes) and Geneva (€16.50, 1¾ hours) via Bellegarde (€12, 1¼ hours).

Yvoire

POP 845

A real sleeping beauty of a medieval village, Yvoire, 16km west of Thonon on the shores of Lake Geneva, makes for a great day trip. The village is a riot of turrets and towers, cob houses and geranium-lined streets. Familiarise yourself with its 700-year history on a 1½-hour guided tour (tours €5.50; ◷10.45am Tue & Thu, 4.45pm Wed & Fri Jul-Aug).

Slumbering in the shadow of a 14th-century castle and enclosed by walls, the Jardin des Cinq Sens (Garden of Five Senses; www.jardin5sens.net; rue du Lac; adult/child €10/5.50; ◷10am-7pm) appeals to the senses through touch, sound (gurgling water), scent (fragrant gardens) and taste (edible plants).

The tourist office (✆04 50 72 80 21; www.yvoiretourism.com; place de la Mairie; ◷9.30am-12.30pm & 1.30-5pm Mon-Sat, noon-4pm Sun) can advise on accommodation.

Annecy

POP 52,161 / ELEV 447M

Even Savoyards spoilt rotten with Alpine views every day of their lives grow wistful at the mention of Annecy. Why? Just look around you: the mountains rise steep, wooded and snow-capped above Lac d'Annecy, so startlingly turquoise it looks unreal; the Vieille Ville (Old Town) is a ludicrously pretty ensemble of pastel-daubed, geranium-strewn houses; the turreted castle – wait, even the old prison – ticks all the medieval-fantasy boxes.

With that phenomenal backdrop, it's no wonder everyone is outdoors – hanging out in pavement cafes, mountain-gazing in gardens, swimming in the lake (among Europe's purest) and cycling around it. Annecy, we think you will agree, really is quite lovely.

◉ Sights

TOP CHOICE Palais de l'Isle MUSEUM
(3 passage de l'Île; adult/child €3.50/1.50; ◷10.30am-6pm) Sitting on a triangular islet in the Canal du Thiou, the whimsically turreted, 12th-century Palais de l'Isle has been a lordly residence, courthouse, mint and prison (lucky inmates!) over the centuries. Today Annecy's most visible landmark hosts local-history displays.

Vieille Ville & Lakefront HISTORIC QUARTER
It's a pleasure simply to wander aimlessly around Annecy's medieval old town, a photogenic jumble of narrow streets, turquoise canals and colonnaded passageways. Continue down to the tree-fringed lakefront and the flowery Jardins de l'Europe, linked to the popular picnic spot Champ de Mars by the poetic iron arch of the Pont des Amours (Lovers' Bridge).

Château d'Annecy CASTLE
(rampe du Château; adult/child €5/2.50; ◷10.30am-6pm) Rising dramatically above the old town, this perkily turreted castle was once home to the Counts of Geneva. The oldest part is the 12th-century Tour de la Reine (Queen's Tower). Its museum takes a romp through traditional Savoyard art, crafts and Alpine natural history.

🏃 Activities

Sunbathing & Swimming
When the sun's out, the beaches fringing Annecy's lakefront beckon.

FREE Plage d'Annecy-le-Vieux BEACH
(◷May-Aug) If you feel like diving straight into those crystal-clear waters, head to this public beach, 1km east of Champ de Mars.

Plage Impérial BEACH
(adult/child €3.90/2.20; ◷Jul & Aug) Closer to town, this privately run beach sits beneath the elegant pre-WWI Palais Impérial.

Annecy

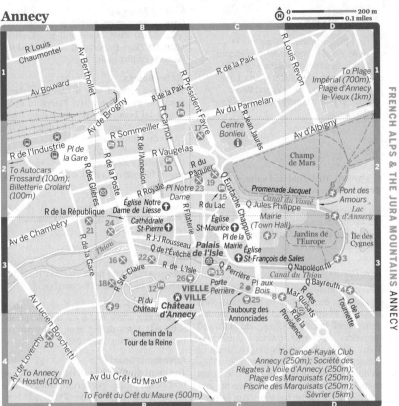

Annecy

FREE **Plage des Marquisats**　　　　　　BEACH
(May-Aug) This sand-and-shingle beach is 1km south of town along rue des Marquisats.

Piscine des Marquisats　　　SWIMMING POOLS
(29 rue des Marquisats; adult/child €4.30/3.30; 10am-7pm May–early Sep) Right next door to the beach is this trio of outdoor swimming pools.

Walking
You can amble along the lakefront from the Jardins de l'Europe to the Stade Nautique des Marquisats and beyond. Another scenic stroll begins at Champ de Mars and meanders eastwards towards Annecy-le-Vieux. Forêt du Crêt du Maure, south of Annecy, has myriad walking trails, as do the wildlife-rich wetlands of Bout du Lac, 20km from Annecy on the lake's southern tip, and Roc de Chère nature reserve, 10km away on the eastern shore.

The tourist office stocks guides and maps, including IGN's *Lac d'Annecy* and *Walks and Treks Lake of Annecy*, listing 15 itineraries in the area (€6.50).

Cycling & Blading
Biking and blading are big, with 46km of cycling tracks encircling the lake. The tourist office and rental outlets have free maps.

Roll'n Cy　　　　　　　　　BLADING
(www.roll-n-cy.org; 8pm Fri) Get your skates on for the jaunts organised by this local rollerblading club. The meeting point is in front of the Mairie (Town Hall) on rue de l'Hôtel de Ville.

Roul' ma Poule　　　　CYCLING, BLADING
(www.annecy-location-velo.com; 4 rue des Marquisats; 9.30am-12.30pm & 2-7pm) Hires out rollerblades (€12/18 per half-/full day), bikes (€12/18), tandems (€25/37) and scooters (€10/15). Can recommend day trips in the area.

Station Roller　　　　　　CYCLING, BLADING
(www.roller-golf-annecy.com; 2 av du Petit Port; 9am-10pm) Bike, blade and kayak outlet near the Plage Impérial at the start of the lakeside cycling path.

Water Sports
The most relaxed way to see the lake is from the water. From late March to October, pedal boats/motorboats can be hired for €15/50 per hour along the quays of the Canal du Thiou (by Quai Napoléon III and Quai Bayreuth) and Canal du Vassé (by Quai Jules Philippe and Promenade Jacquet). In summer check out the following outlets:

Canoë-Kayak Club d'Annecy　　　KAYAKING
(www.kayak-annecy.com; 33 rue des Marquisats; per hr €7) Kayak hire.

Société des Régates à Voile d'Annecy　　　　　SAILING
(www.srva.info; 31 rue des Marquisats) Hires out sailing boats from €30 for two hours.

Annecy Plongée　　　　　　　DIVING
(www.annecyplongee.com; 6 rue des Marquisats) Sells and hires diving gear and arranges two-hour baptism dives (€50).

Adventure Sports
The tourist office has details on a whole host of adventure sports companies on and around Lake Annecy. One of the most central is Takamaka (www.takamaka.fr; 23 rue Ste-Claire). Introductory courses start from €90 for tandem paragliding, €40 for waterskiing or wakeboarding, €42 for rafting, €39 for climbing or freeriding, €49 for canyoning and €65 for bungee jumping.

☞ Tours

Town Tours　　　　　　　WALKING TOUR
(per person €6; 4pm Tue & Thu) The tourist office organises guided tours of the old town; they are in French but some guides speak a little English. If you would prefer to go it alone, pick up the free *Annecy Town Walks* leaflet.

Compagnie des Bateaux　　　　BOAT TOUR
(www.annecy-croisieres.com; 2 place aux Bois; 30min lake cruises €13/17; Feb–mid-Dec) Runs cruises departing from quai Bayreuth. Tickets are sold 15 minutes before departure. From May to September boats also sail across the lake to Menthon-St-Bernard (€5.50), Talloires (€7), Sévrier (€12) and other villages.

⭐ Festivals & Events

Annecy celebrates the flamboyant Venetian carnival in February, the Fête du Lac, with fireworks over the lake, in August, and October's Le Retour des Alpages, when the cows come home from the Alpine pastures, wreathed in flowers and bells. Street performers wow evening crowds at Les Noctibules in July.

🛏 Sleeping

You'll need to book months ahead if you're planning to visit Annecy in July or August, when rooms are gold-dust rare. The tourist office has details of campgrounds and *chambres d'hôte* (B&Bs) scattered around the lake.

Annecy Hostel HOSTEL €
(✆09 53 12 02 90; www.annecyhostel.fr; 32 av de Loverchy; dm/d €22/55; 🛜) Run by two well-travelled brothers, this newcomer makes backpackers' hearts sing with its bright and funky four-bed dorms, shared kitchen, chilled TV lounge and cheap bike rental. Best of all is the garden, perfect for summer games and barbecues. It's a five-minute walk southwest of the old town.

Hôtel Alexandra HOTEL €
(✆04 50 52 84 33; www.hotelannecy-alexandra.fr; 19 rue Vaugelas; s/d/tr/q €55/75/95/110; 🛜) Nice surprise: Annecy's most charming hotel is also one of its most affordable. The welcome is five-star, rooms are fresh and spotless – the best have balconies and canal views – and breakfast (€8) is a generous spread with fresh pastries.

Splendid Hôtel BOUTIQUE HOTEL €€
(✆04 50 45 20 00; www.hotel-annecy-lac.fr; 4 quai Eustache Chappuis; s/d €109/121; 🛜❄🛜) 'Splendid' certainly sums up the lakefront position of this hotel, with breezy views from its boutique-chic, parquet-floor rooms. It's geared up for families: whether you need an extra bed or a babysitter, the friendly staff will oblige.

Hôtel des Alpes HOTEL €
(✆04 50 45 04 56; www.hotelannecy.com; 12 rue de la Poste; s/d/tr €66/75/95/105; 🛜) This bubblegum-pink hotel in Annecy's centre has well-lit rooms with squeaky-clean bathrooms. It's reasonably quiet despite being on a busy street.

Le Pré Carré BOUTIQUE HOTEL €€€
(✆04 50 52 14 14; www.hotel-annecy.net; 27 rue Sommeiller; s/d €178/208; ❄@🛜) One of Annecy's chicest hotels, Le Pré Carré keeps things contemporary with muted colours in rooms with balconies or terraces, a Jacuzzi and a business corner. The staff know Annecy inside out so you're in very good hands.

Hôtel du Château HOTEL €
(✆04 50 45 27 66; www.annecy-hotel.com; 16 rampe du Château; s/d/tr/q €50/75/85/95; 🛜) Nestled at the foot of the castle, this hotel's trump card is its sun-drenched, panoramic breakfast terrace. Rooms are small but sweet, with their pine furniture and pastel tones.

Hôtel du Palais de l'Isle HISTORIC HOTEL €€
(✆04 50 45 86 87; www.hoteldupalaisdelisle.com; 13 rue Perrière; s/d €82/120; ❄🛜) Guests slumber in the heart of old-town action at this 18th-century haunt, where the crisp contemporary decor is soothing after the bustle outside. Rooms sport assorted views of the Palais, the castle or the old town's sea of roofs.

Camping les Rives du Lac CAMPGROUND €
(✆04 50 52 40 14; www.lesrivesdulac-annecy.com; 331 chemin des Communaux; sites €23; ⊙mid-Apr–Sep; 🛜) Pitch your tent near the lakefront at this shady campground, 5km south of town in Sévrier. A cycling track runs into central Annecy from here.

🍴 Eating

The quays along Canal du Thiou are jam-packed with touristy cafes and pizzerias. Crêpes, kebabs, ice cream, patisserie and classic French cuisine – you'll find it all along pedestrianised rue Carnot, rue Pâquier and rue Faubourg Ste-Claire.

⭐ L'Esquisse REGIONAL CUISINE €€
(✆04 50 44 80 59; www.esquisse-annecy.fr; 21 rue Royale; lunch menus €19-22, dinner menus €29-60; ⊙lunch & dinner Mon-Tue & Thu-Sat) A talented husband-and-wife team runs the show at this intimate bistro, with just six tables that fill predictably quickly. Their passion shines through in the service, wine list and, *bien sûr* (of course), the food. The carefully composed *menus* (set meals) sing with natural, integral flavours, from wild mushrooms to spider crab, and are presented with an eye for detail.

Le Denti BISTRO €€
(✆04 50 64 21 17; 25bis av de Loverchy; menus €18-31; ⊙lunch Thu-Tue, dinner Mon & Thu-Sat) Slightly off the beaten track but worth seeking out, this bistro has got a lot going for it: a loyal clientele, a midday buzz and a succinct

menu of ingredient-focused dishes, from asparagus risotto to Atlantic cod with chorizo. The three-course lunch is a bargain at €18.

La Ciboulette
GASTRONOMIC €€€

(☑04 50 45 74 57; www.laciboulette-annecy.com; 10 rue Vaugelas, cour du Pré Carré; menus €35-63; ☺lunch & dinner Tue-Sat) Such class! Crisp white linen and gold-kissed walls set the scene at this Michelin-starred place, where chef Georges Paccard cooks fresh seasonal specialities, such as fillet of veal in a nut crust with cream of *vin jaune*, asparagus and potato-parmesan gnocchi. Reservations are essential.

L'Estaminet
BISTRO €€

(☑04 50 45 88 83; 8 rue Ste-Claire; mains €14-26; ☺lunch Tue-Sun, dinner Tue-Sat; 🖰) With its dark wood and intriguing knick-knacks, this incredibly cosy *estaminet* (Flemish eatery) whisks you to the backstreets of Brussels. Draught Belgian beers pair well with *carbonnade flamande* (rich Flemish beef stew) and *moules* (mussels), with unusual additions like pastis and curry.

L'Étage
SAVOYARD €€

(☑04 50 51 03 28; 13 rue du Pâquier; menus €22-34; ☺lunch & dinner daily) Cheese, glorious cheese... *Fromage* is given pride of place in spot-on fondues and *raclette* (melting cheese, boiled potatoes, charcuterie and baby gherkins) at L'Étage, where a backdrop of mellow music and cheerful staff keep the ambience relaxed.

La Cuisine des Amis
BISTRO €€

(☑04 50 10 10 80; 9 rue du Pâquier; menus €15-31; ☺lunch & dinner daily; 🖰) Opening onto a great people-watching terrace, this charcoal-walled bistro welcomes its clientele like *amis* (friends). Dine well on dishes like *marmite du pêcheur* (seafood stew) and Moroccan-style *pastilla* – crisp puff pastry pie filled with goat's-milk cheese, figs and honey.

La Courette du Faubourg
BISTRO €€

(☑04 50 77 14 03; 4 rue Ste-Claire; menus €15-30; ☺lunch & dinner Wed-Sun) Poised to become an old-town favourite, this new stone-walled bistro keeps it fresh, simple and bursting with flavour – be it beautifully tender braised beef or creamy polenta with basil.

Nature & Saveur
REGIONAL CUISINE €€

(☑04 50 45 82 29; place des Cordeliers; menus €24-44; ☺lunch Tue-Sat) This organic, season-focused restaurant puts a creative spin on farm-fresh legumes and locally reared meat.

Food Market
MARKET €

(Vieille Ville; ☺7am-1am Sun, Tue & Fri) The old-town market is great for picnic fixings.

🍷 Drinking

Annecy needs its beauty sleep, so nights are more about people-watching over relaxed drinks by the canalside than raving it up.

Les Caves du Château
WINE BAR

(6 rampe du Château; ☺Tue-Sun) A sweet little wine bar tucked at the foot of the castle with an excellent array of wines by the glass, tasting plates of cheese and charcuterie (€9 to €14) and a decked terrace for watching the world go by.

Finn Kelly's
PUB

(10 faubourg des Annonciades; ☺4.30pm-3am daily; 🖰) Has live sports, darts and billiards, and regular DJ nights and gigs at weekends.

ℹ Information

Post office (4bis rue des Glières)

Tourist office (☑04 50 45 00 33; www.lac-annecy.com; 1 rue Jean Jaurès, Centre Bonlieu; ☺9am-6.30pm Mon-Sat, to 12.30pm & 1.45-6pm Sun) Has a selection of free maps and brochures, and is the starting point for walking tours of the old town.

ℹ Getting There & Away

BUS From the north terminal of the **bus station** (rue de l'Industrie), adjoining the train station, the **Billetterie Crolard** (www.voyages-crolard.com) sells tickets for various lakeside destinations, local ski resorts and Lyon airport.

Menthon-St-Bernard (€1.50, 20 minutes, hourly)

Veyrier-du-Lac (€1.50, 15 minutes, hourly)

Talloires (€1.50, 25 minutes, hourly)

La Clusaz (one-way/return €8/16, 50 minutes, frequent)

Le Grand Bornand (one-way/return €8/16, one hour, frequent)

Lyon St-Exupéry airport (one-way/return €33/50, 2¼ hours, four to five buses daily)

Next door is **Autocars Frossard** (www.frossard.eu):

Geneva (€10.50, 1½ hours, 16 daily)

Thonon-les-Bains (€14, two hours, twice daily)

Évian-les-Bains (€14, 2½ hours, twice daily)

Chambéry (€6, 1½ hours)

WORTH A TRIP

LAKESIDE LEGENDS

Dining and staying *à la* lakeside legend requires a healthy appetite and bank balance. Book at least a week ahead to snag a table.

At the Michelin-starred La Nouvelle Maison de Marc Veyrat (☑04 50 09 97 49; www.yoann-conte.com; 13 vieille rte des Pensières, Veyrier-du-Lac; menus €77-189, d €350-450, cooking classes with/without lunch €200/145; ⊗closed Mon, Tue, dinner Sun) French celebrity chef Marc Veyrat has handed over his stove, culinary flamboyance and signature use of wild herbs and flowers to his capable successor Yoann Conte. In Veyrier-du-Lac, 5km southeast of Annecy, the baby-blue house by the lake also has a handful of wonderful rooms. If you want to get behind the stove yourself, sign up for one of the morning cooking classes.

Whether alfresco on Lake Annecy's shores in summer or in the classically elegant salon in winter, dining at Michelin-crowned Auberge du Père Bise (☑04 50 60 72 01; www.perebise.com; 303 rte du Port, Talloires; menus €78-175, d €240-300; ⊗closed Tue & Fri lunch, mid Dec–early Feb) is never less than extraordinary. Chef Sophie Bise allows the clean flavours and freshness of local produce to shine in signatures like Annecy lake fish with foie gras and tart Granny Smith apple. The restaurant is 12km south of Annecy in Talloires.

TRAIN Frequent services from Annecy's **train station** (place de la Gare):

Aix-les-Bains (€7.50, 40 minutes)
Chambéry (€9.50, 50 minutes)
St-Gervais (€14.50, 1½ hours)
Lyon (€25, two hours)
Paris Gare de Lyon (€76, four hours)

❶ Getting Around

BICYCLE Bikes can be hired from **Vélonecy** (place de la Gare), at the train station, for €15 per day. People with a valid bus or train ticket only pay €5 per day.

BUS Get info on local buses at **Espace SIBRA** (www.sibra.fr; 21 rue de la Gare), opposite the bus station. Buses run from 6am to 8.30pm and a single ticket/day pass/*carnet* of 10 costs €1/3/9.50.

Around Annecy

On warm summer days the villages of Sévrier, 5km south on Lake Annecy's western shore, and Menthon-St-Bernard, 8.5km south on the lake's eastern shore, make good day trips. South of Menthon, Talloires is the most exclusive lakeside spot. All have wonderful beaches.

In winter, ski-keen Annéciens head for the cross-country slopes of Semnoz (www.semnoz.fr; elevation 1700m), 18km south; or downhill stations La Clusaz (www.laclusaz.com; elevation 1100m), 32km east, and Le

Grand Bornand (www.legrandbornand.com; elevation 1000m), 34km northeast.

Chambéry

POP 58,272 / ELEV 270M

Chambéry has a lot going for it: strategic location at the crossroads of the main Alpine valleys, a scenic setting near Lac du Bourget and two regional parks, and a rich heritage of French, Italian and Savoy rules. The city receives just a trickle of visitors, but those who do venture here are rewarded with crowd-free museums, outdoor cafe life and back-in-time strolls in its arcaded streets.

The city was Savoy's capital from the 13th century until 1563, when the dukes of Savoy shifted their capital to Turin in Italy. The 11th-century castle, which once served as the seat of power for the House of Savoy, now houses the administration for the Savoie *département* (county).

◉ Sights

For up-to-date information on exhibitions, visit http://musees.chambery.fr (in French). Admission to the city's museums is free on the first Sunday of the month.

TOP CHOICE Ville Ancienne   HISTORIC QUARTER
Chambéry has one of the best-preserved medieval old towns this side of the Alps. Its hidden courtyards, cafe-rimmed squares and lanes flanked by tall shuttered townhouses are great for an aimless amble. Streets worth

wandering include rue du Sénat de Savoie, gallery-dotted rue Métropole and cobbled rue Juiverie. Once home to local aristocrats, rue de la Croix d'Or hides the Hôtel du Châteauneuf's rose-draped courtyard, with intricate wrought-iron grilles affording photogenic perspectives of the castle. Winding up to the castle, the 14th-century rue Basse-du-Château is most atmospheric when the afternoon sun warms its caramel-coloured façades.

FREE Les Charmettes   HISTORIC HOME
(890 chemin des Charmettes; admission free; ◷10am-noon & 2-6pm Wed-Mon) Genevan philosopher, composer and writer Jean-Jacques Rousseau, a key figure of the Enlightenment and French Revolution, lived with his lover, Baronne Louise Éléonore de Warens, at this charming late-17th-century house from 1736 to 1742. Discover Rousseau's passion for botany by taking a wander in the landscaped garden full of herbs, flowers and vines. Les Charmettes is 1.5km southeast of town.

Château des Ducs de Savoie   CASTLE
(✏04 79 96 73 73; place du Château; adult/child €2.50/free; ◷tours 2.30pm Tue-Sun May-Sep) Chambéry's trophy sight is this forbidding medieval castle, once home to the counts and dukes of Savoy. Guided tours leave from the Accueil des Guides office, opposite the château, and cover an exhibition tracing Savoy's rich history and the Tour Trésorerie (Treasury Tower). The adjoining Ste-Chapelle was built in the 15th century to house the Shroud of Turin and is famous for its 70-bell Grand Carillon, Europe's largest bell chamber. The chapel was closed for renovation at the time of writing.

Musée des Beaux-Arts   ART MUSEUM
(Place du Palais de Justice; admission free; ◷10am-noon & 2-6pm Wed-Mon) Following a top-to-toe makeover, Chambéry's Museum of Fine Arts reopened to much acclaim in early 2012. Occupying a former corn exchange, the light-flooded gallery showcases 14th- to 18th-century Italian works, with emphasis on Renaissance Florentine and Sienese paintings. Admission to temporary exhibitions is €3/1.50 per adult/child.

Fontaine des Éléphants   FOUNTAIN
(place des Éléphants) With its four intricately carved elephants, this fountain could be the model for an Indian postage stamp. It was sculpted in 1838 in honour of Général de Boigne (1751–1830), who made his fortune in the East Indies. When he returned home he bestowed some of his wealth on the town and was honoured posthumously with this monument. The genteel arcaded street that leads from the fountain to Château des Ducs de Savoie is another of his projects.

Cathédrale Métropole
St-François de Sales   CATHEDRAL
(place de la Métropole; ◷10am-noon & 3-6pm Mon, 8.30am-noon & 3-6pm Tue-Sun) Built as a Franciscan chapel in the 15th century, Chambéry's cathedral hides unexpected treasures, including Europe's largest collection (occupying some 6000 sq metres) of trompe l'œil painting, by artists Sevesi and Vicario, and a 35m-long maze dating from the mid-19th century.

FREE Musée Savoisien   MUSEUM
(sq de Lannoy de Bissy; ◷10am-noon & 2-6pm Wed-Mon) Housed in a Franciscan monastery and linked to the cathedral by cloisters, this museum showcases archaeological finds including a gallery of 13th-century wall paintings. The 2nd floor stages temporary exhibitions concentrating on Savoyard mountain life. The museum closed in late 2012 for renovation and is scheduled to reopen in mid-2014.

🛏 Sleeping

Chambéry's *chambres d'hôte* and self-catering studios are far more appealing than its nondescript chain hotels. Gîtes de France (✏04 79 33 22 56; www.gites-de-france-savoie. com; 24 bd de la Colonne) takes bookings. The nearest hostel is in Aix-les-Bains.

TOP
CHOICE La Ferme du
Petit Bonheur   FARMSTAY €€
(✏04 79 85 26 17; www.fermedupetitbonheur.fr; 538 chemin Jean-Jacques; s/d/tr/q incl breakfast €85/95/115/135) *Bonheur* (happiness) is indeed yours if you stay at this vine-clad farm-

❶ CHAMBÉRY PASS

Pick up the €2 Chambéry Pass at the tourist office from May to October for free entry to temporary exhibitions at the city's museums, substantial discounts on guided tours, 10% reductions at certain restaurants, plus three hours of parking at the central Vinci Park garage.

WORTH A TRIP

KING OF 12 CASTLES

If you love nothing better than a castle, you'll love following in the footsteps of gallant dukes and feudal lords on the Route des Ducs de Savoie (Road of the Dukes of Savoy; www.chateaux-france.com/route-savoie). The route weaves through pristine Alpine landscapes from Thonon-les-Bains to Avressieux, 30km west of Chambéry, and ticks off 12 castles, abbeys and historic sites, including Château de Ripaille, Château d'Annecy and Château des Ducs de Savoie.

For acting out fairy-tale fantasies, nothing beats the silver-turreted, high-on-a-hillside Château de Menthon-St-Bernard (www.chateau-de-menthon.com; Menthon-St-Bernard; guided tours adult/child €8/4; ☺2-6pm Fri-Sun May-Sep), the birthplace of St Bernard (1008). Word has it that the château inspired Walt Disney's *Sleeping Beauty* castle. Tours of the medieval interior, taking in tapestry-adorned salons and a magnificent library, are intriguing, but it's the sparkling Lake Annecy panorama that leaves visitors spellbound.

house in the hills. Your hosts' exquisite taste shows in five countrified rooms and personal touches like homemade croissants for breakfast. In summer there is a fragrant garden for enjoying views of the Bauges massif, while in winter you can snuggle by the wood-burning stove in the salon. La Ferme is a 15-minute walk or two-minute drive south of town; follow the signs for Les Charmettes.

Château de Candie HISTORIC HOTEL €€€
(☑04 79 96 63 00; www.chateaudecandie.com; rue du Bois de Candie, Chambéry-le-Vieux; r €160-260, menus €56-78; @🛜🏊) Landscaped grounds where ornate fountains trickle, old-world elegance in rooms with period furnishings, a swimming pool with dreamy mountain views, and a gourmet restaurant – this sublime 14th-century castle is a taste of the high life for mere mortals. To reach the château by car, take exit 15 on the N201 to Chambéry-le-Vieux.

Art Hôtel HOTEL €
(☑04 79 62 37 26; www.arthotel-chambery.com; 154 rue Sommeiller; d €54-65, tr €75; 🛜) There's nothing artistic about this hotel, with its flag-lined concrete façade, drab rooms and the rumble of trains. That said, it *is* well-run, cheap and central, located halfway between the town's centre and the train station.

Les Pervenches HOTEL €€
(☑04 79 33 34 26; 600 chemin des Charmettes; r €66-87, menus €19-45; 🛜) In a quiet hamlet just 1km from the centre and 200m from Les Charmettes, Les Pervenches has nine cosy rooms with bucolic views of the hills. The restaurant, Le Clos Normand, serves plenty of cheesy goodies but from a different

part of France this time (the owners' native Normandy).

🍴 Eating

Pedestrian-only rue du Sénat de Savoie has butcher, baker and chocolate-maker shops. Hit rue de Lans for crêpes and pizza and place Monge for cheesy treats like fondue and *tartifflete* (potatoes, cheese and bacon baked in a casserole).

Les Halles REGIONAL CUISINE €€
(☑04 79 60 01 95; 15 rue Bonivard; menus €15-29; ☺lunch & dinner Tue-Sat; 🍴) Tucked behind the market hall, this upbeat bistro has gourmet panache and faultless service. Go for regional specialities like chicken stuffed with *diots* (Savoyard sausages) and creamy Beaufort polenta, saving an inch for gooey-centred chocolate molten cake with pecan ice cream.

Bar@Thym CAFE €
(22 place Monge; lunch menus €13; ☺10.30am-3.30pm Mon, to 6.30pm Tue-Sat; 🍴🍴) A lunchtime favourite, this organic cafe gives onto a fig tree–shaded terrace. It's a laid-back place, dishing up vegie fare like spinach tart with sweet potato and feta, homemade patisserie, herbal teas and fair trade coffees. The vibe is cosier in the beamed, stone-walled interior.

L'Atelier INTERNATIONAL €€
(☑04 79 70 62 39; 59 rue de la République; menus €20-28; ☺lunch & dinner daily) Soft light, tightly packed tables and mellow music set the scene in this contemporary bistro. The market-fresh menu changes daily and reveals Italian inflections in dishes like scallop risotto and veal osso bucco. There's a terrace for alfresco dining.

La Maniguette FUSION €€

(📞04 79 62 25 26; 99 rue Juiverie; menus €32-45; ⏱lunch Tue-Sat, dinner Wed-Sat) Everything at this chic bistro goes the extra mile to add a dash of originality: the bread is home-baked, and the menu changes monthly and always adds a far-away twist to local flavours – such as *magret de canard* (duck steaklet) with mango, polenta and Serrano ham.

Le Z INTERNATIONAL €€

(📞04 79 85 96 87; 12 av des Ducs de Savoie; menus €16-30; ⏱lunch & dinner daily; 🍴) This red-kissed, wood-floored brasserie is sleek and contemporary, with its open kitchen and cellar wine bar. The menu is a refreshing break from the norm, with global touches in dishes such as gambas with Thai rice and caramelised ginger and lamb tagine with prunes.

Cafe Botanique TEAROOM €

(193 rue Croix d'Or; lunch menus €10; ⏱11.30am-6pm Wed-Fri, 10am-7pm Sat) Sidling up to a gloriously old-fashioned herbalist's shop, this pocket-sized *salon de thé* does a brisk trade in speciality coffees, fragrant loose teas, and wholesome lunch specials and desserts.

Covered Market FOOD MARKET €

(place de Genève; ⏱7am-noon Tue, Wed, Fri & Sat) Chambéry's covered market is a gastronome's rendezvous, brimming with charcuterie, fromage, patisserie and fresh produce. On Saturday, it spills onto the square, with stalls laden with flowers, fruit, regional treats and (live) hens, rabbits and ducks.

Laiterie des Halles DELICATESSEN €

(2 place de Genève; ⏱7am-12.15pm & 3-7.15pm Tue-Sat) Cheese fiends will go gaga for the Reblochon, Tomme des Bauges and Comté at this dairy shop.

🍷 Drinking

The huge square of place St-Léger is the summertime heart of Chambéry's drinking scene.

O'Cardinal's PUB

(5 place de la Métropole; ⏱10am-1.30am Tue-Sat, 5pm-1.30am Sun & Mon) Leather banquette seating, chipper staff and decent pub grub have turned this into Chambéry students' favourite pub. On warm days the cheer spills out onto cathedral-shaded place de la Métropole.

Le Café du Théâtre CAFE

(place du Théâtre; ⏱7am-1am daily; 🌐) This tiny cafe, right next to Chambéry's 19th-century theatre, has a buzzy terrace for a cold beer, crêpe or ice cream. Students kick-start their evening here.

ℹ Information

Maison des Parcs et de la Montagne (256 rue de la République; ⏱9.30am-12.30am & 1.30-6pm Tue-Sat) Stocks information and exhibitions on the three local parks: national park La Vanoise, and regional parks Les Bauges and La Chartreuse.

Tourist office (📞04 79 33 42 47; www.chambery-tourisme.com; 5bis place du Palais de Justice; ⏱9am-12.30pm & 2-6pm Mon-Sat) Arranges guided old-town tours, including night visits, and has information on the local cheese and wine routes. Can make free room reservations.

ℹ Getting There & Away

AIR There are no-frills flights to regional British airports, including London Stansted, Manchester and Birmingham from **Chambéry-Savoie Airport** (www.chambery-airport.com), 12km north of Chambéry.

BUS From the **bus station** (place de la Gare) there are several daily **Altibus** (www.altibus.com) buses to/from Aix-les-Bains (€2, 30 minutes) and Annecy (€6, one hour).

TRAIN From Chambéry **train station** (place de la Gare) there are frequent trains to/from Paris Gare de Lyon (€82, four hours), Lyon (€17, 1½ hours), Annecy (€9.50, 55 minutes), Geneva (€16.50, 1¼ hours) and Grenoble (€11, one hour). Nine daily trains run through the Maurienne Valley to Modane (€16, 1¼ hours) and onwards into Italy. In town, buy tickets at the **SNCF Boutique** (21 place St-Léger).

ℹ Getting Around

TO/FROM THE AIRPORT Frustratingly, there are no bus services from Chambéry centre to the airport. The 15-minute journey by taxi costs around €20 – call **Allo Taxi Chambéry** (📞04 79 69 11 12).

There are five daily buses to/from Geneva airport (€36, 1½ hours) and Lyon St-Exupéry airport (€22, one hour).

BICYCLE Pick up wheels for €1/5 per hour/day and advice on marked trails and itineraries from Vélostation at the train station. The greater Chambéry area has 66km of cycling lanes.

BUS City **STAC** (www.bus-stac.fr) buses run from 6am to around 8pm Monday to Saturday. A single ticket/24-hour pass/carnet of 10 costs €1/2.50/7.50. They are sold at tobacconists and the **STAC information kiosk** (23 bd du Musée). Buses 3, 5, 6, 7 and 9 link the train station with Fontaine des Éléphants.

CHARTREUSE: THE MONASTIC LIQUEUR

Acid green and yellow, Chartreuse is the traffic-light-bright herb bomb of the cocktail and digestif world. Mixologists sing its praises and in ski resorts it adds a splash of Alpine fire to hot chocolate in Green Chaud. Its surge in global popularity recently might have something to do with it being hailed 'the only liqueur so good they named a colour after it' in Quentin Tarantino's 2007 thriller *Death Proof*. It certainly isn't because the monks have been broadcasting its wonders; this is a liqueur enshrouded in secrecy and silence.

In these parts, Chartreuse has been going strong ever since 1737. It was then that monks at the Grande Chartreuse finally cracked the formula of a bafflingly complex ancient manuscript detailing an elixir of longevity. The vegetal blend of 130 hard-to-find mountain herbs, roots and plants was macerated in alcohol, distilled and then left to age in oak casks.

Today, Chartreuse's exact ingredients remain a closely guarded secret, and word has it only two monks know the recipe. Perhaps closest to the original is the 69% Elixir Végétal, sold as a tonic, but potent, syrupy, chlorophyll-rich Chartreuse Green (55%) and milder, sweeter Chartreuse Yellow (40%) are far better known. You can taste the heavenly liqueur, bone up on its history and tour the barrel-lined cellars at the Caves de la Chartreuse (www.chartreuse.fr; 10 bd Kofler, Voiron; admission free; ☺9am-11.30am & 2-6.30pm) distillery.

CAR & MOTORCYCLE Parking in the centre can be a headache. There are three free P+R car parks on the city fringes; the biggest is in Chambéry-Sonnaz on the D991, linked to bus line 23.

Around Chambéry

PARC NATUREL RÉGIONAL DE CHARTREUSE

The Chartreuse Regional Nature Park (www.parc-chartreuse.net) safeguards the wild forested slopes of the Chartreuse massif, dubbed the 'desert' by monks of the Carthusian Order who settled here in 1084. Today the Grande Chartreuse monastery is home to some 30 monks who have taken a vow of silence. It is off-limits to visitors, but you can see it from above by hiking to the summit of 1867m Charmant Som; follow the signs for 'Col de Porte' on the D512.

The park headquarters (☎04 76 88 62 08; www.chartreuse-tourisme.com) in St-Pierre de Chartreuse, 40km south of Chambéry, has information on visiting the Voiron distillery (p499) where the liqueur is produced. You can also visit the Musée de la Grande Chartreuse (www.musee-grande-chartreuse.fr; La Correrie, St-Pierre de Chartreuse; adult/child €7.70/3.50; ☺10am-6.30pm Apr-Oct), which explores the monastery's 900-year history and the monks' reclusive lifestyle.

PARC NATUREL RÉGIONAL DU MASSIF DES BAUGES

Outdoor enthusiasts can delve into 800 sq km of hiking and biking opportunities in the little-known Massif des Bauges Regional Nature Park (www.parcdesbauges.com), with its endless pastures and plateaus. Several marked trails kick off from the Maison Faune-Flore (adult/child €2.50/1.50; ☺10am-12.30pm & 1.30-6.30pm Tue-Sun) in École, where you can learn how to spot some of the 600-odd chamois and plethora of mouflons inhabiting the park.

Chambéry's favourite weekend retreat for a little snow action is nearby Savoie Grand Revard (www.savoiegrandrevard.com). Downhill skiing is limited to 50km of pistes, but cross-country skiing is superb, with 140km of trails to explore, as is snowshoeing, with 60km of marked itineraries.

Tourist offices in Le Revard (☎04 79 54 01 60; Le Revard), La Féclaz (☎04 79 25 80 49; La Féclaz) and Le Châtelard (☎04 79 54 84 28; www.lesbauges.com; Le Châtelard), which is the main office in the park, have more information.

AIX-LES-BAINS
POP 27,531 / ELEV 234M

With its leafy shores, grand casino and villas, Aix-les-Bains, a small thermal spa 11km northwest of Chambéry, exudes an air of discreet gentility. Come to sail, swim, pedalboat, stroll or skate around France's largest natural lake, Lac du Bourget.

Contact Compagnie des Bateaux (www.compagniedesbateauxdulac.fr; ☺9am-12.30pm & 2-7pm), at the waterfront Grand Port, or the tourist office (☎04 79 88 68 00; www.aixlesbains.com; place Maurice Mollard; ☺9am-12.30pm & 2-6.30pm Mon-Sat), in town, about lake cruises. Both one-hour cruises and trips to the 12th-century Abbaye d'Hautecombe on the other side of the lake cost €12.

ALBERTVILLE
POP 19.774 / ELEV 328M

The main claim to fame of Albertville, an otherwise uninspiring town 52km east of Chambéry, is that it hosted the 1992 Winter Olympics. The highs and lows are colourfully retold at Maison des Jeux Olympiques d'Hiver (www.maisonjeuxolympiques-albertville. org; 11 rue Pargoud; adult/child €3/free; ⊙2-6pm Mon, 10am-noon & 2-6pm Tue-Sat).

Les Trois Vallées

This is the big one you've heard all about: vast, fast and the largest ski area in the world. The snow has never been hotter than in Les Trois Vallées. Some 600km of pistes and 180 lifts zip across eight resorts. Among these are Val Thorens, Europe's highest at a heady 2300m; wealthy and ever-so-British Méribel (elevation 1450m), founded by Scotsman Colonel Peter Lindsay in 1938; and playground of the super-rich Courchevel, which straddles three purpose-built resorts at 1550m, 1650m and 1850m and is a fave of the Beckhams, Prince William and Kate and the Moët-at-five brigade. In between is a sprinkling of lesser-known Alpine villages – Le Praz (1300m), St-Martin de Belleville (1450m) and La Tania (1400m), linked by speedy lifts to their big-sister resorts.

🏃 Activities

Winter Activities

The pull of the pistes in the Les Trois Vallées is irresistible, with some of the world's best skiable terrain appeasing even the feistiest of outdoor-action appetites. Save time queu-ing by buying your pass and lessons online at www.les3vallees.com.

Sunny Méribel is intermediate heaven, with 150km of cruisy (mostly blue and red) runs, 57 ski lifts, two snow parks with jumps, pipes and rails, a slalom stadium and two Olympic runs. The resort is currently gearing up to host the 2015 Alpine Skiing World Cup finals.

In Courchevel there's another 150km of well-groomed pistes, including some knee-trembling black *couloirs* (steep gullies) for the brave, and excellent off-piste terrain. The 2km-long floodlit toboggan run through the forest is a fun-laden après-ski alternative. At the time of writing, the space-age spa Centre Aquatique was taking shape, set to open its doors in 2014.

Watched over by glacier-licked peaks, snow-sure Val Thorens, though smaller, proffers summer skiing on the Glacier de Péclet, abundant winter walking and snow-shoeing tracks, 100km of free cross-country trails and its own snow park. Or bounce down the luge, France's longest at 6km.

For alternative snow action, the key info point is La Croisette (place du Forum; ⊙8.30am-7pm) in Courchevel 1850 (p502), where the ESF (www.esfcourchevel.com) resides in winter. La Croisette is also home to the Maison de la Montagne year-round. The latter takes bookings for guided off-piste adventures, snowshoeing and ski mountaineering and ice climbing, and is home to the Bureau des Guides (☑Courchevel 06 23 92 46 12, Méribel 04 79 00 30 38; www.guides-courchevel-meribel.com).

Summer Activities

Summer in Les Trois Vallées has its own outdoor appeal, with activities like rock climbing, paragliding, canyoning and hiking to peaks, wildflower-strewn pastures, and topaz lakes in Parc National de la Vanoise.

TO THE MANOR BORN

What better way to wake up than in the 19th-century manor house Château des Allues (☑06 75 38 61 56; www.chateaudesallues.com; Les Allues, St-Pierre d'Albigny; d €120-150, tr/q €170/200, dinner menus adult/child €46/25; 🛜), slung high on a hill and proffering sweeping views of the Belledonne range. Painstakingly restored by Stéphane and Didier, the château oozes elegance and originality in five spacious, lavishly furnished rooms, many with four-poster beds, copper fireplaces and antiques. Served at the family dining table, Stéphane's cooking makes excellent use of the herbs, vegetables and fruit that grow in the award-winning garden.

Château des Allues is in St-Pierre d'Albigny, 30km east of Chambéry on the A43, D1006 and D201 roads.

Clip onto vertigo-inducing vie ferrate (fixed-cable mountain routes) in Méribel and Courchevel. The resorts are interlaced with hundreds of kilometres of circuits and downhill runs for mountain bikers; a trail guide and details of bike rental outlets are available at tourist offices.

In July and August Chardon Loisirs (04 79 08 39 60; www.chardonloisirs.com; La Croisette) takes you white-water rafting on the Doron de Bozel River for €40 or downhill dirt scootering (€39 to €49).

Sleeping & Eating

There are accommodation services in Courchevel (04 79 08 14 44; http://reservation.courchevel.com), Méribel (04 79 00 50 00; www.meribel-reservations.com) and Val Thorens (04 79 00 01 06). Most hotels and restaurants open from December to April and July to August. In summer, rates are a fraction of the winter rates quoted below.

Courchevel alone has seven Michelin-starred restaurants, but they are, even by gourmet standards, stratospherically expensive (think upwards of €150 for a *menu* with wine).

Hôtel Les Arolles   CHALET €€
(04 79 00 40 40; www.arolles.com; rte du Laitelet, Méribel-Mottaret; r incl half-board per person €145-200;) This huge mountain chalet gets rave reviews for its perfect ski-in, ski-out location and comfortable, if not fancy, rooms. Classic Savoyard cooking, a log fire burning in the lounge, an indoor pool and a games room all sweeten the deal.

Hotel 3 Vallées   HOTEL €€
(04 79 00 01 86; www.hotel3vallees.com; Grande Rue, Val Thorens; r incl half-board per person €77-132, menus €29-32;) Our pick of Val Thorens' bunch is this friendly abode. The rooms are wonderfully rustic, dressed with Christmassy bursts of red and green and wood reused from old barns. Comforts like flatscreen TVs and DVD players wing you back into the 21st century. Dinner is a treat: consider eating here even if you're not staying.

Hôtel Seizena   HOTEL €€€
(04 79 08 26 36; www.hotelseizena.com; Courchevel 1650; d €230-330;) Contemporary rooms have been spruced up with brushed aluminium, aviation-themed pictures and charcoal and crimson shades at this chalet-style hotel, a quick hop from the slopes. A generous breakfast fuels a day of slope-bashing fun, and there's a lounge and *hammam* (Turkish bath) for après-ski chilling.

La Croix Jean-Claude   HOTEL €€
(04 79 08 61 05; www.croixjeanclaude.com; Les Allues; d €123-156, d incl half-board €186-218;) If you want to escape the madding crowd, this mountain hostelry gives you the best of both worlds – the quaint charm of a village and quick access to Méribel's slopes by free resort bus. Florals lend a homely touch to the cosy rooms, and market-fresh produce features on menus.

Le Farçon   GASTRONOMIC €€€
(04 79 08 80 34; www.lefarcon.fr; La Tania; lunch menus €28, dinner menus €42-120; lunch & dinner daily) At this forest retreat, Michelin-starred chef Julien Machet puts an imaginative spin on Savoyard dishes, with taste sensations like saddle of rabbit stuffed with Beaufort and served with crayfish polenta, and mountain hay and pink grapefruit sorbet. The three-course €28 skiers' lunch would barely buy you a pizza elsewhere.

La Fromagerie   BISTRO €€
(04 79 08 55 48; Méribel-Centre; menus €20-30; dinner daily) Only the tangiest, creamiest Alpine cheeses feature at this deli and bistro duo. Try Méribel's tastiest fondues and *raclette* in the rustic cellar. Book ahead.

Evolution   INTERNATIONAL €
(04 79 00 44 26; www.evolutionmeribel.com; Méribel-Centre; mains €16-21; 8.30am-2am daily;) A funky après-ski bar-cum-restaurant, Evolution is lauded for its monster-sized English breakfasts, Sunday roasts and well-spiced curries. Richard is the man behind the eclectic live music program.

Drinking & Entertainment

Hang out with the rich kids in Champagne-sipping Courchevel or slide down to Méribel for a party-mad après-ski scene. Most places are open only when the flakes are falling.

Le Rond Point   BAR
(Méribel-Rond Point; www.rondpointmeribel.com; 9am-7.30pm daily) Jostle for terrace space, then shimmy in your ski boots to pumping live music between mouthfuls of chips and toffee vodka (hey, don't knock it until you've tried it) at what *seasonaires* (seasonal workers) fondly call 'the Ronnie'.

Jack's Bar   BAR
(www.jacksbarmeribel.com; Méribel-Centre; noon-2am daily;) Jack's makes for one memorable

hangover, whether you come for the cool drinks, the chatty staff or the cracking events line-up – stand-up comedy, air guitar contests, toss-the-bottle Sundays, bring-your-pants parties, you name it...

La Taverne   BAR
(www.tavernemeribel.com; Méribel-Centre; ☺8am-2am; ☎) Ski right up to the terrace, jam-packed with skiers and boarders talking epic descents. Shooters, live music and big-screen sports.

Doron Pub   PUB
(http://doronpub.mountainpub.com; Méribel-Centre; ☺4pm-3am) A loud and lairy Brit-style pub, with live music nightly and a 'happiest hour' from 10pm to 11pm.

Dick's Tea Bar   NIGHTCLUB
(www.dicksteabar.com; rte de Mussillon, Méribel; ☺11pm-5am) Méribel's clubbing mainstay rocks nightly to a stellar line-up of DJs.

❶ Information

Courchevel 1850 tourist office (☎04 79 08 00 29; www.courchevel.com; ☺9am-7pm) Sister offices are at 1650m, 1550m and 1300m.

Méribel tourist office (Maison du Tourisme; ☎04 79 08 60 01; www.meribel.net; ☺9am-7pm)

Val Thorens tourist office (Maison de Val Thorens; ☎04 79 00 08 08; www.valthorens.com; ☺8.30am-7pm)

❶ Getting There & Away

TO/FROM THE AIRPORT Frequent shuttle buses link all three resorts with Geneva airport (€77.50, 3½ hours) and Lyon St-Exupéry airport (€65, three to four hours). There are also regular weekend buses between Chambéry airport and Moûtiers (€30, one hour), where you can catch the shuttles to the resorts.

BUS There are up to 12 regional **Transdev Savoie** (www.transavoie.com) buses daily between Moûtiers and Méribel (€10, 45 minutes), Courchevel (€10, 40 to 60 minutes) and Val Thorens (€10, one hour).

CAR & MOTORCYCLE The four-lane A43 links Chambéry (78km west) with the nearest town, Moûtiers, 18km north of Méribel. All ski resorts are signposted as you approach Moûtiers.

TRAIN Moûtiers is the nearest train station, with trains to/from Chambéry (€13, 1¼ hours) and Paris (€84, 4½ hours).

Eurostar (www.eurostar.com) also operates direct overnight or day trains to/from London on weekends during the winter season (return from €185, seven hours).

Val d'Isère

POP 1643 / ELEV 1850M

Ask any veteran skier why they return winter after snow-filled winter to Val d'Isère and watch their eyes light up. For the challenging skiing and off-piste, say many; for the party vibe and dancing on the slopes, say some; because 'Val Village' is a *real* village with a heart and soul, others tell you. Whatever the reason: one visit and they were wooked.

Lac du Chevril looms large on the approach to Val d'Isère, which is located in the upper Tarentaise Valley, 32km southeast of Bourg St-Maurice. The turquoise reservoir lake and its dam sidle up to Tignes (elevation 2100m), a purpose-built lakeside village that – together with Val d'Isère – forms the gargantuan Espace Killy skiing area, named after French triple–Olympic gold medallist Jean-Claude Killy.

🏃 Activities

Winter Activities

Snow-sure Espace Killy (www.espacekilly.com) has a real mix of beginner, intermediate and advanced skiing on 300km of pistes between 1850m and 3488m, miles of glorious off-piste, and summer skiing on the Pissaillas and Grande Motte glaciers. Ski touring is also fabulous, especially in the nearby Parc National de la Vanoise. Five lifts on the lower slopes give novices a free kick-start, while kids are kept amused on the obstacle-laden Acticross run.

At 2300m, the snowboarders' Oakley Valpark (www.valdiserevalpark.com) is on the back of Bellevarde mountain. Graded from green (easy) to black (experts only), it has rails, jumps, hips, quarters and a boarder-cross. Tignes' runs attract both snowboarders and skiers.

Besides skiing and boarding, winter-sport alternatives range from ice climbing and snowmobiling to mushing, winter paragliding and ice skating.

You can buy lift passes at STVI (www.valdiserepass.com; Gare Centrale; ☺8.30am-6pm). Unusually, Val has five free lifts on the lower slopes, including Les Lanches, Legettaz and Savonette drag lifts.

Centre Aquasportif   LEISURE CENTRE
(www.centre-aquasportif.com; rte de la Balme; adult/child pool €6/5, with spa area admission €14; ☺10am-9pm Fri-Wed, to 10pm Thu) This glass-and-stone complex is great for a postslope unwind. Besides pools with jets and bubble

beds, it harbours first-class sports facilities, a climbing wall, and a spa area with saunas, steam rooms and whirlpools.

ESF   SKI SCHOOL
(✆04 79 06 02 34; www.esfvaldisere.com; Carrefour des Dolomites, Val Village) In slopeside Val Village.

Top Ski   SKI SCHOOL
(✆04 79 06 14 80; www.topski.fr; Immeuble Les Andes, avenue Olympique) France's first and highly regarded independent ski school, dating from 1976, arranges one-to-one and group tuition in on- and off-piste skiing, boarding, ski touring and snowshoeing with expert guides.

Summer Activities

The valleys and trails weaving from Val d'Isère into the nearby Parc National de la Vanoise are a hiker's dream. If you fancy more of a challenge, you can play (safely) among the peaks at La Daille's two vie ferrate fixed-rope routes.

Mountain biking (Vélo Tout Terrain, or VTT) is big in Val, especially since the resort hosted stages of the UCI World Cup in 2012.

Five lifts are open to cyclists, giving access to 16 downhill routes, seven endurance runs and two cross-country circuits. Bike rental is available locally at sport shops.

Stop by the tourist office for details on family-friendly activities, from donkey trekking to farm visits.

Bureau des Guides   OUTDOOR ACTIVITIES
(✆06 14 62 90 24; www.guides-montagne-valdisere.com; Galerie des Cimes, avenue Olympique) Be it hiking, mountain biking, canyoning or rock climbing, this office in the Killy Sport shop can arrange it.

🛏 Sleeping

For self-catering accommodation, contact Val Location (✆04 79 06 06 60). The best beds are booked solid in the high season, making advance bookings a must. Prices vary, with pricey being the common denominator.

Hôtel L'Avancher   HOTEL €€€
(✆04 79 06 02 00; http://avancher.com; avenue du Prariond, Val Village; s €97-170, d €174-210, q €300-320; 🕸) The kind staff make you feel immediately welcome at this homey chalet, which

---

MELTING GLORY

Every restaurant in the Alps worth its weight offers *raclette*, *tartiflette* or fondue. To save cents but maximise the cheese, opt for the DIY option: most dairy shops will lend you the required apparatus provided you buy their ingredients. Here's a 'how to' guide for your own cheese fest.

Fondue Savoyarde

Made with three types of cheeses in equal proportions (Emmental, Beaufort and Comté) and dry white wine (about 0.4L of wine for 1kg of cheese). Melt the mix in a cast-iron dish on a hob, then keep it warm with a small burner on the table. Dunk chunks of bread in the cheesy goo.

Our tip: add garlic to the dish – you'll have cheesy breath anyway, so what the hell.

Raclette

Named after the Swiss cheese, *raclette* is a combination of melting cheese, boiled potatoes, charcuterie and baby gherkins. The home *raclette* kit is an oval hotplate with a grill underneath and dishes to melt slices of cheese.

Our tip: avoid a sticky mess by greasing and pre-heating your grill, and go easy on the ingredients (less is more).

Tartiflette

Easy-peasy. Slice a whole Reblochon cheese lengthwise into two rounds. In an oven-proof dish, mix together slices of parboiled potatoes, crème fraîche, onions and lardons (diced bacon). Whack the cheese halves on top, bake for about 40 minutes at 180°C, and ta-da!

Our tip: more crème fraîche and more lardons (a sprinkle of nutmeg is also good).

shelters large pine-clad rooms with downy bedding. There's a small lounge with magazines, board games and a piano.

Chalet Hôtel Sorbiers   CHALET €€€

(☑04 79 06 23 77; www.hotelsorbiers-valdisere.com; avenue du Prariond, Val Village; s/d/tr/q €155/220/285/324; ☎) A chalet in the traditional Alpine mould, this place has a fire crackling in the salon in winter and a sunny garden in summer. The cosy, well-kept rooms have wood trappings, balconies and some even, ahhh...Jacuzzi bathtubs. Breakfast is the works, with fresh pastries, eggs and bacon.

Hotel La Galise   HOTEL €€

(☑04 79 06 05 04; www.lagalise.com; rue de la Poste, Val Village; s/d/tr €100/170/243; ☎) Right next to the slopes, this family-run, chalet-style hotel keeps it sweet and simple in rustic quarters done up in pine, burgundy fabrics and pictures of the Alps. Many rooms have balconies, and you can grab a drink or a quick bite to eat in the bar.

✖ Eating

Supermarkets, patisseries and assorted snack stops line Val Village. In winter popular tables fill up fast and reservations are recommended. Most places open daily from December to April and have limited hours the rest of the year; if in doubt, call ahead.

⌐TOP⌐ L'Atelier d'Edmond   SAVOYARD €€€
CHOICE

(☑04 79 00 00 82; www.atelier-edmond.com; rue de Fornet, Le Fornet; menus €65-125, cooking courses €145; ☺lunch daily, dinner Tue-Sat) Candlelight bathes the stone walls, low beams and family heirlooms in this gorgeous Michelin-starred chalet in Le Fornet, 2km east of Val Village. Locally sourced ingredients go into imaginative, beautifully presented dishes like roasted scallops with coffee jus and celeriac-walnut tagliatelle. Call for details on the twice-monthly cooking courses, which involve preparing (and eating) a four-course *menu*.

La Fruitière   MODERN FRENCH €€

(☑04 79 06 07 17; www.lafoliedouce.com; rue de la Daille; mains €15-33; ☺lunch daily) At the top of the La Daille gondola, this piste-side oasis of fine dining is legendary, as are its mountain views. The creative cuisine is prepared with farm-fresh produce, paired with *grand cru* (wines of exceptional quality) and served in a hip dairy setting. Save room for the Savoyard cheese plate.

L'Edelweiss   SAVOYARD €€

(☑06 10 28 70 64; www.restaurant-edelweiss -valdisere.com; Piste Mangard, Le Fornet; mains €19-29, 3-course menus €26.50; ☺lunch daily) Slope-side on Le Fornet's Mangard blue run, this wood-and-stone chalet has alluring mountain views from its terrace (reserve your table). The food is above-par, too: duck breast with peaches, risotto with Bourgogne truffles and spot-on *tarte Tatin*.

Le Salon des Fous   CAFE €

(ave Olympique, Val Village; snacks €5-15; ☺8am-9.30pm daily) With its bright-red benches and groovy lighting, this cafe is cool but never pretentious. Homemade tarts, quiches, cakes and crêpes pair nicely with an inventive selection of teas, like *la vie en rose* (vanilla, lemon and rose).

Wine Not   BISTRO €

(☑04 79 00 48 97; ave Olympique, Val Village; mains €12-18; ☺lunch & dinner daily; ☷) Bold colours, exposed stone and smooth contours set the tone at Wine Not. Wok dishes, tapas sharing plates and salads are inspired by the first-class wine list, which does a Tour de France from the Rhône to Bordeaux.

☕ Drinking & Entertainment

Après-ski in Val d'Isère is way up there with the craziest in the French Alps.

La Folie Douce   BAR

(www.lafoliedouce.com; La Daille; ☺3-5pm daily) If you can't wait to party until you're back in the village, DJs and live bands big it up every day on this outdoor terrace at the top of La Daille's cable car. Ibiza in the Alps.

Le Petit Danois   BAR

(www.lepetitdanois.com; Val Village; ☺10am-1.30am daily) Cheap beer, live music and revved-up partygoers; thank God they serve full English breakfast the next morning to mop up the mess.

Moris Pub   PUB

(http://morispub.mountainpub.com; Val Village; ☺4pm-1.30am daily) A buzzy British pub with happy hours, big-screen sports, burger deals and regular gigs. Go easy on the toffee vodka.

Dick's Tea Bar   NIGHTCLUB

(www.dicksteabar.com; Les Crêtes Blanches, Val Village; ☺4pm-5am daily) Val d'Isère's party HQ and the fabled home of the *vodka pomme* (apple vodka). Live music starts at 4pm; DJs follow later on in the night, all night.

DON'T MISS

MILKY WAY

Part of Val d'Isère's charm is that it is a village with year-round residents. Claudine is one of them and she runs the delectable La Fermette de Claudine (www.lafermette declaudine.com; Val Village), selling unpasteurised milk, wonderful cheeses and yoghurts. Her dairy farm, La Ferme de l'Adroit, just 1km down the road in the direction of Col de l'Iseran, is open to the public: you can watch the morning cheese production (Tomme, Avalin, Beaufort) at 8.30am and afternoon milking at 5.30pm. All that dairy goodness lands on your plate in the form of deliciously gooey fondues and dishes made with *raclette* at the neighbouring L'Étable d'Alain (04 79 06 13 02; www.fermedeladroit. com; mains €22-29;), an attractively converted stable where you can feast away while watching cud-chewing cows in the adjacent barn. Book well ahead, especially if you want the popular 'cheese vat' table.

❶ Information

Tourist office (04 79 06 06 60; www.vald isere.com; place Jacques Mouflier, Val Village; 8.30am-7.30pm daily;) Internet access and wi-fi here costs €5 per hour.

❶ Getting There & Away

TO/FROM THE AIRPORT There are no direct services to Val d'Isère, but in Bourg St-Maurice, you can connect to buses for Chambéry airport (one-way/return €30/50, 1½ hours, weekend only). Other high-season bus services from Bourg St-Maurice include Geneva airport (one-way/return €62/106, four hours, three to four daily) and Lyon St-Exupéry airport (one-way/return €65/90, four hours, two to five daily). Advance reservations are essential and can be made online at www.autocars-martin.com or www.altibus.com, or by calling 04 79 68 32 96.

BUS Six daily buses in season link Val d'Isère with Tignes (€3, 25 minutes) and Bourg St-Maurice train station (€10, 40 minutes). Tickets must be reserved 48 hours in advance at the **Boutique Autocars Martin** (www.autocars -martin.com) on the main street in the resort centre. The SNCF desk here sells train tickets.

TRAIN Eurostar (www.eurostar.com) operates direct winter weekend services between Bourg St-Maurice and London (return from €190, eight hours, overnight or day service).

Parc National de la Vanoise

Rugged snowcapped peaks, mirrorlike lakes and vast glaciers are just the tip of the superlative iceberg in the 530-sq-km Parc National de la Vanoise (www.parcnational-vanoise.fr), which fits neatly between the Tarentaise and Maurienne Valleys. This incredible swathe of wilderness was designated France's first national park in 1963. Five nature reserves

and 28 villages border the highly protected core of the park, where marmots, chamois and France's largest colony of Alpine ibexes (there are around 1600 in the park) graze freely and undisturbed beneath the larch trees. Overhead, 20 pairs of golden eagles and the odd bearded vulture fly in solitary wonder.

A hiker's heaven, yes, although walking trails are only accessible for a fraction of the year – June to late September, usually. The Grand Tour de Haute Maurienne (www. hautemaurienne.com), a hike of seven days or more around the upper reaches of the valley, takes in national-park highlights. The GR5 and GR55 cross it, and other trails snake south to the Parc National des Écrins and east into Italy's Grand Paradiso National Park.

You can base yourself in Lanslebourg and Bonneval-sur-Arc, two pretty villages along the southern edge of the park. The Maison du Val Cénis (04 79 05 23 66; www. valcenis.com; 9am-noon & 3-6pm Mon-Fri) in Lanslebourg, and Bonneval-sur-Arc's tourist office (04 79 05 95 95; www.bonneval-sur-arc.com; 9am-noon & 2-6.30pm Mon-Sat) stock practical information on the walking, limited skiing (cross-country and downhill) and other activities in the park. In Termignon-la-Vanoise, 6km southwest of Lanslebourg, the tiny national-park-run Maison de la Vanoise (04 79 20 51 67; admission free; 9am-noon & 2-5pm) portrays the park through ethnographical eyes.

❶ Getting There & Away

CAR & MOTORCYCLE All three mountain passes linking the national park with Italy – the Col du Petit St-Bernard, Col de l'Iseran and Col du Mont Cénis – are closed in winter.

BUS & TRAIN Trains serving the valley leave from Chambéry and run as far as Modane, 23km southwest of Lanslebourg, from where **Transdev Savoie** (www.transavoie.com) runs three to four daily buses to/from Termignon-la-Vanoise (€6, 40 minutes), Val Cénis-Lanslebourg (€10, 50 minutes) and Bonneval-sur-Arc (€10, 1¼ hours).

DAUPHINÉ

Apart from its celebrated *gratin dauphinois* (potato bake), the Dauphiné's other big legacy to the French lexicon is historical. In 1339 Dauphiné ruler Humbert II established a university in Grenoble. A decade later, lacking money and a successor, he sold Dauphiné to the French king, Charles V, who started the tradition whereby the eldest son of the king of France (the crown prince) ruled Dauphiné and bore the title 'dauphin'.

Today, the Dauphiné refers to territories south and southwest of Savoy, stretching from the River Rhône in the west to the Italian border in the east, and roughly corresponding to the *départements* of Isère, Drôme and Hautes-Alpes. It includes the city of Grenoble and the mountainous Parc National des Écrins further east. The gentler terrain of western Dauphiné is typified by the Parc Naturel Régional du Vercors, much loved by cross-country skiers. In the east, the storybook town of Briançon stands sentinel on the Italian frontier.

Grenoble

POP 158,221 / ELEV 215M

With a dress-circle location overlooking the jagged mountains of the Parc Naturel Régional de Chartreuse and the Parc Naturel Régional du Vercors, Grenoble's backdrop is nothing short of extraordinary. That said, the city itself is not an instant heart-stealer, with its tower blocks, run-of-the-mill hotels and traffic. Yet despite initial appearances, Grenoble rewards those who make the detour en route to the slopes: fine museums and restaurants, a quaint *quartier des Antiquaires* (Antiques Quarter) and effervescent nightlife buoyed by some 60,000 students are all here for the taking.

◉ Sights

TOP CHOICE **Musée de Grenoble** ART MUSEUM
(www.museedegrenoble.fr; 5 place de Lavalette; adult/child €5/free; ◷10am-6.30pm Wed-Mon) The glass and steel facade of Grenoble's boldest museum occupies an entire block. Also called the Musée des Beaux-Arts, the museum is renowned for its distinguished modern collection, including star pieces by Chagall, Matisse, Canaletto, Monet and Picasso. The classic collection is equally impressive, spanning works from the 13th to 19th century.

Fort de la Bastille FORTRESS
(www.bastille-grenoble.com) Crowning a hillside above the River Isère, this 19th-century fort is Grenoble's most visible landmark. Built high and mighty to withstand invasions by the dukes of Savoy, the stronghold has long been a focus of military and political action.

Today it lures camera-toting crowds with its far-reaching views over Grenoble and the swiftly flowing River Isère to the peaks of the Vercors and, on cloud-free days, the snowy hump of Mont Blanc. Panels map out trails, from gentle family walks to day hikes.

To get to the fort, hop aboard the riverside **Téléphérique Grenoble Bastille** (quai Stéphane Jay; adult/child one-way €5/3, return €7/4.50; ◷Feb-Dec). The ascent in glass bubbles, which climb 264m from the quay, is almost more fun than the fort itself. Leave early to beat the queues in summer, or take a pleasant hour's walk uphill (half an hour down).

Magasin Centre National d'Art Contemporain ART MUSEUM
(www.magasin-cnac.org; 155 cours Berriat; adult/child €3.50/2; ◷2-7pm Tue-Sun) Ensconced in a cavernous glass-and-steel warehouse built by Gustave Eiffel, this is one of Europe's leading centres of contemporary art. A must-see for its architecture alone, the gallery plays host to cutting-edge exhibitions, many designed specifically for the space. Take tram A to the Berriat–Le Magasin stop, about 2km west of the town centre.

FREE **Musée Dauphinois** REGIONAL MUSEUM
(www.musee-dauphinois.fr; 30 rue Maurice Gignoux; admission free; ◷10am-6pm Wed-Mon) Atmospherically set in a 17th-century convent, this museum focuses on Alpine cultures, crafts and traditions and the region's skiing history. The museum is nestled at the foot of the hill below Fort de la Bastille.

FREE **Musée de l'Ancien Évêché** HISTORY MUSEUM
(www.ancien-eveche-isere.fr; 2 rue Très Cloîtres; admission free; ◷9am-6pm Mon, Tue, Thu & Fri, 1-6pm

Wed, 11am-6pm Sat & Sun) On place Notre Dame, the Italianate Cathédrale Notre Dame and adjoining 13th-century Bishops' Palace (originally home to Grenoble's bishops) form this museum. The rich collection traces local themes from prehistory to the 21st century, and takes visitors beneath the cathedral square to a crypt safeguarding old Roman walls and a baptistery dating from the 4th to 10th centuries.

FREE Musée de la Résistance et de la Déportation de l'Isère   HISTORY MUSEUM
(www.resistance-en-isere.fr; 14 rue Hébert; admission free; ⊙9am-6pm Mon & Wed-Fri, 1.30-6pm Tue, 10am-6pm Sat & Sun) This emotive museum examines the deportation of Jews and other 'undesirables' from Grenoble to Nazi camps during WWII. It also zooms in on the role the Vercors region played in the French Resistance.

🏃 Activities

To jump lift-pass queues in Grenoble's surrounding ski resorts, buy your pass in advance from the tourist office or the *billetterie* (ticket office) inside Fnac (4 rue Félix Poulat; ⊙10am-7.30pm Mon-Sat).

Maison de la Montagne   OUTDOOR ACTIVITIES
(www.grenoble-montagne.com; 3 rue Raoul Blanchard; ⊙9.30am-12.30pm & 1-6pm Mon-Fri, 10am-1pm & 2-5pm Sat) Get the scoop on mountain activities around Grenoble – skiing, snowboarding, ice climbing, walking, mountain biking, rock climbing and more – here. The knowledgeable staff can help plan trips and treks with *refuge* stays, or book activities. It sells an excellent range of maps, walking books and topoguides, and runs a library that is free to consult. For walks around Grenoble, ask for the free SIPAVAG maps and itineraries.

Club Alpin Français
Grenoble Isère   OUTDOOR ACTIVITIES
(www.cafgrenoble.com; 32 av Félix Viallet; ⊙2-6pm Tue-Fri) Runs most of the *refuges* in the area and posts a list of activities in its window.

Bureau des Guides et
Accompagnateurs de
Grenoble   OUTDOOR ACTIVITIES
(www.guide-grenoble.com; Maison de la Montagne, 3 rue Raoul Blanchard) If it's a guide you're after, this outfit runs the whole gamut of sum-

mer and winter activities, from canyoning to ice climbing, paragliding to ski touring.

👉 Tours

The tourist office organises imaginative thematic walking tours (€6-14.50), in French only, including a two-hour stroll in the footsteps of Grenoble-born novelist Stendhal, as well as museum tours and various industry-focused tours. Those who'd rather go it alone can hire a four-hour MP3 audioguide (English available; €5) at the tourist office.

✨ Festivals & Events

Les Détours de Babel   MUSIC FESTIVAL
(www.detoursdebabel.fr) A two-week fest of contemporary world music in spring.

Vues d'en Face   FILM FESTIVAL
(www.vuesdenface.com) The rainbow flag flies high for this gay and lesbian film fest in mid-April.

Cabaret Frappé   MUSIC FESTIVAL
(www.cabaret-frappe.com) Catch poolside concerts in July.

Foire des Rameaux   FUN FAIR
Candyfloss, toffee apples and all the fun of the Easter fair.

🛏 Sleeping

Sleeping in Grenoble is a bit of a let-down. Though good value, hotels tend to be soulless, and the reluctant preserve of passing business people. The tourist office has a list of *chambres d'hôte* in the area.

Le Grand Hôtel   HOTEL €€
(📞04 76 51 22 59; www.grand-hotel-grenoble.fr; 5 rue de la République; r €118-245; ❄@🛜) Right in the thick of things, this newly revamped hotel has raised the bar in Grenoble's style stakes with its slick, monochromatic rooms

---

ℹ **CITY SAVER**

The tourist office sells the money-saving Grenoble multipass, covering the Musée de Grenoble, Fort de la Bastille cable car, guided tours and audioguides. You can pick and mix these, and a two-/three-/four-attraction pass costs €11.50/13.50/15.50.
   Many of Grenoble's museums are free on the first Sunday of the month.

Grenoble

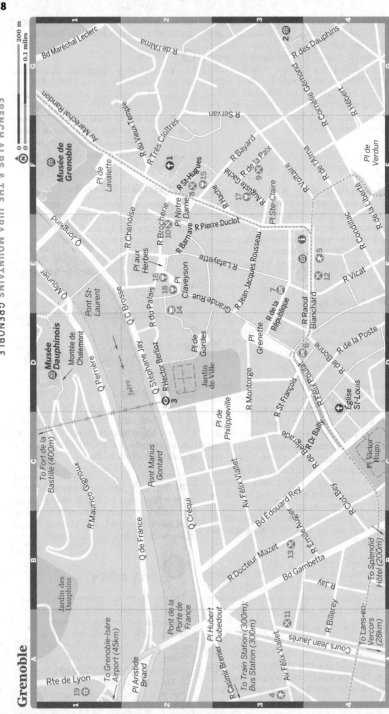

N

0 — 200 m
0 — 0.1 miles

Bd Maréchal Leclerc

R de l'Alma

Av Maréchal Randon

R des Dauphins

R du Vieux Temple

R Très Cloîtres

R Servan

R Cornélie Gémond

R Hébert

Pl de Lavalette

Musée de Grenoble

R St-Hugues

R Bayard

R de la Paix

R Auguste Gaché

Pl de Verdun

R Chenoise

R Brocherie

Pl Notre Dame

R Hoche

R Voltaire

Pl Ste-Claire

R de l'Alma

R de la Liberté

R Colbert

R de la Poste

Q Jongkind

Q Mounier

R aux Herbes

R Barnave

R Pierre Duclot

R Lafayette

Pl aux Herbes

R Chenoise

Pl Claveyson

Grande Rue

R Jean-Jacques Rousseau

R Vicat

Q Perrière

Musée Dauphinois

Montée de Chalemont

Pont St-Laurent

Q C Brosse

R du Palais

Pl de Gordes

Pl Grenette

R de la République

R Raoul Blanchard

R de Bonne

Isère

Q Stéphane Jay

R Hector Berlioz

Jardin de Ville

R Montorge

R St-François

R Dr Bailly

R Félix Poulat

Église St-Louis

To Fort de la Bastille (400m)

Pont Marius Gontard

Pl de Philippeville

Q de France

R de Belgrade

Pl Victor Hugo

R Clot Bey

R Maurice Gignoux

Q Crequi

Av Félix Viallet

Bd Édouard Rey

Jardin des Dauphins

Pont de la Porte de France

R Émile Augier

R Docteur Mazet

Bd Gambetta

R Jay

To Splendid Hôtel (200m)

To Grenoble-Isère Airport (45km)

Pl Aristide Briand

Pl Hubert Dubedout

R Casimir Brenier

Av Félix Viallet

Cours Jean Jaurès

R Billerey

To Lans-en-Vercors (28km)

Rte de Lyon

To Train Station (300m); Bus Station (300m)

Grenoble

FRENCH ALPS & THE JURA MOUNTAINS GRENOBLE

flaunting home-style comforts like flat-screen TVs, wi-fi and bathrobes; the best have balconies looking out across the city to the Alps beyond.

Patrick Hôtel HOTEL €€
(04 76 21 26 63; www.patrickhotel-grenoble.com; 116 cours de la Libération; s/d €97/107; ❄ 🕸) Streamlined and contemporary, the rooms here sport flatscreen TVs and free wi-fi. Rates drop by around 40% at weekends. The hotel is on a busy road 2km south of the centre (just off the A480) and has private parking.

Hôtel de l'Europe HISTORIC HOTEL €
(04 76 46 16 94; www.hoteleurope.fr; 22 place Grenette; s €38-74, d €50-94, tr/q €110/120; 🕸) On Grenoble's liveliest square, this 17th-century haunt retains some charm, with its grand spiral staircase and wrought-iron balconies prime for people-watching. The recently spruced-up rooms are fresh and bright.

Splendid Hôtel HOTEL €€
(04 76 46 33 12; www.splendid-hotel.com; 22 rue Thiers; s €79, d €79-115, tr €95-115, q €145; ❄ 🕸) Colourful, fresh and jazzed up with funky paintings, this is a welcome break from Grenoble's dreary hotel scene. Some of the simple, cosy rooms have hydromassage showers and all have wi-fi.

Auberge de Jeunesse HOSTEL €
(04 76 09 33 52; www.fuaj.org; 10 av du Grésivaudan; dm incl breakfast €21.50; 🕿) Grenoble's ultramodern, ecoconscious hostel is set in parkland, 5km from the centre. The top-notch facilities include a bar, kitchen and sun deck. Take bus 1 to La Quinzaine stop, an easy two-minute walk from the hostel.

Eating

Grenoble's most atmospheric bistros huddle down the backstreets of the *quartier des Antiquaires*. Rue Chenoise dishes up the world on a plate, from Indian and Nepalese to Middle Eastern and Moroccan. As Dauphiné capital, Grenoble is *the* place to sample *gratin dauphinois* (finely sliced potatoes oven-baked in cream and a pinch of nutmeg).

La Petite Idée TRADITIONAL FRENCH €€
(04 76 47 52 95; www.la-petite-idee.fr; 7 cours Jean Jaurès; menus €15.50-28; ☉lunch Sun-Fri, dinner Tue-Sun; 🚸) This sweet bistro had *la petite idée* (the little idea) to drum up business with market-fresh, seasonal dishes, such as rosemary-rubbed lamb with creamy *gratin dauphinois*. The setting is convivial and the €9.50 *plat du jour* great value.

Ciao a Te ITALIAN €€
(04 76 42 54 41; 2 rue de la Paix; mains €16.50-26; ☉lunch & dinner Tue-Sat, closed Aug) Stylish

yet relaxed, Ciao dishes up authentic Italian cuisine: handmade pasta, crispy *panzerotti* (filled pastries), tender veal and the freshest seafood in town. It's a Grenoblois favourite, so book ahead.

Chavant
TRADITIONAL FRENCH €€€

(☎04 76 25 25 38; www.chavanthotel.com; 2 rue Émile Chavant, Bresson; menus €35-115; ☺lunch Tue-Sat, dinner Tue-Fri & Sun) In family hands since 1852, this rustic-chic country manor in Bresson cooks old-school French with a touch of finesse. The wines are drawn from the cellar and the setting is divine, especially in summer when tables are set out under the trees. It's 7km south of Grenoble.

Chez Mémé Paulette
CAFE €

(☎04 76 51 38 85; 2 rue St-Hugues; snacks €4-8; ☺lunch & dinner Tue-Sat) This old curiosity shop of a cafe is crammed with antique books, milk jugs, cuckoo clocks and other knick-knacks. It draws a young crowd with its wallet-friendly grub – from soups to *tartines* (open sandwiches) and homemade tarts.

Le Mandala
INTERNATIONAL €€

(☎04 76 17 14 72; 7 rue Raoul Blanchard; menus €12-29; ☺lunch & dinner Tue-Sat) This choc-mint bistro has a dash of retro flair and a creative menu. Refreshing starters like gazpacho prelude mains such as pollack with basmati rice and *petits pois* (small green pea) jus.

Le Petit Bouche
BISTRO €€

(☎04 76 43 10 39; 16 rue Docteur Mazet; menus €25-28; ☺lunch & dinner Mon-Fri) Full of vintage bric-a-brac, Le Petit Bouche enjoys a loyal following with its endearingly old-world ambiance and classic bistro fare.

La Fondue
FRENCH €€

(☎04 76 15 20 72; 5 rue Brocherie; fondues €17-20; ☺lunch & dinner Mon-Sat) Gorge on fondues laced with kirsch, Génépi and Chartreuse or (double gorge) chocolate. *Raclettes* and *tartiflettes* complete the mountain cheese feast.

🍷 Drinking & Entertainment

Like every good student city, Grenoble does a mean party. Click on to French-language www.grenews.com and www.petit-bulletin. fr for details on what's happening.

Le 365
WINE BAR

(3 rue Bayard; ☺6pm-1am Tue-Sat) If Dionysus (god of wine) had a house, this is surely what

it would look like: an irresistible clutter of bottles, oil paintings and candles that create an ultrarelaxed setting for quaffing one of the wines on offer.

Le Tord Boyaux
WINE BAR

(4 rue Auguste Gaché; ☺6pm-12.30am Tue-Sat) More than 30 flavoured wines, some of them quite extravagant (violet, chestnut, Génépi, fig), and a blind test every Tuesday night to see how many your taste buds can recognise.

Le Couche Tard
BAR

(1 rue du Palais; ☺6.30pm-2am daily) If you're too cool for school, check out the 'Go to Bed Late', a grungy pub that actively encourages you to graffiti its walls. The merrier you become during happy hour (until 10pm daily), the more imaginative those doodles become...

Styx
BAR

(6 place Claveyson; ☺1pm-2am Mon-Sat) Designer cocktails, DJs, soft red light and attitude by the shakerload. The terrace is a favourite hang-out on warm evenings.

Café de la Table Ronde
CAFE

(7 place St-André; ☺9am-midnight daily) Linger over drinks on the square at this historic 1739 cafe, once the beloved haunt of Stendhal and Rousseau.

MC2
THEATRE

(☎04 76 00 79 00; www.mc2grenoble.fr; 4 rue Paul Claudel) Grenoble's most dynamic all-rounder for theatre, dance, opera, jazz and other music. It's 2km south of the centre on tram line A, stop MC2.

La Soupe aux Choux
LIVE MUSIC

(☎04 76 87 05 67; www.jazzalasoupe.fr; 7 rte de Lyon; ☺Tue-Sat) Going strong for some 25 years, 'cabbage soup' stirs live jazz from swing to blues into Grenoble's after-dark mix. Find it a five-minute walk west of Musée Dauphinois.

ℹ Information

Wi-fi is widely available at hotels, cafes and bars in Grenoble; the tourist office has a list of free hotspots.

Post office (rue de la République)

Tourist office (☎04 76 42 41 41; www. grenoble-tourisme.com; 14 rue de la République; ☺9am-6.30pm Mon-Sat, to 2pm Sun) Inside the Maison du Tourisme. Sells maps and guides, and arranges city tours.

ℹ️ Getting There & Away

AIR A clutch of budget airlines, including easyJet and Jet2.com, fly between **Grenoble-Isère Airport** (www.grenoble-airport.com), 45km northwest of Grenoble, and London, Edinburgh, Manchester and Bristol, among others.

BUS The **bus station** (rue Émile Gueymard), next to the train station, is the main terminus for bus companies, including **VFD** (www.vfd.fr) and **Transisère** (www.transisere.fr). There are several services daily to the following:

» **Geneva airport** (€47, two hours)

» **Lyon St-Exupéry airport** (€22, one hour)

» **Chamrousse** (€4, 1¼ hours)

» **Bourg d'Oisans** (€6.50, 55 minutes)

» **Les Deux Alpes** (€6.50, 1¾ hours)

» **Briançon** (€31, 2½ hours)

Eurolines (www.eurolines.com) handles international destinations.

CAR & MOTORCYCLE Grenoble is well connected to motorways including the A48 (Lyon), A41 (Chambéry, Annecy) and the A51 (Marseille). Major car-hire agencies are in the Europole complex underneath the train station.

TRAIN From the **train station** (rue Émile Gueymard), trains run frequently to/from Paris Gare de Lyon (€80 to €100, three to four hours), Chambéry (€11, 50 minutes) and Lyon (€21, 1½ hours). Train tickets are sold at the station and in town at the **SNCF boutique** (15 rue de la République).

ℹ️ Getting Around

TO/FROM THE AIRPORT **Grenoble Altitude** (http://grenoble-altitude.com) shuttle buses run between **Grenoble-Isère Airport** and the bus station (one-way/return €12.50/22, 45 minutes). See the website for timetables.

BICYCLE Underneath the train station, **Métro-vélo** (www.metrovelo.fr; place de la Gare; ⏱7am-8pm Mon-Fri, 9am-noon & 2-7pm Sat & Sun) rents out bikes for €3 per day. Helmets, child seat and locks are free. You'll need ID and €120 deposit per bike. You can also pick up a free map of Grenoble's cycling routes here.

BUS & TRAM Grenoble's four ecofriendly tram lines – A, B, C and D – trundle through the heart of town. A single-trip bus and tram ticket costs €1.50 from ticket machines or drivers. Before boarding, time-stamp your ticket in the blue machines at stops. *Carnets* of 10 tickets (€12.50) and day passes (€4) can only be bought at TAG inside the tourist office or next to the train station. Trams run from around 5am to 1am; bus services run until 6pm or 9pm.

CAR & MOTORCYCLE Grenoble is tricky to negotiate because of its bewildering one-way system, disorientating tram network and expensive, limited parking. Your best bet is to head to one of the 15 **P+R car parks** (www.semitag.com) on the outskirts of town, which are connected to the centre by tram or bus; the supervised ones cost €2 to €3 per day.

Around Grenoble

Grenoble's high-altitude surrounds lure urbanites craving a weekend snow fix. The vast Vercors plateau is laced with a cool 1000km of cross-country trails, many weaving through snow-dusted forests. With sweeping views of the rugged Belledonne massif, **Chamrousse** (elevation 1700m) attracts families with its beginner-level downhill in winter and gentle hikes through marmot-dotted pastures in summer. The **tourist office** (📞04 76 89 92 65; www.chamrousse.com; 42 place de Belledonne) has the full low-down.

Several daily buses link Grenoble with the surrounding resorts (see those sections for details), including Chamrousse (€4, 1¼ hours). For day-trippers, the Skiligne buses operated by **Transaltitude** (www.transaltitude.fr) to 15 different ski resorts in the region are a good deal; rates from Grenoble (€24 to Villard de Lans, €25 to Chamrousse, €36 to Les Deux Alpes and Alpe d'Huez) include a one-day ski pass and return bus fare.

PARC NATUREL RÉGIONAL DU VERCORS

The gently rolling pastures, plateaux and chiselled limestone peaks of this 1750-sq-km nature park, southwest of Grenoble, are great for soft adventure. Quieter and cheaper than neighbouring Alpine resorts, the wildlife-rich park draws families seeking fresh air and low-key activities like cross-country skiing, snowshoeing, caving and hiking.

From pristine, wooded **Lans-en-Vercors** (elevation 1020m), 28km southwest of Grenoble, buses shuttle downhill skiers to the Montagnes de Lans ski area, with 30km of pistes to pound. The postcard-perfect village of **Villard de Lans** (elevation 1050m), 9km up the valley, is linked by ski lifts to **Villard-Correncon** for 130km of winter-wonderland downhill pistes at melting prices (€31 per day). For more snowy fun, the **Colline des Bains** (adult/child 3hr pass €8.50/7.50, sled rental €3), in Villard de Lans, comprises six sledging tracks: pick your vehicle (solo sledge, rubber ring or bobsleigh) and then whiz down.

Mountain Highs

You're tearing down the Alps on your mountain bike, the wind whipping your hair; you're skipping through flowery pastures tinkling with cowbells; you're schussing in Mont Blanc's shadow in Chamonix. Everywhere the scenery makes you feel glad to be alive.

Downhill Skiing

1 Glide to off-piste heaven on the Vallée Blanche (p4800), zigzag like an Olympic pro down black pistes in Val d'Isère (p502), or take your pick of Les Portes du Soleil's 650km of runs (p487).

Magical Views

2 Get close-ups of the shimmering Mont Blanc from Aiguille du Midi (p477) or contemplate the ethereal loveliness of the Cascades du Hérisson from the misty waterfall trail (p526). Lake Annecy spreads out like a mirror before the fairest castle of them all: Château de Menthon-St-Bernard (p497).

Sky High

3 The sky is blue, the mountain air sweet – it's a zip-a-dee-doo-dah kind of wonderful day. Just the day to go paragliding or hang-gliding above glistening Lake Annecy (p492).

Alpine Hiking

4 There's nothing like donning a backpack and hitting the trails in the region's national parks. The rugged wilderness of Parc National des Écrins (p514) and the snow-capped majesty of Parc National de la Vanoise (p505) will leave you breathless.

On the Edge

5 For a buzz, little beats racing down Morzine's heart-pumping mountain-bike track (p488). Not enough of a challenge? Take your intrepid self to Chamonix (p477) for adventure among the four-thousanders.

Clockwise from top left
1. Off-piste skiing at the Vallée Blanche 2. Breathtaking views, Aiguille du Midi 3. Hang-gliding over Lake Annecy 4. Hiking in Parc National de la Vanoise

GREAT ESCAPES

The Vercors has some dreamy chalets and back-to-nature farmhouses. These three are among our favourite escapes; see their websites for maps and directions.

Les Allières (☎04 76 94 32 32; www.aubergedesallieres.com; Lans-en-Vercors; r with shared bathroom incl half-board per person €47, mains €18-30) This 1476m-high forest chalet offers no-frills digs (bunk beds, shared toilets) and wondrous mountain food. The wood-fired raclette (cheese dish) and tarte aux myrtilles (blueberry tart) are divine.

À la Crécia (☎04 76 95 46 98; www.gite-en-vercors.com; 436 Chemin des Cléments, Lans-en-Vercors; s/d/tr/q €58/63/78/93, dinner menus €19) Goats, pigs and poultry rule the roost at this solar-powered 16th-century farm, authentically renovated by Véronique and Pascal. Rooms are stylishly rustic, with beams, earthy hues and mosaic bathrooms. Dinner is a feast of farm-fresh produce.

Gîte La Verne (☎04 76 95 21 18; http://gite.laverne.free.fr; La Verne, Méaudre; apt for 4/8 people per week €500/750) Fitted with fully equipped kitchens, the beautiful apartments at this gîte blend Alpine cosiness with mod cons. Whether you opt for self-catering or half-board, you'll enjoy the hammam (Turkish steambath) and outdoor Norwegian bath as well as owner Edwige's wonderful hospitality.

Villard de Lans' tourist office (www.villarddelans.com; 101 place Mure-Ravaud) has an online service for booking hotels, farmstays and chambres d'hôte, and should be your first port of call for activities from canyoning to mountain biking in the Vercors.

Les Accompagnateurs Nature et Patrimoine (☎04 76 95 08 38; www.accompagnateur-vercors.com) allows you to get in tune with nature on half-day (adult/child €16/10) and full-day (adult/child €26/19) walks, with knowledgeable guides who can point out Alpine wildflowers and animals from marmots to chamois. Half-day snowshoeing tours (adult/child €19/17) are offered in winter.

❶ Getting There & Away

Up to seven Transisère (http://transisere.altibus.com) buses daily link Grenoble with Lans-en-Vercors (€5.20, 45 minutes), Villard de Lans (€5.20, one hour) and Corrençon-en-Vercors (€5.20, 1¼ hours).

PARC NATIONAL DES ÉCRINS

No amount of hyperbole about towering peaks, shimmering cirque lakes and wispy falls can quite do justice to the wild Parc National des Écrins (www.les-ecrins-parc-national.fr). Created in 1973, this is France's second-largest national park (918 sq km). Stretching between the towns of Bourg d'Oisans, Briançon and Gap, the area is enclosed by steep, narrow valleys and sculpted by the Romanche, Durance and Drac rivers and their erstwhile glaciers. It peaks at 4102m with the arrow-shaped Barre des Écrins, a mythical summit for mountaineers.

Bourg d'Oisans, 53km southeast of Grenoble, and Briançon, another 67km in the same direction, are good bases for exploring the park.

BOURG D'OISANS
ELEV 720M

Age-old footpaths used by shepherds and smugglers centuries before – 700km in all – criss-cross the national park, making it prime hiking territory. A gateway to several vertiginous mountain passes, Bourg d'Oisans is also a mountain-biking Mecca. Check out www.bikes-oisans.com for details on trails, maps and bike hire. Kayaking along the Drac's turquoise waters, rock climbing, vie ferrate and paragliding are other activities; tourist and park offices have details.

Bone up on the national park's fascinating geology, flora and fauna, including ibex and chamois, at the Musée des Minéraux et de la Faune des Alpes (place de l'Église, Bourg d'Oisans; adult/child €4.90/free; ⏰2-6pm Wed-Mon).

🛏 Sleeping & Eating

The tourist office in Bourg d'Oisans can provide info on gîtes d'étape (walkers' lodges), open year-round. Cafes and restaurants serving up good honest mountain food cluster on and around avenue de la République.

Au Fil des Saisons   B&B €
(☎04 76 30 07 01; www.chambresdhotes-afs.com; Ferme du Cros, Les Côtes de Corps; s/d

€50/60) This lovingly converted 1731 farm with beamed and vaulted ceilings is a quiet country hideaway, deep in the Parc National des Écrins, 54km south of Bourg d'Oisans. Breakfast is a wholesome spread with organic homemade bread and honey, and farm-fresh cheese. Kids love Hôtesse the draft horse. Find the Ferme du Cros 2km from Corps in Les Côtes de Corps; follow the southbound N85 from Grenoble.

Ferme Noemie   CAMPGROUND €
(☑04 76 11 06 14; www.fermenoemie.com; Chemin Pierre Polycarpe, Les Sables; sites €25-35, apt per week €550-850) A green, mountain-rimmed dream of a campground, family-run Ferme Noemie is a terrific base for cycling, hiking, canyoning and more. Don't fancy roughing it? There's 'camping for softies' in luxury tents with beds. The four- to six-bed, barn-style apartments attract skiers in winter.

La Cascade   CAMPGROUND €
(☑04 76 80 02 42; www.lacascadesarenne.com; rte de l'Alpe d'Huez; sites €21-29; ☺mid-Dec–Sep; ☒) A tree-shaded campground 1.5km from the centre of Bourg d'Oisans.

❶ Information

Maison du Parc (rue Gambetta; ☺9am-1pm & 2-5pm Mon-Thu, 9am-1pm Fri) Sells maps and guides.

Oisans (www.tourisme-oisans.com) This website is an excellent source of information on the area, with accommodation and activities listings.

Tourist office (☑04 76 80 03 25; www.bourgdoisans.com; quai Girard; ☺9am-noon & 3-6pm Mon-Sat)

❶ Getting There & Away

Services from Bourg d'Oisans' **bus station** (av de la Gare):

» **Briançon** (€15.50, 1¾ hours, two to three daily)

» **Les Deux Alpes** (€3, 40 minutes, two to three daily)

» **Alpe d'Huez** (€3, 40 minutes, two to three daily)

» **Grenoble** (€6.50, 50 minutes, eight daily)

LES DEUX ALPES
ELEV 1600M

With year-round skiing on the 3200m- to 3425m-high Glacier du Mont de Lans, glorious powder for off-piste fans, mountain bike terrain parks and a party to rival anywhere in the French Alps, Les Deux Alpes, once two humble farming villages, is now a buzzing

resort with altitude. It's 19km southeast of Bourg d'Oisans.

Freeriders come from far and wide to tackle the breathtaking, near-vertical Vallons de la Meije descent in La Grave (www.la-grave.com), 21km east. The stuff of myth, the run plummets 2150m and is strictly for the crème de la crème of off-piste riders.

◎ Sights

Grotte de Glace   CAVE
(Ice Cave; adult/child €4.50/3.50; ☺10am-3pm) Ice sculptures of metre-tall animals, Alpine flowers and shepherds glisten in this ice cave, carved into the Glacier du Mont de Lans at Dôme de Puy Salié (3425m). To reach it, ride the Jandri Express *télécabine* to 3200m and then the Funiculaire Dôme Express (☺8am-5pm late Nov–Apr, 7am-1pm mid-Jun–Aug) to 3400m. Allow an hour to get there.

La Croisière Blanche   SCENIC RIDE
(The White Cruise; ☑04 76 79 75 03; €8; ☺10.30am-3pm Sun-Fri) Take a panoramic 50-minute ride on this caterpillar-track minibus. Though undeniably gimmicky, it does allow nonskiers to tickle the summit at 3600m and enjoy 360-degree views. Wrap up for subzero temperatures. Cruise plus cable cars plus ice cave costs €33.50. You *must* book before you head off.

🏃 Activities
WINTER ACTIVITIES

Les Deux Alpes pounds the powder on 225km of pistes and a 2600m-high snow park (www.2alpes-snowpark.com) with an 800m-long axe pipe, 120m-long half-pipe, and numerous jumps as well as technical courses along cornice drops, canyons and corridors in the 'slide' zone. The main skiing domain lies below La Meije (3983m), one of the highest peaks in the Parc National des Écrins. Riders wanting to access La Grave from Les Deux Alpes are pulled by a snowcat from the top of the Dôme Express Funicular (p515). In winter, use of the funicular is included in the cost of your ski pass.

Skiing and boarding aside, snow fiends can dart around Les Deux Alpes on ice skates, in an ice-glider (dodgems on ice) or go on a *motoneige* (snowmobile) expedition; the tourist office has details. Contact the Bureau des Guides (p516) for organised ice climbing, snowshoeing and off-piste skiing in winter, and rock climbing, canyoning and biking expeditions in summer.

SUMMER ACTIVITIES

The glacier has Europe's largest summer skiing area, set against the majestic backdrop of Mont Blanc, Massif Central and Mont Ventoux; the season runs from mid-June to August, and a day pass costs €36/29 for an adult/child. Otherwise there are scores of nail-biting descents and cross-country trails for mountain bikers (half-/full-day pass €17/23), numerous hiking trails and plenty of opportunities for paragliding.

🛏 Sleeping & Eating

Hotels and restaurants follow the seasons: most open from December to April and mid-June to August.

Hotel Côte Brune HOTEL €€€

(☑04 76 80 54 89; www.hotel-cotebrune.com; 6 rue Côte Brune; d incl half-board €180-236; ☎) Ski in and out of this slope-side hotel. The homey pine-panelled rooms radiate Alpine charm and come with south-facing balconies; some are geared up for families. Nurse drinks by an open fire or on the terrace before a delicious three-course dinner.

Hotel Serre-Palas CHALET €

(☑04 76 80 56 33; www.hotelserre-palas.fr; 13 place de Venosc; d incl breakfast €58-138) For bright, quiet rooms and marvellous mountain views, you can't beat this spick-and-span chalet. Lionel, your affable host, is a ski instructor and can give you plenty of insider tips.

Le Raisin d'Ours REGIONAL CUISINE €€

(☑04 76 79 29 56; www.leraisindours.fr; 98 av de la Muzelle; menus €25-38) This stylishly rustic bistro outshines most with its relaxed mood, attentive service and creative take on what is available seasonally. Rich, earthy specialities such as beech-smoked salmon with creamy truffle mash and roast cod drizzled with Breton cider jus are perfectly matched with wines.

🍸 Drinking

Les Deux Alpes has a well-deserved reputation for raucous après-ski parties. The resort has a flurry of bars.

Smokey Joe's BAR

(www.smokeyjoes.fr) Live après-ski music, spicy Tex-Mex food and shot slamming are bound to get you grooving in your snow boots at this post-slopes hang-out at the base of Jandri gondola. There are guest DJs, big-screen sports and themed parties aplenty.

Smithy's BAR

(www.smithystavern.com; 7 rue de Cairou; ☎) Vodka, fajitas and nachos, more vodka – that's the scene at this rocking chalet with a long bar for lining 'em up. Smithy's hosts gigs, DJ nights and head-spinning parties.

ℹ Information

Maison des Deux Alpes (place des Deux Alpes) is the key source and home to several helpful groups:

» **Tourist office** (☑04 76 79 22 00; www.les2alpes.com; ☺8am-7pm)

» **Accommodation service** (☑04 76 79 24 38; www.les2alpesreservation.com; ☺9am-noon & 2-6pm Mon-Fri)

» **ESF** (☑04 76 79 21 21; www.esf2alpes.com; ☺8.30am-noon & 4.30-7pm)

» **Bureau des Guides** (☑04 76 11 36 29; www.guides2alpes.com; ☺3.30-6.30pm Mon-Sat, 10.30am-12.30pm & 3.30-6.30pm Sun)

ℹ Getting There & Away

Transisère buses link Les Deux Alpes with Grenoble (€6.50, 1¾ hours, up to 10 daily) via Bourg d'Oisans; return journeys to Grenoble must be booked 72 hours in advance at **Agence Transisère VFD** (112 av de la Muzelle).

There are also services to Lyon St-Exupéry airport (one-way/return €40/58, 3½ hours).

ALPE D'HUEZ

ELEV 1860M

Number of hairpin bends: 21. Length: 14km. Average slope gradient: 7.9%. Record time: 37 minutes and 35 seconds. Portrait of a famous leg of the Tour de France between Bourg d'Oisans and Alpe d'Huez, a purpose-built resort in the Massif des Grandes Rousses. The legendary race whizzes through in July, but heart-pumping sports is the *raison d'être* (reason for existence) of this high-altitude resort year-round. The same slopes that beckon hikers and mountain bikers in summer are given over to skiers and boarders in winter.

🏃 Activities

Apart from legendary cycling, Alpe d'Huez has 250km of well-groomed, south-facing pistes that range from dead easy to death-defying; at 16km the breathtakingly sheer La Sarenne, accessible from the Pic Blanc cable car, is Europe's longest black run. Experienced skiers can also ski in July and August on glaciers ranging from 2530m to 3330m.

Pic du Lac Blanc (3330m) is the highest point accessible year-round by the Tronçons and Pic Blanc cable cars, commanding magical views that reach across the rippling French Alps all the way to neighbouring Italy and Switzerland.

Summer unveils heights threaded through with marked hiking trails leading to jewel-coloured lakes. For mountain bikers this is downhill heaven, with 250km of trails to rattle and roll down and four bike parks. Visit the website www.alpedhuez bike.com for mountain bike or road cycling coaching. A one-day lift pass in summer costs €15.

🛏 Sleeping & Eating

Le Printemps de Juliette   CHALET €€

(☑04 76 11 44 38; www.leprintempsdejuliette.com; av des Jeux; d €125-175; 🐾) View the world through rose-tinted specs at Juliette's very pretty, very *pink* chalet, where vintage teddies and dolls outnumber the guests. It's pastel and floral overload in the spotlessly clean rooms and the *salon de thé*, where you can sip tea and nibble homemade cakes by the fire.

Le Passe Montagne   TRADITIONAL FRENCH €€

(☑04 76 11 31 53; rte de la Poste; mains €15-25; ⊙closed lunch Mon; 🍴) This stylish wooden chalet has service as smooth as its fondue Savoyarde. An open fire burns in the beamed dining room, the place for a tête-á-tête over a juicy rump steak with morels and Roquefort or oxtail in a rich Madeira wine sauce.

ℹ Information

Information hub **Maison de l'Alpe** (place Paganon) sells ski passes and houses the helpful **tourist office** (☑04 76 11 44 44; www.alped huez.com; ⊙9am-7pm), **accommodation reservation centre** (☑04 76 11 59 90) and **ESF** (☑04 76 80 31 69; www.esf-alpedhuez.com).

ℹ Getting There & Away

Transisère (p511) buses link Alpe d'Huez and Grenoble (€6.50, 1¾ hours, up to 10 daily) via Bourg d'Oisans.

TOUR DE FRANCE

No race gets the wheels of the cycling world spinning quite like the Tour de France, or 'Le Tour' as it is known here. It's the big one: one prologue, 20 stages, some 3500km clocked in three weeks by 180 riders, an entire country covered by bicycle. Broadcast in 190 countries and watched by 15 million every July, it is a spectacle of die-hard passion and epic endurance, of thigh-breaking mountain passes and hell-for-leather sprints, of tears and triumph.

The brainchild of journalist Géo Lefèvre, the race was first held in 1903 to boost sales of *L'Auto* newspaper, with 60 trailblazers pedalling through the night to complete the 2500km route in 19 days. Since then, the Tour has become *the* cycling event. And despite the headlines of skulduggery and doping scandals, it's the success stories that really grab you.

The Route

Though the exact route changes every year, the Tour essentially does a clockwise loop of France, takes in a variety of terrains (coast, countryside, mountains) and occasionally dips into other countries (for example, Belgium in 2012). Times are totted up from the day-long stages to get the lowest aggregate time and determine the overall winner, who gets to wear the *maillot jaune* (yellow jersey). The race finishes to much fanfare and victory parading on Paris' Champs-Élysées. See www.letour.fr for a stage-by-stage breakdown.

Spectator Tips

You can watch it on TV, but nothing beats experiencing the Tour first hand. Host towns treat it as a big party, with families turning out for roadside picnics and the publicity caravan of goodie-throwing floats psyching everyone up into carnival mode before the main event. Want to see the race for yourself? You'll need to make travel plans well ahead. The Alpine and Pyrenean stages are terrific, giving you plenty of opportunity to observe riders as they slow down (relatively speaking) to tackle the gruelling inclines. Camping close by and getting up early should snag you a good front-row spot.

Briançon

POP 12,054 / ELEV 1320M

No matter whether you come by bus or car, it's a long, long way to Briançon, but it's worth every horn-tooting, head-spinning, glacier-gawping minute. The road from Grenoble is pure drama and not just because of the scenery. The locals adopt a nonchalant attitude to driving, the general consensus being: overtaking on hairpin bends, *pas de problème*! But brave it behind the wheel and you'll be richly rewarded with views of thundering falls, sheer cliffs and jagged peaks razoring above thick larch forests.

All of this is the drum roll to Briançon. Perched high on a hill and straight out of a fairy tale, the walled old town affords views of soaring Vauban fortifications and the snowcapped Écrins peaks on almost every corner. The centre's Italian look and feel is no coincidence – Italy is just another dizzying 20km away.

◎ Sights

TOP CHOICE Vauban Fortifications   HISTORIC SITE

Briançon's biggest drawcard is its extensive 17th- and early-18th-century Vauban heritage, including the old town's signature star-shaped fortifications, surrounding forts (Fort des Têtes, Fort des Salettes, Fort du Dauphin and Fort du Randouillet) and bridge (Pont d'Asfeld). This architectural ensemble was listed as a Unesco World Heritage Site in 2008, a belated recognition of the pioneering genius of this engineer.

Vieille Ville   HISTORIC QUARTER

Sitting astride a rocky outcrop and surrounded by mighty ramparts, Briançon's old town is a late-medieval time capsule, its winding cobbled lanes punctuated by shuttered town houses in candy colours and shops selling won't-stop-whistling marmots.

The main street is the steep Grande Rue, also known as Grande Gargouille (Great Gargoyle) because of its gushing rivulet. It links the two main gates, Porte de Pignerol in the north, just off the Champ de Mars, and Porte d'Embrun lower down, at the top of av de la République. The coral-pink Collégiale Notre Dame et St Nicolas (place du Temple), another of Vauban's works, is worth a look for its baroque painting.

Fort du Château   FORT

Crowning the old city is the slumbering Fort du Château, affording magnificent mountain views from its battlements. If you can't face the hike up, av Vauban along the town's northern ramparts affords equally spectacular views of the snowy Écrins peaks.

🏃 Activities

Serre Chevalier (www.serre-chevalier-ski.com) ski region, properly called Le Grand Serre Chevalier, links 13 villages and 250km of piste along the Serre Chevalier Valley between Briançon and Le Monêtier-les-Bains, 15km northwest.

The tourist office hands out the excellent booklet *Guide des Itinéraires dans la Vallée de Serre Chevalier* (in French), detailing cultural walks and snowshoeing itineraries for those not so keen on skiing.

Télécabine du Prorel   FUNICULAR

(av René Froger; day passes winter adult/child €44/35, return trips summer €12/9.50; ◷8.45am-5.30pm mid-Dec–Apr & Jul-Aug) It takes just a few minutes to reach the slopes from the Briançon–Serre Chevalier station at 1200m in Briançon's lower town.

École du Ski Français   SKIING

(☏04 92 20 30 57; www.esf-briancon.com; 7 av René Froger; ◷8.45am-6pm Dec-Apr) ESF runs a seasonal office inside the Prorel cable-car station.

Bureau des Guides et
Accompagnateurs   OUTDOOR ACTIVITIES

(☏04 92 20 15 73; www.guides-briancon.fr; Central Parc; ◷10am-noon & 4-7pm Jul-Aug, 5-7pm Sep-Jun) Organises off-piste outings, snowshoeing and ice climbing in winter, with treks, glacier traverses, mountain biking, canyoning and vie ferrate in summer.

Maison du Park   WALKING

(place du Médecin Général Blanchard; ◷2-6pm Mon-Fri) Stop by for information and maps on the outstanding walking opportunities in the mountains of the Écrins national park.

Rafting Experience   RAFTING

(☏04 92 24 79 00; www.rafting-experience.com; ◷May-Aug) White-water fun rafting (€30), hydro-speeding (€36) and air boating (€35) on nearby rivers. Call ahead for times and locations.

☞ Tours

Service du Patrimoine WALKING TOUR
(☎04 92 20 29 49; Porte de Pignerol; adult/child
Mon-Sat €6/4.50, Sun €7/5.50; ⏰2-5.30pm Mon,
9am-noon & 2-5.30pm Tue-Fri) Tucked in one of
the city gates, this organisation offers daily
guided walks at 3pm (in French) of the old
town and fortifications. Walks in English are
few and far between and require advance
booking.

🛏 Sleeping

The tourist-office-run accommodation service, **Briançon Réservation** (☎04 92 24 98
80), can help you find a bed. Hotel parking
in the pedestrian old town is a headache, so
park along the ramparts and walk. Many
places close in the shoulder seasons.

Hôtel de la Chaussée HISTORIC HOTEL €€
(☎04 92 21 10 37; www.hotel-de-la-chaussee.com;
4 rue Centrale; r €70-90; 🖥) The Bonnafoux
family has run this place with charm and
efficiency since 1892. The renovated rooms
fulfil every Alpine chalet fantasy: wooden-
clad, beautifully furnished, subtly scented
and oh so cosy. The restaurant downstairs
follows suit and serves a Vauban *menu*.

Hotel Edelweiss HOTEL €
(☎04 92 21 02 94; www.hotel-edelweiss-brancon.
fr; 32 av de la République; s/d/tr/q €46/61/81/92;
🖥) One of the best of the budget bunch is
this 19th-century manor house turned modest hotel. The no-frills rooms are cosy and
immaculately kept, some with fine views of
the Alps. The helpful owners can arrange
everything from ski passes to babysitters.

**Auberge de Jeunesse
Serre Chevalier** HOSTEL €
(☎04 92 24 74 54; www.fuaj.org; Le Bez, Serre
Chevalier 1400; dm €17; 🖥) Eight kilometres
northwest of Briançon at Serre Chevalier-
le-Bez, this hostel is right at the foot of the
pistes. It's all very collective (big dorms, big
canteen, big parties) and friendly. Take a bus
heading to Monêtier-les-Bains, get off at Villeneuve Pré Long and walk 500m.

✕ Eating

Briançon is milking the Vauban heritage in
every possible way, and that includes eating.
Five restaurants across town have agreed on
a cartel of Vauban menus: no one is allowed
to copy the others' recipes of 17th-century
fare (think pigeon, rabbit stews and never-

heard-of legumes). The tourist office has a
list of participating venues.

Le Valentin REGIONAL CUISINE €€
(☎04 92 21 37 72; www.levalentin.fr; 6 rue de la
Mercerie; menus €18-35; ⏰dinner Tue-Sun year-
round, plus lunch Tue-Sun Jul–mid-Sep; 🍴) Séver-
ine and Arnaud extend a heartfelt welcome
at their softly lit cellar bistro. This is good
old-fashioned home cooking along the lines
of creamy *tartiflettes*, rosemary-infused
lamb with *gratin dauphinois* and calorific
desserts. There's a €9 kids' menu for *les
petits*.

Au Plaisir Ambré REGIONAL CUISINE €€
(☎04 92 52 63 46; 26 Grande Rue; menus €20-
29; ⏰lunch Mon, Tue, Fri & Sat, dinner daily) This
Alpine-chic bistro has carved out a name for
itself with its faultless service and winningly
fresh menu. Mains such as meltingly tender
lamb with artichoke casserole are perfectly
matched by wines and followed by indulgent desserts like chocolate fondue with
seasonal fruits.

Le Pied de la Gargouille REGIONAL CUISINE €€
(☎04 92 20 12 95; 64 Grande Rue; menus €18.50-
22; ⏰dinner Wed-Sun) The Gargoyle's Foot is
an old-town homage to fondue, *raclette* and
tartiflette. Call ahead to reserve the speciality, *gigot d'agneau à la ficelle* (whole leg
of lamb strung over an open fire), and bring
three friends to finish it.

ℹ Information

Tourist office (☎04 92 21 08 50; www.
ot-briancon.fr; Maison des Templiers, 1 place
du Temple; ⏰9am-noon & 2-6pm Mon-Sat,
10.15am-12.15pm & 2.30-5pm Sun) Can help
book accommodation.

ℹ Getting There & Away

Bus

Grenoble-based **VFD** (www.vfd.fr) runs at least
one daily bus to/from Grenoble (€31, 2¾ hours)
via Bourg d'Oisans. Tickets must be booked at
least 72 hours in advance online.

Other services, operated by **SCAL** (www.
scal-amv-voyages.com) and leaving from the
bus stop on the corner of rue Général Colaud,
include seven daily buses (except Sunday) to/
from Gap (€12, two hours), Marseille (€37, five to
six hours) and Aix-en-Provence (€33, five hours).

Car & Motorcycle

The winding Col de Montgenèvre (1850m)
mountain pass links Briançon with neighbouring Italy. It stays open year-round, as does the

nearby Col du Lautaret (2058m), which links Briançon and Grenoble. Both do occasionally get snow-bogged.

Train

The **train station** (av du Général de Gaulle) is about 1.5km from the Vieille Ville.

» **Paris Gare de Lyon** (€124, seven hours, six daily)

» **Grenoble** (€31, 4½ hours, five daily)

» **Gap** (€14, 1½ hours, 10 daily)

» **Marseille** (€42, 4½ hours, three daily)

THE JURA MOUNTAINS

The dark wooded hills, rolling dairy country and limestone plateaux of the Jura Mountains, stretching in an arc for 360km along the French–Swiss border from the Rhine to the Rhône, comprise one of the least explored pockets of France. Rural, deeply traditional and *un petit peu* eccentric, the Jura is the place if you're seeking serenity, authentic farmstays and a taste of mountain life.

The Jura – from a Gaulish word meaning 'forest' – is France's premier cross-country skiing area. The range is dotted with ski stations, and every year the region hosts the Transjurassienne, one of the world's toughest cross-country skiing events.

The region is not short on culture or history either. From heavy metallurgy to precious-gem cutting, its contribution hasn't gone unnoticed in the country's economy; neither has its historical role as the hotbed of the French Resistance during WWII.

Besançon

POP 121,391 / ELEV 262M

Home to a monumental Vauban citadel and France's first public museum, and

VISI'PASS

Besançon's top sights and museums, including the citadel and the Musée des Beaux-Arts et d'Archéologie, can be visited with a good-value Visi'Pass (adult/child €13/10). The pass also includes a one-day bus ticket. You can buy it directly at the sights, online or from the tourist office.

birthplace of Victor Hugo and the Lumière Brothers, Besançon has an extraordinary background and yet, remarkably, remains something of a secret. Straddling seven hills and hugging the banks of the River Doubs, the cultured capital of Franche-Comté remains refreshingly modest and untouristy, despite charms such as its graceful 18th-century old town, first-rate restaurants and happening bars pepped up by the city's students.

It wasn't always that way. In Gallo-Roman times, Besançon was an important stop on the trade routes between Italy, the Alps and the Rhine. This role came full circle in December 2011 when the new TGV station opened in the village of Auxon, 12km north of the centre, putting Besançon firmly back on the global map where it belongs.

◎ Sights

Citadelle de Besançon   CITADEL
(www.citadelle.com; rue des Fusillés de la Résistance; adult/child €9/6; ◷9am-6pm) Besançon's crowning glory is this Unesco World Heritage–listed citadel, a formidable feat of engineering, designed by the prolific Vauban for Louis XIV in the late 17th century. Dominating a hilltop and dramatically lit by night, the citadel commands sweeping views of the city's mosaic of red rooftops and the serpentine River Doubs.

The citadel harbours a trio of museums: the Musée Comtois zooms in on local traditions, the Musée d'Histoire Naturelle covers natural history, and the harrowing Musée de la Résistance et de la Déportation takes an in-depth look at the rise of Nazism and fascism, and the French Resistance movement. The latter is unsuitable for young children.

To boost the citadel's family appeal, there's an insectarium (home to some meaty tarantulas), an aquarium, a pitch-black, ho-hum noctarium and an overly cramped parc zoologique. Citadel admission covers entry to all museums and attractions.

If you don't fancy the uphill trudge, take bus 17 from the riverside Chamars car park on avenue du 8 Mai 1945.

Musée des Beaux-Arts et d'Archéologie   ART MUSEUM
(www.musee-arts-besancon.org; 1 place de la Révolution; adult/child €5/free; ◷9.30am-noon & 2-6pm Wed-Mon) No trip to Besançon is complete without visiting this stately museum.

It is France's oldest, founded in 1694 when the Louvre was but a twinkle in Paris' eye. The stellar collection spans archaeology with its Egyptian mummies, Neolithic tools and Gallo-Roman mosaics; a cavernous drawing cabinet with 5500 works, including Dürer, Delacroix and Rodin masterpieces; and 14th- to 20th-century painting with standouts by Titian, Rubens, Goya and Matisse.

Parc Micaud PARK
(av Edouard Droz) For that must-have snapshot of the hilltop citadel with the swiftly flowing Doubs in the foreground, take a stroll along this leafy riverside promenade, a great spot for a picnic with a view. A carousel, playground and donkey rides keep kids entertained.

Horloge Astronomique ASTRONOMICAL CLOCK
(rue de la Convention; adult/child €3/free; ⊙guided tours hourly 9.50am-11.50am & 2.50-5.50pm Wed-Mon) Housed in the 18th-century Cathédrale St-Jean, this incredible astronomical clock has some 30,000 moving parts, 57 faces and 62 dials and, among other things, tells the time in 16 places around the world, the tides in eight different ports of France, and the time of the local sunrise and sunset.

Porte Noire HISTORIC SITE
(Black Gate; square Castan) A steep 15-minute downhill walk from the citadel, the Porte Noire is a triumphal arch left over from the city's Roman days, dating from the 2nd century AD. It sits on a square where the vestiges of an aqueduct were discovered in the 19th century.

☞ Tours

When the sun's out, a river cruise is a relaxed way to see Besançon. From April to October, vessels dock regularly beneath Pont de la République to take passengers on 1¼-hour cruises along the River Doubs, which include a glide along a 375m-long tunnel underneath the citadel.

Bateaux du Saut du Doubs BOAT TOUR
(www.sautdudoubs.fr; adult/child €13/9; ⊙10am, 2.30pm & 4.30pm Jul & Aug)

Vedettes de Besançon BOAT TOUR
(www.vedettesdebesancon.com; adult/child €11/8.50; ⊙2.15pm, 3.30pm & 5.15pm Apr-Oct, plus 10.45am Jul & Aug)

🎎 Festivals & Events

Festival de Musique
Besançon MUSIC FESTIVAL
(www.festival-besancon.com) Classical music of the highest calibre resounds in Besançon's historic buildings in September.

Marché de Noël RELIGIOUS FESTIVAL
In December get into the festive spirit with twinkling carousels, carols and *vin chaud* in the old town.

🛏 Sleeping

The tourist office makes room reservations for free and hands out the handy *guide des hébergements*, which lists hotels, guesthouses, apartments and campgrounds in the area.

TOP CHOICE Charles Quint Hôtel HISTORIC HOTEL €€
(✆03 81 82 05 49; www.hotel-charlesquint.com; 3 rue du Chapître; d €89-145; ❀◉) This discreetly grand 18th-century town house turned nine-room boutique hotel is sublime, with period furniture, sumptuous fabrics, a garden with a tiny swimming pool and a wood-panelled dining room. Find it slumbering in the shade of the citadel, behind the cathedral.

Hôtel Le Sauvage BOUTIQUE HOTEL €€
(✆03 81 82 00 21; www.hotel-lesauvage.com; 6 rue du Chapître; r €89-220; ❀) Picturesquely straddling a hillside, this convent-turned-boutique-hotel has grandstand views across the city's rooftops and river to wooded hills beyond. The accent is on understated elegance in light-drenched rooms with wood floors and marble bathrooms. Vaulting and a wrought-iron staircase hint at the hotel's historic past.

Hôtel de Paris DESIGN HOTEL €€
(✆03 81 81 36 56; www.besanconhoteldeparis.com; 33 rue des Granges; s €65, d €81-200; @) Hidden down a side street in the old town, this former 18th-century coaching inn reveals a razor-sharp eye for design. Corridors lit by leaded windows lead to slinky, monochromatic rooms, a small fitness room and a shady inner courtyard. Parking costs €7 per night.

Hôtel Granvelle HOTEL €
(✆03 81 81 33 92; www.hotel-granvelle.fr; 13 rue du Général Lecourbe; r €54-68; ❀@❀) You will find 30 neat and tidy, if a bit dated, rooms in this stone building at the back of

Besançon

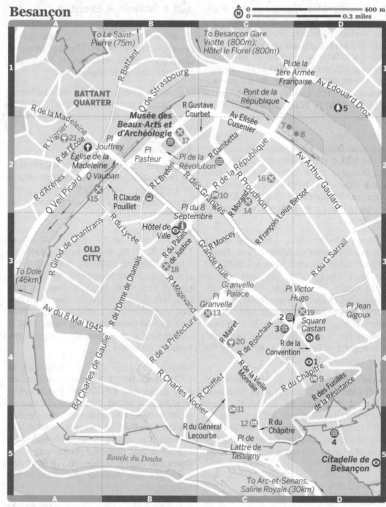

a courtyard below the citadel. 'Interactive' rooms are equipped with internet-linked computers and flatscreen TVs. Wheelchair-accessible.

Hôtel le Florel HOTEL €€
(☑ 03 81 80 41 08; www.hotel-florel.fr; 6 rue de la Viotte; s €59, d €69-109, q €149; ※ ✿) Opened in 1900, this hotel near the station was recently given a complete top-to-toe makeover and now sports bright, contemporary rooms (the best have citadel views) and a pleasant terrace. It is 1km north of the centre of town.

Eating

TOP CHOICE **Le Saint-Pierre** MODERN FRENCH €€€
(☑ 03 81 81 20 99; www.restaurant-saintpierre. com; 104 rue Battant; menus €38-70; ⊙ lunch Mon-Fri, dinner Mon-Sat) Crisp white tablecloths, exposed stone and subtle lighting are the backdrop for intense flavours, such as lobster fricassee with spinach and herb ravioli, which are expertly paired with regional wines. The three-course *menu marché*, including wine and coffee, is excellent value at €38. The restaurant is 500m (a five-minute

Besançon

walk) north of Grande Rue on the opposite side of the river.

Monsieur Victor　　　　　BISTRO €
(✆03 81 82 06 18; 11 rue Victor Hugo; mains €13; ◷noon-7pm Tue & Wed, noon-4.30pm & 6.30-11pm Thu & Fri, noon-4.30pm & 7pm-midnight Sat) Near the House of Victor Hugo is this postage stamp of a bohemian bistro. Stone walls, paintings and a mishmash of retro chairs set the scene for 100% organic mains, all served with Camargue rice infused with garlic and thyme, vegetables and salad. The downstairs *cave* is a cosy place to mellow out with a glass of *rouge*.

La Femme du Boulanger　　　CAFE €
(8 rue Morand; light mains €9.50-16, menus €17; ◷8.30am-btwn 7.30pm & 1am Mon-Sat) This industrial-rustic cafe attracts a regular bunch of locals, who come for its speciality breads, cakes and lunchtime *tartines* and open sandwiches with toppings like smoked salmon and capers. Or go straight for a *café gourmand* (coffee with an array of bite-size desserts).

Brasserie 1802　　　　BRASSERIE €€
(✆03 81 82 21 97; place Granvelle; 3-course menus €24; ◷11.30am-midnight daily; ⛲) With a terrace spilling out onto the tree-shaded place du Théâtre, this contemporary brasserie is ideal for watching the world go by over drinks or dinner. The menu plays the tried-

and-trusted card with a winning hand of classics like hot goat's cheese salad, Charlois beef and pistachio *crème brûlée*.

Le Poker d'As　　　MODERN FRENCH €€
(✆03 81 81 42 49; 14 sq St-Amour; menus €22-55; ◷lunch & dinner Tue-Sat) Warm, woody and as busy as a beehive, Le Poker d'As is a slice of country life in the heart of Besançon. The chef adds a pinch of imagination to expertly cooked seasonal specialities, along the lines of pollack crumble with onion sauce, and farm-fresh chicken cooked with morels and *vin jaune*.

La Petite Adresse　　　　BISTRO €
(✆03 81 82 35 09; 28 rue Claude Pouillet; 3-course menus €17; ◷lunch & dinner Mon-Sat; ✏) A little address worth noting. Big on cheese dishes like *boîte chaude* (hot box) of Vacherin Mont d'Or and *tartiflette*.

Mirabelle　　　　　　CAFE €
(5 rue Mégevand; mains €11-19; ◷lunch & dinner Mon-Fri) This sweet, wholesome cafe has a menu full of gratins, *croûtes au fromage* (melted cheese on bread) and scrummy tarts made with seasonal, mostly organic ingredients.

Marché Couvert　　　FOOD MARKET €
(6 rue Claude Goudimel; ◷8.30am-8pm Mon-Sat) Indoor market with a picnic load of saucisson, cheese, fruit and veg and patisserie.

DON'T MISS

LIGHTS, CAMERA, HUGO

Victor Hugo was an influential national and political figure and one of France's literary treasures, famous for penning masterpieces such as Les Misérables and Notre-Dame de Paris (The Hunchback of Notre Dame). He was born in 1802 in Besançon, and the House of Victor Hugo (140 Grande Rue) is identified by a commemorative inscription. Close by on the same street, look out for the plaque marking the House of the Lumière Brothers (place Victor Hugo). Born here in 1862 and 1864 respectively, the aptly named Auguste and Louis Lumière (lumière means 'light') were among the earliest pioneers of cinema and staged their first screening of motion pictures in 1895.

Drinking

Students spice up the nightlife in Besançon, concentrated in the old Battant quarter, along the river and on rue Claude Pouillet.

Les Passagers du Zinc   BAR
(5 rue Vignier; ⊘closed Mon) A grungy bar-cum-club with battered leather sofas and multi-coloured lights, the regular live bands and music nights keep this place high on the list of best venues in town. Step through the bonnet (hood) of an old Citroën DS to reach the cellar.

Bar de l'U   BAR
(5 rue Mairet; ⊘daily; ⚡) With occasional live music, free wi-fi, a pool table and a relaxed vibe, this is a student mainstay. There is a cheap and cheerful snack menu (€2 to €5) and €7 gets you a glass of wine and tapas.

Information

Post office (23 rue Proudhon) In the old town.
Tourist office (📞03 81 80 92 55; www.besancon-tourisme.com; Hôtel de Ville, place du 8 Septembre; ⊘10am-6pm Mon-Sat, to 1pm Sun) Sells city maps and guides, organises thematic city tours (in French only) and has free internet access.

Getting There & Around

BICYCLE Borrow a bicycle to cruise around town – free with a valid bus ticket – from the local bus company, **Boutique Ginko** (www.

ginkobus.com; 28 rue de la République, Centre St Pierre). Besançon also has the self-service bike-rental system **Vélocité** (www.velocite.besancon.fr), with 30 pick-up and drop-off sites across the city. The first half-hour is free; after that it costs €1/4 per hour/day.

Bus

Boutique Ginko sells bus tickets (€1.50/4/11.50 for a single ticket/day ticket/carnet of 10).

CAR & MOTORCYCLE There is a free outdoor car park on av de Chardonnet, the bank of the Doubs facing the citadel.

TRAIN **Besançon Gare Viotte** is 800m uphill from the city centre. Useful routes:

» **Paris** (€60 to €85, 2¾ hours, 14 daily)

» **Dijon** (€15, 70 minutes, 20 daily)

» **Lyon** (€30 to €45, 2½ to three hours, 25 daily)

» **Belfort** (€16, 1¼ hours, 20 daily)

» **Arbois** (€9, 50 minutes, 10 daily)

» **Arc-et-Senans** (€7, 22 minutes, 10 daily)

Connections to major cities are often cheaper and quicker from the new Gare de Besançon Franche-Comté TGV station, 12km north of the centre and a 15-minute hop by train from Gare Viotte.

Buy tickets at the train station or from the **Boutique SNCF** (44 Grande Rue) in town.

Around Besançon

SALINE ROYALE

Envisaged by its designer, Claude-Nicolas Ledoux, as the 'ideal city', the 18th-century Saline Royale (Royal Saltworks; www.salineroyale.com; adult/child €7.50/3.50; ⊘9am-noon & 2-6pm) in Arc-et-Senans, 35km southwest of Besançon, is a showpiece of early Industrial Age town planning. Although his urban dream was never fully realised, Ledoux's semicircular saltworks is now listed as a Unesco World Heritage Site.

Regular trains link Besançon and Arc-et-Senans (€7, 30 minutes, 10 daily).

ROUTE PASTEUR

Almost every single town in France has at least one street, square or garden named after Louis Pasteur, the great 19th-century chemist who invented pasteurisation and developed the first rabies vaccine. In the Jura it is even more the case, since the illustrious man was a local lad.

Pasteur was born in 1822 in the well-preserved medieval town of Dole, former capital of Franche-Comté, 20km west of Arc-et-

Senans along the D472. A scenic stroll along the Canal des Tanneurs in the historic tanner's quarter brings you to his childhood home, La Maison Natale de Pasteur (www. musee-pasteur.com; 43 rue Pasteur, Dole; adult/child €5/free; ☉10am-noon & 2-6pm Mon-Sat, 2-6pm Sun), now an atmospheric museum housing exhibits that include his cot, first drawings and university cap and gown.

In 1827 the Pasteur family settled in the bucolic village of Arbois (population 3653), 35km southeast of Dole. His laboratory and workshops here are on display at La Maison de Louis Pasteur (83 rue de Courcelles, Arbois; adult/child €6/3; ☉guided tours 9.45-11.45am & 2-6pm, closed mid Oct–Mar). The house is still decorated with its original 19th-century fixtures and fittings.

ARBOIS & THE ROUTE DES VINS DE JURA

Corkscrewing through some 80km of well-tended vines, pretty countryside and stone villages is the Route des Vins de Jura (Jura Wine Road; www.laroutedesvinsdujura.com). Plan your route with the winery guide and map, downloadable from the website.

◉ Sights & Activities

No visit to Arbois, the Jura wine capital, would be complete without a glass of *vin jaune*. The history of this nutty 'yellow wine' is told in the Musée de la Vigne et du Vin (www.juramusees.fr; adult/child €3.50/3; ☉10am-noon & 2-6pm Wed-Mon), housed within the whimsical, turreted Château Pécauld. The 2.5km-long Chemin des Vignes walking trail and the 8km-long Circuit des Vignes mountain-bike route meander through the vines. Both trails (marked with orange signs) begin at the top of the steps next to the Château Pécauld in Arbois; a booklet with more information is available at the tourist office.

High above Arbois is tiny Pupillin, a cute yellow-brick village famous for its wine production. Some 10 different *caves* (wine cellars) are open to visitors.

🛏 Sleeping & Eating

TOP
CHOICE / Closerie les Capucins   B&B €€
(☏03 84 66 17 38; www.closerielescapucines.com; 7 rue de Bourgogne, Arbois; d €115-130, q €235-275; @🛜🏊) A 17th-century stone convent has been transformed with utmost care and taste into this boutique guesthouse. The pared-down elegance of the individually designed rooms accentuates the exquisite

details: a chandelier here, an onyx washbasin there. Breakfasts are copious, with local dairy produce, patisserie, eggs and fruit. Add to that a tree-shaded garden by the river, a plunge pool, sauna, library and terrace overlooking Poligny's rooftops, and this is one special place to stay.

La Balance Mets et Vins   REGIONAL CUISINE €€
(☏03 84 37 45 00; 47 rue de Courcelles, Arbois; menus €16.50-37; ☉lunch & dinner Thu-Mon, lunch Tue & Wed; 🏃) With its lunches favouring local, organic produce, La Balance Mets et Vins provides the perfect coda to a wine-loving trip. Its signature *coq au vin jaune et aux morilles* casserole and *crème brûlée* doused in *vin jaune* are must-tastes, as are the wine menus with five glasses of either Jurassienne wine (€17) or *vin jaune* (€25, including a vintage one). Kids can sniff, swirl and sip, too, with three kinds of organic grape juice (€7.80).

❶ Information

Arbois' **tourist office** (☏03 84 66 55 50; www.arbois.com; 17 rue de l'Hôtel de Ville; ☉9am-noon & 2-6pm Mon-Sat) has walking and cycling information and a list of *caves* where you can taste and buy the local vintage.

❶ Getting There & Away

Trains link Arbois and Besançon (€9, 45 minutes, 10 daily).

Poligny to Région des Lacs

Comté cheese is the indisputable king of the Jura, with small-town Poligny (population 4543) serving as the capital of the industry that produces 40 million tonnes of the venerable cheese a year. Learn how 450L is transformed into a 40kg wheel of the tangy cheese, smell some of its 83 different aromas, and have a nibble at the Maison du Comté (www.maison-du-comte.com; av de la Résistance; adult/child €4/2.50; ☉guided tours 2pm, 3.15pm & 4.30pm, closed Nov-Mar). There are dozens of *fruitières* (cheese cooperatives) open to the public. Poligny's tourist office (☏03 84 37 24 21; www.ville-poligny.fr; place des Déportés; ☉9am-12.30pm & 1.30-5.30pm Mon-Sat) stocks an abundance of info on cheesemakers and wineries in the region.

Heading south, wiggle along the pretty D68 to Plasne, then continue south to **Château-Chalon**, a medieval village of yellow stone surrounded by vineyards known for

LIQUID GOLD

Vin jaune (yellow wine) is renowned for its ageing qualities, with prime vintages easily keeping for more than a century. The oldest bottle sampled was a 1774 vintage, a cool 220 years old when sipped by an awestruck committee of experts in 1994.

Legend has it that *vin jaune* was invented when a winemaker found a forgotten barrel, six years and three months after he'd initially filled it, and discovered its content miraculously transformed into a gold-coloured wine. Almost as miraculous is the price a bottle of *vin jaune*, also dating back to 1774, fetched at a Christie's auction in Geneva in May 2012. The prized bottle, which had been carefully stored in a family's underground cellar, was snapped up for a tidy €38,300.

A long, undisrupted fermentation process gives Jura's signature wine its unique characteristics. Savagnin grapes are harvested late and their sugar-saturated juices left to ferment for a minimum of six years and three months in oak barrels. A thin layer of yeast forms over the wine, which prevents it from oxidising, and there are no top-ups to compensate for evaporation (called *la part des anges*, 'the angels' share'). In the end, 100L of grape juice ferments down to 62L of *vin jaune* (lucky angels), which is then bottled in special 0.62L bottles called *clavelin*. La Percée du Vin Jaune (www.percee-du-vin-jaune.com) festival takes place annually in early February to celebrate the first tasting of the vintage produced six years and three months earlier. Villages take it in turns to hold the two-day celebrations, during which the new vintage is blessed and rated, and street tastings, cooking competitions, cellar visits and auctions keep *vin jaune* aficionados fulfilled.

their legendary *vin jaune*. There is a helpful tourist office (☑04 84 44 62 47; www.tourisme-hauteseille.fr; 3 place de la Mairie; ⊙9.30am-12.30pm & 2-6pm Mon-Fri) in the nearby village of Voiteur, with info and maps on surrounding villages, wine and walking in the area.

Nestled at the foot of lushly wooded limestone cliffs and wedged between three glacial valleys, 20km south of Poligny, is Baume-les-Messieurs, a picturesque village of honey-coloured cob houses and red-tiled rooftops. Its abandoned Benedictine Abbaye Impériale (Imperial Abbey; adult/child €5/3; ⊙guided tours 10am-noon & 2-6pm mid-May–Sep) has an exquisite polychrome Flemish altarpiece dating from the 16th century. Nearby, the 30-million-year-old Grottes de Baume (Baume Caves; adult/child €6/3.50; ⊙guided tours 10.30am-12.30pm & 1.30-6pm Apr-Sep) feature some impressive stalagmites and stalactites.

Immediately east lies Jura's Région des Lacs (Lakes District), a region of wild, lonely heights, dark forests, cave-riddled limestone cliffs and gemstone lakes. This family-oriented region is perfect for low-key outdoor pursuits like hiking, fishing and horse riding. You can take in the enchanting Cascades du Hérisson (www.cascades-du-herisson.fr) waterfalls, including the wispy 65m-high Cascade de l'Éventail, on a walk along the 7.4km circular waterfall trail. For details on sights, activities and events, visit www.juralacs.com.

🛏 Sleeping & Eating

The region is sprinkled with atmospheric *chambres d'hôte* and farmstays, but you'll need your own set of wheels.

Le Relais des Abbesses   B&B €

(☑03 84 44 98 56; www.chambres-hotes-jura.com; rue de la Roche, Château-Chalon; d €75, dinner menus €25) At this turreted *chambre d'hôte* in hilltop Château-Chalon, Agnès and Gérard have attractively decorated the rooms with hardwood floors, romantic canopy beds and Asian antiques. They are both fine cooks and dinner is an absolute treat, whether it's in the elegant dining room or on the terrace overlooking the countryside.

Hôtel de la Vallée Heureuse   HOTEL €€

(☑03 84 37 12 13; www.hotelvalleeheureuse.com; rte de Genève, Poligny; s €95-125, d €125-150, q €175, menus €28-65; ❄) You will indeed be *heureuse* (happy) to stumble across this beautifully converted 18th-century mill, which sits in riverside parkland and affords gorgeous forest and mountain views. The country retreat has tastefully decorated rooms and a restaurant specialising in Jurassien cuisine, plus a mini spa and indoor and outdoor pools.

Le Grand Jardin
B&B €

(☎03 84 44 68 37; www.legrandjardin.fr; rue des Grands Jardins, Baume-les-Messieurs; s/d/tr/q €46/58/72/84, 3-course menus €25-42) Book well ahead in summer to snag one of the three sunny, wood-floored rooms at this delightful *chambre d'hôte*, opposite the abbey in Baume-les-Messieurs. Local cheese, charcuterie and trout appear on the restaurant's appetising menu.

Café Restaurant de l'Abbaye
JURASSIEN €

(☎03 84 44 63 44; place Guillaume de Poupet, Baumes-les-Messieurs; menus €15-25; ⊙lunch Tue-Sun year-round, dinner Fri & Sat Sep-Jun, daily Jul & Aug) Tucked in one of the abbey's old buildings, this stone-walled cafe-restaurant rolls out a feast of regional fare. Try the *vin jaune* terrine or trout fillet in savagnin wine for a real taste of the Jura.

Belfort

POP 51,300

Squeezed between north and east, France and Germany, art and industry, Belfort has grown into its own distinctive identity (it calls itself a *territoire*, not a *département*). Historically part of Alsace, it only became part of the Franche-Comté region in 1921 and is best known today as the manufacturer of the superspeedy TGV train.

◉ Sights & Activities

Citadelle de Belfort
CITADEL

(adult/child €7/free; ⊙10am-6pm Wed-Mon May-Oct) Slung high above the old town, this sturdy citadel, built by the prolific Vauban, is the city's centrepiece. Inside is the Musée d'Histoire, which spells out regional history in artefacts. The citadel stages open-air concerts in summer.

On duty at its foot is a regal 22m-tall lion sculpted in red sandstone by Frédéric-Auguste Bartholdi (of *Statue of Liberty* fame) to commemorate Belfort's resistance to the Prussians in 1870–71. While the rest of Alsace was annexed as part of the greater German Empire, Belfort stubbornly remained part of France.

Musée de l'Aventure Peugeot
CAR MUSEUM

(www.musee-peugeot.com; Carrefour de l'Europe; adult/child €8/4; ⊙10am-6pm) Gleaming old-timers, concept cars and thumb-size miniatures – it's Peugeots *à gogo* at this museum, 12km south of Belfort in Sochaux.

Église du Sacré Cœur
CHURCH

(Carrer del Palau Reial 27; ⊙10am-6pm Tue-Sun) This modernist church, 4km southeast of Audincourt, is an architecture-buff must.

✖ Festivals & Events

Les Eurockéennes
MUSIC FESTIVAL

(www.eurockeennes.fr) Belfort plays host to a three-day open-air rock festival on the last

---

WORTH A TRIP

JURASSIEN HIDEOUTS

Escape civilisation at these more-idyllic-than-idyllic retreats. Advance reservations are essential.

Swiss-run Amondans (☎03 81 86 53 53; www.amondans.com; place du Village, Amondans; s/d/tr incl half-board €85/110/150; ⊙May-Oct) is an 18th-century farm 30km south of Besançon in sleepy Amondans that fuses retro-chic furnishings with centuries-old features. The vast, minimal rooms overlook open fields. Guests are hip, happy, outdoor types who hang out after dinner by an enormous fireplace in a converted barn. Swiss owners George and Geneviève can arrange picnics and all kinds of activities.

Ferme Auberge du Rondeau (☎03 81 59 25 84; http://sebou25.free.fr; Lavans-Vuillafans; s €44-55, d €58-70, q €108-130, menus €25-37; ⊙closed mid-Dec–mid-Jan) is 33km south of Besançon off the N57. Coo over goats, boar and dairy cows at this organic farm, where the friendly Bourdiers keep the snug wood-panelled rooms immaculate and rustle up a fantastic breakfast with homemade yoghurt, jam and fresh-baked bread. Fresh farm specialities like goat's cheese and *sanglier saucisson* (boar sausage) with home-grown vegies are served at lunch and dinner. They also sell fleecy mohair jumpers, hand-knitted from the wool of their angora goats.

weekend in June. In recent years The Cure and Cypress Hill have played here.

Entre Vues   FILM FESTIVAL
(www.festival-entrevues.com) International film festival in late November.

🛏 Sleeping & Eating

Don't leave Belfort without biting into a *Belflore,* a scrumptious almond-flavoured pastry filled with raspberries and topped with hazelnuts.

**Grand Hôtel du
Tonneau d'Or**   HISTORIC HOTEL €€
(☑03 84 58 57 56; www.tonneaudor.fr; 1 rue Reiset; s/d/tr €119/125/140; 🕸🏵) All stucco, sweeping staircases and art nouveau stained glass, this is a grand hotel with a modest price tag. The large rooms are more modern than the lobby would suggest, with creature comforts like minibars and also free wi-fi. Rates drop 40% at the weekend.

Relais d'Alsace   HOTEL €
(☑03 84 22 15 55; www.arahotel.com; 5 av de la Laurencie; s/d/tr/q €40/65/75/80; 🏵) The bright, no-frills rooms are spick and span at this good-value guesthouse on a main road slightly north of the centre. Breakfast is worth the extra €7.50.

❶ Information

Tourist office (☑03 84 55 90 90; www. ot-belfort.fr; 2bis rue Clémenceau; ⊙9am-12.30pm & 2-6pm Mon-Sat) Distributes free city maps and has information on accommodation and activities.

❶ Getting There & Away

TGV connections from Belfort **train station** (av Wilson) include Paris Gare de Lyon via Gare de Besançon Franche-Comté (€73, 2½ hours, 10 daily) and Besançon (€16, 1¼ hours, 14 daily).

Ronchamp

The only reason to rendezvous in Ronchamp, 20km west of Belfort, is to visit Le Corbusier's striking modernist chapel on a hill overlooking the old mining town. Built between 1950 and 1955, the surreal Chapelle de Notre Dame du Haut (Chapel of Our Lady of the Height; www.chapellederonchamp.fr; adult/child €8/4; ⊙9.30am-7pm), with a sweeping concrete roof, dazzling stained-glass windows and plastic features, is one of the 20th century's architectural masterpieces.

A 15-minute walking trail leads uphill to the chapel from the centre of Ronchamp village; the tourist office (☑03 84 63 50 82; 14 place du 14 Juillet; ⊙9am-12.30pm & 1.30-6pm Tue-Fri, 9am-12.30pm Sat, 1.30-6pm Mon) can guide you.

Trains run from Ronchamp to Belfort (€4.50, 20 minutes, nine daily).

Métabief

POP 1033 / ELEV 1000M

Métabief, found 18km south of Pontarlier on the main road to Lausanne, is the region's leading cross-country ski resort. Year-round lifts take you almost to the top of Mont d'Or (1463m), the highest peak, where a fantastic 180-degree panorama stretches right over the foggy Swiss plain to Lake Geneva (Lac

---

DON'T MISS

GRANDE TRAVERSÉE DU JURA

Great for cross-country skiing, mountain biking, walking and snowshoeing, the Grande Traversée du Jura (Grand Jura Crossing; GTJ) cross-country track runs some 200km from Villers-le-Lac (south of Belfort) to Hauteville-Lompnes (southwest of Bellegarde-sur-Valserine). The exact itinerary varies between disciplines, but the track peaks at 1500m near the town of Mouthe (southwest of Métabief) and follows one of France's coldest valleys. To cover the popular, well-groomed track takes 10 days of skiing – a feat even for the ultrafit.

The 76km stretch of the GTJ from Lamoura to Mouthe lures 4000 skiers to the world's second-largest cross-country ski race in February, the Transjurassienne (www. transjurassienne.com), and hundreds of inline skaters to Trans' Roller (www.transroller. com) in September.

For the GTJ low-down, including maps and accommodation details, visit www.gtj. asso.fr.

DON'T MISS

HOT BOX, CHRISTMAS ICE & JESUS

It's hot, it's soft and it's packed in a box. Vacherin Mont d'Or is the only French cheese to be eaten with a spoon – hot. Made between 15 August and 15 March with *lait cru* (unpasteurised milk), it derives its unique nutty taste from the spruce bark in which it's wrapped. Connoisseurs top the soft-crusted cheese with chopped onions, garlic and white wine, wrap it in aluminium foil and bake it for 45 minutes to create a *boîte chaude* (hot box). Only 11 factories in the Jura are licensed to produce Vacherin Mont d'Or.

Mouthe, 15km south of Métabief Mont d'Or, is the mother of *liqueur de sapin* (fir-tree liqueur). *Glace de sapin* (fir-tree ice cream) also comes from Mont d'Or, known as the North Pole of France due to its seasonal subzero temperatures (record low: -38°C). Sampling either is rather like ingesting a Christmas tree. Then there's *Jésus* – a small, fat version of *saucisse de Morteau* (Morteau sausage), easily identified by the wooden peg on its end, attached after the sausage is smoked with pinewood sawdust in a traditional *tuyé* (mountain hut).

Léman) and all the way from the Matterhorn to Mont Blanc.

Métabief is famed for its unique Vacherin Mont d'Or cheese, which has been produced alongside Comté and Morbier by the Sancey-Richard family at the Fromagerie du Mont d'Or (www.fromageriedumontdor.com; 2 rue Moulin; ⊕9am-12.15pm & 3-7pm Mon-Sat, 9am-noon Sun) since 1953. To see it being made, arrive with the milk lorry around 9am.

The closest tourist office (☑03 81 49 13 81; www.tourisme-metabief.com; 1 place de la Mairie, Les Hôpitaux-Neufs; ⊕9am-12.30pm & 1.30-6pm Mon-Sat) open time round is in Les Hôpitaux-Neufs, 2.5km northeast of Métabief. The annexe in Métabief is closed October and November, April and May, much like everything else in the village.

Family-run Hôtel Étoile des Neiges (☑03 81 49 11 21; www.hoteletoiledesneiges.fr; 4 rue du Village; s/d/tr/q €58/84/98/104, with half-board €72/108/150/184; 🖭🌐) has bright, well-kept rooms, including great mezzanine family rooms. There's an indoor pool, a sauna and canteen-style restaurant.

You'll need a car to reach Métabief, along the D9 (just off the N57), 58km east of Arbois and 75km south of Besançon.

Around Métabief Mont d'Or

The closest you'll get to the North Pole in these parts is the Christmassy Parc Polaire (www.parcpolaire.com; adult/child €8/7; ⊕10am-noon & 2-5pm Tue-Fri & Sun, 2-5pm Sat Dec-Oct) in Chaux-Neuve, where the friendly team will introduce you to huskies, reindeer and some mighty hairy yaks on a 1½-hour guided tour.

A real cliff-hanger of a castle, the medieval Château de Joux (☑03 81 69 47 95; www.chateaudejoux.com; adult/child €6.50/3.50; ⊕guided tours 10-11.30am & 2-4.30pm Apr–mid-Nov), 10km north of Métabief, used to guard the route between Switzerland and France. Today it houses France's most impressive arms museum and a 100m-deep well. Guided tours are gripping, full of anecdotes and stories, and available in English (ring ahead). In summer, torch-lit night-time tours are organised for extra spookiness.

Parc Naturel Régional du Haut-Jura

Experience the Jura at its rawest in the Haut-Jura regional park, an area of 757 sq km stretching from Chapelle-des-Bois in the north almost to the western tip of Lake Geneva. Forget about exploring the region's lakes, mountains and low-lying valleys without a car.

A great place to start is the Maison du Parc (www.parc-haut-jura.fr; Lajoux; adult/child €5/3; ⊕10am-12.30pm & 2-6pm Tue-Fri, 2-6pm Sat & Sun), a visitor centre with an interactive sensorial museum that explores the region and its history through sound, touch and smell. The Maison du Parc is found in the east of the Haut-Jura regional park, 19km east of St-Claude and 5km west of Mijoux on the Swiss border.

There's not much to St-Claude – the largest town in the park – bar its illustrious diamond-cutting industry which, unfortunately, is off-limits to visitors.

Les Louvières (☑03 84 42 09 24; www.leslouvieres.fr; Pratz; 2-/3-course menus €32/38;

lunch & dinner Wed-Sat, lunch Sun), a solar-powered mountain farmhouse restaurant to rave about, is a 20-minute drive west of St-Claude in Pratz. The cuisine (foie gras maki zushi with maple syrup, fish in wasabi sauce etc) is strictly fusion.

Le Clos d'Estelle (☎03 84 42 01 29; www.leclosdestelle.com; Hameau La Marcantine, Charchilla; d €68-80, q €125), 12km north, has four *chambres d'hôte* where you can fall asleep to pin-drop silence. The owners, Jura locals through and through, enthusiastically share their knowledge of the area with you.

Les Rousses, on the northeastern edge of the park, is the park's prime sports hub, for both winter (skiing) and summer (walking and mountain biking). The resort comprises four small, predominantly cross-country ski areas: Prémanon, Lamoura, Bois d'Amont and the village Les Rousses. Find out more at the Maison du Tourisme (Fort des Rousses; 9am-noon & 2-6pm Mon-Sat, 9.30am-12.30pm Sun), home to the tourist office (☎03 84 60 02 55; www.lesrousses.com) and the ESF (☎03 84 60 01 61; www.esf-lesrousses.com).

The far-reaching vista from the Col de la Faucille mountain pass, 20km south of Les Rousses, reaches across the Jura Mountains to Lake Geneva and the snow-dusted Alps.

Savour these incredible views (extra incredible at sunset) from the restaurant terrace, or the poolside in summer, of La Mainaz (☎04 50 41 31 10; www.la-mainaz.com; 5 rte du Col de la Faucille; d €87-122, menus €19-49;), a cosy chalet midway along the mountain pass.

As the N5 wriggles down the Jura Mountains past the small ski resort of Mijoux, the panorama of Lake Geneva embraced by the French Alps and Mont Blanc beyond is stunning. For the best views, ride the Telesiège Val Mijoux (chairlift; adult/child return €7/4.50; 10.30am-1pm & 2.15-5.30pm Sat & Sun mid-Jul–late Aug) from Mijoux and continue up to 1533m-high Mont Rond.

Heading a further 25km southeast from Mijoux, you hit the French–Swiss border, passing through Ferney-Voltaire (www.ferney-voltaire.net), 5km north of Geneva, en route. Following his banishment from Switzerland in 1759, Voltaire lived in Ferney until his return to Paris and death in 1778. Guided tours of his elegant home, Château de Voltaire (allée du Château; adult/child €5.50/free; tours in French hourly 10am-1pm & 2-6pm Tue-Sun Apr-Oct), take in the château, chapel and surrounding 7-hectare park. Past visitors include Auden, Blake and Flaubert, all of whom wrote about the philosopher's home in exile.

Massif Central

Best Places to Eat

» Emmanuel Hodencq
(p535)

» François Gagnaire (p552)

» Les Caudalies (p539)

» La Parenthèse (p552)

» Le Sisisi (p536)

Best Places to Stay

» Le Chastel Montaigu
(p545)

» Hôtel Saluces (p547)

» Hôtel Notre Dame (p542)

» Auberge de Jeunesse Le
Grand Volcan (p543)

» Le Moulin Ferme-Auberge
(p554)

Why Go?

In one of the wildest, emptiest and least-known corners of France, the Massif Central, you can feel nature's heavy machinery at work. Below ground, hot volcanic springs bubble up to supply Vichy and Volvic with their famous mineral waters, while high in the mountains trickling streams join forces to form three of France's mightiest rivers: the Dordogne, the Allier and the Loire.

The Massif Central and surrounding Auvergne region remains deeply traditional. Reliant on agriculture and cattle farming, it shelters the country's largest area of protected landscape with two huge regional parks: the Parc Naturel Régional des Volcans d'Auvergne and its neighbour, the Parc Naturel Régional Livradois-Forez. On-tap outdoor activities include heady hiking trails, plunging ski slopes, paragliding off shapely volcanic summits, and setting off on an age-old pilgrimage – sustained by some of the halest, heartiest food in France.

When to Go
Clermont-Ferrand

May & Jun
Experience the region's hiking trails in their full springtime splendour.

Dec–March Max out on winter sports near Le Mont-Dore or catch Clermont-Ferrand's short film festival.

15 August See sacred Vierges Noires (Black Madonnas) paraded on Assumption Day.

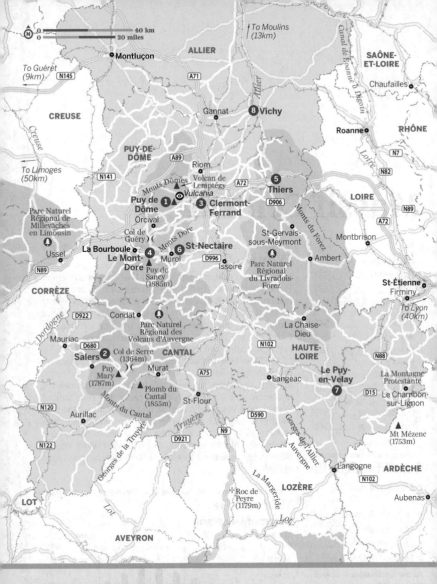

Massif Central Highlights

1 Scale the panoramic summit of **Puy de Dôme** (p541) on the new cog railway

2 Swoon over the pastoral greenery and rugged volcanic scenery around **Salers** (p546)

3 Marvel at the Michelin brothers' influence on travel at the Michelin **museum** (p533) in Clermont-Ferrand

4 Schuss down the slopes, or ride the century-old funicular in **Le Mont-Dore** (p542)

5 Watch artisans at work and tour the world-class knife collection at **Musée de la Coutellerie** (p547) in Thiers

6 Meet the cows who make one of France's most famous cheeses at **St-Nectaire** (p545)

7 Climb the tortuous staircase to the mystical cave-chapel of **St-Michel d'Aiguilhe** (p548), perched atop a pinnacle in Le Puy-en-Velay

8 Soak up the mineral-rich spa waters in belle époque **Vichy** (p537)

History

The historical province of the Auvergne derives its name from a Gallic tribe, the Arverni, who ruled the area until the Romans arrived under Julius Caesar. Arverni chieftain Vercingétorix put up fierce resistance to Caesar's legions, but despite several victories, his armies were crushed near Alésia in Burgundy.

The Romans founded a number of settlements including Augustonemetum (later Clermont-Ferrand). Following the fall of the Empire, the Auvergne entered a period of infighting between rival factions of Franks, Aquitanians and Carolingians, before being split into feudal domains during the Middle Ages under the dukes of Auvergne, whose government was in Riom.

After the French Revolution the capital switched to Clermont-Ferrand, which became a focus of expansion, especially with the Michelin brothers' factories in the late 19th century. Meanwhile aristocrats flocked to the region's fashionable spas, notably in Vichy. During WWII Vichy became the capital of the collaborationist regime under Maréchal Pétain.

Getting There & Around

AIR The region's only airport is in Clermont-Ferrand.

BICYCLE For info on cycling in the region, head to shop.lonelyplanet.com to purchase a downloadable PDF of the Massif Central chapter from Lonely Planet's *Cycling France* guide.

CAR The A75 autoroute (sometimes called La Méridienne) provides high-speed travel to southern France through the viaducts at Garabit and Millau, while the A89 (La Transeuropéenne) travels west to Bordeaux. Elsewhere the region's roads are twisty, slow and highly scenic: you'll need your own car to reach the more remote spots, as the bus network is almost nonexistent.

TRAIN Though the TGV network hasn't yet arrived, regular trains serve all the main towns including a direct service from Clermont-Ferrand to Paris in 3½ hours.

CLERMONT-FERRAND & AROUND

Clermont-Ferrand

POP 142,400 / ELEV 400M

Sprawled around a long-extinct volcano in the middle of the Massif Central, Clermont-Ferrand is the capital of the Auvergne and its only metropolis. Home to the Michelin empire and roly-poly Michelin Man (known to the French as Bibendum), the city has been a thumping industrial powerhouse for over a century. Surrounded by smokestack factories and suburban warehouses, the atmospheric old town is crowned by a soaring twin-spired cathedral.

Sights

The narrow lanes of Clermont-Ferrand's old city twist outwards from the cathedral, and are dotted with mansions dating from the 17th and 18th centuries.

Clermont's three municipal museums can be visited on a combined ticket (€9), available from the tourist office.

L'Aventure Michelin MUSEUM (www.laventuremichelin.com; 32 rue du Clos Four; adult/child €9/5; ⊙10am-6pm Tue-Sun) Next door to Clermont's mammoth Michelin factory, with a 5300kg tyre (the world's largest) out front, this brilliant museum recounts the rubber empire's evolution while also shedding light on Michelin's wide-ranging impact on aviation, rail, maps, restaurant guides and GPS technology. Hugely entertaining for both adults and kids, it's got some great hands-on interactive exhibits and advertising retrospectives. Allow at least a couple of hours; last entry is 1½ hours before closing; audioguides are €2. Take Tram A to Stade Marcel Michelin. The museum's on-site gift shop sells everything from roadmaps to bouncy Bibendum key rings; you can also pick up iconic souvenirs at the city-centre Michelin Boutique (2 place de la Victoire).

Cathédrale Notre Dame CATHEDRAL (place de la Victoire; tower admission €1.50; ⊙cathedral 7.30am-noon & 2-6pm Mon-Sat, 9.30am-noon & 3-7.30pm Sun, tower 9am-11.15am & 2-5.15pm Mon-Sat, 3-5.30pm Sun; 🚻) Carved from the inky volcanic rock of Volvic's quarries, Clermont's jet-black cathedral, with its massive Gothic facade, was constructed between the 13th and 19th centuries. The interior is a striking contrast of light and shade, brilliantly lit by afternoon sunshine. For fantastic views east to Thiers and west to Puy de Dôme, brave the 250 steps to the top of its only transept tower to have survived the French Revolution, the Tour de la Bayette. Two blocks north of the cathedral, the early-16th-century Fontaine d'Amboise also has a panoramic view of the Puy de Dôme and nearby peaks.

Clermont-Ferrand

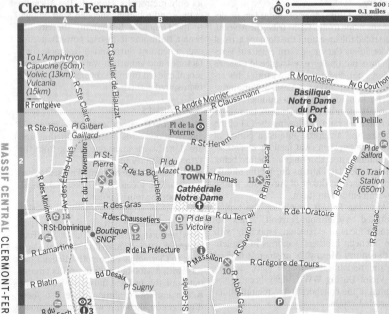

Musée d'Art Roger Quilliot   ART MUSEUM
(museedart.clermont-ferrand.fr; place Louis Deteix; adult/child €5/free; ⊙10am-6pm Tue-Fri, 10am-noon & 1-6pm Sat & Sun) Located in a converted Ursuline convent, the museums has exhibits from the late Middle Ages to the 20th century, including significant works by Delacroix, the Ryckaert family and François Boucher, as well as local artists. Situated northeast of the centre in Montferrand; take tram A from place de Jaude or bus 31 from the train station.

Musée Bargoin   MUSEUM
(museebargoin.clermont-ferrand.fr; 45 rue Ballain-villiers; adult/child €5/free; ⊙10am-noon & 1-5pm

Tue-Sat, 2-7pm Sun) This museum is split into an archaeological department, displaying excavated Roman coins to neolithic wood carvings, and a textile arts department, with a dazzling collection of carpets from Tibet, Iran, Syria, China and beyond.

Musée d'Histoire Naturelle Henri-Lecoq   MUSEUM
(museelecoq.clermont-ferrand.fr; 15 rue Bardoux; adult/child €5/free; ⊙10am-noon & 2-5pm Tue-Sat, 2-5pm Sun) This museum is named for the celebrated pharmacist and natural scientist who lived in Clermont-Ferrand in the 19th century and amassed rocks, fossils, plants

Clermont-Ferrand

◉ Top Sights

◉ Sights

🛏 Sleeping

🍴 Eating

🍷 Drinking

🎭 Entertainment

🛍 Shopping

and stuffed animals from the region. Highlights are the gallery of Auvergnat butterflies and over 50 native orchids.

Basilique Notre Dame du Port   CHURCH
(⊗8am-7pm) A Unesco World Heritage Site, this magnificent example of 12th-century Auvergnat-Romanesque architecture is sparkling after recent renovations. Its black Virgin is venerated with a grand procession in mid-May.

Place de Jaude   CITY SQUARE
At the southwestern edge of the old city, Clermont's monumental pedestrianised square is overlooked by a statue (rue Gonode, place de Jaude) of heroic Celtic chief Vercingétorix.

🛏 Sleeping

As a commercial hub, Clermont has plenty of accommodation, but most places lack character and offer limited value for money.

Hôtel des Puys   HOTEL €€
(☑04 73 91 92 06; www.hoteldespuys.fr; 16 place Delille; d €86-115; ✴@🛜) The exterior has all the charm of a municipal car park, but inside you'll find cool, minimalist rooms, most with a balcony over trafficky place Delille. More cash buys extra space, separate sitting areas and big bathrooms. Best features here include the abundant breakfast buffet (€14) and the panoramic terrace with superb views over Clermont's rooftops.

Hôtel de Lyon   HOTEL €€
(☑04 73 17 60 80; www.hotel-de-lyon.com; 16 place de Jaude; s €64-82, d €78-97; ✴🛜) You'll glimpse the Vercingétorix statue from your window at this ultracentral pad. Despite its classic exterior, soundproofed rooms are motel-modern (pine furniture, country prints). Downstairs, the pub-brasserie is good for a drink.

Hôtel Saint-Joseph   HOTEL €
(☑04 73 92 69 71; www.hotelsaintjoseph.fr; 10 rue de Maringues; s €40-48, d €48-51; @🛜) Behind a facade painted with old-fashioned images of travellers, the double-glazed rooms at this cheerful little hotel near the Friday morning St-Joseph market offer the best budget value in Clermont.

Dav' Hôtel   HOTEL €
(☑04 73 93 31 49; www.davhotel.fr; 10 rue des Minimes; s €61-71, d €64-76; ✴@🛜) Rooms at this central alley hotel are well-equipped, if plainer than the strawberry-and-orange-adorned reception area.

🍴 Eating & Drinking

Place de Jaude and the area north around rue St-Dominique are filled with inexpensive eateries. Cafe terraces ring place de la Victoire, with more on rue Ballainvilliers. Looking like a modern-art experiment gone wrong, the Lego-brick facade of Clermont's covered market (⊗7am-7.30pm Mon-Sat) is on place St-Pierre.

Emmanuel Hodencq   GASTRONOMIC €€€
(☑04 73 31 23 23; www.hodencq.com; 6 place St-Pierre; menus incl drinks €27-150; ⊗lunch & dinner Tue-Sat, closed mid–late Aug; 🍴) Langoustines, locally picked wild mushrooms and truffles are among the stars at chef Emmanuel Hodencq's elegant Michelin-starred affair. To dine in high style without breaking the bank, try the midday 'Le Cercle' *menu*, including main dish, dessert, wine and coffee for €27. Hodencq holds Saturday morning

FILM CENTRAL

One of the world's foremost festivals of short film, Clermont's Festival International du Court Métrage (www.clermont-filmfest.com; ☉Feb) has three competitions for international and domestic shorts, as well as a touring 'Coup de Cœurs' program visiting cinemas across the Auvergne. Tickets are sold at the tourist office.

Year-round, nondubbed feature-length flicks screen at the following cinemas:

» Ciné Capitole (www.allocine.fr; 32 place de Jaude)

» Cinéma Les Ambiances (www.cinema-lesambiances.fr; 7 rue St-Dominique)

cooking classes (€135; book well in advance).

Le Sisisi
BISTRO €

(☎04 73 14 04 28; lesisisi.com; 16 rue Massillon; mains €17-19; ☉lunch Tue-Fri, dinner Tue-Sat) At this laid-back local bistro a mixed crowd sips early evening drinks at the bar, then settles in for delicious, colourful and creative cuisine served at pavement tables or in the high-ceilinged industrial-chic indoor room. From mains like a *mille-feuille* of sirloin steak alternately stacked with olive oil-marinated red peppers to desserts like panna cotta with roasted strawberries and banana-lime coulis, everything is served with artistic flair.

Les Goûters de Justine
TEAROOM €

(11bis rue Blaise Pascal; cakes/lunch €3.90/5.70; ☉noon-7pm Wed-Fri, 2.30-7pm Sat) With its amiable proprietor and cosy jumble of old-fashioned furniture, this is a lovely spot to linger over a light lunch or a cup of tea with homemade cakes from the sideboard – a bit like settling in at your grandma's place.

Le 1513
CRÊPERIE €

(www.le1513.com; 3 rue des Chaussetiers; crêpes €5.50-12; ☉lunch & dinner daily; ☎☁) Through a stone archway inside the vaulted cellars of a 1513-built medieval mansion, local flavours at this cavernous crêperie include its *galette Auvergnate*, a savoury pancake with local ham and St-Nectaire cheese.

L'Amphitryon Capucine
GASTRONOMIC €€€

(☎04 73 31 38 39; www.amphitryoncapucine.com; 50 rue Fontgiève; menus €24-80; ☉Tue-Sat; ☁) Ditch the jeans and dig out your glad rags and you'll be rewarded with splendid seasonal cuisine spread over several courses (including a decadent eight-course *menu gourmand*). Kids' menu available (€15).

Bistrot Bancal
WINE BAR €€

(☎04 73 14 23 92; 15 rue des Chaussetiers; mains €19-25; ☉lunch Wed-Sat, dinner Wed-Sun) This sleek two-level bistro is a local favourite for its hand-picked organic and Auvergnat wines accompanied by authentic *saveurs de terroir* (country dishes), charcuterie and cheese.

☆ Entertainment

For sports and entertainment listings (including news of Clermont's cherished rugby team), pick up the free French-language monthly *Zap* (www.myzap.fr) at the tourist office and elsewhere around town.

La Cooperative de Mai
LIVE MUSIC

(www.lacoope.org; rue Serge Gainsbourg) Cavernous warehouse gig and concert venue. Catch tram A to place du 1er Mai.

Le B-Box
NIGHTCLUB

(www.bboxclub.com; 29 rue de l'Eminée, Le Pardieu; ☉Thu-Sun) Massive (in every sense), this 4000-capacity multilevel warehouse is France's largest indoor club. Take bus 6 or 22 to the Cristal stop.

ℹ Information

Tourist office (☎04 73 98 65 00; www.clermont-fd.com; place de la Victoire; ☉9am-6pm Mon-Fri, 10am-1pm & 2-6pm Sat & Sun) Opposite the cathedral, with free wi-fi and a downstairs multimedia exhibition on the Auvergne's churches.

ℹ Getting There & Away

AIR **Clermont-Ferrand Auvergne airport** (www.clermont-aeroport.com), 7km east of the city centre, is an Air France hub. Domestic destinations include Paris, Nice and Ajaccio; international flights go to Southampton (UK) and Madrid.

CAR The major car-hire companies have branches at the airport and in town.

TRAIN Clermont is the region's main rail hub. You can buy tickets at the **boutiques SNCF** (☎08 92 35 35 35; 43 rue du 11 Novembre) in the city centre.

Long-haul destinations include Paris Gare de Lyon (€56, 3½ hours, six to 10 daily), Lyon (€32.20, 2½ hours, more than 10 daily) and Nîmes (€40.90, 5¼ hours, three direct trains daily).

Frequent short hauls run to/from Riom (€3.20, 10 minutes), Vichy (€9.90, 30 minutes), Volvic (€4.40, 30 minutes) and Thiers (€8.60, 45 minutes), with less frequent service to Le Mont-Dore (€13.20, 1½ hours, two trains and three SNCF buses daily). For Le Puy-en-Velay, the most efficient options involve a train-to-SNCF-bus transfer (€22.50, 2¼ hours, three or four daily).

❶ Getting Around

TO/FROM THE AIRPORT Bus 10 travels to/from the airport several times daily Monday to Saturday; a **taxi** (📞04 73 60 06 00) costs around €15.

BUS & TRAM Clermont's public-transport system is handled by **T2C** (www.t2c.fr; 24 bd Charles de Gaulle; single ticket/day pass €1.40/4.20). Buses (single ticket/10-trip *carnet* €1.40/12.10) link the city and station, while tram A connects place de Jaude with Montferrand.

BICYCLE Moovicité hires out bikes (with deposit, first hour free). You can pick up and drop off bikes at either of its two outlets – **Moovicité Gare** (43 av de l'Union Soviétique) and **Moovicité Renoux** (20 place Hippolyte Renoux).

Riom

POP 18,510

Capital of the Auvergne region during the Middle Ages, Riom has an old quarter with boulevards lined with *hôtels particuliers* (historic mansions), mostly built from dark volcanic stone.

The tourist office (📞04 73 38 59 45; www.tourisme-riomlimagne.fr; 27 place de la Fédération; ⊙9.30am-12.30pm & 2-5.30pm Tue, Wed, Fri & Sat, 2-5.30pm Mon & Thu) is adjacent to the pretty Romanesque church Église St-Amable (rue St-Amable; ⊙9am-7pm).

Climbing 167 steps in Riom's 15th-century Tour de l'Horloge (rue de l'Horloge; adult/child €0.50/free; ⊙10am-noon & 2-5pm Tue-Sun) rewards with wonderful views of the town and mountains.

Customs and traditions of life in the Auvergne are explored at the excellent Musée Régional d'Auvergne (10bis rue Delille; adult/child €3/free; ⊙guided tours 2pm & 4pm Tue-Sun, closed Dec–Mar), which is visitable by guided tour only, while the Musée Francisque Mandet (14 rue de l'Hôtel de Ville; adult/child €3/free; ⊙10am-noon & 2-5.30pm Tue-Sun) displays

a newly acquired decorative arts collection alongside impressive exhibits of classical finds and 15th- to 19th-century paintings.

The 15th-century Église Notre Dame du Marthuret (rue du Commerce; ⊙9am-6pm) holds Riom's treasured relics: a Vierge Noire (Black Madonna) and delicate Vierge à l'Oiseau, depicting the Virgin and Child accompanied by a fluttering bird.

Riom is 15km north of Clermont on the N9, served by frequent trains (€3.20, 10 minutes).

Vichy

POP 25,580

Its belle époque heyday may have passed, but there's still an air of understated grandeur about the stately streets and landscaped parks of Vichy, 55km northeast of Clermont-Ferrand. Famous for its volcanic mineral waters since Napoléon III and his entourage sojourned here during the 19th century, and later infamous as the seat of Marshal Pétain's collaborationist regime during WWII, these days Vichy is a well-to-do provincial hub that remains enduringly popular for its therapeutic waters.

◉ Sights & Activities

Parks   PARKS
The heart of Vichy is the huge Parc des Sources, laid out by Napoléon III in 1812. Filled by chestnut and plane trees, it's encircled by a wrought-iron-canopied colonnade (allowing visitors to perambulate the park without getting wet) and is a beautiful place to stroll.

Other lovely parks include the riverside Parc Kennedy and Parc Napoléon III. Look out for the Swiss-style 19th-century chalet houses along the parks' edge, which once lodged the city's visiting *curistes*.

Springs   MINERAL SPRINGS
Most *sources* for drinking the mineral waters – including the elegant glass Hall des Sources (Parc des Sources; ⊙6:15am-7pm) and the Source de l'Hôpital (Parc des Sources; ⊙8am-8.30pm Apr-Dec), both in the Parc des Sources – require a prescription and are otherwise off-limits. If you're keen, the tourist office has a list of local *médecins* (doctors).

The only place the public can sip is from the brass taps of the Source des Célestins (blvd du Président Kennedy; ⊙8am-8.30pm Apr-Sep, to 6pm Oct-Mar), where filling up is free

Vichy

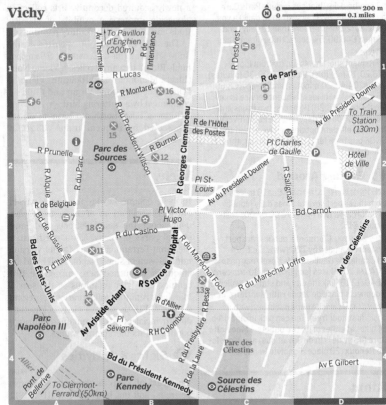

(bring your own bottle). The taps are shut in winter to prevent frozen pipes.

Spas
HEALTH SPAS

Book ahead for treatments at Vichy's spas.

Vichy's most luxurious spa, Les Célestins (☏04 70 30 82 82; www.vichy-spa-hotel.com; 111 bd des États-Unis; ☉9am-8pm Mon-Sat, to 4pm Sun) offers decadent treatments such as the *douche de Vichy à quatre mains* (four-hand hot-spring massage, from €54 for 12 minutes) or the *massage aux pierres chaudes des volcans* (hot lava rock massage, €98 for 50 minutes).

Similar treatments are on offer at Centre Thermal des Dômes (☏04 70 97 39 59; www.destinationvichy.com; 1 av Eisenhower). This once-lavish complex of Moorish arches and tiled towers, much of it now incongruously turned into a shopping arcade, is topped by a Byzantine dome.

Old City
HISTORIC QUARTER

Vichy's old city is small, but a couple of sights merit a visit.

The art deco 1930s Église St-Blaise (rue d'Allier) has 20th-century stained glass and frescos of some of France's famous churches. The original chapel at the rear houses Vichy's Vierge Noire.

The Musée de l'Opéra de Vichy (opera. vichy.musee.free.fr; 16 rue du Maréchal Foch; adult/child €4/3; ☉2-6pm Tue-Sun) houses rotating exhibits that document Vichy's turn-of-the-20th-century opera house.

🛏 Sleeping

Places to stay are plentiful and well priced. Vichy's spas can also arrange pampering accommodation packages.

Aletti Palace Hôtel
HOTEL €€€

(☏04 70 30 20 20; www.hotel-aletti.fr; 3 place Joseph Aletti; d €158-202; ❄❖⊛) A billiards

Vichy

room, wood-panelled bar and outdoor pool flanked by flowers are among the luxurious amenities at this *grande dame* presiding over the Parc des Sources. Palatial rooms come with marble bathrooms and enormous closets. Its glass-canopied **restaurant** (menus €17 to €36) utilises local produce in its classical cuisine.

Hôtel de Naples HOTEL €
(☑04 70 97 91 33; www.hoteldenaples.fr; 22 rue de Paris; d €42-48; @☎) Welcoming and well located, this delightful and recently renovated family-run hotel has clean, good-sized rooms, split between the main building and a quiet rear annexe overlooking the hotel's car park (€4 per day). In summer, breakfast (€6.50) is served on the grassy back terrace.

Pavillon d'Enghien HOTEL €€
(☑04 70 98 33 30; www.pavillondenghien.com; 32 rue Callou; d €75-109; ⊘restaurant lunch Tue-Sun, dinner Tue-Sat; ☎☑) Soothing white and cream rooms in this converted mansion are livened up with splashes of colour. Ask for a room overlooking the interior courtyard and pool, where you can dine alfresco on market-fresh Auvergnat dishes at its **restaurant** (menus €15 to €31). Located just north of Centre Thermal des Dômes; turn left off av Thermale.

Hôtel Arverna HOTEL €
(☑04 70 31 31 19; www.hotels-vichy.com; 12 rue Desbrest; d €55-83; ❀@☎) Completely remodeled in 2012, this comfortable hideaway down a quiet side street has air-conditioning

in all rooms, facilities for disabled travellers and plenty of other new perks, including energy-efficient bedside reading lamps, rain shower heads, heated towel racks and armchairs that convert into kid-sized beds.

✕ Eating

For inexpensive pavement dining, check out the cluster of brasseries at the intersection of rue de Paris and rue Georges Clemenceau. Vichy's **covered market** (⊘7am-1pm Tue-Sun, plus 4-7pm Fri & Sat) is on place PV Léger, 500m northwest of the train station.

Les Caudalies GASTRONOMIC €€
(☑04 70 32 13 22; 7-9 rue Besse; menus €20-71; ⊘lunch Tue-Sun, dinner Tue-Sat) Young chef Emmanuel Bosset creates masterful twists on traditional French cuisine, from starters like 'faux-Caesar' salad with smoked cod, thick slab bacon, romaine tips, anchovies and sun-dried tomatoes in wasabi-crayfish dressing to desserts like Vichy pastille ice cream with poppy wine. The lunchtime *jéroboam* menu, including three courses and a glass of wine, is excellent value at €23.

La Table d'Antoine GASTRONOMIC €€€
(☑04 70 98 99 71; www.latabledantoine.com; 8 rue Burnol; lunch menus €20-22, dinner menus €34-64; ⊘lunch Wed-Mon, dinner Wed-Sun) Abstract portraits and high-backed chairs create a boutique feel at this high-class temple to French fine dining, and the food is seriously fancy, from coconut-poached chicken to langoustines and smoked fish. Reserve ahead.

VICHY SWEETS

Pastilles de Vichy were first created in 1825 using bicarbonate of soda, but the town's mineral waters later inspired its signature sweets. Since 1875 the bicarbonate has been replaced with salts extracted from the local mineral water, which is mixed with sugar and flavoured with mint, aniseed or lemon.

Not all of these octagonal-shaped sweets are the same, however. Those sold in shops and supermarkets have a different composition to those sold in pharmacies, which contain 10% more mineral salts to enhance their digestive properties. And Vichy is the only place in the world where you can buy the sweets stamped with the 'Vichy Etat' logo and packaged in an iconic metal tin, including at the beautiful glass-paned, rotunda-style kiosk Maison des Pastilles (Parc des Sources; ⊙2-6.30pm Mon, 10am-noon & 2-6.30pm Tue-Sun mid-Apr–mid-Oct). To learn more, visit the Pastillerie de Vichy (☑04 70 30 94 70; 94 Allée des Ailes; admission free; ⊙9am-noon & 1.30-3pm Mon-Thu, 9-11pm Fri Apr–mid-Nov) plant, 2.5km north of the centre, for an overview of their history and manufacturing process (and free tastings, too).

Vichy also has a trove of exquisite *confiseries* (sweet shops) and *chocolateries* selling handmade treats. The pastel-pink-framed windows of Prunelle (36 rue Montaret) entice with a rainbow of translucent lollypops, while Aux Marocains (www.auxmarocains.com; 33 rue Georges Clemenceau) is chock-a-block with marzipan, petits fours and caramels.

Brasserie du Casino BRASSERIE €€
(☑04 70 98 23 06; 4 rue du Casino; mains €18-26; ⊙lunch & dinner Thu-Mon) All shiny brass, faded wood and squeaky leather, this timeless haunt has a wall of photos featuring the actors and *chanteurs* (singers) who've stopped by from the opera house. The food is substantial (duck *confit,* rabbit stew) and the feel unmistakably French.

L'Hippocampe SEAFOOD €€€
(☑04 70 97 68 37; 3 bd de Russie; menus €20-56; ⊙lunch Wed-Sun, dinner Tue-Sat) Appropriately enough for a restaurant called the Sea Horse, the menu here features scallops, sole, oak-smoked sardines and a monumental *assiette de fruits de mer* (seafood platter). In summer, the lobster-based *menu homard* (€85 for two, including wine) is a popular tradition.

☆ Entertainment

The free monthly what's-on guide *Vichy Mensuel* (www.editionsducentre.fr/mensuel.html) can be picked up all over town.

Opéra de Vichy OPERA
(☑04 70 30 50 50; www.ville-vichy.fr/opera-vichy; rue du Casino) The Opéra de Vichy stages regular productions. Tickets are sold inside the tourist office.

Casino Vichy Grand Café CASINO
(www.casinovichygrandcafe.com; 7 rue du Casino; ⊙10am-3am) Vichy's casino was one of the first-ever opened in France. Today punters can hit the tables in this annexe of the now-closed original.

ⓘ Information

Tourist office (☑04 70 98 71 94; www.vichy-tourisme.com; 19 rue du Parc; ⊙9.30am-noon & 1.30-6pm Mon-Sat, 3-6pm Sun)

ⓘ Getting There & Around

BICYCLE Near the station, **Cycles Peugeot Gaillardin** (☑04 70 31 52 86; 48 bd Gambetta) rents out bikes.

TRAIN Destinations include Paris Gare de Lyon (€51, 2¾ hours, six to eight daily), Clermont-Ferrand (€9.90, 30 minutes, hourly) and Riom (€7.90, 25 minutes, hourly).

PARC NATUREL RÉGIONAL DES VOLCANS D'AUVERGNE

A vast tract of cloud-shrouded peaks, snowy uplands and lush green valleys, the Parc Naturel Régional des Volcans d'Auvergne (www.parc-volcans-auvergne.com) occupies most of the western Massif Central, stretching some 3950 sq km and 120km from base to tip. Evidence of its volcanic history abounds.

Unsurprisingly, this is fantastic terrain for outdoor enthusiasts, including skiers, hikers and mountain bikers, as well as paragliders who can often be seen drifting around the region's peaks.

Volvic

POP 4740

Just inside the Parc Naturel Régional des Volcans d'Auvergne's northeastern boundary, 13km north of Clermont-Ferrand, you can learn all about Volvic's world-famous mineral water at the company's Espace d'Information (www.volvic.fr; rue des Sources; admission free; ⊗9am-noon & 2-6pm Mon-Fri, 2.30-6pm Sat & Sun), and, of course, taste it, too. Outside, walking trails (from 45 minutes to two hours) fan into the lush surrounds, linking with the GR441. Free hour-long factory tours (☑04 73 64 51 24; ⊗May-Aug, 2-4 tours daily by reservation) of its nearby bottling facility are available between May and August.

Château de Tournoël (www.tournoel.com; adult/child €6/3; ⊗10.30am-12.30pm & 1.30-6pm Jul & Aug), a storybook medieval fortress, is just uphill from the village centre. In summer you can visit the kitchens, kitchen gardens and the castle's 14th-century defensive round tower with its panoramic views.

Volvic's tourist office (☑04 73 33 58 73; www.volvic-tourisme.com; ⊗9am-noon & 2-6pm Tue-Sat), on the village's central square, has details of accommodation.

Frequent trains link Volvic with Clermont-Ferrand (€4.40, 30 minutes).

Puy de Dôme & Around

The shapely summit of Puy de Dôme (1465m) looms 15km west of Clermont-Ferrand. Snowcapped from September to May, the mountain was formed by a volcanic eruption some 10,000 years ago and was later used as a Celtic shrine and Roman temple. You can still see the temple's remains today, along with vistas stretching as far as the Alps.

The traditional path to the summit is the scenic 'mule track' – a steep but exhilarating hour's climb from the Col de Ceyssat, 4km off the D941A; it is 1.8km long, with 400m elevation gain. Train buffs will have a hard time resisting the Panoramique des Dômes (www.panoramiquedesdomes.fr; adult/child €9.50/3.80; ⊗8am-7.30pm, to 11.30pm Thu, Sat & school holidays), a spiffy new cog railway inaugurated in May 2012 that whisks you up top in 15 minutes, departing from a station at the mountain's base, 1km off the D941A. Other new or revamped facilities on the summit include a visitor centre, restaurant and cafe.

The Auvergne's long-extinct volcanoes are brought back to life in spectacular style at Vulcania (☑08 20 82 78 28; www.vulcania.com; adult/child €23.50/16; ⊗10am-6pm, closed Mon & Tue Sep & Oct; ◉) volcanic theme park, 15km west of Clermont on the D941B. Combining educational museum with thrills and spills, it was dreamt up by French geologists Katia and Maurice Krafft, who were tragically killed in a volcanic eruption on Mt Unzen in Japan a year before its 1992 opening. Highlights include the 'dynamic 3-D' film Awakening of the Auvergne Giants, depicting volcanic eruptions complete with air blasts and water spray, and a Dragon Ride – not very scientific, but good fun all the same. In 2012, the park opened a brand new Cité des Enfants (Kids' City), with activities specially geared for three- to seven-year-olds.

At Volcan de Lemptégy (☑04 73 62 23 25; www.auvergne-volcan.com; adult/child €9/7, by train €13/10; ⊗10.30am-6.30pm), just across the D941B from Vulcania, you can set off on foot or aboard a little motorised 'train' to discover volcanic landscapes (chimneys, lava flows and more). The intense 'dynamic 3-D' exploding mine film makes a fitting finale, though it's not suitable for littlies. Last entry is two hours before closing.

Orcival

POP 270 / ELEV 870M

Halfway between Puy de Dôme and Le Mont-Dore, the picturesque slate rooftops and tumbledown barns of Orcival huddle around the banks of the Sioulet River. The birthplace of former French president Giscard d'Estaing, this diminutive village centres on the Romanesque Basilique Notre-Dame (⊗8.30am-5pm Oct-Mar, to 7.30pm Apr-Sep), renowned for its elegant crypt and 12th-century Virgin of Orcival in the choir.

Orcival's tiny tourist office (☑04 73 65 89 77; www.terresdomes-sancy.com; ⊗10am-noon & 2-5pm Tue-Sat), opposite Basilique Notre-Dame, can suggest hikes in the surrounding area.

Fans of French gardens shouldn't miss the 15th-century Château de Cordès (☑04 73 21 15 89; www.chateau-cordes-orcival.com; adult/child €3/free; ⊗10am-noon & 2-6pm daily Jul & Aug, Sun afternoons only May & Jun), with magnificent formal grounds laid out by Versailles' garden designer Le Nôtre. It's just north of the village off the D27.

If you're up for paragliding off the area's peaks, you can arrange tandem jumps with Orcival-based Aero Parapente (📞06 61 24 11 45; www.aeroparapente.fr; per jump incl prep €80; ☺Apr-Oct).

The family-run Hôtel Notre Dame (📞04 73 65 82 02; s €42, d €49-53; ☺Feb-Dec; 🛜) has seven snug refurbished rooms, with pleasant auditory accompaniment from the Basilique's bells tolling next door and the rushing stream out back. Breakfasts include homemade blueberry preserves and a tempting selection of local cheeses. Hearty portions of *chou farci* (pork-stuffed cabbage) and other regional specialities are dished up at its rustic restaurant (menus €13-26).

Orcival is not served by public transport so you'll need your own wheels.

Col de Guéry

South of Orcival, the D27 snakes past the dramatic volcanic crags Roche Tuilière (1288m) and Roche Sanadoire (1286m) up to the lofty pass of Col de Guéry, which offers fantastic mountain views on every side. In winter, cross-country skiing is organised by the Foyer Ski de Fond Guéry-Orcival (📞04 73 65 20 09; www.leguery.fr; day ski pass per adult/child €7.20/3.10).

Beyond the pass is chilly Lac de Guéry – the highest lake in the Massif Central at 1250m and filled with trout and perch. It's a sweet spot for fishing – even in winter! This is the only lake in France that permits *pêche blanche* (ice-fishing); the season kicks off with a big festival the first weekend of March. To buy your fishing licence (€23 per three days in March, €6 per day April to mid-November), visit the cosy inn Auberge du Lac de Guéry (📞04 73 65 02 76; www.auberge-lac-guery.fr; d incl breakfast/half-board/full board €80/128/156). In an unbeatable position right on the lakeshore, the inn serves up fresh fish straight from the lake at its fine country restaurant (menus €21-42).

Le Mont-Dore

POP 1430 / ELEV 1050M

Nestled in a narrow valley 44km southwest of Clermont-Ferrand, and just four kilometres north of Puy de Sancy (1886m), central France's highest peak, Le Mont-Dore, is the Massif Central's main winter-sports base. Considerably quieter than the Alps' adrenaline-pumped resorts, it's a haven for hikers and snow-sports enthusiasts seeking lower-key mountain thrills.

◎ Sights & Activities

Thermes du Mont-Dore   SPA
(📞04 73 65 05 10; 1 place du Panthéon; ☺6am-1pm & 2-5.30pm Mon-Fri, 6am-1pm Sat) Long before anyone thought of hurtling down the hillsides strapped to a pair of wooden planks, Le Mont-Dore was frequented for its hot springs, which bubble out between 37°C and 40°C. The first bathers were the cleanliness-obsessed Romans – you can still see traces of their original baths. In addition to treatments, in low season you can visit the 19th-century neo-Byzantine building on a 45-minute, French-language guided tour (adult/child €3.50/2; ☺2pm & 3pm Mon-Fri).

Funiculaire du Capucin   FUNICULAR
(rue René Cassin; adult one-way/return €3.90/5.20, child one-way/return €3.20/3.90; ☺10am-12.10pm & 2-5.40pm, closed Oct–mid-May) Built in 1898, France's oldest funicular railway (and listed historic monument) crawls at 1m per second up to the plateau of Les Capucins, 1270m above town. Various trails lead off the plateau, including the 2km trail to Pic du Capucin (1450m), the GR30, which wends southward towards the Puy de Sancy, and the steep 1km downhill back to town.

Téléphérique du Sancy   CABLE CAR
(adult one-way/return €6.90/9.10, child one-way/return €5.10/6.90; ☺9am-12.10pm & 1.30-5pm daily Easter-Sep, weekends only Oct) Puy de Sancy's snowcapped summit can be reached by catching the cable car, followed by a short walk along the maintained trail and staircase to the top for fabulous views of the northern *puys* (Auvergne mountains) and the Monts du Cantal.

Snow Sports   SNOW SPORTS
Near Le Mont-Dore, the ski and snowboarding fields Station de Mont-Dore and Super-Besse (p545) encompass 85km of downhill runs for beginners through to experienced, plus countless cross-country trails. A day pass good at both ski runs costs €28.70 for downhill, or €6.80 for cross-country.

There's an abundance of places to hire snow gear in Le Mont-Dore.

Walking   WALKING
Superbly signposted walks around Le Mont-Dore are marked on good trail maps such as Chamina's 1:30,000-scale map *Massif du Sancy* (€10) or the *Massif du Sancy* guide-

TRAIL CENTRAL

The Massif Central is prime walking country, with a network of well-signed trails and as many as 13 GR (long-distance) tracks (including the north–south GR4) criss-crossing the region, supplemented by hundreds of smaller footpaths. Key areas include the Monts du Cantal between Murat and Salers, and the mountainous area around Le Mont-Dore, Puy de Sancy and the Col de Guéry.

Routes range from day hikes to multiweek epics: hard-core hikers tackle the 290km Traverse of the High Auvergne through the Chaîne des Puys; the Robert Louis Stevenson Trail from Monastier-sur-Gazeille, tracing the author's famous routes through the Cévennes; and the Via Podiensis pilgrimage route from Le Puy-en-Velay.

Numerous French-language guidebooks cover walking in the Massif Central, including titles published by Chamina (www.chamina.com).

Online resources abound: www.rando-massifcentral.com (in French) has a database of more than 400 Massif Central walks.

book (€10), which outlines 36 hikes in the area. Both are sold at the tourist office.

Mont-Dore Aventures　　OUTDOOR ACTIVITIES
(☑04 73 65 00 00; www.montdoreaventures.com; Le Salon du Capucin; per 3 hrs adult/child €22/16; ⊗ropes course Apr-Oct) Operates a fun Tarzan-style treetop ropes course. Owner/adventurer Gilles Riocreux is a fount of info on local off-the-beaten-track outdoor activities.

Skating Rink　　SKATING, BOWLING
(☑04 73 65 06 55; allée Georges Lagaye; ice skating adult/child €6.70/5.30, bowling before/after 8pm €5/6; ⊗Jul-Apr) In bad weather, escape to Le Mont-Dore's rink for a skate or skittle.

🛏 Sleeping

Grand Hôtel　　HOTEL €
(☑04 73 65 02 64; www.hotel-mont-dore.com; 2 rue Meynadier; s/d/q €59/69/89; ⊗mid-Dec–mid-Nov; 🐾) Built in 1850 and newly renovated in 2012, this ultracentral Le Mont-Dore landmark provides more comfort and style than its budget prices would imply. Boutiquey bedrooms, including a few with balconies and some nice two-room family suites, come with thick duvets, deep tubs and new wood flooring. The recently added spa (sauna and Jacuzzi) costs €5 extra.

**Auberge de Jeunesse
Le Grand Volcan**　　HOSTEL €
(☑04 73 65 03 53; le-mont-dore@fuaj.org; rte du Sancy; dm/d incl breakfast €18.50/37; ⊗mid-Dec–mid-Nov; 🐾) Always jammed with skiers and hikers, this excellent hostel is right below the Puy de Sancy cable car, 3.5km south of town. Facilities include squeaky-clean two-to six-bed dorms with en-suite bathrooms,

a guest kitchen and laundry, ski and snowshoe rentals, and an in-house bar. Book way ahead in winter, especially for one of the seven double rooms.

**📷 Camping Domaine
de la Grande Cascade**　　CAMPGROUND €
(☑04 73 65 06 23; www.camping-grandecascade. com; rte de Besse; 2-/4-person site €11.40/18.60; ⊗May–Sep; 🐾) At 1250m up, yes, this campground is on the chilly side. But it's a stupendous spot to pitch a tent, near a 30m waterfall, with wondrous views of the surrounding mountains. Head 3km south of town on the D36.

Le Castelet　　HOTEL €
(☑04 73 65 05 29; www.lecastelet-montdore.com; 6 av Michel Bertrand; s €50-74, d €62-90; 🐾🏊) A couple of blocks from the central square, this hotel wins points for its spacious green yard and small swimming pool. Other nice amenities include free parking, ski and bike storage, and an on-site bar and restaurant.

Le Buron de Dame Tartine　　B&B €€
(☑04 73 65 28 40; www.auberge-dame-tartine. com; rte du Sancy; d €89-110) This renovated *buron* (shepherd's hut) has rustic rooms with stripped pine furniture, polished floors and to-die-for mountain views. Stout stone, rough brick and hefty rafters fill the restaurant, which serves hearty mountain fare.

🍴 Eating

Most of Le Mont-Dore's hotels offer half-board, often compulsory during ski season. La Petite Boutique du Bougnat (1 rue Montlosier; ⊗9am-12.30pm & 3-7pm) sells a smorgasbord of local goodies, including sausages, hams and Auvergnat wine, with cheeses available at its fromagerie (4 rue Montlosier) across the street.

Le Petit Paris
BISTRO €

(Chez Mimi; rue Jean Moulin; menus €16; ☺lunch & dinner Fri-Wed) Complete with etched glass, chalkboard menus and art nouveau decor, this atmospheric Parisian-style bistro specialises in reasonably priced French classics, including omelettes, salads and fondue. Convivial owner Mimi is a local fixture, especially famous for her *vin chaud* (hot mulled wine) in wintertime.

La Golmotte
REGIONAL CUISINE €€

(☎04 73 65 05 77; www.aubergelagolmotte.com; rte D996; menus €16-37) The excellent regional cuisine at this mountainside inn is well worth the 3km trek up the main road towards Orcival and Murol, it's a perfect spot to be introduced to *truffade, aligot* and all the Auvergnat classics.

Le Boeuf dans l'Assiette
GRILLED MEAT €

(☎04 73 65 01 23; 9 ave Michel-Bertrand; menus €16-20; ☺closed Mon) Specialising in beef, lamb and pork grilled over a wood fire, this downtown eatery makes a cosy spot on a chilly winter evening.

❶ Information

Tourist office (☎04 73 65 20 21; www.sancy. com; av de la Libération; ☺9am-12.30pm & 2-6pm Mon-Sat, 10am-noon & 2-6pm Sun) Free wi-fi and tons of local info, including hiking maps and guides.

❶ Getting There & Around

Two direct trains and three SNCF buses (fewer on Sunday) connect Le Mont-Dore with Clermont-Ferrand (€13.20, 1½ hours).

In winter a free skiers' *navette* (shuttle bus) plies regularly between Le Mont-Dore and the Sancy cable car.

Around Le Mont-Dore

LA BOURBOULE
POP 2020 / ELEV 850M

Seven kilometres downriver from Le Mont-Dore, you can experience the spa waters of belle époque La Bourboule at a couple of establishments, including the iconic Les Grands Thermes (☎04 73 81 21 00; www. grandsthermes-bourboule.com; 76 bd Georges Clémenceau; treatments €8-72; ☺8am-noon & 6-7pm Feb-Sep).

Sometimes known as '*la station oxygène*', La Bourboule is a lovely place to stroll and to drink in the clear mountain air. From the landscaped Parc Fenestre, filled with giant sequoias, pine trees and open-air games, a télécabine (adult/child return €4.65/2.30; ☺9.30am-noon & 1.45-5.15pm) glides up the Plateau de Charlannes (1300m) to summer hiking trails.

Among the many hotels and restaurants lining the riverbanks, Hôtel Le Parc des Fées (☎04 73 81 01 77; www.parcdesfees.com; 107 quai Maréchal-Fayolle; €59-68, d €72-78, restaurant menus €12-33; @☎) stands out for its belle époque architecture and lovely mountain and river views from the corner rooms.

La Bourboule's efficient tourist office (☎04 73 65 57 71; www.sancy.com; place de la République; ☺9am-noon & 2-6pm) is in the Hôtel de Ville.

Trains and SNCF buses to Le Mont-Dore (€1.60, six daily) take just eight minutes.

MUROL & LAC CHAMBON
POP 550 / ELEV 849M

About 10km east of Le Mont-Dore, the 12th-century Château de Murol (☎04 73 26 02 00; www.chateaumurol.fr; adult/child €6.30/5.20, with guided tour €9.80/8.20; ☺10am-6pm daily Apr-Sep, 10am-5pm Sat & Sun Oct-Mar, closed Jan) squats on a knoll above the surrounding village. Book ahead for medieval guided tours (up to five daily in summer), when costumed guides, scullery maids and jesters recreate daily life in the castle and knights joust beneath the keep.

About 1.5km west of Murol is the water-sports playground of Lac Chambon, where you can hire canoes and windsurfing boards from operators along the pretty lakeshore.

Camping les Bombes (☎04 73 88 64 03; www.camping-les-bombes.com; Chemin de Pétary; sites €9.60-13.70; ☺May–mid-Sep; ☒), west of the lake, is one of several ecofriendly campgrounds in the Lac Chambon area.

BESSE-EN-CHANDESSE & AROUND

Basalt-brick cottages and cobbled lanes make up the mountain village of Besse-en-Chandesse (population 1690, elevation 805m; also known as Besse-et-Saint-Anastaise), 9.4km south of Murol, where life still ticks along at a laid-back country pace. During the Transhumance de la Vierge Noire, local cows are herded to the rich upland pastures on 21 July and back on the first Sunday after 21 September. The cows' September descent is accompanied by street fairs and fireworks.

Besse is best known for its ski resort Super-Besse (www.sancy.com/commune/super besse; downhill/cross-country day pass adult €27.90/7.20, child €22.60/5.50), less than 7km west of the village. Ski passes here also grant access to Le Mont-Dore's slopes.

Also along the D978, 6km southwest of Besse, the near-circular crater lake Lac Pavin makes a scenic starting point for hikes of varying lengths into the surrounding countryside.

In town, skiers will get a kick out of the vintage skis and alpine kit at the Musée du Ski (☑04 73 79 57 30; adult/child €4.50/free; ⊙school holidays 9am-noon & 2-7pm). Call to confirm opening times.

ST-NECTAIRE
POP 750 / ELEV 760M

Six kilometres east of Murol, St-Nectaire stretches out along the river beside the D996, and is famed far and wide for its eponymous Appellation d'Origine Contrôlée (AOC) cheese. The village is split into the newer St-Nectaire-Le-Bas, with a smattering of belle époque buildings remaining from the town's former incarnation as a spa resort; and the much older St-Nectaire-Le-Haut, reached via a steep switchback lane from the main road.

⊙ Sights & Activities

Romanesque Church   CHURCH
(⊙9am-7pm) St-Nectaire's main architectural sight is in the upper village. It has a fine 12th-century statue of the Virgin.

FREE La Ferme Bellonte   DAIRY FARM
(www.st-nectaire.com; rue du 10 août 1944, Farges; ⊙milking 6.30-7.30am & 4.30-5.30pm, cheese-making 8.30-10am Tue-Sat & 6-7.30pm daily, cave tours 10am-noon & 2-5pm) To see how St-Nectaire's famous cheese is made, climb 3km to this multigenerational family dairy farm in the hilltop village of Farges. There's no charge to watch the milking of the cows (early morning or late afternoon) and the pressing of the cheese into moulds; whole cheeses cost €16 in the adjacent shop. Aficionados can also tour (€6.10, in English upon request) the historic cave dwellings across the street where the cheese is aged.

Grottes du Cornadore   ROMAN SITES
(www.grottes-de-cornadore.com; rte de Murol; adult/child €6.50/5; ⊙10am-noon & 2-6pm, closed Nov–mid-Feb) The remains of the town's Roman baths are fascinating.

🍽 Sleeping & Eating

TOP CHOICE Le Chastel Montaigu   B&B €€
(☑04 73 96 28 49; www.lechastelmontaigu.com; d €140-150; ⊙Apr-Oct) Head 11km east of St-Nectaire on the D996 to this fairy-tale castle on its own private hilltop. Rebuilt from ruins using authentic medieval materials, the four rooms are filled with heavy stone, rich fabrics and antique wall hangings. One has its own private turret terrace, and all have blindingly good views across the valley. You'll feel like a true *seigneur* (lord) wandering around the spiral staircases and medieval terraces. There's a minimum stay of two nights or the full duration of public holiday periods.

Villa du Pont Romain   B&B €
(☑04 73 88 41 62; lavilladupontromain.free.fr; Rue Principale; s/d/q €40/50/80) Hosted by a pair of serious runners (he's a world steeplechase champion), this simple three-bedroom B&B is a great budget option, with abundant breakfasts and clean, spacious rooms sleeping up to four.

❶ Information

St-Nectaire's **tourist office** (☑04 73 88 50 86; www.sancy.com/commune/saint-nectaire; av du Docteur Roux, Les Grands Thermes; ⊙9am-noon & 2-6pm Mon-Sat May-Sep) is on the main road in St-Nectaire-Le-Bas.

❶ Getting There & Away

St-Nectaire is on the D996, 25km east of Le Mont-Dore and 35km south of Clermont-Ferrand. You'll need your own vehicle to get here.

Murat & the Monts du Cantal

POP 2120 / ELEV 930M

Tumbling down a steep basalt crag topped by a statue of the Virgin Mary, Murat makes an excellent base for exploring the Monts du Cantal, especially for those traveling by public transport. With a cluster of dark stone houses huddled beneath the Rocher Bonnevie, it's one of the prettiest towns in the region and is a popular hiking and skiing hub.

⊙ Sights & Activities

The twisting streets and wonky stone cottages of Murat's old town make an enjoyable afternoon stroll.

To the west are the lofty peaks of Puy Mary (1787m), Plomb du Cantal (1858m) and Puy de Peyre Arse (1806m), the last remnants of an exploded supervolcano that once covered the Cantal Massif.

Maison de la Faune
MUSEUM

(www.murat.fr; adult/child €4.70/3.10; ◷10am-noon & 2-6pm Mon-Sat, 2-6pm Sun) Budding entomologists should make a beeline for this spiralling stone tower (opposite place de l'Hôtel de Ville), which houses more than 10,000 insects, butterflies and stuffed beasties from the Auvergne to the Amazon.

Rocher Bonnevie
WALKING

For great views, brave the lung-busting climb to the top of Rocher Bonnevie. From the town centre, it's about 1.5km, following the red-and-white GR flashes northwestwards. For drivers, an alternate 10-minute footpath starts from the car park just off the D3 traffic circle, 1km northwest of town.

Le Lioran
SKIING

(www.lelioran.com; day pass per adult/child €25.90/20.80) Skiers can hit the slopes here, 14km west of Murat.

🛏 Sleeping & Eating

La Maison de Justine
B&B €

(☎04 71 20 75 72; www.hotes-cantal-justine.fr; 4 place Gandilhon Gens d'Armes; d €55-70; 🖥) Right in Murat's medieval heart, this charming four-bedroom B&B filled with books and antiques offers the town's most atmospheric accommodation.

Camping Municipal Stalapos
CAMPGROUND €

(☎04 71 20 01 83; www.camping-murat.com; rue du Stade; sites €2.20-5.30, plus €2.60/1.40 per adult/child; ◷May-Sep; 🅿) Beside the Alagnon

River, this pretty campground is 1km south of the train station.

Caldera
DELICATESSEN

(3 rue Justin Vigier; ◷9am-12.15pm & 2.30-7pm Tue-Sat, 9am-noon Sun) Near the tourist office, this deli sells local cheese, cold cuts, sandwiches and regional products including honey, jam and liqueur.

ℹ Information

The **tourist office** (☎04 71 20 09 47; www.officedetourismepaysdemurat.com; place de l'Hôtel de Ville; ◷9am-noon & 2-6pm Mon-Sat, 10am-noon Sun) has a wealth of info on walks and activities in the Cantal area.

ℹ Getting There & Around

Regional trains connect Murat with Clermont-Ferrand (€19.30, 1¾ hours, four to six daily).

The countryside makes for splendid, if taxing, cycling. **Ô P'tit Montagnard** (☎04 71 20 28 40; www.optitmontagnard.fr; 8 rue Faubourg Notre Dame) rents out quality mountain bikes for €22 per day.

Salers

POP 370 / ELEV 830

One of the Auvergne's prettiest towns, Salers sits at the western edge of the Monts du Cantal, looking up towards the Puy Violent (1592m) and Puy Mary, making it the perfect base for exploring the mountains' western slopes. Spreading out from its compact core of 16th-century stone buildings are rolling meadows filled with horned brown cows that create its eponymous Salers AOC cheese.

Salers' picturesque central square, place Tyssandier d'Escous, is named for the

---

FIERY FURNACES

With its peaceful pastures and verdant hills, it's hard to believe that the Massif Central was once one of the most active volcanic areas in Western Europe.

The area consists of three geological bands. The Chaîne des Puys and Monts Dômes, a chain of extinct volcanoes and cinder cones stretching in a 40km north–south line across the northern Massif Central, thrust up around 100,000 years ago. The central Monts Dores are much older, created between 100,000 and three million years ago, while the real grandaddies are the Monts du Cantal, on the Parc Naturel Régional des Volcans d'Auvergne's southern edge, formed by a nine-million-year-old volcano which collapsed inwards, leaving only its caldera (fragmented rim).

Though the volcanoes have been silent for several thousand years (the last serious eruption occurred around 5000 BC), reminders of their turbulent past are dotted across the region – from its mineral waters and geothermal springs to the distinctive black rock often used as a building material across the region.

19th-century agronomist who developed the Salers breed of cattle. Surrounding his statue is a harmonious collection of turreted lava-rock buildings that date from Salers' 16th-century heyday as a regional administrative centre. From here you can walk up to the leafy Esplanade de Barrouze belvedere, or descend into the town's tangle of cobbled streets filled with shops selling cheese, knives and Auvergnat knick-knacks.

Half a block below the square, the delightful Hôtel Saluces (☑04 71 40 70 82; www. hotel-salers.fr; rue de la Martille; d €68-99; @🛜) offers nine spacious and individually decorated rooms with modern amenities in an ancient stone building with a sunny interior courtyard. Hosts Daniel and Jeanette Gil offer excellent advice about the local area.

Also just off the square is the Maison de la Ronade (place Tyssandier d'Escous; teas €2.90; ⊙3.30-6.30pm daily), whose elderly owner serves up 120 varieties of tea in his 15th-century drawing room, giving you a set of three hourglasses to measure the proper brewing time. For solid, reasonably priced Auvergnat dishes (Salers steaks, stuffed cabbage, and the full line-up of meat, cheese and potatoes fare) head downhill to La Martille (www.restaurant-salers.fr; rue de la Martille; menus from €18; ⊙lunch & dinner daily), a venerable eatery with a pleasant outdoor terrace.

The tourist office (☑04 71 63 85 00; www. cantal-tourisme.fr; place Tyssandier d'Escous; ⊙9.30-noon & 2-6pm), on the main square, offers information, maps and books about local hikes.

Salers is on the D680, 43km west of Murat and 21km west of the Pas de Peyrol at the foot of Puy Mary. You'll need your own vehicle to get here.

PARC NATUREL RÉGIONAL LIVRADOIS-FOREZ

Blanketed in pine forest, this nature park is one of France's largest protected areas, stretching from the plains of Limagne in the west to the Monts du Forez in the east. Formerly a centre for logging and agriculture, it's now a haven for nature lovers and weekend walkers.

The Maison du Parc (park information office; ☑04 73 95 57 57; www.parc-livradois-forez.org; ⊙9am-12.30pm & 1.30-5.30pm Mon-Fri, 2-6pm Sat & Sun, closed Sat & Sun early Jun & late Sep) is off the D906 in St-Gervais-sous-Meymont, halfway between Thiers and Ambert. It's stocked with leaflets detailing local honey shops, lace-makers and perfumers, walking trails and mountain-bike routes.

In spring and summer, a lovely if infrequent train touristique (☑04 73 82 43 88; www. agrivap.fr; €9-15, depending on itinerary) – alternately a double-decker *train panoramique* or a vintage steam train – runs through the park from Courpière (15km south of Thiers) via Ambert to La Chaise-Dieu.

Thiers

POP 11,930 / ELEV 420M

Precipitously perched above the Gorges de la Durolle, the industrial town of Thiers has been churning out cutlery for centuries and still produces some 70% of the nation's knives.

For an overview head for the Musée de la Coutellerie (Cutlery Museum; www.musee-coutellerie-thiers.com; rue de la Coutellerie; adult/child €5.50/2.70, combined ticket with Vallée des Rouets €6.80/2.90; ⊙10am-noon & 2-6pm, closed Mon Oct-May), which is split over two buildings along rue de la Coutellerie. No 23 explores the historical side of cutlery-making, while No 58 houses the museum's unparalleled collection of knives past and present. About 4km upstream from Thiers is the Vallée des Rouets (Valley of the Waterwheels; ⊙10am-noon & 2-6pm Jun-Sep), an open-air museum dedicated to the knifemakers who once toiled here in front of water-driven grindstones. Admission includes a shuttle-bus between the two museums.

Knife-sellers are dotted round the town's medieval streets lined with half-timbered buildings – ask at the friendly tourist office (☑04 73 80 65 65; www.thiers-tourisme.fr; 1 place du Pirou; ⊙9.30am-noon & 2-6pm) for recommended shops.

Thiers is easily reached by frequent trains from Clermont-Ferrand (€8.60, 45 minutes).

Ambert

POP 7260 / ELEV 560M

Back in the 16th century, Ambert, 30km north of La Chaise-Dieu, boasted more than 300 water-powered mills supplying the demands of the French paper industry, but the town is better known today for one of the Auvergne's classic cheeses, Fourme d'Ambert.

The tourist office (☎04 73 82 61 90; www.ambert-tourisme.fr; 4 place de l'Hôtel de Ville; ⊙10am-noon & 2-5pm Mon-Sat), opposite the Hôtel de Ville, can help with accommodation.

Around 500 sheets of paper per day are still made using strictly traditional techniques at the restored 14th-century mill Moulin Richard de Bas (www.richarddebas.fr; adult/child €6.90/4.90; ⊙9.30am-12.30pm & 2-6pm). It's 4km out of town on the D57.

In Ambert's pedestrianised centre, the Maison de la Fourme d'Ambert (www.maison-fourme-ambert.fr; 29 rue des Chazeaux; adult/child €5/4; ⊙10am-12.30pm & 2.30-6.30pm Tue-Sat) has displays on the history and manufacture of the town's trademark *fromage* (cheese). Three-cheese tastings cost an additional €3.

Ambert's Thursday morning market, spiralling out around the Hôtel de Ville, is popular with local organic farmers.

SNCF bus-train combos connect Ambert with Clermont-Ferrand (€13.80, 1¾ hours).

La Chaise-Dieu

POP 800 / ELEV 1082M

The centrepiece of historic La Chaise-Dieu, 42km north of Le Puy-en-Velay, is its monumental Église Abbatiale de St-Robert (⊙10am-noon & 2-6pm), built in the 14th century atop an earlier abbey chapel by Pope Clement VI, who served here as a novice monk. Most sights are in the Chœur de l'Église (adult/child €4/1). Highlights include the massive 18th-century organ, Clement VI's marble tomb and some fine 16th-century Flemish tapestries, but the most celebrated relic is the chilling fresco Danse Macabre in which Death dances a mocking jig around members of 15th-century society.

La Chaise-Dieu's prized organ is also a key part (and the origin) of its prestigious Sacred Music Festival (Festival de Musique; www.chaise-dieu.com; ⊙late Aug–early Sep).

PILGRIM'S PASS

Between June and September three of Le Puy's major sights (Chapelle St-Michel d'Aiguilhe, the Rocher Corneille and the Forteresse de Polignac) can be visited on a joint museum pass (€9). Buy it at any of the sights or from the tourist office.

Behind the church is the Salle de l'Echo – an architectural oddity that allows people on opposite sides of the room to hear each other talking, without being overhead by those in between. It's thought to have been built to enable monks to hear lepers' confessions without contracting the dreaded disease.

The tourist office (☎04 71 00 01 16; www.la-chaise-dieu.info; place de la Mairie; ⊙10am-noon & 2-6pm Tue-Sun) has a free English-language leaflet outlining a walking tour of the village.

Peacefully positioned behind the church, Hotel de l'Echo (☎04 71 00 00 45; hoteldelecho@orange.fr; place de l'Echo; s €44-56, d €55-69; ⊙Apr–mid-Nov; ☎) is a refurbished stone town house with prim rooms and a hearty restaurant (menus €19-29) in the old abbey kitchens.

SNCF buses run once or twice each weekday between La Chaise-Dieu and Le Puy-en-Velay (€8.60, one hour).

LE PUY-EN-VELAY & AROUND

Le Puy-en-Velay

POP 20,000 / ELEV 630M

Cradled at the base of a broad mountain valley, Le Puy-en-Velay is one of the most striking sights in central France. Three volcanic pillars thrust skywards above the terracotta rooftops, crowned with a trio of ecclesiastical landmarks – a 10th-century church, soaring Romanesque cathedral, and massive cast-iron statue of the Virgin Mary and Child that has stood watch above Le Puy since 1860. Sacred statues and saintly figurines tucked into niches in the medieval and Renaissance houses lining Le Puy's cobbled streets also attest to its role as a focal point for pilgrims for over a millennium, especially those following the Via Podiensis to Santiago de Compostela.

Throughout the lively pedestrianised old town, shops sell the town's trademark exports: lace; lentils; and vivid green liqueur, Verveine Verte.

◉ Sights & Activities

TOP CHOICE Chapelle St-Michel d'Aiguilhe   CHURCH
(www.rochersaintmichel.fr; adult/child €3/1.50; ⊙9am-6.30pm) Le Puy's oldest chapel (first

THE BLACK MADONNAS OF THE AUVERGNE

The Auvergne has an astonishing number of Vierges Noires (Black Madonnas) in its cathedrals and churches, imbued with considerable sacred significance and miraculous powers.

Usually under 1m tall and carved from cedar or walnut, their origins are a source of constant speculation: some historians believe the tradition began during the Crusades, when Christian soldiers came under the influence of Moorish sculptors. Others believe the figures are part of a much older tradition involving the Egyptian goddess Isis or a pagan Mother Goddess. Still others have suggested that the Black Madonnas are an attempt to depict Mary's original skin colour, which was probably closer to the dark skin of African and Middle Eastern people than the light skin of modern Europeans.

Theories also abound over the figures' colour: that dark woods or varnishes were used to create the dark colouring, or that it's caused by natural ageing or even candle soot.

On Assumption Day (15 August) you'll see the statues paraded throughout Auvergne villages, marking the ascension of Mary's spirit to heaven.

established in the 10th century, and rebuilt several times since) teeters atop an 85m-high volcanic plug reached by climbing 268 stairs. Stepping through its exquisite polychrome doorway into the cavelike interior is a mystical experience – the chapel follows the natural contours of the rock, and the unusual carvings and 12th-century frescos create an otherworldly atmosphere.

Cathédrale Notre Dame & Cloister
CATHEDRAL
(www.cathedraledupuy.org; cloister adult/child €7.50/free; ⊙9am-noon & 2-5pm, to 6.30pm in summer) A Unesco-listed wonder, this 11th-century cathedral's multistoreyed facade, soaring pillars, Romanesque archways and Byzantine domes are a celestial sight. The frescoed portal is framed by porphyry columns shipped in from Egypt; inside, it shelters a statue of St Jacques, patron saint of Compostela pilgrims, and one of the Auvergne's most famous Vierges Noires. The 12th-century cloister indicates the cathedral's Moorish influences with its multicoloured bricks and columns. Upstairs from the cloister (covered by the same admission ticket) is a fine collection of embroidered religious artwork and vestments, newly acquired in 2011.

Rocher Corneille & Notre Dame de France
MONUMENT
(adult/child €4/2.50; ⊙9am-6pm) Staring out across the rooftops from the tiny portholes inside the rust-red statue of Notre Dame de France (aka the Virgin Mary), which crowns the 757m-high pillar of Rocher Corneille, offers dizzying vistas of the town. A creaky spiral staircase winds its way to the top of Le Puy's 22.7m-tall, 835-ton answer to the *Statue of Liberty*, which was fashioned from 213 cannons captured during the Crimean War.

Fortresse de Polignac
CASTLE
(www.forteressedepolignac.com; adult/child €5/3.50; ⊙10am-noon & 1.30-6pm Apr–mid-Nov) Dramatically perched atop a volcanic dome just 5km northwest of Le Puy, this 11th-century castle was built by the powerful Polignac family, who once controlled access to the city from the north. It's ringed by a practically continuous wall dotted with lookout towers and a 32m-high rectangular keep.

FREE Espace Pagès Maison Verveine du Velay
TASTING ROOM
(☑04 71 02 46 80; www.verveine.com; 29 place du Breuil; admission free; ⊙10am-12.30pm & 2.30-7pm Tue-Sat) Visit this tasting room for free samples of Le Puy's fiery green liqueur, Verveine Verte, invented in 1859 using 32 plants and herbs. Despite its potency (55% alcohol by volume), it has a refreshingly sweet taste that sees it used in numerous local desserts. Verveine Jaune (yellow) and Verveine Extra (reddish-brown) varieties are (somewhat) milder at 40% alcohol by volume. Various regional products are sold in the tasting room shop, while the adjacent bar, La Distillerie (⊙10am-11pm), is a fine spot for a drink. In summer you can take a 45-minute guided tour of its distillery (☑04 71 03 04 11; guided tour adult/child €5.50/2; ⊙by reservation Jun & Sep, 10.30am, 2.30pm, 3.30pm & 4.30pm Mon-Sat Jul & Aug), 6km east along the N88 in St-Germain Laprade.

Le Puy-en-Velay

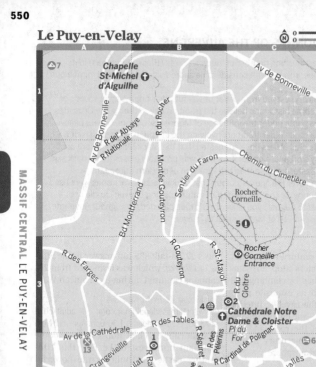

MASSIF CENTRAL LE PUY-EN-VELAY

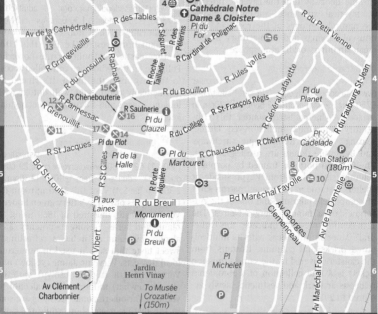

Musée Interactif Hôtel-Dieu MUSEUM (www.hoteldieu.info; 2 rue Becdelièvre; adult/child €6/4; ⊙10am-noon & 2-6pm) The highlight of this brand-new museum inside Le Puy's historic hospital is the 19th-century pharmacy, elegantly panelled in walnut and wild cherry wood. Upstairs, interactive exhibits focus on the architecture, history and natural history of the Haute-Loire region (in French only at the time of research, though English translations were underway).

Le Puy-en-Velay

MASSIF CENTRAL LE PUY-EN-VELAY

Centre d'Enseignement de la Dentelle au Fuseau LACE WORKSHOP
(☎04 71 02 01 68; www.ladentelledupuy.com; 38-40 rue Raphaël; adult/child €4.50/free; ☺9am-noon & 2-6pm Mon-Fri, 9.30am-4.30pm Sat) As a pilgrimage hub, lace was essential for religious clothing and there were once over 5000 lace workshops hereabouts, though only a handful remain today. At this not-for-profit workshop you can watch bobbin lace-making demonstrations, browse temporary and permanent exhibits, or even take a **course** (per hour €17). The tourist office has details of other local workshops.

★★ Festivals & Events

Les Musicales LATIN MUSIC FESTIVAL
(lesmusicales43.com) In mid-July, a week-long extravaganza of tango, flamenco, fado, salsa and more.

Interfolk FOLK MUSIC
(www.interfolk.fr) Week-long folk festival in late July.

Fête du Roi de l'Oiseau STREET FESTIVAL
(www.roideloiseau.com) This mid-September four-day street party – complete with outlandish costumes – dates back to 1524, when the title of *'Roi'* (King) was bestowed on the first archer to shoot down a straw *oiseau* (bird) in return for a year's exemption from taxes.

🛏 Sleeping

The tourist office has a list of *gîtes* (self-catering cottages) and *chambres d'hôte* (B&Bs) in town and the surrounding countryside.

Hôtel du Parc HOTEL €€
(☎04 71 02 40 40; www.hotel-du-parc-le-puy.com; 4 av Clément Charbonnier; d €92-114, ste €159-199; ❄@☎) Minimalist-chic rooms and stylish suites with enormous bathrooms are the norm at this 15-room hotel, adjacent to François Gagnaire's eponymous restaurant. The breakfast buffet (€14) includes Gagnaire's lentil yoghurt.

Hôtel Le Régina HOTEL €€
(☎04 71 09 14 71; www.hotelrestregina.com; 34 bd Maréchal Fayolle; s €58-75, d €65-95, ste €101-123; ❄☎) Topped by a neon-lit art deco turret, the Régina's rooms are individually decorated (our favourite: room 207, with its pop art Chrysler building mural), and some have air-conditioning. Size and style vary considerably depending on price.

Auberge de Jeunesse HOSTEL €
(☎04 71 05 52 40; auberge.jeunesse@mairie-le-puy-en-velay.fr; 9 rue Jules Vallès; dm €11.50; ☎) Inside a former convent, this hostel's monasticlike dorms were undergoing extensive remodelling at the time of research. The new, improved 55-bed layout (scheduled for completion in spring 2013, with an anticipated increase in price) is based around four- to eight-bed dorms, including some equipped for disabled travellers.

Camping Bouthezard CAMPGROUND €
(☎04 71 09 55 09; www.camping-bouthezard-43.com; chemin de Bouthezard; per tent/car/adult/child €2.75/1.80/2.90/1.45; ☺mid-Mar–mid-Oct) Le Puy's campground enjoys an attractive

berth beside the River Borne. Bus 6 delivers you outside.

Dyke Hôtel
HOTEL €

(☑04 71 09 05 30; www.dykehotel.fr; 37 bd Maréchal Fayolle; s €39-51, d €54-58; 🛜) Named for a volcanic pillar (in case you're wondering), this budget hotel is well located if unexciting, with modernish rooms of varying dimensions, some with balconies onto the (very) busy road.

🍴 Eating

The local *lentille verte du Puy* (green Puy lentil; www.lalentillevertedupuy.com) is the sole pulse with AOC classification in mainland France (the only other is the *lentille de Cilaos* on the French island of Réunion). Rich in protein, vitamin B and iron, and gluten-free, Le Puy's lentils are used in dishes ranging from the time-honoured to inventive creations.

La Parenthèse
REGIONAL CUISINE €€

(☑04 71 02 83 00; 8 av de la Cathédrale; menus €19-27; ⊙lunch & dinner Mon-Fri) This cosy spot serves traditional dishes with heartwarming pride. Start with the *tartare de saumon et lentilles vertes du Puy* (smoked salmon with Le Puy lentils), then move on to tasty mains accompanied by sizzling pots of *aligot* (cheesy, garlicky potato purée). Afterwards, don't miss the *coupe Verveine*: Verveine ice cream served in a chocolate cup, a moist emerald-coloured macaron and a shot of liqueur. The rustic farmhouse-style decor includes many local antiques available for purchase.

François Gagnaire
GASTRONOMIC €€€

(☑04 71 02 75 55; www.francois-gagnaire-restaurant.com; 4 av Clément-Charbonnier; menus €28-145; ⊙lunch Wed-Sun, dinner Tue-Sat; 🍴) Book well ahead for a table at the Michelin-starred restaurant of François Gagnaire. Offerings range from the €28 midweek lunch menu to the no-holds-barred *inspiration gourmande*, including wines, for €145. Adventurous little taste buds are even catered for with a 'young gastronome' menu (€25).

Restaurant Tournayre
REGIONAL CUISINE €€€

(☑04 71 09 58 94; www.restaurant-tournayre.com; 12 rue Chènebouterie; menus €25-70; ⊙lunch & dinner Tue & Thu-Sun) Elegantly set in a 16th-century former chapel with vaulted ceiling and stone walls, this refined eatery serves a variety of superb four-course menus, including a good-value lunchtime *menu du marché* (€25).

La Table du Plot
REGIONAL CUISINE €€

(☑04 71 57 05 28; 6 place du Plot; mains €13-25; ⊙lunch Thu-Tue, dinner Mon & Thu-Sat) Enjoying lovely views of the multicoloured historic buildings surrounding Le Puy's market square, the outdoor tables here are great for a drink or a more substantial meal. Specialities include large salads and local beef dishes accompanied by Puy lentils, mashed potatoes, tagliatelle or roasted vegetables.

FRANÇOIS GAGNAIRE: CHEF

François Gagnaire is one of the Auvergne's most renowned chefs and the owner of the eponymous Restaurant François Gagnaire in Le Puy.

Background I was born in Le Puy-en-Velay and trained under three-star Michelin chefs in Paris and worked all over France and in Japan and Chile, but returned to open my restaurant for the quality of life and the quality of produce here.

Culinary philosophy Using traditional regional products in a modern way; with a forward focus. I keep a notebook and try out different things... the *lentille verte du Puy* can be used for the whole meal.

A contemporary lentil-based meal? For the starter, *le caviar du Velay*. Lentils were traditionally known as *caviar du pauvre* (poor man's caviar), which gave me the idea for this dish: first I cook the lentils separately, then in a langoustine bisque, then mix them with the jelly from the bisque and present in a tin – it looks like real caviar! It's spooned onto blinis made with lentil flour and served with lentil soup. For the main course, wholegrain lentils go well with *la Noire du Velay* (locally bred black lamb). For the cheese course, lentil yoghurt, made from lentil pulp. For dessert, Verveine (green local liqueur) soufflé served with lentil confit – cooked with vanilla and sugar – and lentil ice cream.

THE VIA PODIENSIS PILGRIMAGE ROUTE

Ever since the 9th century, when a hermit named Pelayo stumbled across the tomb of the apostle James (brother of John the Evangelist), the Spanish town of Santiago de Compostela has been one of Christendom's holiest sites.

The pilgrimage to Santiago de Compostela is traditionally known as the Camiño de Santiago (Way of St James). There are many different routes from London, Germany and Italy, as well as four that cross the French mainland. But the oldest (and most frequented) French route is the 736km Via Podiensis from Le Puy-en-Velay via Figeac, Cahors, Moissac and Rocamadour, established in AD 951 by Le Puy's first bishop.

Early pilgrims were inspired to undertake the arduous journey in exchange for fewer years in purgatory. Today the reward is more tangible: walkers or horse riders who complete the final 100km to Santiago (cyclists the final 200km) qualify for a Compostela Certificate, issued on arrival at the cathedral.

The modern-day GR36 roughly follows the Via Podiensis route. Plenty of organisations can help you plan your adventure: contact Le Puy's tourist office, or, in Toulouse, the Association de Coopération Interrégionale: Les Chemins de Saint-Jacques de Compostelle (05 62 27 00 05; www.chemins-compostelle.com). Useful online guides include www.webcompostella.com and www.csj.org.uk.

Le Chamarlenc
REGIONAL CUISINE €
(04 71 02 17 72; www.lechamarlenc.fr; 19 rue Raphaël; plat du jour €10, menus €15-19; lunch & dinner Tue-Sat) Crowned world master of *pâté en croûte* cookery in 2009, chef Florian Oriol serves his speciality foie-gras-and-mushroom pies alongside an ever-changing chalkboard menu built around fresh local produce.

Entrez les Artistes
REGIONAL CUISINE €€
(04 71 09 71 78; 29 rue Pannessac; menus €15-28; lunch Tue-Sat, dinner Thu-Sat) Lashings of local lace adorn this cosy place, which dishes up solid local fare, including a €9.90 *plat du jour* (dish of the day).

Self-Catering
Le Puy's Saturday market (place du Plot; 8am-1pm Sat) takes over place du Plot (starting point for the Via Podiensis) every Saturday morning. The town's covered market (place du Marché Couvert; 8.30am-7.30pm Tue-Sat) is just off rue Grenouillit.

Fromagerie Coulaud
CHEESE €
(24 rue Grenouillit; 8.30am-7.30pm Tue-Sat) In the same family since 1925, this excellent cheese shop is run by the delightful Jacques and Jacqueline Coulaud and decorated with their heirloom collection of cheese serving dishes.

ℹ Information
Tourist office (04 71 09 38 41; www.ot-lepuyenvelay.fr; 2 place du Clauzel; 8.30am-noon & 1.30-6.15pm) Offers free internet use on its guest computer, but no wi-fi.

ℹ Getting There & Away
Direct trains link Le Puy with Lyon (€22.80, 2½ hours, three to seven daily). SNCF also operates bus-train combinations to Clermont-Ferrand (€22.60, 2¼ hours, four to six daily).

ℹ Getting Around
TUDIP (www.tudip.fr) operates five local bus lines (single ticket/10-trip carnet €1.20/8.50), all stopping at place Michelet.

For a taxi call 04 71 05 42 43.

Gorges de l'Allier

About 30km west of Le Puy, the salmon-filled Allier River – paralleled by the scenic Clermont–Ferrand–Nîmes rail line – weaves between rocky, scrub-covered hills and steep cliffs. Above the river's east bank, the narrow D301 gives fine views as it passes through wild, wide-open countryside and remote, mud-puddle hamlets.

In the sleepy town of Langeac (population 3943), the tourist office (04 71 77 05 41; www.haut-allier.com; place Aristide Briand; 9am-12.30pm & 1.30-6pm Tue-Sat) has details of walking trails criss-crossing the valley walls as well as companies offering canyoning and white-water rafting.

To explore the area at a gentler pace, book ahead for the scenic Train des Gorges de l'Allier (04 71 77 70 17; www.train-gorges-allier.com; adult €11.50-20.50, child €7.50-12.50; May-Aug), which trundles

CHEESE COUNTRY

With its wide-open pastures and lush green grass, it's not surprising the Auvergne has a long tradition of producing some of France's finest cheeses. The region has five Appellation d'Origine Contrôlée (AOC) and Appellation d'Origine Protégée (AOP) cheeses: the semihard, cheddarlike Cantal and premium-quality Salers, both made from the milk of high-pasture cows; St-Nectaire, rich, flat and semisoft; Fourme d'Ambert, a mild, smooth blue cheese; and Bleu d'Auvergne, a powerful, creamy blue cheese with a Roquefort-like flavour.

To taste them on their home turf, follow the signposted Route des Fromages (www.fromages-aop-auvergne.com) linking local farms and producers. A downloadable map is available on the website.

The area's cheeses figure strongly in many of the Auvergne's traditional dishes, including *aligot* (puréed potato with garlic and Tomme cheese) and *truffade* (sliced potatoes with Cantal cheese), almost always served with a huge helping of *jambon d'Auvergne* (local ham).

through the gorges to/from Langeac. Days and itineraries vary.

Plentiful campgrounds in the valley include Langeac's tree-shaded riverside Camping les Gorges de l'Allier (☎04 71 77 05 01; www.campinglangeac.com; site €12.75; ☺Apr-Oct).

Le Moulin Ferme-Auberge (☎04 71 74 03 09; www.gite-aubergedumoulin.com; St-Arcons-d'Allier; dm incl breakfast/half-board €20/38.50, d incl breakfast/half-board €70/110) has charmingly renovated stone cottages, with dinner served at a big communal table in the 15th-century mill.

La Montagne Protestante

Around 40km east of Le Puy is this sparsely populated highland area, carpeted in rich pastureland and thick fir forest. The area's most distinctive landmarks are the peaks of Mont Meygal (1436m), and Mont Mézenc (1753m), the summit of which is accessible via the GR73 and GR7 hiking trails. On a clear day, sweeping views across southeastern France stretch from Mont Blanc, 200km to the northeast, to Mont Ventoux, 140km to the southeast.

The region around Le Chambon-sur-Lignon (population 2870), 45km east of Le Puy-en-Velay, played a courageous role in WWII, when it sheltered over 3000 refugees, including hundreds of Jewish children, from deportation by the Nazis. Info on local outdoor activities, including horse riding and mountain climbing, is available from the tourist office (☎04 71 59 71 56; www.ot-hautlignon.com; rte de Tence; ☺9am-noon & 2-6.30pm Mon-Sat, 10am-noon Sun).

Limousin, the Dordogne & the Lot

Best Places to Eat

» Le Clos St-Front (p575)
» L'Essentiel (p573)
» La Table du Couvent (p562)
» La Belle Étoile (p591)
» Le Grand Bleu (p581)

Best Places to Stay

» Château les Merles (p593)
» Hôtel La Grézalide (p599)
» Manoir de Malagorse (p602)
» Hostellerie Les Griffons (p577)
» Hôtel Le Saint Cirq (p597)

Why Go?

Together, Limousin, the Dordogne and the Lot are the heart and soul of *la belle France,* a land of dense oak forests, green fields and famously rich country cooking. It's the stuff of which French dreams are made: turreted châteaux and medieval villages line the riverbanks, wooden-hulled *gabarres* (barges) wander the waterways, and market stalls overflow with foie gras, truffles, walnuts and fine wines.

Of the three adjacent areas, the Limousin *région* – encompassing the Haute-Vienne, Creuse and Corrèze *départements* – is the most traditional, strewn with farms and hamlets, as well as a cache of architectural treasures from the Middle Ages in its main hub, Limoges. To the south, the Dordogne *département* has a bevy of *bastides* (fortified towns) and castles, as well as Europe's most spectacular cave paintings. Further south still, the Lot *département* is ribboned with rivers to cruise and subterranean caverns to explore, not to mention the region's most renowned vineyards.

When to Go
Limoges

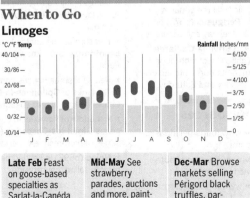

Late Feb Feast on goose-based specialties as Sarlat-la-Canéda celebrates its feathered mascot.

Mid-May See strawberry parades, auctions and more, painting Beaulieu-sur-Dordogne red.

Dec-Mar Browse markets selling Périgord black truffles, particularly in 'truffle capital' Sorges.

RIVER ACTIVITIES

This river-filled region looks its best when seen from the water. Popular villages for boat trips and canoe hire include the following:

» **La Roque Gageac** (p589)

» **Brantôme** (p576)

» **Bergerac** (p592)

» **Beaulieu-sur-Dordogne** (p570)

Fast Facts

» **Population** 1.3 million

» **Area** 31,219 sq km

» **Hotel overnights/yr** 2.5 million

» **Signature drink** *eau de noix* (walnut liqueur)

Atmospheric Markets

» On Saturday, the lanes of **Sarlat-la-Canéda** (p580) spill over with stalls laden with local specialties, like walnuts, wine and foie gras.

» Gourmet delicacies galore fill the squares in **Perigueux** (p572) on Wednesday and Saturday.

» In **Brive-la-Gaillarde** (p568), hectic outdoor markets burst into life every Tuesday and Saturday.

Resources

» www.tourismelimousin.com

» www.tourisme-haute vienne.com

» www.tourismecreuse.com

» www.dordogne-perigord -tourisme.fr

» www.tourisme-lot.com

Regional Parks

This corner of France is renowned for its unspoilt natural beauty, with huge swathes protected in three *parcs naturels régionaux*: Périgord-Limousin (www.parc-naturel -perigord-limousin.fr) in the northwest, Millevaches en Limousin (www.pnr-millevaches.fr) in the east and Causses de Quercy (www.parc-causses-du-quercy.org) in the south. All three regional parks offer a wealth of outdoor activities. Tourist offices throughout the region stock *balades à la journée* (day walks) leaflets and *VTT* (*vélo tout terrain;* mountain bike) guides, while dedicated park Topo-guides detail major walking routes including the GR (Grandes Randonées; long distance) trails. Numerous trails and bridleways can also be explored on horseback.

PREHISTORIC ART

The Dordogne and the Lot Valley are famous for their fabulous prehistoric paintings, which litter many of the region's caves and rock shelters. They were mostly created by Cro-Magnon people between around 15,000BC and 10,000BC, and range in their style, sophistication and artistry from simple scratched lines to complex multicoloured frescoes. Perhaps the most famous of all are the paintings of the Grotte de Lascaux (p587), where the artists depicted a whole menagerie of animals on the walls, including mammoth, horses, ibex, reindeer, aurochs and bulls. Also worth seeking out is the Grotte de Rouffignac (p586), sometimes known as the Cave of 1000 Mammoths, and the Grotte de Pech Merle (p594), which contains many hand tracings and even a set of haunting human footprints.

Picture-Perfect Villages

» Dangling high above the Lot Valley, the red-roofed hilltop village of **St-Cirq Lapopie** (p597) is lined with artists' studios.

» Pleasure-cruise boats ply the waters of riverside **Brantôme** (p576), known locally as the Venice of the Périgord.

» Red sandstone houses and an 11th-century church huddle in the lanes of **Collonges-la-Rouge** (p570), one of France's official *beaux villages* (beautiful villages).

» A muddle of flower-clad cottages and slate roofs, gorgeous **Gimel-les-Cascades** (p569) is also known for a series of picturesque waterfalls nearby.

» **Najac** (p599) is nestled beneath a fairy-tale castle in remote rolling countryside.

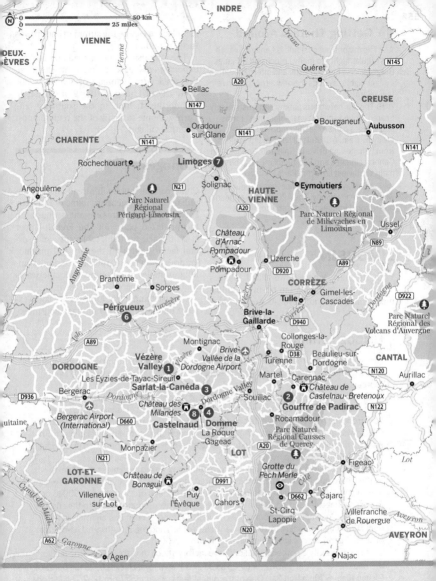

Limousin, the Dordogne & the Lot Highlights

1 Admire the ancient artwork of prehistoric Europeans in the **Vézère Valley** (p584)

2 Descend into the depths on an underground river tour of the **Gouffre de Padirac** (p601)

3 Pick up some foodie souvenirs at Sarlat-la-Canéda's Saturday **market** (p582)

4 Admire the wraparound views from the hilltop *belvédère* in **Domme** (p588)

5 Cruise the waters of the Dordogne River aboard a traditional flat-bottomed **gabarre** (p592)

6 Stroll around an excavated 1st-century Roman villa at Périgueux' **Musée Gallo-Romain Vesunna** (p573)

7 Pick up some French porcelain at one of the renowned china factories of **Limoges** (p558)

8 Wander the ramparts of a quintessential medieval castle at **Castelnaud** (p590)

❶ Getting There & Around

AIR The major transport hub is Limoges, which has regular flights to many French and UK cities. Bergerac also has domestic and international budget flights, as does the new airport at Brive-la-Gaillarde.

BUS The bus network is patchy and frustratingly geared around school timetables; most towns and villages can be reached more quickly and easily by train. A useful rail link runs to Toulouse from Limoges via Brive-la-Gaillarde, Souillac and Cahors; Limoges and Périgueux are both on the main southwest line from Paris.

CAR As always in rural France, having your own wheels is really handy. The A20 motorway heads north from Limoges to Paris and continues south to Toulouse.

LIMOUSIN

With its quiet lanes, flower-filled villages and country markets, Limousin is tailor-made for walkers and cyclists and the per-fect place to escape the summertime crowds further south.

The Limousin *région* is made up of three *départements*: Haute-Vienne, in the west, the *préfecture* (capital) of which is the lively city of Limoges; the rural Creuse, in the northeast; and, in the southeast, the Corrèze, home to many of the region's most beautiful villages.

Limoges

POP 141,287

China connoisseurs will already be well familiar with the legendary name of Limoges. For over 200 years, this elegant city has been the preferred place for the French upper crust to pick up their tableware, and several factories around the city still produce France's finest china. You can see some stunning examples at museums and galleries as well as public spaces around town.

Compact and lively, Limoges is easy to explore on foot. Historic buildings and muse-

---

LIMOGES CHINA

For over 300 years the name of Limoges has been synonymous with *les arts du feu* (literally 'the fire arts'), especially the production of *émail* (enamel) and *porcelaine* (porcelain).

Limoges had been producing enamel since at least the 12th century, but its fortunes were transformed by the discovery of an extremely pure form of kaolin near St-Yrieix-La-Perche in 1768. This fine white china clay, a vital ingredient in porcelain manufacture (along with quartz and feldspar), had previously been imported at huge expense from Asia. Its discovery on home soil led to an explosion of porcelain production in Limoges in the late 18th and 19th centuries.

Three factors distinguish porcelain from other clay-baked ceramics: it's white, extremely hard and translucent. Porcelain is fired three times: first at about 950°C; again, after being covered by liquid enamel, at about 1450°C; and one last time, at 900°C or so, to ensure that the hand-painted or machine-applied decoration adheres to the surface.

While you're wandering around the city, look out for porcelain and enamel tiles on many buildings, including the Halles Centrales (p562) and the Pavillon du Verdurier (place St-Pierre), an octagonal building dating from 1900.

Many of the city's porcelain makers have factory shops that are open to the public:

» Porcelaine Royal Limoges (☎05 55 33 27 30; www.royal-limoges.fr; 28 rue Donzelot; ⊙shop 10am-6.30pm Mon-Sat) One of the oldest factories, dating from 1797. The factory also houses the 19.5m-high Four des Casseaux (www.fourdescasseaux.fr; adult/child €4/3; ⊙10.30am-5.30pm Mon-Sat), the only surviving example of an 18th-century brick kiln. It's 500m southeast of the train station.

» Bernardaud (☎05 55 10 55 91; www.bernardaud.fr; 27 av Albert Thomas; tours adult/child €4.50/free; ⊙9.45am-11.15am & 1-4pm Jun-Sep) Offers guided tours of the porcelain production process, from raw material to finished piece. Tours are run by arrangement outside high season. The factory is 1km northwest of the city centre.

» Haviland (www.haviland.fr; av du Président Kennedy; admission free; ⊙10am-1pm & 2-6.30pm Mon-Sat) Screens a short film and has a small museum. Located 3km southeast of the city centre.

ums cluster in the medieval Cité quarter and radiate out from the partly pedestrianised Château quarter in the city centre. If you come by train you'll be arriving in style: the city's grand art-deco Gare des Bénédictins, completed in 1929, is one of France's most resplendent railway stations, graced by a copper dome, carved frescos and a copper-topped clock tower.

⊙ Sights

CHÂTEAU QUARTER

This bustling corner of Limoges is the heart of the old city. It gets its name from the fortified walls that once enclosed much of the quarter, including the medieval abbey and ducal castle, both long since dismantled.

Rue de la Boucherie   HISTORIC STREET

Just off place St-Aurélien, the pedestrianised rue de la Boucherie – so named because of the butchers' shops that lined the street in the Middle Ages – contains many of the city's most attractive medieval half-timbered houses. The Maison de la Boucherie (36 rue de la Boucherie; ⊙10am-1pm & 2-7pm Jul-Sep) houses a small history museum, and nearby is the tiny Chapelle Saint-Aurélien, dedicated to the patron saint of butchers.

Église St-Michel des Lions   CHURCH

(rue Adrien Dubouché) Named for the two granite lions flanking the door, Église St-Michel des Lions was built between the 14th and 16th centuries. It contains the relics (and head) of St Martial, Limoges' first bishop, who converted the city to Christianity. Its most notable feature is the huge copper ball perched atop its 65m-high spire.

Cour du Temple   SQUARE

Tucked away between rue du Temple and rue du Consulat, this tiny enclosed courtyard was once a private garden belonging to nearby *hôtels particuliers* (private mansions). Look out for various coats of arms and the 16th-century stone staircase around the edge of the courtyard.

Aquarium du Limousin   AQUARIUM

(www.aquariumdulimousin.com; 2 bd Gambetta; adult/child €7.50/5; ⊙10.30am-6pm) Recently saved from closure, this small aquarium houses 2500 fish in the subterranean surroundings of Limoges' old water reservoirs.

Crypt of St Martial   TOMB

(⊙mid-Jun–mid-Sep) All that remains of the once-great pilgrimage abbey of St Martial, founded in AD 848, is a faint outline on place de la République, and an underground tomb dedicated to the city's patron saint.

CITÉ QUARTER

To the east of the Château quarter, la Cité is where you'll find Limoges' main museums.

FREE **Musée des Beaux Arts**   ART MUSEUM

(www.museebal.fr; place de la Cathédrale; ⊙10am-6pm Mon & Wed-Sun) Fresh from a €25-million refurbishment, the city's huge arts museum is lodged inside Limoges' 18th-century bishop's palace. It's a typically impressive affair, with excellent collections of Limoges porcelain and enamel, as well as separate sections dedicated to Egyptian antiquity, fine arts and the city's history.

Musée National Adrien Dubouché   CERAMICS MUSEUM

(www.musee-adriendubouche.fr; 8bis place Winston Churchill; ⊙10am-12.25pm & 2-5.40pm Wed-Mon) One of the main draws to the porcelain capital of France is obviously the chance to check out its famous enamelware. The Musée National Adrien Dubouché has one of France's two outstanding ceramics collections (the other is in Sèvres, southwest of Paris), including 12,000 pieces from Limoges makers as well as Meissen, Royal Doulton, Royal Worcester and others.

Cathédrale St-Étienne   CHURCH

(place St-Étienne) Built between 1273 and 1888, Limoges' Gothic cathedral is worth a visit for the richly decorated Portail St-Jean, as well as a glorious rose window and a Renaissance rood screen.

Jardin de l'Évêché   GARDEN

Near Cathédrale St-Étienne is Limoges' botanical garden, where medicinal and toxic herbs have been grown since medieval times.

FREE **Musée de la Résistance**   WAR MUSEUM

(☑05 55 45 84 44; 7 rue Neuve-Ste-Étienne; ⊙10am-6pm Jun-Sep, 9.30am-5pm Oct-May, closed Tue)

The Limousin was a stronghold of the Resistance during WWII, and this newly reopened museum explores the story of the region's struggle against German occupation

LIMOUSIN, THE DORDOGNE & THE LOT LIMOGES

Limoges

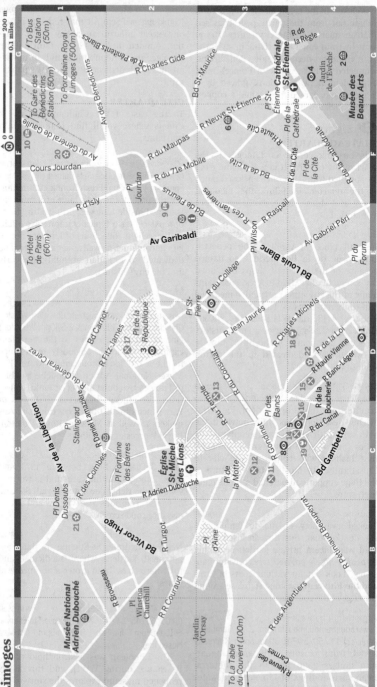

200 m
0.1 miles

To Bus
Station
(50m)

To Gare des
Bénédictins
Station (50m)

To Porcelaine Royal
Limoges (500m)

R de Pénitents Blancs

R Charles Gide

Bd St-Maurice

Av des Bénédictins

R de
la Règle

Cathédrale
St-Étienne

Jardin
de l'Évêché

Musée des
Beaux Arts

Pl St-
Étienne

R Neuve St-Étienne

R Haute Cité

Pl de la
Cathédrale

R de la Cité

Av du Général de Gaulle

Cours Jourdan

R du Maupas

R du 71e Mobile

Bd de la cité

Pl de
la Cité

R de la Cité

R de la Cathédrale

Pl
Jourdan

R d'Isly

Bd de Fleurus

R des Tanneries

R Raspail

Av Gabriel Péri

To Hôtel
de Paris
(60m)

Av Garibaldi

Pl Wilson

Bd Louis Blanc

Pl du
Forum

R du Collège

Bd Carnot

R Fitz-James

Pl de la
République

Pl St-
Pierre

R Jean Jaurès

R Charles Michels

R de la Lot

Pl du
Général Cerez

R du Consulat

R du Temple

Pl des
Bancs

R Haute-Vienne

R Banc-Léger

R de la
Boucherie

Bd Carnot

Pl
Stalingrad

R des Combes

R Daniel Lamazière

R du Temple

R Gonduret

R du Canal

Bd Gambetta

Av de la Libération

Pl Denis
Dussoubs

R des Combes

Pl Fontaine
des Barres

Église
St-Michel
des Lions

Pl de
la Motte

Bd Victor Hugo

R Turgot

R Adrien Dubouché

Pl
d'Aine

R Pétiniaud Beaupeyrat

Musée National
Adrien Dubouché

R Broussea

Pl
Winston
Churchill

R R Couraud

Jardin
d'Orsay

R Neuve des
Carmes

R des Argentiers

To La Table
du Couvent (100m)

Limoges

through a mix of archive film, photography and lots of wartime memorabilia, including photos, letters, diaries and military hardware. Look out for a Free French aeroplane on the upper floors.

Cité des Métiers et des Arts CRAFT MUSEUM
(☏05 55 32 57 84; www.cma-limoges.com; 5 rue de la Règle; adult/child €5/2.50; ☺2-6pm) Showcases work by top members of France's craft guilds.

🛏 Sleeping

The majority of the city's hotels are located around the train station. Rates at most places drop at weekends.

Nos Rev HOTEL €
(☏05 55 77 41 43; www.hotelnos-rev.com; 16 rue du Général du Bessol; s €49, d €53-65; 🛜) This stylish city bolt-hole offers a dozen contemporary rooms, all decorated in zesty colour combos of lime, taupe and cherry red. It's just a couple of streets west of the train station, and the rates are a steal, especially at weekends.

Arthôtel Tendance HOTEL €€
(☏05 55 77 31 72; www.arthoteltendance.com; 37 rue Armand Barbès; s €57-85, d €63-90; 🛜) Globetrotting decor defines this quirky little hotel, with *chambres de thème* including a maple-clad Canadian cabin, a Balinese room with Lombok furniture, and a Grecian room decked out in whites and sea blues. Other overnight destinations include Africa, Egypt, Provence and Morocco. It's around 500m northwest of the train station.

Hôtel Jeanne d'Arc HOTEL €€
(☏05 55 77 67 77; www.hoteljeannedarc-limoges. fr; 17 av du Général de Gaulle; s €68-74, d €82-87; 🛜) The pick of Limoges' plusher options is an old *relais de poste* that's now favoured by business travellers. Shuttered and stylish, it offers spacious rooms, all equipped with elegant furnishings and the odd antique. Private garage parking is available for €5.

Hôtel de Paris HOTEL €
(☏05 55 77 56 96; www.hoteldeparis-limoges. com; 5 cours Vergniaud; s €49-65, d €55-75, f €69-95) A French hotel *à l'ancienne,* offering basic but good-value rooms spread out over several floors of a tall town house. Floors are squeaky, doors are creaky and the spiral staircase will give you a good workout, but it's equally handy for town and station.

Hôtel de la Paix HOTEL €
(☏05 55 34 36 00; www.hoteldelapaix87.fr; 25 place Jourdan; d €53-70; 🛜) This old classic is faded but full of charm. The ground floor is occupied by the owner's Mechanical Music Museum, stuffed with gramophones, rinky-dink record players, barrel organs and other musical oddities, while the upper corridors hide small, serviceable rooms.

✖ Eating

TOP CHOICE La Table du Couvent FRENCH €€
(☎05 55 32 30 66; www.latableducouvent.com; 15 rue Neuve des Carmes; mains €10-20; ⊗lunch & dinner Wed-Sun) As its name suggests, this modish restaurant is housed inside a building that once belonged to a Carmelite convent. These days, it's been converted into one of the city's most popular eateries, with tables set out among rough brick walls, a life-size cow and an open kitchen counter where you can watch your meals being prepared, including locally sourced steaks cooked *à la cheminée* (over an open hearth). Cooking courses are also available.

Le 27 MODERN FRENCH €€
(☎05 55 32 27 27; www.le27.com; 27 rue Haute-Vienne; mains €15-24; ⊗Mon-Sat) A contemporary bistro with quirky decor to match the inventive cuisine. Teardrop lanterns, cream banquette seats and a giant hovering sheep's head set the tone. One entire wall is taken up by the wine selection, while the food revolves around French classics given a contemporary spin.

L'Amphitryon TRADITIONAL FRENCH €€
(☎05 55 33 36 39; 26 rue de la Boucherie; menus €27-46; ⊗closed Sun & Mon) This venerable fine diner has been one of Limoges' top tables for donkey's years, and it's still as esteemed as ever. It's in a delightful timbered building on rue de la Boucherie, and serves classically rich French cuisine, created by renowned head chef Richard Lequet. The dining room makes a suitably smart setting, too, with original beams and period windows.

Les Petits Ventres REGIONAL CUISINE €€
(☎05 55 34 22 90; www.les-petits-ventres.com; 20 rue de la Boucherie; lunch menus €18-26.50, dinner menus €26.50-36; ⊗closed Sun & Mon; ⊕) One for the meat lovers: the 'Little Stomachs' specialises in carnivorous cuts such as *andouillettes* (tripe sausages), *fricassée de rognons* (fried kidneys) and *pieds de cochons* (pig's trotters).

Le Bistrot d'Olivier REGIONAL CUISINE €
(Halles Centrales; menus €12-16; ⊗7am-2pm Mon-Sat) For an authentic lunch in Limoges, you can't do much better than this chaotic little place inside the market, where diners and traders sit at communal wooden tables and share hearty, no-fuss portions of French food chosen straight from the blackboard. If it's full (as it often is), Chez François (Halles Cen-

trales; menus €10-18; ⊗6am-2pm Mon-Sat), also inside the market, offers a similarly lively vibe.

Le Bœuf à la Mode BISTRO €€
(☎05 55 77 73 95; www.leboeufalamode.fr; 60 rue François Chénieux; mains €16-25; ⊗lunch Tue-Fri, dinner Fri & Sat) As you might expect from a restaurant called 'Fashionable Beef', this butcher-meets-bistro prides itself on the quality of its steaks, all of which come from top-quality Limousine beef sourced from local farms. The lamb and veal are excellent, too.

Chez Alphonse REGIONAL CUISINE €€
(☎05 55 34 34 14; 5 place de la Motte; menus €10-25; ⊗Mon-Sat) Checked tablecloths, wooden furniture and blackboards stuffed with regional dishes: what more could you want from a Limoges bistro? The options on offer tend to be meaty, so if you've got an aversion to veal, offal and horse, you might want to look elsewhere.

La Parenthèse TEAROOM €
(☎05 55 33 18 25; www.restaurant-tearoom-parenthese-limoges.com; Cour du Temple; menus €14-16.50; ⊗10am-2.30pm Mon, 10am-6.30pm Tue-Sat; ⊕) Over forty teas and 14 coffees are served at this charming tearoom, hidden in the corner of the Cour du Temple. It's a lovely spot for tea and cake, but there's a good choice of salads and *plats du terroir* (regional dishes), too.

Planetalis ORGANIC €
(www.planetalis.com; place de la République; menus €10-11; ⊗7.30am-8.30pm Mon-Sat; ⊕) If you're a vegetarian and feeling a little unloved about now, drop into Limoges' branch of this organic canteen chain, good for healthy sandwiches and salads.

Halles Centrales FOOD MARKET
(place de la Motte; ⊗to 1pm) Limoges' Halles Centrales runs the gourmet gamut from local cheese to Limousin beef.

🍷 Drinking & Entertainment
The large student crowd keeps Limoges' nightspots ticking; you'll find most of the action around rue Charles Michels and place Denis Dussoubs.

L'Amicale des Parachutistes Belges LIVE MUSIC
(www.myspace.com/parachutistes_belges; 17 rue Charles Michels; ⊗Tue-Sun) Belgian beers and a

buzzy gig scene are the draws at this scruffy boozer.

Le Duc Étienne
BAR

(place St-Aurélien) This long-standing hang-out in the medieval quarter has a hip little bar supplying European beers and late-night coffee to a pre-club crowd. In summer things spill onto the terrace in front of Église St-Aurélien.

La Fourmi
LIVE MUSIC

(www.lafourmi87.net; 3 rue de la Font Pinot) The best place in town for live music, with breaking acts, alternative bands and theatrical spectacles in a twin-floored warehouse-style space. It's about 1km out of town, but worth the trek. Check the website for what's on when.

Le Tabernacle
LIVE MUSIC

(http://limoges.limousin.free.fr/tabernacle; 19 rue de la Loi; ⊕Wed-Sat) Part pub, part club, part grungy gig venue. Bare brick and industrial styling conjure up a lived-in vibe at this late-night venue.

Grand Écran
CINEMA

(www.grandecran.fr; 9-11 place Denis Dussoubs) Multiplex cinema screening nondubbed films.

Cinéma Lido
CINEMA

(www.allocine.fr; 3 av du Général de Gaulle) Artier films.

❶ Information

Tourist Office (☑05 55 34 46 87; www.tourisme-limoges.com; 12 bd de Fleurus; ⊕9am-7pm Mon-Sat, 10am-6pm Sun; ☎)

❶ Getting There & Away

Air

Just off the A20, 10km west of the city, **Limoges Airport** (☑05 55 43 30 30; www.aeroport limoges.com) is a major UK gateway, served by budget carriers including Ryanair and Flybe, as well as Air France.

Domestic destinations include Paris Orly, Lyon, Nice and Ajaccio (Corsica), while UK destinations include London Stansted, London Gatwick, Bristol, Nottingham, Liverpool, Southampton, Manchester, Newcastle, Leeds-Bradford and Birmingham.

Taxis (☑05 55 38 38 38; www.taxis87.com/contact.php) from the airport charge a flat-rate fare of €23 during the day, €31 after 7pm and on Sundays.

Bus

Limoges' bus station is across the tracks from the train station. Buses are geared towards school timetables, so many lines don't run on weekends. Information and timetables are available from **RDTHV** (Régie Départementale des Transports de la Haute-Vienne; ☑05 55 10 31 00; www.rdthv.com; place des Charentes) and the **Haute Vienne en Car** (http://hautevienne encar.cg87.fr) website.

Useful lines:

» **Oradour-sur-Glane** Bus 12, 45 minutes, three daily Monday to Saturday

» **Chalus** Bus 16, 40 minutes, two daily Monday to Friday, one on Saturday

» **Rochechouart** Bus 21, 80 minutes, two daily Monday to Friday, one on Saturday

Car

All the major rental companies are based at the airport. **ADA** (☑05 55 79 61 12; 27 av du Général de Gaulle) and **National-Citer** (☑05 55 77 10 10; 3 cours Bugeaud) also have downtown offices.

Train

Limoges' beautiful Gare des Bénédictins has direct trains all across France. Tickets can also be bought at the town-centre **SNCF boutique** (4 rue Othon Péconnet).

Main destinations include the following:

» **Cahors** €32, 2¼ hours, four daily

» **Brive-la-Gaillarde** €16, one hour, 12 to 15 daily

» **Paris Gare d'Austerlitz** €56, three hours, hourly

» **Périgueux** €16, one hour, at least eight daily

West of Limoges

ROCHECHOUART & CHASSENON
POP 3930

Meteorites and modern art might be an unlikely combination but they're the twin draws of the walled town of Rochechouart, 45km west of Limoges. Rochechouart witnessed one of the most devastating impacts in Earth's history 200 million years ago when a massive 1.5km-radius lump of intergalactic rock slammed into the Earth at 72,000km/h with the force of 14 million Hiroshima bombs.

The impact site, 4km west of town, created a crater 20km wide and 6km deep, but the only visible traces are the unusual rocks, frequently used as local building material, left behind by the massive explosion. The small **Espace Météorite Paul Pellas** (☑05 55 03 02 70; www.espacemeteorite.com; 16 rue

Jean-Parvy; adult/child €4/2; ⊙10am-12.30pm & 1.30-6pm Mon-Fri, 2-6pm Sat & Sun) explores this cosmic cataclysm through minerals, models and video displays. Hours are geared around school holidays, so check ahead to make sure it's open.

Housed in the town's refurbished château, highlights of the Musée Départemental d'Art Contemporain (☎05 55 03 77 91; www.musee-rochechouart.com; place du Château; adult/child €4.60/3, free 1st Sun of month; ⊙10am-12.30pm & 1.30-6pm, closed Tue) include a collection of works by acclaimed Dadaist Raoul Hausmann and an installation of white stones by British artist Richard Long in a room decorated with 16th-century frescos.

About 5km from Rochechouart are the Gallo-Roman baths of Chassenon (☎05 45 89 32 21; www.cassinomagus.fr; entry adult/child €5/2.50, guided tours €1.50; ⊙10am-6.30pm daily). Rediscovered in 1844 and excavated from 1958 to 1988, this luxurious former way station known to the Romans as Cassinomagnus was an important crossroads on the Via Agrippa, the road that crossed France via Saintes, Périgueux, Limoges, Clermont-Ferrand and Lyon. Much of the complex (including a temple and amphitheatre) were plundered for stone, but you can still make out the baths, plunge pools and hypocausts, the Roman equivalent of underfloor heating. Regular events include live entertainment, Roman sports and exhibitions.

Domaine des Chapelles (☎05 55 78 29 91; www.domainedeschapelles.com; restaurant menus €27; 🛜🏊), a converted farm, has been turned into a supremely relaxing rural getaway. Cappuccino-and-cream colour schemes sit alongside exposed stone and rustic tiles in the boutique rooms. Some have private terraces and room 8 even has its own hydromassage bath and sauna. The country restaurant is also very good. It's off the D34 near Vayres, about 9km south of Rochechouart.

There are buses to Rochechouart from Limoges (p558).

East of Limoges

GUÉRET & BOURGANEUF
POP GUÉRET 15,089 / POP BOURGANEUF 3184

Eighty-two kilometres northeast of Limoges, the busy town of Guéret grew up around a 12th-century monastery and the 15th-century Château de Moneyroux, now the administrative HQ of the Creuse *département*, of which Guéret is capital. Guéret itself isn't that exciting, but it's a handy base for exploring nearby attractions. Thirty-two kilometres south of Guéret, bourgeois Bourganeuf is also worth a stop, especially for its atmospheric old town.

◉ Sights & Activities

Le Parc Animalier des
Monts de Guéret   WILDLIFE PARK
(☎05 55 81 23 23; www.loups-chabrieres.com; adult/child €8.50/7; ⊙10am-8pm May-Aug, 1.30-6pm Sep-Apr) At this fascinating wolf sanctuary, black and grey wolves roam free across a 12-hectare park.

Labyrinthe Géant   MAZE
(www.labyrinthe-gueret.fr; adult/child €6.50/4.50; ⊙10am-8pm Jul & Aug, open 2-8pm daily during school holidays, otherwise weekends only) At the Labyrinthe Géant you can get well and truly lost among the hedgerows in what's allegedly the world's largest maze.

FREE Musée de l'Électrification,
de l'Eau et de la Lumière   SCIENCE MUSEUM
(☎05 55 64 07 61; rte de la Cascade; ⊙10am-noon & 2-6pm Mon-Sat Jul & Aug) Bourganeuf's main claim to fame came in 1886, when it became one of the first places in France to be connected to mains electricity. In summer, this museum explores this electrifying event.

Plateau de Millevaches   NATIONAL PARK
(www.pnr-millevaches.fr) South of Bourganeuf, the Limousin is at its lushest, especially around Plateau de Millevaches.

THE LION OF THE LIMOUSIN

The spectre of Richard Cœur de Lion (Richard the Lionheart) looms over the Haute-Vienne *département*. The crusader king waged several bloody campaigns here in the 12th century before meeting his end at the now-ruined keep of Château de Chalûs-Chabrol, 40km west of Limoges, where he was mortally wounded by a crossbowman in 1199.

Many other sites nearby share a Lionheart connection, which are signposted along the Route de Richard Cœur de Lion (Richard the Lionheart Route; www.routerichardcoeurdelion.fr); pick up a free English-language leaflet from tourist offices.

WORTH A TRIP

LE VILLAGE MARTYR

On the afternoon of 10 June 1944, the little town of Oradour-sur-Glane, 21km north-west of Limoges, witnessed one of the worst Nazi war crimes committed on French soil. German lorries belonging to the SS 'Das Reich' Division surrounded the town and ordered the population on to the market square. The men were divided into groups and forced into *granges* (barns), where they were machine-gunned before the structures were set alight. Several hundred women and children were herded into the church, and the building was set on fire, along with the rest of the town. Only one woman and five men survived the massacre; 642 people, including 193 children, were killed. The same SS Division committed a similarly brutal act in Tulle two days earlier, in which 99 Resistance sympathisers were strung up from the town's balconies as a warning to others.

Since these events, the entire village has been left untouched, complete with tram tracks, pre-war electricity lines, the blackened shells of buildings and the rusting hulks of 1930s automobiles – an evocative memorial to a once-peaceful village caught up in the brutal tide of war. At the centre of the village is an underground memorial inscribed with the victims' names. Poignantly, there are also display cases collecting their recovered belongings, including watches, wallets, hairpins and a couple of children's bikes.

Entry is via the Centre de la Mémoire (www.oradour.org; adult/child €7.80/5.20; ⊙9am-5pm), which contextualises the massacre using historical exhibitions, video displays and survivors' testimonies. Various theories have been put forward to try to explain the event – perhaps German panic following the Allied landings four days earlier, or reprisal for sabotage raids committed by the Resistance following the invasion – but it may be one of those terrible events that simply defies any rational explanation.

After the war Oradour was rebuilt a few hundred metres west of the ruins. Bus 12 travels from the bus station in Limoges to Oradour-sur-Glane. By car, take the D9 and follow signs to the *village martyr* (martyred village).

LIMOUSIN, THE DORDOGNE & THE LOT EAST OF LIMOGES

Lac de Vassivière　　　WATER SPORTS
(www.vassiviere.com) The glassy Lac de Vassivière is a popular spot for water sports and afternoon picnics.

🍽 Sleeping & Eating

TOP CHOICE **Hôtel des Estonneries**　　　HOTEL €
(☑05 55 82 14 66; www.hotel-les-estonneries.com; 41 av Georges Clemenceau, Chambon-sur-Voueize; d €59-79; 🕸) This delightful hotel offers lashings more luxury than you'd expect to find in the tiny village of Chambon-sur-Voueize. It's installed in a grand 19th-century *maison bourgeoise* with neatly tended gardens, and has eight gorgeous rooms decorated with real fun and flair: wood floors, retro furniture, vintage lamps, modern art and funky fabrics. Downstairs, there's a super lounge-bar with sofas to sink in and books to browse. Altogether it's well worth the trip, 40km northeast from Aubusson or 46km east from Guéret.

Abbaye du Palais　　　B&B €€
(☑05 55 64 02 64; www.abbayedupalais.com; r €75-135, cottages per week €1100-1600, gypsy wagons per week €500-800; 🖨) Between Bourganeuf and Guéret, this country retreat offers something to suit all comers. Cosy B&B rooms are offered in the main house, once a Cistercian abbey, while around the grounds you'll find lovely *gîtes* (cottages) and vintage gypsy-style caravans that are perfect for longer stays. It's very family friendly and offers lots of activity ideas, from cookery courses to guided hikes.

Le Moulin Noyé　　　HOTEL €€
(☑05 55 52 81 44; www.moulin-noye.com; rte de La Châtre; d from €120) With rooms named after composers, and in shades like raspberry pink and apple green, this backcountry haven overlooks wooded countryside above the Creuse River 9km northwest of Guéret, near the village of Glénic. Its restaurant is a fave of local gourmets for its seasonal local produce, from lake fish to Limousin beef; book ahead.

AUBUSSON
POP 4400

Along with pottery and porcelain, the northern Limousin is famous for its tapestries, which once adorned the walls of aristocratic houses from London to the Loire Valley.

ALL ABOARD!

Clamber aboard the carriages pulled by the 1932 steam engine Chemin Touristique Limousin–Périgord (www.trainvapeur.com) to watch the Limousin's gloriously green fields and forests roll by.

The railway runs between mid-July and mid-August. Reservations are essential and can be made through the Limoges tourist office. There are three main routes, which operate several times a season:

» **Limoges–Eymoutiers** The Vallée de la Haute-Vienne line follows the old upland railway via St-Leonard-de-Noblat to Eymoutiers (adult/child €25/11).

» **Limoges–Pompadour** Full-day excursion, which includes a visit to the stables of Arnac-Pompadour (adult/child €29/15).

» **Eymoutiers–Châteauneuf-Bujaleuf** Two-hour trip (adult/child €14/7), via the plunging Gorges de la Vienne.

They weren't just decorative: in a world before central heating, they provided useful insulation against the cold, especially in draughty castles.

The riverside town of Aubusson was the clacking centre of French carpet production during the 19th century (rivalled only by the Gobelins factories in Paris), producing elegant tapestries known for their vivid colours, fine detail and exquisite craftsmanship. The industry suffered a steady decline following the French Revolution, before being revived between WWI and WWII by inventive new designers, such as Jean Lurçat, Sylvaine Dubuisson and Dom Robert.

⊙ Sights

Today there are around 20 tapestry workshops in Aubusson and nearby Felletin, 10km south. The tourist office, in Aubusson, arranges visits to local tapestry *ateliers* (workshops), and can supply you with a list of local galleries and showrooms, such as Atelier Duché (www.atelier-duche-aubusson.com; 35 Grand Rue; ⊙9am-6pm Tue-Sat).

Maison de Tapissier   TAPESTRY MUSEUM
(http://mtapissier.lacreuse.com; adult/child €5/3; ⊙9.30am-12.30pm & 2-6pm Mon-Sat year-round, plus 10am-noon & 2.30-5.30pm Sun Easter-Sep) Next to the tourist office, this building recreates the atmosphere of a 17th-century weaver's workshop, with tools, original furniture and (of course) vintage tapestries.

Musée Départemental
de la Tapisserie   TAPESTRY MUSEUM
(www.cite-tapisserie.com; av des Lissiers; adult/child €5/free; ⊙9.30am-noon & 2-6pm Mon & Wed-Sun) For a historical overview, head to the Musée Départemental de la Tapisserie,

which houses intricate examples of both antique and modern tapestries produced in Aubusson.

Exposition-Collection
Fougerol   TAPESTRY MUSEUM
(34 rue Jules Sandeau; adult/child €3/free; ⊙10am-1pm & 2-6pm Mon-Sat, 10am-noon & 2.30-5.30pm Sun) The Exposition-Collection Fougerol features some 135 tapestries from the 16th to 19th centuries from Aubusson and Flanders.

🛏 Sleeping & Eating

Hôtel La Beauze   BOUTIQUE HOTEL €
(☑05 55 66 46 00; www.hotellabeauze.fr; 14 av de la République; d €60-70; 🖙) This chic shuttered house on the outskirts of town is one of Aubusson's comfiest places to stay. The stylishly furnished rooms, all of which have peaceful views across a grassy garden, come in shades of beige, cream and slate.

L'Hôtel de France   HOTEL €€
(☑05 55 66 10 22; www.aubussonlefrance.com; 6 rue des Déportés; d €68-100, restaurant menus €20-41; 🖙) This former post inn, now an upmarket Logis hotel, has 21 plush rooms: some modern, some old fashioned and frilly, some tucked into the attic with sloping ceilings and roof beams. Its restaurant is the best in town, with a smorgasbord of Limousin dishes served to the tune of a tinkling piano.

ⓘ Information

Tourist Office (☑05 55 66 32 12; www.ot-aubusson.fr; rue Vieille; ⊙9.30am-12.30pm & 2-6pm)

ⓘ Getting There & Away

Aubusson is 90km east of Limoges. Trains (and SNCF buses) link Aubusson with Limoges

(€14.80, 1¾ hours, around five daily Monday to Saturday, one on Sunday).

South of Limoges

SOLIGNAC
POP 1497

In the thickly wooded Briance Valley, 10km south of Limoges, the tiny medieval village of Solignac was a major stop on the pilgrimage route to Santiago de Compostela. Its 11th-century church is a Romanesque wonder, renowned for its 14m-wide domed roof. The stalls in the nave are decorated with carved wooden sculptures of human heads, fantastical animals and a monk mooning the world, while the columns depict human figures being devoured by dragons.

Five kilometres southeast are the ruins of the Château de Chalucet, a 12th-century keep occupied by the English during the Hundred Years War. The ruins make a fine picnic spot, with valley views from the tumbledown keep.

Nearby in Le Vigen, the Parc Zoologique du Reynou (www.parczooreynou.com; adult/child €13.50/9.50; ⊙10am-7.30pm, last entry 6pm) is a 35-hectare safari park established on land once owned by the Haviland china dynasty. Its exotic denizens include wolves, giraffes, wildebeest, snowy owls and a pair of breeding tigers.

About the only place to stay nearby is Hôtel Le St-Eloi (☑05 55 00 44 52; www.lesaint eloi.fr; 66 av St-Eloi; d €69-96), with 15 sunny rooms inside a shuttered building opposite the church. The ones with jacuzzis and terraces are fantastic value, and half-board is available at the restaurant (menus €29-38; ⊙closed dinner Sun).

The Solignac–Le Vigen train station is linked to Limoges (€2.90, 10 minutes) and Uzerche (€8.70, 40 minutes) by a couple of trains daily.

UZERCHE
POP 3271

On a promontory over the rushing Vézère River, the walled town of Uzerche is one of the Limousin's prettiest hilltop hamlets. Spiky turrets jut out from the walls of the 15th- and 16th-century maisons à tourelles (turret houses) like witch's hats, while the Porte Bécharie, one of the nine original gates that granted access to the village in the 14th century, remains remarkably intact.

Uzerche's single street leads uphill to the Église St-Pierre, a fortified church with an 11th-century crypt – one of the oldest crypts in the Limousin. Out the front, there's fabulous panorama views over the river valley from place de la Lunade, which takes its name from a pagan summer solstice festival (now rejigged as a Christian procession). Nearby, the tourist office (☑05 55 73 15 71; www.pays-uzerche.fr; place de la Libération; ⊙10am-noon & 2-6pm Mon-Fri) sells work by local artists, like patchwork teddy bears and handmade pottery.

Uzerche has just a couple of hotels. Despite the its well-worn exterior, inside Hôtel

LIMOUSIN, THE DORDOGNE & THE LOT SOUTH OF LIMOGES

WORTH A TRIP

LA CITÉ DU CHEVAL

Equine aficionados won't want to miss the château of Arnac-Pompadour, home to one of France's foremost *haras* (stud farms). It was established in the 18th century by the mistress of Louis XV, Madame de Pompadour (born Jeanne-Antoinette Poisson), and has been an Haras National since 1872. It's particularly known for its Anglo-Arab pedigrees.

Based at the château, Les Trois Tours (☑05 55 98 51 10; www.les3tours-pompadour .com) arranges guided visits to the château (adult/child €5.50/4.50), the écuries du Puy Marmont (stallions' stables; adult/child €5.50/4.50) and the jumenterie de la rivière (mares' stables; adult/child €5.50/4); joint passes for two/three tours cost €15/10 per adult and €12/8 per child. Alternatively, you can wander round the château's gardens, carriage house and a small stable for €4/3 per adult/child.

Opposite the château entrance, the tourist office (☑05 55 98 55 47; www.pompadour .net; ⊙10.30am-12.30pm & 2-6pm) has details of forthcoming race meetings, as well as the grand horse show on 15 August and a day dedicated to the humble *âne* (donkey) on 14 July.

Arnac-Pompadour is about 60km south of Limoges, served by train and SNCF bus (€11.60, 1¼ to 1 ¾ hours, two to three daily).

Jean Teyssier (☎05 55 73 10 05; www.hotel
-teyssier.com; rue du Pont-Turgot; d €54-68) you'll
find a comfortable modern hotel. The 14
rooms are fresh and well furnished, with
magnolia walls and checked and striped
fabrics, and the restaurant has a nice river-
view terrace.

Uzerche's other choice, Hôtel Ambroise
(☎05 55 73 28 60; www.hotel-ambroise.com; av
Charles de Gaulle; d €56-64, f €69-78; ⊙closed
mid-Nov–Feb; ☎) has snug, old-fashioned
rooms (some with river views) and a garden
restaurant.

Uzerche is linked to Limoges, 56km to the
north, by train (€10.50 to €13, 40 minutes,
six to eight daily). The train station is 2km
north of the old city along the N20.

Brive-la-Gaillarde

POP 51,629

Busy Brive-la-Gaillarde is the main commercial and administrative centre for the
Corrèze *département*. Apart from its bustling weekly markets, Brive itself is short on
sights, but it's a good base for exploring the
Corrèze as well as the upper Lot and northeastern Dordogne.

◉ Sights

FREE Maison Denoix   DISTILLERY
(☎05 55 74 34 27; www.denoix.fr; 9 bd du Maréchal-
Lyautey; ⊙9am-noon & 2.30-7pm Tue-Sat Sep-Jun)
Since 1839 this traditional distillery has
been producing the favourite firewater of
the Corrèze, *l'eau de noix* (walnut liqueur),
alongside adventurous concoctions such
as chocolate liqueur, quince liqueur and
curaçao.

You can wander around the old copper
cauldrons and stills, and sample the wares
at its shop, including *moutarde violette de
Brive* (purple mustard made with grape
must).

There are free guided tours in French at
2.30pm on Tuesdays and Thursdays during
July and August.

Musée Labenche   HISTORY MUSEUM
(www.musee-labenche.com; 26bis bd Jules-Ferry;
adult/child €5/2.70; ⊙10am-6.30pm Mon & Wed-
Sun) Exhibits at the town's main museum
explore local history and archaeology, as
well as a unique collection of 17th-century
English tapestries, accordions dating from
the late 19th century to 1939, and a piano
that once belonged to Debussy.

Collégiale St-Martin   CHURCH
In the heart of town, the Romanesque Collégiale St-Martin dates from the 11th century,
but it's taken a battering over the years: the
only original parts are the transept and a
few decorated columns depicting fabulous
beasties and biblical scenes.

🛏 Sleeping & Eating

Château de Castel-Novel   CASTLE HOTEL €€€
(☎05 55 85 09 03; www.castelnovel.com; d €120-
415, ste €385-550 restaurant menus €38-105;
❉☎❉) About 10km north of Brive-la-
Gaillarde, this beauty of a château was immortalised by the French author Colette,
who based herself here while writing *Le Blé
en Herbe* and *Chéri*. Topped by turrets, gables and slate tiles, filled with idiosyncratic
rooms (including a turret room and Colette's
Louis XVI apartment) and surrounded by
sweeping lawns and an 18th-century orangery, it's no wonder Madame Colette found it
inspiring. Equally inspired is the château's
Michelin-starred gastronomic restaurant.

Le Manoir de Laumeuil   B&B €€
(☎05 55 87 95 83; www.lemanoirfr.com; 147 rue du
Laumeuil, St Pantaleon de Larche; r €120) These
manorial *chambres d'hôte* on the western
outskirts of Brive are surrounded by three
green acres hosting an orchard, fish pond
and arboretum. There are three rooms and
two apartments, all done with grace and
good taste. The Riverside and Pine apartments feature wood floors and exposed
beams, while the Cream and Sage rooms
go for light fabrics, plush bedspreads and
chaises longues. All have fridges, DVD players and garden views. There's also a lovely
salt-water swimming pool.

La Truffe Noire   HOTEL €€
(☎05 55 92 45 00; www.la-truffe-noire.com; 22 bd
Anatole-France; d €118.80-138.80, restaurant menus
€26-40; ❉☎) If you want to stay in town, this
venerable hotel is the best bet, with comfy but
bland rooms decked out with beige carpets,
big beds and shuttered windows. The restaurant is good for Limousin fare, with dishes
heavy on truffles, duck and wild mushrooms.

Auberge de Jeunesse   HOSTEL €
(☎05 55 24 34 00; brive@fuaj.org; 56 av Maréchal
Bugeaud; dm €14.30; ⊙reception 8am-noon &
5-10pm; ☎) Brive's hostel makes an striking
first impression, with reception housed inside a former mansion accessed by private
gates. However, most of the dorm rooms are

actually in a modern annexe, with a kitchen in the old stables. It's 1.5km from the station.

Food Market   MARKET €

(place du 14 Juillet; ⊙Tue & Sat morning) Brive hosts a bustling market on the main town square, as well as a smaller market on Thursday mornings. It's a great place to stock up on Limousin goodies: look out for local goose products, plum brandy and *galette corrézienne* (walnut and chestnut cake).

ℹ Information

The **tourist office** (☑05 55 24 08 80; www. brive-tourisme.com; place du 14 Juillet; ⊙9am-12.30pm & 1.30-6.30pm Mon-Sat) is housed in a former water tower, locally known as the *phare* (lighthouse), overlooking the market square.

ℹ Getting There & Away

Brive is a major rail and bus junction.

AIR **Brive-Vallée de la Dordogne Airport** (www .aeroport-brive-vallee-dordogne.com), about 10km south of town, has budget flights to Paris-Orly and London City Airport.

BUS The **bus station** (place du 14 Juillet) is next to the tourist office.

TRAIN The **train station** (av Jean Jaurès), 1.3km from the town centre, can be reached via most buses heading south out of town. Regular direct destinations:

» **Cahors** €19, one hour, four daily

» **Limoges** €16 to €19, one hour, hourly

» **Périgueux** €12.70, one hour, six to eight daily

East of Brive

GIMEL-LES-CASCADES
POP 703

A huddle of slate roofs, flower-filled balconies and higgledy-piggledy cottages gather along the banks of a rushing brook in this tiny, typically Corrèzien village. It's a place to wander the lanes, drink in the atmosphere, and stroll along the banks of the river. The three crashing cascades, after which the village is named, are reached via a riverside path at the foot of the village. The local church contains a beautiful enamelled reliquary known as the Châsse de St-Étienne, made in the 12th century by Limoges craftsmen.

Other nearby sights include the remains of the Cistercian Abbaye d'Aubazine (☑05 55 84 61 12; ⊙guided visits 10.30am, 3pm & 4pm Jul & Aug, by appointment Sep-Jun) and the Étang de Ruffaud, a glassy pond that offers a refreshing dip and a shady place for a picnic.

Hotels are in short supply, but the Hostellerie de la Vallée (☑05 55 21 40 60; www .hotel-restaurant-gimel.fr; d from €65; ⊙Mar-Dec) makes for a pleasant stopover, with nine small rooms and a simple country restaurant (*menus* from €18) tucked around the corridors of an old stone cottage in the heart of the village.

Gimel's teensy tourist office (☑05 55 21 44 32; www.gimellescascades.fr; ⊙2-4.30pm Mon-Fri, 10am-noon & 3-6.30pm Sat, 3-6.30pm Sun) shares a space with the post office.

LIMOUSIN, THE DORDOGNE & THE LOT EAST OF BRIVE

TULLE ACCORDIONS

There's nothing more Gallic than the sound of an accordion squeezing out tunes on a street corner. The industrial town of Tulle (population 16,474), 28km northeast of Brive, is renowned as the world's accordion capital. A single accordion consists of between 3500 and 6800 parts and making one requires up to 200 hours' labour, so mass production has never been an option. The very best instruments can fetch upwards of a staggering €9000.

One of the last remaining traditional accordion makers, the Usine Maugein (☑05 55 20 08 89; rte de Brive; admission free; ⊙8am-noon & 2-5.30pm Mon-Thu), runs guided factory tours by reservation, where you can see the craftspeople at work and browse the accordion museum.

The accordion takes centre stage during mid-September's annual four-day street music festival Nuits de Nacre; Tulle's tourist office (☑05 55 29 27 74; 2 place Émile Zola; ⊙9am-noon & 2-6pm Mon-Sat) has details.

More recently, Tulle has become famous for its connections with the new French president, François Hollande. He served as mayor here from 2001 to 2008, before serving as the prefect of the Corrèze department until his election in 2012; tellingly, he chose to make his victory speech on Tulle's main square.

Regular trains run to Tulle from Brive (€5.40, 1 hour and 50 minutes).

South of Brive

Rolling countryside and green pastures unfold south of Brive to the banks of the Dordogne and the border of the northern Lot.

TURENNE
POP 812

Rising up from a solitary spur of rock, the hilltop village of Turenne is an arresting sight: honey-coloured stone cottages and wonky houses are stacked up like dominoes beneath the towering château (☑05 55 85 90 66; www.chateau-turenne.com; adult/child €4.50/3; ☺10am-noon & 2-6pm), built to protect the feudal seat of the *vicomtes de Turenne* (viscounts of Turenne).

The views of the surrounding countryside from the Tour de César, the castle's arrow-straight tower, are so beautiful that you may well find yourself blinking to make sure they're real. Apart from a few ramparts and a 14th-century guard room, the rest of the castle and lordly lodgings have crumbled away, and are now occupied by an ornamental garden.

Turenne's only hotel is La Maison des Chanoines (☑05 55 85 93 43; http://maison -des-chanoines.com; d €70-105; ☺Apr–mid-Oct). Behind its 16th-century Flamboyant Gothic façade you'll find countrified rooms and a good restaurant (menus €34-49; ☺dinner Thu-Tue).

The tourist office (☑05 55 24 12 95; guided visits adult/child €4/free, fire torch €1; ☺10am-12.30pm & 3-6pm Tue-Sun) is at the base of the village, and runs guided visits as well as torchlit night-time promenades in summer.

Public transport is limited: there are usually a couple of daily buses from Brive, but trains (€3.40, 15 minutes) stop at the rather inconveniently located station, 3km southeast of the village.

COLLONGES-LA-ROUGE
POP 475

With its skyline of conical turrets, rickety rooftops and historic buildings built from rust-red sandstone (hence its name), Collonges-la-Rouge is one of the classic postcard villages of the Corrèze. In 1942, thanks to the efforts of villagers, the entire village received classification as a *monument historique*. In 1982, the Plus Beaux Villages (www.les-plus-beaux-villages-de-france.org) association was established here by Collonges' then mayor Charles Ceyrac to celebrate France's most beautiful villages.

Collonges centres on the part-Romanesque church, constructed from the 11th to the 15th centuries on an 8th-century Benedictine priory, which was an important resting place on the pilgrimage to Santiago de Compostela. In a stirring show of ecclesiastical unity during the late 16th century, local Protestants held prayers in the southern nave and their Catholic neighbours prayed in the northern nave. Nearby, the slate roof of the ancient covered market shelters a similarly ancient baker's oven.

Browsing Collonges' artisan shops and pausing at its clutch of traditional cafes and restaurants is an enjoyable way to while away a few hours, but start out early as it steadily fills with tourists as the day wears on.

On the edge of the village, Jeanne Maison d'Hôte (☑05 55 25 42 31; www.jeanne maisondhotes.com; d €95) in a towering 15th-century *maison bourgeoise,* is a real home away from home. The five rooms are stuffed with period features: beams, latticed windows, antique wardrobes and chaises longues. Try to get the Chimney Room, which has its own inglenook fireplace. Home-cooked meals are available for €35.

A couple of kilometres down the road in the village of Meyssac, Relais du Quercy (☑05 55 25 40 31; www.relaisduquercy.com.fr; d €60-72) is a little slate-roofed country hotel with old-time rooms, the best of which look over the rear garden.

Collonges is linked by bus with Brive (€3, 30 minutes, four to six daily on weekdays, one on Saturday), 18km to the northwest along the D38.

BEAULIEU-SUR-DORDOGNE
POP 1326

On a tranquil bend of the Dordogne hemmed in by lush woods and fields, Beaulieu (meaning 'beautiful place') lives up to its name. Once an important stop for Compostela pilgrims, its beautifully preserved medieval quarter is one of the region's finest: a network of curving lanes lined with timber-framed houses and smart mansions, many dating from the 14th and 15th centuries.

☉ Sights

Abbatiale St-Pierre   ABBEY CHURCH
Beaulieu's most celebrated feature is this 12th-century Romanesque abbey church, with a wonderful tympanum (c 1130) depicting scenes from the Last Judgment including dancing apostles and resur-

rected sinners. The nearby Chapelle des Pénitents was built to accommodate pious parishioners – access to the abbey church was strictly reserved for monks and paying pilgrims.

Faubourg de la Chapelle   ARCHITECTURE
A neighbourhood of 17th- and 18th-century houses, near the Abbatiale St-Pierre.

Château de Castelnau-Bretenoux   CASTLE
(http://castelnau-bretenoux.monuments-nationaux.fr; adult/child €7.50/4.50; ⊙10am-7pm Jul & Aug, 10am-12.30pm & 2-5.30pm Sep-Jun, closed Tue Oct-Mar) Not to be confused with the Château de Castelnaud (p590), Castelnau-Bretenoux was constructed in the 12th century and saw heavy action during the Hundred Years War, before being redeveloped in the Middle Ages following the advent of new forms of artillery. The castle is laid out around a roughly triangular courtyard, with stout towers linked by ramparts and bulwarks.

Most of the rooms open to visitors date from the 17th and 18th centuries, when the castle was mainly used as a residential home rather than a defensive fortress. Having fallen into disrepair in the 19th century, the castle was refurbished by Parisian opera singer Jean Mouliérat, before being donated to the state in 1932.

It's about 5km south of Beaulieu-sur-Dordogne along the D940.

🏃 Activities

Aventures Dordogne Nature   CRUISING
(www.adndordogne.org; ⊙May-Oct) Runs *gabarre* (flat-bottomed boat) trips on the picturesque river, ranging from a 1¼-hour spin around Beaulieu (adult/child €6.50/5.50) to a 2½-hour gourmet picnic cruise (adult/child €18/13). They also hire out canoes and kayaks: trips run from various spots upriver, including La Berge Ombragée (90 minutes, 5km, €11 to 18), Monceaux (four hours, 18km, €20 to €32) and Argentat (6 hours, 23km, €21 to €36).

🎊 Festivals & Events

Fête de la Fraise   STRAWBERRY FESTIVAL
(⊙May) Beaulieu's biggest party is the Fête de la Fraise (Strawberry Festival), marking the annual harvest on the second Sunday in May. Strawberry-focused events fill the town's streets, including strawberry auctions, strawberry parades and the eating of a gargantuan strawberry tart to close the festival in style.

🛏 Sleeping & Eating
Beaulieu's market is on Wednesday and Saturday mornings.

TOP
CHOICE
Manoir de Beaulieu   HOTEL €€
(☑05 55 91 01 34; www.hotelmanoirdebeaulieu.com; 4 place du Champ-de-Mars; r €109-159, ste €209; 🖲) Half old-fashioned *auberge*, half modern pampering pad, this smart hotel in the village centre is a find. The rooms mix the best of old and new: wood floors, glass sinks and flat-screen TVs meet solid furniture, velvet armchairs, and the odd vintage piece. The gastronomic courtyard restaurant (menus €24.50 to €64.50) is superb.

Auberge Les Charmilles   HOTEL €€
(☑05 55 91 29 29; www.auberge-charmilles.com; 20 bd Rodolphe de Turenne; d €80-130, restaurant menus €29-42; 🖲) All eight rooms at this lovely *maison bourgeoise* are named after different types of strawberries. The decor's fresh and fruity, with puffy bedspreads, wooden floors and summery bathrooms. Scrumptious home-cooked dishes are served at its peaceful riverside restaurant, overseen by its well-regarded chef Frank Delestre.

Auberge de Jeunesse   HOSTEL €
(☑05 55 91 13 82; beaulieu@fuaj.org; place du Monturu; dm €13.50; ⊙Apr-Oct) Parts of this quirky 28-bed hostel date from the 15th century, and it certainly looks old: latticed windows and a miniature turret decorate the exterior, while inside you'll find a cosy chimney-side lounge, well-stocked kitchen and dinky four-bed rooms, all with private bathrooms.

Camping des Îles   CAMPGROUND €
(☑05 55 91 02 65; www.campingdesiles.com; bd de Turenne; sites for 2 adults, tent & car €23.50-31.50; ⊙Apr-Oct; 🖲🏊) Well-equipped riverside campsite, sandwiched on an island between two branches of the Dordogne.

Camping à la Ferme du Masvidal   CAMPGROUND €
(☑05 55 91 53 14; www.masvidal.fr; bd de Turenne; sites for 2 adults, tent & car €11, d incl breakfast €70; ⊙Apr-Sep; 🖲) This lovely working farm also offers shady camping, B&B rooms and home-cooked meals (€25 per adult) made with their own produce. It's about 10km southwest of Beaulieu in Bilhac.

❶ Information
The **tourist office** (☑05 55 91 09 94; www.beaulieu-tourisme.com; place Marbot;

⊘9.30am-12.30pm & 2.30-6pm Mon-Sat, 9.30am-12.30pm Sun) is on the main square.

ⓘ Getting There & Away

From Monday to Saturday buses link Beaulieu with Brive (one hour, one to three daily).

THE DORDOGNE

Few regions sum up the attractions of France better than the Dordogne. With its rich food, heady history, château-studded countryside and picturesque villages, the Dordogne has long been a favourite getaway for Brits looking for a second home and French families on *les grandes vacances*. It's also famous for having some of France's finest prehistoric cave art, which litters the caverns and rock shelters of the Vézère Valley.

Known to the French as the Périgord, the region has been divided into four colour-coded areas: Périgord Blanc (white) after the limestone hills around the capital, Périgueux; Périgord Pourpre (purple) for the wine-growing regions around Bergerac; Périgord Vert (green) for the forested regions of the northwest; and Périgord Noir (black) for the dark oak forests around the Vézère Valley and Sarlat-la-Canéda.

Périgueux

POP 30,808

Founded by Gallic tribes, and later developed by the Romans into the important city of Vesunna, Périgueux remains the Dordogne's biggest (and busiest) town. Many visitors skip straight past, put off by the suburban sprawl and confusing traffic, but those who press on to the centre will discover a thoroughly charming old town dotted with medieval buildings and Renaissance mansions, radiating out around the Gothic Cathédrale St-Front.

Reminders of the city's Roman past can still be found in the Cité quarter, including a ruined amphitheatre and a triumphal tower, as well as a grand villa inside the city's excellent Gallo-Roman museum.

◎ Sights

PUY ST-FRONT

The area around the cathedral, known as the Puy St-Front, encompasses most of the city's most impressive medieval streets and buildings.

Cathédrale St-Front CATHEDRAL

(place de la Clautre; ⊘8am-12.30pm & 2.30-7.30pm) Périgueux' most distinctive landmark is most notable for its five Byzantine bump-studded domes (inspired by either St Mark's Basilica in Venice or the church of the Holy Apostles of Constantinople, depending on whom you ask). Built in the 12th century, and heavily restored by Abadie (the architect of Paris' Sacré Cœur), the interior is laid out in a Greek cross, with soaring domes supported by svelte arches. The carillon sounds the same on-the-hour chime as Big Ben.

At the time of research, major renovations were underway to restore one of the cathedral's facades, so don't be surprised if there's some scaffold when you visit.

The best views are from Pont des Barris, which crosses the River Isle to the east.

Medieval & Renaissance Buildings ARCHITECTURE

North of the cathedral, Périgueux' broad boulevards give way to a tangle of cobblestone streets lined with medieval houses. The best examples are along rue du Plantier, rue de la Sagesse and rue de la Miséricorde.

Rue Limogeanne has graceful Renaissance buildings at Nos 3 and 12, as well as the elaborately carved Maison du Pâtissier, at the end of rue Éguillerie. Rue Aubergerie is another good street to explore, with several fortified merchant's houses such as the Hôtel d'Abzac de Ladouze (16 rue Aubergerie) and the Hôtel Sallegourde, although the interiors currently aren't open to the public.

Of the 28 towers that formed Puy St-Front's medieval fortifications, only the 15th-century Tour Mataguerre, a stout, round bastion next to the tourist office, now remains.

Musée d'Art et d'Archéologie du Périgord HISTORY MUSEUM

(22 cours Tourny; adult/child €4.50/2.50; ⊘10.30am-5.30pm Mon & Wed-Fri, 1-6pm Sat & Sun) The city's museum offers a mixed bag of exhibits: fine Roman mosaics, prehistoric scrimshaw, medieval stonework from the Cathédrale St-Front, and interesting artworks mainly from the 19th and 20th centuries.

Musée Militaire MILITARY MUSEUM

(32 rue des Farges; adult/child €4/free; ⊘2-6pm Mon-Sat) Eclectic collection of swords, firearms, uniforms and insignia dating from

the Middle Ages until WWII, with sections devoted to WWI and the French Resistance.

LA CITÉ

Périgueux (formerly Vesunna) was among the most important cities in Roman Gaul, but the only remains of this once-thriving outpost are in La Cité, west of the city centre.

Tour de Vésone ROMAN SITES

The Tour de Vésone is the last remaining section of a massive Gallo-Roman temple dedicated to the Gaulish goddess Vesunna.

Roman Amphitheatre ROMAN SITES

Just to the north of the Tour de Vésone are the ruins of the city's amphitheatre. Designed to hold over 30,000 baying spectators, it was one of the largest such structures in Gaul. Today only a few creeper-covered arches remain, and its gladiatorial arena is occupied by a peaceful park, the Jardin des Arènes.

Musée Gallo-Romain Vesunna ROMAN VILLA

(www.perigueux-vesunna.fr; rue Claude Bernard; adult/child €6/4; ☉9.30am-5.30pm Tue-Fri, 10am-12.30pm & 2.30-6.30pm Sat & Sun) Just west of the Tour de Vésone, this museum designed by French architect Jean Nouvel sits above a 1st-century Roman villa uncovered in 1959. Light floods in through the glass-and-steel structure, and walkways circumnavigate the excavated villa; it's still possible to make out the central fountain, supporting pillars and the underfloor hypocaust system, as well as original mosaic murals, jewellery, pottery and even a water pump.

🛏 Sleeping

The choice of hotels in Périgueux leaves a lot to be desired, so you might find it better to visit on a day trip.

Château des Reynats CASTLE HOTEL €€€

(☑05 53 03 53 59; www.chateau-hotel-perigord.com; 15 av des Reynats; r in chateau €132-279, in orangerie €103-115; ☎🐾) This château complex 3km northwest of town is the plushest place to stay around Périgueux. There's a choice of stately rooms: fancy frescos and half-tester beds inside the main château, or functional modern rooms in the adjacent *orangerie*. There's a choice of dining settings, too: either upmarket gourmet in L'Oison (mains €27 to €48), or contemporary French in the conservatory bistro (menus €18 to €22). Both are overseen by the talented young chef Cyril Haberland, who's previously held a Michelin star.

Hôtel L'Écluse HOTEL €

(☑05 53 06 00 04; www.ecluse-perigord.com; rte de Limoges, Antonne-et-Trigonant; d €50-60, half-board per person €48-53; ☎) Rooms at this large waterfront hotel are rather dated, but get one with a river view and you probably won't mind a bit. The style ranges from country and floral to rustic and spartan; ask for one of the suites for the most space. The restaurant serves reliable regional food with a strong Périgord flavour (menus €19.50 to €32). It's 8km northeast of town off the N21.

Hôtel des Barris HOTEL €

(☑05 53 53 04 05; www.hoteldesbarris.com; 2 rue Pierre Magne; s €47, d €53, f €60-80; ✳☎) Beside the broad River Isle with a cute waterside terrace, this Logis hotel is the best value in Périgueux as long as you can get a river-view room (the ones by the main road can be hideously noisy). Rooms at the higher end of the scale have air-conditioning, but only two have cathedral views.

Bristol Hôtel HOTEL €

(☑05 53 08 75 90; www.bristolfrance.com; 37-39 rue Antoine Gadaud; d €62-82, f €86-96; ✳@☎) The Bristol's boxy Lego-like façade has all the appeal of a municipal car park, but look beyond the exterior and you'll find pleasant rooms with all the mod cons, and the odd splash of shades of orange or red to liven up the rather bland decor. Free parking is a definite bonus.

Hôtel de l'Univers HOTEL €

(☑05 53 53 34 79; www.hotelrestaurantlunivers.fr; 18 cours Michel Montaigne; s/d from €50/58; ☎) You won't get more central than the Univers, perched above Le Cercle, a swanky little wine bar and brasserie in old Périgueux. Nine basic rooms, all in sunny yellows, are dotted round the upper floors. The only parking is in the nearby Montaigne car park.

🍴 Eating

The old town is crammed with shops selling local gourmet goodies.

TOP CHOICE L'Essentiel GASTRONOMIC €€€

(☑05 53 35 15 15; www.restaurant-perigueux.com; 8 rue de la Clarté; lunch menus €27-46, dinner menus €40-59; ☉closed Sun & Mon) This Michelin-starred establishment feels like an aristocratic friend's living room, with tasteful table lamps, floral wallpaper and red velour chairs providing a suitably posh setting for some of Périgueux' top gourmet food. Chef

Périgueux

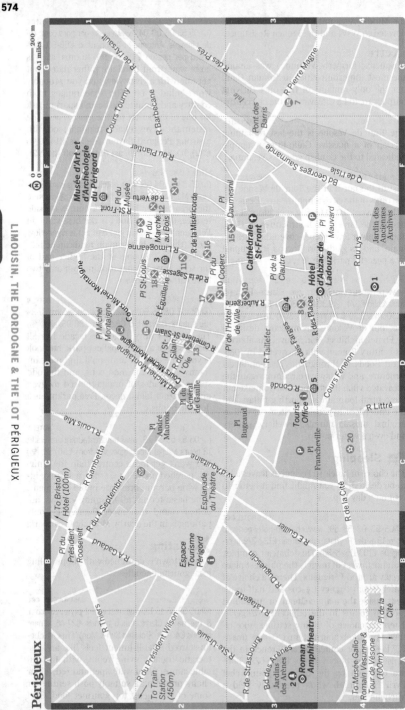

200 m
0.1 miles

Musée d'Art et
d'Archéologie
du Périgord

Cathédrale
St-Front

Hôtel
d'Abzac de
Ladouze

Roman
Amphitheatre

To Train
Station
(450m)

To Bristol
Hôtel (100m)

To Musée Gallo-
Romain Vesunna &
Tour de Vésone
(100m)

Espace
Tourisme
Périgord

Tourist
Office

Jardin des
Anciennes
Archives

Cours Tourny
R de l'Arsault
R des Prés
R Pierre Magne
Pont des
Barris
Q de Georges Saumande
Bd Georges Saumande
Isle
R du Plantier
R Barbecane
Pl du
Musée
R de Vertu
Pl St-Front
Pl du
Marché
au Bois
R Limogeanne
R de la Miséricorde
Pl
Daumesnil
R du
Coderc
Pl de la
Clautre
Pl du Lys
R du Lys
Pl
Mauvard
Cours Michel Montaigne
Pl St-Louis
R de la Sagesse
R Éguillerie
R de
L'Ole
Pl St-
Silain
R Aubergerie
Pl des Places
R des Farges
Cours Fenelon
Pl Michel
Montaigne
Bd Michel Montaigne
Cours Michel Montaigne
R Cimetière St-Silain
Pl de l'Hôtel
de Ville
R Taillefer
R Conde
Cours Fenelon
R Littré
R Gambetta
R Louis Mie
Pl
André
Maurois
Pl du
Général
de Gaulle
Av d'Aquitaine
Esplanade
du Théâtre
Cours 5
Pl
Bugeaud
Pl
Francheville
R de la Cité
R du 4 Septembre
R A Gadaud
R du Président Wilson
R Thiers
Pl du
Président
Roosevelt
R Ste-Ursule
R de Strasbourg
R Lafayette
R Duguesclin
R E Guillier
Bd des Arènes
Jardins
des Arènes
Pl de la
Cité

Périgueux

Eric Vidal is a Tulle native, and he's steeped in local flavours: Quercy lamb, cockerel and local rare-breed pigs regularly feature on the menu, often with a truffly, nutty touch. True gourmets should opt for the €85 *dégustation* menu, which includes two starters, two mains and two desserts.

TOP CHOICE **Le Clos St-Front** GASTRONOMIC €€€
(☑05 53 46 78 58; www.leclossaintfront.com; 12 rue St-Front; menus €27-63; ☷) Set inside a 16th-century *hôtel particulier,* this well-respected restaurant is run by Patrick Feuga, who's known for his creative approach to traditional Périgordine ingredients: roast bream in smoked tea and stinging nettle, or 'black trotter' pork in violet oil and curried lentils. The tree-shaded garden is a dreamy place to eat in summer, and is much sought after; book ahead.

Le Troquet BISTRO €
(☑05 53 35 81 41; 4 rue Notre Dame; mains €8-16; ⊙Tue-Sat) For lunch among the locals, make a beeline for this alleyway bistro, which has attracted a loyal clientele since opening in 2010. It's shoebox small (18 covers inside, 25 on the terrace), but great for authentic market cuisine, such as creamy veal cutlets, duck-leg parmentier and walnut cake.

Café de la Place CAFE, BRASSERIE €
(☑05 53 08 21 11; 7 place du Marché au Bois; mains €14-21) You simply couldn't hope to find a more Gallic spot. All the classic cafe trappings are present and correct – spinning fans, shiny brass fittings, burnished wooden bar – and there's nowhere better in town for people watching over a *petit café*. The food isn't starry, but it's fine for a quick *steak-frites* or *tarte aux pommes*.

Au Bien Bon REGIONAL CUISINE €€
(☑05 53 09 69 91; 15 rue des Places; lunch/dinner menus €11/22; ⊙lunch Tue-Fri, dinner Tue-Sat) Checked tablecloths, chalkboard menus and chipped floor tiles set the earthy tone at this convivial bistro, good for classics such as *confit de canard* (duck leg cooked in its own fat) and *omelette aux cèpes* (omelette with porcini mushrooms).

L'Estaminet REGIONAL CUISINE €€
(☑05 53 06 11 38; 2 Impasse Limogeanne; lunch/dinner menus €18/27; ⊙Wed-Mon Jul & Aug, Thu-Mon Sep-Jun) This small restaurant takes a bit of finding: it's hidden away in a medieval courtyard, right in the middle of the old town. Food is simple but rustic (walnut salad, *confit de canard,* entrecôte with green beans), an ideal match for the dining room's rough stone-and-wood tables. You can eat in the medieval courtyard on sunny days.

Le Cocoon VEGETARIAN €
(☑05 53 53 63 35; 9 place St-Silain; menus €10-15; ⊙lunch Mon-Sat, dinner Mon-Fri; ✐) The rarest of breeds in the Périgord: an exclusively vegetarian restaurant, serving organic omelettes, crunchy salads and wholefood platters in an endearingly boho setting. Inside it's stuffed with jumble-shop furniture; outside there are plastic tables on the square.

Pierrot Gourmet DELI €
(☑05 53 53 35 32; www.pierrotgourmet.com; 6 rue Hôtel de la Ville; mains €9.50, menus €14.50; ⊙11am-6pm Tue-Sat) This lovely deli is Périgueux' equivalent of a posh French takeaway: regional dishes are served canteen

style in the buzzy dining room, or boxed up to go for the perfect gourmet picnic. The choices are mouth-watering: house specialities include cep flans, duck parmentier, Périgueux pâté in a pastry crust, and a truly sinful gingerbread tiramisu.

Covered Market
FOOD MARKET €

(⊙8am-12.30pm daily) You find the covered market in place du Coderc.

Marchés de Gras
FOOD MARKET €

(⊙mid-Nov–mid-Mar) Local delicacies, such as truffles, wild mushrooms and foie gras, are sold on at this lively market on place St-Louis.

Marché du Coderc
FOOD MARKET €

(⊙8am-1.30pm Wed & Sat) Périgueux' wonderful street markets explode into action on Wednesday and Saturday, taking over place du Coderc, as well as place de la Clautre and place de l'Hotel de Ville.

La Ferme Périgourdine
CHEESE SHOP €

(9 rue Limogeanne) For fabulous cheeses stop by La Ferme Périgourdine.

☆ Entertainment

Nightlife is not Périgueux' forte.

CAP Cinéma
CINEMA

(☑08 92 68 01 21; www.cap-cine.fr; place Francheville) The 10-screen CAP Cinéma shows mainly new-release films, some in *version originale* (non-dubbed).

❶ Information

Espace Tourisme Périgord (☑05 53 35 50 24; 25 rue du Président Wilson; ⊙8.30am-5.30pm Mon-Fri) Information on the Dordogne *département*.

Tourist Office (☑05 53 53 10 63; www .tourisme-perigueux.fr; 26 place Francheville; ⊙9am-7pm Mon-Sat, 10am-1pm & 2-6pm Sun)

❶ Getting There & Around

BUS The main local operator is **Peribus** (www .peribus.fr); single fares around town cost €1.25.

Further afield, **Trans Périgord** (☑05 53 02 20 85; 33 rue St-Front) runs school buses to destinations including Sarlat (Line 7A; 1 hour and 45 minutes, two daily Monday to Friday), Montignac (Line 7B; one hour and 55 minutes, one daily Monday to Friday) and Bergerac (one hour, two daily Monday to Friday). Tickets cost a flat rate of €2 per adult, €1 per child.

TRAIN The **train station** (rue Denis Papin), 1km northwest of the old town, is served by buses 1, 4 and 5. Getting to Bergerac (€23.30, 1½ to

2½ hours depending on connections) or Sarlat-la-Canéda (€14.80, 1½ to 3½ hours) requires a change at Le Buisson or Libourne.

Direct services:

» **Bordeaux** €20.50, 1½ hours, hourly

» **Brive-la-Gaillarde** €12.70, one hour, six to eight daily

» **Limoges** €16, one hour, 12 to 15 daily

Brantôme
POP 2169

With its five medieval bridges and romantic riverfront architecture, Brantôme certainly befits its moniker 'Venice of the Périgord'. Set along the banks of the River Dronne and surrounded by grassy parks and willow-filled woodland, it's an enchanting spot to while away an afternoon or embark on a boat ride.

◉ Sights

Benedictine Abbey
ABBEY

Brantôme's most illustrious landmark is the former Benedictine Abbey, built and rebuilt from the 11th to 18th centuries and now occupied by the Hôtel de Ville. Next door is the Gothic abbey church and the tourist office (p580).

Parcours Troglodytique
ABBEY

(adult/child €4/2; ⊙10am-6pm) Behind the modern-day abbey and the tourist office are the remains of Brantôme's original abbey, known as the Parcours Troglodytique, cut from the rock face by industrious monks in the 8th century. Its most famous feature is a 15th-century rock frieze supposedly depicting the Last Judgement. The abbey's 11th-century Romanesque clocher (bell tower) is allegedly the oldest – and arguably most beautiful – in France.

✦ Activities

Canoeing

There are also plenty of places to hire one-person kayaks and two-person canoes for a trip down the Dronne. Brantôme Canoe (☑05 53 05 77 24; kayak/canoe rental per hour €8/11, half-day €14-17, day €25) is located beside the main car-park. The similar Allo Canoes (☑05 53 06 31 85; www.allocanoes.com; kayak rental per half-day/day €15/24) is just along the street from the abbey Both offer half-day trips from Fontaine (4km upriver), Verneuil (8km upriver) and

THE BLACK PEARL OF THE PÉRIGORD

While the Dordogne is famed for its gourmet goodies, for true culinary connoisseurs there's only one ingredient that matters: the black truffle, often dubbed *le diamant noir* (black diamond) or, hereabouts, *la perle noire du Périgord*.

A subterranean fungus that grows naturally in chalky soils (in the Dordogne around the roots of oak trees), this mysterious little mushroom is notoriously capricious; a good truffle spot one year can be inexplicably bare the next, which has made farming them on any kind of serious scale practically impossible. With a vintage crop fetching as much as €1000 a kilogram at the markets, they are a highly sought-after ingredient.

The art of truffle hunting is a closely guarded secret; it's a matter of luck, judgment and hard-earned experience, with specially trained dogs (and sometimes even pigs, which are apparently very partial to truffles) to help in the search. The height of truffle season is between December and March, when special truffle markets are held around the Dordogne, including Périgueux and Sarlat.

If anywhere knows its truffles, however, it's the small village of Sorges, 23km northeast of Périgueux. Known locally as the 'world's truffle capital', the village lives, breathes and sleeps truffles.

The village's Écomusée de la Truffe (www.ecomusee-truffe-sorges.com; Le Bourg, Sorges; adult/child €5/2.50; ⏰9.30am-12.30pm & 2.30-6.30pm daily Jun-Sep, closed Mon Oct-May) has a 3km trail through the local *truffières* (truffle-growing areas), while La Truffe Noire de Sorges (☎06 08 45 09 48; www.truffe-sorges.com; tours €15-25; ⏰by reservation Dec-Feb & Jun-Sep) runs special truffle-themed tours followed by a tasting (English tours are available on request).

The village's renowned Auberge de la Truffe (☎05 53 05 02 05; www.auberge-de -la-truffe.com; Sorges; r €55-81, f €110-145; ✳🛜🏊) even serves a *menu truffe* (€100), where every course features truffles in a different guise – even the desserts!

Bourdeilles (12km downriver), as well as a full-day trip all the way from Verneuil to Bourdeilles (20km). Shorter trips just around Brantôme are also available.

Boat Trips

Pleasure boats depart from the banks of the river in front of the abbey, including Promenade en Bateau (☎05 53 04 74 71; adult/child €7/5) and Bateau Maffioletti (☎05 53 04 74 71; www.bateaumaffioletti.free.fr; adult/child €7/5). Cruises last about 50 minutes, with up to six trips per day from April to mid-October.

🛏 Sleeping & Eating

Brantôme has some enticing places to stay, but prices rocket in summer.

Hostellerie Les Griffons　　　HOTEL, B&B €€
(☎05 53 45 45 35; www.griffons.fr; d €115-143, restaurant menus from €29.50; ⏰restaurant lunch Sun, dinner Mon-Sun; 🛜🏊) In the riverside town of Bourdeilles, 9km southwest of Brantôme along the D78, this converted mill oozes character. Medieval fireplaces, solid beams and higgledy-piggledy layouts characterise the rooms: the ones on the top floor are quite literally squeezed in under

the rafters. Half-board deals are offered by reservation at its riverside restaurant, with French doors opening onto a lovely waterfront terrace.

Hostellerie du Périgord Vert　　HOTEL €
(☎05 53 05 70 58; www.hotel-hpv.fr; 7 av André Maurois; d €54-81, f €105-114, restaurant menus €18-39; 🛜🏊) The ivy-covered façade at this Logis-affiliated inn promises bags of period charm, but inside the rooms are disappointingly modern and bland. Still, the rates are very reasonable, and the restaurant serves reliable *cuisine de terroir* (country cuisine).

Domaine de la Roseraie　　SELF-CONTAINED €€
(☎05 53 02 75 56; www.luxuryholidaydordogne .co.uk; rte d'Angoulême; r per night €99-150, villas per week €499-1499; ✳🛜🏊) This large cottage complex is a good bet if you're planning on basing yourself in Brantôme for an extended stay. Sunny rooms are offered in the main house, but most people rent one of the cottage villas, which come with all mod cons (dishwasher, washing machine, air-con) and sleep from two to eight people. The decor's rather sparse, but the facilities are very family friendly.

Vézère Valley Cave Art

France is renowned for its art – including some of the earliest in European history.

Deep in the Vézère Valley, prehistoric Cro-Magnon artists worked by the light of primitive oil torches, using flint tools for engraving, natural fibre brushes, pads or sponges for painting, and paints derived from minerals like magnesium and charcoal (black), ochre (red/yellow) and iron (red). Usually they painted the animals they hunted, though occasionally left hand-tracings or depicted abstract figures and scenes such as the picture of an injured hunter and bull at Lascaux. But the Cro-Magnon artists' motives remain a mystery.

Some clues come from what they *didn't* draw. There are no landscapes, trees, rivers, skies or rocks in any of the Vézère's caves – only animals, suggesting that the paintings had some kind of ritual or shamanic significance, possibly indicating shrines or sanctuaries. Perhaps most mysterious of all are the geometric shapes and symbols common to many caves, which have been explained as magic markers, tribal signatures or even a primitive form of writing. In reality, no one actually knows what they signified.

Head to some of the valley's extraordinary art sites and ponder these theories yourself.

TOP CAVES FOR VIEWING ART

» **Grotte de Lascaux** (p587)
Breathtaking re-creations of the Vézère's most ornate cave art
» **Grotte de Rouffignac** (p586)
Renowned for its many dramatic friezes of woolly mammoths
» **Grotte de Font de Gaume** (p585) The only original polychrome (multicolour) paintings still open
» **Abri du Cap Blanc** (p586) Flint-carved sculptures

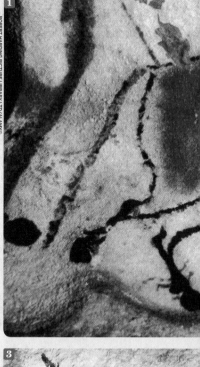

Clockwise from top left
1. Painting at the Grotte de Lascaux 2. Mammoths of the Grotte de Rouffignac 3. Detail of bull's head, Grotte de Lascaux

ROBERT HARDING PICTURE LIBRARY LTD/ALAMY©

CHRIS HOWES/WILD PLACES PHOTOGRAPHY/ALAMY©

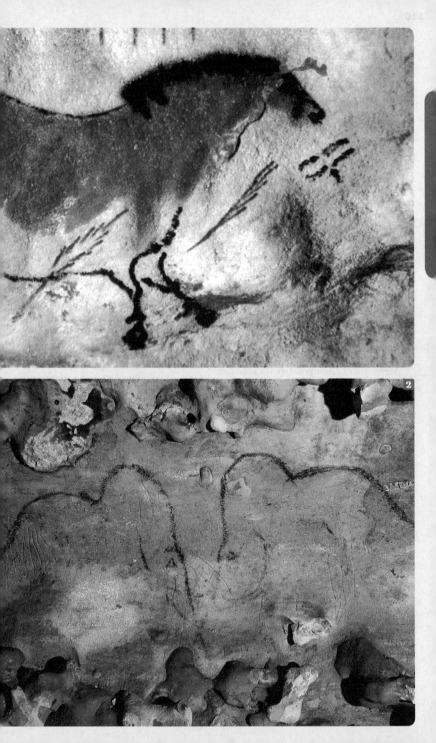

Maison Fleurie
B&B €€

(☑05 53 35 17 04; www.maison-fleurie.net; 54 rue Gambetta; s €45-50, d €65-90; ⚜) Simple, spic-and-span rooms with floral motifs are what to expect at this friendly B&B, which also boasts a sunny courtyard filled with geraniums and petunias.

❶ Information

Tourist Office (☑05 53 05 80 63; www.ville -brantome.fr)

❶ Getting There & Away

Brantôme is 27km north of Périgueux along the D939. From Monday to Friday, two **buses** (www .cftaco.fr) a day run to Périgueux (50 minutes), stopping outside the *gendarmerie* (police station) in the town centre.

Sarlat-la-Canéda
POP 9943

A picturesque tangle of honey-coloured buildings, alleyways and secret squares make up the beautiful town of Sarlat-la-Canéda, which boasts some of the region's best-preserved medieval architecture and makes the perfect base for exploring the Vézère Valley. Unsurprisingly. it's a favourite location for film directors, but it's also firmly on the tourist radar, and you might find it dificult to appreciate the town's charms among the summer throngs.

◉ Sights

Part of the fun of wandering around Sarlat is losing yourself in its twisting alleyways and back streets. Rue Jean-Jacques Rousseau or rue Landry both make good starting points, but for the grandest buildings and *hôtels particuliers* you'll want to explore rue des Consuls. Look out for the medieval fountain, tucked away down steps at the rear of a mossy grotto.

Cathédrale St-Sacerdos
CATHEDRAL

(place du Peyrou) Whichever street you take, sooner or later you'll end up at the cathedral on place du Peyrou, once part of Sarlat's Cluniac abbey. The original abbey church was built in the 1100s, redeveloped in the early 1500s and remodelled again in the 1700s, so it's a real mix of styles. The belfry and western façade are the oldest parts of the building, while the nave, organ and interior chapels are later additions.

Chapelle des Pénitents Bleus
CHURCH

Two medieval courtyards, the Cour des Fontaines and the Cour des Chanoines, can be reached via an alleyway off rue Tourny. Duck down the passage from Cour des Chanoines to the Chapelle des Pénitents Bleus, a Romanesque chapel.

Jardin des Enfeus
PARK

Near the Chapelle des Pénitents Bleus is the Jardin des Enfeus, Sarlat's first cemetery, and the rocket-shaped Lanterne des Morts (Lantern of the Dead), built to honour a visit by St Bernard, one of the founders of the Cistercian order, in 1147.

Maison de la Boétie
ARCHITECTURE

This 16th-century timber-framed house opposite Cathédrale St-Sacerdos is the birthplace of the writer Étienne de la Boétie (1530–63).

Église Ste-Marie
CHURCH

(place de la Liberté) A few steps south of place du Marché aux Oies is the Église Ste-Marie, ingeniously converted by acclaimed architect Jean Nouvel, whose parents still live in Sarlat. It now houses Sarlat's mouth-watering Marché Couvert (p583) (covered market), as well as a spanking new panoramic lift affording 360-degree views across Sarlat's countryside.

Place du Marché aux Oies
SQUARE

A life-size statue of three bronze geese stands in the centre of place du Marché aux Oies (Geese Market Sq), providing a reminder of one of Sarlat's best-known gastronomic goodies. The town's markets sell a smorgasbord of goose-based products, and the town even hosts its own annual goose festival, the Fest'Oie (⊙3rd Sun in Feb), when live birds and food stalls fill the square and Sarlat's top chefs prepare an outdoor banquet.

Château de Puymartin
CASTLE

(www.chateau-de-puymartin.com; adult €7.50, child €3.50-5; ⊙10am-6.30pm Jul-Aug, 10am-11.30am & 2-6pm Apr-Jun & Sep, 2-5.30pm Oct) Heading 8km northwest from town brings you to this impressive turreted château, first built in 1270, destroyed in 1358 during the Hundred Years War, and subsequently rebuilt around 1450. The elegant interior is furnished much as it was during the castle's 19th century refurbishment. Its most famous feature is a 'Cabinet Mythologique', a decorative chamber that can be visited only by reservation; there's also a replica in one of the castle's other rooms. On your way round, keep your eyes peeled for the legendary Dame Blanche, whose restless spirit is said to haunt the castle's corridors.

🛏 Sleeping

Hotel rooms in Sarlat in summer are like gold dust, and budget rooms are thin on the ground at any time.

Villa des Consuls   B&B €€

(✆05 53 31 90 05; www.villaconsuls.fr; 3 rue Jean-Jacques Rousseau; d €82-103, apt €124-184; @🖤) Despite its Renaissance exterior, the enormous rooms here are modern through and through, with shiny wood floors, sofas and original roof trusses. A selection of delightful self-contained apartments are dotted round several buildings in town, all offering the same mix of period plushness – some even have private terraces overlooking the town's rooftops.

La Maison des Peyrat   HOTEL €€

(✆05 53 59 00 32; www.maisondespeyrat.com; Le Lac de la Plane; r €56-103) This beautifully renovated 17th-century house, formerly a nuns' hospital and later an aristocratic hunting lodge, is set on a hill about 1.5km from the town centre. The eleven generously sized rooms are fairly plain, but ooze country charisma; the best have views over the lovingly tended gardens and the countryside beyond. The restaurant's very good, too.

Plaza Madeleine   HOTEL €€

(✆05 53 59 10 41; www.hoteldelamadeleine-sarlat.com; 1 place de la Petite Rigaudie; d €99-179; ❄🖤🏊) Smack bang in the centre of town, this elegant shuttered hotel has benefited from a much-needed decorative overhaul, and it now offers an attractive mix of modern and traditional styles. Classy rooms subtly evoke a bygone era, with vintage phones and shuttered windows, while a solarium and Finnish sauna create a modern boutique feel.

Hôtel St-Albert   BOUTIQUE HOTEL €€

(✆05 53 31 55 55; www.hotel-saintalbert.eu; place Pasteur; d €55-96; 🖤) A small, chic hotel with the barest of boutique touches: chocolate-and-cream tones and posh bath goodies make it feel closer to a metropolitan crash pad than an old-town *auberge*, but rooms are on the small side.

Hôtel Les Remparts   HOTEL €

(✆05 53 59 40 00; www.hotel-lesremparts-sarlat.com; 48 Av Gambetta; d €55-68, tr €68-98; 🖤)

Just outside the old town centre on a busy-ish one-way street, this simple stone hotel has to be one of the best deals in Sarlat. The rooms lack sparkle – white walls, plain furniture and the odd reclaimed roof beam are all you can expect – but the rates are a bargain, even in high summer.

Hôtel Le Mas de Castel   BOUTIQUE HOTEL €

(✆05 53 59 02 59; www.hotel-lemasdecastel.com; rte du Sudalissant; d €68-80, f €88-100; @🏊) This former farmhouse 3km south of town makes a delightful escape from the hectic hum of central Sarlat. Some of its 14 sunny rooms open to the flower-filled courtyard and pool, and one has self-catering facilities.

Hôtel La Couleuvrine   HOTEL €€

(✆05 53 59 27 80; www.la-couleuvrine.com; 1 place de la Bouquerie; d €60-92, tr €92-104, q €104-116; 🖤) Originally part of Sarlat's city wall, this rambling hotel has musty, medieval appeal. Rooms are jammed in awkwardly along creaky corridors: some are sandwiched between solid stone and wooden rafters, while others lurk at the top of the hotel's turret, accessed via their own spiral staircase. The restaurant is in a great hall that partly dates from the 13th century, complete with an enormous inglenook hearth.

Clos La Boëtie   BOUTIQUE HOTEL €€€

(✆05 53 29 44 18; www.closlaboetie-sarlat.com; 95-97 av de la Selves; d €210-280; ❄@🖤🏊) Supremely luxurious rooms in a 19th-century mansion, with a price tag to match.

Hôtel Les Récollets   HOTEL €

(✆05 53 31 36 00; www.hotel-recollets-sarlat.com; 4 rue Jean-Jacques Rousseau; d €49-89; ❄🖤) These budget rooms with an old-town location are set around a pretty hidden courtyard. There's no vehicle access, so you'll have to cart your luggage down lots of cobbled steps.

🍴 Eating

As usual in areas where the tourist turnover is high, Sarlat's old-town restaurants are very hit-and-miss: many are more concerned with packing in the punters rather than keeping their standards high. Choose carefully.

🏆 TOP CHOICE Le Grand Bleu   GASTRONOMIC €€€

(✆05 53 29 82 14; www.legrandbleu.eu; 43 av de la Gare; menus €36-65; ⏲lunch Thu-Sun, dinner Tue-Sat) For a proper supper in Sarlat, this Michelin-starred restaurant is unquestionably

Sarlat-la-Canéda

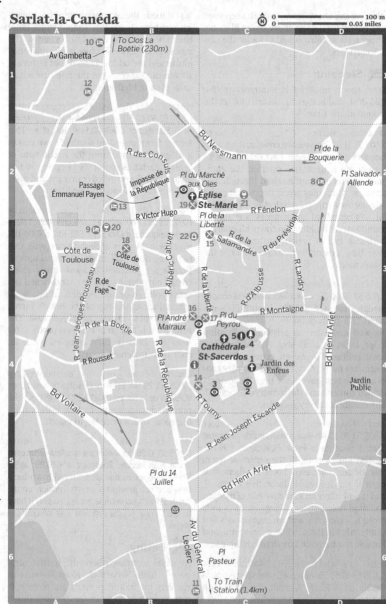

the choice. Run by head chef Maxime Lebrun, it's known for typically creative cuisine that makes maximum use of luxury produce: truffles, lobster, turbot and St-Jacques scallops all feature, and every menu starts with a *mise-en-bouche* treat. Cooking courses are also available. The only downside is the rather out-of-the-way location near the station.

TOP CHOICE **Saturday Market**　　　MARKET €
(place de la Liberté & rue de la République; ⏱8.30am-6pm Sat) For the full-blown French

Sarlat-la-Canéda

◎ Top Sights
Cathédrale St-Sacerdos	C4
Église Ste-Marie	B2

◎ Sights
1	Chapelle des Pénitents Bleus	C4
2	Cour des Chanoines	C4
3	Cour des Fontaines	C4
4	Jardin des Enfeus	C4
5	Lanterne des Morts	C4
6	Maison de la Boétie	B4
7	Place du Marché aux Oies	B2

◎ Sleeping
8	Hôtel La Couleuvrine	D2
9	Hôtel Les Récollets	A3
10	Hôtel Les Remparts	A1
11	Hôtel St-Albert	B6
12	Plaza Madeleine	A1
13	Villa des Consuls	B2

◎ Eating
14	Chez Le Gaulois	B4
15	Fruit & Vegetable Market	C3
16	Jardins de Harmonie	B3
17	Le Bistrot	C4
18	Le Quatre Saisons	B3
19	Marché Couvert	B2
	Organic Market	(see 15)

◎ Drinking
20	Café Léberou	B3
21	Le Pub	C2

◎ Shopping
22	Distillerie du Périgord	B3

market experience, you mustn't miss Sarlat's chaotic Saturday market, which takes over the streets around Cathédrale St-Sacerdos. Depending on the season, delicacies on offer include local mushrooms, duck- and goose-based products such as foie gras, and even the holy *truffe noir* (black truffle). There's also an atmospheric night market (6-10pm) on Thursdays from mid-June to September.

Jardins de Harmonie TRADITIONAL FRENCH €€
(05 53 31 06 69; www.lesjardinsdharmonie.com; place André Malraux; mains €21-35, menus €22-48; lunch & dinner Thu-Mon) This upmarket restaurant has a gorgeous setting, with table lamps, crimson chairs and white linen crammed in among rough stone walls, and a plate-glass window overlooking the cobbled street. The food is classic French laced with contemporary touches: foie gras with Madagascan vanilla, or duck breast smoked in tea.

Le Bistrot REGIONAL CUISINE €€
(05 53 28 28 40; place du Peyrou; menus €18.50-28.50; Mon-Sat) This dinky diner is the best of the bunch on cafe-clad place du Peyrou. Gingham cloths and tiny tables create a cosy bistro feel, and the menu's heavy on Sarlat classics, especially walnuts, *magret de canard* (duck breast) and *pommes sarlardaises* (potatoes cooked in duck fat).

Le Quatre Saisons REGIONAL CUISINE €€
(05 53 29 48 59; www.4saisons-sarlat-perigord.com; 2 côte de Toulouse; menus from €19; Thu-Sun) Another reliable French restaurant, hidden along a narrow alley leading uphill from rue de la République. The food is honest rather than fancy, taking its cue from market ingredients and regional flavours. The most romantic tables have cross-town views.

Chez Le Gaulois SAVOYARD €
(05 53 59 50 64; 3 rue Tourny; platters €10-17; Tue-Sat) Packed plates of smoked sausage, cold meats and cheese are served up on wooden platters at this rather touristy place, which also serves *tartiflettes* (cheese, potato and meat gratin).

Marché Couvert COVERED MARKET €
(8.30am-2pm daily mid-Apr–mid-Nov, 8.30am-1pm Fri-Wed mid-Nov–mid-Apr) Inside the converted Église Ste-Marie (p580), this is the best place for supplies from local producers. The market stays open until 8pm on Fridays in summer.

Fruit & Vegetable Market MARKET €
(8.30am-1pm Wed) This smaller market is held on place de la Liberté.

Organic Market MARKET €
(6-10pm daily) Sarlat's *marché bio* takes place on Thursday evenings on place de la Liberté, with lots of organic products from local suppliers.

Drinking
Sarlat's drinking scene is pretty limited, and most places close completely out of season.

Le Pub BAR
(1 passage de Gérard du Barry) The enclosed courtyard springs to life with alfresco drinkers in summer.

Café Lébèrou BAR
(5 rue Jean-Jacques Rousseau; ⊘Tue-Sat) A local hang-out, with great cocktails.

Shopping

Practically every other shop in Sarlat is stocked with local souvenirs, from *confit de canard* (duck confit) to walnut cake.

Distillerie du Périgord LIQUEUR
(place de la Liberté) Local liqueurs.

Information

There are several banks along rue de la République, all with ATMs.

Tourist office (✆05 53 31 45 45; www.sarlat -tourisme.com; rue Tourny; ⊘9am-7pm Mon-Sat, 10am-1pm & 2-6pm Sun Jul & Aug, shorter hours Sep-Jun) Sarlat's tourist office is very efficient, but it sometimes gets overwhelmed by the sheer number of visitors. Staff can supply several booklets and maps detailing walks around the medieval centre. In summer there is a €2 charge for making hotel and B&B bookings.

Getting There & Away

CAR Cars are banned in the Cité Médiévale from June to September, and rue de la République (La Traverse), the main street that bisects the Cité Médiévale, is pedestrianised in July and August.

There are two large, free car parks on av Général de Gaulle, northwest of the old town.

TRAIN Sarlat's train station is 1.3km south of the old city along av de la Gare. Many destinations require a change at Le Buisson or Libourne.

» **Bergerac** €12, 1¼ hours, six to eight daily

» **Bordeaux** €25.60, 2¾ hours, six to eight daily

» **Les Eyzies** €9.80, 50 minutes to 2½ hours depending on connections, three daily

» **Périgueux** €14.80, 1½ to 3½ hours depending on connections

---

Vézère Valley

Flanked by limestone cliffs, subterranean caverns and ancient woodland, the Vézère Valley is world famous for its prehistoric sites, notably its incredible collection of cave paintings – the highest concentration of Stone Age art found in Europe. The many underground caves around the Vézère provided shelter for Cro-Magnon people, and the area is littered with tangible reminders of their time here. The otherworldly atmosphere is pretty much shattered by the summer crowds and most of the valley's sites are closed in winter, so spring and autumn are definitely the best times to visit.

Most of the key sites are around the towns of Les Eyzies-de-Tayac-Sireuil and Montignac, which are both well set up for visitors. Nearby Sarlat-la-Canéda, between the Vézère and Dordogne valleys to the west, is also a convenient base for exploring this part of the Dordogne.

Getting Around

Public transport is limited, with few trains and even fewer buses. They will get you to most towns but there's usually no transport provided to the caves themselves. Cycling is an option, and hire bikes are often available from campsites, some hotels and rental outlets (ask at tourist offices) but, as always in rural France, having your own car makes things infinitely easier.

LES EYZIES-DE-TAYAC-SIREUIL & AROUND
POP 860

At the heart of the Vézère Valley, Les Eyzies itself makes a fairly uninspiring introduction to the wonders of the Vézère, with postcard sellers and souvenir shops lining the main street. Still, the town has some pleasant hotels and campgrounds and an excellent museum of prehistory, and many major sites are within a short drive.

◎ Sights
LES EYZIES TOWN

TOP CHOICE **Musée National de Préhistoire** PREHISTORY MUSEUM
(✆05 53 06 45 45; www.musee-prehistoire-eyzies .fr; 1 rue du Musée; adult/child €5/3, 1st Sun of month free; ⊘9.30am-6pm Wed-Mon) Inside a marvellous modern building underneath the cliffs, this museum provides a fine prehistory primer (providing your French is good), housing the most comprehensive collection of prehistoric finds in France. Highlights include a huge gallery of Stone Age tools, weapons and jewellery, and skeletons of some of the animals that once roamed the Vézère (including bison, woolly rhinoceros, giant deer and cave bears), as well as a collection of carved reliefs on the 1st floor – look out for the famous frieze of horses and a bison licking its flank. Much of the jewellery is fashioned from bone, antlers and seashells, and intricately marked with chevrons, dots, dashes and other designs.

EARLY ARTISTS OF THE VÉZÈRE

Most of the Vézère Valley's cave paintings date from the end of the last ice age, between 20,000 BC and 10,000 BC, and were painted by Cro-Magnon people – descendants of the first *Homo erectus* settlers who arrived in Europe from North Africa between 700,000 BC and 100,000 BC. These early humans were an entirely separate species from the shorter, burlier Neanderthals who lived in Europe around the same time and died out suddenly around 35,000 BC.

Until around 20,000 BC much of northern Europe was still covered by vast glaciers and ice sheets: Cro-Magnon people lived a loose hunter-gatherer lifestyle, using natural caves as temporary hunting shelters while they followed the migration routes of their prey (including woolly mammoths, woolly rhinoceros, reindeer and aurochs, an ancestor of the modern cow).

The earliest known cave art in the area is from the so-called Gravettian period, consisting of abstract engravings or paintings of female genitalia or 'Venus' figures and developing into complex animal figures and friezes such as those at Lascaux, Rouffignac and Font de Gaume, which date from around 15,000 BC to 10,000 BC. Curiously, the artwork in more recent caves is often less sophisticated than the ones at Lascaux, suggesting that different tribes had differing traditions and levels of artistry, but also indicating that Lascaux seems to have held an unusual significance for its painters. As well as the paintings, these early artists also created jewellery from shells, bones and antlers, and scrimshaw decorated with animal scenes and geometric patterns.

The paintings seem to have come to an abrupt halt around 10,000 BC, around the same time the last ice sheets disappeared and humans hereabouts settled down to a more fixed lifestyle of farming and agriculture.

Abri Pataud   PREHISTORIC SITE

(☑05 53 06 92 46; pataud@mnhn.fr; 20 rue du Moyen Âge; adult/child €5/3; ◷10am-noon & 2-6pm Sun-Thu) About 250m north of the Musée National de Préhistoire is this Cro-Magnon *abri* (shelter) inhabited over a period of 15,000 years starting some 37,000 years ago, displaying bones and other excavated artefacts. The ibex carved into the ceiling dates from about 19,000 BC. The admission price includes a one-hour guided tour (some available in English).

EAST OF LES EYZIES

Grotte de Font de Gaume   PREHISTORIC SITE

(☑05 53 06 86 00; http://eyzies.monuments-nationaux.fr/; adult/child €7.50/free; ◷9.30am-5.30pm Sun-Fri mid-May–mid-Sep, 9.30am-12.30pm & 2-5.30pm Sun-Fri mid-Sep–mid-May) This extraordinary cave 1km northeast of Les Eyzies on the D47 contains the only original polychrome (as opposed to single colour) paintings that are still open to the public. About 14,000 years ago, the prehistoric artists created the gallery of over 230 figures, including bison, reindeer, horses, mammoths, bears and wolves, although only about 25 are included in the tour. Look out for the famous Chapelle des Bisons, a scene of courting reindeer and stunningly realised horses, several caught in mid-movement. Font de Gaume is such a rare and valuable site that there is ongoing talk of the cave being closed for its own protection. Visitor numbers are already limited to 200 per day: it's worth reserving by phone or through the tourist office a few days ahead, and a week or two in advance from July to September. The 45-minute guided tours are generally in French; ask about the availability of English tours when you book.

Grotte des Combarelles   PREHISTORIC SITE

(☑05 53 06 86 00; http://eyzies.monuments-nationaux.fr/; adult/child €7.50/free; ◷9.30am-5.30pm Sun-Fri mid-May–mid-Sep, 9.30am-12.30pm & 2-5.30pm Sun-Fri mid-Sep–mid-May) Rediscovered in 1901, this narrow cave 1.5km east of Font de Gaume is renowned for its animal engravings, many of which cleverly use the natural contours of the rock to sculpt the animals' forms: look out for mammoths, horses and reindeer, as well as a fantastic mountain lion that seems to leap from the rock face. One wall seems to have been used as a kind of prehistoric sketch pad, with many animals and geometric symbols superimposed on one another. Six- to eight-person group tours last about an hour and can be reserved through the Font de Gaume ticket office.

Abri du Cap Blanc
PREHISTORIC SITE

(☑05 53 06 86 00; adult/child €7.50/free; ☉10am-6pm Sun-Fri mid-May–mid-Sep, 10am-noon & 2-6pm Sun-Fri mid-Sep–mid-May) While most of the Vézère's caves contain both engravings and paintings, unusually, this rock shelter contains only carved sculptures, shaped using simple flint tools some 14,000 years ago. The 40m frieze of horses and bison is impressive, but the modern museum built to protect the site means it's tricky to get a sense of how it would have appeared to pre-historic masons. It's 7km east of Les Eyzies.

WEST OF LES EYZIES

Grotte du Sorcier
PREHISTORIC SITE

(☑05 53 07 14 37; www.grottedusorcier.com; adult/child €6.50/3.20; ☉10am-7.30pm Jul & Aug, 10am-6pm Sep-Jun) About 8km west of Les Eyzies, near the hamlet of St-Cirq, this privately owned cave features several animal engravings dating from around 19,000 BC, but it's best known for a male human figure known as the Sorcier (Sorceror), who's endowed with a phallus of truly enormous proportions, possibly indicating his shamanic status, or possibly just a case of prehistoric wish fulfilment...

NORTHWEST OF LES EYZIES

TOP CHOICE Grotte de Rouffignac
PREHISTORIC SITE

(☑05 53 05 41 71; www.grottederouffignac.fr; adult/child €6.50/4.20; ☉9-11.30am & 2-6pm Jul & Aug, 10-11.30am & 2-5pm Sep-Jun) Hidden in woodland 15km north of Les Eyzies, this cave is one of the most complex and rewarding to see in the Dordogne. The massive cavern plunges 10km into the earth through a maze of tunnels and shafts. Luckily, you visit aboard a ramshackle electric train, so there's no chance of getting lost.

Rouffignac is sometimes known as the 'Cave of 100 Mammoths' and you'll see many painted pachyderms on your trip into the underworld, including a frieze of 10 mammoths in procession, one of the largest cave paintings ever discovered. Keep your eyes peeled for scratches and hollows on the cave floor, left behind by long-extinct cave bears.

Tickets are sold at the cave entrance but can't be reserved in advance so arrive early – and wrap up warmly as it's chilly below ground.

Grotte du Grand Roc
CAVE

(☑05 53 05 65 60; www.semitour.com; adult/child €9/4.50; ☉10am-6pm Jul-Nov, 10am-noon & 2-6pm Dec-Jun, closed Fri & Sat Nov-Apr) Around 3km northwest of Les Eyzies along the D47, this cave is decorated by a diverse array of glittering stalactites and stalagmites. The admission price includes entry to the adjacent Abris de Laugerie Basse rock shelter originally occupied by Cro-Magnon people and still used as a natural shelter until recent times.

NORTHEAST OF LES EYZIES

The following sights are situated off the main road linking Les Eyzies with Montignac.

Le Village Troglodytique de la Madeleine
CAVE VILLAGE

(☑05 53 46 36 88; www.la-madeleine-perigord.com; adult/child €5.50/3.50; ☉10am-7pm Jul & Aug, 10am-5pm Sep-Jun) Cro-Magnons weren't the only ones to use the Vézère's caves for shelter. As in the Loire, many of the area's caves were used for storage, defence or protection as recently as the Middle Ages. This cave village 8km northeast of Les Eyzies is a prime example. Carved out from the cliff face above the winding Vézère River, the lower level was occupied by prehistoric people 10,000 to 14,000 years ago, while the upper level was used as a fortified village by medieval settlers. Though it's largely ruined, you can still visit the Ste-Madeleine chapel (after which the Magdalenian era is named), but most of the archaeological artefacts are at the Musée National de Préhistoire (p584) in Les Eyzies.

La Roque St-Christophe
CAVE VILLAGE

(☑05 53 50 70 45; www.roque-st-christophe.com; adult €7.50, child €3.50-4.50; ☉10am-8pm Jul & Aug, 10am-5.30pm or 6.30pm Sep-Jun) On a sheer cliff face 80m above the Vézère, the commanding position of this 900m-long series of terraces and caves makes a practically unassailable stronghold. No wonder, then, that this troglodytic site has been employed as a natural fortress for almost 50 millennia – initially by Mousterian (Neanderthal) people 50,000 years ago, followed by successive generations until the 16th century. The sweeping views are stunning, though the caverns themselves are largely empty and some of the plastic reconstructions are decidedly lame. Located 9km northeast of Les Eyzies.

🏃 Activities

Canoeing on the Vézère is a great way to explore the countryside.

Canoës Vallée Vézère
CANOE RENTAL

(☑05 53 05 10 11; www.canoesvalleevezere.com; 10 promenade de la Vézère; trips €13.50-33; ☉Apr-

Sep) Canoës Vallée Vézère organises self-guided canoe and kayak trips from 10km to 26km including minibus transport. A 5km initiation course costs €8; there are also multiday trips staying at campgrounds or hotels.

🛏 Sleeping & Eating

Les Eyzies has lots of hotels and campsites, but they get heavily overbooked so reserve well ahead.

Hôtel des Glycines   HOTEL €€
(☑05 53 06 97 07; www.les-glycines-dordogne .com; 4 av de Laugerie; d €95-165, ste €195-235, restaurant menus €45-55; ❋🅿️🛜⛱) Les Eyzies' old post house has been converted into this posh pad. Plush rooms range from cream-and-check 'classics' to full-blown private suites, complete with private terrace and garden outlook. Avoid the 'courtyard rooms' if you can, which overlook the main road out of Les Eyzies. The hotel's gastronomic restaurant is a suitably pampering affair – gourmets should go for the *menu truffe* (€95).

Hôtel Le Cro-Magnon   HOTEL €€
(☑05 53 06 97 06; www.hostellerie-cro-magnon .com; 54 av de la Préhistoire; d €82-95; ⊙closed Dec-Feb; 🛜⛱) This wisteria-clad hotel has been around since the 1850s and was often used as a base by pioneering prehistorians. It's more modern these days; although the flowery rooms have a touch of the chain-hotel air about them, the corridors built straight into the rock face add quirky appeal. Dining is good value in the lovely beam-ceilinged restaurant.

Hôtel des Roches   HOTEL €€
(☑05 53 06 96 59; www.roches-les-eyzies.com; 15 av de la Forge; d €60-99, f €120-150; ⊙closed Dec-Mar; 🛜⛱) For a modern feel, try this smart hotel, chunkily constructed from pale stone and decorated in simple pastoral style. The rear rooms overlook the garden and swimming pool.

Camping La Rivière   CAMPGROUND €
(☑05 53 06 97 14; www.lariviereleseyzies.com; sites €6.10-9.80, plus per adult €3.80-6.40; @🛜⛱) The nearest campground to Les Eyzies, a stroll west of town beside the river. Handy facilities include a restaurant, bar, laundry and on-site groceries.

ℹ Information

Tourist office (☑05 53 06 97 05; www .tourisme-terredecromagnon.com; ⊙9am-7pm Jul & Aug, 9am-noon & 2-6pm Mon-Sat, 10am-noon & 2-5pm Sun Sep-Jun)

🚍 Getting There & Away

Les Eyzies is on the D47, 21km west of Sarlat.

The train station is 700m north of town, with connections to Sarlat (change at Le Buisson or Libourne; €9.80, 50 minutes to 2½ hours depending on connections, three daily).

MONTIGNAC & AROUND
POP 2946

The riverside town of Montignac is most famous for its proximity to the Grottes de Lascaux, which are hidden away on the wooded hilltops just outside the town. Huddled along both banks of the Vézère, Montignac is a peaceful, attractive place and makes a less hectic base than Les Eyzies or Sarlat. The old city and commercial centre is on the river's right bank, but you'll find most of the hotels on the left bank around place Tourny.

◎ Sights

TOP CHOICE Grotte de Lascaux
& Lascaux II   PREHISTORIC SITE
(☑05 53 51 95 03; www.semitour.com; adult/child €9.50/6, joint ticket with Le Thot €12.50/8.50; ⊙9am-8pm Jul & Aug, 9.30am-6pm Apr-Jun & Sep-early Nov, 10am-12.30pm & 2-5.30pm early Nov-Dec, Feb & Mar) France's most famous prehistoric cave paintings are at the Grotte de Lascaux, 2km southeast of Montignac. Discovered in 1940 by four teenage boys who were out searching for their lost dog, Lascaux contains a vast network of chambers and galleries adorned with the most complex prehistoric paintings ever found. Far from the comparatively crude etchings of some of the Vézère's other caves, Lascaux' paintings are renowned for their artistry: the 600-strong menagerie of animal figures are depicted in Technicolor shades of red, black, yellow and brown, ranging from reindeer, aurochs, mammoths and horses to a monumental 5.5m-long bull, the largest cave drawing ever found.

Lascaux has often been referred to as the prehistoric equivalent of the Sistine Chapel, and it's a fitting comparison: after a visit in 1940, Picasso allegedly muttered, 'We have invented nothing'. Carbon dating has shown that the paintings are between 15,000 and 17,000 years old, but it's still a mystery why the prehistoric painters devoted so much time and effort to their creation, and why this particular site seems to have been so important.

The original cave was opened to visitors in 1948, but within a few years it became apparent that human breath and body heat was causing irreparable damage to the paintings, and the cave was closed just 15 years later in 1963. A replica of the most famous sections of the original cave was subsequently re-created a few hundred metres away – a massive undertaking that required the skills of some 20 artists and took over 11 years, finally opening in 1983.

Although the idea sounds rather contrived, the reproductions are beautifully done – especially when the lights are turned off and the paintings seem to spring to life in the light of a flickering torch – but, inevitably, they can't quite match the thrill of seeing the original paintings.

From April to October, tickets are sold *only* in Montignac at the ticket office, next to the tourist office (p588). There are several guided tours every hour, including several in English.

Le Thot
ANIMAL PARK

(☑05 53 50 70 44; www.semitour.com; adult/child €7/4.50, joint ticket with Lascaux €12.50/8.50; ☺10am-7pm Jul & Aug, 10am-6pm Apr-Jun & Sep-early Nov, 10am-12.30pm & 2-5.30pm early Nov-Dec, Feb & Mar) In an effort to bring the prehistoric age to life, Le Thot, 7km southwest of Montignac, places displays about Cro-Magnon life and art alongside real-life animals they depicted, including reindeer, stags, horses, ibex and European bison (plus replicas of now-extinct species like mammoths). Perhaps most interesting, though, are the displays showing the recreation of the paintings at Lascaux II.

Château de Losse
CASTLE

(www.chateaudelosse.com; adult/child €7.50/6; ☺noon-6pm May-Sep) A 15th-century moat and battlements surround this grandly furnished château, 5km southwest of Montignac. Allow time for a fragrant stroll in its ornate gardens.

🛌 Sleeping & Eating

Hostellerie La Roseraie HOTEL €€
(☑05 53 50 53 92; www.laroseraie-hotel.com; 11 place des Armes; d €85-185; ☺Apr-Oct; ☺☒) The name's the giveaway: this mansion in Montignac boasts its own gorgeous rose garden, set around box-edged grounds and a palm-tinged pool. Rococo rooms certainly aren't cutting edge, but they're lovely if you like rosy pinks, floral patterns and garden views. Truffles, chestnuts, pork and guinea

fowl find their way on to the seasonal menu in the restaurant, and on warm summer nights the canopy-shaded terrace is an utter delight.

Hotel Le Lascaux HOTEL €€
(☑05 53 51 82 81; http://hotel-lascaux.jimdo.com; 109 av Jean-Jaurès; d €62-92; ☎) Despite the old-timey candystripe awnings, rooms at this family-owned hotel are bang up to date, with cool colour schemes, distressed wood furniture and sparkling bathrooms. The superior rooms have more space, and some overlook the shady back garden. Breakfast is served on a teeny patio on sunny days.

Hôtel de la Grotte HOTEL €
(☑05 53 51 80 48; www.hoteldelagrotte.fr; place Tourny; d €62-66, restaurant menus €12.50-32; ☎) Montignac's former post-house is a sweet place to stay, as long as you don't mind frilly bedspreads and flowery wallpaper. Some rooms feel poky (especially the attic ones, huddled in around the roof beams), but they're reasonably priced and quite comfortable. The restaurant overlooks a pleasant back garden, and the hotel has bikes for hire.

❶ Information
Tourist office (☑05 53 51 82 60; www .tourisme-lascaux.com; place Bertrand de Born; ☺9.30am-12.30pm & 2-6pm Mon-Sat) Around 200m west of place Tourny, next to the 14th-century Église St-Georges le Prieuré.

❶ Getting There & Away
Montignac is 25km northeast of Les Eyzies on the D706, but the buses are inconveniently geared around school times, so you'll need your own car.

Dordogne Valley

To the south of Sarlat, flat meadows and green woods roll out along the meandering banks of the Dordogne, one of France's most iconic and idyllic rivers. In centuries gone by, the valley marked an important frontier during the Hundred Years War, and the hilltops are studded with defensive châteaux, as well as the heavily fortified towns known as *bastides*. These days it's a picture of French tranquillity, perfect country to explore by bike or, better still, by paddle.

DOMME
POP 1037

Commanding an unparalleled view across the surrounding countryside from a dizzying outcrop above the Dordogne, Domme

CAVE OF FORGOTTEN DREAMS

The Vézère Valley might be home to France's best-known prehistoric paintings, but there are many more *grottes ornées* (decorated caves) dotted all over France – particularly around the Pyrenees and the Ardèche.

Many of these are off-limits in order to preserve the paintings, but you don't always have to visit in person to appreciate them. In his 2010 3D documentary *Cave of Forgotten Dreams* (www.caveofforgottendreams.co.uk), the maverick director Werner Herzog managed to gain access to one of the Ardèche's most amazing caves at Chauvet Pont d'Arc, which was discovered in 1994 but has never been open to the public. Containing several hundred paintings of many different animal species, it's considered to be of similar archaeological importance to the ones at Grotte de Lascaux (p587).

As at Lascaux, plans have even been mooted to create another facsimile cave nearby to allow people to experience the paintings in person.

is one of several of France's official *plus beaux villages* in this area. It's also one of the area's best preserved *bastides*, retaining most of its 13th-century ramparts and three original gateways.

Approached via a tortuous switchback road from the valley below, it's the perfect defensive stronghold – a fact not lost on Philippe III of France, who founded the town in 1281 as a bastion against the English. The town's imposing clifftop position is best appreciated from the esplanade du Belvédère and the adjacent promenade de la Barre, which both offer panoramic views across the valley.

◉ Sights

Grottes Naturelles CAVE
(adult/child incl museum €8/5.50; ⊙hourly tours 10am-6pm Apr-Oct) Honeycombing the stone underneath the village is a series of large caves decorated with ornate stalactites and stalagmites. A lift whisks you back up at the end of the 45-minute tour. Tickets are available from the tourist office, opposite the entrance to the caves.

Musée d'Arts et Traditions Populaires HISTORY MUSEUM
(admission included in Grottes Naturelles ticket; ⊙10.30am-12.30pm & 2.30-6pm Apr-Sep) Across the square from the tourist office, artefacts here include clothing, toys and tools, mainly from the 19th century.

⊨ Sleeping & Eating

La Guérinière B&B €€
(☑05 53 29 91 97; www.la-gueriniere-dordogne. com; Cénac et St-Julien; d €80-95; 🗑🏊) Surrounded by its own 6-hectare grounds complete with a tennis court, this family-friendly

B&B's rooms are all named after flowers: our faves are Mimosa, with its sloping roof and chinoiserie wardrobe, and the supersize Blue room. Book ahead for *tables d'hôte* (€25 including wine), using mostly organic produce. It's about 5km south of Domme along the D46.

L'Esplanade HOTEL €€
(☑05 53 28 31 41; www.esplanade-perigord.com; rue du Pont-Carral; d €120-160, restaurant menus €35-70; 🗑🏊) Teetering on the edge of the village ramparts, this family-owned hotel has two main selling points: a top-notch country restaurant and truly mind-boggling valley views. Rooms are frilly and floral, decorated in pastel shades and upholstered armchairs.

ⓘ Information

Tourist office (☑05 53 31 71 00; www.ot -domme.com; place de la Halle; ⊙10am-noon & 2-6pm)

ⓘ Getting There & Away

Domme is 18km south of Sarlat along the D46.

LA ROQUE GAGEAC & AROUND
POP 431

La Roque Gageac's jumble of amber buildings crammed into the cliff-face above the Dordogne have earned it recognition as another of France's *plus beaux villages*, with thanks due to its particular microclimate for its flourishing gardens.

It's an idyllic launch pad for a canoe trip or cruise, while a trio of the region's most famous castles are within a few minutes' drive.

◉ Sights

Fort Troglodyte FORT
(adult/child €5/2; ⊙10am-6pm) A warren of meandering lanes lead up to La Roque's dramatic fort, where a series of defensive

Vézère & Dordogne Valleys

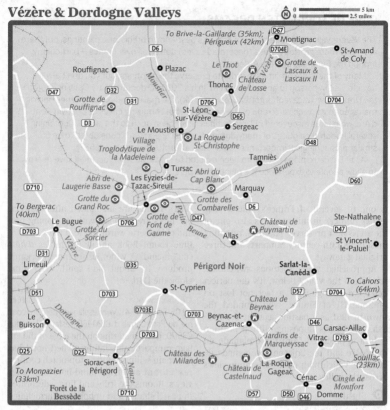

positions constructed by medieval engineers have been carved out of the overhanging cliffs.

Jardins de Marqueyssac
GARDEN

(www.marqueyssac.com; adult/child €7.40/3.70; ⊙9am-8pm Jul & Aug, 10am-6pm Apr-Jun & Sep–mid-Nov, 2-5pm mid-Nov–Jan) Horticulture fans won't want to miss these famous *jardins suspendus* (hanging gardens), overlooking the Dordogne Valley. Signposted paths lead through clipped boxed hedges and decorative topiary to the gardens' breathtaking *belvédère* (viewpoint).

Château de Castelnaud
CASTLE

(www.castelnaud.com/uk; adult/child €8.20/4.10; ⊙9am-8pm Jul & Aug, 10am-6pm Feb-Jun & Sep–mid-Nov, 2-5pm mid-Nov–Jan) The massive ramparts and metre-thick walls of this quintessential castle 4.5km southwest of La Roque are topped by crenellations and sturdy towers. From up here you can see right

across the Dordogne Valley to Castelnaud's arch-rival, the Château de Beynac.

The castle's **museum of medieval warfare** displays daggers, spiked halberds and enormous crossbows. If you fancy seeing them in action, **mock battles** are staged from mid-July to August, as well as one-hour guided **evening tours** by costumed actors – check the events diary on the website.

Château de Beynac
CASTLE

(www.beynac-en-perigord.com; Beynac-et-Cazenac; adult/child €7.50/3.20; ⊙10am-7pm Jul & Aug, 10am-5pm Jan-Jun & Sep-Oct, closed Nov & Dec) Looming ominously from atop a limestone bluff 5km northwest of La Roque, this 12th-century château's panoramic position above the Dordogne made it a key defensive position during the Hundred Years War. Apart from a brief interlude under Richard the Lionheart, Beynac remained fiercely loyal to the French monarchy, often placing it at odds with the English-controlled stronghold of nearby Castelnaud. Protected by 200m cliffs, a double wall and double moat, it presented a formidable challenge for would-be attackers, though it saw little direct action.

Highlights include the château's Romanesque keep, a grand Salle des États (State Room) and frescoed chapel, and the 16th- and 17th-century apartments built to lodge the castle barons. From the battlements, there's a vertigo-inducing view along the Dordogne to the château of Marqueyssac.

Below the castle, a steep trail leads to Beynac-et-Cazenac (population 515), another of France's *plus beaux villages*, 150m below on the river bank, where scenes from the Lasse Hallström–directed movie *Chocolat* (2000), starring Johnny Depp and Juliette Binoche, were filmed along rue de l'Ancienne Poste.

Château des Milandes
CASTLE

(www.milandes.com; Castelnaud-la-Chapelle; adult/ child €9/5.80; ⊙9.30am-7.30pm Jul & Aug, 10am- 6.30pm Apr-Jun & Sep-Oct) This 15th-century château, 8.5km southwest of La Roque, is less famous for its architecture than its former owner: the glamorous African- American dancer, singer and music-hall star Josephine Baker (1906–75), who took the Parisian cultural scene by storm in the 1920s with her raunchy performances. Her most famous stage outfit consisted of a string of pearls and a skirt of bananas, and she often liked to walk her pet cheetah, Chiquita, on a diamond-studded lead around Paris, terrifying her fellow pedestrians.

Baker purchased the castle in 1936 and lived here until 1958. She was awarded the Croix de Guerre and the Legion of Honour for her work with the French Resistance during WWII. She was later active in the US civil-rights movement and is also remembered for her 'Rainbow Tribe' – 12 children from around the world adopted as 'an experiment in brotherhood'.

The château houses a museum documenting the life of the great Ms Baker, and her famous tunes tinkle out from the speaker system as you stroll around. Ask for an English-language leaflet.

Between May and October there are 30-minute-long daily displays featuring the château's birds of prey.

🏹 Activities

Paddling along the river offers a changing panorama of soaring cliffs, castles and picturesque villages. There are several canoe operators around La Roque Gageac, including Canoë Dordogne (☑05 53 29 58 50; www .canoe-dordogne.fr; self-guided canoe & kayak trips €6-24) and Canoë Vacances (☑05 53 28 17 07; www.canoevacances.com; La Peyssière; self-guided canoeing €10-20), which offer self- guided trips of between one and five hours from various points upriver of La Roque.

La Roque's quay also serves as a launch point for short river cruises aboard a traditional gabarre (p592).

🛏 Sleeping & Eating

Accommodation options are limited, with only a handful of hotels in the area, but the tourist offices in La Roque Gageac and Beynac-et-Cazenac have lists of camp- grounds and *chambres d'hôte*.

La Belle Étoile
HOTEL €

(☑05 53 29 51 44; www.belleetoile.fr; Le Bourg; d €55-75, ste €130; ⊙Apr-Oct; 🛜) This riverside hotel has the best position in La Roque, lodged in a solid stone building with views across the water from its higher-priced rooms (cheaper ones overlook the village). The decor is rather staid, with traditional wooden furniture and cream fabrics. The restaurant (menus €26-42; ⊙closed all day Mon & afternoon Wed) is renowned for its sophisti- cated French food, and opens onto a vine- shaded terrace.

ⓘ Getting There & Away

La Roque Gageac is 15km south of Sarlat, via the D46 and D703. There's no public transport.

Monpazier

POP 539

The best-preserved *bastide* in this corner of France, Monpazier was founded in 1284 by a representative of Edward I (King of England and Duke of Aquitaine). It had a turbulent time during the Wars of Religion and the Peasant Revolts of the 16th century, but de- spite numerous assaults and campaigns, the town has survived remarkably intact.

⊙ Sights

Place des Cornières
TOWN SQUARE

From the town's three gateways, Monpa- zier's flat, grid-straight streets lead to the arcaded market square (also known as place Centrale), surrounded by a motley collec- tion of stone houses that reflect centuries of building and rebuilding. In one corner is an old lavoir once used for washing clothes.

GABARRE CRUISES

One of the best ways to explore the gorgeous scenery of the Dordogne River is aboard a *gabarre*, a flat-bottomed, wooden boat used to transport freight up and down the rivers of the Périgord and Lot Valley. *Gabarres* were a common sight in this part of France until the early 20th century, when they were eclipsed by the rise of the railway and the automobile.

From April to October, traditional *gabarres* cruise from several points along the river, including Bergerac, Beaulieu-sur-Dordogne and the quay at La Roque Gageac.

La Roque Gageac's operators include Gabarres Caminade (☎05 53 29 40 95; www.gabarrecaminade.com) and Gabarres Norbert (☎05 53 29 40 44; www.gabarres.com). Standard trips last about an hour and cost around €8.50/6 per adult/child; advance reservations are recommended. Gabarres de Beynac (☎05 53 28 51 15; www.gabarre-beynac.com; Le Port) does slightly shorter, cheaper trips departing from Beynac-et-Cazenac; kids cruise for free in the mornings.

Thursday is **market** day, as it has been since the Middle Ages.

Château de Biron   CASTLE
(www.semitour.com; adult/child €7/4.50; ⊗10am-7pm Jul & Aug, 10am-5pm Feb-Jun & Sep-Dec, closed Jan) Some 8km south of Monpazier, this much-filmed château is a glorious mishmash of styles, having been fiddled with by eight centuries of successive heirs. The castle was finally sold in the early 1900s to pay for the extravagant lifestyle of a particularly irresponsible son.

It's notable for its slate turrets and double loggia staircase, supposedly modelled on one at Versailles.

🛏 Sleeping & Eating

Hôtel de France   HOTEL €
(☎05 53 22 60 06; www.hoteldefrancemonpazier.fr; 21 rue St-Jacques; d €40-70; ⊗Mar-Oct) This honey-stoned *auberge* sits within the *bastide* walls, and parts of the building date back to the 13th century. A wooden staircase dating from the 1400s leads up to snug rooms, with musty carpets, old furniture and shuttered windows overlooking the town's rooftops. The restaurant serves simple regional food.

Hôtel Edward 1er   HOTEL €€
(☎05 53 22 44 00; www.hoteledward1er.com; 5 rue St-Pierre; d €68-134, ste €106-188, restaurant menus €30-40; ⊗dinner Thu-Tue Sep-Jun, daily Jul & Aug; 🕸🏊) Rooms in this tower-topped mansion get more luxurious the more you pay: top-of-the-line suites have a choice of jacuzzi or Turkish bath, and views of the hills. It feels slightly dated, but the owners are full of beans, and there's an excellent restaurant.

Bistrot 2   REGIONAL CUISINE €€
(☎05 53 22 60 64; www.bistrot2.fr; mains €14, lunch menus €14.75-19.75, dinner menu €23.75) Modern dining in an old-town setting, right opposite the medieval gateway. It has an attractive location, inside a stout stone building with a wisteria-covered terrace, and the food is French with an adventurous slant: pork with a cola-soy sauce, or duck in Bergerac wine and cassis.

ℹ Information

The **tourist office** (☎05 53 22 68 59; www.pays-des-bastides.com; place des Cornières; ⊗10am-12.30pm & 2.30-6pm Tue-Sun) is in the southeastern corner of the square.

ℹ Getting There & Away

Monpazier is 50km southwest of Sarlat and 50km southeast of Bergerac.

Bergerac

POP 28,638

Rich vineyards and rolling fields surround Bergerac, capital of the Périgord Pourpre and one of the largest wine-growing areas of the Aquitaine.

The town's main claim to fame is the dramatist and satirist Savinien Cyrano de Bergerac (1619–55), whose romantic exploits – and oversized nose – have inspired everyone from Molière to Steve Martin. Despite the legend (largely invented by the 19th-century playwright Edmond Rostand), Cyrano's connection with the town is tenuous at best – he's thought to have stayed here only a few nights, if at all.

Bergerac's international airport and central location between Périgueux (47km to the northeast) and Bordeaux (93km to the west) makes it a handy gateway to the region.

◉ Sights & Activities

The prettiest parts of Bergerac's old town are place de la Mirpe, with its tree-shaded square and timber houses, and place Pelissière, where a jaunty statue of Cyrano de Bergerac looks up at the nearby church. The town's main museums are dedicated to Bergerac's twin vices: wine and tobacco.

Musée du Vin et de la Batellerie
WINE MUSEUM

(place de la Mirpe; admission €3; ⏰10am-noon & 2-5.30pm Tue-Fri, 10am-noon Sat, 2.30-6.30pm Sun) Wonderfully musty displays of vintage winemaking equipment and scale models of local river boats.

Musée d'Anthropologie du Tabac
TOBACCO MUSEUM

(10 rue de l'Ancien Port; adult/child €4/free; ⏰10am-noon & 2-6pm Tue-Fri, 10am & 2-5pm Sat, 2.30-6.30pm Sun) Inside the 17th-century Maison Peyrarède, the displays span 3000 years of history and include a collection of ornate pipes.

FREE Maison des Vins
WINE TASTING

(www.vins-bergerac.fr; ⏰10am-12.30pm & 2-7pm) Within the walls of the Cloître des Récollets, a former monastery, this wine museum is by far and away the best place to sample some of the area's famous vintages or get the lowdown on touring the local vineyards.

Gabarres de Bergerac
BOAT TRIPS

(☎05 53 24 58 80; www.gabarres.fr; quai Salvette; adult/child €8/5; ⏰Easter-Oct) Offers atmospheric 50-minute cruises from the Vieux Port.

⌂ Sleeping & Eating

Bergerac's town-centre hotels are a bit bland, so it's worth travelling a bit further afield.

TOP CHOICE Château les Merles
BOUTIQUE HOTEL €€€

(☎05 53 63 13 42; www.lesmerles.com; d €150-200, ste €155-240, apt €225-340; @🅿🏊) Behind its 19th-century neoclassical facade, this boutique château 15km east of Bergerac is a study in modish minimalism. Monochrome colour schemes including black-and-white sofas, slate-grey throws and artfully chosen antiques run throughout the rooms, most of which would look more at home in Paris than deep in the Dordogne. It's got wit, style and sexiness in spades: tripod floor lamps, gilt-framed mirrors and objets d'art, along with a nine-hole golf course and an utterly ravishing fusion restaurant (five-/eight-course menus cost €41/49). All in all, a royal retreat.

Château Les Farcies du Pech'
B&B €€

(☎06 30 19 53 20; www.vignoblesdubard.com; Hameau de Pécharmant; d €110; ⏰mid-Mar–mid-Nov) Part of a conglomerate of four renowned wineries, this beautiful château-vineyard is definitely the choice for oenophiles. All five rooms scream rustic chic, with original stonework and hardwoods for vintage character. The owner Marie serves a lovely home-cooked French brekkie in the dining room, and will gladly arrange tours of the vineyards.

Le Colombier de Cyrano et Roxane
B&B €€

(☎05 53 57 96 70; www.samedimidi.com; 17 rue du Grand Moulin; d €64-83; 🅿) One of several sweet *chambres d'hôte* in Bergerac's old town around place de la Mirpe, this 16th-century blue-shuttered stone building has three colourful rooms and a flower-filled terrace where you can doze off in the hammock.

Hotel du Commerce
HOTEL €

(☎05 53 27 30 50; www.hotel-du-commerce24.fr; 36 place Gambetta; d €56-73; 🅿🏊) The best of a rather dull bunch of hotels on place Gambetta. Some of the functional rooms have a view over the tree-lined square.

La Ferme de Biorne
REGIONAL CUISINE €€

(☎05 53 57 67 26; www.biorne.com; menus €19-23; ⏰Tue-Sun Apr-Oct by reservation) This rural *ferme auberge* (farm restaurant), 12km northwest of Bergerac, raises its own birds for the restaurant table, including goose, quail, duck and foie gras. Cosy *gîtes* (€300 to €980 for four people) are also available in coverted outbuildings.

L'Imparfait
REGIONAL CUISINE €€

(☎05 53 57 47 92; www.imparfait.com; 6-10 rue des Fontaines; menus €26-32; ⏰lunch & dinner daily) Chef Hervé Battiston has made this sweet little restaurant a real local's favourite, thanks to artful French food served up in a pretty 12th-century cloister. It's popular, so it's well worth reserving ahead.

ℹ️ Information

Tourist office (☎05 53 57 03 11; www.bergerac
-tourisme.com; 97 rue Neuve d'Argenson;
⏰9.30am-1pm & 2-7pm Mon-Sat; 🛜)

ℹ️ Getting There & Away

AIR Bergerac's **airport** (www.bergerac
.aeroport.fr), 4km southeast of town, is served
by several budget carriers including Flybe and
Ryanair, as well as Air France.

Destinations include Paris Orly, Bristol, Brussels Charleroi, Edinburgh, London Stansted, London Gatwick, East Midlands, Liverpool, Birmingham, Exeter, Leeds Bradford, Southampton and Rotterdam.

TRAIN Bergerac is on the regional line between Bordeaux (€16, 1½ hours, hourly) and Sarlat (€12, 1½ hours, every two hours). For other destinations change at Le Buisson or Libourne.

THE LOT

Southeast of the Dordogne stretches the Lot Valley, a picturesque landscape of limestone cliffs, hilltop towns and canyons carved out by the serpentine River Lot. Formerly the northern section of the old province of Quercy, the valley now stretches along the southern section of the modern Lot *département*.

The valley's main town is Cahors, another area that's celebrated for its vineyards.

Cahors

POP 21,128

In a U-shape *boucle* (curve) in the River Lot, Cahors has the air of a sunbaked Mediterranean town – a reminder that Languedoc lies just to the south. Pastel-coloured buildings line the shady squares of the old medieval quarter, which is criss-crossed by a labyrinth of alleyways and cul-de-sacs, and bordered by the medieval quays.

Slicing through the centre of Cahors, bd Léon Gambetta – named after the French statesman who was born in Cahors in 1838 – neatly divides Vieux Cahors (old Cahors) to the east and the new city to the west.

The city is ringed on three sides by the quays, which once harboured its river-going traffic but are now mostly used by cyclists, rollerbladers and afternoon strollers.

👁️ Sights & Activities

In the Middle Ages, Cahors was a prosperous commercial centre, and the old city is densely packed with timber-fronted houses and galleried mansions built by the city's medieval merchants. Many are marked on the *Itinéraires à Travers la Ville* leaflet from the tourist office. Cahors has just a couple of small museums.

Pont Valentré   BRIDGE

The six-span Pont Valentré, on the western side of the city, south of the train station, is one of France's most iconic medieval bridges, built as part of the town's defences in the 14th century. The parapets projecting from two of its three tall towers were designed to allow defenders to drop missiles on attackers below. On the bank opposite the bridge, numerous Roman coins have been found at the natural spring known as the Fontaine des Chartreux – dedicated to the city's Gallo-Roman goddess Divona – which still supplies the city's drinking water.

WORTH A TRIP

GROTTE DU PECH MERLE

Discovered in 1922, the 1200m-long Grotte du Pech Merle (☎05 65 31 27 05; www
.pechmerle.com; adult/child €9/5; ⏰9.30-noon & 1.30-5pm Apr-Oct) is perched high on the hills above the riverside town of Les Cabrerets, 30km northeast of Cahors.

One of the few decorated caves to be discovered around the Lot Valley, Pech Merle makes a fascinating comparison to those in the Vézère, with several wonderful galleries of mammoths, goats and bison, as well as many haunting hand tracings, creating by artists blowing paint over their splayed hands. The cave's most famous features are a panel featuring two beautiful dappled horses, similar to the pot-bellied 'Chinese horses' on display at Lascaux (p587), as well as a series of beautifully preserved adolescent footprints, clearly imprinted into the muddy clay floor.

Entry is by guided tour (usually in French, but some have an English translation), which includes admission to the museum and a 20-minute film (in French and English). Reserve well ahead by phone if you're visiting in peak season as visitor numbers are limited to 700 per day.

Cathédrale St-Étienne   CATHEDRAL

(⊙cloister Jun-Sep) Similar in style to the Cathédrale St-Front in Périgueux, the airy nave of Cahors' Romanesque cathedral, consecrated in 1119, is topped by two cupolas (at 18m wide, the largest in France). Some of the frescos are 14th century, but the side chapels and carvings in the cloître (Cloister; Cathédrale St-Étienne; ⊙Jun-Sep) (cloister) mainly date from the Flamboyant Gothic period in the 16th century. On the cathedral's north façade is a carved tympanum depicting Christ surrounded by fluttering angels and pious saints.

Tour du Pape Jean XXII   ARCHITECTURE

(3 bd Léon Gambetta) At the top of the old city, the Tour du Pape Jean XXII (closed to the public) is the town's tallest building at 34m high. It was originally part of a 14th-century mansion belonging to Jacques Duèse (later Pope John XXII), who constructed the Pont Valentré and founded Cahors' university.

Mechanical Clock   CLOCK

(place St-Urcisse) Near the Cathédrale St-Étienne, the 1997-installed clock looks like something out of Tim Burton's sketchbook.

Musée Henri Martin   MUSEUM

(Musée Municipal; www.mairie-cahors.fr/musee; 792 rue Émile Zola; adult/child €3/1.50; ⊙11am-6pm Mon & Wed-Sat, 2-6pm Sun) Displays include works by the Cahors-born pointillist painter Henri Martin (1893–1972).

FREE Musée de la Résistance   MUSEUM

(place Général de Gaulle; ⊙2-6pm) Little museum exploring the city's experiences during WWII.

🛏 Sleeping

TOP CHOICE Hôtel Jean XXII   HOTEL €

(☏05 65 35 07 66; www.hotel-jeanxxii.com; 2 rue Edmond-Albé; s €51, d €62-69, tr €76; 🛜) Huddled next to the Tour du Pape Jean XXII, this excellent little hotel mixes original stone, greenery and well-worn wood with a dash of metropolitan minimalism. Smart rooms have muted colours, and there's a reading area on the 1st floor where you can unwind in leather armchairs.

Grand Hôtel Terminus   HOTEL €€

(☏05 65 53 32 00; www.balandre.com; 5 av Charles de Freycinet; d €77-100, ste €130-160; ❄🛜) Built c 1920, Cahors' original railway station hotel evokes an air of faded grandeur. Most of the rooms are large and quite comfortable, with hefty radiators, roll-top baths and king-size beds, but the decor's looking tired. Its chandelier-lit restaurant, Le Balandre (p595), serves classic French food and runs cooking courses.

Auberge de Jeunesse   HOSTEL €

(☏05 65 35 64 71; www.fuaj.org/cahors; 222 rue Joachim Murat; dm €14.70; ⊙reception 10am-1pm & 2-7pm; 🛜) In an old convent, Cahors' hostel is basic but friendly, with 50 beds in four- to 10-bed dorms and a rambling garden.

🍴 Eating

Le Bergougnoux   TRADITIONAL FRENCH €

(☏05 65 35 62 92; 77 rue Bergougnoux; lunch/dinner menus €12/16; ⊙lunch & dinner daily) Country cuisine *de grande-mère* is the speciality of this homely little family-owned eatery, secreted away along a narrow and rather insalubrious backstreet in the old town. With its scruffy tables, an old slate floor and no-frills food, it's not going to win any Michelin stars, but for proper *pot au feu* (hotpot) or *suprême de poulet* (creamy chicken), you won't find anywhere better in town.

Le Marché   FUSION €€

(☏05 65 35 27 27; www.restaurantlemarche.com; 27 place Jean-Jacques Chapou; lunch menus €16-19, dinner menus €23-40; ⊙Tue-Sat) Cahors' most avant-garde cuisine is served at this surprisingly urbane bistro. Puce-and-cream armchairs and razor-edge wood set the designer tone, and the menu dabbles in French-meets-fusion flavours, such as satay tuna, and roast beef in soy marinade.

Le Balandre   GASTRONOMIC €€€

(☏05 65 53 32 00; www.balandre.com; 5 av Charles de Freycinet; lunch menus €18-31, dinner menus €36-75, 6hr cooking class €95; ⊙lunch Tue-Sat, dinner daily) With chandeliers, sparkling glasses and napkins you could cut your finger on, the gourmet restaurant of Grand Hotel Terminus (p595) continues to command a devoted following, especially for its foie gras and *confit de canard*. Ask about its program of cooking courses with chef Gilles Marre.

Le Lamparo   ITALIAN €€

(☏05 65 35 25 93; www.lelamparo.com; 76 rue Georges Clemenceau; mains €12-18; ⊙Mon-Sat; 🖉🖍) Generic wood-fired pizzas, pastas and French staples served in a Med-style dining room.

Cahors

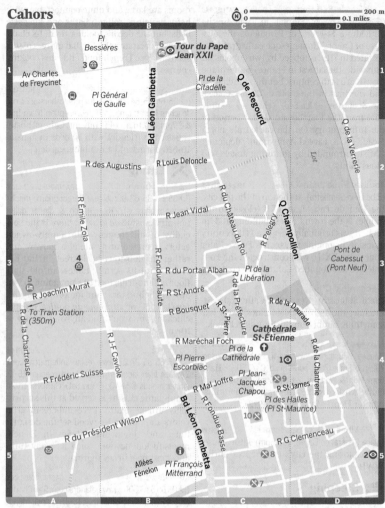

Marché Couvert FOOD MARKET €

(place des Halles) The city's main covered market is usually just referred to as Les Halles. There's an open-air market on Wednesday and Saturday mornings around the covered market and on place Jean-Jacques Chapou. Nearby, food shops can be found around place des Halles and along rue de la Préfecture.

☆ Entertainment

Check with the tourist office what's on in Cahors.

Les Docks CULTURAL CENTRE

(☎05 65 22 36 38; 430 allées des Soupirs; 🕿) Les Docks is a former warehouse turned cultural centre near the Pont Valentré, with regular gigs, theatre, films and a multimedia cafe.

❶ Information

Comité Départemental du Tourisme (☎05 65 35 07 09; www.tourisme-lot.com; 1st fl, 107 quai Eugène Cavaignac; ⊙8am-12.30pm & 1.30-5.30pm) Information on the Lot *département*.

Tourist office (☎05 65 53 20 65; www.tourisme-cahors.com; place François Mitterrand; ⊙9.30am-6.30pm Mon-Sat)

Cahors

❶ Getting There & Away

BUS The tourist office has a booklet of bus timetables, *Les Bus du Lot* (www.lot.fr), but most routes are geared around school-term times, making buses of limited use. Services between Cahors and Figeac (1½ hours, four to five daily) stop at Tour-de-Faure, the nearest access to St-Cirq Lapopie.

CAR Major car-hire companies are located at the train station. Parking is free along the river and at place Général de Gaulle.

TRAIN Cahors is on the main line to Paris Gare d'Austerlitz (€71 to €110.40, five hours, eight to 10 daily), Brive-la-Gaillarde (€19 to €23.40, 1¼ hours), Limoges (€28.90 to €32, 2¼ hours) and Souillac (€13.50, 45 minutes).

From Souillac there are SNCF buses to Sarlat (€2, 40 minutes, two daily).

East of Cahors

The narrow, corkscrew D662 (signposted 'Vallée du Lot') tracks the banks of the River Lot eastwards from Cahors towards Figeac. It's a wonderfully scenic, if hair-raising, drive, with appealing stops and detours along the way. Figeac can also be reached directly from Cahors by the easier D653.

ST-CIRQ LAPOPIE
POP 223

Teetering at the crest of a sheer cliff high above the River Lot, minuscule St-Cirq Lapopie's terracotta-roofed houses and ramshackle streets tumble down the steep hillside, affording incredible valley views.

It's one of the most magical settings in the Lot, but be warned: if it's peace and tranquillity you're looking for, you won't find it in high summer.

⊙ Sights

St Cirq essentially consists of one long main street that leads up to the early 16th-century **Gothic church** and a ruined **château**, where you'll be rewarded with a jaw-dropping panorama across the Lot Valley. Many of the village's houses have been converted into artists studios producing pottery, craftwork and jewellery.

Maison de la Fourdonne   HISTORY MUSEUM
(☏05 65 31 21 51; www.maisondelafourdonne .com; ⊙2.30-7pm) This small town museum and gallery houses a collection of old postcards, pots and archaeological artefacts. It also organises guided visits exploring the village's history and heritage (generally in French).

Musée Rignault   ART MUSEUM
(admission €1.50; ⊙10am-12.30pm & 2.30-6pm Wed-Mon) Houses an eclectic collection of French furniture and African and Chinese art and has a delightful garden.

🍴 Sleeping & Eating

TOP CHOICE **Hôtel Le Saint Cirq**   HOTEL **€€**
(☏05 65 30 30 30; www.hotel-lesaintcirq.com; Tour de Faure; d €68-118, ste €140-160) This luxurious hotel in nearby Tour de Faure boasts one of the best views of St Cirq's hilltop profile. The traditional rooms are lovely, with terracotta-tiled floors and French windows onto the garden, but it's the 'Seigneurale' rooms that really push the decorative boat out, sunken baths, slate bathrooms and all. For a real spoil, ask for Lapopie, with its private lounge and mezzanine bedroom. It's about 1km east of St-Cirq.

Auberge de Sombral   HOTEL **€**
(☏05 65 31 26 08; www.lesombral.com; r €52-80, lunch menus €15-22, dinner menus €28.50; ⊙restaurant lunch daily, dinner Fri & Sat; 🛜) If you want to stay in the village proper, this treacle-stoned house has seven cosy doubles and a titchy attic room crammed in around its narrow corridors. Despite the heritage building, the decor is fairly modern, and the restaurant offers thoughtful versions of Quercy cuisine, especially lamb and trout. Best of all, you'll have the village practically to yourself after dark.

LIMOUSIN, THE DORDOGNE & THE LOT EAST OF CAHORS

La Plage
CAMPGROUND €

(☑05 65 30 29 51; www.campingplage.com; sites for tent & 1 person €10-14; ☺Apr–mid-Oct; 🛜) Riverside campground on the left bank of the Lot near a small swimming beach, with a slew of amenities including canoe and kayak rental.

La Truffière
CAMPGROUND €

(☑05 65 30 20 22; http://camping-truffiere.com; sites €6-8, adult €5.50, child €2-3.50; ▣) Along the D42, 2.5km from St-Cirq in leafy grounds. There's a heated paddling pool, or you can swim in the river nearby.

Le Gourmet Quercynois
REGIONAL CUISINE €€

(☑05 65 31 21 20; www.restaurant-legourmetquercynois.com; rue de la Peyrolerie; ☺lunch & dinner daily) The village's fanciest table offers a menu of biblical proportions, ranging from *nougat de porc* to country *cassoulet* (stew). The tables are packed in tight in the chimney-warmed dining room, but you can escape to the little patio to catch the evening rays setting over town. The in-house deli sells local spoils, including *cèpe* (porcini) mushrooms, gingerbread and chestnut cake.

La Tonnelle
BISTRO €€

(www.brasserie-latonnelle.com; rue de la Peyrolerie; mains €11.80-26.80; ☺lunch & dinner Apr-Oct) Just across the way, Le Gourmet Quercynois' sister bistro, La Tonnelle, specialises in simple, generous *assiettes* (platters) of cheese, meats and salads, served under a clematis-covered pergola.

❶ Information

The **tourist office** (☑05 65 31 29 06; www.saint-cirqlapopie.com; ☺10am-7pm) is in the village hall.

❶ Getting There & Away

St-Cirq is 25km east of Cahors and 44km southwest of Figeac.

BUS Buses between Cahors (45 minutes) and Figeac (one hour, four to five daily) stop at Tour-de-Faure; from here, it's a long 3km uphill walk to the village.

CAR The best idea is to leave the car at the large, free car park at the bottom of the village, and follow the pretty (if steep) trail up from there. There are two other car parks slightly closer to the village, but they're pricey and usually packed in high season.

FIGEAC
POP 10,736

The riverside town of Figeac, 70km northeast of Cahors, has a rough-and-ready charm that comes as a refreshing change after many of the prettified towns in these parts. Traffic buzzes along the river boulevards and the old town has an appealingly lived-in feel, with shady streets lined with ramshackle medieval and Renaissance houses, many with open-air galleries on the top floor (once used for drying leather). Founded by Benedictine monks, the town was later an important medieval trading post and pilgrims' stopover.

◉ Sights

The historic centre of Figeac is place Vival, where the tourist office occupies the ground floor of an arcaded 13th-century building, part of Figeac's lost abbey. Pick up the leaflet *Les Clefs de la Ville* (€0.30) for a guide to the town's medieval and Renaissance architecture. Rue de Balène and rue Caviale have the best examples of 14th- and 15th-century houses, many with wooden galleries, timber frames and original stone carvings, while rue de Colomb has several fine *hôtels particuliers* dating from the Renaissance.

Musée du Vieux Figeac
HISTORY MUSEUM

(adult/child €2/1; ☺10am-12.30pm & 2.30-6pm Mon-Sat, 10am-12.30pm Sun Sep-Jun) Upstairs from the tourist office, the town's historical museum has a collection of antique clocks, coins, fossils and minerals, and a propeller blade made by a local aerospace firm.

Musée Champollion
WRITING MUSEUM

(www.musee-champollion.fr; place Champollion; adult/child €5/2.50; ☺10.30am-12.30pm & 2-6pm daily Jul & Aug, 10.30am-12.30pm & 2-6pm Wed-Mon Apr-Jun & Sep, 2-6pm Wed-Mon Oct-Mar) The museum is named after the Figeac-born Egyptologist and linguist Jean-François Champollion (1790–1832), whose efforts in deciphering the Rosetta Stone provided the key for cracking Egyptian hieroglyphics. The lavishly restored mansion where he was born is now devoted to the history of writing, with exhibits ranging from illustrated medieval manuscripts to Chinese writing tools.

Behind the museum on place des Écritures is a huge replica of the Rosetta tablets, created by artist Joseph Kosuth in 1990.

🛏 Sleeping & Eating

Figeac's lively Saturday-morning market takes place under the 19th-century cast-iron arcade on place Carnot, with stalls also filling place Champollion and place Vival.

TOP CHOICE **Hôtel La Grézalide** HOTEL €€
(☏05 65 11 20 40; www.grezalide.com; Grèzes; d
€77-157, tr €117-137, f €137-177; �wifi☲) You'll need
a car to reach this beautifully rural retreat,
21km west of Figeac in the village of Grèzes,
but it's definitely worth the drive. It's in a
17th-century house set around its own courtyard garden and heated pool. Rooms make
maximum use of the house's architecture,
with solid stone and original floorboards,
and the public rooms are stuffed with pictures and sculptures (the owners are both
art aficionados).

Hostellerie de l'Europe HOTEL €
(☏05 65 34 10 16; www.hotel-europe-figeac.com;
51 allée Victor Hugo; r €59-75, restaurant menus
€14.50-34; ☲restaurant lunch Sun-Thu, dinner Sat-
Thu; ☀wifi☲) Behind the shuttered façade,
up-to-date rooms at this efficient Inter-Hotel
come with spacious bathrooms, although
most are short on character. Its trump
card is gourmet **restaurant** La Table de
Marinette – Figeac's finest for old-fashioned
Quercynois dishes – which offers excellent
half-board deals (€54 to €79 per person).
The hotel is just across the river from the
old town on one of the main exit roads.

Hôtel-Café Champollion HOTEL €
(☏05 65 34 04 37; hotelchampollion@orange.fr;
3 place Champollion; d €45-53; ☎) Right in the
heart of the old town, this modern hotel sits
above a cool and lively cafe. Contemporary
rooms are uncluttered and feature flat-
screen TVs, although some suffer from late-
night noise leakage.

Hôtel des Bains HOTEL €
(☏05 65 34 10 89; www.hoteldesbains.fr; 1 rue Grif-
foul; d €47-52; ☀☎) Basic waterfront hotel,
with 19 rooms in an old public bathhouse.
The best rooms have balconies overlooking
the river.

ⓘ Information
Post office (8 av Fernand Pezet)
Tourist office (☏05 65 34 06 25; www
.tourisme-figeac.com; place Vival; ☲10am-
12.30pm & 2.30-6pm Mon-Sat, 10am-12.30pm
Sun Jun-Sep)

ⓘ Getting There & Away
BUS SNCF buses run west to Cahors (€12.50,
1½ hours, four to five daily) via Tour-de-Faure.

TRAIN Trains run north to Brive-la-Gaillarde
(€13.60, 1¼ hours, six daily) and south to Villefranche de Rouergue (€7, 35 minutes, six to

eight daily) and Najac (€9.50, 50 minutes, six to
eight daily).

VILLEFRANCHE DE ROUERGUE
POP 12,673
Villefranche's origins as a *bastide* are barely
recognisable beneath the main roads, refurbished buildings and busy shopping
streets. But, despite first impressions, it
warrants a brief stop. At the centre of the
timber-framed old town is the arcaded
place Notre Dame – a typical example of a
bastide square – which still hosts the lively
Thursday-morning market. Nearby is the
square-pillared 15th-century Collégiale
Notre Dame, with its never-completed bell
tower and choir stalls, ornamented with a
menagerie of comical and cheeky figures.

Musée Urbain Cabrol (☏05 65 45 44 37;
place de la Fontaine; admission free; ☲10am-noon &
2-6.30pm Tue-Sat Jul & Aug, 2-6pm Tue-Sat Apr-Jun
& Sep), a few blocks to the southwest, has an
eclectic collection of religious art, local folk
art and 19th-century medical equipment.
The fountain out the front, decorated with
14th-century carvings, gushes from a natural spring.

The tourist office (☏05 65 45 13 18; www
.villefranche.com; promenade du Guiraudet; ☲9am-
noon & 2-6pm Mon-Fri, 9am-noon Sat) is next to
the town hall.

Trains travel regularly to Figeac (€7, 35
minutes, every two hours) and Najac (€3.60,
15 minutes, four to six daily).

NAJAC
POP 774
If you were searching for a film set for
Camelot, you've found it. Clustered on a
rocky spur high above the River Aveyron,
Najac is best known for its soaring, turreted
castle, well worth visiting for its medieval
architecture and the superb views from the
central keep.

◉ Sights
Central Place du Faubourg is a beguiling square surrounded by a hotchpotch of
timber-framed houses, some from the 13th
century. Beyond the Forteresse Royale de
Najac is the austere Gothic Église St-Jean,
constructed and financed by local villagers
on the orders of the Inquisition as punishment for their heretical tendencies.

Forteresse Royale de Najac CASTLE
(adult/child €4.50/3; ☲10.30am-7pm Jul & Aug,
10.30am-1.30pm & 3-5pm Mar-Jun & Sep-Nov) On
a hilltop above a hairpin bend in the River

Aveyron, the town's castle looks as if it's fallen from the pages of a fairy tale: slender towers and fluttering flags rise from the crenellated ramparts, surrounded on every side by dizzying *falaises* (cliffs) dropping to the valley floor below.

A masterpiece of medieval military planning, and practically unassailable thanks to its position, Najac was a key stronghold during the Middle Ages, and was hotly contested by everyone from English warlords to the powerful counts of Toulouse. Its architecture is beautifully preserved, and the view from the central keep is unsurprisingly superb.

The castle is reached via a steep 1.2km-long cobbled street from place du Faubour.

🛏 Sleeping & Eating

TOP CHOICE **Oustal del Barry** HOTEL €

(📞05 65 29 74 32; www.oustaldelbarry.com; place du Faubourg; s €49, d €59-77, restaurant lunch menus €19, dinner menus €25-43.50; ❄) The best place to stay in town is this wonderfully worn and rustic *auberge*, with haphazard rooms filled with trinkets and solid furniture to match its venerable timber-framed façade. Definitely get a room with a balcony if you can. Even if you're not staying here, be sure to stop by its country restaurant, renowned for miles around for its traditional southwest cuisine, which you can master yourself during a five-day cooking course (€400 including half-board).

La Salamandre REGIONAL CUISINE €€

(📞05 65 29 74 09; rue du Barriou; menus €18-36) Simple but charming, this little restaurant is a treat for its local dishes and wonderful panoramic terrace overlooking the castle.

ℹ Information

Najac's tiny **tourist office** (📞05 65 29 72 05; www.tourisme-najac.com; 25 place du Faubourg; ⏰9.30am-12.30pm & 2.30-6pm Mon-Sat, 10am-1pm Sun) is on the southern side of the main square.

ℹ Getting There & Away

Trains link Najac with Figeac (€9.50, 50 minutes, two to four daily).

West of Cahors

Downstream from Cahors, the lower River Lot twists its way through the rich vineyards of the Cahors Appellation d'Origine Contrôlée (AOC) region, passing the dams at Luzech, the medieval section of which sits at the base of a donjon, and Castelfranc, with a dramatic suspension bridge.

Sights in this region are few and far between – this is working land first and foremost, and the landscape becomes increasingly industrial the further west you travel from Puy l'Évêque. Along the river's northern bank, the D9 affords superb views of the vines and the river's many twists and turns.

About 15km west of Puy l'Évêque, the imposing feudal Château de Bonaguil (www .bonaguil.org; adult/child €7/4; ⏰10am-7pm Jul & Aug, 10am-12.30pm & 2-5.30pm Mar-Jun & Sep-Oct) is a fine example of late-15th-century military architecture, incorporating towers, bastions, loopholes, machicolations and crenellations.

North of Cahors

Some of the Lot's most striking sights lie north of Cahors near Limousin and the Dordogne, including the celebrated pilgrimage site of Rocamadour. Public transport in this area is pretty much nonexistent, so you'll need your own wheels to get around.

ROCAMADOUR
POP 653

The dramatic silhouette of Rocamadour's steeples and pale stone houses clamped to a vertical cliffside beneath the ramparts of a 14th-century château resembles something out of *The Da Vinci Code*. Rocamadour's miraculous Vierge Noire (Black Madonna) drew a steady stream of pilgrims and worshippers from across Europe in the Middle Ages, and tourist traffic is still going strong several centuries on.

Up top, start by exploring the ramparts of Rocamadour's château (admission €2; ⏰8am-9pm). From here, either follow the switchback staircase down to the old town (which the pious once climbed on their knees) or take the ascenseur incliné (cable car; one-way/return €2.50/4; ⏰9am-7pm) halfway down the cliff to the Sanctuaires, a series of 12th-to 14th-century chapels containing the city's most prized relics, including the spooky Vierge Noire in the Chapelle Notre Dame.

More steps and an ascenseur (elevator; one-way/return €2/3; ⏰9am-9pm) lead from the Sanctuaires further down to the Cité (old city), where you'll find the Cité tourist office (⏰10.30am-12.30pm & 1.30-6pm). Its commercial thoroughfare, the Grande Rue, is crammed (just as in the pilgrims' day) with souvenir shops and touristy restaurants.

One of the city's original medieval gateways can be seen at the street's far end.

The main tourist office (☎05 65 33 22 00; www.rocamadour.com; ◷10am-12.30pm & 2-6pm Mon-Sat, 1.30-6pm Sun) is on the plateau above the cliff 1.5km from the Cité, in the largely modern and touristy suburb of L'Hospitalet. This area is of limited interest, although kids might enjoy the stalactites and stalagmites of the Grotte des Merveilles (www.grotte-des-merveilles.com; adult/child €6.50/4; ◷10am-noon & 2-6pm).

You'd be better off giving the overpriced hotels and restaurants around Rocamadour a wide berth – prices for even the dingiest room skyrocket in summer, and most hotels are booked out well in advance by tour-bus groups.

Rocamadour is 59km north of Cahors and 51km east of Sarlat; there's parking in L'Hospitalet and by the château.

GOUFFRE DE PADIRAC

Discovered in 1889, the spectacular Gouffre de Padirac (☎05 65 33 64 56; www.gouffre-de-padirac.com; adult/child €9.80/6.80; ◷10am-7pm Apr-Nov) features some of France's spangliest underground caverns. The cave's navigable river, 103m below ground level, is reached through a 75m-deep, 33m-wide chasm. Boat pilots ferry visitors along 1km of the subterranean waterway, visiting a series of glorious floodlit caverns en route, including the soaring Salle de Grand Dôme and the Lac des Grands Gours, a 27m-wide subterranean lake.

Just up the road from the cave's main car park, Insectopia (www.insectopia.fr; adult/child €6/3; ◷10am-6pm Easter-Oct) is an interactive bug zoo that will enthral kids and appall mums. Display cases contain a cornucopia of creepy-crawlies, from giant millipedes to scarab beetles, praying mantises and ant farms. If the legs get too much, you can always take refuge in the butterfly house.

From Rocamadour, the caverns are 15km to the northeast.

CARENNAC
POP 401

A cluster of amber houses and brick cottages make up tiny Carennac, secluded on the left bank of the Dordogne. The village's main landmark is the 16th-century Château du Doyen, which now houses a heritage centre and museum, L'Espace Patrimoine (www.pays-vallee-dordogne.com; ◷10am-noon & 2-6pm Tue-Fri), showcasing the art and history of

the region. Above is the square is the Tour de Télémaque, named after the hero of Fénelon's *Les Aventures de Télémaque,* written here in 1699.

Just inside the castle gateway is the priory and the Romanesque Église St-Pierre (◷10am-7pm) with another remarkable Romanesque tympanum of Christ in Majesty, similar to those in Cahors and Beaulieu. Off the cloître (adult/child €2.50/0.80), still beautiful despite being heavily damaged in the Revolution, is a remarkable, late-15th-century Mise au Tombeau (Statue of the Entombment).

Based in Vayrac, 8km northwest of Carennac, canoe and kayak operator Safaraïd (☎05 65 37 44 87; www.canoe-kayak-dordogne.com; self-guided trips €17-30) offers lots of possible routes as well as multiday trips.

With flower-filled hanging baskets and stripy awnings, Hostellerie Fénelon (☎05 65 10 96 46; www.hotel-fenelon.com; r €59-71; ☒) evokes the feel of an Alsatian summer house. The rooms are unremarkable (think pink-tiled bathrooms, flowery bedspreads and sunflower-coloured walls), but the pricier ones overlook the river and tree-covered Île Calypso. Half-board at the downstairs restaurant (menus from €19) is particularly good value.

You'll find the tourist office (☎05 65 10 97 01; www.tourisme-carennac.com; ◷10am-noon & 2-6pm) next door to the church.

MARTEL
POP 1591

Some 15km northwest of Carennac and 15km northeast of Souillac, Martel is known as *la ville aux sept tours* (the town of seven towers) for its turret-topped skyline. This pale-stone, red-roofed village was the ancient capital of the Vicomte de Turenne, and retains much of its medieval architecture.

Activities

Chemin de Fer Touristique
du Haut-Quercy   TRAIN
(www.trainduhautquercy.info; adult/child diesel train €7/4, steam train €9.50/5.50; ◷Apr-Sep) Runs one-hour trips from Martel east along the precipitous cliff face to St-Denis. The tourist office has schedules.

Sleeping & Eating

There's a great market in the village centre on Wednesdays and Saturdays. Truffle markets also take place in the village during December and January.

TOP CHOICE **Manoir de Malagorse**　B&B **€€**

(☎05 65 27 14 83; www.manoir-de-malagorse.fr; d €150-180, ste €280-310) In quiet Cuzance, 8km northwest of Martel, this beauty of a B&B offers a level of luxury normally reserved for top-end hotels. Owners Anna and Abel's period house is a chic combo of sleek lines, soothing colours and fluffy fabrics: some rooms feature worn roof trusses, others polished wood floors, all are gorgeous. It's surrounded by 10 private acres, and the 5-course home-cooked dinner (€42) is superb. Look out for the winter truffle weekends.

Château de Termes　B&B **€€**

(☎05 65 32 42 03; www.chateau-de-termes.com; St-Denis-lès-Martel; r €64-95, cabin per night €59-110, per week €250-490) This family-friendly *gîte* (cottage) complex is set around a cute mini-château, which originally belonged to winemakers and truffle growers. It has something to suit all needs: lovely, spacious rooms with lashings of country charm, and a selection of two- to six-person *gîtes* available nightly or by the week. It's got lots for the kids – badminton, ping pong, skittles, heated pool – and the owners can help organise canoe hire and horse-riding trips.

Relais Sainte-Anne　HOTEL **€€**

(☎05 65 37 40 56; www.relais-sainte-anne.com; d €95-155, ste €185-275; 🐾🏊) The pick of places to stay in the village, with 16 individually decorated rooms that blend country comforts with contemporary flair. Its restaurant utilises produce directly from Martel's markets.

❶ Information

Buried deep within the pedestrianised centre, the **tourist office** (☎05 65 37 43 44; www .martel.fr; place des Consuls; ⊗9am-noon & 2-6pm Mon-Sat) has maps pointing out architectural and historical highlights and can provide details of the area, including working mills that can be visited.

Atlantic Coast

Includes »

Best Places to Eat

» La Ribaudière (p621)

» Hostellerie de Plaisance (p634)

» Marché des Capucins (p630)

» La Bôite à Huîtres (p630)

» Le Cheverus Café (p629)

Best Places to Stay

» Maison Flore (p613)

» Hôtel Pommeraye (p607)

» La Maison Douce (p620)

» Ecolodge des Chartrons (p625)

» L'Hôtel Particulier (p628)

Why Go?

With quiet country roads winding through vine-striped hills and wild stretches of coastal sands interspersed with misty islands, the Atlantic coast is where France gets back to nature. Much more laid-back than the Med (but with almost as much sunshine), this is the place to slow the pace right down.

But the Atlantic coast can do cities and culture as well. There's bourgeois Bordeaux with its wonderful old centre, lively Nantes with its wealth of fascinating museums, and salty La Rochelle with its breathtaking aquarium and beautiful portside setting.

The one thing that unites the people of this area is a love of the finer things in life. The region's exceptional wine is famous worldwide, and to wash it down you'll find ocean-fresh seafood wherever you go and plenty of regional delicacies including crêpes in the north, snails in the centre and foie gras in the south.

When to Go
Bordeaux

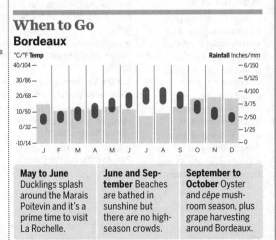

May to June Ducklings splash around the Marais Poitevin and it's a prime time to visit La Rochelle.

June and September Beaches are bathed in sunshine but there are no high-season crowds.

September to October Oyster and cêpe mushroom season, plus grape harvesting around Bordeaux.

TOURING THE WINE COUNTRY

If the Atlantic coast is famous for one thing, it's the pleasure of the grape. The Médoc, St-Émilion, Bordeaux and Cognac are names to set a wine connoisseur's heart aflutter. Visit some of the châteaux to learn the secrets of the grape.

Fast Facts

» **Population** 4,717,460
» **Area** 44,113 sq km
» **Hotel overnights/yr** 11 million
» **Signature drink** Bordeaux wines and cognac

Off the Beaten Track

» Arçais (p613)
» Cap Ferret (p637)
» Cognac (p620)
» Île d'Aix (p616)
» Le Croisic (p607)

Resources

» Insights into the Loire-Atlantique region: www.ohlaloireatlantique.com
» Inspiration for Poitou-Charentes: www.poitoucharentes.visite.org
» Find out about the Gironde region: www.tourisme-gironde.fr
» Become a wine expert: www.bordeaux.com
» For Cognac aficionados: www.cognac-world.com

Top 5 Museums

» Barbie will eat her heart out when she sees the walking, talking, almost living dolls on display in the Musée des Automates (p615).

» The Musée des Beaux-Arts (p606) in Nantes contains one of the most overpowering collections of fine art in the country.

» At the other end of the art scale are the 'out there' collections found in the CAPC Musée d'Art Contemporain (p623) in Bordeaux.

» Pretend you're Alice in Wonderland in a shrunk-down world at the Musée des Modèles Réduits (p615).

» Enrich yourself with knowledge in the Musée d'Aquitaine (p623) in Bordeaux.

GETTING THERE & AWAY

Bordeaux is the main transport hub for the region, three hours by TGV from Paris. From here, trains can take you pretty much anywhere in France. Nantes, Poitiers and La Rochelle are also well served by TGV, and a good rail service links most of the main attractions within the region. A car gives added freedom for the wine-tasting trail.

The region also has good air services, particularly from the UK, with airports at Bordeaux, Nantes, Poitiers and La Rochelle (all served by low-cost operators Ryanair and EasyJet, among others).

Best for Children

The Atlantic coast has plenty to keep youngsters and teenagers happy.

» While the big boys and girls surf the waves, little 'uns can build sandcastles on the beautiful beaches of Cap Ferret (p637).

» From blennies to piranhas and seahorses to giant rays, there's plenty to excite at La Rochelle's high-tech aquarium (p615).

» If the kids have square eyes from watching too much TV, show them the future of film at Futuroscope (p612).

» There's something about a house-sized mechanical elephant that just cannot fail to impress at Les Machines de l'Île de Nantes (p606).

» Spot storks, kingfishers and pond tortoises at Le Teich Parc Ornithologique (p637).

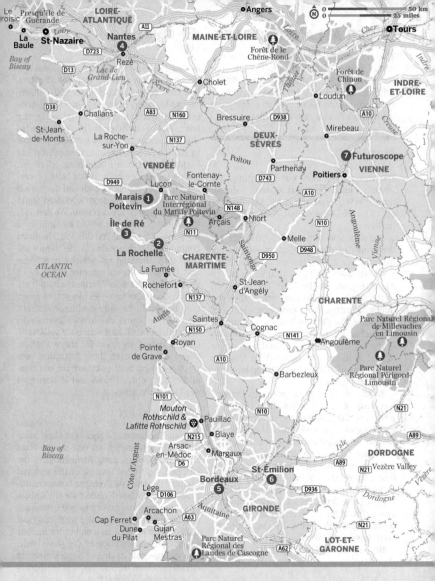

Atlantic Coast Highlights

1 Glide through the emerald-green waterways of the **Marais Poitevin** (p613), otherwise known as the 'Green Venice'

2 Dive deep under the waves and come face to face with wobbly jellyfish and jaw-gnashing sharks at La Rochelle's incredible **aquarium** (p615)

3 Cycle the smooth, flat bike paths criss-crossing the sunbaked **Île de Ré** (p619)

4 Ride a three-storey, 60-tonne mechanical elephant in **Nantes** (p606)

5 Tour the dramatically floodlit buildings and monuments making up the world's largest Unesco-listed urban area in central **Bordeaux** (p622)

6 Satisfy your craving for wine in **St-Émilion** (p632), home to some of the world's most famous wines

7 Hang on to your seat for a wild, cinematically simulated ride at the futuristic theme park **Futuroscope** (p612)

UPPER ATLANTIC COAST

This bite of the Loire-Atlantique *département*, where the Loire empties into the ocean, might as easily be termed 'lower Brittany'. Breton in every sense – cultural, architectural and historical – its centrepiece is Brittany's former capital, Nantes.

Nantes

POP 290,100

You can take Nantes out of Brittany (as when regional boundaries were redrawn during WWII), but you can't take Brittany out of its long-time capital, Nantes (Naoned in Breton).

Spirited and innovative, this city on the banks of the Loire, 55km east of the Atlantic, has a long history of reinventing itself. Founded by Celts around 70 BC, in AD 937 Alain Barbe-Torte, the grandson of the last king of Brittany, established the duchy of Brittany here following a series of invasions. The Edict of Nantes, a landmark royal charter guaranteeing civil rights to France's Huguenots (Protestants), was signed in the city by Henri IV in 1598. Its revocation in 1685 led to a Huguenot exodus from the region.

By the 18th century Nantes was France's foremost port, and in the 19th century – following the abolition of slavery – it became a cutting-edge industrial centre; the world's first public-transport service, the omnibus, began here in 1826. Shipbuilding anchored the city's economy until the late 20th century. When the shipyards relocated westwards to St-Nazaire, Nantes transformed itself into a thriving student and cultural hub. The city centre has now nudged past Bordeaux as the country's sixth-largest metropolis, and it's growing, with one in two Nantais today younger than 40.

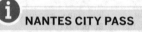

NANTES CITY PASS

The Pass Nantes (€25/35/45; ⊘24/48/72 hours), available from the tourist office, includes unlimited bus and tram transport as well as entry to museums and monuments, and extras like a free guided tour and shopping discounts.

⊙ Sights

TOP CHOICE Les Machines de l'Île de Nantes
THEME PARK

(www.lesmachines-nantes.fr; Parc des Chantiers, Blvd Léon Bureau; adult/child €7/5.50; ⊘10am-7pm Jul-Aug, hours vary rest of year) The quirkiest sight in an altogether fairly quirky city has to be Les Machines de l'Île de Nantes. Inside this fantasy world it's perfectly possible to prance around like a maharajah on the back of a 45-tonne mechanical elephant with a secret lounge inside its belly, or voyage on a boat through rough and dangerous oceans where attacks from oversized squid and giant prawns are common. We can only think that Jules Verne would be smiling in his grave if he could see this lot! The team behind Les Machines de l'Île de Nantes are constantly thinking up whacky new ideas and the latest (open summer 2012) is Le Carrousel des Mondes Marines; a 25m-high, 22m-wide funfair carousel like you've never seen before. In the surrounding waterfront area can be found children's playgrounds, an artificial beach and waterside walkways. Gallery tickets are good for the workshop, where you can watch these fantastical contraptions being built, but there are additional fees for elephant rides and le Carrousel des Mondes Marines.

Château des Ducs de Bretagne
CASTLE, MUSEUM

(www.chateau-nantes.fr; 4 place Marc Elder; adult/child €5/3; ⊘8am-7pm Apr-Oct, shorter hours rest of year) Forget fusty furnishings – the stripped, light-filled interior of the restored Château des Ducs de Bretagne houses multimedia-rich exhibits detailing the city's history. Computer terminals allow you to tour the old medieval city, juxtaposed with images of today. Other exhibits to look out for include sobering documentation of the slave trade, and vintage scale models of Nantes' evolving cityscape. There are also frequent temporary exhibitions (additional fee).

Musée des Beaux-Arts
MUSEUM

(10 rue Georges Clemenceau; adult €3.50; ⊘10am-6pm Wed & Fri-Mon, to 8pm Thu) One of the finest collections of French paintings outside Paris hangs in sumptuous galleries linked by grand stone staircases at the Musée des Beaux-Arts, with works by Georges de la Tour, Chagall, Monet, Picasso and Kandinsky among others. It was closed for renovations until autumn 2013 – prices and

hours may differ from those above when it re-opens.

Musée Jules Verne   MUSEUM
(www.julesverne.nantes.fr; 3 rue de l'Hermitage; adult/child €3/1.50; ⏱10am-7pm Tue-Sun) Overlooking the river, this is a magical museum with 1st-edition books, hand-edited manuscripts and cardboard theatre cut-outs. Child-friendly interactive displays introduce or reintroduce you to the work of Jules Verne, who was born in Nantes in 1828. Signs are in French but Verne's books, such as *Around the World in 80 Days,* are so well known that it's worthwhile visiting regardless. Hours and closing days vary throughout the year – see website. The museum is a 2km walk down river from the town centre.

Musée d'Histoire Naturelle   MUSEUM
(www.museum.nantes.fr; 12 rue Voltaire; adult/student/child €3.50/2/free; ⏱10am-6pm Wed-Mon) The fascinating collection of minerals, fossils and stuffed animals includes a huge whale skeleton and vivariums full of beautiful live snakes. There are frequent temporary exhibitions.

Jardin des Plantes   PARK
Founded in the early 19th century, the Jardin des Plantes is one of the most exquisite botanical gardens in France, filled with flowerbeds, duck ponds, fountains and towering redwoods (sequoias). There are hothouses and a children's playground at the northern end of the gardens. It is opposite the train station.

Cathédrale St-Pierre et St-Paul   CATHEDRAL
(place St-Pierre) Inside the Flamboyant Gothic Cathédrale St-Pierre et St-Paul, the tomb of François II (r 1458–88), Duke of Brittany, and his second wife, Marguerite de Foix, is a masterpiece of Renaissance art.

🛏 Sleeping

Nantes makes a good weekend break, when hotel rates often drop.

TOP⁄CHOICE Hôtel Pommeraye   BOUTIQUE HOTEL €€
(📞02 40 48 78 79; www.hotel-pommeraye.com; 2 rue Boileau; s €54-139 d €59-144; ❄🅿) Sleek and chic, this is more art gallery than hotel. The rooms have shimmering short-pile carpets and textured walls in shades of pale grey, gold, chocolate and violet. The reception and other common areas are adorned in constantly evolving eye-catching art; the last time we visited it all looked like a retro

BESIDE THE SEASIDE

Pack your bucket and spade for any of these worthwhile coastal excursions from Nantes. The classic seaside town of Le Croisic centres on a pretty, half-timbered fishing harbour adjoining its old town, where shrimps, lobsters, crabs, scallops and sea bass are unloaded. From Nantes, an all-day MétrOcéane (www.metroceane.fr) train ticket to Le Croisic costs €20.60 and includes public transport throughout Nantes. En route to Le Croisic, the same ticket allows you to stop at St-Nazaire, where cruise ships – including the *Queen Mary II* – are built and where Airbus has a factory, which can be toured. Also along this stretch of coast is the glamorous belle-époque resort of La Baule, boasting an enormous beach.

art-house cinema, and where you'd normally find ancient gargoyles you instead discover pop-art faces staring back at you.

Hôtel Amiral   HOTEL €€
(📞02 40 69 20 21; www.hotel-nantes.fr; 26bis rue Scribe; s/d from €84/89; 🅿) The rooms at this excellent little hotel are fairly plain but the common areas are funky and the breakfast room a commotion of jungle plants. The family who run it are really helpful.

Hôtel Graslin   HOTEL €€
(📞02 40 69 72 91; www.hotel-graslin.com; 1 rue Piron; r €59-109; 🅿) The unlikely (but very Nantes) marriage of art deco and '70s style at this refurbished hotel includes details like eggplant-and-orange wing chairs in the lounge. Spiffy rooms feature faux timber and edgy colour combinations like peppermint and bone, plus shag-carpeted rooms in the attic.

Hôtel La Pérouse   DESIGN HOTEL €€
(📞02 40 89 75 00; www.hotel-laperouse.fr; 3 allée Duquesne; r €96-146; ❄🅿) Styled to reflect the city's shipbuilding traditions, a wooden gangway entrance leads to this 46-room design hotel's stone-and-wood lobby, with zigzag chairs, canvas sail-like curtains, and glass bathroom basins and wardrobes. This was the first hotel in Nantes to be awarded an EU Ecolabel thanks to its policy of using fairtrade and locally grown items at

Nantes

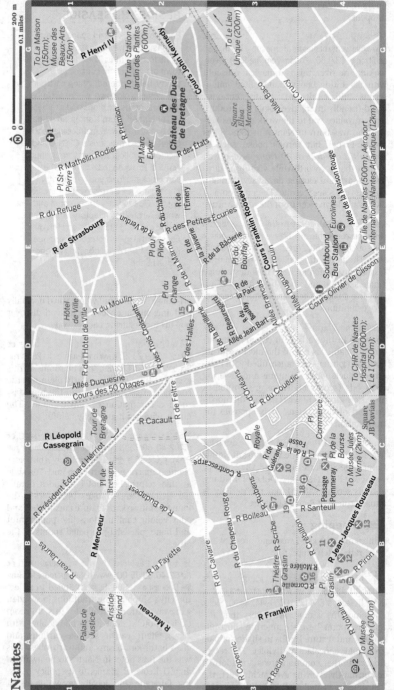

200 m
0.1 miles

To La Maison (150m);
Musée des Beaux-Arts (150m)

R Henri IV

To Train Station &
Jardin des Plantes (600m)

Cours John Kennedy

Château des Ducs
de Bretagne

To Le Lieu
Unique (200m)

R Prémion

Allée Baco

R Cruoy

R Mathelin Rodier

Pl St-
Pierre

R des États

Square
Elisa
Mercœur

R du Refuge

R de Strasbourg

R Château

R de
l'Emery

R des Petites Écuries

la Juverie

R de
la Bâclerie

Cours Franklin Roosevelt

To l'Île de Nantes (500m); Aéroport
International/Nantes Atlantique (12km)

Eurolines

Allée de la Maison Rouge

Pl du
Pilori

R de Verdun

Pl du
Change

R de la Marne

Pl du
Bouffay

R de
la Paix

Southbound
Bus Station

Hôtel
de Ville

R du Moulin

Pl du
Change

Pl du
Change

R des Trois Croissants

R de la Barillerie

R Beaurebaud

R du
Bouffay

R de
la Paix

Allée Duquesny Trouin

Cours Olivier de Clisson

R de l'Hôtel de Ville

R des Halles

R de la Barillerie

Allée Jean Bart Brancas

Allée Brancas

To CHR de Nantes
Hospital (600m);
Le 1 (750m)

Allée Duquesne
Cours des 50 Otages

Tour de
Bretagne

R de Feltre

R d'Orléans

R du Couëdic

Commerce

R Léopold
Cassegrain

R Président Édouard Hérriot

R Cacault

Pl
Royale

R de
la Fosse

Pl de la
Bourse

Pl
Commerce

Square
JB Daviais

Pl de
Bretagne

R de Budapest

R Contrescarpe

R de
Guérande

To Musée Jules
Verne (2km)

R Mercœur

R Rubens

R Boileau

R Santeuil

Passage
Pommeray

R Chapeau Rouge

R Scribe

R Crébillon

R Jean-Jacques Rousseau

R Jean Jaurès

R la Fayette

R du Calvaire

Théâtre
Graslin

R Corneille

Pl
Graslin

R Molière

R Piron

Palais de
Justice

Pl
Aristide
Briand

R Marceau

R Copernic

R Franklin

R Racine

R Voltaire

To Musée
Dobrée (100m)

Nantes

◎ **Top Sights**

breakfast, soap dispensers that do away with packaging, air-con units that switch off as soon as a window is opened and a number of other green initiatives.

Hôtel du Château   HOTEL €

(☎02 40 74 17 16; 5 place de la Duchesse Anne; s €41-53, d €43-6; 🛜) This cosy little establishment opposite the château actually thinks it is a castle. Short histories of various kings and queens grace the doors to the rooms, and the bedrooms themselves have an equally royal flavour with elegant bedspreads and old-fashioned bedside tables. Some rooms have views of the château.

Hôtel St-Daniel   HOTEL €

(☎02 40 47 41 25; www.hotel-saintdaniel.com; 4 rue du Bouffay; r €41-72; 🛜) Peacefully situated overlooking the St-Croix church courtyard in the heart of the old town, this clean, cheery place has a variety of room sizes, in-

cluding some whoppers, and a friendly Labrador dog is thrown in for free!

✕ Eating

For cosmopolitan dining, head to the medieval Bouffay quarter, a couple of blocks west of the château around rue de la Juiverie, rue des Petites Écuries and rue de la Bâclerie. Breton crêperies abound throughout town. West of cours des 50 Otages, rues Jean-Jacques Rousseau and Santeuil are lined with eateries.

TOP CHOICE **Le Bistrot de l'Écrivain**   MODERN FRENCH €€

(☎02 51 84 15 15; 15 rue Jean Jacques Rousseau; menus €14.50-18.50; ⊙Mon-Sat) Splashed in shades of red, with wine bottles lining the walls, Le Bistrot de l'Écrivain is a relaxed and easygoing place with food that's anything but relaxing and easy to make. There's all the Nantaise standards here, but most have an unexpected twist to them – raspberries in crème brûlée and duck dipped in wonderful sauces being just two examples.

Les Pieds dans le Plat   MODERN FRENCH €€

(☎02 40 69 25 15; 13 rue Jean-Jacques Rousseau; menus €13.50-25.50; ⊙11.30am-midnight) This modern French bistro has exposed stone walls, colourful paint work and all your old favourites given a creative new twist. It's a real flavour-of-the-month place at the moment and advance reservations are strongly advised.

Un Coin en Ville   MODERN FRENCH €

(☎02 40 20 05 97; 2 place de la Bourse; menus from €14.95; ⊙lunch & dinner Mon-Fri, dinner only Sat) Expect flickering tea-light candles, soulful jazz and blues, and cooking that combines local produce with exotic styles, such as red curry with prawns and scallops.

Le 1   GASTRONOMIC €€

(☎02 40 08 28 00; www.leun.fr; 1 rue Olympe de Gouges; menus €16.80-25; ⊙9am-11pm daily) Legal eagles from Nantes' gleaming 21st-century law court next door lounge in the ultracontemporary bar and dine on fabulous fusion dishes at this spot overlooking the Loire. The wine cellar is a see-through affair, with over 2000 bottles on stainless-steel racks in a glass cool room.

Crêperie Heb-Ken   BRETON €

(☎02 40 48 79 03; 5 rue de Guérande; crêpes €4.80-18; ⊙Mon-Sat; 🚼) Dozens of varieties of crêpe (such as a delicious trout-and-leek combo, or honey, lemon and almond for dessert) are made with love at this cosy spot. A sure sign of its authenticity: you can order *lait ribot* (thickened milk) by the *bolée* (drinking bowl) or pitcher.

La Bouche à Oreille   BISTRO €€
(🖉02 40 73 00 25; 14 rue Jean-Jacques Rousseau; menus from €19, mains from €12; ⊘lunch & dinner Mon-Fri, dinner Sat & Sun) With checked table clothes and curtains, this is a classic bistro in the heart of Nantes. Although it mixes things up with a few French classics it really specialises in the heavy food of the eastern city of Lyon - so that means things like sausages and pork in lentils. Be warned that portions are of gut-busting proportions.

Brasserie La Cigale   BRASSERIE €€
(🖉02 51 84 94 94; 4 place Graslin; breakfast €11, brunch €20, mains €12.50-24.50; ⊘7.30am-12.30am) No visit to Nantes is complete without joining the high-class old ladies with perfectly manicured hair for fresh seafood or French classics at the 1890s Brasserie La Cigale. Several salons of original gilded tilework and frescoed ceilings are attended by white-aproned waiters.

🍷 Drinking

Nantes has no shortage of lively spots for a drink. Two prime areas are the medieval Bouffay quarter and the Hangar à Bananes (www.hangarabananes.com; 21 quai des Antilles; ⊘daily till late), a former banana-ripening warehouse on the Île de Nantes. Here you'll find over a dozen restaurants, bars and clubs (and combinations thereof), each hipper than the next. The front terraces of most face onto the Anneaux de Buren, a permanent art installation of metal rings that light up at night.

Café Cult   CAFE, BAR
(www.cafe-cult.com; 2 rue des Carmes; ⊘2pm-2am Mon & Sat, from noon Tue-Fri) Squeezed inside a darkened half-timbered house and hung with local art, this bohemian place draws a student crowd and sometimes hosts concerts. During the day it serves mega-cheap but palate-pleasing lunches for €11.

La Maison   BAR
(4 rue Lebrun; ⊘3pm-1.30am) You have to see it to believe this trip of a place, decorated room by room like a home furnished in *bad* 1970s taste, playing (what else?) house music. It's a popular cafe in daylight hours as well.

⭐ Entertainment

A good website where you can find out what's on is www.leboost.com (in French). The tourist office website (www.nantes-tourisme.com) lists upcoming events in English.

[TOP CHOICE] Le Lieu Unique   THEATRE
(www.lelieuunique.com; 2 rue de la Biscuiterie) Within the one-time Lu biscuit factory (crowned by a replica of its original tower, which you can ascend for €2), this industrial-chic space is the venue for dance and theatre performances, eclectic and electronic music, philosophical sessions and contemporary-art exhibitions. Also here is an always-buzzing restaurant (mains a bargain priced €7–8), a polished concrete bar, and a decadent *hammam* (Turkish bath) complex in the basement.

Théâtre Graslin   THEATRE, OPERA
(🖉02 40 69 77 18; www.angers-nantes-opera.com; place Graslin) Constructed in 1788, the beautifully refurbished Théâtre Graslin is the home of the Nantes Opera.

🛍 Shopping

Pedestal statues symbolise traditional Nantais industries inside the ornate three-tiered shopping arcade Passage Pommeray (off rue de la Fosse), built in 1843.

George-Debotté   CHOCOLATE
(9 rue de la Fosse; ⊘9am-7.15pm Tue-Sat) When Jules Verne was a young boy he too was awed by this beautiful chocolate shop's chandeliers, marble floors and circular velvet banquette, where Nantais have waited while their orders were filled since 1823. Handmade specialities include *mascarons* (finely ground chocolates in a dark-chocolate shell) and a rainbow of hard-boiled sweets.

Yellowkorner   GALLERY
(🖉09 63 29 92 92; www.yellowkorner.com; 7 rue Crébillon) It's hard to know whether this is merely a shop or a photographic art gallery. Certainly the photos are for sale, but without doubt they are superb works of photographic art.

ℹ Information

Tourist Office (🖉02 72 64 04 79; www.nantes-tourisme.com) Branches at **Feydeau** and **St Pierre** (🖉08 92 46 40 44; 2 place St-Pierre; ⊘10am-1pm & 2-6pm, from 10.30am Thu, closed Mon).

❶ Getting There & Away

AIR **Aéroport International Nantes-Atlantique** (www.nantes.aeroport.fr) The airport is 12km southeast of town.

BUS The Lila bus web covers the entire Loire-Atlantique *département*. Tickets cost €2 per ride.

Eurolines (☑08 92 89 90 91; www.eurolines.com; allée de la Maison Rouge) Has an office in town.

TRAIN The **train station** (27 bd de Stalingrad) is well connected to most of the country. Destinations include the following:

Paris Gare Montparnasse from €58, two hours, 15 to 20 daily

Bordeaux from €47, four hours, three or four daily

La Rochelle from €19, from 1¾ hours, three or four daily

Tickets and information are also available at the **SNCF ticket office** (12 place de la Bourse, La Bourse; ☺9am-7.15pm Mon-Fri, to 6.30pm Sat) in the city centre.

❶ Getting Around

TO/FROM THE AIRPORT A *navette* bus links the airport with the Gare Centrale bus-and-tram hub and the train station's southern entrance (€7.20, 20 minutes) from about 5.30am until 11.15pm.

BUS & TRAM The **TAN network** (www.tan.fr) includes three modern tram lines that intersect at the Gare Centrale (Commerce), the main bus/tram transfer point. Buses run from 6.45am to 10pm. Night services continue until 12.30am.

Bus/tram tickets (€1.50) can be individually purchased from bus (but not tram) drivers and at tram-stop ticket machines. They're valid for one hour after being time-stamped. A *ticket journalier*, good for 24 hours, costs €4.30; time-stamp it only the first time you use it.

TAXI To order a taxi, call ☑02 40 69 22 22.

CENTRAL ATLANTIC COAST

The Poitou-Charentes region, midway along the Atlantic Coast, scoops up a potpourri of attractions – from the history-rich capital, Poitiers, to the portside panache of La Rochelle, to the languid beaches of Île de Ré, and the eponymous home of Cognac.

Poitiers

POP 91,300

Inland from the coast, history-steeped Poitiers was founded by the Pictones, a Gaulish tribe. The Romans built up the city, and there are numerous reminders still evident, such as extensive ruins uncovered when the large Cordeliers shopping centre was built in the town centre about a decade ago. The city rose to prominence as the former capital of Poitou, the region governed by the Counts of Poitiers in the Middle Ages. A pivotal turning point came in AD 732, when somewhere near Poitiers (the exact site is not known) the cavalry of Charles Martel defeated the Muslim forces of Abd ar-Rahman, governor of Córdoba, thus ending Muslim attempts to conquer France. The city's remarkable Romanesque churches are in part a legacy of Eleanor of Aquitaine's financial support.

Poitiers has one of the oldest universities in the country, established in 1432 and today a linchpin of this lively city.

◉ Sights

Poitiers Churches CHURCHES

Strolling Poitiers' history-trodden streets is the best way to get a feel for the city's past. Along the pavements, red, yellow and blue lines correspond with three self-guided walking tours detailed on a free city map handed out by the tourist office.

Every evening from 21 June to the third weekend in September, spectacular colours are cinematically projected onto the west facade of the Romanesque Église Notre Dame la Grande (place Charles de Gaulle). The earliest parts of the church date from the 11th century; three of the five choir chapels were added in the 15th century, with the six chapels along the northern wall of the nave added in the 16th century. The only original frescoes are the faint 12th- or 13th-century works that adorn the U-shaped dome above the choir.

The 13th-century stained-glass window illustrating the Crucifixion and the Ascension at the far end of the choir of the Gothic-style Cathédrale St-Pierre (rue de la Cathédrale) is one of the oldest in France.

Constructed in the 4th and 6th centuries on Roman foundations, Baptistère St-Jean (rue Jean Jaurès; adult/child €2/1; ☺10.30am-12.30pm & 3-6pm Wed-Mon Apr-Oct), 100m south of the cathedral, was redecorated in the 10th century and used as a parish church. The octagonal hole under the frescos was used for total-immersion baptisms, practised until the 7th century.

Musée Ste-Croix MUSEUM
(www.musees-poitiers.org; 3 rue Jean Jaurès; adult/child €4/free, €2 Sun; ☺10am-noon & 1.15-8pm Tue, 10am-noon & 1.15-6pm Wed-Fri, 10am-noon

& 2-6pm Sat-Sun) Seven signed statues by Camille Claudel are the highlight of this little museum, which also hosts changing exhibitions.

FREE **Palais des Comtes de Poitou** HISTORIC BUILDING
(☑05 49 50 22 00; place Alphonse Lepetit; ⊙8.45am-midday & 1-5pm Mon-Fri) Today it houses law courts, but nearly a thousand years ago this stunning building was the seat of the Counts of Poitou and Dukes of Aquitaine. Its most impressive feature is the dining hall constructed in the late 12th century by that local lass with big dreams, Eleanor of Aquitaine. At its time this 50m-long dining hall was considered one of the largest in Europe. Despite the rather dull proceedings that normally take place here today, it's possible to visit and relive the pomp of the past – but don't expect to be seated for dinner in the great hall!

🛏 Sleeping

In addition to chains such as Ibis, Poitiers has a handful of atmospheric, well-located hotels.

Hôtel de l'Europe HISTORIC HOTEL €
(☑05 49 88 12 00; www.hotel-europe-poitiers.com; 39 rue Carnot; s/d €59/65; 🛜) Behind a dramatically recessed entrance, the main building of this elegant, very un-two-star-like building dates from 1710, with a sweeping staircase, oversized rooms and refined furnishings. It has good wheelchair access, and the annexe has modern rooms for the same price.

Le Grand Hôtel HISTORIC HOTEL €€
(☑05 49 60 90 60; www.grandhotelpoitiers.fr; 28 rue Carnot; s/d from €75/92; ❄🛜) There's nothing fancy about Poitiers' premier hotel. It's just solid, old-fashioned value all the way. Faux art-deco furnishings and fittings fill the public areas with character, and rooms are spacious and well equipped.

Hôtel Central HOTEL €
(☑05 49 01 79 79; www.hotel-central-poitiers.com; 35 place du Maréchal Leclerc; r from €52; 🛜) At the southern edge of a charming pedestrian district of half-timbered houses, this two-star place is a terrific little bargain. It has very snug but sunlit rooms with shower or bath, and, like the square it sits on, has had a recent makeover to make it all shiny and modern.

🍴 Eating & Drinking

Prime dining spots tend to be south of place du Maréchal Leclerc.

Other good dining bets are the atrium-style bistro **La Gazette** (☑05 49 61 49 21; 1 rue Gambetta; menus €11-12; ⊙Mon-Sat) and the green on the outside, green on the inside **La Table du Jardin** (☑05 49 41 68 46; 42 rue du Moulin à Vent; menu from €23.80, mains €13-18; ⊙Tue-Sat), serving exclusively seasonal market-fresh produce.

La Serrurerie TRADITIONAL FRENCH €
(☑05 49 41 05 14; 28 rue des Grandes Écoles; menu €12.50, mains €10-17.50; ⊙8am-2am) Hectically busy, this mosaic-and-steel bistro-bar is Poitiers' communal lounge–dining room. A chalked blackboard menu lists specialities like *tournedos* (thick slices) of salmon, pastas and a crème brûlée you'll be dreaming about until your next visit.

Le Bilbio Café CAFE
(71bis rue de la Cathedral; coffee from €3; ⊙Tue-Sun) If your perfect wet-day entertainment involves a good coffee, a bit of cake and a good book then this small cafe is where we'll find you next time it rains.

ℹ️ Information

Tourist office (☑05 49 41 21 24; www.ot-poitiers.fr; 45 place Charles de Gaulle; ⊙10am-11pm) Near Église Notre Dame.

ℹ️ Getting There & Away

The **train station** (☑36 35; bd du Grand Cerf) has direct links to Bordeaux (from €24, 1¾ hours), La Rochelle (from €19, 1½ hours), Nantes (from €30, 3¼ hours) and many other cities including Paris' Gare Montparnasse (from €47, 1½ hours, 12 daily).

Around Poitiers

FUTUROSCOPE

Futuristic theme park **Futuroscope** (☑05 49 49 59 06; www.futuroscope.com; adult/child €38/28; ⊙9am-11.30pm, closed Jan–mid-Feb) takes you whizzing through space, diving into the deep-blue ocean depths, racing around city streets and on a close encounter with creatures of the future among many other space-age cinematic experiences. To keep things cutting edge, a third of the attractions change annually. Many are motion-seat set-ups requiring a minimum height of 120cm, but there's a play area for littlies with miniature cars and so on.

Allow at least five hours to see the major attractions; two days to see everything. Futuroscope's numerous hotels are bookable through the website, or directly at the lodging desk.

Futuroscope is 10km north of Poitiers in Jaunay-Clan (take exit 28 off the A10). TGV trains link the park's TGV station with cities including Paris and Bordeaux; times and prices are similar to those to/from Poitiers.

Local Vitalis buses 1 and E link Futuroscope (Parc de Loisirs stop) with Poitiers' train station (€1.30, 30 minutes); there are one to two buses an hour from 6.15am until 9.30pm (Sep–Jun) or 11.30pm (Jul–Aug).

MARAIS POITEVIN

Parc Naturel Interrégional du Marais Poitevin (www.parc-marais-poitevin.fr) is a tranquil bird-filled wetland dubbed the Venise Verte (Green Venice) due to the duckweed that turns its maze of waterways emerald green each spring and summer. Covering some 800 sq km of wet and drained marsh, the marshlands are interspersed with villages and woods threaded by canals and bike paths. The whole area is becoming increasingly popular with domestic tourists, and if you want somewhere you can really melt into rural life, the Marais Poitevin waterways are unbeatable. There are two main bases from which to punt out across the waterways: the small honey-coloured town of Coulon and, our favourite, the romantic and pretty village of Arçais.

Boating and cycling are the only way to satisfactorily explore the area and there is no shortage of operators hiring out bikes and flat-bottomed boats or kayaks for watery tours. In Arçais there are three boat operators – Arçais Venise Verte (www.veniseverteloisirs.fr), Au Martin Pecheur (www.aumartinpecheur.com) and Bardet-Huttiers (www.marais-arcais.com) – all of which offer identical services for the same price: kayak per hour/half-day from €13/30, boat per hour/half-day from €15/35; guided tours are also possible. Coulon has even more operators and rates are identical. Bikes can be hired from several operators in both towns for €7/15 per hour/half-day.

Getting to either Coulon or Arçais is difficult in anything other than your own car.

🛏 Sleeping & Eating

TOP CHOICE Maison Flore   BOUTIQUE HOTEL €
(☑05 49 76 27 11; www.maisonflore.com; rue du Grand Port; Arçais; s/d €63/74; ⊙closed Christmas–mid-Feb; @🤶) On the Arçais waterfront, this is a wonderfully romantic 10-room guesthouse in which every room is painted and decorated in the colours and style of local marsh plants such as the pale-green angelica or bright, purple iris. But the environmental connection runs much deeper, with solar hot water, geothermal heating and cooling, and an organic breakfast (€9.50). The hotel also donates a percentage of profits to projects providing fresh water to villages in the developing world. There's a cosy guest lounge with books and board games, and you can rent boats here. The staff also deserve points for the warmth they show to their guests; when we last stayed they staged an Easter egg hunt for the one child staying – ours.

Hôtel-Restaurant Le Central   HOTEL €
(☑05 49 35 90 20; www.hotel-lecentral-coulon. com; 4 rue d'Autremont; Coulon; s/d from €59/71, menus from €14.80-41.50, mains €16-22; ⊙lunch Tue-Sun, dinner Tue-Sat, closed 3 weeks Feb; ❋🤶) Coulon's flashiest accommodation comprises wood-panelled rooms, some overlooking a garden. Sublime dining is to be had at the in-house restaurant, where specialities include crispy eel, sorbet made from angelica, and a mouth-watering cheeseboard.

Hôtel au Marais   HOTEL €€
(☑05 49 35 90 43; www.hotel-aumarais.com; 46-48 quai Lovis-Tardy; Coulon; s/d €70/80; 🤶) Split between two old sandcastle-coloured buildings, this hotel has fairly unexciting rooms but the setting, overlooking the river, is hard to beat.

La Rochelle

POP 77,400

Known as La Ville Blanche (the White City), La Rochelle's luminous limestone facades glow in the bright coastal sunlight. One of France's foremost seaports from the 14th to 17th centuries, the city has arcaded walkways, half-timbered houses (protected from the salt air by slate tiles) and ghoulish gargoyles, rich reminders of its seafaring past. The early French settlers of Canada, including the founders of Montreal, set sail from here in the 17th century.

This 'white city' is also commendably green, with innovative public transport and open spaces. It's kid-friendly too, with lots of activities for little visitors.

La Rochelle

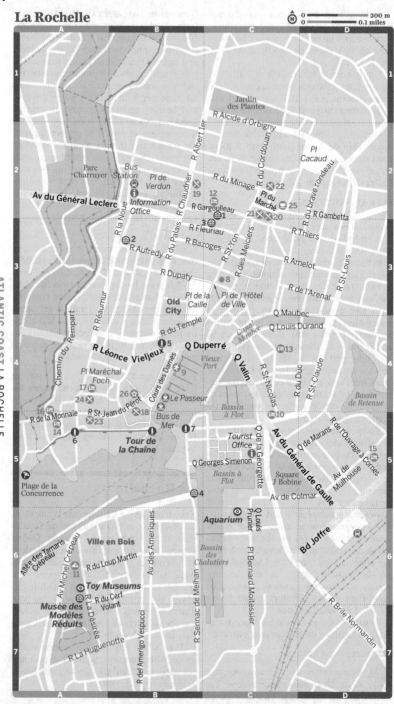

N

0 — 200 m
0 — 0.1 miles

Jardin des Plantes

R Alcide d'Orbigny

Pl Cacaud

R Albert 1er

R Cordouan

R du brave rondeau

Parc Charruyer

Bus Station

Pl de Verdun

Information Office

R du Minage

22

Pl du Marché

25

Av du Général Leclerc

R Chaudrier

19

12

R Gargoulleau

21 20

R Gambetta

R la Noue

3

R Fleuriau

R Thiers

2

R Aufredy

R du Palais

R Bazoges

R St-Yon

R des Merciers

R Amelot

R St-Louis

R Dupaty

8

Pl de la Caille

Pl de l'Hôtel de Ville

R de l'Arenal

Old City

Q Maubec

Canal Maubec

Q Louis Durand

R Réaumur

R du Temple

5

Chemin du Rempart

R Léonce Vieljeux

Q Duperré

13

Pl Maréchal Foch

Cours des Dames

9

Vieux Port

Q Valin

R St-Nicolas

R du Duc

R St-Claude

Bassin de Retenue

17

26

24

Le Passeur

18

R St-Jean du Pérot

23

Bus de Mer

Bassin à Flot

10

16

R de la Monnaie

14

6

7

Tour de la Chaîne

Tourist Office

Q de la Georgette

Av du Général de Gaulle

Q de Marans

R de l'Ouvrage à Cornes

15

Av de Mulhouse

Plage de la Concurrence

Q Georges Simenon

Bassin à Flot

Square J Bobine

Av de Colmar

4

Aquarium

Q Louis Prunier

Bd Joffre

Ville en Bois

Allée des Tamaris Crépeau

Av Michel Crépeau

R du Loup Martin

11

Av des Amériques

Bassin des Chalutiers

Pl Bernard Moitessier

R Brie Normandin

Toy Museums

R du Cerf Volant

Musée des Modèles Réduits

R La Désirée

R Sennac de Meihan

R del Amerigo Vespucci

R La Huguenotte

La Rochelle

La Rochelle's late-20th-century district of Les Minimes was built on reclaimed land, and now has one of the largest marinas in the country. Unlike the Med with its motor cruisers, the 3500 moorings here are mostly used by yachts, which fill the harbour with billowing spinnakers.

◎ Sights & Activities

TOP CHOICE **Aquarium La Rochelle** AQUARIUM
(www.aquarium-larochelle.com; quai Louis Prunier; adult/child €14.50/11, audioguide €3.50; ◎9am-11pm) La Rochelle's number-one tourist attraction is this state-of-the-art family-friendly aquarium. A visit begins by descending in a clunky old 'submarine' to the ocean floor, where you step out into a tunnel of fluoro jellyfish waving their tentacles in time to the classical music that wafts through the aquarium. Other highlights include the huge open-ocean aquarium full of UFO-like rays and fearsome sharks, the jungle area with its tree-level walkways and ponds full of teeth-gnashing piranhas, the elegantly dancing seahorses, timid turtles and the bizarre half-newt, total-fish mudskippers. The aim is to educate visitors to the wonders of the world's waters and the threats our oceans face. You will learn how sea cucumbers spit their guts out when frightened and then just grow another set, and – here's one that all parents can relate to – how poor mummy octopus becomes so tired at the mere thought of bringing up her precious brood that she dies of exhaustion the moment they hatch out! You should allow a minimum of two hours for a visit.

Toy Museums MUSEUMS
(www.museeslarochelle.com; 14 rue La Désirée; adult/child 3-10yrs per museum €8.50/6, joint ticket adult/child €12/9; ◎9.30am-7pm) A treat for kids (and kids-at-heart) is the Musée des Automates (Automation Museum), a small theme-park-style display showing 300 automated dolls from the last two centuries, including a near-life-size recreation of bygone Montmartre in Paris, right down to the Moulin Rouge and the funicular railway. Trainspotters will love the equally appealing Musée des Modèles Réduits (Scale Model Museum) next door, with miniature cars, computer-automated naval battles and a tootling model railway. Both museums are wheelchair accessible.

Defensive Towers LANDMARK
(all three towers adult/child €8.50/free, single tower €6/free; ◎10am-6.30pm) To protect the harbour at night in times of war, an enormous chain was raised between the two 14th-century stone towers at the harbour

entrance to La Rochelle, giving rise to the name Tour de la Chaîne (Chain Tower). There are superb views from the top and a whizz-bang new permanent exhibit about the Canadian voyagers.

Across the harbour it's also possible to climb the 36m-high, pentagonal Tour St-Nicolas.

The conical 15th-century Tour de la Lanterne, so named because of its role as the harbour's lighthouse (lit by an enormous candle), and one of the oldest of its kind in the world, is also referred to as Tour des Quatre Sergents in memory of four local sergeants, two of whom were held here for plotting to overthrow the newly reinstated monarchy before their execution in Paris in 1822. The English-language graffiti on the walls was carved by English privateers held here during the 18th century.

The gateway to the old city, Tour de la Grosse Horloge (quai Duperré) is a steadfast Gothic-style clock tower, with a 12th-century base and an 18th-century top. For safety reasons, it's not possible to enter.

Island Hopping & Beaches ISLAND EXCURSIONS

Several islands are scattered around La Rochelle, including the nearby Île de Ré, as well as a trio further south.

Accessible only by boat, the tiny crescent-shaped Île d'Aix (pronounced 'eel dex'), 16km due south of La Rochelle, has some blissful beaches. Between the Île d'Aix and the larger Île d'Oléron (linked to the mainland by a free bridge) is the fortress-island Fort Boyard, built during the first half of the 19th century.

BIRDWATCHING

An easy 15km drive south of La Rochelle, the Réserve Naturelle Marais d'Yves (www.marais.yves .reserves-naturelles.org; N137) has a free nature centre, where you can pop in and peer through telescopes to watch some of the 192-hectare reserve's 250 bird species amid the wetlands. Depending on the season, you might see flocks of over 20,000 birds fill the sky on their migratory path. The website lists various guided walks and cycle rides through the wetlands (available in English), where you'll also learn about the area's 750 species of frogs, flowers and insects.

Inter-Îles (☎08 25 13 55 00; www.inter-iles .com; cours des Dames) has sailings from Easter to early November to Fort Boyard (adult/child €18.50/11.50), Île d'Aix (€27/17.50) and Île d'Oléron (€27/17.50), plus sailings to Île de Ré (€18.50/11.50) from Easter to September.

La Rochelle's tourist office (p618) also has information about reaching the islands by public and private transport.

If all you want is a quick swim and a blast of sunshine then head to Plage de la Concurrence on the edge of the old town. It's popular with locals but note that the water can be very polluted. For more pleasing beaches head to Île de Ré (p619).

Musée Maritime   MARITIME MUSEUM
(www.museemaritimelarochelle.fr; Bassin à Flot; adult/child €8/5.50; ☉10am-7pm) Moored at Bassin à Flot are the meteorological research ship *France 1*, a *chalutier* (fishing boat) and a tug, which together make up the Musée Maritime. If you think your job is tough, just wait until you see what the crew of these sorts of boats has to put up with on the average working day.

Museums   MUSEUM
(per museum adult/child €4/free; ☉10.30am-12.30pm & 2-6pm Mon & Wed-Sat, 2-6pm Sun) La Rochelle contains a handful of museums including the Musée du Nouveau Monde (New World Museum; 10 rue Fleuriau; adult/child €4/free; ☉10.30am-12.30pm & 2-6pm Mon & Wed-Sat, 2-6pm Sun), which reveals the city's role as a departure point for North America; the Musée des Beaux-Arts (☎05 46 41 64 65; 28 rue Gargoulleau), which is housed inside a stunning neoclassical building and hosts an impressive collection of 15th–20th century art; and the Musée d'Orbigny Bernon (☎05 46 41 18 83; 2 rue St-Côme), which houses an important collection of Asian art.

👉 Tours

Flanked by a 15th-century Flamboyant Gothic wall and a resplendent 17th-century Renaissance-style courtyard, the Hôtel de Ville (Town Hall; place de l'Hôtel de Ville; adult/child €4/1.50) has guided tours in French at 3pm daily in June and September, 3pm and 4pm daily in July and August, and at weekends during the rest of the year. Book tours through the tourist office.

The tourist office (p618) organises a wealth of city tours throughout the summer months (adult/child from €6.50/4.50), often in French only. Reservations are essential.

⭐ Festivals & Events

Festival International du Film   FILM FESTIVAL
(www.festival-larochelle.org) Silent classics, as well as new nondubbed films, are screened during the 10-day film festival in early July.

Francofolies   DANCE FESTIVAL
(www.francofolies.fr) A contemporary-music and performing-arts festival held over four days in mid-July.

Jazz Entre Les Deux Tours   MUSIC FESTIVAL
(www.jazzentrelesdeuxtours.fr) October sees jazz fans jive to La Rochelle's jazz festival.

🛏 Sleeping

During the warmer months, dozens of campgrounds open (and fill up just as quickly) around La Rochelle and Île de Ré. The tourist office has a list of campgrounds outside the town. The closest to the city is Camping du Soleil (☑05 46 44 42 53; av Michel Crépeau; two adults & tent €14.76; ☺late Jun–late Sep).

TOP CHOICE Trianon de la Plage   HISTORIC HOTEL €€
(☑05 46 41 21 35; www.hoteltrianon.com; 6 rue de la Monnaie; r €80-111; ☺closed Jan; 🛜) A fading world of art-deco stained-glass windows, curly-whirly staircases, a grand dining room and multi-hued rooms dominate this character-laden hotel. The owner, who speaks superb English, really looks after his guests and likes to check that everything is just right. The in-house restaurant has high-quality meals for an affordable price (mains around €15–18). It's in a quiet corner of town but only a shipmate's shout from the old town and a mere sandy shuffle from the town beach.

TOP CHOICE Un Hôtel en Ville   BOUTIQUE HOTEL €€
(☑05 46 41 15 75; www.unhotelenville.fr; 20 place du Maréchal Foch; s €70, d €80-100; 🛜) Everything about this smart, bargain-priced boutique hotel screams quality – even the pillows and mattresses are in a league above those of most other hotels in this price range. The admittedly fairly small rooms are painted in a startling white, offset through the use of dark stone furnishings.

La Monnaie Art & Spa Hotel DESIGN HOTEL €€€
(☑05 46 50 65 65; www.hotelmonnaie.com; 3 rue de la Monnaie; r from €159; 🛜) Recently renovated, this is a fabulous boutique hotel whose austere 17th-century exterior hides a virtual art gallery interior of arresting graffati, sparkly light trees, plasticine sculptures,

blurred photos and subtle lighting. The rooms are comfortable in the extreme and the bathrooms futurisitc, hi-tech creations. If you need pampering there's a spa and if not there's a gym.

Axe Hotel   HOTEL €
(☑05 46 41 40 68; www.axehotellarochelle.fr; 5 rue de la Fabrique; s €68, d €75-85; ☺Reception closed 11.30am-4pm; 🛜) This recently renovated old townhouse overlooking the port has modern rooms with red and white furnishings, spotlights and black-and-white tiled bathrooms. It's all very well run and recieves lots of positive feedback; take the low prices into account and it all adds up to a great deal.

Masq Hotel   DESIGN HOTEL €€
(☑05 46 41 83 83; www.masqhotel.com; 17 rue de l'Ouvrage à Cornes; r from €108; 🛜) This designer hotel takes its cue from a chance meeting between owner-creator Michel Dufour and two Balinese brothers, Hindu artists Mantra and Geredeg, whom he commissioned to paint the abstract canvases that hang in all 76 rooms as well as the artistically lit neo-retro foyer. Other conversation pieces include Philippe Starck Carrara marble tables, and Pierluigi Cerri–designed apple-green leather chairs in the breakfast room. A couple of the ultraspacious suites have terraces.

Hôtel St-Nicolas   BOUTIQUE HOTEL €€
(☑05 46 41 71 55; www.hotel-saint-nicolas.com; 13 rue Sardinerie et place de la Solette; r from €110-125; 🛜) This hotel offers smart, clean, minimalist style and beds so soft and welcoming it'll be a battle to get out of them in the morning. The bathrooms have giant rain showers, the service is excellent and the indoor tropical garden is an unexpected nice touch.

Hôtel de la Paix   HISTORIC HOTEL €
(☑05 46 41 33 44; www.hotelalarochelle.com; 14 rue Gargoulleau; s €57, d €73-84; 🛜) In a lovely 18th-century building, the hotel's sweeping staircase of polished wood leads to good-value rooms, some of which have open stone walls and all of which have plenty of splashes of colour and character.

Centre International de Séjour-Auberge de Jeunesse   HOSTEL €
(☑05 46 44 43 11; www.fuaj.net; av des Minimes; dm with breakfast from €17; ☺reception 8am-noon, 2-7pm & 9-10pm, closed Christmas) This popular HI hostel is 2km southwest of the train station in Les Minimes.

✗ Eating

The port has a plethora of restaurants and cafes, especially on the northern side. In summer, the quays in front of the Vieux Port (old port) are closed to traffic from 8pm to midnight Monday to Saturday and 2pm to midnight on Sunday, creating the ambience of a giant street party. Away from the tourist crowds, locals' favoured dining areas are rue St-Jean du Pérot and such streets as rue des Cloutiers surrounding place du Marché.

TOP
CHOICE **Le Soleil Brille pour**
Tout Le Monde   INTERNATIONAL, VEGETARIAN €

(☏05 46 41 11 42; 13 rue des Cloutiers; menus/mains from €13/9.50; ⊙Tue-Sat; ✍) There's a distinctly bohemian air to this excellent little place, decked out in hippy colours. Some highly original (often vegetarian-based) dishes originate from the kitchen, much of them inspired by the tropical French islands of Réunion and Martinique. As much as possible, all the produce used here comes from the nearby market and you can really tell – plus it's one of those all-too-rare French restaurants not afraid to experiment with spices. Advance reservations are essential.

André   SEAFOOD €€€

(☏05 46 41 28 24; 8 place de la Chaîne; menus €32-39, mains €13-30; ⊙noon-4pm & 7pm-midnight) Opened in the 1950s as a small seafood café, André grew so popular it began buying adjacent shops. There's now a maze of interconnecting rooms, each with its own individual ambience (like a portholed cabin) but all serving succulent seafood caught the night before. You can choose your fanciful denizens of the deep from the display tables outside: 'Hello, Mr Crab, you look tasty. I'm going to gobble you up', and with that he'll be thrown into a pan of hot water.

Les Quatre Sergents   GASTRONOMIC €€

(☏05 46 41 35 80; 49 rue St-Jean du Pérot; menus & mains from €18) Set inside a beautifully tiled, historic former greenhouse, it's still a jungle in here today with plants scrambling upward to the height of trees. Don't worry, though; nothing else about this place is as untamed as the Congo. This is the city's premier address for white-tableclothed elegance and classic French gastronomic fare.

Le Bistro du Marché   TRADITIONAL FRENCH €

(☏05 46 27 28 52; 8 rue Gambetta, Échoppe du Marché; mains €10, lunch menu €12.80; ⊙Mon-Sat) Built into the market walls, this family-run place has a convivial atmosphere and draws plenty of regulars with its tasty and filling lunch *menus* comprising all the French bistro standards. Book ahead at lunchtime.

Chez Mah Monir   MIDDLE EASTERN €

(☏05 46 37 50 56; rue Gambetta, Échoppe du Marché; lunch menu/mains from €13/9; ⊙Mon-Sat) As this place is built into the market walls you'd expect the cuisine to be nothing but pure bred traditional French bistro food, but oh how wrong you'd be. Eat here and your taste buds will travel further afield to the souks of Iran and North Africa.

Lulu   MODERN FRENCH €

(☏05 46 50 69 03; 19ter place de la Préfecture; menus/mains from €12/16) Decorated in striking shades of fuchsia, Lulu is La Rochelle's grooviest restaurant, with a hip young team in the kitchen turning out gourmet fare and a lounge vibe that comes into its own during regular piano soirées.

Café de la Paix   BRASSERIE €

(☏05 46 41 39 79; 54 rue Chaudrier; lunch menu €15.50, mains €11-18.50; ⊙7am-10pm Mon-Sat) A visual feast as much as a dining one, this belle-époque brasserie-bar serves up traditional cuisine like beef, duck, foie gras and fish, as well as breakfasts and afternoon teas amid the splendour of soaring frescoed ceilings and gold-edged arched mirrors.

☕ Drinking

There's no shortage of places to drink along the main dining strips, but some of the city's best bars (most open to 2am) are sprinkled along the bohemian-feel rue St-Nicolas.

Merling   TEAROOM

(25 rue Gambetta; ⊙closed Mon morning & Sun) For fresh-roasted coffee, head to this 1st-floor tearoom, which supplies most cafes in town with their brews.

☆ Entertainment

La Coursive   LIVE MUSIC, CINEMA

(☏05 46 51 54 00; www.la-coursive.com; 4 rue St-Jean du Pérot; ⊙late Aug–mid-Jul) The two auditoriums at La Coursive host regular world music concerts, nondubbed art films, theatre and dance performances.

ℹ Information

Tourist office (☏05 46 41 14 68; www.la rochelle-tourisme.com; 2 quai Georges Simenon, Le Gabut; ⊙9am-8pm Mon-Sat, 10am-6pm Sun) Sells the Pass Rochelais, offering various discounts for public transport, sights and activities.

ℹ️ Getting There & Away

AIR **La Rochelle Airport** (www.larochelle.aero port.fr), north of the city centre off the N237, has domestic flights as well as a variety of flights to several UK and Irish airports with Ryanair, EasyJet, Flybe and Jet2. There are also flights to Brussels and Oslo with Ryanair.

BUS **Océcars** (📞05 46 00 95 15) runs services to regional destinations from the **bus station** (place de Verdun).

TRAIN The **train station** (📞08 36 35 35 35) is linked by TGV to Paris' Gare Montparnasse (from €66, 3¼ hours). Other destinations served by regular direct trains include Nantes (€26.90, 1¾ hours), Poitiers (€22, 1½ hours) and Bordeaux (€28.60, 2¼ hours).

ℹ️ Getting Around

TO/FROM THE AIRPORT **Bus 7** (Bus 47 on Sundays) runs from the airport to the town centre (€1.30); schedules are available on the airport website. A taxi costs about €10.

BOAT **Le Passeur** (tickets €1; ⏱7.45am-10pm) is a three-minute ferry service linking Tour de la Chaîne with the Avant Port. It runs when there are passengers – press the red button on the board at the top of the gangplank.

The ferry **Bus de Mer** (€2; ⏱20 minutes) links Tour de la Chaîne with Les Minimes. It runs daily April to September but only at weekends and holidays from October to March. Boats from the Vieux Port depart every hour on the hour (except at 1pm) from 10am to 7pm (every half-hour until 11.30pm in July and August).

BUS Electric buses buzz around town. Local transport system **Yélo Bus** (📞05 46 34 02 22) has a main bus hub and **information office** (place de Verdun; ⏱7.30am-7pm Mon-Fri, 8am-6.30pm Sat). Most lines run until sometime between 7.15pm and 8pm. Tickets cost €1.30.

Bus 1 runs from place de Verdun to the train station, returning via the Vieux Port.

CAR & MOTORCYCLE A free shuttle bus connects the low-cost Park and Ride (P+R) car park off av Jean Moulin.

TAXI Call **Abeilles Taxis** (📞05 46 41 55 55).

Île de Ré

POP 17,600

Bathed in the southern sun, drenched in a languid atmosphere and scattered with villages of green-shuttered, whitewashed buildings with red Spanish-tile roofs, Île de Ré is one of the most delightful places on the west coast of France. The island spans just 30km from its most easterly and westerly points, and just 5km at its widest section. But take note, the secret's out and in the high season it can be almost impossible to move around and even harder to find a place to stay.

On the northern coast, about 12km from the toll bridge that links the island to La Rochelle, is the quaint fishing port of St-Martin-de-Ré (population 2600), the island's main town. Surrounded by 17th-century fortifications (you can stroll along most of the ramparts), the port town is a mesh of streets filled with craft shops, art galleries and salty sea views. St-Martin's tourist office (📞05 46 09 00 05; www.iledere.com; av Victor Bouthillier; ⏱10am-6pm Mon-Sat, to noon Sun) can provide information for the entire island.

The island's best beaches are along the southern edge – including unofficial naturist beaches at Rivedoux Plage and La Couarde-sur-Mer – and around the western tip (northeast and southeast of Phare-des-Baleines). Many beaches are bordered by dunes that have been fenced off to protect the vegetation.

👁 Sights & Activities

Cycling
CYCLING

Criss-crossed by an extensive network of well-maintained bicycle paths, the pancake-flat island is ideal for cycling. A biking map is available at tourist offices; in summer practically every hamlet has somewhere to hire bikes. Year-round Cyland (www.cyland. fr; per day from €12) can deliver bikes to the bridge. Of the numerous cycling trails, an especially fine one links the villages of Ars en Ré with Les Portes en Ré via a maze of marshes and salt pans (bring binoculars because the birdwatching is great). You can then loop back via the Phare des Baleines.

Phare des Baleines
LIGHTHOUSE

(adult/child €3/1.50; ⏱9.30am-9pm Jul-Aug) For an overview of the island, climb to its highest point – the Phare des Baleines, a lighthouse on the island's northern tip.

🛏 Sleeping

Île de Ré is an easy day trip from La Rochelle; however, if you want to spend longer on the island (and you will), each village has a summer tourist office with lists of local accommodation options, including campgrounds and private rooms and houses.

Do note, however, that accommodation here is very expensive – most people camp for a reason!

TOP CHOICE La Maison Douce   BOUTIQUE HOTEL €€€

(☑05 46 09 20 20; www.lamaisondouce.com; 25 rue Mérindot, St-Martin-de-Ré; r from €150; ☜) With weathered-looking ships' timber floors, pastel colour schemes and quality, arty furnishings, the eleven rooms of this magnificent place are as soft and gentle as the *douce* in its name. All the rooms are different but our favourites were those with the bath tubs built into the bedroom walls. Throw in a pretty courtyard garden, a peaceful location and a friendly owner and you get a place that's hard to beat.

La Baronnie Domaine   HISTORIC HOTEL €€€

(☑05 46 09 21 29; www.domainedelabaronnie.com; 21 rue Baron de Chantal, St-Martin-de-Ré; d from €170; ❈☜≋) Attention all kings and queens: this place, which oozes history, is so regal you won't be at all surprised to hear that it was once owned by one of your ancestors – Louis XVI.

Hôtel Le Sénéchal   BOUTIQUE HOTEL €€

(☑05 46 29 40 42; www.hotel-le-senechal.com; 6 rue Gambetta, Ars en Ré; r €90-290; ☜≋) This is a charming family-run place in the centre of the equally charming village of Ars en Ré. When we were visiting, a couple who were checking the rooms commented, 'Oh, isn't it cute.' We couldn't have expressed it better ourselves. The heated courtyard swimming pool is a huge plus.

❶ Getting There & Away

The one-way automobile toll (paid on your way to the island) is €8 (a whopping €16 from mid-June to mid-September).

Year-round excruciatingly slow buses link La Rochelle (the train-station car park, Tour de la Grosse Horloge and place de Verdun) with all the major towns on the island; the one-hour trip to St-Martin costs €4.60 or you can get a special *forfait journée* round trip ticket for €5. There are also intra-island routes.

Cognac

POP 19,500

On the banks of the River Charente amid vine-covered countryside, Cognac is known worldwide for the double-distilled spirit that bears its name, and on which the local economy thrives. Most visitors head here to visit the famous cognac houses; however, it's a picturesque stop even if you don't happen to be a huge fan of the local firewater.

Cognac's cafe-ringed central roundabout, place François 1er, is 200m northeast of the tourist office (☑05 45 82 10 71; www.tourism -cognac.com; 16 rue du XIV Juillet; ⊗9.30am-7pm Mon-Sat, 10am-4pm Sun). It's linked to the river by bd Denfert-Rochereau.

◉ Sights & Activities

Half-timbered 15th- to 17th-century houses line the narrow streets of the Vieille Ville (old city), which sits snugly between the partly Romanesque Église St-Léger (rue Aristide Briand) and the river.

Museums   MUSEUMS

(Joint entry adult/child €4.80/3.50; ⊗10am-6.30pm) At the southern corner of the leafy Jardin Public is the Musée d'Art et d'Histoire (☑05 45 32 07 25; www.musees -cognac.fr; 48 bd Denfert-Rochereau) showcasing the town's history. The Musée des Arts du Cognac (☑05 45 36 21 10; place de la Salle Verte) takes you step by step through the production of Cognac – from vine to bottle.

La Dame Jeanne   RIVER CRUISE

(☑05 45 82 10 71; adult/child €7/4; ⊗May-Sep; ☝) You can float with the sticklebacks down the River Charente on *La Dame Jeanne*, a re-creation of one of the flat-bottomed cargo boats known as *gabarres* that were once the lifeblood of trade along the river. The trip lasts 90 minutes and reservations should be made through the tourist office.

🛏 Sleeping & Eating

Hôtel Héritage   BOUTIQUE HOTEL €

(☑05 45 82 01 26; www.hheritage.com; 25 rue d'Angoulême; s/d €65/70; ☜) It's hard to know what to make of this hotel. It's been renovated in striking shades of lime green, fuchsia and cherry red and looks fantastic. Oh, and the 'medieval' portraits are like none you've ever seen before. But, on the flip side, many people complain of very thin partition walls and when we last visited the reception we received was one of the rudest we've ever encountered in France.

Hôtel Le Cheval Blanc   HOTEL €

(☑05 45 82 09 55; www.hotel-chevalblanc.fr; 6 place Bayard; d from €60; ❈☜) Miniature bottles of Cognac in the vending machine satiate midnight cravings at this hotel, where rooms are set around a courtyard. Although

ATLANTIC COAST COGNAC

not vast, the rooms are immaculate, and there's good wheelchair access.

Bistrot de Claude
BISTRO €€

(☑05 45 82 60 32; 35 rue Grande; menus from €18-29, mains €12-29; ☺Mon-Fri) Set in a lovely old wiggly timber building in the heart of the old town, this character-infused restaurant specialises in oysters and both river and sea fish.

❶ Getting There & Away

Cognac's **train station** (av du Maréchal Leclerc), 1km south of the town centre, has regular trains to/from La Rochelle (from €16, from 1¼ hours).

Around Cognac

Within a short drive of Cognac are some fascinating towns and villages worth seeking out. Just a couple of highlights include the former Gallo-Roman capital of Aquitaine, Saintes, on the River Charente. Dating from the 1st century AD, its Roman legacies include a double arch that served as the town gate, an amazing overgrown amphitheatre built during the reign of Claudius, and an archaeology museum with unearthed statues and even a chariot and harness. Its pedestrianised old town spills over with lively places to shop, eat and drink.

Also straddling the Charente is Jarnac, the 1916 birthplace of former president François Mitterrand. The house where he was born has been transformed into a museum; he's now buried in the town's cemetery. The waters around Jarnac are prime for fishing.

Cognac's tourist office has details of these and other areas in its surrounds.

✗ Eating

TOP CHOICE La Ribaudière
GASTRONOMIC €€€

(☑05 45 81 30 54; www.laribaudiere.com; menus €44-115, mains €39-45; ☺Tue evening, Wed-Sat, Sun lunch) This gastronomic haven is set among orchards overlooking the Charente River, in the tiny village of Bourg-Charente (midway between Cognac and Jarnac). Chef Thierry Verrat grows his own vegetables to accompany his seasonally changing, Michelin-starred creations. If the food sends your taste buds into whirls of excitement,

---

THE HOME OF COGNAC

According to local lore, divine intervention plays a role in the production of Cognac. Made of grape *eaux-de-vie* (brandies) of various vintages, Cognac is aged in oak barrels and blended by an experienced *maître de chai* (cellar master). Each year some 2% of the casks' volume – *la part des anges* (the angels' share) – evaporates through the pores in the wood, nourishing the tiny black mushrooms that thrive on the walls of Cognac warehouses. That 2% might not sound like much, but it amounts to around 20 million bottles a year – if the angels really are up there knocking back 20 million bottles of Cognac a year, then all we can say is roll on our time behind the pearly gates!

The best-known Cognac houses are open to the public, running tours of their cellars and production facilities, and ending with a tasting session. Opening times vary annually; it's a good idea to reserve in advance.

Camus (☑05 45 32 72 96; www.camus.fr; 29 rue Marguerite de Navarre; adult/child from €7/free) Located 250m northeast of the Jardin Public.

Hennessey (☑05 45 35 72 68; www.hennessey.com; 8 rue Richonne; adult/12-18yr/under 12 €9/7/free; ☺closed Jan & Feb) Situated 100m uphill from quai des Flamands; tours include a film (shown in English) and a boat trip across the Charente to visit the cellars.

Martell (☑05 45 36 33 33; www.martell.com; place Édouard Martell; adult/child €7.50/3) Found 250m northwest of the tourist office.

Otard (☑05 45 36 88 86; www.otard.com; 127 bd Denfert-Rochereau; adult/child €9.20/4.10) Housed in the 1494 birthplace of King François I, the Château de Cognac, 650m north of place François 1er.

Rémy Martin (☑05 45 35 76 66; www.visitesremymartin.com) Two locations: the estate (adult/child €15/7; ☺closed Oct-Apr), 4km southwest of town towards Pons; and, in town, the house (adult/12-18yr/under 12yr €25/14/7; ☺by appointment), for intimate tastings in groups of up to eight.

The tourist office has a list of smaller Cognac houses near town; most close between October and mid-March.

you can keep them happy by joining one of the restaurant's cookery courses (€115). See the website for details.

LOWER ATLANTIC COAST

At the lower edge of the Atlantic Coast, the expansive Aquitaine region extends to the Dordogne in the east and the Basque Country in the south. The gateway to the region's wealth of attractions, set amid glorious vine-ribboned countryside, is its capital, Bordeaux.

Bordeaux

POP 240,500

The new millennium was a major turning point for the city long known as La Belle au Bois Dormant (Sleeping Beauty). The mayor, former Prime Minister Alain Juppé, roused Bordeaux, pedestrianising its boulevards,

---

THE MÉDOC

Northwest of Bordeaux, along the western shore of the Gironde Estuary – formed by the confluence of the Garonne and Dordogne Rivers – lie some of Bordeaux's most celebrated vineyards. To their west, fine-sand beaches, bordered by dunes and *étangs* (lagoons), stretch from Pointe de Grave south along the Côte d'Argent (Silver Coast) to the Bassin d'Arcachon and beyond, with some great surf. On the banks of the muddy Gironde, the port town of Pauillac (population 1300) is at the heart of the wine country, surrounded by the distinguished Haut-Médoc, Margaux and St-Julien appellations. The Pauillac wine appellation encompasses 18 *crus classés* including the world-renowned Mouton Rothschild, Latour and Lafite Rothschild. The town's tourist office houses the Maison du Tourisme et du Vin (☑05 56 59 03 08; www.pauillac-medoc.com; ◐9.30am-7pm Mon-Sat, 10am-1pm & 2-6pm Sun), which has information on châteaux and how to visit them.

The lack of a public-transport system to most of the châteaux means this area is best explored in your own car or on one of the tours organised by the tourist office in Bordeaux. There are several different types of tour, which get chopped and changed on a regular basis; at the time of research, half-day Médoc tours taking in two châteaux and including wine tastings left the Bordeaux tourist office at 1.30pm on Thursdays and Saturdays (tours run to other wine regions the rest of the week) at a cost of €31. On Wednesdays the tourist office runs a day-long Médoc 1855 tour (tour including lunch €93; ◐tours 9.15am), which takes in three of the best known châteaux (the actual châteaux visited vary). Day-long La Winery tours also depart from Bordeaux's tourist office on Tuesdays and Sundays at 9.45am. The cost of €53 includes a tasting session and lunch. For any of these tours, advance reservations are essential. Bordeaux Excursions (☑06 24 88 22 09; www.bordeaux-excursions.com) customises private wine-country tours, starting from €190 for one to five people (excluding châteaux fees) for a half-day trip.

If you're travelling under your own steam, the Maison du Vin de Bordeaux (3 cours du 30 Juillet) supplies free, colour-coded maps of production areas, details on châteaux and the addresses of local *maisons du vin* (tourist offices that mainly deal with winery visits). One of the easiest châteaux to visit is Château Lanessan (☑05 56 58 94 80; www.lanessan.com; Cussac-Fort-Medoc), which offers daily hour-long tours throughout the year including ones tailored to children and hard-to-please teenagers; advance reservations required.

The Médoc is an easy day trip from Bordeaux, but should you have wine-heavy eyes at the end of the day there are numerous *chambres d'hôte* in the area or, in the village of Margaux, try Le Pavillon de Margaux (☑05 57 88 77 54; www.pavillonmargaux.com; 3 rue Georges Mandel; d €99-129; ☎), a welcoming, family-run place with rooms styled according to famous local châteaux.

While you're in the area, don't miss Philippe Raoux' La Winery (☑05 56 39 04 90; www.lawinery.fr; Rond-point des Vendangeurs, D1). A first for France, this vast glass-and-steel wine centre mounts concerts and contemporary-art exhibits alongside various fee-based tastings, including innovative tastings that determine your *signe œnologique* ('wine sign') costing from €16 (booking required), and more than 1000 different wines.

restoring its neoclassical architecture and implementing a high-tech public transport system. His efforts paid off: in mid-2007 half of the entire city (18 sq km, from the outer boulevards to the banks of the Garonne) was Unesco-listed, making it the largest urban World Heritage site.

Bolstered by its high-spirited university-student population (not to mention 2.5 million tourists annually), La Belle Bordeaux now scarcely seems to sleep at all.

◉ Sights & Activities

On the first Sunday of every month, Bordeaux's city centre is closed to cars, and attractions often have extended hours.

Cathédrale St-André   CATHEDRAL

Lording over the city, and a Unesco World Heritage site prior to the city's classification, the cathedral's oldest section dates from 1096; most of what you see today was built in the 13th and 14th centuries. Exceptional masonry carvings can be seen in the north portal. Even more imposing than the cathedral itself is the gargoyled, 50m-high Gothic belfry, Tour Pey-Berland (adult/child €5.50/free; ☺10am-1.15pm & 2-6pm Jun-Sep, shorter hours rest of year), erected between 1440 and 1466. Its spire was added in the 19th century, and in 1863 it was topped off with the statue of Notre Dame de l'Aquitaine (Our Lady of Aquitaine). Scaling the tower's 231 narrow steps rewards you with a spectacular panorama of the city.

Museums and Galleries   MUSEUMS

Bordeaux has a healthy collection of museums and galleries. Gallo-Roman statues and relics dating back 25,000 years are among the highlights at the impressive Musée d'Aquitaine (20 cours Pasteur). Upstairs is a small collection of statues and masks from the ex-French African and Oceanic colonies. Ask to borrow an English-language catalogue.

Built in 1824 as a warehouse for French colonial produce like coffee, cocoa, peanuts and vanilla, the cavernous Entrepôts Lainé creates a dramatic backdrop for cutting-edge modern art at the CAPC Musée d'Art Contemporain (rue Ferrére, Entrepôt 7; ☺11am-6pm Tue & Thu-Sun, to 8pm Wed).

The evolution of Occidental art from the Renaissance to the mid-20th century is on view at Bordeaux's Musée des Beaux-Arts (20 cours d'Albret; ☺11am-6pm daily mid-July–mid-Aug). Occupying two wings of the 1770s

Hôtel de Ville, either side of the Jardin de la Mairie (an elegant public park), the museum was established in 1801. Highlights include 17th-century Flemish, Dutch and Italian paintings. Temporary exhibitions are regularly hosted at its nearby annexe, Galerie des Beaux-Arts (place du Colonel Raynal).

Faience pottery, porcelain, gold, iron, glasswork and furniture are displayed at the Musée des Arts Décoratifs (39 rue Bouffard; ☺2-6pm Wed-Mon). For your own decorative treasures, browse rue Bouffard's antique and homewares shops.

Parks   PARKS

Landscaping is artistic as well as informative at the Jardin Public (cours de Verdun). Established in 1755 and laid out in the English style a century later, the grounds incorporate the meticulously catalogued Jardin Botanique, founded in 1629 and at this site since 1855. It's arguably one of the nicest public parks in southwest France.

At the vast square esplanade des Quinconces (quai Louis XVIII), laid out in 1820, you'll see the Girondins monument fountain. Les Girondins were a group of moderate, bourgeois National Assembly deputies during the French Revolution, 22 of whom were executed in 1793 after being convicted of counter-revolutionary activities.

The recently completed facelift of the 4km-long riverfront esplanade incorporates playgrounds, bicycle paths and, everyone's favourite, a wafer-thin 'swimming pool' in which hot and sticky young Bordelaise roll about throughout the summer months.

Pretty place Gambetta, a central open area ringed by shaded benches, also has its share of history – during the Reign of Terror that followed the Revolution, a guillotine placed here severed the heads of 300 alleged counter-revolutionaries.

Palais Gallien   RUIN

(rue du Docteur Albert Barraud; ☺1-6pm Jun-Sep) It was Celtic tribes who first established Bordeaux, but it wasn't until about 200 years later, under the rule of the Romans, that the town started to blossom. Back then it was called Burdigala and today the only remains of Burdigala are the crumbling ruins of the 3rd-century amphitheatre, Palais Gallien.

☞ Tours

The tourist office runs a packed program of bilingual city tours, including a wheelchair-accessible, two-hour morning

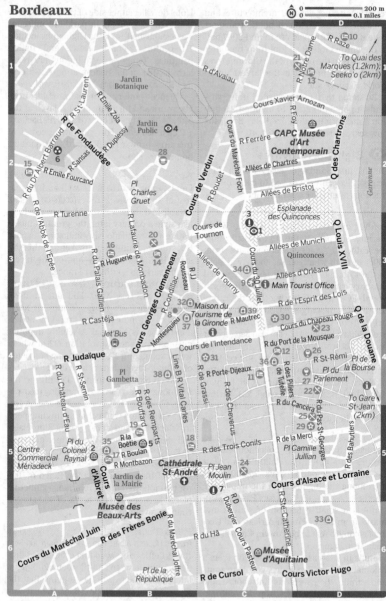

walking tour (adult/child €8.50/6; ☺tours 10am Mon, Tue, Thu, Fri & Sun); a 1.5-hour night-time walking tour (adult/child €16/11; ☺tours 9.30pm Mon-Sat) takes in Bordeaux's floodlit buildings and monuments. Contact the tourist office for details of dozens of other tour options, including gourmet and wine tours as well as river cruises in the warmer months.

There are wine-related tours including day trips further afield, as well as wine courses offered throughout the city to train up your nose and palate (see p628).

Bordeaux

ATLANTIC COAST BORDEAUX

All tours take a limited number of participants; reserve ahead.

🍴 Courses

If you need some food to go with all that wine, sign up for one of Nicolas Frion's highly regarded half-day cookery courses at the **École de Cuisine au Chapon Fin** (☑05 56 90 91 92; www.chapon-fin.com; 5 rue Montesquieu; per person €95).

Other short cooking courses also run periodically and are bookable through the tourist office.

🛏 Sleeping

Accommodation options are plentiful across all categories. The *Découverte* ('Discover Bordeaux') package is a neat little offering from the tourist office that bundles up two nights at your choice of participating hotels along with free public transportation, free access to the city's main monuments and sights, a guided city tour, a vineyard tour including wine tasting (both tours in English and French) and a bottle of wine. Prices start at €220 for a two-night package for two people; kids under 12 stay for free in their parents' room. Book 10 or more days in advance.

TOP CHOICE **Ecolodge des Chartrons** B&B €€
(☑05 56 81 49 13; www.ecolodgedeschartrons.com; 23 rue Raze; s €96-118, d €98-134; 📶) Hidden away in a little side street off the quays in Bordeaux's Chartrons wine merchant district, this *chambre d'hôte* is blazing a trail for ecofriendly sleeping in the city. Owner-hosts Veronique and Yann have added a solar-powered hot-water system, energy-efficient gas heating and hemp-based soundproofing, while preserving the 'soul' of this old wine merchant's house. They've stripped back and limewashed the stone walls, scrubbed the wide floorboards and recycled antique

Wine, Glorious Wine

The countryside around the Bordeaux region is full of renowned vineyards and legendary châteaux, many of which can be visited. Venture a little further north and the Cognac region offers a totally different sort of tipple.

Cognac

1 The Atlantic coast's wine attention might fall on Bordeaux, but it isn't the only wine party in town. Cognac (p620) produces a drink so heavenly that even the angels are said to partake.

St-Émilion

2 The quintessential French wine town, St-Émilion (p632), the oldest French wine region, has a honey glow and its robust and generous wines tickle the taste buds. This is the most rewarding of the wine towns to visit.

Bordeaux

3 No wine-tasting tour of the southwest is complete without a course at the École du Vin (p628). Built on the wealth of the grape, Bordeaux (p622) lives up to its bourgeois reputation, but today an army of students has given the city a lighter edge.

The Médoc

4 The Médoc region (p622) encompasses some of the finest wine territory in France, with such grand names as Mouton Rothschild, Latour and Lafite Rothschild hailing from this area.

Secrets of the Vine

5 Learn some of the secrets of a successful bottle on a château, vineyard or cellar tour in Bordeaux (p625 and p628) and St-Émilion (p633), or on a tour of a Cognac house (p620).

Clockwise from top left
1. Barrels of Hennessy Cognac 2. The medieval village of St-Émilion 3. Rooftop view from Tour Pey-Berland, Bordeaux

ON THE WINE TRAIL

Thirsty? The 1000-sq-km winegrowing area around the city of Bordeaux is, along with Burgundy, France's most important producer of top-quality wines.

The Bordeaux region is divided into 57 appellations (production areas whose soil and microclimate impart distinctive characteristics to the wine produced there) that are grouped into seven *familles* (families), and then subdivided into a hierarchy of designations (eg *premier grand cru classé*, the most prestigious) that often vary from appellation to appellation. The majority of the Bordeaux region's reds, rosés, sweet and dry whites and sparkling wines have earned the right to include the abbreviation AOC (Appellation d'Origine Contrôlée) on their labels, indicating that the contents have been grown, fermented and aged according to strict regulations that govern such viticultural matters as the number of vines permitted per hectare and acceptable pruning methods.

Bordeaux has over 5000 châteaux (also known as domaines, crus or *clos*), referring not to palatial residences but rather to the properties where grapes are raised, picked, fermented and then matured as wine. The smaller châteaux sometimes accept walk-in visitors, but at many places, especially the better-known ones, you have to make advance reservations. Many close during the *vendange* (grape harvest) in October.

Whet your palate with the tourist office's informal introduction to wine and cheese courses (adult €25), held every Thursday (and Saturdays mid-July–mid-August) at 4.30pm, where you sip three different wines straight from the cellar and nibble on cheese.

Serious students of the grape can enrol at the Ecole du Vin (Wine School; ☏05 56 00 22 66; www.bordeaux.com), within the Maison du Vin de Bordeaux (p622), across the street from the tourist office. Introductory two-hour courses are held Monday to Saturday from 10am to noon between July and September (adult €25). To really develop your nose (and your dinner-party skills), sign up for one of three progressively more complex two- to three-day courses (€335 to €600) scheduled between May and October, including châteaux visits.

furniture. Each of the five guest rooms has a bathroom built from natural materials such as basalt. You can curl up with a book in the lounge, access the island kitchen, and start the day with an organic breakfast, served at a long timber table.

TOP CHOICE **L'Hôtel Particulier** BOUTIQUE HOTEL €€€
(☏05 57 88 28 80; www.lhotel-particulier.com; 44 rue Vital-Carles; apt from €97, d from €168; 🖥) When you step into this fabulous boutique hotel with its secret courtyard garden, and find a thousand eyes staring at you from the reception walls and lampshades made only of feathers, you realise you've stumbled upon somewhere special. The rooms don't disappoint and are highly extravagant affairs with huge fireplaces, carved ceilings, free-standing bath tubs and quality furnishings throughout. They also have cheaper, but still very nice, fully equipped apartments ideal for a longer stay.

Les Chambres au Coeur de Bordeaux B&B €€
(☏05 56 52 43 58; www.aucoeurdebordeaux.fr; 28 rue Boulan; s/d from €85/95; 🖥) This recently renovated town house is now a swish B&B run very much along the lines of a small boutique hotel. Its five charming rooms are a very Bordeaux-appropriate mix of the old and the new, and each evening they offer a free *apero* at 7pm.

La Maison Bord'eaux BOUTIQUE HOTEL €€
(☏05 56 44 00 45; www.lamaisonbord-eaux.com; 113 rue du Docteur Albert Barraud; s/d from €145/165; ❄🖥) You'd expect to find a picturesque 18th-century château with a conifer-flanked courtyard and stable house in the countryside, but this stunning *maison d'hôte* is right in the middle of the city. Public areas include a library with shelves of books and CDs for guests' use. A *table d'hôte* is available by arrangement (*menus* €35 to €150 including wine).

Une Chambre en Ville BOUTIQUE HOTEL €€
(☏05 56 81 34 53; www.bandb-bx.com; 35 rue Bouffard; s/d €110/120; 🖥) On a street full of antique and art shops, this stylish place blends in well because each of the five rooms is an individual work of art in its own right. The decoration ranges from the plush reds and spicy pictures of the Oriental room to

the Madame-and-Monsieur classic style of the suites. Une Chambre en Ville is gay-friendly (and all-welcoming).

La Maison du Lierre   BOUTIQUE HOTEL €€

(✉05 56 51 92 71; www.maisondulierre.com; 57 rue Huguerie; s €72, d €72-135, tw €82-145; ☎) The delightfully restored 'House of Ivy' has a welcoming *chambre d'hôte* feel. A beautiful Bordelaise stone staircase (no lift here) leads to sunlit rooms with polished floorboards, rose-printed fabrics and sparkling bathrooms. The vine-draped garden is a perfect spot to sip fresh orange juice at breakfast (from €9.90).

Hôtel de la Presse   DESIGN HOTEL €€

(✉05 56 48 53 88; www.hoteldelapresse.com; 6-8 rue de la Porte Dijeaux; d €69-140; ❄☎) With shoes and letters plastered across the walls and words written across the floors this place has had a seriously hip makeover that helps to make it one of the more memorable hotels in Bordeaux. Service is polished and professional, but some rooms might pick up a little road noise from the busy shopping street outside.

Hôtel du Théâtre   BOUTIQUE HOTEL €

(✉05 56 79 05 26; www.hotel-du-theatre.com; 10 rue Maison-Daurade; s/d from €60/77; @☎) The owners of this recently renovated hotel, just off the main shopping street, have done up some rooms in an entirely classic style and some in the sun-burst colours of the Mediterranean. Our favourites are full of flashy sequins and glitter, and look like they just got home from the disco.

Seeko'o   DESIGN HOTEL €€€

(✉05 56 39 07 07; www.seekoo-hotel.com; 54 quai de Bacalan; d from €199; ❄☎) The monochrome lobby of this iceberg-shaped hotel leads to 45 retro-futuristic vinyl-and-leather-decorated rooms (some with circular beds), fitted out by Bordeaux designers. Unwind in the free Turkish *hammam*, visit the 1st-floor Champagne bar or just peruse the clever modern art throughout.

Hôtel Notre Dame   HOTEL €

(✉05 56 52 88 24; 36-38 rue Notre Dame; s €49-57, d €57-66; ☎) Location is the key selling point of this clean and simple hotel. It's within an easy stroll of the town centre, is sited just back from the river and in the middle of a lovely village-like neighbourhood of antique shops and relaxed cafes. It also has a wheelchair-accessible room.

Hôtel Touring   HOTEL €

(✉05 56 81 56 73; www.hoteltouring.fr; 16 rue Huguerie; s €41-53, d €48-63; ☎) Run with pride by a warm-hearted family, the Touring's rooms are furnished with original 1940s and '50s furniture, like flip-up school-style desks and club chairs. Most have a fridge, TV and telephone. Cheaper rooms share bathrooms.

Auberge de Jeunesse   HOSTEL €

(✉05 56 33 00 70; www.auberge-jeunesse-bordeaux.com; 22 cours Barbey; dm incl sheets & breakfast €22.50; ☺reception closed 11am-2pm; ☎) Bordeaux's only hostel is housed in an ultramodern building with a self-catering kitchen, good wheelchair access and table football to boot. From the train station, follow cours de la Marne northwest for 300m and turn left opposite the park; the hostel's about 250m ahead on your left. At the time of research it was closed for renovations but it will have reopened by the time this book is published.

🍴 Eating

All that fine wine needs fine cuisine to accompany it, and Bordeaux has some excellent restaurants. Place du Parlement, rue du Pas St-Georges and rue des Faussets have a plethora. There are also scads of inexpensive cafes and restaurants around place de la Victoire. The former warehouse district of the Quai des Marques now houses dozens of waterfront restaurants, bars and factory shops. It's a nice place for a sunset meal or drink.

Le Cheverus Café   BISTRO €
TOP CHOICE

(✉05 56 48 29 73; 81-83 rue du Loup; menus from €11.40; ☺Mon-Sat) In a city full of neighbourhood bistros, this one, smack in the city centre, is one of the most impressive. It's friendly, cosy and chaotically busy (be prepared to wait for a table at lunchtime). The food tastes fresh and home-cooked and it dares to veer slightly away from the bistro standards of steak and chips. The lunch *menus*, which include wine, are an all-out bargain. In the early evening it morphs into something of a tapas bar.

La Tupina   REGIONAL CUISINE €€€
TOP CHOICE

(✉05 56 91 56 37; www.latupina.com; 6 rue Porte de la Monnaie; menus €18-65, mains €27-45) Filled with the aroma of soup simmering inside an old *tupina* ('kettle' in Basque) over an open fire, this white-tableclothed place is feted far and wide for its seasonal southwestern

OYSTERS AT CAPUCINS

A classic Bordeaux experience is a Saturday morning spent slurping oysters and white wine from one of the seafood stands to be found at **Marché des Capucins** (six oysters & glass of wine €6; ☺7am-noon). Afterwards you can peruse the stalls while shopping for the freshest ingredients for a picnic in one of the city's parks. To get there, head south down cours Pasteur and once at place de la Victoire turn left onto rue Élie Gintrec.

French specialities such as a minicasserole of foie gras and eggs, milk-fed lamb or goose wings with potatoes and parsley. An €18 lunch *menu* is available on weekdays. La Tupina is a 10-minute walk upriver from the city centre and on a small side street. Any local can point you in the right direction.

La Boîte à Huîtres   OYSTERS €€
(☎05 56 81 64 97; 36 cours du Chapeau Rouge; lunch menu €19, 6 oysters from €10) This rickety, wood-panelled little place feels like an Arcachon fisherman's hut. It's a sensation that's quite appropriate because this is by far the best place in Bordeaux to munch on fresh Arcachon oysters. Traditionally they're served with sausage but you can have them in a number of different forms, including with that other southwest delicacy, foie gras. They'll also pack them up so you can take them away for a riverfront picnic.

Chez Dupont   BISTRO €€
(☎05 56 81 49 59; 45 rue Notre Dame; mains €9-19) Hemmed in by antique shops and small art galleries, Chez Dupont is the kind of cliché neighbourhood bistro you thought you'd only ever see in Hollywood films about France. As seems only right the food is equally traditional old French, but it's of an above-average quality and with an above-average welcome.

Baud et Millet   CHEESE & WINE €€
(☎05 56 79 05 77; 19 rue Huguerie; mains €23-25) If you like cheese or wine, or both of them, then this cute neighbourhood place with over 140 different cheeses served in myriad forms and almost as many wines is unmissable. Serious *fromage* fans should go for the *dégustation* of nine different cheese-based dishes (€45).

Michels Bistrot   BISTRO €
(15 rue du Pas-Saint-Georges; lunch menu €12) In Bordeaux's most bohemian quarter, this buzzing bistro is packed with students and those who wish they were still students. It's renowned for the quality of its beef – whether that be in hamburger form or a more classic steak. It's also a popular early evening *apero* hangout.

Karl   INTERNATIONAL €€
(☎05 56 81 01 00; place du Parlement; brunch from €5; ☺8.30am-7.30pm; ⚑) Simply *the* place in town for a morning-after-the-night-before brunch. These range from a light continental-style affair to the full works with salmon, cheeses, hams and eggs. It's just as good for a snack at any time of the day and is perpetually packed with a young crowd.

Self-Catering
For a taste of Bordeaux (that for once doesn't involve wine!), head to **Baillardran** (www.baillardran.com; place des Grands Hommes), which has several branches in town, including one in the Galerie des Grands Hommes shopping centre, where you can watch the chefs make *canelés*, a local vanilla-infused fluted cake. Nearby, you'll find **Jean d'Alos** (4 rue Montesquieu), a fine *fromagerie* with over 150 raw-milk and farm cheeses.

🍷 Drinking
Considering its synonymy with wine, Bordeaux has surprisingly few bars, meaning restaurants and bistros tend to fill the gap. Student hang-outs ring place de la Victoire.

L'Autre Petit Bois   BAR
(12 place du Parlement; ☺open from 11am) Decorated in an arresting 'modern' baroque and art deco style, this very popular wine bar full of curly-whirly sofas verges on the kitsch but pulls it off with style.

Café Brun   JAZZ BAR
(45 rue St-Rémi) A warm atmosphere and cool nightly jazz make this bar-bistro great for an evening aperitif.

L'Orangerie du Jardin Public   CAFE
(Jardin Public; ☺lunch; ⚑) Bliss out with a drink, light lunch (*menu* €14) and the flowers in this colourful glass-fronted building on the edge of the Jardin Public.

Titi Twister   DRINKING
(☎05 56 91 44 04; 76 rue Leyteire) This tucked-away little bar run by two long-term English expats has cheery waitresses and a fine

selection of Belgian beers (including eight on tap). There's live music on most Fridays. It's about 150m south of place de Victoire and down a side-street on the left.

☆ Entertainment

Details of events appear in *Clubs & Concerts* (www.clubsetconcerts.com, in French), available for free at the tourist office.

Nightclubs & Live Music

Trendy pedestrianised streets like rue St-Rémi are good bets to get the evening started. For zoning reasons, many of the city's late-night dance venues are a few blocks northeast of Gare St-Jean along the river, on quai de la Paludate. Clubs also cluster along the river north of the city centre.

Le Port de la Lune JAZZ CLUB
(www.leportdelalune.com; 58 quai de la Paludate) Gigs at this dark, atmospheric jazz club are posted on the website.

Rock School Barbey LIVE MUSIC
(✆05 56 33 66 00; www.rockschool-barbey.com; 18 cours Barbey) Catch live bands at the rock school, with a stream of up-and-coming French and international indie bands playing as well as various exhibitions. It's almost next door to the Auberge de Jeunesse.

Theatre & Classical Music

Grand Théâtre THEATRE, OPERA
(✆05 56 00 85 95; www.opera-bordeaux.com; place de la Comédie) Designed by Victor Louis (of Chartres Cathedral fame), the 18th-century Grand Théâtre stages operas, ballets and concerts of orchestral and chamber music. Guided behind-the-scenes tours of the building (€3) are possible on Wednesday and Saturday afternoons at 3pm, 4pm and 5pm.

Théâtre Femina THEATRE
(✆05 56 52 45 19; www.theatrefemina.fr; 10 rue de Grassi) Plays, dance performances, variety shows and concerts.

Cinemas

Cinéma Utopia CINEMA
(www.cinemas-utopia.org/bordeaux; 3 place Camille Jullian) Screens nondubbed art-house films.

🔒 Shopping

Europe's longest pedestrian shopping street, rue Ste-Catherine, is probably the city's low point. The southern end, towards place de la Victoire, is the worst half – essentially, an unending shambles of kebab shops. To give the road its dues though, things are better at the northern end where slightly classier chain shops predominate and you'll find the 19th-century shopping arcade Galerie Bordelaise (rue de la Porte Dijeaux & rue Ste-Catherine).

Luxury-label boutiques are concentrated within *le triangle*, formed by the allées de Tourny, cours Georges Clemenceau and cours de l'Intendance.

Antique Market MARKET
(place St-Michel; ⊘Sun am) Stalls of antiques fill the square on Sunday mornings. Located a 700m walk downriver from the city centre.

Bordeaux Magnum WINE
(3 rue Gobineau) Speciality wine shop.

L'Intendant WINE
(2 allées de Tourny) A central spiral staircase climbing four floors is surrounded by cylindrical shelves holding 15,000 bottles of regional wine.

Bradley's Bookshop BOOKS
(8 cours d'Albret) Stacks of English-language books and guides.

Librairie Mollat BOOKS
(15 rue Vital Carles) Books in several different languages.

Lily Blake CLOTHING
(✆05 33 05 41 40; www.lilyblake.fr; 68 rue Notre Dame) This author can't claim to be very knowledgeable on women's clothing boutiques, but his wife and her friends are self-proclaimed experts (and doesn't his credit card know it...) and they rate this independent boutique as one of the better choices in town.

Ballroom Blitz CLOTHING
(✆09 52 22 77 79; 25 rue Saint James) A haven of retro and rock clothing, accessories, gifts and general kitsch.

A TIPPLE WITH THE BEST

When in Rome do like the Romans, and when in Bordeaux drink wine in wine's Holy of Holies. The ultrastylish but very accessible Bar du Vin (3 cours du 30 Juillet; glass of wine from €2, with cheese from €5; ⊘11am-10pm Mon-Sat), inside the hallowed halls of the Maison du Vin de Bordeaux (p622), is the place to come for a tipple with people who really know their wine from their beer.

ATLANTIC COAST BORDEAUX

ⓘ Information

TOURIST INFORMATION **Bordeaux Monumental** (📱05 56 48 04 24; 28 rue des Argentiers; ⊘9.30am-1pm & 2-6pm Mon-Sat, 10am-1pm & 2-6pm Sun) Specialist tourist office dedicated to the city's history. Hosts free multimedia presentations plus temporary exhibitions with a historical theme.

Main Tourist Office (📱05 56 00 66 00; www .bordeaux-tourisme.com; 12 cours du 30 Juillet; ⊘9am-7.30pm Mon-Sat, 9.30am-6.30pm Sun) Runs an excellent range of city and regional tours. There's a small-but-helpful **branch** (📱05 56 91 64 70; ⊘9am-noon & 1-6pm Mon-Sat, 10am-noon & 1-3pm Sun) at the train station.

Maison du Tourisme de la Gironde (📱05 56 52 61 40; www.tourisme-gironde.fr; 21 cours de l'Intendance; ⊘9am-6pm Mon-Fri, 10am-1pm & 2-6.30pm Sat) Information on the Gironde *département*.

Websites

Head to **Lonely Planet** (www.lonelyplanet. com/france/southwestern-france/bordeaux) for planning advice, author recommendations, traveller reviews and insider tips.

ⓘ Getting There & Away

AIR Bordeaux airport (p968) is in Mérignac, 10km southwest of the city centre, with domestic and increasing numbers of international flights to many western European and North African destinations.

BUS **Citram Aquitaine** (www.citram.fr) runs most buses to destinations in the Gironde.

International bus operator **Eurolines** (📱05 56 92 50 42; 32 rue Charles Domercq) faces the train station.

CAR Rental companies have offices in the train-station building and at the airport.

TRAIN Bordeaux is one of France's major rail-transit points. The station, Gare St-Jean, is about 3km from the city centre at the southern terminus of cours de la Marne.

Paris Gare Montparnasse €73, three hours, at least 16 daily

Bayonne €29, two hours

La Rochelle €28.60, 2¼ hours

Nantes €47.70, four hours

Poitiers €38, 1¾ hours

Toulouse from €35.30, 2¼ hours

ⓘ Getting Around

TO/FROM THE AIRPORT The train station, place Gambetta and the main tourist office are connected to the airport (one way €7) by **Jet'Bus** (📱05 56 34 50 50). The first bus leaves the airport at 7.45am from outside Terminal B (last at 10.45pm daily); the first departure to the airport from the train station is at 6.45am Monday to Friday, and 7.30am Saturday and Sunday (last at 9.45pm daily), with buses at 45-minute intervals throughout the day. The trip takes approximately 45 minutes. A taxi costs around €50.

BUS & TRAM Urban buses and trams are run by **TBC** (www.infotbc.com). The company has Espace Bus information-ticket offices at the train station and place Gambetta (4 rue Georges Bonnac) and at esplanade des Quinconces. Tram line C links the train station with the city centre via the riverside.

Single tickets (€1.40) are sold onboard buses, and from machines at tram stops (stamp your ticket onboard). Tickets aren't valid for transfers.

Night buses operate until 1.30am on Thursday, Friday and Saturday nights; line 11 and 16 links place de la Victoire with the nightclub zone on quai de la Paludate.

CAR City parking is pricey and hard to find. Look for free spaces in the side streets north of the Musée d'Art Contemporain and west of the Jardin Public.

TAXI To order a taxi try 📱05 56 32 43 00 or 📱05 56 29 10 25.

St-Émilion

POP 2070

The medieval village of St-Émilion perches above vineyards renowned for producing full-bodied, deeply coloured red wines and is easily the most alluring of all the region's wine towns. Named after Émilion, a miracle-working Benedictine monk who lived in a cave here between AD 750 and 767, it soon became a stop on pilgrimage routes, and the village and its vineyards are now Unesco-listed. Today, despite masses of tourists descending on the town, it's well worth venturing 40km east from Bordeaux to experience St-Émilion's magic, particularly when the sun sets over the valley and the limestone buildings glow with halo-like golden hues.

Note that the cobbled streets and steep hills of the village make it difficult for travellers with disabilities to get around, but three trails that allow mobility-impaired visitors to see at least some of the sites are plotted on free maps available from the tourist office.

◉ Sights

Clocher   TOWER
(Bell Tower; admission €1.25) For captivating views of the hilltop hamlet, collect the

key from the tourist office to climb above the church. The entrance is on place des Créneaux.

Collégiale   CHURCH
(Collegiate Church) A domed Romanesque 12th-century nave dominates the former Collégiale, which also boasts an almost-square vaulted choir built between the 14th and 16th centuries. Cloître de l'Église Collégiale, the church's tranquil 12th- to 14th-century cloister, is the venue for special events.

Porte de la Cadène   CITY WALLS
(Gate of the Chain) Surviving sections of the town's medieval walls and gates include those running off rue Guadet.

FREE **Cloître des Cordeliers**   MONASTERY
(rue Porte Brunet; admission free, Les Cordeliers guided cellar tours with wine tastings €5; ⊙11am-8.30pm May-Sep) Within the ruined monastery, the winery Les Cordeliers has made sparkling wine for over a century. Thirty-minute guided tours of the cellars take place several times daily in high summer. Entry to the gardens and ruins is free (though you might want to consider buying a drink).

La Tour du Château Roy   CASTLE
(admission €1.25; ⊙11am-8.30pm) Climb the 118 steps of the 13th-century donjon known as the Tour du Roi (King's Tower) for exceptional views of the town and the Dordogne Valley.

🏃 Activities

Blind tastings and games (available in English) are a fun and informative introduction to wine tasting at L'École du Vin de St-Émilion (www.vignobleschateaux.fr; 4 rue du Clocher; tasting courses €29; ⊙3pm Apr-Oct, by reservation Nov-Mar). The adjacent Maison du Vin (place Pierre Meyrat; classes €21; ⊙mid-Jul-mid-Sep) also offers bilingual 1½-hour classes starting at 11am.

Eight hiking circuits, from 4km to 14km, loop through the greater World Heritage jurisdiction; the tourist office has maps.

☞ Tours

The only (but highly worthwhile) way to visit the town's most-interesting historical sites is with one of the tourist office's guided tours (adult/child €7-14/free). There are a variety of different tour options – including a lantern-lit evening tour, a secrets of the city tour and family-friendly tours. The standard historical city tour lasts an hour and a half with French-language tours leaving from the tourist office daily at 3pm. English tours are at 11am, weekends only. The St-Émilion Souterrain (Underground St-Émilion; adult/child €7/free) tour takes you beneath the pretty streets and into a fascinating labyrinth of catacombs – highlights are the hermit saint's famous cave, Grotte de l'Ermitage, and the 11th-century church, Église Monolithe, carved out of limestone between the 9th and the 12th centuries. Tours in French depart regularly throughout the day – call ahead to check English tour times (usually 2pm). It's chilly below ground; bring a sweater.

The tourist office organises two-hour afternoon château visits (adult/child €14/free) in French and English. Demand can be heavy so you should reserve in advance. It also runs various events throughout the year, such as Les Samedis de l'Oenologie (€77; ⊙Saturdays), which combines a vineyard visit, lunch, town tour and wine-tasting course.

Note that in all cases tour times and types change frequently.

🎉 Festivals & Events

Les Grandes Heures de St-Émilion   MUSIC FESTIVAL
(www.grandesheuresdesaintemilion.fr; tickets €33) Classical concerts are held at various châteaux between March and December. Tickets must be booked in advance; the program is posted on the tourist-office website.

St-Émilion Jazz Festival   MUSIC FESTIVAL
(www.saint-emilion-jazz-festival.com; tickets €17-77; ⊙mid-July) In July the soothing tones of jazz take over the town during its jazz festival.

Marché du Gout   MARKET
A market selling regional products sets up in the village cloister in mid-October. The cloister is also the venue for free concerts from May to November; the tourist office has the program.

🛏 Sleeping & Eating

The village and its surrounds have some charming, but very expensive, boutique hotels. If you're on a budget and don't want to camp, it might be better to visit on a day trip from Bordeaux. Ask the tourist office for a list of nearby, and much cheaper, *chambres d'hôte*. Many of St-Émilion's best restaurants are attached to hotels.

634

ATLANTIC COAST ST-ÉMILION

VILLAGE CENTRE

Auberge de la Commanderie   HOTEL €€
(☎05 57 24 70 19; www.aubergedelacommanderie
.com; 2 rue Porte Brunet; d €80-120; ⊗mid-Feb–
mid-Jan; ⊛) Inside this hotel's 13th-century
walls, rooms are modernised with massive
murals depicting a Technicolorised pop-art
version of an old black-and-white postcard
of the village. Larger rooms are in an annexe
over the road. Free private parking.

Hôtel-Restaurant du
Palais Cardinal   HISTORIC HOTEL €€
(☎05 57 24 72 39; www.palais-cardinal.com; place
du 11 Novembre 1918; s €71-142, d €88-166; ⊛⊠)
Run by the same family for five generations,
this hotel puts a little more thought into
its dress sense than the other 'cheap' St-
Émilion hotels. The heated pool is set in
flower-filled gardens and framed by sections of the original medieval town-wall
fortifications, dating from the 13th century.
It's well worth partaking in the gastronomic
fare served at its restaurant (closed at lunch
on Wednesday and Thursday, and from December to April).

La Maison d'Aline   B&B €€
(☎05 57 24 65 47; www.alinebb.com; 7 rue Porte
Brunet; d €110-150; ⊗closed Oct-Mar; ⊛) This is
a cosy three-bedroom *chambre d'hôte* with
spacious country-cottage rooms. The largest
room contains a small kitchen and all have
totally modern bathrooms.

Hostellerie de Plaisance   BOUTIQUE HOTEL €€€
(☎05 57 55 07 55; www.hostellerie-plaisance.
com; place du Clocher; incl breakfast r €380-560,
ste €700; ⊗closed Jan; ⊛⊛) With a spice-
coloured bar opening to a wraparound terrace, this intimate gem in the shadow of
the bell tower houses 17 whimsical rooms.
(A glass lift concealed in a gazebo whisks
you through the rock face down to the new
wing.) The rooms are about the size of a castle and look out over a flurry of red terra-

cotta roof tiles and a church tower, but, good
as it is, you can't help feeling that it's very
overpriced.

Hôtel au Logis des Remparts   HOTEL €€
(☎05 57 24 70 43; www.logisdesremparts.com; 18
rue Porte Guadet; r with street/garden view from
€98/140; ⊛⊛⊠) In a thoughtfully restored
town house, the modern rooms are comfortable but lack much sparkle. Much more
exciting is the courtyard garden and swimming pool.

TOP CHOICE Restaurant Hostellerie de
Plaisance   GASTRONOMIC €€€
(☎05 57 55 07 55; www.hostellerie-plaisance.com;
place du Clocher; menus €105-150; ⊗open lunch
only Tue-Fri, lunch & dinner Sat) Award-winning
chef Philippe Etchebest cooks up food like
you've never had before at his double-
Michelin-starred restaurant housed in a
dining room of eggshell blue and white gold
inside the hotel of the same name. The 'discovery menu' allows you to do just that in
about eight courses. Advance reservations
essential.

L'Huîtres Pie   SEAFOOD €€
(☎05 57 24 69 71; 11 rue de la Porte Bouqueyre;
menus €22-52; ⊗open Thu-Mon) Arcachon
oysters and other seafood feature heavily
in the dishes on offer here, but if slippery
shellfish don't do it for you, tuck into one
of the hearty meat or fish dishes. You can
eat inside or outside on the pleasant olive-
shaded courtyard.

AROUND ST-ÉMILION

Grand Barrail   HISTORIC HOTEL €€€
(☎05 57 55 37 00; www.grand-barrail.com; rte de
Libourne/D243; r from €320, menus from €29;
⊛⊛⊠) Grand doesn't even begin to describe
this immense 1850-built château, 3km from
the village, with its decadent on-site spa,
stone-flagged heated swimming pool, free
state-of-the-art fitness room, wheelchair access and, if you happen to be arriving by helicopter, its own helipad on the front lawns.
Undoubtedly the best seat in its restaurant
is the corner table framed by 19th-century
stained glass that would make the average
church green with envy.

Château de Roques   HISTORIC HOTEL €€
(☎05 57 74 55 69; www.chateau-de-roques.com;
d €76-120, menus from €24; ⊛⊠) If you've
dreamed of staying in a romantic countryside château but your budget – or lack
thereof – was a rude awakening, you'll be

OYSTER TASTE TEST

Oysters from each of the Bassin
d'Arcachon's four oyster-breeding
zones hint at subtly different flavours.
See if you can detect these:

» **Banc d'Arguin** – milk and sugar

» **Île aux Oiseaux** – minerals

» **Cap Ferret** – citrus

» **Grand Banc** – roasted hazelnuts

delighted by this affordable 16th-century place in the vineyards, 5km outside St-Émilion. Its restaurant (closed late December to early February) serves delicious regional fare washed down with the château's own wine. The best road is the D122 (north from St-Émilion) – the château is just near the junction of the D21.

Camping Domaine de la Barbanne CAMPGROUND €
(☑05 57 24 75 80; www.camping-saint-emilion.com; rte de Montagne; sites per 2 people, tent & car €38; ☺mid-Apr–Sep; ▣) This family-friendly campground is about 2km north of St-Émilion on the D122. Cabins, sleeping up to five people, are also available.

🛍 Shopping

St-Émilion's sloping streets and squares are lined with about 50 wine shops – one for every eight of the old city's residents. The largest is the Maison du Vin (☑05 57 55 50 55; www.maisonduvinsaintemilion.com; place Pierre Meyrat; ☺9.30am-12.30pm & 2-6.30pm), which is owned by the 250 châteaux whose wines it sells at cellar-door prices. It also has a free aromatic exhibit and sells specialist publications. In August it's open over lunch. If you think St-Émilion is a good place to get a few bottles of cut-price cheapo wine, then think again. It's all quality only, with price tags to match – a very fast perusal of a few shops showed a top-dollar price of €9200 for a bottle of Petrus 1947. Not the sort of bottle you'd want airport customs confiscating from your hand luggage!

Ursuline nuns brought the recipe for *macarons* (macaroons – almond biscuits) to St-Émilion in the 17th century. Specialist shops around town charge €6 per two dozen.

ℹ Information

Tourist office (☑05 57 55 28 28; www.saint-emilion-tourisme.com; place des Créneaux; ☺9.30am-8pm) Stacks of brochures in English and details on visiting more than 100 nearby châteaux.

ℹ Getting There & Away

BICYCLE Year-round the tourist office rents out bicycles for €15 per day.

BUS Getting to St-Émilion from Bordeaux by bus is a bit of a pain as you have to change in Libourne. **Citram Aquitaine** (www.citram.fr) buses run this route. A ticket is €7.30 one-way and there are several buses a day.

CAR From Bordeaux, follow the signs for Libourne and take the D243.

TRAIN It's easier to take a train from Bordeaux, with around half a dozen services a day (€8.60-11.60, 35min-1½ hr). St-Émilion station is a kilometre south of town.

Arcachon
POP 11,750

A long-time oyster-harvesting area on the southern side of the tranquil, triangular Bassin d'Arcachon (Arcachon Bay), this seaside town lured bourgeois Bordelaise at the end of the 19th century. Its four little quarters are romantically named for each of the seasons, with villas that evoke the town's golden past amid a scattering of 1950s architecture.

Arcachon seethes with sun-seekers in summer, but you'll find practically deserted beaches a short bike ride away.

⦿ Sights

Town & Beaches TOWN, BEACHES
(art deco public lift admission free) In the Ville d'Été (Summer Quarter), Arcachon's sandy beach, Plage d'Arcachon, is flanked by two piers. Lively Jetée Thiers is at the western end. In front of the eastern pier, Jetée d'Eyrac, stands the town's turreted Casino de la Plage, built by Adalbert Deganne in 1953 as an exact replica of Château de Boursault in the Marne. Inside, it's a less-grand blinking and bell-ringing riot of poker machines and gaming tables. The sheltered basin in which Arcachon sits means the water is always absolutely flat calm and ideal for families – a far cry from most Atlantic beaches. On the flipside estuary run-off means the water is always a browner colour than the nearby open Atlantic (it's clean, though).

On the tree-covered hillside south of the Ville d'Été, the century-old Ville d'Hiver (Winter Quarter) has over 300 villas, many decorated with delicate wood tracery, ranging in style from neo-Gothic through to colonial. It's an easy stroll or a short ride up the art deco public lift in Parc Mauresque.

Aquarium et Musée AQUARIUM
(2 rue du Professeur Jolyet; adult/under 10yr €5/3.30; ☺9.45am-12.15pm & 1.45-6pm) In a wooden shack opposite the casino, this aquarium has a small collection of Atlantic fish in floodlit tanks.

⚡ Activities

Ocean Roots SURF COURSES
(☎06 62 26 04 11; www.oceanroots.com; 228 bd de la Côte d'Argent; courses from €35; 🚣) The exposed ocean beaches to the south of town generally offer good conditions for surfing. Ocean Roots offers lessons and rents out equipment.

Cycling CYCLING
Cycle paths link Arcachon with the Dune du Pilat and Biscarosse (30km to the south), and around the Bassin d'Arcachon to Cap Ferret. From here, a cyclable path runs parallel to the beaches north to Pointe de Grave.

☞ Tours

Les Bateliers Arcachonnais BOAT TOURS
(☎05 57 72 28 28; www.bateliers-arcachon.com; Île aux Oiseaux (adult/child/under 5yrs €15/10/5), Banc d'Arguin (adult/child/under 3yrs €20/14/8); 🚣) Daily, year-round cruises sail around the Île aux Oiseaux, the uninhabited 'bird island' in the middle of the bay. It's a haven for tern, curlew and redshank, so bring your binoculars. In summer there are regular all-day excursions (11am to 5.30pm) to the Banc d'Arguin, the sand bank off the Dune du Pilat.

🛏 Sleeping

Arcachon has tons of accommodation options. Many are chintzy mid-20th-century time warps, though not without charm.

Hôtel le Dauphin HISTORIC HOTEL €€
(☎05 56 83 02 89; www.dauphin-arcachon. com; 7 av Gounod; s/d from €112/122; 🅿🛜🏊) Don't miss this late 19th-century gingerbread place with patterned red-and-cream brickwork. An icon of its era, it's graced by twin semicircular staircases, magnolias and palms. Plain but spacious rooms are well set up for families. Parking is free.

Park Inn DESIGN HOTEL €€
(☎05 56 83 99 91; www.parkinn.fr; 4 rue du Professeur Jolyet; d from €155; 🚫🛜) Arcachon's version of this chain is utterly distinctive, thanks to its vivid swirled carpet, candy-striped curtains and primary-coloured modular furniture. It's a bit like bouncing around in a preschoolers' playroom. There are three wheelchair-equipped rooms and the staff are a pleasure to deal with.

🍴 Eating

The bay's oysters (served raw and accompanied by the local small, flat sausages, *crepinettes*) appear on *menus* everywhere.

The beachfront promenade between Jetée Thiers and Jetée d'Eyrac is lined with restaurants and places offering pizza and crêpes, plus a couple of standout places serving seafood.

Aux Mille Saveurs TRADITIONAL FRENCH €€
(☎05 56 83 40 28; 25 bd du Général Leclerc; menus €19-50; ☺closed Wed & dinner Sun &Tue) In a light-filled space of flowing white tablecloths, this genteel restaurant is renowned for its traditional French fare artistically presented on fine china.

Chez Pierre SEAFOOD €€
(Cafe de la Plage; ☎05 56 22 52 94; 1 bd Veyrier Montagnères; menus from €30, seafood platters €24-42) This see-and-be-seen restaurant serves up an ocean of seafood.

ℹ Information
Tourist office (☎05 57 52 97 97; www .arcachon.com; Esplanade Georges Pompidou; ☺9am-7pm)

ℹ Getting There & Away
There are frequent trains between Bordeaux and Arcachon (€10.50, 50 minutes).

Around Arcachon
DUNE DU PILAT
This colossal sand dune (sometimes referred to as the Dune de Pyla because of its location in the resort town of Pyla-sur-Mer), 8km south of Arcachon, stretches from the mouth of the Bassin d'Arcachon southwards for almost 3km. Already the largest in Europe, it's spreading eastwards at 4.5m a year – it has swallowed trees, a road junction and even a hotel.

The view from the top – approximately 114m above sea level – is magnificent. To the west you can see the sandy shoals at the mouth of the Bassin d'Arcachon, including the Banc d'Arguin bird reserve and Cap Ferret. Dense dark-green pine forests stretch from the base of the dune eastwards almost as far as the eye can see.

Take care swimming in this area: powerful currents swirl out to sea from the deceptively tranquil *baïnes* (little bays).

Although just a very quick trip from Arcachon, the area around the dune is an enjoyable place to relax for a while. Most people choose to camp in one of the many seasonal campgrounds. Lists and information on all of these (and more bricks-and-mortar-based accommodation) can be found at www.bassin-arcachon.com.

CAP FERRET
POP 7300

Hidden within a canopy of pine trees at the tip of the Cap Ferret peninsula, the tiny village of Cap Ferret spans a mere 2km between the tranquil bay and the crashing Atlantic waves. It's crowned by its 53m-high, red-and-white lighthouse (adult/child €4.50/3; ☺10am-7.30pm), with interactive exhibits and stunning surf-views from the top. If you want to get closer to the waves, the Surf Center (☑05 56 60 61 05; www.surf-center.fr; 22 allées des Goëlands; lesson from €23; ☺Easter-Sep) rents out boards and offers lessons.

Cap Ferret is littered with campgrounds, which can be tracked down on www.bassin-arcachon.com. La Maison du Bassin (☑05 56 60 60 63; www.lamaisondubassin.com; 5 rue des Pionniers; s €120-200, d €140-240, apt €330; ☺closed Jan) has four dreamy rooms the size of suites tucked away in a separate annexe of this quixotic hideaway, while cosy rooms in the main house have details like a muslin-canopied sleigh bed, or a curtained bathtub in the centre of the room. Its restaurant, Le Bistrot du Bassin (menus €25.90 to €39), will make your taste buds very happy indeed.

Les Bateliers Arcachonnais (www.bateliers-arcachon.com) runs ferries from Arcachon to Cap Ferret (adult/child return €11.50/8) year-round. In the warmer months, seasonally operating lines include ferries linking Cap Ferret and the Dune du Pilat, and Cap Ferret and Moulleau. Schedules are posted on the website and available from tourist offices.

Cap Ferret is a scenic drive around Bassin d'Arcachon. Alternatively, to drive here directly from Bordeaux (71.8km) take the D106.

GUJAN MESTRAS
POP 19,400

Picturesque oyster ports are dotted around the town of Gujan Mestras, which sprawls along 9km of coastline.

You'll find the tourist office (☑05 56 66 12 65; www.ville-gujanmestras.fr; 19 av de Lattre de Tassigny; ☺9.30am-12.30pm & 2-6.30pm Mon-Sat, 9.30am-12.30pm Sun) at the western edge of town in La Hume.

Gujan Mestras' train station is on the train line linking Bordeaux with Arcachon.

◉ Sights

Le Teich Parc Ornithologique   BIRDWATCHING
(Bird Reserve; ☑05 56 22 80 93; www.parc-ornithologique-du-teich.com; adult/child €7.60/5.40; ☺10am-8pm Jul-Aug to roughly sunset rest of yr; ☐) A series of trails wind through and around the swamps, lakes and woodlands of the idyllic Parc Ornithologique situated in Le Teich, 5km east of Gujan Mestras. Birds also find the place much to their liking, and some 260 species of migratory and nonmigratory birds call it home. The stars of the show are the white storks, spoonbills, common cranes, marsh harriers and black kites, all of which can be spied on from a network of well-maintained hides. Away from birds, the park is one of the most reliable places in France to see the now-threatened European pond tortoise. The pool just beyond the ticket office is a real hot spot for it.

You can also discover the waterways surrounding the park by canoe or kayak with Canoe sur la Leyre (☑05 56 22 80 93; www.canoesurlaleyre.fr; adult/child from €25.50/19). Tours depart from outside the park gates.

Port de Larros   OYSTERS
Flat-bottomed oyster boats moored to weathered wooden shacks line Port de Larros, the largest oyster port around Gujan Mestras. The small Maison de l'Huître (adult/child €4.50/2.50; ☺10am-12.30pm & 2.30-6pm Mon-Sat) has a display on oyster farming, including a short film in English. They can also supply audio-guides (€3.50) for the whole port area. Locally harvested oysters are sold nearby and served at seafood restaurants with waterside terraces.

French Basque Country

Best Places to Eat

» La Feuillantine (p642)
» Lezetako Borda (p661)
» Buvette des Halles (p658)
» Xurasko (p644)
» Bar Jean (p650)

Best Places to Stay

» Péniche Djébelle (p641)
» La Devinière (p657)
» Maison d'hôte Irazabala (p661)
» Hôtel Mirano (p649)
» Hôtel de Silhouette (p649)

Why Go?

Gently sloping from the foothills of the Pyrenees into the deep-sapphire-blue Bay of Biscay, the Basque Country straddles France and Spain. Yet this feisty, independent land remains profoundly different from either of the nation states that have adopted it.

The Basque Country is famed for the glitzy beach resort of Biarritz, where surfers strut their stuff in the waves and oiled sun-seekers pack the beaches like glistening sardines. But the region offers so much more than the pleasures of sun and surf. Nearby Bayonne is a chocolate box of narrow winding streets full of Basque culture, and St-Jean de Luz, further south, is a delightful seaside fishing port.

Inland, up in the lush hills, little one-street villages and green valleys traversed by hiking trails fan out from the walled town of St-Jean Pied de Port, an age-old stop for pilgrims heading over the Spanish border to Santiago de Compostela.

When to Go
Bayonne

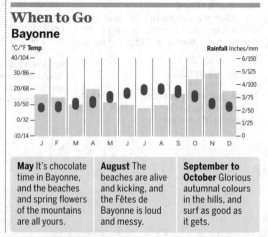

May It's chocolate time in Bayonne, and the beaches and spring flowers of the mountains are all yours.

August The beaches are alive and kicking, and the Fêtes de Bayonne is loud and messy.

September to October Glorious autumnal colours in the hills, and surf as good as it gets.

Bayonne

POP 46,200

Surrounded by fortifications, red-and-white, Bayonne (Baiona in Basque), capital of the French Basque Country, is a delightful, with a perfectly preserved old town (until 1907 it was forbidden to build outside the town's fortifications) and great riverside restaurants.

The Rivers Adour and Nive split Bayonne into three: St-Esprit, north of the Adour; Grand Bayonne, the oldest and most attractive area, on the Nive's western bank; and the very Basque Petit Bayonne quarter on the east. To the west, Bayonne meets the suburban sprawl of Anglet (famed for its beaches) and the glamorous seaside resort of Biarritz.

In addition to chocolates, Bayonne is famous for prime cured ham and for the *baïonnette* (bayonet), developed here in 1640 on rue des Faures (Blacksmiths' Street).

◉ Sights

Musée Basque et de l'Histoire de Bayonne
MUSEUM

(☑05 59 59 08 98; www.musee-basque.com; 37 quai des Corsaires; adult/child €6.50/free; ☺10am-6.30pm) The seafaring history, traditions and cultural identity of the Basque people are all explored at this superb museum through exhibits including a reconstructed farm and the interior of a typical *etxe* (home). Labelling is in French, Spanish and Basque only but English information sheets are available. In July and August free 'nocturnal' visits are possible on Thursday evenings from 6.30pm to 8.30pm.

Cathédrale Ste-Marie
CATHEDRAL

(☺10-11.45am & 3-6.15pm Mon-Sat, 3.30-6.15pm Sun, cloister 9am-12.30pm & 2-6pm) The twin towers of Bayonne's Gothic cathedral soar above the city. Construction began in the 13th century, and was completed in 1451; the mismatched materials resemble Lego blocks. Above the north aisle are three lovely stained-glass windows; the oldest, in the Chapelle Saint Jérôme, dates from 1531. The entrance to the stately 13th-century cloister is on place Louis Pasteur.

Ramparts
CITY WALL

Bayonne's 17th-century fortifications are now covered with grass, dotted with trees and enveloped in pretty parks. You can walk the stretches of the old ramparts that rise above bd Rempart Lachepaillet and rue Tour de Sault.

French Basque Country Highlights

❶ Discover the local chocolate at a factory tour in **Bayonne** (p639)

❷ Tiptoe along the sheer **Iparla Ridge** (p662) in the mist-soaked Pyrenees

❸ Treat yourself to tapas and watch surfers tackle the waves in magisterial **Biarritz** (p645)

❹ Taste traditional Basque seafood dishes at **St-Jean de Luz** (p654)

❺ Browse the farmers market in **St-Jean Pied de Port** (p661)

❻ Explore picturesque villages **Ainhoa** (p660) and **Espelette** (p660), and chug to the summit of **La Rhune** (p659)

❼ Soak up some sun on the sands of **Hossegor** (p645) or **Moliets** (p645) in the region of Les Landes

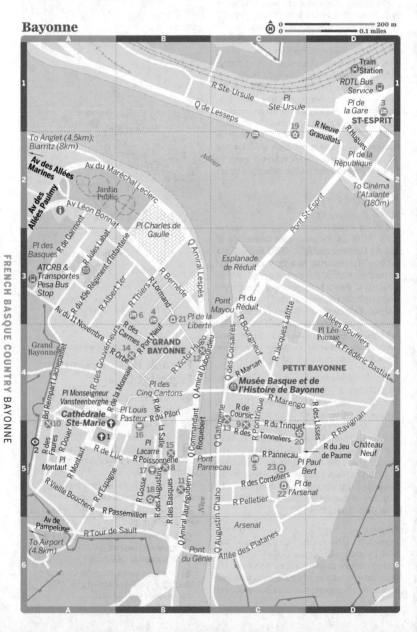 Tours

The tourist office organises a range of city tours (adult €6-10; some in English), from a historical tour of old Bayonne to a chocolate-fiend or museum tour. Departure times and tour type varies by the day.

Festivals & Events

Foire au Jambon FOOD FESTIVAL
(Ham Fair) During Easter week, the town hosts a Ham Fair, honouring *jambon de Bayonne,* the acclaimed local ham. You may think this is just a recently thought up touristy gim-

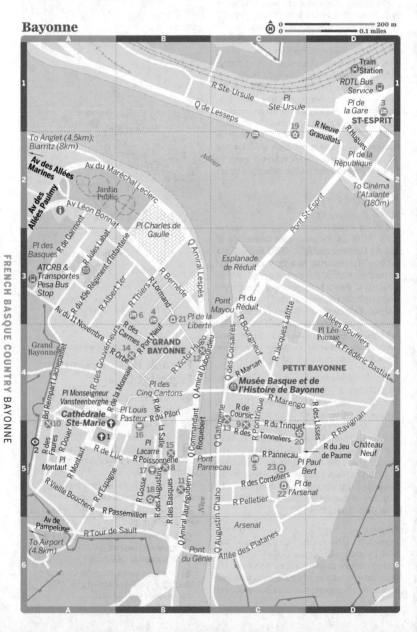

Bayonne

0 _____ 200 m
0 _____ 0.1 miles

mick to sell ham, but no – this fair in March or April has taken place annually since 1462!

Journées du Chocolat FOOD FESTIVAL
Master chocolatiers reveal the secrets of chocolate making (with tastings) in May.

🛏 Sleeping

Even outside the Fêtes de Bayonne, it's tough to find a bed from mid-July to mid-August.

TOP CHOICE **Péniche Djébelle** HOUSEBOAT €€
(📞05 59 25 77 18; www.djebelle.com; face au 17 Quai de Lesseps; d incl breakfast €145; ⊗closed Oct-Apr; 🛜) Now here's something really different! If you stay here you'll have the best river view in the city (and there's a chance your fellow guests will be mermaids or pirates). Yes, this unique *chambre d'hôte* is in fact a houseboat floating in the River Ardour. And don't make the mistake of thinking that because it's a boat it will be uncomfortable; it's quite the opposite. The two vast rooms are imaginatively decorated and absolutley sublime; one has a Moroccan theme and the other, which has the boat's steering wheel built into the bathroom, is full of thoughts of tropical islands. A magnificent breakfast spread is included and there's a pet rabbit and cat to keep you company. Advance booking essential.

Hôtel des Arceaux BOUTIQUE HOTEL €€
(📞05 59 59 15 53; www.hotel-arceaux.com; 26 rue Port Neuf; d €42-76; 🛜) If this hotel, which is

located on one of the prettiest streets in the old town, were a pop star it would surely have to be Lady Gaga or some other flamboyant and over-the-top personality. Its rooms and communal areas are a cacophony of noisy colours and stately antiques, and it's very well run. All the rooms (some of which can accommodate families) are different, so ask to see a few first.

Hôtel Côte Basque HOTEL €
(📞05 59 55 10 21; www.hotel-cotebasque.fr; 2 rue Maubec; r from €75; ❀🛜) Ride the clanky, old-fashioned lift up to your modern room, which has low-slung beds and colourful art on the walls. Sitting opposite the train station, this recently renovated place offers sizzling value for money.

Hôtel Monbar HOTEL €
(📞05 59 59 26 80; 24 rue Pannecau; d from €32; 🛜) Oh la la, what a bargain. Located inside a tall, wobbly, red-and-white Bayonne town house, this hotel is a little slice of old French life. The rooms are basic (as you'd expect for the price), but have attached bathrooms and colourful bed spreads. There's a cafe-bar downstairs.

Le Grand Hôtel HISTORIC HOTEL €€
(📞05 59 59 62 00; www.legrandhotelbayonne.com; 21 rue Thiers; d from €117; ❀🛜) This old building was once a convent, but when they ran out of nuns someone turned it into a hotel. Now its cream-toned, wheelchair-accessible rooms and cosy on-site bar (which probably

FRENCH BASQUE COUNTRY BAYONNE

Bayonne

FÊTES DE BAYONNE

Beginning on either the first Wednesday in August or occasionally the last in July, the Fêtes de Bayonne attracts hundreds of thousands of people from across France and Spain for a five-day-long orgy of drinking, dancing, processions, fireworks and bulls. In many ways it's like a less commercialised version of the famous San Fermín festival in Pamplona (Spain) and, just like in Pamplona, Bayonne also holds bull running. However, here the bulls are actually cows – though they still have horns and they still hurt when they mow you down – and they don't run down the streets, but are instead released on the crowd in front of the Château Neuf. During the *fête*, real bullfights also take place (if you are interested, the tourist office has details).

One of the biggest highlights of the *fête* is the opening ceremony, when huge crowds gather in front of the town hall at 10pm on the Wednesday night for an impressively noisy firework display and the arrival of a 'lion' (the town's mascot).

While the nocturnal activities might be a bit much for children, the daytime processions, marching bands, organised children's picnics and even a children's 'bull' run are tailor-made for the delight of little ones. Thursday daytime has the most child-friendly activities.

If you're planning on attending the *fête*, you'll need to book at least six to eight months in advance for hotel accommodation anywhere in the vicinity of Bayonne. A number of temporary campgrounds (€60 for five days) are erected in and around Bayonne to ease the pressure; otherwise you can just do what most people do and sleep in the back of a car or under a bush (camping outside one of the campgrounds is forbidden). Women would be advised to avoid sleeping rough unless in a group.

Finally, unless you want to stand out like a sore thumb, don't forget to dress all in white with a red sash and neck-scarf. For dates and other *fête* info, see www.fetes.bayonne.fr.

didn't exist when it was a convent) make this friendly business-class hotel a fine place to rest up. Parking is €13.

Auberge de Jeunesse HOSTEL €
(☑05 59 58 70 00; www.fuaj.org/Anglet; 19 rte des Vignes; dm incl breakfast €19.60; ⊙mid-Apr–Sep, reception 8.30am-12.30pm & 6pm-3am; @🖭) In the nearby beach suburb of Anglet, this hostel has reached legendary status for its nonstop international party scene. To keep people well oiled, it comes complete with a basement Scottish pub screening surf films. From the Mairie de Bayonne (Town Hall) bus stop, take bus 4 to the stop for Les Sables, from where it's a 500m uphill walk. In high season they don't accept families (which says a lot about the kind of atmosphere prevalent here). You have to be an HI member to stay (you can sign up on arrival).

🍴 Eating

Bayonne has some superb places to eat, and costs are generally much lower than in nearby Biarritz.

TOP CHOICE La Feuillantine GASTRONOMIC €€
(☑05 59 46 14 94; www.lafeuillantine-bayonne.com; 21 quai Amiral Dubourdieu; menus €25-67, mains €25) This riverside place might be quite small, but it's garnered a huge repuatation for its spectacular Basque gastronomic fare, which is served with flair and style in its colourful dining room. The culinary skills of chef Nicolas Bertegui have recieved virtually universal praise in the mainstream French media.

TOP CHOICE Bar-Restaurant du Marché BASQUE €
(☑05 59 59 22 66; 39 rue des Basques; menus/mains €13/8.70; ⊙lunch Mon-Sat) Run by a welcoming Basque-speaking family, this unpretentious place is an absolute institution where everyone knows everyone (which some people may find slightly intimidating, but don't worry, just dive right in – nobody cares!). Simple but ample home-cooked dishes full of the flavours of the neighbouring market are dished up to all comers.

Chiloa Gurmenta Restaurant BASQUE €
(7 rue des Tonneliers; menus/mains €13/10) As Basque as a game of *pelota*, this simple and rustic little restaurant, located inside a former brothel, serves one thing and one thing only: *axoa*. A Basque farmers' dish, *axoa* originates from the nearby village of Espelette and consists of minced veal with Espelette peppers, rice, potato and whatever

else is lying around. Anne, your host for the evening, could work in show business.

La Grange
FRENCH €€

(☏05 59 46 17 84; 26 quai Galuperie; menus €20.50, mains €15-25; ⊙closed Sun) With a shady outside terrace, this popular place overlooks the River Nive. Basque music plays *sotto voce* in the cosy interior, which is hung with hanks of dried peppers and garlic. Traditional French flavours include plenty of seafood options and the desserts are to die for.

Le Chistera
BASQUE €€

(☏05 59 59 25 93; www.lechistera.com; 42 rue Port Neuf; mains €10-16, menus €15.80; ⊙daily) A local gathering spot, this aromatic, traditional Basque place is named for the *chistera* (scooplike racquet) that *pelota* players strap to their wrists. It's decorated with motifs from the sport, thanks to two generations of owners who are former professional players, and its Basque cuisine is some of the best in town.

Crêperie Harmonika
CRÊPERIE €

(☏05 59 42 20 91; www.creperie-bayonne-harmonika.com; 49 rue des Faures; menus €12; ⊙closed Sun & Mon) Crêpes prepared in the proper Breton fashion are the hallmark of this cute little crêperie well away from the tourist hordes. Breton it might be, but some of the fillings – such as the Irati, which includes serrano ham, egg and brebis cheese – are totally local.

🍸 Drinking

Petit Bayonne is awash with pubs and bars (all generally open from noon to 2am, Monday to Saturday), especially along rue Pannecau, rue des Cordeliers and quai Galuperie.

Chai Ramina
BAR

(11 rue Poissonnerie) In fine weather, rue Poissonnerie is completely blocked by the huge crowds spilling out of Chai Ramina.

Cafés Ramuntcho
TEAROOM

(9 rue du Pilori) To sip no fewer than 380 different teas (reputedly the most in France), take a seat amid the metal canisters of this café, established in 1920. Available for purchase to take home too.

☆ Entertainment

Upcoming cultural events are listed in *À l'Affiche* and the trimestrial *Les Saisons de la Culture,* both available free at the tourist office. Every Thursday in July and August, there's traditional Basque music (admission free; ⊙9.30pm) in place Charles de Gaulle. Between October and June Trinquet St-André (☏05 59 59 18 69; rue des tonneliers; tickets around €9) stages *main nue pelota* (*pelota* played with bare hands) matches every Thursday at 4.30pm and has frequent live music.

Cinéma l'Atalante
CINEMA

(☏05 59 55 76 63; www.cinema-atalante.org; 7 rue Denis Etcheverry) Along with its sister cinema, L'Autre Cinéma (3 quai Sala), l'Atalante screens art-house nondubbed films. Both cinemas are in the St-Esprit neighbourhood.

La Luna Negra Music
MUSIC

(www.lunanegra.fr; rue des Augustins; ⊙7pm-2am Wed-Sat) Catch live jazz, salsa and tango evenings, concerts of world music as well as comedy shows at this alternative cabaret/theatre venue.

🛍 Shopping

For chocolate, head to Daranatz or Cazenave on rue Port Neuf.

Pierre Ibaïalde
FOOD

(41 rue des Cordeliers) To buy Bayonne's famous ham at the lowest prices, visit the covered market or, for the best quality, visit a specialist shop such as Pierre Ibaïalde, a deli

---

BAYONNE CHOCOLATE

Bayonne's long association with chocolate stems from the Spanish Inquisition, when Jews who fled Spain set up their trade in the St-Esprit neighbourhood. By 1870 Bayonne boasted 130 chocolatiers (specialist makers of chocolate), more than in all of Switzerland. Today, 11 are still in business, including Daranatz (☏05 59 59 03 05; 15 rue Port Neuf) and the 19th-century Cazenave (19 rue Port Neuf), which does a sublime *chocolat mousseaux* (rich hot chocolate; €5.70). You can see chocolate being made at L'Atelier du Chocolat (www.atelierduchocolat.fr; 1 allée de Gibéléou; adult/child €5.80/2.90; ⊙9.30am-6.30pm Mon-Sat), including a historical overview of chocolate in Bayonne and, of course, tastings.

Tastings are also the highlight of the weekend-long Journées du Chocolat each May, when master chocolatiers set up the tools of their craft in front of their shops.

For more chocolate heaven, pop by the Planète Musée du Chocolat in Biarritz.

A TASTE OF SPAIN

You know you're getting close to the Spanish border when tapas start cropping up. Bayonne has an increasing number of *pintxo* (tapas in Basque) bars, and in some the quality is every bit as good as the legendary *pintxo* bars of San Sebastián, just over the border in Spain. Two of the best are the bar bodegas **Xurasko** (16 rue Poissonnerie; pintxos from €2.50) and **Ibaia** (45 quai Amiral Jauréguiberry; from €8; ☺closed Sun & Mon Oct-Mar). Tapas start to decorate the bar like little flowers at Xurasko from 7pm and as everyone clocks off work they stop by for a glass of wine and some choice titbits. The golden rule of tapas is to just take one or two (which you pay for when you leave) before moving on to try those elsewhere. And when you do move on from Xurasko you'd best go straight to Ibaia, which, with hams swinging from hooks in the ceiling and a garlic-heavy atmosphere, is a Bayonne legend. Here the emphasis is more on larger plates of hot tapas such as garlic prawns and spicy chorizo sausages, which you order off a blackboard menu. One plate is often enough for two people.

serving only the finest cuts where you can taste a sliver before you buy.

Elkar   BOOKS
(place de l'Arsenal) Elkar has a wealth of books and films on Basque history and culture, on walking in the Basque Country, as well as maps and CDs of Basque music.

ℹ Information

Tourist office (☎08 20 42 64 64; www .bayonne-tourisme.com; place des Basques; ☺9am-7pm Mon-Sat, 10am-1pm Sun) Efficient office providing stacks of informative brochures and free bike rental, plus guided city tours.

ℹ Getting There & Away

Air

Biarritz-Anglet-Bayonne airport (☎05 59 43 83 83; www.biarritz.aeroport.fr) is 5km south-west of central Bayonne and 3km southeast of the centre of Biarritz. It's served by low-cost carriers including EasyJet and Ryanair, as well as Air France, with daily domestic flights and flights to the UK, and regular flights to Ireland, Finland, Switzerland and the Netherlands.

Bus

From **place des Basques**, **ATCRB** (www. transdev-atcrb.com) buses follow the coast to the Spanish border. There are nine services daily to St-Jean de Luz (€3, 40 minutes) and Hendaye (€3, one hour). Summer beach traffic can double journey times.

Transportes Pesa (www.pesa.net) buses leave place des Basques twice a day Monday to Saturday for Bilbao (€19.80) in Spain, calling by Biarritz, St-Jean de Luz, Irún and San Sebastián (€7.75).

Chronoplus (☎05 59 52 59 52; www.chrono plus.eu) buses link Bayonne, Biarritz and Anglet. A single ticket costs €1, while carnets of 10 are

€8. Timetables are available from tourist offices or online. Bus A2 runs between Bayonne and Biarritz about 50 times daily, stopping at the Hôtels de Ville (town halls) and stations of both towns. A couple of other lines link the two towns via Anglet.

Car & Motorcycle

All the big car-rental agencies are represented at the airport; otherwise, close to the train station is **Avis** (☎05 59 55 06 56; www.avis.fr; 1 rue Ste-Ursule).

Train

TGVs run between Bayonne and Paris Gare Montparnasse (€88 to €129, five to six hours, eight daily).

There are five trains daily to St-Jean Pied de Port (€9.20, 1¼ hours) and fairly frequent services to St-Jean de Luz (€4.80, 25 minutes) via Biarritz (€2.40 to €2.60, nine minutes). Trains also go to the French and Spanish border towns of Hendaye (€6.70 to €7.10, 40 minutes) and Irún (€7 to €9.60, 45 minutes). For travel between Bayonne and Biarritz, however, the train station is way out of town so you're better off on the bus.

Other services:

» **Bordeaux** from €29, two hours, at least 10 daily

» **Toulouse** from €42.70, 3¾ hours, five daily

ℹ Getting Around

TO/FROM THE AIRPORT Bus 14 links Bayonne with the airport (€1, buses depart roughly hourly). A taxi from the town centre costs around €20.

BICYCLE Bayonne's tourist office lends out bikes for free (not overnight); you simply need to leave some ID as a deposit.

BUS A free *navette* (shuttle bus) loops around the heart of town.

CAR & MOTORCYCLE There's free parking along the southern end of av des Allées Paulmy, within easy walking distance of the tourist office.

TAXI Call **Taxi Bayonne** (☏05 59 59 48 48)

Biarritz

POP 26,067

As ritzy as its name suggests, this stylish coastal town, 8km west of Bayonne, took off as a resort in the mid-19th century when Napoléon III and his Spanish-born wife, Eugénie, visited regularly. Along its rocky coastline are architectural hallmarks of this golden age, and the belle époque and art deco eras that followed. Although it retains a high glamour quotient (and high prices to match), with some of Europe's best waves it's also a magnet for vanloads of surfers.

◉ Sights

TOP CHOICE Cité de l'Océan   MUSEUM

(☏05 59 22 75 40; www.citedelocean.com; 1 Av de la Plage; adult/child €10.50/7; ⊙10am-10pm) We don't really know whether it's fair to call Biarritz's new show piece a mere 'museum'. At heart it's simply a museum of the ocean but in reality this is entertainment, cutting-edge technology, theme park and science museum all rolled into one spectacular attraction.

BEACHES OF LES LANDES

North of Bayonne is the *département* of Les Landes, a vast semiwilderness of pine forests and lakes. This whole area has a special kind of wild beauty, criss-crossed with excellent cycling and walking trails; maps and route suggestions are available from most tourist offices. The trails are broken up by numerous lakes, the best being at Soustons and the small village of Léon, with opportunities for windsurfing, canoeing and other water sports. But for most people, the reason to visit Les Landes is its beaches. From the mouth of the Ardour at Anglet north to Arcachon and beyond to the mouth of the Gironde stretches a ribbon of shimmering golden sand backed by dunes and basking under a deep-blue sky.

Above all else, this is surf country. Towns such as the twin centres of Capbreton and Hossegor now owe their existence to surfing. Capbreton, which still retains some life beyond the waves, is easily the more appealing of the two and its small port supplies the town's numerous seafood restaurants with delicious fresh fish.

Chez du Camp (☏05 58 72 11 33; 4 rue Port d'Albert, Capbreton; menus €28-38, mains €16) is one of the best places in town to indulge. You can sit at a table overlooking ocean-sized tanks swimming with the imminent contents of your dinner. Or, even better, pick up a serving of the superb house special: mussels and squid; get it all cooked up on the spot and then take it away to have as a picnic.

Brash Hossegor, about 1km north of Capbreton, is renowned for having some of the best beach break waves in the world. It has to be said, though, that this reputation has made it the very definition of a 'hey, dude' surf town, where if you're not wearing just the right T-shirt then you're not welcome at the party. On the plus side, the beaches here are breathtaking and they only get better the further north towards the village of Seignosse you go. For eating you won't do better than La Tetrade (☏05 58 43 51 48; www.latetrade-cote-lac.com; 1187 ave du Touring Club de France, Hossegor; menus €14-39). Set on the banks of Hossegor's shimmering lake, it offers the kind of view to get married to, and a shellfish and seafood menu (including oysters farmed in the lake in front of you) you'd probably marry if you could.

But for the best beach of all, one of the best in France, you have to continue north another 20km to the tiny seasonal village of Moliets. The vast beach here, which sits at the mouth of a sluggish and inky-coloured river known as the Courant d'Huchet, has sand that sparkles like diamonds and is soft as feathers, while the river itself provides safe bathing for children.

Unfortunately, most of the limited hotel accommodation in this region is seriously poor value and most visitors end up camping at one of the dozens of campgrounds or staying at one of the 'surfcamps' along the coast. Local tourist offices can supply details.

From Bayonne's train station, RDTL (www.rdtl.fr) runs services northwards into Les Landes including Capbreton/Hossegor (€5, 40 minutes, six or seven daily).

Biarritz

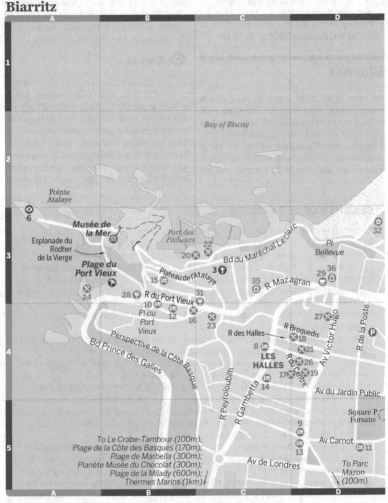

Located inside an eye-catching wave-shaped building south of town, this place will teach you everything about the ocean – from how it was born to the secrets of Gilgamesh – and in between you get to ride to the depths of the ocean in a submarine and watch giant squid and sperm whales do battle. It's all very child friendly but it's equally fascinating and fun for adults. A combined ticket with the Musée de la Mer costs €17.50 for adults and €13 for children. Family tickets are also available. In July and August a free *navette* (shuttle bus) runs between Biarritz and the Cité de l'Océan.

Musée de la Mer MUSEUM
(☑05 59 22 75 40; www.museedelamer.com; Esplanade du Rocher de la Vierge; adult/child €13/9.50; ☺9.30am-midnight Jul-Aug, shorter hr rest of year) Housed in a wonderful art deco building, Biarritz' Musée de la Mer is seething with underwater life from the Bay of Biscay and beyond, as well as exhibits on fishing recalling Biarritz' whaling past. An impressive recent makeover has added many more tanks of fish and it now houses sharks and tropical reef fish, but it's the seals that steal the show (feeding time, always a favourite with children, is at 10.30am and 5pm). In high season

it's possible to have the place almost to yourself by visiting late at night.

Musée d'Art Oriental Asiatica   MUSEUM
(☑05 59 22 78 79; www.museeasiatica.com; 1 rue Guy Petit; adult/student/child €7/5/3; ☺10.30am-6.30pm Mon-Fri, 2-7pm Sat-Sun) Out on the edge of town is this unexpected treasure trove of ancient Indian, Chinese and Tibetan statues, monuments and temple artwork. The layout is a bit haphazard, but the information cards (in several languages) explain the significance of the objects. It's generally considered the finest collection of its type outside Paris.

Planète Musée du Chocolat   MUSEUM
(☑05 59 23 27 72; www.planetemuseeduchocolat.com; 14 av Beau Rivage; adult/student/child €6/5/4; ☺10am-6.30pm) Delve into this real-life *Charlie and the Chocolate Factory* for an indulgent exploration through the world of chocolate, from its earliest beginnings to the mass production of today.

Architecture

From art deco mansions to Russian Orthodox churches and 1970s tower-block disasters, Biarritz has a fantastic potpourri of architectural styles. If the swell's big, you might get a drenching as you cross the twee, toy-town-like footbridge at the end of Pointe Atalaye to **Rocher de la Vierge** (Rock of the Virgin; at the end of Pointe Atalaye), named after its white statue of the Virgin and child. Views from this impressive outcrop extend to the mountains of the Spanish Basque Country.

Tiny Port des Pêcheurs is a tiny fishing port and an atmospheric place for a drink or a meal. Above it, the neo-Gothic **Église Ste-Eugénie** (Blvd du Maréchal Leclerc) was built in the late 1800s for – who else? – Empress Eugénie.

Dominating the northern end of the Grande Plage is the 19th-century **Hôtel du Palais** (1 av de l'Impératrice), also built for Empress Eugénie and now a luxury hotel. Opposite is **Église Alexandre Newsky** (8 av de l'Impératrice), a Russian Orthodox church built by and for the Russian aristocrats who frequented Biarritz until the Soviet Revolution. Eugénie was also the inspiration for the nearby doll's house–sized **Chapelle Impériale** (☑05 59 22 37 10; 15 rue des 100 Gardes; admission €3; ☺2.30-6pm), constructed in 1864.

Climbing the 258 twisting steps inside the 73m-high **Phare de Biarritz** (adult/child €2.50/2; ☺10am-1.30pm & 2-7pm), the town's 1834 lighthouse, rewards you with sweeping views of the Basque coast.

Beaches

Biarritz' raison d'être is its fashionable beaches, particularly the two central **Grande Plage** and **Plage Miramar**, which are lined end to end with sunbathing bodies on hot summer days. Stripy 1920s-style beach tents can be hired for €9.50 per day. The other central Biarritz beach is the tiny cove of **Plage du Port Vieux** which, thanks to its lack of swell, is the best one for young children to splash about on. North of Pointe St-Martin, the adrenaline-pumping surfing

Biarritz

beaches of Anglet (the final 't' is pronounced) continue northwards for more than 4km. Take bus 10 or 13 from the bottom of av Verdun (just near av Édouard VII).

To the south, beyond the long, exposed Plage de la Côte des Basques, some 500m south of Port Vieux, are Plage de Marbella and Plage de la Milady. Bus 10 or 13 heading south will also get you to these.

🏃 Activities

Once the almost exclusive haunt of the rich and pampered, Biarritz is now known more as the capital of European surfing (although, in truth, the real centre of European surfing is the small town of Hossegor around 25km to the north). Grande Plage itself is good from mid-low tide on a moderate swell, whereas the 4km-long stretch of beaches that make up Anglet are more consistent and generally better.

No fewer than nine places around town offer gear and lessons (from €35 per hour); the tourist office keeps a list of most of the surf schools. You should ensure that the school you choose is registered with the

Féderation Française de Surf (FFS; www .surfingfrance.com, in French) as some others are fly-by-night operators whose staff may have only a little more surf knowledge than the pupils. Even with the registered schools, the instructors often seem to use the lessons merely as an excuse to go surfing themselves.

🎉 Festivals & Events

Major surfing competitions take place year-round.

Biarritz Maider Arosteguy   SURFING
A three-day surfing championship is held at Easter.

Festival des Arts de la Rue   CULTURE
Performance artists take to the streets for five days in early May.

Roxy Jam   SURFING
A major female longboarding championship on the ASP (Association of Surfing Professionals) circuit, with spin-off events such as concerts, held over five days in mid-July.

Le Temps d'Aimer DANCE
(www.letempsdaimer.com) A two-week celebration of dance in all its forms is held in mid-September.

🛏 Sleeping

Inexpensive hotels are a rarity in Biarritz, and any kind of room is at a premium in July and August. Outside the high season, however, most prices fall by a good 25%.

TOP CHOICE **Hôtel Mirano** BOUTIQUE HOTEL €€
(☑05 59 23 11 63; www.hotelmirano.fr; 11 av Pasteur; d €68-130; 🎧) Squiggly purple, orange and black wallpaper and oversize orange perspex light fittings are some of the rad '70s touches at this boutique retro hotel. Oh, and there's a flirty Betty Boop in the bar. The staff go above and beyond the call of duty in order to please. All up, this eccentrically funky place offers one of the best deals in town. To get there take the D910 southeast out of town, turn left onto av de Grammont and right onto av Pasteur. It's a good 10-minute walk from the centre.

Hôtel de Silhouette DESIGNER HOTEL €€€
(☑05 59 24 93 82; www.hotel-silhouette-biarritz .com; 30 rue Gambetta; d from €220; ❄🎧) This fabulous new addition to the Biarritz hotel scene has designer rooms with big-city attitude that would feel quite at home in an upmarket Manhattan apartment. In order to remind you that the countryside is close at hand there are a couple of 'sheep' in the garden – as well as frequently changing outdoor art and sculpture exhibitions. The furnishings in the rooms are very high class and the shower heads as big as a rain cloud.

Villa Le Goëland HISTORIC HOTEL €€€
(☑05 59 24 25 76; www.villagoeland.com; 12 plateau de l'Atalaye; r €170-280; ❄🎧) This stunning family home with its château-like spires perched high on a plateau above Pointe Atalaye is one of the most notable buildings in town. Rooms, tastefully furnished with antiques, family photos and mementos, have panoramic views of the town and sea, and across to Spain. There are only four rooms (opt for 'chambre Goëland' with its huge 35-sq-m private terrace), so advance booking is essential.

Hôtel Edouard VII HISTORIC HOTEL €€
(☑05 59 22 39 80; www.hotel-edouardvii.com; 21 av Carnot; d €132-165; ❄🎧) From the ornate dining room full of gently tick-tocking clocks to the pots of lavender carefully colour coordinated to match the floral wallpaper, everything about this beautiful and intimate hotel screams 1920s Biarritz chic.

Hôtel Maïtagaria HOTEL €€
(☑05 59 24 26 65; www.hotel-maitagaria.fr; 34 av Carnot; s/d €76/90; 🎧) Overlooking a park, the spotless modern rooms with art deco furniture, leopard-print furnishings and immaculate bathrooms make this friendly place good value. Not least of its charms is its summer terrace: it opens off the comfy guest lounge, which is warmed in winter by a toasty open fire, and a backgarden filled with flowers and koi carp splashing about in a pond.

Hôtel Palym HOTEL €€
(☑05 59 24 16 56; hotel-palym-biarritz.fr; 7 rue du Port Vieux; d €75-135; ⊘mid-Jan–mid-Nov; ❄🎧) This welcoming, family-run hotel occupies a brightly painted town house on a street packed with hotels. Since our last visit it's been totally renovated and now offers exceedingly smart, colourful and good-value rooms. Add to that a very warm welcome and you've found yourself an ideal Biarritz base.

Maison Garnier BOUTIQUE HOTEL €€
(☑05 59 01 60 70; www.hotel-biarritz.com; 29 rue Gambetta; d €120; ❄🎧) The seven boutique 'rooms' (suites would be a better description) of this elegant mansion are tastefully decorated and furnished in cool, neutral tones; those up at attic level are especially romantic.

THALASSOTHERAPY

Thalassotherapy ('sea healing'), using the restorative properties of seawater (along with seaweed and mud), has been popular in Biarritz since the late 18th century and continues to serve as an antidote to 21st-century ailments such as stress and insomnia.

In Biarritz, put thalassotherapy's curative powers to the test – or simply bliss out – at the following:

» **Thalassa Biarritz** (☑05 59 41 30 00; www.accorthalassa.com; 11 rue Louison-Bobet)

» **Thermes Marins** (☑08 25 12 64 64; www.biarritz-thalasso.com; 80 rue de Madrid)

TAPAS ON THE SEASHORE

Like neighbouring Bayonne, there's a growing number of tapas bars in Biarritz. The area around the covered market, Les Halles, is a real hot spot for character-infused joints with bar tops that are positively loaded with tasty treats. The following spots are our favourites:

» **Bar Jean** (5 rue des Halles; tapas €1-2) The most original – and delicious – selection of tapas in the city is served up with a flamenco soundtrack and a backdrop of blue and white Andalucian tiles. Try the calamari rings wrapped around a stack of lardons and drizzled in olive oil – simply divine. Jean also does larger portions for around €6 to €7.

» **Le Comptoir du Foie Gras/Maison Pujol** (1 rue du Centre; tapas €1) This quirky place morphs from a shop selling jars of outstanding foie gras in the day to a tapas bar in the evening. Needless to say the tapas are foie-gras heavy, but they also have more vegetarian-suitable options such as those made with guacamole. It's so small that you'll probably end up standing outside shouting your order through the bar window.

» **Bar du Marché** (☑05 59 23 48 96; 8 rue des Halles; tapas €1-2.50) First opening its doors in 1938, this is another authentic and high-quality tapas bar beside the market. It also does full meals with great-value lunch menus for €12, which can be eaten out on the sunny terrace.

» **Crampotte 30** (Port des Pêcheurs; tapas €2; ⊗Easter-Oct) It's so small here it pretty much qualifies as a shed. If there's no room indoors to enjoy the short menu of tapas then sit outside and enjoy the views of the pretty port.

» **Bar Basque** (1 rue du Port Vieux; tapas €1.20-7) This rustic-chic hangout serves bite-size Basque tapas washed down with a fantastic selection of wines.

» **La Santa María** (Plage du Port Vieux; tapas plate €12; ⊗closed Nov-Easter & Wed low season) Balanced haphazardly on the rocks at the far end of our favourite Biarritz beach, the cute Plage du Port Vieux, this is a fantastic place for a sunset drink and a plate of tapas (€12). Sadly it knows its positioning is worth gold and so charges likewise!

Hôtel St-Julien　　　　　　　HOTEL €€
(☑05 59 24 20 39; www.saint-julien-biarritz.com; 20 av Carnot; d €160-175; ❀❀) A bright shuttered façade graces this attractive late-19th-century villa, with original parquet flooring inside. Third-floor rooms have views of both mountains and sea. Its undoubted quality means this place fills quickly. The free private parking is a huge advantage. In July and August there's a four night miniumn stay. English is spoken.

Hôtel Les Alizès　　　　　　HOTEL €€
(☑05 59 24 11 74; www.alizes-biarritz.com; 13 rue du Port Vieux; s €62 d €99-115; ❀) With its brash and blushing shades of colour and old-fashioned desks and wardrobes, this family-run hotel is one of the better cheap hotels in town. Its position, just back from the cute Plage du Port Vieux, is spot on.

Auberge de Jeunesse de Biarritz　HOSTEL €
(☑05 59 41 76 00; www.hihostels.com; 8 rue Chiquito de Cambo; dm incl sheets & breakfast €24.20; ⊗reception 8.30-11.30am & 6-9pm, to noon & 10pm May-Sep, closed mid-Dec–early Jan; @❀) This popular place offers outdoor activities including surfing. From the train station, follow the railway westwards for 800m.

Biarritz Camping　　　CAMPGROUND €
(☑05 59 23 00 12; www.biarritz-camping.fr; 28 rue d'Harcet; 2 people & tent €32; ⊗Apr-Sep; ❀) This campground, 2km southwest of the centre, has spacious, shady pitches and lots of facilities. Drawbacks are that it's close to the airport but not that close to anything else.

🍴 Eating

See-and-be-seen cafes and restaurants line Biarritz' beachfront. Anglet's beaches are also becoming increasingly trendy, with cafes strung along the waterfront.

TOP CHOICE Casa Juan Pedro　　　SEAFOOD €
(☑05 59 24 00 86; Port des Pêcheurs; mains €7-10) Down by the old port – something of a hidden little village of wooden fishing cottages and old-timers – is this cute fishing-shack

restaurant. The gregarious atmosphere ensures that you can wash down your tuna, sardines or squid with plenty of friendly banter from both the staff and other customers. There are several similar neighbouring places.

Le Crabe-Tambour   SEAFOOD €€
(☑05 59 23 24 53; 49 rue d'Espagne; menus €13-18) Named after the famous 1977 film of the same name (the owner was the cook for the film set), this friendly local place, a little way south of the centre, offers great seafood for a price that is hard to fault. The prawns in garlic are particularly good.

Bistrot des Halles   BASQUE €€
(☑05 59 24 21 22; 1 rue du Centre; mains €15-17; @) One of a cluster of restaurants along rue du Centre that get their produce directly from the nearby covered market, this bustling place stands out from the pack for serving excellent fish and other fresh modern French market fare from the blackboard menu in an interior adorned with old metallic advertising posters.

Le Clos Basque   BASQUE €€
(☑05 59 24 24 96; 12 rue Louis Barthou; menus €25; ☺lunch Tue-Sun, dinner Tue-Sat) With its tiles and exposed stonework hung with abstract art, this tiny place could have strayed in from Spain. The cuisine, however, is emphatically Basque, traditional with a contemporary twist or two, such as sirloin with green mustard, or stuffed eggplant with saffron. Reserve ahead to secure a terrace table.

Self-Catering
You'll find a picnic hamper of fresh ingredients at the covered market and a tempting array of cheeses, wines and pâtés at nearby Mille et Un Fromages (8 av Victor Hugo). Épicerie Fine du Port Vieux (41bis rue Mazagran) is another excellent delicatessen.

🍷 Drinking
There are some great bars on and around rue du Port Vieux, place Clemenceau and the central food-market area, many of which are tiny hole-in-the-wall places with just enough room for you, your drink, the bartender and a friend or two. Places generally open from 11am to 2am unless noted otherwise.

TOP CHOICE Miremont   CAFE
(☑05 59 24 01 38; www.miremont-biarritz.com; 1bis place Georges-Clemenceau; hot chocolate from €5; ☺9am-8pm) Operating since 1880, this grande dame of a place harks back to the time when belle-époque Biarritz was simply the beach resort of choice for the rich and glamorous of Europe. Today it still attracts perfectly coiffured hairdos (and that's just on the poodles) but the somewhat less chic are also now welcome to come and partake of a fine selection of teas, cakes and views over the bay.

Ventilo Caffé   BAR
(rue du Port Vieux; ☺closed Tue Oct-Easter) Dressed up like a boudoir, this fun and funky place continues its domination of the Biarritz bar scene.

Arena Café Bar   BAR
(Plage du Port Vieux; ☺9am-2am Apr-Sep, 10am-2am Wed-Sun Oct-Mar) Tucked into a tiny cove, this beachfront hang-out combines a style-conscious restaurant (mains €15 to €22) with a fashionista bar with DJs on the turntables and sunset views.

Red Bar   BAR
(9 av du Maréchal Foch; ☺Tue-Sun) You mightn't think a rugby bar would attract trendsetters, but this temple to Biarritz Olympique (their colours are red and white – hence the name), with reggae and '70s rock in the background, will make you think again.

☆ Entertainment
Free classical-music concerts take place in high summer at various atmospheric outdoor venues around town; the tourist office has the program. There are a couple of nightclubs and lounge bars just behind Grande Plage.

Cinéma Le Royal   CINEMA
(www.royal-biarritz.com; 8 av du Maréchal Foch) Screens a good selection of nondubbed films.

Casino Municipal   CASINO
(1 av Édouard VII) Constructed in 1928, Biarritz' landmark casino has 200-plus fruit machines that whirr and chink until the wee hours.

Fronton Couvert Plaza Berri   SPORT
(42 av du Maréchal Foch) Pelota matches are held virtually year-round; ask the tourist office for schedules.

Parc Mazon   SPORT
(av du Maréchal Joffre) From July to mid-September, the open-air fronton (pelota court) has regular matches. Ask at the tourist office for match times.

Basque Culture

Call a Basque French or Spanish and it's almost certain you'll receive a glare and a stern 'I'm Basque!' in return. The Basques have over time developed a culture unique in Europe.

The regional game is *pelote Basque (pelota)* and you'll notice every village has its own court – normally backing up against the village church. *Pelota* is actually the generic name for a group of 16 different native Basque ball games, but the most well known has players using a scooplike basket called a *chistera*. Some players are able to throw the ball at speeds of up to 300km/h.

Throughout France the Basques are also famous for festivals. Some, like La Fête du Thon in St-Jean de Luz (p657), celebrate the region's superlative food. Others, such as the Fêtes de Bayonne (p642), simply celebrate the Basques' sheer joy for life.

Basque festivals are also a good opportunities to see traditional Basque dress. It's said that there are around 400 different Basque dances, many of which require their own special kind of outfit.

But perhaps the most visible symbol of Basque culture is the *lauburu,* also known as the Basque cross and regarded as a symbol of prosperity. It's also used to signify life and death.

HEMIS/ALAMY

HEMIS/ALAMY

TOP BASQUE EATS

» **Piment d'Espelette** This little chilli pepper is an essential accompaniment to many a Basque meal.

» **Fromage des Pyrénées** Cheese – buy it fresh, straight from a shepherd. The best-known cheese is Ossau-Iraty.

» **Jambon de Bayonne** Wafer-thin ham has a fair devoted to it (p640).

» **Axoa** Classic dish – try it at Bayonne's Chiloa Gurmenta Restaurant (p642).

» **Bayonne chocolate** The best chocolate shops in the country (p643).

Clockwise from top left
1. *Pelote Basque* in action 2. Crowds at the Fêtes de Bayonne 3. Gathering at Les Arènes, Bayonne

Parc des Sports d'Aguiléra SPORT

(av Henri Haget) Regular professional *pelota* matches (admission €10 to €20) are held at 9pm at this sports complex, 2km east of central Biarritz, between mid-June and mid-September.

🛍 Shopping

Pare Gabia SHOES

(18 rue Mazagran) Vincent Corbun continues his grandfather's business, established in 1935, making and selling espadrilles in a rainbow of colours and styles (customised with ribbons and laces while you wait). A pair starts from €10.

Robert Pariès CHOCOLATES

(1 place Bellevue) Test your willpower with scrumptious chocolates and Basque sweets.

🅲 Information

Tourist office (📞05 59 22 37 10; www.biarritz .fr; square d'Ixelles; ⊘9am-7pm) In July and August there are tourist-office annexes at the airport, train station and at the roundabout just off the Biarritz sortie (exit) 4 from the A63.

🅲 Getting There & Away

AIR To reach Biarritz-Anglet-Bayonne airport, take Chronoplus (p644) bus 14, which runs every half-hour.

BUS Buses run frequently between Bayonne and Biarritz; they work out much cheaper than taking the train as you'll pay the same to get from Biarritz' train station to its town centre as you will to get from Bayonne to Biarritz directly on the bus.

Ten daily **ATCRB** (www.transdev-atcrb.com) buses travel down the coast to St-Jean de Luz (€2) from the **stop** just near the tourist office beside square d'Ixelles. Buses to Spain also pick up passengers here.

TRAIN Biarritz-La Négresse train station is about 3km south of the town centre; walking to the centre isn't advised due to busy roads without footpaths, so catch bus A1. **SNCF** (13 av du Maréchal Foch; ⊘Mon-Fri) has a town-centre office. Times, fares and destinations are much the same as Bayonne's, a nine-minute train journey away.

🅲 Getting Around

BUS Most services stop beside the Hôtel de Ville, from where route A2 (€1, about 50 daily) goes to Bayonne's Hôtel de Ville and station.

TAXI Atlantic Taxis (📞05 59 23 18 18)

Sea Lifts (📞05 33 52 03 28, for reservations in UK 00 44 (0)203 1371875; www.sea-lifts. com) A private transfer service offering cheap rates from Biarritz airport to Biarritz, Bayonne, Spain, Hossegor, Capbreton and other towns in the region. Staff speak English and reservations can be made online in advance.

St-Jean de Luz & Ciboure

POP 14,200

If you're searching for the quintessential Basque seaside town – with atmospheric narrow streets and a lively fishing port pulling in large catches of sardines and anchovies that are cooked up at authentic restaurants – you've found it.

St-Jean de Luz, 24km southwest of Bayonne, sits at the mouth of the River Nivelle and is overlooked by the lush Pyrenean foothills. The town and its long beach are on the eastern side of Baie de St-Jean de Luz.

Its sleepy, smaller alter ego, Ciboure, is on the western curve of the bay, separated from St-Jean de Luz by the fishing harbour.

To get between St-Jean de Luz and Ciboure you can cross over the Pont Charles de Gaulle on foot or by car, or, for a more fun alternative, take one of the summer ferries that cross the harbour between the two.

⊙ Sights

A superb panorama of the town unfolds from the promontory of Pointe Ste-Barbe, at the northern end of the Baie de St-Jean de Luz and about 1km beyond the town beach. Go to the end of bd Thiers and keep walking.

Église St-Jean Baptiste CHUCH

(rue Gambetta, St-Jean de Luz; ⊘8.30am-noon & 2-7pm) The plain facade of France's largest and finest Basque church conceals a splendid interior with a magnificent baroque altarpiece. It was in front of this very altarpiece that Louis XIV and María Teresa, daughter of King Philip IV of Spain, were married in 1660. After exchanging rings, the couple walked down the aisle and out of the south door, which was then sealed to commemorate peace between the two nations after 24 years of hostilities. You can still see its outline, opposite 20 rue Gambetta.

Église St-Vincent CHURCH

(rue Pocalette, Ciboure) The 17th-century Église St-Vincent has an octagonal bell tower topped by an unusual three-tiered wooden roof. Inside, the lavish use of wood and tiered galleries is typically Basque. The church is just off the main seafront road quai Maurice Ravel.

TOP SURF SPOTS – BASQUE & ATLANTIC COASTS

France's Basque and Atlantic coasts have some of Europe's best surf. Autumn is prime time, with warm(ish) water temperatures, consistently good conditions and few(er) crowds. The big-name spots are Biarritz and Hossegor, where you can watch Kelly Slater and friends battle it out for crucial world-title points in dredging Gravière barrels during September–October's ASP (Association of Surfing Professionals; www .aspworldtour.com) event. In fact, almost anywhere between St-Jean de Luz in the south and Soulac-sur-Mer up in the north by the mouth of the Gironde River has mighty good surf.

Europe's original big-wave spot might have been surpassed by bigger and nastier discoveries, but the reef breaks around Guéthary, just to the south of Biarritz, retain a special sense of magic.

Take a lesson in the mellow waves at Hendaye, just to the south of St-Jean de Luz, where the small, gently breaking waves are tailor-made for learners. The tourist office (☑05 59 20 00 34; www.hendaye-tourisme.fr; 67 bd de la Mer, Hendaye; ⊗9am-7pm Mon-Sat, 10am-12.30pm & 3.30-6pm Sun) can point you in the right direction. Beginners' lessons start at around €35.

Paddle out from the tip of pine-forested Cap Ferret peninsula, or go on surfari to the magnificent beaches around Lacanau, where the surfers of Bordeaux get their kicks.

And for the best waves *away* from the coast, longboarders can attempt the mascaret (http://mascaretgironde.free.fr), a tidal-bore wave travelling inland from the Gironde Estuary. The best place to pick it up is St-Pardon during spring tides.

Maison Louis XIV HISTORICAL BUILDING
(☑05 59 26 27 58; www.maison-louis-xiv.fr; 6 place Louis XIV, St-Jean de Luz; adult/student & child €5.50/3.50; ⊗10.30am-12.30pm & 2.30-6.30pm Wed-Mon, closed Nov-Easter) Sitting on a pretty, pedestrianised square is the so-called Maison Louis XIV. Built in 1643 by a wealthy shipowner and furnished in period style, this is where Louis XIV lived out his last days of bachelorhood before marrying María Teresa. Half-hour guided tours (with English text) depart several times daily in July and August.

Alongside, and rather dwarfed by its more imposing neighbour, is St-Jean de Luz' Hôtel de Ville, built in 1657.

Socoa OLD TOWN
The heart of Socoa is about 2.5km west of Ciboure along the continuation of quai Maurice Ravel (named for the *Boléro* composer, who was born in Ciboure in 1875). Its prominent fort was built in 1627 and later improved by Vauban. You can walk out to the Digue de Socoa breakwater or climb to the lighthouse via rue du Phare, then out along rue du Sémaphore for fabulous coastal views.

Écomusée Basque MUSEUM
(☑05 59 54 15 26; www.ecomusee-basque.com; adult/child €7.50/3.20; ⊗10am-6.30pm, closed Nov-Apr) Around 2km north of St-Jean de Luz beside the N10, Basque traditions are brought to life on one-hour audioguide tours of this illuminating multimedia museum, which has three entire rooms devoted to Izarra (Basque for 'star'), a liqueur made from 20 different local plants.

Château d'Urtubie CASTLE
(☑05 59 54 31 15; www.chateaudurtubie.net; adult/child €6.50/3; ⊗10.30am-6.30) This small château was constructed in the 13th century and has been in the hands of the same family ever since. Rooms are decorated in period style and are stuffed full of antiques and other treasures. If the château catches your fancy you can even stay here as it doubles as a hotel (rooms from €125). There's also an in-house restaurant (menus from €20). To get there follow the D704 and D810 3km southwest of St Jean de Luz in the direction of Spain and you'll find it sitting pretty just off the D810 road.

Joanoenia: Maison de l'Infante HISTORICAL BUILDING
(☑05 59 26 36 82; quai de l'Infante, St-Jean de Luz; adult/child €2.50/free; ⊗11am-12.30pm & 2.30-6.30pm Tue-Sat, closed mid-Nov–May) In the days before her marriage to Louis XIV, María Teresa stayed in this brick-and-stone mansion (like the temporary home of her husband to be, it was owned by a shipowner), off place Louis XIV, which has fine architectural detail.

St-Jean de Luz

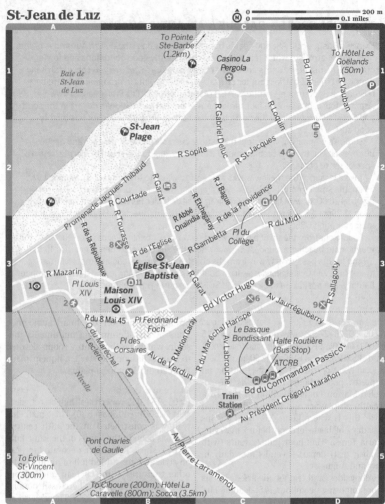

St-Jean de Luz

Beaches

St-Jean de Luz' beautiful banana-shaped sandy beach sprouts stripy bathing tents from June to September. Ciboure has its own modest beach, Plage de Socoa, 2km west of Socoa on the corniche (the D912); it's served by ATCRB buses en route to Hendaye and, in the high season, by boats. Both beaches are protected from the wrath of the Atlantic by breakwaters and jetties, and are among the few child-friendly beaches in the Basque Country.

Activities

Opportunities to get out on, in and under the water abound. As well as the operators listed below the tourist office can put you in touch with surf schools and sailing schools.

Odysée Bleue   DIVING SCHOOL
(06 63 54 13 63; www.odyssee-bleue.com; chemin des Blocs, hangar 4; try dive €50, discovery course €160) Join a diving school in Socoa to dive under the waves to look for starfish and wrasse.

Tech Ocean   DIVING SCHOOL
(05 59 47 96 75; www.tech-ocean.fr; 45 av Commandant Passicot; try dive €60, courses from €115) A diving school in Socoa.

Nivelle Trois   CRUISES
(06 09 73 61 81; www.croisiere-saintjeandeluz.com; quai de l'Infante) From May to mid-September, a boat leaves quai du Maréchal Leclerc for deep-sea fishing trips (adult/child €35/25) and cruises (adult/child from €10/7). Despite the name, the boat currently in use is actually the *Nivelle V*.

Festivals & Events

Fêtes de la St-Jean   CULTURE
Bonfires, music and dancing take place on the weekend nearest 24 June.

Régates de Traînières   BOAT RACES
A weekend of boat races on the first weekend in July.

La Fête du Thon   FOOD
The Tuna Festival, on a July weekend, fills the streets with brass bands, Basque music and dancing, while stalls sell sizzling tuna steaks.

Danses des Sept Provinces Basques DANCE
Folk dancers from across the Spanish and French Basque Country meet in early summer.

La Nuit de la Sardine   CULTURE
The Night of the Sardine – a night of music, folklore and dancing – is held twice each summer on a Saturday in early July and the Saturday nearest 15 August.

Sleeping

July to mid-September are packed and advance reservations are essential; low-season prices can drop significantly. There are a couple of cheap and cheerful places opposite the train station.

Between St-Jean de Luz and Guéthary, 7km northeast up the coast, are no fewer than 16 camping grounds. ATCRB's Biarritz and Bayonne buses stop within 1km of them all.

TOP CHOICE La Devinière   BOUTIQUE HOTEL €€
(05 59 26 05 51; www.hotel-la-deviniere.com; 5 rue Loquin, St-Jean de Luz; d €120-180;) You have to love a place that forsakes TVs for antiquarian books (room 11 even has its own mini-library). Beyond the living room, with its piano and comfy armchairs, there's a delightful small patio equipped with lounges. It's a truly charming place that feels like a little old country cottage that has somehow been sucked into the town centre. The rooms are stuffed full of antique furnishings including old writing desks. It's worth paying the extra for the garden-facing rooms, which have little balconies overlooking the riot of vegetation down below.

Zazpi   DESIGN HOTEL €€€
(05 59 26 07 77; www.zazpihotel.com; 21 bd Thiers, St-Jean de Luz; r/ste from €224/400;) Seriously hip, this wonderful old mansion-turned–designer hotel is one of the most stylish hotels in southwest France. Staying here is like living in a very glam modern-art gallery. There's a rooftop terrace complete with pool and sensational views over an ocean of terracotta roof tiles to the fairy-tale green Basque hills.

Hôtel La Caravelle   BOUTIQUE HOTEL €€
(05 59 47 18 05; www.hotellacaravelle.com; bd Pierre Benoît, Ciboure; d €90-145;) This is a superb option overlooking the water on the other side of the port in Ciboure. Originally this nautical-themed place was two fishermen's cottages; today its very good-value rooms contain old furniture given a coat of paint and a new lease of life. Some rooms have terraces with fake 'gardens' while others have sea views. There's free street parking outside.

Hôtel Les Goëlands
BOUTIQUE HOTEL €€

(☎05 59 26 10 05; www.hotel-lesgoelands.com; 4 & 6 av d'Etcheverry, St-Jean de Luz; s/d with half board from €153/182; 🛜) Accommodation devoted to ecological principles is still a rarity in the French Basque Country, but this place goes all out with a forward-looking recycling and energy-saving policy. The owners haven't skimped on the rooms either – they're large, sunny and comfortable, and look down onto the nicest hotel gardens in St-Jean de Luz, where you can eat your breakfast and lounge about in the sun. They also rent electric bikes to guests and cook meals made from fresh local produce (half board is obligatory in July and August). It's a short walk uphill at the northern end of town.

Hôtel Ohartzia
HOTEL €€

(☎05 59 26 00 06; www.hotel-ohartzia.com; 28 rue Garat, St-Jean de Luz; r with shower/bath €81/91; 🛜) Framed by cobalt-blue shutters, this flower-bedecked Basque house is just a few steps from the beach. Immaculate rooms are well furnished and equipped, and the welcome's friendly. The highlight is its hidden foliage-shaded garden full of well-placed tables and chairs. A couple of the rooms are outside in this garden.

✕ Eating

Seafood is the mainstay of restaurant menus and St-Jean de Luz doesn't disappoint in this department – many people come here as much for the food as anything else. Tempting restaurants line rue de la République, rue Tourasse and place Louis XIV.

TOP CHOICE Buvette des Halles
SEAFOOD €

(☎05 59 26 73 59; bd Victor Hugo, St-Jean de Luz; dishes €7-14; ⏱6am-2pm & dinner, closed Tue Sep-Jun) Tucked into a corner of the covered market, this minuscule restaurant serves goat's cheese, Bayonne ham, grilled sardines, fish soup, mussels and much more. Between June and September you can eat outside beneath the plane trees on the small square; the rest of the year you can eat tucked up inside, but go early for the best pickings.

Grillerie du Port
SEAFOOD €

(☎05 59 51 18 29; quai du Maréchal Leclerc, St-Jean de Luz; mains €7.50-9.50; ⏱mid-Jun–mid-Sep) It won't take long to peruse the menu at this old port side classic. It's essentially a choice of grilled sardines or grilled tuna – all freshly caught that morning and utterly delicious.

Pilpil-Enea
SEAFOOD €

(☎05 59 51 20 80; 3 rue Sallagoity, St-Jean de Luz; lunch mains €10-14, lunch menus €9, dinner menus from €25; ⏱lunch Thu-Tue, dinner Mon & Wed-Sat) Strung with fishing nets, this small, simple restaurant decorated in dark timber and blue-and-white checks is set apart from the tourist throng, and is a firm local favourite for its quality cooking based largely on the aquatic world.

Le Peita
SEAFOOD €

(☎05 59 26 86 66; 21 rue Tourasse, St-Jean de Luz; mains €14.50-20, menus from €26; ⏱Wed-Sun) Dried Espelette chillies and hams hang from the ceiling at this authentic place with crushed-silk tablecloths and friendly owners. For a taste of the local produce on display, order one of the combination plates accompanied by fresh local cheese. There are several other cosy little places on the same street.

☆ Entertainment

In summer frequent *cesta punta* matches take place at **Jaï Alaï Compos Berri** (rte de Bayonne, N10), 1km northeast of the train station. The tourist office can supply times and prices.

🔒 Shopping

Sandales Concha
SHOES

(2 rue Gambetta, St-Jean de Luz) The traditional shoe of the Basque Country is the espadrille and here you can choose from a huge range of locally produced, handmade shoes starting from €10.

Macarons Adam
FOOD

(49 rue Gambetta) Macarons are a regional speciality; try these wonderful biscuit-like delicacies here sold here. Also at 6 rue de la République.

ℹ Information

Tourist office (☎05 59 26 03 16; www.saint-jean-de-luz.com; 20 bd Victor Hugo, St-Jean de Luz; ⏱9am-12.30pm & 2.30-6.30pm Mon-Sat, 10am-1pm Sun, extended hours Jul & Aug) Runs an extensive program of French-language tours around the town and across the Spanish border; ask about English-language tours in summer.

ℹ Getting There & Away

BUS Buses run by **ATCRB** (www.transdev-atcrb .com) pass the **Halte Routière** bus stop near the train station on their way northeast to Biarritz

(€3, 30 minutes, nine daily) and Bayonne (€3, 40 minutes, nine daily). Southwestward, there are around 10 services daily to Hendaye (€1, 35 minutes).

Also passing the Halte Routière is **Transportes Pesa** (www.pesa.net), serving San Sebastián and Bilbao.

TRAIN There are frequent trains to Bayonne (€4.80, 25 minutes) via Biarritz (€3 to €4.10, 15 minutes) and to Hendaye (€3, 15 minutes), with connections to Spain.

ⓘ Getting Around

BOAT The good ship **Le Passeur** plies between the jetty on the northern edge of St-Jean's beach, quai de l'Infante and Socoa (adult/child €2.50/1.80 one way) hourly between April and September.

BUS Between June and September, the Navette Itzulia provides a free local daily bus service, with a skeleton service during the rest of the year.

TAXI Call ☏05 59 47 38 38.

Around St-Jean de Luz
LA RHUNE

The first mountain of the Pyrenees, the 905m-high, antenna-topped and border-straddling La Rhune ('Larrun' in Basque), 10km south of St-Jean de Luz, has always been considered sacred among Basques,

---

CROSS-BORDER ENCOUNTERS: A DAY IN SAN SEBASTIÁN

Spain, and the elegant and lively city of San Sebastián, is now so close it could almost be considered rude not to slip over to see for yourself why people make such a fuss about San Sebastián. Put simply, San Sebastián is stunning. The town is set around two sickle-shaped beaches, at least one of which, Playa de la Concha, is the equal of any city beach in Europe. But there's more to the city than just looks. Cool, svelte and flirtatious, San Sebastián really knows how to have a good time: with more Michelin stars per capita than anywhere else in the world and finer tapas than anywhere else in Spain, San Sebastián's culinary CV is impressive. But it's not just us who think so; a raft of the world's best chefs, including such luminaries as Catalan superstar chef Ferran Adriá, have said that San Sebastián is quite probably the best place on the entire planet in which to eat!

So, how do I get there? By car it's just a short 20-minute jump down the A64 from St-Jean de Luz (and past an awful lot of toll booths!), or you can endure the N10, which has no tolls but gets so clogged up that it will take you a good couple of hours to travel this short distance. Or hop on a bus or a train. Trains run from St-Jean de Luz to Hendaye (and occasionally onto Irun) roughly hourly (€3, 12 minutes), from where you can board one of the frequent Eusko Trens for the ride into San Sebastián (€1.70; 30 minutes). Otherwise, Transportes Pesa (www.pesa.net) buses run twice daily between the two towns (€3, one hour 15 minutes).

And about those tapas? The whole of San Sebastián's old town is crammed with tapas (*pintxo* in Basque) bars, all of which, and we truly mean *all*, have a sublime range of bited-size morsels on offer. However, a couple that really stand out are Bar Borda Berri (Calle Fermín Cabetón 12), where the house special is pigs ears (and they're much better than they sound!) and La Cuchara de San Telmo (Calle de 31 de Agosto 28), a hidden-away bar serving such delights as *carrilera de ternera al vino tinto* (calf cheeks in red wine), with meat so tender it starts to dissolve almost before it's passed your lips.

And if I want to really splash out? With three Michelin stars, Arzak (☏943 27 84 65; www.arzak.info; Avenida Alcalde Jose Elosegui 273; meals around €175; ⊙closed Sun-Mon & Nov & late Jun), run by acclaimed Chef Juan Mari Arzak, takes some beating when it comes to *nueva cocina vasca* (new Basque cuisine). Reservations, well in advance, are obligatory.

And if I want to stay the night? Pensión Bellas Artes (☏943 47 49 05; www .pension-bellasartes.com; Calle de Urbieta 64; s €69-89, d €89-109; 🕸) is our value-for-money hot tip.

And what is there to do there? What? Other than eating, drinking and playing on the beach?! OK, well, there's fantastic shopping, a superb aquarium, a couple of museums and, well, eating, drinking and playing on the beach.

For further information, head to shop.lonelyplanet.com to purchase a downloadable PDF of the Basque Country, Navarra & Rioja chapter from Lonely Planet's *Spain* guide.

LOCAL LINGO

According to linguists, Euskara, the Basque language, is unrelated to any other tongue on Earth, and is the only tongue in southwestern Europe to have withstood the onslaught of Latin and its derivatives.

Basque is spoken by about a million people in Spain and France, nearly all of whom are bilingual. In the French Basque Country, the language is widely spoken in Bayonne and the hilly hinterland. However, while it is an official language in Spain, it isn't recognised as such in France (although some younger children are educated in Basque at primary-school level). The language also has a higher survival rate on the Spanish side.

But you'll still encounter the language here on Basque-language TV stations, and see the occasional sign reading 'Hemen Euskara emaiten dugu' (Basque spoken here) on shop doors. You'll also see the Basque flag (similar to the UK's but with a red field, a white vertical cross and a green diagonal one) flying throughout the region, as well as another common Basque symbol, the *lauburu* (like a curly four-leaf clover), signifying prosperity, or life and death.

though today people come for the spectacular views rather than religious or cultural reasons. The mountain is best approached from Col de St-Ignace, 3km northwest of Sare on the D4 (the St-Jean de Luz road). From here, you can take a fairly strenuous five-hour (return) hike, or have all the hikers curse you by hopping on Le Petit Train de la Rhune (www.rhune.com; single/return adult €14/17, child €7/10; ☉mid-Feb–mid-Nov). This charming little wooden train takes 35 minutes to haul itself up the 4km from col to summit. In July and August departures are every 35 minutes; the rest of the year departures are limited to two to four times a day (see website for exact times). Outside high season prices are a few euros cheaper. Be prepared for a wait of up to an hour in high summer. A free *navette* (shuttle bus) runs from St-Jean de Luz several times daily in summer, and leaves from outside the train station.

GROTTES DE SARE
Who knows what the first inhabitants of the Grottes de Sare (www.grottesdesare.fr; adult/child €8/4; ☉10am-7pm), some 20,000 years ago, would make of today's whizbang technology including lasers and holograms during sound-and-light shows at these caves. Multilingual 45-minute tours take you through a gaping entrance via narrow passages to a huge central cavern. Follow the D306, 6km south of the village of Sare. Le Basque Bondissant (The Leaping Basque; ☎05 59 26 25 87; www.basquebondissant.com) runs buses from St-Jean de Luz to the caves (bus 868) a couple of times a day in summer.

AINHOA
POP 686

'Un des plus jolis villages de la France', says the sign as you enter this, indeed, very pretty village.

Ainhoa's elongated main street is flanked by imposing 17th-century houses, half-timbered and brightly painted. Look for the rectangular stones set above many of the doors, engraved with the date of construction and the name of the family to whom the house belonged. The fortified church has the Basque trademarks of an internal gallery and an embellished altarpiece.

For a memorable Basque meal, stop at the Michelin-starred Ithurria (☎05 59 29 92 11; www.ithurria.com; d from €135, menus €39-62; ❀🛜🛉), established by the Isabal family in an old pilgrims' hostel and now run by Maurice Isabal's two sons (one the sommelier, the other the chef). To make a night of it, Ithurria's rainbow-hued rooms and dreamy swimming pool complement the food perfectly.

ESPELETTE
POP 2013

The whitewashed Basque town of Espelette is famous for its dark-red chillies, an integral ingredient in traditional Basque cuisine. So prized is *le piment d'Espelette* that it's been accorded Appellation d'Origine Contrôlée (AOC) status, like fine wine. In autumn you can scarcely see the walls of the houses, strung with rows of chillies drying in the sun. To learn more about the chillies and to taste and buy chilli products visit l'Atelier du Piment (☎05 59 93 90 21; www.atelierdupiment.com; free admission; ☉9am-7pm) out on the edge of town. The last weekend in October marks Espelette's Fête du Piment, with processions, a formal blessing of the chilli peppers and the ennoblement of a *chevalier du piment* (a knight of the pimiento).

Espelette makes a fine base for both the interior and the coast (assuming you have a car), and an absolutely bucolic place to rest up is the Maison d'hôte Irazabala (☑06 07 14 93 61; www.irazabala.com; 155 Mendiko Bidea; s/d incl breakfast €60/80; ☎), a couple of kilometres out of town (follow signs for the campsite and it's signed just on from there). This beautiful Basque farmhouse is situated in the middle of wild flower meadows and offers breathtaking views over a raised rumple of green mountains. The four rooms are easily the equal of the setting and you'll struggle to tear yourself away from the garden. The owner can advise on walks in the area.

Chillies star on the menu at the renowned Hôtel Restaurant Euzkadi (☑05 59 93 91 88; www.hotel-restaurant-euzkadi.com; menus €18-35; ☎) in dishes such as *axoa* (tender minced veal simmered with onions and fresh chillies).

The tourist office (☑05 59 93 95 02; www.espelette.fr; ◷9am-12.30pm & 2-6pm Mon-Fri, 9.30am-12.30pm & 2-6pm Sat), within a small stone château, shares its premises with the Hôtel de Ville.

Le Basque Bondissant (The Leaping Basque; ☑05 59 26 25 87; www.basquebondissant.com) runs buses between St-Jean de Luz and Espelette a couple of times a day in summer and less frequently in winter.

St-Jean Pied de Port

POP 1700

At the foot of the Pyrenees, the walled town of St-Jean Pied de Port, 53km southeast of Bayonne, was for centuries the last stop in France for pilgrims heading south over the Spanish border, a mere 8km away, and on to Santiago de Compostela, in Galicia in western Spain. Today it remains a popular departure point for hikers attempting the pilgrim trail, but there are plenty of shorter hikes and opportunities for mountain biking in the area.

If you're the sort of person who thinks God invented cars so we didn't have to walk, then St-Jean Pied de Port, with its attractive old core sliced through by the River Nive, is still well worth a visit.

St-Jean Pied de Port makes an ideal day trip from Bayonne, particularly on Monday when the market is in full swing.

◉ Sights

Old Town   OLD TOWN

The walled old quarter is an attractive place of cobbled streets, geranium-covered

FRENCH BASQUE COUNTRY ST-JEAN PIED DE PORT

DON'T MISS

THE BEST OF THE REST

Both people and nature have created scenes of such beauty in the Basque country that it can sometimes all seem a little unreal. But even in a region as well endowed as this, some places are better than others. Discover the best of the rest by visiting the following.

» Guéthary Built onto cliffs overlooking the ocean, this red-and-white seaside village has gained a reputation as the chi-chi resort of choice for the jet set.

» Itxassou Famed for its cherries and for the beauty of its surrounds. Take the long and winding road to the Col des Veux via the Pas de Roland and, for the ultimate in Basque immersion, dine out on baby trout and duck in Lezetako Borda (☑05 59 29 83 65; Col des Veux; menus 19-23; ◷lunch Sat & Sun) (a 20–25 minute drive southeast of Itxassou), a barnlike restaurant sitting a few metres over the border into Spain and atop an often mist-shrouded mountain. You're given little choice in the menu and non-Basque diners are a very rare sight. Call ahead to check it's open.

» La Bastide-Clairence White-washed houses brushed in lipstick red, this is arguably the most beautiful of all Basque mountain villages.

» Bidarray A pretty village famed for its rafting opportunities.

» Forêt d'Iraty A vast beech forest that turns the high mountain slopes fiery orange in autumn. A web of walking trails allows for easy exploration.

» Larrau Nowhere else is the spirit of the Basque mountains as strong as in this quaint village surrounded by giants. There are some astounding walking opportunities here and some nearby gorges.

balconies and lots of quirky boutiques. Specific sights worth seeking out include the Église Notre Dame du Bout du Pont, with foundations as old as the town itself but thoroughly rebuilt in the 17th century. Beyond Porte de Notre Dame is the photogenic Vieux Pont (Old Bridge), the town's best-known landmark, from where there's a fine view of whitewashed houses with balconies leaning out above the water. A pleasant 500m riverbank stroll upstream leads to the steeply arched Pont Romain (meaning

IPARLA RIDGE HIKE

Rising above St-Étienne de Baïgorry are wave upon wave of luminous green mountains, including the sheer-sided ridge of Iparla (1056m), which marks the border with Spain. A breathtaking one-day hike (4½ hours without stopping and an elevation gain of 900m) along the edge of this ridge is easily possible for any moderately fit walker. Many experienced Pyrenean walkers describe this as the finest ridge walk in the entire mountain range. You will need a compass, and a *Rando Éditions 1:50,000 Pays Basque Ouest* map wouldn't go amiss either (this can be obtained at any local bookshop as well as many newsagents). Children may need a helping hand on some of the earlier parts of this walk, but once on the ridge it'll be plain sailing.

The trail begins from the Bordazar Berroa, a traditional Basque farmhouse. To get there, leave St-Étienne de Baïgorry northward on the D9418 and after a couple of kilometres take the narrow turn-off to your left towards Urdos and La Bastide. Continue for around 3km, past the second turn-off for Urdos and past the hamlet of La Bastide.

Walk in a northwest direction along the track signed to Iparla. Fifteen minutes later, at the fork with the concrete track, head right in a due west direction. Ten minutes later, just after a stream and a shepherd's hut, the trail starts to climb steeply. At the next fork, head right in a northeast direction. You now appear to be heading away from the ridge. After another five minutes the path bends around the top of a low ridge and starts to head downhill. There should be a water trough on your left and a dirt trail heading upwards in a northwest direction, back towards Iparla. Follow this dirt trail for around 10 minutes until you get to another shepherd's hut/barn, where you turn right along a narrow track heading north-northwest.

After a quarter of an hour you come to a scree slope and the path, which is marked by the odd rock cairn, zigzags sharply upwards and onto the Iparla Ridge, crossing over a fence on the way (ignore the more obvious trail that continues along the flank of the hill). This is the hardest part of the walk – poles are useful! Fifteen minutes of huffing and puffing, and you emerge onto the Iparla Ridge beside an old BF90 marker stone. You are now on a stretch of the GR10, a highly demanding 45-day trek along the entire length of the Pyrenees, but for now things get much easier.

Turn left, following the obvious path and the red and white paint slashes of the GR10 in a westerly, uphill direction, sticking all the time to the ridge edge. Almost straight away you will start to be rewarded with what you might think are spectacular views: they're nothing compared to those you'll get in a few minutes when you finally reach the summit of Iparla, which is indicated with a marker post. It goes without saying that you'll rest a while here admiring the incredible views across half the French and Spanish Basque Country, but while you're soaking it all in keep your eyes peeled for the numerous huge griffon vultures and various eagles and hawks that circle in the thermals here.

It's impossible to get lost now. Just dance along the edge of the ridge for around an hour (at one point the trail dips down slightly before rising again), following the red and white GR10 paint slashes all the way. Eventually the path drops sharply downhill, off the ridge, in a southwest direction and reaches a signpost marking the Col d'Harrieta.

Leaving the GR10 behind here (which labours upwards again and onto another ridge), turn left (east) and follow the path downhill through the forest. After around 15 minutes you'll reach a fork and a shepherd's hut. Take the left-hand path (the other one leads to Urdos) in a northwest direction towards the Col de Larrarté. The path turns into a concrete road and, ignoring any turn-offs, descends sharply for half an hour until you arrive back at your car.

Roman Bridge, but in fact dating from the 17th century).

Rue de la Citadelle is edged by substantial, pink-granite 16th- to 18th-century houses. Look for the construction date on door lintels (the oldest we found was 1510). A common motif is the scallop shell, symbol of St Jacques (St James or Santiago) and of the Santiago de Compostela pilgrims. Pilgrims would enter the town through the Porte de St-Jacques on the northern side of town, then, refreshed and probably a little poorer, head for Spain through the Porte d'Espagne, south of the river.

Prison des Évêques   MONUMENT
(Bishops' Prison; 41 rue de la Citadelle; adult/under 15yr €3/free; ⊙10.30am-7pm) Dating back to the 14th century, this claustrophobic vaulted cellar gets its history muddled. It served as the town jail from 1795, as a military lock-up in the 19th century, then as a place of internment during WWII for those caught trying to flee to nominally neutral Spain. The lower section dates from the 13th century, when St-Jean Pied de Port was a bishopric of the Avignon papacy; the building above it dates from the 16th century, by which time the bishops were long gone. Inside can be found seasonal exhibitions.

La Citadelle   FORTRESS
From the top of rue de la Citadelle, a rough cobblestone path ascends to the massive citadel itself, from where there's a spectacular panorama of the town and the surrounding hills. Constructed in 1628, the fort was rebuilt around 1680 by military engineers of the Vauban school. Nowadays it serves as a secondary school and is closed to the public.

If you've got a head for heights, descend by the steps signed *escalier poterne* (rear stairway). Steep and slippery after rain, they plunge beside the moss-covered ramparts to Porte de l'Échauguette (Watchtower Gate).

✦ Activities

Escape the summertime crowds by walking or cycling into the Pyrenean foothills, where the loudest sounds you'll hear are cowbells and the wind. Two GRs (*grandes randonnées;* long-distance hiking trails) pass through town: the GR10 (the trans-Pyrenean long-distance trail running from the Atlantic to the Mediterranean over the course of 45 days) and the GR65 (the Chemin de St-Jacques pilgrim route). Outside the summer season, check with the tourist office or hostels for snow reports and possible rerouting, and plan your accommodation ahead as many places on the Spanish side close.

If you speak French, pick up a copy of the excellent *Le Guide Rando: Pays Basque* (€17.90) from local bookshops, which maps walking excursions.

To cycle the easy way while enjoying the best of Nive Valley views, load your bicycle onto the train in Bayonne – they're carried free – and roll back down the valley from St-Jean Pied de Port. If you find the ride all the way back to the coast daunting, rejoin the train at Pont-Noblia, for example, or Cambo-les-Bains.

☞ Tours

In July and August, the tourist office organises an array of different tours – from the historical to countryside rambles.

🛏 Sleeping & Eating

Much of the accommodation is geared towards pilgrims on the long hike to Santiago de Compostela in Galicia, Spain. This sort of accommodation is always very basic; normally it consists of just dorm beds, but it's cheap at around €8 to €10 per person. At many places nonpilgrims will be turned away.

Itzalpea   B&B €
(☎05 59 37 03 66; www.maisondhotes-itzalpea.com; 5 place du Trinquet; incl breakfast s €55-58, d €65-78; 🖇🌐) This friendly and cosy *maison d'hôte* (B&B) has five tastefully renovated rooms (some air-conditioned), all of which differ from one another and are named after local flowers. It's set above a teashop serving some 20 different types of tea.

Maison E Bernat   B&B €€
(☎05 59 37 23 10; www.ebernat.com; 20 rue de la Citadelle; d €79-89; menus from €20; 🌐) There are only four bedrooms in this welcoming 17th-century place with thick stone walls, but they're airy, well furnished and meticulously kept, and each has a double and a single bed. There's a great little restaurant on site, which spills onto a tiny terrace, and the hosts run a program of gourmet-themed weekends (€300 to €340 for two people with accommodation).

Central Hôtel   HISTORIC HOTEL €
(☎05 59 37 00 22; 1 place Charles de Gaulle; r €62-75, menus €20-45; 🌐) Follow the gleaming polished timber staircase up to 12 old-fashioned but disappointingly dull rooms at

this eponymously situated hotel. The owners are welcoming and there's an on-site restaurant opening to a riverside terrace. The rooms are spacious and the hotel overlooks a bubbling river.

Camping Municipal
Plaza Berri CAMPGROUND €
(📞05 59 37 11 19; av du Fronton; emplacement €10, car €2; ⊙Apr-Oct) Beside the river, this smallish campground has ample shade, but gets very busy and cramped.

Chez Arrambide GASTRONOMIC €€
(menus €42-110, mains €30-52; ⊙closed Tue Sep-Jun) This twin Michelin-starred restaurant, inside the (overpriced) Hôtel Les Pyrénées, is where chef Firmin Arrambide does wonders with seasonal market produce, such as truffle and foie-gras lasagne.

Self-Catering
Farmers from the surrounding hills bring fresh produce – chillies, local cheeses and much more – to the town's Monday market (place Charles de Gaulle). In high summer a weekly handicraft and food fair is held most Thursdays in the covered market.

☆ Entertainment

Year-round, variants of *pelota* (admission €7 to €10), including a bare-handed *pelota* tournament, are played at the *trinquet*, *fronton* municipal and *jaï alaï* courts. In summer these tend to take place at 5pm on a Friday.

In high summer, traditional Basque music and dancing takes place in the *jaï alaï* court or the church. Confirm schedules with the tourist office.

❶ Information

Tourist office (📞05 59 37 03 57; www .pyrenees-basque.com; place Charles de Gaulle; ⊙9am-7pm Mon-Sat, 10am-4pm Sun Jul & Aug, 9am-noon & 2-6pm Mon-Sat Sep-Jun)

❶ Getting There & Away

Train is the only option to travel to or from Bayonne (€9.20, 1¼ hours, up to five daily).

St-Étienne de Baïgorry

The village of St-Étienne de Baïgorry and its outlying hamlets straddle the Vallée de Baïgorry. Tranquillity itself after busy St-Jean Pied de Port, the pretty village is stretched thinly along a branch of the River Nive. Like so many Basque settlements, the village has two focal points: the church and the *fronton* (*pelota* court). It makes a good base for hikers, as the spectacular Iparla Ridge hike (as well as several other top-quality walks) starts close by (although you'll still need a car to reach the trailhead). Even if you're not a hiker you can't fail to be impressed by the area's beauty, so an overnight stay is recommended.

🛏 Sleeping & Eating

Hôtel-Restaurant Manechenea HOTEL €
(📞05 59 37 41 68; www.hotel-saint-etienne-de -baigorry.com; s €42, d €52-55, menus €17-30) A couple of kilometres north of St-Étienne de Baïgorry in the hamlet of Urdos, this rural hotel has butter-yellow rooms that overlook green fields and a bubbling mountain-fed brook. You can eat some of the denizens of said brook, such as delicious trout, for lunch at the in-house restaurant.

Hôtel-Restaurant Arcé HOTEL €€
(📞05 59 37 40 14; www.hotel-arce.com; s/d from €75/150, menus €18-48; ⊙closed Nov–mid-Apr; 🛜🏊) This impressive hotel has a stunning riverside location and spacious rooms with old-style furnishings. To reach the pool you must stroll past the orange trees and cross the river via a little humpback bridge. The in-house restaurant is highly regarded by locals.

The Pyrenees

Best Places to Eat

» Le Majestic (p669)

» Au Fin Gourmet (p669)

» Le Viscos (p673)

» Le Sacca (p681)

» L'Héptaméron des
Gourmets (p683)

Best Places to Stay

» Château de Beauregard
(p685)

» Maison des Consuls
(p685)

» Hôtel du Lion d'Or (p680)

» Le Castel de la Pique
(p683)

» Hôtel des Rochers (p673)

Why Go?

They might not be on quite the same lofty scale as the Alps, but the Pyrenees still pack a mighty impressive mountain punch. Crested by snow for much of the year, these high, wild peaks form a natural frontier between southwest France and northern Spain. End to end, they cover a total distance of around 430km, including the 100km strip of protected land known as the Parc National des Pyrénées, created in 1967 and now an important haven for rare wildlife such as eagles, griffon vultures, izards (a type of goat) and some of the last remaining wild brown bears in France.

Needless to say, if you're a hiker, biker or skier, or if you're simply a sucker for views, you'll be in seventh heaven in the Pyrenees. From historic ski stations to isolated valleys, from subterranean caves to snow-dusted peaks, there are enough sights to fill a lifetime of visits. Breathe deep: the wilds are calling.

When to Go

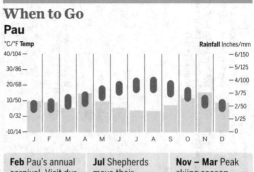

Pau

Feb Pau's annual carnival. Visit during Easter for the Festival International de Musique Sacrée.

Jul Shepherds move their flocks in the Transhumance, and the Tour de France races by.

Nov – Mar Peak skiing season – book hotels well ahead.

The Pyrenees Highlights

1 Marvel at the views from the mountain-top observatory at the **Pic du Midi** (p682)

2 Trek to the face of the amazing **Cirque de Gavarnie** (p682)

3 See some Pyrenean wildlife at the **Parc Animalier des Pyrénées** (p674)

4 See prehistoric artwork by torchlight at the **Grotte de Niaux** (p684)

5 Tackle the trails around Cauterets from the **Pont d'Espagne** (p679)

6 Explore the château and chocolate shops of **Pau** (p667)

7 Trundle high above the Vallée d'Ossau aboard the **Petit Train d'Artouste** (p678)

8 Experience traditional Pyrenean life at the **Forges de Pyrène** (p685)

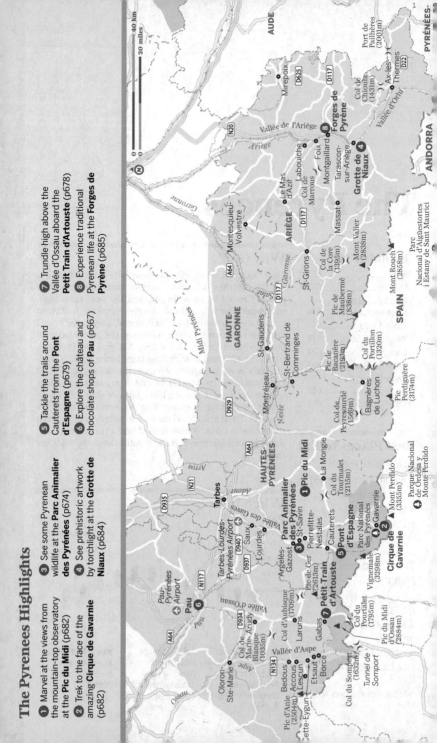

❶ Getting There & Away

The two main towns, Pau and Lourdes, are well served by rail and air. Pau is served by Ryanair flights to and from the UK and Belgium, while Air France handles domestic services, and several other budget carriers fly to European cities. Lourdes' airport has scheduled services to Paris.

Buses are limited, so to properly explore you'll need wheels. Roads are generally well maintained and nowhere near as hair-raising as the Alps.

Pau

POP 80,600

Palm trees might seem out of place in this mountainous region, but its chief city, Pau (rhymes with 'so'), has long been famed for its mild climate. In the 19th century it was a favourite wintering spot for wealthy Brits and Americans, who left behind many grand villas, English-style flower-filled public parks, and promenades with dizzying vistas of the snow-dusted peaks. These days Pau is still an elegant city, and makes an ideal base for exploring the northern reaches of the Pyrenees.

◉ Sights

The town centre sits on a small hill with the Gave de Pau (River Pau) at its base. Along its crest stretches bd des Pyrénées, a wide promenade offering panoramic views of the mountains. A creaky funicular railway dating from 1908 clanks down from the bd des Pyrénées to av Napoléon Bonaparte, allowing you to avoid the uphill slog from the train station.

Pau's tiny old centre extends for about 500m around the château, but despite its minuscule dimensions, it's worth a stroll for its much-restored medieval and Renaissance buildings.

Château de Pau   CASTLE

(www.musee-chateau-pau.fr; adult/18-25yr/child €6/4.50/free, incl temporary exhibitions €8/6.50/free; ◔9.30am-12.30pm & 1.30-6.45pm, gardens longer hours) Originally the residence of the monarchs of Navarre, Pau's castle was transformed into a Renaissance château amid lavish gardens by Marguerite d'Angoulême in the 16th century. Marguerite's grandson, Henri de Navarre (the future Henri IV), was born here – cradled, so the story goes, in an upturned tortoise shell (still on display in one of the museum's rooms).

Much restored, the château is now mainly worth visiting for its collections of Gobelins tapestries and Sevres porcelain, as well as its fine Renaissance architecture.

Within the brick-and-stone Tour de la Monnaie below the main château, a modern lift (free) hauls you from place de la Monnaie up to the ramparts.

Admission includes an obligatory one-hour guided tour in rapid-fire French (departing every 15 minutes), but you can pick up an English-language guide sheet at the reception desk.

Musée Bernadotte   MUSEUM

(8 rue Tran; adult/student €3/1.50; ◔10am-noon & 2-6pm Tue-Sun) This townhouse is the birthplace of one of Napoleon's favourite generals, Jean-Baptiste Bernadotte (nicknamed 'Sergent belle-jambe', apparently on account of his shapely legs). The museum explores the improbable story of how Bernadotte came to be crowned king of Sweden and Norway in 1810, when the Swedish parliament reckoned that the only way out of the country's dynastic and political crisis was to stick a foreigner on the throne. The present king of Sweden, Carl Gustaf, is the seventh ruler in the Bernadotte dynasty.

You'll spot the museum by the blue-and-yellow Swedish flag fluttering outside.

Musée des Beaux-Arts   ART MUSEUM

(rue Mathieu Lalanne; adult/student €3/1.50; ◔10am-noon & 2-6pm Wed-Mon) Works by Rubens and El Greco both figure at Pau's fine arts museum, but the museum's prize piece is a famous Degas canvas, *A New Orleans Cotton Office*, painted in 1873.

✵ Festivals & Events

Carnival Week   STREET CARNIVAL

The prelude to Lent brings street parades and a carnival atmosphere to Pau around late February.

L'Été à Pau   MUSIC FESTIVAL

Lively summer music festival, spanning late July and early August.

🛏 Sleeping

Hôtel Bristol   HOTEL €€

(☎05 59 27 72 98; www.hotelbristol-pau.com; 3 rue Gambetta; s €75-91, d €82-99, f €110-120; 🖥) Definitely the best midrange option in Pau, in a quintessentially French 19th-century building which offers surprisingly modern rooms. Cool whites are the keynote, but

Pau

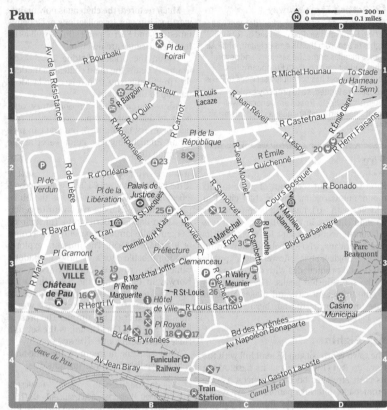

Pau

stripy fabrics, coloured throws and modern art liven things up considerably. The upper rooms are the best: ask for one with a balcony overlooking the mountains.

Hôtel Central
HOTEL €€

(☑05 59 27 72 75; www.hotelcentralpau.com; 15 rue Léon Daran; s €59-67, d €56-79; 🛜) The rambling corridors of this old hotel lead to a selection of higgledy-piggledy rooms, variously decorated in bright stripes and citrus shades, most with tall French windows looking over the street. It's worth asking for one of the larger doubles, as the singles are tiny. Parking's only available on the street outside.

Hôtel Montpensier
HOTEL €€

(☑05 59 27 42 72; www.hotel-montpensier-pau. com; 36 rue Montpensier; s €75-95, d €85-95; ✳🛜) A pastel pink, shuttered facade conceals plain, simple rooms here, all with coir carpets, mix-and-match colour schemes and rather dated bathrooms. The free parking's a real bonus in trafficky Pau.

Hôtel Roncevaux
HOTEL €€

(☑05 59 27 08 44; www.hotel-roncevaux.com; 25 rue Louis Barthou; d €82-160; 🛜) Modern, business-oriented hotel that's part of the Logis chain. There are four categories of room, from 'Confort' to 'Luxe' – higher rates mean much more space and four-poster beds, but the 'Grand Confort' are the best compromise between price and comfort. The decor is a bit eclectic, with some weird colour combos and furniture choices going on, but it's dead central.

🍴 Eating

TOP
CHOICE **Le Majestic**
TRADITIONAL FRENCH €€€

(☑08 92 68 06 89; 9 place Royale; lunch menus €15-24, dinner menus €28-39; ⊙Mon-Sat) A top spot overlooking leafy place Royale, matched by top-notch French cuisine. The feel inside is fairly formal – ice white tablecloths, razor-sharp napkins – but it suits the sophisticated food, heavy on quality ingredients such as turbot, sea bass, Bigorre pork and Pyrenean lamb. Considering the quality, the prices are extremely reasonable, especially at lunch.

TOP
CHOICE **Au Fin Gourmet**
GASTRONOMIC €€€

(☑05 59 27 47 71; 24 av Gaston Lacoste; standard menus €28-39, tasting menus €62-74; ⊙lunch Thu-Sun, dinner Tue-Sat) For old-school fine French dining, this *restaurant gastronomique* is the place in Pau. Run by the Ithurriage

brothers, Patrick and Laurent, it's known for its impeccably presented dishes, heavy on sauces, creams, foams and garnishes. It's in a green setting in the Jardins de Joantho, near the funicular to bd des Pyrénées.

Les Papilles Insolites
BISTRO €

(☑05 59 71 43 79; 5 rue Alexander Taylor; 2-/3-course menu €15/18; ⊙lunch & dinner Wed-Sat) This quirky address is halfway between a wine shop and a bistro. Browse through organic, biodynamic and local wines, then sit at one of the scruffy wood tables to sample the *cuisine du marché* (market cooking). The owner was a sommelier at some of Paris' top restaurants, so quality is high.

Ze Bistrot
BISTRO €€

(☑05 59 27 44 44; 13 rue Henri IV; lunch menu €16, dinner mains €15-20; ⊙lunch & dinner Tue-Sat) Ze wine, ze food, ze ambience – Ze Bistro is hard to fault. It's a creative little diner run by Laurence and Thierry Lassal, who like 'revisiting' traditional French dishes with their own unique spin. Food is very seasonal, so what's on the blackboard is dictated by what's on offer at the market (always a good sign).

Le Berry
BRASSERIE €€

(☑05 59 27 42 95; 4 rue Gachet; menu du jour around €9, mains €13-18) Rough-and-ready brasserie turning out solid grub for a busy local crowd: *steak-frites* (steak and chips), pork cutlets and lamb chops, followed by a good choice of ready-made desserts. There are no bookings, so queue up early.

Le Champagne
BRASSERIE €

(☑05 59 27 72 12; 5 place Royale; mains €10-15; ⊙Mon-Sat) A bustling brasserie on place Royale, ideal for an early-evening beer and a plate of simple bistro fare.

Royal St-André
CAFE €

(26 bd des Pyrénées; ⊙10am-2am May-Oct, 2-7pm Nov-Apr) This popular *café-glacier* is the top spot for ice cream and sorbets, with tables scattered under the trees of bd des Pyrénées, and postcard views of the mountains.

Self-Catering

The lively **Halles de Pau** (Covered Market; pl de la République; ⊙6am-1pm Mon-Sat) is great for general picnic supplies, or there's the **Marché Bio** (pl de Foirail; ⊙Wed & Sat morning) for organic food on Wednesday and Saturday.

🍷 Drinking

Pau's bars generally open from 10am to 2am.

'Le Triangle', bounded by rue Henri Faisans, rue Émile Garet and rue Castetnau, is the centre of student nightlife. Good bets are grungy Le Garage (49 rue Émile Garet) and Péna Muxu (35 rue Émile Garet), which sometimes has live music.

A string of bars (Galway and Australia among them) extends along bd des Pyrénées.

Congenial wine bars near the château include Au Grain de Raisin (11 rue Sully), which also has a good range of draft beers, and Le Bouchon (46 rue Maréchal Joffre), which serves local Jurançon wines.

☆ Entertainment

The free *La Culture à Pau* details forthcoming events; it's available from the tourist office.

Pau's renowned rugby team, Section Paloise (www.section-paloise.com), plays regularly between September and May at Stade du Hameau (☎05 59 02 50 91; bd de l'Aviation).

The town's only cinema is Cinéma Le Méliès (☎05 59 27 60 52; 6 rue Bargoin), which only screens *version originale* (VO, ie non-dubbed) films.

🔒 Shopping

Pau is famous for its *chocolatiers* (chocolate shops): the top names are La Couronne (place Clemenceau), Josuat (23 rue Serviez) and Francis Miot (48 rue Maréchal Joffre).

For an unusual souvenir, stop by Au Parapluie des Pyrénées (12 rue Montpensier), which makes the beech-handled, rattan-ribbed umbrellas traditionally used by Pyrenean shepherds.

ℹ Information

Tourist office (☎05 59 27 27 08; www.pau-pyrenees.com; place Royale; ⏱9am-6pm) Closes early on Sunday.

ℹ Getting There & Away

AIR **Aéroport Pau-Pyrénées** (☎05 59 33 33 00; www.pau.aeroport.fr) is 7km northwest of town. Current direct flights go to Paris Orly, Paris CGD and Lyon (Airfrance), London City, Dublin and Amsterdam (Cityjet) and Marseille (Twinjet).

BUS Bus services are very limited, although there are at least a couple of daily runs to the local towns of Agen and Mont de Marsan. Contact **Cars Région Aquitaine** (☎08 00 64 40 47; http://car.aquitaine.fr) for timetables.

TRAIN Trains are the quickest way to get to Pau. There are two or three direct TGVs daily from Paris. In summer SNCF buses run from Oloron-Ste-Marie into the Vallée d'Aspe.

Bayonne €16.90 to €21.20, 1½ hours

Oloron-Ste-Marie €7.10, 37 minutes

Paris Montparnasse €72 to €96, 5¾ hours

Toulouse €29 to €31, 2¼ to 2½ hours

ℹ Getting Around

TO/FROM THE AIRPORT **Idelis** (☎05 59 14 15 16; www.reseau-idelis.com) runs a shuttle to the train station and town centre in Pau. From the airport, buses run roughly hourly from 7.40am to 7.40pm; from the train station, buses run from 6.30am to 7.50pm. Tickets cost €1, and the journey time is about half an hour. Note that buses don't run on Sundays, so you'll need to reserve a **taxi** (☎05 59 33 33 00); expect to pay between €25 and €30.

CAR & MOTORCYCLE Most streets in central Pau are *payant* (metered), but there's free parking on place de Verdun. Major car-hire firms have kiosks at the airport.

FUNICULAR The quickest way from the train station to the town centre is to catch the antique **Funiculaire de Pau** (⏱every 3 min from 6.45am-9.40pm Mon-Sat, 1.30-8.50pm Sun) from av Napoléon Bonaparte to bd des Pyrénées.

PUBLIC TRANSPORT Public transport in Pau is handled by Idelis. Single/day tickets cost €1/2.50 and can be bought from the driver.

Lourdes

POP 15,700 / ELEV 400M

If you've ever wondered what a Catholic version of Las Vegas might look like, chances are it'd turn out pretty close to Lourdes. This sprawling town, 43km southeast of Pau, has been one of the world's most important pilgrimage sites since 1858, when 14-year-old Bernadette Soubirous (1844–79) saw the Virgin Mary in a series of 18 visions in a rocky grotto. The visions were subsequently confirmed by the Vatican, and Bernadette was beatified in 1933.

Now known as the Sanctuaires Notre Dame de Lourdes, the grotto is considered to be one of the holiest sites in Christendom. Over six million people arrive in Lourdes every year, to pray, pay homage and be doused in the supposedly miraculous waters, but in contrast to its spiritual importance, the modern town of Lourdes itself is a pretty dispiriting experience, with a tatty tangle of neon-signed hotels and souvenir shops selling everything from plastic crucifixes to Madonna–shaped bottles (just add holy water at the shrine).

⊙ Sights & Activities

Sanctuaires Notre Dame de Lourdes   SACRED CAVES
(⊙Porte St-Michel & Porte St-Joseph 5am-midnight, baths 9-11am & 2.30-4pm Mon-Sat, 2-4pm Sun & holy days) The development of the Sanctuaries of Our Lady of Lourdes began within a decade of Ste Bernadette's apparitions in 1858. The main site is approached via one of two gateways: the Porte St-Joseph or the Entrée des Lacets (rue Monseigneur Theas; ⊙24hr).

The most dramatic approach is via the Port St-Joseph, from where a broad boulevard sweeps west towards the Byzantine Basilique du Rosaire, and the Basilique Supérieure, topped by gilded turrets and tiled frescos depicting Bernadette's visions. Beneath the basilica is Lourdes' most revered site, the Grotte de Massabielle (sometimes known as the Grotte Miraculeuse or the Grotte des Apparitions), where Bernadette experienced her famous visions.

The Esplanade des Processions, lined with enormous flickering candles left by previous pilgrims, leads along the river to the grotto's entrance, where people line up to enter the cave itself, or take an icy dip in one of the sacred baths.

From Palm Sunday to mid-October, nightly torchlight processions start from the Massabielle Grotto at 9pm, while at 5pm there's the Procession Eucharistique (Blessed Sacrament Procession) along the Esplanade des Processions.

Château Fort   CASTLE, MUSEUM
(Fortified Castle; adult/child €5/3; ⊙9am-noon & 1.30-6.30pm, open all day in Jul & Aug) Lourdes' imposing castle stands on a sheer hill just behind the town. There's been some kind of stronghold on this site since Roman times, but the present building is largely medieval, including the stout walls and the central keep. The castle was fortified again in the 17th and 18th centuries, and served as a state prison following the Revolution.

Since the 1920s, the castle has housed the Musée Pyrénéen, which owns one of the region's largest collections of folk art, rural artefacts, tools and other exhibits.

Take the free lift (elevator) from rue Baron Duprat or walk up the ramp at the northern end of rue du Bourg.

Pic du Jer   VIEWPOINT
(bd d'Espagne; funicular adult/child return €9.80/7.30; ⊙9.30-6pm or 7pm Mar-Nov) When the crowds of pilgrims get too much, you can take refuge on the rocky 94m-high pinnacle of the Pic du Jer, which offers panoramic views of Lourdes and the central Pyrenees.

There are two routes to the top: a punishing three-hour slog along a signed trail (ideal for penitents and gluttons for punishment) or a speedy six-minute ride on the century-old funicular (ideal for everyone else).

Either way, the summit makes a superb spot for a picnic. There's a choice of routes back down: a black-run mountain-bike trail, or a more family-friendly option along the Voie Verte des Gaves, a decommissioned railway that finishes up at the lower funicular station.

Take bus 2 from place Monseigneur Laurence.

Chemin de Croix   WALKING
The Chemin de Croix (Way of the Cross, sometimes known as the Chemin du Calvaire) leads for 1.5km up the forested hillside from the Basilique Supérieure past 14 Stations of the Cross. Especially devout pilgrims climb to the first station on their knees.

Other Bernadette Sites
Three of Bernadette's former houses can be visited around Lourdes. She was born at the Moulin de Boly (Boly Mill; 12 rue Bernadette Soubirous), but it was while living at the former prison of Le Cachot (15 rue des Petits Fossés; admission free; ⊙9am-noon & 2-6.30pm Apr-Oct, shorter hours at other times) that she experienced her famous visions. The family later moved to more comfortable lodgings, known now as the Maison Paternelle de Ste-Bernadette (2 rue Bernadette Soubirous; admission €2; ⊙9.30am-12.15pm & 2.15-6.30pm Mar-Oct).

For the full back-story, though, the Musée de Lourdes (☑05 62 94 28 00; adult/child €6/3; ⊙9am-noon & 1.30-6.30pm Apr-Oct) details the town's history and Ste Bernadette's life through a mix of exhibits and explanatory panels.

★ Festivals & Events
Lourdes' renowned week of sacred music, Festival International de Musique Sacrée, is held around Easter.

Lourdes

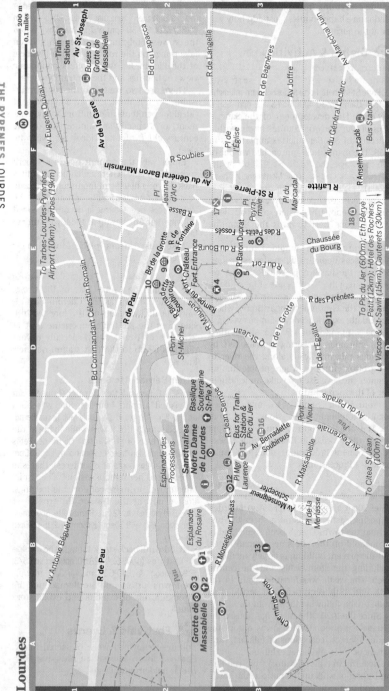

0 — 200 m
0 — 0.1 miles

Train Station
Av St-Joseph
Buses to Grotte de Massabielle 14

Av de la Gare

Bd du Lapacca

R de Langelle

R de Bagnères

Av Joffre

Av du Général Leclerc

Av Maréchal Juin

Av Anselme Lacadé
Bus Station

R Lafitte

R St-Pierre

Pl de l'Église

Av Eugène Duvau

To Tarbes-Lourdes-Pyrénées Airport (10km); Tarbes (19km)

R Soubies

Av du Général Baron Maransin

Pl Jeanne d'Arc

R Basse

R du Bourg

R de la Fontaine

R de la Grotte

Bd de la Grotte

9

10

R des Petits Fossés

R du Bourg

17

i

Pl Peyramale

Pl du Marcadal

Chaussée du Bourg

18

Bd Commandant Célestin Romain

R de Pau

R de Pau

Av Antoine Béguère

R Bernadette Soubirous

R du Château
Fort Entrance

Rampe du Fort

R Baron Duprat

R du Fort

4

5

8

R de Pyrénées

11

R de l'Égalité

To Pic du Jer (600m); Eth Bérye Petit (12km); Hôtel des Rochers, (15km); Cauterets (30km)
Le Viscos & St-Savin (15km);

R des Maurès

Q St-Jean

Pont St-Michel

Basilique Souterraine St-Pie X

R Jean Sempé

Av Peyramale

Pont Vieux

Av du Paradis

R de la Grotte

Pau

To Citéa St Jean (100m)

Esplanade des Processions

Sanctuaires Notre Dame de Lourdes

Pl Mgr Laurence
Bus for Train Station & Pic du Jer 15

16

Av Bernadette Soubirous

R Massabielle

Esplanade du Rosaire

12

Av Monseigneur Schoepfer

Pl de la Merlasse

R Monseigneur Théas

R Jean Sempé

13

Grotte de Massabielle
3
2
7

Chemin de Croix

6

Pau

Lourdes

🛏 Sleeping

Lourdes has an enormous number of hotels (second only to Paris in terms of bed space, believe it or not), but most aren't worth a first glance, let alone a second one. You'll be much better off basing at yourself at a hotel or *chambre d'hôte* (B&B) in a nearby village.

Lourdes

Bestwestern Beauséjour   HOTEL €€
(☎05 62 94 38 18; 16 av de la Gare; d €88-125; 🛜) If you're dead set on staying in Lourdes, this reliable Best Western is a solid choice – but despite the heritage facade and glossy lobby, the rooms are as generic as ever. Still it's businesslike and efficient, handy for the station and it's a lot tidier than many places round town. There's a half-decent bar-brasserie attached to the lobby.

Grand Hotel Moderne   HOTEL €€€
(☎05 62 94 12 32; www.grandhotelmoderne.com; 21 ave Bernadette Soubirous; €136-246) In a

grand art nouveau edifice dating from 1896, this is one of Lourdes' most aristocratic addresses. It makes a memorable first impression, with an elegant lobby, a lavishly mirrored restaurant and a dramatic circular staircase winding up to the upper floors. Sadly the 110 rooms are more chain than chic, with bland decor and boring fabrics – but get one with a balcony and you'll have great views over town.

Hôtel Gallia et Londres   HOTEL €€€
(☎05 62 94 35 44; www.hotelgallialondres.com; 26 av Bernadette Soubirous; d €124-274; ⊙Apr-Oct; ❄@) Another of Lourdes' fancier options, worth a special mention for its chandelier-clad restaurant and wood-panelled lobby, and a lovely garden far removed from the town fizz. The '70s-meets-1700s rooms don't quite live up to the promise, but they're perfectly comfy – if chronically overpriced in the high season.

Around Lourdes

Hôtel des Rochers   HOTEL €€
(☎05 62 97 09 52; www.lesrochershotel.com; 1 place du Castillou; d/tr/f €57/78/95; 🛜) Run by an expat English couple, John and Jane, this St-Savin hotel is a peaceful place to breathe in the mountain air, offering plain rooms, friendly owners and a decent restaurant serving home cooking with outstanding valley views from the dining room.

Eth Béryè Petit   B&B €€
(☎05 62 97 90 02; www.beryepetit.com; 15 rte de Vielle; d €59-64, tr €82) Mountain views unfurl from every window at this idyllic B&B, lodged inside a 17th-century farmhouse. A huge fireplace takes up most of the cosy lounge, while a glorious oak staircase leads up to three country-cosy rooms upstairs. Top of the heap is the Era Galeria room, with its period furniture and French windows leading to a private balcony. The house is 12km south of Lourdes off the N21 near Beaucens.

🍴 Eating

Lourdes' eating options are far from inspirational. Hotel restaurants are generally the best bet – the Grand Hotel Moderne and the Hôtel Gallia et Londres both have decent French restaurants.

TOP CHOICE Le Viscos   GASTRONOMIC
(☎05 62 97 02 28; www.hotel-leviscos.com; 1 rue Lamarque; menus €27-89; ❄🛜) The tiny hamlet of St-Savin, about 16km south, feels a

world away from Lourdes' tourist hordes. This much-lauded hotel-restaurant is one of the top gastronomic spots in the Pyrénées. It's run by celeb chef Jean-Pierre St-Martin, known for his blend of Basque, Breton and Pyrenean flavours, as well as his enduring passion for all things foie gras – choose the €89 *menu gastronomique* and each course gets a personal introduction from Jean-Pierre himself. Upstairs, cosy country rooms offer dreamy alpine views (rooms €99–€123, with full board €67 extra per person).

Restaurant le Magret　　TRADITIONAL FRENCH €€
(☑05 62 94 20 55; 10 rue des Quatre Frères Soulas; lunch menu €12-15, dinner menu €29; ⊙Tue-Sun Feb-Dec) Rustic, sepia-tinted restaurant that's strong on regional cuisine – particularly pork, trout, duck and cheese from the Vallée d'Ossau – but the ambience might be a little dingy for some.

Self-Catering

Lourdes' covered market (place du Champ Commun) occupies most of the square.

ⓘ Information

Forum Information Office (☑05 62 42 78 78; www.lourdes-france.com; Esplanade des Processions; ⊙8.30am-6.30pm) For information on the Sanctuaires.

Tourist office (☑05 62 42 77 40; www. lourdes-infotourisme.com; place Peyramale; ⊙9am-6.30pm)

ⓘ Getting There & Away

AIR **Tarbes-Lourdes-Pyrénées airport** (www. tlp.aeroport.fr) is 10km north of Lourdes on the N21. There are three daily flights to Paris (Air France), plus a few flights a week to Brussels (JetAir), and London and Manchester (Ryanair).

BUS The small **bus station** (place Capdevieille) has services northwards to Pau (though trains are much faster) and is a stop for buses running between Tarbes and Argelès-Gazost (at least daily), the gateway to the Pyrenean communities of Cauterets, Luz-St-Sauveur and Gavarnie.

SNCF buses to Cauterets (€7.40, one hour, at least five daily) leave from the train station.

CAR & MOTORCYCLE Lourdes' one-way system changes direction every couple of weeks to keep the souvenir traders happy. Factor in hordes of tourists and you'll be wise to leave your car on the outskirts; there's free parking near the train and bus stations.

TRAIN Lourdes has regular train connections, including TGVs to Pau and Paris Montparnasse.

Trains to Toulouse tend to connect through Tarbes.

Destinations served:
Bayonne €19.10 to €22.40, 1¾ hours
Paris Montparnasse €75 to €107, 6½ hours
Pau €7.60, 25 minutes
Toulouse €26.80, two hours

Around Lourdes

Grottes de Bétharram　　CAVES
(www.betharram.com; adult/child €13/7.50; ⊙9am-noon & 1.30-5.30pm mid-Mar–Oct) Along the D937, 14km west of Lourdes, is a series of subterranean caverns carved deep into the limestone rock, and covered with impressive stalactites and stalagmites. Guided visits, by minitrain and barge, last 1½ hours, but be warned: the site gets crushingly busy in high summer.

TOP CHOICE **Parc Animalier des Pyrénées**　　WILDLIFE PARK
(www.parc-animalier-pyrenees.com; adult/child €12/8; ⊙9.30am-6pm or 7pm Apr-Oct) This fantastic animal park is home to a menagerie of animals which were once common sights across the Pyrenees, many of which have either been effectively wiped out or are teetering on the brink of extinction. Among the residents are wolves, marmots, lynxes, giant ravens, vultures, racoons, beavers and a few brown bears (known in the US as grizzlies).

Best of all, you can even spend the night in a replica trapper's cabin (double/family €240/290), with toughened glass windows looking directly into the wolves' enclosure. Eat your heart out, Jack London...

It's near the village of Argelès-Gazost, 13km south of Lourdes off the D821.

Parc National des Pyrénées

Sprawling for 100km across the Franco-Spanish border, the Parc National des Pyrénées conceals some of the last pockets of true wilderness left in France. In partnership with the 156-sq-km Parque Nacional de Ordesa y Monte Perdido to the south, this wild mountain landscape is a haven for rare flora and fauna, including golden eagles, brown bears and izards (a close relation of the chamois). It's fiercely proud of its culture and heritage: traditional hill-farming and shepherding are still practised here in much

THE TRANSHUMANCE

If you're travelling through the Pyrenees between late May and early June and you happen to find yourself stuck behind an enormous cattle-shaped traffic jam, there's a good chance you may have just got caught up in the age-old tradition of the Transhumance, in which shepherds move their flocks from their winter pastures up to the high grass-rich meadows of the mountain uplands.

This ancient custom has been a staple fixture on the Pyrenean calendar for hundreds of years, and is still carried on in the time-honoured way – usually on foot, with the able assistance of sheepdogs and an occasional quad bike. It's still regarded as one of the most important events of the year in the Pyrenees, and several of the valleys host lively festivals to mark the occasion.

The whole show is repeated in October, when the flocks are brought back down to the valleys before the snows of winter descend in earnest.

the same way as they were a century ago, although on a much smaller scale.

Within the park's boundaries are the highest peaks in southwest France, including Vignemale (3298m), the Pyrenees' loftiest summit. Unsurprisingly, the park is popular with backcountry hikers and winter skiiers, but even in the high summer you'll still find plenty of quiet trails and pockets of mountain solitude.

🏃 Activities

Walking

Some 350km of waymarked trails (including the Mediterranean-to-Atlantic GR10) crisscross the park; some link up with trails in Spain.

Within the park are about 20 *refuges* (mountain huts), primarily run by the Club Alpin Français (CAF). Most are staffed only from July to September but maintain a small wing year-round.

Each of the six park valleys (Vallée d'Aure, Vallée de Luz, Vallée de Cauterets, Val d'Azun, Vallée d'Ossau and Vallée d'Aspe) has a national-park folder or booklet in French, *Randonnées dans le Parc National des Pyrénées*, describing 10 to 15 walks. Worthwhile for the route maps alone, they're for sale at local parks and tourist offices.

The park is covered by IGN's 1:25,000 Top 25 maps 1547OT *Ossau*, 1647OT *Vignemale*, 1748OT *Gavarnie* and 1748ET *Néouvielle*.

White-Water Sports

Rivers racing from the Pyrenean heights offer some of France's finest white water, since spring snow melt is supplemented by modest (sometimes not-so-modest) year-round rain, bringing a fairly steady annual flow.

The Gave d'Aspe, Gave d'Oloron and Gave d'Ossau offer some of the most reliable white water. There are several companies based around Oloron-Ste-Marie, including Gaïa Aventure (☎06 18 58 08 69; www.gaiaaventure.com; Oloron-Ste-Marie) and Centre Nautique de Soeix (☎05 59 39 61 00; http://soeix.free.fr; quartier Soeix), which both offer a range of canoeing, kayaking and rafting trips. Prices start at around €20 to €30 for a two-hour session.

Mountain Biking

Once the last snows melt around mid-April to May, many of the Pyrenean ski stations open up their trails to VTTs (*vélos tout-terrains*, aka mountain bikes).

Val d'Azun, Bagnères du Bigorre, Barrousse, Barèges, Ax and several other places all have extensive areas of *sentiers balisés* (marked trails). Some are suitable for families, while others specifically cater for hardcore bikers with beams, jumps and other obstacles. The useful Pyrénées Passion (www.pyrenees-passion.info/VTT.php) website lists the main VTT areas.

There's also a large mountain-bike park near Aude, offering over 870km of trails: contact the Aude tourist office (☎04 68 20 07 78; www.aude-pyrenees.fr) for details.

Bikes are readily available for hire, and specialist companies such as VTT Nature (p676) and La Rébenne (☎05 61 65 20 93; www.larebenne.com; 9 chemin de Malet, Foix) offer guided mountain-biking expeditions.

ℹ️ Information

Park visitor centres can be found at Etsaut, Laruns, Arrens-Marsous, Cauterets, Luz-St-Sauveur, Gavarnie and St-Lary-Soulan.

For general information, **PNR Pyrenees** (www.parc-pyrenees.com), the park's official tourist site, is the place to start.

Vallée d'Aspe

The westernmost of the main Pyrenean valleys, the Vallée d'Aspe has been an important thoroughfare through the mountains ever since Julius Caesar's Roman legionnaires marched this way.

Fewer than 3000 people live in the valley's 13 villages, and its upper reaches are still among the most remote corners of the French Pyrenees. But for many people the valley's precious seclusion is already a thing of the past thanks to the Tunnel de Somport, an 8km-long road tunnel across the Spanish border, which opened in 2003 despite howls of protest from local residents.

The small town of Oloron-Ste-Marie stands at the valley's northern end. From here, the N193 runs south, roughly following the course of the River Aspe for about 50km to the Franco–Spanish border, passing through the villages of Sarrance, Bedous, Accous, Cette-Eygun and Etsaut en route.

◉ Sights

FREE Écomusée de la
Vallée d'Aspe   RURAL MUSEUMS
(http://ecomusee.vallee-aspe.com) Life in the Vallée d'Aspe still ticks along at a traditional tilt. Four sites around the valley explore the area's heritage and agricultural traditions, and its connections with the Santiago de Compostela pilgrimage route; they're collectively known as the Écomusée de la Vallée d'Aspe.

There are small folk museums in the villages of Sarrance, Lourdios-Ichère and Borcé, but the most interesting site by far is Les Fermiers Basco-Béarnais (⊙9.30am-1pm & 2.30-7.30pm) in Accous, a farmers' co-operative and thriving *fromagerie* (cheese shop), where you can sample cheese made from the milk of local ewes, goats and cows,

and stock up with cheesy goodies to take home.

Opening hours at the four sites vary depending on the time of year; see the website for details.

🏃 Activities

Hiking
Trails cover much of the upper Aspe Valley, originally tramped by local shepherds, but now busy with hikers and geocachers throughout the summer (as well as a growing number of snowshoers in winter).

The GR10 long-distance trail (part of the iconic Chemin St-Jacques) winds through the valley via the high-altitude village of Lescun, 5.5km from Bedous, which offers westerly views of the Cirque de Lescun and the 2504m Pic d'Anie.

Another popular route follows the GR10 south from Borce or Etsaut to Fort du Portalet, a 19th-century fortress used as a WWII prison.

The Bedous tourist office (p678) can help with route suggestions and general advice on hiking in the valley. It also sells the locally-produced guidebook *Le Topo des 45 Randonnées en Vallée d'Aspe*, as well as detailed hiking maps.

Online route suggestions and planning tools (in French) are available from the Caminaspe website, run by the owner of VTT Nature.

Mountain Biking
VTT Nature (☑05 59 34 75 25; www.caminaspe.fr) in Bedous runs guided mountain-bike sessions in the Vallée d'Aspe for €20/25 per half-/full day, and hires out mountain bikes for €20/95 per day/week. It also offers guided walks and baggage-transfer services (useful if you want to avoid carrying around your backpack).

Also in Bedous, Rando Bike (☑05 59 34 79 11; www.rando-bike.fr) offers mountain-biking trips, guided walks and snowshoeing in winter.

Horse Riding
Auberge Cavalière in Accous runs multiday horseback trips costing €598/1095 for four/seven days. Nearby La Garbure (p678) in Etsaut organises guided hikes and donkey-trekking, with accommodation in local *gîtes* (cottages) and meals included. Prices start from €175/85 per adult/child for a three-day self-guided expedition, or you can hire your own donkey for €27/45 per half-/full day.

MOVING ON?

For tips, recommendations and reviews, head to shop.lonelyplanet.com to purchase a downloadable PDF of the Aragon chapter from Lonely Planet's *Spain* guide.

SKIING IN THE FRENCH PYRENEES

While the Pyrenees' best skiing actually lies across the border (at the Spanish resorts around Baqueira-Beret and Andorra), the French-side resorts still offer plenty of opportunity for downhill skiing and snowboarding, as well as cross-country skiing and, increasingly, snowshoeing. The Pyrenees usually receive much less snow than the Alps, and falls tend to be moister and heavier, making them perfect for learners and intermediates.

The French side has over 20 downhill ski stations, and more than 10 cross-country areas. Following are the major ones:

» **Ax Trois Domaines** (www.ax-ski.com) Above Ax-les-Thermes, gentle runs snake through pine forest and, higher up, the open spaces of Campels. In summer its trails offer superb mountain biking.

» **Barèges-La Mongie** (www.tourmalet.com) This combined resort is the largest in the Pyrenees, with a network of dramatic runs tracing their way around Col du Tourmalet and the foot of the Pic du Midi de Bigorre.

» **Cauterets** (www.cauterets.com) Snow lingers late at this long-established spa town–ski resort; you can still whiz downhill here when other resorts have closed down for the season.

» **Superbagnères** (www.luchon.com) A cabin lift hurtles up from the spa town of Bagnères de Luchon for skiing above the treeline at 1800m.

» **Val d'Azun** (www.valdazun.com) The best cross-country skiing in the Pyrenees, 30km southwest of Lourdes.

Paragliding

One of the most unforgettable ways to explore the valley is from the air. There are several paragliding schools in Accous, including **Ascendance** (☑05 59 34 52 07; www.ascendance.fr) and **Air Attitude** (☑05 59 34 50 06; www.air-attitude.com), which offer introductory tandem rides with an instructor from €65 per session.

⭐ Festivals & Events

The valley holds three annual **markets** in celebration of its local produce, including an Easter market in Bedous, a summer market in Aydius on the first Sunday of August, and an autumn food fair in Sarrance.

Other events to look out for are **Le Transhumance de Lourdios** in early June, and the **Fête du Fromage d'Etsaut**, a cheese fair on the last Sunday in July.

🛏 Sleeping & Eating

Accommodation is mainly geared towards walkers, with seasonal campsites and *gîtes d'étapes* (walkers' lodges) operating on a *demi-pension* (half-board) basis.

Auberge Cavalière   B&B €€
(☑05 59 34 72 30; www.auberge-cavaliere.com; near Accous; s/d half board €60/98; 🐾) You'll really feel part of valley life at this rambling old horse farm 3km south of Accous, which offers five floral rooms and a cosy family *gîte*, as well as guided horse-riding trips round the valley.

Au Château d'Arance   B&B €€
(☑05 59 34 75 50; www.hotel-auchateaudarance.com; near Cette-Eygun; r €60-69; 🐾) One of the valley's only real hotels, lodged inside a 13th-century castle that's reached via a winding 2.25km side road from Cette-Eygun. Although the eight rooms are rather short on charm, the restaurant terrace is a peach, offering superlative valley views and solid *cuisine du terroir* (*menus* €12 to €33).

La Toison d'Or   B&B €€
(☑06 08 70 75 18; www.aubergetoisondor.com; place de l'Église de Cette; s/d/tr/q €45/55/70/80; 🐾) In Cette-Eygun, this homely *auberge* (country inn) is another peaceful retreat, offering a couple of doubles and four family rooms, all furnished in (very) rustic style. Luxury it ain't, but the divine hillside position and pleasant restaurant (with mountain-view patio, *bien sûr*) merit a special mention.

Le Pic d'Anie   B&B €
(☑05 59 34 71 54; http://hebergement-picdanie.fr; s/d €45/60; ⊙Apr-Sep) Heidi-style accommodation perched high above the valley in little Lescun. The stout little shuttered house

conceals spartan rooms that are full of Pyrenean atmosphere: meals are no longer served, but the breakfast is a real mountain feast. The Carrafancq family also own a couple of self-contained *gîtes* round the village.

La Garbure GÎTE €
(☎05 59 34 88 98; www.garbure.net; per person €13, half board €30) Lovely *gîte d'étape* in Etsaut which also organises donkey treks.

Maison de la Montagne GÎTE €
(☎05 59 34 79 14; http://montagne.randonnee. chez-alice.fr; per person €17, half board €35) *Gîte* accommodation in a converted Lescun barn. The owner runs guided walks.

Camping Municipal de Carole CAMPGROUND €
(☎05 59 34 59 19; commune.bedous@wanadoo. fr; Bedous; sites €8-12; ◉Mar–mid-Nov) Small, quiet site sheltered by trees.

Camping Despourrins CAMPGROUND €
(☎05 59 34 71 16; Accous; sites from €8; ◉Mar-Oct) Tiny campsite off the N134, behind the Fermiers Basco-Béarnais cheese centre.

Camping Lescun CAMPGROUND €
(☎05 59 34 51 77; www.camping-lescun.com; adult/ tent/car €3.50/4.50/1.50) Wonderfully secluded site with knockout mountain views, just outside Lescun.

❶ Information

Bedous Tourist Office (☎05 59 34 57 57; www.tourisme-aspe.com; place Sarraillé; ◉9am-12.30pm & 2-5.30pm Mon-Sat) The valley's main tourist office.
Maison du Parc National des Pyrénées (☎05 59 34 88 30; ◉10.30am-12.30pm & 2-6.30pm May-Oct) The main point of information for the park, housed in Etsaut's disused train station.

❶ Getting There & Away

SNCF buses and trains connect Pau and Oloron-Ste-Marie up to 10 times daily. From Oloron there are three to four onward bus connections into the valley via Bedous to Etsaut, the majority continuing to Somport and the Spanish railhead of Canfranc.

Vallée d'Ossau

More scenic splendour awaits in the neighbouring Ossau Valley, which tracks the course of its namesake river for a 60km journey from the watershed at Col du Pourtalet (1794m) to its confluence with the Aspe at Oloron-Ste-Marie. The entrance to the valley

as far as Laruns is broad, green and pastoral, but as you travel south the mountains start to stack up in dramatic fashion, before broadening out again near the hamlet of Gabas.

The valley's main village is Laruns (37km from Pau), which has an excellent tourist office and national park centre, both well stocked with information on outdoor activities, including mountain climbing, canyoning, kayaking and horse riding. There are only a couple of hotels and restaurants: the vast majority of visitors tend to stay in one of the many campsites or walking *gîtes*, so the valley is probably best visited as a day trip unless you're packing a tent.

◉ Sights & Activities

Falaise aux Vautours WILDLIFE RESERVE
(Cliff of the Vultures; www.falaise-aux-vautours. com; adult/child €7/5; ◉10.30am-12.30pm & 2-6.30pm, closed Jan & Mar) The griffon vulture *(Gyps folvus)* was once a familiar sight over the Pyrenees, but habitat loss, hunting and modern farming methods have all taken their toll on these majestic birds. Now protected by law, over 120 nesting pairs roost around the limestone cliffs of this 82-hectare reserve. Live CCTV images are beamed from their nests to the visitors centre in Aste-Béon. There's also a good display on the vultures' life cycle, with captions in English.

Le Petit Train d'Artouste MOUNTAIN RAILWAY
(www.train-artouste.com; adult/child €22.50/18) Six kilometres east of Gabas, the lakeside ski resort of Artouste-Fabrèges (1250m) is hardly the most attractive in the Pyrenees, but it's worth a visit for a quick trip up in the cable car, which soars up the 2032m Pic de la Sagette, and the chance to clamber aboard the open-topped Petit Train d'Artouste, a miniature mountain railway originally built for dam workers in the 1920s.

The train trundles along for 10km from the upper cable-car station to Lac d'Artouste, offering truly heart-stopping views over the valley and the spiky Pic du Midi d'Ossau – don't even think about if you're even vaguely nervy about heights. Unsurprisingly, the train gets busy, carrying over 100,000 passengers in its four months of operation between late May and September. Allow four hours for a visit. Trains run half-hourly in July and August, hourly at other times.

BEARS IN THE PYRENEES

In 2004 in the Vallée d'Aspe, the last native brown bear left in France was shot by a boar-hunter, supposedly in self-defence. The demise of the female bear, known as Cannelle to conservationists, marked the extinction of a species which a century ago was still a relatively common sight in the Pyrenees. France was in uproar; the then-President Chirac declared it 'a great loss for French and European biodiversity'.

The species has since been reintroduced using bears imported from Slovenia. They have bred successfully, and it's thought that between 15 and 20 brown bears now roam across the French side of the mountains. Sadly, several have been killed in recent years, including one that fell from a cliff and another that was hit by a car between Argèles-Gazost and Lourdes.

The plight of brown bears in the Pyrenees has become an important touchstone for French conservationists, but it remains a deeply controversial issue, especially for local shepherds and farmers, who see the bear as a dangerous predator which poses an unwelcome threat to their flocks and livelihoods.

Subsequent reintroductions have been shelved while the debate rages on, leaving the bears in a perilous state: it's thought that their numbers need to at least quadruple in order to establish a viable breeding population, and with no sign of a consensus forthcoming – at least for now – prospects for the Pyrenean brown bear are looking precarious at best.

If you're an experienced mountain biker, you could choose to make the hair-raising BDD (*bicycles de descente*) downhill descent back down the mountain from the Artouste Bike Park. Bikes can be hired for €12/15 for a half/full day: ask at the Artouste cable-car stations.

✦ Festivals & Events

The Vallée d'Ossau is known for its tangy cheese, *fromage d'Ossau,* made here in the high mountains from ewe's milk. You'll see lots of places round the valley selling it in summer, and the valley holds an annual Foire au Fromage (cheese fair) in October.

ⓘ Information

La Maison de la Vallée d'Ossau Office de Tourisme (☑ 05 59 05 31 41; www.valleedossau-tourisme.com; ☺9am-noon & 2-6pm) On Laruns' main square.

National Park Visitor Centre (☑ 05 59 05 41 59; ☺9am-noon & 2-5.30pm) Beside the tourist office in Laruns.

ⓘ Getting There & Around

Citram Pyrénées (☑ 05 59 27 22 22; http://citrampyrenees.fr) runs buses from Pau to Laruns (one hour, four daily).

SNCF trains from Pau stop at Buzy-en-Béarn from where there are a few onward bus connections as far as Laruns (40 minutes).

Cauterets
POP 1300 / ELEV 930M

It might not have the altitude or attitude of its sister ski stations in the Alps, but in many respects Cauterets is a much more pleasant place to hit the slopes. While many of the Alpine resorts have been ruthlessly modernised and crammed to capacity during the winter and summer seasons, Cauterets has clung on to much of its fin de siècle character, with a stately spa and plenty of grand 19th-century residences dotted round town.

Hemmed in by snowy peaks on every side, Cauterets is a superb summertime base for exploring the forests, meadows, lakes and streams of the Parc National des Pyrénées, and in winter it's doused with snow for at least six months of the year. It's nearly always the first of France's Pyrenean ski stations to open and the last to close.

⊙ Sights & Activities

Pont d'Espagne   WALKING
(télécabine & télésiege adult/child €11.50/9.50) Outside the ski season, Cauterets becomes a fantastic summer walking base. Most of the trails leave from the giant car park at Pont d'Espagne (Spanish Bridge; per day €5.50, over 12hr €8), reached via a twisting four-mile stretch of the D920 from Cauterets, known locally as the Chemins des Cascades after

ROAD PASSES IN THE PYRENEES

If you're driving, it's worth knowing that the high-altitude passes around the Vallée d'Ossau, the Vallée d'Aspe and the Vallée de Gaves are often closed due to snow. Signs are posted along the approach roads indicating whether they're *ouvert* (open) or *fermé* (closed); the dates given are approximate, and depend entirely on seasonal snowfall.

» **Col d'Aubisque** (1709m; ☺May–Oct) On the D918, linking Laruns in the Vallée d'Ossau with Argelès-Gazost in the Vallée de Gaves. An alternative that's open year-round is the D35 between Louvie-Juzon and Nay.

» **Col de Marie-Blanque** (1035m; ☺May–Oct) The shortest link between the Aspe and Ossau Valleys is the D294, which corkscrews for 21km between Escot and Bielle.

» **Col du Pourtalet** (1795m; ☺most of year) The main crossing into Spain generally stays open year-round except during periods of exceptional snowfall.

» **Col du Tourmalet** (2115m; ☺Jun–Oct) Between Barèges and La Mongie, this is the highest road pass in the Pyrenees. If you're travelling east to the Pic du Midi (for example from Cauterets), the only alternative is a long detour north via Lourdes and Bagnères-de-Bigorre.

the waterfalls which thunder beside the road.

From the Pont d'Espagne car park, a combination *télécabine* (cable car) and *télésiege* (chair lift) runs up the mountain side, allowing instant access to some of the best-known trails. The most popular destination is the sparkling Lac de Gaube, a brilliantly blue mountain lake cradled by snowcapped peaks; light lunches, snacks and drinks are available at the nearby Hostellerie de Gaube, nestled right beside the lake shore.

Another trail winds up the Vallée de Marcadau to the high-altitude Refuge Wallon-Marcadau (☎05 62 92 64 28; ☺Feb–mid-Apr & Jun–Sep) at 1866m. Allow about five hours for the round trip, or three if you catch the cable car.

Shuttle buses run every couple of hours in July and August from Cauterets (adult/child return €7/4).

Thermal Spas   HOT SPRINGS

It wasn't snow which attracted the first tourists to Cauterets – it was the area's hot springs, which bubble up from deep underground at temperatures between 36°C and 53°C. The waters are rumoured to have numerous healing properties, but miracle cure or not, they're ideal for a soak after a long day's hiking.

The Thermes César (www.thermesde cauterets.com; rue Docteur Domer; ☺Feb-Nov) offers lots of different spa packages starting at around €12 for a soak in a hot tub, up to several hundred euros for a multiday spa package.

Télécabine du Lys   SKIING, CYCLING

(télécabine €8.50, télécabine & télésiège adult/child €11/9.50; ☺Tue-Sun mid-Jun–Sep, daily Dec-Mar) This cable car runs direct from Cauterets to the area's main ski fields at Cirque du Lys, 1850m above sea level. The Télésiège du Grand Barbat (Grand Barbat chair lift) then runs up another 600m to the Crêtes du Lys.

During winter, there are around 36km of ski runs to explore, and in summer the area becomes a popular mountain-bike park, with a 1500m drop in altitude and plenty of downhill trails. A day's bike pass costs adult/child €17/14 including the lifts. Bikes can be hired from various places round town.

FREE **Pavillon des Abeilles**   BEEHIVES

(23bis av du Mamelon Vert; ☺3-7pm Wed-Sat) This educational attraction explores the wonderful world of the bee, with a glass-sided hive, video and honey of every possible flavour. Longer hours in school holidays.

🛏 Sleeping

Cauterets has plenty of big hotels, but the vast majority of people choose to stay in *gîtes* or self-catering apartments during the ski season, so prices tend to be expensive.

TOP CHOICE **Hôtel du Lion d'Or**   HOTEL €€

(☎05 62 92 52 87; www.liondor.eu; 12 rue Richelieu; d €88-147; ☎) This sweet Alpine-style hotel, under the Logis umbrella, oozes mountain character. The exterior's covered in shutters and window boxes, and inside are lots of charming, olde-worlde rooms decked out in candy-stripe pinks, sunny yellows and duck-egg blues. Knick-knacks and curios are dotted throughout the building – an old gramophone here, a stuffed stag's head there – and the restaurant serves up classic Pyrenean cuisine in cosy surroundings. The owner's a ski instructor, so he's full of tips on things to see and do. Rates fluctuate wildly depending on the season.

Hôtel-Restaurant Astérides-Sacca
HOTEL €€

(☑05 62 92 50 02; www.asterides-sacca.com; 11 bd Latapie-Flurin; r €52-76; ☺early Dec–early Oct) This grande-dame hotel is on Cauteret's prettiest street, lined with well-preserved 19th-century buildings and often used as a film set. It's a rambling, reassuringly old-fashioned place: rooms come in a choice of check or floral fabrics, although the bathrooms look rather dated. The restaurant is splendid, and half-board rates are great. Wi-fi is only available in the lobby, and the only parking is on the street outside.

Hôtel Le Bois-Joli
HOTEL €€

(☑05 62 92 53 85; www.hotel-leboisjoli.com; 1 place du Maréchal-Foch; d €98-142; ☺closed May-Jun & mid-Oct–Dec; ☞) Perched above a popular cafe right in the middle of Cauterets, this small town-house hotel offers a surprisingly sweet selection of rooms, cheerily done in bright blues, pinks and yellows, with distant views of the mountains from the upper floors. The €10 breakfast is served in the downstairs cafe, but it's a bit basic. There's no parking, so you'll have to leave the car in Cauterets' main car park.

Camping Le Péguère
CAMPGROUND €€

(☑05 62 92 52 91; www.les-campings.com/peguere; camping €10-14, cabins per week €300-420; ☺May-Sep) Wonderful mountain-view campsite 1.5km north of town on the D920. Aim for one of the riverside pitches, or plump for a chalet for more comfort.

✘ Eating & Drinking

Eating and drinking establishments in Cauterets are generally open from about May until September and again from November to February, but the exact dates can vary; it all depends on when the snowfall and snowmelt happens in any given year.

TOP CHOICE Le Sacca
TRADITIONAL FRENCH €€

(☑05 62 92 50 02; www.asterides-sacca.com; 11 bd Latapie-Flurin; menus €17.50-43; ☺lunch & dinner in season) Rich fussy French food is the staple of this ever-reliable hotel-restaurant. Contemporary it ain't – dishes are dressed with lashings of jus and creamy sauces, and mountain produce features strongly: you'll often see trout, boar and wild game on the menu. The welcome is quite formal (starchy napkins, pastel colours, waistcoated waiters), but it's actually a rather relaxed affair.

En So de Bedau
REGIONAL CUISINE €€

(☑05 62 92 60 21; 11 rue de la Raillère; mains €12-18; ☺lunch & dinner in season) A great bet for hearty Pyrenean *cuisine paysanne* (peasant cooking) such as mountain stew and pork cutlets made from local black Bigorre pigs. It's rustic – wicker chairs, stone walls – but you're bound to make friends with the owners.

La Ferme Basque
BAR

(☑05 62 92 54 32; http://fermebasque.free.fr; rte de Cambasque; ☺lunch & dinner in season) This country farmhouse 4km west of Cauterets has a panoramic mountain view from its terrace, and serves honest, no-frills country food. You can also pick up local goodies from the shop, including locally made honey and strings of sausages.

Self-Catering

Cheese, meats and local sausages line the stalls of Cauterets' covered market (av Leclerc).

À La Reine Margot
SWEETS €

(pl Clemenceau) One of many shops round town selling the sweet fruit-flavoured pastilles known as *berlingots*, a speciality of Cauterets. Drop by in the afternoon and you can often see the sweets being made.

Fromagerie du Saloir
DELICATESSEN €

(av Leclerc) Lots of cheeses, plus meats, hampers and liqueurs (including one called Gratte Cul, or 'scratch arse').

Gailhou Durdos
DELICATESSEN €

(rue de Belfort) Local wines and other specialities.

❶ Information

Maison du Parc National des Pyrénées (☑05 62 92 52 56; place de la Gare; ☺9.30am-noon & 3-7pm) Sells walking maps and guidebooks, and organises guided walks in summer.

Tourist office (☑05 62 92 50 50; www.cauterets.com; place Maréchal Foch; ☺9am-12.30pm & 2-7pm)

DON'T MISS

CIRQUE DE GAVARNIE

The Pyrenees certainly doesn't lack impressive scenery, but your first sight of the Cirque de Gavarnie is still guaranteed to raise a gasp. This breathtaking mountain amphitheatre is one of the region's most famous sights, sliced by thunderous waterfalls and ringed by sawtooth peaks, many of which top out at over 3000m – roughly five times the height of the Eiffel Tower.

The village is about 52km south of Lourdes on the D921. There are a couple of large car parks in the village, from where it's about a two-hour walk to the amphitheatre. Wear proper shoes, as snow lingers along the trail into early summer. Between Easter and October you can clip-clop along on a horse or donkey (around €25 for a round trip).

Another spectacular amphitheatre can be found just to the north at the Cirque de Troumouse, reached via a hair-raising 8km toll road (€4 per vehicle), which snakes its way precariously up the mountainside (there are no road barriers and the drops are dizzying, so take care). Snows permitting, it's usually open between April and October. Look out for the signs near Gèdre, 6.5km north of Gavarnie.

❶ Getting There & Away

The last train steamed out of Cauterets' magnificent station in 1947. It now serves as the **bus station** (☑05 62 92 53 70; place de la Gare), with SNCF buses running between Cauterets and Lourdes train station (€7.40, one hour, around five daily).

Vallée des Gaves & Around

Gentle and pastoral, the Vallée des Gaves (Valley of the Mountain Streams) extends south from Lourdes to Pierrefitte-Nestalas. Here the valley forks: the narrow, rugged eastern tine twists via Gavarnie while the western prong corkscrews up to Cauterets.

TOP CHOICE Pic du Midi   VIEWPOINT
(www.picdumidi.com; adult/child €32/22; ⊙9am-7pm Jun-Sep, 10am-5.30pm Oct-May) If there's one view in the Pyrenees that you simply must not miss, it's the one from the top of the Pic du Midi de Bigorre (2877m). Once accessible only to mountaineers, since 1878 the Pic du Midi has been home to one of France's most important observatories, and on a clear day the views across the snow-capped chain of mountains are simply out of this world.

A cable car climbs to the top of the mountain in around 15 minutes from the ski resort of La Mongie (1800m). At the top, there are several wraparound viewing terraces, as well as a sandwich shop and sit-down restaurant (*menus* €18–€30) in case you're feeling peckish. The site gets busy in summer, and the views are often hazy by midday; aim for an early morning or late evening visit.

If you're visiting in the low season, check the website for seasonal closures – and if you're travelling from the western valleys via the Col du Tourmalet, make doubly sure it's open.

Le Donjon des Aigles   BIRD PARK
(www.donjon-des-aigles.com; adult/child €13/8; ⊙10am-noon & 2.30-6.30pm Apr-Sep) About 15 minutes' drive south of Lourdes in the spectacular surroundings of the 11th-century Château de Beaucens, you can see one of the world's largest collections of birds of prey. Among the taloned residents on display are bald eagles, fish eagles, horned owls, vultures and a collection of colourful parrots: you can visit the park throughout the day, but don't miss the daily flying displays at 3.30pm and 5pm (3pm, 4.30pm and 6pm in August).

Upper Garonne Valley
ST-BERTRAND DE COMMINGES

On an isolated hillock, St-Bertrand and its Cathédrale Ste-Marie (www.cathedrale-saint -bertrand.org; adult/child incl audioguide in English €4/1.50; ⊙9am-7pm Mon-Sat, 2-7pm Sun) loom over the Vallée de Garonne and the much-pillaged remains of the Gallo-Roman town of Lugdunum Convenarum, where you can wander at will for free.

The splendid Renaissance oak choir stalls, carved in 1535 by local artisans, sit below the soaring Gothic east end of the cathedral. It's been an important pilgrimage site since medieval times, and you'll probably still see their modern-day descendants wandering round – although these days they'll be equipped with hiking gear and walking poles.

BAGNÈRES DE LUCHON
POP 3032 / ELEV 630M

Bagnères de Luchon (or simply Luchon) is a trim little town of gracious 19th-century buildings, expanded to accommodate the *curistes* who came to take the waters at its splendid spa. It's now one of the Pyrenees' most popular ski areas, with the challenging runs of Superbagnères right on its doorstep.

◉ Sights & Activities

Thermes   HOT BATHS

(☑05 61 79 22 97; www.thermes-luchon.fr; parc des Quinconces; ⊙Mar–mid-Nov) Luchon's thermal baths are at the southern end of allée d'Étigny. It's €12 to loll in the scented steam of the 160m-long underground *vaporarium,* then dunk yourself in the caressing 32°C waters of its pool, but there's a huge variety of other packages (from mudpacks to hot stones and nasal douches) if you fancy spoiling yourself for a little longer.

Télécabine   SKIING, CYCLING

(adult/child €7.90/5.90; ⊙9am-12.15pm & 2-6pm Jul-Aug, 1.30-6pm weekends May-Jun & Sep, open daily in winter depending on snow conditions) Luchon's ski lift whisks walkers in summer and skiers in winter to Superbagnères (1860m), the starting point for over 250km of walks, ski runs and mountain-bike trails.

The tourist office carries a useful free pamphlet, Sentiers Balisés du Pays de Luchon, and also sells the detailed *Randonnées autour de Luchon* (€10.95).

⌂ Sleeping

Le Castel de la Pique   HOTEL €€

(☑05 61 88 43 66; www.castel-pique.fr; 31 cours des Quinconces; s €59-69, d €64-74; 🔊) This turreted hotel is a charming and enormously welcoming spot. The rooms are chocolate-box cute, with sanded floors, mantelpieces and French windows onto dinky balconies: aim for one with a mountain view. Breakfast is a bargain at just €7.

Hôtel d'Etigny   HOTEL €€€

(☑05 61 79 01 42; www.hotel-etigny.com; 3 ave Paul Bonnemaison; d €72-125; 🔊) Opposite the baths, this swanky establishment oozes plush 19th-century grandeur, with its upholstered armchairs, porcelain pots and elegant public rooms. Rooms are rather less starry, but comfy enough.

✕ Eating

L'Héptaméron des Gourmets   GASTRONOMIC €€€

(☑05 61 79 78 55; www.heptamerondesgourmets.com; 2 blvd Charles de Gaulle; menus €30-60; ⊙lunch Sun, dinner Tue-Sun) Dining out at this smart restaurant feels like dining at a friend's house – albeit a friend with rather classy tastes. It's strong on seasonal produce and fussy French presentation, best sampled on the seven-course degustation menu. Swanky red fabrics, burnished leather armchairs and a lovely conservatory dining room complete the posh package.

Café de la Paix   BRASSERIE €€

(☑05 61 94 74 70; 19 allée d'Etigny; mains €12-18) Luchon's lively streetside brasserie turns out top-quality fare quick as a flash, especially meat and fish *grillée à la plancha* (grilled Spanish-style on a metal plate).

L'Arbesquens   REGIONAL CUISINE €€

(☑05 61 79 33 69; 47 allée d'Etigny; menus €11-25; ⊙closed Wed & dinner Sun) Fondue's what to eat at this timber-beamed restaurant – there are over 18 varieties on offer, most big enough for two to share. Just don't blame us for that ever-expanding waistline...

SELF-CATERING

Luchon's **covered market** (rue Docteur Germès; ⊙daily Apr-Oct, Wed & Sat Nov-Mar) was established in 1897 and is still going strong.

❶ Information

Luchon Tourist Office (☑05 61 79 21 21; www.luchon.com; 18 allée d'Étigny; ⊙9am-7pm summer, shorter hours rest of year)

❶ Getting There & Around

SNCF trains and coaches run between Luchon and Montréjeau (€7, 50 minutes, five daily), which have frequent connections to Toulouse (€16.70) and Pau (€18.50).

Vallée de l'Ariège

On the eastern side of the French Pyrenees, the sleepy Vallée de l'Ariège is awash with prehistoric interest: it's home to some of Europe's most impressive underground rivers and subterranean caverns, many of which are daubed with cave paintings left behind by prehistoric people.

The small towns of Foix and Mirepoix make the most useful bases. For general info and reservations for most of the Ariège

ⓘ PREHISTO PASS

If you're planning on visiting several sights, it's worth picking up the free Prehisto Pass at the first place you visit, which will give you admission discounts at all the subsequent places you go to.

Valley's main attractions, contact Sesta (☑05 61 05 10 10; www.sesta.fr/en).

◉ Sights & Activities

TOP
CHOICE **Grotte de Niaux**   CAVE, HISTORIC SITE
(☑05 61 05 88 37; adult/child €9.40/5.70; ⊗tours hourly 10.15am-4.15pm, extra tours in summer) If you only have time to visit one prehistoric cave in the Pyrenees, it should be the Grotte de Niaux – considered to be of similar importance as the caves in Lascaux in the Dordogne and Altamira in Spain.

Perched high on the mountainside about 12km south of Foix, the cave is home to a spectacular gallery of bison, horses and ibex – most of which adorn a single vast chamber known as the Salon Noir, reached via a 800m underground trek through the inky darkness. There's also one tiny but extraordinary depiction of a weasel – the only cave painting of the animal yet found.

To preserve the paintings, there's no lighting inside the cave, so you'll be given your own torch as you enter. On the way, look out for graffiti left by previous visitors, some of which dates back to the 17th century.

At the mouth of the cave is a striking cast-iron viewing platform designed by the architect Massimilian Fuksas, which features background information on the cave's history (in French).

The cave can only be visited with a guide. From April to September there's usually one English-language tour a day at 1.30pm. Numbers are strictly limited, so bookings are advisable at any time of year.

Parc de la Préhistoire   MUSEUM
(☑05 61 05 10 10; Tarascon-sur-Ariège; adult/child €9.90/6; ⊗10am-6pm) This excellent museum-park provides a useful primer on France's prehistoric past. The centrepiece is the Grand Atelier, an impressive modern building that uses film, projections and an audio-visual commentary to explain the area's history of cave art and human settlement.

There are also some fantastic animal skeletons, including a cave bear and a mature mammoth, as well as full-scale reproductions of the Salon Noir in the Grotte de Niaux, and a fascinating section of the cave that's not accessible to the public, featuring human footprints left behind by a prehistoric family.

Outside, you can follow a trail around the park's grounds, duck inside a selection of prehistoric tents and try your hand with an ancient spear-thrower.

The museum is near Tarascon-sur-Ariège, about 18km south of Foix.

Grotte du Mas d'Azil   CAVE, MUSEUM
(☑05 61 05 10 10; adult/child €6.30/4; ⊗caves 10am-6pm, museum 10am-noon & 2-6pm) This dramatic rock shelter is famous for its rich finds of prehistoric tools, arrowheads and other implements, as well as its complex cave art. Two of the galleries are open to the public: in the Galerie Breuil, you can see engravings of bison, horses, fish, deer and what appears to be a cat, while in the Oven Room, there's a rare – and rather haunting – depiction of a human face. The ticket also includes entry to the site's small museum.

The caves are about 25km northwest of Foix, near the village of Le Mas d'Azil.

Lombrives   CAVE
(☑06 70 74 32 80; www.grotte-lombrives.fr; standard tour adult/child €7.50/4.50; ⊗May-Sep & school holidays) This is Europe's largest cave system, with a maze of over 200 stalactite-lined tunnels, grottoes and rock galleries to explore. Look out for the sandy expanse known as the Sahara Desert, and several limestone columns variously supposed to resemble a mammoth, a wizard and the Virgin Mary.

The standard tour lasts around an hour, but depending on how adventurous you're feeling, longer tours are available on request. The cave is 22km north of Ax-les-Thermes on the N20 near Ussat-les-Bains.

**Rivière Souterraine de
Labouiche**   UNDERGROUND RIVER
(☑05 61 65 04 11; adult/child €9.10/7.10; ⊗9.30am-5.15pm Jul-Aug, shorter hours at other times) Beneath Labouiche, 6km northwest of Foix, flows Europe's longest navigable underground river. It's possible to take an amazing 1500m, 75-minute boat trip along part of its length, taking in some of the huge underground caverns and eerie chambers

carved out over the course of millions of years.

Château des Comtes de Foix CASTLE
(☎05 61 05 10 10; adult/child €4.50/3.30; ☺10am-6pm summer, shorter hours rest of year) The triple-towered Château des Comtes de Foix stands guard above the town of Foix. Constructed in the 10th century as a stronghold for the counts of Foix, it served as a prison from the 16th century onwards.

The interior is rather bare, but there's a small archaeological museum and the view from the battlements is a stunner. There's usually at least one tour daily in English in summer.

Les Forges de Pyrène MUSEUM
(☎05 34 09 30 60; adult/child €8/4.70; ☺10am-7pm summer, shorter hours rest of year) In Montgaillard, 4.5km south of Foix, this 'living museum' explores Ariège folk traditions, with its own blacksmith, a baker, a cobbler and a basket weaver. Spread over 5 hectares, it illustrates a host of lost or dying trades such as glass-blowing, tanning, thatching and nail-making.

🛏 Sleeping & Eating

TOP CHOICE Château de Beauregard HOTEL €€
(☎05 61 66 66 64; www.chateaubeauregard.net; av de la Résistance, St-Girons; d €120-160, ste €160-200; ☎☀) If you've always wanted to play lord of the manor, try this opulent château complex in the little village of St-Girons, halfway between St-Gaudens and Foix along the D117. Topped by turrets and surrounded by 2½ hectares of private gardens, it's full of grand rooms with quirky touches (such as bathrooms hidden away in the castle's corner towers). Throw in a garden pool, a candlelit spa and a superb Gascon restaurant, and you have a castle getaway par excellence.

Maison des Consuls HOTEL €€€
(☎05 61 68 81 81; www.maisondesconsuls.com; 6 place du Maréchal Leclerc; d €99-115; ☎) At this elegant hotel, all the rooms have been decorated to echo a figure from Mirepoix's his-

tory: the nicest are Dame Louise, with its four-poster and fab view over the square, and the Suite de l'Astronome, with a private terrace overlooking the town's red-tiled rooftops.

Hôtel les Remparts HOTEL €€
(☎05 61 68 12 15; www.hotelremparts.com; 6 cours Louis Pons Tarde; r €80-120; ☎) This is one of the area's smartest hotels, a nine-room beauty in Mirepoix that's awash with decorative tics (rough stone, twisted willow, stripped-wood floors), and boasts a delightful breakfast salon with its original beams and chimney. Young chef Nicolas Coutand has turned the brick-vaulted restaurant into a notable dining destination, too.

Hôtel Restaurant Lons HOTEL €€
(☎05 34 09 28 00; www.hotel-lons-foix.com; 6 place Dutilh; r from €55) A traditional and very cosy Logis-affiliated hotel in the middle of Foix, in a super spot overlooking the clattering river. Rooms are fairly functional, but the river-view restaurant (*menus* €18.50–€25.70) serves solid regional cuisine and offers good-value half board.

Auberge les Myrtilles B&B €
(☎05 61 65 16 46; www.auberge-les-myrtilles.com; Salau; r €63.50-67.50, with half board €91.50-96.50; ☎) This mountain retreat in Salau, about 10km west of Foix, is tailor-made for active types: owners Anouk and René are both mad-keen hikers and bikers, and they're full of tips on exploring the surrounding area. Their guesthouse is quaint and cosy, with simply furnished rooms and a lovely beamed restaurant serving filling Ariègeois cuisine: try the local speciality of *azinat*, a hotpot of sausage, duck and vegetables.

ℹ Information
Foix Tourist Office (☎05 61 65 12 12; www.tourisme-foix-varilhes.fr; 29 rue Delcassé; ☺9am-6pm)

ℹ Getting There & Away
Regular trains connect Toulouse and Foix (€13.90, 1¼ hours).

Toulouse Area

Includes »

Best Places to Eat

» Chez Navarre (p694)
» Michel Sarran (p694)
» L'Epicurien (p700)
» Au Fil de l'Eau (p702)
» Le Lautrec (p700)

Best Places to Stay

» Les Loges de St-Sernin (p693)
» La Tour Ste-Cécile (p699)
» L'Echappée Belle (p697)
» Au Château (p703)
» La Lumiane (p707)

Why Go?

Rich food, good wine and slow living: that's what this sun-baked corner of southwest France is all about. Traditionally part of the Languedoc, the red-brick city of Toulouse and the surrounding area has been out on its own since World War II, but scratch beneath the surface and you'll discover the same old southern passions.

The capital city makes the perfect introduction: with its buzzy markets, stately architecture, crackling culture and renowned rugby team, Toulouse is one of France's liveliest provincial cities. Beyond the fringes of La Ville Rose lies a landscape dotted with sturdy *bastides* (fortified towns), soaring cathedrals and country markets, not to mention the historic province of Gascony, famous for its foie gras, fattened ducks and fiery Armagnac. And through it all runs the languid course of the Canal du Midi, the undisputed queen of French canals.

Take things slow: life in this corner of France is all about the living.

When to Go
Toulouse

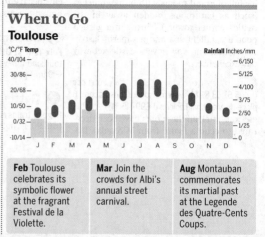

Feb Toulouse celebrates its symbolic flower at the fragrant Festival de la Violette.

Mar Join the crowds for Albi's annual street carnival.

Aug Montauban commemorates its martial past at the Legende des Quatre-Cents Coups.

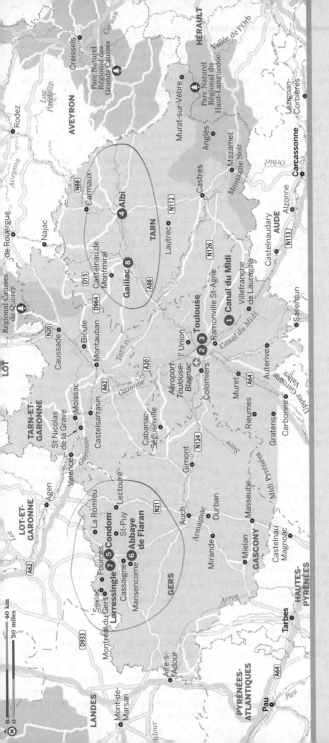

Toulouse Area Highlights

1 Pilot a boat or cycle the towpaths of the historic **Canal du Midi** (p706)

2 Soak up the sights and smells of Toulouse's **covered markets** (p695)

3 Climb inside a replica of the Mir Space Station at Toulouse's **Cité de l'Espace** (p689)

4 Admire the prints, paintings and posters at the **Musée Toulouse-Lautrec** (p699) in Albi

5 Sample some brandy straight from the barrel at a traditional **Armagnac distillery** (p705) in Condom

6 Savour the silence of the **Abbaye de Flaran** (p707), southwest France's loveliest Cistercian abbey

7 Check out some medieval siege weapons at the fortified village of **Larressingle** (p706)

8 Spend a day tasting your way around the vineyards of **Gaillac** (p702)

Toulouse

POP 446,200

Elegantly situated at the confluence of the Canal du Midi and the River Garonne, the vibrant southern city of Toulouse is often known as La Ville Rose, a reference to the distinctive hot-pink stone used to build many of its buildings. Busy, buzzy and bustling with students, this riverside dame has a 2000-year history, but it's a city with its feet very much in the future: it's been a hub for the aerospace industry since the 1930s, and is leading France's drive towards cleaner, greener energies. It's also a city that lives or dies by the fortunes of its rugby team, Stade Toulousain (known simply as *'les rouges et noirs',* the reds and blacks), who have won the European Cup a record four times, most recently in 2010.

With a thriving cafe and cultural scene, a wealth of *hôtels particuliers* (private mansions) and an enormously atmospheric old quarter, France's fourth-largest city simply mustn't be missed.

◉ Sights

Toulouse's city centre is currently the focus of a major urban renovation project. The busy thoroughfare of rue d'Alsace-Lorraine has been pedestrianised, while other key projects (including the redevelopment of Square Charles de Gaulle) are scheduled for completion by 2014. Expect roadworks, bollards and general signs of construction until then.

Place du Capitole   CITY SQUARE

Toulouse's magnificent main square is the city's literal and metaphorical heart, where Toulousiens turn out en masse on sunny evenings to sip a coffee or an early aperitif at a pavement cafe. On the eastern side is the 128m-long facade of the Capitole (rue Gambetta & rue Romiguières; ☺10am-7pm), the city hall, built in the 1750s. Inside is the Théâtre du Capitole, one of France's most prestigious opera venues, and the over-the-top, late-19th-century Salle des Illustres (Hall of the Illustrious).

To the south of the square is the city's Vieux Quartier (Old Quarter), a tangle of lanes and leafy squares brimming with cafes, shops and eateries.

Basilique St-Sernin   CHURCH

(place St-Sernin; ☺8.30am-noon & 2-6pm Mon-Sat, 8.30am-12.30pm & 2-7.30pm Sun) With its soaring spire and unusual octagonal tower, this red-brick basilica is one of France's best-preserved Romanesque structures. Inside, the soaring nave and delicate pillars harbour the tomb of St Sernin himself, sheltered beneath a sumptuous canopy. The basilica was once an important stop on the Chemin de St-Jacques pilgrimage route.

Ensemble Conventuel
des Jacobins   CHURCH

(www.jacobins.mairie-toulouse.fr; rue Lakanal; ☺9am-7pm) The church is the centrepiece of this ecclesiastical ensemble. Indeed the extraordinary Gothic structure of Église des Jacobins, flooded by day in natural light from the huge stained-glass windows, practically defies gravity. Along the nave, a single row of seven 22m-high columns spread their fanned vaulting like palm trees.

Used as an artillery barracks in the 19th century, this is the mother church of the Dominican order. Construction began soon after St Dominic founded the order in 1215, and it took 170 years to complete, including the 45m-tall belfry. Interred beneath the altar are the remains of St Thomas Aquinas (1225–74), early head of the Dominican order.

The Cloître des Jacobins (admission €3) features a box-hedge garden and hosts piano recitals in September. Art exhibitions fill the 14th-century refectory, Les Jacobins (☎05 61 22 23 82; 69 rue Pargaminières; ☺9am-7pm).

Musée des Augustins   ART MUSEUM

(www.augustins.org; 21 rue de Metz; adult/child €3/free; ☺10am-6pm, to 9pm Wed) Toulouse's fabulous fine-arts museum spans the centuries from the Roman era right through to the early 20th century. The highlights are the French rooms, with Delacroix, Ingres and Courbet representing the 18th and 19th centuries, and a few choice works by Toulouse-Lautrec and Monet among the standouts from the 20th-century collection. The museum is in a former Augustinian monastery, and its two 14th-century cloister gardens are postcard-pretty. The entrance is on rue de Metz.

Les Abattoirs   ART MUSEUM

(www.lesabattoirs.org; 76 allées Charles de Fitte; adult/student & child €7/free; ☺11am-7pm Wed-Sun) As its name suggests, this red-brick structure was once the city's main abattoir, but it's now been reinvented as a cutting-edge art gallery and venue for concerts and exhibitions.

Hôtel d'Assézat   MUSEUM

(www.fondation-bemberg.fr; place d'Assézat; ⊙10am-12.30pm & 1.30-6pm Tue-Sun, to 9pm Thu) Toulouse boasts more than 50 *hôtels particuliers*, private mansions built for the city's nobles, merchants and aristocrats during the 16th and 17th centuries. One of the finest is the Hôtel d'Assézat, built for a woad merchant in 1555. It's now home to the Fondation Bemberg, which owns a fine collection of paintings, sculpture and objets d'art; the 1st floor is mainly devoted to the Renaissance, while impressionism, pointillism and other 20th-century movements occupy the upper floor. Guided tours depart daily at 3.30pm.

Château d'Eau   GALLERY

(www.galeriechateaudeau.org; 1 place Laganne; adult/child €2.50/free; ⊙1-7pm Tue-Sun) Photography exhibitions inside a 19th-century water tower.

Musée St-Raymond   MUSEUM

(www.saintraymond.toulouse.fr; place St-Sernin; adult/child €3/1.50; ⊙10am-7pm) The city's archaeological museum houses Roman sculptures, Christian sarcophagi and Celtic torques.

Musée Paul Dupuy   MUSEUM

(13 rue de la Pléau; adult/child €3/free; ⊙10am-6pm Wed-Mon) Toulouse's decorative-arts museum takes in everything from suits of armour to rare clocks.

Museum de Toulouse   MUSEUM

(www.museum.toulouse.fr; 35 allée Jules-Guesde; adult/child €7/5; ⊙10am-6pm) Dinosaur skel-etons, ancient fossils and giant reptiles take centre stage at the natural-history museum.

Cathédrale de St-Étienne   CATHEDRAL

(Cathedral of St Stephen; place St-Étienne; ⊙8am-7pm Mon-Sat, 9am-7pm Sun) The city cathedral dates mainly from the 12th and 13th centuries, and is worth a visit for its glorious rose window.

Église Notre Dame du Taur   CHURCH

(12 rue du Taur; ⊙2-7pm Mon-Fri, 9am-1pm Sat & Sun) This 14th-century church commemorates the city's patron saint, St Sernin, who was reputedly martyred on this very spot.

Jardin des Plantes   PARK

(⊙7.45am-9pm summer, to 6pm winter) Toulouse's two-hundred-year-old botanical garden is a gorgeous place to escape the city hustle when the weather's warm. The entrance to the park is on allée Frédéric Mistral, about 350m south of place St-Jacques.

🏃 Activities

Toulouse is very much a river city. From March to November, boat trips run along the Garonne from the quai de la Daurade. In summer some boats also pass through the St-Pierre lock onto the Canal du Midi and Canal de Brienne.

Trips start at around adult/child €8/5 for an hour's scenic cruising. You don't normally need to book; tickets can be purchased on the boat up to 10 minutes before departure.

The two main companies are Les Bateaux Toulousains (www.bateaux-toulousains.

DON'T MISS

CITÉ DE L'ESPACE

This fantastic space museum (☎08 20 37 72 33; www.cite-espace.com/en; av Jean Gonord; adult €19.50-23, child €14-15; ⊙9.30am-5pm or 6pm, to 7pm mid-Jul–Aug, closed Jan) on the city's eastern outskirts explores Toulouse's illustrious aeronautical history.

The city's high-flying credentials stretch all the way back to WWI, when it was a hub for pioneering mail flights to Africa and South America. Since WWII, Toulouse has been the centre of France's aerospace industry, developing many important aircraft (including Concorde and the 555-seat Airbus A380) as well as components for many international space programs.

The museum brings this interstellar industry vividly to life through hands-on exhibits including a shuttle simulator, planetarium, 3D cinema and simulated observatory. There are even full-scale replicas of iconic spacecraft including the Mir Space Station and a 53m-high Ariane 5 space rocket. Multilingual audioguides allow you to explore at your own pace, but you'll need a full day to do it justice.

To get there, catch Bus 15 from allée Jean Jaurès to the last stop, from where it's a 500m walk. To avoid the queues, buy your tickets in advance online or at the tourist office.

Toulouse

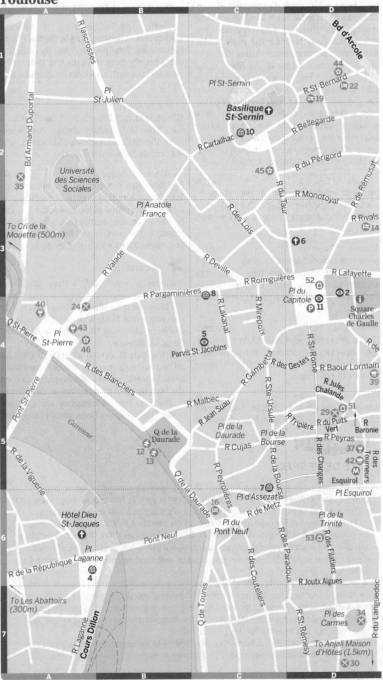

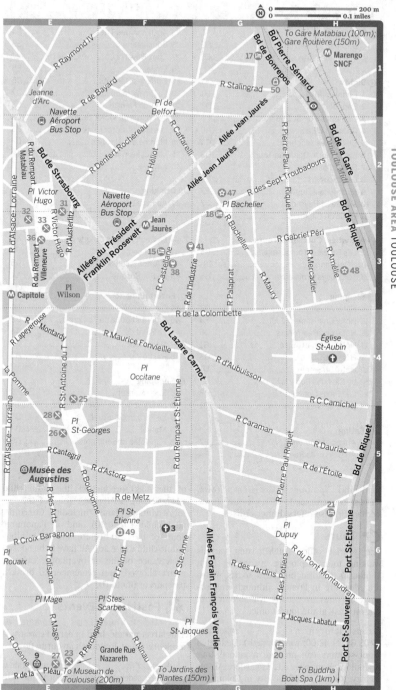

N 0 ——————— 200 m
0 ——————— 0.1 miles

To Gare Matabiau (100m);
Gare Routière (150m)

Marengo
SNCF

Bd de Pierre Sénard
Bd de Bonrepos

17
50

R Stalingrad

1

R Raymond IV

Pl
Jeanne
d'Arc

R de Bayard

Pl de
Belfort

Allée Jean Jaurès

Bd de la Gare
Canal du Midi

Navette
Aéroport
Bus Stop

R Denfert Rochereau

R Héliot

R Caffarelli

Allée Jean Jaurès

R Pierre-Paul Riquet

R des Sept Troubadours

Bd de Riquet

Bd de Strasbourg

R du Rempart Matabiau

Pl Victor
Hugo

R Victor Hugo

R Austerlitz

Navette
Aéroport
Bus Stop

Jean
Jaurès

47

Pl Bachelier

18

R Bachelier

R Gabriel Péri

R des Sept Troubadours

R Mercadier

R Amélie

48

32
33

36

R du Rempart Villeneuve

Allées du Président
Franklin Roosevelt

15

R Castellane

41

38

R de l'Industrie

R Palaprat

R Maury

R d'Alsace–Lorraine

Capitole

Pl
Wilson

R de la Colombette

Église
St-Aubin

R Lapeyrouse

R Montardy

R Maurice Fonvieille

Bd Lazare Carnot

R d'Aubuisson

R C Camichel

R St-Antoine du T

Pl
Occitane

R du Rempart St-Étienne

R Caraman

R Pierre Paul Riquet

R Dauriac

Bd de Riquet

la Pomme

25

28

26

Pl
St-Georges

R de l'Étoile

R Cantegril

R d'Astorg

R Boulbonne

R de Metz

21

Port St-Étienne

Musée des
Augustins

R des Arts

Pl St-
Étienne

49

3

Pl
Dupuy

R du Pont Montaudran

R Croix Baragnon

R Tolisane

R Félmat

R Ste-Anne

Allées Forain François Verdier

R des Jardins

R des Potiers

Pl
Rouaix

Pl Mage

R Mage

Pl Stes-
Scarbes

Pl
St-Jacques

R Jacques Labatut

Port St-Sauveur

R Ozenne

27

23

R Perchepinte

R Ninau

Grande Rue
Nazareth

20

9

Pléau

R de la

To Museum de
Toulouse (200m)

To Jardins des
Plantes (150m)

To Buddha
Boat Spa (1km)

Toulouse

com) and **Toulouses Croisières** (www.toulouse-croisieres.com). **L'Occitania** (www.loccitania.fr) also offers dinner cruises.

⌗ Tours

The tourist office (p696) runs various walking tours exploring everything from Toulouse's historic buildings to its metro art. Most are in French, although English-language ones are usually available in peak season – ask at the tourist office.

Airbus Factory Tours AEROPLANES
(☑05 34 39 42 00; www.taxiway.fr) Dedicated plane-spotters can arrange a guided tour of Toulouse's massive J.L. Lagardère Airbus factory, 10km west of the city in Colomiers. There are three options: the main tour of the A380 production line (adult/child €14.50/11.50), a 'Heritage Tour' of the factory's vintage planes (including Concorde, adult/child €11.50/10), and a 'Panoramic Tour' of the 700-hectare site by minibus (adult/child €10/8.50). All have to be booked in advance online or by phone; cameras aren't allowed, and remember to bring a passport or photo ID.

☆ Festivals & Events

Festival de la Violette FLOWER FESTIVAL
This street parade, held in early February, is a celebration of Toulouse's favourite flower.

Toulouse d'Été MUSIC FESTIVAL
(www.toulousedete.org) Jazz, classical and other music around town in July and August.

🛏 Sleeping

Toulouse's hotels mainly serve the business crowd, so rates often drop at weekends and in July and August.

Les Loges de St-Sernin   B&B €€
(☏05 61 24 44 44; www.leslogesdesaintsernin. com; 12 rue St-Bernard; r €125-150; 🌐) Hidden behind an elegant rosy facade just a hop and a skip from the basilica, Sylviane Tatin's lovely *chambre d'hôte* (B&B) is a home from home. The four rooms are huge, dolled up in shades of pink, lime and butter yellow: try the Capitole room, with its stripy furniture and exposed brickwork, or the Garonne, with its dinky balcony.

Hôtel St-Sernin   BOUTIQUE HOTEL €€
(☏05 61 21 73 08; www.hotelstsernin.com; 2 rue St-Bernard; d from €130; 🌐) This swish number sits right opposite the Basilique St-Sernin, and has been stylishly renovated by a Parisian couple. Slate greys, crisp whites and blonde-wood floors set the metropolitan tone, and the best rooms have floor-to-ceiling windows overlooking the basilica.

Hôtel Albert 1er   HOTEL €
(☏05 61 21 17 91; www.hotel-albert1.com; 8 rue Rivals; d €65-79; ✳🌐) You couldn't ask to be much closer to the city centre than this, on a side street just off the newly pedestrianised section of Rue d'Alsace-Lorraine. Rooms are bright and cosy, with a mix of patterned fabrics, wooden bedsteads and cream-and magnolia colours. If you like your space, it's worth bumping up to 'Supérieure'.

Hotel Castellane   HOTEL €€
(☏05 61 62 18 82; www.castellanehotel.com; 17 rue Castellane; d €82-98, f €120-134) Red-brick and modern it may be, but the Castellane ticks lots of boxes: smart rooms with wood floors, a great position just east of Place Wilson, and an extremely generous buffet breakfast. Rooms are quite variable in size: some have tiny balconies, and the ones overlooking the interior courtyard are quietest. The largest family rooms sleep up to six.

Les Bains Douches   HOTEL €€€
(☏05 62 72 52 52; www.hotel-bainsdouches.com; 4 & 4bis rue du Pont Guilhemery; d €140-210, ste €280-330; ✳) If it's style you want, it's style you'll find at this ubercool establishment, created by Monsieur and Madame Henriette (motorbike designer and interior designer respectively). They've pulled out all the stops to make this Toulouse's design choice par

excellence: shimmering chrome, sleek surfaces, statement light fittings and a salon-bar that wouldn't look out of place in Paris' more fashionable *arrondissements* (city districts).

Anjali Maison d'Hôte   B&B €€
(☏09 54 22 42 93; www.anjali.fr; 86 Grande Rue St-Michel; r €80-130; 🌐) Delphine Cizeau's house dates from the 19th century, but it's full of 21st-century flair. The four rooms all showcase her quirky imagination: Hampi is decked out in Indian colours, Le Poulailler blends brick, beams and spotlights, while Cinema Paradiso takes its inspiration from black-and-white movies. There's a gorgeous garden, too. The B&B is about 1.3km south of place des Carmes or rue du Languedoc.

Hôtel des Beaux Arts   HOTEL €€€
(☏05 34 45 42 42; www.hoteldesbeauxarts.com; 1 place du Pont Neuf; d €115-255; ✳🌐) This heritage hotel sits right beside the Garonne; unfortunately, it's also on one of the city's busiest thoroughfares, so traffic noise can be dreadful. Downstairs, there's a book-lined lobby with armchairs and objets d'art, plus an excellent brasserie; upstairs, rooms boast bespoke wallpaper, snazzy cushions and plush drapes. Breakfast is steep at €14, but two-night weekend stays benefit from a 30% discount for the second night.

Hôtel La Chartreuse   HOTEL €
(☏05 61 62 93 39; www.chartreusehotel.com; 4bis blvd de Bonrepos; s/d/tr €45/51/63) Toulouse's station hotels are definitely on the scruffy side, but this family-run establishment is a welcome surprise: clean, friendly and quiet, with a lovely breakfast room and back garden patio. Sure the rooms are fusty and small, but for this price, what do you expect?

Hôtel St-Claire   HOTEL €€
(☏05 34 40 58 88; www.stclairehotel.fr; 29 place Bachelier; s €63-69, d €69-129; 🌐) This functional hotel is situated on a quiet square just off allée Jean Jaurès. The decor's smart and modern, but some rooms are small and showing their age.

ℹ TOULOUSE CITY PASS

The **Toulouse en Liberté** (per adult/child €10/5) card qualifies you for discounts on museum entries, guided tours, sights, accommodation, shopping and lots of other things. Pick it up at the tourist office.

Le Clos des Potiers HOTEL €€
(☑05 61 47 15 15; www.le-clos-des-potiers.com; 12 rue des Potiers; d €100-220; ☎) It's a bit out of the centre, but this *hôtel particulier* near the Cathédrale St-Etienne is another elegant *chambre d'hôte*. The 10 rooms are cosy and awash with antique rugs and heritage furniture.

Auberge de Jeunesse HOSTEL €
(☑05 34 30 42 80; 2 ave Yves Brunaud; dm from €17; ⊙reception 1-10pm; @☎) Built in 2002, Toulouse's main hostel is as functional as they come (military beds, institutional decor), and it's a pretty long walk from the centre. The hostel is about 1km northwest of Gare Matabiau along ave Georges Pompidou; take care around the station after dark.

✗ Eating

Bd de Strasbourg, place Wilson and the western side of place du Capitole are one long cafe-terrace line-up, but the quality can be variable. Rue Pargaminières is the street for kebabs, burgers and other such late-night student grub.

TOP
CHOICE **Chez Navarre** REGIONAL CUISINE €
(☑05 62 26 43 06; 49 Grande Rue Nazareth; menus €13-20; ⊙lunch & dinner Mon-Fri) Fancy rubbing shoulders with the locals? Then this wonderful *table d'hôte*-style restaurant is definitely the place, with honest Gascon cuisine served up beneath a creaky beamed ceiling at communal candlelit tables. There's usually only one main meal, plus a soup and a terrine, but its informal atmosphere and authentic cuisine make it an experience not to be missed.

Michel Sarran GASTRONOMIC €€€
(☑05 61 12 32 32; www.michel-sarran.com; 21 bd Armand Duportal; lunch menu €48, dinner menu €95-165; ⊙closed Wed lunch & weekends) For a no-expenses-spared, food-as-art kind of dining experience, Toulouse's double-Michelin-starred master-chef Michel Sarran is your man. He's earned an international reputation for his creative but surprisingly classic cuisine, which takes its cue from the traditional flavours of the southwest, then spins off in all kinds of experimental directions. Needless to say, bookings are essential – especially since Michel doesn't even deign to open on weekends.

L'Air de Famille MODERN FRENCH €€
(☑05 61 29 85 89; www.lairdefamille-restaurant. com; 20 place Victor Hugo; mains from €13; ⊙lunch Tue & Wed, lunch & dinner Thu-Sat) You can expect the very freshest of ingredients at this intimate little bistro – it's literally next door to Les Halles Victor Hugo. Chef Georges turns out a small but perfectly formed menu, concentrating on classic *saveurs Toulousiens* (flavours of Toulouse) given his own trademark touch. It's tiny, so you'll need to book.

Les Halles Victor Hugo BISTROS €
(place Victor Hugo; menus €10-20; ⊙lunch Tue-Sun) For a quintessentially Toulousien experience, join the punters at the string of tiny restaurants on the 1st floor of the Victor Hugo food market. They're lunchtime only, and the food is simple and unfussy, but they're full of character and the *menus* (meal deals) are brilliant value. Try Le Louchebem (☑05 61 12 12 52) for fish and seafood, and Le Magret (☑05 61 23 21 32) for classic southwest cuisine.

La Braisière BISTRO €€
(☑05 61 52 37 13; www.labraisiere.fr; 42 rue Pharaon; mains €14-22; ⊙lunch & dinner) Established on the city's dining scene since 1973, this welcoming bistro near the Carmes market is very much a locals' tip. The house speciality is hearty cuts of meat flamed over an open wood fire; take an appetite, as the portions tend to be on the generous side. Quick drinks and tapas are available at its sister venue, L'Annexe, at the same address.

Faim des Haricots VEGETARIAN €
(www.lafaimdesharicots.fr; 3 rue du Puits Vert; menus €11-15; ⊙lunch & dinner; ✍) At this 100% veggie/wholefood restaurant, everything's served *à volonté* (all you can eat). There are five courses to choose from, including a quiche, a salad buffet, a hot dish and a pudding; €15.50 buys you the lot with an aperitif and coffee thrown in. Unsurprisingly, it's usually packed with students.

Au Coin de la Rue BISTRO €€
(2 rue Pargaminières; 2-/3-course menu €20/24; ⊙lunch & dinner) There's nothing remotely fancy about this street-corner bistro, but then that's its charm. Teeny tables, rustic furniture and menus printed on placemats give it a reassuringly relaxed feel, and create the perfect vibe for its brand of honest, no-nonsense Gascon grub.

Anges et Démons CONCEPT DINING €€€
(☑05 61 52 66 69; www.restaurant-angeset demons.com; 1 rue Perchepinte; menus €53-70; ⊙dinner Tue-Sat, lunch Sun) The city's hot

tip for destination dining. The setting is drop-dead trendy – moody lighting, exposed brick, minimal furniture – matched by a smorgasbord of outré ingredients, from pink artichokes and mini-asparagus to back of rabbit and veal liver. Even the pricing's quirky – the main dish dictates the cost of the meal, and includes starter, cheese and dessert.

Emile TRADITIONAL FRENCH €€€
(www.restaurant-emile.com; place St-Georges; mains €28-35, 2-/3-course lunch menu €20/30, 2-/3-course dinner menu €30/40; ⊙Tue-Sat) Long-standing address for old-school French dining, in business since the 1940s. It's especially known for its *cassoulet* (a rich bean, pork and duck stew), touted as the city's best, but its rather starchy atmosphere isn't for everyone.

Self-Catering

Toulouse has two fantastic covered food markets, **Les Halles Victor Hugo** (www.marchevictorhugo.fr; pl Victor Hugo; ⊙around 8am-5pm) and **Marché des Carmes** (place des Carmes; ⊙7am-1pm Tue-Sun). Look out for the long, curly shape of the *saucisse de Toulouse*, the city's trademark sausage, renowned for its meaty flavour and an indispensable ingredient in many local dishes.

Boulangerie St-Georges BOULANGERIE €
(6 place St-Georges; ⊙9am-5pm Mon-Sat) Great sandwich shop; the €7.50 *formule déjeuner* (lunch menu) includes a sandwich, drink and dessert.

Le Fournil de Victor Hugo BOULANGERIE €
(place Victor Hugo; ⊙10am-5pm Mon-Sat) Artisan breads and freshly made sandwiches.

Xavier CHEESE SHOP €
(place Victor Hugo; ⊙9.30am-1.15pm & 3.30-7.15pm Tue-Sat, afternoon only Mon) The city's best cheese shop, bar none.

🍷 Drinking

Almost every square in the Vieux Quartier has at least one cafe, busy day and night. Other busy after-dark streets include rue Castellane, rue Gabriel Péri and near the river around place St-Pierre.

Au Père Louis HISTORIC BAR
(45 rue des Tourneurs; ⊙8.30am-3pm & 5-10.30pm Mon-Sat) This antique bar has been slaking the city's thirst since 1889, and it's crammed with interesting nooks and crannies, not to mention its fair share of colourful characters. There's a huge selection of wines and beers, and it feels very cosy.

Connexion Café BAR, LIVE MUSIC
(www.connexion-cafe.com; 8 rue Gabriel Péri; ⊙from 5pm Mon-Sat) Housed in a converted car park with old oil drums for tables, this lively bar hosts an eclectic line-up of events, from big-screen sports to live weekend gigs. When the weather's warm, they open up the plastic tarps and the action spills out onto the street.

Le Bar Basque BAR
(7 place St-Pierre; ⊙11am-2am Mon-Fri, 1pm-5am Sat, 1pm-2am Sun) Lively sports bar with a huge outside terrace where Toulousiens congregate when the rugby's on.

La Couleur de la Culotte CLUB
(14 place St-Pierre; ⊙9am-2pm) Funky cafe-club decked out in zesty shades of pink, orange and blue. Coffees and light bites by day, with DJs spinning electro and ambient after dark.

TEATIME IN TOULOUSE

Toulouse has a tempting selection of tea shops and streetside cafes where you can take a break and indulge in something sweet and sticky. Here are a few favourites.

L'Autre Salon de Thé (☎05 61 22 11 63; 45 rue des Tourneurs; lunch menu €12-14, Sun brunch €17; ⊙noon-7pm) An old-world tearoom attached to Toulouse's oldest bar, Au Père Louis, with lots of exotic teas and handmade pastries to try.

Flowers Café (6 pl Roger Salengro; cakes €4; ⊙9am-5pm Mon-Sat) With a lovely position beside a tinkling fountain, this busy tearoom has a huge choice of cakes in the window – cheesecakes, lemon pies, strawberry flans, chocolate tarts – all priced at a flat €4.

Au Jardin des Thés (16 pl St-Georges; menus €13.50-15.50, brunch €18; ⊙8am-5pm) *Tartes salées* (savoury tarts) and sinful cakes make the Tea Garden one of place St-George's most popular cafes – arrive early if you want a place on the terrace. There's a second, smaller branch on place de la Trinité.

La Maison
BAR

(9 rue Gabriel Péri; ⏲5pm-2am Sun-Fri, to 5am Sat) 'The House' is a hip, shabby-chic hang-out for students and trendy types, with plenty of scruffy sofas and secondhand chairs dotted around the lounge-style bar.

☆ Entertainment

Cinemas

The city's top places to watch films in *version originale* (VO, ie not dubbed) include the Cinéma ABC (www.abc-toulouse.fr; 13 rue St-Bernard) and the Cinémathèque de Toulouse (www.lacinemathequedetoulouse.com; 69 rue du Taur).

Live Music

Toulouse has a crackling live-music and clubbing scene. Pick up free listings guides at the *billetterie spectacles* (box office) in Fnac (16 allée Franklin Roosevelt), or check http://toulouse.sortir.eu for the latest events.

Le Cri de la Mouette
NIGHTCLUB

(www.lecridelamouette.com; 78 allée de Barcelone) Club-bar and gig venue on a converted canal boat.

Le Bikini
LIVE MUSIC

(www.lebikini.com; rue Hermès, Ramonville St-Agne) Legendary music club that has been rocking for nigh on a quarter-century. At the end of metro line B (Ramonville metro stop).

Le Saint des Seins
JAZZ, LIVE MUSIC

(www.lesaintdesseins.com; 5 place St-Pierre) Hip corner club on place St-Pierre, with regular jam sessions and gigs.

Opus Café
NIGHTCLUB

(24 rue Bachelier) Dance until dawn at this long-standing late-night venue.

Le Zénith
CONCERTS

(11 av Raymond Badiou) The city's big stadium concert venue. Near Arènes and Patte d'Oie metro stops.

Rest'ô Jazz
JAZZ

(www.restojazz.com; 8 rue Amélie; ⏲closed Sun) Dark, atmospheric and (of course) very jazzy.

🛍 Shopping

In addition to the truly fantastic covered markets, Toulouse's outdoor shopping opportunities include a bit-of-everything market (place du Capitole; ⏲Wed), an antiquarian book market (place St-Étienne; ⏲Sat), and a couple of weekend flea markets on place St-Sernin and along the quai de la Daurade.

La Maison de la Violette
SOUVENIRS

(☎05 61 99 01 30; www.lamaisondelaviolette.com; ⏲2-6.30pm Mon-Sat) This button-cute barge sells everything from herbal tea to bath soaps scented with Toulouse's trademark flower, the violet.

Le Paradis Gourmet
GOURMET FOOD

(65 rue des Tourneurs; ⏲10am-noon & 2-7pm Mon-Sat) Biscuits, sweeties and other gastronomic goodies with a Toulousien flavour.

Papillotes et Berlingots
SWEETS

(www.papillotes-berlingots.fr; 49 rue des Filatiers; ⏲noon-7pm Mon, 10am-2pm & 3-7pm Tue-Sat) Candy fans will be in seventh heaven at this olde-worlde sweet shop: make sure you try the violet-flavoured chocolate.

ℹ Information

Tourist office (☎05 61 11 02 22; www.toulouse-tourisme.com; Square Charles de Gaulle; ⏲9am-7pm daily) In a grand building in front of the Capitole on Square Charles de Gaulle.

ℹ Getting There & Away

Air

Eight kilometres northwest of the centre, **Toulouse-Blagnac Airport** (www.toulouse.aeroport.fr/en) has frequent flights to Paris and other large French cities, plus major hub cities in the UK, Italy and Germany.

Bus

As always in France, you'll find it much simpler to use the train to get around; bus services are provided by many operators and mainly operate according to the school timetable. All buses and coaches stop at the **Gare Routière** (Bus Station; bd Pierre Sémard).

Car

Driving in Toulouse, like any large French city, is not for the faint-hearted. Parking in particular is a real headache; some hotels have private garages for an extra charge, or offer discounted rates at city car parks. Otherwise you'll be stuck with expensive on-street parking (which is free from noon–2pm and on Sundays). Count on paying between €18 and €25 for a full day, depending on which car park you choose.

Train

Buy tickets at the **SNCF boutique** (5 rue Peyras) in town or at Toulouse's main train station, **Gare Matabiau** (blvd Pierre Sémard), 1km northeast of the centre. Toulouse is served

WORTH A TRIP

L'ÉCHAPPÉE BELLE

If you're looking for a break from Toulouse's big-city buzz, it's well worth making a pilgrimage 20km west to the village of L'Isle-Jourdain, where you'll find one of the region's sexiest new hotel-restaurants, L'Échappée Belle (☑05 62 07 50 00; www.echappee-belle.fr; rue Fernand Mestre, L'Isle-Jourdain; d €92-160; ☜). Its minimalist decor and experimental design are quite out of keeping with its village location: gleaming wood, curvy furniture, stark walls and giant murals characterise the bedrooms, and the same metro-modern feel runs downstairs, with its stuffed stags heads, globe lights and crazy colour schemes. It's a great place for supper, too – Chef Bernard Bach is a rising star, and a previous holder of Michelin stars. One to watch.

by frequent fast TGVs, which run west to Montauban, Agen and Bordeaux (which has connections to Bayonne and the southwest, plus Paris), and east to Carcassonne, Narbonne, Montpellier and beyond. Smaller towns are served by slower Corail trains.

Destinations include:

Albi €12.80, one hour
Auch €14.60, 1½ hours
Bayonne €42.70, 3¼ hours
Bordeaux €38 via TGV, two hours
Carcassonne €15, 45 minutes to 1 hour
Castres €14.30, 1¾ hours
Montauban €9.30, 30 minutes
Pau €31, 2¼ hours

❶ Getting Around

To/From the Airport

The **Navette Aéroport Flybus** (Airport Shuttle; ☑05 61 41 70 70; www.tisseo.fr) links the airport with town (single €5, 20 minutes, every 20 minutes from 5am to 8.20pm from town and 7.35am to midnight from the airport). Catch the bus in front of the bus station, outside the Jean Jaurès metro station or at place Jeanne d'Arc. The trip takes between 20 and 40 minutes depending on traffic.

Taxis (☑05 61 30 02 54) to/from town cost from €30 to €35.

Bicycle

The city's bike-hire scheme **Vélô Toulouse** (www.velo.toulouse.fr) has pick-up/drop-off stations dotted every 300m or so round the city. Tickets cost €1.20 a day or €5 a week, plus a €150 credit-card deposit. You can buy online, but you'll need a chip-and-pin card to work the automated machines.

Bus & Metro

Local buses and the two-line metro are run by **Tisséo** (www.tisseo.fr), which has ticket kiosks located on place Jeanne d'Arc and cours Dillon. A single ticket costs €1.60, a 10-ticket *carnet*

(book of tickets) is €12.90 and a one-/two-day pass is €5.50/8.50.

Most bus lines run daily until at least 8pm. Night bus lines run from 10pm to midnight.

Albi

POP 48,600

The bustling provincial town of Albi has two main claims to fame: a truly mighty cathedral and a truly marvellous painter. Looming up from the centre of the old town, the Cathédrale Ste-Cécile is one of France's most monumental Gothic structures. Next door is the fantastic Musée Toulouse-Lautrec, dedicated to the mischievous artist Henri de Toulouse-Lautrec, who was born here in 1864 and went on to depict the bars and brothels of turn-of-the-century Paris in his own inimitable style.

Albi's little old town is also well worth a wander, although it's surprisingly small given the town's sprawling suburbs.

◉ Sights & Activities

The **Albi City Pass** (€6.50), sold at the tourist office, gives free admission to the Musée Toulouse-Lautrec and Cathédrale Ste-Cécile's grand chœur, and offers discounts at local shops and restaurants.

Cathédrale Ste-Cécile   CHURCH
(place Ste-Cécile; grand chœur adult/child €2/free; ⊙9am-6.30pm) Right at the heart of Albi is the mighty Cathédrale Ste-Cécile, which was begun in 1282 but took well over a century to complete. Attractive isn't the word – what strikes you most is its sheer mass, rising over town like some Tolkienesque tower rather than a place of Christian worship. Its fortified facade is a result of the many religious wars that marked the medieval era, particularly the persecution of the Cathars during

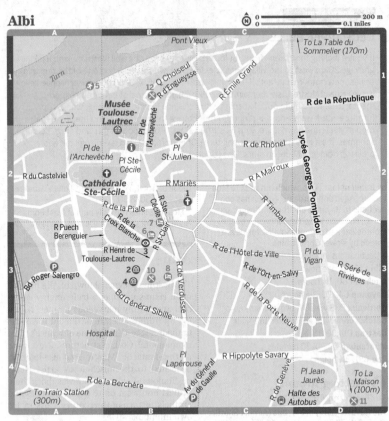

Albi

the early 13th century. The cathedral was intentionally designed as an unmistakable symbol of the might and power of the medieval church, and it certainly makes a statement – it's one of the world's largest brick buildings, and has been cited on Unesco's World Heritage list since 2010.

Step inside and the contrast with the brutal exterior is astonishing. No surface was left untouched by the Italian artists who, in the early 16th century, painted their way, chapel by chapel, along the entire nave. Particularly noteworthy is the grand chœur (great choir) with its frescos, chapels and biblical figures, each carved from stone and painted by hand.

At the western end is *Le Jugement Dernier* (The Last Judgement, painted 1474–1484), a vivid doomsday horror show of the damned being boiled in oil, beheaded or tortured by demons and monsters.

TOP CHOICE Musée Toulouse-Lautrec   ART MUSEUM
(www.museetoulouselautrec.net; place Ste-Cécile; adult/student €5.50/2.50; ⊙9am-6pm Jun-Sep, shorter hrs rest of year) Lodged inside one of Albi's impressive red-brick landmarks, the Palais de la Berbie (built in the early Middle Ages for the town's archbishop), this wonderful museum offers a comprehensive overview of Albi's most celebrated son. The museum owns more than 500 original works by Toulouse-Lautrec (the largest collection in France outside the Musée d'Orsay), spanning the artist's development from his early impressionist influences to his famous Parisian brothel scenes and poster art.

Pride of place goes to two versions of the *Au Salon de la rue des Moulins*, hung side by side to illustrate the artist's subtly different technique. Elsewhere around the museum, look out for a fascinating collection of early portraits – particularly of his mother, the Comtesse Adèle de Toulouse-Lautrec, his cousin Gabriel Tapié de Celeyran and his close friend Maurice Joyant. There are also some surprisingly delicate animal studies that provide a fascinating contrast to his later work.

On the top floor of the museum, there's a small collection of works by some of Toulouse-Lautrec's contemporaries, including Degas, Matisse and Rodin.

A short stroll away is the privately owned Maison Natale de Toulouse-Lautrec (14 rue Henri de Toulouse-Lautrec) where the artist was born. Next door is La Maison de Lapérouse (14 rue Henri de Toulouse-Lautrec), where the Albi-born explorer lived before sailing around the Pacific in 1785. Guided visits can be arranged for groups via the tourist office.

Old Town   ARCHITECTURE
Vieil Albi (Old Albi) is an attractive muddle of winding streets and half-timbered houses, one of which, the Maison du Vieil Alby (1 rue de la Croix Blanche; adult/child €2/free;

⊙10.30am-12.30pm & 2.30pm-6.30pm Apr-Oct, 2.30-6pm Nov-Mar, closed all day Sun & Mon morning year-round), houses a small exhibition on the city's history and its connections with Toulouse-Lautrec.

Also worth a look is the Collegiale Saint-Salvi (Rue Mariès; ⊙9am-noon & 2-6pm Mon-Sat, 9am-10.30am & 2-6pm Sun Jul-Aug, closes 1 hour earlier Sep-Jun), a delicate canons' church with a lovely cloister, and the Pont-Vieux, the 19th-century arched bridge across the River Tarn, which provides a fine perspective over Albi's pink-bricked old town and its landmark cathedral.

Albi Croisières   CRUISING
(www.albi-croisieres.com) Albi Croisières runs various boat trips aboard traditional *gabarres* (flat-bottomed barges). From June to September, there's a regular lunchtime cruise (adult/child €12/8), leaving at 12.30pm from the Berges du Tarn landing stage.

Between April and September, there are also full-day trips (single/return €15/23) between the village of Aiguelèze, near Gaillac, and Albi. Trips depart at 10am and include an afternoon in Albi, arriving back in Aiguelèze at about 7pm.

🎊 Festivals & Events

Carnaval   CARNIVAL
Albi celebrates Carnaval at the beginning of Lent (February or March).

Voix-là   MUSIC FESTIVAL
In May, Voix-là (it's a pun) celebrates vocal music.

Pause Guitare   MUSIC FESTIVAL
Guitar concerts in the sumptuous space of place Ste-Cécile. Held in July.

🛏 Sleeping

TOP CHOICE La Tour Ste-Cécile   B&B €€
(☏05 81 40 51 52; www.toursaintececile.com; 14 bis rue Ste-Cécile; d €130-180; ❀) Built from stout brick with its own turret-tower (hence the name), this enormously attractive *chambre d'hôte* has four regal rooms stuffed with antique furniture and period detail. The Sainte-Cécile Suite looks more like a royal apartment, while the Toulouse-Lautrec room is reached via its own spiral staircase. Rates include a communal breakfast and entry to the Toulouse-Lautrec museum, and there are generous discounts for stays of more than one night. Highly recommended.

TOULOUSE AREA ALBI

HENRI DE TOULOUSE-LAUTREC

Ever the outsider (despite being born into one of Albi's most aristocratic families), Henri de Toulouse-Lautrec (1864–1901) was a fairly unusual character. He was notoriously short as a result of two teenage accidents that broke both his legs, stunted his growth and left him unable to walk without his trademark canes. He also had poor eyesight, brittle bones and a number of other congenital health problems – so it's perhaps unsurprising that he identified with the stranger and seedier sides of the Parisian underworld.

He spent his early 20s studying painting in Paris, where he mixed with other artists including Van Gogh. In 1890, at the height of the belle époque, he abandoned impressionism and took to observing Paris' colourful nightlife.

Perhaps as a result of his own afflictions, he came to identify strongly with the many curious characters he got to know while frequenting the bars, brothels and dance halls. Conversely, he was also entranced by the light, colour and surprising beauty he often encounted on his nocturnal adventures, and it's this juxtaposition of the bizarre and beautiful, which give his works their peculiar energy.

Among his favourite subjects were the cabaret singer Aristide Bruant, the racy can-can dancers from the Moulin Rouge and prostitutes from the rue des Moulins. He liked to work quickly, sketching on whatever was at hand – a scrap of paper, a tablecloth or a handy piece of cardboard. Later in his career, he became a skilled and sought-after lithographer and poster designer, until drinking and general overindulgence (possibly coupled with a syphilis infection) led to his premature death in 1901, aged just 37.

La Maison
B&B €€
(☑05 63 38 17 35; www.chambre-hote-albi.com; 40 blvd Andrieu; s €60-75, d €75-90; 🛜) In contrast to Albi's olde-worle feel, this B&B is a model of modernity. The three lovely rooms are sharp, sexy and swish: the La Velours and La Métal rooms glimmer with gloss-wood floors and designer furniture, while La Ficelle feels more classic with its neutral colours, oil paintings and distressed furniture. It's outside the old city, but you get a garden and parking, not to mention really super rates.

Hôtel St-Clair
HOTEL €
(☑05 63 54 25 66; www.hotel-albi-saintclair.com; 8 rue St-Clair; r €48-75; 🛜) This higgledy-piggledy hotel is slap bang in the centre of town. It's a rabbit's warren – wonky floors, hefty beams and low ceilings galore – but it's quaint and charming, and on sunny days breakfast is served on the enclosed terrace. Private parking (some distance away) costs €8.

Le Vieil Alby
HOTEL €
(☑05 63 54 14 69; www.levieilalby.com; 25 rue Henri de Toulouse-Lautrec; d from €55) Solid, old-school hotel on the fringes of the old city. The rooms are plain but pleasant, but the real draw here is the excellent *terroir* (land) restaurant.

Les Buis de St-Martin
B&B €€
(☑05 63 55 41 23; http://pagesperso-orange.fr/les-buis-de-saint-martin; 11 rue St-Martin, Marssac sur Tarn; d €110) If you don't mind being out in the sticks, this rural *chambre d'hôte* 10km west of town is worth investigating. The house is 19th century, and the two bedrooms (Sophie and Julie) have a cool country charm. There's also a self-contained *gîte* (cottage) for longer stays.

✕ Eating

Albi has loads of places to eat, including a string of places on rue Henri de Toulouse-Lautrec, just downhill from the cathedral.

L'Epicurien
TOP CHOICE
MODERN FRENCH €€€
(☑05 63 53 10 70; www.restaurantlepicurien.com; 42 place Jean Jaurès; menus €19-48; ◷Tue-Sat) The steely grey and glass facade says it all: this establishment is a temple to cutting-edge contemporary French cuisine, run by Swedish chef Rikard Hult and his wife Patricia. Arty presentation takes precedence over copious portions: expect delicate towers of monkfish or lamb noisettes, accompanied by a slash of sauce or just-so sprig of herb.

Le Lautrec
TRADITIONAL FRENCH €€
(☑05 63 54 86 55; 13-15 rue Henri de Toulouse-Lautrec; lunch menus €15-17, dinner menus €28-38; ◷lunch Tue-Sun, dinner Tue-Sat) Housed in

the former stables of the Toulouse-Lautrec family home, this traditional but tempting restaurant specialises in Gascon cuisine, such as a classic rich *cassoulet* spiced with saffron and Tarbais beans. The dining room is a cosy blend of red brick, chimneys and country emphemra.

L'Esprit du Vin GASTRONOMIC €€€
(☎05 63 54 60 44; www.lespritduvin-albi.com; 11 quai Choiseul; menus €60-105; ⊙Tue-Sat) Albi-born chef David Enjalran is one of the region's star names, and his cuisine is as adventurous as it gets. *Menus* are divided into five 'ateliers' (levels), and take their cue from the changing seasons: the approach is very much Michelin-style, so it might be a bit stuffy for some. The lunchtime 'Pause Gourmande' is marginally more affordable at €25/29 for one/two courses. Reservations essential.

La Table du Sommelier BISTRO €€
(☎05 63 46 20 10; 20 rue Porta, lunch menus €14-16, dinner menus €30-48; ⊙Tue-Sat) A quick stroll across the Pont Vieux, this is one for the wine lovers. Owner Daniel Pestre is an experienced sommelier, with an infectious passion for his local vintages: dinner *menus* are themed around the wines, rather than the other way round. The outdoor patio shaded by huge umbrellas makes a great spot for when the sun shines.

Le Vieil Alby GASCON €€
(☎05 63 54 14 69; 25 rue Henri de Toulouse-Lautrec; menus from €17.50; ⊙closed Jan) This hotel-restaurant serves hearty, traditional southwest flavours, heavy on the beef, duck and tarbais beans. House specials include homemade melsat sausages, dried pork stuffed with radishes and (of course) piping-hot *cassoulet*.

Self-Catering
Albi's landmark turn-of-the-century covered market (place St-Julien; ⊙8am-2pm plus 5-8pm Fri & Sat) is a delight – gastronomically and architecturally.

❶ Information
Tourist office (☎05 63 49 48 80; www.albi-tourisme.fr; place Ste-Cécile; ⊙9am-7pm, shorter hours outside summer) Next door to the Toulouse-Lautrec Museum. Ask for one of the themed walking leaflets for old Albi.

❶ Getting There & Away
Useful buses that leave from place Jean Jaurès include Castres (€2.50, 50 minutes, up to 10 daily).

Train destinations include Rodez (€13.60, 1½ hours, six to eight daily) and Toulouse (€12.80, one hour, at least hourly).

Castres
Founded by the Romans as a *castrum* (settlement), this sleepy town is best known as the birthplace of Jean Jaurès, the founding father of French socialism. It's mainly worth visiting for the Musée Goya (goya@ville-castres.fr; rue de l'Hôtel de Ville, Hôtel de Ville; adult/child €3/free; ⊙10am-6pm) and its collection of Spanish art, including works by Goya, Murillo, Ribera and Picasso. The museum's gardens were laid out by Le Nôtre, architect of Versailles' park.

Montauban
POP 53,200

Bastides (fortified towns) litter the landscape of southwest France, and there's no finer example than Montauban, nestled on the banks of the River Tarn. Founded in 1144, Montauban is southern France's second-oldest *bastide* (the oldest is Mont-de-Marsan). All roads lead to its characteristic central square, place Nationale, hemmed in on every side by arcaded walkways and tall pink buildings. Many of the streets around the square would originally have marked the town's fortified walls; the town was badly battered during both the Hundred Years War and the Wars of Religion, and famously withstood an 86-day siege imposed by Louis XIII in 1621 during which the defenders resorted to eating horses, rats and dogs to survive.

◉ Sights
Musée Ingres ART MUSEUM
(13 rue de l'Hôtel de Ville; adult/child €5/2.50, during special exhibitions €7.50/3.50; ⊙10am-6pm, closed noon-2pm outside Jul & Aug) Apart from the pleasure of wandering round Montauban's shady streets, the main focus of a visit is this fine-arts museum, which centres on the work of the neoclassical painter (and accomplished violinist) Jean Auguste Dominique Ingres, who was born in Montauban in 1780. Inspired by Poussin and David, Ingres became one of the most celebrated portrait painters of his day, and the museum houses many of his key works alongside old masters such as Tintoretto, Van Dyck and Gustave Courbet. The entry ticket also admits you

to the nearby Histoire Naturelle (natural history), Terroir (local costumes and traditions) and Résistance et Déportation (with mementoes of WWII) museums.

Another Ingres masterpiece, *Le Vœu de Louis XIII*, depicting the king pledging France to the Virgin, hangs in Montauban's 18th-century Cathédrale Notre Dame de l'Assomption (place Franklin Roosevelt; ⏰10am-noon & 2-6pm Mon-Sat).

🎉 Festivals & Events

Alors Chante   MUSIC FESTIVAL
(www.alorschante.com) A festival of French song in May.

Jazz à Montauban   MUSIC FESTIVAL
(www.jazzmontauban.com) A week-long jam in July.

Légende des Quatre-Cent Coups   STREET FESTIVAL
(400 Blows) This weekend street festival at the end of August commemorates the moment when, says local lore, a fortune-teller told Louis XIII, besieging Montauban, to blast off 400 cannons simultaneously against the town, which still failed to fall.

🛏 Sleeping

Mas des Anges   B&B €
(☎05 63 24 27 05; www.lemasdesanges.com; d incl breakfast €75; 🖩🌐) Wine lovers will love this place, a 4.5-hectare vineyard five miles south of Montauban. It's run by Sophie and Juan Kervyn, a friendly couple who've made winemaking into a lifelong passion. The three ground-floor rooms each have a slightly different theme (African, Latin, Marine).

Tree-filled grounds, a fine pool and guest barbecues are the icing on the cake.

Hôtel du Commerce   HOTEL €
(☎05 63 66 31 32; www.hotel-commerce -montauban.com; 9 place Franklin Roosevelt; s €59, d €59-79; ❄🌐) Montauban's choice of hotels is hardly spectacular, but this is about the best of the bunch. Rooms are floral and old-fashioned, and some overlook the cathedral square.

Château de Seguenville   B&B €€
(☎05 62 13 42 67; www.chateau-de-seguenville. com; r €120-230; 🌐) For aristocratic cachet, this spiky-roofed château *chambre d'hôte* is hard to top. A massive central staircase opens onto a 1st-floor gallery and five boho rooms, each named after aristocratic nobles and each with a different view over the rolling parkland. It's roughly equidistant from Toulouse, Montauban and Auch.

🍴 Eating

Morning farmers markets are on Saturday (place Prax-Paris) and Wednesday (place Lalaque), in addition to a smaller daily one (place Nationale).

Au Fil de l'Eau   GASTRONOMIC €€
(☎05 63 66 11 85; www.aufildeleau82.com; 14 quai du Dr Lafforgue; mains €24-33; ⏰lunch & dinner Tue-Sat, lunch Sun) Ask someone in Montauban where to go for a treat, and they'll point you straight to this riverside restaurant, where the modern art and quirky fixtures are mirrored by the classy *cuisine gastronomique* (gastronomic cooking). There's an €18 lunch *menu* Tuesday to Friday.

GAILLAC WINES

Eat out at any restaurant in this corner of France and you're guaranteed to stumble across the name Gaillac on the menu. The rolling countryside around this little village produces the region's best wines – particularly rosés, light whites and rich, summery reds – which benefit from the area's unique microclimate, positioned halfway between the balmy Mediterranean and the cooling rains of the Atlantic.

Gaillac winemaking stretches right back to Roman times, and the region now boasts several AOCs (Appellation d'Origine Contrôlée), including Gaillac Rouge, Gaillac Blanc Sec and Gaillac Rosé, as well as more unusual ones such as AOC Gaillac Perle (for the area's sparkling or *petillant* white wine) and AOC Mousseux Methode Gaillacacoise (for the Champagne-style wine made by only a few vineyards).

There are lots of châteaux dotted around the area offering *dégustation* (tasting) and cellar visits, connected by a signposted Route des Vins (Wine Route).

Have a look at the useful site www.vins-gaillac.com for more information, or contact the Gaillac tourist office (☎05 63 57 14 65; tourisme@ville-gaillac.fr; pl St-Michel), which can help you arrange vineyard visits.

WORTH A TRIP

TREEHOUSE SLEEPS

It's one thing sleeping under the trees, but sleeping in them is another thing altogether. Arboreal accommodation has developed into something of a minor craze in France, with treetop cabins springing up all over the place in recent years. If you want to try the experience for yourself, Cabane dans les Arbres (☎06 82 41 81 50; www.cabane-spa. com; midweek/weekends €225/245) near Montauban allows you to do so in comparative luxury, with its gorgeous handbuilt treehouse complete with private hot tub, canopy balcony and king-size bed, and a fresh breakfast winched up to you in a wicker basket every morning. It's usually booked out months in advance, though, so you'll have to plan ahead.

Les Boissières   REGIONAL CUISINE €€
(☎05 63 24 50 02; www.lesboissieres.free.fr; menus €22-50; ☺lunch Tue-Fri & Sun, dinner Tue-Sat) If you don't mind driving, this much-recommended restaurant serves excellent *cuisine régionale* in a pleasant village setting in the little hamlet of Bioule. It's about 22km northeast of Montauban.

ⓘ Information

Tourist office (☎05 63 63 60 60; www. montauban-tourisme.com; 4 rue du Collège; ☺9.30am-6.30pm Mon-Sat, 10am-12.30pm Sun Jul-Aug, closes noon-2pm & Sun rest of year)

ⓘ Getting There & Away

From the **train station** (av Mayenne), about 1km from place Nationale across the Tarn, trains serve Toulouse (€9.30, 30 minutes, frequent) and Moissac (€5.80, 20 minutes, six daily).

Moissac

POP 12,300

Riverside Moissac has been an important stop-off on the Santiago de Compostela trail since the 12th century thanks to the glorious Abbaye St-Pierre (place Durand de Bredon), resplendent with some of France's finest Romanesque architecture. It's particularly known for its tympanum, the crescent-shaped frieze above its south portal. Completed in 1130, it depicts St John's vision of the Apocalypse, with Christ in majesty flanked by the Apostles, angels and 24 awestruck elders. If you've got time, it's worth comparing it with the one in Beaulieu-sur-Dordogne's Abbatiale St-Pierre (p570), which is thought to have been carved around the same time, very possibly by the same stonemasons.

Outside, the wonderful cloister (adult/child €5/3.50; ☺9am-7pm) is encircled by delicate marble columns, topped by carved capitals depicting foliage, figures or biblical scenes. Sadly, the Revolution took its toll – nearly every face is smashed.

Entry to the abbey is via the tourist office (www.moissac.fr; 6 place Durand de Bredon; ☺9am-7pm).

⧄ Sleeping & Eating

Au Château   B&B €€
(☎05 63 95 96 82; www.au-chateau-stn.com; St Nicolas de la Grave; r €62-116; ❊☞⊠) This village B&B 10km south of Moissac offers five seriously enormous rooms, which blend modern touches (wood floors, flat-screen TVs, funky fabrics) into the house's 18th-century château shell. It's awash with spoils, including a heated pool and tree-filled grounds, and it's very family-friendly.

Le Pont Napoléon   HOTEL €
(☎05 63 04 01 55; www.le-pont-napoleon.com; 2 allée Montebello; s €49, d €59-70; ☞) Moissac's best hotel occupies a super riverside spot, beside the town's 19th-century Napoleon-built bridge. It's an old building, and some of the rooms are a bit tired, but get one with a view across the Tarn and you won't be complaining. The hotel restaurant, Le Table de Nos Fils (menus €28-45) is run by talented chef Patrick Delaroux, who also runs weekend cooking courses.

Le Moulin de Moissac   HOTEL €€
(☎05 63 32 88 88; www.lemoulindemoissac. com; esplanade du Moulin; d €89-166, restaurant mains €18-55; ☞) Housed in a 15th-century grain mill overlooking the Tarn, this hotel is a riverside treat. In the rooms, distressed wallpaper, wicker chairs and tall French windows open onto river-view balconies. Elsewhere, you'll find a super waterside

restaurant, a smart sauna-spa and a romantic Jacuzzi sheltered under a brick vaulted roof.

❶ Getting There & Away

A few local buses serve Moissac, but it's more convenient to catch a train to or from Montauban (€5.80, 20 minutes, four to eight daily) or Toulouse (€13.30, 50 minutes, four to eight daily).

Auch
POP 23,500

Auch has been a key crossroads since Roman times, and later became the seat of power for the counts of Armagnac. It's now the capital of the Gers *départment*, a busy provincial town made up of a jumble of lanes, steps and courtyards perched above the River Gers. Though scruffy in parts, there are two main reasons to make a detour through Auch.

The first is to see the town's Unesco-listed church, the Cathédrale Ste-Marie (⊘8.30am-noon & 2-5pm), which showcases a peculiar mix of architectural styles from austere Gothic to flamboyant Renaissance (perhaps unsurprising, given that it took over two centuries to complete after the first stones were laid in 1489). The 40m-high Tour d'Armagnac was built to house the archive of Auch's archbishops, and briefly served as a Revolutionary prison.

The second is to walk up the town's fabulous Escalier Monumental, one of France's most impressive public staircases. Built in 1863, it consists of either 275 steps or 370 steps (depending on whether you count the double-flighted section at the top). Halfway up, look out for a statue of d'Artagnan, Alexandre Dumas' swashbuckling hero, who was supposedly based on the local nobleman Charles de Batz.

From the train station, there are regular trains to Toulouse (€14.60, 1½ hours, six to 10 daily). SNCF buses also serve nearby Agen (€12.10, 1½ hours, six to 10 daily).

Condom
POP 7250

Now now, stop sniggering at the back. Poor old Condom's name actually has nothing to do with its namesake contraceptive – it's a derivation of the town's Gallo-Roman name, Condatomagus. Established as a Roman and medieval port on the River Baïse, and later a key stop-off for Compostela pilgrims, these days Condom is a mellow town of yellow stone, surrounded by fertile countryside and orderly vineyards, as well as plenty of prestigious Armagnac producers.

◉ Sights & Activities

Cathédrale St-Pierre   CHURCH
(place St-Pierre) With its lofty nave and elaborate chancel, Condom's cathedral is a classic example of Flamboyant Gothic architecture. On the north side, the 16th-century tentlike cloister was designed to offer wet-weather protection for Compostela pilgrims.

Musée de l'Armagnac   MUSEUM
(2 rue Jules Ferry; adult/child €2.20/1.10; ⊘10am-noon & 3-6pm, closed Jan) In a turn-of-the-century cellar, this museum is dedicated to the fine art of Armagnac-making and houses a modest collection of vintage bottles, agricultural tools and an 18-tonne press dating from the 19th century.

Musée du Preservatif   MUSEUM
(Condom Museum; 2 rue Jules Ferry; adult/child €3/1.50; ⊘10am-noon & 3-7pm summer) Well, if you can't beat 'em... Condom's tiny Musée du Preservatif is attached to the Musée de l'Armagnac and usually opens only in summer. The few displays detail the contraceptive's history from its birth in 1665 to the present day. Some of the exhibits will make you very, very thankful for the invention of latex; if anything's a guaranteed passion-killer, it's a pig's intestine.

Marché aux Gras   MARKET
The weekly Marché au Gras held on Wednesday and Saturday mornings in the covered market is more of an experience than your average shopping trip.

Gascogne Navigation   CRUISING
(☑05 62 28 46 46; www.gascogne-navigation.com; 3 av d'Aquitaine) From April to October, Gascogne Navigation runs 1½-hour river cruises (adult/child €8.50/6.20) and 2½-hour lunch cruises (€36/22) along the Baïse River, departing from quai Bouquerie. It also hires small motorboats (hour/half-day/full day €30/75/115).

🛏 Sleeping & Eating

Les Trois Lys   HOTEL €€€
(☑05 62 28 33 33; www.lestroislys.com; 38 rue Gambetta; d €130-190, menus €40-45; ❄🛜🐾) Pricey it may be, but if it's antiques and architecture you're after, this is the town's

ARMAGNAC

Ask any Gascon: Armagnac slips down just as smoothly as Cognac to the north. Produced from white grapes that ripen in the sandy soils hereabouts and aged in barrels of local black oak, this potent brandy was originally taken for medicinal purposes, but these days it's a popular after-dinner *digestif*. Floc de Gascogne – a liqueur wine made from Armagnac and grape juice – is the aperitif version.

One of the oldest and best-known names is Armagnac Ryst-Dupeyron (36 rue Jean Jaurès; ⊙10am-noon & 2-6.30pm Mon-Fri), lodged inside a turn-of-the-century cellar right in the middle of Condom. It offers regular tours and tasting sessions, and you can buy lots of vintages on site. There are plenty more distilleries in the surrounding countryside: at the 13th-century Château de Cassaigne (☑05 62 28 04 02; www.chateaudecassaigne. com; ⊙10am-7pm Jul & Aug, 9am-noon & 2-6pm Tue-Sun Sep-Jun), 6.5km southwest of Condom on the D931, you can visit the cellars and sample the Armagnac from its 18th-century distillery. The 17th-century Château du Busca Maniban (☑05 62 28 40 38; www.buscamaniban.com; ⊙2-6pm Mon-Sat Apr-Nov) is 5.5km further south along the D229.

premier proposition. There are 10 rooms set around the amber-stoned 18th-century mansion. They range in style and size, but they're all elegantly appointed, and some look over the heated pool. Downstairs, the restaurant dabbles in upmarket dishes such as roast lamb shank and scallop tagine. Classy.

Hôtel Continental HOTEL €
(☑05 62 68 37 00; www.lecontinental.net; 20 rue Maréchal Foch; s/d from €45/49; 🖭) This waterfront hotel offers great value, with spick-and-span rooms and an excellent in-house restaurant (*menus* €21–€29). Front rooms overlook the river, but also suffer from road noise; garden rooms are much quieter.

Le Logis des Cordeliers HOTEL €
(☑05 62 28 03 68; www.logisdescordeliers.com; rue de la Paix; d €53-76; ⊙Feb-Dec; 🖭🖭) The building's bland and boxy and so are the rooms, but this modern hotel makes a useful base in Condom, with its own pool and private gardens. Street-view rooms are the cheapest; garden views command a small premium. It's along a quiet backstreet off ave Général de Gaulle.

Le Relais de la Ténarèze HOTEL €
(☑05 62 28 02 54; www.relais-de-la-tenareze.fr; 22 av d'Aquitaine; d €44-55, f €55-76) Run by its genial *patronne* (owner) Elian Bouvier, this welcoming riverside hotel is a popular stop-off for hikers and bikers on the Compostela route, so it's usually booked out between April and October. Rooms are tiny, simple and dirt cheap, especially when combined with the honest, down-to-earth *demi-pension* (half-board) menu.

La Table des Cordeliers GASTRONOMIC €€€
(☑05 62 68 43 82; www.latabledescordeliers.fr; 1 rue des Cordeliers; menus €25-67; ⊙Tue-Sat) Overseen by Eric Sampietro, one of the region's culinary big-hitters, Condom's *table gastronomique* is housed in a former chapel complete wih vaulted arches and cloister garden. Sampietro's mainly known for his use of fresh flavours and seasonal ingredients, put together in surprising combinations (fish partnered with sorbet, for example).

❶ Information

Tourist office (☑05 62 28 00 80; www.tourisme-tenareze.com; 5 Place Saint-Pierre; ⊙9am-7pm Mon-Sat, 10am-1pm Sun mid-Jul–mid-Aug, 9am-noon & 2-6.30pm Mon-Sat rest of year, earlier closing in winter)

❶ Getting There & Around

The only useful buses from Condom run to Auch (50 minutes, Monday to Friday, three daily) and Agen (50 minutes, Monday to Saturday, three daily).

To park on the street in Condom, you'll need a blue timed disc, available from the tourist office and some shops and hotels.

Around Condom

This corner of the ancient province of Gascon was once wild frontier country, caught between the French, entrenched in Toulouse, and the English, with their power base in Bordeaux. To protect themselves from the crossfire, the better-off villages fortified themselves against attack, creating the many *bastide* towns that now litter the area.

TOULOUSE AREA AROUND CONDOM

THE CANAL DU MIDI

Stretching for 240 languid kilometres between Toulouse and Sète, the Canal du Midi (www.canaldumidi.com) is one of the great waterways of southern France. Built in the 17th century and classified as a World Heritage Site since 1996, the canal links the Étang de Thau in the south with the Garonne River in Toulouse. Along with the Canal de Garonne, it forms part of the 'Canal des Deux Mers' (Canal of the Two Seas), which enables boats to travel all the way from the Mediterranean to the Atlantic.

The canal was essentially a commercial enterprise, designed to open up trading routes and facilitate merchant traffic between major French ports. It was commissioned by Louis XIV in 1666, who delegated the task of the canal's construction to Pierre-Paul Riquet, a farmer turned engineer.

It was a formidable enterprise. To overcome the difficult terrain and the ever-present risk of flooding, Riquet designed an elaborate system of dams, bridges, aqueducts and locks, as well as the first canal tunnel ever constructed in France. The canal finally opened in 1681, but it had taken its toll on Riquet: he died a few months before the official opening, having racked up enormous debts in the hope of recouping costs when the canal finally began to carry traffic.

Eclipsed by the railway in the mid-19th century, these days the canal is almost entirely the preserve of pleasure-boaters, as well as walkers, bikers and horse-riders who stroll along its peaceful towpaths. If you fancy organising your own boating holiday, you'll find comprehensive information at the excellent Canal du Midi website (www.canaldumidi.com), as well as the tourist offices dotted along the canal's route (eg Toulouse, Agde, Béziers, Narbonne and Sète).

There are lots of boat-hire companies, mostly based along the southern reaches of the canal. Locaboat (☎03 86 91 72 72; www.locaboat.com; Argens-Minervois) and Caminav (☎04 67 68 01 90; www.caminav.com; Carnon) hire small motorboats, while the Britain-based Minervois Cruisers (☎01926-811842; www.minervoiscruisers.com; Le Somail, near Narbonne) offers narrowboats; prices vary, but expect to pay somehere around €800 to €1200 a week for a standard four-berth boat. Vintage restored *péniches* (live-aboard narrowboats) are also available, but these tend to be very expensive (upwards of €3000 a week for the nicest ones).

While you're exploring the canal, it's well worth stopping at the Musée Canal du Midi (www.museecanaldumidi.fr; blvd Pierre-Paul Riquet; adult/child €4/2; ⊙10am-7pm), which explores the waterway's history and the life of Paul Riquet. It's in St-Ferréol, between Toulouse and Castres along the D2 and D622.

There are several within easy reach of Condom, all of which can be covered in a leisurely morning's drive or a fine day's bike ride.

◉ Sights

Fourcès   BASTIDE
Some 13km northwest of Condom, Fourcès (the 's' is pronounced) is a picturesque *bastide* on the River Auzoue, worth a visit for its unusual shape – unlike most *bastides*, it's circular rather than square-shaped. The village bursts into colour during the last weekend of April as thousands pour in for its Marché aux Fleurs, more a flower festival than a market.

Cité des Machines du Moyen Age   MUSEUM
(http://larressingle.free.fr; Larressingle; adult/student/child €8/6.80/5; ⊙10am-7pm Jul-Aug, 2-6pm Apr-Jun & Sep-Oct, closed Nov-Mar) Sometimes known locally as 'little Carcassonne', the textbook bastion of Larressingle, 5km west of Condom, must be France's cutest fortified village. Just outside town, this outdoor museum collects together an assortment of replica trebuchets, catapults and siege machines arranged as if they're about to assault the town. You can see several of the machines in action, and kids can clamber around a miniature fort.

Villa Gallo-Romaine   ROMAN SITE
(☎05 62 29 48 57; adult/child €4/free; ⊙10am-noon & 2-6pm Mar-Nov) About 1.5km south-west of the *bastide* town of Montréal du Gers are the excavated remains of a 4th-century Gallo-Roman villa, once part of the agricultural estate of a Roman aristocrat.

Archaeologists so far have revealed the villa's baths, outbuildings and large areas of mosaic floors, still bright despite centuries of being buried underground. Admission includes entry to the small museum within Montréal's tourist office (☎05 62 29 42 85; place Hôtel de Ville; ⊙9.30am-12.30pm & 2-6pm Tue-Sat), which displays artefacts from Séviac.

Abbaye de Flaran
ABBEY

(☎05 62 28 50 19; www.fources.fr/abbayeflaran.html; adult/student €4/2; ⊙9.30am-7pm Jul-Aug, 9.30am-noon & 2-6pm rest of year) Founded in 1151 and guarded by a 14th-century fortress door turned pigeon loft, this Cistercian abbey near Fourcès is the loveliest in southwest France. It was deserted following the Revolution, but the building is remarkably well preserved, with the monks' cloister, refectory and sleeping cells still in situ.

Collegiale St-Pierre
CHURCH

(adult/child €4.90/free; ⊙9.30am-7pm Mon-Sat, 2-7pm Sun Jul-Aug, shorter hours rest of year) Towering over the little village of La Romieu, 11km northeast of Condom, this 14th-century *collegiale* (collegiate church) is famous for its cloister and twin 33m towers. You can climb the 136 steps of one of them for a memorable panorama across the Gers countryside.

Les Jardins de Coursiana
GARDENS

(☎05 62 68 22 80; www.jardinsdecoursiana.com; adult/child €6.80/4; ⊙10am-8pm Mon-Sat mid-Apr–Oct, closed Wed outside school holidays) These landscaped gardens in La Romieu are the handiwork of a local agricultural engineer. More than 700 trees and rare plants flourish in the four main gardens: arboretum, English garden, herb garden and *potager familial* (vegetable patch). A joint ticket with the Collegiale St-Pierre, also in La Romieu, costs €9.70.

Sleeping & Eating

TOP CHOICE La Lumiane
B&B €

(☎05 62 28 95 95; www.lalumiane.com; St Puy; s €49-60, d €58-69; 🛜🍽) Lost in the countryside between Condom and Auch, this bewitching B&B is a rural getaway par excellence. With its stone walls, shutters and beams, the lemon yellow house is a delightful mix of rustic chic and homely style. There are three snug bedrooms and two fantastic suites, accessed by the house's grand central staircase. The setting's beautiful, too – lush garden, tree-shaded pool – and owners Alain and Gisèle lay on a fine country spread for dinner. And at these prices, it's an absolute steal.

Maison Ardure
B&B €€

(☎05 62 68 59 56; http://www.ardure.fr; Terraube; d/ste €94/198; 🛜🍽) About 18km from Condom on the D42 towards Lectoure, this imposing 17th-century Gascon mansion makes an ideal base for exploring the Gers area. It stands in impressive isolation, surrounded by trees, fields, private gardens and its own lovely pool. There are three traditionally furnished rooms, plus two spacious suites; meals are provided and owner Florence will even pack you a picnic on request.

Château de Pomiro
B&B €€

(☎05 62 69 57 99; www.chateaupomiro.com; d from €150) Once a hunting lodge belonging to the Marquis and Marquise de Noë, this château near Montreal-du-Gers now offers five period bedrooms, full of intriguing antiques and creaky features: the Grande Chambre even has its own huge open fireplace. Around the château, there are 10 acres of wooded grounds to explore.

Languedoc-Roussillon

Includes »

Best Places to Eat

» Jardin des Sens (p723)

» Tamarillos (p724)

» Al Très (p749)

» Neptune (p754)

» La Cantine de Robert (p733)

Best Places to Stay

» Le Cheval Blanc (p713)

» Baudon de Mauny (p722)

» Le Relais des Chartreuses (p751)

» Hôtel du Château (p731)

» Château de Creissels (p744)

Why Go?

Languedoc-Roussillon is really three regions rolled into one. Bordered to the east by sun-baked Provence and to the west by the Pyrenees, it's been a strategic border since Roman times, and the area is littered with reminders of its past, from Gallo-Roman aqueducts to lonely Cathar fortresses. It also boasts its own unique culture, cuisine, festivals and languages, making it feel almost like a miniature country in its own right.

Each of the three areas has a different flavour. Bas-Languedoc (Lower Languedoc) is a land of bullfighting, rugby and robust red wines, and is home to the major towns of Montpellier, Nîmes and fairy-tale Carcassonne. To the north is Haut-Languedoc (Upper Languedoc), a wild landscape of hills, caves, valleys and gorges, ideal for outdoor pursuits. In the far southwest is Roussillon, which in many ways has more in common with Spanish Catalonia than it does with the rest of France.

When to Go
Montpellier

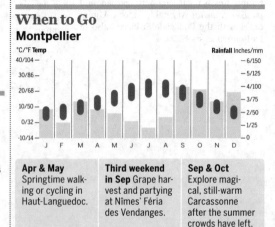

Apr & May Springtime walking or cycling in Haut-Languedoc.

Third weekend in Sep Grape harvest and partying at Nîmes' Féria des Vendanges.

Sep & Oct Explore magical, still-warm Carcassonne after the summer crowds have left.

BAS-LANGUEDOC

The broad, flat plains of Bas-Languedoc boast all of the Languedoc's main towns, as well as its best beaches, richest Roman remains and (arguably) its finest wines.

During the Middle Ages, Bas-Languedoc was largely the property of the counts of Toulouse, but it now forms the modern-day *départements* of Gard and Hérault.

🛈 Getting Around

A single bus journey anywhere within in the Gard *département* costs a flat-rate €1.50. Full timetables are available from **Edgard** (www.edgard-transport.fr).

As always, trains are the fastest way to get between the major towns.

Nîmes

POP 146,500

Nîmes' traffic-clogged, concrete-heavy outskirts provide a pretty uninspiring introduction to this ancient southern city, but push on and you'll discover some of southern France's best-preserved Roman buildings – including a 2000-year-old temple and a magnificent amphitheatre, where bullfights and gladiatorial battles are still staged.

Nîmes has a longstanding rivalry with nearby Montpellier, but it's perhaps best known these days for its contribution to couture – namely the hard-wearing twill fabric known as *serge de Nîmes,* traditionally worn by agricultural labourers right across the Languedoc, and nowadays known to all as denim.

⊙ Sights

Les Arènes   ROMAN SITES
(www.arenes-nimes.com; place des Arènes; adult/child €7.90/6; ⊙9am-8pm Jul-Aug, earlier closing at other times) Nîmes' twin-tiered amphitheatre is one of southwest France's most impressive Roman structures. Built around 100AD, the amphitheatre would have held around 24,000 spectators across four seating tiers; the posher you were, the closer you would have sat to the centre. The arena would have staged gladiatorial contests and public executions, and it's still regularly used for public events – mostly of a less gory nature than in Roman times, although bullfights remain a regular fixture on the calendar.

Inside, the amphitheatre is remarkably well preserved, especially considering its somewhat chequered history of being adapted, modified, plundered for stone and generally abused (the arena even contained a miniature town-within-a-town during the Middle Ages). The seating tiers, interior halls and staircases are still in situ, and there's a small museum which contains replicas of gladiatorial armour. An informative audioguide detailing the building's history is included in the admission price.

A major project is currently underway to clean limescale, lichen and pollution stains from the exterior, and to address some troubling cracks that have appeared in recent years, so there may well be some scaffolding when you visit.

Maison Carrée   ROMAN SITES
(place de la Maison Carrée; adult/child €4.60/3.80; ⊙10am-8pm Jul-Aug, earlier closing at other times) Constructed in gleaming limestone around AD 5, this impressive temple was built to honour Emperor Augustus' two adopted sons. Despite the name, the Maison Carrée (Square House) isn't actually square – to the Romans, 'square' simply meant a building with right angles. The building is beautifully preserved, complete with stately columns and triumphal steps; it's worth paying the admission price to see the building's interior architecture, but it's probably worth skipping the rather lame 3D film on show inside.

Carré d'Art   MUSEUM
(www.carreartmusee.com; place de la Maison Carrée; permanent collection free, exhibitions adult/child €5/3.70; ⊙10am-6pm Tue-Sun) The striking glass-and-steel building facing the Maison Carrée was designed by British architect Sir Norman Foster. Inside is the municipal library and the Musée d'Art Contemporain, with permanent and temporary exhibitions covering art from the 1960s onwards. The rooftop restaurant makes a lovely spot for lunch.

Jardins de la Fontaine   ROMAN SITES
(Tour Magne adult/child €2.80/2.40; ⊙Tour Magne 9.30am-6.30pm) The elegant Jardins de la Fontaine conceal several Roman remains, including the Source de la Fontaine – once the site of a spring, temple and baths – and the crumbling Temple de Diane, located in the gardens' northwest corner.

A 10-minute uphill walk brings you to the crumbling shell of the 30m-high Tour Magne, raised around 15 BC. Built as a display of imperial power, it's the largest of a

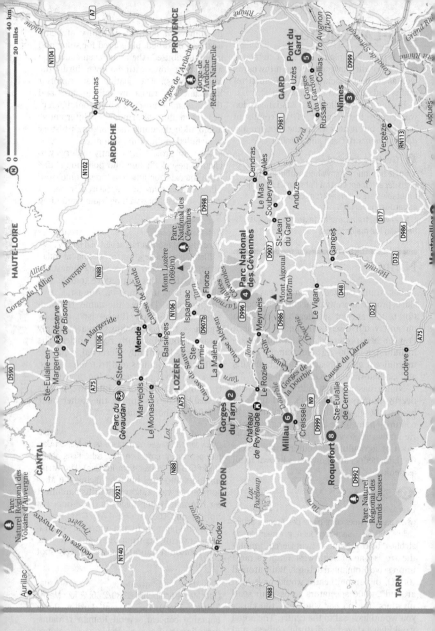

Languedoc-Roussillon Highlights

1 Soak up the art and architecture of Montpellier's renowned **Musée Fabre** (p719)

2 Paddle a canoe through the dramatic **Gorges du Tarn** (p739)

3 Wander around one of France's finest Roman amphitheatres in **Nîmes** (p709)

4 Follow in the footsteps of Robert Louis Stevenson in the **Parc National des Cévennes** (p736)

5 Marvel at the architectural ambition of the **Pont du Gard** (p715) aqueduct

6 Drive across Sir Norman Foster's futuristic **Viaduc de Millau** (p745)

7 Travel back to the Middles Ages among Languedoc's crumbling **Cathar fortresses** (p751)

8 Take a pungent tour around the cheese-filled caves of **Roquefort** (p746)

Nîmes

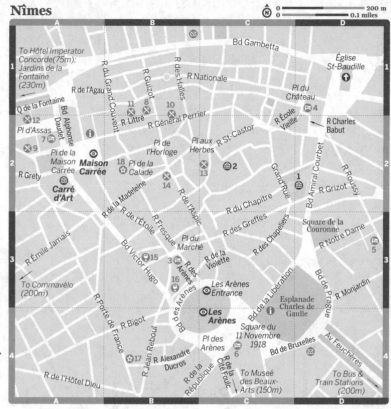

chain of towers that once punctuated the city's 7km-long Roman ramparts. At the top of its 140 steps, there's an orientation table to help you interpret the panorama over Nîmes.

FREE **Musée du Vieux Nîmes**　MUSEUM
(place aux Herbes; ☺10am-6pm Tue-Sun) A mix of old and new at this modest museum: period costumes and furniture, plus pin-ups of denim-sporting celebs such as Elvis, James Dean and Marilyn Monroe. It's housed in the town's 17th-century episcopal palace.

FREE **Musée Archéologique**　ARCHAEOLOGICAL MUSEUM
(13 bd Amiral Courbet; ☺10am-6pm, closed Mon) Nîmes' archaeological museum has a collection of Roman tombs, mosaics and other archaeological artefacts unearthed around the city. The **Musée d'Histoire Naturelle** (Natural History Museum; ☺10am to 6pm, closed Mon) shares the same building.

Musée des Beaux-Arts　ART MUSEUM
(rue de la Cité Foulc; adult/child €5/3.70; ☺10am-6pm, closed Mon) The city's fine-arts museum has a fairly pedestrian collection of Flemish, Italian and French works, although it's worth a look for the fine Roman mosaic that can be viewed from the 1st floor.

✷ Festivals & Events

In summer Nîmes hosts lots of dance, theatre, rock, pop and jazz events; year-round listings are contained in the free *Les Rendez-Vous de Nîmes*.

Les Grands Jeux Romains　EVENT
For two days in mid-April, Romans again take over town with an encampment, staged gladiatorial battles in Les Arènes and a triumphal street parade.

Nîmes

Féria de Pentecôte & Féria des Vendanges   BULLFIGHTING

Nîmes becomes more Spanish than French during its two *férias* (bullfighting festivals): the five-day Féria de Pentecôte (Whitsuntide Festival) in June, and the three-day Féria des Vendanges on the third weekend in September. Each is marked by daily *corridas* (bullfights).

Jeudis de Nîmes   MARKET

Between 6pm and 10.30pm every Thursday in July and August, food markets and live gigs take over Nîmes' squares.

🛏 Sleeping

TOP CHOICE **Le Cheval Blanc**   HOTEL €€

(☎04 66 76 05 22; www.lechevalblanc-nimes. com; 1 place des Arènes; d €115, f €180-210; 🅿) A prime position overlooking Les Arènes and a spare, stripped-back style make this the swishest place to stay in central Nîmes. Bare wood, plaster and stone define the design, and there are several split-level apartments with galley kitchens that are ideal for families or self-caterers. The building itself began life as a textile factory, but it feels deliciously modern now: needless to say, a front room is essential to make the most of the setting.

Hôtel Amphithéâtre   HOTEL €

(☎04 66 67 28 51; www.hoteldelamphitheatre. com; 4 rue des Arènes; s/d €65/85) Tucked away along a narrow backstreet steps from Les Arènes, this tall townhouse hotel has been stylishly renovated in a sleek palette of greys, whites and taupes. The rooms are chic and simple, spread out over several floors and linked by a spiral staircase: some have balconies overlooking place du Marché. It's run by an expat Cornishman and his wife.

La Clapeyrole   B&B, SELF-CONTAINED €€

(☎04 66 26 85 06; 222 Impasse de la Clapeyrole; d per night €120-130, per week €700-900; 🅿) This detached house is a real stunner, lost among the wooded hills above Nîmes, about 10 minutes' drive from the city centre. Modern lines, minimalist decor and a gorgeous pool surrounded by olive trees provide a level of luxury that normally costs twice the price. It's about 7km northeast of town, off the D979.

Royal Hôtel   HOTEL €

(☎04 66 58 28 27; www.royalhotel-nimes.com; 3 blvd Alphonse Daudet; r €60-80; 🅿🛜) This up-market hotel offers both grace and style. Bedrooms have a choice of street views or an outlook over the grand place d'Assas. They're split into standard and superior, all with modern-meets-heritage decor; it's worth bumping up a level for extra space and air-con. The downstairs restaurant, La Bodeguita, offers solid Med-style dining.

Les Jardins Secrets   B&B €€€

(☎04 66 84 82 64; www.jardinssecrets.net; 3 rue Gaston Maruejols; d €195-380, ste €380-450; 🅿) It's wallet-witheringly expensive, but the 'Secret Gardens' is the place to stay in Nîmes if

ⓘ PASS NÎMES ROMAINE

A joint ticket (adult/child €10/7.70) covers admission to Les Arènes, Maison Carrée and Tour Magne, and remains valid for three days.

All three sites have the same closing hours: 8pm in July and August, 7pm in June, 6.30pm in April, May and September, 6pm in March and October, and 5.30pm from November to February.

you're looking for a louche, lavishly over-the-top retreat. It's dripping with 18th-century luxury, from vintage porcelain to antique etchings and upholstered chaise longues. There is a beautiful Romanesque spa and, of course, the gardens are divine – but for these kind of prices, you'd think it would include breakfast and parking (€25 and €20 respectively).

Hôtel des Tuileries   HOTEL €
(☎04 66 21 31 15; www.hoteldestuileries.com; 22 rue Roussy; d €78; 🅿🗲🛜) Look past the boxy exterior and you'll find 11 sweet, candy-coloured rooms at this pleasant hotel, decorated in a mix-and-match palette of creams, crimsons and pistachios. The lift between the four floors is a bit creaky, but the rates are great considering the central location.

Hôtel Imperator Concorde   HOTEL €€€
(☎04 66 21 90 30; http://nimes.concorde-hotels.com; quai de la Fontaine; r €175-260) Expect old-fashioned grandeur at this grande dame, frequented by everyone from famous matadors to literary bigwigs (Hemingway once stayed here). Rooms are filled with hefty drapes and period furnishings, and the elegant restaurant looks over a fountain-filled courtyard.

Hôtel Central   HOTEL €
(☎04 66 67 27 75; www.hotel-central.org; 2 place du Château; d €65-90, f €120) With its squeaky floorboards and floral motifs, this friendly hotel is full of character. Room 20, on the 5th floor, has great rooftop views.

Auberge de Jeunesse   HOSTEL €
(☎04 66 68 03 20; www.hinimes.com; 257 chemin de l'Auberge de Jeunesse, La Cigale; dm/d €15.55/36; ⊙reception 7.30am-1am) It's out in the sticks, 4km from the bus and train stations, but this hostel has lots in its favour: spacious dorms, family rooms, a sweet garden with campsites, and a choice of either self-catering kitchen or cafe. Take bus I, direction Alès or Villeverte, and get off at the Stade stop.

🍴 Eating

Nîmes' gastronomy owes as much to the spicy flavours of Provence as to the meaty richness of the Languedoc.

L'Imprévu   MODERN FRENCH €€
(☎04 66 38 99 59; www.l-imprevu.com; 6 place d'Assas; mains €19.50-27.50; ⊙lunch & dinner) A fine-dining French bistro tucked away in the corner of place d'Assas. The simple, amber-stoned façade looks homey, but the interior is light and contemporary, with swirly modern art, an open-plan kitchen and a cute interior courtyard. There's a posh mix of *terre-et-mer* (surf-and-turf) dishes, mainly served à la carte, although there's usually a limited *menu du jour* chalked on the blackboard outside.

Le Marché sur la Table   MODERN FRENCH €€
(☎04 66 67 22 50; 10 rue Littré; mains €18-22; ⊙Wed-Sun) Warm and welcoming bistro run by husband-and-wife team Éric and Caroline Vidal, with a focus on organic ingredients picked up daily from the nearby market. The interior feels homespun, with plain wooden furniture and stripy table-mats, and there's a quiet courtyard for alfresco dining.

Carré d'Art   GASTRONOMIC €€
(☎04 66 67 52 40; www.restaurant-lecarredart.fr; 2 rue Gaston Boissier; 2-/3-course menu €24/29; ⊙Mon-Sat) Nîmes' top address for gourmet gastronomic dining. Shiny mirrors and moody lighting set the tone in the swish dining room, providing the perfect setting for artfully arranged plates of cod in pepper coulis, or veal in voilet 'essence'.

Au Plaisir des Halles   TRADITIONAL FRENCH €€
(☎04 66 36 01 02; 4 rue Littré; mains €24-30; ⊙Tue-Sat) Unfussy market-fresh dining is the order of the day here, served with an excellent choice of Languedoc wines. The mains are quite expensive, so consider swinging by for the three-course lunch menu (€20). It's in a quiet spot, just along from the covered market.

Self-Catering

There are colourful Thursday evening markets in the old city in July and August. Year-round, Nîmes' covered market (rue Général Perrier) offers riches for the picnic hamper.

Maison Villaret
BOULANGERIE

(13 rue de la Madeleine) This family *boulang-erie* (bakery) makes 25 different kinds of bread, cakes, biscuits and local specialities, such as *caladons* (honey and almond-studded biscuits).

L'Oustaù Nadal
DELICATESSEN

(place aux Herbes; ⊙closed Mon) Goodies such as tapenade, honey and olive oil (including three kinds on tap).

🍸 Drinking

Place aux Herbes, place de l'Horloge and place du Marché are packed with busy cafes.

Grand Café de la Bourse et du Commerce
BAR

(bd des Arènes) This opulent 19th-century cafe opposite Les Arènes is ideal for a leisurely coffee or a pre-dinner cocktail.

Café Olive
BAR

(☎04 66 67 89 10; 22 Blvd Victor Hugo) A lively little nightspot, whose stone walls and dim lighting create a cosy cavern vibe. There are regular gigs and a great choice of wines by the glass.

La Bodeguita
BAR

(place d'Assas; ⊙Mon-Sat) The Royal Hotel's bistro-bar serves Spanish-themed cocktails overlooking place d'Assas.

☆ Entertainment

Les Arènes is the major venue for outdoor spectacles such as concerts, pageants and bullfights.

Ciné Sémaphore
CINEMA

(☎04 66 67 83 11; www.semaphore.free.fr; 25 rue Porte de France) Five screens showing *version originale* (VO, or nondubbed) films.

Théâtre de Nîmes
PERFORMING ARTS

(☎04 66 36 02 04; www.theatredenimes.com; place de la Calade) Renowned venue for drama and music.

ℹ️ Information

Tourist office (☎04 66 58 38 00; www.ot-nimes.fr; 6 rue Auguste; ⊙8.30am-8pm Mon-Fri, 9am-7pm Sat, 10am-6pm Sun Jul & Aug, shorter hours rest of year)

ℹ️ Getting There & Away

AIR Nîmes' **airport** (☎04 66 70 49 49; www.nimes-aeroport.fr), 10km southeast of the city on the A54, is served only by Ryanair, which flies to/from London Luton and Liverpool in the UK.

BICYCLE Commavélo (☎06 07 41 80 61; www.commavelo.com; 28 rue Émile Jamais; ⊙9.30am-1pm & 2-7pm) hires out bikes (per half-day/full day/three days €7/12/30).

BUS The **bus station** (☎04 66 38 59 43; rue Ste-Félicité) is next to the train station. Destinations include the following:

DON'T MISS

PONT DU GARD

Southern France has some fine Roman sites, but for audacious engineering, nothing can top the **Pont du Gard** (☎04 66 37 50 99; www.pontdugard.fr; car & up to 5 passengers €18, after 8pm €10, cyclists & walkers free; ⊙visitors centre & museum 9am-7pm Jun-Sep, to 6pm Mar-May & Sep, to 5pm Oct-Feb, parking lots 9am-1am), 21km northeast of Nîmes. This three-tiered aqueduct was once part of a 50km-long system of water channels, built around 19 BC to transport water from Uzès to Nîmes. The scale is huge: 50m high, 275m long and graced with 35 precision-built arches, the bridge was sturdy enough to carry up to 20,000 cu metres of water per day. Each block was carved by hand and transported here from nearby quarries – no mean feat, considering the largest blocks weight over 5 tonnes.

To put the site in context, the **Musée de la Romanité** provides background on the bridge's construction, while kids can try out educational activities in the **Ludo** play area. Nearby, the 1.4km **Mémoires de Garrigue** walking trail winds upstream through typically Mediterranean scrubland, and offers some of the best bridge views.

There are large car parks on both banks of the river, about 400m walk from the bridge. Parking costs a flat-rate €5.

Crowds can be a real problem in high summer; early evening is usually a great time to visit, especially since parking is free after 7pm and the bridge is stunningly lit after dark.

Several buses stop nearby, including Edgard bus B21 (€6 return, hourly Monday to Friday, four on weekends) from Nîmes to Alès.

OCCITAN

The Languedoc's distinctive language of Occitan is an ancient tongue that is closely related to Catalan. The *langue d'oc* was once widely spoken across most of southern France, while the *langue d'oïl* was the predominant tongue spoken to the north (the words *oc* and *oïl* meant 'yes' in their respective languages).

Occitan reached its zenith during the 12th century, but it was dealt a blow following the Albigensian Crusade (launched in 1208 to suppress the 'heresy' of Catharism), which led to Languedoc's annexation by the French kingdom, and made *langue d'oïl* the realm's official language, effectively banning Occitan from polite discourse and relegating it to the status of a language spoken only by the poor and uneducated.

The *langue d'oïl* subsequently become the basis for modern-day French, but despite the best efforts of the ruling elite to wipe it out, Occitan survived as a distinct language, largely thanks to rural communities keen to hold on to their own regional identity. It enjoyed a literary revival in the 19th century, spearheaded by the poet Frédéric Mistral, who wrote in Occitan's Provençal dialect.

Today Occitan is still widely spoken across southern France, with an estimated 610,000 native speakers, and around a million others who have a basic working knowledge. There are six offically recognised dialects: Languedocien *(lengadocian),* Limousin *(lemosin),* Auvergnat *(auvernhat),* Provençal *(provençau),* Vivaro-Alpine *(vivaroaupenc)* and Gascon *(gascon),* which includes the Aranese subdialect spoken in parts of Spanish Catalonia.

Pont du Gard 30 minutes, five to seven daily in summer

Uzès Bus E52; 45 minutes, four to eight daily

CAR & MOTORCYCLE Avis, Europcar and Hertz have kiosks at the airport and the train station.

TRAIN More than 12 TGVs daily run to/from Paris Gare de Lyon (€52 to €99.70, three hours). Local destinations include the following:

Alès €9, 40 minutes

Arles €8 to €14, 30 minutes

Avignon €9, 30 minutes

Montpellier €9.20, 30 minutes

Sète €13.10, one hour

ⓘ Getting Around

TO/FROM THE AIRPORT An **airport bus** (☎04 66 29 17 27; http://www.nimes-aeroport.fr/en/page/shuttle-car-park-and-access) connects with all flights to/from the train station (€5, 30 minutes). See website for timetables.

TAXI For a cab, call ☎04 66 29 40 11.

Around Nîmes

PERRIER PLANT

Have you ever wondered how they get all the bubbles down into a bottle of Perrier water? Or why the bottle is that distinctive stubby shape? If so, book yourself a tour (in French) of **Perrier's bottling plant** (☎04 66 87 61 01; adult/child €5/2; ⊙tours approx hourly 10am-4pm Mon-Fri) and find out. Located in Vergèze, on the RN113 13km southwest of Nîmes, it fills around 400 million bottles of water each year.

RIVER GARD

The wild and unpredictable River Gard tumbles down from the Cévennes mountains, carving its way through the dramatic Gorges du Gardon before finally emptying out into the Mediterranean. Torrential rains can raise the water level of the river by as much as 5m in a flash, but some sections dry up to almost a dribble during prolonged hot spells.

The best way to explore it is by kayak or canoe. There are several hire companies based in Collias, about 6km upstream from the Pont du Gard, including **Le Tourbillon** (☎04 66 22 85 54; www.canoe-le-tourbillon.com) and **Canoe Collias** (☎04 66 22 87 20; www.canoe-collias.com).

It's an 8km paddle from Collias to the Pont du Gard. Between April and June, you can be dropped further upstream at Russan, and pilot your way for 23km through the dramatic Gorges du Gardon. Count on around €20 for the standard two-hour trip, €35 for the longer ride.

UZÈS
POP 8450

The elegant town of Uzès, 25km northeast of Nîmes, grew fat on the proceeds of three luxurious goods: silk, linen and, bizarrely, liquorice. It's now a major tourist magnet thanks to its graceful renaissance architecture – best seen around the Ducal Palace and the arcaded central square, place aux Herbes, which hosts a lively farmers market every Wednesday and Saturday.

◉ Sights & Activities

Duché CHÂTEAU
(www.duche-uzes.fr; admission €12, incl guided tour adult/12-17yr/7-11yr €17/13/11; ⊙10am-noon & 2-6pm) This fortified château belonged to the dukes of Uzès for more than 1000 years. Its fortified keep, the 12th-century Tour Bermonde, offers a magnificent view across the town's rooftops, and you can take a guided tour (in French) of the ducal apartments and underground cellars.

Jardin Médiéval GARDEN
(Medieval Garden; adult/child €4/2; ⊙10.30am-12.30pm & 2-6pm Apr-Oct) This delightful garden contains a wealth of plants and flowers that served a variety of purposes for their medieval planters: medicinal, nutritional and symbolic.

Musée du Bonbon MUSEUM
(Sweet Museum; Pont des Charrettes; adult/child €7/4; ⊙10am-1pm & 2-6pm Tue-Sun, daily Jul-Sep, closed Jan) Definitely one for the sweet-toothed, this candy museum belonging to Haribo is like a Willy Wonka factory come to life. Take your pick from the rainbow of sweets on offer, or join in with a tasting session – just remember to brush your teeth afterwards, OK?

✤ Festivals & Events

Foire Aux Truffes FOOD FESTIVAL
A full-blown truffle fair, held on the third Sunday in January.

Foire à l'Ail FOOD FESTIVAL
Uzès positively reeks during its garlic fair on 24 June.

Nuits Musicales d'Uzès MUSIC FESTIVAL
An international festival of baroque music and jazz held during the second half of July.

🛏 Sleeping & Eating

Hostellerie Provencale HOTEL €€
(☑04 66 22 11 06; www.hostellerieprovencale.com; 1-3 rue de la Grande Bourgade; d €98-148; 🖹) As its name suggests, this delightful nine-room hotel shimmers with the colours of Provence: terracotta floors, butter-yellow walls, patches of exposed stone. It's a lovely blend of old and new, and the downstairs restaurant, La

Parenthèse, serves good regional cuisine. Breakfast is pricey: €13 in the restaurant or €16 on the terrace.

Château d'Arpaillargues HOTEL €€€
(☑04 66 22 14 48; www.chateaudarpaillargues.com; rue du Château; d €125-240; 🖹🏊) A regal residence, lodged inside an 18th-century château once occupied by Frank Listz' muse, Marie de Flavigny. Rooms range from large to vast, and feature plentiful period features such as fireplaces, beams and flagstone floors: all are decorated in restrained country style. There's a wonderful swimming pool and a very solid restaurant, too. It's 4km from Uzès town centre.

Terroirs DELICATESSEN, CAFE €
(www.enviedeterroirs.com; 5 place aux Herbes; snacks €4-6, platters €10-14; ⊙9am-10.30pm, to 6pm Oct-Mar) This smart deli-cafe has a prime position overlooking the Place aux Herbes. It sells gourmet goods such as honeys, oils, pâtés and foie gras (fattened goose liver), and its platters and sandwiches are perfect lunch fare.

🛍 Shopping

Maison de la Truffe FOOD
(27 place aux Herbes) It's truffles with everything at the Truffle House: oil, rice, vinegar, meats and pâtés are all laced with the pricey tuber. There's even a truffle aperitif.

ℹ Information

Tourist office (☑04 66 22 68 88; www.uzes-tourisme.com; ⊙10am-6pm or 7pm Mon-Fri, 10am-1pm & 2-5pm Sat & Sun, closed Sat afternoon & Sun Oct-May) On Place Albert I, just outside the old quarter.

ℹ Getting There & Away

The bus station – grandly named and in fact merely a bus stop – is on av de la Libération, beside Banque Populaire.

Edgard bus A15 between Avignon (one hour) and Alès (50 minutes) stops in Uzès three to five times daily. There are at least five daily services to/from Nîmes (45 minutes), including the E52.

Alès & Around

POP 41,100

The old industrial town of Alès, 45km from Nîmes and 70km from Montpellier, definitely isn't the most attractive town in the Gard *département*, but it has a good reason for its workaday appearance: it's been a major coal-mining centre since the 13th century, although the last pit closed its shafts back in 1986.

It's looking a lot brighter since the heavy industries moved on, but it probably only warrants a fleeting stop en route to the natural attractions of the nearby Cévennes.

◉ Sights & Activities

Mine Témoin   COAL MINE MUSEUM
(www.mine-temoin.fr; chemin de la Cité Ste-Marie; adult/child €8/5; ☺9.30am-12.30pm & 2-6pm Mar–mid-Nov) To get an insight into the town's long coal-mining heritage, don a safety helmet and take the rattling cage down into the murky tunnels of this disused mine, once used to train apprentice colliers.

The one-hour guided tour explores 700m of underground galleries. It's in French, but English guidebooks are available, although the introductory video is French only. Up top, there are various industrial relics relating to the coal-extraction process,

Remember to wear something warm, since the temperature underground rarely reaches 16°C.

Train à Vapeur des Cévennes   STEAM TRAIN
(www.trainavapeur.com; adult/child return €14/9; ☺Apr-Oct) This atmospheric steam train chugs along a 13km stretch of scenic track between St-Jean du Gard and Anduze. The journey lasts around 40 minutes and there are up to four trains a day in summer.

Bambouseraie de Prafrance   TROPICAL GARDENS
(www.bambouseraie.com; adult/child €8.60/5.10; ☺9.30am-7pm Mar–mid-Nov, closes at 5pm or 6pm in Oct & Nov, closed Dec-Feb) It's over 150 years since the first shoots of this rambling, mature bamboo grove were planted by a spice merchant returning from the tropics. Here in Générargues, 12km southwest of Alès, 150 bamboo species sprout amid aquatic gardens, a Laotian village and a Japanese garden. The Cévennes steam train stops here,.

Musée du Désert   HUGUENOT MUSEUM
(Museum of the Wilderness; www.museedudesert. com; adult/child €5.50/4.50; ☺9.30am-noon & 2-6pm Mar-Nov, open all day Jul & Aug) In the early 1700s, a guerrilla war raged across the Cévennes as Protestant Huguenots took on Louis XIV's Catholic army, in protest of the revocation of the *Edict of Nantes*, which had previously protected many of their rights of religious freedom and worship.

Led by their charismatic leader Roland Laporte, the rebels (known as 'Camisards', after their characteristic shirts, or Camiso in Occitan) fought a valiant two-year battle against the king's better-trained and better-equipped army, but they were eventually crushed, and Laporte and many of his supporters were put to the sword.

Laporte's house in the village of Le Mas Soubeyran, 5.5km north of the Bambouse-raie, now houses the intriguing Musée du Désert, which recounts the history of the Camisard revolt and explores the life and times of its brave young leader. He's still a revered figure for many French protestants: every year thousands of them meet in the village on the first Sunday of September to remember the Camisards' struggle.

La Caracole   SNAIL FARM
(www.lacaracole.fr; adult/child €6/4; ☺tours 4.30pm & 6.30pm Jul & Aug, 3pm & 4.30pm Wed & Sun Apr-Jun & Sep) Only in France could a snail museum actually do good business. Championing itself as a place to explore 'the astonishing, exciting world of the snail', this working snail farm has a museum devoted to the slimy creatures, exploring weighty topics such as the role of snails in religion, art and gastronomy through the centuries.

After the tour (in English and French), there's a free tasting session, or you can pick up takeaway tins of escargots in a choice of tempting sauces.

The farm is in St-Florent sur Auzonnet, 12km from Alès. Take the D904 northwards (towards Aubenas), and look out for the signs.

🛏 Sleeping & Eating

Mas de Rochebelle   B&B €€
(☎04 66 30 57 03; www.masderochebelle.fr; 44 chemin de la Cité Ste-Marie; s €56-66, d €72-92; ✹) Near the Mine Témoin, this welcoming *chambre d'hôte* (B&B) in Alès was once the mine director's residence. It has five attractive rooms and a large garden, where you can wander, swim or simply relax under its magnificent yew tree. No credit cards.

Hôtel Restaurant Le Riche   HOTEL €
(☎04 66 86 00 33; www.leriche.fr; 42 place Pierre Sémard; s/d €57/75; ✹🕲) Alès' hotels leave a bit to be desired, but this is the best of the bunch. It's handy for the train station and has simple modern rooms – but it's mainly worth visiting for its refined restaurant (*menus* €23 to €41), where you can dine on

classic *terroir* cuisine among stucco, cornicing and potted plants.

ℹ️ Information

The Alès **tourist office** (☎04 66 52 32 15; www.ville-ales.fr; place Hôtel de Ville; ⊙9am-noon & 1.30-5.30pm Mon-Sat, also 9.30am-12.30pm Sun Jul & Aug) occupies a modern building set into the shell of a baroque chapel.

ℹ️ Getting There & Away

BUS From the **Gare Routière** (☎04 66 52 31 31; place Pierre Sémard), beside the train station, the A15 bus runs up to five times daily to Uzès (50 minutes) and Avignon (1¾ hours). There's usually one bus daily that heads into the Cévennes in summer, stopping at Florac (1¼ hours).

TRAIN There are regular trains daily to/from Nîmes (€9, 40 minutes), where you can catch fast TGVs on to Montpellier (€16 to €18.80, 1½ hours).

Montpellier

POP 257,100

It might not carry quite the same cachet as some of southern France's cities, but in its own graceful, easy-going way, Montpellier is every bit the equal of Marseille and Nice. With its elegant buildings, grand *hôtels particuliers* (private mansions) and stately boulevards, it's a quietly stylish metropolis with just a hint of Barcelona about its atmospheric old quarter, shady backstreets and leafy squares.

Unlike many other southern towns, Montpellier has no Roman heritage. Instead it was founded in the 10th century by the counts of Toulouse, and later became a prosperous trading port as well as a scholarly centre (Europe's first medical school was founded here in the 12th century).

The population swelled in the 1960s when many French settlers left independent Algeria and settled here, and it's now one of southern France's most multicultural cities – and with students making up over a third of the population, it's also a place that seems eternally young at heart.

Three high-speed tram routes circle around the old quarter before heading out into the suburbs.

⊙ Sights

Montpellier's beating heart is the huge open square of **place de la Comédie**. The city's

ℹ️ CITY CARD

The Montpellier City Card (adult per 1/2/3 days €13/21/27, children half-price), sold at the tourist office, allows free admission to most of the city's main attractions, plus unlimited travel on trams and buses, discounts at many shops, and a place on a guided walking tour.

Note that the standard card doesn't include the Musée Fabre; the version covering the museum's permanent collection costs €16/25/31 for one/two/three days, or €19/27/33 including the Decorative Arts wing.

finest period architecture and *hôtel particuliers* can be found around the old quarter, which lies to the northeast, bordered by the main roads of blvd Henri IV, blvd Foch and blvd Louis Pasteur.

The city's architecture becomes more modern the further you get from the city centre, although it's worth taking a stroll around the neoclassical Antigone housing project, to the east of place de la Comédie. The area was designed by the Catalan architect Ricardo Bofill, but it was the brainchild of the city's controversial mayor Georges Frêche, who remained in power for an impressive 27 years from 1977 to 2004 and inspired admiration and loathing in roughly equal measures.

CITY CENTRE

TOP CHOICE **Musée Fabre** GALLERY
(www.museefabre.fr; 39 bd Bonne Nouvelle; adult/child €6/4, with Département des Art Décoratifs €7/5, 1st Sun of month free; ⊙10am-6pm Tue-Sun) Founded in 1825 by the painter François-Xavier Fabre, and totally renovated to the tune of €61 million between 2002 and 2007, this landmark museum houses one of France's richest collections of European art.

The light, airy galleries are split into three main sections: Old Masters, Modern Movements and Decorative Arts. Highlights of the Old Masters include three paintings by Rubens, a dreamy *Venus & Adonis* by Nicholas Poussin, and a collection of striking works by Jacques-Louis David.

The Modern Movements has a good selection of Romantic paintings by Delacroix, Géricault and Gustave Courbet, and a vibrant, colour-splashed collection by key

Montpellier

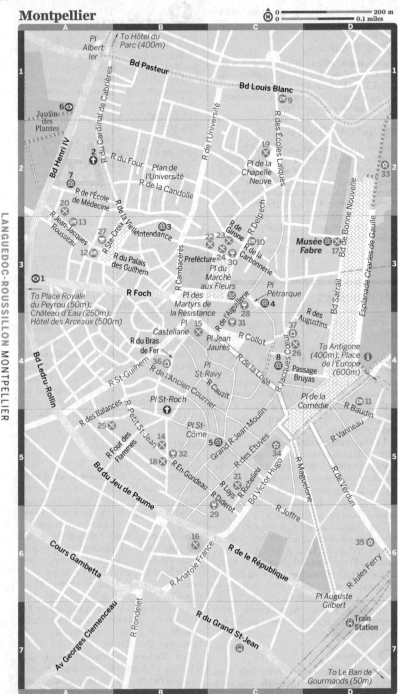

Montpellier

figures including Manet, Degas, Delaunay, Frédéric Bazille and Kees van Dongen.

Ceramics, furniture, faiences and jewellery make up the excellent Decorative Arts section, housed in a lavish former mansion belonging to local notable, Madame Frédéric Sabatier d'Espeyran.

Hôtels Particuliers   HISTORIC MANSION
During the 17th and 18th centuries, Montpellier's wealthier merchants built grand *hôtels particuliers,* often externally quite sober but with resplendent inner courtyards (mostly, alas, closed to the public). The most important houses are marked by a descriptive plaque in French.

Just off place Pétrarque, the Hôtel de Varennes (2 place Pétrarque) is a medieval building given a smart Renaissance makeover, which now contains the city's small history museum, the Musée du Vieux Montpellier (p722).

A short walk south on rue Jacques Coeur is the 17th-century Hôtel des Trésoriers de France (7 rue Jacques Cœur), home to the Musée Languedocien (p722). Just west is

the Hotel St-Côme (Grand Rue Jean Moulin), a suitably grand building for the city's Chamber of Commerce.

Further west near the Cathédrale St-Pierre is the early 17th-century Hôtel de la Vieille Intendance (rue de la Vieille Intendance), built during the reign of Louis XIII for the queen mother and his niece Marie Louise d'Orléans (coloquially known as 'La Grande Mademoiselle'). The house was later occupied occupied by the city's *intendant* (governor), the philosopher Auguste Comte and the Sète-born poet Paul Valéry.

Cathédrale St-Pierre   CATHEDRAL
(bd Henri IV) Montpellier's monumental Cathédrale St-Pierre began life as a church attatched to the 14th-century monastery of St-Benoît, and was raised to cathedral status in 1536. Heavily rebuilt after the Wars of Religion, it's now the seat of the city's archbishops.

Place Royale du Peyrou   ESPLANADE, GARDENS
At the eastern end of this wide, tree-lined esplanade is the Arc de Triomphe (1692). From the Château d'Eau, an elaborate

hexagonal water tower at its western limit, stretches the **Aqueduc de St-Clément**, spectacularly illuminated at night.

Jardin des Plantes GARDEN
(entry on bd Henri IV; ⊙noon-6pm, 8pm Tue-Sun) North of place Royale du Peyrou is Montpellier's delightful botanical garden, France's oldest botanical garden, laid out in 1593 and still used as a research resource by the University of Montpellier.

Musée Languedocien ARCHAEOLOGY MUSEUM
(www.musee-languedocien.com; 7 rue Jacques Cœur; adult/student €7/4; ⊙3-6pm Mon-Sat) This small museum houses a collection of archaeological finds and objets d'art, ranging from ancient Greek and Egyptian statuettes to medieval tapestries and 19th-century faience.

FREE Musée du Vieux Montpellier HISTORY MUSEUM
(2 place Pétrarque; ⊙9.30am-noon & 1.30-5pm Tue-Sat) A storehouse of the city's memorabilia from the Middle Ages to the Revolution.

FREE Musée Atger ART MUSEUM
(2 rue de l'École de Médecine; ⊙1.30-5.45pm Mon, Wed & Fri Sep-Jul) Within the medical faculty of the University of Montpellier, this museum displays a small collection of French, Italian and Flemish drawings.

OUTSKIRTS
There are several attractions to the north of the city centre. Most can be reached by taking tram 1 to the St-Eloi stop, from where a regular shuttle bus (labelled 'La Navette') runs past the zoo gates and on to the Agropolis centre.

FREE Montpellier Parc Zoologique ZOO
(www.zoo.montpellier.fr; 50 ave Agropolis; ⊙10am-6.30pm Easter-Sep, 9am-5pm Oct-Easter) Four kilometres north of the city centre, this excellent zoo – France's second largest – has an enormous population of wild residents that span the world's continents, including African lions, South American spiders, Asian snakes, European deer, Australian emus and more .

Next door to the zoo is the impressive **Serre Amazonienne** (www.zoo.montpellier.fr; 50 av Agropolis; adult/child €6/2.50, audioguide €2; ⊙9am-5pm or 7pm), which replicates the humid world of the Amazon rainforest, complete with prowling piranhas, alligators and

reptiles. Admission to the zoo is free, but there's a charge for the Serre Amazonienne.

Agropolis INTERPRETIVE CENTRE
(www.museum.agropolis.fr; 951 av Agropolis; adult/child €5/free; ⊙10am-12.30pm & 2-6pm Mon-Fri & some weekends) Ten minutes' walk from Montpellier Parc Zoologique, this rather odd agri-museum is all about food and how people around the world grow it. It sounds dull, but it's actually quite interesting, tracing our origins from hunter-gatherer to supermarket shopper.

Odysseum ENTERTAINMENT CENTRE
(www.centre-commercial-odysseum.com; adult/child €12.50/9; ⊙10am-7pm, 8pm or 10pm) This leisure complex has an ice rink, planetarium, multiscreen cinema and the **Aquarium Mare Nostrum** (adult/child €12.50/9; ⊙10am-7pm, 8pm or 10pm), which encompasses 15 different aquatic environments, from polar waters to tropical forests.

⚜ Festivals & Events

Printemps des Comédiens ART FESTIVAL
(www.printempsdescomediens.com) A music, dance and theatre festival in June.

Montpellier Danse DANCE FESTIVAL
(www.montpellierdanse.com) A two-week international dance festival in June or July.

Festival de Radio France et Montpellier MUSIC FESTIVAL
(www.festivalradiofrancemontpellier.com) Top-notch classical music and opera, plus a parallel program of free concerts of all musical genres, in the second half of July.

🛏 Sleeping

TOP CHOICE Baudon de Mauny B&B €€€
(☏04 67 02 21 77; www.baudondemauny.com; 1 rue de la Carbonnerie; d from €150; 🛜) Owners Alain and Nathalie de Bordas have worked magic at this palatial B&B, weaving their taste for modern design seamlessly into the shell of an 18th-century building. Original fireplaces, oak doors and sash windows sit alongside modern furniture and funky angle-poise lamps: the result is a stylish, uncluttered and utterly 21st-century B&B. The most convenient parking is at Parking du Corum, 500m northeast.

Hôtel Le Guilhem HOTEL €€
(☏04 67 52 90 90; www.hotel-le-guilhem.com; 18 rue Jean-Jacques Rousseau; r €96-190; ✳@🛜)

You really couldn't wish to be staying closer to the old quarter than this. Occupying two interconnected 16th-century mansions on a narrow backstreet, this elegant Best Western–owned hotel has rooms split across three 'comfort' categories. The decor's old heritage meets modern boutique – varnished dressers alongside designer fabrics and funky furniture – and Room 100 (€158) has its own little garden terrace. The nearest parking is at Parking Peyrou.

Hôtel du Parc   HOTEL €€
(☑04 67 41 16 49; www.hotelduparc-montpellier. com; 8 rue Achille-Bégé; s €52-89, d €59-105, tr €115; ❄☎) It's a 500m walk from the old quarter, but this charming 18th-century *hôtel particulier* is the place if you're after peace and tranquillity. It's set around its own private garden, and has 19 regal period rooms, accessed via plush carpeted corridors and a sweeping central staircase. There's plenty of parking inside the house's gates, too. Head north from place Albert 1er along av Faubourg Boutonnet.

Mon Jardin en Ville   B&B €€
(☑04 67 64 00 35; www.monjardinenville.com; 23 av de Palavas; s €110-140, d €130-160, tr €185-195; ☎≋) This pamper pad is a trek from the city centre, but the emphasis is on luxury rather than location. The three rooms are glossy-magazine standard: Tulipe Noire is minimalist and monochrome, Orchidée Papillon features blonde wood and neutral tones, and Fleur de Lune has a split-level mezzanine with a mini-office and extra beds. The wooded garden and pool are gorgeous, too.

Hôtel des Arceaux   HOTEL €
(☑04 67 92 03 03; www.hoteldesarceaux.com; 33-35 bd des Arceaux; s €54-65, d €65-70; ❄☎) This delightful town house is in a village-like cranny of Montpellier that's a mere 10-minute walk from the city centre. Enjoy breakfast, brunch or dinner in the tranquil garden.

Hôtel du Palais   HOTEL €€
(☑04 67 60 47 38; www.hoteldupalais-montpellier. fr; 3 rue du Palais des Guilhem; s €72, d €77-92; ☎) An old-town treat offering 26 pretty rooms spread across a tall town house, covered with wrought-iron balconies and window boxes. Warm colours, floral fabrics and arty motifs conjure up a homey feel.

Hôtel de la Comédie   HOTEL €
(☑04 67 58 43 64; www.hotel-montpellier-comedie. com; 1bis rue Baudin; s €49, d €69; ❄☎) The rea-sonable rates belie the fantastically central location here: place de la Comedie is a matter of seconds away. Rooms are plain but perfectly comfy, with crimson bedspreads, double glazing and the odd black-and-white photo, and breakfast (€7) is served in a smart salon next to reception. There's a lift, but no car access.

Auberge de Jeunesse   HOSTEL €
(☑04 67 60 32 22; montpellier@fuaj.org; 2 impasse de la Petite Corraterie; dm incl breakfast €19.60; @) Montpellier's HI-affiliated youth hostel is just off rue des Écoles Laïques. Rooms sleep two to 10 and there's a small garden. Take the tram to the Louis Blanc stop.

🍴 Eating

You'll find plenty of cheap and cheerful eateries on rue de l'Université, rue des Écoles Laïques and the streets interlinking them.

TOP CHOICE **Jardin des Sens**   GASTRONOMIC €€€
(☑04 99 58 38 38; www.jardindessens.com; 11 av St-Lazare; lunch menu €49, dinner mains €45-79, dinner menus €84-173) Loosen that belt buckle: the Jardins des Sens has acquired a mythical status among French foodies. Twice Michelin-starred, it's run by brothers Jacques and Laurent Pourcel, whose passion for contemporary art is mirrored both in their choice of decor and their food, with culinary creations that are as much scuptural as gastronomical. Whether it justifies the stratospheric prices depends on your point of view – but either way, it's an eating experience you won't forget in a hurry.

SMART LIVING

If you're planning on using Montpellier as a base for an extended stay in Languedoc, Smart Living (☑06 76 20 84 70; www.smartliving.fr; apt per night €90-140) offers a selection of swish and very contemporary self-catering apartments around the city. They vary in style, from the sleek, slate-floored 'VIP' apartment, which has its own private wooden-decked patio, to the fancy split-level 'Loft Comédie', set around its own city garden. All come with kitchen, washing machine and wi-fi, and some have private parking. There's usually a two-night minimum; some are only available on a weekly basis.

TOP CHOICE Tamarillos
MODERN FRENCH €€

(📞04 67 60 06 00; http://tamarillos.biz; 2 place du Marché aux Fleurs; lunch mains €18, dinner mains €22-28, menus €38-90) 'A cuisine of fruit and flowers' is the motto of this creative restaurant, and everything on the menu is indeed laced with something fruity or floral: duck in a sauce of acidic fruits, or scallops flavoured with a sprig of violet. Chef Philippe Chapon has twice been named *champion de France de dessert* and taught a young Gordon Ramsay his pastry cooking, so be sure to leave space for the third course – especially if you're ordering the *menus*, which are served by the table, not by the person.

Les Vignes
MODERN FRENCH €€

(📞04 67 60 48 42; www.lesvignesrestaurant.com; 2 rue Bonnier d'Alco; lunch menu €14-22, dinner menus €28-41, tasting menu €75; ☺lunch Mon-Sat, dinner Wed-Sun) Thierry Germain is passionate about two things – the use of local produce and Provençal cooking – and both come to the fore at his smart restaurant in central Montpellier. Cévennes lamb, Mediterranean seafood and bull meat from the Camargue are just some of the ingredients you might find on the menu. The interior is suitably chic – white tablecloths, table lamps, Provençal colours – but the little terrace is the place on a warm summer's night.

Le Grillardin
MEDITERRANEAN €€

(📞04 67 66 24 33; www.restaurantlegrillardin.com; 3 place de la Chapelle Neuve; starters €8 or €12, mains €16 or 22) One of a pocket of attractive bistros in shady place de la Chapelle Neuve, serving zingy Mediterranean cuisine laced with peppers, aubergines, tomatoes, parmesan and basil. One of the house specials is foie gras, served two ways: coated in cereals or covered in honeyed apricots and pine nuts. It's very popular with local diners, particularly for Sunday lunch, so book ahead – especially if you want a prime table on the square.

La Cocotte
BISTRO €€

(📞04 67 86 74 95; 20 rue du Petit St-Jean; menus €21-24; ☺lunch & dinner Thu-Mon) This bolthole bistro is tucked away just off place St-Roch, and makes a reliable spot for bistro dishes served in mini-*cocottes* (earthenware dishes). The salads and *assiette gourmandes* (gourmet platters) are particularly generous, and you can choose to sit on the square or in the brick-vaulted interior. If it's full, try the chaotic Bouchon St-Roch (📞04 67 60 94

18; 14 rue du Plan d'Agde; plat du jour €9.90, menu €14.90; ☺lunch & dinner) across the square.

Le Petit Jardin
FUSION €€

(📞04 67 60 78 78; www.petit-jardin.com; 20 rue Jean-Jacques Rousseau; mains €20-34, 2-course lunch menu €28, 3-course dinner menu €36; ☺lunch & dinner, closed Mon Oct-May) As its name suggests, this lovely bistro overlooks a charmingly green hidden garden, which you can dine in on sunny days, or simply gaze at through big plate-glass windows. It's a sweet setting for modern French food with an Asian flavour.

Thym et Romarin
BISTRO

(📞04 99 61 72 29; 14 rue Roucher; lunch menu €18, mains €14-18; ☺lunch Mon-Fri, dinner Mon-Sat) Homey, no-fuss southern food is what to expect at this streetside bistro, Thyme & Rosemary. Dishes are chalked up daily on the blackboard and take their cue from the market: beef fillet in a garlicky red-wine sauce, perhaps, or meaty *boudin noir* sausage with an apple-mustard sauce. It's simple food in a simple setting, and all the better for it.

Les Bains de Montpellier
SEAFOOD €€

(📞04 67 60 70 87; www.les-bains-de-montpellier.com; 6 rue Richelieu; mains €21-28; ☺Tue-Sat) This former public bathhouse is now a highly recommended restaurant. Tables are set around the old perimeter bathrooms where you can almost hear the gurgle of long-emptied tubs. Seafood is the best choice.

Insensé
BISTRO €€

(📞04 67 58 97 78; Musée Fabre, 39 bd Bonne Nouvelle; menus €22-29; ☺lunch Tue-Sun, dinner Tue-Sat) The Musée Fabre's classy bistro is every bit as tasteful as you might expect: black tables, black tiles and black pepper pots provide a restrained setting, while the menu dabbles in colourful Franco-Mediterranean dishes.

Mesdames Messieurs
MODERN FRENCH €€

(📞04 67 63 49 53; www.mesdamesmessieurs.com; 5 rue de Girone; platters €8-20; ☺lunch Sun, dinner Tue-Sat; 🗲) Stripped floors and moody lighting create a chic ambience at this dressy number, as much wine bar as restaurant. There's a large selection of vintages by the glass, accompanied by tasting platters of Spanish charcuterie, cheese and smoked trout.

Le Ban des Gourmands
TRADITIONAL FRENCH €€

(📞04 67 65 00 85; www.bandesgourmands.com; 5 place Carnot; mains €16-28, menu €28; ☺Tue-Sat) Jacques Delépine serves classic market cuisine at his appealing restaurant, a favourite of locals in the know, tucked away south of the train station.

Tripti Kulai   VEGETARIAN €
(☑04 67 66 30 51; 20 rue Jacques Cœur; mains €4-8, menus €11.50-16; ☺noon-9.30pm Mon-Sat; ☝) A lively veggie-organic cafe with a dining room that's barrel-vaulted. Savoury quiches, salads and gratinées are the mainstays, and the fresh fruit juices are great. It also has a wholefood shop (22 rue Bernard Délicieux) and a takeaway cafe (3 rue Massillian).

Self-Catering
The city's food markets include Halles Castellane (rue de la Loge), which is the biggest, and Halles Laissac (rue Anatole France).

There's a Saturday organic food market under the arches of Aqueduc de St-Clément and a farmers market every Sunday morning on av Samuel de Champlain in the Antigone complex, just east of the city centre.

🍷 Drinking

With nearly 80,000 students, Montpellier has a multitude of places to drink and dance. You'll find dense concentrations around rue En-Gondeau, off Grand Rue Jean Moulin, around place Jean Jaurès and around the intersection of rue de l'Université and rue de la Candolle.

Chez Boris   WINE BAR
(www.chezboris.com; 20 rue de l'Aiguillerie; ☺lunch & dinner Mon-Sat, lunch Sun) Boris' friendly establishment is a mix-and-match place that suits all moods: early-evening aperitif, sit-down dinner or a late-night glass of wine. Rough wood and upturned wine barrels tie in with the oenological atmosphere. There's another branch at 17 bd Sarrail which specialises in locally reared *boeuf d'Aubrac* (Aubrac beef).

Café Latitude   CAFE
(1 rue Ste-Croix; ☺7.30am-8pm Tue-Sat) With its leather chairs and scuffed wood, this chilled cafe overlooking the tree-lined place de la Canourge makes the perfect spot to watch the city roll by over a *café crème*.

L'Heure Bleue   TEAROOM
(1 rue de la Carbonnerie; ☺Tue-Sat) There's a tempting selection of patisseries and fine teas at this refined cafe.

Le Huit   MUSIC BAR
(☑04 67 66 14 18; 8 rue de l'Aiguillerie) Sip cocktails and chilled beers while watching local bands at this hipster hang-out in the old quarter.

In Vino Veritas   WINE BAR
(16 rue Diderot; ☺7pm-midnight) Chandeliers and red-velvet seats create a boudoir vibe here, an ideal setting for sampling Languedoc vintages either by the glass or the bottle.

The Beehive   PUB
(15 rue du Plain d'Age; ☺noon-1am) Brit-themed pub with a French twist and a young crowd. The choice of beers is good, and it gets extra marks for serving proper fish-and-chips in crispy batter.

Le Café de la Mer   GAY BAR
(5 Place du Marché aux Fleurs) One of the city's most venerable gay bars. Ask at the bar for a free map of where else is hot (or not).

☆ Entertainment

For events and gig listings, pick up the weekly free sheet *Sortir à Montpellier*.

Most of the city's big clubs are around Espace Latipolia, about 10km out of town on rote de Palavas. The Amigo (visit www.montpellier-agglo.com & search 'amigo') night bus does a circuit of the main clubs from midnight to 5pm on Thursdays, Fridays and Saturdays, leaving from place d'Europe.

Rockstore   LIVE MUSIC
(☑04 67 06 80 00; www.rockstore.fr; 20 rue de Verdun) You can't miss this long-standing venue – just look out for the tail-fins of the '70s Cadillac jutting out above the entrance. It's one of the city's best places for live gigs, and is often where UK and US indie acts choose to play while on their French tours.

Opéra-Comédie   PERFORMING ARTS
(☑04 67 60 19 80; place de la Comédie) Tickets for Montpellier's theatres are sold at the box office of the Opéra-Comédie.

Le Corum   PERFORMING ARTS
(☑04 67 61 67 61; esplanade Charles de Gaulle) The city's main concert venue and conference centre.

🛍 Shopping

Le Bookshop   BOOKS
(www.lebookshop.com; 8 rue du Bras de Fer) Friendly, well-stocked bookshop with an English-language section.

Les Cinq Continents   BOOKS
(20 rue Jacques Cœur) A specialist travel bookshop.

ℹ Information

Tourist office (✆04 67 60 60 60; www.
ot-montpellier.fr; esplanade Charles de Gaulle;
⊙9am-7.30pm Mon-Fri, 9.30am-6pm Sat &
Sun Jul-Sep, 10am-6pm Mon-Sat, 10am-5pm
Sun Oct-Jun)

ℹ Getting There & Away

AIR Montpellier's **airport** (✆04 67 20 85 00;
www.montpellier.aeroport.fr) is 8km southeast
of town. EasyJet flies to/from London (Gatwick)
and Ryanair to/from Leeds-Bradford.

BUS The **bus station** (✆04 67 92 01 43; rue
du Grand St-Jean) is an easy walk from the train
station.

Most local services provided by **Hérault
Transport** (✆04 34 88 89 99; www.herault
-transport.fr) cost a flat-rate €1.50. Destinations
include the following:

La Grande Motte 20 minutes, half-hourly
Monday to Saturday, every 15 minutes on
weekends. Catch bus 106 from place de France.
Several buses a day continue to Aigues-Mortes.

Palavas-les-Flots 10 to 20 minutes, at least
hourly. Catch the tram to Station Etang l'Or,
then take bus 131.

Sète 55 minutes, hourly Monday to Saturday,
three on Sunday. Bus 102, from Sabines tram
station.

TRAIN

Carcassonne €23.70, 1½ hours, up to 10 daily

Narbonne €15.80, one hour, frequent

Nîmes €8.80, 20 to 30 minutes, frequent

Paris (Gare de Lyon) €49.90 to €108.10, 3½
hours by TGV, at least 10 daily

Perpignan (€21 to 24.70, 1¾ hours, frequent)

ℹ Getting Around

The city's public transport system is run by **TaM**
(✆04 67 22 87 87; www.tam-way.com; 27 rue
Maguelone).

TO/FROM THE AIRPORT The Navette Aéroport (bus 120; one way €5) runs hourly between
the airport and the place de l'Europe tram stop.
Buses from the city to the airport run from
5.50am to 8.30pm, and 8.40am to 11.10pm from
the airport to the city.

BICYCLE Montpellier is hugely bicycle-friendly.
The city's automated bike-hire system, **Vélo-
Magg** (per hr €0.50), has stations across the
city; you'll need a credit or bank card to hire, or
you can buy an access card for €5 from the TaM
office.

CAR & MOTORCYCLE As in most large French
cities, having a car is more a hindrance than a
help in Montpellier. The best idea is to leave your
vehicle in one of the vast car parks beside major
tram stops such as Odysseum; a €4.40 ticket
buys all-day parking and tram tickets into town
for up to five people.

TAXI Ring **Taxis Bleu** (✆04 67 03 20 00) or
Taxis Tram (✆04 67 58 10 10).

TRAM & BUS Christian Lacroix contributed
designs for Montpellier's funky, four-line tram
system. Single tickets (valid on trams and buses) cost €1.40, or a one-day pass costs €3.40.
There are ticket machines at most tram stops, or
you can buy them at the tourist office, the TaM
office or from local newsagents.

Around Montpellier

Strolling around the city centre, it's easy to
forget that Montpellier is actually a coastal
city. Regular buses run to most of the major
beaches.

The closest sand is at Palavas-les-Flots,
12km south of the city and a veritable
Montpellier-on-Sea in summer. Heading
north on the coastal road towards Carnon,
you stand a chance of seeing flamingos hoo-
vering the shallows of the lagoons either
side of the D21.

Carnon itself comes out fairly low in the
charm stakes despite its huge marina. Better to continue hugging the coast along the
D59 (Le Petit Travers) alongside several kilometres of white-sand beach, uncrowded and
without a kiosk or cafe in sight.

About 10km northeast of Carnon is La
Grande Motte, purpose-built on a grand
scale in the 1960s to plug the tourist drain
southwards into Spain. Its architecture, considered revolutionary at the time, now looks
rather heavy-handed, especially compared
to the more authentic nearby fishing port of
Grau du Roi.

Aigues-Mortes, on the western edge of
the Camargue, is another 11km eastwards.

Sète

POP 43,600

Sète is France's largest Mediterranean fishing port and biggest commercial harbour
after Marseille. Established by Louis XIV
in the 17th century, it prospered as the
harbours of Aigues-Mortes and Narbonne,
north and south respectively, were cut off
from the sea by silt deposits.

Huddled beneath Mont St-Clair, Sète has lots in its favour: waterways, beaches and shoals of seafood restaurants, not to mention a network of pretty canals that give it its local nickname, the 'Little Venice of Languedoc' – most notably the Canal du Midi, which ends its 240km journey here from Toulouse.

The town sits at the eastern end of a narrow spit of land, enclosing the saltwater lagoon of L'Étang du Thau and numerous oyster and mussel farms. The town's busy summer beaches unfurl for 12km along the southern side of the lagoon.

◉ Sights & Activities

Musée Paul Valéry   MUSEUM
(www.museepaulvalery-sete.fr; rue François Desnoyer; adult/10-17yr/under 10yr €7/3/free; ⊙9.30am-7pm Apr-Oct, 10am-6pm Nov-Mar, closed Mon year-round) Sète was the birthplace of the symbolist poet Paul Valéry (1871–1945), and the town's main museum houses a huge collection of his works, along with over 700 paintings and 1000 drawings. The local area around Sète features heavily – especially the sea, Valéry's main poetic inspiration. He is buried in the nearby Cimitière Marin.

Musée International des Arts Modestes   ART MUSEUM
(MIAM; www.miam.org; 23 quai Maréchal de Lattre de Tassigny; adult/10-18yr/under 10yr €5/2/free; ⊙9.30am-7pm Apr-Sep, 10am-noon & 2-6pm Tue-Sun Oct-Mar) This offbeat gallery is refreshingly free of big names – here the emphasis is on the art of everyday objects, curated by local artists Hervé di Rosa and Bernard Belluc. From religious icons to kitsch china and travel souvenirs, it's like wandering round a jumble sale curated by an art critic.

Espace Georges Brassens   MUSIC MUSEUM
(67 bd Camille Blanc; adult/child €5/free; ⊙10am-noon & 2-6pm Jun-Sep, closed Mon Oct-May) The town was the childhood home of singer and infinitely more accessible poet Georges Brassens (1921–81), whose mellow voice still speaks at this multimedia space.

BOAT TRIPS
Between April and November, boats chug out around the port and harbour area, and along the southern reaches of the Canal du Midi. Harbour boats also visit the Étang du Thau and the local mussel and oyster farms,

which you can peer at through the boat's glass-bottomed hulls.

The main companies are **Azur Croisières** and **Sète Croisières**, both charging similar prices: around €10/5 per adult/child for a harbour trip, €6/3 for a canal cruise. Canal trips leave from the quai Général Durand, near the boat company's kiosks opposite the tourist office. Harbour trips leave from the Pont de la Savonnerie.

✴ Festivals & Events

Fête de la St-Pierre TRADITIONAL FISHING FESTIVAL
Maritime festival that's also known as the Fête des Pêcheurs (Fisherfolks' Festival). Held over a long weekend in the first half of July.

Fête de la St-Louis TRADITIONAL BOATING FESTIVAL
Six frantic days around 25 August with *joutes nautiques*, where participants in competing boats try to topple each other into the water.

🛏 Sleeping

L'Orque Bleue   HOTEL €€
(☑04 67 74 72 13; www.hotel-orquebleue-sete.com; 10 quai Aspirant Herber; r interior €89-93, canal side €115-125; ⊙closed Jan; ✳🐱) Right on the quayside and prominent among its dowdier neighbours, this hotel occupies a former shipping magnate's mansion, clad throughout in marble. Rooms are reached from the marble-floored lobby via an impressive spiral staircase: the nicest rooms overlook the canal, although you might not appreciate the noise if you're a light sleeper.

Petit-Hôtel Marseillan   B&B €€
(☑06 85 88 95 63; www.petithotel-marseillan.com; 5 bd Lamartine, Marseillan; d €155-195; 🐱🐾) Bright artwork and quirky furniture define this offbeat minihotel, in a former winemaker's house in the neighbouring village of Marseillan, about 9km from Sète's harbour. All five rooms are named after local trees: try Palmier for its spacious layout and Italian shower, or Figuier, with its distressed wood wardrobes and pool-view balcony.

Auberge de Jeunesse   HOSTEL €
(☑04 67 53 46 68; sete@fuaj.org; rue Général Revest; dm incl breakfast €17.20, d €38.50; ⊙Feb–mid-Dec) One kilometre northwest of the tourist office, this hostel has a wooded site with great harbour views and plenty of space for camping. Expect the usual FUAJ

facilities: shop, laundry and self-catering kitchen.

✕ Eating

Fish restaurants line quai Durand and quai Maximin Licciardi all the way from Pont de la Savonnerie to the *criée* (fish market).

La Péniche SEAFOOD €€
(☑04 67 48 64 13; 1 quai des Moulins; mains €13-15, menus €10-22; ☺Mon-Fri, dinner Sat & lunch Sun) Join a mixed crowd of office workers and folks-who-lunch at this converted barge, a fine place for rustic, authentic Sétoise seafood. The four-course *menu du matelot* (sailor's menu; €15) includes the house speciality, *rouille sétoise* – whole baby octopuses smothered in spicy *rouille* sauce (mayonnaise of olive oil, garlic and chillis).

Les Demoiselles Dupuy SEAFOOD €€
(☑04 67 74 03 46; 4 quai Maximin Licciardi; mains €10-18.50; ☺Thu-Tue) This tiny crowded restaurant serves the freshest of seafood at the most reasonable of prices. The oysters, shucked before you, come straight from Les Demoiselles Dupuy's own beds.

❶ Information

Tourist office (☑04 99 04 71 71; www.tourisme-sete.com; 60 Grand' Rue Mario Roustan; ☺9.30am-6pm, to 7.30pm Jul & Aug) Rents out **audioguides** (per route €5) covering six walks (two with English commentary) in and around town.

Agde

POP 21,600

There are really three Agdes: Vieux Agde, the original settlement beside the River Hérault; the fishing port of Grau d'Agde; and Cap d'Agde, a sprawling summer playground, famed for its long beaches and nudist colony.

Of these, Vieux Agde – described by Marco Polo as the 'black pearl of the Mediterranean' – has the most to offer, including some imposing hôtels particuliers and the fortress-like, mainly 12th-century Cathédrale St-Étienne. It's also worth dropping in to the quirky Musée Agathois (5 rue de la Fraternité; adult/child €4.70/1.80; ☺9.30am-6.30pm daily Jul & Aug, 9am-noon & 2-6pm Wed-Mon Sep-Jun), which houses odd artefacts including stuffed birds, antique bedpans and some vintage sextants.

While you're in town, don't miss a meal at the endearingly shabby Lou Pescadou (☑04 67 21 17 10; 18 rue Chassefière; menu €16), which has been serving the same no-fuss five-course *menu* since 1965: fish soup, mussels, pâté, a choice of fish or steak, rounded off with a homemade dessert. There are plenty of fish restaurants along the quay.

Agde's tourist office (☑04 67 62 91 99; www.capdagde.com; ☺10am-noon & 2-6pm daily Jul & Aug, Tue-Sat Sep-Jun) sells tickets for boat trips on the nearby Canal du Midi. Buses run at least hourly to the beaches of Cap d'Agde.

Béziers

POP 74,200

Béziers is a busy provincial town with a long history: founded by the Romans, razed to the ground during the Albigensian Crusade, and now best known at the birthplace of Paul Riquet, the man behind the stately Canal du Midi. There's a fine statue to Béziers' most famous son on allées Paul Riquet, the town's central esplanade, which hosts a flower market every Friday.

Béziers is a bit short on sights, but it's a good place to launch forays along the canal: the 19th-century Pont-Canal aqueduct and the famous stepladder of nine locks known as the Écluses de Fonseranes are both within easy reach.

The town is at its busiest during the weeklong Festa d'Oc, a celebration of Mediterranean music and dance in late July, and the féria, a five-day Spanish-style festival complete with bullfights, held around 15 August.

Of the town's hotels, the Hôtel des Poètes (☑04 67 76 38 66; www.hoteldespoetes.net; 80 allées Paul Riquet; s/d from €45/55; ☎) is the sprucest choice, with feminine, floral rooms spread out over several floors, and a pleasant location down a leafy cul-de-sac.

Regular trains run from Montpellier (€12.30, 45 minutes) en route to Narbonne (€5.40, 15 minutes).

Narbonne

POP 52,500

Once a Roman coastal port but now a whole 13km inland due to silting, Narbonne was once one of the principal cities in Gaul, and the capital of Gallia Narbonensis.

CRUISING ON THE CANAL

The area around Agde, Béziers and Sète makes an ideal place for taking day trips along the stately Canal du Midi, France's most famous man-made waterway.

The traditional way to explore is by barge or narrowboat, but if you just want to do a quick day trip, there are lots of companies offering organised cruises. Bateaux du Soleil (☑04 67 94 08 79; www.bateaux-du-soleil.fr; Port Chassefières, Agde; cruises €10-41) runs commentated trips with or without meals from its base in Agde, while Le Bonpas (☑06 17 54 95 57; www.bonpasmidi.com.sitew.com; Port de Plaisance, Colombiers; per adult/child 1hr cruise €10/7, 2½hr cruise €32/25) offers one-hour, 2½-hour and twilight cruises from Colombiers, just west of Béziers.

If you'd prefer to be your own captain, Eco Canal (☑06 17 64 49 21; www.bateaux-permis-location-34.com) in Villeneuve-lès-Béziers and Rive de France (☑04 67 37 14 60; www.rivedefrance.com; Port de Plaisance) in Colombiers both hire out electric boats from around €25 to €30 per hour for up to five people. They're easy to drive, so you don't need a permit.

The canal's towpaths also make for gorgeous cycling. Most of the main pleasure ports have bike-hire outlets nearby; alternatively, Mellow Vélos (☑04 68 43 38 21; www.mellowvelos.com; 3 place de l'Eglise, Paraza; adult/child per day from €18/9, per week €60/30; ⊗closed Thu) in Paraza near Narbonne will deliver bikes straight to your door (free within a 10km radius, or anywhere in Bas-Languedoc for a small charge).

It's now a fairly uneventful market town, best known for the splendid Cathédrale St-Just (entry on rue Armand Gauthier; ⊗9am-noon & 2-6pm or 7pm) and the ornate art nouveau-era covered market (⊗Mon-Sat). It's also a popular stop-off for boaters on the Canal du Midi.

The town's 2000-year history is explored at the Palais des Archevêques (Archbishops' Palace; ⊗10am-6pm Jun-Sep, 10am-noon & 2-5pm Wed-Mon Oct-May), which houses a collection of interesting archaeological museums. Roman mosaics and stucco paintings are on display at the Musée d'Art et d'Histoire and Musée Archéologique, along with an underground gallery of Gallo-Roman shops in the Horreum, and a collection of impressive Roman masonry in the Musée Lapidaire. The Pass Monuments et Musées (€9 per person) covers all the museums and remains valid for 15 days.

Narbonne's hotels aren't particularly special, but the Demeure de Roquelongue (☑04 68 45 63 57; www.demeure-de-roquelongue.com; 53 ave de Narbonne; d €110-130, f €170; ☎☒) in the nearby village of Saint-André-de-Roquelongue makes a beautiful base, with five royally decorated rooms in a *maison vigneronne* (winemakers' house) dating from 1870.

Frequent trains serve Narbonne en route from Béziers (€5.40, 15 minutes) and Montpellier (€15.80, one hour).

Around Narbonne

Just off the A9, 15km south of Narbonne, is the Réserve Africaine de Sigean (www.reserveafricainesigean.fr; adult/child €28/21; ⊗9am-6.30pm Apr-Sep, earlier closing at other times), where lions, tigers and other 'safari' animals live in semi-liberty. If you arrive by bike or on foot, there's free transport around the reserve.

Carcassonne

POP 49,100

Perched on a rocky hilltop and bristling with zigzag battlements, stout walls and spiky turrets, from afar the fortified city of Carcassonne looks like something out of a children's storybook. It's most people's perfect idea of a medieval castle, and it's undoubtedly an impressive spectacle – not to mention one of the Languedoc's biggest tourist draws.

Sadly, the inside of La Cité, as the old walled town is now known, doesn't quite live up to the fairy-tale façade. With over four million visitors every year, it feels depressingly devoid of any magic and mystery in summer, and the plethora of tacky souvenir shops and cheap cafes does little to contribute to the mystical atmosphere. Time your visit for late in the day, however (or better still for spring or autumn) and the old town

WORTH A TRIP

ABBAYE DE FONTFROIDE

Hidden among woodland 15km south of Narbonne, the magnificent Cistercian abbey of Fontfroide (☑04 68 45 11 08; www.fontfroide.com; abbey, gardens & museum adult/16-25yr/6-15yr €18.50/16/6; ☺10am-5pm) has a history stretching back almost 1000 years. It was founded in 1093 by the Viscount of Narbonne, and during the Middle Ages grew into one of southern France's most powerful ecclesiastical centres. Highlights include the peaceful chapter hall, the refectory and the original monks' dormitory, as well as a terraced rose garden added during the 18th century.

The abbey has been privately owned since 1908, when it was purchased by the French painter Gustave Fayet and his wife Madeleine. Fayet worked tirelessly to restore much of the damage wrought on the abbey during the Revolution, often assisted by his artistic contemporaries such as Odilon Redon, Gaby Bauzil and the musician, artist and *maître-verrier* (glass master) Richard Burgsthal, who contributed some stunning 20th-century stained glass. A small gallery still shows a few of Fayet's works.

Fontfroide also produces its own wine under the Corbières AOC (Appellation d'Origine Contrôlée), which you can sample in the on-site wine shop or, better still, in the refined restaurant, La Table de Fontfroide (☑04 68 41 02 26; latable@fontfroide.com; menus €18.50-38.50; ☺lunch daily year-round, dinner Wed-Sat Jul-Aug).

regains something of its medieval charm – especially along its rickety ramparts, which look out across the Langedoc's sunbaked landscape.

Beneath the old town sprawls the Ville Basse (lower town), an altogether more contemporary grid of grey streets, open squares and busy shops. The two towns are linked by a brace of bridges across the Canal du Midi: the modern Pont-Neuf road bridge and the much older and prettier Pont-Vieux, a pedestrian-only bridge built during the 14th century and rebuilt in the 19th.

◉ Sights & Activities

La Cité WALLED CITY
(Map p734) The hill on which La Cité stands has been fortified countless times across the centuries – by Gauls, Romans, Visigoths, Moors, Franks and Cathars, to name a few. Following the annexation of Roussillon in 1659, the castle's usefulness as a frontier fortress declined and it slowly crumbled into disrepair, but was saved from destruction by the 19th-century architect Viollet-le-Duc, who left his inimitable mark on many of France's medieval landmarks, including Notre Dame in Paris and Vézelay in Burgundy.

The fortified town is ringed by two rampart walls and punctuated by 52 stone towers. The distinctive 'witch's-hat' roofs actually aren't original: they were added by Viollet-le-Duc during La Cite's 19th-century remodelling. The originals would have been much flatter and wouldn't have been topped by slate.

The main entrance to the fortress is beneath the Porte Narbonnaise (Map p734), a great bastion accessed via a cobbled bridge, now home to the Cité's tourist office.

From here, the souvenir-strewn street of rue Cros Mayrevieille leads uphill to place du Château, the heart of the old city, and the imposing Château Comtal (Map p734; adult/child €8.50/free; ☺10am-6.30pm Apr-Sep), built for the viscounts of Carcassonne during the 12th century. The entrance fee includes the castle's rooms, a short explanatory film and a guided tour along the ramparts. Tours are held in English during July and August; at other times you'll have to invest in a multilingual audioguide for €4.50/6 for one/two people.

A little way south of place du Château is the lovely Basilique St-Nazaire (Map p734; ☺9-11.45am & 1.45-5 or 5.30pm), worth a peek for its soaring Gothic transept and vivid rose windows. Haunting plain chant and choral song is provided during the day by an all-male quintet, Le Choeur Doros (Doros Choir).

The tourist office runs 2½-hour guided walking tours (adult/concession €9/7.50; ☺Tue-Sat Apr-Oct) of the old city, leaving from outside the Porte Narbonnaise at 9.30am (in English) and 3pm (in Spanish).

If your pride can bear it, the Petit Train de la Cité (www.petit-train-cite-carcassonne.com; adult/12-17yr/3-11yr €7/6/3; ☺May-Sep) putters around the ramparts and provides an informative mutlilingual commentary, athough a horse-drawn carriage (www.carcassonne-caleches.com; adult/child€7/4; ☉Jul, Aug & school holidays from Apr-Sep) makes a more elegant way to travel.

Canal du Midi Trips   BOAT TRIPS
(Map p732) Down in the Ville Basse, Carcassone Croisières (www.carcassonne-croisiere.com; adult €8.50-11.50, child €6.50-7.50) offers scenic spins along the Canal du Midi, leaving from the quays next to the train station. Trips vary in duration from 1¾ to 2½ hours, and prices vary accordingly. Some trips include a picnic by the river.

Génération VTT   CYCLING
(Map p732; ☎06 09 59 30 85; www.carcassonne.generation-vtt.com; bike hire per 2hr €10-12, per day €18-21; ☉9.30am-12.30pm & 1.30-6.30pm Apr-Oct) Beside the Canal du Midi, this bike-hire outlet runs guided tours covering local culture and gastronomy, or you can rent your own wheels and follow one of the free maps along the canal's peaceful towpaths.

★☆ Festivals & Events

Embrasement de la Cité   BASTILLE DAY
Literally 'Setting La Cité Ablaze', On 14 July at 10.30pm, Carcassonne celebrates Bastille Day with a fireworks display rivalled only by Paris' pyrotechnics.

Festival de Carcassonne   CULTURAL FESTIVAL
(www.festivaldecarcassonne.fr) Brings music, dance and theatre to town for three weeks in July.

🛏 Sleeping

Sleeping inside the old city seems like a romantic idea, but you might think twice once you've lugged your luggage through the summer crowds. Staying outside the walled city is more practical, and there are some super B&Bs and hotels just a stroll away.

TOP CHOICE Hôtel du Château   HOTEL €€€
(Map p734; ☎04 68 11 38 38; www.hotelduchateau.net; 2 rue Camille Saint-Saëns; d €120-280; ❋🛰🏊) You get the best of both worlds at this flashy hotel: knockout night-time views of La Cité's amber ramparts, coupled with the convenience of staying outside the walled city. The 16 rooms are snazzily finished with wood, exposed stone and boutique-style furnishings, and you can admire wonderful castle views from the heated pool and Jacuzzi.

TOP CHOICE La Maison Vieille   B&B €€
(☎04 68 25 77 24; www.la-maison-vieille.com; 8 rue Trivalle; d €85; 🛰) Charm oozes out of every nook and cranny at this amber-stone B&B. The rooms are enormous, and decorated with suprememly good taste: Barbecane in soothing blues, Cité with exposed brick, Prince Noir with a white sofa and in-room rolltop bath. Breakfast is served in the courtyard garden when the sun shines.

Bloc G   B&B €€
(☎04 68 47 58 20; www.bloc-g.com; 112 rue Barbacane; d €90-120; 🛰) Not what you'd expect in Carcassonne – a trendy, minimalist B&B that wouldn't look out of place in Paris' fashionable quarters. It's part bistro, part design gallery, part *chambres urbaines* – the decor's stripped back to the minimum, with stark white walls offset by arty prints and retro bits of furniture, and the downstairs bistro serves excellent regional food and killer coffee. Cosy it isn't – but if you like your sleeps sleek, Bloc G will be right up your boulevard. Best of all, it's right by the Pont Vieux.

Hotel L'Octroi   HOTEL €€
(☎04 68 25 29 08; www.hotel-octroi.fr; 143 rue Trivalle; d €80-115, f €125-210; ❋🛰🏊) One of two sister establishments run by the owners of the Hotel du Château, this is a swish hotel: rooms are resolutely contemporary (punchy puces, acid greens, crazy fabrics) and there's a dinky heated rooftop pool. It's not quite as smart as it thinks it is, but rates are great (at least for Carcassonne).

Hôtel de la Cité   HOTEL €€€
(Map p734; ☎04 68 71 98 71; www.hoteldelacite.orient-express.com; place Auguste Pont; r €300-750; ❋🛰🏊) Prestige with a capital 'p' sums up this neogothic landmark: it takes up almost an entire street of La Cité, features regal rooms crammed with original beams and medieval architecture, and has welcomed numerous film stars, writers and intellectuals over the decades – whether it's actually worth the ludicrous price tag is another matter entirely.

Hôtel Le Donjon   HOTEL €€€
(Map p734; ☎04 68 11 23 00; www.hotel-donjon.fr; 2 rue du Comte Roger; d €135-221, f €250-350; ❋@🛰) Best Western–owned, this former orphanage is one of La Cité's more reasonable options. Comfy rooms overlook either its shady garden or the ramparts, and there's extra space in its sister building, Les Remparts, which has a more modern, city-hotel feel.

Carcassonne

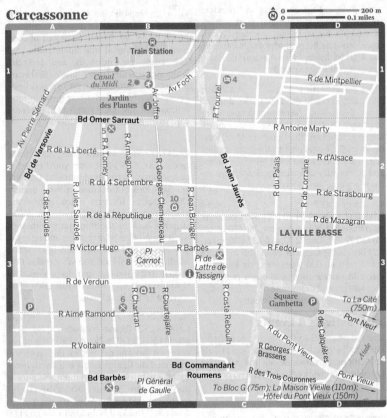

Hôtel du Pont Vieux
HOTEL €€

(Map p734; ☎04 68 25 24 99; www.lacitedecarcas sonne.fr; 32 rue Trivalle; d €66-10, tr & q €114-115, ste €140; 🛜) Creaky, squeaky old stalwart, with musty but cosy rooms hidden behind its battered shutters. Only a few have views of La Cité, and the bathrooms are looking tired; on the plus side, the €7 breakfast is enormous, and there's a garden with olive and fig trees.

Hôtel Astoria
HOTEL €

(Map p732; ☎04 68 25 31 38; www.astoriacarcas sonne.com; 18 rue Tourtel; d €45-72, f €69-99; ✳🛜) Tiny bathrooms and budget bedrooms in pastel colours are what to expect at this modest hotel – but the rates are cheap for Carcassonne, and parking's available for €4 to €6.

Auberge de Jeunesse
HOSTEL €

(Map p734; ☎04 68 25 23 16; carcassonne@ fuaj.org; rue Vicomte Trencavel; dm incl breakfast €21.60; ☉closed Dec; @🛜) This HI hostel is smack-bang in the centre of La Cité – great for atmosphere, not great if you're arriving at the train station. Facilities include four-to six-bed dorms, a spacious kitchen, a lively outside terrace and bike hire. It's very popular, so book well ahead.

🍴 Eating

LA CITÉ

Carcassonne's restaurants are heavy on duck and *cassoulet* (a rich stew of white beans, cubed pork, sausage and sometimes duck). As always in touristy spots, standards can be hit and miss, so it's wise to choose very carefully. Cheap, cheerful cafes line place Marcou.

Au Comte Roger
MODERN FRENCH €€

(Map p734; ☎04 68 11 93 40; www.comteroger. com; 14 rue St-Louis; lunch menu €19-27, dinner menu €38; ☉lunch & dinner) Inside: starched

Carcassonne

white tablecloths, cool grey furniture and sparkling cutlery. Outside: a teeny pergola-covered patio set around an old well. On the table: nouvelle cuisine–style dishes presented with flair by chef Pierre Mesa. The result: just about the best option in La Cité for sit-down dining – just don't expect the portions to be large.

Chez Saskia   BRASSERIE €€
(Map p734; ☑04 68 71 98 71; place Auguste Pont; mains €16-22, menus €40; ⊙lunch & dinner, closed Tue & Wed outside summer) This intimate restaurant next to the Hotel de la Cité offers classic French dining: proper *cassoulet*, lemon sole in beurre blanc, faux filet in a pepper sauce. The walls are covered in photos of the famous faces who have stayed at the hotel: Jacques Chirac, Winston Churchill, Yves Montand and many more.

Auberge de Dame Carcas   TRADITIONAL FRENCH €€
(Map p734; ☑04 68 71 23 23; 3 place du Château; mains €12-15, menus €15-26; ⊙Thu-Tue) Meaty Langedocien fare is the name of the game here – especially lamb, duck *cassoulet* and suckling pig, washed down with plentiful *pichets* (jugs) of local red wine. The grub's not going to win any awards, but the terrace is a pleasantly alfresco place to dine in the heart of La Cité.

L'Écu d'Or   REGIONAL CUISINE €€
(Map p734; ☑04 68 25 49 03; 7-9 rue Porte d'Aude; menus €18-28) Watch your step on the way down to this basement bistro, another

reasonable bet for rustic portions of roast chicken and *cassoulet*. Stone, beams and wonky rafters match the country cuisine.

VILLE BASSE
The restaurants are a lot less touristy down in the Ville Basse.

TOP CHOICE La Cantine de Robert   TRADITIONAL FRENCH €€
(Map p732; ☑04 68 47 37 80; www.restaurant robertrodriguez.com; 39 rue Coste Reboulh; mains €14.50-26; ⊙closed dinner Wed & Sun; ☎) Robert Rodriguez' ramshackle restaurant is just about as French as it gets. It's a retro treat – marble floors, net curtains and Edith Piaf warbling on the stereo – but the organic, locally sourced, pesticide-free ethos is bang on trend. The mustachioed chef loves his Languedocien cuisine, so expect a menu that's heavy on meat, river fish and gamebirds, served with a dash of Michelin flair. He also runs a grocery opposite.

L'Artichaut   BISTRO
(Map p732; ☑04 68 26 56 85; 14 place Carnot; mains €12-16; ⊙lunch & dinner) Lodged in the corner of the Ville Basse's main square, place Carnot, this bright, buzzy bistro offers lots of no-fuss standards, such as classic steak and chips or chicken in a creamy mushroom sauce. It fills up fast with lunchtime workers and predinner drinkers, so arrive early.

Chez Fred   BISTRO €€
(Map p732; ☑04 68 72 02 23; www.chez-fred.fr; 31 bd Omer Sarraut; menus €16-30; ⊙lunch Tue-Fri, dinner daily) Accessed through rickety gates, Fred's cheerful bistro dabbles in a mix of fusion and French flavours, much of which is cooked *à la plancha* (on a hotplate) over ecofriendly coals. There's a sweet courtyard terrace, and the three-course Menu Bistrot Express is super value for lunch at just €11 (the €18 version has more choice).

L'Écurie   TRADITIONAL FRENCH €€
(Map p732; ☑04 68 72 04 04; www.restaurant -lecurie.fr; 43 bd Barbès; mains €14-25; ⊙lunch & dinner Mon-Sat, lunch Sun) Some of the original horse boxes are still in situ at this former stables, all polished woodwork, brass and leather. Expect the usual range of regional cuisine and wines.

Self-Catering
Carcassonne's **covered market** (Map p732; rue Aimé Ramond; ⊙Mon-Sat) is in the Ville

Carcassonne – La Cité

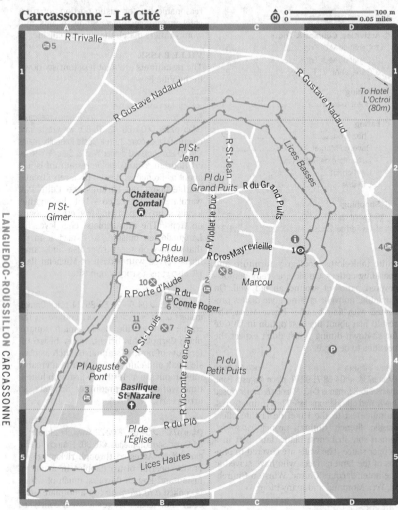

N
0   100 m
0   0.05 miles

Basse, which also hosts an open-air market on place Carnot on Tuesdays, Thursdays and Saturdays.

🛍 Shopping

La Ferme   FOOD & WINE
(Map p732; 26 rue Chartran) A particularly well-stocked delicatessen, piled high with vintage cheeses, wines, sausages and other goods.

Esprit de Sel   HOMEWARES
(Map p732; 10 rue de la République; ⊙Tue-Sat) This eclectic emporium sells everything from retro suitcases to designer lampshades.

L'Art Gourmand   CHOCOLATE
(Map p734; 13 rue St-Louis) Indulge in handmade chocs and umpteen varieties of ice cream at this *confiserie* (confectionery).

ℹ Information

La Cité Tourist Office (Porte Narbonnaise; ⊙9-6pm or 7pm Apr-Sep, only open Sat & Sun Oct-Mar)

Ville Basse Tourist Office (☑04 68 10 24 30; www.carcassonne-tourisme.com; 28 rue de Verdun; ⊙9am-7pm daily Jul-Aug, 9am-6pm Mon-Sat, to 1pm Sun Apr-Jun & Sep-Oct, 9am-12.30pm & 1.30-6pm Mon-Sat Nov-Mar)

Carcassonne – La Cité

❶ Getting There & Away

AIR Ryanair is currently the only airline using Carcassonne's **airport** (☑ 04 68 71 96 46; www.aeroport-carcassonne.com/), 5.5km from town. It serves several UK cities, plus Cork, Dublin, Brussels and Porto.

TRAIN Carcassonne is on the busy main line linking Toulouse (€15, 50 minutes) with Narbonne (€10.50, 30 minutes) and Montpellier (€23.70, 1½ hours). For Perpignan (€19.30, 1½ hours), change in Narbonne.

❶ Getting Around

TO/FROM THE AIRPORT The Navette Aéroport runs to and from the airport (€5, 25 minutes), leaving the train station approximately two hours before each Ryanair departure. By car, take the Carcassonne Ouest A61 motorway exit.

BUS In July and August there's a free shuttle bus between the Ville Basse and the old city every 10 minutes. At other times of year, bus 4 runs roughly every 45 minutes from the train station to La Cité's main entrance.

Kéolis Aude (www.keolisaude.com) runs local buses to destinations including Narbonne (Line 49a, four to six daily Monday to Friday, two or three on Saturday), but schedules are dependent on school timetables, so for most places you're better off catching the train.

CAR & MOTORCYCLE There are several huge car parks around the edge of La Cité (€5 for up to five hours).

HAUT-LANGUEDOC

Haut-Languedoc is a world away from the towns, vineyards and beaches of the broad coastal plain. It's much more sparsely populated, and much of the area is now taken up by the Parc National des Cévennes, a land of craggy gorges, windswept plateaux and dense forest, ideal for those who love being out in the open air.

Parc National des Cévennes

Drier and hotter than the Auvergne to the north, the hills and gorges of the Cévennes have more in common with the climate of the Mediterranean coast than central France. Dotted with isolated hamlets and cut through by rivers and ravines, this vast 910-sq-km expanse of protected landscape was created in 1970, in an attempt to bring ecological stability to an area that had been exploited over several centuries for agriculture, logging, cattle farming and mineral extraction.

The formation of the national park has done a huge amount to protect the Cévennes' astonishing biodiversity. an astounding 2300 plant species and 2410 animal species have been recorded here, and many other previously extinct species have returned here either by reintroduction or by natural migration, including vultures, beavers, otters, roe deer and golden eagles.

Unsurprisingly, the park provides a wealth of opportunity for outdoor activities. In winter there's cross-country skiing on Mont Aigoual and Mont Lozère, while donkey treks are popular in the park in warmer months.

The rest of the park is criss-crossed by over 600km of trails, including a dozen GR (*Grande Randonnée;* hiking) footpaths and 200km of mountain-biking trails: the national park website and the tourist office in Florac are both excellent sources of information. IGN's *Parc National des Cévennes* covers the main area of the park at a scale of 1:100,000.

LANGUEDOC-ROUSSILLON PARC NATIONAL DES CÉVENNES

TRAVELS WITH A DONKEY

The Cévennes were even wilder and more untamed back in October 1878, when Scottish writer Robert Louis Stevenson crossed them with only a donkey, Modestine, for company – a journey recounted in his classic travelogue, *Travels with a Donkey in the Cévennes*.

Accompanied by the wayward Modestine (bought for 65 francs and a glass of brandy), Stevenson took a respectable 12 days to travel the 232km on foot (Modestine carried his gear) from Le Monastier-sur-Gazelle, southeast of Le Puy-en-Velay, to St-Jean du Gard, west of Alès.

» The Stevenson trail is nowadays designated the GR70 and it extends from Le Puy to Alès. The useful Chemin Stevenson (www.chemin-stevenson.org) and GR70 Stevenson (www.gr70-stevenson.com) websites provide planning information, or you can pick up the free pamphlet *Sur Le Chemin de Robert Louis Stevenson* (On the Robert Louis Stevenson Trail) from local tourist offices, which details accommodation en route. The best guidebook is *The Robert Louis Stevenson Trail* by Alan Castle, an indispensable trail companion.

Even better, you don't need a donkey to carry your luggage these days, as the following companies provide baggage-transfer services:

» La Malle Postale (main office ☑04 71 04 21 79, mobile ☑06 67 79 38 16; www.lamalle postale.com; Cussac sur Loire)

» Stevenson Bagages (Taxi Genestier; mobile ☑06 07 29 01 23, office ☑04 66 47 04 66; www.stevenson-bagages.com; Chaudeyrac)

» Transbagages (mobile ☑06 80 06 32 19, office ☑04 66 65 27 75; www.transbagages .com; Mende)

❶ Information

Parc National des Cévennes (eng.cevennes-parcnational.fr) The main park website (English language version), with information on accommodation, activities, nature and much more.

❶ Getting There & Away

Public transport is very limited in the Cévennes: about the only option is the daily bus which shuttles between Alès and Ispagnac, stopping at Florac en route.

By car, the most spectacular route from the east is the Corniche des Cévennes, a ridge road that winds along the mountain crests of the Cévennes for 56km from St-Jean du Gard to Florac.

If you're approaching Florac from Mende and the north, leave the N106 at Balsièges and drive the much quieter, even prettier D31. This crosses the wild, upland Causse de Sauveterre, then descends to Ispagnac, where you turn left to rejoin the main N106.

FLORAC
POP 2000

Sitting in a thickly wooded valley 79km northwest of Alès and 38km southeast of Mende, the rural village of Florac makes a great base for exploring the Parc National des Cévennes and the upper reaches of the Gorges du Tarn.

Lively in summer and moribund for most of the rest of the year, it's draped along the west bank of River Tarnon, one of the tributaries of the Tarn, while the sheer cliffs of the Causse Méjean loom 1000m overhead.

🏃 Activities

Florac is home to the park's main visitor centre, the Maison du Parc National des Cévennes (☑04 66 49 53 01; www.cevennes -parcnational.fr; ⊙9am-6.30pm Jul & Aug, 9.30am-12.15pm & 1.30-5.30pm Mon-Fri Oct-Apr), housed inside the 17th-century Château de Florac. This should be your first port of call for information on activities and general information on things to see and do inside the park. The free *Guide Touristique* covers countless outdoor activities, from short walks to caving and paragliding courses.

WALKING

Florac marks the start of numerous walks. The national-park centre sells around a dozen information kits (€5 each) describing various circular routes, as well as an English-language version of its guidebook *Parc National des Cévennes* (€15).

Ask about Festival Nature, the park's summertime mix of outdoor activities, lectures and field trips.

DONKEY TREKS

Why not follow the lead of Robert Louis Stevenson and hire your very own Modestine? Several companies around Florac are in the donkey-hire business. They include Gentiâne (☎04 66 41 04 16; www.ane-et-randonnee.fr) in Castagnols and Tramontane (☎04 66 45 92 44; www.chevauxdelatramontane.com) in St-Martin de Lansuscle.

Typical prices are €45 to €50 per day and €225 to €250 per week. Though both companies are based outside Florac, they'll transport the donkeys to town or a place of your choosing for a fee (around €1 per kilometre). They can also reserve accommodation – mainly in *gîtes* (walkers' hostels) and B&Bs – along the route.

OTHER ACTIVITIES

Florac's main outdoor activities company is Cévennes Évasion (www.cevennes-evasion.com; 5 place Boyer), which knows plenty of ways to get out and explore the wonderful local landscape. It runs caving, canyon-clambering and rock-climbing expeditions, organises guided or self-guided hiking and cycling trips, and also rents out mountain bikes.

🛏 **Sleeping**

Hôtel Les Gorges du Tarn HOTEL €
(☎04 66 45 00 63; www.hotel-gorgesdutarn.com; 48 rue du Pêcher; d €60-85; ☉Easter-Oct; 🕾) This resolutely modern hotel provides a mix of countrified and contemporary rooms, including a couple of studios that sleep up to four and have cooking facilities. It's fairly functional but affordable. Its restaurant

(*menus* €18 to €29) merits a visit whether or not you're staying here.

Grand Hôtel du Parc HOTEL €
(☎04 66 45 03 05; www.grandhotelduparc.fr; 47 av Jean Monestier; r €52-72; ☉mid-Mar–mid-Nov; 🕾🏊) Shuttered and spacious, this venerable hotel has 55 pleasant rooms, but the main selling points are the gardens, terrace and delightful outdoor pool.

La Carline WALKERS' HOSTEL €
(☎04 66 45 24 54; www.gite-florac.fr; 18 rue du Pêcher; per person €13; ☉Easter-Oct) One for the hikers and bikers: a cute little travellers' *gîte* in an 18th-century house, run by welcoming hosts Monette and Alain Lagrave. Rooms are very simple and share bathrooms, but there are lots of maps and guidebooks to browse, and Alain makes his own jams for the breakfast table.

Camping Le Pont du Tarn CAMPGROUND €
(☎04 66 45 18 26; www.camping-florac.com; sites €14.50-19; ☉Apr-Sep; 🏊) Shady campsite, 2km from Florac beside the D998, where you can swim either in the heated pool or River Tarn, which runs right by.

🍴 **Eating**

In summer pedestrianised L'Esplanade becomes one long dining area where you can eat both well and economically.

La Source du Pêcher MEDITERRANEAN €€
(☎04 66 45 03 01; www.lasourcedupecher.fr; 1 rue de Remuret; menus €16-38; ☉Easter-Oct) One of Florac's prettiest places to dine, with a watery setting and a delightful outside patio. It's

THE GOOD LIFE

Two splendid working farms (both accessible from Florac) make perfect rural retreats, especially for travellers *en famille*.

» La Ferme de la Borie (☎04 66 45 10 90; www.encevennes.com; La Salle Prunet; d €38-47, tr €48-59, q €58-71, meals per adult/child €15/12; ☉Mar-Nov) Run by organic farmer Jean-Christophe Barthes, who cooks up meals using 100% home-grown produce. Depending on the time of year, you can help make traditional cheese or jams, join in with the chestnut and apple harvest, and even learn how to bake the perfect rustic loaf. To get there, turn right onto the narrow C4, signed La Borie, about a kilometre southeast of Florac on the N106.

» La Ferme de Vimbouches (☎04 66 31 56 55; www.causses-cevennes.com/ferme-vimbouches; St Frézal de Ventalon; per adult €53-58, per child €38, incl all meals; ☉Mar-Nov) A bit of a drive from Florac, but worth the trip. It's run by horse trainer Philippe and hostess Cathy, who positively encourage you to join in with life on the farm in a really hands-on way. Borrow a donkey for a day's trekking, visit the pig pen and chicken run, or just get to know the resident horses, rabbits and goats. From Florac, take the N106 towards Alès and, after 27km, turn left onto the D29, following signs for Vimbouches.

CHESTNUT: THE ALL-PURPOSE TREE

As in many rural areas of France, in the Cévennes the humble chestnut tree (known as *l'arbre à pain;* bread tree) once provided the staple food for many families. The nuts were eaten raw, roasted and dried, or ground into flour. Blended with milk or wine, chestnuts were the essence of *bajanat,* a nourishing soup. Part of the harvest would feed the pigs, while the leaves of pruned twigs and branches provided fodder for sheep and goats.

Harvested at ground level with small forks – of chestnut wood, of course – the prickly husks (called *hérissons;* hedgehogs) were removed by being trampled upon in spiky boots. Nowadays chestnuts are the favourite food of the Cévennes' wild boars and still feature in a number of local sauces and desserts.

Nothing was wasted. Sections of hollowed-out trunk would serve as beehives, smaller branches would be woven into baskets, while larger ones were whittled into stakes for fencing or used to build trellises. The wood, hard and resistant to parasites, was used for rafters, rakes and household furniture – everything from the cradle to the coffin.

good for hearty country food – trout fished from local rivers, wild venison, rabbit and game birds shot in the surrounding hills – but as always, the menu tends to be meaty, so vegetarians will struggle. No reservations, so arrive early.

Chez les Paysans REGIONAL CUISINE €
(☑04 66 31 22 07; 3 rue Théophile Roussel; mains €9-14; ☺lunch & dinner May-Oct, lunch Tue-Sat Nov-Apr) No-fuss regional food served in a rustic dining room or a vine-shaded terrace. Its shop has a great selection of produce from small farmers in the local area.

🛍 Shopping

Maison du Pays Cévenol FOOD
(3 rue du Pêcher) Liqueurs, jams, Pélardon cheeses and chestnuts, all with a distinctly local flavour.

Biojour FOOD
(5 rue du Pêcher) Organic produce, from fresh vegetables to hill honey.

ℹ Information
Tourist office (☑04 66 45 01 14; www. vacances-cevennes.com; 33 av Jean Monestier; ☺9am-noon & 2-5pm or 6pm Mon-Sat)

ℹ Getting There & Away
From mid-April to mid-September, one **Transports Reilhes** (☑04 66 45 00 18, 06 60 58 58 10) minibus runs Monday to Saturday from Alès to Florac (€14, 1¼ hours) and nearby Ispagnac (€16). During the rest of the year, it only runs by request on Wednesdays and Saturdays.

MONT LOZÈRE
The 1699m granite lump of Mont Lozère lies about 14km to the northeast of Florac,

and is the highest peak in the Cévennes. It's shrouded in cloud and ice in winter, but in summer thaws out into a land of heather, peat bogs and flowing streams.

It's on the GR68 trail; one of the most popular circular routes begins in Florac and circles round across the mountain's summit via Le Bleymard, Villefort, Génolhac and Saint-Maurice-de-Ventalon, a trip of about six to seven days.

MONT AIGOUAL
About 60km south of Florac is another of the Cévennes' prominent peaks, Mont Aigoual (1567m). It's possible to drive up to the summit and visit the mountain's lofty **observatory** (www.aigoual.fr; ☺10am-7pm Jul-Aug, 10am-1pm & 2-6pm May-Jun & Sep), which affords wraparound views of the central Cévennes – except when the mountain's obscured behind mist and cloud, as it all too frequently is.

Inside, you can learn the science of weather forecasting, cloud formation and lots more. Captions are in French but much of the exhibition is fairly straightforward to follow.

The mountain is about halfway between Florac and Le Vigan, signed off the D18.

Gorges du Tarn

The rushing River Tarn gushes down from the flanks of Mont Lozère, and over the course of countless millennia has carved a series of sheer, craggy slashes into the surrounding rock, known now as the Gorges du Tarn.

Winding southwest for about 50km from the village of Ispagnac, 9km northwest of Florac, this deep ravine marks the boundary between the Causse Méjean to its south and the Causse de Sauveterre to the north.

Until the construction of the riverside road in 1905, the only way to move through the gorges was by boat. Piloting your own kayak is still the best way to experience the amazing scenery – especially in summer, when the road is clogged with almost constant traffic jams.

STE-ÉNIMIE
POP 550

Twenty-seven kilometres from Florac and 56km from Millau, teeny Ste-Énimie is the most convenient base for exploring the gorges. Clinging to the cliffside like a cascade of grey stone, it's a lovely village with a charming cobbled quarter, full of restored timbered houses and stone cottages, as well as the 12th-century Église de Ste-Énimie and the old Halle aux Blés (Flour Market).

Long isolated, the village is now a favoured starting or finishing point for canoe or kayak descents of the Tarn. Many local businesses and B&Bs are only open for the main season between April and October.

Sleeping

Most visitors to the Gorges du Tarn decide to camp, and there are plenty of campgrounds to choose from as you travel down the riverside road.

La Pause B&B €
(05 65 62 63 06; www.hebergement-gorges dutarn.com; rte de Caplac; s €42, d €53-58, f €75-102;) At the gorges' southern end, in the village of Le Rozier, La Pause has three tastefully furnished rooms decorated in pinks and yellows, plus a couple of suites. At breakfast, jams – fig, quince, cherry and more – are all made by your hostess, Pierrette Espinasse. To get there, turn left (signed Capluc) after the village church.

Maison de Marius B&B €
(04 66 44 25 05; www.maisondemarius.fr; 8 rue Pontet; r €65-100) In Quézac, at the northern limit of the gorges near Ispagnac, each of Dany Méjean's delightful rooms has its own character, and you've never tasted sweeter water, drawn from the nearby mineral springs. To get there, skirt the village and follow signs from the church.

Manoir de Montesquiou HOTEL €€
(04 66 48 51 12; www.manoir-montesquiou.com; r €82-117, ste €150;) This turreted manor is a grand affair, in a 16th-century building with a terrace overlooking the bridge in La Malène. The rooms are rather staid in style – half-tester beds, antique furniture – and some are reached via the house's spiral staircase. There's a small cottage annexe in one of the nearby houses, and the manor's refined restaurant serves some of the village's best French food (menus €39 to €50) – ask about the excellent half-board deals.

DON'T MISS

CANOEING IN THE GORGES DU TARN

Riding the River Tarn is best in high summer, when the river is usually low and the descent a lazy trip over mostly calm water. You can canoe as far as the impassable Pas de Soucy, a barrier of boulders about 9km downriver from La Malène (it's possible to carry on further, but you'll have to arrange for your canoe to be transported beyond the barrier).

Tariffs and trip durations depend on how far you want to travel on the river. From Ste-Énimie, destinations include La Malène (€19, 13km, four hours) and Les Baumes Basses (€23, 22km, six hours). If you want an even longer trip, transport can be arranged to enable you to start your trip further upriver in Prades, Montbrun or Ispagnac.

There are scores of companies in Ste-Énimie and La Malène that provide canoe and kayak hire, such as Canoë 2000 (04 66 48 57 71; www.canoe2000.fr), Locanoë (04 66 48 55 57; www.gorges-du-tarn.fr), Méjean Canoë (04 66 48 58 70; www.canoe-mejean .com) and Le Canophile (04 66 48 57 60; www.canoe-tarn.com). It's worth ringing around to ask about seasonal offers and package prices.

If you'd rather someone else did the hard work, Les Bateliers de la Malène (www. gorgesdutarn.com; 4 people €84) will punt you down an 8km stretch of the gorge from La Malène, then drive you back.

❶ Information

The Ste-Énimie **tourist office** (☎04 66 48 53 44; www.gorgesdutarn.net; ☺9.30am-12.30pm & 2-5.30pm or 6pm Mon-Sat, also Sun Jul & Aug) is joined by a small summer-only **annexe** (☺mid-May–Aug) in nearby La Malène.

Mende

POP 13,200

In the northern reaches of the Cévennes, the quiet town of Mende is the capital of Lozère, France's least populous *département*. It's a sleepy, rural town with a lovely medieval quarter that would once have been surrounded by defensive walls.

A few half-hidden towers are all that remains of the ramparts, but the town still boasts some interesting medieval buildings and an improbably large church, the Cathédrale Notre Dame, built in 1368 as the official seat of Mende's bishop. A busy farmers market takes over place Urbain V in front of the cathedral on Saturday mornings.

🛏 Sleeping & Eating

Hôtel de France HOTEL €€
(☎04 66 65 00 04; www.hoteldefrance-mende. com; 9 bd Lucien Arnault; d €78-98; ❄@) Covered in shutters and slate, this classy coaching inn has a tempting assortment of rooms, all huge and some with sweeping views over the garden and valley (two have their own roof terrace). Tiled floors, gleaming bathrooms and plush white-linen beds belie the heritage exterior, and the restaurant (*menus* €29 to €33) is a fine-dining treat.

Hôtel le Commerce HOTEL €
(☎04 66 65 13 73; www.lecommerce-mende.com; 2 bd Henri Bourrillon; s €43, d €52-59; ☎) On the edge of the old town overlooking the busy ring road, this rambling hotel sits above a popular bar, and offers 10 small, simple rooms decked out in gingham checks and beige stripes. The owner Philippe is an ale fanatic, and he keeps up to five different beers on tap at all times.

Le Mazel REGIONAL CUISINE €€
(☎04 66 65 05 33; 25 rue du Collège; mains €14-22, lunch menu €16; ☺closed Wed & dinner Sun) Alongside the restaurant at the Hotel de France, this family-run restaurant is Mende's top place to eat. The menu is small but imaginative, and there's a choice of dining areas: a terracotta-tiled main room and a small conservatory.

Restaurant Les Voûtes GRILL, PIZZA €€
(☎04 66 49 00 05; 13 rue d'Aigues-Passes; menus €25; ☺Mon-Sat) The Vaults enjoys a splendid setting inside an ex-convent. Run by three brothers, it offers salads big enough to fill a fruit bowl, plus the usual range of pizzas and grills.

❶ Information

Tourist office (☎04 66 94 00 23; www. ot-mende.fr; place du Foirail; ☺9am-noon & 2-6pm Mon-Fri, 9am-noon Sat, also Sun Jul & Aug; ☎)

❶ Getting There & Away

BUS Buses leave from the train station, most passing by place du Foirail, beside the tourist office. On weekdays, there's one bus daily to Le Puy-en-Velay (€26, two hours). Three SNCF buses run daily to/from Clermont-Ferrand in the Massif Central (€33, three hours).

TRAIN The train station is 1km north of town across the River Lot. There are two trains daily to Alès (€18.40, 2½ hours).

Around Mende

Parc du Gévaudan NATURE PARK
(www.loupsdugevaudan.com; adult/child €7.50/4.50; ☺10am-6pm or 7pm) Wolves once prowled freely through the Lozère forests but today you'll see them only in this sanctuary, in Ste-Lucie, 7km north of Marvejols. The park sustains around 100 Mongolian, Canadian, Siberian and Polish wolves living in semifreedom.

Réserve de Bisons d'Europe NATURE PARK
(☎04 66 31 40 40; www.bisoneurope.com; ☺10am-5pm or 6pm) Near the small village of Ste-Eulalie-en-Margeride, this nature reserve contains over 40 free-roaming bison. Visits to the reserve are either by horse-drawn carriage (per adult/child €13/7) or, in winter, by sledge (€15.50/8.50). From mid-June to September, you can follow a self-guided 1km walking path (per adult/child €6/4) around the periphery.

Parc Naturel Régional des Grands Causses

The Grands Causses are actually a part of the same geological formation as the Massif Central to the north. Scorched in summer and windswept in winter, these harsh limestone plateaux hold little moisture as water filters through the limestone to form an underground world, ideal for cavers.

The Rivers Tarn, Jonte and Dourbie have sliced deep gorges through the 5000-sq-km plateau, creating four *causses* (plateaux): Sauveterre, Méjean, Noir and Larzac, each slightly different in its geological make-up. One resembles a dark lunar surface, another's like a Scottish moor, while the next is gentler and more fertile. All are eerily empty, save for for the occasional shepherd and his flock – making them perfect for hikers and bikers who like nothing better than to go hours without seeing another soul on the trail.

Millau, at the heart of the park, is a good base for venturing into this wild area. The Gorges de la Jonte, where birds of prey wheel and swoop, skim the park's eastern boundary, rivalling in their rugged splendour the neighbouring and much better known Gorges du Tarn.

◉ Sights

CAUSSE DE SAUVETERRE
The northernmost of the *causses* is a gentle, hilly plateau dotted with a few isolated farms. Every possible patch of fertile earth is cultivated, creating irregular, intricately patterned wheat fields.

CAUSSE MÉJEAN
Causse Méjean, the highest of the *causses,* is also the most barren and isolated. Defined to the north by the Gorges du Tarn and, southwards, by the Gorges de la Jonte, it looms over Florac on its eastern flank. It's a land of poor pasture enriched by fertile depressions, where streams gurgle down into the limestone through sinkholes, funnels and fissures.

This combination of water and limestone has created some spectacular underground scenery. Within the cavern of Aven Armand (www.aven-armand.com; adult/15-20yr /5-15yr €9.45/7.70/6.45; ⊙9.30am-6pm Jul-Aug, 10am-noon & 1.30-5pm Mar-Jun & Sep-Nov), reached by a funicular railway that drops 60 vertical metres, bristles the world's greatest concentration of stalagmites. Guided visits, lasting about 45 minutes (there's an accompanying information sheet in English) head underground about every 20 minutes.

A combination ticket (adult/15 to 20 years/five to 15 years €13.40/10.50/8.65) also includes admission to the gorge at Chaos de Montpellier-le-Vieux in the neighbouring Causse Noir.

CAUSSE NOIR
Rising immediately east of Millau, the 'Black Causse' is best known for the Chaos de Montpellier-le-Vieux (www.montpellierlevieux. com; adult/15-20yr/5-15yr €5.95/4.80/4.20; ⊙9am-7pm Jul-Aug, to 5.30pm Mar-Jun & Sep-Nov), 18km northeast of Millau, overlooking the Gorges de la Dourbie. Water erosion has created more than 120 hectares of tortured limestone formations with fanciful names such as the Sphinx and the Elephant. Three trails, lasting one to three hours, cover the site, as does a tourist train (adult/child €3.85/2.90).

If you're here outside official opening times, there's nothing to stop you wandering around freely.

CAUSSE DU LARZAC
The Causse du Larzac is the largest of the four *causses*. An endless sweep of distant horizons and rocky steppes broken by medieval villages, it's known as the 'French Desert'.

You'll stumble across venerable, fortified villages such as Ste-Eulalie de Cernon, long the capital of the Larzac region, and La Cavalerie, both built by the Knights Templar, a religious military order that distinguished itself during the Crusades.

GORGES DE LA JONTE
The 15km-long Gorges de la Jonte cleave east–west from Meyrueis to Le Rozier, dividing Causse Noir from Causse Méjean.

Just south of the gorge, Dargilan (www. grotte-dargilan.com; adult/child €8.70/5.80; ⊙10am-5.30pm or 6.30pm Apr-Oct) is known as La Grotte Rose (The Pink Cave) for its rosy colouring. The most arresting moment of the one-hour, 1km tour through this vast chasm is a sudden, dazzling exit onto a ledge with a dizzying view of the Gorges de la Jonte way below.

Belvédère des Vautours (Vulture Viewing Point; ☎05 65 62 69 69; www.vautours-lozere.com; adult/child €6.50/3; ⊙10am-5pm or 6pm Apr-Oct) is just west of Le Truel on the D996. Having been all but wiped out by the mid-20th century, these mighty carrion birds have since been reintroduced and nest in large numbers on the sheer cliffs on the opposite side of the valley. You can see the birds gliding through the *causse* from the viewing point, which also has a live video feed from the nesting sites and a multimedia vulture-themed exhibition.

1. Château Royal, Collioure (p753)
The coastal views from this seaside castle, built between 1276 and 1344, are lovely.

2. Pont du Gard (p715)
Built around 19 BC, the huge Roman aqueduct Pont du Gard is a Unesco World Heritage Site.

3. Collioure (p753)
Artistic Collioure provided inspiration for Matisse, Derain, Picasso and Braque.

4. Puilaurens fortress (p752)
The Cathars took refuge in clifftop fortresses during the 13th-century Albigensian Crusade.

ⓘ Information

Parc Naturel Régional des Grands Causses Office (📞05 65 61 35 50; www.parc-grands -causses.fr; 71 bd de l'Ayrolle; ⊙9am-noon or 12.30pm & 2-5pm or 6pm Mon-Fri)

Millau

POP 22,900

Millau (mee-yo) squeezes between the Causse Noir and Causse du Larzac at the confluence of the Rivers Tarn and Dourbie. Though falling just over the border into the Midi-Pyrénées *département* of Aveyron, it's tied to Languedoc historically and culturally. Famous within France for glove-making, it's also the main centre for the Parc Naturel Régional des Grands Causses and a taking-off point for hiking and other outdoor activities – particularly hang-gliding and paragliding, exploiting the uplifting thermals.

⊙ Sights

Le Beffroi BELFRY
(rue Droite; adult/child €3/free; ⊙10am-noon & 2-6pm mid-Jun–Sep) Clamber up this 42m-tall belfry for a great overview of town. From its square base dating from the 12th century, you ascend as it tapers into a 17th-century octagonal tower.

FREE **Causse Gantier** GLOVE MUSEUM
(bd des Gantières; ⊙9.30am-12.30pm & 2-7pm Mon-Sat) Causse Gantier is the only company that still make gloves in Millau (all the rest import their leather goods and trade on their past reputations). You can watch craftspeople at work and buy your very own pair, safe in the knowledge that they're 100% handmade.

Musée de Millau MUSEUM
(www.museedemillau.fr; place Maréchal Foch; adult/chlld €5.40/free; ⊙10am-6pm Jul & Aug, 10am-noon & 2-6pm Mon-Sat rest of year) Small town museum with a mix of fossils, Roman pottery and local history, with plenty of background on Millau's glove-making heritage. A combined ticket (€6.50) includes admission to La Graufesenque archaeological site, or €10 with a trip up the town belfry.

★★ Festivals & Events

Natural Games SPORTS
(www.naturalgames.fr) Festival of outdoor sports such as climbing, canoeing and mountain biking. Held over four days at the end of June.

Millau Jazz Festival MUSIC FESTIVAL
A week of jazz in mid-July.

Mondial de Pétanque PÉTANQUE FESTIVAL
(Pétanque World Series; www.millau-petanque.com) The ultimate pétanque match attracts over 10,000 players in mid-August.

🍽 Sleeping & Eating

TOP CHOICE **Château de Creissels** HOTEL €€
(📞05 65 60 16 59; www.chateau-de-creissels.com; r new wing €71-85, old wing €108; ⊙Mar-Dec) In Creissels, 2km southwest of Millau on the D992, this castle has something of a split personality. Rooms in the 12th-century tower ooze history (parquet floors, fireplaces, oil paintings), while those in the wings exude modern minimalism (sleek showers, stripped-wood floors, designer lamps). The best have balconies overlooking the large garden. The restaurant dishes up excellent regional cusine in a brick-vaulted cellar or on the panoramic terrace. All in all, a spoil.

Hôtel La Capelle HOTEL €
(📞05 65 60 14 72; www.hotel-millau-capelle.com; 7 place de la Capelle; d €39-61, f €49-90; ❄🖂) Budget hotel in a former leather factory, with boxy rooms decked out with crimson bedspreads and generic wallpapers. It's rather short on the wow factor, but the cheap prices will appeal.

La Mangeoire REGIONAL CUISINE €€
(📞05 65 60 13 16; 8 bd de la Capelle; menus €19-48; ⊙Tue-Sun) Millau's oldest restaurant, in the vaults beneath the former city walls, serves hearty regional dishes. Its pride is the open wood-fire barbecue, where hare, partridge and suckling pig roast slowly over the flames.

🛍 Shopping

L'Atelier du Gantier CLOTHING
(21 rue Droite) A wonderful little shop that sells gloves and only gloves of the softest leather. Hit the right moment and you can see staff sewing away at a pair of vintage Singer machines.

ⓘ Information

Tourist Office (📞05 65 60 02 42; www .ot-millau.fr; 1 place du Beffroi; ⊙9.30am-12.30pm & 2-6.30pm, closed Sun Oct-Easter)

ℹ Getting There & Around

BUS Millau's **bus station** (www.gareroutiere demillau.com) is beside the train station; its **information office** (📞05 65 59 89 33) is inside. The R01 bus runs twice daily to Albi (2¼ hours) and Toulouse (3¾ hours). Bus 301/381 runs five or six times daily to Montpellier (2¼ hours), but it's quicker to catch a train.

TRAIN Millau is connected either by SNCF coach or Corail train to destinations including:

Montpellier €27.90, 1¾ hours, one daily

Rodez €12.70, 1¼ hours, five daily

Around Millau

For a bug's-eye view of the world, head for high-tech **Micropolis** (La Cité des Insectes; 📞05 65 58 50 50; www.micropolis-aveyron.com; adult/child Jul-Aug €13/8.90, at other times €11.70/7.90; ⊙10am-7pm Jul & Aug, 10am-6pm Apr-Jun, closed Mon & Tue Feb, Mar & Sep-Nov), where the amazing world of insects is brought fascinatingly to life. You can peer at ant colonies, beehives and fluttering butterflies, see supersized model insects and watch a film about the life of bees in the 3D cinema, then head outside to follow an insect-themed trail.

It's imaginative, informative fun for kids and grown-ups alike: allow at least a couple of hours to do it justice. Follow the signs off the D911, 19km northwest of Millau.

ROUSSILLON

There's a distinctly Spanish flavour about the sunbaked region of Roussillon, with its dusty scrubland, crimson towns and scorching summer temperatures. Sometimes known as French Catalonia, it's really two regions rolled into one: along the coast, busy beach towns and coastal villages sprawl along the Mediterranean, while inland, abandoned abbeys and crumbling Cathar strongholds loom among the fragrant maquis. It's also the land of the Tramontane, a violent wind that howls down from the Pyrenees, cutting to the bone in winter and in summer strong enough to overturn a caravan.

Roussillon's only city is Perpignan, capital of the Pyrénées-Orientales *département*, and a useful base for exploring the wider region.

History

Roussillon's history has been inextricably linked with that of nearby Spain. After flourishing for a time in its own right as the capital of the kingdom of Mallorca, it fell under Aragonese rule for much of the late Middle Ages.

In 1640 the Catalans on both sides of the Pyrenees revolted against the rule of distant Madrid. Peace came in 1659 with the Treaty of the Pyrenees, defining the border between Spain and France once and for all and ceding Roussillon (until then the northern section of Catalonia) to the French, much to the indignation of the locals.

WORTH A TRIP

VIADUC DE MILLAU

France has its share of iconic structures – Mont St-Michel, the Eiffel Tower, the Château de Versailles – but in centuries to come, the majestic **Viaduc de Millau** (www.leviaduc demillau.com; Jul-Aug €8.60, rest of year €6.70) might well stand alongside them in terms of architectural importance. This gravity-defying toll bridge hovers 343m above the Tarn valley, making it one of the world's highest road bridges. Designed by the British architect Sir Norman Foster, it's a work of imagination as much as engineering: seven slender pylons support 2.5km of the A75 motorway, and despite its heavyweight construction (127,000 cu metres of concrete, 19,000 tonnes of steel, 5000 tonnes of cable), the bridge still somehow manages to look like a gossamer thread.

While most people speed across the bridge, it's worth taking the time to explore a little more closely. The **Viaduc Espace** (⊙10am-5pm, to 7pm Apr-Oct), at ground level beneath the viaduct on the D992, explores the story of the bridge's construction and offers 45-minute guided visits (in English on request; per adult/child €6/3.50) around its exhibition garden under the bridge.

For an even more unusual perspective on the bridge, **Bateliers du Viaduc** (www. bateliersduviaduc.com; adult €24, child €9.50-16.50; ⊙every 45 min from 9.45am) runs 1½-hour boat trips along the Tarn from the village of Creissels.

ROQUEFORT

Twenty-five kilometres southwest of Millau, the village of Roquefort is synonymous with its famous blue cheese, produced from local ewe's milk in natural caves around the village. Marbled with distinctive blue-green veins caused by microscopic mushrooms known as *penicillium roquefort* (which are initally grown on leavened bread), this power-fully pungent cheese is one of the region's oldest and most illustrious: it's been protected by royal charter since 1407, and was the first cheese in France to be granted its own AOC in 1925.

Local legend maintains that the cheese was discovered by accident, when a local lad became distracted by a beautiful girl, and left a wheel of cheese behind in one of the villages caves; when he returned, it was covered in mould which fortunately turned out to be surprisingly tasty. It's now France's second-most popular cheese after Comté, with an annual production of around 19,000 tonnes.

There are seven AOC-approved producers in the village, three of which offer free cel-lar visits and tasting sessions. The cellars of four other producers (Roquefort Carles, Le Vieux Berger, Vernières Frères and Les Fromageries Occitanes) aren't open to the public, but they all have shops where you can sample and buy cheeses.

» La Société (www.roquefort-societe.com; adult/child €5/free) Established in 1842, La Société is the largest producer, churning out 70% of the world's supply. One-hour tours of the caves include sampling of the company's three main varieties.

» Le Papillon (www.roquefort-papillon.com; ⊗9.30am-noon & 1-5pm or 6.30pm) Offers free tours of its equally pungent caves, lasting around 45 minutes.

» Gabriel Coulet (www.gabriel-coulet.fr; ⊗9.30-11.50am & 1.30-4.50pm or 5.50pm) You're free to explore the penicillin-streaked caves below the shop, then head upstairs for some tasting.

Parking in Roquefort is a nightmare, so leave your vehicle beside the tourist office (☑05 65 58 56 00; www.roquefort.fr; ⊗9am-5pm or 6pm Mon-Sat, to 7pm daily Jul & Aug), at the western entry to the village.

Although it's no longer officially part of Catalonia, Roussillon retains much of its Catalan identity. The *sardane* folk dance is still performed, and the Catalan language, closely related to Provençal, is still commonly spoken.

❶ Getting Around

Year-round you can travel the length and breadth of Roussillon by bus for no more than €1 per journey. Pick up a leaflet from any tourist office or contact the **Conseil Général Pyrénées-Orientales** (www.cg66.fr/252-les-bus -departementaux.htm; 30 rue Pierre Breton-neau, Perpignan) for route details.

Perpignan

POP 118,200

Nestled in the foothills of the Pyrenees, in many way Perpignan feels as much Spanish as French. Sprawling suburbs radiate out from the tight knot of the old town, with its warren of shady alleys and shabby tene-ments coloured in shades of lemon, peach and tangerine. It feels a little rough around the edges compared to Montpellier or Nîmes along the coast, but it has a distinctly multi-cultural character – Spanish and North Af-rican accents are just as common here as French.

Historically, Perpignan (Perpinyà in Catalan) was capital of the kingdom of Mal-lorca, a Mediterranean power that stretched northwards as far as Montpellier and in-cluded all the Balearic Islands; the Mallor-can kings' palace still stands guard at the southern end of the old town.

The town later became an important commercial centre and remains the third-largest 'Catalan' city after Barcelona and Lleida (Lérida) in Spain.

◉ Sights

Perpignan's old town is surprisingly small, roughly contained within the main ring roads of bd des Pyrénées in the west, bd Thomas Wilson in the north, bd Anatole France in the east and bd Henri Poincaré in the south.

Cars are banned in the town centre, so if you're driving you'll have to park in one of the large municipal car parks on the edges of the old town.

Le Castillet & Casa Païral FOLK MUSEUM
(place de Verdun; adult/child €4/free; ⊙10am-6.30pm Tue-Sun) Perpignan's old town was once encircled by stout walls, designed by the military architect Vauban during the 14th century. Today, all that remains is the red-brick town gate of Le Castillet, located at the northern end of the old town.

Inside the gateway is the Casa Païral, a modest folklore museum which contains various bits and pieces of Catalan ephemera – from traditional bonnets and lace mantillas to an entire 17th-century kitchen.

Place de la Loge TOWN SQUARE
Just south of Le Castillet, the place de la Loge has three fine stone structures, including 14th-century Le Loge de Mer, rebuilt during the Renaissance, which was once Perpignan's stock exchange, then maritime tribunal. Between it and the Palais de la Députation (Place de la Loge), formerly seat of the local parliament, is the Hôtel de Ville (Place de la Loge) with its typically Roussillon red-brick and pebble façade.

Cathédrale St-Jean CATHEDRAL
(place Gambetta; ⊙7.30am-6pm) Perpignan's old town has several intriguing churches, but the most impressive is the Cathédrale St-Jean, begun in 1324 and not completed until 1509. Topped by a typically Provençal wrought-iron bell cage, the cathedral has a flat façade of red brick and smooth, zigzagging river stones.

Inside, the fine carving and ornate altarpiece are characteristically Catalan, and the simple statue of the Virgin and child in the north aisle is a venerated relic for Perpignan believers.

Palais des Rois de Majorque PALACE
(☎04 68 34 48 29; rue des Archers; adult/child €4/2; ⊙10am-6pm Jun-Sep, 9am-5pm Oct-May) The massive brick walls of the Palais des Rois de Majorque (Palace of the Kings of Mallorca) dominates a huge area just to the south of the old town. This grand fortified castle was built in 1276 and was a crowning symbol of Perpignan's late-medieval splendour: it was surrounded by extensive fig and olive groves and a hunting reserve, both lost once Vauban's formidable citadel walls enclosed the palace.

These days the citadel is sparsely furnished, but still its great battlements and strategic defences give a sense of the Mallorcan kings' might – as well as a great view across southern Perpignan all the way to the Mediterranean and the Pyrenees.

The only entrance to the castle is on rue des Archers.

Festivals & Events

As befits a town so close to the Spanish border, Perpignan is strong on fiestas.

Procession de la Sanch RELIGIOUS FESTIVAL
On Good Friday barefoot penitents wearing the *caperutxa* (traditional hooded robes) parade silently through the old city.

Fête de la Sant Joan RELIGIOUS FESTIVAL
A 'sacred' flame is brought down from Mont Canigou. Held around 23 June.

Jeudis de Perpignan STREET CARNIVAL
The streets come alive with stalls, theatre and music of all genres. Thursday evenings, mid-July to mid-August.

Fête du Vin WINE FESTIVAL
To mark this wine festival, a barrel of the year's new production is ceremonially borne to Cathédrale St-Jean to be blessed. During the third weekend in October.

Sleeping

Hôtel de la Loge HOTEL €
(☎04 68 34 41 02; www.hoteldelaloge.fr; 1 rue des Fabriques Nabot; s/d from €47/55; ❄️🛜) On one of the old town's typically narrow streets, this surprisingly spacious hotel feels like an upmarket antique shop: its staircase and hallways are lined with Catalan wood furniture and quirky objets d'art. The rooms are quite variable in size, and they are all furnished in old-fashioned style. Rooms 106 and 206 overlook place de la Loge.

Villa Duflot HOTEL €€€
(☎04 68 56 67 67; www.villa-duflot.com; rond point Albert Donnezan; r €150-190, ste €230-275) It's pricey, but this is the choice for boutique sleeps in Perpignan. The large rooms have a dash of art deco elegance about them, with upholstered furniture, terracotta floors and blocky table lamps. The outside pool is surrounded by parkland filled with conifers and pines, and there's an excellent gourmet restaurant.

Perpignan

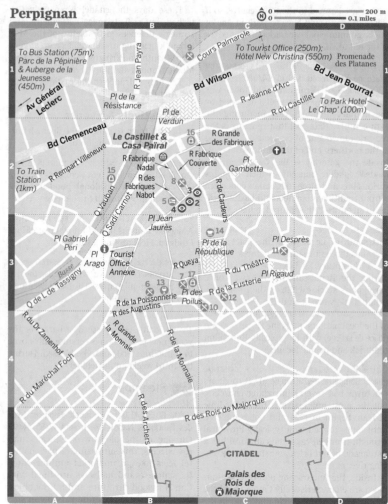

Park Hotel HOTEL €€
(📞04 68 35 14 14; www.parkhotel-fr.com; 18 bd Jean Bourrat; r from €90; ❋@🛜) Each of this pleasant hotel's soundproofed rooms is individually furnished and decorated. The *supérieure* rooms have the most space; numbers ending in 04 and 05 overlook the park. Reputed chef Alexandre Klimenko runs the hotel's Michelin-starred **Le Chap' restaurant**.

Hôtel New Christina HOTEL €€
(📞04 68 35 12 21; www.hotel-newchristina.com; 51 cours Lassus; r €93-105; ❋🛜🏊) The out-side has all the aesthetic appeal of a concrete overpass, but inside this modern hotel are clean, contemporary rooms in blue and beige, with views across a public park from the front. The rooftop pool is a nice surprise, too.

Auberge de Jeunesse HOSTEL €
(📞04 68 34 63 32; perpignan@fuaj.org; allée Marc Pierre; dm incl breakfast €18.60; ⊙Mar–mid-Nov) Perpignan's HI-affiliated youth hostel is just north of Parc de la Pépinière. Facilities include kitchen, lounge and a small garden for barbecues.

Perpignan

✕ Eating

TOP CHOICE **Al Très**   MEDITERRANEAN €€
(☑04 68 34 88 39; 3 rue de la Poissonnerie; mains €19-25, 3-course menu €18; ☺Tue-Sun) This popular alley restaurant is where the locals go for an authentic southern lunch: expect generous portions of steak, shellfish and pork, written up daily on the chalkboard and laced with spicy tomatoes, olives and cayenne pepper. Bustling waiters and buzzy conversation mean the dining room feels cramped when it's busy, but extra tables magically appear in the alley when the weather's warm.

Les Frères Mossés   BISTRO €€
(☑04 68 80 63 31; 14 rue de la Fusterie; mains €16-22; ☺lunch & dinner) Homey bistro with an air of an old-time Parisian diner, with warm colours, tinkling jazz and walls covered in vintage signs. It's a great bet for honest bistro food, and you can watch the chef at work through a hatch into the kitchen.

La Passerelle   SEAFOOD €€
(☑04 68 51 30 65; 1 cours Palmarole; mains €23-30; ☺Tue-Sat & dinner Mon) Seafood is the mainstay at this upmarket place beside the canal, with maritime murals conjuring a shipshape atmosphere. It serves quality oysters and some imaginative fish dishes, but the prices are a bit on the high side considering the somewhat variable quality.

Les Antiquaires   TRADITIONAL FRENCH €€
(☑04 68 34 06 58; place Desprès; mains €14-26, menus €25-44; ☺Tue-Sat & lunch Sun) Old-school in every way – both in terms of the decor, cuisine and clientele. This is one of the old town's oldest addresses for fine French dining, and if you're a sucker for rich, meaty portions of veal, tripe, pork and chicken, liberally doused in wine jus and creamy sauces, you'll be very happy. Beams and vintage bottles contribute to the country ambiance.

Le France   MEDITERRANEAN €€
(☑04 68 51 61 71; place de la Loge; pizzas €10-15, mains €14-25; ☺noon-10pm) Old location, modern style: housed in Perpigan's old stock exchange, this is an attractive cafe-bistro serving wood-fired pizzas and solid, regionally inspired dishes. The interior blends industrial pipes, booth seats and mirrors into the building's brick-vaulted shell.

Laurens'O   ITALIAN €€
(☑04 68 34 66 66; 5 place des Poilus; mains €17-23, lunch menu €17; ☺Tue-Sat) The menu revolves around classic Italian flavours here – foie gras ravioli with truffle cream, or veal Milanese with *beurre noisette* (brown butter) – but the interior is more city diner than country trattoria, with lemon walls, stripy tablecloths and a front terrace sheltered by potted plants.

Casa Sansa   CATALAN €€
(☑04 68 34 21 84; 2 rue Fabrique Nadal; mains €15-21, menus €14-32) Catalan cuisine in a chaotic dining room, secreted along a side alley of the old town. The interior is covered with photos, model ships and chandeliers, but the outside tables feel more convincingly Spanish on a summer's night – perfect for

MOVING ON?

For tips, recommendations and reviews, head to shop.lonelyplanet.com to purchase a downloadable PDF of the Catalonia chapter from Lonely Planet's *Spain* guide.

sampling *baccalà* (salt cod), *riz à l'encre* (squid-ink risotto) and seafood cooked *à la plancha* (on a hot plate).

Espi BOULANGERIE

(43bis quai Vauban) This canalside cafe-cum-*boulangerie* creates delicious chocolates, multicoloured macaroons and tempting ice creams.

Self-Catering

There's a morning fresh fruit and vegetable market on place de la République daily except Monday. Saturday is organic day.

The narrow street of Rue Paratilla is known to locals as 'spice street' thanks to its aromatic delis and groceries, including the family-run **Maison Sala** (1 rue Paratilla; ⊙Tue-Sat & Sun morning), where the shelves are loaded down with bottled olive oils, strings of sausages, pungent cheeses and spicy hams.

Directly opposite, **Les Bonnes Olives** (2bis rue Paratilla; ⊙Mon-Sat & Sun morning) sells olives, anchovies, sundried tomatoes and other Mediterranean goodies, as well as lots of fresh fruit and veg.

🍷 Drinking

The wide open square of place de la République is wall-to-wall cafes, and there's another concentrated cluster overlooking the canal on place Arago.

Républic Café CAFE

(2 place de la République) Arty cafe with a Gaudí-inspired interior, all sinuous shapes and white ceramic fragments.

Les Indigènes WINE BAR

(rue de la Poissonerie) Chilled wine bar, with lots of local vintages served on tables made of upturned oak barrels.

🛍 Shopping

Maison Quinta HOMEWARES

(3 rue Grande des Fabriques; ⊙Tue-Sat) This three-floored town house jumble shop is stacked floor to ceiling with stuff: tasteful, kitsch, utilitarian and antique. it even has its own tearoom.

❶ Information

Tourist office (☑04 68 66 30 30; www.perpignantourisme.com; ⊙10am-7pm Mon-Sat, 10am-4pm Sun mid-Jun–Sep, closes at 6pm weekdays & Sun mid-Sep–Jun) In the Palais des Congrès, off promenade des Platanes.

Tourist office annexe (Espace Palmarium, place Arago; ⊙10am-7pm Mon-Sat, 10am-4pm Sun mid-Jun–Sep, closes at 6pm weekdays & Sun mid-Sep–Jun)

❶ Getting There & Away

AIR Perpignan's **airport** (☑04 68 52 60 70) is 5km northwest of the town centre. Current destinations include Paris (Airfrance); London Stansted, Birmingham, Brussels (Ryanair); Southampton (Flybe); Dublin (Aer Lingus); and Nantes (Volotea).

BUS Buses anywhere in the Pyrénées-Orientales *département* cost a flat-rate €1. Timetables can be downloaded from the Conseil Général Pyrénées-Orientales (p746) website. Perpignan's bus station is on ave Général Leclerc. Destinations include the following:

Côte Vermeille (hourly Monday to Saturday, two on Sunday) Bus 400 trundles to Collioure (50 minutes), Port-Vendres (65 minutes) and Banyuls (80 minutes). A few buses a day continue to Cerbère (1½ hours).

Tech Valley (nine daily Monday to Saturday, two on Sunday) Buses 300/301 and 341 run regularly to Céret (50 minutes).

Têt Valley (every two hours Monday to Saturday) Buses 200/210 and 240/260 run to Prades (one hour) and Vernet-les-Bains (1½ hours).

TRAIN Frequent trains run through the Côte Vermeille towns to Cerbère/Portbou (€8, 35 minutes) on the Spanish border, where you can change for trains to Barcelona (€36.60 to €39, 2½ to 2¾ hours).

In the opposite direction, destinations include Montpellier (€21 to €28, 1¾ hours) via Narbonne (€9.80 to €11.10, 45 minutes) and Béziers (€13 to €15, one hour). For Carcassonne (€19.30, 1¾ hours), change in Narbonne.

Up to nine TGVs run direct to Paris Gare de Lyon (€75 to €110.50, five hours).

❶ Getting Around

TO/FROM THE AIRPORT The Navette Aéroport (bus 7) runs regularly into the town centre for a flat-rate €1.10.

BUS A ticket costs €1.10, a one-day pass is €4.10 and a 10-ticket *carnet* €7.80. Le P'tit Bus is a free hop-on, hop-off minibus that plies a circular route around the town centre.

TAXI **Accueil Perpignan Taxis** (☎04 68 35 15 15)

Around Perpignan

CÉRET

There's one good reason to visit the little town of Céret, settled snugly in the Pyrenean foothills just off the Tech Valley, and that's the excellent Musée d'Art Moderne (www.musee-ceret.com; 8 bd Maréchal Joffre; adult/12-18yr/under 12yr €5.50/3.50/free, incl temporary exhibitions €8/5/free; ☺10am-6pm or 7pm, closed Tue Oct-Apr), with a superb collection including works by Picasso, Braque, Chagall, Matisse, Miró and Dalí – all of whom donated their works for free (Picasso alone donated 53 paintings).

The town also hosts a number of festivals throughout the year, including the Fête de la Cerise (Cherry Festival) in late May, the Céret de Toros Feria (Céret Bull Festival) in early July and the Fêstival de Sardanes in July, which celebrates the traditional Catalan folk dance.

Ten kilometres east of Céret, Le Relais des Chartreuses (☎04 68 83 15 88; www.relais-des-chartreuses.fr; 106 av d'en Carbonner, Le Boulou; s €68-93, d €81-183, ste €200-255) is one of the region's very best places to stay, with gorgeously glossy rooms lodged inside a Catalan-style house dating from the 17th century. The vintage shell of the building is still very much in evidence, but the owners have stripped out all the clutter in favour of a few key antiques, offset by clean lines and soothing colours. A designer outdoor pool and a classy *table d'hôte* (set menu at fixed price) restaurant round off the luxurious ensemble.

Hourly buses run to/from Perpignan (50 minutes). If you're driving, aim for the well-signed Musée d'Art Moderne car park.

TAUTAVEL

The Arago Cave, on the slopes above the village of Tautavel, 27km northwest of Perpignan along the D117, has yielded a human skull, estimated to be 450,000 years old, along with a host of other prehistoric finds. The Musée de Tautavel (Prehistory Museum; ☎04 68 29 07 76; www.450000ans.com; av Jean Jaurès; adult/child incl audioguide €8/4; ☺10am-7pm Jul & Aug, 10am-12.30pm & 2-6pm rest of year) has a full-size reproduction of the cave (in season, cameras show archaeologists excavating the real cave in real time), together with holograms, dioramas, TVs dispensing knowledge from every corner, and lots of fossilised bones and stone tools. The ticket includes entry to a secondary exhibition, at Musée des Premiers Habitants d'Europe, 300m away.

Allow at least 1½ hours to take in both venues.

CATHAR FORTRESSES

When the Albigensian Crusade forced the Cathars into the mountains that once marked the frontier between France and Aragon, they sought refuge in a string of inaccessible strongholds constructed along the border.

Perched on rocky hilltops and flanked by sheer, scrubby cliffs, these crumbling fortresses offer an atmospheric insight into the region's war-ravaged past. Most can be reached after a short, stiff climb from the car park, but this is wild country, and hot as hell in summer – so be sure to pack a hat and plenty of extra water.

You can visit the four major Cathar fortresses in a day's drive from Perpignan.

The Passeport des Sites du Pays Cathare gives reductions to 20 local sites, including several lovely abbeys at St-Hilaire, Lagrasse and Villelongue.

◉ Sights

Château d'Aguilar CASTLE
(☎04 68 45 51 00; Tuchan; adult/child €3.50/1.50; ☺9am-7pm mid-Jun–mid-Sep, 10am-6pm Apr–mid-Jun, 11am-5pm mid-Sep–Nov) Squatting on a low hill near the village of Tuchan, Aguilar features six corner turrets and a hexagonal outer wall. It's the smallest of the castles, and sadly seems to be crumbling fast. The castle is 37km northwest of Perpignan via the D12.

Château de Quéribus CASTLE
(☎04 68 45 03 69; www.cucugnan.fr; Cucugnan; adult/child €5/3, audioguide €4; ☺9am-8pm Jul & Aug, 9.30am-7pm Apr-Jun & Sep, 10am-5pm or 6pm Oct-Mar) Quéribus was the site of the Cathars' last stand in 1255. It's 728m up on a rocky hill, and its interior structure is fairly well preserved: the *salle du pilier* inside the central keep still features Gothic pillars, vaulting and archways. A staircase leads up to the top of the keep, which has a truly mind-blowing view stretching to the Mediterranean and Pyrenees. There's also a small house that has been converted into a theatre, which screens a film documenting

THE CATHARS

Wherever you travel in this corner of France, you'll see references to le Pays Cathare (Cathar Land), a term that harks back to the days when this area was once the main stronghold for the Cathars – a sect of ultradevout Christians known for their strict beliefs and disdain for the teachings of the established church.

The Cathars were the fundamentalists of their day: their name derives from the Greek word *katharos* (meaning 'pure'), and they believed that though humans were fundamentally evil, salvation could be attained through a life of strict religious devotion. Preaching in *langue d'oc*, the local tongue, the sect gained many followers: they believed in a form of reincarnation, rejected the Old Testament and the doctrine of original sin, welcomed women into prominent roles, and remained profoundly critical of the worldliness and corruption of the mainstream church. The most devout of all were the *parfaits* (perfects), who abstained from sex and ate a strictly vegetarian diet.

Inevitably, the Cathars' beliefs placed them on a direct collision course with Rome. In 1208 local lords embarked on a crusade under the instructions of Pope Innocent III, although their motives were as much political as spiritual – crushing the Cathars would enable them to expand their domains by conquering the Languedoc region.

The so-called 'Albigensian Crusade' was a particularly bloody one. After long sieges, the major Cathar centres in Béziers, Carcassonne and Minerve, and the fortresses of Montségur, Quéribus and Peyrepertuse were taken and thousands of people were burned as heretics (in Béziers alone, as many as 20,000 faithful are though to have been slaughtered). The bloodletting continued until 1321, when the burning of the last 'perfect', Guillaume Bélibaste, marked the end of Catharism in Languedoc.

The useful Pays Cathare (www.payscathare.org) website has plenty of background history on the Cathars, and details major sites.

the story of the castle through the eyes of one of the castle's curates.

It's 14km west of Tuchan via the D14.

Château de Peyrepertuse CASTLE
(☑04 68 45 40 55; www.chateau-peyrepertuse.com; Duilhac-sous-Peyrepertuse; adult/child Jul & Aug €8.50/3, rest of year €6/3, audioguide €4; ☺9am-8pm Jul-Aug, to 7pm Apr-Jun & Sep, slightly shorter hours rest of year) Peyrepertuse is the largest of the Cathar castles, teetering on a sheer spur of rock with a drop of 800m on either side. Several of the orginal towers and many sections of ramparts are still standing. In July and August, the castle holds falconry displays and a two-day medieval festival, complete with knights in period armour.

The castle is 6km northwest of Cucugnan via the D14.

Château de Puilaurens CASTLE
(☑04 68 20 65 26; Lapradelle; adult/child €4/2; ☺9am-8pm Jul & Aug, 10am-7pm Jun & Sep, to 5pm or 6pm rest of year) With its tall turrets and lofty hilltop location, Puilaurens is perhaps the most dramatic of the Cathar fortresses. It has the full range of medieval defences: double defensive walls, four corner towers and crenellated battlements. The views from the castle are particularly grand, stretching across sunbaked plains and pine woodland. It's also said to be haunted by the White Lady, a niece of Philippe le Bel.

The castle is about 38km west of Duilhac-sous-Peyrepertuse, via the D117.

Têt Valley

Fruit orchards carpet the lower reaches of the Têt Valley. Beyond the strategic fortress town of Villefranche-de-Conflent, the scenery becomes wilder, more open and undulating as the valley climbs towards Spanish Catalonia and Andorra.

PRADES
POP 6750

Prades is an attractive if uneventful town, with buildings liberally adorned with pink marble from the nearby quarries. At the heart of the Têt Valley and 44km from Perpignan, it's best known for its classical music festival, the Festival Pablo Casals (www.prades-festival-casals.com), held over two weeks in late July or early August, in commemoration of the Spanish cellist Pablo Casals, who settled here after fleeing Franco-controlled Spain.

Prades is mainly a walkers' centre these days, with the most popular target being nearby Mont Canigou (2784m), an emotive symbol for Catalans on both sides of the border. The tourist office (04 68 05 41 02; www.prades-tourisme.fr; 10 place de la République; 9am-noon & 2-6pm Mon-Sat, 10am-noon Sun) on the main square sells various guidebooks and leaflets detailing local walks.

Buses run regularly, departing from Perpignan (p750).

VILLEFRANCHE-DE-CONFLENT
POP 240

The Unesco-listed town of Villefranche sits in a truly breathtaking spot, hemmed in by tall cliffs, at the strategic confluence of the valley of the Rivers Têt and Cady (hence the 'de Conflent' in its name).

It's mainly worth a visit for its dramatic fortress, the Château-Fort Liberia (www.fort -liberia.com; adult/child €7/3.80; 10am-6pm), which dominates the skyline above town. It was originally built by Vauban in 1681, and heavily refortified by Napoléon III between 1850 to 1856. It's still possible to walk along much of the original ramparts, which have survived remarkably intact, with views down the valley through the arrow slits and machicolations.

Apart from the castle, Villefranche's other attraction is the enormously popular Train Jaune (visit www.ter-sncf.com, click on 'Loisirs + Tourisme', select the 'Languedoc Roussillon' region and, under L'offre Ter, choose Le Train Jaune), nicknamed 'The Canary' for obvious reasons, which trundles up from Villefranche-de-Conflent (427m) to Latour de Carol (1231m) through spectacular Pyrenean scenery. It attracts nearly half a million passengers during the peak summer months, and you can't book, so it's wise to arrive a good hour before departure in high summer.

VERNET-LES-BAINS
POP 1550

Busy in summer and a ghost town for the rest of the year, this charming little spa was much frequented by the British aristocracy in the late 19th century. Vernet has the status of *village arboretum* in recognition of more than 300 varieties of trees that flourish on its slopes, many brought here as seeds by overseas visitors.

Vernet is another great base for mountain biking and hiking, particularly for attacking Mont Canigou (2784m). You can get a head start by catching a 4WD up the mountain as far as Les Cortalets (2175m), from where the summit is a three-hour return hike.

The tourist office (04 68 05 55 35; www.ot-vernet -les-bains.fr; 9am-noon & 2-6pm Mon-Fri, also open Sat May-Sep) on place de la République can provide plentiful advice on other local walking and biking routes around Vernet.

Côte Vermeille

The Côte Vermeille (Vermilion Coast) runs south from Collioure to Cerbère on the Spanish border, where the Pyrenees foothills dip to the sea. Against a backdrop of vineyards and pinched between the Mediterranean and the mountains, it's riddled with small, rocky bays and little ports.

Buses and trains run regularly along the coast from Perpignan (p750). If you're driving from Perpignan, leave the N114 at exit 13 and follow the lovely coastal road all the way to Banyuls.

COLLIOURE
POP 3000

Collioure, where boats bob against a backdrop of houses washed in soft pastel colours, is the smallest and most picturesque of the Côte Vermeille resorts. Once Perpignan's port, it found fame in the early 20th century when it inspired the Fauvist artists Henri Matisse and André Derain and later both Picasso and Braque.

In summer Collioure is almost overwhelmed by visitors, drawn by its artistic reputation (there are over 30 galleries and workshops), its wine and the chance to buy the famed Collioure anchovies at source.

Between May and September, leave your car in Parking Cap Dourats, at the top of the hill that plunges down to the village, and take the shuttle bus that runs to the village every 10 minutes. Year-round, there's a large car park behind the castle.

◉ SIGHTS

Château Royal   CASTLE
(04 68 82 06 43; adult/child €4/2; 10am-5.15pm Jun-Sep, to 4.15pm rest of year) Collioure's seaside castle was mostly built between 1276 and 1344 by the counts of Roussillon and the kings of Aragon, and was later occupied by the Majorcan court, although the outer wall was the work of Vauban in the 17th century. The interior displays are fairly unexciting, but the coastal vistas are lovely.

Musée d'Art Moderne
ART MUSEUM

(rte de Port-Vendres; adult/child €2/free; ⊙10am-noon & 2-7pm Jul & Aug, closed Tue rest of year) As befits a town with such long-standing artistic connections, this small museum has a good collection of mainly 20th-century canvases, and holds regular exhibitions by local artists.

FREE Moulin de la Cortina
WINDMILL

This 14th-century windmill is reached after a 20-minute walk through olive and almond groves. Climb to the terrace and admire the Mediterranean vistas of boats, coast and brilliant blue sea.

Fort St-Elme
FORTRESS

(www.fortsaintelme.fr; adult/child €6/free; ⊙10.30am-7pm Apr-Sep, 2.30-5.30pm Oct-Nov) Built in 1552 by the Spanish king Charles V between Collioure and Port-Vendre, this hill-top fort was designed as a key piece of the coastal defence system. It's now mainly used as an exhibition centre.

♣ ACTIVITIES

Le Chemin de Fauvisme
WALKING

'No sky in all France is bluer than that of Collioure. I only have to close the shutters of my room and there before me are all the colours of the Mediterranean.' So effused Henri Matisse (1869–1954), doyen of les Fauves (the Wild Animals), who worked with pure colour, filling their canvases with firm lines and stripes, rectangles and bright splashes.

The Chemin du Fauvisme (Fauvism Trail) is a walking route around Collioure that takes you by 20 reproductions of works that Matisse and his younger colleague André Derain painted while living here. The tourist office carries a French-language guide booklet.

Cellier des Dominicains
WINE TASTING

(☏04 68 82 05 63; www.dominicain.com; Place Orphila; ⊙9am-noon & 2-6pm or 7pm Apr-Sep, closed Sun Oct-Mar) This former monk's cellar now showcases vintages from over 150 local vignerons (winegrowers).

⨼ SLEEPING

Hôtel Casa Pairal
HOTEL €€

(☏04 68 82 05 81; www.hotel-casa-pairal.com; Impasse des Palmiers; r from €89; ❀🐾🕷) Set around a divine courtyard garden with its own fountain, this elegant house was built for a Catalan family in the 19th century, and it has heritage in spades, from the wrought-iron gates right up to the slate-topped roof.

Rooms won't be to everyone's taste, awash with country colours and flock wallpapers, and squeezed into odd shapes to accommodate the antique architecture.

Hôtel Princes des Catalognes
HOTEL €€

(☏04 68 98 30 00; www.hotel-princescatalogne.com; rue des Palmiers; d €58-89, f €120-150; ❀🐾) While it doesn't have much of a sea view, this modern hotel makes up for it by offering some of the most reasonable rates in Collioure – even in summer a double won't set you back more than €90. The decor is clean and fresh, if a touch bland, but with only 15 rooms it doesn't feel crowded even when full.

✗ EATING

TOP CHOICE Neptune
GASTRONOMIC €€€

(☏04 68 82 02 27; www.leneptune-collioure.com; 9 route de Port Vendres; menus €39, €59 or €79; ⊙closed Mon & Tue lunch year-round, also closed Tue dinner & Wed Oct-May) Collioure's long-standing address for gourmet food, Michelin-starred, and with prices and presentation to match. It's especially strong on seafood with a Catalan kick: langoustines, oysters, turbot and monkfish all feature on the three set menus, and the 'Bacchus et Neptune' steps up the gourmet ante with veal, foie gras and four glasses of wine chosen by the sommelier. The dining room may be too fussy for some, so you might prefer to head to the super seaside terrace overlooking the bay.

La 5ème Péché
FUSION €€€

(☏04 68 98 09 76; 18 rue Fraternité; lunch menu €18-24, dinner menu €34) Nippon meets France at this creative fusion restaurant, where classic French seafood is treated with a dash of Japanese flair and flavour. Run by chef Iijima Masashi, it's a creative place to dine, with exotic versions of tuna, swordfish, crab and sea bream finding their way onto the ever-changing menu. The dining room is small, buzzy and busy – book ahead.

❶ Information

Tourist Office (☏04 68 82 15 47; www.collioure.com; place du 18 Juin; ⊙9am-8pm Mon-Sat, 10am-6pm Sun Jul-Aug, 9am-noon & 2-6pm or 7pm Mon-Sat Sep-Jun)

PORT-VENDRES
POP 4500

Three kilometres south of Collioure, Port-Vendres, Roussillon's only natural harbour and deep-water port, has been exploited ever since Greek mariners roamed the rocky coastline. Until the independence of France's North African territories in the 1960s, it was an important port linking them with the mainland.

It's still a significant cargo and fishing harbour, featuring everything from small coastal chuggers to giant deep-sea vessels bristling with radar. There is also a large leisure marina.

PAULILLES

Part industrial relic, part nature walk, this 35-hectare coastal site is found between Port-Vendres and Banyuls. Remote, as befits a one-time dynamite factory, it was set up by the Swede Alfred Nobel, founder of the Nobel prize, and subsequently abandoned for over a quarter of a century.

Haunting photos and text (in English too), inside the former director's house (☺9am-1pm & 2-7pm, closed Tue Oct-Apr) tell of the hard lives and close community of workers, whose explosives helped to blast the Panama Canal, Trans-Siberian Railway and Mont Blanc Tunnel.

BANYULS

POP 4750

At the southern end of Banyul's seafront promenade, Biodiversarium (✍04 68 88 73 39; www.biodiversarium.fr; garden & aquarium adult/child €7.50/4, or per site €5/2.50; ☺9.30am-12.30pm & 2-6pm Jul-Aug, 2-6pm Wed-Sun Apr-Jun & Sep) is part aquarium, part botanical garden. Built in 1885 as the oceanographic research station of Paris' Université Pierre et Marie Curie, the Laboratoire Arago houses an intriguing collection of Mediterranean marine life, from seahorses to sea anemones. The aquarium also oversees a 500m *sentier soumarin* (underwater trail) just off Plage de Peyrefite between Banyuls and Cerbère, where you can see some of the species out in the wild. You can hire fins and masks (€8; from noon to 5pm in July and August) or bring your own gear.

The Jardin Méditerranéen du Mas de la Serre, 3km inland, is a fine place to get acquainted with the local flora, with a huge range of plants arranged around a natural amphitheatre in the hills above Banyuls.

The town is also well known for its wines – particularly robust reds and dessert varieties. You can try some at the Cellier des Templiers (www.banyuls.com; rte du Mas Reig; ☺10am-7.30pm), 1.75km inland from the seafront, and take a guided tour around the 100-year-old oak vats.

LANGUEDOC-ROUSSILLON CÔTE VERMEILLE

Provence

Best Places to Eat

» Restaurant Pierre Reboul (p777)

» Auberge La Fenière (p816)

» Café Véranda (p815)

» L'Atelier (p784)

» Sanglier Paresseux (p816)

Best Places to Stay

» Hôtel La Mirande (p793)

» Le Couvent (p808)

» Relais d'Elle (p817)

» Hôtel Vertigo (p765)

» Le Mas de Peint (p787)

Why Go?

Provence conjures images of lavender fields, gorgeous stone villages, wonderful food and superb wine – most people's idea of a perfect holiday. It certainly delivers on all those fronts, but what many visitors don't expect is Provence's incredible diversity. The Vaucluse and Luberon regions epitomise the Provençal cliché. But, near the mouth of the Rhône, craggy limestone yields to salt marshes, where pink flamingos replace purple lavender. In the south, the light, which captivated Van Gogh and Cézanne, begins to change, a prelude to the Camargue's bleached landscapes. Amid Haute-Provence's soaring peaks and raw wilderness, half-mile-high granite walls lord over a serpentine river at the Gorges du Verdon. The region's other surprises are its cities, sultry Marseille and wonderful Arles.

One thing remains constant everywhere: the food – clean, bright flavours, as simple as sweet tomatoes drizzled with olive oil and sprinkled with *fleur de sel* (sea salt) from the Camargue.

When to Go
Marseille

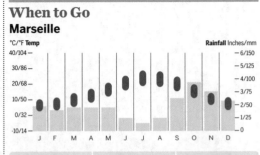

Easter Kick off the bullfighting season with Féria d'Artes.

Jul & Aug Wade through blooming lavender and see performing artists at Festival d'Avignon.

Sep & Oct Wait for cool temperatures and the grape harvest to bike the Luberon's back roads.

The Finer Things in Provence

There are so many ways to treat yourself in Provence. Your budget may not stretch to them all, but a few of our favourites include: spending the night and dining at La Bastide de Moustiers (p820); taking a wine-tasting course (p799) in Châteauneuf-du-Pape (and shipping a case of wine home!); learning to cook in the sumptuous kitchen of Hôtel La Mirande (p793); and enjoying a night of opera in Orange's grandiose Théâtre Antique (p800).

GETTING AWAY FROM IT ALL

It's not too difficult to get off the beaten path in Provence. In the great outdoors, hike along Marseille's rocky coastline at Les Calanques (p775) or picnic in the peaceful Jardins de l'Abbaye (p798) in Villeneuve-lès-Avignon, a world away from Avignon's crowds, but only a tiny hop across the river. Explore the peninsulas and islands of the Parc Naturel Régional de Camargue (p786) or the sublime wilderness of Parc National du Mercantour (p820).

For a few days of peace and quiet, check in at Le Mas Perréal (p813) or La Bouquière (p815) in the Luberon or Relais d'Elle (p817) in Pays de Forcalquier, where good food, select company and big views will ensure you wind down. And when you feel like getting out, track down artists workshops in Oppède-le-Vieux (p814) and Saignon (p815), or go for a scenic drive across the lavender fields of Plateau de Valensole (p817).

Finally, drop in to Prieuré de Ganagobie (p818), where the monks stick by two main tenets, one of which is 'listen': share their serenity.

Provence's Best Markets

Whatever the day of the week, there is a market somewhere in Provence. Mooching around the stalls, tasting local specialities and buying picnic treats and souvenirs is a quintessential part of Provençal life. Here is our list of favourites and their flagship wares:

» Forcalquier (Monday; p816) Lavender products, honey, Banon cheese

» Vaison-la-Romaine (Tuesday; p801) Delicious fruit and veg, charcuterie (pâtés, *saucissons* and more)

» St-Rémy de Provence (Wednesday; p789) Olives, olive oil and a sprinkling of celebrities

» Carpentras (Friday; p806) *Berlingots* (colourful sweets), truffles in winter

» Arles (Saturday; p780) Camargue salt, *saucisson d'Arles* (bull-meat sausage)

» Aix-en-Provence (Sunday; p773) Flower market and a very chic crowd

EUROPEAN CAPITAL OF CULTURE

Marseille, Aix-en-Provence and Arles are European Capital of Culture (p769) in 2013. Hundreds of concerts, exhibitions and events are scheduled – make sure you check out what's on.

Fast Facts

» **Population** 2.66 million

» **Area** 15,579 sq km

» **Hotel overnights/yr** 7.75 million

» **Signature drink** Pastis (aniseed liqueur)

PROVENCE

Planning Ahead

If you're around for the region's biggest festivals, booking tickets and accommodation in advance is essential.

» Féria d'Arles (p783)

» Chorégies d'Orange (p800)

» Festival d'Avignon (p793)

» Festival de Lacoste (p814)

Resources

» En Provence (www.en provence.fr)

» Tourisme PACA (www .tourismepaca.fr)

» Alpes de Haute-Provence (www.alpes-haute-provence.com)

» Bouches du Rhône (www .visitprovence.com)

» Vaucluse (www.provence guide.com)

Provence Highlights

1 Soak up seething, heady **Marseille** (p760)

2 Trail Van Gogh around **Arles** (p780), visiting spots where he painted some of his best-known canvases

3 Spot pink flamingos while riding white horses in the **Camargue** (p786)

4 Canoe, canyon or hike along the vertigo-inducing **Gorges du Verdon** (p818)

5 Take a walk on the wild side in the stunning, remote valleys of the **Parc National du Mercantour** (p820)

6 Stand in awe at the sheer size and magnificence of Orange's exceptional **Théâtre Antique** (p800)

7 Explore winding roads and stone villages like **Roussillon** (p812) amid Luberon's cherry orchards and sunflower fields

ℹ MAX-OUT MARSEILLE

Buy a cent-saving **Marseille City Pass** (one-/two-day pass €22/29) at the tourist office (p772). It covers admission to 15 museums, a city tour, unlimited public-transport travel, boat trips and more.

History

Settled over the centuries by the Ligurians, the Celts and the Greeks, the area between the Alps, the sea and the Rhône River flourished following Julius Caesar's conquest in the mid-1st century BC. The Romans called the area Provincia Romana, which evolved into the name Provence. After the collapse of the Roman Empire in the late 5th century, Provence was invaded several times, by the Visigoths, Burgundians and Ostrogoths.

During the 14th century, the Catholic Church, under a series of French-born popes, moved its headquarters from feud-riven Rome to Avignon, thus beginning the most resplendent period in the city's (and region's) history. Provence became part of France in 1481, but Avignon and Carpentras remained under papal control until the Revolution.

ℹ Getting There & Away

The TGV zips from Paris to Aix-en-Provence (three hours), Arles (four hours), Avignon (2¾ hours) and Marseille (three hours). On Saturdays in July and August, there's a direct Eurostar service from London to Avignon (from €135 return, six hours).

Lignes Express Régional (LER; www.info-ler .fr) runs regional buses. For buses to the Alps of Haute-Provence, see www.cg04.fr (in French), and navigate to 'Transport'.

A smorgasbord of airlines serve Aéroport Marseille-Provence, linked to Marseille and other cities across Provence from the Vitrolles Aéroport station. Ferries sail from Marseille to Sardinia, Tunisia and Corsica.

MARSEILLE REGION

Marseille

POP 858,902

Marseille was for many years the butt of French jokes. No more. The *cité phocéenne* (in reference to Phocaea, the ancient Greek city located in modern-day Turkey, from which Marseille's settlers, the Massiliots, came from) has made an unprecedented comeback, undergoing a vast makeover. The results look rather fabulous: witness the Panier quarter, the new République neighbourhood with its swanky boutiques and Haussmannian buildings, the city's shiny tram line, and the brand new docks and marina around the famous striped Cathédrale de la Major.

Marseillais will tell you that the city's rough-and-tumble edginess is part of its charm and that, for all its flaws, it is a very endearing place. They're right: Marseille grows on you with its history, fusion of cultures, souk-like markets, millennia-old port and *corniches* (coastal roads) along rocky inlets and sun-baked beaches. Their ultimate vindication came with Marseille's selection as European Capital of Culture for 2013.

History

Around 600 BC, Greek mariners founded Massilia, a trading post, at what is now Marseille's Vieux Port (Old Port). In the 1st century BC, the city lost out by backing Pompey the Great rather than Julius Caesar: Caesar's forces captured Massilia in 49 BC and directed Roman trade elsewhere.

Marseille became part of France in the 1480s, but retained its rebellious streak. Its citizens embraced the Revolution, sending 500 volunteers to defend Paris in 1792. Heading north, they sang a rousing march, ever after dubbed 'La Marseillaise' – now the national anthem. Trade with North Africa escalated after France occupied Algeria in 1830 and the Suez Canal opened in 1869.

After the world wars, a steady flow of migration from North Africa began and, with it, the rapid expansion of Marseille's periphery.

⊙ Sights

CENTRAL MARSEILLE

Marseille is divided into 16 *arrondissements* (districts). Sights concentrate around the Vieux Port and Le Panier districts. Dynamic dockland redevelopment is transforming La Joliette to the north.

The city's main thoroughfare, La Canebière (from the Provençal word *canebe*, meaning 'hemp', after the city's traditional rope industry), stretches eastwards from the Vieux Port towards the train station.

Various morning markets fill cours Julien, an elongated square with a forest of palm trees: fresh flowers on Wednesday and Saturday, antique books on alternate Saturdays, and stamps and antique books on Sunday. Cafes on its western side cook up world cuisine.

TOP CHOICE Vieux Port   HISTORIC QUARTER

(Map p766; M Vieux Port) Ships have docked for more than 26 centuries at the city's birthplace, the colourful Old Port. The main commercial docks were transferred to the Joliette area north of here in the 1840s, but the old port remains a thriving harbour for fishing boats, pleasure yachts and tourists. The free Cross-Port Ferry (◎8am-12.30pm & 1-5pm) in front of the town hall is a fun way to get out on the water, however briefly.

Guarding the harbour are Bas Fort St-Nicolas (Map p766) on the south side and, across the water, Fort St-Jean (Map p766), founded in the 13th century by the Knights Hospitaller of St John of Jerusalem. Here, the Musée des Civilisations de l'Europe et de la Méditerranée (MuCEM; Museum of European & Mediterranean Civilisations; Map p766; ✆04 96 13 80 90; www.mucem.org; ◎1pm-7pm Wed, Thu & Sat) will open a brand-new 40,000-sq-metre state-of-the-art museum in 2013.

The port's southern quay has theatres and bars, and restaurants and cafes buzz until the wee hours a block east on place Thiars and cours Honoré d'Estienne d'Orves.

Abbaye St-Victor (Map p766; 3 rue de l'Abbaye; ◎9am-7pm; M Vieux Port) is the birthplace of Christianity in Marseille, built on a 3rd-century-BC Greek necropolis. Nearby Musée du Santon (Map p766; ✆04 91 13 61 36; www.santonsmarcelcarbonel.com; 49 rue Neuve Ste-Catherine; admission free; ◎10am-12.30pm & 2-6.30pm Tue-Sat) and its neighbouring boutique Atelier du Santon (Map p766; 47 rue Neuve Ste-Catherine) are home to handcrafted tiny kiln-fired figures called *santons* (from *santoùn* in Provençal, meaning 'little saint'). The custom of creating a nativity scene with figurines dates from the Avignon papacy of John XII (1319–34).

Perched at the peninsula's edge, the Jardin du Pharo (Map p762) is a perfect picnic spot and is ideal for watching sunsets.

TOP CHOICE Le Panier   HISTORIC QUARTER

(Map p766; M Vieux Port) From the Vieux Port, hike north up to this history-woven quarter, dubbed 'Marseille's Montmartre', as much for its sloping streets as its artsy ambience. In Greek Massilia, it was the site of the *agora* (marketplace), hence its name, which means 'the basket'. During WWII, the quarter was dynamited and rebuilt. Today it's a mishmash of lanes hiding artisan shops, ateliers (workshops) and terraced houses.

Its centrepiece is Centre de la Vieille Charité (Map p766; 2 rue de la Charité, 2e; M Joliette), and nearby Cathédrale de la Major (Map p766) stands guard between the old and new ports with a stripy façade made of local Cassis stone and green Florentine marble.

TOP CHOICE Basilique Notre Dame
de la Garde   CHURCH

(Montée de la Bonne Mère; Map p762; ◎7am-8pm Apr-Sep, to 7pm Oct-Mar) Everywhere you go in Marseille, you see the opulent, domed 19th-century Romano-Byzantine basilica occupying Marseille's highest point, La Garde (162m). Built between 1853 and 1864, it is ornamented with coloured marble, murals

PROVENCE MARSEILLE

MARSEILLE IN...

Two Days

Start at the Vieux Port with breakfast at La Caravelle and a waterside stroll to the brand new Musée des Civilisations de l'Europe et de la Méditerranée. Lunch at La Passarelle then hike up to the Basilique Notre Dame de la Garde or explore Le Panier. Dine at nearby, excellent Le Café des Épices.

On day two, catch a boat to revel in Monte Cristo intrigues at Château d'If. Once back on land, walk or cycle to postcard-pretty Vallon des Auffes and go for bouillabaisse for dinner.

Four Days

Organise a day trip to the wonderful Parc National des Calanques. If you're keen to have an active day, plan a walk and a restorative lunch at Calanque de Sormiou. Otherwise, book one of the scenic cruises.

On day four, go to Aix-en-Provence for the day to retrace the steps of genius painter Paul Cézanne and partake in a spot of shopping in the atmospheric town. Stay for dinner at the outstanding Restaurant Pierre Reboul.

Marseille

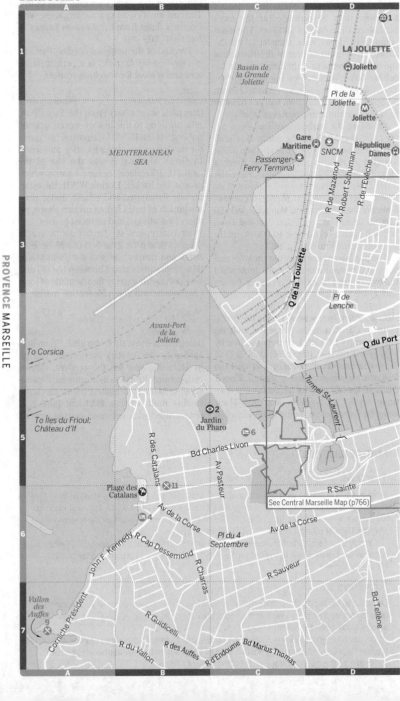

See Central Marseille Map (p766)

0 400 m
0 0.2 miles

E **F** **G** **H**

R Fauchier
R Malaval
Av du Général Leclerc
Pl Victor Hugo
R Honnorat
Bd National
ST-CHARLES

Bus Station

Bd des Dames
R de la République
Jules Guesde Ⓜ
Autoroute Nord
Bd Charles Nédélec
Ⓜ Gare St-Charles
Bd Voltaire
R Flégier
To Palais de Longchamp (450m)

St-Charles
R Bernard du Bois
Pl des Marseillaises

Pl de Lorette
Sadi Carnot Ⓜ
Colbert Ⓜ
R d'Aix
R des Petites Maries
BELSUNCE
Réformés Canebière Ⓜ
Square Léon Blum
🚇13

LE PANIER
Pl Sadi Carnot
Belsunce Alcazar
Allées Léon Gambetta
R Curiol
THIERS

Grand Rue
Jardins des Vestiges Ⓟ
Noailles Ⓜ
Canebière Garibaldi
5
R Sénac de Meilhan
🚇12

La Canebière
R des Trois Mages
Pl Jean Jaurès

Vieux Port Ⓜ
Pl du Général de Gaulle Ⓟ
8✕
14✕
Cours Julien
15☆

Vieux Port
10
Notre Dame du Mont– Cours Julien Ⓜ

Q de Rive Neuve
R Breteuil
R Grignan
Pl Notre Dame du Mont
R de la Loubière
To Mama Shelter (130m)

R Montgrand
Cours Lieutaud

Bd de la Corderie
Estrangin-Préfecture Ⓜ
Pl de la Préfecture
R de Rome
R d'Italie
R de Marengo
R de Lodi

Jardin Pierre Puget
R Roux de Brignoles
Bd L Salvator
R Paradis
R Dragon
R de Village

R Vauvenargues
Bd André Aune
Bd Notre Dame
R Jules Moulet
R Sylvabelle
R Breteuil
7✕
3
R St-Suffren

R du Fort
Pl Castellane
Bd Baille
Bus Stop on Place Castellane Ⓜ Castellane
R de Rouet

Basilique Notre Dame de la Garde ✞
Bd Vauban
Av du Prado
To L'Unité d'Habitation (3km)

Marseille

⊙ **Top Sights**

Basilique Notre Dame de la
Garde E7

⊙ **Sights**

1 Fonds Régional d'Art
Contemporain D1
2 Jardin du Pharo C5

🛏 **Sleeping**

3 Hôtel Edmond Rostand G6
4 Hôtel Le Richelieu B6
5 Le Ryad G3
6 Sofitel Marseille Vieux Port C5

🍴 **Eating**

7 Café Populaire G6
8 La Cantinetta G4
9 L'Epuisette A7
10 Les Pieds dans le Plat H5
11 Restaurant Michel B6

🍷 **Drinking**

12 Au Petit Nice H4
13 Longchamp Palace H2

🎭 **Entertainment**

14 Espace Julien G4
15 L'Intermédiaire H4

depicting the safe passage of sailing vessels and superbly restored mosaics. The hilltop gives 360-degree panoramas of the city's sea of terracotta roofs below.

The church's bell tower is crowned by a 9.7m-tall gilded statue of the Virgin Mary on a 12m-high pedestal. Bullet marks and shrapnel scars on the northern façade evidence the fierce fighting of Marseille's Battle of Liberation (15 to 25 August 1944). It's a 1km walk from the Vieux Port, or take bus 60 or the tourist train.

FREE Palais de Longchamp   PALACE, PARK
(Longchamp Palace; bd Philippon; 👶; MCinq Avenues–Longchamp; 🚋Longchamp) The colonnaded Palais de Longchamp and its spectacular fountains were constructed in the 1860s, in part to disguise a water tower at the terminus of an aqueduct from the River Durance. The northern wing houses Marseille's oldest museum, the Musée des Beaux-Arts, undergoing renovations at research time and slated to reopen in 2013. The shaded park is one of the centre's few green spaces, popular with local families.

La Friche La Belle de Mai   CULTURAL CENTRE
(🖉04 95 04 95 04; www.lafriche.org; 41 rue Jobin; 🚌49 stop Jobin) The site of a former sugar-refining plant and subsequent tobacco factory, the theatre, artists' workshops, cinema studios, radio stations, multimedia displays, alfresco installation art, skateboard ramps and electro-/world-music parties at La Friche la Belle de Mai are the voice of contemporary Marseille. It underwent an enormous renovation in 2012.

Check its program online, view art in the Galerie de la Friche Belle de Mai (admission free; ⊙3-7pm Tue-Sat) or lunch in its cavernous, stylishly industrial restaurant Les Grandes Tables de la Friche (🖉04 95 04 95 85; www.lesgrandestables.com; 12 rue François Simon; mains €10; ⊙8.30am-8pm Mon-Fri).

L'Unité d'Habitation   HISTORIC BUILDING
(La Cité Radieuse; 🖉04 91 16 78 00; 280 bd Michelet; 🚌83 or 21 stop Le Corbusier) Visionary international-style architect Le Corbusier redefined urban living in 1952 with the completion of his vertical 337-apartment 'garden city' also known as La Cité Radieuse (The Radiant City). Along its darkened hallways, primary-coloured downlights create a glowing tunnel leading to a mini-supermarket, an architectural bookshop, Hôtel Le Corbusier (🖉04 91 16 78 00; www.hotellecorbusier.com; 280 bd Michelet; r €70, apt €105-139; 🚌83 or 21 stop Le Corbusier), a restaurant and a rooftop terrace.

Architecture buffs can book a guided tour of a private apartment at the tourist office.

ALONG THE COAST

Mesmerising views of another Marseille unfold along corniche Président John F Kennedy, the coastal road that cruises south to small, sandy, beach-volleyball-busy Plage des Catalans and the fishing cove Vallon des Auffes, crammed with colourful fishing boats.

Further south, the vast Prado beaches are marked by Jules Cantini's 1903 marble replica of Michelangelo's David. The beaches, all gold sand, were created from backfill from the excavations for Marseille's metro, and host a world-renowned skate park.

Château d'If   ISLAND, CASTLE
(www.if.monuments-nationaux.fr; adult/child €5/free; ⊙9.30am-6.30pm May-Sep, to 4.45pm Tue-Sun Oct-Apr) Immortalised in Alexandre Dumas' classic 1844 novel Le Comte de Monte Cristo (The Count of Monte Cristo), 16th-century fortress-turned-prison Château d'If sits on the 30-sq-km island Île d'If, 3.5km west of the Vieux Port. Political prisoners

were incarcerated here, along with hundreds of Protestants, the Revolutionary hero Mirabeau and the Communards of 1871.

Frioul If Express (www.frioul-if-express.com; 1 quai des Belges) boats leave for Château d'If (€10 return, 20 minutes) from the Vieux Port. There are over 15 daily departures in summer, fewer in winter.

Îles du Frioul   ISLANDS

A few hundred metres west of Île d'If are the Îles du Frioul, the barren dyke-linked white-limestone islands of Ratonneau and Pomègues. Sea birds and rare plants thrive on these tiny islands (each about 2.5km long, totalling 200 hectares). Ratonneau has three beaches. Boats to Château d'If also serve the Îles du Frioul (€10 return, 35 minutes).

☞ Tours

Le Grand Tour   BUS TOUR

(Map p766; ☑04 91 91 05 82; www.marseillelegrand tour.com; adult/child €18/9; ☉10am-7pm) Feel the wind in your hair as you travel between key sights and museums aboard a hop-on-hop-off open-topped bus. Tickets are sold at the tourist office or on board, and include a five-language audioguide.

Tourist Train   TRAIN TOUR

(Map p766; ☑04 91 25 24 69; www.petit-train -marseille.com; adult/child €7/4; ☉10am-12.30pm & 2-6pm; Ⓜ Vieux Port) Choose from two circular routes: to Basilique Notre Dame de la Garde (year-round) and Le Panier (April to mid-November). Tours last 65 minutes and depart every 30 minutes, less often in winter.

Guided Tour   WALKING TOUR

(www.resamarseille.com;tour€7;☉2pmSat;ⓂVieux Port) Leaves from the tourist office (p772).

[FREE] Marseille Provence Greeters   WALKING TOUR

(www.marseilleprovencegreeters.com) Free walking tours by locals; advance website registration required.

Croisières Marseille Calanques   BOAT TOUR

(Map p766; www.croisieres-marseille-calanques.com; 74 quai du Port) Runs two-hour return trips from the Vieux Port taking in six *calanques* (adult/child/family costs €22/7/68); three-hour return trips past 12 *calanques* to Cassis (adult/child/family €28/21/85); and 1½-hour trips around the Baie de Marseille (adult €10).

★ Festivals & Events

Carnaval de Marseille   STREET CARNIVAL

(☉Mar) Mad street carnival with decorated floats.

Fiesta des Suds   MUSIC FESTIVAL

(www.dock-des-suds.org; ☉Mar) World music at Dock des Suds.

Beach Volleyball World Championships   SPORTS

(☉Jul) Hosted by Plage du Prado.

Festival de Marseille   PERFORMING ARTS

(www.festivaldemarseille.com; ☉Jul) Three weeks of international dance, theatre, music and art.

Five Continents Jazz Festival   MUSIC FESTIVAL

(www.festival-jazz-cinq-continents.com; ☉Jul) Acid jazz, funk and folk music.

Foire aux Santonniers   CHRISTMAS

(☉Dec) Since 1803 traditional *santon* (figurine) makers have flocked to Marseille for this fair.

🛏 Sleeping

The best rooms in Marseille get snagged fast; reserve ahead. There's also a hotel in Le Corbusier's L'Unité d'Habitation (p764).

[TOP CHOICE] Casa Honoré   B&B €€€

(Map p766; ☑04 96 11 01 62; www.casahonore.com; 123 rue Sainte; d incl breakfast €150-200; ❄ 🌐 ✉; Ⓜ Vieux Port) Los Angeles meets Marseille at this four-room *maison d'hôte*, built around a central courtyard with a lap pool shaded by banana trees. The fashion-forward style reflects the owner's love for contemporary interior design (she has a shop down the block), using disparate elements like black wicker and the occasional cow skull, which come together in one sexy package. One complaint: some bathrooms are partitioned by curtains, not doors.

Hôtel Vertigo   HOSTEL €

(Map p766; ☑04 91 91 07 11; www.hotelvertigo.fr; 42 rue des Petites Maries; dm/d €25/60; @ 🛜; Ⓜ Gare St-Charles) This snappy boutique hostel kisses goodbye to dodgy bunks and hospital-like decor. Here it's 'hello' to vintage posters, designer chrome kitchen, groovy communal spaces and polite multilingual staff. Double rooms are particularly good, some with a private terrace. No curfew (or lift, alas). A second, all-dorm facility is closer to the Vieux Port.

Central Marseille

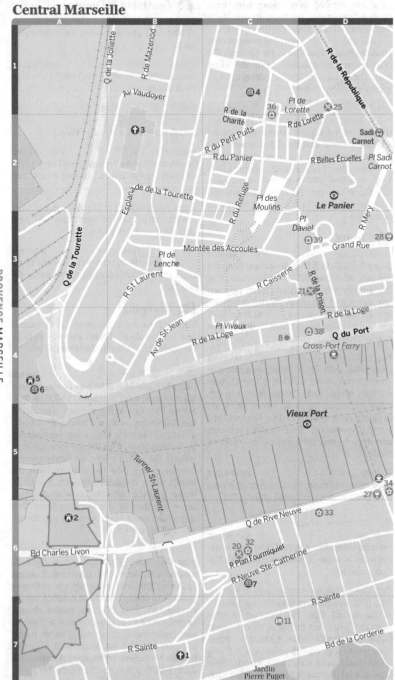

A **B** **C** **D**

R de la République

R de la Joliette

R de Mazenod

Av Vaudoyer

🏛4

36 · Pl de Lorette

✕25

R de la Charité

R de Lorette

Sadi Carnot

✝3

R du Petit Puits

R du Panier

R Belles Écuelles

Pl Sadi Carnot

Esplanade de la Tourette

R du Refuge

Pl des Moulins

◉ Le Panier

R Mery

Q de la Tourette

Pl Daviel

28

🔒39

Pl de Lenche

Montée des Accoules

Grand Rue

R St Laurent

R Caisserie

R de la Prison

21

R de la Loge

Av de St-Jean

Pl Vivaux

R de la Loge

8 ●

🔒38

Q du Port

Cross-Port Ferry

✝5
🏛6

◉ Vieux Port

Tunnel St-Laurent

34

27

✝2

Q de Rive Neuve

✿33

Bd Charles Livon

20 32

R Plan Fourmiquier

R Neuve Ste-Catherine

🏛7

R Sainte

🛏11

R Sainte

Bd de la Corderie

R Sainte

✝1

Jardin Pierre Puget

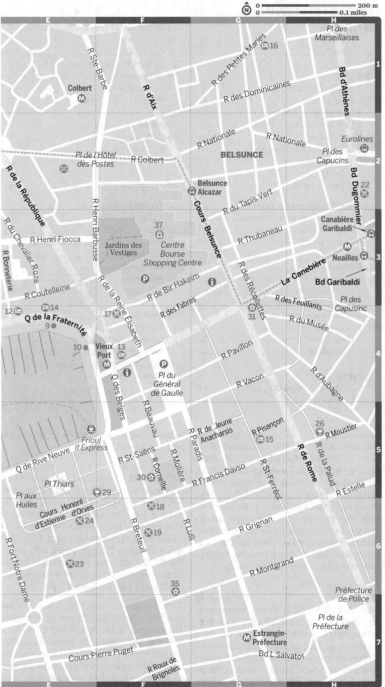

0   200 m
N
0   0.1 miles

Pl des
Marseillaises

R Ste-Barbe

Colbert
Ⓜ

R d'Aix

R des Petites Maries

16

Bd d'Athènes

R des Dominicaines

R Nationale

R Nationale

BELSUNCE

Eurolines

Pl des
Capucins

Bd Dugommier

R de la République

Pl de l'Hôtel
des Postes

R Colbert

**Belsunce
Alcazar**

R du Tapis Vert

22

R du Chevalier Roze

R Henri Fiocca

R Henri Barbusse

37

*Centre
Bourse
Shopping Centre*

Cours Belsunce

R Thubaneau

Canebière
Garibaldi

R Bonneterie

*Jardins des
Vestiges*

R de la Reine Élisabeth

R de Bir Hakeim

R des Récollettes

La Canebière

Ⓜ

Noailles

Bd Garibaldi

R Coutelleine

R des Fabres

R des Feuillants

Pl des
Capusinc

12

14

Q de la Fraternité

9

17

31

R du Musée

10

**Vieux
Port**
Ⓜ

13

Pl du
Général
de Gaulle

R Pavillon

R Vacon

R d'Aubagne

Q des Belges

R Beauvau

R de Jeune
Anacharsis

R Pisançon

26

R Moustier

*Frioul
If Express*

R Paradis

15

R de la Palud

Q de Rive Neuve

R St-Saëns

R Corneille

R Molière

R Francis Davso

R St-Ferréol

R de Rome

R Estelle

Pl Thiars

30

29

*Pl aux
Huiles*

Cours Honoré
d'Estienne d'Orves

24

18

R Breteuil

R Lulli

R Grignan

R Fort Notre Dame

19

R Montgrand

23

35

Préfecture
de Police

Pl de la
Préfecture

Ⓜ **Estrangin-
Préfecture**

Cours Pierre Puget

R Roux de
Brignoles

Bd L Salvato

E   F   G   H

PROVENCE MARSEILLE

Central Marseille

Top Sights
Le Panier ... D2
Vieux Port ... D5

Sights
1 Abbaye St-Victor ... B7
2 Bas Fort St-Nicolas ... A6
3 Cathédrale de la Major ... B2
4 Centre de la Vieille Charité ... C1
5 Fort St-Jean ... A4
6 Musée des Civilisations de l'Europe et de la Méditerranée ... A4
7 Musée du Santon ... C6

Activities, Courses & Tours
8 Croisières Marseille Calanques ... C4
9 Le Grand Tour ... E4
10 Tourist Train ... E4

Sleeping
11 Casa Honoré ... C7
12 Hôtel Belle-Vue ... E4
13 Hôtel Escale Oceania ... F4
14 Hôtel La Résidence du Vieux Port ... E4
15 Hôtel Saint-Ferréol ... G5
16 Hôtel Vertigo ... G1

Eating
17 Jardin des Vestiges ... F4
18 La Casertane ... F6
19 La Part des Anges ... F6
20 La Passarelle ... C6
21 Le Café des Épices ... D3
22 Le Comptoir Dugommier ... H2
23 Le Grain de Sel ... E6
24 Les Arcenaulx ... E6
25 Pizzaria Chez Étienne ... D1

Drinking
26 Caffè Noir ... H5
La Caravelle ... (see 12)
27 Le Bar de la Marine ... D5
28 Les Buvards ... D3
29 Polikarpov ... F5

Entertainment
30 Au Son des Guitars ... F5
31 Espace Culture ... G4
Fnac ... (see 37)
32 La Noche ... C6
33 Le Trolleybus ... D6
34 Pelle Mêle ... D5
35 XY Le Club ... F6

Shopping
36 72% Pétanque ... C2
Atelier du Santon ... (see 7)
37 Centre Bourse Shopping Centre ... F3
38 La Maison du Pastis ... D4
39 Place aux Huiles ... D3

Le Ryad BOUTIQUE HOTEL €€
(Map p762; ☎04 91 47 74 54; www.leryad.fr; 16 rue Sénac de Meilhan; s €80-105, d €95-125, family €170; wi-fi; Ⓜ Noailles, tram Canebière Garibaldi) With high ceilings, arched alcoves, warm colours and minimalist decor, super-stylish Le Ryad draws sumptuous influence from Morocco. Beautiful bathrooms, garden-view rooms and great service make up for the sometimes-sketchy neighbourhood. Despite the four-storey walk up, it's worth booking the top-floor room for its tiny rooftop terrace.

Hôtel La Résidence du Vieux Port DESIGN HOTEL €€
(Map p766; ☎04 91 91 91 22; www.hotelmarseille.com; 18 quai du Port; d €125-200, apt €298; air-con, internet, wi-fi; Ⓜ Vieux Port) Marseille's top-view hotel got a makeover in 2010 in vaguely *The Jetsons*–meets-Mondrian style, with swoop-backed furniture and bold primary colours. Every room looks sharp, and port-side rooms have balconies with knockout views of the old port and Notre Dame.

Mama Shelter DESIGN HOTEL €€
(☎01 43 48 48 48; www.mamashelter.com; 64 rue de la Loubière; d €99-139, q €159, ste €209; air-con, wi-fi; Ⓜ Notre Dame du Monte–Cours Julien) The brainchild of Serge Trigano, son of Gilbert (Club Med creator), this affordable-chic new kid on the block opened with a bang in 2012. It sports design by Philippe Starck, nifty extras like Kiehl's bathroom products and free in-room movies. The rooms are wheelchair accessible and parking costs €17 per day.

Sofitel Marseille Vieux Port LUXURY HOTEL €€€
(Map p762; ☎04 91 15 59 55; www.sofitel-marseille-vieuxport.com; 36 bd Charles Livon; d from €215; air-con, internet, wi-fi, pool; bus 83 stop Fort St-Nicolas) Marseille's top full-service hotel commands spectacular views of the sea and the old port. Rooms have all requisite bells and whistles, from iPod

docks to feather beds; some have double-size soaking tubs. Great spa.

Hôtel Belle-Vue
HOTEL €€

(Map p766; ☑04 91 17 05 40; www.hotel-bellevue-marseille.fr; 34 quai du Port; d €84-135; ❋@✆; ⓜVieux Port) Rooms at this old-fashioned hotel are tastefully decorated with mid-budget simplicity, but have million-dollar port-side views. Bathrooms have occasional mildew spots and there's no lift, but La Caravelle (p771), one of Marseille's coolest cafe-bars, is inside.

Hôtel Escale Oceania
HOTEL €€

(Map p766; ☑04 91 90 61 61; www.oceaniahotels.com; 5 La Canebière; d €91-157; ❋✆; ⓜVieux Port) Though rooms run small (you're buying the excellent Vieux Port location), they're fresh and clean. Spotless bathrooms have big walk-in showers. Rooms on the Canebière side sport wrought-iron port-view balconies.

Hôtel Saint-Ferréol
HOTEL €€

(Map p766; ☑04 91 33 12 21; www.hotelsaintferreol.com; 19 rue Pisançon; d €99-120; ❋@✆; ⓜVieux Port) On the corner of the city's bustling pedestrianised street, this simple hotel has individually decorated rooms, many inspired by artists like Van Gogh and Cézanne, with spotless bathrooms and exceptional service.

Villa Monticelli
B&B €€

(☑04 91 22 15 20; www.villamonticelli.com; 96 rue du Commandant Rolland; d incl breakfast €105; ❋✆; ☐83 or 19 stop Prado St Giniez, ⓜRond-Point du Prado) Colette and Jean are passionate about their city and the five exquisite *chambre d'hôte* rooms in their stunning villa are worth the slightly outer-city location. Breakfast of homemade everything is served on the panoramic-view terrace.

Hôtel Le Richelieu
HOTEL €

(Map p762; ☑04 91 31 01 92; www.lerichelieu-marseille.com; 52 corniche Président John F Kennedy; d €53-88, tr €91-110; ❋@✆; ☐83) An economical seaside choice with odd-shaped rooms, but the owners keep them looking fresh. The best face the sea, lending a beach-house feel. There's an adjacent beach and shared waterview terrace, but no lift.

Hôtel Edmond Rostand
BOUTIQUE HOTEL €€

(Map p762; ☑04 91 37 74 95; www.hoteledmondrostand.com; 31 rue Dragon; s & d €86, tr €127; ❋@✆; ⓜEstrangin-Préfecture) Antique shops surround this good-value hotel in the elegant Quartier des Antiquaires. Though its 16 stylish rooms are a bit worn, some overlook

a tiny private garden, others rooftops and Basilique Notre Dame de la Garde.

✖ Eating

The Vieux Port is packed with restaurants, but choose carefully to avoid tourist traps. The cours Julien and surrounding streets have world cuisine.

Le Café des Épices
MODERN FRENCH €€

(Map p766; ☑04 91 91 22 69; www.cafedesepices.com; 4 rue du Lacydon; 3-course lunch/dinner menu €25/40; ⓧlunch Tue-Sat, dinner Thu-Fri; ⚑; ⓜVieux Port) One of Marseille's best young chefs, Arnaud de Grammont, infuses his cooking with a panoply of flavours...think squid-ink spaghetti with sesame and perfectly cooked scallops, or tender roasted potatoes with hints of coriander and citrus, topped by the catch of the day. The presentation is impeccable, the decor is playful, the staff are friendly, and the place fills up reliably. Don't underestimate the desserts either.

Saturday lunch is particularly family-friendly on the sunny terrace leading onto an olive-tree-lined pedestrianised square. Reservations essential.

La Cantinetta
ITALIAN €

(Map p762; ☑04 91 48 10 48; 24 cours Julien; mains €9-19; ⓧlunch & dinner Tue-Sat; ⓜNotre Dame du

---

DON'T MISS

A RISING CULTURAL STAR

In 2013, Marseille, Aix-en-Provence and Arles will be European Capital of Culture (www.mp2013.fr). As a result, there have been a number of makeovers of local institutions in Marseille such as La Friche La Belle de Mai (p764) and Palais de Longchamp (p764); spectacular facilities were also under construction at the time of writing for Musée des Civilisations de l'Europe et de la Méditerranée (p761) and Fonds Régional d'Art Contemporain (FRAC; Map p762; ☑04 91 91 27 55; www.fracpaca.org; 20 bd de Dunkerque; ⓜJoliette), both scheduled to open in 2013. Performing arts are also gearing up for a year of extravaganzas; the arts organization Marseille Expos (www.marseilleexpos.com) distributes an excellent map of hot galleries and sponsors the festival Printemps de l'Art Contemporain each May. Its website lists what's on.

BOUILLABAISSE

Originally cooked by fishers from the scraps of their catch, bouillabaisse is Marseille's classic signature dish. True bouillabaisse includes at least four different kinds of fish, sometimes shellfish, which is why it's served to a minimum of two people. Don't trust tourist-trap restaurants that promise cheap bouillabaisse. The real McCoy costs about €55 per person and should be reserved 48 hours ahead, enough time to procure the correct ingredients. It's served in two parts: the broth *(soupe de poisson)*, rich with tomato, saffron and fennel; and the cooked fish, deboned tableside and presented on a platter. On the side are croutons and *rouille* (a bread-thickened garlic, chilli and pepper mayonnaise) and grated cheese, usually Gruyère. Spread *rouille* on the crouton, top with cheese, and float it in the soup. Be prepared for a huge meal and tons of garlic.

The most reliably consistent spots for real bouillabaisse include the following:

» **Le Rhul** (☑04 91 52 01 77; www.lerhul.fr; 269 corniche Président John F Kennedy; €50; ☐83) This long-standing classic has atmosphere (however kitschy): a 1940s seaside hotel with Mediterranean views.

» **L'Epuisette** (Map p762; ☑04 91 52 17 82; www.l-epuisette.com; Vallon des Auffes; €60; ☺Tue-Sat; ☐83) The swankest (by far) has a Michelin star and knockout water-level views from an elegantly austere dining room. First courses cost €34 to €45 and desserts €20, though you'll likely not have room.

» **Restaurant Michel** (Chez Michel; Map p762; ☑04 91 52 30 63; http://restaurant-michel-13.fr; 6 rue des Catalans; €60; ☺dinner nightly) Tops since 1946. Alas, the overly bright dining room lacks romance.

Mont–Cours Julien) The top table at cours Julien serves perfectly al-dente house-made pasta, paper-thin prosciutto, marinated vegetables, *bresaola* (air-dried beef) and risotto. Tables in the convivial dining room are cheek by jowl, and everyone seems to know each other, or escape to the sun-dappled, tiled-patio garden. If you're lucky, the gregarious chef-owner, Pierre-Antoine Denis, will regale you with the day's specials. Reservations essential.

La Part des Anges BISTRO €
(Map p766; 33 rue Sainte; mains €15; ☺lunch Mon-Sat, dinner daily) No address buzzes with Marseille's hip, buoyant crowd more than this fabulous all-rounder wine bistro, named after the amount of alcohol that evaporates through a barrel during wine or whisky fermentation: the angels' share. Tables can't be reserved; tell the bartenders you want to eat and take your pick of dozens of wines to try by the glass.

Café Populaire NEO-BISTRO €
(Map p762; ☑04 91 02 53 96; 10 rue Paradis; mains €14-16; ☺lunch & dinner Tue-Sat; ⓂEstrangin-Préfecture) Vintage tables and chairs, old books on the shelves and a fine collection of glass soda bottles all add to the retro air of this 1950s-styled jazz *comptoir* (counter). Plump for a stool at the zinc bar or lounge at a table with a view of the fabulous open kitchen, where simple daily specials like *gambas à la* plancha (fried prawns served on a hot plate) or beetroot and coriander salad are cooked up.

Le Comptoir Dugommier BISTRO €
(Map p766; ☑04 91 62 21 21; www.comptoirdugom mier.fr; 14 bd Dugommier; mains €11-12, 3-course menu with drink €20; ☺7.30am-3.30pm Mon-Wed, 7.30am-1am Thu & Fri; ⓂNoailles, ☐Canebière Garibaldi) Tin moulding, wooden floors and vintage signs make a cosy escape from the busy street outside. The place gets packed for its down-home French fare, like *andouil-lette* sausage stewed with artichokes.

Les Pieds dans le Plat MODERN FRENCH €€
(Map p762; ☑04 91 48 74 15; 2 rue Pastoret; lunch/dinner menus €18/35; ☺lunch & dinner Tue-Sat; ⓂNotre Dame du Mont–Cours Julien) Slip into this intimate, cheery restaurant through a small door surrounded by graffiti. The chef incorporates French Basque and Moroccan influences in his creative, market-fresh cuisine. Reservations essential.

Le Grain de Sel MODERN FRENCH €€
(Map p766; ☑04 91 54 47 30; 39 rue de la Paix Marcel Paul; lunch menu €16, mains €17-22; ☺lunch Tue-Sat, dinner Fri & Sat; ⓂVieux Port) Locals pack this slender bistro for inventive treats like gnocchi with shellfish and fennel or decadent desserts like crème brûlée with rum, chestnuts and orange. Reservations essential.

La Casertane ITALIAN, DELICATESSEN €
(Map p766; ☑04 91 54 98 51; 71 rue Francis Davso;
pastas €11-12; ☺lunch Mon-Sat, deli 9am-3pm Mon,
9am-7.30pm Tue-Sat; Ⓜ Vieux Port) Lunch on a
mind-boggling array of Italian deli meats and
salads, or choose from daily specials, often
with homemade pastas. Convivial staff and a
bustling flow of clientele make for lively meals.

La Passarelle PROVENÇAL €
(Map p766; ☑04 91 33 03 27; www.restaurantla
passarelle.fr; 52 rue du Plan Fourmiguier; mains
€17; ☺lunch Tue-Sat, dinner Thu-Sat; Ⓜ Vieux Port)
Retro vintage tables and chairs sit beneath
lime-green parasols on a terrace between veggie and strawberry beds. Everything growing
in the walled garden goes into something on
Philippe and Patricia's predominantly organic menu, and other products are strictly local.

Les Arcenaulx TRADITIONAL FRENCH €€
(Map p766; ☑04 91 54 85 38; www.les-arcenaulx.
com; 27 cours Honoré d'Estienne d'Orves; lunch
menu €20, mains €17-28; ☺lunch & dinner Mon-Sat;
Ⓜ Vieux Port) Dine in grandiose style in this
cavernous former Louis XIV warehouse with
antiquarian-and-contemporary bookshop
or visit the neighbouring *salon de thé* (tearoom) for savoury tarts, cakes and ice cream.

Pizzaria Chez Étienne MARSEILLAIS €
(Map p766; 43 rue de Lorette; mains €12-15; ☺lunch
& dinner Mon-Sat; Ⓜ Colbert) This old Marseillais haunt has the best pizza in town, as
well as succulent *pavé de boeuf* (beef steak)
and scrumptious *supions frits* (pan-fried
squid with garlic and parsley). Since it's a
convivial meeting point for the entire neighbourhood, pop in beforehand to reserve
(there's no phone). No credit cards.

Jardin des Vestiges ARMENIAN, MEDITERRANEAN €
(Map p766; 15 rue de la Reine Élisabeth; mains €7-
13; ☺9am-6pm Mon-Sat; Ⓜ Vieux Port) A solid
budget choice draws on Armenian, Greek
and Lebanese cuisine in dishes like kebabs,
stuffed eggplant, moussaka and tabouli. Ideal for to-go sandwiches (€4 to €6).

🍷 Drinking

Cafes and bars surround the Vieux Port.
Students and artists congregate near cours
Julien and its surrounding streets. Sundays
are dead.

La Caravelle BAR
(Map p766; 34 quai du Port; ☺7am-2am; Ⓜ Vieux
Port) Look up or miss this standout upstairs
hideaway, styled with rich wood and leather,
a zinc bar and yellowing murals. If it's sunny,
snag a coveted spot on the port-side terrace.
On Fridays, there's live jazz from 9pm to
midnight.

Les Buvards WINE BAR
(Map p766; ☑04 91 90 69 98; 34 Grand Rue;
☺10am-1am; Ⓜ Vieux Port, 🚇Sadi Carnot) Grand
selection of natural wines and munchies.

Longchamp Palace CAFE
(Map p762; ☑04 91 50 76 13; 22 bd Longchamp;
☺Mon-Sat Sep-Jul; 🚇Réformés Canebière) Artsy
bustling bistro and lazy coffee shop.

Le Bar de la Marine BAR
(Map p766; ☑04 91 54 95 42; 15 quai de Rive Neuve;
☺7am-1am; Ⓜ Vieux Port) Marcel Pagnol filmed
the card-party scenes in *Marius* at this Marseille institution, which draws folks from
every walk of life.

Au Petit Nice CAFE, BAR
(Map p762; ☑04 91 48 43 04; 28 place Jean Jaurès;
☺10am-2am; Ⓜ Notre Dame du Mont–Cours Julien)
Cheap and cheerful: €2 beers in a happening courtyard cafe with a youthful, diverse
crowd. (NB: this is *not* the hotel of the same
name.)

PROVENCE MARSEILLE

GAY & LESBIAN VENUES

The website www.gaymapmarseille.com has general coverage of Marseilles and Aix-en-
Provence's gay life. Marseille's small scene is in constant flux, and only converges on
weekends. Gay nights are held at various bars, which are generally straight or mixed on
other nights.
   Caffè Noir (Map p766; 3 rue Moustier; Ⓜ Vieux Port) and Polikarpov (Map p766; 24
cours Honoré d'Estienne d'Orves; Ⓜ Vieux Port) are reliable addresses for a young, mixed,
hard-drinking crowd. Skip Cargo, Caffè Noir's adjoining sauna, for XY Le Club (Map
p766; www.xy-leclub.com; 66 rue Montgrand; Ⓜ Estrangin-Préfecture), which only gets busy
Sunday afternoons; sometimes it throws mixed parties; friendly door staff are an excellent resource for what's happening. Catch-as-catch-can bar Le Trash (www.trash-bar.
com; 28 rue du Berceau; ☺Fri-Wed; Ⓜ Baille) is as its name suggests.

SHOPPING LE PANIER

Le Panier (p761) is home to many of the city's artisans and craftspeople, and is by far the most fun place in the city for stocking up on gifts. Pick up gorgeous AOC (Appellation d'Origine Contrôlée) Provençal olive oils, and jars of tapenade and aïoli at Place aux Huiles (Map p766; www.placeauxhuiles.com; 2 place Daviel; ⊗daily; ⓂSadi Carnot). Brilliantly scented olive soaps, some with chocolate and tomato leaf, and lip-smacking preserves fill 72% Pétanque (Map p766; 10 rue du Petit Puits). Nearby a clutch of ceramic ateliers have shops attached; wander in and say *bonjour*. At the bottom of Le Panier, right on the Vieux Port is La Maison du Pastis (Map p766; 108 quai du Port), where you'll be able to sample over 90 varieties of this aniseed-flavoured aperitif.

☆ Entertainment

Cultural events are covered in *L'Hebdo* (€1.20), available around town, or www.marseille bynight.com and www.journalventilo.fr. Tickets are sold at *billetteries* (ticket counters), including Espace Culture (Map p766; ☑04 96 11 04 60; http://espaceculture.net; 42 La Canebière; ⓂVieux Port), Fnac (Map p766; Centre Bourse shopping centre; ⓂVieux Port) and the tourist office. Alternative theatre and events for kids are held in a trio of venues on Passage des Arts.

Nightclubs & Live Music

Espace Julien   LIVE MUSIC
(Map p762; ☑04 91 24 34 10; www.espace-julien. com; 39 cours Julien; ⓂNotre Dame du Mont–Cours Julien) Rock, *opérock,* alternative theatre, reggae, hip hop, Afro groove and other cutting-edge entertainment all appear on the bill; the website lists gigs.

Pelle Mêle   JAZZ
(Map p766; ☑04 91 54 85 26; 8 place aux Huiles; admission €2; ⊗6pm-1am, closed Sun Oct-Apr; ⓂVieux Port) A 30-something crowd jives to good jazz at this lively port-side bistro.

L'Intermédiaire   NIGHTCLUB
(Map p762; 63 place Jean Jaurès; ⊗7pm-2am; ⓂNotre Dame du Mont–Cours Julien) This grungy venue with graffitied walls is one of the best for live bands or DJs (usually techno or alternative).

La Noche   NIGHTCLUB
(Map p766; 40 rue Plan Fourmiguier; ⊗Fri & Sat; ⓂVieux Port) Downstairs, bands play; upstairs, DJs spin everything from electro to salsa.

Le Trolleybus   NIGHTCLUB
(Map p766; ☑04 91 54 30 45; 24 quai de Rive Neuve; ⊗Wed-Sat; ⓂVieux Port) Shake it to techno, funk and indie at this tunnel-like harbourside club.

Au Son des Guitars   NIGHTCLUB
(Map p766; 18 rue Corneille; ⊗Thu-Sun; ⓂVieux Port) Popular with Corsican locals, this small club has limited dancing, lots of drinking and, occasionally, a Corsican singer. Look sharp to get in.

Sport

Olympique de Marseille   FOOTBALL
Marseille's cherished football team plays at Stade Vélodrome (3 bd Michelet; 1hr guided stadium tours in Jul & Aug €5 ; ⓂRond-Point du Prado). Buy tickets at OM's Boutique Officielle (☑04 91 33 20 01; 44 La Canebière; ⊗10am-7pm Mon-Sat; ⓂNoailles, ⓐCanebière Garibaldi) for as little as €20.

❶ Information

Canebière Change (39 La Canebière; ⊗8am-6pm Mon-Fri, 8.30am-noon & 2-4.30pm Sat; ⓂVieux Port)

Hôpital de la Timone (☑04 91 38 60 00; 264 rue St-Pierre; ⓂLa Timone) About 1km southeast of place Jean Jaurès.

Préfecture de Police (☑04 91 39 80 00; place de la Préfecture; ⊗24hr; ⓂEstrangin-Préfecture)

Tourist Office (☑04 91 13 89 00; www.mar seille-tourisme.com; 4 La Canebière; ⊗9am-7pm Mon-Sat, 10am-5pm Sun; ⓂVieux Port)

❶ Getting There & Away

AIR **Aéroport Marseille-Provence** (www. marseille.aeroport.fr) Also called Aéroport Marseille-Marignane; it is located 25km northwest of Marseille in Marignane.

BOAT The **passenger-ferry terminal** (www. marseille-port.fr; ⓂJoliette) is 250m south of place de la Joliette (1er). **SNCM** (☑08 91 70 18 01; www.sncm.fr; 61 bd des Dames; ⓂJoliette) has services to Corsica, Sardinia and North Africa.

BUS The **bus station** (www.lepilote.com; 3 rue Honnorat; ⓂGare St-Charles SNCF) is at the back of the train station. Purchase tickets from the information desk inside the train station or from the driver. Services to some destinations, including Cassis, use the stop on **place Castel-**

lane, south of the centre. **Eurolines** (www.eurolines.com; 3 allées Léon Gambetta) has international services.

CAR **Avis** (☑08 20 61 16 36; www.avis.com) At the train station.

Europcar (☑08 25 35 83 58; www.europcar.com)

TRAIN **Gare St-Charles** (☺information 9am-8pm Mon-Sat, tickets 5.15am-10pm daily; Ⓜ Gare St-Charles SNCF) is served by both metro lines. The **left-luggage office** (from €3.50; ☺7.30am-10pm) is next to platform A.

In town, buy tickets at the SNCF Boutique inside the **Centre Bourse shopping centre** (Map p766).

From Marseille, trains, including TGVs, go to destinations all over France and Europe, including the following, which all run at least half a dozen times a day:

Avignon €24, 35 minutes
Lyon €50, 1¾ hours
Nice €35, 2½ hours
Paris Gare de Lyon €103, three hours

🛈 Getting Around

For transport information in English: www.lepilote.com.

TO/FROM THE AIRPORT **Shuttle buses** (☑Marseille 04 91 50 59 34, airport 04 42 14 31 27; www.lepilote.com) link the airport with Marseille's train station (€8, 25 minutes, every 20 minutes from 4.30am to 11.30pm).

There are direct **train** services to Marseille, Arles, Avignon and Orange from the Aéroport Marseille Provence Vitrolles station (linked to the airport terminal by a free shuttle).

BICYCLE **Le Vélo** (www.levelo-mpm.fr) Pick up or drop off a bike from 100-plus stations across the city. Free first 30 minutes, €1 for the next 30, and then €1 per hour thereafter. Credit card required to register; instructions in French. Stations dot the centre and the corniche to Pointe Rouge.

FERRY **Cross-Port Ferry** (☺8am-12.30pm & 1-5pm) Runs between the town hall (north side) and place aux Huiles (south side) of the port.

PUBLIC TRANSPORT Marseille has two metro lines (Métro 1 and Métro 2), two tram lines (yellow and green) and an extensive bus network, run by the Régie des Transports Marseillais (RTM).

Bus, metro or tram **tickets** (€1.50) can be used on all public transportation for one hour after they've been time stamped. A **Transpass** for one/three/seven days costs €5/10.50/12.

Bus services stop around 9.30pm, when night buses operate until 12.30am. Most start in front of the **Espace Infos RTM** (☑04 91 91 92 10; www.rtm.fr; 6 rue des Fabres; ☺8.30am-6pm Mon-Fri, 9am-12.30pm & 2-5.30pm Sat;

Ⓜ Vieux Port), where you can obtain information, a great transport map and tickets. **Night shuttles** (☑06 27 06 71 23; www.navettelive.blogspot.com; annual membership €15, rides free; ☺11.45pm-4.30am) operate for people 18 to 30 years old.

The **metro** runs from 5am to 10.30pm Monday to Thursday, and until 12.30am from Friday to Sunday.

Trams run 5am to 1am daily.

TAXI **Taxi Radio Marseille** (☑04 91 02 20 20)

Aix-en-Provence

POP 141,895

Aix-en-Provence is to Provence what the Left Bank is to Paris: an enclave of bourgeois-bohemian chic. It's hard to believe Aix (pronounced 'ex') is just 25km from chaotic, exotic Marseille, and it's no surprise the two remain at odds. Some 30,000 students from the Université de Provence Aix-Marseille, many from overseas, set the mood on the street: bars, cafes and affordable restaurants. The city is rich in culture (two of Aix' most famous sons are Paul Cézanne and Émile Zola) and oh-so respectable, with plane-tree-shaded boulevards and fashionable boutiques. All this class comes at a price: Aix is more expensive than other Provençal towns.

⦿ Sights & Activities

Art, culture and architecture abound in Aix. A stroller's paradise, the highlight is the mostly pedestrian old city, Vieil Aix. South of cours

🛈 DANGERS & ANNOYANCES

Marseille isn't a hotbed of violent crime, but petty crimes and muggings are commonplace. Play it cool. Don't get visibly drunk and stumble home alone at 4am; you may as well wear a target. The tourist office advice is to take taxis at night.

If you're nervous, avoid the Belsunce area (southwest of the train station, bounded by La Canebière, cours Belsunce and rue d'Aix, rue Bernard du Bois and bd d'Athènes). Walking the Canebière is annoying, but generally not dangerous; expect to encounter kids peddling hash.

Solo women travellers should be warned that they will get catcalls from passing strangers.

PROVENCE AIX-EN-PROVENCE

Mirabeau, Quartier Mazarin was laid out in the 17th century, and is home to some of Aix' finest buildings. Place des Quatre Dauphins, with its fish-spouting fountain (1667), is particularly enchanting. Further south still is the peaceful Parc Jourdan, home to the town's Boulodrome Municipal, where locals gather beneath plane trees to play *pétanque*.

TOP CHOICE Cours Mirabeau   HISTORIC QUARTER

No avenue better epitomises Provence's most graceful city than fountain-studded cours Mirabeau, sprinkled with elegant Renaissance *hôtels particuliers* (private mansions) and crowned with a summertime roof of leafy plane trees. Named after the revolutionary hero Comte de Mirabeau, it was laid out in the 1640s. Cézanne and Zola hung out at Les Deux Garçons (53 cours Mirabeau; ⊙7am-2am), one of a clutch of cafes. It buzzes with people watchers.

Among the most impressive *hôtels particuliers* is Hôtel d'Espargnet (1647) at No 38, now home to the university's economics department. Photography and contemporary art get an airing inside Hôtel de Castillon, now the Galerie d'Art du Conseil Général des Bouches du Rhône (☑04 13 31 50 70; 21bis cours Mirabeau; admission free; ⊙9.30am-1pm & 2-6pm Mon-Sat).

TOP CHOICE Musée Granet   ART MUSEUM

(www.museegranet-aixenprovence.fr; place St-Jean de Malte; adult/child €4/free; ⊙11am-7pm Tue-Sun) Housed in a 17th-century priory of the Knights of Malta, this exceptional museum is named after the Provençal painter François Marius Granet (1775–1849), who donated a large number of works. Its collections include 16th- to 20th-century Italian, Flemish and French works. Modern art reads like a who's who: Picasso, Léger, Matisse, Monet, Klee and Van Gogh, among others including the museum's pride and joy: nine Cézanne works. Tickets are sold until one hour before closing.

ℹ AIX-CELLENT

The Aix City Pass (€15), valid five days, includes a guided walking tour, admission to the Atelier Paul Cézanne, Jas de Bouffan and Musée Granet, and a trip on the mini-tram; the Cézanne Pass (€12) covers his three main sights. Buy them at the tourist office, or the two Cézanne sights.

Cathédrale St-Sauveur   CHURCH

(rue de la Roque; ⊙8am-noon & 2-6pm) Built between 1285 and 1350 in a potpourri of styles, this cathedral includes a Romanesque 12th-century nave in its southern aisle, chapels from the 14th and 15th centuries and a 5th-century sarcophagus in the apse. More recent additions include the 18th-century gilt Baroque organ. Acoustics make Gregorian chants (4.30pm Sunday) unforgettable. There are cloister tours.

Fondation Victor Vasarely   GALLERY

(www.fondationvasarely.fr; 1 av Marcel Pagnol; adult/child €9/4; ⊙10am-1pm & 2-6pm Tue-Sun; ◨4 or 6 stop Vasarely) This thrilling gallery and national historical monument, 4km west of the city, was designed by Hungarian optical art innovator Victor Vasarely (1906–97). Though in need of repairs, the building is a masterpiece: 16 interconnecting six-walled galleries, purpose-built to display and reflect the patterning of the artist's 44 acid-trip-ready, floor-to-ceiling geometric artworks.

Thermes Sextius   SPRINGS

(☑04 42 23 81 82; www.thermes-sextius.com; 55 av des Thermes; day pass €45) These modern thermal spas are built on the site of Roman Aquae Sextiae's springs, whose excavated remains are displayed beneath glass in the lobby.

☞ Tours

The tourist office (p779) has DIY walking itineraries and runs a packed schedule of guided walking (€8) and bus tours (from €28) in English, such as a tour retracing Cézanne's steps. Bus tours include Luberon and Alpilles.

Mini-Tram   TRAM TOUR

(☑06 11 54 27 73; www.cpts.fr; tour €6) Leaves from place du Général de Gaulle and winds its way through the Quartier Mazarin, along cours Mirabeau, and around Vieil Aix. Multilingual.

✦ Festivals & Events

The tourist office (p779) has a list of Aix' seemingly continuous festivals.

Rencontres du 9ème Art   ART FESTIVAL

(www.bd-aix.com; ⊙Mar & Apr) Comic books, animation and cartoons.

Festival d'Aix-en-Provence   PERFORMING ARTS

(☑04 34 08 02 17; www.festival-aix.com; ⊙Jul) Month-long festival of classical music, opera, ballet and buskers.

THE CALANQUES: FRANCE'S NEWEST NATIONAL PARK

Marseille abuts the wild and spectacular Parc National des Calanques, a 20km stretch of high, rocky promontories, rising from brilliant-turquoise Mediterranean waters. The sheer cliffs are occasionally interrupted by small idyllic beaches, some impossible to reach without a kayak. The Marseillais cherish the Calanques, and come to soak up sun or take a long day's hike. The promontories have been protected since 1975, and became a national park in April 2012 (www.parcsnationaux.fr).

The best way to see the Calanques, from October to June, is to hike the many maquis-lined trails. During summer, trails close because of fire danger: take a boat tour either from Marseille or Cassis, but be forewarned, they don't stop to let you swim; alternatively, go sea kayaking with Raskas Kayak (www.raskas-kayak.com), drive or take public transport.

Calanque de Sormiou is the largest rocky inlet. Two seasonal restaurants serve lunch with fabulous views, and require reservations. Le Château (04 91 25 08 69; mains €18-24; Apr–mid-Oct) has the best food and Le Lunch (04 91 25 05 37, 04 91 25 05 39; http://wp.resto.fr/lelunch; mains €16-28; Apr–mid-Oct) the better view. By bus, take the 23 from the Rond-Point du Prado metro stop to La Cayolle stop, from where it's a 3km walk. (NB: Diners with reservations are allowed to drive through; otherwise, the road is open to cars weekdays only, September to June.)

Also popular are the *calanques* of Port-Miou, Port-Pin, En-Vau and Morgiou, best accessed from the pretty coastal town of Cassis. A coastal walk from Cassis to Morgiou (about 15km), takes 5½ to 6½ hours and is an absolute stunner. Wear sturdy shoes.

Marseille's tourist office (p772) leads guided walks (no kids under eight) of the Calanques, and has information on walks and trail closures, as does the Cassis' tourist office (08 92 39 01 03; www.ot-cassis.com; quai des Moulins; 9am-6.30pm Tue-Sat, 9.30-12.30 & 3-6pm Sun, shorter hours low season).

Walking aside, the little port town of Cassis makes a postcard-perfect day trip if you have a car. After a glorious morning driving above aquamarine coves, plan to lunch with an obligatory bottle of crisp Cassis white wine at one of the portside restaurants. The tourist office supplies free maps of cellars open for tastings.

Sleeping

L'Épicerie
B&B €€

(06 08 85 38 68; www.unechambreenville.eu; 12 rue du Cancel; s incl breakfast €80-120, d incl breakfast €100-130;) This intimate B&B is the fabulous creation of born-and-bred Aixois lad Luc. His breakfast room and *salon de thé* (tea room) re-creates a 1950s grocery store, and the flowery garden out back is perfect for evening dining (book ahead). Morning meals are veritable feasts. Two rooms accommodate families of four.

Hôtel des Augustins
HOTEL €€

(04 42 27 28 59; www.hotel-augustins.com; 3 rue de la Masse; r €99-250;) A heartbeat from the hub of Aixois life, this former 15th-century convent with a stained-glass foyer has volumes of history: for example, Martin Luther stayed here after his excommunication from Rome. Filled with hand-painted furniture, the largest, most luxurious rooms have jacuzzis; two rooms have private terraces beneath the filigreed bell tower.

Hôtel les Quatre Dauphins
BOUTIQUE HOTEL €

(04 42 38 16 39; www.lesquatredauphins.fr; 54 rue Roux Alphéran; s €55-60, d €70-85;) This sweet 13-room hotel, a former private mansion, was redone in 2010 and is fresh and clean, with excellent new bathrooms. The tall terracotta-tiled staircase (no lift) leads to four attic rooms, with sloped beamed ceilings. Wi-fi costs €5 per 24 hours.

Le Manoir
HOTEL €€

(04 42 26 27 20; www.hotelmanoir.com; 8 rue d'Entrecasteux; d €70-92, tr €98-106, q €124; Feb-Dec;) Atmospherically set in a 14th-century cloister, 'The Manor' sits in a quiet wedge of the old town and has clean and simple, spacious rooms. Friendly staff, free parking and breakfast served alfresco in the vaulted cloister round out its offerings.

Hôtel Cézanne
BOUTIQUE HOTEL €€€

(04 42 91 11 11; http://cezanne.hotelaix.com; 40 av Victor Hugo; d €179-249;) Aix' hippest hotel is a study in clean lines, with sharp-edged built-in desks and lots of light.

Aix-en-Provence

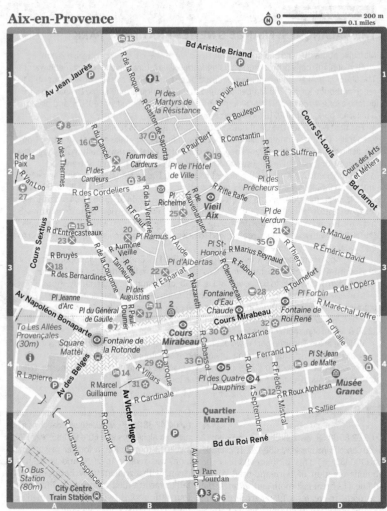

We actually prefer the less expensive 'luxe' rooms, which have the same top-end linens, but more charm. Unfortunately, staff can be surly. Reserve ahead for free parking.

Hôtel Paul　　　　　　　　　　HOTEL €
(☏04 42 23 23 89; http://www.aix-en-provence.com/hotelpaul/; 10 av Pasteur; s/d/tr from €51/52/74; ☏) Just on the edge of Vieil Aix, this bright and cheery little bargain has a sweet garden and a TV lounge. There's fans for summer and wi-fi costs €1.50 per 30 minutes. Free motorcycle and bike parking. No credit cards.

Hôtel Saint-Christophe　　　　HOTEL €€
(☏04 42 26 01 24; www.hotel-saintchristophe.com; 2 av Victor Hugo; s/d/tr/ste from €84/92/132/174; ❄☏) The Saint-Christophe is a proper hotel, with a big lobby and helpful staff. Rooms are styled with a nod to art deco, and have the standard mid-budget amenities, including good bathrooms; some have terraces, some can sleep four. Parking (€12) by reservation.

Hôtel Cardinal　　　　　　　　HOTEL €
(☏04 42 38 32 30; www.hotel-cardinal-aix.com; 24 rue Cardinale; s/d €60/70) Slightly rumpled rooms are quaintly furnished with antiques and tasselled curtains. Six gigantic suites in

Aix-en-Provence

the annexe up the street, each with a kitchenette and dining room, are ideal for longer stays. Wi-fi costs €5 per 24 hours.

✖ Eating

Aix excels at Provençal cuisine and restaurant terraces spill out across backstreet squares. Reservations are essential in the restaurants listed below. Eateries on cours Mirabeau are generally overpriced.

TOP CHOICE / Restaurant
Pierre Reboul GASTRONOMIC €€€
(☎04 42 20 58 26; www.restaurant-pierre-reboul.com; 11 Petite Rue St-Jean; 3-/7-/12-course menus €42/85/142; ⊙lunch Tue-Sat, dinner Wed-Sat, closed late Aug) Aix' newest culinary star invents playful, gorgeous creations that are homages to eating. With a minimalist sensibility, in both the relaxed dining room and on the exquisitely presented plates, Reboul crafts original juxtapositions using fresh but timeless ingredients.

Think perfectly seared duck with a savoury, unexpectedly Asian-influenced broth, sea foam and tender pasta. The lunch special (€50), includes mineral water, coffee and a glass of perfectly paired wine.

Le Petit Verdot FRENCH €€
(☎04 42 27 30 12; www.lepetitverdot.fr; 7 rue d'Entrecasteaux; mains €15-25; ⊙dinner Mon-Sat, lunch Sat) Delicious menus are designed around what's in season and paired with excellent wines. Meats are often braised all day, vegetables are tender, stewed in delicious broths. Save room for an incandescent dessert. Lively dining occurs around tabletops made of wine crates (expect to talk to your neighbour), and the gregarious owner speaks multiple languages.

Charlotte BISTRO €
(☎04 42 26 77 56; 32 rue des Bernardines; 2-/3-course menus €15.50/19; ⊙lunch & dinner Tue-Sat; 🖫) It's all very cosy at Charlotte, where everyone knows everyone. French classics like veal escalope and beef steak fill the handwritten menu, and there are always a couple of imaginative *plats du jour*. In summer everything moves into the garden.

CÉZANNE SIGHTS

The life of local lad Paul Cézanne (1839–1906) is treasured in Aix. To see where he ate, drank, studied and painted, follow the Circuit de Cézanne (Cézanne Trail), marked by footpath-embedded bronze plaques. The informative English-language guide to the plaques, Cézanne's Footsteps, is free at the tourist office. A mobile app, City of Cézanne in Aix-en-Provence (€2), is available online.

Cézanne's last studio, Atelier Paul Cézanne (www.atelier-cezanne.com; 9 av Paul Cézanne; adult/child €5.50/2; ☉10am-noon & 2-6pm, closed Sun winter), 1.5km north of the tourist office on a hilltop, was painstakingly preserved (and recreated: not all the tools and still-life models strewn around the single room were his) as it was at the time of his death. Though the studio is inspiring, none of his works hang here. Take bus 1 or 20 to the Atelier Cézanne stop, or walk 1.5km from the centre. A 10-minute walk uphill from the bus stop is the Terrain des Peintres (opposite 62 av Paul Cézanne), a wonderful terraced garden perfect for a picnic, from where Cézanne, among others, painted the Montagne Ste-Victoire.

Visits to the other two sights must be reserved in advance at the tourist office. In 1859 Cézanne's father bought Le Jas de Bouffan (☏04 42 16 10 91; adult/child €5.50/2; ☉guided tours 10.30am-5.30pm daily summer, less frequent other times; ☒6 stop Corsy), a country manor west of Aix centre, where Cézanne painted furiously: 36 oils and 17 watercolours in the decades that followed depicting the house, farm and chestnut-lined alley.

In 1895 Cézanne rented a cabin at Les Carrières de Bibemus (Bibémus Quarries; ☏04 42 16 10 91; adult/child €6.60/3.10; ☉tours 9.45am daily Jun-Sep, 10.30am & 5pm Mon, Wed, Fri & Sun Apr, May & Oct, 3pm Wed & Sat Jan-Mar), on the edge of town, where he painted prolifically and where he did most of his Montagne Ste-Victoire paintings. Atmospheric one-hour tours of the ochre quarry take visitors on foot through the dramatic burnt-orange rocks Cézanne captured so vividly.

La Mado
MODERN FRENCH €€

(Chez Madeleine; ☏04 42 38 28 02; www.lamado-aix.com; 4 place des Prêcheurs; lunch/dinner menus €18/32; ☉7am-2am daily) This smart daytime cafe and modern restaurant is an unbeatable spot for coffee and fashionable-people watching, or a delicious, relaxed meal. It's been around for years, so the old guard dine while the hipsters shine. The buzzing terrace spills out onto the busy plaza. It also offers oysters and sushi.

Le Formal
MODERN FRENCH €€

(☏04 42 27 08 31; www.restaurant-leformal.fr; 32 rue Espariat; lunch menu €21.50, 3-/7-course dinner menus €38/47; ☉lunch Tue-Fri, dinner Tue-Sat) Chef Jean-Luc Le Formal is making a name for himself in France's foodie circles with his first-class establishment. Impeccably mannered staff serve delicious treats in the vaulted-cellar dining rooms.

Jacquou Le Croquant
BISTRO €

(☏04 42 27 37 19; 2 rue Aumône Vielle; 2-course crêpe menu €16, mains from €10; ☉lunch & dinner daily; ☒) Slide into this tiny, low-key joint for home-cooked, wholesome French basics.

Amphitryon
PROVENÇAL €€

(☏04 42 26 54 10; www.restaurant-amphitryon.fr; 2-4 rue Paul-Doumer; menus €25-40; ☉lunch & dinner Tue-Sat) Run by fiery duo maître d' Patrice Lesné and chef Bruno Ungaro, Amphitryon enjoys a solid reputation among Aix' bourgeoisie, particularly in summer for its market-driven creative cooking and cloister garden. Attached is the Comptoir de l'Amphi (mains €12-18), which serves equally tasty but more informal meals.

Chez Féraud
PROVENÇAL €€

(☏04 42 63 07 27; 8 rue Puits Juif; lunch/3-course menus €22/33; ☉lunch & dinner Tue-Sat Sep-Jul) This elegant, family-run restaurant tucked down a side street is as pretty as a French postcard. The menu features Provençal classics: soupe au pistou (a brothy soup of beans, vermicelli and basil), aubergine en gratin (eggplant gratin), and red peppers stuffed with brandade de morue (salt cod emulsion).

Le Poivre d'Âne
MODERN FRENCH €€

(☏04 42 21 32 66; www.restaurantlepoivredane.com; 40 place des Cardeurs; menus €28-45; ☉dinner Thu-Tue) Locals flock here for affordable, creative, contemporary cuisine in a stylish setting. In summer its designer tables spill across one of Aix' loveliest pedestrian squares.

Drinking & Entertainment

The scene is fun, but fickle. *Le Mois à Aix* (free from the tourist office) and listings on www.marseillebynight.com (in French) cover Aix.

For nightlife, hit rue de la Verrerie and place Richelme. Open-air cafes crowd the city's squares, especially place des Cardeurs, place de Verdun and place de l'Hôtel de Ville.

Aix' student population ensures great cinema options (www.lescinemasaixois.com): Ciné Mazarin (6 rue Laroque; adult/student €7.50/6.50), Cinéma Renoir (08 92 68 72 70; 24 cours Mirabeau; adult/student €7.50/6.50), Le Cézanne (08 92 68 72 70; www.lecezanne.com; 1 rue Marcel Guillaume; adult/student €8.50/6.70).

Le Med Boy GAY BAR
(www.med-boy.com; 6 rue de la Paix; ⊙9.30pm-2am) Aix' only gay bar packs in stand-and-drink 20-somethings.

Le Mistral NIGHTCLUB
(3 rue Frédéric Mistral; ⊙midnight-6am Tue-Sat) If anyone's awake past midnight, chances are they'll wind up at this happening basement club, with three bars and a dance floor. DJs spin house, R&B, techno and rap.

Hot Brass LIVE MUSIC
(04 42 21 05 57; www.hotbrassaix.com; chemin d'Eguilles) Jazz and other live acts, 6km northwest of town.

Grand Théâtre de Provence PERFORMING ARTS
(04 42 91 69 70; www.legrandtheatre.net; 380 av Max Juvénal) State-of-the-art theatre presenting music and opera.

Le Ballet Preljocaj PERFORMING ARTS
(04 42 93 48 00; www.preljocaj.org; 530 av Mozart) Offers performances at the 650-seat Pavillon Noir.

Shopping

Aix' most chic shops cluster along pedestrian rue Marius Reynaud and cours Mirabeau. Les Allées Provençales (www.lesalleesprovencales.fr; av Joseph Villevieille; ⊙10am-7.30pm Mon-Sat) has chain stores.

Place aux Huiles FOOD, DRINK
(59 rue d'Italie) Provençal goodies, like olive oils, chocolates and teas. There's another branch in Marseille (p772).

Cave du Félibrige FOOD, DRINK
(www.aix-en-provence.com/cave-felibrige; 8 rue des Cordeliers) Sells a splendid array of very drinkable wines.

Book in Bar BOOKS
(4 rue Cabassol) Fabulous English bookshop with a cafe.

Information

Centre Hospitalier du Pays d'Aix (04 42 33 50 00; www.ch-aix.fr; av des Tamaris) Medical services.

Police Station (04 42 93 97 00; 10 av de l'Europe)

SOS Médecins (04 42 26 24 00) Medical advice.

Tourist Office (04 42 16 11 61; www.aixenprovencetourism.com; 37 av Giuseppi Verdi; ⊙8.30am-7pm Mon-Sat, 10am-1pm & 2-6pm Sun Oct-Jun, to 8pm Jul-Sep) Has tours, sells event tickets.

Getting There & Away

Consult www.lepilote.com for all transport information, and www.info-ler.fr for some regional buses.

AIR Aéroport Marseille-Provence (p772) is 25km southwest and is served by regular shuttle buses from the bus station.

BUS Aix' **bus station** (04 42 91 26 80, 08 91 02 40 25; av de l'Europe) is a 10-minute walk southwest from La Rotonde. Sunday service is limited. Services:

Arles €9.20, 1½ hours, seven daily
Avignon €17.40, 1¼ hours, six daily
Marseille €5, 25 minutes, every five to 20 minutes
Toulon €12, one hour, seven daily

SWEET TREAT

Aix' sweetest treat since King René's wedding banquet in 1473 is the marzipan-like local speciality, *calisson d'Aix*, a small, diamond-shaped, chewy delicacy made on a wafer base with ground almonds and fruit syrup, and glazed with icing sugar. Traditional *calissonniers* still make them, including Roy René (www.calisson.com; 13 rue Gaston de Saporta), which has a tiny museum. To watch the process firsthand, visit its factory Calissons du Roy René (04 42 39 29 90; tours €1; ⊙10am Tue & Thu by appointment), on the city's fringe.

AIX MARKETS

Food market (place Richelme; ⊘mornings daily): marinated olives, goat's cheese, lavender, honey, peaches, seafood and a bounty of seasonal foods.

Flower markets fill place des Prêcheurs (Sunday morning) and place de l'Hôtel de Ville (Tuesday, Thursday and Saturday mornings).

Flea market (place de Verdun; ⊘Tue, Thu & Sat mornings) Quirky vintage items.

TRAIN Tiny **city centre train station**, at the southern end of av Victor Hugo, serves Marseille (€8, 45 minutes). Aix' **TGV station**, 15km from the city centre and accessible by shuttle bus (€3.70 from the bus station), serves most of France; to Marseille it's 12 minutes (€8, 20 daily).

❶ Getting Around

TO/FROM THE AIRPORT Half-hourly shuttles link Aix' bus station with the airport (€8) from 4.40am to 10.30pm.

BICYCLE **Electric-cycles.fr** (✆04 42 39 90 37; www.electric-cycles.fr; 17bis rue Frédéric Mistral; per 1hr/day/week €4/20/90; ⊘closed Mon morning & Sun) Rents bikes with electrical motors.

BUS **Aix en Bus** (✆09 70 80 90 13; www.aixenbus.fr; 1/10 tickets €1/7, 3-day pass €5) runs local buses. Most run until 8pm. La Rotonde is the main hub. The tourist office also has schedules. Minibus 2 serves the train station, La Rotonde and cours Mirabeau. **Diabline** (www.la-diabline.fr) electric shuttles circle the old town (€0.50, every 10 minutes Monday to Saturday).

There's a **night shuttle** (✆06 26 62 78 33; www.navettelive.blogspot.com; annual membership €15, rides free; ⊘11.30pm-4.15am Tue-Fri), but you must be between 18 and 30 years to ride.

TAXI Outside the bus station.

Taxi Mirabeau (✆04 42 21 61 61)

Taxi Radio Aixois (✆04 42 27 71 11)

ARLES & THE CAMARGUE

Arles

POP 54,088

Arles' poster boy is the celebrated impressionist painter Vincent van Gogh. If you're familiar with his work, you'll be familiar with Arles: the light, the colours, the landmarks and the atmosphere, all faithfully captured.

But long before Van Gogh rendered this grand Rhône River locale on canvas, the Romans valued its worth. In 49 BC Arles' prosperity and political standing rose meteorically when it backed a winner in Julius Caesar (who would never meet defeat in his entire career). After Caesar plundered Marseille, which had supported his rival Pompey the Great, Arles eclipsed Marseille as the region's major port. Within a century and a half, it boasted a 12,000-seat theatre and a 20,000-seat amphitheatre to entertain its citizens with gruesome gladiatorial spectacles and chariot races.

Still impressively intact, the two structures now stage events including Arles' famous *férias* (bull-running festivals), with their controversial lethal bullfights, the less bloody *courses camarguaises* and three days of street parties.

◉ Sights & Activities

Though he painted 200-odd canvases in Arles, there are no Van Gogh artworks here today, and Van Gogh's little 'yellow house' on place Lamartine, which he painted in 1888, was destroyed during WWII. Nevertheless, there are several ways to pay homage to the master. Mapped out in a brochure (€1 or downloadable for free online) from the tourist office (p785), the evocative Van Gogh walking circuit of the city takes in scenes painted by the artist.

Arles will soon be graced with a cultural centre designed by world-renowned architect Frank Gehry. The **Museon Arlaten** is closed for renovations until 2014.

Unless otherwise noted, the last entry to sights is 30 minutes prior to closing. Winter hours are shorter than those listed below; places that close at 7pm in summer usually close at 5pm in winter. Museums are free the first Sunday of the month.

TOP CHOICE Les Arènes ROMAN SITES
(Amphithéâtre; adult/child incl Théâtre Antique €6.50/free; ⊘9am-7pm) Slaves, criminals and wild animals (including giraffes) met their dramatic demise before a jubilant 20,000-strong crowd during Roman gladiatorial displays at Les Arènes, built around the late 1st or early 2nd century AD. During the early medieval Arab invasions the arch-laced circular structure, which is 136m long, 107m wide and 21m tall, was topped with four defensive towers to become a fortress. Indeed, by the 1820s, when the amphithea-

PROVENCE ARLES

CULINARY DETOUR: VENTABREN

A lesser-known hilltop village, Ventabren (population 5000), 16km west of Aix, provides the perfect lazy-day detour. Meander sun-dappled cobbled lanes, peep inside a 17th-century church, and take in panoramic views of Provence from the ruins of Château de la Reine Jeanne before a superb lunch or dinner at La Table de Ventabren (04 42 28 79 33; www.latabledeventabren.com; 1 rue Cézanne; menus €41-50; lunch Wed-Sun, dinner Tue-Sun), reason enough to visit. The terrace looks out to distant mountains, magical on starry summer evenings. Chef Dan Bessoudo, who recently received a coveted Michelin star, creates inventive, wholly modern French dishes and knockout desserts. Reservations essential.

tre was returned to its original use, there were 212 houses and two churches that had to be razed on the site.

Buy tickets for bloody bullfights, bloodless *courses camarguaises*, theatre and concerts at the Bureau de Location (Bureau de Location; 08 91 70 03 70; www.arenes-arles.com; 9.30am-noon & 2-6pm Mon-Fri, 10am-1pm Sat) near the entrance.

Musée Réattu ART MUSEUM
(04 90 49 37 58; www.museereattu.arles.fr; 10 rue du Grand Prieuré; adult/child €7/free; 10am-12.30pm & 2-6.30pm Tue-Sun) This splendid modern-art museum is housed in the exquisitely renovated 15th-century Grand Priory of the Knights of Malta. Among its collections are works by 18th- and 19th-century Provençal artists and two paintings and 57 sketches by Picasso. It hosts wonderfully curated cutting-edge exhibitions.

Fondation Vincent Van Gogh GALLERY
(04 90 49 94 04; www.fondation-vincentvangogh-arles.org; 5 place Honoré Clair; adult/child €6/free; 10am-7pm) This newly renovated gallery houses rotating exhibits and a collection of important modern-day artists, including David Hockney, Francis Bacon and Fernando Botero, paying homage to the artist's distinctive style.

Musée Départemental Arles Antique ANTIQUITIES MUSEUM
(04 13 31 51 03; www.arles-antique.cg13.fr; av de la Première Division Française Libre; adult/child €6/free; 10am-6pm Wed-Mon) This striking, state-of-the-art cobalt-blue museum perches on the edge of what used to be the Roman chariot racing track (circus), 1.5km southwest of the tourist office. The rich collection of pagan and Christian art includes stunning mosaics. Houses a leading mosaic restoration centre; watch work in progress.

Théâtre Antique ROMAN SITES
(04 90 96 93 30; bd des Lices; €4.50, or free with Les Arènes admission; 9am-7pm) Still regularly used for alfresco concerts and plays, the Théâtre Antique dates from the end of the 1st century BC. For hundreds of years it was a source of construction materials, with workers chipping away at the 102m-diameter structure (the column on the right-hand side near the entrance indicates the height of the original arcade). Enter on rue de la Calade.

FREE Église St-Trophime CHURCH
(place de la République) Arles was an archbishopric from the 4th century until 1790, and this Romanesque-style church was once a cathedral. Built in the late 11th and 12th centuries on the site of several earlier churches, it's named after St Trophime, a bishop of Arles during the late 2nd or early 3rd century AD. On the western portal, the intricately sculpted tympanum (more spectacular than the interior) depicts St Trophime holding a spiral staff. Inside the austere church, the treasury contains bone fragments of Arles' bishops who were later canonised. Many of the statues inside were decapitated during the French Revolution.

Next door, the evocative 12th- to 14th-century Cloître St-Trophime (St-Trophime Cloister; 04 90 49 36 36; adult/child €3.50/free; 9am-7pm) was built to accommodate the monks' daily lives. It hosts occasional exhibitions.

Les Alyscamps CEMETERY
(av des Alyscamps; adult/child €3.50/free; 9am-7pm) Van Gogh and Gauguin both painted this necropolis 1km southwest of town. Founded by the Romans and taken over by Christians in the 4th century, the cemetery became a coveted resting place because of the tombs of martyr St Genest and Arles' first bishops.

PROVENCE ARLES

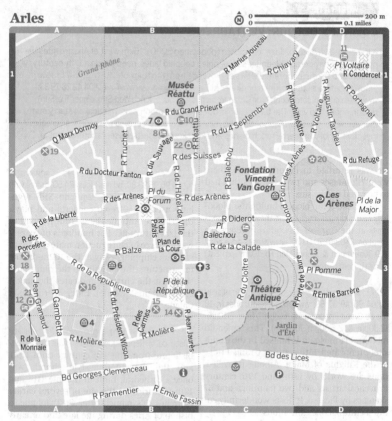

Arles

Arles

◉ Top Sights

◉ Sights

🛏 Sleeping

🍴 Eating

🎭 Entertainment

🛍 Shopping

Espace Van Gogh
GALLERY

(☎04 90 49 39 39; place Félix Rey; ⊙9am-5pm) Housed in the former hospital where Van Gogh had his ear stitched and was later locked up – not to be confused with the asylum Monastère St-Paul de Mausole (p789) – this gallery houses temporary art exhibitions.

Thermes de Constantin
ROMAN SITES

(rue du Grand Prieuré; adult/child €3/free; ⊙9am-noon & 2-7pm) Partly preserved Roman baths were built for Emperor Constantin's private use in the 4th century.

Place du Forum
ROMAN SITES

Just as social, political and religious life revolved around the forum in Roman Arles (spot the remains of a 2nd century AD temple embedded in Hôtel Pinus Nord's facade), so this busy plane-tree-shaded square buzzes with cafe life today.

Beneath your feet are **Cryptoportiques** (adult/child €3.50/free; ⊙9am-noon & 2-7pm), subterranean foundations for the forum and buried arcades (the plaza was lower in Roman times) carved out in the 1st century BC. Access the underground galleries, 89m long and 59m wide, at the **Hôtel de Ville** (Town Hall; place de la République).

🎭 Festivals & Events

Féria d'Arles
BULLFIGHTING

(Féria de Pâques; www.feriaarles.com; ⊙Easter) Festival heralding the start of bullfighting season, with bullfighting in Les Arènes most Sundays in May and June.

Fête des Gardians
CULTURAL FESTIVAL

(⊙1 May) Mounted Camargue cowboys parade and hold games.

Les Suds
MUSIC FESTIVAL

(www.suds-arles.com; ⊙Jul) Vibrant music festival, held over one week in early July.

Les Rencontres d'Arles Photographie
ART FESTIVAL

(www.rencontres-arles.com; ⊙early Jul–Sep) International photography festival.

Féria du Riz
BULLFIGHTING

(www.feriaarles.com; ⊙Sep) Bullfights during this week-long festival mark the start of the rice harvest.

🛏 Sleeping

Arles has reasonably priced, excellent year-round accommodation, which only really fills during *férias;* some hotels only open April to October. Hotels' private parking tends to be pricey.

⌂TOP CHOICE Hôtel de l'Amphithéâtre
HISTORIC HOTEL €

(☎04 90 96 10 30; www.hotelamphitheatre.fr; 5-7 rue Diderot; s/d/tr/q from €57/67/117/137; ❄@🖵) Crimson, chocolate, terracotta and other rich earthy colours dress the exquisite 17th-century stone structure of this stylish hotel, with narrow staircases, a roaring fire and alfresco courtyard breakfasts. The romantic suite (€157) has a dreamy lilac-walled terrace overlooking rooftops. Wheelchair access.

Hôtel Arlatan
HISTORIC HOTEL €€

(☎04 90 93 56 66; www.hotel-arlatan.fr; 26 rue du Sauvage; d €85-157, apt €177-247; ⊙mid-Mar–mid-Nov; ❄@🖵☀) The heated swimming pool, pretty garden and plush rooms decorated with antique furniture are just some of the things going for this hotel. Add to that a setting steeped in history, with Roman foundations visible through a glass floor in the lobby and 15th-century paintings on one of the lounges' ceilings. Wheelchair access.

Le Belvédère Hôtel
BOUTIQUE HOTEL €

(☎04 90 91 45 94; www.hotellebelvedere-arles.com; 5 place Voltaire; s/d from €65/70; ❄🖵) This sleek 17-room hotel is one of the best Arlésian pads. Red-glass chandeliers (and friendly staff) adorn the lobby breakfast area and the super-clean rooms and bathrooms are fitted out in stylish red, chocolate brown and grey.

Hôtel du Musée
BOUTIQUE HOTEL €

(☎04 90 93 88 88; www.hoteldumusee.com; 11 rue du Grand Prieuré; s/d/tr/q from €60/65/90/120; ⊙mid-Mar–Oct; ❄🖵) In a fine 17th- to 18th-century building, this impeccable hotel has comfortable rooms, a checkerboard-tiled breakfast room and a sugar-sweet patio garden brimming with pretty blossoms.

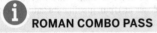

ℹ ROMAN COMBO PASS

Buy a pass for multiple sights at the tourist office (p785) or any Roman site: **Passeport Avantage** (€13.50) covers the museums, both theatres, the baths, crypt, Les Alyscamps and the Cloître St-Trophime; the **Passeport Liberté** (€9) gives you the choice of five sights in total including one museum.

VINCENT

It's easy to forget that Vincent van Gogh was only 37 when he died, as he appears much older in his self-portraits. Born in 1853, the Dutch painter arrived in Arles in 1888 after living in Paris with his younger brother Theo, an art dealer who financially supported Vincent from his own modest income. In Paris he had become acquainted with seminal artists Edgar Degas, Camille Pissarro, Henri de Toulouse-Lautrec and Paul Gauguin.

Revelling in Arles' intense light and bright colours, Van Gogh painted with a burning fervour, unfazed by howling mistral winds. During a mistral he would kneel on his canvases and paint horizontally, or lash his easel to iron stakes driven deep into the ground. He sent paintings to Theo for him to try to sell, and dreamed of founding an artists colony here, but only Gauguin followed up his invitation. Their differing artistic approaches (Gauguin believed in painting from imagination, Van Gogh painting what he saw) and their artistic temperaments came to a head with the argument in December 1888 that led to Van Gogh lopping off part of his own ear.

In May 1889 Van Gogh voluntarily entered an asylum, Monastère St-Paul de Mausole (p789) in St-Rémy de Provence, 25km northeast of Arles over the Alpilles. During his one year, one week, and one day's confinement, he painted 150-odd canvases, including masterpieces like *Starry Night* (not to be confused with *Starry Night over the Rhône*, painted in Arles).

In February 1890, his 1888 work *The Red Vines*, painted in Arles, was bought by Anne Boch, sister of his friend Eugene Boch, for 400 francs (around €50 today) – the only painting he sold in his lifetime. It now hangs in the Pushkin State Museum of Fine Arts.

On 16 May 1890 Van Gogh moved to Auvers-sur-Oise, just outside Paris, to be closer to Theo. But on 27 July that year he shot himself, possibly to avoid further financial burden for his brother. He died two days later, Theo at his side. Theo subsequently had a breakdown, was committed and died, aged 33, just six months after Vincent. Less than a decade later, Van Gogh's talent started to achieve recognition, with major museums acquiring his work.

L'Hôtel Particulier   BOUTIQUE HOTEL €€€

(☑04 90 52 51 40; www.hotel-particulier.com; 4 rue de la Monnaie; d €289-309; ⊙Easter-Oct) This exclusive boutique hotel with restaurant, spa and *hammam* (Turkish steambath) oozes chic charm. From the big black door with heavy knocker to the crisp white linens and minimalist decor, everything about this 18th-century private mansion enchants.

Auberge de Jeunesse   HOSTEL €

(☑04 90 96 18 25; www.fuaj.org; 20 av Maréchal Foch; dm incl breakfast & sheets €18.50; ⊙mid-Feb–mid-Dec, reception closed 10am-5pm) This sunlit place, made up of eight-bed dorms, is just 10 minutes' walk from the centre. Its bar closes at 11pm, just like its gates (except during *férias*).

Camping City   CAMPGROUND €

(☑04 90 93 08 86; www.camping-city.com; 67 rte de Crau; sites €19; ⊙Apr-Sep) Closest campground to town, 1.5km southeast on the road to Marseille. There's bike hire and a laundry, with supermarkets nearby. Take bus 2 to the Hermite stop.

✕ Eating

Arles and its environs are foodie heaven. At Arles' enormous Saturday-morning market (bd des Lices), Camargue salt, goat's cheese and *saucisson d'Arles* (bull-meat sausage) scent the air. The scene shifts to bd Émile Combes on Wednesday morning.

TOP CHOICE L'Atelier   GASTRONOMIC €€€

(☑04 90 91 07 69; www.rabanel.com; 7 rue des Carmes; lunch/dinner menus from €55/95; ⊙lunch & dinner Wed-Sun) Consider this not a meal, but an artistic experience. Every one of the seven or 13 edible works of art is a wondrous composition of flavours, colours and textures, and no two bites are the same. Sit back and revel in Jean-Luc Rabanel's superbly crafted symphony of fresh organic tastes. No wonder this charismatic chef with his own veggie patch has two Michelin stars.

TOP CHOICE L'Autruche   MODERN FRENCH €€

(☑04 90 49 73 63; 5 rue Dulau; lunch menus €18, mains €29; ⊙lunch & dinner Tue-Sat) This modern, inviting restaurant run by husband and wife team Fabien and Ouria assembles market-fresh dishes to perfection. For example, their Michelin-experienced chef layers thin strips of green-apple chutney with a superbly prepared foie gras. Extravagant desserts are a treat.

TOP CHOICE **Le Gibolin** BISTRO €€
(☎04 88 65 43 14; 13 rue des Porcelet; menus €25; ⊙lunch & dinner Tue-Sat Sep-Jun) Sup on peerless home cooking, while the friendly patroness bustles between tables and offers ladies fresh roses, and her Jack Russell terrier nips at her heels. It's a wine bar, really, so the wine pairings are *magnifique*. No credit cards.

L'Entrevue MOROCCAN €
(☎04 90 93 37 28; www.lentrevue-restaurant. com; 23 quai Marx Dormoy; mains €14-18; ⊙lunch & dinner daily; 🖪) Excellent, heaping bowls of organic *tajines* and couscous are briskly served quayside.

Le Cilantro PROVENÇAL €€€
(☎04 90 18 25 05; www.restaurantcilantro.com; 31 rue Porte de Laure; mains €41; ⊙lunch Tue-Fri, dinner Tue-Sat; 🖪) Chef Jérôme Laurent, a born-and-bred local lad, runs this hot spot and combines local ingredients with world spices to create accomplished dishes from fresh fish to duck medallions or steak.

Au Jardin du Calendal TRADITIONAL FRENCH €
(☎04 90 96 11 89; 5 rue Porte de Laure; mains €14-18; ⊙noon-7pm Tue-Sun; 🖪) The leafy courtyard garden of this hotel (d from €120) is perfect for lunching on gourmet salads.

Comptoir du Sud CAFE €
(☎04 90 96 22 17; 2 rue Jean Jaurès; ⊙10am-5pm Tue-Fri) Gourmet sandwiches (tasty chutneys,

succulent meats, foie gras) and divine little salads, all at rock-bottom prices, are served at the counter.

🍷 Drinking & Entertainment

The place du Forum makes for great cafe sitting. Roma bands perform on the city's streets, with past acts including Los Reyes and the Gypsy Kings (from Arles no less, discovered while busking in St-Tropez). The tourist office has lists of what's on.

Patio de Camargue DANCE, MUSIC
(☎04 90 49 51 76; http://patio.chico.fr; 51bis chemin Barriol; ticket incl dinner €55-70) Watch a sangria-fuelled dinner show.

🛍 Shopping

La Botte Camarguaise SHOES
(☎04 90 96 20 87; 22 rue Jean Granaud) Buy a pair of handmade Camargue-style cowboy boots.

La Boutique des Passionnés MUSIC
(☎04 90 96 59 93; www.passionnes.com; 14 rue Réattu) Gig flyers and music by Roma bands.

ℹ Information

Post Office (5 bd des Lices)

Tourist Office (www.arlestourisme.com) Main office (☎04 90 18 41 20; bd des Lices; ⊙9am-6.45pm); train station (☎04 90 43 33 57; ⊙9am-12.30pm & 2.30-5pm Mon-Fri)

ℹ Getting There & Around

BICYCLE **Europbike** (☎06 38 14 49 50; www. europbike-provence.net) rents bikes and has bike tours.

PROVENCE ARLES

A BULLISH AFFAIR

Animal lovers fear not: not all types of bullfights end with blood. The local Camargue variation, the *course camarguaise*, sees amateur *razeteurs* (from the word for 'shave'), wearing skin-tight white shirts and trousers, get as close as they dare to the *taureau* (bull) to try to snatch rosettes and ribbons tied to the bull's horns, using a *crochet* (a razor-sharp comb) held between their fingers. Their leaps over the arena's barrier as the bull charges make spectators' hearts lurch.

Bulls are bred on a *manade* (bull farm) by *manadiers*, who are helped in their daily chores by *gardians* (Camargue cattle-herding cowboys). These mounted herdsmen parade through Arles during the Fête des Gardians (p783) in May.

Many *manades* also breed the creamy white *cheval de Camargue* (Camargue horse) and some welcome visitors; ask at tourist offices in Arles and Stes-Maries-de-la-Mer.

A calendar of *courses camarguaises* is online at the Fédération Française de la Course Camarguaise (French Federation of Camargue Bullfights; ☎04 66 26 05 35; www. ffcc.info), with many occurring at the arena in Stes-Maries-de-la-Mer. *Recortadores* (a type of bull baiting with lots of bull jumping) also happens during the bullfighting season (Easter to September).

BUS From the bus station, there are services to Aix-en-Provence (€9, 1½ hours), Stes-Maries-de-la-Mer (€2.50, one hour) and Nîmes (€1.50, one hour).

Star (📞08 10 00 08 16; ⊘8.30am-noon & 2-5.30pm Mon-Fri) operates local buses from 6.30am to 7.30pm Monday to Saturday, and 9.30am to 5.30pm Sunday. Tickets cost €0.80. Free minibuses called Starlets circle the old city every 25 minutes (7.10am to 7.15pm Monday to Saturday).

TAXI Call 📞04 90 96 90 03.

TRAIN There are services to Nîmes (€7.50, 30 minutes), Marseille (€13, 45 minutes) and Avignon (€7, 20 minutes). The closest TGV stations are in Avignon and Nîmes.

The Camargue

Just south of Arles, Provence's rolling landscapes yield to the flat, marshy wilds of the Camargue, famous for its teeming bird life, roughly 500 species. King of all is the pink flamingo, which enjoys the expansive wetlands' mild winters. Equally famous are the Camargue's small white horses; their mellow disposition makes horse riding the ideal way to explore the region's patchwork of salt pans and rice fields, and meadows dotted with grazing bulls. Bring binoculars – and mosquito repellent.

Enclosed by the Petit Rhône and Grand Rhône Rivers, most of the Camargue wetlands fall within the 850-sq-km Parc Naturel Régional de Camargue, established in 1970 to preserve the area's fragile ecosystems while sustaining local agriculture. On the periphery, the Étang de Vaccarès and nearby peninsulas and islands form the Réserve Nationale de Camargue, a 135-sq-km nature reserve.

The Camargue's two largest towns are the seaside pilgrim's outpost Stes-Maries-de-la-Mer and, to the northwest, the walled town of Aigues-Mortes.

⊙ Sights & Activities

East of Stes-Maries-de-la-Mer, seafront paths like Digue à la Mer are reserved for walkers and cyclists.

Musée de la Camargue   MUSEUM
(Musée Camarguais; 📞04 90 97 10 82; www.parc -camargue.fr; Mas du Pont de Rousty; adult/child €4.50/free; ⊘9am-12.30pm & 1-6pm Wed-Mon Feb-Dec) Inside an 1812-built sheep shed 10km southwest of Arles on the D570, the Camargue Museum paints an exhaustive portrait of traditional life, its exhibitions

covering local history, ecosystems, farming techniques, flora and fauna. A 3.5km trail leads to an observation tower with bird's-eye views of the *mas* (farmhouse) and its protected natural surrounds. The museum is the main information point for the Parc Naturel Régional de Camargue.

Le Parc Ornithologique
du Pont de Gau   NATURE PARK
(📞04 90 97 82 62; www.parcornithologique.com; Pont du Gau; adult/child €7/4; ⊘9am-sunset) Pink flamingos pirouette overhead and stalk the watery landscape at this bird park, home to every bird species known to set foot in the Camargue. Watch them from 7km of beautiful trails meandering through the site. Find the park on the D570 in Pont du Gau, 4km north of Stes-Maries-de-la-Mer.

Domaine de la Palissade   NATURE PARK
(📞04 42 86 81 28; www.palissade.fr; rte de la Mer; adult/child €3/free; ⊘9am-5pm daily Apr-Oct, 9am-5pm Wed-Sun Nov-Feb) This remote nature centre, south of Salin de Giraud, organises fantastic forays into the marshes on foot and horseback; call ahead to book horse treks (1hr adult/child €16/14, 2hr €28/26). They rent binoculars (€2) and have free maps of the estate's three marked walking trails (1km to 8km) through scrubby glasswort, flowering sea lavender (August) and lagoons.

Les Salins de Giraud   SALT PANS
(📞04 42 86 70 20; place Péchiney, Salin de Giraud; adult/child/family €8.20/6/24.20; ⊘10am-12.30pm & 2-6pm Apr-Oct) Learn how *sel* (salt) is produced by local *sauniers* (salt farmers) and tour the salt pans on board a tourist train.

Les Cabanes de Cacharel   HORSE RIDING
(📞04 90 97 84 10, 06 11 57 74 75; www.cabanesde cacharel.com; rte de Cacharel; 1/2/3hrs horse trek €15/28/40) Farms along route d'Arles (D570) offer *promenades à cheval* (horseback riding) astride white Camargue horses, but a more authentic experience can be had at the less tacky Les Cabanes de Cacharel along the parallel rte de Cacharel (D85A). They also have horse-and-carriage rides (€12/20 per one/two hours).

Boating   WATER SPORTS
The marshy Camargue lends itself to exploration by boat, and prices are usually around €10/5 per adult/child per 1½-hour trip. Le Tiki III (📞04 90 97 81 68; www.tiki3.fr) is a beat-up old paddle boat at the mouth of the Petit Rhône, 1.5km west of Stes-Maries.

For canoeing and kayaking on the Petit Rhône, contact Kayak Vert Camargue (☑04 66 73 57 17; www.kayakvert-camargue.fr; Mas de Sylvéréal), 14km north of Stes-Maries off the D38.

🛏 Sleeping & Eating

TOP CHOICE Le Mas de Peint   BOUTIQUE HOTEL €€€
(☑04 90 97 20 62; www.masdepeint.com; Le Sambuc; d/ste from €260/395; ☺mid-Mar–mid-Nov; ❋☎☑☒) Camargue's upmarket *mas* (farmhouse): think chic, gentrified country quarters right out of the pages of design mag *Côte Sud*. The gourmet restaurant (3-course dinner menu adult/child €55/29, lunch from €39, canteen mains €17-30; ☺lunch Sat & Sun, dinner Fri-Wed) with seasonal menus and poolside canteen are open to nonguests. Other offerings include horses and bikes to ride, jeep safaris (€60) and Roma-music dinners in summer. Reservations essential.

Hôtel de Cacharel   FARMSTAY €€
(☑04 90 97 95 44; www.hotel-cacharel.com; rte de Cacharel, D85A; s/d/tr/q from €120/131/142/165; ☺year-round; @☎☑☒) This isolated farmstead perfectly balances modern-day comforts with rural authenticity. Photographic portraits of the bull herder who created the hotel in 1947 give the vintage dining room soul. The priciest rooms look out over the sunrise on the water. There's a friendly owner, fans in summer, and wi-fi in reception. Just north of Stes-Maries-de-la-Mer.

TOP CHOICE La Chassagnette   GASTRONOMIC €€
(☑04 90 97 26 96; www.chassagnette.fr; rte du Sambuc; mains €35; ☺lunch & dinner Thu-Mon Apr-Jun, Sep & Oct, daily Jul & Aug, Thu-Sun Nov-Mar) Inhaling the scent of sun-ripened tomatoes is one of many pleasures at this 19th-century sheepfold – the ultimate Camargue dine. Alain Ducasse prodigy Armand Arnal cooks up a constantly changing 100% organic menu, grows much of it himself and woos guests with a mosquito-protected outside terrace. Look for the fork and trowel sign, 12km southeast of Arles on the southbound D36, just north of Le Sambuc.

Restaurant La Telline   CAMARGUAIS €€
(☑04 90 97 01 75; www.restaurantlatelline.fr; rte de Gageron, Villeneuve; mains €20-25; ☺lunch & dinner Fri-Mon) Jean-Paul and Florence offer rustic home cooking in this locals' favourite. No credit cards.

❶ Getting There & Around

You will need a car to visit the area; it's an easy day trip from Arles. Alternatively, its flat terrain makes Camargue an ideal cycling destination; hire companies based in Stes-Maries-de-la-Mer (p788) can usually drop off bikes at your hotel for free.

Stes-Maries-de-la-Mer

POP 2344

You could be forgiven for thinking you're in Spain at this remote seaside outpost, where whitewashed buildings line dusty streets and dancers in bright dresses spin flamenco. During its Roma pilgrimages, street-cooked pans of paella fuel chaotic crowds of carnivalesque guitarists, dancers and cowboys.

◉ Sights

Tickets for bullfights at Les Stes-Maries' Arènes are sold at the arena.

Église des Stes-Maries   CHURCH
(place de l'Église) This 12th- to 15th-century church, with its dark, hushed, candle-wax-scented atmosphere, draws legions of pilgrim Roma to venerate the statue of black Sara, their highly revered patron saint, during the Pèlerinage des Gitans (p788). The relics of Sara and those of Marie-Salomé and Marie-Jacobé, all found in the crypt by King René in 1448, are enshrined in a painted wooden chest, stashed in the stone wall above the choir. From the church's rooftop terrace (€2), a panorama unfolds.

Beaches   BEACH
Stes-Maries-de-la-Mer is fringed by 30km of fine-sand beaches, easily reached by bicycle. Nudist beaches surround the Gacholle lighthouse off the Digue à la Mer.

🕴 Activities

Camargue Bateau de Promenade   BOATING
(☑04 90 97 84 72; http://bateau-camargue.com; 5 rue des Launes) Trips with this company generally cost around €10/5 per adult/child per 1½-hour trip.

DID YOU KNOW?

The Camargue's animals change colours. Pink flamingos turn white in winter because of the lack of carotene-rich brine shrimp. And the famous white horses are born brown, turning white only at maturity.

Quatre Maries   BOATING
(☎04 90 97 70 10; www.bateaux-4maries.
camargue.fr; 36 av Théodore Aubanel) Boat trips
lasting 1½-hours cost around €10/5 per
adult/child.

Le Vélociste   CYCLING
(☎04 90 97 83 26; www.levelociste.fr; place Mireille,
Stes-Maries-de-la-Mer) Charges €15/28/34 per
one/two/three days of bicycle hire and advises on cycling itineraries. Also organises
cycling-and-horseback (€36) or cycling-and-
canoeing (€30) packages.

Le Vélo Saintois   CYCLING
(☎04 90 97 74 56; www.levelosaintois.camargue.
fr; 19 rue de la République, Stes-Maries-de-la-Mer)
Charges €17/34 for one/three days' bike rental, has tandems (€30 per day) and an English-
language list of cycling routes, and rents
mountain bikes (€15/34 per one/three days).

🛏 Sleeping

Hôtel Méditerranée   HOTEL €
(☎04 90 97 82 09; www.hotel-mediterranee.ca
margue.fr; 4 av Frédéric Mistral; d without/with bathroom €42/55, tr/q €75/80; ☺mid-Mar–Sep; ❄)
Handily located in the centre of town, this
is one of the cheapest and most charming
options, festooned with flowerpots. Simple
rooms seconds from the sea.

L'Auberge Cavalière   BOUTIQUE HOTEL €€
(☎04 90 97 88 88; www.aubergecavaliere.com;
D570; d €140-195) Located approximately
1.5km north of Stes-Maries, this salt-of-the-
earth hotel spreads out over a typical Camargue landscape of wetlands and meadows. Rooms 340 to 345 look over a pond
teeming with bird life; the thatched cabins
offer cosy independent quarters. There are
horse-riding trips and great regional restaurant (menus €18-42).

🍴 Eating

La Cabane aux Coquillages   SEAFOOD €
(rue Théodore Aubanel; menus from €18.50;
☺lunch & dinner daily Mar-Nov) This pocket-size
fish shop has crates of crustaceans piled
high inside and a gaggle of sea-blue chairs
outside. A glass of dry white and a half-doz-
en oysters costs a mere €8.50.

Lou Santen   SEAFOOD €
(☎06 30 17 32 49; 21 rue Sadi Carnot; mains €9-15;
☺May–mid-Sep) Rebuilt each summer for the
new season, this beach restaurant is shaded
by a typical reed *loupio*. The catch of the day
can feel pricey but stick to a finger-licking
bowl of *moules frîtes* (mussels and chips)
and value is guaranteed.

ⓘ Information

Tourist Office (☎04 90 97 82 55; www.sain
tesmaries.com; 5 av Van Gogh; ☺9am-7pm)
Guided walking tours (€7) depart 2pm Tuesday
and Friday.

ⓘ Getting There & Away

Stes-Maries-de-la-Mer has no bus station;
buses to/from Arles (€2.70, 45 minutes,
eight daily) use the shelter at the northern
entrance to town on av d'Arles (the continuation of rte d'Arles and the D570).

Aigues-Mortes
POP 7705

Actually located over the border from Provence in the Gard *département*, the picturesque town of Aigues-Mortes sits 28km

---

THE STORY OF THE MARYS & GITAN PILGRIMAGES

Catholicism first reached European shores in what is now tiny Stes-Maries-de-la-Mer.
The stories say that Saints Marie-Salomé (Mary Salome) and Marie-Jacobé (Mary of
Clopas) – and some say Mary Magdalene – fled the Holy Land in a little boat and were
caught in a storm, drifting at sea until washing ashore here.

Provençal and Catholic lore diverge at this point: Catholicism relates that Sara, patron saint of the *gitans* (Roma Gitano people, also known as gypsies), travelled with the
two Maries (Marys) on the boat. Provençal legend says Sara was already here and was
the first person to recognise their holiness. In 1448, skeletal remains said to belong to
Sara and the two Marys were found in a crypt in Stes-Maries-de-la-Mer.

Gitans continue to make pilgrimages to Pèlerinage des Gitans (Roma pilgrimages)
on 24 and 25 May (often staying for up to three weeks), dancing and playing music in
the streets, and parading a statue of Sara through town. The Sunday in October closest
to the 22nd sees a second pilgrimage dedicated to the two Saint Marys (Stes Maries);
courses camarguaises are also held at this time.

northwest of Stes-Maries-de-la-Mer at the western extremity of the Camargue. Set in flat marshland and encircled by high stone walls, the town was established in the mid-13th century by Louis IX to give the French Crown a Mediterranean port under its direct control. Cobbled streets inside the walls are lined with restaurants, cafes and bars, giving it a festive atmosphere and making it a charming spot from which to explore the Camargue.

Scaling the ramparts rewards you with sweeping views. Head to the top of the tower, Tour de Constance (adult/child €6.50/free; ⊙10am-7pm May-Aug, 10am-5.30pm Sep-Apr); the 1.6km wall-top walk takes about one hour.

L'Hermitage de St-Antoine (☑06 03 04 34 05; www.hermitagesa.com; 9 bd Intérieur Nord; r incl breakfast €84; ✳), inside the walled town, has three exquisitely appointed rooms, one with a small private terrace. Hôtel L'Escale (☑04 66 53 71 14; http://hotel.escale.free.fr; 3 av Tour de Constance; d €40-68, q €75-85) caters fantastically to budget travellers.

The tourist office (☑04 66 53 73 00; www.ot-aiguesmortes.fr; place St-Louis; ⊙9am-noon & 1-6pm) is inside the walled city.

LES ALPILLES

This silvery chain of low, jagged mountains, strung between the rivers Durance and Rhône, delineates a *très chic* side of Provence, notably around upmarket St-Rémy de Provence, known for fine restaurants and summertime celebrity spotting. The entire region is chock-a-block with gastronomic delights – AOC olive oil, vineyards, Michelin-starred restaurants and truffles. History comes to life at magnificent ruined castles, and at one of Provence's best Roman sites, the ancient city of Glanum.

St-Rémy de Provence

POP 10,203

See-and-be-seen St-Rémy has an unfair share of gourmet shops and restaurants – in the spirit of the town's most famous son, prophecy-maker Nostradamus, we predict you'll add a notch to your belt. Come summer, when you may spot Princess Caroline of Monaco at the Wednesday market, the jet set wanders the peripheral boulevard and congregates at place de la République, leaving the quaint historic centre strangely quiet. Many businesses close Mondays; wintertime is dead.

◎ Sights

Site Archéologique de Glanum ROMAN SITES (☑04 90 92 23 79; http://glanum.monuments-nationaux.fr; rte des Baux-de-Provence; adult/child €7.50/free, parking €2.20; ⊙9.30am-6.30pm Apr-Sep, 10am-5pm Oct-Mar, closed Mon Sep-Mar) Spectacular archaeological site Glanum dates to the 3rd century BC. Walking the main street, towards the sacred spring around which Glanum grew, you pass fascinating remains of a once-thriving city, complete with baths, forum, marketplace, temples and houses. Two ancient Roman monuments – a triumphal arch (AD 20) and mausoleum (30 to 20 BC) – mark the entrance, 2km south of St-Rémy.

For a panorama over the ruined city, have lunch or drinks at the Taberna Romana (☑04 90 92 65 97; www.taberna-romana.com; rte des Baux; menus €16-26; ⊙10am-6.30pm Tue-Sun Apr-Oct), whose cooking revives ancient-Roman recipes, including honeyed red wine.

Monastère St-Paul de Mausole HISTORIC SITE (☑04 90 92 77 00; www.cloitresaintpaul-valetudo.com; entry adult/child €4/3, guided tour €8; ⊙9.30am-7pm Apr-Sep, 10.15am-5pm Oct-Mar, guided tour 10am Tue, Thu, Fri & Sat Easter-Oct) Van Gogh admitted himself to Monastère St-Paul de Mausole in 1889. The asylum's security led to his most productive period – he completed 150-plus drawings and some 150 paintings here, including his famous *Irises*. A reconstruction of his room is open to visitors, as are the gardens and Romanesque cloister that feature in several of his works.

For its time, the 19th-century asylum was quite enlightened: Van Gogh was allowed to roam up to a mile away to paint, if accompanied by a staff member. From the monastery entrance, a walking trail is marked by colour panels, showing where the artist set up his easel. The tourist office (p790) runs guided Van Gogh tours in English and French. St-Paul remains a psychiatric institution: an exhibition room sells artwork created by patients.

⨄ Sleeping

TOP CHOICE Sous les Figuiers BOUTIQUE HOTEL €€ (☑04 32 60 15 40; www.hotel-charme-provence.com; 3 av Gabriel Saint-René Taillandier; d €92-154,

PROVENCE ST-RÉMY DE PROVENCE

tr €168; ✻@🛜🏊) Hidden behind a wall, this single-storey country-chic hotel has 14 art-filled rooms facing a leafy garden – lovely for unwinding after a day's explorations. The owner is a painter (who offers classes by request) and has exquisite taste, marrying design details like velvet and distressed wood, Moroccan textiles, and rich colour palates.

Hôtel Canto Cigalo   HOTEL €
(☑04 90 92 14 28; www.cantocigalo.com; 8 chemin Canto Cigalo; r €69-89; ✻@🛜🏊) This excellent-value 20-room hotel is a 10-minute stroll from town. Simple and spotlessly clean, its frilly-feminine rooms are decorated in dusty rose, with wicker and white-wood furniture. Breakfast (€8.50) includes homemade bread and jam. South-facing rooms have air-con.

✗ Eating

Les Filles du Pâtissier   CAFE €
(☑06 50 61 07 17; 3 place Favier; dishes €8-15; ⊙9am-11pm, variable low-season hours) Tables fill the fountain courtyard outside this upbeat, colourful cafe, with a daily-changing menu of market-driven salads and tarts. At night-time, it's a wine bar with charcuterie plates and occasional live music.

La Cuisine des Anges   BISTRO €€
(☑04 90 92 17 66; www.angesetfees-stremy.com; 4 rue du 8 Mai 1945; lunch/dinner menus €14/27; ⊙lunch Mon-Sat, dinner daily Jun-Aug, lunch & dinner Thu-Sat, dinner Sun Sep-May; ✻🛜) Light, simple Provençal dishes are derived from organic local ingredients at this cosy village bistro with wood-floored dining room, textured paintings and zinc-topped tables. Upstairs is the cute-as-a-button *chambres d'hôte*, Le Sommeil des Fées (r incl breakfast €74-94), with five B&B rooms.

Mas de l'Amarine   MODERN FRENCH €€
(☑04 90 94 47 82; www.mas-amarine.com; ancienne voie Aurélia; mains €28-36) Five minutes east of town by car, this fashion-forward *auberge* is filled with contemporary artwork and immaculate details that complement the stylized cooking. Many ingredients come from the magnificent on-site gardens surrounding the former farmhouse. Ideal for a fancy splurge with your sweetheart. Reservations essential. Upstairs are five snappy rooms (€250-360).

❶ Information

Tourist Office (☑04 90 92 05 22; www.saintremy-de-provence.com; place Jean Jaurès; ⊙9am-12.30pm & 2-6:30pm Mon-Sat year-round, plus 10am-12:30pm & 3-5pm Sun Jul & Aug)

❶ Getting There & Away

BICYCLE Rentals and delivery from **Telecycles** (☑04 90 92 83 15; www.telecycles-location.com; 1/3/7 days €19/39/72) and **Vélo-Passion** (☑04 90 92 49 43; www.velopassion.fr).

BUS Allô Cartreize (☑08 11 88 01 13; www.pilote.com) serves Avignon (€3.10, one hour), Les Baux de Provence (weekends May to September, daily July and August; €2.20, 15 minutes), Arles (Monday to Saturday; €2.20), Cavaillon (€1, 30 minutes).

Les Baux de Provence
POP 381

Clinging precariously to an ancient limestone *baou* (Provençal for 'rocky spur'), this fortified hilltop village is one of the most visited in France. It's easy to understand why: narrow cobbled streets wend car free past ancient houses, up to a splendid castle.

OLIVE OIL MILLS

The Alpilles' southern edge contains some of Provence's best-known *moulins d'huile* (oil mills), where four different types of olives, freshly harvested from November to January, are pummelled and pressed into silken AOC Vallée des Baux-de-Provence oil.

In Maussane-les-Alpilles, the cooperative Moulin Jean-Marie Cornille (☑04 90 54 32 37; www.moulin-cornille.com; rue Charloun Rieu; ⊙Mon-Sat) deals directly to the public, though its 200,000L sell out by mid-August. June through September, you can tour the mill at 11am Tuesdays and Thursdays.

At Mouriès, 6km southeast of Maussane, pop in for tastes of exceptional oils, milled at Moulin Coopératif (☑04 90 47 53 86; www.moulincoop.com; Quartier Mas Neuf; ⊙closed Sun mornings). The village celebrates a Fête des Olives Vertes (Green Olive Festival) in mid-September, and the arrival of the year's new oil with Fête des Huiles Nouvelles in early December.

◉ Sights

Château des Baux CASTLE, RUIN
(www.chateau-baux-provence.com; adult/child €7.60/5.70; ⊙9am-6pm Sep-Jun, 9am-8pm Jul & Aug) The town's high point, the dramatic ruins of Château des Baux, crown the village and dominate the landscape. Dating to the 10th century, the castle was largely destroyed in 1633, during the reign of Louis XIII. It's a thrilling place to explore – particularly for rambunctious kids – with maze-like ruins covering 7 hectares.

Climb crumbling towers for incredible views, and descend into disused dungeons. Giant medieval weapons dot the open-air site, and pictograms of knights falling from ledges depict cautionary tales about how high you are on the cliffs. The reconstructed trebuchets, ballistas and battering rams are demonstrated several times daily during summer.

Carrières de Lumières LIGHT SHOW
(☑04 90 54 55 56; www.carrieres-lumieres.com; rte de Maillane; adult/student €8/6; ⊙10am-7pm Apr-Sep, 10am-6pm Oct-Dec & Mar) A high-end sound-and-light spectacular, Carrières de Lumières is an odd, strangely thrilling attraction. In chilly halls of a former limestone quarry, gigantic projections illuminate rough cave walls and floor, accompanied by oration and swelling music in that overly dramatic way the French so love. The show – on Gaugin and Van Gogh at the time of writing – shows famous images in new ways. Dress warmly.

🛏 Sleeping & Eating

L'Oustau de Baumanière GASTRONOMIC €€€
(☑04 90 54 33 07; www.oustaudebaumaniere.com; menus €95-150; ⏸) A legendary table beneath vaulted stone ceilings, L'Oustau serves rarefied cuisine, including a *très* gourmet vegetarian menu, with ingredients plucked from the organic garden outside. Upstairs are luxurious rooms (d from €290). Head chef and owner Jean-André Charial's kingdom also includes the Michelin-starred restaurant and fancy digs at La Cabro d'Or, also in Les Baux. Reservations imperative.

❶ Information

Tourist office (☑04 90 54 34 39; www.les bauxdeprovence.com; ⊙9.30am-5pm Mon-Fri, 10am-5.30pm Sat & Sun) Has information on the few accommodation options.

❶ Getting There & Away

BUS **Allô Cartreize** (☑08 11 88 01 13; www. pilote.com) operates weekends in May, June and September and daily July and August to St-Rémy de Provence (€2.20, 10 minutes) and Arles (€2.20, 30 minutes).

CAR Driving is easiest, but parking is hellish. Find metered spaces far down the hill, at the village's edge; there's free parking outside Carrières de Lumières. Good luck.

THE VAUCLUSE

The Vaucluse is like every Provençal cliché rolled into one: lavender fields, scenic hills, rows upon rows of vineyards, enchanting villages and picturesque markets, traditional stone houses, beating summer sun and howling winter mistral. At the heart of Vaucluse, which means 'closed valley', is the exquisite town of Avignon.

A car is the ideal way to cover the Vaucluse, but it's possible (if not expedient) to get around by bus.

Avignon
POP 92,454

Hooped by 4.3km of superbly preserved stone ramparts, this graceful city is the belle of Provence's ball. Its turn as the papal seat of power has bestowed Avignon with a treasury of magnificent art and architecture, none grander than the massive medieval fortress and papal palace, the Palais des Papes.

Famed for its annual performing arts festival, these days Avignon is also an animated student city and an ideal spot from which to step out into the surrounding region. Avignon is also known for its fabled bridge, the Pont St-Bénézet, aka the Pont d'Avignon.

History
Avignon first gained its ramparts and its reputation as a city of art and culture during the 14th century, when Pope Clement V and his court fled political turmoil in Rome for Avignon. From 1309 to 1377, the seven French-born popes invested huge sums of money in building and decorating the papal palace. Under the popes' rule, Jews and political dissidents took shelter here. Pope Gregory XI left Avignon in 1376, but his death two years later led to the Great Schism (1378–1417), during which rival popes (up to three at one time) resided at Rome and Avignon, denouncing and excommunicating

one another. Even after the schism was settled and an impartial pope, Martin V, established himself in Rome, Avignon remained under papal rule. The city and Comtat Venaissin (now the Vaucluse *département*) were ruled by papal legates until 1791, when they were annexed to France.

◉ Sights

Ticket offices for most sights close up to one hour before overall closing times.

TOP CHOICE Palais des Papes   PALACE

(Papal Palace; www.palais-des-papes.com; place du Palais; adult/child €6/3; ☺9am-8pm Jul, 9am-9pm Aug, shorter hours Sep-Jun) The immense Palais des Papes is the world's largest Gothic palace and a Unesco World Heritage Site. Built when Pope Clement V abandoned Rome in 1309 to settle in Avignon, it was the seat of papal power for 70-odd years. The immense scale, cavernous stone halls and vast courtyards testify to the papacy's wealth; the 3m-thick walls, portcullises and watchtowers emphasise their insecurity.

Today, it takes imagination to picture the former luxury of these vast, bare rooms, but PDA-style audio-video guides show 2-D and 3-D imagery of the once-sumptuous furnishings. Even without these, you see splendour in 14th-century chapel frescos, painted by Matteo Giovannetti; in the intricate walls of the Pope's bedroom; and in the Chambre du Cerf, alive with medieval hunting scenes.

Self-guided tours direct you from lower floors to crenellations: join gargoyles for superb views before stopping for coffee in the sky-high cafe. Exit via a wine cellar, where you can sample 55 Côtes du Rhône wines.

The guided two-hour Visite Palais Secret (Secret Palace Tour) takes you to secret towers, rooftop walkways and hidden chambers; reservations essential. The English-language version (€19.50) runs Fridays in spring and fall; the French-language version (€34.50) runs Saturday and Sunday, September to May, and includes brunch.

Combination tickets (adult/child €13/10) include admission to Pont St-Bénézet.

TOP CHOICE Place du Palais   SQUARE

A golden statue of Virgin Mary (weighing 4.5 tons) stands on the dome of Romanesque Cathédrale Notre Dame des Doms (built 1671–72), outstretched arms protecting the city. Next to the cathedral, the Rocher des Doms gardens provide views of the Rhône,

Mont Ventoux and Les Alpilles. Opposite the palace, the much-photographed building dripping with carvings of fruit and heraldic beasts is the former 17th-century mint, Hôtel des Monnaies.

TOP CHOICE Pont St-Bénézet   BRIDGE

(adult/child €4.50/3.50; ☺9am-8pm Jul, 9am-9pm Aug, shorter hours Sep-Jun) According to legend, Pastor Bénézet had three saintly visions urging him to build a bridge across the Rhône. Completed 1185, the bridge linked Avignon with Villeneuve-lès-Avignon, controlling trade at this vital crossroads. It was rebuilt several times before all but four of its spans were washed away in the mid-1600s. Opening hours are the same as for Palais des Papes; for discount admission, purchase a combination ticket with the palace.

Don't be surprised if you spot someone attempting a dance. In France, Pont St-Bénézet is known as the Pont d'Avignon, from the chirpy nursery rhyme: *'Sur le pont d'Avignon / L'on y danse, l'on y danse...'* (On Avignon Bridge, all are dancing...).

If you don't want to pay to visit the bridge, you can see it free from the Rocher des Doms park, Pont Édouard Daladier or from across the river on the Île de la Barthelasse's chemin des Berges.

TOP CHOICE Musée Calvet   GALLERY

(☎04 90 86 33 84; 65 rue Joseph Vernet; adult/child €6/3; ☺10am-1pm & 2-6pm Wed-Mon) The elegant Hôtel de Villeneuve-Martignan (built 1741–54) provides a fitting backdrop for Avignon's fine-arts museum, with 16th- to 20th-century oil paintings, prehistoric pieces, 15th-century wrought iron, and the landscapes of Avignonnais artist Joseph Vernet.

TOP CHOICE Musée du Petit Palais   ART MUSEUM

(www.petit-palais.org; place du Palais; adult/child €6/free; ☺10am-1pm & 2-6pm Wed-Mon) The bishops' palace during the 14th and 15th centuries houses outstanding collections of primitive, pre-Rennaissance, 13th- to 16th-century Italian religious paintings by artists including Botticelli, Carpaccio and Giovanni di Paolo – the most famous is Botticelli's *La Vierge et l'Enfant* (1470).

Musée Angladon   GALLERY

(www.angladon.com; 5 rue Laboureur; adult/child €6/4; ☺1-6pm Tue-Sun Apr-Nov, 1-6pm Wed-Sun Jan-Mar) Tiny Musée Angladon harbours impressionist treasures, including *Railway*

Wagons, the only Van Gogh in Provence (look closely and notice the 'earth' isn't paint, but bare canvas). Also displayed are a handful of early Picasso sketches and artworks by Cézanne, Sisley, Manet and Degas; upstairs are antiques and 17th-century paintings.

Collection Lambert GALLERY
(www.collectionlambert.com; 5 rue Violette; adult/student/child €7/5.50/2; ⊗11am-9pm daily Jul & Aug, 11am-6pm Tue-Sun Sep-Jun) Opened in 2000, Avignon's contemporary-arts museum showcases works from the 1960s to present – from minimalist and conceptual, to video and photography – in stark contrast with the classic 18th-century mansion housing them.

Activities

One of Avignon's chief joys is to aimlessly wander the photogenic old city. Within its 14th-century ramparts lie crooked streets and leafy squares, medieval churches and handsome houses with ornate doorways. The tourist office (p797) has a free map, outlining four different routes, including the Quartier des Teinturiers, the former dyers' district, where four waterwheels still turn.

Guided Tours WALKING TOURS
(from €15; ⊗10am various days, Sat only Nov-Mar) Two-hour tours of Avignon in English and French depart from the tourist office.

Autocars Lieutaud BUS TOUR
(☑04 90 86 36 75; www.cars-lieutaud.fr; 36 bd Saint-Roch) Themed half- and full-day tours, including wineries, lavender, Roman monuments, and Luberon (€45 to €55). For a vintage experience, book the classic convertible Citroën 2CV (from €145).

Les Grands Bateaux BOAT TOUR
(☑04 90 85 62 25; www.mireio.net; allées de l'Oulle; boat tours adult/child €9/5; ⊗boat tours 3pm & 4.15pm Apr-Jun & Sep, 2-6pm Jul-Aug) Runs 45-minute boat tours, April to September, looping under the famous bridge. For year-round daytime cruises (from €26), *Le Mireio* sails to Arles, Châteauneuf-du-Pape and Tarascon. Summer evenings, the company's dinner cruises (from €51) draw older crowds with dancing and live entertainment.

Avignon Wine Tour VINEYARD TOUR
(☑06 28 05 33 84; www.avignon-wine-tour.com; per person €80) Visit the region's vineyards with a knowledgable guide, leaving you free to enjoy the wine.

Festivals & Events

Festival d'Avignon PERFORMING ARTS
(www.festival-avignon.com; ⊗Jul) The three-week annual Festival d'Avignon is one of the world's great performing-arts festivals. Over 40 international works of dance and drama play to 100,000-plus spectators at venues around town. Tickets don't go on sale until springtime, but hotels sell out by February.

Festival Off PERFORMING ARTS
(www.avignonleoff.com; ⊗Jul) Festival d'Avignon is paralleled by a simultaneous fringe event, Festival Off, with eclectic (and cheaper) experimental programming. La Carte Off (€16) provides 30% discounts.

Sleeping

Avignon is one of the few places in Provence that caters well for budget-conscious travellers. Book many months ahead for a room during the festival, when prices soar.

TOP CHOICE **Hôtel La Mirande** LUXURY HOTEL €€€
(☑04 90 14 20 20; www.la-mirande.fr; 4 place de la Mirande; d €425-610; ❄@🖥) Avignon's top hotel occupies a converted 16th-century palace, with dramatic interiors decked in oriental rugs, gold-threaded tapestries, marble staircases and over-the-top Gallic style. Low-ceiling rooms are small, but still conjure the feeling of staying overnight in someone's private château.

On-site formal restaurant Le Marmiton (mains from €35) offers cooking classes (from €80) and a twice-weekly chef's table (an informal evening akin to a dinner party when the chef cooks in front of guests; €96, reservations essential); afternoon tea is served (albeit slowly) in the glittering lobby or garden.

Le Limas B&B €€
(☑04 90 14 67 19; www.le-limas-avignon.com; 51 rue du Limas; d/tr incl breakfast from €120/200; ❄@) This chic B&B in an 18th-century town house, like something out of *Vogue Living,* is everything designers strive for when mixing old and new: state-of-the-art kitchen and minimalist white decor complementing antique fireplaces and 18th-century spiral stairs. Breakfast on the sun-drenched terrace is a treat – as is bubbly owner Marion.

Hôtel d'Europe LUXURY HOTEL €€€
(☑04 90 14 76 76; www.heurope.com; 12 place Crillon; d €190-540; ❄@🖥) For 200 years, Hôtel de l'Europe has greeted luminaries

Avignon

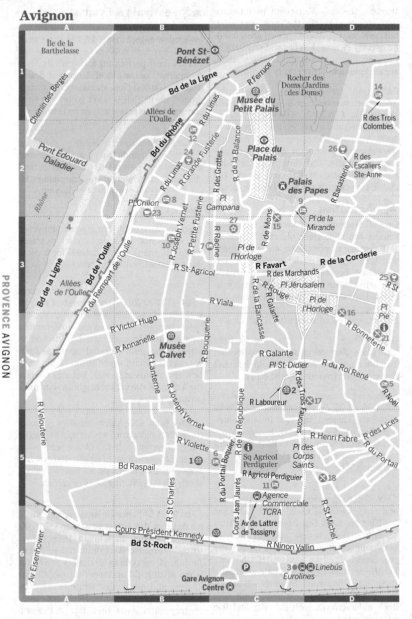

PROVENCE AVIGNON

from Napoléon to Jaqueline Kennedy Onasis. Service remains excellent, but the glamour has faded – rooms need better lighting and fabrics. Still, it's a grand address, paricularly when you score discounted rates.

Lumani   B&B **€€**
(04 90 82 94 11; www.avignon-lumani.com; 37 rue du Rempart St-Lazare; d incl breakfast €100-170; ❄🐾) Art fills this fabulous *maison d'hôte*, a wealth of inspiration for painters. Rooms

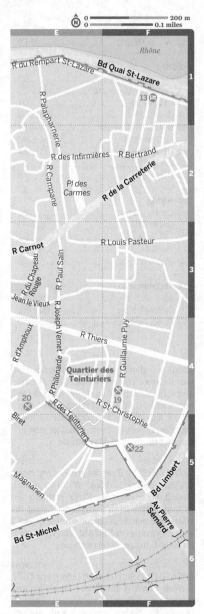

fectious enthusiasm informs this cheerful and colourful, small central hotel; try for themed rooms Morocco or Lavender. Excellent value.

Hôtel de l'Horloge HOTEL €€
(☑04 90 16 42 00; www.hotels-ocre-azur.com; place de l'Horloge; r €95-180; ❄️📶) Most rooms at this super-central 19th-century stone-walled hotel (with elevator) are straightforward (comfortable, all mod cons), but five terrace rooms have the edge with knockout views – room 505 overlooks the Palais des Papes.

Villa de Margot B&B €€
(☑0490826234; http://demargot.fr; 24 rue des Trois Colombes; r incl breakfast €110-190; ❄️📶) A charming, quiet old-city address, this 19th-century private home, converted into an elegant guesthouse, has a walled garden and rooftop views. Rooms are styled like their names – 'Oriental', 'Royal', 'Art Deco' and 'Romantic'.

Autour du Petit Paradis SELF-CONTAINED €€
(☑04 90 81 00 42; www.autourdupetitparadis. com; 5 rue Noël Antoine Biret; apt nightly €105-180, weekly €650-1050; ❄️@📶) Live like a local in a 17th-century stone house, converted into a small apartment hotel. Scrupulously maintained, each apartment has a kitchenette, ideal for travellers who like style, but dislike shelling out for restaurants.

Hôtel Mignon HOTEL €
(☑04 90 82 17 30; www.hotel-mignon.com; 12 rue Joseph Vernet; r incl breakfast €62-84; ❄️@📶) Cute and comfy, with 16 colourful rooms, this good-value hotel within the walled city is tops for no-frills budgeters, despite the tiny baths and steep stairs.

✏️ Hôtel Splendid HOTEL €
(☑04 90 86 14 46; www.avignon-splendid-hotel.com; 17 rue Agricol Perdiguier; s €48, d €68-78, apt €78-98; ❄️📶) Some rooms at this small, cycle-friendly, central hotel overlook the neighbouring park. The ground-floor flat has a private patio.

🍴 Eating

Place de l'Horloge's touristy cafes only have so-so food. Restaurants open seven days during the summer festival season, when reservations become essential. Local treat *Papaline d'Avignon* is a pink chocolate ball filled with potent Mont Ventoux herbal liqueur.

include two suites and there's a fountained garden.

Hôtel Boquier HOTEL €
(☑04 90 82 34 43; www.hotel-boquier.com; 6 rue du Portail Boquier; d €50-70; ❄️📶) The owners' in-

⌖TOP CHOICE Cuisine du Dimanche PROVENÇAL €€
(☑04 90 82 99 10; www.lacuisinedudimanche.com; 31 rue Bonneterie; mains €15-25; ⊘daily Jun-Sep,

Avignon

Tue-Sat Oct-May) Spitfire chef Marie shops every morning at Les Halles to find the freshest ingredients for her earthy flavour-packed cooking, and takes no culinary shortcuts. The market-driven menu changes daily, but specialities include scallops and simple roast chicken with pan gravy. The narrow stone-walled dining room is a mishmash of textures – contemporary resin chairs to antique crystal goblets – befitting the chef's eclecticism. Reserve.

Christian Etienne PROVENÇAL €€€
(☏04 90 86 16 50; www.christian-etienne.fr; 10 rue de Mons; lunch menus €31-150, dinner menus €75-150; ◷lunch & dinner Tue-Sat) One of Avignon's top tables, this much vaunted restaurant occupies a 12th-century palace, with a leafy outdoor terrace, adjacent to Palais des Papes. Interiors feel slightly dated, but the refined Provençal cuisine remains exceptional, notably the summertime-only starter-to-dessert tomato menu. Reserve.

L'Atelier de Damien MODERN FRENCH €€
(☏04 90 82 57 35; 54 rue Guillaume Puy; lunch/dinner menus €13.50/26; ◷lunch Mon-Sat, dinner Wed-Sat) Unframed paintings and worn tile floors lend a rough-around-the-edges look to this off-the-tourist-radar restaurant on Avignon's less-glamorous side. Chef Damien Demazure once cooked under Alain Ducasse, and draws inspiration from market-fresh ingredients, combining French with Asian – ginger, lemon grass and coriander are his favourites. Expect excellent fish, foie gras and caramel-candy cake. Book ahead.

Fou de Fafa BISTRO €€
(☏04 32 76 35 13; 17 rue des Trois Faucons; menus €22-26; ◷dinner Wed-Sun; ▣) The classic French bistro, Fou de Fafa's strength lies in simplicity – fresh ingredients, bright flavours, and convivial surroundings. Expect a warm welcome (in English!) and fresh spins on classic dishes. Reserve ahead.

L'Epice and Love FRENCH €
(☏04 90 82 45 96; 30 rue des Lices; mains €11-12; ◷dinner Mon-Sat) Tables are cheek by jowl at this tiny bohemian restaurant – our favourite for budget dining – with nothing fancy, just straightforward bistro fare: stews, roasts and other reliably good, homestyle French dishes. Cash only.

Numéro 75 MODERN FRENCH €€
(☏04 90 27 16 00; www.numero75.com; 75 rue Guillaume Puy; menus €28.50-34.50, mains €16-

25; ⊙lunch & dinner Mon-Sat) The chic dining room, in the former mansion of absinthe inventor Jules Pernod, is a fitting backdrop for stylized Mediterranean cooking. Menus change nightly and only include three mains, but brevity guarantees freshness. On balmy nights, book the courtyard garden.

Le Grand Café   MEDITERRANEAN €€
(☑04 90 86 86 77; www.legrandcafe-restaurant.fr; cours Maria Casarès; lunch/dinner menus €18/28; ⊙lunch & dinner Tue-Sat Sep-May, Tue-Sun Jun-Aug) Hidden behind the palace, this boho-chic bistro-bar with a big terrace adjoins arty cultural centre La Manutention. Giant mirrors on rough-hewn walls reflect French actors' portraits and rows of vintage tables. Good-value Provençal menus provide an alternative to more touristy places uphill.

Ginette et Marcel   CAFE €
(27 place des Corps Saints; dishes €4-6; ⊙11am-11pm Wed-Mon) *Tartines* (open-faced sandwiches), tarts, salad and soup comprise the menu at this homey cafe, with farm tables, vintage floors and big windows overlooking a happening square.

Les Halles   MARKET €
(www.avignon-leshalles.com; place Pie; ⊙7am-1pm Tue-Sun) Over 40 food stalls showcase seasonal Provençal ingredients. Cooking demonstrations are held Saturdays at 11am.

🍷 Drinking

TOP CHOICE **Utopia Bar**   BAR
(4 rue des Escaliers Ste-Anne; ⊙noon-midnight) Behind Palais des Papes, adjoining an art-house cinema and jazz-music centre, Utopia draws smart crowds to its veranda lined with red-velvet banquettes. Ideal for drinks and light bites pre- or post-theatre.

Cafe la Scène   CAFE
(☑04 90 86 14 70; 19 place Crillon; ⊙9am-1am) On pretty place Crillon, La Scène's outdoor tables are good for drinks and small bites; inside there's a dance floor and cabaret.

Le Cid Café   CAFE
(☑04 90 82 30 38; www.lecidcafe.com; 11 place de l'Horloge; ⊙11am-late) Styled with a nod to the disco era, Le Cid is an upbeat cafe by day, DJ-bar by night. On bustling place de l'Horloge.

L'Esclave   GAY BAR
(☑04 90 85 14 91; www.esclavebar.com; 12 rue du Limas; ⊙11pm-dawn Tue-Sun) Avignon's inner-city gay bar gets busy after 11:30pm.

Red Sky   PUB
(☑04 90 85 93 23; rue St-Jean le Vieux; ⊙10am-1am) A little bit of London in France, this cherry-red English pub has theme nights and TV sports.

☆ Entertainment

Avignon is the theatre capital of France, with dozens of theatres around town. The tourist office has lists.

AJMI   LIVE MUSIC
(Association pour le Jazz & la Musique Improvisée; ☑04 90 86 08 61; www.jazzalajmi.com; 4 rue des Escaliers Ste-Anne; tickets €10-15) Inside La Manutention arts centre, AJMI showcases improvisational jazz at its intimate 2nd-floor (no elevator) black-box theatre. Shows are generally held Thursday and Friday evenings, and Sunday afternoons.

Opéra Théâtre d'Avignon   PERFORMING ARTS
(☑04 90 82 81 40; www.operatheatredavignon.fr; place de l'Horloge; ⊙box office 11am-6pm Tue-Sat) Built in 1847, Avignon's main classical venue presents operas, plays, chamber music and ballet from October to June.

Cinéma Utopia   CINEMA
(☑04 90 82 65 36; www.cinemas-utopia.org; 4 rue des Escaliers Ste-Anne) Four-screen, art-house cinema shows films in their original language.

ℹ Information

Hôpital Général Henri Duffaut (☑04 32 75 33 33; 305 rue Raoul Follereau) Marked on maps as Hôpital Sud, it's 2.5km south of the central train station – take bus 3 or 6.
Police Station (☑04 32 40 55 55; 14 bd St-Roch)
Tourist Office (☑04 32 74 32 74; www.avignon-tourisme.com) main branch (41 cours Jean Jaurès; ⊙ 9am-6pm Mon-Fri, 9am-5pm Sat, 10am-noon Sun Nov-Mar, 9am-6pm Mon-Sat, 10am-5pm Sun Apr-Oct); annex (Les Halles; ⊙10am-1pm Fri-Sun)

ℹ **AVIGNON PASS**

The must-have discount card, *Avignon Passion*, provides discounts on museums, tours, and monuments in Avignon and Villeneuve-lès-Avignon. The first attraction visited costs full price, but each subsequent site discounts admission by 10% to 50%. The free pass covers five sites, and is valid 15 days. Available from the tourist office and tourist sites.

ℹ Getting There & Away

AIR **Avignon-Caumont Airport** (☑04 90 81 51 51; www.avignon.aeroport.fr) About 8km southeast of Avignon. Flybe and Cityjet fly direct from the UK.

BUS The underground bus station is next to the central railway station. Tickets are sold on board. For schedules, see www.lepilote.com and www.vaucluse.fr, both with good mobile sites. Long-haul companies **Linebús** (☑04 90 85 30 48; www.linebus.com) and **Eurolines** (☑04 90 85 27 60; www.eurolines.com) have offices at the far end of the bus platforms. Services:

Arles €7, 1½ hours, eight daily

Carpentras €2, 45 minutes, half-hourly

Nîmes €1.50, 1¼ hours, eight daily

Orange €2, 45 minutes, every 45 minutes

CAR & MOTORCYCLE Find car-hire agencies at train stations (reserve ahead, especially for July). Narrow one-way streets and impossible parking make driving within the ramparts difficult: park outside the walls. The city has 900 free spaces at Parking de L'Île Piot, and 1150 at Parking des Italiens, both under surveillance and served by free shuttle bus (hours at TCRA p798). On directional signs at intersections, 'P' in yellow means pay parking lots; 'P' in green, free lots.

TRAIN Avignon has two train stations: **Gare Avignon TGV**, 4km southwest in Courtine; and **Gare Avignon Centre** (42 bd St-Roch), with services to the following:

Arles €6.50, 20 minutes, half-hourly

Marseille Airport (Vitrolles Station) €16, 1½ hours, half-hourly

Nîmes €8.50, 30 minutes, half-hourly

Orange €5.50, 20 minutes, half-hourly

Some TGVs to Paris (€75, 3½ hours) stop at Gare Avignon Centre, but TGVs to Marseille (€29, 35 minutes) and Nice (€52.50, 3¼ hours) only use Gare Avignon TGV. In July and August, a direct **Eurostar** (www.eurostar.com) service operates on Saturdays to/from London (from €135, six hours).

Luggage storage (*consignes de baggages*; €4.50 per 24 hours) is available only at Gare Avignon Centre.

ℹ Getting Around

TO/FROM THE AIRPORT TCRA bus 21 (€1.50, 20 minutes, Monday to Saturday only) goes to the post office. Taxis to the centre cost about €25.

BICYCLE & MOTORCYCLE **Vélopop** (☑08 10 45 64 56; www.velopop.fr) Shared-bicycle service, with 17 stations around town. Pick up at one, return at another. The first half-hour is free; each additional half-hour, €1. One day/week membership costs €1/3, plus refundable deposit of €150 on your credit card. Sign up by phone, or use credit-card machines at stations.

Provence Bike (☑04 90 27 92 61; www.provence-bike.com; 7 av St-Ruf; bicycles from per day/week €9/39) Rents city bikes (€9/39 per day/week), mountain bikes (€15/75), scooters (from €25/75), and motorcycles (from €59/130).

BUS **TCRA** (Transports en Commun de la Région d'Avignon; ☑04 32 74 18 32; www.tcra.fr) Local TCRA bus tickets, which you can buy on board, cost €1.20. Buses run 7am to about 7.40pm (less frequently on Sundays, from 8am to 6pm). Mains transfer points are Poste (main post office) and place Pie. For Villeneuve-lès-Avignon, take bus 11 (bus 70 on Sundays).

Agence Commerciale TCRA (av de Lattre de Tassigny; ⊙8.30am-12.30pm & 1.30-6pm Mon-Fri) For maps and discounted *carnets* of 10 tickets (€9.50).

TAXI **Taxi-Radio Avignon** (☑04 90 82 20 20)

Villeneuve-lès-Avignon

POP 12,664

Thirteenth-century Villeneuve-lès-Avignon gazes across the Rhône at Avignon like a wistful little sister. Entranced by the bigger city's charm, most visitors barely glance at Villeneuve; yet its monuments rival Avignon's, with none of the crowds. However, the best options for sleeping and eating are in Avignon.

◉ Sights

The Avignon Passion pass (p797) is valid for Villeneuve-lès-Avignon's sights.

TOP CHOICE **Jardins de l'Abbaye**   GARDEN

(☑04 90 25 55 95; www.abbaye-saint-andre.com; Fort St-André; adult/child €5/free; ⊙10am-12.30pm & 2-6pm Tue-Sun) Classed as one of France's top 100 gardens, privately owned Jardins de l'Abbaye is built atop vaults of a 10th-century abbey, within the Fort St-André. Views of Avignon and the Rhône are spectacular. Pathways meander through fragrant roses, iris-studded olive groves, wisteria-covered pergolas, and past ruins of three ancient churches.

Chartreuse du Val de Bénédiction   MONASTERY

(☑04 90 15 24 24; www.chartreuse.org; 58 rue de la République; adult/child €7.70/free; ⊙9.30am-6.30pm) Shaded from summer's heat, three cloisters, 24 cells, church, chapels and nook-and-cranny gardens of the Chartreuse du Val de Bénédiction make up France's biggest Carthusian monastery, founded in 1352 by Pope Innocent VI, who was buried here

10 years later in an elaborate mausoleum. Today La Chartreuse is a retreat for playwrights on residencies.

Fort St-André   FORT

(☎04 90 25 45 35; adult/child €5.50/free; ☉10am-12.30pm & 2-6pm) King Philip the Fair (aka Philippe le Bel) wasn't messing around when he built defensive 14th-century Fort St-André on the then-border between France and the Holy Roman Empire: walls are 2m thick! Today you can walk a small section of the ramparts and admire 360-degree views from the Tour des Masques (Wizards' Tower) and Tours Jumelles (Twin Towers).

Tour Philippe-le-Bel   LANDMARK

(☎04 32 70 08 57; adult/child €2.20/free; ☉10am-12.30pm & 2.30-6.30pm Tue-Sun) King Philip commissioned the Tour Philippe-le-Bel, 500m outside Villeneuve, to control traffic over Pont St-Bénézet to and from Avignon. Steep steps spiral to the top, rewarding climbers with some truly magnificent river views.

Musée Pierre de Luxembourg   MUSEUM

(☎04 90 27 49 66; 3 rue de la République; adult/child €3.10/free; ☉10.30am-12.30pm & 2.30-6.30pm Tue-Sun May-Sep, 2-5pm Oct-Dec, Feb-Apr) Inside a 17th-century mansion, this museum's masterwork is Enguerrand Quarton's *The Crowning of the Virgin* (1453), in which angels wrest souls from purgatory. Rounding out the collection are 16th-to-18th-century paintings.

❶ Getting There & Away

Bus 11 (70 on Sunday) links Villeneuve-lès-Avignon with Avignon (it's only 2km, but dull walking).

CHÂTEAUNEUF-DU-PAPE WINES

Carpets of vineyards unfurl around the tiny medieval village of Châteauneuf-du-Pape, epicentre of one of the world's great wine-growing regions. Only a small ruin remains of the château – a lone wall, high on a hilltop – once the summer residence of Avignon's popes, later bombed by Germans in WWII. Now it belongs to picnickers and day hikers who ascend the hill to scout their lines with a 360-degree panorama.

Thank geology for these luscious wines: when glaciers receded, they left *galets* scattered atop the red-clay soil; these large pebbles trap the Provençal sun, releasing heat after sunset and helping grapes ripen with steady warmth. Most Châteauneuf-du-Pape wines are red; only 6% are white (rosé is forbidden). Strict regulations (which formed the basis for the entire Appellation d'Origine Protégée system) govern production. Reds come from 13 different grape varieties – grenache is the biggie – and should age at least five years. The full-bodied whites drink well young (except for all-rousanne varieties) and make an excellent, mineral aperitif wine, hard to find anywhere else (but taste before you buy, as some may lack acidity).

Sample them at over two dozen wine shops with free tastings (*dégustations gratuites*), or book a two-hour wine-tasting class at École de Dégustation (Tasting School; ☎04 90 83 56 15; www.oenologie-mouriesse.com; 2 rue des Papes; 2hr courses from €40). The tourist office (☎04 90 83 71 08; www.pays-provence.fr; place du Portail; ☉9.30am-6pm Mon-Sat, closed lunch & Wed Oct-May) has a brochure of estates, showing which ones allow cellar visits, have English tours, allow drop-in visitors and offer free tastings.

Perched beneath the ruined château, Le Verger des Papes (☎04 90 83 50 40; 4 rue du Château; menus €20-30; ☉hours vary) has knockout vistas from its leafy terrace. Specialties include succulent rack of lamb for two, and beef entrecôte served with macaroni-and-cheese spiked with cep mushrooms. Park at the château and walk down. Reservations essential.

Make a weekend of it by staying in a 17th-century farmhouse surrounded by vineyards. Each room at Le Mas Julien (☎04 90 34 99 49; www.mas-julien.com; 704 chemin de St Jean; r/apt with kitchen incl breakfast €110/130; ❈@🛜❄) artfully blends contemporary and Provençal style, and there's a studio apartment with kitchen that sleeps three (add €30 for a third person). After a day exploring, nothing beats sprawling by the big pool, glass of wine in hand. Between Orange and Châteauneuf-du-Pape, it's an ideal base for an extended stay.

Orange

POP 30,627

Considering how exceptional Orange's Roman theatre is (if you see only one Roman site in France, make it this one), the ultraconservative town is surprisingly untouristy, and eerily quiet in winter. Accommodation is good value, compared with swankier towns like Avignon, but it's nearly impossible to find an open restaurant on Sunday or Monday night.

The House of Orange, the princely dynasty that ruled Orange from the 12th century, made its mark on the history of the Netherlands through a 16th-century marriage with the German House of Nassau, and then English history through William of Orange. Orange was ceded to France in 1713 by the Treaty of Utrecht. To this day, many members of the royal house of the Netherlands are known as the princes and princesses of Orange-Nassau.

⊙ Sights

TOP CHOICE Théâtre Antique   ROMAN SITES

(www.theatre-antique.com; adult/child €8.50/6.50, 2nd child free; ⊙9am-6pm Mar-Oct, 9am-4.30pm Nov-Feb) Orange's Roman theatre is France's most impressive Roman site. Its sheer size and age are awe inspiring: designed for 10,000 spectators, it's believed to have been built during Augustus Caesar's rule (27 BC to AD 14). The 103m-wide, 37m-high stage wall is one of three in the world still standing in entirety (others are in Syria and Turkey) – minus a few mosaics, plus a new roof.

Admission includes a 10-language audioguide, and access to Musée d'Orange (☑04 90 51 17 60; museum only adult/child €5.50/4.50; ⊙9am-6pm Mar-Oct, 9am-4.30pm Nov-Feb), opposite the theatre, which has unassuming treasures, including portions of the Roman survey registers (precursor to the tax department) and friezes that once formed part of the theatre's scenery.

Come for epic theatrical spectaculars, including the fabulous Chorégies d'Orange (www.choregies.asso.fr; tickets €50-240), an international opera festival in July – balmy nights in this millennia-old venue are magical.

Arc de Triomphe   ROMAN SITES

(www.theatre-antique.com) Orange's 1st-century-AD monumental arch, the Arc de Triomphe, stands on the Via Agrippa, 19m high and wide, and 8m thick. Restored in 2009, its brilliant reliefs commemorate 49 BC Roman victories with carvings of chained, naked Gauls.

Colline St-Eutrope   GARDEN

For bird's-eye views of the theatre – and phenomenal vistas of Mont Ventoux and the Dentelles de Montmirail – follow montée Philbert de Chalons or montée Lambert up Colline St-Eutrope (St Eutrope Hill; elevation 97m), once the Romans' lookout point. En route, pass ruins of a 12th-century château, once the residence of the princes of Orange.

🛏 Sleeping

Hôtel Arène   HOTEL €€

(☑04 90 11 40 40; www.hotel-arene.fr; place de Langes; d €88-132; ✴@🖣🖳) With the best and biggest bathrooms in Orange, the Arène is the closest you'll get to business class. Despite some generic furnishings, the hotel retains some individuality, and has an entire floor of hypo-allergenic rooms. Kids love the two heated pools (one indoors, one out); parents appreciate the family-size rooms. Request a remodelled room – but older ones are also very comfortable.

Le Glacier   HOTEL €€

(☑04 90 34 02 01; www.le-glacier.com; 46 cours Aristide Briand; d €50-110; ✴@🖣) All 28 rooms are individually decorated and impeccably maintained by the charming owners, who pay attention to detail. Also rents bikes (half-day/day €12/16) and has secure, free bike parking.

Hôtel Saint Jean   HOTEL €

(☑04 90 51 15 56; www.hotelsaint-jean.com; 1 cours Pourtoules; s €60-70, d €70-85, t €80-100, q €90-120; ✴@🖣) Simple, spiffy hotel with comfortable proportions and colourful Provençal fabrics. Next to the theatre. Free bike storage, double-pane windows and flat-screen TVs add value.

Hôtel l'Herbier d'Orange   HOTEL €

(☑04 90 34 09 23; www.lherbierdorange.com; 8 place aux Herbes; s/d/tr incl breakfast €59/69/79; ✴@🖣) Friendly, enthusiastic owners keep this small, central, basic hotel looking spick and span, with double-pane windows and gleaming bathrooms. Evening aperitif is included.

Camping Le Jonquier   CAMPGROUND €

(☑04 90 34 49 48; www.campinglejonquier.com; 1321 rue Alexis Carrel; 2 people €20-26; ⊙Easter-Sep; @🖣🖳) Good for active travellers: pool, minigolf, tennis, table tennis, hot tub... From the Arc de Triomphe, walk 100m north, turn left onto rue du Bourbonnais, then right at the second roundabout onto rue Alexis Carrel, then it's 300m ahead on the left.

✕ Eating

Stalls fill the town centre every Thursday for the weekly market.

À la Maison   BISTRO €
(✆04 90 60 98 83; 4 place des Cordeliers; lunch menus €12.50-15, dinner menus €25-32, mains €10-16; ⊗lunch & dinner Mon-Sat) There's no lovelier spot on a warm night than the leafy fountain courtyard at this simple bistro, which serves consistently good homestyle cooking – but it opens sporadically.

Au Petit Patio   TRADITIONAL FRENCH €€
(✆04 90 29 69 27; 58 cours Aristide Briand; lunch menus €18-25, dinner menus €25-35; ⊗lunch & dinner Mon, Tue & Thu-Sat, lunch Wed) A good spot for a lingering lunch (*menus* include wine and coffee) or an indulgent dinner (foie gras is homemade) with excellent service, Au Petit Patio has a charming outdoor terrace, which lacks shade: book a table inside on hot days.

Le Forum   TRADITIONAL FRENCH €€
(✆04 90 34 01 09; 3 rue Mazeau; lunch menus €15-19, dinner menus €29; ⊗lunch Tue-Fri & Sun, dinner Tue-Sun) Classic dishes, like beef filet with morel sauce, are well executed, but the room feels cramped; sit outside if available. Good for a quiet date.

Le Parvis   GASTRONOMIC €€
(✆04 90 34 82 00; 55 cours Pourtoules; lunch menus €12-19, dinner menus €23-44; ⊗lunch & dinner Tue-Sat, lunch Sun) Nobody speaks above a whisper at Orange's top table, which serves excellent food at good value – never mind the frosty reception.

La Roselière   BISTRO €
(3 rue du Renoyer; mains €12-15; ⊗Tue-Sat) Bric-a-brac crowds the ceiling, and the chef-owner shouts jokes at diners' expense, but by your second glass of wine you'll be laughing along, unless you're shy, in which case don't come. Expect classics like lentils and sausages. Cash only.

ℹ Information

Tourist Office (✆04 90 34 70 88; www.ot orange.fr; 5 cours Aristide Briand; ⊗9am-6.30pm, closed Sun Oct-Mar) Hotel bookings.

ℹ Getting There & Around

BICYCLE **Sportaventure** (✆04 90 34 75 08, mobile 06 10 33 56 54; www.velolocation-aven ture.com; place de la République; half-day/day/week €12/18/69) Central bike shop; delivers within 20km radius.

BUS **Bus Station** (✆04 90 34 15 59; 201 cours Pourtoules)

Trans Vaucluse (http://vaucluse.fr) Buses operated by Autocars Lieutaud (p793) serve Avignon (€2, 45 minutes) and Vaison-la-Romaine (€2, 45 minutes).

TRAIN Orange's **train station** (www.voyages-sncf.com; av Frédéric Mistral) is 1.5km east of the town centre. Services:

Avignon €5.80, 20 minutes

Lyon €29.30, 2¼ hours

Marseille €23, 1½ hours

Marseille Airport Vitrolles station; €20, 1½ hours

Vaison-la-Romaine

POP 6392

Tucked between seven hills, Vaison-la-Romaine has long been a traditional exchange centre, and still has a thriving Tuesday market. The village's rich Roman legacy is quite visible – 20th-century buildings rise alongside France's largest archaeological site. A Roman bridge crosses the River Ouvèze, dividing the contemporary town's pedestrianised centre and the walled, cobbled-street hilltop Cité Médiévale – one of Provence's most magical ancient villages, where the counts of Toulouse built their 12th-century castle. Vaison is a good base for jaunts into the Dentelles de Montmirail and Mont Ventoux, but tourists throng here in summer: reserve ahead.

◉ Sights

Gallo-Roman Ruins   ROMAN SITES
(adult/child €8/3.50; ⊗closed Jan-early Feb) The ruined remains of Vasio Vocontiorum, the Roman city that flourished here between the 6th and 2nd centuries BC, fill two central Vaison sites. Two neighbourhoods of this once-opulent city, Puymin and La Villasse, lie on either side of the tourist office and av du Général-de-Gaulle. Admission includes a four-language audioguide, covering the Roman ruins, museum, Cathédrale Notre-Dame and medieval city.

In Puymin, see houses of the nobility, mosaics, workers' quarters, temple, and still-functioning 6000-seat Théâtre Antique (c AD 20). To make sense of the remains (and collect your audioguide), head for the archaeological museum, which revives Vaison's Roman past with incredible swag – superb mosaics, carved masks, and statues that include a 3rd-century silver bust and

Vieux Port

AN ITINERARY

Bold and busy and open-armed to the sea, Marseille is France's oldest city. Standing on the quai des Belges it's hard to get a sense of the extent of the old port, a kilometre long on either side, running down to the great bastions of St-Jean and St-Nicolas, which once had their guns trained on the rebellious population rather than out to sea. Immerse yourself in the city's history with this full-day itinerary.

Go early to experience the **fish market 1**, where you'll swap tall tales with the gregarious vendors. Hungry? Grab a balcony seat at La Caravelle, where views of the Basilique Notre Dame de la Garde accompany your morning coffee. Afterwards, take a **boat trip 2** to Château d'If, made famous by the Dumas novel *The Count of Monte Cristo*. Alternatively, stay landside and explore the apricot-coloured alleys of **Le Panier 3**, browsing the exhibits at the **Centre de la Vieille Charité 4**.

In the afternoon, hop on the free cross-port ferry to the port's south side and wander into the **Abbaye St-Victor 5** to see the bones of martyrs enshrined in gold. You can then catch the sunset from the stone benches in the **Jardin du Pharo 6**. As the warm southern evening sets in, join the throngs on cours Honoré d'Estienne d'Orves, where you can drink pastis beneath a giant statue of a lion devouring a man – the **Milo de Croton 7**.

CAPITAL OF CULTURE 2013

The largest urban renewal project in Europe, the EuroMéditerranée project is rehabilitating the commercial Joliette docks along the same lines as London's Docklands. The city's green-and-white striped Cathédrale de la Major will form its centrepiece. Simultaneously, many of the city's museums and galleries are undergoing ambitious renovations.

GLENN BEANLAND/GETTY ©

Le Panier
The site of the Greek town of Massilia, Le Panier woos walkers with its sloping streets. Grand Rue follows the ancient road and opens out into place de Lenche, the location of the Greek market. It is still the place to shop for artisanal products.

Cathédrale de la Major

4

Fort St-Jean

Centre de la Vieille Charité
Before the 18th century, beggar hunters rounded up the poor for imprisonment. The Vieille Charité almshouse, which opened in 1749, improved their lot by acting as a workhouse. It's now an exhibition space and only the barred windows recall its original use.

Jardin & Palais du Pharo

6

Jardin du Pharo
Built by Napoléon for the Empress Eugénie, the Pharo Palace was designed with its 'feet in the water'. Today it is a private centre, but the gardens with their magnificent view are open all day.

Fish Market

Marseille's small fish market still sets up each morning to hawk the daily catch. Take a lesson in local seafood, spotting sea squirts, scorpion fish, sea urchins and conger eels. Get there before 9am if you're buying.

Milo de Croton

Subversive local artist Pierre Puget carved the savage *Milo de Croton* for Louis XIV. The statue, whose original is in the Louvre, is a meditation on man's pride and shows the Greek Olympian being devoured by a lion, his Olympic cup cast down.

Frioul If Express

Catch the Frioul If Express to Château d'If, France's equivalent to Alcatraz. Prisoners were housed according to class: the poorest at the bottom in windowless dungeons, the wealthiest in paid-for private cells, with windows and a fireplace.

Rue de la République

Quai des Belges

La Caravelle →

3

Quai du Port

1

2

Cross-Port Ferry

Quai de Rive Neuve

7

Cours Honoré d'Estienne d'Orves

Bas Fort St-Nicolas

5

Lunch Break

Pick up sandwiches from Jardin des Vestiges, enjoy portside chic at Une Table au Sud, or go for creative Provençal at Le Café des Épices.

Abbaye St-Victor

St-Victor was built (420–30) to house the remains of tortured Christian martyrs. On Candlemas (2 February) the black Madonna is brought up from the crypt and the archbishop blesses the city and the sea.

marble renderings of Hadrian and wife Sabina.

The Romans shopped at the colonnaded boutiques and bathed at La Villasse, where you'll find Maison au Dauphin, which has splendid marble-lined fish ponds.

Admission includes entry to the soothing 12th-century Romanesque cloister at Cathédrale Notre-Dame de Nazareth (cloister only €1.50; ⊙10am-12.30pm & 2-6pm Mar-Dec), a five-minute walk west of La Villasse and a refuge from the summer heat.

Cité Médiévale HISTORIC QUARTER

Cross the Pont Romain (Roman bridge) in the footsteps of frightened medieval peasants, who clambered to the walled city during valley conflicts. Steep cobblestone alleyways wend beneath stone ramparts and a 14th-century bell tower past romantic fountains and mansions with incredibly carved doorways. Continue uphill to the imposing 12th-century château (guided tours in French €2), where your climb is rewarded with eagle-eye vistas; check with the tourist office for opening hours.

⭐ Festival & Events

Choralies MUSIC FESTIVAL

(www.choralies.fr) Europe's largest choral festival is held in August every three years. Upcoming: 2013 and 2016.

Festival des Chœurs Lauréats MUSIC FESTIVAL

(www.festivaldeschoeurslaureats.com; ⊙late Jul) The best choirs in Europe.

🛏 Sleeping

The tourist office has lists of *chambres d'hôte* and self-contained accommodation.

Hôtel Le Burrhus DESIGN HOTEL €

(☎04 90 36 00 11; www.burrhus.com; 1 place de Montfort; d €55-87; 🐾) On Vaison's vibrant central square, this hotel may look quaint and old, but inside its 38 rooms have ultra-modern decor with designer fittings, original artwork and mosaic bathrooms. No elevator. Parking (€7) by reservation.

L'Évêché B&B €€

(☎04 90 36 13 46; http://eveche.free.fr; rue de l'Évêché; d €92-140) With groaning bookshelves, vaulted ceilings, higgledy-piggledy staircase, intimate salons and exquisite art, this five-room *chambre d'hôte*, in the medieval city, is fabulously atmospheric. Knowledgable owners Jean-Loup and Aude also lend bikes.

L'École Buissonière B&B €

(☎04 90 28 95 19; www.buissonniere-provence.com; D75, Buisson; s €48-52, d €60-70, tr €75-85 q €90-96; 🐾) Five minutes north of Vaison, in the countryside between Buisson and Villedieu, hosts Monique and John have transformed their stone farmhouse into a tastefully decorated three-bedroom B&B, long on comfort. Breakfast features homemade jam, and there's an outdoor summer kitchen.

Hostellerie Le Beffroi HISTORIC HOTEL €€

(☎04 90 36 04 71; www.le-beffroi.com; rue de l'Évêché; d €96-150, tr €180; ⊙Apr-Jan; 🐾) Within the medieval city's walls, this *hostellerie*, dating from 1554, fills two buildings (the 'newer' one was built 1690). A fairy-tale hideaway, its rough-hewn stone-and-wood-beamed rooms are small, but romantic, and its restaurant opens onto a rose-and-herb garden with kids' swings. Parking €10.

Camping du Théâtre Romain CAMPGROUND €

(☎04 90 28 78 66; www.camping-theatre.com; chemin de Brusquet; camping per 2 people €21; ⊙mid-Mar–mid-Nov; 🐾) Opposite the Théâtre Antique. Very sunny, but there's a pool.

🍴 Eating

🔝 Moulin à Huile GASTRONOMIC €€€

(☎04 90 36 20 67; www.moulin-huile.com; quai Maréchal Foch; lunch menus €40, dinner menus €60-70; ⊙lunch & dinner Tue-Sat, lunch Sun) Michelin-starred Chef Robert Bardot showcases gastronomic prowess in a former olive-oil mill beneath the Cité Médievale. Sample a variety of dishes with the €75 tasting menu. In summer, dine outdoors on the riverside terrace (never mind the plastic chairs). Make a night of it in one of three handsome guestrooms (€130-150).

La Lyriste PROVENÇAL €€

(☎04 90 36 04 67; 45 cours Taulignan; menus €18-36; ⊙Wed-Sun) The contemporary Provençal menu at this charming bistro emphasises seasonal and regional ingredients in dishes ranging from *bourride* (fish stew) to a foie-gras tasting menu (€36). In summer, book a table on the terrace.

Terrasses de Ninou BISTRO €

(www.lesterrassesdeninou.fr; 3 place Théodore-Aubanel; dishes €7-24; ⊙lunch & dinner daily Apr-Oct, lunch Feb & Mar) The terrace at this simple bistro has stellar views over the river and medieval city. The menu lists simple seasonal

PROVENCE VAISON-LA-ROMAINE

dishes; between mealtimes, there are crêpes, pizzas and tarts.

ℹ️ Information

Tourist Office (☎04 90 36 02 11; www.vaison -ventoux-tourisme.com; place du Chanoine Sautel; ☺9:30am-noon & 2-5.45pm Mon-Sat year-round, plus 9:30am-noon Sun Apr–mid-Oct) Helps book rooms.

ℹ️ Getting There & Away

Autocars Lieutaud (p793) buses serve Orange (€2, one hour) and Avignon (via Orange; €4, two hours). **Transdev Comtadins** (☎04 90 67 20 25; www.sudest-mobilites.fr) buses serve Carpentras (€2, 45 minutes) and Malaucène (€1, 30 minutes). For schedules, see www.vaucluse.fr. The bus stop is on avenue des Choralies, 400m east of the tourist office.

Mont Ventoux & Around

Visible for miles around, Mont Ventoux (1912m), nicknamed *le géant de Provence* (Provence's giant), stands like a sentinel over northern Provence. From its summit, accessible by road between May and October (the white glimmering stuff you see in summer are *lauzes*, broken white stones, not snow), vistas extend to the Alps and, on a clear day, the Camargue.

Because of the mountain's dimensions, every European climate type is present on its slopes, from Mediterranean on its lower southern reaches to Arctic on its exposed northern ridge. As you ascend the relentless gradients (which regularly feature in the Tour de France), temperatures can plummet by 20°C, and there's twice as much precipitation as on the plains below. The relentless mistral wind blows 130 days a year, sometimes at a speed of 250km/h. So bring warm clothes and rain gear, even in summer.

This climatic patchwork is reflected in the mountain's diverse fauna and flora, which is now actively protected by Unesco Biosphere Reserve status.

Piercing the sky to the west of Mont Ventoux are the spectacular limestone pinnacles of another walker's paradise, Dentelles de Montmirail. On the other side of the Dentelles sits the snug village of Beaumes de Venise, home to France's finest muscat. The village's tourist office (☎04 90 62 94 39; www. ot-beaumesdevenise.com; place du Marché; ☺9am-noon & 2-7pm Mon-Sat, to 5pm winter) has details of local vineyards.

Three principal gateways – Bédoin, Malaucène and Sault – provide services in summer, but they're far apart.

🚶 Activities

Walking

The GR4 crosses the Dentelles de Montmirail before scaling Mont Ventoux' northern face, where it meets the GR9. Both traverse the ridge. The GR4 branches eastwards to Gorges du Verdon; the GR9 crosses the Vaucluse Mountains to the Luberon. The essential map for the area is *3140ET Mont Ventoux* by IGN (www.ign.fr). Bédoin's tourist office (p806) stocks a topographic map (€7), detailing 14 walks for all levels; find corresponding trail markers en route.

In July and August, tourist offices in Bédoin and Malaucène facilitate night-time expeditions up the mountain to see the sunrise (over 15 years only).

Cycling

Tourist offices distribute *Les Itinéraires Ventoux*, a free map detailing 11 itineraries – easy to difficult – highlighting artisanal farms en route. For more cycling trails, see www.lemontventoux.net.

At Ventoux Bike Park (www.facebook.com/ VentouxBikePark; bike-park access before 2pm €14, after 2pm €10; ☺9:30am-4:30pm Mar-Nov), near the summit at Chalet Reynard, thrill-seeking bicyclists ascend via a rope tow, then descend ramps and jumps down three trails, from beginner to advanced. Bring your own mountain bike; helmet and full-length gloves required. Bédoin Location (☎04 90 65 94 53; www.bedoin-location.fr; place Portail Olivier, Bédoin; ☺Mar-Nov) delivers to the summit, and rents equipment. Other rental outlets:

La Route du Ventoux (☎04 90 67 07 40; www.larouteduventoux.com; rte du Ventoux, Bédoin; road bikes/mountain bikes/tandems per half-day from €25/15/30 ; ☺Apr-Nov)

Ventoux Bikes (☎04 90 62 58 19; www. ventoux-bikes.fr; 1 av de Verdun, Malaucène; ☺Apr-Nov)

Albion Cycles (☎04 90 64 09 32; www.albion cycles.com; rte de St-Trinit, Sault; ☺daily Jul-Aug, Tue-Sun Sep-Jun)

ℹ️ Information

Every village in the area has a tourist office, but the following resources are also handy:

Destination Ventoux (www.destination -ventoux.com)

VENTOUX LAVENDER

The isolated but charming village of Sault (population 1285) has incredible summertime vistas over lavender fields. Sault's tourist office (p806) has lists of artisanal lavender producers, such as GAEC Champelle (☑04 90 64 01 50; www.gaec-champelle.fr; rte de Ventoux), a roadside stand northwest of town, selling lavender products galore.

Provence Cycling (www.provence-cycling.com)
Provence des Papes (www.hautvaucluse.com)
Bédoin Tourist Office (☑04 90 65 63 95; www.bedoin.org; Espace Marie-Louis Gravier; ⊙9am-12.30pm & 2-6pm Mon-Sat, 9.30am-12.30pm Sun mid-Jun–Aug) Excellent information source on all regional activities; also helps with lodging.

Malaucène Tourist Office (☑04 90 65 22 59; http://villagemalaucene.free.fr; place de la Mairie; ⊙9.15am-12.15pm & 2.30-5.30pm Mon-Fri, 9am-noon Sat) Stocks info on Mont Ventoux, but (surprisingly) not the Dentelles.

Sault Tourist Office (☑04 90 64 01 21; www.saultenprovence.com; av de la Promenade; ⊙9am-noon & 2-5pm Mon-Sat) Good resource for Ventoux.

❶ Getting There & Around

Reach Mont Ventoux by car from Sault via the D164; or (summer only) from Malaucène or St-Estève via the D974, often blocked by snow until April.

Carpentras

POP 29,709

Try to visit Carpentras on a Friday morning, when the streets spill over with more than 350 stalls laden with bread, honey, cheese, olives, fruit and a rainbow of *berlingots*, Carpentras' striped, pillow-shaped hard-boiled sweets. During winter the pungent truffle market murmurs with hushed-tone transactions. The season is kicked off by Carpentras' biggest fair, held during the Fête de St-Siffrein on 27 November, when more than 1000 stalls spread across town.

Markets aside, this slightly rundown agricultural town has a handful of architectural treats. A Greek trading centre and later a Gallo-Roman city, it became papal territory in 1229, and was also shaped by a strong Jewish presence, as Jews who had been ex-pelled from French crown territory took refuge here. The 14th-century synagogue is the oldest still in use in France.

◉ Sights

Synagogue de Carpentras   SYNAGOGUE
(☑04 90 63 39 97; place Juiverie; ⊙10am-noon & 3-5pm Mon-Thu, 10-11.30am & 3-4pm Fri) Carpentras' remarkable synagogue dates to 1367. The wood-panelled prayer hall was rebuilt in 18th-century Baroque style; downstairs are ancient bread-baking ovens, used until 1904. Although Jews were initially welcomed into papal territory, by the 17th century they were forced to live in ghettos in Avignon, Carpentras, Cavaillon and L'Isle-sur-la-Sorgue. The synagogue is opposite the town hall; its deliberately inconspicuous frontage is marked by a stone plaque inscribed in Hebrew. For access, you must ring the doorbell *only* on the half-hour, or nobody will answer. Closed religious holidays.

Cathédrale St-Siffrein   CATHEDRAL
(place St-Siffrein; ⊙8am-noon & 2-6pm Mon-Sat, closed during services) Carpentras' cathedral was built between 1405 and 1519 in meridional Gothic style, but is crowned by a distinctive contemporary bell tower. Its Trésor d'Art Sacré (Treasury of Religious Art) holds precious 14th- to 19th-century religious relics that you can only see during the Fête de St-Siffrein and on guided walks with the tourist office.

Arc Romain   ROMAN SITES
Hidden behind Cathédrale St-Siffrein, the Arc Romain was built under Augustus in 1st century AD and is decorated with worn carvings of enslaved Gauls.

🍽 Sleeping & Eating

Hôtel du Fiacre   HOTEL €€
(☑04 90 63 03 15; www.hotel-du-fiacre.com; 153 rue Vigne; d €72-110; ⊙reception 8am-9pm; 🖨) The faded grandeur of this 18th-century mansion is charming – from its marble staircase to the canopied beds. Outside there's a lovely sunny courtyard. Good service and value. Parking costs €7.

Hotel le Comtadin   HOTEL €€
(☑04 90 67 75 00; www.le-comtadin.com; 65 bd Albin Durand; s €70-75, d €90-125, tr €120-135; ❄🖨) Formerly a private mansion, now a fresh-looking midrange small hotel under the Best Western banner, Le Comtadin's best rooms face an interior courtyard; less-expensive

rooms face the street, but have double-pane windows. Parking costs €10.

La Ciboulette PROVENÇAL €€
(☏04 90 60 75 00; 30 place de l'Horloge; lunch/dinner menus from €18/24; ☺Tue-Sun) Upmarket La Ciboulette has dramatic wood-beamed ceilings and a flowered outdoor patio. The open kitchen uses local ingredients, breathing new life into old classics – save room for the lavender-flavoured crème brûlée.

Chez Serge PROVENÇAL €€
(☏04 90 63 21 24; www.chez-serge.com; 90 rue Cottier; lunch/dinner menus €17/35; ☺lunch Sun-Fri, dinner Mon-Sat) This smart little courtyard restaurant plays at shabby chic with distressed wood and granite, lending an earthiness complementing the *terroir* cooking: this is the place to sample truffle-based *menus*.

ℹ Information

Tourist Office (www.carpentras-ventoux.com; 97 place du 25 Août 1944; tours adult/child €4/2.50; ☺9.30am-12.30pm & 2-6pm Mon-Sat year-round, plus 9.30am-1pm Sun Jul & Aug) Excellent website; multilingual guided **tours**. The free English-language *Discovery Circuit* brochure details a *berlingot*-themed walking circuit.

ℹ Getting There & Away

BUS The **bus station** (place Terradou) is 150m southwest of the tourist office, which has schedules (or see http://vaucluse.fr). Services operated by **Transdev Comtadins** (☏04 90 67 20 25; www.sudest-mobilites.fr) and **Voyages Arnaud** (☏04 90 63 01 82; www.voyages-arnaud-carpentras.com; 8 av Victor-Hugo):

Aix-en-Provence €11, 1½ hours

Avignon €2, 40 minutes

Cavaillon €3, 45 minutes

L'Isle-sur-la-Sorgue €2, 35 minutes

Marseille €15, two hours

Orange €2, 55 minutes

Vaison-la-Romaine €2, 45 minutes; via Malaucène €2, 35 minutes

CAR There's free parking northeast of the tourist office, along av Jean Jaurès.

Fontaine de Vaucluse

POP 610

France's most powerful spring surges out of nowhere above the pretty little village of Fontaine de Vaucluse. All the rain that falls within 1200 sq km gushes out here as the River Sorgue. The miraculous appearance of this crystal-clear flood draws 1.5 million tourists each year; aim to arrive early in the morning before the trickle of visitors becomes a deluge.

◉ Sights

La Fontaine SPRING
At the foot of craggy cliffs, an easy 1km walk from the village, the River Sorgue surges from the earth's depths. The spring is most dazzling after heavy rain, when water glows azure blue, welling up at an incredible 90 cu metres per second. In drought times the normally surging hole looks like something out of a Harry Potter book, with eerily calm emerald water. Jacques Cousteau was among those who attempted to plumb the spring's depths, before an unmanned submarine eventually touched base (315m down) in 1985 – but the spring's depths remain largely uncharted.

Musée d'Histoire 1939–1945 WWII MUSEUM
(☏04 90 20 24 00; chemin de la Fontaine; adult/child €3.50/1.50; ☺10am-6pm Wed-Mon Apr-Oct & Jan-Feb, Sat & Sun Mar, Nov & Dec) An excellent examination of life in occupied France during WWII. Be sure to request an English-language brochure.

☆ Activities

The glassy Sorgue is a beauty for canoeing on a summer's day. Two companies offer guided or self-guided two-hour trips (adult/child €17/12) to L'Isle-sur-la-Sorgue, 8km downstream, from late April to October. Afterwards, you're returned upstream by minibus to your car. Can also be done in reverse. Contact Canoë Évasion (☏04 90 38 26 22; www.canoe-evasion.net; rte de Fontaine de Vaucluse), on the D24 towards Lagnes, or Kayak Vert (☏04 90 20 35 44; www.canoe-france.com; Quartier la Baume), which is 1km out of town on the D25 toward Lagnes).

⊨ Sleeping & Eating

Hôtel du Poète HISTORIC HOTEL €€€
(☏04 90 20 34 05; www.hoteldupoete.com; r €95-240; ☺mid-Feb–Dec; ❋☏☲) Drift asleep to the sound of rushing water at this elegant small hotel, situated inside a restored mill on the river's banks. By day, lie by the poolside in the sun-dappled shade among the park-like grounds.

Pétrarque et Laure BRASSERIE €€
(☏04 90 20 31 48; place Colonne; lunch/dinner menus from €17/26) Fontaine de Vaucluse's

restaurants tend toward the *touristique;* this one is no exception, but manages to serve reasonably priced, good-quality food (try the local trout). The courtyard has mesmerising river views.

ℹ️ Information

Tourist Office (www.oti-delasorgue.fr; Résidence Garcin; ⏱10am-1pm & 2-6pm May-Sep, Mon-Sat Oct-Apr)

ℹ️ Getting There & Around

BICYCLE The tourist office has English-language brochures detailing three easy backroad biking routes. Bike shops in L'Isle-sur-la-Sorgue (8km west) deliver to Fontaine.

BUS **Voyages Raoux** (www.voyages-raoux.fr) buses serve Avignon (€2, one hour) and L'Isle-sur-la-Sorgue (€1, 20 minutes).

CAR The narrow road to Gordes (14km, 20 minutes) from Fontaine-de-Vaucluse makes a scenic, less-travelled alternative to reach the Luberon.

Parking in town costs €3.50.

THE LUBERON

The picture-perfect area that makes up the Luberon is rectangular on a map, but navigating its bucolic rolling hills, golden-hued perched villages and hidden valleys is a bit like fitting together a jigsaw puzzle. The Luberon is named after its main mountain range, which is split in the centre by the Combe de Lourmarin, a beautiful narrow river valley. Luberon's hues, fragrances and flavours subtly transform in tune with the seasons.

The region's capital, Apt, is a central hub for practicalities, but the heart of the Luberon is in the tiny stone villages fanning out across the countryside, which encompasses the Parc Naturel Régional du Lu-

beron, the Abbaye de Sénanque of postcard fame and ancient, stone *bories* (dry-walled huts). Luberon is best seen with your own wheels (motorised or leg powered; see p817) as there is virtually no public transport.

Apt
POP 11,500

Sleepy little Apt comes alive during its Saturday morning market brimming with local specialities, otherwise it's primarily a hub for shopping.

👁 Sights

Musée de l'Aventure Industrielle du Pays d'Apt   AGRICULTURAL MUSEUM
(Industrial History Museum; ☎04 90 74 95 30; 14 place du Postel; adult/child €4/free; ⏱10am-noon & 3-6.30pm Mon & Wed-Sat year-round, plus 3-7pm Sun Jun-Sep) Gain an appreciation for Apt's artisanal and agricultural roots at this converted candied-fruit factory. The well-curated museum interprets the fruit and candying trade, as well as ochre mining and earthenware production from the 18th century.

FREE **Confiserie Kerry Aptunion**   SWEETS FACTORY
(☎04 90 76 31 43; www.lesfleurons-apt.com; D900, Quartier Salignan; ⏱shop 9am-12.30pm & 1.30-6.30pm Mon-Sat Apr-Jun & Sep-Nov, 8.30am-7pm daily Jul, Aug & Dec, closed Jan-Mar) Thirty tonnes of cherries are candied daily at the Confiserie Kerry Aptunion, the world's largest crystallised-fruit factory, 2.5km west of town. Free tastings and tours.

🛏 Sleeping

TOP CHOICE **Le Couvent**   B&B €€
(☎04 90 04 55 36; www.loucouvent.com; 36 rue Louis Rousset; d €95-130; @🛜🖥) Behind a garden wall in the cobbled town centre, this

---

WORTH A TRIP

GIGONDAS

Wine cellars and cafes surround the sun-dappled central square of Gigondas (population 598), famous for prestigious red wine. The tourist office (☎04 90 65 85 46; www.gigondas-dm.fr; rue du Portail; ⏱10am-12.30pm & 2.30-6.30pm Mon-Sat year-round, plus 10am-1pm Sun Jul & Aug) has a list of wineries. In town, Caveau de Gigondas (☎04 90 65 82 29; place Gabriel Andéol; ⏱10am-noon & 2-6.30pm) represents 100 small producers and offers free tastings – most bottles cost just €12 to €14. Wine tasting here provides an excellent counterpoint to Châteauneuf-du-Pape (p799): both use the same grapes, but the soil is different.

enormous five-room *maison d'hôte* occupies a circa-17th-century former convent, and offers exceptional value and sense of place; breakfast is served in a vaulted stone dining room. One room has air-con.

Hôtel Sainte-Anne HOTEL €€
(☑04 90 74 18 04; www.apt-hotel.fr; 62 place Faubourg-du-Ballet; r €79-109; ❉@🔊) Lovely seven-room hotel in a 19th-century dwelling, completely redone in 2010. Spotless, crisp-at-the-edges rooms mix modern and traditional furnishings, with exceptional beds and big bath-tubs (though small toilets). Little extras include homemade jams and breads, made by the charming owner, served as part of the copious breakfasts (€10). Parking €10.

Hôtel le Palais HOTEL €
(☑04 90 04 89 32; www.hotel-le-palais.com; 24bis place Gabriel-Péri; s/d/ste €55/65/95) Friendly new owners – a young family – are breathing life into this old-fashioned walk-up budget hotel – it's tattered at the edges, but on the up and clean; there's wi-fi in the breakfast room.

✖ Eating

Le Fournil du Luberon BOULANGERIE €
(☑04 90 74 20 52; place de la Bouquerie; ⏱7am-7pm Tue-Sat, 7am-1pm Sun) Apt's best bakery makes rustic bread using local heritage grains, called simply *blé*.

Thym, Te Voilà BISTRO €
(☑04 90 74 28 25; http://thymtevoila.free.fr; 59 rue St-Martin; mains €10-13; ⏱lunch & dinner Tue-Sat; ☑) The earthy, market-driven *menus* at this colour-splashed contemporary bistro are filled with Euro-centric world cooking that reflects the seasons. Tables outside cosy up to a pretty, sunny square.

Le Platane MODERN FRENCH €€
(☑04 90 04 74 36; 29 place Jules Ferry; lunch menus €14-16, dinner menus €29; ☑) Everything is made from scratch at this simple, decent restaurant, which uses quality ingredients in its changing French *menus*. The leafy terrace is good on balmy nights.

ℹ Information

Tourist Office (☑04 90 74 03 18; www.luberon-apt.fr; 20 av Philippe de Girard; ⏱9.30am-noon & 2.30-6.30pm Mon-Sat, 9.30am-12.30pm Sun) Excellent source of information for activities, excursions and walks; makes hotel bookings.

L'ISLE-SUR-LA-SORGUE

A moat of flowing water encircles the ancient and prosperous town of L'Isle-sur-la-Sorgue, 7km west of Fontaine. This 'Venice of Provence' is stuffed to bursting with antique shops: disused mills and factories along the main road contain seven antiques villages (⏱10am-6pm Sat-Mon), which house around 300 dealers. For bargains, the giant four-day antiques fairs held in mid-August and over Easter are the best bet.

Maison du Parc (☑04 90 04 42 00; www.parcduluberon.fr; 60 place Jean Jaurès; ⏱8.30am-noon & 1.30-6pm Mon-Fri year-round, plus 9am-noon Sat Apr-Sep) Information and maps for hikes of the surrounding Parc Naturel Régional du Luberon. Outstanding palaeontology exhibits on the region's natural history.

ℹ Getting There & Around

BICYCLE **Luberon Cycles** (☑04 86 69 19 00; 86 quai Général-Leclerc; bicycle rental half-day/day from €12/16; ⏱9am-noon & 2-6pm Mon-Sat)

BUS The **bus station** (250 av de la Libération) is east of city centre. **Trans Vaucluse** (www.vaucluse.fr) services:

Aix-en-Provence €2, two hours
Avignon €2, 1½ hours
Cavaillon €2, 45 minutes

North of Apt

GORDES & AROUND

Forming an amphitheatre over the Rivers Sorgue and Calavon, the tiered village of Gordes (population 2159) sits spectacularly on the white rock face of the Vaucluse plateau. In the early evenings, the village is theatrically lit by the setting sun, turning the stone buildings a shimmering gold. Gordes has top billing on many tourists' must-see lists (particularly those of high-profile Parisians), so high season sees a cavalcade of coaches.

◉ Sights

Abbaye Notre-Dame de Sénanque CHURCH
(☑04 90 72 05 72; www.abbayedesenanque.com; guided tour in French adult/student/child/family €7/5/3/20; ⏱tours by reservation) Famously

Lavender Trail

Pilgrims come from all over to follow the Routes de la Lavande (www.routes-lavande.com), tracking Provence's aromatic purple bloom. In flower from June to August, it usually hits peak splendour in late July. Cruise the fields, visit mountainside distilleries or scoop up all things lavender at abundant local markets.

Abbaye Notre-Dame de Sénanque

1 Follow the winding D177 north of Gordes to this idyllic 12th-century Cistercian abbey (p809), tucked between hills and surrounded by brilliant fields of lavender. Resident monks tend the crops and stock their shop with monk-made goodies.

Château du Bois

2 Provence is dotted with distilleries, but if you make it to tiny Lagarde d'Apt (p815) you're in for a treat: 80 hectares of Lavande des Alpes de Haute Provence, 'true lavender' (*Lavandula angustifolia*).

Sault

3 The slopes of Mont Ventoux (p805), north of Lagarde d'Apt, make for prime high-altitude lavender. Aim to visit during the Fête de la Lavande (www.saultenprovence.com), usually on 15 August.

Forcalquier

4 Folks come from throughout the region for the booming Monday-morning market in Forcalquier (p816). An embarrassment of riches, the market has venders selling lavender everything, plus mountain honeys, creamy cheeses and handmade sausages.

Plateau de Valensole

5 For sheer heady expansiveness, you can't beat the Plateau de Valensole's carpets of lavender, stretching, dreamlike, as far as the eye can see. Cruise across it on the D6 or D8 east of Manosque, and the A51.

Clockwise from top left
Rows of lavender, Sault; Bunches of lavender for sale at a local market; A carpet of purple blooms, Plateau de Valensole

framed by lavender in July, the exterior of this isolated Cistercian abbey, 4km northwest of Gordes off the D177, appears on every postcard rack in Provence. The abbey was founded in 1148 and it remains inhabited by monks. Reservations are essential to visit the austere interiors; conservative dress and silence are required.

It's a 1½-hour walk from Gordes on the GR6 trail, or a slow, winding drive that is treacherous in rain.

Village des Bories   ARCHITECTURE
(☑04 90 72 03 48; adult/child €6/4; ☉9am-sunset) You'll spot beehive-shaped *bories* (stone huts) while buzzing around Provence – 1610 have been counted to date. At the Village des Bories, 4km southwest of Gordes, explore a whole village of them. Constructed of slivered limestone, *bories* were built during the Bronze Age, inhabited by shepherds until 1839, then abandoned until their restoration in the early 1970s.

Visit early mornings or before sunset for interplay of light and shadow. Tip: the lower parking lot is for buses; continue to the hilltop lot, lest you have to hike uphill in the blazing heat.

Musée de la Lavande   LAVENDER MUSEUM
(☑04 90 76 91 23; www.museedelalavande.com; route D2, Coustellet; adult/child €6/free; ☉9am-7pm May-Sep, 9am-noon & 2-6pm Oct-Apr) Musée de la Lavande – 7km south of Gordes, in Coustellet – showcases top-end fine lavender. An audioguide and short video (in English) explain the lavender harvest, and giant copper stills reveal extraction methods. The on-site boutique is an excellent (if pricey) one-stop shop for quality fine-lavender products, and an easy alternative to driving to distant farms.

🛏 Sleeping & Eating

TOP CHOICE Le Mas de la Beaume   B&B €€
(☑04 90 72 02 96; www.labeaume.com; d €125-180; ☎⊛) In a visually stunning hilltop locale at the village's edge, this impeccable five-room *maison d'hôte* is like a Provençal postcard come to life, with yellow-washed stone-wall rooms decorated with bunches of lavender hanging from wood-beamed ceilings. Beds are dressed in high-thread-count linens, and breakfast is delivered to your room.

Le Mas Regalade   B&B €€
(☑04 90 76 90 79; www.masregalade-luberon.com; D2, Quartier de la Sénancole; d €120-150;

☎⊛) A stone farmhouse on a grassy plain surrounded by oak woodlands, Le Mas Regalade's sexy rooms artfully blend mod cons with playful antiques. Outside, a vintage Citroën peeks from hedgerows of lavender and rosemary, beyond the big pool. It's out in the countryside, 3.5km south of Gordes.

Le Mas Tourteron   GASTRONOMIC €€€
(☑04 90 72 00 16; www.mastourteron.com; chemin de St-Blaise; menus from €49; ☉lunch & dinner Wed-Sat, lunch Sun, closed Nov-Mar) The welcome is warm at this countryside *auberge*, surrounded by flourishing gardens – an ideal destination for a lazy lunch. The stone-walled dining room has a vaguely boho-chic feeling, befitting chef Elisabeth Bourgeois-Baique's stylised cooking. Husband Phillipe selects from over 200 wines to pair with her seasonally changing, inventive menus. Desserts are legendary. Book the garden in nice weather.

It's 3.5km south of Gordes, signposted off the D2. Reservations essential.

ⓘ Information
Tourist Office (☑04 90 72 02 75; www.gordes-village.com; place du Château; ☉9am-noon & 2-6pm)

ROUSSILLON & AROUND
POP 1328

Some two millennia ago, the Romans used the ochreous earth around the spectacular village of Roussillon, set in the valley between the Plateau de Vaucluse and the Luberon range, for producing pottery glazes. These days the whole village, even gravestones in the cemetery, is built of the reddish stone.

⊙ Sights & Activities
Attractions focus on learning more about the region's signature ochreous earth. Roussillon's visual charms are no secret, so arrive early or late in the day.

Conservatoire des Ocres
et de la Couleur   OCHRE MUSEUM
(Ochre & Colour Conservatory; ☑04 90 05 66 69; www.okhra.com; rte d'Apt; guided tours adult/student €6/4.50, combined ticket with Sentier des Ocres €7; ☉9am-7pm Jul & Aug, 9am-6pm Sep-Jun, closed Mon & Tue Jan & Feb; 🐾) This arts centre and historic site examines all things pigment. Occupying a disused ochre factory (on the D104 east of Roussillon), it explores the properties of ochre through indoor-outdoor displays and artwork, fun for kids to run around. There's an excellent art and home-

decor boutique, stocking extensive ranges of powdered pigment. Workshops (some in English) teach colour. Tours happen year-round at 2.30pm and 3.30pm, plus 11am and 4.30pm in summer.

Les Mines d'Ocre de Bruoux HISTORIC SITE
(☑04 90 06 22 59; www.minesdebruoux.fr; admission €7.50; ☺10am-7pm Jul & Aug, to 6pm Apr-Jun, Sep & Oct) In Gargas, 7km east of Roussillon, this former ochre mine has spectacular spire-filled caves, like a serene mineral church. Visits are only by guided tour, so check the schedule on the website; reservations required (book online or by phone).

TOP
CHOICE **Sentier des Ocres** WALKING
(Ochre Trail; adult/child €2.50/free; ☺9am-6.30pm May-Sep, low season closes earlier, closed Jan–mid-Feb) At the edge of Roussillon village, groves of chestnut and pine surround sunset-coloured ochre formations, rising on a clifftop. A 30- to 60-minute walk twists its way through stunning mini-desert landscapes – it's like stepping into a Georgia O'Keeffe painting. Avoid wearing white!

🛏 Sleeping & Eating

Les Passiflores B&B €
(☑04 90 71 43 08; www.passiflores.fr; Les Huguets; d/q incl breakfast €73/120; 🛜🐾) Quiet and friendly, this comme-il-faut *chambre d'hôte* is hidden in the tiny hamlet Les Huguets, 4km south of Roussillon. Spotless rooms are decorated with pretty flourishes of country-Provençal prints, not overdone. The four-person suite is excellent value. Outside, the 'pool' is a small filtered pond. The *table d'hôte* (€28; by reservation) includes wine and coffee.

Les Grands Camps TRADITIONAL FRENCH €€
(☑04 90 74 67 33; Le Chêne; menu incl wine & coffee €28, children's menu €14; ☺lunch Sun; 🖐) This unpretentious working farm serves Sunday lunch – four-course feasts of farm-fresh game and charcuterie – near Gargas' ochre quarry. Make reservations. Take the signposted dirt road north from the hamlet of Le Chêne.

ℹ Information

Tourist Office (☑04 90 05 60 25; www.roussillon-provence.com; place de la Poste; ☺10am-noon & 1.30-5pm Mon-Sat) The tourist office can help with tours and accommodation bookings.

PARC NATUREL RÉGIONAL DU LUBERON

Egyptian vultures, eagle owls, wild boars, Bonelli's eagles and Etruscan honeysuckle are among the species that call the 1650-sq-km **Parc Naturel Régional du Luberon** (www.parc duluberon.fr) home. Created in 1977 and recognised as a Biosphere Reserve by Unesco in 1997, the park encompasses dense forests, plunging gorges and 67 villages with a combined population of 155,000. The GR6, GR9, GR92 and GR97 walking trails all cross it, as does a 236km-long **cycling route**.

Information, maps, workshops and guides are available in Apt at the Maison du Parc.

ST-SATURNIN-LÈS-APT & AROUND
POP 2479
St-Saturnin-lès-Apt is refreshingly ungentrified and just beyond the tourist radar. Shops (not boutiques), cafes and bakeries line its cobbled streets. The village has marvellous views of the surrounding Vaucluse plateau – climb to the ruins atop the village for knockout views. Or find the photogenic 17th-century windmill, **Le Château les Moulins**, 1km north of town off the D943 toward Sault.

🛏 Sleeping & Eating
There are some fine establishments for decadent country dining around St-Saturnin, so make sure you factor in plenty of time for a long lunch.

Le Mas Perréal B&B €€
(☑04 90 75 46 31; www.masperreal.com; Quartier la Fortune; s/d/tr incl breakfast €125/135/175; 🛜🐾) Surrounded by vineyards, lavender fields and cherry orchards, on a vast 17-acre property outside St-Saturnin-lès-Apt, this farmhouse B&B has five charmingly simple rooms, styled with country antiques and Provençal fabrics. Outside there's a heavenly pool and big garden with mountain views. Elisabeth, a long-time French teacher, offers cooking and French lessons (€30 per hour).

TOP
CHOICE **La Table de Pablo** MODERN FRENCH €€
(☑04 90 75 45 18; www.latabledepablo.com; Les Petits Cléments, Villars; weekday lunch menus €17-22, dinner & Sun lunch menus €29-55; ☺lunch

PROVENCE NORTH OF APT

DON'T MISS

PROVENCE'S COLORADO

Luberon's biggest ochre site is just outside the tiny village of Rustrel (10km northeast of Apt), gateway to the other-worldly formations of the Colorado Provençal (☎04 32 52 09 75; www.colorado-provencal.com; ☉9am-dusk). Remnants of a quarry where ochre was mined from the 1880s until 1956, the savage landscape has extraordinary rock formations, notably the fiery upright Cheminée de Fée (Fairy Chimney). It looks like a slice of southwestern US plunked down in France.

Colour-coded trails lead from the car park, signposted south of Rustrel village off the D22 to Banon. Parking costs €4 (free November to March). A cafe serves lunch in high season. The red earth gets blazingly hot in summer: come early, carry water, and wear hiking boots and a hat.

Sun-Tue, Thu & Fri, dinner nightly) Gaining the attention of Michelin, young chef Thomas Gallardo wows diners with inventive gastronomic creations at his tiny, low-key, middle-of-nowhere restaurant. The clean-lined contemporary-style dining room is comfy enough – it's the food that's exceptional. Also offers cooking courses.

Le Restaurant L'Estrade BISTRO €€
(☎04 90 71 15 75; 6 av Victor Hugo; menus from €15) Word of mouth keeps this village restaurant buzzing. The earthy menu showcases the season's freshest ingredients. It's a great destination when taking a road trip around the Luberon. Call ahead.

South of Apt

South of the N100, the deep Combe de Lourmarin carves a north–south divide through the Luberon massif. Le Petit Luberon (Little Luberon) sits on the western side and its rocky landscape is sprinkled with cake-decoration-like *villages perchés* (perched villages) overlooking thick cedar forests and Côtes du Luberon vineyards. To its east, Le Grand Luberon takes in dramatic gorges, grand fortresses and lavender fields.

PETIT LUBERON
The Petit Luberon is famed for its compact hilltop villages overlooking forests, valleys and vineyards.

◉ **Sights & Activities**
One of the highlights of the area are the villages Bonnieux, Lacoste, Ménerbes and Oppède-le-Vieux.

Bonnieux (population 1464) burst onto cinema screens in *A Good Year* (2006) as the village where Russell Crowe's character Max Skinner, a British financier, finds *joie de vivre* in the vineyards of Provence.

Lacoste (population 436) harbours the 9th-century Château de Lacoste, where the notorious Marquis de Sade (1740–1814) retreated when his writings became too scandalous for Paris. The erotic novels penned by the marquis (who gave rise to the term 'sadism') were only freely published after WWII. The 45-room palace remained an eerie ruin until transformed by couturier Pierre Cardin into a 1000-seat theatre and opera stage hosting July's month-long Festival de Lacoste (www.festivaldelacoste.com).

Scaling the steep streets to Ménerbes (population 1159), moored on a hilltop, rewards you with uninterrupted views. The maze of streets conceals a 12th-century village church and the fabulous Maison de la Truffe et du Vin (House of Truffle & Wine; ☎04 90 72 38 37; www.vin-truffe-luberon.com; place de l'Horloge; ☉10am-12.30pm & 2.30-6pm daily Apr-Oct, Thu-Sat Nov-Mar), where the Brotherhood of Truffles and Wine of Luberon represents 60 domaines and sells their wines at rock-bottom prices. April to October there's free daily wine tasting; winter brings truffle workshops.

Ménerbes captured the attention of millions when it was memorably rendered by British author Peter Mayle. The lavishly detailed books *A Year in Provence* and *Toujours Provence* recount renovating a *mas* just outside the village in the late 1980s. Monsieur Mayle now lives in the nearby village of Lourmarin.

Oppède-le-Vieux (population 20), a medieval hilltop village 6km west of Ménerbes, was abandoned in 1910 by villagers who moved down the valley to the cultivated plains to earn their living. Today, a handful of artists lives here among the cool ruins. The Sentier Vigneron d'Oppède, a 1½-hour winegrowers' trail, winds through olive groves, cherry orchards and vineyards.

Sleeping & Eating

TOP CHOICE La Bouquière   B&B €€

(📞04 90 75 87 17; www.labouquiere.com; chemin des Gardioles; d €90-120) Surrounded by orchards and vineyards, with nary a visible neighbour, this rural hideaway 2.5km from Bonnieux has four country-charming rooms dressed with a mishmash of antiques and Moroccan kilims. All open onto flower-filled gardens and share a kitchen, which will save you lengthy restaurant trips at night.

Hôtel La Bastide du Bois Bréant   HOTEL €€

(📞04 90 05 86 78; www.hotel-bastide-bois-breant. com; 501 chemin du Puits-de-Grandaou, Maubec; r incl breakfast €137-218; ✸🏵🛜🏊) Shaded by 200-year-old oaks, this 2-hectare former truffle plantation sprawls behind an iron gate. The 1825 mansion houses 12 romantic rooms, done in upmarket country-Provençal style. Outside are two cosy *cabanes perchées* – bona-fide treehouses (no electricity, but shower and toilet). The expansive grounds have that rarest of treats in Provence: a heated pool. *Table d'hôte* (set menu) costs €28.

Le Clos du Buis   HOTEL €€

(📞04 90 75 88 48; www.leclosdubuis.fr; rue Victor Hugo, Bonnieux; d €120-138; ☉closed mid-Nov-mid-Feb; ✸🛜🏊) Smack dab in Bonnieux village, this stone town house spills onto big terraced gardens, lovely for whiling away the afternoon. The dining room has panoramic views, and there's a self-catering kitchen. One room is wheelchair accessible.

TOP CHOICE Café Véranda   MODERN FRENCH €€

(📞04 90 72 33 33; www.cafe-veranda.com; 104 av Marcellin Poncet, Ménerbes; lunch mains €10-13, dinner menus €38; ☉lunch Tue-Sun, dinner Tue-Sat) High in the village, Véranda feels effortlessly casual, its candy-striped tablecloths a cheerful complement to the sweeping valley views. The kitchen ekes subtle flavours from seasonal and regional produce, like an elegantly simple truffle omelette – superb. Reservations essential.

Le Fournil   MODERN FRENCH €€

(📞04 90 75 83 62; www.lefournil-bonnieux.com; 5 place Carnot, Bonnieux; lunch menus €23-28, dinner menus €45-49; ☉closed Mon & Sat lunch & Nov-Mar) Casual-chic Le Fournil's, set on a quiet, sun-speckled square, sports a contemporary glass-and-steel decor overlooking a carved-rock interior – a moody backdrop for consistently first-rate, inventive cooking that varies seasonally. It's pricey,

but is among Bonnieux' top tables – and you won't soon forget what you ate.

Café du Progrès   CAFE €

(📞04 90 72 22 09; place Albert Roure, Ménerbes; menus €13-16; ☉lunch, bar 6am-midnight) Ménerbes' tobacconist-newsagent-bar, Café du Progrès, run by good-humoured Patrick, hasn't changed much since it opened a century ago. Great for a lunchtime *plat du jour*, but arrive early.

ℹ Information

Bonnieux Intercommunal Tourist Office
(📞04 90 75 91 90; www.tourisme-en-luberon. com; 7 place Carnot, Bonnieux; ☉9.30am-12.30pm & 2-6.30pm Mon-Fri, 2-6.30pm Sat) Has information about the entire area.

ℹ Getting There & Away

The Apt-Cavaillon bus service stops in all four villages three times a day. The best option by far is to have your own transport.

GRAND LUBERON

Purple lavender carpets the Plateau de Claparèdes area between Buoux (west), Sivergues (south), Auribeau (east) and picture-postcard Saignon (north). Cycle, walk or motor through the lavender fields and along the northern slopes of Mourre Nègre (1125m) – the Luberon's highest point. Stop for views of gorgeous Saignon (population 1005) before you wander its streets.

At the base of the Combe de Lourmarin and, unlike many of the Luberon's precarious hilltop townships, easily accessed, the

PROVENCE SOUTH OF APT

WORTH A TRIP

LAGARDE D'APT

In Lagarde d'Apt (population 37), 20km northeast of Apt, beneath some of Europe's darkest night skies, Observatoire Sirene (📞04 90 75 04 17; www. obs-sirene.com; adult day/night €10/15.50, children free; 🚼) shows you the stars and reveals astronomical wonders using high-powered telescopes. Reservations are essential for star-gazing sessions.

The area's other highlight is the 80-hectare lavender farm, Château du Bois (📞04 90 76 91 23; www.lecha teaudubois.com), where a 2km-long lavender trail blazes from late June until mid-July, when the sweet-smelling flower is harvested.

alluring village of Lourmarin makes for a lovely stroll with its charming streets, cafes and a lively Friday morning market.

Sleeping & Eating

TOP CHOICE Auberge du Presbytère HISTORIC HOTEL €€

(09 70 44 64 56; www.auberge-presbytere.com; place de la Fontaine, Saignon; d €65-155; menus €28-38; restaurant closed Tue;) Dating to the 12th century, this former presbytery is now a romantic 16-room village inn, with higgledy-piggledy staircases, low wood-beamed ceilings, and each room (some with air-con) a different style and shape – book well ahead for the top-floor blue room (€130), with its incredible panoramic terrace. The on-site restaurant, overlooking the moss-covered village fountain, serves classic French fare.

La Cordière B&B €

(04 90 68 03 32; www.cordiere.com; rue Albert Camus; r €50-65, studio per week €395-450;) At Lourmarin's village centre, this character-rich house, built 1582, surrounds a tiny flower-filled courtyard, with adjoining summer kitchen for guests. Rooms are ample, with spacious bathrooms, and are filled with atmospheric Provençal antiques. Also rents three great-value studios with kitchens; one has air-con.

TOP CHOICE Sanglier Paresseux MODERN FRENCH €€

(04 90 75 17 70; www.sanglierparesseux.com; Caseneuve; lunch/dinner menus €23/29; lunch & dinner Mon, Tue & Thu-Sat, lunch Sun mid-Jan–mid-Dec) High in the hills above Apt, with jaw-dropping vistas, Sanglier Paresseux tops our list of Luberon favourites. Its easy style is invitingly casual, and there's no better sunset view than from its west-facing terrace (come for lunch or arrive before dark). The chef's disciplined technique and easy personal charm shine through in refined, unfussy creations, which play off the seasons and showcase regional ingredients.

The drive is windy – 10 minutes from Apt, 15 from Saignon.

Auberge La Fenière GASTRONOMIC €€€

(04 90 68 11 79; www.reinesammut.com; rte de Lourmarin, Cadenet; restaurant lunch/dinner menus from €50/90;) The exquisite domain of Michelin-starred Reine Sammut, who grows a kitchen garden for her outstanding six- and nine-course formal restaurant *menus* and more-casual bistro *menus* (€35). Classes (€75 to €145) demonstrate how to make perfect puff pastry or succulent *andouillette* (pork sausage). For an indulgent splurge, consider booking dinner and an overnight stay (rooms from €190).

Information

Lourmarin Tourist Office (04 90 68 10 77; www.lourmarin.com; av Philippe de Girard; 10am-12.30pm & 3-6pm Mon-Thu & Sat, 10am-1.30pm & 3-6pm Fri) Organises guided walks in and around the village.

Getting There & Away

There are a couple of buses a day to Apt, Bonnieux and Aix-en-Provence.

NORTHEASTERN PROVENCE

Haute-Provence's heady mountain ranges arc across the top of the Côte d'Azur to the Italian border, creating a far-flung crown of snowy peaks and precipitous valleys. To the west, a string of sweet, untouristy hilltop villages and lavender fields drape the Vallée de la Durance. Magical Moustiers Ste-Marie is a gateway to the plunging white waters of Europe's largest canyon, the Gorges du Verdon. In the east, the Vallée des Merveilles wows with 36,000 Bronze Age rock carvings. In the far north are the winter ski slopes and summer mountain retreats of the Ubaye and Blanche Valleys. Outside of ski areas, many establishments close in winter.

Pays de Forcalquier

Beyond mass-tourism's radar, Pays de Forcalquier's expansive landscapes comprise wildflower-tinged countryside and isolated hilltop villages. At its heart lies its namesake, Forcalquier.

Sights & Activities

Forcalquier sits atop a rocky perch and its fantastic Monday market draws locals from throughout the region: this is where to stock up on lavender, mountain honey and decadent cured meats and cheeses for picnics. Steep steps lead to its gold-topped citadel and octagonal chapel, where carillon concerts are held most Sundays from 11.30am to 12.30pm. On the way up, peruse the local artists workshops packed with pottery and furniture.

In the village of St-Michel l'Observatoire, a stroll up to the hilltop overlook passes along winding walkways and tiny ateliers. Past the 12th-century Église Haute, there are 360-degree views from the Luberon to the Alps.

TOP
CHOICE **Prieuré de Salagon** HISTORIC SITE
(☑04 92 75 70 50; www.musee-de-salagon. com; adult/child €7/5; ☺10am-7pm daily Jun-Aug, 10am-6pm Wed-Mon Sept-May, closed Jan; ⏹) There are few more peaceful places in Provence than the 13th-century Prieuré de Salagon, 4km south of Forcalquier outside the walled city of Mane. Tour excellent gardens or see concerts and exhibitions in the restored priory.

**Observatoire de
Haute-Provence** OBSERVATORY
(☑04 92 70 64 00; www.obs-hp.fr; adult/child €4.50/2.50; ☺guided visits 2-5pm Tue-Thu Jul & Aug, 2:15-4pm Wed Sep-Jun) Visit this national research centre, near the Église Haute in St-Michel l'Observatoire. Buy tickets for the 30-minute guided tour from the ticket office in St-Michel's village square.

🛏 **Sleeping & Eating**

TOP
CHOICE **Relais d'Elle** B&B €
(☑04 92 75 06 87, mobile 06 75 42 33 72; http:// relaisdelle.com; rte de la Brillane, Niozelles; s/d/tr/q from €55/62/83/104; 🅿🕸) This stately vintage-1802, ivy-covered stone farmhouse, 10 minutes east of Forcalquier, crowns a ridge in big-view countryside. Five rooms (and one studio), each with private entrance, some with beamed ceilings, are decorated in smart country-house style. Reserve ahead for the *délicieux* all-inclusive *table d'hôte* (€28). Huge pool. Limited wi-fi.

Restaurant Le 9 PROVENÇAL €€
(☑04 92 75 03 29; www.le9-forcalquier.fr; av Jean Giono; lunch menus €13-18, dinner menus €20-26; ☺daily Jul & Aug, Thu-Mon Sept-Jun) High in Forcalquier behind the citadel, with panoramic terrace, Le 9 is town's most reliable address for earthy, market-driven cooking, incorporating fresh-from-the-farm ingredients in simple, brightly toned bistro fare, like honey-braised rabbit or grilled lamb with tomato and basil. Fridays there's a *grand aïoli* (boiled vegetables and fish served with a garlic mayonnaise). Make reservations.

ℹ **Information**

Forcalquier Tourist Office (☑04 92 75 10 02; www.forcalquier.com; 13 place du Bourguet; ☺9am-noon & 2-6pm Mon-Sat) The tourist office in Forcalquier is the main information point for the area and has extensive information on walking and cycling. Smartphone users may want to download the app *Visit 04*.

ℹ **Getting There & Away**

There are three daily buses between Forcalquier and Avignon (€18.40, 2 hrs).

Vallée de la Durance

At the western edge of Haute-Provence, the winding waters of the 324km-long River Durance, a tributary of the Rhône, follow the Via Domitia, the road from Italy that allowed the Romans to infiltrate the whole of France. Now it's the autoroute's path, a fast connector between the Alps and the coast.

Come summer, the area's highlight is the Plateau de Valensole, France's lavender capital. Cruise the plateau along the D6 or D8 for arresting views of unfolding purple ripples.

PEDAL POWER

Jaunty blue signs mark the way for the Autour du Luberon, a 236km cycling itinerary through the region that leads from one picturesque village to the next. Tourist offices have maps for this, as well as *Les Ocres en Vélo*, another route through ochre country. Decommissioned railway lines near Apt are being redeveloped into cycling paths; to date 28km of paths are finished. Stay tuned. Bicycle club Vélo Loisir en Luberon (☑04 92 79 05 82; www.veloloisirluberon.com) has extensive info on everything from where to rent bikes and how to arrange transport of luggage, to the location of bathrooms en route.

If you can't bear pedalling up all those hills, Sun-E-Bikes (☑04 90 74 09 96; www. location-velo-provence.com; 1 av Clovis Hugues, Bonnieux; electric bike per day €35), in Bonnieux and Gordes, rents electric bicycles; they're not scooters – you have to pedal – but the motor helps significantly with the ascents.

On the other side of the river, Prieuré de Ganagobie (☑04 92 68 00 04; Ganagobie; ☺3-5pm Tue-Sun), a 10th-century Benedictine monastery, is wonderful for a stroll amongst quiet hilltop woods. The chapel is the monastery's only enclosed section open to visitors. Its 12th-century floor mosaic (depicting dragons) is the largest of its kind in France. The shop stocks monk-made soaps, honey and music, and houses artefacts found on site. The monastery is signposted off the N96 between Lurs and Peyruis.

La Magnanerie (☑04 92 62 60 11; www.la-magnanerie.net; N85, Aubignosc; lunch menus €19, dinner menus €23-29, r €67-91; ☺lunch Tue-Sun, dinner Wed-Sat; @☎) is a convenient roadhouse restaurant-hotel, 10km south of Sisteron. It's a good stopover for proper white-tablecloth dinner and an overnight in contemporary rooms.

Gorges du Verdon

Under the protection of the Parc Naturel Régional du Verdon since 1997, Europe's largest canyon, the plunging Gorges du Verdon, slices a 25km swathe through Provence's limestone plateau.

The main gorge begins at Rougon near the confluence of the Verdon and the Jabron Rivers, and then winds westwards until the Verdon's green waters flow into Lac de Ste-Croix. At a dizzying 250m to 700m deep, the gorge's floors are just 8m to 90m wide, and its overhanging rims are from 200m to 1500m apart.

The two main jumping-off points for exploring the gorges are the villages of Moustiers Ste-Marie in the west and Castellane in the east. The deep floors are only accessible by foot or raft. Motorists, horse riders and cyclists can take in staggering panoramas from two vertigo-inducing cliffside roads.

🏃 Activities

Cycling & Driving

The Route des Crêtes (D952 & D23; ☺closed 15 Nov-15 Mar) corkscrews along the northern rim, past Point Sublime, which offers a fisheye-lens view of serrated rock formations falling away to the river below. The best view from the northern side is from Belvédère de l'Escalès.

Also heart-palpitating, La Corniche Sublime (the D955 to the D71, and then on to the D19) twists along the southern rim, taking in landmarks such as the Balcons de la Mescla (Mescla Terraces) and Pont de l'Artuby (Artuby Bridge), the highest bridge in Europe.

A complete circuit of the Gorges du Verdon via Moustiers Ste-Marie involves about 140km of relentless hairpin-turn driving. Tourist offices have driving itineraries. The only village en route is La Palud-sur-Verdon (930m). In winter, roads get icy or snowy; watch for falling rocks year-round; and heaven forbid that you get stuck behind a caravan in summer – opportunities to pass are rare.

Walking

Dozens of blazed trails traverse untamed countryside around Castellane and Moustiers. Tourist offices carry the excellent, English-language *Canyon du Verdon* (€4.70), detailing 28 walks, plus a map of five principal walks (€2.40).

You can hike most of the canyon along the often-difficult GR4, definitively covered by two IGN maps: 3442 (Moustiers to Rougon) and 3542 OT (Rougon to Castellane) – each €10.50. The full route takes two days, but shorter canyon descents are possible. Bring a torch (flashlight) and drinking water.

Camping on gravel beaches is illegal. Don't cross the river, except at bridges, and stay on marked trails, lest you get trapped when the upstream dam opens, which happens twice weekly. Check with tourist offices before embarking.

Outdoor Sports

Castellane is the main water-sports base (white-water activities generally run April to September, and must be booked); its tourist office has detailed lists of operators.

Des Guides pour l'Aventure   OUTDOOR ACTIVITIES
(☑06 85 94 46 61; www.guidesaventure.com; Moustiers Ste-Marie; ☺year-round) Guides excellent canyoning (€45/70 per half-day/day), rock climbing and rafting (€55/75), and 'floating' (€45/90) – river running with only a buoyancy bag strapped to your back.

Aboard Rafting   WATER SPORTS
(☑04 92 83 76 11; www.rafting-verdon.com) White-water rafting and canyoning trips.

Latitude Challenge   BUNGEE JUMPING
(☑04 91 09 04 10; www.latitude-challenge.fr; jumps €105) Bungee jumps from Europe's highest bungee site, 182m Pont de l'Artuby. Also offers skydiving.

ℹ️ Information

Moustiers Ste-Marie Tourist Office (☎04 92 74 67 84; www.moustiers.fr; ◷10am-12.30pm & 2-6pm daily; 🛜) Free wi-fi. With excellent service, it's the best overall information source. Opening hours vary by half an hour or so depending on the season.

Castellane Tourist Office (☎04 92 83 61 14; www.castellane.org; ◷9am-12.30pm & 2-6.45pm Mon-Sat Mar-Oct, plus 10am-12.30pm Sun Jul & Aug, 9am-noon & 2-5pm Mon-Fri Nov-Feb) Best info source for river trips and eastern side of Gorges du Verdon.

ℹ️ Getting There & Around

Public transport is limited. There's a once-daily **LER bus** (Lignes Express Régionales; ☎08 21 20 22 03; www.info-ler.fr) service between Moustiers, Castellane and Marseille. Daily July and August and weekends April to September, **Navettes des Gorges shuttle buses** (€7; www.lapaludsurverdon.com) link Castellane with Point Sublime, La Palud and La Maline (but not Moustiers), returning hikers to their vehicles. Tourist offices have schedules and detailed information.

CASTELLANE & AROUND
POP 1539

Castellane is the area's main base for watersport companies. It's dead in winter but teeming in summer. Chapelle Notre Dame du Roc is spectacularly perched above town on a needle-like rock.

🛏️ Sleeping & Eating

The nearby river is lined with seasonal camping areas. Hotels and restaurants cluster around the central squares.

Gîte de Chasteuil   B&B €
(☎04 92 83 72 45; www.gitedechasteuil.com; Hameau de Chasteuil; r €58-91; ◷Mar-Nov) Some 12km west of Castellane, this irresistible *chambre d'hôte*, inside a former schoolhouse with gorgeous mountain views, is ideal for hikers along GR4, which passes outside. Excellent *table d'hôte* (€20 to €24); reservations essential.

Mas du Verdon   B&B €
(☎04 92 83 73 20; www.masduverdon.com; Quartier d'Angles; r €55-72; tables d'hôte €22; ◷Apr-Oct) Hidden 1km south of town on the Verdon's banks, this stone-walled 18th-century farmhouse has five inviting rooms and kindly service. *Table d'hôte* by reservation, May to September.

Auberge du Teillon   PROVENÇAL, GASTRONOMIC €€
(☎04 92 83 60 88; www.auberge-teillon.com; D4805, direction Grasse, La Garde; menus €26-38, d €60; ◷lunch Tue-Sun, dinner Tue-Sat Apr-Oct, closed lunch Tue Jul & Aug, closed Nov-Mar) This roadside *auberge* serves the best food this side of Moustiers. Provençal classics include house-made pâtés, tender-roasted pigeon and unusual *tarte tatin au foie gras*. Reservations are essential. Also rents simple rooms. It's located 5km east of Castellane.

MOUSTIERS STE-MARIE & AROUND
POP 635

Dubbed the *Étoile de Provence* (Star of Provence), the charming little village of Moustiers Ste-Marie makes a fair claim to the title. Tucked between two limestone cliffs, it overlooks open fields and far-off mountains. A 227m-long gold chain bearing a shining star is suspended over the town, so legend claims, by the Knight of Blacas, grateful to have returned safely from the Crusades. Beneath the star, clinging to a cliff ledge, 14th-century Chapelle Notre Dame de Beauvoir is built on the site of an AD 470 temple. Moustiers is also known for its decorative faience (earthenware pottery); 15 ateliers (workshops) display their own styles.

🛏️ Sleeping & Eating

📍TOP CHOICE **Le Petit Ségriès**   FARMSTAY €
(☎04 92 74 68 83; www.gite-segries.fr; r incl breakfast €69-79; 🛜) Friendly hosts Sylvie and Noël offer five colourful, airy rooms in their rambling farmhouse surrounded by countryside. Family-style *tables d'hôte* (€21 with wine), which might include fresh lamb, rabbit and mountain honey, is served at a massive chestnut table. Also guides mountain-bike tours (from €65).

La Ferme Rose   HOTEL €€
(☎04 92 75 75 75; www.lafermerose.com; chemin de Quinson; d €80-150; ❄🛜) This inviting converted farmhouse is now a three-star hotel. It contains quirky collectibles – Wurlitzer jukebox, display case of coffee grinders – but its dozen rooms are uncluttered, colourful and airy. Great bathrooms.

Le Petit Lac   CAMPGROUND €
(☎04 92 74 67 11; www.lepetitlac.com; rte du Lac de Ste-Croix; camping per 2 people €15-23, cabins from €47; ◷camping mid-Jun–Sep, cabins Apr–mid-Oct; @🛜🏊) Activity-oriented lakeside campground; also cute, woodsy eco-cabins (two-night minimum).

TOP CHOICE La Bastide de Moustiers

GASTRONOMIC €€€

(☑04 92 70 47 47; www.bastide-moustiers.com; menus €55-75, d from €240; ✳) This splurge-worthy Provençal nest, domain of legendary chef Alain Ducasse, is famous for fine cuisine – hence the helicopter pad in the garden – and provides a chance to dress for dinner, a rarity in Provence. Rooms are sophisticated and smart, and breakfast is served on a garden-view terrace, in view of scampering baby deer.

La Ferme Ste-Cécile

GASTRONOMIC €€

(☑04 92 74 64 18; D952; menus €28-38; ☉lunch Tue-Sat, dinner Tue-Sun, closed Nov–mid-Mar) The delicious culinary surprises, served on the terrace of this authentic *ferme auberge*, may include the thinnest slice of Roquefort and pear warmed in filo pastry, or foie gras wrapped in sweet quince. This is a meal for connoisseurs; the fussy chef demands you linger.

Clérissy

CRÊPERIE €

(☑06 33 34 06 95, 04 92 74 62 67; www.clerissy.fr; place du Chevalier-de-Blacas; dishes €8-12, d/tr incl breakfast €48/58; ☉daily Jul & Aug, Thu-Tue Apr-Jun, Sep & Oct, closed Nov-Mar) Locals gather on the terrace for pizza, salads, crêpes and pastas on hand-thrown pottery. Upstairs are four simple, great-value rooms (reserve ahead). Cash only.

Parc National du Mercantour

Deeply isolated and breathtakingly beautiful, the Parc National du Mercantour (www.mercantour.eu) is one of the last bastions of true wilderness in France. The terrain is mountainous but the sunshine (in excess of 300 days a year) is definitely Provençal. The park spreads across six valleys (Ubaye, Haut Verdon, Haut Var, Tinée, Vésubie and Roya-Béréva).

VALLÉE DE L'UBAYE

Vallée de l'Ubaye is ringed by a roller coaster of rugged mountains. The valley's only town, Barcelonnette (elevation 1135m), has a fascinating Mexican heritage, resulting in some very un-Alpine architecture. From the 18th century until WWII, some 5000 Barcelonnettais emigrated to Mexico to seek their fortunes in the silk- and wool-weaving industries, building mansions throughout the town upon their return.

The area is brilliant for outdoor sports, including white-water rafting, cycling, mountain biking, skiing and, of course, walking. Contact Bureau des Guides de l'Ubaye (☑06 86 67 38 73; www.guides-montagne-ubaye. com; rue Manuel, Barcelonnette) to find independent guides for most sports.

Le Martinet (15km west of Barcelonnette) is a good base for mountain biking and rafting trips – consider outfitter River (☑04 92 85 53 99; www.river.fr). About 10km south of Barcelonnette is the ski resort of Pra Loup (☑04 92 84 10 04; www.praloup.com), the southern Alps' biggest and best snow destination. In summer the lifts are put to good use for brilliant mountain biking.

Outdoor fanatics will find kindred spirits in Babette and Frédéric, the gregarious owners of Les Méans (☑04 92 81 03 91; www.les-means.com; D900, Méolans-Revel; r/apt incl breakfast from €65/98; ☎). Dating to the Middle Ages, this 15th-century farm hides a tunnel where knights once escaped into the mountains. Now it's an incredible B&B – heaven for hikers – surrounded by mountains rising 1000m, echoing the cascading river. Outside there's a wood-fired hot tub.

Pra Loup's tourist office (☑04 92 84 10 04; www.praloup.com; ☉9am-noon & 2-5pm May-Nov, 9am-7pm Dec-Apr) has lists of accommodation. Free shuttles operate between Barcelonnette and Pra Loup.

VALLÉE DE LA VÉSUBIE

A dead-end valley accessed from the south, Vésubie is often referred to as 'Nice's Switzerland' due to its proximity to the Côte d'Azur. In St-Martin-Vésubie, Escapade Bureau des Guides (☑04 93 03 31 32; www.guidescapade.com; place du Marché, St-Martin-Vésubie; ☉Jul & Aug) organises climbs, canyoning and walks into the Vallée des Merveilles. The tourist office (☑04 93 03 21 28; www.saint-martinvesubie.fr; place Félix Faure; ☉9am-7pm daily Jun-Sep, 9am-noon & 2-6pm Mon-Fri Oct-May; ☎) and the Maison du Parc National du Mercantour (Visitor Centre; ☑04 93 03 23 15; rue Serrurier, St-Martin-Vésubie; ☉9am-noon & 2-6pm mid-June–mid-Sept) have loads of information about exploring the surrounding area.

Sustained hunting over 1000 years led to the eventual disappearance of the wolf (*Canis lupus*) from France in 1930. But in 1992 two 'funny-looking dogs' were spotted near Utelle. Since then, wolves have been making a natural return, loping across the Alps from Italy. Set high in the mountains of Le Boréon, Alpha (☑04 93 02 33 69; www.

alpha-loup.com; Le Boréon; adult/child €12/10; 🖶) allows visitors to find out how man is learning to live with the wolf and watch wolves roam wild. Visit year-round, but opening hours vary; call ahead or visit its website for details.

Magical mountain views unfold from the timber terrace of secluded Le Boréon (☎04 93 03 20 35; www.hotel-boreon.com; d/tr/q from €68/99/126, half-board per person €64, menus from €23; ⊗closed Nov-Mar; 🛜), the quintessential chalet. Cosy up in one of its dozen rooms and watch the snowflakes fall outside while dining on Alpine specialities.

For something more stylish, head to Moonlight Chalet (☎06 89 25 36 74; www.moonlightchalet.com; 8 rue Rumplemeyer, St-Martin-Vésubie; r incl breakfast €100-130; 🛏), a hidden boutique hotel on the edge of St-Martin that uses mother nature for interior design.

In nearby La Colmiane, 7km west of St-Martin-Vésubie, is a small ski station that's also good for walking, mountain biking in summer and via ferrata (a mountain course of rope bridges, ladders etc); contact Colmiane Sports (☎04 93 02 87 00; www.colmiane-sports.com) and Ferrata Sport (☎04 93 02 80 56) to hire mountain bikes, ski gear and climbing gear.

Conseil Général des Alpes-Maritimes (www.cg06.fr) buses (€1 flat fee within the département) connect Nice with St-Martin-Vésubie (60 minutes) and La Colmiane (75 minutes).

VALLÉE DES MERVEILLES

The 'Valley of Wonders' contains one of the world's most stupendous collections of Bronze Age petroglyphs. They date from between 1800 and 1500 BC and are thought to have been made by a Ligurian cult. Effectively an open-air art gallery, wedged between the Vésubie and Roya Valleys, it shelters more than 36,000 rock engravings of human figures, bulls and other animals spread over 30 sq km around Mont Bégo (2870m).

The main access is via westbound D91 from St-Dalmas de Tende, in Vallée de la Roya, to Castérino, where there's a summertime national-park office (☎04 93 04 89 79). Alternatively, go via dead-end D171, which leads north from Roquebillière, in Vallée de la Vésubie. The engravings are usually covered in snow in winter; the best time to see them is June to October. Access is mostly restricted: visit with an official guide (inquire at the Mercantour National Park visitor centre or Escapade Bureau des Guides).

The French Riviera & Monaco

Best Places to Eat

» Auberge de l'Oumède (p855)

» Sea Sens (p844)

» La Montgolfière (p865)

» La Colombe d'Or (p840)

» Relais du Vieux Sauvaire (p857)

Best Places to Stay

» Château Eza (p862)

» Les Quatre Saisons (p860)

» Lou Cagnard (p854)

» Hôtel Bellevue (p857)

» Hôtel La Pérouse (p832)

Why Go?

With its glistening seas, idyllic beaches and fabulous weather, the Riviera (known as Côte d'Azur to the French) encapsulates many people's idea of the good life. The beauty is that there is so much more to do than just going to the beach – although the Riviera does take beach-going *very* seriously: from nudist beach to secluded cove or exclusive club, there is something for everyone.

Culture vultures will revel in the region's thriving art scene: the Riviera has some fine museums, including world-class modern art, and a rich history to explore in Roman ruins, WWII memorials and excellent museums.

Foodies for their part will rejoice at the prospect of lingering in fruit and veg markets, touring vineyards and feasting on some of France's best cuisines, while outdoor enthusiasts will be spoilt for choice with coastal paths to explore, and snorkelling and swimming galore.

When to Go
Monaco

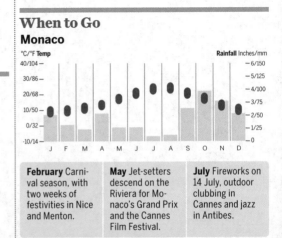

February Carnival season, with two weeks of festivities in Nice and Menton.

May Jet-setters descend on the Riviera for Monaco's Grand Prix and the Cannes Film Festival.

July Fireworks on 14 July, outdoor clubbing in Cannes and jazz in Antibes.

Accommodation Warning

Accommodation can be impossible to find, not to mention prohibitively expensive, during the Cannes Film Festival and the Monaco Grand Prix (both held in May). This applies to the coast between Menton and Cannes but doesn't affect areas beyond Massif de l'Estérel (St-Raphaël, St-Tropez etc).

July and August are busy everywhere, so book well in advance.

MAGICAL MATISSE TOUR

If you're mad about Matisse, you can cherry-pick a Côte d'Azur itinerary that takes in some of the major sites of his life.

Born on New Year's Eve in 1869, Henri Matisse arrived in Nice from Paris in 1917 to recover from bronchitis. He remained here until his death in 1954 at his home and studio in the mansion-lined suburb of Cimiez; this is where the Musée Matisse (p827) is now located.

Matisse's visits to **Renoir's villa** (now the Musée Renoir, p838) in Cagnes-sur-Mer provided further inspiration for paintings, including the 1917 *Oliviers, Jardin de Renoir à Cagnes* (Olive Trees, Renoir's Garden in Cagnes).

During WWII Matisse rented Villa Le Rêve in Vence where he was visited by Picasso and Aragon, among others. It was during his stay in Vence that he designed the Chapelle du Rosaire (p840).

Matisse is buried at the Monastère Notre Dame de Cimiez (p830) in Nice, near the Musée Matisse; signs lead to his grave.

Tourist offices all along the Riviera have an info-packed brochure (available in English) about tracing Matisse's footsteps.

Top Beaches

» **Plage de Pampelonne, St-Tropez** (p853) Sea, sand and celebrity.

» **Z Plage, Cannes** (p841) Glamour and creature comforts on La Croisette.

» **Plage de Gigaro, La Croix-Valmer** (p857) Not too big, along wooded shores, blissful.

» **Calanques, Massif de l'Estérel** (p850) Take your pick from the dozen coves with crystal-clear waters.

» **Île de Port-Cros** (p858) Most beaches on this beautiful island will make you feel like a castaway.

GREAT WALKS

There are superb walks along the Riviera, with great panoramas. Try the well-trodden Cap d'Antibes (p837) or the more-challenging Massif de l'Estérel (p850)..

Fast Facts

» **Population** 2.08 million

» **Area** 10,272 sq km

» **Hotel overnights/yr** 11.8 million

» **Signature drink** rosé wine

Riviera Travel Essentials

» Smart clothes for top-end restaurants, clubs and casinos with strict dress codes

» A penknife and corkscrew for decadent picnics

» Mosquito repellent for a buzz-free night

Resources

» Côte d'Azur Tourisme (www.cotedazur-tourisme.com)

» Tourisme PACA (www.tourismepaca.fr)

» Visit Var (www.visitvar.fr)

THE FRENCH RIVIERA & MONACO

The French Riviera & Monaco Highlights

1. Take a scenic drive along the **Grande Corniche** (p861) for jaw-dropping views of the Med

2. Lose yourself in labyrinthine **Vieux Nice** (p827) and enjoy a panoramic

picnic on **Parc du Château** (p827)

3. Catch a ferry to **Île de Port-Cros** (p858) or **Île de Porquerolles** (p858) for pristine Mediterranean seascapes

4. Enjoy a fabulous day at a **St-Tropez beach club** (p855)

5. Admire seminal 20th-century art at **Fondation Maeght** (p839) in St-Paul de Vence

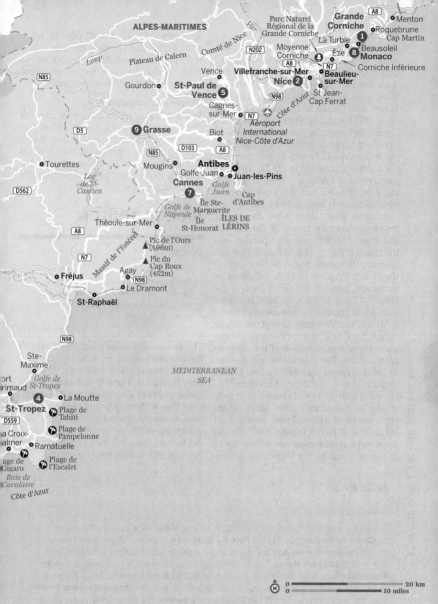

ALPES-MARITIMES

Parc Naturel
Régional de la
Grande Corniche

Grande
Corniche

A8

Menton

Roquebrune
Cap Martin

La Turbie

1

Moyenne
Corniche

Éze

Beausoleil

Monaco

N7

Comté de Nice

N202

8

Corniche Inférieure

Vence

Villefranche-sur-Mer

Beaulieu-
sur-Mer

Plateau de Calern

Loup

Nice

2

N85

St-Paul de
Vence

5

Cagnes-
sur-Mer

N7

St-Jean-
Cap Ferrat

Gourdon

Côte d'Azur

N98

D5

9

Grasse

Aéroport
International
Nice-Côte d'Azur

Biot

N85

D103

A8

Tourettes

Mougins

Antibes

Golfe-Juan

Juan-les-Pins

D562

Lac
de St-
Cassien

Cannes

7

Golfe
Juan

Cap
d'Antibes

Golfe de
Napoule

Île Ste-
Marguerite

Théoule-sur-Mer

Île
St-Honorat

ÎLES DE
LÉRINS

A8

Pic de l'Ours
(496m)

N7

Massif de l'Estérel

Pic du
Cap Roux
(452m)

Agay

Fréjus

N98

Le Dramont

St-Raphaël

N98

Ste-
Maxime

MEDITERRANEAN
SEA

ort
imaud

Golfe de
St-Tropez

La Moutte

St-Tropez

4

Plage de
Tahiti

D559

a Croix-
almer

Plage de
Pampelonne

Ramatuelle

age de
Gigaro

Plage de
l'Escalet

Baie de
Cavalaire

Côte d'Azur

N   0   20 km
         0   10 miles

6 Wind your way through
vineyards and try some of the
area's famed wines at **Maison
des Vins** (p860) in the seaside
town of Bandol

7 Dress to impress and party
the night away in **Cannes** (p840)

8 Try your luck at Monaco's
opulent **casino** (p868)

9 Discover the world of
perfumery in **Grasse** (p847)

History

The eastern part of France's Mediterranean coast, including the area now known as the Côte d'Azur, was occupied by the Ligurians from the 1st millennium BC. It was colonised around 600 BC by Greeks from Asia Minor, who settled along the coast in the areas of Massalia (present-day Marseille), Hyères, St-Tropez, Antibes and Nice. Called in to help Massalia against the threat of invasion by Celto-Ligurians from Entremont, the Romans triumphed in 125 BC. They created Provincia Romana – the area between the Alps, the sea and the River Rhône – which ultimately became Provence.

In 1388 Nice, along with the Haute-Provence mountain towns of Barcelonette and Puget-Théniers, was incorporated into the House of Savoy, while the rest of the surrounding Provençal region became part of the French kingdom in 1482. Following an agreement between Napoléon III and the House of Savoy in 1860, the Austrians were ousted and France took possession of Savoy.

Within the Provence–Alpes–Côte d'Azur *région*, the Côte d'Azur (or Riviera to Anglophones) encompasses most of the *départements* of the Alpes-Maritimes and the Var. In the 19th century, wealthy tourists flocked to the area to escape the cold northern winter, along with celebrated artists and writers, adding to the area's cachet. Little fishing ports morphed into exclusive resorts. Paid holidays for all French workers from 1936 and improved transportation saw visitors arrive in summer, making it a year-round holiday playground. But it's not all play, no work: since the late 20th century, the area inland of Antibes has been home to France's 'Silicon Valley', Sophia Antipolis, the country's largest industrial and technological hub.

Dangers & Annoyances

The Côte d'Azur isn't a dangerous area, but theft – from backpacks, pockets, bags, cars and even laundrettes – is common. Watch your belongings, especially at train and bus stations, on overnight trains, and on the beach. If you're travelling by bicycle, store it off-street overnight.

NICE TO TOULON

Nice

POP 344,460

'Most people come here for the light. Me, I'm from the north. What moved me are January's radiant colours and luminosity of daylight.'

Henri Matisse

The words are Matisse's but they could be those of any painter, or, in fact, of any visitor who comes to Nice, for it's true: the light here is magical. The city also offers exceptional quality of life: shimmering Mediterranean shores, the very best of Mediterranean food, a unique historical heritage and Alpine wilderness within an hour's drive. No wonder so many young French people aspire to live here and tourists keep flooding in.

NICE IN...

Two Days

Spend the morning mooching around atmospheric **Vieux Nice**. Browse the market on **Cours Saleya** and head to the **Parc du Château** for a picnic. Spend the afternoon on the **Promenade des Anglais**, either at the beach or skating along. Settle down for dinner at **Bistrot d'Antoine**. The following day, trace Matisse's artistic evolution at the **Musée Matisse**. Grab some Nice-style tapas at **Chez René Socca** for lunch before immersing yourself in Nice's belle époque history at the beautiful **Musée Masséna**. Finish your day with a long aperitif at **Les Distilleries Idéales** and a flamboyant dinner of Italian fare at **Luna Rossa**.

Four Days

Head to **Èze** for extraordinary views of the Riviera. Walk down **Nietzsche's path** to Èze-sur-Mer and catch the train to **Monaco** for a punt at the Casino de Monte Carlo, a tour of the aquarium at the **Musée Océanographique de Monaco** and a taste of the principality's culinary delights. On the fourth day, go inland to **Grasse** to tour its **perfumeries** or spend the day in **Cannes**: explore unspoilt Île **Ste-Marguerite** before plumping yourself down on a beach lounger on **La Croisette**.

History

Nice was founded around 350 BC by the Greek seafarers who had settled Marseille. They named the colony Nikaia, apparently to commemorate a nearby victory (*nike* in Greek). In 154 BC the Greeks were followed by the Romans, who settled further uphill around what is now Cimiez, where there are still Roman ruins.

By the 10th century, Nice was ruled by the Counts of Provence but turned to Amadeus VII of the House of Savoy in 1388. In the 18th and 19th centuries it was occupied several times by the French, but didn't definitively become part of France until 1860.

During the Victorian period, the English aristocracy and European royalty enjoyed Nice's mild winter climate. Throughout the 20th century, the city's exceptional art scene spanned every movement from Impressionism to new realism. The tram line (customised by local and international artists) and the decision to open all museums for free in 2008 show that art is still very much a part of city life.

⊙ Sights

Nice has a number of world-class sights but the star attraction is probably the city itself: atmospheric, beautiful and photogenic, it's a wonderful place to stroll or watch the world go by, so make sure you leave yourself plenty of time to soak it all in.

VIEUX NICE

TOP CHOICE Vieux Nice   HISTORIC QUARTER
(⊙food markets 6am-1.30pm Tue-Sun) Nice's old town, a mellow-hued rabbit warren, has scarcely changed since the 1700s. Retracing its history – and therefore that of the city – is a highlight, although you don't need to be a history buff to enjoy a stroll in this atmospheric quarter. Vieux Nice is as alive and prominent today as it ever was.

Cue the cours Saleya: this joyous, thriving market square hosts a well-known flower market (cours Saleya; ⊙6am-5.30pm Tue-Sat, to 1.30pm Sun) and a thriving fruit and vegetable market (Cours Saleya; ⊙6am-1.30pm Tue-Sun), a staple of local life. A flea market (cours Saleya; ⊙8am-5pm Mon) takes over on Mondays, and the spill-over from bars and restaurants seems to be a permanent fixture.

Much of Vieux Nice has a similar atmosphere to cours Saleya, with delis, food shops, boutiques and bars crammed in its tiny lanes. Rue de la Boucherie and rue Pairolière are excellent for food shopping. You'll also find a fish market (place St-François; ⊙6am-1pm Tue-Sun) at place St-François.

Much harder to spot because of the narrow lane it sits on is the baroque Palais Lascaris (15 rue Droite; guided visit €3; ⊙10am-6pm Wed-Mon, guided tour 3pm Fri), a 17th-century mansion housing a frescoed orgy of Flemish tapestries, faïence and gloomy religious paintings. On the ground floor is an 18th-century pharmacy.

Baroque aficionados shouldn't miss Nice's other architectural gems such as Cathédrale Ste-Réparate (place Rossetti), honouring the city's patron saint, or the exuberant Chapelle de la Miséricorde (cours Saleya).

Parc du Château   GARDEN
(⊙8am-6pm winter, to 8pm summer) On a rocky outcrop towering over Vieux Nice, this park offers a cinematic panorama of Nice and the Baie des Anges on one side, and the port on the other. The 12th-century castle was razed by Louis XIV in 1706; only the 16th-century Tour Bellanda remains. It is a fabulous place for picnics.

Its other simple attractions include Cascade Donjon, an 18th-century artificial waterfall crowned with a viewing platform, and kids' playgrounds. To get here, ride the Château Lift (Ascenseur du Château; rue des Ponchettes; single/return €1/1.30) from beneath Tour Bellanda, or hike up the staircases on montée Lesage or the eastern end of rue Rossetti in Vieux Nice. From the port, follow montée Montfort.

Port Lympia   ARCHITECTURE
Nice's Port Lympia, with its beautiful Venetian-coloured buildings, is often overlooked, but a stroll along its quays is lovely, as is the walk to get here: come down through Parc du Château or follow quai Rauba Capeu, where a massive war memorial hewn from the rock commemorates the 4000 Niçois who died in both world wars.

CIMIEZ

Cimiez used to be the playground of European aristocrats wintering on the Riviera. These days, it's Nice's affluent residents who live in the area's beautiful Victorian villas.

FREE Musée Matisse   GALLERY
(www.musee-matisse-nice.org; 164 av des Arènes de Cimiez; ⊙10am-6pm Wed-Mon) Located about 2km north of the centre in the leafy quarter

Nice

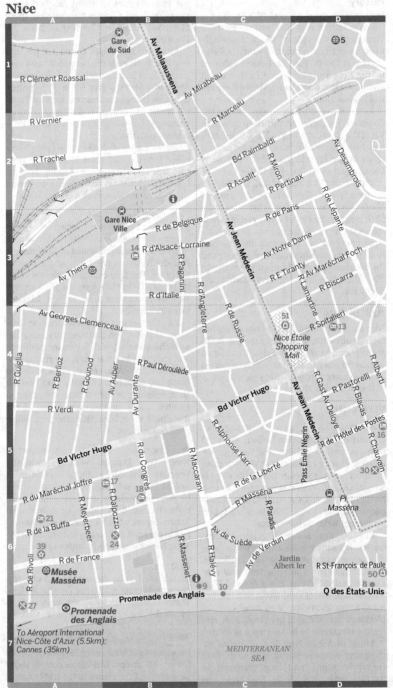

THE FRENCH RIVIERA & MONACO NICE

Gare du Sud

R Clément Roassal

Av Malaaussena

Av Mirabeau

R Vernier

R Marceau

R Trachel

Bd Raimbaldi

R Miron

R Assalit

R Pertinax

Av Désambrois

R de Lépante

Gare Nice Ville

R de Belgique

R de Paris

R d'Alsace-Lorraine

Av Jean Médecin

Av Notre Dame

R E Tiranty

Av Maréchal Foch

Av Thiers

14

R Paganini

R d'Angleterre

R Lamartine

R Biscarra

R d'Italie

R de Russie

R Spitalieri

51

13

Av Georges Clemenceau

Nice Étoile Shopping Mall

R Alberti

R Guiglia

R Berlioz

R Gounod

Av Auber

R Paul Déroulède

Bd Victor Hugo

R Gast Av Deloye

R Pastorelli

R Blacas

R Verdi

Av Durante

Av Jean Médecin

R de l'Hôtel des Postes

R Chauvain

16

Bd Victor Hugo

R du Congrès

R Alphonse Karr

R Maccarani

R de la Liberté

Pass Émile Négrin

30

R du Maréchal Joffre

17

R Dalpozzo

18

R Masséna

R Paradis

Pl Masséna

R Meyerbeer

24

21

R de la Buffa

39

R de Rivoli

R de France

R Massenet

R Massenet

R Halévy

Av de Suède

Av de Verdun

Jardin Albert Ier

R St-François de Paule

8

50

Musée Masséna

9

10

Q des États-Unis

27

Promenade des Anglais

Promenade des Anglais

To Aéroport International
Nice-Côte d'Azur (5.5km);
Cannes (35km)

MEDITERRANEAN
SEA

5

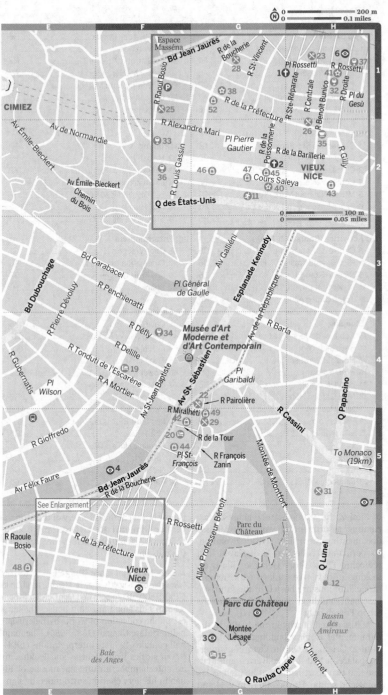

0   200 m
0   0.1 miles

Espace Masséna
Bd Jean Jaurès
R de la Boucherie
R St-Vincent
Pl Rossetti
R Rossetti
Pl du Gesù
R Raoul Bosio
R de la Préfecture
R Ste-Réparate
R Centrale
R Benoît Bunico
R Droite
R Gilly
R Alexandre Mari
Pl Pierre Gautier
R de la Poissonnerie
R de la Barillerie
VIEUX NICE
R Louis Gassin
Cours Saleya
Q des États-Unis

0   100 m
0   0.05 miles

CIMIEZ
Av de Normandie
Av Émile-Bieckert
Av Émile-Bieckert
Chemin du Bois

Bd Carabacel
Av Galliéni
Esplanade Kennedy

Bd Dubouchage
R Penchienatti
Pl Général de Gaulle

R Pierre Dévoluy
R Défly
R Défly
Av de la République
R Barla

R Tonduti de l'Escarène
R Delille
Musée d'Art Moderne et d'Art Contemporain

R Gubernatis
R A Mortier
Av St-Sébastien
Pl Garibaldi

Pl Wilson
Av St-Jean Baptiste
R Cassini
Q Papacino

R Gioffredo
R Miralhéti
R Pairolière
Montée de Montfort

Av Félix Faure
Bd Jean Jaurès
R de la Boucherie
R de la Tour
R François Zanin
Pl St-François
To Monaco (19km)

See Enlargement
R Rossetti
Q Lunel

R Raoule Bosio
R de la Préfecture
Parc du Château
Allée Professeur Bénoit

Vieux Nice
Parc du Château
Bassin des Amiraux

Baie des Anges
Montée Lesage
Q Infernet
Q Rauba Capeu

THE FRENCH RIVIERA & MONACO NICE

Nice

of Cimiez, the Musée Matisse houses a fascinating assortment of works by Matisse documenting the artist's stylistic evolution. Its permanent collection is displayed in a red-ochre 17th-century Genoese villa overlooking an olive-tree-studded park. Temporary exhibitions are hosted in the futuristic basement building. Sadly, all explanations are in French only.

Matisse lived nearby in the 1940s, in the monumental Régina building at 71 bd de Cimiez. Originally Queen Victoria's wintering palace, it had been converted and Matisse had two apartments that he used as his home and studio. He died there in 1954 and

is now buried at the cemetery of the Monastère de Cimiez (Place du Monastère; ⊙8.30am-12.30pm and 2.30-6.30pm), across the park from the museum.

Musée National Marc Chagall GALLERY (www.musee-chagall.fr; 4 av Dr Ménard; adult/child €7.50/5.50; ⊙10am-5pm Wed-Mon Oct-Jun, to 6pm Jul-Sep) This small museum houses the largest public collection of works by Belarusian painter Marc Chagall (1887–1985). The main hall contains 12 huge interpretations (1954–67) of stories from Genesis and Exodus. In an antechamber, an unusual mosaic of Elijah in his fiery chariot, surrounded by signs of the zodiac, is viewed through a plate-glass window and reflected in a small pond.

The excellent audioguide is available in English (you will need a form of ID as deposit). Smartphone users can also download the commentary as an app. It takes about 20 minutes to walk to the museum from the centre (signposted from av de l'Olivetto).

CENTRAL NICE

Promenade des Anglais ARCHITECTURE

Palm-lined promenade des Anglais, paid for by Nice's English colony in 1822, is a fine stage for a stroll. It's particularly atmospheric in the evening, with Niçois milling about and epic sunsets over the sea. Don't miss the magnificent façade of Hôtel Negresco, built in 1912 for Romanian innkeeper Henri Negresco, or art deco Palais de la Méditerranée, saved from demolition in the 1980s and now part of a five-star palace.

The promenade follows the whole Baie des Anges (4km) and has a cycle and skating lane. For a fantastic family outing, rent skates or scooters at Roller Station (www.roller-station.fr; 49 quai des États-Unis; ⊙10am-7pm) and whizz along the Prom. You'll need some ID as a deposit. Rentals include protective gear (helmet and pads).

FREE **Musée Masséna** MUSEUM

(65 rue de France; ⊙10am-6pm Wed-Mon) The beautiful Musée Masséna, housed in a marvellous Italianate neoclassical villa (1898), retraces Nice and the Riviera's history from the late 18th century to WWII. It's a fascinating journey, with a roll-call of monarchs, a succession of nationalities (British, Russians, Americans), the advent of tourism, the prominence of the carnival and much more.

History is told through an excellent mix of furniture, objects, art deco posters, early photographs, paintings and the lovely setting (note, however, that captions are in French only). The city of Nice still uses the ground-floor rooms for official occasions so it can sometimes close at short notice.

FREE **Musée d'Art Moderne et d'Art Contemporain** GALLERY

(Mamac; www.mamac-nice.org; Promenade des Arts; ⊙10am-6pm Tue-Sun) European and American avant-garde works from the 1950s to the present are the focus of this museum. Highlights include many works by Nice's New Realists Christo, César, Arman, Yves Klein and Niki de Saint-Phalle. The build-

ing's rooftop too works as an exhibition space (with panoramas of Nice to boot).

Smartphone users will be able to access audio commentary thanks to flashcodes.

Cathédrale Orthodoxe Russe St-Nicolas CATHEDRAL

(Av Nicolas II) Built between 1902 and 1912 to provide a big enough church for the growing Russian community, this cathedral, with its colourful onion domes and rich, ornate interior, is the biggest Russian Orthodox church outside Russia. The interior was closed to the public at the time of research.

🏃 Activities

Nice Guided Walking Tours WALKING TOUR

The best way to discover Nice's rich heritage is to take a guided walking tour. The Centre du Patrimoine (75 Quai des Etats-Unis; ⊙8.30am-1pm & 2-5pm Mon-Thu, to 3.45pm) runs a two-hour Vieux Nice Baroque tour (Tuesday afternoon), as well as themed tours including art deco, neoclassical and belle époque Nice. The tourist office (p835) runs a 2½-hour Vieux Nice tour in English (adult/child €12/6), at 9.30am on Saturday.

Art with the Tram TRAM TOUR

(www.tramway-nice.org) As well Jaume Plensa's glow-in-the-dark *Conversation* on place Masséna, there are 13 more works of art to discover along Nice's tram route, including original sound bites at each stop, the calligraphy of the tram's stops and more visual works. The best way to appreciate this artistic input is to take the tourist office's two-hour guided tour Art dans la Ville (adult/child €8/3, plus €2 for transport; ☺tours 7pm Fri).

Beaches   BEACHES

Nice's beaches are all pebbly; sensitive behinds should therefore opt for a comfy mattress at one of its 14 private beaches (€15–€20 per day). Out of the free public sections of beach (with lifeguards, first-aid posts and cold showers), Plage Publique des Ponchettes, opposite Vieux Nice, is the most popular (and don't worry about your bottom – many hotels lend you mats!).

Most beaches also offer a raft of activities, from beach volleyball to jetskis and pedalos.

Trans Côte d'Azur   BOAT TOUR

(www.trans-cote-azur.com; quai Lunel; ☺Apr-Oct) To escape the crowds, take a scenic cruise along the coast. Trans Côte d'Azur runs one-hour trips along the Baie des Anges and the Rade de Villefranche (adult/child €16/10) from April to October. From mid-June to mid-September it also runs regular excursions to Île Ste-Marguerite (€35/25, crossing one hour), St-Tropez (€58/44, crossing 2½ hours) and Monaco (€34/ 25, crossing 45 minutes). Reservations are essential.

Nice Le Grand Tour   BUS TOUR

(www.nicelegrandtour.com; 1-day pass adult/child €20/5) With headphone commentary in several languages, the open-topped Le Grand Tour buses (1½ hours) give you a good overview of Nice. You can hop on or off at any one of 14 stops.

🎊 Festivals & Events

Carnaval de Nice   CARNIVAL

(www.nicecarnaval.com) Held each year around Mardi Gras (Shrove Tuesday) since 1294 – highlights include the batailles de fleurs (battles of flowers), and the ceremonial burning of the carnival king on promenade des Anglais, followed by a fireworks display.

Nice Jazz Festival   MUSIC FESTIVAL

(www.nicejazzfestival.fr) France's original jazz festival has taken on a life of its own in its new location off Promenade des Anglais, with fringe concerts popping up all around the venue, from Vieux Nice to Massena and the shopping streets around Rue de France. The festival itself remains as high-brow as ever.

🛏 Sleeping

Nice has a suite of places to sleep, from stellar backpacker hostels to international art-filled icons. Prices jump during summer and also for regional festivals such as Monaco's Grand Prix.

Hôtel La Pérouse   BOUTIQUE HOTEL €€€

(☎04 93 62 34 63; www.hotel-la-perouse.com; 11 quai Rauba Capeu; d from €195; ✳@☎☎) Built into the rock cliff next to Tour Bellanda, La Pérouse captures the vibe of a genteel villa. Lower-floor rooms face the lemon-tree-shaded courtyard and infinity pool; upper-floor rooms have magnificent vistas of the promenade and sea, many with balconies or terraces to make the best of the panorama. Smart accent colours add flair to the traditional decor.

Nice Garden Hôtel   BOUTIQUE HOTEL €€

(☎04 93 87 35 63; www.nicegardenhotel.com; 11 rue du Congrès; s/d €75/100; ✳☎) Behind heavy iron gates hides this little gem of a hotel: the nine beautifully appointed rooms, the work of the exquisite Marion, are a subtle blend of old and new and overlook a delightful garden with a glorious orange tree. Amazingly, all this charm and peacefulness is just two blocks from the promenade.

TOP CHOICE Nice Pebbles   SELF-CONTAINED €€

(☎04 97 20 27 30; www.nicepebbles.com; 23 rue Gioffredo; 1-/3-bedroom apt from €105/320; ☎☎) Have you ever dreamt of feeling like a real Niçois? Coming back to your designer pad in Vieux Nice, opening a bottle of ice-cold rosé and cooking up a storm with the treats you bought at the market? Nice Pebbles' concept is simple: offering the quality of a four-star boutique hotel in holiday flats.

The apartments (ranging from one to three bedrooms) are gorgeous and equipped to high standards (flatscreen TV, kitchen, linen bedding and, in some cases, wi-fi, swimming pool, balcony etc).

Villa Saint-Exupéry   HOSTEL €

(☎04 93 84 42 83; www.villahostels.com; 22 av Gravier; dm €25-30, s/d €45/90; @☎) Why can't all hostels be like this? Set in a lovely converted monastery in the north of the city, this is a great place to put down your bags for a few days. Chill out in the 24-hour common room housed in the old stained-glass chapel, sip a €1 beer on the barbecue terrace and stock up on travel tips.

The villa staff will come and pick you up from the nearby Comte de Falicon tram stop or St-Maurice stop for Bus 23 (direct from the airport) when you first arrive. Rates include breakfast.

Villa Rivoli
BOUTIQUE HOTEL €€

(☑04 93 88 80 25; www.villa-rivoli.com; 10 rue de Rivoli; s/d/q from 85/99/210; ✲🖲) Built in 1890, this stately villa feels like your own pied-à-terre in the heart of Nice. A marble staircase leads to spotlessly clean character-rich rooms, some with fabric-covered walls, gilt-edged mirrors and marble mantelpieces. Take breakfast in the garden's sun-dappled shade, or in the grand belle époque salon.

Villa la Tour
BOUTIQUE HOTEL €€

(☑04 93 80 08 15; www.villa-la-tour.com; 4 rue de la Tour; s/d €79/91; ✲🖲) Small but perfectly formed, the Villa la Tour is delightful, with warm, romantic Provençal rooms, a location at the heart of Vieux Nice, and a diminutive flower-decked roof terrace.

Hôtel Windsor
BOUTIQUE HOTEL €€

(☑04 93 88 59 35; www.hotelwindsornice.com; 11 rue Dalpozzo; d €120-175; ✲@🖲🏊) High-profile artists have decorated more than half the rooms at the Windsor with bold, sometimes unsettling designs. Traditional rooms are more soothing yet still nod to the arts with hand-painted murals.

Hôtel Wilson
BOUTIQUE HOTEL €

(☑04 93 85 47 79; www.hotel-wilson-nice.com; 39 rue de l'Hôtel des Postes; s/d €50/55; 🖲) Many years of travelling, an experimental nature and exquisite taste have turned Jean-Marie's rambling flat into a compelling place to stay. The 16 rooms have individual, carefully crafted decor, and share the eclectic dining room.

Belle Meunière
HOSTEL €

(☑04 93 88 66 15; www.bellemeuniere.com; 21 av Durante; dm/d/t/q €28/78/93/124, without bathroom dm/tr €22/66; 🖲) This jovial hostel, in a 19th-century mansion, is great for unfussy families and groups of friends: rooms are very basic but the price is fair. Rates include breakfast.

Auberge de Jeunesse Les Camélias
HOSTEL €

(☑04 93 62 15 54; www.fuaj.org; 3 rue Spitaleri; dm €25.80; @🖲) This colourful hostel has clean, spacious dorms, a bar, a self-catering kitchen and a laundry. Dorms range from four to eight beds and are single sex. There is a midday lockout (11am to 3pm) but no night curfew.

✖ Eating

Restaurants in Vieux Nice are a mixed bag of tourist traps and genuine good finds. Follow your instincts, or our recommendations.

🔝 CHOICE Le Bistrot d'Antoine
MODERN FRENCH €€

(☑04 93 85 29 57; 27 rue de la Préfecture; mains €13-18; ⊙lunch & dinner Tue-Sat) What's so surprising about this super brasserie is how unfazed it is by its incredible success: it is full every night (booking essential), yet the 'bistro chic' cuisine never wavers, the staff are cool as a cucumber, the atmosphere is reliably jovial and the prices incredibly good value for the area.

Le Chantecler
GASTRONOMIC €€€

(☑04 93 16 64 00; www.hotel-negresco-nice.com; Le Negresco, 37 promenade des Anglais; menu €90, mains €55-68; ⊙dinner Wed-Sun, lunch Sun) In a sumptuous, pink Regency dining room, Le Negresco's two-Michelin-starred restaurant is no ordinary restaurant. Make sure you're in a grand mood if you're going to splash out: every dish is the most exquisite creation, both in cuisine and presentation, and there is a seemingly endless succession of apetisers, palate cleansers and petits fours.

All of this comes complete with the expertise of an exceptional sommelier, who will happily match every course with wine or recommend a bottle for your meal. Service is truly stellar and you'll finish your evening feeling like royalty.

Luna Rossa
ITALIAN €€

(☑04 93 85 55 66; www.lelunarossa.com; 3 rue Chauvain; mains €15-25; ⊙Tue-Fri, dinner Sat) Luna Rossa is like your dream Mediterranean dinner come true: fresh pasta, exquisitely cooked seafood, sun-kissed vegetables and divine meats. Wash it down with one of the excellent bottles of red or rosé from the cellar.

Fenocchio
ICE CREAM €

(2 place Rossetti; ice cream from €2; ⊙9am-midnight Feb-Oct) Dither too long over the 70-plus flavours of ice cream and sorbet at this unforgettable *glacier* (ice-cream shop) and you'll never make it to the front of the queue. Eschew predictable favourites and indulge in a new taste sensation: black olive, rosemary or lavender.

L'Escalinada
NIÇOIS €€

(☑04 93 62 11 71; www.escalinada.fr; 22 rue Pairolière; menu €24, mains €15-23; ⊙lunch & dinner daily) This enchanting old-town *auberge*

TOP 5 REGIONAL SPECIALITIES

Nice's eponymous salad (crunchy lettuce, anchovies, olives, green beans and tomatoes in its purest form) has travelled far beyond its original shores. But there is much more to Niçois cuisine than *salade niçoise*. Here are five local specialities you should try:

» **Stockfish** Dried cod soaked in running water for a few days and then simmered with onions, tomatoes, garlic, olives and potatoes.

» **Socca** A pancake made of chickpea flour and olive oil cooked on a griddle with sneezing quantities of black pepper.

» **Daube** A rich beef stew of wine, onions, carrots, tomatoes and herbs; the sauce is often served with gnocchi or ravioli.

» **Petits farcis** Stuffed vegetables (generally onions, zucchini, zucchini flowers, tomatoes and aubergines).

» **Pissaladière** A pizza-like base topped with onions, garlic, olives and anchovies.

Our selection of Niçois restaurants will see you right on stockfish and daube; otherwise, make a beeline for Chez René Socca (2 rue Miralhéti; dishes from €2; ⊘9am-9pm Tue-Sun, to 10.30pm Jul & Aug, closed Nov) for an informal lunch or aperitif to try the bite-size snacks.

(inn) has been one of the best places in town for Niçois cuisine for the last half-century: melt-in-your-mouth homemade gnocchi with tasty *daube* (Provençal beef stew), grilled prawns with garlic and herbs, Marsala veal stew. The staff are delightful and the welcome kir is on the house. No credit cards.

La Cave de l'Origine   MODERN FRENCH €€
(☑04 83 50 09 60; 3 rue Dalpozzo; mains €15-22; ⊘lunch & dinner Tue-Sat) This sleek new wine bar–restaurant has as much substance as style. As you would expect from a wine emporium, there is a great selection of wines by the glass, many of them local, and fantastic advice about what to try with your food (modern French fare with a touch of fusion).

Le Comptoir du Marché   MODERN FRENCH €
(☑04 93 13 45 01; 8 rue du marché; mains €13-15; ⊘lunch & dinner Tue-Sat) With its vintage kitchen decor and recession-proof prices, it's no wonder the Comptoir does so well. There are five or six daily mains, scribbled on a chalkboard. The cuisine is a modern twist on French traditional recipes with lentil stews, confit rabbit and even *os à moelle* (bone marrow).

La Merenda   NIÇOIS €€
(4 rue Raoul Bosio; mains €12-15; ⊘Mon-Fri) Simple, solid Niçois cuisine by former Michelin-starred chef Dominique Le Stanc draws the crowds to this pocket-sized bistro (you'll be rubbing back and shoulders with fellow customers). The tiny open kitchen stands proud at the back of the room, and the equally small menu is chalked on the board. No credit cards.

Zucca Magica   VEGETARIAN €€
(☑04 93 56 25 27; www.lazuccamagica.com; 4bis quai Papacino; menus €30; ⊘Tue-Sat; ☑) Bursting with vegetarian surprises, the 'Magic Pumpkin' serves a fixed five-course menu, dictated simply by the market and the chef's fancy. Seating is amid a fabulous collection of pumpkins and fairy lights. Bring along a gargantuan appetite.

🍷 Drinking

Vieux Nice's little streets runneth over with local bars and cafes: from a morning espresso to a lunchtime *pastis* (the tipple of choice in the south of France), a chilled evening beer or a midnight cocktail, the choice is yours.

TOP CHOICE Les Distilleries Idéales   CAFE
(24 rue de la Préfecture; ⊘9am-12.30am) Whether you're after an espresso on your way to the cours Saleya market or an *apéritif* (complete with cheese and charcuterie platters, €5.20) before trying out one of Nice's fabulous restaurants, Les Distilleries is one of the most atmospheric bars in town. Tables on the small street terrace are ideal for watching the world go by.

Happy hour is from 6pm to 8pm.

Le Smarties   BAR
(http://nicesmarties.free.fr; 10 rue Défly; ⊘6pm-2am Tue-Sat) We love Smarties' sexy '70s swirly orange style, which draws a hot-looking straight and gay crowd. At weekends, the tiny dance floor fills when DJs spin deep house, electro, techno and occasionally dis-

co; weekdays are mellower. Free tapas with happy hour (nightly 6pm to 9pm).

L'Abat-Jour BAR
(25 rue Benoît Bunico) With its vintage furniture, rotating art exhibitions and alternative music, l'Abat-Jour is all the rage with Nice's young and trendy crowd. The basement has live music or DJ sessions as the night darkens.

Snug & Cellar PUB
(cnr rue Droite & rue Rossetti; ☺noon-midnight) The cellar of this new pub hosts live music (Mondays), a quiz (Wednesdays) and giant screens for sports events. And when there is nothing special going on, it's just a great place for a drink! The atmosphere is more sophisticated than in Nice's other English or Irish pubs and the staff are charming.

Le Six GAY BAR
(www.le6.fr; 6 rue Raoul Bosio; ☺10pm-5am) Primped and pretty A-gays crowd shoulder to shoulder at Nice's compact, perennially popular 'mo bar. The thing to do: climb the ladder to the mezzanine (watch your head!).

Ma Nolan's PUB
(www.ma-nolans.com; 2 rue St François de Paule; ☺noon-2am Mon-Fri, 11am-2am Sat & Sun) This Irish pub is big, loud and *the* pub of reference for all foreigners in town. With live music, a pub quiz, big sport events and pub grub, it's a pretty rowdy place. Happy hour is from 6pm to 8pm.

☆ Entertainment

The tourist office has info on Nice's cultural activities listed in its free publications – *Nice Rendez-vous* (monthly) and *Côte d'Azur en Fêtes* (quarterly) – or consult the weekly *Semaine des Spectacles* (€1), available from newsstands on Wednesday. All are in French.

Chez Wayne's LIVE MUSIC
(www.waynes.fr; 15 rue de la Préfecture; ☺2.30pm-12.30am) Raucous watering hole Chez Wayne's is a typical English pub that looks like it's been plucked out of London, Bristol or Leeds. It features excellent live bands every night and has the best atmosphere in town. The pub is also sports-mad and shows every rugby, football, Aussie-rules, tennis and cricket game worth watching.

Shapko LIVE MUSIC
(www.shapko.com; cnr rue Benoît Bunico & rue Rossetti; cover charge €5; ☺7pm-12.30am Wed-Sun; ☎) The brainchild of Russian jazz musician Dimitri Shapko features plenty of fantastic local and international jazz, soul and R&B bands. Happy hour is between 7pm and 9pm and music generally starts around 9pm.

Les Trois Diables NIGHTCLUB
(☎04 93 62 47 00; 2 cours Saleya; ☺5pm-2.15am) The music is a mix of trip-hop, house and electro at this small local club. Thursday is student night (show your ID); Wednesday is karaoke.

Cinéma Rialto CINEMA
(http://lerialto.cine.allocine.fr; 4 rue de Rivoli) Non-dubbed films, with French subtitles.

🛍 Shopping

Nice is a shopper's paradise: as well as the numerous little boutiques in Vieux Nice, you'll find designers around rue de France and the usual franchises at the enormous shopping mall **Nice Étoile** (www.nicetoile.com; av Jean Médecin).

ℹ Information

Hôpital St-Roch (☎04 92 03 33 33; www.chu-nice.fr; 5 rue Pierre Dévoluy) 24-hour emergency service.

Police Station (☎04 92 17 22 22; 1 av Maréchal Foch; ☺24hr) Non-French speakers can call 04 92 17 20 31, where translators are on hand.

Tourist Office (☎08 92 70 74 07; www.nicetourisme.com; 5 promenade des Anglais; ☺9am-6pm Mon-Sat) There's also a branch at the **train station** (av Thiers, Train station; ☺8am-7pm Mon-Sat).

Websites
Head to **Lonely Planet** (http://www.lonelyplanet.com/france/nice) for planning advice, author recommendations, traveller reviews and insider tips.

ℹ Getting There & Away

AIR Nice Côte d'Azur Airport (NCE; ☎08 20 42 33 33; www.nice.aeroport.fr; ☎) is France's second largest airport and has international flights to Europe, North Africa and even the US, with regular as well as low-cost companies. The airport has two terminals, linked by a free shuttle.

BOAT Nice is the main port for ferries to Corsica. **SNCM** (www.sncm.fr; quai du Commerce, ferry terminal) and **Corsica Ferries** (www.corsicaferries.com; quai Lunel) are the two main companies.

BUS There are excellent intercity services around Nice. All journeys cost €1. The bus station was demolished in 2011 so bus stops are now scattered around the **coulée verte**. There are detailed maps all along the park to help you

GOURMET SHOPS IN NICE

Whether you're looking after original souvenirs or just fancy treating yourself during your stay, the following shops are guaranteed to delight foodies:

» Moulin à Huile d'Olive Alziari (www.alziari.com.fr; 14 rue St-François de Paule) has superb olive oil, fresh from the mill on the outskirts of Nice, for €17 per litre; Alziari also produces a dizzying variety of tapenades (olive spread), fresh olives to nibble (plain, stuffed, marinated etc) and various other snacks.

» More great olive oil and a wonderful selection of liqueurs (anything from absinth to *armagnac*, raspberry liqueur and *crème de cassis*) are to be found at Les Trois Étoiles de St-Paul (rue Pairolière); all are sold in beautiful bottles of various shapes and sizes.

» Buy wine from *cavistes* (wine merchants) who know what they're talking about: Cave de la Tour (3 rue de la Tour) has been run by the same family since 1947.

» Plump for divine macaroons and chocolates from chef patissier Pascal Lac at the mouth-watering Pâtisserie LAC (www.patisseries-lac.com; cnr rue de la Préfecture & rue St-Gaétan).

» Sweet teeth will also love the crystallised fruit sold at the traditional sweet shop Henri Auer Confiserie (www.maison-auer.com; 7 rue St-François de Paule); the recipes date back to 1820 and the shop is a sight in its own right.

locate your bus stop. Smartphone users can also download the very useful app Ligne d'Azur (www.lignedazur.com; 3 place Masséna) or visit the company's office.

» Bus 100 goes to Menton (1½ hours) via the Corniche Inférieure and Monaco (40 minutes)

» Bus 200 goes to Cannes (1½ hours)

» Bus 400 goes to Vence (1¼ hours) via St-Paul de Vence (one hour)

» Bus 500 goes to Grasse (1½ hours)

» Eurolines (www.eurolines.com) serves long-haul European destinations.

TRAIN From Nice, there are services to:

» **Monaco** €3.60, 25 minutes, half-hourly

» **Menton** €4.80, 35 minutes, half-hourly

» **Cannes** €6.40, 40 minutes, hourly

» **Grasse** €9.20, 1¼ hours, hourly

» **St-Raphaël** €14, 1¼ hours, hourly

» **Marseille** €35, 2½ hours, hourly

🛈 Getting Around

Nice is relatively spread out but since the weather is often good and the city beautiful and pedestrian-friendly, walking is the best way to get around. For longer journeys, use the Vélo Bleu (p837).

To/From the Airport

Nice-Côte d'Azur airport is 6km west of Nice, by the sea. A taxi to Nice's centre from the rank outside the terminal will cost around €25.

» Buses 98 and 99 link the airport's terminal with Nice Gare Routière and Nice train station respectively (€4, 35 minutes, every 20 minutes).

» Bus 110 (€18, hourly) links the airport with Monaco (40 minutes) and Menton (one hour).

» Bus 210 goes to Cannes (€14.70, 50 minutes, half-hourly); bus 250 to Antibes (€9, 55 minutes, half-hourly).

Bus & Tram

Buses and trams in Nice are run by Ligne d'Azur (p836). Tickets cost just €1 and include one connection, including intercity buses within the Alpes-Maritimes *département*. A new tram line linking place Masséna with the airport along promenade des Anglais is planned for 2016.

Buses are particularly handy to get to Cimiez and the port. Night buses run from around 9pm until 2am.

The tram is great for getting across town, particularly from the train station to Vieux Nice and Place Garibaldi. Trams run from 4.30am to 1.30am.

Car, Motorcycle & Bicycle

Major car rental companies (Avis, Budget, Europcar, Hertz etc) have offices at the train station. The best deals are generally via their websites.

To go native, go for two wheels (and be prepared for hefty safety deposits).

» **Holiday Bikes** (www.holiday-bikes.com; 23 rue de Belgique) Rents out 50cc scooters/125cc motorcycles for €27/55.

» Vélo Bleu (☑04 93 72 06 06; www.velobleu.
org/ A shared-bicycle service with over 100
stations around the city – pick up at one, return
at another. One-day/week subscriptions costs
€1/5, plus usage: free the first 30 minutes, €1 the
next 30, then €2 per hour thereafter. Stations in
the most popular parts of town are equipped with
special terminals where you can register directly
with a credit card; otherwise you'll need a mobile
phone. The handy Velo Bleu app allows you to find
your nearest station, gives real-time information
about the number of bikes available at each and
can also calculate itineraries.

Taxi

Taxis are prohibitively expensive in France and
Nice is no exception. Find taxi stands outside
the Gare Nice Ville and on av Félix Faure close
to place Masséna; otherwise, call **Taxi Riviera**
(☑04 93 13 78 78; www.taxi-nice.fr).

Antibes & Juan-les-Pins

POP 76,580

With its boat-bedecked port, 16th-century
ramparts and narrow cobblestone streets
festooned with flowers, lovely Antibes is the
quintessential Mediterranean town. Picasso,
Max Ernst and Nicolas de Staël were captivated by Antibes, as was a restless Graham
Greene (1904–91), who settled here with his
lover, Yvonne Cloetta, from 1966 until the
year before his death.

Greater Antibes embraces Cap d'Antibes,
an exclusive green cape studded with luxurious mansions, and the modern beach resort
of Juan-les-Pins. The latter is known for its
2km-long sandy beach and its nightlife, a
legacy of the sizzling 1920s when Americans
swung into town with their jazz music and
oh-so-brief swimsuits.

⊙ Sights & Activities

Vieil Antibes　　　　HISTORIC QUARTER
Vieil Antibes is a pleasant mix of food shops,
boutiques and restaurants. Mornings are a
good time to meander along the little alleyways, when the Marché Provençal (cours
Masséna; ⊘7am-1pm Tue-Sun Sep-Jun, daily Jul
& Aug) (market) is in full swing. Check out
the views from the sea walls, from the urban sprawl of Nice to the snowy peaks of the
Alps and nearby Cap d'Antibes.

Musée Picasso　　　　ART MUSEUM
(www.antibes-juanlespins.com; Château Grimaldi,
4 rue des Cordiers; adult/student/child €6/3/free;
⊘10am-noon & 2-6pm Tue-Sun) 'If you want to
see the Picassos from Antibes, you have to
see them in Antibes.'

Pablo Picasso
Spectacularly positioned overlooking the
sea, 14th-century Château Grimaldi served
as Picasso's studio from July to December
1946. The museum now houses an excellent
collection of the master's paintings, lithographs, drawings and ceramics, as well as
a photographic record of the artist at work.

Particularly poignant is Picasso's *La Joie
de Vivre* (The Joy of Life), one in a series
of 25 paintings from the Antipolis Suite.
The young flower girl, surrounded by flute-
playing fauns and mountain goats, symbol-
ises Françoise Gilot, the 23-year-old lover of
Picasso, with whom he lived in neighbouring Golfe-Juan.

Fort Carré　　　　HISTORIC SITE
(rte du Bord de Mer; guided tour only adult/student/
child €3/1.50/free; ⊘10am-6pm Tue-Sun Jul & Aug,
10am-4.30pm Tue-Sun Sep-Jun) The impregnable 16th-century Fort Carré, enlarged by
Vauban in the 17th century, dominates the
approach to Antibes from Nice. It served as
a border defence post until 1860 when Nice,
until then in Italian hands, became French.
Regrettably, the tours are rather rushed and
the explanations superficial; tours depart
half-hourly, some guides speak English.

Cap d'Antibes　　　　WALKING
Cap d'Antibes' 4.8km of wooded shores are
the perfect setting for a walk-swim-walk-
swim afternoon. Paths are well marked. The
tourist office maps show itineraries.

THE FRENCH RIVIERA & MONACO ANTIBES & JUAN-LES-PINS

PINE CONE TRAIN

Chugging between the mountains and the sea, the narrow-gauge railway Train des
Pignes (Pine Cone Train; www.trainprovence.com) is one of Provence's most picturesque
rides. Rising to 1000m, with breathtaking views, the 151km track between Nice and
Digne-les-Bains passes through Haute Provence's scarcely populated back country.

The service runs five times a day and is ideal for a day trip inland. The beautiful medieval village of Entrevaux is just 1½ hours from Nice (return €20.60), perfect for a picnic
and a wander through its historic centre and citadel.

MUSÉE RENOIR

The city of Cagnes-sur-Mer is nothing to write home about. What is, however, is the exquisite Musée Renoir (04 93 20 61 07; Chemin des Colettes, Cagnes-sur-Mer). Le Domaine des Collettes (as the property was known) was home and studio to an arthritis-crippled Renoir (1841–1919) from 1907 until his death. He lived there with his wife and three children, and the house is wonderfully evocative.

Works on display include *Les Grandes Baigneuses* (The Women Bathers; 1892), a reworking of the 1887 original, and rooms are dotted with photographs and personal possessions. The beautiful olive and citrus groves are as much an attraction as the museum itself. Many visitors set up their own easel to paint.

The museum was closed at the time of research for a major refurbishment and planned to reopen in summer 2013.

★ Festivals & Events

Jazz à Juan   MUSIC FESTIVAL
(www.jazzajuan.fr; ☉Jul) This major festival in mid-July celebrated its 50th edition in 2010. Every jazz great has performed here, and Jazz à Juan, in Juan-les-Pins, continues to attract big music names. The Off fringe festival is the perfect backup option if you haven't managed to get tickets for the main event.

⌂ Sleeping

Hôtel La Jabotte   B&B €€
(04 93 61 45 89; www.jabotte.com; 13 av Max Maurey; s/d €124/142; ❋☎) A hotel with *chambre d'hôte* (B&B) feel, La Jabotte is Antibes' hidden gem. Just 50m from the sea (and 20 minutes' walk from Vieil Antibes), its 10 Provençal rooms all look out onto an exquisite patio where breakfast is served from spring to autumn. Much of the decor is the work of Yves, who runs La Jabotte with Claude.

Le Relais du Postillon   HOTEL €€
(04 93 34 20 77; www.relaisdupostillon.com; 8 rue Championnet; d €73-134; ❋☎) Housed in a 17th-century coach house, the great-value Postillon is in the heart of the old town. The owners did a huge amount of work in 2012: out went the outdated carpet and bathrooms, in came laminate floors and fresh new bathrooms. The decor has thankfully retained its Provençal charm and the welcome is as warm as ever.

Relais International de la Jeunesse   HOSTEL €
(04 93 81 27 63; www.clajsud.fr; 272 bd de la Garoupe; dm €20; ☉Apr-Oct; ☎) In the most perfect of Mediterranean locations, with sea views the envy of neighbouring millionaires, this basic but friendly hostel is particularly popular with 'yachties' looking for their next job in Antibes' port. Rates include sheets and breakfast. There is a daily lock-out between 11am and 5pm.

✖ Eating

TOP CHOICE Le Broc en Bouche   MODERN FRENCH €€
(04 93 34 75 60; 8 rue des Palmiers; mains €15-30; ☉lunch Thu-Tue, dinner Thu-Mon) No two chairs, tables or lights are the same at this lovely bistro: instead, every item has been lovingly sourced from antique shops and car boot sales, giving the place a sophisticated but cosy vintage feel. The charming Flo and Fred have put the same level of care and imagination into their cuisine, artfully combining Provençal and oriental flavours.

La Ferme au Foie Gras   DELICATESSEN €
(www.vente-foie-gras.net; 35 rue Aubernon; sandwiches €3.50-7; ☉8am-6pm Tue-Sun) Now, this is our idea of what a good sandwich should be like: filled with foie gras or smoked duck breast, onion chutney or fig jam, truffle cheese and fresh salad. And many people seem to think the same: a queue snakes down from the tiny counter of La Ferme every lunchtime.

☕ Drinking & Entertainment

TOP CHOICE Balade en Provence   ABSINTHE BAR
(25 cours Masséna; ☉6pm-2am) Flirt with the green fairy at this dedicated absinthe bar in the vaulted basement of an olive oil shop. There is an original 1860 zinc bar, five round tables and all the accessories (four-tapped water fountain, sugar cubes etc).

Pick from 25 absinthe varieties (€4 per glass) and let the knowledgeable staff debunk some of the myths shrouding this much-reviled spirit. And don't worry – if you're really not keen, there are plenty of other beverages on offer.

Pearl La Siesta   NIGHTCLUB
(rte du Bord de Mer; cover €15-20; ☺7pm-5am Thu-Sat) This legendary establishment is famous up and down the coast for its beachside nightclub (Le Pearl) and all-night dancing under the stars. Open from early June to mid-September only, you can still party at the indoor bar–lounge (Le Flamingo) during the rest of the year.

❶ Information

Tourist office (☎04 97 23 11 11; www.antibes juanlespins.com; 55 bd Charles Guillaumont; ☺9am-noon & 2-6pm Mon-Sat, 10am-12.30pm & 2.30-5pm Sun)

❶ Getting There & Away

BUS The Nice–Cannes service (bus 200, €1) stops by the tourist office. Local bus services (€1) for Vence and St-Paul de Vence leave from the bus station.

TRAIN Antibes' train station is on the main line between Nice (€4.20, 30 minutes, five per hour) and Cannes (€2.70, 10 minutes, five per hour).

Biot

POP 9353

From the 16th to 18th centuries, the little hillside village of Biot was famous around the Med for the exceptional quality of its olive-oil jars. Very little remains of that pottery hegemony, but Biot is now famous for another much prettier, but far less pragmatic, art form: bubbled glass.

The famous bubbles are produced by rolling molten glass in baking soda to create a chemical reaction, then trapping the bubbles with a second layer of glass; the latest frosted look uses acid dips. You can watch work under way at the factory Verrerie de Biot (☎04 93 65 03 00; www.verreriebiot.com; chemin des Combes; admission free, 45-min guided tour €6; ☺9.30am-6pm Mon-Sat, 10.30am-1.30pm & 2.30-6.30pm Sun), at the foot of the village.

Biot's tourist office (☎04 93 65 78 00; www.biot.fr; 46 rue St-Sébastien; ☺9am-noon & 2-6pm Mon-Fri, 2-6pm Sat & Sun) is located in the **village** itself, another hilltop warren full of century-old buildings.

Bus 10 (€1, 10 minutes) links the village and the Biot train station half-hourly. In summer, a free shuttle takes in the train station, the glassmakers and the village.

St-Paul de Vence

POP 3540

Once upon a time, St-Paul de Vence was a small medieval village atop a hill looking out to sea. Then came the likes of Chagall and Picasso in postwar years, followed by showbiz stars such as Yves Montand and Roger Moore, and St-Paul shot to fame. The village is now home to dozens of art galleries as well as the exceptional Fondation Maeght.

The village's tiny cobbled lanes get overwhelmingly crowded in high season – come early or late to beat the rush.

◎ Sights

The Village   HISTORIC QUARTER
Strolling the narrow streets is how most visitors pass time in St-Paul. The village has been beautifully preserved and the panoramas from the ramparts are stunning. The main artery, rue Grande, is lined with art galleries. The highest point in the village is occupied by the Église Collégiale; the adjoining Chapelle des Pénitents Blancs was redecorated by Belgian artist Folon.

Many more artists lived or passed through St-Paul de Vence, among them Soutine, Léger, Cocteau, Matisse and Chagall. The latter is buried with his wife Vava in the cemetery at the village's southern end (immediately to the right as you enter). The dynamic tourist office (☎04 93 32 86 95; www .saint-pauldevence.com; 2 rue Grande; ☺10am-7pm) runs a series of informative, themed guided tours (1½ hours, adult/child €5/free) that delve into this illustrious past. Book ahead; tours are also available in English.

Across from the entrance to the fortified village, the pétanque pitch, where many a star has had a spin, is the hub of village life. The tourist office rents out balls (€2) and can organise pétanque lessons (€5 per person).

Fondation Maeght   ART MUSEUM
(www.fondation-maeght.com; 623 chemin des Gardettes; adult/student/child €14/9/free; ☺10am-6pm) The region's finest art museum, Fondation Maeght was created in 1964 by art collectors Aimé and Marguerite Maeght. Its collection of 20th-century works is one of the largest in Europe. It is exhibited on a rotating basis, which, along with the excellent temporary exhibitions, guarantees you'll rarely see the same thing twice. Find the *fondation* 500m downhill from the village.

The building was designed by Josep Lluís Sert and is a masterpiece in itself,

DON'T MISS

MATISSE'S CHAPELLE DU ROSAIRE

'This work required four years of exclusive and relentless attention, and it is the fruit of my whole working life. Despite all its imperfections, I consider it my masterpiece.'

Henri Matisse

An ailing Matisse moved to **Vence** in 1943 where he fell under the care of his former nurse and model Monique Bourgeois, who had since become a Dominican nun. She persuaded him to design this extraordinary chapel (Rosary Chapel; www.vence.fr/the-rosaire -chapel.html; 466 av Henri Matisse; adult/child €4/2; ⊙2-5.30pm Mon, Wed & Sat, 10-11.30am & 2-5.30pm Tue & Thu) for her community.

From the road, all that you can see are the blue-and-white ceramic roof tiles and a wrought-iron cross and bell tower. Inside, light floods through the glorious stained-glass windows, painting stark white walls with glowing blues, greens and yellows (symbolising respectively water/the sky, plants/life, the sun/God's presence).

A line drawing of the Virgin Mary and Child is painted on white ceramic tiles on the northern interior wall. The western wall is dominated by the bolder Chemin de Croix (Stations of the Cross). St Dominic overlooks the altar. Matisse also designed the chapel's stone altar, candlesticks, cross and the way-out priests' vestments (displayed in an adjoining hall).

integrating the works of the very best: a Giacometti courtyard, Miró sculptures dotted across the terraced gardens, coloured-glass windows by Braque and mosaics by Chagall and Tal-Coat.

St Paul's tourist office (p839) runs guided tours (adult/child €5/free); you'll need to book ahead.

🛏 Sleeping & Eating

TOP CHOICE La Colombe d'Or   TRADITIONAL FRENCH €€€
(☎04 93 32 80 02; www.la-colombe-dor.com; place de Gaulle; mains €30-55; ⊙lunch & dinner mid-Dec–Oct; ⚡◍) A Léger mosaic here, a Picasso painting there: these are just some of the original modern artworks at the Golden Dove, the legendary restaurant where impoverished artists paid for meals with their creations. Dining is beneath fig trees in summer or in the art-filled dining room in winter, and the cuisine is surprisingly uncomplicated (terrines, rabbit stew, beef carpaccio). Book well ahead.

The restaurant is also a hotel (d €310) that blends rustic charm and modern artworks in every room. Hotel guests get access to the lovely pool, which is heated year-round and crowned by a Calder mobile.

❶ Getting There & Away

St-Paul is served by bus 400 running between Nice (€1, one hour, at least hourly) and Vence (€1, 15 minutes).

Cannes

POP 74,445

Most people have heard of Cannes and its eponymous film festival. The latter lasts for only two weeks in May, but the buzz and glitz are there year-round – unlike neighbouring St-Tropez, which shuts down in winter – mostly thanks to regular visits from celebrities enjoying the creature comforts of bd de la Croisette's palaces.

However, what people may not know is that, for all its glamour, Cannes retains a genuine small-town feel: just like anywhere in the south, you'll witness pensioners hotly debating who won the last round of *pétanque* (a game not unlike lawn bowls) under the main square's plane trees (in this case, at Sq Lord Brougham). You'll also get a chance to escape to the unspoilt Îles de Lérins, and to become familiar with more than 2000 years of history – from Ligurian fishing communities (200 BC) to one of Europe's oldest religious communities (5th century AD), to the enigmatic Man in the Iron Mask and a stardom born out of anti-fascist efforts.

◉ Sights & Activities

CANNES
La Croisette   ARCHITECTURE
The multi-starred hotels and couture shops that line the famous bd de la Croisette (aka La Croisette) may be the preserve of the rich

and famous, but anyone can enjoy the palm-shaded promenade and take in the atmosphere. In fact, it's a favourite among Cannois (natives of Cannes), particularly at night when it is lit with bright colours.

There are great views of the bay and nearby Estérel mountains, and stunning art deco architecture from the seafront palaces, such as the Martinez or the legendary Carlton InterContinental; its twin cupolas were modelled on the breasts of the courtesan La Belle Otéro, infamous for her string of lovers – Tsar Nicholas II and Britain's King Edward VII among them.

Not so elegant but imposing nonetheless is the Palais des Festivals et des Congrès (Festival Palace; blvd de la Croisette; guided tours adult/child €3/free; 1½ hrs; ⊙guided tours 2.30pm Jun-Apr) at the western end of the prom, host of the world's most glamorous film festival. Climb the red carpet, walk down the auditorium, tread the stage and learn about cinema's most glamorous event and its numerous anecdotes on a Palais des Festivals guided tour (adult/child €3/free; ⊙1½ hr). The tourist-office-run tours take place several times a month, except in May. Check dates on the office's website (visits in English are sometimes available). Tickets can be booked only in person at the tourist office.

After posing for a photograph on the 22 steps leading up to the cinema entrance, wander along allée des Étoiles du Cinéma, a path of celebrity hand imprints in the pavement.

Le Vieux Port & Le Suquet   HISTORIC QUARTER

On the western side of the Palais des Festivals lies the real Cannes. The yachts that frame the Vieux Port (Old Port) are the only reminder that this is where celebrities holiday, but they don't seem to impress the pensioners playing *pétanque* on sq Lord Brougham. Follow rue St-Antoine and snake your way up Le Suquet, Cannes's oldest district, for great views of the bay.

For local folklore, head to Marché Forville (⊙7am-1pm Tue-Sun), a couple of blocks back from port. It is one of the most important markets in the region and the supplier of choice for restaurants (and for your picnic!).

Trans Côte d'Azur   BOAT TOUR

(☎04 92 98 71 30; www.trans-cote-azur.com; quai Max Laubeuf) From June to September, Trans Côte d'Azur runs day trips to St-Tropez (adult/child €44/32 return) and Monaco (€48.50/32), an ideal way to avoid congested roads to these popular spots and relax among scenic landscapes instead. Panoramic cruises (€26.50/16.50) taking in the dramatic contrasts of the Estérel's red cliffs, green forests and intense azure waters are another must.

Beaches   BEACHES

Cannes is blessed with sandy beaches, although much of the stretch along bd de la Croisette is taken up by private beaches (open to all). This arrangement leaves only a small strip of free sand near the Palais des Festivals for the bathing hoi polloi; the much bigger Plage du Midi (blvd Jean Hibert) and Plage de la Bocca, west from Vieux Port, are also free.

Rates for private beaches range from €15-25 at the relaxed and family-friendly Plage Vegaluna (☎04 93 43 67 05; www.vegaluna.com; La Croisette; ⊙9.30am-7pm) (watersports available) to €34/30/38 for the blue loungers on the front row/other rows/pier of the superstylish Z Plage (⊙9.30am-6pm May-Sep), the beach of Hôtel Martinez. Booking ahead is advised.

ÎLES DE LÉRINS

Although just 20 minutes away by boat, the tranquil Îles de Lérins feel far from the madding crowd.

The closest of these two tiny islands is the 3.25km by 1km Île Ste-Marguerite, where the mysterious Man in the Iron Mask was incarcerated during the late 17th century. Its shores are an endless succession of perfect castaway beaches and fishing spots, and its eucalyptus and pine forest makes for a heavenly refuge from the Riviera heat.

As you get off the boat, a map indicates a handful of rustic restaurants as well as trails and paths across the island. It also directs you to Fort Royal (Île Ste-Marguerite; adult/child €6/3; ⊙10.30am-1.15pm & 2.15-5.45pm Tue-Sun), built in the 17th century, and now harbouring the Musée de la Mer. The door

THE FRENCH RIVIERA & MONACO CANNES

ⓘ GOING TO FONDATION MAEGHT

Most tourists take the main road to go to the Fondation, but Chemin Ste-Claire is much more inspirational. It was Chagall's route to the village, and along the way you'll pass three chapels, a convent and two Chagall reproductions, placed roughly on the spot where he created the originals.

THE FRENCH RIVIERA & MONACO CANNES

Cannes

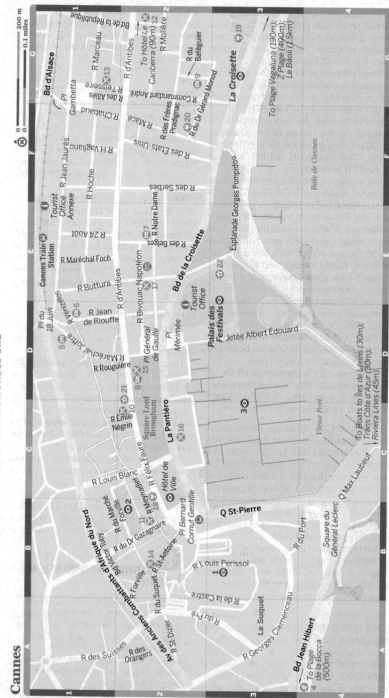

200 m
0.1 miles

Bd d'Alsace

Bd de la République

To Hôtel Le
Canberra (90m)

R Molière

R du
Bateguier

☒12

R Marceau

☒13

Pl
Gambetta

R des Allies

R Teisseire

R d'Antibes

R Chabaud

R Jean Jaurès

R H Vagliano

R des Etats-Unis

R Mace

R des Frères
Pradignac

R du Dr Gérard Monod

R Commandant André

☸19

La Croisette

☒9

To Plage Vegaluna (190m);
Z Plage (490m);
Le Bâoli (1.5km)

Baie de Cannes

Tourist
Office
Annexe

R Hoche

R des Serbes

R Notre Dame

R 24 Août

R des Belges

☒7

☒20

Cannes Train
Station

R Maréchal Foch

R Buttura

R d'Antibes

R Bivouac Napoléon

Bd de la Croisette

Esplanade Georges Pompidou

Pl du
18 Juin

R Venizelos

☒16

R Jean
de Riouffe

Pl Général
de Gaulle

Pl
Mérimée

☸22

Tourist
Office

R Maréchal Joffre

☒5

R Rouguière

☒15

☒8

Palais des
Festivals

Jetée Albert Édouard

R Emile
Négrin

☒10

☒21

Square Lord
Brougham

La Pantiéro

☒16

To Boats to Îles de Lérins (30m);
Trans Côte d'Azur (30m);
Riviera Lines (45m)

☸3

Vieux Port

R Louis Blanc

R du Marché
Forville

R Meynadier

☒18

R F Félix Faure

Hôtel de
Ville

Pl Bernard
Cornut Gentille

Q St-Pierre

Q Max Laubeuf

Q du Port

Bd Victor Tuby

☒2

R du Dr Gazagnaire

R St-Antoine

Square du
Général Leclerc

R des Suisses

R des
Orangers

Av des Anciens Combattants d'Afrique du Nord

R du Suquet

☒14

R Louis Perissol

☸1

Le Suquet

R de la Castre

R du Pré

R St-Dizier

R Forville

Bd Jean Hibert

To Plage
de la Bocca
(500m)

☸4

R Georges Clemenceau

Cannes

to the left as you enter leads to the old state prisons, built under Louis XIV. Exhibits interpret the fort's history, with displays on shipwrecks found off the island's coast.

Smaller still, at just 1.5km long by 400m wide, Île St-Honorat has been a monastery since the 5th century. Its Cistercian monks welcome visitors year-round: you can visit the church and small chapels scattered around the island and stroll among the vineyards and forests. Camping and cycling are forbidden.

Boats for the islands leave Cannes from quai des Îles (along from quai Max Laubeuf) on the western side of the harbour. Riviera Lines (www.riviera-lines.com; adult/child €11.50/6 return) runs ferries to Île Ste-Marguerite (return adult/child €12/7.50), while Compagnie Planaria (www.cannes-ilesdelerins.com; adult/child €12/6) operates boats to Île St-Honorat (return adult/child €13/6).

🎎 Festivals & Events

Festival de Cannes   FILM FESTIVAL
(www.festival-cannes.com; ⊙May) You won't get in, but it's fun because you see all the celebs walking around. And unlike the Oscars, you can get close to the red carpet without tickets. Held in May.

Les Plages Électroniques   MUSIC FESTIVAL
(www.plages-electroniques.com; €8; ⊙Jul & Aug) DJs spin on the sand at the Plage du Palais des Festivals during this relaxed festival. Held July to August, once a week for five or six weeks.

Festival Pantiero   MUSIC FESTIVAL
(www.festivalpantiero.com; 4-night pass €55; ⊙early Aug) Electronic music and indie-rock festival on the terrace of the Palais des Festivals; very cool.

FREE **Festival d'Art Pyrotechnique**   FIREWORKS
(www.festival-pyrotechnique-cannes.com; ⊙Jul & Aug) Around 200,000 people cram onto the Croisette every summer to admire the outstanding fireworks display over the Bay of Cannes. Magical. Held on six nights from July to August.

🛏 Sleeping

Cannes is an important conference centre and hotels fill up with every event (including the Film Festival, when you won't be able to stay in town) so try to plan ahead. There is no hostel in Cannes.

TOP
CHOICE **Hôtel Le Canberra**   BOUTIQUE HOTEL €€€
(☑04 97 06 95 00; www.hotel-cannes-canberra. com; 120 rue d'Antibes; d from €255; ❄@🛜🏊) This boutique stunner, just a couple of blocks back from La Croisette, is the epitome of Cannes glamour: designer grey rooms with splashes of candy pink, sexy black marble bathrooms with coloured lighting, heated pool (Apr–Oct) in a bamboo-filled garden, intimate atmosphere (there are just 35 rooms) and impeccable service. Rooms overlooking rue d'Antibes are cheaper.

Le Romanesque
BOUTIQUE HOTEL €€

(☑04 93 68 04 20; 10 rue du Batéguier; s/d/tr €89/109/149; ❋🛜). Every room is individually decorated at this eight-room boutique charmer in the heart of the Carré d'Or nightlife district (book a back room if you're a light sleeper). Favourite rooms include Charlotte, with its sun-drenched bath; and Elizabeth, the former maids' quarters, with low, sloping beamed ceilings. Gay-friendly. Great service.

Hôtel 7e Art
BOUTIQUE HOTEL €

(☑04 93 68 66 66; www.7arthotel.com; 23 rue Maréchal Joffre; s €68, d €60-98; ❋🛜) Hôtel 7e Art has put boutique style within reach of budgeters. The owners schooled in Switzerland and got the basics right, with great beds, sparkling-clean baths and excellent soundproofing. The snappy design of putty-coloured walls, padded headboards and pop art, and perks like iPod docks in every room, far exceed what you'd expect at this price.

Hôtel Le Mistral
BOUTIQUE HOTEL €€

(☑04 93 39 91 46; www.mistral-hotel.com; 13 rue des Belges; d from €89; ❋🛜) This small boutique hotel wins the *palme d'or* for best value in town: rooms are decked out in flattering red and plum tones, bathrooms feature lovely designer fittings, there are sea views from the top floor and the hotel is a mere 50m from La Croisette.

Hôtel Alnéa
HOTEL €€

(☑04 93 68 77 77; www.hotel-alnea.com; 20 rue Jean de Riouffe; s/d €70/90; ❋🛜) A breath of fresh air in a town of stars, Noémi and Cédric have put their heart and soul into their hotel, with bright, colourful rooms, original paintings and numerous little details such as the afternoon coffee break, the self-service minibar and the bike or *boules* (to play *pétanque*) loans. No lift (elevator).

Hôtel Splendid
BOUTIQUE HOTEL €€€

(☑04 97 06 22 22; www.splendid-hotel-cannes. com; 4-6 rue Félix Faure; s/d from €160/190; ❋) This elaborate 1871 building has everything it takes to rival the nearby palaces: beautifully decorated rooms, vintage furniture, old-world feel with creature comforts, fabulous location, stunning views. A handful of rooms equipped with kitchenettes are ideal for longer stays and families.

✕ Eating

TOP CHOICE Sea Sens
FUSION €€€

(☑04 63 36 05 06; www.five-hotel-cannes.com; Five Hotel & Spa, 1 rue Notre Dame; 2-/3-course lunch menu €29/39, mains €26-55; 🛜🅿🈂) Perched on the 5th floor of the Five Hotel, the Sea Sens is Cannes' latest food sensation. Run by the brilliant Pourcel brothers, with pastry chef Jérôme de Oliveira in charge of desserts, it serves divine food blending French gastronomy and Asian elegance with panoramic views of Le Suquet and Cannes' rooftops on the side.

De Oliveira's signature dessert 'Onde de Choc', a pear-shaped chocolate tower filled with chocolate and praliné, is simply out of this world. Come here for lunch to make the best of the great-value *menus*.

L'Affable
MODERN FRENCH €€€

(☑04 93 68 02 09; www.restaurant-laffable.fr; 5 rue Lafontaine; lunch/dinner menu €26/40, mains €34-38; 🈂) Modern French cuisine has never tasted so good as it does at L'Affable. Everything from the ingredients, the cooking and the presentation is done to perfection, whether it be the roasted veal with its vegetable medley, the seared seabream with white butter and asparagus or the house speciality, the Grand Marnier soufflé, which arrives practically ballooning at your table. Booking essential.

Mantel
MODERN EUROPEAN €€

(☑04 93 39 13 10; www.restaurantmantel.com; 22 rue St-Antoine; menus €25-38; ⊙Fri-Mon, dinner Tue & Thu) Discover why Noël Mantel is the hotshot of the Cannois gastronomic scene at his

---

EXPRESS COOKING LESSONS

Part-restaurant, part-cooking school is probably the best way to describe this boutique kitchen in the heart of Cannes. Cooking classes tend to be short (one to two hours, €32-69) and focus on themes or *menus* (take-away at the end of the class), but the flagship product of Les Apprentis Gourmets (☑04 93 38 78 76; www.lesapprentisgourmets.fr; 6 rue Teisseire) is their express-lunch formula: a €15, 30-minute lesson to cook one main, which you then eat with your fellow cooks on the mezzanine above the kitchen (and they throw in the dessert for free). Great fun, cheap and accessible, even if cooking is your domestic nemesis!

STARRING AT CANNES

For 12 days in May, all eyes turn to Cannes, centre of the cinematic universe where more than 33,000 producers, distributors, directors, publicists, stars and hangers-on descend to buy, sell or promote more than 2000 films. As the premier film event of the year, the festival (p843) attracts some 4000 journalists from around the world.

At the centre of the whirlwind is the colossal, 60,000-sq-metre Palais des Festivals, where the official selections are screened. The palace opened in 1982, replacing the original Palais des Festival – since demolished. The inaugural festival was scheduled for 1 September 1939, as a response to Mussolini's Fascist propaganda film festival in Venice, but Hitler's invasion of Poland brought the festival to an abrupt end. It restarted in 1946 – and the rest is history.

Over the years the festival split into 'in competition' and 'out of competition' sections. The goal of 'in competition' films is the prestigious Palme d'Or, awarded by the jury and its president to the film that best 'serves the evolution of cinematic art'. Notable winners include Francis Ford Coppola's *Apocalypse Now* (1979), Quentin Tarantino's cult film *Pulp Fiction* (1994) and American activist Michael Moore's anti-Bush administration polemic *Fahrenheit 9/11* (2004). More recent winners include *La Classe* (2008), a film by Laurent Cantet about teaching in tough Parisian suburbs, Michael Haneke's *White Ribbon* (2009) about life in pre-WWI Germany, and *Amour* (2012), also by Haneke, about an elderly man caring for his dying wife.

The vast majority of films are 'out of competition'. Behind the scenes the Marché du Film (www.marchedufilm.com) sees nearly $1 billion worth of business negotiated in distribution deals. And it's this hard-core commerce combined with all the televised Tinseltown glitz that gives the film festival its special magic.

Tickets to the Cannes film festival are off-limits to ordinary people. What you can get are free tickets to selected individual films, usually after their first screening. Invitations must be picked up on the day at Espace Cannes Cinéphiles (La Pantiéro; ☺9am-5.30pm) and are limited.

refined old-town restaurant. Service is stellar and the seasonal cuisine divine: try the wonderfully tender glazed veal shank in balsamic vinegar or the original poached octopus *bourride*-style. Best of all, though, you get not one but two desserts from pastry-chef wonder Christian Gonthier, who bakes the bread, and prepares the sweets served with coffee.

Aux Bons Enfants   TRADITIONAL FRENCH €€
(80 rue Meynadier; menus €23; ☺Tue-Sat) A people's-choice place since 1935, this informal restaurant cooks up wonderful regional dishes such as aïoli *garni* (aïoli with vegetables), *daube* (a Provençal beef stew) and *rascasse meunière* (pan-fried rockfish), all in a convivial atmosphere. Make no plans for the afternoon after lunching here. No credit cards and no booking.

PhilCat   DELICATESSEN €
(La Pantiéro; sandwiches & salads €4-6.50; ☺8.30am-5pm) Don't be put off by Phillipe and Catherine's unassuming prefab cabin on the Pantiéro: this is Cannes' best lunch house. Huge salads, made to order, are piled high with delicious fresh ingredients.

Or if you're *really* hungry, try one of their phenomenal *pan bagna* (a moist sandwich bursting with Provençal flavours).

Au Martin Pêcheur   PROVENÇAL €€
(4 rue Émile Négrin; 2-course lunch menu €14, mains €17-25; ☺lunch Tue-Sat, dinner Thu-Sat) This unassuming family-run restaurant is the place to come for great fish. Mother and son duo Christel and Maxime prepare traditional and Provençal recipes with whatever the sea has given them that day, from poached sea bass to grilled sea bream. There are always a couple of meat options, too.

New York New York   BRASSERIE €€
(1 allée Liberté; mains €10-36; ☺8am-2am; ☎⚟📶) The latest venture of the Bâoli nightclub, this new grill house has become a hit with Cannes' young crowd, who love the huge burgers, tender steaks, wood-fired pizzas, budget-friendly prices and the industrial-chic decor.

🍷 Drinking & Entertainment

Bars around the 'magic square' (the area bordered by rue Commandant André, rue des Frères Pradignac, rue du Batéguier and rue du Dr Gérard Monod) tend to be young, trendy and pretty rowdy. For a more sophisticated atmosphere, try the beach or top-hotel bars. Pick up the free monthly *Le Mois à Cannes* for full event listings at the tourist office.

It's worth knowing that going out in Cannes is taken very seriously so dress to impress if you'd like to get into the most sought-after clubs and events.

Le Sun 7
COCKTAIL BAR

(5 rue du Dr Gérard Monod; ◷9pm-2.30am; 🛜) An unpretentious, happening place, Le Sun 7 attracts a pretty young crowd keen to knock back a few drinks and shake their stuff at the weekend. It's more laid-back on week nights.

Le Cercle
BAR

(Le Grand Hôtel, 45 bd de la Croisette; ☏) The bar of Le Grand Hôtel is a great place for a couple of quiet drinks. The lounge is a cosy space (there is a pianist most nights) but it's the garden that really does it: with its giant fairy lights, views of La Croisette and the sea, it is divine on summer evenings.

Byron
PUB

(www.byroncannes.com; 49 rue Félix Faure) There is something of the old traditional pub at the Byron, but the fancy chandeliers, DJ booths and wide screens are definitely more Cannes than the Costwolds. It serves decent food, too.

Le Palais
NIGHTCLUB

(www.palais-club.com; Palais des Festivals, bd de la Croisette; cover charge €25-60; ◷midnight-dawn Jul & Aug) This ephemeral nightclub (it's open for only 50 nights each year) has become the hottest ticket in DJ land, a combination of the most happening names in music and its spectacular setting at the heart of the Palais des Festivals. It's the VIPs' favourite spot so door policy is pretty tight: no guys without girls, and only fabulous-looking people.

Le Bâoli
NIGHTCLUB

(☏04 93 43 03 43; www.lebaoli.com; Port Pierre Canto, bd de la Croisette; ◷8pm-6am Thu-Sat) This is Cannes' coolest, trendiest and most selective night spot. So selective in fact that your entire posse might not get in unless you're dressed to the nines. The Bâoli is part-club, part-restaurant so the only way to ensure you'll get in is to book a table and make a night of it.

Cinéma Les Arcades
CINEMA

(77 rue Félix Faure) Catch a movie in English at Cinéma Les Arcades.

🛈 Information

There is a free wi-fi hotspot at the Hôtel de Ville (town hall).

Tourist Office (☏04 92 99 84 22; www.cannes.travel; Palais des Festivals, bd de la Croisette; ◷9am-7pm) Has a **branch** (☏04 93 99 19 77; Av Jean Jaurès; ◷9am-1pm & 2-6pm Mon-Sat) on Av Jean Jaurès.

🛈 Getting There & Around

BUS **TAM** (http://www.cg06.fr/fr/servir-les-habitants/deplacements/transport-collectifs/lignes-et-horaires/lignes-et-horaires/) runs express services to Nice (bus 200, €1, 1½ hours, every 15 minutes), Nice airport (bus 210, €16.50, 50 minutes, half hourly), Mougins (bus 600, €1, 20 minutes, every 20 minutes) and Grasse (bus 600, €1, 45 minutes). The electric **Elo Bus** (€1) follows a loop that takes in the **bus station** (Place Cornut-Gentille), the Croisette, rue d'Antibes and the train station. It has no set stops; just flag it down as it passes.

CYCLING & DRIVING **Mistral Location** (☏04 93 39 33 60; www.mistral-location.com; 4 rue Georges Clemenceau) rents out bicycles/scooters/cars for €16/35/52 per day. You'll find the usual car-hire companies at the train station, too.

PARKING Street parking is limited to two hours in the centre. Car parks such as **Parking Palais des Festivals** (Palais des Festivals), **Parking Forville** (Rue Forville) or **Parking Gare SNCF** (train station; Rue Jean Jaurès) have no time restrictions but are expensive (€2.70 per hour).

TRAIN Cannes is well connected to Nice (€6.40, 40 minutes), Antibes (€2.70, 12 minutes), Monaco (€8.70, one hour) and St-Raphaël (€6.70, 30 minutes), with services every 20 minutes or so. There are trains to Marseille (€28.40, two hours) half-hourly.

Mougins

POP 19.929

Pinprick Vieux Mougins (old Mougins) looks almost too perfect to be real. Picasso discovered the medieval village in 1935 with lover Dora Marr, and lived here with his final love, Jacqueline Roque, from 1961 until his death.

⊙ Sights & Activities

Mougins' tourist office (☏04 93 75 87 67; www.mougins.fr; 18 bd Courteline; ◷9.30am-5pm Mon-Sat Oct-Jun, to 6pm daily Jul-Sep), located at the entrance of the old village, can give you a map of the historic centre so that you can wander around. Alternatively, smartphone users can download the excellent Mougins Tourisme app (in French only) complete with audioguide, maps and special offers.

Musée d'Art Classique de Mougins
ART MUSEUM

(www.mouginsmusee.com; 32 rue Commandeur, Mougins; adult/student/child €15/8/5; ⊙9.30am-8.30pm daily Apr-Oct, to 7pm Tue-Sun Nov-Mar) The brainchild of compulsive art collector and British entrepreneur Christian Levett, this outstanding museum contains 600 works spanning 5000 years of history. The collection aims to show how ancient civilisations inspired neoclassical, modern and contemporary art; therefore you'll find antiquities juxtaposed with seminal modern works. Not only is it a brilliant idea, it has also been brilliantly executed.

The collection is organised by civilisations – Rome, Greece and Egypt each get a floor – and the top floor is dedicated to armoury. There are fantastic explanatory panels in French and English throughout and excellent interactive displays bringing to life the helmets, spears and shields of the armoury collection.

Les Jardins du MIP
GARDEN

(www.museesdegrasse.com; 979 chemin des Gourettes, Mouans-Sartoux; adult/child €3/free; ⊙10am-6pm Apr-Oct) Opened in 2012 by the Musée International de la Parfumerie (p847) in Grasse, these gardens beautifully complement the museum's collection by offering an insight into the plants used in perfumery. Visitors are actively encouraged to pick, rub and smell their way around. The gardens are organised by olfactive families (woody, floral, ambered, fougère etc); informative leaflets are available and gardeners will happily answer questions.

The gardens are accessible by public transport (stop Les Jardins du MIP): take bus 20 or 21 from Grasse bus station.

🛏 Sleeping & Eating

Les Rosées
B&B €€€

(☑04 92 92 29 64; www.lesrosees.com; 238 chemin de Font Neuve, Mougins; d €220-320; ☎▣) Chic and authentic is its tagline, and it couldn't be more accurate. This stunning, 400-year-old stone manor house with five romantic suites, pool, jacuzzi and century-old olive trees is a gem. The decor is stunning (so much so that the owners now have their own interior-design venture) – a mix of modern and vintage – and breakfast is a copious organic affair.

Le Rendez-Vous de Mougins
MODERN FRENCH €€

(☑04 93 75 87 47; www.au-rendez-vous-mougins.fr; place du Commandant Lamy, Mougins; lunch/ dinner menu €15.80/23.50, mains €16-28; ⊙lunch Mon-Sat, dinner Tue-Sat; ▣) At the heart of the old village, guarded by a mighty plane tree, Le Rendez-Vous is one of the best-value restaurants you'll find in this neck of the woods. The sun-kissed cuisine is fresh, generous and mostly sourced at the Marché Forville in Cannes: think marinated sardines with sundried tomatoes or glacé nougat with lavender honey and citrus coulis. Booking essential.

❶ Getting There & Away

Bus 600 (€1, every 20 minutes) between Cannes and Grasse stops in Mougins.

Grasse
POP 53,150

It is the abundance of water up in the hills that helped turn Grasse into a perfume centre. Tanners, who needed reliable water supplies to clean their hides, first settled here in the Middle Ages. With the advent of perfumed gloves in the 1500s, the art of perfumery took shape. Glove-makers split from the tanners and set up lucrative perfumeries. New irrigation techniques allowed flower growing to boom, sealing Grasse's reputation as the world capital of fragrance.

Today, Grasse is still surrounded by jasmine, centifolia roses, mimosa, orange blossom and violet fields but the industry, which counts some 30 perfumeries, is rather discreet, with only a handful offering tours of their facilities.

◉ Sights & Activities

Musée International de la Parfumerie
PERFUME MUSEUM

(MIP; www.museesdegrasse.com; 2 bd du Jeu de Ballon; adult/child €3/free; ⊙11am-6pm Wed-Mon; ▣) This whizz-bang museum is a work of art: housed in a renovated 18th-century mansion, daringly enlarged with a modern glass structure, it retraces three millennia of perfume history through a brilliant mix of artefacts, bottles, videos, vintage posters, olfactive stations and explanatory panels (in French and English), all beautifully presented. The museum offers interesting insights into how the industry developed in Grasse.

Kids are well catered for with dedicated multimedia stations throughout, a fragrant garden, a film testing your sense of smell and the reproduction of a 19th-century perfume shop.

1. St-Paul de Vence (p839)
Cobblestoned St-Paul de Vence has been home to many 20th-century artists, including Chagall.

2. Èze (p862)
Medieval Èze sits atop a 427m-high peak, with magnificent views across the Mediterranean.

3. Musée Picasso, Antibes (p837)
This museum, which was the artist's studio, has an excellent collection of Picasso's work.

4. Beach at Cannes (p840)
Cannes has glitz and glamour year-round, not only during its famous film festival.

PHOTOSHOT HOLDINGS LTD/ALAMY ©

Musée Fragonard   ART MUSEUM

(www.fragonard.com; 14 rue Ossola; admission free; ⊙10am-6pm) This tiny but fantastic private museum houses France's second-largest collection of works by Grassois painter Jean-Honoré Fragonard (1732–1806). There are 15 major works, beautifully exhibited in a renovated 18th-century townhouse (admire the splendid ceiling fresco in the entrance hall), and complemented by the paintings of Marguerite Gérard (1761–1837), Fragonard's sister-in-law and protégée, and Jean-Baptiste Mallet (1759–1835), another painter native of Grasse.

Perfumeries   PERFUMERIES

Three well-known perfumeries run free guided tours of their facilities: Fragonard (www.fragonard.com; 20 blvd Fragonard; ⊙9am-6pm Feb-Oct, 9am-12.30pm & 2-6pm Nov-Jan), Molinard (www.molinard.com; 60 bd Victor Hugo; ⊙9.30am-12.30pm & 2-6pm) and Galimard (www.galimard.com; 73 rte de Cannes; ⊙9am-12.30pm & 2-6pm). You're taken through every stage of perfume production, from extraction and distillation to the work of the 'nose'. Tours leave every 15 to 30 minutes and are available in a number of languages.

Visits end in the perfumery's showroom where you can buy fragrances (much cheaper than couture perfumes, where 60% of what you pay for is packaging).

✖ Eating

Café des Musées   MODERN FRENCH €

(1 rue Jean Ossola; mains €9-13; ⊙8am-6pm) This gorgeous cafe is the perfect place to stop for a spot of lunch (lovely salads, carefully crafted daily specials, soup or pasta of the day) or indulge in a gourmet coffee break (pastry with coffee or tea €7.50) between sights.

❶ Getting There & Away

BUS Bus 600 goes to Cannes (50 minutes, every 20 minutes) via Mouans-Sartoux (25 minutes) and Mougins (30 minutes). Bus 500 goes to Nice (1½ hours, hourly). All buses leave from the **bus station** (place de la Buanderie); fares are €1.

PARKING If arriving from Nice, park at **Parking Notre Dame des Fleurs** (Place Martelly). If arriving from Cannes, park at **Parking Honoré Cresp** (Cours Honoré Cresp). Allow €1.70 per hour.

TRAIN The station is out of town but linked to the centre by buses 2, 3, 4 and 5 (€1). There are regular services to Nice (€9.20, 1¼ hours, hourly) via Cannes (€4, 30 minutes).

Massif de l'Estérel

Punctuated by pine, oak and eucalyptus trees, the rugged red mountain range Massif de l'Estérel contrasts dramatically with the brilliant blue sea. Extending east from St-Raphaël to Mandelieu-La Napoule (near Cannes), the famous Corniche de l'Estérel (also known as the Corniche d'Or and the N98) coastal road passes through summer villages and *calanques* (coves) that are ideal for swimming.

✦ Activities

Diving & Snorkelling   DIVING

The Estérel is a leading dive centre: with numerous WWII shipwrecks and pristine waters, it's a prime area for underwater exploration. Much of the coast along the

---

LOCAL KNOWLEDGE

CORINNE MARIE-TOSSELLO, PERFUMER IN GRASSE

Corinne Marie-Tosello has two routes to work: one through olive groves, the other one through fields overlooking the sea. Most people would revel in the view, but Corinne revels in their smells: she runs the 'olfactory training' of perfumery Fragonard's staff (scent identification, production process, types of perfumes etc) and also works as an olfactory consultant (she advises on scents for incense, candles and so on).

Apart from the perfumeries, where else can you learn about Grasse's perfume industry? The flower fields around Grasse, such as the Jardins du MIP (p847), are wonderful: you see where the flowers come from and get a chance to meet the people who grow them.

Any fragrant walks in the region? St-Honorat (p841) is an olfactory paradise, with eucalyptus, pine trees, dry wood and vine. I would also recommend the Estérel (p850) in May when the maquis shrub *cistus* is in bloom.

Where would you recommend for lunch? In Grasse, I like the Café des Musées (p850) – the decor is very Fragonard and they have delicious ice-creams. In Cannes, I like Vegaluna (p841): I know the chef – he cooks with fresh, seasonal products – and the atmosphere is very relaxed.

CREATE YOUR OWN SCENT

It can take months, sometimes years, for a 'nose' (perfumers who, after 10 years' training, can identify up to 3000 smells) to create a perfume. And you'll understand why once you sit down in front of a mind-boggling array of essences: the number of combinations is dizzying. Perfume workshops won't turn you into a perfumer overnight, but the olfactory education they offer is fascinating – and great fun.

Molinard (p850) runs a fantastic 90-minute workshop (€69) in its Grasse factory where you can create your own perfume. Perfumer Céline will quiz you about the scents you like - and dislike - talk you through the structure of the perfume (base, heart and head notes), explain the rules of perfume etiquette (banish liberal spraying!) and help you through the more subtle blends of your creations. 'Graduates' leave with a stylish (and refillable) 130mL bottle of their perfume.

Corniche is protected, too, so the fauna and flora is some of the best around. Among the most reputable diving clubs are the multilingual Centre de Plongée Île d'Or (☎04 94 82 73 67; www.dive.fr; 986 bd 36ème Division du Texas, Agay) and the family-friendly Euro Plongée (☎04 94 19 03 26; www.europlongee.fr; Port de Boulouris).

Both clubs offer individual dives as well as courses (Club de Plongée Île d'Or is CMAS and PADI accredited). Euro Plongée also runs great two-hour snorkelling tours (€25); they're fantastic for families: kids will love spotting starfish, sea anemones, urchins and other colourful Mediterranean residents.

Sentier du Littoral   WALKING
Running 11km between Port Santa Lucia (the track starts behind the naval works) and Agay, this coastal path (yellow markers) takes in some of the most scenic spots in the area. It takes roughly 4½ hours to complete, but from May to October, you could make a day out of it by stopping at some of the idyllic beaches scattered along the way.

You can choose to walk smaller sections; the most scenic is around Cap Dramont, crowned by a signal station, which you can do as a loop from Plage du Débarquement. This long sandy beach is where the US 36th Infantry Division landed on 15 August 1944. The large memorial park has a car park easily accessible from the N98.

Walking in the Estérel   WALKING
With its lush green Mediterranean forests, intensely red peaks and sterling sea views, the Estérel is a walker's paradise. Local tourist offices have leaflets detailing the most popular walks, including Pic de l'Ours (496m) and Pic du Cap Roux (452m), but buy IGN's Carte de Randonnée (1:25,000) No 3544ET *Fréjus, Saint-Raphaël & Corniche*

de l'Estérel if you're planning more serious walks.

Access to the range is generally prohibited on windy or particularly hot days because of fire risks, so check with the tourist office before setting off.

Beaches   SWIMMING
With its 36km of coastline, the Corniche has more than 30 beaches running the gamut of beach possibilities: sandy, pebbly, nudist, cove-like, you name it. But wherever you go, the sea remains that crystal-clear turquoise and deep blue, an irresistible invitation to swim.

Fréjus & St-Raphaël

The twin towns of Fréjus (pop 52,953) and St-Raphaël (pop 34,867) bear the hallmarks of the area's history over the millennia.

Fréjus was settled by Massiliots (the Greeks who founded Marseille) and colonised by Julius Caesar around 49 BC as Forum Julii. It was settled thanks to the extension of the Roman road Via Aurelia, which linked Italy with Arles. The town's commercial activity largely ceased after its harbour silted up in the 16th century (Fréjus' town centre is 3km from the sea).

St-Raphaël is better known as the gateway to the Estérel. It was a fashionable hang-out in the 1920s, but the town is rather staid these days.

◉ Sights

Le Groupe Épiscopal   CATHEDRAL
(58 rue de Fleury; adult/child €5/free) Fréjus' star sight is the Groupe Épiscopal, built on the foundations of a Roman temple. At the heart of the complex is an 11th- and 12th-century cathedral, one of the first Gothic buildings

in the region, and a cloister featuring rare 14th- and 15th-century painted wooden ceiling panels depicting angels, devils, hunters, acrobats and monsters in vivid comic-book fashion.

The meaning and origin of these sci-fi like creatures is unknown. Only 500 of the original 1200 frames survive.

Before you enter the cathedral, make sure you take a peek at the octagonal 5th-century baptistery (which incorporates eight Roman columns into its structure) on your left-hand side: it is one of the oldest Christian buildings in France, and is exceptionally well preserved.

Musée Archéologique ARCHAEOLOGY MUSEUM
(place Calvini; adult/child €2/free) The small but fascinating Musée Archéologique features treasures unearthed in and around Fréjus, from everyday objects to rare finds such as a double-faced marble statue of Hermes, a head of Jupiter and a stunning 3rd-century mosaic depicting a leopard.

Roman Ruins ROMAN SITES
Fréjus' Roman ruins are not as well preserved as those found in Arles or Orange, but their abundance bears witness to the importance of Forum Julii at the time, with its strategic location on Via Aurelia and its port. The best way to appreciate this heritage is to join the guided tours (adult/child €6/free) run by the tourist office (☑04 94 51 83 83; www.frejus.fr; 249 rue Jean Jaurès; ☺9.30am-noon & 2-6pm Mon-Sat).

At the southeastern edge of the old city is the 3rd-century Porte d'Orée, the only remaining arcade of monumental Roman thermal baths. North of the old town are the ruins of a Théâtre Romain. Part of the stage and the theatre's outer walls are all that remain. Similarly, crumbling outer walls are all that are left of the 1st century arènes (amphitheatre), which once sat 10,000 and

have now been entirely renovated as a modern outdoor venue.

🛏 Sleeping

L'Aréna HOTEL €€
(☑04 94 17 09 40; www.hotel-frejus-arena.com; 145 rue du Général de Gaulle; d/tr €145/195; ❋🛜🌊) This hotel, with its sienna-coloured walls and lush garden, is a very pleasant option, ideally located to explore Fréjus' Roman ruins. The Provençal decor is starting to age but the rooms remain comfortable. Those in the Jasmine annexe are more spacious but there is no lift in that building. The duplex are ideal for families (with two single beds on a mezzanine).

Auberge de Jeunesse Fréjus-St-Raphaël HOSTEL €
(☑04 94 53 18 75; www.fuaj.org; chemin du Counillier; dm €19.60; ☺Mar-Oct; 🛜) A rambling, pretty basic HI-affiliated hostel set in 10 hectares of pine trees, where you can also pitch your tent. Take Bus 7 from St-Raphaël or Fréjus train stations to stop Les Chênes, then cross the roundabout and take chemin du Counillier on your left (600m). There is a daily lock-out between noon and 5.30pm. Rates include breakfast and sheets.

🍴 Eating

Le Poivrier FUSION €
(☑04 94 52 28 50; 52 place Paul Albert Février; mains €12-16, 2-course lunch menu €17; ☺lunch Tue-Sat, dinner Fri & Sat) Tucked away on one of Fréjus' pretty market squares, you'd never guess from the cute alfresco set up that downstairs is a grandiose vaulted dining room with a monumental fireplace. Nowadays, Le Poivrier is a wonderful address serving exquisitely fresh dishes inspired from local traditions and faraway climes.

Maison de la Tarte BOULANGERIE €
(33 rue Jean Jaurès; ☺7am-7pm Mon-Sat Aug-Jun; 🖋) If you're planning a picnic, stop at this mouth-watering bakery. Tarts of every kind (lemon meringue, pear and chocolate, apricot, almond etc), sold by the slice for €2.60, fill the front window and back shelves.

ⓘ Getting There & Away

BUS Bus 4 links Fréjus' humble **bus station** (Place Vernet) with St-Raphaël (tickets €1.10).
PARKING Parking du Clos de la Tour, on the edge of the old town, is free.
TRAIN The main station in the area is St-Raphaël-Valescure, in St-Raphaël.

St-Tropez

POP 4986

In the soft autumn or winter light, it's hard to believe that the pretty terracotta fishing village of St-Tropez is yet another stop on the Riviera celebrity circuit. It seems far removed from its glitzy siblings further up the coast, but come spring or summer, it's a different world: the town's population increases tenfold, prices triple and fun-seekers come in droves to party until dawn, strut their stuff and enjoy the creature comforts of an exclusive beach.

If you can at all avoid visiting in July and August, do. But if not, take heart: it's always fun to play 'I spy...' (a celebrity).

History

St-Tropez acquired its name in AD 68 when a Roman officer named Torpes was beheaded on Nero's orders in Pisa, and packed into a boat with a dog and a rooster to devour his remains. His headless corpse washed up here intact, leading the villagers to adopt him as their patron saint.

For centuries St-Tropez remained a peaceful little fishing village, attracting painters like pointillist Paul Signac, but few tourists. That changed dramatically in 1956 when *Et Dieu Créa la Femme* (And God Created Woman) starring Brigitte Bardot (aka BB) was shot here, catapulting the village into the international limelight.

◉ Sights

Vieux Port   PORT
Yachts line the harbor and chic visitors stroll the quays at the picturesque old port. In front of the sable-coloured townhouses, the Bailli de Suffren statue, cast from a 19th-century cannon, peers out to sea. The bailiff (1729–88) was a sailor who fought with a Tropezien crew against Britain and Prussia during the Seven Years War. As much of an institution as the bailiff is portside café Sénéquier (p856).

Place des Lices   VILLAGE SQUARE
St-Tropez's legendary and very charming central square is studded with plane trees, cafes and *pétanque* players. Simply sitting on a cafe terrace watching the world go by or jostling with the crowds at its extravaganza of a twice-weekly market (place des Lices; ⊘8am-1pm Tue & Sat), jam-packed with everything from fruit and veg to antique mirrors

and flip-flops (thongs), is an integral part of the St-Tropez experience.

Artists and intellectuals have met for decades in St-Tropez's famous Café des Arts, now simply called Le Café (☑04 94 97 44 69; www.lecafe.fr; place des Lices; lunch/dinner menus €18/30; ⊘lunch & dinner daily) (not to be confused with the newer, green-canopied Café des Arts on the corner of the square). Aspiring *pétanque* players can borrow a set of boules from the bar or buy their own at La Palanquée (☑04 94 97 41 41; bd Louis Blanc). Locals tend to hang on the other side of the square.

Musée de l'Annonciade   ART MUSEUM
(place Grammont; adult/child €6/4; ⊘10am-noon & 2-6pm Wed-Mon Oct & Dec-May, 10am-noon & 3-7pm Wed-Mon Jun-Sep) In a gracefully converted 16th-century chapel, this small but famous art museum showcases an impressive collection of modern art infused with that legendary Côte d'Azur light. Pointillist Paul Signac bought a house in St-Tropez in 1892 and introduced others to the area. The museum's collection includes his *St-Tropez, Le Quai* (1899) and *St-Tropez, Coucher de Soleil au Bois de Pins* (1896), which hangs juxtaposed with a window-view of contemporary St-Tropez.

Citadelle de St-Tropez   HISTORIC SITE
(admission €2.50; ⊘10am-6.30pm) Built in 1602 to defend the coast against Spain, the citadel dominates the hillside overlooking St-Tropez to the east. The views (and peacocks!) are fantastic. Its dungeons shelter a Musée Naval, dedicated to the town's maritime history and the Allied landings in August 1944.

⚓ Activities

Beaches   BEACH
About 4km southeast of town is the start of Plage de Tahiti and its continuation, the famous Plage de Pampelonne, studded with St-Tropez's most legendary drinking and dining haunts. Just east of St-Tropez, Plage des Salins (rte des Salins) is a long, wide sandy beach at the southern foot of Cap des Salins.

Further south, Pointe du Capon (S of La Tête de Chien) is a beautiful cape criss-crossed with walking trails.

Sentier du Littoral   WALKING
A spectacular coastal path wends its way past rocky outcrops and hidden bays 35km

south from St-Tropez, around the Presqu'île de St-Tropez to the beach at Cavalaire-sur-Mer and beyond to Le Lavandou (60km).

In St-Tropez the yellow-flagged path starts at La Ponche, immediately east of Tour du Portalet, and curves around Port des Pêcheurs, past St-Tropez's citadel. It then leads past the walled Cimitière Marin (marine cemetery) to the tiny Plage des Graniers and beyond.

The tourist office has maps with distances and walking times (e.g. to Plage des Salins, 8.5km, 2½hr).

Les Bateaux Verts   BOAT TOUR

(☑04 94 49 29 39; www.bateauxverts.com; quai Jean Jaurès) This boat company offers trips around Baie des Cannebiers (dubbed 'Bay of Stars' after the celebrity villas dotting its coast) April to September (adult/child €9/5) as well as the Calanques de l'Estérel (€20/12), Port-Cros (€35/22) and Porquerolles (€39/25). Shuttles connect St-Tropez with Ste-Maxime (one-way/return €7.10/12.70, 15 minutes, operates year-round).

🛏 Sleeping

St-Tropez is no shoestring destination, but there are plenty of camping grounds to the southeast along Plage de Pampelonne. Most hotels close at some stage in winter; the tourist office keeps a list.

TOP CHOICE Hôtel Lou Cagnard   PENSION €€

(☑04 94 97 04 24; www.hotel-lou-cagnard.com; 18 av Paul Roussel; d €75-156; ⊙Jan-Oct; ❀🖨) Book well ahead for this great-value courtyard charmer, shaded by lemon and fig trees, and owned by schooled hoteliers. This pretty Provençal house with lavender shutters has its very own jasmine-scented garden, strung with fairy lights at night. Bright and beautifully clean rooms are decorated with painted Provençal furniture. Five have ground-floor garden terraces. The cheapest rooms have private washbasin and stand-up bathtub but share a toilet; 15 of the 19 rooms have air-con.

Pastis   HOTEL €€€

(☑04 98 12 56 50; www.pastis-st-tropez.com; 61 av du Général Leclerc; d from €200; ❀🏊) This stunning townhouse-turned-hotel is the brainchild of an English couple besotted with Provence and passionate about modern art. You'll die for the pop-art-inspired interior, and long for a swim in the emerald-green pool. Every room is beautiful.

Hôtel Le Colombier   HOTEL €€

(☑04 94 97 05 31; http://lecolombierhotel.free.fr; impasse des Conquettes; r €84-158, without bath €76; ❀) An immaculately clean converted house, five minutes' walk from place des Lices, the Colombier's fresh, summery decor is feminine and uncluttered, with pale pink bedrooms and vintage furniture. Not all rooms have air-con. Rooms without baths share a toilet, but have bidet, sink and shower, open to the bedroom; rooms with baths may have only a partial wall separating them from the bedroom.

Hôtel Ermitage   BOUTIQUE HOTEL €€€

(☑04 94 27 52 33; www.ermitagehotel.fr; av Paul Signac; r €180-300; ❀@🖨) Kate Moss and Lenny Kravitz favour St-Trop's latest rocker crash pad, which draws inspiration from St-Trop from the '50s to the '70s: disco meets mid-century modern. Rooms designed by celebs (including Chloë Sevigny) and its off-the-beaten-path hillside location up the exclusivity factor, and it has knockout views over town.

B Lodge Hôtel   HOTEL €€

(☑04 94 97 58 72; www.hotel-b-lodge.com; 23 rue de l'Aïoli; d from €140; ⊙Dec-Oct; ❀🖨) Mod-decor rooms are a bit worn but clean, and some have balconies with citadelle views. A two-storey duplex sleeps four (€340). Not all rooms have air-con.

Hôtel Les Palmiers   BOUTIQUE HOTEL €€

(☑04 94 97 01 61; www.hotel-les-palmiers.com; 26 blvd Vasserot; d €89-189; ❀) In an old villa opposite place des Lices, Les Palmiers has simple rooms around a courtyard. Choose one in the main building rather than the annexe.

🍴 Eating

Quai Jean Jaurès on the old port is littered with restaurants and cafes – they have mediocre menus but great portside views. Many establishments close during the winter so your choice may be drastically reduced. In summer, book everywhere.

TOP CHOICE La Tarte Tropézienne   CAFE, BISTRO €

(☑04 94 97 04 69; www.tarte-tropezienne.com; place des Lices; mains €12-17; ⊙7.30am-6.30pm) This cafe and its associated bakery (36 rue Georges Clémenceau), the original creator of the eponymous cake, are the best places to buy St-Tropez's delicacy. Upstairs in the lively, elegant bistro, pick from delicious daily specials, and downstairs salad/sandwich formulas (€6-7).

ST-TROPEZ BEACH RESTAURANTS

St-Tropez' seaside scene is defined by its restaurants (which blanket the sand), and they're all wildly different. Mattresses (€15-20) and parking (€5) are extra. Most open May to September (call ahead); all are marked on the tourist office map. Book lunch (well ahead) at one of the following.

» Club 55 (www.leclub55.fr; 43 blvd Patch, Pampelonne) The oldest-running club dates to the 1950s, and was originally the crew canteen during the filming of *And God Created Woman*. Now it caters to celebs who do *not* want to be seen. Food's nothing special.

» Nikki Beach (www.nikkibeach.com/sttropez; rte de l'Epi, Epi Plage) Favoured by dance-on-the-bar celebs (ie Paris Hilton) who want to be seen. Goes until midnight.

» Plage des Jumeaux (☑04 94 58 21 80; www.plagedesjumeaux.com; rte de l'Épi, Pampelonne; mains €22-29; ⊙lunch Thu-Mon year-round, lunch & dinner daily Jul & Aug; ⊞) First choice for families, with playground equipment and beach toys; tops for seafood.

» Aqua Club (☑04 94 79 84 35; www.aqua-club-plage.fr; rte de l'Epi, Pampelonne; mains €22-29; ⊙Jan-Oct) Friendly mixed gay and straight crowd; the most diverse by far.

» Moorea Plage (☑04 94 97 18 17; www.moorea-plage-st-tropez.com; rte des Plages, Tahiti; mains €15-29) Ideal for conversation and backgammon; tops for steak.

» Liberty Plage (☑04 94 79 80 62; www.plageliberty.com; chemin des Tamaris, Pampelonne; mains €17-19; ⊙year-round) Clothing optional – eat naked.

» Pearl Beach (☑04 98 12 70 70; www.thepearlbeach.com; quartier de la Bouillabaisse; lunch/dinner menus €30/70; ⊙mid-Feb–Dec) and La Bouillabaisse (☑04 94 97 54 00; www.alpazurhotels.com; menus €45; ⊙mid-Feb–Oct), on the way into town on rte de St-Tropez, are family-friendly.

TOP CHOICE **Auberge de l'Oumède**   PROVENÇAL €€€
(☑04 94 44 11 11; www.aubergedeloumede.com; Chemin de l'Oumède; mains €39-59, d from €225; ⊙dinner Tue-Sat May–mid-Sep, dinner daily Jul & Aug; ⊞⊡) Epicureans come from far and wide to sample Jean-Pierre Frezia's Provençal cuisine served in a sea of vineyards: red mullet and spinach cannelloni, grilled catch of the day *aux ceps de vigne* (wood from the vines, which gives grilled food a distinctive flavour) and sensational desserts, all accompanied by some very fine wines. Dining at this isolated *bastide* (Provençal mansion) down a single-lane track is indeed a rare treat. It has seven rooms and a pool, handy should you really not want to leave.

Le Sporting   BRASSERIE €€
(☑04 94 97 00 65; place des Lices; mains €14-24; ⊙8am-1am) There's a bit of everything on the menu at always-packed Le Sporting, but the speciality is the hamburger topped with *foie gras* and morel cream sauce. The Brittany-born owner also serves perfect buckwheat crêpes, honest lunch deals (€13) and a simple salad and *croque monsieur*.

Auberge des Maures   PROVENÇAL €€
(☑04 94 97 01 50; 4 rue du Docteur Boutin; mains €31-39; ⊙dinner) The town's oldest restaurant remains the locals' choice for always-good, copious portions of earthy Provençal cooking, like *daube* or tapenade-stuffed lamb shoulder. Book a table (essential) on the leafy courtyard.

Chez les Garçons   MODERN FRENCH €€
(☑04 94 49 42 67; www.chezlesgarcons.com; 11/13 rue du Cépoun; menus €32; ⊙lunch Tue & Sun, dinner daily mid-Feb–Dec) Super-friendly staff serve delicate specialties like a perfectly poached egg with *foie gras*, all under the watchful eyes of Marilyn, Brigitte and Audrey (art on the wall). Also a lively gay bar next door.

Brasserie des Arts   MODERN FRENCH €€
(☑04 94 40 27 37; www.brasseriedesarts.com; 5 place des Lices; mains €20) Wedged in a line-up of eating and drinking terraces jockeying for attention on St-Tropez' people-watching square, BA, as it is known, is where the locals go. Out of season ask for a table at the back to experience the real vibe. The fixed three-course gourmet *menu* offers excellent value.

🍸 Drinking & Entertainment

Dress to kill. And bring more money than you think you'll need. Many places close in winter, but in summer it's party central

THE FRENCH RIVIERA & MONACO ST-TROPEZ

DON'T MISS

TARTE TROPÉZIENNE

Don't leave town without sampling St-Tropez' signature cake, the *Tarte Tropézienne*. An orange-blossom-flavoured double sponge cake filled with thick cream, it was created by a Polish baker and christened by BB in the 1950s.

seven days a week. To tap into the local gay scene, hit Chez les Garçons (p855).

Sénéquier   CAFE
(☑04 94 97 00 90; www.senequier.com; quai Jean Jaurès) Sartre wrote parts of *Les Chemins de la Liberté* (Roads to Freedom) at this port-side cafe popular with boaties, bikers and tourists, which has been in business since 1887. Look for the terrace crammed with pillar-box-red tables and director's chairs.

Bar du Port   CAFE, BAR
(www.barduport.com; quai Suffren; ⊗7am-3am year-round) Young, happening bar for beautiful people, with chichi decor in shades of white and silver.

Ice Kube   THEME BAR
(☑04 94 97 20 00; Kube Hôtel, 13 chemin de Rogon de la Valette, rte de St-Tropez; admission €30; ⊗6.30pm-1am) Reservations are essential at this bar made of ice. Admission gets you four Grey Goose vodka cocktails, which you must consume within 30 minutes. Then you leave. Best between 11pm and 1am.

Bar at l'Ermitage   BAR
(Hôtel Ermitage, av Paul Signac; ⊗5pm-midnight) Escape the crowds at the laid-back Ermitage, kitted out in distressed '50s-modern furniture. Knockout views.

L'Esquinade   NIGHTCLUB
(☑04 94 97 87 45; rue du Four; ⊗11pm-5am daily Jun-Sep, Sat & Sun only Oct-May) Where the party winds up when you want to dance till dawn. Open year-round, and the Tropéziens' top choice.

L'Octave Café   NIGHTCLUB
(☑04 94 97 22 56; place de la Garonne; ⊗8pm-5am Apr-Oct) Twirl in a cocktail dress at this intimate club with a band that plays standards and pop – ideal on date night.

Les Caves du Roy   NIGHTCLUB
(Hôtel Byblos, av Paul Signac; ⊗mid-Apr–Sep) Star-studded bar of the infamous Hôtel Byblos.

🛍 Shopping

St-Tropez is loaded with couture boutiques, gourmet food shops and art galleries. For designer vintage, browse Le Dépôt (☑04 94 97 80 10; 6 bd Louis Blanc) and De l'Une à l'Autre (☑04 98 12 66 14; 6 rue Joseph Quaranta).

Atelier Rondini   SANDALS
(☑04 94 97 19 55; www.rondini.fr; 16 rue Georges Clémenceau) Colette brought a pair of sandals from Greece to Atelier Rondini (open since 1927) to be replicated. They're still making the iconic sandals for about €120.

ℹ Information

The English-language brochure *Out and About* is available in tourist offices in the area.

Tourist Office (☑04 94 97 45 21; www.ot -saint-tropez.com; quai Jean Jaurès; ⊗9.30am-8pm Jul & Aug, 9.30am-12.30pm & 2-7pm Apr-Jun & Sep–mid-Oct, 9.30am-12.30pm & 2-6pm mid-Oct–Mar) Has kiosk in July and August in Parking du Port.

ℹ Getting There & Away

BIKE Rolling Bikes (☑04 94 97 09 39; www. rolling-bikes.com; 14 av du Général Leclerc; bikes/scooters/motorcycles from €15/40/120 per day, plus deposit)

BOAT Les Bateaux Verts (p854) runs many shuttle-boats.

Les Bateaux de St-Raphaël (www.bateaux saintraphael.com) Connects St-Tropez (Nouveau Port) and St-Raphaël (adult/child €14/9).

BUS VarLib (www.varlib.fr) tickets cost €2 from the **bus station** (☑04 94 56 25 74; av du Général de Gaulle) for anywhere within the Var département (except Toulon-Hyères airport), including Ramatuelle (35 minutes), St-Raphaël (1¼ hours) via Grimaud and Port Grimaud, and Fréjus (one hour). Buses to Toulon (two hours, seven daily, less in summer) stop at Le Lavandou (one hour) and Hyères (1½ hours). Four buses daily serve Toulon-Hyères airport (€15; 1½ hours).

TAXI Boat-taxi Taxi de Mer (☑06 09 57 31 22, 06 09 53 15 47). Car **taxi** (☑04 94 97 05 27) rank is at the Vieux Port in front of the Musée de l'Annonciade.

St-Tropez to Toulon

MASSIF DES MAURES

Shrouded by a forest of pine, chestnut and cork oak trees, the Massif des Maures arcs inland between Hyères and Fréjus. Roamed by wild boars, its near-black vegetation gives rise to its name, derived from the Provençal word *mauro* (dark pine wood).

The village of Collobrières is the largest town in the massif and is renowned for its wonderful chestnut purée and *marrons glacés* (candied chestnuts). The tourist office (☑04 94 48 08 00; www.collobrieres -tourisme.com; bd Charles Caminat; ⊙10am-noon & 2-5pm Tue-Sat, closed Sun & Mon Sep-Jun) has maps, information on guided walks and plenty of tips to make the best of the area. There is no better lunch stop than La Petite Fontaine (☑04 94 48 00 12; place de la République; 3-course/5-course menus €24/31; ⊙lunch & dinner Tue-Sat & lunch Sun Apr-Sep, lunch Tue-Sat & dinner Fri & Sun Oct-Mar): one of southern France's most charming, relaxed village inns, the walls inside are exposed stone, and the fruit tarts for dessert...out of this world. Reservations essential. No credit cards.

The stand-out sight in the region is the majestic 12th- to 13th-century Monastère de la Verne (☑04 94 43 45 51; http://la.verne. free.fr; near Collobrières; adult/child €6/3; ⊙11am-5pm Wed-Mon Feb-May & Sep-Dec, 11am-6pm Jun-Aug), which perches unbelievably on the hip of a mountain deep in the forest, but with a view to the sea. Highlights include the austere Romanesque church, the prior's cell, complete with a small formal garden and workshop, the bakery and the olive mill. To get here, follow rte de Grimaud (D14) east for 6km from Collobrières, then turn right (south) onto the D214 and drive another 6km to the monastery.

Contact the Conservatoire du Patrimoine (☑04 94 43 08 57; www.conservatoiredu freinet.org; Chapelle St-Jean, place de la Mairie, La Garde Freinet; ⊙10am-12.30pm & 2.30-5.30pm Tue-Sat) in La Garde Freinet for various workshops, horse and donkey treks and weekly forest walks to see cork being harvested. Hiking and cycling opportunities abound, especially around La Sauvette (779m), the massif's highest peak.

CORNICHE DES MAURES
This coastal road snakes from La Croix-Valmer to Le Lavandou along the D559. In addition to stunning views, there are some superb spots for swimming, sunbathing and walking.

La Croix-Valmer's Plage de Gigaro is one not to miss, as is the walking path towards Cap Lardier, which is one of the most beautiful, least-trodden bits of the coast.

Domaine du Rayol (☑04 98 04 44 00; www. domainedurayol.org; av des Belges, Rayol-Canadel-sur-Mer; adult/child €8/6; ⊙9.30am-7.30pm Jul & Aug, to 6.30pm Apr-Jun, Sep & Oct, to 5.30pm Nov-Mar) is a wonderful spot. A former seaside estate rescued from ruin, it has been transformed into a stunning 20-hectare botanical garden, with plants from Mediterranean climates around the world. Paths meander down to the sea. In summer, call ahead for snorkelling tours (adult/child €18/14) of the underwater marine garden and botanist-guided walks. One of only a few sights open at lunchtime, there's an on-site cafe.

Le Lavandou (www.ot-lelavandou.fr) is famous for its 12km of fine beaches and 12 types of sand. Boats regularly sail to the Îles d'Hyères from here.

Up in the hills, you'll find the quintessential Provençal village of Bormes-les-Mimosas (☑04 94 01 38 38; www.bormesles mimosas.com; 1 place Gambetta; ⊙9am-12.30pm & 3-6.30pm daily Apr-Sep, Mon-Sat Oct-Mar). The *vieux* (old) village is spectacularly flowered year-round, with the eponymous mimosas in winter and deep-fuchsia bougainvilleas in summer. Old cobbled streets are lined with artists' galleries and boutiques selling traditional Provençal products, natural soap and essential oils. The utterly charming Hôtel Bellevue (☑04 94 71 15 15; www.bellevuebormes. com; place Gambetta; d €48-74, q €114; ✳🐾) has sensational views, pretty rooms and friendly service. For authentic local cuisine, with flavours from the terrois, head to L'Atelier de Cuisine Gourmande (☑04 94 71 27 80; 4 place Gambetta; menus €28; ⊙by reservation).

For breathtaking views of the islands, the Route des Crêtes winds its way through maquis-covered hills some 400m above the sea. Take the D41 as you head out of Bormes-les-Mimosas past the Chapelle St-François; 1.5km up the hill, turn immediately right after the sign for Col de Caguo-Ven to follow 13km of tight bends and spectacular views. Relais du Vieux Sauvaire (☑04 94 05 84 22; rte des Crêtes; mains €18-30; ⊙lunch & dinner Jun-Sep) is the hidden gem of these hills. With 180-degree views you could only dream of, this restaurant and pool (most people come here for lunch and then stay all afternoon) is one of a kind. The food is as sunny as the views: pizzas, melon and Parma ham, or whole sea bass in salt crust.

After the restaurant, Route des Crêtes joins the final leg of the panoramic Col du Canadel road. On the col (mountain pass),

THE FRENCH RIVIERA & MONACO ST-TROPEZ TO TOULON

AU NATUREL

Not a fan of tan lines? This coastal stretch of the Riviera is well endowed with *naturiste* (nudist) beaches. Plage de Tahiti, the northern stretch of Plage de Pampelonne in St-Tropez, is probably the best known. More secluded is Plage de l'Escalet, on the southern side of Cap Camarat on the Presqu'île de St-Tropez, a beautiful but hard to reach spot.

Most isolated is the oldest and largest *naturiste* colony in the region, which occupies half of the 8km-long island Île du Levant.

The coast's laid-back, let-it-all-hang-out attitude was the premise of Jean Girault's cult 1964 farce film *Le Gendarme de St-Tropez,* in which Louis de Funès starred as the policeman of the title, who attempted to crack down on local nudists.

turn left to plunge into the heart of forested Massif des Maures, or right to the sea and coastal Corniche des Maures (D559).

You'll need a car to travel to Bormes and along the rte des Crêtes, but the coastal road is on the itinerary of the Toulon to St-Tropez VarLib bus (www.varlib.fr; €2), which stops in most towns, including Le Lavandou.

HYÈRES
POP 56,020

With its overdose of palm trees, its casino, and medieval Vieille Ville (Old Town) perched on a hillside north of its new town, Hyères retains some of the charm that made it the Côte d'Azur's first resort. The city's real asset, however, is the Presqu'île de Giens (Giens Peninsula), a beach-fringed peninsula that harbours amazing birdlife, including pink flamingos, herons and egrets. Hyères' tourist office (☑04 94 01 84 50; www.hyeres-tourisme.com; 3 av Ambroise Thomas, Hyères; ⊙9am-6pm Mon-Fri, 10am-4pm Sat) runs great guided walks in the old town and the peninsula.

ÎLES D'HYÈRES

For some inexplicable reason, these paradisiacal islands (also known as Îles d'Or – Golden Islands – for their shimmering mica rock) have remained mostly unknown to foreign crowds.

The easternmost and largest of this trio of islands is the little-visited Île du Levant, split into an odd combination of army land and nudist colony. Île de Port-Cros, the middle and smallest island, is the jewel in the islands' crown. France's first marine national park (www.portcrosparcnational.fr) boasts exceptional marine fauna and flora, which makes it a snorkelling paradise. The island is also covered with 30km of marked trails through thick forest, ragged cliff tops and deserted beaches.

The largest and westernmost island is Île de Porquerolles (www.porquerolles.com). Run as a hacienda in the early 20th century, it has kept many of its sprawling plantation features. There are plenty of walking trails, but the best way to get around is by cycling. There are several bicycle-rental places, as well as a few restaurants and hotels.

ⓘ Getting There & Away

Boats to the Îles d'Hyères leave from various towns along the coast. **Vedettes Îles d'Or et Le Corsaire** (☑04 94 71 01 02; www.vedettes ilesdor.fr; 15 quai Gabriel Péri) operates boats to all three islands from Le Lavandou, and between Port-Cros and Porquerolles in summer. Tariffs are:

» **Le Levant** return adult/child €26.50/21.50, 35 minutes or one hour (depending on which island the boat goes to first)

» **Porquerolles** return adult/child €34.20/26.50, 40 minutes

» **Port-Cros** return adult/child €26.50/21.50, 35 minutes

Transport Littoral Varois (TLV; ☑04 94 58 33 76; www.tlv-tvm.com) runs services to Porquerolles (return adult/child €18/16, 10 minutes) from the **La Tour Fondue port** at the bottom of the Giens Peninsula. It also runs services to Port-Cros (return adult/child €26/23, one hour) and Le Levant (adult/child €26/23, 1½ hours) from **Port d'Hyères**.

Toulon
POP 167,813

Built around a *rade* (a sheltered bay lined with quays), France's second-largest naval port provokes the reaction a tramp might get in St-Tropez: Toulon's seedy rough-cut demeanour just doesn't fit in with the glittering Côte d'Azur. It is not quite as terrible as it once was, though most visitors just pass through, since it is a central transport hub.

☉ Sights & Activities

Mont Faron   MOUNTAIN, ZOO
North of the city, from Mont Faron (584m) you can see Toulon's red-roofed houses and epic port. The tourist office has information on walks. Near the summit, Mémorial du Débarquement de Provence (☏04 94 88 08 09; adult/child €4/1; ☉10am-noon & 2-4.30pm Tue-Sun) commemorates the Allied landings, which took place along the coast here in August 1944. Historical displays and a film form part of this museum.

Téléphérique du Mont Faron (cable car; www.telepherique-faron.com; return adult/child €6.80/4.80; ☉10am-7pm) ascends the mountain. Kids love Zoo du Faron (☏04 94 88 07 89; adult/child €9/5.50; ☉10am-6.30pm), a wild-cat breeding-centre. Combination zoo and cable-car tickets cost €13 per adult, €9 for children.

Le Batelier de la Rade   BOAT TOUR
(quai de la Sinse; per person €10) From the port you can take a spin around the *rade*, with a commentary (in French only) on the local events of WWII. In summer the boat goes to the Îles d'Hyères.

⌂ Sleeping & Eating

Hôtel Little Palace   HOTEL €
(☏04 94 92 26 62; www.hotel-littlepalace.com; 6-8 rue Berthelot; s/d €50/62; ✻@☎) The over-the-top Italian-inspired decor lacks authenticity but Little Palace is well run. No lift.

Le Chantilly   BRASSERIE €
(☏04 94 92 24 37; place Puget; mains €10-25; ☉6.30am-11pm) Going strong since 1907, Le Chantilly will sort you out for food, whatever the time of day.

ℹ Information

Tourist Office (www.toulontourisme.com; 12 place Louis Blanc; ☉9am-6pm Mon-Sat, 9am-1pm Sun)

ℹ Getting There & Around

AIR **Toulon-Hyères Airport** (www.toulon-hyeres.aeroport.fr) is 23km east of Toulon, on the edge of the Giens Peninsula. Bus 102 (€1.40) links Toulon-Hyères airport with the Toulon bus station (40 minutes).

BOAT Ferries to Corsica and Sardinia are run by **Corsica Ferries** (www.corsica-ferries.co.uk; Port de Commerce).

BUS **VarLib** (www.varlib.fr) buses (€2) operate from the **bus station** (☏04 94 24 60 00; bd de Tessé), next to the train station. Bus 103 to St-Tropez (eight daily) goes via Hyères (35 minutes) and Le Lavandou (one hour).

The tourist office sells a **one-day pass** (www.reseaumistral.com; €6) that includes unlimited travel on local buses (single fare €1.40) and commuter boats to La Seyne-sur-Mer, and a return ticket for the Mont Faron Téléphérique.

TRAIN Frequent connections include Marseille (€12, 50 minutes), St-Raphaël (€14, 50 minutes), Cannes (€20, 1¼ hours), Monaco (€26, 2¼ hours) and Nice (€24, 1¾ hours).

West of Toulon

SANARY-SUR-MER
POP 17,047

Pretty-as-a-picture seaside Sanary-sur-Mer is a stroller's dream. Watch the fishermen unload their catch on the quay, or admire the traditional fishing boats from one of the seafront cafes. Wednesday's colourful market draws crowds from miles around. Shops line interior streets.

⚓ Activities

Regard du Vivant   DOLPHIN CRUISE
(☏06 10 57 17 11; www.regard-du-vivant.fr; adult/child €75/55) Observe various dolphin species from aboard a boat with naturalist-photographers.

Croix du Sud V   BOAT TOUR
(☏06 09 87 47 97; www.croixdusud5.com) Boat tours serve the Calanques (adult/child from €25/14) and Île de Porquerolles (€36/21).

⌂ Sleeping & Eating

TOP CHOICE **Hôtel de la Tour**   HOTEL €€
(☏04 94 74 10 10; www.sanary-hoteldelatour.com; Port; d incl breakfast €80-130) Some of the excellent, large rooms in this renovated Victorian-era hotel have awesome portside views. Super-modern bathrooms are spacious stone and tile, and the charming decor is clean and inviting. Book ahead.

L'Esplanade   SEAFOOD €€
(☏04 94 74 08 56; www.restaurant-esplanade.fr; near Parking de l'Esplanade; 3-course menus from €36; ☉lunch & dinner Tue-Sat) Dine in portside elegance on the catch of the day.

ℹ Information

Tourist Office (☏04 94 74 01 04; www.sanarysurmer.com; 1 quai du Levant; ☉9am-12.30pm & 2-5.30pm Mon-Sat)

THE FRENCH RIVIERA & MONACO WEST OF TOULON

BANDOL & AROUND
POP 8523

The built-up town of Bandol, a favourite among French holiday-makers, lends its name to the area's excellent wines. The *appellation* comprises eight neighbouring communities including Le Castellet, Ollioules and Evenos.

◉ Sights & Activities

TOP CHOICE / **Maison des Vins**   WINE TASTING

(Oenothèque des Vins du Bandol; ☑04 94 29 45 03; www.maisondesvins-bandol.com; place Lucien Artaud, Bandol; ☉10am-1pm & 3-6.30pm Mon-Sat, 10am-1pm Sun) Bandol's 49 vineyards carefully manage their prized production of red, rosé and white. Pascal Perier, the manager at the Maison des Vins, is a living Bandol encyclopaedia. He provides tastings, keeps a well-supplied shop and can direct you to surrounding vineyards (most require an appointment).

Sentier du Littoral   WALKING

This yellow-marked coastal trail runs 12km (allow 3½ to four hours) from Bandol's port to La Madrague in St-Cyr-Les-Lecques, with the beautiful Calanque de Port d'Alon roughly halfway.

🛏 Sleeping & Eating

TOP CHOICE / **Les Quatre Saisons**   B&B €€

(☑04 94 25 24 90; www.lesquatresaisons.org; 370 montée des Oliviers, rte du Brûlat (D26), Le Castellet; d €90-130; ✸✸) A few hair-pin bends downhill from the medieval hilltop village of Le Castellet, Patrice and Didier have decorated five exquisite rooms in the purest Provençal style. All open onto a central swimming pool, and Patrice's *table d'hôte* (€40) is worth every cent.

Golf Hôtel   HOTEL €

(☑04 94 29 45 83; www.golfhotel.fr; 10 promenade de la Corniche; d/q from €69/116; ☉Jan-Nov; ✸) A prime address for beachside sleeping and dining. Its restaurant, La Chipote (04 94 29 41 62; lunch/dinner menus €19/26; ☉lunch daily, dinner Mon-Sat), with terrace on the sand, cooks up fresh fish and ace desserts.

TOP CHOICE / **La Table du Vigneron**   RESTAURANT €€

(☑04 94 88 36 19; 724 chemin de la Tourelle, Ollioules; lunch/dinner 3-course menus €25/40; ☉lunch & dinner Tue-Sat) In Ollioules, at Domaine de Terrebrune (☑04 94 74 01 30; www.terrebrune.fr; ☉9am-12.30pm & 2-6pm Mon-Sat), you can taste their wines and then dine on delicious seasonal country fare at La Table du Vigneron, the estate's traditional *auberge* with alfresco tables overlooking vineyards. Wine by the glass is expensive, but they throw in the champagne with the dessert course. Their new contemporary restaurant in Ollioules village is L'Atelier du Vigneron (☑04 94 62 42 34; 348 ave de la Résistance, Ollioules).

❶ Information

Tourist Office (www.bandol.fr; ☉9am-noon & 2-6pm Mon-Sat) Has a comprehensive guide in English.

❶ Getting There & Away

Bandol is on the train line between Toulon (€3.60, 15 minutes) and Marseille (€9.30, 45 minutes).

NICE TO MENTON

The Three Corniches

Some of the Riviera's most spectacular scenery stretches between Nice and Menton. A trio of corniches (coastal roads) hugs the cliffs between Nice and Monaco, each higher up the hill than the last. The middle corniche ends in Monaco; the upper and lower continue to Menton.

Grace Kelly, Princess of Monaco, is strongly associated with this part of the world. The Grande Corniche appears in Hitchcock's *To Catch a Thief,* as does the bridge to Èze on the Moyenne Corniche, and Kelly herself died in a car crash on the D53, a road linking the Grande and Moyenne corniches.

CORNICHE INFÉRIEURE

Skimming the villa-lined waterfront, the Corniche Inférieure (also known as the Basse Corniche, the Lower Corniche or the N98) sticks pretty close to the train line, passing (west to east) through Villefranche-sur-Mer, Beaulieu-sur-Mer, Èze-sur-Mer and Cap d'Ail.

❶ Getting There & Around

BUS Bus 100 (€1, every 15 minutes between 6am and 8pm) runs the length of the Corniche Inférieure, stopping at Villefranche-sur-Mer (15 minutes) and Beaulieu-sur-Mer (20 minutes). Bus 81 serves Villefranche (20 minutes) and St-Jean-Cap Ferrat (30 minutes) from Nice.

TRAIN Nice–Ventimiglia (Italy) trains (every 30 minutes, 5am to 11pm) stop at Villefranche-sur-Mer (€1.60, 7 minutes) and Beaulieu-sur-Mer (€2, 10 minutes).

THE FRENCH RIVIERA & MONACO THE THREE CORNICHES

VILLEFRANCHE-SUR-MER
POP 5888

This picturesque, pastel-coloured, terracotta-roofed fishing port overlooking the Cap Ferrat peninsula was a favourite with Jean Cocteau, who painted the frescos in the 17th-century Chapelle St-Pierre (admission €2.50; ⊙10am-noon & 2-6pm Wed-Mon). Steps split the steep cobblestone streets that weave through the old town, including the oldest, rue Obscure, an eerie vaulted passageway built in 1295. Looking down on the township is the 16th-century citadel. Beyond the port is a sandy beach offering picture-perfect views of the town.

ST-JEAN-CAP FERRAT
POP 2047

On the Cap Ferrat peninsula, this fishing-village-turned-playground-for-the-wealthy conceals an enclave of millionaires' villas, with illustrious residents both present and past. On the narrow isthmus of the town, the extravagant Villa Ephrussi de Rothschild (www.villa-ephrussi.com; St-Jean-Cap Ferrat; adult/child €12/9; ⊙10am-6pm Mar-Oct, 2-6pm Nov-Feb) gives you an appreciation of the area's wealth. Housed in a 1912 Tuscan-style villa built for the Baroness de Rothschild, it's full of 18th-century furniture, paintings, tapestries and porcelain. A combined ticket with the Villa Grecque Kérylos in Beaulieu costs €18/13.50 for adults/children.

The peninsula also has three walking trails with glimmering seascapes, and secluded coves for swimming.

BEAULIEU-SUR-MER
POP 3370

Some of the best-preserved belle époque architecture along the coast is in the seaside holiday town of Beaulieu-sur-Mer, including its elaborate 1904 rotunda with Corinthian columns capped by a cupola. Another belle époque beauty is the Villa Grecque Kérylos (www.villa-kerylos.com; av Gustave Eiffel, Beaulieu-sur-Mer; adult/child €10/7.50; ⊙10am-6pm Mar-Oct, 2-6pm Nov-Feb), a reproduction of an Athenian villa built by archaeologist Théodore Reinach in 1902.

MOYENNE CORNICHE

Cut through rock in the 1920s, the Moyenne Corniche – the middle coastal road (N7) – takes drivers from Nice to Èze and Beausoleil (the French town bordering Monaco's Monte Carlo).

Bus 82 goes from Nice to Èze Village (20 minutes, several times daily); bus 112 carries on to Beausoleil (40 minutes, Monday to Saturday).

GRANDE CORNICHE

The Grande Corniche, whose panoramas are the most dramatic of all, leaves Nice as the D2564. Stop at Fort de la Revère in the Parc Natural Départemental de la Grande Corniche for a picnic with stupendous views or a walk in the *garrigue* (Mediterranean scrubs).

Further on, the town of La Turbie, which sits on a promontory directly above Monaco, offers vertigo-inducing views of the principality. The best views are from the town's Trophée des Alpes (18 av Albert Ier, La Turbie; adult/student/child €5.50/4/free; ⊙10am-1pm & 2.30-5pm Tue-Sun), one of only two Roman trophy monuments in the world (the other's in Romania), built by Augustus in 6 BC.

For a sit-down meal, plump yourself on the terrace of Café de la Fontaine (☎04 93 28 52 79; 4 av Général de Gaulle, La Turbie; mains €13-18; ⊙lunch & dinner Tue-Sun), the town's gastronomic bistro.

There is virtually no public transport along the Grande Corniche so you'll need your own wheels.

Monaco (Principauté de Monaco)
POP 32,350 / 377

Squeezed into just 200ha, this confetti principality might be the world's second-smallest country (the Vatican is smaller), but what it lacks in size it makes up for in attitude. Glitzy, glam and screaming hedonism, Monaco is truly beguiling.

Although a sovereign state, the principality's status is unusual. It is not a member of the European Union, yet it participates in the EU customs territory (meaning no bor-

MONACO TRIVIA

» Citizens of Monaco (Monégasques), of whom there are only 7600, don't pay taxes.

» Monaco has its own flag (red and white) and a national anthem, and the national holiday is on 19 November.

» The traditional dialect is Monégasque (broadly speaking, a mixture of French and Italian).

DON'T MISS

ÈZE

On the pinnacle of a 427m peak is the medieval stone village of Èze (pop 2865). Once occupied by Ligurians and Phoenicians, today it's home to one-off galleries and artisan boutiques within its enclosed walls (there's only one doorway in or out of the village). The high point is the Jardin d'Èze (adult/child €4/free; ⊙9am-sunset), a slanting cliff-side garden of exotic cacti with views of the Med all the way to Corsica (on a good day).

To explore the village's nooks and crannies after the tour buses have left, stay at the magnificent Château Eza (✆04 93 41 12 24; www.chateaueza.com; rue de la Pise; d from €440; ❀🐾), which also has a lofty gastronomic restaurant and terrace (lunch menus €49 to €59, dinner mains around €50), with views of the Med on a plate.

You can walk down from the village to Èze-sur-Mer on the coast via the steep chemin de Nietzsche (45 minutes); the German philosopher started writing *Thus Spoke Zarathustra* while staying in Èze and enjoyed this path.

der formalities crossing from France into Monaco) and uses the euro as its currency.

History
Originally from the nearby Genoa region of Italy (hence the Monégasque language's similarity with the Genoese dialect), the Grimaldi family has ruled Monaco for most of the period since 1297, except for its occupation during the French Revolution and its loss of territories in 1848. Its independence was again recognised by France in 1860. Five years later, a monetary agreement with France and the opening of the Monte Carlo casino revived the country's fortunes. Today there are just 7800 Monégasque citizens out of a total population of 32,000 (and 107 nationalities).

Ever since the marriage of Prince Rainier III of Monaco (r 1949–2005) to Hollywood actress Grace Kelly in 1956, Monaco's ruling family has regularly featured in gossip magazines. Albert II, prince since his father's death in 2005, hasn't escaped media scrutiny (he has no legitimate heirs but two illegitimate children), but his achievements as an athlete (he played for the Monaco football team and is a black belt in judo), his charity work and promotion of the arts have earned him favourable press. He married South African Olympic swimmer and former model Charlene Wittstock in July 2011 and Monégasques hope the couple will give them an heir.

◉ Sights & Activities

TOP CHOICE Musée Océanographique
de Monaco   AQUARIUM
(www.oceano.org; av St-Martin; adult/child €13/6.50; ⊙9.30am-7pm) Stuck dramatically

to the edge of a cliff since 1910, the world-renowned Musée Océanographique de Monaco, founded by Prince Albert I (1848–1922), is a stunner. Its centrepiece is its aquarium, with a 6m-deep lagoon where sharks and marine predators are separated from colourful tropical fishes by a coral reef.

Ninety smaller tanks contain a dazzling 450 Mediterranean and tropical species, sustained by 250,000L of freshly pumped sea water per day. Kids will love the tactile basin (which runs during school holidays) – tickets (€3) for the 30-minute feel-the-fish sessions are sold at the entrance.

Upstairs, two huge colonnaded rooms retrace the history of oceanography and marine biology. Displays recount Prince Albert's explorations, and the cetacean skeletons, fossils and other pickled specimens give an insight into the trials of these now-established fields.

Make sure you pay a visit to the rooftop terrace, too, for sweeping views of Monaco and the Med.

Le Rocher   HISTORIC QUARTER
Monaco Ville, also called Le Rocher, thrusts skywards on a pistol-shaped rock. It's this strategic location overlooking the sea that became the stronghold of the Grimaldi dynasty. Built as a fortress in the 13th century, the palace is now the private residence of the Grimaldis. It is protected by the Carabiniers du Prince; changing of the guard takes place daily at 11.55am.

Le Rocher is the only part of Monaco to have retained small, windy medieval lanes; they tend to be overrun with souvenir and ice-cream shops but it does give a sense of what Monaco once was.

To access Le Rocher, visitors can walk up the 16th-century red-brick Rampe Major from place aux Armes in the Condamine area. Alternatively, a path winds from the port up through the shady Jardins St-Martin.

Palais du Prince
ROYAL PALACE

(www.palais.mc; adult/child €8/3.50; ⊙10am-6pm Apr-Sep) For a glimpse into royal life, you can tour the state apartments with an 11-language audioguide. The palace is what you would expect of any aristocratic abode: lavish furnishings and expensive 18th- and 19th-century art.

Cathédrale de Monaco
CATHEDRAL

(4 rue Colonel) An adoring crowd continually shuffles past Prince Rainier's and Princess Grace's graves, located inside the cathedral choir of the 1875 Romanesque–Byzantine Cathédrale de Monaco. The Monaco boys' choir, Les Petits Chanteurs de Monaco, sings Sunday Mass at 10.30am between September and June.

Jardin Exotique
GARDEN

(www.jardin-exotique.mc; 62 bd du Jardin Exotique; adult/student & child €7/3.70; ⊙9am-dusk) Home to the world's largest succulent and cactus collection, from small echinocereus to 10m-tall African candelabras, the gardens tumble down the slopes of Moneghetti through a maze of paths, stairs and bridges. Views of the principality are spectacular and the gardens are delightful. Your ticket also gets you a 35-minute guided tour round the Grottes de l'Observatoire.

The caves are an important prehistoric network inside the hillside; strangely, it's the only cave in Europe where the temperature rises as you descend. It is full of stalactites and stalagmites.

Bus 2 links the gardens with the town centre.

Beaches
BEACH

The beaches in Monaco are definitely not the best on the coast but there are a couple of nice – and, surprisingly, free – options: Esplanade Stefano Casiraghi is a concrete solarium that has been installed on the back of the port's sea defence wall. If you prefer sand, Plage du Larvotto has free as well as paying sections.

☆☆ Festivals & Events

International Circus Festival of Monaco
PERFORMING ARTS FESTIVAL

(www.montecarlofestivals.com; ⊙late Jan) The International Circus Festival of Monaco showcases heart-stopping acts from around the globe.

Tennis Masters Series
SPORTS

(www.monte-carlorolexmasters.com; ⊙Apr) Fast becoming a key fixture on the professional circuit, with all the big players involved.

Formula One Grand Prix
SPORTS

(Automobile Club de Monaco; www.formula1monaco.com; ⊙late May) One of Formula One's most iconic races. If you're dead keen, you can walk the 3.2km circuit; the tourist office has maps.

🛏 Sleeping

Accommodation in Monaco is expensive to say the least, reaching prohibitive levels during the Formula One Grand Prix.

Columbus
BOUTIQUE HOTEL €€€

(✆92 05 90 00; www.columbushotels.com; 22 av des Papalins; d from €230; ❄@🛜🌐) Hi-tech urban chic best describes this large boutique hotel in Fontvieille. Rooms are beautifully

---

SLEEPING FOR LESS

There is no such thing as budget accommodation in Monaco; there are, however, two excellent budget-friendly options in Cap d'Ail, a mere 2km from Monaco. Cheapest of all is the Relais International de la Jeunesse Thalassa (✆04 93 81 27 63; www.clajsud.fr; 2 av Gramaglia, Cap d'Ail; dm €18; ⊙Apr-Oct). This youth hostel has an outstanding location right by the beach (and close to the train station): the dorms are simple but well kept. Rates include sheets and breakfast; half-board is available.

Another good place is Hôtel Normandy (✆04 93 78 77 77; www.hotelnormandy.no; 6 allée des Orangers; d from €89; 🛜). It is run by a multilingual family of artists and it shows: original modern pieces adorn the walls everywhere and the rooms have charm with their simple, old-school furniture (although some of the bathrooms are very dated). Some rooms have sea views. It's just 50m from the bus 100 stop (for Nice, Menton and Monaco) and 20 minutes from the gorgeous beach of La Mala.

Monaco

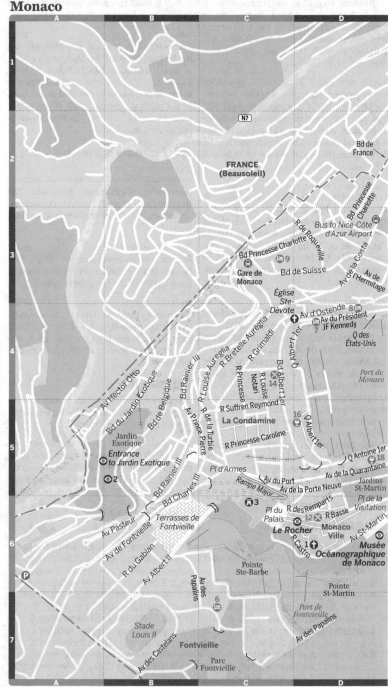

N7

FRANCE
(Beausoleil)

Bd de
France

Bus to Nice-Côte
d'Azur Airport

Bd Princesse Charlotte

Bd Princesse Charlotte 9

Gare de
Monaco

Bd de Suisse

Av de la Costa

Av de
l'Hermitage

Église
Ste-
Dévote

Av d'Ostende 8
Av du Président 7
JF Kennedy

Q des
États-Unis

R de Roqueville

R Bretelle Auréglia

R Grimaldi

Bd Albert 1er

Q Albert 1er

Bd Rainier III

R Louise Auréglia

R Princesse

R Louise
Notari 14

Port de
Monaco

Av Hector Otto

Bd du Jardin Exotique

Bd de Belgique

R Suffren Reymond

La Condamine

16

Q Albert 1er

Av Prince Pierre

R de la Turbie

R Princesse Caroline

Jardin
Exotique

Entrance
to Jardin Exotique

2

Bd Rainier III

Pl d'Armes

Rampe Major

Av du Port

Av de la Porte Neuve

Q Antoine 1er 18

Av de la Quarantaine

Jardins
St-Martin

Bd Charles III

3

Pl du
Palais

R des Remparts

R Basse

Pl de la
Visitation

Terrasses de
Fontvieille

Le Rocher

R Castro

1

12

Monaco
Ville

Av St-Martin

Musée
Océanographique
de Monaco

Av Pasteur

Av de Fontvieille

R du Gabian

Av Albert II

Pointe
Ste-Barbe

Pointe
St-Martin

P

Av des Papalins

6

Port de
Fontvieille

Stade
Louis II

Av des Papalins

Av des Castelans

Fontvieille

Parc
Fontvieille

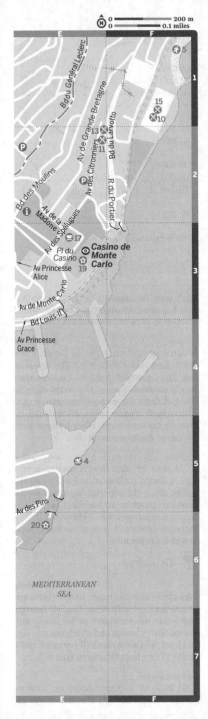

decorated in designer greys, elegant striped fabrics and 'back to nature' bathrooms with bamboo towel racks and elegant wooden furniture. All rooms have little balconies and good views (the higher the better). The outdoor pool is heated only from April to October.

Novotel Monte Carlo   HOTEL €€€

(📞99 99 83 00; www.novotel.com/5275; 16 bd Princesse Charlotte; d from €218; @🛜🎐) Put all your chain-hotel preconceptions aside, for the Novotel Monte Carlo is no ordinary chain hotel. Rooms are bright, spacious and colourful, with bath and shower in every bathroom. Even better, up to two children under 16 can stay for free with their parents (and they throw the breakfast in, too).

Hôtel Port Palace   LUXURY HOTEL €€€

(📞97 97 90 00; www.portpalace.com; 7 av du Président JF Kennedy; r from €249; 🛜) Built into the hillside overlooking the yacht harbor, this discreetly sexy boutique hotel is decked out in fine silks, soft leather and Carrara marble. All rooms have king-sized beds, jacuzzi baths and super views of the port and Le Rocher. The hotel offers a 50% discount on the children's bedroom.

Hôtel Miramar   HOTEL €€

(📞93 30 86 48; www.miramar.monaco-hotel.com; 1 av du Président JF Kennedy; d €145; ❄🛜) This 1950s seaside hotel with rooftop-terrace bar is a great option right by the port. Seven of the 11 rooms have fabulous balconies overlooking the yachts. All rooms were undergoing thorough renovation at the time of research.

🍴 Eating

For those on a budget, a picnic is the best option. There are plenty of parks and benches to sit and take in the atmosphere, and you'll find a raft of sandwich bars and cheap eateries along quai Albert 1er.

TOP CHOICE La Montgolfière   FUSION €€

(📞97 98 61 59; www.lamontgolfiere.mc; 16 rue Basse; mains €21-30; ⊙lunch & dinner Mon, Tue, Thu, Fri, Sun, dinner Sat) This tiny fusion wonder is an unlikely find amidst the touristy jumble of Monaco's historic quarter. But what a great idea Henri and Fabienne Geraci had to breathe new life into the Rocher. The couple have spent a lot of time in Malaysia, and Henri's fusion cuisine is outstanding, as

THE FRENCH RIVIERA & MONACO **MONACO**

Monaco

is Fabienne's welcome in their pocket-sized dining room.

Every day in winter, Henri cooks *bourride*, a salted cod stew typical of Monaco and Nice.

Zelos FUSION €€€
(☑99 99 25 50; 10 av Princesse Grace, Grimaldi Forum; mains €25-30; ⊙dinner; ▥) With enormous chandeliers, intensely blue walls, a ceiling fitted with hundreds of star-like lights and uninterrupted sea views, it's hard to say which makes more of an impression, the setting or the food (modern dishes such as a trio of Carpaccio – sea bass, king crab and salmon). The restaurant also has a huge terrace for magical summer dining.

Café Llorca MODERN FRENCH €€
(☑99 99 29 29; www.cafellorca.mc; 10 av Princesse Grace, Grimaldi Forum; mains €15-26; ⊙lunch; ▥) This new restaurant is Michelin-starred chef Alain Llorca's version of a traditional cafe: the menu is classic French fare (pork loin with sautee potatoes; *daube*, a local beef stew) but elevated to new heights in taste and presentation. In summer, tables are set out on the terrace overlooking the sea.

Mozza ITALIAN €€
(www.mozza.mc; 11 rue du Portier; mains €16-29, lunch menu €14-24; ▤▥) The clue to Mozza's speciality is in the name: mozzarella. You'll find all the traditional Italian fare here, but

don't miss the mozzarella bar: the restaurant has about 10 different varieties, which it serves in platters or as starters.

Cosmopolitan INTERNATIONAL €€
(www.cosmopolitan.mc; 7 rue du Portier; mains €17-31, lunch menu €16-21; ☎▥) The menu of this hip restaurant features timeless classics from all corners of the world such as fish and chips, three-cheese gnocchi or veal cutlets in Béarnaise sauce, all revisited by Cosmo's talented chefs. Wash it down with one of the *many* wines on offer.

Supermarché Casino BOULANGERIE €
(17 bd Albert 1er; pizza slices & sandwiches from €3; ⊙8.30am-10pm Mon-Sat, to 9pm Sun; ▤) It's not so much the supermarket that's worth knowing about as its excellent street-side bakery and pizzeria, which churn out freshly prepared goodies. A saviour for those keen to watch the pennies.

⊒ Drinking

TOP CHOICE **Brasserie de Monaco** MICROBREWERY
(www.brasseriedemonaco.com; 36 rte de la Piscine; ⊙11am-1pm Sun-Thu, 11am-3am Fri & Sat) Tourists and locals rub shoulders at Monaco's only microbrewery, which crafts rich organic ales and lager, and serves tasty (if pricy) antipasti plates. Happy hour runs from 5pm to 8pm.

Cosmopolitan BAR
(☑93 25 78 68; www.cosmopolitan.mc; 7 rue du Portier; ⊙5.45pm-1am; ☎) Whether you're af-

ter cocktails or excellent wine, Cosmopolitan should see you right. With its chocolate-orange decor, contemporary furniture and *The Big Chill* music, it's a nice place to ease yourself into a night out.

Café de Paris CAFE
(www.montecarloresort.com; place du Casino; mains €17-53; ⊘7am-2am) Monaco's best-known cafe has been in business since 1882 and is *the* place to people-watch. Service is brisk and rather snobbish but it's the price you pay for a front-row view of the casino's razzmatazz.

Stars 'n' Bars AMERICAN
(www.starsnbars.com; 6 quai Antoine 1er; ⊘noon-2.30am, closed Mon Oct-May) This Monaco party institution was undergoing a major facelift at the time of our visit but it promised to be back with a bang, with the same American sports-bar atmosphere.

☆ Entertainment

Pack your evening wear for concerts, opera and ballet. The tourist office has a schedule of local events.

Casino de Monte Carlo CASINO
(www.montecarlocasinos.com; place du Casino; Salon Europe/Salons Privés admission €10/20; ⊘Salon Europe noon-late daily, Salons Privés from 4pm Thu-Sun) The drama of watching the poker-faced gamble in Monte Carlo's grand marble-and-gold casino makes the stiff admission fees, stakes and obligatory cloakroom 'tips' almost bearable. To enter the casino, you must be at least 18.

The Salon Europe has English and European roulette and 30/40; the Salons Privés offer European roulette, black jack and *chemin de fer*. A jacket and tie are required for men to enter the Salons Privés and the Salon Ordinaire in the evening.

For more information, see the Monte Carlo Casino illustrated highlight (p868).

Monte Carlo Philharmonic Orchestra CLASSICAL MUSIC
(☑98 06 28 28; www.opmc.mc) Going strong since 1856, the orchestra has maintained the tradition of summer concerts in the Cour d'Honneur (Courtyard of Honour) at the Palais Princier. Tickets (€18 to €80), sold at the Atrium du Casino (☑98 06 28 28; place du Casino; ⊘10am-5.30pm Tue-Sun) in the casino, are like gold dust. The orchestra performs in the principality's various auditoriums the rest of the year.

Open-air Cinema CINEMA
(Chemin des Pêcheurs) Has nightly shows from June to September, specialising in crowd-pleasing blockbusters, mostly in English.

❶ Information

Centre Hospitalier Princesse Grace (Hospital; ☑97 98 97 69; www.chpg.mc; 1 av Pasteur)
Police Station (☑112; 3 rue Louis Notari)
Tourist Office (www.visitmonaco.com; 2a bd des Moulins; ⊘9am-7pm Mon-Sat, 11am-1pm Sun) Smartphone users should download the tourist office's excellent app 'Monaco Travel Guide'.

WORTH A TRIP

ROQUEBRUNE-CAP-MARTIN

Beautiful Cap Martin stretches its languid shores in a sea of crystalline water between Monaco and Menton. The village of Roquebrune-Cap-Martin (pop 13,335) is actually centred on the medieval village of Roquebrune, which towers over the cape (the village and cape are linked by innumerable, *very* steep steps). Roquebrune is delightful, free of tacky souvenir shops. The Château de Roquebrune (www.roquebrune-cap-martin.com; place William Ingram; adult/child €4.50/2.50; ⊘10am-12.30pm & 2-6pm) dates back to the 10th century. It's an atmospheric place, with simple but evocative props of life in medieval times, and the audioguide (available in English) is fascinating.

Of all Roquebrune's steep and tortuous streets, rue Moncollet – with its arcaded passages and stairways carved out of rock – is the most impressive. There are sensational views of the coast from the main village square, Place des Deux Frères. Restaurant Les Deux Frères (☑04 93 28 99 00; www.lesdeuxfreres.com; place des Deux Frères; lunch/dinner menu €28/48; ⊘lunch Wed-Sun, dinner Tue-Sat; ☎) enjoys the same show-stopping views as the square and serves formal, gourmet French fare. It also has a few great value rooms (€75–€110).

Monte Carlo Casino

TIMELINE

1863 Charles III inaugurates the first Casino on the Plateau des Spélugues. **The atrium 1** is a room with a wooden platform from which an orchestra 'enlivens' the gambling.

1864 Hôtel de Paris opens and the area becomes known as the 'Golden Square'.

1865 Construction of **Salon Europe 2**. Cathedral-like, it is lined with onyx columns and lit by eight Bohemian crystal chandeliers weighing 150kg each.

1868 The steam train arrives in Monaco and **Café de Paris 3** is completed.

1878–79 Gambling moves to Hôtel de Paris while Charles Garnier is charged with building a new casino with a miniature replica of the Paris Opera House, **Salle Garnier 4**.

1890 The advent of electricity casts a glow on architect Jules Touzet's newly added **gaming rooms 5** for high rollers.

1903 Inspired by female gamblers, Henri Schmit decorates **Salle Blanche 6** with caryatids and the painting *Les Grâces Florentines*.

1904 Smoking is banned in the gaming rooms and **Salon Rose 7**, a new smoking room, is added.

1910 **Salle Médecin 8**, immense and grand, hosts the high-spending Private Circle.

1966 Celebrations mark 100 years of uninterrupted gambling despite two World Wars.

Salle Blanche
Transformed into a superb bar-lounge in 2012, the Salle Blanche opens onto an outdoor gaming terrace, a must on balmy evenings. The caryatids on the ceiling were modelled on fashionable courtesans like La Belle Otero, who placed her first bet here aged 18.

Salon Rose
Smoking was banned in the gaming rooms after a fraud involving a croupier letting his ash fall on the floor. The gaze of Gallelli's famous cigarillo-smoking nudes are said to follow you around the room, now a restaurant.

Hôtel de Paris

Notice the horse's shiny leg (and testicles) on the lobby's statue of Louis XIV on horseback. Legend has it that rubbing them brings good luck in the casino.

Hôtel de Paris

Salle Garnier
Taking eight months to build and two years to restore (2004–06), the opera's original statuary is rehabilitated using original moulds saved by the creator's grandson. Individual air-con and heating vents are installed beneath each of the 525 seats.

Atrium
The casino's 'lobby', so to speak, is paved in marble and lined with 28 Ionic columns, which support a balustraded gallery canopied with an engraved glass ceiling.

BONNEMAISON JOACHIM ©

Salon Europe
The oldest part of the casino, where they continue to play *trente-et-quarante* and European roulette, which have been played here since 1863. Tip: the bull's-eye windows around the room originally served as security observation points.

COTE D'AZUR/ALAMY ©

Café de Paris
With the arrival of Diaghilev as director of the Monte Carlo Opera in 1911, Café de Paris becomes the go-to address for artists and gamblers. It retains the same high-glamour ambience today. Tip: snag a seat on the terrace and people-watch.

Jardins et Terrasses du Casino

Place du Casino

Salles Touzet
This vast partitioned hall, 21m by 24m, is decorated in the most lavish style: oak, Tonkin mahogany and oriental jasper panelling are offset by vast canvases, Marseille bronzes, Italian mosaics, sculptural reliefs and stained-glass windows.

Terraces, gardens & walkways

Hexagrace mosaic

Fairmont Monte Carlo

Best Views
Wander behind the casino through manicured gardens and gaze across Victor Vasarely's vibrant op-art mosaic, *Hexagrace*, to views of the harbour and the sea.

Salle Médecin
Also known as Salle Empire because of its extravagant Empire-style decor, Monégasque architect François Médecin's gaming room was originally intended for the casino's biggest gamblers. Part of it still remains hidden from prying eyes as a Super Privé room.

❶ Getting There & Away

AIR **Héli-Air Monaco** (☑92 05 00 50; www.heliairmonaco.com) runs helicopter flights between Nice and Monaco's **Héliport** (av des Ligures) several times a day (from €107, 7 minutes).

BUS Bus 100 (€1, every 15 minutes, from 6am to 9pm) goes to Nice (45 minutes) and Menton (40 minutes) along the Corniche Inférieure. Bus 110 (€18, hourly) goes to Nice Côte d'Azur airport (40 minutes). Both services stop at place d'Armes and the **stop** on bd des Moulins. There are also four night services (10pm-3.45am) on Thursdays, Fridays and Saturdays.

CAR Only Monaco and Alpes-Maritimes (06) registered cars can access Monaco Ville. If you decide to drive, park in one of the numerous underground carparks.

TRAIN Services run about every 20 minutes east to Menton (€2, 15 minutes) and west to Nice (€3.60, 25 minutes). Access to the station is through pedestrian tunnels and escalators from 6 av Prince Pierre de Monaco, pont Ste-Dévote, place Ste-Dévote and bd de la Belgique. The last trains leave around 11pm.

❶ Getting Around

BUS Monaco's urban bus system has five lines, bizarrely numbered one to six without the three. Line 2 links Monaco Ville to Monte Carlo and then loops back to the Jardin Exotique. Line 4 links the train station with the tourist office, the casino and Plage du Larvotto. Tickets are €1.

NIGHT BUS The Bus de Soirée (9.20pm-12.30am) follows one big loop around town; it is extended to 4am on Fridays and Saturdays. Tickets are €1.

LIFTS A system of escalators and public lifts links the steep streets. They operate either 24 hours or 6am to midnight or 1am.

TAXI Call **Taxi Monégasque Prestige** (☑08 20 20 98 98; www.taximonacoprestige.com).

FRUITY FÊTE

Menton's quirky two-week **Fête du Citron** (Lemon Festival; www.feteducitron.com; ☉Feb) in February sees sculptures and decorative floats made from tonnes of lemons weave processions along the seafront. Afterwards, the monumental lemon creations are dismantled and the fruit sold off at bargain prices in front of Palais de l'Europe. Each year the festival follows a different theme.

Menton

POP 29,361

Menton used to be famous for two things: its lemons and its exceptionally sunny climate. We're willing to bet our bottom dollar, however, that the city will soon add Cocteau as its third claim to fame, thanks to the opening of the fantastic Musée Jean Cocteau Collection Séverin Wunderman in November 2011.

◉ Sights & Activities

The town's epicentre is pedestrian rue St-Michel, where ice-cream parlours and souvenir shops jostle for space.

TOP CHOICE Musée Jean Cocteau Collection Séverin Wunderman GALLERY
(2 quai Monléon; adult/student/child €6/3/free; ☉10am-6pm Wed-Mon) In 2005, art collector Séverin Wunderman donated some 1500 Cocteau works to Menton, on the condition that the town build a dedicated Cocteau museum. And what a museum Menton built: opened in 2011, the futuristic, low-rise building has breathed new life into the slumbering city and provides a wonderful space to try to make sense of Cocteau's eclectic work.

The museum's collection focuses on Cocteau's graphic works; displays are organised chronologically and thematically, from Cocteau's early works as an illustrator to his cinematographic swansong, the convoluted and abstract *Testament of Orpheus* (in which he stages his own death).

Explanations are in French, English and Italian throughout; audioguides (€2) are also available. The admission fee lets you in at the Musée du Bastion, which Cocteau designed.

Musée du Bastion ART MUSEUM
(quai Napoléon III; combined admission with Musée Jean Cocteau adult/student/child €6/3/free; ☉10am-6pm Wed-Mon) Cocteau loved Menton. It was following a stroll along the seaside that he got the idea of turning the disused 17th-century seafront bastion into a monument to his work. He restored the building himself, decorating the alcoves, outer walls and reception hall with pebble mosaics. The works on display change regularly.

Vieille Ville HISTORIC QUARTER
Menton's old town is a cascade of pastel-coloured buildings. Meander the historic quarter all the way to the Cimetière du

Vieux Château (montée du Souvenir; ☺7am-8pm May-Sep, to 6pm Oct-Apr) for great views. From place du Cap a ramp leads to southern France's grandest baroque church, the Italianate Basilique St-Michel Archange (place de l'Église St-Michel; ☺10am-noon & 3-5.15pm Mon-Fri, 3-5.15pm Sat & Sun); its creamy façade is flanked by a 35m-tall clock tower and 53m-tall steeple (built 1701–03).

Jardin de la Serre de la Madone   GARDEN
(☑04 93 57 73 90; www.serredelamadone.com; 74 rte de Gorbio; adult/student/child €8/4/free; ☺10am-6pm Tue-Sun) Beautiful if slightly unkempt, this garden was designed by American botanist Lawrence Johnston. He planted dozens of rare plants picked up from his travels around the world. Abandoned for decades, it is slowly being restored. Guided tours take place daily at 3pm. Take bus 7 to the 'Serre de la Madone' stop.

🛏 Sleeping & Eating

Accommodation gets booked up months in advance for the Fête du Citron in February (prices also soar) so plan ahead.

TOP
CHOICE Hôtel Napoléon   BOUTIQUE HOTEL €€
(☑04 93 35 89 50; www.napoleon-menton.com; 29 porte de France; s/d from €139/149; ✴@☎✲) Standing tall on the seafront, the Napoléon is Menton's most stylish option. Everything from the pool, the restaurant-bar and the back garden (a heaven of freshness in summer) has been beautifully designed. Rooms come in shades of beige and red; all are equipped with iPod docking stations. Sea-facing rooms also have balconies but are a little noisier because of the traffic.

The two top-floor suites (including one decorated with Cocteau memorabilia) are sensational, with floor to ceiling windows, larger balconies and even sea views from the bath tub!

Ibis Styles Menton   DESIGN HOTEL €€
(☑04 92 10 95 25; www.accorhotels.com; 10 rue Villarey; d/q €110/140; ✴@☎) A great choice in the centre of town, the All Seasons is a minimalist affair, with an all-white decor brightened up by one painted wall in each room (turquoise, red, pink etc, different on each floor). Bathrooms are beautifully designed and the staff are charming. Rates include buffet breakfast.

Rooms from the 2nd floor up have balconies and the family rooms on the top floor have fantastic views.

Hôtel Lemon   HOTEL €
(☑04 93 28 63 63; www.hotel-lemon.com; 10 rue Albert 1er; s/d/tr/q €55/59/75/115; ☎) Housed in a nicely renovated 19th-century villa, Hôtel Lemon has spacious, minimalist rooms in shades of white and funky bright red or lemon-yellow bathrooms. Wi-fi currently works only on the ground floor.

A Braïjade
Méridiounale   TRADITIONAL FRENCH €€
(www.abraijade.fr; 66 rue longue; menu €34, mains €18-25; ☺Thu-Tue) In a beautiful stone-walled dining room framed by heavy wooden beams, A Braïjade is the only restaurant in the old town and has made the best of it. The house speciality is flambé skewers (the kebab is flambéed at your table). The *menu*, which includes an *apéritif*, glass of local wine and *digestif*, is good value.

Sucre & Salés   CAFÉ €
(8 promenade Maréchal Leclerc; cakes/sandwiches €3/5; ☺6.30am-8pm; ☎) Conveniently located opposite the bus station, Sucre & Salés is a contemporary spot to enjoy a coffee, cake or well-stuffed baguette sandwich.

❶ Information

Tourist Office (☑04 92 41 76 76; www. tourisme-menton.fr; 8 av Boyer; ☺9am-7pm)

❶ Getting There & Away

BUS Bus 100 (€1, every 15 minutes) goes to Nice (1½ hours) via Monaco (40 minutes) and the Corniche Inférieure. Bus 110 links Menton with Nice-Côte d'Azur airport (€18, one hour, hourly).

TRAIN There are regular services (half-hourly) to Ventimiglia in Italy (€2.30, 9 minutes), Monaco (€2, 11 minutes) and Nice (€4.80, 35 minutes).

Corsica

Best Places to Eat

» La Sassa (p881)
» Le Lavezzi (p878)
» Le MataHari (p884)
» U Libecciu (p882)
» Au Vieux Moulin (p880)

Best Places to Stay

» A Pignata (p898)
» Domaine de Licetto (p894)
» Hôtel Kallisté (p889)
» Hôtel Restaurant La Corniche (p880)
» Les Roches Rouges (p888)

Why Go?

Corsica is for (beach) lovers...and culture buffs...and hikers ...and divers...and families. It combines vast stretches of shoreline with the beauty of the mountains, plenty of activities for your body and some rich history to engage your mind. Jutting out of the Med like an impregnable fortress, Corsica resembles a miniature continent, with astounding geographical diversity. Within half an hour, the landscape morphs from glittering bays, glitzy coastal cities and fabulous beaches to sawtooth peaks, breathtaking valleys, dense forests and enigmatic hilltop villages. The scenery that unfurls along the island's crooked roads will have you constantly stopping to whip out your camera.

Though Corsica has officially been part of France for over 200 years, it feels different from the mainland in everything from customs and cuisine to language and character, and that's part of its appeal.

When to Go
Ajaccio

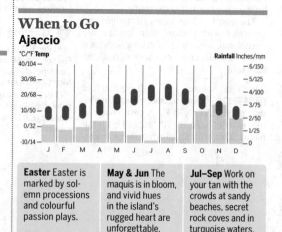

Easter Easter is marked by solemn processions and colourful passion plays.

May & Jun The maquis is in bloom, and vivid hues in the island's rugged heart are unforgettable.

Jul–Sep Work on your tan with the crowds at sandy beaches, secret rock coves and in turquoise waters.

Corsica Highlights

1 Cruise sapphire waters in the **Réserve Naturelle de Scandola** (p886)

2 Explore wild and remote **Cap Corse** (p879) by way of winding coastal roads

3 See red, blazing red, between fantastic rock formations in **Les Calanques de Piana** (p888)

4 Slip into serene turquoise waters at **Plage de Palombaggia** (p895) and **Plage de Santa Giulia** (p895)

5 Admire the work of prehistoric people – see where they lived and what they built – at **Filitosa** (p894)

6 Bone up on Bonaparte around Napoléon's home town, **Ajaccio** (p887)

7 Ride the rickety **Tramway de la Balagne** (p882) along the coast

8 Discover island paradise with a boat trip to the **Îles Lavezzi** (p893)

9 Hike along the **Bonifacio coastal path** (p893) from citadel to lighthouse, with awesome cliff vistas

10 Test your nerves, fitness and head for heights on **Bonifacio**'s (p892) extraordinary 187-step Escalier du Roi d'Aragon down to the sea

NAPOLÉON, SON OF CORSICA?

Despite Ajaccio's endless Napoléonic connections, *le petit caporal*'s attitude to his home island was rather ambivalent. Born to an Italian father and a Corsican mother, and largely educated in France (where he was mercilessly mocked for his provincial Corsican accent), Napoléon actually spent relatively little time on the island, and never returned following his coronation as emperor of France in 1804. But there's no doubt that Napoléon's Corsican roots exerted a powerful hold on his imagination – famously, while exiled on Elba, he is said to have claimed he could recognise his homeland purely from the scent of the maquis.

History

From the 11th to 13th centuries Corsica was ruled by the Italian city-state of Pisa, superseded in 1284 by its arch-rival, Genoa. To prevent seaborne raids, a massive system of coastal citadels and watchtowers was constructed, many of which still ring the coastline.

In 1755, after 25 years of sporadic warfare against the Genoese, Corsicans declared their independence, led by Pascal Paoli (1725–1807). Under Paoli's rule they established the National Assembly and founded the most democratic constitution in Europe.

Corsicans made the inland town of Corte their capital, but the island's independence was short lived. In 1768 the Genoese ceded Corsica to Louis XV, whose troops crushed Paoli's army in 1769. The island has since been part of France, except for 1794–96, when it was briefly under English domination.

A movement for Corsican autonomy was formed in the 1960s to combat what some perceived as France's 'colonialist' policy towards the island. In 1976, the Front de Libération Nationale de la Corse (FLNC) was created, and talk of autonomy increasingly turned to claims for full independence. By the 1990s the FLNC had broken into multiple splinter groups, most armed and mostly violent. This said, relatively few Corsicans support the separatist movements. In 2003 a long-awaited referendum, which would have granted the island greater autonomy, was rejected despite a nail-biting electoral race. Nevertheless, the nationalist issue remains a burning topic, but tourists are always made welcome.

ⓘ Getting There & Away

Air

Corsica has four airports: Ajaccio, Bastia, Calvi and Figari (north of Bonifacio), served by frequent flights year-round from many French mainland airports. From May until September there are also frequent flights to Europe and elsewhere; you'll likely need to fly via mainland France if you're heading internationally at other times of the year.

Boat

TO/FROM MAINLAND FRANCE Corsica's six ferry ports (Ajaccio, Bastia, Calvi, Île Rousse, Porto-Vecchio and Propriano) can be reached from Nice, Marseille and Toulon. Ferry companies:

Corsica Ferries (www.corsica-ferries.fr) Year-round from Nice to Ajaccio, Bastia, Calvi and Île Rousse, and from Toulon to Ajaccio, Bastia and Île Rousse. Crossings last 5½ hours to 6¼ hours.

La Méridionale (www.lameridionale.fr) Year-round overnight sailings from Marseille to Ajaccio, Bastia and Propriano (all take 12 hours).

SNCM (www.sncm.fr) April to September, it operates speedy *navires à grande vitesse* (NGVs) from Nice to Île Rousse (3½ hours), Ajaccio (five hours) and Bastia (4½ hours). Regular ferries run from Marseille to Ajaccio (9¾ hours), Bastia (10 hours), Île Rousse (10 hours), Porto-Vecchio (13 hours) and Propriano (9¼ hours).

Up to 10 boats a day sail in high season, dropping to a single daily sailing in winter; reservations are essential in summer. The fare structure varies dramatically – anything from €25 to €100 for a foot passenger – depending on route, crossing time, class of comfort and size of vehicle (if any). Various discounts and deals are offered throughout the year. In July and August expect to pay around €350 return for a car and two passengers via NGV from Nice to Ajaccio.

TO/FROM ITALY
Corsica Ferries (www.corsicaferries.com) Livorno and Savona to Bastia; Savona to Calvi and Île Rousse (June to August).

La Méridionale (www.lameridionale.fr) Ferries year round between Porto Torres (Sardinia) and Propriano.

Moby Lines (www.moby.it) Seasonal ferries to Bastia from Genoa and Livorno, and to Bonifacio from Santa Teresa Gallura (Sardinia).

Saremar (www.saremar.it) Runs seasonal ferry services between Santa Teresa Gallura (Sardinia) and Bonifacio.

ⓘ Getting Around

By far the best way to get around Corsica is by car, but navigating the island's narrow, twisting roads is not easy. A detailed road map is indispensable. The twin-set of IGN *Cartes de Promenade* maps (map 73 for the north, 74 for the south) at a scale of 1:100,000 is excellent, as is Michelin's yellow-jacketed *Corse-du-Sud, Haute-Corse* (map 345), covering the entire island in a scale of 1:150,000.

Bus services are lean and inconvenient. The train is an attractive, if limited option, running through stunning countryside between Bastia

and Ajaccio, with a branch route to Calvi. **Corsica Bus & Train** (www.corsicabus.org) is a tip-top one-stop website for viewing current bus and train timetables island-wide.

BASTIA & CAP CORSE

Bastia

POP 44,170

Filled with heart, soul and character, the bustling old port of Bastia is a good surprise. Sure, it might not measure up to the sexy style of Ajaccio or the architectural appeal of Bonifacio, but it has an irresistible

---

CORSICAN TEMPTATIONS

Cheese

Gourmands will delight in the flavours and textures of Corsican cheeses, from hard, tangy Tomme Corse (semihard ewe's milk cheese) to the king of the island's cheeses, Brocciu, a crumbly white ewe's or goat's milk cheese that can only be eaten *frais* (fresh) – a real creamy treat – between December and late June; *sec* (dried) or *demi-sec* (half-dried) *are* summertime's consolation prizes. Consume Corsica's signature cheese and revel in the knowledge that Brocciu is the only French Appellation d'Origine Protégée (AOC) cheese made from the milk's whey.

Charcuterie

Prisuttu (ham matured for 18 months), *lonzu* (tender smoked pork fillet, best tasted in springtime), *coppa* (shoulder, air-dried for five months), seasonal *figatellu* (pork liver sausage, always U-shaped, dried and smoked over a chestnut-wood fire, eaten November to April), *salamu* (salami), *terrine de sanglier* (wild-boar pâté): wherever you go, you'll find a wide array of cured meats on offer – several seasonal – made from free-range pigs that feed on chestnuts.

Sweet Treats

From *canistrelli* (biscuits made with almonds, walnuts, lemon or aniseed) and *frappe* (little fritters made from chestnut flour) to *fiadone* (a light flan made with cheese, lemon and egg) and *falculelli* (fried Brocciu cheese served on a chestnut leaf), Corsica's dessert menu is sure to torment the sweet tooth. Oh, and there are devilish ice creams, too, with original flavours such as myrtle, Brocciu or chestnut. Glaces Geronimi (p886) in Sagone, 35km north of Ajaccio, is Corsia's most gourmet *glacier* (ice-cream maker).

Wine & Liqueurs

Corsica has nine AOC-labelled wines and countless fruit liqueurs, including Cap Corse Mattei, a popular aperitif (out of this world when thrown in the pot with mussels). Areas to watch out for are Patrimonio, Cap Corse, Ajaccio, Sartène and Porto-Vecchio.

Olive Oil

La Balagne and L'Alta Rocca produce extremely aromatic olive oils, available direct from the producer.

Seafood

Fish lovers will be in heaven. Lobster, oysters, mussels, squid, sea bass...Corsica has them all, but stick to reputable fish restaurants.

Bastia

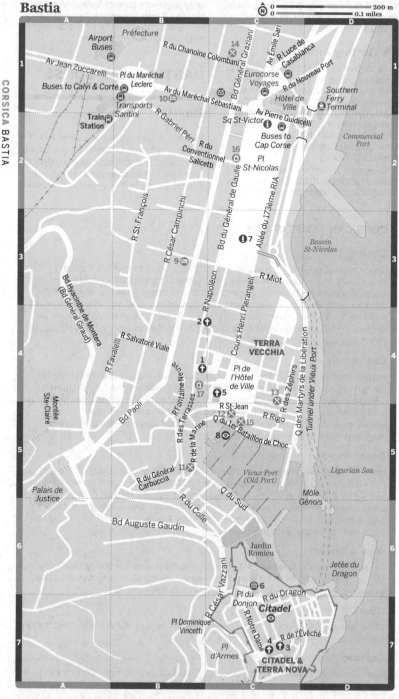

N
0   200 m
0   0.1 miles

Airport Buses
Préfecture
R du Chanoine Colombani
14
Av Émile Sari
R Luce de Casabianca
Av Jean Zuccarelli
Pl du Maréchal Leclerc
Bd Général Graziani
Eurocorse Voyages
R du Nouveau Port
Buses to Calvi & Corte
Av du Maréchal Sébastiani
Hôtel de Ville
Southern Ferry Terminal
Transports Santini
10
Train Station
R Gabriel Péri
Av Pierre Guidicelli
Commercial Port
R du Conventionnel Salicetti
Sq St-Victor
Buses to Cap Corse
R St-François
16
Pl St-Nicolas
R César Campinchi
Bd du Général de Gaulle
9
7
Bassin St-Nicolas
Bd Hyacinthe de Montera (Bd Général Giraud)
R Napoléon
R Miot
R Salvatoré Viale
2
Cours Henri Pierangeli
TERRA VECCHIA
R Favalelli
Montée Ste-Claire
1
R des Terrasses
Pl de l'Hôtel de Ville
13
Allée du 173ème RIA
R Fontaine Neuve
17
5
R des Zéphirs
Bd Paoli
12
R St-Jean
R Rigo
Q des Martyrs de la Libération
15
8
Q du 1er Bataillon de Choc
Tunnel under Vieux Port
R de la Marine
11
R du Général Carbuccia
Vieux Port (Old Port)
Ligurian Sea
Palais de Justice
R du Colle
Q du Sud
Môle Génois
Bd Auguste Gaudin
Jardin Romieu
Jetée du Dragon
R César Vazzani
6
R du Dragon
Pl du Donjon
Citadel
Pl Dominique Vincetti
R Notre Dame
Pl d'Armes
4
R de l'Évêché
3
CITADEL & TERRA NOVA

magnetism. Don't be put off by its hectic traffic, peeling paintwork and ramshackle tenement blocks. Bastia is an authentic snapshot of modern-day Corsica, a lived-in city that's resisted the urge to polish up its image just to please the tourists. Allow yourself at least a day to take in the city's seething old port, compelling museum and dramatic citadel.

◉ Sights

Place St-Nicolas   SQUARE
Bastia's buzzing focal point is the 19th-century square of place St-Nicolas, which sprawls along the seafront between the ferry port and the harbour. Named after the patron saint of sailors – a nod to Corsica's seagoing heritage – the square is lined with plane trees and a string of attractive terrace cafes along its western edge, as well as a statue of Napoléon Bonaparte (place St-Nicolas).

Terra Vecchia   HISTORIC QUARTER
A spiderweb of narrow lanes tangles south towards the old port and Terra Vecchia, a muddle of crumbling apartments and balconied blocks. Shady place de l'Hôtel de Ville hosts Bastia's lively morning market Tuesday to Saturday. One block west, baroque Chapelle de l'Immaculée Conception (rue des Terrasses), with its elaborately painted barrel-vaulted ceiling, briefly served as the seat of the short-lived Anglo-Corsican parliament in 1795. Further north is Chapelle St-Roch (rue Napoléon), with an 18th-century organ and *trompe l'œil* roof.

Vieux Port   HARBOUR
Immediately south of Terra Vecchia is the Vieux Port (Old Port), ringed by pastel-coloured tenements and buzzy brasseries, as well as the twin-towered Église St-Jean Baptiste (4 rue du Cardinal Viale Préla). The best views of the harbour are from the hillside park of Jardin Romieu, reached via a gorgeous old stately staircase that twists uphill from the waterfront.

Citadel   HISTORIC QUARTER
Above Jardin Romieu looms Bastia's amber-hued citadel, built from the 15th to 17th centuries as a stronghold for the city's Genoese masters. Inside the Palais des Gouverneurs houses the Musée d'Histoire de Bastia (☏04 95 31 09 12; www.musee-bastia.com; place du Donjon; admission €5; ⊙10am-7.30pm Tue-Sun Jul–mid-Sep, shorter hours mid-Sep–Jun). A few streets south, don't miss the majestic Église Ste-Marie (rue de l'Évêché) and nearby Église Ste-Croix (rue de l'Évêché), featuring gilded ceilings and a mysterious black-oak crucifix found in the sea in 1428.

⌨ Sleeping

For rural souls who prefer 'in the sticks' to 'urban', the perfect compromise is several lovely addresses accessed via the coastal road that snakes north from the city onto Cap Corse.

TOP CHOICE Hôtel Central   HOTEL €€
(☏04 95 31 71 12; www.centralhotel.fr; 3 rue Miot; s €77, d €90; ☏) From the vintage black-and-white tiled floor in the entrance to the sweeping staircase and eclectic jumble of plant pots in the minuscule interior courtyard, this family-run address oozes 1940s grace. The hotel's pedigree dates back to 1941 and the vintage furnishings inside the 19th-century building don't disappoint.

Bastia

Hôtel Les Voyageurs
HOTEL €€

(☑04 95 34 90 80; www.hotel-lesvoyageurs.com; 9 av Maréchal Sébastiani; s €60-85, d €75-100, q €110-150; ❄🛜) In a city where parking can be tricky, the garage here is a big plus. Combine this with a gorgeous ginger facade, shabby-chic oyster-grey shutters and a modern three-star interior, and you'll be well pleased. Overnight parking costs €7.

Hôtel L'Alivi
HOTEL €€

(☑04 95 55 00 00; www.hotel-alivi.com; rte du Cap; s €80-105, d €95-140, tr €135-235, q €160-235; ⊙mid-Mar–Oct; ❄@🛜🏊) The building is nothing to write home about, but the staggering sea view from its windows is! Smack on the northbound coastal road from Bastia to Cap Corse, this three-star pad spoils guests with a shore-side location wrapped around a glistening pool, stylish rooms and a contemporary restaurant.

🍴 Eating

Tasty breakfast, lunch, dinner and snack-any-time-of-day options abound around the old port and along quai des Martyrs. The old town rabbit warren squirrels away several fabulous addresses. Market stalls packed with local produce spill across place de l'Hôtel de Ville every Saturday and Sunday morning.

Le Lavezzi
MODERN FRENCH €€

(☑04 95 31 05 73; 8 rue St-Jean; mains €20-35, lunch menus €19) A boutique address that design-loving gourmets will love, Le Lavezzi is completely different. Its artsy interior – think polished concrete turquoise floor, white-washed walls and brightly coloured Alexander McQueen–style chairs – is fabulous and funky. But the real heart-stealer is the twinset of 1st-floor balconies above the water with prime old-port views. Modern cuisine injects a fusion zest into classic meat and fish dishes.

Petite Marie
CORSICAN €

(☑04 95 32 47 83; 2 rue des Zéphyrs; mains €16-19; ⊙dinner Mon-Sat) Everything is home-baked at Little Marie, a gem of a bolt-hole hidden away in an alley a couple of blocks from the Vieux Port. Do as locals do and kick-start your feast with *friture de rougets* (battered, fried red mullet) followed by grilled crayfish or a feisty dish of crayfish pasta. No frozen *frites* (fries) – only hand-cut, homemade – and no credit cards.

Chez Huguette
SEAFOOD €€

(☑04 95 31 37 60; rue de la Marine; mains €14-23; ⊙lunch & dinner Mon-Sat, dinner Sun) If fresh seafood is your muse, bag a table by the water at Chez Huguette. It's set a little apart from the line-up of restaurants at the Vieux Port, and rightly so: posher than the rest, this is white-tablecloth dining enjoyed by Bastians since 1969. For a real treat, go for the locally caught *langoustes* (crayfish; €18 per 100g).

🛍 Shopping

LN Mattei
FOOD, DRINK

(www.capcorsemattei.com; 15 bd Général de Gaulle) Iconic boutique for visiting gourmets. Locally milled chestnut flour, *sel à la figue* (fig-scented salt), Corsican *marrons* (chestnuts) preserved in *l'eau de vie* (brandy) or a simple bag of peanuts spiced with *myrte* (myrtle) – the choice of island delicacies is rich, tempting and irresistible.

Santa Catalina
FOOD, DRINK

(8 rue des Terrasses) In season, fresh Brocciu cheese is among the many delicious local delicacies stocked at this packed, pocket-size culinary boutique.

ℹ Information

Tourist office (☑04 95 54 20 40; www.bastia-tourisme.com; place St-Nicolas; ⊙8am-6pm Mon-Sat, to noon Sun)

ℹ Getting There & Away

AIR **Aéroport Bastia-Poretta** (www.bastia.aeroport.fr), 24km south of the city, is linked by

---

DON'T MISS

CORSICAN ICE

Wrapping your lips around a rich Corsican ice cream, flavoured with one of the island's distinctive edible products, is an essential part of the Bastia experience. And no address does it better than Raugi (2 rue du Chanoine Colombani; one/two/three scoops €1.30/2.60/3.90, cups €5-20), an ice-cream house dating to 1937, with its main cafe in town and a waterfront takeaway parlour (quai du 1er Bataillon de Choc) at the old port. Flavours range from bog-standard raspberry, lemon and so on to Corsican chestnut, mandarin, fig, aromatic *senteur de maquis* (scent of Corsican herbal scrubland) and sweet *myrte* (myrtle). Forget the chocolate flake; top it off with a *canistrelli* (local biscuit) stuck in the top.

bus (€9, 35 minutes, 10 daily) with the Préfecture building in town. By taxi, count on around €42/58 by day/night.

BOAT Bastia Port (www.bastia.port.fr) has two ferry terminals; ferry companies have information offices in the Southern Ferry Terminal, usually open for same-day ticket sales a couple of hours before sailings. Ferries sail to/from Marseille, Toulon and Nice (mainland France), and Livorno, Savona, Piombino and Genoa (Italy).

Corsica Ferries (☑08 25 09 50 95; www.corsica-ferries.fr; 5bis rue Chanoine Leschi)

La Méridionale (☑08 10 20 13 20; www.lameridionale.fr; Port de Commerce)

Moby Lines (☑04 95 34 84 94; www.mobylines.com; 4 rue du Commandant Luce de Casabianca)

SNCM (☑32 60; www.sncm.fr)

BUS & TRAIN The **bus station** (1 rue du Nouveau Port) is north of place St-Nicolas and bus stops are scattered around town. Many buses depart from in front of Bastia **train station** (av Maréchal Sébastiani), the departure point for daily trains to Ajaccio (€25, 3¾ hours, four daily) via Corte (1¾ hours), and Calvi (three hours, three or four daily) via Île Rousse.

Autocars Cortenais (☑04 95 46 02 12; www.autocars-cortenais.com) Buses to Corte (€11, 1½ hours, three times weekly) depart from in front of the train station.

Eurocorse Voyages (☑04 95 31 73 76; www.eurocorse.com; 1 rue Nouveau Port) Buses to Ajaccio (€21, three hours) via Corte (€11.50, two hours) depart twice daily except on Sunday from Bastia bus station.

Les Rapides Bleus (☑04 95 31 03 79; www.rapides-bleus.com; 1 av Maréchal Sébastiani) Buses leave from in front of the post office to Porto-Vecchio (€22, three hours) twice daily except Sunday.

Transports Santini (☑04 95 37 02 98) Seasonal buses to Île Rousse (€15, 1¾ hours, six weekly) leave from the train station.

Cap Corse

This spiny northeastern peninsula stands out from the rest of Corsica. About 40km long and 10km wide, Cap Corse resembles a giant geographical finger poked towards mainland France. Beguiling coastal fishing villages and small settlements perched precariously up in the hills seduce time and again, as does a coastline dotted with enigmatic Genoese watchtowers, jagged coves and rocky cliffs. Be prepared for some adventurous driving; although the peninsula is only 40km long, the narrow road that rounds its coast (the D80) crams in 120km

---

of switchback curves and breathtaking drops into the sea.

ERBALUNGA
From Bastia, the coast unfurls through seaside resorts and tiny beaches towards this quaint harbour village, 9km to the north. Wander down to Erbalunga's cute village square and quayside, casually strewn with well-used fishing boats and tempting restaurant terraces. Narrow alleys lead through shady courtyards to a romantic, 16th-century Genoese tower by the water. Each August during the Festival d'Erbalunga, open-air concerts fill the village's central square.

Overlooking the main road through the village, Hôtel Demeure Castel Brando (☑04 95 30 10 30; www.castelbrando.com; rte Principale; d €135-165, ste €149-245; ☺late Mar–mid-Nov; ❄@🛜☂) is a dreamy, creamy, mid-19th-century mansion, with sage-green shutters and lush palm-shaded gardens wrapped around a pool. Guests can rent a bicycle (€15 per day) or sea kayak (€25 per half-day) to explore, or simply flop out after a meal to remember at Le Pirate (☑04 95 33 24 20; www.restaurantlepirate.com; mains €31-55, lunch menus €38, dinner menus €68-90; ☺lunch & dinner daily Mar-Dec, closed Mon & Tue low season), an award-winning restaurant in the village heart, with a terrace overlooking the harbour – magic on starry summer evenings. A Piazzetta (☑04 95 33 28 69; place d'Erbalunga; mains €16-20; ☺lunch & dinner daily Apr-Oct), with chairs beneath an ancient plane tree, is a cheaper choice with a quintessential, traditional village-square vibe.

DON'T MISS

SEA-VIEW SUBLIMITY

No single address leaves guests as smitten as Hôtel Restaurant La Corniche (☎04 95 31 40 98; www.hotel-lacorniche.com; s/d/tr/q €76/80/117/142, 2-/3-/5-course menus €26/30/69; ☺Feb-Dec). Perched high in the hilltop village of San Martino di Lota, 8km north of Bastia, this family-run hotel with a buttermilk façade and olive-green wooden shutters has wooed travellers and gourmets since 1934 with its enormous sea views and fine cooking. An elderly Madame Anziani, whose parents opened La Corniche, lingers endearingly at the front door, while her son runs the front desk and shows guests to their rooms. Summertime ushers in dreamy lounging in the bijou back garden, by the pool or on the front porch terrace that stares out to sea. Perfect the experience with dinner in the much-lauded restaurant, where produce is locally sourced; the *beignets de fromage frais* (battered fromage frais fritters) are, quite frankly, out of this world. Advance reservations recommended.

MACINAGGIO

The hub of the eastern cape, Macinaggio has a pleasant harbour with the island's best moorings and great boat trips: in July and August, the San Paulu (☎06 14 78 14 16; www.sanpaulu.com; port de Plaisance; ☺), which docks opposite the harbourside tourist office (www.ot-rogliano-macinaggio.com; port de Plaisance; ☺9am-noon & 2-5pm Mon-Fri), cruises to the remote village of Barcaggio (round trip adult/child €23/12, two hours). The return trip takes a turn around the nature reserve of Îles Finocchiarola, an important breeding site for seabirds.

Hikers will love the Sentiers des Douaniers (Customs Officers' Trail), a rugged coastal path that laces the northernmost tip of the cape, linking Macinaggio with Barcaggio and Centuri.

CENTURI

Crayfish, anyone? The tiny, boat-crammed harbour of Centuri is home to the most important crayfish fleet on the island: eight boats worked by three rival rock-lobster fishing families. Among the cluster of seafood eateries on the waterfront, two addresses stand out for their legendary *pâtes a la langouste* (crayfish with pasta), a local dish in season early April to early October: get your hands deliciously sticky with a boisterous local crowd at A Macciotta (☎04 95 35 64 12; port de Centuri; menus €19.50-24.50; ☺lunch & dinner daily May-Oct), a buzzing no-frills bistro down at the old harbour; or hobnob with a chichi set at up-market Au Vieux Moulin (☎04 95 35 60 15; www.le-vieux-moulin.net; d €100-230, mains €20-48; ☺lunch & dinner daily May-Oct), a hotel-restaurant at the top of the village. Dining at Au Vieux Moulin is white-tablecloth elegant, double rooms are stylish, and the crayfish pasta is rich, scrumptious and giant. The Old Mill's *araignée de mer,* a (very large) local king crab, translates as gastronomic heaven.

Right by the water at the Vieux Port, Hôtel du Pêcheur (☎04 95 35 60 14; d €65-80; ☺May-Oct) sits snug in an old building with Bordeaux shutters, vintage in age and oozing retro charm. Rooms are without pretension and as cheap as chips for this pricey neck of the woods.

The Oscar for most dramatic location goes to Le Saint Jean (☎04 95 47 71 71; www.lesaintjean.net; Hameau de Botticella; s €70-100, d €75-125, tr €105-140), an isolated ochre-coloured hotel-restaurant on a mountain pass with a top-of-the-world view out to pinprick Île de la Giraglia that simply amazes. Its nine rooms are modern and themed, and dining alfresco on its restaurant terrace is out of this world. Find Le Saint Jean 8km north of Centuri, on the eastern side of the Col de la Serra near Botticella.

NONZA

Clinging to the flanks of a rocky pinnacle crowned with a Genoese watchtower, Nonza is easily the most attractive village on the cape's western coast. With its jumble of schist-roofed stone houses looking ready to tumble down the steep hillside onto the black-pebble beach far below, it fits the picture-postcard ideal. Scramble down the rocky path, past walled lemon groves, to the black beach, a legacy of the asbestos mine that operated on the coast here between 1941 and 1965. The beach's polluted past does little to inspire confidence, but locals certainly do not seem worried about it, given the summertime crowds that pack out its pebbly shoreline.

Sights

Église Ste-Julie
CHURCH

Nonza's picture-postcard church, impossible to miss on the tiny village square, is well worth a peek for its polychrome marble altar created in Florence in 1693.

Tour de Nonza
RUIN

(Nonza Watchtower) From the village church, weave your way up between rocks and sun-warmed cacti to the Tour de Nonza. The old Genoese watchtower, one of Corsica's best kept, boasts staggering coastal views (and, unfortunately, a ticky-tacky souvenir shop inside its thick stone walls).

Sleeping & Eating

TOP CHOICE / Casa Maria
B&B €€

(📱04 95 37 80 95; www.casamaria.fr; chemin de la Tour; d €95-165; ⊘Apr–mid-Oct; ❄️🛜) A bewitching little hideaway in the heart of the village, this five-room *chambre d'hôte* (B&B) sits snug in a coolly refurbished 18th-century mansion. Four of its five rooms revel in sea views, and three – including a great one for families – sit harmoniously beneath the sloping roof. In summer, breakfast beneath a vine-wrapped pergola in the bijou back garden.

Le Relais du Cap
B&B €

(📱04 95 37 86 53; www.relaisducap.com; Marine de Negru; d with shared bathroom €50-80, breakfast €7; ⊘Apr-Oct; 🛜) For the ultimate seaside escape, this is hard to beat. Tucked improbably between a towering cliff and a pocket-size pebble beach, this pert little B&B features four unpretentious yet neat doubles, all with staggering sunset-facing sea views. No air-con here, but who needs it with the sea breezes puffing in? Another draw is the copious breakfast served on a terrace overlooking the sea. It's 4km south of Nonza.

TOP CHOICE / La Sassa
GRILLED MEAT €€

(📱04 95 35 55 26; www.lasassa.com; Tour de Nonza; mains €15-30; ⊘lunch daily mid-Apr–Oct, dinner daily Jul & Aug) Few addresses are as inspirational. Built between rocks in the shade of Nonza's Genoese watchtower, this strictly alfresco diner – it has no interior – cooks up feisty beef steaks on an open grill, while guests look on from rickety tables scattered between olive trees across the rocky-outcrop terrace. Sea views, predictably, are heady and gargantuan.

LA BALAGNE

This striking region blends history, culture and beach, with a dash of Mediterranean glam sealing the deal. Refine your art of sampling *la dolce vita* in Calvi and Île Rousse before venturing inland in search of that picture-postcard-perfect village.

Île Rousse (Isula Rossa)

POP 3127

Sun worshippers, celebrities and holidaying yachties create buzz in the busy beach town of Île Rousse, straddling a long, sandy curve of land backed by maquis-cloaked mountains. Founded by Pascal Paoli in 1758 as a rival port to pro-Genoese Calvi, the town was later renamed after the offshore russet-coloured rock of Île de la Pietra (now home to the town's ferry port and lighthouse).

Sights

Old Town
HISTORIC QUARTER

Get lost in alleyways! Surprise: constructed around 1850, the covered food market (place Paoli; ⊘8am-1pm), with its 21 classical columns, resembles a Greek temple. It abuts Île Rousse's central tree-shaded square, place Paoli, where you can watch nightly boules contests courtesy of the local gents while you sip an aperitif on the terrace of venerable Café des Platanes – it can't get more Île Rousse than that.

DON'T MISS

VILLAGE LIFE

For an authentic taste of rural life, check into Les Caves de Conchiglio (📱04 95 35 10 40; d €80; 🛜), a *chambre d'hôte* (B&B) hidden inside a beautiful, old golden-stone house in Barrettali. The sleepy hilltop village revels in unsurpassable sea views from its handsome perch, 24km south of Centuri on the wiggly and alarmingly narrow D133 (signposted off the coastal D80). Furnishings in the house, an old *miellerie* (honey-maker's workshop), win vintage lovers over with historical romance. The two self-catering *gîtes* (self-catering cottages), available by the weekend or week, are equally enchanting.

Promenade a Marinella BEACH

Île Rousse's sandy beaches stretch along the seafront, known as Promenade a Marinella, for 3km east of town. Less crowded beaches around Île Rousse include plage de Bodri, immediately southwest of town; Algajola, 7km southwest; or the magnificent plage de Lozari, 6km east.

Île de la Pietra PROMONTORY

For an easy stroll, head over the short umbilical causeway that links rocky Île de la Pietra to the mainland, past a Genoese watchtower and up to the lighthouse. Club Nautique d'Île Rousse (☑04 95 60 22 55; www.cnir.org; rte du Port) organises two-hour sea-kayaking trips (€32) around the promontory and its islets.

Parc de Saleccia BOTANICAL GARDEN

(☑04 95 36 88 83; www.parc-saleccia.fr; rte de Bastia, N197; adult/child/family €8/6/23; ⊙10am-7.30pm daily Jul & Aug, shorter hours Apr-Jun, Sep & Oct) Wander the 7 hectares of these landscaped gardens to explore the flora of Corsica – the tough plants of the maquis, pines, myrtles, fig trees and over 100 varieties of olive trees. The gardens are 4.5km from town on the road to Bastia.

🛏 Sleeping

TOP CHOICE Hôtel Le Splendid HOTEL €€

(☑04 95 60 00 24; www.le-splendid-hotel.com; av Comte Valéry; s €60-95, d €74-105, tr €102-145, q €130-184; @🏊) You'll be hard-pushed in Corsica to find better value: Le Splendid is splendid in value, in attitude (all smiles and helpfulness) and in proximity to the beach (footsteps away). Rooms are clean and vary in size and outlook, and those that sleep four – perfect for kid-clad families – are unusually spacious. The tiny pool to dip into out front and the generous breakfast buffet are

the icing on the cake. Look for the pretty pink building and towering palm trees a block from the seafront promenade.

Hôtel Perla Rossa BOUTIQUE HOTEL €€€

(☑04 95 48 45 30; www.hotelperlarossa.com; 30 rue Notre-Dame; ste from €190; ⊙Mar-Oct; ❄@🏊) With its enchanting soft-apricot façade and oyster-grey shutters, this cocoon adds a real touch of glam to the hotel scene. Its refined interior would be right at home in the latest edition of *Elle,* and its 10 rooms – all suites – completely spoil guests. The best have balcony with swoon-inducing sea views.

🍴 Eating & Drinking

Eating and drinking options abound on the beachfront and in the warren of old-town alleys.

TOP CHOICE U Libecciu SEAFOOD €€

(☑04 95 60 13 82; www.ulibecciu.com; rue Notre-Dame; mains €15-28; ⊙lunch & dinner daily Apr-Oct) Named after Corsica's westerly wind, this address is achingly hip, what with its funky interior – think paintings strung crooked on paint-peeling walls, retro heavy-gilded mirrors, see-through glass floor and half-broken plates doubling as bread baskets. Cuisine is equally creative: the *moules au Cap Corse* (gargantuan portions of local mussels) are to die for, as are the extravagant desserts. Should you be wondering what's up with the hundreds of empty 1919 rum bottles lined up on the shelves, just order the house *cocktail du siècle,* a tasty mix of rum, strawberries and basil leaves.

U Spuntinu CORSICAN €

(☑04 95 60 00 05; www.restaurant-spuntinu.com; 1 rue Napoléon; mains €15-22; ⊙lunch daily, dinner Mon-Sat) Footsteps from the central square, this overtly feminine address is known around town for its *cuisine à l'ancienne:*

THE TREMBLER

You may well tremble as the *trinighellu* (trembler) – as the Tramway de la Balagne (☑04 95 60 00 50, 04 95 65 00 61) is affectionately called – trundles periously close to the shore along sand-covered tracks between Calvi and Île Rousse. The dinky little train is the easiest way to access the numerous hidden coves and beaches sprinkled along the coast: no traffic jams and an unforgettable trip alongside getaway beaches. The train runs four to eight times daily from April to September, calling at 15 stations en route, all by request only. Out of season, regular trains run by Chemins de Fer de la Corse (☑04 95 32 80 57; http://train-corse.com) cover the same route. Hop off at an intermediate rocky cove or, for fine golden sand, leave the train at Algajola or Plage de Bodri, the last stop before Île Rousse. It costs €5.40 one-way.

SLEEP ON THE SAND

In high season when the summer crowd is at its worst, consider basing yourself on the sand in Algajola instead. Not only is this enormous stretch of golden sand one of the loveliest for miles around, the beach is an easy train ride to Île Rousse (7km east) and Calvi (16km southwest), and budget accommodation options are superb. Family-run Hôtel de la Plage Santa Vittoria (📞04 95 35 17 03; www.hotelplage-vittoria-corse. com; d €76-128; ⊗Apr-Oct), with history dating back to 1870 and flawless sea views, is the peachy hotel choice. Or go for L'Escale (📞04 95 60 60 80; www.lescale.biz; Plage d'Aregno; d €50-80; ⊗Apr-Oct), a cluster of 20 self-contained apartments and 50 spick-and-span rooms – with bathroom, comfy bed, terrace and five-star sea views – in low-lying cream bungalows at the northern end of Algajola on Alegno beach. There really are few budget addresses more luxurious than this when it comes to dropping off to the grandiose orchestra of crashing waves and then frolicking on the sand in pyjamas fresh out of bed at dawn.

good, old-fashioned cooking that sees *madame* in the kitchen cook up classics such as Brocciu and mint omelette, steak with maquis herbs, and oven-baked aubergine with chestnuts. Want it all? Go for the €24 *assiette Corse,* comprising a taster of every dish.

**Restaurant
Pasquale Paoli**　　GASTRONOMIC CORSICAN €€€
(📞04 95 47 67 70; www.pasquale-paoli.com; 2 place Paoli; mains €20-40, menus €50-85; ⊗dinner daily Jul & Aug, lunch & dinner daily Jun & Sep, shorter hrs rest of yr) The town's most gastronomic restaurant, Michelin star and all, cooks up a sophisticated dining experience inside a whitewashed, vaulted dining room. Or dine alfresco on the wood-decked terrace on place Paoli.

A Siesta　　BEACH RESTAURANT €€
(📞04 95 60 28 74; www.a-siesta.com; promenade A Marinella; mains €15-30; ⊗lunch & dinner daily late Mar–Oct) With its contemporary decor, big windows facing the sea, and sun-flooded decked terrace on the sand, A Siesta can do no wrong. Fish and seafood are the mainstay of Île Rousse's busiest beach restaurant, and the catch of the day baked *en croûte de sel* (in salt crust; €9.50 per 100g) is not to be missed. Or simply indulge in an *apéro* here in the company of *une assiette Corse* (Corsican platter; €14) of island cheese, cold meats and sweet fig chutney.

Tomasini Boulangerie　　BOULANGERIE €
(av Piccioni) For delicious cakes, pastries, bread and other tasty grab-and-go picnic fodder, head for this artisan baker just off place Paoli.

Cave Petra Rossa　　WINE CELLAR
(rue Général Graziani) Fill your water bottle with local AOC wine (€2.80 per litre) or sweet muscat (€8.50 per litre) around the corner from Tomasini Boulangerie.

ℹ Information

Tourist office (📞04 95 60 04 35; www. ot-ile-rousse.fr; av Calizi; ⊗9am-7pm Mon-Sat, 10am-1pm Sun mid-Jun–mid-Sep, shorter hrs mid-Sep–mid-Jun) This excellent information resource on the entire Balagne area stocks transport timetables, sells a lovely collection of walking itineraries with route descriptions in English (€2 per walk), and makes hotel reservations (free).

ℹ Getting There & Away

BOAT Ferries run to Nice, Marseille and Toulon (France), and Savona (Italy).

BUS Buses between Calvi and Bastia stop in Île Rousse.

TRAIN Twice-daily trains to Bastia (2½ hours) and Ajaccio (four hours) require a change of train in Ponte Leccia.

Calvi
POP 5486

Basking between the fiery orange bastions of its 15th-century citadel and the glittering waters of a moon-shaped bay, Calvi feels closer to the chichi sophistication of a French Riviera resort than a historic Corsican port. Palatial yachts and private cruisers jostle for space along its harbourside, lined with upmarket brasseries and cafes, while high above the quay the watchtowers and battlements of the town's Genoese stronghold stand guard, proffering sweeping views inland to Monte Cinto (2706m). Unsurprisingly, Calvi is one of Corsica's most popular tourist spots and in summer it's crammed to bursting.

Sights & Activities

Citadel
HISTORIC QUARTER

Set atop a lofty promontory, Calvi's massive fortified citadel offers superb wraparound views from its five bastions. Built by the town's Genoese governors, Calvi's citadel has seen off several major assaults down the centuries, fending off everyone from Franco-Turkish raiders to Anglo-Corsican armies. Inside the battlements, don't miss the well-proportioned Caserne Sampiero, which was the seat of power for the Genoese administration; and the 13th-century Cathédrale St-Jean Baptiste, whose most celebrated relic is the ebony *Christ des Miracles,* credited with saving the town from Saracen invasion in 1553.

Colombo Line
BOAT TRIPS

(☎04 95 65 32 10; www.colombo-line.com; quai Landry, Port de Plaisance; ☼Apr-Sep) At the marina, Colombo Line runs a bevy of seasonal boat trips along the coast – a fine way to beat the summer traffic. Highlights include day trips to the Réserve Naturelle de Scandola with a beach stopover at Girolata (adult/child €59/28.50) or Ajaccio (€80/40).

Plage de Calvi
BEACH

Calvi's stellar 4km-long sandy beach begins at the marina and runs east around the Golfe de Calvi. Rent kayaks and windsurfing sailboards on the sand, and hook up with local diving schools by the tourist office at the marina.

Festivals & Events

La Semaine Sainte
EASTER FESTIVAL

Easter festival, culminating in street processions on Good Friday.

Calvi Jazz Festival
JAZZ FESTIVAL

(www.calvi-jazz-festival.com; ☼late Jun) Corsica's biggest jazz festival.

Rencontres Polyphoniques
MUSIC FESTIVAL

(☼Sep) Catch traditional Corsican chants at this five-day music festival.

Festiventu
WIND FESTIVAL

(www.lefestivalduvent.com; ☼late Oct) This festival celebrates the role of wind with hundreds of kites on the beach.

Sleeping

At the top of town, right across from the main entrance to the citadel, there is a trio of solid midrange options on place Christophe Colomb and adjoining place Bel Ombra.

Hôtel La Villa
HOTEL €€€

(☎04 95 65 10 10; www.hotel-lavilla.com; Chemin de Notre Dame de la Serra; d low/high season from €110/395; ☼Apr-Jan; ✴@🛜🌊) If you want to do Calvi in style, head straight for this lavish hilltop hideaway, brimming with boutique trappings. Clean lines, cappuccino-and-chocolate colour schemes, designer fabrics and minimalist motifs distinguish the rooms, while the exterior facilities include spas, tennis courts, a Michelin-starred restaurant and one of the most fabulous infinity pools you could ever hope to see.

Hôtel Le Magnolia
HOTEL €€

(☎04 95 65 19 16; www.hotel-le-magnolia.com; rue Alsace-Lorraine; d €70-150; ☼Apr-Nov; ✴@🛜)

DON'T MISS

CORSICAN PARADISE

If there is one crescent of sand in Corsica you must not miss, it's Plage de l'Arinella, a serene, rock-clad cove with dramatic views of the citadel of Calvi across the water and one of the finest beach-dining experiences on Corsica. From the centre of Lumio, 6km south of Algajola on the coastal N197, turn right following the signs and twist 2.6km downhill, past leafy walled-garden *residences secondaires* (holiday homes) to the turquoise water.

Wooden tables, strung along the sand and topped with straw parasols, at Le Mata-Hari (☎04 95 60 78 47; www.lematahari.com; mains €20-30; ☼lunch Tue-Sun Apr, Sep & Oct, lunch & dinner daily May-Aug) immediately evoke a tropical paradise – and rightly so. From the stylish, shabby-chic interior of this hip beach restaurant to the big windows looking out to Calvi beyond the waves, this is one special hideaway. Cuisine is creative: *penne à la langouste,* squid, fresh *morue* (codfish) or a simple tuna steak pan-fried to pink perfection. Opening hours are weather dependent, so call ahead; reservations are essential in high season.

POINTE DE LA RAVELLATA

Thrill your senses with a short scenic motor journey west along the coastal D81b (signposted 'Route de Porto – bord de mer' from the square in front of the citadel in Calvi) to **Pointe de la Ravelleta**, the nearest Corsican point to the French mainland. Within seconds of leaving town you're deep in the hot, sun-baked maquis, a low stone wall being the only separator between white-knuckled passenger and scrubby green drop down to sparkling emerald water far below. Suddenly, after 4km, the magnificent cape, with a toylike white lighthouse at its tip and dusty ginger walking trails zigzagging between dark green scrub to the ocean, pops miragelike into view. Park in the lay-by and indulge in a heady, signposted hike 1.5km inland to **Chapelle Notre Dame de la Serra** or walk sea-bound for 20 minutes for lunch at **Mara Beach** (☎04 95 65 48 30; Plage de l'Alga; mains €15-20; ⌚lunch daily Apr-Oct), a Robinson Crusoe–style beach hut tucked in a turquoise creek on **Plage de l'Alga**.

An oasis from the harbourside fizz, this attractive mansion sits behind a beautiful high-walled courtyard garden pierced by a handsome magnolia tree. Pretty much every room has a lovely outlook - Calvi rooftops, garden or sea - and connecting doubles make it an instant hit with families.

Camping La Pinède CAMPGROUND €
(☎04 95 65 17 80; www.camping-calvi.com; rte de la Pinède; tent, car & 2 adults €34; ⌚Apr-Oct; 🏊) Handy for town and beach; mobile homes and chalets too.

Eating

Calvi's quayside is chock-a-block with restaurants, but many focus more on ocean ambience than quality of food.

A Candella TRADITIONAL CORSICAN €€
(☎04 95 65 42 13; 9 rue St-Antoine; mains €15-25) One of a handful of addresses to eat within the citadel, A Candella stands out for its romantic, golden-hued terrace of stone strung with pretty flowers in pots and olive trees. The food is Corsican hearty, and the sea view is the most marvellous you could hope for.

U Fornu MODERN CORSICAN €€
(☎04 95 65 27 60; www.ufornu.com; bd Wilson; mains €17-24, menus €17.50; ⌚lunch & dinner Mon-Sat, dinner Sun) A surprisingly hip restaurant inside a restored stately house in a quiet cul-de-sac off the main thoroughfare, this cool culinary outpost specialises in creative dishes that stray off the familiar Corsican path. Dishes are elegantly presented and filled with subtle flavours, and the *menu corse* is excellent value. Eat in the sassy grey and red interior, or on the shady terrace.

Le Tire-Bouchon BISTRO €
(☎04 95 65 24 41; rue Clemenceau; mains €15-20; ⌚lunch & dinner daily Jun-Sep, Thu-Tue Apr, May & Oct) This buzzy option, as much wine bar as restaurant, is a gourmand's playground. Perch yourself on the balcony overlooking the crowds milling on rue Clemenceau, then order from the dishes of the day, posted on a chalkboard. Be good to yourself with veal stew, tagliatelle with Brocciu cheese, a cheese platter and luscious local tipples.

Drinking

There are plenty of places around town at which to wet your whistle. The best after-dark buzz is quayside.

TOP CHOICE **Chez Tao** MUSIC BAR
(☎04 95 65 00 73; rue St-Antoine; ⌚Jun-Sep) You won't find cooler than this (or more amazing sea views with cocktail in hand). Up high within the citadel, this supersmooth piano bar is an institution. Find it in a lavishly decorated vaulted room, founded in 1935 by White Russian émigré Tao Kanbey de Kerekoff. Seven decades on, hedonistic hipsters continue to flock here.

Information

Tourist office (☎04 95 65 16 67; www.balagne-corsica.com; Port de Plaisance; ⌚9am-noon & 2-6pm daily Jul & Aug, Mon-Sat May, Jun, Sep & Oct, Mon-Fri Nov-Apr)

Getting There & Away

AIR Count on €20 by taxi from **Aéroport Calvi Ste-Catherine** (www.calvi.aeroport.fr) into town, 7km northwest of the airport.

BOAT From Calvi's **ferry terminal** (quai Landry) regular ferries sail to Nice (France) and Savona (Italy).

BUS Les Beaux Voyages (☎04 95 65 15 02; place de la Porteuse d'Eau) runs a few solitary weekly buses from Calvi to Bastia (2½ hours) via Île Rousse. **Transports Ceccaldi** (☎04 95 22 41 99) serves Porto (2¾ hours).

TRAIN From Calvi train station, south of the harbour, there are at least two departures daily to Bastia (three hours) and Ajaccio (five hours) via Ponte Leccia. April to September, the Tramway de la Balagne (p882) clatters along the coast to Île Rousse (€5.50, 45 minutes).

PORTO TO AJACCIO

The drive from Porto to Ajaccio is a majestic one that is blessed with bags of beaches, wild rock formations aka the iconic Les Calanques de Piana, and, last but not least, the irresistible boutique of Corsica's most famous *maître glacier* (master ice-cream chef), Glaces Geronimi (☎04 95 28 04 13; rte de Cargèse), in the small town of Sagone. Violet tutti-frutti, Camembert or artichoke ice cream (yes, really), anyone?

Porto (Portu)

POP 250

The setting couldn't be more grandiose. The crowning glory of the west coast, the seaside town of Porto sprawls at the base of a thickly forested valley trammelled on either side by crimson peaks. Buzzing in season and practically deserted in winter, it's a fantastic spot for exploring the shimmering seas around the Unesco-protected marine reservation of the Réserve Naturelle de Scandola, the astonshing Les Calanques de Piana (p888)and the rugged interior.

The village is split by a promontory, topped by a restored Genoese square tower, erected in the 16th century to protect the gulf from Barbary incursions.

◎ Sights & Activities

Waterfront   PORT

Porto's main sights are at the harbour. Once you've climbed the russet-coloured rocks up to the Genoese tower (admission €2.50; ⊙9am-9pm Jul & Aug, 11am-7pm Sep-Jun), you can stroll round to the bustling marina, from where an arched footbridge crosses the estuary to an impressive eucalyptus grove and Porto's pebbly patch of beach.

Aquarium de la Poudrière   AQUARIUM

(☎04 95 26 19 24; admission €5.50, joint ticket with Genoese Tower €6.50) Fish fanatics can drop by the Aquarium de la Poudrière, which houses fishy specimens from around the Golfe de Porto.

Réserve Naturelle
de Scandola   NATURE RESERVE

There's no vehicle access or footpath that leads into the magnificent, protected Réserve Naturelle de Scandola – the only way is by sea. Between April and October, several companies based around Porto's marina sail to the base of its cliffs, often taking in Les Calanques and Girolata. Expect to pay around €25 for trips to Les Calanques, or €40 for trips including Réserve Naturelle de Scandola and Girolata. Most offer informative commentaries (usually in French).

Do you see the exceptional coastal wilderness of Golfe de Porto and the crags and cliffs that fret the skyline? It's more or less the same story below the waterline. This gulf boasts an exceptional diversity of underwater wonders, with a jaw-dropping topography – just as on land – and masses of fish due to the proximity of the Réserve Naturelle de Scandola. Porto's three diving outfits, all based at the marina, offer introductory dives, courses for beginners and snorkelling trips.

Gorges de Spelunca   HIKING

The Porto area is a hiking haven. The *Hikes & Walks in the Area of Porto* (€3) brochure from the tourist office details 28 signed walks at all levels of difficulty. Hidden in the hills inland from Porto (follow the D124), the villages of Ota and Evisa offer the best opportunities, within striking distance of Gorges de Spelunca, one of the deepest natural canyons on the island. A path runs along the steep sides of the Spelunca canyon beneath huge, humbling cliffs.

🛏 Sleeping & Eating

Porto is small, with ample eateries jostling for waterside space both at the marina and old harbour; Le Sud and La Mer at the latter are a seasonal twinset with sea views held in high regard locally.

Le Colombo   HOTEL €€

(☎04 95 26 10 14; www.hotellecolombo.com; rte de Calvi; d/tr/q incl breakfast from €75/89/120; ⊙Apr-Oct; ✸) A smart place to rest your head, Le Colombo is built on three levels following the steep slope of the hillside. Most rooms are a soothing sky blue with views of garden, sea and mountain, and corridors are adorned with striking images by local photographer Robert Candela. Mooch around the lovely small garden, shaded by a giant palm and overflowing with bougainvillea.

Camping Les Oliviers　CAMPGROUND €
(☑04 95 26 14 49; www.camping-oliviers-porto. com; adult/tent/car €10/3.50/4; ☺late Mar–early Nov; @☒) Idyllically set among overhanging olive trees, this steeply terraced site climaxes with a swimming pool surrounded by rocks. There are also wooden chalets and *roulottes* (Romany caravans) to rent by the week.

**Hôtel-Restaurant
Le Maquis**　TRADITIONAL CORSICAN €€
(☑04 95 26 12 19; www.hotel-lemaquis.com; cnr D214 & D81; d €94-114, mains €20-30; ☺lunch & dinner daily Apr-Oct) This character-filled eatery in a granite house high above the harbour is much loved by locals and tourists alike. The food's a delight, with a tempting menu based on traditional Corsican cooking. There's a cosy all-wood interior but, for preference, reserve a table on the balcony with brilliant views.

❶ Information

Tourist office (www.porto-tourisme.com; place de la Marine; ☺9am-7pm daily Apr-Sep, 9am-4pm Mon-Fri Oct-Mar)

❶ Getting There & Away

Autocars Ceccaldi (☑04 95 22 41 99) operates up to two buses daily between Porto and Ajaccio (2½ hours) via Piana and Cargèse.

Ajaccio (Aiacciu)
POP 65,000

Ajaccio is all class and seduction. Commanding a lovely sweep of bay, the city breathes confidence and has more than a whiff of the Côte d'Azur. Everyone from solo travellers to romance-seeking couples and families will love moseying around the centre, replete with mellow-toned buildings and buzzing cafes – not to mention its large marina and the trendy rte des Sanguinaires area, a few kilometres to the west.

The spectre of Corsica's general looms over Ajaccio. Napoléon Bonaparte was born here in 1769, and the city is dotted with sites relating to the diminutive dictator, from his childhood home to seafront statues, museums and street names.

◉ Sights

**Palais Fesch – Musée
des Beaux-Arts**　ART MUSEUM
(www.musee-fesch.com; 50-52 rue du Cardinal Fesch; adult/child €8/5; ☺10.30am-6pm Mon, Wed & Sat, noon-6pm Thu, Fri & Sun year-round, to 8.30pm Fri Jul & Aug) One of the island's must-sees, this

(vertical right margin) CORSICA AJACCIO (AIACCIU)

LA BALAGNE INTERIOR

What a difference a few miles can make! Flee the hullabaloo of the coastal fleshpots, grab the steering wheel, jump on a serpentine country road and explore inland Balagne. Hidden among the countless valleys and spurs that slice up the spectacular scenery are cute-as-can-be hilltop villages, Romanesque chapels, olive groves and lush vineyards. The Balagne hinterland is also a source of inspiration for many artisans. A signposted route, the Strada di l'Artigiani (www.routedesartisans.fr), links the region's most attractive villages, and details local workshops; pick up a route map from the Calvi or Île Rousse tourist office.

Particularly charming is Pigna, a mirage of burnt-orange rooftops and blue-shuttered houses 7km south of Île Rousse via the D151. Artisans' workshops are scattered among the sweet cobbled streets both here and in the cute hamlet of Sant'Antonino, precariously perched on a rocky outcrop, a little further south along the D151. What views! And what zesty *jus de citron* (freshly squeezed lemon juice) served at Cave Antonino (☑06 09 58 94 01), a simple wine bar across from the car park at the foot of picture-postcard Sant'Antonino. Its wines and fresh almonds from the Clos Antonino estate are equally tasty.

Should you fancy overnighting, Pigna squirrels away some atmospheric options: Casa Musicale (☑04 95 61 77 31; www.casa-musicale.org; d €77-112) has quirky rooms finished with painted frescos and fabulous valley views, while plush Hôtel U Palazzu (☑04 95 47 32 78; www.hotel-corse-palazzu.com; d €152-240, ste €280; ☺Apr-Oct) languishes inside an 18th-century mansion. Both have romantic restaurant terraces worthy of a milllion and one marriage proposals.

WORTH A TRIP

ICONIC DAY TRIPPER: LES CALANQUES DE PIANA

No amount of hyperbole can capture the astonishing beauty of Les Calanques de Piana (E Calanche in Corsican), sculpted cliffs teetering above the Golfe de Porto that rear up from the sea in staggering scarlet pillars, teetering columns, towers and irregularly shaped boulders of pink, ochre and ginger. Flaming red in the sunlight, this natural ensemble of gargantuan proportions is one of Corsica's most iconic, awe-inspiring sights. And as you sway around switchback after switchback along the rock-riddled 10km stretch of the D81 south of Porto towards the village of Piana (population 500; www.otpiana.com), one mesmerising vista piggybacks another.

For the full Technicolour experience, savour Les Calanques on foot. Several trails wind their way around these dramatic rock formations, unwittingly shaped like dog's heads, dinosaurs and all sorts. Trails start near near Pont de Mezzanu, a road bridge on the D81 about 3km north of Piana. In the village itself, the tourist office (www.otpiana.com; place Mairie; ☾9am-6pm Mon-Fri) stocks the leaflet Piana: Sentiers de Randonnée, detailing six walks. Afterwards, flop on the sand on the idyllic beaches of Ficajola and Arone, 5km and 11km southwest respectively. Or splurge on lunch with a view at Corsica's original luxury hotel, Les Roches Rouges (☎04 95 27 81 81; www.lesrochesrouges.com; D81; s €102-123, d €114-136, tr €156-176, q €177-213; ☾Apr-Oct; ☎). Built in 1912, it remains one of the island's quirkiest vintage addresses. Rambling corridors and musty rooms ooze early-20th-century ambience and, despite the modern(ish) en suites, wi-fi and phone lines, you half expect Hercule Poirot to wander round the corner twiddling his moustache at any given moment. Faded grandeur at its best, a meal in its superb gourmet restaurant (or, should you fancy staying over, a sea-view room) is worth every cent; at the very least partake in a drink on the romantic stone terrace to savour the truly extraordinary vista.

Approaching Piana from the north, find the mythical hotel immediately on the right on the extreme northern fringe of the village. A couple of daily buses link the village with Ajaccio.

superb museum, established by Napoléon's uncle, has France's largest collection of Italian paintings outside the Louvre. Mostly the works of minor or anonymous 14th- to 19th-century artists, there are also canvases by Titian, Fra Bartolomeo, Veronese, Botticelli and Bellini. Look out for La Vierge à l'Enfant Soutenu par un Ange (Mother and Child Supported by an Angel), one of Botticelli's masterpieces. Portrait de l'Homme au Gant (Portrait of the Gloved Man) by Titian matches another in the Louvre. The museum also houses temporary exhibitions. Within the Chapelle Impériale (Imperial Chapel), constructed in 1860 and closed for renovation until 2013, several members of the imperial family lie entombed in the crypt. But don't expect to find Napoléon's remains – he's buried in Les Invalides in Paris.

Maison Bonaparte HISTORY MUSEUM
(☎04 95 21 43 89; www.musee-maisonbonaparte.fr; rue St-Charles; adult/child €7/5.50; ☾10.30am-12.30pm & 1.15-6pm Tue-Sun Apr-Sep, 10am-noon & 2-4.45pm Oct-Mar) Napoléon spent his first nine years in this house. Ransacked by Corsican nationalists in 1793, requisitioned

by English troops from 1794 to 1796, and eventually rebuilt by Napoléon's mother, the house became a place of pilgrimage for French revolutionaries, and visitors are still encouraged to observe suitably hushed tones. It hosts memorabilia of the emperor and his siblings, including a glass medallion containing a lock of his hair. It's closed Monday mornings.

Salon Napoléonien MUSEUM
(☎04 95 21 90 15; www.musee-fesch.com; av Antoine Sérafini; adult/child €2.30/1.50; ☾9-11.45am & 2-5.45pm Mon-Fri year-round, closed Mon morning Jun-Sep) Fans of Napoléon will make a beeline for this museum on the 1st floor of the Hôtel de Ville. It exhibits Napoléonic medals, portraits and busts, as well as a fabulously frescoed ceiling of Napoléon and his entourage.

Musée A Bandera HISTORY MUSEUM
(☎04 95 51 07 34; www.musee-abandera.fr; 1 rue du Général Lévie; adult/child €5/3; ☾10am-7pm Mon-Sat, to 1pm Sun Jul-Sep, to 5pm Mon-Sat Oct-Jun) Tucked away on a side street, this quirky little museum explores Corsican

history up to WWII. Among the highlights are a diorama of the 1769 battle of Ponte Novo that confirmed French conquest of the island, a model of the port of Ajaccio as it was in the same period, and a proclamation by Gilbert Elliot, viceroy of the short-lived Anglo-Corsican kingdom (1794–96). There are also a few worthy panels describing the historical role of women in Corsican society.

Cathédrale Ste-Marie   CATHEDRAL
(rue Forcioli Conti; ⊗8-11.30am & 2.30-5.45pm Mon-Sat, 8-9.30am Sun) The 16th-century cathedral contains Napoléon's baptismal font and the *Vierge au Sacré-Cœur* (Virgin of the Sacred Heart) by Eugène Delacroix (1798–1863).

Citadel   FORTRESS
The 15th-century citadel, an imposing military fortress overlooking the sea, was a prison during WWII and is off-limits to the general public.

🏃 Activities

Kiosks on the quayside opposite place du Maréchal Foch sell tickets for seasonal boat trips around the Golfe d'Ajaccio and Îles Sanguinaires (€27), and excursions to the Réserve Naturelle de Scandola (p886; adult/child €50/35).

Plage de Ricanto   BEACH
Ajaccio's most popular beach, Plage de Ricanto aka Tahiti Plage, is 5km east of town. Heading west, the smaller beaches of Ariane, Neptune, Palm Beach and Marinella culminate at Pointe de la Parata, 12km west of the city, and a grandstand view of the Îles Sanguinaires (Bloody Islands), so named because of their vivid crimson colours at sunset.

Plage de Porticcio   BEACH
Beach bums will prefer the sands of Porticcio to the busier city beaches. It's 17km across the bay from Ajaccio and accessible by seasonal ferry (single/return €5/8, 20 minutes).

Pointe de la Parata   WALKING, CYCLING
The Pointe de la Parata, about 12km west of Ajaccio, is a magnet for walkers and photographers alike. From the car park you'll find a short, much-trodden walking trail that leads around the promontory. A stroll along here rewards you with great sea views and tantalising close-ups of the four islets of the Îles Sanguinaires. Come here at sunset – the scenery is awesome.

To pedal to the point from downtown Ajaccio, pick up two wheels from Loca Cycles (☎06 72 04 77 47; sq César Campinchi; half-day/day/week €10/13/60), or Elec-Evasion (☎06 23 66 64 79; sq César Campinchi; 1hr/3hrs €7/18, half-day/day/week €20/25/150), which has electric bikes; both are across from the water at the port.

✨🎊 Festivals & Events

Festival de la St-Érasme   FISH FESTIVAL
(⊗early Jun) Fishy festival in honour of the patron saint of *pêcheurs* (fishermen).

Fêtes Napoléoniennes   NAPOLÉON FESTIVAL
(⊗15 Aug) Ajaccio's biggest bash celebrates Napoléon's birthday, with military-themed parades, street spectacles and a huge fireworks display.

La Relève de la Garde Impériale   CEREMONY
Watch the pomp and ceremony of the Changing of the Guard, every Thursday at 7pm in summer, in front of the town hall on place du Foch.

🛏 Sleeping

Hôtel Kallisté
TOP CHOICE   HOTEL €€
(☎04 95 51 34 45; www.hotel-kalliste-ajaccio.com; 51 cours Napoléon; s/d/tr €77/95/123; ✳@🖋) Exposed brick, neutral tones, terracotta tiles and a funky glass lift conjure up a neo-boutique feel at the Kallisté, which occupies a typical 19th-century Ajaccio town house. Double-glazing keeps out the traffic hum from cours Napoléon, and the facilities are fab – wi-fi, satellite TV, a copious breakfast buffet for a mere €4 extra served in a spacious room and, the icing on the cake, the convenience of an underground hotel car park in a city where parking can be downright hellish. Unfortunately, the secret's out, so book ahead.

Palazzu u Domu   HOTEL €€€
(☎04 95 50 00 20; www.palazzu-domu.com; 17 rue Bonaparte; d €220-270; ✳@🖋) Bold contemporary design inside the historic 1760 mansion of Duke Pozzo di Borgo makes for an irresistible combo. Indeed, guests at Ajaccio's stylish four-star hotel are treated to swish, neutral-tone furnishings just footsteps from the water. The bijou patio garden in the heart of old Ajaccio is a lovely touch.

CORSICA AJACCIO (AIACCIU)

Ajaccio (Aiacciu)

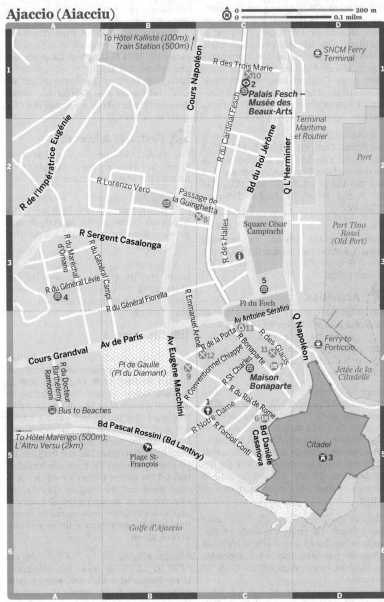

Hôtel Marengo HOTEL €

(☎04 95 21 43 66; www.hotel-marengo.com; 2 rue Marengo; d €65-89, tr €95-115; ⊗Apr-Oct; ❄) For something near the sand, try this charmingly eccentric small hotel near the beach. Rooms have a balconies, there's a quiet flower-filled courtyard and the reception is an agreeable clutter of tasteful prints and personal objects. You can find the hotel down a cul-de-sac off bd Madame Mère.

Ajaccio (Aiacciu)

Hôtel San Carlu Citadelle   HOTEL €
(☎04 95 21 13 84; www.hotel-sancarlu.com; 8 bd Danièle Casanova; s €75-95, d €55-86, tr €90-111, q €105-195; ⊙Feb–mid-Dec) For pure function-ality and location, this cream-coloured town house with oyster-grey shutters, a blink of an eye from the citadel, is a solid bet. Leaving early to catch a ferry at dawn? Opt for the ear-ly-bird €4 *petit dej*, served from 4am to 6am.

✗ Eating

Tiny streetside restaurants cram the old quarter, and eating out on a sultry summer night is an experience not to be missed. Key spots to linger in the shade or sun over a lazy lunch include waterfront quai Napoléon at the old port (aka Port Tino Rossi), main street cours Napoléon, vast car-free place de Gaulle, and the citadel end of beach-bound bd Pascal Rossini.

TOP
CHOICE **Le 20123**   TRADITIONAL CORSICAN €€
(☎04 95 21 50 05; www.20123.fr; 2 rue du Roi de Rome; menus €34.50; ⊙dinner Tue-Sun) This fabulous, one-of-a-kind place started life in the village of Pila Canale (postcode 20123, get it?) and, when the owner upped sticks to Ajaccio, he decided to take the old vil-lage with him – water pump, washing line,

life-sized dolls in traditional dress, central square and all. It sounds a bit tacky, but you won't find many more character-filled places in Corsica. Needless to say, the food is 100% authentic, too: everyone feasts on the same four-course *menu* (set menu), pre-sented orally, built solely from local produce and traditional recipes, and, amazingly, un-changed for 25 years.

Le Bilboq – Chez Jean Jean   SEAFOOD €€€
(☎04 95 51 35 40; 1 rue des Glacis; mains around €50; ⊙dinner daily) In business for decades, this Ajaccio icon is famous for one thing and one thing only: *langouste aux spaghetti* (lobster spaghetti; €12 per 100g), savoured alfresco in a tiny pedestrian street. Knock it all down with a well-chosen Corsican wine, and enter seventh heaven.

L'Altru Versu   GASTRONOMIC €€
(☎04 95 50 05 22; www.laltruversu.com; rte des Sanguinaires, Les Sept Chapelles; mains €20-30; ⊙lunch & dinner daily Jun-Sep, Tue-Sun Oct-May; ✱) Ajaccio's top-notch restaurant belongs to the Mezzacqui brothers (Jean-Pierre front of house, Pierre powering the kitchen), who are passionate gastronomes and excellent singers – they hitch on their guitars and serenade guests each Friday and Saturday night. Their creative cuisine, such as pork with honey and clementine zest, sings to the mouth.

U Pampasgiolu   TRADITIONAL CORSICAN €€
(☎04 95 50 71 52; 15 rue de la Porta; mains €15-30; ⊙dinner Mon-Sat) The rustic arch-vaulted dining room of this Ajaccio institution is packed with punters nearly every night of the week. They come for the first-rate Cor-sican food made from carefully chosen in-gredients. Order à la carte, or choose from the *planche spuntinu* (snack selection) or *planche de la mer* (fish and seafood selec-tion) for a great assortment of Corsican spe-cialities served on wooden platters.

Da Mama   TRADITIONAL CORSICAN €
(☎04 95 21 39 44; 3 passage de la Ghinghetta; lunch menus €12, dinner menus €17-25; ⊙dinner Mon, lunch & dinner Tue-Sat) Staunchly Corsican cuisine aside, the main draw of this unfussy eatery is location in the shade of a magnifi-cent rubber tree down a narrow alley.

Le 58   CRÊPERIE €
(☎04 95 25 96 67; 58 rue du Cardinal Fesch; crêpes €2-5.50, panini €3-6) For a quick bite between museum visits, this simple but stylish,

quick-serve pancake and panini cafe is the perfect address.

A Cantali VEGETARIAN €€
(☑06 22 85 44 26; 6 rue San Lazaro; lunch/dinner menus €15/25; ☺lunch Mon-Fri, dinner Fri & Sat; ☑) Nonmeat eaters will be thrilled to know about this *biovégétarien* (organic vegetarian) address.

🛍 Shopping

For Corsican goodies, there's only one address that matters: U Stazzu (1 rue Bonaparte; ☺9am-12.30pm & 2.30-7pm), famous for its handmade charcuterie and Corsican delicacies crafted by other small producers.

ℹ Information

Tourist office (www.ajaccio-tourisme.com; 3 bd du Roi Jérôme; ☺8am-7pm Mon-Sat, 9am-1pm Sun)

ℹ Getting There & Away

AIR **Aéroport d'Ajaccio-Campo dell'Oro** (☑04 95 23 56 56; www.ajaccio.aeroport.fr), 8km east of town, is linked by bus 8 (€4.50, 20 minutes) with Ajaccio bus station. Count on around €25 for a taxi.

BOAT Ferry services to Toulon, Nice and Marseille on mainland France depart from Ajaccio's **Terminal Maritime et Routier** (☑04 95 51 21 80; www.2a.cci.fr; quai L'Herminier). Buy tickets before sailings inside the combined bus and ferry terminal.

BUS Local bus companies have ticket kiosks inside the terminal building, which is the arrival/departure point for buses. As always in Corsica, expect reduced services on Sunday and during the winter months.

TRAIN From the **train station** (place de la Gare), services include Bastia (four hours, three to four daily), Corte (two hours, three to four daily) and Calvi (five hours, two daily; change at Ponte Leccia).

THE SOUTH

Sartène (Sartè)

POP 3500

With its grey granite houses, secretive dead-end alleys and sombre, introspective air, Sartène has long been said to encapsulate Corsica's rugged spirit (French novelist Prosper Mérimée dubbed it the 'most Corsican of Corsican towns'). There's no doubt that Sartène feels a long way from the glitter of the Corsican coast; the hillside houses are endearingly ramshackle, the streets are shady and scruffy, and life still crawls along at a traditional tilt. It offers a much more convincing glimpse of how life was once lived in rural Corsica than do any of the island's more well-heeled towns.

Notorious for its banditry and bloody vendettas in the 19th century, Sartène has more recently found fame thanks to the annual Procession du Catenacciu, a re-enactment of the Passion that has taken place in the town every Good Friday since the Middle Ages. Barefoot, wearing red robes and cowled (to preserve his anonymity), the Catenacciu (literally 'chained one'; penitent) – chosen by the parish priest to atone for a grave sin – lugs a massive 35kg wooden cross through town in a re-enactment of Christ's journey to Calvary. View the cross and 17kg chain the pentinent wears inside Sartène's granite Église Ste-Marie (place Porta).

Feel like seeing the area on horseback? Domaine de Croccano (☑04 95 77 11 37; www.corsenature.com; rte de Granace, D148; d incl breakfast €79-90; ☺Jan-Nov), 3.5km out of town on the road to Granace, is a lovely old farmhouse B&B surrounded by fields dotted with grazing horses. It runs various guided horse-riding rambles amid the maquis, all with stunnning views over Sartène and the sea. Sartène's tourist office (www.oti-sartenais valinco.com; cours Sœur Amélie; ☺9am-7pm) has a complete list of accommodation and activities in the area.

Don't leave town without stocking up on local cheese, sausages, cold meats, honey, olive oil and Sartène wines – we recommend a Saparale or a Fiumicicoli – at La Cave Sartenaise (☑04 95 77 12 01; place Porta; ☺daily Apr-Oct), an atmopsheric cellar with an old stone vaulted interior by the entrance to the Vieille Ville (Old Town).

Bonifacio (Bunifaziu) & Around

POP 2973

With its glittering harbour, dramatic perch atop creamy white cliffs, and stout citadel teetering above the cornflower-blue waters of the Bouches de Bonifacio, this dazzling port is an essential stop. Just a short hop from Sardinia, Bonifacio has a distinctly Italianate feel: sun-bleached town houses, dangling washing lines and murky chapels cram the web of alleyways of the old citadel;

down below on the harbourside, brasseries and boat kiosks tout their wares to the droves of day-trippers. Bonifacio's also perfectly positioned for exploring the island's southerly beaches and the Îles Lavezzi.

◉ Sights

Citadel (Haute Ville)   HISTORIC QUARTER

Much of Bonifacio's charm comes from strolling the citadel's shady streets, several spanned by arched aqueducts designed to collect rainwater to fill the communal cistern opposite Église Ste-Marie Majeure. From the marina, the paved steps of montée du Rastello and montée St-Roch bring you up to the citadel's old gateway, complete with an original 16th-century drawbridge. Inside the gateway is the 13th-century Bastion de l'Étendard (adult/child €2.50/free; ⊙9am-7pm Mon-Fri, 10am-6pm Sat & Sun Apr-Oct), home to a small history museum. Stroll the ramparts to place du Marché and place de la Manichella for jaw-dropping views over the Bouches de Bonifacio.

From the citadel, the Escalier du Roi d'Aragon (King of Aragon's Stairway; adult/under 12yr €2.50/free; ⊙9am-7pm Mon-Fri, 10am-6pm Sat & Sun Apr-Oct) cuts down the southern cliff-face. Legend says its 187 steep steps were carved in a single night by Aragonese troops during the siege of 1420, only for troops to be rebuffed by retaliating Bonifacio residents at the top. In reality the steps served as an access path to an underground freshwater well.

West along the limestone headland is the Église Ste-Dominique, one of Corsica's few Gothic churches, and a little further, Bonifacio's eerily quiet marine cemetery. At the western tip of the peninsula, an underground passage dug by hand during WWII leads to the Gouvernail de la Corse, a rudder-shaped rock about 12m from the shore.

Îles Lavezzi   ARCHIPELAGO

Paradise! This protected clutch of uninhabited islets were made for those who love nothing better than splashing in tranquil lapis-lazuli waters. The 65-hectare Île Lavezzi, which gives its name to the whole archipelago, is the most accessible of the islands. Savage beauty aside, the island's superb natural pools and scenic stretches of sand beg long-and-lazy sunbathing and swimming sessions. In summer, various companies organise boat trips here; buy tickets at the booths located on Bonifacio's marina and bring your own picnic lunch. Boats also sail to the island from Porto-Vecchio.

MOVING ON?

For tips, recommendations and reviews, head to shop.lonelyplanet.com to purchase a downloadable PDF of the Sardinia chapter from Lonely Planet's *Italy* guide.

🏃 Activities

Don't leave Bonifacio without taking a boat trip around its extraordinary coastline, where you'll get the best perspective of the town's precarious position on top of the magnificent chalky cliffs. The one-hour itinerary (adult/child €17.50/12) includes several *calanques* (deep rocky inlets) with clear aquamarine waters and views of the Escalier du Roi d'Aragon and the Grotte du Sdragonato (Little Dragon Cave), a vast watery cave with a natural rooftop skylight. Longer 1½-hour trips (adult/child €35/17.50) take in the Îles Lavezzi. Numerous companies vie for custom from ticket booths at the marina; they all offer similar deals.

Bonifacio's town beaches are a little underwhelming. Plage de Sotta Rocca is a small pebbly cove below the citadel, reached by steps from av Charles de Gaulle, while plage de la Catena and plage de l'Arinella are sandy inlets on the northern side of Bouches de Bonifacio. On foot, follow the trail from av Sylvère Bohn, near the Esso petrol station.

[TOP CHOICE] Phare de Pertusato   WALKING

If you're after that perfect picture, don't miss the fantastic, easy walk along the cliffs to the Pertusato Lighthouse, from where the seamless views of the cliffs, Îles Lavezzi, Bonifacio and Sardinia are memorable. Pick up the trail just to the left of the sharp bend on the hill up to Bonifacio's citadel. Count 1½ hours for the 5.6km round trip.

Golfe de Sant'Amanza   GULF

There are several lovely beaches around the Golfe de Sant'Amanza, 8km east of Bonifacio, including plage de Maora, with tasty beach dining.

Spérone   BEACH

For fine stretches of sand head east along the D58 to the little cove of Spérone, opposite the islets of Cavallo and Lavezzi.

CORSICA BONIFACIO (BUNIFAZIU) & AROUND

Plage de Piantarella   BEACH, KAYAKING

Plage de Piantarella is popular with windsurfers, and Club Bonif' Kayak (☑06 27 11 30 73; www.bonifacio-kayak.com; ☺10am-1pm & 2-5pm Apr-Sep) on the sand hires kayaks and organises guided sea-kayaking expeditions.

Îles Lavezzi   DIVING

The Îles Lavezzi feature a variety of sites for all levels. At Mérouville, Bonifacio's signature dive site, divers are guaranteed to get up close and personal with big groupers. The tourist office has a list of dive operators; a single dive starts at around €40.

🛏 Sleeping

TOP CHOICE Domaine de Licetto   HOTEL €€

(☑04 95 73 03 59; www.licetto.com; rte du Phare de Pertusato; s €55-85, d €70-105, q €115-175; ☺Apr-Oct) Tucked in the maquis just a couple of kilometres east of Bonifacio, this motel-style address is a lovely surprise. Its seven minimalist rooms sport stylishly modern bathrooms and well-chosen furnishings, and each has a terrace with table and chairs made for lounging alfresco in the surrounding peace and quiet. The restaurant on the estate is a feast in traditional dining and, best of all, Bonifacio town is a short idyllic walk away along the clifftop coastal path.

Hôtel Genovese   HOTEL €€€

(☑04 95 73 12 34; www.hotel-genovese.com; rte de Bonifacio; d €210-250; ☺Mar-Oct; ❉❦⊠) Chic and stylish, this ultracool hotel, built on the ramparts, is hard to resist. Its swimming pool is the last word in pool design, interior furnishings are bright and fresh, and each of its 14 rooms is different. Spoil yourself.

Hôtel Le Colomba   HOTEL €€

(☑04 95 73 73 44; www.hotel-bonifacio-corse.fr; rue Simon Varsi; d €110-180; ☺Mar-Nov; ❉❦) Occupying a tastefully renovated 14th-century building, this beautiful hotel is a delightful address in a picturesque (steep) street, bang in the heart of the old town. Rooms are simple and smallish, but fresh and pleasantly individual: wrought-iron bedsteads and country fabrics in some, carved bedheads and checkerboard tiles in others. Breakfast in a vaulted room is another highlight.

Brise Marine   HOTEL €€

(☑04 95 73 59 72; www.brisemarine.eu; rue de Calalonga; d €130-195) Canopy beds and beach-chic terraces, with big views of the Mediterranean smudged on the horizon, ensure plenty of romance at this contemporary address, nestled on a grassy, 2-hectare estate outside Bonifacio.

DON'T MISS

PREHISTORIC CORSICA

Southern Corsica boasts the island's most astonishing prehistoric sites, which are must-sees for anyone with an interest in Corsica's ancient civilisations. Some time around 4000 BC to 3000 BC, Corsica developed its own megalithic faith (possibly imported by seafaring settlers from mainland Europe); most of the island's standing stones and menhirs date from this period. The most important and impressive site is Filitosa (☑04 95 74 00 91; www.filitosa.fr; adult/child €6/4; ☺8am-sunset Easter-Oct), northwest of Sartène, where a collection of extraordinary carved menhirs was discovered in 1946. The Filitosa menhirs are highly unusual: several have detailed faces, anatomical features (such as ribcages) and even swords and armour, suggesting that they may commemorate specific warriors or chieftains.

About 15km south of Sartène, the desolate and beautiful Cauria plateau is home to three megalithic curiosities: the *alignements* (lines) of Stantari and Renaju, several of which show similar anatomical details and weaponry to those of Filitosa; and the Fontanaccia dolmen, one of Corsica's few burial chambers, with its supporting pillars and capstones. Look out for the turn-off about 8km along the D48 towards Tizzano. What did these strange sites signify for their megalithic architects? Were they ritual temples? Sacred graveyards? Mythical armies? Or even celestial timepieces? Despite countless theories, no one has the foggiest idea.

Inland from Porto-Vecchio, the region of L'Alta Rocca also musters up several megalithic remains. About 7km north of Levie, Pianu di Livia (p898) comprises two sites: the Bronze Age *castelli* (castles) of Cucuruzzu and Capula, connected by a beautiful 3km-long interpretive trail between trees.

Eating

Kissing Pigs   MODERN CORSICAN €
(📞04 95 73 56 09; quai Banda del Ferro; mains €9-15) Soothingly positioned by the harbour, this widely acclaimed restaurant and wine bar serves savoury fare in a seductively cosy interior, complete with wooden fixtures and swinging sausages. It's famed for its cheese and charcuterie platters; for the indecisive, the combination *moitié-moitié* (half-half) is perfect. The Corsican wine list is another hit.

Domaine de Licetto   TRADITIONAL CORSICAN €€
(📞04 95 73 19 48; www.licetto.com; rte du Phare de Pertusato; menus incl drinks €38; ⊙dinner Mon-Sat Apr-Oct, plus dinner Sun Aug) If you're after an authentic Corsican experience, this place is hard to beat. The gargantuan, no-choice, five-course *menu* is a fabulous culinary feast based on local ingredients sourced directly from small-scale farmers. Menu stalwarts include suckling lamb and *aubergines à la bonifacienne*. It's right in the maquis, on the way to Phare de Pertusato.

Cantina Doria   TRADITIONAL CORSICAN €
(📞04 95 73 50 49; www.cantinagrill.fr; 27 rue Doria; mains €10-15; ⊙lunch & dinner daily Apr-Oct) A Bonifacio institution, this cavernous joint has a tantalising menu showcasing the great classics of Corsican cuisine in a rustic setting.

Sorba   BOULANGERIE €
(📞04 95 73 03 64; 3 rue St-Erasme) Down by the water, before setting sail in a boat, visit this artisanal *patisserie-gelateria* and splash out on a bag of sweet lemon- or aniseed-flavoured *canistrelli* (Corsican biscuits), a loaf of *pain du morts* (literally 'death bread' but actually sweet nut-and-raisin bread) or some giant-sized chestnut and orange *fugazzi* (cookies) to nibble aboard.

ℹ Information

Tourist office (www.bonifacio.fr; 2 rue Fred Scamaroni; ⊙9am-8pm Jul & Aug, to 7pm May, Jun & Sep, 9am-noon & 2-6pm Oct-Apr)

ℹ Getting There & Away

AIR A taxi into town from **Figari-Sud Corse airport** (www.figari.aeroport.fr), 20km northwest of town, costs about €40.

BOAT Sardinia's main ferry operators, **Saremar** (www.saremar.it) and **Moby Lines** (www.moby.it), run seasonal boats between Bonifacio and Santa Teresa Gallura (Sardinia); sailing time is one hour.

BUS **Eurocorse** (📞04 95 70 13 83) runs limited daily services to Porto-Vecchio, Sartène, Propriano and Ajaccio.

Porto-Vecchio (Portivecchju) & Around

POP 11,300

Shamelessly seductive and fashionable, Porto-Vecchio is dubbed the Corsican St-Tropez, and it's no wonder. Sitting in a marvellous bay, it's the kind of place that lures French A-listers and wealthy tourists. Its picturesque backstreets, lined with restaurant terraces and designer shops, have charm in spades, and are presided over with grace by the photogenic ruins of an old Genoese citadel. Although there is no beach in the town proper, some of the island's best, and most famous, beaches are close by.

◉ Sights & Activities

When it comes to wishing for the archetypal 'idyllic beach', it's impossible to think past the immense Plage de Palombaggia. This is the Corsican paradise you've been daydreaming about: sparkling turquoise waters, long stretches of sand edged with pine trees and splendiferous views over the Îles Cerbicale. South of Plage de Palombaggia, Plage de la Folacca (also known as Plage de Tamariciu) is no less impressive. Continue a few kilometres further south over a pass called Bocca di L'Oru and you'll come across another gem of a beach, the gently curving Plage de Santa Giulia. From Porto-Vecchio, follow the N198 to the south and turn left onto rte de Palombaggia (it's signposted), which winds around the coast.

To the north, the coast is also sprinkled with scenic expanses of sand. The gorgeous, lucent depths of the beaches at Cala Rossa and Baie de San Cipriana are sure to set your heart aflutter. Further to the north is the stunning Golfe de Pinarello with its Genoese tower and yet more beautiful expanses of sand lapped by shallow waters.

In town at the marina, various operators offer boat excursions to the Îles Lavezzi and Bonifacio.

⌐ Sleeping

A Littariccia   B&B €€
(📞04 95 70 41 33; www.littariccia.com; rte de Palombaggia; d incl breakfast €85-220; ⊠) Find bucolic bliss at this attractive B&B that boasts a *fabulous* location, in the hills overlooking

Plage de Palombaggia. Your heart will lift at the dreamy views over the Med, your soul will find peace in one of the six button-cute rooms, and your body will relax in the small pool. Not all rooms come with a sea view, though.

Le Belvédère HOTEL €€€
(☑04 95 70 54 13; www.hbcorsica.com; rte de Palombaggia; d €210-255; ☉mid-Apr–Dec; ✳@🛜🏊) Built out of an old family estate tucked between eucalyptus, palm and pine on the seashore, this 15-room hotel is quite divine, darling. Decor is modern and exotic: a gregarious mix of traditional stone, wood, marble and wrought iron. Public areas lounge between natural rock and sand and, as for the sea-facing pool, you'll be hard-pushed to move. Rates tumble by 50% in the low season, making Le Belvédère a real bargain.

✗ Eating & Drinking

A Cantina di l'Orriu WINE BAR €
(☑04 95 25 95 89; www.orriu.com; 5 cours Napoléon; mains €14-24; ☉lunch & dinner daily May-Sep) Gourmets will be in heaven at this *bar à vin*, its atmospheric old-stone interior packed to the rafters with sausages and cold meats hung up to dry, cheeses, jars of jam and honey, and other tasty strictly Corsican produce. Lunch platters range from light to feisty, and the *formules apéritives* (pre-dinner drinks with nibbles) are inspired. Don't miss the homemade ravioli for lunch, or the fresh Brocciu cheese sold in season in the adjoining boutique.

Tamariccia MODERN CORSICAN €€
(☑04 95 70 49 89; www.tamariccia.com; rte de Palombaggia; mains €15-32; ☉lunch Apr, May & Sep, lunch & dinner Jun-Aug) Among the various beach restaurants scattered along the Palombaggia sands south of Porto-Vecchio, Tamariccia has that hip St-Tropez-chic touch. With its wooden decking terrace and first-class views of the turquoise surf, dining really does not get better than this. Cuisine is Mediterranean, with lots of grilled fish,

meat dishes and pasta, all beautifully presented. The lunchtime menu also includes pizza served bubbling hot from the oven.

Sous La Tonnelle MODERN CORSICAN €€
(☑04 95 70 02 17; rue Abbatucci; mains €22-28; ☉closed Sun & Mon low season) One of those irresistible shabby-chic addresses that just oozes panache, 'Under the Pagoda' is simply gorgeous. Think wooden floor, industrial floor-to-ceiling windows and a fine selection of contemporary fish and meat renditions of Corsican staples.

Le Séquoïa BAR, BISTRO €
(6 rue Joseph Pietri; wok dishes €15-20, salads & burgers €13) Tucked away by the side of the church, this hybrid bar-bistro is the hipster choice. Hobnob around bar stools outside or on loungy seating inside, while casually quaffing cocktails and scoffing burgers and salads. For a heartier meal, go for one for the one of the wok-cooked daily specials chalked on the blackboard.

ℹ Information

Tourist office (www.destination-sudcorse. com; rue Camille de Rocca Serra; ☉9am-8pm Mon-Sat, to 1pm Sun)

ℹ Getting There & Away

AIR **Figari-Sud Corse airport** (www.figari. aeroport.fr) is about 25km from Porto-Vecchio, near the village of Figari.

BOAT Seasonal ferries sail from Marseille, mainland France, to Porto-Vecchio ferry port at the southern end of Quai Pascal Paoli and its southern continuation, Quai de Syracuse.

BUS **Les Rapides Bleus** (☑04 95 70 10 36; rue Jean Jaurès) operates a daily service to Bastia (three hours) and shuttles to Plage de Palombaggia and Plage de Santa Giulia in summer. **Balési Évasion** (☑04 95 70 15 55; rte de Bastia) has buses to Ajaccio via L'Alta Rocca. **Eurocorse** (☑04 95 71 24 64; rue Pasteur) operates a service to Ajaccio (3½ hours) via Sartène. In the other direction, buses run twice daily to Bonifacio (30 minutes).

HOT NIGHTS OUT

It might seem small and sleepy by day, but, come dark, Porto-Vecchio sizzles in season, as its well-established party reputation dons its dancing shoes and lets rip for a hot night out in town. Hip cafes and bars cluster on place de la République, in the upper town and along the seafront. On the southern outskirts of Porto-Vecchio, Via Notte (☑04 95 72 02 12; www.vianotte.com; rte de Porra; ☉daily May-Sep), with 5000-odd revellers and superstar DJs most nights in summer, is the hottest club in Corsica and one of the most famous in the Med. It has to be seen to be believed.

CORTE AREA

Corte (Corti)

POP 6829

Secretive. Inward looking. Staunchly Corsican. In many ways, the mountain town of Corte feels different to other Corsican cities. This is the heart and soul of Corsica. It has been at the centre of the island's fortunes since Pascal Paoli made it the capital of his short-lived Corsican republic in 1755, and it remains a nationalist stronghold.

Beautifully positioned at the confluence of several rivers, Corte is blessed with an amazing setting. The fairy-tale sight of the citadel atop a craggy mount that bursts forth from the valley is sensational. Despite its isolation, the town oozes atmosphere and student buzz. In summer, it's mainly skittish tourists who make their base here, eager to canyon, hike, rock climb and mountain bike in the nearby Restonica and Tavignano valleys.

Sights

Citadel   HISTORIC QUARTER

Of Corsica's six citadels, Corte's is the only one not on the coast. Jutting out above the Tavignano and Restonica Rivers, and the cobbled alleyways of the Haute Ville, the citadel's highest point is the château – known as the Nid d'Aigle, meaning 'Eagle's Nest' – built in 1419.

The town's finest views are from the belvédère (viewing platform), reached via a steep staircase just outside the citadel's ramparts. Inside the walls are the former barracks and administrative buildings, which previously served as a WWII prison and a French Foreign Legion base. They now house the tourist office and the Museu di a Corsica (Museum of Corsica; 04 95 45 25 45; www.musee-corse.com; adult/child €5.50/3.50; 10am-8pm Jul-Sep, to 6pm Oct-Jun), a must-see for Corsica culture buffs with its outstanding exhibition on Corsican traditions, crafts, agriculture and anthropology.

Place Gaffory   SQUARE

From the citadel, meander downhill to place Gaffory, a lively square lined with restaurants and cafes and dominated by the 15th-century Église de l'Annonciation. The walls of nearby houses are pock-marked with bullet holes, reputedly from Corsica's war of independence.

Cours Paoli   STREET

A gentle wander along the main strip makes a pleasant prelude to an aperitif or a fine meal at one of the town's good restaurants. Start from place Paoli, Corte's focal point, which is dominated by a statue of Pascal Paoli, and stroll down the cours. It's a short walk, but allow plenty of time as there are lots of temptations along the way.

Sleeping

Hôtel du Nord   HOTEL €€

(04 95 46 00 68; www.hoteldunord-corte.com; 22 cours Paoli; s €69, d 82-87, tr €110-115, q €128-133;) Never mind the busy thoroughfare in season and the well-weathered, peeling facade (oh, so cinematic!): this grande dame of Corte's sleeping scene is kept shipshape. It has a cache of cheerful spacious rooms, contemporary colour schemes and a thoroughly homely vibe.

Camping Saint-Pancrace   CAMPGROUND €

(04 95 46 09 22; www.campingsaintpancrace.fr; adult/car/tent €6/3/4; Jun-Sep) The pick of Corte's campgrounds, with lots of pleasant sites sheltering under olive trees and green oak. It's a 20-minute walk north of town, in a peaceful neighbourhood. The owners run a small dairy farm – if you're after local cheese, this place is hard to beat.

Osteria di l'Orta – Casa Guelfucci   B&B €€

(04 95 61 06 41; www.osteria-di-l-orta.com; d incl breakfast €95;) Inside a powder-blue town house on the N193, this peach of a B&B is run by a charming couple with a keen designer's eye. The four rooms (named after local notables) are lovely, with polished wood floors, gleaming walls and great showers, but for real luxury go for the massive Pascal Paoli suite. At the end of the day, make sure you treat yourself to a copious dinner (€25) taken in the dining room, below the main building, with its vast bay windows; the delicious Corsican specialities are made using the finest local produce.

Hôtel Duc de Padoue   HOTEL €€

(04 95 46 01 37; www.ducdepadoue.com; place Padoue; d €75-92;) Don't be deterred by the scruffy façade of this professionally run abode. Renovated throughout a few years ago, the hotel has an inviting interior that offers well-equipped rooms, flat-screen TVs, plump bedding, muted tones and squeaky-clean bathrooms.

DON'T MISS

L'ALTA ROCCA

If you've had a temporary surfeit of superb seascapes, take a couple of days to explore L'Alta Rocca, north of Porto-Vecchio. Here you can really feel a sense of wilderness, a world away from the bling-bling and bustle of the coast. At the south of the long spine that traverses the island, it's a bewildering combination of dense, mixed evergreen-deciduous forests and granite villages strung over rocky ledges.

Leave Porto-Vecchio by the winding D368 that will take you to the calm surroundings of L'Ospédale, at an altitude of about 1000m. The village is close to the Forêt de L'Ospédale, which offers excellent walking opportunities and tranquil picnic spots. Follow signs to Zonza, a mountain village with the iconic Aiguilles de Bavella (Bavella Needles) – granite pinnacles akin to giant skarks' teeth jabbing the skyline at an altitude of more than 1600m – as backdrop. Zonza is a perfect base for exploring L'Alta Rocca, with a good range of restaurants and accommodation options: L'Aiglon (04 95 78 67 79; www.aiglonhotel.com; d €70, with shared bathroom €61; Apr-Dec) is a simple hotel that cooks up refined Corsican cuisine, while Hameau de Cavanello (04 95 78 66 82; www .locationzonza.com; s/d incl breakfast €77/89;), 2km towards the Col de Bavella, has a handful of cosy rooms and a pool nesting in hectares of green meadows and forests. Or plump for a stylish Mongolian yurt between trees on an organic farm at Le Pré aux Biches (06 27 52 48 03; www.lepreauxbiches.com).

Another little charmer is the nearby village of Quenza. It's cradled by thickly wooded mountains, and the Aiguilles de Bavella loom on the horizon. If you're after a typically Corsican atmosphere and the most tranquil location imaginable, at an altitude of 1200m, bookmark Chez Pierrot (04 95 78 63 21; d incl half-board €110), southern Corsica's most idiosyncratic venture. This multifaceted place – gîte (cottage), B&B, restaurant and equestrian centre – is run by charismatic Pierrot, a local character who's been living here since his early childhood. It's on Plateau de Ghjallicu, about 5km uphill from Quenza.

From Zonza or Quenza, it's a short drive to the Col de Bavella (Bavella Pass; 1218m), from where you can marvel close-up at the iconic Aiguilles de Bavella. The Bavella area is also a fantastic playground. Walking, rock climbing, canyoning or simply picnicking... it can all be done in the vicinity of the col (pass). Outdoor action done, feast on a roasted baby goat or wild pig stew at the Auberge du Col de Bavella (04 95 72 09 87; www .auberge-bavella.com; place de la Fontaine; mains €13-21, menu €24; lunch & dinner Apr-Oct), a large Corsican inn on top of the col that serves excellent meat dishes in a comforting rustic setting. Should you want to overnight, it has dorm beds (half-board €36 per person in a four- or six-bedded dorm).

For culture vultures, Levie is worth a pit stop with its well put together museum and superb scenery. The Musée de l'Alta Rocca (adult/child €5.50/3; 9.30am-6pm daily May-Oct, 10am-5pm Tue-Sat Nov-Apr) does a good job of elucidating Corsican geology, climate, flora and fauna. It also features ethnology and archaeology sections. After a visit to the museum, head to the archaeological site of Pianu di Livia (04 95 78 48 21; www .cucuruzzu.fr; adult/child €5.50/3; 9.30am-7pm Jun-Sep, to 6pm Apr, May & Oct), about 7km to the north (it's signposted). Here you can get a feel for what life was like in ancient times in Corsica. Livia has one of Corsica's most attractive accommodation options, A Pignata (04 95 78 41 90; www.apignata.com; rte du Pianu; d incl half-board €180-260, treehouse €300; Apr-Oct;). A real family affair fronted by brothers Antoine and Jean-Baptiste, this boutique farmhouse with vegetable garden and herd of pigs (that end up as the most divine charcuterie) is pure class. Despite its rural setting, its 18 rooms are thoroughly contemporary and its rustic restaurant (menu €40) is among the best in southern Corsica. The icing on the cake is its Zen, pool-clad spa with vast window staring face-to-face with the Alta Rocca mountains, crossed by swirling clouds. Oh, and did we mention the impossibly romantic treehouse for two strung in an old arbre (tree)? Heaven.

From Levie, drive to Ste-Lucie de Tallano, which has a few monuments worthy of interest, including the well-proportioned Église Ste-Lucie and the Renaissance-style Couvent St-François, an imposing building scenically positioned at the edge of the village.

✕ Eating

Café Le Bip's   CORSICAN €
(☑04 95 46 06 26; 14 cours Paoli; mains €12-20)
Want to know where students from Corsica's
only university go when they fancy going out
for dinner? Here, to this old stone candlelit
cellar, famed across town for its gargantuan
portions of traditional Corsican fare. Find
it on the vast square behind cours Paoli. In
winter, by the fireplace is the place to be.

U Museu   CORSICAN €€
(☑04 95 61 08 36; www.restaurant-umuseu.com;
rampe Ribanelle; ☉lunch & dinner daily Apr–mid-
Oct) Just below the entrance to the citadel,
U Museu may look like your typical tourist
trap, but that's deceptive. Dine on its gazebo-
covered terrace and choose from its wide
range of Corsican specialities (the *menu
corse* is excellent value), including *civet de
sanglier aux myrtes sauvages* (wild boar
with myrtle) and *tripettes à la cortenaise*
(tripe with shallots in a red-wine sauce). It
doesn't take reservations and it closes on
Sunday in the low season.

Le 24   MODERN CORSICAN €€
(☑04 95 46 02 90; 24 cours Paoli; mains €15-25;
☉lunch & dinner daily Jul & Aug, closed lunch Sun
Sep-Jun) After something upmarket? Then
swing by this snazzy spot on the main drag.
It boasts contemporary furnishings, a sexy
atmosphere and an innovative menu that
uses top-quality ingredients and changes
with the seasons. The house desserts,
chalked up on the blackboard, hit the right
spot.

🍷 Drinking

There's a lively bar scene along cours Paoli.

Café du Cours   CAFE
(22 cours Paoli) This unfussy cafe is a great
place to watch the world go by.

Le Rex Lounge   BAR
(1 cours Paoli) This sleek place serves excellent
cocktails.

ℹ Information

Tourist office (☑04 95 46 26 70; www.centru
-corsica.com; Citadel; ☉10am-5pm Mon, Wed
& Sat, 9am-7pm Tue, Thu & Fri Jul & Aug,
closed Sat & Sun Sep-Jun)

ℹ Getting There & Away

BUS **Eurocorse** (☑04 95 31 73 76; www.euro
corse.com; 1 rte du Nouveau Port) buses link
Ajaccio with Bastia via Corte (two hours). **Transports Mordiconi** (☑04 95 48 00 44) links Corte
with Porto (2¾ hours) once daily except Sunday
from July to mid-September, leaving from outside the train station.

TRAIN Trains serve Bastia (two hours, three to
four daily) and Ajaccio (two hours, three to four
daily).

Around Corte

In the mountainous area around Corte you'll
find fresh mountain air, deep forests, picturesque valleys and abundant hiking trails.
Enjoy the scenery and rejuvenate mind and
body in a pristine environment.

VALLÉE DE LA RESTONICA
The Vallée de la Restonica is one of the
prettiest spots in all of Corsica. The river, rising in the grey-green mountains, has scoured
little basins in the rock, offering sheltered
pinewood settings for bathing and sunbathing alike. From Corte, the D623 winds
its way through the valley for 15km to the
Bergeries de Grotelle (1375m), where a car
park (€5) and a huddle of shepherd's huts
(three of which offer drinks, local cheeses
and snacks) marks the end of the road. From
them, a path leads to a pair of picture-pretty
glacial lakes – Lac de Melu (1711m), reached
after about one hour, and Lac de Capitellu
(1930m), 45 minutes' walk further on.

There are a couple of tempting sleeping
choices in the early reaches of the valley,
including the fabulous Les Jardins de la
Glacière (☑04 95 45 27 00; www.lesjardinsde
laglaciere.com; Gorges de la Restonica; d €85-100;
☉Apr–mid-Nov; ❄@🊺), an unbeatble budg-
et option with clean, fresh rooms, impeccable communal areas and a fantastic location
(and swimming pool) by the river.

VALLÉE DU TAVIGNANO
If you have a day to spare, do not miss the
opportunity to hike into the car-free (and
much quieter than Restonica) Vallée du
Tavignano. Corsica's deepest gorge is only
accessible on foot and remains well off the
beaten track, despite being on Corte's doorstep. From Corte, the signposted track leads
to the Passerelle de Rossolino footbridge,
reached after about 2½ hours. It's an idyllic spot for a picnic, and there are plenty of
transparent green natural pools in which
you can dunk yourself. The valley can also be
explored on horseback with the outdoorsy
folks behind the lovely B&B and *camping*

à la ferme (at the farm), **L'Albadu** (☎04 95 46 24 55; www.hebergement-albadu.fr; ancienne rte d'Ajaccio; d incl half-board per person/couple €48/96, camping adult/tent/car €5/2.50/2.50).

VIZZAVONA

South of Corte, the N193 climbs steeply in the shadow of Monte d'Oro (2389m) before arriving at the cool mountain hamlet of Vizzavona. A mere cluster of houses and ho-tels around a train station, Vizzavona is an ideal base from which to explore the **Forêt de Vizzavona**, where the 1633 hectares are covered mainly by beech and laricio pines. A magnet for walkers, it features lots of excellent hikes. Look for the signpost indicating a short, gentle path that meanders down through a superb forest to **Cascades des Anglais**, a sequence of gleaming waterfalls.

Understand France

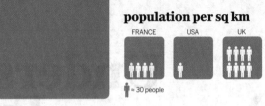

population per sq km

FRANCE USA UK

👤 ≈ 30 people

France Today

A New French President

Presidential elections in spring 2012 ushered in France's first socialist president since François Mitterand left office in 1995. The presidential campaign saw incumbent right-wing president Nicolas Sarkozy vie for a second term in office against left-wing candidate François Hollande (b 1954) of the Socialist party. Sarkozy promised to modernise the French economy, dramatically reduce (by half) the number of immigrants to France, and lower France's budget deficit; but with the electorate tired of the austerity policies of the Conservatives, it was Hollande's ambitious talk of reducing unemployment (at a 12-year high), clearing the country's debts by 2017, upping tax on corporations and salaries over €1 million per annum and increasing the minimum salary that proved the more appealing. In the first round of voting in April 2012, Hollande pipped Sarkozy at the post with 28.6% of the vote against 27.2%. In run-off elections a fortnight later, he landed just under 52% of votes, to become the new French president. Parliamentary elections a month later sealed his grip on power, with the Socialists winning a comfortable majority (273 seats) in France's 577-seat National Assembly, thus paving the way for Hollande to govern France during the biggest economic crisis Europe has seen in decades.

Fast Facts

» Population: 64.3 million

» Area: 551,000 sq km

» GDP: US$2.214 trillion

» GDP growth: 1.7%

» Inflation: 2%

» Unemployment: 10.2%

Cultural Highs

In keeping with the poor economic climate across Europe, 2012 opened gloomily as French hoteliers and restaurant owners shook their heads despairingly over a VAT increase on service products from 5.5% to 7% (one of the Sarkozy government's austerity measures aimed at reducing the public deficit).

Yet within the cultural arena, France is savouring something of a high. Art lovers are bursting with excitement over the reopening in Paris, af-

Faux Pas

» Splitting the bill is deemed the height of unsophistication. The person who invites pays, although close friends often go Dutch.

» Fondle fruit, veg, flowers or clothing in shops and you'll be greeted with a killer glare from the shop assistant.

» Take flowers (not chrysanthemums, which are only for cemeteries) or Champagne when invited to someone's home.

» Never, ever, discuss money over dinner.

Best in Print

The Death of French Culture (Donald Morrison) Thought-provoking look at France's past and present.

Me Talk Pretty One Day (David Sedaris) Caustic take on moving to France and learning the lingo.

belief systems
(% of population)

if France were
100 people

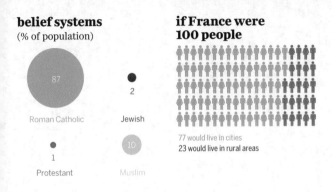

87
Roman Catholic

2
Jewish

1
Protestant

10
Muslim

77 would live in cities
23 would live in rural areas

ter months of painstaking renovation, of both the Musée Picasso and the country's most prestigious theatre, the Comédie Française, where Molière trod the boardwalks. Construction work on Paris' new €336 million philharmonic concert hall, to open in 2014, is back on track after being stalled in 2010 for lack of national funding, while world-renowned Frank Gehry is the architect behind dazzling projects in the capital (a glass crystal-shaped contemporary art gallery in Paris' Bois de Boulogne) and French provinces (a shimmering cultural centre in Arles, southern France). At the 2012 Academy Awards, the French-made silent film *The Artist,* starring the quintessentially French-sexy Jean Dujardin, stole the show by scooping five Oscars. Enter the much-heralded renaissance of French cinema.

Then there is the Louvre-Lens that will see priceless works of art from the original Louvre whisked up north to a striking new gallery space in former coal mining town Lens. Innovative, daring and decidedly bold, it promises to inject new creativity into the conventional French museum experience.

Environmental Lows
The protection of France's lyrical landscapes has never been straightforward, as demonstrated by recent developments at one of the country's most iconic sights, the stunning abbey-crowned mount of Mont St-Michel. A €200 million project is designed to stop the mythical bay silting up by building a dam, ridding the mount of cars and motorised vehicles from its traffic-congested foot, and replacing the original tidal causeway trodden by pilgrims since 1879 with an ultralightweight bridge (by 2014). This would allow the 14m-high tidal waters for which this part of Normandy is famed to swirl without environmental consequence. Yet,

France has always drawn immigrants: 4.3 million from Europe between 1850 and WWI, and another three million between the world wars. Post-WWII, several million unskilled workers followed from North Africa and French-speaking sub-Saharan Africa.

Best Surfs

Paris in Color (Nichole Robertson) No photographic title better captures the extraordinary colours and hues of the French capital.
Stuff Parisians Like (Olivier Magny) Witty vignettes by a Parisian sommelier.

Paris by Mouth (http://paris bymouth.com) Resource for capital dining and drinking.
Wine Travel Guides (www. winetravelguides.com) Practical guides to France's wine regions.
France 24 (www.france24.com/en/france) French news in English.

Lost in Cheeseland (www. lostincheeseland.com) French life through seen the eyes of an American expat wed to a Frenchman.

just as the motorised vehicles go and the 2.5 million annual visitors embrace the final leg of one of France's top tourist pilgrimages on foot or by shuttle, Mont St-Michel risks losing its Unesco World Heritage status. The reason: the proposed construction of offshore turbine farms some 20km out to sea from the priceless mount.

France maintains a rigid distinction between church and state. The country is a secular republic, meaning there can be no mention of religion on national school syllabuses.

Santé!

Swathes of fresh-green vineyards in the Champagne region could be graced with Unesco protection if its bid to become a World Heritage Site in 2013 proves successful. Meantime, such is the global demand for the 320 million bottles of fizz it sells each year that the body regulating where Champagne can be made has agreed to enlarge the production area for the first time since 1927. In 2017 the first new vines will be planted in 40 new Champagne-producing villages. *Santé!* (Cheers!)

Best Films

Les Choristes (The Chorus; 2004) A new teacher arrives at a school for troublesome boys.
La Môme (La Vie en Rose; 2007) Story of singer Edith Piaf.
Midnight in Paris (2011) Woody Allen tale, with standout dream scenes set in 1920s Paris.

Cheese Etiquette

» Cut small circular cheeses into pie wedges.

» Larger cheeses already sliced into a wedge must be cut tip to rind – don't slice off the tip.

» Chop semihard cheeses horizontally.

Tap Water

» Safe to drink, as is water spouting from fountains flagged 'eau potable'.

» If the sign says 'eau non potable', don't drink it!

» Save money by ordering *une carafe d'eau* (a jug of free tap water).

History

The history of France could be said to be a microcosm of the history of much of Europe. As elsewhere, its beginnings involved the mass migration of a nomadic people (the peripatetic Celts), the subjugation by and – dare we say? – the civilising influence of the Romans, and the rise of a local nobility. Christianity would bring a degree of unity, but perhaps nowhere else would such a strongly independent church continue to co-exist under a powerful central authority. From Charles 'The Hammer' Martel and Louis XIV's claim to be the state itself, to the present government's socialist president dealing with '60 million different opinions', this dichotomy is the basis of France's story.

Track France in the news, learn about its history and catch up on stacks more background info with www.discoverfrance.net.

Roman Gaul

What is now France was settled by several different groups of people in the Iron Age, but the largest and most organised were the Celtic Gauls. The subjugation of these people and their territory by Rome was gradual, and within a few centuries Rome had imposed its government, roads, trade, culture and even language. A Gallo-Roman culture emerged and Gaul was increasingly integrated into the Roman Empire.

It began in the 1st millennium BC as the Greeks and Romans established colonies on the Mediterranean coast, including Massilia (Marseille). Centuries of conflict between the Gauls and the Romans ended in 52 BC, when Caesar's legions crushed a revolt by many Gallic tribes led by Celtic Arverni tribe chief Vercingétorix at Gergovia near present-day Clermont-Ferrand – no site better evokes the drama and bloodshed of this momentous point in history than the state-of-the-art, highly insightful MuséoParc Alésia in Burgundy. For the next couple of years, during the so-called Gallic Wars, the Gauls hounded the Romans with guerrilla warfare and fought them in several match-drawn pitched battles. But gradually Gallic resistance collapsed and the Romans reigned supreme.

NEWS

TIMELINE

c 30,000 BC	c 7000 BC	1500–500 BC
During the middle Palaeolithic period, Cro-Magnon people start decorating their homes in the Vézère Valley of the Dordogne with colourful scenes of animals, human figures and geometric shapes.	Neolithic people turn their hands to monumental menhirs and dolmen during the New Stone Age, creating a fine collection in Brittany that continues to baffle historians.	Celtic Gauls move into the region and establish trading links with the Greeks, whose colonies included Massilia (Marseille) on the Mediterranean coast; the latter bring grapes and olives.

HISTORY THE AGONY & THE ECSTASY: MEDIEVAL FRANCE

PRIMITIVE ART

The Cro-Magnons, a *Homo sapiens* variety who arrived in what is now France about 35,000 years ago, had larger brains than their ancestors, the Neanderthals, long and narrow skulls, and short, wide faces. Their hands were nimble, and with the aid of improved tools they hunted reindeer, bison, horses and mammoths to eat. They played music, danced and had fairly complex social patterns.

Those agile hands were not just used to make tools and hunt; Cro-Magnons were also artists. A tour of Grotte de Lascaux II – a replica of the Lascaux cave where one of the world's best examples of Cro-Magnon drawings was found in 1940 – demonstrates how initial simplistic drawings and engravings of animals gradually became more detailed and realistic. Dubbed 'Périgord's Sistine Chapel', the Lascaux cave contains some 2000 paintings of human figures and abstract signs as well as animals and is one of 25 known decorated caves in Dordogne's Vézère Valley.

The Neolithic period produced France's incredible collection of menhirs and dolmens: Brittany's Morbihan Coast is awash in megalithic monuments.

The stone architecture left by the occupiers was impressive and Roman France is magnificent, climaxing with the mighty Pont du Gard aqueduct, built to bring water to the city of Nîmes in southern France, and splendid theatres and amphitheatres dating from this period are still extant in that city as well as at Autun, Arles and Orange. Some Roman remains were reused: in an early form of recycling, the 1st-century Roman amphitheatre at Périgueux in the Dordogne was dismantled in the 3rd century and its stones used to build the city walls.

The Romans' intangible legacy to what would become a new culture was equally great. Sophisticated urban centres with markets and baths of hot and cold running water began to emerge. The Romans planted vineyards, notably in Burgundy and Bordeaux, and introduced techniques to process wine. Most importantly, they introduced the newfangled faith of Christianity, which would eventually beat out the not-dissimilar worship of Mithra in the popularity sweepstakes.

Later the Franks would adopt these important elements of Gallo-Roman civilisation (including Christianity), and their eventual assimilation resulted in a fusion of Germanic culture with that of the Celts and the Romans.

The Agony & the Ecstasy: Medieval France

The collapse of the Roman Empire opened the gates to a wave of Franks and other Germanic tribes under Merovius from the north and northeast who overran the territory. Merovius' grandson, Clovis I, converted to

3rd century BC	121 BC	55–52 BC	c AD 100–300
The Celtic Parisii tribe builds a handful of wattle-and-daub huts on what is now the Île de la Cité in Paris; the capital city is christened Lutetia by the Romans.	The Romans begin taking Gallic territory, annexing southern Gaul as the province of Gallia Narbonensis (in modern Provence and Languedoc), with its capital at the present-day town of Narbonne.	Julius Caesar launches his invasion of Britain from the Côte d'Opale in far northern France; the Gauls defeat the Romans at Gergovia near present-day Clermont-Ferrand.	The Romans go on a building spree throughout France, erecting magnificent baths, temples and aqueducts of almighty proportions such as the Pont du Gard near Nîmes in southern France.

Christianity, giving him greater legitimacy and power over his Christian subjects, and made Paris his seat; his successors founded the abbey of St-Germain des Prés in Paris and later the one at St-Denis to the north, which would become the richest, most important monastery in France and the final resting place of its kings.

The Frankish tradition, by which the king was succeeded by all of his sons, led to power struggles and the eventual disintegration of the kingdom into a collection of small feudal states. The dominant house to emerge was that of the Carolingians.

Carolingian power reached apogee under Charlemagne, who extended the boundaries of the kingdom and was crowned Holy Roman Emperor (Emperor of the West) in 800. But during the 9th century Scandinavian Vikings (also called Norsemen, thus Normans) raided France's western coast, settling in the lower Seine Valley and forming the duchy of Normandy a century later. This would be a century of disunity in France, marked politically by the rise of Norman power and religiously by the foundation of influential abbeys like the Benedictine one at Cluny. By the time Hugh Capet ascended the throne in 987, heralding the arrival of the Capetian dynasty, the king's domain was a humble parcel of land around Paris and Orléans.

The tale of how William the Conqueror and his forces mounted a successful invasion of England from their base in Normandy in 1066 is told on the Bayeux Tapestry, showcased inside Bayeux' Musée de la Tapisserie

HISTORICAL READS

» **The Sun King** (Nancy Mitford; 1966) Classic work on Louis XIV and the country he ruled by acclaimed author and biographer who lived and died in Versailles.

» **Citizens: A Chronicle of the French Revolution** (Simon Schama; 1990) Highly acclaimed and truly monumental work that looks at the first few years of the revolutionary government after 1789.

» **The Discovery of France: A Historical Geography** (Graham Robb; 2008) This much-lauded work is an anecdotal account of France's formation based on 20,000km of research by bicycle around rural France. Don't miss *Parisians: An Adventure History of Paris* (2010) by the same author.

» **The Shameful Peace: How French Artists and Intellectuals Survived the Nazi Occupation** (Frederic Spotts; 2010) This is the book that separates the wheat from the chaff, the saints from the sinners, the 'no' and the 'yes' men.

» **The Greater Journey: Americans in Paris** (David McCullough; 2011) Between 1830 and 1900 dozens of Americans crossed the Atlantic to find inspiration in the 'city of light'. This is their compelling tale.

c 455-70	732	800-900	987
France remains under Roman rule until the 5th century, when the Franks (hence the name 'France') and the Alemanii invade and overrun the country from the east.	Somewhere near Poitiers Charles Martel and his cavalry repel the Muslim Moors. His grandson, Charlemagne, extends the boundaries of the kingdom and is crowned Holy Roman Emperor.	Scandinavian Vikings (also called Norsemen, thus Normans) raid France's western coast and settle in the lower Seine Valley where they later form the Duchy of Normandy.	Five centuries of Merovingian and Carolingian rule ends with the crowning of Hugh Capet; a dynasty that will rule one of Europe's most powerful countries for the next eight centuries is born.

de Bayeux. In 1152 Eleanor of Aquitaine wed Henry of Anjou, bringing a further third of France under the control of the English crown. The subsequent rivalry between France and England for control of Aquitaine and the vast English territories in France lasted three centuries.

Hundred Years War

In 1337 the hostility between the Capetians and the Anglo-Normans degenerated into the Hundred Years War, which would be fought on and off until the middle of the 15th century. The Black Death, which broke out a decade after the hostilities began and lasted more than two years, killed more than a third (an estimated 80,000 souls) of Paris' population alone but only briefly interrupted the fighting.

The French suffered particularly nasty defeats at Crécy and Agincourt. Abbey-studded Mont St-Michel in present-day Normandy was the only place in northern and western France not to fall into English hands. The dukes of Burgundy (allied with the English) occupied Paris and in 1422 John Plantagenet, duke of Bedford, was made regent of France for England's King Henry VI, then an infant. Less than a decade later he was crowned king of France.

Luckily for the French, 17-year-old Jeanne d'Arc (Joan of Arc) came along with the outlandish tale that she had a divine mission from God to expel the English from France and bring about the coronation of French Charles VII in Reims.

The Rise of the French Court

With the arrival of Italian Renaissance culture during the reign of François I (r 1515–47), the focus shifted to the Loire Valley. Italian artists decorated royal castles at Amboise, Azay-le-Rideau, Blois, Chambord and Chaumont, with Leonardo da Vinci making Le Clos Lucé in Amboise his home for three years until his death in 1519.

Renaissance ideas of scientific and geographic scholarship and discovery assumed a new importance, as did the value of secular matters over religious life. Writers such as Rabelais, Marot and Ronsard of La Pléiade were influential as were artist and architect disciples of Michelangelo and Raphael. Evidence of this architectural influence can be seen in François I's château at Fontainebleau – where superb artisans, many of them brought over from Italy, blended Italian and French styles to create what is known as the First School of Fontainebleau – and the Petit Château at Chantilly, both near Paris. This new architecture was meant to reflect the splendour of the monarchy, which was fast moving towards absolutism. But all this grandeur and show of strength was not enough to stem the tide of Protestantism that was flowing into France.

The French invented the first digital calculator, the hot-air balloon, Braille and margarine, not to mention Grand Prix racing and the first public interactive computer network. Find out what else at http://inventors.about.com/od/frenchinventors.

1066	1152	1253	1309
Duke of Normandy William the Conqueror and his Norman forces occupy England, making Normandy and, later, Plantagenet-ruled England formidable rivals of the kingdom of France.	Eleanor of Aquitaine weds Henry of Anjou, bringing a further third of France under the control of the English crown and sparking a French-English rivalry that will last three centuries.	La Sorbonne is founded by Robert de Sorbon, confessor of Louis IX, as a theological college for impoverished students in the area of the Left Bank known as the Latin Quarter.	French-born Pope Clément V moves papal headquarters from Rome to Avignon, where the Holy Seat remains until 1377; 'home' is the resplendent Palais des Papes built under Benoît XII.

The Reformation swept through Europe in the 1530s, spearheaded by the ideas of Jean (John) Calvin, a Frenchman born in Picardy but exiled to Geneva. Following the Edict of January 1562, which afforded the Protestants certain rights, the Wars of Religion broke out between the Huguenots (French Protestants who received help from the English), the Catholic League (led by the House of Guise) and the Catholic monarchy, and lasted three dozen years.

Henri IV, founder of the Bourbon dynasty, issued the controversial Edict of Nantes in 1598, guaranteeing the Huguenots many civil and political rights, notably freedom of conscience. Ultra-Catholic Paris refused

THE VIRGIN WARRIOR

Many stories surround the origins of Jeanne d'Arc (Joan of Arc), the legendary *pucelle* (virgin) warrior burned at the stake by the English, and France's patron saint. Some say she was the bastard child of Louis d'Orléans, King Charles VI's brother. The less glamorous but more accurate account pinpoints Domrémy in northeastern France (Domrémy-la-Pucelle today) as the place where she was born to a simple peasant family in 1412.

Revelations delivered by the Archangel Michael prompted Jeanne d'Arc to flee the fold in 1428. Her mission: to raise a siege against the city of Orléans and see the dauphin (the future Charles VII) crowned king of France. An enquiry conducted by clergy and university clerks in Poitiers tried to establish if Jeanne d'Arc was a fraud or a gift, as she claimed, from the king of Heaven to the king of France. Her virginity was likewise certified. Following the six-week interrogation Jeanne was sent by Charles VII to Tours, where she was equipped with intendants, a horse, a sword and her own standard featuring God sitting in judgment on a cloud. In Blois the divine warrior collected her army, drummed up by Charles VII from his Royal Army Headquarters there. In April 1429 Jeanne d'Arc started her attack on Orléans, besieged by the English from October of the previous year. She entered the city, rallying its inhabitants and gaining their support. On 5 and 6 May respectively the French gained control of the Bastille St-Loup and the Bastille des Augustins, followed the next day by the legendary Fort des Tourelles – a fort guarding the only access to the city from the left bank. This last shattering defeat prompted the English to lay down the siege on 8 May and was a decisive turning point in the Hundred Years War.

From Orléans Jeanne d'Arc went on to defeat the English at Jargeau, Beaugency and Patay. Charles VII stayed at châteaux in Loches and Sully-sur-Loire at this time and prayed to St Benedict with his protégé at Abbaye de St-Benoît in St-Benoît-sur-Loire. Despite Charles' promised coronation in July 1429, battles between the English and the French waged until 1453, by which time the virginal warrior responsible for turning the war around had long been dead. Jeanne d'Arc was captured by the Burgundians, sold to the English, convicted of witchcraft and heresy by a tribunal of French ecclesiastics in Rouen in 1431 and burned at the stake. She was canonised in 1920.

1337	1358	1422	1431
Incessant struggles between the Capetians and England's King Edward III, a Plantagenet, over the powerful French throne degenerate into the Hundred Years War, which will last until 1453.	The war between France and England and the devastation and poverty caused by the plague lead to the ill-fated peasants' revolt led by Étienne Marcel.	John Plantagenet, duke of Bedford, is made regent of France for England's King Henry VI, then an infant; in less than a decade he is crowned king of France at Paris' Notre Dame.	Jeanne d'Arc (Joan of Arc) is burned at the stake in Rouen for heresy; the English are not driven out of France until 1453.

to allow the new Protestant king to enter the city, and a siege of the capital continued for almost five years. Only when Henri IV embraced Catholicism at the cathedral in St-Denis did the capital submit to him.

Arguably France's most famous king of this or any other century, Louis XIV (r 1643–1715), called Le Roi Soleil (the Sun King), ascended the throne at the tender age of five. Bolstered by claims of divine right, he involved the kingdom in a series of costly wars with Holland, Austria and England, which gained France territory but nearly bankrupted the treasury. State taxation to refill the coffers caused widespread poverty and vagrancy, especially in the cities. In Versailles, Louis XIV built an extravagant palace and made his courtiers compete with each other for royal favour, thereby quashing the ambitious, feuding aristocracy and creating the first centralised French state. In 1685 he revoked the Edict of Nantes.

The Seven Years War (1756–63), known as the French and Indian War in North America, was one of a series of ruinous military engagements pursued by Louis XV, the Sun King's grandson. It led to the loss of France's flourishing colonies in Canada, the West Indies and India. It was in part to avenge these losses that his successor Louis XVI sided with the colonists in the American War of Independence a dozen years later. But the Seven Years War cost France a fortune and, more disastrously for the monarchy, it helped to disseminate at home the radical democratic ideas that were thrust upon the world stage by the American Revolution.

From Revolution to Republic

As the 18th century progressed, new economic and social circumstances rendered the *ancien régime* (old order) dangerously out of step with the needs of the country. The regime was further weakened by the anti-establishment and anticlerical ideas of the Enlightenment, whose leading lights included Voltaire, Rousseau and Diderot. But entrenched vested interests, a cumbersome power structure and royal lassitude prevented change from starting until the 1770s, by which time the monarchy's moment had passed.

By the late 1780s, the indecisive Louis XVI and his dominating consort, Marie-Antoinette, had managed to alienate virtually every segment of society, and the king became increasingly isolated as unrest and dissatisfaction reached boiling point. When he tried to neutralise the power of the more reform-minded delegates at a meeting of the États-Généraux (States-General) at the Jeu de Paume in Versailles in May and June 1789, the masses took to the streets of Paris. On 14 July, a mob raided the armoury at the Hôtel des Invalides for rifles, seizing 32,000 muskets, then stormed the prison at Bastille – the ultimate symbol of the despotic *ancien régime*. The French Revolution had begun.

> The Sun King was yet another Louis named after France's patron saint. Paintings in Versailles' Royal Chapel evoke the idea that the French king was chosen by God and was thus his lieutenant on earth.

LOUIS XIV

1491

Charles VIII weds Anne de Bretagne at Château de Langeais in the castle-studded Loire Valley, marking the unification of independent Brittany with France.

1515

With the reign of François I the royal court moves to the Loire Valley, where a rash of stunning Renaissance châteaux and hunting lodges is built.

ESCUDERO PATRICK/GETTY IMAGES ©

» Statue of Joan of Arc, Paris

At first, the Revolution was in the hands of moderate republicans called the Girondins. France was declared a constitutional monarchy and various reforms were introduced, including the adoption of the Déclaration des Droits de l'Homme et du Citoyen (Declaration of the Rights of Man and of the Citizen) modelled on the American Declaration of Independence. But as the masses armed themselves against the external threat to the new government – posed by Austria, Prussia and the exiled French nobles – patriotism and nationalism mixed with extreme fervour, popularising and radicalising the Revolution. It was not long before the Girondins lost out to the extremist Jacobins, who abolished the monarchy and declared the First Republic after Louis XVI proved unreliable as a constitutional monarch. The Assemblée Nationale (National Assembly) was replaced by an elected Revolutionary Convention.

In January 1793 Louis XVI, who had tried to flee the country with his family but only got as far as Lorraine, was convicted of 'conspiring against the liberty of the nation' and guillotined at place de la Révolution, today's place de la Concorde, in Paris. Two months later the Jacobins set up the notorious Committee of Public Safety to deal with national defence and to apprehend and try 'traitors'. This body had dictatorial control over the country during the so-called Reign of Terror (September 1793 to July 1794), which saw most religious freedoms revoked and churches closed to worship and desecrated, cathedrals turned into 'Temples of Reason', and thousands incarcerated in dungeons in Paris' Conciergerie on Île de la Cité before being beheaded.

After the Reign of Terror faded, a five-man delegation of moderate republicans set itself up to rule the republic as the Directoire (Directory).

Napoléon & Empire

It was true happenstance that brought a dashing young Corsican general named Napoléon Bonaparte to the attention of France. In October 1795 a group of royalist youths bent on overthrowing the Directory were intercepted on rue St-Honoré in Paris by forces under Bonaparte, who fired into the crowd. For this 'whiff of grapeshot' he was put in command of the French forces in Italy, where he was particularly successful in the campaign against Austria. His victories would soon turn him into an independent political force.

In 1799 Napoléon overthrew the Directory and assumed power as First Consul, chosen by popular vote. A referendum three years later declared him 'Consul for Life' and his birthday became a national holiday. In 1804, when he crowned himself 'Emperor of the French' in the presence of Pope Pius VII at Notre Dame in Paris, Napoléon's ambitions were obvious.

To consolidate and legitimise his authority, Napoléon needed more victories on the battlefield. So began a seemingly endless series of wars

1530s	1572	1588	1589
The Reformation, spurred by the writings of French Jean (John) Calvin, sweeps through France, pitting Catholics against Protestants and eventually leading to the Wars of Religion (1562–98).	Some 3000 Huguenots visiting Paris to celebrate the wedding of the Protestant Henri of Navarre (the future Henri IV) are slaughtered on 23–24 August, in the so-called St Bartholomew's Day Massacre.	The Catholic League forces Henri III (r 1574–89), the last of the Valois kings, to flee the royal court at the Louvre; the next year he is assassinated by a fanatical Dominican friar.	Henri IV, the first Bourbon king, ascends the throne after renouncing Protestantism; 'Paris vaut bien une messe' (Paris is well worth a Mass), he is reputed to have said upon taking communion.

A DATE WITH THE REVOLUTION

Along with standardising France's system of weights and measures with the almost universal metric system, the revolutionary government adopted a new, 'more rational' calendar from which all 'superstitious' associations (ie saints' days and mythology) were removed. Year 1 began on 22 September 1792, the day the First Republic was proclaimed.

The names of the 12 months – Vendémaire, Brumaire, Frimaire, Nivôse, Pluviôse, Ventôse, Germinal, Floréal, Prairial, Messidor, Thermidor and Fructidor – were chosen according to the seasons. The autumn months, for instance, were Vendémaire (derived from *vendange*, grape harvest), Brumaire (from *brume*, mist or fog) and Frimaire (from *frimas*, wintry weather). In turn, each month was divided into three 10-day 'weeks' called *décades*, the last day of which was a rest day. The five remaining days of the year were used to celebrate Virtue, Genius, Labour, Opinion and Rewards. These festivals were initially called *sans-culottides* in honour of the *sans-culottes*, the extreme revolutionaries who wore pantaloons rather than the short breeches favoured by the upper classes.

While the republican calendar worked well in theory, it caused no end of confusion for France in its communications and trade abroad because the months and days kept changing in relation to those of the Gregorian calendar. The revolutionary calendar was abandoned and the old system restored in 1806 by Napoléon Bonaparte.

and victories by which France would come to control most of Europe. In 1812 his troops captured Moscow, only to be killed off by the brutal Russian winter. Two years later Allied armies entered Paris, exiled Napoléon to Elba in the Mediterranean and restored the House of Bourbon to the French throne at the Congress of Vienna.

In early 1815 Napoléon escaped Elba, landed in southern France and gathered a large army as he marched towards Paris. On 1 June he reclaimed the throne at celebrations held at the Champ de Mars. But his reign came to an end just three weeks later when his forces were defeated at Waterloo in Belgium. Napoléon was exiled again, this time to the island of St Helena in the South Atlantic, where he died in 1821. In 1840 his remains were moved to Paris' Église du Dôme.

Although reactionary in some ways – he re-established slavery in France's colonies in 1802, for example – Napoléon instituted a number of important reforms, including a reorganisation of the judicial system; the promulgation of a new legal code, the Code Napoléon (or civil code), which forms the basis of the French legal system to this day; and the establishment of a new educational system. More importantly, he preserved the essence of the changes brought about by the Revolution.

1598	1635	1643	1756–63
Henri IV gives French Protestants freedom of conscience with the Edict of Nantes – much to the horror of staunchly Catholic Paris, where many refuse to acknowledge the forward-thinking document.	Cardinal Richelieu, de facto ruler during the reign of Henri IV's son, Louis XIII, founds the Académie Française, the first and best known of France's five institutes of arts and sciences.	The Roi Soleil (Sun King), Louis XIV, all of five years old, assumes the French throne. In 1682 he moves his court – lock, stock and satin slipper – from Paris' Palais des Tuileries to Versailles.	The Seven Years War against Britain and Prussia is one of a series of ruinous wars pursued by Louis XV, leading to the loss of France's colonies in Canada, the West Indies and India.

A struggle between extreme monarchists seeking a return to the *ancien régime*, people who saw the changes wrought by the Revolution as irreversible, and the radicals of the poor working-class neighbourhoods of Paris dominated the reign of Louis XVIII (r 1815–24). His successor Charles X responded to the conflict with ineptitude and was overthrown in the so-called July Revolution of 1830. Those who were killed in the accompanying Paris street battles are buried in vaults under the Colonne de Juillet in the centre of place de la Bastille. Louis-Philippe, a constitutional monarch of bourgeois sympathies who followed him, was subsequently chosen as ruler by parliament, only to be ousted by the 1848 Revolution.

The Second Republic was established and elections brought in Napoléon's inept nephew, the German-reared (and accented) Louis Napoléon Bonaparte, as president. In 1851 he staged a coup d'état and proclaimed himself Emperor Napoléon III of the Second Empire, which lasted until 1870.

France enjoyed significant economic growth at this time. Paris was transformed under urban planner Baron Haussmann (1809–91), who created the 12 huge boulevards radiating from the Arc de Triomphe. Napoléon III threw glittering parties at the royal palace in Compiègne, and breathed in fashionable sea air at Biarritz and Deauville.

Like his uncle before him, Napoléon III embroiled France in a number of costly conflicts, including the disastrous Crimean War (1854–56). In 1870 Otto von Bismarck goaded Napoléon III into declaring war on Prussia. Within months the thoroughly unprepared French army was defeated and the emperor had been taken prisoner.

NATIONAL ASSEMBLY

Keep tabs on the moves and motions of France's National Assembly at www.assem blee-nat.fr.

THE KINDEST CUT

Hanging, then drawing and quartering – roping the victim's limbs to four oxen, which then ran in four different directions – was once the favoured method of publicly executing commoners. In a bid to make public executions more humane, French physician Joseph Ignace Guillotin (1738–1814) came up with the guillotine.

Several tests on dead bodies down the line, highwayman Nicolas Jacques Pelletie was the first in France to have his head sliced off by the 2m-odd falling blade on 25 April 1792 on place de Grève (today's place de l'Hôtel de Ville) in Paris. During the Reign of Terror, at least 17,000 met their death by guillotine.

By the time the last person in France to be guillotined (murderer Hamida Djandoubi in Marseille) was given the chop in 1977 (behind closed doors – the last public execution was in 1939), the lethal contraption had been sufficiently refined to slice off a head in 2/100 of a second. France abolished capital punishment in 1981.

1789	1793	1795	1799
The French Revolution begins when a mob arms itself with weapons taken from the Hôtel des Invalides and storms the prison at Bastille, freeing a total of just seven prisoners.	Louis XVI is tried and convicted as citizen 'Louis Capet' (as all kings since Hugh Capet were declared to have ruled illegally) and executed; Marie-Antoinette's turn comes nine months later.	A five-man delegation of moderate republicans led by Paul Barras sets itself up as the Directoire (Directory) and rules the First Republic for five years.	Napoléon Bonaparte overthrows the Directory and seizes control of the government in a coup d'état, opening the doors to 16 years of despotic rule, victory and then defeat on the battlefield.

The Belle Époque

Although it would usher in the glittering belle époque (beautiful age), there was nothing very attractive about the start of the Third Republic. Born as a provisional government of national defence in September 1870, it was quickly besieged by the Prussians, who laid siege to Paris and demanded National Assembly elections be held. The first move made by the resultant monarchist-controlled assembly was to ratify the Treaty of Frankfurt. The harsh terms of the treaty – a huge war indemnity and surrender of the provinces of Alsace and Lorraine – prompted immediate revolt (known as the Paris Commune), during which several thousand Communards were killed and another 20,000 executed. The Wall of the Federalists in Paris' Cimetière du Père Lachaise serves as a reminder of the bloodshed.

The belle époque launched art nouveau architecture, a whole field of artistic 'isms' from impressionism onwards, and advances in science and engineering, including the construction of the first metro line in Paris. World Exhibitions were held in the capital in 1889 (showcased by the Eiffel Tower) and again in 1901 in the purpose-built Petit Palais.

But all was not well in the republic. France was consumed with a desire for revenge after its defeat by Germany, and looking for scapegoats. The so-called Dreyfus Affair began in 1894 when Jewish army captain Alfred Dreyfus was accused of betraying military secrets to Germany; he was then court-martialled and sentenced to life imprisonment on Devil's Island in French Guiana. Liberal politicians and writers succeeded in having the case reopened despite bitter opposition from the army command, right-wing politicians and many Catholic groups, and Dreyfus was vindicated in 1900. This resulted in more rigorous civilian control of the military and, in 1905, the legal separation of church and state.

A full 20% of all Frenchmen – one out of every five males – between 20 and 45 years of age were killed in WWI.

WWI

The Two World Wars

Central to France's entry into war against Austria-Hungary and Germany had been its desire to regain Alsace and Lorraine, lost to Germany in the Franco-Prussian War – but it would prove to be a costly piece of real estate in terms of human life. By the time the armistice was signed in November 1918, some 1.3 million French soldiers had been killed and almost one million crippled. At the Battle of Verdun alone, the French (under the command of General Philippe Pétain) and the Germans each lost about 400,000 men.

In the 1920s and '30s Paris became a centre of the avant-garde, with painters pushing into new fields of art such as cubism and surrealism, Le Corbusier rewriting the textbook for architecture, foreign writers such as Ernest Hemingway and James Joyce drawn by the city's liberal

1815

British and Prussian forces under the Duke of Wellington defeat Napoléon at Waterloo; he is exiled to a remote island in the South Atlantic where he dies six years later.

1851

Louis Napoléon leads a coup d'état and proclaims himself Emperor Napoléon III of the Second Empire (1852–70), a period of significant economic growth and building under Baron Haussmann.

BRUCE BI/GETTY IMAGES ©

» Napoléon and family in wax, Musée Grévin, Paris

THE MAGINOT LINE

The Ligne Maginot, named after France's minister of war from 1929 to 1932, was one of the most spectacular blunders of WWII. This elaborate, mostly subterranean defence network, built between 1930 and 1940 (and, in the history of military architecture, second only to the Great Wall of China in sheer size), was the pride of prewar France. It included everything France's finest military architects thought would be needed to defend the nation in a 'modern war' of poison gas, tanks and aeroplanes: reinforced concrete bunkers, subterranean lines of supply and communication, minefields, antitank canals, floodable basins and even artillery emplacements that popped out of the ground to fire and then disappeared. The only things visible above ground were firing posts and lookout towers. The line stretched along the Franco-German frontier from the Swiss border all the way to Belgium where, for political and budgetary reasons, it stopped. The Maginot Line even had a slogan: 'Ils ne passeront pas' (They won't get through).

'They' – the Germans – never did. Rather than attack the Maginot Line straight on, Hitler's armoured divisions simply circled around through Belgium and invaded France across its unprotected northern frontier. They then attacked the Maginot Line from the rear.

atmosphere (and cheap booze), and nightlife establishing a cutting-edge reputation for everything from jazz clubs to striptease.

The naming of Adolf Hitler as Germany's chancellor in 1933 signalled the end of a decade of compromise between France and Germany over border guarantees. Initially the French tried to appease Hitler, but two days after Germany invaded Poland in 1939 France joined Britain in declaring war on Germany. By June 1940 France had capitulated. The Maginot Line had proved useless, with German armoured divisions outflanking it by going through Belgium.

The Germans divided France into a zone under direct German rule (along the western coast and the north, including Paris), and a puppet-state based in the spa town of Vichy and led by General Pétain, the ageing WWI hero of the Battle of Verdun. The Vichy regime was viciously anti-Semitic, and local police helped the Nazis in rounding up French Jews and others for deportation to Auschwitz and other death camps. While many people either collaborated with the Germans or passively waited out the occupation, the underground movement known as the Résistance (Resistance), or Maquis, whose active members never amounted to more than about 5% of the French population, engaged in such activities as sabotaging railways, collecting intelligence for the Allies, helping Allied airmen who had been shot down, and publishing anti-German leaflets.

Since the end of WWII France has been one of the five permanent members of the UN Security Council. Follow its movements at www.un.org/docs/sc.

WWII

1871	1894	1903	1904
The Treaty of Frankfurt is signed, the harsh terms of which (a 5-billion-franc war indemnity, surrender of the provinces of Alsace and Lorraine) prompt immediate revolt.	Army Captain Alfred Dreyfus is convicted and sentenced to life imprisonment on trumped-up charges of spying for Germany; he is later exonerated despite widespread opposition.	The world's biggest sporting event after the Olympics and the World Cup sprints around France for the first time; Tour de France riders pedal throughout the night to cover 2500km in 19 days.	Colonial rivalry between France and Britain in Africa ends with the Entente Cordiale ('Cordial Understanding'), marking the start of a cooperation that continues, more or less, to this day.

An 80km-long stretch of beach was the site of the D-Day landings on 6 June 1944, when more than 100,000 Allied troops stormed the coastline to liberate most of Normandy and Brittany. Paris was liberated on 25 August by a force spearheaded by Free French units, sent in ahead of the Americans so the French would have the honour of liberating their own capital.

The war ruined France. More than one-third of industrial production fed the German war machine during WWII, the occupiers requisitioning practically everything that wasn't (and was) nailed down: ferrous and nonferrous metals, statues, iron grills, zinc bar tops, coal, leather, textiles and chemicals. Agriculture, strangled by the lack of raw materials, fell by 25%.

In their retreat, the Germans burned bridges (2600 destroyed) and the Allied bombardments tore up railroad tracks (40,000km). The roadways had not been maintained since 1939, ports were damaged, and nearly half a million buildings and 60,000 factories were destroyed. The French had to pay for the needs of the occupying soldiers to the tune of 400 million francs a day, prompting an inflation rip tide.

Rebuilding & the Loss of the Colonies

The magnitude of France's postwar economic devastation required a strong central government with broad powers to rebuild the country's industrial and commercial base. Soon after liberation most banks, insurance companies, car manufacturers and energy-producing companies fell under government control. Other businesses remained in private hands, the objective being to combine the efficiency of state planning with the dynamism of private initiative. But progress was slow. By 1947 rationing remained in effect and France had to turn to the USA for loans as part of the Marshall Plan to rebuild Europe.

One aim of the plan was to stabilise postwar Europe financially and politically, thus thwarting the expansion of Soviet power. As the Iron Curtain fell over Eastern Europe, the pro-Stalinist bent of France's Communist Party put it in a politically untenable position. Seeking at once to exercise power within the government and at the same time oppose its measures as insufficiently Marxist, the communists found themselves on the losing end of disputes involving the colonies, workers' demands and American aid. In 1947 they were booted out of government.

The economy gathered steam in the 1950s. The French government invested in hydroelectric and nuclear-power plants, oil and gas exploration, petrochemical refineries, steel production, naval construction, auto factories and building construction to accommodate a boom in babies and consumer goods. The future at home was looking brighter; the situ-

1905	1918
The emotions aroused by the Dreyfus Affair and the interference of the Catholic Church lead to the promulgation of *läcité* (secularism), the legal separation of church and state.	The armistice ending WWI signed at Fôret de Compiègne near Paris sees the return of lost territories (Alsace and Lorraine), but the war brought about the loss of more than a million French soldiers.

NEIL SETCHFIELD/GETTY IMAGES ©

» WWI cemetery, Verdun

ation of *la France d'outre-mer* (overseas France), however, was another story altogether.

France's humiliation at the hands of the Germans had not been lost on its restive colonies. As the war economy tightened its grip, native-born people, poorer to begin with, noticed that they were bearing the brunt of the pain. In North Africa the Algerians coalesced around a movement for greater autonomy, which blossomed into a full-scale independence movement by the end of the war. The Japanese moved into strategically important Indochina in 1940. The Vietnamese resistance movement that developed quickly took on an anti-French, nationalistic tone, setting the stage for Vietnam's eventual independence.

The 1950s spelled the end of French colonialism. When Japan surrendered to the Allies in 1945, nationalist Ho Chi Minh launched a push for an autonomous Vietnam that became a drive for independence. Under the brilliant General Giap, the Vietnamese perfected a form of guerrilla warfare that proved highly effective against the French army. After their defeat at Dien Bien Phu in 1954, the French withdrew from Indochina.

The struggle for Algerian independence was nastier. Technically a French *département,* Algeria was in effect ruled by a million or so French settlers who wished at all costs to protect their privileges. Heads stuck firmly in the Saharan sands (especially in the south, where the oil was), the colonial community and its supporters in the army and the right wing refused all Algerian demands for political and economic equality.

The Algerian War of Independence (1954–62) was brutal. Nationalist rebel attacks were met with summary executions, inquisitions, torture and massacres, which made Algerians more determined to gain their independence. The government responded with half-hearted reform and reorganisation programs. International pressure on France to pull out of Algeria came from the UN, the USSR and the USA, while *pieds noirs* (literally 'black feet', as Algerian-born French people are known in France), elements of the military and extreme right-wingers became increasingly enraged at what they saw as defeatism in dealing with the problem. A plot to overthrow the French government and replace it with a military-style regime was narrowly avoided when General Charles de Gaulle, France's undersecretary of war who had fled Paris for London in 1940 after France capitulated and had spent more than a dozen years in opposition to the postwar Fourth Republic, agreed to assume the presidency in 1958.

De Gaulle's initial attempts at reform – according the Algerians political equality and recognising their right in principle to self-determination – infuriated right-wingers without quenching the Algerian thirst for independence. Following a failed coup attempt by military officers in 1961,

SUITE FRANÇAISE

Published posthumously, the award-winning *Suite Française* (2004) by Ukrainian-born author Irène Némirovsky, who was murdered at Auschwitz in 1942, evokes the horror of Nazi-occupied Paris from June 1940 until July 1941.

1920s	1939	1944	1949
Paris sparkles as the centre of the avant-garde. The luxurious Train Bleu (Blue Train) makes its first run, and Sylvia Beach of the Shakespeare & Company bookshop publishes James Joyce's *Ulysses*.	Nazi Germany occupies France and divides it into a zone under direct German occupation (along the north and western coasts) and a puppet state led by General Pétain and based in the spa town of Vichy.	Normandy and Brittany are the first to be liberated by Allied troops following the D-Day landings in June, followed by Paris on 25 August by a force spearheaded by Free French units.	France signs the Atlantic Pact uniting North America and Western Europe in a mutual defence alliance (NATO); the Council of Europe, of which France is part, is born.

the Organisation de l'Armée Secrète (OAS; a group of French settlers and sympathisers opposed to Algerian independence) resorted to terrorism. It tried to assassinate de Gaulle several times and in 1961 violence broke out on the streets of Paris. Police attacked Algerian demonstrators, killing more than 100 people. Algeria was granted independence the following year.

The Road to Prosperity & Europe

By the late 1960s de Gaulle was appearing more and more like yesterday's man. Loss of the colonies, a surge in immigration and rise in unemployment had weakened his government. De Gaulle's government by decree was starting to gall the anti-authoritarian baby-boomer generation, now at university and agitating for change. Students reading Herbert Marcuse and Wilhelm Reich found much to admire in Fidel Castro, Che Guevara and the black struggle for civil rights in America, and vociferously denounced the war in Vietnam.

Student protests of 1968 climaxed with a brutal overreaction by police to a protest meeting at the Sorbonne, Paris' most renowned university. Overnight, public opinion turned in favour of the students, while the students themselves occupied the Sorbonne and erected barricades in the Latin Quarter. Within days a general strike by 10 million workers countrywide paralysed France.

But such comradeship between workers and students did not last long. While the former wanted a greater share of the consumer market, the latter wanted to destroy it. After much hesitancy de Gaulle took advantage of this division by appealing to people's fear of anarchy. Just as the country seemed on the brink of revolution and an overthrow of the Fifth Republic, stability returned. The government decentralised the higher-education system and followed through in the 1970s with a wave of other reforms (lowering the voting age to 18, instituting legalised abortion and so on). De Gaulle meanwhile resigned from office in 1969 after losing an important referendum on regionalisation, and suffered a fatal heart attack the following year.

Georges Pompidou stepped onto the presidential podium in 1969. Despite embarking on an ambitious modernisation program, investing in aerospace, telecommunications and nuclear power, he failed to stave off inflation and social unrest following the global oil crisis of 1973 and died the following year.

In 1974 Valéry Giscard d'Estaing inherited a deteriorating economic climate and sharp divisions between the left and the right. Hampered by a lack of media savvy and what was perceived as an arrogant demeanour, d'Estaing proved unpopular. His friendship with emperor and alleged cannibal Jean-Bédel Bokassa of the Central African Republic did little to

PRESIDENTIAL PALACE

Peep into the presidential palace and have a good old nose around at www. elysee.fr.

1951	1946–62	1966	1968
Fear of communism and a resurgent Germany prompts the first steps towards European integration with the European Coal and Steel Community and military accords three years later.	French colonialism ends with war in Indochina (1946–54) followed by the Algerian War of Independence (1954–62), brought to a close with the signing of the Accord d'Évian (Evian Accord) in Évian-les-Bains.	France withdraws from NATO's joint military command in 1966; it has maintained an independent arsenal of nuclear weapons since 1960. A year later NATO moves out of its headquarters near Paris.	Large-scale anti-authoritarian student protests (known since as 'May 1968') aimed at de Gaulle's style of government by decree escalate into a countrywide protest that eventually brings down the president.

THE BIRTH OF THE BIKINI

Almost called *atome* (atom) rather than bikini, after its pinprick size, the scanty little two-piece bathing suit was the 1946 creation of Cannes fashion designer Jacques Heim and automotive engineer Louis Réard.

Top-and-bottom swimsuits had existed for centuries, but it was the French duo who both made them briefer than brief and plumped for the name 'bikini' – after Bikini, an atoll in the Marshall Islands chosen by the USA as the testing ground for atomic bombs in the same year.

Once wrapped top and bottom around the curvaceous 1950s sex-bomb Brigitte Bardot on St-Tropez' Plage de Pampelonne, there was no looking back. The bikini was here to stay.

win him friends, and in 1981 he was ousted by long-time head of the Parti Socialiste (PS; Socialist Party), François Mitterrand.

Despite France's first socialist president instantly alienating the business community by setting out to nationalise 36 privately owned banks, industrial groups and other parts of the economy, Mitterrand did give France something of a sparkle. Potent symbols of France's advanced technological savvy – the Minitel (a proto-personal computer in everyone's home) and high-speed TGV train service between Paris and Lyon – were launched in 1980 and 1981 respectively; a clutch of *grands projets* were embarked upon in the French capital. The death penalty was abolished, homosexuality was legalised, a 39-hour work week was instituted, annual holiday time was upped from four to five weeks and the right to retire at 60 was guaranteed.

However, by 1986 the economy was weakening and in parliamentary elections that year the right-wing opposition, led by Jacques Chirac (mayor of Paris since 1977), won a majority in the National Assembly. For the next two years Mitterrand worked with a prime minister and cabinet from the opposition, an unprecedented arrangement known as *cohabitation*. The extreme-right Front National (FN; National Front) meanwhile quietly gained ground by loudly blaming France's economic woes on immigration.

Presidential elections in 1995 ushered Chirac (an ailing Mitterrand did not run and died the following year) into the Palais de l'Élysée. Whiz-kid foreign minister Alain Juppé was appointed prime minister and several women were placed in top cabinet positions. However, Chirac's attempts to reform France's colossal public sector in order to meet the criteria of the European Monetary Union (EMU) were met with the largest protests since 1968, and his decision to resume nuclear testing on the Polynesian

1981	1989	1994	1995
The superspeedy TGV makes its first commercial journey from Paris to Lyon, breaking all speed records to complete the train journey in two hours instead of six.	President Mitterrand's *grand projet*, Opéra Bastille, opens to mark the bicentennial of the French Revolution; IM Pei's love-it-or-leave-it Grande Pyramide is unveiled at the Louvre.	The 50km-long Channel Tunnel linking France with Britain opens after seven years of hard graft by 10,000 workers.	After twice serving as prime minister, Jacques Chirac becomes president of France, winning popular acclaim for his direct words and actions in matters relating to the EU and the war in Bosnia.

island of Mururoa and a nearby atoll was the focus of worldwide outrage. Always the maverick, Chirac called early parliamentary elections in 1997 – only for his party, the Rassemblement pour la République (RPR; Rally for the Republic), to lose out to a coalition of socialists, communists and greens. Another period of *cohabitation* ensued.

The 2002 presidential elections surprised everybody. The first round of voting saw left-wing PS leader Lionel Jospin eliminated and the FN's Jean-Marie Le Pen – who had infamously dismissed the Holocaust as a 'mere detail of history' and spoke of the 'inequality of races' – scoop 17% of the national vote. But in the subsequent run-off ballot, Chirac enjoyed a landslide victory, echoed in parliamentary elections a month later when the president-backed coalition UMP (Union pour un Mouvement Populaire) won a healthy majority, leaving Le Pen's FN without a seat in parliament and ending years of *cohabitation*.

Sarkozy's France

Presidential elections in 2007 ushered out old-school Jacques Chirac (in his 70s with two terms under his belt) and brought in Nicolas Sarkozy. Dynamic, ambitious and media-savvy, the former interior minister and chairman of centre-right party UMP wooed voters with policies about job creation, lower taxes, crime crackdown and help for France's substantial immigrant population – issues that had particular pulling power coming from the son of a Hungarian immigrant father and Greek Jewish-French mother. However, his first few months in office were dominated by personal affairs as he divorced his wife Cecilia and wed Italian multimillionaire singer Carla Bruni a few months later, and his popularity plummeted.

Unemployment leapfrogged from 8.7% in 2007, to 7.6% during the 2008 global banking crisis (when the government injected €10.5 billion into France's six major banks), to 10% in 2010. Sarkozy's party received a battering in the 2010 regional elections which saw the left scoop 54% of votes and control of 21 out of 22 regions on mainland France and Corsica. Government popularity hit an all-time low.

Riots ripped through the Alpine town of Grenoble in 2010 after a 27-year-old man was shot dead by police while allegedly trying to rob a casino. Violence had also bloodied a Parisian suburb five years earlier – and spread like wildfire countrywide creating a state of emergency – following the death of two teenage boys of North African origin, electrocuted after hiding in an electrical substation while on the run from the police, and the burning cars and street clashes with riot police in Grenoble that echoed this earlier violence was seen as a measurement of just how volatile the country had become.

1998	2002	2004	2005
After resuming nuclear testing in the South Pacific in the early 1990s, France signs the worldwide test-ban treaty, bringing an end to French nuclear testing once and for all.	The French franc, first minted in 1360, is thrown onto the scrap heap of history as the country adopts the euro as its official currency along with 14 other EU member-states.	France bans the wearing of crucifixes, the Islamic headscarf and other overtly religious symbols in state schools.	The French electorate overwhelmingly rejects EU Constitution. Parisian suburbs are wracked by rioting Arab and African youths.

The French

Superchic, stylish, sexy, charming, arrogant, rude, bureaucratic, sexist, chauvinistic... France is a country whose people have attracted more stubborn myths and stereotypes than any other in Europe and, over the centuries, dozens of tags, true or otherwise, have been pinned on the garlic-eating, beret-wearing, *sacrebleu*-swearing French. (The French, by the way, don't wear berets or use old chestnuts such as *'sacrebleu'* any more.) Sit in a cafe some afternoon and you'll soon hear the gentle expressions of surprise favoured by Parisians these days as they slip on dog droppings (a frequent sight on most pavements). *'Merde'* (shit) is quite popular.

Suckers for tradition, the French are slow to embrace new ideas and technologies: it took the country an age to embrace the internet, clinging on for dear life to their own at-the-time-advanced Minitel system. Yet the French are also incredibly innovative – a dichotomy reflected in every facet of French life: they drink and smoke more than anyone else, yet live longer. They eat like kings, but are not fat...how so very enviable.

Superiority Complex

Most people are extremely proud to be French and are staunchly nationalistic to boot, a result of the country's republican stance that places nationality – rather than religion, for example – at the top of the self-identity list. This has created an overwhelmingly self-confident nation, both culturally and intellectually, that invariably comes across as a French superiority complex.

Contrary to popular belief, many French speak a foreign language fairly well, travel and are happy to use their language skills should the need arise. Of course, if monolingual English-speakers don't at least try to speak French, there is no way proud French linguists will let on they speak fluent English! Many French men, incidentally, deem an English gal's heavily accented French as irresistibly sexy as many people deem a Frenchman speaking English. Hard to believe, but true.

Naturally Sexy

On the subject of sex, not all French men ooze romance or light Gitane cigarettes all day. Nor are they as civilised about adultery as French cinema would have you believe. Adultery, illegal in France until 1975, was actually grounds for automatic divorce until as late as mid-2004.

Kissing is an integral part of French life. (The expression 'French kissing' doesn't exist in French, incidentally.) Countrywide, people who know each other reasonably well, really well, a tad or barely at all greet each other with a glancing peck on each cheek. Southern France aside (where everyone kisses everyone), two men rarely kiss (unless they are related or artists) but always shake hands. Boys and girls start kissing as soon as they're out of nappies, or so it seems.

CHILDREN

One of the best sellers addressing French culture in recent years is Pamela Druckerman's *French Children Don't Throw Food* (2012), a witty and entertaining look at how French parents in Paris raise their kids by an American living in the city.

No contemporary writer addresses the natural art, style and panache of French women better than Helena Frith-Powell (http://helenafrith powell.com), an adopted resident of Languedoc in southwestern France for several years who found literary fame with *Two Lipsticks and a Lover* (2007), published in the US as *All You Need to be Impossibly French*. Having exposed the intimate secrets behind many a glam French woman (expensive and matching lingerie, infidelity and the like), Frith-Powell went on to write her first novel *Love in a Warm Climate* (2011), subtitled *The French Art of Love,* in which a mother-of-three finds out her husband is having an affair with a Frenchwoman called Cécile.

Lifestyle

Be a fly on the wall in the 5th-floor bourgeois apartment of Monsieur et Madame Tout le Monde and you'll see them dunking croissants in bowls of *café au lait* for breakfast, buying a baguette every day from the bakery (Monsieur nibbles the end off on his way home) and recycling nothing bar a few glass bottles.

They go to the movies once a month, work precisely 35 hours a week (many French still toil 39 hours or more a week – employers can enforce a 39-hour work week for a negotiable extra cost), and enjoy five weeks' holiday and almost a dozen bank (public) holidays a year. The couple view the web-radio production company their 24-year-old son set up and heads in Paris with a mix of pride, amusement and pure scepticism. Their 20-year-old daughter is a student: France's overcrowded state-run universities are free and open to anyone who passes the baccalaureat, although former president Nicolas Sarkozy had a stab at changing this by giving universities the autonomy to select students and seek outside funding.

Madame buys a load of hot-gossip weekly magazines, Monsieur meets his mates to play boules, and August is the *only* month to summer holiday (with the rest of France). Dodging dog poo on pavements is a sport practised from birth and everything goes on the *carte bleue* (credit or debit card) when shopping. This *is* the society, after all, that microchipped credit cards long before anyone else even dreamt of scrapping the swipe-and-sign system. The couple have a landlord: with a tradition of renting rather than buying, home ownership is low (57% of households own their own home; the rest rent).

Les Femmes

Women were granted suffrage in 1945, but until 1964 a woman needed her husband's permission to open a bank account or get a passport.

TOP FIVE: FROGS VS ROSBIFS

In the finest of traditions, rivalry between *rosbifs* (the English) and frogs (the French) sells like hotcakes. The following are our favourites:

» *1000 Years of Annoying the French* (Stephen Clarke, 2011) A smart comic look at French-Anglo history by the man who launched his career with *A Year in the Merde* (A Year in the Shit).

» *Cross Channel* (Julian Barnes, 1996) Classic short stories set either side of the Channel.

» *More France Please! We're British!* (Helen Frith-Powell, 2004) France from the perspective of Brits who choose to live there permanently.

» *Help, the English Are Invading Us!* (José-Alain Fralon) Slowly but surely the English are invading us...

» *That Sweet Enemy: the French and the British from the Sun King to the Present* (Robert and Isabelle Tombs) Cross-Channel rivalry in a historical context.

FRENCH KISSING

Kissing French-style is not completely straightforward, 'how many' and 'which side first' being potentially problematic. In Paris it is definitely two: unless parties are related, *very* close friends or haven't seen each other in an age, anything more is deemed affected. That said, in certain trendy 20-something circles, friends swap three or four cheek-skimming kisses, as do many young teenagers at school.

Travel south and *les bises* (kisses) – or *les bisous* as the French colloquially say – multiply, three or four being the norm in Provence. The bits of France neighbouring Switzerland around Lake Geneva tend to be three-kiss country (in keeping with Swiss habits); and in the Loire Valley it is four. Corsicans, bizarrely, stick to two but kiss left cheek first – which can lead to locked lips given that everyone else in France starts with the right cheek.

Younger French women in particular are quite outspoken and emancipated. But this self-confidence has yet to translate into equality in the workplace, where women hold few senior and management positions. Sexual harassment is addressed with a law imposing financial penalties on the offender. A great achievement in the last decade has been *Parité,* the law requiring political parties to fill 50% of their slates in all elections with female candidates.

Abortion is legal during the first 12 weeks of pregnancy, girls under 16 not needing parental consent provided they are accompanied by an adult of their choice: 30 abortions take place in France for every 100 live births.

Above all else French women are known for their natural chic, style and class. And there's no doubt that contemporary French women are sassier than ever. Take the Rykiel women: in the 1970s legendary Parisian knit-wear designer Sonia Rykiel designed the skin-tight, boob-hugging sweater worn with no bra beneath. In the new millennium daughter Nathalie created Rykiel Woman, a sensual label embracing everything from lingerie to sex toys and aimed squarely at women who know what they want.

Linguistic Patriotism

Speaking a language other than their own is an emotional affair for the French, memorably illustrated a few years back when the then French president Jacques Chirac walked out of an EU summit session after a fellow countryman had the audacity to address the meeting in English. 'Don't speak English!' was *Le Monde*'s headline the next day, while the French blogosphere seethed with debate on linguistic patriotism: 'Open your eyes, Mr President, you are on another planet' and 'it is a long time since French was the language of the international arena' taunted modern-day French bloggers, most of whom write in English.

Former president Nicolas Sarkozy fared marginally better than his monolingual predecessor. Yet Sarkozy also stuck to what he knew best in public, so much so that the couple of lines he did utter in English were instantly plastered over the internet as a video link and swiftly went viral.

With English words like 'weekend', 'jogging', 'stop' and 'OK' firmly entrenched in daily French usage, language purists might just have lost the battle. One look at the many Anglo-American shop and restaurant signs featured in the online Musée des Horreurs (Museum of Horrors) on the website of the Paris-based Défense de la Langue Française (DLF; Defence of the French Language; www.langue-francaise.org) says it all.

French was the main language of the EU until 1995 when Sweden and Finland came into the EU fold. French broadcasting laws restrict the amount of airtime radio and TV stations can devote to non-French music, but little can be done to restrict who airs what on the internet.

Sixty Million Frenchmen Can't Be Wrong: What Makes the French so French ask Jean-Benoît Nadeau and Julie Barlow in their witty, well-written and at times downright comical musings on the French.

Multiculturalism

The face of France is multicultural (immigrants make up 8.4% of the population), yet its republican code, while inclusive and nondiscriminatory, has been criticised for doing little to accommodate a multicultural society (and, interestingly, none of the members of France's National Assembly represents the immigrant population, first or second generation). Nothing reflects this dichotomy better than the law, in place since 2004, banning the Islamic headscarf, Jewish skullcap, crucifix and other religious symbols in French schools.

Some 90% of the French Muslim community – Europe's largest – are noncitizens. Most are illegal immigrants living in poverty-stricken *bidonvilles* (tinpot towns) around Paris, Lyon and other metropolitan centres. Many are unemployed (youth unemployment in many suburbs is 40%) and face little prospect of getting a job.

Multiculturalism is a dominant feature of French football, with more than half of the 23 players in the last World Cup being of African, West Indian, Algerian or other non-French origin. The country's golden boy of football, Marseille-born midfielder ace Zinedine Zidane (b 1972), now retired, is a classic example. The son of Algerian immigrants, he wooed the nation with a sparkling career of goal-scoring headers and extraordinary footwork that unfortunately ended with him head-butting an Italian player during the 2006 World Cup final. But such was the power of his humble Marseillais grin (since used to advertise Adidas sports gear, Volvic mineral water and Christian Dior fashion) that the French nation instantly forgave him.

PÉTANQUE

France's traditional ball games include *pétanque* and the more formal boules, which has a 70-page rule book. Both are played by men on a gravel pitch.

Good Sports

Most French wouldn't be seen dead walking down the street in trainers and tracksuits. But contrary to appearances, they love sport. Shaved-leg cyclists toil up Mont Ventoux, football fans fill stadiums and anyone who can flits off for the weekend to ski or snowboard.

Les 24 Heures du Mans and the F1 Grand Prix in Monte Carlo are the world's raciest dates in motor sports; the French Open in Paris in late May to early June is the second of the year's four grand-slam tennis tournaments; and the Tour de France is – indisputably – the world's most prestigious bicycle race. Bringing together 189 of the world's top male cyclists (21 teams of nine) and 15 million spectators in July each

A MADAME FROM BIRTH NICOLA WILLIAMS

'About time too', a feminist anywhere else on the planet would argue. Indeed, it is only since 2012 that French women no longer have to tick one of two boxes when filling out official forms and documents – 'Madame' meaning 'Mrs' or 'married' and 'Mademoiselle' meaning 'Miss' or 'not married'. 'Mademoiselle' also implies 'virgin' and 'sexually available' according to Paris-based feminist group Les Chiennes de Garde (meaning 'guard dogs' or, rather, 'guard bitches'), who launched the petition to banish the term 'Mademoiselle' from the administrative and political arena.

'Mademoiselle' originates from the medieval word *'damoiselle'*, meaning a young upper-class girl (male equivalents were called *'damoisel'*). Later merged with *'ma'* to denote an unmarried woman, the term was tantamount to 'sad old spinster who can't find a husband' in the 17th and 18th centuries. In the 19th century, novelist Adolphe Belot borrowed the term to depict a frigid wife in *Mademoiselle Giraud, ma Femme*.

So the fight to become a Madame from birth is won. Although I, already a married Madame, am delighted if someone addresses me as 'Mademoiselle' – as are all my 30-something-with-kids girlfriends. Despite the kids in tow, dirty washing and first wrinkle, it means someone still thinks I look young.

FRANCE'S NORTH–SOUTH DIVIDE

No film better illustrates what southerners think of those from 'the sticks' in the far north than Dany Boon's *Bienvenue chez les Ch'tis* (Welcome to the Sticks; 2008), a poignant commentary on France's north–south divide.

For starters, the weather in the cold rainy north is revolting. So no surprise that post-office chief Philippe, upon setting off north from his native Salon-de-Provence on the sun-drenched Côte d'Azur, dons a puffer jacket and scarf as he bids farewell to bronzed wife Julie. The weather changes when he passes the 'Nord-Pas de Calais' sign – at which point it doesn't just rain but slashes down beyond windscreen-wiper control. Even the gendarme on the autoroute, upon stopping him for driving too slowly, lets him off with a sympathetic smile and his deepest condolences when he hears where he's heading: Bergues, an ex-mining town of 4300 inhabitants, 9km from Dunkirk.

Bienvenue chez les Ch'tis is a kaleidoscope of comic scenes that slowly chip away at the deeply entrenched prejudices surrounding this northern land of redundant coal mines and its unemployed, impoverished, pale, unhealthy and 'uncultured' inhabitants who drink too much beer and speak like this – *Ej t'ermerci inne banes* (that means *Merci beaucoup*).

Yes, their thick Ch'timi dialect (old Picard peppered with Flemish) is incomprehensible to outsiders. Yes, they dunk stinky Maroilles cheese and bread in *chicorée café* (chicory-flavoured instant coffee) for breakfast. Yes, they skip the traditional French three-course lunch for an alfresco round of *frites fricadelle, sauce picadilly* (chips 'n' meatballs) – eaten with their fingers. And yes, their very nickname (*les Ch'tis*) was borne out of prejudice during WWI when French soldiers mocked the thickly accented way their northern comrades spoke – '*ch'est ti, ch'est mi*' (*c'est toi, c'est moi* – it's you, it's me), hence 'Ch'ti'.

The north and its regional characteristics are no mystery to director Boon, a born-and-bred northerner who grew up in Armentières, near Lille. Indeed, if anyone is best placed to speak of *les Ch'tis* and their homeland, it's Boon, whose lovable, huge-hearted character in the film says it all: 'An outsider who comes to the north cries twice: once when he arrives, and once when he leaves.'

year for a spectacular 3000-plus-kilometre cycle around the country, the three-week race always labours through the Alps and Pyrenees and finishes on Paris' Champs-Élysées. The route in between changes each year but wherever it goes, the French systematically turn out in their droves – armed with table, chairs and picnic hamper – to make a day of it. The serpentine publicity caravan preceding the cyclists showers roadside spectators with coffee samples, logo-emblazoned balloons, pens and other free junk-advertising gifts and is easily as much fun as watching the cyclists themselves speed through – in 10 seconds flat.

France's greatest moment in football history came at the 1998 World Cup, which the country hosted and won. But the game has produced no stars since, losing to Italy in the final of the 2006 World Cup. There was also no luck for *les Bleus* in South Africa in 2010, which saw the French team eliminated in the first round – but not before striker Nicolas Anelka was sent home to Paris for arguing with the referee, prompting the rest of the side to 'strike' in protest during a training session. Back home, most French felt deep shame at a team that had clearly not been good sports.

Bon Appétit

Eating well is of prime importance to most French people, who spend an inordinate amount of time thinking about, discussing and enjoying food and wine – with gusto. Yet dining out doesn't have to be a ceremonious occasion or one riddled with pitfalls for the uninitiated. Approach food with half the enthusiasm *les français* do, and you will be welcomed, encouraged and exceedingly well fed.

Two natural factors determine what you eat on your French travels. Season and geography sees the hot south favour olive oil, garlic and tomatoes; the cooler, pastoral regions of northern France turn to cream and butter; and coastal areas are awash with mussels, oysters, saltwater fish and other seafood. Borders are far from firmly drawn, though, and while each region counts a handful of distinctly local dishes, you might well encounter influences of Gascon cuisine in the Atlantic region, an Alsatian-style *choucroute* (sauerkraut with sausage and other prepared meats) in seafaring Marseille or *andouillette* (Lyonnais pig-intestine sausage) in Paris.

Rabelais' phrase *'le jardin de France'* (the garden of France) has been exploited nationwide since he coined it in the 16th century to describe his native Touraine, a green and succulent landscape laden with lush fruit, flowers, nuts and vegetables, west of Paris in the Loire Valley: *pruneaux de Tours* (prunes dried from luscious damson plums) are justifiably famous, and mushrooms polka-dot the forests. In the Loire's unique troglodyte caves *champignons de Paris* (button mushrooms) are cultivated. Yet appropriately, it was the cooking refined in the kitchens of the region's châteaux in the 16th century that became what most today consider to be 'quintessentially French': *coq au vin* (chicken in red wine), *cuisses de grenouilles* (frogs' legs) and *tarte tatin* (upside-down apple tart) all originate from this riverside region encrusted with both agricultural and architectural grandeur. Poultry and game dishes were the pride and joy of the medieval kitchen, and once or twice a year a fattened pig was slaughtered and meat from its neck minced up and fried to make *rillettes*, a tasty cold paste served with small toasts and a standard in every self-respecting French bistro today.

One particularly tasty tradition very much alive and well is *Jour des Rois* (Day of the Kings), or Epiphany, on 6 January when the Three Wise Men paid homage to the infant Jesus. A *galette des rois* (literally 'kings' cake'; a puff-pastry tart with frangipane cream) is placed in the centre of the table and sliced while the youngest person ducks under the table, calling out who gets each slice. The excitement lies in who gets *la fève* (literally 'bean', which translates these days as a miniature porcelain figurine) hidden inside the tart; whoever does is crowned king with a gold paper crown.

For more on regional cuisines in France, see p31.

The Food of France by Waverley Root, first published in 1958, remains the seminal work in English on *la cuisine française*, with a focus on historical development, by a long-time Paris-based American foreign correspondent.

LA CUISINE FRANÇAISE

Bread

The nuts and bolts of French cuisine is *pain* (bread), baked in infinite shapes, sizes and variety, and typically eaten at every meal. Plain old *pain* is a 400g, traditional-shaped loaf, soft inside and crusty out. The iconic classic is *une baguette,* a long, thin crusty loaf weighing 250g. Anything fatter and it becomes *une flûte,* thinner *une ficelle.* When buying bread in a *boulangerie* (bakery), ask for a *demi-baguette* or a *demi-pain* if you only need a half-baguette or -loaf. (Bear in mind, while French baguettes are impossibly good, they turn unpleasantly dry within four hours, rock-hard within 12.)

Cheese

France is cheese land and the *fromagerie* (cheese shop) is the pongiest shop in town. With more than 500 varieties – which can be raw, pasteurised or *petit-lait* ('little-milk', the whey left over after the fats and solids have been curdled with rennet) – buying cheese can be an overwhelming affair. Any self-respecting *fromager* (cheese merchant) will let you taste before you buy – just ask. Say when you intend eating it to ensure the cheese is *fait* (ripe) to a perfect degree.

Charcuterie

Charcuterie, the backbone of every French picnic, is traditionally made from pork, though other meats are used in making *saucisse* (small fresh sausage, boiled or grilled before eating), *saucisson* (salami), *saucisson sec* (air-dried salami), *boudin noir* (blood sausage or pudding made with pig's blood, onions and spices) and other cured and salted meats. Pâtés, terrines and *rillettes* are also considered charcuterie. The difference between a pâté and a terrine is academic: a pâté is removed from its container and sliced before it is served, while a terrine is sliced from the container itself. *Rillettes* is potted meat or even fish that has been shredded with two forks, seasoned and mixed with fat. It is spread cold over bread or toast.

BON APPÉTIT

Foodie Towns

» **Le Puy-en-Velay** for lentils

» **Dijon** for mustard

» **Privas** for chestnuts

» **Cancale** for oysters

» **Espelette** for red chillies

» **Colmar** for chocolate stork eggs

» **Lyon** for piggy-part cuisine

THE PERFECT CHEESEBOARD

Treat your taste buds to the perfect balance of cheese by taking at least one of each type from the cheeseboard:

» **Goat's cheese** *(fromage de chèvre)* Made from goat's milk, this cheese is creamy, sweet and faintly salty when fresh, but hardens and gets saltier as it matures. Among the best are Ste-Maure de Touraine, a mild creamy cheese from the Loire Valley; the classic but saltier Crottin de Chavignol from Burgundy; Cabécou de Rocamadour from Midi-Pyrénées, often served warm with salad or marinated in oil and rosemary; and Lyon's St-Marcellin, a soft white cheese that should be served impossibly runny.

» **Blue cheese** *(fromage à pâté persillée)* 'Marbled' or with veins that resemble *persil* (parsley). Don't miss king of French cheese Roquefort, a ewe's-milk veined cheese from Languedoc.

» **Soft cheese** *(fromage à pâté molle)* Moulded or rind-washed, the classic soft cheese that everyone knows is Camembert from Normandy made from unpasteurised cow's milk. Munster from Alsace and the strong and seriously smelly Époisses de Bourgogne are fine-textured, rind-washed cheeses.

» **Semihard cheese** *(fromage à pâté demi-dure)* Among the finest uncooked, pressed cheese is Tomme de Savoie, made from pasteurised or unpasteurised cow's milk near the Alps; and St-Nectaire, a strong-smelling pressed cheese that has a complex taste.

» **Hard cheese** *(fromage à pâté dure)* Must-taste cooked and pressed cheeses are Beaufort, a fruity cow's-milk cheese from Rhône-Alpes; Comté, made with raw cow's milk in Franche-Comté; emmental, a cow's-milk cheese made all over France; and Mimolette, an Edam-like bright-orange cheese from Lille aged for as long as 36 months.

Then there is consideration of which wine to pair with your cheese. Strong pungent cheeses require a young, full-bodied red or a sweet wine, while soft cheeses call for more quality and age. Classic pairings include Alsatian Gewürztraminer and Munster; Côtes du Rhone with Roquefort; Côte d'Or (Burgundy) with Brie or Camembert; and mature Bordeaux with emmental or Cantal. Even Champagne can get in on the act with mushroomlike Chaource.

French Wine

French wines might not be the world's most venerated, but making them is an ancient art and tradition that bears its own unique trademark. *Dégustation* (tasting), moreover, is an essential part of any French travel experience. Quaff Champagne with friends in a Lille wine bar designed in 1892 by Gustave Eiffel's architectural firm, hike between Alsatian vines with an organic-wine producer, trail walking itineraries in St-Émilion's Unesco World Heritage vineyards, taste with one of the world's top sommeliers to determine your star sign of wine... experiences such as these are the essence of French wine culture.

There are dozens of wine-producing regions throughout France, but the seven principal ones are Burgundy, Bordeaux, the Rhône and Loire Valleys, Champagne, Languedoc, Provence and Alsace. Wines are generally named after the location of the vineyard rather than the grape varietal. Organic and biodynamic wines are increasingly popular.

Quality wines in France are designated as Appellation d'Origine Contrôlée (AOC; literally, 'label of inspected origin'), equivalent since 2012 to the European-wide Appellation d'Origine Protegée (AOP). Both labels mean the same: that the wine has met stringent regulations governing where, how and under what conditions it was grown and bottled. French AOC can cover a wide region (such as Bordeaux), a sub-region (such as Haut-Médoc), or a commune or village (such as Pomerol). Some regions only have a single AOC (such as Alsace), while Burgundy has dozens.

Some viticulturists have honed their skills and techniques to such a degree that their wine is known as a *grand cru* (literally 'great growth'). If this wine has been produced in a year of optimum climatic conditions, it becomes a *millésime* (vintage) wine. *Grands crus* are aged in small oak barrels then bottles, sometimes for 20 years or more, to create those memorable bottles (with price tags to match) that wine experts enthuse about with such passion.

Burgundy

During the reign of Charlemagne, monks began making the wine that gave Burgundy (Bourgogne in French) its sterling reputation for viticulture. Burgundy's *vignerons* (winegrowers) only have small vineyards, rarely more than 10 hectares, and they produce small quantities of very good wine. Burgundy reds are made with pinot noir grapes and the best vintages demand 10 to 20 years to age; whites are made with chardonnay.

Burgundy's most famed winegrowing areas are Côte d'Or, Chablis, Châtillon and Mâcon. Lesser-known Irancy is a charming, local winetasting favourite.

Bordeaux

Britons have had a taste for Bordeaux' full-bodied wines, known as clarets in the UK, since the mid-12th century when King Henry II, who controlled the region through marriage, tried to gain the favour of the locals

Top Self-Drive Wine Itineraries

» Marne & Côte des Bar Champagne routes, Champagne

» Route des Grands Crus, Burgundy

» Route des Vins d'Alsace, Alsace

» Route Touristique des Vignobles, Loire Valley

» Route des Vins de Jura, the Jura

by granting them tax-free trade status with England. Thus began a roaring business in wine exporting.

Bordeaux has the perfect climate for producing wine; as a result its 1100 sq km of vineyards produce more fine wine than any other region in the world. Bordeaux reds are often described as well balanced, a quality achieved by blending several grape varieties. The grapes predominantly used are merlot, cabernet sauvignon and cabernet franc.

Bordeaux' foremost winegrowing areas are the Médoc, Pomerol, St-Émilion and Graves. The nectar-like sweet whites of the Sauternes area are widely considered the world's finest dessert wines.

FRENCH WINE

Côtes du Rhône

Dramatically different soil, climate, topography and grapes in the Rhône Valley region means very different wines in this vast appellation – France's second largest – covering 771 sq km. The most renowned is Châteauneuf-du-Pape, a full-bodied wine bequeathed to Provence by the Avignon popes who planted the distinctive stone-covered vineyards, 10km south of Orange.

Châteauneuf-du-Pape reds are strong (minimum alcohol content 12.5%) and well structured. Winegrowers, obliged to pick their grapes by hand, say it is the *galets* (large, smooth, yellowish stones) covering their vineyards that distinguish their wines from others. Both whites and reds can be drunk young (two to three years) or old (seven-plus years).

Another popular Rhône Valley *grand cru* is red and rosé Gigondas. The medieval golden-stone village of Gigondas, with its ruined castle, Provençal campanile and stunning vistas, is a delight to explore and its reds are among Provence's most sought after. In nearby Beaumes de Venise it is the sweet dessert wine, Muscat de Beaumes de Venise, that delights, enjoyed in equal measure as an aperitif or poured inside half a Cavaillon melon as dessert.

Loire Valley

The Loire's 700 sq km of vineyards rank it as France's third-largest area for the production of quality wines. Although sunny, the climate is humid, meaning not all grape varieties thrive. Still, the Loire produces the greatest variety of wines of any region in the country. The most common grapes are the muscadet, cabernet franc and chenin blanc varieties. Wines tend to be light and delicate. Be sure to sample wines from Pouilly-Fumé, Vouvray, Sancerre, Bourgueil, Chinon and Saumur.

Champagne

Champagne, northeast of Paris, has been the centre of France's best-known wine since the 17th century, when innovative monk Dom Pierre Pérignon perfected a technique for making sparkling wine.

Champagne is made from the red pinot noir, the black pinot meunier or the white chardonnay grape. Each vine is vigorously pruned and trained to produce a small quantity of high-quality grapes. Indeed, to maintain exclusivity (and price), the designated areas where grapes used

Tasting Terms

» bar à vins – wine bar

» cave – wine cellar

» caveau – a small cellar

» dégustation – tasting

» gratuit – free

» maison des vins – literally 'House of Wines'; a place to taste and buy regional wines

» vente – sales

TASTING & BUYING WINE

Wine can be bought direct from the *producteur* (wine producer) or vigneron (winegrower), most of whom offer *dégustation* (tasting), allowing you to sample two or three vintages with no obligation to buy. For cheap plonk *(vin de table)* costing €2 or so per litre, fill up your own container at the local wine cooperative; every wine-producing village has one. Lists of estates, *caves* (wine cellars) and cooperatives are available from tourist offices and *maisons des vins* (wine houses) in main towns in wine-producing areas.

for Champagne can be grown and the amount of wine produced each year are limited. In 2008 the borders that confine the Champagne AOC label were extended to include another 40 villages, increasing the value of their vineyards and its produce by tens of millions of euros (and making partygoers around the world forever grateful). Yet the bulk of Champagne is consumed in France.

If the final product is labelled *brut,* it is extra dry, with only 1.5% sugar content. *Extra-sec* means very dry (but not as dry as *brut*), *sec* is dry and *demi-sec* slightly sweet. The sweetest Champagne is labelled *doux.* Whatever the label, it is sacrilege to drink it out of anything other than a traditional Champagne flute, narrow at the bottom to help the bubbles develop, wider in the middle to promote the diffusion of aromas, and narrower at the top again to concentrate those precious aromas.

Most of the famous Champagne *maisons* (houses) are open to visitors.

Languedoc

Winemaking here is enjoying a renaissance. Following violent protests over Italian imports in the mid-1970s, farmers were subsidised to cut down their vines and replant with better quality AOC grapes, hence Languedoc's splendid wine and gargantuan production today: up to 40% of France's wine is produced in this vast sea of vines.

Of increasing interest are the thoroughly modern table wines made under the Vin de Pays d'Oc (www.vindepaysdoc.com) label. Free of AOC restriction, these wines fly in the face of viticulture tradition as they experiment with new grape blends. The result: creative, affordable wines with funky names and designer labels (and pink neocorks in the case of rosés) to reflect a contemporary lifestyle. Try a Mas de Daumas Gassac (www.daumas-gassac.com) or one of the 'chicken wines' of pioneering viticulturist Sacha Lichine (www.sachalichine.com).

Languedoc's best-known AOC wines are Minervois (drink its white with local sardines!) and Corbières, both known for well-structured reds. An island of six villages in the Minervois produces Minervois La Livinière, a red *vin de garde* (wine suitable for ageing) par excellence. Fitou, the granddad of Languedoc appellations (1948), is another red, easy to keep for four or five years.

APERITIFS & DIGESTIFS

Meals in France are preceded by an aperitif such as a *kir* (white wine sweetened with a sweet fruit syrup like blackcurrant or chestnut), *kir royale* (Champagne with blackcurrant syrup), *pineau* (cognac and grape juice) or a glass of sweet white Coteaux du Layon from the Loire Valley. In southern France aniseed-flavoured pastis (clear in the bottle, cloudy when mixed with water) is the aperitif to drink al fresco; in the southwest, go local with a Floc de Gascogne, a liqueur wine made from Armagnac and red- or white-grape juice. In Corsica, Cap Corse is the choice *apéro.*

After-dinner drinks accompany coffee. France's most famous brandies are Cognac and Armagnac, both made from grapes in the regions of those names. *Eaux de vie,* literally 'waters of life', can be made with grape skins and the pulp left over after being pressed for wine (Marc de Champagne, Marc de Bourgogne), apples (Calvados) and pears (Poire William), as well as such fruits as plums *(eau de vie de prune)* and even raspberries *(eau de vie de framboise).* In the Loire Valley a shot of orange (aka a glass of local Cointreau liqueur) ends the meal.

When in Normandy, do as the festive Normans do: refresh the palate between courses with a *trou normand* (literally 'Norman hole') – traditionally a shot of *calva* (Calvados) or a contemporary scoop of apple sorbet doused in the local apple brandy.

Provence

There is no more quintessential image of daily life in this hot part of southern France than lounging beneath a vine-laced pergola, glass of chilled rosé in hand.

Dating from 1977, Côtes de Provence is the region's largest appellation and France's sixth largest, producing 75% of Provençal wine. Its vineyards carpet 20 hectares between Nice and Aix-en-Provence, and its *terroir* (land) is astonishingly varied. Few other appellations support such a variety of grape varieties – at least a dozen. Its wines are drunk young and served at 8°C to 10°C, and are among the world's oldest. Vines were planted by the Greeks in Massilia (Marseille) around 600 BC.

Smaller appellations include Coteaux d'Aix-en-Provence and Palette around Aix-en-Provence; Côtes du Ventoux (light and fruity reds drunk young); Côtes du Luberon (young reds made trendy by rich foreigners and media stars buying up its vineyards); and Coteaux Varois of Angelina Jolie and Brad Pitt fame (in 2008 the celeb pair rented Château de Miraval, a golden-stone château on a prestigious organic wine-producing estate in Correns, where Pink Floyd recorded part of *The Wall* in 1979).

However, the real star of the Provence show is Bandol, with its own AOC since 1941. Its deep-flavoured reds are produced from dark-berried mourvèdre grapes grown on the coast near Toulon and ripened by oodles of sun, hence its rarity. In Roman times these wines were famous across Gaul, and their ability to mature at sea meant they travelled far beyond their home shores in the 16th and 17th centuries.

A little west along the same coast is Cassis, known for its crisp whites, the dream companion for the bijou port's bounty of shellfish and seafood.

Alsace

Alsace produces almost exclusively white wines – mostly varieties produced nowhere else in France – that are known for their clean, fresh taste and compatibility with the often heavy Alsatian cuisine. Unusually, some of the fruity Alsatian whites also go well with red meat. The vineyards closest to Strasbourg produce light red wines from pinot noir that are similar to rosé and are best served chilled.

Alsace's four most important varietal wines are riesling (known for its subtlety), gewürztraminer (pungent and highly regarded), pinot gris (robust and high in alcohol) and muscat d'Alsace (less sweet than muscats from southern France).

FRENCH WINE

Wine Schools

» Ô Chateau, Paris

» École des Vins de Bourgogne, Beaune, Burgundy

» École du Vin, Bordeaux

» La Winery, the Médoc

» École du Vin de St-Émilion, St-Émilion

» École de Dégustation, Châteauneuf-du-Pape

» Langlois – Chateau, Saumur, Loire Valley

The Arts

Literature

Courtly Love to Symbolism

Troubadours' lyric poems of courtly love dominated medieval French literature, while the *roman* (literally 'romance', now meaning 'novel') drew on old Celtic tales. With the *Roman de la Rose*, a 22,000-line poem by Guillaume de Lorris and Jean de Meung, allegorical figures like Pleasure, Shame and Fear appeared.

French Renaissance literature was great: La Pléiade was a group of lyrical poets active in the 1550s and 1560s. The exuberant narrative of Loire Valley–born François Rabelais (1494–1553) blends coarse humour with encyclopedic erudition in a vast panorama of subjects that includes every existent kind of person, occupation and jargon in 16th-century France. Michel de Montaigne (1533–92) covered cannibals, war horses, drunkenness and the resemblance of children to their fathers and other themes.

The *grand siècle* (golden age) ushered in classical lofty odes to tragedy. François de Malherbe (1555–1628) brought a new rigour to rhythm in poetry, and Marie de La Fayette (1634–93) penned the first French novel, *La Princesse de Clèves* (1678).

The philosophical Voltaire (1694–1778) dominated the 18th century. A century on, Besançon gave birth to French Romantic Victor Hugo. The breadth of interest and technical innovations exhibited in his poems and novels – *Les Misérables* and *The Hunchback of Notre Dame* among them – was phenomenal: after his death, his coffin was laid beneath the Arc de Triomphe for an all-night vigil.

In 1857 literary landmarks *Madame Bovary* by Gustave Flaubert (1821–80), and Charles Baudelaire's (1821–67) poems *Les Fleurs du Mal* (The Flowers of Evil), were published. Émile Zola (1840–1902) saw novel-writing as a science in his powerful series, *Les Rougon-Macquart*.

Evoking mental states was the dream of symbolists Paul Verlaine (1844–96) and Stéphane Mallarmé (1842-98). Verlaine shared a tempestuous homosexual relationship with poet Arthur Rimbaud (1854–91): enter French literature's first modern poems.

Modern Literature

The world's longest novel – a seven-volume 9,609,000-character giant by Marcel Proust (1871–1922) – dominated the early 20th century. *À la Recherche du Temps Perdu* (Remembrance of Things Past) explores in evocative detail the true meaning of past experience recovered from the unconscious by 'involuntary memory'.

Surrealism proved a vital force until WWII. André Breton (1896–1966) captured the spirit of surrealism – a fascination with dreams, divination and all manifestations of 'the marvellous' – in his autobiographical narratives. In Paris the bohemian Colette (1873–1954) captivated and

---

Best Literary Sights

» Maison de Victor Hugo, Paris

» Jean-Paul Sartre and Simone de Beauvoir graves, Cimetière du Montparnasse, Paris

» Oscar Wilde grave, Cimetière du Père Lachaise, Paris

» Musée Colette, Burgundy

» Château d'If, Marseille

» Musée Jules Verne, Nantes

shocked with her titillating novels detailing the amorous exploits of heroines such as schoolgirl Claudine.

After WWII, existentialism developed around the lively debates of Jean-Paul Sartre (1905–80), Simone de Beauvoir (1908–86) and Albert Camus (1913–60) in Paris' Left Bank cafes.

The *nouveau roman* of the 1950s saw experimental young writers seek new ways of organising narratives, with Nathalie Sarraute slashing identifiable characters and plot in *Les Fruits d'Or* (The Golden Fruits). *Histoire d'O* (Story of O), an erotic sadomasochistic novel written by Dominique Aury under a pseudonym in 1954, sold more copies outside France than any other contemporary French novel. In the 1960s novelist Philippe Sollers raised eyebrows with highly experimental novels such as *Le Parc* (The Park; 1961) and *Drame* (Event; 1965); with *Femmes* (Women; 1983) he returned to a conventional narrative style.

Contemporary Literature

Contemporary authors include Françoise Sagan, Pascal Quignard, Anna Gavalda, Emmanuel Carrère and Stéphane Bourguignon. Christine Angot is known as *'la reine de l'autofiction'* ('the queen of autobiography'), while Yasmina Khadra is actually a man – a former colonel in the Algerian army who adopted his wife's name as a nom de plume.

'Beach reading', perhaps, but Marc Levy is France's best-selling writer. The film rights of his first novel were snapped up for the Stephen Spielberg box-office hit, *Just Like Heaven* (2005), and his novels have been

READING LIST

One way of ensuring your beach reading is right up to the minute is to plump for the latest winner of the **Prix Goncourt**, France's most prestigious literary prize awarded annually since 1903. Winners include Marcel Proust in 1919 for *À l'Ombre des Jeunes Filles en Fleurs* (Within a Budding Grove; 1924); Simon de Beauvoir in 1954 for *Les Mandarins* (The Mandarins; 1957); and, more recently, French-Afghan writer/filmmaker Atiq Rahimi (b 1956) with *Syngué Sabour* (The Stone of Patience; 2008), and French-Senegalese novelist/playwright Marie NDiaye with *Trois Femmes Puissantes* (2009). The first black woman to win the award, NDiaye stunned the literary world at the age of 21 with *Comédie Classique* (1988), a 200-page novel comprising – rather mind-bogglingly – just one single sentence. The 2010 winner was *La Carte et Le Territoire* by Michel Houellebecq (b 1958), while the choice of 2011 Prix Goncourt victor reflects French literature's current preoccupation with issues of race, multiculturalism and immigration: Lyonnais biology teacher Alexis Jenni's *L'Art Français de la Guerre* (The French Art of War) portrays 50 years of French military history and colonial wars in Southeast Asia and Algeria. Winning Prix Goncourt works are generally pretty swiftly translated into English.

Add to your reading list the proud laureate of France's other big literary award, the **Grand Prix du Roman de l'Académie Française**, around since 1918, and your holiday reading list is sorted. The 2011 winner, *Retour à Killybegs*, by Sorj Chalandon (b 1952) was inspired by the time the French journalist spent reporting from Northern Ireland in the 1970s for French daily newspaper *Libération*. It was the sequel to Chalandon's earlier novel, *Mon Traitre* (2008), translated into English as *My Traitor* (2011), about a French violin maker's friendship over the course of 25 years with an Irish man ultimately exposed as an IRA traitor. The 2009 Grand Prix winner, *Les Onze*, by French novelist Pierre Michon (b 1945), published in English as *The Eleven* (2013), portrays a humble Parisian painter who decorates the homes of Louis XIV's mistresses and goes on to create a Mona Lisa–type masterpiece. Michon's earlier novels, *Small Lives* (2008) and *Master and Servants* (1997), come equally recommended. *Nagasaki* by Eric Faye (b 1963) was the prize getter of 2010.

translated into 42 languages. *L'étrange voyage de Monsieur Daldry* (The Strange Journey of Mr Daldry; 2011) is his latest.

No French writer better delves into the mind, mood and politics of the country's ethnic population than Faïza Guène (b 1985), sensation of the French literary scene who writes in a notable 'urban slang' style. Born and bred on a ghetto housing estate outside Paris, she stunned critics with her debut novel, *Kiffe Kiffe Demain* (2004), sold in 27 countries and published in English as *Just Like Tomorrow* (2006). Faïza Guène's father moved from a village in western Algeria to northern France in 1952, aged 17, to work in the mines. Only in the 1980s could he return to Algeria. There he met his wife, whom he brought back to France, to Les Courtillières housing estate in Seine-St-Denis, where 6000-odd immigrants live in five-storey high-rise blocks stretching for 1.5km. Such is the setting for Guène's first book and her second semi-autobiographical novel, *Du Rêve pour les Oeufs* (2006), published in English as *Dreams from the Endz* (2008).

Another French writer to address ethnic issues so engagingly is JMG Le Clézio, born during WWII in Nice on the French Rivieria to a Niçois mother and Mauritian father. The bulk of his childhood was spent in Nigeria and as a graduate and post-graduate, he studied in Bristol, England, and Aix-en-Provence. In 2008 he won the Nobel Prize in Literature, confirming France's ranking as country with the most literary Nobel Prize winners. Other contemporary French writers include Jean Echenoz, Nina Bouraoui, Jean-Philippe Toussaint, Annie Ernaux and Erik Orsenna.

Music

Classical

French baroque music influenced European musical output in the 17th and 18th centuries. French musical luminaries – Charles Gounod (1818–93), César Franck (1822–90) and *Carmen* creator Georges Bizet (1838–75) among them – were a dime a dozen in the 19th century. Modern orchestration was founded by French Romantic Hector Berlioz (1803–69). He demanded gargantuan forces: his ideal orchestra included 240 stringed instruments, 30 grand pianos and 30 harps.

Claude Debussy (1862–1918) revolutionised classical music with *Prélude à l'Après-Midi d'un Faune* (Prelude to the Afternoon of a Fawn), creating a light, almost Asian musical impressionism. Impressionist comrade Maurice Ravel (1875–1937) peppered his work, including *Boléro*, with sensuousness and tonal colour. Contemporary composer Olivier Messiaen (1908–92) combined modern, almost mystical music with natural sounds such as birdsong. His student Pierre Boulez (b 1925) works with computer-generated sound.

Jazz & French Chansons

Jazz hit 1920s Paris in the banana-clad form of Josephine Baker, an African-American cabaret dancer. Post-WWII ushered in a much-appreciated bunch of musicians, mostly black Americans who opted to remain in Paris' bohemian Montmartre rather than return to the brutal racism and segregation of the US: Sidney Bechet called Paris home from 1949, jazz drummer Kenny 'Klook' Clarke followed in 1956, pianist Bud Powell did so in 1959, and saxophonist Dexter Gordon arrived in the early 1960s. Jazz in Paris had never been so hot.

Miles Davis never settled in Paris, but it was while he was performing at the city's jazz festival in 1949 that he met French singer and actress Juliette Gréco. The love affair that ensued and the suffering he endured upon returning alone to New York haunted him for the rest of his life.

Cinematic Experiences

» Forum des Images & La Pagode Cinema, Paris

» Musée Lumière & Hangar du Premier Film, Lyon

» Cannes Film Festival, Cannes

» Musée Jean Cocteau Collection Séverin Wunderman, Menton

» American Film Festival, Deauville

» Futuroscope, Poitiers

In 1934 a chance meeting between Parisian jazz guitarist Stéphane Grappelli and three-fingered Roma guitarist Django Reinhardt in a Montparnasse nightclub led to the formation of the Hot Club of France quintet. Claude Luter and his Dixieland band were hot in the 1950s.

The *chanson française,* a French folk-song tradition dating from the troubadours of the Middle Ages, was eclipsed by the music halls and burlesque of the early 20th century, but was revived in the 1930s by Édith Piaf and Charles Trenet. In the 1950s, Paris' Left Bank cabarets nurtured *chansonniers* (cabaret singers) such as Léo Ferré, Georges Brassens, Claude Nougaro, Jacques Brel and the very charming, very sexy, very French Serge Gainsbourg. A biopic celebrating his life, *Serge Gainsbourg: Une Vie Héroïque* (Serge Gainsbourg: A Heroic Life), was released in 2009 to wide acclaim.

In the 1980s irresistible crooners Jean-Pierre Lang and Pierre Bachelet revived the *chanson* tradition with classics such as *Les Corons* (1982), a passionate ode to northern France's miners. Exciting contemporary performers of the genre include Vincent Delerm, Bénabar, Jeanne Cherhal, Camille, Soha and a group called Les Têtes Raides. The next hip crooner on the scene, on Facebook and YouTube, is Arnaud Fleurent-Didier (www.arnaudfleurentdidier.com).

Rap

France is known for its rap, an original 1990s sound spearheaded by Senegal-born, Paris-reared rapper MC Solaar and Suprême NTM (NTM being an acronym for a French expression far too offensive to print). Most big-name rappers are French 20-somethings of Arabic or African origin whose prime preoccupations are the frustrations and fury of fed-up immigrants in the French *banlieues* (suburbs). Take hot-shot rapper Disiz La Peste, born in Amiens to a Senegalese father and French mother: his third album *Histoires Extra-Ordinaires d'un Jeune de Banlieue* (The Extraordinary Stories of a Youth in the Suburbs; 2005) revealed just what its title suggested, as did his album *Disiz the End* (2009), following which he morphed into Peter Punk (www.disizpeterpunk.com) and created a very different rock-punk-electro sound with *Dans La Ventre du Crocodile* (In the Crocodile's Stomach; 2010). In December 2011 the artist announced on Twitter his return to rap as Disiz La Peste, with the release of the much-vaunted album *Lucide* (2012).

Other rappers to listen out for include Monsieur R of Congolese origin, known for his hardcore, antiestablishment lyrics, which have landed him in court in the past; Parisian heavyweight Booba of Senegalese origin; ghetto kid Rohff (www.roh2f.com, in French); and the trio Malekal Morte.

One of France's few female rappers, Cyprus-born Diam's (short for *'diamant'*, meaning 'diamond'; www.diams-lesite.com), who arrived in Paris aged seven, was voted MTV's French Artist of the Year in 2007. Rap bands include Marseille's hugely successful home-grown IAM

FRENCH CINEMA

1920s

French film flourishes. Sound ushers in René Clair's (1898–1981) world of fantasy and satirical surrealism. **Watch** Abel Gance's antiwar blockbuster *J'Accuse!* (I Accuse!; 1919), filmed on WWI battlefields.

1930s

WWI inspires a new realism: portraits of ordinary lives dominate film. **Watch** *La Grande Illusion* (The Great Illusion; 1937), a devastating evocation of war's folly based on the trench warfare experience of director Jean Renoir.

1940s

Surrealists eschew realism. **Watch** Jean Cocteau's *La Belle et la Bête* (Beauty and the Beast; 1945) and *Orphée* (Orpheus; 1950). WWII saps the film industry of both talent and money.

1950s

Nouvelle Vague (New Wave) sees small budgets, no stars and real-life subject matter. **Watch** a petty young criminal on the run in Jean-Luc Godard's *À Bout de Souffle* (Breathless; 1958) and adolescent rebellion in François Truffaut's *Les Quatre Cents Coups* (The 400 Blows; 1959).

1960s

France as the land of romance. **Watch** Claude Lelouch's *Un Homme et une Femme* (A Man and a Woman; 1966) and Jacques Demy's bittersweet *Les Parapluies de Cherbourg* (The Umbrellas of Cherbourg; 1964).

(www.iam.tm.fr, in French), five-piece band KDD from Toulouse and Brittany's Manau trio (www.manau.com, in French), who fuse hip hop with traditional Celtic sounds.

No artist has cemented France's reputation in world music more than Paris-born Franco-Congolese rapper, slam poet and three-time Victoire de la Musique award winner Abd al Malik (www.abdalmalik.fr). His albums *Gibraltar* (2006), *Dante* (2008) and *Château Rouge* (2010) are classics.

Musical Pilgrimages

» Serge Gainsbourg grave, Cimetière du Montparnasse, Paris

» Jim Morrison grave, Cimetière du Père Lachaise, Paris

» La Cigale, Paris

» Château des Milandes, the Dordogne

» Espace Georges Brassens, Sète

» Antibes (for jazz lovers), French Riviera

Rock & Pop

One could be forgiven for thinking that French pop is becoming dynastic. The very distinctive M (for Mathieu) is the son of singer Louis Chédid; Arthur H is the progeny of pop-rock musician Jacques Higelin; and Thomas Dutronc is the offspring of 1960s idols Jacques and Françoise Hardy. And the Gainsbourg dynasty doesn't look like ending any time soon. Serge's daughter with Jane Birkin, songwriter/singer and actress Charlotte, blogs at http://charlotte-gainsbourg.blogspot.com and released her fourth album, *Stage Whisper,* with great success at the end of 2011.

Noir Désir was *the* sound of French rock until its lead singer, Bertrand Cantat, was imprisoned for the murder of his girlfriend and it disbanded. Worth noting are Louise Attaque (http://louiseattaque.com), Mickey 3D and the very funky Nosfell (www.nosfell.com) who sings in his own invented language. The hottest group to emerge in recent years, electro-dance rock-pop Pony Pony Run Run (www.ponyponyrunrun.net), sings in English – a long way from the *yéyé* (imitative rock) of the 1960s as sung by Johnny Hallyday, otherwise known as 'Johnny National' (until he took Belgian nationality for tax reasons). The band released a much-awaited second album, simply titled *Pony Pony Run Run,* in early 2012.

World

With styles from Algerian *rai* to other North African music (artists include Cheb Khaled, Natacha Atlas, Jamel, Cheb Mami) and Senegalese *mbalax* (Youssou N'Dour), West Indian zouk (Kassav', Zouk Machine) and Cuban salsa, France's world beat is strong. One musician who uses world elements to stunning effect is Manu Chao (www.manuchao.net), the Paris-born son of Spanish parents, whose albums are international best sellers.

Postwar Parisian artists worth noting include Jean Fautrier, Nicolas de Staël, Bernard Buffet and Robert Combas, one of whose larger-than-life murals – 120 were commissioned around the city – can be seen in rue des Haudriettes, 4e, in the Marais.

In the late 1980s, bands Mano Negra and Les Négresses Vertes combined many of these elements with brilliant results. Magic System from Côte d'Ivoire popularised *zouglou* (a kind of West African rap and dance music) with its album *Premier Gaou,* and Congolese Koffi Olomide still packs the halls. Watch for the blind singing couple, Amadou and Mariam, and Rokia Traoré from Mali.

In recent years a distinctly urban and highly exportable Parisian sound has developed, often mixing computer-enhanced Chicago blues and Detroit techno with 1960s lounge music and vintage tracks from the likes of Gainsbourg and Brassens. Among those playing are Parisian electro-dance and hip-hop duo Daft Punk (www.daftalive.com), a band originally from Versailles that adapts first-wave acid house and techno to their younger roots in pop, indie rock and hip hop. Daft Punk's debut album *Homework* (1997) fused disco, house, funk and techno, and in early 2012 the internet was abuzz with rumours that Daft Punk would release their first studio LP in seven years.

Electronica duo Air (an acronym for *'Amour, Imagination, Rêve'*, meaning 'Love, Imagination, Dream') bagged a massive loyal following with its sensational album *Moon Safari* (1998) and continued to thrill with its seventh, *Le Voyage dans La Lune* (2012). Then there is

Rachid Taha (www.rachidtaha.fr), a Franco-Algerian DJ-turned-singer whose music mixes Arab and Western musical styles to create an extraordinarily rich fusion of rock, punk, afro-pop, Algerian *rai* and salsa. To add extra appeal there are song lyrics in English and Berber as well as French.

Painting
Prehistoric to Landscape

France's oldest known prehistoric cave paintings (created 31,000 years ago) adorn the Grotte Chauvet-Pont-d'Arc in the Rhône Valley and the underwater Grotte Cosquer near Marseille; neither can be visited.

According to Voltaire, French painting proper began with baroque painter Nicolas Poussin (1594–1665), known for his classical mythological and biblical scenes bathed in golden light. Wind forward a couple of centuries and modern still life popped up with Jean-Baptiste Chardin (1699–1779). A century later, neoclassical artist Jacques Louis David (1748–1825) wooed the public with vast portraits.

While Romantics such as Eugène Delacroix (find his grave in Paris' Cimetière du Père Lachaise) revamped the subject picture, the Barbizon School effected a parallel transformation of landscape painting. Jean-François Millet (1814–75), the son of a peasant farmer from Normandy, took many of his subjects from peasant life, and reproductions of his *L'Angélus* (The Angelus; 1857) – the best-known painting in France after the *Mona Lisa* – are strung above mantelpieces all over rural France. The original hangs in Paris' Musée d'Orsay.

Realism & Impressionism

The Realists were all about social comment: Édouard Manet (1832–83) evoked Parisian middle-class life and Gustave Courbet (1819–77) depicted working-class drudgery.

It was in a flower-filled garden in a Normandy village that Claude Monet (1840–1926) expounded Impressionism, a term of derision taken from the title of his experimental painting *Impression: Soleil Levant* (Impression: Sunrise; 1874). A trip to the Musée d'Orsay unveils a rash of other members of the school – Boudin, Sisley, Pissarro, Renoir, Degas and more.

An arthritis-crippled Renoir painted out his last Impressionist days in a villa on the French Riviera, a part of France that inspired dozens of artists: Paul Cézanne (1839–1906) is particularly celebrated for his post-Impressionist still lifes and landscapes done in Aix-en-Provence, where he was born and worked; Paul Gauguin (1848–1903) worked in Arles; and Dutch artist Vincent van Gogh (1853–90) painted Arles and St-Rémy de Provence. In St-Tropez pointillism took off: Georges Seurat (1859–91) was the first to apply paint in small dots or uniform brush strokes of unmixed colour, producing fine mosaics of warm and cool tones, but it was his pupil Paul Signac (1863–1935) who is best known for pointillist works.

THE ARTS

1970s
The limelight baton goes to lesser-known directors like Éric Rohmer (b 1920), who make beautiful but uneventful films in which the characters endlessly analyse their feelings.

1980s
Big-name stars, slick production values and nostalgia: generous state subsidies see filmmakers switch to costume dramas and comedies in the face of growing competition from the USA. Luc Besson strikes box-office gold with *Subway* (1985) and *Le Grand Bleu* (The Big Blue; 1988).

1990s
French actor Gérard Depardieu wins huge audiences in France and abroad. **Watch** *Cyrano de Bergerac* (1990) and *Astérix et Obélix: Mission Cléopâtre* (2002). Besson continues to stun with *Nikita* (1990) and *Jeanne d'Arc* (Joan of Arc; 1999).

New Millennium
'New French Extremity' is the tag given to the socially conscious, transgressive films of talented Paris-born, Africa-raised filmmaker Claire Denis. **Watch** *Chocolat* (1988) and *Matériel Blanc* (White Material; 2009), scripted by Parisian novelist Marie NDiaye, to explore the legacy of French colonialism.

2012
Renaissance of French film. **Watch** *The Artist* (2011), a silent B&W, French-made romantic comedy set in 1920s Hollywood that scooped five Oscars.

20th Century to Present Day

Twentieth-century French painting is characterised by a bewildering diversity of styles, including cubism, and fauvism, named after the slur of a critic who compared the exhibitors at the 1906 autumn Salon in Paris with *fauves* (wild animals) because of their radical use of intensely bright colours. Spanish prodigy Pablo Picasso (1881–1973) was the man behind cubism, and Henri Matisse (1869–1954) fauvism. Both chose southern France to set up studio, Matisse living in Nice and Picasso opting for Antibes. Cubism, as developed by Picasso and Georges Braque (1882–1963), deconstructed the subject into a system of intersecting planes and simultaneously presented various aspects of it.

The early 20th century also saw the rise of the Dada movement, and no piece of French art better captures its rebellious spirit than Marcel Duchamp's *Mona Lisa,* complete with moustache and goatee. In 1922 German Dadaist Max Ernst moved to Paris and worked on surrealism, a Dada offshoot that drew on the theories of Freud to reunite the conscious and unconscious realms and permeate daily life with fantasies and dreams.

With the close of WWII, Paris' role as the artistic capital of the world ended. The focus shifted back to southern France in the 1960s with new realists such as Arman (1928–2005) and Yves Klein (1928–62), both from Nice. In 1960 Klein famously produced *Anthropométrie de l'Époque Bleue,* a series of imprints made by naked women (covered from head to toe in blue paint) rolling around on a white canvas, in front of an orchestra of violins and an audience in evening dress. A decade on, the Supports/Surfaces movement deconstructed the concept of a painting, transforming one of its structural components (such as the frame or canvas) into a work of art instead.

Artists in the 1990s turned to the minutiae of everyday urban life to express social and political angst, using media other than paint to let rip. Conceptual artist Daniel Buren (b 1938) reduced his painting to a signature series of vertical 8.7cm-wide stripes that is applied to any surface imaginable – white marble columns in the courtyard of Paris' Palais Royal included. The painter (who in 1967, as part of the radical *groupe BMPT,* signed a manifesto declaring he was not a painter) was the *enfant terrible* of French art in the 1980s. Partner-in-crime Michel Parmentier (1938–2000) insisted on monochrome painting – blue in 1966, grey in 1967 and red in 1968.

Paris-born conceptual artist Sophie Calle (b 1953) brazenly exposes her private life in public with eye-catching installations such as *Prenez soin de vous* (Take Care of Yourself; 2007), a compelling and addictive work of art in book form exposing the reactions of 107 women to an email Calle received from her French lover, dumping her. Her most recent work, *Rachel, Monique* (2010), evokes the death and lingering memory of her mother in the shape of a photographic exhibition first shown at Paris' Palais de Tokyo in 2010 and a live reading performance at the 2012 Festival d'Avignon.

Modern Art Meccas

» Monet's garden, Giverny

» Renoir's studio, French Riviera

» Picasso's château studio, Antibes

» Musée Matisse, Nice

» Cézanne's pad, Aix-en-Provence

» Chemin du Fauvisme (Fauvism Trail), Collioure

Contemporary Art Trendsetters

» Palais de Tokyo, Paris

» Centre Pompidou, Paris

» Fondation Maeght, St-Paul de Vence

» Centre Pompidou-Metz, Metz

» Musée d'Art Moderne et d'Art Contemporain, Nice

Architecture

From prehistoric megaliths around Carnac in Brittany to Vauban's 33 star-shaped citadels dotted around France to defend its 17th-century frontiers, French architecture has always been of *grand-projet* proportions.

Prehistoric to Roman

No part of France better demonstrates the work of the country's earliest architects than Brittany, which has more megalithic menhirs (monumental upright stones), tombs, cairns and burial chambers than anywhere else on earth. Many date from around 3500 BC and the most frequent structure is the dolmen, a covered burial chamber consisting of vertical menhirs topped by a flat capstone. Bizarrely, Brittany's ancient architects had different architectural tastes from their European neighbours – rather than the cromlechs (stone circles) commonly found in Britain, Ireland, Germany and Spain, they were much keener on building arrow-straight rows of menhirs known as *alignements*. And, indeed, Carnac's monumental Alignements de Carnac is the world's largest known prehistoric structure.

The Romans left behind a colossal architectural legacy in Provence and the French Riviera. Thousands of men took three to five years to haul the 21,000 cu metres of local stone needed to build the Pont du Gard near Nîmes. Other fine pieces of Roman architecture, still operational, include amphitheatres in Nîmes and Arles, open-air theatres in Orange and Fréjus, and Nîmes' Maison Carrée.

Romanesque

A religious revival in the 11th century led to the construction of Romanesque churches, so-called because their architects adopted many architectural elements (eg vaulting) from Gallo-Roman buildings still standing at the time. Romanesque buildings typically have round arches, heavy walls, few windows and a lack of ornamentation that borders on the austere.

Romanesque masterpieces include Toulouse's Basilique St-Sernin, Poitiers' Église Notre Dame la Grande, the exquisitely haunting Basilique St-Rémi in Reims, Caen's twinset of famous Romanesque abbeys and Provence's trio in the Luberon (Sénanque, Le Thoronet and Silvacane). In Normandy the nave and south transept of the abbey-church on Mont St-Michel are beautiful examples of Norman Romanesque.

Then there is Burgundy's astonishing portfolio of Romanesque abbeys, among the world's finest.

Gothic

Avignon's pontifical palace is Gothic architecture on a gargantuan scale. The Gothic style originated in the mid-12th century in northern France, where the region's great wealth attracted the finest architects, engineers

> Catch up with southern France's prehistoric architects at Marseille's Centre de la Vieille Charité, Quinson's Musée de la Préhistoire des Gorges du Verdon and the beehive-shaped huts called *bories* near Gordes in the Luberon.

BORIES

FRANCE'S MOST BEAUTIFUL VILLAGES

One of French architecture's signature structures popped up in rural France from the 13th century, 'up' being the operative word for these *bastides* or *villages perchés* (fortified hilltop villages), built high on a hill to afford maximum protection for previously scattered populations. Provence and the Dordogne are key regions to hike up, down and around one medieval hilltop village after another, but you can find them in almost every French region. The most dramatic and stunning appear at www.les-plus-beaux-villages -de-france.org (Les Plus Beaux Villages de France, aka France's most beautiful villages).

and artisans. Gothic structures are characterised by ribbed vaults carved with great precision, pointed arches, slender verticals, chapels (often built or endowed by the wealthy or by guilds), galleries and arcades along the nave and chancel, refined decoration and large stained-glass windows. If you look closely at certain Gothic buildings, however, you'll notice minor asymmetrical elements introduced to avoid monotony.

The world's first Gothic building was the Basilique de St-Denis near Paris, which combined various late-Romanesque elements to create a new kind of structural support in which each arch counteracted and complemented the next. The basilica served as a model for many other 12th-century French cathedrals, including Notre Dame de Paris and Chartres' cathedral – both known for their soaring flying buttresses. No Gothic belfry is finer to scale than that of Bordeaux' Cathédrale St-André.

In the 14th century, the Radiant Gothic style developed, named after the radiating tracery of the rose windows, with interiors becoming even lighter thanks to broader windows and more translucent stained glass. One of the most influential Rayonnant buildings was Paris' Ste-Chapelle, whose stained glass forms a curtain of glazing on the 1st floor.

Renaissance

The Renaissance, which began in Italy in the early 15th century, set out to realise a 'rebirth' of classical Greek and Roman culture. It had its first impact on France at the end of that century, when Charles VIII began a series of invasions of Italy, returning with some new ideas.

To trace the shift from late Gothic to Renaissance, travel along the Loire Valley. During the very early Renaissance period, châteaux were used for the first time as pleasure palaces rather than defensive fortresses. Many edifices built during the 15th century to early 16th century in the Loire Valley – including Château d'Azay-le-Rideau and Château de Villandry – were built as summer or hunting residences for royal financiers, chamberlains and courtiers. Red-patterned brickwork – such as that on the Louis XII wing of Château de Blois – adorned the façade of most châteaux dating from Louis XII's reign (1498–1515).

The quintessential French Renaissance château is a mix of classical components and decorative motifs (columns, tunnel vaults, round arches, domes etc) with the rich decoration of Flamboyant Gothic. It ultimately showcased wealth, ancestry and refinement. Defensive towers (a historical seigniorial symbol) were incorporated into a new decorative architecture, typified by its three-dimensional use of pilasters and arcaded loggias, terraces, balconies, exterior staircases, turrets and gabled chimneys. Heraldic symbols were sculpted on soft stone façades, above doorways and fireplaces, and across coffered ceilings. Symmetrical floor plans broke new ground and heralded a different style of living: Château de Chambord contained 40 self-contained apartments, arranged on five floors around a central axis. This ensured easy circulation in a vast edifice that many rank as the first modern building in France.

Renaissance architecture stamped châteaux with a new artistic form: the monumental staircase. The most famous of these splendid ceremonial (and highly functional) creations are at Azay-le-Rideau, Blois, and Chambord in the Loire Valley.

RENAISSANCE STAIRCASES

Mannerism

Mannerism, which followed the Renaissance, was introduced by Italian architects and artists brought to France around 1530 by François I, whose royal château at Fontainebleau was designed by Italian architects. Over the following decades, French architects who had studied in Italy took over from their Italian colleagues.

The Mannerist style lasted until the early 17th century, when it was subsumed by the baroque style.

Baroque

During the baroque period (the tail end of the 16th to the late-18th centuries), painting, sculpture and classical architecture were integrated to create structures and interiors of great subtlety, refinement and elegance. Architecture became more pictorial, with the painted ceilings in churches illustrating the Passion of Christ to the faithful, and palaces invoking the power and order of the state.

Salomon de Brosse, who designed Paris' Palais du Luxembourg in 1615, set the stage for two of France's most prominent early-baroque architects: François Mansart (1598–1666), who designed the classical wing of Château de Blois; and his younger rival Louis Le Vau (1612–70), who worked on France's grandest palace at Versailles.

Neoclassicism

Nancy's place Stanislas in northern France is the country's loveliest neoclassical square. Neoclassical architecture, which emerged in about 1740 and remained popular until well into the 19th century, had its roots in the renewed interest in the classical forms and conventions of Graeco-Roman antiquity: columns, simple geometric forms and traditional ornamentation.

Among the earliest examples of this style is the Italianate façade of Paris' Église St-Sulpice, designed in 1733 by Giovanni Servandoni, which took inspiration from Christopher Wren's St Paul's Cathedral in London; and the Petit Trianon at Versailles, designed by Jacques-Ange Gabriel for Louis XV in 1761. France's greatest neoclassical architect of the 18th century was Jacques-Germain Soufflot, the man behind the Panthéon in Left Bank Paris.

Neoclassicism peaked under Napoléon III, who used it extensively for monumental architecture intended to embody the grandeur of imperial France and its capital: the Arc de Triomphe, La Madeleine, the Arc du Carrousel at the Louvre, the Assemblée Nationale building and the Palais Garnier.

Architect-Buff Sleeps

» Le Pradey, W Paris-Opéra, Five Hotel & L'Apostrophe, Paris

» Les Bains Douches, Toulouse

» Hôtel Le Corbusier, Marseille

» Hôtel Oscar, Le Havre

» Zazpi, St-Jean de Luz

ARCHITECTURE

France's biggest architectural scandals-turned-successes: Renzo Piano and Richard Rogers' Centre Pompidou, and IM Pei's glass pyramid at the Louvre, both in Paris.

VAUBAN'S CITADELS

From the mid-17th century to the mid-19th century, the design of defensive fortifications around the world was dominated by the work of one man: Sébastien le Prestre de Vauban (1633–1707).

Born to a relatively poor family of the petty nobility, Vauban worked as a military engineer during almost the entire reign of Louis XIV, revolutionising both the design of fortresses and siege techniques. To defend France's frontiers, he built 33 immense citadels, many of them shaped like stars and surrounded by moats, and he rebuilt or refined more than 100. Vauban's most famous citadel is situated at Lille, but his work can also be seen at Antibes, Belfort, Belle Île, Besançon, Concarneau, Neuf-Brisach (Alsace), Perpignan, St-Jean Pied de Port and St-Malo. The Vauban citadel in Verdun comprises 7km of underground galleries. Since 2008, 13 sites (www.sites-vauban.org) star on Unesco's World Heritage list under a 'Vauban Fortifications' banner.

The true showcase of this era though is Monte Carlo Casino in Monaco, created by French architect Charles Garnier (1825–98) in 1878.

Art Nouveau

Art nouveau (1850–1910) combined iron, brick, glass and ceramics in ways never before seen. The style emerged in Europe and the USA under various names (Jugendstil, Sezessionstil, Stile Liberty) and caught on quickly in Paris. The style was characterised by sinuous curves and flowing asymmetrical forms reminiscent of creeping vines, water lilies, the patterns on insect wings and the flowering boughs of trees. Influenced by the arrival of exotic objets d'art from Japan, its French name came from a Paris gallery that featured works in the 'new art' style. True buffs should make a beeline for the art nouveau tourist trail in Nancy.

Art Nouveau in Paris

» Hector Guimard's noodle-like metro entrances

» Interior of the Musée d'Orsay

» Department stores Le Bon Marché & Galeries Lafayette

» Glass roof over the Grand Palais

A Beautiful Age

The glittering belle époque, hot on the heels of art nouveau, heralded an eclecticism of decorative stucco friezes, *trompe l'œil* paintings, glittering wall mosaics, brightly coloured Moorish minarets and Turkish towers. Immerse yourself in its fabulous and whimsical designs with a stroll along Promenade des Anglais in Nice, where the pink-domed Hôtel Negresco (1912) is the icing on the cake, or, up north, around the colourful Imperial Quarter of Metz. Or flop in a beautiful belle époque spa like Vichy.

Modern

The Fondation Vasarely, by the 'father of op art' Victor Vasarely (1908–97), was an architectural coup when unveiled in Aix-en-Provence in 1976. Its 14 giant monumental hexagons reflected what Vasarely had already achieved in art: the creation of optical illusion and changing perspective through the juxtaposition of geometrical shapes and colours.

France's best-known 20th-century architect, Charles-Édouard Jeanneret (better known as Le Corbusier; 1887–1965), was born in Switzerland but settled in Paris in 1917 at the age of 30. A radical modernist, he tried to adapt buildings to their functions in industrialised society without ignoring the human element, thus rewriting the architectural style book with his sweeping lines and functionalised forms adapted to fit the human form. Chapelle de Notre-Dame du Haut in the Jura and Couvent Ste-Marie de la Tourette near Lyon are 20th-century architectural icons.

Until 1968, French architects were still being trained almost exclusively at the conformist École de Beaux-Arts, which certainly shows in most of the acutely unimaginative, early structures erected in the Parisian skyscraper district of La Défense and Montparnasse's ungainly 210m-tall Tour Montparnasse (1973).

Contemporary

French political leaders have long sought to immortalise themselves through the erection of huge public edifices (aka *grands projects*). Georges Pompidou commissioned the Centre Pompidou (1977) in which the architects – in order to keep the exhibition halls as uncluttered as possible – put the building's insides out. Valéry Giscard d'Estaing transformed a derelict train station into the glorious Musée d'Orsay. And François Mitterrand commissioned the capital's best-known contemporary architectural landmarks (taxpayers' bill: a whopping €4.6 billion), including the Opéra Bastille, the Grande Arche in La Défense, the four glass towers of the national library, and IM Pei's glass pyramid at the hitherto sacrosanct and untouchable Louvre (an architectural cause célébre that paved the way, incidentally, for Mario Bellini and Rudy Ric-

BUILDING GREEN

A signature architectural feature of the French capital that has since been exported to other European cities is the vertical garden – *mur végétal* (vegetation wall) – especially that of Patrick Blanc (www.verticalgardenpatrickblanc.com). His most famous work is at the Musée du Quai Branly. Seeming to defy the very laws of gravity, the museum's vertical garden consists of some 15,000 low-light foliage plants from Central Europe, the USA, Japan and China planted on a surface of 800 sq metres and held in place by a frame of metal, PVC and nonbiodegradable felt – but no soil.

ciotti's magnificent 'flying carpet' roof atop the Louvre's Cour Visconti in 2012). Jacques Chirac's only *grand projet* was Jean Nouvel's iconic riverside museum, the Musée du Quai Branly.

In the provinces, notable buildings include Strasbourg's European Parliament, Dutch architect Rem Koolhaas' Euralille, Jean Nouvel's glass-and-steel Vesunna Musée Gallo-Romain in Périgueux (a 1920s art deco swimming pool-turned-art museum in Lille) and the fantastic Louvre II in little Lens, 37km south of Lille. Also noteworthy are an 11th-century abbey-turned-monumental sculpture gallery in Angers and Le Havre's rejuvenated 19th-century docks.

Then, of course, there's one of the world's tallest bridges, the stunning Pont de Millau in Languedoc, designed by Sir Norman Foster. Other bridges worth noting for their architectural ingenuity are Normandy's Pont de Normandie (1995) near Le Havre and Paris' striking Passerelle Simone de Beauvoir (2006). Both cross the Seine.

One of the most beautiful and successful of France's contemporary buildings is the Institut du Monde Arabe (1987), a highly praised structure in Paris that successfully mixes modern and traditional Arab and Western elements. It was designed by Jean Nouvel, France's leading and arguably most talented architect. His current project, the ambitious Philharmonie de Paris (2014), will have an auditorium of 2400 'terrace' seats surrounding the orchestra. Equally exciting in the capital is the work going on at the Forum des Halles, a thoroughly unattractive 1970s-eyesore shopping centre in the 1er, currently being transformed into a stunning contemporary creation. The radically curvaceous, curvilinear and glass-topped construction by architects Patrick Berger and Jacques Anziutti, should be complete by 2016.

Daring duo Shigeru Ban (Tokyo) and Jean de Gastines (Paris) are the tour de force behind the very white, bright Centre Pompidou-Metz (2010).

Looking south, Frank Gehry is the big-name architect behind Arles' innovative new cultural centre: all ashimmer in the bright southern sun, rocklike Fondation Luma (2013) evokes the nearby Alpilles mountain range with its two linked towers topped with aluminium. Sir Norman Foster is busy designing a new yacht club for Monaco (2013) and in Lyon in 2014, a shimmering glass-and-steel cloud will rise out of the wasteland at the confluence of the Rhône and Saône Rivers.

Architecture et Musique (www .architecmusique .com) is a fine concept: enjoy a classical-music concert amid an architectural masterpiece; the annual program is online.

ARCHITECTURE ET MUSIQUE

Lyrical Landscapes

The Land

France is a land of art. Fantastic portraits and paintings adorn the walls of galleries big and small, villages throughout the land look like oil paintings of a bygone rural age and the people, with their natural sense of style, could be called works of art themselves. But as gorgeous as the manmade art of France is, it fades when compared to the sheer beauty of the countryside itself.

Hexagon-shaped France, the largest country in Europe after Russia and Ukraine, is encircled by water or mountains along every side except in the northeast.

The country's 3200km-long coastline is incredibly diverse, ranging from white-chalk cliffs (Normandy) and treacherous promontories (Brittany) to broad expanses of fine sand (Atlantic coast) and pebbly beaches (the Mediterranean coast).

Western Europe's highest peak, Mont Blanc (4810m), spectacularly crowns the French Alps, which stagger along France's eastern border. North of Lake Geneva, the gentle limestone Jura Mountains run along the Swiss frontier to reach heights of around 1700m, while the rugged Pyrenees define France's 450km-long border with Spain and Andorra, peaking at 3404m.

Five major river systems criss-cross the country: the Garonne (which includes the Tarn, the Lot and the Dordogne) empties into the Atlantic; the Rhône links Lake Geneva and the Alps with the Mediterranean; Paris is licked in poetic verse by the Seine, which slithers through the city en route from Burgundy to the English Channel; and tributaries of the North Sea–bound Rhine drain much of the area north and east of the capital. Then there's France's longest river, the château-studded Loire, which meanders through history from the Massif Central to the Atlantic.

Wildlife

France is blessed with a rich variety of flora and fauna, although few habitats have escaped human impacts: intensive agriculture, wetland draining, urbanisation, hunting and the encroachment of industry and tourism infrastructure menace dozens of species.

Animals

France has more mammal species than any other country in Europe (around 135 including marine mammals and some introduced species). Couple this with around 500 bird species (depending on which rare migrants are included), 40 types of amphibian, 36 varieties of reptile and 72 kinds of fish, and wildlife-watchers are in paradise. Of France's 40,000

Spotted a bearded vulture? Lucky you! Note down when, where, any distinguishing marks and the bird's behaviour patterns and send the details to the Bearded Vulture Reintroduction into the Alps project at www.wild.unizh.ch/bg.

BEARDED VULTURES

identified insect species, 10,000 creep and crawl in the Parc National du Mercantour in the southern Alps.

High-altitude plains in the Alps and the Pyrenees shelter the marmot, which hibernates from October to April and has a shrill and distinctive whistle; the nimble chamois (mountain antelope), with its dark-striped head; and the *bouquetin* (Alpine ibex), seen in large numbers in the Parc National de la Vanoise. Mouflons (wild mountain sheep), introduced in the 1950s, clamber over stony sunlit scree slopes in the mountains; while red and roe deer and wild boar are common in lower-altitude forested areas. The Alpine hare welcomes winter with its white coat, while 19 of Europe's 29 bat species hang out in the dark in the Alpine national parks.

The *loup* (wolf), which disappeared from France in the 1930s, returned to the Parc National du Mercantour in 1992 – much to the horror of the mouflon (on which it preys) and local sheep farmers. Dogs, corrals and sound machines have been used as an effective, nonlethal way of keeping the growing free-roaming wolf population of the Mercantour and other Alpine areas from feasting on domesticated sheep herds.

The brown bear disappeared from the Alps in the mid-1930s. The 150-odd native bears living in the Pyrenees a century ago had dwindled to one orphaned cub following the controversial shooting of its mother – the last female bear of Pyrenean stock – by a hunter in 2004. However, another 12 to 18 bears of Slovenian origin also call the French and Spanish Pyrenees home, though the reintroduction program has faced fierce opposition from sheep herders.

A rare but wonderful treat is the sighting of an *aigle royal* (golden eagle): 40 pairs nest in the Mercantour, 20 pairs nest in the Vanoise, 30-odd in the Écrins and some 50 in the Pyrenees. Other birds of prey include the peregrine falcon, the kestrel, the buzzard and the bearded vulture, with its bone-breaking habits. The last – Europe's largest bird of prey, with an awe-inspiring wingspan of 2.8m – was extinct in the Alps from the 19th century until the 1980s, when it was reintroduced. More recently, the small, pale-coloured Egyptian vulture (once worshipped by the Egyptians, hence its name) has been spreading throughout the Alps and Pyrenees.

Even the eagle-eyed will have difficulty spotting the ptarmigan, a chicken-like species that moults three times a year to ensure a foolproof camouflage for every season (brown in summer, white in winter). It lives on rocky slopes and in Alpine meadows above 2000m. The nutcracker, with its loud and buoyant singsong and larch-forest habitat, the black grouse, rock partridge, the very rare eagle owl and the three-toed woodpecker are among the other 120-odd species to keep birdwatchers on their toes in highland realms.

Guide de la Nature en France by Michel Viard is an excellent field guide to the most commonly seen plants, birds and animals of France. It's in French but the glossy photos are universal.

HIGH-FACTOR PROTECTION BY THE SEA

Over 10% of the coastline of mainland France and Corsica is managed by the Conservatoire du Littoral (www.conservatoire-du-littoral.fr), a public coastal-protection body that acquires – sometimes by expropriation – threatened natural areas by the sea in order to restore, rejuvenate and protect them.

Among the *conservatoire*'s rich pageant of *espaces naturels protégés* (protected natural areas) are the rare-orchid-dotted sand dunes east of Dunkirk, the Baie de Somme with its ornithological park, several wet and watery pockets of the horse-studded Camargue, and a Corsican desert. (The Désert des Agriates covers 16,000 hectares of wilderness between the towns of St-Florent and La Balagne – not so long ago a highly fertile area but today a barren landscape due to severe soil erosion resulting from human activities.)

France also sports 24 Ramsar Convention wetland sites (www.wetlands.org/rsis).

Elsewhere on the French watch-the-birdie front, there are now 12,000 pairs of white storks – up from seven breeding pairs in 1974; 10% of the world's flamingo population hangs out in the Camargue; giant black cormorants – some with a wingspan of 170cm – reside on an island off Pointe du Grouin on the north coast of Brittany; and there are unique seagull and fishing-eagle populations in the Réserve Naturelle de Scandola on Corsica. The *balbuzard pêcheur* (osprey), a migratory hunter that winters in Africa and returns to France in February or March, today only inhabits two regions of France: Corsica and the Loire Valley area.

Plants

About 140,000 sq km of forest – beech, oak and pine in the main – covers 20% of France, while there are 4900 different species of native flowering plants countrywide (2250 alone grow in the Parc National des Cévennes). In forests in the Champagne region, mutant beech trees grow in a bizarrely stunted, malformed shape in the Parc Natural Régional de la Montagne de Reims.

The Alpine and Pyrenean regions nurture fir, spruce and beech forests on north-facing slopes between 800m and 1500m. Larch trees, mountain and arolla pines, rhododendrons and junipers stud shrubby subalpine zones between 1500m and 2000m; and a brilliant riot of spring and summertime wildflowers carpets grassy meadows above the treeline in the alpine zone (up to 3000m).

Alpine blooms include the single golden-yellow flower of the arnica, which has long been used in herbal and homeopathic bruise-relieving remedies; the flame-coloured fire lily; and the hardy Alpine columbine, with its delicate blue petals. The protected 'queen of the Alps' (aka the Alpine eryngo) bears an uncanny resemblance to a purple thistle but is, in fact, a member of the parsley family (to which the carrot also belongs).

The rare twinflower only grows in the Parc National de la Vanoise. Of France's 150 orchids, the black vanilla orchid is one to look out for – its small red-brown flowers exude a sweet vanilla fragrance.

Corsica and the Massif des Maures, west of St-Tropez on the Côte d'Azur, are closely related botanically: both have chestnut and cork-oak trees (the bark of which gets stuffed in bottles) and are thickly carpeted with *garrigues* and *maquis* – heavily scented scrubland, where dozens of fragrant shrubs and herbs find shelter.

Travellers' Nature Guides: France by Bob Gibbons is the definitive guide to where to watch wildlife in France.

WILDLIFE WATCH

The national parks and their regional siblings offer all sorts of options to visitors who are keen to observe animals in their natural habitat, including nature walks with an expert guide. Other easy-to-reach and highly rewarding areas for wildlife include the Forêt de Fontainebleau outside Paris, the Marais Poitevin on the Atlantic coast, the stunning underwater life between Cerbère and Banyuls, and the central mountains of Corsica, around Corte. The following (at non-national parks) are also worth a gander:

» Ten thousand flamingos in the Camargue, the best-known wetland site in France, as well as over 400 bird species including rollers and glossy ibis.

» Vultures in the Pyrenees at Falaise aux Vautours (Cliff of the Vultures) in the Vallée d'Ossau and in Languedoc at the Belvédère des Vautours in the Parc Naturel Régional des Grands Causses.

» Storks in Alsace at the Centre de Réintroduction des Cigognes, in Hunawihr, and the Enclos aux Cigognes in Munster; on the Atlantic coast at Le Teich Parc Ornithologique and the Parc Ornithologique du Marquenterre; and at the Parc des Oiseaux outside Villars-les-Dombes near Lyon.

National Parks

The proportion of protected land in France is surprisingly low, relative to the size of the country. Seven small *parcs nationaux* (national parks; p955) fully protect just 0.8% of the country. Another 13% (70,000 sq km) in metropolitan France and its overseas territories, with three million inhabitants, is protected to a substantially lesser degree by 45 *parcs naturels régionaux* (regional national parks; p955), and a further few per cent by 320 smaller *réserves naturelles* (nature reserves; www.reserves -naturelles.org), some of them under the eagle eye of the Conservatoire du Littoral.

While the central zones of national parks are uninhabited and fully protected by legislation (dogs, vehicles and hunting are banned and camping is restricted), their delicate ecosystems spill over into populated peripheral zones in which economic activities, some of them environmentally unfriendly, are permitted and even encouraged.

Most regional nature parks and reserves were established not only to improve (or at least maintain) local ecosystems, but also to encourage economic development and tourism in areas suffering from economic hardship and diminishing populations (such as the Massif Central and Corsica).

Select pockets of nature – the Pyrenees, Mont St-Michel and its bay, part of the Loire Valley and a clutch of capes on Corsica – have been declared Unesco World Heritage Sites.

Environmental Issues

As elsewhere in the world, wetlands in France – incredibly productive ecosystems that are essential for the survival of birds, reptiles, fish and amphibians – are shrinking. More than 20,000 sq km (3% of French territory) are considered important wetlands but only 4% of this land is currently protected.

Great tracts of forest burn each summer, often because of careless day-trippers but occasionally, as is sometimes reported in the Maures and Estérel ranges on the Côte d'Azur, because they're intentionally torched by people hoping to get licences to build on the damaged lands. Since the mid-1970s, between 31 sq km and 615 sq km of land has been reduced to black stubble each year by an average of 540 fires. However, as prevention and fire-fighting improve, the number of fires overall is falling, according to the Office National des Forêts (www.onf.fr), the national forestry commission responsible for public forests in France.

Dogs and guns also pose a threat to French animal life, brown bears included. While the number of hunters has fallen by more than 20% in the last decade, there are still a lot more hunters in France (1.3 million) than in any other Western European country.

Despite the 1979 Brussels Directive for the protection of wild birds, their eggs, nests and habitats in the EU, the French government has been very slow to make its provisions part of French law, meaning birds that can fly safely over other countries can still be hunted as they cross France. A good handful of birds – estimated at at least 1000 birds of prey a year – are found to be electrocuted by high-voltage power lines.

The state-owned electricity company, Electricité de France, has an enviable record on minimising greenhouse-gas emissions – fossil-fuel-fired power plants account for just 4.6% of its production. Clean, renewable hydropower, generated by 220 dams, comprises 8.8% of the company's generating capacity but this does affect animal habitats. And no less than 75% (the highest in the world) of France's electricity comes from another controversial zero-carbon source: nuclear power, generated by 59 nuclear reactors at 20 sites. One of the last decisions Nicolas Sarkozy made in

LYRICAL LANDSCAPES

WILDLIFE WATCHING

Butterfly-spotting in Normandy, exploring bird-rich wetlands in the Camargue, or skipping with butterflies between Cathar ruins in Languedoc – UK-based tour company Nature Trek (www .naturetrek.co.uk) organises inspirational watching holidays.

NATIONAL PARKS AT A GLANCE

PARK	FEATURES	ACTIVITIES	WHEN TO GO
Parc National des Cévennes	wild peat bogs, granite peaks, ravines & ridges bordering the Massif Central & Languedoc (910 sq km); red deer, beavers, vultures, wolves, bison	walking, donkey trekking, mountain biking, horse riding, cross-country skiing, caving, canoeing, botany (2250 plant species)	spring & winter
Parc National des Écrins	glaciers, glacial lakes & mountaintops soaring up to 4102m in the French Alps (1770 sq km); marmots, lynx, ibex, chamois, bearded vultures	walking, climbing, hang-gliding, para-gliding, kayaking	spring & summer
Parc National du Mercantour	Provence at its most majestic with 3000m-plus peaks & dead-end valleys along the Italian border; marmots, mouflons, chamois, ibex, wolves, golden & short-toed eagles, bearded vultures; Bronze Age petroglyphs	alpine skiing, white-water sports, mountain biking, walking, donkey trekking	spring, summer & winter
Parc National de Port-Cros	island marine park off the Côte d'Azur forming France's smallest national park & Europe's first marine park (700 hectares & 1288 hectares of water); puffins, shearwaters, migratory birds	snorkelling, birdwatching, swimming, gentle strolling	summer & autumn (for birdwatching)
Parc National des Pyrénées	100km of mountains along the Spanish border (457 sq km); marmots, izards (Pyrenean chamois), brown bears, golden eagles, vultures, buzzards	alpine & cross-country skiing, walking, mountaineering, rock-climbing, white-water sports, canoeing, kayaking, mountain biking	spring, summer & winter
Parc National de la Vanoise	postglacial mountain landscape of Alpine peaks, beech-fir forests & 80 sq km of glaciers forming France's first national park (530 sq km); chamois, ibex, marmots, golden eagles, bearded vultures	alpine & cross-country skiing, walking, mountaineering, mountain biking	spring, summer & winter
Parc National des Calanques	20km of rocky promontories rising out of turquoise water; idyllic coves & beaches, some accessible only by kayak	hiking (Oct-Jun), sea kayaking, swimming, snorkelling	spring & summer

LIFE & DEATH OF THE IBEX

The nippy *bouquetin des Alpes* (Alpine ibex), with its imposingly large, curly-wurly horns (we're talking 1m long and a good 5kg in weight) and a penchant for hanging out on sickeningly high crags and ledges, is the animal most synonymous with the French Alps. In the 16th century, higher altitudes were loaded with the handsome beast, the males spraying themselves with urine and sporting a strong body odour. Three centuries on, however, its extravagant and unusual horns had become a must-have item in any self-respecting gentleman's trophy cabinet, and within a few years the Alpine ibex had been hunted to the brink of extinction.

In 1963 the Parc National de la Vanoise was created in the Alps to stop hunters in the Vanoise massif from shooting the few Alpine ibex that remained. The creation of similar nature reserves and the pursuit of rigorous conservation campaigns to protect the animal have seen populations surely and steadily recover – to the point where today the Alpine ibex is thriving. Not that you're likely to encounter one: the canny old ibex has realised that some mammals are best avoided.

On a less positive note, ibex also used to thrive in the Pyrenees but in a pattern that mirrored that of the Alpine populations, ibex numbers tumbled until, by 1900, only around 100 of them remained. Unlike in the Alps, though, protection measures never worked here and, in 2000, the Pyrenean ibex finally became extinct when the last surviving female was killed by a falling tree. Or did they become extinct? Nine years after the wiping out of the species the Pyrenean ibex became, for seven minutes, the first species in history to become 'un-extinct' when a cloned female was born alive before dying of breathing difficulties.

his final months of office as French president was to guarantee, in February 2012, the life of France's nuclear-power stations for another 40 years.

Meanwhile the world's most ambitious nuclear-power program continues to grow. Costing an extraordinary €6 billion, the country's most recent nuclear reactor, Flamanville 3 on Normandy's west coast near Cherbourg, is due for completion in 2016, two years later than planned.

Europe's largest solar-powered electricity-generating farm sits 1000m-high on a south-facing slope near the tiny village of Curbans in Provence. Since its inauguration in 2011 the farm's 150-hectare array of photovoltaic cells – 145,000 panels in all – have removed 120,000 metric tonnes of carbon dioxide annually from the French energy bill.

Follow the progress of France's precious wolf, bear and lynx populations with Ferus (www .ferus.org, in French), France's conservation group for the wellbeing of these protected predators.

Survival Guide

Directory A–Z

Accommodation

Be it a fairy-tale château, boutique hideaway or floating pod on a lake, France has accommodation to suit every taste, mood and pocket.

Categories

As a rule of thumb, budget covers everything from basic hostels to small, simple family-run places; midrange means a few extra creature comforts such as satellite TV and free wi-fi; and top-end places stretch from luxury five-star palaces with air conditioning, swimming pools and restaurants to boutique-chic chalets in the Alps.

Costs

Accommodation costs vary wildly between seasons and regions: what will buy you a night in a romantic *chambre d'hôte* (B&B) in the countryside may get you a dorm bed in a major city or high-profile ski resort.

Reservations

Midrange, top-end and many budget hotels require a credit card number to secure an advance reservation made by phone; some hostels do not take bookings. Many tourist offices can advise on availability and reserve for you, often for a fee of €5 and usually only if you stop by in person. In the Alps, ski resort tourist offices run a central reservation service for booking accommodation.

Seasons

» Rates listed are for high season.

» In ski resorts, high season is Christmas, New Year and the February–March school holidays.

» On the coast, high season is summer, particularly August.

» Hotels in inland cities often charge low-season rates in summer.

» Rates often drop outside the high season – in some cases by as much as 50%.

» In business-oriented hotels in cities, rooms are most expensive from Monday to Thursday and are cheaper over the weekend.

» In the Alps, hotels usually close between seasons, from around May to mid-June and from mid-September to early December; many addresses in Corsica only open April to October.

B&Bs

For charm, a heartfelt *bienvenue* (welcome) and solid home cooking, it's hard to beat France's privately run *chambres d'hôte* (B&Bs) – urban rarities but as common as muck in rural areas. By law a *chambre d'hôte* must have no more than five rooms and breakfast must be included in the price; some hosts prepare evening *table d'hôte*-style meals for an extra charge of €20 to €30. Pick up lists of *chambres d'hôte* at local tourist offices, or find one to suit your style online:

Bienvenue à la Ferme (www.bienvenue-a-la-ferme. com)

Chambres d'Hôtes France (www.chambresdhotesfrance. com)

en France (www.bbfrance. com) A listing of B&Bs and *gîtes* (self-catering cottages and villas) compiled and written up by property owners.

Fleurs de Soleil (www. fleursdesoleil.fr) Selective collection of 550 stylish *maisons d'hôte* (B&Bs), mainly in rural France.

Gîtes de France (www.gites -de-france.com) France's primary umbrella organisation for B&Bs and *gîtes*. Search for properties by region, theme (charm, with kids, by the sea, gourmet, great garden etc), activity (fishing, wine tasting etc) or facilities

---

BOOK YOUR STAY ONLINE

For more accommodation reviews by Lonely Planet authors, check out http://hotels.lonelyplanet.com. You'll find independent reviews, as well as recommendations on the best places to stay. Best of all, you can book online.

(pool, dishwasher, fireplace, baby equipment, computer etc). Tourist offices often stock local Gîtes de France catalogues.

Guides de Charme (www. guidesdecharme.com) Gorgeous presentation of France's most charming and often-times most upmarket B&Bs, organised by region and/or theme (romantic, gastronomic, green, oenological and so forth).

Samedi Midi Éditions (www.samedimidi.com) Country, mountain, seaside... choose your *chambre d'hôte* by location or theme (romance, golf, design, cooking courses).

Camping

Be it a Mongolian yurt, boutique treehouse or simple canvas beneath stars, camping in France is so in vogue. Thousands of well-equipped campgrounds dot the country, many considerably placed by rivers, lakes and the sea. Gîtes de France and Bienvenue à la Ferme coordinate camping on farms.

» Most campgrounds open March or April to late September or October; popular spots fill up fast in summer when it is wise to call ahead.

» 'Sites' refer to fixed-price deals for two people including a tent and a car. Otherwise the price is broken down per adult/tent/car. Factor in a few extra euro per night for *taxe de séjour* (holiday tax) and electricity.

» Euro-economisers should look out for local, good-value but no-frills *campings municipaux* (municipal campgrounds).

» Many campgrounds rent mobile homes with mod cons like heating, fitted kitchen and TV.

» Pitching up 'wild' in non-designated spots (*camping sauvage*) is illegal in France.

» Campground offices often close during the day.

» Accessing many campgrounds without your own

transport can be slow and costly or simply impossible. Websites with campsite listings searchable by location, theme and facilities:

Camping en France (www. camping.fr)

Camping France (www. campingfrance.com)

Guide du Camping (www. guideducamping.com)

HPA Guide (http://camping. hpaguide.com)

Homestays

One of the best way to brush up your *français* and immerse yourself in local life is by staying with a French family under an arrangement known as *hôtes payants* or *hébergement chez l'habitant*. Popular with students and young people, this set-up means you rent a room and usually have access (sometimes limited) to the bathroom and the kitchen; meals may also be available. If you are sensitive to smoke or pets, make sure you mention this. The following organisations arrange homestays:

France Lodge (✆01 56 35 85 80; www.francelodge.com) Accommodation in private Parisian homes; €32 to €49 a night for a single, €56 to €68 for two people in a double or twin, and from €79/100 for three/four people.

Homestay France Locations (www.homestaybooking. com/homestay-france) Homestays in major French cities from €105 per person per week.

Hostels

Hostels in France range from funky to threadbare: some are little more than a few rooms set aside in a hostel for young workers (*foyer de jeunes travailleurs/travailleuses*), while others are hip hang-outs with perks.

» In university towns, *foyers d'étudiant* (student dormitories) are sometimes converted for use by travellers during summer.

» A dorm bed in an *auberge de jeunesse* (youth hostel) costs about €25 in Paris, and anything from €10.50 to €28 in the provinces, depending on location, amenities and facilities; sheets are always included, breakfast more often than not.

» To prevent outbreaks of bed bugs, sleeping bags are not permitted.

» Hostels by the sea or in the mountains sometimes offer seasonal outdoor activities.

» French hostels are 100% nonsmoking.

HOSTELLING CARD

You'll need to purchase an annual Hostelling International (HI) card (€7/11 for under/over 26s) or a nightly

---

PRICE RANGES

The price indicators refer to the cost of a double room, including private bathroom (any combination of toilet, bathtub, shower and washbasin) and excluding breakfast unless otherwise noted. Breakfast is assumed to be included at a B&B. Where half-board (breakfast and dinner) and full board (breakfast, lunch and dinner) is included, this is mentioned in the price.

CATEGORY	COST
€ budget	< €80 (< €110 in Paris)
€€ midrange	€80–180 (€110–200 in Paris)
€€€ top end	> €180 (> €200 in Paris)

THE FINE ART OF SLEEPING

A château, a country manor, Parisian opulence in the shade of the Eiffel Tower – whether you want to live like a lord, sleep like a log or blow the budget, there's a room with your name on it.

» **Alistair Sawday's** (www.sawdays.co.uk) Boutique retreats and *chambres d'hôte* (B&Bs), placing the accent on originality and authentic hospitality.

» **Châteaux & Hôtels Collection** (www.chateauxhotels.com) Châteaux and other historic properties, now boutique hotels, with a thousand tales to tell.

» **Grandes Étapes Françaises** (www.grandesetapes.fr) Beautiful châteaux-hotels and multistar residences.

» **Hôtels de Charme** (www.hotelsdecharme.com) Abbeys, manors, châteaux – this is a mixed bag of (as the name says) charming hotels.

» **Logis de France** (www.logis-de-france.fr) Small, often family-run hotels with charm and a warm welcome.

» **Relais & Châteaux** (www.relaischateaux.com) Seductive selection of villas, châteaux and historic hotels.

» **Relais du Silence** (www.relaisdusilence.com) Fall asleep to complete silence in a gorgeous château, spa-clad *auberge* (country inn) or vineyard hotel...

» **Small Luxury Hotels of the World** (www.slh.com) Super-luxurious boutique hotels, chalets and resorts.

Welcome Stamp (up to to €3, maximum of six per year) to stay at the two major French hostelling associations: **Fédération Unie des Auberges de Jeunesse** (www.fuaj.org) and **Ligue Française pour les Auberges de la Jeunesse** (www.auberges-de-jeunesse.com).

Hotels

We have tried to feature well-situated, independent hotels that offer good value, a warm welcome, at least a bit of charm and a palpable sense of place.

Hotels in France are rated with one to five stars, although the ratings are based on highly objective criteria (eg the size of the entry hall), not the quality of the service, the decor or cleanliness.

» French hotels almost never include breakfast in their rates. Unless specified otherwise, prices quoted don't include breakfast, which costs around €7/10/20 in a budget/midrange/top-end hotel.

» When you book, hotels usually ask for a credit card number; some require a deposit.

» A double room generally has one double bed (sometimes two singles pushed together!); *deux lits* (a room with twin beds) is usually more expensive, as is a room with a bathtub instead of a shower.

» Feather pillows are practically nonexistent in France, even in top-end hotels.

» All hotel restaurant terraces allow smoking; if you are sensitive to smoke, sit inside or carry a respirator.

Refuges & Gîtes d'Étape

» *Refuges* (mountain huts or shelters) are bog-basic cabins established along walking trails in uninhabited mountainous areas and operated by national-park authorities, the **Club Alpin Français** (French Alpine Club; www.ffcam.fr) or other private organisations.

» *Refuges* are marked on hiking and climbing maps.

» A bunk in a dorm generally costs €10 to €25. Hot meals are sometimes available and, in a few cases, mandatory, pushing the price up to €30 or beyond.

» Advance reservations and a weather check are essential before setting out.

CAMPING CHIC

Farewell clammy canvas, *adieu* inflatable mattress... Camping in France is cool and creative, with *écolo chic* (ecochic) and adventurous alternatives springing up all the time. If you fancy doing a Robinson Crusoe by staying in a tree house with an incredible view over the treetops, visit **Cabanes de France** (www.cabanes-de-france.com), which covers leafy options between branches all over France. Prefer to keep your feet firmly on the ground? Keep an eye out for ecoconscious campgrounds where you can snooze in a *tipi* (tepee) or in a giant hammock.

» *Gîtes d'étape*, better equipped and more comfortable than *refuges* (some even have showers), are situated along walking trails in less remote areas, often in villages.

» Drop by **Gîtes d'Étape et Refuges** (www.gites-refuges.com), an online listing of 4000 *gîtes d'étape* and *refuges* in France.

Rental Accommodation

If you are planning on staying put for more than a few days or are travelling in a group, renting a furnished studio, apartment or villa can be an economical alternative. You will have the chance to live like a local, with trips to the farmers market and the *boulangerie* (bakery).

Finding an apartment for long-term rental can be gruelling. Landlords, many of whom prefer locals to foreigners, usually require substantial proof of financial responsibility and sufficient funds in France; many ask for a *caution* (guarantee) and a hefty deposit.

» Gîtes de France handles some of the most charming *gîtes ruraux* (self-contained holiday cottages) in rural areas.

» Cleaning, linen rental and electricity fees usually cost extra.

» Classified ads appear in *De Particulier à Particulier* (www.pap.fr, in French), published on Thursday and sold at newsstands.

» For apartments outside Paris it's best to search at your destination.

» Check places like bars and *tabacs* (tobacconists) for free local newspapers (often named after the number of the *département*) with classifieds listings.

Activities

From Alpine glaciers, rivers and canyons to the volcanic peaks of the Massif Central – not to mention 3200km of coastline stretching from Italy to Spain and from the Basque country to the Straits of Dover – France's spirit-lifting landscapes beg exhilarating outdoor escapes.

For details on regional activities, courses, equipment hire, clubs and companies, get in contact with local tourist offices.

Organisations

Whether you are a peak bagger, surfer dude or thrill-seeking mountain biker, the following organisations can help you plan your adventure:

CYCLING

Fédération Française de Cyclisme (French Cycling Federation; www.ffc.fr) Founded in 1881, this is *the* authority on competitive cycling in France and mountain biking (VTT), including freeriding, cross-country and downhill.

Fédération Française de Cyclotourisme (French Cycling Tourism Federation; www.ffct.org) This organisation promotes bicycle touring and mountain biking.

Union Touristique Les Amis de la Nature (http://troisv.amis-nature.org) Has details on local, regional and long-distance *véloroutes* (cycling routes) around France.

Véloroutes et Voies Vertes (www.af3v.org) A database of 250 signposted *véloroutes* (bike paths) and *voies vertes* (greenways) for cycling and in-line skating.

GLIDING

Fédération Française de Vol à Voile (French Gliding Federation; www.ffvv.org) Provides details of *vol à voile* (gliding) clubs countrywide.

Fédération Française de Vol Libre (French Hang-gliding Federation; www.federation.ffvl.fr) Groups regional clubs specialising in *deltaplane* (hang-gliding), *parapente* (paragliding) and *le kite-surf* (kitesurfing).

MOUNTAIN & SNOW SPORTS

Club Alpin Français (French Alpine Club; www.ffcam.fr) This highly regarded organisation groups 280 local mountain sports clubs and arranges professional guides for escapades in *alpinisme* (mountaineering), *escalade* (rock climbing), *escalade de glace* (ice climbing) and other highland activities. It also runs many of the *refuges* in the French Alps.

École du Ski Français (ESF; www.esf.net) The largest ski school in the world, operating everywhere in France big enough to have a ski lift and high enough to be snow sure. The tuition is first rate.

WALKING

Grande Randonnée (www.grande-randonnee.fr) A good source of information (in French) on France's long-distance footpaths.

GR-Infos (www.gr-infos.com) Information in many languages, including English, on France's long-distance footpaths.

Parcs Nationaux de France (French National Parks; www.parcsnationaux.fr) This is your first port of call if you are planning a visit to one of France's six national parks.

Parcs Naturels Régionaux de France (French Regional Naure Parks; www.parcs-naturels-regionaux.tm.fr) Has the low-down on activities, accommodation and events

---

WHICH FLOOR?

In France, as elsewhere in Europe, 'ground floor' refers to the floor at street level; the 1st floor – what would be called the 2nd floor in the US – is the floor above that.

PRACTICALITIES

» **Classifieds** Pick up the free **FUSAC** (France USA Contacts; www.fusac.fr) in Anglophone haunts in Paris for classified ads about housing, babysitting, jobs and language exchanges.

» **Laundry** Virtually all French cities and towns have at least one *laverie libre-service* (self-service laundrette). Machines runs on coins.

» **Newspapers & magazines** Locals read their news in centre-left **Le Monde** (www. lemonde.fr), right-leaning **Le Figaro** (www.lefigaro.fr) or left-leaning **Libération** (www. liberation.fr).

» **Radio** For news, tune in to the French-language France Info (105.5MHz), the multi-language RFI (738kHz or 89MHz in Paris) or, in northern France, the BBC World Service (648kHz) and BBC Radio 4 (198kHz). Popular national FM music stations include **NRJ** (www.nrj.fr), **Skyrock** (www.skyrock.fm) and **Nostalgie** (www.nostalgie.fr).

» **Smoking** Smoking is illegal in all indoor public spaces, including restaurants and pubs (though, of course, smokers still light up on the terraces outside).

» **Travel conditions** In many areas, Autoroute Info (107.7MHz) has round-the-clock traffic information.

» **TV & video** TV is Secam; videos work on the PAL system.

» **Weights & measures** France uses the metric system.

---

in France's 48 regional nature parks.

WATER SPORTS

École Française de Kite (www.efk.fr) France's kite-surfing school has dozens of outlets on the Mediterranean and Atlantic coasts, and a couple inland by lakes.

Fédération Française de Voile (French Sailing Federation; www.ffvoile.fr)

WALK THE WALK

The French countryside is criss-crossed by a staggering 120,000km of **sentiers balisés** (marked walking paths), which pass through every imaginable terrain in every region of the country. No permit is needed to hike. Probably the best-known walking trails are the **sentiers de grande randonnée (GR)**, long-distance paths marked by red-and-white-striped track indicators.

Key information source on sailing, for both fun and competition.

Business Hours

French business hours are regulated by a maze of government regulations, including the 35-hour working week.

» The midday break is uncommon in Paris, but common elsewhere; in general, the break gets longer the further south you go.

» French law requires that most businesses close on Sunday; exceptions include grocery stores, *boulangeries*, florists and businesses catering to the tourist trade.

» In many places shops close on Monday.

» Many service stations open 24 hours a day and stock basic groceries.

» Restaurants generally close one or two days of the week, chosen according to the owner's whim. Opening days/hours are only specified if the restaurant isn't open for both lunch and dinner daily.

» Most (but not all) national museums are closed on

Tuesday; most local museums are closed on Monday, though in summer some open daily. Many museums close at lunchtime.

» We give high-season hours for sights and attractions; hours are almost always shorter during the low season.

Customs Regulations

Goods brought in and out of countries within the EU incur no additional taxes provided duty has been paid somewhere within the EU and the goods are for personal consumption. Duty-free shopping is available only if you are leaving the EU.

Duty-free allowances (for adults) coming from non-EU countries (including the Channel Islands):

» 200 cigarettes
» 50 cigars
» 1L spirits
» 2L wine
» 50mL perfume
» 250mL eau de toilette
» other goods up to the

value of €175 (€90 for under 15 year olds)
Higher limits apply if you are coming from Andorra; anything over these limits must be declared. For further details, see www.douane.gouv.fr (partly in English).

Discount Cards

Discount cards yield fantastic benefits and easily pay for themselves. As well as the card fee, you'll often need a passport-sized photo and some form of ID with proof of age (eg passport or birth certificate).

People over 60 or 65 are entitled to discounts on things like public transport, museum admission fees and theatres.

Discount card options:

Camping Card International (CCI; www.campingcardinternational.com; €8) Use as ID for checking into campgrounds; the annual card includes third-party liability insurance and covers up to 11 people in a party; it usually yields up to 20% discount. Available at automobile associations, camping federations and campgrounds.

European Youth Card (Euro<26 card; www.euro26.org; €14) Wide range of discounts for under-26-year-olds. Available online.

International Student Identity Card (ISIC; www.isic.org; €12, online €13) Discounts on travel, shopping, attractions and entertainment for full-time students. Available at ISIC points listed online.

International Teacher Identity Card (ITIC; www.isic.org; €12, online €13) Travel, shopping, entertainment and sightseeing discounts for full-time teachers.

International Youth Travel Card (IYTC; www.isic.org; €12, online €13) Discounts on travel, tickets and so forth for under-26-year-olds.

Electricity

230V/50Hz

Embassies & Consulates

All foreign embassies are in Paris.

» Many countries – including Canada, Japan, the UK, USA and most European coun-
tries – also have consulates in other major cities such as Bordeaux, Lyon, Nice, Marseille and Strasbourg.

» To find a consulate or an embassy not listed here, visit www.embassiesabroad.com or look up 'ambassade' in the super–user-friendly **Pages Jaunes** (Yellow Pages; www.pagesjaunes.fr).

Food

This guide includes options for all tastes and budgets, reviewed in order of preference and categorised according to type of cuisine, or price range, or both.

For the complete taste-bud tour of France's varied regional cuisines and accompanying tipples, see the Bon Appetit (p926) and French Wine (p928) essays. To understand how to eat and drink like a local, see that tip-loaded section at the front of this book.

Gay & Lesbian Travellers

Gay mayors (including Paris' very own Bertrand Delanoë),

STANDARD HOURS

We've only listed business hours where they differ from the following standards:

BUSINESS	OPENING HOURS
Bank	9am–noon & 2-5pm Mon-Fri or Tue-Sat
Bar	7pm-1am Mon-Sat
Cafe	7am or 8am-10pm or 11pm Mon-Sat
Nightclub	10pm-3am, 4am or 5am Thu-Sat
Post office	8.30am or 9am-5pm or 6pm Mon-Fri, 8am-noon Sat
Restaurant	lunch noon-2.30pm (or 3pm in Paris), dinner 7-11pm (to 10pm to midnight in Paris) six days a week
Shop	9am or 10am-7pm Mon-Sat (often with lunch break noon-1.30pm)
Supermarket	8.30am-7pm Mon-Sat, 8.30am-12.30pm Sun

EMBASSIES & CONSULATES IN PARIS

COUNTRY	TELEPHONE	WEBSITE	ADDRESS	NEAREST METRO
Australia	01 40 59 33 00	www.france.embassy.gov.au	4 rue Jean Rey	Bir Hakeim
Belgium	01 44 09 39 39	www.diplomatie.be/paris	9 rue de Tilsitt	Charles de Gaulle-Étoile
Canada	01 44 43 29 00	www.amb-canada.fr	35 av Montaigne	Franklin D Roosevelt
Germany	01 53 83 45 00	www.paris.diplo.de	13-15 av Franklin D Roosevelt	Franklin D Roosevelt
Ireland	01 44 17 67 00	www.embassyofireland.fr	12 av Foch	Argentine
Italy	01 49 54 03 00	www.ambparigi.esteri.it	51 rue de Varenne	Rue du Bac
Japan	01 48 88 62 00	www.amb-japon.fr	7 av Hoche	Courcelles
Netherlands	01 40 62 33 00	www.amb-pays-bas.fr	7 rue Eblé	St-François Xavier
New Zealand	01 45 01 43 43	www.nzembassy.com	7ter rue Léonard de Vinci	Victor Hugo
South Africa	01 53 59 23 23	www.afriquesud.net	59 quai d'Orsay	Invalides
Spain	01 44 43 18 00	www.maec.es	22 av Marceau	Alma-Marceau
Switzerland	01 49 55 67 00	www.eda.admin.ch	142 rue de Grenelle	Varenne
UK	01 44 51 31 00	http://ukinfrance.fco.gov.uk	35 rue du Faubourg St-Honoré	Concorde
USA	01 43 12 22 22	http://france.usembassy.gov	4 av Gabriel	Concorde

artists and film directors, camper-than-camp fashion designers – the rainbow flag flies high in France, a country that left its closet long before many of its European neighbours. *Laissez-faire* perfectly sums up France's liberal attitude towards homosexuality and people's private lives in general, in part because of a long tradition of public tolerance towards unconventional lifestyles.

» Paris has been a thriving gay and lesbian centre since the late 1970s, and most major organisations are based there today.

» Bordeaux, Lille, Lyon, Montpellier, Toulouse and many other towns also have an active queer scene.

» Attitudes towards homosexuality tend to be more conservative in the countryside and villages.

» France's lesbian scene is less public than its gay male counterpart and is centred mainly on women's cafes and bars.

» Introduced in 1999, PACS (civil solidarity pacts) afford same-sex couples most of the rights, legal protections and responsibilities as their married counterparts.

» Gay Pride marches are held in major French cities from mid-May to early July.

Publications

Damron (www.damron.com) Publishes English-language travel guides, including the *Damron Women's Traveller*

PRICE RANGES

Price indicators refer to the average cost of a two-course meal, be it an *entrée* (starter) and *plat* (main course) or main and dessert, or a *menu* (pre-set meal at a fixed price). Lunch *menus* can often yield a better deal.

CATEGORY	COST
€ budget	< €20
€€ midrange	€20–40
€€€ top end	> €40

for lesbians and the *Damron Men's Travel Guide* for gays.

Spartacus International Gay Guide (www.spartacus world.com) A male-only guide to just about every country in the world, with more than 70 pages devoted to France, almost half of which cover Paris. iPhone app too.

Websites

French Government Tourist Office (www.us.franceguide.com/special-in terests/gay-friendly) Information about 'the gay-friendly destination par excellence'.

France Queer Resources Directory (www.france.qrd.org) Gay and lesbian directory.

Gay France (www.gay-france.net) Insider tips on gay life in France.

Gayscape (www.gayscape.com) Hundreds of links to gay- and lesbian-related sites.

Gayvox (www.gayvox.com/guide3) Online travel guide to France, with listings by region.

Tasse de Thé (www.tassede the.com) A *webzine lesbien* with lots of useful links.

Health

France is a healthy place, so your main risks are likely to be sunburn, foot blisters, insect bites and mild stomach problems from eating and drinking with too much gusto.

Before You Go

» Bring your medications in their original, clearly labelled, containers.

» A signed and dated letter from your physician describing your medical conditions and medications, including generic names (French medicine names are often completely different to those in other countries), is also a good idea.

» Dental care in France is usually good; however, it is

sensible to have a dental check-up before a long trip.

» No vaccinations are required to travel to France but the World Health Organization (WHO) recommends that all travellers be covered for diphtheria, tetanus, measles, mumps, rubella and polio, regardless of their destination.

Availability & Cost of Health Care

» Visitors to France can get excellent health care from hospital *(hôpital)* emergency rooms/casualty wards *(salles des urgences)* and at a doctors' office *(cabinet médical)*.

» For minor illnesses, trained staff in pharmacies – in every village and town with a green-cross sign outside that flashes when open – give valuable advice, sell medications, can tell you when more specialised help is needed and will point you in the right direction.

» You will need to pay upfront for any health care you receive, be it at a doctor's surgery, pharmacy or hospital, unless your insurance plan makes payments directly to providers.

» The standard rate for a consultation with a GP/specialist is €25 to €40.

» Emergency contraception is available with a doctor's prescription. Condoms *(les préservatifs)* are readily available.

Insurance

» Comprehensive travel insurance to cover theft, loss and medical problems is highly recommended.

» Some policies specifically exclude dangerous activities such as scuba diving, motorcycling, skiing and even trekking: read the fine print.

» Check that the policy covers ambulances or an emergency flight home.

» Find out in advance if your insurance plan will make payments directly to providers or reimburse you later for overseas health expenditures.

» If you have to claim later, make sure you keep all documentation.

» Paying for your airline ticket with a credit card often provides limited travel accident insurance – ask your credit card company what it is prepared to cover.

EUROPEAN HEALTH INSURANCE CARD

Citizens of the EU, Switzerland, Iceland, Norway or Liechtenstein receive free or reduced-cost state-provided health-care cover with the European Health Insurance Card (EHIC) for medical treatment that becomes necessary while in France. Each family member will need a separate card. UK residents can get application forms from post offices, or download them from the Department of Health website (www.dh.gov.uk), which has comprehensive information about the card's coverage.

The EHIC does not cover private health care, so make sure that you are treated by a state health-care provider *(conventionné)*. You will need to pay directly and fill in a treatment form *(feuille de soins)*; keep the form to claim any refunds. In general, you can claim back around 70% of the standard treatment cost.

Citizens of other countries need to check if there is a reciprocal arrangement for free medical care between their country and France.

» Worldwide travel insurance is available at www.lonely planet.com/travel_services. You can buy, extend and claim online anytime – even if you are already on the road.

Internet Access

» Wireless (wi-fi) access points can be found at major airports, in many hotels and at some cafes.

» Some tourist offices and numerous cafes and bars tout wi-fi hot spots that let laptop owners hook up for free.

» To search for free wi-fi hot spots in France, visit www. hotspot-locations.co.uk or www.free-hotspot.com.

» Internet cafes are becoming less rife, but at least one can still be found in most large towns and cities. Prices range from €2 to €6 per hour.

» If you'll be accessing dial-up ISPs with your laptop, you will need a telephone-plug adaptor, available at large supermarkets.

Language Courses

» The website www.study abroadlinks.com can help you find specific courses and summer programs, while www.edu france.fr/en has information about university study.

» All manner of French-language courses are available in Paris and provincial towns and cities; many also arrange accommodation.

» Prices and courses vary greatly and the content can

CREATIVE LEARNING

Rolling your tongue around French 'Rrrrs' is by no means the only creative-holiday option. In keeping with its generously chic and stylish spirit, *la belle France* cooks up all manner of courses designed to suit every taste and whimsical fancy

» **Cooking** There are courses cooking all over France, many attached to the kitchen of Michelin-starred restaurants or grass-roots farms and *chambre d'hôte*. Paris (p101), Provence and the French Riviera (p844), Burgundy (p402) and Bordeaux (p625) on the Atlantic Coast take the lead with bags of courses to suit every taste and ability – see those chapters for listings. **La Cuisine de Bertrand** (www.lacuisinedebertrand.com) near Paris in Versailles, **Les Apprentis Gourmets** (Map p842; ☎04 93 38 78 76; www.lesapprentisgourmets. fr; 6 rue Teisseire) in Cannes, **Flocons de Sel** (☎04 50 21 49 99; www.floconsdesel.com; 1775 rte de Leutaz, Megève; cooking classes €60-120; ⏰cooking classes 4-6pm Thu-Sat) in Megève, and Anne-Sophie Pic's **Scook** (☎04 75 44 14 14; www.scook.fr; 243 av Victor Hugo; ⏰Tue-Sat) in the Rhône Valley are real favourites.

» **Wine tasting** Paris is the obvious choice with a handful of appealing *dégustation* options (p51), but Bordeaux and Burgundy are where die-hard buffs go; see the French Wine essay (p928) for a list of wine schools.

» **Perfumery** A couple of perfume studios in Paris' trendy Marais district offer perfume-making workshops, but nothing beats a journey south to **Molinard** (www.molinard.com; 60 bd Victor Hugo; ⏰9.30am-12.30pm & 2-6pm) in the French perfume-making capital of Grasse, inland from Cannes on the French Riviera.

often be tailored to your specific needs (for a fee).

» The government site www. diplomatie.gouv.fr (under 'Francophony') and www. europa-pages.com/france lists language schools.

Some schools to consider:
Alliance Française (Map p96; www.alliancefr.org; 101 blvd Raspail, 6e, Paris; Ⓜ St-Placide) French courses

(minimum one week) for all levels; registration takes place in situ five days before (minimum two weeks before online). *Intensif* courses meet for four hours a day five days a week, and cost €180 to €238 per week; *extensif* courses (€85 to €106 per week) involve nine hours of tuition per week.

Centre de Linguistique Appliquée de Besançon (☎03 81 66 52 00; http://cla. univ-fcomte.fr; 6 rue Gabriel Plançon, Besançon) One of France's largest language schools, in a beautiful city, offering a wide variety of language and culture classes.

Centre Méditerranéen d'Études Françaises (www. monte-carlo.mc/centremed; chemin des Oliviers, Cap d'Ail)

WHAT THE ICON MEANS

Only accommodation providers that have an actual computer that guests can use to access the internet are flagged with a computer icon (@). The wi-fi icon (🛜) indicates anywhere with wi-fi access. Where this icon appears, assume the wi-fi is free unless otherwise specified.

Mythical French Riviera school around since 1952, with a stunning open-air amphitheatre, designed by Jean Cocteau and overlooking the sparkling blue Med.

Eurocentres (www.euro centres.com) This affiliation of small, well-organised schools has three addresses in France, in Amboise in the charming Loire Valley, La Rochelle and Paris.

Aix-Marseille Université (www.univ-provence.fr; 29 av Robert Schumann, Aix-en-Provence) A hot choice, also known as Université de Provence, in lovely Aix: semester-long language courses as well as shorter summer classes.

Legal Matters

Police

» French police have wide powers of search and seizure and can ask you to prove your identity at any time – whether or not there is 'probable cause'.

» Foreigners must be able to prove their legal status in France (eg passport, visa, residency permit) without delay.

» If the police stop you for any reason, be polite and remain calm. Verbally (and of course physically) abusing a police officer can lead to a hefty fine, and even imprisonment.

» You may refuse to sign a police statement, and you have the right to ask for a copy.

» People who are arrested are considered innocent until proven guilty, but can be held in custody until trial.

» Because of the threat of terrorism, French police are very strict about security. Do not leave baggage unattended, especially at airports or in train stations: suspicious objects may be summarily blown up.

Maps

Countrywide, road and city maps are available at Maisons de la Presse (large newsagencies), bookshops, airports, tourist offices and newspaper kiosks. Local organisations also produce *topoguides* – map-equipped booklets about major trails (eg GRs) that supply details on trail conditions, flora, fauna and mountain shelters.

Blay-Foldex (www.blayfoldex. com) Produces over 180 orange-jacketed street maps of French cities and towns.

FFRP (www.ffrandonnee. fr) Publishes around 120 *topoguides* in French.

Institut Géographique National (IGN; www.ign.fr) One of France's major map publishers, with regional fold-out maps as well as an all-France volume, *France – Routes, Autoroutes*. Has a great variety of *topoguides* and 1:50,000-scale maps that are ideal for hiking or walking. Its specialised *cyclocartes* (cycle maps) show dozens of suggested bicycle tours around France. The IGN also has themed maps showing wine regions, museums and so on.

Michelin (http://boutique cartesetguides.michelin.fr) Has excellent city maps of Paris and Lyon, and yellow-orange 1:200,000-scale regional maps made for cross-country driving.

Money

ATMs

Automated Teller Machines (ATMs) – known as *distributeurs automatiques de billets* (DAB) or *points d'argent* in French – are the cheapest and most convenient way to get money. ATMs connected to international networks are situated in all cities and towns and usually offer an excellent exchange rate.

Cash

You always get a better exchange rate in-country but it is a good idea to arrive in France with enough euros to take a taxi to a hotel if you have to.

Credit & Debit Cards

» Credit and debit cards, accepted almost everywhere in France, are convenient, relatively secure and usually offer a better exchange rate than travellers cheques or cash exchanges.

» Credit cards issued in France have embedded chips – you have to type in a PIN to make a purchase.

DRUGS & ALCOHOL

» French law does not distinguish between 'hard' and 'soft' drugs.

» The penalty for any personal use of *stupéfiants* (including cannabis, amphetamines, ecstasy and heroin) can be a one-year jail sentence and a €3750 fine but, depending on the circumstances, it might be anything from a stern word to a compulsory rehab program.

» Importing, possessing, selling or buying drugs can get you up to 10 years' prison and a fine of up to €500,000.

» Police have been known to search chartered coaches, cars and train passengers for drugs just because they're coming from Amsterdam.

» *Ivresse* (drunkenness) in public is punishable by a monetary fine.

» Visa, MasterCard and Amex can be used in shops and supermarkets and for train travel, car hire and motorway tolls, though some places (eg 24-hour petrol stations, some autoroute toll machines) only take French-style credit cards with chips and PINs.

» Don't assume that you can pay for a meal or a budget hotel with a credit card – enquire first.

» Cash advances are a supremely convenient way to stay stocked up with euros, but getting cash with a credit card involves both fees (sometimes US$10 or more) and interest – ask your credit card issuer for details. Debit-card fees are usually much less.

LOST CARDS
For lost cards, these numbers operate 24 hours:
Amex (☎01 47 77 72 00)
Diners Club (☎08 10 31 41 59)
MasterCard (☎08 00 90 13 87)
Visa (Carte Bleue; ☎08 00 90 11 79)

Moneychangers
» Commercial banks charge up to €5 per foreign-currency transaction – if they even bother to offer exchange services any more.

» In Paris and major cities, *bureaux de change* (exchange bureaux) are faster and easier, open longer hours and often give better rates than banks.

» Some post-office branches exchange travellers cheques and banknotes in a variety of currencies but charge a commission for cash; most won't take US$100 bills.

Tipping
By law, restaurant and bar prices are *service compris* (include a 15% service charge), so there is no need to leave a *pourboire* (tip). If you were extremely satisfied with the service, however, you can – as many locals do – show your appreciation by

leaving a small 'extra' tip for your waiter or waitress.

WHERE/ WHO	CUSTOMARY TIP
bar	round to nearest euro
hotel cleaning staff	€1-1.50 per day
hotel porter	€1-1.50 per bag
restaurant	5-10%
taxi	10-15%
toilet attendant	€0.20-0.50
tour guide	€1-2 per person

Travellers Cheques
Travellers cheques, a relic of the 19th and 20th centuries, cannot be used to pay French merchants directly – change them into euro banknotes at banks, exchange bureaux or post offices.

Public Holidays
The following *jours fériés* (public holidays) are observed in France:

» **New Year's Day** (Jour de l'An) 1 January – parties in larger cities; fireworks are subdued by international standards

» **Easter Sunday & Monday** (Pâques & Lundi de Pâques) Late March/April

» **May Day** (Fête du Travail) 1 May – traditional parades

» **Victoire 1945** 8 May – commemorates the Allied victory in Europe that ended WWII

» **Ascension Thursday** (Ascension) May – celebrated on the 40th day after Easter

» **Pentecost/Whit Sunday & Whit Monday** (Pentecôte & Lundi de Pentecôte) Mid-May to mid-June – celebrated on the seventh Sunday after Easter

» **Bastille Day/National Day** (Fête Nationale) 14 July – *the* national holiday

» **Assumption Day** (Assomption) 15 August

» **All Saints' Day** (Toussaint) 1 November

» **Remembrance Day** (L'onze Novembre) 11 November – marks the WWI armistice

» **Christmas** (Noël) 25 December

The following are *not* public holidays in France: Shrove Tuesday (Mardi Gras; the first day of Lent); Maundy (or Holy) Thursday and Good Friday, just before Easter; and Boxing Day (26 December).

Note: Good Friday and Boxing Day *are* public holidays in Alsace.

Safe Travel
France is generally a safe place in which to live and travel but crime has risen dramatically in the last few years. Although property crime is a major problem, it is extremely unlikely that you will be physically assaulted while walking down the street. Always check your government's travel advisory warnings.

The France hunting season runs from September to February. If you see signs reading *'chasseurs'* or *'chasse gardée'* strung up or tacked to trees, think twice about wandering into the area. As well as millions of wild animals, some 25 French hunters die each year after being shot by other hunters. Hunting is traditional and commonplace in all rural areas in France, especially the Vosges, the Sologne, the southwest and the Baie de Somme.

Natural Dangers
» There are powerful tides and strong undertows at many places along the Atlantic Coast, from the Spanish border north to Brittany and Normandy.

» Only swim in *zones de baignade surveillée* (beaches monitored by life guards).

» Be aware of tide times and the high-tide mark if walking or sleeping on a beach.

» Thunderstorms in the mountains and the hot southern plains can be extremely sudden and violent.

» Check the weather report before setting out on a long walk and be prepared for sudden storms and temperature drops if you are heading into the high country of the Alps or Pyrenees.

» Avalanches pose a significant danger in the French Alps.

Theft

Pickpocketing and bag snatching (eg in dense crowds and public places) are prevalent in big cities, particularly Paris, Marseille and Nice. There's no need whatsoever to travel in fear. A few simple precautions will minimise your chances of being ripped off.

» On trains, keep bags as close to you as possible: luggage racks at the ends of carriages are easy prey for thieves; in sleeping compartments, lock the door carefully at night.

» Be especially vigilant for bag snatchers at train stations, airports, fast-food outlets, outdoor cafes, beaches and on public transport.

» Break-ins to parked cars are a widespread problem. Never, ever, leave anything valuable – or not valuable – inside your car, even in the boot (trunk).

» Aggressive theft from cars stopped at red lights is occasionally a problem, especially in Marseille and Nice. As a precaution, lock your car doors and roll up the windows.

Telephone

Mobile Phones

» French mobile phone numbers begin with 06 or 07.

» France uses GSM 900/1800, which is compatible with the rest of Europe and Australia but not with the North American GSM 1900

or the totally different system in Japan (though some North Americans have tri-band phones that work here).

» Check with your service provider about roaming charges – dialling a mobile phone from a fixed-line phone or another mobile can be incredibly expensive.

» It may be cheaper to buy your own French SIM card – and locals you meet are much more likely to ring you if your number is French.

» If you already have a compatible phone, you can slip in a SIM card (€20 to €30) and rev it up with prepaid credit, though this is likely to run out fast as domestic prepaid calls cost about €0.50 per minute.

» Recharge cards are sold at most *tabacs* and newsagents.

» SIM cards are available at the ubiquitous outlets run by France's three mobile phone companies, **Bouygues** (www.bouyguestelecom.fr), **Orange** (www.orange.com) and **SFR** (www.sfr.com).

Phone Codes

» **Calling France from abroad** Dial your country's international access code, then 33 (France's country code), then the 10-digit local number *without* the initial zero.

» **Calling internationally from France** Dial 00 (the international access code), the *indicatif* (country code),

the area code (without the initial zero if there is one) and the local number. Some country codes are posted in public telephones.

» **Directory inquiries** For national *service des renseignements* (directory inquiries) dial ☑11 87 12 or use the service for free online at www.118712.fr.

» **Emergency numbers** Can be dialled from public phones without a phonecard.

» **Hotel calls** Hotels, *gîtes*, hostels and *chambres d'hôte* are free to meter their calls as they like. The surcharge is usually around €0.30 per minute but can be higher.

» **International directory inquiries** For numbers outside France, dial ☑11 87 00.

Phonecards

» For explanations in English and other languages on how to use a public telephone, push the button engraved with a two-flags icon.

» For both international and domestic calling, most public phones operate using either a credit card or two kinds of *télécartes* (phonecards): *cartes à puce* (cards with a magnetic chip) issued by Orange (formerly France Télécom) and sold at post offices for €8 or €15; and *cartes à code* (cards where you dial a free access number and then the card's scratch-off code), sold at

STRIKES

France is the only European country in which public workers enjoy an unlimited right to strike, and they avail themselves of it with carefree abandon. Aggrieved truck drivers often block motorways, and farmers agitating for more government support sometimes dump tonnes of produce on major arteries.

Getting caught in one of the 'social dialogues' that characterise labour relations in France can put a serious crimp in your travel plans. It is best to leave some wriggle room in your schedule, particularly around departure times.

tabacs, newsagents and post offices.

» Phonecards with codes offer *much* better international rates than Orange chip cards or Country Direct services (for which you are billed at home by your long-distance carrier).

» The shop you buy a phonecard from should be able to tell you which type is best for the country you want to call. Using phonecards from a home phone is much cheaper than using them from public phones or mobile phones.

Tariffs

Additional charges may apply when calling from a hotel phone or mobile phone.

NUMBER	PER MINUTE
08 00	free
08 05	free
08 10	same as a local call
08 20	€0.12
08 21	€0.12
08 25	€0.15
08 26	€0.15
08 92	€0.34
11 87 12 (directory inquiries)	€1.46 per call, plus €0.45 per minute
11 87 00 (international directory inquiries)	€2-3

Time

France uses the 24-hour clock and is on Central European Time, which is one hour ahead of GMT/UTC. During daylight saving time, which runs from the last Sunday in March to the last Sunday in October, France is two hours ahead of GMT/UTC.

The following times do not take daylight saving into account:

CITY	NOON IN PARIS
Auckland	11pm
Berlin	noon
Cape Town	noon
London	11am
New York	6am
San Francisco	3am
Sydney	9pm
Tokyo	8pm

Toilets

Public toilets, signposted WC or *toilettes*, are not always plentiful in France, especially outside of the big cities.

Love them (as a sci-fi geek) or loathe them (as a claustrophobe), France's 24-hour self-cleaning toilets are here to stay. Outside of Paris – where they are free – these mechanical WCs cost around €0.50 a go. Don't even think about nipping in after someone else to avoid paying unless you fancy a *douche* (shower) with disinfectant. There is no time for dawdling either: you have precisely 15 minutes before being (ooh-la-la!) exposed to passers-by. Green means *libre* (vacant) and red means *occupé* (occupied).

Some older establishments and motorway stops still have the hole-in-the-floor *toilettes à la turque* (squat toilets). Provided you hover, these are actually very hygienic, but take care not to get soaked by the flush.

Keep some loose change handy for tipping toilet attendants, who keep a hawk-like eye on many of France's public toilets.

The French are more blasé about unisex toilets than elsewhere, so save your blushes when tiptoeing past the urinals to reach the ladies' loo.

Tourist Information

Almost every city, town, village and hamlet has an *office de tourisme* (a tourist office run by some unit of local government) or *syndicat d'initiative* (a tourist office run by an organisation of local merchants). Both are excellent resources and can supply you with local maps as well as details on accommodation, restaurants and activities. If you have a special interest such as walking, cycling, architecture or wine sampling, ask about it.

Tourist office details appear under Information at the end of each city, town or area listing.

» Many tourist offices make local hotel and B&B reservations, sometimes for a nominal fee. Some have limited currency-exchange services.

» *Comités régionaux de tourisme* (CRTs; regional tourist boards), their *départemental* analogues (CDTs) and their websites are a superb source of information and hyperlinks.

» French government tourist offices (usually called Maisons de la France) provide every imaginable sort of tourist information on France. Useful websites:

French Government Tourist Office (www.franceguide.com) The low-down on sights, activities, transport and special-interest holidays in all of France's regions. Brochures can be downloaded online. There are links to country-specific websites.

Réseau National des Destinations Départementales (www.fncdt.net) Listing of CRT (regional tourist board) websites.

Travellers with Disabilities

While France presents evident challenges for *handicapés* (people with disabilities) – namely cobblestone, cafe-lined streets that are a nightmare to navigate in a wheelchair, a lack of kerb ramps, older public facilities and many budget hotels without lifts – don't let that stop you from visiting. With a little careful planning, you can enjoy a hassle-free accessible stay.

The Paris metro, most of it built decades ago, is hopeless, but you will be pleased to know that taxi drivers are obliged by law to assist and accept passengers with disabilities (and their guide dogs, where relevant). Choose central accommodation to avoid spending a small fortune on taxi fares.

Whether you are looking for wheelchair-friendly accommodation, sights, attractions or restaurants, these associations and agencies should be able to point you in the right direction:

Infomobi.com (☎08 10 64 64 64; www.infomobi.com) Has comprehensive information on accessible travel in Paris.

Access Travel (☎in UK 01942-888 844; www.access-travel.co.uk) Specialised UK-based agency for accessible travel.

Association des Paralysés de France (APF; www.apf.asso.fr) National organisation for people with disabilities, with offices in every region in France.

Centre du Service Accès Plus (☎08 90 64 06 50; www.accessibilite.sncf.fr) Can advise on station accessibility and arrange a *fauteuil roulant* (wheelchair) or help getting on or off a train.

Mobile en Ville (☎09 52 29 60 51; www.mobile-en-ville.asso.fr; 8 rue des Mariniers, 14e, Paris) Association set up in 1998 by students and researchers with the aim of making independent travel within the city easier for people in wheelchairs.

Tourisme et Handicaps (www.tourisme-handicaps.org) Issues the 'Tourisme et Handicap' label to tourist sites, restaurants and hotels that comply with strict accessibility and usability standards. Different symbols indicate the sort of access afforded to people with physical, mental, hearing and/or visual disabilities.

Visas

For up-to-date details on visa requirements, see the website of the **Ministère des Affaires Étrangères** (Ministry of Foreign Affairs; 37 quai d'Orsay, 7e) and click 'Going to France'. Tourist visas *cannot* be extended except in emergencies (such as medical problems). When your visa expires you'll need to leave and reapply from outside France.

Visa Requirements

» EU nationals and citizens of Iceland, Norway and Switzerland need only a passport or a national identity card in order to enter France and stay in the country, even for stays of over 90 days. However, citizens of new EU member states may be subject to various limitations on living and working in France.

» Citizens of Australia, the USA, Canada, Hong Kong, Israel, Japan, Malaysia, New Zealand, Singapore, South Korea and many Latin American countries do not need visas to visit France as tourists for up to 90 days. For long stays of over 90 days, contact your nearest French embassy or consulate and begin your application well in advance as it can take months.

» Other people wishing to come to France as tourists have to apply for a **Schengen Visa,** named after the agreements that abolished passport controls between 15 European countries. It allows unlimited travel throughout the entire zone for a 90-day period. Apply to the consulate of the country you are entering first, or your main destination. Among other things, you need travel and repatriation insurance and to be able to show that you have sufficient funds to support yourself.

» Tourist visas cannot be changed into student visas after arrival. However, short-term visas are available for students sitting university-entrance exams in France.

Carte de Séjour

» EU passport holders and citizens of Switzerland, Iceland and Norway do not need a *carte de séjour* (residence permit) to reside or work in France.

ACCESSIBILITY INFORMATION

» SNCF's French-language booklet *Guide des Voyageurs Handicapés et à Mobilité Réduite*, available at train stations, gives details of rail access for people with disabilities.

» Michelin's *Guide Rouge* uses icons to indicate hotels with lifts (elevators) and facilities that make them at least partly accessible to people with disabilities.

» *Handitourisme* (€16), a national guide in French, is published by **Petit Futé** (www.petitfute.fr).

» The website www.jaccede.com (in French) has loads of information and reviews.

» **Gîtes de France** (www.gites-de-france-var.fr) can provide details of accessible *gîtes ruraux* (self-contained holiday villages) and *chambres d'hôte* (B&Bs) – search the website with the term 'disabled access'.

» **France Guide** (www.franceguide.com) has a dedicated 'special needs' area with lots of info for travellers with disabilities.

Régions & Départements

ALSACE
67 Bas-Rhin
68 Haut-Rhin

AQUITAINE
24 Dordogne
33 Gironde
40 Landes
47 Lot-et-Garonne
64 Pyrénées-Atlantiques

AUVERGNE
03 Allier
15 Cantal
43 Haute-Loire
63 Puy-de-Dôme

BASSE-NORMANDIE
14 Calvados
50 Manche
61 Orne

BOURGOGNE
21 Côte-d'Or
58 Nièvre
71 Saône-et-Loire
89 Yonne

BRETAGNE
22 Côte-d'Armor
29 Finistère
35 Ille-et-Vilaine
56 Morbihan

CENTRE
18 Cher
28 Eure-et-Loir
36 Indre
37 Indre-et-Loire
45 Loiret
41 Loir-et-Cher

CHAMPAGNE-ARDENNE
08 Ardennes
10 Aube
51 Marne
52 Haute-Marne

CORSE
2A Corse-du-Sud
2B Haute-Corse

FRANCHE-COMTÉ
25 Doubs
39 Jura
70 Haute-Saône
90 Territoire de Belfort

HAUTE-NORMANDIE
27 Eure
76 Seine-Maritime

ÎLE-DE-FRANCE
91 Essonne
92 Haut-de-Seine
75 Paris
78 Seine-et-Marne
93 Seine-St-Denis
94 Val-de-Marne
95 Val-d'Oise
77 Yvelines

LANGUEDOC-ROUSSILLON
11 Aude
30 Gard
34 Hérault
48 Lozère
66 Pyrénées-Orientales

LIMOUSIN
19 Corrèze
23 Creuse
87 Haute-Vienne

LORRAINE
54 Meurthe-et-Moselle
55 Meuse
57 Moselle
88 Vosges

MIDI-PYRÉNÉES
09 Ariège
12 Aveyron
32 Gers
31 Haute-Garonne
65 Hautes-Pyrénées
46 Lot
81 Tarn
82 Tarn-et-Garonne

NORD-PAS-DE-CALAIS
59 Nord
62 Pas-de-Calais

PAYS DE LA LOIRE
44 Loire-Atlantique
49 Maine-et-Loire
53 Mayenne
72 Sarthe
85 Vendée

PICARDIE
02 Aisne
60 Oise
80 Somme

POITOU-CHARENTES
16 Charente
17 Charente-Maritime
79 Deux-Sèvres
86 Vienne

PROVENCE-ALPES-CÔTE D'AZUR
04 Alpes-de-Haute-Provence
06 Alpes-Maritimes
13 Bouches-du-Rhône
05 Hautes-Alpes
83 Var
84 Vaucluse

RHÔNE-ALPES
01 Ain
07 Ardèche
26 Drôme
74 Haute-Savoie
38 Isère
42 Loire
69 Rhône
73 Savoie

International Boundary
Région Boundary
Département Boundary

» Nationals of other countries with long-stay visas must contact the local *mairie* (city hall) or *préfecture* (prefecture) to apply for a *carte de séjour*. Usually, you are required to do so within eight days of arrival in France. Make sure you have all the necessary documents before you arrive.

» Students of all nationalities studying in France need a *carte de séjour*.

Working Holiday Visa

Citizens of Australia, Canada, Japan and New Zealand aged between 18 and 30 are eligible for a 12-month, multiple-entry Working Holiday Visa (Permis Vacances Travail), allowing combined tourism and employment in France.

» Apply to the embassy or consulate in your home country. Do this early as there are annual quotas.

» You must be applying for a Working Holiday Visa for France for the first time.

» You will need comprehensive travel insurance for the duration of your stay.

» You must meet all health and character requirements.

» You will need a return plane ticket and proof of sufficient funds (usually around €2100) to get you through the start of your stay.

» Once you have arrived in France and have found a job, you must apply for an *autorisation provisoire de travail* (temporary work permit), which will only be valid for the duration of the employment offered. The permit can be renewed under the same conditions up to the limit of the authorised length of stay.

» You can also study or do training programs but the visa cannot be extended, nor can it turned into a student visa.

» After one year you *must* go home.

» Once in France, the **Centre d'Information et Documentation Jeunesse** (CIDJ; Youth Information & Documentation Centres; www.cidj.com) can help with information.

Volunteering

Online resources like **Go Abroad** (www.goabroad.com) and **Transitions Abroad** (www.transitionsabroad.com) throw up a colourful selection of volunteering opportunities in France: helping out on a family farm in the Alps, restoring an historic monument in Provence or participating in a summertime archaeological excavation are but some of the golden opportunities awaiting those keen to volunteer their skills and services.

Interesting volunteer organisations:

Club du Vieux Manoir (http://clubduvieuxmanoir.asso.fr) Restore a medieval fortress, an abbey or a historic château at a summer work camp.

Conservation Corps (www.geovisions.org) Volunteer 15 hours a week to teach a French family English in exchange for room and board.

Rempart (www.rempart.com) Brings together 170 organisations countrywide committed to preserving France's religious, military, civil, industrial and natural heritage.

Volunteers For Peace (www.vfp.org) USA-based nonprofit organisation. Can link you up with a voluntary service project dealing with social work, the environment, education or the arts.

World Wide Opportunities on Organic Farms (WWOOF; www.wwoof.org) Work on a small farm or other organic venture (harvesting chestnuts, renovating an abandoned olive farm near Nice etc).

Transport

GETTING THERE & AWAY

Flights, cars and tours can be booked online at lonely planet.com.

Entering the Country

Entering France from other parts of the EU is usually a breeze – no border checkpoints and no customs – thanks to the Schengen agreement, signed by all of France's neighbours except the UK, the Channel Islands and Andorra. For these three entities, old-fashioned document and customs checks are still the norm, at least when exiting France (when entering France in the case of Andorra).

Air

Smaller provincial airports with international flights, mainly to/from the UK, continental Europe and North Africa, include Paris-Beauvais, Bergerac, Biarritz, Brest, Brive (Vallée de la Dordogne), Caen, Carcassonne, Clermont-Ferrand, Deauville, Dinard, Grenoble, La Rochelle, Le Touquet (Côte d'Opale), Limoges, Montpellier, Nîmes, Pau, Perpignan, Poitiers, Rennes, Rodez, St-Étienne, Toulon and Tours.

International Airports

Paris Charles de Gaulle (CDG; www.aeroportsdeparis.fr)

Paris Orly (ORY; www.aeroportsdeparis.fr)

Aéroport de Bordeaux (www.bordeaux.aeroport.fr)

Aéroport de Lille (www.lille.aeroport.fr)

Aéroport International Strasbourg (www.strasbourg.aeroport.fr)

Aéroport Lyon St-Exupéry (www.lyonaeroports.com)

Aéroport de Marseille Provence (www.marseille.aeroport.fr)

Aéroport Nantes Atlantique (www.nantes.aeroport.fr)

Aéroport Nice Côte d'Azur (http://societe.nice.aeroport.fr)

Aéroport Toulouse-Blagnac (www.toulouse.aeroport.fr)

EuroAirport (Basel-Mulhouse-Freiburg; www.euroairport.com)

Land

Bicycle

Transporting a bicycle to France is a breeze.

On **Eurotunnel Le Shuttle** (www.eurotunnel.com) trains through the Channel Tunnel, the fee for a bicycle, including its rider, is UK£16 one way.

A bike that's been dismantled to the size of a suitcase can be carried on board a **Eurostar** (☎in France 08 92 35 35 39, in UK 08432 186 186; www.eurostar.com) train from London or Brussels just like any other luggage. Otherwise, there's a UK£20 charge and you'll need advance reservations. For links relevant to taking your bike on other international trains to France, see **RailPassenger Info** (www.railpassenger.info).

On ferries, foot passengers – where allowed – can usually (but not always) bring along a bicycle for no charge.

European Bike Express (☎in UK 01430-422 111; www.bike-express.co.uk) transports cyclists and their bikes from the UK to places around France.

Bus

Eurolines (☎in France 08 92 89 90 91; www.eurolines.eu), a grouping of 32 long-haul coach operators (including the UK's National Express), links France with cities all across Europe and in Morocco and Russia. Discounts are available to people under 26 and over 60. Make advance reservations, especially in July and August.

The standard Paris–London fare is between €45 and €59, but the trip – including a Channel crossing by ferry or the Chunnel – can cost €13 if booked 45 days ahead.

Car & Motorcycle

A right-hand-drive vehicle brought to France from the UK or Ireland must have deflectors affixed to the headlights to avoid dazzling oncoming traffic. In the UK, information on driving in France is available from the **RAC** (www.rac.co.uk/driving-abroad/france) and the **AA** (www.theaa.com).

A foreign motor vehicle entering France must display a

sticker or licence plate identifying its country of registration.

EUROTUNNEL

The Channel Tunnel (Chunnel), inaugurated in 1994, is the first dry-land link between England and France since the last ice age.

High-speed **Eurotunnel Le Shuttle** (www.eurotunnel.com) trains whisk bicycles (see Bicycle), motorcycles, cars and coaches in 35 minutes from Folkestone through the Channel Tunnel to Coquelles, 5km southwest of Calais. Shuttles run 24 hours a day, with up to three departures an hour during peak periods. LPG and CNG tanks are not permitted, meaning gas-powered cars and many campers and caravans have to travel by ferry.

Eurotunnel sets its fares the way budget airlines do: the further in advance you book and the lower the demand for a particular crossing, the less you pay; same-day fares can cost a small fortune. Fares for a car, including up to nine passengers, start at UK£30.

Train

Rail services – including a dwindling number of overnight services to/from Spain, Italy and Germany – link France with virtually every country in Europe. For details on train travel within France, see p976.

You can book tickets and get train information from **Rail Europe** (www.raileurope.com). In France ticketing is handled by **SNCF** (📞 from abroad 33 8 92 35 35 35, in France 36 35; www.sncf.com); internet bookings are possible but they won't post tickets outside France.

» For details on Europe's 200,000km rail network, surf **RailPassenger Info** (www.railpassenger.info).

» High-speed train travel between France and the UK, Belgium, the Netherlands, Germany and Austria is covered by **Railteam** (www.railteam.co.uk) and **TGV-Europe** (www.tgv-europe.com).

» A very useful train-travel resource is the information-packed website the **Man in Seat 61** (www.seat61.com). Certain rail services between France and its continental neighbours are marketed under a number of unique brand names:

Elipsos (www.elipsos.com) Luxurious 'train-hotel' services to Spain.

TGV Lyria (www.tgv-lyria.fr) To Switzerland.

Thalys (www.thalys.com) Thalys trains pull into Paris' Gare du Nord from Brussels, Amsterdam and Cologne.

Thello (www.thello.com) Overnight train service from Paris to Milan, Brescia, Verona and Venice in Italy.

EURAIL PASS

Rail passes are worthwhile if you plan to clock up the kilometres.

Available only to people who don't live in Europe, the **Eurail Pass** (www.eurail.com) is valid in up to 21 countries, including France. People 25 and under get the best deals. Passes must be validated at a train-station ticket window before you begin your first journey.

EUROSTAR

The **Eurostar** (📞 in France 08 92 35 35 39, in UK 08432 186 186; www.eurostar.com) whisks you from London to Paris in 2¼ hours.

Except late at night, trains link London (St Pancras International) with Paris (Gare du Nord; hourly), Calais (Calais-Fréthun; one hour, three daily), Lille (Gare Lille-Europe; 1½ hours, eight daily) and Disneyland Resort Paris (2½ hours, one direct daily), with less-frequent services departing from Ebbsfleet and Ashford, both in Kent. Weekend ski trains connect England with the French Alps mid-December to mid-April.

Eurostar offers a bewildering array of fares. A semi-flexible 2nd-class one-way/return ticket from Paris to London costs €245/435; super-discount fares start at €50.

For the best deals buy a return ticket, stay over a Saturday night, book up to 120 days in advance and don't mind nonexchangeability and nonrefundability. Discount fares are available for under 26s or over 60s.

Sea

Some ferry companies have started setting fares the way budget airlines do: the longer in advance you book and the lower the demand for a particular sailing, the less you pay. Seasonal demand is a crucial factor (Christmas, Easter, UK and French school holidays, July and August are especially busy), as is the time of day (an early evening ferry can cost much more than one at 4am). People under 25 and over 60 may qualify for discounts.

SAMPLE TRAIN FARES

ROUTE	FULL FARE (€)	DURATION (HR)
Amsterdam–Paris	89	3¼
Madrid–Blois	153	12½
Berlin–Paris	189	8
Brussels–Paris	69	1½
Dijon–Milan	80	7
Paris–Venice	100	11¾
Geneva–Marseille	50	3½
Vienna–Strasbourg	153	9¾

To get the best fares, check **Ferry Savers** (☎in UK 0844-371 8021; www.ferrysavers.com).

Foot passengers are not allowed on Dover–Boulogne, Dover–Dunkirk or Dover–Calais car ferries except for daytime (and, from Calais to Dover, evening) crossings run by P&O Ferries. On ferries that do allow foot passengers, taking a bicycle is usually free.

Several ferry companies ply the waters between Corsica and Italy.

GETTING AROUND

Driving is the simplest way to get around France but a car is a liability in traffic-plagued, parking-starved city centres, and petrol bills and *autoroute* (dual carriageway/divided highway) tolls add up.

France is famous for its excellent public-transport network, which serves everywhere bar some rural areas. The state-owned Société Nationale des Chemins de Fer Français (SNCF) takes care of almost all land transport be-

tween *départements*. Transport within *départements* is handled by a combination of short-haul trains, SNCF buses and local bus companies.

Air

France's high-speed train network renders rail travel between some cities (eg from Paris to Lyon and Marseille) faster and easier than flying.

Airlines in France

Air France (www.airfrance.com) and subsidiaries **Brit Air** (www.britair.fr) and **Régional** (☎36 54; www.regional.com) control most of France's domestic airline industry.

Significant discounts are available to:

» people aged 12 to 24 (26 and under for students)
» people over 60
» couples who are married or can prove they live together
» parents or grandparents travelling with at least one child or grandchild aged 12 to 25 (27 in the case of students). Good deals can also be had if:
» you buy your ticket well

in advance (at least 42 days ahead for the very best deals)
» stay over a Saturday night
» don't mind tickets that can't be changed or reimbursed.

The Air France website posts special last-minute offers.

Budget carriers offering flights within France include **EasyJet** (www.easyjet.com), **Airlinair** (www.airlinair.com), **Twin Jet** (www.twinjet.net) and **Air Corsica** (www.aircorsica.com).

Bicycle

France is great for cycling. Much of the countryside is drop-dead gorgeous and the country has a growing number of urban and rural *pistes cyclables* (bike paths and lanes; see **Voies Vertes** (www.voievertes.com) and an extensive network of secondary and tertiary roads with relatively light traffic.

French law requires that bicycles must have two functioning brakes, a bell, a red reflector on the back and yellow reflectors on the ped-

INTERNATIONAL FERRY COMPANIES

COMPANY	CONNECTION	WEBSITE
Brittany Ferries	England–Normandy, England–Brittany, Ireland–Brittany	www.brittany-ferries.co.uk; www.brittanyferries.ie
Celtic Link Ferries	Ireland–Normandy	www.celticlinkferries.com
Condor Ferries	England–Normandy, England–Brittany, Channel Islands–Brittany	www.condorferries.com
CTN	Tunisia–France	www.ctn.com.tn
Irish Ferries	Ireland–Normandy, Ireland–Brittany	www.irishferries.ie; www.shamrock-irlande.com
LD Lines	England–Channel Ports, England–Normandy	www.ldlines.co.uk
Manche Îles Express	Channel Islands–Normandy	www.manche-iles-express.com
Norfolk Line (DFDS Seaways)	England–Channel Ports	www.norfolkline.com
P&O Ferries	England–Channel Ports	www.poferries.com
SNCM	Algeria–France, Sardinia–France, Tunisia–France	www.sncm.fr
Transmanche Ferries	England–Normandy	www.transmancheferries.com

als. After sunset and when visibility is poor, cyclists must turn on a white headlamp and a red tail lamp. When being overtaken by a vehicle, cyclists must ride in single file. Towing children in a bike trailer is permitted.

Never leave your bicycle locked up outside overnight if you want to see it – or at least most of its parts – again. Some hotels offer enclosed bicycle parking.

Transportation

The SNCF does its best to make travelling with a bicycle easy; see **velo.sncf.com** (www.velo.sncf.com) for full details.

Bicycles (not disassembled) can be taken along on virtually all intraregional TER trains and most long-distance intercity trains, subject to space availability. There's no charge on TER and Corail Intercité trains but TGV, Téoz and Lunéa trains require a €10 reservation fee that must be made when you purchase your passenger ticket. Bike reservations can be made by phone (☑36 35) or at an SNCF ticket office but not via the internet.

Bicycles that have been partly disassembled and put in a box *(housse)*, with maximum dimensions of 120cm by 90cm, can be taken along for no charge in the baggage compartments of TGV, Téoz, Lunéa and Corail Intercité trains.

In the Paris area, bicycles are allowed aboard Transilien and RER trains except Monday to Friday during the following times:

» 6.30am to 9am for trains heading into Paris
» 4.30pm to 7pm for trains travelling out of Paris
» 6am to 9am and 4.30pm to 7pm on RER lines A and B

With precious few exceptions, bicycles are not allowed on metros, trams and local, intra-*département* and SNCF buses (the latter replace trains on some runs).

Bike Rental

Most French cities and towns have at least one bike shop that rents out *vélos tout terrains* (mountain bikes; around €15 a day), known as VTTs, as well as more road-oriented *vélos tout chemin* (VTCs), or cheaper city bikes. You usually have to leave ID and/or a deposit (often a credit-card slip) that you forfeit if the bike is damaged or stolen.

A growing number of cities – most famously Paris and Lyon, but also Aix-en-Provence, Amiens, Besançon, Caen, Dijon, La Rochelle, Lille, Marseille, Montpellier, Mulhouse, Nancy, Nantes, Nice, Orléans, Rennes, Rouen, Toulouse and Strasbourg – have automatic bike-rental systems, intended to encourage cycling as a form of urban transport, with computerised pick-up and drop-off sites all over town. In general, you have to sign up either short term or long term, providing credit-card details, and can then use the bikes for no charge for the first half-hour; after that, hourly charges rise quickly.

Boat

There are boat services along France's coasts and to its offshore islands, and ferries aplenty to/from Corsica.

Canal Boating

Transportation and tranquillity are usually mutually exclusive – but not if you rent a houseboat and cruise along France's canals and navigable rivers, stopping at whim to pick up supplies, dine at a village restaurant or check out a local château by bicycle. Changes in altitude are taken care of by a system of *écluses* (locks).

Boats generally accommodate from two to 12 passengers and are fully outfitted with bedding and cooking facilities. Anyone over 18 can pilot a riverboat but first-time skippers are given a short instruction session so they qualify for a *carte de plaisance* (a temporary cruising permit). The speed limit is 6km/h on canals and 8km/h on rivers.

Prices start at around €580 a week for a small boat and easily top €3000 a week for a large, luxurious craft. Except in July and August, you can often rent over a weekend.

Advance reservations are essential for holiday periods, over long weekends and in July and August, especially for larger boats.

Rental agencies:

Canal Boat Holidays (www.canalboatholidays.com)

France Afloat (www.franceafloat.com) Anglophone, canal-boat specialist in France.

H2olidays (www.barginginfrance.com) Hotel barges, river cruises and self-drive barges.

Worldwide River Cruise (www.worldwide-river-cruise.com) River-cruiser rental, price-comparison website.

Bus

Buses are widely used for short-distance travel within *départements*, especially in rural areas with relatively few train lines (eg Brittany and Normandy). Unfortunately, services in some regions are infrequent and slow, in part because they were designed to get children to their schools in the towns rather than transport visitors around the countryside.

Over the years, certain uneconomical train lines have been replaced by SNCF buses, which, unlike regional buses, are free if you have a rail pass.

Eurolines may soon be permitted to transport passengers between cities within France.

Car & Motorcycle

Having your own wheels gives you exceptional freedom and makes it easy to visit more remote parts of France. Unfortunately driving can be expensive. For example, by autoroute, the 925km drive from Paris to Nice (nine

Trains & Ferries

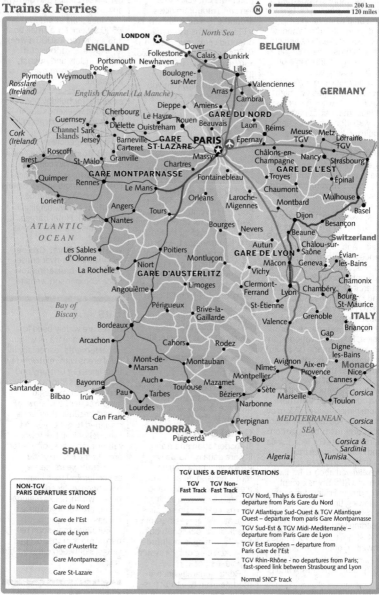

NON-TGV PARIS DEPARTURE STATIONS

- Gare du Nord
- Gare de l'Est
- Gare de Lyon
- Gare d'Austerlitz
- Gare Montparnasse
- Gare St-Lazare

TGV LINES & DEPARTURE STATIONS

TGV Fast Track	TGV Non-Fast Track	
		TGV Nord, Thalys & Eurostar – departure from Paris Gare du Nord
		TGV Atlantique Sud-Ouest & TGV Atlantique Ouest – departure from paris Gare Montparnasse
		TGV Sud-Est & TGV Midi-Mediterranée – departure from Paris Gare de Lyon
		TGV Est Européen – departure from Paris Gare de l'Est
		TGV Rhin-Rhône - no departures from Paris; fast-speed link between Strasbourg and Lyon
		Normal SNCF track

hours of driving) in a small car costs about €75 for petrol and €85 in tolls – by comparison, a one-way, 2nd-class TGV ticket for the 5½-hour Paris to Nice run costs €70 to €150 per person. Also, in the cities, traffic and finding a place to park are frequently a major headache. During holiday periods and over long weekends, roads throughout France also get backed up with *bouchons* (traffic jams).

Motorcyclists will find France convenient for touring, with winding roads of good quality and lots of stunning scenery. Just make sure your wet-weather gear is up to scratch.

France (along with Belgium) has the densest highway network in Europe. There are four types of intercity roads:

» **Autoroutes** (highway names beginning with A) Multilane divided highways, usually (except near Calais and Lille) with *péages* (tolls). Generously outfitted with rest stops.

» **Routes Nationales** (N, RN) National highways. Some sections have divider strips.

» **Routes Départementales** (D) Local highways and roads.

» **Routes Communales** (C, V) Minor rural roads.

For information on autoroute tolls, rest areas, traffic and weather, go to the **Sociétés d'Autoroutes** (www.auto routes.fr) website.

Bison Futé (www.bison -fute.equipement.gouv.fr) is also a good source of information on traffic conditions. Plot itineraries between your departure and arrival points, and calculate toll costs with **Via Michelin** (www.via michelin.com) or **Mappy** (www.mappy.fr).

Note that theft from cars is a major problem in France, especially in the south.

Car Hire

To hire a car in France, you'll generally need to be over 21 years old, have had a driving licence for at least a year, and have an international credit card. Drivers under 25 usually have to pay a surcharge (*frais jeune conducteur*) of €25 to €35 per day.

Car-hire companies provide mandatory third-party liability insurance but things such

as collision-damage waivers (CDW, or *assurance tous risques*) vary greatly from company to company. When comparing rates and conditions (ie the fine print), the most important thing to check is the *franchise* (deductible/ excess), which for a small car is usually around €600 for damage and €800 for theft. With many companies, you can reduce the excess by half, and perhaps to zero, by paying a daily insurance supplement of €10 to €16. Your credit card may cover CDW if you use it to pay for the rental but the car-hire company won't know anything about this – verify conditions and details with your credit-card issuer to be sure.

Arranging your car hire or fly/drive package before you leave home is usually considerably cheaper than a walk-in rental, but beware of website offers that don't include a CDW or you may be liable for up to 100% of the car's value.

International companies:

» **Avis** (☏08 21 23 07 60; www.avis.com)

» **Budget** (☏08 25 00 35 64; www.budget.com)

» **Easycar** (☏in France 08 26 10 73 23, in UK 08710 500 444; www.easycar.com)

» **Europcar** (☏08 25 35 83 58; www.europcar.com)

» **Hertz** (www.hertz.com)

» **National-Citer** (www.nationalcar.com)

» **Sixt** (☏08 20 00 74 98; www.sixt.fr)

French car-hire companies:

» **ADA** (www.ada.fr)

» **DLM** (www.dlm.fr)

» **France Cars** (www.france cars.fr)

» **Locauto** (www.locauto.fr)

» **Renault Rent** (☏08 25 10 11 12; www.renault-rent.com)

» **Rent a Car Système** (☏08 91 70 02 00; www. rentacar.fr)

Deals can be found on the internet and through companies such as the following:

» **Auto Europe** (☏in USA 1-888-223-5555; www.auto europe.com)

» **DriveAway Holidays** (☏in Australia 1300 723 972; www. driveaway.com.au)

» **Holiday Autos** (☏0871 472 5229; www.holidayautos. co.uk)

Note that rental cars with automatic transmission are very much the exception in France and will usually need to be ordered well in advance.

For insurance reasons, it is usually forbidden to take rental cars on ferries, eg to Corsica.

All rental cars registered in France have a distinctive number on the licence plate, making them easily identifiable – including to thieves, so *never* leave anything of value in a parked car, even in the boot.

Purchase-Repurchase Plans

If you don't live in the EU and will need a car in France (or Europe) for one to six months (up to one year if you'll be studying), by far the cheapest option is to

---

CLIMATE CHANGE & TRAVEL

Every form of transport that relies on carbon-based fuel generates CO_2, the main cause of human-induced climate change. Modern travel is dependent on aeroplanes, which might use less fuel per kilometre per person than most cars but travel much greater distances. The altitude at which aircraft emit gases (including CO_2) and particles also contributes to their climate change impact. Many websites offer 'carbon calculators' that allow people to estimate the carbon emissions generated by their journey and, for those who wish to do so, to offset the impact of the greenhouse gases emitted with contributions to portfolios of climate-friendly initiatives throughout the world. Lonely Planet offsets the carbon footprint of all staff and author travel.

ROAD DISTANCES (KM)

	Bayonne	Bordeaux	Brest	Caen	Cahors	Calais	Chambéry	Cherbourg	Clermont-Ferrand	Dijon	Grenoble	Lille	Lyon	Marseille	Nantes	Nice	Paris	Perpignan	Strasbourg	Toulouse
Bordeaux	184																			
Brest	811	623																		
Caen	764	568	376																	
Cahors	307	218	788	661																
Calais	164	876	710	339	875															
Chambéry	860	651	120	800	523	834														
Cherbourg	835	647	399	124	743	461	923													
Clermont-Ferrand	564	358	805	566	269	717	295	689												
Dijon	807	619	867	548	378	572	273	671	279											
Grenoble	827	657	1126	806	501	863	56	929	300	302										
Lille	997	809	725	353	808	112	767	476	650	505	798									
Lyon	831	528	1018	698	439	755	103	820	171	194	110	687								
Marseille	700	651	1271	1010	521	1067	344	1132	477	506	273	999	314							
Nantes	513	326	298	292	491	593	780	317	462	656	787	609	618	975						
Nice	858	810	1429	1168	679	1225	410	1291	636	664	337	1157	473	190	1131					
Paris	771	583	596	232	582	289	565	355	424	313	571	222	462	775	384	932				
Perpignan	499	451	1070	998	320	1149	478	1094	441	640	445	1081	448	319	773	476	857			
Strasbourg	1254	1066	1079	730	847	621	496	853	584	335	551	522	488	803	867	804	490	935		
Toulouse	300	247	866	865	116	991	565	890	890	727	533	923	536	407	568	564	699	205	1022	
Tours	536	348	490	246	413	531	611	369	369	418	618	463	449	795	197	952	238	795	721	593

'purchase' a new one and then 'sell' it back at the end of your trip. In reality, you pay only for the number of days you have the vehicle but the 'temporary transit' (TT) paperwork means that the car is registered under your name – and that the whole deal is exempt from all sorts of taxes. Lonely Planet authors love these plans!

Companies offering purchase-repurchase (achat-rachat) plans:

» **Eurocar TT** (www.euro cartt.com)

» **Peugeot OpenEurope** (www.peugeot-openeurope.com)

» **Renault Eurodrive** (www.eurodrive.renault.com)

Eligibility is restricted to people who are not residents of the EU (citizens of EU countries are eligible if they live outside the EU), and the minimum age is 18 (in some cases 21). Pricing and special offers depend on your home country. All the plans include unlimited kilometres, 24-hour towing and breakdown service, and comprehensive insurance with absolutely no deductible/excess, so returning the car is hassle-free, even if it's damaged.

Extending your contract (up to a maximum of 165 days) after you start using the car is possible but you'll end up paying about double the prepaid per-day rate.

Purchase-repurchase cars, which have special red licence plates, can be picked up at about three-dozen cities and airports all over France and dropped off at the agency of your choosing. For a fee, you can also pick up or return your car in certain cities outside France.

Driving Licence & Documents

An International Driving Permit (IDP), valid only if accompanied by your original licence, is good for a year and can be issued by your local automobile association before you leave home.

Drivers must carry the following at all times:

» passport or an EU ID card

» *permis de conduire* (valid driving licence); most foreign licences can be used in France for up to a year)

» car-ownership papers, known as a *carte grise* (grey card)

» proof of third-party liability *assurance* (insurance)

Fuel

Essence (petrol), also known as *carburant* (fuel), costs around €1.45/L (US$6.80 per US gallon) for 95 unleaded (Sans Plomb 95 or SP95, usually available from a green pump) and €1.30 for diesel (*diesel, gazole* or *gasoil*, usually available from a yellow pump). Filling up *(faire le plein)* is most expensive at autoroute rest stops and often cheapest at hypermarkets.

Many small petrol stations close on Sunday afternoons and, even in cities, it can be hard to find a staffed station open late at night. In general, after-hours purchases (eg at hypermarkets' fully automatic, 24-hour stations) can only be made with a credit card that has an embedded PIN chip, so if all you've got is cash or a magnetic-strip credit card, you could be stuck.

Insurance

Third-party liability insurance *(assurance au tiers)* is compulsory for all vehicles in France, including cars brought in from abroad. Normally, cars registered and insured in other European countries can circulate freely in France, but it's a good idea to contact your insurance company before you leave home to make sure you have coverage – and to check whom to contact in case of a breakdown or accident.

If you get into a minor accident with no injuries, the easiest way for drivers to sort things out with their insurance companies is to fill out a Constat Aimable d'Accident Automobile (European Accident Statement), a standardised way of recording important details about what happened. In rental cars it's usually in the packet of documents in the glove compartment. Make sure the report includes any information that will help you prove that the accident was not your fault. Remember, if it *was* your fault you may be liable for a hefty insurance deductible/excess. Don't sign anything you don't

fully understand. If problems crop up, call the police (🖉17).

French-registered cars have details of their insurance company printed on a little green square affixed to the windscreen.

Parking

In city centres, most on-the-street parking places are *payant* (metered) from about 9am to 7pm (sometimes with a break from noon to 2pm) Monday to Saturday, except bank holidays.

Road Rules

Enforcement of French traffic laws (see www.securite routiere.gouv.fr, in French) has stepped up considerably in recent years. Speed cameras are becoming ever more common, as are radar traps, unmarked police vehicles and saliva drug tests. Fines for many infractions are given on the spot, and serious violations can lead to the confiscation of your driving licence and car.

Speed limits outside built-up areas (except where signposted otherwise):

» **Undivided N and D highways** 90km/h (80km/h when raining)

» **Non-autoroute divided highways** 110km/h (100km/h when raining)

» **Autoroutes** 130km/h (110km/h when raining, 60km/h in icy conditions) To reduce carbon emissions, autoroute speed limits have recently been reduced to 110km/h in some areas.

Unless otherwise signposted, a limit of 50km/h applies in *all* areas designated as built up, no matter how rural they may appear. You must slow to 50km/h the moment you come to a white sign with a red border and a place name written on it; the speed limit applies until you pass an identical sign with a horizontal bar through it.

Most of the speed-limit signs you'll see in cities, towns and villages merely remind you of something you're already supposed to know – that's why they begin with the word *rappel* ('remember'). You can be fined for going as little as 10km/h over the speed limit.

Other driving rules:

» Blood-alcohol limit is 0.05% (0.5g per litre of blood) – the equivalent of two glasses of wine for a 75kg adult. Police often conduct random breathalyser tests and penalties can be severe, including imprisonment.

» All passengers, including those in the back seat, must wear seat belts.

PRIORITY TO THE RIGHT

Under the *priorité à droite* (priority to the right) rule, any car entering an intersection (including a T-junction) from a road (including a tiny village backstreet) on your right has the right of way. Locals assume every driver knows this, so don't be surprised if they courteously cede the right of way when you're about to turn from an alley onto a highway – and boldly assert their rights when you're the one zipping down a main road.

Priorité à droite is suspended (eg on arterial roads) when you pass a sign showing an upended yellow square with a black square in the middle. The same sign with a horizontal bar through the square lozenge reinstates the *priorité à droite* rule.

When you arrive at a roundabout at which you do not have the right of way (ie the cars already in the roundabout do), you'll often see signs reading *vous n'avez pas la priorité* (you do not have right of way) or *cédez le passage* (give way).

» Mobile phones may be used only if they are equipped with a hands-free kit or speakerphone.

» Turning right on a red light is illegal.

» Cars from the UK and Ireland must have deflectors affixed to their headlights to avoid dazzling oncoming motorists.

» Radar detectors, even if they're switched off, are illegal; fines are hefty.

Child-seat rules:

» Children under 10 are not permitted to ride in the front seat (unless the back is already occupied by other children under 10).

» A child under 13kg must travel in a backward-facing child seat (permitted in the front seat only for babies under 9kg and if the airbag is deactivated).

» Up to age 10 and/or a minimum height of 140cm, children must use a size-appropriate type of front-facing child seat or booster.

All vehicles driven in France must carry a high-visibility reflective safety vest (stored inside the vehicle, not in the trunk/boot), a reflective triangle, and (as of 1 July 2012) a portable, single-use breathalyser kit. The fine for not carrying any of these is €90.

If you'll be driving on snowy roads, make sure you've got snow chains (chaînes neige), required by law whenever and wherever the police post signs.

Riders of any type of two-wheeled vehicle with a motor (except motor-assisted bicycles) must wear a helmet. No special licence is required to ride a motorcycle with an engine smaller than 50cc, which is why rental scooters are often rated at 49.9cc.

Hitching

Hitching is never entirely safe in any country in the world, and we don't recommend it. Travellers who decide to hitch should understand that they are taking a small but potentially serious risk. Remember that it's safer to travel in pairs and be sure to inform someone of your intended destination. Hitching is not really part of French culture and is not recommended for women in France, even in pairs.

Hitching from city centres is pretty much hopeless, so your best bet is to take public transport to the outskirts. It is illegal to hitch on autoroutes but you can stand near an entrance ramp as long as you don't block traffic. Hitching in remote rural areas is better, but once you get off the routes nationales traffic can be light and local. If your itinerary includes a ferry crossing, it's worth trying to score a ride before the ferry since vehicle tickets usually include a number of passengers free of charge. At dusk, give up and think about finding somewhere to stay.

Ride Share

A number of organisations around France arrange covoiturage (car sharing), ie putting people looking for rides in touch with drivers going to the same destination. The best known is Paris-based **Allostop** (www.allostop.net), where you pay €3/5/8/10 for a single journey up to 50/100/150/200km. You might also try **Covoiturage** (www.covoiturage.fr) or, for international journeys, **Karzoo** (www.karzoo.eu).

Local Transport

France's cities and larger towns have world-class public-transport systems. There are métros (underground subway systems) in Paris, Lyon, Marseille, Lille and Toulouse and ultramodern light-rail lines (tramways) in cities such as Bordeaux, Grenoble, Lille, Lyon, Nancy, Nantes, Nice, Reims, Rouen and Strasbourg, as well as parts of greater Paris.

In addition to a billet à l'unité (single ticket), you can purchase a carnet (booklet or bunch) of 10 tickets or a pass journée (all-day pass).

Taxi

All medium and large train stations – and many small ones – have a taxi stand out front. In small cities and towns, where taxi drivers are unlikely to find another fare anywhere near where they let you off, one-way and return trips often cost the same. Tariffs are about 30% higher at night and on Sundays and holidays. Having a cab wait for you while you visit something costs about €20 an hour (about €30 in Paris). There may be a surcharge to get picked up at a train station or airport and a small additional fee for a fourth passenger and/or for suitcases.

Train

Travelling by train in France is a comfortable, classy and environmentally sustainable way to see the country. Since many train stations have car-hire agencies, it's easy to combine rail travel with rural exploration by car.

The jewel in the crown of France's public-transport system – alongside the Paris métro – is its extensive rail network, almost all of it run by the state-owned **SNCF** (www.sncf.com). Although it employs the most advanced rail technology, the network's layout reflects the country's centuries-old Paris-centric nature: most of the principal rail lines radiate out from Paris like the spokes of a wheel, the result being that services between provincial towns situated on different spokes can be infrequent and slow. Up-to-the-minute information on perturbations (service disruptions), eg because of strikes, can be found on www.infolignes.com (in French).

Since its inauguration in the 1980s, the pride of SNCF (and the French) is the **TGV** (Train à Grande Vitesse; www.tgv.com), pronounced 'teh zheh veh', which zips passengers along at speeds of 320km/h (198mph).

SNCF FARES & DISCOUNTS

Full-fare tickets can be quite expensive. Fortunately, a dizzying array of discounts is available and station staff are very good at helping travellers find the very best fare. But first, the basics:

» 1st-class travel, where available, costs 20% to 30% extra.
» Ticket prices for some trains, including most TGVs, are pricier during peak periods.
» The further in advance you reserve, the lower the fares.
» Children under four travel for free (€8.50 to any destination if they need a seat).
» Children aged four to 11 travel for half-price.

Discount Tickets

The SNCF's most heavily discounted tickets are known as **Prem's**. They can be booked on the internet, by phone, at ticket windows and from ticket machines a maximum of 90 days and a minimum of 14 days before your travel date. Once you buy a Prem's ticket, it's use it or lose it – no getting your money back or changing the time.

Bons Plans fares, a grab bag of really cheap options on a changing array of routes and dates, are advertised on www.voyages-sncf.com under the title 'Dernière Minute' (last minute).

In an effort to make train travel both affordable and hip for the iPod generation, the SNCF's youthful subsidiary **iDTGV** (www.idtgv.com) sells tickets (online only) for as little as €19 for advance-purchase TGV travel between about 30 cities.

On regional trains, discount fares requiring neither a discount card nor advance purchase:

» **Loisir Week-End rates** Good for return travel that includes a Saturday night at your destination or involves travel on a Saturday or Sunday.

» **Découverte fares** Available for low-demand 'blue-period' trains to people aged 12 to 25, seniors and the adult travel companions of children under 12.

» **Mini-Groupe tickets** In some regions, these bring big savings for three to six people travelling together, provided you spend a Saturday night at your destination.

Certain French *régions* offer great deals on intraregional TER transport for day trips or weekend travel.

Discount Cards

Reductions of at least 25% (for last-minute bookings), and of 40%, 50% or even 60% (if you reserve well ahead or travel during low-volume 'blue' periods), are available with several discount cards (valid for one year):

» **Carte 12-25** (www.12-25-sncf.com; €50) Available to travellers aged 12 to 25.

» **Carte Enfant Plus** (www.enfantplus-sncf.com; €71) For one to four adults travelling with a child aged four to 11.

» **Carte Escapades** (www.escapades-sncf.com; €76) For people aged 26 to 59. Discounts on return journeys of at least 200km that either include a Saturday night away or only involve travel on a Saturday or Sunday.

» **Carte Sénior** (www.senior-sncf.com; €57) For travellers over 60.

Rail Passes

Residents of Europe who do not live in France can purchase an **InterRail One Country Pass** (www.interrailnet.com; 3/4/6/8 days €205/226/288/319, 12–25yr €139/149/190/211), which entitles its bearer to unlimited travel on SNCF trains for three to eight days over the course of a month.

For non-European residents, **Rail Europe** (www.raileurope.com) offers the **France Rail Pass** (www.francerailpass.com; 3/6/9 days over 1 month €242/349/443).

You need to really rack up the kilometres to make these passes worthwhile.

LEFT-LUGGAGE FACILITIES

Because of security concerns, few French train stations still have *consignes automatiques* (left-luggage lockers), but in some larger stations you can leave your bags in a *consigne manuelle* (staffed left-luggage facility) – usually in an out-of-the-way corner of the station – where items are handed over in person and x-rayed before being stowed. Charges are €5 for up to 10 hours and €8 for 24 hours; payment must be made in cash. To find out which stations let you leave your bags and when their *consignes* are open (they're often closed on Sunday and after 7pm or 8pm), go to www.gares-en-mouvement.com, select a station, click 'Practical Information' ('Services en gare') and then the 'Services' tab.

The main TGV lines (or LGVs, short for *lignes à grande vitesse*, ie high-speed rail lines) head north, east, southeast and southwest from Paris (trains use slower local tracks to get to destinations off the main line):

» **TGV Nord, Thalys & Eurostar** Link Paris Gare du Nord with Arras, Lille, Calais, Brussels (Bruxelles-Midi), Amsterdam, Cologne and, via the Channel Tunnel, Ashford, Ebbsfleet and London St Pancras.

» **TGV Est Européen** Connects Paris Gare de l'Est with Reims, Nancy, Metz, Strasbourg, Zurich and Germany, including Frankfurt and Stuttgart. At present, the super-high-speed track stretches only as far east as Lorraine but it's supposed to reach Strasbourg in 2016.

» **TGV Sud-Est & TGV Midi-Méditerranée** Link Paris Gare de Lyon with the southeast, including Dijon, Lyon, Geneva, the Alps, Avignon, Marseille, Nice and Montpellier.

» **TGV Atlantique Sud-Ouest & TGV Atlantique Ouest** Link Paris Gare Montparnasse with western and southwestern France, including Brittany (Rennes, Brest, Quimper), Tours, Nantes, Poitiers, La Rochelle, Bordeaux, Biarritz and Toulouse.

» **TGV Rhin-Rhône** France's most recent high-speed rail route – the first section of which opened in December 2011 – bypasses Paris altogether in its bid to better link the provinces. Six services a day speed between Strasbourg and Lyon, with most continuing south to Marseille or Montpellier on the Mediterranean.

The TGV tracks are interconnected, making it possible to go directly from, say, Lyon to Nantes or Bordeaux to Lille without having to switch trains in Paris or transfer from one of Paris' six main train stations to another. Stops on the link-up, which runs east and south of Paris, include Charles de Gaulle airport and Disneyland Resort Paris.

Long-distance trains sometimes split at a station – that is, each half of the train heads off for a different destination. Check the destination panel on your car as you board or you could wind up very far from where you intended to go.

Other types of train:

Téoz (www.corailteoz.com) Comfortable trains that run southward from Paris Gare d'Austerlitz to Clermont-Ferrand, Limoges, Cahors, Toulouse, Montpellier, Perpignan, Marseille and Nice.

TER (Train Express Régional; www.ter-sncf.com) A train that is not a TGV can be known as a corail, a classique or, for intraregional services, a TER.

Transilien (www.transilien.com) SNCF services in the Île de France area in and around Paris.

Tickets & Reservations

Large stations often have separate ticket windows for *international, grandes lignes* (long-haul) and *banlieue* (suburban) lines, and for people whose train is about to leave (*départ immédiat* or *départ dans l'heure*). Nearly every SNCF station has one *borne libre-service* (self-service terminal) or *billeterie automatique* (automatic ticket machine) that accepts cash and PIN-chip credit cards.

Using a credit card, you can buy a ticket by phone or via the SNCF internet booking, **Voyages SNCF** (www.voyages-sncf.com), and either have it sent to you by post (if you have an address in France) or collect it from any SNCF ticket office or from train-station ticket machines.

Before boarding, you must validate (*composter*) your ticket by time-stamping it in a *composteur*, the yellow posts located on the way to the platform. If you forget (or don't have a ticket), find a conductor on the train before they find you – otherwise you can be fined.

CHANGES & REIMBURSEMENTS

For trains that do not assign reserved seats (eg TER and Corail Intercités trains), full-fare tickets are usable whenever you like for 61 days from the date they were purchased. Like all SNCF tickets, they cannot be replaced if lost or stolen.

If you've got a full-fare Loisir Week-End ticket, you can change your reservation by phone, internet or at train stations for no charge until the day before your departure; changes made on the day of your reserved trip incur a charge of €10 (€3 for tickets bought with a discount card).

Pro tickets (eg TGV Pro, Téoz Pro) allow full reimbursement up to 30 minutes *after* the time of departure (eg by calling 36 35). If you turn up at your departure station up to two hours after your original travel time, you can reschedule your trip on a later train.

Language

WANT MORE?
For in-depth language information and handy phrases, check out Lonely Planet's *French Phrasebook*. You'll find it at **shop .lonelyplanet.com**, or you can buy Lonely Planet's iPhone phrasebooks at the Apple App Store.

Standard French is taught and spoken throughout France. This said, regional accents and dialects are an important part of identity in certain regions, but you'll have no trouble being understood anywhere if you stick to standard French, which we've also used in this chapter.

The sounds used in spoken French can almost all be found in English. There are a couple of exceptions: nasal vowels (represented in our pronunciation guides by o or u followed by an almost inaudible nasal consonant sound m, n or ng), the 'funny' *u* (ew in our guides) and the deep-in-the-throat r. Bearing these few points in mind and reading our pronunciation guides below as if they were English, you'll be understood just fine.

BASICS

French has two words for 'you' – use the polite form *vous* unless you're talking to close friends, children or animals in which case you'd use the informal *tu*. You can also use *tu* when a person invites you to use *tu*.

All nouns in French are either masculine or feminine, and so are the adjectives, articles *le/la* (the) and *un/une* (a), and possessives *mon/ma* (my), *ton/ta* (your) *and son/sa* (his, her) that go with the nouns. In this chapter we have included masculine and femine forms where necessary, separated by a slash and indicated with 'm/f'.

Hello.	*Bonjour.*	bon·zhoor
Goodbye.	*Au revoir.*	o·rer·vwa
Excuse me.	*Excusez-moi.*	ek·skew·zay·mwa
Sorry.	*Pardon.*	par·don
Yes.	*Oui.*	wee
No.	*Non.*	non
Please.	*S'il vous plaît.*	seel voo play
Thank you.	*Merci.*	mair·see
You're welcome.	*De rien.*	der ree·en

How are you?
Comment allez-vous?   ko·mon ta·lay·voo

Fine, and you?
Bien, merci. Et vous?   byun mair·see ay voo

You're welcome.
De rien.   der ree·en

My name is ...
Je m'appelle ...   zher ma·pel ...

What's your name?
Comment vous appelez-vous?   ko·mon voo·za·play voo

Do you speak English?
Parlez-vous anglais?   par·lay·voo ong·glay

I don't understand.
Je ne comprends pas.   zher ner kom·pron pa

ACCOMMODATION

Do you have any rooms available?
Est-ce que vous avez des chambres libres?   es·ker voo za·vay day shom·brer lee·brer

How much is it per night/person?
Quel est le prix par nuit/personne?   kel ay ler pree par nwee/per·son

Is breakfast included?
Est-ce que le petit déjeuner est inclus?   es·ker ler per·tee day·zher·nay ayt en·klew

campsite	camping	kom·peeng
dorm	dortoir	dor·twar
guest house	pension	pon·syon
hotel	hôtel	o·tel
youth hostel	auberge de jeunesse	o·berzh der zher·nes
a ... room	une chambre ...	ewn shom·brer ...
single	à un lit	a un lee
double	avec un grand lit	a·vek un gron lee
twin	avec des lits jumeaux	a·vek day lee zhew·mo
with (a)...	avec ...	a·vek ...
air-con	climatiseur	klee·ma·tee·zer
bathroom	une salle de bains	ewn sal der bun
window	fenêtre	fer·nay·trer

DIRECTIONS

Where's ...?
Où est ...?   oo ay ...

What's the address?
Quelle est l'adresse?   kel ay la·dres

Could you write the address, please?
Est-ce que vous pourriez   es·ker voo poo·ryay
écrire l'adresse,   ay·kreer la·dres
s'il vous plaît?   seel voo play

Can you show me (on the map)?
Pouvez-vous m'indiquer   poo·vay·voo mun·dee·kay
(sur la carte)?   (sewr la kart)

at the corner	au coin	o kwun
at the traffic lights	aux feux	o fer
behind	derrière	dair·ryair
in front of	devant	der·von
far (from)	loin (de)	lwun (der)
left	gauche	gosh
near (to)	près (de)	pray (der)
next to ...	à côté de ...	a ko·tay der...
opposite ...	en face de ...	on fas der ...
right	droite	drwat
straight ahead	tout droit	too drwa

EATING & DRINKING

What would you recommend?
Qu'est-ce que vous   kes·ker voo
conseillez?   kon·say·yay

What's in that dish?
Quels sont les   kel son lay
ingrédients?   zun·gray·dyon

I'm a vegetarian.
Je suis végétarien/   zher swee vay·zhay·ta·ryun/
végétarienne.   vay·zhay·ta·ryen (m/f)

I don't eat ...
Je ne mange pas ...   zher ner monzh pa ...

Cheers!
Santé!   son·tay

That was delicious.
C'était délicieux!   say·tay day·lee·syer

Please bring the bill.
Apportez-moi   a·por·tay·mwa
l'addition,   la·dee·syon
s'il vous plaît.   seel voo play

I'd like to reserve a table for ...	Je voudrais réserver une table pour ...	zher voo·dray ray·zair·vay ewn ta·bler poor ...
(eight) o'clock	(vingt) heures	(vungt) er
(two) people	(deux) personnes	(der) pair·son

Key Words

appetiser	*entrée*	on·tray
bottle	*bouteille*	boo·tay
breakfast	*petit déjeuner*	per·tee day·zher·nay
children's menu	*menu pour enfants*	mer·new poor on·fon
cold	*froid*	frwa
delicatessen	*traiteur*	tray·ter
dinner	*dîner*	dee·nay
dish	*plat*	pla
food	*nourriture*	noo·ree·tewr
fork	*fourchette*	foor·shet
glass	*verre*	vair
grocery store	*épicerie*	ay·pees·ree
highchair	*chaise haute*	shay zot
hot	*chaud*	sho
knife	*couteau*	koo·to
local speciality	*spécialité locale*	spay·sya·lee·tay lo·kal
lunch	*déjeuner*	day·zher·nay
main course	*plat principal*	pla prun·see·pal
market	*marché*	mar·shay
menu (in English)	*carte (en anglais)*	kart (on ong·glay)
plate	*assiette*	a·syet
spoon	*cuillère*	kwee·yair
wine list	*carte des vins*	kart day vun
with/without	*avec/sans*	a·vek/son

Meat & Fish

beef	*bœuf*	berf
chicken	*poulet*	poo·lay
crab	*crabe*	krab
lamb	*agneau*	a·nyo
oyster	*huître*	wee·trer
pork	*porc*	por
snail	*escargot*	es·kar·go
squid	*calmar*	kal·mar
turkey	*dinde*	dund
veal	*veau*	vo

Fruit & Vegetables

apple	*pomme*	pom
apricot	*abricot*	ab·ree·ko
asparagus	*asperge*	a·spairzh
beans	*haricots*	a·ree·ko
beetroot	*betterave*	be·trav
cabbage	*chou*	shoo
cherry	*cerise*	ser·reez
corn	*maïs*	ma·ees
cucumber	*concombre*	kong·kom·brer
grape	*raisin*	ray·zun
lemon	*citron*	see·tron
lettuce	*laitue*	lay·tew
mushroom	*champignon*	shom·pee·nyon
peach	*pêche*	pesh
peas	*petit pois*	per·tee pwa
(red/green) pepper	*poivron (rouge/vert)*	pwa·vron (roozh/vair)
pineapple	*ananas*	a·na·nas
plum	*prune*	prewn
potato	*pomme de terre*	pom der tair
prune	*pruneau*	prew·no
pumpkin	*citrouille*	see·troo·yer
shallot	*échalote*	eh·sha·lot
spinach	*épinards*	eh·pee·nar
strawberry	*fraise*	frez
tomato	*tomate*	to·mat
vegetable	*légume*	lay·gewm

Other

bread	*pain*	pun
butter	*beurre*	ber
cheese	*fromage*	fro·mazh
egg	*œuf*	erf
honey	*miel*	myel
jam	*confiture*	kon·fee·tewr
lentils	*lentilles*	lon·tee·yer
pasta/noodles	*pâtes*	pat
pepper	*poivre*	pwa·vrer
rice	*riz*	ree
salt	*sel*	sel
sugar	*sucre*	sew·krer
vinegar	*vinaigre*	vee·nay·grer

Signs

Entrée	Entrance
Femmes	Women
Fermé	Closed
Hommes	Men
Interdit	Prohibited
Ouvert	Open
Renseignements	Information
Sortie	Exit
Toilettes/WC	Toilets

Drinks

beer	*bière*	bee·yair
coffee	*café*	ka·fay
(orange) juice	*jus (d'orange)*	zhew (do·ronzh)
milk	*lait*	lay
tea	*thé*	tay
(mineral) water	*eau (minérale)*	o (mee·nay·ral)
(red) wine	*vin (rouge)*	vun (roozh)
(white) wine	*vin (blanc)*	vun (blong)

EMERGENCIES

Help!
Au secours!   o skoor

I'm lost.
Je suis perdu/perdue.   zhe swee·pair·dew (m/f)

Leave me alone!
Fichez-moi la paix!   fee·shay·mwa la pay

There's been an accident.
Il y a eu un accident.   eel ya ew un ak·see·don

Call a doctor.
Appelez un médecin.   a·play un mayd·sun

Call the police.
Appelez la police.   a·play la po·lees

I'm ill.
Je suis malade.   zher swee ma·lad

It hurts here.
J'ai une douleur ici.   zhay ewn doo·ler ee·see

I'm allergic to ...
Je suis allergique ...   zher swee za·lair·zheek ...

SHOPPING & SERVICES

I'd like to buy ...
Je voudrais acheter ...   zher voo·dray ash·tay ...

May I look at it?
Est-ce que je   es·ker zher
peux le voir?   per ler vwar

I'm just looking.
Je regarde.   zher rer·gard

I don't like it.
Cela ne me plaît pas.   ser·la ner mer play pa

How much is it?
C'est combien?   say kom·byun

It's too expensive.
C'est trop cher.   say tro shair

Question Words

How?	*Comment?*	ko·mon
What?	*Quoi?*	kwa
When?	*Quand?*	kon
Where?	*Où?*	oo
Who?	*Qui?*	kee
Why?	*Pourquoi?*	poor·kwa

Can you lower the price?
Vous pouvez baisser   voo poo·vay bay·say
le prix?   ler pree

There's a mistake in the bill.
Il y a une erreur dans   eel ya ewn ay·rer don
la note.   la not

ATM	*guichet automatique de banque*	gee·shay o·to·ma·teek der bonk
credit card	*carte de crédit*	kart der kray·dee
internet cafe	*cybercafé*	see·bair·ka·fay
post office	*bureau de poste*	bew·ro der post
tourist office	*office de tourisme*	o·fees der too·rees·mer

TIME & DATES

What time is it?
Quelle heure est-il?   kel er ay til

It's (eight) o'clock.
Il est (huit) heures.   il ay (weet) er

It's half past (10).
Il est (dix) heures   il ay (deez) er
et demie.   ay day·mee

morning	*matin*	ma·tun
afternoon	*après-midi*	a·pray·mee·dee
evening	*soir*	swar
yesterday	*hier*	yair
today	*aujourd'hui*	o·zhoor·dwee
tomorrow	*demain*	der·mun

Monday	*lundi*	lun·dee
Tuesday	*mardi*	mar·dee
Wednesday	*mercredi*	mair·krer·dee
Thursday	*jeudi*	zher·dee
Friday	*vendredi*	von·drer·dee
Saturday	*samedi*	sam·dee
Sunday	*dimanche*	dee·monsh

January	*janvier*	zhon·vyay
February	*février*	fayv·ryay
March	*mars*	mars
April	*avril*	a·vreel
May	*mai*	may
June	*juin*	zhwun
July	*juillet*	zhwee·yay
August	*août*	oot
September	*septembre*	sep·tom·brer
October	*octobre*	ok·to·brer
November	*novembre*	no·vom·brer
December	*décembre*	day·som·brer

Numbers

1	*un*	un
2	*deux*	der
3	*trois*	trwa
4	*quatre*	ka-trer
5	*cinq*	sungk
6	*six*	sees
7	*sept*	set
8	*huit*	weet
9	*neuf*	nerf
10	*dix*	dees
20	*vingt*	vung
30	*trente*	tront
40	*quarante*	ka-ront
50	*cinquante*	sung-kont
60	*soixante*	swa-sont
70	*soixante-dix*	swa-son-dees
80	*quatre-vingts*	ka-trer-vung
90	*quatre-vingt-dix*	ka-trer-vung-dees
100	*cent*	son
1000	*mille*	meel

TRANSPORT

Public Transport

boat	*bateau*	ba-to
bus	*bus*	bews
plane	*avion*	a-vyon
train	*train*	trun

I want to go to ...
Je voudrais aller à ...   zher voo-dray a-lay a ...

Does it stop at (Amboise)?
Est-ce qu'il s'arrête à   es-kil sa-ret a
(Amboise)?   (om-bwaz)

At what time does it leave/arrive?
À quelle heure est-ce   a kel er es
qu'il part/arrive?   kil par/a-reev

Can you tell me when we get to ...?
Pouvez-vous me   poo-vay-voo mer
dire quand   deer kon
nous arrivons à ...?   noo za-ree-von a ...

I want to get off here.
Je veux descendre   zher ver day-son-drer
ici.   ee-see

first	*premier*	prer-myay
last	*dernier*	dair-nyay
next	*prochain*	pro-shun

a ... ticket	*un billet ...*	un bee-yay ...
1st-class	*de première classe*	der prem-yair klas
2nd-class	*de deuxième classe*	der der-zyem las
one-way	*simple*	sum-pler
return	*aller et retour*	a-lay ay rer-toor

aisle seat	*côté couloir*	ko-tay kool-war
delayed	*en retard*	on rer-tar
cancelled	*annulé*	a-new-lay
platform	*quai*	kay
ticket office	*guichet*	gee-shay
timetable	*horaire*	o-rair
train station	*gare*	gar
window seat	*côté fenêtre*	ko-tay fe-ne-trer

Driving & Cycling

I'd like to hire a ...	*Je voudrais louer ...*	zher voo-dray loo-way ...
4WD	*un quatre-quatre*	un kat-kat
car	*une voiture*	ewn vwa-tewr
bicycle	*un vélo*	un vay-lo
motorcycle	*une moto*	ewn mo-to

child seat	*siège-enfant*	syezh-on-fon
diesel	*diesel*	dyay-zel
helmet	*casque*	kask
mechanic	*mécanicien*	may-ka-nee-syun
petrol/gas	*essence*	ay-sons
service station	*station-service*	sta-syon-ser-vees

Is this the road to ...?
C'est la route pour ...?   say la root poor ...

(How long) Can I park here?
(Combien de temps)   (kom-byun der tom)
Est-ce que je peux   es-ker zher per
stationner ici?   sta-syo-nay ee-see

The car/motorbike has broken down (at ...).
La voiture/moto est   la vwa-tewr/mo-to ay
tombée en panne (à ...).   tom-bay on pan (a ...)

I have a flat tyre.
Mon pneu est à plat.   mom pner ay ta pla

I've run out of petrol.
Je suis en panne   zher swee zon pan
d'essence.   day-sons

I've lost my car keys.
J'ai perdu les clés de   zhay per-dew lay klay der
ma voiture.   ma vwa-tewr

GLOSSARY

(m) indicates masculine gender, (f) feminine gender and (pl) plural

accueil (m) – reception

alignements (m pl) – a series of standing stones, or menhirs, in straight lines

AOC – Appellation d'Origine Contrôlée; system of French wine and olive oil classification showing that items have met government regulations as to where and how they are produced

AOP – Appellation d'Origine Protégée; Europe-wide equivalent to *AOC*

arrondissement (m) – administrative division of large city; abbreviated on signs as 1er (1st arrondissement), 2e (2nd) etc

atelier (m) – workshop or studio

auberge – inn

auberge de jeunesse (f) – youth hostel

baie (f) – bay

bassin (m) – bay or basin

bastide (f) – medieval settlement in southwestern France, usually built on a grid plan and surrounding an arcaded square; fortified town; also a country house in Provence

belle époque (f) – literally 'beautiful age'; era of elegance and gaiety characterising fashionable Parisian life in the period preceding WWI

billet (m) – ticket

billetterie (f) – ticket office or counter

bouchon – Lyonnais bistro

boulangerie (f) – bakery or bread shop

boules (f pl) – a game similar to lawn bowls played with heavy metal balls on a sandy pitch; also called *pétanque*

brasserie (f) – restaurant similar to a *café* but usually serving full meals all day (original meaning: brewery)

bureau de change (m) – exchange bureau

bureau de poste (m) – post office

carnet (m) – a book of five or 10 bus, tram or metro tickets sold at a reduced rate

carrefour (m) – crossroad

carte (f) – card; menu; map

cave (f) – wine cellar

chambre (f) – room

chambre d'hôte (f) – B&B

charcuterie (f) – butcher's shop and delicatessen; the prepared meats it sells

cimetière (m) – cemetery

col (m) – mountain pass

consigne or **consigne manuelle** (f) – left-luggage office

consigne automatique (f) – left-luggage locker

correspondance (f) – linking tunnel or walkway, eg in the metro; rail or bus connection

cour (f) – courtyard

crémerie (f) – dairy or cheese shop

dégustation (f) – tasting

demi (m) – 330mL glass of beer

demi-pension (f) – half board (B&B with either lunch or dinner)

département (m) – administrative division of France

donjon (m) – castle keep

église (f) – church

épicerie (f) – small grocery store

ESF – École de Ski Français; France's leading ski school

fest-noz or **festoù-noz** (pl) – night festival

fête (f) – festival

Fnac – retail chain selling entertainment goods, electronics and tickets

forêt (f) – forest

formule or **formule rapide** (f) – lunchtime set similar to a *menu* but with two of three courses on offer (eg starter and main or main and dessert)

fromagerie (f) – cheese shop

FUAJ – Fédération Unie des Auberges de Jeunesse; France's major hostel association

funiculaire (m) – funicular railway

galerie (f) – covered shopping centre or arcade

gare or **gare SNCF** (f) – railway station

gare maritime (f) – ferry terminal

gare routière (f) – bus station

gendarmerie (f) – police station; police force

gîte d'étape (m) – hikers accommodation, usually in a village

golfe (m) – gulf

GR – *grande randonnée*; long-distance hiking trail

grand cru (m) – wine of exceptional quality

halles (f pl) – covered market; central food market

halte routière (f) – bus stop

horaire (m) – timetable or schedule

hostellerie – hostelry

hôtel de ville (m) – city or town hall

hôtel particulier (m) – private mansion

intra-muros – old city (literally 'within the walls')

jardin (m) – garden

jardin botanique (m) – botanic garden

laverie (f) or **lavomatique** (m) – laundrette

libre – vacant, available

mairie (f) – city or town hall

maison du parc (f) – a

national park's headquarters and/or visitors centre

marché (m) – market

marché aux puces (m) – flea market

marché couvert (m) – covered market

mas (m) – farmhouse in southern France

menu (m) – fixed-price meal with two or more courses

mistral (m) – strong north or northwest wind in southern France

musée (m) – museum

navette (f) – shuttle bus, train or boat

occupé – occupied

palais de justice (m) – law courts

parapente – paragliding

parlement (m) – parliament

parvis (m) – square

patisserie (f) – cake and pastry shop

pétanque (f) – a game similar to lawn bowls played with heavy metal balls on a sandy pitch; also called *boules*

petit déjeuner – breakfast

place (f) – square or plaza

plage (f) – beach

plan (m) – city map

plan du quartier (m) – map of nearby streets (hung on the wall near metro exits)

plat du jour (m) – daily special in a restaurant

pont (m) – bridge

porte (f) – gate in a city wall

poste (f) – post office

préfecture (f) – prefecture (capital of a *département*)

presqu'île (f) – peninsula

puy (m) – volcanic cone or peak

quai (m) – quay or railway platform

quartier (m) – quarter or district

refuge (m) – mountain hut, basic shelter for hikers

région (f) – administrative division of France

rond point (m) – round-about

salon de thé – tearoom

sentier (m) – trail

service des urgences (f) – casualty ward

ski de fond – cross-country skiing

SNCF – Société Nationale des Chemins de Fer; state-owned railway company

SNCM – Société Nationale Maritime Corse-Méditerranée; state-owned

ferry company linking Corsica and mainland France

sortie (f) – exit

square (m) – public garden

tabac (m) – tobacconist (also selling bus tickets, phonecards etc)

table d'hôte – set menu at a fixed price

taxe de séjour (f) – municipal tourist tax

télécarte (f) – phonecard

télécabine – gondola

téléphérique (m) – cableway or cable car

téléski (m) – chairlift

téléski (m) – ski lift or tow

terroir – land

TGV – *Train à Grande Vitesse*; high-speed train or bullet train

tour (f) – tower

vallée (f) – valley

VF (f) – *version française*; a film dubbed in French

vieille ville (f) – old town or old city

ville neuve (f) – new town or new city

VO (f) – *version originale*; a nondubbed film with French subtitles

VTT – *vélo tout terrain*; mountain bike

winstub – traditional Alsatian eatery

behind the scenes

SEND US YOUR FEEDBACK

We love to hear from travellers – your comments keep us on our toes and help make our books better. Our well-travelled team reads every word on what you loved or loathed about this book. Although we cannot reply individually to postal submissions, we always guarantee that your feedback goes straight to the appropriate authors, in time for the next edition. Each person who sends us information is thanked in the next edition – the most useful submissions are rewarded with a selection of digital PDF chapters.

Visit **lonelyplanet.com/contact** to submit your updates and suggestions or to ask for help. Our award-winning website also features inspirational travel stories, news and discussions.

Note: We may edit, reproduce and incorporate your comments in Lonely Planet products such as guidebooks, websites and digital products, so let us know if you don't want your comments reproduced or your name acknowledged. For a copy of our privacy policy visit lonelyplanet.com/privacy.

OUR READERS

Many thanks to the travellers who used the last edition and wrote to us with helpful hints, useful advice and interesting anecdotes:

Beebe Bahrami, Rinse Balk & Ilse Harms, Robert Bardolf, Priya Bhagat, Ferdinande Birgsteiner, Roy Bishop, J-I Brussac, Brooke Campbell, Bertrand Camus, Laure Dumas, Mark Dyer, John M Ford, Touché Guimarães, Michele Jones, David Latham, Anne Marie Maclean, Sheila Miller, Anouska Moynagh, Mathilde Recoque, David Rogers, Pablo Ross, Christopher Sacra, Hajime Sasaki, Ariana Scott-Zechlin, Vic Sofras, Sheila Stahl Butler, Mitch Stambler, Didier Tran Ngoc, Tim Van Esch, Andy Wearn, Sin Yen Wang.

AUTHOR THANKS

Nicola Williams

Kudos to my coauthors who resolutely persevered with an ambitious project that, at times, felt akin to scaling the Eiffel Tower on tiptoes in stilettos. On the road, *merci mille fois* to Corsica aficionado Vincent Lehoux (unsurpassable Ajaccio recommendations); Kasia Dietz and Lindsay Tramuta (Corsica tips by way of Paris); Charlie Johnson (best

hidden beach camping); travel-mad husband Matthias and our trilingual tribe (only car sick once during entire 2000km of coastal hairpins covered – at average speed of 38km/h no less).

Oliver Berry

Big thanks as always to Susie, Molly and Gracie. I'd also like to thank the people who helped me during the research of this book, including Jean-Patrique Lafarge, Dominique Dupont, Nadia Durand, Erik Herault and Thomas Goncourt. Lastly huge thanks to Jo Cooke and Nicola Williams for their patience, understanding and moral support throughout, and of course to all my other coauthors on their own French adventures. *Bon courage, mes braves!*

Stuart Butler

First and foremost I want to thank my wife, Heather, for everything she does and my young son, Jake, who has already brought us so much happiness (and sleepless nights!). Thanks also to all Jake's grandparents and aunties for babysitting duties during the course of my research for this book. I would also like to thank Rosie Warren in Bordeaux and the good people of the whole western seaboard of France who knowingly or unknowingly helped out on this project.

Jean-Bernard Carillet
A huge *merci beaucoup* to Nicola Williams, coordinating author *extraordinaire*, who was always a great help throughout this project, as well as being a true pleasure to work with. Huge thanks to the SPP team in Melbourne, to commissioning editor Jo Cooke, to Annelies for her invaluable insight and to the carto team. I'm also indebted to Didier Ferat, Laurent and Béatrice for a fab weekend in Normandy.

Kerry Christiani
A big *merci* goes to all the wonderful interviewees and locals I met on my travels, as well as to the tourist offices who smoothed my path to research, particularly the teams in Chamonix, Val d'Isère, Annecy and Strasbourg. A huge thank you to Leanora Parry for fun times and tips in Les Trois Vallées. Thanks, too, to my great coauthors and the editors at Lonely Planet. Finally, heartfelt thanks to my husband and travel companion extraordinaire Andy.

Gregor Clark
Un grand merci to the countless people who shared their love and knowledge of France with me, especially Alisa, Jean-Philippe, Aline and Andy, Mary, Conor, Gloria, and the two charming retirees in that Lyon *bouchon* whose names I never got. Thanks also to sometime-travelling companions Aideen, Marcel, Lauri, Zara, Maya and Wes. Back home, love and big hugs to my wife Gaen, and to daughters Meigan and Chloe, who helped me immeasurably in researching Loire Valley *châteaux* and *boulangeries*.

Emilie Filou
Big thanks to fellow *Provence & the Côte d'Azur* authors Alexis Averbuck and John Vlahides. Thanks also to my parents for being wonderful travel companions (and sharp critics), all the friends who chipped in with recommendations and offered hospitality and company, the many tourism professionals who went out of their way to help; and finally, thank you to husband Adolfo for always being there.

Catherine Le Nevez
Un grand merci to my Lonely Planet *Paris* City Guide coauthors Nicola Williams and Chris Pitts for their contributions to this book's Paris chapter. *Merci mille fois* to Julian, and to all of the innumerable Parisians who offered insights and inspiration. Thanks too to Jo Cooke, Annelies Mertens, Mandy Sierp, and everyone at Lonely Planet. And, as ever, *merci encore* to my parents, brother and *belle-sœur* for instilling in me and sustaining my lifelong love of Paris.

ACKNOWLEDGMENTS
Climate map data adapted from Peel MC, Finlayson BL & McMahon TA (2007) 'Updated World Map of the Köppen-Geiger Climate Classification', Hydrology and Earth System Sciences, 11, 163344.

Illustrations pp64-5, pp84-5, pp154-5, pp242-3, pp802-3 and pp868-9 by Javier Zarracina.

Cover photograph: Château de Chenonceau; Luca Da Ros/SIME/4Corners.

THIS BOOK
This 10th edition of Lonely Planet's France guidebook was researched and written by Nicola Williams, Oliver Berry, Stuart Butler, Jean-Bernard Carillet, Kerry Christiani, Gregor Clark, Emilie Filou and Catherine Le Nevez. Alexis Averbuck and John A Vlahides contributed to the Provence and The French Riviera & Monaco chapters; Chris Pitts contributed to the Paris chapter. The previous edition was written and researched by Nicola Williams, Alexis Averbuck, Oliver Berry, Stuart Butler, Jean-Bernard Carillet, Kerry Christiani, Steve Fallon, Emilie Filou, Catherine Le Nevez, Tom Masters, Daniel Robinson, Miles Roddis and John A Vlahides.

This guidebook was commissioned in Lonely Planet's London office, and produced by the following:

Commissioning Editor Joanna Cooke

Coordinating Editor Briohny Hooper

Coordinating Cartographer Valentina Kremenchutskaya

Coordinating Layout Designer Kerrianne Southway

Managing Editors Sasha Baskett, Annelies Mertens, Kirsten Rawlings, Angela Tinson

Managing Cartographers Anthony Phelan, Amanda Sierp, Diana Von Holdt

Managing Layout Designer Chris Girdler

Assisting Editors Susie Ashworth, Andrea Dobbin, Cathryn Game, Carly Hall, Amy Karafin, Robyn Loughnane, Anne Mulvaney, Joanne Newell, Rosie Nicholson, Sally O'Brien, Kristin Odijk, Charlotte Orr, Sophie Splatt, Sam Trafford, Fionn Twomey

Assisting Cartographers Hunor Csutoros, Jolyon Philcox

Cover Research Naomi Parker

Language Content Branislava Vladisavljevic

Thanks to Valeska Cañas, Daniel Corbett, Laura Crawford, Melanie Dankel, Ryan Evans, Justin Flynn, Samantha Forge, Larissa Frost, Jane Hart, Jouve India, Elizabeth Jones, Pat Kinsella, Kate Mathews, Kate McDonell, Trent Paton, Jonathan Ricketson, Raphael Richards, Matthew Riddle, Dianne Schallmeiner, Gerard Walker, Juan Winata

BEHIND THE SCENES

how to use this book

These symbols will help you find the listings you want:

👁 Sights	👉 Tours	🍷 Drinking
🏊 Beaches	🎊 Festivals & Events	⭐ Entertainment
🏃 Activities	🛏 Sleeping	🛍 Shopping
🥢 Courses	🍴 Eating	ℹ Information/Transport

These symbols give you the vital information for each listing:

☎ Telephone Numbers	📶 Wi-Fi Access	🚌 Bus
🕐 Opening Hours	🏊 Swimming Pool	⛴ Ferry
P Parking	🥗 Vegetarian Selection	Ⓜ Metro
⊖ Nonsmoking	📖 English-Language Menu	Ⓢ Subway
❄ Air-Conditioning	👨‍👩‍👧 Family-Friendly	🚊 Tram
@ Internet Access	🐾 Pet-Friendly	🚆 Train

Reviews are organised by author preference.

Look out for these icons:

TOP CHOICE	Our author's recommendation
FREE	No payment required
🌱	A green or sustainable option

Our authors have nominated these places as demonstrating a strong commitment to sustainability – for example by supporting local communities and producers, operating in an environmentally friendly way, or supporting conservation projects.

Map Legend

Sights
- 🏖 Beach
- ☸ Buddhist
- 🏰 Castle
- ✝ Christian
- 🕉 Hindu
- ☪ Islamic
- ✡ Jewish
- ◉ Monument
- 🏛 Museum/Gallery
- ⛩ Ruin
- 🍇 Winery/Vineyard
- 🐘 Zoo
- ◉ Other Sight

Activities, Courses & Tours
- 🤿 Diving/Snorkelling
- 🛶 Canoeing/Kayaking
- ⛷ Skiing
- 🏄 Surfing
- 🏊 Swimming/Pool
- 🚶 Walking
- 🏄 Windsurfing
- ➕ Other Activity/Course/Tour

Sleeping
- 🛏 Sleeping
- ⛺ Camping

Eating
- 🍴 Eating

Drinking
- 🍷 Drinking
- ☕ Cafe

Entertainment
- ⭐ Entertainment

Shopping
- 🛍 Shopping

Information
- ✉ Post Office
- ℹ Tourist Information

Transport
- ✈ Airport
- ⊗ Border Crossing
- 🚌 Bus
- Cable Car/Funicular
- Cycling
- Ferry
- Monorail
- P Parking
- S-Bahn
- Taxi
- Train/Railway
- Tram
- Tube Station
- U-Bahn
- Underground Train Station
- Other Transport

Routes
- Tollway
- Freeway
- Primary
- Secondary
- Tertiary
- Lane
- Unsealed Road
- Plaza/Mall
- Steps
- Tunnel
- Pedestrian Overpass
- Walking Tour
- Walking Tour Detour
- Path

Boundaries
- International
- State/Province
- Disputed
- Regional/Suburb
- Marine Park
- Cliff
- Wall

Population
- ★ Capital (National)
- ◉ Capital (State/Province)
- ● City/Large Town
- • Town/Village

Geographic
- 🏠 Hut/Shelter
- 🏮 Lighthouse
- 👁 Lookout
- ▲ Mountain/Volcano
- 🌴 Oasis
- 🌳 Park
-)(Pass
- ⛱ Picnic Area
- 💧 Waterfall

Hydrography
- River/Creek
- Intermittent River
- Swamp/Mangrove
- Reef
- Canal
- Water
- Dry/Salt/Intermittent Lake
- Glacier

Areas
- Beach/Desert
- Cemetery (Christian)
- Cemetery (Other)
- Park/Forest
- Sportsground
- Sight (Building)
- Top Sight (Building)

Jean-Bernard Carillet

Normandy, Burgundy Paris-based (and Metz-born) journalist and photographer Jean-Bernard was delighted to research his own turf. He has clocked up countless trips to all French regions and written extensively about Provence, the Basque Country, Brittany, Alsace, Corsica and, of course, Burgundy and Normandy. As a hopeless French gourmand, he confesses a pronounced penchant for *cuisine du terroir* and robust tipples (Pernand-Vergelesses and Gigondas being two of his favourites). Just after completing this project he set off to Beaujolais and Marais Poitevin.

Kerry Christiani

Champagne, Alsace & Lorraine, French Alps & the Jura Mountains Kerry has been travelling to France since her school days to brush up her *français*, which she studied to MA level. The high-altitude pull of the Alps, Alsace's sweet eccentricities and Champagne's wineries draw her back time and again. Kerry has authored some 20 guidebooks and frequently contributes to magazines, including *Olive*, *Lonely Planet Magazine* and bbc.com/travel. She tweets at @kerrychristiani and lists her latest work at www.kerrychristiani.com.

Read more about Kerry at:
lonelyplanet.com/members/kerrychristiani

Gregor Clark

Lille, Flanders & the Somme, The Loire Valley, Lyon & the Rhône Valley, Massif Central Gregor's love affair with France started on the midnight streets of Paris at age 14, when, jetlagged and culture-shocked, he ordered a crêpe and discovered that his high school Franglais actually elicited a response. He's been feeding his France obsession ever since, picking fruit on summers off from university, leading bike tours, and writing for Lonely Planet since 2000. Highlights of this research trip include sharing his daughters' enthusiasm for their rented Loire Valley troglodyte house, and hiking the Massif Central.

Read more about Gregor at:
lonelyplanet.com/members/gregorclark

Emilie Filou

Provence, The French Riviera & Monaco Emilie was born in Paris but spent most of her childhood holidays roaming the south of France. She left France when she was 18 to go travelling and never quite made it back. She now lives in London, where she works as a freelance journalist specialising in development issues in Africa. She still goes to the Côte d'Azur every summer. See more of Emilie's work on www.emiliefilou.com; she tweets at @emiliefilou.

Read more about Emilie at:
lonelyplanet.com/members/emiliefilou

Catherine Le Nevez

Paris, Around Paris Catherine first lived in Paris aged four and she's been returning at every opportunity since, completing her Doctorate of Creative Arts in Writing, Masters in Professional Writing, and post-grad qualifications in Editing and Publishing along the way. Revisiting her favourite Parisian haunts and uncovering new ones is a highlight of this (and every) book. Catherine's writing on Paris includes numerous Lonely Planet guides to the city, country, continent and beyond. Wanderlust aside, Paris remains her favourite city on earth.

OUR STORY

A beat-up old car, a few dollars in the pocket and a sense of adventure. In 1972 that's all Tony and Maureen Wheeler needed for the trip of a lifetime – across Europe and Asia overland to Australia. It took several months, and at the end – broke but inspired – they sat at their kitchen table writing and stapling together their first travel guide, *Across Asia on the Cheap*. Within a week they'd sold 1500 copies. Lonely Planet was born.

Today, Lonely Planet has offices in Melbourne, London and Oakland, with more than 600 staff and writers. We share Tony's belief that 'a great guidebook should do three things: inform, educate and amuse'.

OUR WRITERS

Nicola Williams

Coordinating Author, Plan Your Trip, Corsica, Understand, Survival Guide Author, travel writer and editorial consultant Nicola Williams has lived in France and written about it for more than a decade. From her hillside house on the southern shore of Lake Geneva, it's a quick and easy hop to the French Alps (call her a ski fiend...), Paris (art buff...), southern France (foodie...). She has worked on numerous titles for Lonely Planet, including *France*, *Discover France*, *Paris* and *Provence & the Côte d'Azur*. She blogs at tripalong.wordpress.com and tweets at @Tripalong.

Read more about Nicola at:
lonelyplanet.com/members/nicolawilliams

Oliver Berry

Limousin, the Dordogne & the Lot, The Pyrenees, Toulouse Area, Languedoc-Roussillon Oliver's French love affair began at the age of two, and he's since travelled right across L'Hexagone while contributing to several editions of Lonely Planet's *France* guide, amongst other books. Research highlights for this edition included hunting for truffles in the Dordogne, canoeing in the Gorges du Tarn and hiking to the Cirque de Gavarnie in the Pyrenees. He lives and works in Cornwall as a writer and photographer. You can see his latest work at www.oliverberry.com.

Read more about Oliver at:
lonelyplanet.com/members/oliverberry

Stuart Butler

Brittany, Atlantic Coast, French Basque Country Stuart's first encounters with southwest France came on family holidays. When he was older he spent every summer surfing off the beaches of the southwest until one day he found himself so hooked on the region that he was unable to leave – he has been there ever since. When not writing for Lonely Planet he hunts for uncharted surf on remote coastlines. The results of these trips appear frequently in the world's surf media. His website is www.stuartbutlerjournalist.com.

Read more about Stuart at:
lonelyplanet.com/members/stuartbutler

OVER MORE
PAGE WRITERS

Published by Lonely Planet Publications Pty Ltd
ABN 36 005 607 983
10th edition – Mar 2013
ISBN 978 1 74220 036 1
© Lonely Planet 2013   Photographs © as indicated 2013
10 9 8 7 6 5 4 3 2
Printed in China